W9-BYX-780

THEOLOGICAL DICTIONARY
OF THE
NEW TESTAMENT

ABRIDGED IN ONE VOLUME

THEOLOGICAL DICTIONARY
OF THE
NEW TESTAMENT

edited by Gerhard Kittel and Gerhard Friedrich
translated by Geoffrey W. Bromiley

ABRIDGED IN ONE VOLUME

by

GEOFFREY W. BROMILEY

WILLIAM B. EERDMANS PUBLISHING COMPANY

Copyright © 1985 by William B. Eerdmans Publishing Company
First published 1985 by
William B. Eerdmans Publishing Company
255 Jefferson Ave. SE. Grand Rapids, Mich. 49503

All rights reserved
Printed in the United States of America

Reprinted, August 1990

Abridged from
THEOLOGICAL DICTIONARY OF THE NEW TESTAMENT, Copyright ©
1964, 1964, 1965, 1967, 1967, 1968, 1971, 1972, and 1974 by
Wm. B. Eerdmans Publishing Company
Vols. 1 (Α-Γ), II (Δ-Η), III (Θ-Κ), IV (Λ-Ν), edited by Gerhard Kittel
Vols. V (Ξ-Πα), VI (Πε-Ρ), VII (Σ), VIII (ΤΥ), IX (ΦΩ), edited by
Gerhard Friedrich

Originally translated from
THEOLOGISCHES WÖRTERBUCH ZUM NEUEN TESTAMENT
Published in nine volumes (1933-1973) by
W. KOHLHAMMER VERLAG
Stuttgart, Germany

Library of Congress Cataloging in Publication Data

Theologisches Wörterbuch zum Neuen Testament. English
Theological dictionary of the New Testament.

Translation of: Theologisches Wörterbuch zum Neuen Testament.
1. Bible. N.T.—Dictionaries. 2. Greek language, Biblical—Dictionaries. 3. Theology—
Dictionaries.
I. Kittel, Gerhard, 1888-1948. II. Friedrich, Gerhard, 1908-   . III. Bromiley, Geoffrey
William. IV. Title.
PA881.T4713   1985   225.4'0321   85-4460

ISBN 0-8028-2404-8

British Library Cataloguing in Publication Data

[Theologisches Wörterbuch zum Neuen Testament. *English*]
Theological dictionary of the New Testament.
1. Bible. N.T.—Dictionaries
I. Title II. Kittel, Gerhard III. Friedrich, Gerhard IV. Bromiley, Geoffrey W.
221.3'21   B82312

ISBN 0-85364-322-9

Contents

Preface

Many years of use have confirmed the value of the *Theological Dictionary of the New Testament* in both the German and the English versions. At the same time its size and the technical nature of much of the material have inhibited many Bible students who might have profited from its essential insights. To overcome these difficulties this single-volume condensation of the nine volumes, this "little Kittel," has been prepared and is being offered to what it is hoped will be a much wider Christian public.

The purpose of *TDNT* is to mediate between ordinary lexicography and the specific task of exposition, particularly at the theological level. The discussion of each New Testament word of religious or theological significance includes comments on the word's secular Greek background; its role in the Old Testament, both in the Hebrew and the Septuagint texts; its usage in such sources as Philo, Josephus, the pseudepigraphal and rabbinical literature; and finally its varied uses in the New Testament and, where pertinent, in the Apostolic Fathers.

In preparing this summary, which amounts to roughly one-sixth of the original, the following changes have been made. All Greek words, including those in the main entries, have been transliterated. And while the order of the entries is the same as in the original (and thus not strictly alphabetical in English), their more prominent (and especially New Testament) meanings have been added in brackets for ready reference. These meanings have also been placed in the running heads at the tops of the pages and in the alphabetized Table of English keywords. An alphabetized Table of Greek keywords replaces the Tables of Contents found at the beginnings of each of the original volumes.

Philological, archeological, and other supporting materials have been drastically reduced, as well as references when fewer are sufficient. Footnotes and bibliographies have both been excluded; interested students can find what they require in the original articles. The focus is on the biblical and especially the New Testament usage, so that the related classical, Hellenistic, apocalyptic, rabbinic, and patristic fields receive more cursory attention. In the biblical sphere itself the emphasis falls on the theological meaning in accordance with the main purpose of the enterprise.

So as to facilitate easy transition for those who might desire more detailed information, the relevant volume and page numbers in the full set are found at the end of each article or section. The names of the authors are also given in recognition that this is not an original work but a condensation of the work of others. But their names are put in brackets (with page references) so as to indicate that these scholars, many of whom are now deceased, bear no direct responsibility for the summarized version. Students might bear this in mind should they wish to refer to this version or to quote from it. Every effort has been made, of course, to reflect the contributors' materials and interpretations as faithfully as the circumstances of condensation permit.

This shorter version is being released in the confidence that these materials can both extend and deepen our understanding of the theology and message of the New Testament, and in this way contribute to the proclamation of the gospel and the edification of the church.

Pasadena, California   GEOFFREY W. BROMILEY

Table of Greek Keywords

The Theological Dictionary of the New Testament treats every New Testament Greek word of theological significance. In the body of the work these words are grouped into families. Here they are listed alphabetically as transliterated, together with the pages on which they are introduced in the boxes.

anthrṓpinos, 59
ánthrōpos, 59
antí, 61
antíchristos, 1322
antídikos, 62
antikaléō, 394
antíkeimai, 425
antilambánomai, 62
antílēmpsis, 62
antiloidoréō, 538
antílytron, 543
antimisthía, 599
antítypos, 1193
anypókritos, 1235
anypótaktos, 1156
AŌ, 1
aóratos, 706
apaídeutos, 753
apaitéō, 30
apallássō, 40
apallotrióō, 43
apangéllō, 10
apántēsis, 64
aparábatos, 772
aparchḗ, 81
apaspázomai, 84
apatáō, 65
apátē, 65
apátōr, 805
apaúgasma, 87
apéchō, 286
apeírastos, 822
apeítheia, 818
apeithéō, 818
apeithḗs, 818
apekdéchomai, 146
apekdýō, 192
apékdysis, 192
apeleútheros, 224
apelpízō, 229
apérchomai, 257
aperítmētos, 831
áphesis, 88
aphíēmi, 88
aphilágathos, 3
aphístēmi, 88
aphomoióō, 684
aphorízō, 728
aphormḗ, 730
áphrōn, 1277
aphrosýnē, 1277
aphtharsía, 1259
áphthartos, 1259
aphthoría, 1259
aphypnóō, 1233
aphysteréō, 1240
apistéō, 849
apistía, 849
ápistos, 849
apodéchomai, 146
apódektos, 146
apodídōmi, 166

apodiorízō, 728
apodochḗ, 146
apodokimázō, 181
apogínomai, 117
apokálypsis, 405
apokalýptō, 405
apokaradokía, 66
apokatallássō, 40
apokatástasis, 65
apokathístēmi, 65
apókeimai, 425
apokóptō, 453
apókrima, 469
apokrínō, 469
apókrisis, 469
apókryphos, 476
apokrýptō, 476
apṓleia, 67
apóllymi, 67
Apollýōn, 67
apoloúō, 538
apolýtrōsis, 543
apophthéngomai, 75
apoplanáō, 857
apoplanáomai, 857
apopnígō, 895
aporíptō, 987
aposkíasma, 1044
apostasía, 88
apostéllō, 67
apostolḗ, 67
apóstolos, 67
apostréphō, 1093
aposynágōgos, 1108
apotássō, 1156
apōthéō, 75
apothnḗskō, 312
apotolmáō, 1183
apotomía, 1169
apótomos, 1169
apotómōs, 1169
apróskopos, 946
aprosōpolḗmptōs, 950
apseudḗs, 1339
ápseustos, 1339
ará, 75
archaíos, 81
archángelos, 12
archḗ, 81
archēgós, 81
archiereús, 349
archipoímēn, 901
archisynágōgos, 1108
árchō, 81
árchōn, 81
arḗn, 54
arníon, 54
areskeía, 77
aréskō, 77
arestós, 77
aretḗ, 77
argéō, 76

argós, 76
arithméō, 78
arithmós, 78
arkéō, 78
arketós, 78
arnéomai, 79
arrabṓn, 80
árti, 658
artigénnētos, 114
ártios, 80
ártos, 80
asébeia, 1010
asebéō, 1010
asebḗs, 1010
asélgeia, 83
ásēmos, 1015
askéō, 84
asōtía, 87
ásōtos, 87
aspasmós, 84
aspázomai, 84
aspháleia, 87
asphalḗs, 87
asphalízō, 87
asphalṓs, 87
áspilos, 85
ásplanchnos, 1067
astatéō, 86
astḗr, 86
astḗriktos, 1085
asthénēma, 83
asthéneia, 83
asthenéō, 83
asthenḗs, 83
astrapḗ, 86
ástron, 86
asýnetos, 1119
ataktéō, 1156
átaktos, 1156
atáktōs, 1156
athanasía, 312
athánatos, 312
athémitos, 25
átheos, 322
áthesmos, 25
athetéō, 1176
athétēsis, 1176
athléō, 25
áthlēsis, 25
augázō, 87
autárkeia, 78
autárkēs, 78
authádēs, 87
autokatákritos, 469
autóptēs, 706
auxánō, 1229
axióō, 63
áxios, 63
ázymos, 302

Babylṓn, 89

baínō, 90
Balaám, 91
ballántion, 91
bállō, 91
báptisma, 92
baptismós, 92
baptistḗs, 92
baptízō, 92
báptō, 92
bárbaros, 94
baréō, 95
báros, 95
barýs, 95
basanismós, 96
basanistḗs, 96
basileús, 97
basanízō, 96
básanos, 96
basileía, 97
basíleios, 97
basileúō, 97
basilikós, 97
basílissa, 97
baskaínō, 102
bastázō, 102
báthos, 89
battalogéō, 103
bdélygma, 103
bdelyktós, 103
bdelýssomai, 103
bebaióō, 103
bébaios, 103
bebaíōsis, 103
bebēlóō, 104
bébēlos, 104
Beelzeboúl, 104
Belíar, 104
bélos, 104
biastḗs, 105
biázomai, 105
biblíon, 106
bíblos, 106
bióō, 290
bíos, 290
blasphēméō, 107
blasphēmía, 107
blásphēmos, 107
blépō, 706
boáō, 108
boḗtheia, 108
boēthéō, 108
boēthós, 108
boulḗ, 108
boúlēma, 108
boúlomai, 108
brabeíon, 110
brabeúō, 110
brachíōn, 110
bréphos, 759
brṓma, 111
brontḗ, 110
brṓsis, 111

Table of English Keywords

In the boxes at the heads of all the main entries, the English keywords (essential meanings) have been placed in brackets next to the entries so that they can be seen at a glance. These keywords are also listed below, together with the pages on which they are found, as a further aid in locating Dictionary discussions.

dog, 494
  house dog, 494
doing, 895
dominions, 486
donkey, 700
  little donkey, 700
door, 340
double-minded, 1342
doubt, 155
dove, 830
down, 422
dragon, 186
draw back, to, 1074
dream, 690, 1233
dream, to, 1233
drink, 841
drink, to, 263, 841
  to cause to drink, 841
drinkable, 841
drinking party, 841
drinking vessel, 841
drunkard, 576
drunkenness, 576
  to be drunk, 576
  to get drunk, 576
dung, 1052
during, 149
dwell, to, 674, 1040
  to cause to dwell, 1040
  to make to dwell, 674
dwelling, 674
  dwelling place, 674

each, 795
eager, 937
eagerness, 937
ear, 744
  outer ear, 744
earlier, 769
earth, 116
  made of earth, 1318
  under the earth, 421
earthly, 113, 459, 1000, 1318
earthquake, 1014
eat, to, 143, 263, 1191
eaten
  moth-eaten, 1025
  worm-eaten, 1054
eating, 111
ecstasy, 217
edible plant, 504
edify, to, 674
edifying, 674
education, 753
elder, 931
  council of elders, 931
  fellow elder, 931
elect, 505
elect, to, 505
elected, 505
elements, 1087
  elemental substances, 1087

Elijah, 306
eloquent, 505
embitter, to, 839
embryo, 759
empty, 426
  empty prattle, 571
  empty prattler, 571
  to make empty, 426
enclose, to, 1098, 1117
encounter, 1191
encounter, to, 846
end, 1161
endurance, 219, 581
endure, to, 58, 417, 581
enlist for military service, to,
    1091
Enoch, 237
enslave, to, 182
enter into, to, 232
entertain, to, 661
entrance, 666
entrap, to, 752
equal, 370
  equal in value, 370
equality, 370
equip, to, 80
equipment, 80
error, 18
Esau, 311
essence, 1237
establish, to, 103, 1085
eternal, 25, 31
eunuch, 277
evangelist, 267
event, 927
everybody, 795
evident, 1244
evil, 391, 912
  to do evil, 391
  evil-doer, 391
  evil speech, 495
  to speak evil, 495
exalt, to, 1241
examine, to, 552
example, 128, 141
exceed, to, 1230
exceedingly, 1230
excellence, 77
excess, 828, 1230
exchange, 40
exchange, to, 40
excommunicated, 1108
exercise, 133
exercise, to, 84
  to exercise authority, 238
  to exercise naked, 133
  to exercise self-control, 196
exhort, to, 778
exhortation, 778
exist, to, 206
exit, 666
exorcist, 729

expect, to, 943
expectation, 943
  eager expectation, 66
expelled from the synagogue,
    1108
experience, to, 116, 798
expiate, to, 362
expiation, 362
  means of expiation, 833
explain, to, 543
explanation, 543
expose, to, 141
  to expose publicly, 318
expound, to, 303
extort, to, 1100
eye, 706
  apple of the eye, 706
  eye-service, 182
eyewitness, 706

fabricated, 862
fabrication, 862
face, 950
  to strike on the face, 1239
faculty, 29
fail to hear, to, 34
faith, 849
  littleness of faith, 849
  of little faith, 849
faithful, 849
faithless, 849
fall, 846, 946
fall, to, 846
  to fall asleep, 1233
  to fall away, 88, 846
  to fall down, 846
false, 1339
  to bear false witness, 564
  bearing a false name, 694
  false apostle, 67
  false prophet, 952
  false teacher, 161
  false testimony, 564
  false witness, 564
falsehood, 1339
falsification, 983
family, 117, 674
  from the family, 805
famine, 820
far off, 549
farewell, to bid, 84
fashion, to, 607, 862
fast, to, 632
fasting, 632
fat, to make, 816
father, 1, 805
  belonging to the father, 805
  from the father, 805
fatherless, 805
fathomless, 58
fault, to commit a, 846
favor, to bestow, 1298

favor, to show, 1298
fear, 275, 1272
   fear of divinity, 137
fear, to, 1272
feature, characteristic, 1308
feel regret, to, 589
feeling for, to have a kindly, 683
feelings, to have similar, 798
fellow captive, 31
fellow disciple, 552
fellow elder, 931
fellow imitators, 593
fellow slave, 182
fellow soldier, 1091
fellow worker, 1116
fellowship, 447
female friend, 1262
female slave, 182
ferment, to, 302
festal gathering, 770
fever, 981
   to have a fever, 981
   intermission of fever, 523
few, 682
fiery, 975
   fiery-red, 975
fig, 1100
   late fig, 1100
   sycomore fig, 1100
fig tree, 1100
fight, 20, 25
   fist-fight, 973
   fighting against God, 573
fight, to, 20, 573, 904
   to fight against God, 573
fighting, 573
figure, 862
fill, to, 840, 867
   to fill completely, 867
   to fill up, 840, 867
   to fill with, 867
filling, 867
finally, 1240
find, to, 278
finger, 140
fire, 975
   to set on fire, 975
firm, 103, 1077
   to make firm, 1077
firmament, 1077
first, 965
   at first, 965
   to be first, 965
   to be the first to hope, 229
   first place, 965
firstborn, 965
firstfruits, 81
fist-fight, 973
fit together, to, 1113
fitness, 361
fitting, 59
   to be fitting, 385

flatter, to, 451, 994
flattery, 451
flesh, 1000
fleshly, 1000
fleshy, 1000
flock, 901
fold, 452
follow, to, 33
   to follow zealously, 177
folly, 636, 1277
food, 111
fool, 983
foolish, 620, 636, 1277
   foolish talk, 620
   to make foolish, 620
foolishness, 620
foot, 925
footprint, 379
footwear, 702
for, 827, 1228
   for the present, 243
forbearance, 58, 119, 550
forbearing, 550
force, to use, 105
forehead, 591
foreign, 43
foreigner, 661
foreknow, to, 119
foreknowledge, 119
foreordain, to, 728
forerunner, 1189
foresee, to, 636, 706
foresight, 636
foreskin, 36
foretell, to, 10
forgiveness, 88
form, 202, 607, 1129
   having the same form, 1102
form, to, 607, 862
formed, 862
fornication, 918
   to commit fornication, 918
fornicator, 918
fortress, 752
forty, 1172
   forty years, 1172
forward, to go, 939
foundation, 322, 418
   to lay the foundation, 322
founder, 81
fountain, 837
four, 1172
fourth, 1172
   fourth day, 1172
fragment, 523
fragrance, 285, 735
free, 224
   to set free, 148, 224
freedman, 224
freedom, 224
fresh, 628
friend, 265

female friend, 1262
friendship, 1262
from, 771
   from a distance, 549
   from above, 63
   from behind, 702
   from the family, 805
   from the father, 805
fruit, 117, 416
fruit, to bear, 416
fulfil, to, 867, 1161
fulfilment, 1161
full, 867, 1161
   full armor, 702
   full of idols, 202
fullness, 867
   supreme fullness, 867
   to bring to fullness, 867

gain, 428
gain, to, 428
   to gain by trading, 927
gate, 974
gateway, 974
gather, to, 1101
   festal gathering, 770
   gathering place, 1108
Gehenna, 113
genealogy, 114
   without genealogy, 114
generous, 447
Gentile, 201
gentle, 243, 929
   to deal gently, 798
gentleness, 243, 798, 929
genuine, 125
ghost, 1244
gift, 166, 459, 1298
girdle, 702
   to gird oneself, 702
   to gird oneself about, 702
give, to, 166
   to give an inheritance, 442
   to give back, 166
   to give freely, 1298
   to give laws, 646
   to give life, 290
   to give offense, 946, 1036
   to give orders, 776
   to give thanks, 1298
giving offense, 946
gladness, 278
   to be glad, 278
gleam, 1293
glisten, to, 1085
glorified, to be, 178
   to be glorified with, 1102
glorify, to, 178
glorious, 178
glory, 178
   to share in glory, 178
gnash, to, 110

to make to dwell, 674
to make valid, 494
to make white, 530
to make wise, 1056
Maker, 895
maker, 149
   tent-maker, 1040
making, 895
   making of money, 1319
malice, 391
mammon, 552
man, 59
   man-pleasing, 77
   the Son of Man, 1215
   violent man, 105
management, 674
manager, 674
manger, 1251
manifestation, 141
manly, to act, 59
manna, 563
manner of life, 20, 666
many, 866
   the many, 906
mark, 1015, 1047, 1085, 1193,
   1308
market, 549
marriage, 111
marry, to, 111
master, 145, 248, 982
   master of the household, 145
matter, 1319
   to handle a matter, 1319
meal, 143, 1187
means of expiation, 833
means of judgment, 469
measure, 590
   beyond measure, 1230
   beyond all measure, 828
   measure, to, 590
meat offered to idols, 202
mediate, to, 585
mediator, 585
meek, 929
meekness, 929
meeting, 64, 1108
Melchizedek, 580
member, 577, 674
memorial, 596
mention, 596
mention, to, 596
merciful, 222
merciless, 1067
mercy, 222
   mercy seat, 362
   to show mercy, 222
message, 10
to send a message, 1074
messenger, 12
Messiah, 1322
mighty, 466
military leader, 1091

military service, 1091
   to enlist for military service,
   1091
milk, 111
mind, 636, 1277
   to be of sound mind, 1150
   to change one's mind, 636
   double-minded, 1342
   to keep in mind, 1174
   of sound mind, 1150
   with one mind, 684
minister, 526
minister, to, 526
ministry, 526
   in ministry, 526
mirror, 27, 264
   to see something in a mirror,
   264
misfortune, to suffer, 798
   to suffer misfortune with, 798
mislead, to, 857, 1093
   to be misled, 857
mixing together, 1113
mock, to, 758
mocker, 758
mocking, 758
model, 1193
moderate, 1150
moderation, 1150
modesty, 26
money, 1319
   money making, 1319
month, 591
moon, 591
   new moon, 591
more than conquerors, to be,
   634
morning star, 1293
mortal, 312
Moses, 622
most varied, 901
moth, 1025
   moth-eaten, 1025
mother, 592
motion, to set in, 435
mountain, 732
mourn, to, 335, 453
mourning, 335, 453
mouth, 1089
mud, 838
mulberry, 1100
multicolored, 901
multiply, to, 866
murmur, to, 125
mustard, 1027
must be, it, 140
mutilate, to, 452
mutilation, 1169
myrrh, 1055
   to treat with myrrh, 1055
mystery, 615
myth, 610

naked, 133
   to exercise naked, 133
nakedness, 133
name, 694
   bearing a false name, 694
name, to, 694
narrative, 303
narrow, 1077
   narrow place, 1077
nation, 201, 499
natural, 1283, 1342
naturally, 1283
nature, 1283
   of the same nature, 684
Nazarene, 625
Nazareth, of, 625
near, 194, 942
   to bring near, 194
   to come near, 194
necessary, it is, 140
need, 1240
need, to, 144
needy, 824
neighbor, 872
new, 628, 950
   new in nature, 388
   new moon, 591
newness, 388
nickname, to, 694
night, 661
nose, to turn up one's, 614
now, 658
number, 78

oath, 729
   to charge under oath, 729
   confirmation by oath, 729
   to swear an oath, 683
obedience, 34
obedient, 34
obey, to, 34, 818
object of worship, 1010
obligation, 746
   to be under obligation, 746
   someone under obligation,
   746
observance, 1174
obsolete, 769
obstacle, 453
obtain, to, 1191
occasion, 730
occupied with, to be, 927
of little faith, 849
of Nazareth, 625
of sound mind, 1150
   to be of sound mind, 1150
of the same nature, 684
offense
   cause of offense, 1036
   to give offense, 946, 1036
   giving offense, 946
   not giving offense, 946

presence, 791
present, for the, 243
present, to, 1176
present, to be, 234, 791
presentable, 278
press, 531
press, to, 334
pressure, 334
presume, to, 1183
presumptuous, 1183
pride, 1231
priest, 349
   to discharge the priestly
      office, 349
   high priest, 349
priesthood, 349
   royal priesthood, 349
prison, 1117, 1280
prisoner, 145
prize, 110
proclaim, to, 10, 430
   to proclaim beforehand, 267,
      430
   to proclaim good news, 267
   to proclaim publicly, 430
proclamation, 430
procreation, 1065
profane, 104
profit, to, 1252
profitable, 1252
progress, 939
   to make progress, 939
prominence, 1230
prominent, 278
promise, 240
promise, to, 240, 687
   to promise beforehand, 238
proof, 564
proper
   it is proper, 238
   what is proper, 385
prophecy, 952
prophesy, to, 952
prophet, 952
   false prophet, 952
prophetess, 952
prophetic, 952
proportion, 56
proselyte, 943
prosper, to, 666
prostitution, 918
protect, to, 988, 1174, 1280
prototype, 1193
proud, 1231
proverb, 790
providence, 636
provoke, to, 394
   to provoke to jealousy, 297
psalm, 1225
public reading, 55
publicly
   to expose publicly, 318

to proclaim publicly, 430
to set forth publicly, 128
publish abroad, to, 10
pulverize, to, 535
punish, to, 451
punishment, 418, 451
pupil, 552
   to become a pupil, 552
pure, 19, 33, 206, 381
purification, 19, 381
purify, to, 19, 381
purity, 19, 206, 381
purpose, 108
purse, 91
put, to
   to put down, 543
   to put in another place, 1176
   to put off, 192
   to put on, 192
   to put on in addition, 192
   to put on sandals, 702
   to put out, 216
   to put to death, 627
   to put to the test, 822
   to put together, 1120
putting off, 192

qualify, to, 361
quarrel, to, 573
quarreling, 573
quarrelsome, not, 573
queen, 97
quench, to, 1009
question, 262
question, to, 262
quick-tempered, 716

rabbi, 982
race, 674
radiance, 87
Rahab, 311
rainbow, 369
raise, to, 60
   to raise the hands, 1308
   to raise to the highest
      position, 1241
   to raise up with, 1102
rank, 1156
ransom, 543
ransom, to, 543
rational, 505
reach out, to, 727
read, to, 55
readiness, 266, 937
reading, public, 55
ready, 266, 937
   to make ready, 266
reality, 1237
reap, to, 332
reason, without, 505
reasoning, 536
rebellion, 839

rebirth, 117
rebuke, 221
rebuke, to, 249
receive, to, 146, 495
   to receive an inheritance, 442
receiving (a guest), 146
recently, 950
reckon, to, 1341
recline at table with, to, 425
recognition, 119
recognize, to, 119
reconcile, to, 40
reconciliation, 40
record, to, 128
red, 975
redeem, to, 19, 543
redeemer, 543
redemption, 543
refresh, to, 1342
refreshing, 1342
refuse, 381, 833, 1052
refuse, to, 79
regret
   to feel regret, 589
   without regret, 589
regulation, 168
reject, to, 30, 75, 181
rejoice, to, 4, 1298
   to rejoice with, 1298
related to, 1097
relation, 1097
relative, 1097
release, 543
release, to, 40, 60, 543
relief, 1342
religion, 137, 337
   self-made religion, 337
religious, 337
remain, to, 581
remember, to, 596
remembrance, 56, 596
remnant, 523
remove, to, 435
renew, to, 388, 628
renewal, 117, 388
repay, to, 166
repayment, 166
repent, to, 589, 636
repentance, 636
reply, to, 469
report, to, 10
reproach, 693
reproach, to, 693
request, 30, 262
require, to, 30
reserve, 1074
residence, to take up, 1040
resident alien, 788
   to live as a resident alien, 788
resolute, 219
resolve, to, 1341
respect, worthy of, 1010

rest, 56, 60, 419
  sabbath rest, 989
rest, to, 419
  to cause to rest, 56
  to rest on, 56, 425, 1085
resting place, 419
restless, 387
restoration, 65, 727
restore, to, 65, 388
  to restore order, 1074
resurrection, 60, 195
retribution, 166, 599
return, to, 543, 1093
reveal, to, 405, 1244
revelation, 405, 1244
  to impart a revelation, 1319
reverence, 275, 1010
  reverence for God, 331
reverence, to, 1272
revile, to, 538, 693
  to revile in return, 538
reviler, 538
revive, to, 1342
revolutionary, 532
reward, 599
rewarder, 599
riches, 873
  to be rich, 873
  to make rich, 873
riddle, 27
right, 238
  right (hand, side), 143
  right moment, 389
  to have the right, 238
righteous, 168
  righteous judgment, 168
righteousness, 168
rise, to, 57, 195
  to rise up, 590
rising, 57
river, 921
road, 666
robber, 532
  robber of temples, 349
  to rob temples, 349
robe, 1088
rock, 833
rod, 982
root, 985
  to cause to take root, 985
rot, to, 1000
rotting, 1000
royal, 97
  royal priesthood, 349
ruin, 1124
rule, 414
  rule of God, 466
rule, to, 81, 97, 110, 938
  to rule one's household, 145
  to rule with, 1102
  to rule with someone, 97
ruler, 81, 186

ruler of the synagogue, 1108
  world rule, 466
run, to, 1189
  to run up against, 1191
rush, violent, 730
  to rush headlong, 730
rust, 368
rust, to, 368
Ruth, 311

sabbath, the, 989
  sabbath rest, 989
sack, 838
sackcloth, 995
sacrifice, 342, 1252
  sacrificed to deity, 349
sacrifice, to, 342
sad-looking, 1053
Sadducee, 992
safeguard, to, 87
salt, 36
salvation, 1132
Samaria, 999
Samaritan, 999
  Samaritan woman, 999
sanctification, 14
sanctify, to, 14
sandal, 702
  to put on sandals, 702
Sanhedrin, 1115
Satan, 150, 1007
satiety, 840
satisfaction, 840
satisfy, to, 840
save, to, 428, 988, 1132
saving, 1132
Savior, 1132
saying, 505
scabby, 529
scale, 529
scales (balance), 301
scaly, 529
scarlet, 450
scatter, to, 1048, 1065
scattering, 1048
school, 27
scoffer, 421
scorn, 758
scourge, to, 571
scribe, 127
Scripture, 128
scroll, 106
Scythian, 1053
seal, 1127
seal, to, 1127
  to seal up, 1127
search, to, 255
seat, 386
  best seat, 965
  mercy seat, 362
secret, 476, 615

to learn the secret, 615
secretly, 476
  to bring in secretly, 786
  brought in secretly, 786
sect, 27
securely, 87
seduction, 857
see, to, 706
  to see something in a mirror,
    264
  to stoop to see, 784
seed, 450, 1065
seek, to, 300
seize, to, 80, 466, 495, 1101
select, to, 1308
self-condemned, 469
self-control, 196, 1150
  to exercise self-control, 196
  lacking self-control, 196
self-controlled, 196, 633
self-disciplined, 1150
self-indulgence, 196
self-made religion, 337
self-seeking, 256
self-willed, 87
sell, to, 846
send, to, 67, 915, 1074
  to send a message, 1074
  to send out, 67
sense, 29
  to bring someone to his
    senses, 1150
separate, to, 728
series, to be in a, 1087
serpent, 186, 748
servant, 152, 331, 526, 1231
  servant of God, 763
serve, to, 152, 331, 503, 526,
    1231
service, 152, 502, 526
  to enlist for military service,
    1091
  in service, 526
  military service, 1091
  to perform holy service, 349
set, to, 386
  to set aside, 1176
  to set before, 1176
  to set forth, 57
  to set forth publicly, 128
  to set free, 148, 224
  to set in motion, 435
  to set on fire, 975
  to set out, 730
seven, 249
  seven times, 249
seven thousand, 249
seventy, 249
  seventy times, 249
severe, 1169
severely, 1169
severity, 1169

stone, 534
  stone of stumbling, 946
stone, to, 533
  to stone to death, 533
stony, 534
stoop to see, to, 784
stop, to, 419
store up, to, 1174
straight, 727
  to cut a straight path, 1169
straightening, 727
strange
  of a strange tongue, 123
  to teach a strange doctrine,
    161
stranger, 661
strangle, to, 895
strangled, 895
stream, swept away by a, 921
strength, 378, 466
stretch out, to, 219
strike, to, 946, 1195
  to strike on the face, 1239
  to strike with a stick, 982
strip, to, 192
strive, to, 25, 727
  to strive after, 297
  to strive against, 20
  to strive side by side, 25
strong, 378, 466
  to be strong, 378, 417, 466
  to become strong, 466
stronghold, 752
study, to, 636
stumble, to, 968
  to cause to stumble, 1036
  to stumble against, 946
stumbling block, 1036
  stone of stumbling, 946
stupor, spirit of, 419
subdue, to, 20
subject
  not subject, 1156
  subject to suffering, 798
subject, to, 1156
subjection, 1156
substances, elemental, 1087
suffer, to, 798
  to suffer before, 798
  to suffer birthpangs, 1353
  to suffer loss, 299
  to suffer misfortune, 798
  to suffer misfortune with, 798
  to suffer pain, 673
  to suffer shipwreck, 627
  to suffer violence, 105
  to suffer with, 798, 1102
suffering, 655, 798
  subject to suffering, 798
  suffering hunger, 632
sufficient, 78, 361
  to be sufficient, 78

suitable, 80
sum up, to, 429
summon, to, 394
superabound, to, 828, 864
superabundant, 828
  to be superabundant, 828
superior, to be, 378
supplication, 362
support, to, 62, 495, 1085
supreme fullness, 867
sure, 87
surpass, to, 1230
surplus, 828
surprise, to, 661
suspect, to, 636
suspicion, 636
swear an oath, to, 683
swept away by a stream, 921
sword, 572, 987
sycomore fig, 1100
sympathetic, 680, 798
  to be sympathetic, 680
sympathize, to, 798
sympathy, 222, 680
synagogue, 1108
  expelled from the synagogue,
    1108
  ruler of the synagogue, 1108

Tabernacles, 1040
table, 1187
take, to, 495
  taking a stand, 1070
  taking offense, 946
  to take down, 380
  to take over, 495
  to take part, 495
  to take up, 495, 1252
  to take up residence, 1040
talk, foolish, 620
Tamar, 311
task, 927
tassel, 466
taste, to, 116
taught, 161
  taught by God, 322
tax collector, 1166
teach, to, 161
  able to teach, 161
  to teach aright, 1169
  to teach strange doctrine, 161
teacher, 161, 753
  false teacher, 161
  teacher of the law, 161
  teacher of what is good, 161
teaching, 161
tearing down, 380
tell, to, 10
temple, 625, 1040
  to rob temples, 349
  the temple, 349
  temple herald, 430

temple of an idol, 202
temple robber, 349
temple treasury, 459
temporary, 389
tempt, to, 822
temptation, 822
  without temptation, 822
ten, 143
tend, to, 901
tender-hearted, 1067
tent, 1040
  pitching tents, 1040
tent-maker, 1040
test, 822
test, to, 181, 822
  to put to the test, 822
testament, 157
tested, 181
testimony, 564
  false testimony, 564
testing, 181, 822
thank, to, 687
  to give thanks, 1298
thankful, 1298
thanksgiving, 1298
theater, 318
thief, 441
think, to, 303, 636, 1277
thinking, 1277
third, 1188
thirst, 177
  to be thirsty, 177
thorn, 1047
thought, 636, 1277
  hidden thought, 339
thoughtful, 1277
thousand, 1316
three, 1188
throat, 503
throne, 338
throng, 750
through, 149
  through and through, 682
throw, to, 91, 987
  to throw on, 987
  to throw oneself, 987
  to throw out, 91
thunder, 110
tie, to, 148
  to tie on, 702
time, 1337
  to have no time, 389
  period of time, 1337
today, 1024
together
  to fit together, 1113
  to groan together, 1076
  holding together, 1117
  to hold together, 1101, 1117
  to join together, 452
  mixing together, 1113
  to put together, 1120

wealth, 552, 873
weapon, 702
wear, to, 1252
weary, to become, 453
wedding, 111
week, 249
weep, to, 436
weeping, 436
weigh down, to, 95
weight, 95, 666
welcome, to, 146
well-disposed, to be, 636
well-mannered, 459
well-pleased, to be, 273
well-pleasing, 77
    to be well-pleasing, 77
well-timed, 389
what is proper, 385
what matters, 1252
whip, 571
whip, to, 571
white, 530
    to make white, 530
whole, 682
wicked, 912
wickedness, 391, 912, 983
widow, 1313
wife, 134
    the wife of Uriah, 311
wild animal, 333
will, 318
    good will, 273
    self-willed, 87
willing, 937
willingly, 221
    unwillingly, 221
wind, 876
wine, 680
winnow, to, 535
wisdom, 1056

wise, 1056
    to make wise, 1056
wisely, 286
wish, to, 279, 318
with, 233
    with one mind, 684
withhold, to, 1240
without blemish, 619
without God, 322
without reason, 505
without regret, 589
without sin, 51
without sorrow, 540
without speech, 505
without spot, 85
without temptation, 822
witness, 564
    false witness, 564
witness, to bear, 564
    to bear false witness, 564
    to bear witness against, 564
    to bear witness beforehand,
      564
    to bear witness with, 564
wolf, 540
woman, 134
    Greek woman, 227
    Samaritan woman, 999
    woman disciple, 552
    young woman, 786
womb, 446
wonder, 316, 1170
wonder, to, 316
wonderful, 178, 316
wood, 665
word, 505
    dispute about words, 505
    to dispute about words, 505
work, 251, 895

work, to, 251
    to work with, 1116
workman, 251
    fellow worker, 1116
works, 927
world, 459
    the inhabited world, 674
    world ruler, 466
worldly, 459
worm, 1054
worm-eaten, 1054
worship, 948, 1010
    object of worship, 1010
worship, to, 1010
worshipper, 948
worthy, 63
    to consider worthy, 63
    worthy of respect, 1010
wrath, 339, 716
wrestling, 770
write, to, 128
    to write beforehand, 128
    to write in, 128
writing, 128
    hand-written document, 1308
wrong, to do, 22
wrongdoing, 22

yeast, 302
yoke, 301
    to be unevenly yoked, 301
young ass, 981
young woman, 786

zeal, 297, 1069
zealot, 297
zealous, 1069
    to be zealous, 1069
Zion, 1028

α α

AŌ [Alpha and Omega]

Peculiar to Revelation, this expression is used by God for himself in 21:6 (cf. 22:13), and by Christ in 1:17 (cf. 2:8). Its use with "first and last" fixes its meaning: God begins and ends all things. While probably taken from Hellenistic speculation, perhaps by way of Palestinian Judaism, it derives its content from the OT. The link with "who is to come" gives it a new dynamic quality. "First and last" occurs in Is. 41:4 LXX; 44:6 MT; 48:12 MT; there are also Mandaean parallels. Number symbolism occurs in both rabbinic Judaism and Hellenism. The former uses the first and last letters of the alphabet to denote completeness, or with numbers for the sake of secrecy. The first letter alone stands for what is best. Truth has God's seal because it consists of the first, middle, and last letters. In view of the link with "first and last" and the reference to Is. 44:6 (in the Hebrew rather than Greek text), Revelation probably took the expression from Palestinian Judaism.　　　　　　　　　　　　[G. KITTEL, I, 1-3]
　→ *prōtos, éschatos*

Aarṓn [Aaron]

1. Heb. 5:1-9. Christ's high priesthood is compared and contrasted with Aaron's. While Aaron is called by God, he has only a partial and transitory ministry, Christ's being of a different order.
2. Heb. 9:4. This verse refers to Aaron's rod, which lay beside the pot with manna and the tables of the law and which miraculously budded (Num. 17:16-26).
3. Lk. 1:5. Elizabeth is of priestly descent; while "daughters of Aaron" is not a Jewish expression, it is formed after the analogy of Lev. 1:5.　　[K. G. KUHN, I, 3-4]

Abaddṓn [Abaddon]

Equivalent to *Apollyṓn,* this name is used in Rev. 9:11 for the king of the scorpions that plague the human race. It is taken from the OT (e.g., Job 28:22), and is a personification of the place of destruction (Job 26:6 etc.). The Gk. *Apollyṓn* is influenced by the LXX use of *apóleia* and the idea of Apollyon as the god of plague and destruction (Aeschylus *Agamemnon* 1082).　　　　　　　　[J. JEREMIAS, I, 4]

abbá [father]

A. In Judaism. This Aramaic word is a familiar term for "father"; it is also a title for rabbis and a proper name, but is almost never used for God.

B. In Christianity. Jesus probably used *abbá* for God not only in Mk. 14:36 but also whenever the Gk. *patér* occurs. It denotes childlike intimacy and trust, not disrespect. In Paul (Rom. 8:15; Gal. 4:6) it may be a liturgical reminiscence, possibly of the opening of the Lord's Prayer. It undoubtedly expresses the new relationship with God proclaimed and lived out by Jesus and then experienced by believers in him.
→ *patér*   [G. KITTEL, I, 5-6]

Ábel – Káin [Abel–Cain]

A. The Tradition in Judaism. The OT does not say why God accepted Abel's sacrifice but rejected Cain's. Josephus and Philo, however, suggest that Abel was religious while Cain was not, so that the former brought an offering of greater value.

B. Cain and Abel in the NT. Mt. 23:35 and Jude 11 reflect the Jewish view when they contrast righteous Abel and wicked Cain. Heb. 11:4 finds faith in Abel (as distinct from Cain). Also in Heb. 11:4, on the basis of Gen. 4:10, the blood of righteous Abel appeals to God for full redress in the consummated kingdom (cf. Rev. 6:9-11). In Heb. 12:24 Abel's blood serves as a type for that of Jesus—the one demanding expiation, the other making it.   [K. G. KUHN, I, 6-8]

Abraám [Abraham]

A. Abraham in Judaism. Abraham is the national and religious hero of the Jews; his tomb is revered and legends cluster around him. He is significant as a. the first proselyte and missionary; b. an observer of the unwritten Torah; c. a model of trust in ten temptations; d. the recipient of the covenant promise that is Israel's basis. His merit avails representatively for Israel, and descent from him is of decisive importance.

B. Abraham in the NT. Abraham's significance is conceded (Mt. 8:11; Mk. 12:26, etc.), but Jesus is superior to him (Jn. 8:52ff.), Peter replaces him as the rock (Mt. 16:18), and mere descent from him cannot help the unrepentant (Mt. 3:9; Jn. 8:33ff.). Though he is still an example of obedience (Jms. 2:21ff.), he is justified by faith (Rom. 4:1ff.) and is thus the father of all who believe, Gentiles as well as Jews (Gal. 3:7, 9; 4:22ff.; Rom. 4:12; Heb. 2:16; 6:13ff.). Spiritual descent, not physical, is decisive.   [J. JEREMIAS, I, 8-9]

ábyssos [abyss]

A term for the underworld as a. the prison of the disobedient (Lk. 8:31; Rev. 9:1) and b. the realm of the dead (Rom. 10:7).

Originally an adjective for an implied "earth," *ábyssos* is used in Greek for the depths of original time, the primal ocean, and the world of the dead. In the LXX it denotes the original flood, then the realm of the dead (e.g., Ps. 71:20).

In the NT it is a prison for antichrist (Rev. 11:7), demons (Lk. 8:31), scorpions (Rev. 9:3ff.), and spirits (Rev. 9:1; 20:1, 3). It is a well-like abyss from which smoke ascends (Rev. 9:1). Satan will be shut up there for a thousand-year period (Rev. 20:1,

3). In Rom. 10:7 it simply denotes the realm of the dead. Descending into the abyss is contrasted with ascending into heaven, but we can do neither to bring Christ to us.
→ *hádēs*   [J. JEREMIAS, I, 9-10]

> *agathós* [good], *agathoergéō* [to do good], *agathopoiéō* [to do good], *agathopoiós* [doer of good], *agathopoiía* [doing good], *agathōsýnē* [goodness], *philágathos* [lover of goodness], *aphilágathos* [despiser of the good]

---

agathós. As both adjective and noun, *agathós* denotes excellence (Plato *Cratylus* 412c). As an adjective it is given specific content by the word it qualifies, e.g., status or quality (cf. Mt. 25:21; 7:17). As a noun it can mean "the good" or "goods," whether material or spiritual.

A. In Greek Philosophy. The good is what gives meaning, e.g., what is pleasant (Sophists), the central idea (Plato), or such things as reason, virtue, the golden mean, and the necessary (Aristotle). People become good through instruction in the good (Plato *Gorgias* 470c).

B. In Hellenism. Being less humanistic, Hellenism gave *agathós* a religious flavor. "The good" is salvation, while "good" is "pleasing to God" in our case and "kind" in God's. In the Hermetic writings God alone is truly good; we humans become good by mortification of material things and by divinization. In Philo the divinity who is the supreme good is the personal God (*Allegorical Interpretation of Laws* 1.47). Piety, faith, and wisdom are goods whereby, with God's help, we may know and serve God (*On the Special Laws* 4.147; *On Abraham* 268; *Who Is the Heir?* 98).

C. In the OT and Judaism. The approach here is religious, as in Hellenism, but the self-revelation of the personal God is now determinative. "God is good" is the basic confession (cf. 1 Chr. 15:34). This God does "good" (cf. Ex. 18:9) in his work in history, which aims at final salvation and gives direction for life through the law. "Good" has already been done but is also awaited (Jer. 32:39, 42). Meanwhile we are shown what is "good" by the revelation of God's will in the law. Those who *do* good *are* good, but whether this is possible without God's help is debatable (Josephus *The Jewish War* 2.163ff.). Qoheleth thinks not (7:20). The rabbis see a struggle between good and evil impulses, works of love being the true good works.

D. In the NT.
a. The basic approach is again religious. Only God is truly good (Mt. 19:17). His goodness is the "kindness" which through Christ confers the "good things" of salvation (Heb. 9:11). Apostles are thus preachers of "good news" (Rom. 10:15; cf. Is. 52:7). Rightly, Matthew sees that God's exclusive goodness does not rule out Christ's sinlessness (Mt. 19:17 and par.).
b. Nothing in this world deserves to be called good (Rom. 7:18-19). The law is good, but even through the law sin works death (7:12-13). Distinctions can be made between good and bad people (Mt. 5:45), or speaking good and being evil (Mt. 12:34). Government can also be called a servant for good (Rom. 13:4). Yet these distinctions are only relative before God.

3

c. Salvation in Christ introduces a new possibility of knowing and doing the good (Rom. 12:2; Eph. 2:10; Col. 1:10). Christians must actualize this possibility (1 Th. 5:15). Its supreme content is love, which is the purpose of the law and the meaning of the Christian life. Grasping this new possibility gives a "good conscience" (Acts 23:1; 1 Tim. 1:5, 19). Yet the good of salvation is still the determinative goal (Rom. 8:28). The "good work" that God has begun will come to "completion at the day of Jesus Christ" (Phil. 1:6).

agathoergéō. This rare word refers to God's kindly action (Acts 14:17) but also to the loving liberality that is required of the rich (1 Tim. 6:18).

agathopoiéō, agathopoiós, agathopoiía. The verb and adjective are used in astrology for stars of benign influence. In the LXX the verb denotes the good in action. It is common in 1 Peter (2:15, 20; 3:6, 17) in the same sense; cf. the "doer of good" who is "of God" (3 Jn. 11). *agathopoiós* in 1 Pet. 2:14 is contrasted with the wrong-doer; the Christian is to be a "doer of right." *agathopoiía* (1 Pet. 4:19) is the right action that alone is the proper preparation for final deliverance.

agathōsýnē. This is the quality, or moral excellence, of the good person. It is the fruit of the Spirit (Gal. 5:22) or of light (Eph. 5:9), the content of the Christian life (Rom. 15:14).

philágathos. This word, found in Aristotle and Philo and used as a title of honor in Hellenistic societies, constitutes one of the qualifications of a bishop: he is to be a "lover of goodness" (Tit. 1:8).

aphilágathos. According to 2 Tim. 3:1ff. the attitude of people in the last time shows how serious this time is. Many of them, as "lovers of self," will be "haters of good[ness]." In that false love, lovelessness will celebrate its triumph.

[W. GRUNDMANN, I, 10-18]

---

agalliáomai [to rejoice],   *agallíasis* [joy]

A. *agállō* in Greek Literature. The underlying term *agállō* is common in Greek prose and poetry. It means "to adorn"; hence the middle *agállomai* means "to plume oneself," expressing joyful pride. Occasionally the reference may be to cultic joy (Euripides *Trojan Women* 452).

B. *agalliáomai* in the LXX and Judaism. This is a new biblical construct. Used mostly for Heb. *gîl*, it denotes cultic joy in God's help and acts, then joy in or before God, and (rarely) God's own joy (Is. 65:19). The cosmos itself is summoned to participate in this rejoicing, which will characterize the last day (e.g., Is. 12:6).

C. *agalliáomai* in the NT. Jn. 5:35 has a more secular joy in view, but the main use is for exulting in God's acts (Rev. 19:7). This joy is eschatological (cf. 1 Pet. 4:13; Jude 24). It is anticipated here and now in faith (cf. 1 Pet. 1:6, 8; Mt. 5:12). The Baptist's joy in the womb, and his parents' joy in him (Lk. 1:44, 58), look ahead to God's saving work in Christ. The community rejoices because it senses that it is the community of the end-time established by God's saving act. Paul does not have the term, but for a parallel cf. 1 Cor. 11:26. The cultic meaning is still present in the NT (cf. Acts 2:46). Christ himself shares the joy (cf. IIcb. 1:9; Lk. 10:21 [rejoicing in the Holy Spirit]).

D. *agalliáomai* in the Early Church. Ignatius of Antioch uses the word eschatologically (*Ephesians* 9.2). The Shepherd of Hermas speaks of the devout rejoicing in spirit (*Mandates* 5.1.2). The Martyrdom of Polycarp gives us the eschatological sense (18.3), while a more general use occurs in Clement of Alexandria (*Paedagogus* 1.8.70.1). [R. BULTMANN, I, 19-21]

---

agapáō [to love], *agápē* [love], *agapētós* [beloved]

A. Love in the OT.

1. In the OT the main Hebrew root for love (*'hb*) can refer to both persons and things in a religious as well as a secular sense. Another fairly common root is *rḥm*, but since this carries the sense of mercy, *eleeín* is more usual for it. Love in the OT is a spontaneous feeling which impels to self-giving, to grasping that which causes it, or to pleasurable activity. It involves the inner person. Since it has a sexual basis, it is directed supremely to persons; love for things or acts has a metaphorical aspect. God's love is correlative to his personal nature, and love for God is love first for his person and only then for his word or law. Yet even in the extended sense love has an element of fervor or passion except in the case of lesser objects. In the secular sphere love is for husband or wife, parents or children, friends, masters, servants, and social groups. This use is more common than the religious use and may thus be taken as the basis of interpretation.

2. *The Secular and Immanent Conception.*

a. Here sexual love comes first and brings the element of impulsion to light. Sexuality can be given a heavy stress, as in Ezekiel (and cf. Hosea and Jeremiah). It is a given factor and contributes to the ennobling of life, as shown by its glorification in poetry (cf. Song of Songs 8:5). Both this love and its opposite can have brutal force, as in the story of Amnon and Tamar, or the saying of Samson's bride in Judg. 14:16. The law takes note of these erotic symptoms (Dt. 21:15ff. etc.).

b. Love in other relationships (e.g., parents and children) takes a different form, but the Hebrews must have felt some kinship, since they used the same term. Perhaps the link lies in love's spontaneous and irrational character, as in the case of Jonathan and David (1 Sam. 18:1, 3; 20:17). David himself expresses something of this in his lament in 2 Sam. 1:26. He is as closely related to Jonathan as to his own soul (1 Sam. 20:17).

c. The same intensity is not always present with more distant relatives and friends, but under the protection of theonomic law love is still the inalienable human element and the norm of social dealings. Relationships need legal definition, but a demand like Lev. 19:18 transcends all law, for it involves an attitude and not mere acts (cf. its opposite in Lev. 19:17). The final concern of the injunction is to foster neighborly feeling as the true basis of legal relations. Purely legal statutes will be only half measures unless informed and empowered by the paradoxical law of love. To interpret love here as mere favoring will not do, for it extends to the resident alien too (Lev. 19:34). This rules out narrow particularism; the neighbor is anyone in the immediate vicinity. Ultimately this means love even for those who from a human standpoint might seem to be enemies, for if Dt. 22:1-4 imposes a duty to help fellow nationals, Ex. 23:4-5 specifically applies this obligation to those who might be hostile. Since the neighbor can thus be foe as well as friend, the human person is set above the legal person as the object of love and consequently as the object of legal action. Joseph offers an example of the love which in obedience to God embraces even those who wrong us (Gen. 50:19). In the OT, of course, there are limits to this love of enemies. Ps. 109 and Prov. 14:20 illustrate this, as does the general attitude to hostile nations. Nevertheless, the nobility of the divinely imposed ethical requirement remains.

3. The Religious Conception.

a. In the light of secular usage, love obviously will have high theological value in the religious realm. The concept of the covenant limits its development, for if the covenant itself is a juridical expression of God's love, its relationship to love is only tacitly recognized. Love runs both ways, embracing both our love for God and God's love for us, but only Deuteronomy seems to link the two (7:9; 10:14ff.).

b. Our love for God is accepted without any attempt at closer definition. It is sometimes connected with fear (Dt. 10:12), but more often it involves delight and striving, a seeking of God for himself (cf. Abraham). Those who love God trust in him and find salvation and assurance. Hence they keep his commandments (Dt. 5:10), serve him (Dt. 10:12), and walk in his ways (Dt. 10:12; 11:22). Yet love itself is no mere externality. It is deeply inward and God-given, a circumcising of the heart (Jer. 31:33). It is certainly made the object of a command (cf. Dt. 6:5), but the law that results transcends law, though those who take it legally might not see this. The aim of the command is to make the most positive force in religion fruitful for covenant faithfulness. In the long run, however, everything depends on the free impulsion of love itself.

c. God's love for us is primarily national rather than individual. Within the nation, however, God loves certain groups such as the pure in heart, the poor, and even resident aliens (Dt. 10:18). God loves us as a father loves his son (Prov. 3:12), but didactic views of the parent-child relation, at least in this context, prevented the development of any deep sense of divine fatherhood.

d. Hosea gives very strong expression to God's love for his people. Official religion has disintegrated, but God's unfathomable love remains, illustrated by Hosea's nonsensical marriage. God's love is thus shown to be the enduring basis of the covenant. This love takes precedence over our love for God, for even when the latter fades (Hos. 6:4), the former does not let go (11:8-9). The threat "I will love them no more" (9:15) would amount, then, almost to God's ceasing to be God; in this light ch. 14 (cf. vv. 4-5) is the appropriate conclusion to Hosea. God is similarly torn between holiness and love in Jeremiah. He hates the rebellion of his people, but he loves Israel with "an everlasting love," and this underlies his faithfulness (Jer. 31:3). In Isaiah God has left Israel for a moment in wrath, but again, although a mother may forget her child, God will never forget or abandon Zion his bride (Is. 49:15). Deuteronomy applies all this pedagogically. God's gracious love is the reason for Israel's election (Dt. 7:7). He has confirmed it by a legal guarantee (7:8), and Israel may thus count on it, but the covenant imposes a demand for faithfulness on Israel's part, so that love can be related to the blessing which is the reward of obedience (Dt. 7:13) in what is close to a contractual sense. Yet the initiative of God's love is strongly stated (Dt. 10:14ff.), and inner circumcision, not just external performance, is necessary for a proper response to it (Dt. 10:16). The legal implications of God's love are expressly worked out in Malachi relative to the particular problems of that later time (cf. Mal. 1:2).

e. God's love for other nations does not find direct expression in the OT. The presentation certainly bears a tendency toward universality, and this comes out clearly in some messianic passages, e.g., Is. 42:5. In context, however, Dt. 33:3 ("all those consecrated to him") does not have a universal sense, while Mal. 2:10 refers to God's creative work rather than his fatherly love. Even messianic universalism is too little developed to affect the main emphasis of God's love in the OT, namely, God's specific love for his people Israel.　　　　　　　　　　　　　　　　[G. QUELL, I, 21-35]

B. The Words for Love in Prebiblical Greek.

1. erán. This is the passionate love that desires the other for itself. The god Eros compels all but is compelled by none. In Plato *érōs* symbolizes fulfilment, in Plotinus desire for union with the one. What is sought in *érōs* is intoxication or ecstasy. Reflection is good, but ecstatic frenzy, while sometimes viewed with horror, is greater. *érōs* masters us and confers supreme bliss thereby. Religion seeks the climax of experience in transmuted eroticism (cf. the fertility cults). But *érōs* can transcend the sensory world. In Plato it issues in creative inspiration. In Aristotle it has (or is) a cosmic function as the force of attraction that maintains orderly movement. In Plotinus it is an impulsion beyond the senses toward the point of coincidence. Even in these forms, however, the original idea is that of erotic intoxication.

2. philein. This signifies solicitous love, e.g., of the gods, or of friends. It embraces all humanity and entails obligation.

3. agapán. This term has neither the magic of *erán* nor the warmth of *philein*. It has first the weak sense "to be satisfied," "to receive," "to greet," "to honor," or, more inwardly, "to seek after." It can carry an element of sympathy, but also denotes "to prefer," especially with reference to the gods. Here is a love that makes distinctions, choosing its objects freely. Hence it is especially the love of a higher for a lower. It is active, not self-seeking love. Yet in the Greek writers the word is colorless. It is often used as a variation for *erán* or *philein* and commands no special discussion. The noun *agápē* occurs very seldom.

C. Love in Judaism.

1. The Background. The normative Hebrew term *'hb* (see A.) covers all three Greek words. But it lacks the element of religious eroticism and denotes a particular, not a universal love. OT love is a jealous love (cf. Song of Songs 8:6). Thus Jacob's love focuses on Rachel and Joseph (Gen. 29; 37:3). Similarly, God loves Israel, but jealously insists on love and loyalty in return. Again, love of neighbor is not cosmopolitan. It does not embrace millions but is love within the nation. The LXX uses *agapán* almost exclusively for the Hebrew term. This word was best adapted to express what was meant, and received a rich new content from the association.

2. Hellenistic Judaism.

a. The OT influence intermingled here with Greek and Near Eastern thought and language. God loves his creation, his people, and those who are righteous, obedient, and merciful. Love is supremely a relationship of faithfulness (as displayed by martyrs). God is the source of love. Love of God includes love of wisdom (Sir. 4:12). In love we turn to true being, overcome fear, and attain to true life (Philo *On the Migration of Abraham* 169).

b. Love of neighbor derives from God and leads to life (unlike hatred, which is of the devil and leads to death). In Philo a more general philanthropy is read into the OT; love extends finally to all creation (*On Virtues* 51ff.). But the movement is still

7

concentric from the compatriot outward by way of the resident alien and proselyte. *érōs* is unfavorably contrasted with *agápē* (Sibylline Oracles 3.171).

3. *Rabbinic Judaism.*

a. Here love is still primarily volitional and religious. It pinpoints the relation between God and humanity, especially Israel. God loves his people with fidelity and mercy. The gift of the law proves this. God's love imposes the obligation of reciprocal love and the related obedience and loyalty. Suffering in particular manifests the mutual love of God and his people. In it God is loved for his own sake. The main stress, however, falls on God's own love. Concealed during suffering, in which it is truly as strong as death, it will finally be gloriously manifest. No one can pluck Israel away from it.

b. Love of neighbor comes to expression in works of mercy. The neighbor is the fellow citizen or proselyte, whether friend or foe. Some, like Hillel, included foreigners, discerning love's missionary force, but others contested this (except for resident aliens). With law and the service of God, love is a foundation of the world. It is the sum of the law as formulated in the negative statement of the Golden Rule (Hillel). Yet it is more than a discharge of duties. It is the power behind all acts of love, and hence it cannot be enforced by legislation.

c. For the rabbis love is the basic principle of the threefold relationship of God, the I, and the Thou. It must determine all dealings within this relationship, or the relationship is broken. As God acts with love, so must we, and by the same token, as we act with love, so will God. A basis is perceived here for assurance of the divine mercy, though not at the expense of the divine righteousness.

D. Jesus.

1. *The New Demand.*

a. In his demand for love Jesus took up previous sayings: Love God; love neighbor; do unto others as you would have them do unto you. But he did so in a startlingly exclusive and unconditional way. Love of God means total commitment and total trust (Mt. 5:29-30; 6:24ff.). In particular, it involves a renunciation of mammon and of vainglory (Mt. 6:24b, 30ff.). It also calls for resistance to persecution, which is a fiery test of the loyalty of love (Mt. 10:17ff.; 5:10ff.).

b. Love of neighbor accompanies love of God (Mt. 22:39). This is no abstract love of humanity. Nevertheless, it transcends any restriction to compatriots; the neighbor is simply the person in need (Lk. 10:29-30), or rather, the neighbor is the person close at hand who acts in neighborly fashion to the one in need. This action derives from a response of the heart and consists of doing in all sobriety what the occasion requires.

c. Love of neighbor definitely includes love of enemies (Mt. 5:43-44). This love is the demand of a new age pointing to grace and applying to "hearers." It is the love of God's new people which they show not merely to one another but even to those of the present age who persecute them. It is thus totally sacrificial. The martyr becomes an intercessor for the hostile world that imposes martyrdom. Jesus makes this demand with full realism but also with full seriousness.

2. *The New Situation.*

a. The demand of Jesus is self-evident because he creates a new situation. He proclaims God's mercy as a new event that changes everything. The forgiveness of sins that he brings releases a new and overflowing love (Lk. 7:47) which fills and directs all life and action. God's new relationship to us puts us in a new relationship to him and to one another (cf. Lk. 6:36ff.). This is a relationship of mercy and reconciliation.

(In the Synoptics Jesus usually speaks about God's forgiveness or mercy and rarely employs either nouns or verbs for love in relation to God.)

b. In regard to us, God's love is a pardoning love. In regard to Jesus, however, it is the preferential love of election and calling. Jesus is the beloved Son (Mt. 12:5) whose death is an exercise of judgment and the establishment of a new order (12:8ff.). Jesus founds the new community into which we enter through relationship with him. Hence love for others is love for him (Mt. 25:31ff.), and he can call for radical commitment to himself (Mt. 10:37ff.). The Son brings remission, calls for an unconditional decision for God, and thus creates a new people who will tread the way of self-sacrificing love that he himself took. A point of interest is that Mark calls Jesus the beloved Son at the beginning of both his ministry (1:11) and his passion (9:7).

E. The Apostolic Period.

1. Paul.

a. Paul sees the new situation clearly. Thus his argument in Rom. 1ff. climaxes in a hymn which moves on from our love for God to Christ's love for us and then to the assurance of God's love in Christ (8:28, 31ff.). He makes three main points: (1) God sent his Son even to the cross in love; (2) God calls his elect in love; (3) God sheds his love abroad in their hearts. God's eternal love is indistinguishable from Christ's love (Rom. 5:8; 8:37), in which it becomes a world-changing event. This love implies election, which includes both pretemporal ordination and temporal calling. The elect community is in fellowship with God, and he endows it with the active and compelling power of love (Rom. 5:5) in fulfilment of his own primary purpose of love.

b. A new humanity is the goal of God's loving action, and he uses acts of human love to attain this end. God is the source of these acts (cf. 1 Cor. 8:3). He awakens the faith which comes into action in love (Gal. 5:6). He pours forth the Spirit who frees us for loving activity (Gal. 5:22). For Paul this new love is supremely brotherly and sisterly love (Gal. 6:10) in a fellowship that is based on Christ's mercy and Christ's death. Love builds up (1 Cor. 8:1); it builds the work of the future. In it the power of the new age breaks into the present form of the world. This is why it is always central when linked with faith and hope (cf. 1 Th. 1:3; Col. 1:4-5). Love is the greatest of the three because it alone stretches into the future aeon (1 Cor. 13:14).

2. James. James shows in practical fashion what it means that faith works by love, e.g., not despising the poor (2:14), or not withholding rights (5:1ff.). Love is the law of the new kingdom (2:8), demanded and made possible by faith. It holds fast to God in trial and is strong in perseverance (1:2ff.).

3. John. John stresses the love of the Father for the Son (Jn. 3:35). The love of God reaches us through him (Jn. 17:23ff.). The death of the Son crowns and releases it. This is a condescending love, yet it achieves victory in moral action. Our own love is here again supremely a love of the brethren. Love of God is the final reality for the fellowship, and abiding in this love is the law of its life (Jn. 15:9-10). The one law of love is constantly repeated in the Epistles of John with no particular specifications except that it be in deed and not in word only (1 Jn. 3:18). In Revelation the main demand is for a love for God that will not be overthrown by persecution (cf. 2:4; 12:11).

F. The Post-Apostolic Period.
Early formulas are handed down here with some infusion of new ideals. 1 Clem. 49–50 demonstrates an ongoing awareness of the

supremacy of love and its practical significance for the community and the world. *Agápē* and *agapán* have become stock terms for God's work and for Christian piety, sometimes as asceticism, more commonly as community love. In a world perishing through *érōs*, and vainly trying to transcend itself by sublimations of *érōs*, the church, being itself totally dependent on the merciful love of God, practices a love that does not desire but gives.   [E. STAUFFER, I, 35-55]

→ *philéō*

Hágar [Hagar]

Hagar, Sarah's maid, is the bondwoman who paradoxically typifies external Judaism (Gal. 4:24-25) in contrast to the freewoman Sarah who typifies the pure Judaism represented by the community. Some rabbis esteemed Hagar for the revelation that God gave her according to Gen. 16:13. She is equated with Sinai either because this is in the land of Ishmael or because of the similarity to the word *hajar* found in some Sinaitic place names.

---

angelía [message], *angéllō* [to announce], *anangéllō* [to tell], *apangéllō* [to report], *diangéllō* [to proclaim], *exangéllō* [to publish abroad], *katangéllō* [to proclaim], *prokatangéllō* [to foretell], *katangeleús* [herald]

"Message" is an important concept in the NT, and the terms for "to tell," "declare," "proclaim," help us to understand the main word *euangelízesthai*. They come from public life (the games and government); this suggests already that the gospel proclaims the rule of God. Respect for government results in a sacral evaluation of the messenger. The cult of the human ruler provides a direct antithesis to the divine lordship. A parallel also exists in the sense of mission (Socrates) and in the missionary word of aretalogies.

Expectation of one coming divine messenger may also be found in Hellenism, though Jesus himself will not be called *ángelos,* since he is above all angels. This expectation is richest in the Mandaean writings, but these are probably post-Christian. Mission is important in the OT too (cf. Isaiah and also the hope of the coming prophet). The difference lies in the content, namely, who sends whom, with what message, and to what end. The NT sums all this up in the name of Jesus. Its emphasis also falls on the act, so that the verbs of sending and telling are more prominent.

angelía.

A. In the NT. This word, rare in the NT, occurs twice in 1 John (John avoids the *euangel-* group). The reference in 1:5 is to the word of Jesus (the reading *epangelía* is a mistaken commentary), while 3:11 has in view the command implied in proclamation (*epangelía* has some support here).

B. Linguistic History. In classical usage the term can mean both "announcement" and "order." The former can cover both the act and the content. In the LXX the reference may be to both good news and bad (Prov. 12:25; 1 Sam. 4:19). Is. 28:9, referring to the prophets, might have influenced 1 Jn. 1:5.

angéllō. The only sure attestation of this in the NT is in Jn. 20:18, where it perhaps has a sacral nuance in the Easter context. Resurrection and proclamation are closely related (Rom. 1:3-4). "Running" is a common feature in secular *euangel-,* and the word has a religious tone in an ancient Eleusis document announcing the approach of a sacred procession.

anangéllō.

A. Outside the NT. This word is common in the Koine for *angéllein* (interchangeably with *apangéllein*). It is used for proclamations of kings, reports of envoys, messages of sorrow, communications of various kinds, and, more weakly, letters, the sense being "to tell." It has a sacral tone in connection with divine festivals and the honoring of divine rulers. It is common in the LXX, often with a religious sense: a. The Lord declares what is to come (Is. 42:9); b. God declares his righteousness, his works, his mercy, and his name to the nations (cf. Pss. 29:10; 63:10; 70:15; 91:3; 95:3; 101:22). In distinction from Hellenism, the OT relates this declaring to God's action and command, as well as to such specifically Hebrew concepts as righteousness and mercy. The same thoughts occur in Judaism.

B. In the NT. The usage is secular in Mt. 28:11 but religious in Jn. 5:15 and Acts 16:38.
1. *Mk. 5:14.* The category here is that of miracle stories (cf. Mt. 28:11; Jn. 5:15).
2. *Acts 14:27; 15:4.* The use here resembles that of the Psalms: the recounting of what God has done. Cf. 2 Cor. 7:7; 1 Pet. 1:12; Rom. 15:21.
3. *Acts 19:18.* There is a rare use here for the confession of sins.
4. *1 Jn. 1:5.* In this verse it is the verb for *angelía,* which declares the perceptible word of life. In Jn. 16:13-15 the Paraclete declares things to come. In 16:25 Christ in that hour will "tell" plainly of the Father. According to Jn. 4:25 (a reminiscence of Dt. 18:18? or a reference to the coming prophet?) the Messiah will "tell" all things.

apangéllō.

A. Outside the NT. This word has much the same range of meaning as *anangéllō,* but tends to be more official. Religiously it is used for Hermes, in honors lists, in aretalogies, and with reference to divine mission (Epictetus). It is common in the LXX. Mainly secular, it can also denote God's message (Is. 44:8) and cultic proclamation, e.g., of God's might (Pss. 145:4; 71:18).

B. In the NT. Used 25 times in the Lucan writings and 14 times elsewhere, this word occurs
1. in accounts of miracles (e.g., Lk. 8:34, 36, 47; Acts 11:13; 12:14, 17);
2. for God's message in the narrowest sense (Lk. 7:22; Acts 26:20; 17:30);
3. with reference to Jesus as God's Messenger (Mt. 12:18; Heb. 2:12).

diangéllō.

A. Outside the NT. Rare in Hellenism, this word can be used for a military pronouncement (Josephus *Life* 98) or imperial proclamation (Josephus *The Jewish War* 6.96), or religiously with reference to Hermes and the Pythia. Its use in the LXX is sacral: reporting a miracle (2 Macc. 1:33), announcing the sabbatical year (Lev. 25:9), and demonstrating God's power (Ex. 9:16).

B. In the NT. Cultic announcement is denoted in Acts 21:26, while declaration of God's acts is the issue in Rom. 9:17 (quoting Ex. 9:16) and Mk. 5:19. In Lk. 9:60 the disciples are to proclaim God's eschatological lordship, which begins with the proclamation (cf. Mt. 11:5-6; Lk. 9:26; Mk. 4:2ff.).

exangéllō. This word occurs only in 1 Pet. 2:9 in the sense of "publishing abroad"; the style is that of aretalogy and there is allusion to Is. 43:21. Historically the word was used in tragedy for imparting something concealed. Religiously it carried the senses of a. publishing conspiracies; b. declaring what is secret (Socrates, Epictetus); c. extolling mighty works (Aesculapius); and d. making official announcements. In the Psalms it has the same sense of cultic declaration as *anang-* and *apangéllō*.

kat-, prokatangéllō, katangeleús.

A. *katangéllō* **outside the NT.** In the secular sphere the term is used for official reports, while in the religious area it announces games and proclaims festivals. Plato has it for philosophical proclamation. The LXX makes no contribution, but Josephus has the word for God's promise to Abraham and through the prophets.

B. *katangéllō* **in the NT.** The word occurs six times in Paul and eleven in Acts. It is always sacral. There is a hint of promise in Acts 3:24, but normally "proclamation" is the meaning. The proclamation is more of acts than of ideas; Jesus has fulfilled what was expected (cf. Acts 4:2; 17:3; 13:38). The language of Acts 26:26 is liturgical. Sometimes there is a missionary thrust, as in Rom. 1:4. Teaching is included (cf. 1 Cor. 11:23; Col. 1:28). This is taken up into the word of the *Kýrios* and shares the dramatic and eschatological character of the message.

C. *prokatangéllō, katangeleús.* The verb occurs in the NT only in Acts 3:18 and 7:52. It describes the word of the prophets through whom God himself gives prior intimation. Josephus uses the term with reference to the birth of Moses, the message to Hagar, and Joseph's prediction to the cupbearer. The noun is found in the NT only in Acts 17:18 and carries the sense of "one who proclaims," more as a herald than a teacher. It thus conforms to the general employment of the group.

[J. SCHNIEWIND, I, 56-73]

ángelos [messenger, angel], *archángelos* [archangel], *isángelos* [like an angel]

ángelos.

A. In the Greek and Hellenistic World.
1. The *ángelos* is a "messenger." His role is sacral and he is protected by the gods. He delivers the message, answers questions, and asks for a reward (cf. Homer, Sophocles). He may also be an envoy, making treaties and delivering official messages. Birds are often messengers of the gods. So, too, are philosophers (Epictetus).
2. Alongside human messengers are heavenly messengers; Hermes is the most prominent. The underworld, too, has its messengers, e.g., Nemesis, Hecate, and lesser beings.
3. Philosophical religion developed the idea of the *lógos*, with which Greek thought linked Hermes and Philo the OT angels.
4. Josephus used the word for the ordinary messenger (*Antiquities* 7.249) but also for the OT angels. He called the angel that met Balaam a "divine spirit" (*Antiquities* 4.108). But he avoided Essene speculations about angels (*The Jewish War* 2.142).

[W. GRUNDMANN, I, 74-76]

B. mal'āk in the OT.

1. Used for both human and angelic messengers, *mal'āk* is often combined with Yahweh to denote a special angelic being: the "angel of the Lord." This angel has a special commission to help and guide Israel or individual Israelites (cf. Ex. 14:19; Num. 22:22; 1 Kgs. 19:7). He is not so much a mere messenger as an instrument of the covenant and personification of divine aid, turning against Israel only in exceptional circumstances (cf. 2 Sam. 24:17). Sometimes (e.g., Gen. 16:7ff.; Ex. 3:2ff.) he is so closely identified with God as to be almost indistinguishable. He is God, as it were, entering human apperception (cf. the alternation in Gen. 21:17ff.).

2. With the angel of the Lord are other heavenly beings, though these are seldom called angels. Forming God's entourage, they seem to have no autonomous functions and are in no sense objects of worship.

3. Angelology increased after the exile, perhaps under outside influences, or to maintain the divine transcendence. In Job the angels, who are not wholly pure (4:17-18), witness creation (38:7), and help in time of need (5:1). In Ezekiel and Zechariah they are interpreters (Ezek. 40:3ff.). Daniel depicts opposing heavenly forces; Michael is the angel of Israel (Dan. 10:13, 20). Myriads of angels surround God's throne (Dan. 7:10). They are depicted in human form and without wings. Strictly the seraphim and cherubim are not angels (though cf. Is. 6). Demons are not presented as heavenly beings and in view of God's omnipotence have no ultimate religious significance.

[G. VON RAD, I, 76-80]

C. The Doctrine of Angels in Judaism.

1. We see here two conflicting trends as developing angelology is opposed by Greek rationalism. The Apocrypha for the most part stays within OT limits. In apocalyptic literature, however, angels mediate the secrets of nature, converse with figures like Enoch, and are grouped more firmly as good and bad angels. The new teaching became part of popular piety (cf. Tobit), and the rabbis accepted it as an outworking of OT belief.

2. The rabbis could accept angels because angels are not themselves divine but serve to represent God's word and will. They are often introduced to give color to OT stories but without modifying the sense, e.g., at creation or at the giving of the law. They are created and are fully subordinate to God. While they speak for God, and present prayers to him, they do not interfere with the direct relation between the righteous and God.

D. ángelos in the NT.

1. The meaning "human messenger" has only a small role in the NT, being applied to the scouts sent by Joshua (Jms. 2:25), the men sent to Jesus by John (Lk. 7:24), those sent ahead by Jesus (Lk. 9:52), and the Baptist as the messenger of the covenant sent by God (Mt. 11:10 and par.).

2. a. The main NT reference is to angels as divine messengers and heavenly representatives (Heb. 12:22; Acts 6:15; Gal. 4:14). As such, angels appeared to Abraham (Heb. 12:2) and Moses (Acts 7:30) and mediated the law (Acts 7:53); perhaps this showed its inferiority (Gal. 3:19).

b. Since God is directly present in Jesus, it is natural that angels should accompany him at high points in his life and ministry: his birth, temptation, passion, and resurrection (Lk. 2:9ff.; Mk. 1:13; Lk. 22:43; Mt. 28:2). But the angels have no independent role, nor do they command interest for their own sakes. Angels will also come with Christ when he returns as Judge (Lk. 12:8-9; cf. 2 Th. 1:7). In Revelation they figure prominently in the events of the end-time. (Among the rabbis Israel rather than the angels will assist God in the judgment.) Thus the angels take a dynamic part in all the processes of salvation history, and show an interest in individual development within it (Lk. 15:10). Similarly the angel of God, or of the Lord, accompanies the church of God in its mission, acting on the apostles' behalf (Acts 5:19; 12:7ff.), showing them God's will (8:26; 10:3ff.), and punishing their enemies (12:23).

c. In the NT Christ is plainly not one of the angels but is superior to them (Mk. 13:32; Heb. 1:4ff.). If he was made lower than the angels, this merely emphasizes the superiority of his commission (Heb. 2:5ff.). In the same vein Paul attaches little importance to angels. As an apostle he is not under orders from angels (Gal. 1:8). Even the tongues of angels are nothing without love (1 Cor. 13:1). As 1 Pet. 1:12 puts it, angels long to look into the gospel; it was not for them but for us that Christ died (Heb. 2:16).

3. In Col. 2:18 there is a strong condemnation of any cult of angels. When angels are divorced from God, they must be reckoned among the hostile forces that threaten us (Rom. 8:38), i.e., as elemental or natural angels that might become demonic. Paul does not contest the reality of these but insists on their subjection to Christ (1 Cor. 15:24) and claims the believer's participation in his eschatological victory (Rom. 8:38).

4. Fallen angels → *daímōn*.

5. The idea of guardian angels is taken over from Judaism. Acts 12:15 assumes a resemblance between the angel and the person. In Mt. 18:10 the angels remind us that little ones are important to God and should be to us. The reference in 1 Cor. 11:10 might be to erotic desires of angels but is more probably to the propriety they require. In Rev. 1:20 and 2–3 the angels of the churches could be bishops but in context are more likely supporting angels, especially since bishops were not exalted above the churches in NT days.

archángelos. The idea of archangels is connected with the singling out of individual angels. Josh. 5:14 mentions a captain or commander of the Lord's army. Michael is a chief prince or angel in Dan. 10:13; 12:1. Later we read of four, six, or seven special angels. The LXX does not use the term *archángelos* but Philo has it for the *lógos*. The NT shows no great interest in the theme. 1 Th. 4:16 says that the call of the archangel will ring out at Christ's coming, and Jude 9 identifies Michael as an archangel.

isángelos. This rare word occurs in the NT only in Lk. 20:36. In the resurrection we shall be "like the angels," knowing neither mortality nor marriage (cf. Mt. 22:30; Mk. 12:25).   [G. KITTEL, I, 80-87]

agenealógētos → *geneá*

---

hágios [holy], **hagiázō** [to make holy, sanctify], **hagiasmós** [sanctification], **hagiótēs** [sanctification], **hagiōsýnē** [sanctification]

In biblical Greek the *hag-* family, which embraces the *hagnós* group, is most extensive and enjoys a very significant history.

hágios.

A. In Greek and Hellenistic Writings. The old Greek term *hágos* denotes an object of awe, the adjective *hagés* means "clean," and the verb *házō* has the sense "to shrink from." *hágios* is used of sanctuaries ("sacred") and later of gods and religious practices, though it becomes common only in the Hellenistic period.

B. The Use of Holiness in the OT. Originally Canaanitic, the root *qds* has a basic cultic reference. The ground around the burning bush is holy (Ex. 3:5), as are Gilgal (Josh. 5:15), the temple (Is. 64:10), days (Is. 58:13), offerings (1 Sam. 21:5-7), and tithes (Dt. 26:13). The adjective may be applied to persons and even to God; this produces an ethical association. The verb is versatile, denoting the expressing of a state of holiness (Is. 5:16), or setting in a state of holiness (Ezek. 36:23), or declaring holy (Ex. 19:10), or entering a state of holiness (Josh. 3:5), or being dedicated.

C. The History of the Term in the OT.

1. Preprophetic Period. The word comes to be connected with God's name, which is the expression of his nature, and thus takes on a moral meaning (cf. Am. 4:2). Profaning God's name even cultically is a sin (cf. Lev. 20:3; Am. 2:7). The name, which cultic invocation acknowledges, gives holiness a personal dimension. But it also fuses it with divinity in contrast to creatureliness. God's holiness expresses his divine perfection. His self-revelation is his self-sanctification (Lev. 10:3 etc.). As God, however, dwells among his people through the covenant at Sinai (Ex. 24:4ff.), Israel is to be a people holy to him (Dt. 7:6). She must shun other cults and worship God alone (Dt. 6:4), allowing no place for pagan shrines and their cultic licentiousness (Dt. 23:18). Cultic purity demands personal purity. The ark as the place of God's presence fills the sanctuary with holiness; in connection with it God is called the "holy God" (1 Sam. 6:20). War and warriors are sanctified through the ark's presence (Num. 10:35-36), as is the camp (Dt. 23:15).

2. Prophetic Theology.

a. The prophet Hosea develops a contrast between the holy God and sinful humanity (cf. Hos. 11:9). Israel has followed pagan cults and thus come into collision with the holy God (14:1). But by destroying false holiness the holy God gives new life (14:8) in his inconceivable love; thus love is incorporated into the divine holiness even in its opposition to unholy human nature.

b. For Isaiah the holiness of God is his secret essence. This evokes holy awe (Is. 6), a sense of moral uncleanness which must be purged (6:7). God himself effects the atonement. Its goal is that the redeemed, too, will be holy (4:3). Though Israel is in herself unholy, God has bound himself to her. He may thus be called the "Holy One of Israel." His holiness consumes what is unholy, but in grace he establishes a remnant as his holy people.

c. In the later chapters of Isaiah the Holy One of Israel is more fully manifested as the God of redemption rather than judgment. God is incomparable (40:25). In his holiness lies his mystery (45:15). This mystery is redemption; hence salvation and holiness are now firmly related (45:18ff. etc.). God's holy ways differ from ours, but for this very reason his holiness issues in a new creation.

3. The Postexilic Period.

a. Two intermingling streams may be seen here, the priestly-cultic and the prophetic-ethical. The law enshrines the former; it endows priests and people with cultic holiness. The Psalms belong to this sphere, but show that it could include a strong spiritual element. Israel is holy because the Holy Spirit is present within her (cf. Ps. 51:11).

b. The apocryphal writings maintain the cultic tradition with frequent references to the holy city, temple, altar, sabbath, garments, candlestick, oil, swords, books, priesthood, people, and covenant. But God, heaven, the angels, and the Spirit are also holy. The LXX translators, in choosing the Gk. *hágios* for the Hebrew term, seem to have tried to give it a distinctive Hebrew nuance, e.g., by using *tó hágion* or *tá hágia* for the temple and avoiding *hierón*.

4. *Philo and Josephus*. Philo adopts the cultic usage of the OT but allegorizes it. In so doing he relates holiness to alien philosophical concepts, e.g., when he calls heaven (the macrocosm), or the mind (the microcosm), or the soul "holy" (largely in the sense of "lofty"). Josephus uses *hágios* sparingly (e.g., in describing the cultus), applying it most often to the temple (also the land). He adopts this course out of consideration for readers to whom *hágios* etc. must have sounded strange.

[D. PROCKSCH, I, 88-97]

D. The Concept of Holiness in Rabbinic Judaism.

a. The rabbis follow OT usage in calling the temple, priests, sacrifices, etc. holy, but with no precise definition. Sometimes systematization is attempted. In a new use the hair of Nazirites and the body can be called holy. "To dedicate to oneself a wife" is a phrase for "to marry."

b. God is holy as Judge and King. But he is known as such by those who draw near in a trust sustained by fear. He is thus the Holy One in Sirach, Enoch, and later rabbinic texts. God's Spirit is also called holy, but above all his name, which led to the replacement of the proper name as well as to the expression "to hallow the name" with God or Israel as subject. Hallowing the name by keeping the law became a chief motive of ethical action.

c. Scripture is holy as God's word, especially the law, though the phrase "Holy Scripture" is infrequent. Reading Scripture is a sacred action. The scrolls, too, are sacred, and writing them is a holy task. The hands must be washed after touching the scrolls.

d. Those who keep the law, and the righteous of the OT, are also holy. Holiness consists negatively of separation, i.e., from the Gentiles, from sin, and especially from licentiousness, so that holy and chaste came to be largely synonymous.

[K. G. KUHN, I, 97-100]

E. *hágios* in the NT.

1. *The Holiness of God*. On an OT basis, holiness is here seen to be God's innermost nature (Rev. 4:8). It embraces omnipotence, eternity, and glory, and evokes awe. In John, God is the holy Father (17:11). The holy God calls for holy people (1 Pet. 1:15-16). God's name, i.e., his revealed but distinct person, is to be hallowed (Mt. 6:9; Lk. 11:12).

2. *Jesus Christ as hágios*. Jesus is seldom called holy (cf. Mk. 1:24; Lk. 1:35; Jn. 6:69; Rev. 3:7; Acts 3:14). But the description is ancient and significant. In Luke it rests on the virgin birth and his being a bearer of the Spirit, confronting evil spirits and inaugurating the pneumatic age. He is confessed as the holy one in Jn. 6:69, sanctified by God and dispensing anointing with the Spirit. In Revelation he has the same predicates of holiness and truth as God. As the holy servant in Acts he has a cultic mission as the holy sacrifice offered vicariously for others. In Hebrews he is priest as well as victim, going into the antitype of the holy of holies for us and achieving our expiatory sanctification *(hagiázein)* (9:25ff.; 2:11; 9:13).

3. *The Holy Spirit*.

a. The Spirit's holiness is inseparable from Christ's.

b. The Spirit is active at the birth and especially the baptism of Christ, which initiates the age of the Spirit. After the resurrection Christ imparts the Spirit to the disciples (Pentecost). The Spirit is now manifest, so that resistance is unforgivable. Baptism is now in the Spirit's name as well as the Father's and the Son's.

c. Luke especially likes the phrase "holy Spirit" in both the definite and indefinite form. He wants to distinguish God's Spirit from other spirits and stresses the charismatic rather than the cultic element.

d. Paul has a more personal emphasis and maintains but spiritualizes the cultic aspect, e.g., the church or Christians as a holy temple indwelt by the Spirit (Eph. 2:21; 1 Cor. 6:19; cf. Rom. 15:16; 2 Cor. 13:13; 1 Th. 4:8). Baptism and the eucharist (1 Cor. 12:13) are signs of the cultic community denoting its fellowship with Christ's death and resurrection.

4. *The Holiness of the ekklēsía.* Again on an OT basis, the Christian fellowship is holy as a temple of the Spirit centered on Christ as the holy servant. As a holy people, Christians are to be holy (1 Pet. 2:9; 1:16). They are sanctified by Christ (1 Cor. 1:2). In him Gentiles are now numbered among the saints (Eph. 2:19). The churches as well as the church are holy (1 Cor. 14:33). Holiness is by the calling of grace in Christ (Rom. 1:6; 1 Cor. 1:24; Phil. 1:1), not by nature. The holy people has a divine inheritance (Eph. 1:18; Col. 1:12; cf. Deuteronomy).

5. *The Holy Life of Christians.* Christians are to offer themselves as holy sacrifices (Rom. 12:1). As a result the cultic impinges on the ethical, and purity is stressed (cf. Mt. 5:8). The mutual service of love gives expression to this (Gal. 5:13; Rom. 15:25; 16:2). The holy kiss seals it (1 Cor. 16:20). Those sanctified in Christ sanctify their family circles (1 Cor. 7:14). Holiness here has a moral content and stands opposed to impurity, especially in Gentile sexuality (Acts 10:14; Eph. 5:5). Its cultic reference keeps it from being mere morality. Holiness in this sense is a principle of judgment (1 Cor. 6:2). Believers will judge—hence faith may itself be called holy (Jude 20).

6. *The Ecclesia triumphans.*

a. The holy angels belong to the church triumphant (Mk. 8:38 etc.); they will return with Christ (cf. 1 Th. 3:13, though this verse may refer to, or include, departed saints, cf. 2 Th. 1:10).

b. Christians also belong to it as the saints (Rev. 14:12; 17:6). The holy will be holy still (Rev. 22:11)—not self-sanctified, but sanctified by God. Holiness is a central determination of Christians as already they worship God, reconciled by Christ's holy offering and constituted the temples of the Holy Spirit.

hagiázō. This is mostly a biblical term and means "to consecrate" or "to sanctify." God is asked to sanctify his name (Mt. 6:9). Jesus sanctifies himself (Jn. 17:19) and his church (Eph. 5:26)—a divine work. The Father sanctifies Christ (Jn. 10:36; cf. 17:19) with a view to sanctifying the disciples (17:19). The latter takes place through Christ's reconciling work (Heb. 2:11; 10:10). For Paul we are thus "the sanctified" (1 Cor. 1:2), and this is a state (1 Cor. 6:11). The sanctified have an inheritance (Acts 20:32). They are to sanctify Christ in their hearts (1 Pet. 3:15), being holy in conduct as Christ makes them holy by indwelling them (1:16).

hagiasmós. Deriving from the verb, this term means "sanctifying." It is rare in the LXX and occurs in the NT only in the epistles. Only a holy person can "sanctify," so divine sanctifying precedes any process of sanctifying (cf. Rev. 22:11). It is God's will (1 Th. 4:3) and finds expression in life (4:4). The body must be yielded to sanctification (Rom. 6:19). Christ and the Spirit effect it (1 Cor. 1:30; 2 Th. 2:13; 1 Pet.

17

1:2). It implies conduct in 1 Tim. 2:15 and is a moral goal in Heb. 12:14. It is thus the moral result of Christ's atoning work.

hagiótēs. This word denotes "sanctification." It is an essential attribute of God that we are to share (Heb. 12:10; cf. 1 Pet. 1:15). In 2 Cor. 1:12 the link with "sincerity" causes difficulty if both refer to God; hence some prefer the reading "simplicity and sincerity," which would confine *hagiótēs* to Hebrews.

hagiōsýnē. This rare word denotes sanctifying as a quality. In the NT only Paul uses it (Rom. 1:4; 2 Cor. 7:1; 1 Th. 3:13). In Rom. 1:4 it refers to a different principle of life from that of "the flesh" (v. 3), i.e., divine, not natural. In 2 Cor. 7:1 and 1 Th. 3:13 the divinely effected condition is to find completion in moral dedication in the form of purity.   [O. PROCKSCH, I, 100-115]

---

agnoéō [to be ignorant],   *agnóēma* [ignorance, error],   *ágnoia* [ignorance], *agnōsía* [ignorance],   *ágnōstos* [unknown]

---

agnoéō, agnóēma. Used with all the nuances of knowledge, these words denote "being mistaken" or "in error" as the character of action (cf. 1 Tim. 1:13). Ignorance of self is meant in Heb. 5:2. "Not recognizing" in 1 Cor. 14:38 means rejection ("not being recognized" by God). Not knowing God is meant in Rom. 10:3, and Christ in 1 Tim. 1:13. This ignorance entails disobedience (Rom. 10:3); hence it is not just pardonable lack of information but a failure to understand that needs forgiveness.

ágnoia, agnōsía.

1. *Philosophical and Legal Usage. ágnoia,* while used of specific ignorance, could also denote ignorance in general as the opposite of wisdom as well as knowledge (cf. Stoicism). Ignorance of self and of God (also of evil) would be included, so that ignorance itself would then be the true evil. In legal usage ignorance of the law is the main point; cf. Lev. 22:14 in the LXX (extended to "unintentional sin" in Lev. 5:18). Philo opposes *ágnoia* to *epistémē* (cf., e.g., *On Drunkenness* 154-61). *ágnoia* can also be equated with heathenism (Wis. 14:22; Josephus *Antiquities* 10.142). Among the rabbis knowledge of the law is a presupposition of piety. The legal use recurs in Hermas *Similitudes* 5.7.3. "In ignorance" is used in the NT only in Acts 3:17; the idea of ignorance of God may be found in Acts 17:30; cf. Eph. 4:17-18; Ignatius *Ephesians* 19.3; Justin *Apology* 61.10. *agnōsía* (Job 35:16 LXX; 1 Pet. 2:15) has the same force as *ágnoia.*

2. *The Dualistic Usage of Hellenism.* Both words occur in Gnosticism for lack of the knowledge essential to salvation. We suffer from this prior to revelation and through bondage to the senses. The NT adopts this usage (cf. Acts 17:30 etc.) but with different ideas of sin and grace.

ágnōstos. Found in the NT only in Acts 17:23, this word denotes "unknown" or "unrecognized." The phrase "unknown God" does not occur in the OT, though the heathen do not know God (Ps. 79:6) and Israel does not know other gods (Hos. 13:4). The rabbis think the Gentiles have some knowledge of God but call God's ways unknown. Neither the Greek nor the Jewish world believes God is unknowable, though Plato thinks he is inaccessible to the senses. An altar to the unknown God would simply imply uncertainty as to the god to which it should apply. Scepticism, of course, questions all knowledge, and Gnosticism thinks God can be known only supernaturally, but Socrates, Aristotle, and the Stoics accept God's knowability.

[R. BULTMANN, I, 115-21]

---

hagnós [pure],   *hagnízō* [to purify],   *hagneía* [purity],   *hagnótēs* [purity],
hagnismós [purification]

---

hagnós. Originally meaning "what awakens awe," this word for "pure" is used cultically in the LXX (2 Macc. 13:8), though also for the inner disposition (Prov. 20:9) and for chastity (4 Macc. 18:7-8). Uncommon in the NT, it signifies "moral purity" (1 Jn. 3:3; 1 Tim. 5:22; Jms. 3:17), "innocence" (2 Cor. 7:11), and "chastity" (2 Cor. 11:2).

hagnízō. Used in the LXX for "cultic qualification," this term occurs in Jn. 11:55 and Acts 21:24; 24:18 for cultic purifying as practiced by Jews and Jewish Christians. It can then relate to moral purifying, as in Jms. 4:8; 1 Pet. 1:22; 1 Jn. 3:3.

hagneía. This denotes cultic purity in the OT, moral purity in 1 Tim. 4:12; 5:2.

hagnótēs. This term, not used in classical Greek or the LXX, denotes moral purity in 2 Cor. 6:6.

hagnismós. This word signifies cultic purification (Num. 8:7) or dedication (Num. 5:5) in connection with a vow (Acts 21:26).   [F. HAUCK, I, 122-24]

---

agorázō [to buy, redeem],   *exagorázō* [to redeem]

A. **The Sacral Manumission of Slaves.** As on Delphic inscriptions, this is a legal form of self-manumission whereby the god purchases the slave, using the slave's own money for the transaction. There was no sacral redemption in the OT temple, but manumission took place in the synagogue and church, and the Jewish world applied the idea of redemption religiously.

B. *agorázō.*
1. Meaning "to buy," this word is used by Paul in 1 Cor. 6:20; 7:23 to signify our being redeemed (and therefore free except in relation to God). In Rev. 5:9 the Lamb has bought us for God with his blood.
2. According to Rev. 3:18 real instead of sham gold is to be bought, i.e., from Christ.

C. *exagorázō.*
1. Not used in the LXX, this term refers in the NT to Christ's redeeming work, the stress now being on purchase to freedom from the law (Gal. 4:1ff.). God, of course, pays the price himself in Christ, meeting the law's claim and thus giving true freedom through justification by faith (Gal. 3:24-25). Redemption is needed because the law is God's holy ordinance and eternally valid. Hence in the transition to freedom sinfulness is exposed and forgiveness is experienced in Christ. Yet redemption is not a transactional "buying" of God's favor. While Christ undoubtedly obeys and serves God, God himself acts in him on our behalf and toward us. Hence redemption is not to be severed from the "we" who by it are put back in fellowship with God by faith.
2. The word means "to buy up" in Eph. 5:16; Col. 4:5, i.e., "make the most" of the time *(kairós),* or the opportunities it offers.   [F. BÜCHSEL, I, 124-28]

agrypnéō → *egeírō, grēgoréō*

---

agōgḗ [manner of life], *parágō* [to pass by], *proágō* [to precede], *proságō* [to approach], *prosagōgḗ* [access]

---

agōgḗ. Used only in 2 Tim. 3:10, this word denotes "orientation," hence "manner of life." In ordinary parlance the word came to have special reference to education or its results, i.e., breeding, behavior. This may well be the background of the use in 2 Tim. 3:10 (cf. "ways" in 1 Cor. 4:17).

parágō. This is found only intransitively in the NT, e.g., in Mt. 9:9, mostly with reference to Jesus "passing by" (perhaps sometimes introductory, e.g., in Mk. 1:16). The sense in 1 Cor. 7:31 (cf. 1 Jn. 2:17) is "to pass away" (cf. Mt. 5:18). The present tense shows that the great eschatological change is already taking place. If *schḗma* means "role," the idea would be that its "part" is played.

proágō. Used both transitively and intransitively, this refers to Christ's "preceding" (Mk. 10:32) and to the preceding of prophecy (1 Tim. 1:18) and the commandment (Heb. 7:18). The sense may just be chronological in the two latter cases, while Christ obviously demands "following" or discipleship. In 2 Jn. 9 "going astray" is a suggested alternative, but perhaps the opponents thought of themselves as "go-aheads" or progressives (cf. 1 Cor. 4:6).

proságō. This is used transitively three times and intransitively once. The main interest arises with the cultic use in 1 Pet. 3:18. a. A general meaning is "to offer," "to sacrifice," in both secular Greek and the LXX (cf. Ex. 29:20). Yet Num 8:9-10 etc. suggest the more specific sense of "presenting for dedication." b. There is also a legal use, e.g., in Ex. 21:6; Acts 16:20 (bringing for judgment); the suggestion here is that Christ leads us to the judgment which is also grace. This merges into the ceremonial sense of "presenting" at court. c. Since God takes the initiative in all this, another idea is that God "brings" us to his side, i.e., reconciles us (cf. Num. 16:5). d. These meanings are not contradictory or artificially read in, but point to the richness of God's saving work, which can be grasped only as different aspects are set alongside or superimposed.

prosagōgḗ. Found three times (Rom. 5:2; Eph. 2:18; 3:12), this word has the same range as *proságein,* but some take it transitively as "introduction," others intransitively as "approach." In Christ, however, this is immaterial, since we "move toward" God as we are "led." "Access" is perhaps the best rendering so long as we recall that Christ himself is our access (the door, Jn. 10).   [K. L. Schmidt, I, 128-34]

---

agṓn [conflict, fight], *agōnízomai* [to fight], *antagōnízomai* [to strive against], *epagōnízomai* [to contend], *katagōnízomai* [to subdue], *agōnía* [conflict]

This group, rare in the LXX and NT, is used frequently in relation to the stadium.

agṓn, agōnízomai, etc.

A. Hellenistic Usage.

a. *agṓn* means place of assembly, then place of contest, then contest, then conflict. It is often applied figuratively to life as a struggle with a prize (Plutarch, Philo; Wis.

4:2). *agōnízomai* means "to carry on a conflict, contest, debate, or legal suit," and can also be figurative.

b. The imagery of the contest also occurs in Hellenistic Judaism, e.g., in Philo *On Husbandry* 112; cf. the martyrs in 4 Macc. 17:10ff. and Job in Test. Job 4 and 27.

B. *agốn, agōnízomai* in the NT.
a. Striving for the goal is the first thought here (Lk. 13:24). Exertion (1 Th. 2:2) and a concentration of forces (Col. 1:29; cf. 2 Tim. 4:7-8) are both necessary.

b. Striving also calls for denial (1 Cor. 9:25), the setting aside of provisional ends (1 Cor. 9:27). This is not asceticism but athletic discipline (2 Tim. 4:5). It is not contempt for the world but a right ordering of priorities.

c. Little reference is made to antagonists, but obstacles and dangers have to be faced (cf. 1 Th. 2:2; 2 Cor. 7:5; Jude 3).

d. Martyrdom is the final conflict (cf. 2 Tim. 4:6; Heb. 10ff.)

e. The goal is not just our salvation but that of others too (Col. 1:29-30). Paul struggles "for" the church (Col. 2:1-2; cf. 4:12-13). Prayer is crucial here (Col. 4; Rom. 15). So is unity in the Spirit (Phil. 1:27ff.). The gospel brings conflict to the entire Christian life, but as we pray and stand together the sign of the cross is a sign of victory.

C. *agốn, agōnízomai* in the Early Church. Pauline ideas recur in 1 Clement. Barnabas summons us to conflict (4.11). 2 Clement depicts the contest in the arena (7). Martyrdom and asceticism are later the leading forms of conflict, especially martyrdom (Tertullian *To the Martyrs* 3).

agōnía. This word means "conflict," "tension," "focusing of powers." In Lk. 22:44 it denotes concern for victory before the decisive struggle (cf. Lk. 12:49-50).
→ *athléō*   [E. STAUFFER, I, 134-40]

Adám [Adam]

A. Early Christian Usage.
1. Adam as the First Man. 1 Tim. 2:13-14 appeals to Adam as the first man when arguing for a right man/woman relation on the grounds that Adam was made first and Eve was deceived first.

2. The NT Typology Adam/Christ. Adam is Christ's antitype in Mk. 1:13; Rom. 5:12-21; 1 Cor. 15:22, 45-49. In Mk. 1:13 Christ reverses Adam's fall and reopens paradise (cf. the genealogy in Lk. 3:38). Paul uses the typology to show the universality of grace (Rom. 5:12-21), to establish the certainty of resurrection (1 Cor. 15:22), and to indicate that we will have spiritual bodies (1 Cor. 15:44ff.; cf. Gen. 2:7 LXX). With respect to our earthly bodies we are like the first Adam, with respect to our resurrection bodies we will be like the last Adam (1 Cor. 15:48).

B. The Origin of the Typology Adam/Christ. The rabbis do not call the Redeemer the last Adam, but the ideas occur that the first man was ideal, that the Messiah will restore the glory lost at the fall, and that the Messiah is preexistent (cf. Philo). Paul adopts these ideas but gives them an eschatological thrust: Adam is the head of this aeon, but Christ is at the head of the new aeon of God's perfect and redeemed creation.
→ *huiós toú anthrōpou*   [J. JEREMIAS, I, 141-43]

21

> *adelphós* [brother], *adelphḗ* [sister], *adelphótēs* [brotherhood],
> *philádelphos* [love of the brethren], *philadelphía* [brotherly love],
> *pseudádelphos* [false brethren]

1. Physical Brotherhood. There are references to the physical brothers of Judah in Mt. 1:2, to brothers among the disciples in Mk. 1:16, 19, to the brother of Mary and Martha in Jn. 11:2ff., to Paul's sister in Acts 23:16, to brothers of Jesus in Mk. 3:31ff., and to various other brothers, e.g., in Mk. 12:19-20; Lk. 15:27; Lk. 16:28; Lk. 12:13; and Mk. 10:29-30.

2. Spiritual Brotherhood. adelphós also refers to fellow believers some 30 times in Acts and 130 in Paul. This usage has an OT and Jewish basis (cf. Acts 3:22; Mt. 5:22-23; Acts 2:29; 3:17, etc.). Jesus uses the term in Mt. 23:8; 25:40. Christians are his brethren (Rom. 8:29) and are to love one another as such (1 Jn. 2–3). *adelphótēs* denotes the brotherhood (1 Pet. 2:17) and means brotherly disposition in Hermas (*Mandates* 8.10). [H. von Soden, I, 144-46]

> *hádēs* [Hades]

A. *hádēs* in Later Judaism.

a. Used for the Hebrew Sheol, the realm of the dead, this term came to denote the place of temporary sojourn prior to resurrection (cf. Is. 26:19).

b. In this place the good were then seen to be separated from the bad (Eth. En. 22; cf. Lk. 16:23, 26).

c. The good were finally thought to be already in bliss (Lk. 16:9, 23ff.).

B. *hádēs* in the NT.

1. The Link with Judaism. The NT view is close to that of Judaism (cf. Lk. 16). a. There is no soul-sleep. b. One goes down into Hades (Mt. 11:23; 12:40). c. The stay is limited (Rev. 20:13). Sometimes all the dead seem to be in Hades (Acts 2:27), but elsewhere believers are in paradise (Lk. 16:9, 23ff.), or with the Lord (2 Cor. 5:8), or under the altar (Rev. 7:9). Hence Hades is sometimes just the abode of the wicked (Lk. 16:23; Rev. 20:13-14).

2. The Early Christian Reconstruction. Faith in the risen Lord gives assurance that believers are secure from Hades (Mt. 16:18) and go to be with Christ (Lk. 23:43). Jesus is the Lord of Hades (Mt. 16:18; Acts 2:31). The descent shows this. Distinctive here is that Christ preaches in Hades (1 Pet. 3:19ff.) and that he has the keys of death and Hades (Rev. 1:18).

→ *ábyssos* [J. Jeremias, I, 146-49]

adiákritos → *krínō*

> *ádikos* [unrighteous], *adikía* [unrighteousness], *adikéō* [to do wrong],
> *adíkēma* [wrongdoing]

ádikos.

A. The Development of the Concept *ádikos*.

1. The term means "violator of the law." What is against custom is usually distinguished from what is impious. The rootage in law forms a link with the LXX.

2. Yet *ádikos* can have a religious connotation, too (Plato *Laws* 4.716d). The OT strengthens this aspect in the Jewish and Christian spheres (cf. Job 16:12 LXX), which makes *ádikos* a synonym of *asebḗs*.

B. The Special Use of *ádikos*, especially in the NT.

1. The NT adopts the OT reference to the "violation of divine law," opposing the wicked to the righteous (cf. Mt. 5:45; Acts 24:15; 1 Cor. 6:1, 9; 2 Pet. 2:9).

2. The word can also mean "unjust" (rulers; God is not unjust [Rom. 3:5]), and "dishonest" (Lk. 16:10), i.e., unfaithful.

3. The reference can be to what is unlawfully gained (Lk. 16:9), or what is of purely illusory value (Lk. 16:11; used with mammon).

4. *ádikos* in 1 Pet. 2:19 means "unjustly."

5. *tó ádikon* in the neuter is the opposite of *tó díkaion* or *alḗtheia*.

adikía.

A. *adikía* outside the NT.

1. The meaning is "unrighteous action," then "unjust act."

2. Further definition is given by the element of lawlessness, the opposing to righteousness, and the opposing to truth or truthfulness.

3. Distinction is made from what is impious, but there is an association, and in the OT *adikía* is primarily "sin against God" (cf. Is. 43:24-25; Jer. 31:33), though it may be "dishonesty," "injustice," "unreliability," or "apostasy."

4. In apocalyptic the last time will be one of general *adikía*, "unrighteousness."

5. *adikía* may be used in the genitive for an adjective (cf. Lk. 16:8; 18:6).

B. *adikía* in the NT.

1. Apart from 2 Cor. 12:13, the instances all give the term basic significance.

a. As the opposite of *dikaiosýnē*, it denotes "violation of the divine law," heading the list of vices in Rom. 1:29. It also means "legal injustice" (Rom. 9:14). It can have, too, the nuance of "unfaithfulness" (Rom. 3:5). In Rom. 6:13 it is a controlling force.

b. As the opposite of *alḗtheia*, it is linked with self-glory in Jn. 7:18. Delight in it is contrasted with believing the gospel (2 Th. 2:12). Love obeys the truth and hence finds no joy in *adikía* (1 Cor. 13:6). In it the truth is suppressed (Rom. 1:18). It involves a denial of correct doctrine (2 Tim. 2:19).

2. a. *adikía* is connected with *asébeia* in Rom. 1; it arises out of false worship, the distinction between law and religion being thus transcended.

b. It is defined as sin against God (cf. Acts 8:23; 1 Jn. 1:9; 5:17).

3. An eschatological reference may be seen in 2 Th. 2:10 and possibly Jms. 3:6; Acts 1:18; 2 Pet. 2:13, 15.

4. The genitive occurs for an adjective in Lk. 16:8; 18:6. Lk. 16:9 perhaps means, not that possessions as such are evil, but that they are gained by trickery (cf. the publicans), or that they are illusory and deceitful.

adikéō.

A. *adikéō* outside the NT.

1. "To do wrong," "to be in the wrong, or mistaken," is the general sense.

2. Relationship to God or the gods may be in view. In the LXX, then, it means "to sin against God" (e.g., 2 Sam. 24:17; 2 Chr. 26:16), sometimes synonymous with

hamartánein and *anomeín*. Josephus has a similar usage (*Antiquities* 4.150; 6.151); so does Philo (*On the Confusion of Tongues* 9-10, 27).

3. The wrongdoing may also be toward others (cf. Gen. 42:22), but in the LXX it is still a breaking of God's command.

4. It may be used with an accusative of object, or person, or both, or passively for suffering wrong or injury or damage.

B. *adikéō* in the NT.

a. The absolute use in the active occurs in 2 Cor. 7:12 ("to do wrong") and in Acts 25:11 ("to be in the wrong"). Judgment for it is held up to view in Col. 3:25.

b. The accusative of person may be seen in Mt. 20:13 and Lk. 10:19. Acts 7:26 echoes Ex. 2:13. In 2 Cor. 7:2 it is a question of hurting in some way; cf. the power of locusts to inflict injury in Rev. 9:10.

c. Revelation often has the accusative of object for judgments on the cosmos (e.g., 7:2-3; 9:4, 19).

d. For the double accusative cf. Acts 25:10; Gal. 4:12; Phlm. 18, and perhaps Lk. 10:19.

e. Examples of the passive are Acts 7:24; 1 Cor. 6:7.

In general *adikeín* is not a strongly nuanced term in the NT, being largely replaced by *hamartánein*.

***adikēma*.**

A. *adikēma* outside the NT. The meaning is "act of wrongdoing." Not common in the LXX, it most frequently means "breach of the law" or "sin against God" (cf. Is. 59:12; Jer. 16:17). It is more common in Josephus and Philo, usually with a sense of action against divine as well as human law.

B. *adikēma* in the NT. The three examples in the NT conform to the use of *adikéō*. In Rev. 18:5 the plural stresses the abundance of wicked deeds. Violation of the Jewish law is meant in Acts 24:20, criminal violation of Roman law in Acts 18:14.

[G. SCHRENK, I, 149-63]

adókimos → *dókimos; adýnatos, adynatéō* → *dýnamai*

ádō [to sing],   *ōdḗ* [song]

ádō. "To sing" is either transitive or intransitive; thus in the NT Rev. 5:9 has "sing a song" and Eph. 5:19 "sing to the Lord." Parallels are *légein* in Rev. 5:13 and *psállein* in Eph. 5:19.

ōdḗ (→ *psalmós, hýmnos*). a. "Song," or b. "a song," not distinguished precisely in the NT (as later) from *psalmós* or *hýmnos*.

The ode is a cultic song of the community sung in worship. It is "spiritual," i.e., has a measure of inspiration (Eph. 5:19). Hence it is not an expression of personal feeling or experience but a "word of Christ" (Col. 3:16). It thus speaks about Christ or God's saving acts in him. It does so for edification rather than evangelism. The "new song" of Revelation (e.g., 5:9) suggests eschatological fulfilment: God's new work is the theme.   [H. SCHLIER, I, 163-65] *ázymos* → *zýmē*

---

aér [air]

For the Greeks the impure air extended to the moon, being then replaced by the pure ether of the starry regions. Spirits inhabited the air. Later Judaism located demons in it, and Paul could thus refer to a prince of the power of the air (Eph. 2:2). Believers will meet Christ in this middle sphere (1 Th. 4:17). "Speaking into the air" in 1 Cor. 14:9 is a proverbial expression, while "beating the air" in 1 Cor. 9:26 is either engaging in a sham fight or striking aimlessly.   [W. FOERSTER, I, 165-66]

athanasía → *thánatos*

---

athémitos [unlawful]

In extra- and post-Attic Greek, "contrary to statute," either cultic or moral and religious. "Lawless" idolatry is a pagan evil in 1 Pet. 4:3. In Acts 10:28 Peter is shown that it is right to do what was previously "unlawful" for him as a Jew, i.e., associate with Gentiles.   [A. OEPKE, I, 166]

átheos → *theós*

áthesmos [lawless]

Originally "illegal" or "impious," of acts, foods, persons. In the NT it is used only as a noun and only in 2 Pet. 2:7 (the Sodomites); 3:17 (heretical leaders).
[A. OEPKE, I, 167]

athetéō → *títhēmi*

---

athléō [to strive],   *synathléō* [to strive side by side],   *áthlēsis* [fight]

---

athléō means literally "to engage in competition or conflict"; it is also used figuratively in 4 Maccabees. *athléō* in 2 Tim. 2:5 suggests the need for exertion, sacrifice, and discipline. *synathléō* in Phil. 1:27; 4:3 carries the idea of striving, suffering, and working together. *áthlēsis* in Heb. 10:32-33 evokes the image of public struggle in the arena. *athlētés* is used by Ignatius (*To Polycarp* 1.3) and 1 Clement (5.1) for leaders and the apostles, while Christ is the supreme *athlētés* in Acts of Thomas 39.
→ *agōn*   [E. STAUFFER, I, 167-68]

---

aídios [eternal]

---

aídios as "everlasting" or "eternal" was common in Aristotle and important to Philo (for God). Rom. 1:20 recalls Philo (and Stoicism) when speaking of God's "eternal" power. Jude 6 ("eternal chains") is the only other instance in the NT. Josephus has the same word for John's imprisonment "for life" (*The Jewish War* 6.434).

[H. SASSE, I, 168]

---

aidṓs [modesty]

A. The Greek Terms for Shame and Disgrace.
a. *aidṓs* was an old term, rare in Hellenism, revived by Stoicism. It denoted reverence, e.g., for God, divine things, rulers, and parents, as well as respect for laws of hospitality, marriage and family, the state and its laws. Applied inwardly, it could then suggest a "sense of shame" but also a "sense of honor" in contrast to shamelessness or insolence.

b. Early on, it was linked with the distinct word *aischýnē,* "shame" at an act, or lowly birth, or humiliation, though also "disgrace" and even perhaps "ignominy."

B. The Hellenistic Use of *aidṓs*. Philo has *aidṓs* in the Greek and later Stoic sense, but in the LXX we find it only in 3 Macc. 1:19; 4:5, though the verb *aideísthai* is more common (e.g., Prov. 24:38), and *anaidḗs* is often used for "insolent," e.g., with face, eye, or mind.

C. The Early Christian Use of *aidṓs*. The only sure instance in the NT is "modest demeanor" in 1 Tim. 2:9. *adeísthai* does not occur at all, nor do the apostolic fathers use *aidṓs*. The reason for this absence of the group is that a Christian's being is not defined by his relation to himself but by his relation to God and neighbor, and the relation to neighbor rests on the neighbor's claim rather than a sense of the state or cosmos.   [R. BULTMANN, I, 169-71]

→ *aischýnē*

---

haíma [blood],   *haimatekchysía* [shedding of blood]

1. The word *haíma* means physical "blood" (Jn. 19:34). We are made of "flesh and blood" and as such are frail (Mt. 16:17; Gal. 1:16; 1 Cor. 15:50; Eph. 6:12; Heb. 2:14). The phrase "flesh and blood" is an established Jewish one (though not OT) for humanity. Blood carries the ongoing life of the species (cf. Jn. 1:13; Acts 17:26). Its use for "descent" or "family" was ancient and widespread.

2. The OT belief in the sanctity of blood underlies the ban on eating it. In sacrifice the life-bearing blood is a means of expiation (Lev. 17:11).

3. "To shed blood" is to destroy life, and the phrase can thus be used for killing (cf. Mt. 27:4, 24; Acts 5:28 [Jesus] and Mt. 23:30, 35; Lk. 11:50-51; Rev. 16:6; 17:6 [prophets, saints, witnesses]). God avenges blood (Rev. 6:10). The Western version of the apostolic decree (Acts 15:9) prohibits murder. Resisting to blood in Heb. 12:4 probably means incurring wounds rather than suffering martyrdom. According to Hebrews blood is shed to ward off the destroying angel (11:28), to institute the divine order (9:18), to consecrate the tent and cultic vessels (9:21), and to effect atonement and purification (13:11).

4. The blood of Christ is supremely significant in the NT (1 Cor. 10:16; Eph. 2:13)—not his material blood, but its shedding in violent death. This guarantees the

new order (1 Cor. 11:25). This order includes forgiveness of sin (Rom. 3:25; Col. 1:20; Eph. 1:7; 1 Pet. 1:2; 1 Jn. 1:7; Rev. 1:5). Legal and sacrificial images are used in this connection but should not be pressed too strongly. Thus Christ's self-offering is expressed by the idea of his sacrificial blood. Hebrews compares this blood with that of animals (9:12 etc.), but the effect of Christ's blood is ethical (9:14). Fellowship with Christ's blood in the eucharist (1 Cor. 10:16) means union with him who died for us and does not involve blood mysticism, though there is some hint of this in Clement of Alexandria *Paedagogus* 2.2.19.4.

5. In apocalyptic, blood may be used for the color red, indicating eschatological terrors such as war (Acts 2:19), hail and fire (Rev. 8:7), and judgment (Rev. 14:20). Ex. 7:17ff. underlies this use. Wine is the blood of grapes in Gen. 49:11; Dt. 32:14, etc., and the wine harvest is an eschatological image in Is. 63:3; cf. Rev. 14:19-20.

haimatekchysía. This word occurs only in Heb. 9:22 (the first instance) and refers to the shedding of blood in sacrifices, though not specifically to pouring or sprinkling. The point is that the giving of life is the necessary presupposition of forgiveness. Only prefigured in the OT, this has now been effected by Christ. Elsewhere the term occurs only in the fathers, e.g., Tatian *Address to the Greeks* 23.2.   [J. BEHM, I, 172-77]

---

ainéō [to praise],   *aínos* [praise]

---

ainéō. Of the two main senses, "to praise" and "to tell," the former alone is important. The eight instances in the NT refer to joyful praise of God in hymn or prayer by individuals (Lk. 2:20; Acts 3:8-9), a group (Lk. 19:37), the community (Acts 2:47; Rev. 19:5), or angels (Lk. 2:13).

aínos. Meaning "story," "resolve," or "praise," this word occurs twice in the NT (Mt. 21:16; Lk. 18:43) for praise in the religious sense.   [H. SCHLIER, I, 177-78]

---

aínigma [riddle],   *ésoptron* [mirror]

---

aínigma occurs only in 1 Cor. 13:12, which contrasts present and future seeing. It means "riddle" and suggests oracular utterances: God speaks to his prophets (except Moses) in riddles (Num. 12:8), which are equated with visions (12:6). *ésoptron* means "to see in a glass." The rabbis speak of the prophets seeing God in nine clouded mirrors, Moses in one clear one. The point here is not that mirrors in antiquity are necessarily indistinct nor that they give only the reflection, but that this is the form of prophetic revelation. Thus *aínigma* and *ésoptron* both refer to prophetic vision but are not tautological; the former stresses its obscure nature, the latter its general form. We see in a mirror, but only indistinctly as in a riddle. Paul here seems to be following the Hebrew text of Num. 12:8 and rabbinic exegesis.   [G. KITTEL, I, 178-80]

---

hairéomai [to choose],   *haíresis* [sect, school],   *hairetikós* [heretical],
hairetízō [to choose],   *diairéō* [to distribute],   *diaíresis* [distribution]

---

hairéomai. *hairéō* means "to take," "to win," "to comprehend," "to select" (middle). The last is the sense in the NT, e.g., selective preference in Phil. 1:22; Heb. 11:25, and God's election of the community in 2 Th. 2:13.

hairesis.

A. *hairesis* **in Classical Usage and Hellenism.** On the basis of *hairéō*, the senses are "seizure," "choice," "resolve." Choice of opinion led to the philosophical use for "teaching," "school," with the associated ideas of delimitation from other schools, the authority of the teacher, specific doctrine, and the private character of these features.

B. *hairesis* **in the LXX and Judaism.** The sense of "choice" occurs, e.g., in Lev. 22:18, but Philo uses it for philosophical schools, e.g., in *On Noah's Work as a Planter* 151, and Josephus for the Essenes and Jewish parties in *The Jewish War* 2.118; *Life* 12. The corresponding rabbinic term was first used for parties in Judaism but later only for those opposed by the rabbis (late 1st and early 2nd cent.) and then for non-Jewish groups (late 2nd cent.).

C. *hairesis* **in the NT.**
1. The usage in Acts resembles that of Josephus and the early rabbis (Acts 5:17; 24:5; 26:5).
2. Yet there is from the outset a suspicion of the *hairesis* within Christianity itself, not through the development of orthodoxy, but through the basic incompatibility of *ekklēsía* and *hairesis* (cf. Gal. 5:20; 1 Cor. 11:18-19). In 1 Cor. 1:10ff. *hairesis* has a sifting purpose. In 2 Pet. 2:1 it affects the church's very basis; a *hairesis* creates a new society alongside the *ekklēsía* and thus makes the *ekklēsía* itself a *hairesis* and not the comprehensive people of God. This is unacceptable.

D. *hairesis* **in the Early Church.** *hairesis* is still a basic threat in Ignatius *Ephesians* 6.2; Justin *Dialogue with Trypho* 51.2. The term has a technical sense, but a sense of basic hostility remains, as when it is used for philosophical schools, Jewish sects, and especially Gnostic societies. Origen, however, surrenders the distinction between *ekklēsía* and *hairesis* when he compares differences within Christianity to those in medicine and philosophy (*Against Celsus* 3.12).

hairetikós. This word can denote "one who can choose aright," but in Christianity it was used always for "adherent of a heresy" (cf. Tit. 3:9-10; *Didascalia* 33.31).

hairetízō. Found only in Mt. 12:18, quoting Is. 42:1 and perhaps reflecting 1 Chr. 28:6; Mal. 3:17, this word means "to choose."

diairéō, diairesis. *diairéō* has five meanings: "to dissolve," "to distinguish," "to decide," "to distribute," "to apportion." The last two are most common in the LXX (Gen. 4:7 etc.), and are the obvious meaning in the NT at Lk. 15:12 and 1 Cor. 12:11, where the Spirit allots various gifts to members of the community as he wills. *diairesis* similarly means "separation," "division," and "distribution," e.g., of property. The context of 1 Cor. 12:4ff. shows that the meaning there is "distribution" rather than "distinction": the one Spirit is seen in the apportionment of spiritual gifts, the one *cháris* in the *charísmata*, *diairesis* covers both the distribution and what is distributed. Later *diairesis* came to be used for the intertrinitarian distinction (cf. Origen *Commentary on John* 1.2.10.74).   [H. SCHLIER, I, 180-85]

---

airō [to lift up, carry off],   *epairō* [to lift up]

---

airō. The meanings are "to lift from the ground," "to lift in order to carry," and "to carry off."

1. The sense "to lift up" occurs for raising the hand in an oath (Rev. 10:5), raising the face in prayer (Jn. 11:41), and raising the voice in prayer (Acts 4:24).

2. "To take up and carry" in Mt. 11:29 means obeying God's will as it is revealed in Jesus in contrast to the yoke of the Torah. Taking up the cross denotes readiness for self-denial (and even martyrdom) in following Jesus (Mk. 8:34).

3. "To carry off" is used of death in Acts 8:33; Jn. 17:15, of depriving of salvation in Mt. 21:43, of taking away knowledge in Lk. 11:52, of removing judgment in Acts 8:33, of taking away guilt by the cross in Col. 2:14, and of the expiation of sin in 1 Jn. 3:5.

Whether the sense in Jn. 1:29 is "to take up and carry," i.e., in a vicarious bearing of penalty, or "to carry off," i.e., to remove by expiation, is debatable. If there is a reference to the Servant of the Lord, the former is more likely, but Lamb of God favors the latter: "takes away the sin of the world" (by the atoning power of his blood; cf. 1 Jn. 1:7).

epaírō. Used most frequently in the LXX for "to set or lift up," *epaírō* has 1. the religious sense of lifting up in prayer (1 Tim. 2:8; Lk. 18:13; Jn. 17:1), sometimes in a gesture of blessing (Lk. 24:50) or of hope (Lk. 21:28). It can also have 2. the figurative sense "to raise up oneself," "oppose," "exalt oneself," in arrogant assertion against God (2 Cor. 10:5) or others (2 Cor. 11:20).   [J. JEREMIAS, I, 185-86]

---

aisthánomai [to perceive, understand], **aísthēsis** [insight], **aisthētḗrion** [sense, faculty]

A. The Linguistic Usage outside the NT. The verb has three main references: a. "sensory perception," b. "perception" or "discernment," and c. "intellectual understanding." The noun follows a similar pattern, being "sense" or "organ of sense," then "discernment," and finally "judgment." For Philo *aísthēsis* is the cause of passions, but it may be trained, and it can even be consciousness, with a hint of moral consciousness. Philo often opposes it to *noús* and religious awareness, but he can also say that in action *noús* is dependent on correct *aísthēsis*. *aisthētḗrion* is "organ of sense" in Philo (even of the *psychḗ*). In the LXX the group is used first for "sensory perception," then "perception" in general (Job 23:5), and finally "judgment" or "understanding" pressing on to decision (cf. Prov. 17:10; Is. 49:26; Is. 33:11). In Prov. 1:7 *aísthēsis* can even be compared with wisdom and instruction.

B. The Word Group in the NT. In Lk. 9:45 *aisthánomai* obviously means "to understand." In Phil. 1:9 *aísthēsis* means "moral discrimination." In Heb. 5:14 *aisthētḗria* (plural) are organs which, when trained, are to distinguish between the good and the bad. Without developed organs of this kind the doctrine of justification (v. 13) will be misunderstood, as by Paul's Judaizing opponents.   [G. DELLING, I, 187-88]

---

aischýnō [to be ashamed], **epaischýnō** [to be ashamed], **kataischýnō** [to put to shame], **aischýnē** [shame], **aischrós** [shameful], **aischrótēs** [shame]

A. The Linguistic Usage in the LXX. Unlike the *aidós* group, this group was in common use and is thus often found in the LXX. The sense is "to shame," "put to shame" (God mostly as subject), "be shamed or ashamed" (personally rather than publicly). The main point of *aischýnē* is not "feeling of shame" but "disgrace," i.e., the shame brought by divine judgment, though sometimes with a stress on "being ashamed."

B. The NT Usage. The same meanings are found here: "to shame" (1 Cor. 11:4-5), "to bring to shame" (1 Cor. 1:27), "to be ashamed" (Lk. 16:3), almost "disillusioned" (Phil. 1:20). *aischýnē* means "disgrace" (Heb. 12:2; Jude 13), with a play on the sexual sense in Rev. 3:18. *aischrós* means "what is disgraceful" (1 Cor. 11:6; Eph. 5:12; Tit. 1:11). *aischrótēs* occurs only in Eph. 5:4 where it refers to "shameful talk."
→ *aidṓs*   [R. BULTMANN, I, 189-91]

---

aitéō [to demand], *aítēma* [request], *apaitéō* [to demand back], *exaitéō* [to require], *paraitéomai* [to reject]

---

aitéō (aitéomai).
1. "To demand." In the NT demands are often given a religious application (cf. Lk. 12:48). The Jews demand accrediting signs (1 Cor. 1:22). People will call us to account for our faith, i.e., demand an explanation of it (1 Pet. 3:15).
2. "To request." Found in both the active and the middle with little distinction, the verb in this sense has both a secular and a religious use. In secular usage we may have a transaction (cf. Mk. 6:24-25) or an official request (e.g., Mk. 15:43; Acts 9:2). In religious usage prayer is the most important reference (sometimes juxtaposed with ordinary requests, Mt. 7:9ff.). Jesus never uses this word for his own prayers (cf. Jn. 16:26), perhaps because it involves requests for self, or has an element of demanding, or is less intimate than *erōtáō* (which is used for the disciples' requests to Jesus and those of Jesus to God). The general use does not support distinguishing the active (for uttered requests) from the middle (for inner requests) in Jms. 4:2-3.

aítēma. "Request," "petition," "desire," especially for individual petitions, with a reference to the content (Phil. 4:6; 1 Jn. 5:15).

apaitéō.
1. "To demand back"—something seized (Lk. 6:30), or "to call in debts"—what is loaned (Lk. 12:48).
2. "To demand"—an account (1 Pet. 3:15).

exaitéō. "To require," "demand the freedom of," "demand the surrender of." The third of these is the most likely sense in Lk. 22:31: Peter is to be handed over for sifting (cf. Job). Jesus allows this, but sustains Peter with his prayer (v. 32).

paraitéomai.
1. "To beg," hence "to beg off" in Lk. 14:18-19 (middle and passive).
2. "To seek to turn aside by asking," suggesting in Heb. 12:19 that what was in Dt. 5:25 a justifiable request (through fear) is a sinful repudiation of divine revelation; in Acts 25:12 Paul will not try to avert punishment by entreaty.
3. "To reject or repudiate" (only in the Pastorals)—myths in 1 Tim. 4:7, controversies in 2 Tim. 2:23, widows under 60 in 1 Tim. 5:11, heretics (excommunication) in Tit. 3:10.

4. "To spurn"—used in Heb. 12:25 of refusing to listen to God.
→ *eúchomai*   [G. Stählin, I, 191-95]

---

aichmálōtos [captive], *aichmalōtízō* [to lead captive], *aichmalōteúō* [to capture], *aichmalōsía* [captivity], *synaichmálōtos* [fellow captive]

---

1. Proper Use. The "prisoner of war" is a miserable person in special need of divine aid (cf. Lk. 21:24). The exile gave the term a religious reference (cf. Ps. 126:1). The messenger of Is. 61:1 proclaims freedom to captives, and Jesus accepts this as a messianic task (Lk. 4:18). Visiting prisoners is a loving duty (Mt. 25:36ff.), and working and praying for release is enjoined (cf. Phlm. 22). God himself grants liberation in Acts 5:19.

2. Figurative Use. Imprisonment may be used to denote subjection to error (2 Tim. 3:6) or sin (Rom. 7:23), but also to Christ (Eph. 4:8; 2 Cor. 10:5). Paul calls his helpers "fellow-prisoners," probably not in a literal sense but in the sense of being similarly subject to Christ (cf. "fellow-servants," Col. 1:7; 4:7).

[G. Kittel, I, 195-97]

---

aiṓn [age, aeon], *aiṓnios* [eternal]

---

aiṓn.

A. The Nonbiblical Use. Meanings are a. "vital force," b. "lifetime," c. "age" or "generation," d. "time," and e. "eternity."

The term is used in philosophical discussions of time, usually for a span of time as distinct from time as such *(chrónos)*, though for Plato it is timeless eternity in contrast to *chrónos* as its moving image in earthly time (cf. Philo). In the Hellenistic world *Aiṓn* becomes the name of the god of eternity.

B. *aiṓn* in the Sense of Prolonged Time or Eternity.

1. The Formulas "from Eternity" and "to Eternity."

a. The concepts of time and eternity merge in the use with prepositions suggesting indefinite time (Lk. 1:70; Acts 3:21; Jn. 9:32; Jude 13). Sometimes the meaning is "from a remote time" (Lk. 1:70; Jn. 9:32— "never"), but sometimes there is a strong hint of eternity (Lk. 1:55; Jn. 6:51). This is especially true of the plural (Mt. 6:13; Lk. 1:33; Rom. 1:25; Heb. 13:8; Jude 25; cf. also with a past reference 1 Cor. 2:7; Col. 1:26; Eph. 3:11). The double formula "for ever and ever" (Heb. 1:8), especially in the plural (in Paul and Revelation; cf. also Heb. 13:21; 1 Pet. 4:11), is designed to stress the concept of eternity, as are constructions like that in Eph. 3:21 ("to all generations for ever and ever").

b. The usage corresponds to that of the LXX (cf. Am. 9:11; Is. 45:17; Ps. 45:6), the only difference being intensification in the NT.

2. The Eternity of God.

a. *aiṓn* means eternity in the full sense when linked with God (Rom. 16:26; 1 Tim. 1:17; cf. Jer. 10:10).

b. In the OT this means first that God always was (Gen. 21:23) and will be (Dt. 5:23), in contrast to us mortals. By the time of Is. 40:28 this comes to mean that God

31

is eternal, the "First and Last," whose being is "from eternity to eternity" (Ps. 90:2). Eternity is unending time, but in later Judaism it is sometimes set in antithesis to time. The NT took over the Jewish formulas but extended eternity to Christ (Heb. 1:10ff.; Rev. 1:17-18; 2:8). Here again eternity could be seen as the opposite of cosmic time, God's being and acts being put in terms of pre- and post- (1 Cor. 2:7; Col. 1:26; Eph. 3:9; Jn. 17:24; 1 Pet. 1:20).

C. *aíōn* in the Sense of the Time of the World.

1. aíōn as the Time of the World; the End of the aíōn. In the plural the sense of *aíōn* is that of a stretch of time. In particular the word is used for the duration of the world. Thus the same term can signify both God's eternity and the world's duration (cf. the Parsee word *zrvan*). The doctrine of creation—an absolute beginning—underlay the distinction in use. *aíōn* for time of the world occurs in the NT in the expression "end of the aeon" (Mt. 13:39 etc.). The plural in Heb. 9:26 and 1 Cor. 10:11 (aeons) represents no essential change; it merely indicates that the one aeon is made up of many smaller aeons, though as yet the word is not used for a particular period.

2. aíōn as World. From "time of the world" *aíōn* easily came to mean the "world" itself (cf. Mt. 13:22; 1 Cor. 7:33) with an equation of cosmos and aeon (1 Cor. 1:20; 2:6; 3:19). The plural can mean "worlds" along the same lines (Heb. 1:2; 11:3).

3. The Present and Future aíōn.

a. If *aíōn* means "duration of the world," and the plural occurs, the idea is obvious that eternity embraces a succession or recurrence of aeons (cf. Eccl. 1:9-10—though here the aeons are periods of the world, and the biblical concept of creation, and hence of the uniqueness of this aeon, ruled out the idea of an unending series).

b. Instead of recurrence the antithesis of time and eternity combined with the thought of plural aeons to produce the belief in a new and future aeon (or cosmos or kingdom) which will succeed this one but will be completely different from it. For the present and future aeons in the NT cf. Mk. 10:30; Lk. 16:8; Rom. 12:2; 1 Cor. 1:20; Gal. 1:4; 1 Tim. 6:17; Eph. 1:21; Heb. 6:5 (and with *kairós* instead of *aíōn*, Jn. 8:23 etc.).

c. The NT took over this concept from Jewish apocalyptic, e.g., Ethiopian Enoch. Similar ideas occur in rabbinic writings and there is hope of a future age in Vergil. In the NT, however, the new aeon is not just future. Believers are already redeemed from this aeon (Gal. 1:4) and taste the powers of the future aeon (Heb. 6:5) which Christ has initiated with his resurrection.

D. The Personification of *Aíōn*.
Important in Hellenistic syncretism, the personification of *Aíōn* is absent from the NT (except for a suggestion in Eph. 2:2).

aíōnios. An adjective meaning "eternal," and found in the LXX in Pss. 24; 77:5; Gen. 21:33, *aíōnios* in the NT is used 1. of God (Rom. 16:26), 2. of divine possessions and gifts (2 Cor. 4:18; Heb. 9:14; 1 Pet. 5:10; 1 Tim. 6:16; 2 Th. 2:16, and 3. of the eternal kingdom (2 Pet. 1:11), inheritance (Heb. 9:15), body (2 Cor. 5:1), and even judgment (Heb. 6:2, though cf. Mt. 18:8; 2 Th. 1:9, where the sense is perhaps "unceasing"). For a more temporal use, see Rom. 16:25; Phlm. 15.

[H. SASSE, I, 197-209]

akatharsía, akáthartos → *katharós; akaíros* → *kairós; ákakos* → *kakós; ákarpos* → *karpós; akátagnōstos* → *ginōskō; akatákritos* → *krínō; akatálytos* → *lýō; akatastasía, akatástatos* → *kathístēmi*

---

akéraios [pure, innocent]

The original meanings of *akéraios* are a. "Unravaged," "unharmed," of a city, walls, country. b. "Intact," "innocent." c. "Pure," e.g., of wine, or gold.

The sense is always figurative in the NT: Christians are to be innocent (Phil. 2:15); to maintain their integrity in face of evil (Rom. 16:19).   [G. KITTEL, I, 209-10]

---

akolouthéō [to follow], *exakolouthéō* [to follow], *epakolouthéō* [to follow], *parakolouthéō* [to accompany], *synakolouthéō* [to accompany]

---

akolouthéō.

A. *akolouthein* **and** *hépesthai* **in Greek Usage.** In Greek the ordinary sense of following led to that of intellectual, moral, and religious following, though for following God, *hépesthai,* not used in the NT, is more common.

B. Discipleship in the OT and Judaism.

1. The Following of God by the Righteous. The more common phrase here is "to go after other gods" (Judg. 2:12; Dt. 4:3; Jer. 11:10, etc.), and this is linked with adultery in Hosea (1:2; 2:7, 13). Going after Yahweh occurs in Deuteronomy (1:36 etc.) but does not receive emphasis (except in 1 Kgs. 18:21); this is because of the association with idolatry. Even when Jer. 2:2 refers to going after Yahweh in the wilderness (Ex. 13:21-22), the thought in view is that of marriage. "Walking in God's ways" is the preferred expression (Dt. 5:30 etc.). The rabbis found it hard to conceive of following God, only his qualities (insofar as this is now possible). Philo adopted Greek usage, and Josephus could link *akolouthía* with the law in the sense of obedience to it.

2. The Following of the Disciple. Following is literal in the OT (cf. Judg. 9:4; Jer. 2:2). This applies when Elisha is said to follow Elijah in 1 Kgs. 19:20-21. The same is true of rabbis and their students; the former go on ahead, and the latter follow them, but with no suggestion of any figurative significance.

C. *akolouthein* **in the NT.** Due to the OT inheritance and the new turn given by Christ's presence, the NT has no reference to "going after" God. The term is reserved for being a disciple of Christ (except when the sense is very general) and is confined to the four Gospels (apart from Rev. 14:4). External following is still involved (cf. Mt. 8:19; Mk. 10:28) but with a total commitment and in an exclusive relation to one who is recognized as not just a teacher but the Messiah. This discipleship brings participation in salvation (Mk. 10:17; Lk. 9:61-62; Jn. 8:12; Rev. 14:4), but also in suffering (Mt. 8:19-20; Mk. 8:34; Jn. 12:25-26). The strength of the figurative use may have been in the presence of sayings like Mt. 10:38, the possibility of discipleship without literally going after Jesus, and the active stress which rules out the use of a noun to express the concept. Since it is the historical Jesus that is followed, it is natural that other terms should be found in the other NT writings to describe the relation to the exalted Lord and his Spirit. Rev. 14:4 simply applies Mt. 10:38 to a particular group.

exakolouthéō. This has only a figurative sense in the NT, where it occurs only in 2 Peter: following "myths" in 1:16, "licentiousness" in 2:2, "the way of Balaam" in 2:15.

epakolouthéō. This, too, has a figurative sense: a. "to follow," e.g., the signs in Mk. 16:20, sin in 1 Tim. 5:24, "in Christ's steps" in 1 Pet. 2:21; b. "to pursue a matter" in 1 Tim. 5:10.

parakolouthéō. a. "To go along with," "accompany," e.g., the signs (Mk. 16:17); b. "to look into" (Lk. 1:3); c. "not to let slip," "to follow what has been grasped" (1 Tim. 4:6).

synakolouthéō. "To go along" with Jesus, though only externally in Mk. 5:37; 14:51, and perhaps in Lk. 23:49. Oddly, the term does not take on the pregnant sense of the simple form *akolouthéō,* as one might have expected in view of its figurative senses "to understand," "to obey," in secular Greek (Plato *Laws* 1.629).

[G. KITTEL, I, 210-16]

---

akoúō [to hear, listen], *akoḗ* [hearing], *eisakoúō* [to obey], *epakoúō* [to listen], *parakoúō* [to fail to hear], *parakoḗ* [disobedience], *hypakoúō* [to listen, obey], *hypakoḗ* [obedience], *hypḗkoos* [obedient]

---

akoúō (→ *blépo, horáō*).

A. The Hearing of Man. The use of the group in the NT reflects the significance of God's word; hearing corresponds to revelation as its form of appropriation.

1. The Hearing of Revelation outside the NT.

a. In the Greek mysteries and Gnosticism more stress is laid on apprehension of God by seeing. Hearing can lead astray, not seeing (Philo *On Flight* 208). If some revelation is by hearing, the true mystery is known to sight. In the Mithras liturgy the God appears. Monuments depicting religious acts show that the climax often comes with vision.

b. The OT and Judaism have a different emphasis. Even when God is said to be seen, the usage is not strict. True vision is dangerous (Gen. 19:26; Ex. 3:6) and unusual (Ex. 33:11, 20). Seeing God is eschatological (Is. 60:1ff.). Even when Moses is face to face with God, they speak (Ex. 33:11). Seeing God is a setting for his word (Is. 6:1ff.). The decisive call is to hear (Is. 1:2, 10; Am. 7:16). Hearing entails action in obedience as true seeking (Jer. 29:13; Mic. 6:8).

c. Symbols are important in apocalyptic, but usually in relation to words (Dan. 7:17ff.; 8:16ff.). For the rabbis hearing is through reading out loud the holy books. Recitation of the Shema brings out the importance of hearing, for the passages used (Dt. 6:4ff.; 11:13ff.; Num. 15:37ff.) show that we know God by studying and keeping his law. The voice from heaven rather than the vision becomes the way of direct, physical apprehension of God.

2. The Hearing of Revelation in the NT.

a. The NT revelation, too, is a word or message. We receive what Jesus did and said by hearing (cf. Mk. 4:24; Mt. 11:4; Lk. 2:20; Acts 2:33; 1 Jn. 1:1). What Jesus looked like is of no interest. Seeing is directed to his acts. Parables like that of the sower are parables of hearing. Things seen take on significance in what is heard (cf.

Mk. 9:7; 2 Cor. 12:3; Acts 18:9). *akoúein* in the absolute can express the true hearing of appropriation (Mk. 4:9). The content of hearing corresponds to that of what is heard. It is the reception of grace and the call to repentance in response to salvation and its ethical demand. Thus faith and obedience are the marks of real hearing (cf. Rom. 1:5; 16:26): the "obedience of faith."

b. This aspect is strong in John but also present in the other Evangelists. Note the message to the Baptist in Mt. 11:4, the blessing in Mt. 13:16, and the condemnation in Mk. 4:12. Yet since Jesus is present in work as well as word, eschatological seeing is also a factor (Mt. 11:20ff.).

B. The Hearing of God. *akoúein* can also refer to God's hearing of prayers, though *eisakoúō* is more common in this regard. *epakoúō* and *epékoos,* common in Hellenism for hearing deity, are largely avoided. For instances of God or Jesus hearing cf. Jn. 11:41-42; Acts 7:34; 2 Cor. 6:2; Heb. 5:7; 1 Jn. 5:14-15.

akoḗ. This common word has the active meaning 1. "sense of hearing" and the passive one 2. "report." In the NT it can mean "preaching" with a stress on the hearing (cf. 1 Th. 2:13; Rom. 10:16ff.; Heb. 4:2). In Gal. 3:2 the point is not "believing hearing" but "preaching of faith," i.e., with faith as the content and goal. In the pagan world *akoaí* was also used 3. for the ears put on sanctuary walls to symbolize hearing deity. The singular *akoḗ* could also be the place of hearing mysterious voices in a temple.

eisakoúō. With the basic senses "to hear" and "consent," this means a. "to obey" in secular Greek and the LXX, and b. "to hear," "answer," always passive in the NT: Lk. 1:13; Mt. 6:7; Acts 10:31; Heb. 5:7 (Christ).

epakoúō. This is the technical word for the hearing of deity, *epékoos* being a popular epiphet for pagan gods. The only NT instance is 2 Cor. 6:2 (cf. Is. 49:8 LXX). Avoidance of the term may reflect a desire to differentiate God from pagan deities.

parakoúō, parakoḗ (→ *apeithéō*). There are three meanings: a. "to overhear," b. "to hear incorrectly," and c. "to disregard." Sense a. seems to be the point in Mk. 5:35-36, sense c. in Mt. 18:17. *parakoḗ* in the NT bears sense c. (cf. Acts 7:57; Rom. 5:19; 2 Cor. 10:6; Heb. 2:2).

hypakoúō (→ *peitharchéō*).
1. "To hear the door," i.e., "open" (Acts 12:13).
2. "To obey." The word is used in this sense for wives, children, and servants (Eph. 6:1, 5; Col. 3:20, 22), for demons and nature (Mk. 1:27; 4:41), for humanity in general relative to good or evil moral powers (Acts 6:7; Rom. 6:12, 16-17; 2 Th. 1:8), and for the community (Phil. 2:12; cf. Acts 5:32). LXX usage shows how strongly the sense of hearing is present in obedience (cf. Gen. 22:18; Jer. 13:10).

hypakoḗ, hypékoos. Except in Phlm. 21, this word always implies religious decision (e.g., Rom. 6:16—over against *hamartía* in Rom. 6:16 and *parakoḗ* in Rom. 5:19). What is obeyed may be the truth (1 Pet. 1:22) or Christ (2 Cor. 10:5), who is himself the subject in Rom. 5:19. The denotation is not the ethical attitude but the religious act from which it derives (1 Pet. 1:14). The obedience of faith (Rom. 1:5; 16:26) implies that the message of faith issues in obedience. *hypékoos* means "obedient"— to God (Acts 7:39), to the apostle (2 Cor. 2:9). Christ himself is *hypékoos* in fulfilling his divine mission (Phil. 2:8).   [G. Kittel, I, 216-25]

---

akrobystía [foreskin]

1. The Etymology of the Word. This word, translated "foreskin," is formed from *ákros* ("running to a point") and *býō* ("to stop up") but may really be based on the medical *akroposthía* ("foreskin" or "male organ").

2. The Occurrence of the Word. It is found only in biblical and ecclesiastical Greek with both a literal and a figurative reference and as the opposite of *peritomḗ*. There are 20 instances in the NT, only in Paul apart from Acts 11:3 (cf. Rom. 2:25, 26, 27; 3:30; 4:9, 10, 11, 12; 1 Cor. 7:18, 19; Gal. 2:7; 5:6; 6:15; Eph. 2:11; Col. 2:13; 3:11). Barnabas has it (quoting the OT, 9.5 and 13.7) among early Christian writers, and so do Justin and Ignatius. [K. L. SCHMIDT, I, 225-26]

→ *peritomḗ*

---

akrogōniaíos → *gōnía; akyróō* → *kyróō; ákōn* → *hekṓn*

---

alazṓn [arrogant], *alazoneía* [arrogance]

The *alazṓn* is "one who makes more of himself than reality justifies," or "promises more than he can perform," often used of orators, philosophers, doctors, cooks, and officials. A link with pride is sometimes seen; hence in Hab. 2:5 the *alazṓn* is one who does not trust in God. The term occurs in the lists in Rom. 1:30 and 2 Tim. 3:2 in its usual sense and with a religious nuance. This nuance is stronger in the case of *alazoneía* in 1 Jn. 2:16 ("thinking one can shape one's own life apart from God") and Jms. 4:16 ("thinking one controls the future"). [G. DELLING, I, 226-27]

---

alalázō [to wail]

Denoting extravagant expressions of emotion, *alalázō* is employed 1. for "lamentation" in Mk. 5:38 and 2. for the "clanging" of cymbals, as in orgiastic cults, in 1 Cor. 13:1. [E. PETERSON, I, 227-28]

---

hálas [salt]

Salt was significant in the ancient world of religion as a symbol of endurance and worth. It was thus used in worship (Ex. 30:35; Lev. 2:13; Ezek. 43:21) and the making of covenants (Num. 18:19). The cultic use dropped away in the NT except figuratively, e.g., disciples must be seasoned with salt like sacrifices (Mk. 9:49). Salt still denoted moral worth, e.g., of disciples (Lk. 14:34-35), or speech (Col. 4:6). The reference to loss of taste (Lk. 14:34-35 and par.) may be based on the fact that Dead Sea salt soon acquired a stale or alkaline taste. [F. HAUCK, I, 228-29]

---
aleíphō [to anoint]

---

aleíphō is used in the LXX for Hebrew terms meaning "to anoint," "to rub over," "to pour an oil offering over," though *chríō* is a more common rendering and carries more significance. Thus the use is for purely outward anointing in the NT, though this can have its own deeper meaning.

1. In Mt. 6:17 anointing is for bodily comfort with a suggestion of joy and festivity not normally associated with fasting.

2. In Mt. 26:7; Lk. 7:38 it is a mark of honor shown to a guest. The woman's anointing of Jesus has the deeper proleptic sense of anointing for burial (cf. Mk. 16:1).

3. Anointing could also be used in cases of sickness, medicinally but with a magical nuance in view of the ascription of sickness to demonic influence. An instance of medical use is in Lk. 10:34. In Mk. 6:13 the disciples anointed the sick as well as preaching and expelling demons in their role as heralds of the inbreaking kingdom. In Jms. 5:14 the elders are to continue this ministry with prayer and the promise of healing and forgiveness. In the later church anointing came to be used at baptism, in exorcisms, and in cases of sickness, producing the medieval sacrament of extreme unction in the west. Ignatius (*Ephesians* 17.1) offers a fanciful exegesis of Mk. 14:3 whereby the ointment signifies the true knowledge with which we must be anointed to be led to immortality.   [H. SCHLIER, I, 229-32]

→ *chríō*

---
alḗtheia [truth], _alēthḗs_ [true], _alēthinós_ [true], _alētheúō_ [to speak the truth]

---

alḗtheia.

A. The OT Term for Truth.

1. The common OT word for truth appears some 126 times. It denotes a reality that is firm, solid, binding, and hence true. With reference to persons it characterizes their action, speech, or thought, and suggests integrity.

2. In law the word is used for a. the actual truth of a cause or process as shown by the facts (cf. Dt. 22:20; 1 Kgs. 10:6; Dan. 10:1). Only rarely is there a more abstract use, e.g., Gen. 4:16 ("whether it is as you say" or "whether there is any truth in you"). Normally the facts establish a matter beyond cavil, as also in the case of God's word (cf. 1 Kgs. 17:24; Jer. 23:28). Regard for facts is indispensable for the right dispensing of justice (Zech. 7:9; 8:16). b. An extension of this usage is to more general facts which demand recognition by all people as reality, as the normal state corresponding to divine and human order.

3. The religious use runs parallel to the legal but is not just a figurative application of it. It often denotes a religious reality that need not be explained by the forensic use. The righteous base their attitude to God on incontestable truth and practice truthfulness as God himself is truthful (cf. Ps. 51:6). Those who are qualified to dwell on God's hill speak truth in the heart, i.e., have their minds set on it (Ps. 15:2). Truth is linked with knowledge of God (Hos. 4:1). If it is fundamentally an attitude, the rational element in the legal use ties it to instruction in the law, i.e., Scripture (Ps. 119:160), for God's ordinances are true (Ps. 19:9). Thus walking in the truth can be

taught (Ps. 86:11). Truth can also be set in opposition to deceit (cf. Mal. 2:6; Prov. 11:8; 12:19). Poetic expressions have truth springing from the ground or falling in the street (Ps. 85:11; Is. 59:14), but when it is said to be dashed to the ground in Dan. 8:12 it seems to be equated with the true religion. Along similar lines God is said to be the true (i.e., the only) God in 2 Chr. 15:3. Yet a parallel phrase in Ps. 31:5 refers to the "reliable" God and thus adds an ethical dimension whereby God guarantees both moral and legal standards. Rich in truth (Ex. 34:6), God is worthy of trust. God does truth (Neh. 9:33), gives true laws (Neh. 9:13), gives valid commands (Ps. 111:7), swears truth (Ps. 132:11), and keeps the norm of truthfulness forever (Ps. 146:6). The element of trust, based on God's character, finds pregnant expression in 2 Sam. 7:28: "Thou art God, and thy words are true."   [G. QUELL, I, 232-37]

B. The Word for Truth in Rabbinic Judaism. The rabbinic use follows that of the OT. Truth is the basis of law, but with a religious reference, since law is a religious function. God's judgment is one of truth, but this is because God's very being is truth, and truth has its being in God. The image of the seal symbolizes this: God's seal is truth, truth meaning that God lives. A problem arises regarding the relationship between God's truth and kindness when truth signifies judgment. If truth is sometimes put first, the two are both seen to be essential qualities in God.

[G. KITTEL, I, 237-38]

C. The Greek and Hellenistic Use of *alḗtheia*. The NT usage is partly determined by the Hebrew term and partly by the nonbiblical use of *alḗtheia*. The two are not coincident, for the LXX had to use such words as *pístis* and *dikaiosýnē* as well as *alḗtheia* for the Hebrew. If it could use *alḗtheia* too, this is to be seen in the light of the flexible Greek usage.

1. The Original Greek Usage and Its Differentiations. Etymologically *alḗtheia* means "nonconcealment." It thus denotes what is seen, indicated, expressed, or disclosed, i.e., a thing as it really is, not as it is concealed or falsified. *alḗtheia* is "the real state of affairs," e.g., the truth in law, or real events in history, or true being in philosophy. Links develop with *lógos,* whose function it is to reveal, and *pístis,* since one may rely on truth and is also trustworthy when speaking it. *alḗtheia* can thus denote "truthfulness" as a personal quality. The philosophical question of absolute truth as distinct from relative truths, while alien to the OT, raises the similar concept of truth as a norm, which in practice yields the sense of "correct doctrine" that indicates the truth.

2. The Usage of Dualism. If in philosophy *alḗtheia* denotes true being, and if this is located in the world of ideas that is hidden from the senses and comprehended in thought, *alḗtheia* comes to mean "genuine reality" in antithesis to appearance. In Hellenism what truly is can then be equated with what is divine or eternal, in which one must share to be saved. Many circles no longer think this can be attained by thought but only by ecstasy or revelation, i.e., from the divine sphere. *alḗtheia* thus comes into relation with *dýnamis* (power) and then with the *gnṓsis* (knowledge) that it mediates and the *zōḗ* (life) and *phṓs* (light) that it gives. Similar connections are made with *pneúma* (spirit) and *noús* (mind) insofar as these concepts describe the divine sphere.

D. The Early Christian Use of *alḗtheia*.

1. *alḗtheia* is "that which has certainty and force": a. as a valid norm (with a hint of what is genuine) in Eph. 4:21; Gal. 1:6; b. as judicial righteousness (in the case of *alēthinós,* cf. Rev. 15:3); c. as uprightness in Jn. 3:21; 2 Jn. 4; 1 Cor. 13:6; Eph. 4:24.

2. *alḗtheia* is "that on which one can rely": a. as trustworthiness (Rom. 3:3ff.; 15:8); b. as sincerity or honesty (2 Cor. 7:14; 11:10; 2 Jn. 1; 3 Jn. 1).

3. *alḗtheia* is "the state of affairs as disclosed" (Rom. 1:18, 25; 2:2; 1 Jn. 3:18).

4. *alḗtheia* is "truth of statement," used with speaking (Lk. 4:25) or teaching (Mk. 12:14).

5. *alḗtheia* is "true teaching or faith" (2 Cor. 13:8; 4:2; Gal. 5:7; 1 Pet. 1:22); thus the preaching of the gospel is the word of truth (2 Cor. 6:7), becoming a Christian is coming to a knowledge of truth (1 Tim. 2:4), the Christian revelation is truth (2 Th. 2:10ff.), the church is the pillar and ground of truth (1 Tim. 3:15), and the *alḗtheia* is Christianity (2 Pet. 1:12).

6. *alḗtheia* is "authenticity," "divine reality," "revelation," especially in John, where this reality, as a possibility of human existence, is out of reach through the fall but is granted to faith through revelation by the word (cf. Jn. 8:44; 1 Jn. 1:8; 2:4). Ambiguity thus arises when Jesus is said to speak the truth, for this means not only that what he says is true but also that he brings revelation in words (Jn. 8:40, 45; 18:37). As revelation, *alḗtheia* is known (Jn. 8:32; 2 Jn. 1). This is not just a knowledge of a complex of statements but an encounter with Christ, who is the truth (Jn. 14:6) and who sanctifies in truth (Jn. 17:17, 19). God himself is disclosed herewith, the incarnate word being "full of grace and truth" (Jn. 1:14; cf. v. 17). Worship in truth is to be understood similarly, i.e., not just in pure knowledge but as determined by God's own reality, in *pneúma* (Spirit), and by the revelation made in Jesus (Jn. 4:23-24). Again, the Paraclete as the Spirit of truth insures ongoing revelation in the community (Jn. 14:17; 16:13; cf. 1 Jn. 5:6), and this comes to expression in right doctrine (1 Jn. 2:21) and a right way of life (1 Jn. 1:6). Thus the church's witness may be equated with that of truth (3 Jn. 12) and Christians are to be fellow workers in the truth (3 Jn. 8), loving one another in the truth and united in truth and love (2 Jn. 1ff.).

alēthḗs.

1. *alēthḗs* means a. "constant" or "valid," as in 1 Pet. 5:12; b. "judicially righteous" (*alēthinós* in the NT); c. "upright" (Phil. 4:5).

2. It also means a. "trustworthy" (Rom. 3:4); b. "sincere" (Mk. 12:14; 2 Cor. 6:8; Jn. 3:33).

3. Another sense is "real" (Acts 12:9; Jn. 4:18; 1 Jn. 2:8).

4. It indicates a "true statement" (e.g., Tit. 1:13; Jn. 5:31).

5. It also indicates "correct doctrine," but the NT does not have this sense.

6. It then means "genuine" (Jn. 6:55; probably Jn. 3:33; 7:18, i.e., he himself is not just truthful but authentic).

alēthinós.

1. This often has the same meaning as *alēthḗs*, e.g., "sincere" (Heb. 10:22). With reference to words it means "true" or "correct" (Jn. 4:37; 8:16), "sure and certain" (Rev. 21:5—with *pistoí*), "real" (Rev. 19:9); with reference to God's ways or judgments "valid" (Rev. 15:3; 16:7; 19:2).

2. As a divine attribute it has the sense of "reliable," "righteous," or "real" (cf. Ex. 34:6; Is. 65:16; 1 Th. 1:9; Jn. 7:28; 1 Jn. 5:20; Rev. 3:7; 6:10); in the NT it can be used of Christ as well as God.

3. In Hellenism it also takes on the sense of "real as eternal" or "real as mediated by revelation." Thus in Heb. 8:2 the heavenly tabernacle is "true" in contrast to the earthly, and in Heb. 9:24 the human sanctuary is a copy of the true one, which is genuine as divine, and as thus containing truth and dispensing revelation. Similarly

the true light of Jn. 1:9 is the light of life of Jn. 8:12, and the true bread from heaven is the bread of life (Jn. 6:32, 35, 48), while the true God of Jn. 7:28 is he who gives revelation, and Christ's true judgment is not merely just or trustworthy but authentic and definitive.

alētheúō. In Gal. 4:16 this may mean "speak the truth" but more probably means "preach the truth." In Eph. 4:15 (with love) it means "be sincere in love," or perhaps "live by true faith in love." [R. BULTMANN, I, 238-51]

---

allássō [to change], *antállagma* [exchange], *apallássō* [to release], *diallássō* [to exchange], *katallássō* [to reconcile], *katallagḗ* [reconciliation], *apokatallássō* [to reconcile], *metallássō* [to exchange]

---

allássō. The basic sense is "to make other than it is," used in both the active and middle for "to alter," "to give in exchange," "to take in exchange," and intransitively "to change." The NT uses only the transitive active and passive.
1. The word has the sense of "to change" in Acts 6:14; Gal. 4:20; 1 Cor. 15:51-52.
2. It means "to exchange" in Rom. 1:23.

antállagma. This means "purchase-money," "equivalent," "substitute." It occurs in the NT only in Mk. 8:37 = Mt. 16:26 (based on Ps. 49:7), not to stress the infinite worth of the human soul, but to show that divine judgment is so serious that in it no exchange or equivalent for a forfeited life is possible.

apallássō. This means "to alter by removal," "to do away," with such nuances as "to dismiss," "to liberate," "to absent oneself," "to withdraw." In the NT it occurs in the transitive active in Heb. 2:15 for "to liberate," and in the middle in Acts 19:12 for "to withdraw," "leave," and in Lk. 12:58 for "to break free," "escape."

diallássō. This word has such varied meanings as "to alter or exchange," "to distinguish oneself," and "to reconcile." It occurs in the NT only in Mt. 5:24 in the sense "to reconcile," i.e., to see to it that the offended brother renounces his anger.

katallássō (→ *di-*, *apokatallássō*, *katallagḗ*). With the thought of "change" predominating, this word can mean "to change," "to exchange," and "to reconcile" or "reconcile oneself."

A. The Religious Use of *katallássō* outside the NT. The group plays no part in pagan expiatory rites, though it has a religious sense in Sophocles *Ajax* 744.

In Judaism God is said to "be reconciled" in the sense that his wrath gives way to grace, e.g., through prayer, confession, or conversion (2 Macc. 1:5; 7:33), but this use is rare. The word corresponds to rabbinic terms for "to placate," "to reconcile oneself," "to be reconciled," "to reconcile," in relations with others or with God.

B. *katallássō* in the NT.
1. Husband and Wife. Greek marriage records have *apallássesthai* for marital separation and *katallássesthai* for reconciliation. Along these lines a separated wife is told in 1 Cor. 7:11 to "be reconciled to her husband," the meaning being, not necessarily that she is at fault, but that she is actively to seek reconciliation.

2. God and Man.

a. In the NT only Paul uses the term for the divine-human relation. God is not reconciled, nor does he reconcile himself, but he himself reconciles us or the world to himself (2 Cor. 5:18-19), while we are reconciled to God (Rom. 5:10) or reconcile ourselves to him (2 Cor. 5:20). *katallássein* denotes a transformation of the state between God and us and therewith of our own state, for by it we become new creatures (2 Cor. 5:18), no longer ungodly or sinners, but justified, with God's love shed abroad in our hearts (Rom. 5:6ff.). God has not changed; the change is in our relation to him and consequently in our whole lives.

b. Reconciliation is through the death of Jesus (Rom. 5:10). He was made sin for us and we are made God's righteousness in him (2 Cor. 5:21). Thus reconciliation is parallel to justification (cf. "not imputing" in 2 Cor. 5:19). In it guilt is removed. Yet reconciliation also entails a change whereby the love of Christ comes to constrain us and we no longer live for ourselves (2 Cor. 5:14-15). On the basis of God's reconciling act in Christ the call goes out: "Be reconciled to God" (2 Cor. 5:20). Reconciliation is not just a transaction but has personal effects which are known to the conscience and may be adduced in answer to opponents (2 Cor. 5:11ff.). These effects are the work of the Holy Spirit (Rom. 5:5) who enables us, even though we are sinners, to walk in the Spirit (Rom. 8:4). By the Spirit we are thus made active in reconciliation through the word of reconciliation that comes to us as a request (2 Cor. 5:20). Yet we are active only in the sense of receiving reconciliation, not of effecting it, so that we may also be said to "be reconciled" (passive) in Rom. 5:10.

c. "We" are said to be reconciled in Rom. 5, and "the world" in 2 Cor. 5, but there is no opposition between them, for the world stands for the same thing as "we" in its widest range. Insofar as the ministry of reconciliation continues, and much of the world has still to hear the word of reconciliation, reconciliation has an ongoing aspect—not, of course, in the sense that its basis in Christ's death is incomplete, but in the sense that people have still to be reconciled to God and thus to become new creatures in whom God's love is shed abroad by the Spirit.

d. The hostility between God and us is not mentioned in 2 Cor. 5 and only alluded to in Rom. 5, but it obviously includes not only our enmity against God but also God's wrath against sin (Rom. 1:18ff.) wherein divine displeasure corresponds to human disobedience (Rom. 8:7-8). Reconciliation is effected by Christ's death inasmuch as this is not just to our advantage, or a revelation of God's love, but a vicarious action (2 Cor. 5:20), an exchange, in which the God who judges is also the God who reconciles. Yet reconciliation is a broader term than justification, for if it embraces forgiveness (Rom. 5:9-10) it also establishes a basis for the appeal of 2 Cor. 5:20 and finds fulfilment in the loving response which this appeal evokes.

katallagē̃. The meaning is first "exchange," then "reconciliation." Used only by Paul, in the NT it denotes a divine dispensation. Paul's word and work are the word and ministry of *katallagē̃* (2 Cor. 5:18-19). They bring God's reconciling action in Christ before people by an appeal which leads believers to "receive reconciliation" (Rom. 5:11). In this sense the reconciliation of the world is a continuing action through the ministry (Rom. 11:15).

apokatallássō. This word does not occur prior to the NT and is found only in Colossians and Ephesians, where it has much the same sense as *katallássō*. Christ is now the subject as well as God or the *plḗrōma* (Col. 1:20, 22; Eph. 2:16). Reconciliation is preceded by human enmity but enables us to stand in the judgment (Col.

1:22). It is connected with the conclusion of peace and a new creation (Eph. 2:15), not merely the removal of guilt. Reconciliation with God brings reconciliation of Jews and Gentiles (Eph. 2:16). It also embraces supraterrestrial beings (Col. 1:20) in what some exegetes see as a restoration of cosmic order, possibly through subjection to Christ (cf. Col. 2:10).

metallássō. "To change," "to exchange." In Rom. 1:25 God's truth, i.e., his self-revelation (1:18ff.), is "changed" into a lie, i.e., the idolatry that sets other things in place of God. This leads in Rom. 1:26 to the "exchanging" of natural relations for unnatural; this sexual perversion is the consequence of the religious perversion.

[F. BÜCHSEL, I, 251-59]

---

allēgoréō [to allegorize]

A. The Use of the Term. This verb, with the noun *allēgoría,* seems to come from the Hellenistic period, probably from Cynic-Stoic philosophy. It means "to speak or to explain allegorically." Thus in Gal. 4:24 the story of Sarah and Hagar is said to be allegorical.

B. The Application of Allegorical Exposition.

1. Allegorizing occurs when traditions are outstripped but not discarded. Thus the Greeks found in it a way to preserve Homeric myths that they found offensive if taken literally. In method, e.g., the handling of names, Jewish and Christian treatment of the OT owed much to the Greek exposition of Homer.

2. Allegorical interpretation of the OT began in Alexandria with Aristobulus (2nd cent. B.C.), who obviously borrowed from the Greeks even though there are some allegories in the OT itself. The Epistle of Aristeas then extracted ethical wisdom from OT ritual. Philo tried to avoid both extreme literalism and extreme allegorizing, but while he did not abandon the literal validity of the text he was notable for the inventiveness of his interpretations. Essential though it was, the literal sense had for him subordinate significance and caused difficulty at points, e.g., in the area of anthropomorphism.

3. Scribal circles in Palestine adopted allegorization too, e.g., in the case of the Song of Songs. Their allegorizing is rarer and less arbitrary than that of Philo. It is narrower in range and closer to the natural sense. But it is not exceptional, and it differs from Philo's, not in principle by retaining historical validity (which Philo also did), but in degree by being less open to Greek rationalism and its criticism of the OT. It finds it consonant with the dignity of Scripture that it should have many meanings, and with this in mind may well have been influenced by Alexandrian developments while taking some steps of its own toward allegorizing. Josephus, who had little occasion to allegorize and could criticize Greek allegorizing (*Against Apion* 2.255), did not hesitate to allegorize the tent and its furnishings along Alexandrian lines (*Antiquities* 3.179ff.).

4. Jesus did not use allegory according to the four Gospels, but Paul did in 1 Cor. 5:6ff.; 9:8ff.; 10:1ff.; Gal. 4:21ff. He followed the Palestinian model, not extracting cosmological or psychological lessons, but still allegorizing in the true sense. Distinctively, however, he did so as one living in the time of fulfilment (1 Cor. 10:11) for whom the veil had been removed (2 Cor. 3:14), so that he could now see the true

sense which found its focus in Christ. Hebrews offers another example of christological allegorizing along these lines (7:1ff.).   [F. Büchsel, I, 260-63]

---

allēlouiá [Hallelujah]

Based on the Hebrew term for "praise the Lord," and found in the LXX as the heading or conclusion to psalms (104-06; 111-13; 115-17; 135; 146-50), *allēlouiá* occurs in the NT only in Rev. 19:1, 3, 4, 6, where it introduces or merges into victory hymns and forms with *amēn* (v. 4) an independent response.   [H. Schlier, I, 264]

állos [other], *allótrios* [alien], *apallotrióō* [to alienate], *allogenḗs* [foreign], *allóphylos* [foreign]

állos. The meaning is "the other," strictly where there are many, as distinct from *héteros* where there are only two, but used interchangeably with *héteros* or for it. In the NT *héteros* does not occur in the genuine Mark, 1 and 2 Peter, or Revelation, and only once in John (19:37). *állos* means "the other" where there are only two, e.g., in Mt. 5:39; Jn. 18:16; 19:32. The two words are interchangeable with no obvious distinction in Mt. 16:14; 1 Cor. 12:8ff.; Heb. 11:35-36. In Gal. 1:6-7 *héteros* is used for "another gospel" and *állos* for "which is not another," i.e., which is no gospel at all but a human teaching.

allótrios. "Belonging to another," "alien," "unsuitable," even "hostile." For the most part it has the first sense in the NT (cf. Rom. 14:4; 2 Cor. 10:15; 1 Tim. 5:22; Heb. 9:25). It is used as a noun in Lk. 16:12. It means "foreign" or "hostile" in Heb. 11:34, but the NT never uses it for hostile to God.

apallotrióō. "To estrange or alienate," found in the NT only in Col. 1:21 and Eph. 2:12; 4:18 for the state prior to reconciliation. It refers only to this state insofar as it is culpable and not to its presuppositions.

allogenḗs. "Alien," "foreign," found only in Jewish and Christian Greek, e.g., Ex. 29:33; Ob. 11 LXX. The only NT instance is in Lk. 17:18, a reference to the Samaritan leper who returned to give thanks. Elsewhere it occurs only on the inscription on the temple barrier, which was almost certainly Jewish rather than Roman in origin, although Josephus omits the term in his accounts of the inscription, probably to avoid offending his non-Jewish readers (*The Jewish War* 6.125; 5.194; *Antiquities* 15.417).

allóphylos. "Of alien descent," "foreign," found from the time of Aeschylus, used in the LXX (Is. 2:6) and Josephus (*Antiquities* 9.102), and adopted in Acts 10:28 to denote the Gentiles.   [F. Büchsel, I, 264-67]

allotriepískopos → *epískopos*; *álogos* → *légō*

hamartánō [to sin],   *hamártēma* [sin],   *hamartía* [sin]

A. Sin in the OT.

1. The Words Used in the OT.

a. The LXX with its summary use of *hamartía, adikía, anomía,* etc. hardly does justice to the rich and flexible Hebrew original and often misses the point, e.g., when "guilt" is in view. The Hebrew terms translated by *hamartía* and the like (for a full list see *TDNT,* I, 268-69) do not have an exclusive religious use, so that it is easy in translation either to import this or to weaken it. No uniform or self-contained concept of sin is present in the OT authors, and detailed questions of linguistic history further complicate the matter.

b. The four main roots which carry the idea of sin have the varied senses of "sin or negligence," "rebelling," "guilt," and "error," enough to show the variety of thinking about sin quite apart from the many other roots.

2. The Legal and Theological Content of the OT Concept of Sin.

a. Statistically the root *ḥṭ'* (with derivatives) is the main term, and this harmonizes with the fact that it offers the best definition. It is basically metaphorical and has the sense of "missing," e.g., the way (Prov. 19:2), what is sought (Prov. 8:36), the mark (Judg. 20:16). While predominantly used for wrong action, the word thus suggests always the idea of going astray. The legal use, of which there are many examples, strengthens the conjecture that the Hebrew term does not have the primary sense of "sin," for what is often in view is transgression of custom, or law, or a treaty, or obligation, with the guilt that this implies (cf. Gen. 43:9).

b. The shift from the legal to the religious use is important inasmuch as it shows that the religious life, too, is seen to be ordered, i.e., that dealings with God must follow a pattern. Yet a root like the term for "to rebel" warns us that a volitional element is involved. In the secular sphere Israel revolts against David's dynasty (1 Kgs. 12:19). As sons rebel against their fathers, so Israel revolts against God (Is. 1:2). What is denoted is a human reaction against the holy and divine. Erring has something of the same dimension, though in its mainly ritual use it describes negligence through ignorance rather than willful transgression (cf. Lev. 4:13). Yet when applied religiously (cf. Job 12:16) it carries the thought that we do not attain to God because we cannot do so. False seers in their quasi-drunken wandering are partly culpable and partly clouded in their minds by God himself (Is. 28:7-8). Seeing no way out of their error, they must suffer the pain of the divine enigma (Job 19:4). For Ps. 119 only study of the law can bring us out of error and its affliction (Ps. 119:67). This darker aspect, however, is not predominant in the OT concept of sin. From a more rational, theological standpoint, sin is what is "unclean." If personal feeling lies behind this concept too, its essential content is failure to keep a norm. The phrase "with a high hand" (e.g., Num. 15:30) assumes that the norm is known (as it was not known, e.g., by the people of Sodom and Gomorrah, Gen. 18:20). Thus in Ps. 32 the one who prays is led to see and confess sin through suffering, i.e., to recognize that even breaches of the ritual, which might not seem to be sin, are really sin against God.

c. The wisdom writings usually have a more intellectual than religious view of sin. By instruction we come to know what is fitting in relation to God and how to apply it to life (as distinct from the fool, Ps. 14:1). Sin is thus folly, to which the righteous are superior. A deeper view occurs in Ex. 20:5; Dt. 5:9, where resistance to God's commands is defined as hatred, and sin is thus an inexplicable process involving such things as abomination, violence, and deception. All this tends to suggest that a theological concept of sin was a later construction. On the other hand, it was also a correct one grounded in firm categories whose validity no one in ancient Israel could contest. Censure, the assertion of guilt, and the knowledge of God's demanding will all meet in it to offer an interpretation of human experience and destiny. If God's will is the supreme law of life, apostasy from God has to come to expression in error, i.e., in terms of what life ought to be and digression from this norm. A connection with the covenant may be discerned at this point. Moreover, whether we regard the aberration as serious or trivial, its character as transgression is established by the concept of God and his order, to which account must be rendered. Violation of God's norm is the substance of the knowledge of sin. In a very bold insight, sin is even seen to serve a purpose by leading to a recognition of the unconditional validity of the divine norm. Human failure is thus ruthlessly set in the divine order and given a religious interpretation as sin (Ps. 51).

d. For the OT as a whole, then, sin is a legal and theological term for what is against the norm. The theological use is prominent but not exclusive. In its rational form it is less a matter of experience than of its theological clarification. The different formulas mediate different theological insights in an attempt to express the underlying religious phenomenon. The concept has many nuances but is not without a certain unity, both being illustrated by the heaping up of synonyms (cf., e.g., Ps. 32:5; Job 34:37; Lev. 16:21). At its root is aberration from the norm, but this may be viewed as either the inner process, the act, or the resultant state. The context rather than the selected root usually shows where the accent lies. In analysis, then, we have to reckon with possibilities ranging from sober intellectual assertion to divine conviction. Yet there will always be a theoretical element which, although of pedagogical value, may tend to reduce multiple religious phenomena to a common denominator. The terms denoting aberration always have a figurative aspect, and it is perhaps the root "to rebel" that brings us closest to the heart of the matter with its stress on motive. Even this, however, imposes a certain intellectual order on the irrational experience. It is thus in prayers that the irrational problem comes out best with their vocabulary of confession or complaint. Significantly, too, the story of the fall avoids the customary terms for sin.

3. Sin and Guilt. Often the terms for sin allude to it in such a way that the translation "guilt" is justifiable or necessary. This is always so when the reference is to the resultant state. Abnormal action and abnormal state are so related that no sharp distinction of vocabulary exists between sin and guilt. The more specific words for guilt belong first to the area of sacral law and bring out its objective character. One could incur guilt unintentionally but the resultant uncleanness (even if not recognized) would be no less a fact than in the case of sin with a high hand, and would need to be set aside by the same ritual as that employed to restore cleanness. Other terms (cf. Ps. 32:1) focus on guilt itself. Emphasis now falls on its intolerable burden (Ps. 38:4). It is the sum of the debts incurred by acts of sin and is manifested in afflictions, which are viewed as punishment for it. The rational or theological character of the OT concept of sin and guilt comes out strongly in the doctrines of expiation and retribution which rest on this basis, though the basis itself is religious.

4. The Story of the Fall (Gen. 3). This story stands aloof from legal concepts and does not influence them. Perhaps using and bending mythological materials, the author depicts the origin and results of sin with childlike force. He does not use the common terms, since these would be out of place in this portrayal of life. Apart from a few hints he lets readers draw their own conclusions, focusing on the events that the terms are meant to explain. He thus brings out far more clearly the sinister reality with which theology and cultus deal.

The basic ideas of the story are the prohibition that expresses the divine will, the clever serpent that sees the apparent disproportion between the transgression and its consequence, the question put to the woman, her readiness for scepticism, the suggestion that the warning is not serious and is only in the divine interest and against human interests, the attractiveness of the fruit, the foolish violation by the woman and the compliance of the man, and the four results: shame at nakedness, hiding from God, subterfuges to excuse the action, and punishment by God.

The stress in this chain of events lies on what is mysteriously indicated by the phrases "being as God" and "knowing good and evil." "Being as God" involves doubt that God's rule is really in the human interest and unconditionally binding. Helped by the serpent, the man and woman see that they can transgress the divine order. Indeed, they believe that practical reason, exalting itself as lord and God, impels them to do so without bothering about religious correctives or divine judgment.

Yet the story also points out that there is no escaping divine accountability. Those who try to be as God finally stand before God like children who have been found out and are full of evasions. The author thus brings out the full absurdity of the Prometheus motif. But he does so with insight into the tragic human situation in which it seems that there is *immanent* justification—in the desire for culture, the work of thought, and sensual longing—for human hostility to God and the attempt to break free from the divine prohibition. The true reality of sin can be grasped only when one perceives that the divine likeness itself opens up the possibilities of deviation and the unfathomable distress which every act of deviation causes when it comes under the pitiless divine glance.

In spite of aetiological features, then, the story in its totality offers a perspective on human existence as a whole. The curses undoubtedly explain common features of human life, just as the realization of nakedness explains the general use of clothing. Nevertheless, the explanations carry weight only because they relate, not to an isolated act, but to an act that is typical of the way that all of us act toward God and incur guilt before him. The aetiology thus extends beyond details—even such momentous details as sorrow, work, shame, and death—to the reality of sin as the real force behind all human unrest and unhappiness. Incidentally, shame at nakedness serves very well to express the shame, the insecurity, and the secretiveness that result from sin, quite apart from the problem of sexuality which it also involves.

A more general aetiological explanation justifies us in building on the story a doctrine of original sin in the sense of universal sinfulness. Sin is motivated by a human impulse that is present in all of us, so that in thousands of variations we will all be tempted similarly and sin similarly. The uncontrolled intellect is in conflict with religion, and freedom of will and thought prepares the ground for sin. By making the serpent the representative of the uncontrolled intellect, the author stresses the demonic character of the thinking which derives from doubt and engages in fanatical striving. This comes over us like an outside force, strengthens existing desires, and thus overpowers uncritical obedience. Our experienced inability to resist at this point compels us to recognize the general validity of the phenomenon. Wishing and to some extent able to be wiser than God and to pierce behind his thoughts, we open up a sphere of mistrust in which we renounce our proper attitude as creatures, regard the Creator with cynicism, and act as though we were ourselves God, responsible only to ourselves.

Since reason and the power of judgment are native to us, the motive for sinning is present just as necessarily as life itself.

The author, however, is not trying to give a theological but a popular account. Piety rather than theology comes to expression in his simple presentation. An unsparing desire for truth gives it its unforgettable impress. Nowhere else in the OT do we find religious discussion that is so penetrating and yet so sustained by piety. The narrator is not spinning a theory but speaking out of the compelling experience of inner tension and trying to give his readers some sense of the serious situation which is inseparable from human existence. Why God made us thus, he does not try to say. His religion is to be found in this silence.   [G. QUELL, I, 267-86]

B. Theological Nuances of *hamartía* in the LXX. This section supplements A. and D. of this article and B. of the article on *hamartōlós* by pointing out some important nuances that are partly deliberate and partly due to difficulties of translation. First of all, the LXX gives greater prominence to arrogance as the chief sin by rendering *arrogant* as *hamartōlós* (Sir. 11:9). Sin is also identified with wealth (Hab. 3:14). Again, it is sickness (Is. 53:4; Dt. 30:3). In Job 42 the LXX stresses the thought of forgiveness, which is only hinted at in the Hebrew, i.e., by substituting the idea of Job's sin for God's wrath in v. 7 and bringing in the idea of remission in v. 9. A similar replacement of God's wrath by human transgression occurs in Judg. 1:18 (cf. Is. 57:17). Sin is equated with apostasy in 2 Chr. 12:2 (cf. 30:7). Folly or ignorance can also be rendered *hamartía* according to the familiar OT thought that folly is sin. The idea of sin is introduced into Is. 66:4 with its reference to the cause of punishment rather than the punishment itself (cf. 24:6). A spiritualization may be found in Ezek. 23:49. The thought of the school of suffering, which presupposes a strong sense of sin, is read into Job 15:11. The thrust of the LXX, then, is to make *hamartía* a general term for sin. In so doing it brings individual sins under the concept of the basic sin which separates us from God and controls us so long as we do not receive God's saving work. For linguistic details, see *TDNT,* I, 286ff.   [G. BERTRAM, I, 286-89]

C. The Concept of Sin in Judaism.
1. The concept of the law is determinative in Judaism. The law as a whole, legal as well as cultic and moral, reveals God's will. Hence every transgression is sin. Two trends develop: one to level down, since even minor infringements are still sin; the other to differentiate, e.g., between flagrant misdeeds, acts of rebellion, and unwitting offenses. Based on this distinction such sins as violence, licentiousness, and especially idolatry are seen to be mortal, since to commit them is to commit every sin, whereas less serious offenses can be expiated by good works, purifications, and sufferings.
2. The tendency in Judaism is to regard sin as individual rather than collective (cf. Ezek. 18:2ff.). Sin as the individual's transgression has individual consequences. The commandment is taken to mean that God visits the fathers' sins on their refractory children to the third and fourth generation. Yet a sense of the general effects of even individual sins remains. The universality of sin finds no opponents. If Israelites sin by breaking the law, the Gentiles sin by breaking the Adamic and Noachic covenants, or even by refusing the law when it is offered to them. Exceptions to universal sinfulness are seen in such saints as Moses and Elijah, and avoidance of sin is possible through freedom and the gift of the law. Furthermore, it is fully expected both that the Messiah will be sinless and that sin will be set aside and sinlessness established in the messianic kingdom.
3. As for the rise of sin, it is traced to Adam and Eve, or at times to the fallen

angels (Gen. 6:1ff.). More basically, sin has its origin in the evil impulse which is implanted by God, which entices to sin, and which may and must be overthrown by observance of the law. If it is not, sin brings such consequences as further sinning, separation from God, disruption of God's gracious purpose, and the punishments of sickness, death, and eternal damnation. But in respect of all these penalties we have the opportunity to repent and return to God. We sin, but God shows us the way of conversion before we die.   [G. Stählin and W. Grundmann, I, 289-93]

D. The Linguistic Usage and History of *hamartánō*, *hamártēma*, and *hamartía* before and in the NT.

1. *hamartánō*, meaning "not to hit," "to miss," occurs from Homer and is also used figuratively for "to fall short intellectually," "to err," or "to fall short morally," "to do wrong." In the LXX the moral sense is predominant.

2. *hamártēma* denotes the result of *hamartánō*, "fault," first due to folly, later, especially in law, in the sense of "offense." In the LXX it usually has a moral or religious sense, "sin," or "punishment of sin." It is rare in the NT.

3. *hamartía*, also used figuratively from the first, refers more to the nature of the act. It is a comprehensive term with intellectual and legal as well as ethical applications, and it can cover all wrong actions from simple errors to crimes. Aristotle defines it as missing virtue because of weakness, accident, or defective knowledge. Later, guilt is associated with it. In the LXX it is synonymous with *hamártēma* and carries the full sense of moral guilt and conscious opposition to God, expressing the Godward reference more clearly and fully than *adikía* or *kakía*. In the NT it stands for "offense against God with a stress on guilt" and is used a. for the individual act (e.g., Acts 2:38; 1 Tim. 5:22; Rev. 1:5; 1 Pet. 2:22; Heb. 1:3), often with the remission of sins in view (Mk. 2:5; Acts 7:60), in Paul usually only in quotations (e.g., Rom. 4:7-8, though cf. Rom. 7:5); b. for sin as human nature in its hostility to God (e.g., Jn. 9:41; 1 Jn. 3:5; 1 Cor. 15:17; Rom. 3:20; Heb. 4:15); and c. for personified sin (e.g., Rom. 5–7; Heb. 12:1). Behind the third use stands the idea of a demon "sin," but what we have in the NT is probably poetic imagery.   [G. Stählin, I, 293-96]

E. Sin and Guilt in Classical Greek and Hellenism.

1. Classical Greek does not have the thought of sin as enmity against God, but only of defect and guilt, i.e., missing the mark by error or by guilt. In view are intellectual and artistic as well as moral senses, i.e., all failures to do what is right. Other terms had to be added to express the idea of guilt.

2. Guilt arises through individual acts, ranging earlier from cultic neglect or perjury to social injustices. It is known by way of misfortunes inflicted by the gods as guardians of law and order.

3. By the sixth century the Greek world becomes aware of the riddle of human destiny and the inevitability of guilt. The mysteries express this with the ideas of original guilt (the soul's exile in the body) and the threat of death. Guilt is now seen as a disruption of order that must be made good by suffering. Guilt is associated with human limitation (e.g., of knowledge) and is thus posited by life itself. It has to be accepted and confessed. To this unavoidable guilt is added personal guilt through failure to heed divine warnings and ultimately through ignorance. Right understanding will thus lead to right action (cf. Socrates and Greek tragedy), although understanding may come only through suffering or paradigms of suffering. Plato, however, lays a greater stress on individual choice, while Aristotle uses the *hamartía* group for mistakes, or for deviations from the mean, and divests it of the association with moral guilt.

4. After Aristotle rationalism destroys the serious concept of guilt. But the idea of fate remains. In the mysteries and Hellenistic mysticism the *hamartía* group is used for predetermined destiny which is the cause of guilt but eliminates personal responsibility, redemption being offered by the rites or by *gnōsis*.

5. Phrygian and Lydian religion offers an exception with the concept of omnipotent deity willing the good and punishing transgressions such as failing to give thanks, cultic violation, and a series of moral offenses. Sickness is a penalty for sin, which consists of the act, not an inner disposition, so that expiation aims at the restoration of health or cultic normalcy.   [G. Stählin and W. Grundmann, I, 296-302]

F. Sin in the NT.

1. The Synoptic Gospels and Acts.

a. In the Synoptics the role of the group is comparatively slight. Jesus does not speak about sin but acts in awareness of it, and is conscious of being the victor over it.

b. His mission is to proclaim the divine lordship in his word and work. This proclamation evokes a sense of distance from God and thus leads to confession and conversion (cf. Lk. 15:18, 21). Sin means guilt toward God and thus demands penitence. Knowing that he has come to call sinners to repentance (Mt. 9:13), Jesus accepts solidarity with them (Mt. 9:10), victoriously bringing forgiveness (cf. Lk. 5:8; 7:37ff.; 19:1-2). His attitude and word of forgiveness are the extraordinary, eschatological breaking in of the divine lordship, as emerges in the Lord's Supper (cf. Mt. 26:28 and Jer. 31:31ff.). Jesus is the servant who by his death and resurrection carries away sin (cf. Is. 53:12). Sin is unforgivable only when people recognize the mission of Jesus by the Holy Spirit but defy and resist it (Mt. 12:31-32).

c. That Jesus is the victor over sin is expressed in his name (Mt. 1:21). The mission of the Baptist prepares his way with its call for confession (Mt. 3:6) and baptism with a view to remission (Mk. 1:4). Jesus himself brings fulfilment with the word and act of forgiveness. The apostles continue his ministry with proclamation of the accomplished salvation. Unlike Jesus, who confers it by fellowship, they summon their hearers to receive it by repentance (Acts 2:38), the difference from the Baptist being that they can now declare a completed, not an awaited basis of forgiveness. The usual sense of sin here is the individual act, hence the normal use in the plural.

2. John.
John, too, presents Christ as the victor over sin, more specifically by taking it away in his death (cf. 1 Jn. 3:5). This atoning work has universal significance (1 Jn. 2:2). It rests on Christ's own sinlessness as the one who does his Father's will (Jn. 8:46). Sin here is action that contradicts the divine ordinance (1 Jn. 3:4). It derives from ungodliness, is universal, involves sins against others, and brings guilt and separation from God (Jn. 9:31; 1 Jn. 3:8) in servitude to demonic power (Jn. 8:34). The mission of Jesus ushers in a new situation expressed in the term *krísis*, i.e., division and decision. Christ's coming shows sin to be hatred of God. In face of him the decision is made that divides people (Jn. 9:41). Those who reject Christ die in sin (1 Jn. 5:16-17). But those who receive him find forgiveness (1 Jn. 1:9) as they confess their sin. The Spirit continues the sifting work of Christ (Jn. 16:8-9). Deliverance from sin is achieved in the community as believers are born of God, receive faith and knowledge, and work out the new situation in love (cf. 1 Jn. 3:6, 9). Tension naturally arises as Christians do in fact sin, but they can maintain a basic sinlessness through the advocacy of Christ (1 Jn. 2:1) and reciprocal intercession (1 Jn. 5:16). In Revelation Christ's loving work delivers us from the sinful world order (1:5). His blood has atoning power. Our task in the end-time is to keep ourselves from the increasing

power of sin (18:4-5). By a final and definitive act God will destroy the universal dominion of sin from which we are already liberated.

3. *Paul.*

a. Paul's view is oriented to God's work in Christ, which (1) comes on us in the specific reality of sin, and (2) rescues us from this reality and reshapes us.

b. Paul's view of sin arises out of his own experience under revelation. From legal blamelessness (Phil. 3:6) he is driven to see and confess the sin of persecuting the church (1 Cor. 15:9) which resulted from attempted self-righteousness and hence from opposition to God even in zeal for his law. Sin for him is thus at its root hostility to God. It entered the world through Adam (Rom. 5) and therefore through freedom, but it subjected us to itself and brought death as its wages (Rom. 6:23). Paul thus connects sin with universal destiny, but does not depict it as a necessity of creatureliness. The act of Adam, death, and the general state of sin are interconnected. Judgment, revealed in Christ, rests on our being as such. The state of sin exists from Adam, but it is made clear only by the law, which actualizes sin and reveals its character (cf. Rom. 8:7), namely, as responsible guilt in enmity against God. Our carnal reality is sinful, not in the sense that sin is equated with the body, but in the sense that we are determined by sin in our carnal being. The law leads to individual sins by stimulating desires that oppose the divine claim. The nerve of individual sins is the failure to acknowledge God (Rom. 1:21). This gives all sins the character of guilt before God and results in sinning as the penalty of sin (Rom. 1:24ff.). Using God's holy will to enhance its power, sin has a demonic quality (Rom. 7:13), enslaving us (7:14) and handing us over to death, so that we cannot fulfil the law (7:15ff.; cf. Eph. 2:1). The law, however, still discharges its holy function by unmasking sin.

c. The Christ event strikes us in this reality of sin. Christ comes from God to judge and destroy sin (2 Cor. 5:21). The sinless Jesus became sin in vicarious atonement through crucifixion and resurrection. Christ can represent us because of our solidarity in sin. Thus the Christ event overcomes sin for us all. Its coming to us releases us from sin and constitutes us anew. Justified by faith, we have remission of sins (cf. Eph. 1:7). By fellowship with Christ in baptism, we are dead to sin (Rom. 6:2). Having died to it, we are free from it (6:7), we are no longer under the law (6:14), we are the servants of righteousness (6:14), and we need not continue in sin (6:1). Freedom from sin means the obedience of faith (cf. 14:23) and is expressed in love of the brethren (1 Cor. 8:12). But tension exists between the somatic life, which is given up to death, and the pneumatic life, which has overcome death (Rom. 8:10). This tension continues until Christ comes again and definitively abolishes sin and death (1 Cor. 15:26).

4. *The Other NT Writings.*

a. Hebrews views sin from the cultic standpoint, presenting Christ as the true and sinless high priest with the one offering for sin in contrast to human high priests with their repeated offerings for themselves and the people. Christ's offering terminates the cultus by bringing forgiveness and initiating the messianic age (10:17-18). Believers in the present time of affliction are to resist sin (12:1) and to avoid especially the deliberate sin of apostasy (10:26).

b. James derives sin from desire, relates it to the will, and finds its end in death (1:14-15). Sin is an act (2:9) and includes failure to do good. Confession and prayer bring forgiveness (5:15-16). To rescue others from sin is a Christian ministry (5:19-20).

c. 1 Peter proclaims Christ as the victor over sin by his voluntary submission and atoning death as the servant of the Lord (2:22, 24; 3:18).

In the NT as a whole the decisive feature is the realization that Christ is victor and that the new age has dawned in and with him. His victory is a victory over sin, which is (1) a reality that determines humanity and (2) a rejection of God's claim in human self-assertion. The victory consists of the saving action by which sin is forgiven and life is constituted anew. [W. GRUNDMANN, I, 302-16]

---

hamartōlós [sinner, sinful], *anamártētos* [without sin]

---

hamartōlós (→ *telṓnēs, asebḗs, ádikos*). Meaning "sinner" or "sinful," this word can be a value judgment for a class of people (cf. Mk. 2:16) as well as a description of our natural relationship to God.

A. *hamartōlós* in the Greek and Hellenistic World.

1. The basic thought is "not hitting" or "missing." It is used for a. the intellectually and b. the morally inferior.

2. On inscriptions it occurs in a sacral context but hardly seems to have the full religious sense of sinner.

3. Neither the Stoics nor Philo and Josephus use the term for the sinner.

4. It seems not to have been fully connected with *hamartía* in the Greek world, nor to have found much literary use, because it was a popular term with an ironical or disreputable flavor. It suggests inordinate negation of right and custom and is strongly derogatory if not an actual term of abuse.

B. *harmartōlós* in the LXX and Its Hebrew Equivalents.

1. In contrast, the term is common in the LXX, mostly for Heb. *rāšaʿ*, either as an adjective or a noun.

2. The occurrence is predominantly for the "sinners" of the Psalms, who are the opposite of the righteous, i.e., Jews boasting of the law and covenant but breaking the commandments (Ps. 10:7), proud of their folly (49:13), trusting in wealth (49:6), oppressing others, and even ignoring God. Basic to this polemical judgment is the insight that these sinners have a wrong attitude to the law and hence to the God whose will it reveals. The righteous, too, may become sinners but are not sinners in this deeper sense in which sin embraces, not just acts, but the whole attitude and the life which it produces. This usage continues in later Judaism with an even stronger emphasis on regard for the law, the study of which alone will keep us from sin, and rejection of which means separation from God. In both the OT and the rabbis the term has something of a contemptuous accent.

3. *hamartōlós* is obviously well adapted to express what is meant by the Hebrew term but in so doing it acquires more of a volitional character, since the law as a revelation of God's will demands decision. It also becomes a religious term, for it now comes into relation with the concept of God.

C. The Development of the Concept of the Sinner in Later Judaism.

1. a. For the rabbis the law is a manifestation of God to Israel and to the whole of humanity. By it the holy God sanctifies his people. This means that those who have the law are by nature holy, whereas those outside it (the Gentiles) are by nature sinners.

b. Those who have and keep the law are kept from sin in an ethical and not just a legal sense, but those who are outside Israel have no similar possibility. This is due to their rejection of the law, and it comes to light in their idolatry, ritual uncleanness, lack of sexual ethics, and general misconduct.

2. This suggests that the righteous, while they may commit sins, do not think of themselves as sinners in an absolute sense. Ideas of general sinfulness and collective sin are present but the possibility of sinlessness through the law is also asserted (cf. Lk. 18:11-12; Phil. 3:6), and there is a sense of distinction from "sinners" through a positive relation to the law. Even the sin of the Gentiles is not an imposed destiny but is by historical decision.

D. The New Testament.

1. The Lexical Evidence. In the NT *hamartōlós,* which is both an adjective and a noun, still has a derogatory nuance and is used a. for those living in conscious opposition to God's will in the law (cf. Mt. 9:10), or the woman in Simon's house (Lk. 7:37), in distinction from respectable people (Mt. 11:19; cf. 1 Tim. 1:9; Jms. 4:8); b. by Pharisees for those who do not keep their ordinances, i.e., most of the people, including Jesus and his disciples (cf. Mt. 9:13; 12:1ff.; 15:2); c. by the Jews for Gentiles (Mt. 26:45; Gal. 2:15), a usage avoided in Acts; d. for guilty humanity as it is yet without Christ and unreconciled (Rom. 5:8; Gal. 2:16ff.); e. for individuals who have fallen into specific guilt (Lk. 13:2; 15:7, 10; Heb. 7:26); and f. adjectivally in all the above senses. In Rom. 7:13 *hamartía* becomes *hamartōlós* beyond measure in the sense that the law gives sin self-awareness and thus brings its character to light and opens up the way to liberation from it.

2. The Attitude of Jesus.

a. Reckoning with sin's reality, though not analyzing it, Jesus adopts current formulas (not ironically) and utilizes them in his mission. He regards those called sinners as true sinners and draws them to himself, a sense of righteousness being the real obstacle rather than a sense of unworthiness, since Jesus has come to meet the need of sin.

b. Mediating total fellowship with himself and God, he thus accepts people as they are, requiring only a confession of need, not of specific sins, opposing the idea that a right relation with God comes by legal observance, and by his kindness, holiness, and majesty inducing renunciation of self-will and readiness for absolute obedience. Only rarely is *hamartōlós* used in self-description (cf. Lk. 5:8; 18:13); Jesus does not demand awareness of sin to the point of abject self-contempt and self-condemnation.

c. The righteous, too, need a new relation to God. Jesus does not call their righteousness sin but judges its inner character as that which meets only human and not divine standards, and leads to complacency, pride, and cruelty, so that the righteous, too, are called to repentance. In this way Jesus transcends the distinction between righteous and sinners, but in so doing he brings a universal offer of forgiveness and of a new and submissive relation to God, the only limit to the removal of sin by Jesus being unwillingness that it should be removed.

3. The Attitude of the NT Writers. This is the same as that of Jesus except that the cross keeps the NT writers from regarding only others as sinners. Hence *hamartōlós* is uncommon outside the Synoptists and does not occur in Acts, while in John only the Pharisees use it. For Paul it is a strong term that he applies to himself, signifying rejection of God's lordship. The new feature is the absence of any frontier between sinners and the righteous, the new frontier being between those who are still subject to sin and those who in Christ are rescued from sin and put in the service of God.

This is a sharper frontier, but it involves no sense of superiority, since believers do not magnify themselves as righteous but magnify the grace by which they are righteous and seek to point all people to this way of grace, since it is for them too.

anamártētos. This word, found from the time of Herodotus, is common and means "without fault," either in a general sense or in a figurative though not necessarily moral or religious sense. It occurs three times in the LXX, in 2 Macc. 8:4 for "guiltless before God." Philo uses it without any Godward reference, but it has this in the one instance in Josephus *The Jewish War* 7.329.

The only NT example is in Jn. 8:7 where Jesus challenges those who are without fault to cast the first stone at the woman taken in adultery. The obvious meaning of *anamártētos* is guiltless before God, but the context seems to rule out any specific reference to sexual sin. Oddly, the word is not used for the sinlessness of Jesus, perhaps to bring out the greatness of his freedom from sin by avoiding any suggestion that it was a mere inability to sin.   [K. H. RENGSTORF, I, 317-35]

ámemptos → *mémphomai; ametanóētos* → *metanoéō*

---

amḗn [Amen]

A. Amen in the OT and Judaism. The OT uses the term in relation to both individuals and the community 1. to confirm the acceptance of tasks whose performance depends on God's will (1 Kgs. 1:36), 2. to confirm the application of divine threats or curses (Num. 5:22), and 3. to attest the praise of God in response to doxology (1 Chr. 16:36). In every case acknowledgment of what is valid or binding is implied. In Judaism Amen is widely used, e.g., in response to praises, to the Aaronic blessing of Num. 6:24ff., to vows, and to prayers. It denotes concurrence, or in the case of a vow commitment, or at the end of one's own prayer the hope for its fulfilment. The LXX mostly renders the Hebrew term by *génoito,* which retains the idea of validity but weakens that of commitment to a claim.

B. amḗn in the NT and Early Christianity. The NT mostly takes over the Hebrew as it stands and uses it in three ways.

1. As an acclamation in worship, it signifies response (Rev. 5:14; cf. Justin *Apology* 65.3; Did. 10.6).

2. At the conclusion of prayers and doxologies (e.g., Gal. 1:5; Eph. 3:21; 1 Tim. 1:17; 1 Clem. 20.12 for doxologies, 1 Clem. 45.8; Mart. Pol. 14.3 for prayers), it expresses the priority of prayer and doxology. Along the same lines it can occur at the end of a prophecy (Rev. 1:7) or book (Gal. 6:18; Rev. 22:20). It can also be put at the beginning of a doxology, especially where a transition is made (Rev. 19:4). In Rev. 1:7 it is set close to the divine Yes, but Rev. 22:20 shows that it is the church's answer to the divine Yes, which is here the basis of the eschatological petition. The sense in 2 Cor. 1:20 is the same, for God's Yes in Christ is the firm foundation for the Amen of the community. Christ himself as the true witness can be called "the Amen" in his own response to the divine Yes that is declared in him (Rev. 3:14).

3. When Jesus places Amen before his own sayings, both in the Synoptics and (liturgically doubled) in John, the point is to stress the truth and validity of the sayings by his own acknowledgment of them. The sayings vary in content but all relate to the

history of the kingdom of God as this is bound up with his own person, so that in the Amen we have all Christology in a nutshell. Acknowledging his word, Jesus affirms it in his life and thus makes it a claim on others.   [H. SCHLIER, I, 335-38]

amíantos → miaínō

---
amnós, arḗn, arníon [lamb]
---

amnós. Attested from classical times and used in the LXX, this word occurs four times in the NT, always with reference to Jesus as the innocent lamb who suffers vicariously for others (Jn. 1:29, 36; Acts 8:32; 1 Pet. 1:19). Since Judaism does not call the Redeemer a lamb, two derivations have been sought: first, in the fact that the servant of the Lord in Is. 53:17 (cf. Acts 3:13; 4:27) is compared to a lamb (cf. Acts 8:32), and second, in that Jesus was crucified at the Passover and thus came to be seen as the paschal lamb (1 Cor. 5:7). The Aramaic might also offer a basis with its use of the same word for both "lamb" and "boy or servant." Thus the Baptist in Jn. 1:29, 36 might have been describing Jesus as the servant of God who takes away the sin of the world in vicarious self-offering (Is. 53). But the writer, in Greek, perceives a reference to the paschal lamb (cf. Jn. 19:36) whose blood blots out sins (→ *aírō*) by expiation. In any case the description of Jesus as *amnós* expresses 1. his patience in suffering (Acts 8:32), 2. his sinlessness (1 Pet. 1:19), and 3. the efficacy of his vicarious death (Jn. 1:29; 1 Pet. 1:19), which like the Passover initiates a new age, brings redemption (from sin), and establishes the people of God (extended now to believers from all nations).

arḗn. This word for "lamb" occurs only in Lk. 10:3, where, in antithesis to wolves, it expresses 1. the dangerous position of the defenseless disciples but also 2. the certainty of divine protection.

arníon. Originally a diminutive of *arḗs* ("little lamb"), and found four times in the LXX (e.g., Jer. 11:19), this word occurs in the NT once in Jn. 21:15 and 29 times in Revelation. "My lambs" of Jn. 21:15 are members of the community as the objects of Jesus' loving care. In Revelation Christ himself is called *arníon* 28 times, and antichrist as his antitype is called *arníon* once. It is sometimes argued that "ram" is here the correct translation in view of the references to the seven horns (5:6) and his wrath (6:16-17) and warfare (17:14). Indeed, a connection is even made with the zodiac. But Dan. 8:3 suggests the seven horns, while there is little philological justification for "ram," and the fact that the *arníon* is "slain" offers a link to the idea of Jesus as the sacrificial lamb *(amnós)*. As Redeemer and Ruler, the lamb of Revelation a. vicariously shed his blood (5:9) and bears the marks of his slaughter (5:6); b. has defeated death (5:5-6) and is omnipotent and omniscient (5:6); c. takes over divine rule, opening the book (5:8ff.), receiving adoration (5:8ff.), establishing a reign of peace (7:9), overcoming demonic powers (17:14), and judging (6:16-17; 13:8); and d. is Lord of lords and King of kings (17:14), holding his marriage feast with the community (19:9) and sharing God's throne in rule over his people (22:1, 3).

[J. JEREMIAS, I, 338-41]

ámpelos [vine]

Jesus compares himself with the "vine" in Jn. 15:1ff. to show the disciples' dependence on fellowship with him and their intensive nurture by God. Jesus is the "true vine," not as distinct from literal vines, but from others who might figuratively be called vines. The image is a common one in the OT, e.g., for Israel (Hos. 10:1) and the wife (Ps. 128:3); it is also used for wisdom (Sir. 24:17), and the Messiah (Syr. Bar. 36ff.). In later Near Eastern texts the term indicates heavenly messengers and beings from the world of light, and it may be in distinction from these that Jesus is called the "true vine."   [J. BEHM, I, 342-43]

ámōmos, amṓmētos → *mṓmos; anabaínō* → *baínō; anangéllō* → *angelía; anagennáō* → *gennáō*

---

anaginṓskō [to read], **anágnōsis** [public reading]

---

anaginṓskō means "to know exactly," "to recognize," and is mostly used to refer to (public) reading, e.g., a letter (Acts 15:31; 1 Th. 5:27) or the title on the cross (Jn. 19:20); usually the OT (Mk. 2:25, etc.), publicly in Lk. 4:16; Acts 13:27; the Daniel apocalypse (Mk. 13:14); the prophecy of Revelation (Rev. 1:3); and the NT (Justin *Apology* 67.3-4). *anágnōsis*, meaning "knowledge" or "recognition," is also used for public reading, as of documents or the OT, and occurs in this sense in the NT (e.g., Acts 13:15; 2 Cor. 3:14; 1 Tim. 4:13) and the early church (e.g., Clement of Alexandria *Paedagogus* 2.10.96.2).   [R. BULTMANN, I, 343-44]

---

anankázō [to compel], **anankaios** [compelling], **anánkē** [compulsion]

A. *anank-* outside the NT. The root refers basically to compulsion and the means of compulsion. As a necessary condition of life this may be 1. a cosmic principle, first personified as the divinity of being, then rationalized as immanent necessity, then repersonified in Hellenism as the inscrutable force controlling all reality. In cosmological dualism it may also be 2. the constraint or constraints which oppose spirit, the main aim in ethical life being to subject these to reason. In the OT the Greek word is used for the Hebrew "constraint" in the sense, not of a natural condition, but of divinely imposed afflictions such as persecution or sickness. Rabbinic theology uses the equivalent for the messianic tribulation.

B. *anank-* in the NT. Since acknowledgment of God as Creator and Preserver of the world leaves no room for necessity, the NT, like the OT, uses the term 1. to express a situation of need, such as a. the messianic tribulation (Lk. 21:23), and b. the afflictions of Paul (2 Cor. 12:10) or the community (1 Cor. 7:26); 2. to describe the apostolic office: it is a divine constraint which Paul cannot escape, being part of God's plan of salvation (1 Cor. 9:16); 3. to denote the divine order (Rom. 13:5; Mt. 18:7).   [W. GRUNDMANN, I, 344-47]

anágnōsis → *anaginṓskō;* '*anadeíknymi* → *deíknymi; anazáō* → *zōḗ; anáthema, anathematízō, anáthēma* → *anatíthēmi; anakainízō, anakainóō, anakaínōsis* → *kainós; anakalýptō* → *kalýptō; anákeimai* → *keímai; anakephalaióō* → *kephalḗ; anakrázō* → *krázō; analambánō, análēmpsis* → *lambánō; anakrínō, anákrisis* → *krínō*

> ### *analogía* [proportion]

análogos, "corresponding to *lógos*"; hence *analogía*, "correspondence," "proportion." In Rom. 12:6 the charism of prophecy is to be in correspondence to faith, not as what is believed (cf. vv. 3, 6), but as the actual believing. There can be no exercise of gifts such as healing without faith, but there may be inauthentic exercise of prophecy (cf. 1 Cor. 12:10; 14:29). Hence the reminder that prophesying is to be in proportion to one's faith. [G. KITTEL, I, 347-48]

análysis, analýō → lýō; anamártētos → hamartōlós

> ### *anámnēsis* [remembrance], *hypómnēsis* [remembrance]

anámnēsis means "remembrance" or "recollection." In Heb. 10:3 the sin offerings cannot remove sins but remind us of them (cf. Num. 5:15). In 1 Cor. 11:24 Christians are to enact the Lord's Supper in a recollection of Jesus which has the form of active re-presentation as the action of Jesus and the disciples is repeated. *hypómnēsis* in 2 Tim. 1:5 and 2 Pet. 1:13; 3:1 has much the same sense. [J. BEHM, I, 348-49]

ananeóō → néos; anáxios → áxios

> ### *anapaúo* [to cause to rest], *anápausis* [rest], *epanapaúō* [to rest on]

anapaúō. a. "To cause to cease"; b. "to give rest," "refresh"; c. "to rest"; d. "to remain at rest"; e. "to rest on." In the NT the word can mean bodily rest (c), as in Mk. 6:31, but more commonly it denotes refreshment (b), as in 1 Cor. 16:18. In Revelation it has an eschatological reference, "to rest from labor" (b) in 14:13, and "to tarry," i.e., await (d) in 6:11. God's Spirit is the subject in 1 Pet. 4:14: "to rest on" (e). Christ's saving work is to give rest (b) in Mt. 11:28.

anápausis. a. "Cessation," "interruption"; b. "rest"; c. "place of rest"; d. "day of rest." Instead of the rest given by wisdom, Jesus offers true rest (b) with the gospel (Mt. 11:28-29). Without "cessation" (a) is the sense in Rev. 4:8, "place of rest" (c) in Mt. 12:43.

epanapaúō. A late and rare word: a. "to rest on," b. "to lean on." Peace will rest on the house (a) according to Lk. 10:6, while rest in possession of the law (a) is meant in Rom. 2:17. [O. BAUERNFEIND, I, 350-51]
→ *katapaúō, katápausis*

anaplēróō → plēróō; anástasis → anístēmi; anastauróō → staurós; anastréphō, anastrophḗ → stréphō

---

anatéllō [to rise], *anatolé* [rising]

---

anatéllō. "To cause to come forth" or (intransitive) "to come forth," used in the NT for "to spring forth" in Heb. 7:14 (cf. Jer. 23:5) or "to shine forth" in 2 Pet. 1:19 (cf. Num. 24:17) with no precise distinction.

anatolé. 1. "Rising of stars"; 2. "sunrise" as a quarter of heaven, i.e., the east, either as a place of good (Rev. 7:2) or of bad (Rev. 16:12); 3. perhaps the Messiah in Lk. 1:78 (cf. Jer. 23:5; Zech. 3:8; 6:12 LXX), or the shining of a star from heaven (cf. v. 79 and Philo *On the Confusion of Tongues* 14). Justin and Melito in the early church see in Christ's advent the rising of a star (Justin *Dialogue with Trypho* 100.4 etc.) or the dawn of heavenly light. [H. SCHLIER, I, 351-53]

---

anatíthēmi [to set forth], *prosanatíthēmi* [to consult], *anáthema* [cursed], *anáthēma* [cursed], *katáthema* [accursed], *anathematízō* [to curse], *katathematízō* [to curse]

---

anatíthēmi (prosanatíthēmi). Used in the NT only in the middle with dative of person and accusative of object, this word means "to set forth one's cause" (Acts 25:14) or "to expound with a request for counsel, approval, or decision" (Gal. 2:2). *prosanatíthēmi* has the latter sense "to submit for approval, consideration, or judgment" in Gal. 1:16 and 2:6. The rendering "to impart something" in 2:6 is linguistically insecure and does not fit the context. "To impose an added burden" is not supported by outside references (cf. Acts 15:28).

anáthema, anáthēma, katáthema. anáthema and *anáthēma* are variants for a. "something dedicated to deity," b. "something put under divine curse."
1. The NT has the first sense only in Lk. 21:5 (temple offerings).
2. Paul uses the term for the object of a curse. Calling Jesus accursed is a self-contradiction for Christians in 1 Cor. 12:3. Handing over to God's judicial wrath is the idea in 1 Cor. 16:22 (cf. Gal. 1:8; Rom. 9:3). Paul's readiness for this on behalf of his people (Rom. 9:3) is a supreme instance of his devotion to the gospel and his race. *katáthema,* a rare word, is equivalent to *anáthema* (perhaps a sharper form) in Rev. 22:3: There will not be "anything accursed" in the New Jerusalem as there was in the first Paradise (Gen. 3:17ff.).
3. In Acts 23:14 the meaning is a vow or obligation whose breach brings under a curse.

anathematízō, katathematízō. "To bring under the anathema," "to curse." Those who plotted against Paul in Acts 23:12, 21 put themselves under a curse, or under God's judgment, if they did not make every effort to fulfil their obligation. Peter in Mk. 14:71 puts himself under a curse if he is lying, or puts the people under a curse if they make out that he is a disciple. *katathematízō* has the same sense in the parallel passage in Mt. 26:74. [J. BEHM, I, 353-56]

anaphérō → *phérō; anápsyxis* → *psyché; andrízomai* → *anér*

---

anénklētos [blameless]

The word *anénklētos* means "blameless," "guiltless," normally in an everyday and even formal sense.

1. The NT uses it in this more general way when Titus is to see that presbyters, and Timothy that deacons, are "blameless" (Tit. 1:6; 1 Tim. 3:10).

2. The word has a more religious sense in 1 Cor. 1:8 and Col. 1:22. Christians are blameless, and will be presented as such at the judgment, on the basis of Christ's reconciling death and resurrection (cf. Rom. 8:33-34). Presupposed are God's help (1 Cor. 1:8) and continuation in faith (Col. 1:23).   [W. GRUNDMANN, I, 356-57]

anektós → *anéchō; aneleḗmōn, anéleos* → *éleos*

---

anexereúnētos [inscrutable]

This postclassical word means "inscrutable" and is used in Rom. 11:33 for the mystery of God's way of judgment with Israel that leads to grace. The term implies that the question of the meaning of this judgment cannot be given any theoretical human answer.   [G. DELLING, I, 357]

anexíkakos → *kakós*

---

anexichníastos [fathomless]

The meaning "indetectable" is found only in biblical and postbiblical usage (e.g., Job 5:9; 9:10 LXX). In the NT the word occurs in Rom. 11:33 and Eph. 3:8. The parallelism in Rom. 11:33 suggests a poetic source (with a Gnostic tinge). Eph. 3:8 in context points in the same direction. Irenaeus (*Against Heresies* 1.10.3) quotes Rom. 11:33 in his anti-Gnostic polemic.   [E. PETERSON, I, 358-59]

anepílēmptos → *lambánō; ánesis* → *aniḗmi*

---

anéchō [to endure],   *anektós* [tolerable],   *anochḗ* [forbearance]

---

1. "To receive," "take up," "bear," "endure." Thus one "receives" the word (Heb. 13:22; 2 Tim. 4:3), "accepts" people (2 Cor. 11:1), "puts up" with them (Mk. 9:19), "receives" or "bears" afflictions (2 Th. 1:4), and "endures" in the absolute (1 Cor. 4:12); cf. in the absolute the verbal adjective *anektós* ("tolerable") in Lk. 10:12.

2. "To restrain oneself." God does this either to our destruction (Is. 64:12 LXX) or in mercy (Is. 42:14 LXX). In Is. 63:15 LXX the sense merges into that of "to tolerate." The noun *anochḗ* in Rom. 2:4 and 3:25 is God's "restraint" in judgment (linked with his kindness and patience in 2:4 and forgiveness in 3:25).

[H. SCHLIER, I, 359-60]

anḗkei [fitting]

anḗkei denotes "what is fitting or seemly," with a suggestion of being "obligatory" in Phlm. 8. In Eph. 5:4 the idea is of "what does not belong" because believers are saints in Christ. The unsuitability may concur with the world's judgment, as in Col. 3:18, or run contrary to it, as in Eph. 5:4.   [H. SCHLIER, I, 360]

anḗr [man, husband], *andrízomai* [to act manly]

A. *anḗr* outside the NT.
1. The word is common for "man" with adjectives or nouns denoting function.
2. It also denotes the human species a. as distinct from fabled monsters or gods and b. in the sense of the inhabitants of a place.
3. It can specifically signify the male.
4. It can also be used for husband (Ex. 21:22 LXX).
5. It may also denote an adult male as distinct from a boy.
6. It may also have the sense of full manhood as an absolutized natural force.

B. *anḗr* in the NT.
1. The term is most common in Luke; for sense 1. see Acts 3:14; 18:24.
2. a. This sense occurs in Lk. 5:8; Jms. 1:20; the main distinction is from spirits or animals. b. This is a common usage either for humans in general, as in Mt. 14:21, or for population of a place, as in Mt. 14:35.
3. Sexual differentiation is usually expressed differently, but cf. Lk. 1:34.
4. The use for husband occurs in Mk. 10:2, 12; Rom. 7:2-3; the household tables in Eph. 5:22ff.; Col. 3:18-19; 1 Pet. 3:1ff.; the rules for officebearers in 1 Tim. 3:2, 12; Tit. 1:6. If wives are to submit to their husbands, husbands are to show the same unselfish love as Christ. The fiancé can already be called *anḗr* (Mt. 1:19; Rev. 21:2).
5. This sense underlies 1 Cor. 13:11. *anḗr téleios* in the NT is figurative (e.g., Eph. 4:13; Jms. 3:2).
6. This does not occur in a sexual sense in the NT, but Luke suggests the dignity of honorable and mature manhood in Lk. 23:50; Acts 6:3, 5; cf. 1:11. *andreía* is not used in the NT, but Paul has *andrízomai* in 1 Cor. 16:13 in the exhortation to steadfastness in the faith.   [A. OEPKE, I, 360-63]

anthomologéō → *homologéō; anthrōpáreskos* → *aréskō*

ánthrōpos [man], *anthrṓpinos* [human]

ánthrōpos.
1. "Man" as a species, a. as distinct from animals (Mt. 12:12), angels (1 Cor. 4:9), Christ (Gal. 1:12), and God (Mk. 11:30); b. as subject to weakness (Jms. 5:17), death (Heb. 9:27), sin (Rom. 3:4), evil (Mt. 10:17), flattery (Lk. 6:26), error (Gal.

1:1). The phrase *katá ánthrōpon* suggests not only analogy to the human sphere and human logic (Gal. 3:15; 1 Cor. 15:32) but also the limited nature of human thinking and conduct compared to God's (Rom. 3:5; 1 Cor. 9:8; Gal. 1:11), with a stress sometimes on its sinful nature (1 Cor. 3:3; 1 Pet. 4:6).

2. The word is used in Semitic fashion with a genitive to suggest relationship (cf. Lk. 2:14; 2 Th. 2:3—man of sin; 1 Tim. 6:11—man of God).

3. Paul has the word in some sets of antitheses: a. the outer man (the physical side) and the inner (the Godward side) (2 Cor. 4:16; Eph. 3:16); b. the old man (unconverted and sinful) and the new (renewed in Christ) (Rom. 6:6; Eph. 4:22ff.; Col. 3:9-10). c. The physical man and the spiritual (1 Cor. 2:14-15).

4. "The man" is a messianic term for Jesus in Rom. 5:15; 1 Cor. 15:21, 47; Eph. 5:32; 1 Tim. 2:5; Heb. 2:6; → *huiós toú anthrṓpou*. For the first and second man of 1 Cor. 15:45, 47 → *Adám* and *huiós toú anthrṓpou*.

anthrṓpinos.

1. This is used of humans as part of the created world; cf. Jms. 3:7, where humans are distinguished from animals; 1 Pet. 2:13, where the sense is more likely "human creature" than "human institution," there being no instance of *ktísis* for the latter.

2. It is also used to distinguish humans from God (Acts 17:25), with a stress on limitation (Rom. 6:19; 1 Cor. 2:13; 4:3—in contrast with God's judgment; 10:13, where the temptation is not said to derive from us, but not to be beyond our puny human strength).   [J. JEREMIAS, I, 364-67]

---

aniēmi [to release], *ánesis* [rest]

The basic idea is that of "relaxation of tension." *aniēmi* means "to release" or "loose" in Acts 16:16; 27:40, figuratively "to give up" in Eph. 6:9.

ánesis has the sense of "mitigation of imprisonment" in Acts 24:23, but elsewhere has the figurative sense of "rest" or "refreshment" (cf. 2 Cor. 2:13; 7:5; 8:13; 2 Th. 1:7; with an eschatological reference, cf. *anápsyxis* in Acts 3:20). *ánesis* is not used in the NT for "remission," nor in the fairly common Greek sense of "license," "self-abandonment."   [R. BULTMANN, I, 367]

ániptos → *níptō*

---

anistēmi [to raise, arise], *exanistēmi* [to raise, arise], *anástasis* [resurrection], *exanástasis* [resurrection]

---

anistēmi, exanistēmi.

A. **Meanings of *anistánai* and *exanistánai*.** In the Bible the words have the general senses a. "to raise up," "awaken," "institute," "deport," "set up," "repair," and intransitively b. "to rise up," "waken," "recover," "rise up" (e.g., to speak, or in enmity).

The words also have the special senses a. "to begin an action," b. "to raise up seed," c. "to introduce" (a personage in history), and d. "to raise up, or rise, from the dead."

B. Resurrection in the Greek World. Apart from transmigration, the Greeks speak of resurrection only a. as an impossibility, or b. as an isolated miracle of resuscitation. They have no concept of a general resurrection; the hearers in Acts 17:18 seem to think *anástasis* is a proper name (cf. 17:31-32).

C. Resurrection in the OT and Judaism. The OT recounts individual restorations to life (1 Kgs. 17:17ff.) and prepares the ground for the hope of a general eschatological resurrection (cf. Ezek. 37:1ff.; Is. 53:10; Job 19:25ff.; Ps. 73), but this becomes specific only in, e.g., Is. 26:19; Dan. 12:2. The Samaritans and Sadducees rejected the hope but it was solidly established in later Judaism, being spiritualized by Josephus (immortality) and Philo (mystical liberation), though neither uses the word *anástasis*.

D. Resurrection in the NT.
1. The NT recounts individual restorations to life (Mk. 5:42; Acts 9:40). The stories are marked by sobriety and solemnity, and the awakenings are not just isolated miracles but messianic signs (Mt. 11:5; Jn. 11:25-26; Mt. 27:53).
2. Jesus predicts his own resurrection (Mk. 8:31; 9:9; 10:34), and his raising is described as the work of the Father exalting the crucified Lord to messianic glory (Acts 1:22; 2:24; Rom. 1:4; 1 Cor. 15:1ff.). On the significance of the resurrection for the kerygma → *egeírō, syzáō*.
3. The resurrection of Jesus is the firstfruits of general resurrection (1 Cor. 15:20; Col. 1:18). The logic of faith is toward resurrection to life (1 Cor. 15:22; Rom. 8:11; Jn. 6:39-40). Yet there is a double resurrection, believers being raised first (perhaps Lk. 14:14; Rev. 20:5-6; possibly 1 Cor. 13:23-24, especially if *télos* means "the rest" rather than "the end"; 1 Th. 4:16-17, though cf. Rom. 2:16; 2 Th. 1:9-10; 1 Cor. 4:5). New life is a present possession but is still the goal of resurrection hope and striving (Phil. 3:11—the only NT instance of *exanástasis*). 2 Tim. 2:18 refutes the Gnostic error that resurrection has already taken place, and 1 Cor. 15 combats denial of the resurrection, possibly as too materialistic.

anástasis, exanástasis. The words are equivalent: a. "erection" of statues, dams, etc.; b. "expulsion" from one's dwelling, then (intransitively) a. "arising," e.g., from bed, or sleep; b. "rising up" or "departure"; c. "resurrection."

In the NT 2. a. occurs in Lk. 2:34: "fall and rising," i.e., judgment and salvation. Elsewhere the terms are used only for Christ's resurrection (e.g., Mk. 2:18; Jn. 5:29; Rom. 1:4; Heb. 6:2; Phil. 3:11). [A. OEPKE, I, 368-72]
→ *egeírō, zōḗ*

ánoia → *noús; anomía, ánomos* → *nómos; anósios* → *hósios; anochḗ* → *anéchō; antagōnízomai* → *agṓn; antállagma* → *allássō; antanaplēróō* → *plēróō; antapodídōmi, antapódoma, antapódosis* → *dídōmi; antapokrínomai* → *krínō; antéchō* → *échō*

---

antí [in place of]

A preposition from the Hellenistic period, *antí* does not have the sense "over against" in the NT but is used for a. "in place of" to denote a replacement or equivalent (Rom. 12:17; 1 Th. 5:15; 1 Pet. 3:9; Heb. 12:16), or a similarity (1 Cor. 11:15). From this develop the senses b. "on behalf of" in Mt. 17:27 or "to the account of"

and c. "for the sake of" or "for this cause" (Eph. 5:31), "because" (2 Th. 2:10—
antí toútou). In Mk. 10:45 the position of *antí pollṓn* ("for many") shows that it goes
with *lýtron* rather than *doúnai* and thus has sense a.: The sacrificed life of Jesus is a
sufficient price to redeem many. Even if we put it with *doúnai* and give it sense b.,
it still carries a vicarious significance, for Jesus is then giving his life "on behalf of"
the forfeited life of the many.   [F. BÜCHSEL, I, 372-73]

---

antídikos [opponent]

A. *antídikos* outside the NT.
1. The basic meaning is "the opponent at law," whether individual or collective
(cf. Prov. 18:17 LXX).
2. Figuratively the term then means "the opponent in a dispute" (cf. Jer. 27:34 LXX).
3. The word then simply means "opponent" (Esth. 8:11 LXX).

B. *antídikos* in the NT. The NT never uses the term in the direct sense 1. Sense 2.
occurs in Mt. 5:25, which is not just prudent advice, since the *antídikos* is the brother
and the background is eschatological. Lk. 12:58 makes the same point with the same
background, but the relation to God rather than to the neighbor is more prominent
here.

The usage in 1 Pet. 5:8 hovers between 2. and 3. The image of a court action is
abandoned, but the idea of Satan as the accuser (Job 1:6ff.; Zech. 3:1; Rev. 12:10) is
still present to give color to the expression. Sense 3. is the obvious meaning in Lk.
18:3, since the widow is not pleading in court.   [G. SCHRENK, I, 373-75]

---

antilambánomai [help], *antílēmpsis* [helpful], *synantilambánomai* [to support]

The main idea is that of "taking up" or "grasping," but with such extensions as
"to help," "to import," and in the LXX "to keep to" (Is. 26:3), "to enter into alliance
with" (Mic. 6:6) as well as, predominantly, "to help."

In the NT *antilambánomai* has the first sense in Acts 20:35 ("take up the cause of")
and the sense of divine "help" in Lk. 1:54 LXX.

antílēmpsis in 1 Cor. 12:28 does not refer to assuming office but to "help" in the
general sense, i.e., not of miracles, but of loving action (cf. Acts 6:1ff.).

synantilambánomai means "to take in hand with," and has a general sense in Lk.
10:40 (Martha and Mary) and a more specific sense in Rom. 8:26, where the Spirit
joins with us in intercession to fashion pneumatic prayers that surpass human comprehension but are searched out by God, who knows the mind of the Spirit.

[G. DELLING, I, 375-76]

---

antílytron → *lýō*; *antimisthía* → *misthós*; *antítypos* → *týpos*; *antíchristos* →
Christós; *anypókritos* → *hypokrínō*; *anypótaktos* → *tássō*

ánō [above],   *anóteron* [above],   *ánōthen* [from above]

---

1. As an adverb of place *ánō* means "above" (or "earlier") and is used of land, mountains, atmosphere, and heaven, heaven in the NT usually in either a material (Jn. 11:41) or a religious sense (cf. *tá ánō* in Jn. 8:23; Phil. 3:14). The above–below distinction was important in the rabbis, with a measure of parallelism between what happens above and what happens below.

2. In Philo the distinction between God and the world is linked with the cosmological distinction between an upper and a lower world, God being at the head and matter at the foot (cf. Gnosticism). Judaism and the NT do not divide the cosmos in this way, since God is its Creator and Lord, and God is thus above and the whole world as his creation is below. Thus the *ánō klēsis* in Phil. 3:14 is God's call in Christ, the *tá ánō* of Col. 3:1-2 refers to where Christ is at God's right hand, and the Father, not "that world," is the opposite of "this world" in Jn. 8:23; 13:1. Similarly, the Jerusalem that is above in Gal. 4:26 is described in religious terms, with "the present Jerusalem," not that which is below, as its counterpart. The NT does offer descriptions of the world to come in Revelation, making use of the idea of a world above and a world below for this purpose, but its basic distinction is not between two worlds but between God as holy and eternal on the one side and the world as sinful and transitory on the other.

ánōthen. Both outside and in the NT *ánōthen* is an adverb a. of place "from above" (Mt. 27:51) and b. of time "from an earlier period" (Acts 26:5). Further senses are then c. "from the first" (Lk. 1:3) and d. "anew" (Gal. 4:9). In Jn. 3:3, 7 the original usage inclines in favor of "from above," which alone links with Job 3:4 and Jms. 1:17 to suggest "of God." John uses *ánōthen* elsewhere in sense a. (3:31; 19:11, 23) and always describes birth in terms of origin (1:13; 1 Jn. 2:29; 3:9; 4:7; 5:18; Jn. 3:5-6). Sense d. helps to make the obtuseness of Nicodemus a little more intelligible and is considered by Origen and Chrysostom, though they both lean heavily toward a. The versions vacillate between a. and d. The suggestion that both a. and d. are meant cannot be proved.   [F. Büchsel, I, 376-78]

áxios [worthy],   *anáxios* [unworthy],   *axióō* [to consider worthy],   *kataxióō* [to consider worthy]

áxios, anáxios. Strictly "bringing into balance," hence "equivalent" (e.g., Rom. 8:18), with such extensions as "being appropriate" (1 Cor. 16:4), "deserving" (Mt. 10:10), "worth," e.g., considering or accepting (1 Tim. 1:15), or praising (Rev. 4:11), "worthy" almost in the sense of "in a position to" (Rev. 5:2), and "corresponding to" (Mt. 3:8).

In the NT the thought of merit is excluded; we are worthy of the gospel only as we receive it (cf. Mt. 10:11, 13; 22:8; Acts 13:46; Heb. 11:38; Rev. 3:4).

In many expressions a genitive or infinitive is put with *áxios* to denote the sphere of correspondence (cf. Rom. 16:2). Paul admonishes his readers to walk worthy of the gospel, their calling, and the Lord (1 Th. 2:12; Phil. 1:27; Col. 1:10; Eph. 4:1; cf. 3 Jn. 6), thus linking the motive and goal of Christian action, the motivating power residing in God's prior action. Hence the warning not to receive the Lord's Supper unworthily (*anáxios*) does not refer legalistically to a moral quality but to an attitude determined by the gospel.

axióō, kataxióō.
1. "To make worthy"—the sense in 2 Th. 1:11.
2. "To regard as worthy," "to value." The NT use of the compound *kataxióō* (Lk. 20:35; Acts 5:41; 2 Th. 1:5) helps to bring out the fact that in ourselves we are not worthy of the divine gift of grace.
3. "To regard as right" (Acts 15:38).   [W. FOERSTER, I, 379-80]

aóratos → *horáō; apangéllō* → *angelía; apaídeutos* → *paideúō; apaitéō* → *aitéō; apallássō* → *allássō; apallotrióō* → *állos*

---

apántēsis [meeting]

In 1 Th. 4:17 there will be, at the Lord's return, a rapture of his people to meet him. The word *apántēsis* was used for the public welcome accorded to important visitors. Similary Christians will welcome Christ, acclaiming him as Lord.
[E. PETERSON, I, 380-81]

---

hápax [once, once for all],   *ephápax* [at once, once for all]

hápax.
1. "Once," a. as a strictly numerical concept, used in the NT for Christ's unique and unrepeatable work (Heb. 9:25-26), with added emphasis through (1) the reference to the last time, (2) the double repetition in vv. 27-28, and (3) the application in v. 28, where Christ is the one offering as well as the one high priest. The term then takes on significance for Christ's second coming as well as the first (Heb. 12:26): "once more," i.e., "for the last time." b. "Once" as an indefinite concept of time, "when," "after," etc., in the NT only in one reading of 1 Pet. 3:20 and perhaps Heb. 6:4; 10:2.
2. "Once for all," used in the NT for the definitive Christian state and the one baptism (Heb. 6:4). "Once . . . tasted" suggests a proverbial saying similar to "having once tasted blood"; it is unnatural to let the gift go again. In Heb. 10:2 the point is that there was no once-for-all cleansing by the old offerings. Jude refers to the definitive nature of Christian teaching ("the faith") by which we know all that is needed for salvation and which we are thus to hold fast.

ephápax.
1. "At once," "together," in the NT (1 Cor. 15:6).
2. "Once for all," with reference to the uniqueness of Christ's death (Rom. 6:10), by which sin and Christ are quits, so that in him we can die to sin in an irreversible turning to God. Heb. 7:27 expresses the same thought in sacrificial language; Christ offered himself once for all in contrast to the high priests with their daily sacrifices, and he thus accomplished a once-for-all cleansing (Heb. 10:10), our sanctification having the same definitiveness as the sacrifice.   [G. STÄHLIN, I, 381-84]

aparábatos → *parabaínō; aparnéomai* → *arnéomai; aparchḗ* → *árchō*

---

apatáō [to deceive],   **exapatáō** [to deceive],   **apátē** [deception]

---

apatáō, exapatáō. Common from Homer, also in the LXX, for "to deceive or entice" (e.g., Judg. 14:15; Jer. 4:10; Gen. 3:10; Job 31:27).

The chief sense in the NT is that of enticing to sin (cf. 2 Cor. 11:3; 1 Tim. 2:14; Rom. 7:11). Eph. 5:6 warns against "deception," and 1 Cor. 3:18 refers to sinful "self-deception."

apátē. a. "Deception or enticement," b. "pleasant illusion," "pleasure." Meaning a. is found in the NT in Col. 2:8; Heb. 3:13; 2 Th. 2:10, while b. is most likely in Mk. 4:19; 2 Pet. 2:13; and perhaps Eph. 4:22, but always with a stress on the evil aspects. It is thus strongly influenced by a.   [A. Oepke, I, 384-85]

apátōr → patḗr; apaúgasma → augázō; apeítheia, apeithéō, apeithḗs → peíthō; apeírastos → peirázō; apekdéchomai → déchomai; apékdysis, apekdýō → dýō; apeleútheros → eleútheros; apelpízō → elpízō; aperítmētos → peritomḗ; apéchō → échō; apistéō, apistía, ápostos → pisteúō

---

haploús [simple],   **haplótēs** [simplicity]

---

haploús. a. "Simple," then b. "open," "with no ulterior motive," then c. "simple" in the negative sense. In the NT, as in Judaism, "simple" is mostly either neutral or positive.

In Mt. 6:22 the meaning might be "healthy," but if there is an ethical reference (cf. the "evil eye" as the possible opposite) "pure" is the meaning (cf. *haplótēs* d.). In Jms. 1:5 "kind" is possible, but "wholehearted" is more likely.

haplótēs. a. "Simplicity," b. "noble simplicity," as of heroes, c. "purity," "singleness of heart," and d. "generosity."

The usual NT sense is c. (Eph. 6:5; Col. 3:22; 2 Cor. 11:3), but d. "liberality" occurs in Rom. 12:8; 2 Cor. 8:2; 9:11, 13.   [O. Bauernfeind, I, 386-87]

apogígnomai → gígnomai; apódektos, apodéchomai → déchomai; apodídōmi → dídōmi; apodokimázō → dókimos; apodochḗ → déchomai; apothnḗskō → thánatos

---

apokathístēmi [to restore],   **apokatástasis** [restoration]

---

apokathístēmi. "To restore," then 1. "to return" (e.g., something borrowed), 2. "to restore" a. buildings etc., b. middle "to heal," e.g., lepers in Ex. 4:7, c. "to renew the world," d. "to reconstitute," e.g., a kingdom.

The biblical and messianic usage derives from 2 d. (and c.). The term is used for God's restoring of Israel to its land (Jer. 16:15; Hos. 11:11). This comes to be understood messianically and eschatologically, but inner restitution is also required (Am. 5:15), effected by the returning Elijah (Mal. 4:5). From the Aramaic for effecting a turn, or returning, the Samaritan Messiah derives the name Taheb. The originally political sense of the term may be seen in the disciples' question in Acts 1:6. The answer accepts the expectation but denies its political significance. Elsewhere in the

NT the verb relates to the forerunner (the Baptist) rather than the Messiah (cf. Mk. 9:12; 8:28; Mt. 11:10; Jn. 1:21). The "all things" of Mk. 9:12 is to be interpreted in terms of the Baptist's mission.

apokatástasis.

A. *apokatástasis* **in Secular Usage.** Found in the NT only in Acts 3:20-21, this word basically means "restoration," and then has special applications 1. in medicine, 2. in law, and 3. in politics. 4. It is also used in astronomy for the return of the constellations, the shining again of the sun or moon, the restitution of the cosmic cycle, and the periods of the phoenix, with the corresponding ideas of eternal recurrence and new creation (as in Stoicism). 5. It is used, too, of individual souls, e.g., when entering again the cycle of generations, and in the Hermetic writings in connection with the release from matter.

B. *apokatástasis* **in Judaism.** The LXX does not have the term, and it is rare in Judaism with little technical input. Josephus uses it for the return from exile, and Philo for the exodus and mystically for the soul. Surrounding cosmological speculation had hardly any influence.

C. *apokatástasis* **in the NT.** The reference in Acts 3:20-21 is strictly to the restitution of that of which the prophets have spoken, or the establishment of what they have spoken. Grammatically the conversion of persons cannot be intended. The relations of which the prophets spoke are restored to the integrity of creation while their promise is itself fulfilled. The times of refreshing mark the beginning of the transformation through the messianic work of Jesus. The text has no bearing on the question of universalism with which it is often linked. Judaism holds out no such hope, and if Paul stresses the comprehensive work of the second Adam (Rom. 5:18; 1 Cor. 15:22; Col. 1:20) he also says that judgment will have a twofold outcome (Rom. 2:7ff.), while God's being all in all will be through the overthrow of opposition (1 Cor. 15:25ff.).

D. *apokatástasis* **in the History of the Church.** From Origen's day the word has often been used for the restoration of all created beings. Irenaeus does not take this view, and Clement of Alexandria only hints at it, but Origen equates beginning and end and hence looks for the ultimate removal of all hostility to God, relying mainly on 1 Cor. 15:25ff. and Jn. 17:11 but taking his term from Acts 3:21 in the medical and political senses rather than the astronomical. His followers include many eastern theologians and such westerners as Scotus Erigena, Hans Denck, J. A. Bengel, and F. D. E. Schleiermacher.   [A. OEPKE, I, 387-93]

apokalýptō, apokálypsis → kalýptō

---

apokaradokía [eager expectation]

Made up of *kára* and *dékomai*, *apokaradokía* denotes stretching the head, e.g., to spy on, or to pay attention. It is linked with hope in the NT (Phil. 1:20) and thus denotes "confident expectation." The same applies in Rom. 8:19, where creation is straining forward, i.e., waiting with eager longing under the stress of conflict.

[G. DELLING, I, 393]

apokatallássō → *allássō; apokatástasis* → *apokathístēmi; apókeimai* → *keímai; apokóptō* → *kóptō; apókrima, apokrínō, apókrisis* → *krínō; apokrýptō, apókrypsos* → *krýptō*

---

apóllymi [to destroy], *apóleia* [destruction], *Apollýōn* [Destroyer]

---

apóllymi.

A. The Literal Use. a. "To destroy," "kill," in battle or prison; b. "to suffer loss or lose"; c. "to perish"; d. "to be lost" (cf. Lk. 15), not sharply distinguished from c.

B. The Figurative Use.
1. In Mk. 8:35 etc., with b. and d. as a background, the soul is an object of value which is not just lost but which we actively lose in trying to save or secure our lives, like the rich fool of Lk. 12:16ff. The ambivalent concept of life gives the sayings their profundity. In Lk. 15 the three parables are told from God's standpoint. The lost sheep has Ezek. 34:4 as a basis, with the idea of wandering and perishing in view. Jesus must seek what is lost and will not lose what the Father has given him (Jn. 6:39).
2. A specific NT usage with sense a. or c. as the basis occurs in 1 Cor. 8:11; Rom. 2:12; 1 Cor. 1:18; 2 Th. 2:10; 1 Cor. 15:18; Jn. 10:28, etc. The meaning is "to be lost," or, more likely, "to perish," active "to destroy" with a human or demonic destroyer (Rom. 14:15), or someone divinely commissioned (Mk. 1:24), or God himself as subject (cf. 1 Cor. 1:19; Jude 5; Jms. 4:12). In view is not just physical destruction but a hopeless destiny of eternal death.

apóleia. Rare in secular Greek, this means a. "destruction," "ruin," b. "perishing," c. "loss." It is common in the LXX in sense b. (cf. Job 26:6). In the NT the curse of Acts 8:20 has an OT ring. Eternal destruction is signified in Mt. 7:13; Rom. 9:22; Phil. 1:28; 2 Th. 2:3; Jn. 17:12; 2 Pet. 2:1; Rev. 17:8, 11.

Apollýōn. In Rev. 9:11 *Apollýōn* is a translation and personification of the Hebrew and means Destroyer (usually seen as a play on Apollo, the god of pestilence, who was regarded as the god of the empire and had the locust as his creature).

[A. OEPKE, I, 394-97]

apoloúō → *loúō; apolýtrōsis* → *lýō; aposkíasma* → *skiá; apostasía* → *aphístēmi*

---

apostéllō [to send out], *(pémpō)* [to send], *exapostéllō* [to send out], *apóstolos* [apostle], *pseudapóstolos* [false apostle], *apostolḗ* [apostleship]

---

apostéllō (pémpō).

A. *apostéllō* and *pémpō* in Secular Greek.
1. *apostéllō* is a strengthening compound of *stéllō* and is common in Greek for "to send forth," differing from *pémpō*, which stresses the fact of sending, by its relating of sender and sent and its consequent implication of a commission, especially in Hellenistic Greek.
2. It thus carries the further thought of authorization, e.g., in the case of official

envoys, but also divinely sent teachers. It is used in the latter sense by the Cynics and Stoics, by Irenaeus (with reference to Menander), and by Philo.

B. *apostéllō* and *pémpō* in the LXX (OT) with Judaism.

1. *apostéllō* occurs over 700 times in the LXX, mostly for the root *šlḥ*; *pémpō* only some 26 times, six with no Hebrew original. *apostéllō/šlḥ* are mostly used where there is commissioning with a message or task. Alone they denote the sending of a special messenger with emphasis on the sender (cf. Is. 6:8), so that the messenger is a kind of plenipotentiary. The message and the one sent are of interest only as they embody the sender, no matter who the sender or the sent may be. Even those who are sent realize that the stress is on the sender (cf. Gen. 24:1ff.).

2. The LXX pursues this thought consistently, even using *apostéllō* for *šlḥ* contrary to the literal sense in order to bring out the authoritative element in the action and the position of the one who acts. The features of the verb in secular Greek are thus taken up and merged with what the OT equivalent contributes. Even in relation to the prophets the use is not just religious; the situation itself gives the religious flavor. Nor does the term denotes self-awareness, as in the case of the Cynic, for there is no place for this alongside unconditional subjection to the will of the sender.

3. Rabbinic Judaism keeps within the sphere delineated by *šlḥ*. Josephus has *apostéllō* some 75 times, more or less synonymously with *pémpō* in some cases, elsewhere to denote official missions or sending by God. Philo has an absolute use similar to that of Cynics and Stoics and not affected by *šlḥ*.

C. *apostéllō* and *pémpō* in the NT.

1. *apostéllō* occurs some 135 times in the NT, mostly in the Gospels and Acts. *pémpō* occurs some 80 times, 33 in John, five in Revelation, 22 in Luke/Acts, only four in Matthew, and one in Mark. Apart from the special use of *pémpō* in John, the Lucan material predominates; it prefers *apostéllō,* yet like Josephus can use *pémpō* as a synonym and has less sense of the specific nature of *apostéllō.* The religious character of the NT material explains the general predominance of *apostéllō,* and in the NT as a whole *pémpō* seems to be used when the stress is on the sending, *apostéllō* when it is on the commission, and especially (in the Synoptists) when it is God who sends.

2. In John, Jesus uses *apostéllō* to denote his full authority, i.e., to ground his mission in God as the One who is responsible for his words and works. But he uses *pémpō,* e.g., in the phrase "the Father sent me," so as to state God's participation in his work by the act of sending. There is a slight parallel here to Cynic usage but with the distinction that the Cynics stress responsibility to God alone, whereas the point in John is the unity of will and action between Jesus and the Father. The terms as such do not shape Johannine Christology, for they are not basically or essentially theological terms. They are given their specific meaning in John by the context. The mission of Jesus acquires its significance and force from the fact that he is the Son, not from its description in terms of *apostéllō.*

3. In the NT *apostéllō* certainly begins to be a theological word for "sending forth to serve God with God's own authority," but only in context and not with any radical departure from its normal sense.

exapostéllō. This has essentially the same meaning as *apostéllō,* with which it is interchangeable in the LXX and Philo. It occurs 13 times in the NT, eleven in Luke, and two in Paul. The idea that in Gal. 4:4 the *ex-* denotes a prior presence with the sender (Zahn) finds no support. Here, too, the term derives it christological flavor only from the context, and the emphasis is on God as the sender.

apóstolos (→ *dṓdeka, mathētḗs*).

A. The Word and Concept *apóstolos* in Classical Greek and Hellenism.

1. The Greek Usage. In older Greek the term is a nautical one denoting a freighter or a naval force with no sense of initiative or authorization. Hence it does not become a term for envoy as in the NT, nor do the LXX, Josephus, or Philo form a link at this point to the distinctive and unusual NT usage.

2. Religious Messengers in Hellenism.

a. Material contacts between the NT apostolate and the Greek world are also slight. The Greek *prophḗtai* serve as mouthpieces for deity, but they do so as anonymous intermediaries, totally subject to the deity and with no specific sense of mission or authority.

b. The Cynics are something of an exception with their awareness of sending, and their use not only of *apostéllō* but also of such words as *ángelos, kḗryx,* and *katáskopos* to describe their work as messengers, heralds, and observers (with a view to helping). The Cynics have an active attitude with a strong sense of commitment to their message and of responsibility both for humanity and toward Zeus, to whom they are ultimately bound and from whom they derive their boldness of speech. In particular the term *katáskopos* offers in their case something of a parallel to the NT *apóstolos,* at least in the formal sense. Their mode of life is also similar, since they move about with their message, dependent on well-wishers for support. They express their awareness of mission by a certain arrogance and by their claim to be "divine men" (a phrase especially used by the Stoics). This claim, however, involves a certain tension with its approximation to the impersonality of the Greek *prophḗtai.* The unlimited claim goes hand in hand with a renunciation of personal significance which does not leave room for development of the concept of the *apóstolos.* The relation of the messenger to the deity does not have the character of an unconditional appointment, there is no clear concept of God or certainty about the revelation of his will, and the message can thus make no claim to absoluteness. For this reason the legal aspect plays little or no role.

B. *apóstolos / šalî(a)ḥ (šālû[a]ḥ)* in Judaism.

1. apóstolos among the Greek Jews. In Greek Judaism the term does not occur much, since the Jews were not a seafaring people. Josephus has it once for the sending of envoys to Rome (involving a journey by sea, but with some influence of *apostéllō*). The LXX has it only in 1 Kgs. 14 to describe Ahijah's commission to give a divine message to the king's wife.

2. The Later Jewish Institution of the šālû(a)ḥ. Judaism takes us a step forward with the term *šālî(a)ḥ,* which is recognized, e.g., by Jerome, to bear some kinship to the NT *apóstolos.*

a. The legal institution of the *šālû(a)ḥ,* which is ancient but takes shape in the first century, involves commissioning with specific tasks and stresses authorization. The legal element of giving and obeying orders is decisive. The person sent represents the sender, e.g., in betrothal, divorce, or purchase. Full adherence to the commission is presupposed. The applicable law is that of the messenger, whose honoring or shaming is an honoring or shaming of the sender (1 Sam. 25:40-41; 2 Sam. 10:1-2). The person sent is as the person who sends.

b. The *šālî(a)ḥ,* however, may represent a group as well as an individual, e.g., a congregation, or the community. It is in this sense that rabbis regulate the calendar in the dispersion, or the high priest acts for the people, or rabbis make a collection for the Palestinian scribes after A.D. 70, or Paul goes to Damascus in Acts 9:1ff.

Laying on of hands for such tasks confers a religious as well as an official character. Jewish missionaries, however, are not called by this term (not even by Justin in *Dialogue with Trypho* 108), since they do not have the authorization of the community. Thus the bearers of the office are better called "authorized representatives" than "apostles," since the latter term, in view of NT usage, would give a wrong impression of the missionaries of Judaism, who were backed by groups rather than the people as such.

c. The term does, of course, carry the idea of divine authorization, e.g., in the case of the priest or of such personages as Moses and Elijah, who are commissioned by God, not the community. The prophets, however, are never given this designation, perhaps because, although they speak about God in God's name, they do not actively represent God, especially as they are for later Judaism instruments of the Spirit.

C. The Use of *apóstolos* in the NT.

1. Statistical Findings. There are 79 instances plus some secondary readings: one each in Matthew, Mark, and John; 29 in Paul plus five in the Pastorals; 34 in Luke/Acts; one each in Hebrews, 1 Peter, and Jude; two in 2 Peter; and three in Revelation—hence 80 percent in the Pauline and Lucan material. The term stands at the head of epistles some eleven times—six in Paul, three in the Pastorals, and one each in 1 Peter and 2 Peter.

2. The Meaning.

a. The NT contains no trace of the common nonbiblical use for the act of sending or, figuratively, the object. Always signified is the person sent with full authority. The Greek gives only the form, the Hebrew the content. The legal element entails that the reference is only to males, although by the course of things women might have been apostles too (see D.2.).

b. There is full identity between *apóstolos* and *šālî(a)ḥ* in Jn. 13:16, where *apóstolos* denotes one who is legally charged to represent the person and cause of another (cf. the juxtaposition of *doúlos* and *kýrios, apóstolos* and *pémpsas*).

c. *apóstolos* can refer to the commissioned representative of a congregation, as in 2 Cor. 8:23 or Phil. 2:25 (Epaphroditus).

d. *apóstolos* also denotes bearers of the NT message, first the twelve (Acts 1:26) sent out by Jesus himself (cf. Mt. 10:2; Mk. 6:30), with Peter their head and Jerusalem their center (Acts 8:1); then the first Christian missionaries, as in Acts 14:4, 14 (Paul and Barnabas), Gal. 1:19 (James), Rom. 16:7 (Junias and Andronicus), and 1 Cor. 15:7 (a wider circle). Paul and Barnabas are sent by the congregation at Antioch (Acts 13:1ff.), but the apostle is properly an apostle of Jesus Christ, and this larger group shares with the twelve the common basis of a meeting with the risen Lord and commissioning by him personally. Hence Apollos and Timothy are not called apostles, but Paul's apostleship is accepted at Jerusalem (Acts 15; Gal. 2:9; cf. 1 Cor. 15:8ff.). Apostles, then, are not officials of the church but officers of Christ for its upbuilding, and in this sense they are comparable to the OT prophets (Eph. 2:20; 3:5). "In the church" in 1 Cor. 12:28 refers to the whole body whose head is Christ (cf. Eph. 1:22; Col. 1:18; Eph. 4:11), not to the local congregation.

e. Heb. 3:1 calls Jesus himself an apostle, obviously in the sense that the definitive revelation of God has taken place in him. Absence of the article before high priest shows that the phrase "apostle and high priest" is a unity. For the church Christ is the Son in whom God has finally spoken and who has made final expiation. Where the Son speaks and acts, God speaks and acts (as it was God who spoke and acted through the OT priest). The confession has absolute authority on the basis of his absolute authorization for word (*apóstolos*) and work (*archiereús*). Another possibility is that the two terms contrast Jesus with Moses and Aaron in virtue of his unique divine sending, but this would involve an unusual NT sense and isolating two terms (*apóstolos* and *archiereús*) which the author is concerned to relate.

D. The Rise and Nature of the Apostolate in the NT.

1. Jesus and the First Circle of Disciples.

a. The rise of the apostolate begins with the first group of disciples. Externally this group resembles similar groups around other leaders. The difference lies in its genesis and outcome. It originates on the initiative of Jesus. The disciples accept his call, listen to him, and learn obedience from his revelation of God as Holy One and Father. The apostles cannot later become mere officebearers because they are under God's orders and acknowledge the supremacy of the rule of love. Only true disciples can have this authoritative part in the work of Jesus. Thus all apostles must be disciples, though not all disciples need be apostles. The phrase "twelve apostles" can be used quite early (Mt. 10:2), yet it does not imply an exclusive equation of "the twelve" and "the apostles."

b. The disciples begin their apostolic work when Jesus makes them co-workers. No reason for this is given. Jesus simply calls the twelve and sends them out (*apostéllein* in Mark) with authority (Matthew, Mark, Luke). Here, then, is authoritative sending in the sense of full delegation, followed by a later return and report. To question the historicity of the sending creates more problems than it solves, but the derivation of the apostolate from Jesus does not depend on this sending in view of Mk. 9:38ff., where the basis of John's complaint about the exorcist is that only the disciples are authorized to use the power of Jesus, and Mt. 10:40ff., where the identification of sender and sent presupposes authorization (the one sent is as the one who sends, and what is done to the former is done to the latter). As the disciples are shown and perceive, their authorization is linked with the person of Jesus. Yet the correction of John in the first passage rules out any claim based on the authorization. If the disciples have full power to speak and act as Jesus does, this does not confer rights but implies the duty of service. The second passage is to the same effect: commissioning by Jesus means humiliation rather than exaltation. Service and humility purge the apostolate of the claims which might accompany its legal authorization. They make it a commission rather than an office. This is also illustrated by the sending out of the seventy (Lk. 10:1) and the fact that when the disciples return to Jesus they do not continue their work but become hearers and ministers again (Lk. 9:49-50). Apostleship as such has no religious character but is just a form. The apostles receive their religious impress from him who commissions them, and in such a way that the commission itself is the main thing, not its bearers.

c. The use of the terms "apostles" and "disciples" in Matthew and Mark supports this. When commissioned, the disciples of Mt. 10:1 become the apostles of 10:2 (cf. Mk. 6:30). But on their return they become disciples again throughout the rest of these Gospels. The situation is a little more complex in Luke, where "apostles" is a fixed term for the first disciples in 22:14; 24:10 but elsewhere is used in connection with actual mission, e.g., 6:12-13; 9:10. In 6:12-13 Jesus himself would use the Aramaic term, which does not have the suggestion of office that later came to attach to the Greek word. Hence it is reasonable enough to believe that the term is not a later assimilation or intrusion so long as we understand that *apóstolos* is simply an objective word to denote a fully accredited representative with a specific commission. Lk. 6:12-13 corresponds to Mk. 3:13ff., though in both cases the true appointment as apostles comes later (Lk. 9:1; Mk. 6:7). The disciples are chosen with a view to their later sending. The apostleship, then, derives from Jesus, and in Aramaic the word itself is also his, not in terms of office, but in terms of authoritative commissioning.

d. Significant, too, is the linking of the apostles with the proclaiming of the word. In Mk. 3:14; Lk. 9:2 the disciples are sent out to preach (cf. Mt. 10:7-8). An objective element, the message, thus becomes the content of apostolate. Full and obedient dedication to the task is demanded. Action accompanies speech in demonstration of authentic commissioning. The works are not a subject of boasting or evaluation but of a joy that expresses a complete ignoring of the person and absorption in the task (Lk. 10:17). The success of the apostles is the success of Jesus himself, and in the report it crowds out any reference to difficulties in the discharge of the task (about which Jesus gives clear warning in, e.g., Mk. 6:11).

2. *The Early Christian Apostolate as a Gift of the Risen Lord.*

a. The first commission to preach the kingdom is for a limited period. The death of Jesus leaves the disciples at a loss, but the risen Lord constitutes them a community and renews the commission. The apostles are now witnesses of the resurrection. On the other hand, not all such witnesses are apostles. Thus women are not included, although women are in fact the first witnesses and the church includes women prophets. Again, not all the "more than 500" seem to have been apostles. Personal commissioning by the risen Lord, as well as personal meeting with him, is the basis of the apostolate. This applies primarily to the twelve (Matthias replacing Judas), who have been prepared for the task but have now to preach Christ as the fulfilment of OT prophecy. They become his authoritative representatives, but the very nature of their commission means that they are now also missionaries. A number of others join with the twelve in receiving and executing this commission (cf. Acts 15:1ff.). The missionary aspect is something new compared to the Jewish *šālî(a)ḥ* institution. The new commission is also of a more lasting character, applying to the whole period between the ascension and the return. Yet there is only one appointment, so that we can hardly think of the apostolate as a continuing office. It is still marked by an endowment with authority and the duty of rendering an account; Paul is a classical example. The Spirit is indispensable, for in the Spirit (Pentecost) the apostles receive assurance of Christ's presence and power and also a standard of what is to be done as the apostles dedicate themselves to God's will and aim at faith in the hearers rather than personal achievement as preachers or healers. The accompanying works are displays of Christ's power which validate the divine message as fact and not just theory. They are indispensable, not to the messengers, but to the message. To dismiss them as legendary accretions is to disclaim the apostolate as a basic religious institution, reducing it to a legal office. The thinking relating to these apostolic signs finds its model in Moses as the divine messenger endorsed by signs (Ex. 3:12). To be sure, Christ as the risen Lord works in the whole community, not just in the apostles. Yet the apostles have special significance as leaders who enjoy the full accreditation of the Lord with a universal commission to what is to be a universal community. The Lord is still behind what they say and do. He himself is the subject of their message. In this new commissioning, however, this is an ongoing message to the world.

b. John's Gospel confirms these findings while not using the term apostle. In it the Easter stories show how the Lord united the disciples to himself and gave them full authority (cf. Thomas in 20:24ff.; Peter in 21:1ff.). Here again obedience and service are the issue, not personal achievement. Believers are Christ's sheep and Peter is to feed them, not rule over them. Commitment and responsibility go with the commission. Only with the Spirit can it be discharged (20:21ff.). The use of *apostéllō* and *pémpō* in 20:21 shows that the work is ultimately Christ's own work in which he gives the disciples a share as he sends them (*pémpō*). The messengers' authorization is subsidiary to that of Jesus. By the same token, however, it is he who sustains them in their office; hence the importance of the *paráklētos* whom he sends (*pémpō*) (14:26; 15:26). Probably the focus on Christ as the one who works with the Father from first to last is what causes John to avoid the term *apóstolos* while not denying that the disciples were fully accredited representatives.

c. It was perhaps in Antioch that *apóstolos* first came to be used for *šālî(a)ḥ,* in the first instance for the mission, then for the missionaries. Paul might have had a hand in it, for he is the first clearly to use it for the individual messenger of Jesus. It could be adopted only because of an existing relation between *apostéllein* and *šālaḥ*. A problem is that of distinguishing between *apóstoloi* in the absolute and the *apóstoloi* of the churches (cf. Acts 13:1), but since Jesus is the principle of the churches' action, since the Spirit has the initiative, since only Paul and Barnabas are sent, and since *apostéllein* is not used for what the church at Antioch does, Paul and Barnabas are obviously apostles of Christ, not of the Christians at Antioch.

d. While the chief basis of the apostolate is the will and commission of Christ under the direction of the Spirit, the election of Matthias shows that eyewitness is also a qualification. The new commissioning is thus a continuation of the old, and the history of Jesus is regarded as supremely important. Paul is inferior in this regard and hence seeks a further basis for his apostolate while entering at the same time into the full stream of the historical tradition (1 Cor. 11:23ff.; 15:1ff.).

3. The Classical Form of the Apostolate in the Person of Paul. Paul offers the classical case of an apostle because of the information he leaves, his unusual position, his special labors, his strong sense of calling and office, and his need to vindicate his apostolate against objections.

a. Paul's entry on the apostolate involves a sharp break in his life which he can trace only to the eternal will and special action of God. His apostolic sense is determined by his meeting with Jesus on the Damascus road. His response to this is one, not of vacillation, but of sudden and resolute commitment to the Jesus he had formerly persecuted. For Paul this meeting is not a visionary experience but an objective act of God speaking through Jesus. He thus becomes an apostle of Jesus Christ, but by the will of God (1 Cor. 1:1; 2 Cor. 1:1; Eph. 1:1). Being an apostle means being "set apart for the gospel" (Rom. 1:1) "before he was born" (Gal. 1:15). The apostolate is thus a sign of divine grace leading to obedient subjection (1 Cor. 15:10). In this regard Paul links up with the OT prophets, especially Jeremiah, in whom we see complete devotion to the message, the predominance of the concept of God, elimination of the ecstatic element, a developed prophetic self-awareness, a determinative union with God, the embracing of his whole life by his calling, and a powerful restriction to the word. Whether or not Paul consciously follows Jeremiah in his sense of mission, he does so in his evaluation of suffering as an element in apostolic life, his concentration on the word, his rejection of any ecstatic basis for the apostolate (cf. 2 Cor. 12:1ff., where Paul can in fact boast of ecstatic experiences but refuses to link them with his apostolate lest grace should be obscured), and his parallel depreciation of apostolic signs (2 Cor. 12:12, where he mentions them only to show the justice of his cause, not the significance of his person). It is in the service of his message (the word of the cross, 1 Cor. 1:18; of reconciliation, 2 Cor. 5:19) that Paul stresses his apostolic authorization. The apostle, like the prophet, is a bearer of divine revelation. Since this revelation is fulfilled in Christ, a new term is needed in place of "prophet"—a term which corresponds to the new situation but still refers to the divine commission. The NT prophets, of course, do not correspond to those of the OT, though they are held in high regard. It is the apostle who has in the new situation the function of the prophet in the old.

b. If the special position of Paul is primarily determined by his calling to be a messenger, one of the reasons that gives him a more developed sense of calling similar to that of the prophets is the objection that he does not have the status or dignity of the other apostles (Gal. 1). But this goes hand in hand with his experience of Jesus and his recognition of the importance of the Spirit. These lead him to see himself as an envoy of Christ (2 Cor. 5:20) working together with him (2 Cor. 6:1). The God who worked in Jesus works through Paul as one who serves God and thus shares in God's own work (1 Cor. 3:8, 11ff.). This is true, however, only on the basis of his commission, not his person. As the servant of this Lord, conscious of God's overruling all history, he can insist with joy on his apostolic responsibility even though the close bond with the Lord imposes present poverty and suffering (2 Cor. 12:10).

E. Jesus as the One Who Was Sent.

1. Only once is Jesus called *apóstolos* (Heb. 3:1), but in John especially the thing itself seems to be present; cf. the use of *apostéllō*. The question arises whether redeemer myths have an influence here with their talk of the messenger, the sending, the ambassador of light, and the imparting of truth. An important point is that spatial movement (from above) rather than authorization is the main issue in such circles.

2. In John, however, the sending brings out the significance of the person of Christ and of what is done in him, namely, that the Father speaks and acts by him. a. In the signs God manifests Jesus as the promised one and himself as the one who works in and through him. b. The destiny of those who meet Jesus is decided by their attitude to him rather than by his doctrine: Jesus represents the Father in person. c. The death of Jesus is inseparable from his word, and his crucifixion and glorification constitute a unity. Thus Jesus is more than the Gnostic ambassadors. If the idea of sending plays a role, it is colored by John's Christology rather than shaping it. For John the whole complex is linked with prophetic sending and acquires its stamp from the fact that this ambassador is not a man, not even primal or preexistent man, but the Son in whom the Father manifests his presence and offers salvation or judgment.

pseudapóstolos. This word occurs only in the NT, and in the NT only in 2 Cor. 11:13, where Paul himself defines it: "disguising themselves as apostles of Christ." These false apostles are not authorized by Christ, as is shown by their lack of exclusive commitment to God or Christ. Their description as "superlative apostles" (11:5) is full of irony, for an apostle already has an incomparable position as such, and yet is marked by humility. Paul has in view his Judaizing opponents who contest his apostleship (cf. Gal. 1:1). Christians, perhaps Paul himself, probably coined the term, which supports the thesis that *apóstolos* in its distinctive sense is also of Christian provenance. For the same idea, though not the word, cf. Rev. 2:2: "who call themselves apostles but are not."

apostolḗ. A fairly common word for a. "dispatch of ships," b. any kind of "sending," also active "separation," "entombment" (of a mummy). In the Jewish sphere it can have such varied senses as "tribute," "present," "dispatch of a gift," or simple "sending."

In the NT it is used with *diakonía* in Acts 1:25, *cháris* in Rom. 1:5, alone in 1 Cor. 9:2 and Gal. 2:8, always with reference to the office of the *apóstolos* of Jesus, being fully controlled now by *apóstolos* in its NT sense.   [K. H. RENGSTORF, I, 398-447]

apostréphō → stréphō; aposynágōgos → synagōgḗ; apotássō → tássō

---

apophthéngomai [to declare]

"To speak out loudly and clearly, or with emphasis" (of philosophers, ecstatics, prophets, singers, and prophets), sometimes in a bad sense. It is used in a good sense in Acts of those who, filled with the Spirit, speak ecstatically (Acts 2:4) or prophetically (Acts 2:14; 26:25).   [J. BEHM, I, 447]

apopsýchō → psychḗ; apróskopos → kóptō; aprosōpolḗmptōs → prosōpolēmpsía

---

apōthéō [to reject]

Used from Homer for "to repel," "to reject," this word occurs in the NT only in the rhetorical question of Rom. 11:1 and the negative answer it demands (v. 2). Israel is God's people, hence he cannot repudiate them.   [K. L. SCHMIDT, I, 448]

apṓleia → apóllymi

---

ará [curse], **kataráomai** [to curse], **katára** [curse], **epikatáratos** [cursed], **epáratos** [accursed]

---

ará. Originally "wish," "petition," but used for "curse" from Homer's time, and found in the NT only at Rom. 3:14.

kataráomai. "To curse," so Lk. 6:28; Jms. 3:9 with accusative of person (mostly dative in nonbiblical Greek).

katára (→ *exagorázō*). Derived from *katarásthai*, "to enchant," *katára* means "curse."
1. *Curse (and Blessing).* Curses, found in almost all religious history, are utterances that are designed to bring harm by supernatural operation. They are made by priests, chiefs, the dying, etc. They often involve special formulas and rites. Sometimes they are linked with prayers. They demand belief in their fulfilment. They play a role in law, e.g., self-cursing for breaches of oaths. Jesus forbade his disciples to curse (Lk. 6:28), giving authority only to withhold remission (Jn. 20:23). God's curse, e.g., through the prophets, reveals his judgment in such a way as to initiate it (cf. Gal. 3:10, 13), the emphasis being on the ineluctability of the consequences of sin.
2. *Gal. 3:13.* This is the curse of the law, since the law expresses it (Dt. 27:26), but as such it is God's curse. It applies to everybody, not just to the Jew or Jewish Christian. To be a sinner is to stand under God's wrath and condemnation. Release comes because Jesus became a curse on our behalf (*hypér*) in a vicarious action which is not relativized but also not merely objectivized as though it were a legal transaction apart from us. Jesus' vicarious work effectively establishes a new fellowship between

God and us, so that redemption is ours through Christ's becoming a curse (v. 13), as reconciliation is ours through his being made sin (2 Cor. 5:17ff.). His being made a curse means that he enters our alienation in order to bring us out of it. Why this is necessary, Paul does not say. He simply accepts the fact. But he also sees that the curse of the law initiates the punishment of sin, so that new fellowship is in fact possible only by Christ's vicarious bearing of the penalty.

epikatáratos, epáratos. epikatáratos occurs in the NT only in Gal. 3:13 and means "cursed." *epáratos* in Jn. 7:49 (on the basis of Dt. 27:26) expresses the scorn of the scribes for the unlearned; not knowing the law, they are "cursed."

[F. BÜCHSEL, I, 448-51]

---

argós [idle], *argéō* [to be idle], *katargéō* [to render inoperative]

---

argós, argéō. argós means a. "indolent," "useless," "unemployed," and b. "incapable of action." It occurs in the NT in the secular sense in Mt. 20:3 ("unemployed"), Mt. 20:6 ("inactive"), and Tit. 1:12 ("idle"). It also has a religious sense in 2 Pet. 1:8, namely, "ineffective," i.e., without works that express faith and hence "unserviceable" or "worthless" (parallel *ákarpos,* "unfruitful"). *argéō,* used in the LXX for "to rest," is used in the negative in 2 Pet. 2:3 to express the latent activity of judgment; it is "not idle."

katargéō. In the NT this word has the secular meanings "to condemn to inactivity" (Lk. 13:7), "to destroy" (1 Cor. 13:11), and "to take out of the sphere of activity" (Rom. 7:2).

1. Religiously Paul uses it for "to make inoperative."

a. When God or Christ is the subject, the effect is beneficial. A transvaluation of values is effected in 1 Cor. 1:28: God "brings to nothing" things that are. In Eph. 2:15 he "destroys" the law of commandments; Christ's work frees us from the legalistic requirements of the law (while not invalidating its ethical demands; cf. Rom. 3:31). God also "robs" this age and its rulers "of their power" (1 Cor. 2:6), including death, and, as Hebrews puts it (2:14), the devil. The body of sin, i.e., our form in subjection to sin, is thus "negated," although our new life has not yet taken on its definitive form, and thus includes things which will be ended, e.g., prophecy and our present knowledge (1 Cor. 13:8). For with the coming of the perfect, the imperfect "loses its point" (v. 10).

b. When we are the subject, the effect is harmful, for by a Judaizing approach to the law we can nullify faith and make the promise void (Rom. 4:14), or by insisting on circumcision we "remove" the offense of the cross (Gal. 5:11).

2. The provisional disarming of demonic powers will issue in their complete destruction at the return of Christ (1 Cor. 15:24; 2 Th. 2:8; 1 Cor. 6:13).

3. The sense in Rom. 7:6 and Gal. 5:4 is "taken out of the sphere of operation," i.e., of the law in the first verse, of Christ in the second.

4. In 2 Cor. 3 vv. 7 and 13 seem to be instances of 2. ("transitory," "evanescent"). The same might apply in v. 14 if the point is that the illusion that the glory of the law remains is "destroyed" in Christ; but if the old covenant is taken to be the subject, the

meaning is that it is "devalued" by Christ, having only a borrowed glory and not its own, and thus losing its relative value when the true glory comes with Christ.

[G. DELLING, I, 451-54]

---

arésko [to please], *anthrōpáreskos* [man-pleasing], *areskeía* [desire to please], *arestós* [pleasing], *euárestos* [well-pleasing], *euarestéō* [to be well-pleasing]

---

arésko. *arésko* originally meant "to set up a positive relation," hence "to make peace," then aesthetically "to please," with such nuances as a. "to be well disposed," b. "to take a pleasant attitude," and c. "to please."

In the NT the word means "to please" in Mk. 6:22; Acts 6:5, "to please oneself" in Rom. 15:1ff., "to please" in expression of an attitude or approach in 1 Th. 2:4; Gal. 1:10; Rom. 8:8; 1 Th. 2:15; 4:1.

anthrōpáreskos. The opposite of an incipient *theáreskos,* this word in Col. 3:22; Eph. 6:6 denotes the norm of those who, out of fear, try to please their superiors. Paul in contrast bases true service to others on service to God.

areskeía. This word denotes the attitude of an *áreskos*; hence the meaning in Col. 1:10 is "every kind of pleasing attitude," toward whom being only implied.

arestós. Meaning "acceptable" or "pleasing," and denoting in the LXX what God (or a person) accepts as pleasing, this word is used for "pleasing" to God in Jn. 8:29; Acts 6:2; to the Jews in Acts 12:3; "things pleasing to God" (par. commandments) in 1 Jn. 3:22.

euárestos, euarestéō. Meaning "well-pleasing," "acceptable," *euárestos* in the NT always (except in Tit. 2:9) refers to God, and is never an evaluation (except in Phil. 4:18, describing the Philippians' gifts) but always the goal of the Christian life (e.g., Rom. 12:1-2; 14:18; Col. 3:20), so that we are constantly to test what is *euáreston* (Eph. 5:10). Of the three senses of *euarestéō*, a. "to be well-pleasing," b. "to take pleasure in," and c. "to walk as is well-pleasing," b. occurs in Heb. 13:16 and c. in Heb. 11:5-6.   [W. FOERSTER, I, 455-57]

---

aretḗ [virtue, excellence]

A. *aretḗ* outside the NT. This word has many senses but primarily means a. "eminence" in either achievement or endowment or both, b. "martial valor," c. "merit," d. in philosophy "virtue," which in Hellenistic Judaism (though not in Philo) can approximate righteousness, e. "self-declaration" on the part of the gods, and finally f. "fame" (its exclusive nuance in the Greek translation of the OT).

B. *aretḗ* in the NT. It is important here that the LXX finds no use for the Greek idea of "virtue" and hence has the term only in the sense of "excellence" or "fame." Not surprisingly, then, it is extremely rare in the NT. In Phil. 4:8 Paul puts it next to "praise" in a series with "what is true" etc., and if the series has mainly a religious ring, what he has in mind is the excellence that the righteous are to maintain in life and death. The same applies in 2 Pet. 1:5 (in spite of a secular parallel that might suggest "virtue"), while in the only other verse (1 Pet. 1:9) the context suggests either "self-declaration" (e.) or "fame" (f.).   [O. BAUERNFEIND, I, 457-60]

arḗn → *amnós*

---

arithméō [to count],   **arithmós** [number]

---

1. These words are often used in the literal senses "to count" and "sum" or "number" (Mt. 10:30; Acts 11:21; Rom. 9:27), but in Rev. 13:17-18 *arithmós* has a special sense which raises the question of sacred numbers. The mystery of regularity seems to have led to the investing of numbers with potency. In the NT new content is given them by events, the inherited symbolism is refashioned, and the symbolism is mainly formal and stylized, 7, 10, and 12 being especially prominent in Revelation.

2. As for Rev. 13:18 the riddle is that of numerical values ascribed to letters, with the added complications that the alphabet might be either Greek or Hebrew, and that 616 is an alternative reading to 666. The various solutions proposed, e.g., Titus, Nero, the Roman empire as such, or simply antichrist, are all unsatisfactory, and it may be that the divine was writing only for initiates of his own day, or that the passage is pure eschatology in the sense that the meaning will be clear only when the mystery is already present.   [O. RÜHLE, I, 461-64]

---

arkéō [to be sufficient],   **arketós** [sufficient],   **autárkeia** [contentment], **autárkēs** [content]

---

arkéō, arketós.
1. In religion these terms, which at first simply express "contentment," can become an ethical demand for contentment with what we have, either out of prudence, or freedom relative to external goods, or (in the NT) confidence in God's adequate provision (cf. Heb. 13:5; 1 Tim. 6:8; also Mt. 6:32ff.; Lk. 3:14).

2. A warning may also be issued against the security of illusory sufficiency (though the NT does not usually have the *arkéō* group for this).

3. Contentment is related by some philosophers to the supreme good, e.g., fashioning life according to nature. In the OT contentment is associated with moderation in 1 Kgs. 3:6ff., and the sense of God's guidance and the readiness for obedience in Ps. 73. Rabbinic exegesis finds religious satisfaction in God in his answer to Moses in Dt. 3:26 (cf. the paraphrase of Gen. 17:1). In Jn. 14:8 being shown the Father confers supreme contentment. In 2 Cor. 12:9 participation in grace is all-sufficient for Paul.

autárkeia, autárkēs.
1. The philosophical sense among the Cynics and Stoics is that of "self-sufficiency" or "self-reliance," while the ordinary meaning is "competence" or "sufficient quantity."

2. In the NT the word is given a new dimension as part of godliness (1 Tim. 6:6). Thus Paul's apparently philosophical contentment in Phil. 4:11ff. finds its center in "him who strengthens me" (v. 13). "Enough" also means having something to give to others too (2 Cor. 9:8).

3. On the basis of the divine name, rabbinic exegesis transfers the ideal of the *autárkēs* to God either in his self-sufficiency, his infinitude relative to the world, his satisfaction with creation, or his saying "Enough" to human suffering.

[G. KITTEL, I, 464-67]

Hár Magedṓn [Armageddon]

This is the name given for the site of the final decisive battle (Rev. 16:13ff.) and world judgment (19:19ff.). The use of Hebrew and absence of interpretation are in the style of apocalyptic. Two explanations have been advanced: a. a link with Megiddo, and b. a Greek rendering of the mount of assembly in Is. 14:13. The problem with a. is that there is no Mt. Megiddo, that Megiddo is not given eschatological significance, and the earliest exegesis does not mention it. The problem with b., which would make *Hár Magedṓn* the demonic counterpart of the mountain of God (cf. Heb. 12:22ff.), is that it is not an exact transliteration of the Hebrew of Isaiah.

[J. JEREMIAS, I, 468]

---

arnéomai [to deny, refuse]

a. "To say no" in answer to a question; b. "to refuse" in relation to a claim or demand.

1. In the NT we find a. in Lk. 8:45; Acts 4:16; Jn. 1:20; Mk. 14:68; Jn. 18:25; 1 Jn. 2:22: "to deny." Examples of b. are Heb. 11:24; Tit. 2:12; Acts 3:13: "to refuse."

2. The main thrust in the NT, however, is that of denying a person, as in Acts 3:13; Jn. 1:20; Mk. 14:68. This contains four elements: a. denial of a person rather than a thing (Jesus in Jn. 13:38; the Master in 2 Pet. 2:11; the Son in 1 Jn. 2:22-23; the name or faith representing the person in Rev. 2:13; 3:8; perhaps that which gives power to godliness in 2 Tim. 3:5); b. prior acknowledgment and commitment (cf. 2 Tim. 2:12; Rev. 3:8); c. unfaithfulness in the three forms of not meeting the claim for confession (Mt. 10:33; Mk. 8:38), not meeting the claims of neighbors (2 Tim. 2:11ff.), and not acknowledging Christ in sound teaching (2 Pet. 2:1ff.; 1 Jn. 2:22); d. a failure of the whole person in respect of total truth before God (Mt. 10:33; 2 Tim. 2:12; 1 Jn. 2:23).

3. The person denied may be the self. Thus God cannot deny himself (2 Tim. 2:13), but the disciples must deny the self (Mk. 8:34) in a radical renunciation, an acceptance of the cross, and the finding of true life in Christ.

aparnéomai. The compound has no greater intensity in the NT but has the same sense as *arnéomai,* as is shown by their interchangeability (Lk. 9:23 and Mk. 8:34), their alternate use in the same passage (Lk. 12:9), and the textual variants (Lk. 9:23; Jn. 13:38). [H. SCHLIER, I, 469-71]

arníon → *amnós*

---

harpázō [to seize],   ***harpagmós*** [something to be grasped]

---

harpázō. a. "To steal," b. "to capture," c. "to snatch," d. "to seize," e. "to take by force," f. "to catch away" (in visions).

Three possibilities exist in Mt. 11:12: a. that the kingdom is taken away and closed; b. that violent people culpably snatch it; c. that people take it forcibly in a good sense. The first has some support in the wording and context, the third is likely because of the irruption of the kingdom with the Baptist and the need for resoluteness to enter it. The second is intrinsically improbable.

harpagmós. Used in the NT only in Phil. 2:6, this word means a. "the act of seizing," b. "what is seized," and c. "something regarded as gain or utilized." In Phil. 2:6 sense a. is impossible due to a lack of object, while sense b. is hardly intelligible. We are thus left with c.: "He did not regard equality with God as a gain, either as not to be let slip, or as to be utilized." Those who favor the former nuance here refer to the temptation of Jesus, but the reference seems to be pretemporal and therefore it is best to translate: "He did not regard it as a gain to be equal with God," the reference being, not to resistance to temptation, but to a free (if unexpected) act of self-abnegation.   [W. FOERSTER, I, 472-74]

---

arrabṓn [deposit, guarantee]

---

arrabṓn is a commercial loanword from the Semitic signifying "pledge" or "deposit." Paul uses it in 2 Cor. 1:22 and Eph. 1:14 for the Spirit who is for us the guarantee of full future possession of salvation.   [J. BEHM, I, 475]

arrḗtos → *erṓ*; *artigénnētos* → *gennáō*

ártios [suitable],   ***exartízō*** [to equip],   ***katartízō*** [to prepare],   ***katartismós*** [equipment],   ***katártisis*** [improvement]

The meanings of *ártios* are a. "suitable," b. "correct" or "normal," and c. "even" (in mathematics). *katartízō* has the senses a. "to regulate" and b. "to equip." In 2 Tim. 3:17 *ártios* means "what is proper or becoming." *exartízō* in 2 Tim. 3:17 means "to equip" and in Acts 21:5 "to end as prescribed." *katartízō* means a. "to order" (the aeons in Heb. 11:3; to destruction in Rom. 9:22), and b. "to confirm" (in unity, 1 Cor. 1:10; the fallen, Gal. 6:1; in everything good, Heb. 13:21), confirmation being a mutual task (2 Cor. 13:11) but finally God's work (1 Pet. 5:10). *katartismós* in Eph. 4:12 denotes equipment for the work of the ministry, while *katártisis* is the inner strength of the organic relationship of the community, or of the character of its members (2 Cor. 13:9).   [G. DELLING, I, 475-76]

ártos [bread]

---

1. This word signifies literal bread in passages like Lk. 24:30; Acts 27:35; Jn. 6:11 (at the Last Supper, Mk. 14:22; the showbread, Mk. 2:26).

2. It then stands for nourishment in general (Lk. 7:33; Jn. 13:18; 2 Th. 3:12).

3. The idea of participation in eternal bliss underlies Lk. 14:15 and Christ as the true bread or bread of life in Jn. 6:31ff.   [J. BEHM, I, 477-78]

archángelos → *ángelos; archiereús* → *hiereús; archipoimḗn* → *poimḗn; archisynágogos* → *synagōgḗ*

árchō [to rule, begin], *archḗ* [beginning, ruler], *aparchḗ* [firstfruits], *archaíos* [old, ancient], *archēgós* [founder, leader], *árchōn* [ruler]

árchō. Active a. "to rule," b. "to begin"; middle "to begin."

1. The active occurs in the NT only in Mk. 10:42; Rom. 15:12 and means "to rule." Jesus relativizes all earthly rule, finding true power only in God.

2. The middle is more common, especially in Luke, usually as a kind of auxiliary verb signifying "indeed" or "moreover," but sometimes in a more pregnant sense, as in Jn. 13:5; 2 Cor. 3:1 (the only instance in Paul); 1 Pet. 4:17.

archḗ.

A. **The General and Philosophical Use of *archḗ*.** The meaning is "primacy," whether in time or rank.

1. In time it denotes the point of a new beginning in a temporal sequence. The relativity of the time sequence is implied, as in the religious statement that God is beginning and end. In philosophy it is used at first for the original material out of which everything evolves, then for the basic laws controlling all evolution. Stoicism views both God and matter (which God permeates) as *archaí*; God is identical with *archḗ* (and *télos*) as *lógos* and *noús*. Philo calls the four elements *archaí*, as he does the atoms, but the number 1 is also *archḗ*, and so is the *lógos* and God.

2. In rank the senses are a. "dominion," b. "realm," and c. "authorities."

B. *archḗ* **in the LXX.**

1. The usual sense is "temporal beginning," sometimes "primeval time."

2. Fairly frequently *archḗ* signifies "dominion," "power," "position of power," "person of influence." In Dan. 7:27 all *archaí* shall serve God's saints; these are earthly kingdoms but with a hint of supraterrestrial powers (ch. 10).

C. *archḗ* **in the NT.**

1. *archḗ* as "beginning" is used in the NT a. in the formula "from the beginning," e.g., of creation (Heb. 1:10), of Christ's appearing (Lk. 1:2), of being a Christian (1 Jn. 2:24), indeterminately of our election (2 Th. 2:13), with the devil as subject ("from all ages," though not in the sense of eternal, Jn. 8:44; 1 Jn. 3:8). 1 John has the phrases "that which was from the beginning" (1:1) and "he who was from the beginning" (2:13-14) for the Logos who has become perceptible to the disciples but is eternally preexistent, since it is God himself who here gives himself to us.

b. "In the beginning" in Jn. 1:1 says this specifically of the Logos; the Logos is before all time, so that no temporal statements can be made about him. Eternal preexistence is plainly implied. Elsewhere "in the beginning" refers to Paul's first evangelistic work in Phil. 4:15 and the early days of the Jerusalem church in Acts 11:15.

c. *tḗn archḗn* is used adverbially in Jn. 8:25 for "all the time."

d. *archḗ* may also denote the first occurrence in a series, as in Mt. 24:8; Heb. 5:12 (the beginning of Christian instruction); Heb. 3:14 (of the confidence of faith); 2:3 (of Christ's own preaching of salvation). In the negative the saying that Christ has no beginning (or end) puts him beyond time (Heb. 7:3).

2. *archḗ* as "power" means a. "dominion" or "power," e.g., Lk. 12:11 for the secular or spiritual authorities, and 20:20 for the power of the Roman procurator (always with *exousía* except in Jude 6); b. (plural) supraterrestrial forces (cf. Daniel) which seem to be hostile to God (Eph. 1:21), which have an overlord (Eph. 2:2), which govern different spheres, e.g., religious (1 Cor. 8:5), sexual (1 Cor. 6:15ff.), vital (1 Cor. 15:26), and social (cf. Eph. 6), which are spiritual (Eph. 6:12), related to angels (Rom. 8:38), and originally meant to be good (Col. 1:16), which are now confined to the lowest heaven (Eph. 3:10), which have been robbed of their power by the cross (Col. 2:15) and are now subject to Christ (Col. 2:15) their Lord (Col. 2:10, 16), but which still engage in conflict with Christians (Eph. 6:12) even though they cannot finally separate them from God (Rom. 8:38) and will ultimately lose all their influence (1 Cor. 15:24).

3. In Col. 1:18 Christ himself is *archḗ* as the image of God and the firstborn of all creation "before" all else. As *archḗ* he is the norm for creation by and for which all things were made (cf. 1:16b). He is also *archḗ* as the firstborn from the dead. Rev. 3:14 probably calls him *archḗ* in much the same sense (cf. 21:6; 22:13). Eschatology with its relativizing of history brought some kinship in philosophical usage: Christ on the throne is pre- and posttemporal (→ *AŌ*).

aparchḗ.

A. *aparchḗ* **outside the NT.** This means a. "firstfruits," then b. "proportionate gift" from earnings and the like, e.g., as a thank offering, then c. "offering" to the deity or sanctuary (cf. the temple tax in Josephus *Antiquities* 16.172). The offering may sometimes be of humans, e.g., for colonization or for temple service. The LXX uses the term for a. "firstfruits," b. "regular offerings," and c. "special gifts," almost always with a cultic reference ("portion" in Dt. 33:21 and "firstborn" in Ps. 78:51 are exceptions).

B. *aparchḗ* **in the NT.**
1. In Rom. 11:16 Paul uses the firstfruits of dough as a comparison to show that Israel's election continues in spite of present apostasy.
2. In 1 Cor. 1:16 the household of Stephanas is called the firstfruits of Achaia either in the sense that they are the first converts, or in the sense that they are Achaia's offering to Christ. Jms. 1:18 has a similar use: God shows his constancy by giving believers new birth so that they are a firstfruits of humanity offered to God. In Rev. 14:4 the 144,000 have become God's both by (temple) redemption and as firstfruits. They are thus the cultic personnel of the heavenly Jerusalem who are always in the Lamb's presence and alone learn the new song.
3. In Rom. 8:23 the relation is reversed, for now it is God who gives us the Spirit as a firstfruits, to be followed by adoption and the spiritual body.

archaíos. This means "from the beginning," then "past" or "old," often with a reference to origins and with something of the dignity of "ancient." In the LXX it can sometimes have the sense of pretemporal, as in Is. 37:26.

In the NT the "ancient world" of 2 Pet. 2:5 is the world before the flood. In Mt.

5:21 the "ancients" are forefathers or predecessors. In Lk. 9:8 the "ancient prophets" are those of repute. In Acts 15:21 the reference is to a "long past," whereas the "early days" of the community are at issue in 15:7. In 2 Cor. 5:17 preresurrection religious relations and attitudes are in view (e.g., to Christ, v. 16). In Rev. 12:9; 20:2 Satan is the "ancient serpent" (cf. Gen. 3).

archēgós. a. The "hero" of a city, its founder or guardian; b. the "originator" or "author" (e.g., Zeus of nature or Apollo of piety); c. "captain." Philo uses the term for Abraham, and once for God, while the LXX mostly has it for "military leader." In the NT Christ is *archēgós* in Acts 5:31: we bear his name and he both looks after us and gives us a share of his glory, especially his life (3:15) and salvation (Heb. 2:10); he is also the *archēgós* of our faith both as its founder and as the first example when in his death he practiced his faith in God's love and its overcoming of the barrier of human sin (Heb. 12:2).

árchōn. The term denotes a "high official," mostly in civil life, rarely in the religious sphere, though Neh. 12:7 refers to archons of priests and Dan. 10 to celestial beings guarding and representing individual states.

The NT uses the term 1. for Roman and Jewish officials of various kinds; 2. for Christ in Rev. 1:5, and 3. for the demonic prince (Beelzebul) who, the Pharisees allege, is behind the exorcisms of Jesus (Mt. 12:24), but whose power is broken (Jn. 12:31), who cannot touch the sinless Christ (Jn. 14:30), and who has already come under judgment (Jn. 16:11); along the same lines Paul speaks of the *árchōn* that works in non-Christians (Eph. 2:2) and of several powers of this age that have lost their force by ignorantly trying to make the Lord of glory their prey (1 Cor. 2:6, 8).

[G. DELLING, I, 478-90]

asébeia, asebḗs, asebéō → sébomai

---

asélgeia [licentiousness]

"License," mostly physical, figuratively spiritual. "Debauchery" or "licentiousness" is the sense in 2 Pet. 2:7 (Sodom and Gomorrah) and Eph. 4:19 (the pagan world). Sexual excess is probably meant in Gal. 5:19 and certainly so in Rom. 13:13; 2 Cor. 12:21; 2 Pet. 2:2, 18.   [O. BAUERNFEIND, I, 490]

---

asthenḗs [weak], *asthéneia* [weakness], *asthenéō* [to be weak], *asthénēma* [weakness]

A. Linguistic Data. This group denotes "weakness" of various kinds, often used for *kšl* in the LXX.

B. Material Data.
1. The first reference is to physical weakness, but in the NT weakness a. extends to the whole person, e.g., the "weaker" sex in 1 Pet. 3:7, Paul's "unimpressive" appearance in 1 Cor. 2:3, the "weakness of the flesh" in Mt. 26:41; Rom. 6:19. It may then be b. a mark of the Christian (in contrast to God's strength): God has chosen the weak (1 Cor. 1:26); Christ himself became weak (2 Cor. 13:3-4; cf. Heb. 5:2);

weakness is a reason for joyful boasting (2 Cor. 11:30); God's power is made perfect in our weakness (2 Cor. 12:10). Yet weakness can be c. something that must be overcome, as in the case of the "weak in faith" of Rom. 14:1 and 1 Cor. 8:9, who are certainly to be protected by the "strong" (Rom. 15:1: the terms are perhaps party slogans), but who are still deficient in knowledge (1 Cor. 8:7), not having fully freed themselves from their pre-Christian past. Weakness also has d. almost the sense of "sin" in Heb. 4:15; 7:28; Rom. 5:6 (the "helpless" here being parallel to the "sinners" of v. 8).

2. A special form of weakness is "sickness," and the group is often used for this in the NT, e.g., in Jn. 5:5 (cf. Acts 28:9); Lk. 10:9; Mt. 10:8. Sickness is seen as a. the work of demons (Mt. 17:18; Lk. 13:11) or b. a punishment for sin (1 Cor. 11:30); Mk. 2:5-6; cf. Jms. 5:16; also Jn. 11:4 and 1 Jn. 5:16). The mighty works of Jesus include healings of sickness (Jn. 6:2; Mt. 8:17, quoting Is. 53:4). So do those of the apostles (Mt. 10:8; Acts 28:9), and later we find the laying on of handkerchiefs (Acts 19:12) and anointing with oil (and prayer) (Jms. 5:14, 16).

3. Figuratively weakness can also have the form of "inner poverty" or "incapacity." Thus we read of the beggarly elemental spirits of Gal. 4:9, the inability of the law to save in Rom. 8:3, and the apparent insignificance of some parts of the body in 1 Cor. 12:22.

4. The weakness may finally be economic, i.e., "poverty," as in Acts 20:35.

[G. Stählin, I, 491-93]

---

askéō [to exercise]

askéō occurs in the NT only in Acts 24:16: "I exercise or exert myself." The term is used by Homer for artistic endeavor but is then applied spiritually from Herodotus and Pindar and occurs in the Stoics for taming the passions, exercise in virtue, and thought control. Philo finds in Jacob the model *askētḗs* on the basis of Gen. 32:24ff. Later fathers like Clement and Origen adopt the same usage and example. Paul has the term only in Acts 24:16, but his self-discipline as he describes it in 1 Cor. 9:25ff. resembles the *askeín* of the spiritual athlete. In Acts 24:16 he devotes much concern or works hard at having a conscience void of offense. It is surprising, but perhaps purely accidental, that the *askéō* group, which is so common in Jewish Hellenism and later Christian literature, is not used more often in the NT (especially in view of the parallel in 1 Tim. 4:7-8). [H. Windisch, I, 494-96]

---

aspázomai [to greet],   **apaspázomai** [to bid farewell],   **aspasmós** [greeting]

A. aspázesthai and aspasmós outside the NT. *aspázesthai* means to effect *aspasmós,* "to proffer a greeting," e.g., on the street, or when entering a house, or when parting. *aspasmós* includes embracing, kissing, offering the hand, and even proskynesis, as well as words of greeting. Homage paid to an overlord is a special form of *aspasmós,* whether a. by paying a ceremonious call, or b. by acclamation. *aspasmós* may also be the greeting in a letter; such greetings were more common in the Near East and less common in the Graeco-Roman sphere in the pre-Christian period. The basic sense seems to be "to embrace" and derived senses are then a. "to like someone," "to pay respects to someone," "to agree with someone," and b. "to give oneself to something," "to welcome something." In the LXX *aspázesthai* occurs only in Ex. 18:7 for "to ask about the welfare" (in greeting); it is more common in the Apocrypha. *aspasmós* does not occur at all.

B. In the NT.

1. Jesus' Rules of Greeting. Greetings were important for the Jews (cf. Mk. 12:18). Once (Mk. 9:15) the crowd greets Jesus himself. (More often we read of the more respectful *proskyneín*.) There is also a mock greeting at the trial (Mk. 15:18-19). Gentiles, too, greet their brethren as a sign of fellowship (Mt. 5:47). Jesus, however, requires his disciples to greet enemies as well as brethren. That he takes greeting very seriously is shown by his command to the disciples, when he sends them out, that they should greet a strange house on entering it, and that the peace of the greeting will either rest on the house or return to them (Mt. 10:12-13). The greeting of the apostles is thus endued with authority. On the other hand, the disciples must not let their time be wasted by casual greetings on the way (Lk. 10:4).

2. The aspasmós in Religious Narrative. In Lk. 1:29 Mary is puzzled by the angelic greeting. In Lk. 1:40ff. her own greeting of Elizabeth causes the child to leap in the womb and leads Elizabeth herself to cry in the Spirit: "Blessed are you among women."

3. The Greeting of the Apostle. In Acts an apostle greets a church on arrival and at parting (cf. 18:22; 21:7, 19). This may simply indicate a visit in 18:22 but receives emphasis in 21:7, 19. In 20:1 it comes at the end of an exhortation and in 21:6 it involves a moving ceremony that no doubt included embracing, kissing, and the wishing of peace.

4. The aspasmós in the Epistles. aspázesthai is the most common form of greeting in letters (47 times). It occurs in all the epistles except Galatians, Ephesians, 1 Timothy, James, 2 Peter, Jude, and 1 John. Paul seems to have regarded the greeting as very important as an expression of affection. In the imperative the writer may a. ask his readers to present greetings from a distance (Rom. 16:3ff.), b. greet all the members of the church (Phil. 4:21), c. tell the members to greet one another (1 Cor. 10:20; 1 Th. 5:26, which implies that the greeting would include embracing), or d. pass on a greeting to friends (2 Tim. 4:19). In the indicative a. absent individual Christians deliver greetings (1 Cor. 16:19; Rom. 16:21ff.: the scribe), b. groups in the church send greetings where there is a special relation (Phil. 4:22; Heb. 13:24), c. the whole church sends greetings, having no doubt asked the apostle to do this (2 Cor. 13:12; Phil. 4:22), d. a general ecumenical greeting is sent (1 Cor. 16:19; Rom. 16:16), and e. a special greeting is sent in the apostle's own hand (2 Th. 3:17; 1 Cor. 16:21; Col. 4:18), this being both personal and a mark of authenticity (2 Th. 3:17), but surprisingly not occurring in all of Paul's letters (though without the *aspasmós* formula it is perhaps to be found in Gal. 6:11ff.; Rom. 16:17ff.).   [H. WINDISCH, I, 496-502]

áspilos [without spot]

---

1. "Without spot," "blameless," cultically "unblemished." In 1 Pet. 1:19 the figure of speech obviously implies that Jesus is an unblemished offering because he is sinless.

2. "Morally pure": this is a biblical usage (Job 15:15) and occurs in the NT in Jms. 1:27; 2 Pet. 3:14; 1 Tim. 6:14. Moral content is thus given to a cultic concept.

[A. OEPKE, I, 502]

---

astatéō [to be unsteady]

"To be unsteady," "restless"; a. active of a flickering glance, an unreliable person, fickle fortune; b. passive "to be set in commotion"; c. either active or passive "to wander around unsteadily" (rare in secular usage). In 1 Cor. 4:11 Paul lists *kaí astatoúmen* as an apostolic burden: "we have no fixed abode," though with no specific stress on "wandering" (cf. 2 Cor. 5:8). [A. OEPKE, I, 503]

---

astḗr, ástron [star]

astḗr denotes a star, *ástron* a star or a constellation. The ancients regarded stars as "beings" and even deities, but in the OT they execute God's command and declare his glory (Is. 40:26; Ps. 19:1), although in so doing they are living creatures (with angels set over them in the pseudepigrapha) (cf. 1 Cor. 15:40ff.). Apocalyptic speaks of stars falling from heaven (Mk. 13:25; Rev. 6:13) or being obscured (Rev. 8:12). A falling star may have destructive effects (Rev. 8:10-11). The seven stars of Rev. 1:16, 20; 2:1; 3:1 may be the planets or the stars of the Great or Little Bear but are more probably related to the lampstands (cf. Josephus and the rabbis), just as the angels are parallel to the churches (1:20). The twelve stars have been connected with the zodiac but more likely refer to the twelve tribes. The morning star of Rev. 2:28 has been understood to be the Holy Spirit, the chief stellar angel, or the dawn of salvation; in 22:16 it seems to be Christ himself. The star which appeared to the Wise Men accords with messianic expectation on the basis of Num. 24:17, but what star it was, and how the wise men interpreted it, we cannot say for certain. [W. FOERSTER, I, 503-05]

---

astrapḗ [lightning, beam of light]

astrapḗ is often used as a comparison in the NT (the Easter angel in Mt. 28:3; the suddenness of the divine working in Lk. 10:18; the visibility and suddenness of the coming in Mt. 24:27). In Rev. 4:5; 8:5; 11:19; 16:18 lightning is linked with OT theophanies, with echoes of the plagues in the last three passages. With thunder, lightning climaxes the series of plagues that display God's supremacy, but it does not occur in the final judgment of 20:11ff. [W. FOERSTER, I, 505]

ástron → *astḗr; asýnetos* → *syniēmi*

asphályeia [certainty], *asphalyḗs* [sure], *asphalyṓs* [securely], *asphalyízō*
[to safeguard]

These words all suggest "firmness" or "certainty." The idea in Lk. 1:4 is the "reliability" of the teachings, in Acts 21:34; 22:30; 25:26 "the truth" (i.e., the facts, the
real reason, something definite), in Acts 2:36 "sure knowledge," and in 1 Th. 5:3
"security" (with *eirḗnē*, "peace and security") in the sense of false security in an
eschatological situation.   [K. L. Schmidt, I, 506]

ásōtos [dissolute], *asōtía* [debauchery]

The original sense is "incurable"; then we have the ideas of dissipation, gluttony,
voluptuousness, and indiscipline. The only OT instances are Prov. 7:11 and 28:7. The
reference in Lk. 15:7 is to the prodigal's life of dissipation, and in Eph. 5:18; Tit. 1:6;
1 Pet. 4:4 to a disorderly life (rather than voluptuousness).
                                                                [W. Foerster, I, 506-07]

ataktéō, átaktos → *tássō*

augázō [to shine], *apaúgasma* [radiance]

augázō. *augḗ* means "radiance" and can be rendered "dawn" in its only occurrence
in the NT (Acts 20:11). *augázō* means a. "to shine forth," b. "to illuminate," and
c. "to see." In 2 Cor. 4:4 b. is impossible, and while older translations and variants
favor a., the parallel in 3:13 strongly supports c. ("that they should not see").

apaúgasma. a. "Effulgence," b. "reflection," used by the LXX of wisdom's relation to eternal light (a.), by Philo of its relation to the world (b.), of our relation to
God (a.), and of the relation of the human spirit to the divine *lógos* (a.). In Heb. 1:3
(of Christ) both senses are possible, but patristic consensus favors a.: Christ is the
effulgence of the glory of God as sunshine is of the sun or light of light.
                                                                [G. Kittel, I, 507-08]

authádēs [self-willed]

a. "Self-satisfied," b. "arbitrary," c. "morose," d. "shameless." In Tit. 1:7 (bishops) the related adjectives favor b., while in 2 Pet. 2:10 (heretics) the context
suggests d.   [O. Bauernfeind, I, 508-09]

autárkeia, autárkēs → *arkéō; autóptēs* → *horáō; autokatákritos* → *krínō;
aphtharsía, áphthartos* → *phtheírō*

> *aphiēmi* [to let go, pardon], *áphesis* [forgiveness], *pariēmi* [to leave], *páresis* [forgiveness]

A. The Greek Usage. *aphiénai*, "to send off," can have such varied nuances as "to release," "to hurl," "to let be," "to pardon." *áphesis*, which is less common, is used for "release" (from office, obligation, debt, penalty). *pariēmi* means "to send by" with such nuances as "to leave behind," "leave off," "let be," "give up," "remit."

B. The Use of *aphiēmi*, *áphesis* in the LXX. In the LXX *aphiénai* is used for a whole series of words denoting a. "to release," "to leave (in peace)," and b. "to remit" (with God as subject, unlike Greek usage). *áphesis* accordingly means "release" (eschatological in Is. 58:6; 61:1), "exemption" (from taxation) (Esth. 2:18), and "forgiveness" (Lev. 16:26).

C. The NT Usage.
1. *aphiénai* means "to let go," "to leave" (Mk. 1:20; 10:28-29; Jn. 4:3; 16:28; 1 Cor. 7:11ff.; Rom. 1:27; Rev. 2:4), or "to leave behind" (Mk. 1:18; Mt. 5:24; Jn. 4:28; Heb. 6:1), or "to let alone" (Mk. 11:6; 14:6; Mt. 3:15; Lk. 13:8; Jn. 11:48; Acts 14:17), or "to allow" (Mk. 1:34; 5:19; cf. the formula in Mk. 7:27; Mt. 3:14; 7:4).
2. *aphiénai* can also mean "to remit," "to forgive" in a secular (Mt. 18:27) or more often a religious sense, e.g., sins (Mk. 2:5ff.), trespasses (Mt. 6:14), iniquities (Rom. 4:7), and the intent of the heart (Acts 8:22). The noun *áphesis* almost always means "forgiveness," usually of sins (Mk. 1:4; Mt. 26:28; Acts 2:38; 5:31; 10:43; Col. 1:14), but of trespasses in Eph. 1:7. *páresis* has the same meaning in its one use in Rom. 3:25. The forgiveness denoted is almost always that of God. It is constantly needed, and is granted when requested so long as there is a readiness to forgive others. Its basis is the saving act of Christ, so that Christ may be said to dispense it (Mk. 2:5ff.) or the community through him (Col. 1:14; Eph. 1:7), through his name (Lk. 24:47; Acts 10:43), or on his commission (Jn. 20:23), especially in baptism (Acts 2:38; Heb. 6:1ff.) and the Lord's Supper (Mt. 26:28). As the community is the holy community of the end-time, forgiveness is an eschatological blessing (Lk. 1:77). Though forgiveness is fundamental, it is not strongly developed conceptually (as the infrequency of *aphiénai* etc. in Paul and John shows). But related concepts make it plain a. that responsibility is maintained to God as Judge, b. that forgiveness is known as his act, not as a theoretical deduction, c. that as an eschatological event forgiveness means total renewal, and d. that forgiveness is received when God's judgment is affirmed in the confession of sins (1 Jn. 1:9; Jms. 5:16; Acts 19:18), penitence (Lk. 24:47; Acts 2:38; Heb. 6:1), and faith (in Paul and John).   [R. BULTMANN, I, 509-12]

aphilágathos → *agathós*

> *aphístēmi* [to fall away], *apostasía* [apostasy], *dichostasía* [dissension]

aphístēmi. Transitive "to remove" either spatially or within a relationship, "to win over," "to seduce," middle "to remove oneself," "to resign," "desist," "fall away." Only the personal use is important theologically, and in the LXX the term becomes almost a technical one for religious apostasy (Dt. 32:15; Jer. 3:14; Is. 30:1), usually from God or the Lord, and leading to idolatry and immorality.

In the NT this sense occurs in Acts 5:37; 15:38; 19:9. Decline from God is the meaning in Heb. 3:12. In 1 Tim. 4:1 apostasy involves capitulation to heretical beliefs as an eschatological phenomenon. An absolute use is found in Lk. 8:13 and cf. Rev. 3:8.

apostasía. Based on *apostátēs* (politically a "rebel," religiously an "apostate"), this term signifies the state (not the act) of apostasy. Paul is accused of apostasy against the law in Acts 21:21. Eschatological apostasy is the issue in 2 Th. 2:3, either with or prior to the man of lawlessness. Resting on Jewish tradition, this will be the decline of Christians into error and sin in the last days (cf. Mt. 24:11-12).

dichostasía. This word for "division" or "dissension" is used for objective disunity in the church in Rom. 16:17, in some readings of 1 Cor. 3:3, and in Gal. 5:20 (probably a reference to party strife within the community).

[H. SCHLIER, I, 512-14]

aphomoióō → hómoios; aphorízō → hóros

β b

Babylṓn [Babylon]

1. Apart from references to the captivity in Mt. 1:11, 12, 17 and Acts 7:43, and the single mention in 1 Pet. 5:13, the term *Babylṓn* occurs only in Revelation, where it denotes the ungodly power of the end-time (14:8; 16:19; 17:5, 18; 18:2, 10, 21). Its destruction is announced in 14:8. When it will fall is shown in 16:19. Seven visions depict the fall in 17:1–19:10. It is presented as a harlot (17:1; 19:2), the abomination of the earth (17:5), sitting on the beast in striking array, with her name on her forehead and drunk with the blood of saints (17:3ff.). God will judge it, to the joy of heaven and sorrow of earth (17:17; ch. 18). The main features in this presentation, including Babylon as a symbol, are taken from the OT (cf. Tyre as a harlot in Is. 23:15ff. and the image of the beast in Dan. 7). But the sayings of Jesus have also had an impact (cf. Mt. 23:25; 24:15ff.). The author, however, weaves the various elements into a totality, perhaps with reference to a city already present (17:18), namely, Rome as the city on seven hills which was often called Babel (as representing ungodly power) in later Judaism.

2. In 1 Pet. 5:13 the greeting is almost certainly from Rome; this is supported by almost all early exegesis and the tradition of Peter's work in Rome. If we accept the identification we must infer that Peter and the churches apply the prophecies against Babylon to Rome and thus expect its destruction.   [K. G. KUHN, I, 514-17]

báthos [depth]

báthos means "depth" as a. the depth of a stratum and b. depth as a dimension, also used figuratively for greatness or inscrutability. Its use in the NT is figurative in relation to God or the world: God's riches etc. in Rom. 11:32 in the sense of unfathomability, his work in 1 Cor. 2:10 as it is accessible only through the Spirit, and the heavenly inheritance in Eph. 3:18 in its comprehensiveness and universality; then depth

as a creaturely power in Rom. 8:39, and as immorality in Rev. 2:24 (the "deep things of Satan"). It may be noted that unlike Gnosticism (in which there are analogies), the NT never calls God himself depth.   [H. SCHLIER, I, 517-18]
→ *hýpsos*

> *(baínō)* [to go away],   *anabaínō* [to go up, ascend],   *katabaínō* [to go down, descend],   *metabaínō* [to change one's place]

(baínō). Not used in the NT or Philo, and used only twice in Josephus and four times in the LXX, this word is mostly intransitive in classical Greek and means "to go," "to stride," then "to go away," "to go on before," "to come."

anabaínō.

1. The primary sense is spatial, "to rise up," e.g., to mount a horse or ship, or to climb a hill, or move from the coast inland, or go to an upper story, or to mount a rostrum, or to rise to address the court. Thus in the NT Jesus climbs a hill (Mt. 5:1; 14:23) or climbs into a boat (Mt. 14:22) or goes up to Jerusalem (Mt. 20:17-18); Joseph goes up from Galilee (Lk. 2:4), the men with the sick of the palsy go up on the roof (Lk. 5:19), and Zacchaeus climbs the tree (Lk. 19:4). *anabaínein* is also used intransitively of the seed springing up in Mt. 13:7 and parallels.

2. More important in the NT is the cultic use (based on the OT and LXX). Jesus' going up from baptism acquires significance through the descent of the Spirit (Mt. 3:16). Going up to the sanctuary or Jerusalem is a stock phrase (Lk. 18:10; Jn. 2:13; 5:1; 7:8, 10, 14; 12:20). For Paul this means not only going to a place but to the mother community (cf. Acts 18:22). Actual ascent is indicated (since the holy city is on a hill) but going to worship is implied, as also in pagan usage due to the common situation of shrines on eminences.

3. The culminating religious use of the term is for ascent to heaven. In Acts 2:34 the claim is made, perhaps against a nonmessianic understanding of Ps. 110:1, that Jesus alone fulfils the prophecy by his ascension and session (possibly also in repudiation of other ascensions depicted in apocalyptic). John's Gospel gives an important role to *anabaínein*. As Jesus has come from heaven, and knows heavenly things, he will go back to heaven (6:62), or to the Father (20:17). Angels ascending and descending keep him in touch with the heavenly world (1:51; cf. Eph. 4:8ff.). In Rom. 10:6-7, which is based on Dt. 30:11ff., the point seems to be that we are not asked to do the impossible, to ascend to heaven or descend to the depths to bring Christ down or raise him up, because through the word of faith he is already present, having himself come down and risen up again. In Rev. 4:1 the command to come up through the open door and see the heavenly throne room denotes prophetic rapture. In Acts 10:4 the prayers of Cornelius have mounted up to God. The odd expression in Acts 7:23 ("it came into his heart") is modeled on the Hebrew (cf. Lk. 24:38: "Why do questionings rise in your hearts?").

katabaínō.

1. This is the spatial, geographical, and cultic opposite of *anabaínō,* used of leaving Jerusalem (also in the absolute), and of rain falling from heaven.

2. Religiously it often occurs with *anabaínō* (cf. Jn. 3:13; 6:33ff.). Jesus has come down to do his Father's will (Jn. 6:38). He is the bread from heaven (6:41-42). This bread comes down from heaven and gives life to the world (6:33). Every good gift

comes down from God (Jms. 1:17). The Spirit comes down on Jesus at his baptism (Jn. 1:32). In baptism one goes down into the water (Acts 8:38). Descending angels keep Jesus in touch with heaven (Jn. 1:51). Christ descends to earth (not Hades), according to Eph. 4:9-10 (though *katábasis* is a term for descent to the underworld).

3. Eschatological events (cf. the parousia in 1 Th. 4:16 and the new Jerusalem in Rev. 3:12; 21:2, 10) start in heaven and come down.

4. Philosophically souls are said to come down into bodies, and Philo speaks of the Spirit and joy descending from heaven.

5. Commercially the term is used for a decline in the value of money.

metabaínō. The usual meaning is "to change place," but the term also denotes change of topic or state. It is mostly topographical in the NT but figurative in John, e.g., for the change from death to life in Jn. 5:24; 1 Jn. 3:14 (which takes place by acceptance of the divine word), or Jesus' transition to his preexistent glory with the Father in Jn. 13:1.   [J. SCHNEIDER, I, 518-23]

Balaám [Balaam]

1. The OT shows Balaam as an instrument of blessing in Num. 22–24 and of seduction and consequent immorality and apostasy in Num. 31:16.

2. Later Judaism tended to interpret the first story in the light of the second, so that Balaam is presented as a wrongdoer (except in Josephus).

3. The NT accepts the Jewish assessment (2 Pet. 2:15; Jude 11; Rev. 2:14). Balaam is the model of the licentious Gnostics who lead the people into apostasy (Rev. 2:14), doing so for gain (Jude 11), and thereby showing his hostility to God.

[K. G. KUHN, I, 524-25]

---

ballántion [purse]

Sometimes spelled *balántion,* this word means "pocket" or "purse," especially for money. It occurs six times in the LXX and is used in later Judaism for money bag. All four NT instances are in Luke (10:4; 12:33; 22:35-36). The point in 10:4 (cf. Mt. 10:9; Mk. 6:8) is that money is not to be taken for the journey, but while Matthew and Mark think of tying coins in the girdle, Luke has in mind a special purse. Hence renunciation of the security of settled life is demanded, as also in 12:33. The situation changes, however, with the death of Jesus (Lk. 22:35-36).

→ *péra*   [K. H. RENGSTORF, I, 525-26]

---

bállō [to throw],   *ekbállō* [to throw out],   *epibállō* [to lay on]

bállō. a. Transitive "to throw, propel," "cast oneself down"; b. "to lay down," "pour in," "lay up (in the heart)"; c. intransitive "to cast oneself on," "sink into (sleep)." We find the sense "to throw" in the NT in Mt. 4:18 etc.; "to cast off" fruit in Rev. 6:18. In connection with judgment we find "to cast" into the fire (Mt. 3:10) or hell (Mt. 5:29) and "to throw out" (Mt. 5:13). "To throw off," i.e., that which causes sin, is the sense in Mt. 18:9. In Mt. 8:6 we find the passive for "to lie" (the sick servant). Other NT senses are "to put in," as wine in wineskins (Mk. 2:22); the finger in the ears (Jn. 20:25); a thought in the heart (Jn. 13:2). There is an intransitive use in Acts 27:4.

ekbállō. a. "To throw out," "expel," "repel"; b. "to send forth," "lead forth," "leave aside." In the NT it is used especially for the expelling or repelling of demons (Mk. 1:34; 3:15, etc.). Judaism had a series of formulas to effect exorcisms, though a word of command might also be enough. Jesus simply uses the word (Mt. 8:16) and has full power over demons (Mk. 1:27; Lk. 11:20). This displays his sovereignty but is also a mark of the inauguration of the kingdom (Mt. 12:28) and accompanies his preaching as such. Jesus commissions his messengers to cast out demons too (Mt. 10:1, 8). He regards the charge that he expels demons by means of demons as a blasphemous misrepresentation (Mt. 12:24). If he himself casts out demons in God's name, they can also be cast out in his own name (Mk. 9:38).

The NT also uses *ekbállein* for expelling a wife (Gal. 4:30), plucking out the eye (Mk. 9:47), expulsion from the Jewish community (Jn. 9:34-44) and the church (by Diotrephes, 3 Jn. 10), the casting out of the name of believers (Lk. 6:22), and the unwillingness of Jesus to "cast out" any who come to him (Jn. 6:22). Other meanings are "to send out" in Mt. 9:38, "to let go" in Acts 16:37, "to lead out" in Mk. 1:12.

epibállō. a. Transitive "to throw over," "lay on"; b. "to cast oneself on," "dedicate oneself to," "break in," "follow," "belong to"; c. middle "earnestly to desire." The term occurs in the NT with the meanings "to lay upon" in 1 Cor. 7:35, "to seize" in Mk. 14:36 (cf. Jn. 7:30, 44: Jesus cannot be seized until his hour comes), "to put one's hand to work" in Lk. 9:62, "to put on" a patch in Mt. 9:16, "to throw oneself on" in Mk. 4:37, "to burst out" (crying) in Mk. 14:72, "to accrue to" in Lk. 15:12.

[F. HAUCK, I, 526-29]

> *báptō* [to dip], *baptízō* [to baptize], *baptismós* [baptizing], *báptisma* [baptism], *baptistḗs* [Baptist, Baptizer]

A. The Meaning of *báptō* and *baptízō.* *báptō,* "to dip in or under," "to dye," "to immerse," "to sink," "to drown," "to bathe," "wash." The NT uses *báptō* only in the literal sense, e.g., "to dip" (Lk. 16:24), "to dye" (Rev. 19:13), and *baptízō* only in a cultic sense, mostly "to baptize."

B. Religious Washings in Hellenism.

1. The General Facts. Sacral baths are found in the Eleusinian cults, in Egyptian religion, in Isis worship, and in the mysteries. Baptisms of blood are post-Christian.

2. baptízein in Sacral and Similar Contexts. This usage is rare; it may be found in some papyri, Plutarch, and the Hermetic writings, but not in any technical sense.

3. The Meaning of the Rites. One underlying theme is that of washing and cleansing. Various liquids, including water, may be used to wash away uncleanness before God. Water, however, gives life, and hence another theme is vivification by way of symbolic drowning, e.g., in the Nile; the drowning connects one who drowns with the god and thus confers divinity. Yet the idea of purification is predominant, though this is cultic, not moral, and thus comes under criticism, e.g., from Plato, Philo, and Josephus. It must be stressed, of course, that the term *baptízein* itself has no great cultic significance.

C. *bapt(íz)ein* **in the OT and Judaism.** In the LXX *báptein* (*baptízein* occurs only in 2 Kgs. 5:14) is used for "to dip" in Judg. 2:14; Josh. 3:15; Lev. 4:6; 11:32. Naaman's dipping in the Jordan in 2 Kgs. 5:14 possibly has some sacramental significance. Later, *baptízein* becomes a technical term for lustrations (cf. Jdt. 12:7). It then comes to be used for the washing of proselytes, though it is hard to say when this practice originated; it seems intrinsically unlikely that it would have started after Christian baptism. Like other lustrations it is a continuation of the OT rites of purification, which are cultic but not magical, having the legal goal of ritual purity. A proselyte is put in a new position and from this point must keep the law. There is no thought here of death and regeneration, and the Hebrew term (*ṭbl*) behind *baptízein* does not signify sinking, drowning, or perishing.

D. The Baptism of John. This baptism (Mk. 1:4ff.; Jn. 1:25ff.; Acts 1:5; 11:16, etc.) is a powerful messianic awakening from which Christianity springs. As presented in the Gospels it does not seem to be a child of Near Eastern syncretism. The nearest analogies are in Judaism, especially proselyte baptism. Like this, John's baptism makes great demands on the elect people. Unlike it, it has a more urgent ethical and eschatological thrust. John is preparing the people for God's imminent coming. His baptism is an initiatory rite for the gathering of the messianic community. He himself actively baptizes, so that the passive use of *baptízein* now becomes more common than the middle found elsewhere. Cleansing, connected with repentance, is the main point, with a suggestion of purification for the coming aeon. The contrast with the baptism of the Spirit and fire shows that there is at least some influence of the idea of life-giving inundation, but the eschatological dimension rules out individualistic death and regeneration.

E. Christian Baptism.
1. Jesus lets himself be baptized but does not himself baptize (cf. Jn. 3:22; Jn. 4:2). The sinlessness of Jesus does not exclude his baptism (Mt. 3:14-15) since his concept of messiahship includes identification with sinners (cf. Jn. 1:29). If Jesus does not personally baptize, he endorses John's baptism (Mk. 11:30) but with a focus on his own death as a "being baptized" (Mk. 10:38-39) (cf. the OT figure in Pss. 42:7; 69:1; Is. 43:2; Cant. 8:7).

2. Christian baptism is practiced from the very first (Acts 2:38ff.). This is not just because John's disciples come into the church. It plainly rests on a command of the risen Lord irrespective of critical objections to Mt. 28:18, 20.

3. Syntactically *baptízein* is linked with *báptisma* in Acts 19:4. The means is expressed by the dative (Mk. 1:8: water; Mk. 1:8: the Holy Spirit, or *en*, "in" (Mt. 3:11 etc.), and once *eis* (Mk. 1:9). The goal is normally expressed by *eis*, "unto" (i.e., "for") or "into," as in Mt. 3:11; Gal. 3:27, etc. "Into" Christ, or the triune name, is not mystical but has a more legal flavor (cf. the commercial use of "in the name" for "to the account" and the invocation and confession of Christ's name in baptism [Acts 22:16; cf. 19:3]).

4. *The Saving Significance of Baptism into Christ.* The goal of baptism is eternal life, but not primarily by way of vivification. In spite of 1 Pet. 3:20-21; Jn. 3:5-6; Tit. 3:5, the thought of the cleansing bath is more fundamental (1 Cor. 6:11; Eph. 5:26; Heb. 10:22). Biblical piety rules out magical evaluations of religious objects and actions. Hence baptism has no purely external efficacy and in itself is unimportant (1 Cor. 1:17; Heb. 9:9-10; 1 Pet. 3:21). As the action of God or Christ, it derives its force from God's reconciling work or Christ's atoning death (1 Cor. 6:11; Eph. 5:25-26; Tit.

3:4-5). It places us objectively in Christ and removes us from the sphere of death (Adam). Imputed righteousness impels us to ethical renewal, for forensic justification (in Paul) leads on to spiritual fellowship with Christ; only a distinction of thought, but no real leap or transition is demanded. Baptism is participation in Christ's death and resurrection which effects a transition to the new creation, though translation into the reality of the present aeon is still a task. Paul may well have taken over the current terminology of the mysteries here, but the content, i.e., the historical relationship, the eschatological new creation, and nonmystical justification, is different. With Christ's death, baptism has a once-for-all character. What we have is more a Christ metaphysics than a Christ mysticism, and if there are spiritual connections there is no magical transformation of human nature. 1 Cor. 10:1ff. combats a materialistic (as distinct from an objective) view, and while 1 Cor. 15:29 seems to suggest a baptism for the dead, this is probably a tactical argument, or even an allusion to some non-Christian practice in the mysteries. The close connection with Christ's death and resurrection is mostly found in Paul, but the connection with the gift of the Spirit is common to Christian thinking. The Spirit may be given prior to baptism (Acts 10:44-45), but more often at or after baptism. The link with forgiveness and the ethical element remain, as in John's relating of baptism to regeneration (Jn. 3:5; cf. Tit. 3:5), since this still stresses faith and retains the connection with salvation history. Infant baptism, which cannot be supported from NT examples, makes sense within this objective interpretation but represents a departure from apostolic Christianity when linked with the later hyperphysical rather than eschatological-christological views.

F. Baptism as a Syncretistic Mystery. After NT days the eschatological context ceased to be a leaven and was treated as an appendage. In consequence baptism tended to become a syncretistic mystery with a primary stress on the matter (Ignatius, Barnabas, Tertullian), the rite (Didache, Hermas), the institutional ministry (Ignatius, Tertullian), the timing (either postponement or in earliest infancy), and the question of second repentance for serious postbaptismal sin.

baptismós, báptisma. "Immersion" or "baptism"; *baptismós* denotes only the act, *báptisma* (not found outside the NT) the institution. *baptismoí* in Mk. 7:4 are Levitical purifications and in Heb. 6:2 all kinds of lustrations. *báptisma* is the specific term for John's baptism (Mt. 3:7; Mk. 11:30; Lk. 7:29; Acts 1:22; 10:37), which is a baptism of repentance for the remission of sins (Mk. 1:4); it is also a term for Christian baptism, which is connected with Christ's death in Rom. 6:4 and with the atonement in 1 Pet. 3:21, and is a basis of unity in Eph. 4:5. Christ's death is itself his *báptisma* in Mk. 10:38-39; Lk. 12:50. As a special term, perhaps coined in the NT, *báptisma* shows us that Christian baptism is regarded as new and unique.

baptistḗs. The nickname for John in Mt. 3:1; Mk. 6:25; Lk. 7:20, etc., apparently coined for him, and thus showing that his appearing as the messianic precursor was unique, a baptizer being indispensable for a baptism to which the word gives its content. (Josephus uses the term for John; the mysteries speak of baptisms by gods and priests, but rabbinic disciples at proselyte baptisms are only witnesses.)

[A. OEPKE, I, 529-46]

---

bárbaros [barbarous, barbarian]

A. The Greek Usage.
1. The basic meaning is "stammering," "stuttering."

2. This gives the sense "of a strange speech," i.e., other than Greek.

3. The next development is "of a strange race," i.e., non-Greek. Alexander's conquests, however, helped to remove the ethnic distinction with extensive Hellenization, and hence to give the term more of a cultural nuance.

4. We thus find a further sense "wild," "crude," "fierce," "uncivilized."

5. The term takes on a positive sense when used of some barbarians (rulers and philosophers) who are highly estimated (cf. the use in the Apologists).

B. *bárbaros* in the LXX, Jewish Hellenism, and the Rabbis. In the LXX *bárbaros* occurs only in Ps. 114:1 (sense 1.) and Ezek. 21:31 (sense 4.). Sense 4. is the most common one in the Apocrypha. Philo follows Greek usage, as does Josephus (who does not reckon the Jews as *bárbaroi*). As a loanword it is used by the rabbis for the Jews as other nations see them, for non-Jewish peoples, and for the uncultured.

C. *bárbaros* in the NT. The term occurs only four times. In 1 Cor. 14:11 Paul has it in sense 1. In Acts 28:2, 4 the reference is to non-Greeks speaking their own language (in Malta). In Rom. 1:14-15 Paul is describing the universality of his apostolic commitment (cf. 1:5); he is to preach to barbarians as well as Hellenes. He includes the Romans among the Hellenes but describes the whole non-Jewish world by the formula. In 1:16 we find the different division "Jews and Hellenes," so that we have finally a three-pronged grouping of Jews, Hellenes, and barbarians. There are hints of this in Col. 3:11 with its reference to Jews and Hellenes, or circumcision and uncircumcision from the biblical standpoint, and barbarians and Scythians. Paul, then, does not include Jews among the *bárbaroi* but by way of the gospel is leading all the groups into a new totality in Christ.   [H. WINDISCH, I, 546-53]

---

báros [weight, burden],   *barýs* [heavy, burdensome],   *baréō* [to burden, weigh down]

---

báros. Originally "weight," then figuratively "suffering," "power."

A. In the Greek and Hellenistic World.

1. From physical weight the meaning is first extended to "tone" or "stress" in speech.

2. The next development is to "thrust," with a nuance of force or violence.

3. A rather different use is for "fullness," "plenitude," "maturity."

4. The next meaning is "oppressive suffering," e.g., illness, depression, and burdensome taxation.

5. Finally we have a common use for "weight" in the sense of "dignity or power," e.g., personal appearance or influence, the power of a state, or the power of arms.

B. The NT Usage.

1. Faith carries with it a changed attitude to affliction and power which is expressed in the changed use of *báros*. Christians are still under the burden of the world's suffering, as in Mt. 20:12; 2 Cor. 4:17; Rom. 8:18, but this is not to be compared with the weight of glory (Rom. 8:18). There is here no thought of merit as in Mandaean parallels. The new glory in affliction is solidly based on grace in Christ (2 Cor. 4:17), in contrast to the Hellenistic viewing of life as a misfortune or the mystical attempt to achieve ascetic or ecstatic liberation.

2. Suffering offers a chance to show love by bearing others' burdens (Gal. 6:2). If

the primary reference in Galatians is to moral lapses, the implications are broader ("fulfilling the law of Christ"). As distinct from Stoic altruism, this bearing of burdens finds focus in the community.

3. A distinctive NT use is for the burden of the law from which Christians are freed (Acts 15:28; Rev. 2:24) as they accept the easy yoke of Christ (Mt. 11:29-30).

4. When *báros* denotes earthly influence or power in the NT, it is something to be opposed. This rather than "financial burden" is probably what Paul has in view in 1 Th. 2:6-7; he does not support his authority by external power or appearance.

barýs. This is parallel to *báros,* being used for "heavy," "deep (in tone)," then "forceful," then "mature," and finally "oppressive" and "significant." The sense "oppressive" is most important in the NT, especially in relation to the law. a. In Mt. 23:4 Jesus accuses the Pharisees of laying "heavy burdens" on the people. b. In 1 Jn. 5:3 we are told in contrast that Christ's commandments are not demanding or burdensome, not so much in the sense that they do not ask too much, but rather in the sense that in keeping them we can draw on Christ's perfect triumph. The sense of "significant" occurs in Mt. 23:23 with reference to the more important commands. "Violent" is the meaning in Acts 20:29.

baréō.

1. The meaning is purely physical in Mt. 26:43; Mk. 14:40. On the other hand, Lk. 21:34 refers to the pressure of desires and cares on the heart.

2. a. The figurative sense of "affliction" occurs in 2 Corinthians. In 2 Cor. 1:8 the troubles in Asia are unbearably severe, so that trust has to be placed in God (v. 9) who gives the necessary strength to endure. In 2 Cor. 5:4 suffering is shown to be under God an expression of our earthly existence as one of hope. Sighing at mortality is a symptom of life in the Spirit. It is unlikely that the sighing is at the prospect of being unclothed. The burden is that of death itself, and the Spirit is the only guarantee of perfection.

b. In spite of similarities with Wisdom, Philo, and Epictetus, which stress the cleavage between body and soul and the consequent burdening of the soul (to be rejected according to Epictetus), Paul accepts the full severity of the burden but in faith and hope focuses on the new life which is provisionally linked with the present mortal body.

3. In 1 Tim. 5:16 the reference is to financial burdens.

[G. Schrenk, I, 553-61]

---

básanos [torment], *basanízō* [to torment], *basanismós* [torment], *basanistḗs* [tormentor]

1. The *básanos* was originally used by inspectors of coins, then the word became a commercial term for checking calculations, later it was used figuratively for testing, and finally it came to signify putting to the test by torture.

2. The group is rare in the LXX, being used mainly a. for "testing afflictions" and b. for "judicial sufferings." *basanízein* occasionally means "to test" but mostly "to torment."

3. In the NT *básanoi* means "pains" in Mt. 4:24 and "torments" (of hell) in Lk. 16:23. *basanízein* means "to plague, torment" in Mt. 8:6 (the servant) and Mt. 8:29

(the demons). The boat is "battered" by the waves in Mt. 14:24. The reference in Rev. 12:2 is to "birth pangs." Lot's "torment" at the sight of wickedness is the point in 2 Pet. 2:8. *basanismós* occurs only in Revelation, and is actively the "torment" that comes on the race in 9:5 and passively the "suffering" of Babylon in 18:7ff. *basanistḗs* is used in Mt. 18:34, not for "tester," but for "tormentor."

[J. SCHNEIDER, I, 561-63]

---

basileús [king], *basileía* [kingdom], *basílissa* [queen], *basileúō* [to rule], *symbasileúō* [to rule with someone], *basíleios* [royal], *basilikós* [royal]

A. *basileús* in the Greek World. *basileús* denotes the lawful king (usually hereditary, later distinguished from the *týrannos,* "usurper"). The king's power derives from Zeus and ideally he is inspired by the Muses. For Plato knowledge of the ideas is a royal art. Plato also depicts the benevolent ruler who knows only his own will as law. This ideal king fuses with the god-king of the Near East to produce the Hellenistic concept of divine kingship. [H. KLEINKNECHT, I, 564-65]

B. *meleḵ* and *malḵût* in the OT.

1. The word *meleḵ* denotes first the king of Israel. Saul arose as a charismatic leader. David, his successor, first ruled over Judah, then the united kingdom. He established a dynasty under covenant with Yahweh (2 Sam. 7; 23:1ff.). The Davidic dynasty lasted some 400 years in Judah, but after the disruption only short-lived dynasties, designated by Yahweh, ruled in Israel. The monarchy was not basic in Israel's religion but came into secondary relation with it and was thus subject to criticism by Yahwism. The stock titles and styles of address of Near Eastern courts were adopted in Israel but incorporated into Yahwistic ideas, as in the Royal Psalms (cf. 2; 20-21; 45; 72; 110; 132).

2. The word can also denote the Redeemer King. Court language forms a bridge to faith in the Messiah. Ideas associated with the king form the soil for messianic expectation. The person of David and the Davidic covenant (the promise of a house for David) are the starting point. Other motifs (e.g., from Gen. 49:8ff.) add their quota to produce the hope of a new aeon of righteousness and peace (Is. 9; 11; Mic. 5:1ff.; Jer. 23:5-6; Ezek. 17:22ff.; 34:23-24); this is projected on Cyrus in Is. 45:1ff. and Zerubbabel in Zech. 6:9ff. Notions of preexistence and paradisal fertility (which may have mythical roots) fill out the picture.

3. Another concept is that of Yahweh as king, which is more prominent than that of the messianic king and hard to relate to it. God as king extends protection and demands obedience (cf. Num. 33:21; Dt. 33:5; 1 Kgs. 22:19). His kingship is eternal (Ex. 15:18; 1 Sam. 12:12; Ps. 145:11ff.). Not being fully visible now, it has an eschatological dimension (Is. 24:23; Zeph. 3:15; Zech. 14:16-17). Yet it is a present kingship. This is perhaps expressed in the so-called Coronation Psalms (47; 93; 96; 99). Messianic beliefs see the coming messianic king as ruling in Yahweh's kingdom (see 1 Chr. 17:14; 28:5; 29:23; 2 Chr. 9:8). Before the exile Yahweh is mostly the king of Israel, bringing peace to his chosen people. Later he is called King of the World, enthroned in Jerusalem and magnified by all nations. But Yahweh can equally well be called Shepherd (Mic. 5:3) or Creator and Redeemer (Is. 43:14-15), so that his kingship has no very specific content.

4. The noun *malḵût* is one of the few older Hebrew abstract terms and denotes

"kingdom" or "kingship." It usually means a political kingdom (2 Sam. 20:31). David's kingdom, however, merges into that of Yahweh (1 Chr. 29:23; 2 Chr. 9:8). In apocalyptic, with its sharper distinction between the aeons, God's kingdom is then more precisely delineated as the final and eternal kingdom of the saints (Dan. 7:16ff.; more strongly nationalistic in later apocalyptic, Eth. En. 84:2; Ass. Mos. 10:1ff.).

[G. von Rad, I, 565-71]

C. The Kingdom of Heaven in Rabbinic Literature.

1. This term, equivalent to "kingdom of God," owes its origin to the tendency of later Judaism to avoid direct statements about God or use of the divine name. Heaven here is not the territory ruled by God. The phrase simply denotes the fact that God is king, i.e., the divine kingship, just as "kingdom" in secular usage implies "rule" or "government" (though "kingdom of heaven" is not merely a religious application of this usage but is an abstract construction of "God is king").

2. The term is comparatively rare but occurs in two important expressions: "accepting the yoke of the kingdom," i.e., confessing by a free decision that the one God is king, and the "manifesting of the kingdom," which points to the future when the time for decision for or against the kingdom will be past.

3. Israel as a people plays little role here. The decision is individual, though rabbinic theology stresses also Israel's privileges, describes God as king of Israel, and finds Abraham the first to confess God as king. The two concepts of individuality and nationality both derive from the OT, and the rabbis see no need to harmonize them. In the case of the kingdom the main stress is individual.

4. The rabbinic kingdom of heaven tends to be more purely eschatological in contrast to the idea of a future messianic kingdom which is a hope for the end of the age. The messianic kingdom is the kingdom of the people of Israel as the goal of God's saving purpose; the kingdom of heaven is the true *éschaton* when God is all in all and the link with Israel is no longer of special significance. The two ideas exist together but are not inwardly related. [K. G. Kuhn, I, 571-74]

D. *basileía (toú theoú)* in Hellenistic Judaism. Where there is a Hebrew original the LXX follows it closely. Elsewhere the kingdom is linked with wisdom (Wis. 10:10 etc.) or ethicized (4 Macc. 2:23). In Philo *basileía* means kingship or lordship, but *basileía* constitutes a chapter in his moral teaching (the true king is the wise person) and is not for him an eschatological entity. Josephus never speaks of God's kingdom, mentioning *basileía* in connection with God only in *Antiquities* 6.60. In general he prefers the *hēgemón* group to the *basileús* group, e.g., the *hēgemonía* of the Roman emperor.

E. The Word Group *basileús* in the NT.

basileús.

1. a. A first use in the NT is for earthly kings, in contrast or subordination to God, e.g., Pharaoh in Acts 7:10, 18; Heb. 11:23; Herod the Great in Mt. 2:1 etc.; Herod Antipas in Mt. 14:9; Herod Agrippa I in Acts 12:1; Herod Agrippa II in Acts 25:13; Aretas in 2 Cor. 11:32. All earthly rulers are kings (1 Tim. 2:2; 1 Pet. 2:13; Mt. 17:25; Acts 4:26; Rev. 1:5, etc.). Kings are not divine: God is king of the nations (Rev. 15:3) and the Messiah is King of kings (Rev. 19:16). Children of the kingdom are set above earthly kings, though they will be haled before them (Mt. 10:18). Kings wear soft clothing (Mt. 11:8) but do not know what the children of the kingdom do

(Lk. 10:24). They make war, but must hear the gospel (Lk. 14:31; Acts 9:15). The kings of the east will cause havoc in the end-time but will then be destroyed (Rev. 16:12 etc.). The kings of the earth will bring their glory into the holy city (Rev. 21:24).

b. Abaddon, an intermediary being, is no more and no less than an earthly king (Rev. 9:11).

c. David and Melchizedek are kings by divine appointment, the former an ancestor (Mt. 1:6) and the latter a type of Christ (Heb. 7:1-2).

2. a. Christ is king in the NT. He is first "king of the Jews" (Mt. 3:2; Mk. 15:2, etc.), accused as such (Lk. 23:2-3), but also treated as a pretender (Jn. 19:12). The people want him as king in a political sense; hence he resists their pressure (Jn. 6:15). Yet in a true sense he is indeed the promised "king of Israel" (Mt. 27:42; Mk. 15:32). He enters Jerusalem as such (Zech. 9:9; Mt. 21:5), and as such will conduct the last judgment (Mt. 25:34). Outside the Gospels the NT seldom refers to Christ as king of the Jews or of Israel (though cf. Acts 17:7). John offers a christological definition of the kingdom in 18:37, and Revelation gives the royal title a cosmological dimension. 1 Tim. 6:16 gives Christ the same title as Revelation: "King of kings and Lord of lords." 1 Cor. 15:24 implies the kingship of Christ when it speaks of the subjection of all other rule, authority, and power until at last the kingdom is handed to the Father.

b. As noted, God the Father receives the kingdom in 1 Cor. 15:24. That God is king is plainly stated in 1 Tim. 1:17: "King of the ages." Matthew, too, describes God as "the great King" (5:35), and many of the parables, especially in Matthew, are parables of the kingdom in which God exercises various kingly functions (Mt. 14:9; 18:23; 22:2, 7, 11, 13).

c. In some readings of Rev. 1:6; 5:10 Christians are called *basileís*; they are certainly said to reign, or reign with Christ, in other passages.

basileía. This term refers to the being or nature or state of a king, i.e., his dignity, and secondarily the expression of this in the territory he governs. The sense of dignity is primary in the LXX, Philo, and the NT.

1. The Earthly basileía.

a. Earthly kingdoms correspond to earthly kings. Sometimes the reference is plainly to kingly dignity, as in Lk. 19:12, 15; Rev. 17:12, sometimes to territory, as in Mt. 4:8; 12:25; 24:7; Mk. 6:23. Earthly *basileíai* are subject to God or even opposed to him (Rev. 11:15). The devil claims a kingdom by seducing the *basileíai*.

b. Hence a kingdom of the devil arises as either reign or realm (Mt. 12:26).

c. There is also a *basileía* of God's chosen people. David represents this (Mk. 11:10). This *basileía* rightly belongs to Israel (cf. Acts 1:6).

2. The basileía of Christ. Christ, too, has a kingdom. The angels will gather wrong-doers out of this (Mt. 13:41). Some will see the Son of Man come in his kingdom (Mt. 16:28). This kingdom will have no end (Lk. 1:33). The disciples will eat and drink in it (Lk. 22:30). The thief asks to be remembered when Jesus comes into it (Lk. 23:42). It is not of this world (Jn. 18:36). It is linked with Christ's appearing (2 Tim. 4:1), and we are to be saved for it (2 Tim. 4:16). Entrance into this eternal kingdom is given to Christians (2 Pet. 1:11). Christ's *basileía* is also God's. Sinners have no inheritance in the kingdom of Christ and of God (Eph. 5:5). The kingdom of the world will become that of our Lord and his Christ (Rev. 11:15). Yet a distinction can also be made. God has handed the kingdom to Christ (Lk. 22:29). God has put us in the kingdom of his Son (Col. 1:13). Having received the kingdom from the Father, Christ will finally hand it back to him (1 Cor. 15:24).

3. *The basileía of God.*

a. In usage, we should note (1) the alternative "kingdom of heaven," found only in Matthew apart from the textually uncertain Jn. 3:5. Matthew also uses "kingdom of God," but the expressions seem to be interchangeable. The nuance "of heaven" suggests that the essential meaning is "reign" and that this kingship does not arise by human effort. "Kingdom of the Father" (Mt. 13:43; 26:29 [cf. 6:10]; 25:34; Lk. 12:32) has essentially the same meaning. *basileía* also occurs sometimes (2) in the absolute (Mt. 4:23; 9:35; 13:19; 24:14; Heb. 11:33; 12:28; Jms. 2:5; perhaps Acts 20:25), but in all these verses the reference is plainly to God's kingdom. Few attributes (apart from "of God" or "of heaven") are supplied (3) to identify or describe the kingdom. It is unshakable in Heb. 12:28, heavenly in 2 Tim. 4:18, and eternal in 2 Pet. 1:11. It belongs to the poor in spirit in Mt. 5:3 and the persecuted in Mt. 5:10. Many synonyms (4) help to bring out its richness. It is related to righteousness in Mt. 6:33, peace and joy in the Holy Spirit in Rom. 14:17, *palingenesía* in Mt. 19:28, tribulation and patient endurance in Rev. 1:9, power in Mk. 9:1; 1 Cor. 4:20, glory in 1 Th. 2:12; Mk. 10:37, promise in Jms. 2:5 (alternative reading), life in Mt. 18:9 (par. Mk. 9:47), and knowledge in Lk. 11:52 (par. Mt. 22:13). These synonyms all show the kingdom to be soteriological.

b. The kingdom is implied in the whole message of Christ and the apostles. The gospel is that of the kingdom (Mk. 1:14; cf. Mt. 4:23; Lk. 4:43; Acts 8:12). Words like *kerýssein* (Mt. 4:23), *diamartýresthai* (Acts 28:23), *peíthein* (Acts 19:8), *laleín* (Lk. 9:11), and *légein* (Acts 1:3) all refer to the kingdom. The mystery is that of the kingdom (Mt. 13:11), and so is the *lógos* (Mt. 13:19). The kingdom also brings with it healings (Lk. 9:2) and exorcisms (Mt. 12:28); the work of the kingdom accompanies its word.

c. The concept of the kingdom was already present when John and Jesus proclaimed it to be near. This concept may be found in the OT and apocalyptic, in the LXX, and in Philo and Josephus.

d. That the kingdom is primarily God's kingly rule emerges in the dominant statement that it is near, or comes, or will come (Mt. 3:2; Mk. 1:15; Lk. 10:9-10; 21:31; 17:20; Mt. 12:28; Lk. 11:20; 19:11; Mt. 6:10; 11:2). Negatively, the kingdom is different, miraculous, not a human product. We cannot arrogantly bring it in but have to wait for it patiently (1 Th. 5:8, 19) like those who sow seed (cf. Mk. 4:26ff.); cf. also the parables of the mustard seed (Mt. 13:31-32), the leaven (Mt. 13:33), and less obviously the wheat and tares (Mt. 13:24ff.), the treasure and pearl (Mt. 13:44-45), the dragnet (Mt. 13:47ff.), the wicked servant (Mt. 18:23ff.), the laborers (Mt. 20:1ff.), the marriage feast (Mt. 22:2ff.), and the virgins (Mt. 25:1ff.). Everywhere the kingdom is shown to be different as it is now overwhelmingly present in the signs given in the ministry of Jesus. In this regard the kingdom is the cosmic catastrophe of apocalyptic (Mk. 13; 14:25), though Jesus refuses to depict the last things, rejects as irrelevant the scorn of the Sadducees (Mk. 12:25-26), and will not give the signs that people ask for (Lk. 17:20-21: the kingdom does not come with signs to be observed but is "among" and "in the midst of" us). With the kingdom, Jesus does not promise political glory for Israel but salvation for the world. There is still some privilege for Israel (Mt. 19:28), but Jews have no particular claim (cf. Rom. 2). The kingdom is not achieved by individualistic ethical achievement but by membership in the community, which stands under the promise. On the other hand, access to the kingdom does not come along Greek lines with spiritual training, ecstasy, or asceticism. Anthropomorphic descriptions do less violence to God's supraterrestrial majesty than the presentation of the kingdom as human self-evolution. The negative point that the kingdom is totally distinct from the world is the most positive thing that can be said about it. The actualization of God's rule is future, but this future determines our present. Setting us before God and his rule, it calls for conversion. A response in faith puts us in touch with this kingdom which comes apart from us, and the gospel is thus glad tidings for us.

e. Many terms describe our dealings with the kingdom. God gives it as a gift (Lk. 12:32). It is taken from some and given to others (Mt. 21:43). Christ gives Peter its keys (Mt. 16:19). He appoints it for us as the Father did for him (Lk. 22:29). God calls us to it (1 Th. 2:12), has set us in it (Col. 1:13), makes us worthy of it (2 Th. 1:5), saves us for it (2 Tim. 4:18), and has promised it (Jms. 2:5). He does not shut it like the Pharisees (Mt. 23:13). We for our part receive it like children (Mk. 10:15; cf. Heb. 12:28), inherit it (Mt. 25:34; cf. 1 Cor. 6:9-10; Gal. 5:21; Eph. 5:5; Jms. 2:5), see it (Mk. 9:1; Jn. 3:3), enter it (Mt. 5:20; 7:21, etc.), or go into it (Mt. 21:31). We are to be its children (Mt. 8:12). We may be "not far from it" (Mk. 12:34), or "trained for it" (Mt. 13:52). As we decide for God we are fit for it (Lk. 9:62). It demands effort; we are to be fellow workers for it (not of it! Col. 4:11), to fight for it (Heb. 11:33), to seek it earnestly (Mt. 6:33). It is destined for the poor (Mt. 5:3), the persecuted (Mt. 5:10), and children (Mt. 19:14). Hence God's invitation demands *metánoia* (conversion). Various parables bring out the sharpness of the decision (cf. Mt. 22:1ff.; 13:44ff.). We must cut out eye or hand (Mt. 5:29-30) or even make ourselves eunuchs (Mt. 19:12) for the kingdom's sake. The latter saying does not demand self-emasculation or even voluntary celibacy but is designed to illustrate the drastic nature of the decision that must be made. Many will be weeded out (Mt. 22:14). Temporary enthusiasm is not enough (Lk. 9:62). The cost must be counted (Lk. 14:28ff.). Hearing without doing will not suffice (Mt. 7:21, 24ff.). Supreme readiness for sacrifice is required (Mt. 10:37).

f. Jesus alone truly fulfils the demands of the kingdom. Hence the kingdom of God is especially linked to Christ. It is in Christ that the kingdom of David comes (Mt. 21:9 par. Mk. 11:10). "For the kingdom's sake" in Lk. 18:29 means "for my sake and the gospel's" in Mk. 10:29 and "for my name's sake" in Mt. 19:29. The kingdom of God in Mk. 9:1 is the same as the Son of Man and his kingdom in Mt. 16:28. For Jesus the invading kingdom of God has come in his person. This equation accounts for the once-for-allness of the mission of the Messiah. Origen's term *autobasileía* aptly sums up the equation, which also explains why the later NT does not refer so much to the kingdom, the phrase "the Lord Jesus Christ" being in itself an adequate substitute.

4. In view of the *autobasileía* the NT refers only once to believers as the kingdom (Rev. 1:6), and the implication here is plain that they are so only in a derivative sense, i.e., as linked to Christ.

basílissa. In Mt. 12:42; Lk. 11:31 we read of the "queen" of the south who will confront impenitent Jews because she came to hear Solomon's wisdom. Acts 8:27 speaks of the Ethiopian queen Candace. In Rev. 18:7 the harlot Babylon sits as a queen and is judged.

basileúō. This word, meaning "to be king," "to reign," is used of Jesus Christ in Lk. 1:33, of God in 1 Cor. 15:25, and of God and his Christ in Rev. 11:5. The called will reign with God (Rev. 5:10) or Christ (20:4, 6) to all eternity (22:5). This reigning with Christ stands behind Paul's ironical statement in 1 Cor. 4:8 (cf. v. 8b). We reign with Christ because we reign through him (Rom. 5:17). By his gift grace reigns (Rom.

5:21) when the usurpers sin and death are destroyed. References to human reigns occur in Mt. 2:22; 1 Tim. 6:15 (cf. Lk. 19:14, 27).

symbasileúō. Christians reign with Christ (cf. 1 Cor. 4:8). This rule implies service, obedience, and patience (2 Tim. 2:12).

basíleios. This word, meaning "royal," occurs in Lk. 7:25 ("palaces"). The "royal priesthood" of 1 Pet. 2:9 (Ex. 19:6 LXX) may refer to its royal dignity, or its being the priesthood of God the King, or its being royal in the same way as royal service, but in any case it is royal, not by inherent quality, but by the calling of God, and by Christ through whom the call comes.

basilikós. This less common word, also meaning "royal," is fairly common in the NT. In Jms. 2:8 ("royal law") the reference is to law as it is given by the king, and thus having royal dignity, rather than to preeminent law. The probable sense in Jn. 4:46, 49 is "royal official."

F. *basileía (toú theoú)* **in the Early Church.** Quotations and original references show that the usage is much the same as in the NT. The kingdom is eternal. It is equated with Christ's promise. We receive it as a gift. We meet, see, and inherit it; we dwell and are glorified in it. It will finally come with Christ's return. In contrast to the NT, however, there is more stress on the need for the sacrament and good works. A degree of ascetic ethicizing may be noted. Sometimes, too, the kingdom is not clearly distinguished from the church. The Apologists make little original use of the concept since they lay more stress on the need for virtuous living with its claim to reward. Quotations, however, prevent the gospel from being transmuted into religious philosophy. In the Alexandrians belief in individual moral progress tends to replace the biblical idea of the kingdom (in spite of Origen's *autobasileía*), while Latin theology thinks increasingly in terms of the active realization of the kingdom on earth.

[K. L. Schmidt, I, 574-93]

---

baskaínō [to bewitch]

From *báskanos, baskaínō* means "to hurt by words," then a. "to bewitch," b. "to revile," and c. "to envy." To a. is added the thought of harming by looks (the evil eye), though sometimes this might be unintentional. In the LXX the sense is "to be unfavorably disposed to." The only NT instance is in Gal. 3:1 ("to bewitch"). The use is figurative, but not without some realism insofar as the power of falsehood stands behind magic. In yielding to these "magicians" the Galatians have come under the power of untruth.   [G. Delling, I, 594-95]

---

bastázō [to bear]

Rare in the LXX, *bastázō* occurs 27 times in the NT for "to lift up" (Jn. 10:31), "to bear away" (Jn. 20:15), and "to pilfer" (Jn. 12:6). External carrying of the cross (Jn. 19:17) symbolizes discipleship (Lk. 14:27). Paul carries the marks in Gal. 6:17 (cf. Rev. 7:2; 9:14, etc.: bearing the seal or name of God, Christ, or antichrist).

Carrying the name in Acts 9:15 denotes confession of Christ in missionary service; there is no idea of a burden.   [F. BÜCHSEL, I, 596]

---

battalogéō [to babble]

Used only in Mt. 6:7, *battalogéō* means "to babble" in the sense of trying to achieve success in prayer by heaping up repetitions. The etymology is much disputed; the word was perhaps formed in analogy to *battarízō,* "to stammer."   [G. DELLING, I, 597]

---

bdelýssomai [to abhor], *bdélygma* [abomination], *bdelyktós* [abominable]

The basic stem means "to cause abhorrence" and the group is often used for an improper or shameless attitude. *bdelýssomai* in the middle passive with the accusative means "to abhor" or "to censure" and is common in the LXX; in the active it means "to make abhorrent" and in the perfect passive "to be abhorrent." *bdélygma* denotes a subject of abhorrence and *bdelyktós* means abhorrent. The biblical point is that God finds some things abominable, e.g., idols (Ezek. 5:9, 11; 6:9) or wickedness (Prov. 8:7; 11:1, etc.). Even when an aesthetic nuance may be discerned, e.g., in respect of unclean animals or incest, what is abhorrent to God is basic. Israel is under obligation to separate herself from everything pagan in her life. In the NT Rom. 2:22 refers to paganism. Pagan abominations are obviously at issue in Rev. 17:4-5; 21:8, 27. The reference is more general in Tit. 1:16. Jesus sounds a strong prophetic note in Lk. 16:15: the holy God abhors what we esteem. The *bdélygma* of Mk. 13:14 is based on Dan. 12:1-2, which refers to the desecration of the temple. In view is the antichrist (cf. 2 Th. 2:3-4).   [W. FOERSTER, I, 598-600]

---

bébaios [firm], *bebaióō* [to establish], *bebaíōsis* [confirmation]

A. *bébaios* etc. outside the NT. *bébaios* means "firm," "steadfast," "steady," "reliable," "certain." *bebaioún* has the sense "to make firm," "to confirm," "to keep truth" (absolute), "to assure for oneself" (middle). In the LXX *bébaios* is rare. It does not occur with *lógos* (a common combination in secular speech), but cf. *bebaioún* in Ps. 119:28.

B. *bébaios* etc. in the NT.
a. The ordinary meaning occurs in Heb. 6:19; 2 Pet. 1:10 (making our present election sure); 2 Cor. 1:7 (unwavering hope); Rom. 4:16 (the sure and valid promise). The same applies to *bebaioún* in Col. 2:6-7 (established in faith); 1 Cor. 1:8 (sustained by Christ); Rom. 15:8 (the validation of the promises); 2 Pet. 1:19 (the prophetic word validated by its enactment); Heb. 2:2 (the angelic message shown to be valid by its efficacy).

b. The group then has the special nuance (taken from the commercial world) of what is legally guaranteed. We find this in Heb. 6:16 (confirmation by an oath); Phil. 1:7 (confirmation as valid witness); Heb. 2:2 (of legal force); Mk. 16:20 (the valid *lógos* takes effect in the signs); 1 Cor. 1:6 (the legal force of the witness is displayed in the *charísmata*); possibly 2 Cor. 1:21 (in connection with *arrabōn*, but in a more baptismal context). [H. SCHLIER, I, 600-603]

---

bébēlos [profane], **bebēlóō** [to desecrate]

bébēlos. This means "accessible," then "what may be said publicly," then in the LXX "what may be used freely," then "of a profane disposition" in Philo, also "ravished." It occurs in the NT only four times in the Pastorals and once in Hebrews.

1. Gnostic myths and chatter (1 Tim. 4:7; 6:20; 2 Tim. 2:16) are "profane"; they claim to offer otherwise inaccessible truth but are in fact remote from God.

2. Certain persons (Heb. 12:16; 1 Tim. 1:9) are profane, i.e., far from God in their immorality and irreligion. As in Judaism, Esau typifies such people.

bebēlóō. "To desecrate," used in the LXX of God (Ezek. 13:19), his name (Lev. 18:21), his day (Neh. 13:17-18), his land (Jer. 16:18), his covenant (Ps. 55:20), and the name of the priest (Lev. 21:9; used also here of a virgin). The only NT instances are in Mt. 12:5 for desecration of the sabbath and in Acts 24:6 for that of the temple, both involving the OT concept of holiness. [F. HAUCK, I, 604-05]

Beelzeboúl [Beelzebub (Beelzebul)]

Used by the Pharisees in Mk. 3:22; Mt. 12:27; Lk. 11:18, this is a name for the prince of demons (cf. Mt. 10:25). Jesus is accused of casting out demons in his name. In his reply Jesus substitutes the name Satan, using *Beelzeboúl* only in Mt. 10:25. *Beezeboúl* and *Beelzeboúb* are alternative forms. The meaning is unimportant in the NT. The god of Ekron possibly underlies the term. There was no necessary equation with Satan (the accuser) in contemporary Judaism. [W. FOERSTER, I, 605-06]
→ *daímōn*

Belíar [Belial]

A name for the devil found only in 2 Cor. 6:15 (originally perhaps a god of the underworld; cf. 2 Sam. 22:5; Ps. 18:4). Why Paul should choose the term is uncertain; possibly, but not very probably, he has antichrist in view. [W. FOERSTER, I, 607]
→ *diábolos*

---

bélos [arrow]

"Pointed weapon," "javelin," "arrow," used also for lightning, rays of the sun, moon, or fire. Greek and Semitic gods are armed with both bows and arrows. In the OT the rainbow is God's bow (Gen. 9:13), lightning is his burning arrow (Ps. 7:13), and the arrows of the sun cause drought and sunstroke (Ps. 90). God shoots the wicked with his arrows (Lam. 3:12; Job 6:4). God's servant is an arrow in Is. 42:9, and Is.

59:17 speaks of ethical and spiritual armament. In the NT *bélos* occurs in Eph. 6:16. The righteous are armed as God's warriors (cf. Is. 59:17). They are attacked by the flaming darts of the evil one but they can parry this assault with the shield of faith, which gives union with God. [F. HAUCK, I, 608-09]

---

biázomai [to use force, suffer violence], *biastḗs* [violent man]

---

biázomai.

A. *biázomai* in Ordinary Greek. The reference of the term is always to "forced" as distinct from voluntary acts. The middle means "to compel," "overpower" (sometimes sexually), the passive "to be constrained." All kinds of compulsion may be at issue.

B. *biázomai* in the NT.
1. In Mt. 11:12 the word occurs in the context of sayings relating to John the Baptist: his position relative to Jesus' works (vv. 1-6); his character (vv. 7-8); his place in God's economy (vv. 9-15); his reception (vv. 16-19). Stress is put on his greatness as the forerunner (v. 10). But he does not belong to the age when the kingdom comes in full power (v. 11). It is in this regard that *biázomai* occurs. a. A first possibility is to take *biázetai* as an intransitive middle: "the rule of God breaks in with power" (cf. the mighty works of Jesus). But this does not go well with the second part of the verse (cf. *biastaí*), which seems to be interpreting the first half. b. To translate "the kingdom of heaven compels" (middle) is no more help in this regard. c. The passive raises other difficulties if taken in a good sense, i.e., that people are pressing into the kingdom, since Mt. 11:1-24 seems to suggest the very opposite (cf. also Mk. 10:17ff.; Mt. 5:3ff. on entry into the kingdom; the striving of Lk. 13:24 is hardly the same as the forcible seizure denoted by *biázetai* and *biastaí*). d. Nor does the rendering "The kingdom is forcibly advanced by God" solve the problem of the second half. e. Another possibility is that the reference is to unprincipled enthusiasts trying to establish the kingdom on their own, but this seems to have no relevance to the general context. f. A final possibility is that Jesus is referring to contentious opponents who attack or hamper the kingdom and snatch it away from others (cf. 13:19). This has the merit of agreement with the fact that John himself is under constraint and that both he and Jesus have met with widespread opposition (cf. 11:2, 16ff., 20ff.).
2. The other instance of the term in Lk. 16:16 has as its context the righteousness of the Pharisees and the validity of the law. John is put in the age of law, while the present age is that of preaching the good news. The subject of *biázetai* here is not the kingdom, but "everyone." Of the various possibilities under 1., f. does not fit the context very well, b. is possible but artificial ("everyone is pressed in"), and a middle active offers the best sense ("everyone presses in"), agreeing with the missionary impulse in Luke and the impression of an ardent and jostling response to the new message. The point of agreement in Matthew and Luke is that with John the Baptist the old age ends and the new begins; Jesus inaugurates the kingdom.
3. Implicit in both uses of the term, then, is the fact that the divine rule, whether present or future, is already here in Jesus, so that all that precedes him is now transcended (cf. Paul's saying in Rom. 10:4; also John's in 1:17). In face of the kingdom, however, opposition intensifies; it has to meet acts of hostility and violence. Never-

theless, the true characteristic of the new age is that people are pressing into the kingdom as in the Lucan saying. If persecution arises, old barriers are also broken down. We thus have both negative and positive signs of the one reality of forceful and decisive change.

biastḗs. *biastás* occurs as an adjective for "strong" or "brave," and we also find words like *biastéon, biazómenos,* and *bíaioi* denoting violence, but *biastḗs* ("violent man") seems to occur for the first time in Mt. 11:12, where it refers most naturally to those who violently assault the divine rule and snatch it away from others.

[G. SCHRENK, I, 609-14]

---

bíblos [book], *biblíon* [book, scroll]

bíblos.

1. General Use. As a loanword from the Egyptian, this first denotes the papyrus. Then, as papyrus replaces wooden tablets for writing, it comes to mean the inscribed paper, the scroll, other writing materials, and finally the writing as book, letter, record, or statute. The form *biblíon* is more common in the LXX.

2. bíbloi hieraí. "Sacred writings" can be used in general for hieratic books (cf. *bíbloi* in Acts 19:19), but in Philo and Josephus they come to denote especially and very frequently the books of Moses and the rest of the OT.

3. bíblos can also be used for individual books of the canon. It can cover the whole law, as in Mk. 12:26. We also read of the book of Psalms in Acts 1:20, the book of the sayings of Isaiah in Lk. 3:4, and the book of the prophets in Acts 7:42.

4. bíblos genéseōs. This phrase in Mt. 1:1 is based on Gen. 5:1; it relates only to the genealogy that follows, not to the whole infancy story.

biblíon.

1. General Use. This diminutive form first means the same as *bíblos* but then is more especially used for a scroll or writing, for nonbiblical writings, for libraries, archives, and chronicles, also for epistles and documents (cf. the bill of divorce in Mk. 10:4).

2. biblíon and biblía for the Canon. With reference to the OT, *tó biblíon* first denotes the law (Gal. 3:10; Heb. 9:19). On the basis of Josephus' use of *biblía* for the law or canon, 2 Tim. 4:13 might mean the OT scrolls. The use of *tá biblía* for the whole canon (for Christians including the NT) follows the same usage. *biblíon* for a single book occurs in Lk. 4:17 (a scroll, as we see from *ptýxas* in v. 20). In Jn. 20:30 the author calls his work a *biblíon,* but this is not in itself a formal claim to canonical authority.

3. The Apocalyptic Use and the Other NT Passages concerning the Book of Life. The word has a special sense in Revelation as a term for the divine secret and as a symbol of God's impregnable purpose. Five nuances may be discerned.

a. The unsealed *biblíon* (22:10) of the Revelation itself contains prophetic sayings and is to be sent to the churches (1:11). b. The *biblíon* with seven seals, which is again a scroll, relates to all the judicial acts that unfold from ch. 6 onward. It is the book of God's purposes of judgment, sealed at first (i.e., hidden from us), but coming into effect as the seals are opened by the only one who is worthy to open them. This is the crucified Lamb who is now enthroned as the Lion, so that the cross is shown to be the basis of divine rule. c. The *biblarídion* which the divine has to swallow (10:9-10) contains visions of the temple and the witnesses, i.e., of God's dealings with Israel in the end-time. d. The *biblíon tḗs zōḗs* in Rev. 13:8; 17:8; 20:12; 21:27, as well as the *bíblos tḗs zōḗs* in 3:5; 13:8; 20:15, is based on the OT truth that the righteous are written in God's book (cf. also Lk. 10:20; Phil. 4:3; Heb. 12:23). The metaphor may be based on family lists, though the common idea of books of destiny may also have played a role (cf. Ps. 56:8). In the NT the idea expresses assurance of salvation (cf. 2 Tim. 2:19). The book is that of the crucified Lamb (Rev. 13:8). God's eternal purpose lies behind his reconciling work; hence the names are written from the foundation of the world. But there must be a human will to persevere if the names are not to be erased (3:5). Abomination and falsehood are to be shunned (21:27), worship of the beast refused (13:8), and obedience rendered. The books of judgment are the opposite of the book of life (20:12). e. These books of judgment—the phrase goes back to Dan 7:10 (cf. also Is. 65:6; Jer. 22:30; Mal. 3:16)—contain all works, both good and bad, but perdition awaits those who are not written in the book of life (20:15). [G. Schrenk, I, 615-20]

bíos → *zōḗ*

---

blasphēméō [to blaspheme], **blasphēmía** [blasphemy], **blásphēmos** [blasphemous]

A. *blasphēmía* in Greek Literature. The word means a. "abusive speech," b. "personal mockery," c. "blasphemy."

B. *blasphēmía* in the LXX and Judaism. In the LXX *blasphēmía* has no fixed Hebrew original. It always has reference to God, e.g., disputing his power (2 Kgs. 19:4), desecrating his name (Is. 52:5), violating his glory (Ezek. 35:12), wicked speech (Is. 66:3), or human arrogance (Lev. 24:11). The religious sense is predominant in Philo. For the rabbis speaking impudently about the law, idolatry, and shaming God's name are blasphemy.

C. *blasphēmía* in the NT.

1. Blasphemy is violation of God's power and majesty. It may be directly against God (Rev. 13:6), his name (Rom. 2:24), the word (Tit. 2:5), Moses (Acts 6:11), or angelic beings (Jude 8-10; 2 Pet. 2:10-12). The concept is a Jewish one; hence Jesus seems to be blaspheming when he forgives sins (Mk. 2:7), or claims to be the Messiah (Mk. 14:64), thus making himself equal to God (Jn. 10:33ff.).

2. For Christians blasphemy includes doubting the claim of Jesus or deriding him (cf. Lk. 22:64-65; Mk. 15:29; Lk. 23:39). Persecuting Christians is also blasphemy (1 Tim. 1:13). The community has to suffer blasphemy (Rev. 2:9; 1 Cor. 4:13; 1 Pet. 4:4). Opposition to Paul's message is necessarily blasphemy (Acts 13:45) because it attacks its basic content.

3. Christians may give cause for blasphemy if they deny Christ, if the weak eat idol meats (1 Cor. 10:30), or if they do not love (Rom. 14:15-16). A bad action is blasphemy either because it resists God's will or brings Christianity into disrepute (1 Tim. 6:1; Jms. 2:7; Rom. 2:24; Tit. 2:5). Yet only blasphemy against the Holy Spirit cannot be forgiven, i.e., the willful and wicked rejection of God's saving power and grace (Mt. 12:32). For this the only remedy is to hand the blasphemer over to

Satan (1 Tim. 1:20). The opposition of the beast (Rev. 13:1) and the harlot (17:3) in the last days is blasphemy. The lists of offenses in Mk. 7:22; Mt. 15:19; Eph. 4:31; Col. 3:8; 1 Tim. 6:4; 2 Tim. 3:2 contain the *blasphēm-* group.

D. *blasphēmía* in the Early Church. The different NT nuances recur in the fathers. Tertullian takes a very serious view of blasphemy. In dogmatic debates opposing views are stigmatized as blasphemy. The exposition of Mt. 12:32 causes considerable difficulty.

[H. W. BEYER, I, 621-25]

blépō → *horáō*

---

boáō [to cry, call]

"To cry," "to call" in such senses as a. "to exult," b. "to proclaim," c. "to call to or call out," d. "to raise an outcry," e. "to utter a cry" (demons in Acts 8:7).

boáō **as Crying in Need to God.** The most significant theological use is for crying out in need, e.g., in the LXX the crying of the oppressed (Judg. 10:10), of innocent blood (Gen. 4:10), of workers (Dt. 24:15), of the field (Job 31:38). God will swiftly answer such cries (cf. Ex. 22:21ff.). The NT contains the same thought in Jms. 5 and Lk. 18: God will redress the wrongs of those who cry to him (cf. Lk. 18:8). On the cross, however, Jesus cries out from the lowest depths of need in dereliction (Mk. 15:34). Biblical crying finds its deepest expression in prayer for God himself, and this leads to a new relationship with God. Prayer is elemental crying. It does not ring out in the void. This mortal cry of the old being is also the first cry of the new being that comes to life with the death of God's Son (cf. 2 Cor. 13:4; Gal. 4:4ff.; Rom. 8:16, 26).

[E. STAUFFER, I, 625-28]

---

boēthéō [to help],   **boēthós** [helper],   **boḗtheia** [help]

boēthéō. The basic meaning is "to run to help," then "to help." The word is often used of doctors. In the NT see Acts 21:28; Mk. 9:22; Acts 16:9; Rev. 12:16; of God, only 2 Cor. 6:2; for help in religious need, Mk. 9:24; Heb. 2:18.

boēthós. The only NT instance is Heb. 13:6 (quoting Ps. 118:6-7): God is the helper of the righteous.

boḗtheia. "Help," used in the NT only in Acts 27:17 (a nautical term) and Heb. 4:16 (God's help). The sparing use of the group in the NT differentiates it from rational piety with its common references to divine help.   [F. BÜCHSEL, I, 628-29]

---

boúlomai [to desire],   **boulḗ** [counsel],   **boúlēma** [purpose]

boúlomai.

A. *boúlomai* outside the NT. In distinguishing *boúlomai* and *(e)thélō*, a. some find more rational as distinct from more impulsive desire, but b. others refer *ethélō* to resolution of spirit and *boúlomai* to inclination of soul. "To prefer," suggesting volition, seems to be the original sense, then "to wish," "to purpose," or, more weakly, "to think." In the LXX *boúlomai* is slightly more common than *ethélō,* with little difference of sense. It means variously "to will," "to resolve," "to desire," "to want," "to purpose," "to seek," even "to be inclined." Josephus has it for "to prefer" but mostly "to desire" or "to resolve." The idea of wishing or intending is to the fore in Philo, especially in connection with God's will or goal.

B. *boúlomai* in the NT. In the contest between *boúlomai* and *ethélō,* the latter has won out by NT days so that little of *boúlomai* remains. a. Mostly it simply means "to wish, desire, intend." b. Three times it is used of apostolic ordering. c. It can still denote the will of God, the Son, or the Spirit (seven times). Thus it expresses God's eternal purpose in Heb. 6:17, his will to save in 2 Pet. 3:9, his will to give new life in Jms. 1:18, his sovereign counsel in Lk. 22:42. Christ's own will (in execution of God's counsel) is the issue in Mt. 11:27 (Lk. 10:22). The Spirit controls the distribution of gifts, according to 1 Cor. 12:11.

boulḗ.

A. *boulḗ* outside the NT.

1. *boulḗ* means first the "process of deliberation" (Prov. 2:11; 8:12), "deliberation" itself (Dt. 32:28), or simply "thought" (Is. 55:7).

2. It then denotes the result: a. "resolve"; b. "intention," "purpose"; c. "plan" (Is. 8:10; 30:1; 44:6); d. "counsel" given to others (Gen. 49:6; 2 Sam. 15:31; 1 Kgs. 12:8; Ps. 1:1).

3. It can also mean the machinery of counsel and resolution: a. the process in general (1 Chr. 12:19); b. the "council" of a city; c. a resolution of state.

4. *boulḗ* may also be "divine counsel" (Job 38:2; Prov. 19:18; Is. 5:19; 14:26; 46:10; Jer. 29:21), or the counsel of wisdom (Prov. 1:25). In Hellenistic mysticism the divine *boulḗ* (or *thélēma*) is important as representing God's transcendence; it is linked with *lógos* as parent or creator of the cosmos, and is sometimes depicted as a goddess separate from God.

B. *boulḗ* in the NT. In 1 Cor. 4:5 the meaning hovers between the weaker "desires" and the stronger "purposes"; "intents" (inward intentions) seems to fit best.

Sense 3.a. is demanded in Acts 27:12, 42: consultation leading to a plan.

In the NT, however, the divine counsel is the main issue, especially in Luke's writings. David died by God's counsel in Acts 13:36. The Pharisees rejected God's counsel in opposing the Baptist (Lk. 7:30). Jesus was delivered up by God's definite plan (Acts 2:23). God's *boulḗ* is the content of the apostolic message (Acts 20:27). Eph. 1:1ff. climaxes in the statement that God does all things according to the counsel of his will, which overarches the choosing and destining of vv. 4-5, and sets in motion the whole grace present in Christ and granted to the church as the reality of salvation. *boulḗ* here strengthens *thélēma*; all God's economy is linked with it (cf. Acts 20:27). God's oath in Heb. 6:17 confirms the unbreakable and unchangeable nature of this counsel.

boúlēma.

1. This rare term denotes the will as "plan" or "purpose" or "intention," with such different nuances as "last will" in the papyri and "preference" in 4 Macc. 8:18.

2. "Purpose" rather than "resolve" seems to be at issue when the reference is to God's *boúlēma* (Josephus *Antiquities* 1.232; Philo *On the Life of Moses* 1.95).

3. The NT follows the common usage. In Acts 27:43 the captain frustrates the design of the soldiers. In 1 Pet. 4:3 Christians used to follow the direction of the Gentiles in ungodly living. In Rom. 9:19 no one can resist the purpose of God, which is described in v. 18 as his twofold will of mercy and severity.

[G. SCHRENK, I, 629-37]

---

brabeúō [to rule], *brabeíon* [prize]

---

brabeúō. This term describes the work of an umpire at the games, then comes to mean "to order" or "control." Paul uses it of the peace which settles strife in the church and maintains its unity (cf. *phrourḗsai* in Phil. 4:7).

brabeíon. This means "prize" in a contest (also used figuratively). Paul has it in 1 Cor. 9:24ff. and Phil. 3:13-14 for the prize of eternal life that we can win only if we throw in all that we have, although only because God first calls us and sets the goal. On the basis of God's call we must break with all that is behind us (Phil. 3:7ff.) and bend all our efforts to attain the end (note the sevenfold "that" in 1 Cor. 9:19ff.), integrating our will into God's (1 Cor. 9:17).   [E. STAUFFER, I, 637-39]

---

brachíōn [arm]

---

brachíōn occurs in the NT only for God's "arm" and in quotations from the LXX or similar expressions (Lk. 1:51; Jn. 12:38; Acts 13:17). In the OT God's arm signifies his power (Is. 62:8; 63:5), which may be exerted on behalf of the righteous (2 Chr. 6:32) but is seen especially in creation (Is. 51:9), the exodus (Dt. 4:34), the preservation of Israel (Dt. 33:27), and the bringing of eschatological salvation (Is. 40:10). In the NT this arm shows its power in the birth of the promised Messiah (Lk. 1:51) and the signs that are done by Jesus before the people (Jn. 12:37-38).

→ *cheír*   [H. SCHLIER, I, 639-40]

---

brontḗ [thunder]

Translated "thunder," *brontḗ* is used for a powerful voice in Jn. 12:29; Rev. 6:1; 14:2; 19:6, and mentioned with other natural phenomena in Rev. 4:5; 8:5; 11:19; 16:18. In the LXX it denotes God's terrifying revelation. The sons of Zebedee are called "sons of thunder" in Mk. 3:17, but there is debate as to the orthography of the Aramaic and its meaning.   [W. FOERSTER, I, 640-41]

---

brýchō [to gnash], *brygmós* [gnashing]

---

brýchō. In the LXX this complex term comes to be used for "to gnash (with the teeth)," as in Lam. 2:16; Ps. 35:16 (in hatred). The only NT instance (Acts 7:54) is in line with LXX usage: Stephen's opponents ground their teeth in rage.

brygmós. This word, used for "chattering of the teeth," "groaning," and "gnashing," occurs in the phrase "weeping and gnashing of teeth" (Mt. 8:12; 13:42, 50; 22:13; Lk. 13:28). The reference is not to despairing rage, nor to a physical reaction, but to the remorse of those who are shut out of the kingdom even though called to it. This special use, which is almost peculiar to Matthew, derives its meaning from the context. [K. H. RENGSTORF, I, 641-42]

---

brṓma [food], _brṓsis_ [eating]

---

1. "Food" in the Strict Sense. The crowds need food in Mt. 14:15; we are to share food in Lk. 3:11; distinctions of food are done away in Mk. 7:19. Food is not significant in the relation to God (1 Cor. 8; Rom. 14), though regard for the weak requires voluntary renunciation of some foods (1 Cor. 8:13; Rom. 14:15). Rules about food have lost their validity in the new covenant (Heb. 9:10). Foods cannot strengthen the heart (Heb. 13:9). All food is God's gift and is thus to be received with thanksgiving (contra false asceticism) (1 Tim. 4:3).

2. "Food" in the Figurative Sense.

a. The term denotes miraculous food from heaven in 1 Cor. 10:3 (cf. Ex. 16).

b. It is used for spiritual food in 1 Cor. 3:2; milk is the first presentation of the gospel, solid food (Heb. 5:12ff.) is the interpretation. For Jesus, doing God's will is his inner nourishment (Jn. 4:34). Jesus also grants spiritual food to others as he fed the multitude (Jn. 6:27). This food nourishes to eternal life and is received by faith in him (6:35ff.), i.e., by the reception of Christ himself (6:51ff.).

[J. BEHM, I, 642-45]

γ g

---

gála [milk]

---

1. In 1 Cor. 3:1-2 "milk" signifies the basic gospel. In Heb. 5:12ff. it is used similarly for the rudiments of Christian teaching (cf. 6:1-2). It is contrasted with the solid food suitable for mature believers.

2. In 1 Pet. 2:2 pure, spiritual milk will help newborn babes to grow up to salvation. The figure of speech may rest on a mythical, magical, or eschatological conception but more probably derives from LXX usage, for in the OT milk is a characteristic of the promised land (Ex. 3:8), is a general mark of blessing (Job 29:6), and has eschatological significance (Joel 3:18). Thus the use of the term in 1 Pet. 2:2 undoubtedly indicates the character of the gospel as mystery or sacrament, but the content of the gospel distinguishes it from the mysteries that used similar terminology.

[H. SCHLIER, I, 645-47]

---

gaméō [to marry], _gámos_ [marriage, wedding]

---

1. Marriage Customs in the NT. The LXX has _gámos_ only in Gen. 29:22; Esth. 2:18; 9:22. Jewish marriages lasted several days and were celebrated far into the night (Lk. 12:36; 14:8; Jn. 2:1ff.).

2. *The New Ideal of Early Christianity.* Gen. 2:24, which speaks of the union of man and wife, forms the starting point. Continued here is the work of creation in Gen. 1:28. For Jesus marriage is the original form of human fellowship. It has its basis in creation, has a history which divides into three periods, and will end with this aeon. Full union is the original state (Mk. 10:6ff.). Sin causes the disruption which leads to the bill of divorce allowed by Moses. Jesus inaugurates a new period marked by a new law of divorce, a deepened ideal, and a fourfold reservation (Mk. 10:9-10). According to this realistic view, dissolution may take place, but not a new marriage, for replacement of one spouse by another is adultery and affects the original union. The cause of marital failure is hardness of heart; hence the need is for a new heart (5:27-28). Inward as well as outward union is demanded. Copulation without communion is fornication. Free love and double standards are both ruled out here, though the initiative of the husband in the conclusion and direction of a marriage is assumed in Lk. 17:27. The four reservations are as follows: (1) In some ages marrying and giving in marriage may be frivolous and irresponsible (Lk. 17:27); (2) marrying may sometimes hamper our readiness for God's call (Lk. 14:20); (3) some people have the gift of celibacy (Mt. 19:12); (4) there will be no more marrying in the new aeon (Mk. 12:25). Though Jesus himself does not marry, and marriage belongs to the passing aeon, Jesus does not warn against marriage or enjoin celibacy, but endorses the institution found in Gen. 2:24. Paul develops the same motifs. In 1 Cor. 6:16-17 he shows how the union of Gen. 2:24 rules out fornication. In 1 Cor. 7 he quotes Jesus in rejection of remarriage after divorce (7:10-11). Once contracted, marriage must be fully carried out with only brief periods of withdrawal (7:3ff.). Paul, however, presses more strongly the fourfold reservation of Jesus. Marriage may hinder true dedication to God (7:5, 32ff.) and is not consonant with the hour (7:26, 28-29). If ascetic experimentation is not approved, and widows are free to remarry (7:39-40), he could wish that all had the gift of celibacy as he himself had for the sake of his unique commission (7:1-2, 7-8; cf. 1 Cor. 9:5, 12, 15ff.). Later, although the ideal is that widows should remain unmarried, young widows are exhorted to remarry rather than engage in questionable activities (1 Tim. 4:3; 5:5ff., 11, 14). Marriage is to be honored according to Heb. 13:4, and if celibacy is also extolled in the case of the 144,000 of Rev. 14:4, this is on account of their special calling. In general, building on the foundation laid by Jesus, the NT finds in *agápē* rather than *érōs* the force that creates and sustains marital fellowship. The ground and measure of human *agápē* lie in the love of God as this comes to expression in Christ's love for his community (Ephesians).

3. *The Messianic Wedding and Christian Marriage. gámos* acquires its deepest meaning when it is used for God's fellowship with us. Ancient religion often speaks about the intercourse of gods with humans or sacred marriages among the gods. Plato thinks that heavenly marriage, as an idea, gives form and meaning to earthly marriage. Israel, too, speaks about the marriage of God and his people, but only as a symbol of the covenant (Hos. 2:19; Is. 54:4ff.; Ezek. 16:7ff.). If Philo allegorizes the concept, the rabbis extol the Sinaitic covenant as God's marriage with Israel, and they look forward to the marriage feast when the covenant will be renewed in the days of the Messiah. Jesus takes up this idea of the messianic wedding in the parable of the virgins (Mt. 25:10ff.) and also when he calls himself the Bridegroom (Mk. 2:19; Jn. 3:29). He himself is now the son for whom the king holds the great feast (Mt. 22:1-2), and the kingdom itself is compared to the feast to which those who are first invited refuse to come, leaving the door open for others (Mt. 22:3ff.). Who is the bride? The covenant people in OT thought, but in the parables the disciples seem to be guests. Yet soon

the new covenant people is presented as the bride (cf. 1 Cor. 6:14ff.; Rom. 7:4; 2 Cor. 11:2; Jn. 3:29). This idea is most vividly depicted in Revelation, where the bride waits with longing (22:17) and the day of consummation is at hand (19:7ff.) when the new Jerusalem will descend as a bride adorned for her husband (21:2). The teaching on marriage in Eph. 5:22ff. is based on the normative union of Christ and the church with overriding love on the one side and self-giving on the other in a relationship that resolves all tensions as the wife is entrusted to the husband and the husband takes responsibility for the wife in mutual service in Christ. In later developments NT teaching conflicts with Hellenistic motifs as Gnostics talk about heavenly syzygies, mystics dwell on the images of Canticles, ascetics despise the body, and ecstatics focus on spiritual union with the heavenly Bridegroom. [E. STAUFFER, I, 648-57]

→ *nymphaíos*

---

géenna [Gehenna]

1. *géenna* is the Greek form of the Hebrew name for the Wadi er-Rababi. This acquired a bad reputation because of the sacrifices offered to Moloch there (2 Kgs. 16:3). Judgment was pronounced on it (Jer. 7:32), and it thus came to be equated with the hell of the last judgment (Eth. En. 90:26). Later it was also used for the place where the wicked are punished in the intermediate state. The LXX, Philo, and Josephus do not have the term; Philo has *tártaros* instead.

2. The NT distinguishes between *hádēs* and *géenna*: a. the former is temporary, the latter definitive (cf. Mk. 9:43, 48); b. the former is for the soul alone, the latter for the reunited body and soul (Mk. 9:43ff.; Mt. 10:28). *géenna* is preexistent (Mt. 25:41). It is manifested as a fiery abyss (Mk. 9:43) after the general resurrection. Those who fall victim to divine judgment (Mt. 5:22; 23:33) will be destroyed there with eternal fire. The ungodly are sons of *géenna* (Mt. 23:15). They go to it with Satan and the demons (Mt. 25:41; cf. Rev. 19:20; 20:10-11). The threat of *géenna* in the NT is used to show the seriousness of sin and to awaken the conscience to fear of the divine anger (Mt. 10:28; 23:33). Even contemptuous words must be avoided (Mt. 5:22); no sacrifice is too costly in the war against sin (Mt. 9:43ff.). [J. JEREMIAS, I, 657-58]

→ *aiṓnios, pýr*

---

gélaō [to laugh],   *katageláō* [to laugh at],   *gélōs* [laughter]

1. The Word Group Applied to Men. The group is common for joyous or scornful laughter, or for its occasion. The note of scorn is stronger in the LXX (cf. Sarah in Gen. 18:12, the enemies in Lam. 1:7). The NT follows OT usage when the people in Jairus' house laugh at Jesus (Mt. 9:24), when a Woe in pronounced on those who laugh (Lk. 6:25) and they are equated with the wealthy who find satisfaction in this aeon, and when James (4:9) demands that laughter should give place to humility before God.

2. The Word Group Applied to the Deity. For the Greeks merry laughter characterizes the gods. In the OT, however, God laughs only because of his superiority over his opponents (Pss. 2:4; 37:13; 59:8; Prov. 1:26). Hence the point of laughter in Ps. 126:2 is really that of victory, although the LXX imports the sense of joy in God by translating the Hebrew as *chará* instead of *gélōs*. This may have a bearing on the eschatological laughter that is promised in Lk. 6:21, which was probably based on Ps. 126:2 unless Luke chose *gelán* with the Greek sense in mind ("joy)" and in order to keep the parallelism with 6:25. [K. H. RENGSTORF, I, 658-62]

---

geneá [descent], *genealogía* [genealogy], *genealogéō* [to trace one's descent], *agenealógētos* [without genealogy]

---

geneá. This means a. "birth," "descent," b. "progeny," c. "race," and d. "generation." In the NT it is common in the Synoptics, rare in Paul, and absent from John. It mostly means "generation" and is often qualified: "adulterous" (Mk. 8:38), "evil" (Mt. 12:45), "unbelieving and corrupt" (Mt. 17:17); the formula "this generation" is very common (Mk. 8:12 etc.). "Crooked generation" in Acts 2:40; Phil. 2:15 is based on Dt. 32:5 (cf. Mt. 17:17 and Dt. 32:20). The use of "generation" by Jesus expresses his comprehensive purpose: he aims at the whole people and is conscious of their solidarity in sin. *geneá* has the sense of "age" in Mt. 1:17; Acts 13:36; Eph. 3:5; Col. 1:26, and of "manner" in Lk. 16:8. In Acts 8:33 there is an allusion to Is. 53:8 in a literal rendering of the obscure original.

genealogía. "Genealogical tree." The only NT instances are in 1 Tim. 1:4 and Tit. 3:9. The meaning here is contested. The texts link the term with (Jewish) myths and therefore with Jewish Gnostics who claim to be teachers of the law (1 Tim. 1:7) but who do not truly keep the law (1:8), teaching human commandments instead (Tit. 1:14). The genealogies, then, are probably human ones taken from the OT and the reference in the phrase "myths and genealogies" is to the biblical history enriched by interpretations and additions.

genealogéō. This derives from *genealógos*, "one who draws up a genealogy." It occurs in the LXX only in 1 Chr. 5:1 and in the NT only in Heb. 7:6: Melchizedek does not "derive his descent" from the descendants of Levi.

agenealógētos. This occurs only in Heb. 7:3, where Melchizedek is said to be "without genealogy." Unlike the Aaronic priests, he was no traceable descent.
[F. BÜCHSEL, I, 662-65]

---

gennáō [to bear, beget], *génnēma* [born], *gennētós* [begotten, born], *artigénnētos* [newborn], *anagennáō* [to be born again]

---

gennáō.

A. "Begetting" as an Image of the Relationship of Master and Disciple. In the LXX and NT, as well as Greek in general, *gennáō* means "to beget" (father) or "to bear" (mother). Already in the OT teacher and disciple are depicted as father and son (2 Kgs. 2:12). The rabbis adopt this usage to express the supremacy of the teacher and the respect of the pupil, but with no thought of actual begetting (cf. Mt. 23:8ff.). Paul actually uses the term *gennán* for the relation in Gal. 4:19, but since he begets through the word (1 Cor. 4:15; cf. Phil. 10), he is obviously not thinking in mystical terms but simply expressing more forcefully the common rabbinic concept.

[F. BÜCHSEL, I, 665-66]

B. The Idea of New Birth by Conversion to the True Religion in Later Judaism. This idea is common in the rabbis. Bringing people to Judaism is like creating them, and proselytes are like newborn children. Winning converts fulfils the command to be fruitful and multiply. This is, of course, only a comparison. Proselytes come from mere existence to true life by conversion. They do so by coming into the holy people; the terms "new" and "holy" are parallel. Regeneration, then, has a forensic rather than a mystical character. Old relations are dissolved; a new relationship begins. Here is the context of Paul's statement in 2 Cor. 5:17. As there is a strong connection between rabbinic and NT holiness, so rabbinic ideas of new birth influence the *gennēthénai* of Christians (Gal. 4:19; 1 Cor. 4:15; Phlm. 10). If there is a difference, it is not because of intrusion from the mysteries but because Christ replaces the law, his perfect sanctification subsumes our imperfect strivings, and relation to him supersedes the more forensic element. Living by the gospel (1 Cor. 4:15) is a new being in grateful response to the divine action in Christ. [K. H. RENGSTORF, I, 666-68]

C. Generation by the Deity.

1. Generation from God in the OT and Judaism. God is rarely said to "beget" in the OT, but the instances are significant. He begets the king in Pss. 2; 110; wisdom in Prov. 8:25. Generation of the king is perhaps a stereotyped formula for institution as heir, though rabbinic exegesis sees in it either affection or new creation out of troubles. What Proverbs says of wisdom is transferred to the law in Sir. 24:6. Philo calls creation a begetting but he does not think of the righteous, or of Israel, as begotten by God.

2. Generation or Adoption in the Mysteries. Sexual images are important in the mysteries but adoption rather then generation applies to initiates (in spite of attempts to prove the contrary).

3. Ps. 2:7 in the NT. This verse is much used in the NT. Its "today" is referred to the resurrection of Jesus in Acts 13:33. On one reading of Lk. 3:22 it applies to his baptism. No point of time is given in Heb. 1:5; 5:5. The birth stories do not quote it (though cf. Lk. 1:35), but on the basis of the resurrection and impartation of the Spirit Jesus is for the church more than a superior human being. The new aeon comes with him. In him we see true generation from God. In faith in him believers are assured of the resurrection and have the pledge of the Spirit. Hence they also see themselves as born of God.

4. gennēthénai in John. John always gives the point of origin of *gennēthénai*: God in 1 Jn. 2:29; Jn. 1:13, the Spirit in Jn. 3:5, water in Jn. 3:5, the flesh in Jn. 3:6, the will in Jn. 1:13. The seed of 1 Jn. 3:9 is the Spirit rather than the word. Birth from God or the Spirit is a reality but also a mystery. Statements about it are not based on experience but are made in faith and are true in virtue of the believer's fellowship with God (1 Jn. 1:3, 6ff.; 3:9). This birth results in doing righteousness (1 Jn. 2:29), in not sinning (3:7ff.), in love (4:7), in overcoming the world (5:4), in faith in Jesus as the Christ (5:1). Birth from above belongs first to Jesus himself (5:18) and then to believers who, as members of the new aeon, have a share in the Spirit and are thus united to Christ, passing from death to life (3:14; 5:24). This concept of divine *gennán* has little in common with what may be found in the mysteries; the view of piety is totally different.

génnēma. "What is born," "fruit," common in the LXX and Philo, but found in the NT only in the phrase "brood of vipers" in Mt. 3:7; 12:34; 23:33.

gennētós. Common in Philo, this occurs in the NT only in the phrase "those born of woman" (Mt. 11:11) to denote humans as distinct from God or angels.

artigénnētos (→ neóphytos). "Newborn," found in the NT only in 1 Pet. 2:2: "newborn babes," the reference being to the newly converted or possibly the newly baptized if the epistle, or 1:3—4:11, is a baptismal address.

anagennáō (→ palingenesía).

A. **The Nonbiblical Usage.** This term is usually connected with the mysteries, but attestation is rare and late. Philo does not use it, although he has *anagénnēsis* for Stoic rejuvenation, and Josephus uses the verb in a general sense.

B. ***anagennáō* in 1 Peter.** In 1 Peter regeneration is God's act (1:3). It is effected by Christ's resurrection (1:3) or the word (1:23). The result is a living hope (1:3). Regeneration is not a state or experience or power. Believers are posited on faith. They are given a nonmystical new beginning which sharpens the tension between present and future as they hope for an inheritance and live in fear of God (1:17). Regeneration is not cultically or sacramentally mediated; baptism is an act of faith in which one is cleansed by prayer for the good conscience received on the basis of Christ's resurrection. It is this resurrection that enables us to speak of regeneration, giving it an eschatological character as a matter of faith (2:6; 1:5; 5:9), hope (1:3; 3:15), and fear of God (1:17; 2:18; 3:2, 15). The background is Jewish, i.e., hope for a new life rather than inner experience. Yet after Christ's resurrection the new aeon has begun and regeneration is also a present reality, though grasped as yet only in faith.

[F. BÜCHSEL, I, 668-75]

---

geúomai [to taste, experience]

1. Strictly "to taste," "enjoy"; 2. figuratively "to come to feel," "to learn by experience" (both good things and bad). "To taste death" is a common Semitic expression; cf. also "to taste something of the world to come." In the NT we find 1. "to taste" in Mt. 27:34, "to enjoy" or "to eat" in Acts 10:10; 20:11. In Acts 23:14 the conspirators vow not to eat, while in Col. 2:21 Christians are to ignore taboos about food. The figurative use 2. occurs in 1 Pet. 2:3: we are to desire the word as those who have already tasted the goodness of Christ. Similar is Heb. 6:4-5, which refers to the tasting of the heavenly gift, the word of God, and the powers of the future aeon, by initial participation in the Spirit. "To taste death" occurs in Mk. 9:1; Jn. 8:52; Heb. 2:9; it expresses very vividly the harsh reality of dying. [J. BEHM, I, 675-77]

---

gē [earth], ***epígeios*** [earthly]

gḗ.
1. The Earth, Land, as a Dwelling Place of Man. a. "Land" (in the geographical sense), as in Mt. 9:26; Mk. 15:33; Acts 7:3, 4 (Palestine); named in Mt. 2:6: Judah;

Acts 7:29: Midian; Acts 13:19: Canaan; Acts 7:36: Egypt etc.; b. the "land of promise" (Acts 7:3; Heb. 11:9, and in an eschatological sense Mt. 5:5); c. the "inhabited earth" (Rev. 3:10; 14:6; Acts 22:22); d. the earth as the theater of history: the past (Rev. 16:18); the work of Jesus (Mk. 2:10; Mt. 10:34; Jn. 17:4—this concept merges into that of the human world); eschatological history (Lk. 18:8; 21:23, and many passages in Revelation).

2. *The Earth as Part of the World.* The ancient phrase "heaven and earth" for the cosmos is common in the NT (cf. Mk. 13:31; Heb. 1:10-11; 2 Pet. 3:7, and for the new heaven and earth 2 Pet. 3:7; Rev. 21:1). Since "sea" is a third component, earth denotes dry land (cf. Acts 4:24; Heb. 11:29; Rev. 8:7ff.). In another triad earth comes between heaven and what is under the earth (Rev. 5:3). There is, however, no consistent cosmology, and cosmological ideas, even in Revelation, are wholly subordinate to theological. Interesting phrases are "from the ends of the earth" for "from abroad" in Mt. 12:42, "to the ends of the earth" for "everywhere" in Acts 1:8, "four corners of the earth" in Rev. 20:8, and "from the margin of earth to the margin of heaven" (i.e., one end of the world to the other) in Mk. 13:27. An echo of personification may be caught in Rev. 12:16.

3. *The Earth in Its Relation to God.* Created by God (Acts 4:24 etc.), the earth shares the world's relation to him as creation. It exists by his will, has a beginning and end, and is his possession (1 Cor. 10:26). God is its Lord (Mt. 11:25), as he is of heaven, although with differentiation, for if things may be valid in both earth and heaven (cf. Mt. 16:19; 18:18-19) and earthly things copy heavenly things (Heb. 8:5), the earth is the place of what is imperfect (Mk. 9:3) and transitory (Mt. 6:19), of sin (Mk. 2:10) and death (1 Cor. 15:47). Christ, then, is not of earth (Jn. 3:31; 1 Cor. 15:47). He comes down and is lifted up again (cf. Eph. 4:9). In contrast to redeemer myths, however, the NT has the incarnation in view and makes no final metaphysical distinction between heaven and earth, since both are God's. The real difference is that the earth is the theater of sin. The Son of Man comes to it to forgive sins (Mk. 2:10), and it is because of the fall that believers are "strangers and pilgrims on earth" (Heb. 11:13) and are "ransomed from the earth" (Rev. 14:3), being exhorted not to "set their mind on what is on the earth" but to mortify their "earthly members" (Col. 3:2, 5).

epígeios. a. "Existing on, belonging to, earth," b. "earthly" (in contrast to heavenly). In Phil. 2:10 the totality of being includes the heavenly, the earthly (not just human), and those under the earth. 2 Cor. 5 refers to the earthly body as distinct from the heavenly; cf. 1 Cor. 15:40ff., where perishable, inglorious, weak, and physical are parallels. Since the earth is the place of sin, "earthly" may have a subsidiary moral sense as in "earthly minded" (Phil. 3:19) and "earthly wisdom" (Jms. 3:15). In Jn. 3:12 the contrast is perhaps between earthly parables and direct instruction on heavenly things (cf. 16:25).   [H. SASSE, I, 677-81]

---

gínomai [to be born], *génesis* [birth], *génos* [kind, family], *génēma* [fruit], *apogínomai* [to die], *palingenesía* [rebirth, renewal]

---

gínomai. This word has little theological interest in the NT apart from the distinction between *gínesthai* and *eínai* in Jn. 8:58. The common Synoptic expression (*kaí*) *egéneto* (as in Lk. 5:12, 17) seems to be consciously based on the style of the OT.

génesis.

1. "Birth," "genesis" (Mt. 1:18; Lk. 1:14), with such derived senses as a. "what has come into being" and b. "life" (cf. perhaps Jms. 1:23).

2. *bíblos genéseos for Genealogy in Mt. 1:1*. This phrase goes back to the OT (Gen. 2:4; 5:1, etc.). The use in the OT varies, and genealogies are named after ancestors, so that one cannot deduce from the OT whether the reference is only to vv. 2-17 or to the whole book. The heading is undoubtedly needed to introduce vv. 2-17 (cf. v. 2 and v. 17).

3. *ho trochós tês genéseos as the Wheel of Life in Jms. 3:6*. This phrase is a technical one in Orphic teaching (cf. also Philo), but there the idea is that of the recurrence of birth and death. The saying in James is closer to the popular idea of the inversion of things which can even be said to bring burning pain. Judaism also speaks about the world as a wheel, although this saying, which is probably the source of the statement in James, itself seems to have been taken from popular Greek sayings about the uncertainty of fortune. The Buddhist idea of the wheel of rotation, becoming and time, which is set on fire by self-consciousness, is too speculative to explain Jms. 3:6. The author is simply adapting a popular expression to a practical end.

génos.

1. "Posterity," "family," as in Acts 17:28 (all are related to God) and, individually, in Rev. 22:16 (descendant, not representative).

2. "People," e.g., the Jewish people in Gal. 1:14; Phil. 3:5, Christians in 1 Pet. 2:9 (quoting Is. 43:20).

3. "Kind," e.g., species of animals or plants, but also tongues (1 Cor. 12:10, 28).

génēma. "Product," "fruit (of the earth)," common in the LXX (to be distinguished from *génnēma*, from *gennán*, for the offspring of humans or animals). In the NT 2 Cor. 9:10 ("harvest of well-doing") follows Hos. 10:12, while Mk. 14:25 is parallel to the blessing of the paschal cup in contemporary Judaism.

apogínomai. This rare term occurs in the NT only in 1 Pet. 2:24, where the reference is to the goal of Christ's saving act, namely, that we might "die" to sin and live to righteousness. The death and resurrection of Christ are thus interpreted in terms of the Jewish concept of destruction and renewal. The goal is at issue rather than an inner or sacramental experience.

palingenesía.

A. The Usage outside the NT. Deriving from *pálin* and *génesis*, and thus meaning either a. "return to existence" or b. "renewal to higher existence," this word takes its distinctive impress from Stoicism with a cosmic and then an individual sense. It then spreads to educated circles with a more general reference, and occurs later in the mysteries, though not in Orphic or Pythagorean writings. Philo has it for restoration of life and the reconstitution of the world after the flood, and Josephus for the reestablishment of the people after the exile, but the only LXX instance is in Job 14:14. In Judaism existence in the new aeon is not just a repetition of this life but an existence in righteousness following the definitive crisis of the last judgment.

B. *palingenesía* in the NT.

1. In Mt. 19:28 the reference is to individual resurrection and cosmic renewal in the Jewish sense (cf. Lk. 22:30: the kingdom; Mk. 10:30: the age to come).

2. In Tit. 3:5 the term embraces both moral renewal and new life, but with a stress on the latter (cf. v. 7). The grace of God works here by instruction and personal fellowship, not by magical incantation; hence the origin of the use is to be found in the Jewish adaptation of Stoicism, not in the mysteries.   [F. BÜCHSEL, I, 681-89]

---

ginōskō [to know, understand], *gnōsis* [knowledge], *[epiginōskō* [to know, recognize], *epígnōsis* [knowledge, recognition], *kataginōskō* [to condemn], *akatágnōstos* [not condemned], *proginōskō* [to foreknow], *prógnōsis* [foreknowledge], *syngnōmē* [forbearance], *gnōmē* [intention, opinion], *gnōrízō* [to make known, to know], *gnōstós* [known]

---

ginōskō, gnōsis, epiginōskō, epígnōsis.

A. The Greek Usage. The ordinary use is for intelligent comprehension ("to perceive," "to understand," "to know"), at first with a stress on the act. As distinct from *aisthánesthai*, *ginōskō* emphasizes understanding rather than sensory perception, and as distinct from *dokeín* it is a perception of things as they are, not an opinion about them. Related to *epistémē*, *gnōsis* needs an objective genitive and suggests the act of knowing rather than knowledge as such. This act embraces every organ and mode of knowledge, e.g., by seeing, hearing, investigation, or experience, and of people as well as things. Supremely, however, knowledge implies verification by the eye; hence the dominant concept is that of knowledge by objective observation. This is related to the Greek view of reality. Reality consist of forms and figures, or of the elements and principles that shape them. The truly real is timeless reality that is constant in every change. Those who see or know this possess and control it. Hence knowledge of what really is constitutes the supreme possibility in life. Those who know participate in the eternal. They are thus capable, as Plato thinks, of right political action, or may achieve the ideal, as Aristotle thinks, of disinterested scientific contemplation.

B. The Gnostic Usage. Hellenistic and Gnostic usage follows the classical development yet also draws on the belief of the mysteries that a secret knowledge may be mediated that leads to salvation. In this area *gnōsis* a. means knowledge as such as well as the act, with a primary stress on knowledge of God. God is the self-evident object of *gnōsis* and distinct from all becoming, so that he can be known only by turning away from the world, i.e., by a special kind of knowledge. This knowledge, then, is not b. an activity of the *noús* but a *chárisma*, i.e., illumination by ecstatic or mystical vision. This knowledge cannot be possessed, although knowledge achieved on the way to it may. In true Gnosticism, however, this preparatory knowledge is an esoteric knowledge acquired by initiatory training, so that the prerequisite is the hearing of faith rather than scientific inquiry. The knowledge that is thus imparted by sacred tradition guarantees the ascent of the soul after death. Its content embraces cosmology and anthropology but always with a view to the knowledge of the self that leads to salvation, i.e., of the self as a soul that comes from the world of light, is entangled in matter, and must return to its true home by turning aside from the physical world. Gnostic knowledge carries with it c. investiture with the divine nature. It is a divine power that drives out death, working almost like a magical fluid identical with light or life, and constituting a mysterious quality of the soul which is made secure by an ascetic mode of life.

C. The OT Usage.

1. The OT view of knowledge comes out most clearly in the use of *yāḏa'* (normally rendered *ginōskein* or *eidénai*). Perception is an integral part of knowledge here too, i.e., coming to know in various ways. Implied are comprehension, ability, and a grasp of what needs to be done. Yet the Hebrew term is broader than the Greek word *ginōskein* and embraces objects such as blows (1 Sam. 14:12), childlessness (Is. 47:8), and sickness (Is. 53:3) that sound odd in Greek. Sexual intercourse may also be denoted (Gen. 4:1 etc.), and while the element of information can be stressed (Ps. 94:11), more attention is paid to the knowing subject, hearing is more important than seeing, and events (as divine or human acts) constitute the reality of knowledge rather than the timeless principles behind things. God himself is not so much that which always is; he is the will that has a specific goal in either claiming, blessing, or judging. Knowledge of God, then, is acknowledgment of his grace, power, and demand, so that we have knowledge, not as mere information or mystical contemplation, but only in its exercise. A movement of will is involved which means that ignorance is guilty. Knowledge is acknowledgment of God's acts (Dt. 11:20), recognition that Yahweh is God (Dt. 4:39), and the honoring of his name and doing of his will (1 Sam. 2:12; Is. 1:3, etc.). Hence knowledge of God is much the same as fear of God (Hos. 4:6). Similarly "known" people are respected people (Dt. 1:13). In the case of God, to know, being an act of will, means to make an object of concern and thus carries the nuance "to elect" (Gen. 18:19; Ex. 33:12, etc.).

2. Among special LXX nuances, *ginōskein* means to know sin in Leviticus, to know something by revelation in Is. 8:9, to know the power of God's wrath in Is. 26:11, and to know God by his self-revelation in Ex. 29:42-43, while in the negative it denotes ignorance of God in Zech. 7:14 and his unknowability in Is. 40:13. When God is said to know us, the sense may be that of standing the test (Gen. 22:12), of election (Num. 16:5; Hos. 5:3), or of God's omniscience in love or mercy. The noun *gnōsis* is rarer than the verb and often denotes a revealed knowledge whose author is the God of knowledge (1 Chr. 4:10), which is a possession of the righteous (Prov. 24:26), and which is taught by the sage or servant of the Lord (Is. 53:11). Sinners, apostates, and idolaters do not have this knowledge (cf. Prov. 13:19; 19:20, etc.). It may be insight into God's plan (Dan. 12:4), and while it surpasses human comprehension (Ps. 139:6), all creation proclaims it to believers (Ps. 19:2). (For details cf. *TDNT,* I, 698-701.)

D. The Jewish Usage.

1. The OT understanding continues in Judaism. For the rabbis knowledge is knowledge of the law, and while the term may denote a thinking, gifted, or learned person, the law and tradition are the basis and theme of instruction. Obedience is regulative in this regard, although liturgically God is still praised for the endowment of knowledge. Hellenistic Judaism finds in knowledge the recognition of God's acts and perception of his ways, but with a special stress now on the confession that there is only one God. In more Hellenic fashion the issue of the possibility of knowledge of God is raised in this field (cf. 2 Macc. 7:28).

2. Philo's use of the group is strongly Hellenistic. He can speak of knowledge of the one God, but this involves only knowledge of the existence or power of God; direct vision that is divinely given is needed to know God's nature. A similar blend of philosophical, Gnostic, and OT views occurs in Philo's thinking about self-knowledge.

E. The Early Christian Usage.

1. Popular Usage. In a general sense *ginōskein* can have such varied meanings as "to detect" (Mk. 5:29), "to note" (Mk. 8:17), "to recognize" (Lk. 7:39), "to learn" (Mk. 5:43), and "to confirm" (Mk. 6:38), with the suggestion of awareness (Mt. 24:50), acquaintance (Mt. 25:24), or understanding (Lk. 18:34). The idea of mastery occurs in Mt. 18:3 and familiarity in Rom. 7:7. *epiginōskein* is often used instead of *ginōskein* with no distinction of sense (cf. Mk. 2:8 and 8:17; Mk. 5:30 and Lk. 8:46). Its general meaning is "to perceive" but it may also mean "to learn" (Lk. 7:37), "to understand" (2 Cor. 1:13-14), or "to know" (Acts 25:10). It should not be pressed too narrowly in the antithesis of 2 Cor. 6:9.

2. The OT and Jewish Usage and Its Influence. The OT view may be seen when a movement of will is required in the phrase: "Be told" (Mt. 24:43; Lk. 10:11; Eph. 5:5; cf. Jms. 1:3; 2 Tim. 3:1; 2 Pet. 1:20). It is clearer still when insight into God's will is at issue, so that knowledge is acknowledgment or obedient submission (cf. Rom. 3:17 [quoting Is. 59:8]; Heb. 3:10 [Ps. 95:10]; Lk. 19:42, 44; Rom. 10:19). Knowledge of God along these lines is the point in Rev. 2:23. Since, however, the Christian message goes out to pagans, knowledge may precede acknowledgment, though the two are linked (Rom. 1:18ff.; cf. 1 Cor. 1:21; Gal. 4:8-9). This knowledge is not speculative (Rom. 11:34). It is a service of God (1 Th. 1:9). The theoretical element is included but is not decisive (1 Cor. 8:4ff.; Jn. 1:10); it becomes more prominent in the apostolic fathers (cf. 2 Clem. 3.1), though not to the exclusion of the practical side (1 Clem. 59.3; Did. 5.2). Another use along OT lines is for God's electing (2 Tim. 2:19). The noun denotes obedient acknowledgment of God's will in Rom. 2:20 (with a suggestion of monotheism). For a liturgical nuance cf. 2 Cor. 2:14; Lk. 1:77. God is the subject in Rom. 11:33; the reference is to his gracious will in the direction of history. The compound *epígnōsis* can take on almost a technical sense for conversion to Christianity, and *epiginōskein* has the same nuance in 1 Tim. 2:4; Tit. 1:1; 2 Tim. 2:25, though not in Rom. 1:28. Strict differentiation from *gnōsis,* however, is hardly possible. In general, the Christian view of knowledge follows closely that of the OT. It involves obedient acknowledgment. It is not a fixed possession. It is a gift of grace that marks the Christian life (1 Cor. 1:5; 2 Cor. 8:7). Practical interests are always implied. Edification rather than learning is the main point (Rom. 15:14; 1 Cor. 14:6). Reflective inquiry must be grounded in love and lead to right action (Phil. 1:9-10; Phlm. 6; Col. 1:9-10; 1 Pet. 3:7). Yet theological knowledge on a biblical basis may also be at issue (Gal. 3:7; Jms. 2:20; cf. 1 Clem. 32.1; 40.1; Barn. 7.1; 14.7). Faith implies knowledge of the mysteries of the kingdom (Mt. 13:1). We know the significance of baptism according to Rom. 6:6. Faith should bring us knowledge of the mystery of Christ (Col. 2:2).

3. The Influence of Gnostic Usage.

a. Christianity developed its view of knowledge in conflict with both polytheism and pagan Gnosticism. It thus ran the risk of permeation by Gnostic ideas, as we see from Jude, 2 Peter, 1 John, Rev. 2:24, the Pastorals, Colossians, Ephesians, and even 1 and 2 Corinthians, where the desire for speculative wisdom, the grounding of authority in knowledge, the ascetic trends, and the denial of bodily resurrection suggest that the opponents of Paul were Gnostics. In answer Paul uses some of their own terms, e.g., *gnōsis* in the absolute in 1 Cor. 8:1 etc. But while he grants that Christians have a special knowledge of the divine plan, he also states that it is knowledge of the plan of salvation and that it demands walking by the Spirit (1 Cor. 2:12; 3:1ff.). As 1 Cor. 8:1ff. shows, this knowledge is not theoretical. It must go hand in hand with a love that is not just a mystical relation to God but finds expression in love of others. It is also grounded in God's knowledge of us (cf. Gal. 4:9). Again, the knowledge of faith in 1 Cor. 13 may be a spiritual capacity (v. 8), but it is set under love and shown to be purely provisional in contrast to faith, hope, and love. Even when Paul uses *epignṓsomai* for a future relationship, he robs it of its Gnostic significance by qualifying it, as in 1 Cor. 8:3 or Gal. 4:9. Paul follows a similar course in 2 Corinthians by putting objective genitives with *gnṓsis* (cf. 2:14; 4:6; 10:5). In Phil. 3:8ff. he calls the knowledge of Christ a mark of the Christian, but this knowledge means renouncing confidence in the flesh (v. 4), involves confessing Christ as Lord (v. 8), and needs constant renewal (v. 12). It is not withdrawal from the world but a being found in Christ and an experience of the power of his resurrection (vv. 9-10).

b. *ginṓskein* plays a bigger role in John and 1 John. It denotes personal fellowship with God or Christ. The relation between Father and Son is a knowing, and so is that between Jesus and his disciples (Jn. 10:14-15, 27). Because the Father and the Son have life, to know them is to have eternal life (5:26; 17:3). Knowing God also means being determined by love (1 Jn. 4:7-8). Love governs the relation between both Father and Son (Jn. 3:35 etc.) and Jesus and his disciples (13:1 etc.). Thus knowledge is neither observation nor mystical vision; it comes to expression in acts. Observing the commandments is a criterion of knowledge (1 Jn. 2:3ff.). Also involved is an awareness of being loved as the basis of loving (cf. Jn. 15:9; 13:34). Thus *ginṓskein* means the recognition and reception of love, i.e., faith. It is not direct knowledge of God (Jn. 1:18) but knowledge through the revelation in Christ, so that all knowledge is tested by Christ's claim. Knowing Christ is more than having information about his life (6:42; 7:28). It is a knowledge of his unity with the Father (10:38), of his obedience and love as the one whom God has sent (14:31 etc.). This knowledge is imparted by the church's proclamation (1 Jn. 4:6). It is the church also that knows the Paraclete (14:17). Johannine *ginṓskein* thus corresponds to the OT view of knowledge but with four distinctive nuances: (1) *ginṓskein* can be combined with verbs of seeing (Jn. 14:7ff. etc.); (2) historical revelation involves the dogmatic knowledge expressed in "that" statements (10:38; 14:20, etc.); (3) obedience is a criterion of knowledge, not knowledge itself; and (4) *pisteúein* and *ginṓskein* are interrelated in such a way that the former is the first and indispensable step (cf. Jn. 5:24; 6:60ff.) and the latter the full and true relation (as of Father and Son), although *ginṓskein* is an element in *pisteúein* and can give it new power (16:30; 17:7-8).

c. In Mt. 11:27, which is unique in the Synoptists, the relation between Father and Son is described as in John and hence the view of knowledge is necessarily the same.

F. The Later Developments of the Usage. The Apologists follow popular usage, using the group for knowledge of God or Christ or the truth, for knowledge attained from Scripture, and for theological knowledge. The Alexandrians find in *gnṓsis* a higher stage of Christian achievement than that of *pístis*, although the latter is never without the former nor vice versa.

kataginṓskō, akatágnōstos. The verb means "to note," "to see something in someone," "to know to be guilty," "to judge," "to take a low view of." It is rare in the LXX, where it means "to condemn" (Dt. 25:1) and "to scorn" (Prov. 28:11). Condemnatory self-knowledge is the point in 1 Jn. 3:20-21. "Detected" (or "condemned") is the meaning in Gal. 2:11. *akatágnōstos* means "one against whom no fault can be alleged or accusation sustained"; it occurs in the NT only in Tit. 2:8.

proginōskō, prógnōsis. The verb means "to know in advance," and in the NT it refers to God's foreknowledge as election of his people (Rom. 8:29; 11:2) or of Christ (1 Pet. 1:20), or to the advance knowledge that believers have by prophecy (2 Pet. 3:17). Another possible meaning is "to know before the time of speaking," as in Acts 26:5. The noun is used by the LXX in Jdt. 9:6 for God's predeterminative foreknowledge and in Jdt. 11:19 for prophetic foreknowledge; Justin uses it similarly in *Dialogue with Trypho* 92.5; 39.2.

syngnōmē. This word has such various senses as "agreement," "forbearance," and "pardon." In 1 Cor. 7:6 "forbearance" or "concession" is obviously meant. The context might support "opinion," but no instances of this exist.

gnṓmē. 1. A first meaning is "disposition," "will," "mind," as in 1 Cor. 1:10; Phil. 2:2; Rev. 17:13. 2. "Resolve," "decision" is a second meaning; this is perhaps the point in Rev. 17:17. 3. "Counsel," "opinion" is the meaning in 1 Cor. 7:25; 2 Cor. 8:10.

gnōrízō.
1. "To make known." As in the LXX the priest or prophet makes things known (cf. 1 Kgs. 6:2 etc.), or God makes known his power or will, or grants secret knowledge (Jer. 11:18), so in the NT the word can be used of God's disclosure of his power (Rom. 9:22-23) or secret counsel (Col. 1:27) and also of the declaration of his acts in preaching (Rom. 16:26; 2 Pet. 1:16). Jesus is the subject in Jn. 15:15; 17:26. Rather different is the making known of our requests to God in Phil. 4:6. For a purely secular use cf. Col. 4:7, 9.
2. "To perceive," "to know." This sense, common in the LXX, Philo, and Josephus, occurs in the NT only in Phil. 1:22, where Paul does not know (or cannot tell?) which to choose when faced by going to be with Christ or remaining in the flesh.

gnōstós. This term means "knowable," "known," "made known" (e.g., Is. 19:21 LXX). The sense seems to be "recognizable" in Acts 4:16, and this is certainly the meaning in Rom. 1:19, though whether the genitive "of God" yields the sense "what may be known about God" or "God in his knowability" (cf. "his invisible nature" in v. 2) may be debated. [R. BULTMANN, I, 689-719]

---

glṓssa [tongue, language, speech], *heteróglōssos* [of a strange tongue]

glṓssa.

A. The General Use of *glṓssa.*
1. The physical organ "tongue" is the first meaning.
2. We then have "speech," or "manner of speech," or "language."
3. "An expression which is strange or obscure and needs explanation" is a third sense.

B. The Use of *glṓssa* in the NT.
1. "Tongue" occurs in the NT in Lk. 16:24; 1:64; Mk. 7:35. Sins of the tongue are given prominence in Jms. 3:1-12. A similar stress may be found in Job, Psalms, Jeremiah, and Sirach, where the bent is practical but the sins are ultimately against God. Figuratively, the tongue can also rejoice (Acts 2:26) and praise (Phil. 2:11). Tongues as of fire symbolize God's descending power at Pentecost (Acts 2:3).

2. "Language" is the meaning in Acts 2:11; "language" is also used figuratively for "nation" in Rev. 5:9; 7:9; 10:11, etc.

3. Glossolalia.

a. Speaking in tongues (1 Cor. 12–14; cf. Mk. 16:17; Acts 2:4) is a gift (1 Cor. 14:2). This speaking is primarily to God (14:2, 28) in the form of prayer, praise, or thanksgiving (14:2, 14-17). Its benefit is for the individual rather than the community (14:4ff.). In it the *noús* is absorbed so that the words are obscure (14:2, 9, 11, 15-16). Since the sounds are not articulated, the impression of a foreign language is left (14:7-8, 10-11), and uncontrolled use might suggest that the community is composed of mad people (14:23, 27). Yet tongues are a sign of God's power (14:22). To make them useful either the speaker or someone else must interpret (14:5, 13, 27-28; 12:10, 30). If parallels may be found in other religions, Paul discerns a difference in the religious content (1 Cor. 12:2-3). He can thus accept and even claim the charisma (1 Cor. 14:18, 39) but demands that it be subject to edification, order, limitation, and testing (1 Cor. 14:26ff.). Prophecy is superior to it, and above all the gifts is love (1 Cor. 13).

b. It should be noted that, while there are Hellenistic parallels for tongues, there is also an OT basis. Thus the seers of 1 Sam. 10:5ff. seem to be robbed of their individuality, and their fervor finds expression in broken cries and unintelligible speech (cf. 2 Kgs. 9:11). Drunkards mock Isaiah's babbling speech (Is. 28:10-11). The later literature, e.g., Eth. En. 71:11, gives similar examples of ecstatic speech (not necessarily speaking in tongues).

c. The event recorded in Acts 2 belongs to this context. Like the speaking in tongues depicted by Paul, it is a gift of the Spirit (v. 4) which causes astonishment (v. 7) and raises the charge of drunkenness (v. 13). But in this case the hearers detect their own languages (vv. 8, 11). Since they are all Jews (v. 9) and an impression of confused babbling is given, it is not wholly clear what this implies. Perhaps there is a reflection of the Jewish tradition that at Sinai the law was given to the nations in seventy languages. In any case, the orderly proclamation of Peter quickly follows (vv. 14ff.).

d. Why *glṓssa* came to be used for this phenomenon is debatable. Speaking (only) with the physical tongue is a most unlikely explanation in view of Paul's *génē glṓssṓn* in 1 Cor. 12:10 and the plural in 14:5. Nor is it likely that the phrase "tongues as of fire" of Acts 2:3 underlies the usage. The meaning "unintelligible sound" might seem to fit the case, but Paul sharply criticizes this aspect and *glṓssa* is for him more than an isolated oracle (1 Cor. 14:2, 9, 11, 26). It seems, then, that "language" is the basic meaning; here is a miraculous "language of the Spirit" such as is used by angels (1 Cor. 13:1) and which we, too, may use as we are seized by the Spirit and caught up to heaven (2 Cor. 12:2ff.; cf. 1 Cor. 14:2, 13ff. as well as the stress on the heavenly origin of the phenomenon in Acts 2:2ff.).

heteróglṓssos. a. "Speaking another language," "of an alien tongue"; b. "speaking different languages." The only NT use is in 1 Cor. 14:21, where Paul applies Is. 28:11-12 (originally spoken of the Assyrians) in his teaching about the use of tongues in the community: As God will speak to Israel by the Assyrians, so he will give the sign of tongues to unbelievers. Paul offers us here an instructive example, paralleled in the rabbis, of his use of the OT.   [J. BEHM, I, 719-27]

---

gnēsios [genuine, legitimate]

Deriving from *gnētós* ("born"), not *génos*, this word means "true born" as distinct from adopted or illegitimate; figuratively it is used for "regular" or "genuine." In the NT, Phil. 4:3 has it for a "true" fellow worker and 1 Tim. 1:2 and Tit. 1:4 describe Timothy and Titus as "genuine" sons of Paul because of their faith. "Genuine" is also the sense in 2 Cor. 8:8 and Phil. 2:20.   [F. BÜCHSEL, I, 727]

---

gongýzō [to grumble, murmur], *diagongýzō* [to murmur], *gongysmós* [grumbling, complaining], *gongystēs* [grumbler]

gongýzō.

A. The Greek Usage.

1. The early instances yield the sense "to be dissatisfied," "to grumble because of disappointed hopes."

2. The idea is that a supposedly legitimate claim is not met. What is denoted is a strong personal attitude. The word is thus well adapted to describe Israel's reactions in certain circumstances.

B. *gongýzō* among Greek Jews.

1. *gongýzō* occurs 15 times in the LXX and *diagongýzō* ten times. Behind the use stands the thought of grumbling based on guilty unbelief and disobedience.

2. The chief root translated by the *gongýzō* group is *lûn,* which means "to murmur" and which is used when the people, discontented after the deliverance from Egypt, murmurs against Moses (Ex. 15:24), Moses and Aaron (Ex. 16:2), and God (cf. Ex. 16:7-8). There are always some grounds for grumbling, e.g., lack of water or the apparent unattainability of the promised land. The fault is that the people is making grace into a claim and then complaining because justice is not done to the claim. God is thus robbed of his sovereignty, and the murmuring is rightly called a tempting (Ex. 17:2) or scorning (Num. 14:11) of God. The basic sense of *gongýzō* is thus maintained but a theological orientation is given.

3. While the term is often avoided, the rabbis, Philo, and Josephus agree with the LXX as to its connotation. a. The rabbis cannot avoid seeing the attitude of Israel as it is depicted in the law but in their exegesis try to soften it by selecting other terms, or to mitigate the guilt by calling it a murmuring before God rather than against him. b. Philo and Josephus not only avoid the word but in their apologetic efforts to present Israel as favorably as possible give a different twist to the actual events. Thus for Josephus the murmuring at Marah is a call for help (*Antiquities* 3.11) and in other instances the complaint is simply against Moses and not against God. Philo construes the murmuring of Num. 14:1ff. as cowardice and restricts it to a majority of the people rather than the totality (*On the Life of Moses* 1.233-34).

C. *gongýzō* in the NT.

1. In Mt. 20:11 the grumbling is simply the ordinary grumbling of workers over their pay. The grumbling of the religious leaders at Jesus' dealings with sinners in Lk. 5:30 is again normal dissatisfaction (cf. *diagongýzō* in Lk. 15:2; 19:7).

2. 1 Cor. 10:10 recalls the guilty murmuring of the people in the desert and transfers at least the possibility of similar murmuring to the church. Paul consistently

carries through here the thought of the church as the covenant people and pinpoints the danger of substituting its own expectations for God's promises.

3. a. In Jn. 6:61 *gongýzō* is used for the scepticism of the disciples regarding the hard saying of Jesus about eating and drinking his flesh and blood to eternal life. At issue is the point that they are measuring Jesus by their own expectations and are disappointed. Since, however, Jesus is the Son of Man (v. 62), their criticism is also criticism of God. The situation is a decisive one, for if the murmuring does not yield to confession, the result is parting from Jesus (vv. 66ff.).

b. In Jn. 6:41, 43 the Jews, repeating their former history, reject Jesus because he does not measure up to their own ideas and desires. The people are in fact mostly Galileans but they represent Israel at a point of crisis similar to that in the desert, not accepting God as God but complaining because he is not the God of their own opinions and hopes. Perhaps because of the repetition of the wilderness situation the term "Jews" is chosen for those who either treat Jesus with scepticism or openly reject him.

c. Jn. 7:32 probably carries the same sense rather than the weaker one of mere discussion. The crowd is vacillating, and while the Pharisees are afraid that the decision might go against them, vacillation is still not acceptance and comes under the judgment of unbelief.

diagongýzō. In the NT this occurs only in Lk. 15:2; 19:7, where it denotes simple dissatisfaction.

gongysmós. The noun corresponds to the verb and has a similar history in secular writings, the LXX, and the rabbis. a. In the NT it occurs in Jn. 7:12 for the vacillation of the people (cf. *gongýzō* in 7:32). b. In Acts 6:1 and 1 Pet. 4:9 it has the ordinary sense of grumbling, i.e., that the claims of Hellenist widows are not met, or that hospitality imposes too burdensome demands. c. In Phil. 2:14 the apostle has general dissatisfaction in view but with a suggestion of the grumbling of desert Israel and a consequent summons to full committal in faith and obedience.

gongystḗs. This word, found only in the LXX and NT, is used by Jude 16 for the false teachers who are discontented with their lot and with God as they follow their own passions.   [K. H. RENGSTORF, I, 728-37]

---

góēs [sorcerer]

---

a. In the strict sense *góēs* means "magician," especially one working with verbal formulas. The *góēs* is a lower practitioner than the *mágos*. b. The term then means "false magician." c. Finally it can denote any "charlatan" (cf. the figurative use in Philo for the confusion and delusion of idolatry or hypocritical and sensual conduct). The only NT instance is in 2 Tim. 3:13, where the sense is the figurative one for the person who entices others to impious action by pious words (cf. vv. 6-7).

→ *mágos*   [G. DELLING, I, 737-38]

---

góny [knee],   *gonypetéō* [to bow the knee]

A. Genuflection in the NT. Except in Heb. 12:12, *góny* is used in the NT only in connection with genuflection. We have *tithénai tá gónata* in Mk. 15:19; Lk. 22:41; Acts 7:60, etc., and *kámptein tá gónata* in Rom. 11:4; 14:11; Eph. 3:14; Phil. 2:10.

Kneeling is linked to prayer in Lk. 22:41; Acts 7:60, etc., to requests to the Lord in Mt. 17:14, to a greeting in Mk. 10:17, to homage in Mt. 27:29, to idolatry in Rom. 11:4, and to acknowledgment of God in Rom. 14:10-11 and the Lord in Phil. 2:10. The gesture expresses supplication, abasement, worship, and subjection.

B. Genuflection outside the NT. The history of the term goes hand in hand with that of *proskynein,* especially since there is not usually any distinction between genuflection and full prostration. We find genuflections of slaves before their masters and of devotees before the gods (although not in the official cult). In the LXX it is a sign of humility in prayer (e.g., 1 Chr. 29:20), or of acknowledgment and homage before God (e.g., Is. 45:23), the king (e.g., 1 Chr. 29:20), or the man of God (2 Kgs. 1:13). In prayer standing is more common (e.g., Gen. 18:22; 19:27; 1 Sam. 1:26). Among the rabbis different words are used for brief falling on the knees, falling on the face, and prostration with outstretched hands and feet. A distinction is also made between inclining, bowing, prostrating oneself, and kneeling. In the early church kneeling becomes customary for individual and public prayer. It expresses subjection, abasement, and petition. Standing, however, is enjoined on the Lord's Day and between Easter and Pentecost. In synagogue worship some place is also found for genuflection and prostration.   [H. SCHLIER, I, 738-40]

→ *proskynéō*

---

grammateús [scribe]

1. Scribes in the NT Period. Once in the NT (Acts 19:35) *grammateús* is used for a higher official in the city of Ephesus (the town clerk). This accords with the early use of the Hebrew word *sôpēr* for royal secretary. But elsewhere in the NT the term denotes the rabbinic scholar or theologian, as the Hebrew does in Nehemiah, 1 Chronicles, and Sirach (although Philo and Josephus do not have *grammateús* in this sense and the rabbis distinguish between themselves and scholars of an earlier time). As we see from the NT, the rabbis are a closed order of qualified scholars who have received the spirit of Moses by succession (Mt. 23:2). They enjoy a high reputation (Mk. 12:38-39) as those who know the law and proclaim God's will by their teaching, preaching, and judgments. As scholars they question Jesus on his message and breaking of tradition, and as members of the Sanhedrin they help to prosecute and condemn him.

2. The Judgment of Jesus on the Scribes. To understand this judgment, we must distinguish between the scribes and the Pharisees, who were not scholars. The accusations against the scribes are kept distinct in Luke (11:46-52; 20:46), and have particular reference to their learning and resultant social claims and privileges. In Mt. 5:21-48 the theologians are again singled out after a common attack in 5:20. The main charges are their lack of humility (Mt. 23:5ff.), unselfishness (Mk. 12:40a), and sincerity (Mk. 12:40b), and their failure to practice what they preach (Lk. 11:46). In doctrine their casuistry defeats God's true will as it is contained in the law of love (cf. Mk. 7:9ff.). Jesus brings out the seriousness of God's true will in the antitheses of Mt. 5:21ff.

3. Paul's Judgment. Himself an ordained scribe, Paul finds in the scribes' rejection of the cross a fulfilment of Is. 33:18 (cf. 1 Cor. 1:20).

4. The Christian Scribe. There is reference to a Christian *grammateús* in Mt. 13:52 (cf. 5:19; 16:19; 18:18; 23:8ff.). Matthew is an example of such a scribe at work, e.g., in his proofs from Scripture.   [J. JEREMIAS, I, 740-42]

> *gráphō* [to write], *graphḗ* [writing, Scripture] *grámma* [letter],
> *engráphō* [to record, write in], *prográphō* [to write beforehand, set
> forth publicly], *hypogrammós* [example]

gráphō.

A. **The General Use of *gráphō*.**

1. The original sense seems to be "to carve," "to engrave" (cf. the carved figures of 1 Kgs. 6:28, the hewn-out chamber of Is. 22:16, and the engraving on stones in Dt. 27:3 in the LXX, and the engraving on wax in Lk. 1:63 and engraving on the ground in Jn. 8:6 in the NT).

2. A further meaning is "to draw," "to paint."

3. We then find the word more generally for "to write" (e.g., in Rom. 16:22; 2 Th. 3:17); this includes writing by dictation (cf. 1 Cor. 4:14; 14:37; Jn. 21:24 [?]), or earlier writing (1 Cor. 5:9; 7:1; 9:15).

4. Another sense is "to set down" or "draw up" (cf. Mk. 10:4; Lk. 16:6-7; Jn. 19:19, 21-22—the title on the cross). This leads to such senses as "to accuse," "to inventory," and "to characterize," not found in the NT.

5. *Composition of a Writing or Inscription in a Scroll or Book.* In the OT writing down is an important mark of revelation. God writes down in Ex. 24:12 etc., Moses in Ex. 24:4, Joshua in Josh. 24:26, Samuel in 1 Sam. 10:25. The king must have God's law written down (Dt. 27:18). The people must write it on the doorposts (Dt. 6:9). The NT endorses the significance of the writing of the OT (cf. Paul's use of *egráphē* in 1 Cor. 9:10; 10:11; Rom. 4:23; 15:4). Jesus himself did not write down revelation, nor cause others to write it (apart from Revelation). Yet writing serves the gospel (Lk. 1:3). It is undertaken with great responsibility (Gal. 1:20). Its goal in Jn. 20:30-31 is that people might believe. Writing is witness (Jn. 21:24). If not all that Jesus did can be written down, what is written is of supreme importance. The things written are *gegramména*—*gegramménon* being also the term used in John to introduce OT quotations. In Revelation the writing is by divine direction (1:11, 19). Those who keep what is written are blessed (1:3). The author is commanded to write to the churches (2:1ff.). A similar command occurs in 14:13; 19:9; 21:5, a prohibition in 10:4. There is also a scroll in heaven (5:1), names are written in the book of life, a new name is engraved on the stone (2:17), and the holy name is written on the foreheads of the victor (3:12) and the 144,000 (14:1). In such ways the divine revelation comes to expression in writing.

6. *gráphein in Legislative Activity.* Another meaning of *gráphein* is "to prescribe," "to decree," used also for God's decrees in the LXX and Philo. The NT refers to what Moses wrote in Mk. 10:5; 12:9; Rom. 10:5. (In Jn. 1:45; 5:46 not law but prophesying of the Messiah is the issue.) A Christian counterpart is 1 Jn. 2:7-8: "I am writing you no new commandment," and for legislation written on the heart cf. Rom. 2:15.

B. **The Special Use of *gégraptai* and *gegramménon*.** *graptós* is "what is fixed in writing" and *tá gegramména* is a stock expression for written laws. When used in the OT (cf. also *gégraptai*) this term denotes the absolute validity of what is written, both legally and religiously. Behind it stands the binding authority of Yahweh as King and Lawgiver. This is first true of the law and then by extension of the prophets and the writings.

1. The Specific Use of gégraptai.

a. The simple use as in Mt. 4:4ff.; Lk. 4:8 corresponds to 2 Esdr. 5:7 and to parallel phrases in Philo, Josephus, and the rabbis.

b. The confirmatory *kathōs gégraptai* (Mk. 1:2; Acts 7:42; ten times in Romans and four in 1 Corinthians) is based on 2 Chr. 23:18 etc. and rabbinic parallels.

c. For *hóti gégraptai* in Gal. 3:13 there are parallels in the papyri.

d. *hós gégraptai* in Mk. 7:6; Lk. 3:4; Acts 13:33 is also based on the LXX and finds parallels in the papyri.

e. *katháper gégraptai* in Rom. 3:4; 9:13, etc. is paralleled in the papyri.

f. *hoútos gégraptai* in Mt. 2:5 finds rabbinic parallels.

g. *gégraptai hóti* in Mt. 4:6; Mk. 11:17 is also found in Philo.

h. *gégraptai gár* in Mt. 4:10; Acts 1:20; Rom. 12:19; 14:11; 1 Cor. 1:19; Gal. 3:10 finds parallels in Philo and the rabbis.

i. *perí hoú gégraptai* in Mt. 11:10; Mk. 14:21; Mt. 26:24 has rabbinic parallels.

2. The Specific Use of gegramménon. There are classical instances of *tá gegramména* for "written laws," and the term is often used in the LXX for the OT itself, as also in Josephus. The NT has it for Scripture mostly in Luke and John (only twice in Paul). Luke stresses that Christ fulfils all Scripture (Lk. 18:31; 21:22; 24:44; Acts 13:29; 24:14). John has the term in Jn. 6:45; 10:34; 15:25 (*éstin gegramménon*); 6:31; 12:14 (with preceding *kathōs*); and 2:17 (with preceding *hóti*). Paul has it only in 1 Cor. 15:54 and 2 Cor. 4:13. Sometimes a reference is made to Jesus by means of a dative or *epí* (cf. Lk. 18:31; Jn. 12:16; Mk. 9:12-13). At issue is what is written concerning Jesus.

graphḗ.

A. *graphḗ* in Secular Greek.

1. The first meaning is "writing," "written characters," or, more broadly, the "art of writing."

2. A second sense is "copy," "drawing," "picture," "art."

3. We then find "written statement," such as a. "letter," b. "piece of writing," c. "record" or "document" (e.g., genealogy or contract), d. "list," e. "decree," f. "accusation."

4. A further meaning is "published work" in the literary sense.

5. Then we have "written law," "statute," sometimes in the LXX with the suggestion of "holy scripture" (1 Chr. 15:15; 2 Chr. 30:5).

B. *graphḗ* as Holy Scripture.

1. graphaí for the (Holy) Scriptures, or the Collection of Individual Books. The rabbis and Philo speak of the Holy Scriptures, but not the OT itself. The NT seldom refers to Scripture as holy. Paul has *graphaís hagíais* (not *hieraís*) in Rom. 1:2. He also calls the law *hágios* in Rom. 7:12. Only 2 Tim. 3:15 has *hierós* in relation to *graphaí*. The plural for the OT as a whole is common in Philo and the rabbis. The NT follows this usage (cf. Mt. 26:54). In Mt. 21:42; 22:29 the reference might be to individual passages, but normally the whole collection is in view (cf. Jn. 5:39; Acts 17:2, 11; 18:24, 28; Rom. 15:4; 16:26; 1 Cor. 15:3-4).

2. graphḗ for Individual Passages of Scripture. *hḗ graphḗ* in the Synoptics, Acts, and John can denote an individual statement, as in Mk. 12:10; Acts 1:16; 8:32, 35, and often perhaps when a quotation follows, as in Jn. 7:38; 13:18; 19:24. In Paul all Scripture is at issue in Gal. 3:8, 22, but in Gal. 4:30; Rom. 4:3; 9:17; 10:11 individual texts are in view, and perhaps also in 11:2, though Paul himself may not have made any clear-cut distinction. Jms. 2:23 obviously has a single passage in view, as does Jms. 2:8.

3. graphḗ for a Single Book. There are no NT instances except perhaps 2 Tim. 3:16, though contemporary parallels suggest that this means "every passage."

4. graphḗ Emphasizing the Unity of Scripture: the Totality of OT Scripture. The use of the singular for all Scripture does not occur in Philo or Josephus and is perhaps based on rabbinic use. Paul has it in the personification in Gal. 3:8 (where the obvious point is that God himself speaks through Scripture), John in 2:22; 10:35; 17:12; 20:9, and Peter in 1 Pet. 2:6; 2 Pet. 1:20. The early church embraced this usage and included the NT canon as well.

C. The Question of Scripture.

1. The Judaistic View of Scripture. According to this view Scripture is sacred, authoritative, and normative. It is God's dictate given by the Spirit. This applied first to the law, then to the prophets and writings. The authors spoke or wrote by a direct inspiration which in Alexandria was construed along the lines of Greek ecstaticism. The concern of rabbinic exegesis was to rediscover and establish the tradition of Scripture by minute examination; it had a tendency to become legal, syllogistic, and scholastic. Alexandrian exegesis took a freer view but surrendered the more easily to Hellenistic allegorizing.

2. The Early Christian Canon. Establishment of the canon accompanied the attempt to consolidate an authoritative tradition. The NT sheds light on this with the reference to Chronicles in Mt. 23:34, the mention of the threefold division in Lk. 24:44, the quotations of Jesus from the prophets, Psalms, and Deuteronomy, the quotations of Paul (older versions of the LXX) from Isaiah, the Psalms, and the law (especially Genesis and Deuteronomy), and the paucity of apocryphal quotations (Jude 14ff. and possibly Lk. 11:49; Jn. 7:38; 1 Cor. 2:9; 9:10; Eph. 5:14; Jms. 4:5). 2 Pet. 3:16 calls Paul's epistles *graphaí*.

3. The Belief of the Early Church regarding Scripture.

a. Inspiration. The early church follows Judaism in searching Scripture to find eternal life (Jn. 5:39). While accepting the Judaic view of inspiration and to some degree the same line of exegesis, it does not attach the same importance to tradition. It modifies OT authority by giving the Lord's sayings equal authority (cf. "I say unto you" in the Sermon on the Mount and 1 Cor. 7:10; 9:14; 11:23). The *graphaí* express God's will, and the authors speak by the Spirit (e.g., David in Mt. 22:43 etc.; the prophets in Acts 18:25; 1 Pet. 1:11; 2 Pet. 1:21; cf. also Heb. 3:7; 9:8; 10:15). 2 Tim. 3:16 formulates inspiration more expressly, but the same conviction underlies Eph. 6:12, as do all the statements that God (Mk. 12:26; Mt. 15:4; 19:5) or the Lord (Mt. 1:22; 2:15; 1 Cor. 14:21; 2 Cor. 6:17) speaks in Scripture. The role of the Spirit, who will bring to mind what Jesus said (Jn. 14:26), presupposes that the words are spirit and life (Jn. 6:63). If there is here more regard for the human authors (cf. Mt. 2:5, 17, 23; 3:3; 4:14, etc.), it is still assumed that God is the true author and this explains why Paul handles the text quite freely (though not capriciously as Josephus does). Paul can also allegorize in rabbinic fashion (cf. Gal. 4:24ff.), but the literal text has far greater importance for him than for Philo, and allegorizing is not his chief mode of exposition. Other rabbinic features in Paul are his combining of quotations from the three groups and his use of catenae.

b. The Thought of Fulfilment as the Heart of the Early Christian Understanding.

All the NT books are convinced that OT Scripture is fulfilled in and by Christ. The Gospels find messianic prophecy in the OT (cf. Mk. 14:49; Mt. 26:54; Lk. 4:21; Jn. 17:12; 19:24, 28, 36; also Acts 1:16). The risen Christ himself shows how his work fulfils and confirms the great message of Scripture (Lk. 24:27, 32, 45). Paul follows this up in Acts 17:2; 28:23, and cf. Apollos in Acts 18:28. It applies not merely to specific predictions but to the OT as a whole, which is thus adopted as Christian Scripture (Rom. 15:4), so that all its teachings may be applied in different ways (cf. Rom. 4:23; 1 Cor. 10:11; 1 Cor. 9:10). John, too, refers all Scripture to Christ (5:39, 47); Abraham may be called his prophet (8:56) and Moses may be said to write about him (5:46-47). Not only his cross and resurrection are prefigured (19:37; 20:9) but also his sabbath freedom (7:22) and his sonship (10:34ff.). Hebrews works out the same thought typologically by showing how Christ both fulfils and transcends the work of Moses and Aaron and the function of the OT cultus, and also by claiming the great heroes of OT faith as Christian witnesses. Revelation takes its symbolism from the OT, so that here, too, the event of Christ sheds a new light on Scripture. In sum, the NT no longer has Scripture without Christ. The fact of Christ is regulative for its use of Scripture. In keeping with this is the truth that while we are to believe Scripture or the prophets (Jn. 2:22; Acts 26:27), we do not believe *in* Scripture.

c. The Twofold Attitude to Scripture in Early Christianity. If Scripture is fulfilled, it no longer exists alone, yet its authority remains (Jn. 10:35). Tension thus arises, for while Jesus finds God's will in the law (cf. Mt. 5:18), he does not hesitate to assert his own authority (cf. Mt. 5:21ff., 31ff.). In Paul we find the same tension, for if we are to live according to Scripture (1 Cor. 4:6), it is by Christ and the Spirit that the *nómos* and *grámma* are given their true validity, as Scripture itself shows us by its permanent soteriological, ethical, and eschatological teaching. Hebrews, too, finds continuity with the OT even as it presents the superiority of Christ. Scripture, then, is not just what is written but God's dynamic declaration climaxing in Christ and the Spirit. Scripture serves Christ but finds its true force only in the revelation of Christ and the Spirit that is more than what is written.

grámma.

A. *grámma* **in Greek and Hellenistic Usage.** Like *graphḗ*, *grámma* has such meanings as 1. "inscription," 2. "picture," 3. "symbol" as a. writing in letters, b. individual letter, c. letters of a book, d. handwritten character, and e. language, 4. "what is written," 5. "grammar" or "academic discipline," 6. "written piece" as a. letter, b. record, c. official report, and d. decree, 7. "written law," and 8. "literature." It is then used 9. for the sacred Scriptures of the OT and NT. In this instance the addition of *hierá* is not necessary but *tá hierá grámmata* is the most common formula, e.g., in Philo and Josephus, then in Origen (who also has *theía grámmata*). Like *graphḗ*, *grámma* can also be used for a specific reference.

B. *grámma* **in NT Usage.**

1. In Lk. 23:38 *grámmata* are written characters, as also in Gal. 6:11; they represent letters in Paul's hand.

2. The meaning in Jn. 7:15 is "learning," the point being that Jesus is not qualified to teach. Paul's learning is what is disparaged by Festus in Acts 26:24.

3. The meaning in Acts 8:31 is "communication by letter" and in Lk. 16:6-7 "bill of indebtedness."

4. In Jn. 5:47 the reference is to the law (the writings of Moses). Since this bears

witness to Christ (v. 46), those who do not believe it will not believe the words (*rhḗmata*) of Christ.

5. *grámma/pneúma*. Paul often draws an antithesis between *grámma* and *pneúma*. In Rom. 2:27 *grámma* is the law as what is demonstrably written. Like the demonstrable sign of circumcision, this does not guarantee observance. Through it (not in spite of it), the Jews are transgressors. *grámma* in this context means more than letter; it has the sense of prescription. The circumcision of the heart or spiritual circumcision is needed (vv. 28-29) to make a true Jew, i.e., one who fulfils the law. The opposing pairs *sárx* and *kardía, en tṓ phanerṓ* and *en kryptṓ,* correspond to the distinction between circumcision *en grámmati* (by the letter of the law) and *en pneúmati* (by a decisive invasion of the personal life). The *grámma* cannot do what the *pneúma* does. The basic antithesis is not between Scripture and the Spirit, but between law as a purely written prescription and the Spirit. Rom. 7:6 makes this point clear. As mere *grámma,* which does not rule in the heart, the law does not enable us to serve. We have to be dead to the law in this sense. Without Christ and the Spirit it is ineffective. But this does not have to mean that there is an absolute antithesis between *grámma* and *pneúma.* It simply means that in and by itself what is written cannot give new life. 2 Cor. 3:6-7 sheds further light on the relation. Here *grámma* is linked with the old covenant and *pneúma* with the new. On the basis of Jer. 31:33 what Paul has in mind is that the law that is merely written can only condemn us, but the law that God writes on the heart by the Spirit gives life. This is by divine purpose and not simply due to a false use of Scripture. God gave Scripture as law with a view to judgment, and he has now given the Spirit with a view to life. In v. 7 *grámmata* (plural) means letters carved on stone and obviously refers to the tables of the law. The letters again point us to the law, so that Paul is not just opposing letter to spirit, or inadequate writing to true meaning, but the older phase of revelation, which is a ministry of death, to the new phase, which through Christ and the Spirit is a ministry of life. The divine purpose behind the old dispensation can be seen, of course, only when Christ removes the veil (vv. 14, 16). It is hidden when he is obstinately rejected (v. 14).

6. *grámma/graphḗ*. Paul's distinction between *grámma* and *pneúma* is not meant to disparage Scripture as such. *grámma* characterizes the law as a written law, while *graphḗ* is Paul's term when he is stressing the positive aspect of Scripture. The word that is near us (Rom. 10:8) is not *grámma* but Scripture self-attested through the Spirit of Christ. Although we are not to focus on the mere letter of the law, we are still under the authority of Scripture as this is regulated by Christ and the Spirit. The new covenant gives life by the Spirit, not because unwritten law now replaces written law, but because the Spirit gives power to fulfil the inner intention of what is written.

engráphō.
1. *Lk. 10:20.* The references of *engráphein* are to a. "writing in a letter or petition," b. "entering in a document," c. "inscribing on a list," d. "inscribing the divine words in the Bible," and e. "entering in the book of life" (Dan. 12:1 LXX). The Lord's saying in Lk. 10:20 carries the thought that those who belong to Christ are enrolled as citizens of the eternal *politeía.*

2. *2 Cor. 3:2-3.* What Paul is saying here is that the Corinthians are letters "inscribed" on his heart. The idea of inscribing on the heart or soul is a common one in antiquity, but Paul is probably influenced more by Jer. 31:33; Prov. 3:3; also Ex. 24:12; 31:18; 34:1; Ezek. 11:19; 36:26.

prográphō.
1. *Eph. 3:3:* "As I have written above," a common use (e.g., when referring to a heading).
2. *Rom. 15:4:* "What was written previously, in earlier times."
3. *Gal. 3:1.* The reference here may be a. to public proclamation, e.g., on placards, or b. to vivid depiction. The latter is less likely both because there is no attestation for this sense and a heart-rending description of the cross is less in keeping with apostolic preaching than its public promulgation.
4. *Jude 4.* The idea here is that of public proscription; the false teachers have been long since listed for condemnation.

hypogrammós (hypográphō). The term *hypográphō* originally means a. "to draw lines for children learning to write," then b. "to show," "depict," "denote," "signify," c. "to demand," d. "to dazzle," e. "to paint" (under the eyes), and f. "to write below," "subscribe." In 1 Pet. 1:21 the rare *hypogrammós* (only biblical and post-Christian Greek) refers to the tracks that Christ has left as examples for us to follow, not in imitation, but in commitment to his way of suffering. This passage influences the Christian use of the term, e.g., in 1 Clem. 5.7; 16.17 and Clement of Alexandria *Paedagogus* 1.9.84.2. [G. Schrenk, I, 742-73]

grēgoréō → egeírō

---

gymnós [naked], *gymnótēs* [nakedness], *gymnázō* [to exercise naked], *gymnasía* [exercise]

---

gymnós.
1. "Naked" in the literal sense of a. "unclothed," b. "badly clothed," c. "stripped by force," or d. "without an upper garment," "partly clothed."
2. "Naked" in the figurative sense of a. "unconcealed," "manifest" (Heb. 4:13), b. "without bodily form." In 1 Cor. 15:37ff. Paul contrasts the bare seed with the future plant or flower in illustration of the transition from the present body to the resurrection body. It should be noted that what is planted is not the naked soul but the present body (which also bears our individuality), so that the bare seed does not simply represent a nonbodily "soul" but that which has not yet received its future form. In 2 Cor. 5:3 a question arises whether Paul is referring to a nonbodily state prior to the parousia of Christ or to the final destiny of the reprobate who will not be clothed with the glorious resurrection body. The latter seems more likely. c. A final figurative sense is "inwardly unprepared," as in Rev. 3:17; 16:15.

gymnótēs. Rare in secular Greek, this term means "nakedness," "poverty," as in Rom. 8:35; 11:27; it is used figuratively in Rev. 3:18.

gymnázō. The literal sense is "to exercise naked." It is used only figuratively in the NT, e.g., for concentration on godliness (as distinct from dualistic asceticism) in 1 Tim. 4:7 (cf. 1 Cor. 9:24ff.; Phil. 2:12); for training in discernment in Heb. 5:24 and in righteousness in Heb. 12:11; for training in greed (perhaps sarcastically) in 2 Pet. 2:14.

gymnasía. "Exercise," also used figuratively (e.g., for "martyrdom" in 4 Macc.

11:20). The term is meant literally in 1 Tim. 4:8, but the context shows that the reference is not to ordinary bodily exercise but to dualistic asceticism (cf. 4:3; 5:23).

[A. OEPKE, I, 774-76]

---

gynḗ [*woman, wife*]

In general *gynḗ* denotes a. "the female" (as distinct from the male), b. "wife" (Dt. 13:6; Mal. 2:14; Lk. 1:5; 1 Cor. 7:2, 27; Eph. 5:22-23; Col. 3:18-19, etc.). By Semitic law a fiancée is already called *gynḗ* (cf. Gen. 29:21; Dt. 22:24; Rev. 21:9; Mt. 1:20). *gynḗ chḗra* means "widow" in 1 Kgs. 17:9; Lk. 4:26.

A. Woman in the Contemporary NT World. The disparagement of women in antiquity finds expression in the common male saying, backed up by anecdotes, that it is a matter of thanksgiving not to be an unbeliever or barbarian, a slave, or a woman. The proverb undoubtedly originated in the Near East.

1. The Greek World and Hellenism. Athenian women were of inferior status, often guarded by dogs, treated as fickle, contentious, and uncultured in comedy, liable to be oppressed if not under male protection. The Doric world gave them more freedom and influence. A high ideal of womanhood persisted even in the Attic world. Plato could demand equality for women, and capable individual women made a surprising impact in both private and public life. Marriage was the rule, but concubinage was common. No laws existed against bigamy but monogamy ruled in practice. Married couples were often affectionate but divorce was common either by consent, by declaration before a judge or third party, or by the unilateral action of the husband. Repeated divorces constituted a form of polygamy. No obstacle existed to remarriage after the death of a partner, though remaining single was sometimes praised, especially on the part of widows. Menander treated marriage cynically, and Neo-Platonism and the mysteries promoted asceticism in the form of total or temporary sexual abstinence, but the older Stoicism valued marriage highly.

2. Rome. In Rome housewives enjoyed a relatively high status. Women were not confined to the home, and Roman Stoicism advocated equal education for them. Many noble as well as rebrobate women figured in Roman history. Sexual intercourse prior to marriage was frowned on, and Roman marriage was strictly monogamous, although this did not exclude intercourse with slaves or harlots. Various ceremonies of marriage were practiced. Divorce was relatively easy for all kinds of reasons and even by mutual repudiation. As in Greece, successive divorces and remarriages became common later, but widows who remained unmarried were highly respected.

3. Women in the OT. In spite of traces of an older matriarchate, women in the OT had few rights. They passed from the protection of one male to another. In Levirate marriage they had no legal choice as the males did (Dt. 25:5ff.). Wives could not claim the sabbath rest (Ex. 20:8ff., though cf. 2 Kgs. 4:22ff.). They depended heavily on their husbands' decisions (cf. 1 Sam. 1:5). Polygamy was a heavy burden for them (1 Sam. 1:5ff.). Stricter fidelity was demanded from them. Yet women could appear in public life (Gen. 24:13ff.). Daughters could inherit property (Num. 27:8). Their wishes were to be consulted in marriage (Gen. 24:39, 58). They could have enormous influence for good or bad (cf. Sarah, Rebekah, Abigail, and Jezebel), and in a few instances played public roles as prophetesses or national leaders (Deborah). The creation stories accord them a high position as helpmeets and lay a firm basis for the close relationship of the one man and the one woman even if they do also show woman to be secondary and focus on her role in the fall.

4. Women in Judaism. The rabbinic writings gave an unflattering picture of women, portraying them as greedy, inquisitive, vain, and frivolous. Their rights and religious duties were restricted and they were assigned a special place in the synagogues. Hellenistic and Palestinian Judaism differed little in this regard. Yet notes of praise are heard too. Women are said to be an adornment to their husbands and to have equal promise with them before God. Some women could be extolled for their learning or piety. Marriage was a duty for loyal Jews. Polygamy was legal but for various reasons (usually financial) was not common. Divorce, however, was rampant, and successive divorces produced a successive form of polygamy. Ascetic ideas were largely alien to Judaism but extramarital intercourse was firmly opposed. Great stress was laid on the physical side of marriage (though not for reasons of carnal desire), yet the personal aspects of the marriage relationship were also valued (cf. Philo). As regards divorce, the initiative lay with the husband, but there was debate whether the main ground ("something scandalous") covered only licentiousness or many other matters, some of them extremely trivial.

B. Woman in Christianity. Two important factors underlie Christian thinking in this area: (1) the establishment of monogamous marriage by creation, and (2) the removal of differentiation of sex by the divine lordship. Yet these principles are not worked out with revolutionary vigor. Christianity is often conservative in practice. Its main advantage is a new adaptability.

1. Jesus. Jesus is no radical social reformer but he comes impartially to help all who are in need. He gives women a role in some of the parables (Mt. 13:33; Lk. 15:8ff.). If he observes Jewish proprieties (cf. Mk. 5:40), he can also break them to speak with a woman (Jn. 4:27), to teach one (Lk. 10:39), or to speak on behalf of women (Mk. 12:40ff.). He also acts decisively to heal sick women (Lk. 13:10ff.; Mk. 1:31). He accepts the ministrations of a band of women (Lk. 8:2-3) who stay with him in his passion (Mk. 15:40-41) and share in his exaltation (Mk. 16:1ff.). Even at a distance he evokes a response from women (cf. Lk. 11:27). He never speaks a derogatory word about women, and by offering them equal salvation he sets them at the side of men as no less the children of God.

2. The Community. Women belong fully to the first Christian community (Acts 1:14). The Christian mission wins them along with men (Acts 16:13-14). As the men are brothers in the family of faith, the women are sisters (Rom. 16:1).

a. A certain tension may be discerned in Paul. By creation woman is a stage further from God (1 Cor. 11:3, 7), and Eve was seduced first (2 Cor. 11:3); on the other hand, differences are transcended in the new aeon (Gal. 3:28). Thus wives are still subject to their husbands (Col. 3:18; Eph. 5:21-22), but husbands are to exercise their leadership unselfishly in a loving service modeled on that of Christ.

b. The same tension may be seen in later writings. The role of Eve in the fall is stressed in 1 Tim. 2:13-14, but 1 Pet. 3:7 demands full recognition of women as joint heirs of life. There is little trace of the ascetic ideals that would emerge strongly in the apocryphal Acts.

C. Sacral and Social Functions of Women.

1. In non-Christian antiquity women take part in worship and the mysteries. Some feasts are for them alone, but they are excluded from other rites. They function as priestesses and sibyls (cf. Delphi).

2. The OT. The OT knows no priestesses, but women are part of the religious community and take part in festivals, sacred dances (Judg. 21:21), sacrificial meals (1 Sam. 1:4), and temple service (Ex. 38:8) as well as having a prophetic ministry (Miriam, Huldah). With children and aliens, they belong, like men, to the covenant people.

3. Judaism. Women have only a restricted role here, being confined to the women's court in the temple, having a special place in the synagogue, not being required to say the Shema or to observe the whole law, and being discouraged from saying grace publicly or publicly reading the law in the synagogue. Destruction of the temple made their earlier participation in festivals impossible, but they were still members of the covenant people with the duty, e.g., of daily prayer.

4. The NT.

a. Jesus has women followers but appoints no women among the twelve.

b. The NT churches include ministering women (Acts 9:36ff.), many of whom are commended for their zeal (Rom. 16:6, 12-13 and cf. Lydia). Phoebe is described as a *diákonos* (probably an office, Rom. 16:1). Women also help in evangelism (Acts 18:26; Rom. 16:3; Phil. 4:2-3). Prophetically gifted women may address the community (1 Cor. 11:3ff.) but only by way of exception (1 Cor. 14:34ff.).

c. As the charismatic element becomes less prominent, women's work may sometimes have to be resisted as heretical (Rev. 2:20), but it can also be given a regular form as older women minister to younger ones (1 Tim. 3:11) as counterparts of the deacons. The relation of these to the widows of 1 Tim. 5:3ff. is complex; the latter are older women who are supported by the church and may have fulfilled some of the duties listed in Tit. 2:3ff. The qualification "wife of one husband" may refer to non-remarriage after the death of the spouse, but in view of the right to such remarriage in Rom. 7:1ff., the commendation of it for younger widows (1 Tim. 5:14), and the general approval of a married clergy (1 Tim. 3), it seems more likely that the reference is to remarriage after divorce (as in 1 Tim. 3:2, 12). The *prótē pístis* of v. 12 is undoubtedly loyalty to Christ rather than fidelity to the first husband.

5. Further Developments in the Church. Women teachers are found mostly in sectarian circles, e.g., the Gnostics and Montanists. We sometimes read of women's choirs in worship. Women engage in charitable service and visitation. Younger unmarried women come to be supported by the church and are reckoned as officebearers, although not ordained by laying on of hands. Deaconesses have a more distinct function, especially in the east, and assist at baptisms, in the visitation of women, and in the presentation of the elements at communion. The right of women to give emergency baptism is debated, and they are not ordained as presbyters. Later they find a new sphere of service in and through monasticism; the abbess is called a deaconess.

[A. OEPKE, I, 776-89]

Gốg kaí Magốg [Gog and Magog]

This phrase occurs in the NT only in Rev. 20:8-9 as the name of the host that after the millennial period wages war against God's people and is destroyed by God. The name is taken from Ezek. 38–39 and the sequences in Ezekiel and Revelation are similar: messianic reign, Gog and Magog and their destruction, the new Jerusalem (in Revelation the resurrection in 20:11ff. followed by the new heaven and earth and the new Jerusalem in 21:1ff.). Some of the rabbis have a similar sequence, although Gog and Magog can precede the messianic reign where this is seen to be the period of absolute consummation. Some apocalyptic works, however, do not mention Gog and Magog at all. One big difference between Ezekiel and Revelation is that Ezekiel is more strictly prophetic whereas Revelation paints a broader eschatological picture. Again, in Ezekiel Gog is the prince (1 Chr. 5:4) and Magog the territorial name (Gen. 10:2), but in Revelation the two form a sinister double-name for the hostile host, as in some rabbinic works and Sibylline Oracles 3.319; 3.512.

[K. G. KUHN, I, 789-91]

---

gōnía [corner], *akrogōniaíos* [cornerstone, capstone], *kephalḗ gōnías* [cornerstone, capstone]

---

gōnía. "Corner" (Mt. 6:5; Acts 26:26), hence the four corners of the earth (Rev. 7:1; 20:8; cf. the four winds and four angels) from which destructive winds blow and the hostile nations come to attack the centrally located holy city (Rev. 20:8-9).

akrogōniaíos (→ *kephalḗ gōnías*). The "final stone" in a building, probably over the gate; used with reference to Christ in 1 Pet. 2:6 and Eph. 2:20. The idea is that the church is a temple, the prophets and apostles are the foundation, and Christ completes the building.

kephalḗ gōnías. This is a Hebraism referring to the final stone in a building and consistently referring to Christ on the basis of Ps. 118:22. In Mk. 12:10 Jesus calls himself the rejected stone which becomes the head of the corner in the new sanctuary (of which he is also the builder, Mk. 14:58; cf. Mt. 16:18). He is thus above the earthly temple (Mt. 12:6). Acts 4:11 finds in Ps. 118:22 a prophecy of the death of Christ (the rejection) and his resurrection (being made the chief cornerstone). 1 Pet. 2:7 relates Ps. 118:22 to Is. 8:14; the *kephalḗ gōnías* is a sharp stone at the corner; against it some stumble and fall in their failure to believe that the rejected stone can be the head of the corner.   [J. JEREMIAS, I, 791-93]

δ *d*

---

daímōn [demon, divinity], *daimónion* [demonic], *daimonízomai* [to be demon-possessed], *daimoniṓdes* [demonic], *deisidaímōn* [religion], *deisidaimonía* [fear of divinity]

---

daímōn, daimónion.

A. *daímōn* in the Greek and Hellenistic World.

1. A persistent animism, which even educated circles had to recognize, underlay the *daímōn* concept in the Greek world. The *daímōn* can be a deity or minor deity but may also be given a philosophical sense. The etymology and original meaning of the term *daímōn* are uncertain.

2. daímōn as a Term for Gods and Divine Powers. Various senses may be noted in this field: a. "god," b. "lesser deity," c. "unknown superhuman factor," d. "what overtakes us," e.g., death, or good or evil fortune, e. "protective deity," and in Stoicism f. "the divinely related element in us," e.g., *noús* or conscience. Stars can also be called *daímones*.

3. The Influence of Popular Religion on the Philosophical Systems. While philosophy interpreted *daímōn* as general divine power, it also introduced *daímones* as personal intermediaries. Heroes and *daímones* are akin, and *daímones* also serve as messengers, supervisors, and mediators. Under the influence of popular belief they are related especially to magic, to misfortune, and to possession. They are also regarded as spatial (especially evil *daímones*), and have a place on the great ladder from God to us as beings that are superior but still imperfect, their wickedness being due to their association with matter.

4. daímōn in Popular Greek Belief. In popular belief *daímones* are a. spirits of the departed, b. shades which appear especially in lonely places at night. They cause all kinds of mischances, are responsible for illness and madness, bear special names, and may be warded off or conjured up by magic.

5. Demon Terminology in the Greek and Hellenistic World. daímōn is the more usual term, while *daímonion* (the neuter of the adjective *daimónios*) has the more indefinite sense of "the divine," especially fate. Parallel terms are *hḗrōs*, *eídōlon*, and *psychḗ*, and later under Judaic influence *ángelos* and *pneúma*.

6. daímōn in Josephus and Philo. Even linguistically Philo follows the Greek. He uses *daímōn* for destiny, a protective spirit, the spirit of a murdered wife, and intermediary beings in the air. Josephus moves in the same world but he approximates the rabbis in speaking of a *daimónion pneúma* and in the main he uses *daimónia* (not *daímones*) for demons.

B. The OT and Later Jewish View of Demons.

1. Belief in Spirits and Demons in the OT. Traces of a belief in spirits occur in the OT in 1 Sam. 28:13 (the witch of Endor) and Is. 8:19. But those who conjured up the dead were to be expelled (Dt. 18:10; 1 Sam. 15:23a; cf. Num. 23:23). Thus the demonic appears only on the margin. Spirits are mentioned to depict the destruction of Babylon and Edom (cf. Is. 34:14; 13:21). Spirits are possibly linked to idolatry in Dt. 32:17; 2 Chr. 11:17. Only once in Ps. 91:6 LXX is there a possible reference to protection against demons. A special word *ángelos* replaces *daímōn* for God's messengers, and God himself is the source of all that happens, including retributive or educative evils. In the main the LXX uses *daimónion* for Heb. *šēḏ,* but can also use *eídōlon* and *mátaia* as equivalents, thus showing that *daimónion* is a contemptuous term for pagan gods. Tob. 6:8ff. offers an example of an evil spirit attacking and destroying humans. But *daimónia* rather than *daímones* is preferred for such spirits, perhaps because it is closer to popular belief and avoids the positive aspects of *daímōn*.

2. Tannaitic Judaism. Here we find a widespread belief in spirits, many of which are named, e.g., Lilith, Bath Chorin; also group names. They have wings and enjoy special knowledge but have sensual needs. Magicians contact them. As spirits of defilement they are in complete antithesis to the Holy Spirit. They are ubiquitous and harmful, and precautions must be taken to avoid them (e.g., at night or in ruined places). They also cause sickness and acts as seducers. They are not connected with Satan. God and his angels can protect against them, as can study of the law, but external precautions are also to be taken. Unlike angels, they are not God's intermediaries, but angels could become hostile demonic powers and there can thus be reference to the angels of Satan in a historical fusion that does not erase the fundamental distinction between angels and demons.

3. Pseudepigraphal Judaism. Linguistically this stands between the OT and rabbinic Judaism as regards demons. We find the idea of fallen angels, and Satan's angels are called demons. We also read of evil or unclean spirits or spirits of Beliar, and of unclean demons in Jub. 10:1 (though *daímones* is seldom used). Only rarely here are demons capricious and hurtful. Their main work is to tempt into witchcraft, idolatry, war, bloodshed, and prying into mysteries. Pagans pray to them when seduced into idolatry. They are in opposition to God and owe their position to a fall which implies sin and guilt. They are depicted sometimes as related or subordinate to Satan, but not consistently so. In general the link with the souls of the dead is broken, and there is no bridge between evil spirits and good. Demonology is adopted because there is found in us a will that resists observance of the law; this evil will is ascribed to demonic influence, and a relation to Satan is thereby suggested.

C. The View of Demons in the NT.

1. The NT usage is similar to that of later Judaism. *Daímōn* occurs only once, in Mt. 8:31. *daimónion* is used elsewhere, as are *pneúma, pneúma akátharton, pneúma ponērón, pneúma álalon, pneúma astheneías,* and *pneúma pýthōn.* Mark is most faithful to Jewish usage, and Luke follows. The Athenians use *daimónion* in Acts 17:18, and Paul has it four times; cf. also *pneúma* in Eph. 2:2 and 1 Timothy. References to Satan's angels are found in Mt. 25:41 etc., and to bad angels in 1 Cor. 6:3; 2 Pet. 2:4; Jude 6; and Rev. 9:11.

2. In the main the NT follows the OT. There is no reference to the spirits of the dead. *daímōn,* which suggests a divine intermediary, is avoided. Angels and demons are basically antithetical. There are few references to demons except in the case of demon possession. Paul does not refer to perils from demons (2 Cor. 11:23ff.), and if he finds in his "thorn" the work of an angel of Satan (2 Cor. 12:7), God overrules this hindrance for good. Because of faith in God, the fear of demons is expelled. Yet Paul regards witchcraft as meddling with demons (cf. the warning in Gal. 5:20), and pagan sacrifices are offerings to demons (1 Cor. 10:20–21). Demonic activity is perhaps alluded to in 1 Cor. 12:2. Revelation also refers to demon worship, in 9:20. A surge of demonic activity is expected in the end-time (1 Tim. 4:1; Rev. 16:13-14). The demonic activity denoted by the swarm of locusts in Rev. 9:1ff. may be eschatological, but it may also be past or even present. We are to arm against spiritual foes in Eph. 6:12, and cf. the devilish wisdom of Jms. 3:15 and the admonition of 1 Jn. 4:1. Demonic powers are reserved for judgment (Mt. 25:41; cf. 1 Cor. 6:3; 2 Pet. 2:4; Jude 6). Demons are subject to Satan (Eph. 2:2) in a kingdom that opposes God's kingdom. They are thus the instruments of Satan (cf. the reply of Jesus in Mk. 3:20ff.). The conflict with demons is for this reason a mortal one, but the main attention focuses, not on demons as such, but on their head. Evil thoughts do not come from seducing spirits but from the heart (Mt. 15:19). Because people do not honor God, he gives them up to a base mind (Rom. 1:28). Sin and the flesh act as evil forces but they are not external to us; they express the sinful self.

3. As regards demon possession in the Synoptics and Acts, it should be noted (1) that while not all sicknesses are said to come from demons, they are all in a sense Satan's work (cf. Lk. 13:11ff.); (2) that the main issue in possession is the distortion of the divine likeness or the impairment of the center of personality (Mk. 5:5) which

Jesus comes to remedy (Mt. 12:28); and (3) that demons have a knowledge about Jesus (and their own fate, Mt. 8:29; Jms. 2:19) which they impulsively utter but which is not the confession that Jesus seeks.

4. In John the people accuse Jesus of having a *daimónion;* this implies total rejection and dishonoring, and Jesus replies to it firmly (Jn. 8:49). When Paul in Acts 17:18 is called a preacher of foreign *daimónia,* this might carry an allusion to the charge against Socrates. OT usage recurs when Babylon is called the abode of *daimonía* in Rev. 18:2. The NT resists Greek divinizing of demons and dispels fear of the demonic, yet it retains a sense of the sinister activity of spirits as they attack us spiritually and physically in the service of Satan. The demonic characterizes the old aeon, but Jesus has gained a decisive victory over it and will keep his people until the final consummation of the new aeon that he has already inaugurated.

daimonízomai. "To be possessed by a *daímōn,*" originally used in all the senses of *daímōn,* not used in the LXX, and found in the NT with relatively the greatest frequency in Matthew.

daimoniṓdes. "Demonic," used in the NT only in Jms. 3:15, which contrasts devilish wisdom with the wisdom from above.

deisidaímōn, deisidaimonía. Made up of *deídō,* "to fear," and *daímōn,* this term normally denotes piety either as religion or (sometimes) as excessive fear of the gods. Since *daímōn* in the Greek world can mean any supernatural power, it is a good neutral expression for religion, and has this sense in Acts 25:19 (Festus) and (the adjective) in Acts 17:22 (Paul of the Athenians).   [W. FOERSTER, II, 1-20]

---

dáktylos [finger]

The only significant NT use is in Lk. 11:20, where Jesus says that he expels demons with the finger of God (denoting God's direct activity). In the OT a. the heavens are the work of God's fingers (Ps. 8:3), b. the tables of the law are written with God's finger (Ex. 31:18), and c. God's finger works miracles (Ex. 8:19).

[H. SCHLIER, II, 20-21]

déēsis → déomai

---

deí [it must be], **déon estí** [it is necessary]

Most common as *deí* (with infinitive) or *déon estí,* this term denotes the element of necessity in an event. It is most precise when linked with the compulsive power, but usually has a weaker sense. In philosophy it expresses logical or scientific necessity. It can also denote ethical or religious obligations (backed sometimes by statute). In the LXX the law must be done as God's will (Lev. 5:17; cf. in the NT Lk. 13:14; 22:7; also Christian duties, 1 Th. 4:1; 1 Tim. 3:2; Tit. 1:7). Fate may often be viewed as the power behind necessity, but the term can also denote the compulsion of magic or the presuppositions essential to its success. In Greek and Hellenistic usage what is expressed is an idea of neutral deity which does not sit well with the OT and rabbinic concept of the personal will of God overruling history and issuing a personal summons to us. The LXX, Josephus, and even the NT adopt the term, but in so doing, while suffering some tension, make it plain that it relates to God's personal will rather than a neutral fate.

2. Lucan usage is important in this regard. Of the 102 NT instances, 41 are in Lucan writings. The usage varies. Sometimes the term expresses God's will in the law (Lk. 11:42; Acts 15:5), with which Jesus may clash as he follows the *deí* of God's will as he himself knows it (Lk. 13:6). The *deí* thus represents for Jesus a rule of life (Lk. 15:32). It is the *deí* of the divine lordship which governs his work (Lk. 4:43) and leads him to suffering and glory (Lk. 9:22; 17:25; cf. Acts 1:16; 3:21; 17:3). Its basis is God's will as laid down in Scripture (Lk. 22:37). His disciples and the church stand under the same *deí* (Lk. 12:12; Acts 9:6, 16; 14:22, etc.). The will of this *deí* is a saving will, so that its demand is a demand for obedient faith in every situation of life.

3. As used by Luke, the term expresses the necessity of the eschatological event. It is well adapted to do this, since the event is known only by revelation and sets us before the inconceivable ineluctability of a historical act that is grounded in God's will. Faith in God's eternal if mysterious plan formulates it. The necessity derives from the very nature of the God who has committed himself to this plan. Daniel stated this already in Dan. 2:28 LXX; Revelation repeats the thought (1:1; cf. 4:1), as does Jesus in Mt. 24:6; Mk. 13:10. The imperative of eschatology is to both judgment and salvation. Everything stands under it from the predicted return of Elijah fulfilled in the Baptist (Mt. 17:10ff.). The messianic age has come; hence the passion and resurrection are under the divine *deí* (Mt. 16:21) of this age. Jesus does not just preach eschatology; his history *is* eschatology. The gospel confirms this by showing that his work is the fulfilment of Scripture (Mt. 26:54; Lk. 22:37; Jn. 3:14; 20:9) and will necessarily, for Paul, issue in Christ's reign (1 Cor. 15:25), the judgment (2 Cor. 5:10), and the resurrection transformation (1 Cor. 15:53).

4. As the divine *deí* shapes Christ's history, it also controls God's work in us, e.g., in the new birth of Jn. 3:7, the need to call on Christ's name in Acts 4:12, the necessity of faith in Christ to salvation in Acts 16:30-31 (cf. Heb. 11:6).

5. Another use of *deí* is for the necessity of prayer in the Christian life. As Jesus taught us, we ought always to pray (Lk. 18:1). The Spirit helps us because we cannot pray as we ought (Rom. 8:26). Worship ought to be in spirit and truth (Jn. 4:20ff.); the divine Spirit sets us in the truth by relating us to Christ who is the truth.

[W. GRUNDMANN, II, 21-25]

---

deíknymi [to point out, reveal], *anadeíknymi* [to show, appoint], *anádeixis* [manifestation, installation], *deigmatízō* [to expose], *paradeigmatízō* [to hold up for contempt], *hypódeigma* [example, copy]

---

deíknymi.

A. The Usage outside John's Gospel.

1. In Mt. 4:8 and parallels the sense is "to point to something," though with little distinction from "to show," "to exhibit," as in Lk. 24:40 (cf. Mt. 8:4 and par.). There are many parallels for this in pagan authors, the LXX, Josephus, and the early fathers.

2. Another nuance is "to point out" (e.g., Mk. 14:15), or even "to bring to pass" in the sense of "to manifest" (1 Tim. 6:15).

3. "To indicate verbally" is another nuance, leading to the sense "to teach," "to explain," "to demonstrate" (cf. 1 Cor. 12:31b; Acts 10:28; Mt. 16:21).

B. The Usage in the Johannine Writings.

1. The term is used in John to show that the works of Jesus are signs; it thus takes on the sense "to reveal," "to disclose" (Jn. 10:32). The Father is shown in Jesus (cf. Philip's request and Jesus' reply in 14:10-11). The unity of Father and Son means that the Father shows all his works to the Son and thus assigns the Son his own actions (5:20). To the showing of the works corresponds a teaching of the things to say (8:28; 12:49).

2. In Rev. 1:1ff. the words of the prophecy represent a revelation of Jesus Christ; God gave him this revelation to show future things to his servants by the mediation of the author, who saw and bears witness to it. Hence *deíknymi* here signifies a. a divine declaration in the form of revelation, b. divine revelation of the future, and c. a fusion of intimation and symbolism. Seeing (v. 2) is the response to the showing (cf. 4:1; 17:1; 21:9-10; 22:1). The general root of this usage is the sense "to cause to see," "to manifest," but instances may also be found, e.g., in 1 Clem. 26:1, of the meaning "to intimate in advance," or, in the LXX, of the theological sense "to reveal" (in 82 of 119 instances, in many of which the LXX itself imports the idea of revelation). In apocalyptic writing, too, we find the senses "to disclose," "to prophesy," and "to refer to mysteriously."

anadeíknymi.

1. In Lk. 10:1 the idea is "to appoint," "to institute," with some vacillation between the idea of ordaining for a task and legally instituting. The word is taken from the political sphere and suggests an official action.

2. In Acts 1:24 the idea is different, for while an appointment is at issue, what is asked is that God will "disclose" or "show" whom he has chosen.

anádeixis. The meaning in Lk. 1:80 is uncertain. Lk. 3:1ff. and 10:1 suggest "installation," as in secular usage relating to official institution. But the meaning might also be "manifestation," which carries the thought that John's appearance is part of revelation.

deigmatízō. This rare word means "to exhibit," "make public," "bring to public notice." In Mt. 1:19 Joseph does not want to expose Mary by having her appear publicly. In Col. 2:15 Christ makes a public exhibition of the vanquished forces, not just by proclamation, but by public display, as in a triumphal procession.

paradeigmatízō. This stronger term, which is more common than *deigmatízō,* means "to expose to public obloquy." It occurs in the LXX in Num. 25:4 (public hanging), in Jer. 13:22 (Heb. "suffer violence"), and in Ezek. 28:17 ("to pillory"). Apart from a variant in Mt. 1:19, the only NT instance is in Heb. 6:6. By apostasy Christ is crucified again and "publicly shamed."

hypódeigma. In Hellenistic Greek this alternative to *parádeigma* means "example" as well as "document" or "proof." The LXX has it (with *parádeigma*) for "model" and "copy." The use for "copy" shows what is at issue in Heb. 8:5 and 9:23-24. What Moses sees on the mountain is the original, and the constructed tent etc. are the copy which reflects the original, yet also the model which points to it. The term "image" is perhaps the best suited to bring out this twofold sense. The OT cultus has a typical character when it is seen in the light of Christ. In this light it points to heavenly things, but it can do so only as a reflection of them. Elsewhere in the NT the term has the sense of "example." The prophets are an example in Jms. 5:10. Jesus offers a prototype of mutual service in Jn. 13:15. The warning of a bad example is offered in 2 Pet. 2:6 and Heb. 4:11.   [H. Schlier, II, 25-33]

---

deípnon [meal, Lord's Supper], *deipnéō* [to eat, dine]

This word, which ordinarily means "meal," "chief meal," "feast," takes on theological significance in the NT when used 1. for the meal consecrated to the Lord (1 Cor. 11:20); the church's table fellowship constitutes divine service. The word also has significance 2. as an eschatological image; the heavenly banquet represents perfect fellowship with God and Christ (cf. Lk. 14:24; Rev. 19:9; 3:20, and the parallel marriage-feast, Mt. 22:2ff. etc.). The terrible counterpart of this feast is "the great supper" of Rev. 19:17 (based on Ezek. 39:17ff.; cf. Mt. 24:28). The use for a cultic meal is common in Hellenistic religion. The idea of an eschatological banquet occurs in the OT (cf. Is. 34:6ff.) and apocalyptic and rabbinic writings.
[J. Behm, II, 34-35]

deisidaimonía, deisidaímōn → daímōn

---

déka [ten]

The number ten, linked originally to reckoning by the fingers, is a favorite round figure in the OT, e.g., the Ten Commandments, the ten plagues, the ten patriarchs before the flood, the tenth as an offering to God, and ten as a measurement in relation to the ark, tent, and temple (Ex. 26–27; 1 Kgs. 6:7). The number is also common in rabbinic Judaism, e.g., the ten temptations of Abraham, the ten divine words at creation, the ten needed to constitute true worship. In apocalyptic, too, we read of the ten epochs of the world, of which the tenth is that of the Messiah. In the NT, ten plays a lesser role. It is a round number, e.g., in Lk. 19:13; Mt. 25:1; Rev. 2:10. Jesus displays his messiahship by ten miracles in Mt. 8 and 9. The genealogy in Mt. 1:1ff. fits into a ten-period schema. The ten horns in Revelation represent a totality of power (as in Dan. 7:20). In Rom. 8:38-39 ten powers are unable to separate us from God, and in 1 Cor. 6:9-10 ten vices exclude from the kingdom of God. On Gnostic speculations about the number cf. Irenaeus in Migne *Patrologia Graeca* 1.17.1; 18.3.
[F. Hauck, II, 36-37]

dektós → déchomai

---

dexiós [right (hand, side)]

From the stem *dek-*, this means "right" a. as the opposite of left; b. as a noun *(hē dexiá)* for God's right hand as a symbol of his power; c. for the favorable or honored side, e.g., birds on the right as a good omen in Greece, the worthy walking on the right, or the law on God's right hand in the OT and rabbis; d. for what is eminent or good, e.g., studying the law on the right hand for proper application to it; and e. in connection with treaties or compacts (on the basis of giving the right hand when concluding agreements).

1. In the NT, Jesus in the parable of judgment says that the sheep will be set at God's right hand and the goats at his left; the right side is that of favor or salvation, as in Plato and the rabbis.

2. The NT depicts Christ himself as exalted to God's right hand. In Acts 2:34 Peter refers to the session at God's right hand, and in 5:31 he says that God exalted Jesus to his right hand. This is a fulfilment of the royal psalm 110 messianically interpreted; cf. Mt. 22:41ff., where Jesus himself shows that Davidic sonship does not exhaust his messiahship but becomes a riddle in view of the greater glory which goes far beyond a mere restoration of David's throne and kingdom. Jesus belongs at God's right hand because he is Lord of the world as well as King of Israel. Throughout the NT his exaltation to God's right hand comes to expression (cf. Rom. 8:34; Eph. 1:20; Col. 3:1; Heb. 1:3, 13; 8:1; 10:12; 12:2; 1 Pet. 3:22). What follows his death vindicates his claim to a place of honor alongside God. In fulfilment of his claim, he has been declared Christ and Lord, the messianic age has dawned, and he shares God's glory and deity, as manifested by his sending the Spirit. Older rabbinic writings refer Psalm 110 to Abraham or David, but later exegesis adopts again a messianic interpretation. Another rabbinic view sets the law at God's right hand but sees the Christ replacing it in the messianic age.   [W. GRUNDMANN, II, 37-40]

> **déomai** [to ask, pray],   **déēsis** [prayer],   **prosdéomai** [to need]

déomai, déēsis.

1. The original meaning of *déomai* is "to lack," "to need," and of *déēsis*, "lack." But there are few traces of this in the LXX and none in the NT.

2. The NT sense is, according to context, "to ask" or "to seek." Formally, in Acts 21:39 and 8:34, it means "please" *(déomaí sou)*. A fuller sense occurs when requests are made to Jesus for help or healing, as in Lk. 5:12; 9:38; cf. also 8:28. Paul uses it in an earnest admonition in 2 Cor. 5:20 (cf. 10:2; Gal. 4:12). Apart from Mt. 9:38 it is exclusive to Luke and Paul.

3. It then comes to be used for "to pray." Jesus prays for Peter in Lk. 22:32 (cf. Heb. 5:7). Paul prays about his plans in Rom. 1:10; 1 Th. 3:10. In Acts 4:31 the reference is to the prayer of vv. 24ff. *déēsis* is intercession in Rom. 10:1, but the element of petition is less strong in Lk. 5:33; Phil. 1:4; 1 Tim. 2:1. Prayer in general seems to be the issue in Acts 10:2; Lk. 2:37; 1 Tim. 5:5. If the answer is uncertain, an *ei* clause is used (Rom. 1:10). The content is denoted by a *hópōs* or *hína* clause, while intercession for someone is *hypér* or *perí tinos*.

prosdéomai. In his address in Acts 17:22ff. Paul says that God does not want worship as though he "had need of something (more)." The *pros-* strengthens an element that is already present in *déomai*, since "to need" carries the thought of something to be added. The real point, of course, is that God does not need anything; Paul is continuing the polemic of the OT (also Stoicism) against anthropomorphic ideas of deity and against the idolatry which worships images that have to be propped up and carried (Is. 40:20 etc.). For Paul the *stoicheía*, too, are weak and ineffectual; the Galatians must not subject themselves to them now that they know the true Lord (Gal. 4:8-9). [H. GREEVEN, II, 40-42]

→ *erōtáō, eúchomai*

déos → *phóbos*

---

desmós [imprisonment], *désmios* [prisoner]

Paul's imprisonment (literally "fetter") has special religious significance in phrases like *désmios Christoú Iesoú* (Eph. 3:1; Phlm. 1:9), *désmion autoú* (2 Tim. 1:8), *désmios en kyríō* (Eph. 4:1), and cf. Phlm. 13 and Phil. 1:13. Actual imprisonment underlies the usage, but the real bondage is to Christ for whose sake it is suffered and to whom self-will is offered in sacrifice. In answer to the idea that Paul borrows here from the concept in the mysteries that *katochḗ* precedes the final dedication, it should be noted that Paul nowhere calls imprisonment a penultimate stage prior to being with Christ (Phil. 1:23). Imprisonment symbolizes his whole life and ministry.

→ *aichmálōtos* [G. KITTEL, II, 43]

---

despótēs [owner, master], *oikodespótēs* [master of the household], *oikodespotéō* [to rule one's household]

---

despótēs.

A. *despótēs* outside the NT.

1. Greek Usage. The first meaning is the domestic one of "owner." This extends to the political sphere when an alien people takes over a land. The word thus acquires such varied nuances as a. master of the house, b. master as distinct from slave, c. absolute ruler (equivalent to *týrannos* in Plato), d. powerful divine being, e. the Roman emperor, and f. (astrologically) planet. While the term expresses social rank or position, it is not one of status; hence the Jews can not only follow normal Greek usage but also link the term with God. In the Greek Bible, while strongly subordinate to *kýrios*, it appears some 56 times (25 times in direct address to God with a special emphasis on his omnipotence). God is *kýrios* because he is *despótēs* of all things (cf. Job 5:8ff.). Elsewhere in the LXX we find all the other nuances except a. and f., but these are less prominent compared to that for God.

*2. The Reason for the Paucity of *despótēs* in the LXX.* The distribution of *despótēs* in the LXX is striking. In the law it occurs only in Gen. 15:2, 8 *(déspota kýrie)*, in the history books only in Josh. 5:14, in Isaiah in 1:24; 3:1; 10:33 *(ho despótēs kýrios* [or *kýrios ho despótēs] sabaōth)*, and in Jeremiah in 1:6; 4:10; 14:13; 15:11, but it occurs more frequently in Wisdom, Maccabees, and Sirach, and still more in other renderings. The reason for this paucity is probably that the term has acquired too abstract a character in its use for absolute power. The God of Israel, however, is the Creator and Lord of all things who is known to his people through acts in history. His omnipotence, then, is a concrete reality and is more suitably expressed by *kýrios*. This explains three characteristics of the use of *despótēs* in the LXX: (a) additions such as "of all things, all creation, heaven and earth" are often made; (b) it occurs more often in later works which display Hellenistic intrusion; (c) in Gen. 15:2, 8 Abraham is appealing to God's omnipotence in a unique way which no doubt suggested the term to the translator.

B. *despótēs* in the NT.
1. Secular Usage. In four of the ten instances the reference is to the master as distinct from slaves, e.g., 1 Tim. 6:1; 1 Pet. 2:18. "Master of the house" is the sense in 2 Tim. 2:21.
2. God as despótēs. Simeon addresses God as *déspota* in Lk. 2:29, and so does the Christian group in Acts 4:24. God is also meant in Rev. 6:10.
3. Jesus as despótēs. A new feature is the description of Jesus as *despótēs* in Jude 4; 2 Pet. 2:1. In 2 Pet. 2:1 the heretics may be known by their rejection of Jesus as *despótēs*. In Jude 4 a double denial, first of one *despótēs*, then of Jesus, might be intended, but this is unlikely in view of 2 Pet. 2:1. The use of *agorázein* in 2 Pet. 2:1 might lead one to expect *kýrios* rather than *despótēs*, but the latter expresses very well Christ's right to his people in virtue of his saving act. It is less likely that the intention is to equate Jesus with God as the Almighty.

oikodespótēs, oikodespotéō. These are not classical words, but occur in astrology and everyday life. In the NT *oikodespótēs* occurs 12 times (especially in Matthew, e.g., 10:25; 13:27, 52, etc.; cf. Lk. 13:25; Mk. 14:14). The meaning is "master of the house" (sometimes with the emphatic addition *ánthrōpos*, Mt. 13:27 etc.). The parables illustrate God's action by that of the householder. The only instance of the verb is in 1 Tim. 5:14: younger widows are to marry and "rule their households," an example of the family virtues that are stressed in the Pastorals.
→ *kýrios* [K. H. RENGSTORF, II, 44-49]

---

déchomai [to accept, receive], *dochḗ* [receiving (a guest)], *apodéchomai* [to welcome], *apodochḗ* [acceptance], *ekdéchomai* [to accept, await], *apekdéchomai* [to accept, await], *eisdéchomai* [to receive, welcome], *prosdéchomai* [to accept, await], *dektós* [acceptable], *apódektos* [acceptable], *euprósdektos* [acceptable]

---

déchomai.

A. *déchomai* outside the NT.
a. The first sense is "to accept," e.g., letters, gifts, payments, even the body by the soul. In pagan religion prophecy is received through, e.g., flights of birds, and offerings are accepted by the gods. In the OT Zephaniah demands an acceptance of God's dealings in punishment and correction (3:7); cf. the cup of wrath in Jer. 25:28. A special use in this regard is for the "bearing away" of sin (Gen. 50:17); punishment for sin is "received," however, in Is. 40:2.
b. "To receive," in the sense "to welcome," "to extend hospitality," is a further use which is common in the NT (cf. Lk. 9:53; Gal. 4:12; 2 Cor. 7:15).
c. "To receive, hear, or understand what someone is saying" is another usage, found in relation to divine commands in the OT, with a volitional as well as an intellectual component.
d. A cultic use in the LXX is for "to receive favorably," e.g., prayer or sacrifice. This adds a theocentric element where the Hebrew equivalent is "to find favor."

B. *déchomai* in the NT.

1. In Mt. 10:40ff. special importance is attached to receiving the disciples, for since they are the envoys of Jesus, receiving them is receiving him, and therefore God. Through the disciples Jesus himself knocks at the heart's door. They are the bearers of Christ. Christ is present in them; they continue and extend his mission. More than simple hospitality is involved, and therefore the love expended on them will bring a special reward. The same applies to receiving a child in Christ's name (Mt. 18:5-6), for Christ himself comes in the person of the child, and what is done for the child is done for him. This gives even such an unassuming act a unique significance.

2. In a related sense the NT speaks about receiving the gospel or the Word of God (Acts 8:14; 11:1; 17:11; cf. Jms. 1:21; 1 Th. 1:6; 2:13). One may also receive its content, i.e., the kingdom of God (Mk. 10:15), the grace of God (2 Cor. 6:1), or love of the truth (2 Th. 2:10). In this sense *déchomai* is equivalent to faith. It brings out the fact that in relation to God we can only receive. In hearing the gospel, however, we are liberated for it. By the Spirit (1 Cor. 2:14), the understanding is opened and we are set in the freedom of decision in which God's grace or kingdom may be ours.

doché. From "receiving a guest," this word comes to denote the "meal" or "feast" that is linked with hospitality. Only Luke uses it in the NT, for the great feast that Levi holds in 5:29, and for the feast to which the poor and needy are to be asked according to Jesus in 14:13. It may be noted that as Jesus accepts hospitality from tax collectors (15:1), he demands that table fellowship be extended to the outcast and needy.

apodéchomai. This compound has much the same sense as the simple form. In the NT it occurs only in Luke, for the welcome that Jesus gives the crowd in 9:11, for the crowd's welcoming of Jesus in 8:40, for the reception of Paul in Acts 18:27; 21:17, and for Paul's welcoming of all who come to him in Acts 28:30.

apodoché. The meaning is "acceptance" with a sense of approval and appreciation. In the NT two sayings which sum up the gospel are said to be sure and worthy of full acceptance or approval, namely, that Christ came into the world to save sinners (1:15), and that godliness has promise both for this life and for the life to come, since it builds on the living God and Savior (4:8ff.).

ek-, apekdéchomai. *ekdéchomai* means a. "to accept" and b. "to await." *apekdéchomai* is also used for "to await," but also means "to deduce (wrongly)." In the NT Paul has *apekdéchomai* for expectation of the end (Rom. 8:25). This expectation is focused on the transformation when the adoption enjoyed by faith will be manifested with the resurrection (8:14, 23) and creation will reach the goal for which it, too, is waiting (8:19). This consummation will come with Christ's return, so that Christ himself is the content of expectation (Phil. 3:20). He is so as the hope of righteousness (Gal. 5:5). On the basis of the gospel that is already received (cf. *déchomai*), *apekdéchomai* thus characterizes Christian life as one of expectation of the great climax which gives not only this life but also the whole of creation its meaning. Hebrews uses *ekdéchomai* as well as *apekdéchomai* for the same eschatological expectation (10:13; 9:28). Jms. 5:7 has the former in the comparison in Jms. 5:7 and 1 Peter, the latter in the reference to God's patient waiting in Noah's day.

eisdéchomai. This means "to receive someone" either to a place or into a circle. The LXX has it for reception of the people into fellowship with God (Mic. 4:6 etc.). In the NT the only instance is in 2 Cor. 6:17 (based on Is. 52:11 and Zeph. 3:20): In the new covenant God's people everywhere are received into fellowship with God, so that the promise of the prophets is fulfilled without national restriction.

prosdéchomai. This has the two senses a. "to receive someone" or "accept something," and b. "to await." The latter is the main sense in the NT.

1. It is used for those who await God's kingdom: Joseph in Mk. 15:43, Simeon in Lk. 2:38. The gospel is that the Messiah has come and waiting is over.

2. It is also used for Christian expectation of the resurrection (Acts 24:15), eternal glory (Tit. 2:13), and Christ's mercy in the judgment (Jude 21). Jesus tells his disciples to be as those who wait for their master (Lk. 12:36).

dektós, apo-, euprósdektos. dektós means "what one can accept," hence in the LXX "acceptable," "pleasing." *apo-* and *euprósdektos* have the same meaning.

1. In the LXX the terms have a cultic reference. Sacrifices that are pleasing to God are effectual (Lev. 1:3), but when the people backslide their offerings are not acceptable (Jer. 6:20) and will become so only in the last time of conversion (Is. 56:7). The acts and prayers of the righteous are also acceptable in Prov. 16:7; so are the righteous themselves (11:20). In the NT Paul says that his ministry is an acceptable sacrifice (Phil. 4:20). So is the fruit of his ministry (Rom. 15:16). The Christian community is a holy priesthood offering acceptable spiritual sacrifices to God through Christ (1 Pet. 2:5). With no cultic association, all who do right are acceptable to God (Acts 10:35). On the other hand, prophets are not acceptable in their own country (Lk. 4:24). What is acceptable is equated with what is good in 1 Tim. 2:3.

2. The word has a messianic sense in Is. 61:2: The messianic age is the time chosen by God as the time of the divine presence and salvation. This time comes with Jesus (Lk. 4:18ff.). The acceptable time of divine election and presence is that of Christ's coming. This is for Paul the time of God's hearing and helping (Is. 48:8ff.), i.e., the acceptable time, the day of salvation (2 Cor. 6:2).   [W. GRUNDMANN, II, 50-59]

---

déō [to bind, tie],   (*lýō* [to untie, set free])

1. *déō* is common in the NT for "to bind" or "bind together" (e.g., Mt. 13:30), "to wrap" (Jn. 11:44), "to chain" (Mk. 5:3-4), and hence "to imprison" (Mk. 6:17 etc.). It expresses supernatural binding in Lk. 13:16; Acts 20:22; cf. the chaining of Satan in Rev. 20:2. It is also used figuratively for the marriage bond (Rom. 7:2; 1 Cor. 7:26, 39). God's word is not bound (2 Tim. 2:9).

2. Behind the *deín* and *lýein* of Mt. 16:19; 18:18 there is no idea of magic, but the rabbinic terminology for declaring forbidden or permitted, and hence for removing or imposing an obligation. On the other hand, the disciples are not to be rabbis (Mt. 23:8), and another if less common use of the rabbinic terms is for imposing or removing a ban. This fits in with Mt. 18:17, offers a parallel to Jn. 20:23, and is the almost unanimous interpretation of the fathers.   [F. BÜCHSEL, II, 60-61]

---

dēlóō [to show, declare]

delóō is the common Greek word for "to show, declare, impart, demonstrate." It can be used for the communication of cultic mysteries and revelation by dreams and visions. In the LXX God declares his name, plans, secrets, and demands (Ex. 6:3;

33:12; Dan. 2:28-29; 1 Kgs. 8:36). It can also indicate the divine act of revelation in judgment and grace (Jer. 16:21). In the NT it denotes the (future) divine act of revelation only in 1 Cor. 3:13, when the day of testing will show the quality of our work. More often it refers to the instruction given by the Spirit (1 Pet. 1:11) or the Lord (2 Pet. 1:14). Yet one cannot make any sharp distinction from *apokalýptein* (cf. Mt. 11:26 and par.; 1 Cor. 14:30; 1 Pet. 1:12). In the Stoics, Josephus, and the fathers we find the sense "to interpret" (the allegorical interpretation of the OT in Barn. 9.8, and the elucidation of puzzling symbols in Hermas *Similitudes* 5.4.1ff.).

[R. BULTMANN, II, 61-62]

---

dēmiourgós [builder, maker]

Strictly "one who pursues public affairs," then "builder, artisan," then "architect of the world." It has only a secular sense in the LXX, and the only NT instance is in Heb. 11:10, where God is the builder and "maker" of the eternal city. For the relation to *ktístēs*, see *ktízō*. [W. FOERSTER, II, 62]

→ *ktízō*

---

dēmos [people], *ekdēméō* [to be abroad], *endēméō* [to be at home], *parepídēmos* [sojourner]

---

dēmos. Originally "portion," then a. "district," b. "territory," c. "people" of a land or city (sometimes, but not always, derogatory: "mob"). In the LXX it first means "race," "family," later "people." In the NT it means the "people" of a place; cf. Acts 12:22 (Jerusalem), 17:5 (Thessalonica), 19:30, 33 (Ephesus).

ekdēméō, endēméō. These two terms denote being abroad and staying at home. Not used in the LXX, they occur in the NT in 2 Cor. 5:6ff. to express the thoughts (1) that bodily existence is absence from the Lord, and (2) that full fellowship with the Lord is possible only apart from this existence. We and the Lord are in separate spheres. Faith overcomes the separation (v. 7) but is not the final reality. We thus desire to be out of the present sphere and at home with the Lord so as to enjoy the full fellowship of sight. Nevertheless, even in the present sphere the desire to please the Lord gives direction to life (v. 9).

parepídēmos. This rare term has the sense of "one who is (temporarily) a resident alien." It occurs in the NT in 1 Pet. 1:1; 2:11: Christians are only temporary residents on earth and must not let their lives be shaped by its interests. They are a Christian diaspora whose true home is the place of their election. Heb. 11:13 applies the same term to the OT examples of faith. Hellenistic thought has a similar idea of earthly life as a sojourn but with a dualistic nuance. [W. GRUNDMANN, II, 63-65]

---

diá [through, during, with, etc.]

A. *diá* with Genitive.
1. Spatial "through" or "through . . . to" (Mt. 7:13; Mk. 10:25; Jn. 10:1; Rom. 15:28).

2. Temporal a. "through a whole period" (Lk. 5:5), b. "during part of a period" (Acts 5:19; 16:9), c. "after a time" (Mk. 2:1; Gal. 2:1). "Within" occurs in Mk. 14:38.

3. Modal a. of manner, "through," "in," "with" (Lk. 8:4; Jn. 19:23; Rom. 8:25), b. of accompanying circumstance "with," "among," "in spite of" (Acts 14:22; 2 Cor. 2:4; Rom. 2:27); the reference in 1 Jn. 5:6 seems to be neither to Christ's baptism and death, nor to baptism and the eucharist, but to baptism as a sprinkling with Christ's blood (cf. 1 Pet. 1:2). There is a personal genitive in 2 Tim. 2:2.

4. Instrumental a. with genitive of cause "by means of," "with," "through" (Rom. 3:27, the law; 3:22, faith; Acts 15:11, grace; Rom. 5:10; Col. 1:20, Christ's death; perhaps 1 Tim. 2:15, childbearing; possibly too Mk. 6:2, Christ's hands; Acts 11:28, the Spirit), b. with genitive of person "through the mediation of" (Mt. 1:22, the prophet; Gal. 3:19, angels; references such as Jn. 1:3; Acts 10:36; Col. 1:20, etc. in which Christ mediates God's action in creation, miracles, judgment, etc., and also Jn. 10:9; 14:6; Heb. 7:25; Rom. 5:2 in which he is a Mediator for us, although not in the sense that it is we who set him in motion; cf. also believing through him in Jn. 1:7; Acts 3:16; 1 Pet. 1:21).

5. Causal a. "in consequence of," "on account of," "on the basis of" (Rom. 8:3, the flesh; 2 Cor. 9:13, the proof of the service; 1 Cor. 1:1, the will of God; Rom. 12:1, the mercies of God; 15:30, Christ and the love of the Spirit; 2 Cor. 10:1, the meekness and gentleness of Christ), b. "by," "for the sake of" with a personal reference (Mk. 14:21; Acts 12:9, etc.), and many references to Christ in which Christ is the author of authority (Rom. 1:5), fruit (Phil. 1:11), comfort (2 Cor. 1:5), peace with God (Rom. 5:1), triumph (Rom. 8:37), acceptance with God (Heb. 13:21), resurrection life (1 Cor. 15:21), final deliverance (1 Th. 5:9); cf. also Rom. 1:8; 2 Cor. 1:20; 1 Pet. 4:11; Heb. 13:15, in which the initiative lies with Christ, so that we never find verbs of asking with the formula "through Christ"; it expresses the constitutive significance of Christ for Christians.

B. *diá* with Accusative.
1. Spatially "through . . . to" (cf. Lk. 17:11, though in view of the order [Samaria and Galilee] "through the borders," i.e., "between," seems more likely here).

2. Modally, Gal. 4:13: "in" bodily infirmity. The genitive would be more correct for this, hence the translation "because of" is sometimes preferred, but it yields no real sense.

3. Causally "on account of," "for the sake of," with a certain final element when the accusative of person is used (e.g., Mk. 2:27; 1 Cor. 8:11), and sometimes the accusative of thing (e.g., Mt. 15:3, 6; 1 Cor. 9:23; Phil. 2:30). The double *diá* in Rom. 4:25 offers some difficulty in view of the tension between a purely causal rendering of the first half and the parallelism of the statement. The point is perhaps that Christ died "because of our sins and in order to expiate them" (cf. 1 Tim. 1:16). In Rom. 11:28 the Jews are enemies in order that salvation may come to the Gentiles but beloved on account of the fathers; the parallelism here is purely rhetorical.

[A. OEPKE, II, 65-70]

---

diabállō [to accuse], **diábolos** [the devil, Satan]

diabállō. The basic sense is "to separate from," "to be set in opposition," "to be hated" (passive), "to accuse," "to repudiate," "to give false information." The only NT instance is with reference to the unjust steward in Lk. 16:1: "accused."

diábolos.

A. Linguistic.

1. The main use is for complaint or calumniation, i.e., "calumniator," "talebearer."

2. Josephus has *diabolé* for calumniation or accusation, but not *diábolos*.

3. The LXX, too, has *diabolé* for calumniation, enmity, and *diábolos* for accuser, and it also uses *diábolos* for the devil as the accuser, adversary, or seducer (1 Chr. 21:1; Job 1; Zech. 3:1ff.).   [W. FOERSTER, II, 71-73]

B. The OT View of Satan.

1. The *śāṭān* is basically the enemy (cf. 1 Sam. 29:4; Ps. 71:13), but specifically the legal accuser (Zech. 3:1) who is placed at the right hand of the accused (cf. Ps. 109:6). Ezek. 21:28-29; 29:16 express the same concept in another term (cf. 1 Kgs. 17:18). On the prophetic view the enemies that God raises up against Israel are also accusers on God's behalf (cf. 1 Kgs. 11:14ff.).

2. Job offers the picture of a heavenly accuser—not a demonic being, but an official prosecutor who comes before God at special times and is part of his entourage. This accuser can act against Job only with God's approval and on God's behalf. A sinister element enters in, however, with his power to use natural disasters and sickness. In Zech. 3:1ff. we again have the accuser at a trial, although here grace overrules law and the accusation is quashed. The OT references to *śāṭān* are infrequent and the concept is not central. Only in 1 Chr. 21:1 (and possibly 1 Kgs. 22:19ff.) does the idea of a tempter occur. The legal element is still present in 1 Chr. 21:1 but Satan (now a proper name) is hostile and harmful. As distinct from Persian dualism, Satan is still under God and the event recorded is not removed from the divine plan of salvation. The OT Satan embodies a threat from God's world, whether as divine prosecutor or as destructive principle. In postcanonical works we find an absolutizing tendency in which Satan is the chief of a hostile kingdom and an absolute principle of evil. Behind this are many motifs, e.g., the ancient dragon, the serpent of paradise, and marriage with angels, in addition to the impact of Persian ideas.

        [G. VON RAD, II, 73-75]

C. The Later Jewish View of Satan. The few OT references undergo considerable development in pre-NT Judaism. The following points may be noted: a. Azazel and his hosts are subjugated to Satan; b. demons are autonomous; c. the main function of Satan is still that of prosecutor; and d. there is no fall of Satan from heaven. In the main, Satan aims to disrupt the relation between God and humanity, or Israel, by temptation (e.g., of Abraham or David), by accusation before God, and by interference in Israel's history. Satan may be resisted by good decisions, human merit or suffering, external aid (Moses, Michael, or the angels), and even by God himself. Satan is not the lord of this world, and although he is sometimes linked with the evil impulse, this is not a force that enslaves us. In some works Satan does not occur at all, being replaced by, e.g., angelic witnesses or several satans. Since all these ideas are fluid, Satan can sometimes be depicted as an exalted angel expelled from heaven, linked with legends about demons and the evil impulse, and even related in Gnostic fashion to the material world, but these are deviations from the main tradition. In this context one should consider names like Sammael and Azazel.

D. The NT View of Satan. As regards names, we find *Belíar* in 2 Cor. 6:15, *Satanás* and *diábolos* in Revelation, and such terms as *ho ponērós, árchōn toú kósmou* *toútou, theós toú aiṓnos toútou, árchōn tḗs exousías toú aéros,* as well as *drákōn* and *óphis. Satanás* is perhaps closer to Palestinian usage than *diábolos;* the two alternate in John and Revelation, while Paul usually has *Satanás* but *diábolos* occurs in Ephesians and the Pastorals. The two main features of the NT concept are the antithesis between God and Satan and the presence of God's kingdom in Christ. In opposition to God Satan is prince or even god of this world (Lk. 4:6; 2 Cor. 4:4), claiming the honor that belongs to God. The unredeemed are under his lordship (Mt. 6:13; Mk. 3:27; Acts 26:18; Col. 1:13). They belong to him (Jn. 6:70; 8:44; 1 Jn. 3:8; Acts 13:10). Their works are works of the *diábolos* (1 Jn. 3:8). His aim is to separate from God. A murderer (Jn. 8:44) and liar (1 Jn. 3:8), he uses various hurtful processes (Mk. 3:23ff.; Lk. 13:11, etc.). The demons are subject to him. His ultimate weapon is death (Heb. 2:14). He is behind paganism and magic (Acts 13:10). If he is still the accuser, the whole of this aeon is finally his. Nevertheless, with Christ the kingdom of God destroys the devil's kingdom, and Satan is cast from heaven (Rev. 12; Jn. 12:31; Lk. 10:18), so that he loses the right of accusation. This does not happen without a struggle against Christ, as at the temptation (Mt. 4:1ff.), and at the end (Lk. 22:31). Conflict continues with the community (cf. Acts 5:3, and the warnings of Rom. 16:20; 1 Cor. 7:5; 1 Th. 2:18; Eph. 4:27, etc.). Satan especially desires to snatch away the seed that is sown (Mk. 4:15). But the battle has been won (1 Jn. 2:13), and the church may thus resist with confidence (Eph. 6:10ff.). In the end-time Satan will summon up antichrist and enjoy some temporary success (Rev. 13:2; 2 Th. 2:9-10), but he will then be bound for the millennial period and after another brief interlude destroyed. While Satan is given certain powers by God, and can prevent journeys (1 Th. 2:18) or tempt believers (1 Tim. 5:15), the community is so secure in faith that the blows of his angel (2 Cor. 12:7) and delivering up to Satan (1 Cor. 5:5; 1 Tim. 1:20) can come within God's gracious operation. In 1 Tim. 3:11 and 2 Tim. 3:3 the meaning is "calumniator." "Devil," however, is the more probable sense in Jn. 6:70 and Eph. 4:26-27. This is also suggested by the use of the article and the singular in 1 Tim. 3:6-7, although "calumniator" is also possible here.

→ *Satanás*   [W. FOERSTER, II, 75-81]

diangéllō → *angéllō; diagongýzō* → *gongýzō; diathḗkē* → *diatíthēmi; diairéō, diaíresis* → *hairéomai*

---

diakonéō [to serve],   *diakonía* [service],   *diákonos* [servant, deacon]

---

diakonéō. This word for service, as distinct from *douleúō* (to serve as a slave), *therapeúō* (to serve willingly), *latreúō* (to serve for wages), and *leitourgéō* (to do public service), carries the basic nuance of personal service.

A. *diakonéō* outside the NT.
1. The concrete sense is basic: a. "to wait at table," b. "to care for," and c. (comprehensively) "to serve." For the Greeks service is undignified; we are born to rule, not to serve. Service acquires value only when it promotes individual development, or the development of the whole as service of the state (or ultimately as service of God). If this demands some renunciation, the idea of self-sacrificial service finds little place.

2. In Judaism, service is not thought to be unworthy; hence a deeper understanding of it develops. The LXX does not use *diakonein,* but has *leitourgein, latreúein,* and even *douleúein.* Philo has *diakonein* for "to serve" with an echo of waiting at table. Josephus has it for "to wait at table," "to obey," and even "to render priestly service." The commandment to love one's neighbor offers a solid basis for sacrificial service, but in later Judaism tends to be weakened by the distinction between the righteous and the unrighteous and the construing of service as meritorious rather than sacrificial.

B. *diakonein* in the NT. By exalting service and relating it to love of God, Jesus both sets forth a completely different view from that of the Greeks and purifies the Jewish concept.

1. The sense "to wait at table" occurs in Lk. 17:8; Jn. 12:2. An astonishing reversal takes place when the returning master rewards his servants by waiting on them (Lk. 12:37). Jesus himself is similarly present as one who serves (Lk. 22:27). Hence when he asks who is greater, the one who sits at table or the one who serves, the obvious answer that the Greeks would give is wrong. Yet Jesus does not substitute an answer that is theoretically opposite. Instead he points to himself, for as the Son of Man who is also Lord of the kingdom, he institutes a new pattern of human relationships which extends even to waiting at table or washing the feet (Jn. 13:4ff.). In Acts 6:2 *diakonein* means "to supervise the meal," i.e., its whole provision, preparation, and organization. This *diakonein* as love in action is set in tension with the *diakonía toú lógou* as the proclamation of love. Most likely what was involved was not just the distribution of portions to those in need but the arranging of common meals, and the radical issue might well have been that of table fellowship rather than wrangling about the better portions; if so, the appointment of the Hellenistic Seven takes on added significance. *diakonein* is also used for Martha's serving in Lk. 10:40 (cf. Jn. 12:2) and that of Peter's mother-in-law in Mt. 1:31. When the angels serve Jesus in Mk. 1:13; Mt. 4:11, they, too, are probably bringing him food after the period of fasting.

2. The wider sense "to serve" reflects the same transvaluation of values as the narrower meaning. Waiting at table may well be included in Lk. 8:3, but the term covers many activities in Mt. 25:42ff. Here service of others is service of Christ and involves personal commitment. Worldly rulers lord it over their subjects but the concern of the disciples is with God's kingdom, the way to which leads through suffering and death that has service as its point. Hence the only path of greatness for Christians is to become the servants and even the slaves of all (Mk. 9:35; 10:44). More than table service is now involved; all kinds of sacrificial activity on behalf of others, as exemplified by Christ's own self-offering, are required. Service of others is service of God, and it may entail service even to the point of death itself (Jn. 12:25-26).

3. The life of the community is thus a life of serving. Every *chárisma* is given (1 Pet. 4:10) in stewardship, and the *charísmata* comprise gifts of word and gifts of action, the latter especially being described as *diakonein.* Timothy, Erastus, Onesimus, and Onesiphorus (Acts 19:22; Phlm. 13; 2 Tim. 1:18) offer examples. The prophets rendered an advance service (1 Pet. 1:10ff.), and the apostles also do service (cf. 2 Cor. 3:3: "a letter *diakonētheísa* by us"). This service cannot be proud, self-righteous service; it is discharged only by God's power and to his glory.

4. A particular service of Paul's is the collection for Jerusalem (2 Cor. 8:19). Thus he uses *diakonōn* when he says that he goes to Jerusalem with help for the saints (Rom. 15:25). This is a single instance of the more general service of the saints which is commended in Heb. 6:10.

5. In 1 Tim. 3:10, 13 *diakoneín* has the official sense "to serve as a deacon."

diakonía.

1. In the NT this first means "waiting at table," "providing for physical sustenance," or "supervising meals" (Lk. 10:40; Acts 6:1).

2. A wider meaning is "the discharge of a loving service." The *diakonía* of Stephanas is an example (1 Cor. 16:15). It is linked with works, faith, love, and patience in Rev. 2:19. All that edifies is covered in Eph. 4:11-12. There are various ministries (1 Cor. 12:4ff.), but all are rendered to the Lord. Acts of care must have been included (1 Cor. 12:28). *diakonía* comes between *prophēteía* and *didaskalía* in Rom. 12:7, but preaching is itself *diakonía* in Acts 6:4, i.e., the offering of the gospel as the bread of life. Preachers, then, have a ministry of reconciliation (2 Cor. 5:18-19). The angels are a model (Heb. 1:14). If trying to live by the law is a ministry of death, faith in the gospel is a ministry of the Spirit or of righteousness (2 Cor. 3:7ff.).

3. A more specific sense is "the discharge of certain obligations," e.g., by the apostles (Rom. 11:13; 2 Cor. 4:1), evangelists (2 Tim. 4:5), or assistants such as Mark (2 Tim. 4:11). Activity in office is the point in Col. 4:17, though whether Archippus is a deacon or not is uncertain.

4. The collection is a *diakonía* (Rom. 15:31; 2 Cor. 8:1ff.; cf. Acts 11:29-30); it is no incidental matter, but a true act of Christian love.

diákonos.

A. **General Uses of** *diákonos.*

1. "Waiter at a meal" (Jn. 2:5, 9).

2. "Servant of a master" (Mt. 22:13). Christians are servants of Christ (Jn. 12:26), but as such must serve one another (Mk. 9:35; Mt. 20:26).

3. Figuratively "servant of a spiritual power" (2 Cor. 11:14-15; Eph. 3:6-7; Gal. 2:17). In Rom. 15:8 the point is that Christ is a servant of Israel. In Gal. 2:17 the idea might be "promoter" (by allowing table fellowship with Gentiles, Christ is extending the realm of lawbreakers), but "servant" is possible if the thought is that of Christ indwelling the believer who is found a sinner.

4. As a *diákonos* of the gospel, the apostle is a servant of Christ (2 Cor. 11:23) or of God in a special way and with special cares and responsibilities (2 Cor. 6:3ff.). Paul often uses *doúlos* in this connection (Rom. 1:1 etc.; Tit. 1:1).

5. By his ministry Timothy, too, is a servant of God (1 Th. 3:1ff.) or of Christ (1 Tim. 4:6). Epaphras is a fellow servant (Col. 1:7), and Tychicus a servant in the Lord (Eph. 6:1).

6. Pagan authorities are servants of God appointed to maintain order (Rom. 13:1ff.).

7. Paul calls himself a *diákonos* of the church (Col. 1:25) because of his divine commission. He and Apollos are servants of God and the church as they use their gifts to bring people to faith (1 Cor. 3:5).

B. **The Deacon as a Church Official.**

1. Sometimes *diákonos* is used for the bearer of a specific office (translated *diaconus*, not *minister*, in the Vulgate) (cf. Phil. 1:1; 1 Tim. 3:8, 12). In Phil. 1:1 deacons are mentioned along with bishops. It is unlikely that these are two terms for the same people, but we are not told what the offices involve. Deacons are also found alongside bishops in 1 Tim. 3, which tells us that they are to be blameless, temperate, with one wife, ruling their houses well, not double-tongued or avaricious, holding the faith with

a clear conscience. That their duties were those of administration and service may be deduced from the title, the qualities demanded, their relation to bishops, and the use of *diakonía* in the NT. That they took their origin from the Seven of Acts 6 is unlikely in view of the work of the Seven in evangelizing and preaching, but there may be an indirect connection. Two offices perhaps arose on the model of the *archisynágōgos* and *hypērétēs* in the synagogue, although these served only in worship, and direction of the synagogue was in the hands of the elders. The terms, unlike the parallel *presbýteros*, were taken from the Gentile world, being adapted from a mainly secular use to describe developing functions in the churches. In the secular world *diákonos* could be used to describe such varied people as messengers, stewards, bakers, assistant helmsmen, and even statesmen. The use in the LXX was also secular, as in Prov. 10:4. Josephus, however, calls himself a *diákonos* of God, and for Epictetus the Cynic is a servant of God. Cultic connections can also be seen on inscriptions, but usually with some reference to the serving of food. In the church this original sense persists, since providing food is a model of practical service and a common meal stands at the heart of worship. Like bishops, deacons emerge fully with the passing of the first apostles, prophets, and teachers (cf. 1 Clem. 42.1ff. and its use of Is. 60:17; also Did. 15.1; Hermas *Visions* 3.5.1). With the development of a single bishop, deacons become more subordinate to the bishop, and a threefold structure is worked out, with more explicit directions for the work of deacons, and in Rome, e.g., the allocation of seven districts to the seven deacons.

2. An order of deaconesses also arises. Phoebe is a *diákonos* in Rom. 16:1; the reference is probably to an office, although some see more general service. In 1 Tim. 3:11 we may have either deaconesses or the wives of deacons. Later an order has in fact developed in which widows play a special part, and in some places virgins. This order was never strong in the west, and decayed in the Middle Ages.

[H. W. BEYER, II, 81-93]

diakrínō, diákrisis → *krínō; diallássō* → *allássō*

---

dialégomai [to converse], *dialogízomai* [to ponder, discuss], *dialogismós* [discussion, doubt]

---

dialégomai. From the basic sense "to converse," we go to a. "to negotiate," b. "to address," c. "to speak." The LXX uses the word for a. "to speak" (Is. 63:1), and b. "to treat with" (Ex. 6:27) or even "contend with" (Judg. 8:1). In Josephus *dialégomai* means a. "to discuss," b. "to make a statement," and c. "to treat of something." In Philo it refers either to conversation or to divine or human speech. Discussion is not at issue in the NT, where 1. Heb. 12:25 has in view God's address, 2. Acts 17:2; 18:4, 19 the public lectures Paul gave, and 3. Mt. 9:34 and Jude 9 disputing— in the former case that of the disciples among themselves, in the latter the dispute between Michael and the devil about the body of Moses.

dialogízomai.

A. *dialogízomai* in the Greek and Hellenistic World. The following are the main senses: 1. "to balance accounts," 2. "to ponder," and 3. "to discuss" (sometimes technically for "to hold a convention" for administrative or judicial purposes).

B. *dialogízomai* **in the NT.**

1. The first meaning is "to ponder" (Mark and Luke). The addition *en taís kardíais* makes this clear in Mk. 2:6; Lk. 3:15; it is unnecessary in Lk. 1:29; 12:17.

2. The second meaning is "to converse, discuss" (e.g., Mk. 8:16; 11:31; Lk. 20:14). The absence of *en taís kardíais* shows that this is the probable sense in Lk. 5:21; in v. 22 Jesus traces back the external utterance to the internal source.

dialogismós.

A. *dialogismós* **in the Greek and Hellenistic World.** The meanings are 1. "reckoning," 2. "deliberation," with the nuances "thought" and "plan," 3. "discussion," 4. "convention," and 5. "judicial inquiry."

B. *dialogismós* **in the NT.**

1. "Evil thoughts" is the predominant sense in the NT (Lk. 2:35; Mk. 7:21; Lk. 9:47; Rom. 1:21). In view of the more flexible LXX use, we see here how deep is the NT conviction that our sinful nature extends to our thinking and our very heart.

2. Sometimes the term denotes "anxious reflection" or "doubt" (Lk. 24:38: torturing doubts; Rom. 14:1: worrying about trifles; Phil. 2:14: murmuring; 1 Tim. 2:8: probably questioning rather than contention).

3. "Discussion" or "argument" is probably the sense in Lk. 9:46.

4. "Bad decisions" rather than deliberations or thoughts fits best in Jms. 2:4.

[G. Schrenk, II, 93-98]

diamartýromai → *martyréō; dianóēma, diánoia* → *noéō*

---

diasporá [dispersion]

A. *diasporá* **outside the NT.**

1. Outside the biblical sphere the only use seems to be for the dispersion that we are to leave behind in a movement toward divine harmony.

2. The LXX uses the term for the dispersion of Israel among the Gentiles (Dt. 30:4; Neh. 1:9), or for the people as thus dispersed. There is no technical Hebrew term corresponding to the technical use of the Greek *diasporá;* such varied expressions occur as leading away, deportation, and exile.

3. The milder Greek term probably developed because passage of time softened the harsh experience, voluntary emigration took place, and the final benefits mitigated the idea of divine judgment (Is. 35:8; Jer. 23:24). Jews are recorded in some 150 places outside Palestine, are enabled to gain new adherents, and thus regain a sense of pride. Only with the loss of a national center after A.D. 70 does the wound of expatriation become more severe again in spite of the attempts of Josephus to gloss over its significance.

4. Philo in his one use of the term seems to be psychologizing the actual situation (as he does Abraham's migration from Ur); he divests the idea of eschatological significance and understands it in an ethical sense.

B. *diasporá* **in the NT.**

1. The NT has the customary use in Jn. 7:35, when it is asked whether Jesus will go to the dispersion and teach the Greeks (either Hellenistic Jews or Greeks among whom the Jews of the dispersion reside).

2. In Jms. 1:1 and 1 Pet. 1:1 a question arises whether the authors have in mind Christian Jews, in which case the sense is literal, or Gentile Christians, or Christians in general, in which case it is probably figurative. In Jms. 1:1 the "twelve tribes" are most likely Christians, who are now the people of God with the heavenly Jerusalem as their true home, so that at present they, too, are dispersed among the nations. If this is the reference, the recipients are simply Christians, both Jews and Gentiles. In 1 Pet. 1:1 the nature of the genitive (without article) causes some difficulty; it may be partitive if Jewish Christians are being singled out, or epexegetical or qualitative if the reference is to all Christians. In any case, the deeper meaning is probably theological, as in Jms. 1:1. "Exiles" and "dispersion" are not tautological; the one word looks to the land in which the recipients are strangers, the other to the land which is their true home. [K. L. Schmidt, II, 98-104]

diastolḗ → *stéllomai; diastréphō* → *stréphō; diatagḗ, diatássō* → *tássō*

---

diatíthēmi [to control, arrange], *diathḗkē* [testament, covenant]

---

diatíthēmi. This word has such varied meanings as "to distribute," "to establish," "to dispose," "to handle," "to put up for sale," "to expound," "to lecture." The only senses that are important in relation to the NT are a. "to control by free choice," b. "to make a testamentary disposition," and c. "to make an arrangement." The LXX mainly has sense c. but with a clear suggestion of disposing (cf. Gen. 9:17).

1. In the NT we find "to determine," "appoint" in the eschatological promise of Lk. 22:29. No idea of making a will is present. As the Father by free resolve has ordained a kingdom for Jesus, so by a similar free resolve he has ordained that the disciples should reign with him. Elsewhere the term is used with *diathḗkē* (Acts 3:25; Heb. 8:10) to denote God's sovereign disposition in salvation history.

2. In Heb. 9:16-17 *ho diathémenos* means "the testator." [J. Behm, II, 104-06]

diathḗkē.

A. The OT Term *bᵉrît.*

1. Equivalents to the LXX diathḗkē. The LXX mostly uses *diathḗkē* (270 times) for Heb. *bᵉrît* and only occasionally for other words, normally where there is the implication of a legal relationship (cf. "testimony" in Ex. 27:21, or "law" in Josh. 4:16).

2. Etymology and Terminology of bᵉrît. Attempts to establish the etymology have been unsuccessful. A connection has been seen with *bārâ,* "to eat bread with," but in actual usage no connection with meals can be established. Nor is there much support for a basis in a similar dubiously attested root meaning "to perceive" or "to determine" (1 Sam. 17:8). The Akkadian *birītu* ("bond") calls for consideration but has no sure backing. Nor does the usage offer much help. "Cutting" suggests a sacrifice. The covenant may be "with" or "between." Terms such as "to be in," "to break," "to transgress" are common but are too colorless to bring out the local sense, and "to establish," "to keep," and "to maintain" show merely that we have something fixed and valid.

3. The Concept of the Covenant in the OT. Two main groups of statements call for discussion, those in which the covenant is between God and humans, and those in which it is between humans. There are also some figurative instances. In view of the two types of covenant, it is tempting to see a distinction between religious and secular covenants, but since the former follow the same legal pattern as the latter, and the latter have sacral assurances, it is better to seek the distinction in the purpose and the resultant nature of the covenants. When humans alone are concerned, the covenant is legally determined; when God is a participant, the legal notion is used to clarify a theological situation. We thus have a legal covenant on the one hand and a theological covenant on the other (although also with a legal aspect). The point of the theological covenant, however, is not merely to bring legal order into religion; to the extent that it does this, it still expresses a genuine insight of faith. Analysis of the covenant leads us to the living basis of OT religion, since it raises the question of our standing with God. The covenant alone, of course, does not answer this question, nor should we use it as a kind of common denominator of Israel's history. Yet it is a distinctive concept, much used by those who, like Ezekiel, have legal interests, less so by the preexilic prophets. Its prominence is due to its simplicity as a concept which crystallizes decisive historical experiences and preserves the truth in them.

4. *The Covenant as a Legal Institution.* As regards human covenants, the example of David and Jonathan is instructive. When Jonathan covenanted "with" David, he placed under legal guarantee a spontaneous love which seemed to demand self-commitment for its definitive confirmation. The legal concept thus supports the deep friendship. While simply giving recognition and confirmation to it, it also makes it a legal fellowship with sacral guarantees. It is thus contracted in the presence of Yahweh and with the taking of a mutual oath. Personal exchange precedes it (1 Sam. 18:4), so that David becomes as Jonathan himself. In many instances, of course, the element of affection is less strong and hence the legal aspect is the more prominent. Thus Laban proposes a covenant with Jacob because of the mutual lack of trust (Gen. 31:44ff.). A cairn is built to record the event. An appeal is also made to God as witness or judge. An oath is taken, and relatives are invited to a sacral meal. The following points are important: a. the use of the word "to cut"; b. the divine attestation; c. details of the agreement; d. the oath; e. the sacrifice; and f. the sharing of a common meal. There might be variations in individual cases, but solemn agreements would always follow a similar pattern. The social significance of the covenant is high, since it was in virtue of it that the tribes came together and the monarchy was established. Blood relationship is the first bond, but this is extended by the legal fellowship embodied in the written covenant. Where blood relationship is plain, the legal bond exists already; where it is less plain or absent, an analogous legal relationship is set up by the covenant, which makes the participants brothers and sisters with a totality no less valid than that of blood relationship. Hence no firmer guarantee of peace, security, and loyalty can be established, especially since regard for the covenant is also a religious duty (cf. Am. 1:9). The significance of blood in the ritual may be connected with kinship (cf. Ex. 24:8; Zech. 9:11). The ritual of Gen. 15:8ff. seems to support this. Here Yahweh himself makes covenant with Abraham to allay the latter's insecurity, but the procedure is similar to that which was probably followed in a human covenant (cf. Jer. 34:18b, where the judgment for falsity to the covenant corresponds to the cutting up of the calf in the ceremony). Whether or not sacrifice is involved here may be debated, but in time the ritual is less important; the covenant itself becomes the true heart of the matter as relations become more complex. The covenant with Assyria in Hos. 12:1 represents an international extension which weakens the original significance, since different divine authorities are appealed to and the responsibility of the participants is consequently diminished. The emergence of the covenantal aspect brings to light the fact that usually the participants are not equals; the granting or

guaranteeing of security plays an important part, and this means that there is often an initiative on the one side whereby an imposition of will takes place. This is especially important when we come to the theological covenant.

5. *The Theological Covenant.* This arises when God is one of the participants and not merely a guarantor. Parallels to the OT exist wherever a family relationship with the deity is discerned (cf. a phrase like "Baal of the covenant" in Judg. 8:33, and also the national or social compacts between kings and gods), but nowhere except in the OT does this ordering of the relation between God and his people become a comprehensive system with ultimately universal implications. The concept arises early, for the confederation that was liberated from Egypt seems to have derived its strength from the idea of a theological covenant with Yahweh with its fixed promises and obligations. Such an idea presupposes an actual event whereby God elected Israel, and Israel in turn elected God (cf. Ex. 24:8; 34:10; Josh. 24). If in Josh. 24 it is Joshua rather than God who takes the initiative, he does so only because God is already the God of Israel who brought Abraham out of Ur, freed the tribes from Egypt, and gave them the promised land. Israel is thus bound to acknowledge Yahweh. When it does so, a covenant is made "with" the people, the terms are written in a book, and a stone is erected in witness. Since God is *king,* this covenant has all the poetry of kingship, the theocracy is legally recognized, and yet at the same time, since it is *God* who is king, the divine initiative and legal obligation have an added force. The transcendent events attending the conclusion of the covenant at Sinai express the added solemnity even though the meal that is held in the divine presence preserves the thought that close fellowship with God is instituted and confirmed. The narrative in Ex. 24 admirably expresses the fact that something new is introduced which runs quite contrary to ordinary religious experience. The basic thought is that God is willing to act to give his people shalom. God gives Israel the assurance that he will be her God if she walks in his ways, and Israel declares that she will be his people, and keep his laws, on the understanding that he will set her high above all nations (Dt. 26:17-18). If a pedagogic element seems to be present here, which almost assumes the parity of the partners, we also find a healthy stress on the knowledge of God that accepts his will and sees that its aim is fellowship, so that God's dealings are not incalculable, and the impulse to approach God is freed from paralysis and referred to the norm of the command. What is echoed here is the experience of Judg. 6:24: The Lord is shalom. This is presupposed even when Hosea transfers the concept to the more emotional sphere of marriage, when Amos questions the privileges of a disobedient Israel, and when Jeremiah (30–31), seeing the danger of clinging to God purely on the ground of legal obligation, looks forward to the new covenant in which the law is written on the heart and its observance is thus self-evident. [G. QUELL, II, 106-24]

B. The Greek Term *diathēkē*.

1. This word is used in classical and Hellenistic Greek for "order," "institution."

2. It is also a technical term in law for "last will and testament"; in the Hellenistic period the testator has full powers and his orders are binding.

3. Aristophanes uses the term once for "agreement" or "treaty."

4. Dubiously attested is "ordinance" or "disposition," but there are hints that this was a common sense before it narrowed down to "last will and testament."

C. The Transition from *berît* to *diathēkē* in the LXX and Jewish Literature.

1. In using *diathēkē* for *berît* the LXX has a covenant or legal compact in view. It seldom uses the real Greek word for "treaty," i.e., *synthēkē*. When God is the author

of a *diathḗkē,* a treaty relationship is at issue, but the link with such words as *nómos, entolaí,* and *krímata* shows that an "ordinance" is often what is really meant. Even when a treaty relationship is suggested, God's disposing is the dominant factor. This is due in part to the meaning of the Greek word, but also to the fact that the translators see that the Hebrew term itself goes beyond the idea of a contract and conveys the idea of a binding expression of the divine will. To be sure, *diathḗkē* brings out this element more strongly, so that the new covenant of Jer. 31:31ff. can be conceived of only as a divine gift of grace, a declaration of God's saving will in relation to which Israel can be only a recipient. We thus have a significant development of the Hebrew term even though its essential content is preserved.

2. The apocrypha and pseudepigrapha present a similar picture, relating *diathḗkē* to the law, using *synthḗkē* for "treaty," construing the holy covenant as God's revealed will, and finding its content in the promised salvation. Thus a combination of legalism and eschatological hope marks the use of *bᵉrît* in the Damascus Document.

3. Philo uses *synthḗkē* for "treaty" and reserves *diathḗkē* for the divine "disposing." In his allegorizing he imports the Greek sense of "last will and testament," but he realizes that this is not the true sense in the LXX, and the LXX concept of God's gracious will (revealed in history) shines through the enveloping imagery.

4. Rabbinic Judaism maintains the legal side, considers the many covenants, relates the covenant to circumcision, reflects on the blood of the covenant, and in connection with Jer. 31:31ff. stresses the writing of the law on the heart.

D. The NT term *diathḗkē*.

1. diathḗkē in Paul. Of the 33 NT instances nine are in Paul. (Seventeen of the others are in Hebrews, four in the Synoptics, two in Acts, and one in Revelation.) In Gal. 3:15ff. the legal language shows that Paul is borrowing an illustration from Hellenistic law; as a valid will cannot be contested or altered, so God's original "testament" cannot be changed by the law. The point is not that God's *diathḗkē* is like a human will, simply that it has the same inviolability. In Rom. 11:27 God's saving disposition in history is obviously the meaning. The covenants of Rom. 9:4 are the declarations of God's will in the OT with their promises and commands. In Eph. 2:12, again, the covenants are covenants of promise. In 2 Cor. 3:6 the new covenant of which Paul is a minister is related to the gospel and marked by the Spirit, so that we are reminded of Jer. 31:31ff. The old covenant, too, is God's. Hence it has its own glory and has been transcended only because its provisional conditions cannot be met. The same comparison occurs in the typology of Gal. 4:24ff.: the slave Hagar represents the Sinai covenant which reduces to bondage, the free Sarah the heavenly covenant which grants liberation. Both are orders in the divine history; they are distinguished only by the different conditions prevailing in them. In Paul, then, the covenant is understood strongly in terms of divine operation and unconditional validity. The one divine will governs salvation history and climaxes in Christ who is both the *télos nómou* (Rom. 10:4) and the fulfilment of every promise (2 Cor. 1:20).

2. diathḗkē in Hebrews. In Hebrews the situation is much the same as in Paul. With other legal terms, *diathḗkē* is used by way of illustration in the popular sense of "last will and testament" in 9:16-17. Yet even here the new covenant of which Christ is a mediator bears the distinctive OT sense, for it involves redemption from the sins committed under the first covenant. The idea of a will is introduced only as a comparison to show why the death of Christ is necessary for the fulfilment of the covenant. Obviously the comparison cannot be pressed, and it certainly does not fix the meaning of *diathḗkē* elsewhere, e.g., in 8:8ff.; 9:15; 12:24. The central concept in Hebrews is that of the new covenant. This replaces the old covenant which was given at Sinai (9:20), was linked to the cultus (9:14), and involved transgressions (9:15). It carries the gifts of salvation whose guarantor is Christ. His blood, then, is the blood of the covenant (10:29; cf. Ex. 24:6). By his heavenly priesthood he fulfils the first and imperfect covenant. The two declarations of God's saving will, in their relationship and distinction, are typologically construed.

3. *diathḗkē in the Synoptists.* Only Luke (including Acts) uses *diathḗkē* to any extent. In Lk. 1:72 the context shows that the reference, as in the OT, is to the declaration of God's will in promise, salvation, and self-commitment. The age of salvation means mercy in remembrance of the *diathḗkē,* and thus testifies to God's rule over time and history. The use in Acts 3:25 is similar; God's saving will is a reality in Jesus. Acts 7:8 bears a reference to circumcision (Gen. 17:10). In Mk. 14:24 (cf. Mt. 26:28; Lk. 22:20; 1 Cor. 11:25) Jesus calls the wine at the Lord's Supper the blood of the *diathḗkē,* or the new *diathḗkē* in his blood. The point is that the blood, or death, of Jesus establishes the new *diathḗkē* and the wine represents it. The saying is based on Jer. 31:31ff. (and possibly Is. 42:6; 49:8). There is no idea of a last will and testament. Jesus by his death effects God's saving will. The new covenant is correlative to the kingdom. As the kingdom expresses God's lordship, the covenant expresses the saving will of God that constitutes its goal and insures its validity. In both form and content, then, the NT use of *diathḗkē* follows the OT use except that we now pass from prophecy to fulfilment. The *diathḗkē* is God's disposing, the mighty declaration of his will in history, by which he orders the relation between himself and us according to his saving purpose, and which carries with it the authority of the divine ordering.

[J. BEHM, II, 124-34]

diaphérō → *phérō; diaphtheírō, diaphthorá* → *phtheírō*

---

didáskō [to teach], *didáskalos* [teacher], *nomodidáskalos* [teacher of the law], *kalodidáskalos* [teacher of what is good], *pseudodidáskalos* [false teacher], *didaskalía* [teaching], *heterodidaskaléō* [to teach strange doctrine], *didachḗ* [teaching], *didaktós* [taught], *didaktikós* [able to teach]

---

didáskō.

A. *didáskō* outside the NT.

1. Common from Homer, this word denotes teaching and learning in the wide sense of imparting theoretical and practical knowledge with the highest possible development of the pupil as the goal. There is little religious use, and the term has a strong intellectual and authoritative bearing. Thus it can also mean "to demonstrate." When used in connection with choral training, it comes almost to have the sense "to perform."

2. It occurs some 100 times in the LXX (mostly for the root *lmd*). While various kinds of instruction can be meant (cf. 2 Sam. 22:35; Dt. 31:19), God's will is the special object, with a volitional as well as an intellectual reference. God himself, the head of a house, or the righteous may do the teaching. As distinct from secular usage, where the aim is to develop talents, the OT relates teaching to the totality of the person.

3. In later Judaism teaching signifies instruction in the law for the right ordering of the relation to God and neighbor. The secular use may still be found (e.g., teaching a trade), but to give teaching in the law, or even to give a scholarly exegetical opinion, is the predominant sense.

B. *didáskō* **in the NT.** Of some 95 instances, almost two thirds are in the Gospels and Acts (and only ten in Paul). The unambiguous meaning is "to teach."

1. The didáskein of Jesus according to the Synoptists.

a. *didáskein* is one of the main functions of Jesus (Mt. 4:23; 9:35; 11:1). He teaches in the synagogues (Mt. 9:35) and the temple (Mk. 12:35) as well as outside.

b. The form of his teaching is that of a typical teacher of the age. At Nazareth he reads Scripture, seats himself, and expounds the passage (Lk. 4:16ff.). He also sits to teach in Mt. 5:1ff.; Mk. 9:35; Lk. 5:3.

c. The material of Jesus is also traditional. He starts from Scripture in Lk. 4:16ff.; Mt. 5:21ff. Yet he does not stop at the law and opposes casuistic exposition. He aims to order all life in relation to God and neighbor (Mt. 22:37ff.), appeals to the will, and calls for decision for or against God. Like the rabbis, he finds a revelation of God's will in Scripture (cf. Mt. 5:17-18). The main difference lies in his own self-awareness as the Son. It is in virtue of his person that his teaching causes astonishment (Mk. 1:22; Mt. 7:28-29). Thus, while he will not absolutize the law, he follows its true line of teaching by claiming the whole person with a view to education and reformation. In this sense he is the end of the law (Rom. 10:4), and the Gospels can refer to teaching in the absolute when they speak of the teaching ministry of Jesus. While this is the common rabbinic use, it would sound odd to Greek ears. Yet even Luke has it, for the connection with Jesus himself gives his teaching an absolute sense.

d. A novel feature in the Gospels is the absence of the intellectual emphasis which is common everywhere else among Greek writers (classical, postclassical, Hellenistic, and even Jewish Hellenistic), and which develops in rabbinic exegesis in an effort to check the disintegrating force of Hellenism, so that in some circles studying the law can be ranked higher than doing it. In this respect Jesus with his total claim represents what is perhaps a truer fulfilment of the OT concept.

2. didáskein in the Johannine Writings.

a. Many of the passages here follow the same pattern of use as in the Synoptic Gospels. There are, however, some distinctive verses. In Jn. 9:34 the idea that the man born blind might teach them is indignantly rejected by the opponents of Jesus. In Rev. 2:14, 20 the reference is to the teaching of Balaam and Jezebel. Other verses, which need separate treatment, deal with the teaching of God and the Spirit.

b. In Jn. 8:28; 14:26; 1 Jn. 2:27 the use of *didáskein* suggests the presence of direct inspiration or revelation. No Hellenistic models have been found for this; it is best to understand it in the light of the teaching of Jesus. Thus the idea in Jn. 8:28 is that of the unity of will of the Father and the Son. In 14:26 the disciples are given a share in this as they continue the ministry of Jesus. In 1 Jn. 2:27 this teaching by anointing (the Spirit) offers a safeguard against false teachers who also raise total claims. If the meaning in these verses verges on "to reveal," it is because the subject of teaching is Jesus himself. Similarly in Lk. 11:1 *didáskein* expresses the thought of a readiness for total subjection to the direction of Jesus and is thus parallel to the confession in Mt. 16:13ff. and Jn. 6:60ff.

3. The *didáskein* of Early Christianity.

a. Even during the life of Jesus, the disciples, too, begin to teach (Mk. 6:30). It becomes part of their commission in Mt. 28:20 as a presupposition of either *baptízein* or *mathēteúein* and with Jesus' own *didachḗ* as its content. In Acts 4 the apostles teach in the name of Jesus (v. 18), proclaiming resurrection (v. 2). If this involves OT interpretation, it culminates in a call to repentance. In outward form, they, too, follow Jewish practice (cf. Acts 5:25). Exegesis and exhortation form the main body of teaching, even at times to the point of instruction in the law (Rom. 2:21; Acts 15:1). In this respect a new beginning has to be made in view of the fulfilment of the law in Jesus (Heb. 5:12).

b. Christian teaching, then, aims primarily to show from Scripture that Jesus is the promised Messiah. In this sense it is "teaching about the Lord Jesus Christ" (Acts 8:31). The combination with *kērýssein* here gives a comprehensive picture of the apostles' work. They impart facts, but in such a way that one must either accept them or reject Scripture. Opponents, of course, saw here a teaching contrary to Moses and the law (Acts 21:21, 28). The word of God that Paul taught in Acts 18:11 probably has the same sense, not of the general message of salvation, but of the message of salvation on the basis and in the light of OT Scripture.

c. If Paul uses the term *didáskein* infrequently, this is probably because he worked in circles where the OT was less known. For him, therefore, teaching is the instruction that is given to churches at their founding (2 Th. 2:15; Col. 2:7; Eph. 4:21) so as to strengthen them against Jewish attacks. In Rom. 12:7 the setting is edification and thus the reference is probably to those who give directions for Christian life. In Col. 1:28; 3:16 *didáskein* occurs with *noutheteín* in a pastoral and ethical connection. It is used similarly in 1 Tim. 4:11; 6:2; 2 Tim. 2:2; Tit. 1:11 except that now there are official teachers. Tit. 1:11 shows that the link with Scripture is still intact. If Paul does not seem to make the OT a book of ethical instruction, he obviously uses it in his own teaching (cf. Rom. 3:31). But he seeks to base his *didáskein* primarily on that of Jesus (cf. Gal. 5:14), on his love and self-sacrifice even to the death of the cross (Phil. 2:1ff.). In this way he prevents disruption through the interposition of particular teachers (cf. Mt. 23:8).

didáskalos (→ *rhabbí*).

A. The Usage and Character of *didáskalos* among the Greeks.

1. The Usage. This word is attested from the Homeric hymns, the feminine also occurring. It means "instructor" as a. "schoolmaster" or b. "chorus master." Since dramatists often acted as players and directors, it also came to have the sense of "poet."

2. The Character of the Word. The rational and technical element is strong from the outset. The teaching of skills and development of aptitudes is especially included. The word is apposite wherever systematic instruction is given. Thus Philo can apply it to a priest giving instructions about leprosy, and for him God, too, is the teacher of the wise, with a strongly intellectualistic bias.

3. The Consequences of the Character of the Word for the Use of didáskalos. The character of the word enables us to see why Socrates rejects the term, Epictetus adopts it, and the LXX for the most part avoids it.

a. Socrates in Plato *Apologia* 33ab will not be called a *didáskalos* because he does not want his statements to be made into a binding system. He does not disparage the intellectual, but aims to carry the person beyond this to moral action. He also seeks to do this for everyone, and thus resists the formation of schools.

b. In contrast Epictetus is proud to be called a *didáskalos*, for as the teacher of a system he is helping to bring his followers to perfection (*Dissertationes* 1.9.12).

c. The LXX has *didáskalos* only in Esth. 6:1 and 2 Macc. 1:10. In Esther the use is the regular Greek one, but in Maccabees Aristobulus is called *didáskalos* as an expositor of the law, so that the word has a special meaning (parallel to *didáskōn*) as one who gives direction in the way of God. The general use for paid or official teachers worked against its more widespread adoption in this sense.

B. *didáskalos* in the NT.

1. *The Usage.*

a. The term occurs 58 times in the NT. 48 instances are in the Gospels, 41 refer to Jesus (29 in direct address), one to the Baptist, one to Nicodemus, one to the teachers among whom the boy Jesus sat, two to the teacher in relation to the disciple. Elsewhere there are references to *didáskaloi* as a group in the churches (Acts 13:1; 1 Cor. 12:28-29; Eph. 4:11). The author calls himself a *didáskalos* in 1 Tim. 2:7; 2 Tim. 1:11. In Rom. 2:20; 2 Tim. 4:3; Heb. 5:12 the context gives us the sense.

b. The usage shows that when Jesus is addressed as *didáskalos*, the term, unlike *kýrios*, does not denote any special respect. The relation between teacher and disciple as set forth in Mt. 10:24-25 is in accord with the usual rabbinic pattern. The teacher here is one who expounds the divine will as laid down in Scripture. When the term is applied to others such as the Baptist or Nicodemus, it consistently means a person who indicates the way of God from the law.

2. *Jesus as didáskalos.*

a. The addressing of Jesus as *didáskalos* shows that outwardly he fits the picture of a rabbinic teacher. He teaches as the latter does, and has a similar band of students around him. The parallel use of *rhabbí* in Jn. 1:38; Mt. 26:25; Jn. 3:2 helps to confirm this. So does the performance by the disciples of many of the duties of disciples, e.g., rowing the boat (Mk. 4:35ff.), handing out food (Mk. 5:37ff.), procuring the donkey (Mk. 11:1ff.), and preparing the Passover (Mt. 26:17ff.). Others, too, honor Jesus as a teacher, e.g., Peter's mother-in-law (Mt. 8:15), Martha (Lk. 10:40), and the ministering women (Lk. 8:3).

b. Jesus, then, does not arouse hostility by his manner or by what he teaches, for even scribal circles recognize that he teaches God's way in truth (Mt. 22:16). To be sure, he has not received official instruction, but he might still have founded a school, debated his opinions, and been widely tolerated. He does not do this, and consequently stirs up violent opposition, because he raises an absolute claim, and does this, not just as a prophet, but in his own name, associating himself directly with God as the responsible bearer of his will who is one with him. He offers himself both as the one who fulfils the law and as the way to its fulfilment (Mt. 5:17, 20).

c. The person of Jesus gives *didáskalos* a new weight. It stamps him as the new Moses who gives the law a universal sweep. This explains why he can simply be called *ho didáskalos* (Mt. 26:18), and why the term is not appropriated by the disciple. Acceptance of the rule of Mt. 23:8 is not just a formality. It is a recognition that salvation is only in Jesus, that he is the absolute *didáskalos*, and that Moses finds himself fulfilled in him (Jn. 5:45-46). If the term plays little part in primitive Christian proclamation, it is because an event (the crucifixion and resurrection) is the central thing rather than a body of teachings.

3. The didáskaloi of the Early Christian Community.

a. The references to Christian *didáskaloi* in Acts and the epistles are in keeping with Jewish and early Christian usage. Thus in Jms. 3:1, especially if the letter is early or derives from rabbinic Judaism, the meaning is the expositor of the law who makes a right fulfilment possible.

b. In 1 Cor. 12:28-29, Eph. 4:1, and Acts 13:1 *didáskaloi* are mentioned after or with (apostles and) prophets. Again they are expositors who edify by their clearer understanding. The order is material, not hierarchical. The apostles are giving way to pastors and the evangelists to teachers. Similarly in 1 Tim. 2:7; 2 Tim. 1:11 the work of teaching constitutes a part of Paul's apostleship which the teachers will continue.

c. A change takes place in the early church when in Alexandria, e.g., a new intellectualization takes place with the invasion of Greek wisdom and the teacher is the one who represents an intellectual Christianity and gives instruction in it.

nomodidáskalos (→ nomikós). This word, not found in secular Greek, the LXX, Josephus, or Philo, occurs three times in the NT. The scribes are "teachers of the law" in Lk. 5:17; so is Gamaliel in Acts 5:34; the term is then used ironically in 1 Tim. 1:7 for legalists who do not know what the law is all about and hence are not really called to teach it.

kalodidáskalos. Not attested outside the NT, this term occurs only in Tit. 2:3; the older women are to be "teachers of what is good," especially to younger women.

pseudodidáskalos. Not found prior to the NT, this occurs only in 2 Pet. 2:1, with *pseudoprophḗtai*. The "pseudo-" suggests that both their claim and their teaching are false, as is shown by their rejection of Christ's dominion over their lives.

didaskalía.

A. *didaskalía* outside the NT.

1. The word is common for "teaching," "teaching activity," "rehearsing," and even "drama"; it has a strongly intellectual character.

2. Philo often has the term for objective teaching.

3. In three instances (Prov. 2:17; Sir. 24:33; 39:8) the LXX uses the word for divine instruction; once in the plural (Is. 29:13) it denotes human teachings that have no claim to absoluteness. (In Prov. 2:17 the LXX misreads the Hebrew.)

B. *didaskalía* in the NT.

1. The plural occurs in Mt. 15:9; Mk. 7:7 when Jesus quotes Is. 29:13 against the Pharisees and scribes. Col. 2:22 and 1 Tim. 4:1 also use the plural for other than divine teachings (i.e., human or demonic).

2. The singular occurs when God's revealed will lies behind the teaching. Thus "teaching" (the activity) serves the community in Rom. 12:7. Scripture was written for our "instruction," according to Rom. 15:4. The point in Eph. 4:14 is that we must be on guard against every variable wind which claims to be teaching, and hence to be God's will. Doctrine here is not the individual error as such.

3. *didaskalía* is common in the Pastorals (15 of the 21 NT instances). The relation to God's historical revelation (attested in Scripture and fulfilled in Christ) is plain in 1 Tim. 4:13; 2 Tim. 3:16 (possibly Tit. 2:10). "Sound doctrine" in 1 Tim. 1:10 etc. also means the teaching that relates to God's saving acts and thus leads to salvation.

"Good doctrine" in 1 Tim. 4:6 has the same sense but with a greater stress on content and practical effect. In general *didaskalía* is not a suitable word in Judaism and the NT, since the *didáskalos* has no *didaskalía* of his own. But it fits well in the Pastorals, where the readers tend to reject the *didáskalos* for false teachers and thus to reject the *didaskalía* which he is commissioned to proclaim and from which he cannot be separated.

4. In the early church the word comes to mean the "sum of teaching" which has come down from the apostles. The kerygma thus tends to ossify into dogma.

heterodidaskaléō. This word, which implies a *heterodidáskalos* (cf. Gal. 1:9), occurs only in 1 Tim. 1:3; 6:3 with reference to those who disseminate a different teaching, making peripheral matters the main issue (1:4ff.) and with a Judaizing stress on the law (v. 7).

didachḗ. This word means "teaching," "instruction" as a fact. Its only LXX use is in the title of Ps. 60. In the NT it refers to the whole *didáskein* of Jesus in Mt. 7:28 etc., i.e., his proclaiming God's will in both form and content. This is also the meaning in Jn. 7:16-17. The same applies when the *didachḗ* of the Pharisees and Sadducees is at issue in Mt. 16:12, of the apostles in Acts 5:28, of those who taught the Roman church in Rom. 6:17; 16:17, and of Paul in 1 Cor. 14:6. 2 Jn. 9-10 follows the same pattern, as does Revelation when speaking of the *didachḗ* of Balaam, the Nicolaitans, and Jezebel in 2:14, 15, 24. In Heb. 6:2, however, *didachḗ* means an established and formulated doctrine, and in 13:4 (plural) specific errors against which a warning is issued. The post-apostolic fathers build on this sense, but in the main the NT stress is on God's teaching through Jesus and the apostles, with a consequent enhancing of the Christian sense of mission in its teaching ministry.

didaktós. This word has three senses: a. "taught," b. "learned," and c. "teachable." It is used in the absolute in Jn. 6:45 (quoting Is. 54:13): "taught by God." In 1 Cor. 2:13 the repeated *didaktós* (not taught by human wisdom but taught by the Spirit) shows that Paul relates his distinctiveness to the source of his teaching.

didaktikós. Outside the NT, this term occurs only in Philo with reference to the learning of Abraham. In 1 Tim. 3:2; 2 Tim. 2:24 it is one of the requirements in a bishop. At a time when false teachers are arising, they must be "able to teach."

[K. H. RENGSTORF, II, 135-65]

---

dídōmi [to give], *dōron* [gift], *dōréomai* [to give], *dōrēma* [gift], *dōreá* [gift], *dōreán* [in vain], *apodídōmi* [to give back], *antapodídōmi* [to repay], *antapódosis* [retribution], *antapódoma* [repayment], *paradídōmi* [to hand over], *parádosis* [tradition]

---

dídōmi. Since love is depicted as a gift in the NT, *dídōmi* is a common term, especially in John. Jesus is what he is by God's gift. God gives him his works (5:36), disciples (6:37), name (17:11), all things (3:35). Jesus himself gives his life (Mk. 10:45), himself (Gal. 1:4), his body (Lk. 22:19).

dōron, dōréomai, dōrēma, dōreá. Philo regards this group as more lofty than *dóma, dósis,* but while the latter are rare in the NT, the distinction is fluid; cf. *dóma* for the divine gift in Eph. 4:8. *dōron* is used for human gifts (Mt. 2:11), sacrifices

(Mt. 5:33), money gifts (Lk. 21:1), and God's gifts (Eph. 2:8). *dōréomai* means "to give" (cf. Mk. 15:45; 2 Pet. 1:3). *dṓrēma* means "what is given" and describes God's gifts in Rom. 5:16; Jms. 1:17. *dōreá* also means "gift" but with a legal nuance. It denotes God's gifts in the NT, e.g., the Spirit in Acts 2:38; 8:20, etc.; Heb. 6:4, or more generally the gifts of God or Christ in Rom. 5:15; 2 Cor. 9:15; Eph. 3:7, but always with an implication of grace.

dōreán. "In vain." The basic sense is "for nothing" (Mt. 10:8; Rom. 3:24; 2 Cor. 11:7; 2 Th. 3:8; Rev. 21:6). Other meanings are "without cause" (Jn. 15:25) and "to no effect" (Gal. 2:21).

apodídōmi.

1.a. "To give or do something in fulfilment of an obligation or expectation," e.g., Mt. 20:8 (reward), 21:41 (fruits), Mk. 12:17 (taxes), Mt. 27:58 (Jesus' body), Heb. 12:11 (fruit). b. "To repay as reward or punishment": divine retribution in Mt. 6:4; Rom. 2:6; Rev. 22:12; human retribution in 1 Tim. 5:4. c. "To give back what has been received or kept" (Lk. 4:20 etc.). d. "To sell" (Acts 5:8; 7:9; Heb. 12:16).

2. The thought of divine retribution in the NT sets us impressively under threat and promise. This retribution is future and carries the promise of love and forgiveness as well as judgment. It brings out the personal nature of the relation with God. We do not do good for good's sake but out of love of God and in recognition that we are his. It thus belongs to our very being to be subject to retribution. It is love that posits a creature that is under retribution. Only because of sin does retribution work against us. But since the root is in love, forgiveness is not incompatible with retribution. How God conjoins the two is the secret of his majesty, with which faith enjoys fellowship, but only in subjection to its holiness.

antapodídōmi, antapódosis, antapódoma. The *antí-* here strengthens the idea of recompense (cf. rendering thanks in 1 Th. 3:9, repaying love in Lk. 14:14, divine repayment in Rom. 12:19; Heb. 10:30). The derived noun *antapódosis* denotes the final divine retribution in Col. 3:24, while *antapódoma* is used for God's repayment in the quotation in Rom. 11:9.

paradídōmi.

1. This word is common in the passion story for the handing over of Jesus, e.g., by Judas in Mk. 14:10, by the Sanhedrin to Pilate in Mk. 15:1, by Pilate to the people's will in Lk. 23:25 and to the soldiers for execution in Mk. 15:15. There are parallels in other trials (cf. Mt. 10:17; Acts 12:4).

2. The word has a similar sense in the formula "to hand over to Satan" in 1 Cor. 5:5; 1 Tim. 1:20. Paul probably adopted this phrase; the idea that Satan executes divine judgment is in accord with Jewish belief.

3. The term also occurs for God's judgment on sinners in Rom. 1:24ff.; Acts 7:42; cf. Eph. 4:19.

4. "To give up one's spirit, body, or self" (Jn. 19:30; 1 Cor. 13:3; Gal. 2:20; cf. Rom. 8:32; 4:25) expresses willingness to die, or sacrificial love. The apostles are also "given up to death" (2 Cor. 4:11), though this is never said of Jesus.

5. In Mt. 11:27; Lk. 10:22 the word expresses the authoritative position of Jesus as Messiah or Son of God. All things (not just knowledge) are delivered to him by the Father; recognition of this is what is hidden from the wise and revealed to babes. Conversely, Christ hands back the kingdom to the Father according to 1 Cor. 15:24.

6. *paradoúnai* is a technical term when the object is teaching, e.g., tradition in Acts 6:14 (cf. Mk. 7:13), Christian tradition in Rom. 6:17; 1 Cor. 11:2, the holy commandments in 2 Pet. 2:21, the faith in Jude 3, the matter of the gospel in Lk. 1:2, the commands of the council in Acts 16:4. This *paradoúnai* is oral.

7. The sense "to commend to" occurs in Acts 14:26 (grace) and 1 Pet. 2:23 (the Judge).

parádosis.

1. This word for "tradition" means "what is transmitted" rather than "transmission" in the NT. It has an unfavorable sense when used of the tradition that is added to the law, e.g., that of the elders in Mk. 7:3, 5, or of men in Mk. 7:8. Jesus rejects the validity of additions to the divine law. The use is more comprehensive in Gal. 1:14, embracing written as well as unwritten traditions.

2. Christian teaching is also tradition in 1 Cor. 11:2; 2 Th. 2:15. It must be adhered to by the churches (1 Cor. 15:2). To be valid it must be handed down (1 Cor. 15:3) and must derive from the Lord (11:23), i.e., it must have divine authority. One may see from 1 Cor. 15:3ff. and 11:23ff. that it is older than Paul and is already acquiring a fixed form in his day.   [F. BÜCHSEL, II, 166-73]

diermēneutḗs, -neúō, -neía → *hermēneúō*

---

díkē [justice], *díkaios* [just, righteous], *dikaiosýnē* [justification, righteousness], *dikaióō* [to justify], *dikaíōma* [regulation], *dikaíōsis* [justification], *dikaiokrisía* [righteous judgment]

The Concept of Law in the OT. This concept influenced all social relationships so strongly that it affected theological reflection on the fellowship between God and man. Law is the basis of the OT view of God, and the religious use of legal concepts helps in turn to ethicize the law. Many terms are used to express the relations between God and man, and the conduct governed by these relations.

1. The richness of the Hebrew usage is well expressed by the *díkē* group, especially *dikaiosýnē* and *díkaios*. (For the relevant Hebrew terms, the statistical distribution, and the equivalents, see *TDNT*, II, 174-75.)

2. It is a basic tenet in the OT that God posits law and is bound to it. Recognition of this is a unifying factor in Israel's faith. All law comes from God, and hence God's authority extends to all Israel's historical relationships. God's law is an order of life that cannot be changed or challenged. It is righteous because he is righteous. His ways are right; they thus give us life and security. He is a righteous ruler and judge, as shown already in the victory celebrated in Judg. 5:11. His righteousness extends to other nations, so that order is seen in the world. The righteous can thus appeal to him with confidence when they are the victims of hostility and oppression (Ps. 5:8).

3. God's righteousness is not just static but dynamic. He establishes as righteous those who seek his righteousness. The righteous, then, are those who show fidelity to God's command (Hab. 2:4) and whom God vindicates against their enemies. This vindication may not be synonymous with success. Misfortunes suggest at times that God's judgment means condemnation. Refuge must then be sought in God. But even from this place of refuge a sense of right may be discerned in God (Ps. 62:7ff.). The torment of doubting God's righteousness constitutes the grief of Job. We have to be

able to take God's right for granted in his dealings with us, even if it must sometimes
be projected into a higher sphere than that of human understanding.

[G. QUELL, II, 174-78]

dikē.

A. The Idea of Law in the Classical and Hellenistic Greek World. Law, religious, political, and ethical, forms the basis and center of Greek thought and society.
The starting point is the goddess Dikē. This goddess then becomes the divine, universal, and triumphant principle of law in Solon. With Theognis righteousness transcends mere justice and comprehends all political and ethical norms. The etymology
of *dikē*, while much debated, seems to support this broader usage. The root means
"to give direction," "to indicate," "to posit," "to establish." Hence *dikē* itself has the
sense both of indicating and of what is indicated or established. We thus have the
following development. 1. What is established becomes a state or manner, so that
dikē means a. what is customary, b. what is proper, and c. what has to be. 2. Legally,
what is established is what is laid down by law as a. law, b. legal case or plea or
decision, and c. punishment.

B. *dikē* in the NT. Apart from the variant in Acts 25:15, *dikē* occurs only three
times in the NT, always for punishment. It is retributive justice (even perhaps Dikē)
in Acts 28:4, and eternal judgment in 2 Th. 1:9 and Jude 7.

díkaios.

A. *díkaios* in the Greek and Hellenistic World.
1. General Usage and Meaning. Linked with *dikē*, *díkaios* suggests a. conforming
to custom, b. fulfilling obligations, and c. observing legal norms. There is also d. an
ethical use whereby *díkaios*, having significance for the whole of life, relates to the
four cardinal virtues. The use here is static; even in Plato it ultimately refers to inner
order. In Josephus *díkaios* means virtuous (with a hint of faithfulness to the law). In
Philo the righteous have achieved a healing righteousness and are the true prop of the
human race. Both Josephus and Philo use *díkaios* to describe the OT saints, and they
can both say (Josephus less frequently) that God himself is *díkaios*. In the further
development of the concept e. comparatives and superlatives become common. The
word is also often used f. to describe things as "good," "right," "legal," or "exact,"
"correct" (weights etc.), and even "fertile" (the earth). g. We also find a neuter use
tó díkaion or *tá díkaia* for "what is lawful or right" (e.g., what is due, or retribution,
or duty). Along these lines the term may characterize OT law, or law in general, or
natural law. h. *díkaios* may be used with several verbs in such phrases as speaking or
doing what is right. i. *díkaión estin* is a common phrase for "it is right, or fitting, or
meritorious."
2. díkaios in the LXX. While the usage here is similar to that elsewhere, OT motifs
also exercise a strong influence. The *díkaios* is the person who fulfils obligations to
God and the theocratic society. We have a righteous cause before God only as we meet
the demands of God. In the background, God himself is righteous; he is consistent in
himself and unswervingly faithful to his covenant promises. He does not merely dispense justice as the righteous God; he also grants salvation (Ps. 116:5).

B. The Righteous in the Synagogue.
1. The Righteous. A distinction is made here between the righteous and the ungodly
which serves the concept of rewards and counts on human ability to keep the law. The

righteous are those whose merits outweigh their faults. A more detailed division lists those who keep the law fully, those who do more bad than good, those who do equal good and bad, and finally the penitent. The patriarchs are put in the first class, and many teachers are listed among the righteous. The prayers of the righteous turn God's thoughts from severity to mercy.

2. *The Messiah as the Righteous.* The Messiah is righteous because his whole nature and action conform to God's will. He is often called "our righteousness." Applied to him are Jer. 23:5; 33:15; Zech. 9:9, and only later Is. 53:11b. The messianic age will be an age of righteousness (Eth. En. 38:2). Revelation in the coming time of salvation will be particularly for the righteous.

C. *díkaios* in the NT. NT use draws on the OT and differs sharply from the Greek use (based on the idea of virtue) except in customary or traditional modes of expression which are not closely connected in any case with the Greek conception.

1. *Greek and Hellenistic Contacts.* When Pilate's wife calls Jesus *díkaios* in Mt. 27:19, she probably means no more than "innocent" or "morally righteous." The same applies to Pilate's saying in Mt. 27:4, that of the centurion in Lk. 23:47, and Herod's saying in Mk. 6:20. Formally Paul echoes Greek terminology in Phil. 4:8 but obviously he has in mind action in accordance with God's will. The same is true in Tit. 2:12. Everyday usage may be found in 2 Pet. 1:13; Lk. 12:57; Mt. 20:4; Phil. 1:7, but added depth is given by "in the sight of God" in Acts 4:19 (cf. 2 Th. 1:6).

2. *The Dependence on the OT and Its Supersession.*

a. In content the NT draws largely on the OT. Thus God is *díkaios* in his judgments (cf. Rev. 16:5; 1 Pet. 2:23; Jn. 17:25). Hence his law is also just (Rom. 7:12). But his justice is shown above all in the atoning death of Jesus (Rom. 3:26). God is thus righteous as he who both judges and saves (cf. also 1 Jn. 1:9). This thought rests on the OT but with Christ's sacrifice as the new factor.

b. When applied to Christ as Messiah, *díkaios* refers first to his fulfilment of God's will (Acts 3:13-14; 7:52). But again his innocent death is supremely in view (cf. Mt. 27:4; cf. Acts 22:14). The vicarious nature of this death ("the just for the unjust") comes out in 1 Pet. 3:18 (cf. 1 Jn. 2:1). Yet those who belong to this righteous one must themselves do right (1 Jn. 2:29). Seeking only God's will, he pronounces just judgment, not going only by appearance (Jn. 5:30; 7:24; cf. 2 Tim. 4:8).

c. *díkaios* can be used for the patriarchs (Mt. 23:35), the OT saints (2 Pet. 2:7), and the prophets (Mt. 13:17); cf. the innocent blood of the martyrs (Mt. 23:35). Fidelity to the law is often at issue, but with a stress on the relationship with God in the parents of the Baptist (Lk. 1:6), Simeon (Lk. 2:25), and Cornelius (Acts 10:22). Joseph deals righteously with Mary in Mt. 1:19. The NT adopts the distinction between the *díkaios* and *hamartōlós* (or *ádikos*) but gives it an ironical twist, since all are called to conversion, and while righteous zeal finds recognition (cf. Rom. 5:7), there is a stern rejection of mere appearance or complacency (Mt. 23:28; Lk. 20:20; 18:9). There will be a resurrection of the just (Lk. 14:14), but the context shows that love constitutes the *díkaios*.

d. *díkaios* sometimes denotes the disciple as a person who truly keeps the law or does God's will. One who receives the righteous receives the reward of the righteous (Mt. 10:41). The *díkaioi* will be separated from the *ponēroí* (Mt. 13:49). The *díkaioi* at the last judgment are those who have practiced love (Mt. 25:37). James has disciples in mind when he says that the righteous are oppressed by the rich (5:6) and that their prayers have great power (5:16). What is said about the OT saints is similarly transferred to Christians in 1 Pet. 3:12; Heb. 12:23; Rev. 22:11. It is Paul who tells us how they become *díkaioi*.

e. Paul can accept the distinction between the righteous and the wicked. The *díkaios* is one who as a doer of the law will be vindicated by God's sentence (Rom. 2:13). On the other hand, no one is righteous by doing the law, for all are under sin (3:10). One becomes *díkaios* by receiving God's *dikaiosýnē* as the power and salvation of God. This reception is by faith. In support Paul adduces Hab. 2:4 (Rom. 1:17; Gal. 3:11). Only the *díkaios* will attain to life; but life can be attained only by faith, hence the *díkaios* is the one who is justified by faith. Rom. 5:19 looks ahead to the judgment, when sinners will be presented or made righteous by God's sentence. In 1 Th. 2:10, however, present conduct is the theme; we are righteous as we act according to divine law. In 1 Tim. 1:9, in contrast to a false use of the law, Christians are *díkaioi* because they use their freedom in a way that comports with the divine norm. The bishop must be *díkaios* (Tit. 1:8) in the same sense, unless the point is that he should reach just decisions.

dikaiosýnē.

A. Secular and General Religious Usage.

1. dikaiosýnē in Greek Ethics. Words with -*sýnē* develop with abstract thought, and *dikaiosýnē*, closely related to the Greek sense of law, occurs commonly as a virtue. It denotes a. the civic virtue of observance of law and fulfilment of duty, b. virtue as such, c. one of the cardinal virtues, and d., in mysticism, the power of virtue with which the initiate is invested.

2. The Legal View of the Term. The idea in law is that of distributive justice, i.e., allotting what is due.

3. dikaiosýnē in Josephus and Philo.

a. Josephus has the term for divine justice and human virtue (as a part of piety).

b. Philo speaks of the righteousness of God in the sense of his revelation when he inquires into what is right. He has a highly developed ethical conception in which *dikaiosýnē* is the chief cardinal virtue which originates in the soul when its three parts achieve harmony, and whose work is healing, peace, and joy. It is meritorious, although in the last resort God himself gives it.

B. Righteousness in the LXX.

1. The Righteousness of God. How far does *dikaiosýnē* do justice to the Hebrew concept of *ṣeḏeq* with its strong legal and covenantal component? In the later chapters of Isaiah the idea of a legal dispute is present; God intervenes judicially for the oppressed, so that salvation is closely linked with righteousness. God's righteousness in his judicial reign means that in covenant faithfulness he saves his people. On the whole the LXX expresses this well with its use of *dikaiosýnē,* while also relating it to divine judgment.

2. The Righteousness of Man. The meaning here is observance of God's will (Is. 5:7). There is a close link with truth, e.g., in Wis. 5:6.

C. Righteousness in the Synagogue.

1. The Righteousness of God. The rabbis do not speak about God's righteousness along the lines of Rom. 3:21. (Dt. 33:21 is construed differently.) The Messiah is called righteousness with a connotation of mercy.

2. Righteousness as Human Action. For the rabbis this is especially almsgiving or benevolence, which is one of the most meritorious of works.

3. The Basis of the Rabbinic View. The underlying idea, discernible in the LXX, is that every observance of the law is meritorious. Standing before God depends on whether the good or bad predominates. Alms and works of charity are especially helpful. The last judgment decides whether merit or transgression is greater.

4. The Relation of the Justice of God to His Mercy. In Psalms of Solomon, Jubilees, and the like God's righteousness and mercy are related. God may exercise unexpected mercy in virtue of his righteousness. The rabbis, too, state that the measure of mercy is greater than that of strict justice. Righteousness, then, is thought of as mercy. As mercy is better than legal rigidity even in human justice, so it is with God. Yet uncertainty remains when divine justice and mercy are balanced against one another, for in the first instance the two are sharply contrasted.

D. *dikaiosýnē* in the Non-Pauline Writings of the NT.

1. dikaiosýnē as Just Judgment and Rule. The word can sometimes denote God's just judgment at Christ's return (Acts 17:31; Rev. 19:11; cf. Mk. 16). In 2 Pet. 1:1 it has the sense of God's just rule in guiding the community. The justice of rulers is the point in Heb. 11:33. An odd use is in Heb. 5:13, which seems to indicate that a child cannot understand correct speech.

2. dikaiosýnē as Right Conduct before God. Except in Paul's formula *dikaiosýnē theoú*, the main use is for right conduct that accords with God's will and is pleasing to him. The fact that the relation to God is in view brings this into line with OT thinking.

a. Matthew. This is the consistent usage in Matthew. Jesus is baptized so as to do what is right with God (3:15). The hungering and thirsting of 5:6 is for a right state before God. Yet this righteousness is God's gift (6:33). It is to be sought with his kingdom. It brings persecution (5:10). It includes the practice of piety (6:1). The way in which the Baptist came is that of right conduct (21:32).

b. Luke. The word has the same sense in Luke. Holiness and righteousness are conjoined in the messianic expectation of 1:75. In Acts God seeks and recognizes uprightness, i.e., what is pleasing to him, even among pagans (13:10; 24:25), although this doing of righteousness does not avail to salvation.

c. Peter. The picture is similar here. Forgiveness is the presupposition of a life of uprightness (2:24). Suffering comes for the sake of this (3:14). Noah represents it (2 Pet. 2:5). The libertines leave the way of righteousness (2:21), but the new world will be governed by it (3:13).

d. Hebrews. The same applies here. Christ's exaltation rewards his righteousness in 1:9. Melchizedek is devoted to righteousness in 7:2 (and thus typifies Christ). Noah inherits righteousness, i.e., an acceptable life as the fruit of faith, in 11:7. Conformity to God's will results from training, according to 12:11.

e. John. The main difference in John is a more consistent christological understanding; all righteousness is linked to Christ the *díkaios* (cf. Jn. 16:8, 10). Doing right in 1 Jn. 2:29 demonstrates what Christ embodies as *díkaios*. Its main content is love for one another (3:10). Thus, as Matthew finds in righteousness a gift of God, and Peter bases it on forgiveness, John finds it to be possible only through commitment to Christ.

3. dikaiosýnē in James. In Jms. 1:20 the righteousness of God is right conduct that is given its distinctive form by God. Life in agreement with God's will is viewed as a fruit in 3:18. How we can be righteous before God is dealt with in 2:23-24. The concern here is to combat a dead orthodoxy that divides faith and works. The works that justify are not legalistic observances but the works of loving obedience that Paul calls the fruit of the Spirit. Abraham was justified by a faith which found fulfilment in works. If Paul could hardly have stated the matter in this way, we have to remember that this formulation is more popular in character, and that the practical concern, namely, that the only valid faith is one that produces works, is very much in line with the total proclamation of the NT, including that of Paul himself.

E. *dikaiosýnē* in Paul.

1. Origin and Presupposition of the Pauline Message of Justification. Legal righteousness forms the starting point. The law is a law of righteousness because it demands righteousness (Rom. 9:30). Those who do righteousness live by it (10:5). But this is impossible except for the relative blamelessness of Phil. 3:6. *dikaiosýnē* cannot be achieved by way of law (Gal. 2:21). Salvation is by divine mercy, not in virtue of deeds that we have done in righteousness (Tit. 3:5). In the struggle to understand this, which leads him into conflict with a legalistic Judaism, Paul comes to a new and comprehensive concept of the righteousness of God which offers a new insight into the relation of the law and Christ. The roots are to be found in the OT teaching concerning the judgment of God, the sinful bondage of humanity, the collapse of synagogue piety, and the dependence on God's gracious intervention in Christ if there are to be righteous people who enter into true fellowship with God.

2. The Meaning of the Pauline Use of dikaiosýnē theoú and the Main Elements in the Doctrine of Justification. As used by Paul, the *theoú* in the term *dikaiosýnē theoú* is a subjective genitive. This is God's righteousness, into which we are set. It is a conjunction of judgment and grace which God demonstrates by showing righteousness, imparting it as forgiveness, and drawing us into his kingdom, as the last judgment will fully manifest.

a. The Whole of Humanity. This righteousness of God is not just an individual experience; it is a universal happening in Christ on behalf of the whole race.

b. The Divine Action. It is not just an attribute but shows God at work with an efficacy no less than that of his wrath (cf. 1:17; 3:5, 17, 25-26).

c. The Center in the Cross. It is in the cross that the saving action takes place. But the resurrection is closely associated with the crucifixion, so that justification is not just a declaration, but has a historical core. For this reason Christ may be called our *dikaiosýnē* (1 Cor. 1:30; cf. Rom. 10:4).

d. God Both Is and Demonstrates Righteousness. God is righteous (Rom. 3:25), but his righteousness is an expression of grace that also displays his justice in the concrete form of an act of atonement (Gal. 3:13; 2 Cor. 5:21; Rom. 8:3). Thus justice and grace are actively united for all time and at the deepest level. This means that antinomian laxity is excluded, for forgiveness is an act of judgment which expresses God's uncompromising No to sin. God's righteousness is judicial and gracious at the same time in the one act of salvation in Christ.

e. Forensic Justification. God's righteousness means justification. Righteousness is forensically ascribed to believers. God's judgment achieves this by remission. The justification is no mere "as if," for God's sentence is sovereign. Nor is it the attainment of moral rectitude. The justified are "right" before God. The forensic element, of course, is only a figure, for we are not in the sphere of human justice, but are dealing with the divine Judge who is also unlimited King. We have thus to transpose the legal aspect into the divine key. An act of grace replaces ordinary legal procedure. But this grace, as the legal concept shows, is not capricious. It conforms to true right. The image of God as Judge is tenable inasmuch as human law does to some extent express imperishable divine norms. But it must be understood in terms of the divine act that strictly finds no human parallel.

f. The Relationship to the Term *áphesis,* the *dōreá* Now Imparted, and the State of Justification. Paul sometimes uses words like *aphiénai* or *katallássein* (Rom. 4:7; 5:9-10), but he uses *dikaiosýnē* to show that forgiveness has its basis in the divine right. *dikaiosýnē* is also given and imparted now (Rom. 3:24-25; 5:1; 8:30; 9:30; 1 Cor. 6:11), so that it is God's action as radical deliverance. It is *dōreá* both imparted and received (Rom. 5:17). This imparting governs the whole life of faith; hence one can call justification a state (Phil. 3:9). At the same time, God's righteousness is always that which he displays as well as that which he imparts. Multiplicity in the use of the phrase is justified because the righteousness is always finally and exclusively God's.

g. *dikaiosýnē* and *pístis*. We are drawn into this righteousness by faith. This is the individual side, though it is not individualistic, for individuals become members of the body, and everything depends on the objective divine act. Thus believers are justified when they are washed and receive the Spirit (1 Cor. 6:11), yet not magically (1 Cor. 1:17), for *dikaiosýnē* precedes the sacrament (Rom. 4:11). God's pardoning *dikaiosýnē* issues an authoritative summons which does not make the divine act dependent on the human response but which means that the divine objectivity of salvation is that of a saving relationship, so that "by faith" is used adverbially to define it (Rom. 3:21; cf. 3:26-27). This faith, of course, is not itself to be set in isolation as a psychological force or a virtue or a meritorious work. It is related to its object and is a gift of divine grace, so that *logízesthai* ("to reckon") implies the very opposite of merit.

h. *dikaiosýnē* as the Object of Hope. Present salvation also implies future salvation. Justification is here already, declared in history and grasped in faith as a present reality. Yet its promise transcends time, so that here and now it has an interim character. Faith, then, involves a hope that looks forward confidently to the final sentence but also impels to resolute action. *dikaiosýnē* is an object of hope in Gal. 5:5, and the verb *dikaióō* is often in the future tense (cf. Gal. 2:16; Rom. 3:20; 5:19), or carries a reference to the last judgment (Rom. 5:19; cf. also 10:4ff.). For Paul a last judgment by works does not contradict justification by faith. Judgment has for him a radical depth as the essential background of justification. He can thus preserve a tension between solid confidence and false security. Justification brings us up against the full seriousness of God as this is expressed at the cross. The absolute norms attested by the last judgment both give the cross its validity and impel us to obedience, thus offering full protection against any antinomian perversion.

i. Justification and Mysticism. Justification and the *pneúma* are closely linked in 1 Cor. 6:11; Rom. 10:8-9; Gal. 5:5; cf. also Gal. 3:2, 5 and Rom. 3:28. Justifying faith is also closely linked with union with Christ (Gal. 2:16ff.; cf. 2 Cor. 5:21), where in virtue of Christ's vicarious work we are God's righteousness "in him." Justification, however, safeguards us against any idea of mystical union with God. The expressions are figurative, like the legal phrases; the linking of legal and mystical phraseology shows us that only pneumatology can fulfil the work of justification.

j. *dikaiosýnē* as the Power of the New Life. God's justifying action is not quietistic. It leads to the rule of grace (Rom. 5:12ff.), which is the rule of righteousness. Believers are drawn into the movement of God's righteous rule. This is a movement toward eternal life, so that *dikaiosýnē* and life are interwoven (Rom. 5:17, 21). Through the Spirit, our spirits are alive on account of righteousness (Rom. 8:10-11). For Paul the process of salvation is not a closed one. There is an obedience that leads to righteousness (Rom. 6:16). The pardoning righteousness that is given commits us to righteousness as a living power that breaks the bondage of sin. Hence, while righteousness is not a state or quality, it becomes right action in Rom. 6:16; cf. 2 Cor. 6:7, 14, the fruit of righteousness in Phil. 1:11, righteousness as the substance of the fruit of light in Eph. 5:9, the breastplate of righteousness in Eph. 6:14, training in righteousness in 2 Tim. 3:16, and the crown of righteousness in 2 Tim. 4:8. Justification means subjection to the living power of the creative divine righteousness.

k. The Relation of *dikaiosýnē* to *aretḗ* in Pauline Writings. The Hellenistic concept of virtue does not occur in the NT, but with the stress on *éthos* as opposed to *gnōsis* the Pastorals bring out the element of truth in it when they list *dikaiosýnē* with such exercises as faith, love, peace, and patience (cf. 1 Tim. 6:11; 2 Tim. 2:22). Faith and love, however, show the difference of content.

dikaióō.

A. *dikaióō* in Greek and Hellenistic Writings (including Josephus and Philo).
1. A first meaning (from Pindar) is "to validate," "to establish as right."
2. We then find the more general meaning "to regard as right," with such nuances as "to judge," "to grant," "to agree," "to desire," "to demand."
3. Another sense is "to treat someone rightly," "to secure justice for someone," either negatively as in "to pass sentence," "to condemn or punish," "to pass sentence of death," or positively as in "to represent someone's cause."
4. In mysticism, we find the sense "to become sinless."

B. *dikaióō* in the LXX, Apocrypha, Pseudepigrapha, and the Synagogue. In the LXX the use is forensic but mostly in the positive sense "to pronounce righteous," "to vindicate." Thus we find 1. "to acquit," "to prove innocent," "to champion someone's cause," and occasionally "to make pure." We also find 2. a use for divine or human vindication. Intransitively in the passive the meaning in Gen. 44:16 is 3. "to justify oneself." (For details see *TDNT*, II, 212-14.)

C. *dikaióō* in the NT. In general we almost always find a legal connection here.
1. An unusual meaning in Rev. 22:11 is "to exercise righteousness."
2. Divine vindication is a common reference (Lk. 7:29; Mt. 11:19; Rom. 3:4; 1 Tim. 3:16).
3. "To justify oneself" occurs in Lk. 10:29 (a weaker application) and Lk. 16:15.
4. "Acquitted" or "declared righteous" is the meaning in Lk. 18:4, and with a clear reference to the last judgment in Mt. 12:37.
5. In Paul we first find a. a legal use. The wicked are justified by faith on the basis of God's gracious action in Christ. This justifying is a saving acquittal which takes place in the present. It has the objectivity of relationship, enacted at the cross and apprehended in faith. The sense in Gal. 2:16-17 is that of being righteous in God's eyes. The idea of judgment is always present, but *dikaioún* is a present act of grace through Christ. Yet Paul's use of the term b. also makes a contribution to the question of experience (cf. Gal. 3:8, 11; Rom. 3:24). Once-for-all justification at the cross and personal justification in faith go together. Justification is a finished work of grace, yet the term "by faith" (cf. Gal. 2:16; 3:8, 11) shows that it is also a continuing present, so that we cannot sever the objective act and subjective apprehension. As regards the last judgment, Paul relates *dikaioún* c. to a sentence that is passed in our favor on the whole of our life's work (cf. 1 Cor. 4:4). Whether or not this is always meant when

the future is used is by no means certain. The reference is undoubtedly to the last judgment in Rom. 2:13, but in context the point here is that no one can stand before God as the righteous Judge. Rom. 5:19 probably has an eschatological reference, but here the divine justification enacted at the cross and known as a continuing gift will be consummated in definitive acquittal (cf. Rom. 8:24, 33). With *apó*, d., the verb has the sense of liberation from, as in Acts 13:38-39 (where forensic justification is again the issue). Paul has this usage in Rom. 6:7: crucifixion with Christ means liberation from sin. The basis here is the rabbinic idea of expiation through death. This shows how closely Paul links justification and atonement. The new feature is that this liberating death is that of identification with Christ in his vicarious death.

6. *dikaióō in James*. James speaks three times about being justified by works. The reference is to present justification. Abraham is a righteous man whose works are recognized. This is not said in polemic against Paulinism but in order to stress that true faith is not idle but active (Jms. 2:21ff.).

dikaíōma.

A. *dikaíōma* outside the NT. This term has such varied (legal) senses as a. "ground or claim," b. "written proof," "document," "validation," c. "decree," "statute," "ordinance," d. "sentence," "punishment," and e. "right action" (sometimes as "restitution").

B. *dikaíōma* in the NT.
1. The most common sense in the NT is "statute," "ordinance," especially the divine ordinances in Lk. 1:6; Rom. 2:26; Heb. 9:1 (cultic regulations), or God's moral decree in Rom. 1:32, or the whole law of God in Rom. 8:4.
2. The word is then used for a "right action" in fulfilment of a legal requirement.
   a. With reference to Christ it occurs in this sense in Rom. 5:18 (materially cf. Phil. 2:8). The idea that the meaning here is "sentence of justification" (as in v. 16) hardly meets the parallelism and would entail a subjectivizing of *dikaíōsis zōés*.
   b. The reference in Rev. 15:4 is to God: his "righteous acts" (or judgments).
   c. The "righteous deeds" of the saints are meant in Rev. 19:8.
3. What is at issue in Rom. 5:16 is the "sentence of justification" (*katákrima* being the opposite). Paul can easily change the sense in v. 18, and thus show that Christ's righteous life underlies our justification, because of the different antonym.

dikaíōsis.

A. *dikaíōsis* in Greek Generally. This rare word denotes the validation of the legal norm by punishment, defense, or demand, or it may denote the execution of personal preference. We thus find it for a. "punishment," b. "vindication," c. "demand," d. "arbitrary judgment," and e. "statute."

B. *dikaíōsis* in the NT. In Rom. 4:25 it has the sense of justification by divine acquittal. The second *diá* here denotes the goal. The point is not that the resurrection is needed to actualize justification. For Paul Christ's crucifixion and resurrection are indissolubly united, so that the parallelism of the statement corresponds to the parallelism of the matter. The death is on account of our sins, the resurrection with a view to our justification. In Rom. 5:18 the sentence of justification is again at issue. It is once more related to life as its goal. This life begins here and now, but carries a forward look to the consummation (just as sin will finally result in condemnation).

dikaiokrisía. This rare and late term denotes "righteous judgment," whether as a quality or with reference to the last judgment. In the NT it occurs only in Rom. 2:5, where it refers very definitely to the day of wrath when God, in contrast to those who do the evils they condemn, will judge righteously. 2 Th. 1:5 has *dikaías kríseōs* as two words. That God's judgment is righteous will be revealed in that the persecuted will be granted rest but their persecutors will receive appropriate retribution.

[G. Schrenk, II, 178-225]

diórthōsis → orthós; dikostasía → aphístēmi

---

dichotoméō [to cut in two]

In Mt. 24:51 the reference is obviously to punishment. Behind the term, which means "to cleave," is the ancient penalty of cutting in two with the sword or saw.

[H. Schlier, II, 225-26]

---

dipsáō [to be thirsty, long for], *dípsos* [thirst, longing]

---

1. Literally "thirsting." "I thirst" in Jn. 19:28 realistically depicts Jesus' desire for refreshment on the cross. We are to help the thirsty (Rom. 12:20). The apostles suffer thirst (1 Cor. 4:11). In heaven there will be no more thirst (Rev. 7:16).

2. Figuratively "passionate longing for a spiritual good" (Mt. 5:6), especially salvation (Jn. 7:37). This longing is met in Christ (Jn. 4:14; 6:35).

The idea that giving drink to the thirsty is an act that is pleasing to God is common in the ancient Near East. For a figurative use in the OT cf. Am. 8:11; Ps. 42:2.

[J. Behm, II, 226-27]

Additional Note: dipsáō and cognates in the LXX.

1. The LXX formulates the idea of yearning for salvation. The typology of God's supply of water in the desert (a thirsty land) is important here.

2. Thirst as a figure for the longing for salvation also occurs in Is. 41:18 etc. with a transition to the idea of eating and drinking in God's kingdom (Lk. 22:30).

3. Thirst also depicts the torments of the damned (cf. Lk. 16:24) on the basis of the idea that thirst, and death from it, is a divine punishment.

[G. Bertram, II, 227-29]

dípsychos → psyché

---

diṓkō [to impel, follow zealously]

---

1. "To impel" as a. "to set in motion" (intransitive "to ride," "march," "row," or, generally, "hasten") and b. "to persecute," "expel," in the papyri "to accuse," common in the Psalms for religious persecution. In the NT we find 1.a. in Lk. 17:23: "Do not run after them," and Phil. 3:12: "I hasten toward the goal." But 1.b. is more common for religious persecution (e.g., Mt. 10:23; 23:34; Jn. 5:16; Acts 7:52). Persecution is a test (Mt. 5:44) and a privilege (Mt. 5:10 etc.).

2. "To follow zealously" as a. "to attach oneself to a person" or b. "to pursue or promote a cause." Only 2.b. occurs in the NT. In Rom. 9:30-31 the Jews, unlike the Gentiles, pursue righteousness. Elsewhere Christians are to pursue righteousness (1 Tim. 6:11), the good (1 Th. 5:15), peace (1 Pet. 3:11), love (1 Cor. 14:1), and hospitality (Rom. 12:13).   [A. Oepke, II, 229-30]

---

dógma [decree, doctrine],   *dogmatízō* [to decree]

The basic meaning is "what seems to be right": a. "opinion," b. "principle," c. "resolution," d. "decree," and e. "the law." The verb means "to affirm an opinion," "to establish a decree," "to publish an edict."

1. In the NT sense d. occurs in Lk. 2:1; Acts 17:7; Heb. 11:23.

2. In Col. 2:14 the reference might be to the new edict of God but in 2:20 we definitely have legal ordinances (sense e.), so that the real point in 2:14 is that Christ has canceled these. Eph. 2:15 carries a similar reference to the ordinances of the law.

3. In Acts 16:4 the term is used for the resolutions of the apostolic council. The apostolic fathers then adopt the term for the teachings of Jesus.

[G. Kittel, II, 230-32]

---

dokéō [to believe, seem],   *dóxa* [glory],   *doxázō* [to glorify],   *syndoxázō* [to share in glory],   *éndoxos* [glorious],   *endoxázō* [to be glorified], *parádoxos* [wonderful, contrary to belief]

The problem with this group in the LXX and NT is that *dokéō* retains the Greek sense but the noun takes on a specific religious sense shared by the verb *doxázō*.

dokéō.

1. The first sense is "to believe," "to think."

2. We then find "to appear," "to have the appearance" (Acts 17:18) (cf. "it seems to me," as in Lk. 1:3; Acts 15:22ff.). *dokeín* is contrasted with *eínai* in Greek thought.

3. A further sense is "to count for something," "to be of repute" (cf. Mk. 10:42; Gal. 2:2, 6b—perhaps here a slogan of Paul's opponents).

dóxa.

A. The Greek Use of *dóxa*.

1. This means "opinion" as a. what I think, and b. what others think of me. As a. it may imply expectation or be a philosophical opinion or tenet, though it can also be a mere conjecture. As b. it usually denotes good standing or reputation, although an unfavorable adjective may change this. *Dóxa* as a name has sometimes been linked with light or radiance (cf. the LXX and NT), but it most likely signifies one who stands in good repute.

2. In Josephus and Philo the word has the senses a. "opinion or tenet," b. "honor or glory," c. "splendor," and d. "divine radiance."

B. The NT Use of *dóxa*, I. Here sense a. ("opinion") has disappeared. Sense b. ("repute") occurs, as in Lk. 14:10; 1 Cor. 11:15; 1 Th. 2:6. Sense c. ("splendor") may be found in Mt. 4:8; 6:29; Rev. 21:24; cf. 1 Pet. 1:24; 1 Cor. 15:40-41. We also find the meaning "reflection" or "image" in 1 Cor. 11:7.   [G. Kittel, II, 232-37]

C. *kābôd* in the OT.

1. The Hebrew term *kābôd* has the root sense of something weighty which gives importance, e.g., wealth (Gen. 13:2; 31:1) or honor (Gen. 45:13).

2. In relation to God it denotes that which makes God impressive. Since God is invisible, it necessarily carries a reference to his self-manifestation.

a. This may be in natural phenomena (cf. Ps. 97:1ff.; Ezek. 1:1ff.; Ps. 29). Yet

God cannot be equated with these as though he were, e.g., the God of thunder and every thunderstorm manifested his glory.

b. Ps. 19 makes it plain that God's *kābôḏ* belongs to the higher regions of heaven. Yet if God dwells in heaven, he comes down to the tent of meeting. Thus in Ex. 40:34ff. a cloud covers the tent and God's *kābôḏ* fills its interior as a kind of radiant substance from which emanates the fire that consumes the sacrifice. In Ex. 24:15ff. God's *kābôḏ* is also like a devouring fire (on the mountain), and Moses' face is radiant after speaking with God.

c. Ezekiel has personal visions of the divine *kābôḏ* in which it is accompanied by the cherubim, rides on a throne, has human shape, bears very strongly the character of light, and both leaves the first temple and returns to the second.

d. In some passages the *kābôḏ* of God has the more general sense of "honor," as in Pss. 24:8; 138:5; 66:2. Often God's glory is linked to his name or there is a demand to give God the glory that is his due, i.e., to recognize the import of his deity. God will not give his glory to another. God's glory is also a theme of hope, as in Pss. 72:19; 57:5, 11; Is. 66:18-19. In this regard God's glory is connected with his act of salvation (Is. 40:3ff.). In this act God will be glory for Israel (Zech. 2:8-9) and Israel will be to God's glory (Is. 43:7).   [G. von Rad, II, 238-42]

D. *dóxa* in the LXX and Hellenistic Apocrypha. In this area *dóxa* is a common word. It represents 25 Hebrew terms, but predominantly *kābôḏ*. It becomes identical with *kābôḏ* and hence does not bear the ordinary senses of *dóxa* in secular Greek usage.

a. In the OT the only possible instance of "opinion" is in Eccl. 10:1. In the apocrypha the only examples, apart from Sir. 8:14, are in 4 Maccabees.

b. "Honor" or "reputation" is also rare in the OT; indeed, it is used less in this sense than *kābôḏ*. The few instances are in Proverbs (cf. also Wisdom, Sirach, Maccabees).

c. We find some instances of the meaning "splendor" (which merges into "honor" as in Is. 17:4) and the use of *dóxa* for other Hebrew words for God's power (cf. Is. 30:30; 40:26). The glory of God's majesty is a well-known refrain in Is. 2:10, 19, 21; cf. also Ex. 33:22; Ps. 102:15.

d. The primary sense, then, is the divine glory which comes to expression in God's acts in creation and history. *dóxa* is the divine nature in its invisibility or its perceptible manifestation, as at the giving of the law, or in the tent or temple. God is the God or King of glory (Pss. 24:7ff.; 29:3). To give him glory is not to impart something he does not have but to acknowledge the honor that is his due (Is. 42). A term that was initially subjective ("opinion") is thus adapted to express something that is absolutely objective, the reality of God.

e. In the apocrypha, LXX usage is followed except for a slight regression in favor of the sense of human honor or magnificence (as in Proverbs).

E. *kābôḏ* in Palestinian Judaism.

1. The Targums translate *kābôḏ* by *yᵉqārā'*, and often have it to avoid anthropomorphisms.

2. *kābôḏ* is important in rabbinic Judaism for either human or divine honor. God recognizes true human honor. In God's case, his glory is his nature. Moses has a share of this, and imparts a lesser share to Joshua. The glory that God grants to rulers or to those who fear him is no more than power or dignity. Yet the first man had a part in God's glory, and if this was lost at the fall, its restoration is the goal of salvation history (cf. expositions of Dan. 12:3). The Messiah in particular will be invested with

God's glory and will restore the radiance lost with the fall. On the other hand, eternal bliss is more commonly depicted as contemplation of the divine glory than participation in it.

3. These various ideas are all particularly strong in apocalyptic: alienation from God's glory, the manifestation of this glory at the judgment, the bliss of contemplating it, the seating of the Messiah on the throne of glory, and the final glory of the righteous.

F. The NT Use of *dóxa*, II.

1. dóxa as the Divine Mode of Being. While the term can denote "reputation" or "power," its main use in the NT is shaped by the OT; it thus becomes a biblical term rather than a Greek one. While individual nuances may embrace divine honor, splendor, power, or radiance, what is always expressed is the divine mode of being, although with varying stress on the element of visible manifestation (cf. Lk. 2:9; 9:31-32; Acts 22:11; Rev. 15:8; 21:23). In the NT again, giving God glory means acknowledging (Acts 12:23) or extolling (Lk. 2:14) what is already a reality. NT doxologies, then, presuppose an *estin* (Gal. 1:5; 1 Pet. 4:11). A peculiarity in John is the almost naive juxtaposition of the use for God's glory and a use for the honor or praise that may be given either by men or God (12:41, 43).

2. The dóxa of Jesus. The NT takes a decisive step by relating *dóxa* to Christ in the same way as to God. *dóxa* then reflects all the dynamism of the relation of God and Christ. Thus Christ is raised by the glory of the Father (Rom. 6:4). He is taken up into glory (1 Tim. 3:16). He is at the right hand of glory (Acts 7:55). Glory is ascribed to him as to God (cf. Lk. 2:14 and Heb. 13:21). He is the Lord of glory (1 Cor. 2:8; Jms. 2:1). The eschatological hope (cf. Is. 40:5) is the appearing of the glory of our great God and Savior Jesus Christ (Tit. 2:13). Most of these references are to the risen Christ, but the revelation of glory at his birth points already to his coming from above (Lk. 2:9). In John, faith also sees the glory of the incarnate Christ (1:14; 2:11; 11:40). This *dóxa* of Christ is not visible in itself. He has to be glorified (Jn. 7:39; cf. 12:23; 13:31; 16:14; the prayer in 17:1, 5). The entry into glory is at the cross (13:31), where God's *dóxa* is acknowledged, but there is also participation in it. It is in the light of the passion that believers, by the Spirit, see Christ's glory.

3. The Believer and dóxa. In the OT the stress lies on seeing the divine *dóxa* (Lev. 9:6; Is. 6:1; 35:2). For the rabbis, too, eternal felicity is contemplation of God's glory. In the NT, however, the emphasis shifts to participation. The righteous will shine, as in Dan. 12:3 (Mt. 13:43). The body is transformed in the resurrection into a body of glory (Phil. 3:21). We are glorified together with Christ (Rom. 8:17; Col. 1:27; 3:4). This is part of the parallelism of Christ's resurrection and ours. Participation in *dóxa* is by participation in Christ. Eternal glory is the goal of our calling (1 Pet. 5:10). In this sinful aeon we fall short of God's glory (Rom. 3:23). But glory is to be revealed to us, and we are to enjoy the glorious liberty of the children of God (Rom. 8:18, 21). What is sown in dishonor is raised in glory (1 Cor. 15:43). Yet the future glory has its roots in the divine purpose and action, so that we may be said to be already glorified (Rom. 8:29-30; 1 Cor. 2:7). The Spirit is the pledge of the new thing that brings glory (cf. Eph. 3:16; 1 Pet. 4:14). This is especially clear in 2 Cor. 3:7ff., which a. contrasts the glory of Moses with the new and greater glory of Christ and b. shows how, beholding the glory of the Lord, believers are changed from glory to glory. The movement here is from present glory to an eschatological consummation of glory. It is effected by the ministry of the gospel as this gives the light of the knowledge of the glory of God in the face of Jesus Christ (4:6). Along the same lines,

Jn. 17 says that the disciples will see the glory of Christ (v. 24), that he is glorified in them (v. 10), and that he gives to them the glory the Father has given to him (v. 22).

4. *The dóxa of the Angels.* As the cherubim bear the divine glory in Ezek. 9:3 etc., and Judaism ascribes glory to the angels, so Heb. 9:5 refers to the cherubim of glory, Rev. 18:1 mentions the glory of the angel, and Jude 8 and 2 Pet. 2:10 call the angelic powers *dóxai* ("glorious ones").

G. **Hellenistic Gnosticism.** The magical papyri and similar writings also use *dóxa* in a special way for "power" or "radiance." That there is a connection between this and biblical usage is most probable, but the later dating of these texts suggests that they depend on Jewish influence (probably in Egypt) rather than vice versa. The same applies to Mandaean and Manichean works. If some Iranian influence may be detected in the whole usage, it will have to be sought in the distinctive OT use of *kābôd,* which is the unquestionable source of the NT view of *dóxa.*

doxázō, syndoxázō. The verb shares the linguistic history of the noun. Outside the Bible it means a. "to have an opinion," "to believe," "to suspect," and b. "to praise," "to value," "to honor." Sense a. does not occur in the LXX, but sense b. is common. The same applies in the NT, where "to honor" occurs in Mt. 5:16; 6:2. But the verb then has the special biblical sense "to give or have a share in the divine glory" (cf. Rom. 8:17, 30; 2 Cor. 3:10; Jn. 17).

éndoxos, endoxázomai. In secular Greek *éndoxos* means a. "according to the customary opinion," a sense which does not occur in the Greek Bible, and b. "honored," "renowned," "magnificent," in which it is used in different ways for honorable people, the glories of Jerusalem, the wonderful acts of God, praise of God, the name of God, and God himself. The verb *endoxázomai,* which is peculiar to the Bible, can refer to human distinction but denotes mainly the magnifying of God's majesty either in those who serve him or in his acts of retribution (Is. 49:3; Ex. 14:4). In the NT the adjective always has the common sense of "honorable" or "magnificent" or "glorious" (clothing in Lk. 7:25; the works of Jesus in Lk. 13:17; the Corinthians in 1 Cor. 4:10; the church in Eph. 5:27). The verb occurs in the NT only in 2 Th. 1, which adapts OT formulas to Christ when it says in v. 10 that Christ will be glorified in his saints and entreats in v. 12 that the name of the Lord Jesus may be glorified in them.

parádoxos. This word, which is common in secular Greek for "an unusual event contrary to belief or expectation," occurs in the NT only in Lk. 5:26, in the ordinary sense, to denote the unusual element in the works done by Jesus.

[G. KITTEL, II, 242-55]

---

dókimos [tested, precious], *adókimos* [inauthentic], *dokimḗ* [testing], *dokímion* [tested], *dokimázō* [to test], *apodokimázō* [to reject], *dokimasía* [testing]

From the stem word *dokḗ* ("watching"), *dókimos* means "tested," and thus a. "reliable," and b. "esteemed," "valuable" (whether persons or things). *adókimos* is the opposite, used of persons. The rare *dokimḗ* means "testing." *dokímion* has the sense of "tested," "genuine," *dokimázein* means "to test," *apodokimázein* "to throw out in the test," and *dokimasía* "testing." The NT gives the group a special application in view of the situation of Christians. Set between salvation on the one side and judgment on the other, they seek attestation.

1. Human life stands under a divine testing which climaxes in the judgment (1 Cor. 3:13; Jms. 1:12). The judgment, however, gathers up the divine testing in history (1 Th. 2:4). The background of this view of testing is to be found in the OT, the last judgment in, e.g., Jer. 11:20, present testing in, e.g., Pss. 17:3; 26:2.

2. The future judgment and the present divine scrutiny fashion a corresponding mode of life. a. Attestation is an urgent question in 1 and 2 Corinthians. The Corinthians do not find in Paul the proof of power that they seek (2 Cor. 13:3). He reminds them that what counts is not human but divine commendation (2 Cor. 10:18). This gives added point to the question of attestation. b. Attestation will be manifested in affliction, i.e., the pressure put on the church in this period when it does not yet see salvation and is exposed to assault from secular and demonic powers. Suffering produces endurance, endurance *dokimḗ,* and *dokimḗ* hope (Rom. 5:3-4). The Macedonians remain joyous and generous in a severe *dokimḗ* of affliction (2 Cor. 8:2). Cf. also Jms. 1:2-3; 1 Pet. 1:6-7: in the former *tó dokímion* is probably "testing," while in the latter it has the more likely sense of "genuineness," but the thought is essentially the same in both. The testing sifts out the *dókimoi* (1 Cor. 11:19), i.e., authentic believers who shun factions, glorify God by obedience (2 Cor. 9:13), attest their love in the collection (2 Cor. 8:8), and, even though the apostle himself may seem to have failed, meet the test themselves by doing good (2 Cor. 13:5ff.). c. The presupposition here is that only believers can meet the test of judgment. Apart from Christ, people are given up to a mind that is *adókimos* (Rom. 1:28), i.e., to an outlook which, since they themselves did not see fit to acknowledge God *(edokímasan),* is unattested or inauthentic.

3. Set under God's searching eye, Christians come under the twofold testing denoted by the verb *dokimázein.* a. They must learn the will of God by testing (cf. Rom. 12:2; Eph. 5:9-10; Phil. 1:10; 1 Th. 5:21). This protects them from caprice and brings them seriously under God's will for their lives. In the same way they are to test the spirits (1 Jn. 4:1). b. At the same time, they are to test themselves (2 Cor. 13:5). In particular, the disorderly Corinthians are to examine themselves when they come to the Lord's table (1 Cor. 11:28). c. Jesus also demands that his followers should test the times, reproaching the people because they can interpret material phenomena but not detect the signs of God's direction of history (Lk. 12:56).

4. In Mt. 21:42 and parallels, quoting Ps. 118:22, Jesus describes himself as the "rejected" stone which has become the head of the corner (cf. 1 Pet. 2:4, 7). We are now exposed to human testing, but what finally counts is the divine test.

[W. GRUNDMANN, II, 255-60]

---

doúlos [slave], *sýndoulos* [fellow slave], *doúlē* [female slave], *douleúō* [to be a slave], *douleía* [slavery], *doulóō* [to enslave], *katadoulóō* [to enslave], *doulagōgéō* [to enslave], *ophthalmodoulía* [eye-service]

---

doúlos, sýndoulos, doúlē, douleúō, douleía. All these words have to do with slavery. In distinction from parallel groups, they denote compulsory service. *oikétēs* comes closest, but it stresses the social position of the slave, while *doúlos* stresses dependence on the lord.

A. The Word Group among the Greeks.

1. Greeks have a strong sense of freedom. Personal dignity consists of freedom. There is thus a violent aversion to bondage. Service may be rendered to the state, but by free choice. Slavery is scorned and rejected. This explains the fierceness with which the Greeks fought for political independence. The only slavery Plato will allow is to the laws. The laws, however, represent the goal of humanity, so that slavery to law is in no way derogatory. Aristotle shows a similar scorn for slavery; for him slaves have no part in the state or true service to it. The Stoics have a broader view of service. Zeus himself summons us to it, so that, while free in relation to all people, we are unconditionally bound to all. Yet the Stoic would never call himself the *doúlos theoú;* he moves through the world as *basileús* and *despótēs,* the very opposite of the *doúlos.* This is the characteristic of the wise. Those who are not wise are slaves, no matter what the form of their bondage (cf. Epictetus, Plutarch, and Philo).

2. This survey shows that the group has no religious significance for the Greeks. It acquires this as Near Eastern religions win new adherents and in so doing change the Greek view of God and our relationship to him. The only apparent exceptions are in Euripides, but these are special instances, e.g., the need to yield to Dionysus, or Orestes' evasion of responsibility by claiming that he is enslaved to the gods. In Greek religion the relationship to the gods is in general a family relationship in which Zeus is father of both gods and humans. Kneeling is no part of religious ceremonial for the Greeks except before chthonic deities, and here only for the sake of proximity. The worshipper is *phílos* rather than *doúlos,* so that it makes no sense to describe service of the gods, or life under the eyes of the gods, as *douleía.*

B. The Word Group on Jewish Soil.
In the Greek Bible, however, the group very largely crowds out the various parallels. The reason lies in its use for the root *'bd.*

1. The relation to this root shows that *doúlos* emphatically denotes the slave and the status of slavery. Thus *país* is used for this root when the normal relationship of a slave is at issue, but *doúlos* when the thought is that of the illegality and unreason of the service. The group then denotes Israel's bondage in Egypt (Ex. 13:3; 14:5; Lev. 26:45, etc.). Jacob accepts the state of a *doúlos* with Laban (Gen. 29:18). When one people falls subject to another, *douleúein* is the proper word to describe it (Judg. 3:8; 1 Sam. 17:9). In contrast, *país* is the proper word in Is. 53 (The Servant of the Lord), since this service is rendered on the basis of an essential relation in the household.

2. Since the group denotes restrictive service, it is the proper term for the relation of ruler and subjects, for it expresses both the power demanded on the one side and the subjection and bondage experienced on the other. Saul's courtiers are his *doúloi* in 1 Sam. 18:5, Joab is David's *doúlos* in 2 Sam. 14:9-10, and the whole people *douleúei* the king in 1 Kgs. 12:7 (where Rehoboam himself is advised to be a *doúlos* to the people in order the more surely to win their *douleía*). An interesting point is that while subordinates use the terms about themselves, rulers do not describe the relationship by the group. An element of decision, whether voluntary or compulsory, is thus assumed.

3. The climax of development is reached when the group comes to be used for the relationship to God. This also involves the sharpest antithesis to Greek and Hellenistic thought. *douleúein* in the LXX is the most common term for the service of God, not just in isolated acts, but in total commitment. The group may also be used for service of Baalim or other gods (Judg. 10:6, 13), but the only right thing for the elect people is exclusive service of the Lord (Judg. 10:16; Ps. 2:11, etc.). For this reason *doúloi*

is a title of honor when conferred on such outstanding figures as Moses (Josh. 14:7), Joshua (Judg. 2:8), Abraham (Ps. 105:42), David (Ps. 89:3), and Jacob (representing Israel, Is. 48:20). The opposite of *douleúein* is disobedience.

4. The Jewish world shares this view of divine service with other Near Eastern peoples, among all of whom the concept of God is one of absolute majesty and supremacy. The uniqueness of Israel is that its whole history is a revelation of God's total claim on the people and on each of its members in virtue of a special status. If the mystery religions also have a concept of slavery to the gods, this is entered into only by the appropriate rituals. Philo adopts the OT view except that for him the use is figurative, the self-sufficiency of God is stressed, and exaltation through the service of God becomes an important factor; the opposite of this service is dependence on creation and a corresponding lack of any spiritual relationship.

C. The Word Group in the NT.
1. Secular Usage.
a. Apart from some instances in the parables, in which the use is hardly a strict one, the word occurs in the ordinary sense only when the position of slaves is at issue, e.g., in Col. 3:22ff.; Eph. 6:8-9. The usage here falls wholly within the contemporary social framework. In the parables this is also true, but the total commitment of *doúloi* and the total claim of the *kýrios* serve here to illustrate the unconditional lordship of God and the unconditional responsibility of believers to him. Thus if slaves have two masters, as might happen, they cannot show the same commitment to both. Similarly, one cannot be a true *doúlos* of God without throwing off mammon (Mt. 6:24).

b. While the NT offers the typical picture of the *doúlos*, it does not hint at scorn or disparagement. It differs in this regard not only from the Greek world but also from Judaism, which tends to accept the lower social, cultic, and ethical status of slaves, to put slaves wholly under the control of their masters, and to regard the term "slave" as a deadly insult.

c. Slaves, then, are fully integrated into the community. If they have the chance of freedom, they are to take it (1 Cor. 7:21). But in any case they come with all believers under the common law of love which in the long run, if applied, necessarily means the end of slavery among Christians. If there is no campaign to abolish slavery, this is not due to otherworldiness, or a situation of eschatological tension, but rather to the fact that redemption, like sin, takes place within existing social structures, so that the first priority is not to change the structures but to achieve a life which is conformable to that of Jesus. Such a life will in due time break down the structures, because the fellowship of a common participation in Christ relativizes social distinctions. Thus Paul points out that Philemon and Onesimus are now brothers (v. 16). He also stresses that the relation to God takes precedence over the mutual relations of slaves and masters (Eph. 6:5ff.; Col. 3:22ff.; 1 Tim. 6:1; Tit. 2:9). Christians lie under this obligation even when their masters (or slaves) are not believers. The overriding freedom of faith that this expresses bears a superficial resemblance to the Stoic's independence of external circumstances, but differs from it in three ways: a. there is no sense of superiority; b. it rests on an act which makes slave and master brothers; and c. this act is the crucifixion and resurrection of Christ for both.

2. Christians as doúloi of God and Christ.
a. The formula *doúlos theoú* is rare in the NT; Christians are mostly called the *doúloi* of Christ. Where used, as in Lk. 1:38 *(doúlē)*; Acts 2:18; Revelation (cf. 10:7; 15:3), it usually has an OT basis. This applies in Acts 16:17 and probably also in

1 Pet. 2:16, since Christians are thought of here as the Israel of God. Jms. 1:1 and Tit. 1:1 are perhaps adopting a prophetic designation rather than describing absolute commitment to God, since in the usage of Judaism the phrase normally covers only outstanding figures (apart from the whole people). *doúlos theoú* becomes more popular in the early church with the development of the idea that the church is the true Israel and a desire to distinguish between Christ as Son and believers as servants, but ideas of merit tend to arise as the phrase comes to denote specially dedicated people.

b. More common is the belief that Christians are the *doúloi* of Christ; Paul in particular represents this conviction. They are already *doúloi* of a sort prior to conversion, i.e., *doúloi* to sin etc. (Rom. 6:6ff., 19; Gal. 4:3, 8, 9), and even to the law (Rom. 7:1ff.). The meaning is that they have totally lost their freedom and are dominated by these forces. Jesus by his saving work rescues them from this *douleía* in a work of liberation (Gal. 3:13; 4:4-5). They thus achieve the freedom of sonship (Gal. 4:5ff.; Rom. 8:15, 23). But sonship does not mean autonomy; it means a new relationship with God. The result is a new service. With his work of redemption Christ has made believers his own possession and now gives them the goals that shape their lives. This new commitment, which is a commitment to righteousness (Rom. 6:19), holiness (1 Th. 3:13), and newness of life (Rom. 6:4), finds expression in the description of Christians as Christ's *doúloi* (1 Cor. 7:22; Eph. 6:6). This entails confession of what Christ has done and acceptance of its practical consequences. It is also a recognition of the freedom which can come only with commitment to Christ, so that there is no contradiction when John speaks of the freedom which the Son brings (Jn. 8:34ff.), or when he has Jesus say that he calls his disciples, not *doúloi*, but friends, for these are friends who do what he commands them (Jn. 15:14-15).

c. The phrase *doúlos Christoú* has a special position when used as a designation, e.g., in the salutations of Paul, James, Jude, and Peter, and also in relation to Epaphras in Col. 4:12. The basis, of course, is the common commitment to Christ, so that the writers, being integrated into the community in subordination to the claim of Christ, cannot seek to dominate it. Yet in this context the term also suggests a specific office (cf. Jms. 1:1; Gal. 1:10) which carries with it the authority of the master himself. In Paul's case (and cf. 2 Pet. 1:1), *doúlos Iēsoú Christoú* runs parallel to *apóstolos Iēsoú Christoú;* the latter describes the outward relation, the former the inner relation which underlies it.

3. Jesus Christ as doúlos.

a. When Jesus washes his disciples' feet, he shows that it is his office, too, to serve, not to seek power or glory, for washing the feet is a servile duty (Jn. 13:1ff.). He also shows, of course, what will be the point of the disciples' own lives as his apostles, for a *doúlos* is not greater than his *kýrios,* nor an *apóstolos* than the one who sends him (Jn. 13:16). Paul gives this lesson a more general application when he tells the Galatians that, just because they are called to freedom, they are to serve *(douleúein)* one another in love (Gal. 5:13).

b. In Phil. 2:7 Jesus is said to take the form of a *doúlos.* The phrase stands in contrast to the form of God in v. 6 and the title *kýrios* in v. 11. It thus shows what the incarnation means for Christ in relation to his inherent glory. It represents the low point on his way of *kénosis* (cf. Jn. 13:1ff.). There is no necessary allusion to Is. 53 (where *país theoú* would be the accepted rendering of the Hebrew). Nor do the terms humility (v. 3) and obedience (v. 8) fully encompass what is involved, for being a *doúlos* involves a new situation (not just an attitude) which is inconceivably different from the prior situation and which carries with it subjection to the death of the cross

(v. 8). Paul's exhortation in vv. 1-5 is thus given a kerygmatic basis in vv. 6ff. This servant form is, of course, the scandal of the gospel, but in God's wisdom it is also its glory (vv. 9-11).

doulóō, katadoulóō. These terms are common from Herodotus and occur in the LXX in the sense "to enslave" both literally and figuratively. Except in Acts 7:6 (quoting Gen. 15:13), the NT use is always figurative. Not "bound" in marriage is the point in 1 Cor. 7:15. A definition of slavery is offered in 2 Pet. 2:19: What overcomes us, enslaves us. Though free, Paul has voluntarily forgone his rights for his work's sake in 1 Cor. 9:9. Commitment to God (or his opponents) is at issue in Rom. 6:18 and Gal. 4:3. Judaizers are trying to enslave believers to their legalistic code in 2 Cor. 11:20. In contrast to being enslaved, Christians are freed by Christ to be responsible *doúloi* of God.

doulagōgéō. This rare word means "to cause to live the life of a slave." Paul uses it in 1 Cor. 9:27 to show that he subordinates his *sóma* to his office and will not allow it to be a hindrance to him in discharging this office.

ophthalmodoulía. Not found outside the NT, this term refers in Eph. 6:6 to a *douleía* of slaves which is outwardly satisfactory but does not express an inner obligation for the sake of God and Christ, so that the eyes of the master are deceived. It also occurs in the plural in Col. 3:22 for the actions that make up this deceitful service.

[K. H. RENGSTORF, II, 261-80]

doché → *déchomai*

---

drákōn [dragon, serpent]

---

drákōn means "serpent," "dragon," or "sea-monster," and is used for Satan in Rev. 12:3 etc. Serpents were commonly regarded as demonic in ancient mythology. They represented the power of chaos as that which opposes God at the beginning or end of things. In the Greek world serpents were also sacred animals. Revelation, however, does not simply appropriate ancient myth. The *drákōn* is the key image for Satan throughout the book, and there is a link with the story of the serpent in Gen. 3. Note: The Greek OT sometimes uses *drákōn* in passages which owe their imagery to the myth of a contest between God and the dragon of chaos, e.g., Job 3:8; Ps. 74:13; Ezek. 29:3; Is. 27:1 (partly perhaps under the influence of Gen. 3:15). Cf. especially Job 26:13 LXX [G. Bertram].   [W. FOERSTER, II, 281-83]

échidna, óphis, Satanás

drómos → *tréchō*

---

dýnamai [to be able], *dynatós* [able], *dynatéō* [to be able], *adýnatos* [unable], *adynatéō* [to be unable], *dýnamis* [ability, power], *dynástēs* [ruler], *dynamóō* [to give power], *endynamóō* [to give power]

Words of this stem all have the basic sense of ability or capability. *dýnamai* means a. "to be able" in a general sense, b. "to be able" with reference to the attitude that makes one able, hence sometimes "to will," and c. (of things) "to be equivalent to," "to count as," "to signify." *dynatós* means "one who has ability or power," "one who is powerful"; the neuter adjective signifies "what is possible or practicable." *dynatéō* means "to have great ability." *adýnatos* means "one who has no ability or strength"; the noun *tó adýnaton* signifies "impossibility" and *adýnatón esti* "to be impossible." *adynatéō* means "not to be able." *dýnamis,* the most important word in the group, means "ability," then "possibility," then "power" both physical and intellectual or spiritual. *dýnastēs* has the sense of "one who can do something" and was early used for "ruler" (including God as ruler). *dynamóō* and *endynamóō* both mean "to give power," "to make strong," "to strengthen."

A. **The Concepts of Power in the Greek and Hellenistic World.** The term *dýnamis* shows that all life in the cosmos is viewed dynamically. *dýnamis* is a cosmic principle. In Pythagorean teaching number is filled with effective force. Plato calls *dýnamis* the absolute mark of being. The Stoics refer to a self-originating and self-moving force. *noús* still underlies *dýnamis* in Aristotle and the Stoics, but *dýnamis* is the basic principle in Poseidonius. In Greek philosophy the cosmic principle is the same thing as God. There is thus little reference to the power of God, for God himself is power. The individual gods are *dynámeis* of the universal force; they personify the capabilities of a neutral deity. In Hellenism the world is a manifestation of the forces that work in and by and on it. To do anything one must know these forces and share in them. Magic is an application of this principle. It seeks contact, not with deity, but with the demonic natural and cosmic forces that stand under deity. Knowing these forces, the magician can mediate them for the good or ill of others. Yet the gods might also intervene directly to help or to heal. This may be seen in the healing miracles of Epidaurus, which are called *dynámeis* ("acts of power"). Acts of divine punishment bear the same name. Humans are outside the forces that rule the cosmos and have to attain to participation in them, especially with a view to salvation from mortality, or from the bondage of matter. The mystery religions are designed to provide the power of salvation in various forms, e.g., by an initiation which will make it possible to be taken up into the cosmic system of forces. The fundamental concept in the Greek sphere, then, is that of a natural force which, imparted in different ways, controls, moves, and governs the cosmos.

B. **The Idea of Power in the OT.** The decisive difference in the OT is that the power of a personal God replaces the neutral force of nature that is equated with deity. Traces of a neutral idea of power may be found in the OT (cf. the power of the ark), but unlike the nature gods, Yahweh is a God of history, so that originally naturalistic elements are all subsumed. Nor is power itself the main thing, but the will which it must execute and serve. The exodus is thus the supreme example of divine power (cf. Ex. 15:6, 13; 32:11; Dt. 9:26, etc.). Dt. 3:24 gives classical expression to the significance of the exodus. God's power is demonstrated in this decisive act at the heart of OT faith and worship. This power is to be declared to the nations, and Israel is to be God's people and to obey and serve him. In time of need, she can confidently seek a further deployment of the same power (cf. Neh. 1:10; Is. 10:33). The description of God as the "lord of hosts" (*dynámeis* is sometimes used for hosts in the LXX) echoes the historical distinctiveness of the OT concept of God and his power, for God is Lord of all the powers, and worship of the powers in the form of astral deities is forbidden (2 Kgs. 17:16; cf. the sharp contrast in Dt. 4:19 and 4:20). To be sure, God manifests himself in the volcano or the storm (Ps. 29), but he does so as the God of history; nature is the theater of his acts and has its origin in his will (cf. Is. 40:26). The same power as fashions history creates and sustains the world (cf. Jer. 27:5; 32:17). It also affects individual destiny. God's superior power (Job 12:13, 16) effects and controls all things, so that in individual need one must look to him for help and draw strength from him (Pss. 46:1; 86:16; cf. Dt. 8:17-18; Is. 41:10). The power of God is not capricious, for it expresses his will and is thus determined by his right-eousness (Is. 5:16). Having the inner energy of holiness, it is effective as the power of judgment and grace, and it serves the manifestation and magnification of his glory (Ps. 24:8). All ideas of magic are thus excluded. We are brought into the sphere of a relationship in which obedience, prayer, and sacrifice replace incantations and rituals. The uniqueness of the OT concept of God and his power issues in doxologies which have parallels in other religions but which are distinguished by their reference to the mighty acts of God in history and by the glow of joy in God, of passion, and of experience of God. For examples cf. 1 Chr. 29:10ff.; Pss. 21:13; 59:16; 2 Chr. 20:6; Dan. 3:27-28.

C. Ideas of Power in Rabbinical and Hellenistic Judaism.

1.a. Awareness of the demonstration of God's power in the exodus persists and indeed is heightened by the Maccabean deliverance. God's greatness is seen in creation and his power in the exodus. Yet creation, too, is the work of the word as an instrument of God's power. Individuals may also rely on God's power.

b. An emphasis develops, however, on the eschatological deployment of God's power. This has an OT basis, as in Is. 2:19; Ezek. 20:33. Many things take place now that are against God's will and are due to subjection to other powers. There is thus hope and longing for a decisive manifestation of God's power in a final conflict. The hostile forces which now lie between God and us are thought of as demons and are sometimes called *dynámeis,* perhaps on the basis of the heavenly hosts of the OT as these are seen in detachment from God. These powers seem to be natural forces personified as angels, i.e., as intermediate beings ruling the realm between heaven and earth. Some are good and magnify God, but others belong to Beliar or Satan, who rules humanity through them. The human race is thus a battlefield of good and bad forces, and paganism worships these intermediate creatures instead of the true and living God. Some influence of Hellenism may be seen in the development of these ideas of demonic *dynámei.*

c. Yet the supremacy of God remains. God's essence is found in his power, so that when the name of God is avoided, power can be used as a designation, as in Mt. 26:64. This is not a hypostatization, but a paraphrase of the divine name. As regards the saving power of God, it is found in the law. The strength that God gives his people is none other than the law. By the law he creates the world, directs his people, and gives sanctification and power to those who obey it. The law is thus saving power as the revelation of God's will.

2. Philo tends more toward Hellenism by viewing God as pure being and thus making a hypostasis of his power. God is the supreme power, but the powers are independent of God, though they belong to his eternal world and are linked to his *lógos* and names. Deriving from the OT an ethical view of God, Philo ascribes ethical functions to the powers. They have their source in God's holiness and they serve the one goal of overcoming human pollution. In Philo, then, the Hellenistic view of power unites with the OT view of God.

D. The Concept of Power in the NT.

1. The Fact of Christ. Like all NT concepts, the NT concept of power receives its decisive impress from the fact of Christ. This fact is obviously linked with the OT view of the Messiah, who is consistently related to the strength of God (cf. Is. 9:5;

11:2; Ps. 110:2; Mic. 5:5). This strength is primarily kingly, but prophetic power is also involved (cf. Mic. 3:8; Acts 7:22 [Moses]; Lk. 1:17 [the Baptist]). The prophetic aspect achieves greater prominence in the NT (cf. Lk. 24:19). Yet Christ is more than a prophet endowed with power; his whole being is a unique one that is peculiarly determined by the power of God. This comes to expression in the parallelism of the Holy Spirit and the power of the Most High in the story of the virgin conception. No attempt is made to describe the mode; the incarnation begins with a conception that transcends normal processes of generation. At the birth of Christ a special and unique act of power rightly gives him the title Son of God (Lk. 1:35). On this basis, Christ is the bearer of the special power of the Spirit in his ministry (Lk. 4:14, 36). As God's essence is power, endowment with power is linked to the gift of the Spirit, and this gift confers on Christ his authority *(exousía)*—an authority which he has the power *(dýnamis)* to exercise in expelling demons or healing the sick (cf. Lk. 5:17; 6:19; 8:46). For this reason the witness of his disciples is that God anointed Jesus with the Holy Spirit and with power (Acts 10:38). The works he does can also be called *dynámeis* (cf. Mt. 11:10ff.; Mk. 6:2; Lk. 19:37; also Acts 2:22). These works differ from similar acts of power in the contemporary world in three ways: a. they have no connection with magic; b. they are done by the word, which is the word of the omnipotent God whose kingdom here enters history and overthrows the rule of hostile forces; c. they presuppose faith both in him who does the work and in those on whose behalf they are done, so that a personal relation is demanded (cf. Mt. 13:58; Mk. 9:14ff.). In faith, all things are possible; there is power (Mk. 9:23). For in faith we share God's rule. The mighty works evoke astonishment and praise (Mt. 13:54; Lk. 19:37), and in Herod, perhaps, an uneasy conscience (Mt. 14:2). John's Gospel does not use *dynámeis*, but with *exousía* and *sēmeíon* employs the verb *dýnasthai*, which shifts the emphasis from the act to the capability (cf. Jn. 3:2). The *sēmeía*, performed in the fullness of messianic power, are unique acts. Jesus can do them only because God is with him, i.e., he has the power of God in fellowship with the Father. In Jn. 9 the blind man, when cured, testifies to the divine *dýnasthai* of Jesus (9:33), and some of the Pharisees agree (9:16). Similarly in Jn. 11, when it is asked whether Jesus could not have healed Lazarus (11:37), he shows his unlimited *dýnasthai* by raising him. It is only in fellowship with Jesus that his disciples also can do things (15:5), but he recognizes at the same time that his own *dýnasthai* has its source in God (5:19, 30). The special features in John are a. that we have in this *dýnasthai* the unique Christ event, and b. that the power in this event is the power of God initiating the new aeon. This power finds particular demonstration in the crucifixion and resurrection. Christ's own resurrection backs up his saying in Mt. 22:29. Peter in Acts 2:24 puts this resurrection power very strikingly in the negative: Christ cannot be held by death. The power of death is broken. As God's power empowered Jesus for acts of power, it empowers him for new life. Paul makes this point in 1 Cor. 6:14 and 2 Cor. 13:4. Christ is declared God's Son in power by his resurrection (Rom. 1:4). We thus preach Christ as God's power (1 Cor. 1:24). The resurrection does not make Christ the Son of God, or give him power as such; what he has by it is sonship in full power in contrast with the apparent weakness of the incarnation (2 Cor. 13:4). If Christ is called God's power in the absolute, it is not because he personifies power, but because in him the power of God works victoriously in history and brings it to its goal. In Hebrews this power is called the power of an indestructible life; it is beyond the reach of mortality. With this power the Son is set at God's right hand where he rules the world (1:3). In Revelation this power is identical with glory (1:16). The Lamb that was slain is worthy to receive power (5:12). Christ's people await his coming in power (Mk. 9:1) which will complete his work and establish God's perfect rule with the subjection of every other force (Phil. 3:21). This coming will be a visible one, and Christ will be accompanied by his mighty angels (2 Th. 1:7).

2. *The Power of God, Demonic Powers, and the Power of Salvation.*

a. The Christ event sheds light on the power of God. Christ's power is God's, so that it is depicted as endowment. Christ shares this power by personal fellowship with God. His power is thus the historical power of an eschatological event, as in the OT. God's omnipotence is manifested in the Christ event (Heb. 11:19; cf. Mt. 22:29). God is the *dynatós* in virtue of his omnipotent rule (Lk. 1:49). All things are possible for him (Mt. 19:26). As faith perceives, all things manifestly declare his eternal power and deity (Rom. 1:20). The NT can thus adopt the OT doxology, as in Mt. 6:13; Rev. 4:11, etc. The doxologies of Rev. 11:17-18 and 12:10 imply acknowledgment that God's power will destroy hostile forces and bring the world to perfection, as the power in the Christ event has already shown.

b. The Christ event also sheds a new light on demonic powers. The NT recognizes these (cf. Mt. 24:29). These are cosmic but also angelic powers. They have lost their force with the resurrection of Christ and will be publicly stripped of it at his return. Between these two events, there is tension. The powers are disarmed, for the new life of believers derives from God and is set under his rule (Eph. 1:20-21; Rom. 8:38-39). Yet they still fight (Rev. 13:2) and have to be brought to submission (1 Cor. 15:24). The antichrist will come with power and spread deception; only Christ's coming again will finally destroy him (2 Th. 2:9).

c. Christ's work also gives a new answer to the question of the power of salvation. When the disciples ask who can be saved, Christ replies that there is no human power to save, only God's omnipotent power (Mt. 19:26). Paul sharply stresses human inability in Rom. 8. Due to our weakness, even the law cannot save from sin and death (v. 3). Hebrews finds the same inability in the cultus (10:1, 4, 11). As Jn. 3:3 says, unless there is a new birth, we cannot see God's kingdom. Of ourselves we cannot bear to hear God's word (Jn. 8:43). No one can come to God unless the Father draws him (6:44). Only God has the power to save, and he puts forth his power in Jesus (Rom. 1:16; 1 Cor. 1:18). This power is not that of mystical initiation or of a mere direction to salvation; it is the power of the word of the cross. It grants salvation by liberating us from the power of darkness and putting us in the kingdom of God's dear Son. It is grounded in the saving act of the Christ event, i.e., in God's mighty work in history. Only in 2 Pet. 1:3-4 do we have a hint of a substantial rather than a dynamic conception when it is said that God's power grants us the things pertaining to life and godliness with a view to our escaping corruption and becoming partakers of the divine nature.

3. *The Power of the Disciple.* As the *dýnamis* of God, preaching continues Christ's saving work, and the apostles, representing Christ, are endowed with his power. Jesus equips the disciples with power when he sends them out in Lk. 9:1. This power overmatches demonic power (Lk. 10:19). The disciples have it only in faith (Mk. 9:14ff.). It is the power of Christ's own presence by the Spirit (cf. Lk. 24:48ff.; Acts 1:8). A special endowment of power takes place at Pentecost which leads to healing as well as preaching in power (Acts 4:7ff., 33; 6:8, 10). Paul's ministry is effective by the power of signs and wonders, by the power of the Holy Spirit (Rom. 15:19).

dynámeis are a mark of the apostolate (Gal. 3:5; 1 Th. 1:5). But the power is that of the Spirit as the mode both of Christ's presence and of the believer's existence. Apostles themselves are witnesses of the cross; they preach in outward weakness but in demonstration of the Spirit and power, so that the faith of their hearers rests in the power of God (1 Cor. 2:1ff.). *dýnamis* relates to the content of the message, not the form. The goal of preaching is the exhibition of Christ's presence by the Spirit and therefore the exhibition of God's saving power in Christ. It is by the same power that Paul is made a minister (Eph. 3:7). In the interests of the community, the power of Christ can also be judicial, as in 1 Cor. 5:3ff. It should be noted here that Satan can have no power over the believer unless the latter is handed over to him, and that even then the purpose is still one of salvation. In the apostle's own life and ministry, the power of Christ means a continual strengthening (Phil. 4:13; 1 Tim. 1:12; 2 Tim. 4:17). This strengthening takes the form of support, and is thus to be construed, not in terms of mana, but in terms of a personal relation between Christ and his servant.

4. The Community. A community that rests in God's saving power is the goal (1 Cor. 2:1ff.). Believers may be strong as they are "in the Lord" (Eph. 6:10). Rescued from Satan's power, yet still beset by perils, they know the power of Christ to protect and preserve. They are guarded by God's power through faith (1 Pet. 1:5). The apostle's prayer is that they may enjoy the greatness of God's power (Eph. 1:19), or that they may be strengthened with all power (Col. 1:11). This power, grounded in Christ's resurrection, creates the hope of their calling and a glorious inheritance. Christians are to know this power with a view to endurance and patience. It is a power that transforms as well as preserves. By the power of the Spirit they abound in hope (Rom. 15:13). Strengthened with might by the Spirit in the inner man, they grow in fellowship with Christ, in comprehension, and in love of Christ (Eph. 3:14ff.). Born of God, they cannot sin (1 Jn. 3:9), but have a new capacity for love (1 Jn. 4:7). Every good resolve and work of faith may be fulfilled by the power of God (2 Th. 1:11). Members of the community may also have the spiritual gift of performing *dynámeis* (1 Cor. 12:10). Furthermore, the power at work in the community is ultimately resurrection power (cf. 2 Cor. 13:3ff.). God raised up the Lord and will raise us up by his power (1 Cor. 6:14). The changing of the body of humiliation into a body of glory is grounded in God's omnipotence (Phil. 3:21). No one can snatch believers out of Christ's hand (Jn. 10:28-29). Paul can give up all things to know Christ and the power of his resurrection—the mighty act which creates new and eternal life for his people. This is the source of real *dýnamis*.

5. Power and Weakness. God's power operates in the weak and corruptible sphere of human existence. It is thus visible only to faith, but for this very reason it is known as divine, not human power. Concealment in apparent weakness is the law of the cross (2 Cor. 13:4). But God's weakness is stronger than men (1 Cor. 1:25), as Paul comes to realize in all the weakness of his apostolic ministry (2 Cor. 12:9-10; cf. Phil. 4:13). The transcendent power belongs to God (2 Cor. 4:7), who gives a spirit, not of timidity, but of power and love and self-control (2 Tim. 1:7). Weakness is the presupposition of the working of divine power. It is the pledge of Christ's presence in which Paul finds freedom from self and reliance on God. By the law of strength in weakness, the resurrection power of God is more abundantly exerted, whether in ministers of the gospel or in the Christian community as a whole. "By the power of God" expresses the reality of faith for the apostolate and all Christian life (2 Cor. 6:7).

[W. GRUNDMANN, II, 284-317]

---

dýō [to go down, arm oneself],   *ekdýō* [to strip],   *apekdýō* [to put off],   *endýō* [to put on],   *ependýō* [to put on in addition],   *apékdysis* [putting off]

---

dýō. "To submerge," also intransitive "to plunge," "go down" (the sun in Mk. 1:32; 4:40), figurative "to arm oneself."

ekdýō. a. "To strip" (cf. Mt. 27:28), b. "to divest oneself," "to take off." In the NT we find *ekdýō* in 2 Cor. 5:4, where it can hardly mean that Paul wants to avoid the nakedness of the intermediate state (cf. v. 5; Phil. 1:23), but perhaps refers to the loss of the earthly body when there is no hope of a heavenly body.

apekdýō. In the NT this occurs only in Col. 3:9, where it has the strong sense "fully to put off" with no possible return to the old state, and Col. 2:15, where it does not mean "to divest oneself of," but "to disarm" (opposite of *dýō,* "to arm oneself").

endýō. a. "To draw on," b. "to put on," "clothe oneself with."
1. In the NT it occurs literally in Mt. 6:25; Mk. 6:9; Acts 12:21; Rev. 19:14.
2. Figuratively we find it in 2 Cor. 5:3; where Paul desires to be clothed with the heavenly body. We also find it with reference to Christian armor in Rom. 13:12; 1 Th. 5:8; Eph. 6:8, 11, investing with qualities in Col. 3:12, and investing with incorruptibility in 1 Cor. 15:53-54. The object is personal in Gal. 3:27: "We have put on Christ," or, as an imperative, in Rom. 13:14: "Put on Christ" (cf. also Col. 3:10: "Seeing . . . you have put on the new man"). Behind this usage stands the concept of Christ as the second Adam.

ependýō. "To put on over." The only NT use is in 2 Cor. 5:2, 4 for investiture with the heavenly body at the parousia.

apékdysis. This occurs only in Col. 2:11, where the sense is figurative (cf. Rom. 6:2-3; Gal. 2:19).   [A. OEPKE, II, 318-21]

---

dṓdeka [twelve], *(hekatón tesserákonta téssares* [144]), *dōdékatos* [twelfth], *dōdekáphylon* [the twelve tribes]

---

dṓdeka means "twelve," a number which was highly esteemed due to the division of the year into twelve months, and in Israel due to the existence of twelve tribes in the sacral union, which is of theological significance even after the disappearance of some tribes and the fusion of the others into a political society.
1. Twelve is a round number in Mt. 9:20; Acts 19:7; 24:11, and perhaps Mt. 14:20, though here the point might be a basket for each of the twelve disciples. It is of interest that in Mk. 5 the woman has been ill twelve years (v. 25) and Jairus' daughter is twelve years old (v. 42), since the two stories are interwoven.
2. In Lk. 2:42 Jesus is twelve years old when he goes to the Passover; the point of the journey seems to have been to familiarize him with the obligations of the feast, since the obligation to keep it came only at the age of thirteen.
3. OT usage is adopted in Acts 7:8; Mt. 19:28 (cf. Jms. 1:1).

4. The use of twelve in Revelation is linked to the OT concept of the twelve tribes as comprising God's people. Thus the twelve stars of 12:1 characterize the woman as a symbol of the daughter of Zion. Twelve also plays an important role in the measurements of the new Jerusalem in ch. 21. Again, in 7:4ff. twelve thousand are sealed from each of the twelve tribes; the figure "twelve" stresses the continuity of the underlying saving will of God, the "thousands" emphasize the size of the community, and the number as a whole brings out the element of order and perfection as God pursues and fulfils his divine way of salvation. These are not just Jewish believers, for the author alters the customary list, leaving out Dan. Interest focuses on the teleology of salvation history as God in faithfulness to himself and his people achieves his purpose in the community as the spiritual Israel. The numbers 12,000 and 144,000 occur in a cosmic sense among the Mandaeans and Manicheans, but if there is a connection, it is more likely that these took the numbers from Revelation, not vice versa.

5. The classical use of *dṓdeka* is in relation to the innermost group of Jesus' followers: the twelve disciples in Mt. 10:1 etc., the twelve apostles in Mt. 10:2; Lk. 22:14, and the Twelve in Mt. 26:14 etc. These are the same people, but while all apostles would be disciples, not all disciples are apostles, only those who are expressly appointed to be such by Jesus. Jesus himself freely chooses these twelve (Mk. 3:13-14; Lk. 6:12-13; cf. Jn. 6:70). To question the historicity of this selection is to make the existence of the Twelve inexplicable, especially as the inclusion of Judas does not fit well with the theory of their emergence after the resurrection, with Paul's reference to them as the first witnesses of the resurrection (1 Cor. 15:5), or with the reference to the eleven in Mt. 28:16; Mk. 16:14; Lk. 24:9. The choice of the number accords with the divine plan of salvation and the preparation of the community as its goal. It looks back to the ancient constitution of Israel and ahead to the final form of the messianic community. In the Twelve Jesus claims all Israel, so that the Twelve have no independent place but serve as the link between Christ and his people. Except as the first witnesses of the resurrection, they then play no special role as a group. The silence of Paul is important in this regard, and their only joint action in Acts is in the advice they give for the selection of the Seven in Acts 6. When James is put to death, they make no attempt to fill his place, mainly because the emphasis has now shifted to Gentile work in which others participate (cf. Acts 8:5ff.), and the time for the Jewish people to make a decision in relation to them has passed, so that they have thus become representatives of judgment upon it (cf. 19:28). The simple form "the Twelve" shows that a special task is at issue rather than a special dignity. It occurs almost always when the group is tested, when a close relationship to Jesus is stressed, or when there is a combination of the two, as in Mt. 20:17. Their function, of course, is finally a positive one, for in Rev. 21:14 the foundation stones of the city bear their names. The Israel that is gathered from all nations is in fact inconceivable without them, so that even if the claim that Jesus makes through them is initially resisted, it comes to a higher fulfilment with the expanded concept of God's people, and they have a vital function in the church's understanding of herself in relation to God's total plan.   [K. H. RENGSTORF, II, 321-28]

→ *apóstolos, Israḗl*

dōreá, dōreán, dōréomai, dṓrēma, dṓron → *dídōmi*

hebdomḗkonta → *heptá; Hebraíos* → *Israḗl; engízō* → *engýs; engráphō* → *gráphō*

ε *e*

éngyos [guarantee]

Formed from *engyáō,* "to pledge," *éngyos* means "offering security" and *ho éngyos* "guarantor." The term occurs figuratively in Heb. 7:22, where Jesus with his life, death, and ascension is the guarantee that the beginning of God's saving work will be followed by its promised completion.   [H. PREISKER, II, 329]

---

engýs [near],   *engízō* [to bring near],   *prosengízō* [to come near]

---

engízō means "to bring near," mostly intransitive "to approach." *engýs* means a. "near" in space, b. "near" in time, c. "almost" (in counting), d. "similar," e. "related," and f. figuratively of a spiritual attitude. *engízō* is very common in the LXX, e.g., for the nearness of God's working, for drawing near to God (Ex. 3:5), for the approach of the time of salvation (Is. 50:8), or for the coming of judgment (Joel 1:15). *engýs* is used for neighbor (Ex. 37:27) or for the relation between God and the righteous (Ps. 33:18). Philo has *engízein* for encounter with God, as in *Allegorical Interpretation of Laws* 2.57.

1. NT usage follows Isaiah in speaking of the nearness of God's kingdom (Mt. 3:2; 10:7; Lk. 10:9, 11) as the time of fulfilment (cf. Mt. 21:34; Mk. 13:28-29). Similarly *engízein* occurs in connection with Christ's death (Mt. 26:45) and the destruction of Jerusalem (Lk. 21:20). *engýs* is significant in Lk. 19:11 inasmuch as the nearness to Jerusalem coincides with the nearness of the decisive event of salvation (cf. Mt. 26:18). The approach of the risen Lord in Lk. 24:15 also has a special significance (cf. Lk. 10:9, 11). In Paul *engízein* denotes a unique aspect of the Christian life: God's coming is at hand (Rom. 13:12). Epaphroditus nearly died for Christ's work in Phil. 3:20. *engýs* occurs in a brief eschatological message in Phil. 4:5 and with reference to the word in Rom. 10:8 (quoting Dt. 30:14). The Gentiles have drawn near to Christ in Eph. 2:13, 17. *engízein* denotes tense expectation in Heb. 10:25; Jms. 5:8; 1 Pet. 4:7, but is used for drawing near to God in Heb. 7:19 and Jms. 4:8. Judgment is imminent *(engýs)* upon apostasy in Heb. 6:8, while the time of God's kingdom is near in Rev. 1:3.

2. *engízein* and *engýs* are used in very different ways to indicate time and space, especially in Luke and John. Thus *engízein* with the dative denotes place and movement in Lk. 7:12; 15:1, etc.; Acts 9:3; 10:9, and similarly with *eis* in Mk. 11:1; Mt. 21:1; Lk. 18:35, with *epí tina* in Lk. 10:9, and in the absolute in Lk. 18:40. As regards times, we read of the approach of the hour (Mt. 26:45), the day (Rom. 13:12), the end (Lk. 21:20). *engýs* is used only for place in Acts (e.g., 1:12), but for time, especially the Passover, in John (2:13; 7:2; 11:55) and for place in John (e.g., 6:19; 11:18, 54; 19:20, 42). Thus the terms have an ordinary sense but also express the hope of the imminent eschatological act of God either in commencement or consummation.   [H. PREISKER, II, 330-32]

---

egeírō [to awaken, rise], *égersis* [resurrection], *exegeírō* [to awaken, rise], *grēgoréō* [to be awake, alert], *(agrypnéō* [to be awake, keep watch])

---

egeírō.
1.a. "To awaken," b. "to arouse," c. "to set up," d. "to awaken the dead"; also intransitive a. "to wake up," b. "to stir oneself," c. "to rise up," and d. "to rise from the dead."
2. All these meanings occur in the Bible, with nuances from the Hebrew. Thus we find a. in Mk. 4:38 etc., intransitively in Mt. 1:24, figuratively in Rom. 13:11. For b. cf. Mk. 13:8, the rising up of prophets (Mt. 11:11), rising in judgment (Mt. 12:42). For c. cf. Jn. 2:19-20; Mt. 12:11; the sick in Mk. 1:37 etc., the intransitive in Mt. 17:7. For d. we have individual raisings as signs of the messianic age and the final resurrection, as in Mt. 9:25; Lk. 7:14; Jn. 12:1. Jesus' own raising is predicted in Mt. 16:21 etc., narrated in Mk. 16:6 etc., and proclaimed in Acts 3:15 etc.; Rom. 4:24 etc.; 1 Cor. 6:14 etc. God has acknowledged and glorified the crucified Lord by raising him (cf. Acts; Rom. 7:4; Phil. 2:9ff.); he has thereby validated his saving work (Rom. 4 and 8; 1 Cor. 15). As distinct from *anistánai, egeírein* expresses the concreteness of the action. For the resurrection as Jesus' own act, cf. Jn. 2:19; 10:17-18. The risen body of Jesus has both material (Lk. 24:39ff.; Jn. 20:25ff.) and spiritual features (1 Cor. 15:47; Phil. 2:6, 9; Jn. 20:17). Even linguistically the myth of the dying and rising redeemer-god neither forms the native soil of the gospel nor offers a parallel, for in it *egeírein* seldom occurs. In addition, the eschatological concept is missing and the NT core is theologically significant history rather than nature myth or speculative myth.
3. The raising of believers with Christ is worked out especially by Paul (cf. Rom. 6:4ff.; Gal. 2:20; Col. 2:12ff.; Eph. 2:1, 5; 2 Cor. 4:10ff.). It is related to justification (Rom. 5:18; 8:28ff.) and depicts the new situation in history into which believers are set with Christ (Rom. 6). The new life is the reality of faith (2 Cor. 4:7ff.). It is not a magical change, lies outside human control, and is a divinely posited reality awaiting consummation (Rom. 8:19ff.). Strictly, the resurrection has not yet taken place (2 Tim. 2:18). Though John stresses present possession (3:18; 5:24; 11:18), this does not mean a complete spiritualizing of eschatology (cf. Jn. 5:28-29; 6:39-40; 21:22; 1 Jn. 2:18; 4:17).
4. For the future resurrection of the dead (Lk. 20:37; Acts 26:8; 1 Cor. 15) see *anístēmi.* The question of the Sadducees in Mk. 12:23 reflects a more materialistic conception; Jesus opposes to it a more spiritual view in vv. 25ff. Paul endorses this in 1 Cor. 6:13; cf. the changing of the *sōma* in 1 Cor. 15:42ff. Similarly, Johannine theology avoids materialistic expressions while presenting a realistic belief in the resurrection.

égersis. This means a. "stimulation," "erection" (of walls etc.), "raising" (of the dead), and b. (intransitive) "awakening," "rising," "recovery." The only NT instance is in Mt. 27:53 where it refers to the resurrection of Jesus.

exegeírō. This has most of the senses of the simple form. It is used in Rom. 9:17 in the sense "to cause to appear in history," "to call into existence," and in 1 Cor. 6:14 in the sense "to raise from the dead."

grēgoréō (agrypnéō).
1. This has the literal sense "to watch" in Mk. 14:34; 24:43; Lk. 12:37.
2. It has the figurative sense "to be vigilant" (especially in relation to the parousia)

in Mt. 24:42; Mk. 13:35; 1 Th. 5:6; Rev. 3:3, linked with sobriety in 1 Th. 5:6, prayer in Mk. 14:38; Col. 4:2, concern for salvation in Acts 20:31. *agrypnéō* (only figurative) is used similarly in Mk. 13:33; Lk. 21:36; Eph. 6:18; Heb. 13:17.

3. The sense "to be alive" occurs only in 1 Th. 5:10.   [A. OEPKE, II, 333-39]

enkainízō → kainós; enkakéō → kakós

---

enkombóomai [to clothe oneself]

---

enkombóomai, meaning "to clothe oneself with," occurs in the NT only in 1 Pet. 5:5, where it has the figurative sense "to make one's essential characteristic." Humility is to be a decisive mark of Christian conduct.   [G. DELLING, II, 339]

---

enkráteia [self-control], **(akrasía** [self-indulgence]), **enkratḗs** [self-controlled], **(akratḗs** [lacking self-control]), **enkrateúomai** [to exercise self-control]

---

1. This group takes its sense from the stem *krat-* denoting power or lordship. Thus *enkratḗs* means "having power over all things and the self," *enkráteia* means "dominion over the self or something," with the nuances of "steadfastness" and "self-control" (opposite *akrasía*), and *enkrateúesthai* means "to compose oneself."

2. *enkráteia* is an important term in philosophical ethics. Socrates regards it as a cardinal virtue, and Aristotle and the Stoics discuss it fully, though the latter subordinate it to *sōphrosýnē*. The idea is that of people who freely control all things, maintaining freedom in self-restraint.

3. Philo has a high regard for *enkráteia* as superiority expressed in self-restraint. He links it to an asceticism deriving from dualism. The Essenes, too, value it highly, and it has religious significance in the Hermetic writings.

4. The term plays little role in the Bible. In the LXX it is found for "restraint" only in such passages as Sir. 18:30; Wis. 8:21; 4 Macc. 5:34. It does not occur in the Gospels. Paul has it in 1 Cor. 9:25 for athletic "self-control" with a view, not to salvation, but to service. Closer to Hellenistic use is 1 Cor. 7:9, where it means sexual "self-control," yet here, too, there is no extolling of asceticism as though marital sex were wrong. The sparse use of this ethical term is due to three things: (1) for Christians life is directed by God's command, so that there is no place for autonomous self-mastery; (2) belief in creation excludes dualism, for all things are good as they come from God; and (3) salvation in Christ leaves no place for meriting salvation by asceticism.   [W. GRUNDMANN, II, 339-42]

enkrínō → krínō

---

egṓ [I]

The NT uses *egṓ* in I-formulas. The term has religious significance in proclamations of God (the theological *egṓ*), the self-witness of Christ (the christological *egṓ*), and self-utterances of the Christian (the anthropological *egṓ*).

A. The Theological *egṓ*.

1. Divine Proclamations in the Ancient Near East and Hellenism. The I-style is common in the ancient Near East, e.g., in Babylonian liturgies, Egyptian papyri, the Avesta, and cf. also the hymnal predication: "I am Isis." The point of such proclamations is the self-representation, self-glorification, and self-commendation of the deity, so that they have a monotheistic thrust.

2. Divine Proclamations in the OT and Apocalyptic Judaism. The I-style acquires a specific ring on the lips of the self-revealing God of Israel. The divine name is paraphrased as "I am who I am" (Ex. 3:14). The decalogue opens with an exclusive "I am" (Ex. 20:2ff.). Even more exclusive is the great revelation of Dt. 32:39ff. In Is. 40ff. God presents himself as the ultimate Subject who will tolerate no other god, whose will is supreme, who has the first and final word, who manifests his omnipotent will and being in incessant action, and upon whose revealing and reconciling grace we are totally dependent. The I-style continues in Jewish apocalyptic, especially in the Apocalypse of Abraham.

3. I-Speeches of God in the NT. The NT maintains the belief that God is absolute Subject, but offers few I-declarations on God's part except in quotations, e.g., Is. 45:23 in Rom. 14:11, Dt. 32:35 in Rom. 12:19, Ps. 2:7 in Acts 13:33; Heb. 5:5, and Ex. 3:14 in expanded form in Rev. 1:8.

B. The Christological *egṓ*.

1. Ruler and Savior Sayings in the Ancient Near East and Hellenism. Ancient Near Eastern rulers, e.g., Hammurabi, Akhnaton, and Cyrus, issue I-proclamations. In Hellenism the Diadochi continue this style. In particular, however, religious saviors use it in their propaganda both in speech and writing. Thus we find it in the Mandaean writings and the Koran, but its overuse by popular prophets and preachers tended to rob it of credibility (cf. Celsus in Origen *Against Celsus* 7.8-9).

2. The I of God's Representatives in the OT and Judaism.

a. Among rulers, Nehemiah lists what he has done for God's people, but self-predications as god or lord are regarded as arrogant and offensive in view of God's sole deity, so that God punishes the pretensions of Tyre (Ezek. 28:2, 9) or Pompey. The prophets call for a hearing as God's mouthpiece, but this is a God-consciousness, not an I-consciousness (though cf. "me Daniel" in Dan. 7:28; 8:1).

b. The I-style of Isaiah is adopted in the I-sayings of heavenly wisdom in Prov. 8; these are imitated by folly in 9:4-5, 16. Angels can use the same style as God's messengers, e.g., in Apoc. Abr. 10; Test. Abr. 13.

c. Others like the Damascus Teacher adopt the same style, as does the Baptist in Jn. 1:23, although in contrast to Simon in Acts 8:9-10 he is not pointing to himself but away from himself to another (Mt. 3:11).

d. The rabbis avoid this style, fighting against the real or apparent pretension of I-sayings in the name of monotheism (cf. Gamaliel's caution in Acts 5:36-37).

3. egṓ in the Synoptic Sayings of Jesus. In the Synoptic Gospels Jesus uses *egṓ* infrequently. It occurs when he quotes Is. 61 in Lk. 4:18, but the three most important instances are in the Sermon on the Mount, where five times he utters a sharp *egṓ dé légō hymín* relating his new demand to his person and mission, in the cry of jubilation in Lk. 10:22, where he is the sole mediator of salvation and knowledge who stands in a unique relation to the Father and through whom all the Father's work is done, and in the Savior's call in Mt. 11:28ff., where he occupies a central place between God and us, gathering up all previous intermediaries into himself as he stands at the heart of the times. The central position of Christ between the Father and believers comes out in other sayings, e.g., when he sends out the disciples with the *egṓ* of divine authority in Mt. 10:16, when he gives the promise of his abiding presence in Mt. 28:20, when he intercedes for his people in Lk. 22:32, and when he commissions the seventy as his representatives in Lk. 10:16. As Christ meets us in his messengers, so he meets us in the lowly (Mk. 9:37). To receive a child is to receive Christ, and to receive Christ is to receive God. Christ himself is the absolute point of intersection between God and us, so that the christological *egṓ* of the Synoptists expresses his claim to absoluteness in brief.

4. egṓ in the Speeches of Christ in John. John carries this line of thought a step further, for here the *egṓ* points a contrast (5:43), is often indispensable (10:25), and gives the sayings of Jesus a solemn, almost liturgical ring (e.g., 9:39). Many of the I-sayings refer to the relation to the Father (cf. "my Father," "I came forth from God" in 8:42, "I do what is pleasing to him" in 8:29, the Father is "with him" in 8:29, the Father is in me and I in the Father in 10:38, I and the Father "are one" in 10:30). The "we" of ch. 17 expresses this relation most fully, and drawing the disciples into this fellowship is the great theme of the discourses in vv. 14ff. Nor is this extension restricted to the Twelve, for a general offer is issued in 7:37. Indeed, the Christ event is shown to have a cosmic reach in a series of I-sayings which go beyond anything that is previously found, even including divine I-proclamations. These are the statements in which the *egṓ* is linked with such impersonal predicative nouns as light, bread, vine, door, way, truth, resurrection, and life. In such sayings Jesus does not equate himself with such things but claims to be such things in an absolute sense, so that everything significant in the world helps to characterize the uniqueness of this *egṓ*. Yet the point of such predication is to bring out his significance for the human race; light, bread, etc. are signs of his power and glory as he brings true light, bread, etc. to those who believe in him and thus sets them in the true reality of fellowship with himself, which means union with God.

5. egṓ in the Sayings of Christ in the Apocalypse. In Revelation, too, we find many christological I-sayings with a solemn ring, as in 22:16. The opening letters are from Christ himself, and if the third person is used in the introductory formulas (2:1 etc.), he can speak directly at the end (2:27-28), and closes the series with the great promise of a share in his own victory (3:21). In Revelation the main thrust of the I-sayings is the union of God and Christ. OT I-sayings are borrowed for this purpose, as in 1:8, 17 (cf. Is. 44:6). What God says in 21:6, Christ can say in 22:13. Yet Christ is not replacing God, nor are the two commingled, nor are there two different gods. Christ has been instituted the bearer of the divine office for the whole of this world and its history.

6. egṓ eimi (→ eimi). The occasional use of *egṓ eimi* without a predicate demands separate notice. It derives from the OT "I am" (Ex. 3:14; Dt. 32:39; Is. 41:4). Sometimes, of course, the meaning is the ordinary one "I am he," as when the blind man identifies himself in Jn. 9:9, or Jesus does the same in Jn. 18:5 and Mk. 6:50, or gives the answer "I am" to the question of Mk. 14:61. On the other hand, there are messianic overtones in the last two instances. *egṓ eimi* has a fixed significance, as we learn from the warning of Mk. 13:6; the "I am he" of messianic pretenders must be rejected and the decisive "I am he" of Christ's own final self-manifestation awaited. This sheds light on the central passage in Jn. 8:24ff. A chain of I-sayings precedes this in vv. 12, 18, 21. Decision for or against Christ means life or death (v. 24). But who is this one who says "I am"? He does not answer directly. The Father will bear witness (v. 18). He who sent him is with him (v. 29). The I of the Son is linked with that of the Father in a unity of action (v. 29). From the very beginning Jesus is the acting Subject of the history of God (v. 58), which contributes at every step to the manifestation and glorification of the Son. The final thrust of the simple *egṓ eimi* is that Christ's *egṓ* is the Subject of this history which is his powerful self-proclamation and in whose every victory Christ calls: "I am he." The I-sayings, then, may well go back to ancient Near Eastern models uniquely modified by the OT, but Christ claims all I-predications for himself and reveals himself to be God's definitive representative in the absolute *egṓ eimi*—the purest and fullest expression of his incomparable significance.

C. The Anthropological *egṓ*.

1. I and We in the Writings of Luke. A personal note is sounded in the prefaces to Luke and Acts (Lk. 1:3; Acts 1:1). Acts also includes some "we" passages which naturally suggest that the author was personally present on such occasions, although some scholars see here a literary device to give the record greater vitality and variety.

2. We and I in the Johannine Writings. In contrast to Luke's preface, that of John contains a confessional "we" (Jn. 1:14, 16). The author is not trying to write a more accurate account but in the name of many believers he is offering testimony. The same "we" occurs in 1 Jn. 1:4, then in 1 Jn. 4:14, 16 etc., and in demarcation from false teachers in 2:19. Above this "we" stands the God who elects, knows, and keeps us (3:19-20). But the author can also write authoritatively in the singular (2:7 etc.). This is very pronounced at the end in 5:13. The author of 2 John begins in the singular but then asserts unity with all who know the truth and blends himself with these in a comprehensive "in us" and "with us" (vv. 1-2). 3 John is wholly in the singular. Revelation cleverly interweaves I and we in 1:9 ("I John, your brother"). This first *egṓ* comes between the I-sayings of God and Christ (vv. 8, 17), and John's last *egṓ* comes after Christ's last *egṓ* in 22:16ff. If the author has a strong self-consciousness, it is a consciousness of office, and ultimately a God-consciousness.

3. We and I in Paul. Many of Paul's letters are personal (e.g., Philemon, Philippians, Romans), but he often associates others with himself either stylistically or with some special nuance, e.g., to add authority in 1 Cor. 11:16. He uses the singular to state his own position or to clarify his status, often with an emphatic *egṓ* which in 1 Cor. 7 differentiates him from the Lord and in Gal. 6:17 asserts his authority over against his opponents. The first person, both singular and plural, is important in exhortation, often in the cohortative, which is less sharp than the imperative (cf. 1 Th. 5:5ff.; Rom. 6:1ff.). Hypothetical "I" and "we" sentences serve the same goal, as in 1 Cor. 13:1ff. Gal. 2:15ff. begins with a statement in "we" style, moves on to a "we" hypothesis in v. 17, then a hypothetical "I" statement in v. 18, but then concludes with "I" statements, not because this is a private opinion, but because Paul has taken seriously the new situation of vv. 15-16 which Peter and the others must accept and work out as he has done.

4. The I of Rom. 7. The common reference of the I of Rom. 7 to the preconversion Paul is challenged by his statement in Phil. 3:6. A general reference to those who are under the law, however, is broken by a closer analysis of the I-style, which is comparable to that of Gal. 2. The context is that of salvation history. To demonic pressure against God, God has given the decisive response of the Christ event which is now being worked out in human will and destiny. Paul (with a "we") refers to this turning point in 7:5-6. He then develops this "we" statement in the "I" statements of vv. 7ff.

Prior to the law, sin is dead (v. 8). The law, in itself holy and good, then enters human history, but what is meant for life proves to be death (v. 10). For evil opposes God and turns the work of the law into its opposite. But God uses this very fact to bring to light our dormant sickness. The law plunges us into a conflict within the *egó*; we want to keep the law, but indwelling sin controls us, so that we break it. We may disclaim responsibility (vv. 17, 20), joyfully assenting to God's law with the *noús,* but we are impotent under the sway of another law that reigns in our members. We are thus forced to issue a passionate cry for redemption from this fatal state—a cry which leads on to a fuller description of the meaning of the Christ event in ch. 8, for our twofold determination by God's law and the law of sin (7:25) has in fact been overcome by God's victorious action in Christ. A new law has thus replaced both the law of God and the law of sin, namely, the law of the Spirit of life in Christ, a law which means freedom, not bondage (8:2ff.). The pneumatic I is the new anthropological fact for Christians. Relative to the Christ event, this implies that Christ has destroyed sin, that he now dwells in us, and that we stand under a new reign and sign in which we are now able not to sin as previously we were not able not to sin. Relative to God, it implies that his plan has been realized, that we are brought to our deepest selves, that we enjoy spiritual fellowship with him, and that we are wholly dependent upon God but find assurance in this very dependence. Relative to our somatic being, it implies that we have as yet only the firstfruits of the new life, that we still await our full redemption, but that this firstfruits is a pledge, so that we may confidently expect our final liberation and the accompanying redemption of creation. The new anthropological situation thus has the scope of a comprehensive renewal which Christ initiates and for which the pneumatic I is the point of departure. There is thus a continuous sequence of thought from 7:7 to 8, but in 8:2 Paul changes from *egó* to *se* and in 8:4 he alternates between "we" and "you," thus showing that the *egó* of ch. 7, while it includes Paul, embraces many others as well. But if Paul is included, what about Phil. 3:6? The difference is one of standpoint. In Phil. 3:6 (and also Gal. 2:15), Paul speaks from the standpoint of a pre-Christian Jew. In Rom. 7 (and Gal. 2:19; Phil. 3:7), he speaks from a Christian standpoint. From this angle the blamelessness is shown to be an illusion which carries the risk of sinful self-glory. In Christ, Paul see the hopelessness of his previous situation. He does so in solidarity with his people. Fulfilling the movement of his people from its real crisis to Christ, he is, as it were, its firstfruits; this gives the *egó* of Rom. 7 its distinctive sense.   [E. STAUFFER, II, 343-62]

---

hedraíos [steadfast],   **hedraíōma** [bulwark]

---

hedraíos means first "seated," "settled," then "steadfast," "solid," and in the OT "permanent," e.g., God's throne, or God himself, or the mountains, or the throne of David, or the human heart if God keeps it, or human work if God accepts it. There are only three instances in the NT. In 1 Cor. 7:37 the self-controlled person is inwardly secure. In 1 Cor. 15:58 Christians are to be steadfast and immovable in the light of the resurrection. In Col. 1:23 believers must be stable and steadfast, continuing in the faith and not shifting away from the hope of the gospel as apostasy threatens. The noun *hedraíōma* occurs in 1 Tim. 3:15. The church is here a solid defense against the confusion of myths, offering individual faith and thought a sure ground with its confession (v. 16).   [E. STAUFFER, II, 362-64]

ethelothrēskeía → *thrēskós*

éthnos [people, nation],   *ethnikós* [Gentile]

A. A People and Peoples in the LXX.

1. The main Hebrew terms for "people," *'am* and *gôy,* both denote human groups, but historically the former comes to be used for the holy people and the latter (in the plural) for the Gentiles. In the LXX *démos* is rare, being used only for smaller clanlike societies. *laós* is the rendering of *'am* and *éthnos* of *gôy.* There is a marked tendency to avoid the plural *laoí,* but *éthnē* is common for the plural "peoples." (For statistics see *TDNT,* II, 365.)

2. In many passages there is intentional differentiation. (For details see *TDNT,* II, 366-67.)

3. When *éthnē* denotes the Gentiles, it often has no sense of a plurality of peoples. The term describes those who do not belong to the chosen people. Yet God is the King of all peoples (Jer. 10:7). They all descend from the first patriarchs (cf. Gen. 10). Their division is by divine ordinance and must not be resisted (Gen. 11; Dt. 32:8). The nations are important in the prophetic view of history as agents of God's wrath (Hos. 8:10) which are themselves under wrath (Is. 8:9) but which will also finally receive salvation. Yet in Jewish piety, and in the hope of universal mission, the specific concept of peoples is merged into the general one of Gentiles (cf. Is. 66:17ff.). In the postexilic period the term can be used for Gentiles dwelling in the land (Ezr. 10:2; Neh. 10:31), and it thus takes on a derogatory sense, i.e., the common people (rendered *óchlos* in Greek) (cf. Jn. 7:49). Nevertheless, even though *éthnē* implies a negative judgment from the Jewish standpoint, this judgment has no final validity in face of the promise of universal revelation (cf. in the NT Mt. 28:19; Rev. 14:6).

[G. BERTRAM, II, 364-69]

B. *éthnos* in the NT.

1. *éthnos,* which probably comes from *éthos,* means "mass," "multitude," "host," and may be used for a "herd" or "swarm" as well as a human group. Applied to humans, it means a "people" but is a weaker term than, e.g., *laós* or *glóssa.* Of some 160 NT instances, 40 are quotations from the OT. This does not affect the general usage but may give a special nuance in context.

2. In 64 passages *éthnos* has no specialized sense. The reference is to a people or peoples (including the Jewish people; cf. Acts 10:22; 1 Pet. 2:9, *éthnos* being used interchangeably with *laós* in this regard). *pánta éthnē* denotes all nations.

3. In some cases, however, one senses that Israel is not included among the nations. Thus in Rom. 15:11 (based on Ps. 117:1) the call to praise God hardly need go out to Israel. Again, Israel does not have to be included in the promise of Gal. 3:8. In other passages too, e.g., Mt. 4:15; Lk. 21:24; Acts 4:25; Rom. 1:5; Rev. 10:11, the reference seems to be to the non-Jewish nations, i.e., the Gentiles, though whether or not *éthnē* is here a technical term for Gentiles may be debated.

4. In some 100 passages *éthnē* is undoubtedly a technical term for the Gentiles as distinct from Jews or Christians. The distinction from Jews is plain in, e.g., Mt. 6:32; Lk. 12:30; Mt. 20:19; Acts 14:16; Eph. 2:12; 1 Cor. 1:23. Gentile Christians are still *éthnē* in Rom. 11:13; Eph. 3:1. Yet a distinction from Christians may also be seen in view of the status of the church as the true Israel, e.g., in 1 Cor. 5:1; 12:2; 1 Th. 4:5; 1 Pet. 2:12; 3 Jn. 7. John does not have *éthnē* for Gentiles, since obdurate Jews are themselves *éthnē.*

5. The quotation of many OT passages shows how the OT influences this primarily

ethico-religious distinction (cf. 1 Th. 4:5 and Jer. 10:25). In this regard, then, the NT differs from the Greeks, for while the latter often use *éthnos* disparagingly to describe non-Greek peoples (as distinct from *Héllēnes*), this is on the basis of national or cultural differentiation, not theological.

6. The biblical view persists in the early fathers (cf. Mart. Pol. 9.2).

ethnikós. This occurs five times in the NT (Mt. 5:47; 6:7; 18:17; 3 Jn. 7; Gal. 2:14). "Gentile" is the obvious sense in Mt. 5:47; 6:7; 18:17. National distinction is not at issue but the inner mark of Gentiles. Adverbially "like Gentiles" in Gal. 2:14 again denotes the religious distinction, but in this instance Paul defends "living like Gentiles" to show that Jews are not justified as such, but both Jews and Gentiles are justified only by the one Lord who summons both to himself.

→ *Héllēn* [K. L. SCHMIDT, II, 369-72]

éthos [habit, custom]

a. "Habit," "use"; b. "custom," "cultic ordinance," "law" (used for Jewish laws in the LXX). The NT has both senses. In Lk. 22:39 the obvious reference is to a habit of Jesus, i.e., to retire to the Mount of Olives for prayer. In Acts 25:16 *éthos* denotes a custom in Roman justice and in Heb. 10:25 the bad custom of nonattendance at community gatherings. The burial law of the Jews is at issue in Jn. 19:40, and this leads on to the common use in Luke for the cultic law of Judaism, whether with reference to individual ordinances (Lk. 1:9; 2:42) or to the whole of the cultic law (Acts 6:14; 15:1; 16:21; 21:21; 26:3; 28:17). [H. PREISKER, II, 372-73]

eídon → *horáō*

---

eídos [form, appearance], *eidéa (idéa)* [form, appearance]

1. "What is visible," "figure," "appearance," whether in persons, objects, or God (cf. Gen. 32:30-31). In Num. 12:8 rabbinic exegesis takes it that Moses saw the speech of God (cf. Jn. 5:37).

2. In 2 Cor. 5:7 "sight" does not seem to be very apposite, since there is no parallel for the presupposed active use. The point is that we are to walk in a sphere in which there is no visible form. But what form? It might be that of the Lord whose *eídos* we shall see only in the next aeon (cf. 1 Cor. 13:12b). More probably it is the form of the Christian which is now only provisional and which will be enjoyed in its full and true sense only when we are at home with the Lord (v. 8; cf. 1 Jn. 3:2).

3. *eídos* often denotes "manner," and this is perhaps the sense in 1 Th. 5:22. The link with v. 21 certainly favors "every form" of evil over "every appearance," especially if v. 21 contains a reference to money changers (as the early church supposed): "As good money changers, test all things; keep the good and reject the bad." (Cf. the use of *eídos* for "mint.") [G. KITTEL, II, 373-75]

---

eídōlon [idol], *eidōlóthyton* [meat offered to idols], *eidōleíon* [temple of an idol], *kateídōlos* [full of idols], *eidōlolátrēs* [idolater], *eidōlolatría* [idolatry]

eídōlon.

1. This means "picture," "copy." It can be used for images of gods, but is not the usual term for cultic images (or human statues). When used for images, the idea is

that of a reflection of the deity. The term can also denote shades or apparitions (beings in the underworld are only copies of people). Another sense is the image evoked by an object (which may be illusory).

2. The LXX uses the term in a derogatory sense for images of the gods, or idols. In this regard it is referring polemically to the deities themselves, which are empty, and which thus express the unreality of pagan belief. The main point is not that another god is worshipped but that this is an unreal god. The Greeks do not follow this usage, so that the LXX here coins a new expression out of a familiar term.

3. NT usage rests on that of the LXX. The word and its derivatives occur only in Acts 7:41; 15:20, the Pauline writings, 1 Jn. 5:21, Peter, and Rev. 9:20. Paul obviously does not regard idols as true gods (1 Th. 1:9). They are not divine by nature but the products of human sin and folly (Gal. 4:8; Rom. 1:23). Demons lie behind them (1 Cor. 10:19; cf. Dt. 32:17), though demons are not what pagans believe their gods to be (cf. 1 Cor. 8:5).

eidōlóthyton. This adjectival noun, the Jewish term for *hieróthyton*, denotes meat deriving from pagan sacrifice (cf. 1 Cor. 10:28). Jews were forbidden to eat this or to trade in it because of its defiling effect. This strict prohibition reflects the firm rejection of every kind of religious syncretism. It does not rest on superstition but on regard for the first commandment. Paul allows such meat to be eaten but only apart from the cultic act (1 Cor. 10:14ff.) and according to the law of love (8:1ff.). He appeals to Ps. 24:1 (10:26) and the overcoming of legalism by faith. The apostolic decree, however, advises against eating meat sacrificed to idols (Acts 15:29; 21:15), and Rev. 2:14, 20 condemns it when it is an expression of the same libertinism as is reflected in licentiousness.

eidōleíon. This term, found only in the Greek Bible and the NT (1 Cor. 8:10), is a scornful word for the pagan temple as a house of idols.

kateídōlos. Found only in Acts 17:16, this word means either "rich in idols" or "idolatrous"; either fits well with vv. 22-23.

eidōlolátrēs, eidōlolatría. These terms occur only in the NT; *eidōlolatría* (which is more correct than *eidōlolatreía*) is the pagan opposite of Jewish *latreía*. The words denote a gross sin and come in the lists of vices in 1 Cor. 5:10-11; 6:9; Gal. 5:20; Eph. 5:5; Col. 3:5; 1 Pet. 4:3; Rev. 21:8. *eidōlolatría* is equated with *pleonexía* in Col. 3:5; Eph. 5:5; cf. mammon as an idol in Mt. 6:24. Participating in pagan feasts is *eidōlolatría* in 1 Cor. 10:7, 14. [F. Büchsel, II, 375-80]

---

eikḗ [in vain]

This adverbial term means "at random," "for no objective reason," "simply," "in vain." The usual NT sense is "in vain" (Rom. 13:4; 1 Cor. 15:2; Gal. 3:4), but "without basis or reason" is the meaning in Col. 2:18. There is good support for *eikḗ* as "without a cause" in Mt. 5:22. [F. Büchsel, II, 380-81]

---

eikṓn [image]

A. The Prohibition of Images in the OT. The belief that God is not to be depicted is intrinsic to the OT (cf. Ex. 20:4). The cultus presents a uniform picture here, and the prohibition is fundamental. God's spiritual nature underlies the belief, yet not in the sense that God is remote from matter, but rather in the sense that he is not under human control. There is thus no literary depiction either (cf. Ex. 24:9-10). The ark has no associated images and is linked only to God's spiritual presence. The dedication of the temple stresses that God dwells in obscurity and governs even the sky's brightest luminary, the sun (1 Kgs. 8:12). God is not equated with such natural phenomena as earthquakes or fires (1 Kgs. 19:11ff.), for again these are his work. The doctrine of creation explains the prohibition of images, for what sense is there in seeking likenesses of God in things that he has made (Ex. 20:4)? Is. 40:12ff. formulates this plainly. A further point is that Israel saw no figure of God when he spoke to her from the fire (Dt. 4:15-16). Making images is thus an act of disobedience (Am. 5:26). The people find this hard to accept, as may be seen from the constant forging of images from the golden calf onward, but the intention is probably to worship God even when praying to idols. The prophets, however, see that making images perverts the religion of Israel, and with the help of such humorous descriptions as that of Is. 44:12ff. they finally establish the prohibition.   [G. von Rad, II, 381-83]

B. Images in Judaism and Christianity.

1. For Jews the prohibition has three practical implications. The first (a.) is the avoidance and removal of all images of alien gods. Jews and Christians have always regarded violation of this rule as apostasy. The pictures of animals and stars on the temple curtain are merely artistic symbols. Similarly, the representation of the sunchariot by Byzantine artists is purely conventional. The second implication (b.) is the absence of depictions of Yahweh in the cultus. At the most we find only pictures of the hand of God at Isaac's sacrifice and in the lifting up of Ezekiel. The third implication (c.) is that depictions of human beings and animals are also partially avoided. Jewish art especially avoids human figures, since humans are made in God's image, but several exceptions have been found in the depiction of biblical scenes. As regards animals, those that are symbols of a deity are strictly avoided, but in other cases animals serve as harmless decoration. Objects used in worship, e.g., the ark of the law, the horn, the knife of circumcision, and the candlestick, may also be depicted. Art thus serves to present God's acts rather than God himself. There is no intrinsic interest in the appearance of God or the exercises of his worshippers, as in pagan art; the focal point is God and his history.

2. Representations of God are just as objectionable for Christians. The NT never even thinks of giving a picture of Jesus (or indeed the apostles). The crucial thing is not worshipping an image but listening to the word. Only in the period after the NT do we have artistic development by way of religious decoration and Christian symbols to depictions of Christ and the apostles. In the NT the absence of any positive interest also means the lack of any negative opposition.

3. The question of images arises in the NT in the following passages. a. Images on coins are at issue in Mk. 12:16. These are offensive to Jews because they violate the commandment and depict alien rulers, but for practical reasons the coins have to be used. b. The image of the beast must not be worshipped according to Rev. 13:14-15 etc. There is a clash here with the widespread ruler cult, as there had been in Dan. 3:5ff. and continually in Jewish history, e.g., when the Alexandrian mob put images of the emperor in the synagogues in A.D. 38, and as there would be for Christians (cf. Pliny's *Letters* 10.96). Rev. 13:15 reminds us of priestly devices to make images move.   [G. Kittel, II, 383-88]

C. **The Greek Use of *eikōn*.** Linked with *eíkō,* "to be like, similar," "to appear," *eikōn* means "image" a. as an artistic representation, b. as a mental image, and c. as a likeness or manifestation.

1. In Col. 1:15 Christ is the image of the invisible God. Since a representation of what is invisible is impossible, the meaning here is a revelation with substantial participation, as in Plato and Philo. The *eikōn* is not alien to the object, nor present only in the mind, but is in fact its reality and illumines its inner essence. Thus in Platonic cosmology the world is the visible image of the intelligible *autozōon.*

2. In popular Greek religion, the god is present in the image, as is shown by the miracles and magic associated with images. The copies have the same powers, feelings, etc. as the originals. Rulers are also gods in visible manifestation.

[H. KLEINKNECHT, II, 388-90]

D. **The Divine Likeness in the OT.**

1. We can understand the divine likeness in the OT only if we remember the distance between God and us. This puts the divine likeness on the margin. Nevertheless it is highly important in relation to human origins, for while we humans are made of earthly materials, God acts more directly in our creation, and precision is given to the special relationship by Gen. 1:28: "Let us make man in our image, after our likeness."

2. Mythical ideas may underlie this, but the only point of mentioning this is to prevent us from taking the phrase in modern terms, e.g., as though it referred to personality or moral capacity. Nor should we read too much into the double statement "in our image and after our likeness." Nor is it a vital question whether spiritual or bodily likeness is at issue. Obviously there is no speculation on God's own form. The main point is to indicate that humans belong by nature to the divine sphere. Yet the image is transmitted by the physical sequence of generations (Gen. 5:1ff.). Ps. 8:5-6 similarly transcends the spiritual/physical alternative, for here humans have a glory of outward appearance, yet their true glory lies, like God's, in the inner force that is native to them. If the OT does not finally say what the divine likeness really consists of, it has much to say about its implications. Humans are to control creation as God's vicegerents (Gen. 1:26). They are thus to represent the divine dominion and majesty (cf. Ps. 8; also Sir. 17:3-4).

3. The OT nowhere speaks about the loss of the divine likeness, but the decline in the length of life suggests degeneration of our native force.

[G. VON RAD, II, 390-92]

E. **The Divine Likeness in Judaism.**

1. In expounding Gen. 1:26-27 rabbinic exegesis tends to focus on the meaning of "let us," whether it refers to consultation with God's own heart, with angels, with the law, or with heaven and earth. No problem is felt with the divine image, nor is there any suggestion of its general loss, only of its diminution or effacement by the sins of specific individuals or groups.

2. The Greek spirit raises the question of the divine image as a metaphysical gift, as in Wis. 2:23-24. Philo associates it with the number seven and also with *noús* and *lógos.* He also makes much of a distinction between "in our image," which applies to the heavenly humanity that has no part in mortality or earthliness, and "after our likeness," which applies to the earthly humanity of Gen. 2:7-8.

F. **The Metaphorical Use of Image in the NT.**

1. In the NT the original is present in the image, which gives it visible manifestation. Thus Heb. 10:1 distinguishes *eikōn* from mere *skiá:* The law has the shadow,

but not the true form of the realities at issue. Rom. 1:23 is to the same effect when it uses *homoíōma* for the copy and *eikón* for the actual figure of the humans, birds, or animals that are put in the place of God (cf. Wis. 13:13).

2. *Christ as the eikón toú theoú*. In this phrase (2 Cor. 4:4; Col. 1:15), the stress is on the equality of the *eikón* with the original. Christ is in the form of God and equal to God (cf. Phil. 2:6). To see him is to see the Father (Jn. 14:9). "Beloved Son" in Col. 1:13 drives home the point. The phrase comes, of course, from Gen. 1:27. But Christ is the second Adam (1 Cor. 15:45ff.). If he thus plays for Paul the role that *lógos* plays for Philo, Paul's interest is not in the least speculative. The point for him is that Christ is given to us as God's image so that we may know what God wills and does. The concept of the image of God also makes it perfectly plain who Jesus himself is.

3. *Man as Image*. In 1 Cor. 11:7 Paul can also apply Gen. 1:27 to the male so as to bring out certain practical consequences for daily conduct. A little later, however, on the basis of Gen. 5:3, he contrasts our present bearing of the image of the earthly man with our future bearing of the image of the heavenly man. The idea here is that our being as the *eikón* of God is restored by union with Christ as *eikón*. This comes out plainly in Rom. 8:29, where our being conformed to Christ is given its distinctive emphasis by the fact that this means participation in his divine likeness. Those who are in Christ's image are in God's image in the true and original sense of Gen. 1:27. This likeness is the goal. 2 Cor. 3:18 carries the same message. Seeing the Lord's glory means sharing it and thus being changed into his likeness. The concern of the Christian life is already the putting on of the new being that is renewed after the image of its Creator (Col. 3:10). When does this restoration of the image in Christ take place? There is undoubtedly an eschatological future in 1 Cor. 15:49b and Rom. 8:29, but this future is linked to something that happens already in 2 Cor. 3:18 and Col. 3:10, so that the restoration is also a goal of ethical action. We have a first instalment of the *eikón*, as of other gifts, so that it now is even though it is still to be.

[G. KITTEL, II, 392-97]

---

heilikrinḗs [pure], **heilikríneia** [purity]

Formed from *heílē* ("warmth or light of the sun") and *krínō* ("to test"), these words mean "tested by sunlight," i.e., "pure," and "purity." In the NT (Phil. 1:10; 2 Pet. 3:1; 1 Cor. 5:8; 2 Cor. 1:12; 2:17) they refer to moral purity.

[F. BÜCHSEL, II, 397-98]

---

eimí [to exist], **ho ṓn** ["I am"]

1. Already in the LXX *ho ṓn* is used for God (Ex. 3:14). Philo has it too, and it is a divine predicate in Josephus. In the NT Revelation uses it in the formulas in 11:17; 1:4, 8; 4:8—formulas of worship, salutation, and self-predication. The non-declinability of *ho ṓn* and the quasi-participial use of *ḗn* preserve the sanctity of the divine self-predication. The formulas express God's deity and supratemporality. Similar formulas occur in Judaism. The Greeks also use two- and three-tense formulas to express eternity (cf. Homer, Plato, and an Eleusinian inscription). These possibly came

into Revelation by way of the Jewish tradition, though a common source may lie behind the Greek and Jewish traditions.

2. *egố eimí* as a self-designation of Jesus in Jn. 8:58 (cf. 8:24; 13:19) stands in contrast to the *genésthai* applied to Abraham. Jesus thus claims eternity. As he is equal to the Father (5:18ff.), what is ascribed to the Father is attributed to him too (cf. Is. 43:10 LXX). The context and the *egố* formulation are both Jewish. The point is not Jesus' self-identification as the Messiah ("I am he") but his supratemporal being.

3. For *egố eimí* with nouns of predication, see *egố*.   [F. BÜCHSEL, II, 398-400]

→ *egố*

---

eirḗnē [peace], **eirēneúō** [to keep peace], **eirēnikós** [peaceful], **eirēnopoiós** [peacemaker], **eirēnopoiéō** [to make peace]

---

eirḗnē.

A. The Greek Concept of *eirḗnē*. For the Greeks *eirḗnē* primarily denotes a state, not a relationship or attitude. It is the opposite of *pólemos* ("war"). It is linked with treaties of peace or the conclusion of peace. It is also the opposite of disturbance. In a negative sense, it may denote a peaceful attitude, i.e., the absence of hostile feelings. In the age of Augustus it carries echoes of redemption, but also implies in everyday reality the legal security of the *pax Romana*.   [W. FOERSTER, II, 400-402]

B. *shālôm* in the OT.

1. This term is in general use but has a strong religious content. To arrive at its theological sense we must look at it in context and also consider the concept even where the term itself is not used. Its basic sense is not the narrower one of "peace" but the wider one of "well-being." It may be used for the good fortune of the wicked, for health, and for national prosperity, which implies stability. In many passages it denotes friendly relationships, whether between states (1 Kgs. 5:26) or individuals (Zech. 6:13). It is thus linked with covenant; a covenant initiates or seals it (Josh. 9:15; Ezek. 34:25). In Ezekiel it is God who makes the covenant that results in peace, so that the term can finally express the relationship between God and his people (cf. Is. 54:10).

2. *shālôm as the Gift of Yahweh.* While there is a material content to *shālôm*, it is always a religious term inasmuch as all blessings are seen to come from God. In all probability, then, the religious significance is primary. This comes to expression in the name of Gideon's altar in Judg. 6:24: "The Lord is peace." God creates peace in the heavens (Job 25:2), but he also pledges peace to us, blesses his people with peace, and wills the welfare of his servants; we are thus to pray for the peace of Jerusalem (cf. Pss. 35:27; 122:6). The peace that God gives is all-sufficient. It carries with it solid blessings, e.g., peace from enemies and wild beasts (cf. Lev. 26:6), but all this is a blessing of salvation in the special sense of occupation of the promised land.

3. *shālôm in the Prophetic Message.* In the history of prophecy *shālôm* is a key term inasmuch as true prophets are in conflict with those who promise a false peace. Micaiah ben Imlah, for example, takes his stand against the many prophets of salvation. Micah accuses such prophets of delivering their message for gain (3:5ff.). Jeremiah comes into dramatic encounter with those who say "Peace, peace," when there is no peace (ch. 28). Ezekiel is engaged in the same struggle (Ezek. 13:16). The problem with the false prophets is not that there is no true message of peace but that they

construe peace as purely political, ignore the sins of the people, and thus fail to see or proclaim impending judgment. The defeats of 597 and 586 B.C. resolve the conflict and open the door to the promise of true peace from God in the larger and fuller sense. Thus Jeremiah proclaims God's plans of welfare in 29:11 and Ezekiel announces God's covenant of peace in 34:25. As may be seen from Is. 48:18 and 54:13, more than political peace is now at issue, for peace is associated with righteousness. The term still embraces welfare and peace, but it has the more comprehensive implication of salvation in its total range and scope.

4. *shālôm as an Element in Eschatological Expectation.* The promise of *shālôm* in the fuller sense brings the term into the orbit of eschatological expectation. The term may not always occur, but when restoration of paradise is prophesied, international peace promised (Is. 2:2ff.), or a humble king of peace awaited (Zech. 9:9-10), we have a proclamation of peace of the widest possible import. No special significance thus attaches to the actual use of the word, as when "prince of peace" is one of the messianic titles in Is. 9:5, for the whole point of the Messiah is that he guards and guarantees enduring peace (cf. v. 7). "He is peace," as Micah says in 5:5 (if this is the correct reading). An interesting point is that for all its wealth of meaning in the OT, *shālôm* nowhere denotes specifically an attitude of inward peace. *shālôm* always finds external manifestation, and in its most common use it is a social rather than an individual term. [G. von Rad, II, 402-06]

C. *eirēnē* in the LXX.

1. Since the LXX mostly uses *eirēnē* for the OT *shālôm*, the content of the Hebrew naturally influences the Greek term, and in turn the LXX usage affects the significance of *eirēnē* for Greek-speaking Christians.

2. *shālôm* comes close to *eirēnē* in its Greek sense when it is contrasted to war (Prov. 17:1) or the reference is to a state of peace (Is. 14:30) or to peace between nations (Judg. 4:17). But even in such cases *eirēnē* can take on a broader sense, as in Zech. 8:12 or 1 Kgs. 2:13 (in contrast to 2 Kgs. 9:17ff.). This is even more true when *shālôm* has nothing to do with peace as the opposite of war but implies well-being as distinct from every form of evil, as in salutations, or in relation to the work of physicians (Sir. 38:8), or in the problem posed by the good fortune of the wicked (Ps. 73:3). In such contexts *eirēnē* has to denote, not merely rest, but a state of well-being or wholeness, so that one can even be said to die in peace (as distinct from suffering violence). Nor is this well-being restricted to material welfare. It covers good in the widest sense, as when Prov. 3:17 says that the paths of wisdom are paths of peace, or when Ps. 34:14 equates the pursuit of peace with the doing of good.

3. The equation of *eirēnē* with ethical good leads on to the use of *eirēnē* for the good that comes from God either in this age or in the age of salvation (cf. Is. 45:7), where *eirēnē* embraces both the blessings of Lev. 26:3ff. and that of Num. 26:6. Peace in this sense is all that is good. It is the peace of those who love the law (Ps. 119:165). When God speaks it, his salvation is at hand (Ps. 85:8-9). Yet it is not just an inner state, for the soul is bereft of peace when it has forgotten what happiness is (Lam. 3:17).

4. The LXX sometimes uses other terms for *shālôm*, mostly in greetings or when external welfare is plainly at issue, e.g., Gen. 26:31; 28:21; 29:6; Josh. 10:21; Ex. 18:7. The aim in such cases is to keep more closely to common Greek usage. *eirēnē* is also used for other Hebrew terms on occasion, as in 1 Chr. 4:40; Prov. 3:23; Ezek. 34:27; 39:6, 26. (For details, see *TDNT*, II, 408.)

D. *shālôm* in Rabbinic Writings. *shālôm* is a common term in rabbinic works. It occurs in greetings in the general sense of well-being. The rabbis also use it for God's gift to his people. Peace is the portion of the righteous and the sum of messianic blessings, although with a stress on concord in Israel. Peace is also the opposite of individual or national strife. Along these lines peacemaking holds a high place in rabbinic estimation. Envy and strife are opposed to God's will, threaten the continuation of the world, and impede the coming of the Messiah. Conflict exists between God and the human race, or even God and Israel when Israel is guilty of idolatry; there is thus a reciprocal relationship with God in which we, too, must act for the establishment of peace.

E. *eirḗnē* in the Pseudepigrapha, Josephus, and Philo. As concerns the religious use of *eirḗnē*, the pseudepigrapha present us with the angel of peace. Peace in this connection is salvation expressed in cessation from war; its opposite is divine judgment, not conflict with God. Peace is thus linked with pardon or mercy, but it is also linked with light and thus has a positive implication. Peace can also mean concord between humans. Josephus follows OT and rabbinic usage. Philo is closer to the Greek tradition in his interpretation of peace as primarily political peace or as the inner rest (or absence of desire) that belongs to God and is to be sought from him.

F. *eirḗnē* in the NT. In the NT *eirḗnē* is first used in greetings, as in the rabbis (cf. Mk. 5:34; Jms. 2:16; Jn. 20:19); with mercy in 1 and 2 Timothy, 2 John, and Jude; Paul uses "grace and peace"; cf. also Rev. 1:4. Peace also occurs in closing greetings, e.g., in 1 Pet. 5:14; 3 Jn. 15. Parallels to the OT "go in peace" occur in Acts 15:33 and 1 Cor. 16:11, and Simeon's saying in Lk. 2:29 has a similar formal sense. The main meaning in the NT is obviously not the Greek one but salvation in a deeper sense. This embraces human concord, as in Acts 7:26 etc., but also peace with God. Closer to the Greek are the use for the opposite of war in Acts 12:20; 24:2; Mt. 10:34 and Paul's use for peace of soul (cf. Rom. 15:13). The OT basis comes out plainly in such expressions as "making peace" in Jms. 3:18 and "giving a greeting of peace" in Jn. 14:27. Lk. 14:32 possibly contains an Aramaism for offering a greeting rather than seeking conditions, but in context it carries the implication of submission and homage. In the material use of the NT we find peace as a feeling of rest, peace as a state of reconciliation with God, and peace as eschatological salvation; the last of these is basic.

1. eirḗnē in Its Widest Sense as the Normal State of All Things. In 1 Cor. 14:33 peace is for Paul the normal state as distinct from the confusion of unruly prophesying at Corinth. This peace is what God wills, not merely for the soul or for the human race, but for his whole creation.

2. eirḗnē as the Eschatological Salvation of the Whole Person.

a. The *shālôm* of the OT is the basis here. Thus in Lk. 1:79 *eirḗnē* is the awaited eschatological salvation. In Lk. 2:14 again peace is the salvation that has now come to the earth. Salvation is also the sense in Lk. 19:42 and 19:38b, and cf. Rev. 12:10; 19:1. In Rev. 12:10 peace is said to have come as a historical event in Christ (cf. Heb. 13:10). Melchizedek as a type of Christ is the king of peace (Heb. 7:2), the gospel is the gospel of peace (Eph. 6:15), and Christ leaves peace with his disciples (Jn. 14:27), the opposite of this being affliction (16:33). When the disciples go out in Christ's name, they offer peace (Lk. 10:5-6; Mt. 10:13). We are to seek this peace (Heb. 12:14). It is a power which protects us (Phil. 4:7) and which rules in the heart

(Col. 3:15), although in human relations it may sometimes result in the very opposite of peace (Mt. 10:34-35).

b. In all these passages *eirēnē* is materially parallel to *zōḗ,* and Paul makes this equation in Rom. 8:6. The striving of the flesh is enmity against God and leads to death (v. 7). Life and peace come when the mind is set on the Spirit; this brings salvation. There is a parallel in 2 Pet. 3:14, where *eirēnē* is neither inner peace nor grace, but the perfect well-being of reconstitution in God's image. Along these lines Paul calls God the God of peace who will crush Satan (Rom. 16:20) and secure our total salvation (1 Th. 5:23; cf. Heb. 13:20-21). Peace, then, embraces the salvation of the whole person, and in Christ this is already present as the power of God.

3. *eirēnē as Peace with God.* Occasionally *eirēnē* denotes peace with God. This is the point in Eph. 2:14ff. As the law has both divided Jews and Gentiles and separated Israel from God, so Christ our peace has healed both relationships, for he has broken down the wall of hostility by reconciling us all to God. Peace with God is solely at issue in Rom. 5:1. It is the relationship in which God places believers by his reconciling work in Christ. The context suggests that the indicative "we have" is the true reading in spite of the better attestation of the imperative "let us have."

4. *eirēnē as Peace with One Another.* When Paul in Rom. 14:17 says that God's kingdom is peace, he is stating that the rule of God is one in which there is no evil or discord; he can thus exhort us to pursue what makes for peace (v. 19), i.e., to avoid squabbling about meats or days. The saying in 1 Cor. 7:15c is to the same effect. If a pagan partner breaks off a marriage, the Christian must accept this, the reason being ("for," not "but") that God has called us to peace. Peace here again means the avoidance of discord, though it also has the positive content of a divinely willed state of normalcy. In 2 Tim. 2:22 we are not just to foster peace with the devout, since *metá* here means "along with"; what is in view is staying out of stupid controversies (v. 23), but with a hint of salvation in the context of righteousness, faith, and love. Concord is the obvious sense in Eph. 4:3 and Jms. 3:18, and probably also in 1 Pet. 3:11.

5. *eirēnē as Peace of Soul.* Peace of soul is meant in Rom. 15:13, although this peace is possible only through the saving work of God which restores our normal state. In contrast to Stoic *galḗnē* it is a positive state inseparably connected with joy and faith.

eirēneúō. a. "To live in peace," "to be at peace" as a state; b. "to keep peace," "to live at peace with" as an attitude; c. "to make peace," "to reconcile." In the NT the word is used only for "to keep peace" with *en* or *metá.* In Mk. 9:50 severity in self-discipline is perhaps contrasted with being at peace with others. In 1 Th. 5:13 the point seems to be that we should be at peace with one another. This is also what is meant in Rom. 12:18 and 2 Cor. 13:11.

eirēnikós. a. "That which relates to peace"; b. "peaceful"; c. more generally the opposite of unrest. Only sense a. occurs in the LXX. Philo uses the term for the wise who have peace of soul. The only NT instances are in Jms. 3:17 and Heb. 12:11. In the former the meaning is "ready for peace," "peaceful," while in the latter, as an attribute of righteousness, the word means "salutary" (cf. *eirēnē* F.2.).

eirēnopoiós. "One who makes peace." The rabbis extol pacification as a work of love and Philo calls God a peacemaker, but the term can also be applied to strong rulers who establish peace by force. The only NT use (Mt. 5:9) is along the lines of the rabbinic view. Blessing is pronounced on those who promote human concord (not general well-being or peace with God); God calls them his children because they are like him.

eirēnopoiéō. "To make peace" (or more generally in Prov. 10:10 LXX "to promote well-being"). In the one NT instance in Col. 1:19 (cf. Eph. 2:14ff.) the idea is that by his reconciling work in Christ God has made peace for all things on earth or in heaven (both with himself and with each other).   [W. FOERSTER, II, 406-20]

> *eis* [in, into, until, etc.]

Originally spatial, this word takes on theological significance in the NT.

A. The Spatial Use of *eis*.

1. The Cosmic and Soteriological Sense. In the NT *eis* expresses the living connection between divine and cosmic realities. In Greek thought the gods belong to the cosmos. Even dualism makes only a static distinction. Hades is another place; it is not God's world. Even in circles which speak of an ascent of the soul, *eis* plays only a minor role. Formally the OT speaks in a similar way, as though, when God comes down, he were simply changing place within the same reality (cf. Gen. 18:21; Ex. 3:8). Yet his superiority over all creatures is strongly asserted, as in Ex. 33:18ff.; Is. 6, so that heaven cannot contain him (1 Kgs. 8:27) and his presence is the willed and gracious address of the covenant God (vv. 28ff.). Judaism thus develops an aversion to anthropomorphic statements and carries the divine transcendence almost to the point of straining the link between God and the world except for a firm belief in providence. Thus the LXX paraphrases Ex. 15:3 and Ex. 24:10, Jubilees omits God's walking in the garden in its rendering of Gen. 3, Palestinian Judaism posits a series of heavens, and apocalyptic works begin to place greater weight on the preposition *eis,* e.g., in the coming of angels to the world, or in relation to apocalyptic vision. The NT inherits the distinction between the divine and human worlds but bridges the gulf with the concept of fulfilment in Christ. In this context *eis* takes on a new significance as follows.

a. "Into the world" delimits earthly creation from all other reality. We all come into the world (Jn. 1:9). Sin and death come into the world (Rom. 5:12); there is perhaps a hint of a transcendent background here, though cf. "through one man."

b. Divine love comes into the world to bring salvation. The NT links this with the preexistent Son, although faith focuses more on the goal than the origin. In this regard *eis* is not present in the Synoptics and is rare in Paul (cf. Rom. 10:6; Phil. 2:5ff.). The thought of God's sending, however, gives it great importance in John (cf. 1 Jn. 4:9), as does that of the Logos himself coming into the world (Jn. 11:27). As the Father sent the Son into the world, so the Son sends his disciples (Jn. 17:18). In the light of the incarnation (Jn. 1:14), this derived mission takes on an eternal quality.

c. The Christ who came down for our salvation passes through humiliation into the heavenly world of God. This receives greater emphasis in the NT than preexistence (cf. Lk. 24:5; Acts 1:11; Heb. 9:24; Eph. 4:8ff., and materially Acts 3:21; Rom. 1:4; Phil. 2:9ff.). A prior journey to the nether regions may be presupposed, as in Rom. 10:7 and especially 1 Pet. 3:19; 4:6 (but not Eph. 4:9).

d. The divine act of salvation forces us to decide where our own path is to lead, either through unbelief and disobedience to destruction (Mt. 7:19; 5:29-30; 3:10; Rev. 19:20; Mt. 13:42; 5:25; 8:12; 25:46), or through faith and obedience to life (Mt. 7:14; 25:21; Lk. 16:22; Mt. 5:20; 2 Pet. 1:11), which is present even now (Jn. 5:24); these references usually contain a spatial as well as a stronger or weaker figurative element.

2. *The Psychological Sense.*

a. *eis* denotes the intrusion of good or bad influences into the center of personality, e.g., demons in Mt. 9:25, evil from Satan in Jn. 13:2, Satan in Lk. 22:3, a wicked purpose from God himself in judgment in Rev. 17:17, the Spirit of God in 1 Th. 4:8; Gal. 4:6, and cf. the prodigal's return to himself in Lk. 15:17.

b. With verbs of sending or speaking, *eis* denotes address; cf. Jesus in Mt. 15:24, God in Acts 2:22, the gospel in Mk. 13:10, and cf. also Lk. 7:1; 2 Cor. 10:16; 1 Pet. 1:25. By its regular use of such constructions, which are good Greek but rest on the Hebrew, Christianity shows itself to be a religion of the word.

c. *eis* may also describe a situation, e.g., being led into temptation (Mt. 6:13), or shut up in disobedience (Rom. 11:32), or having every thought brought captive into Christ's sphere (2 Cor. 10:5). This is perhaps also the point in Rom. 6:17; cf. Rom. 5:2; Gal. 1:6.

B. The Temporal Use of *eis*.

1. When a point of time is given, the sense is "until" (cf. Mt. 10:22; 2 Tim. 1:12). When a period is mentioned, the sense is "for" (cf. Lk. 12:19).

2. More common in the NT is the use in which an action is performed with a view to some end, e.g., caring for the day in Mk. 6:34, being sealed for the day of redemption in Eph. 4:30, being pure or laying a good foundation for the day of Christ in Phil. 1:10; 1 Tim. 6:1; cf. 1 Pet. 1:5; Gal. 3:23-24. In such cases the reference is usually eschatological.

C. The Modal Use. *eis* sometimes denotes intensity, e.g., Jn. 13:1 ("to the utmost" as well as "to the end"); Heb. 7:25; 2 Cor. 10:13 (where the distinction between justifiable and unjustifiable boasting is qualitative); 2 Cor. 4:17 ("in excess to excess" in the sense of beyond all comparison).

D. *eis* in a Logical Connection.

1. Very occasionally *eis* states a reason, e.g., "in view of" in Rom. 4:20; cf. Mt. 12:41; 2 Cor. 10:16; Gal. 6:4 where, after testing, the self, not others, must provide reason for boasting.

2. *eis* denotes appointment, as in Mt. 5:22; 1 Cor. 11:22; Col. 2:22; Jms. 5:3; Rev. 22:2.

a. Divine appointment: the angels are appointed to minister to the heirs of salvation (Heb. 1:14), Moses as a witness (Heb. 3:5), Scripture for instruction (Rom. 15:4), Paul to publish good news (Rom. 1:1), believers to salvation (1 Th. 5:9), sonship (Eph. 1:5), or a living hope (1 Pet. 1:3-4), others to destruction or ignoble use (Rom. 9:21ff.; 2 Tim. 2:20).

b. Human appointment: missionaries are appointed to do God's work (Acts 13:2); believers are to take the bread and wine in remembrance of Christ (1 Cor. 11:24-25), and to do all things to God's glory (1 Cor. 10:31).

3. Consecutive and final *eis*. *eis* may denote the directing of an action to a specific end, whether intentionally or incidentally.

a. With a noun or pronominal accusative it usually has a final sense (cf. D.2.), as in "for a witness to them" (Mk. 1:44) or "in memory of her" (Mk. 14:9). Thus the gospel is God's power "to salvation" (Rom. 1:16), Christ is an expiation "to show God's righteousness" (Rom. 3:25), Paul's mission aims at the obedience of faith (Rom. 1:5), eternal life (1 Tim. 1:16), and edification (Eph. 4:12), and God's praise and glory (Eph. 1:6; Rom. 15:7) are the goals of God's saving action. The use may also be consecutive, as in 1 Cor. 11:17; Rev. 13:3; 2 Cor. 7:9-10; Rom. 10:10; 13:4, where the result, not the purpose, is indicated; cf. Col. 1:11, where endurance and patience are the result of strengthening. Yet the line is a fine one and sometimes precise differentiation is impossible; cf. Rom. 14:1; 1 Cor. 12:13 ("one body" is either the purpose or the result); Rom. 13:4 (wrath is either purpose or result). "To faith" in Rom. 1:17 seems to be final, but "to glory" in 2 Cor. 3:18 is consecutive; neither follows OT analogies such as Jer. 3:9; Ps. 84:7.

b. With nominal accusative or accusative and infinitive *eis* is mainly final though sometimes consecutive. Rom. 12:3; Mt. 20:19, etc. are final, as are Rom. 1:11; Heb. 2:17; Jms. 1:18, but Heb. 11:3 is consecutive (cf. Rom. 6:12; 2 Th. 2:10), and both uses may be found in Rom. 4:11-12 (consecutive), 16 (final), and 18 (consecutive). As regards guilt, the theological question arises whether it is an immanent result or a divine purpose. "To make them believe" in 2 Th. 2:11 might be consecutive but is probably final in view of the final clause that follows, but Rom. 1:20 cannot be final, since the point is to show the ground of the complaint, and we should thus render: "So that they are without excuse."

E. The *eis* of Personal Relationship.

1. *eis* denotes relationship as such in a neutral sense, "with reference to," "relative to" (cf. 1 Cor. 4:6; Eph. 5:32). This is probably the meaning in Lk. 12:21 (rich in relation to God) and Rom. 5:18 (with effect upon all).

2. *eis* may denote hostile relationship, either a. enmity against God, the Son of Man, the Spirit, or God's messengers in the form of sin (cf. Lk. 15:18; Rom. 8:7; 1 Cor. 8:12; Mk. 3:29 [blasphemy]), or b. enmity against others as persecution (Jn. 15:21) or wrongdoing (Mt. 18:15; 1 Cor. 8:12). The NT does not use *eis* for God's reaction to sin or sinners; God is not our enemy.

3. *eis* denotes a friendly relationship a. between believers (Rom. 12:10; 16:6; 1 Cor. 16:3), b. between God and us (Rom. 5:8) or God and believers (2 Cor. 1:11; 1 Pet. 1:10), and c. between us and God: we were created for God (1 Cor. 8:6), and we are to repent toward God (Acts 20:21) and to believe in *(eis)* God or Christ, into whom, or whose name, we are baptized. (It should be noted that believing in Christ is rare in the Synoptic Gospels, Acts, and Paul, but common in John's Gospel, where it is found over 30 times between 2:11 and 17:20.).

F. Individual Points and Questions of Hebraisms.

1. *eis* may occur where one would expect *en*, e.g., when being in a place results from movement to it, e.g., Mt. 2:23; Mk. 1:39; Mk. 1:9 (dipping into the Jordan is suggested here); 2 Cor. 1:21. This interchangeability of *eis* and *en* is not a Hebraism but is Homeric. Most of the instances are in Luke and Acts (Acts 7:12 etc.).

2. *eis* can denote the predicate with verbs of becoming (Mt. 21:42), being (Mk. 10:8), holding (Mt. 21:46), etc., or the result with verbs like gather (Jn. 11:52), perfect (Jn. 17:23), reckon (Rom. 4:3). This again is not just a Hebraism.

3. *eis* can replace the genitive or dative (1 Pet. 1:11; 1:4; Eph. 3:16); this is common usage in the Koine and modern Greek.   [A. Oepke, II, 420-34]

---

heís [one, single]

1. The Understanding of Uniqueness in the NT. Only rarely is *heís* used as a digit in the NT. It usually means "single," "once-for-all," "unique," "unanimous," "one of many," or "only one." Theologically the most important feature is that God is one (as in Dt. 6:4). There is none beside him (Mk. 12:29). The origin and goal of the world are one in him. History and salvation history are a unity in the one Christ. This rules out dualism. We can serve only one Lord (Mt. 6:24). There is an inviolable union with him (1 Cor. 6:17)—the basis of the union of marriage (Eph. 5:31). Hence everything depends on one thing (Mk. 10:21). Keeping the law stands or falls with one commandment (Jms. 2:10). We must be strong for one hour. Disaster strikes in one hour. The NT shows a very strong sense of the significance of the particular. Yet this does not mean individualism. God works through the unity of family or people. God's action sets us in a threefold relation to himself, others, and the world. We are bound to the many. We are saved for their sake (Gal. 1:15ff.). We have to sacrifice what is most individual. Our heart's desire comes to expression in intercession (Rom. 9:3). Conversely, the destiny of others hinges on individuals (Rom. 11:1). NT thinking is organic. The alternative of contingent facts or rational truths is thus irrelevant. All things are determined by the heritage of the past and the dawning of the future, as well as by the decisive character of the present (Gal. 6:7ff.). Past ages, figures, and events decide what is to come. This thought is worked out in two great complexes, that of Adam and the common destiny of the race, and that of Christ and the unity of the church.

2. Adam and the Common Destiny of the Race.

a. Genesis portrays the unity of the race and its destiny in Adam and the fall. Judaism develops this thought, whether in the sense of original sin or of individual sins that start with Adam.

b. In the NT the growth, spread, and history of the race are traced from a single point (Acts 17:26). Adam's history is that of the origin of sin and its consequences (Rom. 5:12). The fall is historically once-for-all, i.e., it takes place once, but does so as the first in a series. It thus becomes the principle of sin that engulfs all members of the race.

c. Knowing the seriousness of this once-for-allness, we appreciate the inescapability of our situation. Death reigns (Rom. 5:14, 17). Our present disposition impels us to sin willingly and thus delivers us up to death. Adam's fall creates a historical fact which implies both external compulsion and inner corruption of the will, so that we all go the way of Adam (Rom. 3:10ff.). Being one with Adam, we are one in responsibility for sin, suffering, and death.

3. Christ and the Unity of the Church.

a. Adam points beyond himself to the second man, Christ (Rom. 5:14; 1 Cor. 15:47). As in Adam all die, in Christ all shall be made alive (1 Cor. 15:21-22). In this antitype of Adam, the race is given a new beginning and principle (Rom. 5:18). He is the head of the new race. Christ is man and more than man; he transcends every analogy. He continues the human line, breaks it, and begins a new line. He is more than those who precede and also than those who follow. Even as the positive counterpart of Adam, he is unique in relation to Adam; he is the divine Son (Mk. 12:6; Heb. 1:1ff.) who endows us, too, with sonship. This uniqueness is established by his special historical position, not by speculation. His work is the center of history. He ends all previous history and gives history a new beginning (Heb. 10:11ff.). He is the one for all (Jn. 11:50; 1 Cor. 15:3). The fact of Jesus is not just one event, nor does it merely illustrate an eternal law; it is all-decisive as the meeting point of all historical lines.

b. The destiny of the new humanity is fixed in Christ as that of the old humanity was fixed in Adam. "In Christ" denotes the unity of God's people (Gal. 3:28; Rom. 12:5). He is the head to which the church as his body is subject (Col. 2:10). Its growth is all from him (Col. 2:19). Its common existence, centered in the Spirit, is from him (1 Cor. 12:1ff.). It has a common destiny under his law; each must intercede for others and suffer and rejoice with them (1 Cor. 12:26; Gal. 6:2). Christ has brought the race together again in himself (Eph. 2:14-15). The church's own unity is thus of paramount importance (Eph. 4:4ff.). A new grouping comes, with those who believe in Christ on the one side, those who do not on the other. Christ himself is in unity with the Father and brings his own into the same fellowship (Jn. 17:23). He is the starting point and center of the new humanity as the Mediator through the historical event of his death and resurrection. The new situation created by this event is now a positive reality in the church—but in the church only as it takes this reality seriously in faith, thought, and action (cf. Eph. 4:3; Phil. 1:27; Rom. 12:6; Acts 4:32).

c. The unity of the church is not that of uniformity; it is organic. Differences exist between the members, i.e., between rich and poor, or men and women. These are not removed but they are transcended. Other differences emerge, e.g., between the strong and the weak. The Spirit also manifests himself in a rich plurality of charisms (1 Cor. 12:11ff.). Paul does not try to establish a Christian cosmopolitanism but is a Jew to Jews even while he resists the Judaizing of Gentiles. He sets himself in the world of his hearers to show how the cross is both offense and fulfilment for the world: the scandal that is the power of God and the foolishness that is the wisdom of God. In this regard Paul follows the divine model, for God brings Jews and Gentiles by different paths to the one salvation. Pentecost expresses this as by one Spirit the apostles preach one message in different tongues. With one saving event as its center, there is one church that is neither national nor universal, but the church of the nations.

→ *hápax, prōtos, mónos, theós*   [E. STAUFFER, II, 434-42]

---

eisakoúō → *akoúō*; *eisdéchomai* → *déchomai*; *eisérchomai* → *érchomai*; *eiskaléomai* → *kaléō*; *eísodos* → *hodós*; *eisphérō* → *phérō*; *hekatón tesserákonta téssares* → *dōdeka*; *ekbállō* → *bállō*; *ekdéchomai* → *déchomai*; *ekdēméō* → *dēmos*

---

ekdikéō [to avenge], *ékdikos* [avenger], *ekdíkēsis* [vengeance]

---

ekdikéō. By assimilation to *ekdikázō*, this acquires the sense "to avenge," "to punish." We find it in the LXX for a. (passive) "to be punished," b. "to avenge" with accusative of cause, c. "to avenge" with accusative of person (or dative), d. "to punish" with accusative of person (or dative), e. "to punish" with *ex, epí,* or more rarely *en* or *pará* of person, and f. "to avenge" with genitive of person or cause. In the OT the usage develops under the influence of the strong sense of the sanctity of blood, whereas a more legal concept affects the usage of the papyri, thus yielding the senses "to decide a case," "to contest a case," "to bring to judgment," and "to help to justice."

1. In the NT we find sense b. in 2 Cor. 10:6 and e. in Rev. 6:10; 19:2. The apostles are ready to punish disobedience; God avenges the blood of martyrs.

2. In Rom. 12:19 the sense is c.: Do not avenge yourselves.

3. Lk. 18:3 carries a reference to legal justice. It is thus closest to the forensic use, while Revelation is closest to the OT.

ékdikos. ékdikos means a. "contrary to the law," b. "avenger." It occurs only in sense b. in the NT. God is the avenger in 1 Th. 4:6, and the authorities are the executors of God's judgment in Rom. 13:4.

ekdíkēsis. ekdíkēsis means a. "revenge," "punishment," "retribution." b. The person on whom revenge is taken is in the genitive, and so c. is the person or cause on behalf of whom it is taken.

1. In the NT *ekdíkesis* can mean (a.) "revenge," "threat," "punishment," e.g., judicial punishment in 2 Cor. 7:11, divine retribution in Rom. 12:19; Heb. 10:30.

2. Magistrates are sent to punish wrongdoers in 1 Pet. 2:14 (b.).

3. In Lk. 18:7-8 God will vindicate his elect by speedy retribution, but in Acts 7:24 the sense is more that of avenging.

4. In 2 Th. 1:8 God will execute vengeance, with the dative of the person on whom it is inflicted.   [G. SCHRENK, II, 442-46]

ekdýō → *dýō; ekzētéō* → *zētéō; ekkathaírō* → *kathaírō*

---

ekkentéō [to put out, pierce]

"To put out" (the eyes), "to pierce" with a lance or sword, "to kill."

1. In the NT Jn. 19:37 is based on the obscure Hebrew of Zech. 12:10, which is interpreted as a prophecy or prefiguration of the completed reality of the death of Christ with the thrust of the spear into his side.

2. Rev. 1:7 relates the same OT verse to the expected return of Christ. Those who crucified him, both Jews and Gentiles, will see him when he comes and will be stricken by tardy remorse and fear of judgment. Closely related to Rev. 1:7 is Mt. 24:30. The pierced Lord is the one who comes with the sign of the Son of Man. At the parousia the cross that the world set up in secret will threaten the world openly as the victorious sign of the Lord who comes back to the world with power and great glory.

       [H. SCHLIER, II, 446-47]

ekklēsía → *kaléō; ekkóptō* → *kóptō; eklégō, eklogḗ, eklektós* → *légō; eklýō* → *lýō; eknéphō* → *néphō; hekoúsios* → *hekṓn; ekpeirázō* → *peirasmós; ekpíptō* → *píptō; ekplēróō, ekplḗrōsis* → *plēróō; ekpnéō* → *pneúma*

---

ekptýō [to spit out]

ekptýō ("to spit out") is a vulgar Koine word used in Gal. 4:14, probably in the literal sense rather than the figurative sense "to despise," "reject." The Galatians did not see in Paul a person demon-possessed because of his sickness, and so they did not spit at him in the ancient gesture of self-defense against demons or misfortune. There are many examples of spitting both in incantations and for the healing of sickness, and spittle came into use in Christian baptism in connection with exorcism. The Galatians, however, received Paul as an angel of God.   [H. SCHLIER, II, 448-49]

ékstasis [ecstasy, distraction],   *exístēmi* [to be astounded]

ékstasis. a. Literally "change of place," then figuratively b. "renunciation of goods," c. "degeneration," "confusion of spirit," "alienation" (often as "convulsive excitement"), and d. "ecstasy." In the OT we find sense c., especially as "illusion" or "terror"; the word is also used for the deep sleep that God sent on Adam in Gen. 2:12 and on Abraham in Gen. 15:12. The NT has c. ("astonishment," "terror") in Lk. 5:26; Mk. 16:8; Acts 3:10, and d. in Acts 10:10; 11:5 (Peter) and 22:17 (Paul).

A. Ecstasy outside the NT.

1. Foundations and Methodical Production of Ecstasy. Exceptional states of soul, whether due to supernatural power or neurotic disturbance, are widespread in antiquity. In detail experiences vary, and there is a fluid line between ecstasy and illusion and ecstasy and possession. In the narrower sense ecstasy denotes beneficial infilling by a substance or person, either by entry or by breathing. Early attempts are made to induce it by narcotics, music, dancing, rhythmic cries, and self-mutilation. In mysticism the goal is an absorption associated with visions and auditions.

2. Ecstasy in the Greek and Hellenistic World. Ecstatic phenomena are found early in the Greek world, as is shown by the Dionysus cult and the related but contrasting cult of Apollo. Dionysus is a union of both the hidden god and the manifested god who shares with his worshippers in a combination of creative desire and destructive frenzy. Wine and dancing and Bacchic cries express this, but also become a means to induce it. The dancing women show vividly how the world is bewitched for ecstatics. Since ecstasy brings vision, a prophetic element is involved which is most clearly reflected in the Delphic cult. A more masculine version may be seen in the Roman Bacchanalian rite in which men engage in prophecy accompanied by wild convulsions. Similar ecstasies occur in the Attis and Isis cults. We also find individual ecstatics both male and female (Bacchants and Sibyls). Ecstasy soon secures a firm place in philosophy. Thus Plato borrows from mystical ecstasy in his description of poetic inspiration. God is in man, or man in God, and there is a separation of body and soul; the soul, like the body, may be a hindrance to ecstasy, but may also be its organ. In Mithraism various ideas are present, e.g., rapture and vision in the body when it is divested of the weight of earth; God's power as our true being or as inbreathed spirit. Philo seems to be the first to use ecstasy in a technical sense. He views rational and mystical-ecstatic knowledge as complementary, but stresses the latter, which carries with it the dawning of divine light. The ecstatic theology of revelation reaches a climax in Neo-Platonism, for which the ecstatic is an organ of deity.

3. The Significance of Ecstasy for OT Religion. Analogous phenomena may be found in the OT sphere, but with important differences. The unusual aspect forms the starting point (cf. Num. 24:15ff.; Ezek. 3:25-26). The root *nb'* means "to speak with frenzy" and prophets are often called mad (2 Kgs. 9:11; Jer. 29:26). At first we find men of God with supernatural powers, seers with supernatural knowledge who can pass on their gifts, and true ecstatics like Deborah (Judg. 4:4) who give oracles for everyday occasions (1 Sam. 9:6ff.) or on political issues (2 Sam. 24:11). In so doing these declare the will of God and enforce his ethical demands. They include both great figures like Samuel and Nathan and many lesser figures (1 Sam. 2:27). Ecstatic groups also develop and wander about to the sound of music, intimating the future and catching up others in their enthusiasm (1 Sam. 10:5ff.). We cannot dismiss these groups as a Canaanite intrusion, for the cultic dance leaves room for them, and they represent the ethical majesty of God (1 Kgs. 18; 21:17ff.), have a strong sense of God's historical direction of his people, show some feeling for eschatology, and claim to work by God's Spirit rather than his direct presence. If classical prophecy holds aloof from the institutionalized *nᵉḇîʾîm*, there are points of connection. Amos is not one of them (7:14), but sees that they are from God (2:11). Other prophets accept the term *nāḇîʾ* (Is. 8:3) and find a place for ecstatic experiences (cf. Is. 6). Yet the role of ecstasy is reduced, and no effort is made to induce it. Visions may be deceptive; what counts is the moral will of God, and the word is the indispensable means to proclaim this. In such later prophets as Ezekiel, Zechariah, and Daniel visions may seem to resume their importance, but they do so only as literary devices.

4. *Ecstasy in Judaism.* Apocalyptic contains many visions but in fact testifies to the decline of ecstatic experience, for here again the visions are artificial products. Judaism endorses inspiration, but places it in the past and the messianic future. Yet ecstatic experiences still occur. Philo claims to be an ecstatic, and many rabbis refer to visions, auditions, fiery phenomena, and visits to paradise. It should be noted, however, that the visits to paradise are not necessarily ecstatic, that the fiery phenomena are usually symbolical, and that the Bath Kol involves a rational element.

B. Ecstasy in the NT.

1. In both appearance and preaching the Baptist probably has conscious links with the *nᵉḇîʾîm*, but he shows no traces of ecstaticism, and while he prays and fasts, does not try to induce it. John is a typical prophet of the word, full of ethical seriousness and eschatological passion, but sober and restrained.

2. Some have tried to portray Jesus as an ecstatic, but while he is unusual, has a developed prayer life, works miracles, and has what might loosely be called ecstatic experiences at his baptism and transfiguration, he is not deranged or possessed (cf. Mk. 3:21-22), avoids sensationalism, puts himself alongside the needy and sinful (cf. Mk. 9:14ff.), and displays a blend of uniqueness and simplicity whose essence lies in his relation to God, his calling, and its fulfilment.

3. Ecstatic features emerge in the primitive church, but the resurrection appearances are not ecstatic experiences, history and eschatology are still dominant at Pentecost, and if the church's prayer life borders on the ecstatic (Acts 4:24ff.) and an ecstatic element gives it direction and strength in its emergencies (Acts 7:55; 10:10ff.; 11:5ff., etc.), it opposes an ecstaticism that is devoid of moral discipline, integrity, and love (Acts 8:9ff.; 1 Cor. 12–14). Paul has ecstatic experiences (1 Cor. 14:18; 2 Cor. 5:13; 12:1ff.) but attaches no great importance to them (2 Cor. 12:1), sees in them an occasion for modesty, orients his higher knowledge to salvation history (1 Cor. 2:10ff.), and shows by his achievements that he is no psychopath. Similarly the divine of Revelation undergoes ecstatic experiences but is a genuine prophet inasmuch as he uses his visions to stir and strengthen the community at a time of serious threat.

C. The Ecstatic Element in the Early Church.
The term does not occur in the apostolic fathers or apologists but we see from the Didache and the Martyrdom of Polycarp that visions do occur. Celsus satirizes Christian ecstatics (Origen *Against Celsus* 7.9), but his account may be due to misconception or generalization from isolated cases. In the main the church, while not totally excluding the ecstatic element, resists unhealthy features and prefers an orderly ministry.

exístēmi (existánō).

1. Transitive "to remove from its place," figuratively "to alter," "to shake," "to set in terror"; in the NT "to confuse" in Lk. 24:22, "to bewitch" in Acts 8:9.

2. Intransitive "to remove oneself," figuratively "to lose one's wits," "go out of one's mind," "be terrified out of one's wits." The verb occurs in the LXX for many Hebrew words to denote the human reaction to God's self-revelation (cf. Ex. 18:9; 19:8; Hab. 3:2). Philo has the term for self-alienation in divinely caused rapture (*On Drunkenness* 146). In the NT we find the meaning "to be beside oneself" in Mk. 3:21 and 2 Cor. 5:13, where the reference is probably to a supposedly eccentric apostolic claim rather than to ecstatic experiences. Astonishment is the point in Lk. 2:47; Mt. 12:23; Lk. 8:56; Acts 2:7; 8:13; 9:21; 10:45; 12:16, i.e., at the child Jesus, at the miracles of Jesus, or at the phenomena displayed in the primitive church.

[A. OEPKE, II, 449-60]

---

ekteínō [to stretch out], *ektenḗs (ektenésteron)* [resolute], *ekténeia* [endurance], *hyperekteínō* [to overextend]

---

ekteínō. In the NT (except in Acts 27:30), the term is always used for stretching out the hand. 1. "Stretching out" is the basic sense, e.g., stretching out in sleep, or stretching a part of the body, or deploying an army, or of words for speech. The use in Acts 27:30 is a technical one; the sailors were trying to flee under cover of "paying out" anchors from the bow. 2. Stretching out the hands is a common expression in the LXX for many Hebrew equivalents. The subject may be God, the messenger of God, or an individual, and the phrase stresses a graphic point in the account. This is perhaps why Lk. 22:53 has the expression for laying hands on Jesus, unless there is simply a reference here to the stretching out of the hand to seize (cf. Mt. 26:51). Mt. 12:49 (cf. Mk. 3:34) describes a gesture that give added point to the saying of Jesus. The graphic significance is also plain in Mt. 14:28ff., where the hand of Jesus reaches out and catches Peter. In Mt. 12:9ff. the point of the command of Jesus is that movement is miraculously restored to the withered hand; by the will and word of Jesus the same movement that serves as a gesture, or is made in grasping, demonstrates his healing power. In Mt. 8:3 it is Jesus himself who stretches out his hand to the leper, thereby manifesting both his will to heal and his power to do so. The action is not necessary to effect the cure, as we see from Lk. 17:14. Thus in Acts 4:29 a particular action of God is not in view but a declaration of his will in active self-demonstration. In contrast the use in Acts 26:1 is technical; Paul introduces his speech with the regular gesture of the orator. In Jn. 21:18, however, we do not have a similar technical use; the variants show that play is made on the stretching out of the hands in crucifixion, the point being that Peter will make a final submission of his own will. In the apostolic fathers the verb occurs for the most part in OT quotations.

ektenḗs, ektenésteron. This term means "tense," "resolute," "eager." It occurs in the NT only in Acts 12:5; 1 Pet. 1:22; 4:8; Lk. 22:44 (*ektenésteron*). The point in 1 Pet. 4:8 is that love should not fail in view of the approaching end. This demands purity of will, so that this earnest love must be from the heart (1:22). Since the term expresses resolute concentration, it is very apt to describe prayer, and is used in this context for the fervent prayer made for Peter in Acts 12:5. The comparative in Lk. 22:44 refers only to the intensity of the prayer of Jesus. Since the problem for him is not death itself, but death as a vicarious death for sin, we do not have here any direct model for us in the hour of death. In the apostolic fathers *ektenḗs* comes to refer more to a Christian attitude than to Christian action (cf. 1 Clem. 62.2), as does prayer itself (59.2), so that later *hē ektenḗs* very naturally becomes a liturgical term.

ektḗneia. This word, meaning "endurance," occurs in the NT only in Acts 26:7. The twelve tribes hope to attain the promise by persistent service; in contrast, Paul points to the event of the divine self-revelation (26:13ff.).

hyperekteínō. Not found prior to 2 Cor. 10:14, Paul uses it here in the negative sense "to overextend"; he does not boast of more than he has actually done.

[E. FUCHS, II, 460-65]

éktrōma [untimely birth]

éktrōma is not a common word; it means "untimely birth," "miscarriage," "abortion." It occurs three times in the LXX (Num. 12:12; Job 3:16; Eccl. 6:3). In the NT the only instance is in 1 Cor. 15:8. As the last to see the risen Lord, Paul calls himself an *éktrōma*. He can hardly be referring to *tardy* birth and probably has in mind his abnormality. He had not been a disciple, was torn out of his former course of life, saw the Lord after the forty days, and was not fit in himself for his new life and calling. Possibly the term is one that his adversaries use to describe his lack of apostolic qualifications and Paul adopts it in relation to his pre-Christian past, but this hardly seems to fit in with the context, in which the stress falls on the abnormal nature of Christ's appearance to him. Ignatius applies the term to himself in *Romans* 9.2, and Eusebius in *Ecclesiastical History* 5.1.45 uses it for Christians who do not confess their faith in time of persecution.   [J. SCHNEIDER, II, 465-67]

---

ekchéō [to pour out],   *ekchýn(n)ō* [to pour out]

Both *ekchéō* and *ekchýn(n)ō* mean "to pour out," a. of fluids (also cultically), with blood "to kill," also "to lavish"; b. of gifts "to lavish."

1. In the NT "to shed blood" is used for the violent slaying of OT or NT martyrs (cf. Mt. 23:35; Rom. 3:15; Acts 22:20; Rev. 16:6). It is also used for the death of Jesus (Mk. 14:24; Mt. 26:28). In the saying about the cup this violent death takes place to save us and to inaugurate the new divine order (cf. Ex. 24:8, though there is no detailed correspondence). Jesus voluntarily accepts this violent death in an act of supreme self-sacrifice.

2. Lavishing divine gifts or powers in fulfilment of Joel 3:1-2 is the point in Acts 2:16ff. As in the OT the outpouring of the Spirit means both ecstatic inspiration and inner renewal (cf. Ezek. 39:29), so the same word occurs both for the giving of tongues (Acts 10:45) and the granting of the Spirit in baptism (Tit. 3:5). In Rom. 5:5-6 the overflowing love of God shown in Christ's death brings us constant assurance by the Holy Spirit.   [J. BEHM, II, 467-69]

ekpsýchō → psychḗ

---

hekṓn [willingly], *(ákōn)* [unwillingly], *hekoúsios* [voluntary]

---

hekṓn (ákōn). a. "Willingly," "intentionally"; b. "voluntarily," "not under compulsion." In philosophy Aristotle thinks the rational will can propose only what is good, but wrongdoing may be intentional or unintentional (due to circumstances). For Stoicism free obedience to the deity is the essence of morality and involves freedom from fate by acceptance of one's divinely imposed lot. In the NT the meaning in 1 Cor. 9:16-17 is "willingly" as opposed to *anánkē* in v. 16 and *ákōn* in v. 17. The point in Rom. 8:20 is that, whereas we sin by our own resolve, creation is subjected to futility through no will of its own.

hekoúsios. This word, too, means "willing," "intentional," "noncompulsory," but usually refers to the thing, not the person, e.g., cultic acts in the LXX. It denotes intentional transgressions in Heb. 10:26, i.e., by those who know saving truth, and "noncompulsory" consent in Phlm. 4: Paul wants willing compliance.

[F. HAUCK, II, 469-70]

élaion [olive oil]

---

1. The production of olive oil is part of a country's merchandise or economy (cf. Rev. 6:6; Lk. 16:6). Oil is an essential of life, used also for food, and as a trading commodity it can be a symbol of wealth (cf. Dt. 32:13). Rev. 6:6 can hardly be an allusion to Domitian's edict in A.D. 92 but is probably the prediction of a partial economic crisis (cf. Dt. 18:38ff.). Intimations of God's judgment are seen in high prices, but as yet there is no total destruction of vital resources.

2. Oil is used for lamps (Mt. 25:3).

3. Oil is also used in various kinds of anointing. In Lk. 7:46 anointing with myrrh is distinguished from anointing with olive oil to point the contrast between the Pharisee who neglects the customary honors to a guest and the sinful woman who performs a menial office in generous response to the Messiah. In Heb. 1:9, the passage Ps. 45:7, which some rabbis take messianically, is referred to the Son. The original speaks of the anointing of the king for marriage. Hebrews says that the Son, having loved righteousness, is exalted to Godhead and becomes the Christ, but there is perhaps a hint of the marriage of the Messiah and the community. The phrase "oil of gladness" (cf. Is. 61:3 LXX) indicates that anointing also expresses festive joy.

4. A final use of oil is for healing, as in Mk. 6:13; Jms. 5:14; Lk. 10:34, and the discussions in Pliny, Galen, etc. [H. SCHLIER, II, 470-73]

→ *aleíphō, chríō*

---

elénchō [to bring to light], *élenxis* [rebuke], *élenchos* [conviction], *elegmós* [rebuke]

---

elénchō.

1. The use outside the NT is complex. In Homer *elénchō* means "to scorn," "to bring into contempt." Later senses are a. "to shame," b. "to blame," c. "to expose," "resist," d. "to interpret," "expound," and e. "to investigate." LXX meanings arc

"to rebuke," "to punish," "to condemn or convict," "to examine," and for the root *ykh* it denotes God's disciplining by teaching, admonition, testing, and correction.

2. In the NT the use is restricted. With the accusative of person it means "to show people their sins and summon them to repentance," either privately (Mt. 18:15) or congregationally (1 Tim. 5:20). The Holy Spirit does this (Jn. 16:8), as also Christ does both now (Rev. 3:19) and at the parousia (Jude 15). No one can do it to Jesus himself (Jn. 8:46). Sinners experience this exposure when faced by the prophetic call (Lk. 3:19), divine instruction (Heb. 12:5), or the law (Jms. 2:9). *perí* is used to denote the fault (Lk. 3:19), with *hóti* for elaboration (Jn. 16:9ff.). Correction as well as exposure or conviction is implied; the corresponding action is *élenxis* (2 Pet. 2:16) or *elegmós* (2 Tim. 3:16).

3. The battle against sin signified by *elénchō* is based on the OT and Judaism. Lev. 19:17 demands correction. Rebuke is an integral part of love for the rabbis. Prov. 3:12; Job 5:17, etc. depict God as One who educates by correction (cf. Heb. 12:5). The Jewish view of the last judgment includes the exposure of wickedness, as in Jude 15. The group plays an important role in Greek philosophy. In Plato and Aristotle the reference is to the controverting of propositions or to negative conclusions, but Epictetus is closer to the NT with his ethical use in connection with the philosophical cure of souls.

elénchos, élenxis, elegmós. elénchos means a. "proof," "convincing," "refutation," and b. "investigation," "account." *elegmós* in 2 Tim. 3:16 and *élenxis* in 2 Pet. 2:16 mean the rebuking of the sinner. In Heb. 11:1, however, the sense of *elénchos* is "persuasion," but not in a subjective sense. Normal usage suggests that "things not seen" is an objective, not a subjective genitive. An *elénchos* is present as the basis of resting on what is hoped for. Faith does not do the convincing, but God, for the whole point in Hebrews is that faith stands on the revelation, word, and promise of God. Faith is the divinely given conviction of things unseen and is thus the assurance of what is hoped for.   [F. Büchsel, II, 473-76]

éleos [mercy], *eleéō* [to show mercy], *eleḗmōn* [merciful], *eleēmosýnē* [sympathy], *anéleos* [unmerciful], *aneleḗmōn* [unmerciful]

éleos, eleéō.

A. The Greek Usage. In Greek *éleos* is a *páthos,* the emotion roused by undeserved affliction in others and containing an element of fear as well as mercy. It is wholly fitting in the noble and plays a part in the administering of justice. For the Stoics, however, it is a sickness and unworthy of the sage, not because the Stoics are cruel, but because they do not think moral relations should be governed by a *páthos.*

B. The OT and Jewish Usage.

1. In the LXX *éleos* is mostly used for *ḥesed* (more rarely *raḥªmîm*). This denotes an attitude arising out of mutual relationship, e.g., between relatives, hosts and guests, masters and servants, those in covenant relation. It is an act rather than a disposition, with trust as the basis and loyalty as the appropriate attitude. An element of obligation is thus intrinsic, e.g., between ruler and subject. On the part of a superior, *ḥesed* also includes grace. This is particularly so on God's part. God has freely bound himself to his people, and the righteous may thus depend on his *ḥesed* as they themselves show

mercy. God's *ḥeseḏ* is his faithful and merciful love which is promised and may thus be expected even if it cannot be claimed. Yet because we are unfaithful, this love takes the form of pardoning grace from which definitive salvation will ultimately come, so that *ḥeseḏ* becomes an eschatological term. An act or expression of love is usually at issue rather than the emotion even in the case of *raḥᵃmîm,* which originally has a physical reference and denotes loving concern.

2. In later Judaism *ḥeseḏ* is used for acts of love, but it refers especially to the divine mercy, often with a stress on faithfulness, but also with a reference to mercy in distinction from wrath. God's *éleos* is upon Israel or those who love and fear him. It is his gracious action which is revealed, expected, and hoped and prayed for. The age of salvation is the age of *éleos*. Philo emphasizes that the law demands *éleos,* and he regards *éleos* as the third of God's mighty works. Being merciful, God is the Savior. For Philo, however, mercy is more an emotion than an act, and it has no eschatological significance.

C. *éleos/eleéō* in the NT.

1. The NT often uses *éleos/eleéō* for the attitude that God requires of us. In Mt. 9:13; 23:23 it denotes the kindness owed in mutual relationships. The LXX phrase "showing mercy" occurs in Lk. 10:37 for the actions of the Samaritan. In Mt. 18:33 the demand for mercy is based on the divine mercy which precedes ours (cf. Jms. 2:13). The new feature here as compared with Judaism is that God's mercy is known in and through Christ. In Jms. 3:17 and Rom. 12:8 *éleos* embraces lovingkindness in general, though pity is included. Concern for eternal as well as temporal welfare may be meant (cf. Jude 22).

2. God's *éleos* in the NT is often his gracious faithfulness (cf. Lk. 1:58; Eph. 2:4; 1 Pet. 1:3; Rom. 11:30ff.). Paul significantly relates God's *éleos* to his salvation; it is God's saving eschatological act in Christ (cf. Tit. 3:5). The opposite in Rom. 9:22-23 is God's wrath. Eschatological awareness may also be seen in Rom. 9:15ff.; 15:8-9; 1 Pet. 2:10; believing Gentiles are now caught up by the divine mercy. The need of mercy in the judgment comes to expression in 2 Tim. 1:18; Jude 21, and cf. Mt. 5:7. In salutations *éleos* may carry only an indirect reference to Christ, as in Gal. 6:16. Mercy may be individual as well as general, as we see from the cry for mercy in Mk. 10:47-78 or the mercy shown to Paul according to 1 Cor. 7:25; cf. Mk. 5:19; Phil. 2:27; 2 Tim. 1:16. In such cases there may not always be a specific reference to God's saving act in Christ.

eleḗmōn. This is an old Greek word for "merciful," "sympathetic"; it is fairly common in the LXX and later Judaism, mostly for God. The NT does not use it for God but has it for Christ in Heb. 2:17, and Jesus praises the *eleḗmones* in Mt. 5:7 (cf. Did. 3.8; Pol. 6.1; 2 Clem. 4.3).

eleēmosýnē. This word for "sympathy" is late in Greek. The LXX speaks of the *eleēmosýnē* by which God judges and which he shows to the righteous, innocent, and oppressed (cf. Dt. 6:25; Pss. 24:4; 103:6). A divine act and not merely an emotion is presupposed. The equivalent in Judaism takes on the sense of benevolent activity and can thus be used more narrowly for almsgiving. This is the meaning of *eleēmosýnē* in the NT (cf. Mt. 6:2ff.; Lk. 11:41; Acts 3:2ff.). Doing works of benevolence and giving alms are common expressions (cf. Mt. 6:1-2; Acts 9:36; Lk. 11:41; 12:33). With fasting and praying, giving alms is a special practice of piety for both Jews (Mt. 6:1ff.) and Christians (Did. 15.4). It is lauded in Acts 9:36 (cf. 10:2), but Jesus warns against its misuse in the service of personal vanity (Mt. 6:2-3) and Did. 1:6 warns against imprudent almsgiving (cf. Sir. 12:1).

anéleos. "Unmerciful." Not attested for certain outside the NT, this term occurs in Jms. 2:13: There will be no mercy in judgment for those who show no mercy.

aneleḗmōn. This is the more common word for "unmerciful." It occurs in the LXX but in the NT it is found only in the list of vices in Rom. 1:31.

[R. BULTMANN, II, 477-87]

> *eleútheros* [free], *eleutheróō* [to set free], *eleuthería* [freedom], *apeleútheros* [freedman]

A. The Political Concept of Freedom in the Greek World. By definition, freedom means self-disposing in independence of others.

1. This sense is partly fashioned by the contrast to slavery. Slaves belong to others, not themselves. Slavery is accepted as an institution; hence freedom arises both theoretically and practically only for those who are politically free. It is the freedom of the *politeía* as an association of the free.

2. Freedom, for Plato and Aristotle, is essential to a state. The best constitution guarantees the greatest freedom (Thucydides). This freedom is freedom within the law, which establishes and secures it. As an embodiment of the claim of the *politeía*, law protects freedom against the caprice of the tyrant or the mass. But freedom means alternation of government as free people both rule and are subjects. Democracy achieves this best by allowing the same rights to all citizens (cf. Plato, Aristotle, Herodotus). It implies equality of voice, honor, dignity, and power. It comes vividly to expression in freedom of speech. As Demosthenes says, there is no greater misfortune for free citizens than to lose this. Yet the concept of freedom in Attic democracy contains the seeds of its own decay, for by promoting individual development it undermines the law on which it rests. Freedom becomes the freedom to do as one likes. The law of the self replaces the law of the *politeía*. Plato perceives this clearly (*Laws* 3.701b/c). It leads to the rise of demagogues and opens the door to tyranny.

3. Freedom also has to be secured against external foes. It means independence and hence the defense of the *politeía* against "barbarians." *eleuthería* can thus be a general expression for the autonomy of the state. At a later stage it becomes a slogan for the common "freedom" of the states which the individual states all claim to champion even in their inner struggles. In this regard it is hardly distinguishable from *autonomía*.

B. The Philosophical Concept of Freedom in Hellenism (Stoicism).

1. In Hellenism, and especially Stoicism, the extolling of freedom increases. The true Cynic prefers freedom to all else. He persistently criticizes tyrants and bewails their fear and misery, which make them slaves too. He also attacks their courtier-parasites.

2. Freedom, however, is now much more than political freedom. It is that of the individual under the law of nature. This is regarded as a reversion to the original meaning. The formal sense is the same, but freedom now takes the form of independent self-determination. To find freedom we must explore our nature. We cannot control body, family, property, etc., but we do control the soul. External things seek to impose

a false reality on us. Hence we have to withdraw from them in a restriction of desires and an abandonment to pressures. This might seem to bring bondage but in fact results in liberation. For true liberation of this kind, there has to be liberation from the passions that represent the world in us. In particular, we must be rid of the dominant fear of death. We find freedom as we neutralize passions and surrender to the ineluctable power of circumstances. That this freedom can seldom be fully attained is recognized. Its fruit is assurance of soul. Those who seek flight in inwardness enjoy the freedom of impassibility and in so doing fulfil what they are as parts of God, or children of God, or God himself.

C. The Concept of Freedom in the NT.

1. The NT sees that the retreat into inwardness does not in fact bring freedom. Existence is inwardly defective, so that to take oneself in hand is simply to grasp a defective existence. Faced with a lost existence, we can come to ourselves only by subjecting our own will to the will of another. We achieve self-control by letting ourselves be controlled. Concretely, *eleuthería* in the NT is freedom from sin (Rom. 6:18ff.), the law (Rom. 7:3-4; Gal. 2:4), and death (Rom. 6:21-22; 8:21). It is freedom from an existence that in sin leads through the law to death. Existing in sin, we are its slaves (Rom. 6:20). The result is anarchy (Rom. 6:19). This means surrender to the craving of the *sárx* that is triggered by the law (Rom. 6:12). The law is intended for good, expressing God's claim, but in our sinful existence it brings sin to light by mediating sinful affections. It is an occasion for the self-seeking love of life that misuses the claim of God. By it there arises not merely the anarchic impulse of Rom. 6:17ff. but also the nomistic impulse of Galatians. Freedom, then, means freedom from the law as well as from sin, i.e., from the need to seek justification by the law. Freedom here is freedom from attempted autonomy, not by breaking the law, but by fulfilling our own interpretation of it in following our own needs, and doing our own will, by what seems to be an honest effort to do God's will. Freedom from the law means freedom from moralism, from self-lordship before God in the guise of serious and obedient responsibility. It thus has the further implication of being freedom from the self-deception in which we see ourselves as God and are thus blind to our true reality (cf. Jn. 8:32; Rom. 2:18ff.). Finally, the freedom that the NT proclaims in Christ is freedom from the death which is the end of human self-seeking in sin. In sin we surrender to an existence that refers to itself and not to God and that is thus severed from life. Sin carries death within it. Death is its power. Living by death (Rom. 6:23), it promotes its life by death (1 Cor. 15:56). Nature, which is subordinate to our historical existence, manifests the reality of separation from God in the process of corruption. In the human sphere, however, the movement of separated existence is to eternal corruption. In life itself we bring about death. Our works have death as their end (Rom. 6:21). We bring it on ourselves and others. As regards this existence that is given up to death, freedom means freedom from self and therefore from the law which delivers up fallen existence even in and of itself to ruin, i.e., the law of sin and death (Rom. 8:2).

2. How is this freedom achieved? The primary answer is: "By the act of Christ." Christ has made us free (Gal. 5:1). The reference here is to the event of the life that he offered up vicariously in obedience to God's will (cf. Gal. 3:13; 4:4). Our freedom is not an existential return to the soul. The Son makes us free (Jn. 8:36). The secondary answer is: "By the gospel call." We are called to freedom (Gal. 5:13). This is a call to the act of Christ which is the basis of a new life in freedom. The life-giving Spirit

of Jesus is present in the call (Rom. 8:2), advancing the claim of God's act in Christ, and making possible a true fulfilment of what the law demands as the will of God (Rom. 8:3ff.). The love of God enacted in Christ's vicarious death and resurrection summons us to recognize it for what it is, so that as we open our lives to the Spirit, by the Spirit and the life and power of Christ there arises in us an unselfish and self-forgetting existence. In the Spirit of Christ's freedom, we find our own freedom. This takes places in the gospel call which already goes out to Israel as promise, and which creates the true and free Israel (Gal. 4:21ff.). The gospel call goes forth in Christ's own word (Jn. 8:31). By the Spirit of truth, it makes the truth known (Jn. 16:13). It does so through ministers who serve the ministry of the Spirit and the Lord in a freedom in which our existence is fashioned into ever increasing glory (2 Cor. 3:17-18). In time, the call is received in baptism. The freed are the baptized (Rom. 6:17). Liberation from sin is by obedience to the baptismal teaching (Rom. 6:17-18). The Spirit of the love of Christ comes with the gospel message, grants liberation from sin, and claims us for the new and free obedience.

3. How do we bring this freedom to expression? The answer is: in love, i.e., not in isolation but in a life with others. We find freedom in service, in yielding our lives to the divinely demanded righteousness of love of God and neighbor (Rom. 6:18ff.). Freedom comes to expression in righteous acts of many different kinds (Gal. 5:22). Being free, we accept civil obedience (Mt. 17:24ff.; 1 Pet. 2:13ff.). We renounce rights for the sake of others (1 Cor. 9:19). We may forgo valid personal claims (1 Cor. 9:1). We do not make of our freedom a basis of superiority (as the strong were doing in Corinth) but in genuine freedom consider the consciences of others (cf. 1 Cor. 8:1ff.). We crucify ensnaring passions and demands (Gal. 5:24). We do not make human status an overriding concern (1 Cor. 7:20ff.), for slaves and free have the same standing with the Lord in whom they are both bound and free, and striving after freedom raises the danger that entanglement with claims will make impossible the unselfish readiness for others for which Christ's sacrifice has freed us. Yet this surrender of desires is not restrictive or self-assertive. Since the gospel assures us that we need not try to attain life by the law, we can fulfil the law freely in works that are not our own but the fruit of the Spirit (Gal. 5:23). Christ has met the claims of the law for us, and therefore, as the law of Christ (Gal. 6:2), it is for us the perfect law of liberty (Jms. 1:25)—a law which now works in the sphere of freedom and constantly mediates freedom. Freedom from sin and the law culminates in freedom from death. Works done in freedom aim at eternal life (Rom. 6:22). They produce the eternity disclosed in the event of Christ's love. Being freed from self-seeking, they make possible for both the self and others the life that is assured by God. They bring in God's future and make it available to others. Our present existence is still subject to death, for in itself it is still fallen. But it knows freedom from death in Christ's resurrection. By word and sacrament this freedom has taken place for it as the basis of life in self-forgetful dying. The disclosed freedom from death is its future enacted in Christ. It will be known here and now only as a sign in the works of freedom that manifest it. Thus those who have the Spirit working freedom in them long and sigh for the release from carnal existence and the manifestation of the children of God which mean that creation itself is set free from bondage and obtains the glorious liberty of God's children.   [H. SCHLIER, II, 487-502]

éleusis → *érchomai*

hélkō [to draw, compel]

The basic meaning is "to draw," "tug," or, in the case of persons, "compel." It may be used for "to draw" to a place by magic, for demons being "drawn" to animal life, or for the inner influencing of the will (Plato). The Semitic world has the concept of an irresistible drawing to God (cf. 1 Sam. 10:5; 19:19ff.; Jer. 29:26; Hos. 9:7). In the OT *hélkein* denotes a powerful impulse, as in Cant. 1:4, which is obscure but expresses the force of love. This is the point in the two important passages in Jn. 6:44; 12:32. There is no thought here of force or magic. The term figuratively expresses the supernatural power of the love of God or Christ which goes out to all (12:32) but without which no one can come (6:44). The apparent contradiction shows that both the election and the universality of grace must be taken seriously; the compulsion is not automatic. [A. OEPKE, II, 503-04]

Héllēn [Greek, Hellenc], *Hellás* [Greece], *Hellenikós* [Greek], *Hellēnís* [Greek (woman)], *Hellēnistēs* [Greeks, Hellenists], *Hellēnistí* [in the Greek]

A. *Héllēnes* in the Greek World.

1. From about 700 B.C. this term comes to be used for the Greek tribes, cities, and states. It develops in opposition to *bárbaroi*. Greek language, race, and culture are virtually absolutized, but on the basis of *paideía*, not a cult. Hence the term can sometimes be restricted to Greeks who share in Greek culture, and at other times be extended to barbarians who embrace Greek language and culture.

2. The process of Hellenizing was accelerated by the incorporation of Macedonia and the conquests of Alexander. Greek culture spread to Asia and Egypt, especially in the cities. In Egypt the term tended to be used only for the ruling caste, but in Asia, with more new cities, native non-Hellenes accepted Greek culture more widely, and even greater integration came with intermarriage. A movement to the west came also by way of Sicily and southern Italy and thence to Rome. Rome continued the process of Hellenization when it took over the Greek kingdoms, although it also brought about its downfall by opening the door to a revival of Near Eastern cultures.

3. The Jews were caught up in the process of Hellenization pushed by the Seleucid rulers. Many worshipped and read the law in Greek. A reaction came in the time of Antiochus Epiphanes but this did not wholly banish Greek culture. The last of the Hasmoneans and Herod and his sons posed as Hellenistic rulers and the incorporation of Judea into the Roman empire strengthened the Hellenizing process. Greek became a second commercial language and Jews met Hellenes in Jerusalem, in the half-Hellenized cities of Galilee, and on the main highways. Jews of the dispersion were affected even more. A rich Hellenistic literature developed to serve those who could speak only Greek and to spread Judaism among the Gentiles. Yet Judaism maintained itself, so that the term Hellene, in a perversion of its original use, came to denote the pagan. Jews rejected the cultus of the Hellenes while accepting their culture. Later a reaction developed even against Greek culture on the ground of its inseparability from idolatry.

B. *Héllēnes* among the Jews. The LXX sometimes uses the word, along with *Hellás* etc. Hellene is the normal sense. But for the Jews the Greek sphere that it denoted was a religious matter, so that the term approximates to Gentile. Thus when the high priest Jason was called Hellenic, it was because he was adopting Greek and abandoning Jewish customs. Hellenism as a specific complex of language, culture, and religion was the most dangerous form of paganism. Distinction was made, of course, between Hellenes and other Gentiles, as by Josephus in *Against Apion* 1.14 (also Philo), so that there is so simple equation of the groups.

C. *Héllēnes* in the NT. *Hellás* occurs for Greece in Acts 20:2, *Héllēn* is found in John, Acts, 1 Corinthians, Romans, Galatians, and Colossians, the feminine *Hellēnís* in Mk. 7:26 and Acts 17:12, *Hellēnikós* in Rev. 9:11 and Lk. 23:38 (some texts), *Hellēnistí* in Jn. 19:20 and Acts 21:37, and *Hellēnistḗs* in Acts 6:1; 9:29.

1. Only Luke and Paul really include *Héllēnes* in their narrative or theology. *Hellēnís* in Mk. 7:26 is ambiguous; it might simply mean Gentile or it could be a cultural term. The Synoptists never emphasize that Hellenes as such came to Jesus. The only parallel is in Jn. 12:20ff., but here the reference is to Greeks who had attached themselves to the synagogue (v. 20). In Jn. 7:35 "among the Greeks" seems to be meant geographically; the suggestion is that Jesus intends to go into the Greek world to teach the Greeks. In fact he does not teach Hellenes, nor does he command his disciples to do so.

2. The mission to Hellenes comes in Acts, where Hellenes denotes a. Greeks and Hellenized residents of Syria and Asia Minor, and b. inhabitants of Hellas and Macedonia. The first evangelism in this sphere is done in Antioch (Acts 11:20), then by Paul and Barnabas in Iconium and Thessalonica (14:1; 17:4), then by Paul in Corinth (18:4) and Ephesus (19:10). The Hellenes in these cities are the non-Jewish inhabitants, especially those who attend the synagogues. Churches of Jews and Hellenes thus arise and Paul picks up some baptized but not circumcised assistants. Whether Luke equates Hellenes and Gentiles may be debated. Acts 14:1-2 might seem to support this, but 17:4 etc. suggest that the Hellenes are mostly "God-fearers" already, so that the distinction is mainly a cultural one.

3. Acts also uses *Hellēnistaí* in 6:1 and 9:29. This is a new term of disputed meaning. In Acts 6:1 it probably denotes Jewish Christians of Greek language (and perhaps culture); Paul himself would be one of these. (In 9:29 it obviously denotes non-Christian Jews of the dispersion; cf. Acts 6:9.) Another view is that the Hellenists of 6:1 are believing Greeks. Arguments for this view are that "Hebrews" denotes race, not language, that Acts does not call such Greek-speaking Jews as Aquila or Apollos Hellenists, and that the names of the Seven favor Greek descent. On the other hand, the story of Cornelius makes little sense (10–11) if there were Greek Christians already in the church.

4. Paul refers to Hellenes in 1 Corinthians, Galatians, Romans, and Colossians, and always in connection with Jews, but also with barbarians. Hellenes are one part of the race to which the gospel is taken. His formulas thus have a national sense. As a Jew Paul is conscious of Jewish precedence. But the gospel is for all, and especially for the peoples that are unified by Greek language and culture. The characteristic of the Hellenes is wisdom, but this is an obstacle because their human wisdom is totally different from the divine wisdom of the gospel (1 Cor. 1:18ff.). If they know God from creation, they have fallen into idolatry and wickedness. They are thus under judgment and are included in the message of salvation (Rom. 1:16). They are not without a moral sense (Rom. 2:12ff.), so that Christians must take their moral judgment into account (1 Cor. 10:32), but they also come under threat for their wrongdoing (Rom. 2:7ff.). Any distinction between Jew and Hellene is resolved in the gospel as

God lavishes his grace on all who believe. The crucified Christ is God's power and wisdom to both Jews and Hellenes if they are called (1 Cor. 1:24). Jews and Hellenes are thus fused into a new unity, the community (1 Cor. 12:13). They are equal as members of Christ's body and bearers of his Spirit. In Christ there is no more Jew or Hellene (Gal. 3:27-28). The Hellene is incorporated into the seed of Abraham (Gal. 3:29). In the new man there can be neither Hellene nor Jew (Col. 3:9ff.). Paul, as the apostle to the Hellenes, develops the implications of the gospel for them, for it is he who has the task of bringing the message to them, who by his preaching brings innumerable Hellenes to Christ, and who resists the imposition of the yoke of the law upon them because he perceives that what counts for believers is not that they are Jews or Hellenes, but that they belong to one and the same body in Christ. For Paul the Hellenes are, of course, Gentiles. He does not equate the two terms, as the distinction between Hellenes and barbarians in Col. 3:11 shows, and as is also plain when wisdom is called their characteristic in 1 Cor. 1:22. Yet there is a close connection between Hellenes and Gentiles. The Gentiles, as the mass of peoples that are drawn into salvation history, include the Hellenes (cf. the parallelism of Hellenes, uncircumcision, and Gentiles in Rom. 1:16ff., or the tendency to use the terms interchangeably in 1 Cor. 1:22-23 and Rom. 9–11). If Hellenes are still a distinct group, they are among the Gentiles and represent them, although Gentiles is still a more general and common term. When Christianity is firmly established on Greek soil (and national distinctions are thus abolished), Hellene and Gentile become full equivalents.

[H. WINDISCH, II, 504-16]

---

ellogéō [to charge to an account]

The term *ellogéō* has a commercial sense in Phlm. 18: Paul will meet any loss suffered through Onesimus. Its use is figurative in the only other NT instance in Rom. 5:13. The argument here is that all are sinners prior to the giving of the law, and death reigns as a destiny posited in Adam, but until God's will is declared in the law sin is not transgression of the law and hence it is not counted or charged in the same way as it is after Moses.

[H. PREISKER, II, 516-17]

---

elpís [hope], *elpízō* [to hope], *apelpízō* [to despair], *proelpízō* [to be the first to hope]

elpís, elpízō.

A. The Greek Concept of Hope.

1. Plato says that human existence is determined not merely by acceptance of the present and recollection of the past, but also by expectation of the future, either good or bad. Hopes are subjective projections of the future. Good *elpídes* are hope in our sense, though later *elpís* is often used for this. Hope for the Greeks is a comfort in distress, but it is also deceptive and uncertain except in the case of the wise who base it on scientific investigation.

2. For Plato, what is at work in hope is the impulse toward the beautiful and the good. Hopes extend beyond the present life, so that one need not fear death. The

mysteries play on hope with their promise of a life of bliss after death, and hope may be grouped with faith, truth, and eros as one of the elements in an authentic life.

3. Earthly hopes are also important. Zeus gives hope, and Augustus is lauded for fulfilling old hopes and kindling new ones. Stoicism, however, has no interest in hope. Thus Epictetus uses the group only in the sense of expectation, and hope is shunned as no more than subjective projection of the future.

B. The OT View of Hope.

1. Normally the LXX uses *elpízein* and *elpís* for *bāṭaḥ*, but also for such terms as *yāḥal, qāwâ,* and *tiqwâ* (for full details see *TDNT,* II, 521-22).

2. In this usage there is no neutral expectation. Hope is expectation of good. It is linked with trust and yearning, and differentiated from fear. So long as there is life there is hope (Eccl. 9:4). It is not a dream that offers comfort but may also be illusory. The life of the righteous is grounded in a hope that implies a future because its point of reference is God. To hope is to trust. It is demanded even in good times. It is not our own projection but confidence in what God will do. God is our hope (Jer. 17:7). It has nothing to do with the calculation that may give a false sense of security. We are not to trust in riches (Job 31:24) or righteousness (Ezek. 33:13) or religious inheritance (Jer. 7:4). God can scatter all our planning (Ps. 94:11; Is. 19:3). Politicians who build on calculable forces will be confounded (Is. 31:1). Hope looks to him whom none can control. It is thus freed from anxiety (Is. 7:4) but must be accompanied by fear of God (Is. 32:11). Hence it must be a quiet waiting on God (Is. 30:15); the fault of Job is that he will not wait (Job 6:11). If God helps in present distress, he will finally put an end to all distress (Is. 25:9 etc.). Hope, then, grasps the provisional nature of every earthly present and is increasingly hope in the eschatological future.

[R. BULTMANN, II, 517-23]

C. Hope in Rabbinic Judaism.

1. Linguistically *elpís* finds little equivalent in the rabbinic world but materially the concept is a common one, especially in the form of messianic hope. The form of this expectation explains the linguistic phenomenon.

2. *Messianic Expectation.* a. Positively this is expectation of the fulfilment of Jewish hopes and negatively it is expectation of judgment on the wicked. The promises belong to the people as a whole; individuals share in them only as members of the people. The basis is that the future belongs to God, but for participation in the promises there must be observance of the law as well as trust in God. The law reveals God's will, but as a way of life, not a theoretical system. This will does not change with the future aeon. The difference is that the Messiah, who keeps and teaches the law, will extend it to the Gentiles. But the messianic age will come only when Israel itself keeps the law. b. The future then, while resting in God's hands, depends on his people's relationship to him. The messianic fulfilment may be hastened or delayed by human action, and an element of uncertainty thus attaches to it, or at least to the time of its coming. Only a strict devotion to keeping the law can dispel this uncertainty, as one may see from the example of Aqiba. c. The resultant attitude, however, differs from what is really meant by hope, for a calculated attempt is made here to guarantee the expectation; the divine sovereignty, which is the basis of true hope, is to that extent abrogated. d. The emphasis on personal achievement which the demand for legal observance entails also brings with it uncertainty as to personal salvation.

3. *The Problem of Assurance of Salvation.* a. Individual expectation accompanies the people's expectation, but since this expectation includes the separation of the

righteous and the wicked, doubt remains as to whether one will qualify for eternal felicity, as the pessimism of some rabbis in face of judgment bears witness. Moses accuses those who do not keep the law (Jn. 5:44). b. Attempts are made to overcome the lack of assurance by pointing to prayer, or noting the manner of death, or developing a theology of suffering whereby the suffering of the righteous pays in this life for the guilt that would otherwise have to be paid for after death. These measures fail to produce true hope, however, for they focus on the self instead of referring to the divine grace and gift which alone can give a true and certain hope.

[K. H. RENGSTORF, II, 523-29]

D. The Hope of Hellenistic Judaism.

1. Hope is part of life and is cut off only by death. We hope for healing when sick, or for reunion when separated. The hope of the wicked is vain. So is the hope fixed in military might. The righteous hope in God, and fearing him need fear nothing else. What is hoped for is his protection, or some special blessing, or help even in death. Eschatologically the restoration of Israel is the theme of hope. See especially Sirach, Wisdom, and 1, 2, and 4 Maccabees for these aspects of hope.

2. Greek psychology influences Philo. Hope for him is neutral expectation, though usually of the good. It is the counterpart of recollection. It offers comfort in distress, but as our own projection of the future. Yet for Philo hope reaches beyond human projection to the perfection of true humanity. In this regard it must be directed to God and his forgiveness and salvation, thus taking on an aspect of trust.

E. The Early Christian Concept of Hope.

1. The NT concept of hope is essentially governed by the OT. Only when the sphere is secular does the group denote (good) expectation; cf. "counting upon" in Lk. 6:34; 1 Cor. 9:10, etc., or with more of an accent on "hoping" Lk. 23:8; 24:21; Acts 24:26; Rom. 15:24; 1 Cor. 16:7. The OT element of trust is strong when the relation is to persons, as in 2 Cor. 1:3; 5:11; 13:6. Trust in persons is the point in 1 Cor. 13:7, though it rests on trust in God (v. 13).

2. When fixed on God, hope embraces expectation, trust, and patient waiting. It is linked to faith, as in Heb. 11:1, which stresses the certainty of what is divinely given. Rom. 8:24-25 makes not only the formal point that we do not hope for what is visibly present but also the material one that what is visibly present offers no basis for hope since it belongs to the sphere of the *sárx*. Hence we have to wait patiently, in hope believing against hope, i.e., unable to count on controllable factors and hence thrown back on God (Rom. 4:18). Patient endurance is the main point in Rom. 5:4; 1 Th. 1:3; Heb. 6:11, but sure confidence is meant in 1 Cor. 15:19; 2 Cor. 1:10; Phil. 1:20; Heb. 3:6; 1 Pet. 1:21. The main difference from the OT is that the act of salvation has now been accomplished in Christ, so that hope itself is an eschatological blessing, and there is every reason for confidence such as Paul has in the Corinthians (2 Cor. 1:12ff.). Hope rests on faith in the act of salvation (Rom. 8:24-25) and is sustained by the Spirit (vv. 26-27). It is an integral part of the Christian life (Rom. 15:13; 12:12). As such it goes closely with faith and love (1 Th. 1:3; 1 Cor. 13:13). It endures even when we attain to sight, for its focus is not on what is to be given but on the God who gives it and will maintain it when it is given. Endurance may be stressed in this life (Rom. 5:2, 4-5), but our waiting is confident, for we are saved by hope (Rom. 8:24).

3. *elpís* occurs only rarely in John (cf. Jn. 5:45; 1 Jn. 3:3), but is embraced here by *pístis,* or by endurance in Revelation. The element of waiting for the eschatological

future is prominent in Col. 1:5; 1 Tim. 4:10; Acts 23:6 (the resurrection), but hope is itself an eschatological blessing in Mt. 12:21; 1 Pet. 1:3, and cf. Christ as our hope in Col. 1:27 and hope as a gift in 2 Th. 2:16. No pictures of the future are given (except in Revelation), so that trust in God's act is always a constitutive element in the Christian's hopeful expectation.

apelpízō. This later word means "not to believe or hope," e.g., that an illness will be cured. In the LXX it can mean "to give up hope." In the NT it occurs in some versions of Eph. 4:19 in depiction of the heathen. There is a singular use in Lk. 6:35, where it means "without expecting to receive again, or to receive any return." The normal meaning would be "without despairing," i.e., "hoping for a heavenly return," but this does not fit the context.

proelpízō. This word means "to hope before or first." In Eph. 1:12 the sense depends on the reference of the "we." If the "we" are Jewish Christians, the point is that they hoped before the Gentiles, or prior to Christ's coming. If the "we" are all Christians, the before refers to the present in relation to the consummation.

[R. BULTMANN, II, 529-35]

---

embateúō [to enter into]

a. "To enter," "go into," usually military occupation in the LXX, entering on an inheritance in the papyri, also used of gods coming to a holy place or a demon indwelling a person. b. The word is used for initiation in the mysteries. c. "To approach with a view to examining," i.e., "to inquire into" is also a possible meaning, as in 2 Macc. 2:30; Philo *On Noah's Life as a Planter* 80.

The only NT instance is in Col. 2:18. Exegetes favor sense b. or sense c. Against b. it should be noted that the inscriptions never use *embateúein* alone (as here) and it always takes place in a sanctuary (unlike here). The sense, then, seems to be c. What the false teachers try to achieve by ecstasy and asceticism is opposed to adherence to the exclusiveness of Christ (2:19). All wisdom is present in Christ, so that there is no need to enter by painful investigation into what is seen in ecstatic visions, as the false teachers require.   [H. PREISKER, II, 535-36]

emménō → ménō; emphanízō → phaínō

---

emphysáō [to breathe on]

In the LXX this denotes the blowing of God's breath into or upon humans (Gen. 2:7), or creation (Ps. 104:29-30), or dead bones (Ezek. 37:5, 14). In the NT it occurs only in Jn. 20:22 for Jesus' breathing on the disciples to impart to them the Spirit who is released by Christ's work and by whom they will continue what he has begun in exercise of his binding and loosing authority. The giving of the keys, the missionary command, and the outpouring of the Spirit are combined here in a single act of creation that denotes the beginning of a new reality of life.

[E. STAUFFER, II, 536-37]

émphytos → phýō

---

en [in, on, with, etc.]

A. *en* with the Impersonal Dative.

1. This use is theologically significant when supraterrestrial localities are denoted, especially "the heavens"; cf. "my or our Father" in heaven in Mt. 10:32-33 etc.; "master" in Eph. 6:9; Col. 4:1; joy, peace, reward, treasure, commonwealth in Lk. 15:7; 19:38; Mt. 5:12; 6:20; Phil. 3:20. In such expressions heaven is God's dwelling. If the visible heaven is referred to in Mk. 13:25 and Acts 2:19, the ideas are close to those in Revelation (cf. 12:1; 4:2; 19:14).

2. Another sense of *en* in this usage is "with," e.g., "with a rod" in 1 Cor. 4:21, "with his kingdom" in Mt. 16:28, "with his blood" in 1 Jn. 5:6.

3. The sense may also be "in virtue of," e.g., "much speaking" in Mt. 6:7, "this retort" in Acts 7:29, boasting "of" in Gal. 6:13-14, "because" in Heb. 2:18, "therefore" in Heb. 6:17.

4. Another meaning is "by," e.g., "by the hand" in Acts 7:35; Gal. 3:19, and especially "by Christ's blood," as in Rom. 5:9; Heb. 9:22; Rev. 1:5. Senses 2-4 are unusual in Greek and betray Semitic influence.

B. *en* with the Personal Dative.

This is a more difficult use. The spatial sense is basic, but other senses, e.g., the instrumental, exert an influence.

1. With Persons in General. a. With a name in quotations, *en* denotes the author (Mk. 1:2) or a character (Rom. 11:2). b. With the plural or collective singular it means "among," as in Rom. 1:12; Gal. 1:16. c. It also denotes the close connection of a possession, attribute, or event with a person (Mk. 9:50; Rom. 9:17). With knowledge it may denote the one who makes known (1 Cor. 4:6) or the one who knows (Rom. 1:19; Gal. 1:16). d. It may express the location within us of psychological processes or qualities (cf. Mt. 3:9; Mk. 2:8; Lk. 12:17; Jn. 6:61; Acts 10:17; Rom. 8:23; in the heart, Mk. 2:6; or in the conscience, 2 Cor. 5:11); especially in the religious or ethical sphere, e.g., fellowship with God in Jn. 2:25, sin in Rom. 7:8 etc., Satan's work in Eph. 2:2, pagan blindness in 2 Cor. 4:4, observance of the law in Rom. 8:4, the effects of preaching in 1 Cor. 1:6, God's work in Phil. 1:6, also anointing, life, joy, faith, witness, etc., or, in relation to Satan, no truth (Jn. 8:44), and, in relation to God or Christ, life (Jn. 5:26), the treasures of wisdom (Col. 2:3), the fullness of deity (1:19). Cf. the phrase "hidden in God" in Eph. 3:9; Col. 3:3. e. The spatial use sometimes passes over into an instrumental (Gen. 9:6; Rom. 9:7; Heb. 11:18; Mk. 3:22; Acts 17:31; cf. 1 Cor. 7:14, and perhaps Acts 17:18), for which parallels suggest a partially local and partially instrumental sense.

2. en with pneúma. a. The concept of the Spirit in us is local (cf. Num. 27:18; Jn. 14:17; 1 Cor. 3:16). b. The converse, that we are in the Spirit (Mt. 22:43; Rom. 8:9; Rev. 21:10; 1 Cor. 12:3; Eph. 6:18), is based on the spatial sense but approximates to the idea of a state (cf. Lk. 4:14; Acts 22:17). In the contrast with "in the flesh" in Rom. 8:8-9 the Spirit is the active principle of the ethical life. The ramifications are important for the preaching of the gospel (1 Th. 1:5) and prayer (Eph. 6:18). The demand of Jn. 4:23-24 stresses the relation between God's personal being and the worship we are to render him. Something of an instrumental use may be seen in Rom. 14:17; 1 Cor. 6:11; 12:9.

3. en Christō̄ Iēsoú, en kyríō̄, and Related Formulas. These formulas are largely peculiar to Paul. a. In general they denote membership in Christ and his church (Phil. 1:13; 2 Cor. 12:2; 1 Th. 4:16; Rom. 8:1; 16:11). b. They may characterize the Christian state or activity (2 Cor. 2:12; Rom. 9:1; 2 Th. 3:4; 1 Cor. 15:31, etc.). c. They may also denote value judgments circumscribing the sphere of reference (Rom. 16:10, 13; 1 Cor. 3:1; 4:10, 17; Col. 1:28). d. They may denote the objective basis of fellowship with God, e.g., with grace in 2 Tim. 2:1, eternal life in Rom. 6:23, love of God in Rom. 8:39, will of God in 1 Th. 5:18, calling in Phil. 3:14, promise in Eph. 3:6, etc. e. They may denote the gathering of many into one, as in Rom. 12:5; Gal. 3:28; Eph. 2:21-22; Col. 1:16-17 (creation); Eph. 1:10 (the cosmos). This rich usage is not just a Hebraism, nor does it rest on a mystically local conception, but it is based on the view of Christ as a cosmically and eschatologically universal personage. Like Adam, Christ initiates a whole race, an order of life instead of death. This differs from the common idea of the primal man by (a) its distinguishing of the first man from the last, and (b) its belief that the author of the second creation is historically present and has thus inaugurated the new creation. We move into a different sphere in baptism, so that the formulas contain a local as well as an instrumental nuance, but with the strong sense of a state.

4. *Christ in Believers.* This less common phrase is also essentially Pauline. Christ, the inaugurator of the new aeon, lives in his people (Rom. 8:10; Gal. 2:20; Col. 1:27). He must be formed in them (Gal. 4:19). This involves suffering (2 Cor. 1:5; 4:10; Col. 1:24). But even if concealed, Christ's life is in our mortal bodies and may be known by faith (Gal. 2:20; 2 Cor. 4:18; 13:5).

5. *The en of fellowship in John.* In John and 1 John we have the *en* of religious fellowship, often with *eínai* (Jn. 10:38; 1 Jn. 2:5b, etc.) or *ménein* (Jn. 6:56; 1 Jn. 2:6, etc.). Reciprocity is frequently stressed (Jn. 6:56; 1 Jn. 3:24, etc.). The Father is brought into the relationship, either with Jesus (Jn. 10:38) or with us (1 Jn. 4:12-13). We thus have a triangle (Jn. 14:20; 17:21; 1 Jn. 2:24). The formulas are neither ecstatic nor eschatological but mystical in a very broad sense with a strong personal and ethical reference (1 Jn. 1:3); cf. constructions with *agápē* and *lógos* (Jn. 15:10; 1 Jn. 2:14). There is no hint of the sacred marriage, nor are there any Hellenistic or Gnostic parallels.   [A. OEPKE, II, 537-43]

endēméō → *dḗmos; endoxázomai, éndoxos* → *dóxa; endynamóō* → *dýnamis; endýō* → *dýō; enérgeia, energéō, enérgēma, energḗs* → *érgon; eneulogéō* → *eulogéō; enthyméomai, enthýmēsis* → *thymós*

---

enístēmi [to be present]

As used in the NT this means a. "to enter" in a temporal sense, hence "to be present," and b. "to intervene." We have sense a. in 2 Th. 2:2; Rom. 8:38; 1 Cor. 3:22; Gal. 1:4; Heb. 9:9. The sense "to threaten," "impend" is improbable in 1 Cor. 7:26, since it is not attested elsewhere. The sufferings of the new aeon have already come (cf. Rom. 8:22). Sense b. is possible in 2 Tim. 3:1 (will "break upon" us), but a. fits well enough (will "come").   [A. OEPKE, II, 543-44]

enkainízō → *kainós; enkakéō* → *kakós; enkrínō* → *krínō; enóptēs* → *horáō; énnoia* → *noús; énnomos* → *nómos; énochos* → *échō*

---

entéllomai [to command, commission], **entolḗ** [commandment, commission]

---

entéllomai. "To command," "commission," mostly with a ruler as subject, though sometimes the deity, or a teacher. The LXX uses it often, with the king as subject, or Moses, but especially God. In the NT we find 1. the general sense "to commission" (Mt. 17:9; Mk. 11:6); 2. the reference to God's commanding, mostly in LXX quotations (Mt. 4:6; Lk. 4:10; Mt. 15:4; Acts 13:47); 3. the *entéllesthai* of Moses (Mt. 19:7; Jn. 8:5); and 4. Jesus' commanding of his disciples in his teaching (Mt. 28:20— where the commands are related to his own ruling presence), his orders immediately prior to the ascension (Acts 1:2), and his specific commanding of love (Jn. 15:14, 17).

entolḗ.

A. *entolḗ* outside the NT.

1. entolḗ in the General Usage of the Greek and Hellenistic World. The meaning is "command," "commission," a. as the command of a king or official, b. as the instruction of a teacher, c. as a commission, and d. as authorization.

2. The Specifically Religious Reference to the entolaí of the Law in the LXX and Hellenistic Judaism. The term acquires a solemn religious sense in the LXX (Hebrew mostly *miṣwâ,* sometimes *piqqûḏîm*) when used for specific requirements of the law. Josephus and Philo, however, rarely use it in this sense, preferring *nómos* or *nómoi.*

3. The Stoic Truncation of the entolḗ Concept in Philo. Philo avoids the term because he finds it too official and historical. He is less concerned with the content of the law than with its ethical substance and its agreement with natural or cosmic law. Like the Stoics, he links *entolḗ* with a lower form of morality. The voluntary act is higher than the commanded act. Commands are given only to the earthly Adam. The true sage knows and practices virtue without them. Commands may be tolerated only for the immature and uneducated.

B. The Synoptic Witness Endorses the Elementary *entolḗ* and Emphasizes Its Central Unity.

In the Synoptics the debate with Pharisaism affects the usage. The synagogue enumerates 613 commands and thus has to try to find some basic principles (cf. Mt. 19:18; Mk. 12:28). Yet no command may be neglected (cf. Lk. 15:29), and *entolḗ* may refer not only to the Ten Commandments but to other provisions of the law (cf. Mk. 10:5; Jn. 8:5). Jesus unconditionally accepts the Ten Commandments (Mk. 10:17ff.). We do justice to the *entolḗ* only as we follow these, amplifying them with the positive command of love (Lev. 19:18) as expressed in giving to the poor. In Mt. 5:19, again, Jesus endorses the smallest commandments, probably the Ten Commandments as those that occupy least space on the scroll. The two tables are an elementary basis of life in the kingdom. Transcending them is the issue in true righteousness (Mt. 5:21ff.). "Least in the kingdom" is a rabbinic turn of phrase that does not suggest rank but stresses how seriously one's destiny depends on decision relating to the commands. The attack on human commandments is not an attack on tradition as such but on casuistic interpretations which overturn the elementary requirement. By concentrating on the main thrust, Jesus gives added force to the divine *entolḗ.* He does this especially when he finds the essence of the commandments in love of God and love of neighbor (Mt. 22:36ff.; Lk. 10:26ff.). This accords with what is actually written in the law itself, so that the scribe and Jesus may give the same answer. The first great command is linked with the Shema, while the second is a common rabbinic compendium. Hence Jesus is not engaging in a creative act; he is simply offering a unitary and central conception taken from the law itself. Yet the combination is distinctive, for it shows that service of God cannot be isolated nor love of neighbor depreciated. The two belong together.

C. The Evaluation of _entolé_ in Terms of the History of Revelation in Paul and Hebrews.

1. Paul interprets the _entolé_ in Rom. 7. While the story of the fall is in the background, he equates it with _nómos,_ relates it to the tenth commandment, raises the question of the relation of law and sin, and bases his exposition historically on Rom. 5. The law, which is linked with Moses, gives the knowledge of sin. By transgressing it, we share in Adam's sin. What is depicted more generally in ch. 5 is applied individually (though not autobiographically) in ch. 7. Sin grasps the opportunity provided by the _entolé_ and by deception leads us eschatologically to death. The _entolé_ makes possible the full development of sin and its consequences, but it is itself good as the righteous requirement of God. God uses it to bring sin out of its obscurity and in this way to open the door to justification. For Paul, then, _entolé_ is the law in its character as divine command, but in itself it cannot bring salvation either by way of its fulfilment or by its preparatory unmasking of sin. From another angle Christ is our peace since he has broken down the barrier of the law of _entolaí,_ i.e., the specific ordinances of the law (Eph. 2:14-15).

2. If _entolé_ cannot save, there is a sense in which Christians must still keep the _entolaí_ (1 Cor. 7:19). The content of this observance is the fulfilment, in the Spirit and on the basis of faith, of the law of love (Gal. 5:6). Paul thus agrees with the Synoptic Jesus and John in summing up all the requirements of the second table in the law of love (Rom. 13:9). This means that the individual commandments are still relevant; the fifth commandment may be cited in Eph. 6:2, and it has special significance due to the annexed promise. In Pauline writings _entolé_ always denotes an OT commandment except in 1 Tim. 6:14 and one reading of 1 Cor. 14:37 ("a command of the Lord").

3. In Hebrews the reference of _entolé_ is always to the law, e.g., the priestly law in 7:5, the institution of the covenant in 9:19; _entolé_ denotes the specific requirement and is always accompanied by _nómos_ as the sum of the whole. The revelation in Christ has shown the old _entolé_ to be external and transitory. Since it cannot lead to fulfilment, its validity has been annulled (7:18).

D. The Christian Message as _entolé_ in the Conflict against Gnosticism and Libertinism (the Johannine Writings and 2 Peter). In John (apart from Jn. 11:57) _entolé_ has these senses.

1. In Jn. 10:18 the Father's _entolé_ to the Son is that he should give his life and take it again, while in 12:49 the Father's _entolé_ underlies the word of the Son as the word of life which the Son mediates by voluntarily accepting the task that the Father commits to him and thus enjoying his loving authorization.

2. Jesus gives his disciples the new _entolé_ of love. This has a christological basis (Jn. 13:34; 15:12). If _entolé_ still entails an imperative, rootage in the love of Christ and decision for him rule out both moralism and mysticism.

3. Keeping Christ's _entolaí_ is a mark of love for Christ (Jn. 14:15, 21). If we love him, we both "have" and "keep" them. In view of the basis, the plural _entolaí_ is not legalistic. The many commands are summed up in the one command of love, which comes to expression in the multiple spheres of the obedient life. In the light of Jn. 15:10 "task" or "commission" might also be embraced by _entolé,_ but _tereín tás entolás_ means "keeping the commandments," not "fulfilling a commission." Comparison of the disciples' keeping of the commandments with the Son's doing of the Father's work

shows that a personal relationship is involved, especially in view of the common abiding in love.

4. In the Johannine Epistles the following features are to be noted. a. The *entolaí* are always related to the one *entolḗ* of love. b. The sharper conflict with Gnosticism leads to a heavier stress on keeping God's commandments (1 Jn. 2:3; 3:22; 5:3; 2 Jn. 4). True understanding of love for God must be opposed to mystical union, and love of God must be strictly related to love of the brethren. c. The description of the *entolḗ* as both old and new is directed against the Gnostic love of novelty. d. Also aimed at Gnosticism is the relating of faith and the *entolḗ* (1 Jn. 3:23) and the insistence that the commandments are not grievous (5:3). The law does not pose a problem, as in Paul, for the *entolḗ* is bound up with faith and the battle is against antinomian Gnosticism. There is no true gnosis without *entolḗ* (1 Jn. 2:3-4), but there are no *entolaí* without the *entolḗ* linked to Jesus, and as in the Gospel, though less explicitly, keeping the commandments is keeping the word. Revelation, too, links God's commands to Jesus and witness to him (cf. 12:17; 14:12). 2 Peter is directed against libertinism and understandably calls Christian teaching *entolḗ* in 2:21 and 3:2. The *entolḗ* of 1 Tim. 6:14, however, is the charge that is committed to Timothy. In the apostolic fathers *entolḗ* takes on a more legal sense. Subjection to God's commandments is the content of the Christian life (Barn. 4.11). Christ fulfilled these commandments (Barn. 6.1). He is the legislator of a new law (Ignatius *Ephesians* 9.2; *Polycarp* 2.2; 2 Clem. 17.1; Justin *Dialogue with Trypho* 12:2-3).

[G. SCHRENK, II, 544-56]

énteuxis → *tynchánō*; *entolḗ* → *entéllomai*; *entynchánō* → *tynchánō*

Enóch [Enoch]

A. Enoch in Judaism. The name comprises a whole group of differing ideas. The title "Book of Enoch" refers to this material. The brief note in Gen. 5:21ff. provides the occasion for its development. Enoch's position as the seventh and his walk with God give him a special importance that leads to his linking with secret knowledge and the primal man, while his 365 years suggest a relation to astronomy. The resultant traditions are deposited in the noncanonical writings; cf. Sir. 44:14ff.; Jub. 4:17ff., etc., where he is the recipient of divine secrets, an ecstatic, a divinely appointed witness, and a heavenly high priest of outstanding righteousness; Ethiopian Enoch, which stresses his knowledge by visions of angelology, astronomy, and eschatology.

B. Enoch Traditions in Early Christianity. Not surprisingly, the NT refers to the Enoch literature but has no Enoch tradition of its own. Lk. 3:37 is based on Gen. 5:21ff. Heb. 11:5 repeats ideas found in Ethiopian Enoch and Jubilees. Jude 14 quotes literally from Eth. En. 7:9. There are probably other allusions to Ethiopian Enoch in Jude 4ff. Revelation also makes use of ideas that occur in Ethiopian Enoch, and there may be indirect allusions in Paul. Jn. 3:13 seems to be opposing the traditions relating to the ascension of Enoch which would make him the exalted Son of Man. 2 Peter seems not to use the materials accepted in Jude, but in early Christian writings we still find Enoch ideas, e.g., in 1 Clem. 9:2-3; Asc. Is. 9:6ff.; Justin *Apology* 2.5; Barn. 16:5.   [H. ODEBERG, II, 556-60]

→ *huiós toú anthrṓpou*

exangéllō → angelía; exagorázō → agorázō; exaitéō → aitéō; exakolouthéō → akolouthéō; exanástasis, exanístēmi → anístēmi; exapatáō → apatáō; exapostéllō → apostéllō; exartizō → ártios; exegeírō → egeírō; exérchomai → érchomai

---

éxestin [it is proper, possible], *exousía* [right, power], *exousiázō* [to have the right or power], *katexousiázō* [to exercise authority]

éxestin. "It is free," denoting a. an action that is possible because there is occasion for it or no obstacle to it, b. an action that is not prevented by a higher norm or court, and c. an action to which there is no psychological or ethical block. In the NT the term mostly refers to God's law or will with its specific demands, especially the OT law. The NT itself does not ask what is permitted in this sense but what is pleasing to God (Eph. 5:10).

exousía.

A. Ordinary Greek Usage.
1. This word denotes first the "ability" to perform an action.
2. It then means the "right," "authority," "permission" conferred by a higher court: a. the possibility granted by government; b. the right in various social relationships, e.g., that of parents, masters, or owners.
3. Since the authority under 2. is illusory without real power, the term approximates at times to *dýnamis,* but with the distinction that *dýnamis* denotes external power but *exousía* has a more inward reference.
4. The term may then denote self-asserted freedom or caprice in antithesis to law (with *hýbris* as a parallel). Yet legal order is usually the context.
5. Derived meanings are "authoritative position," "officebearers" (plural), "laudatory address," "crowd," and "pomp."

B. The Jewish and NT Usage.
1. Jewish usage is parallel to the Greek; the senses are "permission," "authority," or "right." Philo has the term for the absolute power of the king or people, or that of God as seen in his creative activity and his judgments.
2. The LXX uses the term for right, authority, etc. in the legal sense and also as it is given by God, e.g., in the law. In Daniel and Maccabees it may be the power of the king or of God. By using *exousía* for God's power the LXX introduces a term that excellently expresses the concept of God's unrestricted sovereignty, of the God whose very word is power (cf. Dan. 4:14).
3. Formally, NT usage is closest to that of the LXX. *exousía* is God's power, the power given to Jesus, or the power given by Jesus to his disciples. It is also the power of government (cf. Lk. 19:17; Acts 9:14: the Sanhedrin; Lk. 20:20: Pilate), the power of self-determination (Acts 5:4), the power of kings (Rev. 17:12), and "the powers that be" (plural) (Lk. 12:11; Rom. 13:1). It may also denote a sphere of dominion, e.g., the state (Lk. 23:7), the domain of spirits (Eph. 2:2), or the spiritual powers (1 Cor. 15:24; Eph. 1:21; Col. 1:16; 1 Pet. 3:22).
4. The rabbinic parallel *rᵉšût* contributes to the range of meaning that *exousía* displays in the NT, since it embraces such meanings as power of disposal, possession, commission, right, freedom, and government (singular), as well as the monarchical power of God.

5. As regards construction, the classical use is with the genitive; in the NT we also find the prepositions *en, perí, epí,* and *katá* (for details see *TDNT,* II, 566).

C. **The NT Concept of** *exousía*. The NT concept rests on three foundations. First, the power indicated is the power to decide. Second, this decision takes place in ordered relationships, all of which reflect God's lordship. Third, as a divinely given authority to act, *exousía* implies freedom for the community.

1. Primarily *exousía* denotes the absolute possibility of action that is proper to God alone as the source of all power and legality (cf. Lk. 12:5; Acts 1:7; Jude 25; Rom. 9:21).

2. God's *exousía* may be seen in the sphere of nature (Rev. 14:18). Natural forces derive their power from God (Rev. 6:8; 9:3, 10, 19; 16:9; 18:1).

3. God's will also encompasses Satan's sphere of dominion (Acts 26:18; Col. 1:13). The final mystery of evil is not its power but the fact that this hostile power may still be encompassed by God's overruling (Lk. 4:6; Rev. 13:5, 7; Lk. 22:53).

4. In relation to Christ's person and work *exousía* denotes the divinely given right and power to act along with the related freedom (Mt. 28:18; Rev. 12:10). This is a cosmic power but with a special human reference (Jn. 17:2; Mt. 11:27; Jn. 1:12; 5:27: at the judgment). The historical Jesus claims *exousía* within the limits of his commission, e.g., to forgive sins (Mk. 2:10), to expel demons (Mk. 3:15), and to teach (Mt. 7:29; Mk. 11:28; Mt. 9:8; Lk. 4:36). This power is inseparable from the imminence of the kingdom; with the presence of him who exercises it, the kingdom itself draws near.

5. As regards the church, this derives its authority (or enablement) from Christ. Believers receive their right as such from him (Jn. 1:12; Rev. 22:14). The Lord gives the apostles their authority (2 Cor. 10:8); hence they must use it responsibly (cf. Mk. 13:34; 1 Cor. 9:4ff.). But *exousía* also means freedom for the community (1 Cor. 6:12; 8:9; 10:23). *exousía* was perhaps a slogan at Corinth, possibly on the basis of Paul's own teaching about freedom from the law (cf. Rom. 14:14). Some Christians found it hard to apply this in spheres where they might be implicated in paganism, whereas others were perhaps led into startling demonstrations of it (1 Cor. 5:1ff.[?]). Paul radically upholds *exousía,* but relates it to the two principles of what is fitting and what is edifying. *exousía,* then, is not intrinsic autonomy, as, e.g., in Epictetus, but freedom in God's kingdom by faith, so that regard must be had for the perils that lurk in freedom and for the needs of neighbors. In Christian Gnosticism we finds hints of a development of freedom along the lines of the extremists at Corinth, while in apocryphal Acts *exousía* is not God's gift to be used in service but a magically wrested power deployed for one's own ends.

6. A special NT use, usually with *archaí* etc., is for supernatural powers. We do not find this in Hellenism or Gnosticism, but cf. Asc. Is. 1:4; 2:2, etc. and Testaments of the Twelve Patriarchs, as well as Christian Gnostics and the apocryphal Acts. The concept developed on Jewish soil. *exousíai* are cosmic powers, distinct from *daímones* but not clearly different from *archaí.* Paul combines the Jewish idea of the forces that rule nature with the Hellenistic notion of the nexus of destiny embracing the whole cosmos. There are thus various powers that govern human life and stand between God and us. They share the carnal nature of creation but also the fact that it is created in and for Christ (Col. 1:15-16). There is thus tension but no dualism, and the powers can never separate us from Christ.

7. The meaning of 1 Cor. 11:10 is much contested. In context the verse is part of

the discussion of veiling (cf. the *plḗn* of v. 11). The verb *opheílei* implies obligation rather than compulsion and thus suggests a moral duty. It seems, then, that the veil is a sign of subordination and the angels are guardian angels or watchers over the natural order. *exousía* is thus used materially for the veil in a bold image suggesting male dominion. Alternatively it might be due to a confusion or intentional equation of the Aramaic stems for "to conceal" on the one hand and "to rule" on the other.

exousiázō. "To have and exercise *exousía*" as a. possibility, b. right, or c. power. In 1 Cor. 7:4 Paul is saying, not that each partner has a right to the body of the other, but that each forgoes power over his or her own body (c.). The exhortation, then, is to mutual service in marital questions too. Lk. 22:25 carries an allusion to Ecclesiastes (c.). In 1 Cor. 6:12 the point of the passive is that Paul will not let anything win power over him.

katexousiázō. This uncommon word occurs in the NT only in Mk. 10:42 and parallels in the sense of the exercise of political power but with an implication of compulsion or oppression.   [W. FOERSTER, II, 560-75]

exēgéomai → *hēgéomai; exístēmi, existánō* → *ékstasis; exomologéō* → *homologéō; exorkízō, exorkistḗs* → *horkízō; exousía, exousiázō* → *éxestin*

éxō [outside]

---

hoi éxō, "those outside," figuratively "aliens"; *hoi éxōthen,* "the banished"; *hoi ektós,* "the laity" (as distinct from scribes); cf. rabbinic phrases for "heretics," "unrecognized books." *hoi éxō* in Mk. 4:11 means "those who are not disciples" and in 1 Cor. 5:12-13; 1 Th. 4:12; Col. 4:5 "non-Christians"; cf. *hoi éxōthen* in 1 Tim. 3:7. *ho éxō ánthrōpos* in 2 Cor. 4:16 refers to our external or corruptible nature.

[J. BEHM, II, 575-76]

---

epangéllō [to promise], *epangelía* [promise], *epángelma* [promise], *proepangéllomai* [to promise beforehand]

---

epangéllō, epangelía.

A. *epangéllō, epangelía* **with the Greeks.** a. The first sense is "to indicate," "declare," "declaration," "report." b. When the state declares something, it becomes an "order." c. In law we find the senses "accusation" and "delivery of a judgment." d. We then find the senses "to declare an achievement," "to show one's mastery," "to profess a subject." e. Another sense is "to offer," "to promise," "to vow." As regards promises, tension between word and deed is felt, so that promises are often seen as worthless. f. A special type of promise is the "promise of money," and in this sense the idea of a "subscription" or "donation" arises (state liturgies, gifts to rulers at their accession, priests promising gifts in support of their candidature). g. In the Hellenistic period we also find a sacral use for the "proclamation" of a festival. Among all the instances, only one example has been found for the promise of a deity.

B. *epangelía* **and** *epangéllesthai* **in the Jewish World.**
1. There is no prior history in the OT, for the MT and LXX use different words for God's pledges or promises. Paul, however, links *epangelía* and *euangélion* and views

OT history from the standpoint of *epangéllesthai*. We thus think of Heb. *dbr* and LXX *laleín* or *eipeín* (cf. Gen. 18:19) in terms of "promise." The NT usage follows that of Hellenism; we find sense d. in 1 Tim. 4:8 etc. and sense e. in Mk. 14:11 etc.

2. Judaism develops the idea of the promise of God; cf. God's promise to answer prayer, the interrelating of law and promise, the emphasis on the reliability of the divine promises in the rabbis, and the eschatological promises of apocalyptic and rabbinic literature.

C. *epangéllō* in the NT.

1. God is he who promises in Heb. 10:23; 11:11; the reference is to eschatological hope in 10:23 and to the promise of Isaac in 11:11 (cf. 12:26; 6:13).

2. The crown of life is promised in Jms. 1:12 (cf. 2:5). Life (eternal) is also the subject of promise in 1 Jn. 2:25 and Tit. 1:2.

3. Acts 7:5 refers to the promise of the land to Abraham.

4. Paul links the promise to Abraham with the promise of life in Rom. 4 and Gal. 3. The promise of life from death has been fulfilled in Christ for believers (4:15, 17, 21, 24-25). In Gal. 3:18-19 Christ is the promised seed and what is promised is the inheritance, i.e., citizenship in the Jerusalem that is above (4:26 28).

D. *epangelía* in the NT.

1. In Luke. Except in Acts 23:21, the reference is always to God's promise. *epangelía* (often without *theoú*) denotes both the promise and its fulfilment. Abraham is its recipient in Acts 7:17. It is messianic (Acts 26:6-7) and Christ has fulfilled it (13:23, 32-33). The Messiah bears and distributes the Spirit, who is also promised in the OT (2:16ff.), as Jesus has shown the disciples (1:4). Christians live in the age of fulfilment when sins are forgiven and the Spirit is poured out (2:38-39).

2. In Paul. a. Law and Promise. Paul examines the relation between law and promise. He is sure that God can do what he promises (Rom. 4:21) even to the point of raising the dead or creating out of nothing (4:17). But if the promises are to be fulfilled, they must be detached from what we do and related to the gracious will and act of God (4:16). To tie promise to law is to invalidate it by reason of our nonobservance and the resultant judgment (4:13). Promise is no longer promise if it is dependent on law (Gal. 3:18). Covenant promise precedes law. Law cannot give life (3:21) but serves only to lead sinners from works to faith (3:22). Nevertheless, the indicative of the promises carries with it an imperative, as in 2 Cor. 7:1; Rom. 6; Phil. 2:12. The promises are not determined by the believer's conduct; they determine it.

b. The Recipients. Abraham and his descendants are the recipients (Rom. 4:13). The Jews receive the promises of messianic salvation first (9:4); the Gentiles are strangers to them (Eph. 2:12). Jesus is a Jew (Rom. 15:8). From the Jews, however, the promises extend by way of Jesus to the nations, for all who believe like Abraham are his children (Rom. 4:16) in the one seed which is Christ (Gal. 3:16ff.; cf. Eph. 3:6). Those who put on Christ, or are in him, or belong to him, are Abraham's offspring and heirs according to the promise (Gal. 3:27ff.).

c. The Content of the Promise. The content is messianic salvation as inheritance, life, Spirit, righteousness, and sonship (Rom. 4:13ff.; Gal. 3:14ff.; Rom. 9:8; Eph. 1:13). All the promises are fulfilled in Christ as the Yes of God (2 Cor. 1:20) who took the curse of the law (Gal. 3:14) and gave the Spirit as a pledge, deposit, or seal (Eph. 1:13-14).

3. In Hebrews. The author of Hebrews has different concerns. As he sees it, promises are given to Abraham, Isaac, Jacob, Sarah, the patriarchs, the prophets, and the people (6:12-13; 11:9, 11, 33; 4:1ff.). The individual promises, e.g., the land and a posterity (4:1; 6:14), are fulfilled for them, but not the promise in the absolute. All God's promises converge on the messianic salvation which the patriarchs see and greet from afar as strangers and exiles (11:13). The new covenant set up by Christ rests on better promises (8:6). The promises cited are those of Jer. 31; they are now brought to fulfilment (9:15) by Christ's death. The final consummation is still ahead (10:36) but we live already in the *éschaton* (1:2), and we need to persevere in the tension between the already and the not yet lest we finally lose the promise through unbelief (4:1ff.). On God's part, his will to bring the promises to consummation is unalterable; he has pledged fulfilment with an oath, and this should strengthen us in faith (6:12ff.).

4. In 2 Peter. Delay in the parousia has produced scoffers who ask where the promise of Christ's coming is (3:4). The answer is that God's apparent slowness is forbearance (3:9); the prophetic word is sure (1:19ff.).

epángelma. This is not so common as *epangelía* but has much the same range of meaning, e.g., "declaration," "order," "profession," "promise," and in Philo "task." In the NT it occurs only twice in 2 Peter with the same meaning as *epangelía*. In 3:13 we wait for the new heaven and earth according to God's promise. In 1:4 God's promises are called very great and precious, for by them we escape present corruption and become partakers of the divine nature (cf. 1:11).

proepangéllomai. This rare word means a. "to announce beforehand," b. "to exert oneself beforehand" (about an office), and c. "to promise beforehand." We find sense a. in 2 Cor. 9:5 (the gift they have announced in advance) and sense c. in Rom. 1:2 (the gospel promised beforehand in prophetic scripture).

[J. Schniewind and G. Friedrich, II, 576-86]

epagōnízomai → *agṓn*

épainos [praise, approval]

Praise and approval were much sought after in antiquity, though the Stoic tried to achieve freedom from human judgment. In the OT, *épainos* is the recognition that the community gives the righteous, but especially God's approval. In Philo it is the approval of Moses or God, but sometimes public applause in the Greek sense. *épainos* may also be used in the LXX for the community's attitude of praise and worship toward God. God's throne is surrounded by *dóxa* and *épainos* (1 Chr. 16:27).

1. The NT use resembles that of the LXX. Only God's approval counts, not public acclaim (Rom. 2:29; 1 Cor. 4:5). The idea is that of vindication rather than reward. *épainos* is God's saving sentence at the manifestation of Christ (1 Pet. 1:7).

2. Christians should not be concerned, then, about human recognition. Apart from God's recognition, they are to seek recognition only from those whom God has commissioned, i.e., a. the community (2 Cor. 8:18), and b. the government (Rom. 13:3-4; 1 Pet. 2:14). The only instance of classical usage is in Phil. 4:8.

3. *épainos* may also, as in the LXX, denote praise of God (Eph. 1:3ff.; Phil. 1:11). Having experienced salvation, the community can already offer *dóxa* and *épainos* even before the time of consummation. [H. Preisker, II, 586-88]

epaírō → *aírō; epaischýnomai* → *aischýnō; epakolouthéō* → *akolouthéō; epakoúō* → *akoúō; epanapaúō* → *anapaúō; epanórthōsis* → *orthós; epáratos* → *ará; ependýō* → *dýo; epérchomai* → *érchomai; eperōtáō, eperṓtēma* → *erōtáō; epibállō* → *bállō; epígeios* → *gḗ; epiginṓskō, epígnōsis* → *ginṓskō*

---

epieíkeia [gentleness],   *epieikḗs* [gentle]

---

epieikḗs means "what is right or fitting," "what is serviceable," then "equable," "moderate," "reasonable," "gentle." In the LXX the group is used for God's "kindness" as supreme ruler (1 Sam. 12:22; Dan. 3:42), as well as that of earthly rulers or the righteous, e.g., Elisha (2 Kgs. 6:3). Josephus has *epieikḗs* for kings and prophets, as does Philo. *epieíkeia* denotes legal "clemency" or "leniency" in Plato and Plutarch, and cf. the papyri.

In 2 Cor. 10:1 Paul proposes the "meekness" of Christ as a model. As king, Christ has the gentleness that only one with full power may display (Phil. 2:5ff.). *epieíkeia* is thus a complement of heavenly majesty. The weak want to assert their dignity; Christ, having divine authority, shows saving clemency. The community shares his glory and should thus display the same *epieíkeia*. This comes out clearly in Phil. 4:5. Since the Lord is at hand, and the *dóxa* of the community will soon be manifest, it may show forbearance to all. Faith in its heavenly fullness of power finds expression in saving gentleness as the earthly outworking of an eschatological possession (cf. Phil. 2:15-16). As Felix ought to show a clemency befitting his high office (Acts 24:4), Christians should be *epieikeís* in virtue of their divinely given calling. In Jms. 3:17 wisdom is gentle because the attributes of rule are appropriate to it. In 1 Tim. 3:3 the bishop, acting with eschatological assurance as a representative of the community, must also be *epieikḗs* in virtue of its eschatological endowment. On the other hand, the term has a more general reference in 1 Pet. 2:18 (where it refers to non-Christian as well as Christian masters) and Tit. 3:2 (where it comes in a conventional list of virtues).   [H. PREISKER, II, 588-90]

epizētéō → *zētéō; epithyméō, epithymētḗs, epithymía* → *thymós; epikaléō* → *kaléō; epikatáratos* → *ará; epilambánomai* → *lambánō; epilýō, epílysis* → *lýō; epimartyréō* → *martyréō; epiorkéō, epíorkos* → *horkízō*

---

epioúsios [for the present]

In the NT this occurs in Mt. 6:11 and Lk. 11:3. The only instance outside the NT is an incomplete one on a papyrus. The meaning is hard to fix.

1. The Linguistic Derivation. One possible derivation is from *epiénai*, which would give such senses as "regular," "daily," "appropriate." Another is from *hē epioúsa* (*hēméra*), which yields "for the next day," or "for the day already dawning." Derivations from *epí* and *eínai* are possible according to the Koine but cause confusion of sense. The suggestion that *epí tḗn ousían* forms the basis, so that the meaning is "for vital sustenance," is not linguistically feasible. *epí tḗn oúsan* (*hēméran*), "for the present day," makes good sense, but *hē oúsa* has never been found without *hēméra*.

The idea that *epioúsios* is formed in contrast to *perioúsios* and means "not exceeding our need" has little probability.

2. *The Meaning of epioúsios.* a. From the above survey it may be seen that a derivation from *epiénai* (and especially *hē epioúsa*) is perhaps the freest from objections. On this view the meaning is "for the morrow." But this raises material questions, e.g., whether Jesus would teach us to be concerned about the next day, whether the mention of two times in a brief request is to be expected, whether the whole point of asking bread from God is not that he will supply needs as they arise (cf. Ex. 16). In other words, the rendering "for tomorrow" does not yield the attitude that Jesus is teaching.

b. Other possibilities are to take "for the morrow" in either an eschatological or a spiritual sense, but this presents us with a very unusual figure of speech that is out of keeping with the simple diction of the prayer.

c. The idea that *epioúsios* means "sufficient" has little to commend it.

d. The truth may well be that *epioúsios* denotes a measure rather than time. This is possible in two ways. The first is that the prayer is for an amount that is enough for the dawning day. But this forces us to take the Lord's Prayer as a morning prayer and also makes the term tautologous in view of the preceding "this day."

e. *epioúsios* may thus denote the amount in the sense of "sufficient" (cf. Ex. 16; Prov. 30:8). On this view, the unusual Greek word might be due to the difficulty in finding a real equivalent for the Hebrew and Aramaic concept (cf. again Prov. 30:8). Thus, while we cannot say precisely what the derivation and meaning are, the sense conveyed is fairly certainly that we are to pray each day for the bread that we need.

[W. FOERSTER, II, 590-99]

---

episképtomai [to look at, visit],   **episkopéō** [to look at, oversee],   **episkopḗ** [visitation, office of bishop],   **epískopos** [overseer, bishop],   **allotriepískopos** [busybody]

A. *episképtomai, episkopéō* outside the NT.

1. In secular Greek *episképtomai* has the following senses: a. "to look upon," "consider," "have regard to" (something or someone), with such references as inspecting, supervising, having a care to, looking down on, or watching over (the gods); b. "to reflect on," "examine," "investigate" (something), e.g., a document, or virtue; c. "to visit," e.g., the sick (friends or the doctor).

2. The LXX adds some new meanings and intensifies the religious reference. Thus we find a. "to visit," b. "look on," c. "investigate," but also d. "care for" (Jer. 23:2), e. "find out" (Num. 14:34), f. "muster" (Ex. 30:12), and g. "miss" or, passive, "be missed, absent" (1 Sam. 20:6). The term has a religious content only when God is subject, e.g., when he watches over the land (Dt. 11:12) or visits his people in judgment or mercy (Zech. 10:3). Visitation in judgment produces sense h. "to punish" (Ex. 32:34; Job 35:15), and visitation in mercy sense i. "to accept" (Gen. 21:1). A final sense j. is "to appoint," "instal," as in Num. 4:27; Neh. 7:1. Appointment by God in Num. 27:16 is important, since it perhaps influenced the selection of the term *epískopos* for early Christian officebearers. Philo and Josephus use the term in its secular senses but not with any religious significance, and the rabbis, while commending visitation of the sick, add little to the concept of divine visitation.

B. *episképtomai*, *episkopéō* in the NT.

1. Jesus takes up the concern for visiting the sick in Mt. 25:35ff., applies it to people of all nations, and deepens the command a. by asking for an attitude rather than individual acts and b. by relating it to himself and therefore to God. Jms. 1:27 expresses the same concern.

2. Even when the meaning is "to seek out," as in Acts 7:23, the idea of concern is present. Thus Paul in Acts 15:36 proposes a visit to the churches so as to see how they are doing. *episkopéō* has this sense in Heb. 12:14-15. "Seeing to it" that no one fails to obtain God's grace expresses a sense of responsibility for the eternal welfare of all members of the church, and it is a matter not merely for the leaders but for the congregation as a whole. The introduction of *episkopoúntes* into some readings of 1 Pet. 5:2 is to the same effect. Presbyters, in tending the flock, watch over it and show a concern for it (on the model of Christ himself as shepherd and *epískopos* in 1 Pet. 2:25).

3. The word can also mean "to look out" someone with a view to appointment (cf. Num. 27:16; Neh. 7:1), as in Acts 6:3, where for the first time the church makes the selection, though considering only those who are "full of the Spirit and of wisdom."

4. The idea of God's visitation, especially in grace, comes into the NT from the LXX. Thus we have a christological exposition of Ps. 8:4 LXX in Heb. 2:6. Again, in Lk. 7:16 God shows himself to be the Lord in his gracious intervention in earthly affairs. Dependence on the OT may also be seen in Lk. 1:68, 78, except that now visitation is plainly a messianic concept and is related directly to Christ's coming. The visitation of grace now extends from Israel to the Gentiles according to James in Acts 15:14, where the whole content of the term in salvation history supports the rendering "visit (in mercy)."

episkopḗ.

1. This first came into common use in the LXX. In the only instance in secular Greek it means a. "visit." In the LXX, however, it means b. "look," "glance," c. "care," "protection," d. "inquiry," and e. "muster." f. There is no equivalent for the verb "to miss," passive "to be missing." g. The true theological sense is when the term is used for "visitation." More weakly it denotes judicial punishment in Lev. 19:20, but mostly it is used for divine visitation in judgment, as in Num. 16:29; Dt. 28:25. Disobedient nations will be visited by God (Jer. 6:15). Their idols will be broken on the day of visitation (Is. 10:3). Thunder and earthquake will accompany the final visitation (Is. 29:6). h. But the divine visitation may also be in mercy and grace, as in Gen. 50:24-25; Is. 23:16. i. The meaning "office" also occurs in a transition from more general "oversight" to official responsibility (Num. 4:16; Ps. 109:8, where the Hebrew may mean "goods," but the LXX, followed by Acts 1:20, has *episkopḗ* in the sense of "office").

2.a. The NT adopts the eschatological concepts of the hour and day of visitation. Jesus relates the hour of gracious visitation to his own coming to Jerusalem in Lk. 19:44; because the people fails to recognize it, this becomes a visitation of judgment. 1 Pet. 2:12 speaks of the day of visitation when the Gentiles will be brought to glorify God by seeing the good deeds of Christians. The idea here may be that the good conduct of Christians makes this a visitation of grace, or that the Gentiles will be forced to see God's glory manifested therein on the day of judgment when everything is brought to light. Some versions add *episkopḗ* to 1 Pet. 5:6; a visitation of grace changes our time of humiliation into one of exaltation.

b. The NT also has *episkopḗ* for "office": the apostolic office in Acts 1:16ff. and the episcopal office in 1 Tim. 3:1. One should not deduce from this twofold use an equation of the apostle and bishop, for the term occurs in Acts 1:20 because a fulfillment of Scripture is perceived in the replacement of Judas, while in 1 Tim. 3:1 it is probably derived from *epískopos*.

epískopos.

A. *epískopos* in Nonbiblical Greek. The term means "overseer," "watcher," and thus comes to be used a. for "protector," "patron," and b. for various offices involving oversight, but not of a religious nature. The only religious use is for the gods.

1. The Gods as epískopoi. Greek gods are personified forces. They are thus related to the creatures nearest to them, which are under their protection, e.g., springs, groves, cities, peoples, and individuals. Deities watch over these and rule over them, giving sanctity to human life in society. They are thus called *epískopoi*. They watch over treaties, care for cities, and protect markets. They take note of offenses and punish them, e.g., offenses against parents or violations of graves. Pallas Athene watches over Athens and Artemis over pregnant women. Zeus and the gods watch over all good and evil deeds even down to the most secret details. Specific spheres come under different gods; e.g., Zeus and Pallas Athene rule over cities.

2. Men as Overseers, Watchers, Scouts. With the same basic sense, the term can be applied to various human activities, e.g., watching over corpses, overseeing a ship or a business or the market or construction, looking after young married couples, ruling a house. Other meanings along these lines are "protector" and "spy" or "scout."

3. The Cynic as episkopṓn and epískopos. These two terms find a special use in Cynic philosophy. Epictetus, for example, views himself, not as a theoretical thinker, but as a divine messenger acting as God's *katáskopos* to investigate what is good and to test people to see how far they conform to it. *episkopeín* is sometimes used for this testing, but only once, and later, do we find *epískopos* instead of *katáskopos* for the office.

4. epískopos as a Designation of Office. a. Athens uses *epískopoi* for state officials, e.g., supervisors sent by Athens to other cities of the Attic League. b. We also read of similar officials in other states, whether as secret police or as officials with judicial functions, and in one case as the officer over the mint. c. More commonly *epískopoi* are local officials or the officers of societies, but the exact responsibilities are not clear and even when there is a religious connection, e.g., the *epískopoi* of a society for a sanctuary at Rhodes, they have no cultic responsibilities but see to such secular tasks as looking after the funds. The Roman pontiff is *epískopos* only insofar as he has the duty of overseeing the Vestal Virgins. d. An interesting use occurs in Syria in relation to the erection of a public building in which it is clear that those who have the *episkopḗ* are supervisors of the work in the interests of the builders and perhaps with control of the funds. We find similar instances connected with the building of an aqueduct and a temple.

B. *epískopos* in Judaism.

1. God as epískopos. The LXX calls God *epískopos* in Job 20:29 with a clear reference to his judicial function. Philo has the same thought that nothing, good or bad, can be hidden from God. In particular, God sees into the human heart (cf. Wis. 1:6; Acts 1:24: *kardiognṓstēs*).

2. Men as epískopoi. There is no clearly defined office of *epískopos* in the LXX but the term is used for "overseer" in various senses, e.g., officers in Judg. 9:28; Is. 60:17, supervisors of funds in 2 Chr. 34:12, 17, overseers of the priests and Levites in Neh. 11:9, the temple in 2 Kgs. 11:18, and temple functions etc. in Num. 4:16. Philo has the term for "one who knows souls," and Josephus for a "guardian" of morality.

C. *epískopos* in the NT.

1. Of the five NT instances, one relates to Christ. In 1 Pet. 2:25 Christ is called the shepherd and *epískopos* of our souls. Supplementing shepherd, the term suggests the pastoral work of watching over or guarding, but it might also imply that he has the fullest knowledge. In any case, combined with shepherd the word has the implication of his total self-offering in caring for the souls of his people (cf. *episkopéō* in Heb. 12:15).

2. Elsewhere men are called *epískopoi*, and this raises two questions. a. Who are these people called *epískopoi*? The word is not used for itinerant charismatics but only for leaders of settled congregations. For such leaders we quickly find the words *presbýteroi* or *epískopoi* and *diákonoi*. As may be seen from Acts 20:28 (Paul's speech to the Ephesian elders) there is at first no distinction between *presbýteroi* and *epískopoi*. All the *presbýteroi* here are *epískopoi*, their task is that of shepherding (cf. 1 Pet. 2:25; 5:2ff.), there are several *epískopoi* in one church, their calling is from the Holy Spirit (though this does not rule out election or appointment, Acts 6:3ff.; 14:23), and their function is that of the watchful direction of believers on the basis of Christ's work. b. When does the free activity of overseeing become a designation of office? There is from the outset an impulse in this direction, for while Paul describes a function in Acts 20:28 he is also addressing a specific group. The addition in Phil. 1:1 ("with the bishops") also shows that an office and not just an activity is in view even if it does not tell us what this specific office is except in general terms of function. In 1 Tim. 3:1 *episkopḗ* is a definite office that may be sought and for which there are qualifications (though no duties are listed). Since there is here no further reference to the Holy Spirit, everyday needs influence this development, but the qualifications are very soberly stated, embracing moral reliability, a monogamous marriage, disciplined family life, teaching ability, maturity, and blamelessness according to the standards of the non-Christian world. In the parallel passage in Tit. 1:5ff. the qualifications for elders are similar, and the sudden use of *epískopos* in v. 7 shows that the same function is in view, namely, that of guiding and representing the congregation, teaching, and conducting worship when no itinerant minister is present. The use of the singular in 1 Tim. 3:2 and Tit. 1:7 does not mean that there is only one bishop in each church; it is simply a reference to the bishop as a type. The point of the office is service rather than power; the bishop, too, receives admonition and must be sober and disciplined in outlook. His authority is from the Holy Spirit. The singling out of some elders in 1 Tim. 5:17 because of their good rule, especially in teaching and preaching, may hint at early distinctions that would eventually lead to a primacy of bishops. It is hardly likely that the angels of the churches in Rev. 1:20 etc. are bishops.

D. The Origin and Original Form of the Episcopate. We must begin with the distinction between the origin of the episcopal office and that of the designation *epískopos*. None of those called *epískopoi* in the ancient world can have served as a model for the Christian *epískopos*. A formal parallel to the bishop and deacon may perhaps be found in the *archisynágōgos* and *hypērétēs* in the synagogue, especially as the former conducts divine service, supervises external order, and is accompanied by elders, but there seems to be no deeper similarity, e.g., in relation to the task of guiding and caring for the congregation as a fellowship of faith and love. The structure of the Damascus community has also been suggested as a model with its leaders of camps who in addition to external duties have responsibility for admissions and expulsions as well as teaching, preaching, and discipline, and whose title might be rendered *epískopos* in Greek. Yet it is unlikely that this small community offered any direct example for the Christian church, and in addition these leaders are too monarchical for the older Christian episcopate and there is also no mention of deacons. The truth is that we need not seek models, since the Christian church was a new and distinctive thing whose mission required new offices and which had by nature the impulse to create such offices. Jesus had appointed the Twelve and given to them and others an apostolic ministry supplemented by the missionary endeavors of teachers and prophets. Where churches were founded, people with a special charisma (1 Cor. 12:28) had to be put in charge and take responsibility for the common life in such matters as pastoral direction, worship, and preaching (cf. Acts 14:23; 1 Th. 5:12; Rom. 12:8; Gal. 6:6ff.). There thus come into being the *epískopoi* and *diákonoi* of Phil. 1:1, and these remain when the need for itinerants diminishes in a given locality. The title *epískopoi* derives from the function. As *presbýteroi* comes from the Jewish world, the Greek scene offers in *epískopos* a familiar but not precisely defined word which can be given a specific Christian application. Like *diákonos*, it is a modest term, but it has a rich content due to its use for divine being and activity, and the description of Jesus himself as *epískopos* adds to its theological significance. Later, a human claim comes to be associated with the term as 1 Clement opens the door to the idea of apostolic succession with its hierarchical chain: God, Christ, the apostles, bishops (42–44). Did. 15.1 probably gives a better factual depiction of the situation when it shows how itinerants give way to local bishops and deacons. During the second century, however, the single bishop, distinguished from the presbyters, gradually achieves precedence (cf. Ignatius of Antioch). While providing stronger leadership, this system tends to produce authoritarian bishops in direct antithesis to the recommendations to elders in 1 Pet. 5:2-3.

allotri(o)epískopos. This word occurs only in 1 Pet. 4:15. It is formed after the manner of words like *allotriógnōmos*, "a meddler in alien matters." Since it is not found outside the NT, we must deduce its meaning from the context. The context, however, allows of various possibilities: a. "one who has his eye on the possessions of others"; b. "an unfaithful guardian of goods committed to him"; c. "one who meddles in things that do not concern him," and d. "a calumniator or informer."

[H. W. Beyer, II, 599-622]

episkēnóō → *skḗnos; episkiázō* → *skiá*

---

epistátēs [master]

epistátēs occurs in the NT only in the vocative, is peculiar to Luke, and except in Lk. 17:13 is used only by the disciples. Luke chooses it as one of his equivalents for "rabbi" (cf. Mk. 4:38 and par.; 9:5 and par.; 9:38 and par.). Secular Greek has a rich and varied usage; the term can denote a herdsman, a driver of an elephant, a taskmaster, an overseer of public works, the leader of an athletic society or temple, a magistrate or governor of a city, and even a protective deity. The extent of its vocative use is uncertain.   [A. Oepke, II, 622-23] *epistréphō, epistrophḗ* → *stréphō; episynagōgḗ* → *synagōgḗ; epitagḗ* → *tássō; epiteléō* → *teléō*

---

epitimáō [to rebuke],   *epitimía* [censure]

---

epitimáō corresponds to the twofold sense of *timáō,* "to award honor or blame," and comes into use for "to blame," "to reprove." In the LXX it is applied especially to God's rebuke (cf. Job 26:11; 2 Sam. 22:16; Pss. 106:9; 119:21). In a limited way it is also used for human rebuke (Gen. 37:10; Ruth 2:16), but human reproof is often held to be presumptuous, and only judicial, pastoral, or fraternal rebuke is commended. The NT follows the LXX 1. in treating human rebuke with great reserve. Thus the disciples are overhasty with their rebuke in Mk. 10:13, the crowd in Mk. 10:48, and Peter in Mt. 16:22 (Jesus here responds with his own legitimate rebuke). The only acceptable rebuke is that of humility. Thus one of the crucified thieves rebukes the other in Lk. 23:41, and one believer may rebuke another if it is done in a spirit of forgiveness (Lk. 17:3). Rebuke is especially a responsibility of pastoral oversight in 2 Tim. 4:2. The NT also follows the LXX 2. in regarding rebuke as essentially a prerogative of divine lordship. Only God may rightly rebuke the devil (Jude 9). Jesus plainly has the right of rebuke (Mk. 8:33; Lk. 9:55; 19:39-40). In Mk. 8:30 *epitimán* is used to show how strict is his charge to the disciples not to disclose his messiahship at this point. The same term is one of lordship when he commands the demons to keep silence in Mk. 3:12. He displays a similar power when he rebukes and expels the unclean spirit in Mk. 9:25, when he rebukes the fever of Simon's mother-in-law in Lk. 4:39, and when he rebukes even the elemental forces of nature in Mk. 4:39. His unconditional divine power and prerogative are clearly and forcefully revealed in his *epitimán.*

epitimía occurs in the NT only in 2 Cor. 2:6 as a technical term in congregational discipline for the church's "punishment" or "censure."   [E. STAUFFER, II, 623-27]

epiphaínō, epipháneia, epiphanḗs → *phṓs; epiphaúskō* → *phṓs; epoikodoméō* → *oikodoméō; epouránios* → *ouranós*

---

heptá [seven],   *heptákis* [seven times],   *heptakischílioi* [seven thousand], *hébdomos* [week],   *hebdomḗkonta* [seventy],   *hebdomēkontákis* [seventy times]

A. The Background in Religious History.

1. The prominence of the number seven in many cultures is probably due to the observation of the four seven-day phases of the moon rather than to the recognized existence of seven planets, for the number is important even before interest in the seven planets begins, and the moon plays a role in the measuring of time in the Babylonian creation epic.

2. As regards the cosmic significance of seven, the Babylonians make an equation with "fullness" which is also found among the Hebrews. This equation links up with the seven-day period; the seventh day completes the period and thus achieves a divinely ordained totality. The number then comes into cultic use in cleansings, prayers, and the ceremonial of sacrifice. In the OT the seventh day is a holy day, the seventh year is a holy year etc., and there is in the Hebrew year a hebdomadal cycle of feasts.

3. Philo develops a numbers mysticism by which seven determines the rhythms of human life; this goes in seven-year cycles. Like the later rabbis, he believes that a seven-month child may live but not an eight-month child. His interest in this point, however, is not speculative; he simply states it as a fact within his discussion of the number seven.

B. The NT Usage.

1. OT influence may be seen in Rom. 11:4, where Paul quotes 1 Kgs. 19:18 in support of the fact that God has preserved a remnant, i.e., Christian Israel. Perhaps, like 1 Kgs. 19:18, he connects the number 7,000 with the totality of true Israel. Except for Heb. 11:30 this is the only instance of the number in the NT; possibly the NT avoids it in opposition to contemporary speculation. In the references to the seven days of the siege of Jericho in Heb. 11:30 and the seven races in Acts 13:19 the interest is purely factual.

2. "Seven days" is the term for a week in Acts 20:6; 21:4, 27; 28:14, and the "seventh day" is mentioned in Heb. 4:4 (the sabbath).

3. "Seven" is a round number in the feeding of the four thousand (Mt. 15:22ff.; Mk. 8:1ff.). The context offers us no reason to seek a hidden significance.

4. Older ideas of the significance of the number may occur at times. a. When the Sadducees refer to the seven brothers who all marry the same wife, they possibly have in view an infinite series. b. When seven spirits return to the backslider in Mt. 12:45, or seven spirits are driven out of Mary Magdalene in Lk. 8:2, the point is that we have here the worst possible state of corruption. c. In the saying about sinning and forgiving seven times (Mt. 18:21-22; Lk. 17:4), Jesus' point is that there is to be no limit to forgiveness no matter whether readiness for it corresponds to or transcends the measure of guilt. Already in Babylon the number seven is linked with sin and the readiness to forgive, as in penitential psalms which speak of sinning seventy times seven or of asking seven times for pardon. In the OT the blood is sprinkled seven times on the Day of Atonement (Lev. 16:11ff., 15ff.). The point in all such references is the fullness either of sin or of its expiation (cf. the LXX of 2 Sam. 12:6). With the seventy times seven of Mt. 18:22 we may compare Gen. 4:24; whether or not the proper rendering is 490 or 77 makes no difference, since the unlimited nature of forgiveness is obviously the issue. d. A sevenfold principle governs the genealogies of Jesus in Mt. 1:1ff. and Lk. 3:23ff. Here Jesus is shown to be the Messiah by his place in David's lineage as the last in the ninth (Luke) or eleventh (Matthew) group of seven.

5. Seven is a very important number in Revelation. There are seven churches and angels (1:4ff.), seven candlesticks (1:13ff.), seven stars (1:16ff.), seven spirits (1:4; 4:5), seven seals (5:1ff.), seven horns and eyes (the Lamb, 5:6), seven trumpets in the hands of seven angels (8:2ff.), seven thunders (10:3-4), seven heads with crowns (the *drákōn*, 12:3), and seven plagues (15:1ff.). We cannot make seven a formal principle of Revelation, but it pervades the book as the number of fullness, whether this be the perfection of the divine work or the full development and deployment of the forces hostile to God. The individual references are influenced by the various motifs that are suggested by the apocalyptic tradition and the historical situation; cf. the mythical heads of the beast and their relation to the seven hills of Rome (17:9). The seven kings are probably seven emperors. The seven churches comprise the church in Asia Minor, and the cities named are also centers of the imperial cult. The seven stars perhaps carry an allusion to the role of the seven planets in Mithraism or to the images of the

emperors on coins; in context, they imply the unconditional lordship of Christ. The seven thunders are probably based on the seven references to God's voice in the thunder in Ps. 29. The seven candlesticks suggest the seven-branched candelabra, the seven seals the seals attached to a Roman will, the seven horns the common symbol of power, and the seven eyes the Lord's eyes in Zech. 4:10. Seven is also a formal number in Revelation to the extent that it expresses the divine fullness and totality. Hence, even though it is not here a specific apocalyptic form, it serves as a suitable principle of arrangement.

6. Seven men are chosen in Acts 6:2ff. because there were usually seven leaders in a Jewish community. The number shows that the seven are not viewed as mere assistants of the twelve.

7. According to Lk. 10:1ff. Jesus sent out seventy on a mission as well as the twelve. The number suggests the universality of the mission. It is perhaps modeled on the seventy of Num. 11:16, though cf. the seventy-one members of the Sanhedrin, the seventy elders appointed by Josephus in Galilee, the seventy elders of Jerusalem, and also the seventy nations of Gen. 10. The point seems to be that the mission of the seventy denotes the wider claim of Jesus which, unlike the law according to Jewish tradition, will now be embraced by the Gentiles (cf. Mt. 21:43).

[K. H. RENGSTORF, II, 627-35]

érgon [work], *ergázomai* [to work], *ergátēs* [workman], *ergasía* [business], *energḗs* [active], *enérgeia* [activity], *energéō* [to act], *enérgēma* [action], *euergesía* [good deed], *euergetéō* [to do good], *euergétēs* [benefactor]

érgon, ergázomai.

A. General Usage.

1. The Greek Usage. These words, common from Homer, denote action or active zeal. They occur in relation to all kinds of work, working with various materials, building, and technical and cultural activity. They also denote work as a social or ethical task. Hesiod describes work as a divine plan for human life, and Cynic philosophy regards work in the service of humanity as an ideal. Plato relates work to civilization, not nature. For Aristotle a creature is good when it fulfils its *érgon*, so that he extends the concept to all of nature. The passive is common for the work done, i.e., the result of work, or even its reward as wages or profit. In a weak sense the term can also denote a "matter" or "thing."

2. The Linguistic Use of the Bible. In the LXX the term is used for many Hebrew words, so that we have to derive the specific sense from the originals and the context. This is especially important in the ethical and religious sphere, where the reference might be, e.g., to conduct (Job 34:21; Prov. 16:5; Sir. 10:6, etc.). (See *TDNT,* II, 636-37 for details.)

B. The Divine Work and Action.

1. The Divine Work of Creation. The verb *ergázesthai* is infrequent in the LXX with God as subject (cf. Ps. 44:1; Job 33:29). But in Gen. 2:2-3 *érgon* is used for the creative work from which God rests. Elsewhere nature and people are called God's works. While all creation is obviously made by God, the reference is usually to some group of works. Thus natural phenomena, the earth and its creatures, and the human race that is made in God's image all bear witness, as God's work, to his providence and gracious rule (cf. Pss. 8:3; 19:1). God has pity on his works (Pss. 90:16 LXX; 138:8). In particular, God has given humans a special position over the work of his hands (Ps. 8:6). Israel commits herself to God because she is the work of his hands, probably in the sense of his historical rather than creative work (Is. 64:8; cf. 60:21); and as such she also sees the work of his hands (Is. 29:23 LXX). Prov. 20:15 (12) stresses the wonderful nature of God's work. Sir. 43:32 and 16:21 LXX show the relation between God's work in creation and his work in revelation and judgment. In Job 37:15 the LXX imports the thought of creation in the form of a confession. In general, the LXX thinks more of God's works than his work and directs attention a little more than the MT to his work in creation as distinct from his work in history.

2. *God's Activity in the World.*

a. God's work does not cease with creation, although Judaism has to wrestle with the problem of his sabbath rest. One solution is to see that he now works on both the ungodly and the righteous. The general assumption is that he is active by nature (cf. Jn. 5:17). The distinctiveness of the Bible is to show God at work in the specificity of history, i.e., with a people, with individuals, and in particular events (Ex. 34:10; Josh. 24:31; Judg. 2:7, 10). The acts may sometimes be miracles, as at the Red Sea (Pss. 66; 77:11ff.), where the forces of evil are defeated. Even here, however, the stress is on the saving action that establishes Israel as a people, as later generations may see.

b. Less visible is God's present action in judgment and mercy as the prophets perceive it. Present events are also God's acts (Is. 5:12; 22:11; 28:21). Although these mean judgment for the recalcitrant, God's proper work is salvation. Acts 13:41 makes this point on the basis of Hab. 1:5, except that now God's work is the church's mission rather than an ordinary historical event. Yet Rev. 15:3 shows that the NT, too, finds God's work in all events and not just in the upbuilding of the community. Thus even personal events like Hosea's marriage can be significant in God's dealings with his people and the world. Paul sees this in relation to his own life in Col. 1:24 and 2 Cor. 12:7ff. He also integrates historical data into his eschatological understanding in 2 Th. 2:6-7. No prophets grasp this more clearly than Isaiah and Jeremiah; cf. the proclamation of Cyrus as God's anointed in Is. 45:1 and God's claim to all history as the work of his hands in 45:11 (also 41:4). God's saving work for Israel affects the nations in a missionary sense according to Is. 64:4 LXX. In the Psalms the power of God is manifested in his historical work, as shown by the fact that it brings judgment to the wicked and mercy to the righteous (Pss. 28:5; 46:8-9; 64:9, etc.). This thought often comes to expression in expectant prayers for vindication (Pss. 43:1; 86:7-8, etc.).

c. The NT brings the individual acts of God under the comprehensive rubric of the divine work of salvation. The Baptist in Mt. 11:2 finds it hard to correlate the specific works of Jesus and his total mission. In John, however, the works bear witness to Jesus and the salvation that he brings (cf. Jn. 5:20, 36; 7:3, 21; 10:25; 14:10ff.; 15:24). They do so, not just as mighty or glorious works, but as good works that display God's working both as his work in Jesus and as the work he has entrusted to him. The unity of God's saving work is always in the background (cf. 9:3; 17:4). Participation in this work is through faith (6:29). Paul manifests a similar understanding. God's work is the upbuilding of the community (Rom. 14:20; cf. 1 Cor. 3:9). God does this by the Spirit through the apostolic mission (1 Cor. 9:1). Like creation, the church is a work of the Word and Spirit. Paul's helpers have a part in this work of God (1 Cor. 16:10;

Phil. 2:30). Everything done in faith is both the Lord's work and work for the Lord (1 Cor. 15:58; cf. Eph. 4:12). It is all God's working (Phil. 1:6), and this fruitful work alone gives meaning to the Christian life (Phil. 1:22).

C. Human Labor.

1. Human Labor as a Curse. Linked with the fall, human labor is seen as a curse because it is necessary (cf. Gen. 3:17). Hellenistic Judaism stresses this negative side of work in contrast to the work of the eschatological age which will be done without toil. It finds it hard to speak about *érgon* without disparagement (cf. Sir. 30:33; Prov. 31:15 LXX).

2. Human Labor as Sin and Vanity. In Hellenistic Judaism the curse of Gen. 3:17 also has the implication that everything called *érgon* in human life is sin when measured by the final criterion. Thus *érga* as human works (along with the verb) are often linked with wickedness etc. (cf. in the NT Mt. 7:23; Lk. 13:27). The translations of Job 11:4 and 21:16 show this, as do Job 22:3; 33:9. Throughout the OT and on into the NT "works of men's hands" is a stock term for idols (Dt. 4:28; 2 Kgs. 19:18; Is. 2:8; Jer. 1:16; Rev. 9:20). This negative assessment of human work takes on a radically theological character in the NT, where we find such expressions as works of darkness (Rom. 13:12), the flesh (Gal. 5:19), the devil (Jn. 8:41), and ungodliness (Jude 15), as well as evil, lawless, and dead works (1 Jn. 3:8; 2 Pet. 2:8; Heb. 6:1). The context may also give a negative connotation, as in Mt. 23:3; Lk. 11:48; Jn. 8:41; Tit. 1:16.

3. The Righteousness of Works in Later Judaism. Paul's doctrine of the unrighteousness of all human works does not rest merely on the Hellenistic disparagement of work, for it applies even to works that Jewish piety views favorably, e.g., cultic works, or works in fulfilment of the law which form the basis of moral achievement and which may be performed even without the written law, such as the works of Abraham (Jn. 8:39), or works of the law that is written on the heart either in the future age (Jer. 31:33) or in the case of the Gentiles (Rom. 2:15). A decision has to be made between the works of God and the works of self-will; the former are good and the latter bad. A division arises, then, between the righteous who keep the law and sinners who fail to do so. In some texts we even find the idea of works of love that are meritorious because they exceed what the law requires. Yet the hope of God's mercy for the wicked, sometimes through the intercession of the righteous, is not excluded.

4. The Righteousness of Works and the Thought of Reward. That God recompenses us according to our works is a basic concept of Scripture. The stress, however, lies on God's justice rather than our reward. The idea that works make no difference is intolerable (Eccl. 8:14-15) because it seems to throw doubt on the divine justice. Later, however, the thought of a reward for righteousness becomes more prominent. As Aqiba says, the preponderance of good or wicked works will decide our destiny: reward or punishment. Good works will be our advocates.

5. Human Work as a Divinely Given Task. The concept of reward and punishment presupposes that God commissions us to do *érga*. This is the point in Gen. 2:15 (cf. Is. 28:23ff.). God lies behind all the work of civilization, and if Gen. 1 and 2 hardly provide a basis for joy in work or for work as part of the divine revelation, they certainly offer a basis for the belief that work is by divine commission. In part this leads on to the moral concept of redemption by works, of which the planting in paradise is the presupposition, and in part to the work ethic of the rabbis whereby one's earthly avocation is under God's blessing as well as good works, and manual labor is highly regarded. Christianity takes up the same theme with the exhortation to work in 1 Th. 4:11; 2 Th. 3:10ff.; Eph. 4:28, and with Paul's own example of self-support. Here all work serves the community either directly or indirectly and is finally God's work in us. For the NT work is the fruit of faith. Faith works by love (Gal. 5:6). There is a work of faith and labor of love (1 Th. 1:3). God fulfils the work of faith by his power (2 Th. 1:11). Works are thus the basis of judgment (Rom. 2:6). True works are done in God (Jn. 3:21), so that, although we are responsible for them, they carry no merit but are the response to the message of repentance. Only with the apostolic fathers do we begin to find some ambivalence in this regard, i.e., a new nomistic trend.

6. *Word and Act, Faith and Works*. Everywhere in the Greek world we find a certain tension of word and act (*épos* or *lógos* and *érgon*). Philosophy assumes their logical and ethical harmony. The Bible, too, demands that they be in correspondence, as they are with God (Joel 2:11 LXX; Ps. 33:4). The NT agrees (cf. Lk. 23:51; 1 Jn. 3:18). Yet the rabbis are conscious of a discrepancy between preaching and practice (cf. Mt. 23:3). This is perceived also in Jms. 1:25 and 2:17. True faith and works go together. Yet as faith without works is dead, so works that do not proceed from faith are dead (Heb. 6:1); they do not lead to life. As Paul teaches, works of the law must not be an occasion for arrogant seeking of self-righteousness. We must begin with faith, and then the God who works all in all (1 Cor. 12:6) will work by the Spirit in believers. As purely human work, therefore, *érgon* acquires a negative sense. The works of fallen humanity are evil. Yet salvation restores the situation by producing in us the good works that are the *érga toú theoú* (not *nomoú*) of the new covenant, i.e., the work of faith that is active by love (Jn. 6:29). Of ourselves, we cannot really see the divine work of salvation, e.g., in the miracles or the resurrection. We view it only in terms of earthly goals (Jn. 6:26) or even as the work of demons (Mk. 3:22). Only by faith do we pierce the ambivalence of God's saving *érgon,* and then we find that everything that promotes life, while it may be abused, is really God's good work (cf. the law in Rom. 7:12-13), serving the faith in Christ that leads to the good works that are done in and by us also.

energéō, enérgeia, enérgēma, energḗs. *enérg(e)ia* in the sense of "activity" or "energy" occurs at an early date. *enérgēma* means "act" or "action," and *energḗs* "active." The verb *energéō* means "to act," "to be at work." The group is used in Hellenism for the work of cosmic or physical forces, but mostly in the OT and NT for the work of divine or demonic powers. Only in Phil. 2:13 do we find *energeín* for human activity. Evil powers are the subject in Eph. 2:2; 2 Th. 2:7, 9. Yet God is finally behind even this activity (2 Th. 2:11). God, by the Spirit, is more directly the subject in the discussion of gifts (1 Cor. 12:6, 10-11). God also works through Peter and Paul (Gal. 2:8); his mighty working gives force to their ministry (Gal. 3:5). The door for work in 1 Cor. 16:9 also has to do with the apostolic mission, as does the active word of God in Heb. 4:12. Phlm. 6 uses the same adjective as Heb. 4:12 for the faith that promotes knowledge. Always, of course, it is God who is ultimately at work (Phil. 2:13; Eph. 1:11). The power of his working is resurrection power (Eph. 1:19-20; Col. 2:12). The middle *energeísthai,* which occurs only in Paul and Jms. 5:16, has such varied subjects as the word in 1 Th. 2:13, comfort in 2 Cor. 1:6, faith in Gal. 5:6, divine power in Eph. 3:20, and prayer in Jms. 5:16. *enérgeia* is related to Christ in Eph. 4:16; it is he who gives the power of growth to members of his body. Hostile forces are the subject of *energeísthai* in Rom. 7:5 (passions), 2 Cor. 4:12 (death), and 2 Th. 2:7 (the mystery of lawlessness).

euergetéō, euergétēs, euergesía. This group denotes favors, benefits, benefactors, etc., whether human or divine. The OT speaks of God's beneficence, but the Greek renderings tend to avoid the group. We find it four times in the NT. In Acts 4:9 the healing of the cripple is a divine benefit mediated through the apostles. In Acts 10:38 the Savior's work is described similarly. In 1 Tim. 6:2 the relation between believing slaves and their masters is viewed in terms of benefit. In Lk. 22:25, however, Christians are to reject the title *euergétēs,* for God alone is the true benefactor from whom all blessings come, and God's saving work does not really come under the rubric of *euergesía,* which suggests the meeting of human desires, but under that of saving power (Rom. 1:16). [G. BERTRAM, II, 635-55]

---

ereunáō [to search],   *exereunáō* [to inquire carefully]

The general sense is "to search after": a. "to sniff out" (animals), b. "to search," e.g., a house or a crime, c. "to investigate," either legally or more generally, and d. "to test, examine." Plato and Philo use the term for academic, scientific, and philosophical inquiry; Philo also has it for the rabbinic study of Scripture. In the LXX we find senses b.-d., as well as "to discover," "invent."

1. In John the study of Scripture is the point in 5:39 (with a view to finding God's revelation) and 7:52 (rabbinic study, also relating to the Messiah).

2. The sense "to look into" occurs in 1 Pet. 1:11; the prophets searched for the time or person indicated by their predictions of messianic suffering and glory.

3. The "searching" of the Spirit enables believers to see something of God's purpose and work in 1 Cor. 2:10. Christ himself searches the hearts and minds of his people according to Rev. 2:23, while in Rom. 8:27 God searches the hearts of those who pray, but through the Spirit graciously accepts their prayers.

[G. DELLING, II, 655-57]

érēmos [abandoned],   *erēmía* [waste],   *erēmóō* [to lay waste],   *erḗmōsis* [desolating]

érēmos, erēmía, erēmóō. The reference of the group is to "abandonment," and it thus denotes a desolate or thinly populated area, and then a "waste" in the stricter sense.

1. A first use in the NT is for a "lonely place" (cf. Lk. 8:29; 2 Cor. 11:26).

2. Jesus seeks an "uninhabited place" when he wants to be quiet with God or his disciples (Mt. 14:13; Mk. 1:45; 6:31ff., etc.). What he primarily seeks is stillness for prayer (Mk. 1:35). This is the point of the forty days (Mk. 1:12-13). The forty days need not be related to the forty years in the desert (Dt. 8:2), since this was more a period of disobedience than testing. There are parallels in the fasts of Moses (Ex. 34:28) and Elijah (1 Kgs. 19:5, 8), though the details differ, and Elijah in particular is seeking refuge.

3. The desert wandering of Israel is stressed in the NT as an instructive time of disobedience (Heb. 3:8-9; Acts 7:41ff.), yet also of God's gracious working (Acts 7:36; Jn. 3:14; 6:31, 49) and speaking (Acts 7:38). Judaism gives this period a special

emphasis, leading to the belief that the last age will begin in the desert (cf. Acts 21:38; also Mt. 24:26; Rev. 12:6, 14).

4. The Baptist begins his work in the desert, so that he is seen to be "the voice crying in the wilderness" of Is. 40:3 (Mt. 3:3; Mk. 1:3; Lk. 3:4; Jn. 1:23).

5. A city or country may be devastated by enemy action (Mt. 12:25) or divine wrath (Mt. 23:38; Rev. 17:16; cf. Is. 6:11; Lam. 5:18, etc.). Yet there is also promise for waste places, according to the OT (Is. 32:15-16; 35:1ff.; 41:18-19, etc.).

erémōsis. This occurs in Mt. 24:15; Mk. 13:14; Lk. 21:20 (cf. Dan. 9:27 etc.) in the phrase "desolating sacrilege." The point is that the sacrilege causes worshippers to shun the sanctuary and thus deprives it of any useful purpose.

[G. KITTEL, II, 657-60]

---

eritheía [self-seeking]

1. From *eritheúō*, "to work as a day-laborer"; this has to do with the work or disposition of the day-laborer.

2. It then comes to denote the attitude of self-seekers, harlots, etc., who demean themselves for gain. Aristocratic contempt for daily wage earners seems to have brought about the devaluation of meaning.

3. The result is that later translators and expositors of the NT often fail to understand the term.

4. As a complex term in everyday usage, it can be given different senses according to context. "Contentious" is perhaps too specialized in Rom. 2:8, where it refers to the "despicable nature" of those who do not obey the truth but seek immediate gain. This also fits the context in 2 Cor. 12:20; Gal. 5:20; Phil. 1:17; 2:3. The idea is "base self-seeking," the "baseness" that cannot shift its gaze to higher things.

[F. BÜCHSEL, II, 660-61]

---

hermēneúō [to interpret], *hermēneía* [interpretation], *hermēneutḗs* [interpreter], *diermēneúō* [to interpret], *diermēneía* [interpretation], *diermēneutḗs* [interpreter]

A. Linguistic Data. The basic sense is a. "to interpret," "expound," "explain" (e.g., Scripture), b. "to indicate," "express" (e.g., thoughts), then c. "to translate." *diermēneúō* occurs in senses a. and c.

B. Material Data.

1. In the OT the view may be found that ordinary people cannot understand visions, so that Yahweh must provide the interpretation (Gen. 40:8; Dan. 2:27-28).

2. The Greeks regard interpretation as a creative gift along with perception and reason. Poets and seers utter things that come from the gods and need expositors who can pass on the *hermēneía* of what they say.

3. Philo applies this concept to the prophets as interpreters of God, e.g., Moses. Those who expound dreams (e.g., Joseph) have the same office. Sometimes the inspired mediator of God's truth needs an interpreter, as in the case of Moses and Aaron.

The name of God serves as God's *hermēneús,* and speech (not very reliably) plays the same role for the human *noús.*

4. The *hermēneía* of tongues which is a charisma in 1 Cor. 12:10 is more likely interpretation than translation, and the *diermēneutḗs* of 1 Cor. 14:28 is probably an interpreter of ecstatic speech in the interests of edification. Concern for *hermēneía* is a concern for the true and disciplined operation of the Word and Spirit through the charism of tongues.

5. Lk. 24:27 presents Jesus on the road to Emmaus as an expositor of the OT prophecies of his passion and exaltation. The messianic understanding of the OT which is established here, and which early Christianity develops, rests on an exposition of Scripture which is new in content, if not method, as NT revelation gives a christological meaning to OT sayings.   [J. BEHM, II, 661-66]

érchomai [to come, go], *éleusis* [coming], *apérchomai* [to go away], *diérchomai* [to pass through], *eisérchomai* [to come, go], *exérchomai* [to go out], *epérchomai* [to come to], *parérchomai* [to pass by], *pareisérchomai* [to come in], *periérchomai* [to wander about], *prosérchomai* [to come to], *synérchomai* [to go with, come together]

érchomai.

A. The General Use of *érchomai.*

1. The classical meaning is "to come" or "to go," with nuances supplied by prepositions or context, and with such varied references as to natural events, states of mind, letters, transfers of property, or making agreements.

2. The cultic use, e.g., in prayer for the coming of deity, is significant.

3. In the LXX the term is used for 35 Hebrew words, mostly in a spatial sense, but sometimes cultic, e.g., for coming to God's house, or the coming of prayer to God, or prayer for the coming of God's mercy, or the coming of God, his word, angels, the Messiah, the ages, the day of salvation, the Spirit, or the coming of the nations to God's inheritance. In the Psalms, Job, etc. both good and bad things come, especially bad.

4. The basic NT sense is "to come" or "to go," often with a reference to people coming on the scene or to decisive events or natural phenomena, and sometimes in the sense of hostile approach (Lk. 14:31). Interesting phrases with *eis* are "to come into disrepute" (Acts 19:27), "to come to oneself" (Lk. 15:17), and "to move on to a new subject" (2 Cor. 12:1); cf. also "to grow worse" in Mk. 5:26 (*eis tó cheíron eltheín*).

B. The Special Use of *érchomai* in the NT.

1. The Synoptists.

a. The Coming of Jesus. With reference to the coming of Jesus as the Messiah, the group takes us to the heart of the divine epiphany. The *élthon* sayings of Jesus in the first person derive from his messianic consciousness and state his messianic task. He has come to proclaim the kingdom (Mk. 1:38), to call sinners to repentance (Mk. 2:17), to set up a new order of life (Mt. 5:17), to kindle a fire (Lk. 12:49), and to enforce division (Mt. 10:34ff.). Son of Man sayings are of the same order. The Son of Man has come to seek and save (Lk. 19:10), to give his life as a ransom (Mk. 10:45), but to do so eating and drinking (Mt. 11:18-19). The demons describe his coming similarly in Mk. 1:24; Lk. 4:34 when they see that it involves their own destruction.

b. Coming to Jesus. Often in Matthew and Luke great crowds come to Jesus, but true coming involves a cultic action (e.g., *proskyneín*), as we see from certain individuals (Mt. 8:2; 9:18; Mk. 5:33; cf. Mt. 2:2), and a willing commitment by embracing and doing Jesus' words and by denying the self (Lk. 6:47; 9:23; 14:27). The parables of the supper and the marriage feast depict coming (or not coming) as the response to divine invitation. In the parable of the prodigal coming is also coming home to God out of lostness and alienation (Lk. 15:20, 30).

c. The Coming of God's Kingdom. We are to pray for the coming of the kingdom (Mt. 6:10). Praise is offered for its coming on the entry into Jerusalem (Mk. 11:10). The kingdom comes in power (Mk. 9:1). The future kingdom is identical with the coming aeon which means eternal life (Mk. 10:30; Lk. 18:30). The future kingdom will come with the parousia; Jesus comes in and with his kingdom (Mt. 16:28; Lk. 23:42).

d. The Coming of the Messiah. Judaism often refers to the Messiah as the coming one who inaugurates the age of salvation and whose coming will be preceded by the return of Elijah (cf. Mt. 11:14; 17:10; 27:49). The Baptist asks whether Jesus is this coming one (Mt. 11:3). The crowd hails Jesus as "he that comes in the name of the Lord" (Mt. 21:9). But there is still to be a coming in glory (Mt. 16:27). No time is set for this, but it will be sudden (Mk. 13:36). False prophets claiming to be the Messiah will come first (Mt. 24:5).

e. God's Coming in Judgment. The parables of the wicked husbandmen (Mt. 21:40), the fig-tree (Lk. 13:6-7), and the talents (Mt. 25:19) refer to a coming in judgment.

f. The Coming of Days of Decision. Many sayings refer to coming days when something significant will happen (cf. Lk. 17:22; 21:6; 23:29). Significant, too, is Simeon's coming into the temple in Lk. 2:27 and the coming of the hour of the passion in Mk. 14:41.

2. *The Johannine Writings.*

a. The Coming of Jesus. *érchesthai* has an even stronger theological content here, along with a wider figurative use. In the first person, the "coming" sayings of Jesus, both positive and negative, have a polemical edge. Jesus has not come of his own accord (Jn. 7:28). His claim rests on his divine sending (8:42). He comes in the Father's name (5:43) to bring light (10:10) and to save the world (12:47). Though he has not come to judge (12:47), his coming means judgment (9:39), since with the coming of light those who love darkness reject it (3:19). He has come to bear witness to the truth (18:37) and will be heard by those who are of the truth. His messianic claim is directed against those who think they know his origin (7:27) and those who think the Messiah must still come (cf. 4:25). It is supported by the Baptist, who has come to bear witness (1:7) and who recognizes Jesus as the coming one (1:15) whose way he prepares (1:31) with a baptism that has eschatological significance as his manifestation. Others who come before Christ are thieves and robbers (10:8).

b. Coming to Jesus. Here again we find a general coming (3:26; 6:5; 10:41). Jesus invites people to come (7:37). Those who respond come in a special sense (6:35) by becoming disciples (cf. 1:47). Disciples can also issue the invitation (1:46). Jesus will not reject those who come (6:37) but give them life (6:35). Yet only those whom the Father draws (6:65) and who are taught by him (6:45) can come. Coming means believing in Jesus as the coming one (11:27), and believing means deliverance from judgment (5:24) and new birth by the Spirit (3:8). The opposite is a refusal to come to Jesus (5:40) or to come to the light (3:20).

c. The Coming of the Risen Lord. *érchomai* is an important word in the resurrection appearances in John. It occurs in the coming to the disciples in 20:19, in the coming to Thomas and the others in 20:26, and in the coming by the lake in 21:13.

d. The Coming Again of Christ. Jesus bears witness to this in 14:3, and there is also reference to it in 21:22-23. Between the comings, however, the Paraclete comes, or Christ himself comes by the Paraclete in a pneumatic rather than a personal coming (Jn. 15:26; 14:28). The Paraclete enables people to come to Jesus even though they cannot come where he now is (7:34; 8:21-22; 13:33).

e. The Coming of the Hour. The formula "the hour is coming" is important in John. The hour (*hóra*) is the future age of salvation, yet this has already dawned (cf. 4:21, 23, "and now is"). The same applies to the hour of resurrection in 5:25. Especially significant is the hour of the passion, which is God's hour (not yet come in 7:30; 8:20; come in 12:23; 13:1; 17:1). The hour is also coming for the disciples, i.e., the time of persecution which begins with Jesus' own hour (cf. 16:2, 4).

f. The Epistles. 1 John speaks of the coming of Christ in the flesh (1 Jn. 4:2) and by water and blood (5:6). Antichrist comes with the last hour (2:18).

g. Revelation. The eternal God is he who was and is and is to come (1:4, 8; 4:8). Christ will come quickly (2:5); the church lives for his coming (22:17) and makes it an object of expectant prayer (22:20). Christ will come as a thief (16:15) with the clouds (1:7). The coming will bring judgment (6:17 etc.), but after messianic tribulation (3:10) it will also bring rejoicing (19:7).

3. *Paul.* References to Christ's first coming occur only in Eph. 2:17 and 1 Tim. 1:15, but there are many references to the coming again, which is imminent (1 Cor. 4:5; 16:22), is proclaimed at the Supper (1 Cor. 11:26), will be like that of the thief (1 Th. 5:2), will be in glory (2 Th. 1:10), and will bring perfection (1 Cor. 13:10) but also judgment (Col. 3:6), being preceded by apostasy (2 Th. 2:3). Paul also uses "coming" for significant events, such as the coming of the commandment in Rom. 7:9, and of faith in Gal. 3:23. As an apostle he himself comes with the blessings of the gospel (Rom. 15:29); he comes not with lofty words (1 Cor. 2:1), but to preach the gospel (2 Cor. 2:12). He wants to come with meekness (1 Cor. 4:21), not with sorrow or to punish (cf. 2 Cor. 2:1, 3), and he is ready to suffer humiliation at his coming though he hopes to find repentance (2 Cor. 12:20-21).

4. *The Other NT Writings.* Here the eschatological use predominates: the coming again of Christ in Acts 1:11, the coming of judgment day in Acts 2:20, the coming of the age of salvation in Heb. 8:8, the coming of scoffers in 2 Pet. 3:3. The coming of the Spirit in Acts 19:6 shows that the age of salvation has already dawned (cf. Acts 2:17-18).

éleusis. This word, meaning "coming," is rare outside the Bible. It occurs in the NT only in Acts 7:52 for the coming of the Righteous One proclaimed by the prophets, probably with a reference to the coming again in judgment.

apérchomai. opísō apérchesthai is common in the Synoptists for discipleship. Mk. 9:43 expresses the seriousness of decision; if anything hinders, we go (*apelthein*) to hell. *apelthein* is also the opposite in Jude 7 (indulging in unnatural lust). It is used for the end of the first and fallen creation in Rev. 21:4.

diérchomai. In Rom. 5:12 this word denotes the extension of death to everybody, while in Heb. 4:14 it signifies Christ's passing as High Priest through the heavens to the heavenly sanctuary.

259

eisérchomai. "To go," "to come," with such varied references as to the entry of a chorus, the movement of money, going to court, entry on an office, the onset of hunger. It occurs cultically for invocation of deities. In the LXX it can have a sexual as well as a local reference, but is commonly sacral: a. God or his glory or Spirit comes to us; b. worshippers go into the temple, purity being demanded; c. believers bring their prayers to God; d. Israel enters the promised land.

1. In the NT we often find such phrases as going into the temple (Acts 3:8), God's house (Mt. 12:4), or the synagogue (Mk. 1:21), or entering Jerusalem (Mk. 11:11), and the angel coming to Mary (Lk. 1:28).

2. The most significant theological use is with *eis*. The Synoptists speak about entering the kingdom, for which the following requirements are found: becoming as little children (Mk. 10:15), keeping the commandments (Mt. 19:17), doing God's will (Mt. 7:21), a new beginning (Mt. 5:20), a clean break (Mt. 18:8-9), vigilance (Mt. 25:10), and fidelity (Mt. 25:21ff.). Jesus and the disciples summon people into the kingdom; they are to enter by the strait gate (Mt. 7:13), but may be hindered by wealth (Mk. 10:23) or by the self-righteous (Lk. 11:52). John adds the need for regeneration by water and the Spirit (3:5) and stresses that access is only through Christ (10:2, 9). Tribulation precedes entry (Acts 14:22).

3. In general religious use we find Jesus coming to sinners and the risen Christ to the disciples (Lk. 19:7; 24:29). The ascension is an entry into glory (Lk. 24:26). But Satan enters into Judas (Lk. 22:3), and Jesus commands the spirit not to enter the boy again (Mk. 9:25). The disciples must pray not to enter into temptation (Mk. 14:38) and enter their rooms to pray (Mt. 6:6). Paul has the word for unbelievers coming into Christian gatherings in 1 Cor. 14:23-24, for the coming of sin in Rom. 5:12, and for the coming of the fullness of the Gentiles in Rom. 11:25. Hebrews uses the word for the entry of the high priest into the holy of holies (9:25), the entry of the heavenly High Priest into the heavenly sanctuary (6:19 etc.), the coming of Christ into the world for sin (10:5), and the entry of believers into eternal rest (3:11, 18; 4:1ff.). Revelation says that only those who are written in the book of life can enter the holy city (21:27), and Christ says that he will come in when people open the door for him (3:20). Some readings of 2 Jn. 7 refer to deceivers going into the world, while Jms. 5:4 says that the cries of the economically oppressed go up to God.

exérchomai. "To go out," e.g., sickness, time, also "to issue," "to come up," "to leave," even "to stand out." The LXX uses the word for the issue of the earth, body, or lips, for what proceeds from God, but also for our fleeting breath, and cultically for the divine epiphany and coming to prayer.

In the NT the word denotes resurrection (Jn. 11:34, 41). It also occurs for going forth to do things (Mk. 6:12), for what comes forth from a person, e.g., the decree of Lk. 2:1, rumors (Mt. 9:26), utterances (Jms. 3:10), evil thoughts (Mt. 15:19), but also God's word (1 Cor. 14:36) and news of faith (1 Th. 1:8). Other uses are for descent (Heb. 7:5), leaving a fellowship (1 Jn. 2:19), going out on missionary work (3 Jn. 7), and the going forth of angels (Rev. 14:15ff.) or Satan (20:8). Demons go out when expelled (Mk. 1:26). Peter asks Jesus to leave him (Lk. 5:8). Jesus has come out to preach (Mk. 1:38), and power goes out of him when he heals (Mk. 5:30). Jesus has come forth from God (Jn. 8:42; cf. 16:30), and he is the door through which the disciples go in and out to pasture (10:9). Judas goes out in Jn. 13:30-31. Jesus goes out of Jerusalem to be crucified in 19:17, and disciples are to go out with him in Heb. 13:13. Abraham goes out in an act of faith (Heb. 11:8), but believers are not to leave the world (1 Cor. 5:10). Angels will come forth to divide the good from the bad according to Mt. 13:49.

epérchomai. a. "To come to," "draw near," used of people, events, time, etc. b. "To come with hostile intent," "to attack," "to accuse." c. In the papyri we also find "to enter illegally," d. "to be due," e. "to contest the validity," and f. "to make claims," "oppress with demands." The LXX uses the word with reference to things, events, conditions, etc. that bring evils, or, less frequently, blessings.

Except in Eph. 1:7 and Jms. 5:1 the word occurs in the NT only in Luke and Acts. Figuratively it means coming on someone, e.g., the stronger on the weaker in Lk. 11:22. The Holy Spirit as the power of God comes on Mary in Lk. 1:35 and on the disciples in Acts 1:8. Disasters will come at the end, according to Lk. 21:26, 35 (cf. Jms. 5:1). But in Eph. 2:7 the ineffable generosity of divine grace will be shown to coming ages.

parérchomai. a. "To go by," "to pass" (time), "to come to an end." b. "To outstrip," "surpass." c. "To pass over," "disregard," "miss," "transgress." d. "To come to, arrive at," "come forward," "attain to," "enter into" (an inheritance). The LXX has the term for human mortality, for breaking or deviating from the commandments, and for theophanies.

When Lk. 18:37 says that Jesus "passes by," this might be just a topographical note, but it carries a hint of epiphany. In Lk. 15:29 Jesus condemns the complacency that thinks it has left no commandment "unfulfilled," and in 11:42 the practice that "overlooks" the essentials. In 1 Pet. 4:3 the pre-Christian life is "past," in Jms. 1:10 all earthly things are "fleeting," and in Mt. 5:18 etc. heaven and earth will "pass away," but not the word of Jesus (Mt. 24:35). In Mk. 13:30 this generation will not "pass away" until the events depicted take place. For Paul in 2 Cor. 5:17 the old has "passed away" and the new has come.

pareisérchomai. This is a significant word in Rom. 5:20, where the law has "come in" as it were parenthetically (to increase sin), and in Gal. 2:4, where false brethren (the Judaizers) have slipped into the churches to spy out and reverse their freedom.

periérchomai. This word is used in 1 Tim. 5:13 for the gadding about of younger widows and in Heb. 11:37 for the wanderings of persecuted heroes of faith.

prosérchomai. "To come to or go to," "approach (also hostilely)," "apply oneself," used for such things as income, going in to a woman, going to work or market, taking up a matter or cause, appearing before a judge or tribunal, also cultically coming before a deity. The LXX uses it sexually and militarily and also for appearing in court (Dt. 25:1) and being occupied with a matter; we also find the cultic sense of coming before God (Jer. 7:16), and cf. the warning not to draw near to sin (Sir. 21:2).

In the NT the word is most common in Matthew and denotes the coming to Jesus of angels (4:11), the tempter (4:3), and various human groups: a. the disciples (5:1), the women (28:9), and Peter (18:21), b. the crowds seeking help (15:30), the sick (8:2; 9:28, etc.), and their relatives (8:5); c. people with special requests (19:16; 20:20; 26:7), d. opponents, the scribes etc. (8:19; 15:1; 16:1), Judas (26:49), those who arrest Jesus (26:50), the false witnesses (26:60), the soldiers (Lk. 23:36). A few times Jesus himself comes to people, e.g., to heal in Mk. 1:31, to raise the dead man in Lk. 7:14, to expel demons in Lk. 9:42, and to give the great commission in Mt. 28:18. In Acts the term denotes important events (8:29; 10:28; also in Paul's life, 9:1;

18:2; 24:23). In Hebrews and 1 Peter the sense is cultic. Christians have drawn near to God through Christ (Heb. 7:25) and by faith (11:6). They have come to Mt. Zion (12:18), and should draw near to the throne of grace (4:16) or to Christ (10:22) as worshippers under the law draw near to sacrifice (10:1). The decision of faith is a coming to the Lord in 1 Pet. 2:3-4.

synérchomai. In Acts 15:38 this word means "to journey with someone" on missionary work. In 1 Cor. 11:17 it denotes the coming together of the congregation, which here is not for the better. The sense is the same in 1 Cor. 14:23, 26, where Paul is giving direction for the proper use of spiritual gifts in the church.

[J. SCHNEIDER, II, 666-84]

---

erōtáō [to ask, request], *eperōtáō* [to ask, question], *eperōtēma* [request, question]

---

erōtáō.

1. The first sense is "to ask," "seek information." The rich young ruler is asking Jesus about the good (Mt. 19:17), Jesus asks his disciples about the loaves available (Mk. 8:5), or about people's views of him (Mt. 16:13), and he asks his opponents about John's baptism (Mt. 21:24). The disciples ask the meaning of the parables (Mk. 4:10) and also ask when God's kingdom will be set up (Acts 1:6). Most of the instances are in John. The disciples will no longer need to ask when they have the perfect knowledge of fellowship with Christ (16:23). Gaining an insight into his vicarious ministry, they no longer need to question him (16:30). Yet it is by asking that fuller fellowship is achieved (16:5). Outside the Parting Discourses the word is used in John only for the questions of opponents (except in 9:2, where the disciples ask whose sin was responsible for the man being born blind).

2. "To request," "demand." Apart from Acts 1:6, this is the chief meaning outside the Gospels. It can denote the disciples' request to Jesus (Mt. 15:23), that of the Jews to Pilate (Jn. 19:31), and the invitation to a meal (Lk. 14:18-19). John has it for requests to God, but only by Jesus except in 1 Jn. 5:16. The LXX uses *erōtáō,* "to ask," and *aitéō,* "to pray," for the same Hebrew word (*šā'al*), but secular Greek offers a cultic use, so that the use for "to pray" need not be a Semitism.

eperōtáō. "To ask," "to question," "to inquire"—a favorite word in Mark. It may suggest an urgent asking (Jn. 18:7). It is used for judicial examination (Mk. 14:60-61), investigation (Mk. 15:44), asking for a decision as in probing questions (Mk. 10:2; 12:18), and perhaps disputing rather than merely asking questions (Lk. 2:46; cf. v. 47). In Mt. 16:1 the sense is "request" or "demand." In 1 Cor. 14:35 wives are to ask their husbands at home, but in Rom. 10:20 God has shown himself to those who did not ask for him.

eperōtēma. This word means "question." The only NT instance is in 1 Pet. 3:21, which perhaps rests on the use in the LXX for an oracular question addressed to God, so that we are to translate "request." Baptism does not confer physical cleansing but saves as a request for forgiveness; the author perhaps avoids the idea of spiritual cleansing so as to stay clear of magical conceptions.   [H. GREEVEN, II, 685-89]

→ *aitéō, déomai, eúchomai*

---

esthiō [to eat, drink]

A. *esthiō* outside the NT.

1. "To eat and drink," a stock term that occurs in connection with the sick needing to eat, the righteous not being concerned about eating, giving the hungry to eat, etc.; it is sometimes a mark of pleasure-seeking, but also suggests table fellowship (cf. the rabbis).

2. The OT and Judaism have cultic rules about eating, e.g., washing before eating, not eating idol-meats, ascetic abstinence from eating and drinking.

3. Eating and drinking are linked to the vision of God (cf. Ex. 24:11, which the rabbis spiritualize). In the mysteries there is eating and drinking of the divine essence.

4. Judaism has hopes for eating and drinking with God in the eschatological banquet (cf. rabbinic and apocalyptic writings and Lk. 14:15).

5. Figuratively the word means a. "to enjoy" (Job. 21:25; Prov. 9:5). For spiritual eating cf. Philo *Allegorical Interpretation of Laws* 1.97. b. The Hebrew term (usually *katesthíein* in the LXX) can denote consuming by the sword (2 Sam. 2:26), fire (Num. 16:35), heat (Gen. 31:40), hunger and sickness (Ex. 7:15), and divine wrath (Am. 5:6). c. In warnings or laments we also find "to destroy" (Ps. 14:4; Prov. 30:14).

B. *esthiō* in the NT.

1. Eating is necessary for life (Mt. 6:35). Having something to eat is a pressing concern (Mt. 6:36ff.). Jesus and the disciples hardly have time to eat (Mk. 3:20). Eating and drinking is a formal expression for meeting basic needs (Mt. 6:31). After raising from the dead, it is a sign of life (Mk. 5:43; Lk. 24:41ff.). As workers are worthy of their hire (Mt. 10:10; cf. 2 Th. 3:12; 1 Cor. 9:7), missionaries should be supported (Mt. 10:8ff.). Those who will not work should not eat (2 Th. 3:10). But the hungry must be given to eat (Mt. 25:34ff.). As servants first give their masters something to eat, so the disciples are to render unselfish service (Lk. 17:7ff.). Eating is a sign of festive joy (Lk. 15:23) but also of fatal materialism (Lk. 12:19). Jesus, in eating and drinking, seems to be too worldly for a true man of God (Mt. 11:19). Eating with people is a mark of close fellowship (Mk. 14:18). Refusal of *synesthíein* expresses repudiation of fellowship (1 Cor. 5:11).

2. Apart from the references to eating manna in Jn. 6:31 etc., ritual matters are mostly at issue in the religious use. Paul refers to priests partaking of the offerings in 1 Cor. 9:13. Jesus quotes David's eating of the showbread in Mk. 2:26 to support the eating of ears of grain on the sabbath. He also defends eating without ritual washing (Mk. 7:1ff.) and risks defiling table fellowship (Mk. 2:16). Yet an ascetic abstinence from eating and drinking may be practiced on occasion (cf. Mt. 11:18; Acts 9:9; 23:12). Eating idol-meats raises a problem. The strong are free to do this, for fellowship with God does not depend on eating and drinking (1 Cor. 8:1, 7ff.). Yet it is better to renounce this freedom than sin by wounding the weak (vv. 11ff.; cf. 10:23ff.). A similar question is that of abstinence from certain foods (Rom. 14:2ff.). Paul favors the strong on this issue too, for both eating and not eating are good in God's sight, but again loving responsibility for others demands restraint: It is wrong to make others fall by what we eat (v. 20). A ritual question is involved here (v. 14) as well as the more general practice of abstinence and vegetarianism.

3. The church comes together to eat (1 Cor. 11:33). In rectifying abuses at Corinth, Paul stresses the cultic character of the Lord's Supper. Eating bread and drinking wine are part of a sacred action that demands restraint and that is incompatible with profane

and selfish eating (vv. 22ff.). The OT manna is a model (1 Cor. 10:3). Using the same example, Jesus offers himself as the true bread from heaven; by eating this bread we may live forever (Jn. 6:50-51).

4. Eating and drinking with the heavenly King corresponds to the messianic banquet referred to in Lk. 14:15. Jesus will eat the fulfilled Passover in God's kingdom (Lk. 22:16), and he assures the disciples that they will eat and drink at his table (22:30). Eating of the tree of life means sharing in the life of the age of salvation (Rev. 2:7). In contrast, the birds will eat the flesh of the defeated hosts of antichrist (Rev. 19:17-18).

5. The divine of Revelation eats the rolls of a book (10:9; cf. Ezek. 2:8; Jer. 15:16) in token of inward filling with his prophetic message.

6. We find figurative use a. ("to enjoy") when Jesus refers to his spiritual food in Jn. 4:32, and b. ("to consume") in Heb. 10:27 and Jms. 5:3.

→ *trógō*   [J. Behm, II, 689-95]

ésoptron [mirror],   *katoptrízomai* [to see something in a mirror]

ésoptron. In the figure of speech in Jms. 1:23, the obvious point is that those who are hearers and not doers are like people getting only a fleeting reflection of themselves in a mirror.

katoptrízomai. This means a. "to show in a mirror," "to reflect" (passive "be reflected"), b. middle "to see oneself in a mirror," and c. "to see something in a mirror." The only NT instance is in 2 Cor. 3:18, where we have sense c.: "We see the Lord's glory as in a mirror." The idea here is that of a mirror that makes the invisible visible and in so doing changes us into the likeness of what we see. This is all the work of the Spirit (cf. 1 Cor. 13:12). There are no examples to support the rendering "reflect" that some exegetes have favored.   [G. Kittel, II, 696-97]

éschatos [last]

1. The general use is for what is last materially (Mt. 5:26), spatially (Acts 1:8), or temporally (Mt. 12:45). Theologically significant is the last resurrection appearance to Paul. This closes the series, and the association with "least" gives Paul his character as "one untimely born" (1 Cor. 15:8-9).

2. The eschatological use derives from what is last in time (cf. the influence of the prophetic "day of Yahweh"). The end begins with Jesus' coming (Heb. 1:2). That the present is the last time is shown by the outpouring of the Spirit (Acts 2:17) and by the coming of scoffers, antichrist, etc. (2 Tim. 3:1; Jms. 5:3; 2 Pet. 3:3; Jude 18; 1 Jn. 2:18). Yet the last day is also awaited; cf. the last plagues of Rev. 15:1, the last enemy of 1 Cor. 15:26, the last trumpet of 1 Cor. 15:52, and the last hour or time of resurrection, judgment, and salvation in Jn. 6:39-40; 1 Pet. 1:5. Christ is the last Adam (1 Cor. 15:45ff.); he is also the first and the last (Rev. 1:17).

3. A figurative sense is "last in rank" (opposite of first) (cf. 1 Cor. 4:9; Mk. 9:35; 10:31). The last place is the place of least honor (Lk. 14:9-10), but disciples are willingly to take this place in unselfish service to others.   [G. Kittel, II, 697-98]

ésō [in, inside]

1. *hoi ésō* in 1 Cor. 15:12 are those who are in the community in distinction from pagans.

2. *ho ésō ánthrōpos,* parallel to *egō* and *noús,* is used in Rom. 7:22 for our spiritual side which gives us self-awareness and enables us to make moral judgments. By reason of it we are open to the claim of revelation but contradict it in our conduct. In 2 Cor. 4:16, however, the phrase denotes our determination by God as those who are new creatures (5:17) and who experience daily renewal through the Spirit (5:5); the opposite is the "outer man," our being in its creaturely mortality. In Eph. 3:16 the reference is again to believers as the object of God's working or the place where God's Spirit meets and shapes them. Like the parallel phrase in 1 Pet. 3:4 it carries a hint of God's hidden operation. The term is materially parallel to "heart" in the OT, and we may thus compare the sayings of Jesus in Mk. 7:21 and Lk. 11:39.   [J. Behm, II, 698-99]

---

hetaíros [friend]

This term is used for a. "companion," b. "fellow-soldier," c. "member of the same party," d. "religious society," e. "pupil," f. "friend," and g. "colleague." It is not common in the LXX but is used in later Judaism for a qualified but not yet ordained member of the scribal body, and more widely for one who seeks to live strictly by the law, especially its ritual requirements.

1. The only NT use is in Matthew, where the owner of the vineyard (20:3) and the king (22:12) employ it when addressing the grumblers and the man without a wedding garment, and Jesus has it in greeting Judas (26:50). The meaning is "friend" but in each case with the implication of a distinct relationship in which there is generosity on the one part and abuse of it on the other.

2. The absence of the word elsewhere in the NT shows that it is not thought to be appropriate to Christians, for in relation to Christ *doúlos* is the proper term for believers, and in relation to one another *adelphoí*. The use of *adelphoí* shows that God has invaded the sphere of human egoism and that Christians have a new relationship with one another in virtue of their common relatedness to the one Lord.

[K. H. Rengstorf, II, 699-701]

heteróglōssos → *glōssa; heterodidaskaléō* → *didáskō; heterozygéō* → *zygós*

---

héteros [other, another]

In the NT *héteros* is used in much the same way as *állos,* but does not occur in several books (e.g., Mark, 1 and 2 Thessalonians, 1 and 2 Peter, Revelation). It denotes the new member in a series that either continues (Lk. 14:18ff.) or concludes it (Acts 15:35). It may denote others either of the same kind (Acts 17:34; Lk. 4:34) or of another kind (Lk. 23:32). It may compare or contrast two groups (Acts 23:6), but can also simply denote the next day (Acts 20:15). At times there may be the hint of a qualitative distinction, as in Mt. 11:3 ("Shall we look for another?"); Mk. 16:12 ("another form," i.e., that of a traveler); Lk. 9:29 (Jesus' transfigured face). The "other tongues" of Acts 2:4 may simply refer to tongues as in 10:46; 1 Cor. 12:10; 14:1ff., but in this case "other" would seem to be superfluous, and we should have to assume that, since the later tongues are unintelligible, the true miracle is that the people are granted a gift of understanding, which, in spite of Acts 2:6, 11, is not very convincing. Thus the alternative view that they spoke in foreign languages seems alone to do full justice to the phrase, especially in the light of v. 11 (though cf. the contemptuous reference in v. 13). In Acts 17:7 the point of the charge against Paul is that he is proclaiming a rival to the emperor. In Rom. 7:23 the other law which differs from the holy law of God, and the law of reason that assents to it, is the law of sin that dwells in our members and enslaves us. 1 Cor. 15:40 refers to the different glory of celestial and terrestrial bodies. Eph. 3:5 contrasts the present age of salvation with all preceding generations. Phil. 3:15 may refer either to failure to attain to the preceding insights or to more general divergence from Paul. In Heb. 7:11ff. Jesus is the other priest who, as is shown in detail, both fulfils and transcends Melchizedek. What has come in Jesus is different in the sense that it excludes any other way of salvation (1 Cor. 8:4; Acts 4:12), so that decision is demanded. "Another gospel" (Gal. 1:6) is not really another, let alone a better; it is no gospel at all (cf. 2 Cor. 11:4). *ho héteros* can also be used for the neighbor, a Thou as distinct from the I (cf. Rom. 2:1). The law of Christ is to seek the other's good (1 Cor. 10:24). Self-giving to others fulfils the law (Rom. 13:8). The other here is not a collective concept but denotes the person who in a specific situation crosses my path and whose edification is my concern (1 Cor. 14:17).   [H. W. BEYER, II, 702-04]

> *hétoimos* [ready], *hetoimázō* [to make ready], *hetoimasía* [readiness], *proetoimázō* [to prepare beforehand]

The meaning of the group is (active) "making ready" and (passive) "readiness."

1. In relation to God the words denote his living and active work of creation and preservation a. in nature and history, relative to heaven and earth (Prov. 3:19), natural processes (Job 38:25), individuals (Ps. 119:73), their needs (Ps. 65:9), their destiny (Gen. 24:14), God's throne (Ps. 103:19), the people of Israel (2 Sam. 7:24) in the desert (Ps. 78:19-20), the conquest (Ex. 23:20), and the history of the monarchy (1 Sam. 13:13; 2 Sam. 5:12), but also in judgment (Zeph. 1:7). b. The group refers to God's work, too, in salvation history. God prepares good things for those who love him (1 Cor. 2:9). This salvation is the heart of the kerygma. It is present in Christ (Lk. 2:30-31). In him the feast is prepared (Mt. 22:4, 8). But it is also future. We are to enter into a prepared kingdom (Mt. 25:34). Jesus is preparing a place for us (Jn. 14:2). His death and resurrection prepare salvation (cf. 1 Pet. 1:5). God is also preparing us for salvation (Rom. 9:23). He has prepared the good works in which we are to walk (Eph. 2:10). Yet God prepares destruction too (Mt. 25:41). The angels are held ready for the decisive time (Rev. 9:15). The group expresses the ineluctable certainty of perdition no less than salvation.

2. In relation to us, corresponding to God's preparation, the terms denote both preparing and preparedness. The Baptist prepares the way of the Lord (Mt. 3:3). Individuals must prepare for fellowship with God (Ps. 108:1). Amos summons the people to prepare to meet their God (4:12). Israel, like Moses, must be ready to receive God's revelation (Ex. 19:11ff.). In the NT readiness is demanded as readiness

for good works (Tit. 3:1), readiness for witness (1 Pet. 3:15; Eph. 6:15), and readiness for the Lord's return (Mt. 24:44). Readiness gives the Christian life a distinctive dynamic character as expectation of the goal of salvation and openness to the possibilities of action determined by this goal. [W. GRUNDMANN, II, 704-06]

---

euangelízomai [to proclaim good news], *euangélion* [good news, gospel], *proeuangelízomai* [to proclaim beforehand], *euangelistēs* [evangelist]

---

euangelízomai.

A. *bśr* in the OT. This word means "to proclaim good news" (1 Kgs. 1:42). In view of 1 Kgs. 1:42 the basic sense might seem to be simply "to deliver a message," but the stem itself contains the element of joy, so that announcing a victory is a common use and the messenger views himself as the bearer of good tidings (2 Sam. 4:10). Transition to a religious use may be seen in 1 Sam. 31:9 where the proclamation of victory in the land of the Philistines has a cultic character. Parallels are Ps. 68:11, where the women proclaim victory in a song that God himself has given, and Ps. 40:9, where deliverance is declared in the congregation. The term is especially significant in Is. 40ff., where the messenger comes to Zion to proclaim the worldwide victory of God which initiates the age of salvation (52:7). This declaration is not just human word and breath, for God himself speaks through it, bringing to pass what is said by his own creative word. Ps. 96:2ff. is to the same effect. The great eschatological hour has come, and the message of God's acts of power goes out to the nations. Indeed the Gentiles themselves will proclaim it (Is. 60:6). The messenger takes on cultic significance with this effective proclamation of God's royal dominion, and the prophet shares this significance as one who is anointed to bring good tidings to the afflicted (Is. 61:1). All these themes—eschatological expectation, the embracing of the Gentiles, and the links with salvation, righteousness, and peace (Pss. 95:1; 40:9; Is. 52:7)—point forward to the NT.

B. *euangelízomai* with the Greeks. This verb, usually in the middle, with dative or accusative of person, a *perí* to introduce the message, and sometimes a preposition denoting the recipient, is used for bringing news, especially of a victory or some other joyous event, in person or by letter. Often, especially in war, the news may be false. Words like salvation may be combined with it, but also, in secular Greek, the idea of fate or luck. The messenger may come with an oracle, and this yields the thought of "promise" or even "threat." We also find the term used for announcing in the royal palace the arrival of the divine man Apollonius. The ideas of victory and liberation provide links with the NT, but the NT knows nothing of luck, and Jesus, unlike the divine man, is himself the content of the message. Furthermore, in both the OT and NT the term has an actuality of pronouncement that is not found in the secular sense of revealed promise.

C. The Septuagint, Philo, and Josephus.
1. The LXX uses the group for *bśr* (though it has *paidárion* for the messenger with bad news in 1 Sam. 4:17). It prefers *euangelizómenos* to *euángelos* for the messenger in a more literal rendering of the Hebrew. On the other hand, it weakens the Hebrew in Is. 40:9, Ps. 68:11, and Is. 52:6-7 by generalizing the concept, minimizing the efficacy of the divine word, and losing the idea of the dawn of divine rule. It links

euangelízesthai more frequently to salvation (cf. Is. 60:6) and also links it with *dóxa* (Ex. 15:11), *areté* (Is. 42:12), and *aínesis* (Ps. 106:47).

2. Philo is close to the Greek world of thought. He has the verb for announcing good news, sometimes poetically as when an almond tree announces a good crop. In an allegory on Ex. 14:30 the sense is "to promise." We also find in him the terminology of the emperor cult.

3. Josephus uses the word, like Philo, for announcing good news, and also in the sense "to promise," as in *Antiquities* 5.24, 277. In neither writer is there any sense of salvation history or eschatology; individual experiences replace the great history of God, and there is thus no place for the bearer of good tidings in the sense of Is. 40ff.

D. Palestinian Judaism. *bśr* here normally means "to proclaim good news," but sometimes bad news too. With a future reference we also find the sense "to promise." Yet the idea of the messenger of Is. 40ff., with whom the messianic age dawns, may also be found even if the tradition regarding this messenger is not uniform (he may be anonymous, or Elijah, or the Messiah, or there may be many messengers). Expectation of the great age of God's saving rule is alive, and if the message is for Israel first it is also for the Gentiles, and for the dead as well as the living, since the God of Israel is also Lord of the whole world.

E. *euangelízomai* in the NT. This verb (along with *euangélion*) is common in Luke and Acts and fairly common in Paul, but it does not occur in the Johannine writings (perhaps because the primary concept in John is that of fulfilment). We also do not find the verb in Mark, James, 2 Peter, or Jude, and it occurs only once in Matthew, twice in Hebrews, and three times in 1 Peter (*euangelízein* twice in Revelation).

1. Jesus. Jesus brings the good news of the expected last time (Mt. 11:5). The message carries with it the fulfilment. The works of Jesus are signs of the messianic age. At Nazareth Jesus applies Is. 61:1 to himself (Lk. 4:18). With him the good news of God's kingdom is preached (Lk. 16:16). Lk. 8:1 sums up the entire ministry of Jesus when it calls him a herald and messenger of the kingdom. His whole life proclaims the gospel. His birth is good news (Lk. 2:10). His coming, work, and death are the great proclamation of peace (Eph. 2:14ff.). He preaches the good news even to the dead (cf. 1 Pet. 3:19 and 4:6).

2. John the Baptist. Lk. 3:18 says of John that he preached good news to the people. As Elijah, he proclaims God's imminent kingdom (Lk. 1:17; Mt. 11:14; 17:12). Though belonging to the old age, he is more than a prophet. Hence an angel brings the good news of his birth (Lk. 1:19), he prepares the way of God, and as the precursor of the Messiah he is an evangelist whose story is the beginning of the gospel (Mk. 1:1).

3. The Host of Witnesses. Rom. 10:15 refers Is. 52:7, not to the Messiah, but to the messengers of the gospel, even though both the MT and LXX are in the singular. The reason for this is that Jesus had sent out the twelve to preach the gospel (Lk. 9:1ff.) and then given the task of evangelizing (telling the good news about himself) to the church (cf. Acts 5:42; Philip in 8:12, 35, 40). The message goes to both Jews and Gentiles (Acts 11:20). Paul is especially called to be the evangelist to the Gentiles (Gal. 1:16; Rom. 15:20; 1 Cor. 15:1; 2 Cor. 10:16; Acts 14:10; 17:18). This is his grace (Eph. 3:8). His whole ministry is *euangelízesthai* (1 Cor. 1:17). The same message goes out to both Christians and pagans (Rom. 1:15; Acts 14:15), for God himself speaks through it to all people. The content is Jesus himself (Gal. 1:16), his passion and resurrection (1 Pet. 1:11ff.; Acts 17:18), the kingdom (Acts 8:12), the OT in its witness to Christ (Acts 8:35), the word (Acts 15:35), and the faith (Gal. 1:23). Parallel terms are preaching, teaching, and witnessing. *euangelízesthai* is not just speaking but proclaiming with power to the accompaniment of signs. It thus brings healing (Mt. 4:23), joy (Acts 8:8), salvation (1 Cor. 15:1-2), and regeneration (1 Pet. 1:23ff.) as God's own word in the power of his Spirit (1 Pet. 1:12). Being proclamation of the good news of God, it carries with it both the offer and the power of salvation. Two special uses may be noted: In 1 Th. 3:6 the faith and love of the Thessalonians are the theme of the good news brought by Timothy, and in Heb. 4:2, 6 OT proclamation is included with its element of promise.

4. God. Twice God is the subject of evangelizing. In Acts 10:36 he causes peace to be proclaimed through Christ; the story of Jesus is God's good news of peace and joy. In Rev. 10:7 God has announced the good news of his coming rule to his servants the OT and NT prophets.

5. Angels. Gabriel gives the good news of the Baptist's birth in Lk. 1:19, and the angel announces the Savior's birth in Lk. 2:10. In both cases the message is evangel because the time of salvation has come and great joy may thus be proclaimed.

euangélion.

A. *euangélion* outside the NT.

1. b^eśōrâ in the OT. The noun, much less common than the verb, occurs only six times in the OT and means 1. "good news" (2 Sam. 18:20, 25, 27; 2 Kgs. 7:9) and 2. "reward for good news" (2 Sam. 4:10; 18:22). The spoken word is equated with its content; bad news brings sorrow and good news joy. The bearer of bad news is thus guilty and may be punished for it (2 Sam. 1:15-16), while the bearer of good news is rewarded. The use in the OT is purely secular.

2. euangélion among the Greeks.

a. This word is an adjective as well as a noun and means "what is proper to an *euángelos*," i.e., either good news, or the reward for it. The term becomes a technical one for "news of victory." A whole ritual surrounds the coming of the messenger who bears this news, e.g., decking his spear with laurels and crowning his head. Sacrifices are also offered when the news comes, the temples are garlanded, an *agón* is held, and the offerings are crowned. Good fortune is contained in the words; hence the reward for the messenger. The first messenger receives a higher reward, a dilatory messenger may be punished. Yet, since lying reports circulate, rewards are given only after verification. An *euangélion* can also be an oracular saying. Thanksgivings are offered for such an *euangélion*, though when the Ephesians do not believe an oracle of Apollonius he orders them to postpone the sacrifice until what he has said comes to pass.

b. *euangélion* is particularly important in the emperor cult. The emperor is a divine ruler who controls nature, dispenses healing, serves as a protective god, and brings good fortune, his birth being accompanied by cosmic signs. Imperial messages, then, are joyous ones, since what he says is a divine act implying good and salvation. The first *euangélion* is news of his birth, then his coming of age, then his accession. Offerings and yearly festivals celebrate the new and more hopeful era that dawns with him. His accession to the throne is a gospel for his subjects. This imperial *euangélion*, like that of the NT, has a Near Eastern source, but to the many imperial messages the NT opposes the one gospel, and to the many accessions the one proclamation of God's kingdom. Again, the NT may use familiar language, but it associates it with the scandal of the cross (1 Cor. 1:17), penitence, and judgment, so that it must have seemed ironical to some (Acts 17:32). Caesar and Christ confront one another. They

269

have much in common, for both claim to be gospel, but they belong to different worlds.

3. The Septuagint and Josephus.

a. The LXX does not have *euangélion* in the singular. In the plural the word occurs only in 2 Sam. 4:10 as "reward for good news"; *hē euangélia* is used in 2 Sam. 18:22 etc. This term is rare, and a distinction between it and *euangélion* is not found elsewhere. The NT use of *euangélion* clearly does not derive from the LXX, since the NT never has either the plural or the sense of reward.

b. Philo does not use the noun, but Josephus has *hē euangélia, tó euangélion,* and *tá euangélia* for "glad tidings," especially in connection with the emperor cult.

4. Rabbinic Judaism. This does not help much regarding the noun. The rabbis use the Hebrew term for good news (or sometimes sad news), and it may have a religious sense, but they do not employ it for eschatological good news. The reason seems to be that while they expect the eschatological act, and the messenger who announces it, the message as such is not a new one and hence is not so important. The stress on the act is significant, however, since it influences the NT understanding of *euangélion* as denoting action as well as content, which would be most unusual in Greek. The fact that *euangélion* seems to be a loanword to describe the NT gospel, and open as such to malicious punning, does not prove the contrary, for Palestinian Judaism was largely bilingual.

B. *euangélion* in the NT. Mark has the noun eight times, Matthew four, and Luke (preferring the verb) none at all. There are two instances in Acts, sixty in Pauline works, and one each in 1 Peter and Revelation.

1. The Synoptists. Except in the title (1:1) and the general summary in 1:14, Mark has *euangélion* only in sayings of Jesus. Doubts have been expressed as to the actual use of the word by Jesus himself except perhaps in Mk. 14:9. The real question, however, is whether it is true to the matter itself. The proclamation of Jesus is undoubtedly good news, and he himself is its proclaimer, so that we have an obvious transition from the verb to the noun. Furthermore, with his messianic consciousness, Jesus realizes that he is not just bringing a new teaching but bringing himself as the content of his message, so that for the disciples *euangélion* implies disclosure of the messianic secret. Thus, while the verb might be the better term for Jesus himself, the noun is apt for the direct continuation of his proclamation by the community. The question whether the word is original in Jesus' own teaching is consequently of secondary importance, as is also the question whether "gospel of the kingdom" or "gospel of Jesus" is more authentic, or whether the genitive in 1:1 is objective or subjective. Jesus both proclaims the gospel and is and actualizes it. Its content is the fulfilment of the time and the nearness of the kingdom. Being contrary to appearances, it demands repentance and faith. During his lifetime Jesus restricts it to Israel, but all nations are to come in with the messianic age (Mt. 8:11), so that when Jesus is exalted as Lord in the resurrection, proclamation extends to the Gentiles as itself an eschatological event (Mk. 13:10).

2. Paul.

a. Most of the NT references to *euangélion* are in Paul. His use of *tó euangélion* shows that the concept is now a fixed one both for himself and his readers. As one may see from 2 Cor. 8:18; Phil. 4:3, 15, it refers to the act of proclamation, but 1 Cor. 9:14 shows that it may also refer to the content. This twofold sense is especially plain in Rom. 1:1: "set apart for the gospel of God," for while Paul is set apart to preach the gospel, the clause that follows (vv. 2-3) describes its content.

b. Verbs of speaking and hearing indicate that a specific message is to be declared (cf. 1 Cor. 15:1; 9:14; Gal. 2:2; 1 Th. 2:2; 2 Tim. 1:11; Col. 1:5, 23; Gal. 1:12). Two passages summarize the content (Rom. 1:1ff. and 1 Cor. 15:1ff.), and cf. Rom. 2:16; 16:25; 2 Tim. 3:8. From Rom. 1:1ff. we learn that the preexistent Son has become man, is as such the expected Davidic Messiah, and has been exalted as *kýrios* with his resurrection. The resurrection presupposes the death and passion. As the message of Jesus, the gospel brings peace (Eph. 6:15), but judgment is also part of its content (Rom. 2:16). The gospel also brings strength (Rom. 16:25) as the revelation of God's saving counsel concurrent with the preaching of Jesus. No break with the OT is implied, for the gospel is the fulfilment of promise (Rom. 1:1ff.) both in its preaching and message. Bearing witness to Christ, the OT belongs to the gospel and serves to make it known to the nations (Rom. 16:26). The new thing is what the message effects. If the content is to be summed up in a single word, that word is Christ (cf. Rom. 15:19; 1 Cor. 9:12; 2 Cor. 2:12; Gal. 1:7; Phil. 1:27, etc.; also 2 Th. 1:8 and Rom. 1:9). Whether the genitive is objective or subjective in the phrase "gospel of Christ" is of little moment, since Christ is both author and content as the Exalted and Incarnate Lord in one.

c. The gospel records a historical event, but this event transcends ordinary history. Similarly, it consists of narratives and teachings, but it also relates to human reality and shows itself to be living power. The "for our sins" of 1 Cor. 15:3 makes it a message of judgment and joy. The "resurrection from the dead" of Rom. 1:4 shows it to be the initiation of the general resurrection. If the gospel is witness to salvation history, it is itself salvation history, for it comes into human lives, refashions them, and constitutes the communities. It cannot be grasped in the ordinary way (2 Cor. 4:3); divine revelation takes place in it. Through the gospel God calls us to salvation through the preacher (2 Th. 2:14), summons us to decision, and claims our obedience (Rom. 10:16; 2 Cor. 9:13). We shall be judged by our attitude to it (2 Th. 1:8). The gospel is no empty word; it effects what it says, since God is its author (Rom. 1:1 etc.). It is everywhere at work (Col. 1:5), and brings the Gentiles into the promise (Eph. 3:6). There must be no hindrance to either its proclamation or its operation (cf. 1 Cor. 9:12). It is fulfilled when it takes effect (Rom. 15:18ff.). It brings salvation (Eph. 1:13; Rom. 1:16). It reveals God's justifying righteousness, combining judgment and grace (Rom. 1:16-17). Faith arises through it and is directed to it (Phil. 1:27). It gives new life (1 Cor. 4:15); the life achieved through Christ's death and resurrection comes to actuality through it (cf. 2 Tim. 1:10). It mediates the presence of something future (Col. 1:5) and is thus an eschatological event, fulfilling hope (cf. Col. 1:23). Effecting what it proclaims, it can be a term for salvation itself (1 Th. 2:8). Fellowship in it is not just cooperation in evangelism but fellowship in the salvation it brings. The divine glory of Christ shines in it (2 Cor. 4:4). Christ is himself present in it (cf. 1 Th. 2:12; Col. 1:10; Phil. 1:27). Paul is in prison both for Christ and the gospel (Phlm. 9, 13). Message and content are one (2 Cor. 10:14). It forces service upon us (Col. 1:23) as its fellows (1 Cor. 9:23). It is a cultic foundation where Paul offers priestly service in Rom. 15:16, but as distinct from election it is an order of salvation in Rom. 11:28 and a declared mystery in Eph. 6:19.

d. Paul can speak of "our" (2 Cor. 4:3) or "my" gospel (Rom. 2:16). He can also refer to the gospel which "he" preached (1 Cor. 15:1; Gal. 1:11; cf. 2:2). He does not mean that he has a special gospel. He shares with others only the one gospel of Christ

(Gal. 1:6). It is his because he is entrusted with its proclamation (1 Th. 2:4; 1 Tim. 1:11). He is its herald, apostle, and teacher (2 Tim. 1:10). He is called to preach it (Rom. 1:1) to the Gentiles (Gal. 1:16). He serves Christ as an evangelist (Rom. 1:9). He is a partner of the gospel (1 Cor. 9:23), and as such a priest (Rom. 15:16) and servant (Eph. 3:7). Suffering with him is suffering with the gospel (2 Tim. 1:8). But if he is in bonds, the gospel is not (2 Tim. 2:8ff.). His imprisonment is for its defense and confirmation (Phil. 1:7). What happens to him promotes it. Those who serve him, serve it (Phil. 2:22). He is Timothy's father through the gospel (1 Cor. 4:15).

e. The gospel teaches the right use of the law, revealing God's glory (1 Tim. 1:11). Law and gospel are not in direct antithesis. The Judaizers see their teaching as gospel too. For them, however, the gospel becomes proclamation of law. What Paul opposes to law is promise, not gospel. Promise predates law, and even in the OT is the true ground of acceptance. It comes to fulfilment in Christ and discloses the real purpose of law. Paul's gospel is the same as that of the others (Gal. 1:11; 1 Cor. 15:1ff.). The risen Lord is its author (Lk. 24:19ff.). But as the apostle to the Gentiles Paul is the one who faces the question of law and gospel. Jewish Christians keep the law while being free regarding it. Paul himself will do this (1 Cor. 9:20). But salvation is in Christ alone for both the circumcised and uncircumcised (cf. Gal. 2). Christ allows us to be neither legalists nor libertines. The gospel demands obedience. It is a criterion of conduct (Phil. 1:27). We are obedient to it when active in the ministry of love (2 Cor. 9:13ff.).

3. *Revelation.* In Rev. 14:6-7 an angel proclaims the gospel, the gospel is everlasting, and there is no article. Since the content seems to be judgment, it is thought by some that this is not the gospel of Christ. An angel proclaims it, however, because the time is short. This preaching is a sign of the end. The real content is not judgment but fear of the Lord (Mk. 1:14-15) and worship of the Creator (Acts 14:15).

C. Transition of the Term *euangélion* to Designation of a Book. In the NT *euangélion* is oral preaching. The apostles' writings are not *euangélion*; they declare it (cf. 1 Cor. 15:1). Soon, however, the works that contain the words and deeds of Jesus are themselves called gospel. Missionaries thus acquire both a verbal and a written mission. The gospel is both preached and read. Ignatius still uses "gospel" in the dynamic sense of Christ as the center and goal of salvation history. In the Didache it comprises the whole tradition. Irenaeus can speak of the Prophets and Gospels, i.e., the OT and the NT. But he also refers to the four Gospels, which all, of course, proclaim the same gospel. "Gospel" is used by Eusebius for the whole collection as well as each individual book, and Clement of Alexandria says "in the gospels" when he quotes a saying that is in fact found only in one Gospel.

euangelistḗs. Except in church writings, this is a rare word. It occurs three times in the NT: for Philip in Acts 4:11, Timothy in 2 Tim. 4:5, and evangelists as a group in Eph. 4:11. The evangelist does not proclaim oracles, as among the Greeks, but the good news (Rom. 10:15). The term denotes a function which apostles also exercised, though not all evangelists would be apostles, and the function is a lower one than that of the apostles in all three references. Congregational as well as missionary proclamation is denoted (cf. 2 Tim. 4:5). In the early church evangelists continue the apostles' work. The word also comes to be used for the author of a Gospel.

proeuangelízomai. Not found in classical Greek, this word is used in Gal. 3:8 to show that the promise given to Abraham is an advance preaching of the gospel. The *proeuangélion* becomes *euangélion* when the promise is fulfilled in Christ (3:16) and justification by faith is secured for the Gentiles   [G. FRIEDRICH, II, 707-37]

euarestéō, euárestos → aréskō

---

eudokéō [to be well-pleased],   **eudokía** [good will, good pleasure]

---

eudokéō.

A. *eudokéō* outside the NT. Developed from *eú dokeí tiní ti,* this popular Hellenistic word occurs in papyri and inscriptions as well as the LXX in various constructions.
a. Its usual sense is "to take pleasure or delight in," e.g., God in his people, or in the righteous, or in an offering, but also humans in the sanctuary, or the sabbath, or the truth. b. A further sense is "to decide for," "to select," "to prefer," and even "to adopt." c. From this evolves the sense "to want," "to will," "to be willing or ready." d. A more social meaning is "to agree," "consent," "acquiesce," "concede," "comply." e. Outside the Bible we often find "to be satisfied," "happy."

B. *eudokéō* in the NT.
1. With the dative of person we find the term in the declarations at the baptism and transfiguration of Jesus (Mt. 3:17; 17:5), where it indicates that the Son is the recipient of God's elective good pleasure (cf. Mt. 12:18; 2 Pet. 1:17). Of the various words for election, this one brings out most strongly the emotional side, i.e., God's love for the one whom he chooses. In view of the total presentation in Matthew and Luke, the aorist does not support an adoptionist understanding of the baptismal statement. In 1 Cor. 10:5 the negative ("God was not pleased") implies rejection (cf. Heb. 10:38 for a similar use).
2. *eudokeín ti* with object occurs only in the LXX quotation in Heb. 10:6, 8 with reference to God's taking no pleasure in offerings. The object with dative or *en* and dative appears twice in Paul: in 2 Th. 2:12 with reference to those who take pleasure in wickedness, and in 2 Cor. 12:10 with reference to Paul's acceptance of weaknesses, insults, etc. for Christ's sake.
3. With infinitive or accusative and infinitive, the word carries a clear hint of choice or resolve, i.e., what is preferred in 2 Cor. 5:8; decision in 1 Th. 3:1 and Rom. 15:26-27; readiness in 1 Th. 2:8; God's free and gracious counsel in Lk. 12:32. The divine decision in Gal. 1:15-16 confers independence on Paul, while God's resolve in 1 Cor. 1:21 stands in antithesis to the wisdom of the world. In Col. 1:19, where one should take God as the subject, God resolved that his whole fullness should dwell in Christ and that all things should be reconciled through him. The divine resolve accompanies the revelation in Gal. 1:15 and the preaching in 1 Cor. 1:21, but it has a plain supratemporal reference in Lk. 12:32 and Col. 1:19.

eudokía. This is not a classical word; it occurs for the first time in the Greek Bible.

A. *rāṣôn* in the OT.
1. This word, used some 56 times in the OT, mostly denotes God's good pleasure:
a. in sacrifices (Lev. 19:5 etc.), b. more generally as God's "favor" (Ps. 5:12 etc.), e.g., God's blessings (Dt. 32:33), and c. as the divine "will" (Ps. 40:8).
2. Less commonly the term expresses a human disposition, either a. bad, "caprice,"

"arrogance," or "partiality" (cf. Gen. 49:6; Dan. 8:4) or b. good, royal "favor" (Prov. 14:35) or mutual "delight" (Prov. 14:9), and cf. c. the setting of the will of the righteous on God (Ps. 145:19; 2 Chr. 15:15).

B. *rāṣôn* and *eudokía* in Jesus Sirach. The term reaches its full development in Sirach in 23 instances, some for *rāṣôn* and some with no Hebrew equivalent. 1. When *rāṣôn* is not rendered *eudokía*, it means a. God's "favor," b. God's "will," and c. human "caprice." 2. When *eudokía* is used for *rāṣôn* or without equivalent, the main sense is a. "God's good pleasure," but we also find b. "God's resolve," c. human "desire" or "will," and d. "satisfaction."

C. *eudokía* in the Septuagint and Hexapla. There is little that is new here. *eudokía* occurs only eight times in the LXX in the senses of divine "favor" and "good pleasure." One version has Eudokia for the name Tirzah in Cant. 6:3, i.e., Satisfaction. The other translations use the word more often but add nothing to its development.

D. Rabbinic Examples of *eudokía*. The rabbis use *rāṣôn* for God's favor and will, and also speak of favor before God. There are also expressions denoting human good pleasure in the sense of doing things willingly and not by constraint.

E. *eudokía* in the NT.
1. eudokía in Paul. In the NT there are only two references to human will. In Rom. 10:1 the will of the heart becomes petition to God. In Phil. 1:15 the idea is that of good will, directed toward Paul but by implication toward his mission as well. The other references in Paul are all to God's good pleasure or counsel. It is just possible that good human resolve is at issue in 2 Th. 1:11, but this is unlikely. In Eph. 1:5, 9, 11, where *thélēma*, *próthesis*, and *boulḗ* accompany *eudokía*, the term brings out the element of free good pleasure in the divine counsel.
2. eudokía in the Synoptists.
a. The prayer of Jesus in Mt. 11:26; Lk. 10:21 describes it as God's decree that the knowledge of the Son is hidden from the wise and revealed to babes.
b. In the Christmas saying in Lk. 2:14 we have two versions: "to men of good will" and "good will to men," but the former is better attested, and the latter may have arisen through a failure to understand the Hebrew form of the original. The meaning of the declaration is that God is glorified in heaven with the sending of Christ and the implication for earth is peace (i.e., salvation) for the people of good pleasure now that the turning point of the ages has come. These people of good pleasure are not, of course, those who have the good will to open themselves to God's grace or who do acts that will arouse a response of divine favor. *eudokía* can indeed have the meaning "consent," and the idea of divine favor in human offerings may be found in the OT, but the dominant use of *eudokía* shows plainly that the people of good pleasure are the recipients of God's grace by his free and unfathomably sovereign choice or counsel. Who are these people? We must obviously include Israel in view of 2:10, but 2:14 itself suggests a broader eschatological reference to all the elect who are redeemed in virtue of God's saving act in Christ. The word *eudokía* plays an important role in Gnosticism as a name for the Savior. It is common, too, in the fathers, usually with a reference to God, the Logos, or the Spirit, and with explanations that reflect Greek uncertainty as to its precise connotation.   [G. SCHRENK, II, 738-51]

euergesía, euergetéō, euergétēs → *érgon; eúkairos* → *kairós*

> *eulabés* [devout], *eulabeísthai* [to be afraid, reverence], *eulábeia* [fear, reverence]

A. The Non-Christian Usage. a. This group denotes an attitude of "caution" or "circumspection," e.g., regard for the *kairós,* vigilance, provision, concern, then conscientiousness, in religion scrupulosity or awe, more generally fear or anxiety. b. In the LXX the verb means "to be on guard," but mostly "to fear," especially fear of God. c. In Josephus and Philo the group is used for "nervousness," "caution," "fear," "prudence," "religious awe."

B. NT Usage. The group is rare in the NT. It characterizes Simeon in Lk. 2:25, the Jews of Acts 2:5, those who bury Stephen in Acts 8:2, and Ananias in Acts 22:12, always in the sense of "devout" or "pious." In Heb. 12:28 *eulábeia* probably means "anxiety" (cf. Phil. 2:12). In Heb. 5:7 it may mean "fear of God," in which case *apó* means "by reason of." Another possibility is that the reference is to liberation from "anxiety," but this hardly does justice to the sonship of v. 8. The group is perhaps used mostly for devout Jews because of the element of nervous caution, which is most appropriate where regard must be had for the law. Later it achieves a new prominence for religiosity in the Eastern Church and monasticism.　　　[R. BULTMANN, II, 751-54]

> *eulogéō* [to speak well of, bless], *eulogētós* [blessed], *eulogía* [blessing], *eneulogéō* [to bless]

eulogéō, eulogía.

A. *eulogéō* and *eulogía* in Greek Literature. The literal sense is "speaking well." This yields the meaning "to extol." We also find a use for "advocacy" in the papyri. The term may be used for the praise of humans by the gods, but more often for praise of the gods. The idea of blessing is extremely rare.

B. Blessing in the OT. Blessing is a most important concept in the OT and Judaism. Like cursing, it involves a transfer by acts and words. The Hebrew group *brk,* translated by *eulogéō* etc. in the LXX, denotes blessing, being blessed, and the individual blessings.
1. A father has a power to bless which he may transmit to his heirs (cf. Gen. 27:1ff.; 48:15; 49:25-26).
2. This blessing takes the form of prayer to God (Gen. 49:25). Since God is personal, the blessing is not magical, but relates to his free and gracious giving. Creation depends on divine blessing (Gen. 1:22). Man and woman are blessed from the outset (Gen. 1:28). God sustains his work by sending showers of blessing (Ezek. 34:26). He blesses the sabbath (Gen. 2:3) as well as crops and cattle (Dt. 28:1ff.). Specific blessings are related to salvation history (cf. Gen. 17:7-8; 26:3). The history of the chosen people stands under blessing or cursing (Dt. 11:26ff.; 30:1ff.). Blessing becomes cursing if the commandments are not kept. The righteous who trust in God and do his will find blessing, but sinners cursing (Jer. 17:5, 7; Ps. 24:4-5).
3. The reminder of God's blessings takes cultic forms (cf. the blessings given by Melchizedek in Gen. 14:19, by Moses in Dt. 33:1ff., by Joshua in Josh. 14:13, by Eli in 1 Sam. 2:20, by David in 2 Sam. 6:18, and by Solomon in 1 Kgs. 8:14). It gradually becomes the priest's prerogative to bless (cf. Lev. 9:22-23; Num. 6:22ff.; Dt. 10:8). The prayer of Ps. 3:8 echoes constantly in the temple liturgy.

4. An important use of the group is also for the blessing of God by believers in the sense of giving him praise and glory.

5. The Hebrew verb can be used for blessing in the general sense of greeting.

6. The term may also be used euphemistically where cursing is intended (cf. Job 1:11; 2:5, 9; 1:21).

7. The use of the *eulogeín* group for the *brk* group does not change the sense by ruling out magical ideas, for the OT itself removes blessing from the sphere of primitive mana, and the Greek terms simply set the seal on this development.

C. Blessing in Judaism at the Time of Jesus.

1. Philo uses *eulogéō* frequently either with the thought of reward or in connection with the contemplative life. Noting the presence of *lógos* in the word, he gives the praise of God a rational basis; it is most fitting that we should magnify God, unuttered thoughts rather than words being the true norm.

2. The rabbis work out specific rules for blessing. a. The Aaronic blessing has a firm place in the cultus. b. Only a priest may pronounce it in the synagogue. c. All forms of prayer that begin with praise of God are blessings. d. Ascriptions of praise etc. are common in other contexts (cf. the blessing of the law, temple, etc. on the Day of Atonement). Blessings must also precede all meals in recognition that all things come from God (Ps. 24:1). A concluding thanksgiving makes an *eulogía* of the whole meal. e. Table blessings play an important part in the Passover, e.g., the blessing of the bread, and the cup of blessing after the eating of the lamb.

D. *eulogéō* and *eulogía* in the NT.

1. The use of the group in the NT is heavily influenced by the OT. Thus Heb. 7:1 uses the story of the blessing of Abraham by Melchizedek to show the superiority of Christ's high priesthood, while Heb. 11:20-21 and 12:17 reflect the OT concept of parental blessing.

2. The NT also recognizes the duty of blessing God (cf. Lk. 1:64; 2:28).

3. Blessing within salvation history may be seen in the case of Mary (Lk. 1:28, 42) but especially the Messiah himself (cf. the greeting of Mk. 11:9-10; Jn. 12:13).

4. The Messiah adopts the religious practices of his day, so that we find him blessing the bread in Mk. 6:41; 8:7, though with an upward rather than the prescribed downward look, and with something distinctive that made him recognizable in Lk. 24:30. At the last supper Jesus blesses the bread and hands around the cup of blessing (Mk. 14:22; cf. "the cup of blessing which we bless" in 1 Cor. 10:16).

5. Jesus also blesses people, e.g., the children in Mk. 10:16, and the disciples in Lk. 24:50ff. He brings a fullness of blessing (Rom. 15:29). This is a spiritual blessing (Eph. 1:3) which fulfils what was promised to Abraham (Gal. 3:8-9) and means eternal joy for the blessed of the Father (Mt. 25:34).

6. Those who are thus blessed are no longer to repay evil with evil but to bless even those who curse them (Lk. 6:28; cf. Rom. 12:14).

7. Springing out of unconditional love, *eulogía* can be used by Paul for the gifts that he seeks as a collection for Jerusalem (2 Cor. 9:5-6).

8. In 1 Cor. 14:16 *eulogeín* denotes ecstatic praise. As distinct from the curse *anáthema Iēsoús,* confession of Jesus as Lord is true *eulogía* (1 Cor. 12:3).

9. The citation in Rom. 16:18 for the flattering words of seducers reflects Greek usage, but perhaps with a Palestinian suggestion of false promises.

10. Revelation shows that the eternal world of the last time includes the magnifying of him that sits on the throne and the Lamb (5:12-13; 7:12).

eulogētós.

1. In the OT believers may be the blessed of God (Gen. 12:2; Dt. 28:6), but more commonly God is the blessed one (Gen. 14:20, where Abram is also blessed by God, v. 19).

2. In Jewish writings outside the OT, liturgical formulas call God blessed.

3. Only God is the blessed one in the NT in such doxological formulas as occur in Lk. 1:68; Rom. 1:25; 2 Cor. 1:3; 11:31; Eph. 1:3; 1 Pet. 1:3. Christ is the Son of the Blessed in Mk. 14:61; this may echo Jewish concern to paraphrase God's name.

eneulogéō. This compound form occurs in Gen. 12:3; 18:18 to stress the fact that the blessing embraces all races and peoples. In the NT we find it in the quotation in Gal. 3:8 and the rather free rendering in Acts 3:25.　　　[H. W. BEYER, II, 754-65]

eunoéō, eúnoia → noús

---

eunoúchos [eunuch], *eunouchízō* [to make a eunuch]

---

1. Outside the NT *eunoúchos* is used not only for men but also for castrated animals and for fruits or plants with no seed or kernel.

2. Castration is alien to the Greeks but is found in the Near East. Eunuchs here are overseers of women and confidants of rulers, often in places of power. Eunuch priests play a role in many cults; perhaps the idea is that of assimilation and dedication to the deity.

3. The OT forbids the castration of men or animals as contrary to the Creator's will (cf. Dt. 17:16ff.; 23:2ff.). The desire for a healthy cultic order may play some part in the prohibition. Yet the prophets insist that God's boundless love covers eunuchs too (Is. 56:3ff.). The OT term *sārîs* denotes a military or political official as well as a eunuch (cf. 2 Kgs. 25:19). The LXX rendering *eunoúchos* may imply emasculation but does not have to do so. By the time of Jesus Hellenistic influences strengthen a more lenient attitude toward eunuchs in some circles, e.g., in Herod's court, where Josephus tells us the three chamberlains were eunuchs.

4. Rabbinic Judaism, however, insists on the duty of marrying and having children. In view of this Jeremias believes that Paul must have been a widower (though cf. 1 Cor. 7:7).

5. Jesus transcends the rabbinic view by differentiating three groups of eunuchs (Mt. 19:12): those who are so from birth, those who are castrated, and those who emasculate themselves for the kingdom's sake. In the latter case the sense is obviously figurative; the reference is to those who renounce sex in order to focus on the higher goal of the kingdom, as Jesus himself does. The gospel affirms the natural order but may require its denial for the sake of the new and higher order.

6. In Acts 8:27ff. Is. 56:3-4 comes to fulfilment as the eunuch of Queen Candace comes to faith and is baptized.

7. The early church mostly takes Mt. 19:12 figuratively (though cf. the young Origen) and excludes from the ministry any who are castrated except through no fault of their own (cf. canons 21ff. of the *Apostolic Constitutions*).

　　　[J. SCHNEIDER, II, 765-68]

euprósdektos → déchomai; euprosōpéō → prósōpon

heurískō [to find]

This word means "to find": a. "to find after search," b. "to find accidentally" (passive "to be struck by"), c. "to fetch or get" (of goods), d. "to procure," e. (figuratively) "to gain perception or insight, to discover," and f. "to show or prove oneself," "to be found as." All these nuances but c. occur in the NT, sometimes with reference to ordinary facts, but mostly with reference to things relating to God's work and kingdom, e.g., surprising events (Mt. 1:18; Lk. 9:36; Acts 5:10), or miracles (Mt. 17:27; Mk. 7:30; Jn. 21:6), or supernatural gifts (Mt. 7:7-8), or the gift of God's kingdom (Mt. 13:44), or encounter with Jesus (Mk. 1:37), or experience of God (Lk. 4:17; Rom. 10:20), or gifts of salvation such as pasture in Jn. 10:9, grace in Acts 7:46, mercy in Rom. 4:1, and redemption in Heb. 9:12, or God's call and salvation (Mt. 18:13; 24:46; Lk. 15:5-6), but also with a suggestion of responsibility (Lk. 13:6-7; 17:18) and of the seriousness of divine judgment (Mt. 24:46; 2 Pet. 3:14; Rev. 12:8; 16:20; 18:14; 20:15).   [H. PREISKER, II, 769-70]

eusébeia, eusebéō, eusebḗs → *sébomai*

eúsēmos [clear, distinct]

A compound of *sḗma, eúsēmos* means a. "favorable" (giving good signs) and b. "evident" (giving clear signs). It occurs in the NT only in 1 Cor. 14:8-9, where Paul demands clarity of proclamation in view of the serious import of the message in questions of eternal destiny.   [W. GRUNDMANN, II, 770]

eúsplanchnos → *splanchnízomai*

euschḗmōn [presentable, prominent]

1. "Honest," "orderly," "becoming." Paul uses the term in this sense when exhorting to Christian conduct that the non-Christian world will also find blameless. Thus in 1 Th. 4:12 his point is that outsiders can make judgments on this basis and should be given no occasion for offense. In Rom. 13:13 the underlying idea (in context) of "suitable attire" merges into that of "becoming conduct." The external aspect of Christian life is at issue, and therefore, from the Greek standpoint, the aesthetic element may sometimes be what counts, as in 1 Cor. 12:23-24.

2. "Noble," "honorable," "excellent," "prominent." Joseph of Arimathea is a "respected" man in Mk. 15:43 (rich in Mt. 27:57, good and righteous in Lk. 23:5). The women who are incited against Paul in Acts 13:50 are "prominent," as are those in Acts 17:12. They belong to a higher social stratum.   [H. GREEVEN, II, 770-72]

euphraínō [to be cheerful, glad], *euphrosýnē* [joy, gladness]

1. *euphraínō* means "to cheer," "to gladden," and (middle or passive) "to be glad," "to rejoice." *euphrosýnē* means "joy" with an emphasis on the mood. The objects of

joy may be physical happenings, festivals, or intellectual and spiritual things (as in Plato and the Stoics).

2. Alternation in translation shows that in the LXX the group has no specific sense as distinct from other terms for joy. It may denote cultic joy, joy at God's help, or eschatological joy in the last time as a time of celebration.

3. Judaism follows the same usage, and since obedience to the law has a cultic character even the fear of the Lord can be described as *euphrosýnē*. Philo distinguishes between true and false festive joy. True joy characterizes the sphere of God and comes from God as the supreme divine blessing.

4. The terms play no great role in the NT. Theologically they are overshadowed by *chará*. *euphraínesthai* is used for secular joy. This may be simply worldly merriness (Lk. 12:19; 16:19) or even wicked jubilation (Rev. 11:10), but it may also be social jollity (Lk. 15:29) or the joy of the father at the return of his lost son (Lk. 15:23-24). The term may thus denote a gladness that pagans experience as recipients of God's natural bounties (Acts 14:17). The joy of fellowship comes to expression in 2 Cor. 2:2 (the good side of the joy of Israel when sacrificing to the golden calf in Acts 7:41). Rev. 12:12 and 18:20 echo the OT demand for joy at God's eschatological judgments. But the nations may rejoice already at the message of God's saving act in Christ (Rom. 15:10). The Christian community brings fruitfulness to Jerusalem and is thus an occasion of rejoicing in fulfilment of Is. 54:1 (Gal. 4:27). The resurrection of Christ is also an occasion for the joy foreseen in Ps. 16 (Acts 2:25-26). In the early Christian writings we find cultic joy in Barn. 15.9, joy at the preaching of the word in Did. 12.9, and eschatological joy in Justin *Dialogue* 80.1 etc. (quoting the OT).

[R. BULTMANN, II, 772-75]

eucharistéō, eucharistía, eucháristos → *cháris*

---

eúchomai [to wish, pray], *euchḗ* [prayer, vow], *proseúchomai* [to pray], *proseuchḗ* [prayer, place of prayer]

---

eúchomai, euchḗ.

A. The Usage of *eúchomai, euchḗ.* In nonbiblical Greek these are the most comprehensive terms for invocation of the deity. The sense "to vow" is present as well as "to ask, pray." The LXX has the word, but here, and even more so in the NT, *proseúchomai* becomes the main term.

1. "To pray, ask, beseech," "prayer, petitionary prayer, invocation." Both noun and verb occur in this sense in Jms. 5:15-16, thus ruling out any magical operation and perhaps implying prayer for forgiveness as well as healing. In 2 Cor. 13:7, 9 Paul uses the term when praying God that the Corinthians may not do wrong and may show improvement. His courteous wish of Acts 26:29 also becomes a prayer when he adds the words "to God": only God can bring about the conversion of Agrippa and his hearers.

2. "To vow, dedicate," "vow." Only the noun occurs in this sense in the NT. We find it in Acts 18:18 and 21:23. The shaving of the head indicates that this is a Nazirite vow (cf. Num. 6:7, 9, 19).

3. The cultic connection weakens with time and *eúchomai* can thus take on the more general sense of "to wish" or "to ask." The salutation in 3 Jn. 2 reflects this. So does Paul's statement in Rom. 9:3, where he could wish (not pray) that he himself

might be cut off from Christ for his fellow Israelites. In Acts 27:29 again the ship's company wish rather than pray that day may come.

B. Prayer in the Greek World.

1. Greek prayer accords with Greek religion, which nonanimistically finds in the gods restricted forces of destiny, so that incantations are secondary in prayer, and sacrifice and prayer have a place in every sphere of life.

a. The Homeric prayers, though often stylistic devices, express this clearly. Homer's heroes are conscious of their dependence on the gods, ascribe to them human impulses and emotions, and come to them in need, e.g., before battle. The favors sought show that humans have some control of life, and even in areas where the gods rule they may be swayed by prayers and offerings that impose an obligation on them, or by promises of future offerings if the prayers are answered. Cultic and moral demands are made, however, in the approach to the gods, though the approach itself is one of intimacy rather than fear.

b. In tragedy we find a greater concern for moral and spiritual blessings, e.g., honesty and piety. Prayer for revenge becomes prayer for just retribution. The stress on moral as well as cultic requirements is stronger.

c. Lyric poetry and philosophy combine eudaemonistic and more purely ethical concerns, e.g., wealth but also protection against pride. Philosophy tries to reduce the eudaemonistic element but in so doing robs prayer of its vitality. Yet Plato reaches a new moral depth, and we begin to find prayer for the remission of moral guilt. In later philosophy prayer becomes more general petition for the good, sometimes as intercession for others. But a note of skepticism arises. A failure of Zeus to answer displays his impotence.

2. Hellenism combines Greek features with Near Eastern influences. The literature again reflects popular thinking and practice.

a. In the Stoic-Cynic diatribe we see that practical monotheism has replaced the earlier polytheism. If prayer is offered to many gods, these represent the one God. Since this God is impersonal, there is no real petition. The requests simply reflect the ideal that is to be sought, and since one can attain this oneself, there is no final need to pray. Prayer for health is repudiated; the gods do not give this, and therefore we should not pray for it. The Zeus of Cleanthes is little more than fate, and the *apátheia* of the wise makes it impossible for them to invoke the deity. Later we find some return to concrete petition in Marcus Aurelius, but in general he, too, extols prayer for inner development as alone appropriate for the true sage.

b. The mysteries rest on a basis of individual religious life, and in their prayers initiates experience with awe the nearness of the deity to whom they belong by their dedication, who controls their destiny, and from whom they expect salvation. Yet prayer is only penultimate; the vision of God is ultimate. Hence prayer is primarily adoration, then thanksgiving. Prayers for mundane things are rare, there is little concern about guilt, the great aim is to seek escape from natural frailty in ecstasy, and intercession for others focuses on their ignorance (cf. in contrast 2 Cor. 12:1ff.).

c. In Philo and the Wisdom of Solomon the Jewish elements predominate. For Philo only those who pray truly live. The high priest's task is to intercede for the people, humanity, and all creation. The people's strength lies in the presence of the God who answers prayer. Prayer must be with purity and penitence. The prayer for mercy is always heard. But in general God grants only what is good for us. Prayer should be more for moral than material blessings. In Wisdom, prayer gives the soul true freedom, all may pray without fear of rejection, and we have all received so many gifts that thanksgiving is always in order.

d. Inscriptions add little to our knowledge of Greek prayer. We find public petitions for prosperity, thanksgivings for healings, and formulas that seek to use divine power for the purposes of exorcism, medicine, and eroticism.   [H. GREEVEN, II, 775-84]

C. Prayer in the OT.

1. OT Usage. For "to pray" the OT uses the not very common word *'tr,* and sometimes *pll,* but several other words belong to the sphere of prayer.

a. Proper Verbs. For *'tr* an original sense "to sacrifice" has been proposed, but in the OT it always means "to pray (to God)" or "to ask (God)." *pll* also denotes either "to pray" or "to ask for."

b. Other Words. The idea of prayer may also be suggested by terms denoting "to wish," "to present oneself," "to induce God's favor," by various words for speaking or crying, and also by words for sighing, groaning, roaring, and weeping.

c. Prayers of praise and thanksgiving are very common and therefore terms for "to extol," "to magnify," and "to confess" belong to the area of prayer. So, too, do verbs denoting "to murmur," "to meditate," "to reflect," and the group signifying "to exult," "to rejoice," "to make merry."

d. Words for music and singing must also be mentioned, e.g., singing, leading, playing instruments, and making music.

e. *hsthwh,* the term for respectful greeting, describes the disposition as well as the attitude of prayer. Even when not followed by prayer, it often denotes the worship of God (Lev. 26:1; 2 Kgs. 5:18, etc.). Prayers of different kinds follow in Gen. 24:26; Ex. 34:8; 1 Sam. 1:28, etc. For its use at great festivals, cf. 1 Chr. 29:20; 2 Chr. 7:3; Neh. 8:6, etc. Kneeling is mentioned as a similar gesture (1 Kgs. 8:54), and we also find standing in prayer (1 Sam. 1:26; Jer. 18:20). The hands may be stretched out to God (Is. 1:15; Jer. 4:31) or lifted up (Ps. 28:2). (For a detailed survey of the Hebrew terms, cf. *TDNT,* II, 785-90).

2. The Main Features of OT Prayer.

a. Prayer and Faith in Yahweh. The OT demands the exclusive worship of Yahweh; hence all prayer is directed to the one God, the covenant God of Israel. Israel is conscious of the might, wisdom, goodness, and faithfulness of this God, but also of his holiness and righteousness. Individuals with their faith share in the faith of the people and therefore in God's relationship with the people. This governs their prayer life, gives it the necessary confidence, and embeds it in the people's history as the history of the ongoing action toward them of their gracious, faithful, and merciful God from whom they may expect future salvation. Faith in this God, however, is faith in the God who is also the world's Creator and Sustainer and disposes of all things in heaven and earth. Yet faith in God does not give overconfidence in prayer. Petitions are supported by confession, appeals to the past, and remembrance of God's mercy. God cannot be taken for granted. He is a living person in his love and wrath. Seeing and hearing all things, he is always the sovereign Lord. Answers, then, depend on his personal counsel and decision.

b. The Content of Prayer. What do Israelites pray for? Since all good things come from the Creator God of Israel, one may ask him and thank him for all things. Bodily affairs play a big role in OT prayers, e.g., in the Psalms. Body and soul being so closely related, bodily goods merge into spiritual. Prayers for the overthrow of enemies are common, whether the enemies are personal or national. These prayers are the outbursts of an oppressed or exiled people (cf. Ps. 137 or Ps. 149), and they express, not just a human desire for revenge, but a concern for divine justice, i.e., the triumph of the good represented by Israel, and the defeat of wickedness represented by her foes. Alongside these requests, we find, of course, passionate cries for such spiritual blessings as forgiveness and the bliss of fellowship with God.

c. Prayer and the Cultus. Prayers are closely related to sanctuaries, sacrifices, feasts, and solemn days (cf. Gen. 12:8; 1 Sam. 1; Dan. 12:11; Is. 56:7). The temple forms a special focus; hands are stretched out to it or to the holy city (Ps. 5:7; Dan. 6:11). Yet prayer is tied neither to the sanctuary nor to the land. It may be offered in foreign countries (Gen. 21:32; 1 Kgs. 17:20) and in one's own home (Gen. 25:21). Daniel prays three times a day (6:11; cf. Ps. 55:17), and we find morning and evening prayers in Pss. 4 and 5. While prayer may accompany sacrifice, it can be rated above it (Pss. 50:23; 69:30-31; 40:6ff.), and songs may be described as spiritual sacrifices (Ps. 107:22). Yet there is no absolute antithesis. Abraham sets up altars when he calls on God (Gen. 12:8 etc.), forms of prayer are given for the offering of firstfruits (Dt. 26:13ff.), the Psalms often refer to sacrifices in connection with prayers (Ps. 22:25-26), and we find prayers along with sacrifices in Neh. 12 etc. Fasting may also accompany prayer (Jer. 14:12; Neh. 1:4; Ezr. 8:23). Vows of praise as well as sacrifice are made, and Hannah makes a vow of dedication (1 Sam. 1:11).

d. Prayer and Magic. In a few passages words or acts might suggest magical concepts, e.g., Moses stretching out his rod in Ex. 17:9, or Joshua addressing the sun and moon in Josh. 10:12-13, or Elijah stretching himself on the child in 1 Kgs. 17:21, but in all cases prayer to God divests the words or acts of any magical character. Faith in Yahweh crowds out magic, replacing it by true prayer (cf. 1 Kgs. 18:41ff. and Jms. 5:18).

3. Review of Prayer in the OT.

a. Prayer in the History Books. Specific references to prayer are comparatively few, but it is often implied (Gen. 30:6, 17, 27), and we have some beautiful examples (Gen. 24; 32:10ff.). Moses is depicted as a great intercessor (Ex. 32:11ff. etc.). The short prayers of Samson are forceful and fervent (Judg. 15:18), and Hannah's prayer is a fine instance of quiet outpouring even if couched in more general terms. The David stories contain a magnificent prayer by David in 2 Sam. 7:18ff., and music and song accompany the bringing up of the ark in 2 Sam. 6. From Solomon we have the royal prayer at Gibeon (1 Kgs. 3:6ff.) and the great prayer of dedication (8:23ff.). In the Elijah stories the powerful prayer of 1 Kgs. 18:36-37 stands in contrast to the empty crying of the priests of Baal. In 1 and 2 Chronicles we have many instances of both liturgical prayer (e.g., 1 Chr. 16) and individual prayer (cf. the prayers of Asa and Manasseh). Nehemiah is also a man of prayer (1:4 etc.), and Ezra makes a great impression with his prayer of penitence concerning mixed marriages (Ezr. 9:6ff. and 10:1ff.).

b. The Wisdom Literature. All three friends tell Job to pray (5:8 etc.), and Job himself is faithful, if sometimes critical, in prayer (12:4 etc.; 9:16 etc.; 42:2ff.). Proverbs commends the prayer of confession in 28:13, assures the righteous of God's answer in 15:29, and puts prayer above the sacrifice of the wicked in 15:8. Eccl. 5:2 warns against wordiness in prayer.

c. Prayer in the Prophets. We find here less material than might be expected. The prayers of sinners weary God (Is. 1:15; cf. Am. 5:23-24). He will not hear them (Mic. 3:4). Amos himself prays for the forgiveness of the people and is heard (Am. 7:1ff.), and Hosea issues a call for penitent prayer (14:2ff.). Jeremiah, too, prays for the people

(10:23ff.) but is forbidden by God to do so (7:16). He also prays for God's righteous judgments (17:12ff.). True seeking of God, he claims, will lead to finding (29:13-14; cf. Is. 55:6; 58:9; 65:24). Joel calls for a day of penitential prayer (1:14ff.; 2:17), while Jonah offers a prayer of thanksgiving for his deliverance (2:3ff.), summons Nineveh to prayer (3:8), and utters a discouraged prayer for death (4:2-3).

d. The Psalter. This is the great treasury of OT prayer, combining beauty of expression with wealth of content. The prayers are more commonly those of individuals than of the community, but they stand against a cultic background and their highly developed personal piety is embedded in the collective awareness of belonging to God's people. Few of the psalms offer clear evidence of their original cultic use, but all of them show that even when piety is no longer closely tied to cultic observance, it still has its source in public worship. Dominant themes are complaint and grief and the earnest seeking of help from God, but hope and assurance arise out of complaint, and the note of praise and thanksgiving is almost always sounded. The forms and imagery, of course, are in many cases stylized, as may be seen from comparison with Babylonian and Egyptian psalms, but these prayers have a supreme religious force that can derive only from the psalmists' God and that makes the Psalter a universal Christian possession which new converts easily appropriate and from which they learn not only to pray but also to set themselves in the saving history which through the Psalms reaches out into all the world.   [J. HERRMANN, II, 785-800]

D. Prayer in the Synagogue. Destroying the temple, the Babylonians helped to force prayer into the center of Jewish piety. Only regular prayer could replace regular worship. This might make prayer superficial, but formulas etc. are regarded less highly by the Jews than other peoples, and a vigorous life pulses through all the forms. Praying two or three times a day is attested (cf. Acts 3:1). Rehearsal of the Shema is a prayer as well as a confession. The chief prayer, which develops early, consists of eighteen benedictions, beginning with three thanksgivings, moving on to petitions for knowledge, penitence, restoration, etc., and closing with a thanksgiving for God's loving rule and prayers for peace. The we-form gives evidence of a continuing sense of community. Prayers are to be offered two or three times a day, and shorter times develop (and may also be earlier). Prayers at table also pre-date the Christian era, but we cannot be too sure about the dating of other fixed forms. There is plenty of scope, of course, for independent prayer, though it is debated whether individual petitions should be put in the eighteen benedictions. Casuistry develops at times regarding individual points, but the prayers of Jesus stand firmly in the context of Judaism, and if he censures the prayer of the time it is only when he finds impure motives (Mt. 6:5), or sees prayer to be a pious mask (Mk. 12:40), or detects in it an impenitent heart (Lk. 18:10ff.). Hardly a clause in the Lord's Prayer either does not or could not stand in Jewish prayers, and the effective prayer life of Jesus, as the first disciples record it, clearly has its human roots in the rich prayer life of his people.

E. Prayer in the NT.

1. Review, Presuppositions, and Content. In prayer believers draw on the powers of the new aeon as Jesus did in the garden and on the cross. That Jesus was a man of prayer may be seen from his withdrawals for prayer, his blessings at meals, and his prayers at exorcisms and healings. He finds assurance in prayer, prays for his disciples, and gains help in prayer during the passion. In John his prayer at the raising of Lazarus (11:41-42) convinces those around him of his divine mission. His praying is so much an attitude that individual acts are secondary. In view of his unique relation to the

Father, his prayers are not put on the same level as those of the disciples. Distinctive of Christian prayer is the certainty of being heard in virtue of God's love, so that all things may be brought to him (Mk. 11:24). Indeed, the answers exceed the asking (cf. 2 Cor. 12:7ff.). Confidence in prayer lies behind the addressing of God as Father (and even Abba). Prayer for the kingdom is fundamental, but future salvation is so close to present life that one may at the same time pray for daily bread, remission of sins, and deliverance from temptation. Constant prayer is needed because the filial relation to God needs constant renewal. Jesus in giving the Lord's Prayer does not mean to restrict freedom and yet the text has a certain normativeness, since Jesus is not hostile to formal prayer and the disciples require and request guidance in prayer (Lk. 11:1ff.). In prayer Christians are to avoid selfishness (Jms. 4:2ff.), to remember that this aeon is coming to an end (1 Pet. 4:7), and to honor each other (1 Pet. 3:7). External things can have a place in prayer (Mk. 13:18; Rom. 1:10). Intercession is important, e.g., for the sick and imprisoned (Jms. 5:14ff.; Acts 12:5). Prayer is to be offered for the brethren and even for enemies (cf. Jesus on the cross). Thanksgiving is also an integral part of prayer (cf. the graces at meals, the greetings in epistles, and Paul's cry in Rom. 7:25). The Spirit is at work in prayer, attesting to us that we are God's children, and interceding for us in our frailty (Rom. 8:15, 26). Prayer may be offered kneeling (Acts 21:5) or standing (Mk. 11:25). Common as well as private prayer is in order (1 Cor. 14:13ff.; Mt. 18:19 with its special promise for the two or three). Prayer may be offered to Jesus as well as the Father in view of his identification as *kýrios,* whether in invocation of Jesus when praying to the Father or in direct prayer to Jesus. Except in Rev. 5:8, 14, however, *proseúchesthai* and *proskyneín* are not used with reference to such prayer.

2. *The Words Used. aitéō* ("to want something") is not used for Jesus' own prayers but occurs when Jesus summons his disciples to pray. *erōtáō* is used in John with an emphasis on intimate fellowship with God; only in 1 Jn. 5:16 does it refer to believers' prayers. *parakaléō* also posits closeness to the one addressed, e.g., in Mk. 5:10; 2 Cor. 12:8; Mt. 26:53. As in Jewish usage, *eulogéō* occurs in grace at meals. *eucharistéō* is the term for thanksgiving. *krázein* in Rom. 8:15 expresses fervency in prayer. *epika-léomai,* often used with *ónoma,* stresses the element of confession (invoking the name) (Acts 9:14; 22:16). But since prayer commonly means petition, the words used most frequently are *déomai* and *déēsis.* The former, which may also have a secular sense, almost always denotes petition (Acts 10:2 is the exception); *déēsis* is more general (cf. Lk. 5:33; Phil. 4:6). A more exclusively religious word group now demands separate treatment.

proseúchomai, proseuchḗ. The construction may be with accusative of object, with *hína,* or with *hypér* and *perí.* The genitive with *proseuchḗ* usually refers to the one praying, but in Lk. 6:12 to the one addressed. James uses the strong *proseuchḗ proseúchesthai* in 5:17.

1. "To pray," "to pray to," "to ask," "prayer," "petitionary prayer." While *deísthai* almost always denotes asking, *proseúchesthai* contains no narrower definition of content and refers to calling on God. The nouns are harder to distinguish. Both may denote prayer as a habit or a single act (Lk. 22:45; Phil. 1:4; cf. the plural in Rom. 1:10; Lk. 5:33). The difference seems to be in content; *déēsis* is more specific (cf. Lk. 1:13 and Acts 10:31). Yet this should not be pressed in view of the *deéseis* and *proseuchás* of 1 Tim. 2:1.

2. *proseuchḗ* can also denote a "place of prayer," as in Acts 16:13ff., which prob-

ably refers to a synagogue (synagogues were often built near water). This use is rare in secular Greek but has been found on an inscription. It occurs in Philo but not in the canonical books of the LXX.   [H. GREEVEN, II, 800-808]

→ *aitéō, déomai, epikaléō, erōtáō, eulogéō, eucharistéō, proskynéō*

---

euōdía [fragrance]

In secular Greek *euōdía* has the literal sense of "sweet smell," "scent," e.g., of plants, fruits, wine, ointment, atmosphere, incense, breath. The LXX uses it for the sweet savor of the burnt offering. Philo compares the good influence of the wise to the invisible outflowing of a sweet scent.

1. In the NT Eph. 5:2 and Phil. 4:18 employ the figure of the sweet savor of sacrifice—Christ's offering in the former, the gift of the congregation in the latter—which also contains the thought of acceptability to God.

2. The meaning is not so clear in 2 Cor. 2:14-15. The idea of the sweet savor of a triumphal procession makes the expression purely metaphorical and does not explain the thought of the scent being to salvation or perdition. Nor can we simply see here the thought that Paul himself is a living sacrifice to God in view of the reference to the fragrance of knowledge. Judaism uses the image of "savor" for the power of the preached word, and since the *euōdía* is that of Christ, and "to God" rules out the view that *euōdía* might be a term for God's manifestation, the best explanation is that the aroma is a palpable mark of God's invasion of the world, in grace and judgment, through the sacrificial self-offering of Christ as this is proclaimed by the apostles.

[A. STUMPFF, II, 808-10]

ephápax → *hápax*

---

echthrós [hostile],   **échthra** [hostility]

While *mísos* denotes the disposition of hostility and *pólemos* war, *echthrós* means "hostility" itself. Hebrew usage is similar.

echthrós.

A. *echthrós* outside the NT. In classical Greek we find a varied use for personal or impersonal enmity, first only in the passive, then the active. The main LXX use is for Heb. *'ōyēḇ,* which itself is almost always rendered *echthrós.* Yet while the Hebrew denotes both personal and national enemies, *echthrós* has a more personal reference a. to enemies in war or daily life, b. to enemy nations, the opponents of Israel or its king, c. to the enemies of the righteous, and d. to God's enemies. Basic to the usage is that Gentiles do not alternate between hostility and friendship but are in constant opposition to both Israel and God (Ex. 23:22), so that defeat of Israel dishonors God (Josh. 7:8), and David's adultery causes the Lord's enemies to blaspheme (2 Sam. 12:14). The opposition becomes more purely religious in Is. 1:24 when foes within Israel are at issue. Liberation from enemies is Israel's hope (Is. 62:8), but ongoing hostility between the righteous and the wicked is a common theme (Ps. 6:10 etc.). For the rabbis opponents include idolaters, apostate proselytes, renegades, and wicked Israelites. Unjustifiable hatred is forbidden but there is a legitimate hatred of foes in the OT sense as those who disrupt the covenant relationship. Josephus speaks of hatred of God in more general Greek terms, while the pseudepigrapha often call the devil *echthrós* and the rabbis construe the enemy of Prov. 25:21-22 as the evil impulse.

B. *echthrós* in the NT. The term is used in the NT for personal enemies (Gal. 4:16), but as in the OT and LXX it is used for the foes of Israel (Lk. 1:71), of Jerusalem (Lk. 19:43), of the NT witnesses (Rev. 11:5), and of believers within their own families (Mt. 10:36). *echthrós* refers, too, to hostility to God and Christ (Lk. 19:27; Phil. 3:18; Acts 13:10, and cf. the quoting of Ps. 110:1 in Mk. 12:36; Acts 2:34-35; 1 Cor. 15:25; Heb. 1:13; Paul in 1 Cor. 15:25 refers to all the forces that are hostile to God, including death). The reference of Mt. 5:43-44 is to love for the enemies of God and his people (in contradistinction to the older hatred), and the same view may be reflected in 2 Th. 3:15. By nature we are all God's enemies (Rom. 5:10; 11:28; Col. 1:21; Jms. 4:4). The point is that we hate God (active), although in Rom. 11:28 Jews are both hated (passive) because of the gospel and loved on account of the fathers. The *echthrós* is the devil in the parable of Mt. 13:24ff. and Lk. 10:19; the devil is the absolute enemy both of us and of God and his kingdom.

échthra. "Hatred," "hostility" is a disposition, objective opposition, and actual conflict. In the LXX canon the word mostly denotes individual hostility, in the apocrypha national enmity. In the NT hatred is one of the works of the flesh in Gal. 5:20 (cf. Herod and Pilate in Lk. 23:12). Christ, however, has broken down the wall of human hostility (Eph. 2:14). The carnal mind means enmity against God (Rom. 8:7; cf. Jms. 4:4). [W. FOERSTER, II, 811-14]
→ *miséō*

échidna [viper]

An *échidna* is a "poisonous serpent" (adder or viper). The only NT instances are in Acts 28:3 and Mt. 3:7; 12:34; 23:33. Paul shakes off the viper unharmed in Acts 28:3. Poison is essential to the comparisons in Matthew, and since the viper is by nature destructive it has to be asked who gave warning of coming wrath, or how good can be spoken, or hell escaped. We should not press the idea of the serpent in paradise or the cunning, self-concealment, or deceptive smoothness of the snake, though there may be some suggestion of its repulsiveness. [W. FOERSTER, II, 815-16]

échō [to have, hold], *antéchomai* [to hold fast], *apéchō* [to keep away], *enéchō* [to hold fast], *énochos* [held fast], *katéchō* [to hold fast], *metéchō* [to share], *metochḗ* [sharing], *métochos* [sharing in], *nounechṓs* [wisely], *symmétochos* [sharing with]

échō (nounechṓs).

A. *échein* in Secular Usage. This term means "to have" in various senses, "to have in, on, around, over, or with," "to own," "to enjoy," "to possess." In Greek philosophy it is used with abstract terms, e.g., with qualities or with fellowship, which may be with gods or demons as well as other people (for Christians with Christ or God).

B. *échein* in the LXX. Hebrew has no single term for "to have," so that *échein* is comparatively rare in the LXX (some 500 times), mostly with no originals. The use of *échein* covers all the meanings in classical and Hellenistic Greek, including the having of power, spirit, hope, etc., as well as virtues and fellowship with others or with God. When there is no object, the meaning is "to have property."

C. *échein* in the NT.

1. The word is common in the NT but its distribution is uneven. It does not occur in Lk. 1–2 or the Sermon on the Mount, is used with above-average frequency in Mark, is less common in the epistles, and is most common in 1 John and Revelation. Almost every meaning found elsewhere is found in the NT.

2. *Spiritual Possession.* In the Greek world having *noús* or *lógos* ("thought or understanding") differentiates humans from animals, which also have *psyché* ("life"). Later we are said to have a part in *noús* or *lógos* as a world spirit is thought to pervade the cosmos. In other circles we share in the world spirit (*lógos*) and have an individual spirit (*noús*). Another view is that participation means mystical possession. Rev. 8:9 attributes having *psyché* to sea creatures, and Rev. 13:18 uses the noun *échein* for having understanding (cf. 17:9; Mk. 12:34). In general, then, the NT views the human creature as a trichotomy, but while all have *noús,* only believers have *pneúma.* Yet *pneúma échein* is rare; the point is that we share in the one divine Spirit (cf. *métochos* in Hebrews). The *échein pneúma Christoú* of Rom. 8:9 has a strong ethical note, while in 8:11 the Spirit is a pledge of final redemption (cf. 8:23; 2 Cor. 1:23). Ethical and eschatological concerns are also present in 1 Cor. 6:19 and 2 Cor. 4:13. The point of the slightly ironical 1 Cor. 7:40 is that having the Spirit means knowing God's will. If Paul cannot quote Christ himself here, his view carries weight because he is a bearer of the Spirit. In Jude 19 *pneúma échein* echoes the Gnostic distinction between psychics and pneumatics, possibly turning the Gnostics' own slogan against them. One might have expected *pneúma* rather than *noús* in 1 Cor. 2:16 (the "mind" of Christ). Where *lógon échein* occurs in the NT, the basic sense of *lógos* is word rather than reason. In Acts 19:38 the thought is that of alleging something, in Col. 2:23 standing at the call of something, and in 2 Pet. 1:19 holding fast the prophetic word. In Jn. 5:38 having God's word means believing and receiving him who is the Logos, the personal revelation of God.

3. *Demonic Possession.* Greek religion and thought also postulate a daemon active within humans. If this daemon is good, we possess it; if bad, it possesses us. Magical papyri suggest means to secure good daemons, ultimately by having their names. In the NT Christ has the seven spirits of God (Rev. 3:1, in the sense of having authority over them; they are "sent out" in 5:6). Mostly, however, having demons means demon possession, i.e., not having authority over them, but bearing them in oneself. Sometimes these are spirits of sickness, e.g., in Mk. 3:22; 5:15; Lk. 4:33; 13:11; Acts 8:7. Jesus is accused of having Beelzebul (the chief demon) in Mk. 3:22. 1 Cor. 2:12 speaks of not receiving the spirit of the world but God's Spirit. *daimónion échein* in Jn. 7:20; 8:48-49 has the weaker sense "to be out of one's mind."

4. *To Have God.* This phrase is rare in the NT but is distinctively Christian. The Greek world speaks of fellowship with God as a having, and also says that we are God's possession. Classical texts also contain such phrases as "to have the deity gracious" (cf. the Jewish "to have God as a covenant partner"). The OT refers to Israel as God's possession (Jer. 10:16) and to God as the portion of the Levites (Dt. 10:9). The Psalms are full of similar phrases for the righteous. Jewish writings in

Greek develop this into "to have God" (cf. Esth. 4:17). In the NT the Jews say that they have only one Father (God) (Jn. 8:41), though the stress here is on Father. The point in Rom. 1:28 is that the wicked see no value in really knowing God (having him in their knowledge). Col. 4:1 speaks of having a master in heaven, but acknowledgment is again the issue. Only in 1 Jn. 2:23 and 2 Jn. 9 does *échein* express a distinct relation to God. This relation depends on having Christ (1 Jn. 5:12) and includes reaching God in prayer, enjoying the blessings of forgiveness and grace, and sharing eternal fellowship with him. It comes through having Christ as advocate (1 Jn. 2:1) and high priest (Heb. 4:14-15). The phrase "having God or Christ" is a common one in the apostolic fathers (1 Clem. 46.6; 2 Clem. 16.1; Ignatius *Magnesians* 12.1), and Ignatius speaks of attaining to God by martyrdom. In Clement of Alexandria and Origen the phrase takes on a mystical sense, and it later becomes integral to Christian mysticism.

5. *Having Hope.* The eschatological orientation of NT Christianity comes out in the phrase "to have hope." Pagans are without hope, but Christians have a solid hope that is grounded in Christ's work and gives a good conscience, boldness, and comfort (cf. Acts 24:15; 1 Th. 4:13; Heb. 10:2; Acts 24:16; Eph. 3:12; Heb. 6:18), for through Christ's advocacy they have redemption and access to God (Col. 1:14; Eph. 2:18). Present possession is a foretaste of eternal salvation (Rom. 8:23; Eph. 1:13). It takes the form of having a reward (Mt. 5:46; Heb. 10:35) or heavenly treasure (Mt. 19:21) or inheritance (Eph. 5:5). All this is summed up in having eternal life (Mt. 19:16; Jn. 3:15; 5:24; 6:40; 10:10; 1 Jn. 3:15; Rom. 6:22). This is the overcoming of death by resurrection (only God has immortality, 1 Tim. 6:16), but it has already dawned (Jn. 5:24; 6:53) as we receive it through the eternal Son (Jn. 5:26; cf. 1 Tim. 4:8). The new dwelling is already prepared (2 Cor. 5:1), so that we may have absolute certainty of hope backed by the Spirit as guarantee (v. 5).

6. *Johannine Having.* In John we have eternal life even here and now. This concept expresses the richness of the Christian life as not just life in hope but as present possession. It is having God's love (Jn. 5:42), peace (16:33), grace (17:13), light (8:12), life (3:15 etc.), indeed, God himself and fellowship with him (1 Jn. 2:23). We have all these in Christ or as we have Christ (Jn. 5:38).

7. *Christianity as Having.* In the NT as a whole Christianity is a religion of having and not just seeking. The Jews have the law (Jn. 19:7), knowledge of the truth (Rom. 2:20), and zeal for God (Rom. 10:2), but Christians have Christ, the Spirit, the gifts of righteousness, redemption, peace, and the fellowship with God that means true knowledge. Materially poor, they are thus immeasurably rich (Acts 3:6; 2 Cor. 6:10; Jms. 2:5; 1 Tim. 6:17) in a transvaluation of all values. Yet Christian having is not a merit but a gift that is constantly sought from God and renewed by him. The idea of merit (having something to show) occurs in Rev. 2:6, 25; 3:11, but the thought is different in the proverb in Mt. 13:12 etc., where those who have heard will be granted fuller understanding so long as they also give out what they get (cf. Mk. 4:21ff. and the parable of the talents, Mt. 25:29).

antéchō (-omai). In the active this means "to hold against" and in the middle "to do this in one's own interest," then "to cleave to," "to concern oneself with," "to hold fast." The NT uses only the middle but the concern is for the interests of others (1 Th. 5:14; cf. servant and master in Mt. 6:24). In Tit. 1:9, with a material object, it means "to hold fast."

apéchō. In classical Greek this means a. "to hold off," b. "to have received (what is owed)," and c. "to be distant" (middle "to keep away"). The LXX has b. twice and

c. frequently. The NT has b. five times and c. six (also the middle six times). "To receive back" in Phlm. 15 is a special use of b. (cf. Phil. 4:18). The idea of full receiving is important in Mt. 6:2, 5, 16; Lk. 6:24: the disciples await full possession. There are no parallels for the use in Mk. 14:41 (usually rendered with the Vulgate: "It is enough"—but what is enough?). Perhaps the meaning is: "It is out of place."

enéchō, énochos. The classical meaning of *enéchō* is "to hold fast to something," and of *énochos* "held fast," "liable," "subject to" (with dative of a law, offense, or penalty), middle "to strive after," "be entangled," LXX "to pursue." In the NT we find "to press" in Lk. 11:53, and "to entangle oneself," "subject oneself" in Gal. 5:1. *énochos* means "subject" in Heb. 2:15, "guilty" in Mk. 3:29, with genitive of the law or principle in 1 Cor. 11:27; Jms. 2:10 and the penalty in Mt. 26:66, and dative of the local court in Mt. 5:21-22, the progression being from a local court to the supreme court and then to hell (v. 22).

katéchō. This more emphatic form means 1. "to hold fast or back," 2. "to occupy spatially," 3. "to occupy legally," "to possess." A nautical sense is "to steer toward" or "land at." Religiously the term denotes inspiration or rapture with a stress on human passivity. But the group can also be used for imprisonment in service of the deity. The main sense in the LXX is 1. It may be used for states that possess us, and once for spirit possession. Sense 1. also predominates in the NT: a. for one person holding another (Lk. 4:42; Phlm. 13); b. for holding fast values, instruction, or attitudes (Lk. 8:15; 1 Cor. 11:2; 15:2; 1 Th. 5:21; Heb. 3:6, 14): Christians already have spiritual blessings but have to hold them fast to the end; c. for holding illegally (Rom. 1:18; 7:6); d. for restraining (2 Th. 2:6-7, where the restraining force, though first neuter and then masculine, is the same but cannot be identified for certain). Sense 2. occurs only in Lk. 14:9 (occupying the lowest place). Sense 3. may be found in 1 Cor. 7:30 (free for God as though there were no goods), 2 Cor. 6:10 (in poverty possessing all things), and Jn. 5:4 (passive, possessed by illness).

metéchō, metochḗ, métochos, symmétochos. The point of this group is sharing or participation. In Greek thought, it is used for sharing in the "idea," the universal spirit, the higher world, or the deity (as seen in spiritual life, inspiration, and fellowship with God, sometimes extended to the whole cosmos, sometimes after death). The group is rare in the LXX. *métochos* here often means "companion"; in Prov. 29:10 it means "participant in (guilty of)" the blood of another. Sharing is still the dominant sense in the NT: sharing the fruits in 1 Cor. 9:10, the bread in 10:17, the table in 10:21, our flesh in Heb. 2:14, a right in 1 Cor. 9:12. The NT never speaks of sharing God or Christ, but hints at participation in Christ in Jn. 13:8 ("you have no part in me," *ouk écheis méros met' emoú*), where one must accept service from Christ to have fellowship with him. In Jn. 14:30 *en emoí ouk échei oudén* might mean that the ruler of this world has no part in Christ, but the more likely sense is that he has no power over him. *metochḗ* in 2 Cor. 6:14 means fellowship rather than participation; partnership brings out the idea. *métochos* in Lk. 5:7 has the LXX sense of colleague. Elsewhere only Hebrews uses it. 1:9 quotes Ps. 45:6-7, where the reference is to Christ's fellows. Christians are his fellows (*métochoi*) in 3:14 as they share his heavenly call (3:1) and partake of his Spirit (6:4), whereby partnership in the world to come (which belongs strictly to the angels, 1:9), is brought into this period between the aeons.

H. HANSE, II, 816-32]

→ *anéchō, anektós, anochḗ, schḗma, héxis*

ζ z

---

záō [to live], *zōḗ* [life], *(bióō* [to live], *bíos* [life]), *anazáō* [to come to life again], *zṓon* [living creature], *zōogonéō* [to give life], *zōopoiéō* [to make alive]

---

záō, zōḗ (bióō, bíos).

A. *zōḗ* in Greek Usage.

1. *Classical Usage.*

a. *zōḗ (zḗn)* denotes the physical vitality of organic beings. Life is not a thing but the vitality that characterizes all living things. The whole cosmos can be called a *zṓon*. Life involves self-movement with its source in the *psychḗ*, though only *sṓmata* are living and *zōḗ* is thus a natural phenomenon like its antithesis, death. The gods have immortal *zōḗ*. Where the cosmos and deity are equated, the vitality of the whole takes shape in specific organic phenomena. For Aristotle the deity stands outside the cosmos as *noús*, but even so its *enérgeia* is still *zōḗ*.

b. If the *zōḗ* of deity is related to the *noús*, this means that *zōḗ* transcends as well as includes natural vitality. The supreme human possibility is also *noús*, and this can be achieved only in distinction from the body, though not apart from it. Thus true human *zōḗ* is not the *zōḗ* in virtue of which one becomes a *zṓon* by the unity of body and soul. *Psychḗ* is the principle of vitality in matter but it is also the principle of selfhood in humans as opposed to matter. Similarly *zōḗ* is life as a natural phenomenon but also the specifically human life whose possibilities are not fulfilled in organic nature and which has a meaning beyond perpetuation of the species. Human life has its own destiny, knows happiness or unhappiness, is aware of its own possibilities, and is thus faced with the question of what is appropriate to it.

c. In humans *zōḗ* is thus accompanied by *bíos*, i.e., manner of life or character (closely related to *éthos*). Relative to animals, *bíos* denotes species, but relative to humans it denotes individual forms of the species. It can thus be used for the writing of a life (biography) and also denotes life's duration or the means of supporting it. *bíos* is lived in the *pólis* and in this respect stands under law (*nómos*). While *bíos* is individual, it is not strictly unique; the various *bíoi* may be classified as types, so that a leading question is that of the normal *bíos*. Both as *bíos* and as natural vitality, *zōḗ* belongs to this world; it is not eschatological except as intermittent achievement of the blessed life of godhead.

2. *Hellenistic Usage.*

a. Stoicism. For Stoicism *zōḗ* is the physical life of organic creatures. The whole cosmos is an organism; in humans the general vital force takes individual form. Yet the fulfilment of human life depends on intelligent resolve. The *ánthrōpos*, being more than *zṓon*, is asked whether his life is true life or not. Those who do not achieve true humanity are "dead." Natural life has value for us only as the presupposition for the attainment of virtue. The life of rational *zóa* may be called *bíos,* and the question of true *bíos* is thus a live one, but the *pólis* is now less important and the *bíos* of the sage is the norm.

b. Neo-Platonism. With Near Eastern dualism, the anthropological dualism of Plato has an impact here. *zōḗ* belongs to cosmic *psychḗ*, yet the human *psychḗ* has come from above, is a stranger in the body, seeks its true home, and survives death. Thus, while *zōḗ* derives from *noús* as *psychḗ* does, it is a lower rung on the ladder of totality. True life has to be attained by turning from the body in the contemplation in which we are *zōḗ* and do not just have it. This true *zōḗ* belongs to the other world. It is not achieved in historical life, yet it is an actual determination to the degree that life is a constant striving for the good.

c. Gnosticism. In Gnosticism *zōḗ* without attributes characterizes the divine life. The connection with natural life is severed. Life is not the vitality of cosmic being but a basic force of unending duration. It flows down from the divine world and is present in us by means of *pneúma*, the divine breath. Behind this concept stands the primitive idea of life as a divine fluid that flows into earthly beings from the godhead. In Gnosticism, however, this otherworldly power cannot be received in the earthly world. God is life, living denotes relationship to God, and the divine power of life flows into believers. With light, life belonged to primal humanity, but after the fall into matter it is hampered by the body; only as revelation brings liberation from the body can there be a return to light and life. Life as divine vitality comes as a new birth when there is union with God. It can be experienced in ecstatic vision and in this sense is a physical state, but it is still awaited as the blissful vision of God. If it has to have the character of individuality, liberation from the mortal body severs it from the possibilities of historical human life. As my *zōḗ*, it can be regarded only as a psychological state, and negatively it can be achieved only by negation. The Odes of Solomon, relating light and life to revelation in the word, sound a more positive note whereby life comes to concrete fulfilment as knowledge of God, joy, and love.

[R. BULTMANN, II, 832-43]

B. Life and Death in the OT. In the OT the ideas of life and death stand in the context of Near Eastern ideas but are given a distinctive shape by Israel's faith in God.

1. Life in the OT. The term *ḥayyîm* covers only physical, organic life, yet it contains a value judgment. Life is good—the supreme good (Job 2:4; Prov. 3:16)—as the presupposition of all else (cf. Eccl. 9:4). Long life is a special grace (cf. Gen. 25:8 etc.), a reward for keeping the commandments (Dt. 5:16 etc.). Life itself comes from God, who breathes the breath of life into our nostrils (Gen. 2:7). The center of life is in the blood (Gen. 9:4). Life, however, has been disrupted. On the one hand it has been shortened (Gen. 6:3), on the other made bitter, by reason of human sin. The tree of life signifies a destiny of eternal life that was forfeited with the fall and expulsion from the garden. More important than the origin of life is the actual relation of life to God, who is Lord of both life and death, who controls the book of life (Ex. 32:32), and who, having given the covenant, determines the preservation or loss of life by the response to his word. Life is not secured by magical rites but by a decision for obedience (Dt. 30:15ff.; 32:47). It does not depend on bread alone but on God's word (Dt. 8:3). Ezekiel develops this theme most sharply with his call for repentance and the associated promise of life. Life is thus understood solely in terms of grace. It is the very basis of salvation and may be had only by faith, by cleaving to the saving God (Hab. 2:4). While it is the enjoyment of blessings on the one side, it is fellowship with God on the other, but either way it is understood as God's gift. The Wisdom books make it their chief aim to offer life, or to lead to life, by a right decision concerning the true order of life. The only difference is that wisdom now replaces God or the word as the source or giver of life. If the view that the word or wisdom confers life in a physical and not just a spiritual sense involves some contradiction with the harsh realities of experience, the OT is aware of this, but can provide a solution only as death is not seen as the irrevocable end of life.

2. *Death in the OT.* The termination of life by death in old age is accepted as regrettable but natural. The state expected after death is cheerless. Individuality is lost and no reunion is expected. Sacral quality is denied to graves, and corpses are unclean (Dt. 21:23). The dead are excluded from the praise of God (Ps. 115:16-17). Severance from the God of life is the true sting of death (Is. 38:18). If life comes by relation to God, death is characterized by the lack of any such relation. The perpetuation of the nation, even by restoration (Ezek. 37), is guaranteed by the covenant, but the spell of death rests on individual life.

3. *The OT Conquest of Death.* Although God is always seen to rule over higher spheres to which he may snatch up the righteous (Gen. 5:21ff.; 2 Kgs. 2:9-10), it is out of stress, and faith in the divine righteousness, that fulfilment of the covenant promise comes to be expected after death (Pss. 16:9-10; 49:16; 73:23ff.; Job 19:25). The concept of grace underlies the assurance stated here. The same concept lies behind Is. 26:19 and Dan. 12:2, though here the righteousness of God means retribution for the wicked as well as ongoing fellowship with God for believers.

[G. von Rad, II, 843-49]

4. *The Concept of Life in the OT.* If Heb. *ḥayyîm* corresponds more to *bíos* (as duration) than to *zōḗ*, the word *nepeš*, denoting the potency on which life rests, stands closer to *zōḗ*. The essence of *ḥayyîm* may be seen in the expressions of life whose subject is *nepeš*, e.g., hunger and thirst, wishes and desires. Yet *nepeš* is not also the subject of the intellectual life, for the concept of life is linked with that of flesh, all living creatures come under the rubric of *nepeš*, and soul and flesh can be used as parallels or combined. While *nepeš* is in us, or in the blood, it cannot be investigated, for it is subject only to God's control (Gen. 6:3, 17 etc.). We have life only as a loan. God is the Lord of life (Ps. 104:29-30). He is its Giver, killing and making alive (Ps. 36:9; Dt. 32:39). He alone has life in himself. We who are mortal can only sustain it by food and toil. For us life is temporal and implies movement, possibility, orientation, and desire. Striving and hope characterize it, as well as hunger and thirst. Mere existence is not life. Sickness is as bad as death (Job 27:15), and healing is life. True life is long and happy. Life is the supreme good; the worst suffering is "unto death" (Jon. 4:9). Death ends life; it cannot fulfil it. Life means self-knowledge; hence the link with light (cf. Eccl. 11:8). Life is individual; death equalizes (Job 3:19). This individuality is present with life itself; it does not not have to be attained by the way one lives, nor does it survive death. Death is a rest (Job 3:17-18), and one may die content when full of days. This present life is true life if long and happy, and by obedience to the law or wisdom one may fashion a long and happy life, thus choosing life and not death.   [R. Bultmann, II, 849-51]

C. *zōḗ* and *bíos* in the LXX. Almost always the LXX uses *zḗn* and *zōḗ* for the Hebrew terms. *bíos* does not occur at all in the law and the prophets, and is used in Job, Prov. 3:2, 16, Wisdom, and 2 and 3 Maccabees only for length of life. It acquires an ethical sense only in 4 Maccabees. *zōḗ* occurs some 278 times, 191 in the canon, 10 times with no original, and 19 times in a free rendering. It first means length of life or vitality as distinct from sickness and death. God is the lord of life and history who smites and heals. Later the life that is a divine gift is eternal life (cf. 4 Macc. 18:18). On earlier burial inscriptions the references are to earthly life, but sometimes OT texts are adduced to support belief in the afterlife (cf. 1 Sam. 25:29; Gen. 3:22ff.;

Job 19:25 for LXX suggestions along these lines; also Is. 26:19; Lev. 18:5; Ps. 119; Ps. 49:7). (For a full survey cf. *TDNT*, II, 851-54.)   [G. BERTRAM, II, 851-54]

D. The Concept of Life in Judaism.
1. *Palestinian Judaism.*
a. Life and Death. Palestinian Judaism maintains the OT concept of life. Humans, as the primary subjects, are living. Life is an extension of natural existence. It depends on nourishment, but God is Lord of life and death, gives life, has put in us the spirit of life, and is invoked as the Father of life. Life is a blessing; it is health and salvation. Long life rewards obedience, but death is better than a miserable life. Since death ends all things, one should use life wisely. God's commands are the commands of life, his words the words of life, the law the tree of life, and we must choose between the ways of life and death. Death is the common lot and does not tarry. All of us fear it, but it brings rest and may at times be desired. Yet it is also a penalty for sin, having come into the world through the first sin and being brought by the devil.

b. Life after Death. Death contradicts individual life. Hence the conviction grows that true life must be eternal as God creates it anew in resurrection. Beliefs vary as to whether the wicked are also raised, what forms the new life will take, and how it fits in with the awaited age of salvation. The Pharisees defend the resurrection academically, while apocalyptic takes it for granted. Eschatological life is not life in a wholly new sense. Freedom from suffering is in keeping with the OT view of true life. The only truly new features are liberation from sin and from present conditions. If there is no dualism, we find a tendency to stress the otherworldly aspects.

2. *Hellenistic Judaism.*
a. Linguistically *zēn* is used for natural life—"to be alive," etc. *zōḗ* and *bíos* are sometimes but not always distinguished. One may both *bíon zēn* and *zōḗn bioún*, and both *bíos* and *zōḗ* may denote sustenance.

b. The understanding of life is Jewish with Hellenistic modifications. God, the living God and Lord of life and death, gives life. The soul as the bearer of life is immortal. Both *zōḗ* and *bíos* denote the leading of life (a Hellenistic modification). True life must accord with a transcendent norm. Death is rest, but in martyrdom it may be a deliberate act and therefore good or glorious. It may even be a liberation of the soul (cf. Josephus *The Jewish War* 344ff.).

c. Expectation of life after death is widespread, but while the idea of heavenly being is similar to that of Palestinian Judaism, belief in immortality of the soul partly replaces the concept of resurrection, and judgment comes immediately at death.

d. Philo uses *zōḗ* philosophically for the vital force that is active in the *psyché*. This is common to all *zóa*, but humans also have the rational force of inbreathed *pneúma*. True life is life in knowledge and virtue. Life in the body is bad and a hindrance to the soul, so that true life is apart from the body and will culminate in life after death or ecstatic vision.

E. The Concept of Life in the NT.
1. *Natural Life.*
In the NT *zōḗ* and *zēn* refer first to natural life as distinct from natural death. This life is corruptible and limited but involves movement and ability. To live sometimes means to be healthy (Mk. 5:23; cf. Rom. 7:8). Figuratively things that are efficacious may be called living, e.g., words (Acts 7:38), hope (1 Pet. 1:3), and sacrifice (Rom. 12:1). Power is of the essence of life. Life is a supreme good (Mk. 8:36-37). Jesus puts forth his power to save or restore it (Mk. 5:23; Mt. 9:18). Sinners lose it (Acts 22:22). It is sustained but not assured by food, resting also on

the *pneúma* as the power of the God who has life intrinsically (Jn. 5:26), who lives eternally (Rev. 4:9-10; cf. 1 Tim. 6:16), who is Lord of life and death, who judges the living and the dead (1 Pet. 4:5), and who makes alive through his life-giving Spirit (1 Cor. 15:45). Life is thus dependent on God. It is fulfilled, however, in the manner of leading it, and may thus be qualified adverbially (cf. Lk. 15:13; Gal. 2:14; Tit. 2:12, etc.). *bíos* can be used for *zōé* in this sense (1 Tim. 2:2), but *zōé* does not first take on meaningful content in *bíos* (as in Greek thought), for it is responsible before God. Believers do not live for self but for God or the Lord (Rom. 14:7-8). Living for self is living for sin and death (Rom. 6:2). Life stands always under the question of its origin and goal.

2. *True Life according to the General NT View.* Death is not just a natural phenomenon. It is not self-evident but a punishment for sin. True life, the life of God, is indestructible. Thus the life that is subject to death is only provisional (1 Cor. 15:19). It is life in the flesh (Gal. 2:20). Those who are bound to it are "dead" (Mt. 8:22-23; Eph. 5:14; Rev. 3:1). The true life is future (1 Tim. 4:8). This is *zōé* in the absolute (Mk. 9:43), or *zén* (Rom. 1:17). Being indestructible, it is eternal (Mk. 10:17; Rom. 2:7; Gal. 6:8, etc.), and is linked with salvation. It is inherited, received, or entered (Mk. 10:17; 10:30; 9:43-44). If we may be worthy of it (Mt. 7:13-14), we have no control over it; as natural life is given by creation, true life is given by resurrection. There is no immortality of the soul. God sovereignly ordains to eternal life (Acts 13:48, and cf. the book or books of life in Rev. 13:8; 17:8).

3. *The Grounding of Life in Jesus Christ.* The new feature in the NT is that the future act of awakening is grounded in the enacted resurrection of Christ. The heart of the Christian gospel is the Easter message that he who was dead now lives (Lk. 24:9; Rom. 6:10; 14:9; 2 Cor. 13:4). This life of his is eternal (Rev. 1:18), and death is thus robbed of its power. Faith in a future *zōé* no longer rests merely on a general concept of God. The concept of God is radicalized, the result of sin is shown to be deeper, and the claim of humanity is more sharply negated. God's gift of new and true life is by a free and gracious act of salvation (Rom. 5:15; 1 Pet. 3:7) without which we would be lost. Hope rests on faith in this act (Rom. 1:17). To believe in Jesus is to have life (Jn. 3:15-16). Jesus has brought life and immortality to light (2 Tim. 1:10). He is the author of life (Acts 3:15). We are saved by his life (Rom. 5:10). He is our life, a life hidden with him in God (Col. 3:3-4). In him is life (Rom. 8:2). He is the resurrection and the life (Jn. 11:25), the way, the truth, and the life (Jn. 14:6), the true and eternal life (1 Jn. 5:20).

4. *Life Future and Present.* If future *zōé* is established by Christ's work, this work has already taken place and the resurrection of the dead is simply the consummation of the replacing of the old aeon by the new. Thus *zōé* is not just hoped for; we have it already. It is still future in the teaching of Jesus and throughout the NT. Yet the present is seen in the light of it, and since it is grounded in a completed act, our hope is sure and living (1 Pet. 1:3). In Rev. 2:7, 10 the present is sustained by this certain hope. In Col. 3:3-4 *zōé* is already present but hidden as yet in God. In 2 Tim. 1:1 it is given in Christ. In 1 Tim. 6:12 we are to lay hold of it; it is manifested in the gospel (2 Tim. 1:10). Earthly conditions no longer apply to it (Mk. 12:25). It is a life of joy and glory (Mt. 25:21; 2 Tim. 2:10), free from suffering and decay (Rev. 21:4). Yet it is not wholly different from life as it now is.

5. *Paul's View of Life as Present.*

a. Paul uses present terms to describe life. The old aeon has given way to the new. Christ is the second Adam, the author of a new humanity, its firstfruits or firstborn

(1 Cor. 15:20; Rom. 8:29). If there is a future fulfilment (1 Cor. 15:20ff.), there is also present renewal (Rom. 5:12ff.). The *pneúma* is a pledge of the future (Rom. 8:11ʃ. Yet the *pneúma* also means a new manner of life as Christ is present and active in believers, so that their *zōḗ* is a historical reality here and now. The life-giving *pneúma* differs from the living *psyché* (1 Cor. 15:45) and is already present, so that if we hope for *zōḗ* (Rom. 5:1ff.), we also have it, like *dóxa* (Rom. 8:30; 2 Cor. 3:6ff.).

b. *zōḗ* is not present in an ideal *bíos* (as in Stoicism), nor as a substance conferring immortality (as in Gnosticism). For Paul the *pneúma* is not the *noús* but the power of God, and the presupposition of reception of the *pneúma* and *zōḗ* is the word that proclaims a historical event and that belongs to this event. The word, as God's power to salvation (Rom. 1:16), is the word of life (Phil. 2:16; cf. Acts 5:20). Hence the gospel destroys death and manifests immortality (2 Tim. 1:10). Faith corresponds to the word; it grasps the righteousness of God and the remission of sins which are necessary for life. Thus the *pneúma* is not our possession but implies that we cannot live on our own. Our true life is Christ living in us (Gal. 2:20). His life is in us (2 Cor. 4:20-21). We live in him (Rom. 6:11). Christ is our life (Rom. 8:2). We have life in relation to his work for us.

c. This true life in the Spirit is at work in the concrete possibilities of life (1 Cor. 7:29ff.). It is freedom from death by identification with Christ's vicarious death. This freedom comes to expression in daily dying, for "dying, behold we live" (2 Cor. 4:8ff.). By living and dying we glorify Christ; our death is gain and our life in the flesh is fruitful labor (Phil. 1:20ff.). Since we belong to God and serve him, our living and dying are relativized, and our possibilities are only mediately such through faith. We walk in newness of life (Rom. 6:4), i.e., righteousness (6:12ff.). The first fruit c life in the *pneúma* is *agápē* (Gal. 5:22-23). The walk itself, of course, is not *zōḗ*, for *zōḗ* propagates itself by the word and is not limited in time, the *télos* of *zōḗ* being also *zōḗ* (Rom. 6:22). If right conduct alone makes us worthy of eternal life, this conduct springs from the life that is already given and that confers freedom from the law (2 Cor. 3:17), and from sin (Rom. 6:18). Thus *zōḗ* is both present life and future blessing. The implied transformation (2 Cor. 3:18; 4:16) is not by natural process but by divine action (1 Cor. 15:36ff.) linked to a dramatic cosmic event (1 Th. 4:13ff.).

d. As future life, *zōḗ* defies full definition. It is both salvation (Rom. 5:10) and glory (2 Cor. 3:6ff.). Transcending earthly possibilities, it is still somatic (1 Cor. 15:35ff.). It brings with it righteousness, peace, and joy (Rom. 14:17), face-to-face vision (1 Cor. 13:12), perfect knowledge, and being with Christ in abiding faith, hope, and love.

6. *John's View of Life as Present.*

a. As the eternal Son and Logos, Christ has life in himself (Jn. 1:4), for he is God's creative power. He yields up his human *psyché* to death (10:11) but his *zōḗ* (which is the light of men, 1:4) cannot be destroyed. As himself *zōḗ*, he reveals the God whose command is eternal life (12:50). Giving life to believers, he is the bread of life (6:35) and the light of life (8:12), he gives the water of life (4:10-11), his words are spirit and life (6:63) or the words of life (6:68), and he has come to give life to the world (6:33).

b. Believers in Christ already have life in faith (3:25). They have passed from death to life (5:24). With his word, the hour comes (5:25). He is the resurrection and the life, so that believers in him will live though they die (11:25). He has already given them glory (17:22). Yet this *zōḗ* has an eternal future (4:14; 6:27) and there is the promise of a new vision of glory (17:24). Express references to an eschatological future occur in 5:28-29 and 6:51ff.

c. By depicting life as present, John does not spiritualize it but radicalizes it. Christ's coming is the decisive event. Life comes by commitment to him. It thus stands under the command of love, for abiding in him is abiding in love (15:1ff., 9ff.). Our love is grounded in God's love (13:34; 1 Jn. 4:7ff.). Love of the brethren shows that we have passed from death to life (1 Jn. 3:14-15). Inwardly, life means an assurance or confidence that drives out fear (1 Jn. 4:18) and a joy of asking (Jn. 16:20ff.) that overcomes sorrow. These are part of the abundance (Jn. 10:10) that comes with the life that is knowledge of God in Christ.

d. If this view seems to resemble the Hellenistic concept, it does so only in a complete radicalizing and restructuring (as in the related issues of truth and knowledge). For it points away from speculation and mysticism to the historical revelation of God in Christ. The *egṓ eimi* sayings are significant in this regard. If the *zōḗ* of creation is light, it is so in actuality even though the cosmos resists it (Jn. 1:4-5). The question of *zōḗ* is an urgent one even in darkness, for all things owe their being to the Logos. People may wrongly think they have found life (5:39-40), but revelation leads from false life to true life. Thus common necessities and metaphors of life (water and bread) are adopted, and the fact that in themselves these do not satisfy the quest for authentic life turns them into a question that the incarnate Logos answers as the one in whom alone real life is to be found.

anazáō. This rare word, meaning "to become alive again," "to rise again," is used figuratively in Lk. 15:24 (the prodigal) and Rom. 7:9 (sin), and literally with reference to Christ's resurrection in Rom. 14:9 and that of the dead in Rev. 20:5.

zṓon. This word for "living creature" (whether the animal or human) is used for animals in Gen. 1:21; Ps. 104:24; Ezek. 47:9; Heb. 13:11. Heretics are compared to irrational creatures (animals) in Jude 10; 2 Pet. 2:12. A special use is for the four heavenly creatures of Ezek. 1:5, 13ff. and Rev. 4:6ff.; 5:6ff.

zōogonéō. Attested from the time of Aristotle for "to make alive," this word normally has reference to nature or animals, and ultimately to deity. God makes alive in 1 Sam. 2:6. Another use, with humans as subjects, is for "to leave alive" (Ex. 1:17-18; Judg. 8:19; 1 Sam. 27:9ff.). God gives life to all things in 1 Tim. 6:13, while the LXX sense "to leave or keep alive" occurs in Lk. 17:33; Acts 7:19.

zoopoiéō. This word, too, means "to make alive" (animals, plants, deity). God is the usual subject in the LXX (2 Kgs. 5:7; wisdom in Eccl. 7:12). In the NT the term acquires a distinct soteriological sense. The law cannot give life (Gal. 3:21). God gives life to the dead (Rom. 4:17). He will give life to our mortal bodies (Rom. 8:11; cf. 1 Cor. 15:22). He raises Christ (1 Pet. 3:18). This life-giving can have a present reference: God (and Christ) in Jn. 5:21; Col. 2:13; the Spirit in 1 Cor. 15:45; 2 Cor. 3:6; Jn. 6:63.   [R. BULTMANN, II, 855-75]

| *zéō* [to boil],   *zestós* [hot],   *(chliarós* [lukewarm],   *psychrós* [cold]) |

---

zéō. The basic sense is "to well up," then "to boil" (cf. the stormy sea, fermenting wine), also "to glow" (figuratively: desire). The LXX has the word for the manna going bad in Ex. 16:20, for a stormy spirit in Job 32:19, for the seething pot of judgment in Ezek. 24:5. In the NT the term finds a special use for being stirred in the Spirit (Rom. 12:11; Acts 18:25). Boiling or glowing seems to be the basis of the metaphor. In Rom. 12:11 we are to develop our energy as Christians, although we can do so only as we are impelled by God's Spirit. In Acts 18:25 some exegetes see a reference to Apollos' ardent spirit or fiery eloquence, but in view of the prior mention of his gift of speech (v. 24), what is in view is probably his fervor in the Holy Spirit (as in Rom. 12:11).

zestós (chliarós, psychrós). Apart from *psychrós* in Mt. 10:42, these three terms occur only in Rev. 3:15-16. The rare word *zestós* occurs for "cooked" meat, "glowing" sand, and "boiling" water. It has the sense of "hot" as distinct from "tepid" or "cold." It is unlikely that the sense of *zéō* in Rom. 12:11 underlies the usage in Revelation. Perhaps the fact that the hot springs of Hierapolis are lukewarm at Laodicea suggests the metaphor, but rabbinic distinctions between the hot and tepid, or sinners, righteous, and lukewarm, are materially more relevant. The point is that the gospel calls for unconditional self-offering to the Lord who even now knocks at the door. A commitment that is rendered lukewarm by secular concerns is worse, and harder to overcome, than complete alienation.   [A. OEPKE, II, 875-77]

---

zḗlos [zeal], *zēlóō* [to strive after], *zēlōtḗs* [zealot], *parazēlóō* [to provoke to jealousy]

---

zḗlos.

A. *zḗlos* in Greek Usage. The usual translation of this term is "zeal": a. as the capacity or state of passionate commitment; b. comprehensively for the forces that motivate personality (e.g., interest, taste, imitative zeal, rivalry, fame, enthusiasm); c. in the bad sense jealousy, envy, competition, contention.

B. Zeal in the OT and Judaism.
1. *zḗlos* as a human emotion occurs only in the later parts of the OT; all sense of zealous striving to ennoble personality is alien to the underlying Hebrew. a. The term characterizes the living in Eccl. 9:6. It has a derogatory sense in Sir. 30:24 etc.; Prov. 27:4; perhaps Eccl. 4:4. The feeling that gives rise to national hostility is the point in Ezek. 35:11; cf. Is. 11:13. b. Marital jealousy is the reference in Prov. 6:34; Cant. 8:6. c. A special OT sense is that of zeal for God and his will (Pss. 69:9; 119:139).
2. In half of the LXX instances the term denotes the intensity of God's action, whether this means good or ill for those concerned. It is linked with anger in Dt. 29:20, with fire in Zeph. 1:18, and with compassion in Is. 63:15. God's zeal (*qin'â*), which is more commonly mentioned in the OT than *zḗlos* might suggest, relates primarily to Israel. Expressing God's holiness, his zeal turns against the apostasy of Israel (as jealousy at her adultery), but when the nations seek to disrupt his plan for Israel, his zeal is displayed either historically or eschatologically on her behalf (cf. Ezek. 16:38 on the one side; Ezek. 36:6; Is. 9:7; 26:11; Zech. 1:14; Zeph. 1:18 on the other). Its combination with "Lord of hosts" (Is. 9:7; 2 Kgs. 19:31) shows that *zḗlos* is closely related to the concept of Yahweh as the Lord of history.
3. Philo uses *zḗlos* for human striving after things along the lines of Greek ethics. The term may be predicated of God only for the sake of those of lesser intelligence.

4. The rabbis, too, find it hard to speak about God's zeal for fear of anthropomorphism. God is a jealous God, not because he envies idols as rivals, but because he cannot allow his honor to be infringed by idolatry.

C. *zḗlos* in the NT.

1. In the NT the word is in the singular except in Rom. 13:13 and Gal. 5:20. It occurs in the Gospels only in Jn. 2:17 (quoting Ps. 69) for the zeal of the righteous. This is also the point in Jewish zeal against Christianity in Acts 5:17 and possibly 13:45 (cf. 17:5). Zeal for God is what Paul has in mind in Rom. 10:2, though when misplaced this turns against itself (v. 3). Paul earlier shared this zeal when persecuting the church (Phil. 3:16).

2. In 2 Cor. 11:2 we find a sense similar to that of the OT (cf. 1 Cor. 10:22). As God seeks with holy zeal to keep his people from idolatry, so Paul jealously watches over the church lest it fall into error.

3. Elsewhere *zḗlos* has the ordinary Greek senses: a. enthusiasm for the collection in 2 Cor. 9:2 and an ardent desire to restore good relations in 2 Cor. 7:7; b. in connection with such words as quarreling, anger, etc., competitive envy or jealousy (Rom. 13:13; 1 Cor. 3:3; 2 Cor. 12:20; Gal. 5:20); c. consuming ardor (of fire) (Heb. 10:27).

In the apostolic fathers, *zḗlos* (envy) is an important word in 1 Clement and Cyprian, who depict the evils of envy, but Chrysostom in his homily on 2 Cor. 12:21, while condemning divisive *zḗlos*, finds high ethical value in imitative *zḗlos*.

zēlóō, zēlōtḗs.

A. The Greek Usage. In Greek *zēlóō* is mostly in the active and means "to admire or commend," with such nuances as "to be enthusiastic for," "to seek to imitate," "to envy" in a good sense; yet we also find the bad sense of "to envy" and an occasional use for jealousy in marriage.

B. The Usage in the OT and LXX.

1.a. The most consistent use is in Proverbs, where it means "to strive after," though commonly with a warning not to do so (3:31; 4:14, etc.; but cf. 6:6). b. Wrathful indignation is the point in 1 Macc. 2:24 (cf. Ps. 73:3, 21-22), envy in Gen. 26:14, and zeal on behalf of the people in 2 Sam. 21:2. c. The only instances of jealousy in marriage are in Num. 5:14, 30.

2.a. God is jealous in Ex. 20:5; 34:14. This jealous zeal is not a mood but belongs to God's very essence. It turns against Israel in case of disobedience (Dt. 32:19) but may also work in her favor (Ezek. 39:25). It is bound up with the manifestation of God's omnipotent reality (Ezek. 39:28). b. The righteous may be zealous on God's behalf, not in mood, but in specific action (Num. 25:11; 1 Kgs. 19:10, 14; 2 Kgs. 10:16; 1 Macc. 2:24).

C. Zealotism.

1. Zeal for God and his law and honor is in keeping with the basic orientation of Pharisaism and comes to violent expression in the movement of Zealotism. The Zealots make active zeal for God the determinative factor in their whole conduct.

2. The origins of Zealotism are obscure. It derives from Pharisaism and takes shape when Judas of Galilee joins Zadok in resistance to Roman rule. Phinehas is taken as the prototype of the Zealot. At first Pharisaism tends to side with Zealotism but diverges from it when Zealotism becomes a more revolutionary and anarchical movement.

3. The fact that the first disciples include a Zealot points to some link between Zealotism and Palestinian Christianity (though not in respect of social action). Gamaliel adopts the same principle in relation to both (Acts 5:34ff.). The distinction may be seen when Zealots plot to murder Paul in Acts 23:12ff. Zealotism is activist, seeking to set up the rule of God by revolt, displaying a readiness to suffer to this end, and passionately trusting that God will intervene to insure success. A saying like Mk. 8:34-35 is immediately understandable in the context of Zealotism, and a question like that of Mk. 12:13ff. arises in the same context, though Zealots would reply with a definite negative. The sons of Zebedee manifest Zealot traits in Lk. 9:54 and Mk. 10:38-39 (cf. their name in Mk. 3:17). Rev. 13:4ff. also reflects a Zealot hostility to alien domination. The application to Rome of OT prophecies concerning Edom and Babylon may also indicate Zealot influence (cf. Rev. 18:2-3, 9ff.). Yet Christians could not stay in Jerusalem when Zealot rule was established, not merely because the Zealots were now becoming revolutionary fanatics, but because of basic incompatibilities, e.g., the Christian command to love one's enemies, or Christ's understanding of his crucifixion as the fulfilment of his divine mission.

D. *zēlóō* **and** *zēlōtḗs* **in the NT.**

1. A first meaning is that of zeal for God. a. The disciple Simon is called *zēlōtḗs* in Lk. 6:15; Acts 1:13; this denotes membership in the Zealot party. b. This zeal may find expression in hostility to Christian preaching (Acts 17:5). Paul had been one of these zealous Jews (Gal. 1:14). Christian Jews may still be zealous for the law (Acts 21:20).

2. *zēlóō* may also denote the apostle's personal attitude to the community, as in 2 Cor. 11:2. Paul's strong concern is to woo believers to obedience to the gospel. In Gal. 4:17 Paul's opponents manifest zeal for the welfare of the Galatians, but only for a selfish purpose; in contrast, the apostolic zeal of Paul is good, for it is for a good purpose.

3. The usual Greek sense "to strive after something" may be seen in Tit. 2:14 and 1 Pet. 3:13, not along the lines of individualistic ethics, but with a view to edification (cf. striving after gifts in 1 Cor. 12:31; 14:1). In 1 Cor. 13:4 and Jms. 4:2, however, there is no thought of edification and thus the sense of envious or passionate striving is apposite.   [A. STUMPFF, II, 877-88]

---

zēmía [loss, hurt],   *zēmióō* [to suffer loss]

zēmía originally meant "disadvantage" and *zēmióō* "to disadvantage."

1.a. Disadvantage may take the form of monetary or material "loss" or "damage." b. It may also be moral or spiritual in the sense of "hurt" or "ruin," with a subjective nuance of "unpleasantness." c. Legally *zēmía* early takes on the sense of "penalty" and *zēmióō* "to punish."

2.a. Underlying 2 Cor. 7:9 is sense 1.b. Paul is responsible for the welfare of the church, and it should not suffer hurt through his fault. The same sense is probable (rather than "penalty") in 1 Cor. 3:15 in contrast to the reward of v. 14. What is at issue is "hurt" or "loss" in a general sense, not in a financial sense or as loss of salvation (cf. the continuation). The point in Phil. 3:7-8 is not objective loss but subjective loss of value. For Paul all value now lies in Christ, and therefore things that were once highly estimated (his zeal and legal righteousness) are now regarded as worthless. The idea is not that they are harmful to his new Christian life, and there is certainly no thought of punishment.

b. In the one instance in the Synoptics (Mt. 16:26; par. Mk. 8:36; Lk. 9:25), the antithesis "gain" suggests the commercial figure of profit and loss. To gain the whole world one must lose (i.e., pay the price of) the self—a poor exchange. Gaining the world may refer to material goods (cf. Mt. 4:8-9) or just possibly to missionary success (cf. Mt. 6:2). The loss takes place here and now, but if final judgment is also implied the term carries some sense of punishment (though cf. the equivalent "to forfeit" in Lk. 9:25).   [A. STUMPFF, II, 888-92]

---

zētéō [to seek],   *zétēsis* [debate],   *ekzētéō* [to seek],   *epizētéō* [to seek]

---

zētéō.

1. Religiously this term denotes first the seeking of what is lost by the Son of Man with a view to saving it (Lk. 19:10; Mt. 18:12; Lk. 15:8). But it can also refer to God's requiring much from those to whom much is given (Lk. 12:48), or fruit from the tree (Lk. 13:6-7), or faithfulness from the steward (1 Cor. 4:2), or true worship from the righteous (Jn. 4:23). From this twofold use we see that the divine seeking involves at the same time a divine claiming. In John 8:50 the point seems to be that the Father looks after the glory of the Son and will judge those who refuse him recognition.

2. In many instances human seeking is the point. The basis here is the Greek use of *zētéō* for philosophical inquiry (cf. 1 Cor. 1:22; Acts 17:27) and the LXX use for seeking God (cf. Rom. 10:20). The seeking of God in prayer in Mt. 7:7ff. follows LXX usage. Seeking covers the broader orientation of will: the seeking of God's kingdom and righteousness (Mt. 6:32-33), the seeking of things above (Col. 3:1), the seeking of the great goal of life (Mt. 13:45), the seeking of justification (Gal. 2:17). Such seeking can be perverted into the request for a sign whereby the demand of the gospel may be evaded (Mk. 8:11-12).

zétēsis. On the basis of the Greek use for philosophical investigation, this word occurs in the NT for "debate" or "dispute," the accent now being on the manner of inquiry. In Jn. 3:25; Acts 15:2, 7; 1 Tim. 6:4 we seem to have an exchange of words rather than true search. General disputing is at issue in 2 Tim. 2:23, and here (as in 1 Tim. 6:4 and Tit. 3:9) the disputes are useless, foolish, harmful, and incompatible with true faith and assurance. The context in Acts 25:20 suggests a legal sense ("investigation"). There are no clear instances of the use for "clash of opinions" in the pre-Christian era, and the word does not occur in the LXX or apostolic fathers.

ekzētéō. This compound means the same as the simple form. As in the LXX, seeking God is the point in Acts 15:17; Rom. 3:11; Heb. 11:6. The element of search is stronger in 1 Pet. 1:10, but the seeking is more general in Heb. 12:17. Eschatological requiring or demanding of justice is the point in Heb. 11:50-51. The eschatological element distinguishes it here from the Hebrew usage on which it is based (e.g., 2 Sam. 4:11).

epizétéō. This word, too, means the same as *zētéō.* Thus the Gentiles seek material things (Mt. 6:32), while the Jews seek righteousness (Rom. 11:17), and Sergius Paulus seeks to hear God's word (Acts 13:7). In Hebrews the OT saints seek a heavenly country (11:14) and Christians an eternal city (13:14). "Look for" and "desire" are the meanings in Acts 12:19 and 19:39.   [H. GREEVEN, II, 892-96]

---

zygós [yoke, scales],   *heterozygéō* [to be unevenly yoked]

---

zygós.

A. *zygós* in the LXX.

1. The normal LXX use is for "scales" or "yoke." For scales in the secular sense cf. Ezek. 5:1 (division), Is. 46:6, and Jer. 32:10 (weighing). God weighs the universe in Is. 40:12, and demands just weights in Lev. 19:35; Ezek. 45:10; Hos. 12:7; Am. 8:5; Prov. 11:1; 16:11. Scales symbolize justice when given to Dan (cf. Gen. 49:16). For a moral use cf. Sir. 21:25; 28:25 (the measuring of words).

2. A significant figurative use is found for destiny and human worth. Job's sufferings weigh more than the sand (i.e., they cannot be measured) (6:2). We ourselves are to be weighed (Job 31:6; cf. Mic. 6:11). We count for nothing in God's sight (Ps. 62:9; cf. Is. 40:15). Belshazzar's kingdom, when weighed, is found wanting. Though the LXX translates this differently, the idea of weighing in judgment occurs in many apocryphal and apocalyptic texts.

3. The image of the "yoke" is also common in the LXX. It denotes political tyranny in 2 Chr. 10:4ff. (cf. Gen. 27:40) and alien rule in Is. 19:10; 14:29; 47:6; Dan. 8:25. Deliverance is the taking away of the yoke in Is. 9:3 and its breaking by God in Lev. 26:13 (cf. the false prophecy in Jer. 28:2, 4, 11). In the moral sphere, slaves must be under the yoke (Sir. 30:35), one must avoid the yoke of the tongue (28:19), but it is good to accept the yoke of wisdom (51:26). Sinners do not want to bear God's yoke (Jer. 2:20) but finally the nations will bear it gladly (Zeph. 3:9). The suffering of the righteous is construed as God's yoke (cf. Mt. 11:29-30).   [G. BERTRAM, II, 896-98]

B. *zygós* in the NT.

1. In Rev. 6:5 the third horseman (on the black horse) has "scales" in his hand. He symbolizes scarcity as a sign of impending judgment (cf. Lev. 26:26).

2. Elsewhere in the NT *zygós* means "yoke," but is used only figuratively in the general sense of absolute dependence. a. In 1 Tim. 6:1 the word expresses the situation of slaves; where the masters are Christians, the legal situation is the same but the personal relation is determined by their love as brethren, which adds a new dimension to service. b. The yoke of slavery has figurative significance in Gal. 5:1: Having escaped bondage to the elemental spirits (4:8ff.), believers should not submit to the yoke of the law but enjoy the freedom of sonship that Christ has conferred. The use in Acts 15:10 is similar: Gentile Christians are not to be put under the yoke of the law. c. In Mt. 11:29-30 Jesus invites those who labor and are heavy laden to take his easy yoke upon them. The apparent paradox (how can a yoke be easy?) vanishes when one considers that this is the yoke of the Messiah who offers free access to God to all who accept his call. Parallel rabbinic sayings refer to the putting off of the yoke of government by acceptance of the yoke of the law, or of coming under the yoke of earthly rule by breaking the yoke of heaven, but with the distinction that human achievement is here presupposed (though the divine yoke is regarded as a privilege rather than a burden), and that the yoke of Christ does not stand in such absolute

antithesis to that of earthly government (cf. Mt. 22:15ff.). d. The apostolic fathers adopt the metaphor of the yoke, e.g., in Did. 6.2 (more legalistically) and Barn. 2.6 (characterizing the new law of Christ as gift rather than obligation).

heterozygéō. This word derives from *heterózygos,* "unequally yoked" (e.g., the yoking of an ass and ox). It occurs for the first time in 2 Cor. 6:14, where Paul uses it to describe the abnormal situation that results when Christians fail to maintain their distinction from unbelievers.   [K. H. RENGSTORF, II, 898-901]

---

zýmē [yeast, leaven],   *zymóō* [to ferment],   *ázymos* [unleavened]

1. The NT usage rests on the Feast of Unleavened Bread and its rules in Ex. 12:18 (cf. 13:6-7; Num. 28:16-17; Dt. 16:3-4). The origin and meaning of this feast and its precise relation to the one-day Passover are hard to determine.

2. The feast itself is mentioned in Mk. 14:1, 12 (cf. Mt. 26:17; Lk. 22:1,7) and twice in Acts (12:3; 20:6). The *ázyma* are the seven days following the evening of the Passover, though the Passover itself is sometimes called the first day of an eight-day feast (Mk. 14:12). It is not clear why the accounts of the last supper do not mention the eating of unleavened bread which was part of the Passover ritual (cf. Ex. 12:18). Is *ártos* used instead?

3. The *ázyma* ritual underlies 1 Cor. 5:6ff., where Paul (perhaps writing at the Passover season) gives the cultic demand a moral significance. *zýmē* denotes the moral impurity of the old life, *ázyma* liberation from this and therefore the truth and purity of the new life. The ideas of oldness and newness are introduced by the thought of conversion (cf. Rom. 7:6; Col. 3:9-10), while allegorizing suggests the idea of sin as leaven in the dough, and the whole metaphor opens up exciting vistas, e.g., the *ázymoi* as the new festal community, the new life as the feast, and Christ as the paschal lamb who both demands renewal and makes it possible. We have a good example of Paul's combining indicative and imperative in v. 7. Philo has several allegorical interpretations of *ázyma* and *zýmē.* Thus eating *ázyma* symbolizes asceticism, and *tá ázyma* is a symbol of humility and *zýmē* of pride or sinful lust. But Philo has no powerful injunction to cleanse out *zýmē* (which on occasion may indeed denote the lawful elevation of the soul). Plutarch, too, finds in *zýmē* a symbol of uncleanness and compares the process of leavening to defilement, so that Paul's metaphor would be readily understandable to Gentile Christians not so well versed in the OT.

4. In the parable of the leaven in Mt. 13:33 (Lk. 13:21), Jesus makes the more general point that a little cause can have great effects (cf. Jms. 3:3ff.). Here the kingdom itself is compared to *zýmē.* Though quantitatively small, it can penetrate the whole earth (cf. the salt in Mt. 5:13).

5. In contrast is the figurative warning of Mk. 8:15; Mt. 16:6; Lk. 12:1 against the *zýmē* of the Pharisees (and Herodians and Sadducees). The reference here is obviously to the corrupt and corrupting element in the teaching of these opponents of Jesus, though in itself *zýmē* is possibly neutral, the emphasis being on the qualifying genitive or genitives. There is no parallel for this kind of use in the LXX, which employs the group only in rules for the feasts and sacrifices (Ex. 12:15; 23:18; Dt. 16:3-4, etc.).

→ *ártos, páscha*   [H. WINDISCH, II, 902-06]

zōḗ, zōogonéō, zóon, zōopoiéō → *záō*

η ē̄

---

hēgéomai [to lead, think],   *exēgéomai* [to expound],   *proēgéomai* [to outdo],
diēgēsis [narrative]

---

hēgéomai.
1. This word means a. "to lead," b. "to think," "believe," "regard as." In the NT it occurs in sense a. only in the present participle (see 2.), but is widespread in sense b. (though not found in the Johannine writings). "To esteem" is the point in 1 Th. 5:13 (as in Thucydides 2.89.9).
2. a. *hēgoúmenoi* (mostly plural) is used for community leaders in Heb. 13:7, 17, 24. These are examples of faith (v. 7) and pastors responsible to God (v. 17); they are thus to be obeyed (v. 17), and are mentioned before the saints (v. 24). Yet according to Lk. 22:26 the *hēgoúmenos* is to be as one who serves—a necessary check on officialdom. Judas and Silas are called "leading men" among the brethren in Acts 15:22.

b. *hēgoúmenoi* can also be leaders outside the community, e.g., military leaders in 1 Macc. 9:30, national leaders in Ezek. 43:7, princes in 1 Clem. 5.7, leading priests in the papyri. Quoting Mic. 5:1ff., Mt. 2:6 has the term for a national ruler, and Acts 7:10 has it for Joseph as the governor of Egypt. A common predicate of Hermes is adopted when Paul is called the *hēgoúmenos toú lógou* in Acts 14:12 (cf. Hermes as *theós ho tṓn lógōn hēgemṓn*).

exēgéomia. Of the two meanings a. "to introduce," "adduce," and b. "to expound," "recount," the NT uses only b. (Jn. 1:18; Lk. 24:35; Acts 10:8; 15:12; 21:19). The word is a technical one for the exposition of poetry, law, oracles, etc. In Jn. 1:18, where there is no object, the sense is "to reveal."

proēgéomia. This occurs in the NT only in Rom. 12:10. Since it can hardly mean "to take the lead" or "to go first," we do best to see it in analogy to Phil. 2:3 and render "to esteem more highly" (cf. 2 Macc. 10:12).

diēgēsis. In Lk. 1:1, Luke refers to those who have undertaken to compile a "narrative" of the things concerning Jesus. The word is used from the time of Plato for an oral or written "record." Attempts to give *diēgēsis* a special sense in support of the theory that random extracts form the basis of the present Gospels have met with little success.   [F. Büchsel, II, 907-09]

---

hēdonḗ [pleasure],   *philḗdonos* [lover of pleasure]

In the NT *hēdonḗ* is one of the many forces of unsanctified carnality that work against God and drag us back into evil.

A. General Greek Usage.
1. Semasiological Development.
a. Derived from the root *hēdýs* ("sweet," "pleasant," "delightful"), *hēdonḗ* first means what is pleasant to the taste, then to the senses in general, then what gives

pleasure. b. The word then comes to mean the "desire for pleasure" (cf. Jms. 4:1 and perhaps Tit. 3:3). c. A final development is for that which kindles desire or pleasure (e.g., good news), or for pleasure with an enumeration of the pleasures at issue, with a tendency in the NT period to take on the sense of "sensual lust."

2. *Ethical Evaluation.* For the Greeks, *hēdonḗ* is ambivalent. It belongs to *bíos* and enriches it, yet it may also threaten and dissolve its true meaning. In Plato and Aristotle it may be noble pleasure in the good, true, and beautiful, and thus equivalent to *chará* (joy). But it may also be sensual pleasure, and *hēdonokrasía* is surrender to a life of dissipation. The restriction of meaning brings a decline in estimation and makes it the opposite of *aretḗ*.

B. *hēdonḗ* in Greek Philosophy.

1. In philosophical anthropology *hēdonḗ* (as the opposite of *lýpē*) is one of the emotions or a result of one of the emotions.

2. In philosophical ethics the basic question is whether it is a virtue, whether it may be the goal of life, whether it conforms to what is rational, or whether it promotes virtue. For Socrates, it is part of the felicity based on virtue so long as it remains within self-control and is in harmony with other forms of the good. For Aristotle, too, *hēdonḗ* is good if it springs from a virtuous life. Others, however, regard *hēdonḗ* either as wholly good (Aristippus and later Epicurus), or as wholly bad (Antisthenes). The Stoics, who keep it on the periphery, prefer to call the pleasure that results from virtue either *chará* or *euphrosýnē*.

3. Conformity to nature, reason, or virtue is the criterion when value is assigned to *hēdonḗ*. Aristotle posits harmony between true *hēdonḗ* and nature, reason, and virtue; yet he makes *hēdonḗ* subsidiary to all three. The Cyrenaics and Epicureans ascribe a higher role to *hēdonḗ* as the fulfilment of nature, reason, and virtue. The Stoics question whether *hēdonḗ* is really in accord with nature and reason. Aristotle, of course, has to distinguish between higher and lower *hēdonaí*, and while Epicurus states that bodily pleasure is the original seat of spiritual joy, he, too, recognizes that sensual pleasure is not at all the true goal of life. The critical attitude of the Stoics, along with increasing pessimism, helps to produce later a mostly negative evaluation.

C. *hēdonḗ* in Jewish Literature.

1. In the LXX, the term is rare. "Pleasant taste" is the sense in Num. 11:8; Wis. 16:20. The closest to the usual sense is Prov. 17:1. "Sexual desire" is the point in Wis. 7:2.

2. 4 Maccabees is an exception, forming a bridge to the use in Greek philosophy. *hēdonḗ* here may be ethically neutral pleasure, but Stoicism is evident where it is the seat of evil impulses, as in 1:25. Yet along OT lines *hēdonḗ* refers to both body and soul (1:28).

3. Philo is close to 4 Maccabees. For him the seat of *hēdonḗ* is the body. As the source of many evils, it is in antithesis to the *lógos* and consists primarily of sensual pleasure.

4. In the rabbis there is no exact equivalent for *hēdonḗ*, but teaching on the evil impulse offers interesting similarities to the extent that both cover the element of desire and the pleasures of the evil impulse are sweet.

D. The Nonbiblical Use of *philḗdonos*.

1. In relation to persons this means "intent on pleasure," with nuances similar to those of *hēdonḗ*. Philo, thinking theologically, contrasts *philḗdonos* and *philótheos*; Epictetus, thinking anthropologically, contrasts *philḗdonos* and *philánthrōpos*.

2. In relation to objects the meaning is "bringing pleasure."

E. *hēdonḗ* in the NT. The following secular meanings may be found in the NT too: a. "pleasure" (2 Pet. 2:13); b. "desire for pleasure" (Jms. 4:1); c. "sensual pleasure" (Jms. 4:3; Lk. 8:14).

1. The Origin and Nature of hēdonḗ. hēdonḗ marks a non-Christian orientation to life. It belongs to the sphere that is ruled by ungodly forces: *bíos* in Lk. 8:14, this aeon in Mt. 13:22. In Jms. 4:1-2 *hēdonaí* are in the service of sin and stand in contrast to the *chará* which is the fruit of the Spirit (Gal. 5:22). *hēdonḗ* comes under the same judgment as fallen human nature. It is one of the basic NT antitheses.

2. hēdonḗ and Man's Relationship to God.

a. *hēdonḗ* stands opposed to God. Those who disrupt the church in 2 Tim. 3:4 are lovers of pleasure (*philḗdonoi*) rather than lovers of God (*philótheoi*). Love of the world is enmity against God, and yielding to *hēdonaí* is disloyalty to him (Jms. 4:1ff.). It influences our relation to God's will and word and to prayer.

b. Human *hēdonḗ* opposes God's will, for we live either according to this will or our own desires (cf. 1 Pet. 4:2). Cf. the evil impulse in the rabbis.

c. It struggles, then, against God's word (Lk. 8:14), which *epithymíai* are said to choke in Mk. 4:19. Cf. again the rabbinic evil impulse.

d. What is said *to* God (in prayer) is also adversely affected by *hēdonḗ,* as we read in Jms. 4:3, where we ask amiss if we make carnal *hēdonaí* the object of prayer. The attitude of unbridled earthly desire is contrary to the attitude of true prayer, which waits on God and seeks only what can be asked in the name of Jesus. The prayer that is based on *hēdonḗ* moves in a futile circle which leads only to new *hēdonḗ* and ends only with death (Jms. 4:1, 3).

3. hēdonaí and Man.

a. *hēdonaí* are the enemy of man no less than God, as we learn from the three biblical images that describe their operation: conflict, slavery, and thorns. *hēdonaí* bring constant conflict (Jms. 4:1ff.) instead of the peace (peace with God and peace of soul, Rom. 5:1; 15:13) that we have in Christ. This conflict is with God (Jms. 4:4), with others (v. 1), and probably with the self as well (v. 2; cf. Gal. 5:17; 1 Pet. 2:11; Rom. 7:23). Parallels for this inner conflict may be found in Thucydides, the rabbis, Philo, and Hermas among the apostolic fathers. In James, however, the main stress is on the conflict with others.

b. If we will not fight *hēdonaí,* or are defeated by them, we become their slaves (Tit. 3:3). They are masters that rule instead of God or Christ. The same image of bondage to *hēdonḗ* may be found in Plato, the rabbis, and Philo, all of whom advocate resistance to desire, which may take the form of *logismós* in 4 Maccabees, study of the law in the rabbis, or prayer and submission to God in the NT.

c. The third image brings out the destructive nature of *hēdonḗ* (Lk. 8:14), for, as thorns choke the seed, so *hēdonaí* bring death to those who yield to them (cf. Rom. 6:23; Hermas *Similitudes* 8.8.5, and rabbinic teaching on death as the final end of the evil impulse).

4. The Bearers and Victims of hēdonḗ.

a. Among the three groups that fall victim to *hēdonḗ* in the NT, non-Christians are the most numerous (Tit. 3:3). *hēdonḗ* is one of many terms that the NT uses to describe the state prior to faith (cf. *ágnoia, átheoi,* without hope, etc.). The lists of vices enumerate what is covered by the term.

b. The second group consists of double-minded Christians as these are best described in Jms. 4:1ff. Parallel to this group are the people in Lk. 8:14 who for a time are open to the work of the word but then fall away, not now because of external pressures, but because of the opposing impulses to which they submit.

c. Finally, there is the group of false teachers who are characterized more by bad living than bad doctrine (2 Tim. 3:4) and whose presence is an indication of the last time (cf. Jude 18). 2 Pet. 2:13 offers the most exact delineation of this third group. *hēdonḗ* here is more than pleasure in a general sense. It is voluptuousness—taking delight in revelings by day, i.e., in carousing and intemperance (cf. Phil. 3:19). This stands in the sharpest possible contrast to the joy which in the NT, too, is a supreme thing both in this life and the next, but which is promoted, not by *hēdonaí,* but by the fellowship with Christ in trials and afflictions (Jms. 1:2) that has perfection and eternal bliss as its end.   [G. STÄHLIN, II, 909-26]

---

hḗkō [to come]

Formally a present, this word denotes a state and thus has the force of a perfect, although still used in the present for "to come." An aorist was constructed in the Hellenistic period (*hḗxa*). In the papyri we find the meanings "to come to," "to turn to," "to resolve on," and "to attain." The term is important cultically for the coming of deity, especially to cultic participants, and conversely for the coming of these participants to deity. Cultic as well as local use may be found in the LXX, e.g., coming to God in prayer or sacrifice, and God's coming (sometimes eschatological) to redeem or to judge (cf. Ezek. 7:2). In the age of salvation the Gentiles will come and see God's glory (Hag. 2:7). The last time also comes (Ezek. 7:2ff.). Heavy blows (and good things too) come on us during our lives. Josephus has the word for the coming of a point in time (*Jewish War* 7.323). The main use in the NT is for the final coming of God in salvation and judgment. Jesus looks forward to the future of the kingdom in which Gentiles will share (Mt. 8:11; Lk. 13:29). The end will come after the gospel is preached (Mt. 24:14). Christ will come like a thief (Rev. 3:3; cf. 2:25). 2 Pet. 3:10 refers to the terrible events that will accompany the Lord's coming, and Rev. 18:8 speaks of the plagues that come on Babylon. Days of destruction will also come on Jerusalem (Lk. 19:43). In John *hḗkein,* like *érchesthai,* is used to express epiphany. Jesus has come forth from God (8:42). In 2:4 his hour has not yet come. We know that the Son has come (1 Jn. 5:20). At the same time those whom the Father gives will come to him (Jn. 6:37). The Jews in Rome come to question Paul (Acts 28:23). The term has a cultic ring when linked with *proskyneín* (Rev. 3:9)
                                                                [J. SCHNEIDER, II, 926-28]

Hēl(e)ías [Elijah]

A. Elijah in Later Judaism. No biblical figure influenced later Judaism more than Elijah (cf. 1 Kgs. 17–18; 2 Chr. 21:12ff.; Mal. 3:23-24; Sir. 48:1ff.; Eth. En. 89:52, etc.; 1 Macc. 2:58; Philo, Josephus, rabbinic writings, and Elijah apocalypses). The reasons for Elijah's prominence are his mysterious rapture (2 Kgs. 2:11) and the prophecy of his return (Mal. 4:5-6). His miracles provide rich material for legend, and his rapture offers assurance that he gives supernatural aid. In apocalyptic he has the role of a heavenly scribe as well as Israel's intercessor.

3. The Return of Elijah.

a. In the oldest passage (Mal. 4:5-6) Elijah will return as a messianic figure who prepares the way of the heavenly King (3:1) by purifying the priesthood (3:2ff.) and establishing peace (4:6). In Sirach he will restore the twelve tribes (48:10). For the rabbis Elijah will come from Gad as a military deliverer.

b. Later, Elijah prepares the way of the Messiah rather than God (cf. many rabbinic passages and Justin *Dialogue* 8.4). The Damascus Document expects the coming of a teacher of truth (the term for its own founder) who is equated by some with Elijah. It also speaks of a past and coming Messiah, and there is a possibility that the Messiah, not Elijah, is the expected teacher of truth.

c. Another common view is that Elijah is the high priest of the last time (cf. Zech. 4:1ff.). Probably underlying this idea is a combination of Mal. 3:1 and 4:5-6 with 2:4-5 (the angel of the covenant and the covenant with Levi). In the NT it may be noted that the Baptist is of priestly descent and that in Rev. 11:3ff. Elijah and Moses are two olive trees (cf. Zech. 4:3, 11ff.); the olive trees of Zechariah are usually expounded as representing the priesthood and monarchy.

4. The Task of the Returning Elijah. Elijah's coming announces the age of salvation. His task is the restoration of the people: a. inner restoration, setting up peaceful relations by preaching repentance, solving disputed issues of the law; b. outer restoration, establishing purity of blood and regathering the scattered people; c. proclamation of salvation, conflict with antichrist, and introduction of the Messiah (though the two latter functions occur only outside the older rabbinic literature).

B. Elijah in the NT.

1. The Historical Elijah in the NT. Mentioned some 29 times in the NT (behind only Moses [73 times] and David [59]), Elijah receives attention a. for proclaiming the 3½-year drought and famine (Lk. 4:25; Jms. 5:17; Rev. 11:6; cf. 1 Kgs. 17:1), which he both starts and ends by his effective prayer as a righteous man (Jms. 5:16-17), not by some special endowment; b. because he offers a model of ministering to Gentiles (Lk. 4:25-26); c. because of the assurance he is given of the 7,000 who have not bowed the knee to Baal (Rom. 11:2ff., and cf. Lk. 22:43 for resemblances to 1 Kgs. 19:5, 7); and d. because of the divine judgment that he brings down on opponents in 2 Kgs. 1:10, 12, and that is probably in the minds of the sons of Zebedee in Lk. 9:54 when Jesus shows them that such an act is incompatible with his saving mission.

2. The Later Jewish Conception of Elijah in the NT.

a. The idea of Elijah as a helper in time of need is recognized only as a popular belief in the NT (Mk. 15:35-36; Mt. 27:47, 49). When Jesus cries "Eli, Eli," some spectators think he is appealing to Elijah for help, and when this help does not come his messianic claim is disproved. For Christians, Christ is himself the one intercessor whose help is to be sought in time of need.

b. The expectation that Elijah will return is everywhere apparent in the Gospels (Mk. 9:11 etc.). There is speculation whether the Baptist is Elijah (Jn. 1:21) or even Jesus (Mk. 6:15), especially in view of his miracles (Lk. 9:7-8). Elijah is expected as the forerunner (Mk. 9:11) with a task of restoration (Mk. 9:12) through preaching repentance (Rev. 11:3). The "must" of Mk. 9:11 shows that this expectation is thought to have a biblical basis.

3. The NT Understanding of Expectation of Elijah and Its Fulfilment in the Baptist.

a. Whether the Baptist thought of himself as Elijah is hard to say. He certainly does not view himself as Elijah's forerunner. In support of self-identification with the returning Elijah one might cite his preaching of repentance, his clothing (Mk. 1:6), and the views expressed in Lk. 1:14ff. On the other hand, the hairy mantle is a common prophetic garment (Zech. 13:4), and the views of the people and even his disciples are not necessarily his own (cf. Jn. 1:20-21). What John seeks to be is probably just the anonymous voice in the wilderness (Jn. 1:23; cf. Is. 40:3).

b. A scribal argument against the messiahship of Jesus is that Elijah has not yet returned (cf. also the disciples in Mk. 9:11). Jesus answers this by hinting in Mk. 9:13 and stating openly in Mt. 11:14 that the Baptist has fulfilled the prophecy of Malachi, though the "if you are willing to accept it" of Mt. 11:14 suggests that this is a new interpretation which is significant because Jesus places himself under Scripture, views the restoration as religious rather than political, sees the closeness of the end, and with the execution of John faces his own imminent crucifixion. In accepting the fact that John fulfils the expectation of Elijah (Mk. 1:2), the NT consciously confesses Jesus' own messiahship.

4. Elijah's Appearance on the Mount of Transfiguration. This story (Mk. 9:4-5 and par.) is interesting because older rabbinic sources do not associate Moses and Elijah in this way. Various theories have been advanced in interpretation, e.g., that the two represent law and prophecy, or the unveiling of the heavenly world, or the harbinger and forerunner, or two escorts of an oriental king, or two Iranian messengers, precursors, companions, or deities. Pre-Christian apocalyptic certainly refers to two forerunners (cf. Mk. 9:4-5), but these are usually Enoch and Elijah, not Moses and Elijah as in Mk. 9:4 and Rev. 11:3ff. At the transfiguration, Moses and Elijah are probably precursors whose appearance proclaims the inauguration of the end-time. As suffering figures, they also intimate the passion (cf. Mk. 8:31ff. and Lk. 9:31).

5. The Suffering Elijah. Only once in the NT is Elijah's coming still future, i.e., in Rev. 11:3ff., where Elijah and Moses are the two preachers of repentance who will be killed by the beast and rise again after 3½ days (in identification cf. the drought and the changing of water into blood in 11:6 [1 Kgs. 17:1 and Ex. 7:17]). A parallel to this may be found in the Elijah Apocalypse, which also speaks of the conflict with antichrist, the martyrdom, the shaming of the corpses, and the rising again, but with Enoch rather than Moses as the second figure. A distinction is that in Revelation the two witnesses do not return to kill antichrist. The tradition is important, however, for it shows that the idea of a suffering forerunner (Mk. 9:12-13) was not unknown in the time of Jesus; the historicity of Jesus' predictions of his own passion is thus supported.

[J. JEREMIAS, II, 928-41]

---

hēlikía [age, stature]

1. This word first means "age," especially of maturity, collectively "contemporaries." 2. It then means "generation." 3. A final sense is "physical size," "growth," though this does not occur in the papyri, where the word often has the legal sense of "maturity." The meaning "age" is the most common one in Philo and the LXX. In the NT "stature" is the sense in Lk. 19:3. This might be the meaning in Mt. 6:27 and Lk. 12:25, but the context favors "span of life." Maturity is the point in Jn. 9:21, 23, age of virility in Heb. 11:11, and "years" rather than "stature" in Lk. 2:52. Eph. 4:13 is theologically significant when it posits maturity as the goal of the Christian life. Whether we think of age or physical growth is immaterial here. The church is to achieve its perfect form as "all" come to the stature of the fullness of Christ through

the ministry (vv. 11-12). Christ's fullness is represented in the church when it achieves its divinely ordained form by upbuilding into Christ's body through the ministry of evangelism and edification.   [J. SCHNEIDER, II, 941-43]

---

hēméra [day]

A. "Day" in the OT.

1. The ancient Hebrew day consisted of day and night beginning in the evening (Ex. 12:18). Thus light is created (as distinct from darkness) and day results from the separation of light and darkness (Gen. 1:5). God himself recognizes day and night. Time and its rhythm are God's creation, and all that takes place within the bounds of temporality is under his control (Ps. 31:15).

2. All days are God's, but the secular nature of life demands that special days (the sabbath and cultic feasts) be set apart for God. Other days apart from cultic may also be specially related to God (e.g., the day of Midian in Is. 9:3). There is expectation, too, of a special future "day of the Lord" when his might, his readiness to save, and his judicial power will be manifested. This is not necessarily a final day. Thus the overthrow of Jerusalem is a day of God which can be looked back on in Lam. 1:21. The day of the Lord is similarly a historical rather than an eschatological day in Ezek. 34:12. In Am. 5:18ff. the popular hope is obviously for a great day of salvation, and this day has eschatological features for the prophet when he refers to the cosmic changes it includes. But here again there is a mixture of the political and eschatological. The prophets, however, revise the original idea that the day of the Lord will mean judgment for the Gentiles and salvation for Israel by showing that this day will mean judgment for Israel too (cf. especially Zephaniah).

3. The day of the Lord is not the dominant feature in all prophecy. It is very subsidiary in Hosea, and even predictions of judgment or disaster do not have to refer to it (e.g., Is. 28:14ff.). The fall of Jerusalem is a turning point, for after this judgment the day of the Lord is to be a day of deliverance (cf. the precisely dated change in Ezek. 33:21ff.). Thus the later prophets again view the day of the Lord as a day of judgment for the Gentiles but protection (Zech. 12:1ff.), purification (Mal. 3:2), cleansing (Zech. 13:1-2), endowment with the Spirit (Joel 3), and paradisal waters (Joel 4:18) for Israel. This eschatological prospect is sometimes called the end of days (Is. 2:2; Jer. 23:20, etc.). An eschatological belief is firmly embedded in the OT and in essentials it is identical to this postexilic day of the Lord.

4. The use of the term, while not restricting what takes place to a calendar day, signifies the occurrence of an event. There is a time when God hides his face or visits Jerusalem or when all know him in the new covenant. Yet the term may refer to conditions rather than a specific span of time. Jeremiah, for example, uses the phrase "that time" or "those days" but not the "day of the Lord." Ezekiel combines "time" and "day" in 7:12. Eschatologically the day of the Lord denotes the inauguration of a new era. In Daniel we find a different set of expressions (cf. 8:17; 9:26; 10:14; 11:27; 12:13). A time of affliction will here precede the end of the old aeon and the inauguration of the new.   [G. VON RAD, II, 943-47]

B. General Greek Usage.

1. "Day" as a. "daylight," b. "full day" (24 hours), and c. "day" of the week.

2. "Time" (not common) a. as "time of youth, age, etc.," b. as determined by events, experiences, situations, or moods.

3. Very rarely personified in religion or art (e.g., the daughter of Helios) in sense 1.a.

C. LXX Usage.

1. The word is common in the LXX in senses 1.a. (Gen. 1:5) and 1.b. (Gen. 25:24; Ex. 29:36).

2. Sense 2. is also common in the LXX. We find 2.a. first for lifetime or extended times as historical periods, then in connection with the future as the time of God's action either historically or eschatologically. 2.b. is especially common in the Psalms, e.g., the "day of trouble" in 27:5.

D. NT Usage.

1. hēméra as Day.

a. The time of "daylight"; with *gínesthai* of dawn (Luke and Acts) and *klínein* of sunset (only Lk. 9:12; 24:29); with *báros* for the burden of the full sun (Mt. 20:12); as distinct from night (2 Pet. 2:13); restricted in Rev. 8:12.

b. "Day" as a measure of time from sunrise to sunset or sunrise to sunrise (Lk. 9:37; Acts 21:26), with a number (Mt. 26:2), the "third day" relative to Christ's resurrection (Mk. 8:31 and par.; 9:31 and par., etc.). That Christ rose on the third day is an early part of the tradition (1 Cor. 15:3), so that the influence of mystery religions on the number is unlikely. Three might be used simply as a small number, but the "according to the scriptures" (1 Cor. 15:4) suggests that its significance derives from the fulfilment of Hos. 6:2 (which Jewish exegesis blunted by suppressing the number, changing the days to millennia, or referring the passage to the final resurrection). The difference between the *tē̂ . . . trítē* of Matthew, Luke, and Paul and the *metá treís hēméras* of Mark may be explained by the difference between Greek and Jewish modes of reckoning (cf. Mt. 27:63-64). "Day" is relativized in 2 Pet. 3:8 (cf. Ps. 90:4). For "every day" see 1 Cor. 15:31, and "day by day" 2 Cor. 4:16.

c. For "day of the week" cf. Mk. 16:2, date Rev. 9:15, day of judgment 1 Cor. 4:3, day of fasting or feasting Rom. 14:5-6, day of the Lord Rev. 1:10, sabbath day Lk. 4:16, day of unleavened bread Lk. 22:7, day of preparation Lk. 23:54.

2. hēméra as Time.

a. "Lifetime" etc. (Heb. 5:7; 7:3; 12:10), "period of time" (Rev. 10:7, of future events; Acts 15:7, the early days; 2 Pet. 3:3, the last time prior to judgment; Acts 2:17, the last time as already present; 2 Tim. 3:1, the last time as the time of judgment; Lk. 17:22, the days of the Messiah; Mk. 2:20, the time after Jesus' death). In the singular the word denotes the last age. The stress is on the divine action along the lines of apocalyptic, but still with different nuances as in the Jewish world. Thus in Lk. 17:24 the day of the Son of Man refers to his final coming in glory (cf. Jn. 8:56). In 2 Pet. 3:12 the reference is to the day of God as a day of final conflagration, while in Rev. 16:14 the great day of God is that of conflict with the kings of the earth. In Paul the "day" is the great day of judgment for the church (1 Cor. 1:8) or himself (2 Cor. 1:14) as well as non-Christians; it serves as an ethical incentive. In 2 Th. 2:2 the manifestation of Christ is the primary concern; the day of the Lord here is equivalent to the day of Christ in Philippians. In the absolute, "day" is the day of judgment in 1 Th. 5:5; 1 Cor. 3:13; Heb. 10:25 (cf. "that day" in Mt. 7:22 etc., and "great day" in Jude 6; Rev. 6:17, etc.). The day of Christ's manifestation and the day of judgment are, of course, the same. The content may sometimes be denoted by phrases like day of judgment in Mt. 11:22, wrath in Rom. 2:5, and redemption in Eph. 4:30. The last day is also used for the day of resurrection in Jn. 6:39-40 etc. But day may simply denote a point of time, as in Col. 1:6, 9, or a period as in Jms. 5:5; 1 Pet. 2:12— these two passages are probably not eschatological.

b. With further definition we have the evil day of Eph. 6:13, the day of testing in Heb. 3:8, birthday in Mk. 6:21, and good days in 1 Pet. 3:10.

3. In Rev. 11:9, 11 days are used figuratively for years. Day is also figurative in Jn. 9:4 (2.a.) and Jn. 11:9b (1.a.). In Rom. 13:12-13 the time after Christ's resurrection is the time of daylight when Christians, as those who share its brightness (1 Th. 5:5), must shun the works of darkness. In 2 Pet. 1:19 the word of God, like a lamp in a dark place, brings the day which scatters the powers of darkness.

[G. DELLING, II, 947-53]

Ēsaú [Esau]

---

1. Paul uses Esau's rejection typologically in Rom. 9:13 to show that God's counsel does not depend on human privilege or merit. Esau is also a descendant of Abraham but is not chosen even though he is born first and has done neither good nor evil. There are no parallels for this use of the story; Jewish exegesis tends to explain Esau's rejection by his evil works.

2. In Heb. 11:20 Isaac invokes blessings on Esau as well as Jacob. Again Jewish exegesis thinks Jacob has precedence because God foresees Esau's wickedness.

3. In Heb. 12:16 Esau is given as an example of the immoral and irreligious person who wants, too late, to reverse his wrong decision.   [H. ODEBERG, II, 953-54]

ēchéō [to sound]

---

a. Intransitive "to sound," "ring," "boom," "peal"; b. transitive "to cause to sound"; middle "to sing." The word finds varied use in the LXX for the sounding of a zither (Is. 16:11), the roaring of the sea (Is. 51:15), the tumult of enemies (Ps. 83:2), the howling of a dog (Ps. 59:6), the tinkling of the priestly bells (Sir. 45:9), and blowing on trumpets (Sir. 50:16). The only NT instance is in 1 Cor. 13:1: Ecstatic speech without love is like a clanging cymbal, which may attract attention and enthuse the hearers but has no moral or spiritual worth. The *chalkós* is usually taken to be the gong that hung in temples or on sacred trees and whose long and booming notes were struck by orgiastic cults to induce ecstasy.   [J. SCHNEIDER, II, 954-55]

θ *th*

Thamár [Tamar],   *Rhacháb* [Rahab],   *Rhoúth* [Ruth],   *hē toú Ouríou* [the wife of Uriah]

---

1. The inclusion of women in Jesus' genealogy is surprising, but even more so is the substitution of these four women (Mt. 1:3, 5, 6) for the four ancestral mothers of Israel. The point is that these women have a place here, even though they are sinners and aliens, because the history of the people of the Messiah is one of grace working

through the fall and making the last first (cf. 1 Cor. 1:27ff.). Rabbinic exegesis may sometimes excuse these women, but Matthew does not do this, nor is he producing them merely as types of Mary, and certainly not to justify a supposed illegitimacy of Jesus.

2. Rabbinic exegesis does in fact mitigate the sins of Tamar etc. a. In Gen. 38 the OT itself attributes the sin to Judah more than to Tamar (Gen. 38:26), though rabbinic exegesis tends (not without dissent) to excuse Judah too. b. Rahab is extolled as a proselyte and tool of the Spirit (cf. in the NT Heb. 11:31; Jms. 2:25), who is the ancestress of many priests and prophets (e.g., Jeremiah), though she is nowhere put in the Davidic line. c. That David had an alien as ancestress might be regarded as a serious blemish, but rabbinic exegesis stresses her conversion and the divine overruling; the suggestion is also made that the implied humiliation makes for a more lasting exaltation. d. Various reasons are advanced in some circles to exculpate Bathsheba and David, e.g., that Uriah might have divorced Bathsheba on going to war, or that he was in revolt against David. On the other hand, Shammai and others freely admit David's guilt. [G. KITTEL, III, 1-3]

> *thámbos* [astonishment],   *thambéō* [to be astonished],   *ékthambos* [utterly astonished],   *ekthambéomai* [to be amazed]

---

1. The basic meaning of the group is "to be astonished," then "to be affrighted." Thus divine manifestations or miracles can cause astonishment or fear and trembling. Plutarch links *thámbos* and superstition; true piety flourishes only on rational soil.

2. The group is not much used in the LXX, nor does it have a fixed Hebrew original. (For the various words rendered by it see *TDNT,* III, 5.) In general the psychological element is dominant in instances of the group, but the element of the occasional is less prominent; something mysterious and impalpable is at work in human *thámbos*.

3. Astonishment is again linked with sight in the NT: Mk. 9:15; 16:5-6; Acts 3:10-11, etc. Yet the element of epiphany rather than the external form arouses astonishment or fear. With cognate expressions, the terms stress the revelatory content and christological significance of incidents (cf. Mk. 1:27). The words also serve to accredit the miracles (Lk. 4:36). But Jesus' strict demand for discipleship also kindles astonishment and fear because of our human inability to meet it (Mk. 10:24ff.; cf. Lk. 5:9-10). The fact that the disciples are in the hands of the Lord probably causes their amazement and fear in Mk. 10:32. This pious awe is a preparatory stage of faith. In Mk. 14:33 we are perhaps to see a christological understanding of, e.g., Ps. 31:22. The incident not only sheds light on the historical character of Jesus (contrary to Docetism) but brings out the element of epiphany in Gethsemane by presenting the "fearful" Christ as the bearer of divine revelation. [G. BERTRAM, III, 4-7]

> *thánatos* [death],   *thnḗskō* [to die],   *apothnḗskō* [to die],   *synapothnḗskō* [to die with someone],   *thanatóō* [to kill],   *thnētós* [mortal],   *athanasía* [immortality],   *(athánatos* [immortal]*)*

---

thánatos, thnḗskō, apothnḗskō, synapothnḗskō.

A. *thánatos* in Greek Usage.

1. Classical Usage. Death destroys life; the shadowy existence of the dead in Hades is no true life. The most that may be expected is the survival or transmigration of the soul. All must die, so that death casts a shadow on life and its meaning. Yet death brings release from the dubious boon of life. Thus suicide may be liberation. Yet no one wants to die, and there is no knowledge of what comes after it. Heroes live on immortally in their renown, for it is good to die for the *pólis*. Death is seen as a natural phenomenon. The *psyché* lives on as the vital force in the cosmos, but only as the birth of one is the death of another. This does not solve the riddle or remove the terror of individual death. Plato lifts the issue to another plane by giving precedence to the question of right and wrong. The point, then, is to die a good death. Indeed, death can be the fulfilment of life by rising above the mortal body. On this basis the hope arises that the soul will live on. Aristotle follows the same reasoning, except that for him it is the *noús* that survives in some obscure way.

2. Hellenistic Usage.

a. Stoicism. For the Stoics, death is a natural phenomenon. It has to be accepted as such and in this way may become an ethical act. Death as well as life is a matter of individual decision, and since life is indifferent, and its goods are viewed pessimistically, responsible suicide is justifiable. Death serves a useful purpose as a test of right conduct, i.e., whether we turn from external things, accept our destiny, and are thus ready when death strikes. Death does not have the character of judgment, but those who focus on external things have no true life and may thus be described as already dead.

b. Neo-Platonism. Bodily life is here regarded as involving death for the *psyché*. The soul attains true life only by progressive release from the body. Death is good inasmuch as it completes this release, but suicide is an illegitimate way of hastening the process.

c. Gnosticism. Here again true life cannot develop in the body, but true life is now the immortality of divine life, and transition to it is made with ascetic mortification, or in the mystery religions with sacramentalized experiences of a mystical or ecstatic nature. Life is finally attained with the putting off of the soul in transmigration or the ascent to heaven.

d. Philo. Philo follows Stoicism and Neo-Platonism in describing the wicked as already dead. Physical death itself is either indifferent or good. But there is also a death that is eternal destruction.

B. The Concept of Death in the NT.

1. In the NT *thánatos* means "dying" (Heb. 7:23) or "being dead" (Phil. 1:20). Death is our human lot, remote only from God (1 Tim. 6:16). It is never presented in heroic terms, not even as self-sacrificial death (2 Cor. 4:12) or martyrdom (Rev. 2:10). Death is a terrible thing that makes *zōḗ* improper *zōḗ*, and the work of Christ is that of destroying death (2 Tim. 1:10). Death is the last enemy; with its overthrow salvation will be complete (1 Cor. 15:26; Rev. 20:14). It is nowhere neutralized as merely a natural process. It belongs together with sin, and stands opposed to *zōḗ* as the true being of God.

2. Death is the consequence and punishment of sin. Its origin is not treated speculatively, for even if Paul views it as a cosmic power, it results from a responsible act (Rom. 5:12ff.). That Adam was created only a "living soul" might perhaps imply natural mortality, but *thánatos* came into the world through Adam's sin (Rom. 5:12, 17). This does not excuse us, for we are responsible for our own sin and our own death. The ineluctability of sin and death serves merely to bring out the fact that there is salvation only in Christ. The law is what effects death, for as Adam disobeyed God's

command and pagans transgress his just requirement (Rom. 1:32), so in Israel the law awakens slumbering sin and enforces death as its penalty (cf. Rom. 7; 2 Cor. 3:7). Our sinful being is what Paul calls *sárx*. This is neither matter, nor a prison of the soul, nor a demonic power, but the lost self seen in terms of the corruptible sphere (Rom. 2:28-29). Wanting to live for ourselves, we are subject to death, and all self-efforts to escape this entangle us in the same vicious circle (Rom. 7:10). The message of John is materially the same. Outside the revelation in Jesus we are all sinful and thus rightly given up to death. Sin is seeing the self in terms of the self instead of God. Thus the self sets up its own criteria (5:31ff.), imagines it is free (8:33), and has its own standards of glory (5:41ff.).

3. The NT sometimes portrays death as purely destructive and sometimes as involving future torment (cf. Mk. 9:48). Yet God or Christ judges both the living and the dead, so that physical death is followed by judgment and resurrection. No detailed teaching is given on the intermediate state, but physical death becomes definitive death (the second death, Rev. 2:11; 20:6, 14; 21:8) through judgment. Even now, however, death robs life of its true quality. It imposes fear (Heb. 2:15). It casts a shadow and darkness (Lk. 1:79). It reigns over what is carnal (Rom. 8:6). Outside Christ, we might as well eat and drink, for tomorrow we die (1 Cor. 15:32). Death brings uncertainty (Mt. 6:25ff.). Human works are dead from the outset (Heb. 9:14). As sinners, we are already dead (Mt. 8:22; cf. Rom. 7:10, 24; Jn. 5:21).

4. Christ's death and resurrection are the eschatological event by which death itself is destroyed (2 Tim. 1:10; Heb. 2:14). Christ's death is unique. It is not a death to sin; God made him sin for us (2 Cor. 5:21; Rom. 8:3; Gal. 3:13-14), and he died for us. In him God deals with us, takes death to himself, and thus makes it a creative divine act. This removes sin and death, and from it life springs, for Christ is not held by death (Acts 2:24), comes to life again (Rom. 8:34), and now has the keys of death and Hades (Rev. 1:18). Giving his life, he takes it again (Jn. 10:18). Humbling himself, he is divinely exalted (Phil. 2:6ff.). He thus overcomes death for those who make his death their own in faith. He is the firstborn from the dead (Col. 1:18; Rev. 1:5). Believers still die, except for those alive at Christ's coming (1 Th. 4:15ff.). But they will finally overcome death at the resurrection (1 Cor. 15:26; Rev. 21:4), so that even now death has lost its sting (1 Cor. 15:55). As impending death negates life for unbelievers, awaited resurrection gives it a new character for believers. They will not die (Jn. 6:50). They have passed from death to life (5:24). This life is not their own possession (2 Tim. 2:18; cf. the probable belief of the Corinthians). But death's destruction is already present in hope on the basis of the gospel. It takes place in the obedience of faith, which is acceptance of Christ's death, i.e., dying with Christ (Rom. 6:3-4) worked out in a new way of life which we must grasp with intelligent resolve (Rom. 6:11). Thus the destruction of sin and death manifests itself in mortification and the fulfilment of God's righteous demand (Rom. 8:2ff.). Believers no longer live for self but for the Lord who died for all, so that all are dead in him (Rom. 14:7ff.; 2 Cor. 5:14-15). In the cross the world is crucified for believers and believers for the world (Gal. 2:19-20; 6:14). Proclamation of Christ's death in the Lord's Supper demands worthy conduct (1 Cor. 11:27ff.; cf. 5:7-8). Yet this conduct does not itself overcome death. The goal is already reached with Christ's death, so that boasting is ruled out (Rom. 3:27) and we are dead to the law (7:6); its reimposition robs the death of Christ of its effect (Gal. 2:19ff.). The Christian walk is participation in this death (Phil. 3:9, 14). This participation also gives a new meaning to sufferings as a daily dying in which the message is brought to others (cf. especially Col. 1:24) or an

example is given to them (1 Pet. 2:18ff.). Union with Christ in dying is a sure ground of comfort. We die in Christ (1 Th. 4:16). We are thus blessed (Rev. 14:13). We die for the Lord's name (Acts 21:13). This is to God's glory (Jn. 21:19). Death is not taken idealistically here. The new walk and understanding do not themselves defeat death. Based on the event of Christ's death and resurrection, they are part of a movement of consummation. We are dead, but our life is hidden (Col. 3:3). Our present life being provisional, we long for physical death or the parousia (2 Cor. 5:1ff.). Yet this provisional life is service of the Lord (even if to die is gain, Phil. 1:21). Both death and life are thus relativized (Rom. 8:38), but only for believers, for Christ's work has made death final for those to whom the gospel spreads death (2 Cor. 2:16) and who thus abide in death (1 Jn. 3:14).

thanatóō. This word means "to kill," "to give up to death," "to condemn to death." It has these senses in the NT: "to kill" in Mk. 13:12; 1 Pet. 3:18; "to give up to death" in Rom. 8:36; "to condemn to death" in Mk. 14:55. The use is figurative ("to mortify") in Rom. 8:13.

thnētós. This word, meaning "mortal," is used by the Greeks to characterize humans in contrast to the gods (cf. in the LXX Job 30:23; Prov. 3:13). Paul uses it as a comprehensive term for human nature in 1 Cor. 15:53-54. In 2 Cor. 5:4 he longs for the swallowing up of what is mortal by life. In particular the *sárx* or *sōma* is mortal (2 Cor. 4:11; Rom. 6:12; 8:11). The apostolic fathers and Apologists similarly see in *thnētós* a typical human attribute; the latter can also apply the term to pagan deities in polemical sections (e.g., Tatian 21.2).

athanasía (athánatos) (→ zōḗ, thánatos).

1. *athanasía* is primarily a literary term meaning "immortality." This belongs properly to the gods. Whether the soul is immortal is debated. The school of Plato adopts this view. In Hellenism the demand for it is great but belief in it meager. Pantheistic Stoicism finds impersonal immortality in the cosmos, while individual immortality is sought in the mysteries, magic, and mysticism. This immortality is more than duration; it is participation in the blissful divine nature, i.e., divinization. Anything superhuman may thus be called immortal, e.g., seers, rulers, and all things pneumatic (e.g., Christian knowledge in 1 Clem. 36.2). A supposed food of immortality or medicine of life is a common notion (cf. Sir. 6:16 and Ignatius *Ephesians* 20.2).

2. The OT has no equivalent for *athanasía,* but the LXX uses it for the future life of the righteous (Wis. 3:4; 4 Macc. 14:5). The word is common in Philo, and occurs in Josephus in references to Eleazar, Titus, the Essenes, and the Pharisees.

3. In the NT *athánatos* does not occur, and we find *athanasía* only in 1 Cor. 15:53-54 (the incorruptible mode of existence in the resurrection) and 1 Tim. 6:16 (God alone has immortality in himself). In both instances the form of expression shows the influence of Hellenistic Judaism.   [R. BULTMANN, III, 7-25]

→ *zōḗ*

---

tharréō (tharséō) [to be confident, courageous]

1. In its two forms (*tharséō* is the older) this word has the basic sense "to dare," "to be bold," "to be of good courage," "to be cheerful or confident," and then a. "to trust in," "rely on," and b. "to be bold against someone or something," "to go out

bravely to." The LXX always has the basic sense. While Plato suggests that boldness in face of death is possible only where there is awareness of the soul's immortality, the LXX uses the term as a summons in time of stress or emergency, and God's readiness to help is the basis. God himself issues the summons in Hag. 2:5; Zech. 8:13; he stakes himself by way of guarantee.

2. In the NT Jesus issues the summons to be of good courage (Mt. 9:2, 22; 14:27). What he gives or is backs the summons. His own claim lies behind it; in encounter with him God's is a liberating action. The gospel thus gives joy and confidence, chasing away anxiety, bringing us into God's fatherly goodness. The risen Lord issues the same summons to Paul in prison (Acts 23:11). The disciples live in a threatening world, but they may be of good courage because Christ has overcome it (Jn. 16:33). Their boldness does not rest on a dubious theory of the soul's immortality, nor on a process of initiation and deification, but on the historical event of Christ's victorious death and resurrection. History replaces myth, and fulfilment longing. Though we are now separated from Christ, we are still of good courage (2 Cor. 5:6, 8), for we have the pledge of the Spirit (v. 5) and move toward the consummation. Heb. 13:6 finds a ground for courage during persecution in the fact that the Lord is our helper. An instance of "to have confidence in" occurs in 2 Cor. 7:16, and Paul is "bold against" the Corinthians when absent according to his ironic statement in 2 Cor. 10:1.

[W. GRUNDMANN, III, 25-27]

---

thaúma [wonder],   *thaumázō* [to wonder],   *thaumásios* [wonderful], *thaumastós* [wonderful]

A. The Use of the Word Group in Secular Greek. The group has first the sense of astonishment, whether critical or inquisitive, then admiration, with a nuance of awe or fear at what is unusual or mysterious, e.g., miracles or oracles in religion, also magical acts or media, and certain phenomena (prior to their explanation) in philosophy.

B. The Use of the Word Group in Greek Judaism.
1. The Greek OT. The group finds varied use here for many unconnected Hebrew words. It serves to denote religious experience face to face with what transcends human possibilities. a. In the negative (Prov. 6:30, no MT) it introduces something self-evident. The group also finds a use for God's nonrespecting of persons (Dt. 10:17), or having respect to someone in prayer (Gen. 19:21). In human relations, judges should not be guilty of respect of persons (cf. Is. 9:14). Partiality is also the issue in Lev. 19:15 etc., while the point in Job 22:8 is flattery. b. At times the LXX uses the group for astonishment so as to stress the effect of a fact or event on those who see it (cf. Job 11:13; 42:11). In particular, it brings out the wonderful and inexplicable ways of God in relation to problems of theodicy. Yet it may express horror at divine judgment (as in Job 17:8; cf. Lev. 26:32) as well as wonder at divine direction (Ex. 34:10; cf. Job 42:3 and especially the Psalms, e.g., 45:4). In 2 Sam. 1:26 the reference is to the wonderful love of friends, and in 2 Chr. 26:15 to the miraculous help of God. In Sir. 39:20 the idea is that nothing is impossible for God, but while the wonderful thing may be what is humanly impossible, it may also be something great or glorious (cf. Ex. 34:10; Job 5:9). The element of the dreadful in miracle comes out at times (cf. Job 41:1; Am. 3:9). Verbs of seeing may be linked with the group to bring out

the idea of startled astonishment (Hab. 1:5). A negative sense may be seen in Is. 52:14, where the offense is caused by God but the verb brings out the human reaction of those who do not understand. God, who is wonderful in his works (Ps. 68:35), does wonders of salvation and judgment (Ex. 3:20 etc.), and everything connected with him—his name, house, etc.—can have the attribute of the wonderful. c. This attribute may also apply to his people, the saints, the righteous, and especially martyrs, although it is only in the Hellenistic writings that we find this usage with its dangers of exaggeration and profanation (cf. the heroine cult of Jdt. 10:19 and the martyr motifs of Maccabees). The canonical books, in contrast, forbid us to enter of ourselves into the sphere of divine wonder (Ex. 19:12; cf. the sign-seeking of the NT in Mt. 12:38ff.). The proper attitude is not to occupy oneself with things that are too marvelous (Ps. 131:1). The title *thaumastós* is also one that is intrinsically unbiblical. (For a detailed linguistic study, see *TDNT,* III, 29-36.)

2. In Philo and Josephus the secular and legendary motifs are stronger. Stress is placed on the wonderful events of OT history. For Philo, wonder at creation may lead to admiration of its Creator, though it may also remain fixed on the world. Either way, there is little true sense of awe at divine revelation. The terms are used within a rational view of things, may be applied to sages and prophets, and in general promote religion rather than magnifying God.

C. **The Use of the Word Group in the NT.** While the NT use agrees externally with that of the OT, the secularizing of the group in the Hellenistic period means that it cannot have the same linguistic or theological significance, that the instances are neither so numerous nor important, and that there are strong differences in the different sections of the NT.

1. a. Most of the passages occur in the Synoptists (especially Luke) in relation to the miracle stories. The purpose of the term is to describe the effect on the spectators (e.g., Mk. 5:20; Lk. 11:14). In Mt. 9:33, however, what is brought out is the significance of the event as part of NT salvation history. The same is true of Mt. 15:31. In Mt. 9:8, where *ethaúmasan* is a variant reading, the term serves to express joyful astonishment that Jesus not only gives himself for sin but himself personally forgives our sins. The stilling of the storm also causes astonishment (Mt. 8:27; Lk. 8:25), but Matthew finds this too weak at the walking on the water and substitutes "worship" (Mt. 14:33). The astonishment at the withering of the fig tree in Mt. 21:20 perhaps carries an element of doubt in view of the reply of Jesus in vv. 21-22. The teaching of Jesus causes astonishment as well as his deeds. In Lk. 4:22 the hearers are surprised by the charm but also by the gracious content of Jesus' sermon, though they remain critical. In the tax debate the astonishment is at the wisdom of the answer (Mt. 22:22), but surprise is the point in Lk. 11:38 (the Pharisees), Mk. 15:5 (Pilate when Jesus will not defend himself against such flimsy charges), and Mk. 15:44 (Pilate again when he hears that Jesus has died so quickly). Doubt and wonder intermingle in the *thaumázein* of Lk. 24:12 and 24:41 relative to the resurrection. In the infancy stories in Luke the use of *thaumázein* (1:21, 63; 2:18, 33) gives a sense of the divine action and revelation in the events. In Mk. 12:11 Jesus himself quotes Ps. 118:22-23 to denote the response to God's working—a response which is only preliminary to faith, since it may contain elements of surprise, doubt, or mere admiration as well as awe at the manifest operation of God.

b. Twice Jesus himself is astonished, first at the lack of belief in Nazareth (Mk. 6:6), and second at the faith of the Capernaum centurion (Mt. 8:10; Lk. 7:9).

c. Acts follows Synoptic usage, linking the group with miraculous events in 2:7; 3:12; 7:31 (the burning bush). Hab. 1:5 is quoted as a warning in 13:41 with the accent on the negative element.

3. John does not use the term for individual miracles or for the psychological response but for the impact of Jesus' works (5:20; 7:21). It indicates the disciples' misunderstanding in 4:27, 33. There is exhortation not to marvel in 3:7; 5:28 (cf. 1 Jn. 3:13); they are not to doubt or take offense.

4. In Paul *thaumázein* is a literary form in Gal. 1:6; 2 Cor. 11:4. In the passive in 2 Th. 1:10 the reference is to the eschatological manifestation of God's glory in which the community shares; the word is here parallel to "glorified."

5. Jude 16 follows OT usage for flattery, while 1 Pet. 2:9 has a more Hellenistic ring when it speaks of our calling into God's "marvelous" light.

6. Revelation uses the group six times. In 13:3 the earth follows the beast with wonder (probably a first step to cultic adoration in view of v. 4; cf. the imperial cult of Rome). It is because of the close relation to worship that the seer is forbidden to marvel in 17:6-7. In 15:1 a sign from heaven is called great and wonderful, and God's works are great and wonderful in 15:3. The usage here is similar to that of the Psalms.

D. The Word Group in Early Christian Usage. There is nothing distinctive here except in the dominical saying preserved in Clement of Alexandria *Stromateis* 2.9.45.4 (cf. 5.14.96.3), which echoes a motif in Platonic philosophy and thus suggests a mystical misunderstanding of the biblical concept. The provisional nature of wonder is lost in 1 Clem. 1.2 when the wonderful in a weaker sense is linked to Christian blessings, but theological particularity is maintained is 2 Clem. 2.6; 13.3-4. The use in early martyrology is similar to that of 4 Maccabees.   [G. BERTRAM, III, 27-42]

theáomai → *horáō*

---

theatron [theater, spectacle],   **theatrízomai** [to expose publicly]

The word *théatron* (not in the LXX) denotes a. "theater or amphitheater," b. "audience," and c. "play" or "spectacle." The Stoics use it in sense c. (also *théama*) to express the thought that the sage in conflict with destiny is a spectacle for gods and men. This usage is echoed in 1 Cor. 4:9 (cf. Heb. 10:33), but 1. there is also here recollection of the public sufferings of Job, 2. this *théatron* is a sorry one rather than a proud one, and 3. the stress is not on human autonomy but on divine operation, so that unbelievers might very well miss the point of this *théatron*.

[G. KITTEL, III, 42-43]

theíos, theiótēs → *theós*

---

thélō [to wish, desire],   **thélēma** [will],   **thélēsis** [will]

---

thélō. On the relation to *boúlomai,* see *boúlomai* above. In secular Greek and the LXX the word *thélō* has such varied meanings as "to purpose," "to be ready," "to resolve," "to desire," "to wish," "to prefer," and negatively "to refuse." It may be used for the divine will or the royal will. It is common in the OT in the negative.

A. The Common Greek Meaning of *(e)thélō*.

1. A first sense is "to be ready" (with a nuance "to consent") or "to like."

2. We then find "to want," sometimes in an erotic sense leading to "to come together" and even "to conceive," but also, with no erotic sense, "to like," "to take pleasure in," primarily, in the LXX, with a human subject.

3. Expressing intention, the word may then denote "to wish," "to be about to do something," "to be used to doing something," "to intend."

4. The word also expresses resolve as free or weighed decision, sometimes with the idea of choice or preference, and religiously with the nuance of resolute willingness (considered or stubborn refusal in the negative).

5. *thélein* may also denote the will that commands, e.g., God's rule and purpose in creation and history, or the rule, decrees, or orders of rulers, officials, and military leaders.

B. Significant Features in the NT Use of *thélein* from the Standpoint of Biblical Theology.

1. The thélein of God. God's *thélein* is characterized by definiteness, assurance, and efficacy. In Mt. 27:43 (quoting Ps. 22:8) it expresses divine desire or delight, but elsewhere it refers to God's sovereign will in creation (1 Cor. 12:18) or salvation (Jn. 3:8; 1 Tim. 2:4). In the parable in Mt. 20:14-15 God's freedom of disposal is the point. Paul shows how this works out in salvation and judgment in Rom. 9:18, 22. The saving will of God is declared to the Gentiles in Col. 1:27. In contrast stands the pseudoclaim of the devil in Lk. 4:6. God's *thélein* also expresses his demands upon his people, especially mercy rather than sacrifice (Mt. 9:13; Heb. 10:5, 8). It further denotes God's direction in the lives of his people; thus we are to suffer for doing right if that is God's will (1 Pet. 3:17).

2. The thélein of Jesus.

a. The disciples accept the power of Jesus' will, as in the request of Lk. 9:54, or the readiness to follow in Mk. 14:12. This will initiates the miracle of Mt. 15:32ff. It may be seen in his choice of the disciples in Mk. 3:13 and his healing work in Mk. 1:40-41; Mt. 8:2-3. It extends to raising the dead in Jn. 5:21, or (in prayer) to granting the disciples a vision of his glory in Jn. 17:23. The whole future of the disciples rests upon this omnipotent will of the Son (21:21).

b. Yet the will of Jesus in his earthly calling bears witness to his sharing our humanity. Thus his will may be thwarted in Mk. 7:24. Indeed, human rejection can frustrate his saving purpose (Mt. 23:37; Lk. 12:49). The prayer in Gethsemane implies the possibility of an independent human will that is set aside in voluntary submission to the divine will (Mk. 14:36; Mt. 26:39).

3. The thélein of Paul in His Authoritative Apostolic Dealings with the Churches. Paul is fond of *thélein* either when stressing points of teaching (1 Th. 4:13; 1 Cor. 10:1; 12:1; Rom. 11:25), making personal statements (Rom. 1:3), expressing intention in controversy (Gal. 3:2), or giving pastoral direction (1 Cor. 7:32).

4. Religious thélein and Its Opposite in the NT.

a. In the Synoptists *thélein* may express religious striving, e.g., that of Jewish piety in Mt. 19:17, or the will for discipleship in Mk. 8:34. A misguided wish is at issue in Mk. 10:35 and Gal. 4:21. On the other hand, the wish of Mt. 15:28 implies faith with its orientation to Christ's power (cf. Mk. 10:51). In Jn. 7:17 we have a readiness to do God's will which becomes effective prayer in 15:7, a will for sanctification in Heb. 13:18, and a will for true life in 1 Pet. 3:10 (cf. the determinative role of *thélein* in Mt. 7:12). In Rev. 22:17 the desire for the water of life may be met by coming to Christ, i.e., by faith.

b. In Paul religious *thélein* is linked with verbs of doing. God himself wills and does in Phil. 2:3. Giving follows a ready will in 2 Cor. 8:10-11. Desires and doing interact in Gal. 5:17. In Rom. 7, however, *thélein* under the law, apart from faith and the Spirit, cannot be put into action. What is willed is not done; what is not willed is done. This impotent *thélein* consents to the law and even delights in it (vv. 16, 22), but cannot get beyond the intention to do it. A cleavage is at issue here which is a matter, not merely of keeping specific commands, but of life and death. Yet the perversion of being in legalism also involves concrete transgression. Only the Spirit, not the law itself, can give force to the will and enable it to meet the law's just demand (8:4). In attempts at self-righteousness, the will is enslaved to *sárx*; in Christ it is liberated by the Spirit. Parallels to Rom. 7 may be seen in Epictetus, who argues that there is something in life that does not conform to what is desired, and that while we will to be free, we are bound by the body. But in Epictetus the first problem is mostly one of ignorance, while the body, being a secondary matter, need not be the serious obstacle that *sárx* is in Paul, for whom true freedom of the will comes only as the spiritual will replaces the legal will through the ministry of Christ and the Spirit. As Rom. 9:16 puts it, will and effort are to no effect without the divine will and mercy (cf. vv. 18, 22).

c. Refusal as the opposite of religious willingness may be seen in the parable of Mt. 21:30, the resistance of Jerusalem in Mt. 23:37, the blunt rejection of Lk. 19:14, the refusal to come to Jesus in Jn. 5:40, the disobedience of Acts 7:39, and the refusal to repent in Rev. 2:21. A resolute will to do evil is denoted in Jn. 8:44 and an orientation to mistaken values in Mk. 8:35.

thélēma.

A. *thélēma* in the Greek World, in Hellenism, and in the Synagogue.

1. A first use of *thélēma* is for "wish" or "purpose," then "desire" (also sexual).

2. In the LXX it occurs for the divine "will" and "pleasure," then for human "desire," the royal "will," and "self-will."

3. In the Hermetic writings there is considerable use for the will of God as good, sovereign, creative, and all-determinative.

4. In rabbinic writings the will of God, often linked with his name and rule (as in the Lord's Prayer), is that which is to be done.

B. *thélēma* in the NT. The plural form (common in the LXX) occurs in the NT only in LXX quotations (Acts 13:22) and for carnal desires (Eph. 2:3). God's will is a unity and is thus put in the singular (apart from the variant reading in Mk. 3:35).

1. thélēma as God's Will.

a. Christ as Doer of the Divine Will.

(i) The third petition of the Lord's Prayer expresses a consent to God's will that Christ himself exemplifies in Mt. 26:42. It is because he lives by the divine will that he calls the one who does this will his brother, sister, and mother (Mk. 3:35).

(ii) John makes the same point with christological depth. Jesus does the will of the divine Sender, executing and thereby mediating it (4:34; 5:30, etc.). The essential union of Son and Father comes to ethical expression. Jesus is the eternal Son (7:28) who is one with the Father (1:18 etc.) and hears his words (5:20). He demonstrates this by his constant openness to the Father's will. His very life is to do this will (4:34).

The content of this will is to lead believers in him to eternal life (6:39-40). Obedience, however, is neither a natural process nor a miracle. It entails a willing subjection of his own will which enables him to claim that his mission, word, and work are all from God (7:28 etc.). This guarantees that his judgment is just (5:30), and it insures his power in virtue of the divine hearing (9:31). Yet it also involves his self-giving (cf. 12:25) in fulfilment of his saving mission.

(iii) In Heb. 10:7, 9 the whole life of Christ, in contrast to animal sacrifices, is a self-offering to God's will whereby believers in him are sanctified.

b. The Conception of the Will of God as the Basis and Purpose of Salvation.

(i) Except in Rev. 4:11, God's will in the NT is always his will to save. In Mt. 18:14 this will is protective of little ones. It is a fatherly will in Mt. 6:10 etc. As such, it is normatively commanding (cf. 21:31).

(ii) Paul expresses the saving character of God's will by his use of *katá* when speaking of Christ's work (cf. Gal. 1:4). In Eph. 1:5ff. we have *en* Christ, *katá* God's will, and *eis* the praise of God's glory. God's will is related here to his *eudokía* and *boulḗ,* and it is a published *mystḗrion* in v. 9. If we expound the divine *thélēma* in terms of these equivalents, we see that it is the source, basis, and norm of the whole work of salvation, the resolve which demands action and which alone can provide the impulse for execution of what is planned.

c. The New Life of Believers and the Divine Will.

(i) The Basic Attitude. (a) The Jews know God's will in the sense of his requirements (Rom. 2:18), but only those who are taught by Jesus truly recognize it (Lk. 13:47-48). Thus Paul acquires a wholly new knowledge of God's will at his conversion (Acts 22:14). This will must be tested (Rom. 12:2) on the basis of nonconformity to this aeon and renewal of the mind. What is needed is a practical knowledge in wisdom and spiritual understanding (Col. 1:9). The Spirit teaches us how to conduct ourselves as God desires (cf. Eph. 5:17). (b) Prayer, too, should be according to God's will on the model of Jesus (Mk. 14:36). Such prayer may be sure of a hearing (1 Jn. 5:14).

(ii) The Doing. (a) Doing is decisive for following Jesus (Mt. 12:50). Only where there is a resolve to do can one know the *didachḗ* of Jesus (Jn. 7:17) and perceive its true conformity with Scripture (Jn. 5:46-47). Doing is also a condition for entering the kingdom (Mt. 7:21; cf. 1 Jn. 2:17). Reception of what is promised follows only on endurance in doing (Heb. 10:36). (b) If doing is a condition, it is also the content of the Christian life under God's own enabling (cf. Heb. 13:21; Rom. 12:2; Phil. 2:12-13). 1 Pet. 4:2 contrasts the new living by God's will with the former living by human passions. Even slaves will now render their service as a doing of God's will from the heart (Eph. 6:6). (c) Definitions. We are rarely told what God's will specifically involves, since it is supposedly no secret. Sanctification and thanksgiving are commended in 1 Th. 4:3; 5:18, and submission to rulers in 1 Pet. 2:15. In 2 Cor. 8:5 we are to give ourselves to the Lord. Glorifying God is a common denominator. (d) Detailed Directions. God's will is to be worked out in detail (cf. Col. 4:12). Thus Paul is an apostle by God's will (1 Cor. 1:1 etc.), and as such he declares God's will and is ruled by it (cf. Rom. 1:10). The community, too, sees the operation of God's will in what befalls it (cf. 1 Pet. 3:17; 4:19).

2. *thélēma as Human and Demonic Will.* Apart from Mt. 21:31 (in a parable), the only Synoptic instances of human will are in Luke, e.g., 22:42; 23:25. Human self-will is the point in 2 Pet. 1:21; as Scripture was not written by human impulse, so we are not to expound it arbitrarily. The will of the flesh in Jn. 1:13 is sexual desire (and the will of man here is perhaps the desire for a son and heir, while blood might just

conceivably be a reference to the female contribution). The same sense occurs in 1 Cor. 7:37, which can hardly refer to a father or guardian, nor to a spiritual marriage, but seems most naturally to have in view a purpose of marriage. In Jn. 1:13 and 1 Cor. 7:37 sexual desire is meant in a purely psychological and nonderogatory sense, but this is not so in Eph. 2:13, where the passions of the flesh in pagan life embrace sexual lusts and carry a hint of enslavement to the *sárx*. 2 Tim. 2:26 refers to the will of Satan which opponents do as they are ensnared and captured by him.

C. *thélēma* **in the Early Church.** In the apostolic fathers *thélēma* is used biblically for the will of God which underlies salvation (Ignatius *Smyrneans* 11.1), gives direction for service (Ignatius *Ephesians* 20.1), and is the power that begets Christ (Ignatius *Smyrneans* 1.1 etc., taking Jn. 1:13 in the singular). The term is important in the Monothelite controversy, but with a non-NT stress on the *thélēma* as an organ of volition instead of its content.

thélēsis. This is a late Koine word related to *thélēma* but less common. It occurs in the LXX for the divine will or good pleasure, for human desire, for the royal will, and in a special usage for "delight" or "sweetness." The only NT instance is in Heb. 2:4: Along with the attestation of the Lord's hearers, God also gave testimony by signs etc. and gifts distributed according to his own will.   [G. SCHRENK, III, 44-62]

---

themélios [foundation], *themélion* [foundation], *themelióō* [to lay the foundation]

---

1. Found from Homer, the adjectival noun *ho themélios* means "basic stone" or "foundation" (masculine in 1 Cor. 3:12; 2 Tim. 2:19; Heb. 11:10; Rev. 21:19, neuter in Acts 16:26). The use may be literal for the foundation of a house, tower, or city (cf. Lk. 6:48-49; Heb. 11:10; Rev. 21:14, 19), or it may be figurative for the foundation of churches (Rom. 15:20) or teachings (Heb. 6:1; cf. 1 Tim. 6:19). Christ is the foundation in Rom. 15:20; 1 Cor. 3:11, while the apostles and prophets are the foundation and Christ the cornerstone in Eph. 2:20 (cf. also 2 Tim. 2:19). Behind this use is the concept of edification. The church is a house that is built by God or Christ, or in God or Christ by its leaders and members. Christ is the foundation, but the apostles are associated with him (cf. Mt. 16:18). The house is the house of God; there are OT roots for this concept and for the related idea of the *themélios* (cf. Is. 28:16 and Rev. 21:14, 19).

2. The verb *themelióō* in Mt. 7:25; Lk. 6:48; Heb. 1:10 means "to provide with a foundation." The sense is figurative in Eph. 3:17; 1 Pet. 5:10, i.e., "to strengthen," "to confirm," but with the implicit thought that when God confirms us in faith and love he establishes his house or church on its sure foundation in Christ.

[K. L. SCHMIDT, III, 63-64]

theodídaktos → *theós; theómachos, theomachéō* → *máchomai; theópneustos* → *pneúma*

---

theós [God, god], *theótēs* [divinity], *átheos* [without God], *theodídaktos* [taught by God], *theíos* [divine], *theiótēs* [divinity]

---

theós (→ *kýrios, patér*).

A. The Greek Concept of God.

1. theós in the Usage of Secular Greek. The word *theós* is used in both singular and plural, definite and indefinite, often with little distinction of sense between the gods, god, the god, and the godhead. The term does not denote a specific personality but the unity of the religious world in spite of its multiplicity. The Greek concept is essentially polytheistic in the sense of belief in an ordered totality of gods. Zeus as the father of gods and men brings this to expression. Since he has the first and last word, piety often associates him quite simply with god. Out of the plurality a hierarchy develops with families of gods and a pantheon. Zeus, Apollo, etc. are called gods, but so is the cosmos, and elemental forces may also be given the name. The deepest reality is god (the Greeks would have to reverse 1 Jn. 4:16 and say that love is God). But reality is manifold; hence the plural *theoí*. Heroes, unusual people, and outstanding rulers are also gods, so that in the emperor cult *theós* is a designation of office. Finally, philosophers use the word for metaphysical forces, so that often they use as equivalents the divine, the good, the existent, and destiny. We see here a spiritualizing and moralizing of mythical figures which enhances their dignity but robs them of proximity. Through every change of form, however, the inner structure of the concept remains constant.

2. *The Content of the Greek Concept of God.* The gods are a given factor. Though eternal, they have come into being. They have not created the world but are its form or meaning. They are thus identified with human order, e.g., in the state. Their eternity includes eternal youth. They enjoy superior power and felicity, but lack moral seriousness. They are infinite beings, but of the same kind as ourselves. Unlike impersonal fate, which even they cannot alter, they represent meaningful plan and purpose. They have human form (their majesty being that of the highest living creature), and their emotions and customs are human.

3. *The Development of the Greek Concept of God.*

a. Two motifs in Homer govern the development of the concept, the natural and the ethical. These motifs lead to nature mysticism on the one side and rational ethics on the other. The philosophers subject the Homeric gods to rational criticism, replacing anthropomorphism with cosmomorphism. The presence of divinity in the world is not denied, but its unity is stressed, and the idea of the unmoved mover is introduced. The regularity of being and the principle of compensation or cosmic justice represent the ethical aspect. Thus in tragedy divine justice rules inscrutably in the dialectic of human existence. Zeus is a redeeming power as he teaches us moderation through suffering. The Greek concept thus achieves a certain objectivity, but there is no direct relationship with the deity, for state and society stand between, and we know deity only from its works in nature and history.

b. Plato carries the ethicizing and spiritualizing further by attacking false religiosity, denying divine intervention in the form of physical relationship, and completing the separation between deity and humanity by postulating only a resemblance of being and no true unity. In Plato myth serves only to elucidate philosophical themes. Final reality is impersonal, and divinity means its actualization in space and time as a moving reflection of eternity. In this regard deity plays the role of architect, not creator. In Aristotle, too, deity is the necessary condition of a world order, the cause of each thing existing as it does. One cannot pray to this deity, nor does it will anything, and if there is love for it, this is simply the attraction which impels us to strive for a higher form of being.

c. Hellenism transforms the mythical gods into metaphysical and cosmic concepts. Thus Stoicism finds in Zeus the comprehensive law of the world which is operative in all things and to which one must adapt. An impersonal pantheistic view thus develops, stressing the providential aspect, though later Stoicism takes a more personal and ethical line with its father and provider who is the original of all virtues and who through the *noús* may be in us too. In contrast, the atomism of Epicurus leaves no true place for deity except at the level of our views about it or consciousness of it. Over against constant increase in the number of gods, Hellenism attempts unification by equation on the principle that only names differ and realities are the same. Non-Greek deities are fused with Greek, and syncretistic trends lead to the worship of a chief or universal god, Zeus or Jupiter, though not in any truly monotheistic sense.

d. Philo tries to mediate between the OT concept and the Greek ideas of Platonism and Stoicism. God for him is transcendent, the unique, incomprehensible, and almighty Creator who first fashions the ideas and then makes of them the visible world. Alongside God is the *lógos* of whom the ideas are begotten. The *lógos*-concept depersonalizes God, yet, while the work of the Greek deity is simply the interrelating of idea and being, for Philo the idea itself is a creation and emanation from God.

e. In Neo-Platonism the concern is with an ultimate *one* from which and to which all things flow. The one is the first and fatherly deity from which *noús* proceeds as architect and then *psyché* as the link between the worlds of ideas and experience. We thus have the one and all, but the one does not merge into the all. The one is the underlying force of all that is, and for it being and creating are all the same. The world timelessly evolves from it as its objectification, so that the deity becomes the world. On this view prayer is pointless except as self-reflection with a view to elevation to purer heights.

f. A mystical pantheism may be found in the Hermetic writings. The deity fills all things, and is bi-sexual, and self-creating, the one and all; mystics who reflect on the merging of cosmic unity into the unity of the spiritual ego are themselves *theoí*. It is noteworthy that in none of these developments is there a place for a personal, monotheistic view of God as the Creator with whom there may be personal relationship. The basic orientation is to eternal being and law, with the deity as the power or essence that insures permanence.   [H. KLEINKNECHT, III, 65-79]

B. *El* and *Elohim* in the OT.

1. The Usage of the LXX. theós is the usual LXX equivalent for ʼ*ēl* and ʼ*ᵉlōhîm*; other words such as *kýrios* and *ischyrós* occur at times, but infrequently (*kýrios* being the usual word for the divine name Yahweh). *theós* itself occurs only some 330 times.

2. The OT Belief in God in the Form of Faith in Yahweh. What the OT authors believe about God comes out in what they say about him and to him. Though individual experience and teaching vary, the underlying reality is the same. Simple expressions bring out its basic character, though these are complicated by the random use of such terms as El, Elohim, and Yahweh. God and Yahweh are obviously the same, but there is an initial tension between the divine person of Yahweh and the sum of cosmic forces; this is resolved only as the prophets promote confidence that Yahweh is the Creator and Ruler of the world in whom divine power is concentrated into an omnipotent will and beside whom there are no other deities. As the canon shows, the people move on only slowly to a recognition that the national God is the Lord of all things. The starting point is with faith in Yahweh as the covenant God. Moses takes this concept and gives it its uniquely impelling force by linking it with the God of the fathers (Ex. 3:15), the exclusive God (Ex. 20:5; 34:14, etc.).

3. The Tradition concerning Belief in God prior to the Rise of the Community of Yahweh. Due to the nature of the material, it is hard to say with certainty what was the precise form of the pre-Mosaic concept. The name Yahweh is brought into the material, but Ex. 6:3 displays an awareness of distinction. Nevertheless, the combination "Yahweh God" in Gen. 2:4 identifies Yahweh as the God who created all things and whom the patriarchs knew and worshipped. The fuller apposition in Ps. 50:1 has the evident nature of a confession of faith.

4. *El and Elohim as Appellatives.* Neither '*ēl* nor '*ᵉlōhîm* has originally the same meaning as Yahweh. They both denote God generically rather than personally, are of polytheistic derivation, and need qualification to denote God individually. '*ēl* as a name outside Israel is secondary and does not help us to understand biblical usage. When used alone for Yahweh (Is. 40:18 etc.), or as a parallel to Yahweh (Num. 23:8), the point is that Yahweh alone is '*ēl,* though not necessarily with a polemic against other gods.

5. *The Content of the OT Belief in God.* The thesis that God is Israel's God is fundamental. This God is God in the absolute (cf. 1 Kgs. 18:21), so that as the name merges into the appellatives, the words '*ēl* and '*ᵉlōhîm* come to contain the vital heritage of faith. a. '*ēl,* of course, is not peculiar to Israel. Ishmael has '*ēl* in his name, and Balaam and Job both speak of '*ēl.* Parallels may be found among many peoples. In the OT '*ēl* is the simplest form for the divine as distinct from the human (Ezek. 28:2; Hos. 11:9). '*ēl* is holy (Hos. 11:9), spirit (Is. 31:3), ethically superior (Num. 23:19), and thus worthy of trust. Through every nuance '*ēl* is a personal object of religious awe and knowledge even if the concept of God is introduced only by the usage and is not the original meaning. As may be seen from the expression "It is in my power" (Gen. 31:29), the root idea may be one of power, but in the ultimate religious sense of power that is superhuman. Parallel terms for God, e.g., Owner, Lord, and King, support the connection with power. b. The etymology, of course, raises several difficulties (see *TDNT,* III, 84-85 for details). c. Nor can the linguistic data be explained in terms of '*ᵉlōhîm* and '*lô(a)h,* even if we have a plural and related singular (which some contest). Certainly one need not suppose that these terms have a different basic sense, i.e., "he who is to be feared." d. But if they are related and carry the sense of power, the use of the singular and plural raises a question. Since '*lô(a)h* is mainly later, and is common only in Job, its significance is fixed by the other two terms. '*ᵉlōhîm* is clearly a numerical plural only in a very few instances (cf. Ex. 15:11). Even a single pagan god can be meant by the word (e.g., 1 Kgs. 11:5). In the main, then, we have a plural of majesty. There is no sense of treating God as one among many gods. The point is that God has all that belongs to deity.

6. *The Historical Continuation of the OT Belief in God.* If Yahweh is called '*ēl* or '*ᵉlōhîm,* this implies that he is a concrete manifestation of divine reality. The concept does not have the dynamism of the name, but forms a basis for its development as a basic religious experience. This experience differs for Israel inasmuch as Israel's God is truly God, i.e., sovereign, creative, and self-revealing as distinct from the natural forces that pagans symbolize in images or cultic actions. Such forces are inactive; they can neither help nor impel, and are therefore vain (Is. 44:9; 1 Sam. 12:21). If they can be explained rationally as cosmic or sexual, only faith in Yahweh and obedience to his commands can break their numinous power. God made us in his own image (Gen. 1:26); we cannot make God. Hence God's word comes as a reality that transcends and shapes human will and action. This reality may be partial or inadequate (cf. 1 Sam. 28:13). It can be properly filled out only as God himself commands and acts and guides. But one cannot count on this, for God hides himself (Is. 25:1; 45:15), and confusion is caused by experience of other cults, whose gods may be puny (Ps. 31:6; 1 Chr. 16:26), but can point to great triumphs and prodigality (Jer. 7:18; Am.

5:26; Dt. 12:2), so that the people yields allegiance (Jer. 5:7) and is conscious of their power (cf. 2 Kgs. 3:27). That there are real divine powers is admitted in Dt. 6:12. The exclusivism of Yahweh (Ex. 20:5) is finally directed, not against those who turn to other gods, but to the gods themselves. Whether in her own fellowship or in external dealings, Israel is conscious of the reality of a territorial pantheon. Only belief that God is the Mighty One (Josh. 22:22), supreme over the whole pantheon, can prevent relapse into idol worship. Yet a monarchical monotheism is seen to imply (Jer. 2:11) that for all the sincerity of paganism, the gods of pagans have no true reality; and if Israel looks to them she is guilty of infidelity and falls victim to inner discord (Jer. 2:13ff.). Later writings can thus make a clear distinction between the one God and foreign gods (cf. Dan. 11:36; Mal. 2:10-11; Ps. 82), but these distinctions rest on the recognition of God's deity in his help or faithfulness or comfort, as in the Psalms with their personal motif "my God." God is known as the living God who is active on his people's behalf (Hos. 2:1). As Is. 40–41 shows, he manifests himself as God by doing what is worthy of God in his works of creation and redemption.

[G. Quell, III, 79-89]

C. The Primitive Christian Fact of God and Its Conflict with the Concept of God in Judaism.

1. The Usage. a. In the LXX *theós* is the usual term for *'ĕlōhîm. ho theós* is the God of Israel, while *theós* is mostly appellative. *tó theíon* does not occur. Judaism prefers not to speak of God, adopting instead such expressions as the Lord, the Almighty, the Most High. Hellenistic Judaism, adopting philosophical style, refers to the deity, providence, etc. Philo uses the adjective *theíos, ho theós* for the God of Israel (or *ho kýrios* to denote his power), *theós* for the *lógos,* and *theoí* at times for humans, but his favorite term is *tó theíon.* Josephus has *ho theós* and *theós* without distinction, but likes *tó theíon* and *hoi ouranoí,* and seldom uses *kýrios.* Apocryphal and pseudepigraphal works, adopting older styles, use *kýrios* (for Yahweh) along with many other expressions, e.g., Most High, Most Merciful, Almighty, Holy One, Creator, Unbegotten, etc. Jesus uses *theós* freely and more rarely has *kýrios, ouranós, dýnamis* (cf. Mk. 14:61-62), or *sophía* (Lk. 7:35). *patér,* however, is his true name for God. Elsewhere in the NT *theós* is the normal word. From Paul onward *kýrios* is more often used for Jesus, as *theós* is in, e.g., Jn. 1:1. *theós* usually has the article in the nominative, but in other cases may be with or without article with no distinction. *theós* may also denote pagan deities (cf. Acts 19:37; 1 Cor. 8:5) and even humans (Jn. 10:34-35 quoting Ps. 82:6).   [E. Stauffer, III, 90-92]

b. The Rabbinic Terms for God. Later rabbinic Judaism avoids the divine name and adopts formal substitutes. It distinguishes between the proper name (Yahweh), generic names (*'ēl, 'ĕlô(a)h, 'ĕlōhîm),* and descriptive names (the Most High, the King, etc.). Since the divine name must not be taken in vain, its use is restricted to the cultus, and eventually it comes to exist only as a written symbol and not a living word. The substitutes vary according to whether the usage is religious or secular, and as these take on the full concept of God, they in turn tend to become too holy for secular use and give way to others. *'ĕlô(a)h* and *'ĕlōhîm* cause no initial difficulty and become taboo only in medieval times. Terms or nouns expressing qualities and the like are freely used, and an abstract group (holiness, power, etc.) also becomes popular. (See *TDNT,* III, pp. 92-94 for details.)   [K. G. Kuhn, III, 92-94]

2. The Uniqueness of God.

a. Prophetic Monotheism as the Starting Point of True Monotheism. True monotheism is not a product of polytheism but its negation. Its God is not a new idea of unity but ultimate and true reality. The one God is the decisive reality for Moses and as such claims sole validity (Ex. 20:2-3). This God is the only God of the whole world. He is revealed and worshipped, however, only in Israel. Hence his uniqueness must be asserted against both false gods and the other forces that dominate the people (Is. 26:13). The later triumph of monotheism in Islam owes much to biblical concepts. Elsewhere monotheistic formulas have little impact. Zoroaster expounds a dualistic philosophy of history with a monotheistic orientation (in view of the final triumph of light).

b. Dynamic Monotheism in Later Judaism.

(a) Judaism may sometimes use *theoí* for humans or for pagan gods. The OT basis for the description of humans as gods is slight, and in passages like Ps. 82:1; Ex. 21:6 the reference is to judges as God's representatives. The rabbis resist strongly the pagan pretensions of humans to deity (cf. Dan. 11:36-37). Where the OT calls heavenly beings '*ĕlōhîm*, the LXX usually has angels or sons of God. This is part of the great polemic against the idea that the idols of paganism are gods in any true sense, as in Bel and the Dragon, Wis. 13:1ff., Josephus, and the attacks of the rabbis on star worship, animal worship, and the emperor cult. Sometimes demonic forces are seen behind idols, sometimes they are dismissed as things of nought. But there is a united front against polytheism.

(b) Judaism gives a primary place to the confession of one God, whether in faith, formulas, or practice. The formulas vary and may take confessional or polemical form. The original meaning is best preserved in the Shema (Dt. 6:4). To the uniqueness of God corresponds the uniqueness of the people, for while the one God will one day be God of the whole world, he is now the only God only for Israel, which is ready to suffer and die in confession of his uniqueness.

(c) God works, of course, through intermediaries, i.e., angels or hypostases (word, spirit, truth, etc.), but these are not independent or of the same rank. They serve God as his deputies. Their numbers increase from Daniel on. Angels subject their own wills wholly to God's will, daily receiving and executing orders, proclaiming God's will in the first person, but only as God's representatives, so that they cannot accept human worship. In extreme emergencies, only God's direct help avails.

(d) The one God is in conflict with demonic forces. Satan has rebelled against God and commands a host of demons. But Satan is God's creature, has fallen from heaven, and, while still powerful, is held in check by God, who overrules the evil acts of demons to his own purposes of good and to their destruction. Thus a dynamic monotheism overcomes both automatic monotheism and static dualism.

(e) In this conflict, apocalyptic finds a role for the Savior King, the Messiah, the Son of Man, who, whether heavenly or earthly, is God's representative, not himself God, but armed with a divine power to which all enemies must submit. This Savior King is God's decisive representative, not replacing God, but effecting a universal acknowledgment of God's glory and uniqueness.

c. *theoí* in the NT. Acts vividly depicts the polytheism that the apostles encountered in Ephesus (19:27), Athens (17:23), Malta (28:6), and Lystra (14:11ff.); cf. also Herod in Caesarea (Acts 12:22). The monotheistic answer is always the same (Acts 19:26; 17:23-24; 14:15; 12:23). Idols are nothing (1 Cor. 8:4), but idolatry is a sin (10:7), for it is a failure to worship the true God and involves subjection to demonic forces; the *theoí polloí* are not true gods but they impose terrible bondage.

d. *heís theós* in the Confession and Practice of Primitive Christianity. Jesus himself quotes the Shema in Mk. 12:29-30, and the scribe can only endorse this (12:32-33). Similar monotheistic formulas occur in, e.g., Rom. 3:29-30; 1 Tim. 1:17. We believe (Jms. 2:19) or know (1 Cor. 8:4) that there is only one God. As yet not all peoples perceive this; hence the NT refers to the God of the fathers, of Israel, of Abraham, etc., or to our God or my God in true OT fashion. As the church has inherited the promises, the God of Israel is now the God of the church (cf. Acts 15:14). Yet the church must not only believe that God is one; it must believe in God (Rom. 4:3) and hope in him (1 Pet. 1:21). Zeal must accompany knowledge (Rom. 3:11). Recognition of his sovereignty means that he is not to be tempted (Mt. 4:7). The first commandment takes on new seriousness in its exclusion not only of idols but of mammon, belly, cosmic forces, state authorities, or even the emperor. The confession of one God imposes the constant task of trusting and obeying this one God alone.

e. God and His Angels in the NT. Angels play no big role in the NT. They come from God (Acts 12:11) and he acts through them (Acts 7:35). They are nothing without God and everything with him. They will not accept worship (Rev. 19:10).

f. Monotheism and Christology in the NT. Christ confirms monotheism by depriving the prince of this world of his power. He himself sharpens the monotheistic confession (Mk. 10:18), is consumed by zeal for God's house (Jn. 2:17), prays constantly to God, and calls him exclusively "my Father" (Jn. 20:17). As the Son he has power to forgive sins, will sit on God's throne and judge the world, bears the name Logos, mediates creation (Jn. 1:3) and salvation (1 Cor. 10:4), and precedes angels (Heb. 1). He battles the devil (Lk. 22:28; 1 Jn. 3:8), resisting his temptations, driving out demons, binding the strong man, turning the apparent defeat of the cross into victory, and establishing the dominion of the one God (1 Cor. 15:28). God has sent, instituted, accredited, confirmed, anointed, and exalted him. God is with him, empowers him, and works with and through him, reconciling the world to himself (2 Cor. 5:19). He comes from God and returns to him. Faith in him and faith in God are the same (cf. Jn. 14:1, 9; 10:30; 17:11). The forerunner of God in Mal. 3:1 is the forerunner of Jesus in Mk. 1:2. Jesus uses the divine *egṓ eimi*. He is first Judge and then God in 1 Cor. 4:4-5. All things are by and to him as well as God (Rom. 11:36; 1 Cor. 8:6; Col. 1:16). He is the First and the Last (Rev. 1:17; cf. v. 8). Yet God is his God and Head and Father (Eph. 1:17; 1 Cor. 11:3; Jn. 5:18). He, too, is "of" God (1 Cor. 3:23). His titles, with the article, express his uniqueness (the holy one, elect, anointed, son, etc.), but the genitive "of *theós*" shows his derivation from God. The exception is *kýrios*.

g. Christ as *theós* in Primitive Christianity. In Jn. 10:30ff. Jesus proves that the use of *theoí* for humans is not unbiblical, though he himself claims only to be God's Son. In Heb. 1:8-9 the designation of the OT king as *theós* is transferred to Jesus. In Rom. 9:4-5 Christ is called *theós* directly unless we have in the last clause an independent doxology. In Jn. 1:1 "the Logos was God" (and cf. some readings of 1:18). Thomas recognizes Jesus as his God in Jn. 20:28 (cf. the blind man in 9:38). Cf. also Tit. 2:13 and outside the NT Did. 10.6, Ignatius *Ephesians* 18.2 etc., and Pliny *Letters* 10.96.7. Christ as *the* representative of God is himself the bearer of the divine nature and office.

h. The Threefold Relation of God, Christ, and Spirit. The relation between God and Christ finds expression in formulas that state both their unity and God's primacy (1 Cor. 8:6; 1 Tim. 2:5; Mt. 23:8ff.). Triadic formulas occur which include angels

(Lk. 9:26), and cf. the spirits of Rev. 1:4-5. But the usual triad is God, Christ, and the Spirit, who stands in a special relation to both God (Jn. 4:24) and Christ (Mk. 3:29-30; Lk. 1:35; Jn. 3:34; Rom. 8:27, 34; Jn. 16:14), but who also continues Christ's work (Jn. 14:26; Gal. 4:4ff.). We thus find triadic formulas embracing God, Christ, and Spirit in 1 Cor. 12:4ff.; 2 Cor. 13:13; Mt. 28:19. These formulas express the indissoluble threefold relationship but do not actually speak of triunity. The clear-cut statement of 1 Jn. 5 is brought into the text only in the sixth century.

3. *The Personal Being of God.*

a. *The Conflict with Anthropomorphism in the Jewish World.* The LXX tries to purify the concept of God by minor alterations, e.g., bringing in a divine messenger in Ex. 4:24, or putting "power" for "hand" in Josh. 4:24, or speaking of seeing God's place instead of God in Ex. 24:10, or saying that God becomes gracious for his repenting in Gen. 6:6-7. Later Hellenists go further by allegorizing the OT, finding abstract content in anthropomorphisms, and substituting philosophical concepts. Yet faith in the personal God remains. Thus Josephus uses alien terms but is still speaking of the living God of his fathers. The rabbis avoid allegorizing but explain anthropomorphisms as divine accommodation to human frailty, though they themselves in prayer call God Father, speak of his ear and hand for their needs, and think of him as weeping over Jerusalem. Stressing God's will, they do not equate him with his attributes but bring out his personal character. Thus, while both Greeks and Jews eliminate anthropomorphism, the former regard personality as itself anthropomorphic but the latter distinguish between anthropomorphism and faith in the personal God. God is not as we are, but he wills, speaks, and hears.

b. *The Personal God of the NT.* Anthropomorphism is a dead issue in the NT. God's personal nature is here a living reality disclosed in Christ and the Spirit (2 Cor. 4:6; Rom. 8:27; cf. the prayer "Abba" in Rom. 8:15). We respond to God's Thou to us with our Thou to God. God is the living God of will and purpose to whom we may come with prayers and cries for aid. He is known to be faithful and true (Rom. 11:29; Jn. 3:33; Tit. 1:2), gracious (Rom. 2:4), righteous (Rom. 1:18), holy, and perfect (Mt. 5:48). These are not abstract descriptions but historical attestations. They are expressed by attributive or predicative adjectives (Rom. 16:27 etc.), by a genitive of *theós* with noun (Rom. 3:3) or *theós* with genitive (Rom. 15:5 etc.), by bold equation (1 Jn. 4:8, which makes God the origin and norm of love), by predications referring to his nature (Rom. 16:26; 1 Tim. 1:11), and by equation with neutral predication (Jn. 4:24; 1 Jn. 1:5).

4. *The Transcendence of God.*

a. *The Power of God as Ruler in Semitic Religion.* (1) In the Semitic world deities are defined by their power and thus bear titles of rule. In relation to people they are masters, protectors, judges, fathers, kings. In relation to the world they are rulers who control its destiny. (2) Magical ideas, fertility cults, and astral mythologies dissolve this concept in syncretism, but in Israel the prophets deepen it. Israel's God is the absolute Creator and Ruler of all things. The LXX expresses this by stressing the term *kýrios* and such related words as *despótēs* and *basileús*.

b. *God and the World in Later Judaism.* God is above the world and uses intermediaries to execute his commands. He is immortal, but dynamically so as Ruler. He is not outside the world but above it, and hence omnipresent rather than distant. He is the all, but as its Creator and not in any pantheistic sense. We are not "in" God by natural or ecstatic union, but we come "from" him. He is "with" us in virtue of his covenant, so that in every need we may pray to him, knowing that the Ruler of all things will extend his powerful protection. Apocalyptic descries an opposition of will that distorts the form of this world but God can omnipotently bend all things to his own purpose, so that one may confidently expect his final triumph and dominion.

c. The Transcendent God of the NT. In the NT, too, God is *kýrios* etc. He is not outside the world but above it. Heaven and earth are together God's creation, though heaven is superior as God's throne (Mt. 5:34-35), and earthly forces oppose God's lordship in heaven (cf. Mt. 6:10). The Christ event is the decisive encounter between heaven and earth that apocalyptic awaited (Lk. 17:20, which means that the kingdom is present in Jesus). In Jesus God is with us—Immanuel (Mt. 1:23; cf. Is. 7:14). His heavenly form and nature find earthly manifestation in servanthood and crucifixion (Phil. 2:6ff.). The Word became flesh (Jn. 1:14). The encounter does not mean human enlightenment or divinization, nor a divine-human marriage, but a heightening and overcoming of the tension by Christ's death and resurrection. The tension is not that of infinite and finite or eternity and time, as in Hellenistic philosophy. God is not restricted by metaphysical relations (cf. Lk. 3:8). No natural or historical power can thwart God (Rom. 11:23-24). His word is life and death (Lk. 12:20). All life's changes and chances are from him. God is with his people as its Ruler and Protector, but with a new certainty in Christ that Paul expresses with his *hypér* in Rom. 8:31-32. In virtue of this "God for us" the cosmic anxiety of antiquity is resolved. Words like *moíra* do not occur in the NT. Along with this transcendence, there is, of course, a certain immanence as well. Believers are the house in which God dwells. God is among them (cf. 1 Cor. 14:25: *en hymín*). He is the Father who is in all, though this "in all" is to be understood in terms of the preceding "above and through all" (Eph. 4:6; cf. 1 Cor. 12:6; Col. 1:17). 1 Jn. 4:16 refers to a mutual abiding, though more in the sense of faithfulness than metaphysical union. This accords with the important role of prayer in the Johannine writings. Prayer has no place when immanentism dissolves the I-Thou relation. Prayer presupposes a God who is above the world and to whom we may turn with confidence in time of need. Various terms for prayer occur in the NT. It is addressed *to* God. Made in the name of Jesus, it has purpose as well as assurance. Its climax is petition for the definitive actualizing of God's rule whose victory the Christ event has already decided (Lk. 11:2). Even after the Christ event, this actualizing is still an object of faith, not sight. The first encounter will come to completion when all conflict is removed (Rev. 21:3-4) and God is all in all (1 Cor. 15:28).

theótēs (→ *theiótēs*). This word, meaning "divinity," occurs in the NT only in Col. 2:9 (cf. 1:19-20). The one God, to whom all deity belongs, has given this fullness of deity to the incarnate Christ.

átheos. There were seven basic forms of atheism in antiquity: 1. the practical atheism of the ignorant, careless, and hedonistic (cf. Is. 22:13; Rom. 1:30); 2. the secularized religion of the state-cult (Ezek. 28:2; Dan. 11:36; Rev. 13); 3. belief in fate (cf. Col. 1); 4. metaphysical reinterpretation of beliefs; 5. religious doubt (cf. Ps. 73); 6. defiance of the omnipotent God (cf. Moses in Ex. 32:32; Jeremiah; Job); 7. any denial of God or the gods (Jews and Christians are accused of atheism by polytheists, whose gods they reject, while Eph. 2:11-12 calls pagans *átheoi*, and cf. Mart. Pol. 9.2).

theodídaktos. Unlike *theópneustos*, which is used for canonical Scripture (2 Tim. 3:16), *theodídaktos* ("taught by God") is used in 1 Th. 4:9 for Christians as members of the new community (cf. Jer. 31:34; Is. 54:13; Jn. 6:45).

[E. STAUFFER, III, 94-121]

theíos. a. Adjective of *theós,* this means "divine" relative to all that bears the stamp of deity, e.g., as predominant power, final reality, supreme meaning, or philosophical conception. The educated like the term and often use the impersonal *theía phýsis* for God. Humans may also be *theíos,* e.g., seers, priests, singers, saviors, and rulers. b. The noun *tó theíon* is a common term for "deity." The NT uses *theíos* only in passages under Hellenistic influence (2 Pet. 1:3-4; Acts 17:29), but with no surrender of faith in the personal God.

theíotēs. Formed from *theíos,* this, too, means "divinity" in the sense that something is divine, whether a god or imperial majesty. The only NT instance is in Rom. 1:20: God's deity may be perceived in creation.   [H. KLEINKNECHT, III, 122-23]

---

theosebḗs [God-fearing],   *theosébeia* [piety, reverence for God]

A. Usage outside the NT. 1. True piety is the point behind this compound of *theós* (i.e., honoring the gods), but in a critical sense it means "superstition," and more generally it simply denotes "religion." 2. The group is rare in the LXX (though *eusébeia* is common in 4 Maccabees), but when used (e.g., in Job 1:1; Ex. 18:21), it has the sense of true religion. The noun occurs only in Prov. 1:29. 3. *theosebḗs* may be found on a few inscriptions to describe the Jews as holding the true religion. The Jews themselves like the term "God-fearers" for themselves and Gentile adherents, since it implies that they are worshippers of the true God.

B. NT Usage. The NT avoids the group, using *theosebḗs* and *theosébeia* only once each. The adjective occurs in Jn. 9:31: God hears those who fear him, which is defined as doing his will (cf. Prov. 15:29; Job 27:9). The noun comes in 1 Tim. 2:10, which teaches that women professing religion (i.e., Christianity) should substantiate their confession with good deeds.

C. Early Christian Usage. The terms are still infrequent in the apostolic fathers. In Mart. Pol. 3 *theosébeia* is obviously Christianity (cf. 2 Clem. 20.4). The words are more common in the Apologists. In Justin *Dialogue* 110.2 *theosébeia* comes through the apostolic preaching. In Athenagoras *Supplication* 37.1 Christians are the true God-fearers. Diognetus charmingly describes the *theosébeia* of Christians. Origen *Against Celsus* 3.59 and 81 tries to bring out the uniqueness of the *theosébeia* of Jesus. In this instance, however, the use of the general term "religion" tends to surrender the point at the outset. The restricted Jewish and NT use for true worship in contrast to idolatry is thus threatened by the invasion of a more general anthropocentric use which is intrinsically alien to the biblical revelation.   [G. BERTRAM, III, 123-28]

---

therapeúō [to heal, serve],   *therapeía* [healing],   *therápōn* [servant]

therapeúō.
1. This word, in secular Greek, means a. "to serve," "to be serviceable," and b. "to care for the sick," "to treat," "to cure" (also figuratively).
2. The same senses may be found in Judaism (cf. "to serve" in Esth. 1:1b and "to heal" in Sir. 18:19). Philo refers to healing of both body and soul.

3. In view of the miracles of Jesus, one might expect many parallels among the rabbis of his day, but in fact we have only isolated instances.

4.a. In the NT *therapeúō* never means "to serve" in a secular sense, and only once in Acts 17:25 does it denote worship. Paul's point here is that the true God has no cultic dwelling and does not need a cultic ministry, so that the *therapeúein* that is suitable for idols is inappropriate to him.

b. A much more common use is for "healing," not merely in the sense of medical treatment, but in the sense of the real healing that the Messiah brings. Jesus has power to heal the sick (Lk. 7:21ff.). This is no less a part of his ministry than preaching (Mk. 4:23). No sickness can resist him. He heals many (Mk. 3:10) or all (Mt. 12:15), whether they be ill, lame, blind, maimed, or deaf and dumb, and whenever the need arises even though it be on the sabbath (Mt. 12:10 etc.). Driving out demons is one form of healing. This is done by the word in what is sometimes a violent struggle (cf. Lk. 4:40-41; Mk. 3:10-11). The word also cures ailments or defects, though Jesus will often touch the sick (Mk. 1:41), take their hand (1:31), lay on hands (5:23), or perform acts like those of doctors (7:33; cf. Jms. 5:14). The sick may simply touch him or his garment (Mk. 3:10; 5:28; cf. Peter's shadow in Acts 5:15 and Paul's clothing in Acts 19:12). The healing is total as Jesus, initiating the age of salvation, takes away the sicknesses of the people (Mt. 8:17; cf. Is. 53:4). The actual processes may have parallels in Greek and Jewish records, but the important point is the demonstration that with Jesus God's kingdom has already broken into our suffering world. The real miracle, then, is not the breaking of natural law but victory in the conflict for world mastery. Following up this victory, Jesus commands his disciples to heal the sick. The command itself, received in faith, grants them the power (Mt. 10:1 etc.). The risen Lord repeats the commission, and in Jesus' name the apostles heal the sick and demon-possessed (Acts 5:16; cf. Peter in Acts 3:1ff., Philip in Acts 8:7, Paul in Acts 28:8-9). Healing may be blocked, however, by a false attitude: skepticism in Nazareth (Lk. 4:23; Mk. 6:5), and the weak faith of the disciples in the case of the epileptic boy (Mt. 17:14ff.).

c. The serious wound that is inflicted on the beast is healed according to Rev. 13:3, 12. The event to which this refers cannot be fixed with certainty.

therapeía. This word means a. "household" and b. "healing." For a. cf. Mt. 24:45 and for b. Lk. 9:11 (medical) and Rev. 22:2 (eschatological). The LXX has the term for "divine worship" (e.g., Joel 1:14), but the NT never has this sense.

therápōn. Common in the LXX, this word is used in the NT only for Moses in Heb. 3:5. The point is that Moses is a servant in contrast to Jesus the Son (cf. Gal. 4:1ff.).　　　　　　　　　　　　　　　　　　　[H. W. BEYER, III, 128-32]

---

therízō [to reap, harvest],   **therismós** [harvest]

---

therízō. a. Literally "to reap," b. figuratively "to reap a harvest" (cf. a moral action and its consequences either ethically or eschatologically in the LXX and Philo). The NT uses the word literally in Mt. 6:26 and figuratively in Jms. 5:4 (with an eschatological thrust). What is reaped corresponds necessarily to what is sown (Gal. 6:7ff.). This provides a motive for right conduct. The results of mission, too, are a harvest based on what is sown (Jn. 4:36ff.). But here one may have the joy of reaping what others sow. Material support is also a harvest related to the spiritual seed that is sown (1 Cor. 9:11).

therismós. The LXX uses this word for "harvest" literally in Gen. 8:22 and figuratively for world judgment (the separation of the elect people from the nations) in Joel 4:1ff. An ethical sense may be found in apocalyptic (eschatological) and Philo (psychological). The literal sense occurs in the NT in Jn. 4:35, the figurative (God's eschatological decision) in Mt. 13:30; Mk. 4:29; Rev. 14:15. The hour of this decision is imminent (Mt. 9:37-38) and the criterion is ethical (Mt. 13:41ff.). Both promise and threat are implied (Mt. 3:12; 13:30), for the decision entails separation in consequence of present action.   [F. HAUCK, III, 132-33]

theōréō → *horáō*

---

theríon [wild animal, beast]

A diminutive of *thḗr*, *theríon* means "wild animal," sometimes including birds and insects, and later any animal. The LXX uses the term only for land animals, usually wild, and if Tit. 1:12 adds *kakós*, no addition is needed to convey the sense of a wild beast. The figurative sense (humans as beasts) also occurs. Wild animals are with Jesus (as well as angels) in the desert in Mk. 1:12. The sense here is literal; there is no need to think of Gen. 2 or of a mythological conflict. The *theríon* of Rev. 13:2 links Revelation to Dan. 7, but one cannot simply equate the beast of Revelation and the fourth beast (Rome) of Dan. 7. Since there is antithetical parallelism between God and the dragon, Christ and the beast, and the seven spirits and the second beast (Rev. 13:11ff.), the first beast is antichrist. This wounded beast stands in contrast to the slain Lamb (5:6). The beast, which is wounded but not slain, enforces worship by violence, persecutes believers, and dishonors God by serving as the dragon's representative; the Lamb, on the other hand, gives himself up in service to a self-sacrificial death, receives honor and power, and brings glory to the Father. The second beast is the false prophet of the last time who acts like a true prophet but whose prophecy is a devilish temptation to worship the first beast (13:11ff.). Elsewhere in the imagery of Revelation demonic powers are commonly depicted as beasts: the locusts of 9:1ff., the horses of 9:16ff., and the frogs of 16:13-14. One may see here a distinction from *zóon*, which includes humans. In a fallen creation the beasts seem to signify the perversion of our calling as those who are made in God's image. They can thus symbolize the demonic element that corrupts what is truly human into what is subhuman.   [W. FOERSTER, III, 133-35]

---

thēsaurós [treasure, treasure chest], **thēsaurízō** [to keep, lay up]

---

thēsaurós. a. "What is deposited," "store," "treasure." b. "Place of storage," "warehouse," "treasure chamber or chest" (e.g., temple treasury). The LXX has both a. (Josh. 6:19 etc.; also figuratively in Is. 33:6) and b. (Am. 8:5; figuratively in Jer. 51:16 etc.). In Judaism good works are a treasure laid up with God; interest may be paid now, but the capital is kept for the judgment. Eternity is also a treasure house to which the righteous go (cf. Lk. 23:46; Rev. 6:9). The NT has a. "treasure" in the literal sense in Mt. 13:44, with a figurative use in Mt. 12:35 (the heart's treasure), Mt. 6:19ff. (heavenly in contrast to earthly treasures, but with a new urgency and no thought of merit), Col. 2:3 (the treasures of true wisdom and knowledge hidden in Christ), and 2 Cor. 4:7 (the treasure of the new life in Christ that we have as yet only in earthen vessels). The NT also has sense b. ("treasure chest") in Mt. 2:11; 13:52. In sense a. *thēsaurós* is important in Gnosticism for the treasure of light and Christ as treasure and pearl. Perhaps Gnostic terminology influenced Col. 2:3, but cf. Is. 45:3.

thesaurízō. "To keep," "hoard," "lay up," especially valuables. In the LXX see 2 Kgs. 20:17 and figuratively Am. 3:10. Christ forbids the heaping up of earthly goods as materialistic and egotistical (Lk. 12:21). They may be lost if not renounced, for they carry no security (Mt. 6:19ff.). Acts of love are a storing of treasure in heaven (Mt. 6:20). Paul uses the word literally for the setting aside of weekly offerings in 1 Cor. 16:2 (cf. 2 Cor. 12:14), but in Rom. 2:5 the use is figurative for the storing up of wrath by the impenitent (cf. God's keeping of the present world for judgment in 2 Pet. 3:7).   [F. HAUCK, III, 136-38]

---

thlíbō [to press, afflict],   *thlípsis* [pressure, affliction]

A. *thlíbō, thlípsis* in Secular Greek.
1. *thlíbō* means literally "to press," "squash," "hem in," then "to be narrow." *thlípsis* means "pressure" in the physical sense, e.g., medically of the pulse.
2. *thlíbō* figuratively means "to afflict," "harass" with the nuances a. "to discomfit," b. "to oppress" or "vex." Philosophically the group is used for life's afflictions.

B. *thlíbō, thlípsis* in the LXX.
1. The theologically significant figurative use is common in the LXX for various Hebrew terms meaning a. "to distress," b. "to treat with hostility," c. "to afflict," d. "to oppress," and e. "to harass," "be hostile to," and even "destroy," or, in the case of the noun, a. "trouble," b. "distress," c. "oppression," "tribulation," etc. 2. Both internal and external afflictions are in view, the former covering both distress and anxiety, the latter the afflictions of slaves or aliens, oppression by enemies, and such troubles as illness, desert wandering, and shipwreck. 3. Inner fear or anguish may be intended (cf. Gen. 42:21). 4. The terms acquire theological significance because the reference is usually to the distress of Israel (or the righteous), e.g., in Egypt (Ex. 4:31), or exile (Dt. 4:29). Often such distress is seen as a divine visitation on the people, so that we read of a present or future day of affliction (Is. 37:3; Hab. 3:16). 5. Yet the righteous also suffer various afflictions (enemies, sickness, etc.) from which God delivers them (cf. Pss. 9:9; 32:7, etc.). In later Judaism afflictions are said to bring about repentance, increase merit, or achieve expiation for the self or others.

C. *thlíbō, thlípsis* in the NT.
I. The Nature of Tribulation.
1. The terms are common in the NT (especially in Paul), and are mostly figurative. Both believers and apostles undergo affliction. It is factual (Acts 11:19 etc.) but also unavoidable (Jn. 16:33). Israel is a type in this regard. Paul as an apostle suffers particular affliction (cf. 1 Th. 3:3-4; Acts 20:23; 2 Cor. 1:4-5; Col. 1:24).
2. These sufferings are Christ's own sufferings, which, not yet exhausted (Col. 1:24), continue in the apostle. The apostle experiences Christ's own passion as he is

given up to death for the church (2 Cor. 4:10-11). In proclaiming the word, he exemplifies it. The martyrs of Rev. 7:14 bear similar witness to Christ's own sufferings. The church's sufferings are Christ's in a representative capacity. Christ suffers in his people on the basis of his own suffering.

3. Christian suffering, then, is inseparable from the Christian life, is Christ's own suffering, and is eschatological in view of its occurrence in the aeon that Christ has ended (cf. 1 Cor. 7:26ff.; Mt. 24:4ff., 9ff., 15ff.; Rev. 1:9, where present afflictions are set in the light of the great end-time tribulation). Judaism, too, expected eschatological tribulation, but new features in the NT are (a) that this final tribulation has begun, (b) that the Messiah's own passion initiates it, and (c) that it is suffered by his scattered people.

4. There is also an affliction associated with the last judgment, when the unrighteous and those who afflict the church will come under God's wrath (Rom. 2:9; 2 Th. 1:6). The church anticipates this judgment as it is associated with Christ in his vicarious suffering of divine judgment. In this sense Christian affliction is for faith a true demonstration of God's righteous judgment (2 Th. 1:5).

II. The Experience of Tribulation.

1. Christian afflictions are of different kinds (cf. the synonyms in Rom. 2:9; 1 Th. 3:7; Jn. 16:21; Mk. 4:17). Specific references are to persecution in 1 Th. 1:6, imprisonment in Acts 20:23, derision in Heb. 10:33, poverty in 2 Cor. 5:13, and perhaps sickness in Rev. 2:22 (cf. also the lists in Rev. 8:35 and 2 Cor. 11:23ff.). We also find inner distress and sorrow (Phil. 1:17) or anxiety and fear (2 Cor. 7:5).

2. The common power of affliction is that of the death that works in it (2 Cor. 1:8-9; 4:10-11; 11:23). Christ's suffering in his members is an experience of the effects of the death that he has defeated (cf. Phil. 3:10). Affliction leaves its external mark on our present life with its contingency and corruptibility (2 Cor. 4:16). It thus brings us under the test whether we will champion the gospel at the risk of life, whether we will see life in terms of its own possibilities or of those opened up by the divine promise (cf. 2 Cor. 1:8-9). Faith accepts the divine judgment in affliction and offers life back to God. It thus leads to patient endurance (2 Th. 1:4) which in hope focuses on what is not seen, thus giving comfort (2 Cor. 1:5-6) and the assurance that coming glory far outweighs present suffering (2 Cor. 4:17-18). We have, then, a virtuous circle whereby the promise gives hope, hope accepts suffering, suffering nourishes endurance, and endurance augments hope, fulfilling thereby the joy of the Spirit's promise.

3. With this acceptance of affliction Christians edify the community. In it the word becomes a relevant promise of comfort to others (2 Cor. 1:4ff.). In his people's suffering Christ himself builds up the church, thus showing that in fact he has already broken the power of affliction.   [H. SCHLIER, III, 139-48]

thnḗskō, thnētós → *thánatos*

---

thrēnéō [to mourn, lament],   *thrḗnos* [mourning, lamentation]

From Homer on *thrḗnos* is a technical term for "mourning" and may even mean "lament" or "dirge." The verb, however, is not restricted to lamenting for the dead.

A. *thrḗnos* in Graeco-Roman Culture.

1. In Greece mourning is an essential part of burial during the display of the corpse and the actual interment. The dirge serves as homage to the departed. Women play

a prominent part, but men also sing laments. Professionals are often used. Solon tried to restrict excesses connected with the related growth of a burial industry, e.g., by laying down that mourners must be relatives.

2. Near Eastern influences reduced the effectiveness of Solon's reforms. These may be seen in the use of lamentations to bewail the death of the cult-god in the mysteries.

3. The Romans follow the Greeks in the singing of dirges by close female relatives during the showing of the corpse and burial.

B. *thrēnos* in Near Eastern Culture. Near Eastern customs allow a place for more violent lamentation. Here again women play a more important part than men.

1. The OT. The LXX normally uses *thrēnos* for the lament rather than more spontaneous mourning. Mourning takes place in the house and then during interment. Relatives are the first to mourn, though there may be national mourning for outstanding figures (cf. Gen. 50:3, 10). Professional mourners are found, and the formal dirge replaces the original less formal lamentation (cf. Gen. 23:2). Inspired poets like David (2 Sam. 1:17ff.) and Jeremiah (Jer. 9:9) take the place of the paid threnodists of Greece. Women are again prominent (Jer. 9:10; Ezek. 32:16), especially virgins (Joel 1:8; Jer. 9:20). No cultic lamentation occurs in the OT. Instead of mourning for a dead god, the living God himself, through his prophets, calls for lamentation on account of judgment on his people or the destruction of other peoples. Thus *thrēnos* becomes an important prophetic word, whether it refers to the *thrēnos* of the prophet, of those affected, or of spectators (cf. Is. 14:4). The circle widens as the divine judgments become universal. *thrēnos* may cover the whole land (Am. 5:16), especially the high places (Jer. 7:29 etc.). For examples of Hebrew *thrēnoi* see Lamentations; 2 Sam. 1:19ff.; Am. 5:1ff.; Is. 14:4ff.

2. Judaism. In postbiblical Judaism mourning customs are fixed and codified. Lamentation takes place in the house and at the interment. Flutes are played, but their use is restricted (e.g., not in the house or procession or on certain days). Dirges are sung by women, who also clap their hands. Women relatives play little part, but the men eulogize the dead, beating their breasts and heads and stamping their feet. Paid speakers deliver orations near the grave. Burial inscriptions *(epitáphioi thrēnoi)* are referred to by Josephus in *Antiquities* 7.42.

C. *thrēneō* and *thrēnos* in the NT. The noun occurs only in Mt. 2:18 (uncertain) and the verb only in Mt. 11:17 (Lk. 7:32); Lk. 23:27; Jn. 16:20. Except in John the reference is strictly to mourning but not to the formal lament.

1. The use of *thrēneō* bears witness to Jewish customs at the time of Jesus (cf. weeping, beating on the breast, and the lamenting of the women on the way to Golgotha).

2. An inner continuation of OT trends may be seen in Mt. 2:17-18 (quoting Jer. 31:15). The NT fulfilment corresponds here to the OT prophecy inasmuch as God accomplishes a miraculous deliverance amid complete destruction. The *thrēnos* of the mother of Israel (Rachel) is taken up by the mothers of Bethlehem, but over both rings out the voice of the *éleos* of God, so that with the proleptic preservation of the Savior Jesus the voice of lamentation becomes the voice of joy. The women of Israel lament similarly as Jesus marches to the cross in a burial procession (cf. the anointing). But Jesus forbids this, for he himself is on the way to life and Jerusalem to destruction, so that it is for themselves and their children that the women should mourn. We thus have here another instance of the prophetic intimation of *thrēnos*. In Jn. 16:20 there is a reference, of course, to the lamenting of the disciples at the death of Jesus, but

the term now has a broader reference to the lamenting of his people during the whole period of affliction prior to his parousia (cf. v. 21). At the same time, as Israel's mourning is turned into joy by Christ's first coming, so the mourning of the church will be turned into joy by his second coming. His people passed through the night of sorrow and death to the day of joy and life. In Mt. 11:17 (Lk. 7:32) the mourning, like the piping, is an attempt to tell God what he ought to say through his messengers. The people's leaders, like the children, want to give orders to God (cf. Ahab in 1 Kgs. 22:8ff.). They will not accept the divine singularity of the messengers and they evade the claim of God thereby (cf. Mk. 3:22, 29-30). God's acts are accompanied by human *thrénos,* but in the NT this centers on Jesus himself, the messenger of joy. There is *thrénos* at his birth and death, and during its time of tribulation with him his church also knows *thrénos.* Yet since he is the messenger of joy, we are not to expect *thrénos* from him personally, and the *thrénos* of the church militant will finally be the *chará* of the church triumphant.   [G. STÄHLIN, III, 148-55]

→ *klaíō, klauthmós, kóptō, kopetós, lypéō, lýpē, penthéō, pénthos*

---

thrēskeía [religion], *thrēskos* [religious], *ethelothrēskeía* [self-made religion]

1. This group, rare in the LXX and NT, is common in Greek.

2. The etymology is disputed; early suggestions were derivation from Thrace or *thréomai* ("to tremble"), while modern scholars favor a link with *therap-* ("to serve").

3. Distinction of meaning may also be noted. The good sense is "religious zeal" (for which Thracian women were noted), "worship of God," "religion" (cf. Josephus *Antiquities* 1.13.1). This seems to be meant in Acts 26:5 and Jms. 1:26-27.

4. But there is also a bad sense, i.e., "religious excess," "wrong worship"; this is the point in Col. 2:18 with its attack on the cult of angels.

5. The bad sense is not intrinsically necessary but is added by the genitive. In itself *thrēskeía* is a colorless word rather like cultus. It has to do mostly with the externals of worship, and makes them a matter of taste or choice. Synonyms like *therapeúō, epiméleia,* and *hierourgía* are similarly rare in the NT. This indicates that expressions denoting a religious attitude to God find little place in NT Christianity, for here one's attitude to God is the response to God's claim, and in distinction from cultus the Bible speaks of faith as the obedience of the whole person to God (cf. the phrase *leitourgía tḗs písteōs* in Phil. 2:17).

6. The word *ethelothrēskeía* in Col. 2:23 seems to have been coined by the author to denote, not an affected piety, but a piety that does not keep to its true reality, to Christ, but is self-ordered.   [K. L. SCHMIDT, III, 155-59]

---

thriambeúō [to lead in triumph]

The basis of "triumph," *thriambeúō* means a. "to triumph over" and b. "to lead in triumph." In the NT it occurs in sense b. Christ's way to the cross is paradoxically God's triumph march in which he leads the powers (Col. 2:15). Christians, too, are led in triumph (2 Cor. 2:15), but for them, as Christ's servants, it means grace and ministry.   [G. DELLING, III, 159-60]

---

thrónos [throne]

A. The Throne outside the NT.

1. On the Usage. This word, related to seat and footstool, denotes a high stool with back, arms, and footstool. It is a seat for elders, teachers, etc., and is later reserved for kings and gods. In the plural (cf. Col. 1:16) it may denote royal or divine power. The LXX, which has it for *kisē'*, often adds genitives, e.g., throne of glory (1 Sam. 2:8), of the kingdom, i.e., royal (1 Kgs. 9:5), of wickedness (Ps. 94:20); cf. throne of glory in Mt. 19:28 and of grace in Heb. 4:16.

2. The Throne in the Greek World. The royal throne comes to Greece from the Near East. The divine throne is the prerogative of Zeus, though there is sometimes a double throne for Zeus and Hera. Thrones also occur in the cult of the dead. There is no equivalent to a real divine throne in the OT, though cf. heaven as God's throne. The ark is never spoken of as the empty throne of God.

3. The Throne in the OT. The throne is the seat of the king (Gen. 41:40), the queen mother (1 Kgs. 2:19), and the governor (Neh. 3:7). The firstborn of Pharaoh shares the throne (Ex. 11:5), and Solomon sits on David's throne (1 Kgs. 1:13). The throne is thus a symbol of rule. David's throne is to last forever (2 Sam. 7:12ff.). It is the Messiah's throne in Is. 9:6. Since David's kingship implies that of God, the throne is that of Yahweh's kingdom (1 Chr. 28:5) or of Yahweh himself (1 Chr. 29:23). References, then, to the throne of God (cf. Is. 6:5; Ezek. 1:26) or to God's throne in heaven (Is. 66:1) are meant to express the majesty of the divine Ruler. This majesty manifests itself on earth; the coming age of salvation is the Lord's throne in Jer. 3:17 (cf. the link with the name and covenant in 14:21). Majesty and presence also come together in the address in Jer. 17:12-13. The power of God's throne extends over the Gentiles (Ps. 47:8). It is eternal (Ps. 93:2; Lam. 5:19). It carries with it the administration of justice (Ps. 9:4, 7). Thrones are depicted in the judgment scene in Dan. 7:9ff. The throne of the Ancient of Days is fiery flames, and myriads of angels surround it.

4. The Throne in Hellenistic Judaism. In Wis. 18:15 the word comes down from God's throne to judge Egypt. Wisdom itself is the occupant of the throne in Wis. 9:4. The martyrs are near the throne in 4 Macc. 17:18. Josephus mentions the throne in *Antiquities* 3.137, but he and Philo avoid the idea of God's throne as too anthropomorphic.

5. The Throne in Palestinian Judaism. The rabbis show great interest in the throne. It is a precosmic work. The righteous dead are under it, the martyrs being closest. Of the angels, the throne angels are nearest. The thrones of Daniel are for the great men of Israel. The Son of Man sits on the throne of judgment in Eth. En. 45:3 etc.

B. The Throne in the NT. The NT refers freely but nonspeculatively to God's throne and associates the throne of Christ with it.

1. Heaven as God's Throne. On the basis of Is. 66:1ff. Jesus calls heaven the throne of God (Mt. 5:34). Swearing by it is swearing by God. Stephen quotes the same verse to show that God cannot be enclosed in a human temple (Acts 7:49).

2. The Throne of David. David's throne is the throne of the Messiah King in Lk. 1:32. Heb. 1:8 refers Ps. 45:6 to Christ as the eternal Son. The Davidic monarchy reaches its true fulfilment with the sovereign majesty of the Messiah.

3. The Throne of Glory. This phrase occurs often in Synoptic sayings with reference to the future rule of the Messiah over Israel, in which the disciples share (Mt. 19:28).

This rule extends to the Gentiles (Mt. 25:31-32), though others do not now have a part. In Revelation, too, there are thrones at the beginning of the millennial rule (20:4), but at the end there is only the great white throne of world judgment and the one who sits on it (20:11).

4. *The Throne of Grace.* Now that Jesus, our great High Priest, is seated at God's right hand, the throne may be called the throne of grace, for God's sovereignty is manifested in mercy rather than condemnation (Heb. 4:14ff.).

5. *The Throne of God and of the Lamb.* In the vision in Rev. 4 the throne, though not described, is central. Worship is addressed to him who sits on it (4:8ff.). The exalted Christ shares the throne (cf. 5:13; 6:16). It is the Lamb that feeds the host before the throne (7:15ff.). The stream of 22:1 issues from the throne of God and the Lamb. The throne of God and the Lamb is in the city (22:3). Already in 3:21 Jesus shares this throne with his Father and promises the fellowship of the throne to overcomers. The elders have their own thrones in 4:4, but these are not autonomous, for they worship him who sits on the throne. In contrast, God's own throne itself is finally the throne of the Lamb. This twofold throne represents the same eternal dominion.

6. *The Throne of Satan and of the Beast.* There is an ungodly counterpart to the throne of God and the Lamb. The throne of Satan in Rev. 2:13 may contain an allusion to the cult of Aesculapius at Pergamos, or more narrowly to the altar to Zeus in the fortress there. The dragon gives a throne to the beast in 13:2, and an angel pours out a vial on the throne of the beast in 16:10. This results in darkness for his kingdom; the throne and dominion are related.

7. *The Throne as a Class of Angels.* Col. 1:16 mentions "thrones" among the supraterrestrial powers (cf. Slav. En. 20:1). The reference seems to be to the highest class of angelic powers.   [O. SCHMITZ, III, 160-67]

---

thymós [passion, wrath], *epithymía* [desire], *epithyméō* [to desire], *epithymḗtēs* [one who desires], *enthyméomai* [to consider], *enthýmēsis* [hidden thought]

---

thymós (→ *orgḗ*). *thýō* denotes violent movement (of air, water, the ground, or living creatures). From the sense "to boil up" comes "to smoke" and then "to sacrifice." *thymós* means what is moved or moves, i.e., vital force, and it may then denote such varied things as desire, impulse, spirit, anger, sensibility, disposition, and thought. In the NT *thymós* occurs five times in Paul, once in Hebrews, twice in Luke, and ten times in Revelation (five with *toû theoú*). The meaning is always "wrath," human in Paul, Hebrews, and Luke but not in Rom. 2:8, divine in Revelation except in 12:12 (the dragon's wrath). Symbols are wine and cup (from the OT), as well as vials (cf. Rev. 14:10, 19; 15:7). In Rev. 14:8; 18:3 Babylon has brought the nations into ungodliness, so that they have fallen into sin and under God's wrath (cf. Jer. 25:15ff.). *thymós* is the same as wrath, and the phrase the *thymós* of wrath *(orgḗ)* occurs in Rev. 16:19; 19:15.

epithymía, epithyméō (→ *hēdonḗ*).

1. This group denotes desire, especially for food or sex. This desire is morally neutral at first, but philosophy, holding aloof from the sensory world, regards it as reprehensible, and in Stoicism *epithymía* is one of the four chief passions. Epicurus

distinguishes between natural and illicit desires, subdividing the former into the purely natural and those that are necessary to happiness.

2. The OT condemns the evil will as well as the evil act, e.g., coveting. Sexual self-discipline is demanded (cf. 2 Sam. 11:2). In Judaism fasting, regulation of meats, and strict keeping of the sabbath are important. Desire is sometimes viewed as the main sin, for *epithymía* conflicts with supreme devotion to God.

3. Stoicism and Judaism combine in the Hellenists. The LXX has *epithymía* for base desire in, e.g., Num. 11:4 (though *epithymeín* can denote pious striving in Is. 58:2). Philo summons us to conflict with *epithymía*. 4 Maccabees demands the rule of reason over impulse and numbers *epithymía* (arising out of sensuality) as one of the chief impulses alongside *hēdonḗ*, *phóbos*, and *lýpē*.

4. Rabbinic equivalents are to much the same effect, e.g., in such phrases as "doing one's desire."

B. The Usage in the NT. The group is more common in the epistles than the Gospels. It may denote hunger (Lk. 15:16), longing (Lk. 22:15), or a desire for the divine mysteries (Mt. 13:17) or for anything good (Phil. 1:23; 1 Tim. 3:1). But it usually denotes evil desire as indicated by the object (a woman in Mt. 5:28, other things in Mk. 4:19), by the orientation (cf. Gal. 5:17), by the instrument (the heart in Rom. 1:24, the body in Rom. 6:12, the flesh in Eph. 2:3, the eyes in 1 Jn. 2:16), or by the manner (carnal in 1 Pet. 2:11, worldly in Tit. 2:12, defiling in 2 Pet. 2:10, etc.). A Jewish model for Paul's use of the term for the tenth commandment is found in Rom. 7:7. Hence one need not postulate Stoic influence except perhaps in 1 Th. 4:5. In any case, disobedience, not irrationality, is the evil in *epithymía*. Desire is a manifestation of sin. Under the prohibition of the law, it discloses our carnality, our apostasy from God, and our subjection to wrath (Gal. 5:16; Rom. 1:18ff.). In James it is the root of individual sins (1:14-15), while in John it arises out of the world, constitutes its nature, and perishes with it (1 Jn. 2:15ff.). NT statements about *epithymía* belong to the message of repentance and self-denial. *epithymía* is impulse, lust, or anxious self-seeking. It shows us what we really are. Even after reception of the Spirit, it remains a danger.

epithymḗtḗs. In the NT the only instance is in 1 Cor. 10:6 (alluding to Num. 10:34).

enthyméomai. From *énthymos,* which means "brave," "spirited," this word has many senses, of which only "to weigh," "consider" occurs in the NT (Mt. 1:20; 9:4).

enthýmēsis. This rare word is used in Mt. 9:4; 12:25; Heb. 4:12 for the hidden thoughts of the heart which only God can discern. *énnoia* is parallel in Heb. 4:12 and *téchnē* in Acts 17:29. What is foolish or wicked may be implied.

[F. Büchsel, III, 167-72]

---

thýra [door]

A. The Literal and Figurative Use.

1. Strictly *thýra* is used in the NT for "door," especially in a house, whether outer door or door into a room (cf. Mk. 1:33; 2:2; Lk. 11:7; Acts 5:19; Jn. 18:16; Mt. 6:6). It may also denote the "gate" of the temple (Acts 3:2; 21:30), and a third use is for the "entrance" to a tomb (Mt. 27:60; Mk. 15:46).

2. Figuratively, to be "at the door" is to be very near (Mk. 13:29 etc.). To "open

a door" is a common metaphor for opportunity. God opens a door by granting the chance for missionary work (Col. 4:3), or the possibility of faith (Acts 14:27); believers open the door to Christ in repentance (Rev. 3:20). In contrast, to "close the door" represents the irrevocable loss of opportunity (Rev. 3:7; Mt. 25:10) and thus carries an implication of judgment. That Christ has power to open and shut (Rev. 3:7) shows that grace and judgment are both in his hand.

B. The Door Miracles of the NT.

1. Three times in Acts (5:19; 12:6ff.; 16:26-27) liberation comes through the miraculous opening of doors. The motif of the self-opening door is a common one in the OT and beyond, but there is only a restricted connection with freeing from prison. The details in Acts, the ancient parallels, and the inner similarities suggest to some scholars that Luke is stylizing the accounts, but no specific influences can be established. The lesson of the stories is that no bonds or prisons can check the course of the gospel, since God's arm is strong enough to break every lock and remove every obstacle.

2. In Jn. 20:19, 26 the risen Lord twice passes through locked doors. His transfigured corporeality is no longer subject to earthly restriction.

C. The Heavenly Door.

The idea of a solid firmament carries with it the thought of a door or doors into heaven. Though there are only two references in the OT (Gen. 28:17; Ps. 78:23), the notion is common in classical writings, mysticism, Gnosticism, and later Judaism. The only express reference in the NT is in Rev. 4:1, but the same figure lies behind the verses that speak about the shutting of heaven (Lk. 4:25) or its opening either (1) in God's self-revelation (Mk. 1:10; Jn. 1:51; Acts 10:11; Rev. 19:11) or (2) in disclosure to the saints of the mysteries of the coming aeon as they have access by vision (Acts 7:55ff.) or in the Spirit (Rev. 4:1ff.) to God's heavenly palace.

D. The Eschatological Use of the Image of the Door.

Eschatologically the opened or closed door denotes the granting or refusing of a share in salvation. In this instance, the door is not the door of heaven. Entry into the kingdom, whether a door is mentioned (Mt. 25:10) or not, usually implies entry into the festive hall for the eschatological banquet (Mt. 7:7-8; 22:12; 25:10, 21ff.; Lk. 13:24-25; 14:23). In context, the opened door of Rev. 3:8 also signifies access to eschatological glory rather than missionary success. The image of Rev. 3:20 has an eschatological thrust as well; the returning Savior (cf. Lk. 12:37) seeks entry as a guest so as to enjoy table fellowship in the great festal meal.

E. "I Am the Door" (Jn. 10:7, 9).

The context seems to force us to take this I-predication rather differently in v. 7 (the door to the sheep) and v. 9 (the door for the sheep). But this is not very likely, and we do best to interpret the ambiguous v. 7 by v. 9. The origin of the metaphor has been much debated. Some scholars see a misreading of the Aramaic "shepherd of the sheep" as "door of the sheep." Others trace the influence of pre-Christian Gnosticism. Yet OT models for the shepherd image, for going in and out, and for door-predication (especially in the messianic context of Ps. 118:19ff.) form a more obvious basis. In analogy to "I am the way" in 14:6, "I am the door" develops the thoughts in 10:1-2. The lesson of v. 9 is that Christ alone mediates membership in the messianic community and reception of its blessings of salvation and eternal life. The lesson of v. 7 is that he alone mediates the authentic pastoral office.   [J. JEREMIAS, III, 173-80]

→ *kleís, pýlē*

thyreós → *hóplon, panoplía*

---

thȳō [to sacrifice],   *thysía* [sacrifice],   *thysiastḗrion* [altar]

A. Linguistic Data.

1. thȳō. a. The basic sense is "to sacrifice," at first only burnt offerings, then all kinds. The LXX uses it for sacrifices both to God (Gen. 31:54) and to alien gods (Ex. 34:15), the NT only for pagan sacrifices (Acts 14:13: 1 Cor. 10:20). b. In connection with burnt offerings, the word also means "to immolate," then "to slay" (cf. in the NT Lk. 15:23; Acts 10:13). It is used for killing the Passover lamb in Mk. 14:12 (cf. 1 Cor. 6:7: Christ, our paschal lamb, has been slain). c. A third sense is then simply "to murder."

2. thysía. a. The "act of sacrifice." b. "Sacrifice" (a) literally, both pagan and OT (cf. in the NT Lk. 2:24; 1 Cor. 10:18), and (b) figuratively for the death of Christ as an offering to God (Eph. 5:2), and the Christian life as an offering of the self (Rom. 12:1), whether in gifts (Phil. 4:18), praise (Heb. 13:15-16), or sharing and doing good (Heb. 13:16).

3. thysiastḗrion as God's Altar. a. Literally for the temple altars (Lev. 4:7 and in the NT Mt. 5:23-24; Lk. 11:5-6; 1 Cor. 9:13; Heb. 7:13; Rev. 11:1), for other cultic altars (Gen. 22:9-10; Jms. 2:21), and for the heavenly altar (Rev. 6:9 etc.); b. figuratively, but with no very specific reference, Heb. 13:10.

B. The Concept of Sacrifice in the NT.

1. The OT Presuppositions. The root of the OT concept of sacrifice is to be found in the reality of the covenant order. God in his historical self-revelation wills to have personal dealings with his people through sacrifice. Whether sacrifice be a gift to God, means of atonement, or expression of fellowship, it is oriented to God's presence in grace and judgment. The prophets contest it (Am. 5:21ff.; Is. 1:10ff.) and the Psalms reject it (40:6ff.; 50:8ff.) only when human achievement replaces personal encounter. If praise, obedience, faithfulness, and love are seen to be the true sacrifices (Pss. 40:6ff.; 50:14, etc.), these do not invalidate the cultic sacrifices, which may also be sacrifices of righteousness (Ps. 51:19).

2. The NT Evidence. In the Gospels Jesus does not pronounce judgment on the cultus. He accepts the altar and sacrifices as given factors in Mt. 5:23-24; 23:18ff. The call for mercy and not sacrifice simply follows the prophetic line (Mt. 9:13; cf. Hos. 6:6). If the temple and the cultus are secondary and will come to an end (Mt. 12:6; 26:61; Jn. 2:19), it is because Jesus himself will set up a new covenant which finds no place for cultic offerings. Paul realizes that fellowship with deity is the goal of sacrificial meals (1 Cor. 9:13; 10:18ff.), but in 1 Cor. 10:11ff. he gives no hint that the eucharist, in which we have fellowship with Christ's body and blood, is for him a sacrificial meal. In keeping with his theology of history and its schema of the old order and the new, he compares Christ as the paschal lamb of the new community to the paschal lamb of Israel (1 Cor. 5:7). Christ's atoning death is the antitype of the death of the lamb. Both in its nature and its effect, this death is pleasing to God. The figure of sacrifice, so familiar to Paul, helps him to understand it as the basic event of salvation. The same figure helps him to understand the Christian life. As believers we are to offer thanksgiving, or to offer ourselves as *logikḗ latreía* (Rom. 12:1). All that we do in faith, e.g., in ministry (Phil. 2:17b) or giving material help (Phil. 4:18), becomes *thysía* and *leitourgía*. 1 Peter is to the same effect when it calls Christians a holy priesthood (2:5) whose gifts are spiritual sacrifices as they offer back their lives to God (cf. 1:15). Hebrews uses the cultic concepts of the OT when it calls Christ the High Priest who makes expiation by his free self-offering. For all the parallels, however, the epistle sees a qualitative distinction inasmuch as the sinless and eternal Son, by his once-for-all and personal self-giving, accomplishes the inward cleansing and eternal redemption which fulfil the original purpose of OT sacrifice, i.e., personal fellowship with God. For this reason, the unique self-sacrifice of Christ abolishes as well as transcends the OT ritual. If the author uses the ritual as a means to portray Christ's work, he also finds that in the new covenant the literal offerings of the ritual are replaced by the obedience of Christ (10:5ff.; cf. Ps. 40) and the Christian ministry of praise and mutual service (13:15-16; cf. Ps. 50). In other words, total self-giving, first that of Christ, and then, on this basis, that of his people, is the true meaning of sacrifice.

3. The Historical Background: Later Judaism and Hellenism.

a. Later Judaism is strict in observing the laws of sacrifice but voices criticism as well as commendation. Sacrifices are good because they involve obedience to God's commands. Doing good, however, is also obedience and may indeed be regarded as sacrifice (cf. also fear of God and suffering on his behalf). Thus cultic sacrifice loses its special place and the way opens for Judaism to continue unshaken without it. If the cultus is second only to the law as one of the things on which the world rests, synagogue piety (i.e., repentance, a broken spirit, study of the law, benevolence, and prayer) is also sacrifice, and even though sacrifices cease, the sacrifice of thanksgiving will not cease to all eternity.

b. Hellenism inherits from the classical world, not the old view of sacrifice nor its spiritualizing, but the philosophical criticism of it. If only the good are worthy to sacrifice, and a pious life is more pleasing than a great offering, there is no thought that right conduct bears any relation to literal sacrifice. For some, true worship takes place in the sphere of the *noús*. For others, mystical prayer replaces offerings. Hellenistic Judaism adopts a figurative concept, regarding moral obedience as better than cultic observance in a possible fusion of philosophical and prophetic influences. Philo allegorizes the law of sacrifice and thereby spiritualizes it on mystical lines. If a right attitude of soul is necessary, the true point is that the outward form points beyond itself.

4. The NT Concept and the Early Church. In the first post-NT writings sacrifice is a plastic image for self-giving to God. The Epistle of Barnabas finds in Christ's death the counterpart of OT sacrifices, while the Martyrdom of Polycarp regards martyrdom as a sacrifice; fasting, benevolence, and prayer are sacrifices in the Shepherd of Hermas. Justin, with his typological view of OT and NT worship, calls the sacramental elements *thysíai* (*Dialogue* 41), though for him only prayers have the character of true sacrifices (117). The praise of creation is the supreme sacrifice in Athenagoras *Supplication* 13. Did. 14.2 alludes to Mt. 5:23-24 and Mal. 1:11 in connection with the eucharist, but an approach to eucharistic sacrifice emerges only with Irenaeus.

[J. BEHM, III, 180-90]

thṓrax → *hóplon, panoplía*

ι ι

Iakṓb [Jacob]

---

1. In the NT the formula "Abraham, Isaac, and Jacob" denotes the special relation to God on which Israel prides itself. God made his covenant with these three patriarchs, and the expression symbolizes true and faithful Israel. The Pharisees apply it to themselves as those who have accepted God's will and are thus sure of the kingdom. Those who have the patriarchs as their fathers are sons of the kingdom; hence the offense of the saying in Mt. 8:11-12 that outsiders will sit down with Abraham, Isaac, and Jacob in the kingdom while the sons are cast out. Later Judaism finds in the formula a guarantee of God's dealings with the covenant people that is included in the patriarchs. This line of thought lies behind Mk. 12:26 and parallels: If God is still the God of the patriarchs, then they must have been raised to life again, and we shall be raised with them. In Acts 3:13, since it is the God of the patriarchs who raised up Jesus, Israel denies its own God in rejecting Jesus. The inclusion of the three names has a restrictive purpose, for only the descendants of Jacob, not all the descendants of Abraham, are the covenant people (cf. Acts 7:2ff.; Heb. 11:9).

2. Paul finds an abandonment of the restriction in the gospel, for all who believe are true children of Abraham and heirs of the promise. If Jacob represents national Israel in Rom. 11:26, he also illustrates that grace is by election and not by right of birth (Rom. 9:13).

3. The use of "house of Jacob" for Israel (Lk. 1:33; Acts 7:46) is again restrictive.

4. 1 Clem. 31.4-5 remains within this circle, seeing in Jacob the epitome of national Israel to which Jesus belongs by the flesh and as High Priest.

[H. ODEBERG, III, 191-92]

Iánnēs [Jannes],   **Iámbrēs** [Jambres]

---

1. These two names are corrupt even in rabbinic texts, where they figure as the chief magicians of Egypt who try to compete with Moses and Aaron (Ex. 7:11ff.). They are said to have continued their opposition at the Red Sea and in the desert, where they instigated the worship of the golden calf and later worked with Balaam.

2. In 2 Tim. 3:8 they are mentioned only in a general way as opponents of Moses who typify opponents of the gospel.

3. Traces of a work recounting their story are found in Origen and the *Decretum* of Gelasius.   [H. ODEBERG, III, 192-93]

---

iáomai [to heal],   *iasis* [healing],   *iama* [healing],   *iatrós* [healer]

A. Sickness and Healing outside the Bible.

1. Primitive Views. In early times the only physical ailment that can be understood is a wound in battle. Sicknesses that are not understood are thus seen as attacks by alien powers which can be overcome by magic or sacrifices. But the healing properties of plants and animals are also discovered and play a role in treatment.

2. Rationalization of the Art of Healing in Ancient Medicine. The Egyptians were among the first to develop medicine, using a strange blend of research and theory (2600–1600 B.C.). They lanced sores, set bones, stitched wounds, filled teeth, and used drugs, but also found a place for magic. The Greeks put the art of healing on a more empirical basis (6th cent. B.C. on). Doctors formed a guild bound by the Hippocratic oath, and were trained in schools. Specialists in eyes, teeth, ears, and women's complaints emerged in Rome, and many physicians became wealthy.

3. Miracles of Healing, Gods of Healing, and Savior Gods in Hellenism. Religion and superstition merged with medicine. Sickness was often seen as a punishment, and we find gods of healing, especially Apollo and Aesculapius. Temple sleep supposedly had healing value in such shrines as Epidauros, which were very well appointed. Whether surgery was performed during sleep is debatable, but there was no rift between priest and doctor except in detail, e.g., on the nature and treament of epilepsy. Miraculous healings are reported, such as the curing of the blind and lame by Vespasian and Hadrian. The gods are healers and saviors in both an inward and a cosmic sense. Thus Aesculapius is seen as the founder of medicine and Eros as the patron of gymnastics and agriculture as well as medicine. The gods mediate the healing presence of Zeus, whose goal is human happiness in a predominantly natural sense.

4. The Literal and Figurative Use of the Words. a. The literal sense is most frequent, but b. the Greeks extend the terms to other fields in the general sense "to restore," e.g., by removing intellectual defects, or avenging wrongs, or correcting evils. Along these lines Epictetus thinks of the philosophical school as *iatreíon*.

B. Sickness and Healing in the OT and Judaism.

1. The Religious Evaluation of Sickness. In Israel some ailments, such as mental illness, leprosy, and mortal sickness, are associated with demons, but we also find the beginnings of hygiene, and the conviction develops that God sends or withholds sickness. Thus it may be a sign of divine wrath (Is. 38), but this raises problems for the righteous (e.g., Job) when there is no obvious cause. When there is, repentance is a way to healing (2 Sam. 12:15ff.). Judaism tries to assign particular ailments to particular sins, but recognizes that sickness may also be a chastisement of love or a means of alleviating eternal pains.

2. Magic and Medicine; God the Healer (Literally). Belief in God discredits magic, but relics continue (cf. conjurations in Judaism). Egyptian and Greek influences (Gen. 50:2) produce more empirical medicine (cf. Is. 3:7; Jer. 8:22; hygienic rules in Sir. 19:2-3, etc.). Anatomy and surgery command respect. But God is the true Doctor. The priest is put in charge of health (Lev. 13:49ff.). If physicians are praised as the work of God (Sir. 38), prayer plays an important role (38:13-14); cf. the censuring of Asa for resorting to physicians rather than God (2 Chr. 16:12). Philo is no less ambivalent, recognizing good doctors but pointing to God as the true Healer. In later Judaism warnings against doctors go hand in hand with the training of many rabbis as physicians and the use of physicians in the temple. Prayer is the chief means of healing, as in many psalms with their sequence of complaint, petition, and thanksgiving (Pss. 6; 16:10; 38; 107:17ff.). If the terms may at times be figurative, the literal sense is original. The relation between prayer and miraculous healing is fluid (cf. Naaman in 2 Kgs. 5 and the raising of the dead in 2 Kgs. 4).

3. Healing in the Figurative Sense. God heals by withdrawing judgment, which may take the form of either sickness or other calamities. Thus healing has a broader sense, especially in Jeremiah (3:22 etc.). Repentance and remission of sins are prerequisites, so that healing and forgiveness go closely together. *iásthai* denotes God's gracious turning, with the binding up of a wound in the background. Thus restoration of fellowship is the crucial thing from which physical or mental restoration flows. The prophet is anointed by God to bind up the broken in heart (Is. 61:1) by announcing good tidings. The Servant of the Lord undergoes vicarious suffering to make expiation, so that the paradoxical conclusion is reached that "by his stripes we are healed." Philo favors the figurative use, but more for inner healing than for forgiveness, though this healing comes from God, the *lógos,* or the divine *énnoia.*

C. Sickness and Healing in the NT.

1. Sickness and the Art of Healing in the Light of the NT. At times the NT relates sickness to demons (cf. possession and Mt. 12:22ff.), but it also sees it as judgment (Rev. 6:8), although not in terms of a rigid dogma of retribution (cf. Mk. 2:5; Jn. 9:3-4; 11:4). Paul, then, can classify it with all other sufferings (Rom. 8:28) even under the burden of what was perhaps a physical ailment that God did not remove (2 Cor. 12:7ff.). Sickness in the NT is seen to contradict God's plan for creation, so that in spite of Mk. 5:26 there can be no opposing any effort to free us from it (cf. Lk. 10:34; Col. 4:14; 1 Tim. 5:23).

2. Jesus the Physician. The Use of the Terms in the Gospels. Jesus made a great impression as the Healer. All the Gospels, especially Luke, use *iásthai* for his work. *iasis* is literal in Lk. 13:32, and figurative only in quotation. Jesus calls himself "physician" more than once (cf. the parabolic saying in Mk. 2:17 and the proverbial saying in Lk. 4:23).

3. Jesus' Miracles of Healing in the Light of the History of Religion. Stories of similar healings to those of Jesus raise many questions.

a. Tradition. Many accounts of healing come from excavations at Epidauros. Some of the healings are grotesque, but others seem to be authentic. The stories of healings in Judaism contain legendary accretions, but often the essentials may well be historical. When two or more recensions are present, these confirm the tenacity of popular tradition. No original testimony exists to the miracles of Jesus, nor can one trace an unbroken tradition (in spite of Papias), so that expansion may well have taken place in some instances (cf. Mk. 5:21ff.; Lk. 7:11ff.; Jn. 11:1ff.). Yet there can hardly have been substantial change after the first century. The tradition took its basic form before the written record (cf. 1 Cor. 15:6) and authenticates itself by vividness and simplicity (as compared to apocryphal stories). The community arose under the impress of mighty acts which could hardly be replaced and which Christians themselves showed no eagerness to imagine (cf. the fact that the Baptist is credited with no miracles, and the matter-of-fact account of what happened to Paul in Acts 14:20 and what he said in Acts 20:10). Common features of miracle stories are (1) the failure of medical skill, (2) an encounter, and (3) the quickness and sureness of the miracle. Motives in telling the stories vary, e.g., to give confidence at Epidauros, to show the power of keeping the law among the rabbis, and to lead to faith in Christ in the Gospels.

b. The Nature of the Miracles. Nature miracles are recounted at Epidauros and in Judaism. A few occur in the Gospels, but healings are more common. The ailments cured include more than nervous disorders, and there are also exorcisms. The stories are told, not from the standpoint of the patients or self-seeking priests, but from that of the mercy of Jesus, so that love, not egoism, is the central force. There are no animal healings, no payments, no punishments, and no burlesque elements. Jesus will not use miracles to cause a sensation and the only demand he makes is for discipleship, so that spiritual blessing may be enjoyed as well as physical healing.

c. The Cures. The mode of healing in the Gospels is simple and involves no empirical therapy. There must have been some special reason for the use of spittle in Mk. 7:33; 8:23; Jn. 9:6. We find no healing sleep, and laying on of hands replaces cruder contacts. Some healings are at a distance. Healing is often by word, not in the sense of magic, but by Jesus' word of command in answer to appeals for help and in virtue of the power received in prayer (Mk. 9:29; cf. the rabbis). A precondition and consequence is faith. Jesus himself has faith, demands it of those whom he heals, and promises power to the disciples only as they have faith. The faith required, however, is not a belief in the credibility of the miracles but faith in Jesus himself. It involves a relationship of trust, a conviction of God's power, and the resultant commitment of obedience. This faith, which is well illustrated in Mt. 8:5ff. (the centurion), receives not merely physical healing but the full health of salvation (Mk. 5:34; Lk. 7:50).

d. Theological Appraisal: The Uniqueness of Jesus' Healings. Miracles of healing are well attested from various sources, and natural "laws" are relative, so that one cannot rationalistically rule out the healings of Jesus. The impact of the personality and special powers of Jesus must also be taken into account. Since these are put in the service of God's own work in history, we should not measure them by ordinary standards. Compared to other healings, those of Jesus are unique by reason of his own holy and merciful love, which is both supremely intensive and supremely comprehensive, and which embraces both the outer and the inner being. Jesus does not sever the connection between evil and sin, yet he does not view sickness as retribution nor believe that freedom from sickness is a primary goal. His chief concern is to free from sin, and while he may use healing as a first step in this direction, he may also give forgiveness first (Mt. 9:2) or even confer forgiveness where there is no need of healing (Lk. 7:47ff.). The healings may also sometimes serve a pastoral point, e.g., when performed in the context of a dispute (the sabbath in Mt. 12:9ff., the right to forgive in Mt. 9:1ff.). The miracles are not spectacles, but they are signs (Jn. 2:11, 23; 4:48, etc.). They are simple but powerful demonstrations that the promised age of fulfilment has come (cf. Mt. 11:5 and Is. 35:5-6). From them the Baptist should perceive that God's rule is present (Mt. 12:28). Failure to see this is guilty obtuseness (Lk. 12:54ff.). The miracles are proleptic victories—a foretaste and pledge of the final victory. Jesus invades Satan's kingdom with power (Lk. 10:18). Nothing can resist him, for even though he is put to death, the kingdom comes thereby. This messianic and eschatological context gives the healings of Jesus a uniqueness in religious history which is the uniqueness of his whole person and mission.

4. *Healing in the Apostolic Age.* If Jesus gives his disciples power to heal (Mk. 3:14-15), this is not an endowment for selfish use but an equipment for effective witness by act as well as word. The power may reach a limit (Mk. 9:18), is not to be used for profit (Mt. 10:8), and may be exercised even outside the apostolic circle when the name of Jesus is invoked (Mk. 9:38ff.). With their eschatological faith in Jesus, the first witnesses take up the fight against bodily suffering (Acts 3:1ff. etc.). If primitive features occur, especially on the part of the healed, the acts of power, like the healings of Jesus in missionary preaching (Acts 2:22), awaken faith (Acts 2:43 etc.) and further the progress of preaching (Rom. 15:18-19 etc.). The gift of healing is an operation in the name of the exalted Lord (Acts 3:16), or an operation of the Lord himself through the Spirit (Acts 9:34). It is a special charism, given particularly

to commissioned witnesses, but confers no claim or magical exemption from serious or persistent sickness (cf. Phil. 2:26; 2 Tim. 4:20). Healing may be a gift, but it is still a theme in godly intercession (2 Cor. 12:8; Jms. 5:13ff.). The figurative use of the group occurs in the NT only in OT quotations (except in Heb. 12:13). Thus the warning of Acts 28:27 quotes Is. 6:10, and 1 Pet. 2:24 quotes Is. 53:5. In both instances the reference is to restoration through forgiveness and the resultant saving benefits. The use in Heb. 12:13 is ethical. In an exhortation to Christian conduct, this is compared to the making of straight paths so that what is lame may be healed.

D. The Gospel of the Healer and Healing in the Early Church. The missionary vigor of Christianity owes much to the power with which it brings release from bondage to demons and destiny and to the selfless love with which believers take up the cause of the sick and needy. With an emphasis on liberation from sin, the figurative use (partly under OT influence) becomes more prominent again, as when Jesus is called *iatrós* (cf. the similarity of sound of Jesus and *iásthai*) and Hellenistic motifs are transferred to him. Literal use of the group is rare. It occurs in OT quotations in 1 Clement and Barnabas, and the figurative use is especially common in Hermas (e.g., *Visions* 1.1.9; *Mandates* 4.1.11; *Similitudes* 5.7.3) with a hint of infusion of grace as well as remission of sins. [A. OEPKE, III, 194-215]

→ *dýnamis, therapeúō, sōtḗr, hygiḗs*

---

idiṓtēs [layman, outsider]

A. *idiṓtēs* outside the NT.
1. In Greek usage we find the following senses: a. "private individual" as distinct from public person; b. "layman" as distinct from expert, and c. "outsider" as distinct from member. The term takes on its distinctive sense from the context.
2. The rabbis take over *idiṓtēs* as a loanword in the three senses: a. "private person" as compared to the king; b. "layman" in contrast to expert; and c. "human being" as distinct from God.

B. *idiṓtēs* in the NT.
1. The word has in Acts 4:13 the general sense of "uneducated" and in 2 Cor. 11:6 the similar sense of "unskilled" (in eloquence)(cf. Justin *Apology* 1.39.3; 60.11).
2. In 1 Cor. 14:16 the context suggests a person who does not have the gift and hence is not edified. In 1 Cor. 14:23-24, however, the combination with *ápistos* shows that the reference is to a nonmember attending the church's gatherings. In both cases, then, unbelievers are in view, i.e., outsiders who have neither the gift of tongues nor faith, and whom exercise of the gift will not help. [H. SCHLIER, III, 215-17]

Iezábel [Jezebel]

Jezebel is seldom mentioned in later Judaism, and usually only in repetition of the OT stories in 1 and 2 Kings. Rev. 2:20 obviously uses the name symbolically, possibly for a movement or a pagan prophetess, but more likely for a woman leader in the Christian community, i.e., a libertinistic prophetess. [H. ODEBERG, III, 217-18] *hierateía, hierateúō, hieráteuma* → *hierós*

Ieremías [Jeremiah]

A. **The Prophet Jeremiah in Later Judaism.** Sources of the Jeremiah tradition are 2 Chr. 35:25; 36:12, 21-22; Ezr. 1:1; Dan. 9:2; Sir. 49:6-7; 2 Maccabees; also Philo and Josephus, a fragment transmitted in Eusebius *Preparation for the Gospel* 9.39, and various apocrypha. Most of the tradition relates to the historic personage, adding to the scanty data of Scripture legends about his birth, his hiding of the ark, and his martyrdom by stoning.

B. **The Prophet Jeremiah in the NT.**
1. The only express NT references are in Mt. 2:17; 6:14; 27:9, though there are probable allusions in Mt. 23:37 and Heb. 11:37. 2. A saying of Jeremiah is expressly quoted in Mt. 2:17 (Jer. 31:15). 3. Recollection of Jer. 32:9 may explain the attributing of Zech. 11:13 to Jeremiah in Mt. 27:9. 4. Mt. 16:14 says that some people saw in Jesus a reappearance of the prophet Jeremiah. This is puzzling inasmuch as there is no record of eschatological expectation relative to Jeremiah. Possibly Jeremiah occurs as a representative name (cf. Mk. 8:28; Lk. 9:19) because of the canonical position of the Book of Jeremiah at the head of the latter prophets.

[J. Jeremias, III, 218-21]

---

hierós [holy], *tó hierón* [the temple], *hierōsýnē* [priesthood], *hierateúō* [to discharge the priestly office], *hieráteuma* [royal priesthood], *hierateía (-ía)* [priestly office], *hierourgéō* [to perform holy service], *hieróthytos* [sacrificed to deity], *hieroprepḗs* [holy], *hierosyléō* [to rob temples], *hierósylos* [temple robber], *hiereús* [priest], *archiereús* [high priest]

---

hierós.

A. **Etymology.** Various suggestions have been made but there is no certainty except that the word is pre-Greek.

B. *hierós* **in Common Greek Usage.**
1. Synonyms and Antonyms. There is no fixed distinction from such terms as *theíos, hágios, hósios,* etc. On the one side it denotes the power of the divine sphere, on the other the sanctity of what belongs to deity, whether by nature, primal law, or custom. It is the most common sacral and cultic term in the Greek world.
2. The Main Groups of Usage.
a. Relative to things it denotes (1) what belongs to the divine sphere (2) as this is experienced in the form of consecration, e.g., (3) countries and cities under divine protection, but (4) especially cultic things like temples, feasts, etc., yet also (5) anything dedicated religiously to deity.
b. Persons are *hieroí* (1) when as heroes or kings they stand under divine protection, or (2) are sacrosanct like the emperor, or (3) are initiates in the mysteries (cf. also poets, philosophers, and priests).

C. *hierós* in the LXX. Feeling the pagan sense of the term, the LXX prefers *hágios* for *qdš* and has *hierós* only rarely, e.g., the sacred trumpets in Josh. 6:8 and vessels in Dan. 1:2.

D. *hierós* in the Rest of Hellenistic Judaism.

1. Josephus senses the distinctiveness of *hágios* but still makes lavish use of *hierós* in the general literary sense.

2. Philo, too, has *hierós* frequently, e.g., for holy Scripture or a holy commandment, but with a stronger moral significance than in ordinary Greek usage.

3. In Josephus, Philo, and the Apocrypha, the word describes (1) Scripture and the law, (2) holy things pertaining to the tabernacle and temple, and (3) holy days, especially the sabbath.

4. We also find such speculative connections as to (1) nature and the cosmos (Philo), (2) the *lógos* and the *noús* (Philo), (3) the mystical in the broad sense, especially relating to numbers and allegorical meanings (Philo), and (4) persons such as priests, angels, and occasionally virtuous people (Josephus and 4 Maccabees).

E. *hierós* in the NT. The infrequent use in the NT shows that Christianity shares the LXX shunning of this sacral term of paganism. The one concession is the description of the OT scriptures as *hierá* in 2 Tim. 3:15, and cf. the use of *tá hierá* in 1 Cor. 9:13.

F. *hierós* in the Early Church. In the apostolic fathers and Apologists *hierós* occurs for Scripture in 1 Clement, for the right use of money in Hermas *Similitudes* 1.10, and once for God in 1 Clem. 33.4. Clement of Alexandria uses the term only rarely (for Moses in *Stromateis* 1.12.4), but Origen has it frequently, e.g., for incense, the resurrection, and especially angels, prophets, the apostles, and friends devoted to sacred study.

tó *hierón*.

A. tó *hierón* and tá *hierá* as General Cultic Terms. a. A first use is for "sacrifices," especially burnt offerings and sacrificial meals and customs. b. Cultic objects and actions in general may also be denoted. c. A more comprehensive use is for the cultic as such (cf. 1 Cor. 9:13: "the temple ministry").

B. The Use of tó *hierón* for Temple.

1. General Greek Usage. While *naós* is normally the inner shrine, and *témenos* the precincts, *tó hierón* may be used more comprehensively for either, or for any consecrated grove or place of sacrifice, including pagan shrines, the Jerusalem temple, and even synagogues.

2. The Jerusalem Temple in Judaism.

a. The LXX and Apocrypha. (1) While the priest is *ho hiereús*, the LXX avoids *tó hierón* for the temple, preferring *oíkos* or *naós*. (2) In the Apocrypha, however, we often find *tó hierón* or *tó hierón toú theoú* (or *toú kyríou*) for the temple.

b. Josephus and Philo. (1) In general Josephus offers a full account of Herod's temple (*Jewish War* 5.184ff.). (2) As regards usage, both Josephus and Philo use *tó hierón* for the tabernacle, Solomon's temple, and pagan shrines. In Josephus *hierón* can denote the whole court or the temple hill, while *naós* is used for the temple proper, as are *tó hágion* and *tá hágia,* which put a special stress on the holiness of the place (cf. Philo's allegorical use), with a distinction between *tá hágia* and *tá hágia tôn hagíōn* (the holy of holies).

3. *The Use of tó hierón for the Temple in the NT.*

a. The General Usage. While the LXX avoids *hierón* for the OT temple, the NT finds no reason not to use the term now that the age of the OT temple has gone. *oíkos* may be used, as in Mt. 12:4 *(toú theoú)* and Jn. 2:16 *(toú patrós mou),* and *naós* is also found in a general sense (cf. Mt. 27:5; Jn. 2:19), but *tó hierón* is the common term for both the precincts and the inner sanctuary.

b. *tó hierón* as a General Term. With a general reference *tó hierón* occurs in such passages as Mt. 12:6; Acts 24:6; 1 Cor. 9:13; Lk. 22:53; Mk. 13:3.

c. As the Temple Hill. *tó hierón* denotes the temple hill or outermost court in verses like Mt. 21:14; 21:12 and parallels (the cleansing of the temple).

d. *tó pterýgion toú hieroú.* The exact reference in Mt. 4:5; Lk. 4:9 is uncertain. Schlatter suggests an overhanging balcony and Dalman the southeast corner jutting out over the valley of Kidron.

e. Teaching in the *hierón.* When we read of Jesus or the apostles teaching in the temple (e.g., Mk. 14:49; Jn. 7:14; Acts 5:20; cf. Lk. 2:46), the site is either the house of instruction or a pillared hall in the outer court.

f. The Beautiful Gate. The site of the healing in Acts 3:2ff. is the bronze Corinthian gate at the eastern entrance to the Court of Women (Josephus *Jewish War* 2.411).

g. *tó hierón* as the Court of Women. This is where Anna prays in Lk. 2:37. Jesus watches the widow here in Mk. 12:41ff., teaches here in Jn. 8:20, and probably has here the encounter of Jn. 8:2ff. Mothers bring their purificatory offerings here (Lk. 2:24).

h. As the Inner Court. This is the reference in Lk. 18:11; Lk. 24:53; Mk. 11:11; Jn. 7:37-38; Acts 21:26.

i. As the Temple Proper. Only the priest may enter this. Curtains cover the entrances to the sanctuary and the holy of holies (cf. Mt. 27:51).

C. Impulses toward a Spiritualization of the Temple in the Greek World.

1. *The Enlightenment.* The Ionic enlightenment protests against the Homeric anthropomorphizing of the gods, speaks of a single God, and shows some understanding of inward prayer. Criticism of the cultus develops in Zeno. Seneca finds the cultus salutary for the people but reinterprets it for the sage.

2. *The Spiritualizing of the Concept of the Temple.* Seneca suggests that the world or the soul is the true temple of God. Dualistic contempt for the body does not allow the body to be called God's temple. Later the image of the temple is used for the indwelling of the spirit or of magical power.

D. The Way from OT Prophecy to Jewish Apocalyptic and Hellenistic Judaism.

1. *The Temple in OT Prophecy.* Prophets like Amos and Isaiah do not stand in a cultic tradition, but while they criticize cultic acts when there is injustice or lack of love (Am. 5:21ff.; Mic. 6:6ff.; Is. 1:10ff.), they are not against the cultus as such. Even if the temple cannot embrace God's majesty (Is. 66:1ff.), the nations will still come to Zion (Is. 60:1ff.). Similar themes occur in Proverbs (e.g., 15:8; 21:27) and Psalms (cf. 50:8ff.; 51:16ff.), but with no rejection of the cultus as such. The temple will be destroyed (Mic. 3:12) but it will also be rebuilt (Ezek. 40ff.; cf. Hag. 2:9 and Is. 2:1-4). The smallness of the new temple, the absence of the ark, and the desecration by Antiochus Epiphanes influence later temple apocalyptic.

2. The Temple in Apocalyptic.

a. Sayings Prior to A.D. 70. A more glorious temple is expected in the messianic period, though whether the Messiah builds it is unclear.

b. The New Temple. There is a legend that the sanctuary is buried and hidden prior to restoration. With the liberation of Israel will come a bigger Jerusalem with a new temple as the sanctuary of the nations.

c. The Heavenly Temple. References to a heavenly city and temple as the pattern of the earthly city and temple and as the abode of the blessed also occur.

d. The Catastrophe of A.D. 70. The destruction of the city and temple in A.D. 70 intensifies the above expectations. Special consolation is found in the idea of a heavenly Jerusalem (which in 4 Esdras will appear at the end).

e. The Spiritualizing and Criticism of Sacrifice. For some rabbis, acts of love and keeping the commandments are the true sacrifices, and we even find the view that there will be no sacrifices in the world to come.

3. The Temple in Josephus and Philo.

a. Josephus. Josephus values the temple and the cultus highly. God sends a portion of his Spirit into it, though without actual localization. For Josephus, however, virtue is the worthiest service of God and the cosmos is God's eternal house which survives even when the temple perishes.

b. Philo. Philo attacks a perverted religiosity which neglects inner purification. To make God a house of wood or stone is sinful; the cosmos is God's true *hierón,* as well as the *logikḗ psyché,* the *noús,* and the *logismós* of the wise. The *lógos* reigns as true priest of the soul. Yet Philo can find a place for temple worship both in allegorizing and in the sense that it offers scope for the valid impulse to bring thank offerings and to seek expiation.

E. The Attitude of Jesus and Primitive Christianity toward the Temple.

1. The Emphasis of the Witness of Jesus and the Primitive Christian Attitude in the Gospels. The sayings in the Gospels reflect the church's conflict as well as Jesus' own position, but what Jesus says undoubtedly influences the church's decisions.

a. The Twofold Attitude of Jesus. Jesus affirms temple worship as divinely appointed, and yet claims superiority over the temple. He prays in the temple and teaches in it as the public center of Judaism (cf. Mk. 14:49; Jn. 7:14, etc.). He also heals there (Jn. 5:14; Mt. 21:14). Children's lips praise him there (Mt. 21:15).

b. The Temple as the Place of the Divine Presence. By making the temple the place of his self-manifestation, Jesus fulfils and transcends the prior divine history. The tabernacle and the temple are the house of God (Mt. 12:4) and a house of prayer (Mk. 11:17). To swear by the temple is to swear by the indwelling God (Mt. 23:21). As the place of God's presence, the temple sanctifies all that is in it (Mt. 23:16-17). The temple tax is to be paid (Mt. 17:24ff.).

c. The Cleansing of the Temple. This is a purification, not an interruption, of worship. Holiness extends to the precincts as a whole. The protest expresses the prophetic conviction that the temple is not a place of gain, that it is to be a place of prayer for all nations, and that prayer takes precedence over sacrifice. The action may also have a messianic aspect but can hardly be political.

d. The Saying concerning the Destruction and Rebuilding of the Temple. Garbled at the trial, this saying seems to have been to the effect that new worship, associated with the person of Jesus, will replace the old. Worship will be perfected in the messianic age of salvation. Jn. 2:18ff. also relates the saying to the body of Jesus (cf. Jn.

1:14b). As Mt. 12:6 puts it, a greater than the temple is here. The full import of this comes out after A.D. 70.

e. The Prophecy of Its Destruction. The Synoptic apocalypse contains a prediction of the overthrow of the temple in a judgment which is also a sign of the parousia. While the disciples admire the temple, Jesus sorrowfully foretells its devastation. The abomination of Dan. 12:11 is given a wider reference: Gentile armies in Lk. 21:20, and the antichrist in 2 Th. 2:3-4.

f. Sayings from Later Strata of the Tradition. The infancy stories offer prophecies from temple devotees to whom it is important that the new revelation is given on the ancient site. Jesus as a boy shows reverence for the temple, especially as a place of teaching. In the passion story the rending of the temple curtain shows that Christ's death gives free access to God (Mk. 15:38).

2. *The Attitude of Other NT Writings toward the Temple as tó hierón.*

a. Acts. In Acts the disciples pray in the temple (2:46), and Paul has a vision there (22:17) and brings the offering of purification (21:26). Yet Stephen argues that the Most High does not dwell in houses (cf. Is. 66:1-2) and insists that the temple is only temporary.

b. Other NT References. In other NT references *naós* or *tá hágia* is used rather than *tó hierón*. The central point is that such terms as temple, people, and priesthood now apply to Christ's universal community. In 1 Pet. 2:4ff. the image of the temple is combined with that of Christ as the living stone. The community itself is the temple in 1 Cor. 3:9; 2 Cor. 6:16-17; Eph. 2:19ff. In 1 Tim. 3:15, however, the *oíkos theoú* is God's household (cf. 1 Pet. 4:17; Heb. 3:6; 10:21).

c. The Images of Revelation. Revelation develops the new imagery. Overcomers will be pillars in God's temple. The new Jerusalem comes down as the universal city, and the temple is God's eternal presence on the throne (7:15; 11:19; 14:15; 15:5-6; 16:1, 17). In the consummation there will be no more temple (21:22).

hierōsýnē.

1. More abstract than the later *hierateía,* this means "priesthood," "priestly office," "priestly dignity," or (more rarely) "priestly ministry." It occurs only once in the canon (1 Chr. 29:22) for the priestly office, but is common in the Apocrypha, Josephus, and Philo for the priesthood or priestly office or dignity (and occasionally activity).

2. The only NT instances are in Heb. 7:11-12, 24. This passage contrasts the Levitical priesthood, which cannot bring perfection, with Christ's priesthood after the order of Melchizedek. In the fathers we find the term for the Levitical priesthood (1 Clem. 43.2), the pagan priesthood (Athenagoras *Supplication* 28.3), Christ's priesthood (Origen *Commentary on John* 1.28), and the Christian ministry (Chrysostom).

hierateúō.

1. This word means "to discharge the priestly office" and occurs in the Koine, the LXX, the Apocrypha, and Josephus, but not Philo.

2. In the NT we find it only in Lk. 1:8 (Zacharias). 1 Clement has it for the Levitical ministry (43.4), and Justin for that of pagan priests (*Apology* 1.62.2).

hieráteuma. This word seems to occur only in the LXX and dependent writings. It is coined in exposition of the revelation at Sinai (Ex. 19:6; cf. 23:22).

1. The underlying Hebrew means "kingdom of priests" and implies that all members of the people have a priestly function (cf. Num. 11:29; Is. 61:6).

2. The LXX translates very freely and brings out the priestly side more strongly.

3. 2 Macc. 2:17 alludes to Ex. 19:6 with its reference to Israel's divinely conferred dignity, which is both royal and priestly. But here and in Philo the exact meaning is uncertain, for strictly *basíleion* means "royal residence."

4. In 1 Pet. 2:5, 9 salvation and dignity are transferred to the community, which, based on Christ as the living stone, is built up into a spiritual temple for a consecrated priestly ministry. The community is a priesthood because it offers spiritual sacrifices. As a priestly company it is immediate to God, but there is no priestly caste, for the whole people is a priestly fellowship. It is royal inasmuch as it belongs to the King, serves him, and shares his glory in a ministry of witness (v. 9).

hierateía (-ía).

1. Deriving from *hierateúō*, this word may denote priestly activity, but more commonly relates to the office, or to the priesthood in general (cf. Ex. 40:15; Josh. 18:7).

2. In Lk. 1:9 it refers to the temple ministry (burning incense), but in Heb. 7:5 it denotes the priestly office received by the descendants of Levi.

hierourgéō.

1. This term means "to perform sacred or sacrificial ministry." In Josephus and Philo it always means "to offer sacrifice" and often has no object. (*hierourgía* means "sacrifice" and *hieroúrgēma* the "act of sacrifice.")

2. In Rom. 15:16 Paul calls his service of the gospel a cultic ministry. As Christ's minister he brings the Gentiles as an acceptable offering. He protects the metaphor from cultic misunderstanding by showing that the true sacrifice, sanctified by the Spirit, is the offering of life in obedience.

hieróthytos.

1. This word means "consecrated or sacrificed to deity"; the use is mainly cultic.

2. In 1 Cor. 10:28 the reference is to cultic meat that has been offered in pagan sacrifice. For Paul it is *eidolóthyton* (food sacrificed to idols; cf. 8:1).

hieroprepḗs.

1. The idea here is "that which corresponds to the *hierón*," whether as temple, temple ministry, sacred action, or deity. The term may refer to anything religious or cultic, but can also have a moral reference, and in Philo may take the more general sense of "solemn," though for him what is consonant with God is the usual sense. Other possible meanings are "worthy of respect" and "costly."

2. Tit. 2:3 exhorts the older women of the church to be *hieroprepeís* in conduct. With a cultic background, the point is that, since they belong to God by faith in Jesus Christ, they should live and act accordingly, i.e., with the consonant reverence.

hierosyléō.

1. The reference of this term is to the robbery of temples, which is a most serious offense in Greek and Roman eyes, on a par with treason and murder, and involving drastic penalties. In the OT Dt. 7:25-26 forbids the people to take anything from pagan shrines. Josephus reinterprets this as an expression of the tolerance of the OT law for other religions. The rabbis view temple robbery more leniently than, e.g., murder, and impose less stringent penalties. Some rabbis allow idols to be possessed if they are deconsecrated by Gentiles, and the associated gold, clothing, and vessels may be put to positive use.

2. Literally the term means "to commit temple robbery" but it may also be used less strictly, e.g., for the taking of the temple gold from the Jews.

3. In Rom. 2:22 Paul accuses the Jews of despising idols yet also robbing temples. The use of the verb in a kind of list shows that a literal sense is in view. At issue is probably not so much the actual robbing of pagan temples as making a profit out of votive offerings. The suggestion that robbing the Jerusalem temple by not paying the temple tax is all that Paul means is not very convincing in view of the antithesis: abhorring idols.

hierósylos.

1. Literally this refers to the removal of the gold vessels from the temple by Lysimachus or to the stealing of sacred books and funds from the Jews according to an edict of Augustus. The noun may also be used for sacrilege in general and for the category of punishment *(hōs hierósylos)* applying to similar offenses. In comedy it becomes a common term of abuse ("rascal").

2. In the Ephesian riot the town clerk defends the apostles on the ground that they are not offenders against religion; they have committed no sacrilege (Acts 19:37).

hiereús.

A. The Priest in the Greek World.
1. The Facts of Religious History.

a. *hiereús* occurs in Homer in much the same sense as *mántis*; both priest and seer have indwelling powers equipping them to mediate dealings with the gods. b. But we also find the idea that all people may pray and sacrifice. c. Shrines, however, require official priests serving the local deities. d. There is thus a priestly vocation, and if there is no definite caste, some priestly functions are hereditary.

2. Philosophical Reflections on the Priesthood in Stoicism.

a. For Zeno the priest must have correlative knowledge and piety that put him in touch with the power at work in all things. b. Only the sage is truly equipped for what the priest is and should be. c. Epictetus may thus use the figure of the priest for the philosophical ministry.

3. The Particular Form of Such Reflection in Hellenistic Judaism (Philo).

a. In Philo the priest symbolizes the *lógos* or reason. In the temple of the soul the true man reigns as priest (cf. the phrase *ho hiereús lógos*). b. The priestly office is supreme for Philo. Physical freedom from blemish denotes spiritual blamelessness. The priest avoids sensual entanglements and looks exclusively to God. All righteous sages are priests. c. The Jewish people has priestly rank through the law, which is a preparatory school for priesthood, although only the sage, not the Jew, is the true priest.

B. The Priest in the History of Israel.
1. From the Early Period to Josiah's Reform. The original priestly function is to deliver oracles (Ex. 17:9; 33:7ff., etc.); cf. the derivation of *khn* from Arab. *kahin* ("seer"). The family head may offer sacrifices. Moses and Aaron are Levites, linked with a priestly clan, which has guest status in the national organism. The cultus is at first decentralized inasmuch as the Levites act as house priests alongside their functions at Shiloh (giving oracles, offering sacrifices, and ministering to the ark). A full cultus is established with the official temples under royal control, and in these sacrifice becomes more important than giving oracles or instruction in the law.

2. From Josiah to Ezra. Centralization is enforced by Josiah, and idolatry at local shrines is suppressed. This reform promotes the one priesthood of the one sanctuary, that of the Zadokites, and other Levites perform only lesser duties at the temple. In spite of prophetic criticism, which stresses the deeper requirements of God, sacrifice tends to overshadow instruction. The exilic period is one of codification; the priesthood emerges with exclusive cultic control. After the exile, Ezra reconstructs the community on this basis. The priesthood becomes a self-enclosed order, but scribes are also needed for the exposition of the law. If the priests, as organs of the temple ministry, become an influential caste, the scribes achieve increasing authority as they declare the law and direct religious instruction, even teaching the priests, who are only cultic ministers and often of poor reputation.

3. The Priests and Levites at the Time of Jesus.

a. A social gulf separates ordinary priests and higher priests. Traced back to Aaron, the priesthood is hereditary. It is divided into 24 classes or courses, each of which serves a week at a time and is itself subdivided into four to nine houses. On duty only two weeks a year and at the feasts, priests pursue secular callings.

b. The Levites, who are also hereditary, have charge of more lowly temple duties and the music, but have no access to the altar or sanctuary. J. Jeremias estimates that the priests and Levites, with their families, number about 10 percent of the people.

4. The Priest after the Destruction of the Temple. After the destruction of the temple, priests may read Scripture, impart blessings, and receive firstfruits, but the scribes become the true center of the community as the law and its study offer a replacement for the temple and its sacrifices (in spite of hope for restoration of the temple and priesthood).

C. The Use of *hiereús* in Jewish and Christian Writings.

1. For lack of any other word, *hiereús* is freely used for priest and high priest in the LXX. 2. *hiereús* is also used for pagan priests, but often with a qualification, e.g., *tōn eidólōn*. 3. Josephus often distinguishes ordinary priests from high priests.

D. *hiereús* in the NT.

As distinct from the chief priests and high priest, the priests play only a minor role in the NT. Jesus, while not hostile to the priestly ministry, does not call himself or his disciples priests, and shows more of a prophetic spirit.

1. Jesus accepts the role of the priest when he tells cleansed lepers to show themselves to the priest (Mt. 8:4 etc.) and offer the prescribed gift.

2. In Mt. 12:4ff. he defends his healing on the sabbath on the twofold ground that in an emergency David breached priestly law and that the priests themselves break the sabbath. Scripture itself justifies these breaches, and there is now something present that is greater than either temple or priesthood.

3. In Lk. 1:5 a priest receives the new revelation, and in Acts 6:7 many priests become believers, but the priest and Levite show up badly in Lk. 10:31-32.

4. In Rev. 1:6; 5:10; 20:6; 22:5 (on the basis of Ex. 19:6) all Christians are priests as they are redeemed by Christ, and as such they have a share in Christ's royal dominion. The church is the new community consisting wholly of priests of God and Christ.

archiereús.

A. Linguistic Observations.

1. This word occurs only from the third century B.C. and seems to have been adopted in Judaism from 150 to 50 B.C. Derivatives such as *archiéreia* (high priestess) are common. 2. OT equivalents may be found in Lev. 21:10; 2 Kgs. 25:18; Lev. 4:5.

3. *archiereús* is rare in the LXX. It occurs only five times (e.g., Lev. 4:3); elsewhere the high priest is *ho hiereús mégas* or just *ho hiereús*. 4. *archiereús*, however, is more common in the Apocrypha (41 times).

B. The *archiereús* in the Greek and Hellenistic World.

1. In Egypt and Tyre and in Theoretical Discussion. The term occurs first in Herodotus for the chief priest in Egypt, who ranks next to the king. A chief priest is also documented for Tyre. Plato's ideal state includes an annual high priest at the head of the priests officiating for the year.

2. Under the Seleucids and Ptolemies. Under the Seleucids the term is used for royally appointed high priests of satrapies and also for the chief priests of local shrines. The Ptolemies also appoint high priests, and high priests are among the various classes of priests in Egypt.

3. After Augustus. a. Provincial chief priests of the imperial cult are given the title. b. There is also a chief priest in Egypt to whom Greek and Egyptian cults seem to be subject. c. Provincial temples (e.g., in Pergamos, Smyrna, etc.) are under high priests. d. Hereditary priests of artistic and other societies are *archiereís*. e. So are many chief priests of specific gods and local shrines.

4. As pontifex maximus. The term also applies (without *mégistos*) to the emperor himself. Caesar bears the title, and with Augustus it becomes part of the imperial style.

C. The High Priest and Chief Priests in Judaism and the NT.

1. The History of the High Priesthood.

a. From the Exile to the Hasmoneans. After the exile, the high priest, claiming descent from Aaron by way of Zadok, stands alongside the governor. The Zadokite line is broken by Antiochus. Onias III goes to Egypt, and from 160 to 153 B.C. Jerusalem has no high priest.

b. From the Hasmoneans to the Time of Jesus and the Apostles. Jonathan, an ordinary priest, takes the high priesthood in 153 B.C. and later the Hasmoneans assume the royal title as well. Under Herod and the Romans arbitrary appointments and depositions take place, and influential families arise (e.g., that of Annas), though legalists still argue for Zadokite legitimacy. Political manipulation, simony, and the increasing power of the Pharisees weaken the role of the high priests, but they are still Israel's supreme religious representatives.

2. The Dignity, Rights, and Tasks of the High Priest.

a. The Dignity. With the fall of the monarchy, the high priest is not only God's plenipotentiary but also the people's chief representative. He has an indelible character of sanctity transmitted by investiture.

b. The Rights. These include a seat in the Sanhedrin and prerogatives in relation to sacrifice.

c. The Tasks. The duties are primarily cultic and culminate with the unique privilege of entering the holy of holies once a year to offer sacrifice on the Day of Atonement. The high priest ministers during the week prior to this day and must carefully protect his ritual purity at this time. Ritual regulations (e.g., avoiding a corpse) are especially strict in his case. The succession is guarded by very strict rules concerning his bride (age, virginity, legitimacy, etc.).

3. The archiereús (Singular) in the NT.

a. The high priest most often mentioned in the NT is Caiaphas, son-in-law of Annas, who was high priest in the memorable year of Christ's death (Jn. 11:49-50).

b. Annas, who had been replaced at this time, was still influential; five of his sons and his grandson, as well as his son-in-law, held the office. The references in Jn. 18:15, 19ff. (and cf. Lk. 3:2; Acts 4:6; Jn. 18:13) may be to him.

c. Ananias is high priest in Acts 23:2; 24:1.

d. The *archiereús* presides over the Sanhedrin (Mt. 26:57; Mk. 14:53; Lk. 22:54).

4. The archiereís (Plural) as Chief Priests.

a. The Significance of Higher Priestly Offices. The chief priests seem to have been a priestly college that controlled the temple and its treasury and had seats in the Sanhedrin. This college included the ruler of the temple, the heads of weekly and daily courses, the temple proctors, and the temple treasurers.

b. The *archiereís* in the NT. There are more references in the NT (and Josephus) to chief priests than high priests. Often they are mentioned alone (Mt. 26:3-4 etc.); the probable reference here is to officeholders or to the whole Sanhedrin. They are also mentioned with one or more other groups in the Sanhedrin (Mt. 27:1-2 etc.). Chief priests and scribes is a general term for the religious authorities (Mt. 2:4), and cf. chief priests and elders (Mt. 21:23 etc.), or rulers (Lk. 23:13; 24:20), or principal men of the Jews (Acts 25:2). *génos archieratikón* in Acts 4:6 (cf. Josephus *Antiquities* 15.40) denotes membership in the priestly aristocracy that occupies the higher posts. Sceva in Ephesus (Acts 19:14) is a chief priest in the diaspora. The common references to the chief priests in the NT show that opposition to Jesus comes from the religious authorities in general and not from single individuals. The official religious representatives of the people resist his ministry.

D. Speculation concerning the High Priest in Philo.

1. The Concept of Mediator.

a. In Philo the high priest represents the people, and is identified with them in expiation. Yet he also stands in a special relationship to God, and his role is thus mediatorial. b. For Philo, however, the *lógos* is central in mediation. Thus Moses, the primary *lógos*, stands behind Aaron. *lógos* speculation alone makes possible the exaltation of the *archiereús* when he enters the holy of holies (cf. Lev. 16:17).

2. The Concept of Sinlessness.

a. Philo goes beyond Lev. 16:6 in postulating the sinlessness of the high-priestly mediator, whose mistakes fall back on the people and are easily made good. b. The Stoic ideal of the sage has an influence here. c. The *lógos* doctrine controls the formulation of this absolute sinlessness. d. Also at work is the fluid concept of the man of God—a phrase which may be used for the priest or prophet, as well as for Moses, the *lógos*, or archetypal man.

3. Cosmic Speculation. The *lógos* is high priest in the temple of the cosmos, which is God's exalted world. Reflecting the cosmos, the high priest, serving the Father, brings the cosmos into this service. As he prays mediatorially for the cosmos, it enters with him into the sanctuary. The high priest should fashion his life accordingly.

E. The High Priest in Hebrews.

1. The Basic Elements in the Scheme.

a. The view of the high priest in Hebrews rests on the powerful impression made by Christ's life and death.

b. It is illumined by such OT texts as Ps. 110:4, the Melchizedek story in Gen. 14, and covenant passages such as Jer. 31:31ff. The use made of Melchizedek is typological, the main point being that of superiority to the Levitical priesthood. The prophetic passages give dynamism to the cultic image with their stress on fulfilling God's will, fellowship with God, and forgiveness.

c. Christ's high priesthood is a way that we are also to tread. It leads through sacrificial death to the throne. It comprises both saving action and continuing intercession. The ministry on earth is denoted by a "once-for-all" (cf. Rom. 6:10); the present ministry is in heaven (8:4).

d. The Son fulfils the cultus but also transcends it. He is God's complete self-manifestation in person; the truth of sonship controls that of high priesthood. This entails a predicate of eternity that gives the high priesthood its impress and force. The prophetic category of inviolable covenant promise stresses the eternal character of this new and final revelation.

e. Focus on the cultic image not only will prevent readers from flirting with the old cultus but also does justice to the fact that the ancient theocracy is built on the Levitical priesthood personally represented by the high priest.

2. *The Levitical High Priest.*

a. The Deepest and Eternally Significant Dimensions and Tasks of the Priestly Ministry. The priest is divinely called, represents the people, is in solidarity with them, is also a sinner, and has as his chief task the offering of sacrifices in expiation (Heb. 2:17; 5:1ff.; 9:7).

b. The Office of the OT High Priest Finds Its Limit in Sin. The OT priest has to offer for his own sins (7:27), his mediation does not cover willful sins (5:2), and continuing guilt creates a constant need for fresh offering, so that the cultus is in fact a reminder of sin (10:3).

c. This failure is rooted in the earthly nature of the cultus. The priest is mortal, the sacrifice must be repeated, the purification is external, and the sanctuary belongs to corruptible creation. The temple curtain expresses the indirect and provisional nature of the relationship to God (9:9).

3. *Christ the Exalted High Priest.*

a. Solidarity with Humanity. The synthesis of Son and high priest entails first the lowliness of the historical Jesus in compassionate solidarity with those he comes to help (4:15). In this regard he corresponds to the earthly high priest, yet with the exception of sinlessness (4:15; 7:26).

b. The Eternal High Priesthood Arises by Attestation of the Sonship. Jesus qualifies as high priest by showing himself to be the Son in loyal obedience through suffering (3:2; 5:7-8). His calling and institution rest on declaration of the sonship (Ps. 2:7) which he accredits by his perfection (7:28).

c. The Sinless High Priest. As high priest Jesus is unblemished like the OT high priest (7:27), but being also sinless he need not offer for himself (7:27-28), having demonstrated his sinlessness in an obedience that gives him the right to represent and save those with whom he is in solidarity (2:17).

d. The Contrast with the Carnal Offering. The sacrifice of this high priest is a supremely personal self-offering in which the priest is also victim (7:27). The offering of blood is also an offering of life which is made definitive by the eternal Spirit (9:14). This vicarious offering is once-for-all (7:27; 9:24ff.) in the double sense of being historically unique and eternally definitive.

e. The High Priest Christ Effects Access to the Throne, to God's Full Presence. This high priest passes into heaven as the earthly high priest does into the holy of holies. He thus makes the place of God's presence accessible to hope (4:14ff.; 6:17ff.). Christ the priest is also seated on the throne as king. He is eternally and omnipotently priest (7:16, 24-25). No change or chance, not even death, can interrupt his work.

4. Radical Deductions from the Christological Interpretation of the Cultus. A radical break with the ancient order occurs. The first offering ceases with the eternal validity of the high priest who brings fulfilment (10:9). God annuls the former commandment (7:18) and replaces the earlier covenant (8:13).

5. The Saving Efficacy and Practical Implications of the Truth Proclaimed.

a. The saving benefit is total redemption (cf. 9:12, 15; 10:18). This covers not only forgiveness but purifying of the conscience and sanctifying to God.

b. This salvation is a possession (4:14), an access (12:22), and a confessed reality (3:1) which the community may freely enjoy (4:16; 10:19, 22).

c. The only offerings that need now be made are those of thanksgiving and loving fellowship (13:15ff.). We must neither continue nor replace the ancient cultus, for Christ has definitively fulfilled it, and he alone abides.

F. *archiereús* and *hiereús* in the Early Church.

1. Christ as High Priest or Priest. Ignatius, 1 Clement, Justin, Clement, and Origen all reflect the language and thinking of Hebrews.

2. The General Priesthood of the Community. Irenaeus, Tertullian, and Origen refer in different connections to the general priesthood, and Justin can even use the term "high-priestly" for the church (*Dialogue* 116.3).

3. The Clergy as Priests. Did. 13.3 calls prophets "your high priests," 1 Clement uses the OT orders as a model for the church (40–41). Tertullian calls the bishop the chief priest, and Eusebius in *Ecclesiastical History* 10.4.2 has a passage in which the clergy are addressed as *hiereís*.   [G. SCHRENK, III, 221-83]

hieróthytos,   hieroprepḗs,   hierosyléō,   hierósylos,   hierourgéō → *hierós;
Hierousalḗm, Hierosólyma* → *Siṓn; hierōsýnē* → *hierós*

Iēsoús [Jesus]

---

1. *Iēsoús* is the Greek form of the OT Joshua (the name of the son of Nun in Exodus etc., of the high priest in Haggai and Zechariah, of two men in 1 Sam. 6:14 and 2 Kgs. 23:8, and of a Levite in 2 Chr. 31:15).

2. *Iēsoús* is a common name up to the early second century A.D. The NT uses *Iēsoús* for Joshua in Acts 7:45; Heb. 4:8, and cf. *Iēsoús* in Lk. 3:29, *Iēsoús Barabbás* in Mt. 27:16, *Bariēsoús* in Acts 13:6, and *Iēsoús* in Col. 4:11. After the second century *Iēsoús* disappears as a proper name, probably due to conscious avoidance.

3. The name *Iēsoús* expresses Christ's humanity. He goes by this name and is addressed and discussed by it. To distinguish him from others who bear it, we find such additions as "from Nazareth of Galilee" (Mt. 21:11) or "the son of David" (Mk. 10:47-48) (cf. also Mk. 1:24; Mt. 27:37; Jn. 18:5, etc.). The Christian community confesses this *Iēsoús* as the prince of life (Acts 3:15), as the Christ of God, as Lord and Savior, and as God's Son. But it makes no separation between *Iēsoús* and *ho kýrios*; *Iēsoús* is himself the one whom God has made both Lord and Judge (cf. Phil. 2:7; Gal. 3:1; Acts 17:31). In the Synoptic Gospels and Acts the simple *Iēsoús* is commonly used, though we also find *ho kýrios* (e.g., in Luke) and such fixed expressions as *Iēsoús Christós* and *ho kýrios Iēsoús Christós*. In the rest of the NT, however, the simple *Iēsoús* is rare. Paul has it mostly when thinking of Christ's life and death, as in 1 Th. 4:14; 2 Cor. 4:11ff.; Phil. 2:10. In Hebrews and Revelation, too, *Iēsoús*

indicates that the history of Jesus forms the basis of faith (e.g., Heb. 2:9; 6:20; 10:19; Rev. 1:9; 14:12; 20:4; 22:16).

4. Matthew and Luke claim that the name is no accident; it is given because Jesus is to save his people from their sins (Mt. 1:21). The full name in Hebrew is a sentence name: "Yahweh saves." Some fathers link *Iēsoús* with Gk. *iáomai*, and a modern theory is that Jesus is a masculine form of *Iasó*, the goddess of salvation, but Eusebius recognizes the Hebrew basis, and the use of *Iēsoús* predates Christian contacts with the Hellenistic world.

5. The name Jesus is important from the standpoint of Christ's historicity. Those who deny this must show that there is a Jewish myth of a dying and rising God, that the Gospel records are nonhistorically intelligible, that Jesus is the name of a mythological figure, and that there is a pre-Christian Jesus cult (possibly related to Joshua the son of Nun, though arguments for this are purely speculative, as are suggestions that there was a Jesse sect, or that the Therapeutae worshipped a cultic god called Jesus). As regards Joshua, for later Judaism the exodus period is pivotal, yet the entry under Joshua is secondary to the giving of the law, and Joshua is nowhere a prototype of the Messiah. Furthermore, the law has in the NT only interim significance between Abraham and Christ, and if Joshua is mentioned it is only in relation to historical events (Heb. 11:30-31; Acts 7:45) or to show that the exodus did not bring fulfilment (Heb. 3:7ff.). If they were pre-Christian, the Naassene Psalm and magic papyri might point to a Jesus cult, but these texts are later and simply testify to the impact of the historical Jesus. The simple use of the name Jesus in the Gospels and Acts bears convincing (and wholly unintentional) testimony to the historicity of Jesus.

→ *ónoma*   [W. FOERSTER, III, 284-93]

---

hikanós [sufficient], **hikanótēs** [fitness], **hikanóō** [to qualify]

---

hikanós has the basic sense of "sufficient," "enough," "large enough." It occurs in the NT for a large group, for a long period of time, or for a quality (cf. Mk. 10:46; Lk. 8:27; Mt. 3:11). It occurs mostly in Luke and Acts.

1. Among verses in which *hikanós* has theological significance is Mt. 3:11. That the Baptist is not "worthy" to carry the sandals of the Messiah denotes his servant status. He can give the baptism of repentance, but the coming Christ is the absolute Lord before whom there can be no claim and in whom God will act beyond all human measure. The centurion in Mt. 8:8; Lk. 7:6 makes a similar confession of the majesty of Jesus when recognizing his own unworthiness. In 1 Cor. 15:9 Paul is acknowledging his lack of qualifications for the apostolic office (cf. 2 Cor. 2:16). Yet recognition of personal inadequacy goes hand in hand with recognition of God as the source of all adequacy (2 Cor. 3:5-6; cf. 1 Cor. 7:25; 2 Cor. 4:1; Gal. 2:7; 1 Cor. 15:10; Col. 1:12).

2. In the Lucan passion story, when the disciples produce two swords, Jesus says: *hikanón estin* (Lk. 22:35ff.). The meaning is contested. One suggestion is that the two swords are all that is needed. But many exegetes see an implied censure, whether of the disciples' general lack of understanding, this specific misconception, or their foolish reliance on weapons. In this case the saying terminates the discussion: "That's enough." Another possibility is that Jesus is ironically pointing out the inadequacy of such arms. A final interpretation is that Jesus is trying to wean the disciples from trust in temporal weapons even while recognizing the love and loyalty which cause them

to produce the swords. He must go to the cross alone, yet the *hikanón estin* points to his continuing fellowship with his followers. Boniface VIII uses this passage allegorically (*Unam sanctam* 1302) to prove that both the temporal and spiritual powers (the two swords) are under papal control.   [K. H. RENGSTORF, III, 293-96]

---

hiketēría [supplication]

Deriving from *hiktḗr*, "one who asks protection," *hiketēría* denotes the request for protection, then, more generally, "urgent supplication." In Heb. 5:7 (with "prayers") it obviously has the more general sense in what is probably a conventional phrase.
[F. BÜCHSEL, III, 296-97]

---

hilarós [cheerful], *hilarótēs* [cheerfulness]

1. Meaning "glad" or "cheerful," *hilarós* can be used of daylight, songs, messages, and especially people. A later sense is "benevolent."
2. Common usage in the LXX is for the "cheerful countenance" or the "favor" of a ruler. "Cheerful" is the common meaning in Philo, whether in relation to feasts, sages, or the face.
3. In 2 Cor. 9:7 (in loose allusion to Prov. 22:9) Paul refers to the cheerfulness of generosity. The sense approximates to liberality (cf. Rom. 12:8). This cheerfulness contrasts with the grumbling and questioning of Phil. 2:14. Reception of God's gift provides the motivation (cf. 1 Pet. 4:9-10).
4. Among the apostolic fathers only Hermas has *hilarós* and *hilarótēs*. Nature and the human countenance are cheerful, generosity is a cheerful service, and the commandments are cheerful, while *hilarótēs* is contrasted with *lýpē* in *Mandates* 10.3.
[R. BULTMANN, III, 297-99]

---

híleōs [gracious], *hiláskomai* [to expiate], *hilasmós* [expiation], *hilastḗrion* [mercy seat]

híleōs. A predicate of persons, *híleōs* means "happy," "friendly," "gracious." It is used especially of rulers and deities. In the LXX it is a predicate of God alone, e.g., in phrases for "to forgive," "to have pity." The only NT instances are in Heb. 8:12 (quoting Jer. 31:34) and the negative protestation in Mt. 16:22.
[F. BÜCHSEL, III, 300-301]

hiláskomai, hilasmós.

A. Expiation and Forms of Expiation in the OT.
1. kipper in the LXX. Mostly (83 times out of 100) the LXX has *exiláskomai* for Heb. *kipper.* Other terms (e.g., *hagiázō*) are used by way of variation or on account of special content.
2. The Meaning of the Root kpr. The etymology of *kpr* is obscure. Gen. 32:21 favors the basic sense "to cover," though "to wash away" and "to propitiate" are also possible.

3. kipper and Ransom. In Ex. 21:30 there is reference to the noncultic expiation by which an injury may be made good and the injured party reconciled (cf. Num. 35:31; Ps. 49:8; Ex. 30:12). A relation between this and *kipper* is rightly perceived.

4. Noncultic kipper. a. In its general use *kipper* signifies expiation by the substitution of human or animal life (Dt. 32:43; Ex. 32:30), or the averting of threatened destruction by gifts (Prov. 16:14) or, before God, by God's own action (Jer. 18:23; Ps. 78:38).

b. In one or two passages the word occurs with sacrifice. Thus God is pleased in Gen. 8:20ff., and he abandons his wrath in 2 Sam. 24:25, but there can be no expiation by sacrifice for the serious sins of the sons of Eli in 1 Sam. 3:14.

5. The Cultic Use.

a. In relation to substitutionary expiation or ransom we may refer again to Ex. 30:15-16, as well as to Num. 35:33-34; 35:11ff.

b. Mostly, however, the use occurs in relation to the offerings prescribed by the law and along with such terms as "to free from sin," "to purge," and "to sanctify." While expiation is clearly linked with blood, the usage is fluid. Among the offerings we read in 2 Kgs. 12:16 of guilt offerings, which seem here to be expiatory payments (cf. 1 Sam. 6:3ff.). To these are added the special offerings of Lev. 5 whereby those guilty of certain offenses must confess their fault and bring a specific sacrifice so that the priest may make atonement for them. This expiation is effected by blood on the basis of Lev. 17:11: "The life of the flesh is in the blood; and I have given it for you on the altar to make atonement for your souls; for it is the blood that makes atonement, by reason of the life."

c. In the sin offering of Lev. 4 the manipulation of blood and burning of fat constitute the climax, with forgiveness as the goal. The same applies in the trespass and guilt offerings of Lev. 7 and Lev. 5 (and cf. the priestly consecration in Ex. 29 and Lev. 8; also Lev. 9; Num. 8:5ff.; Lev. 12; 15:2ff.; Lev. 14). The concepts of purification and consecration may both be seen in the ritual of the Day of Atonement. If this includes burnt offerings, the blood of the sin offering lies at the heart of the expiation as the priest offers for himself, the people, and the sanctuary. The ritual in Ezek. 43:18ff. builds on that of the law but with the distinction that expiation is here the goal of all cultic actions (43:13ff.). The strength of the concept of expiation may be seen from the fact that in Num. 28–29 the sin offering now accompanies all other offerings. It should be noted that expiation and forgiveness are only for nondeliberate transgressions (Lev. 4:2; Num. 15:30). This obviously covers more than cultic offenses but none that are committed willfully and with evil intent. Purification goes hand in hand with expiation.

6. Conclusion. Among the people of God nothing is to be left unexpiated. God himself has provided the means of expiation. Expiation restores the disrupted relation with God except where sinners cut themselves off from the community by willful transgression. Whatever is affected by sin or uncleanness needs expiation, for it cannot stand before the holy God and his threatened judgment. Expiation is made supremely by the blood of offerings. God has ordained that this should be so, and blood is appropriate in view of the life that it contains. Life is threatened if expiation is not made, and preserved if it is. Since life is thus saved by life, the idea of vicariousness is undeniably present in some sense. [H. HERRMANN, III, 301-10]

B. *hilasmós* and *katharmós* in the Greek World. *katharmós* is purification from cultic or moral defects, *hilasmós* the propitiation of deities, demons, or the departed. While the two are not coincident, they constitute two aspects of the same process.

The former is more important, since cleansing is essential to a right relation to deity. *katharmoí* may take the form of washings or rubbings, but they also include sacrifices (animal or human) in which the stains are transferred to the victim and hence removed. *hilasmoí* include such cultic acts as prayers, sacrifices, purifications, dances, and games. These are repeated annually, and are for both ritual and moral offenses. They cleanse as well as atone, and while they originally have the aim of appeasing the gods (whose anger is sometimes capricious), the stress in philosophy is on moral conduct and the essential benevolence of deity, so that *katharmoí* and *hilasmoí* lose their significance or undergo psychological reinterpretation.

C. Ideas of Expiation in Judaism.

1. The concept of sin is an urgent one in rabbinic theology. Sin is the chief obstacle to a right relation with God, and its removal or expiation is thus essential. This is achieved by the cultus and personal piety. The Day of Atonement, the sacrifices, and cultic objects all have atoning significance. So, too, do penitence, suffering, works of love, study of the law, fasting, martyrdom, and death. The suffering of the righteous can atone for the sins of the people or ward off suffering from others.

2. Jews of the dispersion hold essentially the same views as Palestinian Jews. They pay the temple tax and have an interest in its rituals. They also see the expiatory value of penitence, and Philo speaks of vicarious suffering.

D. *hiláskomai.*

1. From the same root as *híleōs* come the verbs *hílēmi*, "to be gracious," and *hiláskomai* (or *exiláskomai*), "to make gracious." In the latter case humans are the subjects and deities or the deceased the objects (except when the sense is "to bribe"). The passive aorist has the meaning "to be made gracious," i.e., "to show mercy." But in the prayer *hilásthēti*, the deity is active: "Be merciful."

2. In the LXX *hiláskomai* is rare; it bears the sense "to be merciful" or "to be or become gracious" (cf. Ex. 32:14; Lam. 3:42; 2 Kgs. 5:18). *exiláskomai*, however, is common for priestly acts in the purging or expiation of sin (*kipper*). It can have both the personal sense "to make gracious" and the cultic sense "to purge (the stain of sin or guilt)."

3. Philo makes little use of either term. For him *hiláskomai* usually means "to placate" (with persons as subject and God or persons as object) or "to atone" (by cultic or moral actions). While stating that good works atone for sin, Philo (on a cultic basis) perceives that it is God who acts in us to effect true purity; he thus gives expiation a personal dimension.

4. In the NT *hiláskomai* occurs only in Lk. 18:13; Heb. 2:17, *exiláskomai* not at all. In Lk. 18:13 *hilásthēti* is a cry to God for mercy. In Heb. 2:17 the task of Jesus as High Priest is to expiate sins before God. The idea is not to make God gracious nor to conquer sins ethically.

5. The interesting thing in the construction and meaning of *hiláskomai* and *exiláskomai* is the addition to the sense "to propitiate" (with accusative of the person propitiated) of the sense "to purge" (with accusative of the person or object purged) and "to expiate" (with accusative of the guilt expiated or with *perí*, *apó*, etc.). This was a natural development, since that which makes God gracious also purges from sin and expiates its guilt. No less striking, however, is that words that originally denote our human action in relation to God are now used instead for God's divine action in relation to us and on our behalf.

E. *hilasmós*. This is the action of propitiation and expiation. In the LXX, which also has *exilasmós*, it denotes cultic expiation and divine forgiveness. Philo also uses it for purging from sin. The only NT instances are in 1 Jn. 2:2; 4:10. Here it is God's own gracious action, and hence denotes the removal of guilt (cf. the confession of sin in 1:8, 10, and *paráklētos* in 2:1). The result in us is confidence in the judgment (4:17) and victory over the sense of sin. Demonstrating love, *hilasmós* begets love (4:7, 11, 20-21). Because Jesus has come for the removing (*hilasmós*) of sin, the regenerate cannot sin. When they do so, they are against the truth, and they have to come back again to Jesus as *hilasmós*. This *hilasmós* is not linked specifically to Christ's death but to his total mission (cf. 1:7; 3:16; 5:6). *hilasmós* is necessary in view of approaching judgment. It is not just a doctrine but a reality by which we live.

[F. Büchsel, III, 310-18]

hilastérion.

1. hilastérion in the LXX.

a. The OT refers to a golden *kappōret* over the ark (Ex. 25:17ff.). The cherubim are at the ends with their faces toward it (v. 20). God meets Moses there (v. 22; cf. Num. 7:89; Lev. 16:2). The high priest burns incense before it on the Day of Atonement (Lev. 16:13), and then sprinkles blood on and before it.

b. The *kappōret* is no mere cover, nor is it part of the ark (cf. Ex. 26:34; 30:6). In Ex. 25:17 the LXX first calls it *hilastérion epíthema* ("an atoning handpiece"), then *hilastérion* ("place of expiation"), and once *exilasmós* (1 Chr. 28:11). The Hebrew term probably derives from the word "to cover," not "to expiate," but 1 Chr. 28:11 favors an equation with *hilastérion*, and the exegetical tradition supports this.

[J. Herrmann, III, 318-19]

2. *tó hilastérion* is a neuter noun from the adjective *hilastérios*. It could be an accusative masculine in Rom. 3:25, but there are no other instances of this.

3. The neuter noun is common for *kappōret* in the LXX (Ex. 25:16ff.; 31:7; Lev. 16:2ff.; Num. 7:89). The sense is that of agent rather than place of expiation: "that which makes expiation." The altar of burnt offering is *tó hilastérion* in Ezek. 43:14 (probably because of the sprinkled blood). Technically, however, the term denotes the *kappōret*, though outside the LXX and related works the sense is the more general one of "oblation."

4. *Rom. 3:25*.

a. Whether Paul has the *kappōret* in view in Rom. 3:25 is not wholly certain, but he undoubtedly means "that which expiates sin" and thus reveals God's righteousness and brings redemption. God himself is the subject of the action, so that divine expiation rather than human propitiation is the point. "By faith" is to be taken with *hilastérion*. The object of faith is Jesus crucified and risen, who is thus our *hilastérion* as we believe in him, and the theme of the word of reconciliation (cf. the "put forward," which seems to refer to apostolic preaching rather than divine selection). "In his blood" clearly relates to *hilastérion* rather than to faith. It is as the one who died for believers that Jesus is their *hilastérion*. The revelation of divine righteousness in Jesus as *hilastérion* is linked with the passing over of former sins, in which the *kappōret* plays an important role. The point, then, seems to be that Jesus is a higher *kappōret* which works through faith, not external observance, which is sprinkled with Jesus' own blood, not that of animals, and which is open to view, not hidden in the holy of holies. In this way Paul personalizes and spiritualizes the concept of the *kappōret* as elsewhere he does that of cultic service or of circumcision (Rom. 12:1;

Col. 2:11). If he has the actual *kappōret* in view, he reorients it to Jesus as the one in whom true and full expiation has been made.

b. The *hilastérion* does not make God gracious, for God's grace is its presupposition. Those who are under God's wrath are also under his patience (Rom. 2:4). The *hilastérion* reveals this. Yet this revelation comes only with God's vicarious action. What is revealed is not just patience but the holiness of God which punishes sin (v. 26) and yet in so doing separates sin and sinner and thus brings the sinner to faith and repentance. Required to accomplish this is one who both reveals God to us and at the same time represents us to God by vicariously bearing the divine judgment and thus bringing us to the self-judgment of faith. Without this vicarious work the revelation could not bring true redemption. It is in the unity of divine revelation and human representation that Jesus is by faith an expiation in his blood, and thereby brings redemption.

5. Heb. 9:5 simply follows LXX usage when it speaks about the *hilastérion* in connection with the ark.   [F. BÜCHSEL, III, 319-23]

---

hína [in order that]

If the final significance is not always too strict (cf. the Johannine writings), the NT does not follow the Koine in giving the word consecutive or causal significance. *hína* clauses are common in the NT chiefly because of its teleological understanding of God's ways with us and of our human destiny.

A. Theological Final Clauses.

1. In Judaism.

a. The LXX uses *hína* to denote the point of God's action (e.g., in not abandoning Israel or championing the suffering), namely, to manifest his nature, power, and glory. The Wisdom literature sees God's purposeful work in all reality and events (cf. Sir. 39). Final clauses are important in Sir. 44ff. If God's historical action serves different ends, the final goal is still that he be acknowledged and glorified.

b. Apocalyptic broadens and deepens this view. It interprets everything (e.g., the law) teleologically. Much takes place to fulfil what is predicted. Individuals are sent to do specific works. Nations have their own destinies, especially Israel, whose present visitation is a means to a further end. True servants of God recognize God's teleological direction (cf. Joseph, and Mordecai's question to Esther in Esth. 4:14). The ultimate goal is eschatological; all historical goals point forward to the divine consummation when God's righteousness and majesty will be victoriously displayed and the goal of creation will be achieved in the future world and the righteous who inherit it. Teleology, of course, raises acutely the question of theodicy. One solution is that only a minority will reach the goal and the rest of human and other creatures will perish. Judaism in general, however, prefers to contrast the purposes of God for the Gentiles and for Israel by arguing that the Gentiles are now let loose with a view to later discipline, while Israel is now disciplined with a view to future forgiveness.

c. Rabbinic theology accepts the teleological principle that all that God does is for good. After A.D. 70 this is a defiant nevertheless, though it can easily become a facile slogan. The phrase "that it might be fulfilled" also occurs. As in all teleological thinking, fanciful reasons are sometimes found for God's actions.

2. In the NT.

a. The Christ event gives new life and meaning to the older teleology. Jesus himself speaks of his unique office in terms of commission (Mt. 5:17ff.; Jn. 3:17, etc.). The mighty works serve his revelation (Mk. 2:10 etc.). They thus bring about a crisis of decision. They will lead either to faith or to hardening (cf. Lk. 2:34). The *hína* clauses are final even when the reference is to hardening (Mk. 4:11-12). Jesus has come into the world for judgment (Jn. 9:39). Supremely, the cross itself has teleological signif- icance even down to the fact that the prophets have to be fulfilled (Mt. 26:56).

b. The first Christian preaching borrows the Joseph formula and extols God's pur- poseful overruling at the cross (Acts 2:36 etc.). Paul puts this in the form of a paradox: Jesus has become poor so that by his poverty we might become rich (2 Cor. 8:9; cf. 5:21; Gal. 3:13-14, etc.). Along the lines of martyrdom theology, he does not die merely to be exalted but in order to save. The cross is thus seen in the light of the *télos,* and the *télos* concept permeates the total Christian understanding of God, the world, and history. Creation, the call of Abraham, the law, and the history of Israel all move forward to Christ, in whom alone the ancient witnesses and martyrs are made perfect (Heb. 11:40). The cross, however, does not rule out a future consummation. Like the martyrs, Christians undergo present suffering with a view to future glory (Rom. 8:17; 1 Pet. 1:6-7). God treads the way of conflict with his people, working everything for good to those who love him (Rom. 8:28; cf. Phlm. 15). Even the hardening of Israel is the means to a final end of grace and glory: "that they also may receive mercy" (Rom. 11:31); "that he may have mercy upon all" (v. 32).

c. The end of all God's ways is justification by faith, salvation, God's self-revelation, but above all the divine glorification in the victory, not of wrath, but of grace, when all things will be subject to God (1 Cor. 15:28) and his creation will achieve its original destiny (Rom. 11:36). This can be stated with confidence because already in the cross of Christ God has carried history to its goal through conflict, destroying human self- glorification and thereby establishing the divine glory in the *soli deo gloria* of the new creation.

B. Ethical Final Clauses.

1. In Judaism.

a. In ethical final clauses (cf. Ex. 20:12 and especially Proverbs), the good or bad results of conduct are stated. In the last resort, however, seeking to do God's will is the goal of right action (cf. Prov. 3:21-22). The basic form of blessings accords with this. God's action has specific human action as its goal.

b. Apocalyptic makes these theological concepts the basis of ethics. We have been made for a divine purpose. God has given us the law to show this. He intervenes to lead us to righteousness. We are shown the final reason or goal for acts and not just their immediate consequences. This comes out plainly in prayers that conclude with final clauses.

c. Rabbinic theology accepts the same principle, but with a tendency to formalize and trivialize it. The result can be a utilitarian moralism even though fulfilment of God's will is perceived as the goal of creation.

2. In the NT.

a. Jesus often uses imperatives with final clauses. These clauses direct our will and actions to the eschatological goal of salvation, to which our present life must be oriented in preparation, conflict, and sacrifice (Mt. 19:12, 23ff.). The supreme goal of conduct is entry into the kingdom (Lk. 16:9), or forgiveness (Mk. 11:25), or the glorifying of God (Mt. 5:16).

b. The divine action supplies the impulse for all human action. Creation is a divine calling and God's historical work a word of summons. Thus statements about God's action lead on to final clauses about human tasks and possibilities. Predestination (Rom. 8:29; 9:11-12) points to our final goal, not fatalistically, but in orientation to our human will. God wills this will, and directs it to its goal by liberating and governing it. He does this in the Christ event as his supreme word and work (cf. Eph. 2:8-9). The indicatives of this event lead on to imperatives (cf. 1 Cor. 5:7; 2 Cor. 5:15 etc.; Rom. 8:3-4). A final *eis* or *hína* brings out the force of the cross for the Christian life (cf. Rom. 7:4; Gal. 2:19). This applies especially to the apostolate (2 Cor. 4:10).

c. Final clauses in Paul also refer to the divine goals for us (1 Cor. 9:22ff.; 9:12ff.). Since these goals demand supreme self-sacrifice, utilitarianism is excluded. We are not just to pursue personal salvation. In a hierarchy of goals, the glorifying of God is again supreme (2 Cor. 4:15 etc.). This transcends our own ability; hence NT ethics is an ethics of prayer. Exhortations merge into blessings and petitions that are introduced by *hína* (cf. Jesus in Lk. 22:32; 21:36, and Paul in Col. 4:3-4; 1:9ff.). It is not just a stylistic device that Paul's epistles begin with requests and thanksgivings and close with blessings, for the apostle has more trust in God than in human goodwill or power. That God may be glorified is again the final goal of our ways as well as God's (cf. Phil. 1:9ff.; 2 Th. 1:11-12; 2 Cor. 1:8ff.; Eph. 1:17ff.).

→ *eis, diá*   [E. STAUFFER, III, 323-33]

Iordánēs → *potamós*

---

iós [poison, rust],   *katióomai* [to rust]

Of the two words *iós,* the first (meaning "arrow") does not occur in the NT, while we find the second (meaning "poison" or "rust") in Rom. 3:13; Jms. 3:8; 5:3.

1. *iós as "Poison."* In the OT the poison of snakes is a metaphor for the malicious speech of enemies (cf. Ps. 140:3). Evil, too, is compared to the gall of asps (Job 20:12ff.). Wine, though pleasant to the taste, has the sting of an adder. In the NT Paul uses the same comparison to describe sin: Our tongues are deceitful, our lips have the poison of serpents, and our mouths are full of cursing and bitterness. Sin produces enmity and makes words into treacherous weapons that bring destruction. Due to the power of the word, sins of the tongue are particularly sinister. James agrees when he calls the tongue a restless evil full of deadly poison (3:8). The tongue does not just bring evil; it is itself evil. Death lurks in its violent and deceitful word. Cf. also Hermas *Similitudes* 9.26.7; Ignatius *Trallians* 6.2.

2. *iós as "Rust."* In Jms. 5:3 *iós* as rust offers a warning against heaping up worldly wealth. The rust will not merely rot this but will serve as a testimony against its owners and sear their flesh like fire. The point is not just that rust proves the transitoriness of riches but that it accuses the rich for letting things rot rather than give them to the poor. As in Ezek. 24:3ff., rust is an indictment, though a warning against trust in transitory things may also be present (cf. Mt. 6:19-20). In the same verse the verb *katióomai* occurs for "to rust."   [O. MICHEL, III, 334-36]

Ioudaía, Ioudaíos, ioudaízō, Ioudaismós → *Israḗl*

---

híppos [horse]

---

1. The Horse in Palestine, the OT, and Judaism. The horse is very early of military importance in Egypt, and from there (or Asia Minor) it comes into Palestine. Solomon receives horses as presents (1 Kgs. 10:5) and also buys them from Egypt (10:29). Horses and chariots form the core of the armies of Israel, Syria, Assyria, and Persia. Horses are lauded for their speed and strength (cf. Job 39:19ff.). God's power is depicted in terms of horsemen and chariots (2 Kgs. 2:11; 6:17). But the horse also denotes the alien power in which one is not to trust (Ps. 76:6; Hos. 1:7). It symbolizes carnal confidence (Is. 30:16). Thus the king of peace chooses an ass, not a horse (Zech. 9:9). The horse plays a special role in visions. Joel describes the locusts as chariots and horses (2:4-5). Zechariah sees horses of various colors (1:8ff.). 2 Macc. 3:25ff. tells of an avenging horse and rider, while in 10:29ff. we read of horsemen that protect the army of Judas.

2. The Horse in the NT.

a. Jesus rides into Jerusalem on an ass, not on the warlike horse (Mk. 11:1ff.). Faith discerns here the coming of the messianic king of peace in fulfilment of Scripture and in disclosure of the messianic secret (cf. Mt. 21:5; Jn. 12:15).

b. Jms. 3:2-3 compares Christian mastery of the body to control of a horse.

c. Revelation follows apocalyptic in the use of horse imagery. The four horses of 6:1ff. represent conquest, civil strife, hardship, and pestilence. The demonic locusts of ch. 9 are compared to horses with heads like lions and the ability to kill with both head and tail. In 14:20 the terrible nature of the judgment is shown by the fact that there is blood to the horses' bridles. At the end, however, the Messiah and his host will appear on the white horses of victory (19:11ff.), though the Messiah alone "judges and makes war" (v. 11); he does this with the sword of his mouth (v. 15).

[O. MICHEL, III, 336-39]

íris [rainbow]

A. Outside the NT.

1. *íris* is the usual word for "rainbow," though it can also mean "halo," "iris" of the eye, or "play of colors." The goddess Iris personifies the bow in reflection of the religious concepts and experiences associated with it.

2. In the OT the rainbow is a sign and witness of the covenant of Gen. 9:9ff. The Hebrew term can also denote the bow of the hunter or warrior; the underlying idea, then, might be that God's bow is laid up in the clouds. But in Ezek. 1:28 the bow demonstrates God's grace and glory, and in Sir. 43:11 it testifies with all creation to the Creator's power. The LXX always uses *tózon*, not *íris*.

3. The rabbis warn against looking at the rainbow both for fear of being blinded by the divine glory and also because of the danger of desecrating the divine name. They express the opinion that the rainbow appears only when there are no righteous on the earth; the existence of the righteous guarantees the world's preservation, and thus makes the rainbow unnecessary.

B. The NT.

1. Unlike the LXX, the NT, like Josephus and Philo, uses *íris* for rainbow so as to make the meaning clear to Greek readers.

2. The word occurs in Rev. 4:3 and 10:1. In 4:3 an emerald halo encircles the divine throne. In 10:1 the cloud and sun show that the emblem of the angel with the prophetic book is a rainbow. In both instances there is probably an allusion to the covenant sign of Gen. 9. Even when God judges, the rainbow is a reassuring indication of his good and gracious will. If God in 4:1ff. is the holy and transcendent God (cf. v. 6), the iris around the throne bears witness that he is also the near and loving God whose book of destiny is opened by the slain Lamb (ch. 5) and whose judgments still stand under the rainbow sign (10:1ff.). The covenant sign of Gen. 9 is thus given a christological reference and fulfilment. The enacted salvation of God, which precedes all human works, forms the basis of legitimate assurance in the judgment.

[K. H. RENGSTORF, III, 339-42]

Isaák → Iakṓb; isángelos → ángelos

ísos [equal], *isótēs* [equality], *isótimos* [equal in value]

A. *isótēs* as a Quality.

1. Quantitative Equality.

a. The equality denoted by *ísos* is primarily one of size or number, or of value or force in a quantitative sense (as distinct from *hómoios,* which suggests quality). It may thus be used for equal sums, lengths of space or time, shares, pieces, or an equal voice (cf. Ex. 30:34; Ezek. 40:5ff.).

b. In Rev. 21:16 the three equal sides of the heavenly city, especially as three times twelve thousand, denote perfection. While cubes occur in antiquity (cf. the cubic tower of Marduk in Babylon and the cubic shape of the holy of holies in the temple), the idea is probably that the new Jerusalem fills both heaven and earth.

c. In Lk. 6:34 the basic thought is clear but not the precise sense, for *tá ísa* might be (1) the capital without interest, (2) the corresponding total of capital with interest, (3) a similar service, or (4) interest amounting to the original capital. In any case, giving in order to get is shown to be incompatible with unselfish love. Calculating exact correspondence (whether in repayment or revenge) is alien to the true Christian attitude (cf. 1 Cor. 13:5).

2. Equality of Content or Meaning. As *ísos* may denote exact equality in mathematics, so it may be used for precise agreement of content, e.g., in a duplicate or transcript. Thus the content of the witnesses in Mk. 14:56 is not consistent in detail, as the law requires.

3. Human Equality: the Greeks. The concept of human equality is important for the Greeks, especially as the necessary basis of law. Only legal equals can enter into legal relationships. Though different in nature, they may enjoy the same rights. This equality reflects or is a part of the equality which is for Plato the essential dynamic of the cosmos and the basis of order. Equality is a fundamental principle of democracy (along with freedom), not as essential equality, but as equality of position and rights (cf. 2 Macc. 9:15). It also underlies the personal society of friends, in whom is achieved a true blending of spirits. Legal equality also demands justice, i.e., the administration of law without respect of persons. At this point there is approximation to *díkaios.* Finally, *isótēs* is important in contracts in the sense that signatories accept equally the agreed rights and obligations.

4. Human Equality: Christians. Over against legal equality stands the Christian equality based on grace and love. This is an equality of spiritual possessions (Acts

11:17) and eternal salvation (Mt. 20:12) that God has set up without regard for origin, prior history (Acts 11:17), achievement, or merit (Mt. 20:12), and that demands equality in relationship. Paul uses an appeal to the Greek sense of equality when promoting the Jerusalem collection (2 Cor. 8:13-14). This is no mere appeal for giving in hope of return but an application of the golden rule of Lk. 6:31. The *hína* of v. 14 states the divine objective rather than the human motive. *isótēs* as a principle of mutual assistance serves the divine goal of *isótēs*. God himself establishes this equality by giving the same gift to Gentiles as to Jews, i.e., the Holy Spirit (Acts 11:17). 2 Pet. 1:1 uses the words that denote the same rank and status in civic life (*isótimos* and *isotimía*) to describe the equal faith by which we are equally righteous in the kingdom of God. Jesus in the parable of the laborers (Mt. 20:12) brings out the eschatological nature of this equality. Here is no legal principle involving equality of rights or achievement but an act of divine righteousness against which the sense of human justice protests (vv. 11-12). The equal reward is equal felicity such as we find expected in many rabbinic statements and stories. This equality does not exclude present differences in faith (Rom. 12:3), receptivity (Mk. 4:24), and charisms (1 Cor. 12). The NT presupposes differences in God's kingdom (Mt. 5:19; 10:41-42, etc.). Yet equality of eternal life and salvation remains.

5. *Equality by Nature and Equality with God outside the NT.* While *ísos* refers first to quantitative equality, it quickly acquires a qualitative aspect. It may thus be used for equality of character, or, in Stoicism, of good and bad actions, or, in the LXX, of our human equality in birth and death (Wis. 7:3). Human equality contrasts with God's equality only with himself (Is. 44:7 etc.). The divine image does not imply equality by nature. In Judaism God will finally establish a fuller likeness (cf. 1 Jn. 3:2), but to seek equality with God (Gen. 3:5; Is. 14:14) is a fundamental sin. Thus the Bible avoids such common Greek expressions as "godlike" (*isótheos*).

6. *The Equality of Jesus with God in the NT.*

a. In Jn. 5:18 Jesus is accused of making himself equal to God. While he does not expressly make the claim (cf. v. 19), he stresses the identity of works. In Jn. 1:1; 10:30 the unity of Father and Son is plainly stated even alongside the subjection of the Son to the Father; hence the accusation in 10:33 that "you, being a man, make yourself God." In this context *ísos* in 5:18 has a new depth and fullness, for with its inherent element of exactness, and its added dimension of quality, it denotes an essential equality which the later term *homooúsios* was designed to state and defend.

b. This is also the meaning of *ísa* in the difficult verse Phil. 2:6. The problems of the verse are whether being equal with God is a reality or a possibility and whether the action is that of the preexistent or the historical Christ. The first answer is that equality with God is a possession that can neither be renounced nor lost; it is the beginning of Christ's way (v. 6) and it will also be the end (vv. 9ff.). But Christ temporarily ceases to make use of it, taking the form of a servant, exercising his lordship in this strange form of humiliation, and thereby attaining to its public recognition. Because he does not have regard for himself—the point of the exhortation— the divine nature that is demonstrated in his humility is confirmed in his glory. The action, then, is that of the eternal Christ, and the emptying implies no loss of essential equality with God.

B. *isótēs* as Equity. Since *isótēs* approximates to *dikaiosýnē* ("justice"), the group takes on the sense of equity or fairness. The just judge is *ísos* (impartial), but the righteous person is also *ísos* (upright). Col. 4:1 reflects this usage when enjoining masters to treat their slaves both justly and fairly (*tó díkaion kaí tến isotết a toís doúlois paréchesthe*). Their Master in heaven, who is unconditionally just and fair, is the one to whom they must give account (though Clement of Alexandria [in *Stromateis* 3.6.1; 6.47.4] has God's grace rather than judicial *isótēs* in mind when he uses the term with reference to God).   [G. STÄHLIN, III, 343-55]

→ *díkaios, heís, hómoios*

Israēl [Israel], *Israēlítēs* [Israelite], *Ioudaíos* [Jew], *Ioudaía* [Judea], *Ioudaikós* [Jewish], *ioudaízō* [to live as a Jew], *Ioudaismós* [Judaism], *Hebraíos* [Hebrew], *Hebraikós* [Hebrew], *Hebraís* [Hebrew (language)], *Hebraistí* [in Hebrew]

A. Israel, Judah, and Hebrews in the OT.

1. Israel and Judah. Israel is the name of the sacral tribal league of Josh. 24. It denotes the totality of God's elect and embraces their central beliefs. With the monarchy it still covers the whole group under Saul, but under David it comes to denote the northern tribes as distinct from Judah. David and Solomon hold the league together in spite of tensions, but with Rehoboam Israel breaks away and we have the two kingdoms of Israel and Judah. Judah is simply a political name for the tribe and then for the southern kingdom, and has no sacral significance. With the collapse of the northern kingdom, Israel again becomes the name for the whole people in the spiritual sense (as it had been for the prophets; cf. Is. 8:14), and this becomes the normative usage. In practice, of course, Judah is now Israel, but the concept of a greater Israel embracing all the tribes is never lost. Josiah attempts an actual restoration of the full Davidic kingdom, and reconstitution of the twelve tribes becomes a form of eschatological expectation.

2. Hebrews. The name Hebrews seems at first to be a legal rather than an ethnic term (perhaps connected with *ḥabiru*) (cf. Ex. 21:2ff.; Jer. 34:8ff.; 1 Sam. 14:21). But the term then becomes a more general one that is used by foreigners to denote Israel (often critically; cf. Gen. 39:14 etc.), or by Israelites to distinguish themselves from foreigners (Gen. 40:15; Ex. 1:19, etc.). It thus has almost a national sense in, e.g., Gen. 14:13 and Jon. 1:9.   [G. VON RAD, III, 356-59]

B. *Israēl, Ioudaíos, Hebraíos* in Jewish Literature after the OT.

1. Israēl—Ioudaíos.

a. The Basis. In postexilic times two terms come into use for the people, the sacral term Israel(ite) and the political term Jew. Both denote the people in terms of religious confession as well as national allegiance. Israel is the fellowship of those who worship the true God and who have been chosen by him to do so. Every Jew stands in relationship to God, and outsiders can enter into this relationship only by becoming members of this people. Of the two designations, Israel is preferred by the people and stresses the religious aspect, while Jew is the non-Israelite usage (freely adopted by Jews of the dispersion) and carries at times (though infrequently) a disparaging nuance.

b. The Usage of Palestinian Judaism. (i) In 1 Maccabees Israel is the author's own term but *Ioudaíoi* is used (a) when non-Jews are speaking, (b) in diplomatic letters, treaties, etc., (c) by Jews themselves in diplomatic communications, (d) and by Jews also in official domestic documents (cf. 1 Macc. 13:42; also Hasmonean coins). (ii) Religious works like Sirach or Judith naturally use Israel with its religious orientation. The same applies to rabbinic works. (iii) When the rabbis do use *Ioudaíos*, it is mostly on the lips of non-Jews, or in adoption of the usage of non-Jews or Jews of the dispersion. How unusual the term is may be seen from the attempt to find a play on the word monotheist in the description of Mordecai as a Jew in Esth. 2:5.

c. The Usage of Hellenistic Judaism. (i) In 2 Maccabees Israel occurs only five times and always in strongly religious contexts, e.g., 1:25-26. *Ioudaíos* is freely used even in self-designation. We also find *Ioudaismós* for the Jewish religion (cf. 8:1). 3 Maccabees follows a similar pattern (cf. Israel in 2:6 etc., *Ioudaíos* elsewhere). (ii) The testimony of inscriptions is to the same effect. Even Jews call themselves *Ioudaíoi*. Cf., too, the Aramaic documents from the Elephantine colonists. (iii) 4 Maccabees may also be cited in this context, though the religious contents here give greater scope for Israel.

2. *Hebraíos*.

a. As a Term for the Language and Script. (i) *Hebraíos* is less common than *Israēl* and *Ioudaíos*, and in the rabbis denotes the language (as distinct from Aramaic or Greek) and the script (as distinct from the Assyrian and Greek scripts). Only rarely are Hebrew and Aramaic lumped together. (ii) The Apocrypha and pseudepigrapha also use the term for Hebrew, but occasionally, and more commonly in Josephus and the NT, Aramaic is included. Josephus also extends the term to cover coins, measures, names of the month, and various national characteristics.

b. As an Archaic Name and Lofty Expression for the People of Israel. (i) The OT uses the word for the earliest period, and this leads to its use in references to the remoter past or in works cultivating an archaic style. (ii) As an archaic term, *Hebraíos* acquires dignity and thus comes into use as a lofty or polite term that will avoid the derogatory nuances of *Ioudaíos*, e.g., in the martyrdom stories in 4 Maccabees (5:2, 4 etc.) or in Judith. (iii) Possibly this is the point on some inscriptions, although in view of the accepted use of *Ioudaíos* here the reference may well be to national characteristics, primarily by clinging to the use of Aramaic.

[K. G. Kuhn, III, 359-69]

C. *Ioudaíos, Israēl, Hebraíos* in Greek Hellenistic Literature.

1. *Ioudaíos*.

a. In Pagan Writers. (i) Postclassical Greek writings contain many references and mostly have *Ioudaíos* for the individual Jew and *Ioudaíoi* for the people (less commonly *Hebraíoi*). Historians take note of the people and show an interest in its history and politics (e.g., Hecataeus of Abdera, or Agatharchides). (ii) The term *Ioudaíos* also has a decisive religious connotation, e.g., in Megasthenes, Plutarch, etc. Plutarch describes Jewish rituals and festivals. (iii) A significant point is that *Ioudaíos* may denote religious adherence irrespective of nationality (cf. Plutarch).

b. Among Jews and Jewish Writers. (i) Dispersion Jews adopt the Gentile custom and soon come to call themselves *Ioudaíoi*. (ii) Philo follows this usage, with a stress on religious as well as national unity (though he does not go so far as to speak of Jews not belonging to the nation). (iii) Josephus rarely has *Ioudaíoi* for early Israel but uses nothing else when he comes to the postexilic and contemporary period. He interweaves the national and religious aspects and can sometimes call proselytes *Ioudaíoi*.

2. *Israēl*.

a. In Pagan Writers. Since Israel is a specifically Jewish term, it is no surprise that pagan writers never use it for either past or present Israel. It occurs in papyri only under direct Jewish or Christian influence.

b. In Philo and Josephus. (i) Philo. With reference to the early period, Philo follows the OT in using Israel, often in quotations. (ii) Josephus. Josephus, too, uses Israel only with a past reference. Unlike Philo, who gives the term figurative significance, Josephus seems not to attach any particular religious meaning to it. He prefers *Israēlítai* for the whole people, and shows acquaintance with the Palestinian use of this for ordinary people as distinct from priests and Levites.

3. *Hebraíos*.

a. In Pagan Writers. (i) Rare in Greek literature, this word usually has a national, geographical, or linguistic sense. (ii) Sometimes it is selected as a more ancient term. (iii) Once it plainly denotes the language. (iv) For Pausanias the term means inhabitant of Palestine.

b. Among Jews: Philo and Josephus. (i) Philo. Philo uses the word for Jews of ancient times, and also for that which, though Jewish, is not common to all Jews, e.g., the language. (ii) Josephus. We have here a similar usage for ancient Israel and for such things as language, script, coins, etc. that are peculiar to the Jews as a nation. (iii) On inscriptions the term denotes Aramaic-speaking Jews from Palestine.

D. *Ioudaíos, Israḗl, Hebraíos* in the NT.

1. *Ioudaíos, Ioudaía, Ioudaikós, ioudaízō, Ioudaismós*.

a. *Ioudaíos* in the Synoptists. *Ioudaíos* is rare in the Synoptists. It occurs for the people only in the plural and only on the lips of foreigners (cf. Mt. 2:2). It has a national and geographical but especially a religious sense. In the passion story, as in that of the Wise Men, Jesus is called "king of the Jews," but Pilate obviously does not take the religious side seriously, and the crucifixion plainly strikes at any political claim (cf. Mt. 27:11, 29, 37). In contrast the leaders of the people mock Jesus as the "king of Israel" (Mt. 27:42). In Mt. 28:15 there is no article and the reference is to Jews who refuse to trust in Jesus. In Mk. 7:3 the explanatory note is for non-Jews and the word has a religious connotation. In Lk. 7:3 and 23:51 the author may well be adopting his own usage. The Synoptic use corresponds to that of 1 Maccabees: *Ioudaíoi* is used for the people either by non-Jews or by Jews in their dealings with them, while *Israḗl* is the proper Jewish term.

b. John. (i) Among the many uses in John, we note first a similarity to that of the Synoptics in the passion story (18:33, 39; 19:3), where "king of the Jews" occurs on non-Jewish lips (cf. also 18:35). It is also a Samaritan woman who speaks in 4:5, and distinction is made from the Samaritans in 4:22. (ii) John also uses *Ioudaíos* for inhabitants of Palestine, especially in explanation of Jewish customs or circumstances. The aim is obviously to make things clear to foreigners (cf. 2:6, 13; 5:1; 7:2). In such contexts the use is objective and nonemphatic. The same applies to 1:19; 3:1, etc. Some of these Jews may well be believers in Jesus (8:31; 11:45; 12:11). This usage corresponds to that of Josephus and need not imply that the author himself is distant in time or nationality. (iii) In some passages the Jews in John are opponents of Jesus, though opposition arises from the context and is not implicit in the term. Thus certain Jews criticize Jesus as such because he seems to reject the temple in 2:18ff., or calls himself the bread of life in 6:41ff., or claims unity with the Father in 10:31 (cf. also 5:16ff.; 8:48; 13:33). Some "Jews" take up an ambiguous attitude for fear of the "Jews" (7:13; 9:22). The point in all this is not that the Jews as a whole reject Jesus, or that a specific group of Zealots does so, but that opposition arises on the grounds of the Jewish religion (cf. 9:29). A gulf is thus implied between the Christian understanding of the OT and the Jewish understanding which resists it. For John the Jews are often those who adopt this Jewish understanding in rejection of Jesus. At the same time, the national basis remains. Not all Jews reject Jesus, and those who do so are first Jews by nationality, and only then Jews in opposition to Jesus.

c. Acts. The usage in Acts is like that in John. It differs, however, inasmuch as dispersion Jews are now included (but not proselytes except perhaps in 2:5). *Ioudaíos* is the normal term on the lips of non-Jews (18:14; 22:30) or of Jews in their dealings with them (21:39; 23:20; 24:5). Sometimes there is a religious connotation (cf. 10:22 and perhaps 16:20). There is no unfavorable implication in passages like 13:6; 18:4; 19:10, 17. Commitment to the law typifies the Jews in 10:28. This can yield a usage (as in John) for those who oppose Christ and his community (cf. 16:3; 9:23; 12:11; 13:50; 17:5, 13). Yet this aspect is not indissolubly linked to the term, for there are Jews who believe (14:2) and these Jews are at odds with *Ioudaíoi* who are opponents.

d. Paul. Paul more commonly has *Ioudaíos* in the singular, and often without the article. This suggests that he has in mind a religious type. Even in 1 Th. 2:14, which refers to Palestinian Jews, those who reject both Christ and the prophets are in view. But the type includes the true Jew, who keeps the law, as distinct from the merely outward Jew (cf. Rom. 2:17ff.). Devotion to the law is what characterizes the Jew (cf. 1 Cor. 9:20). Thus the Jew of Gal. 2:13 is the adherent of the law. This contrasts with the "Jew by nature" of v. 15. It is because the Jew has the law that he differs from the Hellenes and the Gentiles (Rom. 3:1-2; 9:4-5). By the will of God the Jew has an inherent advantage, and the gospel is preached to the Jew first. Yet since the Jew does not keep the law (Rom. 2:17ff.), and God is also the God of the Gentiles and will bless all peoples in Abraham (Gal. 3:8), the radical distinction of Jew and Hellene no longer applies to those who are justified by faith in Christ (Gal. 3:28; Col. 3:11; Rom. 9:24), though historical distinctions remain (1 Cor. 7:17ff.).

e. Revelation. In the two instances in Revelation (2:9; 3:9) those who are Jews only in claim and name are said to be the synagogue of Satan. They stand in implied contrast to true Jews who are committed to God and his will (cf. Rom. 2:18ff.). It does not have to follow, however, that the latter are Christians.

f. *Ioudaía, Ioudaikós*. *Ioudaía* as the name of the country is primarily adjectival (Mk. 1:5). More narrowly, it denotes Judea (cf. Mt. 3:5; 19:1), but it may also be used for all Palestine (cf. Rom. 15:31; 2 Cor. 1:16). It is a geographical word and has no theological significance. *Ioudaikós*, which occurs only in Tit. 1:14, has the sense of "related to," but the point is not that the *mýthoi* are Jewish by nature, but that they circulate among the Jews.

g. *ioudaízein, Ioudaismós*. Outside the NT *ioudaízein* means either conversion to Judaism or the partial adoption of Jewish customs. In the single NT passage in Gal. 2:14 the word has the latter sense. *Ioudaismós* occurs only in Gal. 1:14. In 2 Maccabees it means Jewishness in either an objective or a subjective sense. The sense is subjective in Gal. 1:14: Paul surpasses his contemporaries in the Jewishness of his life and thought.

2. *Israēl, Israelítēs*.

a. The Patriarch *Israēl*. While there is no direct reference to the patriarch *Israēl* in the NT, there are possible allusions in Phil. 3:5 and Rom. 9:6, though the people is probably meant (as also in Mt. 10:6; Lk. 2:32; Heb. 11:22; Rev. 7:4, etc.).

b. The People of God. (i) In Matthew and Luke *Israēl* is the usual word for God's people on Jewish lips. In Mt. 2:20 it occurs generally for the land and in Lk. 1:80; Mt. 10:23 it refers to the people in a purely objective sense. Usually, however, it has a religious connotation: *Israēl* is in a special sense God's people. Thus God is the God of *Israēl* in Mt. 15:31 and Jesus the true king of *Israēl* (even if mocked as such) in

Mt. 27:42 (cf. Lk. 2:25; 24:21). Because of her status as God's people, Jesus expects to find faith in *Israēl* (Mt. 8:10). He is sent to her lost sheep (Mt. 10:6). God cares especially for *Israēl* (Lk. 1:16). He brings her to decision through Christ (Lk. 2:34). The disciples will judge her twelve tribes (Mt. 19:28). Everywhere the historic people is in view.

(ii) John. *Israēl* and *Israelítēs* are rare in John. In the four instances of the former it always denotes Israel as the people of God (e.g., 1:31, 49; 12:13). Nicodemus as a teacher of Israel ought to understand God's working (3:10). The one use of *Israelítēs* (for Nathanael) shows that one may be an external member of God's people but not a genuine *Israelítēs* (1:47; cf. Rom. 2:28-29; 9:6). There is no extension of the term, however, beyond the historic people to all believers.

(iii) In Acts *Israēl* occurs mostly in the first part, *Ioudaíos* in the second. The use is neutral in Acts 5:21, though with the implication (as in 2:22; 3:12; 5:35; 13:16) that those who come face to face with the gospel face a special decision regarding her as the people of God. It is as this people that Israel is summoned to see what God has done in 2:36; 4:10; 13:24. A contrast between unbelieving Israel and the church may be found in 4:27 and 5:21, but it is to Israel that Christ will restore the kingdom (1:6; cf. 28:20), and this implies an extension of the term to cover the new people of God. Yet there is an identity of the old people and the new (cf. 13:23, in which the Israel of promise and the Israel of fulfilment are the same).

(iv) Paul mostly uses *Israēl* specifically for God's people, especially in Rom. 9–11. God has not rejected his people, for Paul is an *Israelítēs* (11:1). Even carnal Israel enjoys the blessing of the law etc. (9:4). Seeking righteousness through the law (9:31-32), she is now in disobedience (10:21) and subject to a partial hardening (11:25). Yet in fulfilment of the promise all Israel will be saved (11:26), for she is more than the totality of her members. A similar use may be seen in Eph. 2:12. In neither case does the term cover the Christian community. There are, however, movements in this direction in Rom. 9:6 and 11:17ff., and it seems to be implied, though not specifically stated, in the *Israēl katá sárka* of 1 Cor. 10:18, and also in the *Israēl toú theoú* of Gal. 6:16, which comprises all those who follow Paul's rule, whether circumcised or uncircumcised.

3. Hebraíos, Hebraikós, Hebraís, Hebraistí.

a. The Derived Forms. (i) *Hebraikós*. This occurs in the NT only in some versions of Lk. 23:38. Elsewhere it normally denotes the language. (ii) *Hebraís*. In Acts 21:40; 22:2 we read that Paul spoke to the crowd in Aramaic. The brief sketch of his education in ch. 22 explains his knowledge of both Hebrew and Aramaic. He also hears the heavenly voice in Hebrew or Aramaic (26:14), probably because this is his mother tongue unless there is an allusion to Hebrew as the language of heaven. (iii) *Hebraistí* occurs only in John and Revelation. It is used either when a Greek expression is to be put in the original or when it is desired for some reason to give an original name. In contrast to *hermēneúein,* which implies clarification (cf. Jn. 1:38; 4:25), *Hebraistí* is designed to give greater historical precision (cf. Jn. 19:13, 17, 20; 20:16). In Revelation, which uses Hebrew in contrast to the Aramaic of John, the idea in 9:11; 16:16 may be to increase the element of mystery and strangeness. Alternatively, the Hebrew term may already be a familiar one.

b. *Hebraíos*. (i) In Acts 6:1 one of the two groups is called *Hebraíoi*. It seems unlikely that as distinct from the Hellenists these were just Aramaic speakers. More likely they were native Judeans, already well known to one another, whereas the Hellenists were from abroad, and were thus neglected simply because they were not well known, not out of ill-will. There might, of course, have been linguistic problems as well. (ii) In Phil. 3:5 Paul has descent in mind when he calls himself a Hebrew of the Hebrews. He is not a proselyte nor is he hellenized; he is of the tribe of Benjamin and has Aramaic as his mother tongue. (iii) *Hebraíos* has the same sense, and is not just a stylistic variation, in 2 Cor. 11:22. Like his opponents, Paul is of Palestinian descent, a full member of God's people, an heir of the promise, and a servant of Christ. (iv) The title of Hebrews is to the same effect. The recipients are not just Aramaic speakers but Palestinian Jews, even though they are probably living in Italy at the time (13:24).   [W. GUTBROD, III, 369-91]

---

histōréō [to investigate, visit],   *(historía* [information, visit])

---

1. *historéō* seems to derive from *hístōr,* "one who knows and puts this knowledge to effect." The verb thus means "to investigate," "to bear witness." In tragedy and philosophy "inquiry" is usually the sense. *historía* comes to mean "information" based on research. From the time of Aristotle, and probably Herodotus, it then means "history."

2. In Greece poetic sagas at first fulfil the function of history. The conflict against Persia inspires Herodotus to write true history. Both he and Thucydides seek to bring out the greatness of what they have experienced. Having plumbed the depths of life, they are no longer content to present the heroic past in poetic form. Truth is interesting as such, and they set out to investigate the truth in all life, both past and present. They cannot see the present as poetry, but only as it happens, though an artistic element unavoidably intrudes. In the work of Thucydides the Greeks achieve scientific history. Due to their primary interest in nature they fail to enter into human differences, and they also lack methodical source criticism whereby to correct the legendary pictures handed down from the past. Yet they point in the right direction.

3.a. The first Christian preaching is proclamation of Jesus as the risen Lord who sits at God's right hand, whose coming again is awaited, and whose historical words and acts are recalled. Even as regards the historical element it is witness in the service of God and the truth. The accuracy of the historical information is important (1 Cor. 15:3ff.). Relatively precise timings are given (1 Cor. 11:23). Since believers cannot verify the events for themselves, the witness must be accredited and credible. Yet the Gospels show little influence of Greek history. They consist of sayings and stories in rabbinic fashion. At first oral, these are collected and recorded as an account of the earthly activity of the Messiah who is now exalted. In origin and standpoint, they are totally different from Greek biography.

b. Only in Luke do we find some contact with Greek historical writing. His prologue, the speeches in Acts, and the accounts of Paul's travels give evidence of literary culture in the Hellenistic sense. What Luke offers is genuine history within the limits of his material and purpose. In the gospel he cannot write a biography, and obviously the story of Jesus and the apostles differs from that of a nation. He is thus content to fit Jesus into world history (3:1-2), to investigate the tradition very closely, and to write better Greek, using at times the technical terms of historical research and composition (*lógos, prágma,* etc.).

c. As noted, Paul is interested in historical accuracy (1 Cor. 11:2, 23 etc.), and it is his aim to set forth Christ crucified to the churches (Gal. 3:1). Yet he uses *historéō* in Gal. 1:18—the only instance in the NT—merely in the popular sense "to visit in order to get to know." He has nothing in common with the Greek historians. Nor has John, though John has a great gift of presenting characters (Martha, Thomas, etc.), bringing out the drama of conflict, depicting the mood of crowds (7:11 etc.), and sketching situations (13:30 etc.).   [F. BÜCHSEL, III, 391-96]

---

ischýō [to be strong, able], *ischyrós* [strong, powerful], *ischýs* [strength, ability], *katischýō* [to be strong, superior]

---

1. The group *ischy-* has the sense of "ability," "capacity," "power," or "strength." It overlaps with the *dyna-* group, but with greater stress on the power implied. Thus *ischýō* is "to be strong, healthy, able," *katischýō* "to be strong," "to be superior," "to strengthen," *ischyrós* "strong, powerful," and *ischýs* "strength," "ability." *ischýs* is common in earlier Greek and is liked in the LXX, but fades out in Hellenism and hardly occurs at all in the papyri or on inscriptions.

2. The NT follows the common pattern. a. *ischýō* means "to be able" and occurs often in Luke but also in Matthew, Revelation, and Hebrews. In Mt. 5:13 it describes the salt that has lost its savor: it is good for nothing. In Acts 19:20 God's word prevails mightily. In Gal. 5:6 circumcision and uncircumcision have no power in relation to the hoped-for righteousness, only faith working through love. Jms. 5:16 reminds us of the power of fervent prayer in times of distress. In Phil. 4:13 Paul points us to the source of all strength for the Christian life; he has in Christ a power that makes all things possible for him.

b. *katischýō* occurs in Lk. 23:23 in the sense "to be strong," "to prevail," and in Lk. 2:36 in the sense "to be strong," i.e., to be able to survive the depicted disasters and hence to be able to stand before the Son of Man. In Mt. 16:18 the meaning is "to overcome"; the realm of death cannot prevail over the church as the community of him who is stronger.

c. *ischyrós* is used in the absolute in the NT for both persons and things (Lk. 15:14; 1 Cor. 4:10; 10:22; 2 Cor. 10:10; Heb. 5:7; 11:34; Rev. 18:2, 21). In 1 Cor. 1:25 we read that God's weakness is "stronger" than men. Human ethics and religion have no power relative to salvation. The apparent weakness and folly of the cross are more powerful than human wisdom and might. Heb. 6:18 refers to the strength of the comfort or encouragement that is grounded in Christ's saving act as our high-priestly forerunner. In 1 Jn. 2:14 the young men are strong because of God's word dwelling in them. God himself is a mighty Judge in Rev. 18:8; he judges mighty Babylon (v. 10). We read of a mighty angel in Rev. 5:2; 10:1; 18:21.

d. *ischýs* refers to human ability in Mk. 12:30; we are to focus it all on God. The might of the Lord is the basis of Christian strength in Eph. 6:10. Judgment is to be executed in the glory of God's power according to 2 Th. 1:9. God has power to do what we cannot do (Lk. 12:4-5). Yet this power is put forth on behalf of Christian ministry too (1 Pet. 4:11). It is ascribed to God and his Christ in the doxologies of Rev. 5:12 and 7:12.

3.a. In Mt. 9:12 Jesus uses *iatrós* to describe his saving work. He has come to heal the sick. The *ischýontes,* i.e., the strong or healthy, who do not perceive their need, can make nothing of him or his mission.

b. In Mt. 3:11 and parallels the Baptist speaks of a mightier one who is coming after him. He himself can give only the water baptism of repentance with a view to the kingdom, but this mightier one will baptize with the Spirit and fire. Jesus calls himself the stronger one in Lk. 11:20ff. The context here is the debate about the exorcisms of Jesus. His opponents attribute these to Beelzebul, but Jesus in reply compares them to the despoiling of a strong man (Satan) by a stronger. Satan has a certain dominion, but the history of Jesus is the history of a successful attack on this dominion and its overthrow. Behind the statement stand passages like Is. 49:25 (the release of the prisoners of the strong) and Is. 53:12 (the suffering servant dividing the spoil with the strong). Similar passages may be found in the pseudepigraphal and rabbinic writings, and in the NT (cf. Lk. 4:6; 13:16). The common point is that Satan enslaves us to sin, sickness, demonic possession, and death, but that Christ views it as his mission to break this dominion, conquer Satan, and bring us liberation. The mighty power of Jesus displayed in this liberating mission is that of the kingdom of God. Jesus puts forth this power, not merely in his death and resurrection, but already in his life, in his triumph over temptation, in his healings and exorcisms, in his raising of the dead. Yet Is. 53:12 maintains the link with his vicarious death (cf. also the metaphor of ransom). With Is. 53:12 and Mt. 20:28, Lk. 11:22 forms a nexus embracing Christ's life, death, and resurrection as the decisive act of human liberation.

c. In Eph. 1:18-19—a passage which heaps up words for power—the faith of the community is traced back to God's mighty power. For similar formulas cf. Is. 40:26; 44:12, and in the LXX Dt. 9:26; 26:8. The use of two or three terms for divine power is a common and intentional one that is designed to bring out its greatness. In Eph. 1:19 it is preceded by the threefold statement: "the riches of the glory of his inheritance."

→ *dýnamai*   [W. GRUNDMANN, III, 397-402]

íchnos [footprint]

1. *íchnos* may denote either an individual footprint or a track. It is used figuratively for the trace that is left by life or conduct and that others may mark and follow. In 2 Cor. 12:18 Paul and Titus have followed the line of responsible conduct in their handling of the collection. In Rom. 4:12 the faith of Abraham has left its impress by which circumcised believers may take their bearings and faith may also be accessible to the uncircumcised. "Features" is a possible rendering here, but it might suggest imitation of special aspects of Abraham's life, whereas the real point is that all faith is a following in the steps of Abraham.

2. In 1 Pet. 2:21 the implied sense of "example" is more apposite. Yet here again the idea is more that of a trail to follow than acts to imitate. The *hypér* of Christ's passion ("for you") removes it from the sphere of repetition. Believers suffer as disciples of him who has trodden the path of suffering, in fellowship with him, following the same direction, but not in detailed imitation. But does suffering exhaust the meaning of following in this sense? The immediate situation, being one of suffering, might seem to say so (cf. also 1 Pet. 4:1; Mt. 20:20ff.). Yet the disciples also receive commission and authority from Christ (Mt. 10:1ff.), and Paul speaks of being glorified with him (Rom. 8:17; cf. also Jn. 13:15; 15:12; Jms. 5:10-11).

3. The NT never suggests that the Christian life is to be an exact imitation of that of Christ. There may be echoes of this, e.g., in the healings, or in the death of Stephen (Acts 7:58ff.). Again, Paul often holds up Jesus as an example (Phil. 2:5ff.; Rom.

15:1ff.; Col. 1:24; Gal. 6:17). But discipleship is always the goal, not imitation. The apocryphal Acts hardly go beyond this. The early church, however, tends to move toward imitation, especially when it finds true discipleship in martyrdom (cf. Ignatius *Ephesians* 12.2; Mart. Pol. 22.1).

4. *íchnos* can also mean "sole" or "foot" (cf. in the LXX Dt. 11:24; 28:35; Josh. 1:3; 2 Sam. 14:25; 2 Kgs. 19:24; Dan. 10:10). There is reference to the foot of God in Ezek. 43:7. In pagan religions we find votive offerings with engraven footprints; these either commemorate the visits or healings of pilgrims or bear witness to visits by the gods. Obviously, however, such practices are alien to the NT, nor do we find there the idea of enduring footsteps (cf. Paul in Rom. 11:33 on the basis of Ps. 77:16ff. and Job 11:7 LXX: "Canst thou find the trace of the Lord?").

→ *anexichníastos*   [A. STUMPFF, III, 402-06]

Iōnás [Jona, Jonah]

A. Jona, the Father of the Apostles Peter and Andrew. In Mt. 16:17 Simon Peter is called *Bariōná,* while in Jn. 1:42; 21:15ff. his father's name is *Iōánnēs. Iōná* occurs as a variant of *Iōán(n)ēs* in the LXX (2 Kgs. 25:23). Elsewhere there are no first-century examples of *Iōná.* Hence it is probably a shorter form of *Iōánnēs,* unless John substitutes the more common form. Nothing else is known of Simon Peter's father.

B. The Prophet Jonah.
1. The Later Jewish View of Jonah. Jonah was greatly magnified in later Judaism. He was supposedly the son of the widow of Zarephath, fled in the interests of Israel, and offered his life for his people.

2. The Prophet Jonah in the NT. The stay in the great fish (Mt. 12:40) and the preaching in Nineveh (Mt. 12:41; Lk. 11:32) are mentioned in the NT. There are also echoes of the story in the stilling of the storm (Mk. 4:35ff.). The repentance of Nineveh is presented as a warning now that one greater than Jonah is here. The double contrast between Gentiles and Jews and Jonah and Jesus gives point to the threat. What is meant by the sign of Jonah is much debated. Some have tried to find an original reference to John the Baptist, but this is linguistically dubious. The context of Lk. 11:29ff. has suggested that the preaching might be the sign, but it would be unusual for human preaching to be a divine sign. It thus seems that the sign is the deliverance after three days and nights (Mt. 12:40) which accredits Jonah as a preacher in the same way as the resurrection will accredit Jesus (Lk. 11:30). The contemporary concept of the self-offering of Jonah might be included. Jesus may validly give this enigmatic sign because it is not abstracted from his person and does not soften the offense and the related call for decision.   [J. JEREMIAS, III, 406-10]

---

kathairéō [to take down, destroy],   **kathaíresis** [tearing down, destruction]

kathairéō. This verb has the four main senses a. "to take down," b. "to tear down," c. "to destroy," and d. "to dethrone." The LXX uses it in all these senses for various

Hebrew equivalents, e.g., taking down the brazen sea, tearing down houses etc., destroying cities, and dethroning rulers. In the NT we find a. for taking down from the cross in Mk. 15:36 (while living) and Mk. 15:46; Lk. 23:53; Acts 13:29 (when dead). Regard for the Passover did not allow Jesus and the thieves to be left on the cross. Sense b. occurs in Lk. 12:18: In his folly the rich farmer tears down the barns he has in order to build bigger ones. For sense c. we turn to Acts 13:19 (cf. Dt. 7:1), where God gives Israel the land by destroying seven nations. The word also has this sense figuratively in 2 Cor. 10:4. Lk. 1:52 has sense d.: God overthrows the powerful who do not do his will; the context here is eschatological. In Acts 19:27 the verb has the same sense in a different connection. The Ephesian silversmiths argue that Artemis may be deprived of her majesty through the ministry of Paul.

kathaíresis. This noun has the same senses as the verb. In 2 Cor. 10:4 Paul's preaching will lead to the destruction of the bulwarks of human sophistry (cf. Prov. 21:22). In 2 Cor. 10:8 and 13:10 *kathaíresis* is the opposite of *oikodomḗ* (edifying). Once Paul tore down, but his commission now is not destroying but building up (cf. Jer. 1:10; 24:6).   [C. Schneider, III, 411-13]

---

katharós [clean, pure],   *katharízō* [to cleanse, purify],   *kathaírō* [to make clean],   *katharótēs* [purity],   *akáthartos* [unclean, impure],   *akatharsía* [impurity],   *katharismós* [cleansing, purification],   *ekkathaírō* [to cleanse], *perikátharma* [offscouring, refuse]

---

katharós, katharízō, kathaírō, katharótēs.

A. The Usage. The group denotes physical, religious, and moral cleanness or purity in such senses as clean, free from stains or shame, and free from adulteration. In the LXX it is mostly used for *ṭāhôr* and *zāḵaḵ* with the usual connotations of clean, free, or innocent (cf. Ezek. 36:25; Ps. 51:10; Ex. 25:11, etc.).

B. Clean and Unclean outside the NT: Part I.
1. In Primitive Religion. Ideas of power are dominant in primitive thinking about cleanness. After coming into contact with power, e.g., in birth, sex, and death, cleansing is necessary to fit one for ordinary life. But since the numinous power may be deity as well as demon, cleansing is also needed for dealings with it. Cleanness and uncleanness are viewed quasi-physically, but the association of cleanness and holiness offers a starting point for moral spiritualizing.

2. In Greek Religion. At its primitive stage Greek religion follows the customary pattern. At the historical stage, however, the gods are seen as friendly forces, though they must be approached with cultic purity. Rules are thus devised to ward off what is demonic and to protect the holy nature of the gods. These rules are primarily cultic but in personal religion, and especially in philosophy, a sublimation takes place which affects the cultic sphere too. Moral purity as well as ritual purity is demanded in the approach to deity.

3. In OT Religion. The OT reflects the same general development. Uncleanness, which may be contracted in contact with birth or death (Lev. 12; Num. 19:11), is a positive defiling force. So is anything linked to a foreign cult. Animals formerly devoted to deities are disqualified (cf. Lev. 11). Hygiene, of course, plays a role (Lev. 11:29-30). Stress also falls, however, on the holiness of God, so that the concept of purity develops with special force. Purifications by washing, sacrifice, or transfer restore forfeited purity and open up access to God. As God's holiness has moral content, ritual purity symbolizes moral purity. The prophets emphasize this aspect even to the point of castigating purely ritual conceptions, though not of totally rejecting them. Some groups in later Judaism tend to the opposite extreme, but Hellenistic Judaism (cf. Philo) strongly spiritualizes the older cultic concept. The cultic rules of cleansing are upheld, but their significance is primarily symbolical; moral purity is what God requires.   [F. HAUCK, III, 413-17]

C. Clean and Unclean outside the NT: Part II: Judaism.

1. Cultic Uncleanness.

a. For Judaism uncleanness clings to the unclean person or thing and can be transferred to others. The source and what is infected are distinguished, and there are four degrees of uncleanness, the intensity weakening at each stage of transmission.

b. Transmission is by touch, carrying, pressing, entry (e.g., of a leper), or place (e.g., being in the same house as a corpse).

c. Various degrees of exclusion result from the different degrees of uncleanness. One presentation distinguishes ten degrees, and divides up the land itself into ten areas of holiness, e.g., cities, the temple hill, the inner courts, etc.

d. As regards vessels, the degree of defilement depends not only on the kind of infection but also on the make and material. The use to which material is put (e.g., leather) may also determine its defilement.

e. Stricter sects view other groups as deficient from the standpoint of their view of purity. These groups include ordinary Jews and half-Jews as well as Samaritans and Gentiles. Gentiles are shut out from the temple, and strict Jews must avoid contact with pagan temples or vessels and purify what they buy from Gentiles.

f. Oddly enough, the canonical Scriptures are also thought to defile the hands. The original explanation of this puzzling fact is probably that they are devoted to deity and thus taboo. But a later explanation is that they were pronounced unclean for purposes of distinction.

2. Cultic Cleansing.
Restoration of cleanness is primarily by water (washing, sprinkling, or bathing), though sin offering may also be required. Vessels, too, are cleansed by water (dipping or scalding); sometimes they may have to be destroyed. The most common act of cleansing is washing the hands (e.g., at grace or times of prayer). Purity is also demanded for the study of the law, but the rules vary. Prayer should cease if defilement takes place in the course of it.

3. The Attitude of the Rabbis to the Law.
Rabbinic theology recognizes that the rules of purity are important only because it is the King of all kings that ordains them. At many points there is also a readiness for relaxation. Levitical uncleanness should not stop the reading of the law, since the law itself has purifying force. Yet the laws of purity may also be applied with legalistic stringency.

4. Inward Purity.
The stress on ritual purity is accompanied in rabbinic Judaism by a strong and consistent requirement of moral purity. We have received the soul pure from God and must keep it so. The demand for inner purity covers the whole of life from such things as speech on the one hand to the administration of justice on the other. We are to keep our mouths from every sin and sanctify ourselves from all sin and guilt; God then gives us the promise of his enduring presence.

[R. MEYER, III, 418-23]

D. Clean and Unclean in the NT.

1. Physical Cleanness. This sense is present in passages that follow the traditional view that what is physically clean is adapted for cultic (Heb. 10:22) or ritual (Mt. 23:26) or respectful (Mt. 27:59) use. Closest to Judaism are the statements about the new Jerusalem in Revelation (21:18, 21; cf. 15:6; 19:8, 14). What is clean is adapted for fellowship with God; what is profane is shut out (cf. 21:27).

2. Cultic Cleanness and Cleansing. The term has this reference when used for the ritual cleansing of vessels (Mt. 23:25), the cleansing of lepers (Mt. 8:2-3), or blood as a means of cleansing (Heb. 9:22). Yet Paul asserts the basic cleanness of all created things (Rom. 14:14, 20). Peter learns the same lesson in the vision of Acts 10 (cf. v. 15 and 11:9). If animals are clean, however, Gentiles are not debarred from the gospel by cultic impurity. The purification that counts is the cleansing of the heart by faith (Acts 15:9). Jesus himself points the way here with his teaching that the true defilement is inward (thus declaring all foods clean, as Mark comments; cf. Mk. 7:14ff.). Tit. 1:15 advances the principle that it is the person who makes things clean or unclean: To the pure all things are pure, to unbelievers nothing is pure. According to 1 Tim. 4:5 grace at meals sanctifies all foods, so that we may enjoy them without scruple. In the NT, then, the idea of material or purely cultic impurity drops away; the concept of moral and spiritual purity transcends and replaces it.

3. Moral Purity. Jesus shows us that a cultic purity that is concerned only with externalities is inadequate (Mt. 23:25-26; Lk. 11:41). The purity required of the NT community is moral and personal. It consists of a dedication to God that renews the inner being. Purity of heart—which is far above purity of hands—is what counts before God. Yet purity becomes a primary motif only in such writings as the Pastorals, Hebrews, John, James, and 1 Peter. Jms. 1:27 claims that pure religion consists of practical love, while Jms. 4:8 demands a purifying of the heart as well as a cleansing of the hands (cf. Is. 1:16-17). 1 Pet. 1:22 calls for a purifying of the soul in the obedience of faith and a sincere love. Eph. 5:26 uses the symbolism of baptism to portray the moral purification by Christ which determines future conduct. The death of Christ is above all the sacrifice that expiates sin and creates a new purity of life. By this death we are his people and zealous for good deeds (Tit. 2:14). We receive a pure heart and a good conscience that issue in love (1 Tim. 1:5). Hebrews opposes to the older ritual purity the superior moral purity of the new order (9:13). Cleansing is still needed (cf. 9:22), but only Christ's blood can achieve this with its cleansing from sin (1:3) and liberation from sinful impulses (9:14). It is by the death of Christ, then, that we have access to holiness and may live in God's presence. Purity is also an important theme in John. The disciples are clean through their association with Jesus (Jn. 15:3). This cleansing is by the word (cf. 17:14ff.). In Jn. 13 the foot-washing both serves as a symbol, pointing to baptism (Jn. 13:10), and offers an example, denoting Christ's loving service in daily forgiveness. 1 John attributes the power of this ongoing cleansing to the blood of Jesus (1:7). It is in virtue of this purifying that believers may attain to purity (3:3, 6). Revelation insists on the ritual purity of the new Jerusalem but obviously only as a symbol of its perfect inner sanctity.

akáthartos, akatharsía. These two terms are used for physical, cultic, and moral impurity, which are closely intertwined. The use in the LXX is mostly cultic. Uncleanness clings like an infection and renders cultically unserviceable. Objects, animals, places, vessels, and people may be unclean, e.g., by contact, through sexual processes, or through idolatry. Priests decide what is unclean and conduct the rites of purification (cf. especially Lev. 7, 11, 13ff.; Num. 9, 19). Hellenistic Judaism deepens the concept along moral lines. In the NT 1. the sense of cultic impurity may be seen in Mt. 23:27; Acts 10:14, 28; Gal. 2:11-12, and cf. the term "unclean spirit." But the NT also has the term 2. for Gentile alienation from God in the form of licentiousness (cf. Rom. 1:24ff.; 1 Th. 4:7; Eph. 4:19; 2 Cor. 6:17). *akatharsía* is a work of the flesh, i.e., of the unregenerate person who is subject to natural desire (Gal. 5:19). Christian sanctification, however, covers the children of Christians so that they are no longer unclean (1 Cor. 7:14).

katharismós. This term means "physical," then "cultic cleansing." It is used in the LXX for ritual purification (cf. Lev. 15:13; Ex. 29:36; 30:10). The sense of cultic cleansing may be found in the NT in Mk. 1:44; Lk. 2:22; Jn. 2:6, but the term also denotes here cleansing from sin, in baptism (Jn. 3:25; Eph. 5:26; 2 Pet. 1:9), through Christ's death (Heb. 1:3; cf. 1 Jn. 1:7ff.). For the same concept Paul has *hagiasmós* in 1 Cor. 1:30; 1 Th. 4:7; Rom. 6:19—a more dynamic term.

ekkathaírō. "To cleanse," "to purge," "to separate": Paul uses this word in 1 Cor. 5:7 for purging out the leaven, i.e., removing all abominations, and in 2 Tim. 2:21 for setting aside what is shameful.

perikátharma. This more intensive form of *kátharma* is common in secular Greek for a. the expiatory offering, b. the unworthy and destitute, and c. what is thrown out after purification. All three senses are apposite in Paul's self-description as *perikátharma toú kósmou* in 1 Cor. 4:13.   [F. HAUCK, III, 423-31]

---

katheúdō [to sleep]

A. The General Usage.
1. Of Humans.

a. The primary sense is "to sleep." Sleep is highly rated in antiquity, but the activism of the Greeks and Romans finds too much sleep distasteful; the early hours up to sunrise are the main periods of intellectual production (lucubrations). Peaceful sleep in time of peril (cf. Socrates) is a mark of greatness.

b. Sleep is also viewed as an incursion of the suprasensual, so that antiquity pays great attention to dreams. Attempts are made to interpret these scientifically; they mostly have to do with such material things as prosperity or poverty, health or sickness, etc. Some religious significance attaches to temple sleep.

c. Figuratively sleep has a derogatory reference, e.g., to deficient concentration or the inactive or vegetative life.

d. Since sleep embraces the ambivalence of human life and death, the question arises whether life itself is not a sleep, and its activity a mere dream. But sleep and death are also equated, with immortality as the inference.

2. Of Gods and Heroes.

a. Homer finds it natural that the gods should sleep the secure sleep of heroes, but philosophy finds the idea meaningless, whether the reference be to personifications of nature or to God in the supreme sense.

b. The idea of sleeping gods persists in less intellectualized religion and stands closely related to the problem of death (cf. the lifeless but incorruptible Attis, sleeping Endymion with his eyes open, and the Cretan cult of the dying and reborn Zeus).

B. Sleep in the OT and Judaism.

1. Of Humans.

a. The OT, too, values sleep highly. It refreshes us (Jer. 31:26), and God protects it (Ex. 22:25-26). Even in sleep the righteous can meditate on the law (Ps. 1:2), and their sleep is sweet (Prov. 3:24), for God does not sleep (Ps. 121:3), and they are thus secure (Ps. 3:5). Indeed, God gives his beloved sleep (Ps. 127:2). On the other hand, too much sleep is culpable indolence (Prov. 10:5), the luxurious beds of the rich are condemned (Am. 6:4), and diligent servants do not sleep.

b. Visions from God come in sleep (Gen. 15:2; 1 Sam. 3:1ff.). These may take the form of dreams needing interpretation; cf. Jacob's ladder (Gen. 28:10ff.), Joseph's dreams (Gen. 37:5, 9) and interpretations (Gen. 40:5ff.; 41:1ff.), and the dreams of Zechariah and Daniel. Prophetic dreams denote divine favor, but dreams may also deceive (Num. 12:6-7; 1 Sam. 28:6; Joel 2:28). In divine judgment sleep may also be stupefaction (Is. 51:20).

c. The OT does not use *katheúdein* for laziness, but it has the term neutrally for death (cf. Dan. 12:2).

2. Of Idols Which Sleep and God Who Does Not. Elijah taunts the priests of Baal: Perhaps their god is asleep and has to be awakened (1 Kgs. 18:27). In contrast, the God of Israel "will neither slumber nor sleep" (Ps. 121:4). Only the mode of expression, not the concept, is mythological in, e.g., Pss. 44:23; 78:65.

C. The NT.

1. The Literal Sense.

a. The NT accepts sleep as a natural fact (Mt. 13:25; Acts 20:9), but shows more interest in activity than sleep (cf. Lk. 6:12; 1 Th. 2:9). In Gethsemane the disciples should not sleep but watch (Mt. 26:40ff.). Yet Jesus sleeps peacefully in the storm (Mk. 4:38), trusting implicitly in the Father's care and thus secure in his fellowship with God (cf. the little faith of the disciples).

b. God gives directions in sleep, e.g., to Joseph (Mt. 1:20), the Wise Men (Mt. 2:12), Pilate's wife (Mt. 27:19), and Paul (Acts 16:9). Yet dreams are only marginal in the NT, and there may be morally dangerous dreams (Jude 8).

2. The Metaphorical Sense.

a. The term occurs for death in 1 Th. 5:10. An authentic raising from the dead is at issue in Mt. 9:24. It is not taught that death is really only a sleep.

b. There is a specialized use in 1 Th. 5:6, where sleep is the opposite of the concentration and energy of faith in an eschatological situation. The wise as well as the foolish virgins sleep in Mt. 25:5, but the former are ready at the decisive moment.

D. The Early Church. *katheúdō* does not occur in the immediate post-NT writings. Legends like that of the seven sleepers, which borrow from ancient myth and Jewish concepts, arise only in the fifth century at the earliest.   [A. Oepke, III, 431-37]

→ *hýpnos, egeírō*

---

kathḗkō [to be fitting], *(tó kathḗkon* [what is proper]*)*

---

1. Popular Usage. a. "To come down or to," b. "to be proper, fitting, appropriate."

2. Philosophical Usage. From popular use *tó kathḗkon* comes into philosophical vocabulary in the sense of "what is fitting or demanded," e.g., by nature, custom, or piety.

3. The LXX. The LXX has the term in all its shades of meaning; cf. Gen. 19:31 ("after the manner"), Ex. 5:13 ("daily task"), Lev. 5:10 ("according to the law"), and cf. Sir. 10:23; 2 Macc. 6:4; 3 Macc. 4:16.

4. The NT. The only NT instance (plural) is the negative one in Rom. 1:28, where Paul has in mind what is offensive even to natural human judgment. The decision against God leads to a complete loss of moral sensitivity, the unleashing of unnatural vices, and hence the type of conduct that even healthy pagans regard as improper.

[H. SCHLIER, III, 437-40]

---

káthēmai [to sit],   *kathízō* [to set, seat],   *kathézomai* [to sit]

1. The Neutral Sense. Sitting is usually on a stool (2 Kgs. 4:10) or couch (Gen. 48:2; Ezek. 23:41), or outdoors on a stone (Ex. 17:2), preferably under a tree (Judg. 4:5), or on a hilltop (2 Kgs. 1:9) or the edge of a well (Ex. 2:15). Jesus sits by the shore (Mt. 13:1) or on mountains (Mt. 5:1). Peter sits in the court (Mt. 26:58; cf. Esth. 5:13). Oddly the soldiers sit at the foot of the cross (Mt. 27:36). In the OT sitting is common at meals (Gen. 27:19; Ezek. 44:3), but in the NT reclining (Mt. 9:10; Jn. 13:23, etc.).

2. Sitting as a Mark of Distinction.

a. Gods. Archaeology depicts gods as sitting while humans stand to pray. Thus the ark is thought of as God's throne (1 Sam. 4:4; 2 Sam. 6:2, etc.). In Is. 19:1 God sits, or rides, on a cloud. For Jesus the throne expresses divine dignity (Mt. 5:34-35). Revelation depicts God on the throne (4:2ff.; 5:1ff., etc.; cf. Is. 6), but antichrist can also sit on a throne (2 Th. 2:4).

b. Rulers. In antiquity rulers are often godlike figures and hence the throne is also their prerogative (Ex. 11:5; 1 Kgs. 1:17ff., etc.). The queen and royal favorites also sit on thrones. Rulers may even sit in God's presence (Ps. 110:1). The ornamentation of thrones symbolizes royal power (1 Kgs. 10:18ff.). In the NT the messianic king is enthroned alongside God, and he grants a seat with him to believers who conquer (Rev. 3:21). Influential in this regard are Ps. 110:1 and Dan. 7:13 (cf. Mt. 26:64; Mk. 14:62; Col. 3:1; Heb. 1:3; 8:1; 12:2).

c. Judges. As the Egyptian gods sit for judgment, so human judges sit in token of their dignity (cf. Mt. 27:19; Acts 25:6; 12:21; 23:3). The divine Judge sits at the last judgment (Mt. 19:28; 25:31).

d. Teachers. Like many teachers in antiquity, Jesus sits to teach (Mt. 5:1; 13:1-2, etc.), thus following rabbinic custom (Mk. 2:6; Mt. 23:2; Lk. 5:17).

e. Assemblies. Ancient assemblies are depicted as sitting, e.g., the senate, the Sanhedrin, Christian synods. Rev. 20:4 refers to a heavenly senate (cf. 4:4), though there the picture merges into one of worship.

f. For precedence in seating → *dexiós.*

3. Sitting as a Psychological Attitude.

a. As a Gesture of Grief. In the OT sitting is a sign of mourning. Denoting pathetic abandonment, it is the position in which to bewail oneself or others (Job 2:8ff.). Sitting in darkness is a technical term for mourning (Is. 9:1; Lk. 1:79). Beggars also sit (2 Kgs. 7:3; Mt. 20:30, etc.). The women who weep for Jesus sit (Mt. 27:61) (cf.

those who mourn for Adonis in Ezek. 8:14). Penitents also sit to express sorrow (Jon. 3:6; Lk. 10:13).

b. For Practical Reasons. Some people sit for practical reasons, e.g, scholars (Mk. 3:32), tax gatherers (Mt. 9:9), fishermen (Mt. 13:48), money changers (Jn. 2:14), and children at some games (Mt. 11:16; Lk. 7:32).

4. *Sitting at Divine Service.* Standing was customary in ancient temples, but sitting became necessary with the long mystery services. In the synagogue Jesus (Lk. 4:20) and Paul (Acts 13:14) both sit, and sitting is general in the church (Acts 2:2; 20:9; 1 Cor. 14:30; Jms. 2:3, and perhaps Rev. 4:4).

5. *Figurative Meanings.* The verb can also mean a. "to stay" (Mt. 26:36), b. "to dwell" (Gen. 23:10; Lk. 21:35), c. "to ride, journey" (Mk. 11:2, 7; Jn. 12:14-15; Acts 8:28), d. "to instal" (1 Cor. 6:4; Eph. 1:20), e. "to sit to consider" (Lk. 14:28, 31), and f. "to alight, rest" (the tongues as of fire at Pentecost in Acts 2:3).

[C. SCHNEIDER, III, 440-44]

> *kathístēmi* [to bring, make, cause], *akatastasía* [disorder], *akatástatos* [restless]

kathístēmi. From the basic sense "to set down," the following significant meanings develop.

1. "To conduct," "bring," "lead to" (Acts 17:15).

2. "To set in office," "instal," a. with accusative (Heb. 5:1), b. with accusative and *epí* and genitive (Mt. 25:21), dative (Mt. 24:47), or accusative (Ps. 8:6), c. with double accusative (Heb. 7:28), and d. with final infinitive, also in the genitive or with *eis* (Mt. 24:45; Heb. 8:3).

3. "To make someone something" (double accusative). Theologically important in this regard is Rom. 5:19. The question arises how far our becoming righteous through the obedience of the one is a fact, and how far it is a judgment. The forensic element is present in the context (cf. v. 18) and the dominant nature of the creation is what counts for God rather than the nature of the individual (vv. 13ff.). Yet God's sentence decides both destiny and quality, so that while all became sinners in Adam, in Christ all virtually, and believers factually, become righteous, and will stand as such in the judgment. Pronounced righteous, they will be so in fact as well (Rom. 8:3-4), though the emphasis is on the judicial sentence. The theory that Paul has linked senses 1. and 2. in an eschatological riddle is too artificial.

4. In Jms. 3:6: "the tongue is a fire," the word expresses the aspect of affirmation better than a mere *estín.* Similarly in Jms. 4:4 the friend of the world proves to be an enemy of God.

akatastasía. This word signifies "disorder" a. as "political turmoil," b. as "personal unrest." Sense a. occurs in Lk. 21:9, sense b. in 2 Cor. 6:5. We also find in the NT a further sense c. "disruption" in the community through disputes (Jms. 3:16) or charismatic exaggeration (1 Cor. 14:33).

akatástatos. The meaning of this word is "restless" either a. as "exposed to unrest" or b. as "unsettled." We find only b. in the NT: The "unstable" person cannot pray effectively in Jms. 1:8, and the tongue is a "restless" evil in Jms. 3:8.

[A. OEPKE, III, 444-46]

Káin → *Ábel*

> *kainós* [new (in nature)], *kainótēs* [newness], *anakainízō* [to renew, restore], *anakainóō* [to make new], *anakaínōsis* [renewal], *enkainízō* [to renew]

kainós.

1. Linguistic Data. As distinct from *néos,* "new in time," *kainós* means "new in nature" (with an implication of "better"). Both words suggest "unfamiliar," "unexpected," "wonderful," and the distinction fades with time. The NT has *kainós* for "not yet used" in Mt. 9:17, "unusual" in Acts 17:21, and "new in kind" in Mt. 13:52; Eph. 2:15; 2 Jn. 5; Heb. 8:13 (though an aspect of time is also present in 2 Cor. 5:17; Heb. 8:13, etc.).

2. Theological Data. kainós denotes the new and miraculous thing that the age of salvation brings. It is thus a key teleological term in eschatological promise: the new heaven and earth in Rev. 21:1; 2 Pet. 3:13, the new Jerusalem in Rev. 3:12; 21:2, the new wine in Mk. 14:25, the new name in Rev. 2:17; 3:12, the new song in Rev. 5:9, the new creation in Rev. 21:5. This new creation, which is the goal of hope, finds expression already in Christian life (2 Cor. 5:17). The new aeon has come with Christ. In him Jews and Gentiles are one new man (Eph. 2:15). Believers are to put on the new nature that they are given (Eph. 4:24). God's saving will is worked out in the promised new covenant that Jesus has now set up (Lk. 22:20; 1 Cor. 11:25; Heb. 8:8ff.; 9:15). This is a better covenant (Heb. 7:22), infallible (8:7), everlasting (13:20), grounded on higher promises (8:6). The fact that the old and the new cannot be mixed (Mk. 2:21-22) stresses the element of distinctiveness. The new commandment of love has its basis in Christ's own love (Jn. 13:34); it is new without being novel (1 Jn. 2:7-8). The immediate post-NT writings retain the qualitative sense of *kainós* but with a legalistic tendency, especially in the idea of Christianity as a new law (cf. Barn. 2.6: Justin *Dialogue* 11.4; 12.3).

kainótēs. "Newness," with a secondary suggestion of the unusual. Only Paul uses the term in the NT. In accordance with the NT senses of *kainós* we are to walk in "newness" of life and serve in "newness" of the Spirit (Rom. 6:4; 7:6). New creation by the Spirit releases from bondage to sin and law and gives a new quality to life and service.

anakainízō (→ *anakainóō, ananeóō*). The meaning of this word is "to renew," "restore." It occurs in the NT in Heb. 6:4, which issues the warning that those who commit apostasy cannot be restored again to repentance, i.e., brought back to conversion (*metánoian*). In early Christian writings the term is a common one in connection with regeneration and baptism (Barn. 6:11; Hermas *Similitudes* 8.6.3 etc.).

anakainóō (→ *anakainízō, ananeóō*). This word means "to make new." Paul uses it in 2 Cor. 4:16, not for a process of moral change, but for the daily renewing and strengthening by the Spirit which lifts him above external pressures. Moral renewal, however, is the point in Col. 3:10, for with the gift of the new life in Christ there is continual renewal according to the standard of the divine image.

anakaínōsis. This word, meaning "renewal," is used in Rom. 12:2 for the renewal of mind and will that we must undergo, through the work of the Spirit (Rom. 8:9ff.), if we are to show that we belong to the new aeon. The reference in Tit. 3:5 is to the first and unique renewing, the creation of a life that was not there before, which is the work of the Holy Spirit associated with baptism.

enkainízō. Rare outside the Greek Bible, this word also means "to make new, renew." In Heb. 10:19-20 it occurs in connection with the new way into the sanctuary: Jesus has opened or dedicated this way, treading it himself for the first time. In the other instance in Heb. 9:18, with reference to the covenant, the idea is that of bringing into effect, or consecrating. As an ordinance in salvation history, the old covenant, like the new, is put into effect by death (Ex. 24:6ff.).   [J. BEHM, III, 447-54]

---

kairós [decisive point], *ákairos* [untimely], *akairéō* [to have no time], *eúkairos* [well-timed], *eukairía* [right moment], *próskairos* [temporary, transitory]

---

kairós.

A. **The Nonbiblical Use.** In its basic sense *kairós* seems to refer to a decisive point in place, situation, or time.

1. The spatial sense is rare.

2. The idea of a decisive situation develops after Hesiod with many nuances, e.g., danger, effect, favor, opportunity, advantage, success, or goal.

3.a. The term then has the sense of a "decisive moment," again with positive, neutral, or negative implications, though the positive one of fortune is the most common. Fortune in this sense is not fate, but the chance that must be boldly grasped. A connection with ethics thus arises, e.g., in Stoicism, which stresses responsibility of meeting the demands of the *kairós*. A cult of the god Kairos is also found; the god is depicted with a lock of hair at the front, so that even religiously a summons to action is implied. b. Yet *kairós* can also become a weaker term for time, (i) as a short space of time, and (ii) as a stretch of time.

B. **The Use in the Septuagint.**

1. Used mainly for Heb. *'ēt* and *mô'ēd* (also Aram. *zᵉnān*), *kairós* first means "decisive point in time," but with more stress on divine appointment than ethical demand. The reference, then, is to God's time (cf. Job 39:18; Num. 23:23; Eccl. 3:11; Dan. 2:21). God gives the final time of felicity, fixes the time of death (Eccl. 7:17), and brings the last time or the time of judgment (Lam. 1:21). Ecclesiastes discerns God's hand in the *kairoí* through which the author passes (3:10ff.). A more secular use occurs in 1 Chr. 12:23 etc. ("critical situation") and Sir. 4:20 ("right moment") (cf. Hag. 1:2).

2. A purely temporal sense is more common, e.g., point of time in Gen. 17:21, 23 etc. or stretch of time (cf. Ezek. 12:27 etc.). We thus find a use for festivals, or for regular biological or meteorological times. Sections in life may also be indicated. In general, however, this more common use is of less theological interest.

C. *kairós* in the NT.

1.a. The spatial use does not occur in the NT, and the situational use only in Heb. 11:15 ("opportunity"), but the temporal sense of "decisive point" is common, often with a stress on the fact that it is divinely ordained. Jerusalem does not recognize the unique *kairós* when Jesus comes to save it (Lk. 19:44). The masses fail to see the decisive character of the *kairós* that is present with Jesus (Lk. 12:56). The presence of this *kairós* is God's fulfilment of OT prophecy (Mk. 1:15). The seriousness of decision is thus given a new intensity. The simultaneity of end and present fulfilment poses a demand and confers an ability for recognition and outworking in love (Rom. 13:11; Gal. 6:10; Eph. 5:16; Col. 4:5). Jesus' own life stands under the claim of the *kairós*. He discerns the moment and decides accordingly (Jn. 7:6, 8). This *kairós* is not just a favorable opportunity. Jesus awaits it from the Father and thus enjoys true certainty. His end especially stands under the *kairós*. He himself says when it has come (Mt. 26:18), but only as he sees and grasps and accepts the *kairós* that is given by God. It is thus the "right time" (Rom. 5:6).

b. The stress may sometimes be on the content, so that the element of human decision is weaker, but that of God's ordination is no less clear. Thus God fixes the time for the manifestation of the Logos (Tit. 1:3), for the attestation of divine love in Jesus (1 Tim. 2:6), for the epiphany of Christ (1 Tim. 6:15) and the reaping of his people (Gal. 6:9). Among other *kairoí* of this kind, i.e., specific points in the development of God's plan, are the beginning of messianic power over demons (Mt. 8:29), of imminent judgment (1 Pet. 4:17), of the removing of the power of the *katéchon* (2 Th. 2:6), and of the final judgment (1 Cor. 4:5; Rev. 11:18). Christians cannot calculate the times (Mk. 13:33; Acts 1:7); God has sovereign control over them. *kairós* can become a technical term for the last judgment (cf. Lk. 21:8; 1 Pet. 5:6; Rev. 1:3). Yet it may also denote individual points in the believer's life (cf. 2 Tim. 4:6; Lk. 1:20).

2.a. Among many instances of the use for a "short space of time," cf. Lk. 21:36; Eph. 6:18; Rom. 9:9; Mt. 24:45; Mk. 12:2; Mt. 13:30; Gal. 4:10 (with various references).

b. For a "stretch of time" (again with various references), cf. 1 Th. 2:17; 1 Cor. 7:5; Lk. 8:13; Heb. 11:11; Acts 17:26; Rom. 3:26; 2 Cor. 8:14; sometimes for a general indication of time, e.g., Mt. 11:25; Acts 12:1; 7:20; 1 Tim. 4:1.

ákairos, akairéō, eúkairos, eukairía. *ákairos* has the meanings a. "excessive," b. "unwelcome," and c. "unseasonable." *akairéō* can mean "to have no time." In the LXX we find *ákairos* only in Sirach for "untimely." In contrast *eúkairos* and *eukairía* denote what is "propitious," the "favorable" or "right" time (cf. Ps. 104:27). In 2 Tim. 4:2 the point of *eúkairōs akaírōs* is "whether convenient or not." In Heb. 4:16 *eúkairos* denotes the "divinely appointed time"; the sympathy of our High Priest insures that this will also be the right time for us. *eukairía* occurs in Mt. 26:16: Judas has to seek a "favorable opportunity" to hand over Jesus (cf. Lk. 22:6). *akairéō* occurs only in Phil. 4:10: "to have no opportunity."

próskairos. This late word means "temporally conditioned," "temporally limited," "unusual," "transitory" (also in a qualitative sense). In the LXX it denotes "temporal" as distinct from "eternal," i.e., belonging to this world (only 4 Macc. 15). In Mt. 13:21 the reference is simply to time ("for a while"), but Heb. 11:25 contains a moral judgment: sinful pleasures are fleeting. In 2 Cor. 4:18 we find the contrast between the temporal, which is also transitory, and the eternal, which is definitive.

[G. DELLING, III, 455-64]

---

kaíō [to light, burn]

kaíō is theologically significant in Lk. 24:32 and 1 Cor. 13:3. 1. In Lk. 24:32 the idea of the heart burning within seems to rest on OT usage (Ps. 39:3), though there are also Greek and Latin parallels. 2. In 1 Cor. 13:3 various interpretations have been offered for giving one's body to be burned. a. Martyrdom. Paul would have been familiar with the idea of martyrdom by fire (cf. Dan. 3:23ff.; rabbinic references; 2 Macc. 7:3ff.; 4 Maccabees; Heb. 11:34). Such martyrdom involves heroism, but Paul views it with reserve if it is oriented to self, since it opens the door to pride, offers a ground of self-righteousness, and may even obscure Christ's cross. Paul is certainly not opposing love to faith here. b. Self-burning. Self-immolation by fire is sometimes extolled in antiquity as a supreme act of sacrifice or freedom (cf. Stoicism; also the Indian self-burning of widows). If this is what Paul has in view, he has against it the same objections as against a. c. Branding as a Slave. On this view Paul's thought is that of giving the self to slavery on behalf of others. This is an unlikely interpretation, for most slaves were not branded (usually only runaways and criminals), and in any case this course would involve a measure of self-sacrificial love. We do best, then, to follow a., or b., or both.   [K. L. SCHMIDT, III, 464-67]

---

kakologéō [to abuse, curse]

This rare word means "to abuse," "calumniate," "curse." The negative version of the fifth commandment in Mk. 7:10; Mt. 15:4 is based on Ex. 21:16 LXX. Jesus gives the commandment added depth by applying it to the withholding of what is due to parents on a hollow religious pretext (Mk. 7:11-12). In Mk. 9:39 we probably have a popular type of saying containing subtle humor. In Acts 19:9 Paul's opponents deride (not curse) his message.   [C. SCHNEIDER, III, 468]

kakopátheia, -théō → *páschō*

---

kakós [evil], *ákakos* [upright], *kakía* [wickedness, trouble], *kakóō* [to hurt], *kakoúrgos* [evil-doer], *kakoḗtheia* [malice], *kakopoiéō* [to do evil], *kakopoiós* [evil-doer], *enkakéō* [to treat badly], *anexíkakos* [long-suffering]

---

kakós. This word, expressing a lack, has the meanings a. "unserviceable," "incapable," b. "morally evil," "bad," c. "weak," and d. "ruinous." The presence of what is *kakós* raises the difficult question of the origin and purpose of evil in relation to God and human and cosmic destiny, i.e., the question of theodicy.

A. *kakós* in the Greek World. Two views of evil develop in the Greek world: first, that it comes from deity by divine necessity, and second, that it is partially caused by us. These views overlap in tragedy in the themes of guilt and fate. Philosophy suggests that ignorance is the reason for evil, but dualism is also present, e.g., in the thought that good necessarily implies evil, or in the theory that souls have been plunged into this earthly state as a punishment and have to rise up out of it to the supraterrestrial world of good. Socrates and Plato develop the concept that we do evil involuntarily through ignorance, but Plato also finds an emotional and even a cosmic dimension to evil in the form of a dialectical necessity connected with the matter which the deity used in fashioning the world (cosmological dualism of spirit and matter). Aristotle stays more closely with the idea that ignorance, itself culpable, is the cause of moral evil. Stoicism, too, rejects the idea of metaphysical necessity, attempting to bring evil into its monistic system by relativizing it as a counterpart of good, attributing it to a false view of the world, or arguing that the perfection of the whole excludes that of the individual. It cannot avoid a psychological dualism (cf. Epictetus).

B. *kakós* in Hellenism. For Philo evil is a possibility from birth. Even if we choose good, we are always in conflict with it in this life. It is a reality linked to the earth. It has, however, a religious dimension as sin, and is overcome by union with God. Plutarch offers a more metaphysical view, ascribing evil to an evil world soul. The Hermetic writings pose an absolute contrast based on having or not having *noús*. Plotinus finds the principle of evil in matter, which is at the farthest remove from the One. The soul, though sunk in matter, is still divine, and has an impulse toward a union with deity that it achieves in ecstasy and death. Evil is a reality, but it is so as a lack of true being.

C. In the Evil Principle in Parseeism. In Zoroastrianism we find two antithetical wills (or deities) rather than two opposing principles. The spirits of falsehood and truth fight for mastery in us. We work out in this life the choice that we make between them in pretemporal existence. All evil comes from the wicked spirit, which has the help of demons. A final judgment will separate the good and the bad, and in a last conflict evil and the wicked will be destroyed and perfection established.

D. *kakós* in the OT (LXX). In the OT the questions relating to *kakós* arise mainly in connection with such concepts as *hamartía* and *adikía*. *kakós* corresponds to the Hebrew stem *ra'*, though it is used for other terms as well; it brings out impressively the moral judgment of Judaism on wickedness. There are 371 instances.

1. tó kakón as Evil. In the history books the LXX has the term for "disaster." Two thoughts are present here. First, evil in this sense is a punishment for sin, especially for idolatry and apostasy (cf. Dt. 21:17-18; Jer. 6:19). Second, God saves from evil in this sense (Jer. 26:13) when his people repents. Evils have, then, a political or national dimension. They come from God, the Lord of history, as the penalty for a walk that leads away from him. Yet God's final intentions are good, for even as evils are the response of his righteousness to human guilt, they are also expressions of his merciful seeking inasmuch as through them he recalls his people to true faith, obedience, and worship. This insight underlies the statement of Job in 2:10. It gives the concept of God a solemn and mysterious character, but carries with it the assurance that in its depths his being is peace and love.

2. tó kakón as an Ethical Concept. tó kakón is also an ethical concept (cf. Mic. 2:1; Ps. 28:3). Evil in this sense has its seat in the human heart (Jer. 7:24). In this regard the term is an important one in Proverbs (95 times). Often the translator substitutes it for different Hebrew originals (cf. Prov. 1:18; 2:16; 3:31). The point made is that we may choose good with the help of wisdom. If we do, we shall also find good. If, however, we willingly choose evil, through ignorance or ungodliness, evil results will follow (cf. 4:27; 13:10; 25:19). Often the term is used very generally, e.g., for strife in the Hebrew, and in many cases it is introduced by the translator (cf. 19:6, 27; 21:16, etc.). While noncommittal in itself, the term expresses the moral judgment of the period.

E. *kakós* in the NT. The term *kakós* is not a significant one in the NT, for the saving work of God in Christ robs the problem of theodicy of its main point, and *kakós* as a moral concept is far less important than *hamartía* and *ponērós*.

1. Jesus regards the heart as the seat of evil (Mt. 7:21), though behind it stands the *ponērós*. God himself is apart from everything evil (Jms. 1:13). The tongue (Jms. 3:8) and the love of money lie at its root (1 Tim. 6:10).

2. The NT uses *tá kaká* for the temporal or eternal ruin that might come upon us. Lazarus has *tá kaká* now, Dives later (Lk. 16:25). God's lordship decides the issues of perdition and salvation, but the divine decision is not fully worked out in this life. The point of the parable is not one of mechanical redress (evil for good and good for evil) but of response to the divine summons to trust and obedience, with eternal and not just temporal destiny at stake.

3. Paul in Rom. 13:3-4 recognizes that there is evil in the world and points out that God has committed to the state the task of restraining it.

4. In Rom. 7:19, 21 Paul realistically faces the fact that, while God wills the good from us, on our own we cannot do it. We thus come under the judgment of 2:9. Evil here is more than moral; it involves nonacknowledgment of God and self-assertion before him, i.e., ungodliness. Ambivalence obtains in this regard, for inwardly we consent to the good—we are God's creation and cannot negate our origin—but we cannot translate our good intentions into action, and thus fall victim to sin and death. Deliverance comes only when we are united by faith with Christ, who has borne our guilt.

5. When we are united with Christ in this way, the previous impossibility becomes a possibility that we are to grasp (Col. 3:5). The new reality of life in Christ means that we may be guileless as to what is evil (Rom. 16:19). In love we may now overcome evil with good (Rom. 12:21), for love neither thinks evil (1 Cor. 13:5) nor does it (Rom. 13:10). If evil is a force that disrupts fellowship, the love that derives from Christ makes true fellowship possible again.

ákakos. This word, the opposite of *kakós,* means "upright," "innocent." Philo uses it for newborn infants. Job is upright in 2:3 (cf. 8:20). The sense of innocent leads on to that of "guileless" (cf. Jer. 11:19). This is the point in Rom. 16:18: Those who cause divisions deceive the "simple-minded." In Heb. 7:26, however, the meaning is "upright." Religiously our High Priest is holy, cultically without defect, and morally innocent. The final qualifications denote his majesty.

kakía. This word expresses the quality of *kakós;* it is the outworking of *kakón* or the principle of evil, mostly in the ethical field, though it may also denote incompetence, or, in a religious sense, guilt. *kakíai* play an important part in Philo's ethics. A possibility of human life, they cannot stand before God. In the LXX *kakía* may be an individual misdeed (1 Kgs. 2:44). Every *kakía* is *kakía* before God (Jer. 1:16). Yet *kakía* may also be a synonym of *tó kakón* in the sense of misfortune or disaster (1 Sam. 20:7).

In the NT *kakía* means "trouble" in this sense in Mt. 6:34. All work that caters to natural needs imposes a burden, though this should not oppress those who know God as a caring Father. Elsewhere the use is ethical. The word denotes a single sin in Acts 8:22 (the offense of Simon Magus), but Paul uses it more generally for the evil which is a penalty of sin and which is disruptive of fellowship (Rom. 1:28-29; Tit. 3:3). Christians may put off this evil (1 Pet. 2:1; cf. Jms. 1:21; Eph. 4:31). Yet the new freedom must not become a pretext for license (1 Pet. 2:16). We are to be babes in *kakía* (1 Cor. 14:20). In the main, the NT views *kakía* as a force that is destructive of fellowship.

kakóō. The meaning of this verb is "to hurt," "to maltreat," "to injure." The NT uses it for the oppression of Israel in Egypt (Acts 7:6, 19), for the persecution of the church (Acts 12:1; 14:2), and for averted attacks on Paul (Acts 18:10). Where there is zeal for the right, no true harm can be done (1 Pet. 3:13).

kakoúrgos (→ *lēstḗs*). The *kakoúrgos* is "one who does wrong," "malefactor," "villain." The NT uses the word for the two thieves crucified with Jesus (Lk. 23:32-33, 39). In 2 Tim. 2:9 the apostle finds a likeness between himself and his master when he speaks of being in fetters like a *kakoúrgos*.

kakoḗtheia. This word, found in Esth. 8:12-13 and meaning "wickedness," is part of the series in Rom. 1:29, where its position shows that it means "intentional wickedness" or "malice."

kakopoiéō, kakopoiós. The verb means "to do evil" and the noun "one who does evil." Instances in the LXX are in Gen. 31:7; Prov. 6:18; Jer. 4:22. In the NT the two words occur especially in 1 Peter (2:12; 3:17; 4:15). Believers will be regarded as evil-doers (2:12). They should respect rulers, whose office is to punish evil-doers (2:14). If they themselves suffer, it should not be for doing wrong (3:17). Suffering as a Christian and not as a wrongdoer is to God's glory (4:15-16). 3 Jn. 11 makes a basic distinction. When we see God, there arises in us the power for good action in love and mercy. Where evil is done, there is no vision of God. We see God, of course, when we see Christ (cf. Jn. 14:9).

enkakéō. This word has two senses, "to act or treat badly" and "(wrongly) to cease." In Lk. 18:1, just after the apocalyptic discourse in ch. 17, the point is obviously that, with a view to the end, the disiciples should not grow slack in prayer. The meaning is the same in 2 Cor. 4:1: Paul will not let any difficulties cause him to fail or grow weary. In virtue of the eternal purpose of God, Paul in Eph. 3:13 asks his readers not to be discouraged by the pressures of his present situation, which are in fact their glory. Similarly, there is an exhortation not to grow weary in well-doing in 2 Th. 3:13; Gal. 6:9, with the promise of an ultimate reaping of eternal life (Gal. 6:8).

anexíkakos. This word, meaning "long-suffering," occurs in the NT only in 2 Tim. 2:24, which states that the Lord's servant must not be contentious but kindly, apt to teach, and "forbearing" even with opponents.   [W. GRUNDMANN, III, 469-87]
→ *agathós, hamartánō, ponērós*

> *kaléō* [to call], *klḗsis* [calling], *klētós* [called], *antikaléō* [to invite back], *enkaléō* [to accuse], *énklēma* [accusation], *eiskaléō* [to invite], *metakaléō* [to bring], *prokaléō* [to provoke], *synkaléō* [to call together], *epikaléō* [to call out, appeal], *proskaléō* [to invite, summon], *ekklēsía* [assembly, church]

---

kaléō.

1. Data. kaléō, meaning "to call," appears often throughout the NT, especially in Luke and Acts, less frequently in Mark and John. It may always be rendered "to call," but often has the special nuance of divine calling or vocation.

a. In the active with accusative and vocative we find it in Lk. 6:46: "Why do you call me 'Lord, Lord'?" With accusative of object and predicative accusative it means "to name" in, e.g., Mt. 10:25; Lk. 1:59; Mt. 1:21, 23; Lk. 1:13. It also occurs in the passive in this sense in various constructions (cf. Mt. 2:23; Mk. 11:17; Lk. 1:32; Jn. 1:42; Acts 1:12, etc.).

b. Another fairly common use is for "to call to," "to invite," e.g., in Mt. 20:8; 22:4; Mk. 3:31; Lk. 7:39; Jn. 2:2; Acts 4:18 and 24:2 (in a legal sense); 1 Cor. 10:27.

c. Often it is God or Christ who calls. God calls his Son (Mt. 2:15). Jesus calls the disciples (Mt. 4:21). He calls sinners to repentance (Mt. 9:13). God calls us to himself or to salvation (Rom. 8:30). He has called the seed of Abraham (Rom. 9:7). He has called both Jews and Gentiles (Rom. 9:24). He has called Christians to fellowship with his Son (1 Cor. 1:9). He has called us to peace (1 Cor. 7:15), in grace (Gal. 1:6), to freedom (Gal. 5:13), to his kingdom and glory (1 Th. 2:12), in holiness (1 Th. 4:7; cf. 2:13-14), to eternal life (1 Tim. 6:12), to light (1 Pet. 2:9), yet at the same time to suffering (1 Pet. 2:20-21). Christ himself is called (Heb. 5:4). As Abraham is called (11:8), he is a type of Christians, who may simply be described as "the called" (9:15), and who are as such invited to the marriage feast of the Lamb (Rev. 19:9). If Jesus does the calling in the Gospels, he does so in fulfilment of a divine function, and the proper response is faith, which carries with it not only discipleship but also the blessings of salvation. Behind the term, then, stands the whole work of God, through Christ, in judgment and grace. This takes place either directly with Jesus' own calling or in the gospel ministry (cf. 2 Th. 2:14). In this use of the term there is thus a technical element even where this is not explicit.

2. Parallels.

a. For "to name" we find parallels in Gen. 17:19; 1 Sam. 1:20, etc. Names are important in the OT world. To be called something is equal to being it (cf. the parallelism in Lk. 1:32).

b. The use of the word for "to invite" is common from Homer and occurs in the papyri and LXX.

c. We also find parallels for the idea of God calling us with a view to our obedience (cf. in addition to more general parallels Prov. 1:24; Philo *On the Special Laws* 4.187; 1 Clem. 32.4 etc.; Hermas *Similitudes* 9.14.5; *Mandates* 4.3.4).

3. Origin.

a. The main origin of the NT usage is to be sought in the LXX. The richest source is to be found in Is. 40ff. (cf. 41:9; 42:6; 46:11; 48:12; 51:2; cf. also naming in 43:1; 45:3).

b. The Hebrew term is usually *qārā'*. The objective force of *kaleín* may also be seen from its use for words meaning "to take" and "to be."

c. The idea of invitation or summons to salvation is a common one in rabbinic writings. An ordinary word thus acquires special significance through the fact a. that God is the subject and b. that salvation is the goal.

klḗsis.

1. Data. In Rom. 11:29 God's *klḗsis* is his call or calling. In 1 Cor. 1:26 the Corinthians are to consider their call; God "chose" the foolish and weak etc. (v. 27). In 1 Cor. 7:20 they are to remain in the state of their calling. This is not their secular "vocation," for they were called in the Lord and their *klḗsis* is with God (vv. 22ff.). In Eph. 1:18 the hope of one's calling is the hope to which one is called (cf. 4:4). Eph. 4:1 speaks of a life worthy of calling, Phil. 3:14 of a prize of calling, 2 Th. 2:11 of being worthy of God's call, 2 Tim. 1:9 of a holy calling, Heb. 3:1 of a heavenly call, and 2 Pet. 1:10 of the confirming of one's call and election. In all these passages there is a technical nuance, so that "calling" is usually a better rendering than "call," though call is always possible. The element of grace in calling comes out especially well in 2 Tim. 1:9.

2. *Parallels.*

a. There are a few instances of *klḗsis* for "naming" or "name."

b. Invitation is more common (cf. Jdt. 12:10; 3 Macc. 5:14; Jer. 31:6 LXX).

c. The religious sense of "calling" occurs in Epictetus *Dissertationes* 1.29.49 (the imposing of a difficult task); Barn. 16.9 (the calling of the promise); Hermas *Mandates* 4.3.6 (great and august calling, i.e., baptism). [In a distinctive secular usage we find *klḗsis* or *kalḗseis* for the Roman classes.]

3. *Origin.* Since *klḗsis* as a verbal noun is equivalent to *kaleín*, the origin of its use in the NT is the same. Its absence from the LXX may be accidental, or may be due to the influence of Hebrew, which has fewer verbal nouns than verbs.

klētós.

1. *Data.*

a. This verbal adjective occurs ten or eleven times in the NT. It is sometimes a verb and sometimes a noun referring to Christians. Examples are Rom. 1:1, 6-7; 8:28; 1 Cor. 1:1, 2, 24; Jude 1; Rev. 17:14; Mt. 22:14, and some versions of Mt. 20:16.

b. *klētós apóstolos* in Rom. 1:1 might suggest a call to office, but for Paul calling as a Christian and as an apostle is the same thing.

c. Mt. 22:14, unlike other NT passages, seems to distinguish between the called (*klētoí*) and the elect (*eklektoí*) (cf. Rev. 17:14). To get the point we really need to know the Aramaic original. The saying may also be dialectical; its aim is perhaps to show that calling cannot be taken for granted, so that there is no real distinction between calling and electing. Similar paradoxes may be found in Jesus' attitude to prayer and his description of opponents in Mt. 8:12 as sons of the kingdom.

2. *Parallels.* While the word goes back to Homer, parallels are few. a. The LXX has it for "named" in Ex. 12:16. b. Homer uses it for "invited," "welcome," in the *Odyssey* 17.286. c. "Divinely called" occurs only in the Christian sphere, e.g., 1 Clement.

3. *Origin.* The origin is similar to that of *klḗsis*. Ex. 12:16 probably lies behind the combination of *klētós* and *hágios*. There is no evidence that *klētós* was a cultic term in pagan religion.

anti-, enkaléō, énklēma, eis-, meta-, pro-, synkaléō. These compounds are not of theological significance in the NT. *enkaléō* occurs in a legal sense ("to accuse") in Acts, as does the noun *énklēma*. *meta-* for "to have brought" occurs only in Acts, *syn-* for "to call together" in Mk. 15:16; Lk. 15, 6, 9, *eis-* for "to invite" in Acts 10:23, *anti-* for "to invite back" in Lk. 14:12, and *pro-* ("to provoke") in Gal. 5:26.

epikaléō.

1. *Data.*

a. A first meaning is "to name" (cf. Mt. 10:25 [active]; Lk. 22:3; Acts 1:23, etc.; Heb. 11:16; Jms. 2:7 [passive]).

b. The middle use for "to appeal to someone" is a common legal one (cf. Paul's appeal to Caesar in Acts 25:11-12). Less technically, cf. the appeal to God in 2 Cor. 1:23. Often, too, there is appeal to God in prayer (cf. Acts 2:21; 7:59; 9:21; 22:16; Rom. 10:12; 2 Tim. 2:22: calling on God).

2. Parallels. There are many Greek parallels for the sense a. "to name" and also for b. "to appeal," whether in literature, the papyri, or Josephus. Calling on God is found in the LXX, but also in classical authors and the papyri.

3. Origin.

a. While NT usage reflects the general use, LXX influence is strong. Thus in Acts 15:17 naming the Gentiles by God's name implies that they are his by his self-revelation to them (cf. Jms. 2:7).

b. LXX influence is also strong in the idea of calling on God in prayer (cf. Pss. 50:15; 53:4; 86:5; 89:26; 91:15, etc.).

c. The usage in the LXX and NT suggests that calling on the name of the Lord is almost a technical term (cf. Gen. 13:4; 21:33; Ps. 79:6, etc.).

d. Often the LXX translates the Hebrew original by *krázein,* perhaps because of some similarity of sound. That we have in the Hebrew as well as the Greek equivalents a technical term for prayer may be seen from the absolute use.

e. In the NT "calling on the name of the Lord" (in prayer) may refer to God the Father (Acts 2:21) but also to God the Son (Acts 7:59; Rom. 10:12ff.; 2 Tim. 2:22). Those who "call on the name of our Lord Jesus Christ" (1 Cor. 1:2) are Christians. Directing prayer to Jesus is a mark of faith in him as the Messiah.

proskaléō.

1. Data. Only the middle occurs in the NT and the term rarely has theological significance; it is simply used when people call another, or others, to them (cf. Mk. 15:44; Lk. 7:18; 15:26; Acts 5:40; 6:2; 13:7, etc.; Jms. 5:14). God does the calling in Acts 2:39, the Holy Spirit in Acts 13:2, and Jesus in Mt. 10:1; Mk. 3:13, etc.

2. Parallels. Greek writings show that the middle is preferred, and it may be a legal term for "to bring to judgment" (cf. some of the instances in Acts).

3. Origin. LXX influence is plain in Acts 2:39 (Joel 2:32) and 16:10. In Matthew and Mark the style suggests that when Jesus calls to himself he is fulfilling the divine calling as the Christ (cf. the more or less fixed opening to the accounts).

ekklēsía.

A. Introduction. General dictionaries define *ekklēsía* as 1. "assembly" and 2. "church." NT lexicons then distinguish between church as a. the whole body and b. the local congregation or house church. The emphasis differs according to denomination, although sometimes the basic unity is perceived. Since the NT uses a single term, translations should also try to do so, but this raises the question whether "church" or "congregation" is always suitable, especially in view of the OT use for Israel and the underlying Hebrew and Aramaic. It must also be asked why the NT community avoids a cultic term for itself and selects a more secular one. "Assembly," then, is perhaps the best single term, particularly as it has both a concrete and an abstract sense, i.e., for the assembling as well as the assembly.

B. The NT. An important question is why *ekklēsía* does not occur in such books as Mark, Luke, John, and 1 and 2 Peter. (Its absence from Jude is less significant, as also that from 2 Timothy and Titus in view of 1 Timothy, and 1 and 2 John in view of 3 John.)

1. Acts. The first passages in Acts (2:47; 5:11; 7:38; 8:1, 3; 9:31) are important in view of the use not only for the Jerusalem church (8:1) but for the church throughout Judea and also for OT Israel (7:38). The singular predominates, but later we also find

397

the plural (possibly 9:31, probably 15:41, certainly 16:5). A pregnant saying is 20:28: "the *ekklēsía* of the Lord which he bought with his own blood." In all these verses the local church is called *ekklēsía* with no question of precedence or of local emphasis. The singular and plural are interchangeable. Two or more churches do not make the church, nor are there many churches, but one church in many places, whether Jewish, Gentile, or mixed. The only descriptive term that is added is *toú theoú* (or *kýriou*), which clearly marks it off from a secular society (denoted in 2:47 by *laós*). In three instances there is a purely secular use (19:32, 39, 40), which shows that what matters is not assembling as such but who assembles and why. In the case of the church it is God (or the Lord) who assembles his people, so that the church is the *ekklēsía* of God consisting of all those who belong to him (cf. *hólē* in 5:11; 15:22). Applied to believers, the term is essentially a qualitative one, the assembly of those whom God himself gathers.

2. *Pauline Epistles, I.* The usage in Paul is similar; cf. the free use of singular and plural (Rom. 16:23; 16:4, 16; Gal. 1:13, 22), the use of *hólē* (Rom. 16:23), and the references to a place (Rom. 16:1) or district (1 Cor. 16:19). Occasional omission of the article shows that *ekklēsía* is almost a proper name (cf. 1 Cor. 14:19; 2 Cor. 8:23). Even a small house church may be called *ekklēsía* (Rom. 16:5). Each local church represents the whole church (2 Cor. 1:1: "the church which is at Corinth"), so that what applies in it (1 Cor. 6:4; 11:18; 14:34) will apply everywhere. For Paul, too, *toú theoú* is the main definition, whether in the singular (1 Cor. 1:2) or the plural (1:16). (This shows that he does not differentiate church and churches, as is sometimes done.) Since God acts in Christ, *en Christō* (Gal. 1:22) or *toú Christoú* (Rom. 16:16) may also occur; "Christian" is too colorless a rendering for this. We also find "churches of the saints" in 1 Cor. 14:33—natural in view of the equation of the *ekklēsía* with the "sanctified in Christ Jesus" in 1:2. Materially, Paul shares his conception of the church with the early disciples. The church is still the *ekklēsía toú theoú* as in the OT, but with the new thing that God has fulfilled the covenant in Christ, and that Christ has manifested himself to his disciples and commissioned them to assemble a people in his name. The church is constituted and authorized by the appearances of the risen Lord, not by the charismatic experiences that are also enjoyed by the disciples and Paul. Paul thus recognizes the privileges of the first community and its leaders, as may be seen in his organizing of the collection for Jerusalem (which is not just a matter of benevolence or strategy) and his description of James etc. as "pillars" in Gal. 2:9 (even if there is irony here in view of their human fallibility and the mistaken desire of some to overexalt authoritative persons). Paul has no desire to impose a new view of the church, but rather to protect the original view against incipient innovations. For him the church stands or falls with its sole foundation in Christ, its acknowledgment of him alone as Lord, and the rejection of overemphasis on persons or places. No description of the church is given, but Paul gets to the heart of the matter with his understanding of it (parallel to that of Acts) as an assembly which is the assembly of God in Christ.

3. *Pauline Epistles, II: Colossians and Ephesians.* A more specific doctrine of the church unfolds in these epistles. It is Christ's body, with Christ himself as head (Col. 1:18, 24; Eph. 1:22; 5:23). There is a relation of coordination and subordination between it and Christ (Eph. 5:24-25, 29). The church is to be holy and without blemish (5:27). Through it God's wisdom is to be made known (3:10). The human statements here circle around a divine mystery (3:4-5). All that concerns Christ and the church is God's doing. The mystery of their union forms a model for that of husband and

wife even as it is also illustrated by this (5:25ff.). The images are taken from the contemporary world: the Redeemer overcomes hostile powers on his heavenly ascent (Eph. 4:8ff.), breaks down the wall of division (2:14ff.), creates the new man (2:15), loves and cherishes the church as his spouse (5:22ff.), and builds it up as his body (2:19ff.). Yet while these ideas are related to the world of Gnostic speculation, and can hardly be either derived from such passages as Rom. 12:4ff. or fused into a consistent picture, their import is practical rather than theoretical or esoteric. For a. they express the strict relation between Christ and the church, and thus serve a christological ecclesiology, and b. they protect an exalted Christology in the difficult situation caused by false teaching and the tensions between Jewish and Gentile Christians. These concerns are wholly Pauline even if a new set of concepts has to be used to meet the Jewish devaluation of the church by focusing on place and person and the Gnostic exaggeration which postulates a marriage between Christ and wisdom rather than between Christ and his people. Indeed, even the ideas of these letters are present materially, if not formally, in epistles like Romans and 1 and 2 Corinthians, where the church is the body in its interrelationships (1 Cor. 12) and Paul's aim is to present it as a pure bride to her husband (2 Cor. 11:2). The language may be Gnostic, but the point is to show that the church is not just a human society but is defined in terms of Christ. Ecclesiology is Christology and vice versa. All human distinctions are thus transcended (Col. 3:11; cf. Gal. 3:28). Yet this is no Christ mysticism, for the church can be Christ's body only by obeying God's call in Christ, and the God who calls in Christ is the God of the old covenant who has now established the new, so that the NT assembly is the fulfilled OT assembly. If holiness is ascribed to this community, it is not as a quality but in virtue of God's justifying and sanctifying work in Christ, on the basis of which the word of promise to Israel is now the word of fulfilled promise to Christians.

4. *The Rest of the NT.* The other NT passages add little to what has been said. Revelation uses the plural 13 times and also speaks of the church of Ephesus, Smyrna, etc. 3 John has the term twice with and once without the article. Jms. 5:4 mentions the elders of the church, probably referring to the whole community. Heb. 2:12 quotes Ps. 22:22, and Heb. 12:23 refers to the assembly of the firstborn, probably not in a technical sense, but simply in that of a festal gathering in heaven (cf. v. 22).

C. **The Greek World.** The Greek world uses *ekklēsía* for a popular assembly (cf. Acts 19:32, 39-40). The OT and NT give it its specific sense by adding *toú theoú* or *en Christó*. Did they choose this word because it had a cultic sense? It denotes the assembly of *ekklētoí* in Greek cities, but there is no sure evidence of use for a cultic society. The secular *ekklēsía* offers a formal parallel, and may have a religious undertone, as in the offering of prayers, but NT usage derives from that of the LXX. This explains why Latin adopts *ecclesia* rather than such renderings as *curia, civitas Dei,* or *convocatio*. The term *ekklēsía* has a sacred history in the sacred writings. It stresses the distinctiveness of Christianity as compared to cultic societies, for which there are special terms like *thíasos*. Hellenistic Jews are probably the first to apply the term to the church, preferring it to *synagōgé* because the latter was acquiring a more restricted sense, and perhaps because there is some similarity of sound between *ekklēsía* and Heb. *qāhāl*.

D. **Parallel Expressions.** Often *ekklēsía* may not be present, but the matter itself is presented under different terms. 1 Peter especially offers such expressions as "spiritual house" (2:5), "chosen race" etc. (2:9), and "God's people" (2:10). Gal. 6:16

speaks of the "Israel of God," Gal. 3:29 of "Abraham's offspring," and Jms. 1:1 and 1 Pet. 1:1 of the "twelve tribes" or "exiles" in the dispersion. Less closely related terms are the saints, the brethren, disciples, etc. In Jms. 2:2 the church can also call itself *synagōgḗ,* which also derives from the OT. The question arises which term might have been used by Aramaic-speaking Christians, and before that by Jesus himself.

E. Matt. 16:18 and 18:17.

1. The Problem. There are several difficulties relating to these two passages: their coordination with other *ekklēsía* passages, their authenticity, their Semitic equivalents, and their correct exposition. Complexity arises because the answers to these questions all affect one another.

2. The Relation of the Two Passages. A specific problem is that 16:18 seems to refer to the whole church and 18:17 to the local church, for which we might have expected *synagōgḗ.* Is *qāhāl* the underlying term in both instances?

3. Textual and Literary Criticism. Neither verse offers real textual problems. Literary criticism points out that there are no parallels to 16:18 in Mark or Luke, but it can supply no cogent arguments for the theory of interpolation (and in any case even an interpolation might rest on a genuine tradition).

4. Material Criticism. Mt. 16:17ff. has a Semitic flavor, but the two questions of Jesus and the church and the position of Peter involve statistical, eschatological, historical, and psychological problems. a. The statistical problem is the absence of *ekklēsía* elsewhere in the Gospels, but as in 1 Peter this fact is not decisive in view of the parallel "flock" in Mt. 26:31 and Jn. 10:16, the gathering of the Twelve as the nucleus of the true people of God, and Jesus' description of himself as the Son of Man, i.e., the representative of the people of the saints (Dan. 7). Furthermore, the messiahship of Jesus and his institution of the covenant (the Lord's Supper) show that he must be regarded as the founder of what is later most frequently called the *ekklēsía.* b. The eschatological problem is whether founding an *ekklēsía* fits in with the preaching of the kingdom. While the *ekklēsía* is obviously not the *basileía,* it is itself plainly an eschatological entity, and regards itself as such. c. The historical argument is that Peter does not occupy the position that he is given in 16:18 (cf. 1 Cor. 3:11; 10:4). On the other hand, he plays a part which is hard to explain on purely historical or psychological grounds, and if he may be challenged, as in Gal. 2 or Jn. 20:2ff., it is hard to see how 16:18 can have arisen and established itself if not authentic. d. The psychological objection is that Peter does not prove to be a rock. But this is only a special aspect of the miracle of grace that is seen in the election of Israel, or indeed of the church itself.

5. Hebrew and Aramaic Equivalents. A separate question is whether the Hebrew original of *ekklēsía* is *qāhāl* or the corresponding Aramaic loanword, which is in any case rare. Jesus and the disciples must have known Hebrew, but the rabbis do not necessarily use *qāhāl* for the Jewish congregation, whether national or local, and the normal Aramaic term (*kᵉništā'*) suggests a specific group which might be regarded as a sect. The point, perhaps, is that Jesus might have used this term, but with the clear implication that this separated group represents the true Israel as the people of God. If this is so, in 18:17 the original reference might well be to the OT community, but rightly the church then applies it to itself with the rendering *ekklēsía.*

F. The OT and Judaism.

1. Greek Judaism. a. The LXX uses *ekklēsía* about 100 times, mostly for *qāhāl.* The term *ekklēsía* has the basic sense of "assembly" (cf. Dt. 9:10; 1 Kgs. 8:65); only the addition *kyríou* gives it a theological sense (cf. Dt. 23:2ff. etc.), or an expression like "of Israel" (1 Kgs. 8:14) or "of the saints" (Ps. 89:5 etc.). The use of *synagōgḗ* is similar. It, too, is often used for *qāhāl*, and it has both a general sense ("assembly") and a technical sense ("congregation of Israel"). b. In Philo and Josephus the position is much the same, but there is more reference to national assemblies, and the technical sense is also more pronounced.

2. *The Hebrew Text.* While *ekklēsía* is almost always used for *qāhāl*, *qāhāl* is rendered *ekklēsía* only in some books (e.g., Deuteronomy, Joshua, Judges, Samuel, Kings, Chronicles, Ezra, Nehemiah, Psalms). Elsewhere *synagōgḗ* is the equivalent, or occasionally other terms like *óchlos* or *sýstasis. synagōgḗ,* unlike *ekklēsía,* is also used for *'ēḏâ,* which is common in Exodus, Leviticus, and Numbers.

G. Etymology. Since the NT *ekklēsía* is given its specific impress by the OT, the history is more important than the etymology, especially as neither *ekkaleín* nor *ékklētos* occurs in the NT, and both are also very rare in the LXX. The NT writers are unlikely to have had the idea of "called out" in mind when they spoke about the *ekklēsía* (though cf. Eph. 5:25ff.; 1 Tim. 3:15; Heb. 12:23). If the church does in fact consist of those whom God has called out of the world, this relates to material rather than linguistic considerations. What is always meant is the "assembly (of God)." The word "church" suggests the universal aspect, and etymologically its belonging to the Lord (*kyriakón*), but it has the disadvantage of having acquired a hierarchical nuance. The word "congregation" makes the point that the small fellowship is already the church, and it stresses the aspect of gathering together, but it has the disadvantage of drawing attention to the individual group, sometimes in a sectarian sense. "Church community" might be commended as a possible alternative to both.

H. The Apostolic Fathers and Early Catholicism. In the early church we find signs of a shift in the use of adjectives and the rise of speculation. In the first works *ekklēsía* is common only in Hermas with its vision of the *kyría,* who is *hagía* and *presbytéra,* the *morphḗ* of a holy spirit (cf. *Visions* 1.1ff.). 1 Clement in three instances has a use similar to that of 1 Pet. 1:1 and Jms. 1:1. Ignatius has imposing epithets in his epistles, many of them quite extravagant. In *Ephesians* 5.5 God, Christ, and the church are presented as one entity to believers. The churches have single bishops, and the word *katholikḗ* appears in *Smyrneans* 8.2. In the Martyrdom of Polycarp the church is holy and catholic, sojourning in the different places. In the Didache the church is scattered but is to be gathered into the kingdom (9.4). An obscure phrase here speaks of the worldly mystery of the church enacted by the true prophet (11.11). 2 Clement stresses the dimension of mystery in 14.1. With its reference to the preexistence of the church, this links up with speculation about the aeon of the church and statements about the ideal church in contrast to the empirical church (cf. Augustine, and the later distinction between the invisible church and the visible).

J. Conclusion. The development of "Catholicism" as distinct from primitive Christianity is plainly apparent in the area of the church with the rise of Gnostic speculation and the influence of Platonism. The NT itself makes no distinction between an invisible triumphant church and a visible militant church. The church, as the individual congregation representing the whole, is always visible, and its righteousness and holiness are always imputed through faith. Luther recognizes this when he prefers the term "congregation" to "church" in his rendering of Scripture. Yet if the ideal is not to be played off against the reality, no more is the whole church against the local congregation. Every congregation represents the whole church, that at Corinth no less than that at Jerusalem. The development of larger organizations does not alter this basic truth. If there is an element of constitutional change, e.g., with the greater stress on bishops and deacons than on charismatics, this does not in the NT represent an essential change from a pneumatic to a juristic form. Such a change comes only later when lofty speculation about the church attributes divine significance to historical developments and thus makes possible the step from primitive Christianity to early and later "Catholicism."   [K. L. SCHMIDT, III, 487-536]

→ *anénklētos, parakaléō, paráklētos, symparakaléō*

kalodidáskalos → *didáskō*

---

kalós [beautiful, good]

A. The Meaning of *kalós*. Related to Indo-European words for "powerful," "excellent," "strong," *kalós* has the sense of a. "healthy," "serviceable," e.g., sterling metal, suitable place, or right time, b. "beautiful," "attractive," "lovely," and c. "good." All these senses may be brought together under the idea of "what is ordered or sound," and with this basic sense *kalós* is a key term in Greek thought. The noun *tó kalón (tá kalá)* means a. "the good," "virtue," and b. "the beautiful," "beauty."

B. *kalós kaí agathós*.
1. This combination occurs from the fifth century, at first with a political and social sense. The *agathoí* are the worthy or outstanding, and the *kaloí kaí agathoí* are leading citizens who also display some qualitative superiority related to character and culture. The phrase may be used for non-Greeks too.
2. Socrates then adds to the term a spiritual and ethical dimension. The *kalós kagathós* is a worthy citizen who has become such by instruction in virtue. *kalokagathía* begins inwardly and then expresses itself outwardly. Education is the secret, and the ordered life that results will bring happiness.
3. The influence of philosophical thinking on political life may be seen in the orators, e.g., Demosthenes, for whom the *kalós kagathós* is the ideal politician who considers only the public welfare and not his own interests or enmities.
4. The phrase later becomes stereotyped. Epictetus stresses the relating of desire to renunciation and the integrating of one's will to that of the deity. Philo follows the older philosophy.

C. *kalós* and *tó kalón* in the Greek World and Hellenism.
1. Plato relates the *kalón* very closely to the *agathón*. It is an aspect of it, or its form. The *kalón* is the moving force of the striving for harmony and fulfilment. It underlies education as the prototype of a higher image. An eternal idea of the *kalón* lies behind the earthly form. *érōs* is the ability to perceive the *kalón*. From the vision or knowledge of the *kalón* through *érōs,* come virtue and immortality. The *kalón* fuses deity, cosmos, and humanity, and in art and virtue it brings meaning, fellowship, and eternity into life.
2. Aristotle divides the *kalón* into the naturally beautiful and the morally beautiful. Defined by order, the *kalón* is the good in an absolute sense. Stoicism accepts this ethicizing of the concept. The main meaning now becomes "the virtuous," and the concept is that of a norm.

3. The religious aspect emerges again in Hellenism. Philo, influenced by the OT as well as Stoicism, gives the term a religious sense. The divine is the *kalón,* and the world is conjoined with it. Those who seek and achieve the *kalón* are God's children.

4. Plotinus revives the view of Plato. He begins with perceptible beauty, but presses on to the idea of the beautiful as true being. The beauty of this world reveals the glory and goodness of the spiritual world, where true beauty belongs. To see this transcendent beauty brings happiness. It is the goal of life, since the beautiful is the good and vice versa. We achieve it through beauty of soul attained in purification and in such virtues as self-discipline, courage, magnanimity, and wisdom.

5. In the Hermetic writings the *kalón* belongs to God's world. The ideal cosmos is the *kalós kósmos.* The *kalón* is here a transcendental thing like deity. Dualism shuts us off from it except by the knowledge of revelation and the corresponding piety.

D. *kalós* in the OT (LXX) and Judaism.

1. Used in the LXX for *yāpeh,* "beautiful" (e.g., Gen. 12:14), and *ṭôb,* "useful" (Gen. 2:9) or "morally good" (Prov. 17:26), *kalós* plays only a meager role in the OT. The more personal concept of the *dóxa* of God replaces much of what the Greek philosophers meant by it, and in an ethics determined by the law the ideal of life and education expressed in the *kalós kagathós* has no place. Where *kalós* means the good it denotes conformity to God's will, and while the sense of ordered beauty may be present in the creation story (cf. Gen. 1:4, 10, 12, 18, 21, 25, 31), the aesthetic dimension is usually absent.

2. In the sense of "morally good," i.e., in accordance with the law, *kalós* is a synonym of *agathós* and occurs in Num. 24:1; Dt. 6:18; 2 Chr. 14:1; Is. 1:17; Mic. 6:8.

3. In parallelism *kalós* has the sense of "lovely" or "pleasing" in Ps. 135:3 (cf. also 1 Macc. 4:24).

E. *kalós* in the NT.

1. Synoptists. In the message of the Baptist and the preaching of Jesus we find the metaphor of "good fruit" (Mt. 3:10; 7:17ff.). The summons here is to *metánoia* with a view to becoming the good tree that produces good fruit. In the parables we also read of "good seed," i.e., the word of the kingdom of God (Mt. 13:24, 27, 37-38), and "good fish," i.e., those who come under the lordship of God by *metánoia.* Always, here, *kalós* is oriented to God's *basileía.*

2. The *kalá érga* to which Jesus summons us (cf. Mt. 5:16; 25:35ff.) are works of love and mercy such as we find in the OT (Is. 58:6-7) and the rabbinic writings, where God's own works of love and mercy are the model, e.g., his clothing of Adam and Eve (in Gen. 3:21), or visiting the sick Abraham (in Gen. 18:1), or comforting Isaac (in Gen. 25:11), or burying Moses (in Dt. 34:6). Jesus requires mercy and not sacrifice (Mt. 9:13), and displays this himself by coming to save sinners. Yet such good works are integrated into the divine lordship, so that even a work like burying one's parent must not be an end in itself (Lk. 9:59). Furthermore, all good words are now done to Jesus himself (Mt. 25:40). As he is our advocate with the Father, he is also an advocate with us for others. He comes to us in the needy, and seeks to pursue his saving work through us. The reward for this saving work is that God is glorified thereby (Mt. 5:16). All thought of reciprocity is thus eliminated (cf. Lk. 14:12ff.). Inheritance of the kingdom is the only recompense, and in this kingdom there is no scale of payment. The Good Samaritan is the model of the divinely willed mercy that acts spontaneously and seeks no reward (Lk. 10:30ff.). The anointing in Mk. 14:3ff. is extolled as a memorable work of love—more important than the almsgiving on

which the disciples would have used the money (vv. 4-5)—because it meets the need of the moment and is proleptically performed for one who faces a criminal's death and the related threat of a criminal's grave without anointing.

3. *John.* A significant use in John is in the description of Jesus as the "good shepherd." This carries with it a unique claim in opposition to the shepherd gods of Hellenism and the shepherds (leaders) of the people. The basis of the claim is the shepherd's knowledge of his flock, and his giving his life to save it from the wolf. Taking up the flock into his own fellowship with the Father thereby, he proves himself to be the true shepherd, good, competent, and worthy of praise. In 10:31-32 Jesus asks for which of his good works the people wants to stone him. These works are good because they are works of God. As such, however, they carry with them a messianic claim that the people cannot or will not accept.

4. *Paul.* At times Paul uses *tó kalón* in the absolute as a synonym of *tó agathón.* Thus in Rom.7:18, 21 *tó kalón* is the good that we want to do but cannot. In 2 Cor. 13:7 doing *tó kalón* is the new Christian possibility. We are not to tire of doing it (Gal. 6:9). The term may also denote specific things that are good or praiseworthy, e.g., sexual restraint (1 Cor. 7:1, 8, 26), or respecting the consciences of others (Rom. 14:21). As an adjective it characterizes the law in Rom. 7:16 but cannot be used for the Corinthians' boasting in 1 Cor. 5:6. Paul demands good works in the sense of works of love and mercy (cf. Rom. 12:13, 20; 1 Cor. 16:11), but he does not use *kalá érga* for these.

5. *The Pastorals. kalós* is a much more important term in these epistles. We read of *kalá érga* in 1 Tim. 5:10, 25; 6:18; Tit. 2:7, 14; 3:8, 14, and *kalón érgon* in 1 Tim. 3:1. Good works are Christ's intention for us (Tit. 3:8). To pray for all people is good (1 Tim. 2:3). We are to wage a good warfare (1 Tim. 1:18), and be good soldiers (2 Tim. 2:3). The author has fought a good fight (2 Tim. 4:7). Like Christ, we are to make a good confession (1 Tim. 6:12-13). We must also be rich in good works (1 Tim. 6:18). The law is *kalós* (1 Tim. 1:8). Bishops must have a good report (3:7), and deacons will gain a good standing by good service (3:13). The good minister teaches good doctrine (4:6). Finally, everything created by God is good (4:4). In these passages, *kalós* has for the most part the philosophical sense of "right," "orderly," or "excellent," manifested in such things as right conduct, correct teaching, and a proper attitude to the world. All this, however, is in orientation to Christ and the gospel. The usage in James, 1 Peter, and Hebrews is similar (cf. Jms. 2:7; 1 Pet. 4:10; Heb. 13:18; also Jms. 1:27; 1 Pet. 4:9; Heb. 13:2-3; 3 Jn. 5).   [W. GRUNDMANN, III, 536-50]

F. *kalós* in Christological Statements in the Early Church.
1. The Influence of Is. 53 on the Early Church View of an Ugly Christ.
a. Is. 53 is one of two main passages that govern the early concept of Christ. Especially significant (with Is. 52:14) is Is. 53:2b in the LXX version. The actual terms play no role in the NT itself, which stresses Christ's humility rather than any lack of beauty, and which does not have outward appearance in view when it calls Jesus either God's image (2 Cor. 4:4) or Son of Man (Heb. 2:6-7). 1 Clem. 16 agrees with the NT when quoting Is. 53 and Ps. 21: Christ's humility is the point at issue.

b. Justin shows a similar concern to that of 1 Clement in his use of Is. 53 in *Apology* 50.1ff.; *Dialogue* 100.2, etc. Outward appearance is not the issue, but the renunciation of divine glory. This does lead, however, to human dishonoring, so that the heavenly powers, at Christ's ascension, have to ask: "Who is this king of glory?" (*Dialogue* 36.6). The theme of nonrecognition finds a basis in 1 Cor. 2:8.

c. That Christ's humility involves ugliness comes out in Acts of Thomas 45, though again divine glory rather than human beauty is the opposite. In similar works this is linked with a dualistic depreciation of humanity which ignores the biblical doctrine of the divine image.

d. In its striving against docetic trends the church is led to lay more stress on the physical appearance of Christ, and it turns to Is. 53 for guidance. Thus many Christians accept the view that the Lord intentionally does not appear in a beautiful form so as not to distract from his teaching. Origen, replying to Celsus' objections in this regard, discounts the relevance of Is. 53. Among other fathers there is vacillation and disagreement; the only consensus is that Is. 53 refers to the lowliness of Christ, and supremely to his passion.

2. *The Concept of a Beautiful Christ in the Early Church.*

a. Another influential passage is Ps. 45. The idea that beauty is intrinsic to deity predisposes many theologians to claim outstanding beauty for Christ in spite of Is. 53. This Hellenistic idea finds echoes in Wis. 13:5; Sir. 39:16, in obvious allusion to the creation story. In the LXX we also find such passages as Pss. 49:1, 96:6. Christian apologists like Athenagoras refer to the beauty of creation (*Supplication* 10.1 etc.), and 1 Clement speaks of the beauty of the bond of divine love (49.1). This view of beauty makes an ugly Christ unthinkable.

b. In this light we can understand the messianic application of Ps. 45:2-3. Jewish writers take the passage messianically too. Types of Christ are also found in the handsome Moses (Ex. 2:2) and Joseph (Gen. 39:6). The bridegroom of the Song of Songs serves as a messianic type, and sometimes Is. 33:17 (where the LXX has *dóxa*) is given a messianic interpretation.

c. Gnostic depictions go beyond the OT data with their depiction of the eternal youth and beauty of the exalted Lord. While human terms are used, these depictions lack historical realism, so that the total result is docetic.

d. In the art of the catacombs we also find a young and beautiful Christ, usually in connection with the good shepherd (though perhaps on the basis of Ezek. 34:23; Zech. 11:7ff. rather than Jn. 10:1ff.). The divine shepherd is an ideal embodiment of the Christian view of salvation even if formally religious and secular models from the contemporary world have had some impact. Popular piety takes up the thought of the beautiful Christ, in spite of gruesome depictions of the passion, and gives it expression in both art and song.   [G. BERTRAM, III, 550-56]

→ *agathós, kakós, ponērós*

---

kalýptō [to cover, hide], *kálymma* [covering, veil], *anakalýptō* [to uncover], *katakalýptō* [to cover, veil], *apokalýptō* [to uncover, reveal], *apokálypsis* [revelation]

---

kalýptō. The basic meaning seems to be "to bury," and this yields "to hide," "to cover." The main use in classical Greek is poetic. The word is common in the LXX (cf. Ex. 14:28; 27:2). The cloud covers the tent in Ex. 24:15-16, and priests cover themselves when ministering. A figurative use for the covering of sin occurs in Ps. 32:5. In the NT we find the literal use in Mt. 8:24; Lk. 23:30 (with a hint of "to bury"); Lk. 8:16. Mt. 10:26 has the term in a figurative sense: God will see that the message is declared in spite of all attempts to suppress it. In 2 Cor. 4:3 Paul faces the charge that his message is obscure; he accepts this in the case of unbelievers, whose minds are blinded by the god of this world. Jms. 5:20 and 1 Pet. 4:8 are based on Prov. 10:12 when they speak about the covering of sin by loving action. Love insures access to divine forgiveness (though the rabbis sometimes refer the love of Prov. 10:12 to God's love or to the law). A parallel thought is perhaps that only those who forgive will be forgiven (Mt. 6:15) if the sins that are covered are those of the one who loves.

kálymma.

1. In early classical works this word, too, is poetic. One meaning is "veil" or "head covering." Veiling is linked with sorrow, the warding off of evil, fruitfulness (in a bride), and the presence of the numinous (masking).

2. In the OT Moses wears a "cover" over his face in Ex. 34:33ff. Attempts to explain this comparatively (e.g., in terms of a cultic mask) are speculative. Whether the cover is to protect the people from the divine glory or to protect the divine glory from profanation may be debated. Perhaps there is an element of both. God's glory can be seen only as he himself wills.

3. In 2 Cor. 3:7ff. Paul uses the story of Moses in his comparison of the OT revelation and the gospel. *kálymma* is literal in v. 13. The application is then twofold. a. The veil conceals the fading splendor, glorious though this was. If the transitory splendor is so glorious, how much more so is the lasting splendor of the gospel (cf. vv. 7ff.). b. The veil symbolizes the veil that now rests on the minds of obdurate Israelites when they read the old covenant. What they ought to see there is the glory of Christ, and only when they turn to the Lord will the veil be removed by Christ so that they not only see the Lord's glory but are themselves changed into its likeness. (The experience of Moses in the tent seems to underlie the thought of vv. 16ff.; cf. Ex. 34:34-35.)

anakalýptō.

This word means "to uncover" a. with an impersonal object (a package, character, etc.), and b. with an inner object "to remove." Sense b. occurs in 2 Cor. 3:14: The veil remains "unremoved" or "unlifted." On the other hand, the sense in 2 Cor. 3:18 is a. (a figurative use of the literal sense): We all with "unveiled" face (in contrast to vv. 13 and 15). The term expresses here the directness of revelation and of fellowship with God in the NT.

katakalýptō.

1. Outside the NT the word means "to veil (oneself)." In the LXX Moses hides the ark behind a curtain (Ex. 26:34), the seraphim cover their faces (Is. 6:2), and while women customarily veil themselves, a muffled up woman by the wayside is a harlot (Gen. 38:15).

2. In the NT the term occurs only in 1 Cor. 11:6-7. Here Paul requires women to wear a covering for prayer or prophecy. There is no evidence to support the view that Greek women were under any compulsion to be veiled in public. In Tertullian's day Jewish women were prominent in North Africa because they wore veils on the streets. The custom seems in fact to have belonged to the Near East, as in the Assyrian law that married women and widows should be veiled in public, and harlots (slaves) unveiled. Paul's hometown Tarsus, being on the frontier of the Near East, is stricter in this regard than Greece or most of Asia Minor, but even here there are many exceptions. The practice that Paul commends, then, derives from the Near East, and he restricts it to the sphere that is under church jurisdiction, i.e., worship.

3. In the Christian era the veiling of women for worship has had a mixed history.

The catacombs depict women at prayer only partially veiled, and we often find Mary and holy women depicted without covering. Veils have been regarded as obligatory for nuns and sometimes for other women workers in the church. Many women, especially Roman Catholics, will also use some covering when at worship. But there neither has been nor is a universal application of the rule.

apokalýptō, apokálypsis. These terms raise special problems because dogmatic ideas may easily be imported into the NT passages with the usual renderings "to reveal" and "revelation." Yet one cannot take refuge in purely philological exposition by using such translations as "to disclose" or "to unveil." The terms are to some degree ambivalent, but they have a good measure of inner unity that is best brought out by "revelation" as the manifestation of deity, so long as this is first put on a broader basis.

A. The Idea of Revelation in Religious History. Modern religious inquiry, while not neglecting phenomena, looks behind them for an objective element. Religion has to do with the manifestation of deity. Deity is hidden; there is no direct access. Yet there can be no dealings with it if it remains hidden. It is a general view, then, that deity manifests itself. Religion seeks the right method to bring this about. To this end we find the use of fetishes, dreams, oracles, astrology, auspices, etc. These things, when institutionalized, may be counterbalanced by the word of gifted individuals, who sometimes become the founders of religion and whose teachings take on more permanent form as writings.

B. Revelation in the Greek World and Hellenism.
1. Popular Religion. While the Romans stress regularity in revelation, the Greeks find deity primarily in the unusual. Common means may be used, however, to declare the forces of destiny. Dreams and their interpretation are important, but above all the oracle. The Greeks do not use *apokalýptein* for divine revelation. For them deity is as open and hidden as the reality of which it is the basic form; one may thus see it or miss it. If it is still of the essence of deity to manifest itself, there is no unique revelation. The gods only give hints, and they are as fickle as fortune, having no standard of an inviolable moral will. Greek religion knows revelations but is not a religion of revelation.

2. Believing and Unbelieving Criticism. Antiquity can be critical of revelations. It does not accept myth as history, allegorizes its objectionable features, and contests miraculous signs (cf. the Epicureans, and the stress of Epictetus that we should be guided by duty). Plutarch, discussing the oracle, accepts the fact that the soul may be an instrument of deity but points out that it is an imperfect instrument. The deity uses inspired people, but does not enter into them bodily or use them involuntarily. Physical phenomena may stir up the mantic gift, however, so that if we understand the matter correctly we are not to dismiss the oracular as undeserving of confidence.

3. The Turning to History. Although magical conceptions may form the starting point, the idea of the "divine man" marks a turning to history. Outstanding rulers, statesmen, poets, physicians, scholars, and philosophers (cf. Empedocles, Pythagoras, and Apollonius; also Socrates, Plato, and even Epicurus) make such an impress on their own and succeeding generations that they are seen and honored as divine revealers.

4. The Rationalization of the Idea of Revelation. Greek philosophy inclines toward causal and immanent explanations. This might seem to exclude the idea of revelation. But meaning, embraced by thought, is injected into nature. Being and thought form a unity, whether as *lógos, noús,* or idea. The cosmos manifests thinking spirit, and when Poseidonius gives this a religious turn, the idea of natural revelation results. Thus Cicero infers from creation that it must have either a creator or a governor. Hidden from the senses, the deity, like the human spirit, may be grasped by the *noús,* with no need for a special revelation.

5. *Mysticism and Gnosticism.* Mysticism accepts the hiddenness of deity and the occurrence of special revelations. Initiates, however, know the deity, if only step by step, so that deity is veiled only by lack of initiation, not by essence. The roots of mysticism are in magic. An enhancement of life by divinization is postulated, and this is attained by the use of the right methods or formulas. This rules out historical singularity in revelation. As the sacral actions are spiritualized, they gradually yield to vision and contemplation, which may be purely inward and cognitive rather than emotional. A compact may thus be made with Gnosticism and philosophy, as in the Hermetic writings. These embody the esoteric knowledge entrusted to Hermes Trismegistos. God has given the word of revelation which leads to regeneration, which is to be received with reverence and thanksgiving, which must be kept secret, but which also impels to witness. In spite of the terms, here again is no historical revelation but simply the handing on of knowledge of the factually but not intrinsically hidden ground of the world that may just as well be impersonal as personal.

6. *The Use of Terms.* When the Greeks speak of something analogous to revelation, they mostly use other words. The Hermetic corpus has *apokalýptein* for the illegitimate disclosure of mysteries, which is worthy of execration. Iamblichus, however, has it for beneficial exposition. The noun usually has such ordinary senses as uncovering the head or finding hidden springs. It is, however, a technical term in soothsaying, finds a place in astrology and alchemy, and may signify cultically the revealing of secret matters. Theological use of either verb or noun is fundamentally alien to the Greeks and perhaps derives from the Greek Bible, though this is philologically debatable.

C. Revelation in the OT.

1. *The Basis in Religious History.* OT religion, too, knows such means of revelation as signs (Gen. 24:12ff.), seers (1 Sam. 9:6ff.), dreams (Gen. 28:12ff.), oracles (1 Sam. 14:37ff.), priestly directions (Dt. 17:9, 12), and ecstasy and prophecy. Fasting may be preparatory (Dan. 9:3).

2. *The Revelation of the Living God.* The new factor is that the God of Israel is the living God (Josh. 3:10; Is. 37:4; Dt. 5:23) in distinction from dead idols. As true God, he is hidden (Is. 45:15). He reveals himself as he himself wills. We thus have true revelation, which is worked out in three main directions.

a. God reveals himself as Lord of history. The exodus is basic here (Ex. 14:18). By it God separates Israel for himself (Ex. 19:4ff.). This confers no claim, for he rules over all nations (cf. Am. 9:7). Yet it is constitutive for the covenant. What counts is not so much what is as what happens. History is God's work (Is. 7:1ff.). The kingdoms are subject to him and his purposes (Is. 7:18ff.). He uses Assyria and breaks it; he makes Cyrus an agent of restoration from exile (Is. 45:1ff.). Revelation, then, is not just the imparting of knowledge, though knowledge comes through it. It is God's action as he removes essential concealment and offers himself for fellowship on a moral basis.

b. God reveals himself as gracious and holy. He is holy in the ethical sense (the Ten Commandments). The people often inclines to natural or cultic religion, but the prophets constantly issue a call to obedience, without which the cultus is an abomination (2 Sam. 12:7ff.; 1 Kgs. 17:1; Am. 2:6ff.; Hos. 6:6; Is. 1:10ff., etc.). In his holiness God is concerned for his glory (Ex. 20:5). He is not governed by an abstract idea of goodness. His will is good, even though its goodness may not always be apparent (cf. Ps. 73; Job). Yet God is also gracious. He shows mercy and forgives (Ex. 34:6-7). His overruling leads through judgment to blessing (Is. 40:1ff.; 53; 61:1ff.). In this is manifested his almighty power as Creator and Lord.

c. God reveals himself as the world's Creator and Sustainer. He made heaven and earth (Is. 37:16). From the fact that he acts in power it may be seen that the world has its origin in his will and word. Mythological cosmogonies are thus radically purified in the creation stories. The world exists by the word, and by the same word it is upheld and ruled (cf. Pss. 18:7ff.; 19:1ff.; 29; 33; 96:10ff.; 97:1ff.; 104; 148; Is. 40:12ff. etc.; Am. 5:8; Job 38–39). In contrast to the Greek conception, which involves a mastering of the world by thought, God is central here. It is not we who unveil God, but God who reveals himself to us.

3. The Delimitation of Revelation. While the Greek view moves between compression into a mystery and cosmopolitan extension, worship in the OT is neither a mystery nor a world religion. God is the God of his freely chosen people (Ex. 19:4ff.). As such he is the God of the world who declares himself to other nations as well in his judgments (Is. 13ff.) and blessings (Am. 9:7). He can summon other peoples to repentance (Jon. 3:4ff.), and by leading his own people to salvation will share his revelation with them (Is. 41:1ff.; 45:4ff.; 49:1ff., etc.). Yet all this takes place within the covenant relation to his people and as God's own act to which no one has a claim. It is because revelation is God's own act that he may reveal himself outside Israel and that false revelation as well as true may be found in Israel (cf. 1 Kgs. 22:19ff.). Due to the people's sinfulness, indeed, a conflict with false prophecy, which seems to take institutional form, rages for centuries (1 Kgs. 22:5ff.; Jer. 2:26; 6:13ff.; 18:18ff., etc.). God himself may even use such prophecy in judgment (1 Kgs. 22:19ff.). So acute is the problem that the OT advances criteria whereby to distinguish true prophets from false (Dt. 18:21): a. motivation (cf. Mic. 3:5; Am. 7:14, though also 2 Kgs. 4:8ff.); b. reception, with the powerful impact of reception of the word (rather than dreams) as the decisive point (Jer. 23:28; Ex. 33:11; Am. 3:8; linked to visions, Is. 6; Am. 7–9; Zech. 1ff.); c. fulfilment (1 Sam. 3:19; 1 Kgs. 8:56; Dt. 18:22), though God's will is not unalterable and will adjust to a changing situation (Is. 28:23ff.); d. content, which in true prophets will always be faithful rather than pleasing, whether it be a message of judgment or salvation (1 Kgs. 22:5ff.; Mic. 3:5; Is.7:1ff.). True prophecy, while not moralistic, will always have a moral orientation (Jer. 23:21-22). It does not reflect our own judgment but puts us under God's judgment and then leads on through judgment to grace. God makes himself known to his messengers both inwardly and historically. They often have inner qualms (Jer. 20:7ff.) but revelation imposes constraint upon them and confers the confidence they need.

4. Revelation and Eschatology. OT revelation is especially distinctive in relation to the future. It does not refer to what always is but to what is to be. This future is not the utopia of natural optimism. God's day is first a day of darkness (Am. 5:18ff.) and only then a day of final salvation (Am. 9:11-12; Is. 9:1ff.). Apocalyptic develops with the disclosure of future glory (cf. already Ezek. 40ff.; Pss. 46–47; 96–99).

5. The Usage. apokalýptein first has the ordinary sense "to uncover" (Ex. 20:26 etc.) or figuratively "to initiate" (1 Sam. 20:2). It has theological import only when God is the subject (Num. 22:31; 1 Sam. 2:27; 2 Sam. 7:27). Yet there is no fixed term for revelation, and *apokálypsis* is not used in this sense. The verb finds an important use in Is. 56:1, where it denotes the eschatological manifestation of the existent divine deliverance.

D. The Attitude of Judaism to Revelation.

1. General Points. Judaism no longer expects direct revelation. The focus is on past revelation in the law, prophets, and writings. Oral tradition is meant only as exposition. God's will is now known, and is to be done. New revelation will come in the last time, but in part as new exposition. In Hellenistic Judaism the terms *apokalýptein* and *apokálypsis* are rare; Philo does not use either.

2. Apocalyptic. Apocalyptic forms a substitute for revelation (the term comes from the last NT book). It is distinctively Palestinian, though hard to link with any specific group and popular also in Hellenistic Judaism. The genre is pseudepigraphal; the revelations supposedly derive from great figures of the past. Divine transcendence is stressed. The new aeon already exists, and when evil reaches a climax it will break in with power. For the seers the veil has already been lifted in visions, and they impart these so as to encourage God's struggling servants. The seriousness of the themes, the concept of world history, and the dynamic understanding of revelation make apocalyptic an important force.

3. Natural Revelation. Partly for apologetic and partly for polemical reasons, Hellenistic Judaism inclines more to immanentism. Philo and Wisdom (e.g., 13:3ff.) discern God in the beauty and teleology of the world, so that idolatry, while inexcusable, is also pitiable. The problem here is that in Philo, as in Greek philosophy, the movement is from below upward, so that Philo finds it hard to ward off the threat of pantheism. A parallel development is the equation of revealed law and natural law.

E. Revelation in the NT.
The NT inherits and presupposes OT revelation. It thus bypasses Judaism except for the eschatological impact of apocalyptic. The distinctive dynamic of its view of revelation arises from the relationship between history and eschatology.

1. Revelation in the Synoptists. The Baptist's witness (Mt. 3:2) and the initial message of Jesus (Mk. 1:15) imply that God is coming and will manifest his kingdom. We must prepare for this revelatory divine act. Yet it soon becomes apparent that Jesus himself is the kingdom. It is present in him as an eschatological reality. He grants revelation (Mt. 11:27), embodies it, and will finally manifest it (Mk. 8:38) as he himself is manifested (Lk. 17:30). By the Father, believers may see him already as he is (Mt. 16:17). The making known of the revelation that is present in Jesus is itself an act of revelation. Human knowledge on its own is a hindrance here (Mt. 11:25). Yet even for the simple, revelation is equivocal (cf. Mk. 4:11ff.). The parables may conceal even as they reveal. If use is made of such general presuppositions as God's rule in nature and a sense of the good; if the law may be summarized (Mk. 12:28ff.) and wisdom sayings find a place (Lk. 14:7ff.), a cosmic ground of being does not crowd out the living God, nor natural morality God's holy will, as these may be known in Scripture. The aim of Jesus is the honoring and fulfilment of the revelation of the covenant God (cf. Mk. 7:8ff.; Mt. 5:17). This revelation is for all people (Mt. 8:11), but only in the sense of God's self-offering to all sinners and with a view to their response in obedient faith and confession.

2. The Understanding of Revelation in the Primitive Community. Here we find an even stronger orientation to the future. The Messiah who has come will come again. Concealed in heaven, he will one day be manifested (Acts 3:21). The earthly words and works fulfil the OT promises but the goal will be reached only with this manifestation in glory (10:36ff.). The giving of the Spirit is the present link between past and future. While Hellenists have a freer attitude to the cultus (cf. Stephen), we have no documentation for a Hellenism, whether Jewish or Gentile, that might have replaced historical revelation with mystical ecstaticism, as in later Gnosticism.

3. Revelation in the NT Epistles.

a. In the epistles revelation is primarily the historical coming of God that is fulfilled in Jesus and will be consummated in the last day. The OT is the sacred letter of revelation, not itself called revelation, but set in the service of the NT fulfilment (Rom. 4:23-24). The true locus is eschatology, i.e., the manifestation of Christ (1 Cor. 1:7), of God's judgment (Rom. 2:5) or wrath (1:18), of antichrist (2 Th. 2:3), but also of God's righteousness (Rom. 1:16), of his children (Rom. 8:19), of their glory (8:18) and salvation (1 Pet. 1:5). The destiny of believers through God's grace is a mystery that is disclosed through Christ's self-revelation and is known to Christ's messengers (Eph. 3:3ff.; Rom. 16:25-26; Gal. 1:12, 16). By divine overruling, faith is revealed as the means of salvation (Gal. 3:23). Proclamation and reception are revelation as well as the message (cf. 1 Th. 2:13). We cannot teach or learn the decisive thing; the Spirit reveals it (1 Cor. 2:10-11), not mystically, but in orientation to God's historical self-offering to us in Christ. Paul does not use *apokálypsis* for Jesus' earthly life. This has the character of concealment. Yet God's revelation is now by way of this concealment (1 Cor. 1:18ff.). Even in concealment, the earthly life is eschatological revelation. The preexistence of Christ, while not stressed, makes this apparent (cf. Phil. 2:6ff.; Gal. 4:4; 2 Cor. 8:9). Christ is present even with Israel in the desert (1 Cor. 10:4). His Spirit inspired the prophets (1 Pet. 1:11-12). All salvation history is thus set in the morning light of the revelation that will climax with the parousia. There may, of course, be direct revelations too (cf. Acts 16:9-10; 2 Cor. 12:1, 7; Gal. 2:2). Yet this more general use is integrated into the narrower use, for these special revelations of Christ are for confirmation, direction, or edification. They must meet the test of Christian love and service.

b. The question of natural revelation in Paul is a difficult one. He plainly states that God makes himself known in creation, that the Gentiles know God, and that they do by nature what is written in the law (Rom. 1–2; cf. Acts 14:15ff.; 17:22ff.). Yet he also argues that this makes them inexcusable because of their sin and idolatry (Rom. 1:20, 32; 2:12ff.). This explains why he can say that the Gentiles do not know God (Gal. 4:8), that the world does not know God through wisdom (1 Cor. 1:21), and that knowledge of God's decree does not mean its observance (Rom. 1:32). God plainly intends that all people should know him, but they frustrate his purpose by resistance and hence become guilty of inexcusable disobedience and ignorance. Paul's use of such terms here is not systematic but missionary and polemical. His theological assessment lies in 1 Cor. 2:14. The natural thinking of sinners cannot grasp the things of the Spirit. Only when it passes under the judgment of the cross does it attain to true knowledge. Even in Rom. 1 Paul speaks from within the knowledge of revelation, and he never uses the present terms when he speaks about what the Gentiles either know or can know about God. The only revelation is that of the judgment of God and the concurrent righteousness of God which means salvation for believers.

4. Revelation in the Johannine Literature.

a. The Gospels and Epistles. Johannine theology does not use the present terms, yet it is a supreme theology of revelation. By claiming the term *lógos* for Christ, it binds all creation to revelation in Christ and thus makes an exclusive claim for Christ. If the Logos is cosmic (Jn. 1:3), it is also personal and, in Jesus, historical (1:14). All concerns, whether messianic or mystical (light, life, joy, spiritual union with God), are met in the incarnate Logos. Yet this is not by syncretism or natural revelation, but by the one, absolute, historical revelation. The supreme note is love. Eschatology is not excluded, but hope now rests on possession. Pre-Christian salvation history is linked to the Preexistent (cf. 8:58). The earthly work of Jesus is seen primarily from the angle of manifestation (1:14; 1 Jn. 1:1ff.). Dividing, the reality of God shines into the world of sin and death in the person of Jesus (Jn. 3:14ff.). Hidden from unbelievers, he is seen in all his grace and truth by believers (1:14).

b. Revelation. This book calls itself *apokálypsis*. It shares with John the use of the term *lógos*, but the orientation is now to the future in an unveiling of the heavenly world. In spite of some affinities to Jewish apocalyptic, it is closer to prophecy and has more of the content of biblical revelation. It is designed to strengthen the church in its clash with the self-absolutizing power of the state. Above both brutal state and suffering church stands the world of eternity which is the world of the final conquest and the kingdom of God and his Christ.

5. *The Limitation and Confirmation of Revelation.* Fulfilling the OT covenant, the NT recognizes that Israel is the locus of saving revelation (cf. Jn. 4:22) even though God has nowhere left himself without a witness (Acts 14:16-17). Yet this revelation is now more fully directed to all humanity (cf. Mk. 13:10; Acts 1:8, etc.). At the same time, the NT is concerned to confirm true revelation against false. Signs indicate it (Mt. 11:5-6; Jn. 5:36; 1 Cor. 2:4), but demonic miracles also exist (Mk. 13:22-23; 2 Th. 2:9-10). Even an angel cannot be the guarantee of an authentic revelation (Gal. 1:8; cf. 2 Cor. 11:14). A better test is to be found in the fruits (Mt. 7:15ff.). The Holy Spirit has also given the charisma of discernment (1 Cor. 12:10). Confession of Jesus as Lord is the clearest standard (1 Cor. 12:3). But love must accompany this (13:1ff.). The office of the Spirit is to glorify Christ (Jn. 16:13ff.), i.e., the incarnate Christ (1 Jn. 4:1ff.). Revelation must thus verify itself by commitment to Christ, but again with the backing of love (1 Jn. 4:8; cf. Jn. 13:35). Love protects the confession from formalism, and the confession protects love from moralism.

6. *The Terms in the NT.* For divine manifestations the NT uses in ascending order the groups *gnōrízein, dēloún, phaneroún,* and *apokalýptein.* The first of these finds the greatest secular use, the last two occur mostly in a religious sense, usually in the passive. The distribution of *phaneroún* and *apokalýptein* varies. The former occurs in the Synoptics only in Mk. 4:22 and not at all in Galatians, Philippians, 1 and 2 Thessalonians, James, or 2 Peter. It is common in John, 1 John, 2 Corinthians, Colossians, and the Pastorals. *apokalýptein* is common in the Synoptics, most of Paul, and 1 Peter, but does not occur in John (except in the quotation in 12:38), 1-3 John, or Colossians. These two terms are less intellectual than the first two, but *phaneroún* is more neutral and *apokalýptein* more Jewish. Thus *phaneroún* suggests that what is seen is in principle accessible, *apokalýptein* that there is disclosure only by an act of divine will. The latter term is closer to the core of the biblical concept. The former is perhaps adopted in the missionary encounter to show that the gospel meets all human concerns, but in this adoption it takes on much of the sense of the basic term, namely, that God reveals what is otherwise hidden by his own historical speech and acts that climax in Christ.

7. *Theological Summary.* In the NT revelation denotes the unveiling of hidden facts and the manifestation of the transcendent God. It is God's gracious turning to those who are lost in sin. Prepared in the OT, it is actualized in Christ's life, death, and resurrection, and awaits consummation at the parousia. But it is then also the message

that transmits this content, i.e., its effective transmission. In this way it becomes revelation for individuals, too, but only because it is already revelation with a claim to be heard and the power to make itself heard. In sum, it is the Father's self-offering for fellowship in Christ.

F. Historical Survey. The terms are fairly common in the early church. In Hermas they denote visionary experiences. Justin uses them mostly for individual directions (*Dialogue* 78.2ff.). A more central use is when he quotes Mt. 11:27, but his understanding is intellectualistic (*Apology* 63.3ff.). Ignatius is closer to the NT view when he speaks of entry into knowledge of the divine economy regarding Christ (*Ephesians* 20.1). Diognetus is even closer in 8.11. Origen includes knowledge of future things in his definition. Theologians like Irenaeus discern the cleft that runs across creation through the fall, and show an acute awareness that only God's saving work in Christ can and does bridge it.   [A. OEPKE, III, 556-92]

---

kámēlos [camel]

Common throughout the Near East, the camel is used in the OT by the patriarchs (Gen. 24:10ff.) and is favored by bedouins (cf. Judg. 6:5; 7:12).

1. In the NT the word occurs only in the Synoptics. The Baptist wears a garment of camel's hair (Mk. 1:6). This is cheap, hard-wearing, and distinctive (cf. Mt. 11:8). People of faith will see the prophet behind the rough exterior (cf. Zech. 13:4). A desert motif is present (cf. the food); God is again speaking to his people in the wilderness (Hos. 2:14-15). Perhaps there is also some assimilation to Elijah (2 Kgs. 1:8: the hairy garment and leathern girdle).

2. In Mt. 19:24, after the interview with the rich young ruler, Jesus uses a typical Near Eastern image to stress the fact that entry into the kingdom is normally impossible for the rich, though this does not rule out God's gracious action (Mk. 10:27). A large animal and a small aperture are chosen to stress the impossibility, as in several rabbinic parallels (often an elephant).

3. The denunciation of the scribes and Pharisees contains a similar image in Mt. 23:24. In anxious legalism they will strain out dead insects from their drinks but will be virtually swallowing camels with their unconcern for righteousness and mercy and their sins of extortion and rapacity (23:23, 25). They have lost all sense of proportion relative to the law, and this loss is their judgment.   [O. MICHEL, III, 592-94]

---

kámptō [to bend, bow]

Used with *góny*, this word signifies bending the knee in submission and worship. It is linked with universal recognition of God in Rom. 14:11 and Phil. 2:10. Not yielding to Baal worship is the point in Rom. 11:4. The attitude of prayer is denoted in Eph. 3:14. Paul derives the formula from the LXX (cf. Is. 45:23; 1 Chr. 29:20, etc.). Secular Greek uses *kámptein* with *góny* for bending the knees to sit or rest, but not as a formula for prayer.   [H. SCHLIER, III, 594-95]

→ *góny, proskynéō*

> ## *kanōn* [rule, standard]

A. *kanōn* outside the NT.

1. The underlying sense is "reed." In the LXX the word is not used for the Hebrew term for measuring rod, but occurs only in Judith for "bedpost," in Mic. 7:4 with no clear sense, and in 4 Macc. 7:21. Philo has it for "statute" and Josephus for "model," "measure."

2. In secular use the basic sense of "reed" yields to that of "straight rod." a. Literally it may be used for a weaver's beam, or for scales, or in building for a measuring rod. b. Figuratively it then becomes a "norm" or "ideal." c. In sculpture it denotes the perfect human frame. d. In music it is the controlling monochord. e. In grammar there is a canon of model writers. f. In law it is the binding ideal. g. In philosophy it is used by Epicurus for the basis by which to know what is true or false, what is to be sought or avoided. *kanónes* are criteria of truth and value, or rules for the right use of free will. h. The word may finally denote a "list" or "table," e.g., a mathematical list or a historical timetable.

B. *kanōn* in the NT.

1. Paul uses *kanōn,* though rarely, as a measure of assessment for the self or others. Thus in Gal. 6:16 Christians have only the one "canon"; they see that all previous concepts and standards are set aside and they must now live by the new reality of the freedom that Christ gives. This will both determine their own conduct and enable them to see whether others truly belong to the Israel of God. The word has a similar sense in some readings of Phil. 3:16.

2. The threefold use in 2 Cor. 10:13ff. is more difficult. In contrast to his opponents' claims, Paul advances here a canon for his own apostolic ministry. It lies in his pioneering work under God's direction. This probably does not mean that he has in view either a measuring line of God or the allocation of a geographical district giving him exclusive rights. The point is rather that it has been divinely granted to him historically to come to Corinth and then to press on when his ministry is successful. He will not stop where the gospel is already known; this would involve boasting beyond limit in the labors of others (v. 16). The law of his canon lies in Is. 52:15b, which he expounds in Rom. 15:20-21 in support of his preaching where Christ is not yet named.

C. *kanōn* in the Christian Church.

1. If in the NT *kanōn* is used only in Gal. 6:16 for what is normative for Christians, the idea of norm, whether for life, doctrine, worship, or accepted Scripture, becomes a primary one in the early church due to constant disputes. 1 Clement has it in an ethical sense in 7.2; it is the measure of allotted service in 41.1. The phrase "canon of truth" occurs in Irenaeus 1.9.4-5 for the binding truth of the gospel (cf. canon of faith and the ecclesiastical canon). The canon is thus the norm, to canonize is to recognize as such, and *ekklēsiazómenos* is a synonym of *kanonizómenos.*

2. After the fourth century we find the following uses. (i) First, the canon is the collection of the sacred writings of the OT and NT. The concept of norm rather than model or list is primary here. (ii) Rulings of church councils are also canons. (iii) Canon law is the collection of such rulings, along with papal decretals. (iv) There is a canon of ordained clergy, as well as of monks and nuns, in the sense of list. (v) The term can also be used for a rule of life, and consequently may denote clergy living according

to such a rule, e.g., in cathedrals or colleges. (vi) The fixed central part of the mass comes to be called the canon. (vii) Saints are said to be canonized from A.D. 993; it is hard to say which sense predominates in this use.

[H. W. BEYER, III, 596-602]

---

kapēleúō [to peddle, trade]

1. The Greek Usage. This word means "to engage in retail trade" and carries a nuance of trickery and avarice. In philosophy it denotes the selling of teaching for money.

2. The Usage in the LXX and Philo. The verb does not occur in the LXX, but *kápēlos* ("retailer") in Is. 1:22 has the usual derogatory ring. Philo has *kapēleía* ("retail business") for the conduct of the Essenes but uses other words for the merchandising of false prophets.

3. kapēleúein in the NT. The only NT instance is in 2 Cor. 2:17, where Paul protests that he is not one of those who make merchandise of God's word (cf. Acts 20:33; 1 Th. 2:3ff.). What he has in mind is (i) offering the word for money (as distinct from receiving gifts in return for it, 1 Cor. 9:14) and (ii) adulterating the word (cf. the parallel in 2 Cor. 4:2). While Paul accepts the Lord's rule in Mt. 10:10, he himself forgoes his right to support lest he be accused of avarice and false dealing. The preacher must be governed by commitment to the word, responsibility before God, and allegiance to Christ.   [H. WINDISCH, III, 603-05]

---

kardía [heart], *kardiognôstēs* [knower of hearts], *sklērokardía* [hardness of heart]

kardía.

A. *lēb* and *lēbāb* in the OT.
1. The literal meaning is a. "breast" and b. "seat of physical vitality."
2. Figuratively the heart stands a. for courage (2 Chr. 17:6) in various expressions, b. for the seat of rational functions (Dt. 29:3), c. for the place of willing and planning (Jer. 23:20), and d. for the source of religious and ethical conduct (1 Sam. 12:20). (For details see *TDNT,* III, 606-07.)
3. Another figurative use is for the midst of the sea.

[F. BAUMGÄRTEL, III, 605-07]

B. *kardía* among the Greeks.
1. Physiologically *kardía* denotes the central bodily organ.
2. Figuratively it is a. the seat of the emotions and b. the seat of thought.
3. Another figurative use in nature is for the central part, e.g., the core or kernel of a plant or tree. (For details cf. *TDNT,* III, 608-09.)

C. The LXX and Hellenistic and Rabbinic Judaism.
1. For Heb. *lēb* and *lēbāb kardía* is the true equivalent, though we also find *diánoia, psyché,* and, rarely, *noús, phrénes,* and *stéthos. kardía* in the LXX is the chief organ of human life, including the intellectual, the volitional, and the religious.
2. Hellenistic Judaism, e.g., Philo, can adopt the same usage, though for Philo

kardía is an inexact term, since a physical organ cannot be the seat of the higher life. In Josephus *kardía* is simply the physical organ, though he uses *eukardíōs* figuratively for "of good courage."

3. Rabbinic Judaism follows the OT in its use of *lēḇ* and *lēḇāḇ*.

D. *kardía* in the NT.

1. The thought that the heart is the central organ and the seat of physical vitality occurs in the NT only in Lk. 21:34 and Jms. 5:5.

2. There is in the NT a rich usage of *kardía* for a. the seat of feelings, desires, and passions (e.g., joy, pain, love, desire, and lust; cf. Acts 2:26; Jn. 16:6; 2 Cor. 7:3; Rom. 10:1; 1:24); b. the seat of thought and understanding (cf. Mt. 7:21; Jn. 12:40; Acts 8:22; Mk. 11:23; Rev. 18:7; Rom. 1:21); c. the seat of the will (e.g., Acts 11:23; 2 Cor. 9:7; Lk. 21:14); and d. the religious center to which God turns, which is the root of religious life, and which determines moral conduct (e.g., Lk. 16:15; Rom. 5:5; 8:27; Eph. 3:17; Heb. 8:10; 2 Pet. 1:19; as the heart of the sinner, Mk. 7:21; Jn. 12:40; Eph. 4:18; Jms. 1:26; as the heart of the redeemed, Mt. 11:29; 1 Tim. 1:5; 1 Th. 3:13; Col. 3:22; 1 Pet. 3:15; Jms. 4:8, etc.).

3. The meaning "inward part of the earth" occurs in Mt. 12:40.

kardiognṓstēs. This term, first found in the NT, applies to God as the one who knows the heart (Acts 1:24; 15:8). It expresses the familiar thought that God (or Christ) can see into the innermost being where decision is made concerning him (cf. Lk. 16:15; Rom. 8:27; 1 Th. 2:4; Rev. 2:23, and in the OT 1 Sam. 16:7; 1 Kgs. 8:39, etc.).

sklērokardía (→ *sklērós, sklērótēs, sklērýnō*). "Hardness of heart" is the sense of this LXX and NT word (coined from Heb. *'orlāṯ lēḇāḇ*). Found in Mk. 10:5 (and par.) and 16:14 (with *apistía*; cf. Rom. 2:5), it denotes persistent unreceptivity to the declaration of God's saving will.   [J. BEHM, III, 608-14]

> *karpós* [fruit], *ákarpos* [unfruitful], *karpophoréō* [to bear fruit]

---

karpós. In secular Greek we find a. the literal sense "fruit" and b. the general sense "product" or "gain." LXX usage is similar; cf. a. in Num. 13:27; Dt. 11:17, and b. in Prov. 12:14; Am. 6:12; Hos. 10:13; Ps. 104:13. In Iranian writings the soul is compared to a plant that is to bring forth fruit. Later Judaism often calls the result of an action its fruit, and in a financial image this might express the idea of retribution (sometimes simply as interest, i.e., the consequences in this life as distinct from the capital which will be credited only in the judgment).

In the NT we find the literal sense (a.) in Jms. 5:7, 18; Mt. 21:19; Mk. 4:29; Rev. 22:2; Lk. 1:42 (children). The general sense (b.) first denotes the results of human actions, as in Mt. 3:8 (as a test of *metánoia*); Mt. 7:16 (an expression of the inner nature); Mt. 21:43. Fruits here are a decisive standard for judgment. The power which produces them is either the power of sin in the case of bad fruits (Rom. 6:20-21), or fellowship with Christ (Jn. 15:2ff.) or the Holy Spirit (Gal. 5:22) in the case of good fruits (cf. Rom. 6:22). But *karpós* in this sense may also be the result of ministry (Rom. 1:13; Phil. 1:22). The collection for Jerusalem is a fruit in this sense (Rom. 15:28). Support for Paul will bring fruit to the Philippians (Phil. 4:17). Righteousness is the fruit of God's discipline (Heb. 12:11) or the fruit that God gives to those who seek wisdom (Jms. 3:18). Christ's death is the precondition of a rich harvest in Jn. 12:24.

ákarpos. This word, meaning "unfruitful" (cf. Jer. 2:6), is always figurative in the NT except in Jude 12. Christians are to translate their commitment into righteousness; hence they must not be unfruitful at the judgment (Tit. 3:14; 2 Pet. 1:8). Bad works are unfruitful since they bring no salvation (Eph. 5:11). The *noús* is unfruitful in tongue-speaking (1 Cor. 14:14), and the word itself may be unfruitful when it falls among thorns (Mt. 13:22). In Jude 12 the false teachers are compared to fruitless trees.

karpophoréō. This word, meaning "to bear fruit," has the literal sense in the parable in Mk. 4:26ff., but elsewhere the use is figurative. Those who accept the word bear fruit in Mk. 4:20. Works are the fruit of the righteous in Col. 1:10 (cf. Rom. 7:4 in contrast to 7:5). The word of gospel truth bears fruit in the Colossians and throughout the world (Col. 1:6).   [F. HAUCK, III, 614-16]

---

karteréō [to be strong, endure], *proskarteréō* [to persist, hold fast], *proskartérēsis* [perseverance]

---

karteréō. This word has the two senses a. "to be strong" and b. "to endure steadfastly." It has the meaning "to endure" in the LXX in Job 2:9 and Is. 42:14 ("to cry out" in Hebrew). It also has this sense in 4 Macc. 9:9, 28; 10:1, etc. in connection with martyrdom. It means "to persevere" in 2 Macc. 7:17.

The only NT instance is in Heb. 11:27, where Moses, having left Egypt, endures by the faith that reaches to him who is invisible but efficacious. This faith in the invisible God is the presupposition of NT faith in the God who has revealed and given himself in Jesus Christ.

proskarteréō. This word finds two uses: 1. with persons "to be devoted to," and 2. with objects a. "to focus on," b. "to hold fast to," and c. "to be in continually." In the LXX it is a stronger form of *karteréō* in Num. 13:20. In the NT sense 2.c occurs in Mk. 3:9 ("to be continually ready") and Acts 2:4, and sense 2.a. in Rom. 13:6, where the authorities focus constantly on their divinely given task. An instance of sense 1. may be found in Acts 10:7 (the loyal soldier; cf. also Acts 8:13, where Simon Magus attaches himself to Philip). Sense 2.b. is theologically significant in Acts 1:14, where the disciples hold on in prayer. This persistent praying precedes the choice of a replacement for Judas in 1:15ff. Jesus himself prays similarly, e.g., when in night-long prayer he brings his decisions before God. He directs his disciples to pray in this way (Lk. 11:1ff.) and to persist in prayer (Lk. 18:1ff.), not just observing set times, but enjoying continuing fellowship with God in the obedience and confidence of children. The apostles accept this as part of their primary task in Acts 6:4, and the community as a whole devotes itself to teaching, fellowship, breaking of bread, and prayer in Acts 2:42. Apostolic exhortations to persistence in prayer occur in Rom. 12:12 and Col. 4:2. In *proskarterein*, then, we find expressed one important aspect of the vitality and power of the NT church.

proskartérēsis. This word occurs only in Eph. 6:18. Perseverance in prayer and intercession is part of the spiritual warfare. Prayer, which has its roots deep in the life and power of God, knits the church together with a firm bond. It is not just a pious discipline but serious work which demands persistence.

[W. GRUNDMANN, III, 617-20]

katabaíno → *baínō*

---

katabolḗ [foundation, beginning]

---

1. This word, which means "laying down," is used for, e.g., the casting of seed, human begetting, the sowing of war, and the establishment of government. In the NT the word means "foundation" of the world, either to denote time (Mt. 13:35; Lk. 11:50), or, more often, to denote the eternity of God's plan of salvation (Mt. 25:34; Rev. 13:8). With *pró* it is used for God's pretemporal love of the Son (Jn. 17:24), election of the Son (1 Pet. 1:20), and election of believers (Eph. 1:4). This concept is found in the rabbis.

2. A second meaning in Heb. 11:11 relates to the sexual function of the male. The verse might refer to Sarah, but the context, especially v. 12, suggests that Abraham is the subject and that *kaí auté Sárra* is due to textual corruption.

[F. HAUCK, III, 620-21]

katangeleús, katangéllō → *angelía; katageláō* → *geláō; katagōnízomai* → *agṓn*

---

katadikázō [to condemn],   **katadíkē** [condemnation, punishment]

---

katadikázō.

A. Outside the NT.

1. In the active this verb means "to condemn," either in the absolute or with person (genitive or accusative) and object (accusative or dative), with the ground of condemnation in the genitive.

2. In the passive *katadikastheís* is common. The meaning in the passive is judicial condemnation, judgment by default, or losing a case.

3. In the middle the plaintiff achieves condemnation of an opponent, or wins a case (cf. Ps. 94:21).

B. In the NT. Except in Mt. 12:7 the use is always in the absolute in the NT. The *ek* in Mt. 12:37 gives the ground or proof. In Lk. 6:37 the opposite is *apolýein*, "to acquit." Jms. 5:6 complains of the hard-hearted rich who secure the condemnation of the innocent poor by an abuse of justice.

katadíkē. 1. "Condemnation," a. in the judicial sense (to exile, crucifixion, etc.), and b. in the moral sense (Philo *On the Special Laws* 3.116).

2. "Punishment," a. financial, and b. of the dead, in fanciful depictions. The only NT use is in Acts 25:15: Festus tells Agrippa that the chief priests and elders at Jerusalem want Paul's condemnation. [G. SCHRENK, III, 621-23]

katadoulóō → *doúlos; katáthema, katathematízō* → *anatíthēmi; kataischýnō* → *aischýnō; katakaucháomai* → *kaucháomai; kataklēronoméō* → *klḗros; katákrima, katakrínō, katákrisis* → *krínō; katakyrieúō* → *kýrios; katalaléō, -lalía, -lalos* → *laléō; katalambánō* → *lambánō; kataleípō, katáleimma* → *leípō; katalitházō* → *litházō; katalýō, katályma* → *lýō; katamanthánō* → *manthánō; katamartyréō* → *martyréō*

---

katantáō [to arrive at],   **_hypantáō_** [to come to meet],   **_hypántēsis_** [coming to meet]

---

katantáō. This word, which means literally "to come down to a meeting," usually has the sense "to reach a goal" (with *eis*), which may be set or ordained. It occurs in the NT only in Acts and Paul. In Acts 26:7 the twelve tribes hope to attain to the promise, though for all their zeal they do not achieve true knowledge (Rom. 10:2). Paul in Phil. 3:11 shares Christ's sufferings, and therefore the likeness of his death, with resurrection as the goal. In Eph. 4:11 the goal of the community is unity of faith and of knowledge of God's Son. Here again God has set the goal, and likeness to Christ in his unity is its content. As in Acts 26 and Phil. 3, the goal is eschatological, but it also poses a task for the ministry of the word. Linked with unity are maturity, totality, and perfection. Individuals have a share in this with the community. A slightly different use occurs in 1 Cor. 10:11, where Paul says that the end of the old aeon and the dawn of the new have come upon us. Here again, however, we have God's action with a teleological and eschatological implication. In 1 Cor. 14:36 Paul reminds the Corinthians that God's word did not start with them nor are they the only ones that it reached. They should thus pay attention to what other churches do, and test their own practices accordingly.

hypantáō, hypántēsis. The idea behind these words is that of "encounter." Thus we find "come out to meet" in Mt. 8:34; 25:1; Jn. 12:13, and "meet" in Mt. 8:28; Mk. 5:2; Lk. 8:27; Jn. 4:51, etc. A hostile encounter is in view in Lk. 14:31.
→ *apántēsis*   [O. MICHEL, III, 623-26]

---

katanýssō [to pierce],   **_katányxis_** [spirit of stupor]

The noun occurs in the NT only in Rom. 11:8 (quoting Is. 29:10). The hardening of Israel (apart from the elect) is God's work; he gave them a spirit of stupefaction. The related verb occurs in Acts 2:37 (based on Ps. 109:16) in the sense of "pierced to the heart."   [H. GREEVEN, III, 626]

kataxióō → áxios; katapatéō → patéō

---

katapaúō [to stop, rest],   **_katápausis_** [rest, resting place]

---

katapaúō. This word means "to cause to cease" with the nuances a. "to end" (actions or conditions), b. "to restrain" (persons), also "to dismiss," "to kill," c. "to give rest" (i.e., cause suffering to cease), usually with God as subject in the LXX, and d. "to rest" (cf. Ex. 20:11). In the NT we find b. in Acts 14:18. Heb. 4 relates Joshua's bringing the people to rest (c. in v. 8) and God's resting (d. in v. 4). The OT is thus seen to point beyond itself; in a true fulfilment God will bring a rest that properly corresponds to his own rest. Those who have a share in Christ today are summoned to persist with a view to this final goal (3:14).

katápausis. This word, meaning "resting" (active) or "rest" (passive), is common in the LXX for God's rest (Is. 66:1), the people's rest (1 Kgs. 8:56), or the sabbath rest (Ex. 35:2 etc.). In Acts 7:49 (based on Is. 66:1) it denotes God's rest, i.e., the place where he fixes his presence. In Heb. 3–4 (cf. Ps. 95:11), the reference is to the rest (or resting place) that God gives to his people. As the OT promise points beyond Moses to Christ, so the rest of God in Gen. 2:2 points beyond Joshua and David (4:7-8) to the final rest to which believers in Christ will attain if they hold fast to their faith.   [O. BAUERNFEIND, III, 627-28]

→ *anapaúō, anápausis, epanapaúō*

---

katapétasma [curtain]

A. Outside the NT.
1. Literally meaning "that which spreads out downwards," this word seems to have been used as a technical term for temple curtains. Thick and gaily colored, these curtains covered images that were displayed only at high feasts, and often had symbolical significance.

2. The LXX uses the term similarly for curtains in the tent or temple, e.g., between the holy place and the holiest of all (Ex. 26:31ff. etc.), or between the sanctuary and the forecourt (Ex. 26:37 etc.). The outer curtain has no cultic significance, but the inner one, traditionally depicting the two cherubim, is an important dividing mark. Whether there was a single curtain (Josephus) or a double (Talmud) is debatable.

3. The inner curtain has cultic significance, for it conceals the holiest of all, and only the high priest may pass it on the Day of Atonement, when it, too, is sprinkled with blood.

4. Synagogues probably had curtains from an early period, e.g., in front of the ark of the law, but these were not supposed to copy the temple curtains.

B. In the NT.
1. The temple curtain that was torn on Jesus' death (Mk. 15:38 and par.) is the inner curtain. Implied is that Jesus opens up access to the holiest of all.

2. Heb. 6:19; 9:3; 10:20 interprets the inner curtain theologically. Jesus has passed through the heavenly curtain which is its prototype. He has done so as a forerunner on our behalf. The curtain is identified as his flesh, which serves as a veil (cf. 2 Cor. 5:16) but which is also the way into the holiest of all. On this basis the Greek Orthodox Church finds a place for the *katapétasma* in its liturgy.

[C. SCHNEIDER, III, 628-30]

katapínō → *pínō; katapíptō* → *píptō; katára, kataráomai* → *ará; katargéō* → *argós; katartízō, katártisis, katartismós* → *ártios; kataskēnóō* → *skḗnos; kataskopéō, katáskopos* → *skopéō; katastéllō, katastolḗ* → *stéllō*

---

katastrēniáō [to grow wanton]

This compound of *strēniáō,* "to burn," "to be covetous" (cf. Rev. 18:7, 9), noun *strḗnos* ("arrogance"; cf. 2 Kgs. 19:28; Rev. 18:3), occurs in the NT only in 1 Tim. 5:11, where the idea is that younger widows may "grow wanton" against Christ and are not, therefore, to be put on the official list. The concept is figurative, as we see from v. 14. No moral condemnation of remarriage is involved, nor is asceticism commended. The point is simply that a conflict may arise between ministry for Christ and the desire to remarry.   [C. SCHNEIDER, III, 631]

katasphragízō → *sphragís; katatomḗ* → *témnō*

---

kataphronéō [to despise], *kataphronētḗs* [scoffer], *periphronéō* [to despise, disregard]

---

kataphronéō. With genitive, double genitive, accusative, or *epí,* this verb means "to despise," "to disparage," "to treat with disinterest." The NT warns us against despising God's goodness (Rom. 2:4), the church (1 Cor. 11:22), little ones (Mt. 18:10), younger leaders (1 Tim. 4:12), and masters (1 Tim. 6:2). Positively, Jesus despises the shame of the cross (Heb. 12:2). Common proverbial use underlies Mt. 6:24. In 2 Pet. 2:10 opponents despise angels, or Christ's lordship.

kataphronētḗs. Acts 13:41 quotes Hab. 1:5 in a warning to Jewish and proselyte hearers (v. 26) not to be "scoffers" when they hear the gospel of forgiveness through Christ.

periphronéō. Originally meaning "to consider," then "to dismiss," "to despise," this word occurs in the NT only in Tit. 2:15. Titus is to let no one disregard or disparage him.   [C. SCHNEIDER, III, 631-33]

---

katachthónios [under the earth]

---

katachthónios is common in secular Greek relative to the underworld. In the NT it occurs only in Phil. 2:10 in a phrase denoting, without further specification, the totality of beings (cf. Rev. 5:13). To attempt classification, e.g., by seeing in the *katachthónioi* the dead who rest in the earth, is to miss the poetical-liturgical nature of the passage.
                                                                [H. SASSE, III, 633-34]

kateidōlos → *eídōlon*

---

katergázomai [to overcome, accomplish]

---

katergázomai means a. "to overcome," then b. "to work at, make" (also "to prepare, equip"). Its main use in the NT is in Romans and 2 Corinthians, but it is found once each in 1 Corinthians, Ephesians, Philippians, and 1 Peter, and twice in James. It has a bad sense in Rom. 1:23; 1 Cor. 5:3 (to do a wrong action) and 2 Cor. 7:10 (to cause death); cf. also Rom. 7:8 (sin works covetousness). But it may also have a good sense, as in Rom. 7:18 (doing good); 5:3 (working endurance); 2 Cor. 7:10 (producing repentance to salvation), etc. In Eph. 6:13 it may refer to preparation for battle or the overcoming of opposition. The ultimate subject of the word in this good sense is God or Christ (cf. Rom. 15:18; 2 Cor. 12:12), for it is he who makes the gift of salvation and fashions us for new and eternal life (2 Cor. 5:5).
                                                                [G. BERTRAM, III, 634-35]

katéchō → *échō*

---

katḗgoros [accusing], **katḗgōr** [accuser], **katēgoréō** [to accuse], **katēgoría** [accusation]

---

katḗgoros, katḗgōr. katḗgoros, meaning "speaking against," "accusing," is used judicially in the NT in Acts 23:30, 35; 26:16, 18; Rev. 12:10, though this should probably be *katḗgōr,* "accuser," i.e., the devil. The devil as *katḗgōr* occurs in Job 1:6ff.; Zech. 3:1ff., and the idea is common in Judaism. In the NT, see Jn. 12:31 as well as Rev. 12:10. In Rom. 8:33 Paul refers only to accusation.

katēgoréō. This means "to accuse," or, more broadly, "to betray," "to make known," "to declare." In the NT it has mostly the judicial sense (Mk. 3:2; 15:3, 4; Lk. 23:10; Jn. 5:45; Acts 22:30, etc.). More general accusation is the point in Rom. 2:15. We never find the meaning "to declare" in the NT.

katēgoría. This means judicial "accusation" (also "predicate" in grammar and "category" in logic). In the NT it means "accusation" in Lk. 6:7; Jn. 18:29; 1 Tim. 5:19; Tit. 1:6. [F. BÜCHSEL, III, 636-37]

---

katēchéō [to instruct]

---

1. This rare and late word means "to sound from above" (e.g., in address from a stage), then a. "to recount something" and b. "to instruct someone."

2. In the NT we find a. ("to tell something," passive "to receive news") in Acts 21:21, 24 with reference to the false rumor about Paul. Paul himself uses the word in sense b. Thus in Rom. 2:18 the Jew is "instructed" in the law. In 1 Cor. 14:19 Paul prefers to speak five words with the mind so as to "instruct" others. Gal. 6:6 points out that those who are taught should support those who teach. It may be that Paul chooses this rare word (rather than *didáskein*) so as to stress the distinctive nature of Christian instruction (cf. our present use of "catechism"). In Acts Apollos has been "instructed" in the way of the Lord, i.e., the will of God, with its claim and promise, as manifested by and in Jesus (18:25). In Lk. 1:4 two thoughts are possible: 1. the stories "reported" to you, and 2. the doctrines in which you have been "instructed." In context 1. seems more likely. Theophilus has received information, and the aim of the author is to confirm its truth. [H. W. BEYER, III, 638-40]

---

katióomai → iós; katoikéō, katoikízō, katoikētḗrion, katoikía → oíkos; kati-schýō → ischýō; katoptrízomai → ésoptron

---

kátō [below, down], **katōtérō** [under], **katṓteros** [lower, lowest]

---

katṓ, katōtérō. katṓ is an adverb denoting "below," "down" (in the NT cf. Mk. 14:66; Acts 2:19 for "below" and Mt. 4:6; Jn. 8:6; Acts 20:9 for "down"). "Below" denotes the earth as the abode of sinners and "above" heaven as the abode of the holy God (cf. Acts 2:19; Jn. 8:23). *katōtérō* in Mt. 2:16 means two years old or "under."

katṓteros. This comparative (or superlative) of *kátō* occurs in the NT only in the much debated passage Eph. 4:9. The redeemer who has now ascended first descended to "the lower (or lowest) parts" of the earth. This might refer to the realm of the dead (the underworld as the lowest part) or simply to the earth itself. The reference to "above all the heavens" in v. 10 suggests that "under the earth" is in view here, and Christ's death rather than his incarnation offers a better antithesis to his resurrection and ascension. Ephesians also stresses the saving significance of Christ's death (1:20; 2:16; 5:2). The idea of leading captives is not so much that he liberates the dead in Hades as that he subdues the spirits that kept us captive (1:21; 2:1ff.). The descent and ascent make possible the imparting of gifts (4:7ff.) for the equipping of the saints to withstand false teachings (4:14), behind which stand the evil forces of 6:12, and for bringing the community to the fullness of Christ (4:13), who by his ascent and descent has traversed the whole cosmos from the place of the dead to the right hand of God. [F. Büchsel, III, 640-42]

---

kaúma [burning heat], *kaumatízō* [to burn (up)]

---

kaúma. This word means "burning heat," or, figuratively, "heat of fever" or "fire of love." In Rev. 16:9 it denotes God's fierce wrath. In the age of salvation the saints are protected from scorching heat (Rev. 7:16).

kaumatízō. This word means "to wither up" (figuratively "to suffer from fever"). In Rev. 16:8-9 God's anger burns up sinners like fire or fierce heat.

[J. Schneider, III, 642-43]

---

kaúsis [burning], *kaúsōn* [heat], *kausóomai* [to burn up], *kaustēriázomai* [to brand]

---

kaúsis. This word, meaning "burning," "consuming," occurs in the NT only in Heb. 6:8. The unfruitful earth will finally be given up to burning; similarly, apostate believers will fall victim to the fire of divine wrath.

kaúsōn. This word might mean either "heat" or "hot wind" (LXX). "Heat" is the sense in Mt. 20:12; Lk. 12:55. "Hot wind" is possible, but not so likely, in Jms. 1:11.

kausóomai. Meaning "to suffer from heat (or fever)," this word is used apocalyptically in 2 Pet. 3:10, 12 for the dissolving of the elements with fire in a final conflagration.

kaustēriázomai. This rare term, which means "to burn with glowing iron," occurs figuratively in 1 Tim. 4:2, where false teachers are said to have "branded" consciences. The thought seems to be that they are the slaves of demonic forces. Runaway slaves and criminals were branded in antiquity; also sometimes prisoners of war, workers in the mines and munitions, and army recruits. This practice underlies the metaphor.

[J. Schneider, III, 643-45]

---

kaucháomai [to boast], *kaúchēma* [boast], *kaúchēsis* [boasting], *enkaucháomai* [to boast], *katakaucháomai* [to boast against]

---

kaucháomai, kaúchēma, kaúchēsis.

A. Greek Usage. The meaning of this group is "to boast," "boasting," usually in a bad sense, so that we find warnings against it in the philosophers and satirists.

B. The OT, LXX, and Judaism.

1. The LXX uses the group for various Hebrew terms for self-glorying. While the OT finds a place for justifiable pride (Prov. 16:31; 17:6), there are many proverbs against boasting (1 Kgs. 20:11; Prov. 25:14). It is the basic attitude of fools and the ungodly (Pss. 52:1; 74:4). To boast of wealth is to trust in it (Ps. 49:6). There can be no boasting before God (Judg. 7:2). Yet one may glory in the knowledge of God (Jer. 9:23-24). God deals with Israel to his own glory (Dt. 26:19). Thus the righteous may boast of his help (Ps. 5:11). To boast in this sense is equivalent to "to rejoice" and it has eschatological significance, since it will finally be actualized in the last time (Zech. 10:12). This glorying goes hand in hand with looking away from self and confident confession of God.

2. Judaism maintains the same tension between false boasting and true boasting, but with a tendency to stress the law as a reason for true boasting (Sir. 39:8).

3. The rabbis find a source of boasting in the law, or even in its fulfilment, but they emphasize that the law must not be observed in self-interest, warn against pride, and find in righteous suffering, too, an occasion for boasting.

4. For Philo self-glorying is wrong because in it we do not acknowledge God as the Giver of all good but forget him and usurp his glory. The righteous, by humbly submitting to divine grace, stand high with God and thus achieve true glory.

C. The NT and Early Christianity.

1. Paul.

a. The Basic Christian Attitude. Paul, who almost exclusively uses the group in the NT, opposes to self-assured boasting the appropriate attitude of faith which is made possible and demanded by Christ. Faith precludes boasting (Rom. 3:27); Abraham, the father of faith, has nothing to boast about before God (4:2). The valid boasting of Judaism has become a false boasting in the law (2:17, 23). Our only legitimate boasting is in Christ (5:11), who has negated all the greatness of both Jews and Gentiles (1 Cor. 1:18ff.). Believers, boasting in Christ alone (Phil. 3:3), have left off all self-boasting (3:7ff.). They glory only in the cross (Gal. 6:14). On this basis, by God's grace, they may stand before God, yet only as recipients of the divine gift (1 Cor. 3:21; 4:7). Paradoxically, then, believers may glory in their sufferings, not because they are ascetic achievements, but because the power of God is manifested in them (2 Cor. 11:23ff.; 12:9; 4:10-11), so that, rejoicing in them, they rejoice also in the hope of God's glory (Rom. 5:2).

b. Apostolic Self-Boasting. Rejection of self-boasting does not exclude for Paul a valid boasting in his apostolic work (2 Cor. 7:4, 14 etc.), partly because this expresses trust in the churches, but chiefly because what he does rests on what Christ does through him (Rom. 15:17-18; 1 Cor. 15:10). Thus the work depends on grace rather than merit, and the boasting is only within the assigned limits of the work (2 Cor. 10:13) and is not by comparison with the work of others (10:12ff.). Paul can commend himself only because God commends him, and he measures himself only by his own commission (2:14–7:4). We are not even to measure ourselves against unbelieving Israel (Rom. 11:18ff.) but to boast only on the basis of self-scrutiny (Gal. 6:4). Boasting will then be an occasion for thanksgiving and joy, since it will be acknowledgment of God's grace. In this sense Paul finds his glory in the churches (1 Th. 2:19-20). Indeed, he himself should be the boast of these churches (2 Cor. 1:14), for his work strengthens their faith and they thus have greater cause to glory in Christ (Phil. 1:26). The fact that all is by grace explains why it is that for Paul refusal of the right to support is paradoxically an occasion for boasting (1 Cor. 9:15-16); this right has no basis in human achievement. At the same time, Corinthian resistance to Paul's valid authority as an apostle forces him into self-boasting, not in his own cause, but in Christ's (2 Cor. 10:8ff.). He recognizes that this is foolish (11:16), and when he has listed all his natural advantages (11:22), he switches quickly to a listing of his sufferings (11:23ff.). If he goes on to speak of visions and revelations (12:1ff.), he does not pursue this theme. Instead, he returns at once to the theme of weakness (12:5ff.). He finally closes the discussion with the statement that, while he is not in fact inferior to others, this is all folly, for in himself he is nothing (12:11).

2. *Early Christianity after Paul.* The basic theme of Paul occurs briefly also in Eph. 2:8-9 and 2 Th. 1:4. Boasting in God may be seen in Heb. 3:6. Jms. 1:9 expresses the OT theme that the lowly should boast in their exaltation by God, while the rich should boast in their humiliation, trusting in God alone (cf. 4:13ff.). In later writings outside the NT, 1 Clement warns against boasting and admonishes to humility (13.1; 21.5), Hermas lists boasting as a vice in *Mandates* 8.3, Ignatius follows Paul in *Ephesians* 18.1 and *Trallians* 4.1, and Jesus is a model in Justin *Dialogue* 101.1. The valid boasting of the righteous in God comes to expression in 1 Clem. 34.5.

enkaucháomai. This word, sparsely attested, means the same as *kauchásthai* (2 Th. 1:4; cf. 1 Clem. 21.5).

katakaucháomai. This word expresses the element of comparative superiority in boasting (cf. Rom. 11:18; Jms. 2:13 [figurative]; Jms. 3:14). The context shows with whom there is comparison (unbelieving Jews in Rom. 11:18, judgment in Jms. 2:13).

[R. BULTMANN, III, 645-54]

---

keímai [to lie], *anákeimai* [to rest on], *synanákeimai* [to recline at table with], *antíkeimai* [to confront], *apókeimai* [to be laid up], *epíkeimai* [to lie on], *katákeimai* [to lie down], *parákeimai* [to lie ready], *períkeimai* [to lie around], *prókeimai* [to lie in front of]

---

keímai. This word means "to lie" with reference to either the fact or the result, and may be figurative as well as spatial. In the NT it is usually spatial, "to lie" or "to be laid or set" (Lk. 2:12, 16; Mt. 5:14; 28:6; Rev. 4:2), but may also be figurative, "to be appointed" (Lk. 2:34), "to be laid down" (1 Tim. 1:9), "to lie in" (1 Jn. 5:19).

aná-, synanákeimai. This verb means "to be laid up" (votive offerings), "to rest on," "to recline (at table)." In the NT it has the third sense (Mk. 14:18; Mt. 9:10; 22:10-11; Lk. 22:27; Jn. 6:11). In antiquity people reclined to eat, resting on the left side (though women, children, and slaves ate standing or in other ways). Reclining at the Passover symbolizes the freedom achieved at the exodus.

antíkeimai. From "to confront," this word takes the sense "to be opposed," as in Gal. 5:17; 1 Tim. 1:10. *ho antikeímenos* is "the adversary" (Lk. 13:17; 1 Cor. 16:9; Phil. 1:28).

apókeimai. This word, which has such varied senses as "to be laid up," "to come upon," and "to be despised," means "to be laid aside or up" in Lk. 19:20; Col. 1:5; 2 Tim. 4:8, "to be appointed for" in Heb. 9:27. In the last three references what is expressed is the certainty of the divinely ordained future.

epíkeimai. In the NT this word means "to lie on" in Jn. 11:38, "to beat upon" in Acts 27:20, "to throng" in Lk. 5:1, and "to be imposed" in Heb. 9:10; 1 Cor. 9:16.

katákeimai. This compound means "to lie down" (e.g., in sickness, at sleep, or at meals); cf. Mk. 1:30; 2:4; Jn. 5:3, 6; Acts 9:33 (the sick), Mk. 2:15; 1 Cor. 8:10 (at table).

parákeimai. The only use of this word in the NT is in Rom. 7:18, 21: "to lie ready, at hand."

períkeimai. This word, meaning "to lie around" (passive "to have around"), is used for the millstone in Mk. 9:42, Paul's chain in Acts 28:20, and figuratively weakness in Heb. 5:2 (cf. also 12:1).

prókeimai. This word means "to be displayed" in Jude 7 and "to be before one" in Heb. 12:2 (the appointed joy) and 6:18 (the promised hope).

[F. BÜCHSEL, III, 654-56]

> ## *kéleusma* [cry of command]

With a basic sense of "what is impelled," *kéleusma* has such meanings as "command," "summons," "cry of encouragement," and "cry." In ordinary speech it tends to be replaced by *kéleusis,* which becomes a technical term for a government decree. It is used in the NT only in 1 Th. 4:16 for the shout of command, though it is not clear who gives this or what is its relation to the archangel's call. The command, the call, and the trumpet sound seem to relate primarily to the awakening of the dead, but they also intimate the end in a general sense (cf. 1 Cor. 15:52). The "first" and "then" of vv. 16-17 have qualitative rather than chronological significance; the goal is that all believers should be with the Lord.   [L. SCHMID, III, 656-59]

> ## *kenós* [empty], *kenóō* [to make empty], *kenódoxos* [boaster], *kenodoxía* [conceit, delusion]

kenós.

A. Outside the NT.
1. Literally the meaning is "empty"—usually things, but also persons.
2. Figuratively the reference is to vain or frivolous persons or futile things, e.g., opinions, boastings, speech, and cf. the expression *eis kenón,* "in vain."

B. In the NT.
1. The literal sense occurs in Mk. 12:3; Lk. 1:53; 20:10-11. In Lk. 1:53 (cf. 1 Sam. 2:7-8) we have the thought of the great reversal when the rich go away empty (cf. Mt. 5:3ff.).
2. Jms. 2:20 has the figurative sense for persons: an "empty" or "foolish" person. Mostly, however, the NT uses the word figuratively for things, e.g., empty words in Eph. 5:6 (cf. Jms. 4:5), empty deceit in Col. 2:8, futile grace in 1 Cor. 15:10, futile work in 1 Cor. 15:58. In saying that neither grace nor our service is in vain, Paul

expresses a strong sense of confidence in God's gift and of the resultant responsibility this imposes on us. His visit (1 Th. 2:1) was not "in vain" both because there was no guile or self-seeking in it and because it was successful in the power of God at work in it (1:5-6). In contrast, his preaching would be *kenós,* i.e., without content and also ineffective, if Christ were not risen (1 Cor. 15:14).

kenóō. This word means "to make empty" (passive "to be desolate") and "to nullify" (passive "to come to nothing"). The first sense occurs in the NT only in Phil. 2:6-7 (of Christ). This can hardly mean that Christ negated himself, nor is it suggested that he aspires beyond his existing state. The point, then, is that Christ does not selfishly exploit his divine form but lays it aside to take the form of a servant. The preexistent Lord is the subject. He remains himself, but changes his mode of being (cf. 2 Cor. 8:9). For the second sense, we turn to 1 Cor. 9:15 and 2 Cor. 9:3. Paul would rather die than allow anyone (by supporting him) to nullify his ground of boasting, and he presses the collection lest his boasting about the Corinthians come to nothing. In Rom. 4:14 inheritance by the law would invalidate faith. Similarly, in 1 Cor. 1:17 a synthesis of content and brilliance of technique would rob the cross of its force, i.e., of its saving content, its consequent offense, and its related divine efficacy.

kenódoxos. This word means "one who talks big," "boaster," as in Gal. 5:26.

kenodoxía. This word has the two senses a. "delusion," and b. "conceit." Only b. occurs in the NT (Phil. 2:3), though we find both in the apostolic fathers (a. in Hermas *Similitudes* 8.9.3, and b. in Hermas *Mandates* 8.5).   [A. OEPKE, III, 659-62]

---

kéntron [goad, sting]

A. Outside the NT. With the basic sense of "something that pierces," this word is used 1. for animal claws, 2. for such human instruments as spurs, goads, scourges, or nails, 3. figuratively for torments or incitements, 4. for authority (cf. the common expression "to kick against the goads"), and 5. mathematically for the point of a compass or the center of a circle. The LXX uses the term for goad (e.g., Prov. 26:3). Philo compares God to a charioteer with rein and whip, but he also uses the term for center (the earth as the center of the cosmos). Josephus refers to the *kéntron* of passion (cf. *Antiquities* 7.169) (Amnon for Tamar) or attraction (cf. *Jewish War* 2.385).

B. In the NT.
1. In Acts 26:14, in Paul's conversion story, Christ tells Paul that it hurts him to kick against the goads. Although the idea of the goad for oxen is common in the Jewish world, Paul (or Luke) seems to be adopting the Greek proverb here; this is most suitable in an address to the Hellenist Agrippa. It is hardly possible to prove a direct quotation (by Luke) from Euripides, who has the saying (with the plural goads) in a similar situation. In any case, the proverb (also in the plural) is a stock quotation by the first century A.D.
2. In 1 Cor. 15:55ff. Paul quotes Is. 25:8 and Hos. 13:14, and then adds that the *kéntron* of death is sin. The idea here is not so much that death is a tyrant with a goad, or a soldier with a lance or arrow, or a beast with a poison tip, but rather that

it is like an insect with its sting. When sin, on which its power rests, is vanquished by Christ, the sting is withdrawn and death becomes impotent.

3. In Rev. 9:10 the locust-scorpions that arise from the abyss when the fifth trumpet sounds have poisonous stings in their tails with which they torment those who do not have God's seal.   [L. SCHMID, III, 663-68]

---

kéras [horn]

A. The Horn outside the NT. This word, used for animal horns, is also a symbol of divine or human strength. In the OT it depicts God's power in a prophetic action (1 Kgs. 22:11) and is also a direct term for power (Zech. 2:1ff.). A common OT metaphor is that of exalting or destroying a horn, which is God's prerogative, not ours (cf. Ps. 75:4-5). In later Judaism we read of the growing of horns on lambs to denote their increasing power, and the Messiah is a white bullock with big, black horns. The horns of the altar (Ex. 27:2) are its hornlike corners (cf. Rev. 9:13).

B. The Horn in the NT.
1. Lk. 1:69 uses OT terminology when it speaks of God raising up a horn of salvation (cf. Ps. 18:2). God is here the Lord of history putting forth his power to help and bless through his Messiah ("in the house of his servant David").
2. The horn is an important symbol in Revelation. The second beast in 13:11 has two horns like a lamb but speaks like a dragon (cf. wolves in sheep's clothing). The seven horns of the Lamb express the divine plenitude of his power. The ten horns of the dragon and the beast (cf. 12:3; 13:1, etc.) are ten future kings (cf. Dan. 7:7, 24). Some commentators have seen in these kings Parthian satraps who would support the returning Nero in his attack on Rome. Others have suggested a list of Roman emperors, and yet others demonic powers. It is to be noted that these are kings of the whole earth (16:14, 16) and that they do not war against Babylon (Rome?) but against the Lamb in a final open battle. The serpent with ten horns is Satan, who uses the amassed power of the race in the last struggle.   [W. FOERSTER, III, 669-71]

---

kérdos [gain],   *kerdaínō* [to gain, save]

kérdos means "gain," "advantage," "profit," with the desire for it as a derived sense, also crafty counsels in the plural. *kerdaínō* is "to procure gain, advantage, or profit," but more generally "to win something" or "to save oneself something." Neither word occurs in the LXX. In the NT Tit. 1:11 refers to those who give false teaching for "gain" (in the bad sense). In Phil. 1:21 Paul reckons that it will be "gain" to die and be with Christ. In contrast, he reckons the "advantages" of his pre-Christian life to be loss for Christ's sake (Phil. 3:7). The verb means "to get profit" in Jms. 4:13, "to spare oneself something" in Acts 27:21, and "to win something" in Mt. 25:16-17 (more talents) and Phil. 3:8 (Christ). In 1 Cor. 9:19ff. it has the sense "to win" (for Christ) (cf. 9:22: "to save"). A parallel is winning the erring brother in Mt. 18:15. In Mt. 16:26 winning the cosmos might just conceivably mean winning humanity by missionary endeavor, but the more obvious sense is winning dominion over the world as the sphere of earthly power, resources, and possibilities.

       [H. SCHLIER, III, 672-73]

---

kephalḗ [head],   *anakephalaióomai* [to sum up]

A. *kephalḗ* outside the NT.

1. Denoting what is first, supreme, or extreme, *kephalḗ* is used for the human or animal "head" but also for a "point," "tip," or "end," e.g., prow of a ship, top of a wall, mouth of a river (or source), start of an era, point of departure. A further sense then develops, what is "prominent" or "outstanding," and in yet another development the *kephalḗ* denotes the "whole person," e.g., in such phrases as *phílē kephalḗ* or *megálē kephalḗ* (dear or great person).

2. The LXX adopts the Greek usage for "head" and "point" or "top," along with the sense of the whole "person," but also adds a new meaning: the "head" or "ruler" of a society (cf. Dt. 28:13; Is. 9:13-14). Comparison of the people with the body lies in the background in Is. 1:4ff. (cf. 7:20).

3. Judaism sometimes follows this usage in Dt. 28:13. We also find such phrases as "head of the priesthood" or "of the world's idolaters," and Adam is called the "head of all created things."

4. In Hellenistic and Gnostic circles the word acquires a special sense in connection with the aeon and the primal man. The cosmic aeon embraces the totality of all things in its head and body. In Gnosticism the divine aeon becomes primal man embracing the substance of the cosmos, but also redeemer man embracing the remaining substance of a fallen world. Primal man, who bears the cosmos, recovers from the fall as redeemer man, who gathers the cosmos to himself. In this scheme the *kephalḗ* is both apart from (and superior to) the body but also in unity with it. Elements of this view may be seen in Philo's commentary on Exodus, where the *lógos* is the *kephalḗ* which rules the cosmos and in which the cosmos finds its fullness. Gnostic texts are more complicated but in various combinations contain the idea of the primal man and/or the redeemer as the *kephalḗ* (sometimes equated with Christ).

B. *kephalḗ* in the NT.

1. The term often means here the human or animal "head" with no theological significance (cf. the head of Jesus in Mt. 8:20; Lk. 9:58), and especially in the passion narrative (Mt. 26:7; 27:30, 37; Mk. 15:19; Jn. 19:2, 30; 20:7, 12); the head of the risen Lord (Rev. 14:14; 19:12).

2. In 1 Cor. 11:3, Christ is the head of man, man of woman, and God of Christ. Hence man should not cover his head, since he is the image and glory of God, but woman should do so, since she is the glory of man. The distinction between man and woman is seen here to have an ontological ground, for while man is God's reflection directly, woman is so only indirectly, having her life from man and for man. It is by reason of this basic distinction that charismatically gifted women should cover the *kephalḗ* when praying or prophesying. Not to do so is to offend against the head in the twofold sense; the long hair that *phýsis* gives women for a covering is an indication of this.

3. a. In Eph. 1:22-23; 4:15-16; 5:23; Col. 1:18; 2:10, 19 Christ is the head of the church, which as his body grows up into him to form the new and perfect man. In a distinctive application of primal man-redeemer thinking, the stress here is on the unity of Christ and his church. He, as the heavenly head, is present in earthly form in the church, while the church, as his body, is present in heavenly form in Christ. As head Christ directs the church's growth to himself and to its fulfilment in him. He is its

archḗ or principle (Col. 1:18). He is also its goal (Eph. 2:15). This goal is attained in faith and knowledge, and consequently in subjection to the head (Eph. 5:23-24).

b. As head of the church, Christ is also before all things and hence the head of creation as well (Col. 1:15ff.; 2:20). The first man is at work in the redeemer, displaying the body of creation in the body of the church. Things cohere only in him. The gospel, then, discloses the mystery hidden before time inasmuch as God's wisdom in creation (i.e., Christ) is made known through the church. In the plḗrōma of the church which is his body Christ draws all things into the plḗrōma. Christ is the Lord of the world, and as the risen Lord he takes control over it through the church, which is thus relevant to all things.

anakephalaióomai. This rare term means "to bring to a *kephalḗ,*" "to sum up," or "to divide into the main portions." Other nuances are "to bring to a conclusion" and "to recapitulate." In the one NT use in Eph. 1:10 the context suggests that there is a definitive, comprehensive, and recapitulatory summation of the totality of things as the church receives it head. In Christ, this head, the totality is comprehended afresh as its sum.   [H. SCHLIER, III, 673-82]

---

kḗryx [herald, preacher], *(hierokḗryx* [temple herald]*)*, **kērýssō** [to announce, proclaim], **kḗrygma** [proclamation], **prokērýssō** [to proclaim publicly or beforehand]

---

kḗryx (hierokḗryx).

A. The *kḗryx* in the Greek World.

1. The Dignity and Social Position of the Herald. The herald has a high place in Greek antiquity; he belongs to the court, carries a sceptre, and is renowned for cleverness and wisdom. Yet he also performs menial tasks and runs very ordinary errands. Later there are heralds of mysteries, games, festivals, and markets. As state officials heralds come to be poorly regarded but still render important services, belong to the higher classes, and are often given high honors and rewards.

2. The Qualities Demanded of a Herald. A strong and resonant voice is the basic requirement, since the herald has to issue summons, keep the peace, and make announcements. The games include contests to test the strength and diction of heralds. To restrict garrulity and exaggeration, it is important that heralds deliver news or pass on messages strictly as these are given to them. In negotiations they seldom act on their own initiative but simply deliver short messages, put a few questions, and report back for further instructions. In the assembly or in court they act only as the voice of the chairman or president.

3. The Religious Significance of the Herald.

a. His Inviolability on Diplomatic Missions. Since politics and religion are inseparable for the Greeks, heralds on foreign missions are regarded as under the protection not only of their country but also of the gods. To violate them is to bring down divine wrath. Even if their message is unwelcome, they must be hospitably received. They have a special sanctity which enables them to speak without fear or favor. For this reason they often accompany envoys. Even in war they may go to the enemy camp to open up negotiations for peace. Similarly, they may go to an enemy capital to declare war.

b. *His Participation in Cultic Life.* Heralds offer prayers at the opening of assemblies or the mustering of the army. They invoke divine blessing on their cities and cursing on traitors and public offenders. They also have a part in preparations for sacrifices and lead in prayer at the actual sacrifices. They have a part, too, in the religious act of making treaties. Their intimation of festivals and games may also have a cultic aspect, and some heralds are specifically employed by cultic societies (cf. their role in the Eleusinian mysteries, in which they issue the call to worship, lead in prayer, help in the sacrifices, and make important announcements).

4. *The Herald of the Gods.* While all heralds stand under the protection of the gods, the gods have their own special heralds. Hermes is the herald-god who plays the herald role in the divine assemblies. Birds are also at times heralds of the gods. So, too, are Stoic philosophers, who, according to Epictetus, go through the world in simple style with the task of presenting divine teaching with its truth and claim, bringing a higher peace than even the emperor can grant, but also issuing a call for decision, chiding error, and summoning to emulation. Formally one sees a close parallel here to the work of early Christian missionaries. A primary distinction is that the Stoic sees himself as a *katáskopos,* an inspector of people who declares his message on the basis of his observations. The Stoic starting point, then, is human need or wickedness, whereas the Christian starting point is God's gracious presence in Christ. This points to the fundamental difference, namely, between the god whose heralds the Stoics are and the Father of Christ whose message the apostles declare. The message itself differs in consequence, for while the Stoics have high ideals, they can finally hope only to quicken a slumbering seed of morality, whereas the gospel ushers in the new age of the kingdom which involves radical conversion and renewal. Philosophical heralds proclaim human development and divinization, apostolic messengers the incarnation, the forgiveness of sins, and the gift of eternal life.

B. The Herald and the Jewish World.

1. *Josephus and Philo.* The use in Josephus seems mainly to be in connection with war and diplomacy; Philo avoids the term.

2. *The LXX. kḗryx* occurs only four times in the LXX. In Gen. 41:43 there is no Hebrew original. In Dan. 3:4 Nebuchadnezzar's herald commands the people to worship. The use in 4 Macc. 6:4 is similar (the herald of Antiochus). Sir. 20:15 has the word in a comparison. That there is no true equivalent shows that the idea is an alien one.

4. *The Rabbis.* In the rabbis, however, the herald is again prominent with the adoption of the loanword *kārôz.* The origin of this term is disputed (Greek? Persian?), but it finds frequent and varied use for town criers, court heralds, temple criers to awaken the priests, the announcers of rabbinic judgments, and God's angelic or human heralds (e.g., Noah in the generation of the flood).

C. The *kḗryx* in the NT.

The herald is strangely unimportant in the NT. There are only three instances of the term. Noah is a herald of righteousness in 2 Pet. 2:5 (cf. 1 Clem. 7.6; 9.4), and Paul is a herald and apostle (and teacher) in 1 Tim. 2:7 and 2 Tim. 1:11. (Some texts also have the word in Col. 1:23.) Since the word might seem to be so suitable for the NT preacher, this paucity of use is surely intentional. There are perhaps two main reasons for it. First, the focus of the NT is on the message rather than the messenger, or on God himself as the real messenger. Second, the Greek concept is too precisely defined; NT preachers are not sacral personages who can claim inviolability. Rather, they are like sheep among wolves (Mt. 10:16), will be persecuted as their Master was (Jn. 15:20), and are as it were dedicated to death (Rev. 12:11). Yet this does not prevent the message from taking its irresistible and victorious course through the world (2 Tim. 2:9; 2 Th. 3:1). The stress, then, falls on the verb *kerýssō,* not the noun *kḗryx.*

kērýssō.

A. *kērýssō* in the Greek World.

1. Shades of Meaning and Synonyms. The verb is a much less significant word in Greek than the noun. It means "to cry out loud, declare, announce." It may carry such nuances as "to offer, order, forbid, ask," and commercially "to offer for sale, auction." A general sense is "to make known," though specifically it may also mean "to herald."

2. kērýssō in Passages of Religious Significance.

a. A first religious use is for announcements relative to games and feasts, e.g., in proclaiming contests, announcing winners, conferring honors.

b. Another use is in aretalogies for declaring the works of deity by divine instruction and, in spite of hesitation, by divine constraint.

c. In the Hermetic writings we find close parallels to the NT in the concept of prophetic proclamation. The message, however, is not that of forgiveness and liberation from sin, but of liberation from the body and divinization. Nor is there any declaration of God's rule and act; the proclamation is instruction in what to do, and exhortation to do it, in order to move from error to knowledge.

B. *kērýssō* in the OT. In the Greek OT the word occurs 33 times for various Hebrew equivalents. It may have the general sense "to cry" but also denotes proclamation, either by a herald (Gen. 41:43) or in a more general sense (Ex. 36:6; 2 Chr. 24:9). The proclamation may even be in writing (2 Chr. 36:22). Only rarely does *kērýssō* describe the work of prophets, e.g., false prophets in Mic. 3:5, Jonah in 1:2; 3:2, and Jeremiah in 20:8. Is. 61:1 refers to the proclamation of liberty to the captives in an efficacious, eschatological event (fulfilled by Jesus in Lk. 4:21). In Hos. 5:8 the sense is to "sound the alarm" in face of the approaching enemy. This is also the point in Joel 2:1, except that now it is the day of the Lord that is imminent. In Joel 3:9, however, we have a summons to arms, while in Zeph. 3:14 and Zech. 9:9 the call is to exultation because the salvation of God has come. In the OT *kērýssō* never has the prominent place it has in the NT.

C. *krz* in the Rabbis. In rabbinic writings we find four main uses of *krz:* to clear the way for an important person, to give legal findings validity by proclamation, to make cultic intimations, and (with God as subject) to reveal, either directly or through Scripture.

D. *kērýssō* in the NT.

1. kērýssō and Other Words for Proclamation. The NT uses many words for the proclaiming of the Christian message, e.g., *légein, laleín, martyreín, didáskein.* It is a mistake simply to render such terms, and *kērýssein* itself, by "to preach." Fundamentally *kērýssein* is the declaration of an event. Except in Rev. 5:2 we do not find it in the Johannine writings, which prefer *martyreín,* nor in Hebrews. It occurs 61 times in the NT (nine in Matthew, 14 in Mark, 17 in Luke-Acts, 19 in Paul, once in 1 Peter, and once in Revelation.) Its greater importance than *kḗryx* or *kḗrygma* shows that the stress is on dynamic proclaiming.

2. The Use of kērýssō. The use is mainly active. The content is denoted by an accusative noun, an infinitive, *hóti* or *hína,* a relative clause, or direct speech (at times with *légōn*). The person addressed is in the dative, and place may be indicated by *en* or *eis.* The verb also occurs in the absolute (e.g., Mt. 11:1; Mk. 1:39).

3. The Secular Meaning in Lk. 12:3. The reference in Lk. 12:3 is not to the work of the disciples; Jesus is here adducing a popular saying to indicate that the hidden designs of the Pharisees will be made public.

4. Proclamation by Different Preachers.

a. The Jews. These proclaim the law (Rom. 2:21). Moses is proclaimed in the synagogue (Acts 15:21).

b. The Baptist. John heralds the messianic age in the desert (Mk. 1:4 and par.). He does not preach the law but calls for repentance, and points prophetically to Christ in a promise that is sure of immediate fulfilment. His baptism seals those who await God's rule and anticipates messianic remission (Acts 13:24).

c. Jesus Christ. (i) Incarnate. Proclaiming God's word is Jesus' mission in Mk. 1:38. He delivers the same message as the Baptist (Mk. 4:17), but does so as the prophet of fulfilment, so that the declaration is itself the event (Lk. 4:18ff.). In him the word is a creative force; it gives what it declares. (ii) Crucified. Between Good Friday and Easter Day Jesus proclaims remission in the realm of the dead (1 Pet. 3:19-20). The spirits are probably the souls of the dead rather than the OT righteous or fallen angels. The prison seems to be a special place in Hades. The timing falls between the death (v. 18) and the resurrection and ascension (vv. 21-22). The preacher is Christ. The content of the message is not given but is surely the gospel, as the immediate context in vv. 18-22 suggests. (iii) Risen. The risen Christ is also present in the word of his messengers (cf. Lk. 10:16), though only believers hear his summons in it (cf. Rom. 10:14ff.). Paul relates Christ and his message very closely in 2 Cor. 1:18-19. The NT word is God's act as Christ himself speaks through it.

d. The Healed. Those who are healed by Jesus tell others what has happened even though he orders them not to do so (Mk. 1:44). Since they do not do so by commission, their action is witness (cf. Mk. 1:44-45) rather than proclamation in the true NT sense (even though *kērýssō* is used). The prohibition seems designed to prevent astonishment at the miracle taking the place of faith. Where the miracle is opposed, as in Mk. 5:17ff., Jesus authorizes the cured person to tell what has been done, and so he begins to proclaim it.

e. Disciples and Apostles. The disciples are sent out to proclaim repentance and the nearness of the kingdom, and also to heal. They are to proclaim fearlessly what they have heard from Jesus (Mt. 10:17). The end will come when the whole world has heard (Mt. 24:14). Like the life, death, and resurrection of Christ, this proclamation is part of God's saving plan. It is the declaration of the saving facts in order that they may be also a saving reality for believers. The word of the cross, as well as the cross itself, is God's power (1 Cor. 1:18). Sinners are commissioned to declare it. The efficacy does not depend on them, whether on their skills, or on their purity of motive (1 Cor. 1:22-23; Phil. 1:15). The Christ whom they preach is greater than they are; they proclaim him, not themselves (2 Cor. 4:5). Although there should be no discrepancy between their message and their conduct, they do not act in their own interests but seek to win people to Christ, presenting themselves only as servants for his sake.

f. An Angel. In Rev. 5:2 an angel puts to the world the question who is worthy to open the book with seven seals.

5. *The Content of the Specific NT Message.* While the stress in the NT is on the act of proclamation, the content is by no means secondary. If the word enacts what it proclaims, the content is indeed of supreme importance. It is not determined either by the situation of the hearers or by the ideas of the proclaimer but by the divine kingdom or lordship that Jesus himself announces and brings. The imminence of the kingdom poses the demand for *metánoia* as the possibility of participation. With this demand goes the declaration of forgiveness as a divine act of judgment and grace that will mean condemnation for some and deliverance for others. Which it will be depends on the response to Christ (1 Cor. 1:23-24). The king is intrinsic to the kingdom: the total Christ who is Lord by death and resurrection, and who is proclaimed as such (2 Cor. 4:5). Here is no myth of a dying and rising god, for the reference is to the factual event of a life in history. Yet the mere life, edifying though it might be, has significance only in the light of the resurrection. What is proclaimed, then, is not just a human history any more than it is merely human dogma. Salvation history is proclaimed, and its proclamation is itself saving event. At work here is not just the content of what is proclaimed, but God himself. For this reason, it is God's power (1 Cor. 1:24), it will permit no adulteration (Gal. 5:11), and it must be proclaimed in season and out (2 Tim. 4:2). As in the Greek world, *kērýssein* stands linguistically in close relation to *euangelízesthai* (cf. also *kēryx* and *euángelos*), although with the special nuances and content which the NT gives to both terms.

6. *The Hearers.* The goal of proclamation is faith rather than understanding. Jesus does not bring a teaching but a message. People of all cultures resist it (1 Cor. 1:21ff.) but believers accept it. Proclamation is important because through it faith arises. True hearing brings the faith that is also obedience; this is effected by the word (Rom. 10:8). Since faith comes by proclamation, the two have the same content (1 Cor. 15:14).

7. *Sending and Proclamation.* Proclamation demands messengers, and messengers imply commissioning. During his life Jesus commissions the Twelve and the Seventy (Mt. 10:7; Lk. 9:2; 10:1). He renews the commission after the resurrection (Mk. 16:15). The sending is now to the world and not just to Israel (Mk. 13:10; Col. 1:23). If the sending entails restriction, it also confers authority. Those who are sent proclaim what they are commissioned to proclaim (Mt. 10:27). They do not report their own experiences but declare the acts and will of him who sends them. If there were no sending, there would be no divine proclamation, only human propaganda.

8. *Teaching and Proclamation in the Synoptists.* In the NT, especially the Synoptists, *kērýssein* and *didáskein* often go together (Mt. 4:23; 11:1; cf. Acts 28:31). In the main, teaching is synagogue exposition that is designed for believers, while proclaiming may take place anywhere as a call to sinners. Yet Jesus "proclaims" in the synagogue, too, for his teaching is no mere exposition. Even as exposition, it takes the form of an address that demands decision in the light of God's present action (cf. Mt. 7:29).

9. *Miracles and Proclamation.* If proclamation is God's active word, and God's rule is a present reality, signs and wonders occur, accompanying and confirming the word (Mk. 16:20; Heb. 2:3-4). For believers miracles demonstrate the reality of the message, but signs are refused to unbelievers, for they are not meant to force faith on people. Jesus himself plays them down (cf. Mt. 4:3ff.; Mk. 5:43). After the healings of Mk. 1:32ff., he moves on to preach in other towns, for that is why he has come (v. 38). Proclamation is what counts; the mighty acts are simply signs that God's kingdom has indeed come therewith (Mt. 11:5).

kērygma.

A. Outside the NT.

1. The Greek World. This word denotes both the act and the content of proclamation. It can have such senses as "news," "declaration," "decree," "announcement," etc.

2. Philo. Philo often uses the term for the herald's "cry," a "decree," or especially the "publication" of honors or victories (figuratively).

3. The LXX makes little use of the word (cf. 2 Chr. 30:5; Jon. 3:2).

4. The rabbis have it for court proclamations or in connection with property.

B. In the NT.

In Mt. 12:41 par. Lk. 11:32 Jonah's preaching is meant. The act is at issue in 1 Cor. 2:4; it is effective, not as oratory, but in the spirit and power. What is meant in Mk. 16 is the content or message, but this in itself is powerful to save in 1 Cor. 1:21. It includes the resurrection in 1 Cor. 15:14. Paul's gospel is the same as the preaching of Jesus in Rom. 16:25. The act is again meant in Tit. 1:3; by it the divine Word comes to us, and it is entrusted to the apostle by divine command. The preaching office comes into view in 2 Tim. 4:17. God has strengthened the apostle to fulfil the office of a preacher (cf. 4:5, 7). He does not stand as a defendant but as a herald, so that representatives of all nations hear the word through him.

prokērýssō. *pro* in Greek can mean either "forth" or "before," thus yielding the sense "to speak forth" or, rarely, "to proclaim beforehand." "To offer publicly" (i.e., "auction") and "to promise" are other meanings. In the one solid use in the NT in Acts 13:24 the addition of *pro* suggests that John is the last of the prophets before the time of fulfilment, although even here John preaches rather than foretells the baptism of repentance. Due to the imminence of the kingdom, this is no mere promise but anticipation. [G. FRIEDRICH, III, 683-718]

kephalḗ gōnías → *gōnía; Kēphás* → *Pétros*

---

kīnéō [to set in motion, cause],   *metakīnéō* [to remove, shift away]

---

kīnéō. This word means "to set in motion," "to stir," "to cause," with such nuances as "to disturb," "to move," "to instigate," and in the papyri "to demand," "to bring a suit or complaint." In Mt. 23:4 it stresses the contrast between the burdens laid on others and the failure to move a finger to help them. Ephesus is warned in Rev. 2:5 that its lampstand will be removed if it does not repent. Paul in Acts 17:28 uses Stoic terms to prepare the ground for the gospel; in God we live and move and have our being. Elsewhere only two of the terms occur together but the underlying thought is a common one. It goes back to Plato's idea of the world soul from which all movement comes. Philo has the same thought: God, himself unmoved, sets all things in motion. Paul in his own theology would no doubt prefer to say "through God," but finds in the statement a starting point for his missionary address.

metakīnéō. This uncommon word means a. "to remove" and b. "to alter." In the Greek OT it is used for "to remove (a landmark)" (Dt. 19:14) and "to put to flight" (Is. 54:10). In the only NT instance the use is figurative; the Colossians in 1:23 are not to shift away from the hope of the gospel. [J. SCHNEIDER, III, 718-20]

---

kládos [branch]

kládos means "shoot," "bud," "branch," and is used figuratively for children. In Rom. 11:16ff. Paul uses the term for the branches that are grafted into the one olive tree. Paul accepts the continuity of the community, but for him Christ is the "seed" of Abraham (Gal. 3:16), and hence the community consists of believers in Christ, both Jews and Gentiles. Faith in Christ, and God's saving work in him, is the one qualification of membership. A relationship of faith replaces that of blood. The tree remains, but some branches are broken off, and new ones replace them. In Ignatius *Trallians* 11.2 Christians are called *kládoi* of the cross, in Hermas *Simitudes* 8.1ff. there is an allegory of engrafting, and in Justin *Dialogue* 110.4 we find a parable of the vine and its continual shoots.   [J. SCHNEIDER, III, 720-22]

---

klaíō [to cry, weep],   *klauthmós* [crying, weeping]

klaíō. This word, meaning "to cry" or "bewail," expresses grief at parting, remorse, sorrow for the dead, but sometimes also joy (cf. Gen. 46:29). Jesus in Lk. 6:21 blesses those who weep and promises them laughter, whereas those who laugh shall weep. As in the rabbis, laughter before God denotes human self-affirmation and self-confidence, but weeping expresses acknowledgment and acceptance of God and his rule. At the end, however, those who now ignore God will see their lostness and those who trust in him will enjoy his grace and fellowship. This transvaluation of all values will manifest the difference between true and false security. OT examples of this type of weeping may be found in 2 Kgs. 20:3ff. and 22:18-19 (Hezekiah and Josiah). Other references are Judg. 15:18; Hos. 12:4; Ps. 126:5-6. Included in the biblical usage is the idea of tears of remorse due to a sense of guilt. This is alien in the Greek world, where what is bewailed is fate rather than one's own sinful deeds. Behind the distinction stands the different relationship to God, in whom there may be humble trust because he directs human destinies to salvation. Where judgment is expressed by *klaíein*, its full severity is denoted by the use of milder terms (*penthein, thrēnein*, etc.) to denote the actual lamenting (cf. Lk. 6:25; Jms. 4:9; Rev. 18:11; Jn. 16:20). Disclosure of God will mean both subjection to him and the grief of realizing what this entails. In Lk. 23:28 the women bewail and lament Jesus; they are full of grief because they see the irreversibility of the march to the cross. But Jesus tells them not to weep, for he is fulfilling God's plan, and this is his glory. By their weeping they show their lack of understanding, and Jesus responds by another call to repentance as he tells them that they should weep for their children, who will suffer the consequences of what is being done. He himself weeps for Jerusalem in Lk. 19:41-42.

klauthmós. This word is used literally for lamentation or grief in Mt. 2:18 and Acts 20:37. Elsewhere it occurs with "gnashing of teeth" to denote the terror of God's self-manifestation for those who reject his invitation (Mt. 8:12; 13:42, 50; 22:13; 24:51; 25:30; Lk. 13:28). Gnashing of teeth suggests racking remorse.

[K. H. RENGSTORF, III, 722-26]

---

kláō [to break off], *klásis* [breaking off], *klásma* [piece, crumb]

A. General Usage.

1. *kláō* means "to break," "to break off" (cf. Rom. 11:19-20 [variant reading]), "to shatter," *klásis* means "breaking off" (of shoots of the vine), and *klásma* means "fragment" or a "bite" or "piece" of bread.

2. The word group is used in the NT for the common custom of breaking bread at meals which initiates the sharing of the main course. Jesus follows the practice at the feeding of the multitude (Mk. 6:41), the Last Supper (Mk. 14:22), and the Emmaus meeting (Lk. 24:30). For Paul cf. Acts 20:11; 27:35. The common church meal is called the *klásis* of bread in Acts 2:42 and cf. 20:7. The fragments that remain in Mt. 6:42 and Jn. 6:12-13 are *klásmata*; according to custom Jesus orders that they be gathered up after the meal.

B. Breaking of Bread as a Term for the Lord's Supper.
Breaking of bread is not as such a cultic act, even at the Last Supper; it is part of the initiatory process. Thus the breaking of bread in Acts 2:42 (cf. 20:7) is simply a term for ordinary meals in which the believers find table fellowship in recollection of Jesus' own table fellowship with the disciples. Yet within the ordinary meal we also find a special, cultic breaking of bread (1 Cor. 11:20). Thus, as we learn from Ignatius *Ephesians* 20.2 and Did. 14.1, breaking of bread becomes perhaps the first title for the new liturgical meal, the Lord's Supper. This usage continues, but the title is later replaced by *eucharistía,* and the breaking of bread becomes a special part of the celebration, symbolizing Christ's violent death.

C. The Lord's Supper in Primitive Christianity.

1. Sources.

a. Survey. In addition to 1 Cor. 11:23ff.; Mk. 14:22ff.; Mt. 26:26ff.; Lk. 22:15ff., we have to consider 1 Cor. 10; 11; 16:20, 22; Acts 20:7, 11; Jn. 6, especially vv. 51ff.; and passages in Ignatius, the Didache, and Justin.

b. Appraisal. The accounts of institution are of three types: Pauline, Markan, and Lucan. Paul and Mark share the narrative, the word of interpretation, and an eschatological saying, but with variations in the cup saying. Luke both abbreviates by ending with "This is my body" and expands by putting the institution more firmly in the Passover setting and giving a more specific eschatological context.

2. The Last Supper.

a. Traces of the Passover Setting. The Last Supper is in all probability the Passover, since many details fit in best with the external forms of the Passover.

b. The Jewish Passover of the Time. The meal at the time was held on the 14th of Nisan in Jerusalem, with at least ten persons present. After blessings of the feast and the wine, a first cup was drunk, the food was served, and instruction was given with a call to thanksgiving and hope. The first part of the Hallel was then sung, the second cup drunk, bread taken, blessed, and broken, and the meal started. The Passover concluded with the third cup (of thanksgiving), the rest of the Hallel, and a fourth cup.

c. Traces of the Passover in the Tradition. The following details may be discerned: (1) the drinking of the cup; (2) the linking of interpretative sayings with parts of the meal; (3) the eschatological reference; (4) the express equation in Lk. 22:15 (cf. v. 17); (5) the time (evening); (6) the place (Jerusalem); (7) the careful preparation; (8) reclining, which is prescribed for the Passover; (9) the multiple cups (Lk. 22:17,

19); (10) the cup of thanksgiving (1 Cor. 11:25; cf. 10:16); and (11) the concluding hymn (Hallel). Remarkably, however, there is no reference to the paschal lamb.

3. The Meaning of the Sayings of Jesus at the Supper.

a. The Groups of Sayings in the Oldest Texts. There are two groups, those about the present and future Passover (Lk. 22:15ff.; Mk. 14:25), and those about the bread and wine (1 Cor. 11:24-25; Mk. 14:22ff.; Lk. 22:19). The sayings of the first group relate to the opening blessings and the first cup, those of the second to the distribution of the broken bread and the sharing of the cup of thanksgiving.

b. The Passover Sayings. The first saying (Lk. 22:15-16) expresses joy at the feast and the coming consummation along with the solemnity of parting and imminent death. The second (22:18) presupposes that the disciples will hold table fellowship without Jesus but looks ahead to the consummating banquet when the kingdom comes.

c. The Sayings about the Bread and Wine. These sayings in the second group refer to Jesus himself. They are parabolic, but this time the parable is accompanied by an action, so that the disciples do not just hear but partake as well. Within the Passover the sayings are widely separated. As regards the first saying, the Aramaic original that was probably used for "body" does not denote the physical body as such but the person: "This bread, I am myself." The saying is thus a pledge of Christ's presence when the disciples hold future table fellowship. The second saying relates the cup to the new *diathḗkē*, the new divine order that is based on the shed blood of Christ. The saying is thus a pledge that the Master who is going to a violent death is present with the fullness of enacted salvation. Taken together, the sayings direct attention away from the past to Jesus himself, who now fulfils the divine will to save, and who offers the promise of his personal presence as Savior (in virtue of his self-sacrificial death) during the period up to the establishment of definitive fellowship at the final banquet.

d. Alterations and Additions. The cup saying in Mk. 14:24 relates Christ's death to Is. 53:12, while Mt. 26:27 suggests Jer. 31:34. The forms of distribution in Mark and Matthew stress the handing out of the elements. Paul with his "do this" (1 Cor. 11:24) expresses the presupposition that the disciples are to repeat the action as Israel celebrates the deliverance of the Passover.

e. Maranatha. This phrase in 1 Cor. 16:22 ("Our Lord, come") is a cry of longing for the parousia but also a eucharistic prayer for a foretaste of the final fellowship in the Supper (cf. Did. 10.6; also Rev. 22:20).

4. The Lord's Supper in Paul.

a. Relation to the Lord's Supper in the Primitive Community. Since Acts 2:42, 46 can hardly refer to the Lord's Supper, we have no direct information about its observance in the primitive church. The phrase "breaking of bread," which denotes a common meal, does not justify communion in bread alone.

b. 1 Cor. 10 and 11. The evening meal of 1 Cor. 11:20 (held on Sunday in Acts 20:7; cf. 1 Cor. 16:2; 11:20ff.) is no longer connected to the Passover. The association of the Lord's Supper with the bread and wine, not the lamb, makes the dissociation easier. The rite takes place in the context of a shared meal, which gives rise to scandals in Corinth. As a remembrance of Christ's death it demands appropriate seriousness (1 Cor. 11:23ff.). Judgment falls when there is failure to realize this (vv. 28ff.). Fellowship with the Lord rules out fellowship with demons at idol feasts (1 Cor. 10:14ff.).

c. Paul's Thinking about the Supper. The meaning is personal fellowship with Christ (1 Cor. 10:3-4, 16-17; 16:22). Fellowship with Christ creates fellowship with one another (1 Cor. 10:16-17). Christ's vicarious death is the central content of the eucharistic sayings (11:26); by it a new covenant is set up. The Supper is observed between the times; in it we look back to the first coming and ahead to the second (11:24ff.). There is a strong focus on the elements as these represent Christ's body and blood. If the feast is a feast of remembrance, it is so in the same sense as the Passover, i.e., as a re-presentation, as the proclamation of the present reality of God's saving act in history. The Supper is a solemn cultic action, yet it differs from pagan feasts inasmuch as sacrificial ritual is excluded and the fellowship is not crassly sensory. Participation in Christ's presence relates, not to eating and drinking alone, but to the whole action. The union is not a result of a mere observance of the rite but comes through Christ's own action by the word and Spirit, so that the Supper is neither spiritualized not materialized, but given a realistic yet historical and spiritual interpretation. It demands an appropriate attitude, which is to be tested by self-examination and which may be corrected by divine chastisement. Participants must ask whether they are as they should be according to the indicative and imperative of the gospel.

5. *The Lord's Supper in John.*

a. The Discourse in Jn. 6. Instead of an account of the institution, John offers reflections on it in connection with the feeding of the five thousand (Jn. 6). Jesus is the bread of life, his bread is his vicariously offered flesh, and taking his flesh and blood brings fellowship with him and eternal life. Yet it is not the actual flesh and blood, but the Spirit, that gives life.

b. John's Understanding. When bread and wine are taken, Christ is present. The bread and wine represent the flesh and blood that constitute his person. They mediate eternal life by union with Christ. The elements themselves do not do this, for it is the living, spiritual, exalted Christ who is present and who imparts himself. The concepts of presence and fellowship agree with the earliest traditions. John's realism is remote from either a symbolical or a magical view; the presence of Christ by the Spirit confers the gift of saving fellowship.

6. *The Lord's Supper in the Post-Apostolic Age.*

a. Didache. In this work the Supper is to be celebrated on Sunday, within a common meal, and with specified prayer and eschatological expectation (cf. the use of Maranatha). The idea of fellowship is present. Qualifications are given for participation, and new elements include the concept of sacrifice and the inclusion of immortality and knowledge among the gifts (9–14).

b. Ignatius. In scattered references, Ignatius finds the risen Christ at work in the eucharist, warns against unworthy reception, and sees in the Supper a representation of unity. He tends, however, to hellenize the concept of life and to materialize the operation with his understanding of the eucharist as the medicine of immortality. The eucharist is called a sacrifice of prayer and the bishop ought to preside at it (cf. *Ephesians* 13.1; *Philadelphians* 4; *Smyrneans* 7.1; 8.1; *Ephesians* 20.2).

c. Apocryphal Acts. These slip over into magical sacramentalism and cult mysticism, making the eucharist into a Gnostic mystery (cf. Acts of John 109; Acts of Thomas 27; 49–50; 121; 133; 158).   [J. BEHM, III, 726-43]

---

kleís [key]

A. The Different Applications of the Image of the Keys in the NT.

1. Common in antiquity is the idea that heaven is closed off by doors and that certain deities or angels have the keys to it. In later Judaism we also find a few

references to angels (e.g. Michael) as keepers of the keys. God himself may be said to carry the key. In another figure he keeps the key of rain. Lk. 4:25 alludes to the key of rain when it says that heaven was shut up in Elijah's day. The two witnesses of Rev. 11:6 also have the power to shut heaven.

2. *The Keys of the Underworld.* Antiquity also depicts the underworld as sealed off by gates to which various keepers have the keys, e.g., Nedu, Pluto, Kronos, or Isis. Judaism makes only isolated use of this concept. Revelation in 9:1 and 20:1 refers to the sealed abyss to which God or an angel has the key. The risen Christ himself has the keys of death and Hades (1:18); the idea here is probably that Christ has taken over the keys of the underworld from personified death and Hades; he thus has the power to open the doors of this world and to summon the dead to resurrection (cf. 1 Pet. 3:19-20; Acts 2:25ff.). Since the rabbis allot to God the key of quickening the dead, Christ is thus given here a divine predicate.

3. *The Key of (to) Knowledge.* In Lk. 11:52 Jesus complains that the scribes have taken away the key of knowledge. The meaning may be that they have taken away either a. knowledge as the key to the kingdom, or b. the key to knowledge. In the original the former is more likely (cf. Mt. 23:13), although in the Hellenistic world the latter would be more natural. Either way the thought is that the scribes hold the key of theological knowledge, but instead of opening the door of salvation they withhold the key and thus keep the door closed.

4. *The Eschatological Use.*

a. The Key of David. In Rev. 3:7 the risen Christ has the key of David (cf. Is. 22:22). As the promised shoot of David, he has the key to God's eternal palace, controlling judgment and grace.

b. The Keys of God's Royal Dominion. In Mt. 16:19 Jesus grants to Peter the keys of the kingdom of heaven. In the Gospels this can hardly mean that Peter has the key to the doors of the heavenly world, for the kingdom of heaven is God's royal dominion in the end-time (cf. Rev. 3:7). In what sense does Peter have the key to this?

B. The Power of the Keys.

1. *Mt. 16:19.*

a. This passage is strongly Semitic in vocabulary, style, and rhythm. This is important as regards both its authenticity and its interpretation.

b. In biblical and Judaic usage handing over the keys does not mean appointment as a porter but carries the thought of full authorization (cf. Mt. 13:52; Rev. 3:7).

c. The scribes claim the power of the keys and exercise it (or fail to do so) by declaring God's will in Scripture, i.e., by preaching, teaching, and judging. The implication is that Jesus takes away this authority from the scribes and grants it to Peter.

d. The latter part of Mt. 16:19 equates the power of the keys with binding and loosing. Among the rabbis this has the sense of rendering decisions as to what is allowed or forbidden, but originally the terms denote acquittal or condemnation, and they may be used for executing or averting divine judgment by prayer. The authority of Mt. 16:19, then, covers the pronouncing of judgment on unbelievers and the promising of forgiveness to believers, i.e., dispensing the word of grace and judgment.

2. *The Extension of the Power of Binding and Loosing to the Apostles.* Mt. 18:18 and probably Jn. 20:23 refer back to Mt. 16:19. Jn. 20:23 extends the right to the eleven. Mt. 18:18 might seem to have the congregation in view (v. 17), but the address is to the disciples, and after vv. 12ff. the section vv. 15ff. is designed to show that there is a ministry of discipline as well as love (cf. Tit. 3:10).

3. The Exercise of the Power of Binding in the Primitive Community. Exercise of the power of binding involves a threefold process that culminates in public rebuke and excommunication when there are serious moral lapses or falsifications of the gospel (1 Cor. 5:1ff.; Acts 8:18ff.; Gal. 1:8-9; Tit. 3:9-10). Excommunication carries with it cursing (Gal. 1:8-9) and handing over to Satan (1 Cor. 5:3-4). In Jn. 20:23 God's judgment is intimated.

4. The Power of Loosing. This is the power to promise forgiveness. In Jn. 20:23 it is perhaps associated with baptism (cf. Mt. 28:16ff.; Lk. 24:47). It rests on the imparting of the Spirit, who equips the apostles for their ministry when Jesus sends them out. Through the Spirit Christ himself is at work as the one who forgives.

→ *thýra, pýlē*   [J. JEREMIAS, III, 744-53]

---

kléptō [to steal],   *kléptēs* [thief]

kléptō means a. "to steal" (either objects or people), b. "to cheat" or "bewitch," and c. "to conceal." *kléptēs* means a. "thief," and b. "one who acts with subterfuge." While stealing may sometimes be excused in the Greek world, it is a chief sin in the OT (Ex. 20:14; Dt. 5:19), whether the objects stolen be valuable articles, idols, animals, or words of God. As a sin against God (Ex. 20:14), it incurs punishment (Ex. 22:2). Even need or poverty does not excuse it (Prov. 30:9). The locusts of Joel 2:9 are compared to thieves, and Obad. 5 suggests that God's judgment is more destructive than burglary (cf. Jer. 49:9). Stealing takes place by night (Job 24:14) and by force (24:16); its marks, then, are secrecy and violence. In the NT the new life of love in the Spirit means that the Ten Commandments are given added seriousness and that a new power is available to keep them (cf. Mk. 10:19; Mt. 19:18; Lk. 18:20; Rom. 13:9; Eph. 4:28). Stealing is a breach of fellowship (cf. Jn. 12:6); work in the service of others replaces it. Yet the NT often uses *kléptēs* with reference to the breaking in of the messianic age. The disciples must watch, for their Lord will come as unexpectedly as a thief (1 Th. 5:2ff.). This coming will take unbelievers by surprise, but believers, who live in the light of the new age, should be ready (cf. Mt. 24:43; 2 Pet. 3:10; Rev. 3:3; 16:15). If the Lord comes as a thief, thieves also break in and steal earthly treasures (Mt. 6:19-20), and those who raise false claims to lordship are thieves and robbers (Jn. 10:8, 10). The use of the simile of a thief for the Lord at his coming shows a. that only one point in a parable is important (here the suddenness of the coming), and b. that the freedom of faith rids the church of fear of such comparisons.   [H. PREISKER, III, 754-56]

---

klḗma [branch]

klḗma, meaning "shoot," "twig," "slip," usually denotes the shoot of the vine in the LXX (Joel 1:7; Nah. 2:3; Ezek. 17:6ff.; also Mal. 3:19). In Jn. 15:1ff. the parable indicates the vital organic relation between the vine and the branches. To bear fruit, the branches must abide in the vine and must undergo the discipline of pruning. If they do not abide they are discarded and wither.   [J. BEHM, III, 757]

> *klḗros* [lot, inheritance],   *klēróō* [to appoint by lot],   *prosklēróō* [to allot],
> *holókleros* [complete],   *holoklēría* [completeness],   *klēronómos* [heir],
> *synklēronómos* [joint heir],   *klēronoméō* [to inherit],   *kataklēronoméō*
> [to give or receive an inheritance],   *klēronomía* [inheritance]

klḗros.

1. Greek Usage. The basic sense of *klḗros* is "lot" (in drawing lots), then "portion," and finally "inheritance" (also in Egyptian papyri "land in fee").

2. klḗros and klēronomía in the LXX. klḗros means "lot" (cf. Jon. 1:7; Josh. 18:7) and then "lot of land" (Num. 16:14). *klēronomía* means "inheritance," but because of the mode of apportionment of Canaan (e.g., in Josh. 17:4), *klḗros* is an equivalent. Thus we find *klēronomeín klḗron* in Num. 18:24, and the Lord is the Levites' *klḗros* in Dt. 10:9. Indeed, *klēronomía* may take on originally alien senses of *klḗros.* Nevertheless, the land as a whole is never said to be Israel's *klḗros, klḗros* can be used in the plural (Num. 32:19), but not *klēronomía,* and we can read of a *klḗros tḗs klēronomías* (Num. 36:3: "lot of inheritance") but not vice versa. When the whole land is said to be given *en klḗrō,* it is unlikely that this means "in fee." The probable meaning is that it is given for apportionment into individual *klḗroi* (Num. 36:2). The assignment guarantees the legitimacy of possession. *klḗros* and *klēronomía* both recognize that the land is not Israel's by conquest but by God's gift. *klḗros* stresses assignment and *klēronomía* the validity of possession. As the whole land is assigned to Israel, individual portions are assigned to tribes, clans, and families. A figurative use then develops whereby Israel is God's *klḗros* (Dt. 9:29), or *klḗros* (like *merís*) is the "destiny" or "lot" of nations (Is. 17:14) or individuals (Prov. 1:14). With the rise of the hope of resurrection, *klḗros* can finally denote one's allotted portion after death (Dan. 12:3). The whole usage is rooted in the sense of God's overruling of history.

3. klḗros in Later Judaism. In Judaism we still find the two senses of "lot" and "portion." Thus in A.D. 67 the Zealots choose a new high priest by lot, and Josephus tells us that Philip went to Rome "to acquire a share (in the inheritance)" (cf. Josephus *Jewish War* 4.153ff.; 2.83). In the pseudepigrapha Israelites have a portion in Moses (his blessings) and the phrase "the portion of the righteous" denotes eternal life.

4. klḗros in Philo. Philo stands on OT soil when he uses *klḗros* for "lot," "portion," "inheritance," or "patrimony." He also calls the righteous God's *klḗros* and vice versa. He explains that God is the Levites' portion in the way that art is the portion of artists. He can say, too, that nobility is the *klḗros* of the soul in a spiritual participation which is not without a natural basis.

5. klḗros in the NT. A first meaning in the NT is "lot," as in Mk. 15:24 (with emphasis on the humiliation of Christ) and Acts 1:26 (with emphasis on seeking the will of God). The main sense, however, is "allotted portion." Thus Judas has a share in the apostles' ministry in Acts 1:17. Simon Magus has no share in God's word or gift in Acts 8:21, and there is reference to an eschatological portion in Acts 26:18; Col. 1:12. Ignatius expands on this sense in *Ephesians* 11.2 etc. and Polycarp in Polycarp 12.2. In 1 Pet. 5:2-3 what is meant is not the elders' personal possessions, and certainly not offerings on their behalf, but the portions assigned to them (i.e., to their charge).

klēróō. This means first "to appoint by lot" and then "to apportion." The only plain use in the LXX is in 1 Sam. 14:41. Philo has the word for orderly appointment in the natural and moral world. The only NT instance is in Eph. 1:11-12, where it does not denote a pretemporal act but God's determination as this affects our being and assigns us a goal, namely, "to live for the praise of his glory."

prosklēróō. Meaning "to distribute by lot," then just "to distribute," this is a common word in Philo for the natural ordering of things to God, and then for the self-ordering of the righteous. The only NT use is in Acts 17:4, where the meaning might be "they were assigned (by God) to," but the preceding persuasion supports an active sense: "they joined Paul and Silas."

holóklēros (→ hygiḗs). This word denotes "complete" in extent or compass. In the LXX it is used for whole (i.e., unhewn) stones in Dt. 27:6, a whole vine in Ezek. 15:5, and whole weeks in Lev. 23:15. Elsewhere the term may denote animals or men that are without defect, or a true people, or full righteousness, or in Philo the unadulterated world of God. In the NT the idea in 1 Th. 5:23 is that believers may be kept whole in every respect; the reference to the body may suggest a wish that they be kept alive for the parousia. It is the God of peace who can do this; peace here embraces the wholeness (the total bodily and spiritual salvation) which God alone can bring but which he can and does bring even to those who are broken in spirit, soul, and body. In Jms. 1:4, the only other NT instance, the achievement of "completeness," which will include curbing the tongue (3:1ff.), is the goal of our various trials or testings.

holoklēría. Meaning "completeness," this word occurs in Acts 3:16 for the physical wholeness or intactness which is restored to the lame man.

klēronómos, synklēronómos, klēronoméō, kataklēronoméō, klēronomía.

A. Greek Usage of the Group. In Greek the central point of the group is inheritance. The *klēronómos* is the "heir," the *synklēronómos* is the "joint heir," *klēronoméō* is "to be heir," "to inherit," and *klēronomía* is "inheritance," then "possession." It may be noted that in Greek, Egyptian, Hellenistic, and Jewish law children were always heirs, but Roman law allowed parents a freedom of testamentary disposition.

[W. FOERSTER, III, 758-69]

B. The OT.

1. Linguistic Survey. While *klḗros* occurs 129 times, *klēróō* occurs only three times, *synklēróō* not at all, and *klēronómos* four times. *klēronoméō,* however, occurs 163 times, *kataklēronoméō* 59 times, and *klēronomía* 143 times (mostly for Heb. *naḥ"lâ*). (For details and full Hebrew equivalents see *TDNT,* III, 769.)

2. The Promise of Possession of Canaan to the Patriarchs. The patriarchal stories begin with the command and promise of Gen. 12:1ff. On this basis Israel believes that possession of Canaan is by divine promise and ordination. The land is "the land of their fathers" (Gen. 31:3; 48:21).

3. The Promise of Possession of Canaan in the Moses Stories. The story of Moses opens with the same promise (Ex. 3:7-8). If this is at first presented independently, it is later taken up into the patriarchal promise as a renewal of it (cf. Ex. 32:13; Dt. 34:4).

4. Canaan as Israel's Inheritance in Exodus to Numbers. In Exodus to Numbers the thought that God gives Israel the land is common, but the idea of inheritance is less prominent than that of apportionment except when the reference is to the tribes (cf. Num. 26:52ff.; 33:50ff.; 36:2ff.; 18:20ff.; 27:1ff.).

5. Canaan as Israel's Inheritance in Deuteronomy. Since Deuteronomy presents Moses' last addresses prior to entry into the land, it is not surprising to find many references to the land which God promised to give to the patriarchs and their descendants (cf. 1:7ff.; 2:12, 29; 3:18ff.; 4:1ff., etc.). In this context the inheritance comprises both the whole land and individual portions (cf. 19:14). Possession is possible only because God has given the land and will drive out the Canaanites (3:20; 9:4-5).

6. *Canaan as Israel's Inheritance in Joshua.* Joshua receives and repeats the divine command (Josh. 1:2, 10-11), takes the land, and then divides it by lot (13:1, 7). The division is by families and individuals as well as tribes (19:49; 24:30), and it is the basis of the rulings protecting inheritance in Num. 27.

7. *Canaan as Israel's Inheritance in Judges to Nehemiah.* In the books that follow we find the common themes that God gives Israel the land (1 Kgs. 8:36), that she should keep the commands of God in order to maintain possession (1 Chr. 28:8), that the whole land is Israel's inheritance (Judg. 20:6), and that the tribes are allotted portions (Judg. 2:6) and must occupy these in detail (1:3), which the Danites fail to do (cf. 1:34 and ch. 18). Ezra sums up the general understanding in his great prayer in Neh. 9:8ff.

8. *The Land of Canaan and the People of Israel as God's Inheritance.* The land is called God's inheritance in 1 Sam. 26:19; 2 Sam. 21:3; 1 Kgs. 8:36; 2 Chr. 20:11; cf. Ex. 15:17. More commonly Israel herself is God's possession (Ex. 19:5; cf. Dt. 7:6; 1 Kgs. 8:51; 2 Kgs. 21:14; 1 Sam. 10:1; 2 Sam. 14:16; 20:19). When God gave the nations their portions, he chose Israel as his own portion and heritage (Dt. 32:8-9).

9. *The Prophets.* In general the prophets make little use of the theme. Amos refers only to the taking of Canaan in possession (2:9-10). Micah calls the land the people's portion (2:4). Jeremiah says that God has given Israel the most beautiful heritage (3:19). They will possess it forever if they do God's will (7:7), but in fact they have made it an abomination (2:7) and he has thus handed it over to their enemies (12:7ff.). Ezekiel presents similar thoughts (20:5-6; 37:25; 35:15), but with the promise of new and eternal possession after the exile (36:12; 27:25; cf. 40ff.). At the end of Isaiah the righteous will possess the land (60:21), and there is reference to God's heritage in 63:17. In Zechariah God will inherit Judah as his portion (2:12), and he will cause the righteous to possess all Judah (8:12). Joel calls Israel God's people and heritage (2:17), and the land is also his (2:18).

10. *The Psalms.* In the Psalms consolation and strength are found in a rehearsal of God's saving acts, so that we often find references to the promise (105:9ff.), the winning (44:2ff.), the giving (135:12), and the allotment of the land (78:55). Israel, too, is God's own heritage (28:9 etc.), although all nations are his possession inasmuch as he is universal Lord and Judge (82:8). The land is God's inheritance only in 79:1; elsewhere it is Israel's in both recollection (37:18 etc.) and hope (37:18). God is himself the lot of the writer in 16:5-6, and God's law in 119:111.

11. *Conclusion.* a. The references show that the Hebrew terms denote allotment, and possession only on this basis. They thus express the element of divine ordination. b. The sense of apportionment is also present. Tribes, families, and individuals have their own shares by sacred lot, and hence also by divine appointment. c. The basic concept is that of possession of land, and the law takes various steps to safeguard this (Ex. 20:17; Lev. 20:5; cf. Is. 5:8; Mic. 2:2). d. Since God promised the land to the patriarchs, it could be called an inheritance even though it was not possessed or handed down, but given by God at the conquest. The individual portions then become inheritances, as in the case of Naboth in 1 Kgs. 21:3. While an inheritance may embrace goods, it consists primarily of land (Num. 27:1ff.; Ruth 4:5ff.). e. The above developments explain why Israel may be called God's portion and heritage. f. They also

explain the use for destiny as one's "lot"—a lot which may be equated with God himself (Ps. 16:5-6). [J. HERRMANN, III, 769-76]

C. The Group *klēronómos* in the LXX.

1. Linguistic Data. As noted, *klēronómos* is rare in the LXX; it means "heir" in 2 Sam. 4:7 and "owner" in Mic. 1:5. *synklēronómos* does not occur. *klēronoméō* is common and has such varied senses as "to inherit," "to possess," "to take" (cf. Gen. 22:17; 1 Kgs. 20:15ff.), and "to hold." *kataklēronoméō* is fairly common, especially for "to divide an inheritance" or "to cause someone to inherit or take possession." *klēronomía,* another common word, means "inheritance," "possession," but also merges with *klḗros* in the sense of "share" or "portion."

2. Material Data. Important in a material survey are the relations of the group to the Hebrew originals (for details see *TDNT,* III, 777). From these we gather that the main point of *klēronoméō* and *klēronomía* is not so much inheritance as enduring possession (Josh. 18:3). This is based on the promise (Dt. 30:5) and established by violent seizure. Incidentally, then, it also entails inheritance (Num. 27:8), for the seizure of the land is an irreversible process that carries with it tribal and family rights to the portions that are allotted. On this basis the description of land or people as God's *klēronomía* expresses a lasting relationship that has its basis in the divine gift.

D. The Group in Later Judaism.

1. Linguistically the terms have here the legal sense of inheritance, but the religious usage of the OT still exerts a strong influence.

2. Materially the idea of the seizure and possession of the land is important, especially with an eschatological reference. The promise to Abraham is extended to cover permanent possession of the whole earth, e.g., in a messianic fulfilment of Gen. 28:14. The thought of inheriting eternal life is also prominent, although with no particular reference to God as Father and Israel as son. Conversely, hell is the portion of the wicked. *klēronomía* can sometimes be used for Israel as God's heritage or possession, and the law is a precious possession for Israel.

E. The Group in the NT.

1. The Usage. klēronómos means "heir" in Mk. 12:7, "heir" religiously in Gal. 4:1; Rom. 8:17, and "recipient" of the divine promises in Rom. 4:13-14; Tit. 3:7; Heb. 6:17; Jms. 2:5. *synklēronómos* occurs for "fellow heir" in Rom. 8:17; Heb. 11:9; 1 Pet. 3:7; Eph. 3:6. *klēronoméō* means "to inherit" in Gal. 4:30; Heb. 1:4 (Christ) and "to receive" God's gifts or promises in Mt. 5:5; 19:29; Lk. 10:25; 1 Cor. 6:9-10; Gal. 5:21; Heb. 1:14; 6:12. *kataklēronoméō* means "to give in possession" (Acts 13:9). *klēronomía* means "inheritance" in Mk. 12:7 and Gal. 3:18, "possession" in Acts 7:5; Heb. 11:8, and "eternal inheritance" in Acts 20:32; Eph. 1:4, 18; Col. 3:24; Heb. 9:15; 1 Pet. 1:4.

2. The Theological Usage. A special NT sense may be seen in the parable of Mk. 12:1ff., where the Son is the heir and the inheritance is the kingdom. This links sonship and inheritance much more closely than in the OT and Judaism. Paul expresses the same thought when he relates inheritance to sonship in Rom. 8:17-18 (cf. Gal. 3:29; 4:7). Similarly Heb. 1:2 says that the Son is appointed heir of all things. In the parable inheritance does not yet denote actual possession; only the risen Lord enters upon this (Mt. 28:18). Inheritance is expressly linked with the kingdom in Mt. 21:43; this frees it from earthly limitations and equates it with the new world of God's sovereign rule. If Christ is heir, his people are fellow heirs, yet only by divine call and appointment. The children of the kingdom are shut out (Mt. 8:11-12). Inheritance is by a new creation (1 Cor. 15:5), or by adoption (Rom. 8:23), and as such it is an object of hope. Salvation (Heb. 1:4), glory (Rom. 8:17), redemption (8:23), grace (1 Pet. 3:7), blessing (3:9), in sum, eternal life (Tit. 3:7), constitutes the content of the inheritance. Spatial ideas are unimportant, even in Mt. 5:5. Reigning with God is the issue (Rom. 5:17; Rev. 5:10). Rev. 21:2ff. indicates clearly what is meant by the inheritance (cf. v. 7). The heavenly portion (1 Pet. 1:4) does not denote a spatially distinct part of heaven but a part in God's eternal rule. Inheritance is not acquired but rests on filial relationship to God, and there is no reference to a parallel inheriting of hell. In Galatians Paul meets the Judaizing view that only those who keep the law may rank as the children of Abraham who inherit the promises. This involves the contradiction that inheritance is no longer by promise but by law (Gal. 3:18). In fact, however, this promise precedes the law, faith makes Abraham its recipient, Christ is the seed to whom the promise is given, and all those who belong to him by faith are the true progeny of Abraham, not by natural descent but by adoption (4:5ff.). The emphasis here is on the eschatological promise to Abraham which has found initiatory fulfilment in Christ. Similar lines of thought occur in Rom. 4:13-14 and Eph. 3:6. Hebrews, too, regards *klēronomía* as the content of the OT promise (9:15). Christians are heirs of the promise (6:17) as those who have taken it over and attained to it. Yet the promise, guaranteed by God, is set before the readers in order that by faith and patience they may receive it. Like the fathers (cf. 11) they live in the "not yet" of the inheritance. They are not to be irreligious as Esau was, who, when he desired to inherit the blessing, was rejected (12:16-17).   [W. Foerster, III, 776-85]

klēsis, klētós → *kaléō*

---

koilía [belly, womb]

A. Outside the NT.

1. Meaning "hollow," *koilía* is used for a. "the hollow part of the body," b. "the belly," "entrails," "intestines," and c. (rarely) "the womb."

2. In the LXX it is used for "belly" (Jon. 2:1), fairly commonly for the "womb" (Gen. 25:24; Dt. 28:4, 11), as well as for the male sex organ (Ps. 132:11), and figuratively for the "underworld" (Jon. 2:3) and for "hidden thoughts" (Job 15:35). In Philo it is the digestive system, which, as in Greek philosophy, is regarded as the seat of desire. Josephus uses it for the diseased lower part of the body.

3. The rabbinic equivalents have the usual senses "belly" and "womb," and we find a figurative use for the "vault" of a house.

B. In the NT.

1. In the NT "belly" is the sense in Mk. 7:19; Lk. 15:16; 1 Cor. 6:13; Rev. 10:9-10, "womb" in Mt. 19:12; Lk. 1:15 etc.; 2:21; Jn. 3:4; Acts 3:2; Gal. 1:15, and "inward part" in Jn. 7:38.

2. In Mk. 7:14ff. Jesus explains sin in terms of the difference between the *koilía* and the *kardía*. What is external does not disrupt our relationship to God. Evil is rooted in the evil heart. In 1 Cor. 6:13 Paul accepts the thesis of the libertines that the *koilía* is corruptible. But he does not agree either that it is morally indifferent or that it is the seat of sinful desire. Belonging to the creaturely world, it will perish, but the

body (*sóma*) belongs to the risen Lord, and hence it must not be surrendered to licentiousness (vv. 13-14). In Rom. 16:18 and Phil. 3:19 it might be that Paul is referring to unbridled licentiousness and gluttony (cf. the rendering "appetites"), but another possibility is that he has in mind Judaizers who lay too much stress on dietary regulations.

3. The sense of "inward part" is present in Jn. 7:38. When Jesus quenches the inner thirst of believers, their refreshed inner being becomes a source of wider refreshing (cf. Is. 58:11; Zech. 14:8; Ezek. 47:1ff.) in an outflow to others.

[J. BEHM, III, 786-89]

---

koinós [common], *koinōnós* [companion, participant], *koinōnéō* [to share in], *koinōnía* [fellowship, participation], *synkoinōnós* [partner], *synkoinōnéō* [to participate in, share], *koinōnikós* [generous], *koinóō* [to make common]

---

koinós.

A. In Secular Greek.

1. This word means "common" a. in the sense of common ownership, property, ideas, etc., b. in the sense of what concerns all, e.g., societies, monies, resolves, and c. in the sense of what is of little value.

2. A second line of use is for "fellows," "participants."

B. In the OT and Judaism.

1. The general sense of common is found only a few times in Proverbs (e.g., 1:14; 15:23; 21:9; 25:24).

2. Another sense (Heb. *ḥōl*) has reference to what is in general or ordinary use as distinct from what is consecrated (though the LXX uses *bébēlos* in such cases). Thus the rabbis use *ḥōl* for working days, or for ordinary ground, money, or food, or for animals slaughtered for common use. Only in apocryphal works (e.g., 1 Macc. 1:47) and Josephus do we find *koinós* as an equivalent for this.

C. The Individual and Society, Theories and Forms of Society.

1. The Greeks value individuals and individual rights, yet with a strong sense of the duty to society and of integration into it, since order is the principle of all reality. Common ownership of the land underlies society, but except where military needs demand a degree of communal economy (as in Sparta), private property soon develops with the resultant distinction between rich and poor. Theories of society seek to redress the balance. Thus Pythagoras establishes a communal society for his followers. Plato in his portrayal of the ideal state suggests that rulers and soldiers should be put on a public basis, and in his modified proposals he advocates nationalization of the land and strict economic supervision. Aristotle preserves private ownership but with the proviso that one portion of the land be held in common, and that the nearest possible equality of ownership be achieved. Poets like Hesiod depict an ideal state in either past or present. The Cynics believe that common possession of all things is the true order of nature. The Stoics seek the best possible realization of a better age by fostering the spirit of brotherhood. The Neo-Pythagoreans renew the ideal of a common life and a community of goods (for the earth is a common mother) in which one may possess nothing and yet be the owner of all things.

447

2. Apart from the Pythagoreans, the Greeks only theorize about common ownership, but Jewish groups like the Essenes practice it, sharing both meals and property. The Therapeutae also live communally and in ascetic isolation for the intenser study of Scripture.

D. *koinós* in the NT.

1. Tit. 1:4 speaks of the "common" faith and Jude 3 of the "common" salvation. In Acts 2:44; 4:32 the disciples live a "common" life, following the example of Jesus (Lk. 8:1ff.) and anticipating the last days (Dt. 15:4). This life in community is not based on economic theory, legal socialization, or philosophical imitation of nature, but expresses the loving fellowship which renounces ownership (cf. Lk. 12:33) in order to help others (Acts 2:45). The phrase in Acts ("having all things or everything in common") is a Hellenistic one.

2. The sense "profane" occurs in Rev. 21:27; Heb. 10:29 ("profaning the blood of the covenant"); Mk. 7:2 ("cultically unclean hands"). The NT denies that anything that God created is ritually profane (cf. Acts 10:28; Rom. 14:14). Weaker brethren may still think in these terms, and allowance must be made for them, but they are objectively mistaken (Rom. 14:14).

koinōnós, koinōnéō, koinōnía, synkoinōnós, synkoinōnéō.

A. The Meaning and Construction of the Terms. *koinōnós* means "fellow," "participant." *koinōnéō* means 1. "to share in" and more rarely 2. "to impart." It is used in the absolute, or with genitive of object, dative of person, or both. *koinōnía* means "participation," "impartation," or "fellowship." It is used with the objective genitive (what is shared), the subjective genitive (the person or thing sharing), the recipient being in the dative or with a preposition and the objective genitive (the person in whom there is sharing).

B. The Group in Secular Greek.

1. Human Life. Sharing occurs in many fields, e.g., enterprises, legal relations, and marriage. Friendship is for the Greeks a supreme expression of fellowship. Citizenship is also important, since the preservation of society, and indeed of the cosmos, depends on political or cosmopolitan sharing.

2. Sacral Speech. Sharing in divine power through common meals is an ancient idea which persists in the Greek concept of communion with the gods at sacrificial feasts or even by sexual union. Philosophy purifies the idea. Thus for Plato communion with God is the supreme form of fellowship, while Stoicism with its idea of an integrated universe stresses human fellowship and the fellowship of all humanity with deity. Mysticism replaces communion with union.

C. The Group in the Israelite-Jewish Sphere.

1. The OT. The group is not common in the OT (less so than the equivalent Hebrew group *ḥbr,* which denotes association with other people for various purposes, or association with idols, but never with God). *koinōnía* occurs only in Lev. 6:2 for "deposit," and in Is. 44:11 those who worship idols are their "fellows." In Sirach *koinōnós* may be used for table fellowship (6:10) but also for association in unlawful acts (41:19). *koinōnéō* denotes close comradeship with the wicked or the rich in Sir. 13:1. *koinōnía* is used for material participation in Wis. 8:18.

2. The OT: God. The absence of the group for fellowship with God marks off the OT from the Greek world. The righteous in the OT depend on God and trust in him, but do not regard themselves as his fellows. This is surprising in view of the fact that the cultus expresses the entry of God into sacral fellowship. A sense of distance rather than association prevails even where there is rejoicing before God (cf. Dt. 12).

3. *Rabbinic Literature.* Among the rabbis the basic sense of "fellow" carries such nuances as "companion" (in good or evil), "person in a legal relation," "member of a society," and, among the rabbis themselves, "colleague." "Fellowship" has a general sense but also has religious overtones when it denotes table fellowship, e.g., at the Passover.

4. Philo distinctively uses the group for human fellowship with God, e.g., in the cultus. He also has it for the ideal common life of the Essenes. He gives *koinōnéō* and *koinōnía* the rare sense of "giving a share" or "imparting."

D. The Group in the NT.

1. The Sense "To Share in Something."

a. In Lk. 5:10 the point is partnership in work. In Heb. 2:14 the children share a common mortality which Christ himself partakes of in order to overcome death and the devil. In 2 Pet. 1:4 redemption brings participation in the divine nature. In Rom. 11:17 the engrafted branches share the total life of the cultivated tree. Participation in what is holy has an exclusive character (2 Cor. 6:14). As the children of light Christians cannot have a part in sin (Eph. 5:11). Participating in the sins of others entangles one in a common guilt and judgment (Mt. 23:30; cf. 1 Tim. 5:22; 2 Jn. 11). God's people must leave Babylon lest they share her sins and judgment (Rev. 18:4).

b. Paul often gives the group a religious content. In 1 Cor. 1:9 Christians are called to fellowship with God's Son. Since there is no mystical absorption, this fellowship is by faith, which identifies their life with his. If it is a present possession, it awaits future consummation (cf. 1 Th. 4:17). It carries with it participation in the gospel (1 Cor. 9:23; cf. Phil. 1:5) and a sharing of faith (Phlm. 6).

c. In this regard the fellowship of the Lord's Supper is important as an enhanced expression of fellowship with Christ (1 Cor. 10:16ff.). For Paul sacrificial feasts denote divine fellowship (vv. 18, 20). Those who share the Supper are companions of Christ; for this reason they should shun idolatrous feasts. By taking bread and wine they share with Christ in an inward communion which carries with it the blessing of the forgiveness won by his death. This communion extends to all the participants, as represented by the one loaf (v. 17).

d. Fellowship with Christ also means living, suffering, dying, inheriting, and reigning with him (Rom. 6:8; 8:17; 6:6; 2 Tim. 2:12; cf. also 2 Cor. 7:3; Col. 2:12-13; Eph. 2:5-6). There are here two phases of fellowship, the first with Christ's humiliation and the second with his exaltation. In his life and work Paul has a share in Christ's total sufferings (Phil. 3:10; Col. 1:24), but he hopes to share analogously in his glory (Phil. 3:10; Rom. 8:17). 1 Pet. 4:13 makes the same point. For Paul individual sufferings are part of the burden that rests on the whole community according to the law of fellowship (Col. 1:24; 2 Cor. 1:5, 7).

e. Believers also share in the Spirit (2 Cor. 13:13) by whom Christ comes to them. In Phil. 2:1 this is a participation in the Spirit rather than the Spirit's gift.

f. Fellowship with Christ means fellowship with other Christians in a partnership of faith (cf. Phlm. 17) and service (2 Cor. 8:23). Since Gentile Christians share the same blessings as Jewish Christians, they should share their material goods with them (Rom. 15:27; cf. 12:13). Sharing each other's sufferings, they share each other's grace

449

(Phil. 1:7; cf. 4:14). Even when they themselves do not suffer, they are partners of those who do (Heb. 10:33).

g. *koinōnía* is a favorite term in 1 John for the living bond that unites Christians. It begins as fellowship with the Father and the Son (1:3, 6) by an abiding that commences here and is fulfilled hereafter (3:2, 24; 4:13). It issues in the family fellowship of believers (1:3, 7).

2. *The Sense "To Give a Share in Something."* This rare Greek meaning is fairly common in the NT. We find it in the reciprocal sharing of Phil. 4:15 and Gal. 6:6 (cf. 1 Cor. 9:11). Paul also has it in connection with the collection for the Jerusalem church, which gives a definite form to the fellowship between the two parts of Christianity (Gal. 2:9; Rom. 15:26). The collection has the significance of fellowship in service (2 Cor. 8:4) in a sincere and ready sharing (2 Cor. 9:13). Active sharing is also the point in Heb. 13:16.

3. *The Absolute Sense: "Fellowship."* In Gal. 2:9 shaking hands expresses the full fellowship of common faith in Christ. In Acts 2:42 *koinōnía* denotes, not the Christian society nor its community of goods, but the family fellowship established and expressed in the church's life.

koinōnikós. a. A first sense of this word is "belonging or appointed to society." b. Another meaning is "gladly giving others a share." The word does not occur in the LXX, and in the NT it is used only in 1 Tim. 6:18 in sense b.

koinóō. This word, meaning "to make common" or "to share," is not used in the LXX but occurs in three senses in the NT. 1. In Acts 21:28 it means "to profane" the temple. 2. In Mt. 15:11, 18, 20 it means "to defile," not by ritual impurity, but by personal sin. 3. In Acts 10:15; 11:9 it means "to declare profane, unclean."

[F. HAUCK, III, 789-809]

---

kókkos [seed],   **kókkinos** [scarlet]

kókkos.

1. This word, meaning "seed," occurs in the NT in the parables of Jesus. The mustard seed that grows into a great shrub (Mt. 33:31-32 and par.) stands for the unassuming preaching of Jesus which as the divine action has all-embracing significance. The tree in whose branches birds nest (cf. Ezek. 17:22-23) symbolizes a rule that will extend to all peoples. In Lk. 17:6 the mustard seed is small compared to the solid sycamine tree, but it can uproot and remove it (cf. Mt. 17:20). The point here is not so much the power of even a tiny faith, but the fact that God's power is not proportionate to human faith. Faith, then, should look away from itself, and then the impossible becomes possible.

2. Paul and John both find in the grain of wheat (1 Cor. 15:37; Jn. 12:24) a sign of divine action and creation. Paul perceives in the burying and coming to life of the seed a symbol of the continuity of the old corporeality and the new, while John finds in it a symbol of the necessity of Christ's death and resurrection and of the divine law that links Master and disciple. The eschatological picture takes on christological urgency in John.

3. Outside the NT *kókkos* also denotes the scarlet berry and the color scarlet (cf. 1 Clem. 8.3).

kókkinos. This word means "scarlet" (cf. the furnishings of the sanctuary in Ex. 26:1 etc., the scarlet stuff in Lev. 14:4, and the scarlet clothing of 2 Sam. 1:24). In the prophets scarlet is linked with sin, either as the opposite of white (Is. 1:18) or as a sign of luxury (Is. 3:23; Jer. 4:30). In the NT 1. Jesus is clothed in a scarlet robe in Mt. 27:28. This was probably a soldier's cloak; the king of peace, in a mocking misrepresentation, is thus clothed in warlike garb. 2. In Heb. 9:19 scarlet wool is mentioned in connection with atonement under the law (cf. Lev. 14:4, 6). 3. Scarlet and purple denote the pomp of Babylon's demonic power in Revelation. Arrayed in purple and scarlet, the woman sits on a scarlet beast (17:3-4). The fiery red of 6:4; 12:3 differs from the scarlet here, which epitomizes demonic abomination, lasciviousness, and ungodly power. The Messiah's army is clothed in white linen and rides on white horses (19:11ff.); the robes are made white in the atoning blood of the Lamb (7:14). We thus have a striking contrast to the woman who is clothed in scarlet and rides on a scarlet beast.   [O. MICHEL, III, 810-14]

---

kolázō [to cut short, punish], *kólasis* [punishment]

---

kolázō. This means "to cut short," "to lop," "to trim," and figuratively a. "to impede," "restrain," and b. "to punish," and in the passive "to suffer loss." A common use is for divine chastisement. In inscriptions the deity punishes those who violate cultic laws. Some classical authors regard evil as divine retribution. Philo finds in beneficence and retribution the two primary powers of being, though God would rather forgive than punish, and punishes only those who are not amenable to reason. Punishment brings blessing by freeing from a false frame of soul. The NT uses *kolázō* in Acts 4:21 and 2 Pet. 2:9. Only the latter refers to God's punishment. The wicked will be under punishment between death and judgment, i.e., until their destiny is finally fixed.

kólasis. This word, meaning "punishment," is used for divine punishment in 2 Macc. 4:38; 4 Macc. 8:9. In the NT it occurs in Mt. 25:46: Those who fail the practical ethical task will go away to eternal punishment. The only other instance is in 1 Jn. 4:18, which says that fear is its own punishment (cf. 3:18). This fear is driven out by love, which is free from every fear.   [J. SCHNEIDER, III, 814-17]

(kolakeúō) [to flatter], *kolakía* [flattery]

The word *kolakía* derives from *kolakeúō* ("to flatter"), which does not occur in the NT. *kolakía* is not found in the LXX but is common in Philo. The one NT example is in 1 Th. 2:5, where Paul says that he does not use flattery in his preaching (unlike many Hellenistic orators).   [J. SCHNEIDER, III, 817-18]

---

kolaphízō [to buffet]

This rare term occurs a few times in the NT and Christian writings. It means "to buffet," "to ill-treat," "to revile." The sense is literal in the passion story (Mt. 26:67).

Spiritual pain is also involved in 1 Cor. 4:11; 1 Pet. 2:20 (which reflects the passion of Christ, vv. 21ff.). In 2 Cor. 12:7 Paul is buffeted by an angel of Satan. The thorn in the flesh can hardly refer to persecution or the temptation to licentiousness, but may have to do with intense pain accompanying Paul's visions. Various diagnoses have been attempted in explanation of such pain, e.g., an eye ailment, epilepsy, neurasthenia, migraine, malaria, etc., but none is fully convincing. Paul himself comes in prayer to the realization that his affliction has profound meaning. Christ, too, was buffeted by Satan and his agents, but Christ is still the victor, and his power is made perfect in Paul's weakness.   [K. L. SCHMIDT, III, 818-21]

---

kolláō [to join together, unite],   *proskolláō* [to join, unite]

---

kolláō.

1. In the NT *kolláō,* meaning "to glue or join together," occurs only in the middle or passive. Thus in Lk. 10:11 it means figuratively "to touch" and in Acts 8:29 "to join" (the chariot). In Rom. 12:9 Christians are to "hold fast" to what is good, while in Lk. 15:15 the prodigal "joins" a citizen in the far country, and in Acts 5:13 none dared "join" the apostles.

2. A specific sense of *kollásthai* is for sexual intercourse; cf. Mt. 19:5 (quoting Gen. 2:24); Eph. 5:31 (quoting Gen. 2:24 more literally with *proskollḗthḗsetai*); 1 Cor. 6:16 (where the opposite is union with the Lord, v. 17).

proskolláō.

1. One reading has this word in Acts 5:36 in the sense "to join."

2. In Eph. 5:31 and one reading of Mt. 19:5 it denotes marital union.

[K. L. SCHMIDT, III, 822-23]

---

kolobóō [to mutilate, cut short]

---

kolobóō occurs in the NT in Mt. 24:22 in the figurative sense "to cut short." God has cut short the time of affliction, i.e., made it less than the oppressors purpose, so that the elect may be preserved from *physical* destruction (as indicated by the "all flesh" of Mk. 13:20, the physical nature of the sufferings, and the presence of the elect at the parousia, Mk. 13:27).   [G. DELLING, III, 823-24]

---

kólpos [bosom, fold]

---

kólpos has the senses "bosom," "fold" (of a garment), and "arch" or "hollow," e.g., the floor of a valley or bosom of the sea. The LXX uses it to express marital fellowship (Dt. 13:7), for the fold of a garment (Ex. 4:6-7), and for the bottom of a chariot (1 Kgs. 22:35) or the altar (Ezek. 43:13). In the NT the beloved disciple takes the place of honor by reclining on Jesus' "breast" (Jn. 13:25; cf. the Son and the Father in Jn. 1:18). "Fold" of a garment is the sense in Lk. 6:38 and "bay" of the sea in Acts 27:39. In Lk. 16:22-23 the point may be that Lazarus has the place of honor on Abraham's "bosom," but it is also possible that what is expressed is loving fellowship. Both ideas are present in rabbinic Judaism.   [R. MEYER, III, 824-26]

koniáō [to whitewash]

koniáō means "to daub with lime," "to plaster," "to whitewash" (Dt. 27:2). Paul in Acts 23:3 calls the high priest Ananias a "whitewashed" wall to denote his carefully concealed wickedness. In Mt. 23:27 Jesus similarly calls the hypocritical scribes and Pharisees "whitewashed" tombs. The irony of the saying is that they represent the very thing they avoid. They are not what they appear to be, and they are to be avoided as unclean (even though they claim to be clean).   [J. SCHNEIDER, III, 827]

kópos [labor, trouble],   *kopiáō* [to become weary]

In secular Greek *kópos* means a. "beating" or the "weariness" caused by it, and b. the "exertion" (e.g., of manual work) that brings on physical tiredness. *kopiáō*, then, means "to tire," "to wear oneself out." The LXX uses it for tiring in battle (2 Sam. 23:10), for exertion in work (Josh. 24:13), and for the groans of the afflicted (Ps. 6:6). *kópos* is the human lot in the OT (Job 5:7; Ps. 25:17-18). Present toil is contrasted with future rest (Is. 65:23). God, who never wearies (Is. 40:28ff.), will grant rest to the righteous (33:24). In the NT 1. the sense "to weary" occurs literally in Jn. 4:6 and figuratively in Rev. 2:3. 2. "To tire oneself out" occurs literally in Mt. 6:28; Lk. 5:5; Eph. 4:28; 2 Tim. 2:6, and figuratively in Mt. 11:28-29 (fainting under the legal burden). *kópos* has a general sense in Mt. 14:6 and an eschatological reference in Rev. 2:2. Paul as an apostle accepts troubles as normal (2 Cor. 6:5; cf. Mt. 5:11-12). His special troubles strengthen his assurance (2 Cor. 11:23); *kópoi* take precedence in his appeal to things that show him to be a true servant of Christ (*loc. cit.*).

3. A distinctive NT use is for Christian work in and for the community. Paul has it for his own work in 1 Cor. 15:10 etc. It describes his manual work in 1 Cor. 4:12, but, since he is not under obligation to do this, it forms part of the work that he does for Christ (1 Th. 2:9; 1 Cor. 9:15ff.). All his service for Christ may indeed be regarded as strenuous work, though it is also his pride and joy (2 Cor. 11:23). His aim is to present mature Christians to Christ (Col. 1:29). He shows concern for the success of this work (Gal. 4:9) and aims at an eschatological reward (1 Th. 3:5; Phil. 2:16). Paul uses the *kop-* group for the work of others too (1 Cor. 15:58), which as labor in the Lord (Rom. 16:12) deserves the highest esteem (1 Cor. 16:16). Love is the mainspring of this labor (1 Th. 1:3), which is carried on especially by officebearers (1 Th. 5:12). The same usage may be found in 1 Tim. 4:10; 5:17; Jn. 4:38; Acts 20:35, but it becomes less prominent in later Christian authors, who perhaps think that *kópos*, with its nuance of manual work, is not a fitting term for ministry.

[F. HAUCK, III, 827-30]

kopetós [beating, mourning],   *kóptō* [to beat, mourn],   *apokóptō* [to cut off, castrate],   *enkopḗ* [obstacle],   *enkóptō* [to block],   *ekkóptō* [to cut off, cut down]

kopetós, kóptō.

A. The General Custom of Mourning.

1. In Greek, as in many other tongues, "to beat" takes on the specific sense "to mourn." Women especially beat their breasts in mourning (men beat themselves in

remorse or pain). The idea is probably to give bodily expression to grief, though there may be an underlying cultic (even sacrificial) concept.

2. Lamentation for the dead takes other external forms, e.g., outcries punctuating individual laments (often by paid mourners supplementing women relatives).

3. The common posture of mourning is sitting on the ground. We also read of a death dance in which women may beat their cheeks to the wail of tambourines.

4. The reasons for noisy lamentation are varied, e.g., frightening off demons, cultic honoring of the dead, and the kindling of sympathy.

B. Mourning in the Greek and Roman World.

I. Popular Mourning.

1. Beating the body and loud crying are customary in Greece from early days. They probably come to Greece from the Near East.

2. Solon legislates against extreme violence and extravagance at funerals, as does Roman law, but the customs continue at the showing of the corpse and the interment, and in Rome burial societies are formed to meet the high costs. Philosophy expresses abhorrence of exaggerated mourning.

3. As a chief part of mourning, beating the body (*kopetós*) comes to be used for mourning itself. The verb, originally used with the part of the body beaten, is thus found in the absolute or with the accusative of the person lamented.

4. In the Near East women are the main mourners (either relatives or paid professionals). Their purpose is to express grief, to honor the dead, to stir up sympathy, and to ease the grief of relatives with consoling thoughts. Women are the mourners in Greece too. Solon tries to restrict them to relatives, but we find paid mourners in Athens. These may include both sexes in both Greece and the Near East, and sometimes we find men as well as women beating their breasts, rumpling their hair, and scratching their cheeks in mourning.

II. Mourning in the Cultus.

1. Mourning takes a violent form in cults that focus on the dying and rising again of deity; cf. the Babylonian cult of Tammuz (Ezek. 8:14), the Syrian cult of Adonis, the Phrygian cult of Attis, and the Egyptian cult of Osiris, in which the goddesses Ishtar, Astarte, Cybele, and Isis, along with the devotees, weep for the dying gods at the great annual festivals.

2. Similar rites may be found in the Greek mysteries, in which the repeated cultic dramas (Persephone and Dionysus) involve wild lamentation and rejoicing. The mourning feast for the hero Achilles may also be mentioned.

C. Mourning in the OT.

I. Popular Mourning.

1. Linguistic Data. The exact equivalent of *kóptomai* in Hebrew is *spd,* though the Greek is also used for other terms. Mourning is normally the sense, and other words such as *klaíō* (2 Sam. 1:12), *alalázō* (Jer. 4:8), *penthéō* (Jer. 16:5), and *thrēnéō* (Mic. 1:8) often accompany *kóptomai*; cf. also *klauthmós* (Is. 22:12) and *thrḗnos* (Jer. 9:9) with *kopetós*. The verb is often used either for or with such gestures of grief as cutting off the hair, tearing the clothes, and donning sackcloth. *kóptomai kopetón* is the phrase for instituting mourning.

2. Practices. In the OT one finds various mourning customs, e.g., going barefoot, rumpling or cutting the hair, tearing clothes, scattering ashes, fasting, lamenting, and beating the breast or hip. Mourning begins with death (or very soon after) and continues up to interment. A mourning period of fasts and laments follows burial and lasts seven days (or longer in the case of prominent people). Sometimes there might be annual mourning (Jephthah's daughter and Josiah).

3. *The Mourners*. These are first the immediate family (husband, wife, bride, father, etc.; cf. the cries "Alas, sister" etc. in passages like Jer. 22:18). Others are then included (friends etc.), and sometimes the whole nation, as for Moses, Samuel, Abner, and Josiah. Women are prominent, and we find choruses of women or even all the women of a town or country (e.g., 2 Sam. 1:24). Professional mourners play a part (Jer. 9:16; 2 Chr. 35:25).

4. *Expressions of Grief*. Grief first comes to expression in formless cries (Lam. 1:1 etc.). These cries then become brief laments for the departed ("Alas my brother" in 1 Kgs. 13:30). Out of these develop the fuller laments for which the professional mourners train (cf. the lament for Josiah in 2 Chr. 35:25). Some such laments come down through the generations and serve as models for others. They might be sung responsively or antiphonally (2 Chr. 35:25; Zech. 12:10ff.). The dead are often addressed in the second person (Ezek. 27:3ff.), and the lament is uttered on behalf of the relatives (Lam. 1:12ff.) or even the dead (Jer. 9:18). Abuses arise through violence of outcry and extravagance, as in Greece and Rome.

5. A distinctive feature of the OT is that full mourning is a sign of normality. Divine judgment carries with it the curse of death without proper burial or mourning (Jer. 8:2; 22:18; Job 27:15). This is humiliation to the status of a beast (Jer. 22:19). It is a fate that overtakes all of Jeroboam's house apart from Abijah (1 Kgs. 14:10ff.).

II. *Prophetic Lamentation (→ thrēnéō)*.

1. Mourning has a specific form in the OT, but this is prophetic rather than cultic. It consists partly of public acts and partly of spoken or written laments. The laments follow popular models (Ezek. 32:19ff.; Jer. 9:20-21). The aim, however, is not to comfort but to startle, not to excite sympathy but to bring to repentance. Prophetic mourning, uttered in God's name, is usually for future death in the form of national destruction. The main concern, however, is with the nation's rebellion rather than its overthrow. This mourning does not accept death; it seeks renewal of life (cf. Am. 5:14) and carries the assurance of restoration.

2. The lament of Am. 5:1-2 is typical. The fact that it is for the virgin daughter awakens the deepest sense of loss, since unfulfilled purpose is expressed hereby. The laments of Micah (1:8), Jeremiah (9:18), and Ezekiel (ch. 19) should also be noted; also the ironical and scornful laments for Egypt (Ezek. 32) and Babylon (Is. 14). Such laments rise to great poetic heights.

3. A secondary aspect is that the prophet may have to forgo ordinary mourning (Ezek. 24:16; Jer. 16:5). The aim of such symbols is to portray the terrible state when there will be no mourning because of divine judgment (Ezek. 24:22ff.; Jer. 16:4ff.).

4. Prophetic activity also includes the declaration of mourning or the need for it. The lamentation may be for sin (Joel 2:12) or for the destruction that God's judgments bring (Is. 22:12). It can take an ironical form, as in the lamentation for universal catastrophe in Jer. 25:34, or for the dispossession of the god Milcom in Jer. 49:1ff.

5. Assurance of restoration comes with intimation of disaster; this will mean the replacement of mourning with dancing (Ps. 30:11). Yet mourning for the Messiah (Zech. 12:10ff.) is part of the message of salvation; here is a sorrow which issues in life.

D. Mourning in Judaism.

1. Sources and Usage. Various tractates bear witness to the mourning customs of Judaism. The usage is much the same as in the OT.

2. Customs and Times. The first part of mourning is during the funeral procession. It consists of lamentation and beating the breast. A second part follows interment; this is divided into a one-day period, a main period of seven days (three very strict), and a longer but not so strict period of thirty days (a whole year for parents). Extra commemorations, encouraged by wandering orators, might follow.

3. The Mourners. Hired women with their cries, banging of instruments, and beating the breast play a large role in the funeral procession, though restrictions are put on their activity. Only lamentation is prescribed after interment. Family members, both men and women, join in the funeral procession and express their grief by stamping the feet, wringing the hands, and beating the breast. Male orators honor the dead with eulogies at the grave. Larger groups of friends are also found, and there is national mourning for important leaders, especially rabbis.

4. Significance and Motifs. Mourning is regarded as a duty of love (Ex. 18:20). It has atoning force (1 Kgs. 14:13) and consoles the deceased. Fear of demons, which are potent and dangerous near tombs, may also be a reason for it.

E. Mourning in the NT.

I. Popular Mourning.

1. The case of Jairus' daughter gives evidence of the first period of mourning, which begins with death, and which takes a conventional form, involving the presence of relatives, condoling acquaintances, flute players, and mourning women (Mk. 5:38; Mt. 9:23; Lk. 8:52). The case of Lazarus (Jn. 11:17) puts us in the second period of seven days, when the three strictest days are over, and visits are the most important feature according to the ceremonial of Judaism.

2. The children's game of Mt. 11:16-17 reflects burial customs of the day. It presupposes that a leader strikes up the lament and that the others should join in with hand movements, probably beating the forehead or breast.

3. Jesus himself experiences in anticipation the first stage of mourning when the women of Jerusalem weep over him on the way to the cross (Lk. 22:37). This is a symbol of national mourning in spite of the prohibition of such mourning in cases of execution. Either courageous confession that Jesus is no criminal, or involuntary recognition that he is truly Israel's King, finds expression in it. The Gospels, however, mention no second period of mourning for Jesus.

4. The disciples follow Jewish customs in the burial of Stephen (Acts 8:2). Here men, who have a role in Greek mourning but are more prominent in that of Judaism, seem to play an exclusive part. The "devout men" are probably Jewish Christians who by public mourning protest against Stephen's condemnation. In Acts 9:39 it is the women (widows) whom we find weeping for Dorcas.

5. Mourning has really lost its point with the resurrection triumph of Christ, but in the early church custom lags behind faith. Hence mourning remains a seat of tenacious paganism against which, e.g., Chrysostom protests, and even much later governments (cf. Venice) have to pass restrictive laws.

II. Mourning in the Life, at the Death, and on the Coming Again of Christ.

1. Jesus, when he meets mourning, resists it. As the Victor over death, he turns it into joyful awe in Mk. 5:42, grateful faith in Jn. 11:45, and cheerful praise in Lk. 7:16. There is no sense in expecting mourning from the Messiah (Lk. 7:30). The

Pharisees who do so have a false picture of the Messiah as a pitiless Judge who prefers to kill on the sabbath and fasts with no less severity than they do. Ironically they have no more liking for John the Baptist, for they are unwilling to follow him in serious repentance. Their answer to the Savior Messiah is to deal him a mortal blow which brings a lamentation they do not desire.

2. Before this, however, comes the proleptic mourning for Jesus himself, for it is through death that he gains the decisive victory over death. In this mourning there is perhaps a fulfilment of Zech. 12:10, which carries the motifs of sorrow for the martyrdom of the divine prophet and concern for the misfortune which comes on the people in consequence (cf. Barn. 7.5). Jesus himself tells the women, however, not to weep for him but to weep for themselves and their children. In so doing he takes up the prophetic demand for lamentation but also manifests his self-forgetful love.

3. The NT speaks, too, of an eschatological mourning in which there is no longer a place for repentance. Zech. 12:10 is usually interpreted as a prophecy of this final mourning (cf. Mt. 24:30; Rev. 1:7). This mourning, which is now universal, combines remorse for the death of Jesus with grief at personal loss in the judgment. Realization of the truth comes with the manifestation of the exalted Christ, but it comes too late. The lament for Babylon in Rev. 19 is a special form of this intimation of eschatological mourning. The sinful world has to bewail the fall of its representative, and in so doing it laments its own fate (vv. 11, 15).

4. *Summary.* The witness of Scripture is that death belongs to the world that is against God, that it cannot be where God is, and that it thus entails distance from God. It is in death, therefore, that pagan hopelessness finds its fullest manifestation. Pagan mourning vividly symbolizes this. Even in paganism, however, there is a sense that it ought not to be, and this is even more true in the biblical sphere. Here lies the ultimate reason for the many attempts to check excessive mourning. Yet legislation alone cannot do it. Only the death and resurrection of Christ, which overcome the alienation of sin and replace death with life, can rob pagan lamentation of its point. Grief at parting remains, but it is now illumined by the assurance of new life with God (Rev. 21:4). Violent mourning may thus yield to a quiet sorrow whose very quietness anticipates the blessed rest when sorrow is changed forever into the fullness of joy.

apokóptō (→ *ekkóptō, eunoúchos, eunouchízō*). This word means literally "to cut off," "to chop," "to break," "to hew down," symbolically "to mourn," and figuratively "to remove," "to conclude abruptly" (in rhetoric), and "to omit letters" at the end of a word (in grammar). There are two important instances in the NT.

1. *Jesus' Saying in Mk. 9:43, 45.* In secular Greek the term is used for "cutting off" members of the body in battle, in amputations, and in punishment (of prisoners of war, cf. Judg. 1:6-7; for various offenses, cf. Dt. 25:11-12; Ex. 21:23-24, etc.). The cutting off of members in punishment probably underlies the metaphor in Mark. Prevention of further temptation can hardly be the point. Self-punishment inflicted on the erring member will weaken the force of sin, but above all it will anticipate future punishment and thus prevent eternal judgment.

2. *Paul's Saying in Gal. 5:12.* A special sense of *apokóptō* is "emasculation." The participle, then, can be used for "eunuchs." In the Near East eunuchs served as chamberlains at court and as ministers in various cults (cf. in the OT 1 Sam. 8:15; 2 Kgs. 8:6, etc.). The OT excludes eunuchs from the people (Dt. 23:2): emasculation is a sin against the Creator, is alien to the life of the covenant people, and is an offense

against the pure worship that demands no blemish. A place is found for faithful eunuchs, however, in Is. 56:3ff. (cf. Jer. 41:16); in the NT cf. Acts 8:27. The reference in Mt. 19:12 is, of course, a figurative one; Jesus has celibacy in view. In Gal. 5:12, where emasculation is probably in mind, Paul is not commending it. There is thus no reason to weaken the sense to "separation" or even to the more general but vaguer "mutilation." In an ironical play on his opponents' demand for circumcision, Paul is suggesting a radical surpassing of circumcision that would bring exclusion from the community instead of entrance into it—an exclusion which is already the true situation. The wish is obviously not meant to be taken literally. [Some rabbis advocate celibacy, but they condemn pagan self-emasculation; the Romans also repudiate it.]

enkopḗ, enkóptō (→ proskopḗ, próskomma). The basic idea expressed by this group is that of "blocking the way." This yields the sense of "obstacle."

1. In the NT the obstacles denoted by the group are always religious. What is hindered is the course of the apostle (Rom. 15:22), the progress of the gospel (1 Cor. 9:12), the walk of Christians (Gal. 5:7), or the ascent of prayer (1 Pet. 3:7).

2.a. The one who primarily impedes is Satan (1 Th. 2:8). Since Paul elsewhere finds other reasons for changes of plan (cf. 2 Cor. 1:15ff.; Rom. 1:13; Acts 16:6-7), and since he does not view Satan as the lord of nature, what he probably has in mind in 1 Th. 2:18 is the devil's opposition through human action (cf. perhaps vv. 14ff.). Satan may also be the one who hinders in Gal. 5:7. This time, as the opposite of the one "who called you," he works through the Judaizers.

b. Since the NT finds the source of evil in the human heart as well as the devil, humans, too, can be the ones who hinder. Even the apostle himself might become an obstacle by using his right to support, i.e., by giving the impression that he was doing his work for personal profit, or by frightening away the poor (1 Cor. 9:12). Paul's supreme concern is that there be no *enkopḗ* to the *prokopḗ* of the gospel (Phil. 1:12). In 1 Pet. 3:7 human sin in the form of a perverted marital relation may constitute a hindrance to prayer. We have here the specific form of a general problem—sin impedes prayer—that only Christ's saving work has solved.

ekkóptō.

A. **General Greek Usage.** a. The first sense of *ekkóptō* is "to strike out" (e.g., the eyes, branches in pruning, etc.). b. A second sense is "to break open" (doors, locks, etc.). c. A third meaning is "to hew down" (trees; cf. Jer. 22:7; Mt. 7:19). d. Figuratively we then have the sense "to drive out" or e. "to exclude" or "repel." f. Another figurative meaning is "to extirpate" or "destroy" (cities etc., but also states of mind, impulses, claims, etc.; cf. 2 Cor. 11:12).

B. **Radical *ekkóptein* in the Sayings of Jesus.**

1. In the repeated parable of the unfruitful tree (Mt. 7:19; Lk. 13:7, 9), hewing down denotes irrevocable destruction either temporal or eternal (Mt. 3:10; 7:19). The warning against Gentile arrogance in Rom. 11:22 is a parallel.

2. The demanded cutting off of an offending member in Mt. 5:30; 18:8 denotes the seriousness of the decision that discipleship requires. The principle of punishing the sinning member is often found in rabbinic writings. In the sayings of Jesus, however, we have self-punishment rather than a judicious penalty. Against the eschatological background of the teaching of Jesus, the thought is that it is better to lose members in this life, or even this life itself, if that is the only way to avoid eternal loss and attain to eternal life (cf. Mt. 16:26).   [G. STÄHLIN, III, 830-60]

---

korbán [gift], **korbanás** [temple treasury]

---

1. *korbán* is the loanword from the Hebrew. It is a technical term which Josephus explains as referring to advantages that accrue from the dedication of oneself to God (*Antiquities* 4.72-73). The form *korbanás* denotes the temple treasury as the repository of what is offered as *korbán* (*Jewish War* 2.175).

2. *korbán in the OT and Later Judaism.* In the OT *korbán* is "what is offered," more particularly to God (cf. Num. 7:3). All kinds of offerings, not just sacrifices, are included. We find the same general use in later Judaism, but now the term is also a vow formula when something is offered to God, either in sacrifice or by a transfer of use, i.e., a withdrawal from secular use and control. The "something" may be objects, foods, etc., but it may also be individuals or groups or even the whole people. It does not mean that the people or objects are made over to the temple but simply that they are subject to a transfer of control. *korbán* may take the form of personal renunciation but it may also be a means of denying to others the use of one's person or possessions (whether to exert pressure, to take revenge, or to inflict injury). It can thus lead to a breach of relations even within the marriage or family, and in view of the simplicity but drastic consequences of the process the rabbis try to find ways to reverse the vow or to soften the consequences, though the date of such efforts is much disputed.

3. *korbán in the NT.*

a. In Mt. 27:6 the chief priests rule that the silver pieces that Judas wants to return are not suitable for the *korbanás*, i.e., the temple treasury, even though Judas has put them in the temple and they probably come originally from the treasury. The reason given is that they are blood money and hence unclean.

b. *korbán* occurs only in Mk. 7:10ff. in the debate with the scribes and Pharisees. Mt. 15:3ff. uses *dóron* in the sense of "offering" (cf. 5:23-24; 8:4, etc.; also Heb. 5:1; 8:3-4; 9:9; 11:4). The argument of Jesus is that the scribes uphold a vow (*korbán*) taken by a son even though it releases him from all obligations to his parents. The scribal argument (based on Num. 30:2-3) is that vows to God always take precedence. In reply Jesus quotes Is. 29:13. The scribes cannot truly do justice to their concern for fulfilment of the law because they forget that God's love and justice coincide and that God's concern is for human welfare. Jesus does not wish to weaken the validity of Scripture but to put it in its full context in which the goal may be sanctification but sanctification itself leads on to lovingkindness. The fourth commandment expresses this, but the defended practice of *korbán* becomes a means of evasion.

4. *The Early Church.* Early exegesis takes the saying only along the lines of Lk. 21:4 (which has *tá dóra*); the Latin *corban* is the poor box, and almsgiving is viewed as a sacrifice that is brought to God. Later this usage drops away.

[K. H. RENGSTORF, III, 860-66]

---

kosméō [to order], **kósmos** [world], **kósmios** [well-mannered], **kosmikós** [earthly, worldly]

---

kosméō. This verb means "to order," hence "to command" or "to regulate," also "to adorn," "to furnish," and "to bring honor to." The LXX has it for "to adorn" (e.g., Jer. 4:30; 2 Chr. 3:6); we find "to order" in Sir. 29:26. In the NT the only instance of "to put in order" is in Mt. 25:7; elsewhere the sense is "to adorn," e.g., women (1 Tim. 2:9), the temple (Lk. 21:5), graves (Mt. 23:29), and figuratively the doctrine (Tit. 2:10).

kósmos.

A. Nonbiblical Usage.

1. Of uncertain etymology, *kósmos* has various senses connected with "order." It thus denotes "what is well assembled or constructed from its individual parts."

2. When what is constructed consists of people, we find the sense of "human order," e.g., of rowers, of an army, or of a city or state.

3. The general sense of "order" (e.g., "right order") is also common.

4. Since what is well ordered is also beautiful, *kósmos* may denote "adornment" (women, buildings, walls, cultic actions, etc.).

5. *kósmos* as "World." I. The Greek View.

a. The senses previously mentioned all merge in that of the cosmic order. The use of *kósmos* for the universe is widespread and goes back to an early period. The idea is that there is an order of things that corresponds to the order of human law. Individual things are at odds, as people engage in disputes, but an immanent cosmic norm holds things together as law does society. The world itself is thus viewed as an ordered society.

b. The first use of *kósmos* for the universe refers to the order that constitutes it a totality rather than to the universe itself. Only later does the term come to mean the totality that is constituted by this order. When exactly the word acquires the spatial sense is much debated. The idea of a cosmos in the spatial sense is undoubtedly present in the fifth century B.C.; questions of space and infinity arise already in the natural philosophy of this period.

c. Plato uses *kósmos* in the spatial sense, though with an underlying sense of order. For Plato the *kósmos,* manifesting the "idea" in space, is a living creature. Embracing the visible, it reflects what can be known only by reason. An interesting point in Plato, as in other authors, is the merging of the ideas of cosmic space and heavenly space, so that heaven and cosmos tend to be exchangeable terms.

d. Aristotle makes the same equation of heaven and cosmos, but in this connection he is not using heaven in its narrower sense. The cosmos is the totality of things. It is for Aristotle a spherical body with the unmoved spherical earth at its heart. Embracing time and space, the cosmos is itself infinite. But it has no soul or reason; reason controls only the heavenly spheres, and only what is supracosmic enjoys the perfection that is incorruptible and impassible. There can be no plurality of worlds, whether successively or simultaneously.

e. After Aristotle Near Eastern influences affect ancient cosmology. The Aristotelian view prevails in philosophy in NT times. This puts the earth at the center of things. Firm and unmoved, it is the source and home of living creatures. The universe is above it on every side, and what is above all is the abode of the gods that is called heaven.

f. The distinctive features of the Greek view are as follows. (i) Unity characterizes the cosmos. Even though individual things might be called *kósmoi,* each of such *kósmoi* is a perfect unity of individual constituents. (ii) This cosmic unity derives from an immanent norm that integrates the individual things into a totality. Various attempts are made to describe this norm, e.g., in terms of the social order, mathematics, or the *lógos* that is also the norm of human thought and conduct. (iii) Beauty is a feature of the ordered cosmos. Its form and movement express this; to contemplate it is supreme bliss. (iv) Human beings stand in unique relation to the cosmos; law and *lógos* are special connecting points.

6. *kósmos* as "World." *II. God and the Cosmos for the Greeks.*

a. Greek philosophy discusses the theologically important questions of the origin and duration of the cosmos.

b. Heraclitus postulates an infinite cosmos, with no beginning or end, but with periodic glowing and dying down. What he opposes is not the creation of the cosmos but its formation from original matter.

c. In contrast Plato accepts the ordering or fashioning of the cosmos in space in accordance with an idea of perfect being. There is here no true distinction between Creator and creature, for Plato's demiurge is not truly God and the cosmos itself is in a lower sense divine.

d. For Aristotle the cosmos is eternal and God is not a demiurge (or architect of the world) but *noús,* pure form, the unmoved mover, the object and not the subject of love.

e. In Stoicism we find a becoming and perishing of the world but also the idea of eternal recurrence, so that the genesis is not an absolute beginning nor the perishing an absolute end. God is here neither demiurge nor unmoved mover but the world soul that permeates all things, the reason that rules all things. In later Stoicism, however, this pure pantheism yields to a new belief in transcendental divine power.

f. Philo, heir to both Judaism and Hellenism, makes great use of the term cosmos. On the basis of Gen. 1:1-2 he distinguishes the noetic cosmos and the empirical cosmos; the former is a spiritual model of the latter, and it is this world of ideas that is created on the first day. The empirical cosmos is a perfect world of order whose beauty Philo extols. God is the transcendent Creator, but Philo does justice to Stoic concerns by means of the mediating *lógos*. While speaking of a beginning of the cosmos, he seems to assume that it is made out of formless matter, and it has no apparent end. Like Plato, he calls God the Father of the cosmos, but develops this concept in Near Eastern fashion when he teaches the birth of the cosmos from God.

g. Plotinus postulates two worlds, the intelligible and the phenomenal. While both are ordered and beautiful, the former, which is the archetype, is far more so. It contains nothing finite, evil, imperfect, or discordant. The phenomenal world is beautiful as its copy or reflection.

h. The term *kósmos* also makes its way into religious and cultic speech. Although it banishes earlier nature myths, syncretistic Gnosticism combines it with cosmogonic materials from Near Eastern religions. The cosmos becomes here a kind of mythological personage and the subject of fantastic speculations, e.g., as a living creature with a soul, as the image of God, or even as the body of a god with its parts or elements as the members. The cosmos is also integrated with such entities as God, aeon, and time into a ladder of being.

7. *kósmos* as World in the Sense of Earth, Inhabited World, Humanity. As the term *kósmos* might mean "heaven," so it can be used for "earth" as distinct from heaven or the underworld. It can also denote the totality of creatures inhabiting the world, or the human inhabitants, i.e., humanity.

B. *kósmos* **in the LXX. The Concept of the Cosmos in Judaism.**

1. The adoption of the term *kósmos* by the LXX is an important event in its history, for this makes of it a biblical as well as a philosophical concept. The LXX uses *kósmos* for (a) the "host (of heaven)" (cf. Gen. 2:1; Dt. 4:19), thus combining such ideas as

order, adornment, world, heaven, and stars; (b) "adornment" as the equivalent of various Hebrew terms, as in Ex. 33:5; Prov. 20:29; Is. 3:24; Nah. 2:10; (c) "adornment" with no Hebrew equivalent, as in Is. 49:18; Prov. 28:17; Sir. 6:30, etc.; 1 Macc. 1:22; 2:11; (d) "universe," substituting it in such books as Wisdom and Maccabees for the older term "heaven and earth."

2. Since *kósmos* for "universe" becomes common only in the later Greek works, it is obviously adopted by Hellenistic Judaism from contemporary usage and bears some imprint of philosophical teaching. The fact that God can be called the Creator, Lord, and King of the cosmos shows that it has probably come into liturgical use. The phrase "to come into the world" is a stereotyped one.

3. Under the influence of the use of *kósmos* a Hebrew term like *'ôlām* takes on a new spatial sense (cf. the rabbinic adoption of *kosmikós* as a loanword). The Greek idea of humanity as microcosm also finds entry into rabbinic thinking.

C. *kósmos* in the NT.

1. General. kósmos in the Sense of Adornment. In the NT *kósmos* never means "order," and it occurs for "adornment" only in 1 Pet. 3:3 (women). In all the other references the meaning is "world." The distribution is uneven: 78 references in John, 22 in 1 John, one in 2 John, three in Revelation, 46 in Paul, 15 in the Synoptists, five each in Hebrews, James, and 2 Peter, and one in Acts. Jesus himself constantly uses "heaven and earth" for the cosmos. Whether *kósmos* ever means "totality" depends on the exposition of Jms. 3:6, which might mean that the tongue is the "epitome" of unrighteousness, but is more likely calling it a "world" of iniquity, or the evil "world" among our members.

2. kósmos as World. I. The Universe, the Sum of All Created Being.

a. As "universe," *kósmos* is synonymous with the OT "heaven and earth" (Acts 17:24). It is the place where all creatures dwell, and has a spatial reference (cf. Jn. 21:25). It may still be distinguished from the things that fill it (Acts 17:24; cf. 4:24), and under OT influence, which does not yet see the universe as a unity, it may be indicated by its constituent parts (Rev. 10:6). Yet the idea that the cosmos is the totality of all created things finds expression in verses like Jn. 1:10, where *kósmos* is the equivalent of "all things" (cf. 1 Cor. 8:6; 15:27-28; Phil. 3:21; Col. 1:16-17; Eph. 1:10; Heb. 1:2-3).

b. The *kósmos* is of limited duration. Thus we read of its beginning (Mt. 24:21), creation (Rom. 1:20), or foundation (Lk. 11:50; Heb. 4:3), and also of its end as the end of the age (Eph. 2:2). Transitoriness characterizes all that is created (2 Pet. 1:4). The world passes away (1 Jn. 2:17); it is thus "this world" in contrast to the imperishable world to come (1 Cor. 3:19; cf. 2:6; Jn. 12:31; 16:11). The NT, however, avoids *kósmos* when speaking of the world to come. The present *kósmos* is alienated from its Creator. It is thus thought that the term is unsuitable to denote the eternal world of eschatological hope. The term *aión* is preferred for this. Similarly, the NT usually avoids *kósmos* in relation to God (apart from Acts 17:24). Thus it never calls God the King or Lord of the cosmos but has instead King of the ages (1 Tim. 1:17) or Lord of heaven and earth (Mt. 11:25; cf. Acts 17:24). For the present, this world stands in the power of the ruler of this world (Jn. 14:30); the fulfilment of God's lordship over it is the object of eschatological expectation. Only when the victory is fully won will it be sung that the kingdom of the world has become the kingdom of our Lord and his Christ (Rev. 11:15).

c. In detail it may be noted that the *kósmos* is a system of spheres, notably heaven and earth, with the sea or the underworld as a third sphere. The spatial aeons of Heb. 1:2; 11:3 are to be taken in this sense.

d. Various cosmological conceptions are linked with the term *kósmos* in the NT (cf. the elements or elemental spirits of Gal. 4:3; Col. 2:8, 20). It should be noted, however, that (1) these may be clearly indicated but they are not the theme of proclamation; (2) there are no distinctive NT conceptions, only such as are shared with contemporary systems; (3) the various pieces cannot be fitted into a coherent NT cosmology or worldview on account of the differences in different books (cf. Mk. 13; 1 Cor. 15; Revelation; John); and (4) there is already in the NT (Pastorals; 2 Peter; 1 John; Jude) an incipient demarcation from Gnosticism and its cosmological interests.

3. *kósmos as World. II. The Abode of Humanity, the Theater of History, the Inhabited World, the Earth.*

a. When seen as the theater of human life, the *kósmos* is the "inhabited world." This is the sense in Mt. 4:8; Lk. 12:30; Mk. 8:36; Rom. 4:13 (merging into the "nations"); Rom. 1:8, etc.

b. There is an approximation to the sense of "humanity" in phrases like "to come into the world" (e.g., Jn. 1:9; 3:19; 11:27; 1 Tim. 1:15; 1 Jn. 4:1; 2 Jn. 7), "to be in the world" (Jn. 1:10; 9:5; 13:1; 1 Jn. 4:17; 2 Cor. 1:12; 1 Jn. 4:3), and "to go out of the world" (1 Cor. 5:10; Jn. 13:1). What is suggested in such phrases is the theater of human life. The same applies when it is said that we brought nothing into this world (1 Tim. 6:7) or when death is a departing from this world. Only when Christ is said to come into or to be in the world does a greater stress fall on cosmos, for it now has a new and distinctive NT sense as the setting of God's saving work.

4. *kósmos as World. III. Humanity, Fallen Creation, and the Setting of Salvation History.*

a. As the inhabited world, the cosmos can narrow down yet again to the "human world" or "humanity" (cf. the LXX, the Koine, and the rabbis). This sense occurs, e.g., in the great commission in Mk. 16:15; cf. Lk. 2:10; Acts 1:8. In Mt. 26:13 *kósmos* might still be taken in a spatial sense, but in Mk. 16:15 the main idea is that of preaching to all the dwellers on earth. The meaning "human world" is also the main point in verses like Mt. 5:14; 13:38; 18:7; 2 Pet. 2:5; Heb. 11:7; 1 Cor. 4:13; 4:9 (angels are included here). The human world that is hostile to God is implied in 1 Cor. 1:27-28; Heb. 11:38.

b. Since the Bible regards the *kósmos* as the object of divine creation, the OT view of God as its Judge necessarily comes to bear upon it once it is regarded as the human world (cf. Gen. 18:25; Ps. 94:2). The implication is that the human world falls victim to divine judgment because it is the evil world. Judaism develops this thought to some extent, especially in apocalyptic, which shows some influence of Persian dualism. Yet Hellenistic Judaism, which inherits Hellenistic joy in the world, maintains a more optimistic view on the basis of the fact that the cosmos is God's creation. The NT, in spite of some difference in usage, e.g., between the Synoptists and John, or Paul and John, presents a new view which puts the *kósmos* in a different light, for it is now the theater of salvation history and Christ is its Savior (Jn. 4:42; 1 Jn. 4:14).

c. Paul equates the *kósmos* and this aeon. Thus the spirit of the cosmos is the antithesis of the Spirit from God (1 Cor. 2:12). The wise of the world do not understand God's wisdom (1 Cor. 2:6ff.). Godly sorrow leads to salvation but that of the world does not (2 Cor. 7:10). It is sin that has brought this deep gulf between God and the cosmos (Rom. 5:12). The whole cosmos (humanity) is thus guilty before God (Rom. 3:19) and under his judgment (3:6) and condemnation (1 Cor. 11:32). Only the saints, who will judge the cosmos, are outside this condemnation (cf. 1 Cor. 6:2). It was the rulers of the cosmos who crucified the Lord of glory (1 Cor. 2:8). Yet as the death of Christ brings the antithesis most fully to light, Christ also removes the antithesis, for God was in Christ reconciling the cosmos to himself (2 Cor. 5:19). The reference here is primarily to humanity, yet as the cosmos is the theater of God's saving work, the term takes on a broader significance. Christ's history is true human history, but the whole universe (Rom. 8:22; Col. 1:16) has a part in it. The final goal is the destruction of every other power and the handing of the kingdom to the Father (1 Cor. 15:24-25). This view yields a full unity of concept; the cosmos comprises the universe, all individual creatures, nature and history, humanity and the spirit world. When reconciled and redeemed, the cosmos ceases to be cosmos; it is the kingdom of God, the coming aeon, the new heaven and earth. Christ comes into the cosmos to save sinners (1 Tim. 1:15); the saved are taken out of the dominion of darkness and put in the kingdom of the Son (Col. 1:13). Believers live in the cosmos (1 Cor. 5:10), honor its Creator (Acts 17:24), receive his gifts (14:15ff.), and care for things of the cosmos (1 Cor. 7:32ff.), but their true life is no longer in the cosmos (Col. 2:20). The cosmos is crucified to them and they to the cosmos (Gal. 6:14). The cosmos, then, epitomizes unredeemed creation. Believers are not to be conformed to it (Rom. 12:2; cf. Jms. 1:27). To be its friend is to be God's enemy (Jms. 4:4).

d. These thoughts come to full development in the Johannine writings. The cosmos is the universe of which Christ is the light (Jn. 8:12) and to which he comes or is sent (3:17; 10:36; 11:27, etc.). Christ and his kingdom are not of it (8:23; 18:36). In divine love he has come to save it (3:16-17). As the Lamb of God he takes away its sin (1:29). But the cosmos knows neither him nor God (1:10; 17:25). Outwardly it goes after him (12:19), but it really meets him with hatred (7:7). Hence his mission entails its judgment (12:31; 16:11). In such references the cosmos is as it were a collective person represented by its prince. Christ and the cosmos are thus opponents (14:27; cf. 1 Jn. 4:4; 5:18-19). Salvation history is a struggle between Christ and the cosmos, or the evil one who rules it (1 Jn. 4:3; 5:19). Christ is victorious in this conflict (Jn. 16:33). Believers are elected out of the cosmos (15:19; 17:6). In them the cosmos is to see that the Father in love has sent the Son (17:21). The cosmos will turn its hatred on them (15:18-19; 17:14; 1 Jn. 3:13). But they will overcome the cosmos (16:33; cf. 1 Jn. 5:4-5). They are in the world as Christ was (Jn. 17:11; cf. 9:5), but, born of God, they are no longer of it (17:16). Thus, although they are sent into it (17:17), they are not to love it, i.e., as the world of the lust of the flesh and the eyes, and the pride of life. This is not negation of the world, or contempt for it; it is the faith that overcomes the evil world.

kósmios. At first a philosophical term for the well-ordered and balanced person, this term later takes on a weaker social sense, "well-mannered" or "honorable." In the NT the only instances are in 1 Timothy. In 1 Tim. 2:9 the women are to adorn themselves in a decorous manner, and in 3:2 bishops should be disciplined and honorable.

kosmikós. This word means "cosmic," i.e., "pertaining to the world." In Heb. 9:1, 11 the OT sanctuary is "earthly" in contrast to that which is perfect; the suggestion here is that what belongs to the cosmos is transitory. In Tit. 2:12 God's grace trains us to renounce "worldly" passions, i.e., those that belong to this world and are thus hostile to God (cf. 1 Jn. 2:16). In postcanonical works the martyrs despise "earthly" torments (Mart. Pol. 2.3). Did. 11.11 refers, in a difficult phrase, to the "earthly" mystery of the church, perhaps the ascetic life that symbolizes the mystery of Eph. 5:32, or prophetic actions that represent supernatural truths.

[H. SASSE, III, 867-98]

kosmokrátōr → krátos

---

krázō [to cry], *anakrázō* [to cry out], *kraugḗ* [outcry], *kraugázō* [to cry]

Suggesting a croaking sound, *krázō* means a. "to croak or cry," and b. "to demand with cries." *anakrázō* means "to cry out," *kraugḗ* "outcry," and *kraugázō* "to cry."

A. The Use of the Terms outside the NT.

1. In the Greek world the group has religious significance in connection with the demonic sphere (invoking the gods of the underworld) and magic (incantations). The Greeks and Romans mostly felt that such crying was unworthy of the gods. The verbs also occur for proclamation, e.g., of the mysteries of Eleusis.

2. The Greek OT uses the group for crying to God in times of need. God graciously hears such crying (Ex. 22:22; Judg. 3:9; Pss. 22:5; 34:7, 17, etc.), but he will not hear the cries of the wicked (Mic. 3:4; Jer. 11:11). In the Psalms this crying takes on a special form which expresses a confident appeal for a hearing and an answer (Pss. 27:7; 28:1). There is here no magical attempt to force God; the crying to God may be both sorrowful (Ps. 22:2) and joyful (Ps. 55:17). A different usage occurs in Is. 6, where the seraphim cry "Holy, holy, holy" (v. 3). Different again is Is. 42:2, where the Servant will not cry or lift up his voice. Jeremiah, however, is to cry to God, and he is granted a great vision of restoration (33:3ff.).

3. In Judaism Josephus uses the group for the proclamation of the prophets, while the rabbis use the equivalents to introduce quotations, i.e., in the formula: "The Holy Spirit (or a prophet) cries and says. . . ."

B. The Use of the Terms in the NT.

1. In the NT the demons cry out when Jesus expels them. These are either inarticulate sounds (Mk. 5:5; 9:26) or cries of recognition (Mk. 3:11 etc.). They express the demonic resistance that Jesus overcomes. Cries for help are also addressed to Jesus, e.g., by the blind men in Mt. 9:27, the Canaanite woman in Mt. 15:22, the father of the possessed boy in Mk. 9:23, Peter on the lake in Mt. 14:30. Cries of jubilation meet Jesus on his entry into Jerusalem (Mt. 21:9, 15); if the disciples were silent, Jesus says that even the stones would cry out (Lk. 19:40). In contrast are the cries that demand his crucifixion (Mt. 27:23) and seek the release of Barabbas (Lk. 23:18). Jesus himself cries with a loud voice at his death (Mt. 27:50); this is not an inarticulate cry but a final prayer to God (Lk. 23:46). The ministry of Jesus bears the marks of the Servant of Is. 42:2 according to the quotation in Mt. 12:17ff.: "He will not wrangle or cry aloud."

2. John uses *kraugázein* rather than *(ana)krázein* for the rejoicing on Christ's entry (12:13), the demand for crucifixion (19:6), the cry that Pilate would not be Caesar's friend if he let Jesus go (19:12), and the cry: "Away with him" (19:15). Jesus himself cries with a loud voice when he raises Lazarus; he puts forth all his resources to rob death of its prey (11:43). *krázein* has a special sense in John. It denotes the declaration of the message in spite of opposition (1:15; 7:28, 37-38; 12:44-45). The mysteries of Jesus' person and work are solemnly intimated by it.

3. In Acts 19:28 the group is used for the tumultuous outcries of the mob, while in 7:60 it denotes Stephen's final prayer (cf. Lk. 23:46), in 14:14 it is crying to make oneself heard, in 23:6 it is crying to say something at a crucial point, and in 16:17 it is the crying of the possessed girl. In Revelation *krázein* has the various senses of calling on God (6:10), jubilation (7:10), proclamation (18:2), command (7:2), and lamentation (18:18-19).

4. Rom. 8:15 and Gal. 4:6 refer to the special cry of sonship, i.e., crying "Abba, Father." The point in both passages is that Christ's work results in a new relation to God in which believers are led by the Spirit (Rom. 8:14). The difference is that in Gal. 4:6 it is the Spirit who cries, whereas in Rom. 8:15 believers themselves utter the cry. There is no suggestion in either case that this is an ecstatic outcry; indeed, Rom. 8:16 implies full self-awareness. This crying is more likely that of a calling on God in which the Father of Jesus is now addressed as the Father of believers, possibly in the words that Jesus himself taught his disciples. The reference to the Spirit reminds us of the rabbinic formula ("The Spirit cries and says. . . ."), but the Spirit is now known in his dynamic reality and gives the full confidence of a hearing as believers come to God, not as servants, but as children.

5. The noun *kraugé* occurs as a cry of joy when Elizabeth greets Mary (Lk. 1:42), and when the bridegroom comes at midnight (Mt. 25:6). In Acts 23:9 it is used for the clamor after Paul's speech; believers are to avoid this kind of *kraugé* in Eph. 4:31. In Rev. 21:4 it is the anxious crying that is banished from God's eternal kingdom (cf. Jesus' prayers on the way of suffering in Heb. 5:7).

[W. GRUNDMANN, III, 898-903]

---

kráspedon [hem, border, tassel]

Originally meaning "tip of the head," this word is used for "hem," "border," and "wing" (of an army). In the NT it is used for the "tassels" which were worn on the corners of outer garments as a reminder of the commandments. Jesus accuses the Pharisees of making these unduly long in self-righteous display (Mt. 23:5). The word is also used for the "hem" of Jesus' own garment which the sick woman touches (Mt. 9:20; Lk. 8:44). Although the action verges on the magical, Jesus perceives her faith and assures her of healing. [J. SCHNEIDER, III, 904]

---

krátos [power, strength], *(theokratía* [rule of God]*)*, *kratéō* [to be strong, to seize], *krataiós* [strong, mighty], *krataióō* [to be(come) strong], *kosmokrátōr* [world ruler], *pantokrátōr* [the Almighty]

---

krátos (theokratía).

1. This word, denoting the presence of strength, means a. "natural strength," b. the "power" that one has, or with which one is invested (e.g., divine power, political power, especially in the legal sense), c. "control," and d. "supremacy," "superiority," "victory."

2. In the LXX only 20 of 50 instances are in the Hebrew canon. The reference may be to human strength (Dt. 8:17) or the strength of the bow (Ps. 76:3) or even the sea (Ps. 89:9), but mostly it is to God's strength (Ps. 62:11).

3. *krátos* occurs in Philo but is less common than *dýnamis* and *ischýs*. It usually means "strength" or "supremacy" and is often used for God's "might," with adjectives to denote its uniqueness. For Philo all things are subject to God's power; all other power is lent or derived. Knowledge of God's power induces both fear and trust.

4. The NT never says that humans can either have or gain *krátos*. In Heb. 2:14 the devil has the power of death; he controls it and uses it as an instrument (cf. 1 Cor. 15:24, 26). Elsewhere in the NT *krátos* always refers to the power of God (although in Acts 19:20 *katá krátos* is an adverbial phrase for "mightily"). The only Synoptic use is in Lk. 1:51, which stresses God's overwhelming might. Eph. 1:19-20 finds a demonstration of this power in believers on the basis of Christ's resurrection, while in Eph. 6:10 believers are to be strong in the strength of Christ's might. Col. 1:11 refers to the effective working of the divine glory in the lives of believers. In doxologies *krátos* occurs alone in 1 Pet. 5:11, with time in 1 Tim. 6:16, with *dóxa* in 1 Pet. 4:11; Rev. 1:6; 5:13, and with *exousía* in Jude 25. It denotes God's supreme and victorious power.

5. *theokratía*, which does not occur in the NT, is a term that we owe to Josephus. He coins it in analogy to aristocracy, democracy, and plutocracy. It is not, then, a term for the kingdom of God (which Josephus does not use), but has a narrower sense than what is meant by God's rule in the OT. By it he tries to describe the constitution of the Jewish state in terms familiar to his readers. Although the divine kingdom and what Josephus calls theocracy obviously overlap, so that one cannot over-rigidly distinguish the two concepts, it is important to see that for Josephus theocracy has a distinctive constitutional reference which is alien to the NT understanding of the kingdom. Since Josephus himself has *theokratía* only once in *Against Apion* 2.164-65, and the term is not immediately taken up by others, it is of no direct significance on the NT scene.

kratéō.

1. This verb, meaning "to be strong," has such nuances as "to conquer," "to seize," "to arrest," "to have the use of," and "to distrain."

2. It occurs some 170 times in the LXX in such senses as "to be strong," "to have power," "to rule," "to take control," and "to hold." The meanings in Philo are "to rule," "to conquer," and "to be lord over."

3. In the NT the main sense is "to seize." The term is used for the arrest of the Baptist (Mk. 6:17), the attempt of Jesus' family to seize him (Mk. 3:21), the attempts of his enemies to arrest him (Mk. 12:12), and the arrest of Paul (Acts 24:6). A common NT phrase is "to take by the hand" (Mk. 1:31 etc.; cf. Gen. 19:16; Is. 42:6). In Lk. 24:16 the eyes of the two disciples were "held" so that they did not recognize Jesus. Death could not "hold" Jesus (Acts 2:24), but the sailors thought that they had "obtained" their purpose with a south wind (Acts 27:13). In Revelation we find such nuances as "holding on" to a possession in 2:25, and "holding" a teaching in 2:14. "Holding fast" is the point in Mk. 7:3-4; 2 Th. 2:15; Heb. 4:14, "grasping" in Heb. 6:18. In Jn. 20:23, as the opposite of *aphíēmi*, *kratéō* means "to retain."

krataiós. This word, meaning "strong," "mighty," occurs 68 times in the LXX, 31 times with *cheír*, usually in connection with God's mighty hand, especially in the election and deliverance of Israel. The only NT instance is in 1 Pet. 5:6, which exhorts us to submit to the mighty blows of God (cf. Job 30:21).

krataióō. This word, which means "to make strong," occurs 64 times in the LXX.

In the NT we find only the passive "to become strong." In Lk. 1:80; 2:40 it denotes childhood growth. In 1 Cor. 16:13, with *andrízesthe*, the exhortation is to "be strong" (cf. 2 Sam. 10:12). Eph. 3:16 traces such strengthening to the inward operation of the Holy Spirit (cf. 2 Sam. 22:33).

kosmokrátōr. This rare and late word is used for the gods, and in astrology for the planets, as heavenly rulers. In Eph. 6:12 it is one of the terms used to describe the evil forces with which believers have to contend. It denotes the force and comprehensiveness of their designs.

pantokrátōr. This word, meaning "the almighty," "the ruler of all things," is used occasionally for the gods. The LXX adopts it as an equivalent for *ṣeḇā' ôṯ* or *šadday*. Philo has it only twice and Josephus not at all, but we find it in Jewish prayers. In the NT it comes after a series of OT quotations in 2 Cor. 6:18, and Revelation uses it for God (or Christ) in 1:8; 4:8; 11:17; 15:3; 16:7, 14; 19:6, 15; 21:22. The reference is to God's universal supremacy, but in a static sense as compared with the more dynamic sense of omnipotence.　　　　　　　　　　　　　　　[W. MICHAELIS, III, 905-15]

---

kremánnymi [to hang on, from],　　*(kremáō* [to hang]*),*　　*krémamai* [to hang], *ekkrémamai* [to hang out, on]

These words have the basic sense of "to hang on or from," and are used for the hanging of vessels, e.g., shields, helmets, quivers, as well as amulets (Ezek. 13:18). The earth hangs on nothing (Job 26:7). Absalom hangs in the branches of the tree (2 Sam. 18:9-10). The snake hangs from Paul's hand (Acts 28:4).

1. Mt. 18:6. The reference here is to a millstone hanging from or around the neck. This is not a Jewish punishment. Only God can establish this fault and impose the penalty. It is debatable whether the sense is comparative: "It would be better," or positive: "It is fitting." The suggestion seems to be that this terrible earthly punishment is preferable to the loss of eternal salvation (cf. vv. 8ff.). Salvation at the cost of life is found in rabbinic teaching (cf. also 1 Cor. 5:5).

2. Gal. 3:13. A common use of the verb in the Bible is for judicial hanging. Corpses are hung up after stoning (Dt. 21:22-23). But the term may cover not only this hanging up of the dead but also putting to death by hanging, impaling, or crucifixion (cf. Gen. 40:19, 22; Lam. 5:12). Thus it is used for the crucifixion of Jesus in Lk. 23:39; Acts 5:30; 10:39. This is what makes possible Paul's reference to Dt. 21:23. The rabbinic tradition makes the same identification when it places Jesus under a curse (like Haman or Absalom). Paul accepts the fact that Jesus comes under the curse of Dt. 21:23, but by his vicarious bearing of this curse he redeems us from the curse of the law and brings the promised blessing of Abraham to all peoples.

3. Mt. 22:40. The verb has here the figurative sense "to be dependent on." There are parallels for this sense in the Greek world (usually with a preposition), and we also find efforts to reduce moral laws to basic principles both in classical and rabbinic authors. In the NT the law of love is everywhere regarded as preeminent (cf. Rom. 13:9; Gal. 5:14). The fact that love of neighbor is sometimes mentioned alone, sometimes made secondary, and sometimes set alongside love of God, is of no essential significance. The metaphor of Mt. 22:40 makes all other commands depend on the law of love as on a nail. They are not ways of fulfilling this command, nor are they judged by their closeness to it. Rather, this command is their sustaining basis. God is the God of love, and his children must be impelled by his love and reflect it in their lives. The many commands do not derive logically from the one, nor may they be logically reduced to it. The one command of love is the fundamental law of all action in faith. Acting in the power of love, believers are freed from other demands and enjoy the liberty of sonship.

4. *Lk. 19:48.* The sense here is that of close attention ("hanging on Jesus' words"). We have in this alternative to Mt. 22:23 one of the human touches in Luke.

[G. BERTRAM, III, 915-21]

---

krínō [to judge], *krísis* [judgment], *kríma* [decision], *kritḗs* [judge], *kritḗrion* [means of judgment], *kritikós* [able to judge], *anakrínō* [to investigate], *anákrisis* [hearing], *apokrínō* [to answer], *antapokrínomai* [to reply], *apókrima* [decision], *apókrisis* [answer], *diakrínō* [to judge], *diákrisis* [discernment], *adiákritos* [impartial], *enkrínō* [to class with], *katakrínō* [to condemn], *katákrima* [condemnation], *katákrisis* [condemnation], *akatákritos* [uncondemned], *autokatákritos* [self-condemned], *prókrima* [prejudgment], *synkrínō* [to interpret]

A. **Linguistic Data.** The word *krínō* means "to sunder," then "to select," "to decide," "to judge," "to assess," "to go to law," "to seek justice," also "to expound," then "to believe," "to resolve." The LXX mostly has *krínō* for legal terms, though it may also denote deliverance for the oppressed (Ps. 72:2). The NT sense is usually "to judge" with God or man as subject and in either an official or a personal sense. We also find "to determine" in Acts 16:4, "to value" in Rom. 14:5, "to regard as" in Acts 13:46, "to think" in Acts 15:19, and "to rule" in Mt. 19:28 (a biblical sense). Theologically the most important use is for divine judgment (e.g., Rom. 2:16).

[F. BÜCHSEL, III, 921-23]

B. **The OT Term** *mišpāṭ.*

1. *The Stem špṭ.* This stem carries the double sense "to rule" and "to judge." In judging the point is not to reach a decision but to restore a relationship (Gen. 16:5). This is the emphasis in Is. 2:4 (though cf. 1 Sam. 24:13). Ruling and judging go together (1 Sam. 8:20; 2 Sam. 15:4); it is hard to say which has priority (cf. Ex. 2:14). To do justice is part of the royal office. The noun, formed with *m*, denotes judgment as a decision but also as a process. It carries the nuances of legal use, norm, and claim, but with a distinctive transition to the concepts of divine grace and salvation.

2. *God as the Giver and Guardian of mišpāṭ.* It is an ancient OT idea that God is Judge. He is both legislator and legal partner, watching over the relationships of the people and acting for it against its enemies. As the people's Ruler, God is also its Judge. His judging manifests his lordship and gives it an ethical orientation. God has made a covenant with the people. Hence all law is referred to him. The historical relation makes it possible to use legal terms theologically; this is not possible with nature gods, to which such attributes as justice and righteousness are fundamentally alien. The historical situation presupposed by "I am the Lord thy God" means that

God has taken the initiative and bases covenant commands on the covenant promise. There is no place for secular law in Israel; all legal enactments have their source in the covenant. As Judge, God is also the Guardian and Helper of his people against foreign threats (Judg. 11:27; 2 Sam. 18:31; Dt. 33:21). Israel's victories are his judgments. His protection of Israel is the universal establishment of his just rule.

3. mišpāṭ as a Relationship. Divine *mišpāṭ* is not just a legal principle or moral norm. It regulates the relationships in a specific society. God is involved with his people. He is concerned both to keep his promise and to enforce the observance of his command. His judicial decisions serve his covenant purpose, which is a purpose of salvation. Other peoples may have similar relations with other gods (cf. 1 Kgs. 18:28; 2 Kgs. 17:24ff.), but these stand in sharp contrast, as is seen in their modes of worship.

4. The Ethical and Religious Meaning of mišpāṭ. In the covenant God makes the people his own people. All the legal enactments expound the basic decision: "I will be your God, and you shall be my people." The revelation of this *mišpāṭ* underlies the obligations, but also the claims, that arise for the whole people and for each individual within it. Although there is no abstract norm of morality, God's judging necessarily means justice. The prophets give this implication ethical concreteness, especially in the ability to differentiate between right and wrong (cf. 1 Kgs. 3:9; Mic. 3:1-2; Is. 1:17; Am. 5:7), or in the championing of the cause of the poor and needy (Dt. 10:18; Is. 10:2; Am. 5:11; Jer. 5:28; Ezek. 22:29), who may not be morally superior but are at least in the right against their oppressors. A corollary is that, since the ways of God are upright, all that opposes him will finally be made subject (cf. Is. 2). God will bind up the broken and destroy the strong (Ezek. 34:16). Yet the primary orientation of *mišpāṭ* is religious; it goes forth as light, demanding that the people do right on the basis of God's self-revelation (Hos. 6:5-6; cf. Mic. 3:8; Zeph. 3:5). Jer. 9:23-24 expresses the same thought: One's only boast should be to know God, but to know God is to know his *mišpāṭ*, with an implication of an obligation to execute it too. In this light one can understand the prophetic summons to repentance. If God's judgments reveal his will, the full seriousness of commitment becomes clear. The people is set under God's blessing and curse; failure to keep God's revealed judgment means the possibility of breaking covenant. Hence the day of the Lord may be a day of judgment on Israel instead of victory over its foes (Am. 1; Hos. 4:1ff.; Is. 1:2, 18ff.; Zeph. 3:8). Judgment on Israel is at the heart of universal judgment. The only privilege of election is that of judgment with special severity. At the most only a remnant survives, and the covenant is so broken that it can continue only if God in his grace and mercy reinstitutes it.

5. The Change in Meaning of mišpāṭ. That *mišpāṭ* may thus come to mean grace and mercy is evident in Is. 30:18ff. Here it signifies salvation for an afflicted remnant. This ties in with the existing sense of judgment for the needy and oppressed. Yet this is now an act, not of justice, but of love. If *mišpāṭ* means destruction for the proud, it means help for the weak (Ex. 34:16). The Israel of the exile is weak. It may thus claim the *mišpāṭ* that protects the weak (Dt. 32:4). Yet it recognizes that meeting this claim is an exercise of mercy as well as justice (Dt. 10:18). This alters the legal content of *mišpāṭ*, for forgiveness is in tension with retribution, and judgment is shown to the people even though it has not kept the judgments of God. The lordship of God defies purely legal categorizing. As may be seen from Job, God's justice is beyond human comprehension. No one teaches God the path of justice (Is. 40:14). Yet this is not just a matter of omnipotence; it is a matter of God's faithfulness to the covenant of grace. This is his *mišpāṭ* (Dt. 32:4; Pss. 105:5ff.; 111). The elect people is judged for its sin. For this reason *mišpāṭ* is far from it (Is. 59:9ff.). The presence of righteous individuals does not alter this. The only hope is divine *mišpāṭ* which will cancel sin and set up the covenant afresh (cf. Jer. 30–31; Hos. 2:20ff.; Is. 28:17). The Messiah will establish the kingdom with justice and righteousness (Is. 9:6ff.). The people, having God's Spirit, will observe his judgments (Ezek. 36:27). Judgment of the wicked is the reverse side of this saving *mišpāṭ* (Is. 1:27-28), but this is not a causal succession, since the only basis of salvation is pardoning grace. Tension remains, however, in view of the fact that *mišpāṭ* denotes both salvation and judgment.

6. *mišpāṭ in Its Relation to the Nations.* God's *mišpāṭ* is part of his rule. It thus applies to the nations that have observed their own judgments instead of God's (Ezek. 5:6ff.). In a sense such judgments come from God (Ezek. 22:25) in execution of his negative judgment. Yet God's *mišpāṭ* may also be positive in relation to the nations. Thus God puts his Spirit on his Servant so that he may bring *mišpāṭ* to the nations. In a universal extension this means salvation for the nations and mercy for the oppressed. God himself sends forth his *mišpāṭ* as a light for the peoples (Is. 51:4); this will mean deliverance and salvation for them (v. 5). *mišpāṭ*, then, is the gracious revelation of God which is the basis of his relationship not merely to the chosen people but to all peoples.   [V. HERNTRICH, III, 923-33]

C. The Concept of Judgment in the Greek World. For the Greeks the gods are the guardians of right and custom. At first, they are themselves capricious, so that they have to be placated. They are also the executors of fate. But the belief develops that Zeus rules as judge and causes right to triumph and wrong to be punished in this world. There is at first no thought of future judgment; death is the common lot. The Orphics, with their belief in transmigration, are the first to proclaim a judgment in the underworld, although this is not final retribution but assignment of the next transitional stage. Adopted by Pindar, Plato, etc., the idea of future judgment becomes part of the philosophical tradition. The enlightenment destroys the belief in gods of judgment, but the concept of judgment after death persists in both popular belief and philosophical teaching.

D. The Concept of Judgment in Judaism. It is a cardinal article of Judaism that God judges, that he resists evil and rewards good, that he upholds the law, and enforces it in spite of infractions. Individual judgments are seen for individual sins, but since this does not always work out, there develops an expectation of future judgment on sinners (both Jewish and Gentile) which will also bring salvation to Israel. Since judgment will fall on individual Jewish sinners, Pharisaic groups experience some tension between fear of judgment and the confidence granted by scrupulous observance of the law. On the details of judgment, there is the widest possible variety of views. The hope of forgiveness, of course, never dies.

E. The Concept of Judgment in the NT.
1. The Baptist. John the Baptist proclaims the direct imminence of divine judgment and therefore the urgent need to repent and be baptized with a view to divine forgiveness and the amendment of life (Mt. 3:7ff.).

2. The Synoptic Preaching of Jesus. Jesus issues a similar call to repentance because of the seriousness of sin and of God's judgment on it (cf. Mt. 5:22ff.; 7:21ff.; 10:28, 33; 13:47ff.; 24:50-51; 11:20ff.; 23:13ff.). Merits are of no avail (Lk. 17:7ff.). The law is the standard, i.e., the law of love. Judgment may be executed by God (Mt. 10:32-33) or by Jesus himself (Mt. 7:22-23), and it falls on both Jews and Gentiles

(Mt. 25:32), for all are responsible to God. The ground of deliverance is forgiveness. A gift of grace, this is promised by Jesus (Mk. 2:9; Lk. 7:36ff.), so that his disciples may look forward to the last day, and pray for the coming of the kingdom (Mt. 6:10). Forgiveness is enjoyed only in personal fellowship with Jesus. It must be prayed for (Mt. 6:12) and involves a readiness to forgive others (Mt. 6:14). This does not mean that divine forgiveness is made conditional on our human forgiveness; it means that the absence of human forgiveness is meaningless and nonsensical where divine forgiveness is known. The fact that the preacher is the judge (cf. Mk. 14:62) gives a unique urgency to the message of Jesus. It means that the message itself entails eternal decision. If rejected, it leaves no other ground of hope at the last judgment. If accepted, it brings true liberation from judgment. Jesus' opponents cannot understand this assurance of liberation (Mk. 2:7), and they thus bring Jesus to the death by which this liberation is effected. Jesus' concept of judgment is crucial. If it is wrong, his ministry has no relevance for our relationship with God. If it is right, our situation is hopeless and intolerable apart from his forgiving word.

3. Paul. Paul proclaims the coming day of God's righteous judgment (Rom. 2:1ff.). All must come before God's judgment seat (2 Cor. 5:10). God's wrath on wicked works is already manifest (Rom. 1:18ff.), but his goodness leaves space for repentance (Rom. 2:4). The final decision is still future, and this makes the question of justification the critical one in human life. The answer lies in God's justifying grace set forth in Christ (Rom. 5:9-10). On this basis sinners can have assurance of salvation in the judgment (Rom. 8:31ff.; 1 Cor. 3:15).

4. John. John, too, expects a last judgment when the dead shall be raised (Jn. 5:28-29; 1 Jn. 4:17). Judgment is committed to the Son (Jn. 5:22). Jesus has come to save, not to judge (Jn. 3:17), but his word will still judge on the last day (12:48). Indeed, judgment takes place already on unbelievers (3:18-19). Similarly, believers will not come into judgment (5:24). They need have no fear of the last day (1 Jn. 4:17). This world and its ruler are also judged already (Jn. 12:31; 16:11) with the self-dedication of the Son (12:27ff.). In the assurance of faith, the eternal is present in time.

5. Revelation. Revelation presents a terrifying picture of judgment (20:11ff.) and issues serious warnings to the churches (2–3). Christ himself has a crucial role in the judgment which establishes God's rule and initiates the new heaven and earth.

6. Peter and Hebrews. 1 Peter urges fear of God as Judge (2:17) and warns that judgment must begin in God's house (4:17). Hebrews has a plea against taking judgment too lightly (10:26ff.) and an exhortation to serve God with reverence and awe, for he is a consuming fire (12:28-29).

7. Human Judgment. In the light of God's judgment, we should not judge one another (Mt. 7:1-2; Jms. 4:11; Rom. 14:4, 10; 1 Cor. 4:5). This does not mean flabby indifference to moral wrong but recognition of solidarity in guilt. Thus church discipline must not be harsh and condemnatory; it must use the methods of edification and pastoral care. The very seriousness of divine judgment preserves the church from legalistic judgmentalism.

8. Conclusion. In the NT judgment does not have the capricious and emotional aspects that mark divine judgments in myth. All human acts are a sowing (Gal. 6:7-8). God's judgment is a repayment (Rom. 1:27). There is an organic relation between act and consequence. God judges in holy wrath, not in mere passion. As Creator he has established a moral order of being. His demands correspond to the very structure of human life and thus decide its destiny. Obedience or disobedience to them will mean integration with the created order or friction with it. If obedience brings life, disobedience means restriction of life and finally death (Rom. 6:23). This judgment begins in this life and is consummated in the next (Rom. 1:18ff. and 2:3ff.). The restriction is not just external; it is primarily internal, leading to the hollowness portrayed by Jesus in Lk. 16:19ff.; 18:10ff.; 12:16ff., and the impoverishment depicted by Paul in Rom. 1:21ff. It is God who has established the relation between the order of being and his demands, and it is God, therefore, who may justly judge. The images associated with judgment may be traditional, but judgment itself lays bare our hidden essence (Rom. 2:16), exposing the hypocrisy of acting only for show, for hope of reward, or for fear (cf. Mt. 6:1ff.; 1 Cor. 4:5-6), and summoning us to true love of God on the basis and in the power of God's love for us. The very proclamation of God's love presupposes that without God's saving work we are moving hopelessly to judgment. To excise or restrict the thought of divine judgment is thus to destroy the gospel.

krísis. This word, denoting an act, has such senses as a. "estrangement," "conflict," b. "selection," c. "decision," "judgment," "verdict," even "accusation," and d. "decision" in a battle or illness.
1. In the NT it means first "judicial decision," "judgment."
2. In John it is the world "judgment" of Christ, future (Jn. 5:28-29), yet already present (3:18ff.). The sense of "decision" is included, but this does not wholly replace that of "judgment."
3. The LXX uses *krísis* for the "right" of the oppressed (Ps. 101:1), and this explains the use in Mt. 23:23; Lk. 11:42, where the reproach is not that the Pharisees neglect judgment but that they are indifferent to the rights of the poor (cf. Mt. 12:18ff. quoting Is. 42:1ff. and Acts 8:32-33 quoting Is. 53:7-8).

kríma. This word means the "decision" of a judge a. as an action (Jn. 9:39; Acts 24:25, etc.) and b. as a sentence, usually condemnation (human as well as divine). In 1 Cor. 6:7 the reference is to a legal action or process. In Rev. 18:20, on an LXX basis, the thought of a legal claim is present (cf. Zech. 7:9; Jer. 21:12).

kritḗs. In the NT the *kritḗs* is usually a judge, whether official (Mt. 5:25 etc.) or not (Jms. 2:4). The OT judges are *kritaí* in Acts 13:20. God is *kritḗs* in 2 Tim. 4:8; Heb. 12:23; Jms. 4:12, and Christ in Acts 10:42.

kritḗrion. This word denotes the means of judging, the place of judgment, or judgment. The sense in 1 Cor. 6:2, 4 is "legal process."

kritikós. This word has reference to the manner, ability, right, or action of a judge. In Heb. 4:12 it describes God's word as able to judge inner thoughts and intents.

anakrínō, anákrisis. *anakrínō* means "to investigate," and refers mostly to judicial interrogation (Lk. 23:14; Acts 4:9; 12:19, etc.). Paul uses it ironically in 1 Cor. 4:3. In 1 Cor. 14:24 it means "to inquire into." It can be used for the searching of Scripture in Acts 17:11 and for spiritual discernment in 1 Cor. 2:14-15. The spiritual judge all things and are judged by none, not in superiority, but because they are subject to the Lord and are thus the servants of others. They respect the consciences of others (Rom. 14) but correct them when they live after the flesh (2 Cor. 12:19ff.). The communities are united only through Christ; they are thus pneumatic organisms with a unity of love and not of compulsion.

apokrínō, antapokrínomai. *apokrínō* has such senses as "to separate," "to secrete," "to dedicate," and "to condemn," while *apokrínomai* means "to separate oneself," "to vindicate oneself," and "to answer." The NT has *apokrínomai* only for "to answer" (a question, request, etc.), usually with *légein* etc. Often there is no answer to anything that has just been said, so that the force is "to begin to speak" (an idiom of the LXX based on the Hebrew). *antapokrínomai* is a stronger form in Lk. 14:6; Rom. 9:20; it carries the implication that the objections raised are groundless.

apókrima. This rare word denotes an official resolution that decides a matter. This is the point in 2 Cor. 1:9. From a human angle Paul is like a person who has received a sentence of condemnation. He does not name the author of the decision; he is condemned *to* death, not *by* it.

apókrisis. This common word means a. "separation," "secretion," and b. "answer." The NT has it only in sense b. (Lk. 2:47; 20:26; Jn. 1:22; 19:9).

diakrínō.

1. A stronger form of *krínō,* this word has many senses. In the NT it means "to distinguish between persons" (Acts 15:9), then "to judge" (1 Cor. 6:5; Mt. 16:3). In the middle *diakrínomai* means "to contend" (Jude 9) and "to doubt" (Mk. 11:23; Mt. 21:21; Jms. 1:6; Rom. 4:20).

2. NT doubt comes to expression in prayer and action, not in thought. What is doubted is God's word. Doubt is not philosophical skepticism nor is it the uncertainty of conflicting motives. In Mk. 11:23 it is a final lack of faith that God can really do what is requested. It involves wavering or inconstancy (Jms. 1:6). Abraham is an example of truth faith; he accepts God's promise without distrust or wavering (Rom. 4:20). The element of inner division is apparent in Rom. 14:23, where the doubter has no certainty of faith that what is done is right (cf. Acts 10:20). Inconsistency is the point in Jms. 2:4. Despising the poor is at odds with the faith that is professed by going to the assembly.

3. This kind of doubt does not appear in the OT, where rejection of God's word is a deliberate attitude rather than a lack of certainty or consistency. Job is a fighter rather than a doubter. Later Judaism censures pusillanimity in prayer (cf. Mk. 11:23), but doubt in the NT sense comes only with the full unconditionality of grace in Christ, which intensifies the demand for a full committal of faith.

4. Greek normally uses *distázō* for "to doubt" (cf. in the NT Mt. 14:31; 28:17). The NT has *dialogismós* in the same sense. *diakrínesthai* for "to doubt" is rare even in later Christian writings, which prefer *distázō*. The Semitic originals express the thought of "divided or divergent opinion."

diákrisis. This word has such varied meanings as "separation," "distinction," "strife," "appraisal," and "exposition." In the NT it usually means "discernment" or "differentiation" (between spirits in 1 Cor. 12:10, between good and evil in Heb. 5:14). In Rom. 14:1 the point is obscure. The meaning might be "not for disputes," but another possibility is "not for evaluation."

adiákritos. This word, too, has many senses, e.g., "indistinguishable," "imprecise," "obscure," "impartial," "without distinction." In the only LXX instance (Prov. 25:1) it perhaps means "uncertain." In Jms. 3:17, the one occurrence in the NT, it means "without doubts or hypocrisy." In the apostolic fathers we find it in Ignatius for "unshakable" (*Ephesians* 3.2; *Trallians* 1.1, etc.).

enkrínō. Found in the NT only in 2 Cor. 10:12, this word means "to count among," "to class with."

katakrínō, katákrima, kátakrisis. katakrínō means "to condemn." In human judgment it is the verdict as distinguished from its execution, but the two converge in divine judgment (cf. Mk. 16:16; 1 Cor. 11:32; 2 Pet. 2:6). Both sentence and execution seem to be in view in Rom. 8:3; Paul has in mind the totality of what God has done and does through Christ, i.e., the whole movement from the incarnation to the imparting of the Spirit (v. 4). The condemnation is universally valid but is efficacious only for those who are in Christ (cf. 2 Cor. 5:17). It is the removal of the enmity between God and us (Rom. 8:7). The law condemns us and we perish, but in Christ God condemns sin and we are free.

katákrima, too, refers in the NT to the total divine "condemnation" (Rom. 5:16, 18; 8:1). In Rom. 8:1 it covers the results as well (cf. v. 2).

katákrisis, "condemnation," is used in the NT only by Paul in 2 Cor. 3:9; 7:3. By reason of sin the old covenant is one of condemnation that can only bring death (3:6ff.). Paul does not speak in condemnation but in self-sacrificial love (7:2ff.).

akatákritos, autokatákritos. The former of these words occurs in the NT only in a legal connection in Acts 16:37, where Paul protests that he and Silas have been badly treated while still "uncondemned." The later term, meaning "self-condemned," occurs in Tit. 3:11 for the person who is unrepentant even after a twofold admonition.

prókrima. This word occurs in the NT only in 1 Tim. 5:21. It has here, not the stricter legal sense of a "precedent," but the more general moral sense of "prejudgment."

synkrínō. This word has the varied senses "to unite," "to compare," "to measure," "to evaluate," and "to interpret." In 2 Cor. 10:12 it means "to compare." Paul will not be compared with the arrogant pseudo-apostles; let them compare themselves with one another. The sense in 1 Cor. 2:13 is hard to fix. "To unite" is too weak, "to compare" brings in an alien thought, "to evaluate" hardly fits the context, and it thus seems best to render "to interpret" or "to expound": interpreting the truths revealed by the Spirit.   [F. Büchsel, III, 933-54]

> ## *kroúō* [to knock]

kroúō means "to strike," "to knock" in various contexts, e.g., driving in nails, or knocking at doors. The NT has the secular sense of knocking at a door in Acts 12:13, 16, but it also makes double use of knocking at the door as a metaphor.

1. In Mt. 7:7-8 and Lk. 11:9-10 knocking signifies the seeking of entry by believers. Seeking and knocking stress the material content of asking. The point is not the general one that prayer may count on an answer, or that action is the presupposition of fulfilment, but the specific one that God's promise of salvation gives us the assurance in faith that when we knock the door will be opened and access made possible. In contrast, there is a useless knocking in Lk. 13:25. This knocking is a tardy attempt to gain entry after an earlier refusal to knock in faith (cf. v. 24) when the door would have been readily opened. Those who engage in this futile knocking do not trust in him who opens and shuts (Rev. 3:7). Refusing to knock and enter when they should, they have shut themselves out.

2. In Lk. 12:36 and Rev. 3:20 the Lord himself knocks. Lk. 12:35-36 is an exhortation to watchfulness, so that there may be an instant readiness to receive Christ at his coming. In Rev. 3:20 it is the risen Lord who speaks. On the basis of Cant. 5:2,

6 this is often taken to refer to personal union with Christ, but in context it carries a serious admonition and promise to the church of Laodicea. The saying transcends both eschatology and mysticism and proclaims the gospel of the coming of Christ, both present and future, with the decision that this demands and the life that it brings for those who receive him. [G. BERTRAM, III, 954-57]

> *krýptō* [to hide], *apokrýptō* [to hide], *kryptós* [hidden, secret], *kryphaíos* [hidden], *kryphḗ* [secretly], *krýptē* [cellar], *apókryphos* [hidden]

A. Occurrence and Meaning. *krýptō* has the basic sense "to cover," "to conceal" (either protectively or for selfish reasons). It then means a. "to bury," and b. "to set" (of constellations, also used in eclipses). Figuratively it means "to keep secret" (with accusative, double accusative, or preposition, often shameful things), but also "to overlook" and hence "to pardon." *krýptein* may also denote the keeping of entrusted secrets, as in the mysteries. *apokrýptō* means "to cover," "to conceal," and figuratively "to keep secret" (usually in a good sense). Intransitively both terms may be used for "to disappear from sight." *kryptós* means "covered," "hidden," and figuratively "secret." The *kryptoí* are secret police in Sparta, and the word at times acquires a nuance of cunning. Secret sins are particularly shameful or abominable. *kryphaíos* is a rare word for "hidden," *kryphḗ* means "secretly," *krýptē* is a "vault" or "cellar," and *apókryphos* means "hidden" (e.g., treasure) or "secret."

B. Theological Significance of the Terms.

I. The Greek and Hellenistic World.

1. Popular Religion. The hiddenness of deity produces a numinous element in Greek religion. The riddle of death and the related cult of chthonic deities and heroes strengthens this. Yet the numinous aspect should not be overrated, for the deity does not have absolute knowledge or control (being subject to fate). Indeed, the Greeks show great familiarity with their gods (who finally may become affable and even impotent), so that the group is not at first common in religious contexts.

2. Mysticism, Gnosticism, and Philosophy.

a. The mysteries do not stress secrecy. The Eleusinians are like a private cult society. Alien mysteries make a difference, but often with more reference to the secrecy of the cult than to the concealment of the deity.

b. Orphism teaches a deity that is visible in all things but also hidden inasmuch as the universal body of the deity is an esoteric doctrine. Greek and Near Eastern influences converge in Gnosticism with its concepts of hidden but self-revealing deity and of esoteric knowledge. *apókryphos* becomes here a technical term for secret books or inscriptions (written in cryptograms). Astrologers make much use of the group; thus *apókrypha* are dark affairs (either criminal or mantic) which *mýstai* alone can penetrate; these *mýstai* are grouped with mathematicians and athletes.

c. At a later period Greek philosophy is connected with the secret wisdom of the Near East. There is some truth in this, and although natural philosophy seeks a scientific explanation of things, it accepts the inscrutability of nature and the gods. The element of hiddenness increases as antiquity declines, but the *krýptō* group is rare. The term "to conceal" is important in Stoic ethics; the Cynic differs from others in living an open life and having nothing to hide.

II. The Old Testament.

1. Hebrew has seven roots (see *TDNT*, III, 967) to express the idea of concealment, and their use is extremely loose and varied. A first theological use is to denote the essential distinction between God and us. God may show himself but he wills concealment (1 Kgs. 8:12), his works are hidden (Sir. 11:4), he knows hidden things (Dt. 29:28), and to see him is fatal (Is. 6:5).

2. Nothing is hidden from God (Dan. 2:22). Sinners cannot remain hidden (Jer. 16:17). God has total knowledge of his human creatures (Ps. 139).

3. Sinners try to flee from God. They lurk in darkness (Ps. 10:8), offend in secret (Ezek. 8:12), set up images in secret (Dt. 27:15), avoid God (cf. Adam, Cain, and Achan), and when judgment comes try to hide in the rocks (Is. 2:10).

4. The righteous disclose everything, and this opens the way to the restoration of fellowship (Pss. 32:1ff.; 19:12). The penitential psalms are formally parallel to those of Babylon, but the latter are polytheistic, ritual, and pessimistic.

5. When fellowship is restored, the righteous take comfort in knowing that their ways are not hidden from God. No less than their sin, their sighing is not hidden (Ps. 38:9). Only those of little faith think the contrary (Is. 40:27).

6. God gives the elect a share in his own hidden life. He covers them in his tent in times of trouble (Ps. 27:5; cf. Is. 49:2; 4:6). Even in Sheol Job thinks he might be hidden by God (Job 14:13). God teaches wisdom in the secret heart (Ps. 51:6). Yet there is no occultism; one must keep to what is revealed (Dt. 29:29).

7. God comes out of hiddenness in self-revelation to chosen individuals (Gen. 18:17; Is. 29:10) and to the whole people once this self-revelation is available in the law (Ps. 119:19). But he hides himself from the Gentiles (Is. 45:15).

8. God controls his self-revelation. He may hide his purposes even from the prophets (2 Kgs. 4:27). There is judicial self-concealment from a sinful people (Is. 29:10). The righteous, too, experience the hiding of God's face (Job 13:24; Pss. 10:11; 44:24, etc.). This hiddenness can become intolerable (Lam. 3:6). But grace is not at an end (Lam. 3:22). One may still flee from the hidden God to the revealed God.

9. Since God's word is a treasure, one must hide it in oneself (Ps. 119:11; Prov. 2:1). What is hidden is not cosmic gnosis but the historically given word.

10. Yet what is hidden in oneself is also to be declared to others (Ps. 40:10). Jeremiah finds it impossible to stop speaking about God (Jer. 20:9). God's words and deeds are to be published among the nations (Ps. 96:2-3).

III. Judaism.

1. *Palestinian Judaism.* In the main, Palestinian Judaism thinks that present revelation has ceased. Apocalyptic tries to fill the gap, linking the discovery of hidden guilt or divine purpose with eschatology. In spite of their love for what is hidden, the rabbis have a strong sense of God's presence in nature and history and of his revelation in the law. Yet the ways of God are mysterious, especially after A.D. 70. The tension of the secret and open comes out in exegesis. Secret guilt is to be openly punished and the secret hallowing of God's name will be publicly recognized.

2. *Hellenistic Judaism.* Mystical influences may be seen in the theological use of the group in Hellenistic Judaism. Thus Reuben wants to reveal the hidden things of his heart in the Testaments of the Twelve Patriarchs, while Philo stresses God's hiddenness, uses mystical terms for the knowledge that he reads into the OT, describes God as a mystagogue, and brings the group into his ethics.

3. *Gnosticism Influenced by Judaism.* The Essenes move in a Gnostic direction with their oaths of secrecy and secret writings. In later Jewish Gnosticism the idea that

hiddenness confers honor, and the accessibility of deity only to a few elect, is a common theme. The Mandaeans speak of hidden mysteries and also of the offering to God of hidden prayers.

IV. The New Testament.

1. The Synoptists. In general the NT adopts the presuppositions of the OT, and in part of Judaism, but with the difference that eschatological expectation is now fulfilled. The kingdom is compared to hidden treasure (Mt. 13:44) or leaven (Lk. 13:21), for only God can reveal himself. Yet it has come out of concealment and God will publicly declare it (Lk. 12:2-3). Human unreceptivity forms an impediment (Lk. 18:34). God judicially withholds knowledge of himself from those who do not seriously seek it (Lk. 10:21; 19:42). This is stressed with grim severity in Mk. 4:11-12; cf. Mt. 13:34-35. Those who do find the treasure hide it again with joy (Mt. 13:44). In contrast to the Pharisees, for whose display of piety there is much rabbinic evidence, they give and fast and pray in secret, so that their Father who sees in secret may reward them openly (Mt. 6:4, 6, 18). On the other hand, they are not to conceal the talents that they receive (Mt. 25:18), but are to be like cities on a hill, or lamps on a stand, so that others may see their good works and glorify their Father in heaven (Mt. 5:16).

2. John's Gospel. This gospel mentions secret disciples (19:38; cf. 3:2; 7:50; 19:39), but with understanding rather than reproach. In the main, however, the terms are used here for the mission of Jesus, who puzzlingly seems to work in secret while seeking to be known openly (7:4). Thus he visits the feast secretly (7:10), and hides when the people wants to stone him (8:59; cf. 12:36), yet he can also claim with truth that he has spoken openly and said nothing secretly (18:20).

3. The Other NT Writings. In 2 Cor. 4:2 Paul avoids anything underhanded. The wicked, however, try to hide from God (Eph. 5:12). In the last time rulers will try in vain to seek a hiding place in the rocks (Rev. 6:15-16). God the Judge will bring all hidden things to light, both good and bad (1 Tim. 5:25; 1 Cor. 4:5). God is hidden by nature, but he gives his people a share in his hidden life (cf. the hidden manna of Rev. 2:17). The mystery concealed for aeons is now manifest to the saints (Col. 1:26). The hidden treasures of wisdom are present in Christ (Col. 2:3). The gospel proclaims God's hidden wisdom (1 Cor. 2:7ff.). Paul's language here is well suited to those with Gnostic leanings but it has its basis in the OT. This hidden wisdom relates to the plan of salvation that finds historical fulfilment in Christ (1 Cor. 2:6ff.). If true faith is a hidden matter of the heart (Rom. 2:29), the true hiddenness of Christians is eschatological, i.e., their hiddenness with Christ in God (Col. 3:3).

4. Conclusion. NT usage is rooted in OT usage; the ten aspects noted under II. all recur in it. Echoes of Gnosticism may be heard, but the true NT distinction is between Creator and creature, not between Gnostic and non-Gnostic, and the concept of the hidden but self-revealing God leads to world mission, not to esotericism. Election is present, but it bears strongly the character of decision.

V. Transition to Church History. The first writings after the NT use the group mostly in biblical quotations. For the rest, God discloses what is hidden and we find the twin thoughts of revelation and judgment. A singular use occurs in Diog. 9.5 when the death of Jesus is said to hide the sin of many.   [A. Oepke, III, 957-78]

C. Supplement on the Canon and the Apocrypha.

I. The Canon and the Apocrypha in Judaism.

1. The Term Canon. In Judaism one may speak of a closed and normative canon from the beginning of the second century (A.D.). This is the result of a process of collection, evaluation, and selection.

2. *The Early History of the Canon.*

a. The Law. This is fixed from 300 B.C. From the temple it comes into the synagogue, where it has a central role in worship, and functions as a normative code on which there can only be commentaries.

b. The Prophets. The rabbinic order lists Joshua to 2 Kings with all the prophetic books (except Daniel) in a second canonical group, but there is considerable freedom relative to them in the pre-NT period, and in the later cultus only selected portions are used, liberties are taken in reading, and edification is the primary goal in their use.

c. The Writings. These are the other books of the OT (mentioned in the Prologue to Sirach) as they are finally listed by the rabbis. At an earlier point Ruth and Lamentations are sometimes grouped with Judges and Jeremiah, Job and Daniel are reckoned as prophets, and Chronicles and Esther are also put among the historical prophets. In general, there is no fixed canon in the late second century B.C. Only the law has a secure place. This is accompanied by works of edification that are partly history and prophecy and partly poetry and instruction.

3. *The OT in the First Century A.D.* By this time we find the concept of a normative Scripture based on the law, although the full consequences of this idea are not yet drawn.

a. Canonical Works. Philo and the NT bear witness to the idea of Scripture as a totality. Philo refers to sacred writings, and the NT authors use the term "scripture" or "scriptures," also "law" for the whole of the OT. Other titles are "law and tradition," "law and prophets," and "law, prophets, and psalms" (Lk. 24:44; cf. 24:27). Mt. 24:15 numbers Daniel among the prophets, and Mt. 23:35 is perhaps putting Chronicles at the end of the canon.

b. The Later Apocrypha. In NT times the line between canon and Apocrypha is not rigidly fixed. Philo puts Proverbs and Sirach on the same level, Josephus quotes from apocryphal works, Palestinian Judaism has a high regard for Sirach and apocalypses, and early Christian authors quote apocryphal works (cf. Jude 14).

c. The LXX as a Preliminary Stage. The LXX rests on the idea of OT Scripture as a totality, although it still includes 1 Maccabees and Sirach.

4. *The Closing of the Canon by the Rabbis.*

a. The Restriction of the Prophetic Age. A sense of decline after the exile promotes the formation of the canon (cf. Zech. 13:2ff.). The rabbis (also Josephus) see prophecy as ending in the fifth or fourth century B.C., with some debate about the status of Sirach. It is also postulated that no written work precedes Moses. Possible patriarchal writings are enshrined in the law.

b. The Sacramental Holiness of the Scriptures. The idea of a material holiness indwelling Scripture, associated in part with the holiness of the divine name, gives rise to the notion that true scriptures defile the hands. Defiling the hands becomes a technical term for the concept of canonical validity. A similar notion is that of the hiding of Scripture, i.e., its abandonment to natural corruption when it becomes unserviceable or is desecrated or has a blemish. In the case of a noncanonical work, e.g., Sirach, the concept has the different sense of a withdrawal from cultic use, i.e., in reading and exposition.

c. The Battle for Individual Writings. The closing of the canon is not without friction. Thus Ezekiel has to meet the objection that it is contrary to the law and that Ezek. 1 opens the door to theosophical speculation. Ecclesiastes is also attacked as antinomian and self-contradictory. Proverbs runs into a charge of inner contradiction.

Canticles seems to be too worldly until its allegorical interpretation prevails. Esther is thought by some to be too nationalistic. In each case, however, the objections are finally overcome.

d. The Canon and Apocryphal Literature. With the closing of the canon there is discussion as to the number of books. The usual number is 24, but some favor 22, not treating Ruth and Lamentations separately. The division into the three groups of law, prophets, and writings establishes itself, but with initial debate as to the place of Job, Daniel, Chronicles, Lamentations, and Ruth. Excluded books are not necessarily heretical but their religious use is forbidden in order to make a clean break between the canon and other works. These other works may be used only for secular reading.

5. *The Influence of the Noncanonical Writings.* Although the apocryphal writings lose their equality with canonical works, they still exert an expository influence. Thus we find quotations from Sirach in the rabbis. Motifs from apocalyptic works, e.g., the rapture of the Messiah, or from apocryphal history, e.g., the martyrdom of the mother and her seven sons, also occur. [R. MEYER, III, 978-87]

II. *bíbloi apókryphoi in Christianity.*

1. *The LXX and Hebrew Canon in the Early Church.* Since Christianity develops in the Greek-speaking world, the LXX is its first OT canon. The NT mostly uses the LXX in quotations, as do the fathers. The NT, however, hardly ever quotes from the noncanonical works included in the LXX. The early fathers are less discriminating, but doubts about such works soon arise and quickly grow.

2. *Apocryphal Quotations in the NT.* The surest NT instance of reference to a noncanonical work is Jude 14 (cf. also Jude 9; Heb. 11:37). A possible apocryphal quotation occurs in 1 Cor. 2:9, but this is much debated and we perhaps have here a paraphrase of Is. 64:4. Gal. 6:15 is also debatable, and Eph. 5:14 is more likely a bit of ancient Christian poetry. The names in 2 Tim. 3:8 derive from apocryphal tradition. Jms. 4:5 contains a quotation of uncertain provenance, while Jn. 7:38 seems to be a paraphrase of a passage like Is. 58:11. Mt. 27:9 undoubtedly seems to have in mind Jer. 18:3 and Zech. 11:13, so that there is no need to postulate a Jeremiah apocryphon. As regards Lk. 11:49, cf. Jer. 7:25-26.

3. *The Apocrypha in the Fathers.*

a. The Apostolic Fathers. We should distinguish in these works between inexact OT quotations and genuine apocryphal quotations, of which there are a few instances, e.g., in Barn. 4.3; Hermas *Visions* 2.3.4.

b. Later Fathers. Justin, Irenaeus, and especially the Alexandrians Clement and Origen make use of apocryphal works (e.g., Justin *Dialogue* 120; Irenaeus *Against Heresies* 4.6.2; Clement of Alexandria *Stromateis* 1.23.153.1; Origen *Commentary on Matthew* 10.18 [13:57]). Origen defends the use of the Apocrypha in exposition of the NT, but after his day there is a sharp decline in the estimation of noncanonical works.

4. *The Christian Preservation, Revision, and Canonization of the Jewish Apocrypha.* Since the Jews tend to scorn Christian use of the Apocrypha, the church plays a big part in preserving noncanonical works, although not without revising them. Some such works pass into the canonical lists of various churches.

5. *Christian Apocrypha.* During the first centuries Christianity itself produces various Gospels, Acts, Epistles, and Revelations that have been called apocryphal. The attitude of the church to such works is not wholly consistent. Hermas commands some early support, while Clement of Alexandria seems to accept the Gospel of the Egyptians

(*Stromateis* 3.5.45.3). Yet apocryphal Acts are never thought to be valid, and even works that have initial support never gain entry into the canon.

6. *The Term Apocryphal.* In Judaism apocryphal works are noncanonical writings that are not only not to be read publicly, but are excluded totally from religious use. In the early church, on the other hand, the term occurs first in the struggle against false teachers and refers to their esoteric writings, with an implication of obscurity of origin and falsification. Later, the church comes to appropriate the term for Jewish works (especially apocalypses) that do not belong to the OT canon. When reaction against such works comes, the way is open for the application of the term to works that do not belong to the Hebrew OT but are acceptable because of their place in the LXX. But while Jerome and others offer a basis for this distinction, it is only in Protestantism that this usage establishes itself. In the patristic period the term finds varied use for prohibited Jewish and NT pseudepigrapha and for works that are not condemned as such but are simply not regarded as canonical (e.g., 1 and 2 Clement, Ignatius, and Polycarp). By this final distinction, which does not necessarily amount to total avoidance, the church recognizes that it has all that is necessary in the canon and it protects itself from possible doctrinal danger.   [A. OEPKE, III, 987-1000]

---

ktízō [to create], *ktísis* [creation], *ktísma* [creature, creation], *ktístēs* [Creator]

Since the question of the "whence" of the world also involves the questions of its goal and purpose, the concept of creation plays a leading part in philosophical discussion.

A. Historical Review. In many religions chaos stands at the beginning of all things as formless matter, devoid of true being or quality but constituting the seed or mother from which all nature comes into being. A psychological parallel is the idea that longing, *érōs,* or the like underlies organic processes. The Egyptian notion of the self-copulation of the original god shows that beginnings of this kind are never more than relative. Natural processes, of course, suggest forces of order that are in conflict with chaos, and inasmuch as humanity sides with such forces a transcendent goal arises for the human race, though not without the recognition that chaos finally triumphs in the form of fate. In Greek and Indian thought another notion is that matter is the original principle of all life. Thus the world is for Stoicism a harmonious circular movement into which the task of humanity is to integrate itself, although here again it seems that things will ineluctably take their course no matter what may be the human response. A certain ambivalence arises with the references to creator-gods. These are sometimes given precedence, receive the supreme attributes that elsewhere are given to chaos, and have unlimited power over nature, humanity, and the world of the gods (cf. Aristides' "Hymn to Zeus"). Along the same lines are attempts to construe creation as a miracle or act of power, whether by word or ecstasy. Such views move in the direction of a personal Creator, but are prevented from reaching this goal either through magical conceptions, through abstractions whereby the world owes its origin to the idea of the good or supreme being, or through the concept of emanations. Where emanations are presupposed, a dualism may result between the original deity (negatively conceived) and the material creation. Alternatively, Zoroastrian dualism advances the view that the two original forces of good and evil are in conflict.

B. Belief in Creation in the OT.

1. The Development of the OT Belief in Creation. Belief in creation is very old in Israel, but there are few preexilic statements (Gen. 1:1ff.; 2:4ff.; 14:19). References become more common nearer the exile (cf. Jer. 5:22ff.; Ezek. 28:13). Earlier the main stress is on God as the Lord of history and election. The movement is from the God of Israel to the Creator, not vice versa. Israel's God is the true and personal Subject of historical action. He acts with will and purpose. He moves in time and space, so that his action is action in nature too. All nature is the sphere of his operation (Am. 9:2ff.). He has established the order of nature (Jer. 5:22ff.). Thus his absolute power in history and nature may be traced back to the fact that he is the Creator (Jer. 27:5). Indeed, history itself is a creation or fashioning (Is. 22:11; 27:11). The word that becomes a technical one for creating can thus occur in the context of God's extraordinary action in history (Ex. 34:10). With this term *bārā'* and the idea of action by God's almighty word, the concept of creation is fully present.

2. Creation Terminology and Conceptions in the OT. Various terms are used in connection with creation. These carry the senses "to make for oneself" (Ps. 78:54), "to fashion" (e.g., the potter and the clay, though the use is often figurative), "to make," and "to create" in the strict sense that is reserved for God. Various poetic expressions also occur relative to God's creative work, e.g., stretching out the heavens, making heaven, the earth, the stars, the mountains, etc. fast, or basing the earth on pillars. Anthropomorphic images are also found, e.g., references to God's right hand or to his calling, but with clear indications that God is not just a giant person (cf. Is. 51:13). Finally, there are mythological allusions, although only in a theological use which assumes that the monsters of myth are mere objects of the divine action (Ps. 89:10). (For details, cf. *TDNT*, III, 1007-09.)

3. The OT Belief in Creation.

a. All the statements about the Creator relate to the God of Israel.

b. In Gen. 1 creation is creation out of nothing by the word (cf. Ps. 33:9). As in Rom. 4:17, God makes what is out of what is not. His word is not an incantation but a word of command in a personal act of will. Creation of this kind is proper only to God and stresses the distinction between Creator and creature. Creature cannot become Creator as son becomes father. For the basic nature of this distinction cf. Ex. 33:23; 1 Kgs. 19:13; Is. 6:5; 45:15. It is because God is so superior that all nature praises him (Pss. 8; 95; 104; 19). His creation manifests his transcendent majesty. God can destroy as he creates (Pss. 102:26ff.; 104:29). Between creation and its dissolution lies his preserving, i.e., his continuing creativity in nature and history. In nature his power may be revealed in violent activity, but his decrees are also to be seen in the orderliness of natural processes.

c. Creation by the word best expresses the OT view of creation; it is not emanation, but a personal act. Word expresses conscious will and act and at the same time brings out the spiritual and transcendent character of what is done (cf. Is. 41:4; 48:13; Am. 9:6; Pss. 33:6; 148:5, etc.). Creation by the word is creation out of nothing. If Gen. 1:2 begins with chaos, Gen. 1:1 precedes it. God always is; creation comes into being. The beginning, then, is that of creation. God is subject to no prior conditions. Creation displays his wisdom and omniscience (Jer. 10:12; Ps. 104:24). It establishes his right to the creature (Ps. 24:1-2). It is the basis of his historical action (Jer. 27:5), and of the human duties of trust and obedience (Is. 17:7; Ps. 119:73). By reason of it the creature cannot escape God (Ps. 33:14). Creation distinguishes Israel's God from idols (Jer. 10:12ff.). It insures that all his works are right (Job 34:12-13). It gives purpose and meaning to all things (Is. 44:6; 48:12). Human creatures in particular have a divinely willed task. This includes work (Ps. 104) but it comes to its climax in praise (Is. 43:21; 45:23).

d. The creation stories move on to the fall and a relapse into disorder with the expulsion from the garden and the deluge. God's creative action then takes the form of restoration with the promise of Gen. 9:2-3 and the call of Abraham. The idea of a fallen creation is implied with the hopes of Is. 11 and 66:22 but not clearly stated. The distinction of foods does not teach dualism. Yet the praise of creation can be loud and clear because it is the Creator who is glorified, not the creature.

e. The OT view of creation fixes the role of humanity as both part of creation and yet distinct from it because of a special relation to God (Gen. 1:26ff.; 2:7). Being in the divine image is not lost at the fall (cf. Gen. 9:6), and no matter how it is understood it involves a particular relation to God whereby people are constituted persons who both confront nature and transcend it in a manner analogous to God. As animals should know humans as their masters, so humans should know God (Is. 1:3). That they do not is unnatural. This mystery of sin has its root in the heart (Jer. 17:9; Gen. 6:5). Restoration promises a new heart (Ezek. 36:26ff.; cf. Jer. 31:33ff.; Ps. 51:10). Even in the changed situation after the flood, however, God's blessing still rests on his works (Gen. 9:1ff.; Ps. 8).

C. The Doctrine of Creation in Later Judaism.

1. Terminology. The rabbis use the same terms for God's creative work as the OT. A common metaphor is that of building a palace or city. The term "creation" is found both for all creatures and specifically for humanity. Greek works have *ktízein* and *poieín* for "to create" or "to make," *ktísis* for "creation," and *ktístēs* (or *ho ktísas*) for "Creator."

2. God as Creator of the World. God is often stated to be the sole Creator by his word. Sometimes, though not always, it is clear, or at least implied, that this is a creation out of nothing. The rabbis reject speculation that seeks to go behind creation. Even preexistent things like the throne of God or the law of God are created. As in the OT, creation and preservation go hand in hand. The God who has commanded still commands. Although God rests, he still renews creation each day. He does not entrust the keys of rain, birth, and resurrection to anyone else. There is much reference to the Creator in petitions and thanksgivings. The thought of creation gives confidence in affliction and establishes the duty of obedience. Creation distinguishes the living God from dead idols. The Creator is, of course, the God of the fathers. As such, he protects and avenges his people. In later conflicts refuge is sought in his transcendent power.

3. The World as God's Creation. The world depends on God, is directed by him, and owes him obedience. God's will (expressed in the law) constitutes its meaning. It is created for the fathers in the sense that Israel is to receive the law. Creation provides the setting for the doing of God's will. Sin has brought no ontic change but a state of sickness, e.g., shorter life for humans, less fertility for the earth, a diminished intensity of light in the sun and moon. The pseudepigrapha, however, offer a darker view of the fall with their stress on the distinction of the aeons, the activity of Satan, and the totally new form of being in the coming aeon. Yet this does not mean an identification of the world with sin.

4. Humanity as God's Creation. The divine likeness is a decisive determination of humanity. A proof of God's love, it finds expression in speech. It means that all people are confronted with God's demands. By free decision Israel accepts the law, and some Israelites fulfil it. The divine likeness provides a motive for respecting others. If an evil impulse is present, this does not represent an ontic change. Indeed, the impulse consists of natural strivings that must be held in check, and God has given the law to make this possible. In the pseudepigrapha there is greater stress on the fall and the resultant judgment. Only a few will painfully find their way to final restoration. The promise of a renewed creation runs through all the writings. Renewal of the relation to God (e.g., by circumcision, conversion, or forgiveness) means a new creation, although the word in this case is not necessarily to be taken in its literal sense.

D. *dēmiourgéō* and *ktízō* in Greek and the Linguistic Contribution of the LXX. In Greek the main words for God's creative work are *poieín, plássein,* and *themelioún.* The LXX uses these words but avoids the *dēmiourgéō* group. *dēmiourgós* is a general word in Greek for a doctor, builder, or any kind of craftsman. The suggestion is that of action on something already there. The movements of the sun and moon are the *dēmiourgoí* of day and night. The *dēmiourgoí* of feasts are those who win the victories that are the occasion for them. Later the term is used mainly for artisans, who are not highly regarded. When applied to the Creator, it implies that God makes the world out of existing materials. The LXX avoids it for this reason. *ktízō,* which the LXX adopts, is put to varied use for settling a land, establishing groves or temples, instituting festivals, etc. It expresses the resolve to take the action, and hence is often followed by *dēmiourgeín.* Other uses are for invention and the founding of philosophical schools, but in NT days the main use is for the founding of cities or the settling of countries, with an emphasis on the personal resolve (e.g., that of rulers in the founding of cities) which initiates the actual work. It is probably because of the reference to resolve, and to avoid the association of *dēmiourgeín* with artisans, that the LXX prefers the *ktízō* group to the more obvious *dēmiourgéō* group. At the same time, the LXX uses *ktízō* in only 17 out of the 46 instances in which it reads *bārā'* as "to create," and the only such use in the Pentateuch is in Dt. 4:32. Indeed, there are only four (or five) instances in the Pentateuch, none in the historical books, 15 in the prophets, and nine in the writings, with 36 in the apocryphal books. The findings suggest that the term takes on theological significance only gradually and has not yet done so when the first works are translated. *ktísis* means the settling or founding of cities, but does not have this sense in the LXX, where it means "creature" or "creation." *ktísma* is what is founded, and it, too, means a creature in the LXX. The *ktístēs* is the founder, e.g., of a city; the LXX uses it as a divine attribute in 2 Sam. 22:32 to show God's power and to differentiate him from idols.

E. **Creation in the NT.**

1. Terminology. The most common group in the NT is the *ktízō* group, then *poiéō* and *plássō.* We find *dēmiourgós* only with *technítēs* in Heb. 11:10. The *ktízō* group in the NT applies only to God's creation. *ktístēs* occurs only in 1 Pet. 4:19. *ktísma* means "creature," "the creature," or "creation" as the totality of created things, sometimes humanity as in Mk. 16:15, sometimes nature as in Rom. 1:25.

2. God as the Creator of the World. Many verses in the NT state that God is the Creator of all things. Some of these refer back to the beginning (e.g., Mk. 10:6; Rom. 1:20; 2 Pet. 3:4; Jn. 8:44; Lk. 11:50); these imply that there is no preexistent matter, but that creation means an absolute beginning by God's word (cf. Rom. 4:17; 2 Cor. 4:6). Again, it is affirmed that God created all things (cf. Eph. 3:9; Col. 1:16; Acts 17:24). This excludes emanation. Heaven as well as earth is part of creation. God's will is done there and its creatures worship God (cf. Rev. 4:8ff.) in voluntary, personal expression. The Son himself gives thanks to his Father as Lord of heaven and earth (Mt. 11:25-26). God has willed the existence of all creatures with a divine purpose in view. All things are from and through and to him (Rom. 11:36), and the final goal is that he should be all in all (1 Cor. 15:28). Thus the vision of God the Creator, enthroned in his majesty and surrounded by the living creatures and the elders, precedes the revelation of his historical acts (Rev. 4–5). God's Spirit permeates and sustains all things (4:5), although the lightnings, voices, and thunders remind us of fallen creation (4:15).

3. Fallen Creation. The NT makes a distinction between what is made with hands and the place of God's presence (Heb. 9:11, 24), or between what is in the flesh and what is in the spirit (Eph. 2:11), or between the transitoriness of this world and the eternity of the world to come (Heb. 1:12). Heaven is used both for God's dwelling and for a part of this world. Similarly, the angels are creatures but do not belong to this creation (cf. the song in Rev. 5:8ff. with its widening circles). Nor does Satan belong to this creation. This creation, according to Rom. 8:19-20, is that which, in some connection with the human fall, is subject to decay, revolving in a gigantic circle of futility. The futility takes the form of temporality which offers both space for repentance and the possibility of offense. Creation displays God's deity but it also tempts us as cosmos. It is the place of revelation but its form is that of the flesh, so that only in Christ can one truly see God in nature. In and for itself the revelation in nature leads on ineluctably to the exposition of human guilt (Acts 14:17; Rom. 1:19-20). In Rev. 5 only the Lamb can open the sealed book which contains God's will for the world. This implies that the world lies in Satan's power and that the Lamb has freed it. The opening of the book means a new heaven and earth when the orders imposed with time and space will be lifted (cf. Mk. 12:25; 1 Cor. 15:26, 42ff.). As the world was created in Christ (1 Cor. 8:6), so its meaning lies in its redemption through him. All God's counsel is epitomized in him (Eph. 1:4; 1 Pet. 1:20). The form of this world is determined by the fall of humanity but also by its calling to glory. In it we have all that we need, and since all that is necessary to life is good (Mk. 7:14ff.; Rom. 14:14; 1 Cor. 7ff.), we are to use it with thanksgiving to God (1 Tim. 4:4), neither honoring the creature instead of the Creator nor dishonoring the Creator by rejecting or despising the creature.

4. Humanity as Creature and New Creation. Humanity is creation's goal, yet also the starting point of evil. The human creature is a living being (1 Cor. 15:45), and its natural life involves the tension of a being in God's image that is accompanied by subjection to sinful impulses. As God's creatures, people have no claim on God. They belong to this creation, with *psychḗ,* not *pneúma,* as their life's principle. With the gospel there is a new creation (2 Cor. 5:17; Gal. 6:15; cf. Eph. 2:10, 15; 4:24; Col. 3:10). This is creation by the Word and Spirit (cf. Jms. 1:18) to new life in the Spirit (Rom. 6:1ff.). The entry of the Spirit through Christ's word and work (Mt. 12:28) means that the new aeon breaks into the course of this aeon in a creative work of God which unites divided humanity into one new humanity (Eph. 2:15). The goal is the totally new creation, the new heaven and earth, in which death will be abolished, Christ will be fully manifested as the pneumatic man, and the glorious liberty of God's children will be fulfilled with the redemption of the body (Rom. 8:21). (The use of *ktísis* in 1 Pet. 2:13 poses a special problem. The word is usually rendered "order" or "institution," with special reference to the state. There are, however, no real parallels for this, and another possibility is that with "human" the word simply refers to "humanity," i.e., that we should be subject for the Lord's sake to all kinds of people.)

[W. FOERSTER, III, 1000-1032]

---

kybérnēsis [government]

1. *kybernáō* means "to steer," then "to rule," and the *kybernḗtēs* is the "helmsman" (Acts 27:11), then the "statesman." God is sometimes called the *kybernḗtēs* as the one who directs the world. *kybérnēsis* means literally "steering" and figuratively "government" and "divine direction."

2. In the LXX *kybérnēsis* occurs three times in Proverbs for right or wise direction (1:5; 11:14; 24:6).

3. In 1 Cor. 12:28 the reference is plainly to the special gifts that qualify a Christian to give good direction to the community. The bishops and deacons are probably the bearers of the gift. It may be noted that the questions of v. 29 do not apply to this gift. This seems to suggest that the offices are elective, although they cannot be discharged properly without the divine charism.

4. In the fathers the church is often depicted as a ship and Christ as the Helmsman or Pilot. The stilling of the storm and the ark provide a starting point. The symbolism is that Christ steers his church safely to port through the storms of life or across the sea of sin.

[H. W. BEYER, III, 1035-37]

---

kýmbalon [cymbal]

kýmbalon, found in the NT only in 1 Cor. 13:1, denotes the shallow metallic basin which gives a resounding note when struck against another. The LXX has it frequently in Chronicles, Ezra, and Nehemiah (cf. 1 Chr. 13:8). In 1 Sam. 18:6 the reference may be to a plucking instrument or triangle, in 1 Chr. 15:19 striking instruments are denoted, and bells is possibly the meaning in Zech. 14:20 (or perhaps bosses). Paul would be familiar with the cultic instruments of Judaism, although in writing to Corinth he might have had pagan instruments in mind. The clanging cymbal also seems to have been a term for an empty prattler. The point is that the gifts favored at Corinth can only produce empty noise unless there is within them the inner force of *agápē.*

[K. L. SCHMIDT, III, 1037-39]

kyránion → *kýōn*

---

kýrios [Lord, lord], *kyría* [lady], *kyriakós* [the Lord's], *kyriótēs* [lordship, dominion], *kyrieúō* [to be(come) lord], *katakyrieúō* [to lord it]

kýrios. Historically the concept of lordship combines the two elements of power and authority. A true realization of the unity of the two arises only in encounter with God, who creates us with absolute power but is also the absolute authority before which it is freedom rather than bondage to bow. In the biblical revelation the humanity that rejects subordination to its Creator meets the one who with the authority of God's ministering and forgiving love woos its obedience and reconstructs and reestablishes the relations of lordship.

A. The Meaning of the Word *kýrios*.

1. The adjective *kýrios*, from a root "to swell," "to be strong," means a. "having power," "empowered," "authorized," "valid." The power denoted is a power of control rather than physical strength. Laws are valid, persons are authorized or competent, and rulers may have a powerful impact. A second meaning b. is "important," "decisive," or "principal."

2. The noun *kýrios*, rare at first, takes on two fixed senses: first, the owner, e.g., of slaves, a house, or a subject people, and second, the legal guardian of a wife or girl. Both senses carry the implication of what is legitimate. In Attic, however, *despótēs* is a much more common word. In the Koine the two become almost interchangeable, although *kýrios* has a stronger element of legality and suggests more the power of disposal than of possession. The closer we come to NT times, the more emphatic the legal element becomes and the more *kýrios* tends to replace *despótēs*. At first officials are not called *kýrioi*, but gradually the habit develops of attaching the word as a title, and the term is then used for philosophers, doctors, members of an audience, husbands (by wives), fathers (by sons), and finally even sons (by fathers). In the early period neither kings nor gods are called *kýrioi*; the first use of *kýrios* for God is to be found in the LXX.

B. Gods and Rulers as *kýrioi*. The concept of God necessarily contains an element of legitimate power. If legitimacy is lacking, religion yields to fear of capricious spirits, whereas if power is lacking, the deity is a mere idea. The combination of might and right, however, involves personality. The Greek use of *despótēs* for deity bears witness to a personal element, but the Greeks do not fundamentally regard their gods as lords, primarily because their view of God allows no place for the personal act of creation.

1. kýrios for Gods and Rulers in Classical Antiquity. The word *kýrios* is first applied to the gods as an adjective to describe their spheres of control. But the gods are not, as in Egypt or Babylon, the lords of these spheres. They are the forms of reality, not its creators or designers. With humans, they are organically related members of the same reality. For this reason, there is no personal responsibility to them; even prayer is fundamentally illogical. Religious disintegration results, therefore, when the gods are viewed in this way. The political implication is democracy, in which individuals freely give themselves to the right. Since, however, the right stands above them, and is not merely that which they decree, an impulse toward monarchy is present. The ruler has a special measure of virtue. As such he is inspired law, although not *kýrios*.

2. Gods and Rulers in the Near East and Egypt. In the Near East the gods are the lords of reality. They control destiny, and individuals, created by them, are responsible to, and may be punished by them. Rightly, then, they may be called lords. It is they who give the laws which rulers declare to their subjects and which subjects must simply obey. The Near East has a strong sense that laws need personal authorization. This leads to the cult of the ruler as the administrator of law who is closer to the gods and who may thus make unconditional demands on others. Personal confrontation with the gods stands at the heart of this understanding.

3. The Hellenistic kýrios.

a. Chronology. The use of *kýrios* for gods and rulers develops in the first century B.C. At this time the phrases *kýrios basileús*, *kýrios theós*, and *kýrios stratēgós* come into common use. The available data from Egypt and Syria show that all this seems to happen within a single life span. It is probably the adaptation of an older Egyptian and Syrian development.

b. Location. In Egypt *kýrios* is used for various gods, and this usage spreads to Asia Minor, Crete, Italy, Rome, and Spain. In Syria a similar use develops for which there are parallels in Arabia and Spain. Other deities are called *kýrios* or *kyría* in Asia Minor and Italy (e.g., the Ephesian Artemis). It may be noted that the usage never becomes widespread. It is common only where it corresponds to native usage, and in Syria *kýrios* is comparatively much less common than its Semitic equivalent.

c. Tendency. While indigenous usage fixes the main content, a certain tendency may be discerned in the Greek examples. The term *kýrios* is not used for outstanding gods, nor only for those that are particularly venerated. It denotes a personal relationship, e.g., in petitionary prayer, votive dedication, or thanksgiving. *kýrios* denotes an order under which people stand and which is connected with the idea of dominion over nature and destiny. Correlative to *kýrios* is the term *doúlos* ("slave"), which implies personal authority as well as relationship, but with a strong guarantee of protection as well (cf. Semitic names which contain the names of gods). In Egypt the concept of lordship gives stronger linguistic expression to the dominion of deity over nature, but there is no doubt that the transfer of *kýrios* to the gods on the basis of existing native usage takes place independently in Egypt and Syria.

d. Rulers. As regards rulers, phrases like *kýrios basileús* are adaptations of native usage which always seem alien to the Greeks and later drop away. In the imperial period *kýrios* becomes a brief summary of the emperor's position, mostly for the purpose of dating. We find it a few times under Nero but it is more common later, and after Trajan gradually finds its way into the full imperial style. It also occurs in the absolute (cf. Acts 25:26), although at first the Latin *dominus* is shunned because of its obvious suggestion of absolute monarchy (cf. Augustus). Under the cover of democracy, however, a Near Eastern style of autocracy triumphs. This explains why the term *kýrios* establishes itself. Initially it has no connection with the emperor cult, but if the emperor is not *kýrios* as god, he can easily be god as *kýrios,* i.e., in virtue of his universal rule. Sometimes, then, we find the phrase *dominus et deus.* Nevertheless, this is not the main emphasis. Hence Tertullian can accept *dominus* in one sense and not another, and whereas the Zealots, for political reasons, cannot accept either, the Jews in general do not find it difficult to call civil rulers their *kýrioi.*

[W. FOERSTER, III, 1039-58]

C. The OT Name for God.

1. The Name for God in the LXX.

a. The LXX uses *kýrios* for the divine name Yahweh in an effort to bring out its meaning. Since the term has to be used for human lords too, or even as a respectful form of address, the effort is perhaps not wholly successful. Yet in the religious sphere *kýrios* is reserved for God. In this sense it is used regularly, i.e., over 6,000 times, and except in a few instances always for Yahweh in such forms as *kýrios theós, kýrios ho theós,* and *ho kýrios theós.*

b. Although a little capricious, the use or nonuse of the article seems to be meant to relate to the significance of the name. Whether or not *kýrios* is a creative attempt of the translators or the rendering of a Hebrew substitute like Adonai cannot be determined. Its justification derives less from ordinary Hebrew originals than from the divine name itself.

2. "Lord" as a Designation for Yahweh. In the history of the Bible the use of "Lord" has been no less influential than that of Yahweh. Like the usual Hebrew terms, it carries a recognition of the power of the divine will. The title corresponds to the divine nature. God is Lord of the land and people, but also of all things (Mic. 4:13). In replacement of the divine name, or in addition to it, the term implies the divine majesty (cf. Is. 6:11; Ezek. 2:4, etc.). Why the term for Lord is completely substituted for Yahweh in later Judaism is not wholly clear, nor is it clear whether the LXX *kýrios* comes first or is a translation. It certainly has important missionary implications, for the witness to God as Lord shows that, as the Creator, God is the exclusive holder of power over humanity and the cosmos. The term Lord states in practice who God is and what he means for us as the one whose personal will intervenes with all the force that is the distinctive mark of the name Yahweh.

3. The Name Yahweh as a Concept of Experience. The OT belief in God is grounded in historical experience and develops in constant contact with history. The name Yahweh is thus distinguished by a specific content. God is not just any deity but a distinct divine person. This still applies even when he is more generally called Lord. Behind statements like "the Lord is God" (1 Kgs. 18:39) or "the Lord is his name" (Ex. 15:3) stand the more specific expressions "Yahweh (or Yahweh of hosts) is his name." There is encounter here with the definite person of God. Only Gentiles can make nothing of his name. While Yahweh may have been used in different ways before, in the OT it always has reference to a specific encounter. It is the name of the revealed God and leaves no room for speculation. Use of the name suggests the essential and indelible features of the picture of God which the biblical tradition paints in the inner history of his people.

4. The Mosaic Institution. Yahweh religion is an instituted religion. It is not a reformation of Canaanite animism but a new beginning. There is a prehistory in the stories of the patriarchs but Moses is the virtual founder of Yahweh religion. With him it truly enters the state of history and becomes a norm of conduct and a spur to political action. On the basis of God's revelation to him, the tribes come into a relation of covenant obligation. Their life is dominated by trust in the guiding will and power of the God who knows no natural restraint and who has proved his majesty at the exodus. A tradition of common worship begins at this time. Theophorous personal names come into use and the wars of Yahweh begin with the invasion of Canaan. With acceptance of the name Yahweh Israel makes an exclusive confession of God and puts itself under active obedience to his will (Ex. 15:11; cf. Josh. 24:16ff.).

5. The Origin of the Divine Name. The name Yahweh is given by God himself in Ex. 3. Whether Moses is the first to use it or it has been taken from tradition is hard to say. Parallels have been sought (cf. Ras Shamra and Egypt), and an original home of Yahweh has been postulated among the Kenites or in Edom. The only thing that is certain is that from the time of Moses the name has a new and specific content.

6. The Form and Manner of the Name Yahweh. a. The form of the name presents problems even regarding the consonants, let alone the vowels, for variations exist in the tradition. b. Attempts to interpret the name philologically produce no certain results. On the basis of the longer form we are possibly led to a root that might mean either "to fall" or "to be." On the basis of the shorter form we perhaps have an interjection, a cry to God. We are not even certain that the two forms are originally the same word, and in any case it is difficult either to relate them or to derive any definite meaning from them.

7. The Reasons for Reticence in Relation to the Name. a. Interpretation is made harder by the fence that the tradition builds around the name. This reticence is due in part to the power that is associated with the name. The name epitomizes the person (cf. 1 Sam. 25:25). It is thus feared as God himself is feared (Dt. 25:58). b. On the other hand, the bibilical authors, freely using the name, have a positive sense of the divine reality and power that protect them, so that it is only later, in redaction and translation, that the sense of distance grows. c. Another contributory factor is the sense that the divine person is so unique that one cannot distinguish him from other persons by the simple method of using names.

8. *The Name of God in the Account of Yahweh's Revelation to Moses (Ex. 3:14).* a. In Ex. 3:14, when Moses asks God his name, a puzzling answer is given which either tries to explain the name by alliterative paraphrase or seeks to avoid its use by close approximation to its form. b. If it is an explanation, the name bears some reference to existence, although in what sense is not wholly clear. c. The Hebrew certainly does not have the speculative profundity of the LXX rendering (*egố eimi ho ốn*). There are also various linguistic arguments against etymological explanation, and the style of revelation is the least adapted for etymology. d. The other possibility is that God is refusing to give a name that would make him merely one among the many gods of the period, although cf. 3:14b.

9. *The Name Yahweh as the Basic Form of the OT Declaration about God.* a. OT statements about God take different forms and the constant link to history works out in different ways. The theme that God is Lord, however, is always the same. One can neither invoke him by magic nor influence him except as a servant. The revelation is that of the vital power of God oriented to salvation. Hence the name Yahweh is the sum of all that the OT says about God, and the figure of Yahweh is the original form of biblical revelation. If the name does in fact set Yahweh among the gods, so that under mythical pressure there is a felt difficulty in serving God or singing his songs in a foreign land (1 Sam. 26:19; Ps. 137), and the rivalry of other gods causes recurrent crises of faith (1 Kgs. 18:17ff.; 2 Kgs. 21:3; Jer. 2:28), nevertheless there is a strong sense of the uniqueness of Yahweh and a sharp rejection of the reality of false gods (Pss. 58; 82; Am. 5:26; Ex. 20:3ff.). b. The receptivity to alien myths, which is particularly marked in Northern Israel (Hos. 11:2 etc.), is accompanied by, or finds expression in, a widespread bourgeois complacency that does not sense the true reality or power of God (cf. Jer. 48:11; Zeph. 1:12; Is. 5:12; Jer. 29:26). The prophets fight against this limited view of God, however, with the assertion of God's unconditional authority in every sphere of life. Am. 5:4 sums up the demands and promises of God in a way that allows no place for mythical forms of thinking. c. For the prophets God is no abstract concept but the personal God who lays hold of them with compelling force (Ezek. 1). Although anthropomorphic expressions have to be used to describe him, the resolution of the prophets and the fervor of the psalmists have their root in personal encounter with Yahweh and his will. This is why their messages convey the grandeur, power, and reality of God with imperious force. d. Attempts to discern God's rule in time (Ps. 90) and space (Ps. 139) push us to the limits of the concept of personality but do not surrender it. These thoughts arise out of a sense of responsibility that leads to anxiety, guilt, and panic (cf. Am. 9:2; Job 7:16ff.) but finally leads back to confident praise and prayer (Ps. 139:24). e. Naive conceptions may be present in the we-style of Gen. 1:26-27 etc., or in the idea of creation in the divine image, but these are set in a context of demythologization. f. The same applies to the depiction of God as a warrior (Ex. 15:3 etc.), in which the stress lies, not on divine savagery, but on the loyalty and love of God in protecting his people and providing for it. In much the same way the jealousy of God (Ex. 20:5) carries the implication

that the people owes him unconditional love and loyalty in return. What comes out in such statements, then, is the personal nature of the whole relationship. Yahweh is no static Baal. Loving, he may be wounded and provoked. He puts feeling into his actions and directions, a man, as it were, and yet no man but God. The imponderable element of the dynamic is thus restructured as the imponderable element of the divine person to whose wrath one might fall victim but whose mercies are great (2 Sam. 24:14). g. Yahweh is the Lord in his directions. These are total. The divine I addresses the Thou of the community or the individual with a demand for the practical exclusion of other gods which implies the decisive reality of the one God and a compulsion to bow to his will. The lordship of God means that God gives direction which imparts meaning to life and demands loyal and obedient action. Recognition of this (Ex. 24:7) is perhaps the most valuable legacy of the OT inasmuch as the universal validity of this knowledge of Yahweh comes clearly to light in the moral requirement (cf. Mic. 6:8). The dynamic of the divine commission suggests that the demand of Yahweh refers not merely to Israel but to humanity in general. Amos calls the nations to account precisely because they, like Israel, are responsible to the one transcendent God whose voice he hears from Zion (1:2; cf. 9:12).

10. *The Confession of Yahweh in Dt. 6:4.* Yahweh religion is not monotheistic in a speculative sense. It is monotheistic in its energizing of the will of those who confess him. This is true in the Shema, where love for Yahweh is expressed in order to strengthen love for him. The four words in Dt. 6:4 are thus introduced by the formula: "Hear, O Israel" (cf. 5:1; 9:1, etc.). Possibly hymnic, they perhaps consist of two clauses: "Yahweh is our God," and "Yahweh is one." If so, the repetition of the name suggests that the point is that in Yahweh all that he is is exhaustively and exclusively present (cf. 4:35; 7:9; Is. 45:6). The difficulty in postulating two clauses is that the second clause seems to be a trite mathematical one which is less far-reaching than the first and can hardly be justified as a protest against the view that there might be many Yahwehs as there are many Baals. On the other hand, to take the words as one clause adds little to the sense: "Yahweh, our God, Yahweh is one," or, in a paraphrase: "Yahweh is our God, Yahweh as the only one." Analysis shows that the words defy precise interpretation but for that reason, in their very sweep and majesty, are an eloquent testimony to the power of faith in Yahweh. The active dynamic of the national religion comes up against the problem of adequate expression, but the confession makes it plain that Yahweh as the sum and center of religious experience is the source of a single historical revelation.   [G. QUELL, III, 1058-81]

D. Lord in Later Judaism.

1. The Choice of the Word kýrios in the LXX. Why the LXX chose *kýrios* is debated. One theory is that it really means "superior" rather than "one who has power or control." But this is not the Greek usage of the time. The LXX probably chooses *kýrios* because it stresses the fact that as the Liberator from Egypt, or as the Creator, God has a valid right to control over his people and the universe. He is sovereign in the absolute sense.

2. Lord in the Pseudepigrapha. Whether the use of Adonai for Yahweh is older than the LXX is also debated. Other renderings of the OT follow different courses, as do the pseudepigrapha, which offer several substitute terms. In circles open to Hellenism *kýrios* is avoided, as it might lead to misunderstanding. Philo, finding *kýrios* in the LXX, allegorizes it by discerning in it a reference to royal power.

3. Lord in Rabbinic Judaism. By the time of the rabbis Yahweh is seldom pronounced literally and Adonai is little used in ordinary speech. The rabbis use various terms for Lord in such senses as the master of slaves, the owner of goods, or the master of passions, and also in polite address. *rb* denotes the teacher but also the master of slaves. In the Hebrew and Aramaic use of lord we never find the absolute without a dependent noun, and there is occasional doubling in address. As regards God, he is for later Judaism both Lord and Governor of the world and Lord and Judge of the individual. Creation provides the final basis for this lordship. The election of Israel is seen as its creation by God.

E. *kýrios* in the NT.

1. Secular Usage. In the NT *kýrios* is used for the owner of the vineyard (Mk. 12:9) or of animals (Lk. 19:33; Mt. 15:27), and for the master of the steward (Lk. 16:3) and slaves (Eph. 6:5-6). It also refers to the one who controls something, e.g., the harvest (Mt. 9:38) or the sabbath (Mk. 2:28). Polite usage occurs in Lk. 1:43, but superiority is suggested in 1 Pet. 3:6; Mk. 12:36-37; Acts 25:26. Slaves and workers use the address *kýrie* (cf. Lk. 13:8). The Jews use the same address to Pilate in Mt. 27:63, Mary to the gardener in Jn. 20:15, the jailer to Paul and Silas in Acts 16:30 (cf. also Mt. 21:29; Acts 10:4). The double form occurs in Mt. 7:21-22; 25:11; Lk. 6:46. We find genitive combinations in 1 Cor. 2:8 (glory) and 2 Th. 3:16 (peace). *despótēs* is used only in prayer or for the master of slaves or owner of a house (1 Tim. 6:1-2; 2 Tim. 2:21).

2. God as Lord. God is called *kýrios* in the NT mostly in OT quotations or allusions (Mk. 1:3; 12:11, etc.; for a full list see *TDNT*, III, 1086-87). In the basic Synoptic material God is *ho kýrios* only in Mk. 5:19. *kýrios* is very common in the prologue to Luke (cf. also the epilogue to Matthew). LXX influence may be seen in expressions like the hand, name, angel, spirit, or word of the Lord (Lk. 1:66; Jms. 5:10; Mt. 1:20; Acts 5:9; 8:25). *kýrios* also means God in 1 Cor. 10:9; 1 Tim. 6:15; Heb. 7:21, etc., and Revelation has such formulas as *kýrios ho theós* (1:8 etc.; cf. 11:15; 22:6). The data suggest that *kýrios* is not a common term for God apart from OT use, but that its content can at any time be given full weight (cf. Mt. 11:25, which implies free assent to the free divine decision; Mt. 9:38, where the lord of the harvest is the Lord of world history; 1 Tim. 6:15, which ascribes total sovereignty to God; and Acts 17:24, where God is Lord as Creator). In Revelation God is Lord as the Almighty (1:8 etc.), but the elders call him "our Lord" (4:11). Lord has a special emphasis in the prayer of Acts 1:24 and it underlies the obligation of worship in Jms. 3:9.

3. Jesus as Lord.

a. Paul in 1 Cor. 12:3 contrasts *anáthema Iēsoús* and *kýrios Iēsoús*. The parallel is not exact, for *anáthema* may be pronounced against many persons or things but *kýrios* applies to Jesus alone. In Phil. 2:6ff. the name *kýrios* is given to Jesus as the response of God to his obedient suffering. It implies a position equal to that of God. That the risen Jesus is Lord is stated also in Rom. 10:9; Acts 2:36, and for parallels cf. Heb. 2:6ff.; Mt. 28:18, and the use of Ps. 110:1 (Acts 5:31; Rom. 8:34; 1 Cor. 15:25ff.; Col. 3:1; Eph. 1:20-21). In 1 Cor. 11:3 the world is related to God only indirectly through Christ its Head. In Col. 2:6, 10 Christ the Lord is the Head of all authority and power. In 1 Cor. 15:28 the Son exercises the lordship of God the Father in order to subject all things to him. In Rom. 14:9 lordship over humanity is central as the lordship of the crucified and risen Lord (5:6; 6:4, 9; 1 Cor. 1:23-24; Gal. 3:13, etc.). The gospel is the gospel of Christ and involves being crucified with him or baptized into him. Paul comes to Rome with the blessing of Christ, and the church is one body in Christ. Believers serve the Lord (Rom. 12:11), stand or fall before him (14:4ff.), and are to walk worthy of him (cf. 1 Cor. 11:27). It is the Lord who comes (1 Th. 4:15ff.), from whom Paul is absent (2 Cor. 5:6ff.), who gives powers to his servants (2 Cor. 10:8), and whose work is being done (1 Cor. 15:58). This Lord is the Spirit (2 Cor. 3:17). As there is one God, the Father, so there is one Lord, Jesus Christ (1 Cor. 8:6). It is through him that all things are, and that Christians exist as such. There is no set pattern for the alternation of *Christós* and *kýrios*. Often we find combinations such as *ho kýrios Iēsoús* or *ho kýrios hēmṓn Iēsoús* (*Christós*). The use of the name Jesus gives emphasis and solemnity to the formula, and the personal pronoun stresses the personal relationship, which as that of the whole church implies the interrelationship of Christians (Rom. 15:30; 1 Cor. 1:2) but also their separation from others (Rom. 16:18).

b. *kýrios* may also be used for the historical Jesus (cf. 1 Cor. 7:10, 12; 1 Th. 4:15; 1 Cor. 9:5; Heb. 2:3; Acts 11:16; 20:35). Luke has *kýrios* for Jesus 13 times, John has it five times, and cf. Mk. 11:3; Jn. 21:7 (though in Mk. 11:3 the reference might be to God). In address to Jesus we find *didáskale, rhabbí,* and *rhabbouní* as well as *kýrie*. In Mark *kýrie* is used only once by a Gentile woman, but the doubling in Lk. 6:46; Mt. 7:21-22 suggests a Semitic original. If *didáskalos* is more commonly used by Jesus himself as well as others (cf. Mk. 14:14; Mt. 10:24-25), *kýrios* in Luke and John has its roots in the life and work of Jesus. The resurrection is decisive, for it shows that Jesus is still the Lord and casts a new light on his teaching (cf. the use of Ps. 110:1 in Mk. 12:35ff.). The word *kýrios* is thus seen to be a proper one for the comprehensive lordship of Jesus. In him God acts as the *kýrios* does in the OT.

4. Earthly kýrios Relationships. Earthly relationships take on a new aspect in the NT. Slaves will render wholehearted service because they are now serving the Lord and not men (Col. 3:23-24). The whole problem of earthly relationships finds its solution in the transcendent lordship of Christ (cf. Col. 4:1).

kyría. The only NT use of the feminine *kyría* is in 2 John. The reference to vv. 1 and 5 is a symbolical one to the church (cf. the plural in v. 6). John does not simply call the church *kyría* as the bride of the *kýrios*; he does so in respectful address, perhaps because this is not a church that he himself has founded. On this view the churches are sisters and the members are their children (v. 13).

kyriakós. This adjective, meaning "of the lord or owner," occurs in the NT in 1 Cor. 11:20 and Rev. 1:10 for the Lord's Supper and the Lord's Day. As regards the former cf. the *kyríou* (genitive) of 1 Cor. 10:21. As regards the latter, the day of Christ's resurrection takes on special significance (cf. Jn. 20:1; Acts 20:7; 1 Cor. 16:2). Already the first day is important in Judaism as the day when creation began, and it becomes a special day of Christian assembly as the beginning of the new aeon.

kyriótēs. Meaning "power or position as lord," this word is used in Col. 1:16 for the members of a class of angels. In Jude 8 (cf. 2 Pet. 2:10) the reference seems to be, not to angels, but to the divine majesty (i.e., God himself), whom the false teachers despise with their libertinism.

kyrieúō. Meaning "to act as *kýrios*," then "to be or become *kýrios*," this word occurs in Lk. 22:25 for the use of power by rulers, in Rom. 6:9, 14 for the broken rule of death and sin, in Rom. 7:1 for the validity of the law, and in Rom. 14:9 for the lordship of Christ. In 1 Tim. 6:15 God is the Lord of lords (*kyrieúontes*), and in 2 Cor. 1:24 Paul explains that he is not lording it over the Corinthians.

katakyrieúō. Although the force of the *katá* is mostly lost in ordinary usage, it conveys the sense of rule to one's own advantage in Mk. 10:42 (Gentile rulers), Acts 19: 16 (the evil spirit), and 1 Pet. 5:2-3 (the admonition to the elders).

[W. FOERSTER, III, 1081-98]

---

kyróō [to validate], *akyróō* [to invalidate], *prokyróō* [to make valid in advance]

---

kyróō. This word means a. "to enforce," "to validate," b. "to resolve," and c. "to bring into force." In Gal. 3:15 the point is that the will is ratified and comes into force, although there is a certain tension in the equation of will and promise. In 2 Cor. 2:8 Paul is begging for a reaffirming of love in an effective linking of a legal term with the basis ethical principle of *agápē*.

akyróō. This is a legal term for "to invalidate" which is also used more generally for "to render inoperative." It has a legal nuance in Mk. 7:13 (the commands of God invalidated by human traditions) and Gal. 3:17 (the ratified will that cannot be annulled—an illustration of the promise that cannot be made void by the law).

prokyróō. This word, meaning "to make valid in advance," is used in Gal. 3:17 to make the point that the promise is ratified by God prior to the giving of the law and is thus of incontrovertible validity.   [J. BEHM, III, 1098-1100]

---

kýōn [dog],   *kynárion* [house dog]

---

kýōn.

1. This word, meaning "dog," is mostly used disparagingly in the OT for despicable street dogs (cf. 1 Sam. 17:43; 2 Kgs. 8:13; 1 Kgs. 14:11; Ps. 22:16, 20; Prov. 26:11). The rabbis display similar contempt for dogs when they compare the ungodly or Gentiles to them.

2. What distinguishes Israel is possession of the law, which is not to be given to the unclean. Jesus takes up this thought in Mt. 7:6. In view of the majesty of the gospel the disciples must not address it to the wrong people, i.e., where they cannot break through opposition in their own strength. The cultic form of the saying suggests an application in worship too. In Lk. 16:19ff. the licking of the sores of Lazarus by dogs describes the supreme wretchedness of his position.

3. Paul's warning in Phil. 3:2 has a sharp edge. He is perhaps referring Mt. 7:6 to those who disturb the community, or thinking of the hostility of his opponents in reminiscence of Ps. 22 or Ps. 59:6-7. 2 Pet. 2:22 takes up Prov. 26:11 to describe believers who fall back into sin. The influence of the OT may also be seen in Rev. 22:15 with its exclusion of dogs from the holy city, i.e., those who reject the truth and are hardened against grace (cf. Ignatius *Ephesians* 7.1).

kynárion. This diminutive of *kýōn* means "house dog" and is probably chosen by Jesus in Mk. 7:27; Mt. 25:26 to show that there is a distinction between Jews and Gentiles but still to give the Gentiles a place in the house. The woman in her reply accepts the distinction but in so doing takes the place that is offered and finds the help she seeks.   [O. MICHEL, III, 1101-04]

λ *l*

---

lanchánō [to allot, receive]

1. In Jn. 19:24 *lanchánō* has the unusual sense "to cast lots." The soldiers cast lots for the coat of Jesus, thus fulfilling Ps. 22:18 *(ébalon kléron)*.

2. In Lk. 1:9 we find the more common sense "it was his lot." Offering incense is a special privilege, granted each priest only once, and decided by lot.

3. Acts 1:17 is similar, except that in this instance God makes the decision, and thus the thought is that of the allotment of a share in the apostolic ministry.

4. In 2 Pet. 1:1 the common idea of attainment is present, but with the usual sense of allotment in the background. Attainment to faith is not a human achievement but is by divine allotment (cf. Acts 13:48; 17:31; Rom. 12:3; Jude 3). God does not merely grant the possibility of faith; he effects it (cf. Eph. 2:8). As a divine gift, faith is the epitome of grace; hence attaining to faith is by God's gracious decision, yet closely linked with his righteousness. [H. HANSE, IV, 1-2]

---

laktízō [to kick]

laktízō, meaning "to kick," occurs in the NT only in the proverbial saying in Acts 26:14. [H. HANSE, IV, 3]

laléō → légō

---

katalaléō [to speak against, speak evil], **katalaliá** [evil speech, slander], **katálalos** [slanderer]

katalaléō has such senses as "to importune with speeches," "to prattle," "to blurt out," "to accuse," and "to calumniate." In the LXX it is used for hostile speech, especially slander. It does not occur in the ethical lists of the secular world, and is infrequent for malicious gossip even in Psalms and Proverbs. In the NT the main stress is on the malicious nature of the speech; and the importance of resisting this vice, which is a violation of the law (Jms. 4:11) and contrary to the new life in God (1 Pet. 2:3), may be seen from its high placing in lists of vices or its being made the subject of special exhortation (2 Cor. 12:20; Jms. 4:11). Its frequent occurrence in the apostolic fathers shows how seriously it is taken in the early church, but also how rampant it is. [G. KITTEL, IV, 3-5]

---

lambánō [to take, receive], **analambánō** [to take up], **análēmpsis** [death, ascension], **epilambánō** [to grasp], **anepílēmptos** [irreproachable], **katalambánō** [to seize, attain], **metalambánō** [to take part, change], **metálēmpsis** [sharing], **paralambánō** [to take over], **prolambánō** [to anticipate], **proslambánō** [to receive], **próslēmpsis** [acceptance], **hypolambánō** [to take up, support]

lambánō.

1. From the basic sense "to take," *lambánō* acquires the active senses a. "to take to oneself," "to receive," "to collect," and b. "to seize."

2. It also takes on the more passive sense "to acquire" and middle "to hold or grasp something or someone." Sense 2. is less common in the LXX, which also has such special uses as "to take life," "to take a census," "to take guilt," "to fetch," and "to strike up" (a song).

In the NT we find sense 1. in such contexts as taking up one's cross (Mk. 10:38), accepting the witness (Jn. 3:11) or messengers of Jesus (13:20) or Jesus himself (1:12), and collecting what is due (Heb. 7:8). Sense 2. is predominant in theological passages. Thus Jesus takes our infirmities (Mt. 8:17), God receives praise (Rev. 5:12), and even Jesus has only what he receives from God (cf. 1 Cor. 4:7; 2 Pet. 1:17). Believers receive God's Spirit (Jn. 7:39; Acts 10:47) and the gifts of the Spirit (1 Pet. 4:10). They do so by faith (Gal. 3:2) and as a gift (cf. Rom. 1:5). Indeed, they receive even earthly things from God (1 Tim. 4:4), and they are invited to ask in order that they may receive (Jn. 16:24). Beyond this life lies the imperishable crown of life that they are also to receive (1 Cor. 9:25). Receiving may be by way of the church (1 Cor. 4:7), but it is from Christ himself that the gospel is finally received (Gal. 1:12).

analambánō, análēmpsis (→ *anabaínō*). This word, meaning first "to take up," has in the LXX such senses as "to load," "to set on the feet," "to raise" (a song), "to lift up" (in prayer), "to receive" (instruction), and "to keep upright." It can also become a term for rapture. In the NT we find "to take up" in Acts 10:16, "to take with" in 2 Tim. 4:11, "to take on board" in Acts 20:13-14, and "to put on" (weapons) in Eph. 6:13, 16. For the ascension the term occurs only in Mk. 16:19 and 1 Tim. 3:16, where the focus is not on the process (quickly hidden by a cloud even in Acts 1:2, 11) but on endowment with divine majesty. *análēmpsis* comes to be used for death in later Judaism, and this is the sense in Lk. 9:51, perhaps with a hint of the taking up or back to God that is completed with the ascension.

epilambánō, anepílēmptos. epilambánō means "to grasp," "to seize," "to lay firm hold," and also "to add to." In Lk. 14:4 it is used of the healing hand of Jesus, while in 1 Tim. 6:12, 19 it refers to the firm grasping of eternal life. *anepílēmptos,* meaning "inviolable," "unassailable," has the sense "beyond reproach" in 1 Tim. 3:2; 5:7; 6:14.

katalambánō. This term has such senses as "to seize," "to light upon," "to understand," and "to hold fast." One sees from the NT that the *katá* gives the term the character of intensity or surprise (Mt. 9:18; 1 Th. 5:4). The word is used epistemologically only in Luke and Acts. "To attain definitively" is the point in Rom. 9:30. An important use is in Phil. 3:12-13: the Christian must seek fellowship with Christ but will finally possess it only in the last day (cf. 1 Cor. 9:24). In Jn. 1:5 the sense is negative: the darkness does not overpower the light. For the sense "to perceive," "to comprehend," cf. Acts 10:34; Eph. 3:18.

metalambánō, metálēmpsis. This compound has the two senses "to take part" and "to change." In the NT we find the first sense in 2 Tim. 2:6; Heb. 6:7 (cf. Mt. 13:3ff.). The point in Acts 24:25 is the changing of an unfavorable time for a favorable one. *metálēmpsis* in 1 Tim. 4:3 forbids rules about foods. All foods, given by God, are ordained for the glad participation of believers in Christ, who are no longer subject to evil forces.

paralambánō.

A. *paralambánein* in the Greek and Hellenistic World. This compound has such senses as "to take over," e.g., a position, and "to inherit," especially intellectual things, e.g., a student from a teacher. It is important in philosophy, for most knowledge is handed down orally, and since it is practical, the teacher is an authoritative leader whose goal is the formation of character and who will still be respected even should the students strike out on their own (cf. Socrates). The handing down of questions, and of certain religious doctrines, is also significant, and we also find *paralambánō* in the mysteries for the inheriting of special rites and secrets, although with a stress on oral impartation rather than supernatural revelation.

B. The Question of Tradition in Judaism. In Judaism the material rather than the teacher is the binding link. Students may be grateful to teachers, but the authority rests with the law (as handed down by the prophets and exegeted by the rabbis). If there is an esoteric element, it relates to the withholding of some doctrines from the immature.

C. *paralambánō* in the NT.

1. With a personal object the term is used for the reception of Christ by the world (Jn. 1:11) and for acceptance into the kingdom of Christ (Jn. 14:3; Mt. 24:40-41).

2. With a material object we find "to take over" an office in Col. 4:17, "to inherit" the kingdom in Heb. 12:28, "to adopt" traditions in Mk. 7:4, and "to receive" Christian teachings in 1 Cor. 11:23; 1 Th. 4:1, but always with a close attachment in personal life and faith to Christ himself as their Author (cf. Gal. 1:12). Only in the light of the ultimate relationship to Christ, not of the historical or doctrinal content, can one understand the exclusive claim of what is received (cf. Gal. 1:9) and the final attributing of *paralambánō* to God himself (1 Th. 2:13). Christian understanding is at root a receiving of Christ himself (Col. 2:6).

prolambánō.

1. In 1 Cor. 11:21 this means "to anticipate" (cf. also Mk. 14:8, where the anointing is an intimation of Jesus' death).

2. In Gal. 6:1 the point is surprise, i.e., being betrayed into a fault unawares. In this case loving restoration is demanded, not unloving censure.

proslambánō, próslēmpsis. In the NT *proslambánō* occurs only in the middle (as in the LXX) in the sense "to take to oneself" (Acts 17:5; 18:26), "to take aside" (Mk. 8:32), or "to receive" (Rom. 14:1ff.). As God has received us, so we are to receive one another. The noun, not found in the LXX, occurs in Rom. 11:15 for "drawing to oneself."

hypolambánō.

1. With the basic sense "to take up," this means "to support" in 3 Jn. 8.

2. The idea in Lk. 10:30 is "to take up the words," i.e., to reply.

3. In Lk. 7:43 the meaning is "to suppose." The supposition is right here, but false in Acts 2:15.

4. In Acts 1:9 Jesus is taken up out of the disciples' sight.

[G. DELLING, IV, 5-15]

---

lámpō [to shine, light up], *eklámpō* [to shine out, blaze up], *perilámpō* [to shine around], *lampás* [torch, lamp], *lamprós* [bright, shining]

A. Meaning. *lámpō* has the primary sense "to shine," or transitively "to light up." The compounds are stronger forms. *lampás* means a "torch" or "lamp," and *lamprós* "bright," "shining."

B. The Moral and Religious Sense of the Words outside the NT.

1. The Greek and Hellenistic World.

a. Used with a human reference, *lámpō* may denote fighting power or an ideal, e.g., right.

b. Theologically the Greek world does not specifically associate light with deity, although light has a numinous character (e.g., in Homer). Torches are first used cultically in connection with chthonic deities. This explains their presence at birth, marriage, and burial. They seem also to have had purifying significance. A connection may perhaps be seen between protection against danger and the promotion of life. Because the torch symbolizes life, the torchbearer is especially close to the deity in the mysteries. The worship of light is more common in Egypt and the Near East, where light is the substance of deity and is related to life and knowledge. Along with the Persian cult of fire, the religious exalting of light in the Near East has an impact on such movements as Mithraism with its extensive use of lamps and torches and its stress on the stars, and on Manicheism with its dualism of light and darkness and its hope for a reconcentration of scattered light in the victorious consummation.

2. "To Shine" in the OT. The OT has many references to light, both natural and religious, yet it nowhere deifies light. God is the Creator of light (Gen. 1:3), he wraps himself in it (Ps. 104:2), he causes his glory to shine in the starry heaven (Is. 40:12), he makes the people like a flaming torch (Zech. 12:6), he seals the covenant with a torch (Gen. 15:17), he shines in the cloud at night (Ex. 13:21), he is depicted as a flaming fire (Ex. 24:17), he is (actively) a lamp to the psalmist (Ps. 18:28), he causes his face to shine on his people (Num. 6:25), and in his light they see light (Ps. 36:9), for he is the fountain of life (note life and light together).

3. Judaism. Judaism works out the OT concept of the luminous glory of God. The Shekinah is radiant light illumining the blessed. God's light shines through Adam, the Messiah, Israel, Jerusalem, the law, and its expositors. God will finally make his light visible, and the faces of the righteous will shine as the sun. In Philo one cannot by nature grasp the light of God; the shining of divine knowledge in the human spirit is like the creation of light or the sunrise.

C. *lámpein* etc. in the NT.

1. General Presuppositions. These correspond to the OT and Judaism with some Hellenistic influence. The NT content gives the terms their specific sense. The world of God is a world of light (cf. the images in Revelation). God's light is unchangeable (Jms. 1:17) and unapproachable (1 Tim. 6:16). But it relates itself to us. In Jesus God's world comes to us as a manifestation of light in antithesis to darkness.

2. The Theological Use of the Words.

a. *lámpein* and compounds are used of messengers from God's world (Acts 12:7; Lk. 2:9).

b. They are used of the Messiah at his coming (Lk. 17:24). There is an anticipation at the transfiguration (Mt. 17:2), and cf. the appearance to Paul (Acts 26:13).

c. They are used of the dawn of the experience of salvation (2 Cor. 4:6). A new creation of light corresponds to the first creation as the knowledge of God's glory shines in the heart and then shines out into the world. The linking of God, light, and saving knowledge is Hellenistic, but not the relating of knowledge to the historical act of salvation in Jesus Christ.

d. The words are used of the disciples (Mt. 5:15-16); they are to cause the light that they receive from God to shine out in the world to God's glory.

e. They are used of believers eschatologically (Mt. 13:43).

f. In Revelation they are used of the seven torches (Rev. 4:5, an OT phrase; cf. Zech. 4:2), of the star blazing like a torch (8:10), of the bright river (22:1), of Jesus as the bright morning star (22:16), and of the raiment of the angels (15:6) and the bride of Christ (19:8) (cf. Acts 10:30). As regards the clothing, the point is that it is white and radiant in contrast to the bloody finery of the harlot of 19:8. There is also a suggestion of heavenly transfiguration (19:8).

D. The Church.

1. The words are rare in patristic writings but there is a sense of possessing a unique light. The Hellenistic religion of light continues in Gnosticism.

2. The liturgical use of lamps develops by the fourth century, due partly to necessity, partly to contemporary examples and the general symbolism. Lamps are first placed around the altar, then on it.   [A. OEPKE, IV, 16-28]

→ *phṓs*

---

laós [people, crowd, nation]

laós, common in the Greek poets but not in prose, becomes a very important word in the LXX in a specific sense that recurs in the NT.

A. *laós* in Nonbiblical Greek.

1. The Form of the Word. The form is Doric-Aeolic. The Ionic form is *lēós,* the Attic *leṓs.*

2. The Etymology. This is uncertain. A link has been seen with *láas* ("stone"), but a connection with Old High German *liut (Leute)* is doubtful.

3. The Use in Homer. The first use in Homer is for "people" as a plurality ("crowd," "population," "group"), especially in distinction from rulers. The *laós* consists of *laoí* (the individuals). A special use is for soldiers in the army, sometimes denoted by nationality.

4. The Use in the Post-Homeric Period. The word is still used for "crowd" but may now denote the totality of a population (Pindar). The reference may still be to the public as distinct from rulers, and *laoí* may be used for *ánthrōpoi.*

B. *laós* in the LXX.

1. Hebrew Equivalents. In the LXX *laós* occurs some 2,000 times, seldom in the plural, and with a specific reference to Israel as God's people. In most instances the Hebrew original is *'am.* The LXX inclination is always to use *laós* when the reference is to Israel and to use *éthnos* even for *'am* when the reference is to another people, although this is not a consistent principle.

2. The Main and Popular Use of laós in the LXX. The first and decisive point is that *laós* now refers, not to people in general, but to a people as a unit (cf. Gen. 34:22; a city in Gen. 19:4; a tribe in 49:16; including the dead in 49:19). The *laoí* are not individuals but peoples. There is still a distinction between *laós* and rulers (Gen. 41:10; Ex. 1:22). The looser usage for people continues (e.g., "many people" in Num. 2:6; Josh. 17:14; "the oppressed people" in Ps. 18:27; "much people" in Gen. 50:20), and the LXX has *laós* for soldiers (cf. Ex. 14:6), but not in the plural.

3. The Specific LXX Use of laós for Israel.

a. Israel as *laós theoú.* While *laós* may denote any unit, the LXX mostly reserves the term for Israel, just as the Hebrew prefers *'am* for Israel. The stress is on the special position of Israel as God's people. *laós* is probably chosen for this purpose because, as a solemn and slightly archaic poetic term, it is more suitable than *éthnos* to express the distinction between Israel and other peoples.

b. The Nature of the Relation. Passages like Ex. 19:4ff.; Dt. 4; 7:6ff.; Ps. 135 show the nature of the relation. All nations belong to God, but he has allotted other nations to the angels and kept Israel for himself; she is a holy people by reason of this distinction.

c. The Basis of This Relation. God's free choice and act is the basis of the relation (Dt. 4:37; 7:6). It has no special advantages (Dt. 7:7). He has chosen her in love and faithfulness (7:8). He has freed her to serve him (Ex. 7:16, 26). In the plagues he clearly distinguishes her from Pharaoh's people (Ex. 8). This liberation from alien domination by God's mighty act, along with the institution of the covenant at Sinai (Dt. 4:7ff.), is what makes Israel a nation.

d. The Two-Sided Nature of This Relation. The relation is a reciprocal one of love and obligation. As God has separated Israel to himself (Lev. 20:26), he expects her to separate herself for him. She is holy, and is to be holy (Lev. 19:2). Her love for God must be her response to God's initial love for her (Dt. 7:9).

e. The Battle of the Prophets for Its Actualization. Because Israel does not live up to her obligations, the prophets wage their great battle (cf. Hos. 1:9; Is. 1:10). They threaten the judgment which falls at the exile (Dt. 4:27). But God remains faithful (Dt. 4:31). He waits only for repentance to treat Israel, or a remnant of Israel, once more as his people. The remnant represents the true Israel (Is. 10:20ff.). The present of possession becomes the future of promise linked to obedience (Jer. 7:23 etc.). The people is holy only by future sanctification (Is. 62:12). There is also a universalist extension to the nations (Is. 11:10; 62:10; Zech. 2:10-11, etc.) with the development of an eschatological messianic hope.

f. Prophecy as the Climax of the History of the Word *laós*. Prophecy brings to full expression the unique relation denoted by *laós*. But since Israel fails to live up to her status, the relation becomes judgment and its certainty can be maintained only by a faith in God's faithfulness that looks beyond present contradictions and extends its sweep beyond Israel's own frontiers.

C. *laós* in Hellenistic Judaism outside the Bible.

1. Josephus. Josephus in *Jewish War* uses *éthnos* for Israel and *laós* for "people," "population," "crowd." In the *Antiquities,* however, he often uses *laós* for Israel, largely because he makes considerable use of the LXX in this work.

2. Philo. Philo, who has *leós* as well as *laós,* engages in speculative allegorizing of the concept on the basis of its use in the Pentateuch (cf. Gen. 35:29; Dt. 7:7).

3. Inscriptions. Inscriptions, which have both *éthnos* and *laós,* apply the term to individual groups of Jews as representative of the whole people.

[H. STRATHMANN, IV, 29-39]

D. People and Peoples in Rabbinic Judaism.

I. The People.

1. God's Possession.

a. Israel as *laós theoú.* The basic motif that Israel is God's people finds expression in the idea that God has given the other nations to angels but kept Israel for himself. In some statements the national angels of the peoples seem to be their gods.

b. The Father-Son Relation between God and Israel. Another concept is that Israel is God's firstborn with special privileges as such. While the sonship is natural, it has ethical implications: Israelites are to behave as sons.

c. The People as the Bride of God. The theme of marital love also occurs in description of the relationship. As yet there is only betrothal, with small gifts, but with the Messiah will come the marriage and the fullness of gifts.

d. The Jews as Friends and Brothers of Their God. Along with marital love we also find the idea of friendship or brotherhood between God and his people. God is a brother in adversity (Prov. 17:17), and he invites his friends to eat with him (Cant. 5:1).

2. *The Holy People.* As God's people, Israel is holy by reason of her separation from idolaters and the gift of the law.

3. *The People as the Center of the World.* Judaism has a strong sense of the centrality of God's people. It will rule the world, if not in this aeon, then in the next. The main thought, however, is that the world is created for Israel, and it is only because of God's delight in Israel that the race is kept from perishing.

4. *The Meaning and Duration of Suffering.*

a. Suffering the Result of Sin. The disastrous situation of Israel after A.D. 70 is interpreted as the result of sinful conduct.

b. Suffering as a Means of Testing. With judgment goes the idea of testing. Only by way of this present world can one enter the future aeon. It is by suffering that Israel enjoys the three special gifts of the law, the land, and the world to come.

c. Suffering with a View to Purification for the Coming Aeon. Another thought is that of the atoning power of suffering. The people falls to temptations but penal suffering purges it for the future aeon.

5. *The Eternal Character of the People.* The peoples enjoy present success but Israel's great day will come with the Messiah, the final aeon, and world judgment, through which Israel will pass unscathed. Israel may thus hope for collective salvation. Some individuals may be excluded, others may need purgatorial cleansing to participate, and a few righteous pagans may find a place. Hence collective salvation does not necessarily embrace all (or merely) those of patriarchal descent.

II. The Peoples.

1. *The Remoteness of the Peoples from God.* The relation between Israel and other peoples is especially acute during and after the exile and involves tension between particularism and universalism. The assigning of the nations to guardian angels (or gods), who are, of course, inferior to God, entails a remoteness from God, a deprivation of the honors granted to Israel, and even at times a sense that God is hostile to other peoples.

2. *The Sinful Character of the Peoples.*

a. Transgression of the Adamic Commands. The conflict between God and the nations is ethical, not mythical. The first charge against them is failure to keep the six commands given to Adam.

b. Violation of the Noachic Commands. More common is the charge of failure to keep the seven commands given to Noah.

c. Rejection of the Law. The main charge is rejection of the law, which the peoples once knew but against which they rebelled, so that their ignorance is culpable.

3. *The Success of the Gentiles.* The political success of the nations is interpreted as a limited rewarding of transgressors for the good works they have done. In the last judgment it will be replaced by definitive punishment, for then there will be no more claim to reward.

4. *The Mass of Perdition.* The general thought is that the nations, being sinfully

remote from God, are for the most part excluded from the future aeon, and thus constitute a mass of perdition.

III. The Election and Privilege of the People.

1. Universalism. In the struggle between universalism and particularism, universalism assumes that the peoples have some share in God's salvation, and it is thus imbued with missionary zeal. Universalism is most at home in Hellenistic Judaism, which believes that Israel has a priestly and prophetic mission to pray for the human race and to spread the knowledge of the law among it. Balancing the more hopeful view of the nations, however, is a sense of superiority and privilege.

2. Particularism. With the disasters of A.D. 70 and 135 particularism tends to triumph with its view that the nations are God's enemies, that Israel is a privileged people, and that Israel will thus be given her rights as the only nation of the future aeon after the great world judgment. [R. Meyer, IV, 39-50]

E. *laós* in the NT.

1. Occurrence. The word occurs some 140 times in the NT (only eight in the plural). It is most common in Luke and Acts (36 times in Luke and 48 in Acts), and very rare in John.

2. The Popular Meaning. In the NT the predominant use is for "crowd," "people," "population." This use is rare in Mark and Matthew but common in Luke, where there is also distinction between the Sanhedrin and the *laós* (Lk. 22:2; cf. Acts 6:12), or the leaders and the *laós* (Acts 13:15).

3. The National Meaning. laós is parallel to *éthnē* in Lk. 2:30-31 (plural), and cf. Rom. 15:11; Rev. 7:9; 10:11, etc. In Acts 4:25, 27 there is transition to 4.; the plural comes from Ps. 2:1.

4. The Specific Meaning: Israél. We find this sense where there is antithesis to *éthnē* (Lk. 2:32) or there are additions like "Israel" (Acts 4:10), or "of the Jews" (Acts 12:11). *éthnos* may also denote Israel (cf. Lk. 7:5; 23:2; Acts 10:22; 24:10; Jn. 11:48ff.). In Luke-Acts this is mostly used either by or before non-Jews. *laós* may also denote Israel with no addition (cf. Acts 10:2; 28:17). In contrast, Acts uses *óchlos* when referring to non-Jewish crowds. It is specifically as God's people that Israel is *laós* (cf. Mt. 1:21; Lk. 1:68; Rom. 11:1-2; 15:10; Heb. 10:20; Acts 7:34; Lk. 24:19).

5. The Figurative Meaning: The Christian Community. The NT goes beyond the LXX by using *laós* for the church (cf. Acts 15:14; Rom. 9:25-26; 2 Cor. 6:16; 1 Pet. 2:9-10; Heb. 4:9, etc.). A basis for this lies in Lk. 1:17 (cf. 3:8). The saying of James in Acts 15:14 signifies the revolution whereby the *laós* has a new center in the gospel, so that it now comprises all believers, both Jewish and Gentile. This concept underlies Paul's mission, e.g., in Corinth (Acts 18:10). A spiritual *laós* replaces the biological *laós;* Paul adduces Hos. 2:23 in support (Rom. 9:23ff.). What has previously applied to Israel now applies to the church (1 Cor. 6:14ff.). Tit. 2:14 claims the phrase "a people of his own" for the church, and 1 Pet. 2:9-10 adds to this Israel's other titles of honor. Hebrews finds in the OT *laós* a type of the Christian community (cf. 2:17; 4:9, etc.). In Rev. 21:3 the church is the *laós theoú* of the prophecies of Zech. 2:14 and Ezek. 37:27.

6. The Significance of the Metaphorical Use. In the OT tension arises between the national and religious aspects of *laós,* which are meant to be in harmony (cf. Ex. 19:5; Hos. 1:9). Prophecy announces judgment on the national *laós* but also additions to the *laós* from the *laoí* or *éthnē.* This finds fulfilment in the church with the rise of a purely spiritual *laós* which is fashioned by God's saving act in Christ and in which faith is normative. This is one *laós;* it transcends all the frontiers of the *laoí,* although not eliminating them. The Judaizing element in the church resists this concept, insisting that Gentile believers must also become members of the older *laós* by circumcision. But Paul contends for the unity of the new *laós* simply on the basis of faith in the one Lord. Nationality is not a condition of belonging to God.

7. *Related Transfers.* As the true *laós* of God, the church is the true Israel (Gal. 6:16), the true seed of Abraham (Gal. 3:29), the true circumcision (Phil. 3:3), and the true temple (1 Cor. 3:16). These phrases all bind the church to the OT as its true fulfilment.

F. *laós* **in the Usage of the Early Church.** In the early church we find *laós* used for "crowd," "nation," "Israel," and "the church." There is a strong sense of the church as the new people of salvation (cf. Clement of Alexandria *Stromateis* 6.5.4.2.2). *laós* may also be used for the congregation at worship (1.1.5.1). When the congregation is distinguished from the leaders, this gives rise to the later idea of the "laity."

[H. STRATHMANN, IV, 50-57]

---

lárynx [larynx, throat]

---

lárynx, meaning "throat," occurs in Rom. 3:13 (quoting Ps. 5:9). The point here is that words uttered through the throat express inner depravity just as the breath of corruption issues from the entrance to a tomb (cf. Mk. 7:15, 18ff.).

[H. HANSE, IV, 57-58]

---

latreúō [to serve], *latreía* [service]

A. **In Nonbiblical Greek.**
1. latreúō.
a. Etymology. From *látron,* "reward," "wages," *latreúō* means "to work for reward," then "to serve."
b. Use. The word is used literally for bodily service (e.g., workers on the land, or slaves), and figuratively for "to cherish." We also find it for the service of the gods, but not in a technical sense.
2. latreía. The noun is more common than the verb and has such connotations as "service for reward," "labor," "bodily care," and "service of the gods."

B. **In the LXX.**
1. latreúō.
a. Occurrence. The verb, unevenly distributed, occurs some 90 times in the LXX, mostly in Exodus, Deuteronomy, Joshua, and Judges. The Hebrew original is *'bd,* which is usually rendered *douleúein* when human relations are at issue and *latreúein* when the reference is to divine service. *latreúein* always has a religious sense except in the play on words in Dt. 24:48.
b. Use. The religious use of *latreúein* is specifically a cultic use (Ex. 3:12; 4:23; 7:6, etc.). Cultic acts are obviously in view in 2 Sam. 15:8. The worship at issue may be worship of idols as well as God (cf. Ex. 20:5; 23:24; Dt. 4:28, etc.). The demand of the OT is that Israel should worship God alone, but the outward act is to express inward commitment (cf. Dt. 10:12ff.). The term has the same implications in Josh.

503

24:19. Unlike *leitourgeín, latreúein* does not refer only to priestly functions but to the religious and moral conduct of the whole people.

2. latreía. This occurs only nine times in the LXX and refers generally to cultic worship (Josh. 22:27) or to a single cultic act (Ex. 12:25: the Passover). In Maccabees it has the sense of religion except in 3 Macc. 4:14 (forced labor).

3. Comparison with Nonbiblical Usage. The LXX focuses on the cultic sense but with no restriction to priestly ministry. Secular Greek prefers *therapeúein* for cultic worship, but the LXX usually has this for healing or cherishing (except in Is. 54:17; Dan. 7:10), and it reserves *douleúein* for service in a general sense.

4. Philo's Usage. Philo uses the verb only once and the noun only six times. The verb denotes cultic worship but the noun embraces the ministry of virtue and spiritual service of God.

C. In the NT.

1. latreúō.

a. Occurrence. The verb occurs in the NT 21 times, eight of which are in Luke and Acts, six in Hebrews, four in Paul, two in Revelation, and one in Matthew. Three of the verses come from the OT.

b. LXX Influence. The service denoted by the verb is always rendered to God (or to the gods) (cf. Rom. 1:25; Acts 7:42).

c. The Sacrificial Ministry. As in the LXX, *latreúein* refers to the sacrificial ministry in Acts 7:7, 42; Heb. 8:5; 9:9; 10:2; 13:10. Hebrews, however, departs from the LXX by using the term for the ministry of the priests, thus equating *latreúein* and *leitourgeín.*

d. The Ministry of Prayer. Elsewhere the reference of *latreúein* is to the general ministry of prayer and praise, e.g., adoration in Mt. 4:10; Rev. 7:15; 22:3, prayer and supplication in Lk. 2:37; Acts 26:7.

e. The Generalized Figurative Sense. The verb has the general sense of righteous conduct in Lk. 1:74; Acts 24:14; Heb. 12:28; perhaps Heb. 9:14. Paul's missionary work comes under the heading of *latreúein* in Rom. 1:9; 2 Cor. 8:18; it is an act of religious service with an inward ("with my spirit") as well as an outward dimension. The Christian life in the Spirit is also a serving of God in Phil. 3:3. This more spiritualized rather than cultic *latreúein* is the main point in the NT.

2. latreía. Three of the five NT instances of *latreía* refer to the sacrificial ministry, i.e., Rom. 9:4; Heb. 9:1, 6. In each case the OT is in view. In Jn. 16:2, too, the word carries a hint of sacrifice. The same applies in Rom. 12:1, although here it is the living sacrifice of inner life and outer conduct that constitutes the *logikḗ latreía,* i.e., a service of God which conforms to human reason, and in which the divine reason is also at work. This statement is the climax of the process of internalizing and more comprehensive externalizing which begins with Dt. 10:12ff.

[H. STRATHMANN, IV, 58-65]

> ### *láchanon* [edible plant, vegetable]

In Mk. 4:32 the mustard seed becomes the greatest of plants (a parable of the divine rule). In Lk. 11:42 the tithe on all garden plants goes beyond the demands of the law (Dt. 14:22-23), although Jesus does not forbid it as such. In Rom. 14:2 Paul describes the "weak" as vegetarians; he probably has some Jewish group in view (cf. v. 5;

15:8ff.), but we know nothing of the details of the group or of its reasons for vegetarianism. Paul does not argue the rights or wrongs of the practice but contends for freedom, love, edification, and concern for the conscience of others.

[G. BORNKAMM, IV, 65-67]

---

legión [legion]

Borrowed from Lat. *legio, legión* is used for the Roman legion, which consists of about 6,000 infantry, 120 cavalry, and supporting special troops. The only NT instances are in Mk. 5:9 (referring to demons) and Mt. 26:53 (referring to angels). The underlying idea is that of extremely powerful demonic or angelic forces. But Jesus, as the Son of God, can drive out the demonic legion and has the angelic legions at his command. [H. PREISKER, IV, 68-69]

---

légō [to speak], *lógos* [word, Logos], *rhēma* [statement], *laléō* [to babble, prattle], *lógios* [eloquent, learned], *lógion* [saying], *álogos* [without speech, reason], *logikós* [rational, spiritual], *logomachéō* [to dispute about words], *logomachía* [dispute about words], *eklégomai* [to choose, elect], *eklogē* [chosen, elected], *eklektós* [chosen, elect]

---

légō, lógos, rhēma, laléo.

A. In the Greek World.

1. légō.

a. The basic sense of *légō* is "to gather" with the twofold nuance of repetition and separation.

b. The meaning "to gather" is often present, as is the middle "to assemble."

c. "To count" is a derived sense as the mental gathering of similar things.

d. Along similar lines we find "to enumerate," "to draw up," "to enter on a list."

e. From enumeration we move on to narration, which then yields the sense "to say," with such various nuances as "to speak," "to mean," and in compounds "to contradict," "to foretell," "to proclaim." There is approximation here to *eipeín* and the root *rhē*.

2. lógos.

a. Like *légō, lógos* has first the sense of "collection."

b. A second sense is "counting" with the nuances (i) calculation, (ii) account, (iii) consideration, or evaluation, and (iv) reflection, or, in philosophy, ground or reason.

c. Counting also gives the sense of "list" or "catalogue."

d. We then find "narrative," "word," "speech." In this sense, supplanting *épos* and *mýthos, lógos* acquires the most varied nuances, e.g., legend, proverb, command, promise, tradition, written account, conversation, sentence, prose, even thing.

3. rhēma. The root of *rhēma* has durative significance. What is denoted is something definitely or expressly stated, i.e., "statement." This may be an announcement or even a treaty. While distinguished as word from deed, *rhēma* as active word later comes to be used in grammar for the verb, and it lives on only in this sense.

4. laléō, laliá.

a. This word, like "lull," imitates childish babbling, and thus means "to prattle," "to babble." It is also used for the sounds of animals and musical instruments. As regards speech, it may denote sound rather than meaning, but also the ability to speak. In compounds the meaning is always "to prattle."

b. *laliá.* The point here is excessive speech, i.e., chatter or garrulity.

[A. DEBRUNNER, IV, 69-77]

B. The Logos in the Greek and Hellenistic World.

1. The Meaning of the Word lógos in Its Multiplicity. Although little used in epic, *lógos* becomes important with the rise of Greek rationality. As mental activity, it still has the basic sense "to reckon" or "to explain." It can thus be a. "an account" as narrative, speech, or saying, b. the result of reckoning as a principle, argument, or explanation (commercially an account), c. mathematically "proportion," "relation," then more generally "measure" or "order," and d. subjectively human reason, mind, or thought. For Socrates it combines the ideas of expression, enumeration, and definition. It necessarily stands related to such words as truth, knowledge, virtue, law, life, nature, and spirit. While it has a wealth of meanings, it nowhere has the sense of a word or address of creative power. The stress is on the rational element in speech; *rhḗma* carries the emotional and volitional emphasis. For Aristotle *lógos* denotes the showing of something for what it is, and orientation thereto. Only in magic does the term become a technical one for incantation.

2. The Development of the lógos Concept in the Greek World.

a. The Two Sides. On the one side *lógos* means speech or revelation as the clarification or explanation of something. It is the content of a thing in terms of its law, meaning, basis, and structure. On the other side is a metaphysical reality, the primary and intelligible law of things, which makes clarification possible and determines life. In this sense *lógos* can later be a cosmological hypostasis.

b. Heraclitus. As that which constitutes the being of both cosmos and humanity, *lógos* connects humanity with cosmos, with itself, and with deity. It thus establishes humanity in its true being. *lógos* here is both word and meaning evoking human words and works. As the law or principle of things, it transcends human opinion, grounds the *psychḗ*, and poses a claim which we see to be our own claim.

c. The Sophists. The *lógos* now becomes predominantly human reason, i.e., the power of thought and speech, and in politics the power of persuasion. It is the basis of pedagogy and culture as well as political life.

d. Socrates and Plato. With Socrates and Plato the thought develops that the *lógos*, through a common tongue, has the power to establish fellowship by way of agreement on the reality of things. Presupposed is a harmony between the *lógos* of reason and the *lógos* of reality. Truth is achieved when the *lógos* interprets things, but the *lógos* must proceed from them. The *lógos* makes philosophy possible because it is linked to being. *lógos* interrelates thought, word, matter, nature, being, and norm.

e. Aristotle. For Aristotle the *lógos* is the source of human virtue and piety, for actions are determined by the understanding, and we come to understanding by speech.

3. The lógos in Hellenism.

a. Stoicism. In Stoicism *lógos* expresses the ordered and teleologically oriented nature of the cosmos. It can thus be equated with God and with the cosmic power of reason of which the material world is a vast unfolding. Human *lógos* is a particular part of the universal *lógos*. The latter achieves awareness in us, thus combining God and humanity into a great cosmos. A later development is the equation of *lógos* and *phýsis* (nature) in a fusing of rational and vital force.

b. Neo-Platonism. Here, too, *lógos* is shaping power, whether in art or nature. The whole world is *lógos* as the pure power of form, while things in the world are also *lógos* in admixture with matter. The one *lógos* may thus divide into antitheses, but humanity, by its *lógos*, may attain to true *lógos*, i.e., the truth of being.

c. The Mysteries. In relation to deities of revelation *lógos* takes on a special sense as sacred history, or holy doctrine, or revelation. Gods like Osiris and Hermes are personifications of the *lógos* or the son of God. The sacred *lógos* leads to union with deity in which the initiate is also *lógos theoú*. Another use of *lógos* is for prayer, the only way whereby one may enter into relation with God.

d. The Hermes-Logos Theology. In the personification of *lógos* as Hermes (also Pan, Isis, etc.), there is no incarnation but an equation of the revelatory and cosmogonic principle with a deity, i.e., its hypostatizing as a god. Hermes serves as a mediator or herald of the divine will but also as the great force of conception. Thus *lógos* is creative potency, the guide and agent of knowledge, increasingly represented as a doctrine of revelation. We see this in the speculations of Hermeticism on creation and revelation, in which *lógos* is the son of God, the demiurge, which plays the role of an intermediary as an image of deity of which humanity is itself an image, and which forms a trinity with the divine purpose and the cosmos as the seed which the former fashions into the latter.

4. *The lógos of Philo of Alexandria.* A common term in Philo, *lógos* gives evidence of his attempt to unite Jewish religion and Greek philosophy. For Philo the divine *lógos* is a mediating figure which comes from God, forms a link between the transcendent God and the world, and represents humanity as a high priest and advocate before God. It is the sum and locus of God's creative power, and as such it orders and governs the visible world. If this conception shows Hellenistic features, it is distinctive inasmuch as the *lógos* is specifically the *lógos theoú* (or *theíos lógos*), it is personal, and its origin and mode of operation are described in figures taken from the sphere of procreation.

5. *Hellenistic lógos Speculation and the NT.* Differences between the *lógos* of Hellenistic speculation and the NT *lógos* are as follows. In the NT concepts like *lógos* and law are not important in themselves; what counts is what God has to say to us, the *lógos theoú*. The Greek *lógos* concept is an attempt to master the world. It is governed by the human *lógos*, which is found again in the cosmic *lógos*. To shape life according to the latter is to come to one's true being. Revelation is simply the perception of the inner law of self and all reality. In the NT, however, *lógos* expresses the specific divine address with which God comes to us here and now with his outside demand and claim. A related point is that the Greek *lógos* can divide up into individual *lógoi* in the phenomena which invest the world with reality. If it is the principle of harmony, it is not a mediator between God and humanity. Nor is it historically unique. It does not come in time but releases and reclaims forces in an eternal process which is not the outworking of a divine resolve but a continuous unfolding of things. Along these lines, it may be called the son of God, but only in equation with the world, not as the only-begotten who becomes one historically unique man, *sárx*.

[H. KLEINKNECHT, IV, 77-91]

C. The Word of God in the OT.

1. The Hebrew Equivalents of the Greek Terms for "Word." The roots '*mr* and *dbr* are the main equivalents for *lógos, lógion, rhḗma,* and *rhḗsis*. The former has a more poetic reference when used for "saying" (cf. Pss. 19:2-3; 68:11; Job 22:28), and the latter offers the classical terms for "word" in history, law, prophecy, and poetry. Etymologically the root sense seems to be "back." The reference, then, is to the background or content or meaning of what is said. In speech the content stands for the thing. The thing thus takes on a historical element in its word. The word *(dābār)* contains a thought. It makes a thing known, so that to grasp the word is to grasp the thought. But the word is also dynamic. It is filled with a power which is felt by those who receive it but which is present independently of such reception. As the prophets see and proclaim, these two aspects are most forcefully to be seen in God's word.

2. *The General Use of dābār for lógos and rhḗma.* The LXX treats *lógos* and *rhḗma* as synonyms and uses both for *dābār. rhḗma* is more common in the Pentateuch, Job, Joshua, Judges, and Ruth, but *lógos* takes the lead in the other historical books and the poetical books, and it occurs eight times more often than *rhḗma* in the prophets. When it is given such attributes as true, good, right, etc., *lógos* (or *rhḗma*) remains readily understandable to Greeks, but other combinations, e.g., hoping in the word in Ps. 119:74, or looking to it for life in Ps. 119:154, give evidence of the dynamic concept of the Hebrew original. Furthermore, since the meaning of a thing is implied in the word, so that word and thing are co-extensive, the most important quality of word is truth. As God's word is truth (2 Sam. 7:28), so ours must be (Gen. 42:16). An Amen must be uttered to give a word validity (Dt. 27:15ff.). The sum of God's word is truth (Ps. 119:160). Relating meaning and reality, and also speaker and hearer, the word belongs to the moral sphere as a witness to something for the persons concerned.

3. *The dābār of Prophetic Revelation.*

a. Revelation in Sign. In 2 Sam. 23:1ff. David is seized by God's Spirit and word, and he himself speaks God's word in an early messianic prophecy (for similar direct speech cf. Balaam in Num. 24:4, 16). In prophetic rapture the speaker has an eye and ear for the suprasensory picture and can thus impart the mystery. There is a relation between image and word. The messianic picture contains the prophetic word; the picture is to be put into words. The later prophets are familiar with a similar relation between picture and word; cf. the calls of Isaiah (ch. 6) and Ezekiel (ch. 1), the visions of Amos (chs. 7ff.), and the visions of Zechariah (chs. 4–5), although sometimes even the prophet needs an interpreter who can translate the picture into words (cf. Zech. 1:9; 2:4; 4:4; 6:4).

b. Revelation in Sign and Word. In the writing prophets, however, the pictorial revelation is less significant. The voice that speaks is not their own but God's. Puns (cf. Am. 8:2; Jer. 1:11-12) bring out the relation of image and word, but the word does not have to be combined with an image. Whether long or short, the speech finds its vital nerve in the word received from God, so that the complete address can itself be called God's word. Reception of the word is a spiritual process. This is implicit, although there are few express references to the Spirit (cf. 2 Sam. 23:2; Num. 24:2; Hos. 9:7).

c. Dissolution of the Sign. The word increasingly frees itself from the sign and becomes a pure expression of revelation. As in the call of Samuel (1 Sam. 3), God himself speaks, and this speech is a summons which empowers Samuel himself to speak God's word (1 Sam. 9:27) with its promise, its demand, and its judgment (1 Sam. 15:23, 26). The word thus becomes a force in Israel's history. Made known by the prophets, it comes to pass (1 Kgs. 2:27; Judg. 13:12), it is irresistible (2 Kgs. 1:17), and it stands forever (Is. 40:8).

d. The Writing Prophets. The formula "The word of the Lord came" at the head of prophetical books (Hos. 1:1; Mic. 1:1; Zeph. 1:1) implies that the whole book is God's word, with no distinction between the divine voice in the prophet and its written expression. The idea of revelation is present in the concept, and there is a transition to the understanding of the entire OT as God's word. If this word is teaching, it has a dynamic aspect as blessing (Is. 2:3; Am. 8:11-12) and constraint (Am. 3:8). The word is put on Jeremiah's lips (Jer. 1:9). It is his joy and delight (15:16), but it also puts him under compulsion (20:7ff.). It is no idle dream, for even when clothed in vision, it is an irresistible force (23:29) which is known because it infallibly comes to pass (28:9). Clarity concerning it comes only with prayer either as self-subjection (15:10ff.) or intercession (42:7ff.). In Is. 40ff. the word endures forever (40:8) and carries its fulfilment within itself, accomplishing its mission no less than the rain and snow (55:10-11). Coming from God, it is the effectual force which epitomizes all true prophecy.

4. *The Word as the Revelation of the Law.* As revelation, the word establishes a personal relation between God and the prophet which reorients the prophet's life and work. But the law as revelation may also be called word (often in the plural), and while the prophetic word is more topical, the legal word has permanent validity for the people. Thus the commandments are the words of the covenant in Ex. 34:28 (cf. Dt. 4:13) and the words of the book of the covenant (Deuteronomy) are read to the people in 2 Kgs. 23:2. Indeed, the commandment of Dt. 30:11 is equated with the word of 30:14; the reference in both cases is to the sum of the book. This word may be easily grasped, it is present revelation, and it carries within it the power of performance as the mouth speaks it and the heart receives it.

5. *The Divine Word of Creation.* Since the word always contains revelation, denoting the revealed will of God, it also applies in the sphere of revelation in creation. Thus in Gen. 1 the world has its origin in the divine word. The same concept of the creative power of the word occurs in Ezek. 37:4; Is. 40:26 etc.; Ps. 147:15ff. "By the word of the Lord the heavens were made" (Ps. 33:6ff.) is an apt summary.

6. *The Word in Poetry.* In poetry, too, revelation is by the word (Job 4:12). Ps. 119 is a treasury in this respect with its many nuances. The word stands in heaven, is truth, is a light, gives life, grants understanding, carries power, evokes trust and obedience, and is the object of hope. Here again the word has both a noetic and a dynamic aspect.

[O. PROCKSCH, IV, 91-100]

D. Word and Speech in the NT.

1. *Basic and General Aspects of the Use of légō/lógos.* The NT stress on hearing presupposes speaking. The main Greek word for speech is thus the vehicle of many important statements. Even at the baptism and transfiguration the word gives the event its theme and content. Yet *légō* and *lógos* carry various senses ranging from the everyday to the most pregnant. Indeed, one can even read of empty words (Eph. 5:6), or evil words (3 Jn. 10), or false words (2 Pet. 2:3), or flattering words (1 Th. 2:5). Human words are full of error (Jms. 3:2), and the words of human wisdom are impotent for all their eloquence and plausibility (1 Cor. 1ff.). The terms can also be used in a neutral sense, as in Mt. 7:28; Mk. 7:29; 2 Th. 2:2. *lógos* may denote a letter, address, account, or rumor (cf. 2 Cor. 10:11; Acts 2:41; 1:22; Lk. 5:15), or the partial record in a book (Acts 1:1). In tongue-speaking it may even be inarticulate (1 Cor. 14:19), for wherever there is *légein* there is *lógos*. It is because the stress is on saying something that the same term may be put to such varied use, e.g., for the word of

knowledge or the opposite, or for the word of power or the empty word. Even in the pregnant use for the word of the gospel the same sentence may contain the term in a looser or opposing sense (cf. 1 Cor. 2:4). The context provides the specific content, but the basic meaning is the same, namely, a spoken word. This is true even in John 1 with its reference to God's revealing word, for the word is no independent entity but points to him who in living reality speaks it. Jesus' use of *légō* in the emphatic *egō légō hymín,* which may also be used by the Baptist (Mt. 3:9), Paul (Gal. 5:2), and even Gamaliel (Acts 5:38), carries an authoritative note, not because of the *légō,* but because of the person of the speaker.

2. *More Specific and Technical Meanings.*

a. In the NT *lógos* may mean an "account" or "reckoning." The use is secular in Acts 19:40 but contains the idea of eschatological responsibility and judgment in the parables of Jesus (Mt. 18:23; 25:19; Lk. 16:2) and in the general stress on Christian accountability (1 Pet. 3:15; Mt. 12:36; Heb. 13:17). Paul plays on the commercial sense in Phlm. 15ff. "Having to do" with God in Heb. 4:13 carries a sense of relationship involving responsibility.

b. "Ground" or "reason" is the sense in Acts 10:29; 18:14.

c. "Matter" or "subject" is the point in Acts 8:21; 15:6.

d. In the Hebraic phrases in Mt. 5:32; Lk. 4:36 we find a similar meaning to b. and c. The reference in Mt. 5:32 is probably to a form of licentiousness, and in Lk. 4:36 the substance of what is said is at issue.

3. *The Sayings of Jesus.*

a. The Quotation of the Sayings. Since Jesus himself did not write down his sayings, the record refers constantly to his speaking or his *lógoi* or *rhḗmata.* The reference may be to a single saying (Mk. 10:42), a group of sayings (Mt. 26:1), or his total message (Mt. 24:35). Various formulas are used (cf. Mt. 26:75; Mk. 14:72; Jn. 18:9; Acts 11:16; Lk. 22:61: 1 Th. 4:15, etc.). Although there is no fixed formula, and differing versions of the same sayings may be freely given, the sayings of Jesus clearly have an authoritative character (cf. 1 Cor. 7:10). The authority is that of genuine words that are spoken, heard, and recounted; it is in the word made flesh that the glory is seen.

b. The Authority of the Sayings of Jesus. In the Gospels the sayings of Jesus often arouse displeasure (Mk. 10:22) and offense (Mt. 15:12), not just because they are hard (Jn. 6:60), but because they carry such an unheard-of claim (Mk. 2:7). Yet they also cause astonishment by reason of their authority (Mt. 7:28). The reaction to his word is eternally decisive (Mk. 8:38), for it demands faith in him. His word, however, goes hand in hand with his work. It is an active word which effects healing (cf. Mt. 8:8), exorcism (Mt. 8:16), raising the dead (Lk. 7:14-15), and ruling the elements (Mk. 4:39). The preservation of the Aramaic (cf. Mk. 5:41; 7:34) shows that power is seen in this word, not in the sense of a magical formula, but in virtue of its efficacious authority (cf. Acts 3:6; 1 Cor. 7:10). Similar data occur in John (cf. 4:41ff.; 6:60ff.; 8:51; 12:48; 14:24; 15:3, etc.). It is because Jesus is the Christ and the Son that his word has this authority (Jn. 14:24; 6:63, 68). It may thus be put on the same footing as Scripture (2:22). To grasp it is to be grasped by it (Jn. 6:65; cf. Mt. 19:11; Mk. 4:11; Lk. 9:45), although this does not absolve from responsibility when there is failure to do so.

c. The Appeal to Jesus' Word outside the Gospels. Outside the Gospels there are only a few direct quotations, but there are many allusions, and in any case the words are seen as part of the total christological reality. They are thus viewed with the works, related to the cross and resurrection, and set in the context of Christ's present ministry (cf. Heb. 1:3; Rom. 10:17).

4. The OT Word in the NT.

a. The NT quotes the OT as both Scripture and word. In verbal forms we find several words, including *légein*, in both the active and the passive. The speakers may be human (Moses, David, etc.), superhuman (Scripture, the preexistent Christ), divine, or indefinite. Sometimes God himself is called the speaker when we have sayings from the prophets or Psalms (Mt. 1:22 etc.). But this implies no elimination of the human subjects. No antithesis is seen between divine and human speaking. The indefinite and passive often imply divine speech (cf. Mt. 5:21ff.).

b. Both *lógos* and *rhḗma* may be used for human words, whether individual or collective, and also for divine sayings, usually with reference to OT verses or passages, although God's word comprises the totality of his revelation in Col. 1:25 and Heb. 4:12. Oddly, "word of the Lord" is not used in NT quotations from the OT, and "the Lord spoke" occurs only within quotations, though cf. Mt. 1:22; 2:15.

c. Sometimes it is hard to say whether the divine word is the OT or the Christian message (cf. Heb. 4:12; Eph. 6:17; 13:7). There are not, of course, two words, but one (cf. Heb. 1:1-2).

5. The Special Word of God to Individuals in the NT.

a. Simeon and the Baptist. Both Simeon and John are put in the category of OT prophets when it is said that God's *rhḗma* came to them (Lk. 2:29; 3:2).

b. The Apostolic Period. While the phrases *lógos theoú* and *lógos* (or *rhḗma*) *toú theoú* are common, they are not used again for special directions. These are now given by the Spirit, or Christ, or an angel, or the divine voice. The reason for the change is that there has been a definitive coming in the incarnate Word.

c. Jesus. The word of God is never said to come to Jesus himself, not even at the baptism or transfiguration. While we have a voice from heaven at these events, the words spoken are not words of direction but of ratification to the hearers. To speak of God's word coming to Jesus is inappropriate in view of the unity with the Father that is implied in, e.g., Mt. 11:27.

6. The Early Christian Message as God's Word (outside John).

a. Statistics. Word of God, word of the Lord, and word are all used for the Christian message with no discernible difference apart from statistical distribution. The first term occurs 30 times, the second eight, and the third 40.

b. Content. The content is apparent when we compare Acts 6:1ff. and 1:21ff. The word is witness to Jesus. Lk. 1:2 confirms this, and cf. Acts 17:11; 18:5, etc. To receive the word is not just to receive the OT but to receive the message of Jesus which is the fulfilment of the OT. The usage of Paul is the same (1 Th. 1:6; 1 Cor. 14:36; Gal. 6:6; Col. 4:3-4). Tit. 1:2-3 plainly states the content of the Pauline *lógos*. Similarly it is the message of Jesus that gives life in 1 Pet. 1:23, 25 and Jms. 21. *rhḗma* is much less common in this sense (Heb. 6:5; Eph. 5:26; 1 Pet. 1:25).

7. The Character and Efficacy of the Early Christian Word (outside John).

a. As the gospel, the word is the word of the cross, reconciliation, grace, life, and truth. It is so because the speaker is God. Explicitly or implicitly *toú theoú* controls the *lógos* statements of the NT (cf. 1 Th. 2:13). Paul is its minister, and must guard it against corruption (2 Cor. 2:17), but it is God who speaks through him (cf. 2 Cor. 5:19-20). This insures its efficacy (Jms. 1:18). Because it is the power of God (1 Cor. 1:18), it cannot be bound (2 Tim. 2:9). Prayer must be made that God give it free course (2 Tim. 3:1) or open a door for it (Col. 4:3; cf. Acts 6:4 for the relating of the word and prayer). Not magical, its efficacy is concrete, overriding obstacles and human opinions, and grasping and sanctifying believers. As the word of grace, life, or salvation, it does not just preach these things but effects them.

b. Initially, then, the human response to the word is passive, as in a new birth (1 Pet. 1:23). God's choice precedes its hearing (cf. Acts 15:7), and the Holy Spirit seals those who hear and believe (Eph. 1:13), not by intellectual agreement alone, but by appropriation in faith (Acts 4:4). Receiving the word, when authentic, involves doing (Jms. 1:22). Disobedience blasphemes it (Tit. 2:5); obedience glorifies it (Acts 13:48).

c. The *lógos* is always, concretely, a spoken word, not a mere concept. There is no word, and hence no reception, faith, or Christian life, without proclamation (Rom. 10:17). The norm of teaching is faithfulness in transmitting the word spoken in the Christ event (cf. Lk. 1:1ff.; Tit. 1:9).

8. The Word in the Synoptic Account of Jesus.

a. In the Synoptists the word is plainly linked to the person of Jesus. It is the word of Jesus himself, and also the word about him.

b. Jesus himself preaches the word (Mk. 2:2; 4:33; Lk. 5:1). Yet this is said only rarely, for Jesus is no mere teacher or prophet. The whole work of Jesus is the word which others are to speak (cf. Mk. 11:4).

9. The Word in the Synoptic Sayings of Jesus.

a. The term *lógos* is infrequent in Jesus' own sayings. In Lk. 8:21 Jesus says that his mother and brethren are those who hear the word of God and do it, while in Lk. 11:28 he pronounces blessing on those who hear the word of God and keep it. Matthew and Mark have "will" for "word" in the first case.

b. "Word" is used in all three gospels in the interpretation of the parable of the sower (Mk. 4:13ff. and par.). Some scholars doubt whether Jesus offered the interpretation himself, but the use corresponds to what we find elsewhere in the NT.

c. In this light the term is legitimate in this context, whether or not it is authentically used by Jesus himself.

10. lógos/lógoi (toú theoú) in Revelation.

a. The use of *lógoi* at the beginning and end of Revelation (words of the prophecy, 1:3; of this book, 22:9; etc.) shows it to be authentic revelation. *lógoi toú theoú* is used relative to the promise in 19:9 and to prophecies about the beast in 17:7.

b. Apart from 19:13 the singular *ho lógos toú theoú* is always linked with witness (cf. 1:2, 9; 6:9; 12:11; 20:4). This is the witness of Christ himself, and it entails suffering. The word, then, may be apostolic preaching, the testimony of martyrs, or the revelation itself, which is an elucidation and illustration of the *lógos* that is spoken by God and by the witness of Jesus. Only in the light of 19:13 can one say whether *lógos* and *martyría* are two things or one.

11. Jesus Christ the lógos toú theoú.

a. Preaching the Christ event is preaching the word, and to receive it is to have faith in Christ. The ministers of the word are eyewitnesses (Lk. 1:2). The word is not just what Jesus said but the mystery of God disclosed in Christ (Col. 1:25ff.). An event, not a concept, underlies this use. Christ is God's "Yes" in his historical person (2 Cor. 1:19; cf. Rev. 3:14). This shows that Rev. 19:13 is expressing something integral to the whole Christian message when it says that his name is the Word of God.

b. We have here the filling out of an old term with a new content that catches up rather than negates the old; cf. for parallels such terms as *ktísis, entolé,* and *diathḗkē* (2 Cor. 5:17; Jn. 13:34; Lk. 22:20). One sees from 1 Jn. 1:1 that the use of "word" for Jesus is dynamic. A real word is spoken; hence the use of the neuter "that which" along with the masculine *lógos*. This protects the equation of Jesus and *lógos* from mythological personification.

c. Rev. 19:13 declares the name that no one knows, relating the *lógos* to the King of kings but still linking the historical and eschatological Christ (cf. 1:7).

12. 1 Jn. 1:1ff.

a. The *lógos* here is the historical Christ in a dynamic equation that preserves the idea of a real word, avoiding mythical personification.

b. Yet 1 Jn. 1:1ff. introduces new elements, comparable to Jn. 1:1, with the phrases "from the beginning" (v. 1) and "with the Father" (v. 2).

13. The Distinctiveness of the lógos Saying in Jn. 1:1.

a. John uses *lógos* in many combinations, e.g., "of God" in 10:35, "of Isaiah" in 12:38, "of Jesus" in 18:32, "my" in 5:24, etc. Only in the Prologue do we find *ho lógos* in the absolute.

b. There is in John no hesitation to present Jesus as a teacher of the *lógos*, for the basis of the whole gospel is the unity of Christ's speech and action. Jesus gives the *lógos*, but he also is the *lógos*. This fact controls the use.

c. Yet after the Prologue Jesus is never again called *lógos*, for the preexistent *lógos* (1:1) has now become flesh (1:14), i.e., Jesus.

d. The identity of Jesus and *lógos* emerges here as the kernel of all the NT sayings that use *lógos* in a specific sense; the new thing is the preexistence of the *lógos* and its transition to history. This appears at several points in the Gospel (cf. 1:30; 6:33ff., 46, 50ff., 62; 8:23, 38, etc.). Preexistence is stated by Paul too (Rom. 1:4; Phil. 2:6ff.; Col. 1:16; cf. 1 Cor. 8:6). What it expresses is a manifest reality that is of ethical or soteriological concern. It is the necessary presupposition of Jesus' awareness of his sonship and his adoption of the title Son of Man. The distinctive thing in Jn. 1:1ff. is that preexistence is now put thematically at the head and expressed in the term *lógos*.

14. The Concern and Derivation of the lógos Sayings in John: I.

a. Lack of Speculative Concern. While the sayings have a speculative ring, they arise out of the historical figure of Jesus and the historical process of seeing and hearing him. Hence we do not have the personifying of a concept. The interest is not in ideas but in an event, which is now given its eternal context. Basic is seeing the eternal glory in this *sárx*, i.e., in the historical Jesus.

b. Allusion to Gen. 1:1. Since the word goes back to the beginning with God, a link naturally arises with the creative word in the beginning which is the origin of all things. The *en archḗ* is intentional (Jn. 1:1); it leads on to the truth of v. 3 that the word and "God spoke" of Gen. 1:1ff. are the same. The word cannot be detached from God; it always goes forth as God's word. Yet the word is no mere function; it is personal, identical with the person in whom it was made flesh. The preexistence of the *lógos* is that of Christ himself.

c. Other Connections. While messianic teaching contributes to Jn. 1:1ff., this does not contain preexistence statements. We find these, however, in relation to such concepts as the Gnostic *lógos*, the Gnostic primal man, the Hellenistic Jewish *sophía*, and the Palestinian Jewish law. Attempts have thus been made to find parallels in Jn. 1:1 to all four of these. The "primal man" parallel is too indirect to be considered seriously, but *lógos* calls for discussion even though there might be an Aramaic original for Jn. 1:1ff.

d. Relations to Contemporary "Word" Speculations. The author may well be adapting a concept common in contemporary speculation, but he relates it specifically to the preexistent word which is uttered in creation and which becomes a historical and personal event in Jesus. Nor does he do this polemically or apologetically. Only the term itself forms a connection; the concern and the context are quite different.

15. *The Interest and Derivation of the lógos Sayings in Jn. 1:1ff.: II: Logos and Law.* In view of the antithesis of word and law (cf. 1:17), there is a more direct relation to the Palestinian concept of the law. Unlike contemporary *lógos* speculation, this is a basic question throughout John. The law, too, is a word (cf. Ps. 119). To it, too, preexistence and majesty are ascribed. But what the rabbis say about the law is now said about Christ, in whom God's word is not just transmitted but enacted. Jesus does not merely teach the law; he is the law. In him the disciples see the true and final law. As Jesus Christ, the personal word, is the new temple, or the new covenant, so, as the eternal word that has become an event, he is the new law. Similarly, he might be described as true wisdom, although wisdom speculations bear no direct relation to Jn. 1:1ff.

lógios. This word has two meanings, a. "eloquent" and b. "educated" or "learned." Sense b. is more common in Philo and Josephus. The only NT instance is in Acts 18:24, where Apollos is called *lógios.* In the light of v. 25 and 1 Cor. 1:12 "eloquent" is often preferred here, but the accompanying clause would also justify "learned."

lógion.

A. **The Pre-Christian Use.**
1. This word means "saying," "pronouncement," "oracle."
2. The LXX uses it for God's word in, e.g., Num. 24:4; Dt. 33:9; Is. 5:24; Ps. 19:14. It is more or less equivalent to *lógos* in this use.

B. *lógion* **in the NT.**
1. In Acts 7:38 the reference is plainly to the revelation at Sinai, i.e., to the law which Moses received and was to pass on to the people.
2. In Rom. 3:2 the divine *lógia* are specifically but not exclusively God's promises to Israel (cf. the promises of Rom. 15:8).
3. In Heb. 5:12 the main emphasis is on the revelation of God in Christ, although God's prior revelation in the OT is included (cf. 1:1-2). The readers have become so hard of hearing that they need to be taught the first principles of this afresh.
4. In 1 Pet. 4:10-11 the good steward, bearing a divine charisma, utters Spirit-filled pronouncements. The usage here is closest to the nonbiblical (A.1.), but the "as" makes it plain that strictly only God can speak *lógia theoú.*

In the NT, then, the term may refer to past sayings but it may also be used for the proclamation of what God has said in Jesus Christ, which will, of course, include the individual sayings of Jesus.

C. *lógion* **in the Usage of the Early Church.**
1. The term may still denote an individual saying (cf. 2 Clem. 13.3-4; Justin *Apology* 32.14).
2. It is also used, however, for a number of such sayings, or for the sum of them (cf. 1 Clem. 13.4; 19.1; 62.3; Clement of Alexandria *Stromateis* 1.31.124.2, etc.).
3. In some passages which refer to the *lógia toú Kyríou,* there is thus doubt whether individual sayings are meant or the whole gospel (cf. Pol. 7.1; Irenaeus *Against Heresies* 1, Preface 1).

4. The title of Papias' work *(logíōn kyriakṓn exergḗseis)* is obviously not meant to refer only to sayings. Similarly, when Papias speaks about the composition of Mark, *tá kyriaká lógia* is obviously equivalent to "what the Lord said and did." The same applies to *tá lógia* in connection with Matthew. This plainly includes dominical sayings, but a more comprehensive meaning is also possible. The passage offers no support, then, for the argument that Papias is a witness in favor of a special book of sayings (Q).

álogos. This word means a. "without speech," "dumb," and b. "without reason or basis." Sense b. occurs in Acts 25:27, but the meaning in 2 Pet. 2:12; Jude 10 might be either a. or b. ("dumb" or "irrational" animals).

logikós. This means either a. "belonging to speech" or b. "belonging to reason." Sense a. does not occur in the NT but we find sense b. in 1 Pet. 2:2 ("spiritual"). Perhaps *logikós* is used here rather than *pneumatikós* (cf. v. 5) because, like milk, it is a familiar term in philosophy and mysticism. Parallels show that it may express the spiritualizing of the cultic, and this is its function in Rom. 12:1, where our bodies are to be offered, not in immolation, but in spiritual worship (cf. 1 Pet. 2:5). In Judaism, too, one finds moral spiritualizing of the cultus. In Paul, however, this is christological as well as ethical. It is based on the mercies of God in Christ (Rom. 12:1), and the norm of conformity to the *lógos* lies in the Spirit of Jesus Christ.

logomachéō, logomachía. The verb occurs in 2 Tim. 2:14, which says that "disputing about words" is of no profit. The noun is used in 1 Tim. 6:4, which issues the warning that those who do not keep to sound words have a liking for "disputes about words," which can have only harmful results.   [G. KITTEL, IV, 100-143]

eklégomai.

A. The Common Greek Meaning. In the middle *eklégō* means "to make a choice," with various objects, e.g., slaves, payments, or abstract things. The perfect passive means "choice" or "chosen."   [G. SCHRENK, IV, 144]

B. Election in the OT.
1. The LXX Rendering of the Hebrew. The verb is mostly used in the LXX (108 times) for the Hebrew root *bḥr*. Where it translates other roots this is for the sake of variety or theological association. Greater caprice may be seen in the use of the verbal adjective *eklektós*, which may carry such meanings as "choice," "desirable," "costly," etc. The root *bḥr* may itself be rendered by other Greek words. (For details cf. *TDNT*, IV, 144-46.)
2. bḥr and Related Expressions. The verb *bḥr* ("to choose," "to elect") occurs 164 times in the OT. In 92 cases God is the subject, and divine election is also the theme in 13 instances of the passive. Human choice may be of God or his law, will, etc., although naturally the word also has a common use. When God is the subject, the term has very definite doctrinal significance. It expresses a resolve of the divine will with an element of insistence (cf. 1 Sam. 12:22). Related terms bring out the implied element of taking, separating, appointing, and knowing. Congruent with election are the concepts of redeeming, liberating, and delivering, or, from another angle, those of people and inheritance, although such terms are either historically oriented or refer more specifically to the covenant than to election. The belief in election is bound up closely with *bḥr*, which is well adapted to provide an interpretation of historical revelation.

3. bḥr in Current Usage. Like the word "to choose," *bḥr* denotes choice among possibilities. When objects are chosen, purpose is implied, e.g., land, stones, wood, animals, etc. for specific ends (cf. Is. 7:15-16; Ps. 118:22). The same applies in the choice of persons (Gen. 6:2; Ex. 18:25), which also carries an element of approval. While emotion has a part in the choice, intelligence is a more important factor.

4. bḥr as an Act of Religious Confession. The rational element is present when the choice is of God or false gods (Josh. 24:15, 22), of God's law or way (Ps. 119:30, 173), of the fear of God (Prov. 1:29), or of the sanctuary (Ps. 84:10). God shows the way (Ps. 25:12), and instruction brings the conviction that it is right. Yet choosing what is pleasing to God means keeping the covenant and is thus an act of confession (Josh. 24:22). A rationally grounded act of will underlies the commitment to the covenant God. In Josh. 24 only those who leave Yahweh can choose among other gods (v. 15). But this is plainly regarded as an absurdity. Hence it may be that there is some sarcasm in the idea of "choosing" God in v. 22. To be sure, it is not unprofitable to do so, but there is no real thought here of the establishment of a contract, for God has called Abraham and liberated the people, so that there is no real choice but to serve him. In this regard the element of selection plays only a minor role and has little influence in the rest of the OT. One possible explanation of the story of Josh. 24 is that it represents an act of political resolve whereby the tribes bind themselves to unity on a sacral basis, i.e., on the common confession of Yahweh. There is perhaps allusion to something similar in Dt. 35:5.

5. The Election of Individuals by God.

a. Only rarely does the divine choice refer to individuals (apart from kings). One of David's sons in 2 Sam. 5:15 bears the name Ibhar, which means "God elects" or "May God elect." The idea is probably that the bearer of the name, or his family or people, is the recipient of divine favor.

b. Surprisingly the prophets do not specifically equate their calling with election. In Is. 49:7 the Holy One has "chosen" the servant of rulers, and in 42:1 the servant is "elect" ("called" in v. 6). Here election is linked to calling in connection with a mission that is divinely given to the people (42:6). In general, however, election and calling are regarded as distinct; the former stresses the subject, the latter the action. Thus the call of Amos is a summons to go and prophesy (7:15). The call of Jeremiah is close to Is. 49:1ff., but the prophet says that he is "known" rather than "chosen." As in the case of Isaiah (Is. 6) or Amos (7:14), the point is that the idea of selection by God is meaningless for the prophets. It is not as though he were choosing among many possibilities.

c. National heroes such as Abraham (Neh. 9:7), Moses (Ps. 106:23), and David (Ps. 78:70) are sometimes said to be chosen, but these references are few and late.

d. The same applies to election to the priestly office. The choice of Eli is earlier (1 Sam. 2:28) but has little independent theological significance.

e. In general the election of individuals occurs in the context of the election of the community. Those who pray (cf. Ps. 65:4) are conscious of their election, which they experience as divine grace that is renewed in the cultus. If in this experience they are marked off from the wicked among the people (Ps. 5:5ff.), it is as personal representatives of the elect nation. What is said about individuals exemplifies the one concept that derives from the common heritage of faith.

6. The Choice of the King. The same applies to the king. He is not a divine ruler in pagan style but is elected by God to guarantee the divine direction of the people's destiny on a religious basis. It is for the sake of Israel that God establishes David

(2 Sam. 5:12); the king's people is God's people (Ps. 28:8). There are, of course, more direct references to anointing than to election, and there is a political element in the making of a king which means that the people can also be said to choose their ruler (1 Sam. 8:18; 12:13). Note, however, that there is a skeptical element in these references. If a popular element cannot be avoided, it is disapproved except insofar as God himself makes a decision in favor of the one whom the people chooses, so that the bearer of the kingly office may be regarded as the elect of Yahweh. This explains why a secular monarchy without sacral sanction is impossible in Israel (cf. Eshbaal in 2 Sam. 2:8-9 and Adonijah in 1 Kgs. 1:38ff.). Even though Saul is chosen by the people, and gains his victory over the Ammonites, there has to be the ratification by the divine choice in 1 Sam. 10:17ff. and by the anointing in 1 Sam. 10:1, in which Samuel serves as a representative of nabiism with its charismatic emphasis (cf. 10:5ff.). The law of monarchy in Dt. 17:14ff. thus distinguishes between divine choice and human institution. The stress lies on God's decision. God appoints, the anointing ratifies the divine choice, and the people adds its own ratification (2 Kgs. 10:5), although this ratification may also at times be called the choice of the people (2 Sam. 16:18).

7. *The Election of the People.*

a. The thought of national election finds clear formulation in Dt. 14:2 but it is implicit in the basic idea that Israel is God's people (cf. Judg. 5:11). In secular terms this idea expresses a sense of nationality strengthened by common experience. Belief in God, however, is the impulse behind the development of nationality and can sustain it even when political identity is lost (Jer. 31:10). God's supremacy is linked to Israel's power and loyalty but it also confers uniqueness on this people (Num. 23:9). Only on the basis of faith in God's omnipotence can the people maintain itself among alien cultures and their resources.

b. The encounter between national election and the universal rule of God poses the question of God's purpose in choosing Israel. A clash thus arises in which the prophets oppose unconditional ethical commitment to nationalistic self-awareness, and even propose the concept of a mission of the elect people to the nations.

c. In Israel particularly (as distinct from Judah) a religious nationalism is fostered which evades the unconditional authority of the ethical and finds easy assurance in the thought of God's cultic presence (Mic. 3:11). The cry "Peace, peace" (Jer. 6:14) when there is no political peace except in the balance of the great powers serves only to blind this theologically perverted nationalism to the inner moral crises which, in spite of temporary military successes, will finally bring disaster.

d. The prophetic message does not dispute the election of Israel but shows that it involves special responsibility rather than primacy or privilege. Thus Amos points out that the elect nation is subject to special scrutiny and judgment (Am. 2:4ff.; 4:12), for God's interest in his people is in its righteousness (5:24), not its greatness.

e. In Deuteronomy (cf. 4:37; 7:6; 10:15) the election of the people rests on the love of God, not on any national qualities, and it carries with it a commitment to holiness. Rational thought blends here with the certainty of faith. The idea of election, like that of the covenant, is both logically clear and theologically fruitful. Love and faithfulness determine the divine choice.

f. From one standpoint election establishes the special status of the elect as a holy people that must serve God's purposes. From another standpoint the concept sustains the idea of history as the place of God's revelation. The Lord of the earth makes his will known in a historical process which encompasses all people.

g. This raises the problem of the Gentiles. Election means rejection. A judgment on false religions is pronounced (Dt. 7:5, 25). Israel can have no part in the worship of idols, which gives rise to unworthy customs (Dt. 9:5). This implies that God alone is the true Lord of the world. But it must not lead to arrogance (Dt. 9:6ff.), for the covenant is an ongoing thing (5:2-3), and the sense of election must rise above emotional nationalism and serve the observance of covenant demands.

h. An emotional element may still be found in Deuteronomy in the form of love. God elects Israel because he loves her, not for her greatness (7:7) or purity (9:5), but as a free gift. Deuteronomy does not draw the inference that this love of Israel means lack of love for the nations. The reference is to his love of Israel as a fact.

i. Election means education. Israel is to be what she is by God's will (Dt. 8:5). God's action in election is purposeful. The education, however, is not abstractly pedagogical but personal. In this regard, then, election uniquely intertwines theology and faith in statements of distinctive charm and didactic value.

j. The patriarchs are embraced by election both as the fathers of the people and as the bearers of blessing to all peoples (Gen. 22:18; 26:4). Abraham bears the promise because he follows the call of God in simple trust and obedience through all the crises of his history from his alien status to the unexpected gift of a son and the adventures in Egypt. The way of God is a way of salvation, for he wills by Abraham to lead to righteousness and judgment (Is. 51:2).

k. Understanding the national history by means of the concept of election does not come easily, for election as prerogative comes into collision with election as responsibility (cf. Am. 7:10ff.; Jer. 7:26; 28; 37–38). Political and religious leaders find it hard to accept that God may judge his elect people. They are thus ready to fight to the last for Israel's national interests in the belief that these are identical with the divine purposes.

l. Election as responsibility develops into the concept of election as mission. The elect people is to bear witness to the nations that God is God (Is. 42:1; 43:10). Israel is to be restored but only in order that through her a light may shine to the Gentiles. Indeed, even in suffering the chosen witness carries the truth of divine love to the world. The love of God is the heart of election, the power of God is seen in the mystery of it, the experience of the people derives from it, and in its light the nations shall walk (Is. 60:3).   [G. QUELL, IV, 145-68]

C. *eklégomai* in the LXX and Jewish Hellenistic Writings.

1. General. In the LXX *eklégesthai* occurs with the genitive, dative, and more commonly the accusative, and also with *en*. In the middle an emphatic *heautó* is often used. To stress the preferring of one thing over another we find *hypér* plus the accusative, and *ek* or *apó* denotes selection from.

2. The Nature of the Selection. Selection may be of articles (wood, stone, etc.), persons, or abstract things (e.g., light and darkness). It may be between two or three things (cf. David in 2 Sam. 24:12).

3. Religious Election.

a. This may be the selection of a place, e.g., Jerusalem (2 Kgs. 21:7 etc.) or the temple (Dt. 12:5ff.).

b. It may also be the choice of individuals, e.g., Abraham, Moses, the king, the priest, and the elect servant of Is. 43:10.

c. Commonly it is the election of the people, although not in Josephus.

d. Only a minor part is played by rejection as its opposite. Ps. 78:67 simply means that God does not choose the king from Ephraim.

e. The thought of purpose is often added with an *eís ti* or *hína* and infinitive (cf. 1 Kgs. 8:16; 1 Chr. 28:4).

f. The word may sometimes have the sense of "picking out" or "sifting," of "trying" the heart (Prov. 17:3), of "being pleased" (2 Sam. 19:39), of "deciding" (Josh. 24:22), or of "determining" (Job 29:25).

D. The Idea of Election in Apocalyptic and the Damascus Document.

1. Eschatology promotes the sense of election in times of conflict, rallying resistance but also fostering the pride of privilege and submerging the concept of mission in a spirit of revenge.

2. The Damascus Document takes an even narrower view by confining election to a righteous remnant that will inherit eternal life and all human glory. In contrast, God knows the works of sinners even before their creation.

E. *eklégomai* in the NT.

1. The Synoptists. In Lk. 14:7 and 10:42 the word has the general sense of choosing among two or more possibilities. In Mk. 13:20 the verb supports the noun *eklektós*. Elsewhere the use is for the choosing of the apostles. This is selection from a larger number *(ap' autôn)* in Lk. 6:13.

2. The eklégesthai of the Disciples in John. The use in John resembles that of the Synoptists. A special problem is how Judas can be chosen (cf. Jn. 6:70). His inclusion is for the fulfilment of Scripture (13:18-19). When Judas has left, election is given fuller weight (15:16ff.). It is Jesus who elects (6:70 etc.), but the Father stands behind the choice (6:65). Election is worked out in the sphere of faith and obedience (6:63ff., 68). If Judas is not given by the Father, this is shown by his failure to do what Jesus says (13:17). The goal is bringing forth fruit in love (15:16-17). It should be noted that Judas is nowhere said to be foreordained as *diábolos,* although the betrayal itself is divinely foreseen and determined. It is only after the departure of Judas that the true purpose of election emerges. Because election is from the world, the world will hate and fight the disciples (15:18ff.). Only as election originates with Christ is fruit-bearing possible. Election is the basis and source of fruitful service. What applies specifically to the apostles in these passages has a wider reference to the community as a whole. From Judas it learns that even the severest conflicts find their solution in the Lord's decision. The worst that can happen is perfectly apprehended by Jesus in judgment and grace.

3. eklégesthai in Acts. Acts uses the term (1) for selection, whether of the apostles (1:24), the Seven (6:5), or the delegates to Antioch (15:22), (2) for the election of the patriarchs (13:17), and (3) for the choice of Peter to initiate the Gentile mission (15:7).

4. eklégesthai in Paul and James: The Election of the Community. In 1 Cor. 1:27ff. the threefold use expresses the fact that the members of the community, in all their human weakness, serve the purpose of manifesting the divine strength. In Eph. 1:4 the accent is on eternal choice, the purpose is adoption in Christ, and the result is a consecrated walk, not in selfishness, but in love. Jms. 2:5 is parallel to 1 Cor. 1:26ff. but in the context of a polemic against discrimination. The needy become rich by election; the two accusatives express the gift bound up with election (cf. Eph. 1:5-6).

5. The Idea of Reprobation. The NT does not expressly bring *eklégesthai* into contrast with reprobation. In Rom. 9:13 the "love" and "hate" come from the quotation (Mal.

1:2-3) and seem to refer to historical role rather than eternal destiny. *eklégesthai* is more closely related to words of calling than to words of foreknowing or foreordaining.

eklogḗ.

A. General Greek Usage. The idea of "selection" is predominant in Greek usage, e.g., of rulers, guardians, officials, etc. The stress is on the act, not the result, and the basis is aptness for a specific purpose. The principle of selection may be added, e.g., by birth, income, etc., although this is left out when it is obvious. In papyri and inscriptions we read of the selection of a bride, field, gift, etc. In Stoicism the reference may be to a choice in practical life. Epictetus lays down the rule that one should choose what is in accordance with nature.

B. Aquila, Symmachus, and Theodotion. *eklogḗ* does not occur in the LXX, but the other renderings of the OT have it in a few cases, e.g., Is. 27:7; 37:24.

C. Other Jewish Hellenistic Writings. The element of free choice is predominant in these works. In Ps. Sol. 18:6 *eklogḗ* is God's sifting choice within Israel, while in 9:4 it is the free choice of the human will. Josephus has the term for the choice that Abraham gives Lot (*Antiquities* 1.169) and for the choice that David must make between famine, plague, and war (7.322). Free human decision is the point in *Jewish War* 2.165.

D. The NT.
1. Acts. In Acts 8:15 the Lord tells Ananias that Paul is a chosen instrument (in Hebraic fashion the genitive is used adjectively here). The choice is for the apostolic task of carrying Christ's name to Gentiles, kings, and the people of Israel.
2. Paul.
a. Paul first uses *eklogḗ* for divine selection in the history of the patriarchs (Rom. 9:11). The choice is not for salvation as such but for historical mission. Similarly, God has now chosen the Gentile church to fulfill his purpose. The stress is on God's free decision but not to the exclusion of human responsibility.
b. In Rom. 11:28 *eklogḗ* denotes the election of the whole people in the patriarchs.
c. In 1 Th. 1:4 the reference is to the choice of the Christian community. This takes place in the power of the Spirit (v. 5) and is equivalent to being loved by God.
d. Another use (Rom. 11:5) is for the gracious selection of a believing remnant out of the totality of Israel. The NT does not speak of a similar selection out of the church, and the OT concept of the remnant controls the application to Israel.
e. *eklogḗ* is used in a passive sense in Rom. 11:7 for those who are selected according to 11:5. The chosen number has attained what Israel as a whole was seeking.
3. eklogḗ in Peter. 2 Pet. 1:10 refers to the election and calling of the community (cf. Rev. 17:14). *eklogḗ* is only apparently a more dogmatic term, for the word is used in a movement of responsibility with regard to teleological ordination. Believers must confirm their election; their action is thus to be taken with full seriousness relative to the divine rule (cf. the promises and the corresponding acts in 1:3ff.).

E. The Early Church.
1. Apostolic Fathers and Apologists. Diog. 4.4 says that circumcision is for the Jews a witness to *eklogḗ*. 1 Clem. 29.1 says that God has made the church his chosen portion. Mart. Pol. 20.1 applies the term specifically to martyrs in a way which suggests selection within the community, i.e., an elite.

2. *Origen and Gnosticism.* Origen follows Paul's use in Romans. Expounding Eph. 1:4 he makes of *eklogḗ* almost a dogmatic term in a static sense not found in the NT. But for him it may also be the future goal. In Gnosticism we find a sectarian use for an elite, e.g., the *pneumatikoí* as distinct from the *psychikoí*.

eklektós.

A. Ordinary Greek Use. The ordinary use of the adjective is for "choice," "select(ed)." It refers in the papyri to things of the best quality.

B. The Greek Bible and Jewish Hellenistic Writings.

1. In the LXX the general meaning is for choice products, e.g., plants, animals, or minerals. With reference to persons we find it for select troops. The term becomes more prominent in Ezekiel with a figurative reference to Israel in ch. 19.

2. The religious use takes three forms. a. The term may refer to what is sacred or pure (cf. 1 Sam. 10:3). It can even be used for God in the sense of pure (Ps. 18:26). b. Cultically the term has the sense of "consecrated" and is used for the sacred vessels, for people dedicated to judgment (2 Sam. 21:6), and for the stones used in building the temple (cf. Is. 28:16; 54:12). c. In its use for the election of Israel, we find the term for Abraham (Philo), Moses, Joshua, David, etc., as well as for the land (Zech. 7:14), for the city of Jerusalem (Tob. 13:13), and, of course, for the people (cf. Is. 43:20; Ps. 106:5).

3. There is a marked growth in the use of *eklektós* as compared with the Hebrew equivalent. This is not necessarily due to a liking for the religious concept of election, yet there is an increasing inclination to stress the fact that Israel is the elect or chosen people.

C. Apocalyptic.

1. Israel or Her Elite as the Elect. In a further extension of use, mostly with an eschatological thrust, *eklektós* often occurs in apocalyptic either for Israel or for the righteous within it. The struggle against Hellenism strengthens the tendency to restrict the term to those who keep the law. The idea of a definite and divinely predetermined number appears.

2. The Messiah as the Elect. In the OT the only basis for a reference to the Messiah is the description of the servant as elect in Isaiah. Apocalyptic, however, relates the one elect to the many elect. As the elect the Messiah is righteous, kept by God, sent out with power, and set on the throne of glory, where he makes a final choice of the elect to share his glory to all eternity.

3. The Angels as Elect. In a few instances the angels are God's holy and elect children.

D. Mandaean Writings.

1. In the Mandaean literature the adjective elect is applied to such concepts as life and light.

2. From elect life comes the elect messenger or helper who joins himself to the elect.

3. The process of redemption produces elect persons, i.e., the perfect who are chosen from the world, roused from sleep, and illumined by the mysteries, so that their liberated souls go to the house of life.

4. In the battle for the title of elect the idea of rejection also seems to be present.

E. The NT.

1. The Synoptists.

a. In the Synoptists the term always has an eschatological reference. The cryptic saying in Mt. 22:14 is to be seen in the light of the parables in Mt. 21–22, where an invitation is issued to many, but those who reject it in disobedience (cf. 21:31, 43) are not chosen. Here is a dynamic view of election in which God's eternal pronouncement does not enslave history fatalistically but establishes responsible decision. The reading which has the same saying in Lk. 14:24 is in keeping with the thrust of 14:7ff., which uses the *kaleín* group eight times. The different forms of the parable, which seem to derive from independent sources, do not affect the meaning of *eklektós* in Matthew.

b. The use in Lk. 18:7 is equally practical, for it leads to trust on the one side and obedience on the other. The elect can have an effect on history by their prayers, but this is no ground for self-confidence, for the final question whether the Son of Man will find faith when he comes poses the issue of responsibility while not conflicting with faith's looking to God and his goal. Election is set in the context of exhortation. An appeal to the conscience accompanies the confidence it gives.

c. The term occurs again in Mk. 13:19ff.; Mt. 24:21ff. Here it has an eschatological content but with no sectarian slant. The elect that are gathered from the four winds are believers from all lands. The theme is the final threat that confronts them, their preservation, and their final salvation. The preservation comes only through the shortening of the days, the threat is that of unprecedented *thlípsis,* false messianism, and false prophecy (Mk. 13:19ff.), and the final salvation is by grace. If election is a basis of confidence, it again carries with it a warning.

2. *Christ as the Elect in Luke.* In Lk. 9:35 and 23:35 the term elect is applied to Christ himself, first by God at the transfiguration, then by those who deride him at the crucifixion. It is by the cross that he enters into his glory, so that he is elect not merely in or in spite of the passion but by his ordination thereto. His claim to election does not rest on outward success. Although Luke has both *eklektós* and *eklektoí,* he does not expressly relate them as Paul does in the case of *huiós,* e.g., in Gal. 3:26.

3. *eklektós in Paul.* Paul makes little use of the term. At the climax in Rom. 8:33 it sums up all that he says in 8:14-15 about the bearers of the Spirit. There is no condemnation for the elect, for they have a salvation that begins and ends in eternity with the love of God. Similarly in Col. 3:12 the elect are holy and beloved, and as such they should and can show love. That each believer is elect appears in Rom. 16:13 (Rufus). The relation of election to the final goal is the point in 2 Tim. 2:10, while 1 Tim. 5:21 carries a reference to elect angels.

4. *eklektós and syneklektós in 1 Peter and the Johannine Epistles.* The word has thematic significance in 1 Peter. The readers, who are called exiles of the dispersion, are chosen, destined, and sanctified (1:1-2) in a work of Father, Spirit, and Christ. Predestination (cf. 1:20) is the basis of election, while *en* denotes the means (sanctification by the Spirit) and *eis* denotes the goal (obedience to Christ). The theme is developed in 2:4ff. with the transfer of the OT promises and predicates from Israel to the community. This passage links the choice stone (Christ) to the chosen community (cf. Eph. 1:6). What marks the elect people is faith in contrast to unbelief and disobedience. Thus, even though faith has an eternal basis and unbelief displays God's judicial action (v. 8), responsibility is presupposed. The aim of election is ministry; foreordination is an ordination to declare God's gracious acts (2:10). As the whole church is a *génos eklektón* consisting of *eklektoí,* so the local congregation is an *eklektḗ,* and that at Babylon is thus *syneklektḗ* (5:13). The usage in 2 Jn. 1, 13 is similar if, as seems likely, the elect lady and the elect sister are here personified churches.

5. *Summary.*

a. The NT gives a new turn to the concept as it finds the basis in Christ and has in view a worldwide community.

b. It discerns in election the eternal foundation of salvation but without eliminating responsibility.

c. Far from viewing election as preferential treatment it relates it strictly to mission in the service of the divine teleology.

F. *eklektós* **in the Apostolic Fathers.** There is a great growth in the use of *eklektós* in the apostolic fathers, especially in 1 Clement and Hermas, with a rather greater interest in the number of the elect in 1 Clement. [G. SCHRENK, IV, 168-92]

---

leíos [smooth, level]

leíos has such varied meanings as "smooth," "level," "fine," "tender," and "sweet." The only instance in the NT is in Lk. 3:5 (quoting Is. 40:3), which says that the rough ways will be made smooth. The express quotation identifies the Baptist as the messenger of joy, intimates a reversal of human standards, declares the universal scope of salvation, and fixes the place of the Baptist in its enactment.

[G. BORNKAMM, IV, 193]

---

leímma [remnant], *hypóleimma* [remnant], *kataleípō* [to leave behind], *(katá-* [descendant, remnant], *perí-* [fragment], *diáleimma* [intermission (of fever)]*)*

A. Greek Usage.

1.a. With the general sense of "what is left over," *leímma* may be used for human remains, for fragments left over at a meal, etc. b. It also denotes an interval in music. c. In the LXX it is used for survivors, and more specifically for the remnant of the people.

2. The compounds display a similar usage. *hypóleimma* denotes what is left on the sale of wine, the remains of food, burned wood, etc., the remnants of rebellion, and in the LXX the prophetic remnant. *katáleimma* may be used for descendants, but also for what is left of Jerusalem, or the remnants of the house of Ahab, or the prophetic remnant. *períleimma* is found for the fragments of an oration. *diáleimma* occurs in medicine for arrest in growth or the intermission of fever.

[G. SCHRENK, IV, 194-96]

B. The Remnant in the OT.

1. Usage. a. The OT uses four roots for remnant, especially *š'r* and *ytr*. It often uses these in combination or in parallelism.

b. For the *š'r* group, which is theologically the most important, the LXX has forms of *kata-* or *hypoleípein*.

c. The main use of the terms is secular, e.g., for wood left over, land still to be taken, remaining nations. That nothing remains can denote the greatness of judgment (2 Kgs. 13:7 etc.), but remnant may also be used positively for those who escape (Gen. 14:10 etc.). The remnant of the people, historically, is the portion that survives a national disaster (cf. Is. 37:4; 2 Kgs. 25:11, 22). The term may also be used for those that return from exile (Hag. 1:12, 14).

d. Since historical disasters may signify eschatological judgment, the term sometimes has for the prophets a fluid sense in which it may denote those who survive either the disaster or the judgment (cf. Am. 5:15; Mic. 2:12; Jer. 6:9).

e. The idea of the remnant clearly belongs at times to the context of expectation of judgment and salvation (Is. 1:8-9; 4:2ff.; 7:3; Jer. 23:3; Joel 2:32; Zeph. 2:9; Zech. 14:16). It becomes a fixed term in this sense, and has a double reference to sifting and deliverance with an implied stress on the greatness of the judgment but also a comforting orientation to salvation.

2. *The Rise of the Remnant Concept.* The concept develops with the eschatological message of the prophets, which has (cf. Amos) the three elements of destruction, salvation, and responsibility. Some scholars believe that the remnant is a bridge between the organically unrelated factors of judgment and deliverance, although the prophets clearly adjust their message to the shifting historical scene. Others find a basis for it in the idea of Israel herself as the remnant that is saved from hostile attacks—an idea which is modified when it is God himself who brings disaster to Israel and a converted remnant is delivered. In the OT itself, however, the concept stands in the context of three acts of divine revelation: the election of the people, the calling of the prophets, and the promise of the Messiah. Is. 6 (cf. 8:16ff.) plainly relates the calling of the prophet to the fashioning of a remnant. With this calling God himself comes into history as the Holy One. This means destruction for sin, but on the far side of destruction lies salvation for those who are called and believe (Is. 6:8; 7:9). Retrospectively, it may be seen that the basis of the remnant is the election of Israel (Is. 46:3). From the very first, God has carried the house of Jacob, and he has eternally set up his rule over it in Zion (Mic. 4:7). The connection with the Messiah occurs in the Servant concept of Is. 53 and the son of man concept of Dan. 7. Chronologically the concept occurs already when 1 Kgs. 19:18 states that God has left 7,000 worshippers for himself in Israel. Amos has it both in dialectical passages in which he opposes a false remnant belief (9:1) and in the debated verse 5:15, which may be using "remnant of Joseph" for the northern kingdom, and may thus have in view a possible national repentance, but which also has an eschatological thrust whereby the remnant is the group that God preserves when judgment falls. The core of the concept occurs in Gen. 7:23 with the preservation of Noah and in Gen. 45:7 with the gracious preservation through Joseph.

3. *The Remnant Established by God.*

a. The survival of the remnant is not due to its virtue but to divine grace. This is very clear in Mic. 2:12; 4:7; 5:6-7. Again, God gives the prophet his disciples in Is. 8:16ff. The Lord of hosts leaves the people a remnant in Is. 1:8-9 (cf. 7:3). It is God who gathers the people (11:12), who makes the highway (11:16), who will be the crown of the remnant (28:5), who lays a foundation for it (28:16). The only question concerns membership of the remnant, and since faith is the answer to this question, the message of the remnant is a summons to believe (7:2, 9; 28:16). The teaching of Zephaniah is similar (3:12-13), and in Ezekiel the remnant exists by an act of God which displays the justice of his judgment (8:6; 14:21ff.). The zeal (2 Kgs. 19:31), righteousness (Is. 10:20ff.), grace (Jer. 31:2), mercy (Jer. 31:7), and forgiveness of God (Jer. 50:20) are the basis.

b. That there is a remnant only by divine action is set in relief by the totality of judgment (Ezek. 7:7; Am. 3:12, etc.). It is also implied in the comparison with the exodus (Is. 4:2ff.; 11:16; Jer. 23:5ff.; 31:31ff.).

c. Since the remnant is preserved by God's act, it does not have to be small. In

Mic. 4:7 it is to be made a strong people, and in Jer. 23:3 the regathered remnant has the promise that it will be fruitful and multiply.

d. The eschatological orientation of the prophets means that the remnant is both a present and a future entity. It is a present entity in Am. 5:15; Is. 8:16ff.; Ezek. 9:8; 11:13. After the exile it may thus be equated with those who come back from exile (Zech. 8:6; Ezr. 9:8, 13).

e. As a present entity, the remnant may be linked to Zion or Jerusalem (Is. 1:8; 28:16-17; Mic. 4:1ff.; Zeph. 3:11ff.; Jer. 31:6-7; Zech. 14:2). Yet the concept resists too strict an equation. Its use in the absolute (cf. Is. 7:3) shows that it transcends every restriction. The promise is to believers, who cannot be limited to historical entities like Judah or Jerusalem. The individualizing of the concept also means its extension (Is. 1:9; 4:2ff.; 7:2ff., etc.). The Servant of Is. 40ff. may bring an exclusive relation between the deliverer and the community, but by its very nature this restriction entails extension (Is. 52:13ff.).

4. The Conversion of the Remnant. Since the remnant rests on God's gracious action, conversion is not a precondition. Deliverance comes first; the call to conversion follows (cf. Is. 10:20-21; even 2 Chr. 30:6). Faith and holiness are the other side of God's establishment of the remnant (cf. Is. 28:16-17; Zeph. 3:12-13). This point is aptly summarized in Joel 2:32. Indeed, there can be no remnant without divine pardon and cleansing (Mic. 7:18; Jer. 50:20). The remnant, too, is sinful in itself; God saves it only by forgiving, sanctifying, and creating anew (cf. Zech. 13:8-9). Conversion is the response to God's act (Zeph. 3:12-13). The renewal of the remnant is the work of the divinely imparted Spirit (Ezek. 36:24ff.; 37:23-24; Joel 2:28ff.).

5. The Remnant and the Nations. As an entity in the world the remnant stands in relation to the nations. It will rule over them (Mic. 5:6) but the nations will go to it to receive instruction (4:1ff.). With the judgment of the nations, there will also be a Gentile remnant (Is. 45:20ff.). The remnant of Israel has a mission to declare God's glory and to bring Gentiles, too, into God's service (Is. 66:19ff.). In this light we are to construe the remnant of the Philistines in Zech. 9:7, the worshipping remnant of the nations in Zech. 14:16, and perhaps the more formal references to the rest of the nations in Ezek. 36:3, 5, 36.

6. The Remnant Community and the Messiah. Although the relation is not worked out in detail, a link between the Messiah and the remnant is implied in the name Immanuel, in the "us" of Is. 9:6, in the statement of Is. 10:21 (cf. 9:6), and in the promises of Jer. 23:3ff. and Mic. 5:1ff. The lines here lead up to Is. 28:16ff., with its hint that the stone is the Messiah on which the remnant with its faith is built, and more especially to Is. 40ff. and the message of the Servant who bears the sins of many, so that the remnant community has its life in him.

[V. Herntrich, IV, 196-209]

C. The Remnant Concept in Paul in Comparison with Apocalyptic and the Rabbis.

1. The Remnant in Rom. 9–11.

a. In Rom. 9ff. Paul adapts the prophetic concept of the remnant so as to show its present fulfilment. The obduracy of Israel confirms the distinction between carnal and spiritual Israel. As seen in Jacob and Moses, the latter exists by God's gracious calling. It now consists of believing Jews and Gentiles.

b. Believing Israel within the new community is the remnant. The cutting away of merely natural Israel displays God's judgment, but the preservation of a remnant of

Jews among believing Gentiles displays his mercy and faithfulness. The focus is on God's free action, but in view of the general unbelief of Israel a place is also found for the responsibility of Israel (9:30–10:21).

c. This responsibility consists of the stubborn attempt to establish self-righteousness in spite of the message of divinely given justification by faith. In contrast, the remnant attains to true righteousness by responding to the gospel. The existence of this remnant is a message of hope to Israel. Jewish Christians resemble the 7,000 of the days of Elijah and are thus in a special sense a remnant of Israel.

d. This remnant carries a promise of the future salvation of all Israel when the fullness of the Gentiles has come in. It may be small now, but it is not an unchangeable minority. At the end it will become the totality.

2. *Comparison and Summary.*

a. Israel. In apocalyptic the remnant is what will finally be left of the whole people. In rabbinic theology the emphasis is on total salvation; only a few Jews are rejected and only a few Gentiles saved. In Paul the remnant consists of believing Jews of his own time, which is, proleptically, an eschatological fulfilment of remnant prophecies.

b. Election. In apocalyptic the election involves a restriction of salvation to a sectarian remnant. In Paul faith in God's salvation through Christ leaps sectarian boundaries. The remnant confirms the inviolable election of Israel, but in such a way as to embrace the Gentiles as well.

c. The Messiah. Apocalyptic assigns an important place to the Messiah in its hope for the salvation of the remnant. The new turn in Paul is that the Messiah has already come in Christ, that the remnant has its whole life in him, and that it consists of those who find in him the righteousness of faith.

d. Faith. Apocalyptic stresses foreordination, but still has too strong a stress on work-righteousness. The same is true of rabbinic theology with its concern for study and observance of the law. What matters for Paul, however, is conversion to Christ and the new life which comes therewith. God brings us to faith, but faith is then our own act by grace. Faith is not a meritorious work, yet it is still a human act. God does the grafting in, but it is those who do not persist in unbelief who will be grafted in (Rom. 11:23).

e. The Nations. Apocalyptic tends to see the destruction of the nations as parallel to the preservation of the remnant. Paul, however, discerns a divine teleology whereby the general hardening of Israel serves the salvation of both the Gentiles and Israel (Rom. 11:13ff.). For Paul, then, the remnant concept involves no narrow sectarianism. It has a place in the mission which summons all people under the dominion of grace. The remnant is the root of a perfected community, and the judgment which it displays is for the purpose of a broader mercy.   [G. SCHRENK, IV, 209-14]

---

leitourgéō [to serve, minister], *leitourgía* [service, ministry], *leitourgós* [servant, minister], *leitourgikós* [in service, ministry]

---

leitourgéō, leitourgía.

A. Nonbiblical Greek.

1. *Form of the Word.* The older form is *lēitourgeín;* the shift comes about 300 B.C.

2. *The Basic Meaning.* Etymologically the word carries the sense of doing things for the body politic, or discharging a task for society.

3. Usage.

a. Technical Political. Politically the term refers to the rendering of specific social services at one's own expense, either out of patriotism or vainglory, or under compulsion. According to Aristotle many democratic states fleece the wealthy by means of "liturgies."

b. Extended Political. Later, especially under imperial government, the term covers all kinds of compulsory services and official tasks. There are many discussions of the relevant obligations and many complaints about the associated burdens.

c. Popular. A weaker sense develops whereby the group simply applies to any rendering of service, e.g., slaves to masters, friends to friends, mothers to young, members to the body, courtesans to patrons, etc.

d. Special Cultic. The group also comes into use in a cultic sense for the performance of various cultic actions. While this is another form of communal service, there is here no particular idea of serving the body politic through the cultus. The main concept is that of rendering service to the deity.

B. The LXX and Hellenistic Judaism.

1. leitourgéō.

a. Occurrence and Equivalents. The term occurs some 100 times in the LXX, mainly in cultic passages (Ex. 28ff.; Ezek. 40ff., etc.). It is mostly used for *šērēt* when this occurs in cultic contexts; in other cases other Greek terms are used. The LXX thus reserves *leitourgeín* for divine service (including the service of idols; cf. Ezek. 44:12); there are few exceptions to this rule (cf. 1 Kgs. 19:21; 1 Chr. 27:1). The reference is nearly always to the worship of God by the priests and Levites in the tent or temple.

b. As a Technical Cultic Term. The term may be used in various combinations (cf. Num. 8:22; 2 Chr. 11:14; Joel 1:13), but there is also a common use in the absolute (Ex. 28:35; 35:19; 36:33, etc.). A spiritualizing trend appears in Sirach when it speaks of serving wisdom (4:14), and angelic service is at issue in one rendering of Dan. 7:10.

2. leitourgía. The noun, too, becomes a technical term for priestly ministry. The only secular use is in 2 Sam. 19:19. The reference is either to priestly functions and actions (Num. 16:9 etc.) or to cultic vessels (1 Chr. 9:28).

3. The LXX and Nonbiblical Usage. There is in the LXX no trace of the political use and only a relic of the popular use. The LXX has chosen the group almost exclusively for priestly ministry. Why the translators fixed on this group for the purpose is debatable. Perhaps it is an expansion of cultic use elsewhere, or perhaps there is some thought of a legally ordained and solemn service that is rendered on behalf of the whole people.

4. Greek-Speaking Judaism. Josephus has the words only for the cultus, although he also has *latreía* and *hierourgía* for this. Philo, too, uses the words for the cultus, but he has an extended use for the spiritual worship of God, and he also mentions *leitourgíai* in the sense of official public functions. [H. STRATHMANN, IV, 215-22]

C. Cultic Ministry in Rabbinic Judaism.

1. Lexical Survey. The rabbis use various roots, some of which seem to come into later Hebrew by way of Aramaic. (For details see *TDNT,* IV, 222-23.)

2. The Idea of Cultic Ministry.

a. Verbs. These may be used for the priestly ministry but also for the cultic actions of the laity.

b. Nouns. The reference is mainly to the temple worship, or the worship of God, although we also find expressions for pagan worship.

c. Spiritualization. The rabbis speak of ethical as well as cultic service of God. Synagogue worship extends the use to the ministry of the word and of prayer. With the destruction of the temple, expiatory significance may be ascribed to prayer. Study of the law is also divine service for the rabbis.   [R. Meyer, IV, 222-25]

D. The NT.

1. Occurrence and Use. *leitourgeín* occurs only three times in the NT (Acts 13:2; Rom. 15:27; Heb. 10:11), and *leitourgía* only six times (Lk. 1:23; 2 Cor. 9:12; Phil. 2:17, 30; Heb. 8:6; 9:21). *leitourgós* and *leitourgikós* add another six instances, three in Hebrews. The predominance of use in Hebrews is natural in view of its christological interpretation of the OT cultus. Thus Christ has a more excellent ministry in 8:6, the liturgical vessels are sprinkled in 9:21, and the OT priests have to offer daily service in 10:11. The use in Lk. 1:23 is also within an OT context. In Acts 13:2, however, the term seems to have a more spiritualized reference to prayer (cf. v. 3). It is the first instance of a use for specifically Christian worship. Rom. 15:27 and 2 Cor. 9:12 both refer to the collection, and cf. Phil. 2:30. It may be that monetary gifts here are seen as public service or are given a cultic significance, but the use is more likely the popular one of A.3.c. There is, however, a plain cultic nuance in Phil. 2:17 in view of the associated reference to libation. The point is either that the Philippians' faith is the offering (to which Paul will add the libation of his martyrdom), or that Paul's work in establishing their faith is the offering. Either way, the term *leitourgía* has here the sense of a cultic or priestly ministry.

2. Findings. The sparse use in the NT is connected partly with OT and partly with popular use. Movement toward a new Christian use occurs only in Acts 13:2 with reference to prayer. The end of the OT cultus with Christ means that the terms are not suitable for the functions of Christian ministers, whose task is to proclaim the *leitourgía* that has been fulfilled once and for all in Christ. The new community has no priests; it consists of priests, for all can enter the sanctuary through Christ's blood (Heb. 10:19).

E. Transition to Later Ecclesiastical Use. The position is similar in the apostolic fathers, who use the group for the ministry of OT priests, or for righteous conduct. The comparison of Christian ministry with that of the OT opens the door for a more specific use of the terms for the ministry of bishops and presbyters (1 Clem. 40ff.). In this way the terms finally come to be used for the Christian cultus, especially the eucharist; hence the common meaning of "liturgy" today.

leitourgós. This term is rare in Greek. It occurs occasionally in the papyri and inscriptions for liturgical officials, for workers, and for cultic ministers. It is also uncommon in the LXX, and has a cultic sense only in Is. 61:6. Of the five NT instances only Heb. 8:2 and Rom. 15:16 have cultic significance. In the one Christ is a minister of the true sanctuary, in the other Paul has a priestly ministry inasmuch as by his missionary work he presents the Gentiles an acceptable offering to God. In other NT verses the angels are servants of God in Heb. 1:7, rulers are servants of God in the execution of justice in Rom. 13:6 (cf. *diákonos* in v. 4), and Epaphroditus is a minister to Paul's need in Phil. 2:25. If there is a religious coloring in Heb. 1:7 and Rom. 13:6, it is because the service is rendered to God. 1 Clement has the term for OT priests (41.2), prophets (8.1), and angels (36.3).

leitourgikós. This rare term is used in the papyri with reference to cultic taxes and services, and in the LXX with reference to cultic vessels and vestments. The only NT use is in Heb. 1:14, which calls the angels ministering spirits that are sent to render *diakonía* to believers. This use is obviously noncultic.

[H. STRATHMANN, IV, 226-31]

---

lepís [shell, scale]

lepís has two meanings: a. "shell" (e.g., of a nut) and b. "scale" (e.g., of fish, snakes, or, figuratively, metal plates). The only NT use is in the story of Paul's conversion, when Ananias lays hands on the blinded Saul and "something like scales fell from his eyes" (Acts 9:18). The term comes from the medical world of the day which speaks of descaling the eyes, i.e., removing a growth of skin that causes blindness. The author needs no special medical knowledge to use the term, and the passage must not be thought to support the view that Paul suffered from an eye affliction (cf. Gal. 4:15). The metaphor suggests that, as the Lord has overcome Paul's enmity, so he has given him the witness that he is to go to the Gentiles "to open their eyes" and turn them from darkness to light (Acts 26:18).   [G. BORNKAMM, IV, 232-33]

---

lépra [skin ailment], *leprós* [scaly, scabby]

leprós means "scaly," "scabby," and with *lépra* is used for various skin ailments. Whether these are always (or ever) the same as what we call "leprosy" is debated, but Jesus' public healing of lepers (Mt. 11:15; Mk. 1:40ff.; Lk. 17:12ff.) is an effective sign that the age of messianic salvation has come.   [W. MICHAELIS, IV, 233-34]

Leu(e)í [Levi],   *Leu(e)ís* [of Levi]

1. This name occurs in the genealogy of Jesus for the great-grandfather of Joseph and then again between David and Zerubbabel (Lk. 3:24, 29).

2. In Lk. 5:27, 29 a tax collector named Levi is called to be a disciple and holds a great supper to which he invites Jesus. In Mk. 2:14 this Levi is said to be the son of Alphaeus, which has led some to identify him with the James of Mk. 3:18, although another suggestion is that he is the Matthew of Mt. 9:9. The story shows that even hated tax collectors may have a place among the disciples of Jesus and that there is no need to hide their shameful past, since faith does not look to the greatness of believers but to the greatness of the Lord to whom all believers own their life and pardon.

3. The three other NT passages (Heb. 7:5, 9; Rev. 7:7) all refer to the son of Jacob and Leah.

a. Many questions have been raised about the development of the priestly status of the tribe of Levi, but according to the dominant OT view it is plainly charged with the priesthood (Ex. 2:1ff.; 6:20; 32:25ff.; Dt. 33:9ff.).

b. Later Judaism evinces a strong interest in the tribe, giving it a princely as well as a priestly and prophetic role. The basis of this evaluation is the fact that the

Hasmonean dynasty is of Levitical descent. For Philo Levi is the type of a lover of God who leaves everything to cleave to God.

c. The NT verses, however, simply follow the OT tradition. In Rev. 7:7 Levi has no special position among the tribes. In Heb. 7 the priesthood of Jesus is shown to be superior to that of Levi on the ground that he is a priest after the order of Melchizedek, who is without genealogy and to whom even Abraham pays a tithe. The perfect priesthood of Jesus, notwithstanding his descent from Judah, replaces the imperfect and transitory priesthood of Levi.

4. In the early church we find some efforts to trace a descent of Jesus from Levi by way of Mary (cf. the relationship to Elizabeth in Lk. 1:36). The NT, however, establishes no such descent and attaches no importance to the point.

[H. STRATHMANN, IV, 234-39]

Leu(e)ítēs [Levite]

This word occurs in the LXX, Philo, and Josephus, and denotes both a member of the tribe of Levi and a subordinate cultic officer serving with the Zadokite priesthood (cf. Ezek. 44:6ff.). According to the account in Chronicles the Levites play an important liturgical role (as singers etc.), and rivalry develops with the more exclusive priestly caste in which the Levites secure the right to wear the same linen garments but lose their tithes. Their duties include 1. singing (for which they are divided into 24 classes), 2. policing (for which there are 24 posts, the three in the inner court being manned by priests), 3. keeping the doors, and 4. helping in the sacrifices. In the synagogue they read the law—a reflection of their teaching office. In the NT a Levite passes by the wounded man in Lk. 10:32, Levites are among those who come to John the Baptist in Jn. 1:19, and Barnabas, the Cypriot Christian who befriends Paul, is of the tribe of Levi.

[R. MEYER, IV, 239-41]

---

leukós [white], *leukaínō* [to make white]

1. *leukós,* whose root means "bright," is used for various shades of "white." It commonly describes such things as milk or snow, and occurs in the phrase "as white as." On inscriptions it is the color of sacrificial animals and priestly garments. The verb *leukaínō* means "to make white"; thus time makes the hair white. White is the color of joy or victory, and is regarded as pleasing to the gods; helpful deities are themselves called white.

2. In the Hebrew world, too, white is an important color, due partly to the importance of light but more to the prominence of the concept of holiness. The Hebrew terms, like the Greek, are not precise, and *leukós* may be used for various words (cf. *TDNT,* IV, 243 for details).

3. Philo often has white and black as antitheses along with life and death, good and bad, etc. In allegories it is the color of truth. Josephus tells us that the Levites secured the right to wear white linen clothes and that the Essenes always went about clothed in white.

4. Rabbinic sources display a fondness for white clothes. They are a mark of joy or distinction. They also denote purity. From the first century A.D. the dead are buried

in white linen; the main thought seems to be that of transfiguration to heavenly glory (cf. Dan. 7:9).

5. The eschatological use dominates the field in the NT.

a. Other possibilities hardly arise; indeed, the NT shows little interest in color of any kind. Jesus must have worn the ordinary garb of the people, for only at the transfiguration does he have a brightness in keeping with his heavenly dignity, and there is nothing distinctive about his robe to prevent its being diced away by the soldiers. The only noneschatological references in the NT are in Jn. 4:35, where the ripe ears are white or golden, and Mt. 6:36, where the fact that God alone can make the hair white or black shows how limited human power is.

b. In Rev. 1:14 (cf. Dan. 7:9) the whiteness of the head and hair of the risen Lord denotes, not his age, but his heavenly glory. The garment of v. 13 seems to be a priestly one, and if so, it, too, will be white. The same point applies at the transfiguration, where the clothing becomes, not pale, but radiant, so that we have here an anticipation of the resurrection of Christ and his heavenly glory (cf. Mk. 9:1; Lk. 9:31-32; Mt. 17:2). Implied is a transfiguring of the whole nature, as in other NT references to new and heavenly clothing (cf. 2 Cor. 5:2ff.; Phil. 3:21).

c. The closest parallel to the transfiguration accounts is to be found in the references to the angel or angels at the tomb whose faces and clothes shine with heavenly radiance (see Mt. 28:3; Mk. 16:5; Lk. 24:4; Jn. 20:12; Acts 1:10). The white clothes alone are enough here to indicate the transcendental character of their glory. But the implication is not that Jesus is shown to be an angel at the transfiguration, for the elders of Rev. 4:4 are also clothed in white, and so are the overcomers of 3:4 etc. In the case of Christ the radiance signifies his unique position, in the case of the angels it denotes their heavenly character, and in the case of the overcomers it symbolizes the gift of eternal fellowship with the exalted Lord (3:4-5) by way of his cleansing work (cf. 6:11; 7:13-14). White is also significant in Revelation; cf. the white stone of 2:17, the white horse of 6:2 and 19:11 (cf. 19:14), the white cloud of 14:14, and the great white throne of 20:11. In all these verses the reference is plainly eschatological.

[W. MICHAELIS, IV, 241-50]

---

léōn [lion]

léōn is used both literally and figuratively, e.g., for the constellation, the sign of the Zodiac, or a brave or violent person. The lion plays a role in religion; thus in the OT lions are depicted on the temple stands (1 Kgs. 7:9) and the cherubim have lions' heads (Ezek. 1:10ff.). The word occurs some 150 times in the LXX, often in comparisons. In all the NT instances we find OT allusions. Thus Heb. 11:33 is based on Dan. 6:17ff. Again, Rev. 4:7 reflects Ezek. 1:10ff. (and cf. Rev. 9:17; 13:2). A messianic understanding of Gen. 49:9 underlies Rev. 5:5, and one may compare 10:3 with Hos. 11:10 and Am. 3:8. For the warning against apostasy in 1 Pet. 5:8 cf. Ps. 22:13, and for 2 Tim. 4:17 cf. Ps. 22:21. The promise that lions will be peaceful in the last time (Is. 11:6-7) finds no echo in the NT.   [W. MICHAELIS, IV, 251-53]

---

lēnós [vat, press], **hypolḗnion** [trough]

1. *lēnós* means a "vat" or "press," usually for oil or wine. Grapes are pressed with great jubilation (Is. 16:9-10; Joel 2:24). The contrast is all the sharper, then, when

God treads the press in judgment (Jer. 25:30; Lam. 1:15; Is. 63:1ff.). In Joel 3:13 a call goes out for helpers to join with God in treading the overflowing press of retribution.

2. The NT references to the press all stand under OT influence. Thus the parable of Mk. 12:1 (Mt. 21:33) is based on Is. 5:2 and has allegorical features.

3. Similarly Rev. 14:19-20 and 19:15 use prophetic images in their depiction of divine judgment. The first vision raises some problems by giving a role to the "other" angel, by mentioning the city, by mixing the motifs of winepress and battle, and by its seeming finality. It is probably meant to point forward to the definitive depiction in 19:15, where it is the Messiah Judge who treads the winepress of divine wrath. The location is in keeping with the OT message (cf. Joel 3:2), and the reference to the angel of fire may be in harmony with the idea that the mouth of Gehinnom is at the holy city. If some of the details in ch. 14 and ch. 19 seem to vary, it may be noted that 19:15 combines the motifs of 14:8, 10, 19-20, that the mention of the beast in 19:20 corresponds to 14:9, 11, and that in 14:9ff. and 20:15 those who worship the beast are consigned to the lake of fire as the beast and the false prophet are in 19:17ff.

[G. BORNKAMM, IV, 254-57]

---

lēstḗs [robber, revolutionary]

A. Outside the NT.

1. From a root meaning "to win," "to seize," come words for "prey," and "to seize as prey," and hence *lēstḗs* for "one who seizes prey." This word is used in antiquity for a soldier or mercenary who has an implicit right to booty (cf. in the LXX Jer. 18:22). But it usually has a bad sense, e.g., for undisciplined troops, then for robbers, bandits, etc., with an implied use of force (cf. Jer. 7:11).

2. Josephus uses the term for the Zealots, who under such leaders as Hezekiah and Judas of Galilee revolt against Roman rule, perhaps with messianic pretensions. For many Jews the Zealots are patriots rather than bandits, even though they often take what they need from their own people. But Josephus takes the Roman view, for although the Romans execute the Zealots as political offenders (by crucifixion), they contemptuously describe them as bandits. It is interesting that Josephus does not use *lēstaí* for the Jews as a whole when they rebel in A.D. 66, but reserves the term for Zealot individuals and factions that in his view misuse the religious cause.

3. Rabbinic Judaism adopted the terms *lēstḗs* and *lēsteía* from the Greek and used them both for robbers and originally, perhaps, for the Zealots, which suggests that the Zealots themselves regarded the term of reproach as a title of honor, but also that the rabbis to some degree repudiated them.

B. In the NT.

1. In 2 Cor. 11:26 Paul uses the term when listing the perils to which he was subject; he has bandits in mind.

2. In Mt. 21:13 Jesus accuses the priestly aristocracy of turning the house of prayer into a den of robbers. He has in view the temple trade which serves personal enrichment and satisfies cupidity. The saying brings the priesthood under the threatened judgment of Jer. 7:8ff.

3. In Lk. 10:30, 35 the *lēstaí* are probably bandits but they could also be Zealots, who preyed on the population in self-support. If they are Zealots, the parable perhaps contains an indirect criticism of the Zealot movement.

4. The use of the term is similar in Jn. 10:1ff., where it covers those, including Zealots, who try to bring in the kingdom without regard for Jesus, and who thus bring the flock into serious danger (cf. Mt. 24:4ff.).

5. The saying of Jesus to those who arrest him in Mt. 26:55 carries a clear messianic reference. To reject the claim of Jesus is to rank him with Zealot leaders. Pilate, indeed, lets the people choose between the freedom fighter Barabbas, whose first name was probably Jesus, and Jesus of Nazareth, as though they are both men of the same stamp (Mt. 27:15ff.; cf. Jn. 18:40, where Barabbas is called a *lēstḗs*, or, in some versions, an *archilēstḗs*). Two *lēstaí* are also crucified with Jesus. The title on the cross identifies Jesus as a Zealot leader, although, handed over by his own people, he is one whom the people rejects. This explains why Celsus later calls Jesus a *lēstḗs*, i.e., a false Messiah (Origen *Against Celsus* 3.59).   [K. H. RENGSTORF, IV, 257-62]

---

líbanos [incense], *libanōtós* [censer]

Incense, made from the resin of various trees, is widely used in antiquity both generally and cultically. In Mt. 2:11 it is one of the costly gifts brought by the Wise Men to the infant Jesus, and in Rev. 18:13 it is an important item in the trade with fallen Babylon. *libanōtós* has in Rev. 8 the unusual meaning "censer"; it is associated with the prayers of saints in v. 3 and filled with fire from the altar (which is cast down as a sign of divine wrath) in v. 5. The normal word for censer is *thymiatḗrion,* though this means "altar of incense" in Heb. 9:4.   [W. MICHAELIS, IV, 263-64]

Libertínoi [Libertines]

Among Stephen's opponents in Acts 6:9 are those of the synagogue of the so-called *Libertínoi*. The double *tṓn* divides the opponents into two groups, and to the first group belong the Cyrenians and Alexandrians along with the Libertines. *Libertínoi* is a term borrowed from Roman law and denotes slaves who have gained their freedom, or the descendants of such slaves. The reference here might well be to the descendants of Jewish prisoners whom Pompey had taken to Rome. Persecution of the infant church begins, then, with Hellenistic groups settled in Jerusalem (cf. Acts 8:1ff.). This agrees with the divisive attitude of Hellenistic Judaism and with what we know of its ideal of piety.   [H. STRATHMANN, IV, 265-66]

---

litházō [to stone], *katalitházō* [to stone to death], *lithoboléō* [to stone to death]

The reference of these terms is to stoning, which is a common penalty in antiquity, associated with expulsion as well as execution. In Mt. 21:35 *lithobolein,* and in Lk. 20:6 *katalitházein,* carry the sense of "killing." In Jn. 10:31ff. and 11:8 attempts are made to stone *(litházein)* Jesus for blasphemy (cf. also Jn. 8:5). In Acts 5:26 "throwing stones" is the point of *litházein,* but stoning is meant in 7:58 and 14:5 (both *lithobolein*). The stoning of Paul in 14:19 *(litházein;* cf. 2 Cor. 11:25) seems to be due to mob action without trial. Hebrews has *litházein* in the list in 11:37 and *lithoboleín* (quoting Ex. 19:13) in 12:20.   [W. MICHAELIS, IV, 267-68]

---

líthos [stone], *líthinos* [stony]

A. **The Literal Sense.** In the NT *líthos* means a. "stone" (hewn or not), b. "rock" (cf. Mk. 15:46), and c. "stone image" (Acts 17:29). As an enduring material, stone is used for writing (the tablets of the law, 2 Cor. 3:3, 7). It is also used to block up sepulchres (Jn. 11:38-39). Not being subject to impurity, it is also suitable as a ritual vessel (Jn. 2:6). As something inert, it may be contrasted with God (Acts 17:29), humans (Mt. 3:9), flesh (2 Cor. 3:3), and bread (Mt. 4:3). Precious stones symbolize wealth (Rev. 17:4; 21:18ff.). The saying about Christ being in the wood and stone may mean that he is immanent in all things, but it may also mean that his presence sanctifies manual labor with wood and stone.

B. **Living Stones.**
1. Lk. 19:40 refers to the stones crying out. This might mean that inorganic nature will praise Christ if humans do not, but more probably it means that the stones will accuse the disciples if they withhold their praise (for other lifeless objects that demand retribution see Gen. 4:10; Job 31:38; Jms. 5:4).
2. The striking saying in Mt. 3:9 is to the effect that God can give even stones the power to raise up progeny (cf. Is. 51:1-2, which is understood by the rabbis to refer to Isaac's birth from Abraham when he had lost the power to pass on life). The figure of the rock that produces children rejects the idea that salvation depends on natural descent. God can bring forth spiritual life from the spiritually dead (the Gentiles?).

C. **Christ as *líthos*.**
1. The Verses. Several verses compare Jesus to a *líthos,* e.g., Mk. 12:10; Lk. 20:18; Acts 4:11; 1 Pet. 2:4ff.; Rom. 9:32-33, and cf. Eph. 2:20; 1 Cor. 10:4-5; Jn. 7:37ff.; possibly Lk. 2:34; also the quotations from Is. 28:16 in Rom. 10:11 and 1 Tim. 1:16, though the image of the stone has faded from view in these verses.
2. The Reference of OT líthos Statements to the Messiah in Later Judaism. The NT verses mentioned above come almost entirely from the OT. Many of the OT originals are also linked to the Messiah in later Judaism (cf. the LXX addition to Is. 28:16, rabbinic references to the stone of Dan. 2:34ff., and rabbinic interpretation of the stone of Gen. 28:18). The OT use of "Rock" for God prepares the ground for the messianic understanding of the OT *líthos*.
3. Christ the Stone.
a. The Keystone and Foundation Stone of the True Temple. Primary in the description of Christ as the stone is the thought of the true temple of which he is the cornerstone or foundation stone. Jesus himself uses the figure in Mt. 12:10 and Lk. 20:18; according to these verses he will be rejected but God will then exalt him as the keystone, i.e., the Head of his community. The setting of the saying is eschatological. Acts 4:11 takes up the same thought but finds the exaltation of Christ as the keystone already fulfilled in the resurrection. Eph. 2:20ff. links the idea with that of the ongoing upbuilding of the community until it reaches completion in the final stone that is Christ. But Christ is ultimately the foundation stone as well. Thus 1 Pet. 2:4ff. refers

Is. 28:16 to Christ. God has laid this foundation, and those who build on it in faith will not be put to shame.

b. The Stone Which Crushes and the Stone of Offense. Lk. 20:18 adds to Ps. 118:22 an eschatological threat which is based on Dan. 2:31ff. (which the rabbis view messianically) and possibly on Is. 8:14 and on the proverbial saying about the pot which is broken whether it falls on the stone or the stone on it. The point of the saying is that those who run up against the stone will be shattered, but so, too, will those on whom it falls in judgment. A decision has to be made regarding Christ the stone, for his ultimate supremacy is guaranteed.

c. The Significance of Christ the Stone for Salvation or Perdition. The stone metaphor contains both promise and threat, for in Christ both divine goodness and divine wrath are revealed. Rom. 9:32-33 brings out the double significance. Those who seek self-righteousness stumble on the stone, but those who believe will be saved. 1 Pet. 2:4-5 is to the same effect. Christ the stone means salvation for the community of faith (Is. 28:16), but unbelievers will stumble and fall over him (Ps. 118:22; Is. 8:14). The lesson of Lk. 2:34 is similar.

d. The Dispenser of Living Water. 1 Cor. 10:4 finds the preexistent Christ in the rock that provides water for Israel. Jn. 7:37-38 carries the same thought in connection with the pouring out of water at the Feast of Tabernacles, which is taken to symbolize both the provision of rain and the outpouring of messianic blessings. Jesus seizes on the ritual of the feast (and its meaning) to point to himself as the one who gives the water of life to needy believers.

e. Christ as Stone in Post-NT Writings. The stone sayings quoted in the NT are often combined in later works as part of the christological proof from Scripture. Thus Barn. 6.2ff. combines Is. 28:16; 50:7; Ps. 118:22, Justin *Dialogue* 70.1; 76:1; 114.4 refer Dan. 2:34; Gen. 28:18; Ex. 17:12, etc. to Christ, and Cyprian has a collection of stone passages in *Testimonies* 2:16-17.

D. Christians as Living Stones. As Christ is *líthos zṓn* in 1 Pet. 2:4, Christians are *líthoi zṓntes* in 2:5. As such they form a spiritual house (cf. Eph. 2:20). The term "living" suggests that they owe their life to Christ, the living stone. Ignatius in *Ephesians* 9.1 develops the metaphor rather fancifully by comparing Christ (the cross) to the lifting beam and the Spirit to the rope. Hermas in *Visions* 3 and *Similitudes* 9 works out the comparison in exhaustive detail. He finds two types of stones, the serviceable and the unserviceable. His concern is with the latter, which can become serviceable by repentance.   [J. JEREMIAS, IV, 268-80]

→ *gōnía (akrogōniaíos, kephalḗ gōnías), pétra*

---

likmáō [to winnow, pulverize]

likmáō means a. "to winnow," b. "to scatter," and c. "to pulverize." In the OT winnowing is a common figure for temporary (Ezek. 36:19ff.) or final (Jer. 15:7) judgment. The only NT instance is in Lk. 20:18 par. Mt. 21:44, where the meaning is "to pulverize" and the point is the ineluctability of the judgment which the rejected stone will bring on unbelief (cf. Dan. 2:34-35; Is. 8:14).

[G. BORNKAMM, IV, 280-81]

> ### *logeía* [collection]

logeía (like *logeúō*) is a popular term meaning "collection" (sometimes sacral). It occurs in the NT only in 1 Cor. 16:1-2, where Paul asks for an orderly gathering of the gift for the Jerusalem church so that there need be no special effort when he comes. While the word can denote an extraordinary tax, there is here no thought of an assessment. Accompanying terms such as ministry and fellowship show that it is a gift comparable to the voluntary love offerings of the diaspora to Jerusalem rather than to the obligatory temple tax (cf. Rom. 15:26, 31; 2 Cor. 8:4ff.; 9:1ff.).

[G. KITTEL, IV, 282-83]

> ### *logízomai* [to calculate, deliberate], *logismós* [calculation, reasoning]

A. The Word Group Outside the NT.

1. logízomai. In secular Greek this word is used a. commercially for "to reckon," "to charge," and b. more generally for "to deliberate," "to conclude." In the LXX it takes on the nuance a. of an emotional and even volitional act, e.g., devising, or counting in the subjective sense (see *TDNT,* IV, 284-85 for details). It also b. enters the religious sphere for God's purposing of evil against a sinful people, or for the purposing of evil against the Lord (cf. Jer. 18:8; Nah. 1:9, 11). Rather different is the reckoning of faith as righteousness in Gen. 15:6, the imputing of sin in Ps. 32:2, and cultic crediting in Lev. 7:18 and 17:4. In cultic imputing the basis is God's will but there is also something of the commercial sense of charging.

2. logismós. The noun has the same basic senses as the verb but finds special applications in mathematics and logic. It thus comes to denote the supreme human function, with an ethical orientation in Stoicism. It is reason in its concrete form in the consciousness and as worked out in action. The law is its basis in 4 Maccabees. In the LXX the word also has the common sense of "plan," good when it is God's plan to save, but usually bad (Ezek. 38:10). In Wisdom it is self-vaunting reason apart from God (1:3).

B. The Word Group in the NT.
Paul uses *logízesthai* in all its nuances, though bending it to his own purposes. *logismós* occurs only twice in Paul. In the rest of the NT *logízesthai* is rare and weak, and *logismós* is never used at all.

1. Thought Taken Captive to Christ. Paul expresses the popular philosophical idea of thought in his use of *logismós.* In Rom. 2:15, where he stands on common ground with the diatribe, he has *logismós* in a positive sense for the thoughts which, on the basis of moral law, either accuse or excuse. Its function, however, is only judicial. In 2 Cor. 10:4, where the *logízesthai* of v. 2 is hostile to Paul and reflects an overestimation of reason, the situation is different. The *logismoí* are the thoughts of arrogant reason which can be subdued, not by reason's own weapons, but only by God's power as this is set forth at the cross (cf. Lk. 22:37 quoting Is. 53:12). The *logismoí* are not destroyed but reoriented to divine reality. Hence *logízesthai* can become a term for the judgment of faith in Rom. 3:28; Phil. 3:13. This is an obedient *logízesthai* in which we judge on the basis of the justifying efficacy of Christ's work (Rom. 3:28) or consider that present suffering is not to be compared with future glory (8:18). It is also unconditionally valid; there can be no objection when Paul thinks he is not inferior

536

as an apostle (2 Cor. 11:5), or when he considers that he has not yet achieved perfection (Phil. 3:13), or when he calls us to consider that we are dead to sin and should act accordingly (Rom. 6:11), or even when the weak think things to be unclean (14:14).

2. *logízesthai in the Apostle's Ministry*. In the estimation of his work in 2 Cor. 3:5 Paul uses *logízesthai* in a broader sense than that of thought. As in 1 Cor. 13:11 and 2 Cor. 10:2, judgment involves commitment to action.

3. *logízesthai in the Community's Life*. In Phil. 4:8 Paul is not asking for mere reflection but for the practical consideration that leads to action. The same applies in 1 Cor. 13:5, where what is at issue in this very un-Greek combination is not reflecting on a principle but living according to the fact of salvation (Phil. 2:5ff.). When Christ is normative, *logízesthai* involves the power to live. It is not arbitrarily or aimlessly impelled to action, but unfolds in the community and comes to fulfilment in the edification of the community (1 Cor. 12 and 14).

4. *logízesthai as God's Saving Act*.

a. God imputes faith (cf. Jms. 2:23; Rom. 4:3ff.; Gal. 3:6). This imputing sets up a relation between salvation and faith and raises the question of merit. In Gen. 15:6 God reckons faith as righteousness because he is pleased to do so and not because it has intrinsic worth. Yet a tendency develops, especially among the rabbis, to remove the judgment from God's personal will and turn it into general recognition. The Greek term *logízesthai* fits in with this trend, for while it embraces the idea of imputation, it also carries with it the idea of recognition, which implies that faith is also a merit. Jms. 2:23 breaks with this trend by stressing, not the meritoriousness of faith, but its commitment to action. Paul makes an even more decisive break in Rom. 4:3ff., where he is plainly playing off the Hebraic *logízesthai* of the LXX against the Greek use, as may be seen by his contrasting of gift and debt (v. 4). The presupposition here is that the very question why faith should be reckoned for righteousness is a false one unless an answer is sought in the grace of the cross. The point of faith is that in it believers subject themselves to divine judgment and mercy and are ready to live by divine grace. On the basis of the cross righteousness is now the true reality, so that this imputation is no fiction. The reality of God's assessment thus serves as a norm of action. Believers become new creatures by God's *logízesthai*, which carries with it the imparting of the Spirit (Gal. 3:2ff.). Paul, then, restores Gen. 15:6 to its true sense, corrects the trend supported by the Greek sense of *logízesthai*, and presents *dikaioún* and *logízesthai* as complementary terms whereby God the Judge is also God the Father.

b. The reverse side of the imputing of faith is the nonimputing of sin (Rom. 4:7-8; 2 Cor. 5:19; cf. Ps. 32:2). The intrusion of grace into divine justice offends the Greeks linguistically and the Jews materially. The cross is the point of union, for if God does not impute sin *to* us, it is because Christ has been made sin *for* us. *logízesthai* is here again a judgment of grace, but it is the only connecting point between Gen. 15:6 and Ps. 32:2, for the imputing of faith obviously embraces much more than the nonimputing of sin. Justin *Dialogue* 141.2-3 rather misses the point when he suggests that repentance is the ground of nonimputation (cf. faith in 1 Clem. 10.6).

[H. W. HEIDLAND, IV, 284-92]

logikós, lógios, logomachéō, lógion, lógos → *légō*

> *loidoréō* [to revile, abuse], *loidoría* [abuse], *loídoros* [reviler],
> *antiloidoréō* [to revile in return]

This common word group has the secular sense of reproach, insult, calumny, and even blasphemy. In the LXX it carries the nuance of wrangling, angry remonstrance, or chiding as well as the more usual calumny. Philo has it for mockery or invective. In the NT the verb occurs four times and the noun and adjective twice each.

1. *loídoros* occurs in lists of vices in 1 Cor. 5:11 and 6:10. In Acts 23:4 Paul is asked why he reviles the high priest, and in his reply he recognizes a religious duty not to do so. In Mart. Pol. 9.3 the aged Polycarp cannot revile Christ; to do so would be blasphemy.

2. Christians should try to avoid calumny (1 Tim. 5:14), but when exposed to it (cf. Mt. 5:11) they should follow Christ's example (1 Pet. 2:23; cf. Mt. 26:63; Jn. 18:23), repaying railing with blessing (1 Pet. 3:9). This is the apostolic way of 1 Cor. 4:12: "When reviled, we bless" (cf. Diog. 5.15). By this answer to calumny the reality of the new creation is manifested. [H. HANSE, IV, 293-94]

→ *blasphēméō, oneidízō*

> *loúō* [to wash, bathe], *apoloúō* [to wash oneself], *loutrón* [bath, place for bathing]

A. The Terms in Hellenism.

1. General Usage. Bathing in Antiquity and the Church's Attitude. loúein normally refers to washing or bathing the body, middle "to take a bath." A *loutrón* is a place for bathing. From early days the Greeks bathe in the sea, in rivers, and in swimming pools. Baths are an established feature, more for nursing and strengthening than for cleansing. The Romans adopt the Greek habit and make bathing a luxury with their heating systems. Bathing includes successive warm and cold baths and various anointings. The church does not oppose the practice but protests against its excesses.

2. Sacral Baths and Purifications. In primitive times such processes as birth and death are thought to involve impurity through demonic action or a material *míasma*. Those affected are a danger to themselves and others and thus need purification. At first the notions are purely physical, but moral judgments develop too. Cultic purifications play a big part in religious life in Egypt, Greece, etc. Lustrations are important in cases of birth, marriage, madness, homicide, death, cultic participation, and private devotion. Even the gods need purification; cf. the washing of idols, and in Egypt the idea that the progress of the sun through the ocean is a purifying and vivifying bath. Later there is a growing demand for moral purity rather than external purification, but this can easily fall into the error of moralization.

B. The Group in the OT and Judaism.

1. In the OT *loúein* is commonly the rendering of Heb. *rāḥaṣ*, which means "to wash," "to bathe." Bodily care is the first reference, but ritual purification is also important (cf. Lev. 11:40; Dt. 23:12, etc.). In the OT, however, recognition of the moral element rules out purification for, e.g., intentional homicide. The prophets make it plain that there can be no easy washing away of guilt. Hence purifications for moral faults are given figurative significance. True washing is by repentance (Is. 1:16). It is the promised, saving act of God himself (Is. 4:4; Ps. 51:7). This act embraces human

repentance even as it transcends it (cf. Is. 43:25). The prophets thus maintain the moral demand and yet avoid moralization.

2. Judaism lays stress on ritual washings but uses other terms. It remains aware that washing with water does not result in remission. Yet concern for the law brings great scrupulosity, so much so that even God is said to bathe after burying Moses, not, of course, because he contracts impurity, but because he observes the law. Philo uses the group in the everyday sense, but also uses it for both OT and Gentile purifications. He allegorizes outward washing as inward cleansing. The latter is a favorite theme, and he distinguishes those who are being purified from those who are fully purified.

C. The Group in the NT.

1. The Secular Sense. Only *loúein* bears the secular sense in the NT, e.g., in Acts 9:37 (semi-sacral?) and Acts 16:33. The use in 2 Pet. 2:22 is figurative. All the other references are to freeing from sin (in baptism) (cf. *loutrón* in Eph. 5:26; Tit. 3:5).

2. Theological Reflection. Jesus protests sharply against confusing ritual and moral purity and against trust in external observances (Mk. 7). The rest of the NT develops this insight. Even a moral break with the past does not itself purify. The proper starting point is the forgiveness of sins by a merciful God. If full cleansing comes only with the consummation, eschatological fulfilment is already a reality in Christ (1 Pet. 1:2). Entrance into this is at baptism, which is thus a *loutrón,* not in the old sense of a ritual cleansing, but in a new and distinctive sense that derives its content from the saving work of Christ.

3. Pertinent Passages.

a. If *loúsanti* is the correct reading in Rev. 1:5, this gives a true NT thought indirectly related to baptism. But *lýsanti* ("freed") is better attested.

b. In many verses there is a clear reference to baptism. In Acts 22:16 Ananias tells Paul to be baptized and wash away his sins. In 1 Cor. 6:11 Paul reminds his readers that, being washed, they are to avoid fresh defilement. In Eph. 5:26 Christ purifies the church for bridal union by the washing of water with the word (i.e., the divine word of the gospel). In Heb. 10:22 the outward washing is related to the inner purifying. In Tit. 3:5 the washing of regeneration is on the basis, not of our own works, but of God's mercy. In 2 Pet. 2:22 the point of the proverb (Prov. 26:11) is that the false teachers, after baptism, return to sin and incur unforgivable guilt (Heb. 6:4ff.; 1 Jn. 5:16).

c. The reference to baptism is less clear in Jn. 13:10. The story of the foot-washing has two points, i.e., cleansing by Jesus and the example of ministering love. In view of the distinction between total and partial washing, the former *(lelouménos)* probably refers to the baptismal cleansing and the latter *(toús pódas nípsasthai)* to the renewed cleansing of daily forgiveness. The relation between cleansing and service is that the love of Jesus which confers forgiveness is the source of power for the disciple's own ministry of love.

D. *loúein* in the Early Church. In the apostolic fathers we find only *loúesthai* in the sense "to bathe" (Hermas *Visions* 1.1.2; 1 Clem. 8.4). The group is uncommon in the Apologists but is favored by Justin, who quotes Is. 1:16 in *Apology* 1.44.3, refers to pagan washings in 1.62.1, and has direct references to baptism in 1.61.7; *Dialogue* 12.3, etc. Later, although the church resists the idea that bodily washing is of value without inner cleansing, sacral washing finds a place, e.g., in washing the hands before prayer and the liturgical use of consecrated water.

→ *baptízō, katharízō*   [A. OEPKE, IV, 295-307]

---

lýkos [wolf]

A. Outside the NT. The wolf is commonly mentioned in antiquity as a terrible beast of prey. Common themes are its fierceness, its appetite, its cunning, its hostility to sheep, and the terror it inspires by its sudden appearances. The wolf figures largely in mythology and superstition as the symbol of the fugitive or the epitome of demonic power. The main use in the OT is in metaphors (Gen. 49:27; Ezek. 22:27, etc.). The wolf's lying down with the sheep symbolizes the peace of the messianic age in Is. 11:6; 65:25. In rabbinic writings there is a distinctive use of the term in the reported blasphemy when God is called a wolf to his people; this seems to involve a play on the words *locus* (the place of God's presence) and *lýkos*.

B. NT Usage. *lýkos* occurs in the warning of Jesus against false prophets in Mt. 7:15. These teachers might produce notable achievements (the distinction is not merely that of word and deed) but they do not do the one thing that matters, i.e., the Father's will. This is the criterion by which to differentiate appearance and reality. Paul has a similar saying in Acts 20:29, although it is impossible to say what false teachers he has in mind. As distinct from the church's own teachers in v. 30, they come from outside. In Mt. 10:16; Lk. 10:3 Jesus warns his disciples of the dangers they will face on their mission. The contrast between their authority and the persecutions they suffer characterizes their eschatological relation to the world. Jn. 10:12 again shows that the community is under mortal threat, but the focus is on the fact that Jesus, unlike the hireling, sees the threat, protects the flock with his life, and thus averts the danger. Faced with the threat, the flock may thus see to whom it truly belongs.

[G. BORNKAMM, IV, 308-11]

---

lymaínomai [to harm, destroy]

lymaínomai has such senses as "to treat disgracefully," "to injure," "to hurt," "to imperil," and "to destroy." The only NT occurrence is in Acts 8:3, where, in the sense "to ravage," "to lay waste," it describes Saul's relentless persecution of the church (cf. 9:1; 22:4).   [W. MICHAELIS, IV, 312]

---

lýpē [pain, sorrow], *lypéō* [to grieve], *álypos* [without sorrow], *perílypos* [profoundly sorrowful], *syllypéomai* [to sorrow with]

lýpē, lypéō.

A. The Greek Understanding of *lýpē*.

1. *lýpē* means "pain," "sorrow," *lypeín* is "to cause pain," and *lypeísthai* "to experience sorrow." Both physical pain and mental anguish are covered by the words. Physically the pain is especially that caused by hunger, thirst, heat, cold, or sickness, while mentally it is especially the anguish of misfortune, death, annoyance, insult, or outrage.

2. Pain alternates with joy *(hēdoné)* in the Greek view of things. There is a natural desire to live without it, yet life in mere *hēdoné* would be vegetating. The things that

bring joy also bring pain (e.g., children). We also bring sorrow on ourselves by our deeds. Carousing offers brief *hēdonaí* and many *lýpai*.

3. Dealing with *lýpē* only in relation to *hēdonḗ*, philosophy sees that there can be no *hēdonḗ* without it. Plato thinks *hēdonaí* and *lýpai* belong to the lower part of the soul but differentiates true and spiritual *hēdonaí* from others. Yet even here there is the possibility of deception by a false evaluation of things or by trying to have joy by the concealment of pain. True *hēdonḗ* comes with the perception of goodness, truth, and beauty. But this poses a limitation for *lýpē* and raises the question of its purpose. For Aristotle *hēdonḗ* is a good, but not absolutely so. Stoicism groups *lýpē* with the passions (including *hēdonḗ*, fear, etc.) from which sages free themselves. It really arises from within as an emotion based on error, and it serves no positive purpose.

4. At the same time, there are some beginnings of a positive view in the Greek world. Thus *lýpē* leads to sympathy, to knowledge, and in that sense to salvation. Some circles also see in *lýpē* a divine punishment which leads to penitence, although the prevailing belief in ineluctable fate hampers true self-accusation. Some forms of Gnosticism find a place for *lýpē* as a valuable means of discipline for the imprisoned soul. Plotinus, too, suggests that through *lýpē* one might learn the alienation of the soul and its relationship to deity.

B. The Understanding of Sorrow in the OT and Judaism.

1. In the LXX *lýpē* is the rendering of various Hebrew terms. Its meaning varies, covering such things as physical exertion, trouble, pain, sorrow, anxiety, and annoyance.

2. Proverbs (14:13) accepts the fact that joy and pain intermingle in human life (cf. Eccl. 3:4). But one is not to surrender to sorrow (Prov. 31:6; Eccl. 9:7). The real focus of the OT, however, is not psychological but practical, i.e., on the things that cause joy or grief. God imposes pain (Gen. 3:16-17), but in the last age it will vanish (Is. 35:10; 51:11). Pain is not merely a penalty but also a means of divine instruction, so that faith sees in it a firm relation to joy (Ps. 126:5).

3. Philo adopts to a large extent a Stoic view of *lýpē*. Although full joy belongs to God alone, pain should have no place for the righteous, since God does not will that we be just tormented by *lypaí*. The *lýpē* of remorse can serve a more positive purpose.

C. Christian Writings.

1. The NT contrasts *lýpē* and *chará* (Jn. 16:20ff. etc.) rather than *lýpē* and *hēdonḗ* (cf. also *lypeín* and *euphraínein* in 2 Cor. 2:2). The main sense of *lýpē* is sorrow or grief (cf. Jn. 16:6; Rom. 9:2; Phil. 2:27).

2. The NT does not discuss whether *lýpē* is good or bad. The desire to be spared it is right (cf. 2 Cor. 2:1ff.), and at the end it will be done away (Rev. 7:17). We are not to cause *lýpē* to others (Rom. 14:15) except it be in love and with a view to repentance (2 Cor. 2:4). Divine correction is perceived in it (Heb. 12:4ff.; 1 Pet. 1:6).

3. In another sense, however, *lýpē* is an integral part of the Christian life. Conversion involves a godly *lýpē* which is essential to the ongoing life of faith (2 Cor. 7:9ff.). The consequent break with the world exposes Christians to *lýpē* which they now regard, not as a hindrance, but as an opportunity for growth in the power of Christ's death and resurrection. Acceptance of *lýpē* is acceptance of the cross (Gal. 6:14; Phil. 3:10-11; 2 Cor. 4:8-9). In John Christ's departure plunges the disciples into the *lýpē* not merely of mental sorrow but of vulnerability in the world (Jn. 16:6-7, 20ff.). They must experience this if they are to know the true meaning of belonging to Jesus. Yet this *lýpē* is the source of their joy (16:21-22). The very isolation from

Jesus brings out the significance of fellowship with him and the resultant victory over the world (Jn. 16:33).

4. 1 Pet. 2:19 develops a similar thought. The pain of unjust suffering carries a rich reward when accepted in commitment to God and separation from the world, with Christ again as a model (v. 21). Eph. 4:30, however, has the rather different warning that believers are not to grieve the Spirit, presumably in a strengthening of the admonition against evil talk in v. 29.

5. Among the apostolic fathers Hermas uses *lýpē* for sorrow over sin in *Visions* 1.2.1-2. At the same time *lýpē* is one of the twelve vices of *Similitudes* 9.15.3, and the *lypērós* person wounds the Spirit. There is little of note in the Apologists apart from a Stoicizing reference in Tatian *Address to the Greeks* 11.1.

álypos. This word, meaning "without sorrow or care," is common in the papyri and plays an important role in Stoicism. It occurs in the NT only in Phil. 2:28.

perílypos. This word means "extremely afflicted" or "profoundly sorrowful." The NT uses it of the rich young ruler in Lk. 18:23, Herod in Mk. 6:26, and Jesus in Gethsemane in Mk. 14:34.

syllypéomai. Having the common sense "to sorrow with," "to feel sympathy," this word (used by the LXX in Is. 51:19) occurs in the NT only in Mk. 3:5 to express the strong grief of Jesus at the hardness of heart of his opponents.

[R. BULTMANN, IV, 313-24]

lýtron etc. → *lýō*

---

lýchnos [lamp],   *lychnía* [lampstand]

The *lýchnos* is a lamp, originally an open bowl, then a closed lamp in various forms, usually put on a stand to give better light, the *lychnía* being the stand. Both words are common in the LXX (cf. the seven-branched candelabra, a *lychnía* with seven *lýchnoi*). The lamp is a common metaphor in the OT. It denotes length of life (2 Sam. 21:17), the source of divine help (Job 29:3), and the law (Ps. 119:105). The lamp of the wicked will be put out (Job 18:6). In the NT Jesus makes figurative use of the fact that to give its light a lamp must be put on a stand. In Mt. 5:15 this seems to suggest that the disciples must give open witness, although a reference to Jesus' own ministry is not excluded. In Lk. 11:34 Jesus calls the eye the lamp of the body; we must be open to the light of the gospel if we are to know full health. The exhortation in Lk. 12:35 presents the burning lamp as a symbol of readiness. The woman in Lk. 15:8 lights a lamp in her search for the lost coin, a token of her great anxiety to find it. In Jn. 5:35 Jesus honors the Baptist by calling him a burning and shining lamp; he cannot be called the light itself (cf. 1:8) but he has given faithful witness to it. Rev. 11:4 describes the two witnesses as *lychníai* (cf. Zech. 4:2, 11), while the seven churches are seven golden *lychníai* in 1:12-13 etc. (cf. Zech. 4 and Mt. 5:15), and the Lamb himself is the lamp of the heavenly city in 21:23. Heb. 9:2 refers to the temple lampstand, and 2 Pet. 1:19 calls the prophetic word a lamp shining in a dark place until the day dawns. [W. MICHAELIS, IV, 324-27]

> *lýō* [to loose, destroy], *analýō* [to depart, return], *análysis* [departing], *epilýō* [to release, explain], *epílysis* [explanation], *katalýō* [to put down, destroy], *katályma* [inn, guestroom], *akatálytos* [indestructible], *lýtron* [ransom], *antílytron* [ransom], *lytróō* [to ransom, redeem], *lýtrōsis* [redemption, liberation], *lytrōtḗs* [liberator, redeemer], *apolýtrōsis* [release, redemption]

A. The Word Group in the OT.

1. lýō and Compounds. The simple *lýō*, "to loose," is rich in compounds that add nuances to the meaning. In the LXX we find *apo-, dia-, ek-, epi-, kata-, para-, peri-, syl-*, and *hypo-*; all but the last three of these occur in the NT. *lýō* is used for release from prison, the opening of what is closed, the destroying of foundations, and the putting off of fetters. The compounds carry such senses as "to leave," "to loosen," "to relax," "to become slack," "to break off," "to untie," and "to part," i.e., those engaged in a struggle.

2. lýtron.

a. Theologically more important than *lýō*, *lýtron* has three Hebrew originals, of which the first is *kpr*. Derived by some from an Assyrian word meaning "to wash away," this more likely has the basic sense "to cover," and it then denotes "to atone." As a cover, *kpr* carries the idea of an equivalent, so that when a fault is covered it is not by cancellation but by a vicarious offering. What is at forfeit is human life, and for this a *lýtron* is presented which may be accepted or refused. There can be no *lýtron*, e.g., for willful murder (Num. 35:31-32).

b. A second term is *g'l*. This belongs to family law. The *g'l* must redeem family lives or goods that have fallen into bondage (Lev. 25:48; Jer. 32:7; Ruth 2:20), and must also be the avenger of blood (Num. 35:12 etc.). In virtue of the bond between God and his people, God himself is the *g'l* for Israel (Is. 41:14; 43:14, etc.). As Creator, he is also Redeemer. He has sold Israel into bondage because of her sin, yet her redemption is assured because of his status as her *g'l*. The same thought occurs in Job 19:25. God has smitten Job, but the same God is Job's *g'l* and will thus enter the lists against himself when he causes Job to see him after death. The slain and risen Job is in the hands of the same God.

c. A third Hebrew term is *pdy*, which lays the stress on payment, although again for animate, not inanimate objects. Thus in sacral law the Levites are a payment for the firstborn of Israel (Num. 3:12 etc.), and cf. the payment for Jonathan (1 Sam. 14:45). In the story of David God himself functions as the Redeemer (2 Sam. 4:9); this thought is prominent in Dt. 7:8; 13:6; 15:15, etc., and it is given a personal turn again in Jeremiah (e.g., 15:16). As distinct from *g'l*, *pdy* carries a stress on the action rather than the subject.

3. lytroústhai and Derivatives.

a. From *lýtron* comes *lytroún*, "to free for ransom." Since *kpr* involves expiation by sacrifice, *lytroústhai* is used mostly for the other two terms. The main use for *g'l* is in Is. 40ff. The idea is first suggested that God gives Egypt etc. as a ransom for Israel (45:13), but then the bolder thought emerges that God need give no ransom to Cyrus but gives alien peoples to Israel as a voluntary acquisition. Redemption is thus an act of free grace with no ransom price. When used for *pdy*, *lytroústhai* denotes either the redeeming of the firstborn by a vicarious offering or liberation from bondage, especially at the exodus (Dt. 7:8 etc.). As in Isaiah, so in Deuteronomy God pays no ransom when he frees Israel from Egypt, so that *lytroústhai* can adequately cover the two different Hebrew terms. It does duty for both in Psalms, which speaks a great deal about the redemption of both Israel and righteous individuals (Pss. 144:10; 26:11; 31:5, etc.), although mostly from affliction, not from sin. Death is the last emergency, and redemption from it may have the sense of being kept from it (Ps. 103:4), but it may also be redemption out of it (Ps. 49:7ff.). No ransom avails here, but God can snatch the soul from the underworld. The sparseness of the idea of redemption from sin is due to the fact that the *kpr* group applies in this field with the added factor of sacral expiation.

b. *lýtrōsis*. Various nouns and adjectives develop from *lytróō*. The rare *lýtrōsis*, which is active outside the Bible, is passive in the LXX and NT and has the sense "release." It is connected with the Year of Jubilee in Is. 63:4 and with substitution for the firstborn in Num. 18:16 (cf. Ps. 49:8).

c. *lytrōtḗs*. This word, meaning "redeemer," is twice used of God in the Psalms (19:14; 78:35). The passive *lytrōtós* means "redeemable" in Lev. 25:31-32.

d. *apolýtrōsis*, which means "ransom" or "ransom payment" in nonbiblical Greek, becomes a significant term for "redemption" in the NT.

[O. PROCKSCH, IV, 328-35]

lýō (→ *déō*). This common Greek word, which can denote the redemption granted by deity, has two main senses in the NT: a. "to loosen," "release," or "free," in various connections, and b. "to dissolve," "to destroy," "to break up," "to invalidate." Sense b. can be an important one; cf. relaxing or invalidating the law in Mt. 5:19; Jn. 5:18; 7:23, dismissing Jesus as the Christ in 1 Jn. 4:3, and destroying the works of the devil in 1 Jn. 3:8. Theologically important instances of a. are in Rev. 1:5 (redeeming from sin) and Acts 2:24 (loosing the pangs of death).

analýō, análysis. From the literal sense "to undo again" develops the sense "to leave," which is a euphemism for "to die" in Phil. 1:23. *análysis* means departing in the same sense of death in 2 Tim. 4:6. In Lk. 12:36 *analýō* has the special sense "to return."

epilýō, epílysis. Literally meaning "to release," *epilýō* means "to resolve" (an issue) in Acts 19:39 and "to explain" in Mk. 4:34. *epílysis* means "exposition" or "interpretation" in 2 Pet. 1:20.

katalýō, katályma.

a. From the basic sense "to put down," *katalýō* means "to destroy" in various contexts (Mk. 14:58; 2 Cor. 5:1; Gal. 2:18). It can also have the nuance "to frustrate," as in Acts 5:38-39.

b. A second meaning is then "to invalidate," e.g., the law in Mt. 5:17.

c. A third meaning is "to unyoke," "to rest," "to lodge" (Lk. 9:12; 19:7). Hence *katályma* means "place of lodging" or "inn" (Lk. 2:7), although it may also be used freely for a guestroom (Mk. 14:14; Lk. 22:11).

akatálytos. This word, meaning "indissoluble," "indestructible," occurs in the NT only in Heb. 7:16, where it carries the nuance of "eternal." The risen Jesus (vv. 25ff.) is superior to the Levitical priest because he now has in fullness the indestructible life that he has already as the historical man Jesus. As 9:14 points out, the eternal Spirit is at work in him, so that even in his mortal humanity he enjoys a fellowship with God that means eternal life. In his death, then, he is upheld by the same Spirit. Under no compulsion to die, he offers himself in priestly sacrifice, and in so doing he remains above death. In virtue of this indestructible power, his sacrifice, too, is of eternal validity.

lýtron.

A. *lýtron* and Ideas of Ransom outside the NT.

1. Formed with *-tron*, which usually denotes a means of doing something, *lýtron* has the sense of releasing by payment. It refers to money paid to ransom prisoners of war, to release slaves, to redeem a bond, or, infrequently, to cover a debt to deity. The cultic use is more common in the LXX and Philo. Josephus has it often for ransom for prisoners of war or war booty.

2. The payment in a ransom is a matter of agreement, either by law (Ex. 30:12) or by negotiation. In negotiations, law tends to protect the purchaser, but fixing an equivalent is a subjective matter. A legal form is needed to make sure that the person ransomed is truly freed. In the cultus the deity or the tradition of the sanctuary can fix the price, although changes are always possible, and since acceptance of a ransom is an act of grace the payment may be refused (cf. Num. 35:31-32; Ps. 49:7).

3. The Jews share the general view but move easily from the thought of ransom to that of expiation.

B. The *lýtron* Sayings in the NT.

1. In the NT *lýtron* occurs only in Mk. 10:45 and Mt. 20:28.

2. In Mk. 10:45 Jesus is the Son of Man, and his messianic work is a service in which he finally gives himself (cf. Jn. 10:11, 15, 17). He does this in willing obedience and for the sake of the many, an indefinite number with at least a suggestion of universality. The liberation is fairly obviously from sin, although this is not stated; there is no mention of any recipient of the ransom.

3. The saying clearly gives the work of Jesus a vicarious dimension. The *antí* ("for") means "in place of" as well as "to the advantage of." Jesus does for the many what they cannot do for themselves and what no other can do for them. Yet one cannot interpret the saying exclusively in the light of any single OT passage (e.g., Is. 53) nor detach it from the history narrated in the Gospels. Accepting the Father's gracious will, Jesus vicariously suffers death on behalf of the many who have fallen victim to death, and thereby initiates the new covenant with his blood (Mk. 14:24). His vicarious ministry involves the necessity of dying.

4. Since it is God who demands that this vicarious offering be made, the ransom is obviously paid to God, not Satan. If God is not mentioned, it is out of reverence for his name. The God of this saying is the God of Ps. 90 whose judgment is the reality of our being as sinners and with whom we can speak only out of the depths (Ps. 130).

5. The saying does not explain why God requires a ransom instead of liberating us freely. God owes explanations to no one but follows his own wise and righteous will. Jesus accepts this, and in so doing discloses to us that his death is the obedient service to God on the one side and the vicarious service for us on the other whereby freedom from sin is secured.

6. Jesus himself, of course, has previously forgiven sin (Mk. 2:5). But he has done so as one who accepts God's holy judgment on it (cf. Mk. 9:42ff.), who sees that forgiveness is a divine miracle (Mk. 10:27), and who demonstrates the seriousness of sin, the full reach of obedience, and the true reality of forgiveness by his atoning death. By his death he fulfils the condition of forgiveness by lifting sinners out of

disobedience into his own obedience and thus bringing renewal instead of merely lulling a feeble sense of guilt. To see that the willing acceptance of death by Jesus is the inner condition of his right to forgive is to understand why a ransom is demanded. It is also to understand why this cannot be explained in advance but is evident only in the light of his death.

7. While Jesus expects to find Gentiles in the kingdom (Mt. 8:11; cf. 5:45), he sees no other valid forgiveness than that which he himself dispenses as Christ and Judge (Mt. 25:31ff.). The Father's grace is grace through him (Lk. 15:11ff.). There is joy in heaven over one sinner repenting, but Jesus is the one who pronounces pardon. Even those who may enter the kingdom without knowing him (Mt. 25:37ff.) will do so only in his name and in virtue of his forgiving work.

8. Speculative constructions, both objective and subjective, tend to miss the decisive significance of the relation between God and us in the atonement. This relation is grounded in the living unity of God's judgment and blessing. In Christ God has shown himself to be the reality of this unity by the self-sacrificial obedience that combines the divine justice and the divine grace. This ransom opens up forgiveness for believers and frees them for obedience on their part in genuine love for both God and others.

antílytron. This rare and late word occurs in the NT only in 1 Tim. 2:6. Based on Mk. 10:45, this verse has *heautón* for *psychḗn, pántōn* for *pollṓn,* and the elegant compound for the simple *lýtron.* Tit. 2:14 contains the same thought.

lytróō. This word means "to free by ransom," "to let free for ransom," middle "to purchase for ransom," and passive "to be set free by ransom." Rabbinic equivalents are used for the exodus, for deliverance from Antiochus Epiphanes, and for the final redemption for which prayer is made. There is no thought of redemption from sin. In the NT only the middle occurs; it is used for the redeeming act of God or Christ. There is no idea of an actual ransom in Lk. 24:21, but ransom is plainly at issue in Tit. 2:14 and 1 Pet. 1:18-19, where the understanding of Christ's death as a ransom (Mk. 10:45) obviously has an impact.

lýtrōsis. This word means "redemption," or "release from an obligation." In Lk. 1:68; 2:38 it means "liberation" from the yoke of enemies (cf. Lk. 24:21). In Heb. 9:12 it means redemption in a more general sense, including redemption from sin. The idea is more cultic than legal, so that one should not press the idea of ransom.

lytrōtḗs. Meaning "liberator," this word is used to describe Moses in Acts 7:35.

apolýtrōsis. Sparsely attested elsewhere, this noun is common in the NT. It means "freeing for ransom," but it may also have the more general sense of "release." In Lk. 21:28 it means the definitive eschatological redemption of the new aeon for which the disciples are to watch expectantly. This is also the point in Eph. 1:14 and Rom. 8:23. In the latter verse it is specifically the redemption *of* (not *from*) the body, i.e., its transformation after the model of the risen Lord (Phil. 3:21; cf. 1 Cor. 15:42-43). In the former (cf. Eph. 4:30) it is entry into the full inheritance of which we now have a first instalment by the Spirit. Yet redemption is also itself a present possession (Eph. 1:7; Col. 1:14). It consists of forgiveness as the act of God which is now enjoyed by promise but which will bring full renewal at the last day. The historical reality of redemption is that of the crucifixion and resurrection of Christ, who as the second Adam, divine Son, and human Brother is the middle point of God's history with us. Now hidden with him in God, our redemption will come to consummation when we attain to union (1 Th. 4:17) and glorification (1 Cor. 15:49) with him. He himself is made *apolýtrōsis* for us (1 Cor. 1:30). Hence it may be had only in fellowship with him, i.e., in virtue of his work (Gal. 2:20), and in the sphere of his lordship (Col. 1:13). It is not won from God, for God himself has made him our redemption. It is a gift of grace (Rom. 3:24). In Hebrews the word has the common Greek sense of "release" in 11:35, but the meaning is "remission" in 9:15. It may be noted that in none of the NT passages is the idea of an actual "ransom" expressly present. The closest to a direct reference is Rom. 3:24, but in 3:25 the thought is cultic rather than commercial, and if justification is a legal concept in 3:24, law does not demand payment for release from a penalty. *apolýtrōsis* is not, in fact, a key term in the NT. It does not occur in many books, and is less important than, e.g., *dikaiosýnē* in Paul. It has become a more general term which has to be given its specific content by other facts or concepts. Its most significant use is eschatological, as in Lk. 21:28; Eph. 1:14; 4:30; Rom. 8:23.   [F. Büchsel, IV, 335-56]

μ *m*

---

mágos [magician, Magus],   **mageía** [magic],   **mageúō** [to practice magic]

---

mágos.

1. The Greek World. This word has four consistent senses: a. "member of the Persian priestly caste," b. "possessor and user of supernatural knowledge and power," c. "magician," and d. (figuratively) "deceiver."

2. Judaism. For Philo the *mágos* is subreligious. Philo accepts the Persian *mágoi* only as they do *mageía* as scientific research. The rabbis adopt *mágos* as a loanword for "magician"; Jews must avoid *mágoi*. The LXX has the term only in Dan. 2:2 for those who have magical and religious arts in Babylon.

3. The NT. In Mt. 2:1, 7, 16 the reference seems to be to those who have special wisdom in reading the stars. In Acts 13:6, 8 *mágos* is parallel to *pseudoprophḗtēs* (cf. the Jewish exorcists of 19:13). The reference seems to be to a house philosopher, who is possibly tempted to use the name of God magically, but who is confounded when he encounters Christian truth.

mageía, mageúō. *mageía* is the activity of a *mágos,* and *mageúō* means either "to belong to the order" or "to do the work of a *mágos.*" The words occur in the NT only in connection with Simon Magus (Acts 8:9, 11). Simon started a movement in Samaria (perhaps as a supposed predecessor of the Messiah) by the use of extraordinary powers but not in the power of the true Spirit of God. His rapid conversion points to a messianic interest but his subsequent offer (vv. 18-19) shows that he views the operation of the Spirit as a higher (and hence desirable) form of magic.

→ *góēs*   [G. Delling, IV, 356-59]

Magṓg → *Gṓg kaí Magṓg; mathēteúō, mathētḗs* → *manthánō*

---

maínomai [to rage, be furious]

---

maínomai, meaning "to rage," "to be furious," is used of warriors, strong drink, sorrow, desire, rapture, etc. In the LXX it denotes the raging of the nations under the terror of the divine judgment of war. In 4 Macc. 8:5; 10:13 the fidelity of Eleazar and his sons seems to be madness to the king. Philo uses the word only for delusion, and in Josephus (*Antiquities* 1.116) the building of the tower of Babel is madness to God. In the NT Jesus seems to be out of his mind to those who reject his message (Jn. 10:19ff.), Rhoda is thought to be mad when she says that Peter is at the door (Acts 12:15), Festus tells Paul that his learning is making him mad (Acts 26:24), Paul in his reply states that he is not mad but speaking sober truth (v. 25), and divinely inspired glossolalia necessarily appears to be madness to those who do not understand the gift (1 Cor. 14:23). Consistently, then, the NT uses the term for the judgment of unbelief on the divine work of salvation and Christian witness to it.

[H. PREISKER, IV, 360-61]

---

makários [blessed, happy], *makarízō* [to consider blessed], *makarismós* [blessing]

A. Greek Usage. *makários* is at first a poetic word and refers to the blessedness of the gods. Later it comes to be used for the freedom of the rich from normal cares and worries. The verb *makarízō* means "to extol as, or declare to be, blessed," while *makarismós* means "extolling as blessed," and is first used by Aristotle as a technical term for "beatitude" (macarism).

B. The Stylistic Form of the Beatitude. A set form develops in Greek to extol the good fortune that accrues to a person. Using *makários* (or *trismakários*), it takes on a gnomic quality, and is often found, e.g., on epitaphs. Themes are varied, e.g., material goods, children, a marriage partner, bachelorhood, riches, a good understanding, fame, righteousness, the release of death, and mystic initiation. Happy are those who enjoy such things.   [F. HAUCK, IV, 362-64]

C. The LXX and Judaism. The main Hebrew term is *'ašrê,* but the LXX extends the range by using *makários* for various other terms. The predicative *makários* is most common, with the content in a relative clause, participle, or *hóti* clause. *makarízein* as a finite verb is rare. In the OT macarisms always refer to persons, never to things or states. God is not called *makários* (though in the NT cf. 1 Tim. 1:11; 6:15). Blessedness is fullness of life and relates to such things as a wife, beauty, honor, wisdom, and piety. The OT contains many warnings against purely external judgment, so that the true blessedness is that of trust in God, forgiveness of sins, righteousness even in affliction, and final deliverance. Formal beatitudes are not common in Philo. For him God alone is truly blessed, and humans can know blessedness only as they share the divine nature in their bearing of earthly sorrows and their philosophical endeavors. Rabbinic Judaism, however, stays closer to the usage of the OT.

[G. BERTRAM, IV, 364-67]

D. The Word Group in the NT.
1. The special feature in the NT is use of the term for the distinctive joy which comes through participation in the divine kingdom. The verb *makarízō* occurs only

twice, first in Lk. 1:48 for the blessing of the mother of the Messiah by all generations, and second in Jms. 5:11 with reference to those who endure. The noun *makarismós* occurs three times—in Gal. 4:15 for the blessing of receiving the gospel, and in Rom. 4:6, 9 for that of forgiveness of sins. *makários* is very common, usually in direct beatitudes. The reference is to persons, and the macarism, in the third person, consists of a predicative *makários*, then the person, and finally the reason in a subsidiary clause. Set in the context of eschatological salvation, the NT macarisms have great emotional force. Often there is a contrast with false happiness, but now all secular values are secondary to the one supreme good of the kingdom. Often, then, we find sacred paradoxes (Mt. 5:3ff.; Lk. 6:20ff.). God effects a reversal of all human values. True happiness is not for the rich and secure, but for the poor and oppressed who are rich only in pity, purity, and peace. Blessing is also for the persecuted, for those who hear the message of the kingdom (Mt. 13:16), for those who meet it with faith (Lk. 1:45), for those who make no false demands (Jn. 20:29), for those who watch (Lk. 12:37) and stand fast (Jms. 1:12), and for those who understand the words and acts of Jesus (Jn. 13:17). The mother of the Messiah is blessed (Lk. 11:27), but childless women are also blessed in an age of impending judgment (Lk. 23:29). Paul in Rom. 4:7-8 calls those who know forgiveness blessed, while in Rom. 14:22 he refers to the blessedness of those who see their way clearly in ethical decisions, and in 1 Cor. 7:40 he thinks widows who do not marry again are more blessed. Revelation contains seven macarisms (and fourteen woes). Five are pronounced authoritatively from heavenly lips (14:13; 16:15; 19:9; 22:7, 14) and refer to the blessedness of martyrs, of those who persevere, of those who are invited to the feast, of those who share in the first resurrection, and of those who may enter the holy city.

2. The secular concept of counting someone fortunate occurs in Acts 26:2 (Paul).

3. In 1 Tim. 1:11; 6:15 *makários* describes the blessed transcendence of God. Eschatological hope belongs to this sphere, and may thus be called blessed in Tit. 2:13.

[F. HAUCK, IV, 367-70]

---

mákellon [market]

mákellon means "enclosure," then "market." Markets are rectangular courts with a dome-shaped roof, a fountain in the middle, booths at the side, and perhaps a room for sacrificial repasts. In 1 Cor. 10:25 Paul uses the word when he tells the Christians at Corinth how to act relative to meat sold on the market, which might well come from pagan temples but might also be the only meat readily available. Paul's advice is that one is to eat without asking questions, for everything is the Lord's. Only when unbelievers say that the meat has been offered in pagan sacrifice should one refrain for their sake.

[J. SCHNEIDER, IV, 370-72]

---

makrán [far off, long], *makróthen* [from a distance]

makrán means "far off" in space or "long" in time. God is sometimes said to be not *makrán*. *makróthen* is an abverb of place only. The LXX uses both words spatially. Theologically they may denote the remoteness of God (Ps. 10:1) or his salvation (Is. 59:11) or righteousness (Is. 59:14), or they may denote human distance from God

(Jer. 2:5). Aloofness from sin may often be the theme (cf. Prov. 4:24; Ps. 119:155; Prov. 15:29). *makrán* refers to length of time in 2 Sam. 7:19; Ezek. 12:22. *makrán* is used as a preposition with genitive in Sir. 15:8, and Josephus has it both for space (God's presence) and time (*ouk eis makrán,* "in brief").

1. The NT has both words in the spatial sense in Mt. 8:30; Jn. 21:8; Acts 22:21; Mk. 5:6; 8:3; 11:13; 14:54.

2. The use of *apó makróthen* in Mk. 14:50 and parallels has a figurative aspect. The women at the cross stand "afar off" in pious awe and in aloofness from the scoffing. In Lk. 16:23 the *apó makróthen* depicts the great gulf between the rich man and Lazarus. In Rev. 18:10, 15, 17 it expresses horror at the sight of the judgment on Babylon. This sense of distance is also strong in Lk. 18:13, where the publican, conscious of his unworthiness, stands afar off. *ou makrán* is common in the NT to denote the overcoming of the gulf between God and us. The scribe is "not far" from the kingdom in Mk. 12:34, God is "not far" from each of us in Acts 17:27, Gentiles who were "far off" are brought near in Eph. 2:17 (cf. Is. 57:19), and if the father sees the prodigal "afar off," it is only to run quickly to him (Lk. 15:20).

[H. PREISKER, IV, 372-74]

---

makrothymía [patience, forbearance], *makrothyméō* [to have patience], *makróthymos* [patient, forbearing], *makrothýmōs* [patiently]

A. Nonbiblical Greek. At first *makrothymía* means "resignation" or "forced acceptance." It then takes on such nuances as "desperate acceptance," "procrastination," and "endurance."

B. The OT (LXX) and Later Judaism. The group has theological depth in the OT when it is used for God's "longsuffering" or "forbearance" (Heb. *'erek 'ap*). The majestic God graciously restrains his righteous wrath, as in his saving work for Israel (cf. Ex. 34:6 etc.). He does so in covenant faithfulness but also out of regard for human frailty. Divine forbearance imposes a demand for human forbearance too. Forbearance, of course, is not renunciation but postponement with a view to repentance (cf. Nah. 1:2ff.). In this light God's *makrothymía* is a gift. Nor is it confined to Israel or the righteous; this is why it can arouse complaints in, e.g., Jeremiah (15:15) and Jonah (4:2). In some passages, however, forbearance with the Gentiles is merely postponement until they fill up the measure of their sins (2 Macc. 6:14ff.). In the divine *makrothymía* there is always the tension of grace and wrath.

C. The Rabbis. Various considerations are found in rabbinic writings. Thus forbearance is distinguished from indulgence. Its purpose for the wicked is that they might repent or at least produce righteous children. It might vary according to the measure of guilt or merit. It imposes an obligation of forbearance on us.

D. The NT.
1. Synoptic Gospels. In the parable of Mt. 18:23ff. an appeal is made for the forbearance, first of the king, then of the servant. The parable presupposes a wrathful judgment with full exaction of a debt that can never be repaid. Disregarding the amount, the *kýrios* cancels the whole debt, not in indulgence or postponement, but in the generosity of grace. Forbearance of this kind demands an answering forbearance in the servant. The absence of this response will call it into question. The divine

forgiveness does not become a law which one may then plead against God; it is always God's free grace, and it may be withdrawn if the overflowing love of God does not evoke the response of a pardoning love of neighbor. An echo of the same point may be heard in Lk. 18:7. The righteous may be sure of their vindication by God. Why, then, does God delay? Not, of course, because God is like the unjust judge of the parable (18:1ff.), but because the elect themselves need an interval of grace for the faith and prayer with which alone they can move into the day of reckoning (cf. v. 8).

2. *Paul.*

a. God's Longsuffering. Paul relates God's forbearance to his wrath (Rom. 2:4; 9:22). Already manifest, divine wrath will reach a climax only on the day of wrath (2:5). Longsuffering obviously does not mean irresolution or compliance. It is not swayed by emotion but has the end in view. The delay may allow time for repentance but it also increases the wrath. It leaves no room for a claim on God's goodness but makes God's purpose plain in its eschatological dimension. The goal, however, is not just passive, for even vessels of wrath serve to bring into relief the mercy of God displayed in vessels of mercy (9:22ff.).

b. The Christian's Longsuffering. God's forbearance pledges Christians to a similar forbearance (1 Th. 5:14) which, as a fruit of the Spirit controlled by love (Gal. 5:22), issues in mutual correction. Love itself is forbearing (1 Cor. 13:4). Forbearance is a necessary quality in the service of God (2 Cor. 6:6), linking knowledge and kindness. It is a spiritual force that has its origin in the divine glory and works itself out in joyful endurance (Col. 1:11). The elect put it on as their new garment in Christ (Col. 3:12-13). It corresponds to their calling to the one body of Christ (Eph. 4:1ff.).

c. The Pastorals. In 1 Tim. 1:16 Christ himself exercises forbearance toward Paul. He thus offers a model for us in dealing with opponents. No one is to be given up easily. The divine forbearance leads naturally to praise (v. 17). It imposes an obligation in missionary service (2 Tim. 3:10). The best way to meet error is by the longsuffering which, while not retreating, leaves the decision with all confidence to the divine Judge (4:1-2).

3. *The Catholic Epistles.*

a. James. In unjust suffering, *makrothymía* is perseverance in expectation of Christ's coming (5:7ff.). Awareness of the nearness of Christ quenches angry feelings, produces triumphant steadfastness, and confers the certainty of fruit.

b. Hebrews. The emphasis here lies on the connection with faith (6:11-12). *makrothymía* is the steadfastness of faith and hope which is not vexed by waiting. Its basis is the promise of the righteous God.

c. 1 Peter. In 1 Pet. 3:20ff. God's forbearance in Noah's day allows for the development of the obedience and disobedience that will be manifested in deliverance and destruction. It is characterized today by the work of Christ through proclamation and baptism.

d. 2 Peter. In this epistle God's *makrothymía* is a central concept. It explains why the parousia has not yet come (3:4). Its purpose is wholly positive, namely to allow space for repentance. Judgment will finally fall on the wicked (v. 7), and Christians must be zealous to be found without spot (v. 14). Yet we are to count the Lord's forbearance as salvation (v. 5).

makrothýmōs. This adverb occurs in the NT only in Acts 26:3 in the secular sense of "patiently." [J. Horst, IV, 374-87]

---

mamōnás [wealth, mammon]

---

1. The Gk. *mamōnás* seems to come from an Aramaic noun which most probably derives from the root *'mn* ("that in which one trusts").

2. The word does not occur in the OT but is used in Jewish writings in the senses a. "resources," b. "gain" (especially dishonest), and c. "compensation" or "ransom," but also "bribe." In general it has an ignoble sense, is often called unrighteous, and is a target of ethical censure and admonition.

3. In the NT the word occurs only on the lips of Jesus. It denotes "earthly goods," but always with a stress on their materialistic character. When people trust in it (Lk. 12:15ff.) or give their hearts to it (Mt. 6:21), they cannot love God. Believers, then, must break out of enslavement to it and learn to depend on God (Mt. 6:24). From the unjust steward they must learn to use it in the service of love for others (Lk. 16:1ff.). Faithfulness with even a modest amount of mammon is the presupposition of God's entrusting the true riches to them (Lk. 16:10-11).   [F. HAUCK, IV, 388-90]

---

manthánō [to learn],   **katamanthánō** [to examine, consider],   **mathētḗs** [pupil, disciple],   **symmathētḗs** [fellow disciple],   **mathḗtria** [woman disciple],   **mathēteúō** [to become a pupil, to make disciples]

---

manthánō.

A. The Greeks.

1. Ordinary Use.

a. From the basic sense "to direct one's mind to something," *manthánō* comes to be used for (1) "to accustom oneself to something," (2) "to experience," (3) "to learn to know," (4) "to understand," (5) "to learn under instruction," and (6) "to receive direction from a deity by oracle." In the phrase *tí mathṓn* (7) it means "why?" (often with an ironical note).

b. The use consistently implies an intellectual process that always has external effects and involves a conscious or unconscious intellectual initiative. Hence other terms may elucidate it but cannot replace it.

2. Philosophical Use.

a. Beginnings. As the intellectual element in Greek life develops, *manthánō* is well adapted to serve in theories of knowledge. Already before Socrates, and to some extent in tragedy, it is part of the process by which knowledge arises. Knowledge comes by learning. *manthánein,* of course, is not the only way. Indeed, it may become purely mechanical reception. Yet this does not rule out its necessity. In tragedy *manthánein* is used for those who seek to live in harmony with the whole. The point of events is that men and even gods should learn from them to see themselves in all their limitation as part of cosmic reality.

b. The Metaphysics of Learning in Socrates/Plato.

(1) The transition to a speculative use takes place in Socrates. Learning is for him essential to moral development. Traditional forms of education do not prepare citizens to deal with the issues of the day, as the Sophists believe. Instead of gathering around him a paying group, Socrates uses dialectical conversation to kindle a moral sense. Learning has a suprapersonal accent. He himself is always learning, and in so doing

becoming, and in becoming fulfilling his divinely ordained destiny. Plato sees the value of formal education. He thus proposes compulsory education for both sexes from the years 10 to 18. This will include reading, writing, music, mathematics, and astronomy, along with physical education. But as in Socrates, this is all secondary or rudimentary.

(2) On the basis of the preexistence of the soul, Plato thinks all learning is recollection. The point of the teacher is to bring his pupils from unconscious to conscious knowledge, and in this way to kindle in them a moral sense. The Socratic dialectic serves this purpose by bringing to light what is already latent in the soul. For this reason Plato insists that we are always active in learning, that it is more demanding than gymnastics since it engages the whole being, and that we ought to learn by play so as the better to establish our aptitudes. Mathematics *(tá mathémata)* is especially important for Plato.

c. The Intellectualizing of the Learning Process. Later philosophers intellectualize and rationalize *manthánein*. Xenophon again speaks of *mathētaí* and thinks there should be restriction of some subjects. Aristotle posits the importance of the *noús* in the reception of knowledge; its receptive part is for him an empty slate. Epictetus uses *manthánein* for mastering technical skills, for learning to think, and for adopting philosophical insights. The best way for him to learn is from others, especially in ethics, in which example is important.

3. *manthánō as a Special Cultic Term in Hellenism.* A special use of *manthánō* is for reception of the "holy word" by initiates. One may see here a clear trend toward the intellectualizing of piety. The mysteries contain symbolical formulas which can hardly be understood or used without thorough instruction. Hence teaching and learning necessarily have a place when the mystery cults lead to the formation of proselytizing religious societies.

B. *manthánō* in the OT and Judaism.

1. The OT (LXX).

a. *manthánō* occurs in the LXX and other translations of the OT some 55 times, almost 30 of which are for the root *lmd*.

b. The usage, however, is by no means uniform. This is partly due to the character of *lmd* and partly due to the penetration of the ordinary use of *manthánō* into the LXX. Yet the divine revelation, as the declaration of the divine will, gives a special nuance to *manthánō*. Thus in Deuteronomy the fear of God is its object (4:10 etc.). Learning the commandments involves obeying them (Ps. 119:71, 73). What is learned is righteousness (Is. 26:9). The will as well as the intellect is engaged, and since it is God who wills what is to be learned, all learning revolves around him.

2. The Rabbis.

a. The rabbis sometimes use *lmd* in a secular sense, e.g., for learning a trade, or getting information about something, or drawing knowledge from a book.

b. Mostly, however, learning means study of the law with a view to knowing and doing God's will. The OT is the basic text, then its traditional exposition. In view of the exegetical task this poses, the word can also be used for learning hermeneutical method. Learning is a mark of the righteous. Members of the people are ordained to learn the law, and as learners are a holy people.

c. Under Greek influence a certain intellectualizing takes place in rabbinic Judaism, e.g., in the opinion that learning is of higher rank than doing. This is disputed, of course, especially with reference to moral rather than ritual observance. There is also the distinctive point that for the Greeks learning and teaching are different things, whereas the same Hebrew term covers both. Furthermore, the basic feature remains that in Judaism, as in the OT, the revealed will of God in the law is the content and goal of all learning.

3. Josephus. The formal aspect is to the fore in Josephus. *manthánō* can mean "to experience," but primarily it is "to appropriate intellectually." This applies even in relation to the law, which one learns in the same way as human laws.

4. Philo. manthánō is rare in Philo and shows no special features. Philo personalizes Plato's view that learning is *anámnēsis* and puts it in the context of a philosophy of revelation. With Scripture as its basis, *manthánein* is the perception of ultimate reality in God. Direction is given by persons, words, or objects. *máthēsis* leads to knowledge and faith, and in the process discipline and example play a part. Scripture is the normative text.

C. The NT.

1. The General Situation. In the NT *manthánō* occurs only 25 times and is far less prominent than *didáskō*. We find it only three times in Matthew, once in Mark, two times in John, and none at all in Luke (once only in Acts). *mathētḗs,* of course, is a fundamental term, but *akoloutheín* rather than *manthánein* is the true mark of the *mathētḗs.* Jesus does not seek to impart information but to awaken commitment to himself. That this involves *manthánein,* too, may be seen in Mt. 11:29, but true *manthánein* means continuing in his word (Jn. 8:31).

2. Ordinary Use.

a. In the one instance in Acts (23:27) the tribune in his letter says that he had "learned," i.e., "found out," that Paul was a Roman citizen.

b. In Rev. 14:3 it is possible that the learning of the new song is simply learning in the ordinary sense, but certain passages (cf. 2 Cor. 12:4) suggest that this is learning of a higher kind, especially since none but the 144,000 can learn the song.

3. Learning from Scripture.

a. The word occurs twice in disputations. In Mt. 9:13 Jesus tells the Pharisees to learn from Hos. 6:6 why he ranges himself with sinners. [Mt. 12:7 shows us what such *manthánein* involves.] In Jn. 6:45 hearing means learning, and learning from God necessarily means accepting Jesus. As in the OT, learning has the will of God as its object, but God's will is one great reference to Jesus as the Christ.

b. In Jn. 7:15 *manthánein* denotes the academic study of Scripture. The Jews question the right of Jesus to teach in view of his lack of formal training. He replies that the will of God is done in his person and teaching. Paul uses the term in a somewhat similar way in Gal. 3:2, where he is not seeking information but wants to learn from the Galatians the saving will of God as the law itself, to which they make appeal, proclaims it. Only through the life and death of Christ does *matheín* cease to be a purely human affair. Yet it is from Scripture, as it thus testifies to Christ, that we must learn to live (1 Cor. 4:6).

4. The New Learning.

a. In Mt. 11:29 Jesus sets his own authority over against that of the scribes. We are to learn *ap' emoú.* Jesus is no mere teacher, but a sign of the coming of God's kingdom in which God's holy will is done. From him one can learn that fulfilling this will is no burden but brings joy and rest to those who come to him.

b. Mt. 24:32 rests on the truth that for the disciples everyday things express the eternal law of God declared in the prophets. Paul in 1 Cor. 14:31 finds a similar principle in the gift of prophecy, by which the Spirit gives guidance in specific situations.

c. Eph. 4:20 uses *manthánein* in the full sense of accepting Christ and his work with all its implications for life. True *manthánein* is not just by the law but by the gospel, i.e., by Christ himself. A similar use may be seen in 2 Tim. 3:14; Rom. 16:17; Phil. 4:11 (where Paul has learned to be content because he has learned Christ; cf. vv. 10, 13).

5. *The Pastorals*. In the Pastorals *manthánō* is more common. It is used in answer to a threat that is presented to faith through false teaching of an intellectualistic and legalistic type. Thus warnings are issued to women to learn in silence (1 Tim. 2:11) and to children to learn family obligations at home (5:4). True learning means applications to good deeds, genuinely following in the spirit of Christ (Tit. 3:14).

6. *Heb. 5:8*. There is here a play on the words *émathen* and *épathen*. The suffering of Jesus is not due to outside forces but to his own acceptance of the righteous will of the Father. It is from Scripture that he learns that this suffering is grounded in God's will and cannot be divorced from his calling. The saying bears witness, then, to the conscious demonstration of total obedience which is a mark of the Son in his saving ministry. Explanations which refer to increasing capacity for obedience, or to developing maturity in it, miss the point that learning in the OT and the NT is through the study of Scripture as God's revealed will. The new thing in Hebrews is not the learning of obedience but the learning of its nature and manner as denoted by the reference to the passion. This is where the accent lies. The context of the sonship of Jesus supports this (cf. v. 7). Formally, "although he was a Son" may go with what precedes, but materially it prepares the way for what follows, and comes to completion with the perfecting of v. 9, which refers to God's validating of his filial attitude and his associated designation as a high priest. Formally, again, learning may seem to go with perfecting, but materially it is the suffering that leads to this goal (cf. 2:10). For this reason there is no need of a conjectured "not" in v. 7. The contrast is not between sonship and not being heard, but between sonship and the paradoxical course of suffering that it entails. Since Jesus suffers according to God's word, God's ear is open to him even in this suffering.

D. The Early Church. A certain intellectualizing takes place in the church. A moral attitude is the object of *manthánein* in Ignatius *Romans* 4.3. Learning through allegorical exegesis or special revelation is the point in Barn. 6.9; 9.7ff., etc. Christianity itself becomes the object in Diog. 1.1. Learning saving truths is at issue in Justin *Apology* 1.13.3. The term can then be used for the imparting of truths to catechumens (Hippolytus *Against Noetus* 1). Finally *máthēma* becomes a common term (with *pístis* and *sýmbolon*) for the baptismal confession.

katamanthánō. This intensive form means "to examine," "to learn," "to grasp," "to note." It may be used in various ways, e.g., for the probing of wounds or the watching of spies. In the LXX it is used for words of seeing or scrutinizing, often in respect of moral conduct. The only NT instance is in Mt. 6:28, where Jesus invites the anxious, not merely to contemplate, but to "consider" the lilies, because in them they will see the fullness of the Creator's resources and realize that they may have unbounded confidence in his ability to provide.

mathētēs.

A. The Greek World.

1. General Use.

a. *mathētēs* is used for those who direct their minds to something. It then denotes the "pupil," not as a tyro, but as one engaged in learning.

b. In the sense of "pupil," *mathētḗs* implies relationship to a teacher. It may thus be used in various ways, e.g., for the apprentice to a weaver, a student physician, or the disciple of a philosophical school.

c. In a broader sense *mathētḗs* denotes an intellectual link between those who are distant in time, e.g., Socrates as a true *mathētḗs* of Homer. The emphasis here is not on formal relationship but on inner fellowship.

2. Pupil or Disciple?

a. When the stress is on the more formal or technical side, *mathētḗs* carries no more than the sense of gaining knowledge or skill under expert direction. Because of this restriction, Socrates dislikes the term for his own followers. The philosophical schools, however, favor the word in view of their cultivation of *mímēsis* of the master.

b. Various words, e.g., *gnṓrimos, akólouthos, hetaíros,* are used along with *mathētḗs* to suggest the independence and dignity of the student. Of these *gnṓrimos* is the most widespread in later writers. Socrates likes *syngignómenoi,* and Xenophon *synóntes.*

c. While Xenophon avoids *mathētḗs,* his occasional use of *manthánontes* shows that he does not fully grasp the concern of Socrates to get beyond the commitment of the hearer to the teacher and to emphasize the commitment of both to the object of study.

3. Master and Disciple.

a. Socrates, Plato, and the Academy. We first meet the master/disciple relation in the philosophical sphere when Socrates fosters it to replace the teacher/pupil relation of the Sophists. Plato and the Academy develop it as an ideal fellowship between those who give and those who receive. In contrast to Protagoras, who imparts information for a fee, Socrates refuses payment and offers himself rather than his knowledge. Common meals are an expression of the resultant fellowship. This becomes a feature of Plato's Academy, in which each member is called *hetaíros,* and the director is viewed as the first among equals.

b. The Mystery Religions. The mystery religions need a master/disciple relation in order that the initiate may learn the secrets and become a member of the cultic society. In this case, however, the master is a functionary and remains anonymous. Learning is also secondary; the goal is fellowship with the deity. Thus the society is regarded as a family rather than a school, and the term *mathētḗs* is not used.

c. The Master/Disciple Relation with a Religious Aspect. The relation has a religious side in such cases as Pythagoras, Epicurus, and Apollonius. The followers of Pythagoras constitute a religious and moral community. The heart of this is the word and person of the philosopher, who thus takes on a divine aspect. Epicurus, too, binds his disciples to his own person and is honored as the founder of a religion and even as a god. Apollonius makes a strong impression by his personality. He is said to have performed many miracles, and his disciples, who regard him as more than human, proclaim his fame when he goes on his great journeys.

4. The Fellowship of Disciples and the Principle of Tradition.

a. The Fellowship of Disciples. The solid groups associated with great teachers continue when the teachers die, with the concerns of the teachers as their point of unity and the added responsibility of presenting these concerns as the impelling motive. The oldest schools are religious unions. Sometimes the original teachers appoint their own successors, but the schools, too, may appoint future leaders, since the emphasis is on the schools as such rather than their directors.

b. The Principle of Tradition. Loyalty to the teaching of the master finds expression in the principle of tradition, i.e., the desire to fulfil his intentions and preserve his sayings. This principle operates dynamically rather than statically. If the school lives by its tradition, the school itself is the soil in which the tradition is renewed. The strongest orientation to the master is among the Epicureans, who very carefully hand down the sayings supposedly formulated by Epicurus. Things are similar in Stoicism, in which Chrysippus presents his own teaching as a development of that of Zeno, so that the Stoics are often simply called the school of Zeno. The actual word *parádosis* is rarely used in connection with the philosophical schools, but the principle of tradition is generally accepted in practice.

B. The OT and Judaism.

1. mathētḗs in the OT (LXX).

a. The LXX. *mathētḗs* does not occur in the established LXX tradition.

b. The OT. The Hebrew equivalent *talmîd* occurs only in 1 Chr. 25:8 (LXX *manthánontes*).

2. The Material Problem in the OT.

a. Reason for Absence of the Terms. As seen previously, the OT relates the group *lmd* to the revealed will of God; other terms are used for human instruction (Gk. *paideía*). Again, God has chosen the whole people to learn his will and serve him. Individuals are chosen only in order that they may perform special tasks on behalf of the whole. It is thus inappropriate to use a word of the *lmd* group (or *mathētḗs*) to differentiate a special group from the whole people.

b. Absence of the Relation. (a) Individual relations in the OT, e.g., that between Moses and Joshua, differ from the relations found in the Greek and Hellenistic world. Thus Joshua is the servant of Moses, succeeds him only by divine proclamation (Num. 27:15ff.), and thus enjoys full authority in his own right (Josh. 1:2ff.). (b) The OT prophets have no disciples. The seers are organized in guilds, but charismatic endowment rather than devotion to a leader is the focus of their unity. Elisha is more an assistant of Elijah than a disciple (cf. Gehazi and Elisha). When Elijah casts his mantle over him, this is more an appropriation for service than a designation to succession. Like Joshua, Elisha receives his appointment directly from God and hence has his own authority, not that inherited from Elijah (2 Kgs. 2:9ff.; 3:11). Baruch, too, serves as an assistant of Jeremiah, especially as a scribe and interpreter (Jer. 36:4ff.). He works with him very closely (cf. 43:3), but in no sense does he succeed him. In fact, he disappears from the scene along with Jeremiah. (c) Scribes. The presence of scribes in the OT (1 Chr. 2:55) possibly gives some impulse to the formation of schools, but the most that we can say with confidence is that there are scribal guilds.

c. Absence of the Principle of Tradition. The OT gives no evidence of a principle of tradition similar to that found in the Greek world. The OT is consciously Mosaic. All who follow stand on the shoulders of Moses. The life of the people is rooted in his work. Yet Moses is never venerated as a liberator or as the founder of a religion. He is, indeed, seldom mentioned in the prophets. Tradition in the form of orientation to a person is alien to the OT. It is no surprise, then, that no religious or moral traditions are linked to individual prophets. Even Is. 8:16 seems to refer, not to a group of disciples, but to a new community gathered around the prophet.

3. The Reason for These Absences. The religion of Israel is a religion of revelation. Human speakers are the agents by which God proclaims himself and his will. They do not speak for themselves or champion their own causes. They are stewards passing on God's word to God's people. The commitment they seek is commitment to God. No place remains for the authority of a great personality or for the resultant master/disciple relation. What counts is God's continuous and dynamic speaking, whether by Moses or by those who follow him. Moses himself is presented as God's minister (Ex. 4:10ff.) whose concern is the declaration of God's will (Ex. 5) and whose legislation comes from God after God's own act of liberation (Ex. 19:20ff.). When the prophets seek to win back the people, they do not appeal to Moses himself but to the days of Moses. God, not Moses, is the Master or Teacher in whose name they speak, so that they can have no desire to pose as masters for others.

4. *The Rabbinic Use of talmîḏ.*

a. Meaning. The rabbis do not use *talmîḏ* for "apprentice" but solely for "student" of Scripture and its interpretation.

b. Different Groups. The rabbis distinguish two groups of biblical students. First come beginners who are under the tutelage of accepted rabbis. Ideally all Israelites should be qualified students of the law with God himself as the Teacher. For the moment, however, rabbis are needed to instruct the rest, and under their immediate guidance are those preparing for the office. The second group consists of those who are demonstrably successful in their initial studies. These form a kind of guild to which admission is by ordination and which can give authoritative decisions in disputed matters.

c. Men. Only males can be students at either level. Women are not allowed to do the work of teaching or learning in the law.

d. High Honor. Students of the law share the glory of the law and are thus highly regarded. Many statements and rulings bear witness to this.

e. Targumic Usage. In the Targum the Aramaic equivalent of *talmîḏ* can be used for terms which denote one who receives, or is influenced, in a personal relation.

5. *The talmîḏ as the Member of a School or Tradition.*

a. As Pupil. There is no student without a teacher; independent study is not enough. The student is under external submission to the teacher, even to the point of doing menial tasks for him, which express reverence for the law and offer practical training.

b. As Listener. Learning is by listening to what is said and appropriating it. The teacher sits and lectures, with opportunity for questions that serve to open up discussion and promote critical reflection, since the law, not the teacher, is the final authority.

c. The School. The prominence of the teacher means that groups develop under the influence of individual teachers. These may take opposing views (cf. the famous schools of Hillel and Shammai). Within the larger schools subgroups may also form around particular rabbis.

d. Tradition. The individual rabbi represents the tradition of his school and is a link in the teaching chain. Oral teaching enhances the role of tradition. Yet the great teachers earn respect in their own right and not merely as voices of the past. In particular, they teach by example, for life and not mere learning is the goal.

e. The Rabbinate as the School of Moses. The dominating element beyond every school is always the law, so that Moses is the absolute teacher. The law limits the authority of individual rabbis. Agreement with it is the decisive point.

6. *The Origin of Rabbinic Views.*

a. The OT. The main contribution of the OT is belief in the supremacy of the law (as the revelation of God's will) to those who teach it. Detailed derivation of, e.g., a school or tradition is hardly possible.

b. Hellenistic Influences. (a) The rabbinic tradition derives from the Maccabean period of conflict with Hellenism when Judaism has to insure its survival in the traditional form. (b) Hellenism influences the forms in which instruction is given (e.g., the dialectic) even in the apologetic against it. (c) The appeal to authoritative sayings is parallel to what we find in, e.g., Stoicism. (d) The new focus on Moses is in line with the treatment of the founders of the philosophical schools, although it is still recognized that Moses is a hero only as the mediator of the divine will. (e) The acceptance of fees, at least in some instances, is another possible token of Hellenistic influence.

c. The Adoption of *talmîḏ* from Hellenistic Teaching. (a) Linguistically the use of *talmîḏ* corresponds to that of *mathētēs* in the Greek world. Josephus calls Joshua the *mathētēs* of Moses and Elisha the *mathētēs* of Elijah. Elisha himself then has *mathētaí*. Furthermore Josephus describes the three trends in Judaism as philosophical schools. (b) Materially, we find that one of Hillel's teachers came from a Greek background; he might well have brought Greek elements into Jewish teaching.

7. *The Theology Implied in the Later Jewish talmîḏ.*

a. Dependence on Hellenism may be taken as certain.

b. The Greek form is integrated into the central concern for the law, so that the rabbinic *talmîḏ* always stands within the community and seeks to serve it.

c. The rabbinate makes an absolute claim over against all schools insofar as the will of God laid down in the law contains the answer to all questions.

d. This claim finds expression in the assertion of a chain of tradition going back to Moses and the inclusion in it of the great figures in the national history.

8. *Philo.* Philo uses *mathētēs* in the ordinary Greek senses. He often associates the term with *gnōrimos,* and sometimes distinguishes *mathētēs* (the ripe scholar) from *manthánōn* (the beginner). In general, however, he is in the main scholastic tradition of Judaism.

C. The NT.

1. Usage.

a. Statistical Data. In the NT *mathētēs* occurs only in the Gospels and Acts. It is attested some 250 times, almost always for those who follow Jesus. Acts has it in the absolute for a disciple of Jesus. Occasionally we read of the disciples of the Baptist and of Paul. In Mk. 2:18; 22:16 we read of *mathētaí* of the Pharisees and in Jn. 9:28 of *mathētaí* of Moses.

b. Uniformity of Usage. In each instance we find attachment to a person. Jesus as the head of the group is expected to give the ruling in Mk. 2:18ff., 23ff. It is he who, like the Baptist, teaches his disciples to pray (Lk. 11:1ff.). The destiny of the disciples is bound up with his.

c. Relation to *talmîḏ.* NT usage manifests a close linguistic relation to the rabbinic use of *talmîḏ.*

d. Peculiarities of Usage. Luke commonly has *mathētaí* for the personal disciples of Jesus but never uses the term in the Gospel after 22:45. He starts using the term again in Acts 6:1, but this time for all believers.

2. Jewish mathētaí in the NT.

a. The phrase "disciples of the Pharisees" (Mk. 2:18 and par.) causes some difficulty in view of the fact that the Pharisees are practical exponents of the law (as distinct from the scribes). The point, perhaps, is that many scribes might be Pharisaic leaders, for the boundaries between the theoretical and the practical are fluid. It may be noted, too, that the rabbis teach by example as well as word.

b. In Jn. 9:28 the opponents of Jesus, by calling themselves the disciples of Moses, argue that they belong to the chain of tradition that stretches back to Moses, whereas

Jesus is a new and unknown teacher whom they cannot accept merely on his personal authority.

3. *The Disciples of Jesus.*

a. The Call. (a) The Initiative of Jesus. A basic feature of NT discipleship is that it begins with a call in which Jesus takes the initiative (Mk. 1:17; Mt. 4:19; Lk. 9:49; Jn. 1:43). This differs sharply from rabbinic practice, in which it is the student's duty to find a teacher. A further point is that Jesus calls those who seem to lack the necessary qualifications (Mk. 2:13ff.). (b) Exceptions? Some passages suggest, of course, that the wider circle of *mathētaí* included many who simply began to follow with no specific call. A few names are given with no corresponding stories of calling, e.g., Cleopas in Lk. 24:18. Jesus also seems to be ready to accept people into fellowship without a summons if there is true readiness to follow (Lk. 9:57, 61). On the other hand, the larger group in, e.g., Jn. 6:60, 66 seems to consist of a great number who were only interested and not fully committed.

b. The Disciples in Their Relation to Jesus. (a) Commitment to His Person. A unique aspect of NT discipleship is that it is commitment to the person of Jesus. His teaching has force only when there is first this commitment to his person. Peter probably knows Jesus, and has heard him speak, prior to the incident in Lk. 5:1ff., but it is the impact of the person of Jesus that makes him a *mathētés* (cf. Nathanael in Jn. 1:45ff.). This personal commitment explains the deep depression of the disciples after the crucifixion (Lk. 24:19ff.). It is not enough that they have the legacy of his word. They have lost Jesus himself. The crucial importance of the resurrection reinforces this. Jesus himself reinstitutes the group (in spite of initial resistance, Lk. 24:36ff.; Jn. 20:24ff.), restores personal fellowship, and sends the disciples out, not to transmit his teaching, but to bear witness to his resurrection (Lk. 24:48). To mark the break in fellowship Luke ceases to use *mathētés* after Gethsemane and begins to use it again only for the wider community in Acts. John after 6:66 prefers to speak of the *dōdeka (mathētaí)* in order to show that faith in Jesus (cf. 6:64) is an essential mark of the true disciple. As distinct from the customary rabbi, or indeed the Greek teacher, Jesus offers himself rather than his outstanding gifts, and claims allegiance to himself rather than to a cause that he represents. (b) Obedience to Jesus. Many rabbis give up a great deal to study the law, but later they enjoy fame and authority in the strength of the law that they study and teach. Jesus, however, requires that his disciples leave all things for his sake alone (Mt. 10:37ff.). In so doing, they are not merely to believe in him; they are to obey him as *doúloi* obey their *kýrios* (Mt. 24:45ff.). The services they perform go beyond those that students perform for their teachers (cf. Mk. 14:12ff.). They obey him because they see in him the Messiah. Whereas rabbinic students will one day be rabbis themselves, the disciples of Jesus are simply his disciples. Their lives are permanently stamped and fashioned by him. Jesus himself follows the normal course of a teacher, but the disciples are simply listeners who ask questions only for clarification and for whom the decisive thing is not just to appropriate intellectually but to obey. The true disciple in John (8:31) is the one who abides in the words of Jesus and keeps his commands (13:34-35 etc.). This disciple is not just a *doúlos*. But he is also not a *gnōrimos* or *hetaíros,* terms which imply equality. By Jesus' own gift, he is his *phílos* (15:14ff.). (c) The Obligation to Suffer. Drawn into fellowship with Jesus, the disciples are set on the way of the cross. Suffering is unavoidable for the apostles (Mt. 10:17ff.; Jn. 15:18ff.). It also applies, more generally, to all disciples (cf. Mk. 8:34ff.; Lk. 14:26-27).

c. The Disciples, the Twelve, and the Apostles. The relation between these terms in the NT is a complicated one. If not all disciples are apostles, all apostles are disciples, and the Twelve are the inner circle as compared to wider groups.

d. The Band of (Twelve) Disciples. (a) Failure to Understand. By choosing the Twelve, Jesus manifests his claim to be divinely sent to save his people. The disciples, however, fail to understand either his mission or his message. This is shown by their fears (Mt. 8:23ff.), their quarrels (Mt. 20:20ff.), their protests against the passion (Mt. 16:22-23), their eventual flight (Mt. 26:55-56), and their doubts about the resurrection (Lk. 24:11). Only when they recognize the risen Lord do they finally achieve the understanding that sends them out as his primary witnesses. Jesus himself obviously feels this lack of understanding as a severe burden (Jn. 14:9), but he handles it with matchless patience (Lk. 22:31-32) in his concern to bring the disciples to salvation and service. (b) Composition. Jesus chooses men of all types to make up a representative inner group. We find Zealots, a publican, a Judean, Galileans, and men with Greek as well as Semitic names. The selection shows that he has a realistic understanding of the contemporary situation and seeks to serve the people as it is, with all the inherent tensions as well as the possibilities.

e. The Disciples' Share in Jesus' Work. The call to discipleship is a call to partnership in service (Lk. 5:1ff.). This comes out in sayings (Mt. 5:13ff.; Jn. 17:13ff.), parables (Mt. 25:14ff.), and specific directions (Mt. 10:5ff.). The sending out of the disciples two by two (Mk. 6:7ff.; cf. Lk. 10:1ff.) is for the purpose of doing the work of Jesus on his authority and according to the principle that, as they have freely received, so they should freely give (Mt. 10:8). In Jn. 3:22, 26; 4:1-2 this ministry includes baptizing on his behalf.

f. The Principle of Tradition in Jesus' Band of Disciples. (a) Lack of a Principle. Obviously there are similarities in Christianity to the principle of tradition that one finds in Greek and Jewish teaching. Paul refers to tradition in 1 Cor. 15:3ff., and the gospel material clearly derives from tradition. Yet it is debatable whether there is any true principle of tradition. Recollection of Jesus as a teacher is always secondary. The story of the cross and the resurrection is the heart of the message, and the sayings of Jesus are handed down with considerable freedom. For the disciples Jesus is not the head of a school but the living Lord. Again, the primary emphasis is on witness (Acts 1:21-22). To support his apostleship Paul has to argue that he has in fact seen the Lord (1 Cor. 9:1). Furthermore, Jesus plainly takes a different course from that of rabbinism, for he chooses ordinary people, and warns them that they will always be *mathētaí,* never rabbis (Mt. 23:8). Love is to be a sign of the *mathētés* to the world (Jn. 13:34-35). (b) Reasons for the Lack. The disciples are witnesses rather than bearers of a tradition because their attachment is to Jesus and because Jesus himself brings tradition to a definitive end. As the fulfilment of his people's hope, who is the truth itself (Jn. 14:6), Jesus cuts across all traditions (cf. Mk. 3:1ff.). He calls his disciples, not to the mediation of insights, but to the obedient giving of testimony (cf. Lk. 24:48; Acts 1:8; Jn. 19:35; 21:24).

g. Summary. (a) For all the formal similarities, there is no inner relation between the *talmîd* of the rabbis and the *mathētés* of Jesus. Jesus is *kýrios,* not rabbi. (b) Witness to Jesus rather than transmission of his teachings or imitation of his life is the primary task of the *mathētés.*

4. The mathētaí of John the Baptist.

a. In John's Lifetime. John, too, has a solid band of disciples who must have been fairly numerous (Jn. 4:1), who have a rule of fasting and prayer (Mt. 9:14; Lk. 11:1), who engage in discussions (Jn. 3:25), and who visit John in prison, come to Jesus with his question, and finally bury him (Mt. 11:2; 14:12). Jesus' own first disciples seem to come from this group, but it is highly doubtful whether Jesus himself does so. One might ask why all John's disciples do not become followers of Jesus. Possibly John consolidates his group more than he first intends.

b. After John's Death. The group goes on after John's execution. In Acts 18:24 and 19:7 we read of conversions from among those who know only John's baptism. The transition to faith in Jesus presents little difficulty but has not taken place en bloc. What finally happens to the remaining disciples of John is not known. There is no direct link with the Mandaeans.

5. *mathētḗs as a Term for Christians in Acts.*

a. The Linguistic Problem. The term occurs in Acts only in specific sections and according to no systematic principle. The textual tradition tends to increase the use. It is found in the "we" passages only in 21:4, 16. Normally it has no explanatory addition (*toú kyríou* in 9:1); this suggests that it derives from the term used for Christians by Palestinian believers. It applies to all believers, e.g., Timothy in 16:1, converts in 13:52; 14:20ff. This usage is peculiar to Acts but *mathētḗs* is not the only term Acts uses for Christians (cf. believers, brethren, saints, etc.).

b. The Material Problem. Materially the primary point is that Acts uses *mathētaí* for those who come to believe in Jesus (cf. Jn. 8:31). True faith means abiding in the word of Jesus and thus enjoying personal fellowship with him even across the generations. The presence and operation of the Holy Spirit makes this possible (cf. Acts 19:1ff.). The Greek communities, however, do not continue to use *mathētḗs* in this sense, probably because it tends to suggest that Christianity is simply a philosophical movement rather than personal fellowship with Christ as Lord.

6. *mathētaí of Paul in Acts 9:25?* The reference to Paul's *mathētaí* in Acts 9:25 might mean that Paul as a recognized rabbi has a group of his own disciples, but it is more likely that these *mathētaí* are either Christians whom he brought to faith in Damascus or those who were in his party on the way to Damascus and who were converted through his witness.

D. *Early Church Usage.* Hellenistic influences strengthen the use of *mathētḗs* for intellectual adherence or imitation of Christ, so that Ignatius can say that only the martyr is a true disciple (*Romans* 4.2; 5.3).

symmathētḗs. This word, rare outside the NT, occurs in Jn. 11:16 for "fellow disciple" (of Jesus). The context stresses the element of fellowship with Christ and one another.

mathḗtria. This feminine form is rare, for women are outside organized education, both in Greece and among the rabbis. The one NT instance is in Acts 9:36 (Tabitha). The meaning is either that Tabitha is one of the disciples (which is possible though not probable; cf. Mk. 15:40-41), or that she is a Christian (cf. the use of *mathētḗs* in Acts).

mathēteúō. Intransitively this word means "to be or become a pupil." One reading of Mt. 27:57 has it with reference to Joseph of Arimathea; he is said to be a disciple of Jesus. In a distinctive transitive use (Mt. 13:52; 28:19; Acts 14:21) the NT also uses the term for "to make disciples." Behind this sense possibly stands the NT belief that a call is the basis of discipleship of Jesus.   [K. H. RENGSTORF, IV, 390-461]

Mánna [manna]

1. Linguistic Data. mān is the OT term for the food by which Israel is fed in the desert (Ex. 16:31 etc.). Other terms for the food are "heavenly bread" (Ps. 105:40), "bread from heaven" (Ex. 16:4), "grain from heaven" (Ps. 78:24), and "angels' bread" (Ps. 78:25). *hē mánna* in Greek is used for "morsel," "grain," and especially "grain of incense." The LXX uses manna in Num. 11:6-7, Philo adopts the term, and the NT has *tó mánna* in Jn. 6:31, 49.

2. Manna in the OT. With water and quails, manna is part of God's provision for Israel in the desert. In Ex. 16:4 it falls like dew, is a granular deposit like frost, resembles coriander seed, tastes like honey, and must be gathered each day. It may be baked after being ground down (Ex. 16; Num. 11), and becomes uneatable if kept (Ex. 16).

3. Manna in Later Literature. The rabbis believe that God created manna just before the seventh day. As the people owes the well to Miriam and the pillar of cloud to Aaron, it owes the gift of manna to Moses. Another view sees manna as a reward for keeping the law. With water, it accompanies Israel on her wanderings. The ark contains a little basket with manna which disappears when the ark is hidden and which Elijah will restore. Manna is now the heavenly food of the righteous. Although not needed, it will again fall from heaven in the age of messianic salvation. The messianic generation will enjoy the same food and drink as the wilderness generation.

4. NT Views of Manna.

a. The manna motif occurs in Jn. 6:31, 49. The term alternates with "bread from heaven." After the feeding of the 5,000, the Jews want Jesus to give a sign which will accredit him as the Messiah as manna accredited Moses. Jesus, in his reply, points out that the messianic age transcends the wilderness age. Moses could not give true bread from heaven, for the people who ate manna still died. In contrast, the bread that Jesus gives confers eternal life. Jesus himself is this living bread (6:35, 48).

b. Heb. 9:4 refers to the manna which is contained in a golden urn in the ark along with Aaron's rod and the tables of the law. This agrees with rabbinic tradition, but cf. 1 Kgs. 8:9.

c. Rev. 2:17 also reflects rabbinic tradition with its promise of hidden manna to those who triumph (cf. also the living water of Rev. 7:17).

[R. MEYER, IV, 462-66]

maranathá [Lord, come; Our Lord is (has) come]

1. maranathá occurs in the NT only in 1 Cor. 16:22 in Paul's greeting. It also appears at the end of the eucharistic prayers in Did. 10.6. It is more common in later ecclesiastical use, often to give added weight to *anáthema.*

2. The term is undoubtedly Aramaic but the exact meaning is debatable. Linguistic research suggests three equally possible meanings: a. "Lord, come," as a prayer for Christ's return; b. "Our Lord has come," as a confession of his coming in humility, and c. "Our Lord is come," i.e., is present in worship. (For linguistic details see *TDNT,* IV, 467-68.)

3. Paul uses the Aramaic term most probably because it has already become a recognized formula in the first Palestinian community. As such it shows that Jesus is

confessed as Lord and that petition is made to him as such. The idea that *maranathá* comes from bilingual Antioch rather than Jerusalem hardly explains why it spreads into Greek-speaking churches.

4. In Did. 10.6, where *maranathá* does not come directly in the eucharistic prayer, it seems to carry the sense "Our Lord is present" as a warning against participation by the unholy. The context of 1 Cor. 16:22 supports this understanding. Yet Rev. 22:20 strongly suggests that "Lord, come" is the real point, for *érchou kýrie 'Iēsoú* seems to be a translation of *maranathá*. If this is Paul's meaning in 1 Cor. 16:22, he is impressing on the church the urgency of its hope. Either way, there is a link to the eucharist, which carries the certainty of the Lord's presence but also the expectation of his return (1 Cor. 11:26). Confession of Christ's coming in the incarnation is less likely in context. We may thus conclude that *maranathá* is either a confession of the presence of the exalted Christ or a fervent and expectant cry for his coming again in glory.   [K. G. KUHN, IV, 466-72]

> *margarítēs* [pearl]

Pearls are usually regarded as precious stones in antiquity. They come from the Red Sea, the Persian Gulf, and the Indian Ocean. They are brought into the west through Alexander's conquests, and are used for necklaces and other ornaments. The word for pearl becomes a figure of speech for what is of supreme worth. The word *margarítēs* does not occur in the LXX, but Judaism uses "pearl" figuratively for a valuable saying. Thus a series of biblical verses is compared to a string of pearls. Eschatology refers to great pearls that serve as gates for the celestial city. The NT has the term a. for the incomparable saving benefits of the kingdom (Mt. 7:6; 13:45-46), b. for costly ornaments (1 Tim. 2:9; Rev. 17:4; 18:16), and c. for the twelve gates of the new Jerusalem (Rev. 21:21). Gnosticism calls Christ himself the pearl, and Mandaean writings use the pearl as a figure for the soul that comes down into the vile body from the divine world.   [F. HAUCK, IV, 472-73]

> *mártys* [witness], *martyréō* [to bear witness], *martyría* [witness, testimony], *martýrion* [testimony, proof], *epimartyréō* [to attest], *symmartyréō* [to bear witness with], *synepimartyréō* [to confirm], *katamartyréō* [to bear witness against], *martýromai* [to affirm], *diamartýromai* [to charge], *promartýromai* [to bear witness beforehand], *pseudómartys* [false witness], *pseudomartyréō* [to bear false witness], *pseudomartyría* [false testimony]

mártys, martyréō, martyría, martýrion.

A. Form and Etymology.

1. Form. The ancient epic form is *mártyros,* and we also find *mártyr. ho* or *hē mártys* takes the genitive *mártyros,* the accusative *mártyra* (or *mártyn*), and the dative plural *mártysi.*

2. Etymology. The root would seem to be *smer,* "to bear in mind," "to be concerned." The *mártys* would thus be one who remembers and can tell about something, i.e., a witness. The verb *martyreín* means "to be a witness," *martyría* means "bearing witness" or "the witness borne," and *martýrion* means "witness" as proof.

B. Use in Nonbiblical Greek.

1. Legal Witness to Facts. The proper sphere of the terms is the legal one, e.g., in trials or legal transactions. What is signified is personal testimony to events, relations, persons, etc. The verb may mean "to come forward as a witness," but with the dative it can mean testifying for somebody, and with the accusative, *perí* and genitive, or a *hóti* clause, it may denote giving witness to something specific. *martyría* signifies both the act and the actual witness. The more objective *martýrion* comes into more general use for anything that may be adduced to confirm a fact or statement.

2. Witness to Facts, Truths, and Views. The whole group finds a more general use. In so doing, it may still refer to facts of which there is direct personal knowledge. But it may also refer to truths or views which are proclaimed with conviction but cannot be verified empirically. Aristotle makes this distinction between witness as objective statement and witness as personal conviction. He also refers to witness to future events, which by its very nature is based on faith rather than fact.

3. Application of the General Use in the Sense of Witness to Facts. Along these lines appeal is made to the gods as witnesses to oaths, treaties, etc. Another common use is for the witness of the senses. We also find instances of the citing of impersonal witnesses. The poverty of Socrates is a witness that he is not a philosopher for gain.

4. Application of the General Use in the Sense of Witness to Truths or Views. Plato offer many instances of this kind of witness in respect of such matters as happiness, homosexuality, etc. The life of Socrates in particular is a witness to the truth of his teaching. In Epictetus the philosopher is the divinely called witness to practical wisdom not only by his teaching but above all by his equanimity in misfortune and affliction. The use is not technical, however, for health bears witness to the truth of the Stoic lifestyle, and while death may be a witness to truth, it does not have to be, for Epictetus does not call Socrates a *mártys*.

C. The LXX.

1. Hebrew Terms.

a. *mártys* occurs some 60 times, almost always for Heb. *'ēḏ*.

b. *martýrion* is more common (some 250 times) and more complex, since it stands for various Hebrew terms, and is at times a very mechanical rendering.

2. The Use.

a. Legal. The first use in the LXX is legal. The *mártys* is the witness (for the prosecution) (Num. 5:13 etc.). False witness is severely punished (Dt. 19:16ff.). *martyreín* means judicial witness in Num. 35:30 and witness to an agreement in Ruth 4:9-10. God himself is a witness in the pact between David and Jonathan (1 Sam. 20:23, 42). He is also a witness to the integrity of Samuel in 1 Sam. 12:5-6 and to the innocence of Job in Job 16:19. The people are witnesses against themselves in Josh. 24:22, and the song of Moses bears witness against Israel in Dt. 31:19, 21.

b. Religious. Of particular significance are the passages in Is. 43:9ff. and 44:7ff. Here God arranges a trial which will show who is truly God. The nations are spectators but they are also witnesses on behalf of their various candidates. Idols, however, are impotent and will thus be put to shame. In contrast, the people of Israel are God's witnesses (43:10, 12; 44:8). On the basis of God's acts of calling and redemption Israel will declare the reality and uniqueness of her God. The content of this witness is God's saving work; this may not be demonstrable to unbelief (Is. 43:8) but it is an incontestable certainty to faith. If there is some similarity here to the concept of Epictetus, there are also decisive differences. The witness is primarily given by word, and it is witness to the self-manifestation of the living God, not to a philosophical code. At the same time, there is no developed witness theology in Isaiah. The goal of evangelizing the nations shines before the prophet (42:4; 49:6), but the idea of witness is here a figurative rather than a technical one. In particular, one cannot connect it too closely with the picture of the Suffering Servant in Is. 53.

3. *martýrion.* As objective witness, the act in Ruth 4:7 confirms the transaction. The seven lambs in Gen. 21:30 serve a similar purpose of *martýrion,* as does the cairn of 31:44 (Jacob and Laban). The altar of Josh. 22 is a *martýrion* to the agreement between the tribes (vv. 26-27), and David is a *martýrion* to God's grace and power in Is. 55:4. God himself may be a *martýrion* against the people in Mic. 1:2; the meaning here is that his judgment will irrefutably establish the people's guilt. The tent of meeting is a tent of witness inasmuch as the law is kept in it (cf. Ex. 25:15-16, 22). The plural *tá martyría* occurs in Ex. 30:6, 36 etc.; it refers to the concrete statutes of the divine attestation which are the basis of the law. God himself is here the subject of the *martyreín* contained in *martýrion.* This *martyreín* consists of God's self-revelation to Moses, of which the commandments are the content.

D. The Martyr in Later Judaism; Josephus and Philo. Judaism is a religion of martyrdom, born out of the sufferings of the Maccabean age. Indeed, even prior to this time, the figure of the prophet or righteous person who suffers calumny and even death is familiar in Israel (cf. Elijah [1 Kgs. 19:10] or Uriah [Jer. 26:20ff.]). The prophets have to preach whether they are heard or not, and the righteous maintain their integrity even in persecution (Ps. 44:22). This experience comes to a climax in the Maccabean period. 4 Maccabees reads the whole of the OT as a series of examples of the martyr spirit. Later, Josephus extols the Essenes for their patient acceptance of suffering, and various rabbis display the same loyalty to the faith in persecution or death. Yet the group *mártys* is nowhere used in this connection, for the suffering of persecution is a work of piety rather than a work of witness, except, of course, in the most general sense. In this regard it may be noted that both Josephus and Philo use the *mártys* group in the normal way for legal witness or for the attestation or proof of facts, events, or ideas. There is in them not the slightest impulse toward the specific Christian use.

E. The NT.

1. *Occurrence. mártys* occurs 34 times in the NT, 13 of which are in Acts and nine in Paul (none in John). There are 76 instances of *martyreín,* 33 of which are in John, eleven in Acts, eight each in Paul and Hebrews, and ten in 1 and 3 John. *martyría* is found 37 times, 14 of which are in John, seven in 1 and 3 John, and nine in Revelation. *martýrion* occurs 20 times, nine of which are in the Synoptics and six in Paul. A noteworthy fact is that *martyreín* occurs 47 times in the Johannine writings, and *martyría* 30 times, but *mártys* and *martýrion* not at all in the Gospel.

2. *mártys.*

a. General Use: Witness to Facts. This use occurs in Mk. 14:63 when the high priest finds no need of any other witnesses after Jesus' confession. The sense is the same in Acts 6:13; 7:58, and cf. Heb. 10:28 and Mt. 18:16, where the demand of Dt. 17:6 and 19:15 for more than one witness is cited or adopted. The accusation of an elder must be in accordance with the same principle in 1 Tim. 5:19, and Paul appeals to it also in 2 Cor. 13:1, in which he compares his two visits to two witnesses that have plainly established the facts. A slightly different use is when Paul calls on God as a witness to his unceasing prayers etc. (Rom. 1:9), or when he calls upon the Thessalonians (and God) as witnesses to his blameless conduct (1 Th. 2:10). In 2 Cor. 1:23 he makes this appeal a call on God to witness against him if he is not telling the truth. Human witness to facts is the point in Lk. 11:48, where the cult of the graves of the prophets bears witness to their persecution. *mártys* bears a similar sense in 1 Tim. 6:12: Timothy's confession is made before many witnesses (cf. 2 Tim. 2:2). In Heb. 12:1 the witnesses watching the race seem to be confessing witnesses (cf. 11:2), but this does not exclude the element of factual witness.

b. Special Lukan Use. Luke's usage in Lk. 24:48 and Acts embraces witness to facts concerning Jesus that are directly known. But this witness can be given only if the meaning of the facts is appreciated, so that the witness takes the form of believing, evangelistic confession. Since the gospel is a historical revelation, the witness to facts and the witness to truth are the same. Facts, not ideas or myths, are at issue. Those who bear witness to these facts have lived through them (Lk. 24:47; Acts 1:8). They have also understood them. When endowed with the Spirit, they are thus equipped to go out as witnesses to the world. Those who have seen the risen Lord are in a special sense his witnesses (Acts 13:31) as compared to the evangelists Paul and Barnabas (v. 32).

c. Incipient Separation of Factual and Confessional Witness in Luke. Luke, however, can still call Paul (Acts 22:15) and Stephen (22:20) witnesses. Paul in his missionary work is a witness to facts, even if not in the precise sense of Acts 1:8 (except insofar as he meets the risen Lord in 9:3ff.). Above all, he is a witness to the meaning of the facts, namely, as a witness *for* Jesus rather than *to* him (22:15). The confessional element is now stronger than the factual element, although naturally the confession itself embraces the historical facts of Christ's life, death, and resurrection. Stephen, too, is predominantly a confessional witness, and he is so in a distinctive way because he proves the seriousness of his confession by his death. Thus the usage in 22:20 prepares the ground for the later use of *mártys* for the one who is a witness by blood, i.e., the martyr.

d. 1 Pet. 5:1. There is a distinctive and ambivalent use in 1 Pet. 5:1. The first and obvious sense is eyewitness, but the continuation suggests participation as well. The author knows from his own experience what the sufferings of Christ entail (cf. 4:13).

e. *mártys* in the Johannine Writings. Of the Johannine writings, only Revelation uses *mártys*. Jesus himself is the *mártys* in 1:5 and 3:14, the two prophets are witnesses in 11:3, Antipas is a witness in 2:13, and there is reference to the blood of "martyrs" in 17:6. In all these instances death is involved, but "martyrdom" here clearly involves bearing witness to the truth as well as dying (cf. Acts 22:20). Jesus is the faithful and true witness not simply as the one who is crucified but as the one who passes on his *martyría* or testimony (Rev. 1:2) and who has borne witness to the truth (Jn. 18:37).

3. *martyréō*.

a. The Human Declaration of Facts. *martyreín* is not used in the NT for legal witness, but it often connotes the declaration or confirmation of facts or events (cf. Mt. 23:31; Rom. 10:2; Gal. 4:15; 1 Cor. 15:15; Acts 22:5; Jn. 2:25; 2 Cor. 8:3, etc.). The event is a future one in Jn. 13:21, and the fact is a general fact of experience in Jn. 4:44.

b. The Good Report. In the absolute, *martyreín* means "to give (or receive) a good report" (Lk. 4:22; Acts 6:3; 1 Tim. 5:10). The thought is always that the person(s) can be vouched for on the basis of direct observation.

c. The Witness of God, the Spirit, or Scripture. In a special group, God, the Spirit, or Scripture guarantees judgments or statements (Acts 13:22; Heb. 11:2; 7:8, 17). In Acts 14:3 the confirmatory witness of miracles supports apostolic proclamation.

d. Religious Witness. A special use develops when the facts to which witness is given are divinely established facts, and the witness is thus also witness to revealed truth. Acts 23:11 is a good example.

e. Special Johannine Use. In John witness is especially the witness that is given, not specifically to the facts of Jesus' history, but to the person of Jesus (Jn. 1:15; 5:31ff.; 8:13ff.) as the eternal Son of God (1:15, 34). Thus the Baptist has come to bear witness to the incarnate Logos as the light (1:8; cf. 8:12). As the Son, Jesus is the truth, so that to witness to the truth is to witness to him (3:26; 5:32-33). Witness is given to him by the Baptist (1:7-8), by Scripture (5:39), by God (5:32), by his works (5:36), by himself (8:13-14), and later by the Spirit (15:26) and by his disciples (15:27). The three that bear witness in 1 Jn. 5:7 seem to be baptism, the Lord's Supper, and the Spirit, though possibly with an allusion to Jn. 19:34-35. Witness in John is confession. To be sure, the author of John and 1 John stresses eyewitness (1 Jn. 1:1-2). But the witness is also a witness of Christ's glory (Jn. 1:14; 1 Jn. 5:9-10). Hence witness can still be given even by those who are not eyewitnesses, i.e., by those who confess who Jesus was and what he signified. The term is in no way reserved for those who are put to death for their witness. Nor is this true of *martyreín* in the four instances in Revelation, in which *martyreín* means bearing witness to the prophetic word (1:2; 22:20) or bearing witness to the threat which protects the prophecy (22:18).

f. 1 Tim. 6:13. In 1 Tim. 6:13 Timothy is admonished in the presence of Christ, who himself made a good confession in his witness to Pilate. At issue is Jesus' acknowledgment of his messianic mission by his declaration, or his death, or both.

4. martyría.

a. Outside the Johannine Writings. Of the seven instances outside the Johannine writings, six are religiously neutral, e.g., for court witness in Mk. 14:55, a good report in 1 Tim. 3:7, and the witness of the pagan poet in Tit. 1:13. The exception is Acts 22:18, where Paul's *martyría* is evangelistic witness.

b. In the Johannine Writings. In contrast, a Christian use dominates the 30 instances in the Johannine material. Human witness is at issue in Jn. 8:17, a good report in 3 Jn. 12, and the testimony of men in 1 Jn. 5:9, but elsewhere the reference is to evangelistic witness to the nature and significance of Christ. This is the active bearing of witness in Jn. 1:7 and Rev. 11:7, but in all the other instances it is the witness that is given, e.g., by the Baptist (Jn. 1:19), by Jesus (3:11 etc.), by God (5:32), or by the author (19:35). God's witness is also the point in 1 Jn. 5:9ff. "Having the witness" is a distinctive phrase in 1 Jn. 5:10 and Rev. 6:9; 12:17; 19:10. Revelation also speaks about the witness of Jesus (1:2, 9; 12:17; 19:10; 20:4), which is identical to the word of God. In 1:2 the testimony of Jesus refers to the book, and this is perhaps the point in 19:10 as well: the testimony of Jesus is their witness as Christian prophets. Elsewhere this testimony is revelation in general. Because of this witness the author is exiled (1:9), the martyrs are slain (6:9), and the dragon fights against them (12:17). The special use of *martyría 'Iēsoú* as a formula for the gospel is perhaps linked with the fact that Jesus is the faithful witness even to the point of death (cf. 1 Tim. 6:13). The term "witness" is thus beginning to take on a martyrological nuance. "Having the witness" in Revelation supports this, for it always applies to those who suffer for their testimony. Similarly, the witness of the two prophets is oral testimony sealed by death (and cf. 12:11). *martyría* undoubtedly means evangelistic confession and not just the testimony of blood. But it is the specific evangelistic confession that culminates in death.

5. *martýrion.*

a. Occurrence. This word, which is less common than the other three (20 times), occurs in the Johannine material only in Rev. 15:5 ("the tent of witness"), and is found most often in parallel passages in the Synoptics.

b. Witness for the Prosecution. In the NT, as in common Greek usage, *martýrion* means objective proof. This may be seen in the phrase "for a testimony (or evidence) against" in Jms. 5:3; Mk. 6:11, and cf. Mk. 1:44-45. In Mk. 13:9 the disciples will bear testimony as they are whipped in the synagogues and arraigned before rulers, and in Mt. 24:14 the gospel will be preached as a testimony to all nations. In these instances a chance to believe may be offered, but the preaching will also be evidence in case of unbelief.

c. Witness to Something. *martýrion* may also denote witness to something with a genitive of subject (2 Cor. 1:12) or object (Acts 4:33). In such instances *martýrion* is equivalent to gospel, message, or teaching (cf. 1 Tim. 2:6).

d. Active Witness. *martýrion* has the active sense of attestation in Heb. 3:5, in which Moses is said to be a faithful servant in the attesting of what he receives from God and has then to speak to the people. Neither here nor elsewhere does *martýrion* move in a martyrological direction.

F. Specific Martyrological Use in the Early Church.

1. *Survey.* The second century, under persecution, develops certain impulses in NT usage. The ordinary use lives on, as does the NT use for evangelistic witness. But full witness is now witness under threat. Witness, then, becomes a special term that is reserved for the one who seals the seriousness of witness by death.

2. *Usage.* The usage is still fluid in 1 Clem. 5.4, 7, and neither Hermas nor Ignatius uses the *mártys* group technically for martyrdom. It is in the Martyrdom of Polycarp that we first find all four words used in this special sense. Interestingly, this work comes from the area that is the home of Revelation. Other writers also use the terms for those who risk their lives without actually suffering death (cf. Hippolytus). Hegesippus uses the term *martyreín* for the death of James, the Lord's brother, but he also has *martyría* for oral witness to the faith. In South Gaul the victims clearly reserve *mártyres* for those who suffer death; the rest, even though they suffer terrible tortures, are confessors. The account itself is not so precise in its usage, for *martyreín* refers to all who suffer, whether killed or not. Gradually, however, the distinction gains ground. Thus Clement of Alexandria says that *mártyres* are perfect in confession (*Stromateis* 4.21.133.1), and Tertullian calls those who are not yet condemned *mártyres designati* (*To the Martyrs* 1). It is in this specialized sense that Latin adopts the Greek term instead of using its own word for the witness (*testis*).

3. *Understanding.* Into the idea of martyrdom comes the concept of a struggle with the devil in an imitation and continuation of Christ's sufferings in which Christ himself grants support and in which some may even have a vision of his glory. Such thoughts go back to the NT (cf. Mt. 5:11-12; 10:17ff.; Acts 5:41; Col. 1:24; Rom. 5:3; 8:17; 1 Pet. 2:21ff.; 4:13). The difference is that the NT does not associate these factors with the concept of the *mártys*. The martyrological sense is in fact a consequence of the suffering which the church actually experiences in bearing its witness.

epi-, sym-, synepi-, katamartyréō. All these compounds stand in close relation to the popular sense of *martyréō. epimartyreín* occurs in the NT only in 1 Pet. 5:12, where it means "to attest (a preceding assertion)." Witness or proof in the strict sense is not at issue. *symmartyreín* is a common term for "to bear witness with" others, and then, more generally, "to confirm," or, with the dative, "to agree." Paul has the term in Rom. 2:15 for the confirmatory witness of conscience. The same usage occurs in Rom. 9:1: Paul's conscience, in the Spirit, confirms his concern for Israel. In Rom. 8:16 it is the Holy Spirit who adds his confirmatory witness to our spirit that we are children of God. In this last verse "our spirit" is probably not just the soul but the ego as it is shaped already by God's Spirit, so that the statement of faith that this ego makes is confirmed by God's Spirit. *synepimartyreín* occurs in the NT only in Heb. 2:4, which says that the salvation declared by the Lord and attested by his hearers is confirmed by God through signs etc. *katamartyreín* carries the sense of bearing hostile witness. It occurs in the NT in Mk. 14:60 and Mt. 27:13, where first the high priest, then Pilate, asks Jesus about the things that are testified against him.

martýromai, dia-, promartýromai. *martýresthai* first means "to invoke as a witness," then "to affirm," "to attest." In the NT it occurs twice in Acts and three times in Paul. In 1 Th. 2:11-12 and Eph. 4:17 it is used to suggest an emphatic demand. In Gal. 5:3; Acts 20:26; Acts 26:22 the sense is that of emphatic affirmation, whether in relation to a truth, a fact, or the gospel. *diamartýresthai* has much the same meaning. Ten of the 15 NT instances are in Luke's works (nine in Luke). "To declare emphatically" (in admonition) is the point in Lk. 16:28; 1 Tim. 5:21; 2 Tim. 4:1; "to charge" brings out the sense. Elsewhere what is meant is "affirmation" (cf. Acts 20:23; Heb. 2:6; 1 Th. 4:6). In Acts 2:40 the context supplies the content, while in 10:42 we have a *hóti* clause, and in 18:5 the phrase "that the Christ was Jesus." *promartýresthai* occurs in the NT only in 1 Pet. 1:11 in the sense "to attest something in advance as a fact." The Spirit of Christ in the prophets predicts the sufferings and the subsequent glory of Christ.

pseudómartys, pseudomartyréō, pseudomartyría. The *pseudómartys* is a "false witness," i.e., a witness who declares something that is untrue. Mt. 26:60 employs the term for those who give false evidence against Jesus at his trial. Paul has it in 1 Cor. 15:15 in his argument that if Christ is not risen the apostles are false witnesses. The "of God" which he then adds is not a subjective genitive (witnesses whom God has appointed), but an objective genitive (witnesses who misrepresent God, claiming that he has done something which he has not, i.e., raised Jesus from the dead). *pseudomartyreín* occurs in Mt. 19:18 and parallels (quoting the ninth commandment from Ex. 20:16 and Dt. 5:20 LXX). Some MSS include the commandment in Rom. 13:9 as well. The only other NT instance is in connection with the trial of Jesus in Mk. 14:56-57. *pseudomartyría,* which is not found in the LXX, occurs in the list of vices in Mt. 15:19 and then again in the trial of Jesus in Mt. 26:59. The meaning is "false witness" (which is usually *pseudomartýrion* in a legal context).

[H. Strathmann, IV, 474-514]

---

masáomai [to bite]

---

masáomai means "to bite," "to chew," "to eat." The one LXX instance is in a free rendering of Job 30:4. In the NT we find it only in Rev. 16:10. Men "gnaw" their tongues for pain when the angel pours out the fifth vial and the kingdom of the beast is in darkness. The mixed imagery reflects the confusion and anguish.

[C. Schneider, IV, 514-15]

---

mastigóō [to whip, lash, torment], *mastízō* [to scourge], *mástix* [whip, lash, torment]

---

mastigóō, mastízō. mastigóō means "to whip," "to beat with a lash," then figuratively a. "to lash with words," and b. "to torment." In the LXX it occurs literally in Ex. 5:14; Dt. 25:2-3; Prov. 27:22, and figuratively in, e.g., Job 15:11; Prov. 3:12.

1. Mt. 10:17 and 23:34 say that the disciples will face whippings in the synagogues. This punishment is prescribed for various offenses and follows an established procedure. The number of strokes is not to exceed thirty-nine and may be reduced in case of physical weakness. The instrument is the *mástix*, "the lash." Women may be whipped as well as men. The synagogue servant does the whipping.

2. The scourging of Jesus in Jn. 19:1 is the Roman punishment which precedes execution and which is of far greater severity. In the prediction in Mt. 27:26 and Mk. 15:15 the loanword *phragellóō* is used instead of *mastigóō*. Lk. 23:16 has the milder *paideúsas*.

3. The whipping of Paul in Acts 16:22ff. is perhaps a primary punishment, but that with which he is threatened in Acts 22:24-25 is for the purpose of examination, i.e., in order to wrest a confession. Roman law protects citizens from beating, but exceptions are found.

4. We find a figurative use in Heb. 12:6 (quoting Prov. 3:12): "to impart corrective punishment." As parents may correct children whom they love, so God corrects by means of sufferings.

mástix. This word first means "horsewhip," then any "whip" or "lash," and figuratively "trouble" or "suffering." It is used especially in the LXX for God's scourge (Job 21:8) or punishment (Ps. 89:32), and cf. afflictions in Ps. 32:10.

1. In the NT it occurs literally in Acts 22:24 (the Roman scourge) and Heb. 11:36 (the synagogue strap of four thongs).

2. A figurative use may be found in Mk. 3:10 for the diseases that Jesus cures (cf. Lk. 7:21) and in Mk. 5:29, 34 for the specific ailment of the woman with a hemorrhage.

→ *mólōps, plēgḗ, rhabdízō*   [C. SCHNEIDER, IV, 515-19]

---

mátaios [vain, deceptive], *mataiótēs* [vanity, deception], *mataióō* [to deceive, be delivered to vanity], *mátēn* [in vain], *mataiología* [empty prattle], *mataiológos* [empty prattler]

---

mátaios.

A. Outside the NT.

1. The word *mátaios* carries the senses of "vain," "deceptive," "pointless," "futile." While *kenós* means "worthless," *mátaios* means "worthless because deceptive or ineffectual." *mátaios* implies antithesis to the norm, which may at times be liberating but is more often harmful. Tragedy raises the ultimate question whether everything is not *mátaios*. Religion offers a partial answer by pointing to the divine world, but the plurality and mutability of the gods undermine this answer. Later Greek thought makes little use of the group, perhaps because it raises so unsettling a question, and involves such practical self-contradiction.

2. The OT, however, does not evade the question. Many Hebrew words pour their

negative content into Gk. *mátaios*. Ps. 60:11 states baldly that human help is vain (*mátaios*), Ps. 62:9 describes the children of men as vain, and Prov. 31:30 characterizes beauty as vain. Above all, the OT points out that the gods of the nations are vain. Only the one true and living God, who is known as he makes himself known, can save us from futility. It is faith in God, however, which enables the OT bluntly to extend the sphere of the *mátaios* to all values, not in a spirit of negativism, but with positive confidence. It may be pointed out that the sayings of false prophets are also called *mátaia* in Ezek. 13:6ff., and that "taking in vain" is a phrase for misuse of the name of God in Ex. 20:7.

B. The NT. The NT accepts the ruthless judgment of the OT on the human sphere. The thoughts of the wise are empty (1 Cor. 3:20), and so are controversies and dissensions (Tit. 3:9). Indeed, even Christian faith itself is futile if it does not rest on the historical fact of the resurrection. Idols and idolatry are vain things (Acts 14:15), and pagan ways as a whole are described as futile (1 Pet. 1:18) even though they may be valued because they are inherited from the fathers. As Christian faith is vain if it does not accept the reality of the resurrection, so Christian religion is vain if it ignores the divine command in arrogant self-deception (Jms. 1:26).

mataiótēs. This rare word is used in Greek for human nothingness. The LXX has it more often, e.g., in Pss. 39:6; 144:4. Eccl. 1:2 calls everything vanity; for this reason we must look to God, with whom alone is no *mataiótēs*. Rom. 8:20 takes up the thought of Eccl. 1:2. Creation is subject to futility, but God lies before and after it, so that the subjection is in hope of final glory. Eph. 4:17 describes the effect of vanity in human society (cf. 2 Pet. 2:18).

mataióō. This biblical word is used once in the active in the LXX ("to deceive") but mostly in the passive ("to be delivered up to vanity"). The meaning in Rom. 1:26 is that those who do not honor and thank God are betrayed into futile thinking (cf. 1 Cor. 3:20).

mátēn. This adverb means a. "in vain," b. "pointlessly," and c. "deceitfully." It has sense a. in Mt. 15:9 and Mk. 7:7, which quote Is. 29:13.

mataiología. This word, meaning "empty prattle," is used in 1 Tim. 1:6 for those who forsake sincere faith.

mataiológos. This word occurs in the plural in Tit. 1:10 for "empty prattlers."

[O. Bauernfeind, IV, 519-24]

---

máchaira [sword]

máchaira means the "knife" used in sacrifice, cooking, gardening, etc., then the "small sword," e.g., the saber or dagger. In the LXX it is the knife in Gen. 22:6; Josh. 5:2-3, but mostly the dagger or small sword.

In the NT the word is used 1. for the swords at the arrest of Jesus (Mt. 26:47, 55). When one of the disciples draws his *máchaira*, Jesus tells him to put it back, for those who take the *máchaira* will perish by it (Mt. 26:51-52). In Heb. 11:34, 37 some of the heroes of faith escape the sword but others are killed with it (cf. 1 Kgs. 19:10), while in Lk. 21:24 the people of Judea will fall by the edge of the sword, and in Acts

12:2 James is killed with the sword. A great *máchaira* is given to the rider on the red horse in Rev. 6:4.

2. In Mt. 10:34 the use is obviously figurative. Those who follow Jesus must be prepared for hostility even in their own families. Figurative, too, is the use in Lk. 22:35ff., where Jesus is not asking for armed defense but warning his disciples to be ready for final sacrifice.

3. In Eph. 6:17 the *máchaira* is part of the spiritual armor of Christians. The sword is God's word.

4. A similar thought occurs in Heb. 4:12, except that here the *máchaira* is more likely the knife of the priest, butcher, or surgeon, since the function is not that of destroying or punishing but of piercing and disclosing.

[W. MICHAELIS, IV, 524-27]

---

máchomai [to fight, quarrel], *máchē* [fighting, quarreling], *ámachos* [not quarrelsome], *theomáchos* [fighting against God], *theomachéō* [to fight against God]

---

máchomai, máchē, ámachos. This group is used for physical combat, especially of a military kind. The military use predominates in the LXX. In the NT, however, only Acts 7:26 relates for certain to physical conflict. Strife of words is the point in Jn. 6:52. Physical threats are perhaps involved in 2 Cor. 7:5, and Jms. 4:1-2 is debatable. Strife is wrong for Christians (2 Tim. 2:23; Tit. 3:9: legal disputes). Bishops (1 Tim. 3:3), and indeed all Christians (Tit. 3:2), are not to be quarrelsome (*ámachos*). Where there is strife, it is due to passions. Hence other words are used for the necessary spiritual warfare of believers, e.g., *agōnízesthai.*

theomáchos, theomachéō. These rare words denote striving against God. In Acts 5:39 Gamaliel warns the council to proceed cautiously lest they be found opposing God. Luke follows Euripides in this usage, although without suggesting that the march of the gospel is in any way similar to that of Dionysus (whom it is fatal to oppose).

[O. BAUERNFEIND, IV, 527-28]

---

mégas [great], *megaleíon* [greatness], *megaleiótēs* [greatness], *megaloprepḗs* [greatness], *megalýnō* [to magnify], *megalōsýnē* [majesty], *mégethos* [greatness]

---

mégas.

A. Outside the NT.

1. The basic sense of *mégas* is "great" or "big" (either people or inanimate objects). We then find such nuances as "high," "wide," or, figuratively, "powerful" (gods, rulers, natural forces, dangers, emotional states, impressions, etc.). The word is used in epiphanies and also in courtly style. It may at times have a censorious ring, i.e., "arrogant."

2. In the LXX *mégas* is mostly used for the root *gdl*, which covers much the same range as the Greek term. Other Hebrew terms for which *mégas* is used express par-

ticular aspects of greatness. In Isaiah *mégas* is used for *gdl* only 13 out of 32 times. In the other passages we have free renderings or interpretations.

B. The NT.

1. General Use. In the NT *mégas* conforms to the usual Greek and Hellenistic usage. Worth noting is its use for the great supper of Rev. 19:17 and the great faith of the Canaanite woman in Mt. 15:28. God is the great king in Mt. 5:35. Greater judgment awaits the teacher in Jms. 3:1. The Baptist is to be great before God in Lk. 1:15 (cf. Jesus in 1:32). The mighty God (*dynatós*) has done great things (*megála*) for Mary in 1:49. Love is for Paul the greatest of the triad in 1 Cor. 13:13. Prophecy is a greater gift than tongues because it does more to edify the church (1 Cor. 14:4-5). The relation between Christ and the church is a great mystery in Eph. 5:32. In 1 Timothy the mystery of our religion is great (3:16), and godliness is great gain (6:6). Cf. the great reward of confidence in Heb. 10:35. The day of eschatological judgment is the great day in Jude 6 and Rev. 6:17 (cf. Zeph. 1:14).

2. Great and Small in the Kingdom of Heaven. Among the disciples of Jesus there is a struggle for rank (Lk. 9:46) which is even projected into the kingdom of God (Mt. 18:1). They obviously think of the kingdom after the model of an earthly state with its distinctions. Judaism underlies this concept with its conviction that there will be small and great in the future world. Those who make themselves small for the law will be great in the world to come. Jesus, however, takes a child as an example. The answer to the question of greatness is the simple trust which marks the children of God as they accept their heavenly Father's gifts. Mt. 20:26 brings out another aspect of the true greatness that is required in disciples. Answering the request of the sons of Zebedee, Jesus points out that loving service is the order of life for his disciples. To ask about greatness is to ask about ministry. Lk. 22:26 adds the nuance that the greatest is to act as the youngest. Mk. 10:43ff. offers the example of Jesus himself, who is obviously the greatest, but has come to serve rather than to be served. In Mt. 5:19, of course, Jesus himself does talk about the greatest and the least in the kingdom. The point here, however, is that position in the kingdom is bound up with the total fulfilment of God's will in its embracing of the whole person and its orientation to truth and trust. Those who erode the law while supposedly protecting it will not even enter the kingdom (5:20). A similar issue arises in Mt. 11:11, where John the Baptist is among the greatest born of women, but the least in the kingdom is greater than he. Since the kingdom is open to the patriarchs and prophets (cf. Mt. 8:11), this can hardly be meant to exclude John from the kingdom (the one who is more than a prophet, v. 9). The probability is, then, that Jesus has himself in mind when he refers to the least in the kingdom who is still greater than John. If this is so, the saying may be compared to Mt. 12:6, in which Jesus says that something greater than the temple is here, and 12:41-42, in which he says someone greater than Jonah or Solomon is here.

3. The Greatest Commandment. In the disputes preceding the passion, a scribe raises the question of the greatest commandment. In reply Jesus combines Dt. 6:5 and Lev. 19:18 to give the commandment of twofold love for God and neighbor. This inseparable love embraces all else. Palestinian piety distinguishes weightier and lighter commandments among the 248 commands and 365 prohibitions of the law. Rabbis also raise the question of a principle of the law. Thus Hillel finds it in a negative form of the golden rule. The general insistence, however, is that observance of the whole law is obligatory. Jesus, then, takes an independent course in finding the sum of the law in the twofold love of God and neighbor. Love is the commitment to God in divine sonship which comes to expression in commitment to others. It is the one essential thing, embracing in itself both law and sacrifice. It finds its fullest illustration in the cross, which is the almost unavoidable outcome of Jesus' challenge to more nomistic views.

4. *The Johannine Use.* In Jn. 1:50 Jesus tells Nathanael that he will see greater things, namely, the glory of Jesus (v. 51) into which he, too, will be drawn. In 5:20 Jesus says to the disciples that the Father will show the Son even greater works for their sake, i.e., giving life to the dead (v. 21). Indeed, even believers themselves will do greater works when Jesus goes to the Father (14:12). Jesus is greater than all who precede him (cf. the questions of 4:12 and 8:53, and the confession of 5:36, where Jesus has the greater witness of God and Scripture; cf. 1 Jn. 5:9). A textual question arises in Jn. 10:29, where it is either the Father who is greater than all or Jesus himself in virtue of the power that the Father has given him. While Jesus is one with the Father, direct equation is avoided, so that Jesus can say that the Father is greater than he (14:28). The same God is greater than the accusing heart (1 Jn. 3:20) and greater than he who is in the world (4:4). Not being greater than their master, the disciples must love and serve as he does (Jn. 13:16); this will involve similar persecution (15:20). The greatness of God is that with forgiveness he grants the needed power for this.

5. *Tit. 2:13.* The question posed in Tit. 2:13 is whether Jesus is the great God and Savior, or the great God is distinguished from the Savior Jesus, or God is the great God and Savior and Jesus is in apposition to glory. Elsewhere in the NT the goddess Artemis is called great (Acts 19:27-28). God is great in the OT (cf. Ex. 18:11; 2 Chr. 2:4). Other religions in the Near East also call their gods great, and the phrase "the great god" occurs everywhere in Hellenism, often in acclamation and without the clear monotheistic thrust of the OT. The statement in Tit. 2:13 obviously belongs to this total context, but who is the great God of the statement? Since Jesus is called Savior elsewhere in Titus, this term plainly refers to him, and the position of the article, the reference to the *epipháneia* (the return of Jesus), and the stereotyped nature of the expression support the view that Jesus is here the great God as well.

6. *Acts 8:10.* Acts 8:10 calls Simon the power of God that is called great. "Great power" and "great god" commonly go together. Even in Judaism God is called Power (cf. Mt. 26:64). Thus when Simon is called the great power of God he is characterized as a divine man, a mediator of revelation, an embodiment of divine power. He himself makes the same claim when he calls himself "somebody great" (v. 9).

megaleíon. This word, meaning "greatness," is used in the plural for "mighty acts" (Dt. 11:2). In Acts 2:11 *tá megaleía* are the mighty acts of God in the story of Christ.

megaleiótēs. This word means "greatness," "majesty," or "glory." In Jer. 33:9 God's work for Jerusalem is to the glory of his people (LXX; the Hebrew has "to his glory among the peoples"). Some versions have the Greek term in Ps. 130:1 (wicked pomp) and Ps. 71:21 (the greatness of the righteous). In the NT the expulsion of the demon in Lk. 9:42-43 results in astonishment at God's majesty, while the majesty of Jesus at the transfiguration is the point in 2 Pet. 1:16, and in Acts 19:27 Demetrius refers to the magnificence of Artemis of Ephesus.

megaloprepēs. This word has the sense of "greatness," "magnanimity," or "nobility." It is used for God in Dt. 33:26. The only NT instance is in 2 Pet. 1:17, which refers to God as the "excellent glory."

megalýnō. This word means "to make great," "to magnify." In the NT it means "to make great" in Mt. 23:5 and Lk. 1:58 and "to extol" in Lk. 1:46; Acts 10:46; 19:17. In Phil. 1:20 Paul's whole aim is the magnifying of Christ by life or death. In 2 Cor. 10:15 he hopes to be magnified with the increase of the Corinthians' faith.

megalōsýnē. This word, meaning "majesty," is used for the divine name in Heb. 1:3. It also occurs with glory etc. in the great doxology of Jude 24-25.

mégethos. The noun of *mégas*, this word means physical or spiritual "greatness." In the LXX it usually means "height" or "growth." The only NT instance is in the petition of Eph. 1:19 that the recipients may know the incomparable "greatness" of God's power.   [W. GRUNDMANN, IV, 529-44]

---

méthē [drunkenness], *methýō* [to be drunk], *méthysos* [drunkard], *mesthýskomai* [to get drunk]

A. Outside the NT. In the literal sense this group denotes intoxication. *methýō* is "to be drunk," *methýskō* "to make drunk" or passive "to be drunk," *méthysos* "drunkard," *méthē* "drinking," "drunkenness." Figuratively the words are used for being drunk with sleep, frenzied with fear, etc. (although *méthysos* is not used figuratively). The LXX uses the group literally in, e.g., Gen. 9:21; Prov. 23:21; Is. 28:7. Figurative use of *methýskō* occurs in Is. 34:5; Cant. 5:1; Nah. 3:11; blood is the drink in Is. 34:5ff., love in Cant. 5:1, divine wrath in Nah. 3:11. *methýskō* may also denote a refreshing drink. Philo has the literal sense; he links drunkenness to ignorance, but commends moderate drinking for the relaxation and cheerfulness that it brings. In a figurative use he refers to the beautiful intoxication of the ascetic and the sober intoxication of union with deity.

B. The NT.
1. In the literal sense *méthysos* and *méthē* occur in the lists of vices in 1 Cor. 5:11; 6:10; Rom. 13:13.
2. *methýō* and *methýskomai* mostly have the literal sense "to drink" (cf. Jn. 2:10) or "to be or get drunk." In 1 Th. 5:6 Paul warns believers, as those who belong to the new aeon, to be vigilant and sober; drunkenness belongs to the night. In the parable in Mt. 24:45ff. the bad steward, not living in eschatological tension, gives way to selfishness and hedonism, drinking with the drunkards. In 1 Cor. 11:21 the Corinthians disrupt the fellowship of the Lord's Supper; some are hungry while the wealthy are drunk. Unlike the feasts of Dionysus, the Lord's Supper is no place for intoxication. Intoxication is the direct opposite of spiritual drink. Thus Peter in Acts 2:15 resists strongly the accusation of drunkenness, and Paul in Eph. 5:18 contrasts orgiastic enthusiasm with the infilling of the Spirit that comes to expression in praise, thanksgiving, and love (vv. 19ff.).
3. A figurative use occurs in Rev. 17:2, 6. In 17:2 the dwellers on earth are drunk with the wine of fornication (idolatry); in 17:6 the woman (who epitomizes the ungodly world) is drunk with the blood of saints and martyrs.   [H. PREISKER, IV, 545-48]

methodía → *hodós*

mélas [black]

mélas means "black" or "dark," dark blue, red, grey, etc. It suggests what is sinister or unlucky, and in the pagan world finds a cultic use in mourning. The LXX uses the term similarly apart from the cultic side. Philo often has the antithesis of black and white. Josephus mentions dyeing the hair black, and he also refers to the black clothing of accused persons, debtors, and mourners. *mélas* is rare in the NT. In Mt. 5:36 the black hair of youth is contrasted with the white hair of age. One of the horses in Rev. 6:1ff. is black (v. 5; cf. Zech. 6:2, 6). In Rev. 6:12 the sun is said to become as black as sackcloth when it is darkened. In the apostolic fathers 1 Clem. 8.3 describes sins in the same image, while Hermas treats black as an apocalyptic color (cf. the black beast of *Visions* 4.1.10, the black hill of *Similitudes* 9.1.5, the black stones of *Similitudes* 9.6.4, etc.). The devil is black in Barn. 4.9.   [W. MICHAELIS, IV, 549-51]

méli [honey]

The ancients use honey as a preservative, for sweetening, and also in medicine and cosmetics. Comparison with honey (for sweetness) is common. With milk, honey is offered to the dead and to deities, and it is said to be the food of the gods. The LXX mentions *méli* some 60 times. The promised land is a land flowing with milk and honey (Ex. 3:8 etc.); the honey is that of wild bees, or sometimes perhaps of grapes or fruit, since beekeeping comes only later. Philo compares the divine wisdom to honey. In his exposition of the prohibition of honey as an offering, however, he equates it with excessive and unholy joy. In the NT the scroll that the divine eats in Rev. 10:9-10 is bitter and yet as sweet as honey (cf. Ezek. 3:1ff.). John the Baptist eats wild honey (Mk. 1:6), which is here the honey from wild bees, not the sweet exudations from certain trees. Some MSS add "and of a honeycomb" in Lk. 24:42. This is hardly an original reading that was dropped because of the Gnostic use of honey, nor is it an addition for cultic reasons. It reflects the contemporary custom of adding a sweet dessert to the main fish course.   [W. MICHAELIS, IV, 552-54]

mélos [member, part, song]

A. Secular Greek.
1. This word has the senses a. "member of the body," and b. "song." In Parmenides it takes on an abstract sense akin to "elements." Plato relates it to *méros* ("part") and also uses it in the singular for "melody" or "song" (cf. Pindar). Prior to Aristotle it is always in the plural for bodily members, but Aristotle also uses it in the singular in this sense, while Epictetus uses both singular and plural for songs. In the singular *mélos* takes on the nuance of an organism which may be compared, e.g., to an integrated *pólis*. In inscriptions the plural may denote the whole body from which the life departs at death.
2. In Orphic myth the consumed members of Dionysus are found in humans as the most noble legacy at creation. In Gnosticism individuals are members of the primal

man which the redeemer gathers from dispersion and which receive from him a new form.

B. Jewish Use.

1. The LXX uses the term for bodily members (both human and animal, Job 9:28; Ex. 29:17), and also for songs or melodies (Ezek. 2:10). *melízō* is used for cutting up offerings into parts (Lev. 1:6). The body is made by God and is subject to death. The stress is on the function of the individual members, which serve the will, not on the whole body as an integrated organism.

2. Philo begins with concrete functions but gives these allegorical significance in an attempt to show that philosophical thought is already present in the OT. For him, as for the LXX, the head is the chief member; it denotes the ruler of a society. God himself has neither parts nor passions. Like Plato, Philo uses the phrase *mélē kaí mérē* for members of the body. He also has *métra kaí mélē* for verse and melody. Josephus compares the suffering of all Judea with Jerusalem in the Jewish war to the effect of the inflammation of an important member on the whole body.

3. Rabbinic theology relates the 248 commands of the law to the 248 members of the body (and the 365 prohibitions to the 365 days of the year). As regards the most important member, it suggests the head, but also the heart or reins. The tongue may also be the mistress of all others (cf. Ps. 39:1). Supernatural powers strive for mastery over the members, but these, albeit few, may be saved by the good impulse. The hands, feet, and mouth are contrasted with the eyes, ears, and nose as particularly under God's power.

C. The NT.

1. The Synoptists. In Mt. 5:29-30 Jesus contrasts the single members and the whole body. The eye and hand are members with very important functions. They are treated here as the subjects of actions, and if the actions are bad, then the right member (the privileged one) should be sacrificed. The actions are not just adulterous glances etc. (v. 28) but anything that might run counter to the demands of the kingdom or of faith in Jesus (cf. Mk. 9:43ff. and Mt. 18:8-9). Obviously Jesus is not demanding self-mutilation (cf. the general demand for self-sacrifice). What he demands is that these members be renounced as regards sinful actions or functions. Judgment rests on the body, but it is saved from hell when there is this radical *metánoia*. The juxtaposition of the members and the body shows that life is more than the perfection of the members; the whole body has an eternal destiny even though individual members perish. Yet Jesus heals individual members as a sign that in the coming aeon there will be a renewed existence in the resurrection body.

2. Pauline Epistles.

a. In Paul the members are not under our autonomous control but are responsible to the Creator. We are set in a conflict which involves the members, since they may be instruments of either iniquity or righteousness (Rom. 6:11-12, 19). Sin needs the members of the mortal body in order to actualize itself. The members are its slaves. Christ, however, has brought liberation and set them in a new service. It may be noted that the reference here is to all the members; Paul makes no ascetic differentiation. The slavery of the members to sin brings no profit; it issues in death, which is the heavy destiny of being in the flesh (6:21; 7:5). Sin imposes its will on our members even against our better knowledge (7:23). The reference to the *mélē* shows that it is the real person who is sinning in concrete acts of sin. Yet the new sanctification in Christ also consists of concrete acts of righteousness by the members which demonstrate the justifying faith that gives the members a new master. In Rom. 12:4-5 and 1 Cor. 12:12 Paul compares the community to a body and its members. The underlying thought here is not that of an integrated organism, as in Greek thinking; the stress is on the functions of the members, as in the OT. The unity of body and members is the ongoing act of God's creative will (1 Cor. 12:18). Because God confers this unity, no member can argue that it does not belong (vv. 15ff.). Each has its own function, thus giving richness to the body. From the very first, the body at issue here is the body of Christ. Along with national, religious, or social differences, there are functional differences according to the charisms, but the creative Spirit permeates the whole as life does the body and unites the different members, so that they suffer and rejoice together (v. 26). In virtue of their common life in the Spirit, the members are Christ's body. Yet individuality remains: "You are the body of Christ, and individually members of it" (v. 27). Unity is already present, so that the great need is not to achieve integration but to avoid arrogance (Rom. 12:3). We belong together as we belong to Christ (12:5). We are to work this out in our different functions (12:4). It is not that Christ is one body of which we are members, but that we are one body in Christ and hence members of one another. As persons, the members themselves have bodies, so that these can be called Christ's members in 1 Cor. 6:15. Christ does his work through the bodies of Christians. As natural bodies, these will be destroyed, but as bodies that are meant for the Lord (and the Lord for them) they are appointed to resurrection (6:13-14). To give the body to a harlot is to take it from the Lord and make it a member of the harlot in a carnal relation that stands in sharp contrast to the spiritual relation to Christ (vv. 16-17). The fact that believers are one spirit with Christ shows that what is said transcends the limits of the comparison to the body and its members. On the other hand, this comparison serves a useful purpose and cannot be arbitrarily replaced.

b. In Col. 3:5 the reference is again to members that constitute active corporeality under sin (cf. deeds of the body in Rom. 8:13). The "seeking" of 3:1 and the "putting off" of 3:9 show what is meant by "putting to death" in 3:5. The example of the tongue adds clarification; we are to renounce lying (3:8). In Eph. 4:25, as in Rom. 12:5 and 1 Cor. 12:25, the stress is on reciprocal ministry. In Eph. 5:30 we have the reverse of 1 Cor. 6:15. As the members become members of a harlot in fornication, so the members are members of Christ in the lawful marriage of Christ and his church. In Eph. 4:16 the complex metaphor has some new features. Yet it is Christ who gives unity to the whole by his creative lordship, for Christ is head as well as body in a headship that transcends what can be ascribed to the merely physical head. In Colossians and Ephesians, probably in conflict with incipient Gnostic trends, Christ plays an increasing role. As Christ is before all things, so he is the head of his body, the church (Col. 1:18). Yet the starting point is still the older Pauline use and the realistic biblical view of the members. Being a member of Christ means being saved by his death and resurrection (Col. 1:7, 20) and brought into the community that stands obediently and actively at his disposal for service to others (3:12ff.).

3. James. Jms. 3:5ff. discusses the harmful working of a powerful member, the tongue, which affects the whole body (vv. 3, 6). As in Paul, other forces control the member and initiate division by it (cf. 4:1). The use of *mélē* here is similar to that of later Judaism.

D. Apostolic Fathers. 1 Clem. 37.5 shows dependence on 1 Cor. 12:12ff. The comparison in Diog. 6.2ff. reflects Greek dualism with its distinction between the soul and the body with its individual members. Ignatius reduces the creative role of God by introducing works (in the context of agreement with the bishop) as a basis for acknowledgment as a member of Christ (*Ephesians* 4.1ff.). He uses the term for the physical members at martyrdom in *Romans* 5.3.   [J. Horst, IV, 555-68]

Melchisedék [Melchizedek]

1. Melchizedek is the priest-king of Salem, the contemporary of Abraham, in Gen. 14:18. Ps. 110:4 refers to this story in relating kingship to priesthood. The idea of the priest-king is important (Simon) in the Maccabean period. Apocalyptic awaits a priestly monarchy with the overcoming of sin and the opening of paradise. Rabbinic interest shifts the interest to Abraham, to whom the priestly dignity is supposedly transferred. Melchizedek is seen as a link between Noah and Aaron. Josephus calls him the founder and first priest of Jerusalem. Philo thinks he is a type of the kingly mind or *lógos* and an example of one who is taught by God.

2. On the basis of Ps. 110, the NT finds in Christ fulfilment of the high priesthood of Melchizedek (Heb. 5:6, 10; 6:20; 7:1ff.). Melchizedek's name and dignity point to the messianic gifts of righteousness and peace. His mysterious appearance indicates the eternity of Christ. The fact that Abraham pays him tithes shows his superiority to Levi. Ps. 110 predicts the beginning of a new order which ends the legal covenant and cultus. The account in Hebrews is marked by great vividness, christological depth, and acceptance of the offense of nonintegration with the Aaronic ministry.

3. Both in the church and in Gnosticism there is much later speculation about Melchizedek. He figures as one of the Gnostic redeemers, and the sect named after him seems to have put him above Christ and paid him cultic homage.

[O. Michel, IV, 568-71]

---

mémphomai [to blame], *mempsímoiros* [grumbler], *ámemptos* [blameless], *momphḗ* [blame]

mémphomai means "to blame, scold, upbraid, chide." *mempsímoiros* denotes "one who bemoans his fate," a "grumbler." *ámemptos* means "blameless," *mémpsis* means "censure," and *momphḗ* "blame" or "reproach." In the NT we find *memphómenos* in Heb. 8:8, where God finds fault with Israel for breaking the covenant, and for this reason gives promise of a new covenant. In Rom. 9:19 Paul raises the question why God finds fault if God is sovereign, all things serve his purpose, and no one can resist his will. But Paul rejects the question; we have no right to dispute with God. In Phil. 3:6 Paul says that he was blameless touching the law (cf. Gal. 1:14). But his very zeal for the law leads him into the sin of persecuting the church, thereby showing that righteousness is not possible by the law. Phil. 2:15 and 1 Th. 3:13 show that it is God's will that his people should be blameless at the judgment. This is possible by reason of justification and the sanctifying work of the Spirit. It is a motive in admonition and sums up the purpose of Christian life. Paul displays this blamelessness in his apostolic ministry (1 Th. 2:10), and it is his prayer that body, soul, and spirit may be kept blameless at the coming of Christ (5:23). *momphḗ* means a "reproach" or "complaint" in Col. 3:13, and in Jude 16 the false teachers are *mempsímoiroi*, i.e., they are dissatisfied with God, with his guidance, with his purpose for them.

[W. Grundmann, IV, 571-74]

ménō [to stay, await],   *em-* [to persevere],   *para-* [to remain, endure],   *peri-* [to await],   *prosménō* [to stay on, with]   *monē* [staying, place to stay],   *hypoménō* [to hold out, wait on],   *hypomonē* [patience, endurance]

ménō.

1. This word means a. "to stay in a place," figuratively "to remain in a sphere," b. "to stand against opposition," "to hold out," "to stand fast," c. "to stay still," and d. "to remain," "to endure," "to stay in force."

2. There is also a transitive use "to expect someone."

In the NT the word is an important one relative to the permanence of God in contrast to human and earthly mutability. As the OT says, God is the eternal God whose counsel and word abide forever (Is. 7:7; 14:24; 40:8), whose eternal city will also remain in the new heaven and earth (Zech. 14:10; Is. 66:22), and who gives the righteous a share in his enduring (cf. Ps. 112:3, 9). The NT repeats these points. God's counsel endures (Rom. 9:11), his word endures (1 Pet. 1:23, 25), the new covenant endures (2 Cor. 3:11), and faith, hope, and love endure (1 Cor. 13:13). In Jn. 12:34 Christ himself remains forever, and in 1:32 the Spirit does not just visit him but remains on him. Another line of thought occurs in 1 Tim. 2:15 and 2 Tim. 2:15 with their references to the perseverance of believers in faith, love, and holiness, or in what they have learned and believed. In the Johannine writings this becomes a more personal abiding in Christ or in God as the converse of God's abiding in Christ or Christ in them (cf. Jn. 6:56; 15:4ff.; 14:10; 1 Jn. 2:6, 24, 27). In this abiding, eschatological promise is already possession, but the concept of abiding rules out mystical or ecstatic identity. Other uses in the Johannine writings are for abiding in God's word (1 Jn. 3:15), in love (3:17), in truth (2 Jn. 2), in the anointing (1 Jn. 2:27), in God's house (Jn. 8:35), in light (1 Jn. 2:10), and in doctrine (2 Jn. 9). Unbelievers, however, abide in darkness (Jn. 12:46) and death (1 Jn. 3:14).

emménō. This word means a. "to abide in something" and b. "to keep to something," e.g., an agreement. The LXX also has it in Is. 30:18 for waiting on God. In the NT Acts 28:30 uses it for staying in a place. Religiously it denotes perseverance in faith (Acts 14:22) and continuing in covenant with God (Heb. 8:9). In Gal. 3:10 Paul refers to the judgment which rests on those who do not keep to the law.

paraménō. This word means a. "to remain in place," "to stand firm," "to endure," b. "to stand by someone," and c. "to stay in an occupation or state." In the NT Paul tells the Corinthians in 1 Cor. 16:6 that he will stay with them, devoting the time to his work among them. In Phil. 1:25 he prefers continuing at work among believers to the union with Christ for which he longs. Heb. 7:23 uses the term in the negative to contrast the impermanent OT priesthood with the abiding high priesthood of Christ. Jms. 1:25 has in view an abiding in the law which means readiness to do it as compared with a mere glance that results in no transformation of life.

periménō. This word has the sense of expecting, awaiting, or waiting. The only NT instance is in Acts 1:4, where Jesus tells the disciples to wait for the promise of the Father.

prosménō. This word means a. "to stay on," b. "to stay with," and c. "to wait." The NT uses it in sense a. in Acts 18:18. Sense b. occurs in Mk. 8:2, where the crowds stay with Jesus in their desire to hear his teaching and see his works. Acts

11:23 refers to going on with the Lord, with a hint of perseverance in spite of opposition. This faithful continuing in grace stands in contrast to the vacillation that easily lets go (Acts 13:43; cf. Mk. 4:17). In 1 Tim. 5:5 righteous widows, unlike the giddy younger ones, set all their hope in God and thus continue in prayer.

monế. *monế* means a. "staying," "tarrying," "abiding," and b. "place to stay," e.g., inn or watchhouse. In the NT the word occurs only twice in John. In 14:2 it denotes the abiding dwelling (in contrast to our transitory earthly state) that Christ prepares for his people in his Father's house. In 14:23, however, the abode is on earth, for Christ and the Father will come to believers and make their home with them. God's dwelling with his people finds cultic expression in the OT (Ex. 25:8). It is promised for the last time (Ezek. 37:26-27). It has now come to spiritual fulfilment in Christ. In both 14:2 and 14:23 the reference is individual rather than universal or eschatological. Salvation consists of union with God and Christ through their dwelling in believers and their taking believers to dwell with them. The *monế* brings out the indestructibility of the union. The idea of a heavenly dwelling for the righteous is found in Iran and then in Talmudic and Mandaean writings. Plato, too, speaks of heavenly dwellings to which the soul returns. The NT reflects the concept in Lk. 16:22; 23:43. As regards indwelling, Philo speaks of the *noús,* the *lógos,* or, indeed, God himself dwelling in us.

hypoménō, hypomonế.

A. The Greek World. *hypoménō* has the senses a. "to stay behind," "to stay alive," b. "to expect," c. "to stand firm," and d. "to endure," "to bear," "to suffer." *hypomonế* means a. "standing fast" and b. "expectation," "waiting." While *hypoménō* is at first ethically neutral, *hypomonế* becomes a prominent virtue in the sense of courageous endurance. As distinct from patience, it has the active significance of energetic if not necessarily successful resistance, e.g., the bearing of pain by the wounded, the calm acceptance of strokes of destiny, heroism in face of bodily chastisement, or the firm refusal of bribes. True *hypomonế* is not motivated outwardly by public opinion or hope of reward but inwardly by love of honor. In the Stoic system it is an important branch of *andreía.*

B. The OT and Later Judaism.
1. Toward God: Waiting on God or Cleaving to God. Distinctive to the LXX is the use of *hypoménein* with an accusative or dative of person, so that the idea is not that of standing against but waiting on. In this sense it is used for Hebrew terms expressing tense, steadfast, or patient expectation (cf. Job 3:9; Ps. 37:7; Job 32:4). The noun *hypomonế* similarly denotes either confidence or tense expectation. It is a mark of the righteous in the OT that they wait on God. In distress and opposition, they look to God for deliverance (cf. Ps. 37:9; Mic. 7:7). God is the almighty covenant God on whom they can rely (Is. 51:5; Zeph. 3:8). As the God of Israel (Jer. 14:8), he is also the God of Israelites (Ps. 39:7). Only the wicked abandon hope in him (Sir. 2:4). The final deliverance is eschatological (Hab. 2:3). Those who endure to the end will be saved (Dan. 12:12). The focus here is neither on the hostile forces nor on inward strength but on the power and faithfulness of God. Yet this divinely oriented *hypomonế* confers courage (Ps. 27:14). This is the strength of cleaving to God or waiting for him (Is. 40:31). There need be no fear of weakening it by a link with hope. It focuses on hope and issues in it. What sustains the righteous is that God will establish justice (Ps. 140:12).

2. *Toward the World: Enduring, Standing Fast, Bearing Patiently.* Standing fast against evils plays a secondary role in the OT. Job is an example, and *hypomonḗ* plays an important part in this book (for various Hebrew words). Humans cannot endure in their own strength (6:11). They cannot stand against God (9:4). God shatters their expectations (14:19). God himself reminds Job that no one can stand against him (41:3). Yet Job waits for God to intervene (14:14). Later Judaism, taking Job as a model, develops the idea of pious steadfastness more strongly, Abraham, too, is an example of one who stood fast in ten temptations. 4 Maccabees extols the endurance of Noah, the prophets, and the Maccabean martyrs. This endurance shares Stoic features, but it is ultimately higher because it comes from God and evidences fear of God.

C. The NT. *hypomonḗ* is naturally a basic attitude of NT believers in view of the eschatological orientation of their faith. Over against a hostile world, they wait confidently for the fulfilment of the kingdom and their own salvation. Yet the NT does not describe them in the OT phrase as those who "wait on the Lord" (or "for God"), possibly because of the concentration on faith and hope. The term *hypoménein* is mostly used in the absolute for "to endure," and only rarely for "to wait on," "to expect."

1. *Toward God: Expecting, Waiting.* A use similar to that of the LXX may be found in 2 Th. 3:5, where steadfast expectation of Christ, balancing love of God, is the point. The sense is probably the same in Rev. 1:9. Pious waiting for Jesus is the heartbeat of the Christian community.

2. *Toward the World: Standing Fast, Perseverance.*

a. Synoptic Gospels. Jesus uses the term three times. In Lk. 8:15 *hypomonḗ* characterizes true believers; it is here an active force that finally bears fruit. In Mk. 13:13 endurance will be needed in the trials of the last period if one is to be saved. Lk. 21:19 offers an active formulation of the same thought (cf. Acts 14:22).

b. Paul. Paul sketches the main features of *hypomonḗ* as a Christian attitude. It does not derive from bravery or insensitivity but from faith and hope (Rom. 8:25). It displays endurance in the present aeon of wickedness and injustice (Rom. 12:2; 1 Cor. 3:7). Actively it produces good works (Rom. 2:7), passively it endures under suffering (2 Th. 1:4; cf. 1 Pet. 2:20). Unlike Greek ethics, which regards the passive suffering of evil as shameful, Christians know that they are called to suffer (Acts 14:22), and they show their faith by persevering all the same (cf. 2 Tim. 2:10). Affliction produces endurance, and endurance character (Rom. 5:3-4). This endurance, which differs from God's forbearance, since God is subject to no external pressure, is never a complaining or despondent endurance. It is given by God (Rom. 15:5) and is closely related to faith and love (1 Tim. 6:11; 2 Tim. 3:10). Tit. 2:2 has the triad faith, love, and (hoping) steadfastness. If hope focuses on the future, the steadfastness of hope is its expression in the present time of affliction. It has the promise that those who die with Christ, if they endure, shall also reign with him (2 Tim. 2:11-12).

c. Hebrews. Written to a persecuted church, Hebrews strongly exhorts to *hypomonḗ* (10:32, 36; 12:1). The gaze of Christians should be on Christ, who himself endured the cross (12:2). Endurance of trials serves as divine discipline (12:7).

d. James. James, too, shows that trials confirm faith and thus strengthen the steadfastness that makes complete (1:3-4). Job is the great example (cf. the prophets too in 5:10). As in Job's case, the Lord will prove to be compassionate to believers if they are steadfast (5:11; cf. 1:12; Mt. 5:12).

e. Revelation. Revelation, the book of the martyr church, extols *hypomonḗ* as right

583

and necessary for believers. On the one side, it is waiting for Jesus (1:9; 3:10). On the other, it is the enduring of suffering and persecution (2:2-3; 19). The final clash is the supreme test and demands supreme steadfastness if all is not to be for nought (13:10; 14:12). It is worth noting that in contrast to Revelation, John and 1-3 John do not use *hypomonḗ* or *hypoménein*; the focus there is on *ménein*.

[F. HAUCK, IV, 574-88]

> ***merimnáō*** [to be concerned, anxious], ***promerimnáō*** [to be anxious before-hand], ***mérimna*** [concern, anxiety], ***amérimnos*** [unconcerned]

merimnáō, promerimnáō, mérimna.

1. Greek Usage. This group covers much the same range of meaning as the English "care": a. "to care for someone or something," b. "to be concerned or anxious," c. "to be intent on or strive after," d. "to be anxiously expectant," e. "to be solicitous," and f. "to brood, speculate, or inquire." The plural *mérimnai* is often used for the cares of life which disturb sleep, from which refuge is sought in love or drink, and which only death can end.

2. Hellenistic Jewish Use. The group is used in the LXX for intentness, for pondering, and for anxiety or anxious care. Only Ps. 55:22 has theological significance. Philo and Josephus do not use the group.

3. The NT.

a. *mérimna* and *merimnán* occur several times in the NT but only rarely in post-NT works. The usual Greek meanings are to be found, e.g, caring for in Mt. 6:25ff., intentness in Mt. 6:31, anxiety in 1 Pet. 5:7, sorrow in Lk. 8:14, and pondering in Mt. 10:19.

b. The NT realizes that life is swayed by care. Concern is unavoidable but it is given a new orientation. Liberation from it comes as one casts it upon God, not because God grants every wish, but because prayer grants freedom from care. To be anxious about food or clothing is opposed to concern for the kingdom of God (Mt. 6:26ff.). Naturally we have to work (1 Th. 2:9 etc.), but we cannot secure life by care; our concern must be for the kingdom. To care for the world is to fall victim to it. If care gains control over us, it leads to apostasy (Lk. 21:34). We must focus on the one thing needful (Lk. 10:41-42), confronting worldly ties with a *hōs mḗ* (1 Cor. 7:29ff.). We belong to the coming aeon and must be ready for it (Lk. 21:34). But this entails care for others as members of the same body (1 Cor. 12:25).

c. In Mt. 6:25ff. *merimnán* is self-concern relative to the future. The questions show that worry is what is meant. It is this that makes a proper concern foolish by fostering the illusion that concern for the means of life can grant security to life itself. The future is not in our hands. We cannot add one cubit (either length of days or stature) by worrying. The right course is to seek first the kingdom, and God will see to other things, not removing uncertainty, but taking the worry out of it. A bit of secular wisdom drives home the point in v. 34. It is ridiculous to add tomorrow's worry to that of today.

amérimnos. This word, meaning "without care," "unconcerned," occurs in the NT only in 1 Cor. 7:32, where Paul wants his readers to be free from worries, and Mt. 28:14, where the story of the theft of the body will keep the soldiers out of trouble.

[R. BULTMANN, IV, 589-93]

---

méros [part]

A. Outside the NT.
1. Secular Greek. From the root *(s)mer,* "to get or have a share," *méros* means "part" in such varied senses as "district," "department," "army division," "political party," "party at law," "portion," "allotted destiny," and "fixed time or place." It is often used with prepositions in the sense of "partially," e.g., *apó, ek, epí, katá.*

2. The LXX and Philo. méros is common in the LXX for various Hebrew words and in various senses, e.g., architecturally, topographically, sociologically, and mathematically. Thus it may denote the parts of a country, the sides of the altar, the sides of a road, the divisions of an army, and shares or portions, e.g., an inheritance. The LXX does not use it for human or animal parts of the body, but Philo has it in this sense, as well as for parts of the soul or the world. Accepting the unity of the cosmos, Philo teaches the Stoic harmony of the parts. The parts share in the totality only for the sake of the totality, and the truly perfect good is a whole. As a part, man cannot be the direct image of God, only an image of the *lógos.*

B. The NT.
1. Usage.
a. Part. The NT uses *méros* for parts of the body (Lk. 11:36), of a competence (15:12), of a garment (Jn. 19:23), of a fish (Lk. 24:42), or of a city (Rev. 11:13). The meaning may also be district (Mt. 2:22 etc.), or side of a ship (Jn. 21:6: the right side.) Another use is for a theological party (Acts 23:6), and we also find *méros* for a "trade" in Acts 19:27, i.e., part of the business life of the city.
b. Share. One can have a share in Jesus (Jn. 13:8), in a group (Mt. 24:51), in a thing (Rev. 22:19), or in an event (Rev. 20:6).
c. Adverbial Phrases. The NT uses various adverbial phrases, e.g., "after one another" in 1 Cor. 14:27, "partially" in Rom. 15:5, "a little" in Rom. 15:24, "in this case or matter" in 2 Cor. 3:10 and 9:3, and "in detail" in Heb. 9:5.
2. Theologically Important Statements. In 1 Cor. 13:9, 12 the adverbial *ek mérous* indicates that our present knowledge and prophesying are only partial. The future aeon will bring in what is complete. In Rom. 11:25 a partial hardening has come on Israel while the Gentiles are brought to salvation; only at the end will all Israel be saved. In 1 Cor. 12:27 individual believers belong to the fellowship and therefore their individuality is part of the whole. Eph. 4:16 shows that each part has a contribution to make to the growth of the total body. Jn. 13:8 teaches that only the cleansed disciple can have any part in Jesus. At the end of the aeon fellowship with Jesus will mean participation in the first resurrection (Rev. 20:6) and a share in the tree of life (22:19). The unfaithful, however, have a place with the hypocrites (Mt. 24:51), and the ungodly are allotted a share in the lake of fire (Rev. 21:8). The "lower parts" of Eph. 4:9 may mean the earth, or possibly the realm of the dead. [F. Büchsel, IV, 594-98]

---

mesítēs [mediator], **mesiteúō** [to mediate]

A. Occurrence and Meaning.
1. Hellenistic Usage. 1. A first use of *mesítēs* is for the trustworthy neutral, e.g., the umpire or guarantor. Thus we find the word for a. the legal arbiter, b. the witness,

c. the sequester, d. the pawnbroker, e. the guarantor, and f. a warehouse official. More general senses are 2. "intermediary," and 3. "negotiator." *mesiteúō* means 1. "to act as umpire," 2. "to occupy a middle place," and 3. "to establish a relation between two hitherto unrelated entities."

II. The Term and Concept in Israelite-Jewish Usage.

1. The OT. *mesiteúō* does not occur in the LXX and *mesítēs* only in Job 9:33. Hebrew has no single term for "mediator" but we find words meaning "interpreter" and "negotiator."

2. Rabbinic Judaism. The business world brings the idea of the negotiator or broker into rabbinic thought, in which it takes on a figurative sense.

3. Hellenistic Judaism. Josephus uses the terms only in a secular sense. Philo starts with this but gives added depth to the idea of the "mediator," using both noun and verb mostly in a religious sense.

B. The Theology of Mediatorship outside the Bible.

1. The Deity as Guarantor of Human Agreements. The gods are often viewed as guarantors of agreements. This idea underlies the oath. Mithra is often mentioned in this connection (cf. God in Philo and the rabbis).

2. Cosmic Soteriological Intermediaries. A common idea in ancient thinking is that one's country is the middle point of the earth and that the local deities are thus middle deities who grant temporal or eternal benefits. More spiritually the deity may then be seen as the heart of the cosmos. Another concept is that the middle deities keep heaven and earth apart (cf. Atlas). Philo views the *lógos* as that which keeps the world in harmony. The title *mesítēs* is early assigned to Mithra, although there is debate whether this means primarily that he occupies a middle place or that he is personified agreement. Both ideas may well be present. As the middle cosmic force, Mithra is the arbiter between opposing forces, and by the law of sacrifice (i.e., that life comes through death) he is the mediator of salvation to believers in him. Hellenism then assumes that the gods of the cults are mediators between the supreme god and their devotees. We also find impersonal mediators, e.g., sacral fire, and in Gnosticism there are semipersonal hypostases (cf. the complex Manichean system, which, however, uses the term "sent one" rather than mediator). The task of these mediators is to bring saving knowledge, which has an ethical and spiritual component. They do this by fighting darkness and binding evil influences. Often present in such speculation is the idea of the primal man who bears the life of light, falls victim to darkness, and is freed by the redemptive process. Yet the concept of the mediator is not necessarily bound to that of the primal man. Pantheistic notions, too, find a place for personal mediators, although fundamentally pantheistic mysticism rules out mediation.

3. Men as Mediators. Various human beings are also regarded as mediators. Kings are such in view of their divine origin, and priests in view of their sacrificial and intercessory ministry. Above all, founders of religions do a lasting mediatorial work and are usually invested with legendary features. Often the actual founders make no claim to mediate eternal salvation. Their followers develop their sober sense of mission into a supreme mediation of saving wisdom.

C. Mediatorship in the OT.

1. Divine Mediatorship. The OT finds no place for cosmic mediatorship. Even Gen. 1:6-8 does not teach this, for God comes first, not chaos, and God acts with supreme power by the word. Jerusalem may be at the center of the world (Ezek. 5:5; Is. 2:2), but God is not confined to any place (cf. Am. 5:8 etc.). Places receive honor from him, not he from places (Dt. 12:5). As the almighty ruler of the world, God is not its middle point but its supraterrestrial Sovereign (Jer. 23:23-24). As such, however, he serves as an arbiter for Job in the latter's battle against the concept of God in the dogma of retribution. In Job 9:33 Job laments that there is no umpire who might decide in his suit. He decides to press his case in 13:3, achieves the confidence that he has a witness in 16:18-19, and knows that he has a living Redeemer in 19:25ff. God himself, apart from human instruments of revelation, has his own mediators in the angels, the Spirit, and wisdom or *lógos*.

2. *Human Mediators*. The OT finds a place for human mediators. Kings play a lesser role except in the future figure of the Messiah. Priests and especially prophets are more important. A tendency develops for the priest and king to flow together, and when the prophet is added the stage is set for the threefold NT mediator. A special mediator at the beginning of Israel's history is Moses. Uniquely called, Moses is a mediator as the divinely commissioned spokesman (cf. Ex. 4:15-16). As such he gives the law and stands between God and the people (cf. Ex. 19:3ff.; 20:19, etc.). As intercessor, Moses includes himself in the prayer for forgiveness and expresses a readiness to be cut off for his people (Ex. 32:11ff.; 34:8-9). The first of the prophets, he is unique as the one with whom God speaks face to face (Ex. 33:11). He fasts for the people (Dt. 9:8-9), wrestles with God for them (9:26ff.), and dies as it were vicariously for them outside the land of promise (3:23ff.). Another special figure in the OT is the Servant of the Lord in Is. 42:1ff., 49:1ff., 50:4ff., and 52:13–53:12. This Servant seems to be a historical figure who has a mission of gentle preaching to Israel and the nations, replacing as such the whole people when it proves deaf and blind to the divine call (42:19). He meets with opposition that he endures vicariously even to the point of a miserable death, but in all this suffering God fulfils his purpose of salvation, so that the suffering itself is a means of blessing for Israel and for the world. Moses, Ezekiel, and Jeremiah are prophetic forerunners in the development of the concept of vicarious mediation (cf. Ezek. 13:5; 22:30; Jer. 15:16ff.; 20:7ff.). The OT problem, of course, is that the mediators themselves are involved in guilt. Yet mediatorship is at the heart of the OT. We cannot approach God as we will. His moral demand is the unconditional basis of fellowship. Yet fellowship means election as well as demand. Thus the mediator carries a twofold but related claim. At the side of the community, he stands in the gap when the people fails to meet God's demand, first by intercession, then by vicarious self-offering. The presupposition of this divinely appointed ministry is the being of God and his saving rule. There can be no glorifying of the mediator as such. The focus is on God, and for this reason the mediatorship finally embraces not merely Israel but all peoples.

D. The Theological Concept of the Mediator in Judaism.

1. *Rabbinic Judaism*. Judaism introduces the term "mediator" in its theological sense. The basis is the concept of the negotiator or broker or interpreter, and in essentials the term is used exclusively for Moses as God's commissioned agent. Moses is the go-between who brings God and his people together. He is at times associated with Miriam and Aaron, and it is noted that he, too, is fallible, and has to suffer for the people's sins. The Servant of the Lord is taken messianically in early exegesis but with little place for vicarious mediation, since the emphasis (apart from intercession) is on the exalting of Israel and the victory over the nations. This is strange, since the idea of vicarious suffering is not alien to Israel, nor is the thought of a suffering and

dying Messiah. In apocalyptic the Messiah serves as an intermediary, but this is a transcendent Messiah developed out of Dan. 7:13ff.

2. Hellenistic Judaism. In Philo angels are heavenly mediators (*lógoi*) connecting heaven and earth. Moses is also a mediator for Philo either at the human or the cosmological level. Under Hellenistic influences there is a tendency to exalt the mediator of the covenant (e.g., the high priest) almost to semidivine status. The wealth and depth of the OT understanding are grasped only in part.

E. The NT Concept of the Mediator.

1. The Use of the Terms. The words are both rare in the NT. In Gal. 3:19-20 Paul uses the noun in a much debated phrase. He has been showing what is the purpose of the law. It is given by God in order to lead to faith in Christ. But it is ordained by angels through an intermediary. Paul mentions angels here to denote the lesser status of the law rather than its high significance. The intermediary is no doubt Moses. The point of v. 20 is not so much that Moses is the intermediary between two parties but that he is so on behalf of a plurality, i.e., the angels. The law, then, does not come directly from God. This explains the question of v. 21 and the need to show how the law fits in with the divine promises. In 1 Tim. 2:5-6 we find a Christianized use. The one God wills that all people be saved, and there is one Mediator representing God to them and them to God, i.e., Christ Jesus in his sacrificial death (v. 6; cf. Rom. 3:30). The term takes a more Hellenistic turn in Heb. 8:6; 9:15. Linked with *diathḗkē*, it has the nuance of guarantor as well as mediator. This is also the point of the verb in 6:17, where God is not merely one of the parties but vouches for the promise with an oath. It may be noted, however, that Christ is still the mediator. He does not merely guarantee salvation but also accomplishes it by his vicarious death.

2. The Theology of Mediatorship in the NT.

a. Jesus. Jesus does not use the terms but the concept is present in his demands (Mt. 10:37ff.), his claims (Mt. 11:27), his remission of sins (Mk. 2:1ff.), and his relating of human destiny to confession of himself (Mt. 10:32-33). The Sermon on the Mount reflects Moses' giving of the law at Sinai, and the Last Supper has the exodus as its background. The main form of Jesus' sense of mediatorship is messianic divine and human sonship but in a unique combination of majesty and humility that is strongly oriented to the Servant of Is. 53 (cf. Mk. 10:45).

b. The Primitive Community. The faith of the primitive community plainly rests on Jesus' own synthesis of the Son of Man and the Suffering Servant as this is fulfilled at Good Friday, Easter, and Pentecost and will be consummated at the expected Second Advent. The portrayal is not a creation of the community but accords with the historical actuality.

c. Paul. On his conversion Paul adopts the faith of the primitive community. His gospel is one of mediation with the focus on the cross and resurrection. Baptism is the end of the old aeon and the inauguration of the new as fulfilled in the Mediator (Rom. 4:25; 6:1ff.). The preexistent Christ plays a role in creation (1 Cor. 8:6). A parallel is also drawn between Christ and Adam, but Christ is the last Adam. While Adam, the first man, mediates ruin, Christ, the last Adam, mediates salvation, not as some timeless heavenly man, but as the incarnate Son. His mediation is cosmic (Eph. 1:10), but the *plḗrōma* is the church. The cosmos, then, is bound to salvation, not salvation to the cosmos.

d. John's Gospel and Epistles. Though the term is not used, these works are full of the belief that Christ fulfils all mediatorship. In contrast to all others (Jn. 10:8),

Christ is the way, truth, and life (14:6). Mediation culminates in his intercession (v. 17) and death (10:11), whose atoning significance finds emphasis in 1 John (1:7; 2:2).

e. Other NT Writings. James finds little place for mediation, but tacitly presupposes it. Hebrews uses the concept to show that the church is God's true people in the age of salvation. 1 Peter refers to the sprinkling of Christ's blood and the new birth through his resurrection (1:2-3), and then moves on to the election of the priestly nation (2:9). 2 Peter and Jude contain formulas which prove how deeply rooted the concept of the mediator is (cf. 2 Pet. 1:1, 11; 2:20; Jude 1, 21, 25). In Revelation Christ is the Lion and the slain Lamb, uniting power and humility. Cosmic symbols (the numbers of the planets, the signs of the zodiac, and the glory of the sun, moon, and morning star) are applied to him (1:12ff.; 12:1ff.; 21:14; 22:16). He stands at the center of the cosmos and leads his people through the epochs.

F. The Church. The terms are surprisingly rare in the first writings. *mesítēs* does not occur until Clement of Alexandria (*Paedagogus* 3.1.2.1), who also uses *mesiteúō* (*Protrepticus* 12.122.3). Even later, although the matter is present, theologians stress other concepts. In the Middle Ages the church ascribes mediatorial functions to its priests, but the Reformation brings a new focus on Christ himself as the one Mediator.

[A. OEPKE, IV, 598-624]

---

mesótoichon [dividing wall]

This uncommon term occurs in the NT only in Eph. 2:14, where vv. 16-17 seem to show that the "partition" or "dividing wall" is not merely the barrier between Jews and Gentiles but ultimately that between God and us. It is when this barrier is removed that earthly barriers fall too.   [C. SCHNEIDER, IV, 625]

Messías → *Christós; metabaínō* → *baínō; metáthesis* → *títhēmi; metakaléomai* → *kaléō; metakinéō* → *kinéō; metalambánō, metálēmpsis* → *lambánō; metallássō* → *allássō*

---

metamélomai [to feel regret, repent],   *ametamélētos* [without regret]

1. Unlike *metanoeín*, which means "change of heart," *metamélesthai* means the "experiencing of remorse." The two may, of course, converge. Aristotle criticizes the latter as a sign of inconstancy, and the Stoics reject both on similar grounds. The preaching of the Cynics and Pythagoreans, however, gives them positive force as it arouses guilt and summons to conversion.

2. The LXX hazards the phrase that God repents, using both words in this connection (1 Sam. 15:35; Am. 7:3). Yet God's repentance does not overthrow his judgment (Num. 23:19 etc.). He may reject in spite of his grace (1 Sam. 15:35) no less than renew his grace in spite of his judgment (1 Chr. 21:15). This tension continues in Judaism, in which God is the God both of judgment and of mercy. In humans the LXX distinguishes between remorse, which may not be pleasing to God (Ex. 13:17), and repentance, although with some assimilation (cf. Jer. 4:28 and 20:16). Remorse sees the bitter end of sin, repentance breaks free from it. The result of sin brings remorse, a divinely commissioned call brings repentance.

3. In general, Judaism distinguishes the narrower *metánoia* from the more general *metaméleia*. Philo can call the latter the presupposition and proof of forgiveness, but Josephus senses that *metánoia* goes further with its implication of a change of will.

4. *metanoeín* and *metánoia* take precedence in the NT. The only instances of *metamélomai* are in Mt. 21:29, 32; 27:3; 2 Cor. 7:8; Heb. 7:21 (quoting Ps. 110:4). In Mt. 21:28ff. the son who refuses to work changes his mind and goes, but the opponents of Jesus refuse to do so when they hear the call of the Baptist. In Mt. 27:3 Judas suffers remorse when he sees the result of his betrayal. His suicide shows that this is no true repentance. In 2 Cor. 7:8ff. Paul does not "regret" sending a severe letter (although he had regretted it), because it has led to "repentance" (*metánoian*) in the readers—a "repentance" which brings "no regret" (*metánoia ametamélētos*). In this passage "being sorry" is plainly distinguished from repenting. Paul uses *ametamélētos* again in Rom. 11:29, where he says that God's gifts and calling are irrevocable. The same thought of God's faithfulness occurs in Heb. 7:21: God has pledged with an oath that the institution of the eternal high priest is unchangeable, and he will not change his mind. The NT, then, has a clear sense of the distinction between the terms; it reserves *metánoia* for the divinely effected change of heart which leads to salvation.

[O. MICHEL, IV, 626-29]

metamorphóomai → *morphḗ*; *metanoéō, metánoia* → *noús*; *metapémpomai* → *apostéllō*; *metastréphō* → *stréphō*; *metaschēmatízō* → *schḗma*; *metatíthēmi* → *títhēmi*; *metéchō* → *échō*

---

meteōrízomai [to rise up, be anxious]

In the active *meteōrízomai* means "to lift up," "to suspend," and figuratively "to buoy up," "to encourage," "to stir." In the more common middle and passive we find the two different figurative meanings a. "to rise up," "to exalt oneself," "to be arrogant or greedy," and b. "to be anxious," "to hover between fear and hope." The LXX has only a., and this only in the bad sense (e.g., Ps. 131:1). Indeed, sense b. is generally less common. In the one NT instance in Lk. 12:29 choice is difficult, for "do not be arrogant" yields good sense as well as "do not be anxious." In support of the former one might refer to Rom. 12:16 and 1 Tim. 6:17ff. as well as LXX usage. Yet the context, with the oldest versions, favors the latter. God lavishes even his temporal gifts, and the ultimate gift of his kingdom is secure. There is thus no reason for torturing anxiety (cf. Phil. 4:4ff.).   [K. DEISSNER, IV, 630-31]

métochos, metochḗ → *échō*; *metriopathéō* → *páschō*

---

métron [measure], **ámetros** [immeasurable], **metréō** [to measure]

1. Outside the NT. métron means a. "measure," b. "proportion," c. "measure of verse," and d. "what is measured" (both literal and figurative). In philosophy the *métron pántōn* is the absolute measure of all things (which Protagoras finds in humanity, Plato in God). The LXX uses the term in cultic measurements, for weights and measures, for the measures of the world, and in threats of destruction. *metréō* means "to measure" and figuratively "to evaluate."

2. The NT. In the NT sense a. occurs in the Gospels, e.g., in the prohibition of judging in Mt. 7:2, or the reference to the measure of sin in Mt. 23:32. We do not find senses b. and c., but d. (figurative) is common (cf. Rom. 12:3; 2 Cor. 10:13; Eph. 4:7, 13). *ámetros*, meaning "immeasurable," occurs in 2 Cor. 10:13, 15 for "immoderate" boasting. *metréō* is used symbolically in Rev. 11:1-2; 21:15ff. for the measuring of the temple and the city, and there is a figurative use in 2 Cor. 10:12. In Mt. 7:2 Jesus gives seriousness to the prohibition of judging by referring to the corresponding divine judgment. In Lk. 6:38 forgiveness carries with it the promise of a good measure in return, but judging will bring a corresponding measure of judgment. In Eph. 4:7 and Rom. 12:3 *métron* expresses the diversity of the gifts that God gives to his people, while in Eph. 4:13 it is then used for the fullness that the gifts are meant to achieve. Christ himself receives the gift of the Spirit without measure or limitation (Jn. 3:34). According to the symbolism of Rev. 11:1-2 what is measured is what is to be preserved.   [K. DEISSNER, IV, 632-34]

---

métōpon [forehead]

---

métōpon, meaning the "brow" or "forehead," occurs in the NT only in Revelation. In 7:3; 9:4; 14:1; 22:4 God's servants bear on their foreheads the seal of God, or the name of Christ and God, which protects them through the apocalyptic woes. In 13:14; 14:9; 20:4 God's enemies have the mark of the beast stamped on their hands and foreheads. This will bring them temporal prosperity but will also expose them to God's wrath and exclude them from the millennial kingdom. There would seem to be in these double markings—on the positive side, allusions to Ezek. 9:4 and Ex. 12:13, and less probably to the mark of Cain, and on the negative side to the marks signifying cultic adherence and also to the branding of slaves as a punishment. In 17:5 the harlot, who signifies worldly abomination, bears a mark that expresses her true nature in an allusion to Babylon. The basis here is the custom whereby Roman harlots had their names on bands around their foreheads.   [C. SCHNEIDER, IV, 635-37]

---

mēlōtḗ [sheepskin]

A *mēlōtḗ*, or "sheepskin," is a prophetic garment in Heb. 11:37 (cf. Zech. 13:4). The harsh clothing bears witness to the life of loneliness and affliction which God's servants endure (cf. the Baptist in Mk. 1:6). Monasticism later interprets *mēlōtḗ* as the skin of the goat.   [O. MICHEL, IV, 637-38]

---

mḗn [moon, month],   *neomēnía* [new moon]

---

1. *mḗn* is the word for the "moon," then for the "month," which originally begins with the new moon. The new moon (*neomēnía*) takes on religious significance, for the swelling of waters and ripening of fruits are ascribed to the moon. Those born at the new moon are regarded as lucky, and a cult of the moon (*Mḗn*) develops which is very common in Asia Minor. Stoicism adopts the popular view of the moon, finding

the universal soul or world principle in it. The moon is also supposed to be a transitory station for souls on the way to and from earth.

2. In the LXX *mḗn* and *neomēnía* are used for the Hebrew word for "month" or "beginning of the month." The feast of the new moon is one of the biblical feasts, and with the sabbath it is a day to consult the prophets (2 Kgs. 4:23). The community assembles for the offerings of the feast (Ezek. 46:3), and Philo offers a moral rationale for keeping it. In later Judaism the time is set by the observation of as many witnesses as possible. The new moon is then consecrated and proclamation is made by wind instruments. The OT forbids veneration of the moon (Dt. 4:19). Penalties for infringement are severe because of the danger presented by surrounding moon cults (Judg. 8:21, 26). Yet moon worship creeps in (2 Kgs. 23:5) and its enticement is felt (Job 31:26-27). The righteous, however, view the moon only as a measure of time (Ps. 104:19) under the rule of God (Gen. 1:16).

3. The NT.

a. The NT mentions the moon in measurements of time (Lk. 1:24; Acts 7:20). Matthew, Mark, and John never mention months, and if Luke shows more interest in dates, this does not extend to detailed events. The NT focuses on the facts rather than the dates, and presents history as a sum of forces rather than a stream of events, i.e., from the standpoint of energy rather than continuity.

b. Revelation engages in calculations of the future but in veiled rather than literal references, as in 9:5, 10. In 11:2 and 13:5 the 42 months are the 1,150 days of Dan. 8:14. The dates may be concealed but they have also been fixed (9:15). The image of the trees bearing fruit each month depicts the wealth of joys in the kingdom.

c. In Gal. 4:10 *mḗn* occurs in connection with Judaizing errors. *neomēnía* in Col. 2:16 is parallel, for observation of months goes hand in hand with the new moon festival. Judaizing naturally carries with it regard for the OT feasts, and the new moon festival might well be a special temptation in Asia Minor with its strong cult of the moon god. For Paul, then, the moon is one of the elements from which Christians are liberated (Gal. 4:3, 9; Col. 2:8, 20), and there must be no relapse into its veneration.

[G. DELLING, IV, 638-42]

---

mḗtēr [mother]

The position of mothers in antiquity does not wholly coincide with the general evaluation of women. Stoicism has a high regard for mothers, and the cult of mother deities exerts a strong influence. Traces of matriarchy may be found. The OT mentions many important mothers. *mḗtēr* may indeed personify the people (Hos. 4:5), and the LXX uses *mētrópolis* for a city in 2 Sam. 20:19. In Philo wisdom is the mother of the world and matter is the mother of all things. In the NT Jesus strongly endorses the OT commandment to honor mothers (Mt. 15:4). The demand that we should love Jesus more than father or mother no more negates the fifth commandment than the first commandment does (Mt. 10:37). The Synoptists mention Jesus' own mother only in the infancy stories apart from Mt. 12:46ff. and parallels; Mt. 13:55. In John Mary is present at the wedding in Cana and at the cross, though the name is not given. The only other NT reference to Mary is in Acts 1:14. Other mothers mentioned are the mother of James and John in Mt. 20:20 (the Mary of 27:56); Mary the mother of John Mark in Acts 12:12; the mother at the deathbed in Mk. 5:40; the mother at the bier in Lk. 7:12; and Herodias in Mt. 14:8. The OT phrase "from the mother's womb" occurs in Mt. 19:12; Lk. 1:15; Acts 3:2; Gal. 1:15. Paul never mentions his parents, but respect for one's mother is expressed in Rom. 16:13 (cf. 1 Tim. 5:2; Gal. 4:26). The important religious role of the mother may be seen in the succession from Lois and Eunice to Timothy in 2 Tim. 1:5.   [W. MICHAELIS, IV, 642-44]

---

miaínō [to stain, defile], *míasma* [defilement], *miasmós* [defilement], *amíantos* [undefiled]

---

miaínō. a. Neutrally this word means "to paint in color." b. Censoriously it means "to stain," first literally, then in a cultic sense, i.e., with guilt or demonic processes. Washings are designed to remove such stains. In the OT defilement is with alien cults, dead bodies, etc., and unclean persons can stain others or holy objects. The LXX uses *miaínō* for "to declare unclean." Since the NT no longer thinks in cultic terms, the word is very rare. A reference to Jewish practice occurs in Jn. 18:28. Heb. 12:15 develops a figurative sense; apostates may defile others. Inner defilement is at issue in Tit. 1:15, i.e., the defilement of the mind and conscience. Jude 8 carries a reference to licentious sex acts that defile the flesh.

míasma. This means "defilement" as a result of an action, especially cultic pollution, then moral defilement. The only NT instance is in 2 Pet. 2:20, where the world seems to be the ungodly world; hence its defilements are pagan practices.

miasmós. This is "defilement" as an action or state, first cultic, then moral. The one NT use is in 2 Pet. 2:10, in which it is licentious passion that defiles.

amíantos. This word means "undefiled," first physically, then morally. In the NT it has the narrower sense of sexual purity in Heb. 13:4. The sense is broader in Jms. 1:27 (pure religion), 1 Pet. 1:4 (a pure inheritance), and Heb. 7:26 (the moral purity of Christ as high priest).   [F. HAUCK, IV, 644-47]

---

mikrós [small], (*eláttōn* [smaller], *eláchistos* [smallest]*)*

---

1. In the Greek world *mikrós* means a. "small in size," b. "small in compass," c. "small in significance," and d. "short in time" (or "young" in age).

2. The LXX uses *mikrós* for various Hebrew terms denoting smallness of size or insignificance. The phrase "small and great" is often used for "all." Stress is laid on smallness (Judg. 6:15; 1 Sam. 9:21) in a humility that also stresses the freedom and majesty of God (cf. also Solomon's reference to his youth in 1 Kgs. 3:7).

3. The rabbis often refer to young scholars as "little" or "insignificant," perhaps in connection with the use of the term "little ones" for children.

4. *NT Use I.* There is a general use in the NT. Zacchaeus is "short of stature" in Lk. 19:3. James the *mikrós* in Mk. 15:40 is either "short of stature" or "the younger." The phrase "small and great" occurs frequently. Jesus calls people "these little ones" with no hint of disparagement (cf. Mt. 10:42; 18:6, 10, 14). The reference is not necessarily to children but is more likely to be to disciples (cf. Mt. 10:42). Far from being disparaging, the description hints at a hidden or future dignity. The term "little"

implies insignificance in human terms but also conversion (here is the link with children, Mt. 18). God calls the mean and the poor (Mt. 11:25, 29). Those whom he calls become lowly as children (Mt. 18:4). But the small in this aeon will be great in the future aeon (Mt. 18:1; cf. 5:19). The least in the kingdom is greater than the Baptist (Mt. 11:11). Although the reference here is probably to Jesus himself, the saying is in accord with the general teaching of Jesus that greatness in the kingdom differs radically from greatness in human estimation. The change from small to great is the mystery of God's working (Mk. 4:31). Though the flock is little, it need not fear, for the Father will give it the kingdom (Lk. 12:32; cf. 9:48). The sense of littleness is the true humility of conversion that corresponds to the humility of Christ (Mt. 18:4; cf. 11:29). Jesus, then, resists the striving for human greatness but at the same time blunts the temptation implicit in littleness. Paul takes up the message in Phil. 2:3, 8. He sets Christ himself under this rule and adopts it for himself (4:12). Small things can be big with meaning (cf. the little leaven of 1 Cor. 5:6, but also the little member of Jms. 3:5).

5. *The NT Use II (Comparative and Superlative).* The comparative *eláttōn* and the superlative *eláchistos* (Jn. 2:10; Eph. 3:8) correspond to the positive *mikrós*. Insignificant Bethlehem is by no means least among Judah's rulers (Mt. 2:6). Those who trifle with the least of the commmandments will be least in the kingdom (5:19). Jesus identifies himself with the least of the brethren (25:40, 45). In Luke the superlative expresses human weakness (12:26). It also appears in the rule that faithfulness (or the reverse) in what is least means the same in what is much (16:10; cf. 19:17). Paul calls himself the least of the apostles in 1 Cor. 15:9 and the least of the saints in Eph. 3:8. The phrase in 1 Cor. 4:3 means "it is a very small thing" (i.e., "it makes no difference"), and the reference in 1 Cor. 6:2 is to "trivial" cases. The use for very small things (e.g., animals or parts of the body) recurs in the apostolic fathers, where we again find the rule that very little things can exert great force. In Hermas, however, believers are viewed as innocent children in a theme which is common in antiquity but hardly corresponds to what the NT teaches with its sayings about "little ones."

[O. MICHEL, IV, 648-59]

---

miméomai [to imitate], *mimētḗs* [imitator], *symmimētḗs* [fellow imitator]

1. *Secular Usage.* This group, which arises in the sixth century B.C., means "to imitate," "to mimic." Culture is said to arise with the imitating of animals. Art is called an imitation (in a derogatory sense in Plato). The term can have a bad sense for what is unoriginal. In ethics imitation of good people is a way to goodness, but there is also a danger of imitating wicked people.

2. *The Cosmological Concept.* In Plato reality is an imitation of the idea, time of eternity, and the visible of the invisible. The creation of living creatures involves imitation, and humans, too, must engage in imitation. The controlling concept here is that of analogy, i.e., the relation between original and copy. Imitation is not, then, the obedient following of a model in ethical responsibility. The thinking of Plato has great influence, e.g., on the Neo-Pythagoreans, the Stoics, and Philo. Later, the more ethical concept seems to break free from the cosmological understanding, e.g., when Seneca says that one should take God as a model.

3. *The LXX and Pseudepigrapha.* The group is rare in the LXX and occurs only in

the Apocrypha. In general the idea of imitation is alien to the OT and there is no thought of imitating God. The situation changes in the pseudepigrapha, which demand that we imitate exemplary people like Joseph, and also that we imitate God by keeping his commandments. Kings should take God as their example in dealing with their subjects.

4. *Philo and Josephus.* Philo, who often uses the group, is influenced by Plato's view that the heavenly and the earthly worlds correspond. The verb may denote conscious imitation, but it may also be used where there is only comparison. Moses is set up as a model to follow, and children should imitate their fathers. When the *lógos* imitates God, the idea of original and copy is present. Imitating God is fitting in with his plan at creation, but Philo recognizes that there are limits to this imitation. Resemblance rather than conscious imitation is the point when Joshua is said to be an imitator of the attractive character of Moses. Josephus uses the group in the common sense of copying, imitating, and resembling. He does not speak of imitating God but suggests that creation is a model with its order and regularity.

5. *The Word Group in the NT.* In the NT we find *miméomai*, *mimētḗs*, and *symmimētḗs*. In 3 Jn. 11 we simply have a general admonition; in context it means taking Demetrius rather than Diotrephes as a model (vv. 9ff.). In Heb. 13:7 (cf. 11:4ff.; 12:1ff.) imitating faith means not merely striving to live up to the faith of others but a readiness to take the same way of faith in full commitment to Christ. In Heb. 6:12 *mimētaí* has a strongly active thrust, unless the point is a simple comparison, namely, that the readers should inherit the promises like those who have shown faith and patience. Comparison is the point in 1 Th. 2:14; what happened to the churches in Judea has now happened to the Thessalonians and is no exception to the rule. In 2 Th. 3:7, 9 Paul offers himself as an example of earning his own bread and not being a burden to others. *týpos* here is more than a pattern; it is an authoritative model. *týpos* also occurs in Phil. 3:17, which demands that the readers join in imitating Paul and also mark those who so walk. Here again Paul is not only a pattern but also an authoritative example. They are to walk as he does, but in so doing to obey. This element of obedience is very clear in 1 Cor. 4:16, for Paul has sent Timothy to remind the Corinthians of his "ways" in Christ, i.e., not merely his conduct but his directions. The same applies in 11:1. To be sure, Paul offers himself as a model in 10:32-33. He himself follows the same criterion that he enjoins on his readers. But imitation involves obeying the rule as well as copying Paul's example. This is why Paul adds: "As I am of Christ." If he simply meant that Christ is a model for him, then he would surely have pointed the Corinthians themselves directly to Christ and explained in what sense Christ is a model. Christ is, of course, a model in this sense in Rom. 15:1ff. and Phil. 2:4ff. But in these passages Paul develops the thought, and in any case it is not certain that Christ as model is really the central concept in Phil. 2:4ff. The point, then, is rather that the Corinthians should imitate Paul by heeding his word as he imitates Christ by understanding the apostolic ministry as Christ wishes. Paul's own authority rests on the superior authority of Christ. (Along these lines 11:2 stands in a closer relation to 11:1 than is sometimes thought.) In 1 Th. 1:6 "and of the Lord" is an intensifying, and the next phrase shows to what degree the Thessalonians are imitators. A question arises, of course, whether the stress in this added phrase is on receiving the word or on much affliction and joy. If it is on the former, then the idea is that in receiving the word the readers become imitators by obeying, and they become a *týpos* (v. 7) simply by becoming believers and turning to God (v. 8). If the emphasis falls on the affliction and joy, imitation has more of the nature of a comparison. In Eph. 5:1 "therefore" points back to 4:32 and

ahead to 5:2. If the point is that God is to be an example, then the same applies to Christ in 5:2. But 5:2 (cf. 4:32) seems rather to be supplying the ethical motive. The point of 5:1, then, is that as children we are to follow God's fatherly will, showing that we are children thereby. To take God as a model is not to be equal with God but to live by his pardoning love. In general, Paul uses the group in three senses: (1) comparison (1 Th. 2:14), (2) following an example (2 Th. 3:7, 9), with a plain implication of Paul's authority, and (3) obeying directions (1 Cor. 4:16; 11:1; 1 Th. 1:6; Eph. 5:1). The NT as a whole does not teach imitation in the primary sense of imitating an example but rather in the predominant sense of discipleship, i.e., of obedience to the word and will of the Lord either directly or by way of the apostles.

6. *The Apostolic Fathers.* The group is more common and more important in these writings. The usage is fluid in Ignatius and 1 Clement and still contains the thought of obedience. Ignatius stresses discipleship in suffering, but without restricting the idea of imitation to martyrdom. The imitation of the passion, even externally, is a key concept in the Martyrdom of Polycarp. Polycarp himself (1.1) calls imprisoned brethren *mimémata* of true love either in a portrayal or a copying of Christ.

[W. MICHAELIS, IV, 659-74]

---

mimnéskomai [to remember], *mneía* [remembrance, mention], *mnémē* [remembrance], *méma* [memorial, grave], *mnēmeíon* [memorial, grave], *mnēmoneúō* [to remember, mention]

---

mimnéskomai.

1. This word, meaning "to remember," is an important one in the LXX, for when God remembers people in grace and mercy (Gen. 8:1; 19:29, etc.), this is a creative event. God remembers the covenant (Gen. 9:15ff.; Ex. 2:24) and the patriarchs (Ex. 32:13). The converse is that Israel remembers God's past acts and commandments (Num. 15:39-40). She is summoned to remember the visitation in Egypt (Dt. 15:15 etc.), not remembering the fleshpots (Num. 11:5), but remembering her own guilt (Dt. 9:7) and God's mercy. In prayer she may call on God to remember (Judg. 16:28; Job 7:7; Ps. 74:2, etc.). If he remembers his people, he also remembers her foes and punishes them (Ps. 137:7). The prayers of Nehemiah combine various facets of remembering (1:8ff.; 5:19, etc.). God can summon Israel to remember and therefore to repent (Mic. 6:5), and one person can ask another to remember and return a favor (Gen. 40:14).

2. In the NT "to remember" is not just a mental act. A word or action serves to kindle the memory. Recollection may strike (Mt. 5:23) or be continually present (1 Cor. 11:2). The Lucan infancy stories link God's remembering and his saving acts, as in the OT (1:54 etc.). In Heb. 8:12 God no longer remembers sin. In Acts 10:4 he remembers the prayers and alms of Cornelius. On the other hand, his remembering means judgment for Babylon in Rev. 16:19. Abraham tells Dives to remember the good things he had enjoyed in this life (Lk. 16:25), and the dying thief asks Jesus to remember him in his kingdom (23:42). The word of Jesus is alive in the disciples through recollection (Mk. 14:72 etc.). At Easter remembrance means understanding (Lk. 24:6, 8). Indeed, as new and true knowledge, remembrance belongs to the work of the Spirit (cf. Jn. 2:22; 12:16; especially 14:26). The gospel also demands recollection (1 Cor. 4:17). The church is to remember the apostle and his teaching (11:2).

This remembering is not just intellectualistic (cf. 2 Pet. 3:1ff.). To remind others is to bear witness to the word of God; to remind oneself is to place oneself totally under this word. Recollection of the sayings of Jesus is central (Acts 11:16), not out of purely historical concern, but in self-judgment, self-dedication, and concern for the brethren (Heb. 13:3).

mneía. This word means "recollection" or "mention." It often occurs in the phrase "to make mention" (Rom. 1:9) or "to have in remembrance" (1 Th. 3:6). Mentioning in prayer is part of Paul's apostolic ministry. The kindly remembering of 1 Th. 3:6 denotes unruffled relationship.

mnḗmē. An important word in Greek thought, *mnḗmē* occurs in the NT only in 2 Pet. 1:15 in a general phrase: "to recall or recollect these things."

mnḗma. This word means "memorial," and may even mean the grave. In antiquity the grave or tomb is a lonely and sinister place. Judaism forbids living in tombs. To lodge in them is a sign of madness or of sacrificing to demons, and brings defilement. In Mk. 5:3 the Gerasene demoniac lives in the tombs. In Mk. 15:46 Jesus is buried in a new tomb hewn out of the rock. It is situated in a garden according to Jn. 19:41. The empty tomb confirms the gospel message of the resurrection of Jesus (Mk. 16:2ff.). Acts 2:29 and 7:16 refer to the tombs of David and the patriarchs; these tombs are memorials for later generations. In Rev. 11:9 (cf. Ps. 79:3) the two witnesses are dishonored by being left unburied.

mnēmeíon. This word means "memorial" and then "grave." The graves of the righteous are adorned (Mt. 23:29); the scribes honor the prophets in their tombs but reject their word. The opponents of Jesus are like whitewashed tombs (Mt. 23:27; Lk. 11:44). Those resting in their graves will hear the voice of Jesus and rise again at the resurrection (Jn. 5:28). The raising of Lazarus anticipates and confirms this (Jn. 11:1ff.). Many come out of their tombs after the death of Jesus (Mt. 27:52-53). While Mark and Luke use *mnḗma* and *mnēmeíon* together, Matthew and John prefer the latter (though Matthew sometimes has *táphos* in the same sense).

mnēmoneúō. This word means "to remember," "to mention." God's works are remembered in the OT in praise and confession (cf. Ps. 6:5). The feasts are appointed for remembrance (Ex. 13:3). God's remembrance will be to all generations (Ex. 3:15). Words and narratives assist it (Ex. 17:14). God protects the remembrance of the righteous but blots out that of sinners (Pss. 112:6; 9:5-6). In the Gospels the disciples are to remember not only God's past acts but also the words and acts of Jesus (cf. Jn. 15:20; 16:4). A new cultic action is appointed for remembrance (*mnēmósynon*, or *anámnēsis*, Mk. 14:9; Mt. 26:13; 1 Cor. 11:24-25; Lk. 22:19). Paul recalls the sayings of Jesus (Acts 20:35). The church is to remember Jesus (2 Tim. 2:8) and its leaders (Heb. 13:7). It should also remember the poor (Gal. 2:10). Remembrance of God's saving acts (Eph. 2:11-12) ought to lead to confession in penitence and gratitude. Faith itself is remembrance. In the apostolic fathers remembrance takes various forms. One is to remember God's commandments, Jesus' words, others in prayer, and Christ and his messengers. [O. MICHEL, IV, 675-83]

---

miséō [to hate]

1. Secular Greek. This term is found from an early period in the sense "to dislike," "to hate." The idea of being hated by the gods is ancient. In Aeschylus the gods hate evil deeds and those who do them. Comedy does not take this so seriously but still retains the thought that the gods are averse to disreputable passions. As a human impulse, hatred can and should be overcome according to Epictetus. Prohibitions of hatred occur in the Mandaean writings along with the golden rule that what is hateful to us we should not do to our neighbor.

2. *The OT and LXX*.

a. Human Aversion and Hostility. The group is common in the LXX for human dislike or hatred. This may come out in overt acts (Gen. 26:27; Dt. 4:42; 21:15). It can take a political form (Dan. 4:16). To love is its opposite (Dt. 21:15). Love can turn into hatred (Judg. 14:16; 2 Sam. 13:15). God commands that hatred should be overcome (Lev. 19:17). The Psalms often refer to the hatred of enemies and ask God, or praise God, for deliverance from it (25:19; 106:10). The wicked hate the righteous without a cause (34:21; 35:19), but they will suffer for it (34:21). Hatred of God's people is hatred of God himself (Num. 10:35).

b. God's Hating. God hates various things, e.g., alien worship (Dt. 12:31), the true cultus without heart worship (Am. 5:21), wickedness in all its forms (Prov. 8:13), and the members that commit it (Prov. 6:16ff.). The righteous hate what God hates (Ps. 97:10; Am. 5:15, etc.). This is not an emotional hatred but a disowning of evil and of those who commit it. As the wicked love evil and hate the good, so the righteous love the good and hate evil (Mic. 3:2). Implied is a rejection in will and deed.

c. Hatred of God and the Righteous. To this hatred of the wicked by God and the righteous corresponds the hatred of the wicked. God visits sins to the third and fourth generation of those who hate him (Ex. 20:5). Hating God means ignoring his commands and persecuting his people. Those who hate God may be strong, and they show their hatred by repaying evil for good, but in the long run their opposition to God is doomed to failure (Pss. 34:21; 35:19; 38:19-20; 69:4; 86:17).

d. Fraternal Hatred. This is forbidden by the OT (Lev. 19:17) and the rabbis. Hating one's neighbor is equivalent to the shedding of blood (cf. Dt. 19:11). God blotted out Sodom because its inhabitants hated one another.

3. *Palestinian Judaism*. Like the OT, the rabbis are aware of a hatred that is both legitimate and imperative. Thus one must hate seducers, traitors, and freethinkers. Yet hatred within the people is a heinous sin that brings down divine punishment. The battle against its poison is important in apocalyptic. Hatred is wicked, sides with falsehood, and fights against the truth. But it will ultimately be overthrown.

4. *Philo*. Philo's usage is close to the Greek. God has declared desire and the body to be worthy of hate. Humans hate virtue but God honors it. There is a forbidden hate, but also a proper hate of the passions of youth and the vices of age. By amendment sinful hate may be turned into love.

5. *The NT*.

a. Human Hatred. Only *miséō* occurs in the NT. This can denote ordinary human hatred, as in Mt. 5:43. Hating one's enemy is not actually commanded in the OT, and Jesus enjoins love instead (Lk. 6:27). In Mt. 6:24 and Lk. 16:13 loving and hating express the thought of preferring the one master to the other.

b. Hatred of God's Community. There is a present and future hatred of the community. The righteous are hated in Lk. 1:71. The disciples will be hated according to Lk. 6:22, 27. Hatred is an apocalyptic sign (Mt. 10:22; Lk. 21:17). The coming of Jesus delivers from it (Lk. 1:71) but also increases it (Mt. 10:22).

c. Hatred in Discipleship. To be a true disciple one must hate all others for Jesus' sake. This is not psychological hatred but a total commitment that gives absolute priority to Jesus. It is to be understood pneumatologically and christologically.

d. God's Hatred. Rejection by God is described as being hated by God in Rom. 9:13 (cf. Mal. 1:2-3). At issue is God's office as Judge. This is a hatred that disowns what is evil (cf. Rev. 2:6). Jesus himself loves righteousness but hates, i.e., repudiates, iniquity (Heb. 1:9 quoting Ps. 45:7).

e. Love and Hate in John. In John divine love conflicts with cosmic hate. The world's hatred for God, Christ, and God's people is sin. The world is blinded and impelled by darkness and therefore hates the light (Jn. 3:20). Since Jesus is the light, the world hates Jesus (7:7). In so doing it hates God (15:23-24). It also hates the disciples (15:18). To live in the light is to be a target of hate. To hate the brethren is to live in darkness (1 Jn. 2:9, 11). Yet there is a proper hatred, as in Jn. 12:25, which states that one must hate one's life in this world in order to keep it for eternal life.

f. Rom. 7:15. In this verse "to hate" is the negative equivalent of "to will." We are forced by sin (7:17), and hence we have no power either to do what we will or not to do what we hate (i.e., do not will).

g. Various Facets. In Lk. 19:14 and Rev. 17:16 hatred means political enmity. The sense in Rev. 18:2 is "hateful." Eph. 5:28ff. shows how unnatural it is not to love one's wife, for people do not hate their own bodies. In Tit. 3:3 hatred is of the very essence of the old aeon. Jude 23 warns against contact with false teachers, probably with licentiousness in view. Whether the hatred extends to those guilty of it as well as their works may be debated, but since the cause of Christ differs so radically from the wickedness of the present aeon, false teachers are certainly to be shunned.

h. Distinctive Elements. Jesus forbids his disciples to hate (Lk. 6:27). Hatred means bondage to the old aeon (1 Jn. 2:9). There is still a holy hatred in the sense of the repudiation of evil, but this is directed primarily against the wrong, not the person (cf. Rev. 2:6). The unconditional claim of Jesus means that earthly ties must be put second, but obviously this is not to be construed as psychological hatred. In the NT even holy repudiation is embraced by divine love. It thus involves a repudiation of all personal hatred.

6. *The Post-Apostolic Age.* The apostolic fathers preserve the NT emphasis. Did. 2:7 forbids hate (cf. Ignatius *Ephesians* 14.2 and Hermas *Similitudes* 9.15.3). There is perhaps a new stress on the beneficial results of loving others, as in Did. 1.3. The church realizes that it is hated by the world and prays for deliverance (1 Clem. 60.3). Wickedness and error are to be hated (Barn. 4.1; 19.2). A new trend, however, appears in 2 Clem. 6.6 which contrasts transitory things (which are to be hated) with eternal things (which are to be loved). Diog. 6.5-6 uses a dualistic image to explain the world's hatred for the church, comparing it to the hatred of the flesh for the soul. But the soul repays this hatred with love.   [O. MICHEL, IV, 683-94]

---

misthós [reward], *misthóō* [to hire], *místhios* [day laborer], *misthōtós* [hired hand], *misthapodótēs* [rewarder], *misthapodosía* [reward, retribution], *antimisthía* [reward, penalty]

A. The Use of the Group.
1. Outside the NT.
(1) The Graeco-Roman World. a. *misthós* means first "reward for work." b. It then means professional "fee." c. A third sense is soldiers' "pay." d. We then find the

meaning "rent." e. Another use is for the "honorarium" of a priest. f. "Payment" for visiting an assembly is another meaning. g. We also find the sense "expenses." h. "Bribe" is sometimes the meaning. i. Human or divine "reward" is another sense, although the Greeks do not normally use the term outside the commercial sphere. j. Divine reward may take the form of "punishment." The verb *misthóō* means "to hire or let." The *misthōtós* is "one who is hired for pay." *místhios* means "hired" or "hired hand." *misthapodótēs* means "one who hires for service."

(2) The LXX. The LXX contains examples of *misthós* in most of the senses listed above. God rewards the righteous in this life as a sign of his grace and blessing (Gen. 15:1; Is. 40:10). "Penal recompense" occurs in Ezek. 27:33. *misthóō* means a. "to hire for reward" (Judg. 9:4), b. "to bribe," and c. "to buy." We find *misthōtós* for "hired hand" in Ex. 12:45 etc., also for "mercenary." *místhios* means "hired worker" in Lev. 19:13 (A).

(3) Philo and Josephus. Philo uses *misthós* for "payment" and "priestly honorarium." He also has *misthōtós* for "laborer." Josephus has *misthós* mostly for ordinary payments, though occasionally for divine rewards based on God's justice.

2. The NT.

(1) *misthós*. The NT uses *misthós* for "pay" in Lk. 10:7 and 1 Tim. 5:18. The laborer is worth his pay (cf. Mt. 10:10). Wages not paid are an accusation against the rich (Jms. 5:4). Wages are paid at the end of the day in Mt. 20:8. The "reward of iniquity" is a fixed expression in Acts 1:8 etc. The iniquity is greed for money in 2 Pet. 2:15. The false teachers want to profit from their wrongdoing, and judgment will overtake them. The use in Jn. 4:36 is figurative, i.e., the reward of fruit for spiritual labor (cf. 1 Cor. 9:18), where Paul finds his reward in making the gospel free to those to whom he brings it. Divine reward is the point in Mt. 5:11-12. This does not come through seeking earthly gain or recognition, but through pure, unselfish obedience (Mt. 6:2ff.). There is a great reward in heaven only where there is unlimited love (Mt. 5:46; Lk. 6:35). Paul sees a relation between the reward of service and the inner commitment to it (1 Cor. 3:8). This is an eschatological reward, not the reward of outward success. Those whose work endures will be rewarded (1 Cor. 3:14). Reward for Paul is not a matter of achievement but of grace (Rom. 4:4). 2 Jn. 8 and Rev. 11:18 both express expectation of reward. But there may also be reward in the sense of punishment for the wicked (Rev. 22:12).

(2) Derivatives. *misthóō* occurs twice for "to hire" in Mt. 20:1ff. *misthōtós* means a "hired sailor" in Mk. 1:20 and a "hired shepherd" in Jn. 10:12. *místhios* means "day laborer" in Lk. 15:17. *misthapodótēs* in Heb. 11:6 refers to the God who rewards those who seek him, i.e., who accept his transcendent reality. *misthapodosía* in Heb. 10:35 means "recompense of reward," i.e., the promise of salvation which is given to those who confidently persevere. In Heb. 11:6, 40 this reward is integrated into the divine purpose. In 11:26, therefore, it is a powerful motive in the moral struggle. Moses can prefer Christ to the treasures of Egypt because he has the promise of eschatological glory. Yet the same word can bear a negative sense in Heb. 2:2, where transgression of the law is said to bring a just punishment or "retribution." *antimisthía*, too, is an ambivalent term. It means "recompense" or "return" in 2 Cor. 6:13, where Paul asks his readers to open up their hearts in childlike response to him. In Rom. 1:27, however, it is the just "penalty" for unnatural conduct. 2 Clem. 6.13 uses it in the good sense as the response to Christ or God for his saving work. In 2 Clem. 11.6 it has the sense of the final reward for righteous acts.

B. The Concept of Reward.

1. The Graeco-Roman World.

(1) The Basic View of Greek Ethics. Greek ethics teaches that goodness and happiness coincide. Happiness is the supreme good, and good acts contribute to it. Harmony is of the essence of happiness, and this may be achieved in this life. Just kings enjoy it, the gods promote it, and knowledge leads to it. Evil acts are punished by madness, lightning, sickness, etc. Retribution here and now makes the belief in future reward or punishment unnecessary. True goodness is sought for its own sake.

(2) Absence of the Biblical Concept of Reward. In rejecting the idea of reward, or of doing good for the sake of reward, the teaching of Socrates and Plato differs from that of the OT and NT. Plato may refer to rewards, but only along the lines of the immanent laws of being, and not in the context of motive. Aristotle, too, believes that reason leads the soul to virtue, supported by the indwelling desire for happiness. For Stoicism morality is obedience to deity as cosmic law. Omnipresent deity sees all things, but happiness resides in virtue, and there is neither reward nor punishment beyond virtue or vice. The only reward is to fulfil the goal of this life; there is no other.

(3) The Mysteries. In contrast, the mysteries are oriented to a future life and reward. Eternal salvation is assured by cultic participation. In Orphic circles asceticism is demanded as a test, but a final judgment will decide between heavenly reward and eternal torment.

(4) The Hellenistic Cults. These cults find a considerable place for future rewards. Egypt in particular shows great concern for the after-life. Whether good or evil deeds predominate will decide the soul's destiny. In Mithraism, too, those whose merits outweigh their sins will be conveyed safely to the heavenly spheres of light.

(5) Roman Religion. Roman religion makes much of a contractual relation to the gods in which there are vows and offerings in return for assistance. In sacrifice worshippers remind the deity of their gifts and expect to be heard in return.

(6) Death as Reward. In antiquity supreme recognition by the deity takes the form of being taken up to the deity. Early death may thus be seen as a reward. Death may also entail deification by a mystical vision that comes to a climax in the heavenly journey.   [H. PREISKER, IV, 695-706]

2. The OT Belief in Recompense.

(1) The Origin. The OT belief in recompense is an ancient one that perhaps has its origin in the idea that good actions bring happy results and bad ones unhappy results. The belief in a personal God gives this thought the shape of recompense in the stricter sense. It is God who relates acts to destiny. A just God, he accords to deeds the due rewards or punishments.

(2) The Meaning and Significance. In Judg. 9:23-24 the quarrel between Abimelech and the Shechemites is interpreted as divine retribution for the sin against the sons of Jerubbaal. In 1 Sam. 15:2-3 the war on Amalek is construed as a divine visitation. In both cases God uses human instruments to serve the purpose of recompense. The concept links and explains historical events. God is at work in these events, and their inner justification thus comes to light. History is not arbitrary. As one may see from Gen. 2:4–11:9, human sin is responsible for the pitiable state of humanity, for it comes up against the divine righteousness. The main thought, then, is not so much that God rewards good acts as that he punishes evil ones. God's saving initiative in the call of Abraham goes far beyond the idea of recompense.

(3) The Belief in the Prophets. In the prophets the holy God is against all sin and his annihilating judgment falls upon it. God never overlooks sin, not even in his elect

people (Am. 1:3–2:16). The relation between God and Israel is a personal relation in which obedience and disobedience mean decision, and recompense rules out a frivolous view of election. The divine retribution proclaims the reality of God and the unconditional nature of his claim. Acceptance or rejection of this claim signifies decision for the future. Since Israel is a unit, recompense is at first collective, falling on the innocent as well as the guilty and children as well as parents. Yet, if applied too strictly, this principle can inhibit repentance. Hence the prophets proclaim that God, too, will "repent" of his judgments if the people repents (Jer. 18:1ff.). Ezekiel carries this thought to the point of an individual retribution that does not permit any blaming of others for one's own fate (Ezek. 18:21ff.). Yet this is not a doctrinaire position but an assurance that God is always willing and ready to deliver the penitent from impending disaster.

(4) Twofold Recompense. The thought of reward as well as retribution is strong in Deuteronomy (cf. ch. 28). The stress is now a positive one, i.e., so to live as not merely to escape judgment but to receive blessing. The history of Israel as told in Judges and Chronicles illustrates the principle. Even the wicked Manasseh is allowed a long life in view of his tardy repentance (2 Chr. 33).

(5) The Wisdom Literature. The idea of twofold recompense is an important one in Proverbs (cf. 11:21, 31; 19:17). Happiness is the goal here, and obeying God is the way to it. Job, however, shows that there is a danger of serving God with the ulterior motive of achieving happiness (Job 1:9). If Ecclesiastes points out that ultimately the good may suffer and the wicked flourish (8:14), Job makes it plain that God himself is not to be bound by the principles of recompense, and Ps. 73 totally transcends the principle with its faith that fellowship with God means more than all recompense in either heaven or earth (73:25-26). [E. WÜRTHWEIN, IV, 706-12]

3. *The Concept of Reward in Later Judaism.* Later Judaism adopts the principle of recompense and combines it with eschatological expectation. Eternal life is promised to the righteous as a reward. There are already rewards and penalties in this life, but death also serves to punish the wicked and to atone for the sins of the righteous. Sometimes the idea of recompense is presented in commercial images, but the thought of divine grace and mercy is also present. Reward provides a strong incentive for keeping the law, although some rabbis insist strongly that the law is to be kept for its own sake and not just for the rewards it brings. While salvation will ultimately depend on God's forgiveness, the stress on human achievement introduces a common note of uncertainty and leads in some circles to the legalistic piling up of merits in order to counterbalance offenses.

4. *The Concept of Reward in the NT.*

(1) The Synoptists.

a. The Synoptic Gospels refer freely to both rewards and punishments. To do God's will is to lay up treasure in heaven (Mt. 6:19ff.). Faithful disciples will be rewarded (Mt. 5:12). The rich young ruler may find treasure in heaven (Mk. 10:21). Rewards are offered for service (Mt. 20:2; 24:45ff.; 19:27). Reward is either recompense for achievement (Mt. 5:7) or compensation for what is renounced (Mt. 10:39). The reward is God's kingdom. Like the punishment that is also threatened (cf. Mt. 11:20ff.; 18:23ff.; Mk. 12:9), it is future; the lot of disciples in this life is persecution. The one exception is in Mk. 10:29-30, where those who give up family for the gospel will find a new family in the community of faith. The community is the sign of the irruption of God's lordship with the coming of Christ and his raising from the dead.

b. Many of the sayings about reward and punishment have obvious parallels in

Judaism. Scholars have thus raised the question how far they derive from Jesus himself and how far they may be fashioned or adapted by the community. Mk. 10:29-30; 11:25, Mt. 13:36ff.; 25:14ff., and Lk. 16:19ff. have all been subjected to minute analysis. Yet sayings like Mk. 9:43ff.; 3:28-29; 12:1ff., Mt. 7:13-14; 10:28; 18:23ff., and Lk. 13:1ff. seem to be undeniably authentic.

c. The concept of reward is important for Jesus. Yet God rewards as a father, not as a judge (Mt. 6:1ff.; 25:34). He demands obedience, but the reward far exceeds what is deserved, and it is thus a matter of divine generosity rather than human merit. This lifts the concept out of the sphere of calculation. In Mt. 20:1ff. the equal treatment of the laborers shows that reward is not according to achievement but according to the prodigality of love. Lk. 17:7ff. makes it plain that the concept of merit is totally repudiated. The promise of the kingdom to children in Mk. 10:15 strengthens this thought. God alone is good (Mk. 10:18), and this means that like children we must simply let the kingdom be granted to us. In Jesus the kingdom has already broken into time and it catches up the disciples in its living power, so that their moral actions are not autonomous achievements that deserve a reward but manifestations of a divine power that moves on to future fulfilment. For Jesus, disciples stand under the eyes of a holy God and owe obedience to him, but salvation is God's own work and in his generosity God grants to receptive hearts a reward which finds in the kingdom its commencement and consummation. The concept of reward is thus taken up into that of the kingdom as the divine glory undeservedly received.

(2) Paul.

a. Paul, too, speaks of twofold recompense (cf. 2 Cor. 5:10; Gal. 6:7-8; Rom. 2:1ff.). He adds promises and threats to his admonitions (cf. Gal. 5:21). He compares himself to a runner seeking a prize (1 Cor. 9:24ff.). Judgment is according to works (1 Cor. 3:13ff.). Paul himself seeks praise from God (1 Cor. 9:14-15). At the same time, the day of judgment is for Paul a day of victory and joy, for the reward is according to grace (Rom. 4:4). The fact that justification is by faith, and that faith itself is God's work, rules out any idea of merit. A new reality has come with Christ's life, death, and resurrection. The Spirit imparts this reality to believers, so that Christian life and work are no longer a matter of their own volition or achievement but of the Spirit's infilling and impulsion (Rom. 8:14; Gal. 5:22; Phil. 2:13). Thus, if Paul does more than all others, it is not he, but the grace of God that is with him (1 Cor. 15:10). There is no place for human boasting (Rom. 3:27). God in his grace gives the incomparable reward of his kingdom (1 Cor. 15:50), of the glory of Christ (Col. 3:4).

b. If a certain tension may thus be seen in Paul, it should be noted that he still speaks of reward and retribution because God is the holy God who demands obedience, because the Spirit manifests himself primarily in the ethical rather than the ecstatic sphere (Gal. 5:22), and because justification itself implies the seriousness of divine judgment. For Paul, then, twofold recompense is a safeguard against libertinism, ecstaticism, and moral passivity. Yet within the framework of grace and faith it involves no dependence on merit. It can accompany, then, a joyous assurance of salvation which need not add up achievements but even in the midst of moral struggle knows the grace of God and stands in the living power of his kingdom. Paul often speaks in traditional terms, but he lifts the concept of reward into the pure air of grace and faith, of the Spirit and joy, where no place remains for externalism or legalism.

c. Ephesians is wholly Pauline in its thinking about reward. The life of believers is grounded in God's saving work (2:5). Only as children of light can they do the works that God expects of them (2:8-9). Only in Christ is there power for truth and love (4:13). The divine election rules out all idea of claim or merit (1:4). Assurance of the inheritance rests on the indwelling of the Spirit (1:13-14). It is in this context that the admonition of 6:8 contains the thought of a divine recompense.

d. The Pastorals. These epistles, too, emphasize that God did not send the Savior because of works (Tit. 3:5; 2 Tim. 1:9). Yet the reverse of works is now God's pity rather than faith (Tit. 3:5). Practical moral concerns, then, are more prominent. God judges on the basis of works (1 Tim. 5:24-25) and there is a reward both in this world (1 Tim. 4:8) and the next (4:16). Yet works are possible only on the basis of the relation to Christ (1 Tim. 2:15).

(3) The Johannine Writings.

a. An echo of the idea of recompense may be caught in Jn. 9:31, but in general all thought of reward is transcended, for the resurrection corresponds to the life that is already present (6:39-40), eternal life fulfils the new birth from above (3:3, 6), all that disciples achieve derives from grace (1:12, 16), and sin and death are overcome by the gift of divine life (1 Jn. 3:9-10; Jn. 5:24ff.).

b. In Revelation judgment is the eschatological expression of the divine majesty. Sinners receive punishment on earth (2:22-23), but supremely at the judgment (11:18 etc.), when the righteous will receive the full blessings of the kingdom (2:7; 7:15-16; 11:12, etc.). Judgment is by works (20:12-13), and good works follow those who die in the Lord (14:13; cf. 7:9ff.; 14:4; 2:19). Yet Revelation is not legalistic, for the names of believers are in the book of life from all eternity (17:8), and already on earth they are kings and priests (1:6) and witnesses. Works, then, are an outworking of redemption and the reward is a public declaration of what they are. Being sealed, they do not fear the judgment but await the manifestation of the glory of God and their hidden kingship.

(4) Post-Pauline Writings.

a. Acts. Acts speaks of the reward of the Spirit for obedience (1:5; 2:1ff.). The presence of the same Spirit brings punishment even on earth to those who set themselves in deceitful and selfish opposition (5:4-5, 9-10; 8:20ff.). Judgment is proclaimed (10:42; 17:31; 24:15), but the Christian life rests on Christ's life, death, and resurrection, and on the ministry of the Spirit, so that grace replaces merit. The inheritance of 24:32 is God's gift rather than an earned payment (cf. the role of forgiveness and faith in 26:18).

b. Hebrews. As Hebrews warns its readers against relapse, the idea of recompense takes on great importance. There is punishment for apostasy, but rest is the reward of faithfulness (4:3), along with salvation (9:28) and the kingdom (12:28). Faith insures a part in the consummation. As faithfulness, it is rewarded; as hope it becomes fulfilment. Yet faith has already experienced the future reality (6:19). Christians live by the Spirit of grace (10:29) and bear the powers of the new aeon (6:5). For them the last judgment is grace (4:16), so that they move toward it with confident joy (10:19ff.). They do not have to rely on meritorious achievement but rest on grace (4:16).

c. James. Christians are regenerated by the word of truth (1:18). It is faith that expresses itself in works (2:14ff.), leads to prayer (1:6), and is confirmed in affliction (1:2). Suffering, not reward, comes in this life, and although faith is futile without works, there is no place for merit, since faith is God's gift (2:5), election is the basis of the reward (2:5), and salvation rests on the implanted word (1:21) and the indwelling Spirit (4:5).

d. 1 Peter. This work, designed to strengthen believers in face of persecution, refers to the future inheritance as a recompense (5:6) and issues a plain reminder of the judgment. Yet again the basis of the Christian life is faith in Christ (1:3), Christians are regenerate (2:2) and set in the reality of the resurrection (1:3-4), and their salvation (1:9) or glorification (1:11) is the consummation of their calling rather than a merited payment.

e. Jude and 2 Peter. In their warnings against heretics, these epistles stress divine judgment (Jude 4, 6-7; 2 Pet. 2:3, 9) and expectation of the kingdom (2 Pet. 3:13). Here too, however, divine power is the basis of godliness (2 Pet. 1:3-4), and as partakers of the divine nature (1:4) believers may be at peace (3:14). In faith, prayer, and the love of God they look forward to being presented faultless before the presence of God's glory with rejoicing (Jude 20ff.).

(5) The Meaning of Reward for Jesus and Primitive Christianity. The NT speaks freely of reward but transcends the concept. Strict recompense would mean judgment for all of us. Reward, then, is a term for God's gracious generosity. It reminds us that we are set before God and it gives us an awareness of the gift of the kingdom. It implies, however, the indwelling of the Spirit, so that calculation is ruled out, and the reality of faith and the Spirit is the true incentive to moral action. Reward is the loving gift of the Father toward which believers may move with confident and childlike trust in the love that will perfect their calling in the glory of the kingdom.

[H. PREISKER, IV, 712-28]

mneía, mnémē, mnéma, mnēmeíon, mnēmoneúō → mimnḗskomai

---

moicheúō [to commit adultery],   *moicháō* [to commit adultery],   *moicheía* [adultery],   *moíchos* [adulterer],   *moichalís* [adulteress, adulterous]

A. Use of the Group. *moicheúō* in the active means "to commit adultery" or "to seduce," and in the passive or middle "to be seduced" or (in the case of a woman) "to commit adultery" (cf. Mt. 5:27-28, 32). *moicháō* means "to commit adultery" or "to adulterate." *moicheía* is "adultery," "illicit intercourse," while *moíchos* means "adulterer" or "lover," and *moichalís* "adulterous" and as a noun "adulteress," "mistress," "harlot."

B. Adultery in the OT and Judaism.

1. The Decalogue protects marriage (Ex. 20:14; Dt. 5:18) and thus forbids its violation by adultery; death is the penalty for transgression (Dt. 22:22). Where a wife is suspected of adultery, the husband may request trial by bitter water (Num. 5:16ff.), but he is not obliged to take steps against her (cf. Mt. 1:19).

2. Hosea compares the apostasy of Israel against God to adultery (2:4ff.; 3:1-2; 4:12ff.). Jeremiah uses the same comparison in 2:1; 5:7; 9:1. Israel breaks the marriage bond, and Jerusalem will bear the punishment of an adulteress (13:22). Ezekiel interprets Israel's history as a story of constant adultery (16:32; 23:37ff.).

3. Proverbs contains many warnings against marital infidelity (2:16ff.; 6:26ff.). Wine and strange women are to be avoided (23:31ff.; 7:5ff.). In Sirach the adulteress is a threefold transgressor: against God, her husband, and the children she may bear to another. Adulterous old men are especially offensive. Philo thinks adultery corrupts the soul as well as the body and sows a blameworthy seed.

4. Judaism gives more precise definitions of the act and the penalties. It distinguishes between adultery with Jews and non-Jews, and lays down that there must be warnings and witnesses if there are to be penalties. Divorce replaces death as the main

punishment, and confession replaces the ceremony of bitter water. Adultery is a serious sin, the thought is equated with the act, and eternal judgment is the final penalty.

C. Adultery in the Greek and Roman World. Greek law strictly forbids adultery by women and grants to the husband or family the right of revenge (though this is limited by public law, and may be waived in favor of a public complaint). Guilty wives are to be put away. Ideally, moralists urge fidelity on husbands too, but in practice intercourse with the *hetaíra* is accepted. Roman law allows the husband to punish an adulterous wife (even by death), and a father has similar rights of punishment or revenge. Later, adultery becomes a penal offense with banishment as the punishment, but in the moral degeneration of the imperial period the infidelity of both husbands and wives is common.

D. The Group in the NT.

1. Literal Use. The NT puts the husband as well as the wife under the obligation of fidelity. Marriage is a lifelong partnership, divorce is contrary to God's original purpose (Mt. 19:6ff.), and remarriage after divorce is adultery (Mt. 5:32; 19:9; Mk. 10:11-12; Lk. 16:18). Adultery is present even in the desire (Mt. 5:28), so absolute is the divine requirement. Yet Jesus rejects hypocritical self-righteousness and proclaims forgiveness even for the adulterer (cf. Jn. 8:1ff.), although on the plain presupposition of repentance, and therefore without sapping the validity of the divine command (Jn. 8:11). Paul upholds the teaching of Jesus in the lax Hellenistic world (1 Cor. 5:1ff.; 6:9). Adultery is not just a matter of civil law but conflicts with God's holy will (1 Th. 4:3). Women are joint heirs of life and thus have the same honor as men (1 Pet. 3:7). Adultery excludes from the kingdom (1 Cor. 6:9), and marital fidelity must be kept intact (Heb. 13:4). Even the lustful glance is sinful (2 Pet. 2:14). The love of spouses is the positive relation that the prohibition of adultery protects (Rom. 13:9).

2. Figurative Use. The NT, too, uses the group figuratively for infidelity to God. Those who resist Jesus are an adulterous generation (Mt. 12:39). Love of the world is adultery against God (Jms. 4:4). Adultery is a figure for acceptance of the false teaching of the prophetess in Rev. 2:20; the children are her followers.

[F. HAUCK, IV, 729-35]

---

mólis [hardly],   *mógis* [hardly]

Both *mólis* and *mógis* mean "hardly," "with difficulty" (the two forms are interchangeable). In Rom. 5:7 *mólis* occurs in a parenthetical note. In human life people are unlikely to die even for the good, though perhaps some would do so. In contrast, Christ offers his life even for the ungodly. In 1 Pet. 4:18 we have a quotation from Prov. 11:31 LXX. The sufferings of the age make great demands on believers, so that it is only with difficulty that they will survive the test and stand in the judgment. The author's aim is to spur them on to faithfulness and impress on them their responsibility.

[J. SCHNEIDER, IV, 735-36]

---

molýnō [to soil, defile],   *molysmós* [defilement]

---

molýnō. a. This means "to soil," "to smear." b. Religiously it means "to defile." It occurs three times for religious or cultic defilement in the NT. Contact with paganism defiles the conscience of the weak in 1 Cor. 8:7. In Rev. 3:4 and 14:4 the reference is not just to sexual continence in the strict sense but to the faithfulness of the community (cf. 14:1) as the bride of Christ (cf. 2 Cor. 11:2).

molysmós. This word means "defilement" in either a physical or a religious sense. In the one instance in the NT (2 Cor. 7:1) the reference is to defilement by sharing a pagan way of life; believers are to separate themselves from paganism (6:14ff.).

[F. HAUCK, IV, 736-37]

morphḗ → *mémphomai; monḗ* → *ménō*

---

monogenḗs [only begotten]

A. The Usage outside the NT. In compounds with *genḗs,* adverbs describe the nature rather than the source of derivation. Hence *monogenḗs* is used for the only child. More generally it means "unique" or "incomparable." The LXX has the first sense in Judg. 11:34 and the second in Ps. 22:20. *agapētós* occurs in Gen. 22:2, 12 where *monogenḗs* might have been used (cf. Mk. 1:11), but while the only child may be "beloved," the terms are not synonymous. Philo refers to the *lógos* as *prōtógonos* rather than *monogenḗs.* Ps. Sol. 18:4 refers to God's chastisement coming on Israel as his firstborn and only-begotten son.

B. The Use in the NT.
1. In the NT the term occurs only in Luke, John, and Hebrews. Isaac is *monogenḗs* in Heb. 11:7, and the son of the widow at Nain (Lk. 7:12), the daughter of Jairus (8:42), and the demoniac boy (8:42) are all only children.

2. Only John uses the term for Jesus. John calls Christians the *tékna* of God rather than his *huioí* (cf. 1:12; 11:52; 1 Jn. 3:1). Jesus is the only *huiós;* his unique relation to God is thus given emphasis. God is the *patḗr ídios* of Jesus; no others stand in the same relationship (Jn. 5:18). It is thus that Jesus is *monogenḗs* (Jn. 1:14; 3:16; 1 Jn. 4:9). Because he is the only-begotten Son, his sending into the world is a supreme proof of God's love (Jn. 3:16). But it also means that decision for life or death takes place in relation to him (3:18). As the only-begotten Son he shares all things with the Father. His glory is not merely like that of an only child; it is that of the only-begotten Son (1:14). He is not just unique; he is the Son, for combined with *huiós* the term describes his origin. The risen Lord is also the preexistent Lord, who is with God, is loved by him, and shares his glory from all eternity (17:5, 24). Whether or not this implies actual begetting by God is debated by some, but 1 Jn. 5:18 definitely teaches this, for sonship is here presented in terms of begetting. John does not lift the veil of mystery that lies over the eternal begetting, for he aims to awaken faith rather than give systematic knowledge. Yet eternal begetting is an implication of *monogenḗs* in its distinctive application to Jesus.   [F. BÜCHSEL, IV, 737-41]

---

morphḗ [form], *morphóō* [to form, fashion], *mórphōsis* [form], *metamorphóō* [to transform]

morphḗ.

A. Greek Usage.
1. The Meaning. morphḗ means a. "form," "external appearance" (humans, animals, plants, statues, etc.), b. "good pleasure," and c. "kind," "manner."

2. Synonyms. In its basic meaning *morphē* is synonymous with *eídos, idéa,* and *schḗma,* but as the form proper to a being in its objective reality it has its own nuance for all the interchangeability.

3. Philosophical Use. morphē has no unequivocal sense in philosophy. Thus it is used for light and darkness as forms of being, for the forms of appearance of numbers, or for distinctive forms of a concept. Aristotle distinguishes between form and matter, but there is a relation between essence (or nature) and form, and ultimately there is a unity of form and matter. Aristotle can also use form for the various kinds of a virtue like courage. The term never achieves any fixity that influences ordinary usage, and from Stoicism onward it is rare in philosophy. Philo contrasts unformed matter with the creation, in which all things have received their forms. In general *morphē* in all its nuances represents what may be seen by the senses and not what is mentally apprehended.

4. The LXX. morphē is rare in the LXX. It occurs for "form" in Job 4:16 and "expression" in Dan. 3:19. Another rendering has it for "color" (of the face) in Dan. 5:6.

B. *morphē theoú* in the Greek World.

1. The idea that deity has form occurs frequently in Greek religion (cf. the concept of epiphany). The gods take shifting forms in Homer, and legends narrate the presence of gods or spirits or heroes in bodily form. In magic, spiritual forces are asked to take bodily form, and in Hermes mysticism the primal man, as the son of the father of all things, is of the same form.

2. Doubts. Doubts soon arise as to whether one should think of deity assuming bodily form. While popular belief retains the concept, philosophy censures such anthropomorphism as unworthy of the gods. Socrates looks for deity in its works, and Plato argues that the gods remain in their own perfect forms. With the belief in immortality, the idea is present that the gods have a supraterrestrial form that believers will share after death. Thus, while there is criticism of the idea that gods take various terrestrial forms, philosophy sublimates the concept by ascribing to gods their own forms.

C. The Form of God in the OT and Judaism.

1. In the OT the idea of God having a perceptible form is totally alien. For this reason anthropomorphisms may be used freely. The theomorphic view of humanity is more important than the anthropomorphic view of deity. When God manifests himself in sensory form (cf. Gen. 15:17; Ex. 1:26ff.), this sets limits as well as giving expression. Not even the prophets may see God face to face, and no image of God may be made. The personal and ethical concept of God resists sensory objectification.

2. Judaism, too, finds no place for statements about the form of God. Philo says emphatically that God is not *anthrōpómorphos,* and Josephus accepts the philosophical criticism of Greek anthropomorphisms and scoffs at attempts by painters or sculptors to depict the deity. The rabbis have a clear sense that one can speak about the form of God only in a figurative way.

D. The *morphē* of Christ in the NT.

1. The "another form" of Mk. 16:12 is a human form but different from that which Jesus bore during his earthly life (cf. Lk. 24:16).

2. Jesus undergoes a change of form at the transfiguration.

3. Phil. 2:6-7 speaks in hymnic style of the "form" of Christ. Exhorting to unselfish humility, the passage says that Jesus took the form of a *doúlos* in an act of exemplary

renunciation. Prior to the incarnation he is in the form of God, i.e., he bears the image of the divine majesty, and after the incarnation he is exalted again as the *kýrios*. In antithesis to the earlier and the later glory, his incarnation is a time of humble service when he bends his own will to that of others. His self-denial is not just the opposite of a selfish exploitation of his position but stands in the sharpest possible contrast to his former mode of being in divine power and splendor. He comes down from the height of glory to the abyss of lowliness as the Redeemer who is both above history and in history. There is here no mythical concept of a god in human form, nor is there any idea of a metamorphosis. Materially the phrase *morphḗ theoú* is wholly in the biblical tradition; it is not the same as the *eikṓn toú theoú* of, e.g., 2 Cor. 4:4; Col. 1:15.

morphóō. In the active this word means "to form," "to fashion," e.g., artists their materials, and in the passive "to take on form" (especially in the womb). The only NT instance is in Gal. 4:19, where the growth of Christ in believers is compared to development in the womb. This growth is an ongoing process, both open and secret, and both a gift and a task, with maturity as the goal.

mórphōsis. This word means "forming" or "shaping" (e.g., shaping trees), and then, as the result of this activity, "form" or "figure." In Rom. 2:17ff. the law is the representation or embodiment of knowledge and truth in Jewish eyes. In 2 Tim. 3:5 the reference is to an external form of religion with no inner power, i.e., a mere appearance without the corresponding reality.

metamorphóō.

A. Linguistic Data. This word, predominantly middle or passive, means "to change into another form." The change may be an external one, or a change of state, or an inner change.

B. Comparative Religion. A common religious belief is that the gods can change into other forms. In apocalyptic and mysticism humans change into a supraterrestrial form. In Judaism such a change is a gift of eschatological salvation. In the mysteries it involves liberation from the body and deification. Magic promises a change into divine form, and magicians claim a godlike nature through union with the divine form.

C. The NT. A transformation into supraterrestrial form takes place at the transfiguration in Mk. 9:2 and Mt. 17:2. The context is eschatological. What is promised to believers takes place already for Jesus as the bearer of a unique call. It does so as the anticipation and guarantee of the new reality. It shows that the glory of consummation is the goal of his way of suffering and death. As regards believers, transformation begins already in this life. Seeing the glory of the Lord in the Spirit, they are changed into the image of him whose glory they see (2 Cor. 3:18). This is not mystical deification but a reattainment of the divine likeness. It does not take place by rituals but by the ministry of the Spirit. It is not for an elite few but for all Christians. It is not just a hope for the future (cf. 1 Cor. 15:44ff.) but begins already with the coming of the Spirit as a deposit. It carries with it an imperative (Rom. 12:2). Set in the new aeon, Christians must reshape their conduct in accordance with it. This takes place as their minds and wills are renewed by the Spirit. They are thus to become what they are.   [J. Behm, IV, 742-59]

→ *sýmmorphos, symmorphízō, symmorphóō*

---

móschos [calf]

The calf figures a good deal in the sacrificial rules of Leviticus. The making of a golden calf is the great sin of Israel at Sinai (Ex. 32:4). One of the creatures of the vision of Ezek. 1:4ff. has the face of a *móschos* (cf. also *taúros* in Dt. 32:14; Is. 1:11; Heb. 9:13). In Lk. 15:11ff. a fatted calf is killed in honor of the returning prodigal. The blood of goats and calves is mentioned in Heb. 9:12, 19 (bulls in 9:13 and 10:4). The scene in Rev. 4 is based on Ezek. 1:4ff. (cf. also Is. 6:1ff.). The creatures are angelic powers attesting to God's presence in the visible world. 1 Clem. 52 quotes Pss. 7:16; 50:14-15, etc. to show that God prefers confession to the offering of bullocks. Barn. 8.1ff. tries to give a christological sense to the red heifer of Num. 19 and to relate the rite as a whole to the saving work of Christ and the apostolic preaching.   [O. MICHEL, IV, 760-62]

---

mýthos [myth]

A. Problems Raised by the Term.
a. The word *mýthos,* or myth, can be highly regarded when it is taken to express a total view of things or to have the dignity of supreme religious value. Basic here is the opinion that life can be expressed only in terms of myth.

b. Myth also enjoys high regard when, as a unity of form and content, it is viewed as a symbol whereby philosophical systems can be found in primitive antiquity.

c. Divorced from history, myth may also be accorded high religious value when it is seen as the absolute expression of religious institutions, experiences, or ideas.

d. For those who think that historical reality and truth are essential to genuine revelation, myth has no religious value. Thus the NT opposes myth to history (2 Pet. 1:16) and truth (2 Tim. 4:4), and declares it to be incompatible with the divine *oikonomía* and with true piety (1 Tim. 1:4; 4:7). Many skeptics who dismiss the NT stories themselves as myths agree with this evaluation.

B. The Development of the Meaning.
1. *"Thought."* The etymology is much debated. Derivation from *mýō* ("to close"), *myéō* ("to initiate"), or the cry *mý!* does not commend itself. The stem is probably an Indo-European word with the basic meaning "thought." The use of the verb *mythéomai* supports this theory, as does the use in Homer.

2. When they are merely thought, *mýthoi* may be intentions, opinions, ideas, reasons, or counsels.

3. Thoughts, however, have an urge to express themselves. The term *mýthos* can thus take on the senses a. "saying" (with such nuances as proverb, statement, reply, proposal, speech, report, or discussion), b. "word," and c. "story" (either as a story of facts, i.e., a report etc., or as an unauthenticated story, i.e., a rumor, legend, fairy tale, fable, plot of a play or poem, or myth in the narrower sense of a story about the gods).

C. Myth in the Greek World and Hellenism.
1. *The Many Senses.* Writers sense the tension in a word that can mean both factual story (or even fact) on the one side and invented story on the other. This tension comes to light in translation and involves the possibility of mistranslation.

2. Antonyms. On the analogy of *épos, mýthos* becomes an antonym of *érgon.* On the other hand, it also stands in antithesis to *lógos,* which is more closely associated with truth (*alḗtheia*). As distinct from *lógos, mýthos* is a. the fairy story in contrast to credible history, b. the mythical form of an idea in contrast to its dialectical presentation, or c. popular myth in contrast to the kernel of truth that it contains.

3. mýthoi in the Intellectual World of Greece.

a. The Cultus and Religious Teaching. Cultus and myth are originally a unity as religious experience takes shape both as cultic action that represents deity and as stories that proclaim it. The guardians of cultus and myth are the priestly theologians and the poets (in religious drama). Yet the poets, like the philosophers, treat the myths with some skepticism (cf. the humorous scenes in Homer and the rough handling in Euripides and Aristophanes). Aristotle finds in myths a symbolic expression of pantheistic theology, but the ideas of fate and right tend to dispel their authority. The enlightened thus treat myths either as crafty inventions or as exaggerations of real history. Yet myths retain their religious force even into the Hellenistic period.

b. Poetry. Even when it loses its religious power myth can evoke fear and pity and it thus remains the raw material of poetry. As Plato says, there is no poetry without myths. Myth dies only when it loses, not its credibility, but its force as an ideal and example.

c. Philosophy. Philosophers, too, make use of myths. Plato refuses to scorn them; they are for him the symbolical reality of the sphere that is accessible only to faith. He does not accept them as they are, for only fragments fit into this view. With great inventive power he uses these fragments to create new philosophical statements. He also produces new mythical constructs as vehicles for his rich and varied thinking. Myth carries the line of *lógos* beyond the frontiers of conceptual knowledge. The union of *mýthos* and *lógos* is linked to the fact that Plato's philosophy is also a doctrine of salvation concerned with human destiny.

d. Spiritual Direction and Education. Both traditional and newly invented myths serve an educational purpose. This is true in Hesiod and Plato. It is less true in Aristotle, who gives a higher place to *lógos,* and later *mýthos* is used only in the interests of morality or as a first stage in rhetorical instruction. Plato finds a special place for the fairy tale, which with its mixture of the invented and the true is well adapted for the teaching of children.

4. The Allegorical Interpretation of Myth. Whereas Plato uses myths to embody truths, a later age seeks to discover truth in traditional myths, thereby warding off attacks on their irrationality and immorality. Stoicism in particular produces masters in the art of allegorizing.

5. The Evaluation and Use of Myth.

a. Stoicism. The Stoics present myths as primitive philosophy in historical dress. They find in them their own natural philosophy and ethical instruction.

b. For Stoicism myth is valid as a symbol. Poseidonius goes further, regarding it as the expression of the higher needs of the mind which thought alone cannot meet.

c. The mystery religions treat myth as the representation of experiences that either cannot or should not be given rational expression. Later, however, even the mysteries put the meaning of myth in words by means of allegorical exposition.

d. In connection with the mysteries mythical themes play a symbolical role on monuments and sarcophagi.

e. Gnosticism dethrones both ancient myth and history alike. Allegory is here a revolutionary instrument for the transvaluation of all values, both pagan and biblical. It blends the two in the new myth of Gnostic speculation.

6. Criticism and Repudiation of Myth. Plato is openly critical of traditional myths, and will allow mythical poets no place in his ideal state. Aristotle, Epicurus, Plutarch, and others follow a similar line and disqualify even allegorical exegesis. In their eyes myth is childish, untrue, and of little moral worth.

7. Conclusion. The ancient world treats myth in many different ways including joyous acceptance, profound interpretation, allegorical exegesis, and frivolous mockery, but there is no basic repudiation on religious grounds outside the biblical sphere.

D. *mýthos* and Myths in the OT (LXX) and Judaism.

1. The word *mýthos* is an alien one to the OT.

2. Whether myth itself is alien has been much debated. Some scholars think the stories of Gen. 1ff. are myths, but if the OT adopts mythical materials it historicizes them, or, as in the case of the prophets, simply uses them as poetic images (cf. Is. 14; Ezek. 29). Apocalyptic relates several myths to the last time, and Wisdom literature possibly has a hidden basis in the Sophia myth. The rabbis use even Greek myths as parables.

E. *mýthoi* in the NT.

1. Myth as an Alien Body in the NT. The NT uses the term only in the negative statements of 1 Tim. 1:4; 4:7; Tit. 1:14; 2 Pet. 1:16; 2 Tim. 4:4. The gospel proclaims God's great acts in history (Acts 2:11). It is thus *lógos,* not *mýthos* (cf. 2 Pet. 1:19).

2. The Problem of NT mýthoi. What are the *mýthoi* that the NT repudiates?

(1) A first question is whether one is to distinguish between the *mýthoi* of present and future heretics (1 Tim. 4 and 2 Tim. 4). There is no good reason to do so. A further question is whether the *mýthoi* of 1 and 2 Timothy and those of Titus are the same. Both seem to have the same derivation, both threaten the truth of the gospel (2 Tim. 4:4; Tit. 1:14), and both involve moral defects (1 Tim. 4:7; Tit. 1:16).

(2) But are these Hellenistic or Jewish *mýthoi?* Some commentators think they are stories of the gods in the Greek sense, others think they are of a Gnostic type, relating the genealogies to the Gnostic aeons, but it is more likely that we are to see in them Jewish fables, most likely connected with a Jewish Gnostic sect.

(3) The reference in 2 Peter is eschatological, and here again it seems that we have *mýthoi* of a Jewish type which the author contrasts with the apostolic proclamation of Christ's coming glory.

3. Myth, Truth, and History.

(1) Myth and Truth for the Greeks. The Greeks can speak of the truth in *mýthos,* but Plato, while regarding *mýthos* as a reflection of truth, thinks that it is in itself only an uncertain or false *lógos.* Hence the term comes to be regarded as the opposite of truth.

(2) Myth and History in Antiquity. At first myth is regarded as a first stage of historical writing, and even later it is seen as an element in history, and history itself is turned into myth (cf. the exploits of Alexander).

(3) Myth, Truth, and History in the NT. The NT gives new depth to the distinction between myth and truth by way of the historical actualizing of truth in Christ. Truth is here divine fact with the force of historical reality. A word or history cannot contain truth if it has no relation to reality. There is thus a sharp antithesis between myth and truth.

4. Designations and Relations of NT mýthoi.

(1) 2 Tim. 4:4. Myths here, scornfully called "the" myths, are opposed to the *lógos* of the gospel and are spread by people who cater to human likings. The *lógos* is the incarnate word; if it is replaced by myth, all is lost, and even if it is only linked with myth, it is betrayed. The teachers now are philosophers rather than the original poets of antiquity.

(2) 1 Tim. 4:7. Myths here are called ungodly and foolish. They have nothing to do with the true God and are indeed unholy and immoral, as the Greeks themselves come to perceive (cf. Plato). They are also silly, i.e., old wives' tales rather than education-ally valuable fairy stories.

(3) 1 Tim. 1:4. The point in this verse is that interest in *mýthoi* and genealogies, while possibly harmless in itself, does not serve the divine work of salvation that builds on faith but leads to speculation, perhaps by way of allegorical exposition.

(4) Tit. 1:14. This sharp warning identifies the *mýthoi* as Jewish (probably the allegorical development of haggadic and halakic pieces), and argues that they are a human wresting of the truth which turns away from sound faith.

(5) 2 Pet. 1:16. The author has himself seen the glory of the Lord which will one day be manifested to the world. He thus rejects proclamation in the form of self-invented speculation and resists the accusation that the apostolic message, based on OT prophecy and the gospel history, itself contains *mýthoi*. As regards the first point, it is a feature of myths that they are poetic inventions, and that as such they may be freely altered or adapted by philosophers and priests. As regards the second point, Philo, too, sees that biblical religion differs from pagan religion by reason of its basis in history rather than myth, although he himself, with his allegorizing, treats the biblical history as though it were myth when he finds difficult passages. Origen follows a similar course, especially in answer to the charge of Celsus that the biblical stories are inferior and valueless even as myths (the common accusation of educated pagans; cf. Porphyry and Julian). 2 Peter, however, insists on the historical reality of the Christian message on the basis of the prophetic word and the apostolic eyewitness.

5. Myths in the Gospel? In the light of comparative religion, it is sometimes argued that there are mythical elements in the Gospels and that causal connections exist between the ideas of Paul and John and the mythical concepts of the age. The NT authors obviously make use of the ideas and vocabulary of their time, but there is more analogy than borrowing. Furthermore, as in the OT, what is analogous is his-toricized, or integrated into the sphere of God's kingdom. The apostles preach the mighty reality of Christ by which all else is transformed.

F. The Evaluation of Myths in the Early Church.

1. The Apologists mock pagans for their own myths and reject their right to alle-gorize them. Origen argues that pagan myths are inseparable from a pagan view of God. Ancient church orders view teachers with great reserve because they have to teach myths, and a primary objection to Gnosticism is that its stories are *mýthoi*.

2. Christian (like Jewish) art makes some use of pagan myth, e.g., in the depiction of the Good Shepherd as Hermes. Here, then, is some impulse, by way of allegorizing, toward the development of a Christian mythology. In the main, however, the church insists that there is no relation between NT *lógos* and myth.

G. Conclusions.

1. Myth as a Form of Religious Communication. Antiquity uses myth to teach children (the fairy story) and then to teach adults (philosophical allegorizing). The NT, however, is from first to last the narration of facts. The form may vary (cf. the Synoptists and John), but the theme is always what God says and does.

2. *Myth as Parable*. In its later stages paganism uses myths as parables. The NT, too, is full of illustrations, but these are pure parables that never lay claim to historical truth but are likenesses of the kingdom. In the long run, they can be dispensed with (Jn. 16:25).

3. *Myth as Symbol*. Paganism finally regards myth as a symbol of eternal realities. In the NT, however, the central symbol is the harsh reality of the cross, which cannot be divorced from its personal representative and its historical setting, with which no myth can be integrated, and on which no myth can be imposed.

4. *A New Use of the Term?* In two ways an attempt might be made to bring myth into the context of the biblical data. The first is by construing myth as an account of facts in the divine realm. But this involves an almost impossible reorienting of the term. It also carries with it the risk of a dehistoricizing which will negate the incarnation, i.e., the intersection of divine and earthly history, on which everything depends. The second way is to regard the gospel as fulfilled myth. But this is to presuppose that myth is not just a product of human longing and to bring the mythical theologians of paganism into dubious proximity to the prophetic theologians of the old covenant. Can one truly say, in the light of Jn. 14:6, that there are traces of the Logos in myth?

→ *alḗtheia, genealogía, lógos, paramythéomai*   [G. Stählin, IV, 762-95]

> *myktērízō* [to turn up one's nose],   *ekmyktērízō* [to sneer]

myktērízō. This word, which literally means "to suffer from nose-bleeding," takes on the sense "to turn up one's nose." It is thus a common term for scorn in the LXX, e.g., scorn of enemies in 2 Kgs. 19:21, of the slothful in Prov. 12:8, of pagan gods in 1 Kgs. 18:27. It is a sin when directed against God's messengers (2 Chr. 36:16) or chastisements (Prov. 1:30) or against parents (Prov. 15:5). The only NT instance is in Gal. 6:7, where it is a term for the mocking of God by a life that will not accept the lordship of the Spirit (cf. 5:25). The reference is not to verbal scoffing but to despising God by a whole way of life.   [H. Preisker, IV, 796]

ekmyktērízō.

A. **In the LXX.** This word, too, means "to turn up one's nose." In the LXX it is the rendering of many Hebrew originals. It relates 1. to the scorning of God and his messengers and followers by the ungodly (cf. Prov. 1:30; 23:9). Fools are scoffers, and this is their real offense (Prov. 11:12; 15:5, 20). 2. There is then a scorning of the wicked by the righteous and even by God himself (cf. Is. 37:22; Ps. 2:4; Prov. 1:26). 3. The present situation is that the righteous are exposed to the scorn of the wicked, partly as chastisement, partly as blessing.

B. **In the NT.** Lk. 23:35 quotes Ps. 22:7-8 in the story of the passion. It thus gives historical concreteness to a general phenomenon. Mt. 27:41 and Mk. 15:31 use *empaízein* (cf. Lk. 23:36), which refers more to the outward action, while *ekmyktērízein* denotes the inward attitude. Another instance is in Lk. 16:14, where the Pharisees scoff at the sayings of Jesus about mammon. While the Pharisees are lovers of money, they can hardly be scoffing at the fact that Jesus, although poor, teaches about poverty and wealth, or at the idea that wealth and piety are incompatible. More probably (cf.

v. 15) they are expressing an attitude of conceited superiority which a priori rejects the bearer of revelation. The point is not, then, a psychological one, but rather that (as in the OT) mockery is an integral burden of discipleship, or, in this instance, of the messianic mission of Jesus and the suffering it entails.

[G. BERTRAM, IV, 796-99]

---

mýron [ointment], *myrízō* [to anoint]

The use of ointment (vegetable oil to which sweet-smelling materials are added) is of great antiquity, e.g., in medicine, the cultus, magic, embalming, feminine adornment, and festal decoration. The main NT use is in the stories of anointing. The costly ointment is spikenard in Mk. 14:3 par. Jn. 12:3. The head of Jesus is anointed in Matthew and Mark, while Mary anoints the feet in John (cf. also Lk. 7:6ff.). The ointment is carried in the customary alabaster box, and this is probably opened at the neck (Mk. 14:3). Jesus explains that the anointing points ahead to his burial (Mt. 26:12; Mk. 14:8; Jn. 12:7). In Lk. 23:56 the women prepare spices and ointments to give fragrance to the tomb. In Rev. 18:13 *mýron* is included in the cargo of the great fleet. The verb *myrízō* occurs only in Mk. 14:8 in the sense "to anoint."

[W. MICHAELIS, IV, 800-801]

---

mystḗrion [mystery, secret], *myéō* [to be initiated, learn the secret]

---

mystḗrion.

A. The Mysteries in the Greek World and Hellenism.
1. The Cultic Concept.
a. The word *mystḗrion* is used for many mystery cults which enjoined silence on their devotees, so that our knowledge of them is fragmentary. They are cultic rites portraying the destinies of a god in such a way as to give the devotees a share in them.

b. Those who wish to participate must undergo initiation in a ceremony which embraces various offerings and purifications, which may itself be called a mystery, and which involves certain conditions and new relationships.

c. The mysteries promise initiates salvation (*sōtēría*) by the dispensing of cosmic life. The deities are chthonic deities, the mysteries are connected with the seasons, and in general the gods undergo sufferings that are enacted in cultic dramas expressing joy and sorrow, birth and death, ending and new beginning. The priests and initiates enter into the drama and effect union with the gods by various sacramental actions, e.g., meals, fertility rites, baptisms, investitures, and symbolical journeys. What is denoted is a change which, by way of participation with the deity, insures them of future salvation. The mysteries are rituals of death and life that prepare the devotees for the life to come. Examples from Eleusis, the Dionysus rite, and the Attis and Isis mysteries all support this.

d. In all mysteries the vow of silence expresses the distinction between initiates and others. This vow is an essential feature, as all the evidence goes to show. It does not seem to extend to the essential message, but rather to the rites, symbols, formulas, etc. These must be protected against profanation, e.g., by frivolous imitation. The special sanctity of the cultic actions is thus the true reason for the command of silence.

2. The Mysteries in Philosophy. Plato adopts the ideas and terminology of the mysteries when he speaks of a divinely appointed way to the goal of the vision of true being. In Plato mysteries are hidden teachings rather than cultic actions. This opens the door for philosophy to represent itself as a special way of knowledge whereby initiates are given an understanding of doctrines that are concealed from others. The aim in this mystagogic philosophy is to distinguish between real truth and its symbolical appearance. The knowledge itself is divinely inspired and its theme is the allegorical interpretation of names, rites, myths, etc. The mysteries express the truth that the divine cannot be declared openly but only symbolically. This establishes the new use of the term *mystḗria* for secret teachings. The cultic mysteries are no longer true *mystḗria,* for what the term really implies is the divine ground of being rather than cultic encounter with deity.

3. The Mysteries in Magic. The magical texts offer a rich use of the term *mystḗria* for magical actions, for formulas that effect magic, for magically potent mystery writing, and for other means employed in magic, e.g., ointments, animals, and amulets.

4. The Mysteries in Secular Usage. By way of figurative usage based on the cults, the term comes into the secular sphere for private secrets, family secrets, and secrets or mysteries in general. But instances are rare and late. The religious use maintains its dominance.

5. The Mysteries in Gnosticism. Gnosticism presupposes and fosters an intermingling and interpreting of ancient mystery cults. A redemption myth governs the understanding of the mysteries and makes possible the adoption of their various symbols. The mystery remains inasmuch as only special people can receive the divine message. But it is also disclosure inasmuch as the message may be imparted to others. Everything belonging to the heavenly world, to human origin and redemption, is mystery. In contrast to the mystery religions, however, the cultus is now the by-product of the myth, not the myth of the cultus. Mystery belongs to the heavenly sphere. The bringer of it to us is the redeemed Redeemer. The disclosure is itself an enactment of redemption; hence the supreme significance of *gnṓsis.* The concept of the mysteries may then find an extended use in relation to sacred books, rites, and conjurations. These are powerful secret instruments which lose their potency if they are disclosed. They are opposed by the mysteries of evil forces; the Redeemer brings these mysteries to light and thus robs them of their power.

B. *mystḗrion* in the LXX, Apocalyptic, and Rabbinic Judaism.

1. LXX Usage. In the LXX the word occurs only in the Hellenistic period. It may refer to the mystery cults (Wis. 14:15) or show their influence (Wis. 6:22; 8:4, etc.). The secular sense also occurs, e.g., in Tob. 12:7 (the secret plans of a king) or Sir. 22:22 (the secrets of a friend). The word takes on a special sense in Daniel, namely, as the concealed intimation of future events that will be disclosed or interpreted only by God or by those whom he inspires (2:28-29; 4:9).

2. Apocalyptic. Apocalyptic is the disclosure of divine secrets. Hence the concept of *mystḗrion* is important in it. God's being and rule are unsearchable. Apocalyptic speaks objectively of prepared and hidden realities that are shown to the seer as he is led through the heavenly spheres by an angel. As the hidden basis of reality, the mysteries are those of heaven, creation, the aeon, storm, etc., as well as of the law, the righteous, and sinners. Disclosure of the mysteries involves names, measurements, times, etc. The seer has a vision of what will come to pass and of the final destinies of sinners and the righteous. The mysteries are God's present counsels that will ultimately be manifested. They are made known to the seer by signs or rapture, but only in enigmatic visions. The mysteries made known by prying angels are responsible for human possession of forbidden powers and magical arts. Common to the mystery cults and apocalyptic are the demand for silence, the role of the angel (or mystagogue), and the heavenly journey. But in apocalyptic the mysteries deal with a destiny that the deity ordains rather than suffers, reception of the mysteries does not bring deification, and the orientation of the mysteries is to eschatological revelation on a cosmic scale.

3. *Rabbinic Judaism*. Rabbinic Judaism has little time for apocalyptic after the fall of Jerusalem in A.D. 70, but earlier we find some discussion of secret doctrines, the understanding of oral tradition, circumcision etc. as a mystery, the promise that the secrets of the law will be revealed to those who study it for its own sake, and the obligation laid on Israel to keep its secrets.

C. *mystērion* in the NT.

1. *The Mystery of the Divine Lordship in Mk. 4:11-12 and Parallels*. The only Synoptic use of *mystērion* is in the saying about the purpose of the parables that comes between the parable of the sower and its interpretation. The saying distinguishes the disciples from those who are without comprehension and are thus taught in parables alone. This method conceals the mystery of the divine rule from all but the disciples, who are also taught in parables, but to whom an explanation is given. The context shows what the mystery is that is generally intimated in the parables. It is the fact of the coming of the kingdom, which only faith can grasp. The eyes of the disciples are open to the dawn of the messianic age (Mt. 13:16-17). Hence the parables teach them about the incursion of God's rule in the word and work of Jesus. By grace they perceive that the mystery is Jesus himself as the Messiah. The parables are ultimately a veiling of the mystery because they are so simple. The fact of the sower going out to sow is itself the new world of God.

2. *The Mystery of Christ*. In Paul the *mystērion* is connected with the *kērygma* (1 Cor. 1:23; 2:1, 7). Paul uses Gnostic terminology but links the *mystērion* to the word of the cross which is the divine wisdom (*sophía*). The *mystērion* is the eternal counsel of God which is hidden from the world but eschatologically fulfilled in the cross of the Lord of glory and which carries with it the glorification of believers. This *mystērion* is before the world (1 Cor. 2:7), hidden from the aeons (2:8), hidden in God (Eph. 3:9), but fulfilled in Christ. The times reach their end with its manifestation (Eph. 1:10). The *mystērion* embraces the historical enactment of God's purpose. In Christ the heavenly reality breaks into this world. It not only achieves the victory of the cross but carries with it an indwelling in believers (Col. 1:27). It also unites Jews and Gentiles in the one body of Christ (Eph. 1:9-10; 3:4ff.). The *mystērion* is not itself revelation; it is the object of revelation. It does not declare itself; God in his free grace discloses it to his elect. The term thus occurs with terms for revelation (Rom. 16:25; Eph. 3:3, 5; 1 Cor. 2:10, etc.). Its proclamation belongs to the event of the *mystērion* and its manifestation. The apostolic *oikonomía* is part of the *oikonomía* of the mystery (Eph. 3:2, 9). The apostles, then, are bearers of revelation. In the reception of their message the calling of believers and their setting in the heavenly sphere take place (Eph. 2:5-6). The concealment of the *mystērion* is also present with its manifestation

in an antithesis of the then and the now (Rom. 16:25), the rulers of this world and believers (1 Cor. 2:6ff.), and the now and the one day. Even as it is now revealed, the *mystērion* conceals the consummation (cf. Col. 1:24-25; Eph. 3:13). The more formal use in 1 Tim. 3:9 and 3:16 (the mystery of faith and religion) derives its point from the reference to the eschatological enactment in Christ, as the rest of v. 16 shows.

3. The General Use in Paul and the Rest of the NT.

a. To penetrate the mysteries of God is the special gift of the prophet (1 Cor. 13:2). The contents of tongue-speaking are also mysteries (1 Cor. 14:2). The destiny of Israel is a mystery (Rom. 11:25). The present obduracy of Israel has eschatological significance. The transformation that takes place at the parousia is a mystery, too, in 1 Cor. 15:51.

b. In Eph. 5:31-32 the *mystērion* is not marriage itself but the prophecy of the relation between Christ and the church which lies hid in Gen. 2:24.

c. The *mystērion* of lawlessness in 2 Th. 2:3ff. is eschatological; the mark of the present time is that in hidden form the lawless one, who will finally be manifested, is already at work in it. Rev. 15:5, 7 speaks similarly of the *mystērion* of the harlot Babylon, whose name holds the mystery of her power, but the unmasking of whose secret shows that she is marked for destruction. There is a *mystērion* of ungodly forces only because the hidden plan of God moves to its fulfilment (cf. 10:7). In the light of this fulfilment the divine understands the mystery of the seven stars in the right hand of Christ (1:16, 20). Christ, who holds the symbol of dominion, will be the Lord of the new world. It may be noted that in the NT *mystērion* always has an eschatological reference, is never a secret discipline that is to be protected against profanation, and carries no express connections with the mystery cults.

D. *mystērion* in the Early Church.

1. The Apostolic Fathers. In these works *mystērion* is rare. The reference in Ignatius (*Ephesians* 19.1) is to the arrangements for salvation that are prepared in heaven and then revealed. Did. 11:11 is a difficult passage; the allusion is perhaps to the spiritual marriage of a prophet that represents the heavenly mystery of the marriage between Christ and the church.

2. The Apologists.

a. The Apologists use the term for the mystery cults (e.g., Justin *Apology* 1.25.27), or for the secret teachings of the Gnostics (cf. Irenaeus *Against Heresies,* Preface).

b. They also apply it in various ways to Christianity, e.g., for the facts of salvation (Justin *Apology* 1.13), or for OT types (Justin *Dialogue* 44) such as the name of Joshua (111) or the Passover lamb (40).

3. Alexandrian Theology. Adopting the Greek concept, this theology regards Christian truths as mysteries. Believers are led by Christ through the little mysteries to the great ones that are to be passed on only in veiled form (Clement *Stromateis* 4.162.3; 4.3.1; 5.57.2; 6.124.6). Thus we move through Proverbs and Ecclesiastes to the hidden truths of Canticles (Origen *Homily on Canticles*). Later, dogma is sometimes called *mystērion* because it is not fully disclosed and is profaned by discussion.

4. mystērion as a Term for the Sacraments. Cultic ideas return with the use of *mystērion* for the sacraments, although pagan mysteries are naturally seen as a demonic imitation. The sacraments represent the saving acts of Christ in a hidden form, and many mystery terms come to be used when the equation is fully made in the fourth century. Both the saving acts and the cultic representation are called *mystērion,* and by the latter believers are taken up into the former, since it contains the reality of these saving acts.

5. mystḗrion and sacramentum. In the Latin Bible *sacramentum* is at first the rendering of *mystḗrion.* As the soldier's oath, the *sacramentum* is an initiation (the mysteries, too, impose an oath). Tertullian preserves the military use by seeing a commitment to the rule of faith (cf. also Cyprian), but in later usage *sacramentum* becomes a full-scale equivalent of *mystḗrion,* may be used for it (along with *mysterium*) in the Vulgate, and becomes the preferred term for baptism and the Lord's Supper.

myéō. This word, meaning "to initiate into the mysteries," occurs in the NT only in Phil. 4:12. The use here is possibly general, but more likely there is an ironical echo of the mysteries. Paul learns the secrets of faith, i.e., he experiences the power of Christ, in the everyday gifts and stresses of daily life.

[G. BORNKAMM, IV, 802-28]

---

mṓlōps [bruise]

mṓlōps, which is commonly used for "weal" or "welt," or "swelling" from a sting, is found in the NT only in 1 Pet. 2:24 (quoting Is. 53:5). When Christian slaves are unjustly beaten, they should remember that paradoxically it was by the blows he received that the *doúlos* Christ effected their salvation.   [C. SCHNEIDER, IV, 829]

---

mṓmos [blame, blemish],   *ámōmos* [without blemish, blameless],   *amṓmētos* [blameless]

mṓmos. This word has such senses as "censure," "reproach," "insult," and "ignominy." It still has these senses in the LXX (Sir. 11:33) but also takes on here the meaning "physical blemish" or "moral blemish." The only NT instance is in 2 Pet. 2:13, where heretics, because of their moral libertinism, are said to be "blemishes" (and *spíloi*) in the sacred table fellowship of believers.

ámōmos. This means "irreproachable," "blameless," "without blemish." It is a cultic term in the LXX, denoting the physical perfection of the priest or offering. But it may also be used for the absolute blamelessness of God (2 Sam. 22:31). The NT adopts the term for the perfect piety to which believers are obligated by membership in the eschatological community (cf. Eph. 1:4; 5:27; Phil. 2:15; Col. 1:22). They are to manifest this at the judgment (cf. Jude 24). 1 Pet. 1:19 and Heb. 9:14 build on the cultic use but give it a moral thrust; the OT requirement that there be no blemish finds its fulfilment in the moral blamelessness of the Redeemer who offers himself (Heb. 4:15; 7:26).

amṓmētos. This word, which means "blameless," "without reproach," is used in 2 Pet. 3:14 (with *áspiloi*) to denote the blamelessness of believers at the judgment.

[F. HAUCK, IV, 829-31]

---

mōrós [foolish], *mōraínō* [to make foolish], *mōría* [foolishness], *mōrología* [foolish talk]

A. The Group in Classical Greek. *mōrós* and cognates denote deficiency, e.g., physical sloth, but more especially mental dullness. We find such varied uses as for insipid foods, animals that are sluggish in winter, or people suffering from fatigue. With a human reference the main use is psychological. What is meant is a weakness of understanding or judgment, sometimes through stupidity, sometimes through confusion, but always demanding censure. Along with a more rationalistic view, the Greeks suggest at times that folly of this nature is a fate.

B. The Group is the Greek OT. The group is not common in the LXX (*áphrōn* is the usual term for the fool). Where it occurs, more is meant than lack of understanding. What is missing is true knowledge of God (cf. Dt. 32:6; Jer. 5:21). The people is hardened and its folly is apostasy. A more intellectualistic view occurs in Sir. 4:27 (cf. Is. 32:5), and in Sir. 21:22 *mōrós* simply refers to those who disregard good manners. In Ps. 94:8 the folly consists of practical atheism, i.e., not thinking that God really sees and controls events. That we are to honor the truth against foolish people of this kind (especially rulers) is taught in Sir. 4:27. In Is. 19:11 the fact that the rulers of Egypt have become fools is a sign of divine judgment. In some versions we also have the group when David confesses his foolishness in 2 Sam. 24:10. In general, although there is a certain secularization at times in Sirach, the group has a strong religious orientation in its biblical use. Folly may be in some ways a general social and moral affair, but at root it implies a practical denial of God as the Judge of good and evil. (For a full discussion of the Hebrew originals and the various references see *TDNT,* IV, 833-36.)

C. The Group in Philo. Philo retains the religious emphasis of the OT. His use of the group implies criticism of worldly wisdom. Humanity is ensnared in a folly that is linked with arrogance. In God's eyes we are childish in relation to truth (cf. Dt. 32:6). Even the people of the OT falls victim to ungodly folly. True wisdom comes only to the Jewish philosopher who has a deeper understanding of the world and life.

D. The Concept of Folly in the NT.

1. The Salt of Mt. 5:13; Lk. 14:34. In the NT, unlike the LXX, the main weight of the concept of folly rests on *mōrós*. A first use of the group is in the saying about salt losing its taste in Mt. 5:13 and Lk. 14:34 (cf. also Mk. 9:50). How this might happen has been much debated (an impure salt has been suggested, or salt used by Arab bakers to help burning). The main point, however, is surely that salt does not lose its taste, and neither does the gospel. We thus have here a kind of parable of the kingdom which denotes the indestructibility of God's gift in Christ. In the exhortations that accompany the saying, the corresponding responsibilities of the disciples are stressed. But whereas they themselves might fail—and exegesis that finds the main point in their response can easily make the word of grace a word of judgment—the word of God can never lose its efficacy.

2. "Fool" as an Insult. Mt. 5:22 raises the question what is meant by *mōrós* in this context and why its use as an insult merits such severe condemnation. Exegesis has suggested that what the term implies is either recalcitrance, ungodliness, the insulting of the righteous as fools, or simple stupidity. In context, anger relates to the disposition, the charge of empty-headedness is a charge of frivolity, and the charge of folly implies a lack of capacity for right thought or action. But since Jesus is hardly making casuistical distinctions, the two latter terms are to be seen as explanatory additions to the saying about anger. Anger and terms of abuse are closely related (cf. Jms. 1:19) and equally reprehensible. Since there is no real crescendo in the passage, since the two terms of abuse are virtually synonymous, and since the first court (*krísis*) comprises the supreme human and ultimate divine judgment, what we have is a threefold statement which achieves its effect by repetition. In the world of Jesus injury by words is of the utmost seriousness. Where there is anger and vilification, Jesus sees that the true problem is that there is no fellowship (cf. his own condemnation of the scribes and Pharisees as fools and blind in Mt. 23:17). Hence he is not just issuing a moral warning against anger and abuse but establishing by commitment to himself the true fellowship which excludes anger and the insults that express it.

3. The "Fool" in Parables. In the parables of Mt. 7:24ff. and 25:1ff. the contrasting of the "wise" and the "foolish" rests on the use in everyday life, but with an orientation to the last judgment (cf. also the rich fool in Lk. 12:13ff., the clever steward in Lk. 16:1ff., and the foolish guests in Lk. 14:15ff.). The point in the parable of the virgins is readiness. The fault of the foolish virgins is a lukewarmness that takes participation for granted and thus brings down judgment on itself. To make light of salvation is to exclude oneself from it.

4. Foolish Words and Thoughts (Eph. 5:4; 2 Tim. 2:23; Tit. 3:9). Eph. 5 warns against various sins of the tongue. These include *mōrología*, i.e., offensive and foolish speech, and in view of v. 6 heresy may also be meant. This is the point in 2 Tim. 2:23 and Tit. 3:9, where the teaching of Jesus contrasts sharply with stupid controversies, i.e., speculations and subtle questions that do not relate to the truths of salvation. Occupation with such matters is not just foolish but culpable. False teaching is in view, but with its nature rather than its content as the main point of contention.

5. "Folly" in Paul (Rom. 1:22; 1 Cor. 1:18ff.; 2:14; 3:18-19; 4:10). Paul's use is determined by the gospel's transvaluation of all values. The group expresses the world's judgment on believers; the word of the cross is foolishness to those who are lost (1 Cor. 1:18, 23; 2:14). The philosophers at Athens mock Paul (Acts 17:32), Gallio regards the disputes at Corinth as *mōrología* (18:15), and Festus thinks Paul is out of his mind (26:24). Even to speak about a crucified man is a breach of etiquette in Hellenistic eyes. But in his saving work God has reversed the situation. Ignoring the world's assessment, he has made its wisdom the real folly (1 Cor. 3:19). Paul accepts the fact that from the human standpoint his message and preaching are foolishness. God does not need human wisdom, for his foolishness is wiser than the world's wisdom (1:25). In their presentation of the gospel, then, Christians must be ready to be fools for Christ's sake (4:10). On the basis of the divine work of salvation, a radical break with human culture is thus made. The world has no true understanding of either wisdom or folly, just as it has no true understanding of either strength or weakness. Like strength, wisdom is a gift of God that is manifested precisely in what seems to be foolishness to human eyes.   [G. BERTRAM, IV, 832-47]

Mōysēs [Moses]

A. Moses in Later Judaism.

1. The View of Moses in Later Judaism.

a. Hellenistic Judaism. Moses is seen as the most important figure in the people's history, his person is magnified, and his life and work are surrounded by legends. Thus in Hellenistic Judaism we find various legendary elements, e.g., the prediction of his birth, his trampling on the crown of Egypt, his victories as an Egyptian general, and his leading role in Egyptian culture. Much of this glorification is a defense against the antisemitic presentation which depicts Moses as a leprous priest who became the leader of expelled lepers. For Philo Moses is the ideal sage who lives in harmony with nature and the prophetic ecstatic who mounts up to God. All in one, he is mediator, reconciler, legislator, prophet, high priest, king, and personification of the law.

b. Palestinian Judaism. *The Book of Jubilees* is often called the *Apocalypse of Moses* and supposedly rests on a revelation given to him at Sinai. The *Assumption of Moses* contains a disclosure of Moses to Joshua on Mt. Nebo. Other works relating to Moses are *The Life of Adam and Eve, The Greatness of Moses, The Midrash of the Decease of Moses,* and *The Chronicle of Moses.* The main point in these works is that Moses is the mediator of revelation. He is the faithful servant of God who sees God's glory and mediates the law. He is also a prophet for the whole world, a deliverer, and a man of prayer who vicariously accepts Israel's sin.

c. The Death and Ascension of Moses. In legends based on Dt. 34:5ff. Moses resists death. He dies through the kiss of God, Michael contends for his body, he is buried by God and the angels, corruption has no power over him, and atoning power is ascribed to his death. A few references, in spite of Dt. 34:5, suggest a rapture. Hellenistic Judaism is the probable home of this notion.

d. The Distinction between the Hellenistic and the Palestinian Views. The Hellenistic view reflects the concept of the divine man, i.e., the superhuman genius or the ideal of human righteousness. The Palestinian view embodies redeemer expectation. It accepts Moses' fallibility but extols him as the mediator of the law.

2. Moses in the Eschatological Expectation of Later Judaism: The Return of Moses. There are few references to Moses' return in the end-time. Mk. 9:4-5 suggests that there was a tradition that Elijah and Moses (rather than Enoch) would be the precursors of the Messiah. Elsewhere Moses is said to die so that he may come at the head of the wilderness generation (Dt. 33:21), which on this view is given a share in the resurrection. Moses is never presented as the Messiah.

3. Moses as a Type of the Messiah.

a. The Coming Prophet like Moses. As Moses is seen to be the ideal man, so he comes to be viewed as a prototype of the Messiah. A starting point for this view is Dt. 18:15, 18. This is referred at times to a historical prophet. It is also seen as the prophecy of a special prophetic forerunner of the Messiah. Only a few passages (e.g., Jn. 6:14-15 and references in Josephus, the Damascus Document, and the *Testaments of the Twelve Patriarchs*) suggest that this prophet is himself the Messiah. This might well have been a more popular view that finds little documentation.

b. The Messiah as the Second Moses. Quite apart from Dt. 18:15, 18 there is evidence that the Messiah is expected to bring a second redemption and is thus seen as a second Moses. A rabbinic principle is that the final redeemer will be like the first, and there is expectation that he will give miraculous water and manna, that he will be brought up at Rome, that his age will last forty years, and that he will be accompanied by Elijah as Moses was by Aaron. The Damascus Document rests on the view that the wilderness period is a prototype of the age of salvation, that the Damascus sect is the new covenant people, and that its leader is a teacher and lawgiver who has called them to a new exodus. The false messiahs depicted by Josephus all follow Moses' example by leading their followers into the desert and promising signs and wonders. The witness of the NT is to the same effect, whether in relation to the Egyptian of Acts 21:38, the false messiahs against whom Jesus warns in Mt. 24:26, the hope that the Baptist might be the Messiah in Lk. 3:15, or the expectation of the people regarding Jesus in Jn. 6:14-15. The Samaritans, too, look for a Messiah who will be like Moses.

c. The Second Moses as a Figure of Suffering. Since Moses is described as a model of patient endurance, it is no surprise that elements of suffering are linked with the second Moses. Thus he will stay for a time at Rome, will come in lowliness on an ass (cf. Ex. 4:20), will be hidden as Moses was, and will endure hardships in the wilderness. In Rev. 11:3ff. the second Moses, with Elijah, will suffer martyrdom, and one theory is that, since Elijah is sometimes viewed as the Aaron of the Messiah, the second witness here (the second Moses) is the Messiah himself (cf. Mk. 9:12-13).

B. Moses in the NT.
1. The Historical Moses.
a. As Mediator of the Law. For the NT Moses is supremely the messenger and servant (Acts 7:35; Rev. 15:3) whom God validated by miracles (Jn. 6:32) and through whom he gave the law (cf. Acts 7:33-34). So strongly is Moses linked to the law that the law can simply be called Moses (2 Cor. 3:15; Acts 15:21). As teachers of the law, the scribes sit on Moses' seat (cf. Mt. 23:3; Jn. 9:28). Their fault in the eyes of Jesus is that they do not practice what they preach.

b. As Prophet. Moses is also a prophet, and especially a prophet of Christ (Lk. 24:27), of his suffering (Acts 26:22-23) and resurrection (Lk. 20:37), of the Gentile mission (Rom. 10:19), and of the election of grace (9:15). Belief in Moses, then, involves belief in Christ (Jn. 5:46-47).

c. As the Suffering Messenger of God and Model of Faith. Acts depicts Moses as God's suffering messenger (7:17ff.), and Hebrews presents him as a model of faith (11:23ff.) in his renunciation of worldly dignity (vv. 24ff.), his defiance of Pharaoh (v. 27), his keeping of the Passover (v. 28), and his crossing of the Red Sea (v. 29).

d. The Moses Legend. At a few points the NT goes beyond the OT account; cf. Moses' learning in Egyptian wisdom (Acts 7:22), his age when going to Midian (Acts 7:23), the opposition of Jannes and Jambres (2 Tim. 3:8), the role of angels in the giving of the law (Gal. 3:19), and the dispute about his body (Jude 9). In general, however, the NT presentation stays close to the OT, and the additional features are of Palestinian, not Hellenistic, origin.

2. Moses as a Figure of the Last Time.
Moses has only a peripheral eschatological function in the NT. He appears at the transfiguration (Mk. 9:4-5) and he will testify against unbelieving Jews in the judgment (Jn. 5:45).

3. The Moses/Christ Typology.
Like Adam, Abel, and others, Moses is a type of Christ in the NT. This typology is plain only in Acts, Hebrews, and John, is briefly hinted at in Paul and Revelation, and is presupposed in Mark and Matthew.

a. The Baptist. The appearing of John in the desert raises the hope that the Messiah is coming as the second Moses. The people think that John himself might be the Messiah (Lk. 3:15), but John apparently expects another to manifest himself as such.

b. Jesus. Jesus compares himself to Moses as the bearer of God's message (Mk.

10:1ff.; Mt. 5:21ff.) and as the mediator of the new covenant (Mk. 14:24), but his refusal to make bread in the desert (Mt. 4:3-4) or to repeat the miracle of the manna (Jn. 6:30ff.) shows that there might be a false identification.

c. The Primitive Community. The first community refers Dt. 18:15, 18 to Christ (Acts 3:22-23). Stephen, with Christ in view, depicts Moses as the misunderstood deliverer (Acts 7:14ff.). The suffering Moses is a type of the suffering Messiah. 1 Cor. 10:1ff., Mk. 9:2ff., and Mk. 6:32, 35 (cf. Jn. 6) show that this is an authentic understanding and not a mere thesis developed by the author of Acts.

d. Paul. Paul develops the typology in the form of a contrast in 2 Cor. 3. Moses as the officebearer of the old covenant exercises a ministry of death with a veil on his face, whereas the officebearers of the new covenant have a ministry of the Spirit and may speak openly and in such a way that the community sees the imperishable glory of the Lord. In 2 Tim. 3:8 Moses is again a type of the community rather than Christ, this time in the sense that heretics oppose the community as Jannes and Jambres opposed Moses. In 2 Cor. 10 Paul compares Christian baptism to the baptism of the wilderness generation in the Red Sea. Judaism finds in the Red Sea crossing a type of proselyte baptism, but the idea of baptism "into Moses" is unique (and finds a parallel in the formula "into Christ"). The subordination of Moses to Christ is evident in Rom. 10:4-5, Gal. 3:19ff., and Eph. 4:8.

e. Matthew. In Mt. 2 the infancy story shows similarities to legends that develop around the birth of Moses. The fast for 40 days and 40 nights (Mt. 4:2) corresponds to the fast of Moses in Ex. 34:28. The Sermon on the Mount offers a counterpart to the giving of the law at Sinai (cf. "the" mountain in 5:1 and the references in 5:17 and 5:21ff.).

f. Hebrews. Moses is a type of faithfulness in Heb. 3:1ff., but as a servant, not a son. He is also a type as the mediator of the old covenant (cf. 9:15ff.; 12:24), but again the fulfilment is incomparably higher than the type (7:22; 13:20, etc.). As Moses renounces his glory in Egypt to suffer affliction with God's people (11:24-25), so Christ leaves his heavenly glory and accepts vicarious abasement and suffering (2:7, 9, 14; cf. 12:2) in infinitely greater self-sacrifice.

g. The Johannine Writings. The seer in Rev. 15:3 compares the triumph by the crystal sea to the triumph on the far side of the Red Sea; Moses as the divinely sent liberator is a type of Christ. In Jn. 3:14 the lifting up of the serpent by Moses is a figure of the lifting up of Christ, and in Jn. 6:32ff. the manna is a type of the heavenly bread, although here in sharp contrast (cf. Jn. 10:11, 14 if this saying has in view the description of Moses as the faithful shepherd). In Jn. 1:17 the parallelism is probably synthetic. Moses mediates divine revelation in the preliminary form of the law and is thus a type of him who mediates it fully in the form of grace. The emphasis in John tends to fall on the antithesis.

h. The Suffering Moses as a Type of Christ. In the NT there is a heavy stress on the suffering Moses (cf. Acts 7:17ff.; Heb. 11:24ff.; Mt. 2; Lk. 9:31). Orientation to the cross means that the prototype is set in the light of the fulfilment, although later Judaism itself opens the door to this understanding. The Moses/Christ typology is not a controlling influence on NT Christology but as a common motif it helps to shape it. Moses and Christ are both divine messengers, they are both misunderstood and rejected, and together they stand for the combination and contrast of the law and the gospel.

624

C. **The Post-Apostolic Age.** The story of Moses is used in exhortation in 1 Clem.
4.10.12; 17.5, etc. Barn. 4.6ff.; 6.8ff.; 10.1ff. offers allegorical interpretations of the
story of Moses. Thus his arms outstretched in prayer signify Christ's arms outstretched
on the cross.   [J. JEREMIAS, IV, 848-73]

ν *n*

Nazarēnós [of Nazareth],   *Nazōraíos* [Nazarene]

Jesus is called *Nazarēnós* in Mk. 1:24; 10:47; Lk. 4:34, and *Nazōraíos* in Mt. 2:23;
26:69; Lk. 18:37. Paul is linked to the sect *tōn Nazōraíōn* in Acts 24:5. A connection
with Nazareth is presupposed in Mark, Luke, and John (also *Nazarét* and *Nazará*; cf.
Mt. 4:13; Lk. 4:16). Comparison of Mt. 26:69 and 26:71 shows that *Nazōraíos* and
Galilaíos mean much the same thing (cf. Acts 1:11). The terms seem to derive from
the outside world and have a derogatory nuance as applied to Jesus and the disciples.
Paul does not use them, and *Christianoí* becomes the common designation in the
Gentile world (Acts 11:26). Whether or not the use of *Nazarēnós* or *Nazōraíos* for
Jesus and the first Palestinian Christians underlies the term adopted by Christians in
Syria, Persia, Armenia, etc. is much debated, and attempts have beeen made to trace
an earlier sect of *Nasaraíoi*. As regards the prophecy of Mt. 2:23 we have the content
rather than the exact wording, and the explanation probably lies in the similarity of
Nazōraíos to *Naziraíos* (Nazirite; cf. Judg. 13:5, 7). The pre-Christian Jewish sect of
Nasarenes is known only from Epiphanius (*Against 80 Heresies* 18; 29.6), who carefully distinguishes them from the Jewish Christian *Nazōraíoi*. It is possible, however,
that there never was any sect of this kind at all, but that Epiphanius is confused by
a Jewish list that really has Christians in view. According to his depiction, they have
little in common with John the Baptist, Jesus, or later Jewish Christianity. One may
conclude that the term *Nazōraíos* derives from the city of Nazareth as the hometown
of Jesus. Neither linguistic nor material objections to this view are convincing.
                                                                            [H. H. SCHAEDER, IV, 874-79]

---

naós [temple]

---

1. Nonbiblical Usage. *naós*, from *naíō*, "to dwell," means "abode of the gods,"
"temple." Unlike the verb, it has a cultic nuance. House, altar, and statue are the
essential features. The "house" may be a small one that can be transported, but is
more generally a building. The *naós* is strictly the sanctuary as compared to broader
terms for the precincts as a whole. It can be used even more narrowly for the innermost
shrine that houses the god.
    2. Biblical Usage. *naós* is relatively common in the LXX. It usually refers to the
temple at Jerusalem (cf. Ps. 45:15). Ezekiel uses *tá hierá* for pagan sanctuaries, but
this distinction is not maintained in Maccabees. Josephus has *naós* for both the temple
itself and the precincts. The NT uses *naós*, *hierón*, and *hágion* with no sharp distinc-

tion. *naós* refers in particular to the Jerusalem temple but has a more general reference in Acts 17:24 and is used for silver shrines of Artemis in Acts 19:24. A special development that gives *naós* precedence in the NT is its use for the spiritual temple. The reasons for this development are the LXX interest in the term, the fact that it goes well with the idea of upbuilding, and the rich potential of the word. In the Gospels Mt. 23:16ff. mentions the custom of swearing by the temple or by its gold adornment. The casuistic distinction rests on the fact that the gold is consecrated and is thus supposedly more fully God's, but Jesus cuts through the casuistry by showing that God is invoked with whatever belongs to him, so that there can be no nonbinding oath. In Mt. 23:35 the slaying between the temple and the altar is particularly heinous, since this is a place of refuge (Ex. 21:14). The Zechariah intended is probably the son of Jehoiada (2 Chr. 24). At the trial Jesus is accused of saying that he would destroy the temple (cf. Mk. 14:58; Mt. 26:61; Acts 6:14; also Jn. 2:19, 21). Mark states that the witness is false. He also contrasts the temple made with hands and the wonderful new temple of the eschatological community, whereas Matthew and John stress the person and power of Jesus. An enigmatic saying underlies the accusation. Its context is the cleansing of the temple, it links the coming of the Son of Man and the temple, and it makes the point that Jesus is the builder of the messianic temple (which the church relates to itself as the messianic community of which Jesus is the head of the corner). In Mt. 27:5 Judas brings the thirty pieces of silver into the temple before hanging himself; *naós* here presumably means the precincts. In Mk. 15:38 one of the signs at the death of Jesus is the ripping of the temple curtain. We are not told whether this is the inner or outer curtain or what is the precise meaning of the sign. In Luke and Acts *hierón* tends to be more common than *naós,* which in Luke occurs only in the infancy stories (1:9, 21, 22). Notable points in Acts are the distinction between the earthly and heavenly temple in 7:48 (cf. Is. 66:1) and the use of *naós* for the miniature representations of the pagan shrine made by Demetrius in 19:24. In the epistles Paul impresses on the Corinthians that they are temples of God in which the Spirit dwells (1 Cor. 3:16; 6:19; 2 Cor. 6:16-17). This seems to rest on a saying of Jesus in a form related to Mk. 14:58. There are parallels in Philo and Stoicism but not for the description of the *body* as God's temple. The presence of an idol in God's temple is an abomination according to 2 Kgs. 21:7 etc.; Paul gives this cultic principle a moral application. In 2 Th. 2:3-4 the lawless one will try to usurp God's temple, possibly the historical temple at Jerusalem but more likely the Christian community. The community, with the apostles and prophets as a foundation and Christ as the head of the corner, is being built up into a holy temple (Eph. 2:20), or, as 1 Peter puts it, a spiritual house in which the members are living stones, and Christ, the stone that the builders rejected, is the cornerstone (2:5; 4:19). The idea of "pillars" in Gal. 2:9 (cf. Rev. 3:12) may be part of the same comparison. In Revelation *naós* is sometimes the historical temple (cf. 11:1). In 7:15 those who are cleansed serve as priests in God's temple. In 11:19 the heavenly temple is opened, in 14:15, 17 angels come out of it, in 15:8 it is filled with the smoke of God's glory, and in 16:1 the word of fulfilment is spoken from it. This temple is the abode of God's majesty and the source of his commands. The temple may also be the community, as in 3:12. In the new Jerusalem there is no temple, for God himself is the temple (21:22). The point is that God is now present in person.

3. *Postapostolic Usage.* The term *naós* is an important one in the postapostolic period. Barn. 4.11 demands that believers become a perfect temple for God. The heart is a holy temple in 6.15. This is the true temple, not the historical temple

(16.1ff.). Yet we are also being led to God's heavenly dwelling as a temple. Ignatius has an elaborate depiction of the building of the temple with the cross as the pulley and the Spirit as the rope (*Ephesians* 9.1). He also calls believers temple bearers, perhaps on the basis of pagan processions with their representations of shrines (9.2). We are to act with a sense of God's indwelling (15.3). We are especially to keep the flesh as God's sanctuary (*Philadelphians* 7.2; cf. 2 Clem. 9.3). This admonition has an anti-Gnostic thrust. The whole community is a temple in *Magnesians* 7.2, which exhorts believers to come together as one temple of God.

[O. MICHEL, IV, 880-90]

---

nauagéō [to suffer shipwreck]

---

nauagéō means "to suffer shipwreck," and figuratively "to fail," "to be put to shame." It occurs literally in 2 Cor. 11:25, where Paul says that he has been shipwrecked three times. A figurative use occurs in 1 Tim. 1:19. Timothy must fight a good fight; those who do not do this fall into error and bad conduct, i.e., they suffer shipwreck in the faith, or make shipwreck of it.   [H. PREISKER, IV, 891]

---

nekrós [dead],   *nekróō* [to put to death],   *nékrōsis* [death, deadness]

---

nekrós. In Greek *nekrós* is a common noun for "dead person or body" and a common adjective for "dead." Inanimate things may be called *nekrá*; also the things of the sensory world (e.g., the body), or the false philosopher and his teaching. The main LXX use is for a deceased person or a corpse. As an adjective *nekrós* occurs in the NT for dead persons (Acts 5:10; Rev. 1:18) and for inanimate objects (Jms. 2:26). As a noun it is the opposite of the living. Christ will judge both the living and the dead (Rom. 14:9). Christ has power to raise the dead (cf. Mt. 10:8). The *nekroí* are often the dead in Hades. As Christ is raised from the dead, so the dead will finally be raised (1 Cor. 15:35) or will arise (Mk. 12:25). The sea, death, and Hades will give up their dead (Rev. 20:13). Figuratively the prodigal is dead and then comes to life again (Lk. 15:24, 32). The church at Sardis is dead (Rev. 3:1). Dead works mark the pre-Christian period (Heb. 6:1), and faith without works is dead (Jms. 2:17, 26). The whole pre-Christian life is dead (Col. 2:13; cf. Eph. 2:1-2). In Mt. 8:22 those who resist the call of Jesus are treated as the dead. Jesus' call comes to the dead in Jn. 5:25; Eph. 5:14. A sacramental use of the adjective may be seen in Rom. 6:11. By identification with Christ believers are dead to sin in baptism and they are to live as those who are already raised from the dead (v. 13). For a variation on the same thought see also Rom. 8:10.

nekróō. This means "to put to death" and is used medically for atrophy. Rom. 4:19 says that Abraham is as good as dead (cf. Heb. 11:12) in a literal sense. Col. 3:5 has the command that we should figuratively put earthly things to death (cf. the sacramental use of *nekrós*).

nékrōsis. This Hellenistic term is used medically for the mortification of a member or the body. Rom. 4:19 uses it for the deadness of Sarah's womb, Mk. 3:5 has it figuratively for the deadness of the heart, and in 2 Cor. 4:10 Paul uses it sacramentally for the death of Jesus in himself as a process of dying in the form of his afflictions.

[R. BULTMANN, IV, 892-95]

---

néos [new, fresh],   *ananeóō* [to renew]

---

néos.

1. Linguistic and Historical Data. Meaning "belonging to the present," *néos* has the nuances of "fresh" and "young." As what is fresh or new, it may denote the odd or unexpected but also a new state or position, e.g., new converts or converts as new people. In the sense of young we find it for children and young people, and it can denote younger men as a group. In the LXX Proverbs has *país néos* for a youth in 1:4. In the NT *néos* is less common than *kainós*. It is used for fresh dough in 1 Cor. 5:7 and new wine in Mk. 2:22. The *néos* is contrasted with the *palaiós* in Col. 3:9-10, and Heb. 12:24 differentiates the new covenant from the old. The reference is to a new age, whereas *kainós* would suggest a new nature. The only instance of "young" is in Tit. 2:4 ("young women"), but we find the comparative in Tit. 2:6; 1 Pet. 5:5; 1 Tim. 5:1-2 (also Lk. 15:12-13), i.e., younger people (or the younger son).

2. Theological Implications. Unlike *kainós, néos* does not have an eschatological content in the NT. It refers to the new reality of present salvation. The new wine of Mk. 2:22 represents the unheard of element in the person and message of Jesus (cf. Mt. 12:6, 41-42; Lk. 4:21; Mk. 10:6ff.). The old age and the new are opposites. The community, as the new leaven, must keep itself pure from earlier sins (1 Cor. 5:6ff.) so as to be in its conduct what it really is. As Christ, the new man, is present, so is the new person of the Christian, and this must express itself in daily renewal (Col. 3:9-10).

ananeóō (→ *anakainízō* and *anakainóō* under *kainós*). This word means "to renew" and in the passive "to be renewed." In Eph. 4:23, which is asserting obligations, the infinitive has an imperative sense. But the renewal is not a self-renewal. It is accomplished *on* rather than *by* believers. They are set in a field of renewal in which they are to let themselves be renewed by Christ (v. 20). The *anakainoústhai* of Col. 3:10 is to the same effect, and *ananeoústhai* in Eph. 4:23 gives a nuance that connects the verse with vv. 22 and 24, namely, that through inner renewal by Christ Christians are freed from their old being and free for their new.   [J. BEHM, IV, 896-901]

---

nephélē [cloud],   *néphos* [cloud]

A. The Terms in General Religious and Moral Imagery.

1. In an Emphatically Low Sense. These words, meaning "mist," "haze," or "cloud," occur in the name of Aristophanes' city of the birds, Cloud-Cuckoo-Land, i.e., the sophistry that introduces new gods. In the OT the cloud signifies what is transitory. Salvation slips from us like a cloud (Job 30:15). Israel's love of God is like a cloud (Hos. 6:4). Boasters are like clouds and wind with no rain (Prov. 25:14). God blots out sins like a cloud (Is. 44:22). Gnostic heretics are like waterless clouds (Jude 12). To take note of clouds but not of God's time is hypocrisy (Lk. 12:54).

2. In an Emphatically Lofty Sense. The chariots of the destroyer are like clouds (Jer. 4:13), and so are those that bring tribute (Is. 60:8). The king's benevolence is like a spring cloud (Prov. 16:15), as is God's mercy (Sir. 35:24). In the age of salvation the clouds will pour down righteousness (Is. 45:8). God is as incomprehensible as a high cloud (Job 35:5). Arrogance reaches to the clouds (Is. 14:14), but so does God's faithfulness (Ps. 36:5).

B. The Cloud as an Embodiment and Attribute of Deity.

1. The Greek and Hellenistic World. Clouds have a religious significance because of human dependence on them and the fear of sinister thunderclouds. The Harpies personify storm clouds, and there is a goddess Nephele. The cult of the clouds does not occur in Greece, but Orphism includes invocation of the clouds at the offering of incense. Aristophanes parodies Orphic worship in his *Clouds*; the clouds represent the new gods of sophistry. The cloud is an attribute of deity; Orphism itself often places the clouds in the service of the supreme god. Gods watching battles hide in clouds. They hide their assistants or favorites in clouds. The cloud is also the chariot of the gods that leads the hero to them. In later Hellenism the cloud has a stylized part in divine appearances or journeys.

2. The OT.

a. The Cloud in Theophany. The OT takes a similar course to that of the Greek world but with a distinctive concept of God. God appears in the storm in Judg. 5:4-5 (cf. Ps. 18). Dark clouds are his tent (Ps. 18:11). He comes from the clouds (Ezek. 1:4). The cloud fills the temple (1 Kgs. 8:10-11), and is his chariot (Is. 19:1) or the dust of his feet (Nah. 1:3). In all this, however, God is the one God and it is only in subordination that heavenly beings share his glory in the clouds. The one like the son of man who comes with the clouds of heaven in Dan. 7:13 receives his power from the Ancient of Days.

b. The Cloud in Rapture. The stories of rapture in the OT (Enoch in Gen. 5:24 and Elijah in 2 Kgs. 2:1ff.) do not mention clouds, although the storm cloud probably stands behind the heavenly chariot of the second story.

c. The Cloud in the Story of the Covenant. It is the covenant God who conceals and manifests himself in the cloud. The pillar of cloud plays an important part in the exodus and the desert journey (Ex. 13:21-22; 14:19ff.; 33:9-10; 40:36-37). At Sinai the dark cloud on the mountain conceals and manifests God's presence (Ex. 19:16 etc., and cf. Pss. 77:18; 78:14; 99:7; 105:39). A parallel cloud is promised for the age of salvation (Is. 4:5).

d. The Cloud in Belief in the Creator. Dependence on the cloud gives it acute religious significance (1 Kgs. 18:44-45). There thus develops a view of nature that sees in it the power and glory of the covenant God. God gathers the clouds (Jer. 10:13) and controls them (Job 36:27ff.; 37:11, 16, etc.). Mythology is ruled out, not by rationalism, but by the personality of the historical God of the covenant.

3. Judaism (and the Mandaeans). In Judaism interest focuses on the cloud of the wilderness and the last days. Philo links the plagues to the clouds. By the pillar of cloud God separates the good from the bad. The cloud at Sinai, reaching from earth to heaven, shows that all things serve God. Josephus tries to play down the miracle of the divine cloud but in so doing achieves the absurdity of a special and highly unusual cloud over the tent. The rabbis ascribe additional properties to the pillar of cloud, e.g., smoothing the ground and smiting scorpions. The Messiah will come on clouds if the people has merits; if not, he will come on an ass. Israel will mount up on a cloud to the throne of glory. It will also be brought back on the clouds to its own land for worship in the age of salvation. For the Mandaeans the great cloud of light is the place of original life. The clouds serve as seats for exalted beings, and the redeemed are wrapped in clouds of glory. Dark clouds conceal the guardhouses of evil. This differs sharply from the OT presentation, in which dark clouds are a sign of the inaccessible God who graciously discloses himself.

4. The NT.

a. The Cloud in Nature Theology. This aspect hardly figures in the NT, but God in his all-embracing love sends rain on both the just and the unjust (Mt. 5:45). By this self-attestation he issues a summons to conversion (Acts 14:17).

b. The Cloud in the Wilderness. The only mention of this cloud is in 1 Cor. 10:1ff., which views it as a type of baptism into Christ. The stress is on personal encounter with God. Sacramental grace is not a talisman but sets us before decision. Even those who are baptized in the cloud perish if they are disobedient.

c. The Cloud in Theophany. The garment of the angel of revelation is a cloud in Rev. 10:1 (cf. Ex. 13:21). At the transfiguration of Jesus a cloud overshadows "them," probably Jesus, Elijah, and Moses, since the voice comes to the disciples out of the cloud (Mk. 9:7). This bright cloud (Mt. 17:5) is God's answer to the saying of Peter in Mk. 9:5 and manifests the divine presence that is promised for the last time. The taking up of Jesus into it means that he will bring final salvation.

d. The Cloud in Apotheosis. The cloud at the ascension gives plasticity to the event but its role is that of a veil rather than a means of ascent. The cloud covers only the external form, so that a personal relation to Jesus persists.

e. The Cloud in Eschatology. The old motifs are now linked to the person of Jesus. He himself is the Son of Man who will come with the clouds of heaven (Mk. 14:62). The linking of the Daniel theme with Zech. 12:10ff. (a threat) is traditional. In Rev. 14:14ff. Christ already sits on the cloud and its white color denotes heavenly triumph. Believers will come on clouds at the parousia (1 Th. 4:17). The application to Christ gives a new thrust to ancient motifs in the NT. The cloud is a sign of the Father of Jesus Christ who in concealment offers himself for fellowship and victoriously establishes it. But this new meaning exhausts the symbolical value of the term. The known reality so far transcends the figure that it plays little further role in the church.

[A. OEPKE, IV, 902-10]

---

nephrós [kidney]

The word *nephrós,* for "kidney," is common in the OT laws of sacrifice and is also used figuratively for the "inner parts" where grief is bitter (Job 16:13), the conscience sits (Ps. 16:7), and there is deep distress (Ps. 73:21). Only God sees these inner parts (cf. Ps. 7:9 etc.). He is far from the inner parts of the wicked (Jer. 12:2). Philo thinks the kidneys are appropriate for offering to God because they sift out waste material. The only instance of *nephrós* in the NT is in Rev. 2:23 (quoting Jer. 11:20). By the afflictions that fall on false prophets and their followers the church may see that God demands ultimate truth and purity. The OT saying that God "searches mind and heart" expresses the total claim that he makes on the community.   [H. PREISKER, IV, 911]

---

nḗpios [child, childish], *nēpiázō* [to be as a child]

A. *nḗpios* in General Greek Usage. This word means "immature," "foolish." It is used in medicine for small children in various stages. We also find it on burial inscriptions for small children aged 1 to 10. It may also be used for orphans (denoting their helplessness), and then comes into use for legal minors. It often occurs for children as members of the family along with the wife or mother. (It can also be used for the young of animals or plants.) But the main sense in Greek is "foolish," "inexperienced," or "childish" with no necessary reference to children. A person is *nḗpios* who is immature in conduct, who shows a foolish confidence in fortune, who does not take account of reality, or who does not heed the advice of philosophers.

B. *nḗpios* in the OT. In the LXX *nḗpios* is used in Prov. 23:13 for the young man who is undergoing education. It is a simple term for youth in Hos. 11:1. When Israel was a youth, God loved her. The term expresses the childlike innocence of the wilderness age prior to the apostasy of later times. In Hos. 2:17 *neótēs* expresses the same thought. The LXX prefers *áphrōn* when the reference is to folly, although other versions sometimes have *nḗpios* in the censorious sense. *nḗpios* has a good reference when it denotes the simple person in the Psalms. The simple are the righteous to whom God gives wisdom (Ps. 19:7) and whom he protects (116:6) and enlightens (119:130). In other words, the LXX does with *nḗpios* what Paul does with *mōrós,* accepting and transmuting the word with the derogatory nuance that it has in the pagan world.

C. *nḗpios* in the NT.

1. Paul and Hebrews. The use in Paul and Hebrews is primarily ethical and pedagogic. Paul links the term with children but in specific connections. The Corinthians are childish to stress outwardly impressive gifts (1 Cor. 14:20). They are to be children in malice. Maturity, however, is the chief goal for Paul (Eph. 4:13-14), since children are easily led astray. From one standpoint childhood is a state that is already left behind (Gal. 4:1ff.). The reference here is to the heir who is still a minor and for whom the law is a pedagogue. Now that Christ has come, the full rights of sonship are bestowed. Paul also compares the child and the adult in 1 Cor. 13:11. Our present knowledge is the imperfect knowledge of childhood, which will yield to full understanding when the age of maturity comes. If *nḗpioi* is the reading in 1 Th. 2:7 ("we were infants among you"), this is a straightforward and nondialectical self-designation, but *épioi* ("gentle") is to be preferred. In the churches Paul accepts his role as a teacher of children (cf. Rom. 2:20). The Corinthians, being still *sárkinoi,* are *nḗpioi,* i.e., they are children who are not yet ready for deeper instruction and therefore must be fed with milk (cf. 1 Cor. 3:1-2). The situation dealt with in Heb. 5–6 is similar. The readers ought to be teachers but they have remained *nḗpioi* who know only the basic doctrines (cf. 6:1-2) and have not yet learned to put what they have been taught into action (6:11). For Paul, of course, knowledge alone carries the danger of evaporating into speculation. In the long run the cross is the one theme of Christian preaching, and the decisive thing is that God's power, which is folly in human eyes, is granted to *mōroí* or *nḗpioi* (1 Cor. 1:18ff.).

2. Little Children in the Message of Jesus. In this regard Paul is at one with Jesus, who in different ways insists that the gospel is for children or little ones. The term *nḗpioi* occurs only in Mt. 11:25 (par. Lk. 10:21) and Mt. 21:16 (quoting Ps. 8:2). In the latter passage small children would be at the feast with their parents, but with the literal sense there is probably an extended reference to the lowly, the disciples, and the masses (just as rabbinic exegesis finds in Ps. 8:2 a reference to Israel as a weak and helpless people). Those whom the world does not notice acknowledge Jesus. God has disclosed to them who he is (Mt. 16:17). To them it is given to know the mysteries (13:11). The story of OT revelation continues as a story of revelation to the simple (cf. Ps. 25:14). This is the special point in Mt. 11:25. The cry of jubilation is not just the result of experience but expresses a basic insight into the nature of revelation as God himself wills it. Jesus, who is lowly, has come to *nḗpioi*. This manifests the greatness of divine grace. Being gentle and lowly, Jesus invites the *nḗpioi* to himself (v. 29). "These things" in v. 25 is to be taken christologically. The reference is to Jesus himself as the revelation of God. Recognition of Jesus, the presupposition of the acceptance of revelation, is fulfilled in the *nḗpioi*. The church, attracted to pedagogic models, has always found it hard to stand by this truth. The fact that it includes concealment from the wise enhances the difficulty. This is why Paul's understanding in 1 Cor. 1:19-20 is so important. It is also why the idea of Jesus himself as a child has been significant even though it has produced apocryphal traditions that reflect the childhood stories of the age. In spite of their stress on learning, then, even theologians like Clement and Origen of Alexandria find it impossible to abandon the principle that revelation is to the simple. Origen defends the self-description of believers as *nḗpioi* against the scorn of Celsus, and Clement not only allows that the gospel is for *nḗpioi* but sees that through Christ, childhood's revealer, all Christians are *nḗpioi* notwithstanding the educational distinctions between them. [G. BERTRAM, IV, 912-23]

---

nḗstis [hungry, fasting], *nēsteúō* [to hunger, fast], *nēsteía* [suffering hunger, fasting]

1. *The Meaning of the Word.* *nḗstis* means "one who has not eaten," "who is empty," then "who fasts." *nēsteúō* means "to be without food or hungry," but mostly "to fast." The noun *nēsteía* means "suffering hunger," usually "fasting."

2. *Fasting in Antiquity.* Fasting is found in all religions. It is the temporary abstention from nourishment on religious grounds. At first it is more common among the Greeks than the Romans, but it spreads over the whole of the ancient world. Fear of demons plays a role in it; it is also seen as a means of preparing for dealings with deity. The mourning fast is due to fear of demonic infection. Egyptian priests fast before entering the sanctuary. Fasting also prepares the way for ecstatic revelations. There is little relation between fasting and ethics in antiquity.

3. *Fasting in the OT and Judaism.* The OT uses various terms for fasting. Many aspects of OT fasting are the same as elsewhere. There is a mourning fast for the dead that expresses sorrow (1 Sam. 31:13). Moses fasts before receiving the commandments (Ex. 34:28), as does Daniel before receiving his visions (Dan. 9:3). Fasting also expresses submission to God, whether in the case of individuals (2 Sam. 12:16ff.) or the people (Judg. 20:26 etc.). Prayer accompanies fasting (Jer. 14:12), especially penitential prayer (1 Sam. 7:6). The one who fasts often takes the posture of a mourner (cf. 1 Kgs. 21:27). Fasts last one day (Judg. 20:26); three days in Esth. 4:16. In the seven-day fast of 1 Sam. 31:13 the actual fasting is only during the day. The only cultic fast is on the Day of Atonement (Lev. 16:29ff.). Special fasts are set up to remember the fall of Jerusalem (Zech. 7:3, 5; 8:19). The prophets protest against the

view that purely external fasting gains a hearing with God (cf. Jer. 14:12; Is. 58:1ff.). For them true fasting is a bowing down of the soul that leads to moral action. Judaism finds an important place for fasting. Apocalyptists prepare for revelation by it. Fasting confirms vows and prayer. It has efficacy with God for forgiveness, healing, and exorcism, although true fasting necessarily involves repentance. The devout make the second and fifth days of the week into additional fasts, but there is never fasting on special feast days, days of preparation, or the sabbath. Longer fasts of up to 40 days occur, and much stress is laid on gestures of mourning in fasting. The Pharisees, the disciples of the Baptist, and the Therapeutae all observe fasts. Philo extols *nêsteía* as ascetic restraint. Rules are set up for the public fasts, and individual fasting tends to replace sacrifice after the destruction of the temple, since it grants expiation, guarantees a divine hearing, and produces sanctity. Yet there are warnings that penitence is also required, and students are advised against excessive fasting.

4. Fasting in the NT. Jesus opens his ministry with a 40-day fast corresponding to that of Moses. But Jesus as the Mediator of the new covenant has already received God's revelation, and he fasts in order to be equipped to confirm his messianic dignity and power. He seems not to engage in special fasting during his ministry, but he would naturally observe the public fasts, and he does not forbid his hearers to fast. For Jesus, however, fasting is service of God and a sign of true conversion. It must be done in secret and not accompanied by open signs of mourning. His disciples do not fast like those of the Baptist (Mk. 2:18ff.), for the presence of the Messiah means rejoicing as at the presence of a bridegroom. The new age is an age of joy. Only the age of waiting (which will begin again after his death) is a time of fasting (cf. Jn. 16:20). The eschatological message of Jesus transcends fasting, but since there is a gap between the dawn of salvation and its consummation there is room for fasting, not as a pious work, but as the sign of an inner attitude. The sayings about the patch and the wineskins are linked to the question of fasting in Mk. 2:18ff. This link preserves the insight that the new age has come as an age of joy. Yet fasting goes hand in hand with prayer in Acts 13:2-3 and 14:23, when missionaries are sent out and elders are appointed. The epistles do not mention fasting; it is not listed even in Heb. 13:16.

5. Fasting in the Early Church. Voluntary fasting on specific days returns in the early church (Wednesday and Friday in Did. 8.1). The Easter fast is laid on all Christians in the second century (Eusebius *Ecclesiastical History* 5.24.12ff.). Fasting before baptism also comes into vogue (Did. 7.4), as does fasting before communion. Reasons given for fasting are to strengthen prayer, to prepare for revelation, to express sorrow, to help the poor with the food saved, and to reconcile penitents with God. Criticisms of fasting are based on the OT prophets (Barn. 3.1ff.), and there is a tendency to subordinate the rite to inwardness and to the ethical (Hermas *Similitudes* 5.3.5ff.). But the early church shows little awareness of Jesus' distinctive approach to fasting.

[J. BEHM, IV, 924-35]

---

nêphō [to be sober], *nēphálios* [sober, self-controlled], *eknêphō* [to become sober]

nêphō.

1. Sobriety in a Literal Sense. The thought behind *nêphō* is a negative one, i.e., the opposite of intoxication. This is first meant literally either in the strict sense of complete abstemiousness or the relative sense of temperance.

2. *Sobriety in the Figurative Sense.*

a. When the word is used figuratively the subject is a person or the human *logismós* and what is meant is the opposite of every kind of fuzziness. Sober judgment is highly valued in both individual and public lfe.

b. In the OT world the readiness to bear the burdens of obedient service to God is denoted by the group. For Philo the sober regulation of given powers is a self-evident requirement in dealings with God. *paideía* is a guide in this regard. Every form of fuzziness (including intoxication) usurps the place of God, and awakening from it is a conversion.

c. Psychologically Philo sees that intoxication and sobriety overlap. In the literal sense this involves a concession, but figuratively, while a softening takes place, Philo endorses the synthesis.

The NT uses *nḗphō* only in the figurative sense. It does not equate the endowment of the Spirit with Dionysiac-type intoxication (as onlookers might do, Acts 2:12ff.; cf. Eph. 5:18), but in the five instances (1 Th. 5:6, 8; 2 Tim. 4:5; 1 Pet. 1:13; 4:7; 5:8) *nḗphō* means acknowledgment of the reality of revelation and discharge of the resultant ministry in worship, hope, love, and conflict.

nēphálios.

1.a. This word means "holding no wine"; the reference is to (cultic) materials or offerings. b. It then describes cultic objects (e.g., fuel) that are not to be made of the wood of the vine, and, by extension, things that remind us of cultic actions without wine.

2.a. The neuter singular denotes "what is sober," "soberness." b. In relation to ecstasy, Philo takes a positive view, using the phrase *nēphálios méthē*. But Philo also applies *nēphálios* to men when he regards abstemiousness as a priestly obligation, not just in a literal sense, but in the sense of sobriety of judgment. The word still belongs at this point to the sacral sphere. In the NT the term occurs in the listed requirements for bishops (1 Tim. 3:2), women (3:11), and elders (Tit. 2:2). If 1 Tim. 3:2 and 1 Tim. 3:8 are parallel, the meaning might be "temperate in the use of wine." But the term is probably a cultic one and refers to the self-control and clarity of mind that are needed in the service of God (though with a hint of the literal sense too).

eknḗphō. This word, meaning "to become sober," occurs in 1 Cor. 15:34. Paul has just mentioned the confused thinking about life and death that leads to loose conduct. Appropriately, then, he summons the Corinthians to come to their senses in a true sobriety of thought centered on God's message in the raising again of Christ.

[O. BAUERNFEIND, IV, 936-41]

---

nikáō [to conquer, overcome], **níkē** [victory], **níkos** [victory], **hypernikáō** [to be more than conquerors]

A. **Usage outside the NT.**

1. This group denotes "victory," "supremacy," or "success." It is assumed that the success is palpable and achieved by an action, but two questions remain, a. whether the human eye can distinguish true victory from false, and b. whether mortals can ever really achieve true victory. In answer to the first question, it is argued that true victory may be hidden, while in answer to the second the mystery religions hold out the promise of ultimate victory.

2. The Greek renderings of the OT yield no striking data regarding the use of the group. The LXX employs it variously for standing in the judgment and for military success. Israel's victory (2 Macc. 10:38), or that of the prophet (Ezek. 3:8), is viewed as God's victory. 4 Maccabees speaks about victory over inner passions and external assaults. Yet the martyr's victory is a divine gift no less than a moral achievement.

B. NT Usage. In the Lucan version of the parable of the strong man, the stronger "overcomes" him (Lk. 11:22; "binds" in Mt. 12:29). This is an obvious victory, but the victory of Jesus which it illustrates is not obvious to his opponents, who advance a theory that would mean discord in the kingdom of evil. The same decisive victory of Jesus is in view in Jn. 16:33. Revelation talks about provisional victories of evil, e.g., in 6:2; 11:7; 13:7. But these victories are "allowed" and therefore restricted. Terrible though they are, the Lion has won the final victory (5:5; cf. 17:14). The beast may thus seem to be victorious, but by the crystal sea are those who have overcome him (15:2). Promises may thus be given in all the churches to those who overcome (2:7, 11, 17, 26; 3:5, 12, 21). This victory will be achieved in the new heaven and earth (21:7). The victory is eschatological, but Christ has won it already with his blood (3:21; 12:11), and it is already present (1 Jn. 5:4-5). The young men have overcome the evil one (1 Jn. 2:13-14), and evil is overcome by good (Rom. 12:21). The use of *níkē* is similar to that of *nikáō*. On the basis of Is. 42:1ff., Mt. 12:20 speaks of the victory of God's servant Christ, while on the basis of Is. 25:8 Paul in 1 Cor. 15:54ff. refers to the victory over death. Faith itself is *níkē* in 1 Jn. 5:4. So great is the victory that is secured by the loving work of Christ that Paul in Rom. 8:37 finds *nikáō* too weak a term. He thus adopts the rare *hypernikáō*. In every test we win the supreme victory; we are "more than conquerors."

[O. BAUERNFEIND, IV, 942-45]

---

níptō [to wash],   *ániptos* [unwashed]

---

níptō (→ *baptízō, loúō, katharós*). This word means "to wash" both generally and cultically. Running water, especially from springs, is preferred for washing. Partial washing of people is at issue. Ritual purity in the approach to deity imposes the need for cultic washing. This is important in the OT (cf. Ex. 30:18-19; Dt. 21:6). Judaism extends the OT rules, e.g., by requiring washing of the hands before meals. In the NT *níptō* means partial washing but is of no great significance. It denotes ordinary washing in Jn. 9:7, 11, 15 and Jewish ritual washing in Mt. 15:2. Jesus defends the disciples when they are attacked for not washing before eating, and he exposes the hypocrisy of those who deliberately refrain from washing when fasting (Mt. 6:17). In the foot-washing *níptō* is partial washing (the feet) as distinct from *loúō* (Jn. 13:5-6, 8 etc.). By his action here Jesus sets an example of menial service. But the action also has symbolical significance. Christ's death gives full cleansing (cf. baptism), so that there is no need of partial washing (if we omit "except for his feet"), or need only of cleansing from daily sin (if we include it).

ániptos. This word means (cultically) "unwashed." It does not occur in the LXX, but the OT stresses the need for clean hands in ministry and prayer (Lev. 15:11; Ex. 30:19ff.). Judaism brings in the custom of washing the hands before meals, but when the disciples are attacked for eating with unwashed hands (Mk. 7:2; Mt. 15:20) Jesus exposes the formalism of the requirement.   [F. HAUCK, IV, 946-48]

---

noéō [to perceive, think, know], *noús* [mind, understanding], *nóēma* [thought], *anóētos* [inconceivable, foolish], *ánoia* [folly], *dysnóētos* [hard to understand], *diánoia* [mind, understanding], *dianóēma* [thought], *énnoia* [thought, insight], *eunoéō* [to be well-disposed], *eúnoia* [goodwill], *katanoéō* [to ponder, study], *metanoéō* [to change one's mind, repent], *metánoia* [repentance, conversion], *ametanóētos* [unrepentant], *pronoéō* [to foresee, care for], *prónoia* [foresight, providence], *hyponoéō* [to suspect, conjecture], *hypónoia* [suspicion, conjecture], *nouthetéō* [to instruct, admonish], *nouthesía* [instruction, admonition]

---

noéō.

1. Linguistic Data. The verb *noéō* means "to direct one's mind to." At first it is used in the broad sense "to perceive," but later it means only "to perceive mentally" and then "to think," "to understand," "to intend," and "to know" as a function of the mind (*noús*). In the LXX the organ of *noeín* is often the heart (*kardía*), but the sphere of *noeín* is always mental. In the NT the verb has such senses as "to note," "to grasp," "to recognize," "to understand," and "to imagine."

2. Biblical Theology. Jn. 12:40 takes the biblical view that the heart is the center of *noeín*. Knowledge has religious and moral significance. Rom. 1:20 states that God's power and majesty may be apprehended in his works. From visible things we can and should work back (in an intellectual process) to the invisible reality of the Creator. We are thus responsible when we fail to do so. Heb. 11:3 argues that by faith we do in fact perceive that the universe is ordered by God's word. To acknowledge that God's creative will is the basis of all reality is to think in terms of faith. Faith sees that the invisible is the true reality, but this reality is the reality of salvation. Hence knowledge of God as Creator is rooted in the knowledge of God as Savior.

noús.

A. The Meaning of the Term.

1. The original meaning of *noús* is "(inner) sense directed on an object," and from this come such meanings as "sensation," "power of perception," and "mode of thought." The main nuances are "mind," "insight," "understanding," "judgment," and "meaning."

2. The word is rare in the LXX, since *kardía* is there the main organ of understanding. The usual meaning in the Apocrypha is "mind" or "disposition."

3. The term is imprecise in postbiblical Jewish works, having such senses as "moral nature," "mode of thought," and "power of spiritual perception."

B. The Term *noús* in Greek Philosophy and Religion. The transition to philosophy gives the term *noús* more pregnancy but in so doing restricts it. The *noús* is now the "reason" or "spirit" with a more theoretical orientation. In Anaxagoras *noús* is the cosmic reason that orders the universe and links perception and creativity. Plato thinks the *noús* is the most excellent part of us. As it rules the world, so it controls moral action. With truth, it is the product of the marriage of humanity with pure being. Aristotle sees in the *noús* our characteristic *enérgeia*. Theoretical *noús* is the power of logical thought and practical *noús* sets goals for the will. The *noús* is immortal and comes into the body from outside. Yet this applies only to the active, not the passive or potential *noús*. In Zeno God is cosmic reason, in Epictetus God's being is *noús*, and in Marcus Aurelius the *noús* is our *daímōn*. Philo uses *noús* for reason (as distinct from *pneúma* as spirit), but while *noús* is the best in us, it is earthly and can attain to truth only as divinely instructed. The *noús* of the first man far surpasses ours. When the *noús* serves God purely, it is divine and rises up to heaven in an initiation into the divine mysteries. In ecstasy, it is replaced by the *pneúma*. God himself is *noús* in the deepest sense. In contrast, the human *noús* is limited, but because cosmic *noús* has created the universe, it has the promise that it will finally come to know God and itself. In Plotinus the *noús* is the thinking substance and the supreme hypostasis in the intelligible realm. It works in the lesser suprasensual and sensual spheres and is in us the chief force alien to the world of sense. In the Hermetic writings God is *noús* in the supreme sense and then there is a second *noús*. The divine *noús* is a unique human property that brings knowledge and insight, although in some texts it seems to belong only to the righteous. In Gnosticism and magic *noús* is hypostatized as the god *Noús* or as an emanation among the aeons. The aeon *Noús* still plays a part in Manicheanism.

C. *noús* in the NT.

a. Used only by Paul (apart from Lk. 24:45; Rev. 13:18; 17:9), *noús* is imprecise in the NT, though never equated with *pneúma* or *psyché*. It first means "mind" or "disposition" in the sense of inner orientation or moral attitude (cf. Rom. 1:28; Eph. 4:17; Col. 2:18; 1 Tim. 6:5; Tit. 1:15). In the disposition of the believer there should be constant renewal (Rom. 12:2). Unity is achieved when members of the community are of the same *noús* (1 Cor. 1:10).

b. A second sense is "practical reason," i.e., the moral consciousness that determines will and action. Thus in Rom. 7:23 the *noús* affirms the law to be God's, and in 7:25 Paul serves this law with his *noús*.

c. The word then means "understanding"; in this sense it is the faculty of knowledge whether as state or act. Thus the *noús* understands the OT in Lk. 24:45 and penetrates secrets in Rev. 13:18; 17:9. God's peace grants a liberation far beyond our care-ridden understanding (Phil. 4:7). The *noús* produces intelligible words and clear thoughts in 1 Cor. 14:14-15, 19. It commands a sure power of judgment when faced with extravagant ideas (2 Th. 2:2).

d. A final sense is "thought," "judgment," or "resolve." We are to be established in our own judgment (Rom. 14:5). God's saving resolve answers the question put in Rom. 9–11 (11:34). This is also the meaning in the first occurrence in 1 Cor. 2:16 ("the mind of the Lord"); in the second occurrence ("the mind of Christ") the sense is more that of disposition (a.).

D. *noús* in the Oldest Christian Literature after the NT.
The word is rare and imprecise in the apostolic fathers, but Gnostics find in Christ the first-begotten *Noús*, the Apologists think God and Christ are by nature *noús* and may be known only by *noús*, and Clement of Alexandria suggests that God is *noús*, that Christ is the Son of *noús*, that the word illumines the soul as it pierces to the depths of the *noús*, and that the human *noús*, when purified, can in some sense receive God's power. Thus philosophical ideas give to the use of *noús* a thrust that it does not have in the NT itself.

nóēma. This word denotes the result of the activity of *noús*, i.e., "what is thought," "thought," "concept," "point," "resolve," or "plan." Only Paul uses it in the NT, and always in a bad sense (except in Phil. 4:7). Thus, in the plural, it means corrupt thoughts in 2 Cor. 3:14; 4:4; 11:3, the devices of Satan in 2 Cor. 2:11, and opposing thoughts that are captured and brought into Christ's service in 2 Cor. 10:5. In Phil. 4:7 (also plural) the reference is to thoughts that proceed from the hearts of believers.

anóētos. In the rare passive this word means "unthought of," "unsuspected," "unintelligible," or "inconceivable," and in the more common active it means "unwise," "irrational," or "foolish," with a moral as well as an intellectual nuance. In Rom. 1:14 the plural is used for those whose power of thought is undeveloped. Elsewhere in the NT the word involves an adverse moral or religious judgment (Gal. 3:1; Tit. 2:3). In 1 Tim. 6:9 the many desires that assail the rich are *anóētoi* because they are morally suspect as well as making no sense or having no substance.

ánoia. This word means "unreason" or "folly," and has a moral slant. In Lk. 6:11 a mad fury is denoted. 2 Tim. 3:9 refers to the dreadful folly of new and old errors.

dysnóētos. This word means "something that is hard to understand." 2 Pet. 3:16 refers to such things in Paul's epistles; the ignorant and unstable twist them. Possibly in view are what Paul says about freedom, about flesh and spirit, or about eschatology.

diánoia.
1. Use outside the NT. This common word for "thought" has such varied senses as (1) thought as a function, (2) the power of thought, the thinking consciousness, (3) the way of thought, (4) the result of thought, e.g., thought, idea, opinion, or judgment, (5) resolve or intention, and (6) the meaning of words or statements. The LXX uses it as an equivalent of *kardía,* and the usage is much the same in other Jewish works.
2. NT Usage. Though not common, *diánoia* occurs in most NT books in the popular sense, with some LXX influence. In the Synoptics and Hebrews the main sense is "mind" or "understanding" (cf. Mk. 12:30; Heb. 8:10; 10:16; an arrogant disposition in Lk. 1:51). In Eph. 4:18 the defect of *noús* is traced back to a defect of *diánoia* (moral and spiritual understanding). In Col. 1:21 the pre-Christian mode of thinking is in view, and the impulses of the will are meant in the plural in Eph. 2:3, i.e., evil thoughts or inclinations. The metaphor of 1 Pet. 1:13 is a summons to readiness of mind and soul, while in 2 Pet. 3:1 a pure disposition is meant. The only instance in the Johannine writings is in 1 Jn. 5:20, where the reference is not to specific knowledge, nor to a natural disposition, but to thinking (given by the Son of God) that is oriented to God. In the apostolic fathers we find a use similar to that of the NT, e.g., for faculty of thought or for mind (evil thoughts in 1 Clem. 39.1). The word is less common than *noús* and *kardía* in the Apologists, but Clement of Alexandria uses it in all the current Greek senses.

dianóēma. This word denotes the result of *dianoeísthai,* namely, "thought," "opinion," "resolve," "judgment." The only NT instance is in Lk. 11:17 where, in a bad sense, it is used for the hostile reservations regarding Jesus and his power.

énnoia.
1. Use outside the NT. This word means "what takes place in the *noús,*" i.e., "deliberation." It can then mean "what arises in the *noús,*" and it is used in philosophy for "idea" or "concept." Thus in Stoicism all thought rests on empirical *énnoiai* (concepts). Such concepts come by experience or observation. They are common to all people, but not innate. They include notions of God, immortality, providence, and good and evil. In the LXX *énnoia* occurs often in Proverbs for "insight," "perception," "consideration," etc. (cf. 1:4; 3:21; 4:1; 16:22; 18:15; 23:4). In the plural it denotes ethical thoughts in 23:19. Elsewhere in Jewish works the term is rare. Philo can use it in the everyday sense, but usually for him it denotes the thoughts with which reason

fructifies the *noús*. In Gnosticism it is hypostatized as the aeon *Énnoia*.

2. *NT Use*. The term is rare in the NT and the use is popular. In Heb. 4:12 the *énnoiai* that God's word discerns are morally questionable thoughts. In 1 Pet. 4:1 the truth expressed in Christ's passion is a "thought" with which believers are to arm themselves so as to have no more dealings with sin (cf. Rom. 6:2ff.).

eunoéō, eúnoia. eunoéō means "to be well-disposed to," "to meet halfway," and *eúnoia* means "goodwill." In Mt. 5:25-26 the advice to the debtor is to meet his adversary halfway, i.e., to come to an arrangement with him. In the light of the last judgment, disciples should be conciliatory with a view to settling wrongs. In Eph. 6:7 the admonition that slaves should serve with *eúnoia* (goodwill) corresponds to a general view of antiquity but is given a new basis, namely, that the service is now rendered to the Lord. Mart. Pol. 17.3 transfers the loyalty or self-sacrifice of subjects directly to the relation between Christians and Christ.

katanoéō. This compound intensifies the simple *noéō*; it means "to immerse oneself in." This may be in the field of sensory perception, but critical examination is also denoted, and in literary Greek the idea is that of apprehension by pondering or studying. In the NT visual perception is usually the point, e.g., scrutiny of an object (Jms. 1:23-24), or the observation of facts or processes (Lk. 12:24, 27; Rom. 4:19; Acts 7:31-32). Sensory contemplation may lead to intellectual apprehension, and this is indicated in Lk. 20:23, where Jesus takes note of the craftiness of his questioners. In Hebrews Christians are to focus on the moral example of Christ (3:1-2) or to consider how they can stir up one another to loving actions that will demonstrate their faith (10:24).

metanoéō, metánoia.

A. Greek Usage.
1. *metanoéō*. (1) This word, which is fairly rare, has first the sense "to note after or late" (often with the sense "too late"). (2) It then means "to change one's *noús*," i.e., opinion, feelings, or purpose. (3) If it is perceived that the former *noús* was wrong, it then takes on the sense "to regret," "to rue," in various constructions, and often with an ethical nuance.
2. *metánoia*. (1) The noun, too, can mean "later knowledge" or "subsequent emendation." (2) More commonly it denotes "change of *noús*," whether in feelings, will, or thought. (3) It then means "remorse" or "regret" if there is dissatisfaction with the previous *noús* and the pain etc. it might have caused.
3. *Historical Significance of the Data*. At first the two words bear a purely intellectual sense. When the idea of change of *noús* establishes itself, emotional and volitional elements come in, but the change is not necessarily ethical; it may be from good to bad. Only when the idea of regret is present is a moral component plainly included, and even now there is no total change in life's direction, for the regret is only for a specific act or attitude, not for a whole way of life. Philosophers use the terms mainly in the intellectual sense, though not without a moral nuance. Fools become wise when they reconsider, but the wise are above *metánoia*, since it would pillory them as the victims of error and show them to be lacking in inner harmony. The Greek world offers no true linguistic or material basis for the NT understanding of *metanoéō* and *metánoia* as conversion.

[J. BEHM, IV, 948-80]

B. Repentance and Conversion in the OT.

1. Cultic and Ritual Forms of Penitence.

(1) The Occasion and Development of Penitential Observances. Although the OT has no special terms for repentance, the concept is present in cultic and prophetic forms. The cultic forms develop out of national emergencies, which are traced to the wrath of God even when no specific offenses are perceived. The fast that is used as an occasion for accusing and robbing Naboth is an example, although often common afflictions will not be attributed to the sins of individuals but to public guilt. As Joel portrays it, the priests summon to the fast, the people assembles on the blast of the ram's horn, and there is common lamentation (Joel 2:15ff.).

(2) External Forms. Along with fasting, sackcloth and ashes are penitential forms. We also read of scratching (Hos. 7:14) and pouring out water (1 Sam. 7:6). Cattle may also fast and be garbed in sackcloth (Jon. 3:7-8; cf. Esth. 4:16).

(3) Liturgies. Calling on God with the confession of sin is also a feature in the fast. Fixed liturgies develop to this end (Hos. 6:1ff.; Jer. 3:21ff.; Neh. 9; Dt. 9:4ff.). Neh. 1:5ff. contains a strong sense of sin, but later we also find protestations of innocence (cf. Ps. 44). No reference is made to offerings in this connection, but one may perhaps infer from Mic. 6:6-7 that they would be made. Indeed, it has been suggested that the human sacrifices which the prophets condemned might be made on such occasions.

(4) Days of Penitence. General days of penitence seem to have been common in preexilic times (1 Kgs. 8:33ff.). During the exile fasts are established for the fall of Jerusalem. Defeats, droughts, famines, fires, etc. are the reasons for these special days.

(5) Prophetic Criticism of Cultic and Ritual Penitence. Since cultic forms might become purely external, they are subject to prophetic criticism. Thus Amos complains that the people does not truly repent (Am. 4:6ff.) even though it most likely engages in cultic practices. Hos. 6:1ff. depicts the people doing outward service, but in 6:4ff. God sees no serious penitence in it, for it has no moral force. Zechariah raises again the ancient prophetic cry for an inner fasting that will issue in righteousness (7:5ff.). Joel adds to the summons to weeping a call for the rending of the heart and not the garment (2:12-13). The prophets are not rejecting external forms but are insisting that serious penitence carries with it a turning from sin to righteousness. Without this the external forms might easily come to be viewed as magical ways of dealing with national disasters rather than as ways to establish a new and true relationship with God. This is why they protest against them.

2. The Prophetic Concept of Conversion. The prophets do not invent a special word for true repentance but make do with the common word for return (*šûḇ*). This carries with it a sense of turning back, i.e., after relapse, but not exclusively so, for sometimes the idea is that of turning from. In general, what is meant is an about-face. The turning is mostly to God (once in Neh. 9:29 to the law), and what is turned from is evil conduct, previous conduct, violence, idols, or sin. The concept of conversion stresses positively the fact that real penitence involves a new relation to God that embraces all spheres of life and claims the will in a way that no external rites can replace. The question of standing before God is the question that really matters. All other things, relations with others, the cultus, and the state, depend on it. Implied here is a strongly personal view of sin whereby individual faults are seen to result from a wrong attitude to God, e.g., infidelity in Hosea, rebellion in Isaiah, forsaking God in Jeremiah. This wrong attitude is the more serious because of Israel's special relationship to God as the covenant people. In line with the personal view of sin is a personal view of repentance as turning to God with all one's being. This turning, or returning as the prophets often call it, has three facets. (1) It means obedience to the will of God, i.e, unconditional recognition of God in conduct corresponding to his will (Hos. 6:1ff.; Jer. 34:15). (2) It means trust in God in rejection of all human help and all false gods (Hos. 14:4; Jer. 3:22-23). (3) It means turning aside from everything that is ungodly. This third aspect seems to be taken for granted in the older prophets but comes to expression in Jeremiah and especially in Ezekiel (Jer. 26:3; Ezek. 18:26, etc.). The call to conversion presupposes its possibility. This aspect is less prominent in Amos, whose message is predominantly one of ineluctable judgment (7:8; 8:2). Hosea, too, appreciates the seriousness of the situation, but he believes that judgment itself will open the door to conversion, not because the latter is a human possibility, but because it is the goal of God's direction of history (2:8-9; 3:5). Isaiah accepts the fact that conversion is a consequence of God's own saving action, but only for a remnant, not for the whole people. Jeremiah in his many appeals seems to assume that by repentance the people may avert judgment, but he expects a comprehensive renewal only as God writes his law in the hearts of the people (31:33). In general, the prophets do not state that the people has a possibility of its own whereby it may repent and avert judgment. On the other hand, judgment is not for it a blind fate. It preserves the living quality of the relation to God and the validity of the moral order.

3. _The Exilic and Postexilic Period._ The later chapters of Isaiah and Ps. 51 maintain the prophetic witness with their orientation of both sin and conversion to God (Is. 44:2) and their insistence on inner renewal (Ps. 51:10). Ezekiel stresses the individual aspect, accords more prominence to the forsaking of sin, gives conversion enhanced significance as a means to salvation, and counts far more on its possibility, although in the last resort he, too, sees the need for a new heart that only God can give (cf. 18:21ff.; 33:12ff.; 36:26). A stronger orientation to the law may be seen in the sins from which Malachi demands conversion (3:7-8), or in the call of Neh. 9:29 for conversion to the law (cf. the role of the Passover in 2 Chr. 30:6ff.). Yet inner repentance is still seen to be the central point (cf. Joel 2:12ff.; Jon. 3:8ff.) even if the thought is not expressed with its original grandeur and profundity.

[E. WÜRTHWEIN, IV, 980-89]

C. _metanoéō_ and _metánoia_ in Hellenistic Jewish Literature.

1. The LXX.

(1) _metanoéō._ This word is rare in the LXX. It is used for "to regret" and "to change one's mind"—with both God and man as subject. The LXX prefers _epistréphō_ or _apostréphō_ for religious and moral conversion, but _metanoéō_ can have much the same sense (Jer. 8:6) when used for Heb. _šûḇ._ _metanoéō,_ then, can acquire the sense of a lasting change that it does not have in the secular sphere.

(2) _metánoia._ The LXX does not use this word in translating the OT.

2. Other Literature.

(1) Apocrypha and Pseudepigrapha. These works have _metanoéō_ and _metánoia_ for conversion in the full sense (Sir. 48:15 etc.). The usage echoes the prophetic call for conversion as a gift and task from God. God himself grants it as a means whereby sinners may come to eternal life. But while a total change is the goal, there is a tendency to stress individual sins that are left and individual laws that are kept. Thus a petty legalistic zeal tends to crowd out the true concept. On the other hand, when conversion is related eschatologically to the final goal of faith and hope, it is seen in the prophetic sense as God's gift and work for Israel.

(2) Philo. In Philo one sees the synthesis of Greek culture and Jewish religion.

Philo uses the terms for "change of mind," but he also gives them the religious nuance of religious and moral conversion, i.e., the total change of turning to God and turning from sin that affects all life and conduct. Without such conversion there is no salvation. In his depiction Philo does, of course, adopt philosophical and mystical elements, e.g., when he says that conversion fulfils the Stoic ideal, or when he shows that it brings harmony in thought and word. Yet he does not agree with the Stoics that the sage needs no *metánoia,* and in his total view the OT concept retains its distinctive flavor.

(3) Josephus. Like Philo, Josephus uses the terms both in the common sense and in the religious and moral sense. His statements, however, are echoes with little profundity. He attaches significance to external forms, focuses on individual vices and virtues, and relates conversion to the averting of punishment. Yet the goal of a new life stands behind the individual manifestations.

D. Conversion in Rabbinic Literature. The rabbis give linguistic expression to the OT view of conversion with their frequent use of terms for "to convert" or "conversion." While they do not work out the theology of conversion systematically, they have an inner religious concern for the matter. They extol conversion as great, and accord it saving significance. Its gates are always open. It is a break with wicked acts and where necessary entails restitution. It comes to expression in penitential prayer. Its positive side is obedience to the law. Although God must give it, humans achieve it, partly in the form of cultic exercises. It is often repeated since there are new violations of the law. By obstinate sinning, one may forfeit it and incur final punishment. Some rabbis think that Israel's conversion is a condition of the coming of the Messiah but others think that the time is set by God. Another hope is that the Messiah will lead all people to God by conversion. The core of the rabbinic view is much the same as that of Hellenistic Jewish teaching.

E. *metanoéō* **and** *metánoia* **in the NT.**

1. The Linguistic Understanding. The two words are most common in the Synoptics and Acts (the verb 21 times, the noun 14). Paul has the verb only once, and the noun four times. The verb occurs 12 times in Revelation, the noun three times in Hebrews and once in 2 Peter. The popular sense occurs in Lk. 17:3-4 and 2 Cor. 7:9-10 ("regret" or "remorse"). The usual meaning is "change of mind" or "conversion" with the full OT nuance. This nuance is important, for it makes a big difference whether the call of Jesus to repent is a call to total conversion or simply a call to sorrow for sin, a change of mind, or acts of restitution.

2. The Concept of Conversion.

(1) John the Baptist. Conversion is the core of the message of John, who proclaims the imminence of judgment and demands a turning to God as God is turning to us. The summons acquires new urgency inasmuch as it stands in the light of eschatological revelation. This is a once-for-all conversion, an inner change, that is required even of the righteous and must find expression in acts of love. A baptism of conversion signifies that God is at work to change our nature for the new aeon. God himself grants conversion as both gift and task; it is for us to let it be given and to authenticate it as the divine basis of a new being.

(2) Jesus. In the teaching of Jesus *metanoeíte* is the imperative that is implied in the indicative of the message of the kingdom. Conversion is a basic requirement that follows from the reality of the eschatological kingdom as it is present in Jesus' person. The preaching and miracles are a call to conversion in a final and unconditional

decision, in a once-for-all turning to God in total obedience (cf. Mk. 1:15; Mt. 12:39ff.; 11:20ff.; Mt. 4:17). This is the point of Jesus' teaching even when the terms are not used. Not merely evil, but anything that might be put before God must be renounced (Mt. 5:29-30; 10:32ff., etc.). Conversion applies to all people, demanding a complete commitment that seeks forgiveness in full trust and surrender. Faith is its positive aspect (cf. Mk. 1:15). It is not a human achievement, for it involves becoming small and receptive like a child (Mt. 18:3). It is God's gift, but as such a binding requirement. By the baptism of the Spirit Jesus imparts the divine power that creates those who are subject to the divine rule, i.e., converted people. In all its severity, then, the message is one of joy. *metánoia* is not law, but gospel.

(3) Primitive Christianity.

a. General. In the apostolic kerygma conversion is a total requirement. The disciples preach it in Mk. 6:12 and are directed to summon people to it in Lk. 24:47. *metánoia* is at the heart of their message in Acts (5:31; 8:22; 11:18, etc.). It is a basic article in Heb. 6:1. Peter's sermon connects it with baptism (Acts 2:38). It is a turning from evil to God (8:22; 20:21). It is both a divine gift and a human task (5:31; 2:38). It embraces all life (cf. Acts 3:19 etc.). Its basis is Christ's saving work (5:31). The Spirit effects it (11:18). Faith goes with it (26:18). The imminent end gives urgency to its proclamation (Rev. 2:5, 16; 3:3). The goal is remission of sins (Acts 3:19) and final salvation (11:18).

b. Paul. In Rom. 2:4 *metánoia* in view of the judgment is what God in his goodness seeks for us. It is God's gift (2 Tim. 2:25). It means a radical break with the past (2 Cor. 12:21). Psychologically it involves remorse (2 Cor. 7:9-10), but more deeply it is God's saving work. For Paul, the concept of faith embraces conversion with its implication of death and renewal. This explains his sparing use of the terms.

c. John. In John, too, faith includes conversion. So does the new birth from God. The sharp line drawn between light and darkness etc. means that believing in God necessarily carries with it a turning from evil.

d. The Impossibility of a Second *metánoia* in Hebrews. Hebrews stresses the total seriousness of conversion. We cannot command it at will (12:7). There is no renewal of it for apostates. What is at issue is not daily repentance but the decisive change that is a new creation. Those who are set in the circle of eschatological salvation, if they consciously arrest the movement and turn back from God, are exposed to eschatological judgment. Conversion is a totality, and hence its surrender is a total surrender.

F. *metanoéō* and *metánoia* in the Ecclesiastical Writings of the Postapostolic and Early Catholic Period. The apostolic fathers make frequent use of the terms in the full sense (1 Clem. 8.3; Justin *Dialogue* 109.1; Hermas *Mandates* 4.3.2). Greek ideas are interfused (Hermas *Visions* 3.7.3; Justin *Apology* 61.10; Mart. Pol. 9.2), but Christian influence is apparent (Did. 10.6; 1 Clem. 7.4; Hermas *Similitudes* 9.22.3; Justin *Apology* 15.7-8), and there is a strong orientation to the OT (1 Clem. 8; Justin *Dialogue* 25.4; 30.1; 107.2). Jewish ideas make some impact. Thus keeping the commandments is part of conversion (Hermas *Visions* 5.6-7), and penitence with weeping and wailing is required (Justin *Dialogue* 141.3). This leads to the development of a penitential discipline and the equation of *metánoia* and penance. The teaching of Hermas opens the door for this with its message of a second repentance. The first conversion is unique (*Mandates* 4.3.1-2), but a second repentance is possible which consists of moral achievement in accordance with the mandates (*Mandates* 1-12).

Asceticism and penal suffering are the school of this conversion (*Similitudes* 7.4-5; *Mandates* 4.2.2).

ametanóētos (→ *ametamélētos* under *metamélomai*). This word means "exposed to no change of mind," "beyond repentance or recall," "unshakable." The Stoics use it to express their ideal of never repenting. Paul, however, poses the Christian antithesis to this ideal by using the word in Rom. 2:5 for the hardened mind and heart of the self-righteous who resist conversion.

pronoéō, prónoia.

A. The Usage.

1. pronoéō. This word means "to perceive in advance," "to note beforehand," "to foresee"; also "to know in advance," then "to care for," "to make provision for," "to take thought for." "To care for" is the meaning in 1 Tim. 5:8, while "to have regard for" is the sense in 2 Cor. 8:1 and Rom. 12:17 (cf. Prov. 3:4 LXX).

2. prónoia. This word means "prior vision or knowledge" but usually has the sense of "forethought" or "provision." When the term is applied to the gods the meanings converge in foreknowledge, foresight, and foreordination. The stress is on the temporal and rational elements. In philosophy *prónoia* is used for divine providence and itself becomes a term for deity (especially in Stoicism). The NT never alludes to divine *prónoia*. *prónoia* is rhetorically ascribed to Felix in Acts 24:2, and in Rom. 13:14 Paul warns believers not to care for the body in such a way as to give entry to sinful lusts.

B. The Concept of Divine Providence.

1. Greek and Roman Antiquity. Beginning with the idea of the rule of cosmic reason, Greek thought develops the concept of a divine *prónoia* that works in nature for human good. The wise and just care of the gods binds us to obedient trust. Providence is at the heart of Stoic belief. Nothing is contingent; immanent divine power harmonizes all things and works them for good. Destiny may be ineluctable, but it expresses a benevolent concern. Moral as well as physical events are under divine control, and a rational humanity is the goal. Since the gods cannot fail, a joyous confidence results.

2. The OT. The only direct expression of providence in the OT is in Job 10:12, but the belief that the God of creation upholds and directs the world is everywhere present (cf. Pss. 65:6ff.; 104; Hos. 2:10; Job 9:5ff.). God sees to it that his purposes are achieved (Ps. 19:6; Job 38:33; Prov. 8:29; Jer. 5:22). We have here no neutral or abstract idea but the personal God who overrules the history of his people (Dt. 32:39; 2 Kgs. 19:25ff.) and shapes the destiny of all peoples (Am. 2:1ff.; 9:7; Gen. 11:1ff.; Is. 41:2ff.). Displaying his presence by miracles (1 Sam. 12:16ff.), God foresees history (Is. 22:11) and chooses instruments to effect his purposes in it (Is. 49:1ff.). Believers are caught up in the events that God directs and hence they experience his guidance and see that their lives are in his hands (Prov. 20:24; Job 5:18ff.; Ps. 16:5ff.). Even evil is a means in God's hands (Am. 3:5-6; Is. 45:7). Incomprehensibly it serves his plan of salvation (cf. Gen. 50:20). The OT view of providence is strongly theocentric and volitional.

3. Judaism. Through all the pressures of history Judaism maintains the OT belief in God's providence. This is apparent in the great apocalypses in which persons and events serve foreknown ends and history follows a predetermined course with the rule of God as the final goal. The law is a providential guarantee of God's dynamic presence and its commandments are tools of providence. God controls all situations, so that one may commit oneself always to him in prayer, although providence in this sense does not negate human freedom. To express the idea of providence Hellenistic Judaism takes over the term *prónoia*. It is natural that God as Father should be concerned for his children. He thus works to avert what is harmful and to achieve what is beneficial (cf. Philo and Josephus). The habit even develops of calling God *prónoia* (4 Macc. 9:24), and Philo can describe providence in Stoic terms (cf. *On the Special Laws* 3.189).

4. *The NT.* That the NT does not express the concept of providence illustrates its distinction from philosophy. The belief is implicitly present but along OT lines. God as Creator is Lord of heaven and earth (Mt. 11:25). He directs history's course to his own goal (Rom. 11:36). Predominant is the love of God enacted in Christ. This is what is reflected in God's sending sunshine and rain on all people (Mt. 5:45) and in his care for all creatures (6:26ff.). God works all things for good for those who love him (Rom. 8:28), and nothing can separate them from his love (8:35ff.; cf. Phil. 2:13). This faith gives individuals their place in God's teleological control of history (Rom. 9–11) with the establishment of his kingdom as the goal. The foreseen plan of salvation, manifested in history in Christ, reaches its consummation beyond history.

5. *The Early Church.* The apostolic fathers inherit the concept of providence. The sprouting of seeds attests to the resurrection (1 Clem. 24.5) and the church is the work of divine providence (Hermas *Visions* 1.3.4). Philosophical ideas intermingle with the primary soteriological concern (Athenagoras *Supplication* 1.1). If Irenaeus ascribes providence plainly to the God of salvation (*Against Heresies* 4.36.6), Clement of Alexandria views it as a rational truth, to doubt which is unchristian (*Stromateis* 1.52.1ff.). Philosophy itself is for him a work of providence preparing the way for the gospel (1.18.4; 6.128.3). The tendency, then, is to split providence and salvation into distinct branches of the divine operation that are related, but not organically so.

hyponoéō, hypónoia. The verb means "to think in secret," "to suspect," or, more generally, "to conjecture." In the NT only Acts uses it, and with no theological significance. It means "to suppose" in 13:25, "to suspect" in 27:18, and "to conjecture" in 27:27. The noun has such senses as "secret opinion," "conjecture," "illusion," and "hidden meaning" (e.g., of metaphors or allegories). In 1 Tim. 6:4, which depicts the liking of false teachers for wars of words, the reference is to the wicked suspicions or insinuations with which they try to discredit those who oppose them.

nouthetéō, nouthesía. The verb means "to impart understanding," "to set right," "to lay on the heart." The stress is on influencing not merely the intellect but the will and disposition. The word thus acquires such senses as "to admonish," "to warn," "to remind," and "to correct." It describes a basic means of education. Philo and Clement of Alexandria speak about God or Christ warning, censuring, and encouraging us in this way. The idea is not that of punishment but of a moral appeal that leads to amendment. In this sense it takes on the meaning "to discipline." Philosophy, however, does not use it technically for its own work. The LXX makes little use of it; it means "to reprimand" in 1 Sam. 3:13, "to admonish" in Job 4:3, and "to correct" in Job 30:1; 36:12. The noun, which means "admonition" or "correction," is common in Philo, for whom it represents divine warnings as distinct from divine punishments. The only LXX use is in Wis. 16:6 (the desert plagues as a warning), but Job 5:17 has the synonymous *nouthétēma*. The group occurs in the NT only in Paul. In Eph. 6:4 the noun represents a means of Christian upbringing, i.e., the admonition or instruction which will correct but not provoke. In 1 Cor. 10:11 God's OT judgments have pedagogic significance; they are written for our instruction. The verb denotes a pastoral function. Paul warns and teaches (Col. 1:18) with a view to bringing believers to maturity in Christ. Admonition is a central part of the cure of souls (Acts 20:31). Criticisms are fatherly words of correction (1 Cor. 4:14-15). The churches are to correct one another through their pastors (1 Th. 5:12) or their reciprocal ministries (1 Th. 5:14). This may be a correcting of the refractory (2 Th. 3:15), but it may also be a last attempt to reclaim heretics (Tit. 3:10). The pastoral use remains a common one in the apostolic fathers (1 Clem. 7.1; Ignatius *Ephesians* 3.1; Hermas *Visions* 2.4.3), and the reference may also be to admonitory sermons (2 Clem. 17.3; Justin *Apology* 67.4).

[J. BEHM, IV, 989-1022]

---

nómos [law], *anomía* [lawlessness], *ánomos* [lawless], *énnomos* [lawful], *nomikós* [lawyer], *nómimos* [lawful], *nomothétēs* [lawgiver], *nomothesía* [the law], *nomothetéō* [to give laws], *paranomía* [lawlessness], *paranoméō* [to transgress the law]

---

nómos.

A. The Greek and Hellenistic World.

1. The Meaning of nómos.

a. From *némō,* "to allot," *nómos* first means "what is proper." It thus comes to apply very broadly to any norm, rule, custom, usage, or tradition. The concept is religious but embraces all aspects of life (e.g., marriage, family, schools, and meals, not just the cultus). Even the gods have *nómoi.*

b. Politically a specialized use develops in the sphere of law, although *nómos* may still denote more generally the absolute as well as the political law, e.g., cosmic law, natural law, or moral law.

c. By the fifth century B.C. the term comes to be used for written laws in a legal sense.

d. It then denotes "contracts" or "conventions."

e. It has a musical application as "mode of singing" or "melody." *Nómos* is personified as a divine figure in poetry and later in theology.

2. The Nature and Development of the Concept in the Greek World. Rooted in religion, *nómos* always retains its relation to the cultus in the Greek world. Even written law expresses the will of deity. *nómos* always has an author, either deity or an inspired legislator. It is thus a work of supreme skill. Only when laws come to be made by consent does the concept lose its strength.

a. In the earliest period *nómos* is a creation and revelation of Zeus. It is thus firmly anchored in the divine sphere and expresses what is right or just. The city-states give constitutional form to established usage. The state represents *nómos*; hence the people must fight for its *nómos* as for the state itself. It is the ruling power (the *basileús* or *despótēs*) in the city.

b. By the sixth century B.C. Zeus comes to be viewed as a divine principle. The cosmos is ruled by *nómos,* and human *nómos* reflects this. It is a specific instance of divine law. One can no more live without it than without the *nómos* that rules the cosmos. Some authors (e.g., Heraclitus) understand cosmic law in terms of national law, but others (e.g., the Stoics) lay more stress on cosmic law, a basis for their cosmopolitanism.

c. Greek tragedy tackles the question of conflicting laws. Sophocles in *Antigone* depicts the confrontation between the law of the state and ancient unwritten law. The inability to keep the law arises, therefore, from an irreconcilability that may be traced right back to God, and a tragic outcome is thus unavoidable. Violation of the law is not due to human sinfulness in this instance. Out of the dilemma more stress comes to be put on unwritten law, either as the original usage of a state, or more commonly as universally valid natural or divine law (cf. the natural law of the Sophists and the cosmic law of the Stoics). This unwritten law embraces ethical and social as well as ritual commands.

d. In the fifth century B.C. the authority of law is shaken by the discovery of other laws and the conclusion that humans are the authors of specific laws. Conflict results not only between laws but between what is right by law and what is right by nature. An attack on religion is also the consequence. From one standpoint, law alone forms a basis for belief in deity. From another (that of the Sophists), the divine origin of law is a clever invention of lawgivers to add sanctions to their laws. Laws, then, can be overthrown only by an attack on religion. On the other hand, they can be protected only by showing that they are truly divine. This is what Plato attempts, first by proving the existence of the gods and second by affirming that *nómos,* as a child of *noús,* is related to the soul.

e. The thinking of Socrates begins with the positive content of the state. The law of the state is for him the law of life. It may be unjustly manipulated, but he dies rather than resist it. Laws are parents that sustain and instruct us, and they are still valid in the face of death and beyond.

f. Socrates does not oppose his individual conscience to *nómos,* for what is important for the Greeks is not the subjective moral sense but objective knowledge of right and wrong. This knowledge is law, and obedience to law is righteousness, which includes all virtues. The goal of education (Aristotle) is instruction in the spirit and ethos of laws, with law itself as a teacher, and obedience as a valid form of servitude that distinguishes free citizens from real slaves. (The only other valid form of *douleía* is respect for the gods.) The rule of law guarantees the preservation of the state and the possibility of human life.

g. Plato regards the death of Socrates in obedience to the law as the transition of norm and law from the institution to the soul. He finds a cosmos and order in the soul itself. This is *nómos.* The inner *nómos* is the order that is controlled by the norm of the soul, i.e., righteousness and self-control. The spirit gives law a new validity and force (Aristotle finds this in the *noús*). In this way a fresh link is formed with the divine world. Yet the ideal for Plato is no longer the dominion of law but the rule of a righteous and kingly figure who has true knowledge. In Aristotle, too, the person of outstanding virtue is above law and is indeed law itself for the self and others.

3. nómos in Hellenism.

a. This theory becomes a reality in Hellenism. The king himself is now *nómos.* As divine, he is the source of law. He is the visible manifestation of eternal law in the cosmos.

b. Stoicism replaces political law with cosmic law. It does not use the term for the laws of state. True divine law is to be sought only in the cosmos, where one law rules that is the basis of society and the union of divine and human beings. As reason, this law pervades nature and determines moral conduct. Zeus is identified as this cosmic law in a concession to popular religion. To decide for this *nómos* is to come to one's true self. It is thus a reasonable possibility, and it leads to a happy life. Law is written on the soul.

647

c. In Neo-Platonism law is less significant but the law of providence upholds humanity by relating morality and happiness.

d. Later antiquity adopts for the most part Orphic Platonic views seen in the light of cosmic theology.

4. The Greek Concept of nómos and the NT. For the Greeks *nómos* comes from the spirit rather than by revelation. Hence it is no mere imperative. It has power over those who try to evade it and brings salvation to those who obey it. It produces, however, no awareness of the inability to keep it, and in the long run fails to carry conviction because of a lack of historical objectivity. All this is in marked contrast to the NT understanding of *nómos*.   [H. KLEINKNECHT, IV, 1022-35]

B. The Law in the OT.

1. The Law in Ancient Israel. In ancient Israel thc first laws are rooted in the doctrine of the covenant. The basic principle is that the whole life of the people belongs to God. Laws are not an adjustment of human interests that receives divine sanction nor are they conditions of the divine relationship. They are the requirements of the God to whom Israel belongs in virtue of the exodus and they come directly from God at Sinai. Thus a. their demand is unconditional, as their form shows; b. they take a negative turn, forbidding that which destroys the covenant relationship; c. they make a persuasive appeal to the will; d. they are brief but comprehensive; and e. they are addressed to all Israel, their aim being to fashion the whole people as the people of God.

2. The Understanding of the Law in the Older Historical Books. The true climax of the older histories is the giving of the law. Israel is a graciously elected people. Hence the law is itself a gift of grace that shows the people what is in accord with its status. As faith in God impregnates the law, there is no distinction between law and morality. Ritual legislation fits into the same pattern, for God's requirement is the principle, and the priests are the guardians of the law. All law is the will of God and rests on God's active choice of the people and his desire to see it live accordingly.

3. The Attitude of the Prophets toward the Law. Prophecy rests on a new encounter with God. The prophetic preaching of repentance presupposes a knowledge of the law (cf. Mic. 6:8). The prophets may put God's demand in a new way, but they do not pose a new demand. For them Israel is still God's people, and violation of the law is apostasy (cf. Am. 2:9; Is. 1:27-28). The prophets see, however, that appeal to the law may go hand in hand with a refusal of true obedience (Am. 2:6). They radicalize and interiorize the law, and in so doing bring out its real thrust. In view of the people's disobedience, they do not expect salvation from a legal order; for this reason they proclaim a new act of God which will establish righteousness and bring the law to the Gentiles (Is. 1:26; 2:3). They attack the cultus when it is used to gloss over disobedience (Jer. 7:11; Hos. 4:6), but while they may regard the contemporary cultus as beyond remedy (Am. 5:25), they clearly do not advocate noncultic worship.

4. The Deuteronomic Understanding of the Law. A distinctive feature of Deuteronomy is the urgency with which the requirement of the law is grounded in God's liberating act. The law must be safeguarded as the link between Israel and God. A further point in Deuteronomy is the concern to impart the blessing of the relation with God to all members of the people. We thus find that in Deuteronomy a. proclamation of the law is preaching; b. the law encompasses all areas of life; c. the neighbor is of central concern; d. distance from God is maintained by upholding the divine supremacy and contesting all submoral worship. Blessing is promised for observance of the law in the form of full enjoyment of the divine purpose and gift. The problem, of course, is the disruptive fact of sin, which only a new covenant, not the law itself, can remedy (Jer. 31:31ff.).

5. *The Understanding of the Law in the Priestly Writing and Related Works.* The priestly legislation presents the law with great austerity. Stress falls here on the divine transcendence and the role of Israel in establishing divine order. Yet the basis is still in history, for the holy God is personal will, not impersonal power. It is by God's calling that Israel is God's people and by his creative action that she knows how to live. Moral and cultic norms find a higher unity in the divine will, so that the cultus stands within the total revelation of the law to Moses. The austerity of this presentation does not rule out elements of joy, reverence, and self-sacrifice (cf. Pss. 19; 119). Legalism is thus avoided. In Lev. 17–26 supreme dignity lies in subjection to God's will with a stress on obligation to one's neighbor and less emphasis on the historical validation of the law.

6. *The Law in the Postexilic Period.* Prophetic judgment falls at the exile, and after it the people knows that it must obey God's will if it is to live. Election is still the basis. Keeping the law does not establish the relation to God but upholds it. Yet the latter aspect comes to the fore and gives the law a certain independence as the means whereby the people may keep itself in grace. Important points (e.g., in Chronicles) are a. that a legal norm governs Israel's history, even the prophets being commandeered by the law; b. Israel becomes a religious community centered on the law (Ezra); c. worship acquires importance primarily as a fulfilment of the law; and d. a new class (the scribes) takes over the religious leadership of the people (Ezr. 7:10). Genuine piety remains (cf. Pss. 19; 37; 40; 119), but by a certain inner logic there is now pressure toward casuistry, the loss of the neighbor as a person, and the exploiting of attachment to the law as an evasion of authentic obedience and as a false means of security.

7. *The Meaning of Torah.* In the OT Torah is the most comprehensive term for law. It occurs some 220 times in various senses. Its administration is at first a task for the priests, but the prophets use the term both for written commandments and for God's word to them (Is. 8:16). The essential point, then, is always divine authority even though the term may often be used for specific cultic or ritual directions. Later it may denote moral instruction as well (Prov. 28:4; 29:18). In Deuteronomy the whole corpus is the Torah, and this embraces the curses as well as the legal provisions. The law may also be equivalent to divine revelation or to general instruction (Ps. 1:2; 2 Chr. 17:9), but always with a strong sense of authoritativeness. In later works a specific reference to the Pentateuch may be discerned.

8. *nómos in the LXX.* The LXX mostly has *nómos* for Torah (some 200 times), and in all it uses *nómos* some 240 times. In general it gives *nómos* the fuller sense of later usage. Where other terms are adopted, the reference is usually to plural laws, to human directions, or to individual statutes. In virtue of its equation with Torah, *nómos* expands its meaning beyond the boundaries of normal Greek usage.

C. The Law in Judaism.

1. *The Law in the Pseudepigrapha and Apocrypha.* In these varied works, law is always the basis, and some of them specifically apply, defend, or commend the law.

a. Linguistically we find *ho nómos* (or *nómos*) in the absolute. Also used are *ho nómos kyríou, toú theoú,* or *Mōyséōs,* and such less typically OT expressions as *hoi nómoi, ho patróos nómos,* and *ho theíos nómos.*

b. Interesting features are (a) the unconditional divine validity and supremacy of the law, as illustrated by the Maccabean revolt, the rise of the Pharisees, the stress on the sabbath and circumcision, and the relating of reward to observance; and (b) the equating of the law and wisdom, with the Torah as a universal law that timelessly expresses the divine will, is itself preexistent, and occupies a mediatorial position (although inability to keep it may give rise to despair in spite of the recognition of its eternal divine validity).

2. Josephus.

a. Josephus usually has *nómos* for the religious law of Israel (although he often has *hoi nómoi*). He may also use *ho nómos* for the Pentateuch or the OT. Sometimes he employs *nómos* for the laws of other nations or for the natural order. Another use is for the norm of something, but this is rare.

b. For Josephus the law is dominant. He accepts its divine origin even while making accommodations to his Gentile readers by pointing to the wisdom of Moses, the antiquity of the law, and the rationality of its provisions. The law makes a happy life possible but it also prevents the excusing of sin. For Josephus rewards and punishments play a great part as motives for keeping the law, but Josephus also stresses early instruction in the law and the constraint of conscience. The essential material basis of his view is Jewish, but with an apologetic orientation to the rationalistic and moralistic world of Hellenistic culture.

3. Philo of Alexandria.

a. In usage Philo resembles Josephus, but Philo employs *nómos* more broadly for the order or law of nature and for norm.

b. Materially, the law is not central in Philo. He seeks to show the agreement between OT law and cosmic law in nature and reason. The unity of God means the unity of creation and revelation. Hence the patriarchs can keep the law by nature. The law itself is of supernatural origin, but, while it must be kept literally, it has allegorical significance. Philo is also concerned to show the rational point of its various provisions, e.g., circumcision. He also stresses the voluntary nature of the law, which encourages rather than commands. We are to meditate on the law, but in the long run the perfect do it by nature, so that for them the law is external and alien. Philo presses for observance, but the thrust of his presentation is to dissolve the law in favor of Hellenistic speculation and moralism.

4. The Law in Rabbinic Judaism.

a. The Torah in rabbinic writings is primarily the Mosaic law. Specifically, but by no means exclusively, it may be the Decalogue. It may also be the Pentateuch. The OT as a whole may also be called the Torah in virtue of its agreement with the Pentateuch. Valid teaching is Torah in a more general sense, as is revelation. Finally, Torah may denote study of the law.

b. Materially, the rabbinic understanding rests on the principles that God has revealed himself once and for all in the Torah and that we are related to God only by relation to the Torah. Special features are (a) that all other authoritative writings depend on the law as contained in the Pentateuch, of which they are the explanation and application; (b) that the law is authoritative because of its divine origin, implications being that the Torah is preexistent, that Moses is passive in its mediation, that it must be copied with great care, and that its sanctity is so great that one must wash the hands before turning from it to secular activities; (c) that reasons are not to be sought for the provisions of the Torah; (d) that the authority of the Torah is so high that God himself is bound by it and that the Messiah will study and keep it; (e) that all relationships are subject to the Torah; (f) that the Torah has diffentiating force in human relationships, distinguishing between Israel and the Gentiles and between individuals within Israel; (g) that the Torah shows us what to do or not do with a view to God's approval and eternal life, great danger being incurred by disobedience to it; and (h) that casuistical development almost necessarily follows, although not without a stress on inward piety as a prerequisite of true study.

D. The Law in the NT.

I. Jesus and the Law in the Synoptic Gospels.

1. The Word nómos. nómos occurs only eight times in Matthew, nine in Luke, and not at all in Mark. It normally denotes the Pentateuch, though it may comprise the OT as a whole. The law is primarily that which governs conduct, but promise is also denoted (cf. Lk. 24:44). It is never used for the oral Torah or the teaching tradition (cf. Mk. 7:5, 8).

2. Jesus' Negation of the Law. Jesus affirms the law but also negates it by replacing its mediatorial office. The answer to breaking the law is conversion and forgiveness, not obedience to the law (cf. Lk. 15). Keeping the law does not insure a right relation to God (Lk. 15:25ff.). The attitude to Jesus determines the relation to God (cf. Mt. 10:13ff.). Rest is achieved by coming to Jesus (Mt. 11:28ff.) and justification by repentance (Lk. 18:14). The law is still valid but a new aeon has come (Lk. 16:16-17) which is bound up with the word and person of Jesus (Mk. 2:21), who himself is free relative to the law.

3. Jesus' Affirmation of the Law. (a) While Jesus negates the mediatorship of the law, he affirms the law in the judgment on sin that his forgiveness implies. Breaking the law brings death, and it is this situation that the act of eschatological pardon remedies. (b) Conversion restores sinners to obedience to the law and is in this sense its affirmation (cf. Mt. 5:20; 7:16ff.; 11:29). (c) Jesus affirms the law by himself observing it (cf. Mt. 9:20; Lk. 2:22ff.). His whole coming is indeed a fulfilment of the law (Mt. 5:18). (d) Jesus states specifically that doing God's good will and keeping the commandments are the same thing (Mk. 10:18ff.). A right disposition demands obedient action expressive of self-sacrificial love of God and neighbor. Those who see this are not far from the kingdom (Mk. 12:34). (e) Detailed criticisms, e.g., of sheltering from disobedience behind the law, or of appealing to the law to evade discipleship, or of putting legal observance above loving service, are in fact a radical affirmation based on the focusing of the law on love of God and neighbor. This concentration restores the law to its original OT sense of a claiming by God in orientation to the neighbor. The difference is that Jesus brings in person the divine act that creates true obedience. When Jesus attacks casuistry, the primary point is that the divine demand on the whole person is taken seriously. Thus the law is open to criticism when it does not expose sin at the root by condemning the attitude and not the act alone. It also fails inasmuch as it can restrain sin (cf. Mt. 5:21ff.) but cannot set it aside as Jesus himself does by establishing the obedience of love. Nevertheless, by bringing the divine forgiveness and sonship, Jesus makes possible a genuine fulfilment of the law, not as a means of self-justification, but as an expression of the new relationship.

4. The Interrelation of Negation and Affirmation of the Law. Jesus' acknowledgment of the law calls for full repentance, which acquires depth and concreteness from the law's demands. It also exhibits true obedience, which rests on the restoration of fellowship by God's new creative act. Confrontation with God's unconditional demand

and liberation from the mediation of the law mutually promote and control one another. God's new act establishes the demand, and those who receive forgiveness thereby offer the true obedience of love.

II. The Conflict Concerning the Law.

1. The Primitive Community.

a. At first the primitive community keeps the law without greatly reflecting on it. The extension of the gospel to the Gentiles raises the question, and a first position is reached at the apostolic council (Gal. 2; Acts 15). This council accepts the agreement between Paul's message and that of the Jerusalem church by stating that observance of the law is not necessary to salvation. At the same time, it agrees that Jewish Christians should keep the law, and this leaves unclarified the question of table fellowship with Gentiles that becomes an issue at Antioch (Gal. 2).

b. Implicit in the resultant debate is the question why even Jews have to keep the law if salvation is by faith in Jesus. The main reason given is concern for the Jewish mission (cf. 1 Cor. 9:20-21). To solve the issue of fellowship the apostolic decree adopts measures that can be defended before the Jewish world, which itself permits fellowship with the uncircumcised in synagogue worship.

c. The primitive community obviously regards faith in Christ as its main distinctive, viewing observance of the law as obedience for love's sake in the service of the gospel. It derives this position from Jesus himself, since historically it can hardly have read back its own attitude into the acts and teaching of Jesus: messianic Judaism offers no basis for this by any inner logic of development, and Hellenistic Judaism provides no true parallels (cf. the story of Stephen in Acts 6:9ff.).

d. Further developments arise out of the apostolic council. The radical Judaizers zealously resist the council's decision and claim that circumcision is necessary to salvation and to membership in the community. In some cases this is perhaps due to fear of trouble in the Jewish world (cf. Gal. 6:12-13), but in others it may well be through devotion to the law. Arguments in support are the command of the law, the example of Jesus, the dubious apostolic authority of Paul (cf. Gal. 3; 2 Cor. 11), and the possibility of antinomianism.

e. The main Jewish body represented by James and Peter keeps to the lines laid down by the council. The law is not necessary to salvation, but should be observed by Jewish Christians in the service of the Jewish mission. Fellowship with Gentile Christians is accepted so long as these Christians observe such points as make the fellowship defensible in the Jewish world.

2. The Usage of Paul. Paul starts with the traditional sense whereby the law is the OT law, though his usage is not uniform. The Decalogue is the gist of the law (Rom. 13:8ff.), but *nómos* comprises other laws and it may be used for a single law (Rom. 7:2). The law demands action; one *does* it (Rom. 2:25). It represents God's living will. Even those who do not know the law, but do it, are "the" law to themselves (not a law of their own choosing) (Rom. 2:12ff.). The law is the one revealed will of the one God. It can thus be personified (Rom. 3:19; 7:1). On occasion the *nómos* may be the Pentateuch (cf. Rom. 3:21; Gal. 4:21). A figurative use may also be seen, as when Paul refers to the law of faith (Rom. 3:27). The law of Rom. 7:21 is perhaps to be taken in this way, i.e., the rule that when we want to do right, evil is close at hand. Other instances are the law of sin (Rom. 7:25), the law of the spirit of life (8:2), and the law of Christ (Gal. 6:2).

3. The Material Understanding of the Law in Paul.

a. The cross dominates Paul's material understanding. This explains his otherwise inexplicable negation and affirmation of the law.

b. The law is the good will of God, so that to oppose it is to oppose God (Rom. 8:7). It is oriented to human acts, not just knowledge (cf. Rom. 2:17ff.). To do it is to have a life based on achievement, but this gives rise to boasting, and in fact the law cannot give life (Gal. 3:21), for no one truly keeps it. The law must be affirmed because it is identical with the good. If a distinction is made between Jews who have it and Gentiles who do not, the Gentiles assent to its verdict and all fall under its judgment (Rom. 1–2). Hence all are referred to faith in Christ for salvation (Gal. 3:28).

c. In relation to human sin, the law first forbids it (Rom. 7:7 etc.), then unmasks it as revolt against God (Rom. 7:9), then condemns it (5:13), so that there can be no further appeal to the law, then nails us to it with divine authority (Gal. 3:22ff.), ruling out all attempts at self-righteousness, and finally brings us to death (Rom. 7:9-10). This is the weakness of the law, which causes Paul to reckon it among the elements, the constitutive features, of the present order (Gal. 4:3), not in spite of, but precisely because of its holiness as a revelation of the divine will.

d. This negation rests on the affirmation of God's pardoning act in Christ (Rom. 3:21ff.; 8:1; Phil. 3:9). Outside faith in Christ, people are still under law (Col. 2:20), but by Christ's death and participation in it there is translation from the sphere of law (cf. Rom. 10:4) into the relation of sonship. Christ, then, replaces the law as the way of salvation; for those who still seek righteousness by law, Christ has died in vain (Gal. 2:21).

e. Yet the cross accepts the verdict of the law (Gal. 2:19; 3:13). It fulfils the condemnation (cf. 2 Cor. 5:21; Rom. 5:6ff.). It is a fulfilment of the law in perfect obedience (Phil. 2:5ff.) and love (Rom. 8:34ff.). Faith recognizes the condemnation implicit in the law, and with it comes the new obedience whereby the law comes to fulfilment in the fruit of the Spirit (Gal. 5:22-23). This is the law of Christ (Gal. 6:2) in which the true intention of the law is realized, so that Paul can say that the gospel establishes rather than abolishes the law (Rom. 3:31). On this ground Paul himself can freely keep concrete provisions of the Mosaic law in ministering to Jews (1 Cor. 9:20ff.), and he can advise Jews not to renounce their circumcision (1 Cor. 7:18ff.). Indeed, the law is the place where Paul seek guidance in community life, not as the decisive argument, but in confirmation of what is known in the obedience of faith.

f. Paul's view seems to derive not so much from personal experience of the law as from a consistent application to the law of faith in the crucified and risen Lord, although it may be debated whether he works out his view independently or in debate with the answers proposed by others around him. Certainly he sees from the outset the antithesis between the way of law and the way of faith.

III. The Period after the Conflict.

1. Hebrews.

a. In Hebrews *nómos* is usually the OT law. In content it mostly has to do with the priestly law as that which gives the OT priesthood its dignity and force. The main focus, of course, is on the relation between the OT priesthood and that of Christ (cf. 7:16).

b. Although validated by law, the OT priesthood cannot make perfect, nor can its law (7:11, 19). This is because of human weakness (7:18ff., 24ff.) and the externality of this ministry (9:9-10). The law is weak here, not because humans do *not* do it, but because *humans* do it. Only the priesthood of Jesus can bring true sanctification, for here we have a sacrifice of pure obedience.

c. Along these lines Hebrews teaches that the law is not meant to bring us to the goal on its own but rather to point us to Christ and his authentic high-priestly ministry (cf. 10:1ff.).

d. We thus find a striking similarity to the negation and affirmation of the law in Paul.

2. James. This epistle raises the question of faith and works rather than faith and law. When it uses the term *nómos,* it often adds a qualification (1:25; 2:8, 12) as though to warn against legalism while guarding against misinterpretaticns of Paul's teaching. In 1:25 the perfect law of liberty is much the same as the implanted word of v. 21. It is the gospel in its application to life, a law, but in contrast to legalistic law a law of liberty. In 2:8ff. *nómos* is commandment but hardly in the sense of the whole OT law (notwithstanding v. 10), for the royal law is the law of love, which the rich, too, must take with full seriousness and not expect any partiality. In v. 11 an example is given to back up v. 10, but this does not alter the general equation of *nómos* with the law of love, which is, as in 1:25, the word of the gospel oriented to specific action. In 4:11-12 the point seems to be that the *nómos* is God's will for the individual—the law of liberty—which we judge if we judge those who act according to it. The freedom, of course, is the freedom of obedience to the commandment of love.

3. John's Gospel. nómos is more common in John (14 times) than Matthew (eight), but less significant. What is meant is the law, especially in the Pentateuch (1:45), but also in the OT as a whole (10:34). But *nómos* may also be a single commandment (7:19) or ordinance (7:51). John shows interest in the law, not as a norm of conduct, but as revelation. Thus a. Jesus is compared and contrasted with the law as the perfect revelation of God (cf. 1:17; 8:12, etc.). Yet b. there is an inner connection between Jesus and the law (1:45), for the law witnesses to Jesus (5:39-40), and he fulfils it (8:17), so that one cannot quote the law against him (7:19ff.). Thus c. Jesus and the disciples are not bound by the law as such (5:19; 13:34-35), and yet Christ is imparted to those who do it (1:47ff.). True hearing of the law leads to faith, for Christ both replaces and fulfils the law. In John the law is never a rule for conduct, and *nómos* does not occur in the epistles or Revelation.

anomía. The prefix gives to *anomía* the sense of either absence of law or nonobservance of it, i.e., lawlessness. The word is common in the LXX, sometimes in the plural for lawless acts (Gen. 19:15). In the NT it denotes sinful acts in Rom. 4:7 and Heb. 10:17, not necessarily with the law in view. In Rom. 6:19 the condition is also meant, i.e., alienation from the law. In 2 Cor. 6:14, where righteousness and *anomía* are mutually exclusive, the sense is the general one of iniquity (cf. 2 Th. 2:3). There is perhaps a stronger relation to the law in Mt. 23:28, although less so in Mt. 7:23; 13:41; 24:12. In 1 Jn. 3:4 sin is shown to be serious because it is *anomía,* i.e., revolt against God, or transgression of the commandment of love as the true law.

ánomos. This word has the objective sense of "having no law" and the subjective sense of "paying no heed to law." The Jews often use the term for the Gentiles with some vacillation of sense. In the NT the reference is to the absence of law in Rom. 2:12 and 1 Cor. 9:21 (cf. also Lk. 22:37; Acts 2:23: the Gentiles). Yet there is an element of judgment in 1 Cor. 9:21, for Paul adds that he is not *ánomos theoú.* With no specific reference to the OT law, *ánomos* implies judgment in 1 Tim. 1:9 (lawless); 2 Pet. 2:8 (lawless deeds); 2 Th. 2:8 (the lawless one).

énnomos. The opposite of *ánomos,* this word implies adherence to the law. When used of persons, it thus means "upright." In Acts 19:39 the reference is to a properly constituted assembly. In 1 Cor. 9:21 Paul says that he is not *ánomos theoú* but *énnomos Christoú,* i.e., under Christ's law.

nomikós. This word, meaning "according to law," comes to be used for "lawyer." In Tit. 3:9, as an adjective, it denotes wranglings about the law, either as a norm of life, or, more likely, as a general source of teaching. In Matthew and Luke the word occurs as a noun for Jewish leaders concerned about the administration and understanding of the law (cf. Mt. 22:35; Lk. 7:30; 14:3). The general sense of "lawyer" fits best in Tit. 3:13.

nómimos. This word means "according to rule or order"; *tó nómimon* is "what is right or fair." The NT has *nómimos* only as an adverb in 1 Tim. 1:8 and 2 Tim. 2:5. In the latter the meaning is "according to the rules," or, perhaps, "well." In the former the meaning is "appropriately": the law is good if properly used.

nomothétēs. This word, meaning "lawgiver," occurs in the NT only in Jms. 4:12 with reference to God. The preceding verse controls the sense.

nomothesía. This word denotes the result rather than the act of legislation, i.e., the law, constitution, etc. The one NT instance is in Rom. 9:4, where one of Israel's privileges is the possession (not the giving) of the law.

nomothetéō. This word means either a. "to give laws" or b. "to settle matters legally." In the passive in Heb. 7:11 the point is receiving the law—the whole law and not just cultic legislation. In Heb. 8:6 the reference is to the general enactment of either the ministry (*leitourgía*) or the covenant (*diathékē*)—most likely the former, although nothing essential is at stake.

paranomia. This word may denote either a condition or an act conflicting with a (legal) norm. The only use in the NT is in 2 Pet. 2:16, where the reference is to Balaam's wrong act with no specific connection with the OT law. A question arises whether the rebuke here refers to punishment or warning.

paranoméō. This word, meaning "to transgress a law," occurs in the NT only in Acts 23:3; the antithesis *katá tón nómon* shows that breaking the OT law is at issue.
→ *nomodidáskalos (didáskō)*   [W. GUTBROD, IV, 1036-91]

---

nósos [sickness], *noséō* [to be sick], *nósēma* [sickness], *(malakía* [weakness, sickness], *mástix* [suffering], *kakós échō* [to do badly]*)*

---

nósos, of uncertain etymology, means "sickness," "plague," "epidemic"; also "calamity," "licentiousness." *noséō* means "to be sick" and figuratively "to be full of (unhealthy) ambition" etc.

A. Sickness and Sin.
1. Primitive Near Eastern and Greek Thinking. Primitive thinking connects sickness and impurity under the concept of *míasma,* which is a kind of substance that one should avoid. Later, demons are thought to convey it or to be stirred up by it, or gods are thought to avenge offenses (mostly cultic) by means of it. Many Babylonian words for sin also denote sickness, and Babylonian penitential psalms often complain about disease and destruction. Expiations are designed to restore the body. In Greece Apollo avenges wrongs by inflicting pestilence, and Egypt offers examples of sickness as a punishment for offenses.
2. The Equation of Defect and Sickness in Greek Philosophy. Greek philosophy hints at the derivation of immoral acts from physical degeneration but also relates defect

and sickness more strictly by calling for both physical and mental training to overcome evil.

3. *Sickness and Sin in the OT.* The OT never describes sin as a spiritual sickness. If the penitential psalms bear resemblances to those of Babylon, the difference is that guilt before God is moral. The sickness of Ps. 103 is a real one, and if it is hopeless like sin, the OT starting point is the connection between guilt and judgment. A sense of innocence (Job) protests against a rigid causality of sin and sickness, and Is. 53 solves the resultant problem by the concept of vicarious suffering.

4. *Sickness and Sin in Judaism.* Judaism works out the doctrine of retribution but avoids a direct equation of sin and sickness except for some Greek influence in Hellenistic Judaism. If the sick are to make special confession, it is more because of the imminence of death than some special sinfulness. Illnesses may be chastisements of love, and God is especially near the sick, so that they are to be visited and helped, not shunned. The role of medicine is honored as early as Sir. 38:12.

5. *Sickness and Sin in the NT.* The NT views sickness as contrary to God's creative will, sees demonic power at work in it, and traces a general connection between sin and sickness (Mt. 12:22ff. etc.). But Jesus, transcending the dogma of retribution, grants both healing and forgiveness (Mk. 2:5ff.), so that Christians may now see sickness as a divine correction (1 Cor. 11:32) and at the same time take steps to deal with it by prayer, healing, etc. (2 Cor. 12:8; Jms. 5:13ff., etc.). In Mk. 2:17 Jesus accepts sickness as a figure of speech for sin, but he does so only to proclaim that he has come to save sinners. The figurative use in 1 Tim. 6:4 is more Hellenistic with its suggestion that ignorance is the source of aberration (cf. the description of error as a cancerous growth in 2 Tim. 2:17). Being sick denotes here an abnormal inward state.

B. Sickness as Vicarious Suffering.

1. *The Suffering Hero in the Greek World.* The sick hero or heroine (Orestes, Ajax, Antiope, especially Hercules) is a common figure in Greek mythology. The sicknesses are finally due to a demonism of destiny, which alone can bring human life to full richness. The tragedy, then, has saving significance, but the vicariousness is not that of historical expiation.

2. *The Suffering Servant of God in the OT and Judaism.* The Bible reflects a tension that only the eschaton can solve, yet in prophetic figures one finds an understanding of sickness in terms of vocational burden. Thus Ezekiel with his cataleptic type of sickness bears the burden of Israel's iniquity (3:22ff.; 4:4ff.), and above all the Servant of Is. 53 bears the sin of the people in vicarious expiation. Only later and in part does Judaism relate this passage to the Messiah, but out of it arises the idea of the Messiah as a leper.

3. *The Suffering Man of God in the NT.* The NT refers Is. 53 to Jesus, although more in terms of violent death than sickness. Mt. 8:17 specifically quotes Is. 53:4 in relation to the fact that in bearing away illnesses Jesus also bears them, i.e., takes the needs of the sick to himself (cf. 15:30ff.). Sickness is a vocational burden for Paul (cf. 2 Cor. 12:7ff.), though he does not call it vicarious. His sufferings mostly take the form of persecution but do not exclude ill health. In Col. 1:24 the thought is not that Paul's sufferings supplement or complete the vicarious work of Christ but that Christ, present with his "body" in this aeon, still undergoes a measure of suffering which hastens the final redemption. Himself present as Head in the heavenly aeon, Christ has died vicariously once and for all at the cross.

C. The Church and Sickness.

1. Visiting and Caring for the Sick. Visiting and caring for the sick is an important ministry in the early church (1 Clem. 59.4; Pol. 1.3). The bishops and deacons pray over the sick, and in times of plague believers devote themselves sacrificially to the sick and dying.

2. The Influence of Is. 53 on the Concept of Christ. The early church does not depict a sick Christ. It refers Is. 53:4 to the crucifixion and sees in the healing and teaching Christ the mighty Helper. A sign of increasing Hellenization is the growing tendency to take the infirmities and diseases of Mt. 8:17 figuratively.

→ *asthenés, iáomai*   [A. OEPKE, IV, 1091-98]

---

nýmphē [bride, daughter-in-law],   *nymphíos* [bridegroom, son-in-law]

The meaning of *nýmphē* is "bride," "marriageable young woman," or "young wife," while *nymphíos* means "bridegroom" or "young husband." Jewish Greek also uses the terms for "daughter-in-law" and "son-in-law." The NT always uses the words for bride or bridegroom except in Mt. 10:35, where the strife is between daughter-in-law and mother-in-law living in the same house.

A. Background Material.

1. The Bride as gynḗ. In the NT the bride is often called *gynḗ* (Mt. 1:20; Rev. 19:7). This accords with Palestinian usage whereby betrothal constitutes a valid marriage and the bride can become a widow, be divorced, or be punished for adultery.

2. The Escort for the Bridegroom. Since marriages are held in the bridegroom's house, the bridegroom comes for the bride and takes her there. The point in Mt. 25:1 is perhaps that the virgins are friends of the bride who meet the bridegroom when he comes for the bride, although on the longer reading ("and the bride" in v. 1) they more likely form an escort on the way to the bridegroom's house.

3. lampádes in the Bridal Procession. Mt. 25:1 presupposes an evening wedding, and the *lampádes* are either torches or lamps, probably lamps on poles or lanterns.

4. The Best Man. Jn. 3:29 refers to the friend of the bridegroom. At weddings there are two best men who take the bridegroom to the bride and superintend the sexual union. Rejoicing at the success of the bridegroom is taken as a figure for the unselfish delight of the Baptist at the success of Jesus.

B. Christ as Bridegroom in the Parables of Jesus.

1. The Allegory Bridegroom/Messiah Unknown to the OT and Later Judaism. In the parables of Mk. 2:19-20 and Mt. 25:1ff. the bridegroom seems obviously to stand for the Messiah. There is no OT basis for this equation, although Hosea and Jeremiah depict God as the bridegroom or husband of Israel (cf. also Is. 62:5), and later Judaism often uses this image, as in the interpretation of the Song of Songs.

2. The Two nymphíos Parables of Jesus.

a. "Can wedding guests mourn?" (Mt. 9:15 and par.). This is a genuine metaphor, perhaps even a secular proverb, which shows that fasting is out of place now that the age of salvation is present. The secondary clause carries the implication that, since this age is present with Jesus, he is the bridegroom. The addition, predicting the passion, limits the time of nonfasting to Jesus' earthly life.

b. "The bridegroom comes" (Mt. 25:1ff.). This statement comes in a parable of judgment warning of the unexpected end of the age. It refers directly to the suddenness of this end. Implied is the point that the Messiah is the bridegroom and that his coming is delayed. It may be noted that in his own preaching Jesus compares the disciples to the guests rather than to the bride (Mt. 9:15; 22:1ff.).

C. The Development of the Bridegroom/Bride Imagery. This occurs first in 2 Cor. 11:2, where Christ is the bridegroom, the community the bride, and the apostle the best man. Further development comes in Eph. 5:22ff., which on the basis of Gen. 2:24 stresses the loving union between Christ and the church, with self-sacrifice on the one side and obedient dedication on the other. In the Synoptists, of course, the wedding days are at first the days of Jesus' earthly life, but in Revelation the consummation is the wedding (19:7ff.; 21:2, 9; 22:17) and the bride is the heavenly Jerusalem (cf. 21:2 and Is. 61:10). Final fulfilment is depicted here in what is said about the Lamb and his bride.   [J. JEREMIAS, IV, 1099-1105]
→ *gaméō, gámos*

---

nýn [now],   (*árti* [now])

A. The Presuppositions of the NT Concept of *nýn*.
I. The Forms of the Word (nýn, nyní, árti). In the Koine *nyní* is as common as *nýn*, but less so in the biblical Koine. In the LXX *nyní* is more common in literary books like Job, while in the NT it occurs mostly in Paul and Hebrews. *nýn* occurs mostly in Paul, Luke, and John. *árti* is less common in the NT and is not found at all in Mark, Luke, Acts, the Pastorals, or Hebrews.
II. The Forms of Use.
1. A transitional form to use as a noun occurs when *nýn* or *árti* is dependent on prepositions, e.g., "from now on" (Mt. 23:39), "now" (Jn. 13:19), "until now" (1 Jn. 2:9).
2. More commonly in such cases *nýn* is a noun.
3. As an accusative of time, the noun *nýn* is more common in the plural either in a temporal sense or with a very weak meaning (Acts 17:30; 4:29).
4. The words may also serve as attributive adjectives between articles and nouns (cf. 1 Tim. 6:17; Rom. 3:26; 2 Pet. 3:7; Acts 22:1; 1 Cor. 4:11).
III. The Nontemporal nýn.
1. As a Connecting Particle. While *nýn* mostly has temporal significance, it is sometimes used very weakly as a connecting particle.
2. As a Particle of Logical Antithesis. *nýn* has greater force as a particle when the NT opposes something factual to a hypothetical but erroneous supposition, e.g., human ungodliness in Jn. 8:40 etc., or divine reality in Jn. 18:36 etc. The sense of *nyn(í) dé* in such cases is "in fact."
3. A similar expression is *kaí nýn,* which has the force of "nevertheless" (Jn. 11:22).
IV. The Temporal nýn.
1. As a Limit.
a. At the End. *nýn* is a limiting concept expressing boundaries. At the end the boundary may be that of a provisional end (Mt. 24:21), that of human life (Gen. 46:34), that of the age of grace (Num. 14:19), or that of hardening (cf. 2 Cor. 3:14). *árti* has this sense in the NT only in Jn. 16:24.
b. At the Beginning. Since the *nýn* pushes it back, the ending boundary is fluid. In contrast, the beginning boundary is more sharply fixed. What begins is usually a divinely appointed period, e.g., the new aeon, the time of salvation, or the time of

personal blessing (Lk. 1:48; 5:10). The end of Jesus inaugurates the time between the comings, a time of distress but also of Christ's lordship (Lk. 22:18, 69).

2. *As a Period of Time.* The point may become a line, e.g., the period between the comings, or the now that extends to eternity (2 Pet. 3:18).

3. *With Reference to Past and Future.*

a. With the preterite, *nýn* and *árti* may refer to what has just happened (Mt. 9:18; 26:65, etc.), but also to a state or process initiated by it (Jn. 8:52; Acts 7:52).

b. But *nýn* may also refer to the near future (Jn. 12:31; Rom. 11:31) in expression of the certainty of faith.

B. The NT Now.

I. Now as the Divine Hour. *nýn* denotes only a moment, but such a moment may become a *kairós* as God chooses it (cf. Lk. 5:10; Acts 18:36; 20:32). This is especially true of the *nýn* of the departure of Jesus (Jn. 12:27; 13:31; Lk. 12:52; 22:18). In this now Jesus anticipates his glorifying, which begins even with his humiliation.

II. Now as the Divinely Delineated Period.

1. *The History of Christ as Present.* The NT claims that God once gave a new turn to human history, but this new turn has present power. It has full weight for Christians as a *nýn* (Rom. 5:9; Col. 1:22, etc.). They experience history as present, and, since this present has eternal significance, in it they also experience the future as present.

2. *The NT nýn between the Comings.*

a. Intimations. The prophets give intimations of a future already present by declaring the judgments or blessings that they prophesy. In their case, however, each Now becomes a Then and looks ahead to a new Now. The use of the concept of the two aeons gives further intimation of the specific NT *nýn* (cf. 2 Tim. 4:10; 1 Tim. 6:17; Gal. 4:25).

b. The Uniqueness of the NT *nýn*. This concept of the two aeons gives to *nýn* the value of an interim period from which one may survey the two comings and in which believers belong to both, being *still* in the old aeon but *already* in the new. Paul has for this the expression *ho nýn kairós,* i.e., the time of the remnant of grace for Israel (Rom. 11:5), of suffering between the presence and the return of the Bridegroom for Christians (8:18), but also of the unique revelation of God's righteousness prior to final judgment (3:26). *ho kairós hoútos* is the term for this interim period in Lk. 12:56 and Mk. 10:30. The present of Heb. 9:9 is also the time of Christ, with a stress on the contrast between the time of fulfilment and that of prefiguration.

3. *The NT Still.*

a. The unique NT present is part of the old aeon as God's creation (Jn. 5:17), which is now fallen creation (Rom. 8:21-22; cf. 1 Jn. 2:9).

b. The darkness of this aeon is part of the structure of Christ's time between the comings (Lk. 6:21, 25; Jn. 16:20, 22). The *nýn* begins with Christ and brings division (Lk. 12:52) and suffering (22:36); it also ends with Christ (Rom. 8:18). In this time the world is still the world, and Christians share in this still (Gal. 2:20). Yet the world presses on to Christ's victory (2 Th. 2:6ff.). In it there is thus the possibility of conversion (Acts 17:30). The *nýn* carries with it an urgent "now at last."

4. *The NT Already.*

a. *nýn* in Parallelism with the Past. If the NT *nýn* also stands in sharp tension with this aeon, there is, of course, an element of correspondence, as in a typological reading of the OT (Gal. 4:29; Heb. 12:26; 1 Pet. 3:21). Yet even here we find a measure of antithesis.

b. *nýn* in Antithesis to the Past. The antithesis comes out in Paul's *tóte/nýn,* which stresses the newness and splendor of the present as (a) the now of a new relation to God (Rom. 5:10-11; Col. 1:21-22; Eph. 2:12; 1 Pet. 2:10), (b) the now of the new life in righteousness, freedom, and the power of the Spirit (Rom. 3:21; 6:22; 7:6; cf. Eph. 2:1ff.), and (c) the now of new knowledge in which God has fully revealed himself (Col. 1:26; Eph. 3:5, 10; Rom. 16:26) and believers enjoy the radically transforming knowledge of love (Gal. 4:8-9; 2 Cor. 5:16).

c. *nýn* as an Anticipation of the Last Things. The day of the Lord has come in this *nýn* (Lk. 4:19, 21; 2 Cor. 6:2). It expresses the certainty of eschatology already realized: judgment (Jn. 12:31), salvation (2 Tim. 1:10), and even the vision of God (Jn. 14:7). Especially in John (cf. also Revelation) the *nýn* of the life of Jesus, and more narrowly of his final crisis, anticipates the last things, for in it one is aware of being in transition, of the presence already of the end (cf. the singular *nýn* of Lk. 16:25 and the *ap' árti* of Rev. 14:13).

d. *nýn* as a Proleptic First Stage of the Last Things. If the last things are anticipated in the *nýn,* the NT still looks ahead to a consummation, so that the now means hope as well as possession (Rom. 5:8-9; 1 Jn. 3:2; 1 Tim. 4:8). While there is present participation, there will also be future fulfilment (cf. Eph. 1:13-14).

5. *Stages of the NT nýn.* Within the one *nýn* of the day of salvation there is a progression of moments. Jesus is aware of the *nýn* of work in, e.g., Jn. 13:19; 16:1, 4; cf. Lk. 22:36. Within the *nýn* the disciples are incomplete, and they may thus make progress (cf. the *íde nýn* of Jn. 16:29). Paul senses the movement of the eschatological clock from *nýn* to *nýn* in Rom. 13:11-12; 2 Th. 2:5ff.; cf. the *nýn* of 1 Cor. 3:2.

6. *Once and Now in the Lives of Individual Christians.* As Paul shows in Gal. 1:23, the once and now of salvation history apply also to believers (cf. Rom. 5:9; 7:6, etc.). This is a matter of objective fact and not merely of personal experience (Rom. 6:21-22; 11:30-31). The pun of Phlm. 11 brings out its basic significance (cf. also Lk. 2:29; Acts 13:31; Lk. 1:48).

III. nýn with the Imperative.

1. *In NT Exhortation.* The already of the NT includes renewal, but since the principle of NT ethics is "Be what you are," a *nýn* with the imperative corresponds to the indicative. There are classical and Hellenistic models for this. In the NT we find it (a) in missionary proclamation (although here the emphasis is more indicative; cf. Acts 17:30-31), and (b) in edificatory exhortation, which stresses that the time of liberation and tension is the time for righteousness and abiding in Christ (Rom. 7:6; Col. 3:8; 1 Jn. 2:28).

2. *In NT Prayer.* In many urgent crises there rings out the *nýn* of prayer to God (cf. in the LXX Jon. 4:3; Is. 64:8). Acts 4:29 is an example. The supreme instance, however, is in Jn. 17:5, in which Jesus accepts his most difficult hour as that of divine glorifying.

IV. The Significance of the NT View of the Now. The ancient world suffers under the ineluctable transitoriness of time. The OT proclaims teleological movement but only in a preparatory way. In the NT, however, the Christ event, the historical past of Christ's life, death, and resurrection, is also present as God's breaking into time. History is thus made contemporaneous in a unique way. As grasped by faith, the past is also the present and it carries the hope of the future. For individuals, this involves decision. The NT evokes the *nýn* as a fact but also teaches us to live in terms of it as the divinely given *kairós.* What has been done once and for all is still at work in the *nýn* of the time of Christ. Moreover, as the *tóte* of the past stands behind it, the *tóte* of the future is ahead of it. Believers live in hope because the present of Christ gives them ground for hope. When the reality of faith comes to the consummation of sight, the *tóte* of 1 Cor. 13:12 will be the new and eternal *nýn*.

→ *aiṓn, hēméra, kairós, sḗmeron, hṓra*   [G. Stählin, IV, 1106-23]

---

nýx [night]

nýx means "night," "darkness," "the dark," and figuratively "blindness," "harm," or "death." In mythology deified *Nýx* is a dreadful figure. Night is a time for demons and hence for magic. But it is also a time for revelations, especially by dreams as the consciousness is released from the empirical world.

1. In the NT *nýx* has first the literal sense of "night" (divided into three or four watches or 12 hours). Nicodemus comes to Jesus by night (Jn. 3:2). The reference to 40 days and nights (Mt. 4:2 etc.) stresses the length of time (unless it is OT pleonasm). Jesus does not fear the night, but spends nights in converse with God (Lk. 6:12). The NT introduces dreams only where they mediate divine commands (Mt. 1) or instruct or exhort (Acts 16:9; 18:9; 23:11; 27:23). It may be the Lord or a messenger who issues the directions, and the revelation is at night because there is greater openness to it during the night. Since darkness is sinister, Revelation associates the darkening of the stars with judgment (8:12), and declares that there will be no darkness in the end-time (21:25).

2. Figuratively, night is a time when there can be no work (Jn. 9:4) and also a time of defective spiritual understanding (11:10). In Paul it is the time before the consummation of God's rule (Rom. 13:12). Believers already stand in the light (1 Th. 5:5ff.) in contrast to those who are spiritually asleep or are drunk. As children of light, they are to walk in the light (cf. Rom. 13:11ff.).   [G. Delling, IV, 1123-26]

---

nōthrós [sluggish]

The word *nōthrós*, meaning "sluggish," "obtuse," occurs in the NT only in Hebrews. In 5:11 the author cannot deal with profounder themes because his readers are slow to hear and receive. This is because they lack the vitality of assured and persevering faith (6:12). Those who are exhausted in both breathing in (hearing) and breathing out (confident believing) are *nōthroí*.   [H. Preisker, IV, 1126]

ξ *x*

---

xénos [foreigner, stranger, guest], **xenía** [hospitality, guestroom], **xenízō** [to surprise, entertain], **xenodochéō** [to show hospitality], **philoxenía** [hospitality], **philóxenos** [host, hospitable]

A. The Tension in the *xénos* Concept.

1. Words of the *xen-* stem can mean "foreign" or "strange" but also "guest." The former is the main sense in the NT, though the less common "host" is the meaning

in Rom. 16:23. The verb *xenízō* in the NT means "to surprise," "to be strange" (Acts 17:20; 1 Pet. 4:4), but also "to entertain" (Acts 10:23; Heb. 13:2).

2. Strangeness produces mutual tension between natives and foreigners, but hospitality overcomes the tension and makes of the alien a friend. Historically foreigners are primarily enemies or outlaws who should be killed. It is then found, however, that hospitality is a better way to deal with strangers, and they thus become the wards of law and religion.

B. The Judgment of Antiquity.

1. Greeks and Romans.

a. The Treatment of Foreigners. Homer divides the nations into the savage and the hospitable. Greece prides itself on hospitality to strangers, although at first it treats them with reserve and grants them no rights. Religion puts strangers under the protection of Zeus and gradually their rights are defined. In ethics mistreating aliens is a serious offense, but aliens themselves incur specific obligations, e.g., military service. Rome at first grants no rights to aliens unless they have patrons, but the situation changes by the imperial period. In the cosmopolitan cities of Hellenism natives and aliens live side by side with no palpable distinctions.

b. Religious Evaluation. While the Bible opposes and condemns alien cults, Hellenism may deride them but is also interested in them. This is reflected in Acts 17:18ff., where some mock Paul's message but others are curious about it.

2. Israelites and Jews.

a. Foreign Peoples, Resident Aliens, and Aliens Temporarily Present.

(a) Terms. Hebrew has different words for foreigners denoting (1) the alien, (2) the resident alien, (3) the resident without rights, and (4) the alien temporarily present. For these the LXX usually has the terms *allótrios* or *allogenḗs, pároikos,* and *prosḗlytos. xénos* is not as such the direct equivalent of any of the Hebrew words.

(b) Basic Judgment. (1) Foreigners are primarily enemies both politically and religiously. (2) Yet if it is a wretched thing to be an alien (Gen. 19:4ff.), kindness is shown to foreign visitors. (3) Resident aliens come under protection (Ex. 22:20). They might at first be treated with contempt or even violence (cf. Gen. 12:26), but religious law takes them under its wing (cf. Dt. 10:18-19) and gradually integrates them into the people.

b. Historical Survey.

(a) The OT Period. The monarchy is a period of openness to foreigners (1 Kgs. 8:41ff.; 11:7-8), but the prophets head a reaction against foreign influences and especially foreign religions. Aliens are representatives of their religions, i.e., Gentiles. Their foreignness may be overcome either by exclusion or by full inclusion. Exilic prophecy calls for universal mission (Is. 42:6ff.; 66:19), but ungodly Gentiles are to be destroyed (Jer. 46ff.). After the exile the attitude hardens with the campaign against mixed marriages (Ezr. 9–10) and the opposition to the Samaritans. But resident aliens may still be full members of the community, since this is religiously rather than racially defined. The attitude to foreigners has a theological basis. It is for God's sake that mercy is to be shown to aliens and that efforts are to be made to win them, but it is also for God's sake that Gentiles are to be bitterly opposed.

(b) Later Judaism. Later Judaism practices strict separation from everything foreign. Yet there is a broader party (cf. Philo and Josephus) that is more open to foreigners and foreign influences. Missionary zeal appears on both sides. Yet semi-proselytes enjoy only limited civil and religious rights, and after A.D. 70 a stricter approach to Gentiles tends to prevail, the missionary impulse weakens, and even full proselytes, who are sharply distinguished from others, meet with some reserve. Since neighborly love need be shown only to members of the people, hostility to others increases except for the sake of peace. It may be noted that the rejection of aliens is thought to have eternal as well as temporal significance.

c. Graves of Foreigners. A question arises as to Mt. 27:7: Who are the strangers that are to be buried in this field? Of the various suggestions—Israelites temporarily in Jerusaelm, proselytes temporarily resident there, or Gentiles—the most likely one is that the field was meant for unclean Gentiles, who are thus set apart from members of the people even in death.

3. *The Attitude of Christians to Foreigners.* Christians share the dislike of the OT and Judaism for what is foreign in religion, but love of the *xenós* is a special form of love of neighbor, as Jesus shows (1) in the parable of the Good Samaritan and (2) in the parable of judgment in Mt. 25. That kindness to strangers has a bearing on eternal destiny is a theme in Parsee and Greek religion, and the thought occurs in Judaism too, but the new thing in Mt. 25 is that Jesus himself is the *xenós,* so that the deciding factor is one's relation to Jesus. The stranger representing Jesus might, of course, be anyone, and not just some other Christian. Thus all the ethical concepts of humanity regarding kindness to strangers come to fulfilment here; in the most alien of aliens Jesus himself is loved. The point is 3 Jn. 5, of course, is the different one that hospitality is to be shown to brethren from abroad.

C. The Custom of Hospitality.

1. *Greeks and Romans.* While aliens may have no rights, hospitality provides some compensation. Based on a sense of mutual obligation, this has divine sanction. Aliens are guests of deity, and sanctuaries are the primary places of hospitality. (a) There is, of course, private hospitality among the Greeks and Romans. Motives for this are the divine requirement, sympathy, and hope of return. (b) Hospitality may also take a more public or official form. (c) With increasing commerce, the need arises for inns or hospices, some of which are associated with temples, synagogues, or places of pilgrimage.

2. *Israelites and Jews.* The biblical stories extol hospitality (cf. Job 31:32). This is a duty as a work of mercy. In later Judaism the tradition continues, but with some emphasis on the meritoriousness of the work and some restriction to members of the people.

3. *Christians.* a. The NT.

(a) Terms. *philoxenía* is the term for hospitality, the *philóxenos* is the host, and the guestroom is the *xenía* (Phlm. 22).

(b) The Story and Message of Jesus. Hospitality is important in the Gospels. Jesus depends on it (Mk. 1:29ff.; 2:15ff., etc.). He regards it as important in the parables (Lk. 10:34-35; 11:5ff., etc.). God's hospitality is an essential part of his message (cf. the divine generosity in Lk. 14:16ff.; 12:37; 13:29, etc.).

(c) Exhortation. *agápē* implies *philoxenía.* The latter expresses *agápē* in Rom. 12:9ff. It is linked to *philadelphía* in Heb. 13:1-2. It is to be shown *by* all (Mt. 25:35ff.), but especially bishops etc. (1 Tim. 3:2). It is also to be shown *to* all (Rom. 12:13-14), although in fact it will be shown most to fellow believers (Gal. 6:10; 1 Pet. 4:9).

(d) Motives. While *agápē* is the ultimate motive, there is also a charismatic motive—hospitality is a charism; an eschatological motive—Christians are strangers and pilgrims going through affliction; a metaphysical motive—the hope of entertaining angels unawares (Heb. 13:2); and above all a missionary motive—aiding itinerant evangelists (cf. Mt. 10:11ff.; Acts 10:6, 18, 32; Phlm. 22; 3 Jn. 8), which in the case of genuine messengers plays a big part in the spread of the gospel and may lead to the baptism of whole families (cf. Acts 16:15, 33; Rom. 16:4-5).

b. The Early Church. Hospitality becomes a prominent feature in the early church (cf. 1 Clem. 1.2), although Origen complains of the gap between preaching and practice (*Homily 5.1 on Genesis*). Hermas *Mandates* 8.10 includes hospitality in the list of Christian virtues. With missionary increase, organization is needed, and in the fourth century Antioch cares daily for 3,000 widows, sick, and strangers. Bishops and widows are especially expected to be hospitable both privately and officially. Bigger churches and sanctuaries later set up hospices, and where care focuses on the sick these develop into hospitals.

4. *Christ the Host.* While Christ comes to earth as a guest, he is also depicted as the heavenly Host. In the OT God is often presented as the Host (cf. Pss. 15:1; 23:5), and as in the judgment, so in the related eschatological banquet, Jesus is the Host alongside God or in his place (cf. Mt. 22:2ff.). At this feast, which is for sinners, Christ offers lavish entertainment (Mt. 6:41ff.), he himself serves his guests (Lk. 12:37), washes their feet (Jn. 13:1ff.), and crowns his service by offering himself as their eternal nourishment (Mk. 14:22ff.).

D. Foreign as a Religious Concept.

1. The Greek and Biblical Views.

a. The Greek View. Foreignness has a religious aspect in Greek thought. But the approach is primarily anthropological. The soul belongs to the noetic world and by divine appointment is temporarily lodged as a stranger in the body. It is anxious in this alien world and longs for its heavenly home.

b. The Biblical View. The biblical approach is theological. The world belongs to God but has been estranged from him by an alien power, so that the antithesis of humanity is not with the world but with God. God's action, whether in grace or judgment, is alien to us. Israel, however, has been put in God's land as a resident alien under his protection, and as such, keeping God's law, she becomes a foreign body in the world of humanity.

2. Hellenistic Judaism. As represented by Philo, Hellenistic Judaism brings Greek ideas into the biblical world. The souls of the wise are of heavenly origin and hence are strangers on earth. The wise prefer heavenly citizenship even if this means that they are strangers here. Hillel calls his soul a guest in the body.

3. The NT.

a. God and Christ. The NT follows the OT pattern. God and the world are alien to one another because of human estrangement from God (cf. Acts 17:23; Eph. 4:18). This estrangement means hostility. On account of it Christ comes to the world as a stranger (Mk. 12:1ff.; Jn. 8:14, 25ff.). He comes from the unknown God (Jn. 7:27ff.). He lives as in a tent (Jn. 1:14). He is subject to misunderstanding (3:4). Even his disciples must ask who he is (21:12). His dominion is not of this world (18:36). He must go back to heaven to take his kingdom (Mt. 25:15; Lk. 19:12).

b. Christians.

(a) Legal Terminology. Christians, too, are strangers in the world, for God has given them a new home in heaven (Heb. 11:15-16; Eph. 2:6; Phil. 3:20). In legal terms, they belong to the city of God (Heb. 11:10, 16; 12:22-23). Formerly outlaws, they now have civil rights there (Eph. 2:19). They are thus aliens in the world (Jn. 15:19; 17:14, 16). They live as sheep among wolves (Mt. 10:16). The world is offended by them (1 Pet. 4:4). They can only reside as aliens in it (2:11). In the apostolic fathers Diog. 5.5 makes this point with impressive force, and cf. Hermas *Similitudes* 1.1; 2 Clem. 5.1.

(b) OT Prototypes. For this position of Christians in the world, models are found in (1) the patriarchs (Heb. 11:8ff.), (2) Israel in Egypt (Acts 7:6), and (3) the Jewish dispersion (Jms. 1:1; 1 Pet. 1:1).

c. Foreignness and Foreigners. Christians have to be on guard against making this world their homeland. They must therefore avoid all strange ways and doctrines. Yet they must offer the gospel freely to foreigners (in contrast to Greek, Roman, and Jewish exclusiveness).

d. The Devil as Foreigner. Behind the world stands the devil, who in relation to God and believers is the supreme alien and enemy (Mt. 13:39; Lk. 10:19). In the early church *ho xenós* is thus one of the names for the devil.

4. Fusions of Biblical and Greek Views.

a. Gnosticism. Hellenization effects a fusion of the very different biblical and Greek views of foreignness. Thus Gnosticism makes a big point of the foreignness of the soul, its longing for another world (the strange world of God), and its redemption by the stranger from heaven. A complication is that the soul, astray in a strange world, becomes alien from its true home. The redeemer-stranger, however, does not let himself be alienated, rekindles in the soul homesickness for heaven, and by attaching it to himself makes it foreign again in the world. In some versions the redeemer, by clothing himself in earthly garments, runs the risk of alienation and has thus to be redeemed by a letter from home and a heavenly voice. In distinction from the NT this complex does not see that it is sin that brings estrangement or that Christians become strangers in the world only when Christ brings redemption. Gnosticism thinks anthropocentrically. It starts with the experience of foreignness, whereas the Bible starts with the holy and gracious God.

b. Marcion. For Marcion humans, as creatures of the just God, are alien to the good God. This alien God brings them into the new Father's house. Marcion, then, thinks theocentrically, but in contrast to the NT his stranger God comes in merciful love to redeem those who are not his concern, since he has not created them. In other words, God is *essentially* a stranger. In the Bible, however, estrangement is due to the fall. God's world has become an alien world, and by God's saving action believers become alien in and to it.   [G. STÄHLIN, V, 1-36]

→ *allogenḗs, allóphylos, bárbaros, éthnos, parepídēmos, pároikos, prosḗlytos, phílos*

---

xýlon [wood, cross, tree]

---

xýlon means living or dead "wood," anything made of wood, e.g., a "stick," "cudgel," or "club," also a "bench" or "table." As an instrument of punishment or restraint it is a kind of wooden collar. It is also used for the "stake" or "tree" to which malefactors are fastened. Figuratively *xýlon* is an "unfeeling" person. The LXX often uses *xýla* for trees, but also has *xýlon* for wood, used for cultic or secular purposes.

1. Wood. The NT offers instances of the use for both living and dead wood. Thus in Lk. 23:31 we have the contrast between green wood and dry. If God has not spared the green wood (Jesus), how will it be with the dry (the impenitent)? In 1 Cor. 3:12 Paul lists wood among the materials which might be used in the building that God will examine on the judgment day. Scented wood has a place in the cargo that merchants can no longer sell after the fall of Babylon (Rev. 18:12); this is wood from North Africa used to make costly vessels and inlaid work.

2. *Cudgel.* Those sent to arrest Jesus carry cudgels *(xýla)* according to Mt. 26:47, 55.

3. *Stocks.* Paul and Silas are put in stocks when arrested at Philippi (Acts 16:24).

4. *The Cross.* A distinctive use of *xýlon* in the NT is for the cross. The basis is Dt. 21:22, which stresses the shame of being exposed on a tree. Acts 5:30; 10:39, etc. make the point that crucifixion is the greatest possible insult to Jesus, but that God has displayed his majesty by raising him from the dead. Paul in Gal. 3:13 shows that Christ has redeemed us from the curse by being made a curse for us according to Dt. 21:22. A curse lies on those who break the law, but Christ, who has not broken the law, voluntarily and vicariously becomes accursed, as his death on the accursed wood makes plain. He thus releases us from the curse and from the death that it entails. 1 Pet. 2:24 is to the same effect when it says that Christ bore our sins in his own body on the "tree" (with a plain reference to Is. 53:4, 12). The vicarious element is prominent here. Human sins are laid on Christ, crucified in him, and thus set aside. Christ does not lay sins on a scapegoat, but takes them to himself and cancels them on the cross, so that sinners, dead to sin, may live to righteousness.

5. *Tree (of Life).* Revelation speaks of the tree or trees of life in paradise or the heavenly Jerusalem (2:7; 22:2, 14, 19). A share in their fruit is granted to those who are cleansed by Christ and who conquer, but it is withheld from those who reject the prophetic word. In this regard Revelation takes up the apocalyptic notion of salvation as restoration. Yet perhaps there is also some association between the tree of life and the cross, as in early Christian art.   [J. SCHNEIDER, V, 37-41]

O o

ónkos [weight, burden]

ónkos means "mass," "weight," "compass," and figuratively "burden." In Heb. 12:1 it obviously means the "weight" that contestants must put off if they are to finish the race. The use of "every" shows that the author has no specific hindrance in mind. Believers must not let anything hamper them.   [H. SEESEMANN, V, 41]

---

hodós [way, road, manner of life], *hodēgós* [leader, guide], *hodēgéō* [to lead, guide], *methodeía* [craftiness], *eísodos* [entrance, access], *éxodos* [way out, death], *diéxodos* [outlet, exit], *euodóō* [to guide well, prosper]

---

hodós.

A. *hodós* for the Greeks.

1. *General.* This word means "way," "path," "road," "route," also "course," "journey," "march," and figuratively "means," "procedure," "manner." Life is often com-

pared to a way, as in phrases that speak about the path of life or the manner of life. A technical philosophical use is for a "way of inquiry" or "method."

2. *The Prodicus Fable.* In view of the importance of the two ways in Jewish and Christian writings, note should be taken of the fable of Hercules at the crossroads. Earlier Hesiod speaks about two ways, a short and easy one to evil and a long and steep one to virtue. In the case of Hercules there is no contrasting of the ways, and the main point is the vision of the two women who seek to win him for good or evil. Only in later versions do the two ways take on the greater significance that justifies the idea of a crossroads.

3. *hodós in Religiously Significant Statements.* A common idea is that there are two ways after death, but it should be noted that these are ways of destiny, not decision, and that sometimes we find three ways. *hodós* also occurs in connection with the ascent of the soul. The way to truth (right thinking) is a way to heavenly light. In Hermetic writings *gnôsis* is a way. In Gnosticism the soul takes the way from heaven to earth and then at death from earth back home to heaven. But the idea of the way is not an essential one in Gnosticism.

B. *hodós* in the LXX and Judaism.

1. The LXX. hodós occurs some 880 times in the LXX (mostly for *drk*). Often what is denoted is literally a path, road, or street, whether well constructed or not. It is a bad sign when streets are deserted (Lev. 16:22) or when one must resort to byways (Judg. 5:6). Verbs are used in phrases that do not refer to a specific road, e.g., "to go one's way" (Gen. 32:1). One may pass people on the way (Job 21:29) and should not deviate from it (Num. 22:23). Animals also have their ways (Prov. 30:19; figuratively 6:6). Thunders take a divinely ordained course (Job 28:26). God takes his way in judgment (Nah. 1:3) but also in saving grace (the Red Sea, Ps. 77:19). Figurative use is common (cf. Dt. 8:2; Prov. 1:31). Life itself is viewed as a way (cf. passages like Prov. 4:10; Is. 40:27; Job 3:23), and dying is a way that all must go (1 Kgs. 2:2) and from which none can return (Job 16:22). Another common use is for "manner of life" or "conduct" (cf. Ex. 18:20; 1 Sam. 18:14; 8:3, 5 etc.; 2 Kgs. 22:2 etc.). More frequently we read of the way or ways of God. These may be God's own dealings, but they may also be the ways that he commands for us (Jer. 7:23). The ways are thus equivalent to the commands (Ps. 119:15 etc.). Yet these ways do not have to relate to specific commandments of the law (cf. 1 Kgs. 11:33 with Dt. 5:33). Various descriptions are offered: they are good ways (1 Sam. 12:23), right ways (1 Sam. 12:23), the way of truth (Ps. 119:30), the everlasting way (Ps. 139:24), etc. Some passages assume that people can follow these ways (Job 23:11; Ps. 17:4, etc.), but others state that people neither observe (Mal. 2:9) nor know them (Jer. 5:4-5). Mostly they leave the right way (Prov. 2:13) and follow their own ways (Is. 56:11), which may seem right to them (Prov. 12:15). The self-chosen way is a wicked one (Is. 65:2); cf. such expressions as the way of the wicked (Ps. 1:6) or of sinners (1:1), or the ways of darkness (Prov. 2:13). The cry of the prophets is that we should return from our evil ways (Zech. 1:4 etc.). God sees all our ways (Prov. 5:21) and punishes wicked ways (Hos. 4:9). Yet we cannot turn from such ways unless God helps us. He has promised this help, teaching us his ways, and leading us in the way we should go (Is. 48:17). Yet if the thought of divine assistance is always present, the many imperatives show that we are responsible for our ways and for taking God's way. Knowing the ways of the Lord, we should also proclaim them (Ps. 51:13; 1 Sam. 12:23). What is said about human ways presupposes an antithesis between God's ways and self-chosen ways, but only rarely do we find the metaphor of the two ways. The most important instance is in Ps. 1:6, and cf. also Prov. 4:18-19; 15:19; Pss. 119:29-30; 139:24; Prov. 11:20. Included in the contrast are the thoughts of light and life on the one side and darkness and death on the other. The range is narrow, however, and we find neither any reference to the two ways as such nor any attempt to integrate all the hortatory material into this schema. As regards the ways that God himself takes, the combination with *érga* shows that *hodoí* may mean "dealings" and that with *boulaí* (Is. 55:8-9) the reference may be to "purposes" or "plans." God's ways are mercy and truth (Ps. 25:110). They are also right (Hos. 14:10) and perfect (Ps. 18:30). God is righteous in all his ways (Ps. 145:17). His ways are beyond human criticism, for we can know only the outskirts of them (Job 26:14). Is. 55:8-9 gives classical expression to this thought when it states categorically that God's ways are not ours, but are higher than ours. Distinctive concepts in the LXX usage are that there is no human way to virtue, that an attainable human goal does not control the metaphor, and that the divine commandment stands at the beginning of the true way.

2. *The Influence of OT Usage on the Pseudepigrapha and Rabbinic Writings.* When the pseudepigrapha speak about two ways, OT influence is plain. The literal use of "way" is rare. References occur to the "course" of years or the stars, and to the "way" of angels. The sense of "walk" is common, and we also read of God's "ways," either his dealings or his commands. A contrast is drawn between the ways of this world and those of the next. The image of the two ways occurs in Eth. En. 91:18-19, which enjoins the way of righteousness and warns against that of violence, but the image is not as yet a fixed part of catechetical instruction. It is found at times in the rabbis on the basis of Dt. 11:26; 30:19; God has set before his people the ways of life and death. Here it might refer either to the destiny that God has appointed or to the decision that we must make. Again, however, there is no generally accepted schema.

3. *Philo and Josephus.* Philo makes great use of *hodós* in many senses, e.g., for the Red Sea "passage," for the "ways" of the sea or stars, for "procedure," for "human life," for the "paths" that we should take, for the "way" to virtue or to God, for the "two ways" (of vice and virtue) between whch choice must be made (although with little schematic content), for the "royal way" that is identical with God's word or with wisdom (cf. Num. 20:17; 21:22; Dt. 28:14), or for the "right way," which is in general the broad or smooth one as distinct from the slippery way of wrong. Philo stresses that we need a guide on the right way, i.e., Moses, the *lógos,* or God himself, who as a merciful Savior leads the *noús* to virtue. In Josephus the word mostly has the literal sense of road, street, corridor, passage, journey, march, etc., although at times we find the sense "manner of life" and less commonly "means," "purpose," or "possibility."

C. *hodós* in the NT.

1. *The Literal Sense.* Most instances of the literal use are in the Synoptics. We are not told what roads Jesus used. Only two roads are mentioned, from Jerusalem to Jericho in Lk. 10:31 and from Jerusalem to Gaza in Acts 8:26. Some incidents take place "on the road" (cf. Mk. 8:27; 10:32; Mt. 20:17). The reference in Mk. 9:33 is a general one, but Lk. 9:57 is more narrowly topographical. Mk. 10:52 adds an "on the way" to indicate that the man who has received his sight follows Jesus on the path to Jerusalem. *hodós* occurs in certain parables but with no special emphasis. Thus seed falls along the path (Mk. 4:4, 15), which runs either through or alongside the field. In Lk. 14:21ff. the servant who has gone first to the lanes is then to go to the

highways. In Lk. 11:6 the friend who comes is on a journey. Other uses are for the way leading to the Gentiles in Mt. 10:5, the way of the sea (toward the sea?) in Mt. 4:15, a way that is taken in Mk. 2:23, and a day's journey in Lk. 2:44.

2. *The Metaphorical Use.* This important use of *hodós* is found throughout the NT. How far the idea of a road is present is not always clear; cf. Mk. 1:3, where the meaning might be "plan" or "work" as well as "way" (cf. Mt. 11:10).

a. The Two Ways in Mt. 7:13-14. Jesus uses the image of the two ways in Mt. 7:13-14 (cf. Lk. 13:24). The first thought is that of entering by the narrow gate, but this seems to be a parallel metaphor—the gate does not lead on to the way. Thus the way is narrow (or broad) as well as the gate, in contrast to other descriptions of the right way. There are no exact parallels to Jesus' presentation, although gate and way are sometimes brought together, e.g., the little gate that leads on to a difficult way, or the narrow path or entrance. It is unlikely that Mt. 7:13 is directly related to 7:12 (the golden rule), nor is the door to be seen as entry into God's kingdom (as in Lk. 13:24). Again, the narrow way is not just that of piety in contrast to the broad way of vice and frivolity, although such an understanding might fit in with the call of Jesus for conversion. Furthermore, the saying is not primarily polemical, i.e., directed against the Pharisaical view of the law. What we have is a summons to discipleship. Jesus' demands are severe. Hence the gate is narrow and the way is hard. But there is no other way to life. If there are few on this way, it is not because it is too small, but because people like an easier path. The few of v. 14 are disciples; the many of v. 13 are those who refuse discipleship. "Way" does not denote the way of life of disciples but what Jesus expects of them. Like "gate," "way" has the connotation of entry. The destination, then, is mentioned, either life or destruction. "Finding" in v. 14 does not imply choice among many ways, or trying to find a path in difficult terrain, or coming across a narrow entry after a lengthy search. It involves the mystery of the divine action whereby those who seek will find. Although Mt. 7:13-14 does not explicitly say so, the way is found in Christ himself; it is he who makes possible our entry on it.

b. The Way into the Sanctuary (Heb. 9:8; 10:20). The uses of *hodós* in Heb. 9:8 and 10:20 are related. In 9:8 *hodós* clearly has a topographical connection with the temple, yet in the light of 10:19 the thought is more that of access than of way *(eísodos)*, although still not without a certain spatial reference. Even if it is not stated, the way is obviously a way to (fellowship with) God. Jesus is not said to be the way, but the term "living" shows that the way is closely connected with his person. That Jesus is the way is thus a fairly clear implication.

c. Jesus as the Way (Jn. 14:4ff.). The statement in Jn. 14:4 grows out of the context. Jesus is talking about the situation of the disciples. The dwellings of 14:2 represent the goal of salvation. Jesus is going and will prepare a place for them. The disciples are not said to be going with him (e.g., to martyrdom); he will finally take them to be with himself (v. 3). The way of 14:4 is thus the way of Jesus, which the disciples ought to know because he has told them. But this way includes the promise for the disciples that Jesus has given in v. 3. Thus the question of Thomas refers to the significance of the way of Jesus for his followers, and the same is true of the answer of Jesus in v. 6. The secondary clause ("no one comes . . .") makes the sense plain. It stresses the importance of the "I am," and if it rules out other attempts to get at the Father (especially by the disciples), its thrust is positive. Thomas is asking about the one way, and Jesus replies that he himself is that way. One should note that, while v. 7 might imply a general attaining to fellowship with God, v. 3 links the way more closely to the coming again of Jesus. A question thus arises whether 14:6 is exclusively eschatological or whether 14:4 prepares the way for a general reference as well. The terms "truth" and "life" in v. 6 have a bearing on this. These might represent the goal of the *hodós,* but in view of vv. 2ff. *hodós* itself refers to both way and goal. Hence the function of "truth" and "life" is more likely one of elucidation: Jesus is the way as he is the truth and the life. While "life" has an eschatological flavor in John (11:25), these terms serve to effect the redirection to the present that one finds in v. 7, although they do not involve any conflict with what precedes. No direct models have been found for linking the three terms. At most, we read of the way(s) of truth or life in the OT, and the law is separately called way, truth, and life in rabbinic works, though this does not warrant any antithesis of Jesus and the law in this or other passages. The Gnostic idea of the heavenly journey of the soul can hardly have had much influence, for elsewhere in John *hodós* occurs only in 1:23, there is no reference to the heavenly origin of souls or to their return, the orientation is to the coming again of Jesus rather than the death and subsequent journey of the disciples, and John lays little stress on the function of the Redeemer as guide. The passage might be directed against rival contemporary claims, but since *hodós* is adequately explained by the context, it undoubtedly has its own unique and positive significance.

3. *The Figurative Use.* In the figurative use the spatial idea is often strong. Thus in Lk. 1:79 "way" rather than "means" is the obvious point (cf. the verb "guide"). In contrast to Is. 59:8 (cf. Rom. 3:17) the reference of peace here is to messianic salvation rather than a life at peace with others. In Acts 2:28 (cf. Ps. 16:10-11) *hodós* might refer to the "means" or "possibility" of the resurrection, and "means" seems to be the point in Acts 16:17. In 1 Cor. 12:31 the context does not support "means" as the means of seeking the best gifts. On the other hand, one does not have to think in terms of "manner of life" or "attitude." The "way" is probably the means of reaching the goal that is elsewhere sought by the earnest desiring. The idea of "walk" or "conduct" is often plain enough, e.g., in Jms. 1:8; Acts 14:16; Rom. 3:6; Jms. 5:20; 2 Pet. 2:2 (though this might denote true teaching); probably Mt. 21:32. Another sense is the "divinely commanded walk" (cf. 2 Pet. 2:21; Heb. 3:10). This is the obvious sense in Mk. 12:14. It might also be the meaning in Acts 13:10, although in the light of OT parallels (Dan. 3:27; Hos. 14:10) the reference here is perhaps to God's dealings. In 1 Cor. 4:17 Paul is thinking of the ways that he teaches, not his own manner of life. In the light of Rom. 2:16, these ways correspond to the walk that God requires. Hence the reference could well be to the "principles" or "commands" that Paul imparts. On the other hand, in Acts 9:2; 19:9, 23; 22:4, 14, 22 what is meant is the mode of life expressed in Christian fellowship. In the absolute, the singular *hodós* is here the Christian equivalent of what others would call *haíresis* (cf. Acts 24:14). Implied is the teaching or view that others might disparage but Christians believe to be the right one. "This way" in 22:4 does not imply that there might be other ways but is simply giving precision to what is in view. How this special use of *hodós* develops is hard to explain. Acts 18:25-26 is of little help, for here the "way of the Lord" is the divine plan or work of salvation. Nor are we aided by 2 Pet. 2:2, 21, for these verses do not permit us to give to *hodós* a single absolute sense. The OT and later Jewish use offer no parallels for the specific usage in Acts, and it is unlikely that Luke develops it out of the use of *hodós* for philosophical "method" (and hence "system"). Furthermore, there is only a tenuous link with the Damascus description of apostates as "those who deviate from the way." In Acts 18:25-26 and 13:10 the divine plan of salvation and its fulfilment in the Christian mission are at issue. Rom.

11:33 and Rev. 15:3 also refer to the divine plans, which are inscrutable, but just and true.

D. Early Christian Usage. In the apostolic fathers *hodós* is fairly rare in the literal sense. It occurs in the confusing allegory in Hermas *Visions* 4.1.2, where leaving the way proves no way at all, although the stones that fall from the tower are said to fall on the way. In Ignatius *Romans* 9.3 the way is obviously the way that Ignatius takes; the *katá sárka* indicates that he is not a free agent on it. The idea of a journey also occurs in 1 Clem. 12.4 (the story of Rahab). Figurative use is more common. *agápē* is a way in Ignatius *Ephesians* 9.1, while the ways of 1 Clem. 31.1 seem to be ways of achieving blessing, and in 36.1 *hodós* has the sense of conduct (cf. Hermas *Visions* 2.2.6). Along similar lines we read of the way of truth or righteousness (cf. Barn. 1.4; 2 Clem. 5.7). *hodós* has the sense of command in Apoc. Pet. 1. This Apocalypse (2.2) also employs *hodós tḗs dikaiosýnēs* for what is virtually the gospel or the Christian faith. The metaphor of the two ways is important in the apostolic fathers. In addition to brief references, e.g., in Barn. 10.10, the two main passages are Barn. 18–20 and Did. 1–6. Of these, Didache integrates the hortatory material more consistently with its antithesis of the ways of life and death (as compared to light and darkness in Barnabas). It may be noted that in Didache the ways lead to life or death, whereas in Barnabas they are controlled by light or darkness. Didache is closer to Mt. 7:13-14, but neither refers to a gate nor uses the descriptions "broad" and "narrow." Barnabas possibly rests on Prov. 4:18-19, and Didache may also reflect Jewish influence. The angels of Barn. 18.1 hardly form a parallel to the women of the Prodicus fable. The two ways are also described in Hermas *Mandates* 6.1.2ff., where the sense of walk is prominent. Here there are no paths on the crooked way, but the straight way is level and smooth. *hodós* is of no significance in the Apologists. Justin has it mostly in biblical quotations. He also refers to the way of the stars and to the way of the Baptist (*Dialogue* 85.5; 88.2). The letter of the churches of Vienne and Lyons (Eusebius *Ecclesiastical History* 5.1.48) uses "way" for Christian teaching, but this is not common.

hodēgós, hodēgéō. hodēgós has the sense of "leader" or "guide," while *hodēgéō* means "to lead," "to show the way," "to instruct." The noun is rare in the LXX. It occurs for guides in 1 Macc. 4:2 and for the pillar of fire in Wis. 18:3. The verb is more common; mostly it is God who leads or guides or instructs (cf. Ex. 13:17; Josh. 24:3; Pss. 25:9; 78:72, etc.). The spatial sense comes out when *hodēgéō* is used with *hodós* or *tríbos*, but when it is parallel to *didáskō* the meaning "to teach" is strong. Wisdom is the subject in Wis. 9:11 etc., but OT parallels make it clear that God is in view. Philo has *hodēgós* only once and *hodēgéō* not at all (though we do find *podēgetéō* in *On the Unchangeableness of God* 182 etc.). The idea of guiding angels is common among the rabbis; they fetch the souls of the righteous after death. In the NT *hodēgós* has a literal sense in Acts 1:16 (Judas is the guide who leads the police to Jesus). The sense is also literal in the figure of speech in Mt. 23:16, 24 (the Pharisees are leaders of others but are themselves blind). Paul's use is similar in Rom. 2:19. *hodēgéō* has a literal sense in Mt. 15:14 and Rev. 7:17, and a figurative sense ("to instruct") in Acts 8:31. In Jn. 16:31 the idea might be that of "leading" to the goal of full truth, but one might ask whether the thought is not that of the Spirit's instruction complementing and completing that of Jesus, i.e., in the whole sphere of truth (cf. 14:26). If the thought is that of "leading," then the suggestion is that the Spirit (and Jesus before him) is a *hodēgós*, for which there would be nonbiblical parallels. If, however, the sense is "to teach," alien influence is less likely. *hodēgós* does not occur in the apostolic fathers but we find *hodēgéō* in Did. 3.2ff., where the point is that sinful impulses may seem trivial but they lead to great offenses. *hodēgós* does not occur in the Apologists, and *hodēgéō* is rare (cf. Justin *Dialogue* 38.3).

methodeía. This word is not attested prior to the NT. We find *méthodos* for "treatment," "procedure," or, in a bad sense, "deception," and *methodeúō* for "to treat methodically," "to handle according to plan," also "to handle craftily," "to deceive." In the NT *methodeía* occurs only in Ephesians. In 4:11 we have a warning against those who act craftily, while the word again has a bad sense in 6:11, where believers are to put on the whole armor of God against the machinations of the devil. In the apostolic fathers only *methodeúō* occurs, the sense being "to distort."

eísodos, éxodos, diéxodos. *eísodos* and *éxodos* often occur together. Literally they mean "entrance" and "exit." Figuratively we find them for "access" and "exodus" (in such varied senses as going away, banishment, dissolution, or conclusion). Commercially they denote "income" and "expenditure." *eísodos* occurs some 50 times in the LXX for "entrance," "gate," "door," "entry." *éxodos* occurs in over 70 verses, sometimes for a way out, then for leaving, departing, exporting, and often for the exodus from Egypt. "Going out and coming in" is a common phrase to denote fellowship (1 Sam. 29:6) or total activity (2 Sam. 3:25). In Wis. 7:6 the two words denote birth and death. The terms are rare in Philo in a spatial sense, but we often find them for coming and going, and Philo also uses *éxodos* for "death" in the sense of departure on a journey. Josephus makes common use of the two words both spatially, e.g., for "entrance," and verbally, e.g., for "marching in," or "visiting prisoners," or for "riding out," "setting off," and even "escaping." The terms are rare in the NT, never occur together, and do not have the spatial sense. *eísodos* in Heb. 10:19 means "entry" or "access" rather than "entrance" (even though it is not used with *eis*). This is also the point in 2 Pet. 1:11 (with *eis*). In 1 Thessalonians (with *prós*) the idea is that of a welcome in 1:9 and a first appearance or visit in 2:1. In Acts 13:24 the Baptist is said to have preached before the public appearance of Jesus, i.e., not his coming into the world, but the beginning of his ministry. *éxodos* occurs only three times. It refers to the exodus from Egypt in Heb. 11:22. In Lk. 9:31 and 2 Pet. 1:15 it means the end of life in the sense of "conclusion" rather than "departure." Thus Lk. 9:31 is not speaking of Jesus' going out of the world but of the conclusion of his life and work. There is certainly no reference to his coming out of the grave (though the resurrection may well be in view in the light of 9:22). In the apostolic fathers *eísodos* occurs only once in Hermas *Similitudes* 9.12.6 (for "entrance") and *éxodos* only once in Hermas *Visions* 3.4.3 for "end." Of the Apologists Justin uses both terms frequently both independently and in quotations. *diéxodos* occurs in the parable in Mt. 22:9, most likely in the sense of "end"; the *diéxodoi tōn hodōn* are the points where the town streets give way to country roads. Mt. 22:9 thus seems to combine Lk. 14:21, 23 and supports the view that Jesus means the gospel for the Gentiles too. Outside the NT *diéxodos* means "gate," "passage," "exit." The LXX has it for the endpoints of boundaries (Num. 34; Josh. 15–19). It can also denote a "spring," and figuratively it has such varied meanings as "escape," "result," and "exposition" or "elucidation."

euodóō. This rare term means "to lead on a good path," "to guide well," "to bring on to the right path." Its attestation prior to the LXX is dubious, but it is common in the LXX, where it takes on the sense "to bring to a good conclusion," "to succeed." In some 40 instances God is the one to whom success is ascribed either directly or indirectly, and this finds a counterpart in the use of the stronger compound *kateuodóō*, mostly in the passive. (For details of LXX usage see *TDNT,* V, 110-12.) The only NT instances are in Rom. 1:10, 1 Cor. 16:2, and 3 Jn. 2 (twice). All these are in the passive and LXX influence is plain. The fairly obvious meaning in Rom. 1:10 is "I will succeed," although with a hint perhaps that God will make a way, or provide the opportunity. In 1 Cor. 16:2 it might seem at first as though we have in *hó ti* an accusative of object, but it is more probably the material subject, so that the sense is "as much as possible." It is unlikely that there is reference to "profit"; the idea of success is linked to saving, which each is to accomplish with genuine weekly sacrifice. In 3 Jn. 2 we have a customary wish for health, but the stress is on *euodoústhai* rather than *hygiaínein,* probably because this is a less secular term and carries the thought that all health and success, both material and spiritual, depend on God, and that we may have confidence in him. In Hermas *Similitudes* 6.3.5 the point seems to be success in business ventures, while Justin in *Dialogue* 14.6 quotes Is. 55:11 and in *Epitome* 7.8 uses *euodoún* in the sense "to be well advised."   [W. MICHAELIS, V, 42-114]

---

odýnē [pain, distress], **odynáomai** [to suffer pain]

odýnē means a. "physical pain" and b. "mental distress." *odynáō* is "to cause pain or sorrow," passive "to feel pain," "to suffer." The main LXX use is for deep grief of soul, as in Zech. 12:10; Is. 38:15; Am. 8:10; Prov. 17:25; Ezek. 21:11. In the NT Paul uses *odýnē* in Rom. 9:2 for his distress that his compatriots are shut off from salvation. In 1 Tim. 6:10 the reference is to pangs of conscience that afflict those who defect through love of money. *odynáomai* occurs four times in Luke and Acts. In Lk. 4:28 it is anxiety for a beloved child, in Lk. 16:24 torment at eternal loss, in 16:25 the anguish of remorse, and in Acts 20:38 the sorrow of final parting from the apostle.

[F. HAUCK, V, 115]

(odýromai [bewail, lament]**)**, **odyrmós** [lamentation]

odýromai means transitively "to bewail" and intransitively "to wail," "lament," "grieve." It occurs in the LXX only in Jer. 31:18. *odyrmós* means "lamentation" or "weeping." It occurs in the LXX in Jer. 31:15 (cf. also 2 Macc. 11:6). Only the noun occurs in the NT, first in Mt. 2:18 quoting Jer. 31:15, then in 2 Cor. 7:7. In the former it expresses Rachel's grief; in the latter the Corinthians' remorse.

[F. HAUCK, V, 116]

---

oída [to know, understand]

1. *oída,* which means "to know" and is more or less synonymous with *ginóskō,* is often used in the NT in a general way, e.g., to know a person in Mk. 14:71, to be able to understand in Mt. 7:11, to apprehend in Eph. 1:18, and to recognize in 1 Th. 5:12.

2. Theologically significant is the phrase "to know (or not to know) God or Christ."

Not knowing God is culpable, as in the OT (cf. Gal. 4:8; Tit. 1:16; 1 Th. 4:5). Demons know Jesus (Mk. 1:24), but try to defend themselves by declaring his true name. Over against the Gnostics in Corinth Paul is determined to know only the crucified Christ (1 Cor. 2:2). Over against Judaizers he insists on more than the knowledge of Jesus on earth (2 Cor. 5:16).

3. In John Jesus is said to know God (7:28-29). This is not abstract knowledge but a knowledge of mission that produces obedience (8:55). Jesus knows that this mission will issue in his death (13:1ff.). The Jews, however, do not know Jesus (8:23). The Baptist is aware of this (1:26). Even the disciples do not know him (4:32; 14:7). Yet they are not of the world, and hence knowledge is promised to them when Jesus departs and the Paraclete comes (14:15ff.; 16:7ff.).   [H. SEESEMANN, V, 116-19]

---

oíkos [house, family, household, race], *oikía* [house, family], *oikeíos* [member], *oikéō* [to live, inhabit], *oikodómos* [builder], *oikodoméō* [to build, edify], *oikodomḗ* [building, edifying], *epoikodoméō* [to build on], *synoikodoméō* [to build together], *oikonómos* [steward, manager], *oikonomía* [management, administration], *katoikéō* [to dwell], *oikētḗrion* [dwelling place], *katoikētḗrion* [dwelling place], *katoikízō* [to make to dwell], *oikouménē* [the inhabited world]

---

oíkos (→ *oikía*).

1. General Greek and Hellenistic Usage. oíkos means "house" or "dwelling." The dwelling may be a cave, a temple, a palace, or even a grave. In the papyri *oíkos* can also mean "domestic affairs," "wealth," or "property." In astrology it is used for the "station" of the planets.

2. "House" and "House of God" in the OT. oíkos, mostly for Heb. *bayit,* is a common word in the LXX. It may mean "family," but with *theoú* is often used for "sanctuary." Like *oikía,* it also means "house"; cf. the house that wisdom builds in Prov. 9:1 (and rabbinic references to the house of the law).

3. "House of God" in Jesus and the Gospels. The NT uses both *oíkos* and *oikía,* but usually links *toú theoú* to *oíkos,* reserving the phrase for the temple (or the Christian community, Heb. 3:6; 1 Pet. 4:17). Jesus speaks about the house of God in Mk. 2:26 and in Mk. 11:17 (based on Is. 56:7), where the temple is holy because it is a house of prayer for the nations (cf. Jn. 2:16, which recalls Zech. 14:21). While Jesus uses "my Father's house" for the temple, as in Lk. 2:49, his phrase may also denote the heavenly home (Jn. 14:2). The house also suggests the kingdom, as in Jn. 8:35.

4. The Heavenly "Father's House" in Gnosticism and Philo. Gnosticism favors the picture of the "house." The world is a lower dwelling in Mandaean writings. The elect are promised a place in the Father's house, for which they long. Philo, too, speaks of the return of the soul to the Father's house (*On Dreams* 1.256). He spiritualizes and individualizes the concept of the house of God (1.149). The divine house is not spatial but represents God's care. When the cosmos is viewed as a house, God is obviously its builder or Creator. For Philo, the body may also stand as the house of the soul, and the soul itself is a house which lodges holy and pious thoughts (*On the Confusion of Tongues* 27) or receives the *lógos* (*On the Unchangeableness of God* 135).

5. Primitive Christian Sayings about the Earthly Temple and Contacts with Near Eastern Symbolical Use. In Lk. 11:51 Zacharias is struck down between the altar and the *oíkos.* In Acts 7:2ff. Stephen distinguishes between the tent and the *oíkos,* perhaps viewing the tent more favorably, unless v. 47 applies to the tent as well. In Mt. 23:38 Jesus may be alluding to the temple, but it is also possible that he has the whole city or people in view. Relative to Mt. 12:44; Lk. 11:24, Babylonian and later Jewish texts speak about demons pursuing their unnatural activities in shrines and houses.

6. *"House of God" as a Primitive Christian Image for the Community.* Heb. 3:1ff. calls Moses a faithful servant in all God's house, while Christ in contrast is faithful over God's house as a son. In the OT "my house" refers to Israel, so that the NT passage recalls the equation of house and community. The glory of Moses relates to that of Christ as building does to builder. Christ as the son builds the OT community and is thus set over it. Believers are this house if they hold fast their confidence. Earlier Paul refers to the church as God's temple (1 Cor. 3:16). Primarily the whole church rather than the individual is God's house. This line of thought is fully developed in Eph. 2:19ff. and 1 Pet. 2:3ff. It leads on naturally to the usage in 1 Pet. 4:17 and 1 Tim. 3:15. The meaning of *oíkos* in this connection is not "family" but "dwelling" (cf. the comparison of Christ and Christians to stones in 1 Pet. 2:4ff., and the introduction of the thought of priesthood and sacrifice in 1 Pet. 2:5, 9). 1 Pet. 4:17 takes up the prophetic concept that purifying judgment will first smite the sanctuary and people (cf. Ezek. 9:6), while 1 Tim. 3:15 expresses the fact that the church as God's house is the bastion of truth inasmuch as the Spirit dwells in it.

7. *The Related Symbolism of Later Jewish Apocalyptic and the Rabbinate.* "House" is a common metaphor in the historical allegories in En. 83ff. It may stand for the sanctuary, for Jerusalem, or for the new and heavenly Jerusalem. In the rabbis the highest of the seven heavens is the dwelling of God. This is hidden by a curtain, but the righteous dead and ministering angels may approach, although they do not see God face to face.

8. *"House" as Family and Race.* On an OT basis the NT uses the phrase "house of Israel" (Mt. 10:6; 15:24; Acts 2:36, etc.). "House of David" also occurs (Lk. 1:27, 69; 2:4—the royal race of David). Two OT quotations refer to the "house of Jacob" (Lk. 1:33; Acts 7:46). Another quotation speaks of the "house of Judah" (Heb. 8:8ff.). Cf. also Acts 7:10.

9. *The "House" as a Group in the Structure of the Christian Community.* The NT church structured its congregations in families and houses. The house is both a fellowship and a place of meeting (cf. 1 Cor. 1:16; Phlm. 2; Acts 11:14; 16:15, 31, 34; probably Acts 18:8; 2 Tim. 1:16). In Acts 2:46 the first believers break bread in their houses (cf. 5:42). The conversion of the head of a house brings the whole family to the faith (16:15). The bishop must rule his house well (1 Tim. 3:4), and so, too, the deacons (3:12), while false teachers lead whole houses astray (Tit. 1:11). Paul addresses house meetings according to Acts 20:20. For similar references in the apostolic fathers, cf. Ignatius *Smyrneans* 13.1; *Polycarp* 8.2.

oikía (→ oíkos).

1. In Greek a distinction is first made between the broader *oíkos* and the narrower *oikía,* whereby the latter denotes only the "house." The NT, however, uses *oikía* not only for "house" (Mt. 5:15; 7:24ff.) but also for "family" (Mt. 10:12; 12:25) and even for "possessions" (Mk. 12:40). Mk. 3:24-25 associates *oikía* with the kingdom, and cf. Mt. 12:25, which brings together kingdom, city, and family to show that Jesus does not invade the domain of Satan with Satanic power (cf. also Jn. 8:35). Mk. 6:4 links three circles that deny recognition to the prophet: his city, kin, and family *(oikía).*

2. A distinctive saying is that of Jesus in Jn. 14:2-3. There are rabbinic parallels for the phrase "my Father's house." The point is that God's house has places of rest for the afflicted disciples; Jesus will take them there at his coming.

3. In 2 Cor. 5:1ff. Paul contrasts the earthly body with the future heavenly body. The use of "house" for body is common, and denotes perishability (cf. Job 4:19). "Tent" stresses the transitory nature of our stay in the body (cf. 2 Pet. 1:13; Is. 38:12). In Gnosticism the body is a house, but it is the abode of evils.

4. Phil. 4:22 refers to members of Caesar's house, most likely the imperial staff, both slave and free. The phrase suggests that Paul wrote from Rome.

5. Hermas *Similitudes* 1.1-2.8-9 objects to Christian possessions in this world; we should win fields and houses of another kind.

oikeíos. This adjective means "belonging or related to the household," then "intimate," and finally "fitting" or "suitable." In the NT it is partly used as a noun and is controlled by the understanding of the church as a house (Heb. 3:1ff.). Thus Gal. 6:10 requires that good be done especially to members of the household of faith. Eph. 2:19 tells the readers that they belong to the household of God (note the combination of *oíkos* and *pólis* in this verse). A more general sense applies in 1 Tim. 5:8, which gives divine sanction to the common moral norm that we should provide for relatives, and especially for our own families.

oikéō. This word means "to live," "to dwell," and transitively "to inhabit." In the LXX it can mean "to live with a woman." Important in the NT is the use for spiritual indwelling. Thus Paul says in Rom. 7:18 that nothing good dwells in him, and in 7:20 that sin dwells in him. Yet the Spirit of God dwells in the new man (1 Cor. 3:16; Rom. 8:9, 11). As sin previously enjoyed lordship, so the Spirit impresses the human spirit into service, not effacing it in ecstatic rapture. The common formula in 1 Cor. 3:16 and Rom. 8:9, 11 suggests that this is a stock theme in Paul's teaching. God is said to dwell in inaccessible light in 1 Tim. 3:16 (cf. the apocalyptic depictions of God's heavenly throne in En. 14:10ff., although here the stress is on glory and fire rather than light). In Diog. 6.3 Christians live in the world as the soul does in the body.

oikodómos. This word means "builder of the house," "architect." The only NT instance is in Acts 4:11 quoting Ps. 118:22.

oikodoméō.

A. *oikodoméō* **outside the NT.** This word means literally "to build" houses, temples, etc., but it soon acquires a figurative sense, as in Ps. 28:5. To plant and to build are related concepts in the LXX. The image of building is also common among the rabbis. God builds the world, the righteous build by doing good works and learning the law, and students build up the world by studying the law. In Mandaean works believers are chosen, planted, and built up (integrated into the fellowship of life). Philo says that the body is built on the heart, that fools build untenable doctrine like a tower, and that good thoughts and teaching are the foundation stones of a solid house. Josephus has *oikodoméō* only in a literal sense.

B. *oikodoméō* **in the NT.**
1. The NT uses *oikodoméō* literally with various objects, e.g., house in Lk. 6:48, tower in Mk. 12:1, sepulchres in Lk. 11:47. This word is common in the similitude of the tower in Hermas *Similitudes* 9.3.1; 9.12.6; cf. *Visions* 3.2.4ff. Building is an

apocalyptic and messianic concept. By the resurrection or the return Christ will build the heavenly temple. In Mt. 16:18 (cf. Mk. 14:58) the reference might be either to the resurrection or to the return, but Acts 2:1ff. seems to suggest the former. The future tense points to an act of eschatological power, but with a spiritual element. For the temple not made with hands of Mk. 14:58 cf. Acts 7:47, 49. Although messianic, *oikodomeín* is also an ecclesiastical term, as in Acts 9:31; 20:32; 15:16 (which borrows from Am. 9:11 and Jer. 12:15ff.). In such verses God is the subject and the community the object; the building itself is spiritual and eschatological.

2. *The Pauline Concept.*

a. An Apostolic Task. In Paul's letters *oikodomeín* is important. It denotes first an apostolic activity (2 Cor. 10:18; 12:19; 13:10). Paul may destroy when necessary, but his true work is to build up. In 1 Cor. 3:10ff. one apostle lays the foundation and another builds on it. The community is the object, although not without a hint of the spiritual temple (3:16). Planting is also mentioned in this connection (3:6ff.). It is Paul's special pride that he himself does not build on the foundation of others (Rom. 15:20), although this is not an absolute rule (1:11, 14-15).

b. A Community Task. Important also for Paul is the fact that the Spirit builds up the community. Edification for him has a charismatic and spiritual bearing. In 1 Th. 5:11 we note a relation of individuals to the whole, a mutual interrelationship of individuals, and the charismatic nature of the process. Edification goes hand in hand with exhortation (or encouragement), and also with consolation (1 Cor. 14:3). Unbelievers may be won by the prophetic word (14:24). The edification is at the same time that of the community and that of individuals. Knowledge alone does not edify, as some seem to have thought at Corinth (cf. 1 Cor. 8:1, 10; 10:23). Eating idol meat might be lawful, but it could destroy rather than build up. Love, however, always serves to edify. Self-edification by tongue-speaking is not enough (1 Cor. 14:4). It is not directed to the community as prophecy is. Prophecy builds up both by strengthening believers and winning unbelievers, although this, too, must be understood in terms of Christ, the Spirit, and faith.

c. *oikodomeín* and *katalúein.* Paul contrasts building up and tearing down in Gal. 2:18. The partition between Jews and Gentiles has been torn down, but Peter is building it up again by his vacillation. The same contrast occurs in rabbinic writings, but the usage in Gal. 2:18 is unique.

d. 1 Pet. 2:5. This passage takes up the thought of building on a foundation. Using Is. 28:16; Ps. 118:22; Is. 8:14; Ex. 19:6, it combines Pauline and Synoptic motifs. On the cornerstone that is also a stone of stumbling, a house is built that is also a household as individuals are integrated into the church. The eschatological temple is the new community.

C. *oikodoméō* in Postapostolic Writings. The word is common in these works. It occurs especially in the allegory of the tower in Hermas, where angels do the building, the church is the tower, and the time of building is the time of conversion (cf. *Similitudes* 9.3.1ff.; *Visions* 3.2.4, etc.). Barnabas also uses the term. In 11.1 it is said that Israel rejects baptism and builds for itself, while 16.1ff., dealing with the temple, says that the true temple is gloriously built in the name of the Lord (i.e., by spiritual conversion). In *Polycarp* 3.2 we find the common use of the term for building up in the faith. Ignatius has the word mostly with a purely individual reference.

D. Summary. *oikodomeín* is a community concept that is understood teleologically, spiritually, cultically, and ethically. Paul plays a key role in its development. Various influences are discerned by various scholars, e.g., architecture, apocalyptic, the OT, Gnosticism, and even Stoicism.

oikodomḗ.

1. This word first denotes the act of building (Hermas *Similitudes* 9.5.1). In Paul spiritual furtherance is primarily in view (1 Cor. 14:12). Everything, including apostolic authority, should serve this (2 Cor. 10:8). Individuals give and receive it. Whether they edify is the chief criterion in assessing charismata (1 Cor. 14:5).

2. *oikodomḗ* can then mean the finished building. The temple is in view in Mk. 13:1-2; Mt. 24:1. In 1 Cor. 3:9 the reference is to the church, but a special turn is given to the thought in 3:10ff. In Eph. 2:21 the church is God's temple, with the apostles and prophets as the foundation and Christ as the cornerstone. Related thoughts include that of the heavenly temple and the church as Christ's body. Hermas *Visions* 3.2.6 combines mythological motifs and the Christian concept. In the tower passages *oikodomḗ* may sometimes denote the act of building, but its predominant use is for the building itself. (For details cf. *TDNT,* V, 146).

3. Paul uses *oikodomḗ* as a figure of speech for human corporeality. When the present tent dissolves, we have a house from God not made with hands, eternal in heaven (2 Cor. 5:1). "We know" shows that this apocalyptic belief is part of the tradition (cf. Mk. 14:58). There are Hellenistic parallels for the image of the tent, though cf. also Is. 38:12. Judaism does not use the thought of a building anthropologically. Mandaean writings make a similar switch from the metaphor of a building to that of clothing (v. 4).

epoikodoméō. This word means "to build on something," "to build further." It occurs in the NT in 1 Cor. 3:10 for building on a foundation that is already laid, with all the responsibility that this entails. Another use is in Eph. 2:20: believers are built on the foundation of the apostles and prophets (cf. some versions of 1 Pet. 2:5). The *epí* has very little force in Col. 2:7, which again combines the thoughts of building and planting. Jude 20 emphasizes that the holy content of faith should be the foundation of individual Christian lives.

synoikodoméō. This word means "to build together," passive "to be built together." In Eph. 2:22 we do not have an imperative, nor is mutual fellowship the point. The reference is to the unity and totality of the structure in which Christ and the apostles are united with believers. The same image occurs in Hermas *Similitudes* 9.16.7.

oikonómos. In Greek this word means "steward." It may then denote the head of a particular branch of a great house, e.g., the chief cook. As a loanword it can denote a city official (cf. Rom. 16:23). It may also be used for an estate manager or accountant as well as a housekeeper. In the rabbis Moses is God's steward. In parables the loanword usually has the sense of treasurer. In the NT *oikonómos* first occurs in the parables of Jesus. In Lk. 12:42 and Mt. 24:45ff. the *oikonómos* is a steward from among the slaves who is set over the house and property of the owner. In Lk. 16:1, 8 the *oikonómos* seems to be a free treasurer. Paul in Gal. 4:2 links the *oikonómos* with the guardian as the one who has charge while the heir is a minor. *oikonómos* here is perhaps meant to amplify and elucidate *epítropos* (the guardian). The apostle himself is an *oikonómos* in 1 Cor. 4:1: as a minister of Christ he is entrusted with the treasures of the gospel, and the first requirement is trustworthiness. Tit. 1:7 describes the bishop as God's steward, and 1 Pet. 4:10 calls on every Christian, as a recipient of a gift, to be a good steward of God's varied grace. Ignatius *Polycarp* 6.1 takes up the same theme.

oikonomía. In Greek, applying to household administration, this word has the sense of "direction," "provision," "administration." In the NT it means 1. the office of household administration, and discharge of this office (Lk. 16:2ff.). Paul applies the thought to the apostolic office (1 Cor. 9:17; Col. 1:25; Eph. 3:2), which he holds by divine commission and in service to the churches. A second NT use is for the "divine plan" of salvation, its order and administration. This is the point in Eph. 1:10′ and 3:9, and there is a hint of it in 3:2 and Col. 1:25. Ignatius follows this usage in *Ephesians* 18.2; 20.1. A final NT use occurs in 1 Tim. 1:4, where false teachers are said to promote speculations rather than godly "instruction" (or training) in faith (*oikonomían theoú en pístei*). We find this sense in the fathers, e.g., Clement of Alexandria *Paedagogus* 1.8.64.3.

katoikéō. This common Greek word means "to dwell." It often has a figurative sense, as in Philo, who speaks of man dwelling in God, or of the sage dwelling like an alien in the body but like a native in virtues. The NT uses the word transitively for "to inhabit" in Lk. 13:4 and intransitively for "to dwell (in)" in Acts 1:20. The stock phrases "dwell upon earth" and "inhabit the earth" occur in Rev. 3:10; 6:10; 8:13; 17:2, etc. Figuratively demons dwell in humans (Mt. 12:45). God dwells in the heart (cf. 1 Cor. 3:16), God dwells in the temple (Mt. 23:21, though cf. Acts 7:48), Satan dwells where Antipas was killed (Rev. 2:13), Christ dwells in his people by faith (Eph. 3:17), the fullness of God dwells in Christ (Col. 1:19), the fullness of deity dwells in him bodily (2:9), and righteousness dwells in the new heaven and earth (2 Pet. 3:13). In Hermas God dwells in patience (*Mandates* 5.1.3), the Holy Spirit dwells in believers (5.2.5), and God causes the Spirit to dwell in a selected fleshly nature (*Similitudes* 5.6.5).

oikētḗrion. This word means "abode," "dwelling place." Paul uses it in 2 Cor. 5:2 in relation to the building we have from God. We long to put on our heavenly "dwelling."

katoikētḗrion. This term is common in the LXX and seems to have come from there into the NT. In Rev. 18:2 fallen Babylon has become an "abode" of demons (cf. Is. 13:21-22). In Eph. 2:22 believers are built into the temple as a "dwelling place" for God. As in 2 Cor. 5:1-2, the concept takes up here the figure of the building and temple with reference to the edification of the whole community. Barnabas individualizes the concept in 6.15; 16.7-8.

katoikízō. This verb means "to make to dwell," "to assign a dwelling." It is almost a formula in Jms. 4:5: "the Spirit whom God has made to dwell in us" (cf. Hermas *Mandates* 3.1: *Similitudes* 5.6.5). On the basis of creation and/or conversion the Holy Spirit is regarded as sent into us by God.

hē oikouménē. This word, having the sense of a noun, denotes the "inhabited world" and then comes into use for the Roman empire. In Philo it has primarily a general rather than a political sense. It is fairly common in the NT. In Mt. 24:14 the use is general; the gospel is for all nations. In Lk. 2:1, however, the reference is more political. The inhabited world is the point in Lk. 4:5 (Mt. 4:8 has *kósmos*) and Lk. 21:26 (cf. Acts 11:28; Rev. 3:10). Acts 17:6 and 19:27 are in accord with current Greek usage. Paul uses the term only in quoting Ps. 19:4 (Rom. 10:18). Heb. 1:6 and 2:5, however, reflect Hellenistic usage. The NT never contests the Roman claim that equates the *oikouménē* with the empire. 1 Clem. 60.1 perhaps includes the spiritual and angelic world in the concept.   [O. MICHEL, V, 119-59]

---

oiktírō [to be sympathetic],   *oiktirmós* [sympathy],   *oiktírmōn* [sympathetic]

A. Greek Usage. *oíktos* is first "lamentation," then "sympathetic lamentation," "sympathy." Hence *oiktírō* means "to be sympathetic." Sympathy in grief may be regarded as a sign of weakness, but compassion as such is not reprehensible and may be sought from deity.

B. The LXX and Judaism. *oiktírō* is mostly used in the LXX for *ḥnn* and *rḥm,* although sometimes it has no original. *oiktirmós* and *oiktírmōn* are common, and we also find *oiktírēma* and *oiktrós*. The meaning is always sympathy or pity, mostly with reference to God, whose compassion is invoked in prayer. The group is most common in the Psalms.

C. Primitive Christian Writings. The verb *oiktírein* occurs in the NT only in Rom. 9:15 (quoting Ex. 33:19), where it is parallel to *eleeín*. The noun *oiktirmós* is always in the plural and denotes God's compassion in Rom. 12:1 and 2 Cor. 1:3. In the latter verse God is the Father from whom all compassion comes and is then imparted to all. Human sympathy is at issue in Phil. 2:1 and Col. 3:12, specifically the mercy of the judge or the law in Heb. 10:28. The only adjective used in the NT is *oiktírmōn*. This refers to God in Jms. 5:11 (cf. Pss. 103:8; 111:4; also 1 Clem. 60.1). It also denotes the divine mercy in Lk. 6:36, where it serves as the basis of an admonition (cf. Justin *Apology* 15.13; *Dialogue* 96.3). [R. BULTMANN, V, 159-61]

---

oínos [wine]

The vine was cultivated from prehistoric times, and wine comes into early use both socially and cultically. The god Dionysus is equated with wine, and it has a special place in his cult. Noah cultivates the vine in Gen. 9:20. Many OT texts praise wine (Judg. 9:13; Ps. 104:15). Fullness of wine is a divine blessing (Gen. 27:28). The Rechabites abstain from wine (Jer. 35), and Hos. 2:10ff. links it to Baal worship. There are also warnings against overindulgence (Is. 5:11-12; Prov. 20:1). Wine has cultic significance in the OT (Ex. 29:38ff.). The vine also serves frequently as a metaphor. In the NT *oínos* has a literal sense and never occurs in a cultic connection. The Baptist abstains from it (Lk. 1:15); his mission demands that he be controlled solely by the Spirit. Jesus partakes of wine (Mt. 11:19), for the time of the bridegroom's presence is a time of festivity (Mk. 2:18ff.). The new wine of the new age demands new skins. At Cana (Jn. 2:1ff.) Jesus turns a great amount of water into wine. If the nature of Johannine miracles as signs is considered, a deeper meaning must be sought. Thus law and gospel may be contrasted as water and wine, or wine may be equated with Logos (Philo). While *oínos* is not used in the accounts of the Last Supper, it is obvious that the cup contains wine, and with the cup (Mk. 14:25 and par.) Jesus is triumphantly looking ahead to the consummation (cf. Mt. 8:11). On the cross Jesus is handed a mixture of wine and myrrh (Mk. 15:23) to dull his senses (cf. Mt. 27:34). Paul recommends abstinence should weaker believers be upset about eating and drinking (Rom. 14:21). In Eph. 5:18 he warns against excess (cf. Prov. 23:31), and calls instead for infilling with the Spirit. A moderate use of wine may be beneficial to health (1 Tim. 5:23), but overindulgence is to be avoided (3:3, 8). In Revelation *oínos* is one of the commodities that the fleet can no longer sell when Babylon falls (18:13). The term denotes the crop in 6:6; this is to be spared when the yield of wheat and barley falls short. In 14:10; 16:19; 19:15 *oínos* denotes the wrath of God in a figure that is taken from the OT (cf. Jer. 25:15-16; 49:12, etc.). In 14:10 "poured unmixed" indicates the great and terrible nature of the divine wrath. The metaphor is rather different in 14:8 (cf. 17:2; 18:3), where the wine is that of impure passion. But the figures merge into one another inasmuch as those who drink this wine fall victim to God's wrath.

[H. SEESEMANN, V, 162-66]

---

oknērós [slothful]

oknērós describes a. those who are slow to act through hesitation, anxiety, negligence, or sloth, and b. things that awaken suspicion, dislike, or fear. In the OT it is used for the slothful (Prov. 6:6, 9) who let inconveniences stop them (20:4) or never move on from the will to the deed (21:25). In the NT sense a. occurs in an eschatological context in Mt. 25:26. Slothful servants represent disciples who hesitate to put their gifts to work in the testing period of earthly life, and who thus fail to live up to their eternal responsibilities. Another instance is in Rom. 12:11, where yielding to indolence is contrasted with being inspired and directed by the Spirit. Sense b. occurs in Phil. 3:1, where Paul says that under the impulsion of the Spirit he overcomes his dislike of repeating the same admonitions.   [F. HAUCK, V, 166-67]

---

olethreúō [to corrupt, destroy], *ólethros* [corruption, destruction], *olothreutēs* [destroyer], *exolothreúō* [to destroy completely]

olethreúō. This term means "to corrupt," "to destroy." Philo uses it for the corruption of the soul. It occurs 18 times in the LXX in its usual sense. The only NT instance is in Heb. 11:28, where by faith Moses sprinkles the blood so that the destroyer *(olethreúōn)* might not touch his people.

ólethros. This word means a. "corruption," especially "death," and b. "that which brings corruption." It is common in the LXX; the prophets use it often for eschatological "destruction" (Jer. 48:3). The sense is eschatological in two NT instances. In 2 Th. 1:9 eternal destruction will come on those who reject the gospel when Christ is revealed from heaven. In 1 Tim. 6:9 the conscience of those who seek wealth is seared, and they are thus in danger of falling into temptations that will plunge them into complete ruin. The point is rather different in 1 Cor. 5:5, where Paul seems to be saying that physical destruction (i.e., death) will follow when the congregation, with whom Paul will be present in spirit and with the power of the Lord, delivers the incestuous person to Satan (cf. Acts 5:5, 10; also Ignatius *Ephesians* 13.1 for the divine power at work when the church gathers).

olothreutēs. This word occurs in the NT only in 1 Cor. 10:10, where the reference is to the OT angel of destruction. This may be a specific avenging angel (cf. the definite article), or it may be more generally an angel of Satan (cf. 2 Cor. 12:7).

exolothreúō. This word means "to destroy completely." It is very rare except in the LXX, in which it refers to God's extirpation of sinners or of the disobedient. The only

NT instance is in Acts 3:23, where Peter, after healing the lame man, quoting Lev. 23:29 and Dt. 18:19, tells the people that those who will not listen to the predicted prophet (i.e., the Messiah) will be rooted out from among the people. The apostolic fathers often use the term in OT quotations (cf. 1 Clem. 14.4; 15.5; 53.3).

[J. SCHNEIDER, V, 167-71]

oligopistía, oligópistos → *pisteúō*

---

oligos [few, little]

---

oligos means a. "small" or "few," i.e., in number, and infrequently b. "little" (in quantity). The idea of "little" is important in the LXX. God can work with few means (1 Sam. 14:6), and so can the righteous with God's help (cf. Job 8:7). A poor man who is wise can do much with little (Eccl. 9:14-15), and a little wisdom means much (10:1). Such sayings may express practical experience, but they also denote the eschatological transvaluation of all values. Rather different is the thought that we are limited by a short span of life (Job 10:20). This is a punishment for sinners (Ps. 37:10). It is also a punishment that only a few remain in times of distress (Dt. 4:27), or that little is left of the harvest (28:38). The suffering of the righteous, however, is of little account (Zech. 1:15). The NT gives the term something of the same theological stress as the LXX. In Lk. 7:47 Jesus answers the critical Pharisee by telling him that those who are forgiven little, love little. The saying seems to be aimed at the self-righteous who hold aloof from sinners and whose love, in transgression of the chief commandment, is consequently small. In Mt. 25:21, 23 the point is that those who are faithful in small things will have greater things entrusted to them. Lk. 12:48 makes a distinction between greater and smaller punishments. Those who know the master's will but do not do it will be more severely beaten than those who do not know or do it. Whether Jesus has the common people in mind here, or possibly the Gentiles, one cannot say.

[H. SEESEMANN, V, 171-73]

oligópsychos → *psychḗ; holoklēría, holóklēros* → *klḗros*

---

ololýzō [to cry out, wail]

---

ololýzō means "to make a loud, inarticulate cry" in expression of great stress of soul. It is common in sacral contexts, e.g., at sacrifices or divine epiphanies, usually denoting jubilation (along with dancing etc.). In the LXX it denotes the effect of judgment on those smitten by it (Ezek. 21:17; Zech. 11:2). In crying of this type there comes to expression both horror at oneself (Am. 8:3) and dread at the destruction of worldly power. Hos. 7:14 demands the prayer of the heart in place of such cries. Jms. 5:1 is in line with the prophetic use except that now the fulfilment has come with Christ, and the last and total possibility of repentance will have gone.

→ *alalázō, threnéō, kóptō*   [H. W. HEIDLAND, V, 173-74]

---

hólos [whole, complete],   **holotelḗs** [through and through]

---

hólos. This word means "whole," "complete," "intact," "undivided." In the NT it is used with nouns to denote their totality (cf. Acts 21:30; Mt. 5:29-30; Lk. 11:36).

It has theological significance in Jn. 7:23, where the reference is not just to the contrast between healing the whole man and one member (by circumcision) but more broadly to the healing of the whole being (cf. 13:10). The point is similar in Mk. 12:30 and parallels: the chief commandment demands that we dedicate ourselves wholly and utterly to God, with all our being. In keeping, too, is the negative admonition to stake everything on not being cast totally into Gehenna (Mt. 5:29-30), and also the positive admonition to see to the integrity of the whole person (Mt. 6:22-23), since only those who serve God in this totality can render true service (6:24).

holotelḗs. This is a stronger form of *hólos* meaning "through and through." The only NT example is in 1 Th. 5:23, where Paul's use of this rare term gives emphasis to his prayer that God may grant total sanctification. In the apostolic fathers Hermas has the word four times for "unbroken" (*Mandates* 9.6) or "complete" (*Visions* 3.6.4).

[H. SEESEMANN, V, 174-76]

---

homeíromai [to have a kindly feeling for]

The meaning of this rare word is not wholly clear, but it obviously expresses intensity of feeling. Paul uses it in 1 Th. 2:8 to show that he does not serve the church merely in obedience to his commission but out of heartfelt love for it.

[H. W. HEIDLAND, V, 176]

---

omnýō [to swear an oath]

omnýō means "to swear," "to affirm by oath." It is mostly used with the accusative of the person or object by which the oath is taken. Those to whom one swears are in the dative, and the matter sworn is in the accusative or infinitive. In the LXX a common oath is by the life. When God swears by himself the first person is used. In the ancient world swearing is usually by the gods, who are invoked as witnesses. Later, with the concept of divine monarchy, swearing may be by kings. Oaths are common in public life, but the stronger forms show that their force was declining.

1. In the NT the most important passage theologically is Mt. 5:33ff. In the law the oath is an essential element in spite of the tendency to abuse it in daily life. The law prohibits false oaths and insists that oaths and vows be kept. Jesus, however, sets up a new order of life in the kingdom which leaves no place for oaths since there is no reason here to suspect human veracity. Those who belong to the kingdom must always be truthful, and hence do not need to swear. Jesus does not limit this prohibition to promises or to common swearing. The Sophists, Pythagoreans, Stoics, and Essenes all agree that consistent truthfulness should obviate the need for oaths, and some of them forbid their followers to use them. Judaism forbids frivolous swearing, and Philo demands that we either avoid oaths or use them only with great circumspection. We should never swear by God. Jesus himself follows up his prohibition by exposing the insincerity of substituting equivalents for the name of God (5:34-36). He then issues the positive command that his disciples should use a simple "yes" or "no" (5:37); the double form here does not indicate a simplified form of oath, as in some rabbinic

statements, but is obviously by way of confirmation. Anything more than this either proceeds from the evil one (if *toú ponēroú* comes from *ho ponērós*) or is a consequence of the evil that is present in the world (if it comes from *tó ponērón*, as is more likely).

2. Jms. 5:12 offers another and perhaps more original form of the saying. The second half brings out its absoluteness. Truthfulness is the norm in the Christian community; hence taking oaths is totally unnecessary.

3. The sayings in Mt. 23:16ff. are aimed at the casuistical treatment of oaths and vows. There is no rabbinic instance of the distinction between the gold and the temple or altar, but parallels exist, and we find examples of oaths by the covenant, the law, the temple, and its ministry. An oath by the temple, Jesus says, is also an oath by everything in it, and by the God who dwells in it.

4. Heb. 6:13, 16 and 7:20ff., following the OT, regard it as natural that God should take an oath. The oath confirms the promise. God, unlike us, swears by himself, since there is none higher to whom he can appeal. His oath is thus a guarantee that removes all doubt. It gives his word unconditional validity. The oath that confirms Christ's priesthood shows its superiority to the priesthood that it replaces.

5. Peter at his denial ignores the prohibition of Jesus and swears with an oath that he does not know Jesus (Mk. 14:71). Jesus confirms his own sayings by a solemn but simple *amḗn*. When adjured (Mt. 26:64), he answers with a plain declaration. Paul avoids direct oaths, but comes near when he invokes God (Rom. 1:9) or his conscience (9:1) as witness. The saying in 1 Cor. 15:31 is also close to an oath ("by my pride in you").

6. Herod swears in the manner of a great Near Eastern ruler at his birthday feast, and his frivolous oath seals the fate of John the Baptist.

[J. Schneider, V, 176-85]

> ### *homothymadón* [with one mind]

homothymadón denotes the unity of a group and may be translated "with one mind." It often occurs with words denoting number (e.g., "all" in Acts 1:14) and place (Acts 2:1). The *thymós* may be anger, fear, or gratitude, but the most common use later is political (cf. Acts 15:25), or, in Judaism, religious. The term denotes common interest rather than personal feeling and expresses reaction to some outside event. In the NT it stresses inner unanimity in response to teaching (Acts 8:6) or in prayer (1:14). Tensions exist, but unanimity is achieved in the magnifying of the one Lord (Rom. 15:16). It is a response to God's action for the community and the world (cf. Acts 1:4; 4:24). It is thus a gift of God to the praise of God.   [H. W. Heidland, V, 185-86]

homoiopathḗs → *páschō*

> ### *hómoios* [of the same nature, similar], *homoiótēs* [similarity], *homoióō* [to be like], *homoíōsis* [likeness], *homoíōma* [likeness, copy], *aphomoióō* [to be like, copy], *parómoios* [similar], *paromoiázō* [to be like]

hómoios. This word means a. "of the same kind," b. "of like disposition," c. "belonging equally," and d., in geometry, "similar" (of figures). In the LXX it is common in the question "Who is like?", presupposing a negative answer. In the papyri it mostly means "similar." It is common in the NT, e.g., in images and parables. In Jn. 8:55 Jesus alone has true knowledge of God; if he were to deny this he would be "like" the Jews, who do not know God. In Acts 17:29 Paul says that as God's offspring we should not think the deity is "like" gold etc. In 1 Jn. 3:2 believers will reach fulfilment when they are "like" Christ; this will come about at the parousia. In Rev. 1:13 the figure is "like" the Son of Man—a messianic designation (cf. Dan. 7:13). In Mt. 22:39 the command to love one's neighbor is of the same importance and validity as the command to love God. In Gal. 5:21 Paul ends his list with the phrase "and the like," which enables his readers to continue the list in thought.

homoióō. This word means a. "to make like or equal," b. "to liken," and c. (passive) "to be like." In Matthew it usually serves to introduce parables. The introduction may be in the form of a stereotyped question (cf. 11:16; Mk. 4:30; Lk. 13:18, 20). In Mt. 6:8 Jesus tells his disciples not to "be like" the Gentiles when they pray. Heb. 2:17 tells us that in his humiliation Jesus is "made like" his brethren so as to be able to do his high-priestly work. But this is not mere equality (cf. 9:14).

homoiótēs. This word means "likeness" or "similarity." The only NT instances are in Hebrews. In 4:15 the temptation of Jesus bears a "similarity" to ours; the difference is that he does not sin. In 7:15 Christ is a priest in the "likeness" of Melchizedek, not on the basis of law and descent, but by the power of an indestructible life.

homoíōsis. This uncommon word means a. "making like or similar," b. "being like," and c. (in grammar) "comparison." In the LXX it mostly means "similarity." The only NT example is in Jms. 3:9 (cf. Gen. 1:26), where cursing those who are made in God's "likeness" is in sharp contradiction to blessing God himself. In this sense the term is an important one in the fathers. The Alexandrians distinguish between *eikōn* as something *in* which we are created (and which thus remains after the fall), and *homoíōsis* as something *for* which we are created (and which we are thus to strive after).

homoíōma. This rare word means "what is similar," "copy," with a stress on the aspect of "similarity." In the LXX it also takes on the sense of "form" (Dt. 4:12). This is the meaning in Rev. 9:7.

1. In Rom. 1:23 cultic "images" are contrasted with the glory of God; they are made in the form of human or animal bodies.

2. In Rom. 6:5 the baptized are in the "likeness" of Christ's death and resurrection. Much debated is whether Paul's point is that baptism is just a representation of Christ's death or whether it is a likeness that contains the original. A first view is that it is a similitude or reproduction of Christ's death and resurrection. A second view relates the "likeness" to our own death in baptism; we have grown together with a baptismal death that is like Christ's death, which is the type that is reflected in the death experienced at baptism. A third view is that the word *homoíōma* denotes the mystical and sacramental death of the baptized with Christ; in Roman Catholic thinking Christ's death is directly present in the sacrament. A fourth view is that we are sacramentally but not mystically integrated into Christ's death as it is present in baptism. As concerns the likeness of the resurrection, there is debate as to whether this refers to mystical resurrection with Christ at baptism or to the future resurrection of the baptized. The two main lines of exegesis are a. that the baptized experience a mystical resurrection

corresponding to that of Christ, and b. that they share sacramentally in Christ's own resurrection. It may be noted (1) that since Paul speaks of the likeness rather than the event of Christ's death and resurrection, he can hardly be referring to a mystical relation to the historical acts, (2) that since he has in view an organic link, he can hardly be saying that our experiences are copies of Christ's, and (3) that we are thus led to the conclusion that the likeness in question is that of the death and resurrection of Christ, as they are now sacramentally present, to the historical acts, and that by means of this likeness we ourselves are thus closely linked with these saving realities.

3. In Rom. 5:14 Paul says that death holds sway even over those who did not sin like Adam, i.e., who did not copy Adam's sin.

4. In Rom. 8:3 and Phil. 2:7 Paul uses the word with reference to Christ's earthly life. In Rom. 8:3 he stresses the reality of Christ's humanity by saying that he came in the "likeness" of sinful flesh; he entered the nexus of human sin but without becoming subject to the power of sin, as would be implied if Paul had simply said "in sinful flesh." The *homoíōma* denotes likeness in appearance but distinction in essence. With the body the intrinsically sinless Christ becomes the representative of sinful humanity in order that by destroying this body God might cancel human sin. The term *homoíōma* is clearly an attempt to overcome the difficulty of having to say that the Christ in whom human sin is condemned is not himself a sinner. The word may well be an inadequate one, face to face with the mystery of Christ's person and work, but it is not docetic as some suppose. Christ is not just a heavenly being with an external human form; he is fully and truly human, but not a sinner. The point is similar in Phil. 2:7, where Christ, taking servant form, is born in human "likeness." The sense here is closer to that of form, but in the background are the two thoughts that he who is the full image of God becomes the image of man, and that the image means likeness rather than full identity, since Christ differs from all others by his consistent obedience (v. 8). Behind the statement lies the message of Jn. 1:14, namely, that God has entered human history. It is not implied that he has ceased to be God; even in his humanity Christ is at the same time a being of another kind. In the fathers Ignatius refers to the resurrection of believers corresponding to Christ's "likeness" (*Trallians* 9.2), and an early sacramentary calls the bread the "likeness" of Christ's body.

aphomoióō. This verb means "to copy," rarely "to compare," and in the passive "to be or become like" or "make oneself out to be like." The only NT instance is in Heb. 7:3, which says that Melchizedek "is like" the Son of God. The point may be that the Son of God is the prototype, or that the OT text is taken to be a messianic prophecy, i.e., a sign that points forward to Christ.

parómoios. This word means "similar," or "mostly alike." In Mk. 7:13 Jesus has shown how the Pharisees invalidate God's word by their tradition in the matter of corban, and he adds that they do many similar things.

paromoiázō. This verb means "to be like"; it occurs in Mt. 23:27 when Jesus tells the scribes and Pharisees that they are like whitewashed tombs.

[J. SCHNEIDER, V, 186-99]

---

homologéō [to confess, promise, praise], *exomologéō* [to confess, promise, praise], *anthomologéomai* [to praise, thank], *homología* [confession], *homologouménōs* [confessedly]

A. The Group in Secular Greek Usage.

This group is common in law and religion. The literal meaning of *homologeín* is "to say the same thing." We thus get the senses a. "to agree to something" (an affirmation, a charge, etc.), b. "to confirm receipt," c. "to agree or submit to a proposal," and d. "to agree to a wish," "to promise." In a transferred sense it may denote the agreement of words and deeds, or of customs. The noun *homología* is important in Socratic dialogue as indicating consent to what is found to be valid followed by the appropriate resolve and action; theoretical assent is not enough. In the Stoics there is a shift from the thought of actual conduct to the idea of an integrated state of life. In the papyri the word takes on the sense of a "compact" or "agreement" of a legal character. In religion we find varied use, e.g., for commitment to vows and especially for the confessing of sins.

B. The OT-Near Eastern and Hellenistic-Gnostic Liturgy of Thanksgiving.

a. Biblical homology develops out of the cultus and takes the form of confession of sins and praise of God. Many psalms (e.g., 22; 30; 116) and many other passages (e.g., 1 Sam. 2:1ff.; Is. 38:9ff.) are thanksgivings after deliverance. Job 33:26ff. describes how God has brought restoration, and a response is made in confession and acknowledgment. There are parallels of confession in psalms of complaint outside Israel. The persons afflicted confess their faults, invoke divine mercy, promise a song and offering, and then fulfil the vow. The song of thanksgiving (cf. Ps. 116) describes the distress, utters a prayer, and depicts the saving action. It often associates true sacrifice with thanksgiving and calls for praise from those present (cf. Jer. 33:11). Sacred words are used, but there may be a call for a new song (Pss. 33:2; 40:3).

2. Liturgies of thanksgiving also occur in the Hellenistic religions of redemption. These focus on the redeemer myth and the theme of union with the redeemer. The cultus enacts the soteriological drama. In the Hermetic corpus the idea of *logiké thysía* is an important one. It comprises the whole life of thanksgiving, but especially the hymn of thanks.

C. The Group in the LXX and Postbiblical Judaism.

1. The LXX prefers the compounds *exomologeísthai* and *exomológēsis,* which in secular Greek denote public admission or acknowledgment. On the basis of Heb. *yāḏâ,* however, the idea of praising God is added to that of confessing sin (cf. 1 Kgs. 8:33, 35; Neh. 9:3 for the linking of the two). *homología* may still denote the confession of sin; public confession is presupposed. In the sense of extolling or praising, the group takes its place with other terms, e.g., invoking and reciting. It carries the thought of magnifying God by confessing or rehearsing his mighty acts.

2. In later Judaism the group carries the thought of the confession of sin with penitential prayer. The great men of the past publicly acknowledged their guilt (Dan. 9:1ff.; Jdt. 9:1ff., etc.). Even the ungodly Manasseh humbled himself (2 Chr. 33:12-13). Prominent in this type of confession is the concept of divine judgment, which both inspires it and is averted by it. Josephus refers to acknowledgment of the emperor in *Jewish War* 7.418; its opposite is confession of the one God (2 Macc. 7:37).

3. Philo gives evidence of philosophical influence, e.g., of Stoicism in his demand for integrity and harmony of soul. Confession of God is for him a transcendent virtue.

True confession is the work of God and belongs to the immaterial sphere. *homologeín* can also denote both God's declarations in Scripture and human promises to God. Other meanings are confession of sin and agreement or affirmation, as well as engagement or contract in the secular sense.

4. The praise of God plays a role in apocalyptic. In En. 61:9ff. it will accompany God's righteous judgment. Such praise may be a sign of human transformation (71:11-12).

D. The Group in the NT.

I. homologeín.

1. A first use of this verb is for "to assure," "to promise," "to admit," or "to concede." In Mt. 14:7 (cf. Acts 7:17; Heb. 6:13) it binds the speaker to his word. The use is Hellenistic, but in Jn. 1:20 there is a distinctive Christian note. In John solemn declarations belong to the circle of witness to Christ (1:7, 15, 19). Similarly in Heb. 11:13 the idea of a solemn declaration of faith is added to that of admission or confirmation. Similarly, admission of sin in 1 Jn. 1:9 (cf. the opposite in 1:8) carries with it the idea of confession.

2. A second use is for "to make a statement" or "bear witness" in a legal sense. Shaped by the gospel tradition, this is perhaps the most important NT use. It occurs in Lk. 12:8; Mt. 10:32. Jesus demands confession of himself, and he will confirm it to the Father as the eschatological witness. Important here is the correspondence between earthly conduct and the eschatological word. Rev. 3:5 takes up the theme, and cf. Mt. 7:23 for rejection by the eschatological witness or judge. In Jn. 9:22 the Jews expel those who publicly confess Jesus as Messiah. To confess Jesus means honor with God; refusal to confess him is based on the desire for human honor (5:44; 12:43). Judicial confession is also the point in Acts 24:14, where Paul acknowledges that as a Christian he serves the God of the fathers.

3. A third use is for "to make solemn statements of faith," "to confess something in faith." Rom. 10:9-10 (cf. Dt. 30:14) links faith and confession (cf. 2 Cor. 4:13). Confession and proclamation grow out of faith. Confession stands under eschatological responsibility (2 Cor. 4:14) and has the promise of eschatological salvation (Rom. 10:9-10). The eschatological aspect is evident in Acts 23:8. We are perhaps to take Heb. 13:15 in the same way, and also Tit. 1:16, where the words of the false teachers confess God but their works deny him. 1 John, too, contrasts denying and confessing. Those who deny Christ are liars and antichrists (2:22). Confessing, then, implies acceptance of a specific christological understanding. Only the spirits that affirm this understanding are from God (4:2-3). That more than intellectual understanding is at issue may be seen from 4:15. This type of *homología* causes division (cf. 2 Jn. 7). The aim of John is to bring about decision by a firm formulation of the gospel that expresses its saving significance. 1 Tim. 6:13 views the witness of Jesus at his trial as confession. This good confession, ordained and confirmed by God, stands in sharp contrast to the false witness of his opponents (Mk. 14:56). It consists of his admission that he is the Son of God (cf. Mt. 16:16; Mk. 15:39). It is a model for disciples (Mt. 10:32). Such confession should be public (1 Tim. 6:12), binding (6:12-13), and definitive (Mt. 10:32). It may come as the answer to a question (Mt. 16:13ff.; Jn. 1:19ff.; Acts 8:37: at baptism). The authentic confession rules out other possibilities, and even though the question is put personally the answer is given representatively (cf. the link between Peter's confession and the church in Mt. 16:13ff.). Knowledge does not

necessarily include confession (Mt. 10:19; Jn. 12:42), and present confession does not rule out future denial (Peter). But confession means taking sides, and confession of Christ means confession of the risen and exalted Lord (set side by side with the one God in 1 Cor. 8:6). Proclamation and teaching are forms of confessing and witnessing. They start from an event in history, which they proclaim and interpret, they carry with them a commitment and a claim, and they integrate those who accept them into eschatological fellowship with God.

II. homologouménōs. This adverb means "by common consent." It occurs in the NT only in 1 Tim. 3:16, which says that the mystery of the faith is "confessedly great." Christ is vindicated in the Spirit, seen by angels, preached among the nations, and believed on in the world.

III. anthomologeísthai and exomologeísthai tō̂ theō̂.

1. *anthomologeísthai* has many meanings in secular Greek, e.g., "to agree," "to admit," "to express thanks." In Lk. 2:38 (on an OT model) Anna's thanksgiving combines acknowledgment, obedience, and proclamation.

2. *exomologeísthai* also has such senses as "to admit," "to confess," and "to promise." The NT adopts especially the cultic sense "to confess," "to extol." Paul's use in Rom. 15:7ff. recalls the Psalms, and cf. Rom. 14:11 and Phil. 2:11 (Is. 45:23), where the Christian confession, which is to God's glory, broadens out into that of the last time (cf. the songs of Rev. 4:8, 11; 5:9ff.; 12:10ff., which pledge final victory and are a summons to rejoicing; also the angels' song in Lk. 2:14 and the blessing of Simeon in Lk. 2:29ff.). As many OT Psalms begin with praise (111:1; 138:1), so Jesus' cry of jubilation refers to a rejoicing in the Spirit (Mt. 11:25). The threefold division here combines praise of God, disclosure of the authority of the Son, and a summons to accept eschatological wisdom (or, in Lk. 10:23-24, a blessing of eyewitnesses). This wisdom is not that of the law or tradition, but of the gospel; this is why the scribes reject it (1 Cor. 1:19-20).

IV. exomologeísthai tás hamartías. While Phil. 2:11 construes the confession of Is. 45:23 as praise of God, Rom. 14:11 relates it to the eschatological confession of sins before God's judgment throne. The two go closely together. From the time of the Baptist public confession of sin is integral to conversion (cf. Mk. 1:5; Mt. 3:6; Acts 19:18). According to Jms. 5:16 it is also a custom in times of sickness.

V. homología. This word denotes a free act of confession of the gospel or a liturgical form of confession in the community. As a response in 2 Cor. 9:13 it implies acceptance, commitment, and obedience. It is thus an occasion for thanksgiving and for praise of God (9:12-13). At issue here is an act of sharing, so that the use is very broad. In Heb. 3:1; 4:14; 10:23, however, the reference is to the ecclesiastical or baptismal confession of faith to which the hearers are committed, or to a liturgy of praise connected with the various predicates of Christ. In Hebrews, too, the word expresses commitment, but with a fixed *homología* in view. In 1 Tim. 6:12-13 the reference seems to be to a gathering for ordination, and it may be that the verse which follows gives the content of Timothy's confession, echoing both its legal and its cultic form. The hymn in 2 Tim. 2:11ff. recalls Mt. 10:32-33: the Christ who summons us to confession himself makes confession and is faithful. The concept of witnesses is important in 1 Tim. 6:12; Heb. 12:1; Rev. 1:5, for, like Christ, they hear the commitment and will speak for or against those who make the confession at the last judgment. In 2 Tim. 2:11ff. it is Christ himself who is the witness. The first two members are oriented to the eschatological promise and the last two to the attitude of Christ. The third member adopts the concept of correspondence as a warning, but the last breaks it in view of God's greater faithfulness (cf. Rom. 3:3), unless the point is that Christ will be faithful to his word. The point of Jms. 2:14ff. is that confession does not release from obedience but demands it.

E. The Group in the Postapostolic Writings.

1. homologeín. This word occurs in the senses a. "to promise," "to admit," "to concede" (cf. Diog. 2.1), b. "to make legal statements," "to bear witness" (Ignatius *Smyrneans* 5.1; Hermas *Similitudes* 9.28.1ff., which presents confession as a duty of servant to master; 2 Clem. 3.1ff.; Mart. Pol. 6.1), c. "to make solemn statements of faith" (Ignatius *Smyrneans* 5.2; 7.1, where contradiction of the confession of the Lord's Supper as Christ's flesh means exclusion and death; *Polycarp* 7.1; 2 Clem. 3.2ff., which demands honoring with the whole heart and mind).

2. exomologeísthai tō̂ theō̂ or tás hamartías. exomologeísthai tō̂ theō̂ finds a place in the liturgy (1 Clem. 52:1ff., which extols the resurrection; 61.3, where it takes a christological form; Hermas *Mandates* 10, which argues that the sorrowful cannot give God thanks). *exomologeísthai tás hamartías* is recommended (cf. 1 Clem. 50–51, where it is closely related to praise; 2 Clem. 8.1ff., which says it will come too late after death; Did. 4.14, where it should precede intercession; Hermas *Similitudes* 9.23.4, which may hint at formulas of remission).

3. homológēsis, exomológēsis. These words, denoting confession and praise of God, do not occur in the NT but are found in Hermas *Similitudes* 9.28.7 and 2.5.

4. homologouménōs. Diog. 5.4 uses this term in the sense "admittedly."

5. Clement of Alexandria. Clement uses *homologeín* in the various senses "to agree," "to concede," "to promise," "to confess," and *homología* in the senses "agreement," "assent," "acceptance." He offers an exposition of the Lord's sayings about confession in *Stromateis* 4.9.70ff.   [O. Michel, V, 199-220]

ónar [dream]

Used only in the nominative and accusative, and of uncertain etymology, *ónar* means "dream." It does not occur in the LXX, which mostly uses *enýpnion*. In the NT only Matthew and Luke mention dreams, and Luke (in Acts) has *hórama* (16:9-10; 18:9), and *hórasis* and *enýpnion* (2:17).

A. The Dream in Antiquity.

I. Dreams and Their Interpretation.

1. The Problem. Belief in the significance of dreams is common in antiquity (as it still is today), but not without criticism. Distinction is made between significant dreams and others. A problem is whether some dreams might be caused by deceiving powers or by purely physical causes (wine etc.). Dietary rules are established. Aristotle and Cicero are mostly critical. Cicero argues that it is unworthy of deity to use dreams for revelation, that interpretation is uncertain, and that there are too many dreams to prove by observation that they come true.

2. The Most Important Books of Dreams. In spite of recent findings, knowledge of the field is far from complete. In Babylonian texts it is hard to differentiate dreams and omens. From Egypt we have a hieratic book and various demotic texts. Greek books date from the time of Socrates but the first to come down in full is that of Artemidorus. The later book of Synesius takes a platonic turn. The Byzantine book of Achmet derives from Arabian sources. Other books are apocryphal.

3. The Importance of Dreams in Antiquity.

a. The Cultic Dream. Cults and sanctuaries are set up through dreams, e.g., a temple in Hierapolis, and the cult of Sarapis in Alexandria. Directions are also given by dreams, and the gods threaten punishment for neglect or encouragement for devotion. The sick are healed as they dream of the gods. Domitian dreams of the disarming of his protective goddess Minerva before his death. Votive offerings are made on the basis of dreams.

b. The Political Dream. Dreams supposedly intimate the birth of great leaders, e.g., Pericles and Augustus. Generals are promised victories in dreams, e.g., Xerxes and Caesar. But dreams may be equivocal, coming to fulfilment in reverses rather than successes. Critical events are intimated by dreams, e.g., the end of Nero, or the accessions of Hadrian and Marcus Aurelius.

c. The Personal Dream. Ordinary people as well as leaders have dreams that relate to events in their lives. Such dreams are usually symbolical or allegorical. They often have to do with death or with the consequences of evil acts.

4. The Metaphysics of Dreams. Primitive people feel that in dreams they are caught up into the suprasensory world. Thus in Egypt dreamers supposedly enter the world that the sun god traverses by night, and what they experience there is unquestionably true. In Greece, too, there is a connection between dreams and the world of the dead. The dead often appear in dreams, and dreams are seen as messages from the hereafter in the form of rapture. They are common on the approach of death.

5. The Interpretation of Dreams as a Science. When directions are given in dreams, interpretation is not needed. But other dreams are more obscure and various efforts are made to interpret them. These might be intuitive, but as regular patterns are sought, supported by examples, interpretation is put on a more scientific basis, and a class of scholars develops that collects and studies dreams and undertakes their interpretation, e.g., in Babylon and Greece. Since the same dream may have different interpretations according to age, sex, health, and situation, one needs ability, wit, and experience to fit it to a given case. Pleasant dreams usually indicate pleasant things and vice versa, but the reverse may be true. Animals denote characters, e.g., the crocodile a rapacious official, pirate, or murderer. Puns help in view of the divine nature of language. Keywords come under scrutiny, and Artemidorus has a well-arranged system relating to such things as birth, the arts, contests, washing, food, sleep, the chase, fishing, voyages, and heavenly phenomena. The harvest usually refers to progeny (wheat to sons and barley to daughters), and fruits in husks are miscarriages. This is a bizarre world, although modern study of dreams shows that there may be elements of truth in the belief that dreams are significant.

6. The Dream as a Literary Form. The dream also becomes a form of literary composition. Cicero makes effective use of this, as does Lucian when he describes his life in the form of a vision, or when he invents the witty dialogue between the cobbler Micyllos and his cock.

7. Dream Life as a Mirror. The people of antiquity are seen unadorned in their dreams. Books of dreams enable us to construct a mosaic of their culture. We find harmless dreams presenting life as work or depicting good fortune. But in the main the picture is one of riotous and perverted fantasy in which the dominant concern is not for higher things but for the trivialities of daily life, e.g., money, health, safety, and sexual fulfilment. If unfavorable interpretations show a sober realism, they also manifest a pitiless lack of concern. The total picture is one of fatalism, superstition, and corruption; nowhere is antiquity so unmasked as in its dreams.

II. Dreams and the Interpretation of Dreams in the OT.

1. The Dream and History. In the OT we again find cultic, political, and personal dreams. Thus Jacob's dream is cultic (Gen. 28:11ff.), those of Joseph and Solomon are political (Gen. 37:5ff.; 1 Kgs. 3:5ff.), and those of the butler and baker are personal (Gen. 40:8ff.). Dreams are mostly allegorical, so that interpretation is important, and it follows traditional lines. Joseph and Daniel replace the Egyptian and Babylonian soothsayers, even using some of their equations. Yet OT dreams have certain distinctive features. They move on a more sober, indeed a higher level. Stress is laid on the evanescent character of dreams (cf. Ps. 73:20). They do not come from the realm of the dead, which is in no sense an abode of God, but from God himself (Gen. 20:6; 28:10ff.; Judg. 7:13ff.; Dan. 2:1ff.). They are not needed for revelation, but God can use them if he so chooses, and he alone can give the true interpretation to selected people (Gen. 40:8; Dan. 2:17ff.). On these conditions dreams are integrated into the history of God with his people (cf. Gen. 41:1ff.; Judg. 7:13ff.). Even personal dreams are told because the persons concerned have a part in salvation history. The God who gives dreams is the God of history from whom sanctifying power goes forth. Dreams, then, are given a distinctive stamp.

2. The Dream as a Regular Means of Revelation. Job and his friends all regard dreams as messages from God (cf. 4:13ff.; 7:14). Dreams are associated with shrines (Gen. 28:10ff.), and revelations are sought there (1 Sam. 3:1ff.). Prophecy is linked with dreams (Num. 12:6-7). Dreams will be a feature of the age of salvation when God pours out his Spirit (Joel 2:28).

3. The Prophetic Criticism of Dreams. Yet there is also criticism of dreams. God speaks to Moses directly (Num. 12:6ff.). Revelations by dreams may be untrustworthy even when accompanied by signs and wonders (Dt. 13:2ff.). Jeremiah struggles with prophets who appeal to dreams (23:25ff.). It is on the basis of the true word of God, not of rationalism, that dreams are suspect. Eccl. 5:3, 7 comes to a similar conclusion. Words and dreams are cheap; it is better to fear God.

III. Dreams and Their Interpretation in Judaism.

1. Philo. The prophetic criticism is lost to view in Hellenistic Judaism. Philo knows the emptiness of dreams, but he still thinks that God gives knowledge of heavenly things through them, e.g., the beauties of virtues. In some dreams God speaks directly, in others through immortal souls, in yet others through the souls of the dreamers. Dreams of the last group are obscure and need authentic interpreters, although Philo himself allegorizes biblical interpretations.

2. Hagiography and Apocalyptic. Popular religious literature evinces a strong belief in dreams. In Esther the LXX adds a dream by Mordecai, and in 2 Macc. 15:11ff. Judas Maccabeus tells a dream to encourage his troops. In apocalyptic there is a fluid border between dream and vision. Many visions are literary constructs.

3. Josephus. Josephus shows considerable credulity. He adds new dreams to the OT and adorns postcanonical history with dreams, e.g., those of Jaddus, Hyrcanus, Archelaus, and Josephus himself, who has dreams disclosing the future destiny of the emperors before going over to the Romans.

4. Rabbinic Judaism. The rabbis show some skepticism, e.g., in the saying that dreams neither exalt nor abase. They sometimes interpret dreams psychologically, but also distinguish between valid and invalid visions, i.e., those that come from angels and those that come from demons. There is an angel of dreams, and dreams constitute a tiny fraction of prophecy. In practical life the concerns in dreams are the common ones of money, health, marriage, etc. Those who have corrupt dreams should seek reason and wisdom. There are both expert and popular interpreters, and fixed interpretations develop; thus wheat denotes peace, barley forgiveness, a white horse good, an ass messianic salvation. Puns are common in exposition. Peculiar to Judaism is the belief that a dream has force only by interpretation. Interpretation is thus a valuable art, and dreams may be evaded by seeking a favorable interpretation (as also by reciting Scripture, prayer, almsgiving, and penitence). Attempts are made to apply dreams morally. Thus God is said to give the wicked bad dreams to lead them to repentance.

B. The Dream in the NT.

1. The Tradition. Paul's dreams in Acts 16:9-10 and 27:23-24 bear the stamp of authenticity, and we may thus accept 18:9 and 23:11 as well. Elsewhere the only dreams are in Matthew (1:20-21; 2:12; 2:13ff.; 27:19). The formula *kat' ónar* shows that these are from the same hand, although some scholars think they are legendary and apologetic.

2. The Uniqueness of the NT Understanding.

a. Paucity. If the NT seldom mentions dreams, this is because it regards fewer dreams as significant. It does not rule them out, for it quotes Joel 2:28 with approval. But it resists the Hellenistic interest. Thus Paul never mentions the dreams of Acts in the epistles, and he refers only hesitantly to his visions and revelations (2 Cor. 12:1). Jude, indeed, condemns the carnal dreamings of heretics (v. 8).

b. Absence of Allegorical Dreams and Interpretations. There are no allegorical dreams in the NT. God appears, or an angel, or a messenger, or a man, and gives plain directions about what is to happen or what is to be done (cf. Acts 27:23; Mt. 1:20, etc.). There is thus no interpretation of dreams in the NT. When God speaks through dreams, he does so unambiguously.

c. Lofty Nature of NT Dream Life. On the basis of the OT, the dreams of the NT compare most favorably with those of secular antiquity. There is nothing vulgar, disgusting, sexually unnatural, or egocentric about them. They are not concerned with personal fate but with Christ and the Christian mission. They do not terrify, but by means of them God directs his people. The tension between superstition and enlightenment is resolved.

C. Dreams and Their Interpretation in the Postapostolic Period. The terms do not occur in the apostolic fathers and are rare in the Apologists. The Gnostic Acts abound in dreams and visions. Martyrs like Polycarp have dreams (Mart. Pol. 5.1-2; cf. Perpetua, Saturus, and Cyprian). Synesius works out a system of interpretation on an eclectic philosophical basis. He advocates keeping a book of dreams and daydreams, and follows the principle that like follows like. Achmet makes use of the dreams of the OT, and traces interpretation to God, but he also draws on various sources, and his detailed suggestions are often trivial, e.g., that cutting side hairs denotes poor management of income. Thus the muddy waters of antiquity bring in a new flood of superstition.   [A. OEPKE, V, 220-38]

onárion → *ónos*

óneidos [disgrace, reproach],   *oneidízō* [to reproach, revile],   *oneidismós* [abuse, reproach]

óneidos. This word seems to come from a root meaning "to revile," and it means "disgrace," "abuse," or "object of disgrace or shame." In the LXX the fact of sin means that earthly life is marked by shame, so that all of us despise and are ourselves despised. Release from shame is part of divine deliverance (Is. 25:8; Joel 2:19). The wicked despise God, but he in turn heaps shame on them. Sin is a reproach to a people (Prov. 14:34), yet God may also bring reproach on the righteous as a test, and when accepted in God's name (Ps. 69:7-8) this brings joy and courage (cf. 73:23ff.). In the NT the only instance is in Lk. 1:25, in which Elizabeth rejoices that God has taken from her the "reproach" of childlessness.

oneidízō. This word means "to upbraid," "to revile," "to bring reproaches or complaints." In the Psalms enemies revile God, Israel, the righteous, etc. Jesus has authority to reproach in Mt. 11:20 (cf. Mk. 16:14). In his passion, however, he himself is reviled (Mk. 15:32). The disciples will be reviled too (Mt. 5:11). Yet blessing comes upon them when they are reviled in Christ's name, i.e., as Christians (1 Pet. 4:14). God's generosity is such that he gives without reproaching (Jms. 1:5). Paul in Rom. 15:3 quotes Ps. 69:9 in holding up Christ as a model of unselfishness. The word is also a variant in Mk. 15:34, where it softens the "forsaken," and in 1 Tim. 4:10, where it hardly seems to fit the context.

oneidismós. This word means "insult," "abuse," "reproach." It is fairly common in the LXX. In the NT the bishop must be well thought of lest he fall into "reproach" (1 Tim. 3:7). In Heb. 10:33 the readers were formerly exposed to "abuse," in 11:26 Moses prefers "abuse" for Christ's sake to the treasures of Egypt, salvation history providing the link between Moses and Christ, and in 13:13 the readers are to go outside the camp with Christ, bearing "reproach" for him as messianic bearers of the cross who have a share in their Lord's sufferings.   [J. SCHNEIDER, V, 238-42]

ónoma [name, person], *onomázō* [to name], *eponomázō* [to nickname], *pseudṓnymos* [bearing a false name]

A. Historical Background. It is a common belief of antiquity that the name is not just a label but part of the personality of the one who bears it. Various rites are used to find names for children. New names are often given in puberty. The name carries will and power. One must know the names of gods to have dealings with them or power over them. The name conjures up the person; there is thus a desire to know it and a reluctance to give it. Possession of secret names is a safeguard of freedom.

B. The Greek World and Hellenism.
1. Usage. *ónoma* means a. "name" of a person or thing. Names are given by parents, and strangers must give their names when seeking hospitality. Common expressions are "to call by name," "to give a name," "in the name," "under the name," and "with mention of the name." *ónoma* also means b. "repute." It may be used c. as the opposite of a thing, but also d., with the genitive, for the person or thing. In grammar e. it is used for a "noun" or "word." In the papyri f., on the basis of names in books or on lists, it may denote such things as "legal title," "item in an account," or, in banking, the actual "account," e.g., when money is paid to the name (credit or account) of someone.
2. The Significance of ónoma in Greek Thought. Epic poetry shares the belief in the significance of names, although it also shares the philosophical doubt whether human names truly reflect reality. Many things have both divine and human names. Skeptical

philosophy suggests that human names express false notions and concepts, since they are conventional and relate only to experience. Thus the Sophists contrast the name with the work, reality, or nature. The nature is what counts; names cannot change it. Plato accepts the view that, while names are not capricious, and are undoubtedly necessary, they do not convey true knowledge and simply act as signs. Aristotle attaches importance to the thought behind the mere sound. The name is a verbal sign, but a limited one since words have to indicate more than one thing, some ideas can hardly be put into words, and words change their meanings. Linguistic research is needed, then, to serve logic. For the Stoics, language arises from the human soul, and hence words represent things according to their nature in a fusion of thing, concept, and word. Etymology has the task of showing the truth of words *(etymótēs)* in their agreement with the objects they denote. By this art the Stoics take over popular religion, for they find truth and wisdom in it by etymologizing the names of the gods.

3. *The Name of God.* Originally the Pelasgians are thought not to have named their gods. The divine names come from Egypt; Homer and Hesiod play a big part in naming the gods of Greece. Strabo also mentions a tribe that sacrificed to an unnamed god. Later Greek religion, however, attaches great importance to the divine names and tries to learn about their being and nature from their names by way of etymology. Philosophy has doubts about the correspondence of name and nature. Etymology can yield only human thoughts about the gods. Yet the names are still commonly regarded as significant. Indeed, names are heaped on the gods to pay them greater honor and to be sure of gaining control over them. Stoicism thinks Zeus should be known by many names in view of his many functions and characteristics. In the Hermetic writings God is too lofty to have a name; no name fits him and all names fit him. The anonymity of deity is related to its incorporeality, for language is corporeal. Again, names differentiate distinct things, but the deity is the one and all. Celsus thinks along these lines, as do the Gnostics, and even some Christian authors.

4. *The Magic Papyri.* The magic papyri believe in the power and efficacy of names. Knowledge and utterance of them give power over their bearers by invocation and even mystical identification. Magicians know the right acts and times to gain this power. They use names from all possible languages; barbarian names have great force if pronounced correctly. In Egypt even the name of Yahweh is used. The name has to be the one that the deity itself has given. In invocation it is honored by many predicates. The name works by its own power, for the deity is itself the name. Christian magic papyri mention the names of Mary, the Baptist, and the Trinity as efficacious along with Yao, Sabaoth, etc. Antiquity has, of course, its skeptics like Lucian.

C. The OT.

1. *Lexical and Statistical Data.* The common Heb. *shēm* (some 770 times in the singular and 84 in the plural) is used for the names of gods, humans, and animals, also of such geographical features as rivers, mountains, and towns, then of things or times. With reference to acts it may also be used for a good or bad "reputation," and then for "memory" or "fame" after death, although there is debate as to whether it is used metonymically for the person or in the sense of "memorial" or "sign." A common expression is "for the name" (usually God), and familiar verbs used with the name (of God) are "to invoke," "to speak," "to bless," and "to prophesy."

2. *The Significance of the Name.* Israel believes in the significance of names. Thus Adam exercises dominion by naming the animals (Gen. 2:19-20). To name a city is to establish control over it (2 Sam. 12:28). Women seek the name of a man in times

of distress (Is. 4:1), i.e., to put themselves under his protection. God names the stars (Ps. 147:4) and Israel (Is. 43:1). His name is named over Israel (Is. 63:19), and also over the temple, the ark, and Jerusalem. He knows Moses by name (Ex. 33:12, 17). Names live on in children (Gen. 21:12). The names of those without children are blotted out. The names of the righteous are written in the book of life (Ex. 32:32-33; Ps. 69:28).

3. *Proper Names and Meaningful Names.* Proper names establish identities. Thus it may be said of Nabal (1 Sam. 25:25) that as a man is named, so he is. Etymologies are given for such names as Eve (3:20), Cain (4:1), Noah (5:29), and cf. Babel (11:9). The name may express the whole person or a single feature. Many names are theophorous, expressing either a relation to God or a Godward wish. The names of the 12 patriarchs bear witness to God's help (Gen. 29:31ff.). Second names are sometimes given (cf. Gen. 41:45; 2 Kgs. 23:34; Dan. 1:7). These express new status. God himself may give new names (Gen. 32:29). As in Abraham's case, the name may have meaning for more than its bearer (Gen. 12:2-3). This applies to the symbolical names in Hos. 1 and Is. 7:3; 8:3.

4. *The Name Yahweh.* Knowing the name of God is important in the OT (Gen. 32:30). God reveals his name to Abraham (Gen. 17:1) and Moses (Ex. 6:2). Invocation of his name is common, but incantation is forbidden (Ex. 20:7). God promises to hear when properly called upon, but his name is a gift of revelation, not an instrument of magic. Yet invocation of his name implies faith in his power, as in swearing (1 Sam. 20:42), cursing (2 Kgs. 2:24), or blessing in his name (2 Sam. 6:18). The name may indeed stand for the person (Lev. 18:21; Am. 2:7). If the name is in the angel of Ex. 23:21, this means that God himself is present in revelatory action. While he himself is in heaven, he chooses a place for his name to dwell (Dt. 12:11; 2 Sam. 7:13; 1 Kgs. 3:2). This is the pledge of his saving presence. It assures a high estimation for the temple and yet also a low estimation, for God is not tied to the temple by causing his name to dwell there. After the exile, the name often denotes the glory of God. A common idea is that God will be gracious to Israel so that his name may not be dishonored among the nations. Much more frequently, however, the name now stands for the person, and this leads to the hypostatizing of the name whereby it stands alongside God as an acting subject or an instrument in his hand (cf. Ps. 20:1; Prov. 18:10; Mal. 1:11). If there is often parallelism here, there is also a more conscious use of the term.

5. *In the Name.* A formula that is often used is that of "in the name." Sometimes this is much the same as "by name" (Judg. 18:29). Elsewhere it means "under the name" (cf. 1 Kgs. 21:8). More strongly it means "on the commission" (cf. Esth. 2:22; 1 Sam. 25:9). Most commonly we find the phrase with reference to God. Cultically it has the significance of calling "on the name" (Gen. 4:26; 12:8), or swearing or blessing "by" or "in the name" of God (Dt. 6:13; 10:8). David meets Goliath "in the name" of God (1 Sam. 17:45), Elijah builds an altar "in his name" (1 Kgs. 18:32), and one may be strong or set up a banner "in his name" (Ps. 20:5, 7). In Dt. 18:18-19 the sense is probably "on the commission of God," but in 18:20; Jer. 14:14 false prophets either name the name of God, speak only ostensibly on his commission, or make an appeal to his name.

D. Hellenistic Judaism.

1. *The LXX.* *ónoma* occurs over 1,000 times in the LXX, mostly for *shēm*. (For details of the Hebrew and Greek words see *TDNT*, V, 261-62.) The concept "in the

name" causes problems. The LXX uses *ek* (Esth. 8:8), *diá* without *ónoma* (3:12), *epí* (1 Sam. 25:5), and *en* (25:9; *en tō onómati* is literal, but unusual in classical Greek). (For details cf. *TDNT,* V, 262-63.) The verb *onomázein* is rare in the LXX; *kaleín* usually replaces it, perhaps because *shēm* has no related verb. *eponomázein* occurs some 36 times.

2. *Philo.* Philo calls the name a kind of shadow accompanying the reality (*On the Decalogue* 82). Clear thoughts find suitable terms, as in the case of Moses, but there are no fitting expressions for obscure concepts. The LXX is praised because its renderings harmonize so well with the original that they correspond to the things denoted. Giving names is a task for the first man rather than many people, and this means that confusion is avoided. Philo allegorizes many OT names, building partly on OT expositions and partly on Stoic etymologizing. Words are important for Philo, but we must not spend our whole lives on them and ignore the realities. Idolatry gives false names to things, and in so doing obscures the true God (*On the Decalogue* 53). As regards God's name, Philo borrows from Ex. 3:14 LXX. But as "he who is" (i.e., being itself), God cannot be named (*On the Life of Moses* 1.75). He is the Lord God, or the God of Abraham etc., but he has no proper name. The powers of God have many names (cf. Stoicism), as does the *lógos,* and these names are to be held holy. Philo warns against false swearing and also against the blasphemous heaping up of many names instead of simply praising God (*On the Special Laws* 2.8).

3. *Josephus.* The use in Josephus is more Greek than Semitic. For "in the name" he mostly has *ex* or *ep.* He is reserved about God's name; he avoids mention of "name" in his version of the third commandment, and says that God showed Moses his *prosēgoría* (not *ónoma*), about which it is not permissible to say anything. God's name is dreadful. It may be invoked in crises, and coins are marked by his name (as alien temples are named for their gods). One must honor fathers because they bear the same name as God. On the other hand, part of God's Spirit rather than his name dwells in the temple. Writing for Greeks, Josephus perhaps thought they would regard it as odd to speak about God's name dwelling in the temple.

E. Later Judaism.

I. Pseudepigrapha. These works are not rich in statements about the name. Slavonic Enoch expounds the meanings of human names, e.g., Adam. In Ethiopian Enoch the wicked are under threat that their names will be blotted out of the book of life (108:3). The names of saints and believers are related to stars and lightnings (43). An interest is shown in the names of fallen angels (6:7 etc.). As regards God's name, seven divine names are known. God will protect Israel for his name's sake. To know God's name is to praise him, but sinners deny his name. The Son of Man is named before the Lord of spirits prior to the creation of the stars. In affliction, believers will overcome in God's name. Often the name seems to be the same as God himself, but in other passages it seems to be a mysterious force that is revealed by angels.

II. Rabbinic Sources.

1. Usage. The rabbis take over the meanings of the Hebrew term from the OT. They speak of three names: the family name, the given name, and the acquired name. When Scripture doubles a name, it points to a share in both this world and the next. "In the name" means "in virtue of," "on the basis of," or "with appeal to the name." "In the name of a teacher" is a phrase used when citing an authority. Circumcision is given "in the name of the covenant," denoting both entry into the covenant and commitment to it. Doing things "in God's name" may sometimes have the force of doing them "for his sake."

2. *The Name of God.* In the synagogue reading of the OT the divine name Yahweh is read as Adonai. Yahweh is the special name of God, his secret proper name that is mostly not to be uttered. To curse parents with this name is a capital offense. Originally used in temple worship, it is gradually replaced and becomes an ineffable name that lays itself open to magical use. Lev. 24:11, 16 is adduced in support. A technical term for it is "the name of four letters."

3. *Belief and Magic.* We find many accounts of the wonder-working power of the divine name, e.g., the deliverance of Isaiah, or the binding of Asmodai the demon-prince. Knowledge of the future may be gained with its help. In syncretistic magic God's name is used along with others. By linking the name "el" with angels and Israel, God has made over power to them. If official Judaism struggles against magic, the Talmud ascribes force even to the individual letters of the divine name, and Hebrew Enoch (42:2ff.) believes that divine names hold together the polar forces in the cosmos, thus insuring its harmony.

F. The NT.

1. Usage.

a. Name of a Person. In the NT proper names are usually integrated into sentences (Mk. 3:16; Acts 27:1, though cf. Rev. 9:11). Hebrew influence may be seen in Lk. 1:5; Mt. 1:21, 23; Lk. 1:59, etc.

b. Name as "Reputation." This occurs in Mk. 6:14 and Rev. 3:1.

c. Name for Person. Three examples of this are Acts 1:15; Rev. 3:4; 11:13. Perhaps one might also add Acts 18:15.

d. Name with Prepositions. This usage shows strong Semitic influence. Along with *epí, diá, perí, kat'*, and *prós, en* is very common. It is used with various verbs and in such senses as "with invocation of," "with proclamation of," "on the commission," "in fulfilment of the will," "in obedience to," "in the power of," or "in the presence of." (For details cf. *TDNT,* V, 271.)

2. *ónoma as the Name of God or Jesus Christ.* In the NT the name, person, and work of God are inseparably linked to those of Christ. This applies even to OT quotations or allusions, e.g., Mk. 11:9-10; Mt. 23:39; Acts 15:17.

a. The name of God relates to revelation, and in this sense it is linked to "glory," thus expressing a specific approach and relationship. In Jn. 12:28 God glorifies his name in the life and work and then again in the death and resurrection of Jesus (cf. Jn. 17:6). Jesus discloses the obscure name of God to his disciples, giving it the specific content of "Father." To be received in the name is to stand in the sphere of the love of Father and Son (17:11, 12, 21). When the name is declared it awakens new life in believers (1 Jn. 4:7) as the Son is present in them in the Father's love. Glorifying God's name is supremely Christ's work as a work of revelation and reconciliation. Grounded on Christ's work, the church has the promise that this work will continue in it (Jn. 17:26).

b. The fullness of Christ's being and work may be seen in his name. The divinely given name "Jesus" expresses his humanity and his mission (Mt. 1:21). It implies "God with us" (1:23). The exalted name he receives is that of Son (Heb. 1:4). He is also called Lord (Phil. 2:9-10), which denotes divine equality and is the name above all others. Hence Jesus is Lord of lords. Revealing the divine dominion, he is also King of kings (Rev. 19:16). The unity of nature and name may be seen in Rev. 19:13

and Jn. 1:1. He alone knows his name in the sense that he alone knows the fullness of his relationship with God (Rev. 19:12). Jesus acts in God's name as the Christ (Jn. 10:24-25). His coming again completes his work (Mt. 23:39). His name, then, embraces the whole content of God's saving acts (1 Cor. 6:11). Justification and sanctification in his name relate not to the mere pronouncing of the name but to baptism in the sense of Rom. 6:1ff. Forgiveness is in his name (Acts 10:43; cf. 1 Jn. 1:7; 2:12). Life is given in his name, i.e., by entry into his sphere of action or the sphere of his person (Jn. 20:31). As Peter says, salvation is only in his name (Acts 4:12). Those who enter into it are to do all things and to give thanks for all things in this name (2 Th. 1:12; Col. 3:17; Eph. 5:20). His name is the hope of all peoples, although it may mean judgment as well as salvation (Jn. 3:18). The Father sends the Spirit in the name of Jesus (Jn. 14:16).

c. In Mt. 28:19 Father, Son, and Spirit come together and thus give fullness to the Father's name. Baptism in this name means entering into fellowship with the Father through the Son and coming under the operation of the Spirit. The phrase *eis (tó) ónoma* is difficult. It sometimes has the force of "with regard to" or "because" (cf. Mt. 10:41-42; Mk. 9:41). Gathering in Christ's name means meeting "on the basis of" Christ (Mt. 18:10; cf. Heb. 6:10). Yet this does not seem to be the sense in Mt. 28:19 (cf. Acts 8:16; 1 Cor. 1:13, 15). After the rabbinic model, the force is final rather than causal, expressing a specific end or intention, and with forensic rather than mystical implications. Without the use of *ónoma*, Paul has similar phrases in 1 Cor. 1:13, 15; Rom. 6:3; Gal. 3:27, and cf. 1 Cor. 10:2. It is Semitic in origin rather than Hellenistic (e.g., charging to the account). In Acts 2:38 the *epí* with dative may denote the basis, and the *en* of Acts 10:48 is perhaps to be taken in the same way.

d. The first petition of the Lord's Prayer (Mt. 6:9) relates to the dawn of the kingdom and is thus a prayer, primarily that God will sanctify his own name in spite of all sin and opposition. The disciples of Jesus are to pray in the name of Jesus (Jn. 14:13-14), i.e., according to his will, on his commission, and with invocation of his name. Presupposed here is faith that he has come from his Father and that the Father will hear the prayer for his sake. The unity of Father and Son is shown in the fact that the Son will himself do what is asked (14:13).

e. Believing in His Name. In Jn. 2:23 believing in the name of Jesus is believing in him as the Christ, the Son of God (3:18). Belief arises through his acts of power (10:25). It confers a right relation to the Father (1:12). God commands it (1 Jn. 1:23).

f. Believers in this name can act on its commission and in its power (Lk. 10:17). Even nondisciples find power in it (9:49). Works of mercy, too, are done in it (Mt. 18:5). It is the force in the healing of the lame man (Acts 3:6, 16). Paul drives out the spirit of soothsaying in the name (16:18). It is no magic formula but stands for Christ's presence (9:34). Adjurations are used only by demons (Mk. 5:7) and the Jewish exorcists (Acts 19:13ff.). The name has power only where there is faith and obedience (cf. Mk. 9:38-39). This power is in answer to prayer (Acts 4:30; Jms. 5:14-15).

g. The name of Jesus is the basis and theme of proclamation (Acts 8:12). Repentance is preached to the Gentiles in it (Lk. 24:47). Missionaries go out for it (3 Jn. 7). Saul persecutes it (Acts 26:9), but when converted, he proclaims it (9:27-28). He speaks on its commission (Rom. 1:5 etc.). He beseeches in it (1 Cor. 1:10).

h. Belief in the name leads to confession of it (Heb. 13:15), which is linked to suffering for it (Mk. 10:29; Jn. 15:21). The disciples are put to shame for it (Acts 5:41), and Paul and Barnabas risk their lives for it (15:26). The church at Pergamum holds fast to it (Rev. 2:13) and that at Philadelphia does not deny it (3:8). Reproach for the name means blessing (1 Pet. 4:14). Fulfilment for the church comes with reverence for the name (Rev. 11:18) and praise of it (15:4). Calling on it is salvation (Acts 2:17ff.), and it is named over believers, so that they are called Christians (11:26; Jms. 2:7). In the new creation the victors will bear the name of the Lamb with that of God and the new Jerusalem (Rev. 3:12). Investing with the new name marks entry into the new world order (cf. Is. 56:5). Unbelief is blaspheming the name (Rom. 2:24; 1 Tim. 6:1).

3. *Other References*.

a. In the case of the beast, the name expresses ungodliness, for the beast usurps the names and titles of God (Rev. 13:1). What the number signifies is hard to determine. The name or number is a mark denoting the beast's sphere of power. In the case of the harlot, too, the name expresses ungodliness (17:1). Babylon violates the divine purity and majesty. The names Death, Hades, Abaddon, and Apollyon (6:8; 9:11) denote forces that are opposed to life as God's true nature. Spirits have names. The name Legion suggests not only the nature and greatness of the spirit but also the fullness of the power of Jesus.

b. Jesus gives three disciples new names. These do not denote natural qualities but future promises. Thus Simon is called Peter, and James and John are Sons of Thunder. Jesus will build his church on Simon, and he gives James and John a mighty power of witness. The names of the apostles are the foundation stones of the new Jerusalem (Rev. 21:14). Note here the link with the OT community (21:12). Jesus knows his own people by name (Jn. 10:3). These names are written in heaven (Lk. 10:20; cf. Rev. 3:5; Phil. 4:3). Christ promises those who overcome that he will not blot out their names (Rev. 3:5). The names stand because Jesus confesses them. With the white stones, the victors receive a new and secret name (2:17), which expresses a new nature and inexchangeable fellowship with Christ.

onomázō. This word, meaning "to name," "to call by name," "to number," "to denote," and "to promise," occurs nine times in the NT. Jesus calls the 12 apostles; their name and ministry come from him (Lk. 6:13). He calls Simon "Peter" (6:14). Those who bear the name but act unworthily are to be denied table fellowship (1 Cor. 5:11). Sins are not even to be named, i.e., mentioned, by the saints (Eph. 5:3). Every family in heaven and earth is named by God (Eph. 3:14-15), for he is the common Father.

eponomázō. This word means "to give a second name" or "nickname." The only NT instance is in Rom. 2:17, where Paul overturns any pride associated with the mere name of Jew, since Jews and Gentiles are both under judgment and are both referred to grace.

pseudṓnymos. This word means "bearing a false or incorrect name." The one NT instance is in 1 Tim. 6:20, where the apostle warns Timothy against a movement that gives the lie to its name, since it leads to error, not knowledge.

[H. BIETENHARD, V, 242-83]

ónos [ass, donkey],   *onárion* [little donkey]

A. The Ass in Palestine and Judaism.

1. There are early references to the *ónos* (diminutive *onárion*), or "ass," in Egypt

and Palestine (cf. Gen. 12:16 and figuratively 29:14). The ass is used for riding, carrying, plowing, etc. (Num. 22:22ff.; 1 Sam. 25:18; Is. 30:24). Only in dire need is it eaten (2 Kgs. 6:25). The wild ass loves its freedom (Job 6:5). The burial of an ass is a shameful burial (Jer. 22:19). A calumny against Jews and Christians is that they worship the head of an ass.

2. In Gen. 49:11 and Zech. 9:9 the eschatological ruler who will establish peace rides on an ass, or, as the parallelism shows, a young male animal. The verse in Genesis stresses the fruitfulness of the reign, that in Zechariah its righteousness. Rabbinic exegesis relates the second redeemer to the first, i.e., Moses (cf. Ex. 4:20). Some scholars argue that he will come on an ass only if Israel has no merits, while others think that riding on an ass is for the sake of the wicked, and recalls the merit of the fathers, e.g., Abraham in Gen. 22:3.

B. The Ass in Antiquity, Hellenism, and Gnosticism. In Egypt the ass is dedicated to the god Typhon. It seems to come to Greece from Asia Minor. Ajax is compared by Homer to an ass. Dionysus and his followers ride on asses. There are accounts of sexual intercourse with asses. Epiphanius calls the Gnostics worshippers of Typhon, and the Mandaeans refer to the mystery and sacrament of the she-ass with four bones, in an attack on Christianity.

C. The Ass in the NT.
1. While Mk. 11:1ff. does not quote Zech. 9:9, as Mt. 21:2ff. and Jn. 12:15 do, it is full of allusions. Mark and Luke stress the fact that no one has yet sat on the foal that Jesus uses (cf. Num. 19:2; Dt. 21:3). Matthew mentions both ass and colt. This seems to create difficulties (even of a practical kind), and it is hard to see why both should be mentioned. Jn. 12:14ff. uses *onárion* for the colt, and expressly says that the disciples do not at first understand the incident. Surprisingly, perhaps, he relates the prophecy to the messianic event rather than the messianic character (v. 16).

2. The OT often mentions the ox and the ass together, and Jesus does the same in the saying in Lk. 13:15. In Lk. 14:5 the true reading might be "a son or an ox," but "an ass or an ox" is also attested. Some Jewish rulings allow pulling a man out of a well on the sabbath, but not an animal.   [O. MICHEL, V, 283-87]

óxos [sharp, sour]

"Sour wine" is a popular drink, and "very sour wine" (vinegar) a popular seasoning. Doctors recommend sour wine for fevers, as well as for refreshment and for digestion. In Ps. 69:21 (cf. Jn. 19:29) the complaint seems to be that only a sour drink is given instead of wine. The passion story (Mk. 15:36 and par.) says that the wine of the people was offered to Jesus on the cross. Some commentators suggest that a sharp drink would produce nervous stimulation and prolong the agony, but no such effect is known, and Mk. 15:36 implies that it is given for refreshment after the cry of v. 34. Mt. 17:48-49 supports this view, although Lk. 23:36-37 finds an element of mockery when the soldiers hand Jesus sour wine. Jn. 19:28ff. attributes the initiative to the saying of Jesus: "I thirst," and traces in the incident a fulfilment of the saying in Ps. 69:21 that the innocent sufferer is given vinegar to drink. The stupefying drink in Mk. 15:22-23 and Mt. 27:34 is quite a different one.   [H. W. HEIDLAND, V, 288-89]

---

opísō [behind, later],   **ópisthen** [behind, from behind]

---

1. *opísō* has such meanings as "behind," "after," "later," and "again." As a noun in Phil. 3:13 it denotes "what lies behind." The reference in Jn. 6:66 is to "withdrawal" and in Lk. 9:62 to "looking back." Like the LXX, the NT uses *opísō* as a preposition with the genitive, mostly of person.

2. *ópisthen* as an adverb and preposition means "behind." The NT has it seven times. As an adverb it means "from behind" in Mk. 5:27 (Mt. 9:20; Lk. 8:44) and "behind" in Rev. 4:6; 5:1. As a preposition it means "behind" in Mt. 25:23; Lk. 23:26.

3. *opísō* is theologically significant when it is combined with a genitive of person and verb of motion (though there are exceptions, e.g., Lk. 9:14; Rev. 12:15). Thus in Mk. 1:17 it binds the disciples to Jesus. In the OT "going after" God (or other gods) means obedience (or apostasy). Hence Jesus does not just ask his disciples to follow him. He demands total commitment with a view to entry into the kingdom. This means self-denial (Mk. 8:34; cf. Mt. 26:24; Lk. 9:23) in cross-bearing and self-surrender. When the call to "go after" is heard (Mk. 1:17), there can be no going back (Lk. 9:62; cf. Mk. 13:16). Discipleship means belonging exclusively to Christ. A warning is issued to avoid going after false Christs (Lk. 21:8). On the other hand, the Pharisees complain that the world has gone after Christ (Jn. 12:19). In other verses Gamaliel refers to Judas drawing people after him (Acts 5:37), Paul warns against false teachers who draw disciples after them (20:30), 1 Tim. 5:15 says that some believers go astray after Satan, Rev. 13 refers to following the beast, Jude 7 and 2 Pet. 2:10 describe licentiousness and indulgence in unnatural lust, and Paul in Phil. 3:13 says that in pressing on to what lies ahead, he forgets what lies behind, his commitment to Christ involving abandonment of all that he has previously valued.

[H. SEESEMANN, V, 289-92]

---

hóplon [tool, weapon], **hoplízō** [to prepare, arm], **panoplía** [full armor], **zṓnnymi** [to gird oneself], **diazṓnnymi** [to tie on], **perizṓnnymi** [to gird oneself about], **zṓnē** [girdle], **thṓrax** [breastplate], **hypodéō** [to put on sandals], **(hypódēma** [footwear], **sandálion** [sandle]), **thyreós** [long shield], **perikephalaía** [helmet]

---

hóplon. Originally meaning "implement," this word comes to be used for 1. "ship's tackling," "cable," "rope," 2. "tool," 3. "weapon," and 4. "troops," or "camp." It is used figuratively for weapons of both offense and defense. In the LXX the general term often replaces more specific Hebrew words, e.g., for "spear" in Ps. 46:9. It is rare in the LXX in a figurative sense (cf. Ps. 57:4). God may use human weapons, but when he wishes he destroys these (Ps. 46:9), and lends his people his own weapons (Ps. 35:2). In Philo the figurative use predominates. The NT always has the word in the plural for "weapons." Paul, describing his work as warfare, stresses the efficacy of his weapons (siege-engines) in 2 Cor. 10:4. Moral qualities seem to be the weapons of 2 Cor. 6:7, and in Rom. 6:13 the members of believers are to be weapons of righteousness. In Rom. 13:12 (cf. 1 Th. 5:8) the nearness of the parousia does not mean inertia but arming for the conflict, not merely with what is unnatural or immoral (cf. 1 Cor. 11:13ff.), but with satanic forces. The early fathers follow the NT closely (cf. Ignatius *To Polycarp* 6.2; Clement of Alexandria *Protrepticus* 11.116.3-4), but with a moralizing rather than an eschatological thrust.

hoplízō. This word means "to prepare," e.g., provisions, meals, sacrifices, ships, lamps, or, in the case of soldiers, weapons. It then means "to prepare oneself," "to train," "to arm," and figuratively, "to arm oneself with courage." The only NT use (1 Pet. 4:1) is figurative; here the idea is that of arming oneself with a mind or thought in preparation for suffering.

panoplía.
1. Linguistic Data. This word is used variously for the soldier's full equipment, for war material, for booty, and for the prize in contests. The only figurative use is in the biblical field.

2. Archaeological Data. The soldier's equipment remains much the same for centuries but with minor variations, e.g., in the size of shields or the weight of armor. The Roman legionary carries a lance or spear, a shield, javelins, helmet, and breastplate or coat of mail. In the OT we read of shields, helmets, armor, shoes, spears, bows and arrows, and slings.

3. Religious Data.
a. Deity. Gods are often depicted as armed, e.g., with bows and arrows, clubs, nets, helmets, mail shirts, and chariots. The reference is often to such phenomena as storms and lightning. In Greece clouds are the shield and helmet of Zeus and lightning his sword. Apollo has a bow and arrows. In the OT God's breastplate is righteousness and his helmet salvation (Is. 59:17). In Ps. 35:1ff. and Is. 34:6 etc. we read of the spear, javelin, bow, and shield of God in poetic references.

b. Human Share in the Divine Equipment. The idea of invincibility because of divinely given weapons is an ancient one (cf. Odin's helmet as a cap of invisibility, or Achilles' armor, or Siegfried's sword). In the OT God protects his people with his own weapons (cf. Pss. 7:11ff.; 35:1ff.). His faithfulness is a shield and buckler (Ps. 91:4). He gives power to the javelin of Joshua (Josh. 8:18, 26). The concept is moralized in the Iranian sphere. Philo believes that God has given rational speech to humans as a protection.

c. The Community *panoplía.* The Qumran Community sees itself in a situation of conflict in which the sons of light war with the sons of darkness. The community is God's covenant people engaged in a military action in which it uses lances, spears, darts, and slings. The depiction gives new vividness to the parallel passages in Rom. 13:12 and Eph. 6:16.

4. panoplía in the NT. The word is used only figuratively in the NT. Luke has it in the parable of the overcoming of the strong man in 11:22. It occurs twice in the allegory of the Christian's spiritual armor in Eph. 6:10ff. Here Paul takes his verbs from military speech, and he lists six items of equipment, i.e., girdle, breastplate, shoes, shield, helmet, and sword. He has in view the actual equipment of the Roman soldier along with OT models. Since the enemy is spiritual, the whole *panoplía* of God is needed. The background is the mythological one of God giving his own equipment, but the concept is spiritualized. In an ethical context, the apostle is describing a religious and moral battle. The weapons, however, are not moral qualities but divine realities. One's whole existence depends on the outcome of this battle with the forces of evil, and one can triumph in it only in the Lord and the power of his might (v. 10).

5. The Early Church. Ignatius *Polycarp* 6.2 uses *panoplía* in a passage that contains several military terms, but here the word seems to mean "armor," and the passage is less vivid and more moralistic than Eph. 6. Clement of Alexandria has the term in *Stromateis* 2.20.109.2 in a Stoic context.

zōnnymi (zōnnýō), diazōnnymi, perizōnnymi (perizōnnýō), zōnē.

I. Girdle and Girding in Graeco-Roman Antiquity.

1. The girdle is used in antiquity to fasten articles of clothing. In the passive the verb means "to be fastened"; the middle, "to gird oneself," "to tie on something," is common.

2. Richly decorated girdles are worn for adornment, especially by women.

3. The girdle serves as a pocket, e.g., for money, valuables, daggers.

4. The girdle is an item of military equipment, e.g., as a broad leather band for protection, as an apron under the armor, as a belt studded with metal, or as a sign of rank.

5. In a transferred sense the girdle is a sign of virginity among women. Loosing it can denote intercourse, and hence we have a use for marriage. The word also denotes the ocean as the girdle of the earth, and it carries a reference to the zones of the earth, the planetary spheres, and the angels of the zones. *zōnnýnai* may be used for an embrace in wrestling or of the ocean.

II. Girdle and Girding in the OT and Judaism.

1. The girdle is an article of clothing made of linen or leather. To gird up one's loins is to be ready for hasty departure (cf. Ex. 12:11) or for work (Prov. 31:17) or prophetic ministry (Jer. 1:17). Elijah wears a distinctive leather girdle (2 Kgs. 1:8; cf. 1 Kgs. 18:46).

2. Girdles are used for adornment (cf. the royal marshal in Is. 22:21, the high priest in Ex. 39:29, and the angel in Dan. 10:5). But they may also signify sorrow or disgrace, e.g., when made of sackcloth (Is. 3:24; 2 Sam. 3:31).

3. Girdles also serve as pockets (cf. Ezek. 9:2ff.).

4. Girdles serve as items of military equipment, e.g., to fasten underclothes, to distinguish officers, to protect the lower body (1 Kgs. 22:34), and to carry swords (1 Sam. 17:39).

5. Figuratively God binds Israel to himself as with a girdle. But he delivers it up to judgment in the form of Jeremiah's girdle (Jer. 13:11). The wicked are girdled by a curse (Ps. 109:19). God himself is girded with might (Ps. 65:6), and he girds the righteous with strength (Ps. 18:32) and joy (30:11). He also girds the hills with rejoicing (65:12). The messianic king will be girdled with righteousness and faithfulness (Is. 11:5). People gird themselves for battle or for work. Judaism refers to God's girding himself with mercy, love, and grace, and to Moses' girding himself with prayer.

III. Girdle and Girding in the NT.

1. In the NT the girdle is an article of clothing in Mt. 3:4, which tells us that the Baptist wears a leather girdle. Girding one's undergarment for work occurs in several parables (cf. Lk. 17:8; 12:37). In Lk. 12:35 disciples are to be ready for their master's unexpected return (cf. Ex. 12:11). In Jn. 13:4-5 Jesus girds himself to wash his disciples' feet. Peter fastens on his clothes in Jn. 21:7. The idea of preparing to set out is present in Acts 12:8. The contrast in Jn. 21:18 is between acting on one's own initiative and being bound and carried off by others (cf. Acts 21:11).

2. The angels wear girdles for adornment in Rev. 15:6, and Christ similarly wears a high girdle like that of the high priest in 1:13.

3. In Mk. 6:8 the disciples are to carry no money in their girdles.

4. The only use for armor is the figurative one in Eph. 6:14. The reference is probably to the breechlike apron of the Roman soldier. The truth here is neither reliability, nor subjective truthfulness, nor real fighting, nor even the gospel, but the divine reality that has come in the gospel and is put on by believers.

IV. Girdle and Girding in the Early Church. The words are uncommon in the early church. The aged Polycarp looses his girdle before execution (Mart. Pol. 13.2). Hermas refers to the girding of abstinence (*Visions* 3.8.4), virgins (*Similitudes* 9.2), and vices (*Similitudes* 9.9.5). Clement of Alexandria cites the girdles of Jeremiah, the Baptist, and Jesus as models of humility and contentment (*Paedagogus* 2.3.38.1; 10.112.3-4; *Stromateis* 3.6.53.5). The liturgical girding of the tunic is an admonition to sexual abstinence.

thṓrax.

1. Armor. In Greece we find various forms of armor from leather doublets (with metal studs) to bronze armor conforming to the body. The Romans also use coats of mail combining lightness and strength. Armor comes into Egypt from abroad. Goliath the Philistine wears a heavy coat of mail. In Israel armor is at first a privilege of the nobility but comes into general use under Uzziah (2 Chr. 26:14).

2. Chest, Trunk, Thorax. In a transferred sense *thṓrax* is used for the part of the body covered by armor.

3. The Metaphorical Use in the Bible.

a. The OT. The biblical metaphor originates in Is. 59:17 with its statement that God has put on righteousness like a breastplate, i.e., that he will deploy his full moral integrity to destroy evil and bring salvation in the sense both of justice (Am. 5:7) and of help (Ps. 5:8 etc.). Why the image of armor is chosen is not clear. Possibly putting it on denotes military initiative, and if so we are to think more of offensive than defensive action.

b. The NT. Paul alludes to Is. 59:17 in 1 Th. 5:8 and Eph. 6:14. In the former the breastplate is that of faith and love (and the helmet that of hope). The emphasis here, too, is on preparing for battle rather than on defense. In Ephesians the situation is different, for offensive weapons are also named. The breastplate is now that of righteousness, and what is in view is most likely the righteousness that we have before God by faith in Christ (Rom. 3:22). Enclosed in this, we are secure against all evil assaults (8:38-39). It issues, of course, in righteousness of life, and for this reason protects against temptation.

hypodéō (hypódēma, sandálion). The verb *hypodéō* means "to furnish with footgear," middle "to put on sandals." In the Near East and Greece people usually go barefoot or wear sandals. Sandals are put off for worship, mourning, and fasting. Slaves tie and untie them, and carry them when not needed. Assyrian soldiers wear laced boots, the Roman legionaries wear half-boots with strong soles, and in Rome shoes of leather, often expensive, are worn. John the Baptist is not even worthy to carry or untie the sandals of the mightier one who is to come (Mt. 3:11 and par.). The disciples are not to use *hypodḗmata* according to Mt. 10:10; Lk. 10:4, though Mk. 6:9 seems to permit *sandália,* which longer journeys make necessary. If it is hard to reconcile the two accounts, the point is that full commitment demands renunciation of all nonessentials. In Eph. 6:15 shoes are a necessary part of the believer's armor. They represent a readiness to take the gospel of peace to the nations. The paradox that this message is the best way of fighting evil powers is in full keeping with the general outlook of Ephesians. Later Hermas sees the bride of Christ arrayed in white robes and sandals (*Visions* 4.2.1). Clement of Alexandria demands that women should avoid richly embroidered shoes, and that men should go barefoot; he also compares talkative Sophists to old shoes that are weak except for the tongue (*Paedagogus* 2.7.59.3; *Stromateis* 1.2.22.5).

thyreós. The *thyreós* is the ancient four-cornered long shield. The long shield comes in various shapes, but the reference is to the rectangular Greek shield which is almost a portable wall, which covers the whole person, and which poses the hard problem of reconciling strength and lightness. The Romans take over a later form of the long shield around 340 B.C. and retain it until the days of Constantine, who reverts to the round or oval form. The only NT use is the figurative one in Eph. 6:16. Describing faith as a shield, this verse has in view the divinely given reality (1 Cor. 13:13; 1 Th. 5:8) rather than a subjective attitude. Believers have a fellowship with God that hurls back all the attacks of the enemy (cf. 1 Jn. 5:4; 1 Pet. 5:9).

perikephalaía. This word, meaning "head covering," is used in a military sense for the "helmet," which in gladiatorial conflict is medically suspect because of its pressure, and which is a prize in some contests. Earlier times know only a leather cover with metal plates (cf. 1 Sam. 17:5). Metal helmets come into Israel later (2 Chr. 26:14). Greek soldiers wear bronze helmets, as do the Romans. The helmet is slung on a strap during marches and put on for battle. The only NT use (in 1 Th. 5:8 and Eph. 6:17) is figurative. Both are based on Is. 59:17, where God, or the Messiah, is the subject. In these verses believers are the subjects, the OT indicative becomes an imperative, and salvation has a more passive sense. The eschatological thrust is strong in 1 Th. 5:8, and in Eph. 6:17, too, the final deliverance that is assured to believers encompasses their heads like a helmet, so that they may confidently commit themselves to the battle against the sinister powers that would harass them. Ignatius *Polycarp* 6.2 also compares faith to a helmet, but with reference to the human attitude rather than the divine gift.   [A. OEPKE, V, 292-315]

→ *máchaira, stratiṓtēs*

---

horáō [to see, perceive],   *eídon* [to see, perceive, visit],   *blépō* [to see, watch], *optánomai* [to appear],   *theáomai* [to behold],   *theōréō* [to view, contemplate],   *aóratos* [invisible],   *horatós* [visible],   *hórasis* [sight, vision], *hórama* [vision],   *optasía* [appearing],   *autóptēs* [eyewitness],   *epóptēs* [spectator, overseer],   *epopteúō* [to view, inspect],   *ophthalmós* [eye, apple of the eye],   *kathoráō* [to see, perceive],   *prooráō* [to foresee],   *proeídon* [to foresee]

---

horáō, eídon, blépō, optánomai, theáomai, theōréō.

A. Usage among the Greeks.

1. The Words.

a. *horáō.* While *akoúō* is virtually the only Greek word for hearing, there are various words for seeing. The first of these is *horáō,* which means "to look," "to see," "to experience," "to perceive," "to take note, "to see to," "to take care." The range of *ideín* is much the same, although, since it suggests presence, with *tina* it can also mean "to visit or meet someone."

b. *blépō* also means "to see" with a stronger emphasis on the function of the eye, so that it serves as the opposite of "to be blind." It can also be used for intellectual or spiritual perception, and in the absolute for insight.

c. *optánomai* is rare and late and has the sense "to be visible," "to appear."

d. *theáomai* suggests spectators and denotes attentive seeing, i.e., "to behold." Having a certain solemnity, it is used for visionary seeing and the apprehension of higher realities.

e. *theōréō* has primary reference to spectators at a religious festival, and thus means "to look at," "to view," with such additional senses as "to review (troops)," "to discover," "to recognize," and figuratively "to consider," "to contemplate," "to investigate."

2. *Seeing in the Greek World and Hellenism.* The Greeks are a people of the eye, and seeing is important to them. It has strong significance in their religion, which is a religion of vision. (If *theōréō* is derived from *theós,* and first means "watching over" the god, this is even more true, but that derivation is unlikely.) Quite early there is a transition from sensory to intellectual and spiritual perception. The two are seen to be linked, but there is also a sense of the limits of sensory seeing. Mythology allows that the gods can be seen, but only in a visionary manner to a few, and then in a frightening way. Philosophy stresses the invisibility of the gods, and Plato with his world of ideas finds an antithesis between *horán* and *noeín.* True reality is accessible only to the *noús;* this alone can comprehend God. Yet this comprehension is still viewed as a kind of seeing, especially in the form of *theōreín.* For Aristotle seeing is the most spiritual sense, since it gives access to light. As Plato thinks that we contemplate God with the eye of the soul, so for Aristotle the true goal of life is contemplative self-giving to God, for God's own mode of being and working consists of pure *theōría.* The divine is something to be contemplated, not heard and believed. Thus philosophy transposes into an intellectual key something that is a historical reality in Greek religion. The visual is important in the mysteries as well. True bliss is to see the rites and enjoy visionary experiences. Gnosticism accepts the invisibility of God but believes that deification by *gnósis* brings the vision of God. In the Hermetic writings this comes only with death, although it may be possible in this life for a few Gnostics. Hearing the teacher is merely a preparation for ecstatic vision. In magical papyri formulas and actions are offered for forcing gods and demons to manifest themselves and thus come under control.

B. Usage and Concept in the LXX and Judaism.

I. LXX.

1. Meaning of the Terms.

a. *horáō.* With *eídon* (930 times), *horáō* (520 times) covers most of the references to seeing. The future *ópsomai* is common (178 times), while the present (110) and perfect (97) are balanced. The main Hebrew original for both verbs is *rā'āh* (over 400 times for *horáō,* and 670 times for *eídon*). Figuratively water, the sea, and the earth may be said to see (Pss. 77:16; 114:3; 97:4). The dead will never again see the light (Ps. 49:19). When seeing and hearing occur together, the reference is usually to recognition or understanding (Job 13:1). Either may come first, for God has created both (Prov. 20:12). Yet seeing may be contrasted with mere hearsay (Ps. 48:8; Job 42:5). In the intransitive passive sense ("to show oneself," "to appear"), the meaning is usually "to be present" (cf. the fixed expression "to appear before God"). The thought of seeing God's face is rare (cf. Ex. 33:20), and the LXX normally has in view a spiritual encounter, though cf. Ps. 17:15. In ordinary use "seeing the face" usually means "to visit," "to meet," or, at court, "to be granted an audience." *horáō* and *eídon* often denote spiritual perception in such senses as "to observe" (Gen. 16:4-5), "to perceive" (26:28), "to experience" (Jer. 5:12), and "to encounter" (God's works in history, Ex. 34:10). Thus "seeing God's glory" means receiving the revelation of God in his glory (Ps. 97:6; Is. 26:10). The more concrete *ophthḗnai* is used in Ex. 16:10 because the glory appears in a cloud, but the cloud is only a veil, so that the verb denotes the presence itself, not the manner of the presence. The parallelism of Ex. 16:6 and 16:7 ("to know" and "to see the glory") shows that sensory perception of the glory is not the issue (cf. Is. 40:5).

b. *blépō* occurs over 130 times, 38 in Ezekiel (35 of these for geographical or architectural directions; cf. Num. 21:20; Josh. 18:14). In the main the Hebrew original is the same as for *horáō*. Ability to see is mostly in view, including ability to perceive. God is the subject in Ps. 10:11. Prophetic vision is at issue in Am. 8:2; Zech. 4:2; 5:2.

c. *optánomai* is rare. It occurs in 1 Kgs. 8:8 (the poles could not be "seen from outside"). We also find the intransitive passive in Num. 14:14 (God "is seen").

d. *theáomai* occurs eight times (with a Hebrew original only in 2 Chr. 22:6: "to visit"). The sense is that of seeing with astonishment, of contemplating God's acts, and of seeing Jerusalem's future glory.

e. *theōréō* occurs some 56 times, often with other verbs of seeing as alternative readings. In Daniel (13 times) the reference is usually to visionary seeing, but sense perception is the point in Josh. 8:20; Judg. 13:9-10, and "to live" is what is meant in Eccl. 7:11. Watching as a spectator is the meaning in Judg. 16:27 and Ps. 68:24. Actual seeing is less prominent in Ps. 73:3, but only in Wis. 6:12; 13:5 does the term mean "to perceive."

2. *The Significance of Seeing in OT Proclamation.* As regards the distinction between sensory and spiritual seeing, the compass of verbs of seeing is much the same in Greek and Hebrew. When God is said to see, sensory perception is not in view; there are few anthropomorphisms in the narrower sense (cf. Gen. 6:12; Ex. 12:13), for it is only poetically that the Psalms and prophets refer to God's seeing. The verbs of seeing, like those of hearing, embrace many meanings that have little to do with actual seeing, although in the main it seems that in the relationship with God and his revelation hearing is regarded as more important than seeing. The main uses are as follows.

a. Visionary Prophetic Seeing. *horáō* and *eídon* are the words for prophetic visions. Prophets are called seers, and for this term *ho horṓn* is used in 2 Sam. 24:11; 2 Kgs. 17:3, etc. The OT, however, does not record visions in the case of the seers; their revelations are by word (2 Sam. 24:11). The dreams in Gen. 37:9 etc. are purely visual and need interpretation. If they are accepted as impartations of the divine will, they are not manifestations of God. The visions of Zechariah are inner perceptions. The mark of authentic visions is that in them the prophets are recipients, not authors; they cannot induce them by prayer, sacrifice, etc. There is no specific term for auditions, and *hórasis* may apply to more than visual elements, possibly because seeing is more important at first, then yields to hearing as the great prophets hear God's own word but never see God himself in their visions, only creatures or creaturely processes. Ezekiel sees the glory of God but does not describe it. Dan. 7:8 mentions the Ancient of Days but again without description, for the fate of the empires is the real point of the vision. Am. 9:1 is purely introductory. If Is. 6:1 is unique, here again there is no description, and in 1 Kgs. 22:19 the real reference is to the true word of God that Micaiah is to deliver to Ahab.

b. Theophanies. Num. 12:6, 8 makes it plain that there is a difference between prophetic vision and the more direct theophany in Moses' case. Yet even Moses does not see God directly (Ex. 33:11). In Ex. 3:2 the angel (or God himself) appears to Moses in the bush, but Moses veils his face, and if 3:16 says that God has appeared to him, this simply means that he has manifested himself as present, as also to Abraham etc. In Ex. 24:10 a select group ascends the mountain and sees God, but the LXX softens the realism. In Ex. 33:18ff. the basic principle is that to see God directly is to die because of the divine holiness; hence Moses is permitted only an indirect vision. The same principle appears in Ex. 19:21, and cf. Gen. 32:30; Judg. 6:22ff., where it is only by God's special grace that the rule does not apply. In instances like Gen. 12:7; 17:1, etc. God is simply heard, and the introductory *ōphthē* indicates the presence of the God who reveals himself in his word. These are not, then, attenuated theophanies.

c. Seeing God in a Transferred Sense. Often seeing God is in a transferred sense. Thus Ps. 17:15 refers to the certainty of God's proximity, while in Sir. 15:7 the meaning is perception. In Job 23:9 Job sees no sign that God is taking note of him, in 34:29 seeing God means certainty of his grace, and in 42:5 the reference is to spiritual understanding. Job 19:26-27 raises the question of seeing God after death. 23:9 and 35:14 suggest that the point might be seeing God's grace again in this life, but even if the reference is to the future the idea is probably that God's grace still sustains Job after death. In Is. 60:2 there will be a future vision of the divine glory, but again with reference more to God's revealing presence than to eschatological vision.

II. *Philo and Josephus.*

1. *Philo.*

a. Words. *horáō* (with *eídon*) is for Philo the most important verb of seeing. The future and the passive are rare, and there is *ophthḗnai* of God only in OT quotations. *horáō* may denote sensory seeing (except in the case of God), but its main use is for spiritual perception. The words and voice of God are visible in this sense, and *horáō* (with *theōréō*) may thus be used for "seeing" God. *blépō* has primary reference to sense perception and is seldom used of God. In a transferred sense it may be applied to the *noús,* and Philo can use *ho blépōn* for Israel and *hoi blépontes* for the prophets. *theáomai* is used for intensive looking and occurs in relation to visions and seeing God. *theōréō* mostly means "to consider," "to perceive," and passive "to show." *theōría* is common for "perception" and also as the opposite of *práxis,* while *theōrēma* (almost always plural) has the meaning "view" or "doctrine."

b. The Significance of Seeing. Adopting Plato's dualism, Philo has a poor view of the senses. The chief of these are seeing and hearing. Seeing as perception of the noetic world is superior to hearing, but as an agent in human development, not as a response to revelation. Does this mean that Philo has in view a vision of God? His exposition of the OT passages is inconclusive, and his references to deification and vision are counterbalanced by references to the divine invisibility and unknowability. Since the latter references are more common, and Philo says that we see only the fact and not the nature of God's existence, he seems to speak of the vision of God only with qualifications.

2. *Josephus.* In Josephus the primary emphasis is on sensory seeing and the related mental perception. *blépō* and *theōréō* are less common; the former is often used figuratively for "to note," "to observe," while the latter signifies "to view" (as a witness), "to be present" (as a spectator). When directions are received in dreams, this is not a seeing of God, for God is intrinsically invisible for Josephus.

III. The Pseudepigrapha and Rabbinism.

1. The Pseudepigrapha. In apocalyptic seeing is important, but angels explain the visions, so that hearing is the climax. Even when God is seen, as in Eth. En. 14:15ff., this leads up to God's word. The vision of God is not an end in itself. God's glory is seen in heavenly wonders. The eschatological vision hinted at in places is vision of God's glory, or face, or salvation. In Jub. 1:28 God will appear to all eyes in the last time.

2. Rabbinism. The rabbis lay the stress on hearing, as the OT does. They are thus opposed to the idea of ecstatic vision. At most they speak of seeing the face of the Shekinah. This is eschatological vision, but it may come in the days of the Messiah. God himself is invisible, so that even angels cannot see him. Greeting the face of the Shekinah may take place in this life through attending the temple or synagogue, studying the law, or giving alms.

C. Usage and Concept in the NT.

1. Review of the Words.

a. *horáō* and *eídon.* In the NT *horáō* and *eídon* are the most common verbs of seeing. The former occurs some 113 times, the latter some 350 times in the Gospels, Acts, and Revelation. *eídon* is less common in John, mainly because the perfect *heóraka* is preferred. John uses *theōréō* instead of the present *horáō,* which is generally uncommon, being replaced elsewhere by *blépō.* The two verbs *horáō* and *eídon* have a broad range of meaning. God is said to "see" in Acts 7:34. *horáō* is used for "seeing" Christ in Jn. 3:11; 6:46; 8:38. To see means to "speak to" in Jn. 12:21. The distinction in Phil. 1:27, 30 does not imply any antithesis between seeing and hearing, and if seeing is more highly estimated in Jn. 8:38, seeing and hearing constitute the totality of perception in Mk. 4:12; Mt. 13:14-15; Acts 28:26-27; Rom. 11:8. For the most part seeing comes first in such cases, but hearing is first in Lk. 2:20; Jn. 5:37. For brevity seeing alone is mentioned in, e.g., Jn. 12:40; Rom. 11:10. Seeing signs is equivalent to hearing the message in Acts 8:6 (and cf. Jn. 11:45), but the desire to see signs may also denote resistance to the message (Mt. 12:38; Lk. 23:8). Often the verbs mean "to perceive" in such senses as "to experience," "to note," "to establish," "to realize," "to know," "to judge," "to mark," "to heed."

b. *blépō.* This word occurs some 137 times, mostly in the present. It first denotes ability to see as distinct from blindness (Mt. 12:22; 15:31; Mk. 8:23-24; Lk. 7:21; Jn. 9). Seeing the book in Rev. 5:3-4 includes reading. Scrutiny is implied in Mt. 22:16. God's seeing in Mt. 6:4 is a secret one. Jesus sees the Father's works in Jn. 5:19 (cf. 8:38). Angels see the face of God in Mt. 18:10. Empirical seeing is the point in Rom. 8:24-25; 2 Cor. 4:18; Heb. 11:1ff. Figuratively *blépō* can mean "to note," "to perceive" (Rom. 7:23; Col. 2:5). It is rare for visionary seeing (Acts 12:9; Rev. 1:11-12). It is not used for appearances of the risen Lord or for eschatological vision; in Acts 1:9, 11 it denotes full participation rather than mere sensory perception, and in 1 Cor. 13:12 the image of the mirror shows that the use is metaphorical even in the second half of the statement, which also does not mention God as the object. Only in Mt. 18:10 and Jn. 5:19 is *blépein* used for seeing God.

c. *optánomai.* This word occurs only in Acts 1:3 with reference to the resurrection appearances. It is used because an appearing comprising many proofs demands a present participle.

d. *theáomai.* This word occurs 22 times. It suggests a more intimate visit in Rom. 15:24 (compared to *ideín* in 1:11). It means "to look over" in Mt. 22:11, is more graphic than *ideín* in 11:7-8, stresses the element of loving regard in 28:1, and brings out the importance of the meeting in Lk. 5:27. Attentive regard is implied in Acts 21:27. The use in John has a certain solemnity in 6:5, and the same applies in 1:14, where it denotes not just the seeing of witness but the seeing of faith. *theáomai* is never used in the NT for seeing God.

e. *theōréō*. This verb occurs 58 times (24 in John and 14 in Acts). In John the present *theōréō* seems to be used instead of *horáō*. It has the original sense "to watch" in Mt. 27:55. The chief sense in Acts is "to perceive" (4:13; 17:16, etc.). In Jn. 6:19; 20:6, 12, 14 sense perception is at issue, but "to perceive or recognize" is the point in 4:19; 12:9, and "to know or experience" in 8:51, and possibly in 17:24 in an eschatological sense.

2. *The Significance of Seeing in NT Proclamation.*

a. General. As in the LXX, there are in the NT more instances of verbs of seeing (680) than of hearing (425), yet hearing is more important. The NT has little interest in the physiology or psychology of seeing, and since it makes no distinction between the sensory and the spiritual, it readily accepts seeing as a function in revelation. If more blind people than deaf people are healed in the Gospels (Mt. 9:27ff.; Mk. 8:22-23, etc.), this is most likely because eye afflictions are more common, not because sight is more important or Jesus wants eyewitnesses.

b. Eyewitness: Faith and Sight. Mt. 13:16 seems to commend eyewitness, but the reference to eyes and ears (cf. Lk. 11:27) does not necessarily stress sense perception. The point is rather that those who have the privilege of seeing and hearing should not fail to attain to true seeing and hearing (cf. Mt. 13:14-15). Underlying the saying is the conviction that the age of salvation has come with Jesus, and that a right decision must be made in the light of it. Lk. 1:2 bases the truth of the gospel on a tradition that goes back to eyewitnesses. Eyewitness here includes ministry of the word and thus comprises both seeing what took place and understanding its significance as revelation (cf. Jn. 20:31). It is authentic, then, only when the imperative of faith is present as well as the privilege of sight. The stress on eyewitness in 2 Pet. 1:18 is unusual, and the statements in Jn. 1:14 and 1 Jn. 1:1 include more than eyewitness, for what follows is no mere report but proclamation. The Gospels omit many details (the appearance of Jesus, scenery, etc.), for their focus is on the words (hearing) and acts (seeing) of Jesus. Word and work (hearing and seeing) constitute the full historicity and totality of the event of revelation. Hearing is primary, but seeing is a kind of hearing, for if dependence on a certain kind of seeing is unbelief (Mk. 15:32), seeing, too, can and should lead to faith (Jn. 11:40). In Jn. 20:24ff., while the reference is to seeing the risen Lord, the statement in v. 29 has more general validity (cf. 1 Pet. 1:8). As the first eyewitness is oriented to proclamation, so proclamation rests on the first eyewitness as a safeguard of historicity. Thus the seeing of the disciples becomes the hearing of later believers (1 Cor. 15:3; Rom. 10:16ff.). It is no longer essential that those who preach the gospel should be themselves witnesses. A contrast arises between what is seen and what is not seen (2 Cor. 4:18). What is seen is perishing, but what is not seen—and this includes not merely what is yet to come but inner renewal by the operation of the Spirit and the powers of the coming age—is eternal. Similarly the object of faith and hope in Rom. 8:24-25 is not yet seen, for otherwise faith and hope would be unnecessary. Believers have a present sonship in faith, but they are still hoping for eschatological sonship as a visible entity. In Heb. 11:1 the things not seen, qualifying the things hoped for, are future things. In incidental contrast is the visible world of v. 3, which is created, as faith perceives, by the nonvisible word of God.

c. Visionary Prophetic Seeing. Dream-revelations are rare in the NT. In Mt. 1:20 etc. Joseph is given verbal directions by the angel, so that these are not true visions. The same applies in Lk. 1:11; Acts 7:2-3; 9:10; 18:9; 23:11. God does not speak directly here, as in OT parallels, but either an angel or the Lord (Acts 9:10 etc.). There is no ecstatic element, nor are there any theophanies except in the quotation in Acts 7:2. A voice speaks in Mt. 3:17 and parallels, but only in Acts 7:31 do we have direct mention of the voice of God. Angels appear in the infancy stories (Lk. 1:11-12), but only as heralds of the divine action. In Lk. 22:43-44 the appearing of the angel simply implies that an angel comes to help Jesus, not that he has a vision of an angel. In the resurrection stories angels are seen again, this time as agents of proclamation. Jn. 20:12 is the only angelophany in John (unless we include the thunder of 12:29). Acts 1:10 belongs to the resurrection group. The angel that comes to Cornelius in 10:3 bears a message (cf. 8:26). In 5:19-20; 12:7ff. angels bring release from prison and explanatory messages. 12:9 shows that what takes place is real even though it belongs to the suprasensory realm. In Acts 10:10ff. we are specifically told that Peter is in a trance, so that we have a parallel to the prophetic visions of the OT. Visions of future events occur in Revelation, but we learn from 1:3; 22:7, etc. that what is intended is prophecy rather than apocalyptic, and in the last analysis the word predominates (22:6, 8). Paul has ecstatic experiences, but to clear up eschatological questions he appeals to words (1 Th. 4:15) or disclosed mysteries (1 Cor. 15:51). In 2 Cor. 12:1ff. "revelations" seem to be the key term (v. 7), and the stress is again on things that Paul heard (v. 4). What the revelations are, Paul does not say, but he does not include the Damascus experience. If Paul does not mention the Spirit in this connection (cf. Rev. 1:10; 4:2), this aspect is plain in Acts 7:55 when Stephen sees heaven opened and the Son of Man standing at God's right hand. In the life of Jesus the only visionary element is in the baptism story, in which he sees the Spirit descending (Mt. 3:16) and hears the voice from heaven (3:17). We have here two sides of a common event. On the one side is the assurance that Jesus is the divine Son and Messiah; on the other the perceived imparting of the Spirit at the beginning of his ministry as such. Materially the revelation by word is primary. The transfiguration is not to be regarded as an ecstatic experience of Jesus himself. The terms used leave open what form of seeing is intended. Lk. 9:32 shows that the disciples are awake during the experience. Neither the transfiguration nor the voice is for the sake of Jesus himself, so that we might have here a shared visionary process, although a real transfiguration is not to be ruled out. The eschatological form and orientation make it unlikely that the transfiguration is an emergence of preexistent glory; the primary reference is more probably to the form that Jesus will have as Messiah–Son of Man at the parousia.

d. The Resurrection Appearances. We have accounts of resurrection appearances in Mt. 28:9-10, 16ff.; Lk. 24:13ff., 36ff., 50ff.; Jn. 20:14ff., 19ff., 24ff.; 21:1ff.; Acts 1:4ff., and cf. Paul's conversion. The appearances are all isolated, and in Acts 9:3; 22:6 Jesus seems to come from heaven. No appearance is said to have occurred during sleep, so the appearances are not dream-visions. Indeed, they do not take place by night. Again, they are always linked with revelations by word. At times the Lord's corporeality is viewed more literally (Lk. 24:39-40), at times more spiritually (Lk. 24:36). In 2 Cor. 12:1 Paul does not include the Damascus experience among his visions (in spite of the *optasía* of Acts 26:19; cf. 22:17-18). If he sees the Lord according to 1 Cor. 9:1, it is because God reveals his Son to him (Gal. 1:16). In 1 Cor. 15:3ff. Paul says that Jesus "appeared" (cf. Lk. 24:34; Acts 9:17). The stress is on revelation rather than on actual seeing; Jesus shows himself, and those to whom he does so experience his presence. The Damascus experience is for Paul similar to the prior experiences during the 40 days. The object of the appearances is the risen and exalted Lord, who is thus the basis of faith and the community. The disciples do not mistake the appearances for the parousia. Hence one should not stress the analogy of the visual element in the two cases. In the case of the parousia, the important thing is the coming rather than the seeing; the visual element in the appearances, which is stronger, is neither proleptic of eschatological events nor influenced by them.

e. Johannine Seeing. Jn. 6:62 does not refer to the ascension as such, but to the exaltation of Jesus by way of the cross. It thus has in view the spiritual perception that demands decision. When this seeing achieves its goal, it means faith and eternal life (6:40). In 16:10, 16-17, 19, however, the reference is to seeing the earthly life and then the resurrection (or parousia). Yet in view of the mention of the Spirit this seeing, too, denotes encounter through the Spirit's ministry. The world does not see Jesus because it resists the Spirit's work (14:19). When Jesus and his disciples are said to see the Father, this seeing cannot be integrated into the usual parallelism of seeing and hearing in John. There is, of course, a distinction between Jesus' seeing of the Father and the disciples' seeing of the Father, for it is Jesus himself who reveals the Father to the disciples (12:45; 14:9). Jesus reveals the Father in a unique way (12:45); hence seeing the Father involves submission to his revelation in Jesus (14:9). Both the historicity of the event and the pre- and postexistence of Jesus are involved. For John seeing is the seeing of faith; indeed, it *is* faith, although this does not have to mean that it is an anticipation of eschatological seeing. Its more probable significance is that for John verbs of seeing bring out the personal element in the encounter with Jesus.

f. The Vision of God. Since God is seen in the Son, Jn. 1:18 is not contesting previous theophanies but simply saying that God reveals himself exclusively through the Son. The Son has immediate access to the Father (6:46); others know God, whether through hearing or seeing, by means of the Son. The point is not that the invisible God becomes visible, but that God reveals himself. 1 Jn. 4:12 (cf. v. 20; 1 Tim. 6:16) maintains the intrinsic invisibility of God. God makes himself known through his works (Rom. 1:19-20), but supremely through the Son who is his image (Col. 1:15). At the end there will still not be direct vision but complete revelation. Future vision will differ from present possibilities (cf. the seeing of 1 Cor. 13:12 which goes hand in hand with faith), but God is not named in 1 Cor. 13:12 as the direct object of sight. Vision and sonship are related in Mt. 5:18 and (eschatologically) in 1 Jn. 3:2. Vision and sanctification also go hand in hand in these verses, so that the presupposition is full divine likeness (not deification by vision) at the consummation. In a book that is oriented to the visual Rev. 22:4 also refers to a final seeing of the face of God (and cf. the exhortation in Heb. 12:14). The NT speaks of the vision of God only with great restraint and in the light of the saving revelation of God in Christ. This promise is so unsurpassably great that it is not lightly repeated and thus rings out the more joyfully, as in 1 Jn. 3:2.

D. Usage and Concept in the Apostolic Fathers. The apostolic fathers use verbs of seeing (some 265 instances compared to 170 of hearing) in much the same way as the NT. God sees (1 Clem. 28:1), but we humans cannot see God except figuratively (Diog. 8.5-6). We may know God from his visible works (1 Clem. 60.1), and God reveals himself by way of the incarnation because we could not have stood direct vision (Barn. 5.10). Jesus will be seen at the parousia, and eschatological fellowship with him is a form of seeing (Barn. 7.9.11).

horatós, aóratos.

1. These words, meaning "visible" and "invisible," are important words in Greek philosophy as they become slogans for the sensory world and the world of ideas.

2. Both terms are very rare in the LXX. *horatós* means "handsome" in 2 Sam. 23:21 (and cf. Job 37:21; 34:26). *aóratos* is used in Gen. 1:2, and we find *aorátous* in Is. 45:3, but God is not called *aóratos*.

3. Philo has *horatós* over 70 times (often with a negative), and *aóratos* over 100 times. He adopts and extends the view of Plato. Invisible powers are at work in the cosmos. The *noús* is invisible. But so especially are God and the divine nature and spirit. Josephus uses *aóratos* for places that are not, or ought not to be, seen. The soul cannot be seen, but it moves the body. There are no direct rabbinic equivalents for the terms.

4. The NT uses *horatós* only in Col. 1:16 (with *aóratos*). *tá horatá* here seems to denote the whole earthly sphere, including the stars, and other heavenly phenomena, while *tá aórata* are the heavenly powers which, while created, share God's invisibility and seek dominion in the human sphere (cf. Eph. 6:12). Elsewhere *aóratos* relates only to God. Invisibility is a divine predicate in the doxology in 1 Tim. 1:17. It is the invisible God who is seen in Heb. 11:27; faith enables Moses to accept him as the supreme reality in his demands and promises. Paul in Rom. 1:20 refers to the invisible nature of God which is manifested in his works. Creation does not make God visible, but reveals him. This is also the purpose of Christ as the image of God in 2 Cor. 4:4.

5. In the apostolic fathers God is invisible in 2 Clem. 20.5; Diog. 7.2; Ignatius *Magnesians* 3.2. The earthly life of Jesus makes visible the preexistent Christ (Ignatius *Polycarp* 3.2). In Diog. 6.4 the invisible soul is guarded by the visible body. Ignatius *Polycarp* 2.2 makes a distinction between things phenomenal and things invisible, and Ignatius *Smyrneans* 6.1 refers to visible and invisible angelic powers.

hórasis. This word means "seeing," "sight" (plural "eyes"), later "appearance," and in the biblical sphere "vision." It is common in the LXX (some 110 times, 38 in Ezekiel and 18 in Daniel) in such senses as "sight," "appearance," "vision." Philo has it over 70 times for the sense or process of "sight." He often prefers *ópsis,* as does Josephus. The NT uses it twice for "appearance" in Rev. 4:3, and also for "vision" (Rev. 9:17; Acts 2:17; cf. Joel 2:28). In the apostolic fathers it means "eyesight" (2 Clem. 1.6), "spectacle" (7.6), and "vision" (Hermas *Visions* 2–4).

hórama. This word means "what is to be seen," "spectacle," "appearance," "vision." The LXX uses it 43 times, often for "vision" (cf. Daniel). In the NT it occurs in Mt. 17:9 for what the disciples have seen at the transfiguration. In ten instances in Acts (9:10, 12; 10:3, 17, 19; 11:5; 12:9; 16:9-10; 18:9) it means "vision," but often with only a formal emphasis on the visionary aspect (9:10, 12, etc.). In the apostolic fathers the phrase in Hermas *Visions* 4.1.3 is reminiscent of 2 Cor. 12:1. The only other examples are in Hermas *Visions* 3.4 (twice plural; at night in 3.10.6).

optasía. This noun is an uncommon one. It occurs only four times in the LXX in the sense "appearing" (cf. Esth. 4:17; Mal. 3:2). In Lk. 1:22; 24:23 it refers to angelophanies, and the Damascus appearance is called a heavenly *optasía* in Acts 26:19. There is little emphasis on the visionary aspect in either Luke or Acts; the stress lies on the revelation by word and the demand for obedience. Paul himself does not use the term for the Damascus incident. In the apostolic fathers Mart. Pol. 5.2 records a vision of Polycarp (cf. 12.3).

autóptēs. This term has the sense of "eyewitness" ("seeing for oneself"). It does not occur in the LXX but Josephus uses it. The only NT instance is in Lk. 1:2. Stylistically there are parallels for this, but materially the statement shows that for the tradition it is an inner necessity that eyewitnesses should be mentioned as normative carriers.

epóptēs, epopteúō. The noun has such meanings as "spectator," "observer," then "overseer." In the mysteries it denotes "one who comes to have a share in vision." The verb means "to view," "to inspect," "to consider," and in the mysteries "to have the rank of an *epóptēs*." The noun occurs in the LXX to indicate that God takes note of things (cf. Esth. 5:1; 2 Macc. 3:39), but the verb is not used. Philo uses neither noun nor verb, and Josephus has only compounds. The NT uses the verb in 1 Pet. 2:12; 3:2. Gentiles take note of the conduct of Christians, and when they see their good deeds they will glorify God or be won over. There is no relation here to the use in the mysteries, nor is *epóptēs* in 2 Pet. 1:16 dependent on this use, for the sense of "spectator" or "observer" is adequate enough in context; the specific element of "eyewitness" is not too strongly emphasized by the word in isolation. God is *epóptēs* in 1 Clem. 59.3 and *pantepóptēs* in 55.6; he sees and knows all human deeds.

ophthalmós.
1. This word means "apple of the eye," "eye" (mostly plural), and figuratively "what is most dear." Many phrases bring out the importance of the eye, and we also find references to seeing with the eyes of the *noús* or *kardía* (mind or heart).
2. The LXX uses the word some 700 times, often for human perception or judgment, or for divine perception (cf. Dt. 11:12). The eyes can be the seat of evil impulses (cf. Prov. 6:17; 10:10; 30:13; Job 31:1, 7).
3. Philo uses the word some 130 times, over 100 literally for "seeing" or "sight." He seldom speaks about the eyes of God and mostly uses *ómma* figuratively for the mental eyes. The pseudepigrapha refer to the eyes of God, but also say that human eyes may reveal an adulterous or covetous nature. The rabbis, too, speak about evil or good eyes and refer to seeing the seducer in the eye.
4. The NT employs the word some 100 times. As the organ of sight it occurs in relation to the blind and their healing (cf. also the blinding in Acts 9:8). The eyes are heavy in Mt. 26:43, and tears are wiped off them in Rev. 7:17. The parable of the mote and the beam (or the speck and the log, Mt. 7:3ff.) is a warning against judging others. The OT rule of an eye for an eye is quoted in Mt. 5:38, but with an admonition to replace strict justice with love. The function of the eye is the basis of the image in Mt. 6:22-23, which considers the possibility that the eye might be sound or unsound, with a moral reference (cf. Test. Iss. 4:6). That the eyes may entice to sin is stated in 1 Jn. 2:16, and cf. 2 Pet. 2:14. The eye may also be a cause of offense according to Mt. 5:29. Under OT influence the eye is associated with eyewitness in Mt. 13:16; Lk. 2:30; 1 Jn. 1:1; Rev. 1:7. In connection with the resurrection appearances there is no special singling out of sight (cf. Lk. 24:16, 31; Acts 1:9); the crucial point is spiritual rather than sensory perception. God grants enlightenment to the eyes of the heart (cf. Acts 26:18; 1 Jn. 2:11; Eph. 1:18). Only rarely does the NT refer to the eyes of God (cf. 1 Pet. 3:12; Heb. 4:13).
5. In the apostolic fathers *ophthalmós* is rare except for ten references in 1 Clement. The Martyrdom of Polycarp applies "eyes of the heart" to martyrs. 1 Cor. 2:9 is quoted in 1 Clem. 34:8; 2 Clem. 11:7; Mart. Pol. 2:3. *ómmata* occurs only in 1 Clem. 19.3.

kathoráō.

1. This word means "to look down," then more generally "to view," and figuratively "to perceive," "to note," "to look over," "to give attention to."

2. The LXX uses *kathoráō* four times and *kateídon* four times, usually for sense perception, or anthopomorphically for God's looking down from heaven (Job 10:4).

3. Philo uses *kathoráō* 34 times with a greater emphasis on intellectual perception, as is shown by the objects, by the fact that God may be the subject, and by the link with *diánoia* (although not with *noús*). In Josephus, on the other hand, sense perception is mostly at issue, although we also find the transferred meaning "to perceive," "to inspect."

4. The only NT use of *kathoráō* is in Rom. 1:20. Since the construction here rules out sense perception prior to intellectual apprehension, what seems to be meant is sense perception that is at the same time apprehension (*nooúmena kathorátai*). Hence the *poiēmata* are not just empirical phenomena but phenomena or processes that must be considered in a way that combines sensory and intellectual perception, e.g., God's works in history. The context seems to make it plain that true perception of these is not a possibility that is naturally available to sinners (cf. v. 19); it depends on the divine action in self-revelation. This is no less necessary at the level of general revelation than special revelation.

prooráō, proeídon. This word means "to see before, ahead, earlier, in advance," and hence "to provide for." The middle means "to have before one's eyes," "to have seen in advance" (cf. God's advance knowledge of human ways and deeds). Philo uses the term for foreseeing the future. This is possible for God but not for us. Josephus agrees (except in the case of the prophets), but he also uses the term for foreseeing and taking precautions against dangers. In the NT Acts 2:31 says that David as a prophet has advance knowledge of the resurrection of Jesus. Acts 2:25 quotes Ps. 16:8 to the same effect. The meaning in Acts 21:29 is "to have seen earlier." Gal. 3:8 refers to the foreseeing of Scripture. *problépomai* has the same sense of "foreseeing" in Heb. 11:40 (with God as subject). In the apostolic fathers the sense in Ignatius *Trallians* 8.1 is that of foreseeing dangers and taking precautions against them.

[W. MICHAELIS, V, 315-82]

---

orgē [anger, wrath], *orgízomai* [to be angry], *orgílos* [angry, quick-tempered], *parorgízō* [to make angry], *parorgismós* [anger, wrath]

A. Wrath in Classical Antiquity.

1. The Meaning of orgē.

a. *orgē,* which denotes "upsurging" (of sap or vigor), comes to be used for "impulsive nature." This is a tragic element in drama, since it inclines people to decisive acts. A demonic excess of will combines with fate to bring disaster.

b. A second and resultant meaning is "anger" as the most striking manifestation of impulsive passion. Unlike *thymós,* a complementary term, *orgē* is especially oriented to revenge or punishment. Thus it is applied to rulers who must avenge injustice.

c. There then develops the sense of "punishment." Apart from this legitimate form, however, *orgē* is recognized to be an evil, or the source of other evils. Some philosophers regard it as natural and necessary, although only in moderation, but Stoicism lists it as a primary passion that should be completely eradicated.

II. The Wrath of the Gods in the Greek World. Wrathful and avenging deities have a firm place in Greek religion. The Furies call for retribution when the ties of nature (e.g., blood and family) are broken. Anger may be between the gods when there are conflicting claims, but it is also directed against humans when they are arrogant, or when they neglect such duties as sacrifice, hospitality, and honoring the dead. This anger, to which one had best submit, is not just blind rage but rests on a claim. In an odd sense it confers a negative dignity on its victims by marking them out or setting them within specified limits. At first words like *chólos, kótos,* and *ménis* are used for this divine anger, but tragedy begins to use *orgé,* making a distinction between divine and human wrath. Philosophy has some difficulty with the concept of divine wrath in view of its teaching that there must be no passion in deity. Yet Plato refers to the sufferings that fall on various races because of divine anger, and later philosophers, while critical of mythological conceptions, accept the idea of divine punishments. In popular belief the divine anger has a cultic connection as attempts are made to placate it, and phenomena such as storm and pestilence, as well as deformity and sickness, are accepted as plain evidences of the wrath of the gods or of demons.

III. The Wrath of the Gods in the Roman World. The Romans hold much the same views about the wrath of the gods as the Greeks, and their philosophers express the same reservations. Prodigies in particular manifest the divine wrath, and it results in famine, sickness, and plague. Cultic neglect is the common cause of the anger, and expiatory rites are devised to avert disaster. Prayers may be made for the direction of divine wrath against enemies, and those who take oaths call down divine wrath on themselves in case of perjury. Wrath falls especially on the impious, and this is one reason why, superstitiously, the Romans are ready to recognize the most varied cults. Political evils such as civil war and mutiny are also regarded as manifestations of divine wrath, and conquered cities or defeated enemies are seen as its victims. Should sacrifices and other rites be ineffectual in averting divine wrath, a voluntary sacrifice of the self is the supreme mode of expiation. Divine wrath plays a very significant role in Roman history and literature. For Tacitus the fortunes of Rome are bound up with it, and in the *Iliad* divine wrath is a controlling force that leads Aeneas to Rome. Wrath and fate are two sides of the same coin. The wrath of the gods, and its appeasing, give expression to the opposition and reverses, and their overcoming, which mark the fulfilment of historical destiny. This historical reference is the distinctive factor in the Roman view.   [H. KLEINKNECHT, V, 382-92]

B. Human and Divine Wrath in the OT.

I. The Hebrew Terms. Hebrew is rich in terms for anger. a. The most common is *'ap,* which has the basic sense of snorting; it is mostly used for divine anger (170 times), but also for human (40 times). b. Another word is *ḥēmâ,* which carries the sense of "heat" or "passion," and is often used for divine (90 times) or human (25) rage. c. Used only for God's wrath is *ḥārâ* in the phrase *ḥᵃrôn 'ap.* d. Another word is *'ebrâ,* and other terms include *kā'as, zā'am,* and *zā'ap;* all these express facets of wrath such as rage, indignation, chiding, etc. (For full details cf. *TDNT,* V, 392ff.)
[O. GRETHER and J. FICHTNER, V, 392-94]

II. Human Wrath.

1. Against Others. While the same terms may denote divine and human wrath, there are important material differences in the two cases. The objects of human wrath are usually individuals, groups, nations, or their rulers. The wrath of other nations is a threat to Israel (Am. 1:11), but puny in face of God's protection (Is. 7:4). Human wrath is directed mostly against other people, and it is justified when not concerned only with self-interest (cf. 2 Sam. 12:5; Neh. 5:6). This is especially true when the cause of God is championed (cf. Moses in Ex. 16:20; Lev. 10:16, Elijah in 2 Kgs. 13:19, Elihu in Job 32:2, and Jeremiah in Jer. 6:11). Yet human anger may also be self-interested (e.g., Cain in Gen. 4:5, Esau in 27:44-45, Balak in Num. 24:10, Saul in 1 Sam. 20:30, Potiphar in Gen. 39:19).

2. *Against God*. Human anger may be directed against God when his dealings seem to be enigmatic or unjust (cf. Samuel in 1 Sam. 15:11, David in 2 Sam. 6:8, Job in 11:2-3 etc., and Jonah in Jon. 4:1ff.). The anger of the righteous at the prosperity of the wicked is finally directed against God (Ps. 37:1, 7-8; Prov. 3:31-32).

3. *Evaluation*. Proverbs measures human anger in terms of practical wisdom. It is dangerous in the light of its results (6:34; 15:1, etc.). We should wait for God to judge the wicked (24:19-20; cf. Ps. 37:7ff.). Patience is the true wisdom (Prov. 14:29), and anger is folly (14:17, 29). The wise see that human anger leads to injustice (14:17; cf. Jms. 1:20). Job's friends condemn his anger because it damages him (Job 18:4), undermines fear of God (15:4), and attacks God's justice (8:2-3). God endorses the verdict, although at much greater depth (38ff.), and Job himself repents (42:6).

III. Divine Wrath.

1. *Linguistic Data*. In the OT terms for wrath more commonly denote divine than human anger, especially in combinations which distinguish the wrath of God by its power. Wrath is consistently linked with Yahweh, the covenant God. Later there is a tendency to loosen the tight link with God. The absolute use of "wrath" in Chronicles calls for notice. Is. 63:5 distinguishes Yahweh and the wrath of Yahweh, but the next verse shows that this is poetic personification.

2. *Objects*. Israel knows only one God, with whom she stands in a special covenant relationship. The concept of divine wrath is thus controlled by the knowledge of faith with its historical perspective of past, present, and future. Israel does not deal with an irrational, impersonal force but with the personal divine will. This gives shape and vitality to what is said about wrath. A strong sense of the distance of God keeps the involved anthropopathism within proper limits. Wrath is not the same thing as judgment, for it has to do with a process or emotion within God. Yet this emotion affects, not his intrinsic being, but only his being in relation to the world and its entities.

The divine wrath is directed a. against Israel. It is a recurrent factor in the wilderness wanderings, the conquest, and the subsequent history. Where it falls on individuals such as Moses, Aaron, Miriam, kings or prophets (Ex. 4:14; Dt. 9:20; Num. 12:9; 1 Sam. 15; Jer. 21:1ff.), their representative function is usually at issue. But it may also fall on the people as a whole because of individual sins (cf. Achan in Josh. 7 or David in 2 Sam. 24). For some prophets, divine wrath is a primary theme, though they do not all use the word (cf. Amos). The aim of these prophets is to shatter a false sense of security (cf. Am. 3:2; Hos. 13:9ff.; Mic. 3:11; Zeph. 2:2). In particular Jeremiah and Ezekiel are prophets of the wrath of God. Wrath is less prominent after the exile, but cf. Hag. 1:5ff.; Zech. 1:3, 12.

b. Other nations and their rulers are also subject to divine wrath. Most of the prophets proclaim this (cf. Is. 13:3ff.; Jer. 50:13, 15; Ezek. 25:14). Psalms also sing of it (cf. 2:5, 11; 110:5). When it breaks forth, it affects the whole earth (Dt. 32:22).

3. *Exercise*. Various means are used to depict God's wrath, but it always threatens the existence of those concerned. The figures used express its destructive and irresistible force. Fire is a common metaphor (cf. Jer. 15:14). The storm is another symbol (cf. Jer. 30:23). Commonly it is said to be poured out like a fluid (Hos. 5:10). At

times it is poured out like fire or burning pitch (Is. 30:33); at other times it is to be drunk (Jer. 25:15). God may vent his wrath through the nations (Is. 10:5; 13:5), but his own arm is also said to be the agent of his anger (Is. 30:30). His wrath is variously said to be kindled and stilled (Ezek. 5:13), brought or sent (2 Chr. 36:16; Job 20:23), and executed (1 Sam. 28:18). When it ends, God ceases from it (Ex. 32:12), or it is turned aside (Jer. 4:8), though the latter expression might denote only suspension. The final aim of divine wrath is total destruction in the form of historical defeat and banishment from the land. More detailed manifestations are temporary oppression, famine, plague, and drought. In its eschatological dimension it stands for the complete triumph of God. The day of God will be a day of wrath even for Israel (Am. 5:18ff.). Only by divine grace and forgiveness will some escape the judgment that will inevitably fall on the nations and on the wicked in the land (Pss. 9:16-17; 7:6, etc.). In the lives of the righteous divine wrath takes the form of various problems such as sickness, persecution, the threat of early death, and a sense of remoteness from God (Pss. 88:16; 90:7ff.; 102:8, 10-11, 23). Job is an example of the righteous undergoing an apparently inexplicable manifestation of divine wrath.

4. Motives. In some instances there seem to be no reasons for God's wrath. It simply comes with primal force (cf. Gen. 32:23ff.; Ex. 4:24-25). It is a death-dealing intervention when God's holiness is violated (Ex. 19:9ff.). No real explanation can be given for God's opposition to David's census (1 Sam. 24) or for the sufferings inflicted on Job or the righteous of the Psalms. It seems as though we have here an incalculable factor that borders on the arbitrary. Yet at other times the reasons for wrath are plain. The covenant God smites his people, or groups within it, when they resist his saving will and fail to make the response of trust and obedience (cf. Num. 11:1; 17:6ff.; Josh. 7:1; 1 Sam. 15, etc.). Apostasy is an obvious reason for divine wrath (Ex. 32; Num. 25, etc.). In the prophets the context of wrath is the gracious and faithful love that God displays to Israel. All her offenses are a despising of this love. Hence wrath, as wounded love, is correlative to grace. It is a jealous zeal that will not tolerate the disloyalty of the chosen people. The same zeal, however, will protect Israel when as a faithful husband God destroys the nations that oppress his people and brings his people deliverance (Zech. 1:14-15; Neh. 1:2). An attack on Israel is an attack on God himself, on the honor of God (Is. 48:9ff.). Yet God's wrath against the nations has a broader dimension. It is directed against human arrogance and wickedness in assertion of the claim of God to lordship over the cosmos. God may use Assyria as the rod of his anger against Israel, but he also turns his wrath against Assyria when she exceeds her commission (Is. 10:5ff.; Ezek. 25:15ff.; Zech. 1:15). The aim of divine wrath is the establishment of the divine rule of holiness. In this connection the whole burden of human life after the fall is in itself an expression of divine wrath (cf. Gen. 3; 4; 6–8; 11). As Job 14:1ff. vividly puts it (cf. Ps. 90:7), all human life stands under the constant operation of the wrath of God.

5. Outbreak, Duration, and Turning Aside. Historically, as distinct from eschatologically, God's wrath falls on individuals or peoples in the form of afflictions. Often it will flash down like lightning (Ex. 19:12; Num. 11:33; 1 Sam. 6:7). Yet God does not give free rein to wrath but is long-suffering (Ex. 34:6-7; Num. 14:18, etc.). He warns the people to repent, as the prophets bear witness. He is quick to show clemency. He can even exercise restraint in the case of Nineveh, to the disgust of Jonah (Jon. 4:2). This restraint may sometimes be for the sake of testing his people or bringing out the fullness of guilt. The question of the duration of wrath is a constant one in the exilic period and the Psalms. There is hope that it will be short (cf. Is. 54:8ff.). The conviction arises that the day of wrath must run its course and then the time of grace will come. Yet the divine wrath against the nations will be final (Nah. 1:2). This is the reverse side of God's love for Israel. The aim of the law and the prophets is to bring the people to the conversion and obedience that will avert wrath (cf. Dt. 6:15). No rites can placate God's wrath when it falls. God himself decides its duration, and the only course is to seek the divine mercy in prayer or intercession (cf. Moses in Ex. 32:11-12; Num. 12:13; Amos in 7:2, 5; Jeremiah in 14:7ff.; and Job in 42:7-8). God hears such petitions (Num. 11; 14), but the time may come when he will not do so or may even forbid them (Jer. 7:16). The grounds of intercession are God's own faithfulness and the weakness of his creatures (Num. 14:18; Am. 7:2, 5). Job especially stresses his weakness and asks God to leave him alone (7:1ff.; 9:18ff.; 13:13ff.), not realizing that there is a special reason for the severity of his lot. Since the wrath of God manifests the divine holiness, it can cease when punishment is executed on transgressors (cf. Num. 25:1ff.; Josh. 7:1, 25-26). Expiatory offerings sometimes play a role (Num. 16:46; 2 Sam. 24:17ff.), but in the prophets the only hope for an aversion of wrath is total repentance (Jer. 4:4, 8). The exiled people will see the end of wrath when it has emptied the cup of wrath and received double for its sins (Is. 51:17, 22; 40:2).

6. *God's Wrath and His Holiness, Righteousness, and Pity.* While wrath is only once called an essential trait in God (Nah. 1:2), it is an integral part of the OT message. The wrath of God is God's onslaught in assertion of his claim to dominion. Materially, if not linguistically, it is closely linked to his holiness. It is presented as the work, not of objective fate, but of a personal will. It is God's attack on all forces that resist his holy will. It is not the same as God's justice even though it is aimed against transgressions of the divine demands. To Job it may even seem to be unjust, for there is an inscrutable element in it. Thus Job can even appeal from the God of wrath to the God of justice (16:20-21), and Jeremiah can ask for correction in just measure rather than in anger (10:24). Nevertheless, in relation to Israel wrath is no mere caprice but is the reverse side of God's faithful and zealous love. The sins of Israel bring tensions, as it were, to God as his pity restrains his wrath (Is. 54:8ff.). Confession of the divine mercy provides no reason for thinking that judgment will not fall, especially on the nations and the wicked. Yet it nourishes the belief that for God's righteous people God's anger is but for a moment and his favor for a lifetime (Ps. 30:5).

[J. Fichtner, V, 394-409]

C. The Wrath of God in the LXX.

I. Usage.

1. *orgē and thymós.* In rendering the various Hebrew terms the LXX uses *orgē* and *thymós*. Etymologically *thymós* denotes the emotion and *orgē* the expression, but this distinction is lost in the LXX. a. The two are often used together (cf. Dt. 9:19). b. They are used interchangeably in parallelism (cf. Hos. 13:11; Is. 34:2). c. Also interchangeable are the genitive constructions *thymós tēs orgēs* and *orgē toú thymoú* (Ex. 32:12; Num. 32:14, etc.). d. We also find *thymoústhai orgē* (Gen. 39:19), and more rarely *orgē thymoútai* (1 Sam. 11:6). e. There are many expressions with either *orgē* or *thymós* but far fewer with just one of the terms (for details cf. *TDNT,* V, 409-10).

2. *orgízō, (thymóō), parorgízō, parorgismós.* Active forms of *orgízō* and *thymóō* occur only once each ("to make angry"), but passive forms are common ("to become or be angry"). The nouns *parorgismós* and *parórgisma* ("provocation to anger") are rare.

3. orgílos and thymṓdēs. These words, meaning "angry," "wrathful," occur mostly in the Wisdom literature, and in every case but one refer only to the human attribute.

4. (kótos), chólos, and mênis. These words, common in secular Greek for "anger," are not used for God's wrath in the LXX. *kótos* does not occur at all, *chólos* only five times (*cholán* once) with reference to human anger, and *mênis* only four times (*mêniama* or *mênima* once and the verb *mêniein* five times), again with reference to human anger except for the verb in Jer. 3:12; Ps. 103:8. The translators perhaps avoid using for God's wrath terms that are associated with the anger of the Greek gods.

II. Interpretations and Paraphrases. In general the LXX correctly renders the Hebrew, although it is mechanical at times, e.g., in using *thymós* when the Hebrew reference is to "poison" or *orgḗ* when the Hebrew means "vexation." When the Hebrew refers anthropomorphically to the nose of God, the LXX prefers the anthropopathic *orgḗ*. It sometimes replaces the wrath of God with the sin that provokes it, and it chooses to paraphrase (and alters the sense) in Mal. 1:4, Is. 66:14, and Zech. 1:12. In a verse like Dt. 32:22 it offers the rendering that a fire is kindled as a result of (not in) God's anger. A direct treatment of the revelation of God's anger occurs in Sir. 48:1. (For full details cf. *TDNT,* V, 411-12.)

[O. GRETHER and J. FICHTNER, V, 409-12]

D. The Wrath of God in Later Judaism.

I. Apocrypha and Pseudepigrapha.

a. Later Jewish writings continue along the same lines as the OT, using some of the same Hebrew terms, and in the Gk. *orgḗ* and *thymós* (and derivatives).

b. Human anger is judged in different ways. There may be righteous anger, e.g., at transgressions of the law. The anger of pagan rulers against offenders is also justifiable, and may even serve as an illustration of the wrath of God. Mostly, however, anger is regarded as a passion that leads to sin and ruin. The fierce anger of pagan rulers (e.g., against Israel) is condemned. Strictly, anger is proper to God alone; human anger particularly arouses God's anger. Even by secular criteria anger is contrary to wisdom, although reason can also control it.

c. Since the judgment on anger is predominantly negative, it is perhaps surprising that almost all these works speak uninhibitedly about God's anger. Even the Hellenistically tinged 4 Maccabees reckons with God's righteous wrath. *orgḗ* denotes the passion itself as an expression of God's nature and of his righteous opposition to evil. It may also denote its effects as wrathful judgment. This is especially true of eschatological wrath. Personification of anger serves to preserve the personal aspect while detaching it to some degree from God himself. Apocalyptic tends to stress the divine mercy and gives as reasons why wrath is held in check the small number of the righteous, the ignorance of the masses, the universality of sin, and the subjection of evil itself to the divine will. Where wrath breaks out, it has first a historical phase in which it is directed against individuals and nations, including Israel (with limitations). Historical wrath, however, is a type of eschatological wrath. This is directed against the nations and against all impenitent sinners. The objects of wrath, e.g., rulers, may also be its instruments, as are angels. Ways to avert wrath are worship, righteous conduct, intercession, vicarious suffering, and God's own saving advocacy.

[E. SJÖBERG and G. STÄHLIN, V, 412-16]

II. Rabbinism. The rabbis have no problem with the idea of divine wrath. They can even depict it in human terms, although they condemn human anger apart from righteous indignation. Sometimes they hypostatize anger in angelic forms. Divine anger is never divorced from God's essential righteousness. Even in anger God continues his merciful care for the world. Punishing the wicked, he is kind to the righteous and merciful to the penitent. Indeed, he still gives good gifts to sinners. This does not weaken, however, the terror of his wrath. The day of judgment is a day of wrath, although with a greater emphasis on justice. [E. SJÖBERG, V, 416-17]

III. Philo. Philo recognizes a righteous anger at sin and sinners, but under Stoic influence he views anger as a passion that should be suppressed. He speaks about God's anger as chiding, and finds its outworking in earthly events, but he suggests that anger is ascribed to God rather than being a divine reality, and he explains biblical references as a divine accommodation to the capacities of the hearers.

[E. SJÖBERG and G. STÄHLIN, V, 417-18]

IV. Josephus. Josephus uses *orgē* for divine and human anger, and he also uses *chólos, mḗnima* and *mḗnis,* but not *thymós.* He relates divine wrath to violations of the law. The criterion of *orgē* is *díkē,* so that he sometimes uses *díkē* instead. In his own time he regards the Romans as the instrument of divine *díkē.*

[O. PROCKSCH, V, 418]

E. Human and Divine Wrath in the NT.

I. Human Wrath.

1. Relative Justification. Apart from *orgē* itself, words of the stem *org-* are used in the NT only for human anger, although *thymós* is preferred for sudden rage (Lk. 4:28; Acts 19:28). Since the NT takes divine wrath seriously, it cannot be wholly negative toward human anger. It accepts a holy anger that hates what God hates and that is seen in Jesus himself (Mk. 3:5) or in Paul (Acts 17:16). Nevertheless, it does not think love and wrath are intrinsically compatible in us as they are in God (cf. 1 Cor. 13:5). The divinely provoked anger of Israel is good in Rom. 10:19, and so is the indignation that is the fruit of the true repentance in 2 Cor. 7:11.

2. Negative Appraisal. Elsewhere in the NT human anger is a fault. The anger of the elder brother is wrong in Lk. 15:28. So is the anger of Jesus' hearers in Lk. 4:28. So, too, is the anger of the Gentiles in Rev. 11:18. Such anger is finally directed against God, and it comes to full focus in the anger of the devil in Rev. 12:17. Herod is a human prototype in Mt. 2:16. It is anger of this sort that James describes in 1:20, and that Jesus perhaps has in mind in Mt. 5:22, where it is a first step to murder. Paul takes a similar view. Anger is one of the sins of Col. 3:8 and Eph. 4:31. To refrain from it is to give place to God (Rom. 12:19); to yield to it is to give place to the devil (Eph. 4:26-27). If it leads to revenge, it is an infringement of the divine prerogative of judgment (Rom. 12:19). God's wrath is the response to it (Col. 3:6, 8). We are neither to be angry nor to provoke to anger (Col. 3:8; Eph. 6:4). Anger is out of place in divine service (1 Tim. 2:8; Tit. 1:7). Eph. 4:26 allows that even believers might be angry at times, but if they are, they must be careful not to sin. Jms. 1:19 teaches a forbearance that, like God's, is more ready to forgive than to yield to anger, for anger does not advance true righteousness.

II. Divine Wrath.

1. Differentiation from the World Around.

a. Linguistic. The NT never uses *mḗnis* and *chólos* for God's wrath but only *orgē* and *thymós,* and the latter only in Rom. 2:8 and Revelation. The linking of *orgē* with *ekdíkēsis* (Lk. 21:22) and *dikaiokrisía* (Rom. 2:5) rules out the idea of unbridled explosions of anger, and the use of words like *stenochōría* as parallels shows that the stress is more on the effects than on the emotion.

b. Material. The message of the Baptist, Jesus, Paul, and Revelation includes wrath as well as mercy. Hence the NT does not stand opposed to the OT in an antithesis of love and wrath. Love and wrath are present in both. If, however, human arrogance is the occasion of divine wrath (cf. Rom. 2:4ff.), it does not cause eternal hostility between God and humanity, for God's love stands alongside and above his wrath. Hence God's wrath is never depicted in the NT as an emotional or irrational outburst. A theological concept outweighs the psychological concept.

2. *Wrath in the NT View of God.*

a. Wrath is an inalienable element in the NT view of God. It is a fearful thing to fall into his hands (Heb. 10:31). He can destroy both body and soul in hell (Lk. 12:5; cf. Jms. 4:12).

b. *orgḗ* might sometimes seem to be present almost as an independently operating force (cf. Paul's use of *orgḗ* without a qualifying *toú theoú*). Yet the NT finds no place for transcendent embodiments (as distinct from instruments), refers to the coming of wrath only as to the coming of the last things, and rejects the fatalism that would be implied if *orgḗ* were an automatic principle. Paul's use of *orgḗ* corresponds to his use of *cháris;* he takes it for granted that God's *orgḗ* is in view.

c. Is *orgḗ* an emotion, however, or is it a punishment? In most instances it undoubtedly denotes the divine work of judgment, yet God's serious displeasure at evil is also implied (cf. Rom. 1:18; Rev. 6:16; Heb. 3:11).

d. In the NT, as in the OT, love and wrath are not mutually exclusive in God. It is by wrath that the greatness of mercy is measured, and by mercy the greatness of wrath. Where love is confronted by ungodly resistance, it has the form of wrath (cf. Mk. 3:5; Mt. 18:34). Those who accept mercy are freed from wrath, those who despise mercy remain under it (Lk. 2:34; Mt. 3:12; Mk. 4:12). The two malefactors who are crucified with Jesus vividly illustrate this truth (Lk. 23:39ff.).

e. What is the relation of God's *orgḗ* to his *makrothymía* (patience)? On the one side *makrothymía* is an instrument of mercy that gives sinners space for repentance (cf. Rom. 2:4; Rev. 2:21; 2 Pet. 3:9); it thus serves the manifestation of the riches of glory in the vessels of mercy. On the other hand, when it is despised, it is an instrument of wrath that confirms the power of God in the destruction of the vessels of wrath. The revelation of wrath is the indispensable foil of that of mercy, as in Rom. 1:17-18; 3:23.

f. The NT sees that God's wrath is directed against human *adikía,* yet its message is that of the triumph of divine *dikaiosýnē* over human *adikía.* If, then, human wickedness serves God's righteousness, is God unjust to inflict wrath (Rom. 3:5)? Indeed, can there be any justice at all in God's wrath when God himself abandons humanity to the chaos of wickedness (Rom. 1:18ff.)? Paul's first answer is that those who realize that they are sinners deserving nothing at God's hands are fully aware that God's wrath is his just judgment of the world. Only impious thinking can reason otherwise (3:7-8). His second answer is that God's wrath and righteousness are united in a humanly inconceivable way. It is precisely because God has to be wrathful against all of us that he grants righteousness from faith to faith and in this very way vindicates his righteous judgment (3:26). The vicarious work of Christ is God's solution to the apparent tension or dilemma.

3. *The Revelation of Divine Wrath.*

a. In Jesus and His Message. Although direct references are infrequent (Mk. 1:43; 3:5; Mt. 9:30; Jn. 11:33, 38), wrath is an integral characteristic of Jesus himself. His anger displays his humanity and yet its objects point to his deity. He is angry at forces that oppose God, e.g., Satan (Mt. 4:10), demons (Mk. 1:25), leprosy (Mk. 1:41), the wicked and hypocritical (Jn. 8:44; Mt. 12:34), the disobedient (Mk. 1:43), and the unbelieving (Jn. 11:33). His angry sorrow at the Pharisees is that of the merciful Lord whose love encounters only a legalistic hate that wants law, not love, and thus reacts with merciless hostility (Mk. 3:5-6). Especially severe is the wrath shown in the parable against the wicked servant who is so freely forgiven but then refuses to forgive (Mk. 18:34). Terrible, too, is Jesus' anger at the cities which reject the call to conversion (Mt. 11:20ff.) and at the merchants who desecrate the temple (Mt. 21:12ff.). In a strange parabolic action he also displays his wrath against those who withhold the fruits of repentance (Mk. 11:14; cf. Lk. 13:7). This is the wrath of the eschatological Judge who can cut off from fellowship (Mt. 21:12) and cast into Hades (11:23). By word and act Jesus manifests God's eschatological wrath. He is the Lord of the last judgment (Ps. 2:12) who denies evildoers (Mt. 7:23), destroys enemies (Lk. 19:27), and casts into the furnace of fire (Mt. 13:42). Rev. 19:15 offers a similar picture. So does Rev. 6:16 when it refers to the wrath of the Lamb. The same Lamb that comes under human judgment will finally exercise divine judgment on those who despise his vicarious self-offering.

b. Historical and Eschatological Outworking. Like such concepts as kingdom and salvation, *orgḗ* can have both an eschatological and a historical reference.

(a) Accompanying words and images (e.g., such words as coming and day, and such images as fire and cup) give *orgḗ* an eschatological thrust. The NT opens with the Baptist's message of coming wrath and liberation from it (Mt. 3:7ff.). Jesus seldom uses the terms *orgḗ* and *orgízomai* but he finds a place for eschatological *orgḗ* in the last tribulation (cf. Lk. 21:23) and in the last judgment. In Rom. 2:5 the last day is the day of wrath, and this is the setting of the drama of wrath at the end of the NT in Revelation (cf. the great day of wrath in 6:17).

(b) Yet there is also a historical wrath that is already present. Jesus himself is present as the holy Judge. He portrays the historical outworking of wrath in Lk. 13:2ff. Paul discerns an operation of wrath in Rom. 1:18ff. Related to the operation of righteousness, this is bound up with Christ, whose coming means both grace and judgment. In the light of the gospel the wrath of God may be seen in the world's sinfulness. This temporal manifestation points ahead to the full and final manifestation, so that one must preach both present and future wrath (2:8) as well as present and future justification. The two aspects go together in Rom. 2:5ff.; 3:5; 4:15; 13:4-5; 1 Th. 2:16. In Rom. 3:7 present wrath is in view but the term *krínomai* confers an eschatological quality.

(c) Wrath is delayed in the NT; God is slow to wrath. There are parallels for this thought in the Greek world, the OT, and the rabbis. As noted already, the delay has a double function (Rom. 9:22; cf. 2:4). We should not anticipate God's delayed wrath by exercising retribution ourselves (12:19).

(d) Faith sees a period of wrath and a period of grace, but these overlap in Christ, so that in the present time both righteousness and wrath are manifested (Rom. 1:17-18). The law, when violated, brings wrath, but this is the reaction of spurned love, for the law, like the gospel, is a gift of love.

(e) The anticipation of eschatological wrath means that there is a present state of wrath (Jn. 3:36). This does not eliminate the eschatological element, but it raises the question whether wrath will finally be eternal. Greek thinking accepts this, the OT seems to question it in Jer. 3:12, and Judaism is uncertain. In the NT many passages support an eternal duration (Mt. 3:12; 18:34; Rev. 14:10), although the reference is to the punishment rather than the wrath. God's wrath is undoubtedly lasting as his holy resistance to everything unholy (Rev. 20:10, 14; 21:8). Eternity of wrath, however, is definitely not meant in 1 Th. 2:16 (cf. Rom. 9–11), where the *eis télos* might mean "forever" in the sense of "eternally" but has here a weaker rhetorical sense, and may even mean up to the dawn of the last time.

4. *Divine Wrath in NT Imagery.*

a. In the parables of Jesus we find the human images of the wrathful king (Mt. 18:34) and judge (Mt. 25; Lk. 13:6ff.).

b. For those smitten by divine wrath we find the image of vessels into whom it is poured (Rom. 9:22). A family image is also used in Eph. 2:3 with its reference to children of wrath. In both cases there are opposites, i.e., vessels of mercy and children of God by adoption.

c. For wrath itself we find the image of (a) fire, which unites judgment, torment, and the fires of hell; (b) flood, which as in the OT carries the thought of the water that both saves and destroys (cf. the baptism of John); (c) the cup or vial, which carries the double thought of punishment and stupefaction (Rev. 14:8ff.), and which is accompanied by the image of the winepress (14:19-20); and (d) the capital (Rom. 2:5) that is stored up in heaven and will be paid back at the last judgment (cf. the opposite treasure in Mt. 19:31).

5. *The Objects and Instruments of Wrath.*

a. Objects. In the NT wrath is not of the essence of God but always has objects. God is wrathful with Israel (Mt. 3:7; Lk. 21:23; 1 Th. 2:16). He is wrathful with all sinful humanity (Eph. 2:3) and all nations (Rev. 11:18; 14:8; 18:3). He is wrathful with the mighty and the rich (Rev. 6:15ff.). He is wrathful with the whole earth (especially Babylon) because of its worship of antichrist (Rev. 14:8ff.; 16:1, 19). He is wrathful with the demonic world which opposes its own wrath to God's (cf. Rev. 12:17).

b. Instruments. God uses demonic forces as instruments of his wrath (Rev. 11–12). These forces bring disasters, but dualism is avoided by their subordination to God. Even in opposition to God, the devil unwittingly and unwillingly serves him (1 Cor. 2:8). Like the great powers of the OT, even as an instrument he is also an object (i.e., a vessel in the twofold sense). Political power also serves as a tool of divine wrath (Rom. 13:4). Like the devil, it can do so even when it is itself ungodly and thus becomes subject to the very wrath which it executes (cf. Rev. 13).

c. The Christian. All are under the wrath of God (Rom. 3:23). Christians, however, are liberated from it (1 Th. 1:10). In retrospect they thus see that they were not destined for wrath but prepared as vessels of mercy (Rom. 9:23).

6. *The Causes and Effects of Wrath.*

a. Causes. The root cause of wrath is despising God. The world stands under wrath because it disregards his revelation in creation and transgresses his will in ungodliness and wickedness (Rom. 1:18ff.). *orgé* is God's displeasure at false worship (cf. Paul in Acts 17:16 and Jesus in Jn. 2:15ff.) and evil (Rom. 12:19). Sin, apostasy, and hatred of God are the reasons for wrath (Rom. 5:8, 10). Apostasy stirs up God's wrath especially in its form as worship of the beast (Rev. 14). But alongside despising of the law, despising of God's holy love and forbearance is a decisive cause of *orgé* (Lk. 14:16ff.; Rom. 2:4). A rejection of Jesus is answered by rejection in divine wrath (1 Th. 2:14ff.). Despising of God may also take the form of a lack of love or compassion (Mk. 3:5; Mt. 18:23ff.) which easily takes the form of judging others (Rom. 2:5). Despising of God's love and lack of love for others, at root the same, are both reasons for wrath. Behind all other causes lies the will of God as the truly normative basis. Thus Rom. 9:22 and 1 Th. 5:9 hint at an ordination to wrath. The law is given in order to set sinners unequivocally under wrath (Rom. 3:19). The divine will does not mean human exculpation. Divine ordination and human guilt are no less inextricably interwoven than devilish temptation and human transgression (Eph. 2:2-3).

b. Causes and Effects. The most serious causes of divine wrath are also its effects, so that the great acts of wrath are occasions of new wrath. If sin and unbelief are causes of wrath, they are also its effects (Rom. 1; 9:22). Sin and punishment converge, for God repays like with like. The acts of sinners fall on their own heads.

c. Effects. Like the OT, the NT sees the working of divine wrath in death (Rom. 1:18ff.). Eschatological wrath brings destruction (Rom. 9:22), as is typified in the overthrow of Jerusalem (Lk. 21:23). Destruction is not annihilation but eternal torment (Rev. 14:10-11; 20:10). The most proper outworking of wrath, however, is further sin (Rom. 1–2). The moral chaos of the race is an effect of divine wrath, not in a causal nexus, but by God's answering of the threefold human "exchange" by a threefold "handing over" (1:23ff.).

7. *Liberation from Wrath.*

a. General. Antiquity at large seeks escape or deliverance from divine wrath.

b. Conversion and Baptism. The Baptist offers repentance and baptism as a means of deliverance by a figurative anticipation of judgment. This is no automatic process but depends on an authentic conversion that finds demonstration in fruits (Mt. 3:8ff.). It is thus a valid way of escape from judgment.

c. Jesus the Deliverer. The apostolic message finds in Jesus the one who delivers his followers from coming wrath (1 Th. 1:10; Rom. 5:9), since in him they have already a present and future salvation that grants assurance that they are not destined for wrath (1 Th. 5:9-10). Jesus delivers from wrath because, justified and reconciled in him, they are no longer enemies or under condemnation (Rom. 5:9-10; 8:1). He brings this about by tasting the cup of wrath for them (cf. Mk. 14:36; Lk. 22:43-44). His acceptance of baptism, the sign of judgment, points in this direction. He takes away God's wrath from others by bearing it himself, for even as he voluntarily comes under wrath the good pleasure of the Father rests upon him in view of his righteousness and self-sacrificial obedience. His vicarious work solves the tension between divine wrath and divine love. If, however, deliverance from eternal wrath is in Christ, then everything depends on one's response to him. To reject him is to abide under wrath; to receive him is to be free. We must either "fear future wrath or love present grace" (Ignatius *Ephesians* 11.1). In faith in Christ the eschatological gift of freedom from wrath is a present reality. Water baptism is an anticipatory judgment. As a type of outpoured wrath, it saves from wrath as in it we receive a portion in Christ who bore and cancelled wrath (cf. Rom. 6:2ff.). Deliverance from wrath by grace is not, of course, a possession on which we can count irrespective of our own conduct (cf. Mt. 18:23ff.). Yet the final testimony of the NT is not to the fiery lake of wrath but to the wellspring of mercy in Christ.   [G. Stählin, V, 419-47]

→ *hágios, thymós, krínō, makrothymía*

---

orégomai [to reach out, strive],   *órexis* [desire, longing]

---

orégō means "to reach out," "to reach for." It is used figuratively for 1. intellectual or spiritual striving, either generally, e.g., for fellowship, or philosophically, e.g., rational or irrational aspiration, or, in Philo, homesickness for the world of ideas; and 2. physical craving, e.g., for nourishment.

The group occurs only four times in the NT and only twice in formal analogy to the philosophical use. Thus in Heb. 11:16 faith desires a better country; it is oriented, not to nature or the *lógos* as in philosophy, but to the promise (11:8, 17). A total attitude is at issue, for those who turn aside from the promise crave after money instead (1 Tim. 6:10). The difference from philosophy lies in the eschatological focus of the seeking. In Rom. 1:27 Paul uses *órexis* for the sexual impulse. This is not to be dualistically disparaged as such. It becomes corrupt only because the truth of God is perverted (vv. 24-25). In the justified, it integrates itself into the service of God to which the body is dedicated. Faith, then, has a decisive bearing on physical needs too.

[H. W. HEIDLAND, V, 447-48]

---

orthós [straight, upright], *diórthōsis* [straightening, correction], *epanórthōsis* [restoration, correction], *orthopodéō* [to stand erect, not to waver]

---

orthós.
a. This word first means "upright," "standing." b. It then means "moving in a straight line." c. A next sense is "right," "correct," "true." d. We then find the meaning "stretched," "taut." The LXX offers examples of a. in Mic. 2:3 (figurative), b. in Jer. 38:9, and c. in Prov. 8:6 etc. In the NT Paul in Acts 14:10 tells the cripple to stand up "straight" on his feet. Heb. 12:13 quotes Prov. 4:26 but changes the idea from that of right conduct to that of moving "straight" toward the goal in an eschatological rather than a more purely ethical sense. With their eyes fixed on Jesus, believers pursue paths that lead straight to the goal.

diórthōsis. This word, which originally means "straightening," is variously used for "correction," "arrangement," "setting up" states, and "settlement" (debts or taxes). Heb. 9:10 argues that the OT cultus, which can have only temporary and external effects, is set up only until the time of the true order *(diorthṓseōs).* When this comes, the cultus finds its own fulfilment in the dawning age of consummation.

epanórthōsis. This word means "restoration," "reestablishment," "correction," "reformation." It occurs in the NT in the sequence in 2 Tim. 3:16. Scripture is given for teaching and reproof, then for *epanórthōsis,* and finally for instruction. Placed as it is, the word seems to mean "amendment," i.e., the restoration that means salvation (v. 15) and that only God can give.

orthopodéō. This word means "to stand erect," "not to waver or tumble." First found in the NT, it is used negatively in Gal. 2:14 to describe the conduct of Peter and the followers of James at Antioch. Denying freedom from the law, they do not walk firmly according to the truth of the gospel, i.e., in obedience to the reality of the salvation accomplished in Christ. Like the rest of the group, the word deals with the new relationship to God and the implied conduct. It has in view the eschatological determination of the human situation.   [H. PREISKER, V, 449-51]

orthotoméō → *témnō*

---

horízō [to limit, appoint],   **aphorízō** [to separate],   **apodiorízō** [to divide],
proorízō [to foreordain]

---

horízō. This word (from *hóros*, "boundary") means "to limit" and then figuratively "to fix," "to appoint." Time as well as space can be limited. A literal use occurs in the LXX (cf. Num. 34:6; Josh. 13:27). We find limitation of time in Heb. 4:7 and of time and space in Acts 17:26-27. Elsewhere the sense is "to appoint" or "determine" (cf. Lk. 22:22; Acts 2:23; 10:42; 11:29; 17:31). In Rom. 1:4 Jesus is instituted the Son of God in power. Whether the reference here is to a declaration or an appointment is not a matter of great urgency, since a divine declaration is also a divine appointment. In the light of Acts 10:42 and 17:31 what Christ is now declared or appointed to be is to be equated with what he already is from all eternity by divine ordination (hence the addition of a *pro-* in some readings of Rom. 1:4). Apart from Acts 11:29, the *horízō* passages in the NT are all emphatically christological; they relate to the person and work of Jesus Christ.

aphorízō. This compound means "to separate," "to sever." It is used in the NT for the divine separation for service (Rom. 1:1; Gal. 1:15) which goes hand in hand with divine calling. By divine commission the Son of Man will separate the good and the bad (Mt. 25:32; cf. the angels in 13:49). Believers, then, must already separate themselves as a people of salvation (2 Cor. 6:17; cf. Is. 52:11). The Holy Spirit demands separation for special tasks (Acts 13:2). In Acts 19:9 Paul and his followers separate themselves from the synagogue, but Peter wrongly reverses the process by separating himself from Gentile believers (Gal. 2:12). The world for its part retaliates by excluding and reviling the followers of Christ (Lk. 6:22). In the OT separation for God and the separation of the unclean (e.g., lepers) are important models for NT separation for service or separation from the world.

apodiorízō. This rare double compound means "to define more exactly" in Aristotle. It might bear this sense in Jude 18-19 if the sense is that false teachers engage in endless definition. But the more likely meaning is that they cause divisions in antithesis to the true task of edification (v. 20). Thus in 2 Pet. 2:1 the heretics introduce destructive teachings, and often the NT castigates the spirit of contention or division (Gal. 5:20; 1 Tim. 4:1ff.).

proorízō. This rare and late word has in the NT the sense "to foreordain." It is parallel to "to foreknow" in Rom. 8:29. God has ordained everything in salvation history with Christ as the goal. Hence Herod, Pilate, and the Gentiles can only do what God has predetermined (Acts 4:28). Herein lies the hidden wisdom of God (1 Cor. 2:7). Divine sonship in Christ is the goal of God's ordaining (Eph. 1:5). Our assurance of inheritance rests on it (1:11).   [K. L. SCHMIDT, V, 452-56]

---

hórkos [oath], *horkízō* [to adjure], *horkōmosía* [confirmation by oath], *enorkízō* [to adjure, invoke], *exorkízō* [to charge under oath], *(exorkistḗs* [exorcist]*)*, *epíorkos* [perjured], *epiorkéō* [to commit perjury]

---

hórkos. This word means a. "oath" (usually taken by the gods, who are invoked as witnesses) and b. the god that punishes false swearing and perjury. In the papyri we find oaths by rulers, and later by relics and the Trinity. Oaths steadily increase in intensity and compass.

A. The Oath in the Greek World and Judaism.

1. The Greek World. Oaths are primarily self-cursing should one not be speaking the truth. Higher beings, usually deities, are invoked as witnesses and guarantors. Oaths may be simple or highly complex. In public life the formulas and deities are fixed by law. When Greece comes under the Roman empire, oaths are also sworn by the genius of the emperor. Judges give force to their sentences by oaths. Penalties for perjury are often included in oaths. The weakening of oaths leads to their multiplication but also to attempts at reform; the movement to abolish oaths, however, does not prevail.

2. Judaism. The OT has two words for the oath, the one having the basic sense of "seven" (perhaps because seven animals are offered when oaths are taken; cf. Gen. 21:31 with 15:10 and Jer. 34:18), the other literally meaning "cursing." The two may be used together (cf. Num. 5:21). The law lays down that the oath must be taken by God (Dt. 6:13). It is thus a solemn confession of God. False swearing and swearing by other gods are forbidden (Ex. 20:7; Jer. 5:7). Self-cursing adds force to oaths, and penalties may be mentioned (Is. 65:15; Jer. 29:22). God himself may swear by himself (Num. 14:21ff.). He backs his will and word with his oath. Divine cursings and blessings are highly significant (Num. 14:21ff.). God's relation to his people is a solemn marriage by oath (Hos. 1:ff.). which he upholds in spite of Israel's apostasy. Oaths of witness do not occur in the OT but there is an oath of purification which the accused take when there are no witnesses to their innocence (Ex. 22:8ff.). Trespass offerings are demanded when ill-considered oaths are sworn (Lev. 5:44ff.). Perjurers are left to divine retribution, though Talmudic law prescribes penalties. The prophets complain about a growing laxity in relation to oaths (Jer. 5:2; Zech. 5:3-4; Mal. 3:5). In the Damascus Document only judges may demand the oath of cursing to unmask a thief. The Mishnah mentions various kinds of oaths, e.g., the oaths of witness and deposition, and the judicial oath. It imposes the penalty of scourging for intentional perjury.

B. The Oath in the NT.

1. In Jms. 5:12 *hórkos* is the object of *omnýō*. The final member of the statement shows that James has in view an absolute prohibition of oaths.

2. Twice *hórkos* appears in OT quotations. In Lk. 1:73 God has given Abraham a sworn promise which is now being fulfilled in Christ. In Acts 2:30 Peter sees in Christ's resurrection a fulfilment of the sworn promise to David (Ps. 132:11). Mt. 5:33 refers to the demand of the law that oaths should be taken only by God.

3. In Heb. 6:16-17 the definitive nature of an oath is invoked in order to show that the purpose of God will not change.

4. Mt. 14:7 and 26:72 link statement and oath by the expressions "promise" and "deny" "with an oath." Mk. 6:26 brings out the serious consequences of oaths lightly taken.

horkízō. This word means "to cause someone to swear" and "to adjure someone by something." In Mk. 5:7 the demoniac adjures Jesus by God in an effort to rob him of his power, but to no avail, since Jesus is the Son of God. In Acts 19:13 the exorcists try to cast out demons by adjuring them in the name of Jesus. Using the name as a magical formula, however, has the opposite effect to what they desire, for the name of Jesus has force only when spoken in faith and on his commission.

horkōmosía. This rare word means "confirmation by oath." It occurs in the NT only in Heb. 7:20-21, 28. Contrasting the imperfect priesthood of the OT with the perfect priesthood of Christ, these verses make the point that the former is instituted by the law but the latter by the divine oath of Ps. 110:4, which makes Jesus the surety of a better covenant.

enorkízō. This word means "to adjure someone by something" and "to invoke in petition." In the NT it occurs only in 1 Th. 5:27, where Paul adjures his readers by the Lord to read the letter to all the brethren.

exorkízō (exorkistḗs). This word has such senses as "to put on oath," "to invoke," and "to deny upon oath." The *exorkistḗs* is one who expels demons by magical formulas; it is used in the NT only in Acts 19:13. In Mt. 26:63 the high priest adjures Jesus by the living God to tell the truth about his messianic claim, and Jesus answers with a simple affirmation. Some exegetes take his reply to amount to a declaration on oath, others construe it as no more than a declaration, others see in it an evasion, and a few even find in it a rejection of the oath. The most likely interpretation is that Jesus makes a simple declaration which at the most involves tension, but not contradiction, with Mt. 5:33ff. In the post-NT period baptism is regarded as a kind of exorcism (cf. Justin *Dialogue* 30; 85).

epíorkos. This word means "perjured." The one NT instance is in 1 Tim. 1:8ff., which states that the law is good but is not given for the justified but for sinners, among whom are perjurers.

epiorkéō. This word means "to be a perjurer," i.e., "to commit perjury," "to break a vow." It occurs in the NT in Mt. 5:33. Formerly false swearing was forbidden, but now there is to be no swearing at all. The Didache seems to reverse this by simply forbidding perjury (2.3).   [J. SCHNEIDER, V, 457-67]

→ *omnýō*

> *hormḗ* [impulse],   *hórmēma* [violent rush],   *hormáō* [to set out, rush head-long],   *aphormḗ* [impulse, occasion]

hormḗ, hórmēma, hormáō.

A. **Extrabiblical Usage.**

1. From a root meaning "flowing," *hormḗ* has various senses denoting the start of a rapid movement. The verb *hormáō* means "to set in rapid motion," "to impel," and intransitively "to go out," "to storm out," "to originate." Psychologically the words find common use for impulses, strivings, inclinations, longings, or even demonic impulses. The strivings may be good, but in Stoicism they may also be contrary to reason or nature.

2. Philo is fond of the concept. *hormḗ* distinguishes beings with souls, and is good so long as it is under the control of the *lógos*, e.g., as a striving for piety, virtue, or immortality.

B. The Word Group in the OT. There is little psychological use of the group in the LXX. Its original sense comes out best when it is used for flowing water (Prov. 21:1) or other forms of movement (often violent). (For details cf. *TDNT*, V, 469-70.) Even where the LXX uses the group for emotion, it denotes a power of violent effort which goes beyond the conscious will. It is thus used sometimes to describe divine intervention in a way which accords well with the OT concept of God.

C. The Word Group in the NT. Like the LXX, the NT does not put the group to psychological use. In Mk. 5:13 and parallels it describes the senseless flight of the swine into the water under the grip of demonic impulsion. In Acts 7:57; 19:29 it is aptly used in relation to mob action. In Acts 14:5 a stroke is planned but no subject is given. In its one NT occurrence in Rev. 18:21 *hórmēma* obviously bears a connection to the wrath of God but its immediate reference is to the storm against Babylon or to the city's violent fall. Behind Jms. 3:4 stands neither the pressure on the rudder nor the purpose of the helmsman but an element of caprice. The images of the bit and the rudder are common ones in antiquity (cf. Philo) and often bear an optimistic sense. In James the point seems to be the more realistic one that as the horse cannot resist the bit or the ship the rudder, so we humans are helpless against the *hormḗ* or caprice of that little but powerful member, the tongue.

D. The Postapostolic Period. *hormḗ* and *hormán* are rare in the first Christian writings outside the NT. We find the sense of caprice in Diog. 4.5 and that of striving in Justin *Apology* 58.3; *Dialogue* 8.3. The verb occurs for "to derive from" in Athenagoras *Supplication* 2.2.

aphormḗ. This word has such various senses as "start," "origin," "cause," "stimulus," "impulse," "undertaking," "pretext," "possibility," "inclination," "opportunity," and even "aversion." Its use in the LXX in Ezek. 5:7 alters the sense by establishing a connection of the people with the Gentiles. It is added in elucidation in Prov. 9:9. In the NT it occurs only in Paul except for an alternative reading in Lk. 11:54, where it has a derogatory sense. In 2 Cor. 5:12 the term has the neutral sense of "cause" or "occasion," but in 11:12 it has more of the sense of "pretext": Paul hopes by his conduct to counter the deceptive pretexts that his opponents seek against him. What he probably has in view is that he is blamed for not claiming support, but would be no less blamed, i.e., accused of avarice, were he to claim it. In Gal. 5:13 the flesh (*sárx*) seeks a pretext, or starting point, or opportunity, in Christian freedom, as does the enemy in widowhood in 1 Tim. 5:14, and sin in the law in Rom. 7:8, 11. It may be noted that the things that offer occasion are themselves good but they may be turned to evil. In 1 Tim. 5:14 remarriage is recommended because it offers some safeguard, but in Rom. 7:8ff. the law is used by God to unmask the true nature of sin inasmuch as sin is incited by it to open resistance against God. This does not mean that the law instigates sin any more than that God's prohibition in Eden instigates the disobedience of Adam and Eve, or Christ's coming instigates the sin of his rejection. It simply means that the flesh, or sin, or the devil uses the good gifts of God as deceitful occasions for leading people astray. Yet God is in no sense defeated thereby, for in his inscrutable counsel his good gifts serve in this way to unmask sin by offering it a fresh impetus. Thus the rather formal concept of *aphormé* takes on a more material character in the NT, finding a place alongside such terms as "offense" and "temptation," and such figures of speech as "nets" and "snares."

[G. BERTRAM, V, 467-74]

óros [mountain]

tó óros means "mountain" or "mountain range," plural "mountains" or "mountain range."

A. The Mountain in Antiquity.

1. As striking natural phenomena, mountains have always been honored as gods or as abodes of the gods. Gods of light and life are connected with their peaks, those of darkness and death with the inner parts of mountains or with mountain woods or deserts. A common mythological concept is that of the primal mountain.

2. In the Near East mountains are often figures for power. To the Babylonians mountains are remote and inaccessible, and there are eastern and western mountains on which the arch of heaven rests (cf. the two pure and two dark mountains of the Mandaeans). Various references are made to the mountains where gods were born, to the mountain of assembly where they meet, to the mountain of winds whose top reaches the heavens and whose base is in the sea, etc.

3. The Greeks praise their wooded mountains as an adornment of their land. They derive from them a sense of power and associate them (especially Olympus) with the gods. Soaring up to heaven, Olympus symbolizes natural and ethical perfection.

4. In Asia Minor worship of the great mother is linked to a mountain. The mother of nature is sensed in the storm and experienced in ecstatic dancing in the woods by night. The mountain belongs here to the darker side of life (cf. Cybele's link with mountain caves).

5. In Syria and Palestine divine honors are paid to mountains as such, and cultic worship takes place on them. Mountains are also abodes and places of assembly for the gods. Here, too, they are used as symbols of power.

B. The Mountain in the OT and Judaism.

1. The LXX almost always uses *óros* for Heb. *har,* which also means either a single mountain or a range. In 2 Sam. 1:6, 21 the MT and LXX vacillate between the singular and the plural for Mt. Gilboa.

2. There are many references to hills in the OT. Later the hills are denuded of trees (earlier cf. Josh. 17:18). We thus read mainly of pastures (Ps. 147:8). The hills are suitable for beacons (Is. 13:2). Messengers can be seen on them from afar (Is. 52:7). They offer extensive views (Dt. 34:1ff.). Voices carry across them (2 Sam. 2:25-26). But they hamper travel (2 Kgs. 19:23). Lonely (1 Sam. 23:14), they are a shameful place to die (Ps. Sol. 2:26) but also a refuge (Judg. 6:2).

3. In prophecy and poetry mountains display God's power. God establishes them (Ps. 65:6), weighs them (Is. 40:12), crushes them (41:15), turns them (Job 9:5), and levels them (Is. 40:4). They tremble before him (Judg. 5:5), are consumed by him (Dt. 32:22), and melt before him (Mic. 1:4). The mountain may also symbolize political power (Jer. 51:25; Dan. 2:44). In Eth. En. 18:13 etc. the fallen angels are burning mountains, and in 52:2, 6-7 iron and gold mountains represent the power of

iron and gold. In rabbinic writings the evil impulse is presented as a great mountain that the righteous must overcome, and mountain is used as a title of honor for eminent people. Authoritative sayings are also compared to mountains.

4. Topographical changes are expected in visions of the last time. The mountains will drip with wine (Am. 9:12). They will be levelled for the returning exiles (Is. 40:4). At the end the Mount of Olives will disappear (Zech. 14:4) and Mt. Zion will be higher than all other hills (Mic. 4:1).

5. The OT associates mountains with God's proximity. Isaac is to be offered on a mountain (Gen. 22:2). Moses prays on a hill (Ex. 17:9-10). Blessings and curses are issued from the two mountains (Dt. 11:29). Elijah prays on Carmel (1 Kgs. 18:42). Circumcision takes place on a hill (Josh. 5:3), the ark is set on a hill (1 Sam. 7:1), and Samuel sacrifices on a high place (9:12ff.). David captures Jerusalem, and Solomon builds a temple on a projecting height. Zion then becomes the sign of God's presence and the only legitimate place of sacrifice. Yet God is not specifically a mountain God (1 Kgs. 10:23, 28-29), and Sinai and Zion are not holy places as such. Zion is the hill that God has chosen. Prophecies are uttered from mountains (Balaam in Num. 23:7, and cf. 1 Sam. 10:5), but the great writing prophets have no particular mountain connections.

6. There is little mountain mythology in the OT. Poetic allusions or echoes may perhaps be found in Gen. 49:26; Pss. 68:15; 48:2; Zech. 6:1. Is. 14:12ff. and Ezek. 28:11ff. make ironical use of the myth of a mount of the gods in songs that mock the downfall of pagan rulers. The pseudepigrapha take up mythical themes more strongly, e.g., in equating paradise and the mount of God (Eth. En. 24–25). The reason why mythological imagery is less important in the OT is not that it opposes a spiritual to a sensory depiction but that its concern is with the God who acts in history.

C. The Mountain in the NT.

1. In the NT, too, the *óros* is either the single mountain (Jn. 4:20-21) or the range (Mk. 5:11). The plural denotes a range in Mt. 18:12; Mk. 13:14, etc.

2. Many sayings reflect Palestinian geography, e.g., the city on a hill (Mt. 5:14), the sheep left on the hills (18:12), the faith that moves mountains (Mk. 11:23), the cry to the mountains to give cover (Lk. 23:30), and the warning to flee to the mountains (Mk. 13:14). Mountains named are Gerizim (Jn. 4:20-21) and Olives (Lk. 19:37), and cf. the hill on which Nazareth lay (Lk. 4:29).

3. Jesus often goes up into mountains (Mt. 5:1; Mk. 3:13; Mt. 15:29, etc.). He prays in the mountains, perhaps for solitude (Mk. 6:46; 1:35). He teaches on a mountain in Mt. 5:1ff., possibly because the voice carries well there, possibly to make the crowds decide whether to follow him, possibly to gain the effect of withdrawal from everyday surroundings, possibly to offer a parallel to the giving of the law on Sinai.

4. Traditionally the transfiguration takes place on Mt. Tabor. The name is not important for the NT authors, and it is not so likely that Jesus would go to Tabor from Caesarea Philippi. The mention of a high mountain perhaps suggests that Jesus uses the evocative significance of the mountain to attune the disciples to the world of God. The mount of temptation (Mt. 4:8) cannot be pinpointed with accuracy. Surveying all the kingdoms of the world is represented as looking out from a high mountain; Luke simply says that "the devil took him up." There is a parallel in Rev. 21:10 (cf. Ezek. 40:2), where looking out from a high mountain symbolizes the surveying of eschatological events in the Spirit.

5. The NT contains some important eschatological sayings about mountains. Lk.

3:4-5 gives wider range to Is. 40:3ff. The image in Rev. 8:8 is that of destructive power. The shaking of the mountains in Rev. 6:14 announces the shaking of heaven and earth. The mountains and islands disappear in 16:20, and then heaven and earth perish at the climax in 20:11. The islands are places of security for the Gentiles and the mountains are symbols of power. The point, then, is the shaking and then the destruction of pagan power and security. No new mountain replaces the old ones in Revelation, just as there is no new temple or altar in the new world where God dwells among us (Rev. 21:3). Revelation also uses óros for the seven hills on which the woman is seated. These are probably not the seven hills of Rome in any specific sense, since Babylon represents secular power and culture in a more general way, and the number seven denotes this totality. The world (cf. 1 Jn. 2:16) is enthroned on all the world powers, the hills, and antichrist, the beast, has the nature of these powers (17:11).
→ Siná, Sión   [W. FOERSTER, V, 475-87]

> *orphanós* [orphan]

1. This word means "bereaved," "without parents or children," "orphaned," "orphan." In the LXX it is usually associated with "widow" (Is. 1:17). Occasionally it has the figurative sense of "abandoned," "deprived."
2. The word occurs twice in the NT. Jms. 1:27, echoing the OT, calls for the protection of widows and orphans (cf. Ex. 22:21). This is in accord with the teaching and legal practice of Judaism, and similar exhortations occur in Barn. 20.2; Hermas *Mandates* 8.10, etc. The second NT instance is in Jn. 14:18, where the use is figurative. Jesus will not leave his disciples "orphaned," i.e., "abandoned" or "unprotected."
[H. SEESEMANN, V, 487-88]

> *hósios* [holy, devout],   *hosíōs* [devoutly],   *anósios* [impious],   *hosiótēs* [holiness]

hósios, hosíōs.
1. Greek Usage.
   a. A first reference of these terms is to actions that are regarded as "sacred," "lawful," or "dutiful," i.e., good from the standpoint of morality and religion, no matter whether they are based on divine precept, natural law, ancient custom, or inner disposition. When combined with *díkaios,* what is indicated is that which corresponds to both divine and human law.
   b. A second reference is to persons who feel awe before the gods and eternal laws, i.e., "pious" or "devout." A narrower use is for initiates. Only rarely is the term applied to God himself.
   c. A third reference is to "pure" or "sanctified" things.
2. LXX. In the LXX *hósios* is plainly distinct from words like "righteous," "pure," or "devout." In its primary human reference it denotes those who are pledged to obedience to God. Originally this covers the whole people, but since the people includes some who are ungodly, it comes to characterize those who are ready to fulfill covenant obligations. What counts here is dutiful acceptance of the relations to God and others. Toward the end of the OT, the term is thus used for the quiet in the land

who are faithful to the law, who oppose Hellenization, and who will finally take up the struggle for freedom in the Maccabean revolt, but then withdraw when this struggle loses its religious emphasis.

3. *The NT. hósios* occurs only eight times in the NT (five in quotations), and once as an adverb in 1 Th. 2:10. It is common (with *anósios*) in the Pastorals. It is obviously not a leading concept in the church's vocabulary, nor do believers use it for themselves.

a. In quotations (Dt. 32:4; Ps. 145:17), Rev. 15:4 and 16:5 use it of God. God is righteous and holy in vindicating persecuted believers and judging malefactors.

b. *hósios* occurs three times in quotations in Acts. In 2:27 and 13:35 (quoting Ps. 16 and Is. 55:3) it refers to Christ; he is "the holy one of God" and the "holy" blessings of David are promised to him. Jesus is also called *hósios* in Heb. 7:26. In mind and conduct he perfectly fulfils the divine requirements, and therefore he does not need to make an offering for himself, as the OT priests do.

c. The group mostly has a human reference in the NT, four times with *díkaios*. Paul in 1 Th. 2:10 has satisfied divine and human law by his "holy" and righteous conduct in his apostolic work. Bishops must be upright and "holy" if they are to do their work properly (Tit. 1:8). Hands that are lifted up to God in prayer should be "holy," thus symbolizing freedom from ungodly thought or action.

4. *hósios* and *anósios* occur in the apostolic fathers only in 1 and 2 Clement.

anósios. This word refers 1. to "impious" acts that transgress ancient laws and 2. to "impious" persons. It occurs twice in the NT for impious persons who impiously reject sacred obligations. "Ungodly" might fit the context of 1 Tim. 1:9, but "devoid of piety" is obviously meant in 2 Tim. 3:2 (cf. the sequence).

hosiótēs. This word denotes personal "piety," whether toward God or parents, as a disposition that has regard for eternal ordinances. In the NT it occurs twice in the phrase "in holiness and righteousness." In Lk. 1:75 it refers to the life of believers in the age of salvation, and in Eph. 4:24 to the new nature that results from regeneration.

[F. HAUCK, V, 489-93]

---

osmē [smell, fragrance]

A. The Meaning outside the NT.

1. The meaning of this word is "smell," either good, bad, or neutral. In antiquity it is thought that the scent of water can give new growth to a withered tree (cf. Job 14:9). Odors are regarded as exhalations of mist and air that have the power to give either life or death.

2. Along these lines divine savors play an important role in theophanies. An inscription speaks about a deified boy giving off sweet scents that give life to flowers growing out of his grave. A tree with a sweet smell will give life to the righteous (Gk. En. 25:4, 6).

3. The OT refers to the sweet savor of sacrifice that causes God to be favorably disposed to worshippers (Gen. 8:21). Lack of savor is a sign of rejection (Lev. 26:31). In offerings to idols (cf. Ezek. 6:13) there is perhaps some thought that the scent gives power to the gods. Tob. 8:2-3 reflects the notion that scents can serve as a safeguard against hostile forces. Wisdom gives off a scent, i.e., vitality for righteous living (Sir.

24:15), and the righteous are summoned to give out a sweet savor in praise of God (39:14).

B. The NT.

1. The literal sense occurs in Jn. 12:3.

2. A figurative use of the idea that the scent of sacrifice is pleasing to God occurs in Eph. 5:2. The combination with love suggests that God's pleasure is in the loving and vicarious self-offering of Jesus. Paul also calls the gift of the Philippians a fragrant offering in Phil. 4:18. As a demonstration of love, it is a pleasing sacrifice to God.

3. The idea of scents dispensing life and death occurs in 2 Cor. 2:14ff. The knowledge of God in Christ gives life to the apostle. Carrying the savor of Christ, he brings life (in the power of God) to those who believe, but judgment to those who do not. On the one hand, then, we have life from life, but on the other, for those who do not find freedom from the power of death at work in them, death from death.

[G. DELLING, V, 493-95]

> *osphýs* [hip, loins]

osphýs, meaning "hip," is common in the LXX, e.g., in the phrase "to gird up one's loins," for travel, work, battle, etc. (used of the Messiah in Is. 11:5). Under OT or LXX influence it occurs eight times in the NT. In relation to the Baptist in Mk. 1:6 and Mt. 3:4, a comparison with Elijah is suggested. In Lk. 12:35ff. the thought is that of vigilant readiness. Eph. 6:14 applies Is. 11:5 to the warring believer in a figurative sense. Also figurative is 1 Pet. 1:13 with its admonition to be ready and watchful. Another OT usage stands behind Heb. 7:5, 10; Acts 2:30 (cf. Gen. 35:11; 2 Chr. 6:9; Ps. 132:11), namely, that for descent. "Prior to his birth" is thus the point in Heb. 7:10.   [H. SEESEMANN, V, 496-97]

> *ouranós* [heaven], *ouránios* [heavenly], *epouránios* [heavenly], *oura-nóthen* [from heaven]

ouranós.

A. Greek Usage.

1. The Basic Idea. *ouranós* in the singular means "heaven" either as the overarching firmament or as that which embraces all things. This duality is already present in the notion of the cosmic egg, in Homer's view of a solid heaven on pillars which can yet be called the abode of the gods, or in Plato's use of heaven for both the cosmos and the perfect or the absolute (cf. also Aristotle, the Stoics, and the Gnostics). There is one heaven, but it is given both a natural and a divine reference, with a realistic, symbolical, or figurative link. Up to a later period we find representations of the god Uranos.

2. The Cosmological Sense. In Homer heaven is a solid vault or half-globe (of iron or brass). An effort is made later to understand heaven in terms of thought and experience. The phrase "heaven and earth" is common, and "under heaven" also comes into use. Heaven is the cause and prototype of all being and may be equated with the universe or cosmos. For Plato it is the starting point for the contemplation of being and for absolute knowledge.

3. *The Mythological Sense.*

a. The God Uranos. Uranos is a god of pre-Homeric religion. He is emasculated and overthrown by his son Cronos, who is then replaced by Zeus, but depictions of Uranos continue into the period of the empire.

b. The Abode of the Gods. Heaven in this sense is Olympus; the Olympians are dwellers in heaven. The lord of heaven is the lord of the universe (Zeus). Prayer is made to heaven, oaths are taken by heaven, and crimes can reach to heaven.

c. Orphic Writings. These integrate heaven and earth (cf. the cosmic egg, of which heaven is the upper shell). Initiates recapture this unity by becoming divine. Heaven is also presented as the mantle of the world.

d. The Magic Papyri. Heaven is important in these papyri, e.g., in invocations.

4. *Gnosticism.* In the Hermetic writings heaven is divided into seven "cycles." It is created by the demiurge and serves as his dwelling. It lies above ether, air, and earth. The heavenly god is a bad god; mysteries are shut up in heaven, necessity rules there, and its inhabitants have demonic souls. Light brings liberation from it. The upward journey leads through the heavenly spheres. In general, heaven is a sign of dualism; the view of it is profoundly pessimistic.

5. *Philo.* Philo combines Plato, Stoicism, and the OT. Heaven and earth for him are God's votive offering. Heaven, which is noncorporeal, represents the cosmos, although it has a material counterpart. The heavenly man is the prototype of the earthly, but man himself is a heaven with starlike natures. Heaven for Philo is a sign of cosmic unity and helps to effect it.   [H. TRAUB, V, 497-502]

B. The OT.

1. *Heaven in Ancient Israel.* The Hebrew term for heaven is *šāmayim* (a plural word of obscure etymology). It is first depicted as something fixed, with windows, pillars, and foundations. It is largely equivalent to "firmament." Above it is the heavenly ocean which can bless with rain or destroy with flood. Heaven can also denote the atmosphere, but is not limited to this sense. Heavenly spheres are sometimes suggested (cf. the "ends" of heaven), but the phrase "heaven of heaven" is largely hyperbolical. "Days of heaven" is a phrase that denotes lasting duration (Dt. 11:21). The cosmos consists of heaven, earth, and the lower waters (Ex. 20:4), but often only heaven and earth are mentioned. Only fragments of mythical ideas occur. In poetic imagery heaven is a tent (Is. 40:22), or a stretched out scroll (34:4). It has chambers for snow, hail, wind, and water (Job 37:9; 38:22, 37). It is also a place of signs and calendar references. In general it is presented on the basis of simple observation.

2. *God and Heaven.* God created heaven (Gen. 1:1). He dwells in it, although he also dwells in the sanctuary, the ark, etc. Possibly the twofold dwelling reflects Near Eastern ideas of temples of dwelling and temples of manifestation. While the ark, e.g., is a place of temporary presence, heaven is the real abode of God. Yet the OT presentation is complex. The belief that God is the God of heaven is undoubtedly ancient, as is the concept of the heavenly court and the heavenly host (1 Kgs. 22:19ff.; Job 1:6ff.). There may be some influence here of the Canaanite pantheon, but the depiction is fluid, for the heavenly host may consist of spirits (1 Kgs. 22:19), but it may also be the heavenly army (Josh. 5:14), or simply the stars (Gen. 2:1). The cult of the host of heaven is sternly resisted (2 Kgs. 17:6; cf. Jer. 7:18). Because God dwells in heaven, hands are lifted up to heaven in oaths (Dt. 32:4) or prayer (Ex.

9:29), and God is asked to look down from heaven (Dt. 26:15). Deuteronomy explains that in the Sinai revelation God really speaks from heaven, not from the mountain (4:36), and if God dwells in the sanctuary, it is as he sets his name and causes it to dwell there, the name representing God's turning to Israel in self-revelation (cf. Dt. 12:5, 11; 14:23-24; 26:2). In cultic practice, of course, the main concern is with the manifestation. Ezekiel depicts the throne-carriage coming forth from heavenly transcendence, but his message has to do with the revealed God. Earth is God's sphere of dominion (Dt. 4:39), but heaven itself cannot contain him (1 Kgs. 8:27). Enthroned on high, he rules on earth (Ps. 113:5-6). In times of affliction he seems to be wrapped in clouds (Lam. 3:44), and prayer is made that he will rend the heavens and come down (Is. 63:19). Eliphaz accuses Job of thinking that thick clouds cover him so that he cannot see (Job 22:13). Ecclesiastes warns against foolish talk in view of the divine transcendence (5:2). In the main, however, the OT links God's dwelling in heaven with his mighty works on earth. The "God of heaven" of the later period is the God who in historical omnipotence controls the destinies of empires and works out his plan for the world.

3. *Heaven as the Place of Salvation.* As the dwelling of God, heaven is the source of blessing, the setting of life, and the place where God's planned salvation is already present. The isolated idea of rapture (2 Kgs. 2:11) relates to this concept. The thought of God's word being fixed in heaven (Ps. 119:89) has a more general application (cf. 89:2). There is a model of the earthly tabernacle in heaven (Ex. 25:9, 40), and Ezekiel (2:1ff.) refers to a roll that is preexistent in heaven. In the visions of Zechariah the kingdom of God is already prepared in heaven. In Dan. 7:13ff. the kingdom of the Son of Man is one that comes down from heaven in contrast to the earthly empires that come up from below (v. 17). Since heaven is also created, it, too, may be shaken (cf. Am. 8:9; Jer. 4:23ff.). A cosmic collapse is foreseen in Is. 51:6, and a new heaven and earth will be created according to 65:17. Thus heaven itself is drawn into the circle of soteriology. But heaven is never of primary interest in the OT; even when salvation comes from heaven, the central point is that it comes to earth. Only once (Dan. 4:23) is heaven substituted for the name of God, though cf. Ps. 73:9; Job 20:27.

[G. von Rad, V, 502-09]

C. The LXX and Judaism.
I. The LXX.
1. Additions.

a. *ouranós* is used 667 times in the LXX, sometimes in additions. These may be designed to give greater vividness (cf. Josh. 8:21; Ex. 9:29; Dt. 9:15; Job 7:9, etc.).

b. Another reason for adding *ouranós* may be to give greater concreteness (cf. Is. 8:21; 24:18, 21; 38:14).

c. At times the belief that God the Creator is linked with heaven is the reason for adding *ouranós* (cf. Ps. 91:1; Is. 14:13; Job 22:26). There may be anticipations here of the substitution of heaven for the name of God, or the point may be to protect the divine transcendence.

2. *The Plural ouranoí.* The LXX has the plural 51 times. It is alien to secular Greek and follows Hebrew usage. It occurs mostly in the Psalms or similar pieces (cf. 1 Sam. 2:10; Dt. 32:43). The only prose use is in 2 Chr. 28:9, but it becomes more common in 2 and 3 Maccabees, Wisdom, etc. The phrase "heaven of heavens" (Dt. 10:14; 1 Kgs. 8:27) reflects the idea of a plurality of heavens but it is used to suggest the comprehensiveness of the universe and of God's dominion over it.

II. Judaism.

a. Judaism engages in speculation about heaven which leads to the idea of various heavens. These are usually seven in number, each with its own name and all loved by God. Other texts, however, speak of two, three, five, or ten heavens. En. 71:5ff. offers a vivid description of the heaven of heavens with the Ancient of Days, the seraphim, angels, etc. in a house of crystal stones with living fire running between them.

b. Another development in Judaism is the widespread use of heaven instead of God.

c. Judaism expects a new creation in the last time in the form either of a transfiguration or of a complete destruction and replacement of the old creation.

D. The NT. *ouranós* occurs 284 times (94 in the plural) in the NT. It is most common in Matthew (84 times) and Revelation (54). It is chiefly used in Matthew in the formulas "Father in heaven" and "kingdom of heaven" (plural in both instances). The plural usage of the NT derives mainly from Jewish sources, although Hellenistic Gnosticism might have had some influence on Eph. 1:10; 4:10; 6:9; Col. 1:16, 20, and just possibly Heb. 4:14; 7:26; 9:23. NT usage in general reflects on the one side the ancient view of heaven as a vault and on the other side the belief that heaven is the divine sphere from which God comes down. These ideas go together, for the relation to God involves the cosmological sense, and the cosmological sense the relation to God. The cosmos is "heaven and earth," with heaven as the controlling part. The integration of the two is God's work. Their relationship symbolizes that of Creator and creation (cf. Is. 55:9).

1. Heaven and Earth.

a. With earth, heaven was created by God (Acts 4:24; Rev. 10:6; cf. Acts 17:24). The creation of a new heaven and earth is promised (Rev. 21:1). Sin has disrupted the old creation, but the new creation is already prepared in God's saving purpose (2 Pet. 3:13; cf. Rom. 8:21ff.).

b. Heaven will pass away as well as earth (Mk. 13:31; Rev. 21:1; Heb. 12:26). Both are kept for destruction (2 Pet. 3:7), and they flee before God in terror (Rev. 20:11). The law is valid so long as the first heaven and earth remain (Mt. 5:18), but the word of Jesus will remain even when these perish (Mk. 13:31). The judgment of God on heaven and earth is the background to the true message of the NT, i.e., the intimation of what is enduring and unshakable (Heb. 12:27).

c. With earth, heaven stands under God's lordship. God is Lord of heaven and earth (Mt. 11:25; cf. Gen. 24:3). He is so not merely as Creator (cf. Rev. 17:24) but as Father, i.e., as God of the covenant. With Is. 66:1, Mt. 5:34 and Acts 7:49 describe heaven and earth as the absolute sphere of God's dominion. When the Son of Man comes, he will gather his elect from the ends of earth to the ends of heaven—an intentional paradox designed to indicate universal gathering.

d. Heaven and earth are given a new relation by Christ's saving work. This is expressed by the "in heaven and on earth" of Eph. 1:10 and Col. 1:16, 20. With "all things," this phrase denotes absolute comprehensiveness and yet also makes "all things" more concrete. Heavenly things are probably to be equated with the "invisible" things of Col. 1:16. The universe in this total sense is strictly related to Christ. Its very being is grounded in him through whom the work of reconciliation and peace is done. The formula serves as a basis for the idea of the body in Col. 1:18. Everything in heaven and on earth is integrated as a body whose head is Christ (Eph. 1:10, 21-22). In 1 Cor. 8:5-6 the many gods in heaven and on earth may be called lords but they have no reality. What is real is defined only by the one God and the one Lord. In Eph. 3:15

all families in heaven and on earth derive not merely from God the Creator but from the God who is the Father of Jesus Christ. In Rev. 5:3 Christ is the only one in heaven and on earth who can open the book, and in 5:13 all creation, in heaven, on earth, and under the sea, praises the Lamb. In Acts 2:17-18 the outpouring of the Spirit means signs and wonders in heaven above and on earth beneath. In Mt. 28:18 the risen Christ has all *exousía* in heaven and on earth; in virtue of his saving work, no entity exercises autonomy. The unity of heaven and earth that Christ's work effects finds expression in the petition of Mt. 6:10 that God's will be done on earth as it is (already) in heaven. Earth is taken up to heaven, or heaven descends to earth, yet heaven is superior because God's will is done there and his throne is set there (cf. Heb. 8:1, 4). To be sure, what is decided on earth is ratified in heaven (Mt. 16:19), yet only in the eschatological community in which God's will is already done and there is thus a unity of earth and heaven. In Lk. 15:18, 21 "heaven and you" represent heaven and earth, although here heaven probably stands for God. The *eis* means "against," not "up to heaven."

2. *God in Heaven.*

a. God is called the "God of heaven" only in Rev. 11:13; 16:11. This denotes an affinity of God to heaven but not vice versa, for heaven is God's work. What is implied is not just divine transcendence but divine dominion. God rules from heaven and initiates his saving work in heaven. "Father in heaven" in Matthew (5:16, 45; 6:1, 9, etc.) and Mark (11:25) has the same thrust but with more stress on the approach to humanity. Father is not just a substitute for God. Where "in heaven" is not added we mostly have statements of Jesus about his Father. Parallel sayings show that "in heaven" denotes God's freedom from restriction; he knows, sees, and can do all things. The "from" of Lk. 11:13 shows that God acts from heaven.

b. "Heaven" is sometimes thought to be used as a substitute for God, e.g., in the phrase "kingdom of heaven." Yet the NT shows no fear of using the name of God, and while heaven obviously relates to God, it may also help to define God's lordship as that which comes down from heaven. Heaven, then, carries a reference to God's saving work. God's kingdom sets heaven in motion (Mt. 3:2) and breaks in from it.

c. God's throne is in heaven, or is heaven itself (Heb. 8:1; Mt. 5:34). "Throne" here denotes government. The point is not that heaven is God's location but that it expresses his absolute and inviolable lordship.

3. *Heaven and Jesus Christ.*

a. Jesus Christ is awaited from heaven (1 Th. 1:10). He will come with the clouds of heaven (Mt. 14:62; 24:30); the expression implies apotheosis. His sign will be visible in heaven. Session at God's right hand is linked with coming from heaven (Mk. 14:62). In 1 Th. 1:10 Christ's raising from the dead is related to his coming from heaven (cf. 1 Cor. 15:23, 47). His resurrection is the basis of the parousia. When the Lord descends from heaven, the dead in Christ will rise (1 Th. 4:16). There will be a manifestation of what is concealed in heaven (2 Th. 1:7). In this concealment lies the *políteuma* of believers as they await their Savior from heaven (Phil. 3:20). Christ's coming means eschatological manifestation.

b. Since Jesus comes from heaven, it is natural to refer to Christ as the lord or master in heaven (Col. 4:1). This is not so much a reference to location as to rule. Christ is lord over believers and the ruler who sees and knows all things.

c. In Acts 2:32ff. raising up and exalting at God's right hand imply ascension (v. 34). One reading of Lk. 24:51 intimates ascent. In Acts 1:10-11 the disciples see Jesus go up as far as the sky, which is here the margin of the heaven that receives and conceals him. Heaven also stands for God's sovereignty that has still to be consummated on earth (2:35; 3:21). The determinative factor is that heaven is seen from the standpoint of the right hand of God (1 Pet. 3:22; Mk. 16:19). In Acts 3:21 heaven receives Christ in virtue of its concealing function. In Eph. 4:9-10, however, the picture differs. Christ ascends above the heavens, shattering the isolation imposed by evil forces. The ascent is Christ's triumphal procession through the subjugated zones of heaven. A similar thought is present in Rom. 10:6-7. In Jn. 3:13 only he who comes from heaven can mount up to it. God's saving will characterizes the heaven from which Jesus comes and to which he returns. The divine will and plan are "heavenly things" (3:12). The incarnation does not interrupt fellowship with the Father, for heaven is open to the Son (1:51), and he has his true existence there (15:16, 19; 1 Jn. 4:6). Coming from heaven, he is the true bread from heaven (6:41, 50-51). Only God can give this bread; it is uniquely the bread of God that gives life to the world (v. 33). Hebrews refers to Christ's session at God's right hand in heaven (8:1) and also to his passing through the heavens (4:14), or into heaven as the innermost sanctuary (9:24). Where heaven is the innermost sanctuary, it is thought of eschatologically as the perfect tent not made with hands. It is here in the presence of God that he has offered his once-for-all sacrifice of himself. Before God's face there are no more types or shadows but fulfilment. God is both high above heaven and yet also in heaven. In Col. 3:1 heaven is where Christ is, but only in the sense that this defines the purpose rather than the nature of heaven, i.e., to denote the right hand of God. In 1 Cor. 15:47 Christ is the second man from heaven in contrast to Adam as the first man from earth. Behind the phrase lies the idea of the primal man that is also found in Philo (with Platonic links). But Paul's use is different, for he stresses *sōma,* and his man from heaven belongs to the eschatological present understood as the last time. He thus selects the phrase more from the standpoint of exaltation, i.e.., the victory over death, than from that of eternity. The Christ who rose in the *sōma,* and is awaited from heaven, is the Christ who has come already in the incarnation. He is the initiator of the aeon of resurrection.

4. *Heaven Opened.* At the baptism of Jesus opened heaven corresponds to eschatological expectation. God is at hand in him (cf. Mt. 3:16). In Jn. 1:51 heaven is always open to Jesus. He is Bethel, the gate of heaven on earth. Opened heaven enables faith to see his glory (cf. Acts 7:56). Christ's messianic work is the basis of the opening of heaven. Hence the vision of open heaven in Rev. 19:11 is the revelation of Jesus Christ (1:1). Heaven is here a temple into which a door is opened (4:1). Peter receives his vision, too, from this opened heaven (Acts 10:11, 16; 11:5).

5. *Heaven as the Starting Point of the Event of Revelation.* God's revelations come from heaven. The voice at the baptism (Mk. 1:11) is God's authoritative voice initiating the eschatological aeon. The same applies to Jn. 12:28 and cf. Mk. 9:7; Rev. 10:4, 8; 11:12, etc., although in Revelation the voices are probably those of angels speaking with divine authority. Heb. 12:25 is perhaps referring to God's speaking from heaven. Like the voice, the Spirit also comes from heaven (Mk. 1:10; cf. Jn. 1:32). He is sent from heaven in 1 Pet. 1:12 (cf. Acts 2:2). Heaven denotes origin and authority. John's baptism is from heaven; hence its validity (Mk. 11:30). Not to acknowledge this baptism is to render futile the seeking of a sign from heaven (Mk. 8:11). The light from heaven in Acts 9:3 is a light from the Lord that leads to faith and knowledge. Jn. 3:27 says that we can receive only what is given from heaven; the reference is to the exclusiveness of God's saving lordship (cf. 6:65; 19:11). All giving is from the dominion of the Father of Jesus and beyond human control or influence. In Rom. 1:18

God's wrath is also revealed from heaven in and with the revelation of righteousness. OT figures are used to depict wrath concretely, e.g., fire from heaven (Lk. 9:54), or hailstones from heaven (Rev. 16:21). Closed heaven may also be a form of wrath, i.e., the withholding of rain and fruitfulness (Lk. 4:25; Jms. 5:18; Rev. 11:6).

6. *Heaven and the Blessings of Salvation.* As God's throne and the place from which Christ comes and to which he returns, heaven is a focus for present and future blessings in the new aeon, e.g., citizenship (Phil. 3:20), dwelling (2 Cor. 5:1), inheritance (1 Pet. 1:4), reward (Mt. 5:12), and treasure (6:20). Being in heaven, these blessings are with God or Christ, with whom believers already are, although incomprehensibly. The new Jerusalem is also present in heaven in the same reality and concealment (Rev. 3:12; 21:2, 10; cf. Heb. 12:22, 25).

7. *Heaven and the Angels.* Heaven is the sphere of angels and is served by them (Mt. 18:10). They come from it and return to it (Mt. 28:2; Lk. 2:15). The divine in Rev. 10:1 etc. sees them there. Their heavenly origin denotes their divine authority. If evil powers also seem to live in heaven (1 Cor. 8:5; Acts 7:42), the reference here seems to be to the firmament (though cf. Lk. 10:18; Rev. 12:7ff.). Satan's fall from heaven means that he can no longer stand in God's presence (Rev. 12:10). Since God's will is done in heaven, it is summoned to rejoice with those who overcome (12:12). Heaven is defined here in terms of the perfect service of God.

8. *Heaven as the Firmament.* This is the meaning when Jesus and others lift up their eyes to heaven (Mk. 6:41; Jn. 17:1; Acts 1:11). The sky hides God's throne but also signifies his ruling presence. Oaths and prayers are directed to it, i.e., to God. It also denotes the height of human arrogance (Mt. 11:23). Hypocrites interpret the signs in it but not the signs of the times (Lk. 12:56). Birds fly in it (Mt. 6:26). Stars falling from it are apocalyptic signs (Mk. 13:25). The final catastrophe is a collapse of the vault of heaven that shakes its powers (Mt. 24:29; Mk. 13:25).

9. *Heaven in the Plural.* Paul speaks of a rapture to the third heaven in 2 Cor. 12:2 (cf. v. 3) but says nothing specific about the three heavens. The things he hears are *árrēta*: they may not and cannot be uttered. The heavens of Hebrews are filled with ministering angels.

E. The Apostolic Fathers. The use in the apostolic fathers is much the same as that of the NT (and the LXX in 1 Clement). 1 Clement usually quotes in the singular but itself has the plural. There are OT and even Stoic echoes in what it says about God's creating and sustaining the heavens. Barnabas has OT quotations and touches on the ascension. In Hermas *Visions* 1.1.4 heaven opens and closes for the vision. Its unattainable height plays a role in *Mandates* 11.18. Did. 8.2 has the singular in the Lord's Prayer, and in 16.6 the opening of heaven is an apocalyptic sign. In Mart. Pol. 9.1 Polycarp hears a voice from heaven, and in 14.1 he prays toward heaven. Gnostic influences may be seen in 2 Clem. 1.16.3. Diog. 5.9 says that while Christians live on earth they are citizens of heaven. God sends down his truth and Logos, the Creator of the heavens, from heaven (7.2). In Ignatius *Smyrneans* 11.2 the work of believers is to be perfect on earth and in heaven, and in *Ephesians* 19.2 a star in heaven marks the incarnation.

ouránios. This word means "heavenly" with reference either to the sky or to the abode of the gods or to the gods themselves. With the latter reference, it has the sense of "divine." The immortal gods (especially Zeus) are heavenly beings. With the former reference, the word is used for the sun, the stars, the course of the stars, the pole, etc. Plato also connects the term with his ideas. In Gnosticism heavenly beings are intermediaries furnished with bodies. Philo speaks of the heavenly man by participation in whom we all dwell in heaven. "Heavenly" for him denotes divine origin; he can thus speak of heavenly virtue, insight, word, message, etc. For Josephus the word is imprecise. Pagan gods are heavenly, but so is the theme of philosophy. The LXX hardly uses the term, though there are a few instances in the pseudepigrapha. God opens the heavenly gates in 3 Macc. 6:18, and his host is heavenly in 4 Macc. 4:11. God is the heavenly Lord in 1 Esdr. 6:14. His children are heavenly in 2 Macc. 7:34, but in the sense that they have entered the heavenly sphere. The main NT use is in the phrase "your or my heavenly Father" (Mt. 5:48; 6:14; 15:13; 18:35). What is stressed here is the Father's openness and power as he effects the saving transition of the aeons. In Lk. 2:13 the host is heavenly; it consists of servants of God proclaiming from heaven God's saving work in the Savior's birth. Paul's vision in Acts 26:19 is heavenly; the vision is from the Lord and displays his resurrection power. In the apostolic fathers the only instance is in Mart. Pol. 22.3, which calls Christ's kingdom heavenly (cf. Diog. 10.2).

epouránios. *ep-* in this word means "at" or "in" rather than "upon." The term is used for the gods who dwell in heaven and come from it. It also has the sense of belonging to heaven. The divine word is said to be *epouránios*, and so is God, according to the Hermetic writings. *epouránia* are heavenly things. The term is rare in the LXX, but Philo uses it. In the NT it occurs both as an adjective and as a noun. Ephesians has the phrase "in the heavenlies" in 1:3, 20; 2:6; 3:10; 6:12. In some instances the meaning is much the same as "in the heavens." God's throne, government, and right hand belong here; this is the world of God and Christ. Yet in 4:10 Christ is exalted above the heavenly world and reigns over it. This world is filled with spiritual forces that constitute and dominate it. Christians share in Christ's rule over it (2:6), and in Christ they have blessings in it (1:3). They can withstand its forces as they follow Christ in his march through it (4:9-10). Through them God's mystery is disclosed to it (3:10). The phrase "in the heavenlies" brings out the cosmic significance of the event of revelation. In Hebrews the word is given its stamp by the idea of the heavenly sanctuary which the heavenly high priest enters to do his work (8:5; 9:23). The heavenly things are the truly real and eschatologically future things (8:2; 10:1). They stand for the consummation, and are not set in antithesis but simply in comparison (8:5; 9:23). Their essence lies in God's presence, from and to which alone there is reality (9:24). The inheritance is heavenly in virtue of its origin and goal (3:1). The heavenly gift (6:4) is eschatological salvation. The country (11:16) and Jerusalem (12:22) are heavenly because they are the final aim. The broad canvas of 12:22ff. also includes innumerable angels, the festal gathering, the firstborn enrolled in heaven, God the Judge, and Jesus the Mediator. In 2 Tim. 4:18 the kingdom of Christ is called heavenly with an emphasis on its consummation. In Phil. 2:6ff. "every knee" of Is. 45:23 is said to apply to heaven, earth, and under the earth. Heavenly powers, too, will recognize Christ's lordship, whether angels or hostile forces. In 1 Cor. 15:40 heavenly bodies exceed earthly bodies in glory. In vv. 48-49 the meaning is that as we have borne the image of the earthly one, so we shall bear the image of the heavenly one, i.e., we shall have membership in the risen Christ. In Jn. 3:12 the heavenly things embrace the descent and return of the Son of Man (vv. 13ff.) as these are grounded in the love of God and effected by the obedience of Jesus. They express the divine secret of revelation in the Son. In the apostolic fathers the plural noun occurs only in

Ignatius for "heavenly spirits" (*Smyrneans* 6.1). The term is used for God in 1 Clem. 61.2 and for Jesus in Mart. Pol. 14.3, both times with "eternal."

ouranóthen. This word means "from heaven" in the various senses of heaven. The LXX has it only in 4 Macc. 4:10. Philo uses it once in allegorical exposition of Ex. 22:25. The two NT instances are both in Acts. In 14:17 rain comes down from heaven both as falling from the sky and as sent from God. In 26:13 the light shines from the sky but it also shines forth from the Revealer. Pouring forth from him, it pierces the firmament.   [H. TRAUB, V, 509-43]

Ourías → *Thamár*

---

oús [ear],   ōtíon [outer ear],   ōtárion [outer ear],   enōtízomai [to hear]

---

oús.

A. Outside the NT.

1. Greek Usage. In Homer this word means the "ear" and also the "handle" of vessels. It is common later for the human or animal "ear." It occurs in various phrases, e.g., to bring to the ear, to strike the ear, to lend one's ears, to stop one's ears. The movement of air is thought to have a role in the hearing process, but the will can open or close the ears. The ear has a place in revelation as the organ for divine communications. Depictions of the ears of the gods may imply a request for hearing. Other votive ears may be ears cured of deafness or they may denote the hearing of requests. The Greeks, however, lay less stress on the ears of deity than Near Eastern lands. The use for "handle" as well as "ear" may be found in the papyri.

2. The OT.

a. The "ear" (Heb. *'ōḇîḇ*) is first the natural "ear" both human and animal (Gen. 35:4). Ears are adorned with pendants and rings. The ears of perpetual slaves are bored (Ex. 21:6).

b. The ear also denotes the function of hearing. By it statements and orders are noted. "Before the ears" for "in the presence" is a phrase that shows its importance (Gen. 23:10). Being heard, the spoken word is not just the expression of a thought but a concrete process (Gen. 20:8). The written word is meant to be heard (cf. Ex. 17:14; Dt. 31:11). When something important is revealed, the ear is uncovered (1 Sam. 20:2). The righteous stop their ears from hearing bloodshed (Is. 33:15). The ear is itself a subject in its critical activity (Job 12:11).

c. God has created the ear (Ps. 94:9), and we are thus responsible for its proper use. The greatest thing we can hear is God's word as it comes to and through the prophet (Is. 22:14). Yet more than natural hearing is needed for this; the ear may hear and yet be deaf (Is. 6:9-10). God himself decides whether to open the ear for understanding and faith (Is. 48:6ff.). Deaf ears will be opened in the messianic age (35:5). In priestly consecration the ears are important organs of priestly action and receive a sacred character by smearing with the sacrificial blood (Ex. 29:20).

d. The OT often refers to God's ears (e.g., Num. 14:28; 1 Sam. 8:21). Since the futile ears of idols are ridiculed (Ps. 135:17), the emphasis is on God's hearing and answering of prayer. That the thought is seen to be anthropomorphic emerges plainly in Ps. 94:9. The NT avoids such expressions except when quoting the OT.

3. Philo and Josephus.

a. Philo follows the OT pattern as regards the creation and use of the ear, but also attempts a natural explanation of hearing and a teleology of the ear along the lines of Greek philosophy. Greek influence may also be seen in his concern lest things heard by the ear should have a disruptive effect, in his giving precedence to the eye over the ear, and in his theory that the soul really hears rather than the physical organ.

b. Josephus, too, adopts the Greek differentiation of the soul from the body, and he thus offers a different presentation of the scene in Ex. 17:14 (*Antiquities* 3.59-60); cf. also Dt. 21:11 (*Antiquities* 4.210). The prophetic word comes through the souls of the prophets rather than their eyes or ears.

4. The Rabbis. The ear is of basic significance for the rabbis. God speaks into the ears of the prophets as we shout into the ears of neighbors. He has to incline to our weak ears. Human ears should be attuned to the law. Those who expound the law must bend their ears to it so that their hearers will hear aright. When God's voice sounds forth, it is not mystical but is heard with the actual ear; however, this rarely occurs. God judges the ear; hence one should not listen to unprofitable talk.

B. The NT.

1. The Synoptic Gospels and Acts.

a. Like the OT, the NT thinks of hearing in terms of the physical ear. Jesus heals real ears in Mk. 7:33; Lk. 22:50-51.

b. It is to the ear that Jesus speaks his message. He seeks to strike the real ears of hearers in their specific time and situation. His message is "today" an eschatological event (Lk. 4:21). The warning is given to hearers that they should have ears to hear (Mt. 11:15; 13:43; Mk. 4:9). The point is not just good hearing but right hearing.

c. In Mk. 7:31ff. a messianic sign is given (Is. 35:5-6) with the opening of the ears of the deaf man. In this instance Jesus does not shun using popular medicine to show on what members the miracle may be expected.

d. The ears of the disciples are blessed because they hear the proclamation of the age of salvation (Mt. 13:16). Jesus himself is the mystery of this age, and what they hear from him they are to tell on the housetops (Mt. 10:27). They must first be hearers before they can be preachers. The warning in Lk. 9:44 points to the mystery of the messianic way of suffering which only believing ears will later understand. In Lk. 1:44 the Holy Spirit has to open Elizabeth's ears to the true meaning of Mary's greeting; both women are in the sphere of the messianic event and the operation of the Spirit.

e. The true mystery of the divine rule of Jesus lies hidden in parables that some people hear only with the natural ear (Mk. 4:1ff.). Faith and understanding are connected with true hearing (cf. Mk. 4:20; Mt. 13:23; Lk. 8:15). In Lk. 4:21 the point is that the fulfilment is in the person of the one who puts it in their ears, so that it ought to penetrate their hearts as a living word. But hearing may bring hardening instead of faith (cf. the free rendering of Is. 6:9-10 in Mt. 13:11ff.; Lk. 8:10). While John (12:40) refers this prophecy to all the teaching of Jesus, the Synoptists refer it specifically to the parables. What distinguishes those who hear with faith and understanding from those who hear only with the natural ears is an awareness of the dawn of the divine lordship as it is visibly and audibly set before them in the person of him who proclaims it. The *hína* has the force of a very serious "in order that," but the *mépote* ("unless perhaps") leaves open a possibility of grace and conversion. Only God can open the ears, but the challenge to hear retains its full seriousness if the ear is to grasp this most astonishing of all messages. The disciples who do hear are like the remnant of Isaiah, and their ears are therefore blessed (Mt. 13:16). Yet even their ears have no certainty of true hearing (Mk. 8:18). They cannot take their understanding for granted but must strive to hear responsibly.

f. In Acts uncircumcision of the ears is connected with resistance to the work of the Holy Spirit (7:51). The stopping of the ears so as not to hear blasphemy is really a closing of the ears to the Spirit (v. 57). In Acts 28:25ff. Paul applies the saying in Is. 6:9-10 not merely to Jesus' own ministry but to the apostolic ministry. In contrast to unbelieving Jews, the Gentiles to whom he has been sent will listen.

2. *Paul's Epistles.* In Rom. 11:8, which quotes Dt. 29:3 supported by Is. 29:10, Paul echoes Is. 6:9-10. Trying to understand why Israel does not believe, he finds a divine stupefying that results in unseeing eyes and unhearing ears. In 1 Cor. 2:9 (which echoes Is. 64:3; 65:17; Jer. 3:16) eye, ear, and heart must first be freed by the Spirit if they are to see the good things that God has prepared for those who love him (cf. v. 10). The ear is one of the parts of the body listed in 1 Cor. 12:16.

3. *The Catholic Epistles.* In these epistles we have references to God's ears in OT quotations (Jms. 5:4 quoting Is. 5:9 and 1 Pet. 3:12 quoting Ps. 34:15). 1 Pet. 3:12 links the assurance of being heard with calling (v. 9) and obedience (v. 8).

4. *Revelation.* In each of the seven letters Revelation issues the challenge of Jesus to hear what the Spirit is saying (2:7, 11, 17, 29; 3:6, 13, 22). By the Spirit the risen Lord has a message for the readers and hearers of the prophecy (1:3). In 13:9 the shortened form of the common warning gives urgency to the threat and to the call for vigilance.

ōtíon. This diminutive means the "lobe" or "little ear." In the NT it occurs only in Mt. 26:51 (the cutting off of the ear at the arrest of Jesus). Lk. 22:50 uses *oús* and adds that it is the right ear. The healing love of Jesus stands in contrast here to the violence of a disciple who has not grasped the hour (Lk. 22:51).

ōtárion. This is another diminutive. It occurs in the NT in Mk. 14:47 and Jn. 18:10 in the story of the cutting off of the (right) ear at the arrest.

enōtízomai. This word, which means "to hear," "to listen," occurs in the NT only in Acts 2:14, where Peter asks his hearers seriously to listen to what he has to say.

[F. HAUCK, V, 543-59]

> *opheílō* [to owe, be under obligation],   *opheilḗ* [debt, obligation],   *opheílēma*
> [debt, obligation],   *opheilétēs* [debtor, someone under obligation]

opheílō.

A. Outside the NT.
1. Etymologically obscure, this word means "to owe someone something," e.g., loans, debts, sums, or rents. The things owed may be spiritual, and the word is also used with the infinitive for "to be under obligation to," "to have to." The word is common in respect of revenge or law. Transgressors are in debt to injured parties. Secular and sacral penalties are owed. God's goodness also makes people debtors. This gives rise to the idea of moral obligation.

2. Rare in the LXX, *opheílein* is used for owing money (Dt. 15:2), for owing offerings (Prov. 14:9), and for owing penalties (Job 6:20). The sense "I ought to"

occurs in Wis. 12:15; 4 Macc. 11:15. Only in the basic sense of owing money is there a Hebrew original. The OT thinks more in terms of obedience to the divine law than of inner obligation, but the idea develops that sin is indebtedness to God.

3. Philo follows Greek usage in speaking about inner moral obligation. This derives from the relation to God, from creation, and from law and sacred custom. Thus priests are under obligation to set aside secular things, the Gentiles owe worship to God, parents and children are under mutual obligations, physical cleanness is demanded as a sign of moral purity, and judges must be just to dispense justice.

4. Later Judaism often applies the idea of indebtedness to God, e.g., through falling into arrears in good works. Debt, then, becomes a common term for sin, and one's record with God is presented in financial terms. God will remit part of the debt in consideration of fasting, and payments can be made to offset arrears in the hope of a final balance.

B. The NT.

1. The *opheil-* group is common in the NT, and the use in Matthew is close to that of Judaism. Jesus often speaks about people being debtors to God (Mt. 6:12; 18:23ff.; Lk. 7:41; 17:10), but only in Mt. 6:12 is sin specifically equated with debt. Jesus uses the illustration of debt to explain the human situation vis-à-vis God. The debt is so great that no good deeds can offset it. We are totally dependent on the divine mercy. Remission is a matter of grace, but it imposes a corresponding obligation to forgive others. Refusal to do this brings with it the severe judgment of God. In Mt. 6:12 the readiness to remit the debts of others does not constitute a claim for divine remission but simply shows that no implacability on our part stands in the way of remission. In Mt. 23:16, 18 the oath imposes an obligation to God. Jesus uses *opheílein* with the infinitive only in Lk. 17:10 and Jn. 13:14. In general he does not refer to human obligations but speaks in direct imperatives, thus giving his demands an unconditional character.

2. In Phlm. 18 the word bears the literal sense. In Jn. 19:7 the point is that he "ought" to die (cf. Mt. 26:66). In Heb. 5:3 the reference is to the priest's legal duty. In 1 Cor. 11:7, 10 Paul finds in the Jewish custom something that is grounded in creation. In Rom. 13:8 he puns on the word; we are to owe nothing but love, which places us under an infinite obligation. In Rom. 15:1 we should support the weak, and in 15:27 we should repay spiritual goods with material goods. In 2 Th. 1:3; 2:13 thanksgiving is an obligation, and various other obligations are parental duty (2 Cor. 12:14), marital love (Eph. 5:28), sanctification (1 Jn. 2:6), self-sacrifice (3:16), love (4:11), and hospitality (3 Jn. 8). In the main these obligations toward others develop out of the preceding act of God or Christ, as the sentence construction shows (Rom. 15:3; Eph. 5:28, etc.).

3. A weaker sense of obligation may be found in Acts 17:20; 1 Cor. 5:10; Heb. 5:12.

opheilē. This word is common in the papyri for financial debts. In the NT it is used for debts in Mt. 18:32, for taxes and obligations (e.g., honor) in Rom. 13:7, and for the mutual obligations of spouses in 1 Cor. 7:3.

opheílēma.

1. This word means "debt" and in a broader sense "obligation." It occurs in the LXX for "debt" in Dt. 24:10. In later Judaism it is a common term for "sin." In the NT it occurs in Mt. 6:12 for "debt" in the sense of "sin" (cf. *hamartía* in Lk. 11:4). Paul uses it in Rom. 4:4: The reward for works is "something that is due."

opheilétēs.

1. This word first means "debtor." It has this sense in the NT in Mt. 18:24. In Jewish usage it also denotes one who is guilty of a fault (cf. Mt. 6:12; Lk. 13:4).

2. The word then means "someone who is under an obligation." Paul owes the gospel to Greeks and barbarians (Rom. 1:14), Gentile Christians owe the mother community material support (Rom. 15:27), those who accept circumcision are debtors to the whole law (Gal. 5:3), and those who trust in Christ are no longer debtors to the flesh.   [F. HAUCK, V, 559-66]

ophthalmodoulía → *doúlos; ophthalmós* → *horáō*

óphis [snake, serpent]

A. The Serpent in Antiquity.

1. As an Animal. As an alien animal the snake kindles similar reactions of aversion in various peoples. Its form of movement, its gliding, its stare, its sudden appearances, and its association with poison give rise to the idea that it is cunning, malicious, and hostile, although house snakes are often almost domestic pets.

2. As a Hostile Animal in Religious History. The snake as a hostile animal is often depicted in attempts to create fear, e.g., in descriptions of the underworld, or on the headband of the Egyptian king. From this it is only a step to the use of the dragon for chaos. The primal sea encompasses the earth like a serpent. In dualistic religions the serpent is a demonic animal in a narrower sense.

3. The Earthly Nature of the Serpent in Religious History. Creeping on the ground, the snake is a chthonic animal. It is dedicated to the gods of inner earth or connected with the god of ocean depths. In Greece it is associated with earth deities (Hecate, Demeter, and Kore) and with the realm of the dead. It is thus also a mantic animal which appears in dreams and gives oracles.

4. As an Animal of Life. By association with the resources of the earth the serpent can also become a symbol of fertility or a phallic symbol, thus appearing in birth stories. The sloughing off of its skin denotes rejuvenation. In places it is worshipped as divine. Egyptians keep snakes in their temples and domestic snakes are venerated. From ancient times serpents have connections with the worship of Zeus, and the serpent has an important role in Orphic cosmogony.

5. Summary. By a circular route the serpent of chaos becomes the primal serpent. This duality corresponds to that of nature, which gives life and also destroys life. Its alien character gives the serpent its preeminent role in religion. In the light of Scripture, however, the elevation of this cunning and harmful creature into a symbol of deity is a sinister indication of the intermingling of God and the devil.

[W. FOERSTER, V, 566-71]

B. The Serpent in the OT.

1. Linguistic Data. Snakes are common in Palestine, and the OT uses various terms for them, not all of which can be translated with zoological precision. In addition to ordinary snakes we find supernatural references or allusions in Is. 14:29; Ex. 7:9-10; Job 7:12; Is. 51:9; Ps. 104:26, etc. The snake is unclean in Israel because of its veneration by other peoples; it is not, then, to be used in sacrifice. (For details cf. *TDNT*, V, 571-72.)

2. The Nature of the Serpent. The OT observes the serpent with some precision, noting its strange progression, its hissing, its sudden attacks, its dangerous bite and poison (Gen. 3:14; Jer. 46:22; Gen. 49:17; Num. 21:6). Protection against it is a vivid metaphor for the divine protection (Ps. 91:13). It is a cunning animal that stands under God's curse (Gen. 3:1, 14-15). It thus symbolizes malignity (Dt. 32:33). It serves God when he punishes his people (Num. 21:6). In the last days peace with the snake is one of the marks of the messianic kingdom (Is. 11:8).

[O. GRETHER and W. FOERSTER, V, 571-73]

3. Gen. 3. The serpent has an important role in Gen. 3. The story is not a snake myth, for the serpent's role is secondary and is only that of a creature. Yet supernatural elements are used in depicting the serpent, e.g., its cunning, its knowledge of hidden things, and its hostile intentions. There are parallels elsewhere for the serpent's hostility to God and its purpose to destroy life. There is no actual parallel, however, to the biblical story of the fall, which engages in a measure of demythologizing by making the serpent so plainly a creature and asserting the sole deity of God as Creator and Lord. The tension in the story arises out of the tension in the human situation as the original harmony with God has been lost through apostasy. This apostasy is the result of a human decision, yet the impulse toward it comes from outside, and the serpent serves very well to suggest that behind the insoluble mystery of the entrance of evil into the good world of God lies the presence or activity of a force that is inimical to God. According to the sentence of Gen. 3:15 the cooperation between the serpent and humanity is turned into hostile confrontation. The reference is not simply to the natural threat of snakes but to the profounder threat presented by the power which is hostile to God and which continually presses humanity toward sin and death. Gen. 3:15 does not clearly predict an end to this conflict, but in the light of the new creation Christ may be validly seen as the serpent's conqueror.

4. Num. 21. The story of the brazen serpent (Num. 21:4ff.; Dt. 8:15) is theologically important. In contrast to other stories of murmuring, this story does not depict God as helping the whole people but only those who look at the symbol. The meaning is not, of course, that the looking has a quasi-magical effect, but that God has set up a sign of salvation that all can see and that can thus bring help to all who will turn to him.

[J. FICHTNER, V, 573-76]

C. The Serpent in Later Judaism.

1. The LXX.

a. Linguistic Data. The LXX uses various words for the many Hebrew terms, e.g., *óphis, drákōn, aspís, ékgona, aspídōn, basilískos, kerástēs.* Oddly, the rams of Jer. 50:8 become serpents (*drákontes*) in the LXX version. (For details cf. *TDNT*, V, 576.)

b. Material Data. In dealing with mythological allusions the LXX sometimes takes the way of excision (Is. 51:9), sometimes leaves names like Rahab as they stand (Ps. 87:4), and sometimes makes an ethical and religious application (Job 26:13; Ps. 89:10).

2. The Apocrypha, Pseudepigrapha, and Rabbis.

a. Metaphors. In these works serpents are often used for metaphorical purposes. The rabbis allude to the cunning of serpents. Their crooked ways are compared to those of government. The serpent illustrates cunning temptation in 4 Macc. 18:8, and Gentile kings display the poison of dragons and venom of asps in Damascus Document 8:9ff.

b. Mythological Echoes. Bel and the Dragon alludes to the temple snakes of Babylon. Slavonic Enoch depicts the gates of Hades as great serpents. Hades itself is a serpent in Apoc. Abr. 31:7. In the pseudepigrapha and rabbinic works Leviathan and Behemoth will be food for the righteous in the messianic age.

c. The Serpent of Paradise. At first no clear relation is seen between Satan and the serpent, but later the serpent is called an instrument of the devil, and then the two are equated. Attempts are made to supply motives for the serpent's actions, e.g., jealousy of Adam, refusal to bow to his rule, the desire for world dominion, and sexual desire.

d. Num. 21. One interesting comment on this story associates the healing, not with the brazen serpent as such, but with sincere subjection to the heavenly Father.

e. The Serpent and the Demonic. In the rabbis the serpent is close to the demonic world, as in occasional statements to the effect that demons and dragons howl in the desert, or that a dragon is the form in which an evil spirit is manifested. In view of the prodigal use of serpents in pagan religion the rabbinic aversion to snakes is understandable.

D. The Serpent in the NT.

1. In Similitudes. In Mt. 22:33 the serpent represents what is dangerous and malevolent. In Mk. 16:17-18 taking up serpents is a sign of the new aeon (cf. Lk. 10:19, where that which is menacing in natural as well as human life belongs to the kingdom of Satan). In Mt. 7:9-10 (cf. Lk. 11:11) the second member is sharper than the first, for a stone is useless but a serpent harmful. The point of the saying is that what is given in answer to prayer will be good. As regards Mt. 10:16 there are rabbinic parallels and the saying may well be proverbial. A direct reference to the fall is unlikely. The memorable feature in the exhortation is the unexpected combining of a serpent's cunning and a dove's innocence. Rev. 9:19 describes horses with tails like serpents. Their power to poison is thus worse than the power of the locusts (8:7ff.) to sting.

2. The Serpent of Paradise. Rev. 12:9 and 20:2 use the rabbinic expression "the ancient serpent," equating the *óphis* (or *drákōn*) with Satan. 2 Cor. 11:3 alludes to the deceiving of Eve by the serpent. It is unlikely that he has sexual temptation in view. In 1 Tim. 2:14-15 the point is the woman's receptivity to cunning arguments, and it is probably against this that Paul is warning the community in 2 Corinthians. The promise of Rom. 16:20 obviously rests on Gen. 3:15.

3. The Brazen Serpent. Paul refers to the brazen serpent in 1 Cor. 10:9 (perhaps with Ps. 78:18 in mind). Jesus uses the story in Jn. 3:14-15 to bring out the significance of his lifting up. The christological reference is distinctive.

E. Gnosticism. In Gnosticism the serpent plays a varied role, mostly as a symbol of evil. The *drákōn* is Satan, the tempter. *Óphis* is one of the devil's names. The *drákōn* is also equated with matter, which drags humanity down. Yet some sects call wisdom a serpent and oppose it to the demiurge.   [W. FOERSTER, V, 576-82]

→ *drákōn, échidna*

óchlos [crowd, throng, common people]

A. Nonbiblical Usage.

1. *óchlos* first means "crowd," a. as a "throng," b. as "the public" as distinct from private persons or small groups, and c. as "the mass" or "mob."

2. A second meaning is "host," "troop," "army," used especially for a. "lightly armed troops," b. the "baggage train," c. "common soldiers," d. "mercenaries," and e. "an irregular armed mass."

3. The word also has the sense of "people" or "population."

4. As a measure *óchlos* is a "great number."

5. A final sense is "unsettlement" or "harassment."   [R. MEYER, V, 582-84]

B. OT Usage.

1. Canonical Books. Almost completely absent from the older books, *óchlos* occurs later in such senses as a. "crowd," "assembly," b. "camp followers," "troops," "levy," or "armed mob," and c. "great number."

2. Apocrypha. The word has here such customary senses as a. "crowd," b. "army" or "camp followers," and c. "population."

C. *óchlos* as a Rabbinic Loanword. The rabbis use *óchlos* as a loanword (both Hebrew and Aramaic) for a "crowd," an "army," a "train" (of stars), and a "great number."   [P. KATZ, V, 584-85]

D. NT Usage.

I. The Meaning.

1. Crowd of People.

a. Except for Rev. 7:9; 19:1, 6, *óchlos* occurs only in the Gospels and Acts. In the former it usually denotes the crowd that runs to Jesus (Mt. 13:2), seeks him or goes to him (Lk. 8:40; Jn. 12:9), and accompanies him (Mk. 5:27; Lk. 7:9). Jesus calls it to him (Mk. 7:14) and pities it (Mk. 6:34). It wants to see his miracles (Lk. 6:19). Sometimes it throngs him (Mk. 3:9). It is closer to him than his family (Mk. 3:31ff.). It expresses joy, admiration, astonishment, and fear (Mt. 7:28; 9:8).

b. After Jesus finishes his acts or addresses, he leaves the people (Mt. 13:36). He then deals more specifically with the disciples (cf. Mk. 6:45). He heals the deaf mute away from the crowd in Mk. 7:33. The crowd argues about him (cf. Lk. 9:18). It welcomes him in Mt. 21:1ff.; the reference here is to Galilean pilgrims as distinct from the population of Jerusalem (v. 10). He is the subject of debate in Jn. 12:43 and prays for the people in Jn. 11:42.

c. The masses are at times distinguished from the rulers (cf. Mt. 14:5; Mk. 15:15), although the latter have to take them into account (cf. Mk. 11:18; Mt. 21:26). Jesus is accused of inciting the masses (Jn. 7:12; cf. Acts 24:12, 18). The rulers' scorn of the crowd comes out in Jn. 7:49. Fickle and easily swayed by propaganda, the crowd is induced to condemn Jesus (Mk. 15:11; cf. Lk. 23:48). The relation of the crowd to the apostles is similar (cf. Acts 8:6; 13:45; 14:11, 19; 17:8, 13, etc.).

2. "Host," "troop." This is the meaning in Mk. 14:43.

3. "People." The plural means "hosts of peoples" in Rev. 17:15.

4. Only Luke uses the term as a measure (Lk. 5:29; 6:17; Acts 1:15; 6:7; 11:24, 26).

II. óchlos and 'am hā'āreṣ.

1. The Johannine óchlos. The word has a special sense in John. It may have different references, e.g., to a Galilean crowd in 6:2 etc., or to the Jewish public in 7:11-12, or to the masses as distinct from the rulers (7:49), or to pilgrims at the feast (12:12), or to the many who believe because of Lazarus (12:9; cf. v. 11). In general, however, John has in view the common people, many of whom believe, many are opposed, and many also believe at first but then fall away.

2. The 'am hā'āreṣ. The judgment of the Pharisees in 7:49 stamps this crowd as a rabble that does not really know or keep the law. It is the *'am hā'āreṣ*. This term goes back to the OT and is at first a sociological one for the nobility or land-owning class. Later, however, it becomes a religious term for ordinary people who irrespective of social position do not live strictly according to the demands of the law. After A.D. 70 the Pharisees, by their ideological and organizational superiority, take advantage of political events to subjugate the *'am hā'āreṣ* to the rabbinate. Jn. 7:49 still contains a measure of social as well as religious contempt. This is probably because the common people, and especially Galileans, are more attracted to the message of Jesus in view of their eschatological hopes and their dislike of legalism. When Jesus disappoints these hopes his influence on the people wanes, and after the failure of major and minor revolts, and the destruction of the temple hierarchy, they fall under rabbinic control.

[R. MEYER, V, 585-90]

---

ochýrōma [stronghold, fortress]

This is a military term for a "fortified place." It is used only in the literal sense in secular Greek, but the LXX introduces a figurative usage (2 Sam. 22:2; Prov. 10:29). Here God is the stronghold. Philo then employs the term for the bastion of vaunting human reason (*On the Confusion of Tongues* 129-30). This is close to Paul's use of the term in 2 Cor. 10:4. Like Philo, he may have the tower of Babel in view, but he certainly wishes to stress both the strength of philosophical structures and even more so the power of spiritual weapons (under God) to lay them low.

[H. W. HEIDLAND, V, 590-91]

---

opsṓnion [wages]

This word means literally "what is appointed for buying food," then "money," then "military pay," then more generally official "salaries or wages."

1. In Lk. 3:14 the Baptist tells the soldiers to be content with their pay, putting God's command above claims that they can make good only by force.

2. In 2 Cor. 11:8 Paul uses the word for the support that is given him by the churches, thus suggesting that his work is a form of warfare, that he has a valid claim to support (even though in a venture of faith he does not assert it), and possibly that any support given can never be adequate recompense but only an "allowance."

3. In Rom. 6:23 the use of the word brings out three important points: a. that sin is a deceiver, promising subsistence but delivering death; b. that as wages are not a single payment, so death already casts its active shadow on life in an ongoing process; and c. that in contrast to the gift of life we have here a right, but a right that carries only judgment with it.

[H. W. HEIDLAND, V, 591-92]

π p

---

pagís [trap],   *pagideúō* [to entrap]

pagís. This word means "what fastens" or "holds fast." It is often used for a "net" or "snare," as well as for a "mousetrap." A vivid expression is "snatching at bread."

Figuratively the word is often used in connection with seductive women. The Trojan horse is also called "wooden *págis.*" A religious phrase is "to be caught in the net of Ate" (delusion or perdition or guilt). The LXX uses the term for snares, often figuratively (Ps. 69:22). The transferred sense stresses the crafty or destructive element (cf. Ps. 35:7). Often the suddenness of the destruction is to the fore. Later the usage is more stereotyped, e.g., for idolatry and for the "snares of the ungodly" (Jeremiah, Psalms, Proverbs). In Prov. 13:14 the reference seems to be to the divine punishment itself. The term is rare in the NT. In Lk. 21:34-35 Jesus warns his disciples to be on guard lest the last day come on them like a snare. 1 Tim. 3:7 warns bishops that bad conduct will bring them into disrepute and make them easy victims of the devil's wiles, so that they will be unfit for further service. 2 Tim. 2:25-26 shows that those who resist the Christian message are still in the snare of the devil; deluded by him, they are trapped into doing his will. The idea of gods and demons being equipped with traps and nets is ancient and widespread. The devil is not just an accuser but an active opponent who is at work to capture and destroy people. 1 Tim. 6:9 deals with the danger of the craving for wealth. This leads people into a snare. In the context of desires and destruction, this is clearly again the snare of the devil. In Rom. 11:9 (quoting Ps. 69:22), Paul uses *pagís* in connection with divine judgment. All that the people lives by and does is a snare, offense, and recompense. In the apostolic fathers Did. 2.4 uses the LXX phrase "snare of death" for a double-dealing tongue, and Barn. 19.8 uses it for the mouth in general.

pagideúō. This word occurs only in the biblical sphere and is perhaps coined by the LXX for "to lay a snare," "set a trap," "entice into a trap." The LXX uses it only in 1 Sam. 28:9 and Eccl. 9:12. Other versions of the OT have it in Ezek. 13:20-21; Is. 8:15; Prov. 6:2; 11:15. The only NT instance is in Mt. 22:15 where the Pharisees try to trap Jesus by asking him about paying taxes to Rome.

[J. Schneider, V, 593-95]

páthēma, pathētós, páthos → páschō

---

paideúō [to train, instruct], *paideía* [education, instruction], *paideutḗs* [teacher], *apaídeutos* [untrained, uninstructed], *paidagōgós* [attendant, guide]

The words *paideía* and *paideúō* relate to the upbringing of children, who need direction, teaching, instruction, and discipline. Both the way of education and the goal are indicated by *paideía*. Other words in the group are *paídeuma, paídeusis,* and various compounds.

A. The Orientation of the Concept in the Greek World. The group characterizes Greek culture and has remained a basic one in the development of all Western civilization.

1. Home Education among the Greeks.

a. Up to the Sophists. *paideía* is not known in Homeric Greece, where nobility rules, *aretḗ* is a divine gift, upbringing is physical, and education is simply the handing down of uses and customs according to rank. The Sophists challenge the aristocratic principle and advance the idea that culture can be acquired by teaching, thus giving the *paideía* concept its orientation.

b. The Classical and Later Periods. Plato distinguishes vocational training from *paideía* but includes music and gymnastics. Parents are primarily responsible, but they need direction. Aristotle distinguishes age groups and regards reading and writing as essential. The goal of personal education is virtue, and happiness is brought by culture. In Stoicism the aim, by way of self-scrutiny, is Hellenistic cosmopolitanism. The Roman ideal of firmness of character as the goal of education has an impact here (cf. also the Spartan system). A heroic attitude to fate offers freedom in relation to worldly values and makes even the renunciation of life easy. Plutarch argues that education is only for free males. The child is like the earth, the teacher like a farmer, the teaching like the seed. Boys are in the hands of carefully screened pedagogues, who, though slaves, are private tutors giving instruction in fear of God, uprightness, self-discipline, and courage. Parents must supervise, for culture is all-important, being divine and permanent. Above all, parents must teach by example. Fate itself plays a role in *paideía* by its chastisements, but the word is not used in nonbiblical Greek for corporal punishment.

2. *The Legislator and paideía.* Education in Greece is a public affair, for the relation to the state is at issue. Hence even ideas about family education are presented as legal demands. Man is by nature ordained for *paideía,* and *paideía* serves the security of the state and individual integration into society. Laws, then, order education. *paideía* is what distinguishes humans from animals or Greeks from barbarians. Lying myths, Plato thinks, must be set aside, and virtue is of the essence of culture, which requires personal commitment. Aristotle argues that the state must impose education on all free men, although rulers will be marked by superior culture as well as riches. Law is for Aristotle the true pedagogue. Education serves a social end, i.e., integration into the political relations set up by law.

3. *Religious Education.* Greek *paideía* is fundamentally anthropocentric, each person being the measure of all things (Protagoras). Plato, however, introduces a transcendent absolute, thus giving *paideía* a theological aspect. Education presupposes knowledge of the good, which is theology. Reason may control education, but the cultivation and even the salvation of the soul is finally at issue. Aristotle, too, finds a place for theology, and his successors think *paideía* sets us on an equality with the gods. The anthropocentric element remains, but *paideía* rounds out human nature and fulfils its destiny by directing its strivings to the good.

B. Education in the OT.
1. *God's Discipline by Law and Wisdom.* Originally the biblical tradition has no pedagogic vocabulary. God is holy, and he demands holiness from his chosen people. Breaches of holiness are either punished or expiated. Since holiness has a moral dimension, moral commandments are an obligation. God helps the covenant people to keep them by way of instruction, punishment, and reward. The record of God's acts, along with law and prophecy, stamps and fashions the people. The law especially is an educative force (Ps. 119). The father is its guardian, charged to teach the younger generation (Gen. 18:19). Its purpose is to serve as a standard for growth in faith and order. Of the many words for instruction, *ysr* (with *musr*) is the one that comes closest to the idea of education. It combines the ideas of moral "rearing," correction, and culture. It carries the thought of interpersonal relations and may refer to the training of the people as well as personal upbringing. It also carries the thought of censure, admonition, and disciplinary measures. Even corporal chastisement is included (Prov. 13:24), for it keeps from worse things (23:13) and gives hope of amendment (19:18).

Yet it must be in love and not in anger. Fathers and mothers have a primary responsibility (1:8). Cultivation of the character of adults as well as the education of children is also at issue in Proverbs. The fear of God is the beginning of wisdom (1:7). The goal of instruction is wisdom, understanding, discipline, and integrity (1:2ff.). The law is a lamp and wisdom a light (6:23). What is sought is moral education. Poverty and shame pursue those who neglect it (13:18; 24:32). God is the ultimate source of all training. Trust in him is the content of instruction (3:11). God himself disciplines and corrects (Ps. 16:7). His absolute correction would destroy; hence the request for moderation (6:1; 38:1). This moderate chastisement is a blessing (94:12). It is that of a loving Father. It extends even to the Gentile world (94:10).

2. *God's Discipline in the Prophetic Revelation.* The prophets relate God's discipline to his historical acts rather than to teaching. As the point of the law, this discipline serves the whole people (cf. Hos. 10:12). The prophet has insight into the divine direction of events (cf. Is. 8:11), which may take very different turns (28:26). God teaches Israel by destroying Jerusalem (Zeph. 3:2, 7). Instruction is futile, however, in face of obduracy (Jer. 2:30; 5:3, etc.). Even so, God preserves his people and there is hope of renewal (Jer. 30:11; 31:18). Along similar lines, the sense of warning is present in Ezekiel (5:15; 23:48). The desert experiences are an example of divine instruction (Dt. 11:2). Since Israel is depicted as an individual, the intrinsically individual concept of education applies to it quite easily, though there is an application to righteous individuals as members of the covenant community.

3. *The Reconstruction of the Concept in the Greek Translation of the OT.* The depiction of God as Educator gives an anthropocentric turn to the theocentric character of the OT revelation. Problems of theodicy strengthen this trend, although the idea of testing preserves a more theocentric view. The notions of education and development remain on the margin in Scripture, and while the term *paideía* enables the translators of the OT to give a pedagogic interpretation of OT history, it acquires the new sense of chastisement in the process.

a. The Wisdom Literature. Here parental discipline is the setting for pedagogic thinking. The Greek term adapts itself to the original and often means "chastisement" (Prov. 29:19). Education by suffering is presupposed in Prov. 3:11-12. Yet the group also brings in cultural notions that are more characteristic of Hellenistic Judaism, e.g., that of intellectual instruction (Prov. 1:8; 4:1, 13, etc.). Wisdom is the ultimate teacher, working both through the law and through life, and comprising more than human reason. Later the thought of educative punishment is present (cf. Wisdom and Psalms of Solomon), though it is not easy to differentiate the disciplinary sufferings of the righteous from the penal sufferings of the wicked. The solution to the problem of theodicy is that a merciful God is in various ways, not always evident, the Educator of his people.

b. The Psalms. The references here are to correction by God or instruction in his will. The noun tends to have more of the Greek sense of culture, the verb more of the biblical sense of discipline. In the main the relevant verses belong to the Wisdom tradition.

c. The Prophets. More plainly than the original, the LXX here presents God's dealings as correction. The LXX assumes that the prophet's true task is to instruct the people by means of the divine wisdom he is given (cf. Ezek. 13:9; Am. 3:7). Education by God is a gracious gift to the covenant people, not a privilege of the human race as such. The Gk. *paideúein* may mean "warn," "correct," "chastise," or "educate," but the upbringing of children is always in the background, and the concept comes to embrace both the law and all Israel's experiences after the exodus (cf. Hos. 5:2).

d. The Presentation of History. Here all God's dealings, including the giving of the law and wisdom, are seen as the work of God the Teacher. If God teaches through suffering, he also teaches through the law and its statutes. The law becomes the basis of the culture of Judaism and is viewed as the book of education for Israel and the race. With it Judaism confronts the world with a supreme claim to culture. In its discipline, it finds life and bliss (Sir. 24:27).

C. The *paideía* Concept in Hellenistic and Rabbinic Judaism.

1. paideía and nómos in Philo. Philo finds in *paideía* a bridge between the OT revelation and Greek culture. In it he sums up the intellectual content of the OT tradition for educated people. He also uses the group to prove the superiority of the OT revelation. It denotes the education and culture of the individual and people. It has character formation and self-fulfilment as the goal. A clear worldview and practical wisdom are included. *paideía,* as a gift of God, develops the human spirit. OT content pours into this Greek form. *paideía* is the agent of OT revelation in the Greek world. Parents are the primary educators. They give an education that ends at maturity, although *paideía* also embraces the self-education of adult life. If education is primarily for boys, Philo thinks a suitable education should be provided for girls as well. The synagogue gives training in piety. It teaches educated people to choose the right from the triple standpoint of love of God, of virtue, and of others. *paideía* is a divine jewel of the divine soul. The Greek "know thyself" is seen in terms of the biblical "take heed to thyself" (Ex. 34:12). Self-education is thus referred back to the divine commandment. Concern for the one God and Creator gives Jewish culture its superiority. The staff of Ex. 12:11 signifies *paideía.* As a sceptre, it symbolizes the rule of God, the one king who stands behind all *paideía. paideía* brings salvation. The soul attains to good gifts only by exercise in virtue. *paideía* is a well or source with saving significance, although only with the goodness of God as the ultimate basis. Most people can attain only to the ordinary *paideía* (represented by Hagar) that brings them under the positive laws of nations. Yet this bears healthy fruit, for the good is imperishable, and *paideía* marches on, constantly rejuvenated, blooming with eternal blossoms. In the last resort, *paideía* means for Philo a life that is led under the direction of the *lógos* from which all potentialities of wisdom and culture proceed.

2. Jewish-Hellenistic Education in Josephus. Josephus, too, raises a claim to culture and knows educational theory. Education for him embraces both teaching and practice, and religion is its goal. The law offers the best combination of teaching and practice. Obedience to the law, as even outsiders see, is the basis of Jewish education. This gives it a volitional as well as an intellectual slant. Yet fundamentally Josephus accepts the Greek norm of culture. He does not try to give the group its OT sense of discipline or correction. At the most parents discipline by admonition.

3. Discipline through Suffering in Later Jewish Theology. The rabbis develop a view that sees God's education as essentially correction. The Maccabean period exerts an influence here. Correction is a filial privilege; ungodly nations are left in temporal prosperity which will lead to final ruin. Correction may take the form of direction as well as chastisement. In rabbinic statements chastisement presupposes guilt. Those on whom it falls should scrutinize their actions or ascribe it to neglect of the law. In some instances it may be simply the chastisement of love. Even this concept, however, does not wholly solve the problem of theodicy. The pedagogic solution is an anthropocentric one that does not fit in too well with the theocentric claim of the OT that God's revelation is unconditional.

D. The *paideía* Concept in the NT.

1. Greek and Jewish Culture in the NT. Two verses in Acts, which have no theological significance, give evidence of Hellenistic usage. Acts 7:22 says that Moses was nurtured in all the wisdom of the Egyptians. This accords with similar biographical notices about great figures. Acts 22:3 has Paul say of himself that he was brought up in Jerusalem and educated in the law. He can thus understand the importance of this education, but as a Christian and an apostle he must dispute the claim of the Jews to be directors of the foolish and teachers of children. At issue in Romans is not just an intellectual understanding but the shaping of life according to a consistent study and application of the law. The word *paideutḗs* suggests practical guidance, and *áphronōn* denotes those who need direction.

2. The Law as Taskmaster. Jesus rejects the claim of the scribes and Pharisees to be educators for the world (Mt. 23:15), and Paul takes the same position, quoting Is. 52:5 and Ezek. 36:20 (Rom. 2:24). For Paul the law has only limited validity (Gal. 3:24). Its time ends with Christ. It is a *paedagōgós* while we are minors. During our minority we are under it and virtually in the position of slaves. With faith, however, we achieve adult sonship and a new immediacy to the Father which is far better than dependence on even the best "pedagogue." Although Paul here associates the law with the "elemental spirits," he is not against the law. It is a taskmaster with an educational role. He thus continues to appeal to it when decisions must be made in congregational life, interpreting the OT in the light of Christ.

3. Education by God. In Lk. 23:16, 20 *paideúein* is twice used for "to chastise" in the passion story. This usage is not attested in the nonbiblical world, but whipping forms part of the Greek upbringing of children, and the word has this sense in popular, if not in literary, usage. Heb. 12 deals with the discipline of suffering. Suffering is disciplining by the Father in responsible love. In the light of Christ's passion, it is the guarantee of sonship and hence of divine grace and forgiveness. It is not just athletic training but association with Christ. "For *paideía*" in 12:7 hardly means that Christian "culture" is the goal. *paideía* is not the goal but the way; believers are to endure for the purpose of education. As earthly parents exercise discipline for the good of their children, so the heavenly Father disciplines believers with a view to holiness (v. 10). If *paideía* is painful at first, it brings the peaceful fruit of righteousness (v. 12). An eschatological understanding lifts this view above that of practical wisdom, for the end is participation in the eternal worship of God in heaven. The letters of Revelation teach the same message. Those whom God loves he rebukes and chastens (3:19). The two verbs here express friendly testing, censuring, chastising, and educating, not in a moralizing sense, but in terms of the divine dealings. In Tit. 2:12, too, God's loving will as Father stands behind the training. The goal is salvation (v. 11), and the word of God educates for this by summoning to renunciation of ungodliness and nourishing the hope of Christ's appearing. In 1 Cor. 11:32 Paul takes up the thought that God's chastisement of his people is not one of condemnation, since it is for the world. This chastisement is an outflowing of fatherly love. 2 Cor. 6:9 is to the same effect. The blows Paul experiences as an apostle are the *paideía kyríou* (cf. 11:23). They have a negative appearance but the reality is life, victory over death, and rejoicing.

4. Christian Discipline in the NT. The basic rule of Christian upbringing is stated in Eph. 6:4. The Lord himself does the educating through the parent. He uses the ordinary means of discipline and instruction to this end. In 2 Tim. 3:16 Scripture plays a key role; it is profitable for teaching, correction, and instruction in righteousness. This does not contradict Gal. 3:24. Taught by Christian leaders, members of the churches are to actualize righteousness under the guidance of Scripture. Timothy in 2 Tim. 2:25 is to correct those who are in error with meekness, not entering into stupid controversies that do not promote spiritual development, but exerting an educative influence that under God can bring repentance and enlightenment. In 1 Tim. 1:20, where there is no human subject, chastisement rather than destruction is the point. If the stress is more on punishment than education, the aim is amendment, and in this sense we have Christian *paideía* (cf. the edificatory discipline in Acts 5:1ff.; 13:6ff.).

[G. BERTRAM, V, 596-625]

paidíon → país

---

paízō [to play, dance, mock],   *empaízō* [to mock, deceive],   *empaigmonḗ* [mocking],   *empaigmós* [mocking, scorn],   *empaíktēs* [mocker]

---

paízō. Deriving from *país,* this word means "to act as a child," e.g., "to play," "to dance," "to jest," "to mock."

1. Greek Usage. Homer uses the group for games and dancing. Lack of seriousness is sometimes meant, e.g., when it is asked whether Socrates is speaking in jest. Ships are seen to be playthings of the winds, and humans of fate or the gods. Mockery may be suggested, or the thought of what is frivolous or futile. Aristotle finds a valid place for play as a means of relaxation, but it is not the best use of leisure. Play has a universal role in the education of children.

2. The OT and LXX. Like the world around, the OT attests to religious dancing (Ex. 15:20; Ps. 26:6, etc.), though this may at times tend to be orgiastic (2 Sam. 6:16ff.) and can also have pagan associations (1 Kgs. 18:26). Eschatologically Jer. 31:4 promises joyful dances and Zech. 8:5 looks forward to the streets being filled with children at play. In Judg. 16:25 playing a musical instrument is perhaps meant, while children's play is the point in Gen. 21:9 (Ishmael and Isaac). Dancing is the sense in Is. 3:16, with possibly a hint of frivolity.

3. The Sense of Play, Scorn, Bravado. In Wis. 15:12 the Gentiles treat life as a game. In Jer. 15:17 the Hebrew refers to merrymakers, but the LXX brings in the thought of an arrogance that scorns revelation. Prov. 8:30-31 and Ps. 104:26 give play a theological reference, but the group is more ironical when it denotes God's mocking of human pretension (cf. Wis. 12:26). As God himself scorns human bravado, his people may mock enemies, dangers, and temptations (2 Kgs. 19:21).

4. paízō in the NT. The only NT instance is in 1 Cor. 10:7 (quoting Ex. 32:6). The reference is to idolatry in the form of cultic dancing and the associated licentiousness. For Corinthian believers pagan feasts offer temptations to similar idolatry.

empaízō.

1. Mockery in the Greek OT. empaízō means "to make sport with," "to dance around," "to mock," "to deceive," "to defraud." It is one of many words denoting disparagement, scorn, ridicule, etc. The scorn may be justifiable and constructive, or it may be a negative expression of arrogance, aversion, or hostility. In the OT the Greek term does not always correspond exactly to the various Hebrew originals, for which various other Greek words are also used. Common ideas in the OT are Jacob's mocking of his father, the scorning of idols, the contempt God brings on Jerusalem, mocking punishment, despising and derision, outwitting and overreaching, etc. (cf. for details *TDNT,* V, 630-33).

2. *Mockery in the Martyr Piety of Judaism.* In the Apocrypha a distinct vocabulary of mocking develops in connection with Jewish passion piety. The reference may be to human arrogance or to God's derisive punishments. The mockery of the wicked is a test for the righteous. It takes the form of abominations committed against the city, the temple, and the people. Actions and not just words are in view.

3. *empaízō in the NT.* The verb *empaízō* occurs in the NT only in the Synoptics. In Mt. 2:16 Herod is outwitted by the Wise Men. In Lk. 14:29 the imprudent builder exposes himself to ridicule because he cannot finish what he begins, whether through weakness, rashness, arrogance, or sheer incompetence. In predictions of the passion Jesus himself is to be mocked (Mt. 20:19; Mk. 10:34; Lk. 18:32). Spitting and scourging go along with the mocking, all at the hands of the Gentiles. The passion story itself gives accounts of the mocking (cf. Mk. 15:16ff.; Mt. 27:27ff.). The various actions, which include the scourging in Jn. 19:1ff., show plainly that the messianic claims of Jesus are being held up to derision. Something similar occurs in Mt. 26:67-68; Mk. 14:65; Lk. 22:63ff., though only Luke uses *empaízein* as a comprehensive term for this incident. In Matthew and Mark the judges themselves treat Jesus with scorn and derision, although this time as a prophet rather than a king. Luke also uses the term *empaízein* in relation to the mocking before Herod (23:11). Finally, Matthew and Mark use the verb for what takes place during the crucifixion itself (Mk. 15:31; Mt. 27:41; cf. Lk. 23:35). The chief priests, scribes, and elders mock Jesus as the pretended king who saved others and trusted in God, but who is now helpless on the cross between two malefactors. Here, as in the passion piety of Judaism, violence against the righteous is mockery. It expresses sinful arrogance against the instrument of revelation in the form of cruel contempt.

empaigmonḗ, empaigmós, empaíktēs. While *empaízein* is in the main restricted to the passion narrative, Hebrew gives *empaigmós* a wider reference to the righteous of the OT who suffered mocking and scourging like Christ (11:36). *empaigmonḗ* and *empaíktēs* occur in the NT only in Jude 18 and 2 Pet. 3:3. Here the scoffers, who may be Gnostic libertines, are people who are hostile to revelation and to godliness, although their scoffing may take specific forms, e.g., scoffing at delay in the parousia. Such mockers are enemies of the cross of Christ (Phil. 3:18; cf. Gal. 5:11; 6:12; 1 Cor. 1:23). This is the general reference in Jude, and the scoffers of 2 Peter fit into the same basic understanding, since the concept of mockery receives its basic NT imprint from the passion narratives.   [G. BERTRAM, V, 625-36]

> *país* [child], *paidíon* [small child], *paidárion* [small child], *téknon* [child], *tekníon* [small child], *bréphos* [embryo, infant]

A. Lexical Data.

1. *bréphos.* This word has such senses as "embryo," "young," "infant," "small child."

2. *país.* This word means "child" (usually "boy" but also "girl"), and with reference to descent "son," or to social position "servant." Another use is for a class, e.g.,

orators or doctors (*paídes rhētórōn, paídes Asklēpioú*). Figuratively an author's works are his "children."

3. paidíon. This word means "small child" with reference to age or descent, and it may also denote "servant" (social position). Figuratively it carries the sense of undeveloped understanding but is also used in affectionate address (cf. Jn. 21:5; 1 Jn. 2:18).

4. paidárion. This is another diminutive denoting "little boy" or "young slave."

5. téknon. This word means "child" (or "son") in the sense of progeny (also spiritual progeny in Mt. 3:9; Gal. 3:7; 1 Pet. 3:6; cf. Gal. 4:21ff.; 2 Jn. 1; Lk. 7:35). The inhabitants of Jerusalem are its "children" in Joel 2:23; Mt. 23:37; Lk. 13:34. We also read of "children of light" (Eph. 5:8), "wrath" (2:3), "obedience" (1 Pet. 1:14), and the false prophetess (Rev. 2:13).

6. tekníon. This is a nursery term for a "small child." In the NT it occurs only in affectionate address (Jn. 13:33; 1 Jn. 2:12, 28; 3:7, 18; 4:4; 5:21).

B. The Child from the Natural and Ethico-Religious Standpoint.

I. Antiquity.

1. Original Positive Estimation. Children, especially sons, are valued highly in early antiquity because they enhance the strength of a family and the state. Their birth is greeted with feasting. Rome takes a similar view, but with little personal feeling.

2. Decline and Countermeasures from the Classical Period. Cultic and genetic factors lie behind the exposure of children, but economic considerations are also important. Depopulation comes with abortions and the prevention of pregnancies. Children are regarded as unimportant. Laws are passed favoring larger families but with no great success. Philosophers tend to shun marriage, poetry magnifies free love, and the novel depicts adultery, jealousy, procuring, and pederasty. Another trend is toward continence even in marriage.

3. The Rediscovery of the Child in Hellenism. Parental love continues, provision and prayer are made for children, and their loss is bewailed. Poetry revives ancient motifs, e.g., the divine child of the golden age (Vergil). Drama makes some use of children (in boyish pranks), and art gives better depictions of children. But taste is sentimental and perverse; the rich often amuse themselves with slave children. On the other hand, there is no bar to children becoming emperors.

4. Ethico-Religious Evaluation. Antiquity rarely speaks of the innocence of children. The child has no sexual complications, has little comprehension of joy or suffering, and cannot deceive (though mainly because of intellectual immaturity). The idea of the wonder child is strong in Egypt. Ideas of universal imperfection and guilt also occur. Thus Orphism detects a nexus of evil that initiatory rites must overcome. The concept of the body as a prison moves in the same direction. But these thoughts are marginal. The main feature of the child is immaturity or childishness. The child lives for the moment and simply plays at things. Education has the task of making something out of this raw material, and with normal gifts and the right techniques can succeed at the task, but with little love for the child or regard for its developing personality.

5. The Child in the Cultus.

a. Children have a part in the cultus from birth. They are placed under divine protection, are present at cultic rites, and may be lifted up to kiss the household gods.

b. The children of priests and other privileged groups serve the sacrifices. Temple schools exist. Conscious or unconscious manticism is ascribed to children. Children engage in intercessory processions. They also perform certain cultic actions. Thus a boy at the games cuts the victors' leaves from the sacred olive. Boys and girls assist the vestal virgins. The vestal virgins themselves are appointed as small girls. To guarantee chastity, many Greek cults entrust priestly functions solely to children.

c. Children have a place in the mysteries too. They join in the processions of Eleusis. Their initiation is customary. They officiate in the mystery ritual.

II. The OT and Judaism.

1. The Religious Evaluation of Progeny. In the OT increase is an order of creation (Gen. 1:28). To be childless is a source of sorrow and vexation (Gen. 15:2). Children are a gift from God (Ps. 127:3ff.). The family lives on in them. Judaism stresses this aspect with reference to the people. Levirate marriage provides for those who die childless. Contraception is infamous. Intercourse is for the sake of children. Pure marriages are pleasing to God. Abortion and exposure of children are pagan abominations. Ascetic inclinations are rare (cf. the Essenes) except in warnings against immoderation.

2. The Estimation of the Child.

a. The OT stresses parental love (Gen. 22:2; 1 Kgs. 3:26) but demands obedience from children (Ex. 20:12). The babbling of children glorifies God (Ps. 8:2). A few children have prophetic gifts (1 Sam. 3:1ff.). Children may be ignorant and self-willed (Is. 3:4; Eccl. 10:16; cf. Gen. 8:21), and they need discipline (cf. 2 Kgs. 2:23ff.), but the messianic child is highly estimated (Is. 7:14ff.).

b. The OT does not see children as innocent. Though individual responsibility may be stressed (Jer. 31:29-30; Ezek. 18:2ff.), there is a nexus of sin, guilt, and punishment (cf. Ps. 51:5; Gen. 3) that only God can break. Judaism develops a full doctrine of original sin, although each person affirms Adam's deed afresh. Rabbis argue that children are not personally responsible in the first years, but the evil impulse is present, and children soon yield to it. Where dualism has an influence, the soul is pure, but unwillingly or by its own fault it is chained to matter. Children in any case are open to sensual desire.

3. The Participation of the Child in Religious Exercises. Circumcision initiates into the cultic fellowship. Firstborn males belong to God and must be redeemed by offerings. Children attend family offerings and planned instruction is given (cf. 1 Sam. 1:4; Dt. 4:9; 11:19; Prov. 4:1ff.). Early dedication to the sanctuary is possible but rare (1 Sam. 1:28). There are no child priests. Judaism lays the main stress on instruction in the law. Boys, who alone must keep the law in its entirety, are taught from an early age and must attend the great feasts as soon as possible. Circumcision is seen as a duty owed to the child, and the children of proselytes are baptized with their parents (although attestation of this is late).

III. The NT.

1. Affirmation of the Child as a Creature of God.

a. Jesus. Inheriting the OT belief in the Creator and the implied affirmation of human life, Jesus finds some place for ascetic concerns (Mt. 19:11-12) but he also endorses and sanctifies parental love (Mt. 5:36; 9:19; 7:9ff.).

The community obviously agrees with the teaching of Jesus in the sayings that it transmits. It supports missionaries and their dependents (1 Cor. 9:5). Paul accepts marriage as an order of creation in spite of an ascetic inclination (1 Cor. 7). The family teaching in Eph. 6:1ff. displays a positive attitude to children and their upbringing. 1 Tim. 2:15, which does not mean that childbearing is a basis of salvation or a means of doing penance, calls the bearing (and nurture?) of children a work that promotes salvation.

2. *Affirmation of the Individuality of Children?*

a. Jesus evaluates children highly (Mt. 18:2ff.; 19:13ff.). This is not because of a Hellenistic sense of their relative innocence, but because their littleness, immaturity, and need of help keep the way open for God's fatherly love.

b. Paul alludes to childlike innocence in 1 Cor. 14:20, but mostly his comparisons stress the immaturity and inferiority of children (3:1; 13:11; Gal. 4:1). Heb. 5:13 is to the same effect. In regard to regeneration, however, the relative innocence of children is an important motif in exhortation (1 Pet. 2:1).

3. *The Child in God's Saving Counsel.* Jesus' teaching is explicable only on the assumption that children have a place in God's saving counsel. Paul's objective view of God's saving work has a similar implication (Rom. 5:18-19; 11:25). The need for faith raises a question, but faith does not effect salvation; it receives it. The transmission of the infancy stories and of the account of the blessing of children is hardly conceivable if children are excluded from God's plan (cf. also Acts 2:39).

b. Children are numbered with the community, take part in crucial events (Acts 21:5), are present at services (20:9, 12), and are under instruction (Eph. 6:1ff.).

c. Whether children are baptized is debated. The household baptisms and contemporary custom (cf. Jewish proselyte baptism) favor infant baptism. So do the relationship to circumcision (Col. 2:11), the concept of eschatological sealing (Ezek. 9:4, 6), the common participation of the whole people (1 Cor. 10:1-2), and patristic testimony. The story of the blessing of the children (Mk. 10:13ff.) might well have been seen as an answer to objections.

IV. *The Later Church.*

1. *The Child as a Creature of God.* Eschatological hopes and ascetic inclinations militate against the high view of children, but the church maintains the biblical doctrine of creation. It thus protects marriage and fights licentiousness, contraception, abortion, and the exposure of children. Clement of Alexandria offers a fine presentation which combines the best of antiquity with the Christian legacy. He sees the lack or loss of children as a heavy burden and commends marriage for the sake of the nation, the children, and the good of the world so far as it rests in our hands (cf. *Stromateis* 3.3.22ff.; 9.67.1, etc.).

2. *The Relation to the Child.* The church depicts childish innocence but does not forget the nexus of evil. Children are immature and even foolish but also fresh and friendly, so they must not be scorned. Christ is lauded as the divine child. Augustine tends to stress infant sin but is led to conversion by the prophetic voice of a child.

3. *The Child in the Cultus.*

a. Clerical Functions. The prayers of children are thought to be efficacious and we read of choirs of boys and choir schools, as well as of boy lectors.

b. Infant Baptism and Communion. Infant baptism is said to be an apostolic tradition, and the delay in baptism dates only from the fourth century. For infant communion there is witness from the time of Cyprian (*On the Lapsed* 9).

C. **Divine Sonship.**

1. Religious History. The motif of divine sonship arises mainly in connection with the word *téknon,* which suggests a closer personal relationship. Greek religion thinks of divine sonship in natural terms. In the mysteries it comes by initiation, with deification as the goal. The OT applies the thought nonmythologically to the people (Hos. 11:1). Salvation history controls the relation, and God is more often depicted as King than Father. Individualism comes to the fore later, but divine sonship is not at the heart of Jewish piety.

II. The NT.

1. Jesus puts divine sonship in the center. It rests on grace, and since the original relation has been broken, there has to be reacceptance into it. Jesus bears God's definitive offer, not simply because he enjoys a unique divine sonship, but because he is sent for this purpose. His own sonship differs from ours, and he is never called the *téknon theoú*. *téknon* either denotes descent from Abraham as a precondition of divine sonship (Mk. 3:9), or it denotes divine sonship in parables (Mk. 7:27; Mt. 21:28).

2. For Paul believers have divine sonship through Christ's work. It does not come by creation or physical descent but involves true descent from Abraham (Gal. 3:6ff.; Rom. 4). It has a universal sweep and carries with it freedom and adulthood (Gal. 3:25ff.; 4:1ff.; Rom. 8:31ff.). *tékna theoú* is used as well as *huioí*, but Christ is never *téknon*. Full sonship is still hoped for (Rom. 8:23).

3. In John only Christ is *huiós*; believers are *tékna* (1:12; 11:52; 1 Jn. 3:1). Sonship means being born of God but with a reference to fellowship rather than individual deification. The thought of the people and eschatological hopes are still present (Jn. 11:51-52; 1 Jn. 3:2), but there is a victorious possession that drives out fear. A break with sin and love of others are demanded (1 Jn. 3:9ff.).

4. Other NT writings do not use *téknon* for believers, but James and 1 Peter relate sonship very clearly to regeneration (Jms. 1:18; 1 Pet. 1:23).

III. The Church. While the church never forgets the truth of divine sonship, it tends to be overgrown by alien naturalistic and moralistic concepts.

→ *huiós*   [A. OEPKE, V, 636-54]

---

pais theoú [servant of God, child of God]

A. The OT.

I. The Secular Use of 'ebed.

1. The Hebrew original of *pais* in the phrase *pais theoú*, i.e., *'ebed*, carries a stress on personal relationship and has first the sense of "slave." OT law offers some protection to slaves, for Israel itself is redeemed from bondage, slaves are part of the cultic fellowship, and they can act representatively for their masters.

2. The word then comes to be used for the "paid soldier" and even more broadly the "court official"; these are the king's servants.

3. A third use is to denote general political subjection.

4. On the basis of court usage the term is then used in polite phrases like "your humble servant."

5. A special use is for servants of the sanctuary (Josh. 9:23).

II. The Religious Use of 'ebed.

1. The term serves as an expression of humility used by the righteous before God. Different emphases in this regard are self-abasement, the implied claim on God for help, and grateful self-commitment when help is received. These elements are present in other nations too, but distinctive in the OT are the exclusiveness and totality involved in being God's servant, the gracious decision of God which makes it possible, and the historical character of the relationship. These factors give the status of the *'ebed* a unique security. God himself calls Moses his servant (Num. 12:7-8; cf. Ps. 119:76).

The divine call is the basis of confidence even though enemies arise against God's servant (Ps. 109:28).

2. In the plural the term becomes a designation for the righteous, those who seek refuge in God (Ps. 34:22), those who love his name (Ps. 69:36), his saints (Ps. 79:2), his people (Ps. 105:25). The two poles of the concept are election and obedience.

3. In the singular "servant of God" is a term for Israel. Is. 41:8ff. seems to initiate this usage. Abased by the exile, Israel is elected, created, and gathered by God (41:8-9; 44:2, 21). The role of the people as God's servant here is the passive of reception. It is summoned only to "convert" (44:22).

4. "Servant of God" may also be a term for distinguished figures. Among these are the patriarchs, who stand in a gracious relationship to God and are pledges of his will to save. Then comes Moses (Ex. 14:31; Num. 12:7-8), who specifically embodies God's words and works as an active servant who enjoins the law, orders the conquest, regulates the cultus, and promises rest; to obey Moses is to obey God, for God has chosen him as his minister. Later the kings are servants of God with the special role of securing the people against its enemies. David, chosen by God, is a special instance who is also a sign of promise in darker days (cf. 1 Kgs. 11:34; Ps. 89:3; Jer. 33:21-22). In certain circumstances even a pagan ruler may act as God's servant, e.g., Nebuchadnezzar in Jer. 27ff. Alongside the king is the prophet, the servant of God who has a unique office as God's messenger (1 Kgs. 18:36). God himself is present in such messengers, so that the phrase "my servants the prophets" becomes almost a fixed one. The prophets warn the people and show it the true meaning of its history. The older writing prophets for the most part avoid the term "servant," probably because of its associations with the cultic and courtly piety which they castigate. Nevertheless, it aptly denotes their function. In the prose sections of Job, God calls Job his servant even though he does not belong to Israel. Job belongs to God as his creature and in virtue of his uprightness and his refusal to renounce God with cursing when subjected to testing.

5. A special question arises with the references to the suffering servant of the Lord in Is. 42:1ff.; 49:1ff.; 50:4-9; 52:13–53:12. There is no reason to isolate these passages from their general context, but the problem arises how the figure of the *'ebed* is to be understood in them, whether collectively or individually. 49:3ff. seems to support an individual reference. The individual may be either a royal or a prophetic figure, and of these the latter is the more likely, for ear and tongue (50:4-5) are the organs of this servant's work, and prophets may judge and liberate as well as kings (42:1ff.). In the immediate context the author himself may well be intended; anonymity is preserved because the important point is that the servant belongs to God, being fashioned, elected, grasped, called, and equipped by God (cf. 42:1ff.). The task of the servant is to publish justice, not perhaps in the general sense of a proclamation to the nations, but in the special sense of the restoration of Israel, which itself will put idols to shame, glorify God's name, and thus bring light and salvation to the whole world (42:1; 49:5-6). Yet this task cannot be accomplished without suffering (cf. Jeremiah), though whether this is persecution by his own people, oppression by Babylon, or a mortal(?) sickness is not clear from the text, and the depiction in 52:13–53:12 transcends biographical features and may not unjustly be seen as pointing to the true Servant of the Lord who is yet to come. Meaning is found in the suffering, for it has a vicarious character and is thus obediently accepted by the servant as divinely ordained (53:6, 10). This is not just blind obedience, nor does it relate only to the vicarious ministry effected by the suffering, for the servant of Is. 53 triumphantly believes that God will

confess him even beyond the tomb (50:7ff.), that he will receive from God his right (49:4) and his reward (53:12). This is not just a private transaction, for it will be seen by the rulers of the nations, and will thus serve to promote God's honor and to proclaim his faithfulness in the world at large.

B. The LXX Translations.

1. Translations of 'ebed. *'ebed* occurs 807 times in the Hebrew and is translated by the *país* group 340 times, the *doúlos* group 327 times, the *oikétēs* group 36 times, the *therápōn* group 46 times, and *huiós* and *hypērétēs* once each; there are no equivalents or very free renderings in 56 instances. *país* predominates in Genesis, but *therápōn* in Exodus. In Leviticus, Numbers, and Deuteronomy various terms are used, but *país* is to the fore again in Joshua. *doúlos,* however, hardly appears at all in the Hexateuch. From Judges to 2 Kings, however, *doúlos* alternates with *país, doúlos* being "slave" in the stricter sense and *país* the "free servant" of the king, i.e., the soldier or official. The service of God is expressed by *doúlos* even in the case of Moses or Joshua, since this is not a service into which one may freely enter. The differences between the renderings in the first group and this later group are probably due to the fact that the first group is an older translation which reflects more of the Greek sense of the nearness of God and man, while the later group uses the harsher *doúlos* for the relationship with God in order the better to emphasize the divine sovereignty. After Judges to 2 Kings, the groups begin to interfuse except that *therápōn* fades from the picture. Psalms prefers the sterner *doúlos,* as do the Minor Prophets, but Isaiah and Daniel opt for *país.* Alternation occurs in Jeremiah, and the omission of any rendering at all in many cases shows that the translator(s) find it hard to decide on the proper equivalent. The same alternation occurs in Ezra and Nehemiah.

2. The Servant of the Lord Passages in Isaiah. The LXX of Is. 42:1 inserts Jacob and Israel into the text, showing that a collective interpretation is held. On the other hand, the LXX of 52:13–53:12 might well have an individual reference. *paidíon* is used in 53:2, and in view of 9:5 this might suggest a messianic understanding (cf. the future in 52:14-15 and the recurrent use of the term *dóxa* with no real original). As distinct from the Hebrew, the LXX states that divine retribution is exerted on the wicked for putting the servant to death. This is regarded as part of the servant's exaltation.   [W. Zimmerli, V, 654-77]

C. *país theoú* in Later Judaism.

I. The Twofold Meaning of país theoú.

1. Child of God. *país theoú* is rare in Judaism after 100 B.C. It may mean either "child" or "servant" of God; the context usually shows which. The plural *paídes theoú* occurs for Israel or the righteous in Wisdom. Since Wisdom also depicts the righteous in terms of suffering, the servant of God of Is. 52:13ff. has here become the child of God.

2. Servant of God. After 100 B.C. *país theoú* more often means "servant of God," e.g., when applied to Moses, the prophets, or the three children (Bar. 1:20; 2:20; Dan. 9:35 Θ).

II. Persistence of the Religious Use of 'ebed.

1. Self-Designation in Prayer. In addition to *país,* other words such as *doúlos* and *diákonos* are used for *'ebed,* and these alone occur when what is expressed is abasement before God in prayer.

2. Servants of God. This phrase is often used for Israel, the prophets, the righteous, priests, and even proselytes, parents, and angels.

765

3. Collective Use. The collective use of the singular for Israel lives on after 100 B.C. but is not common.

4. As a Title of Honor. A few instances may be found of *país* as a title of honor for such figures as Moses, David, Noah, Abraham, Isaac, Jacob, Aaron, Elijah, etc. The title is solidly established only for Moses, next for David.

5. The Messiah. The Messiah is "my servant" in the OT in Ezek. 34:23-24; 37:24-25; Zech. 3:8. This usage continues only in 4 Esdr. 7:28 etc.; Syr. Bar. 70:9, and the Targums on Is. 42:1; 43:10; 52:13; Zech. 3:8; Ezek. 34:23-24; 37:24. The rabbis use the term only in OT quotations. The form is always "my servant"; God is the speaker.

III. Interpretations of the Servant of the Lord Passages in Isaiah. Apart from the references to Isaiah, Eliakim, and David in Is. 20:3; 22:20; 37:35, the singular "servant of God" occurs 19 times in 41–53. The rabbis do not isolate these chapters from the rest of the book, nor the Servant Songs from these chapters. Nor do they think that there has to be a uniform interpretation. One must also distinguish between mere allusions and solid exposition, and between the Palestinian tradition and that of the diaspora, which develops independently, partly as a result of divergent LXX readings.

1. Hellenistic Judaism. At first *país* is the usual word for *'ebed,* and it carries the sense of "child" as well as "servant." In the second century A.D. the picture changes and *doúlos* is preferred as closer to the original. On the basis of the LXX the collective interpretation becomes more general. Thus Hellenistic Judaism (unlike Palestinian) refers 42:1ff. to Israel. It also takes Is. 53 collectively; the servant here is a type of the righteous (as Origen testifies in *Against Celsus* 1.55). This is an interpretation that does not occur in Palestinian Judaism until the eleventh century A.D.

2. Palestinian Judaism. Palestinian Judaism advances three different interpretations in the different passages. The first is a collective one on the basis of the Hebrew (e.g., Is. 41:8-9; 44:1ff.; 45:4; 38:20; 49:3ff.). In the collective sense, the servant is mostly Israel. In allusions the righteous or the prophets may be perceived, and in exegesis there are occasional references to penitent sinners or sufferers, to the prophets, or to upright teachers. Qumran does not clearly apply the "servant" to the community. The second interpretation refers the sayings to Isaiah himself (49:5), although not in the case of 53:7-8. Individual verses are sometimes referred to other figures, e.g., Jacob (41:8), David (43:10), Noah (49:8-9), and Moses (53:12). The third interpretation, which applies to 42:1; 43:10; 49:6; 52:13; 53:11, is messianic. Sir. 48:10 applies a phrase from 49:6 to the work of the returning Elijah. Ethiopian Enoch describes the Messiah in language based on Is. 42:1 (the elect), 53:11 (the righteous one), 42:6 (light of the nations), etc. It fuses the Son of Man and the Servant, although only in respect of the Servant's exaltation. The Peshitta refers Is. 53 to the future Messiah. In the NT the rulers in Lk. 23:35 mockingly call Jesus the Chosen One (Is. 42:1). The translation of Is. 53:8-9 in Aquila has the servant exercise judgment, and the idea of a leprous Messiah, also inferred by some rabbis, is read into 53:4. Theodotion's translation also takes Is. 53 messianically, especially in the understanding of 53:9ff. as referring to final judgment. The Targum, which rests on older material, interprets the whole of 52:13–53:12 messianically. In it only weak traces of the sufferings remain, and the passage is taken to describe the establishment of messianic rule over Israel. The rabbis apply 42:1ff. and 52:13ff. to the Messiah, including the passion sayings in ch. 53. As regards the suffering Messiah, the first witness is textually uncertain, Justin's testimony in *Dialogue* 36.1 etc. is secondary, and incontestable examples date only from around A.D. 200. After this period opposition to Christianity leads to the avoidance of such terms as Servant of the Lord or the Elect for the

Messiah, and textual alterations and tendentious reinterpretations occur in renderings of Is. 53, e.g., referring Is. 53:12 to Moses. Nevertheless, a distinctly nonmessianic interpretation of Is. 53 does not occur even though it might seem to have been natural for the rabbis to link the chapter more generally with current ideas of the atoning power of death, e.g., in the case of criminals, or the righteous, or martyrs, or children. In sum, Is. 42:1ff.; 43:10; 49:1ff.; 52:13ff. are taken messianically, the messianic understanding is constant in the case of 42:1ff. and 52:13ff. (with reference especially to judgment), and a messianic interpretation of the passion sayings of 53:1ff. fairly certainly goes back to the pre-Christian period.

D. *país theoú* in the NT. Of eight instances of this phrase, one refers to Israel (Lk. 1:54), two refer to David (Lk. 1:69; Acts 4:25), and the other five to Jesus (Mt. 12:18; Acts 3:13, 26; 4:27, 30). Lk. 1:54 has righteous Israel in view. The references to David are liturgical and are taken over from later Judaism.

I. país theoú as a Title of Jesus.

1. The Provenance. In the few instances in which Jesus is called *país theoú* we obviously have early tradition. Indeed, *país theoú* may also underlie other passages, e.g., Mk. 1:11; 9:7, where the basic quotation may well be Is. 42:1 (cf. the imparting of the Spirit, the textual vacillation between *agapētós* and *eklelegménos,* and the version in Jn. 1:34). In Jn. 1:29, 36, too, the unusual *amnós* may go back to an original Aramaic that might mean "boy" or "servant" as well as "lamb," and if so the use of *país theoú* in the church could well originate in Aramaic-speaking circles. After the NT there are only eleven instances in three works, but these instances are all in liturgical contexts (Did. 9.2-3; 10.2-3; 1 Clem. 59.2ff.; Mart. Pol. 14.1ff.; 20.2), and in all but two cases the same liturgical formula is used. In the light of the usage in Acts 4:27, 30, this suggests that we have here an ancient title that never becomes as common as *kýrios, Christós,* or *huiós theoú,* but lives on in the eucharistic prayer, in doxology, and in confession. The provenance of the title is to be sought in the Palestinian community; the Gentile churches do not favor it (preferring *huiós*) because it seems not to do full justice to the majesty of the risen and glorified Lord.

2. The Meaning. The reserve of the Gentile churches suggests that "servant" rather than "child" is the original meaning (cf. the juxtaposition with David in Acts 4:25, 27, 30 and Did. 9.2-3, and the references to Is. 52:13ff. in Mt. 12:18; Acts 3:13ff.).

3. The Change in Meaning. In Gentile churches *país theoú* signifies "child of God" from at least Mart. Pol. 14.1 and possibly from 1 Clem. 59.4. It is unlikely, however, that "son" is the meaning in Acts, and "servant" persists as the sense in Didache. If *país* can have at times a distinguished, archaic ring, it has a lowly ring as well, and for this reason it does not commend itself to Gentile Christians.

II. Christological Interpretation of the Isaianic Servant in the NT.

1. The References. Only in Mt. 8:17; 12:18ff.; Lk. 22:37; Jn. 12:38; Acts 8:32-33; Rom. 15:21 are verses from Isaiah referred directly to Jesus, but many direct and indirect allusions fill out the picture. Thus we find obviously pre-Pauline tradition and formulas, e.g., in 1 Cor. 15:3ff.; 11:23ff.; Phil. 2:6ff.; 1 Tim. 2:6; Gal. 1:4, etc. (the *hypér* formula); Rom. 5:16, 19; 10:16; perhaps 8:32. Pre-Synoptic formulas may also be cited, e.g., Mk. 14:24; 10:45; 1:11; Lk. 2:32; Mt. 12:18ff.; Mk. 9:12. Acts also contains obvious tradition and formulas, e.g., 8:32-33; the title *ho díkaios* in 3:14; 7:52; 22:14. Primitive formulas may also be traced in 1 Pet. 2:21ff.; 3:18; 1:11; Heb. 9:27-28; 7:25. The same applies to the Johannine works, e.g., Jn. 1:29, 34, 36; 1 Jn. 2:1, 29; 3:7; Jn. 10:11, 15, 17-18; 16:32. Paul himself quotes Is. 52:15 in Rom.

15:21, but with a missionary rather than a christological slant. Matthew contributes an obvious allusion to Is. 53 in 26:54. The lack of references in James, 2 and 3 John, Jude, 2 Peter, and Revelation and the paucity of references in Paul, Hebrews, and John support the conclusion that like *pais theoú* the christological interpretation of Isaiah belongs to the oldest stratum of tradition and quickly takes on fixity of form. Of the Isaiah passages only 42:1ff.; 49:6; 52:13ff. are expounded messianically, as in the case of Palestinian Judaism.

2. *The Setting in the Primitive Church.*

a. Scripture Proof. In the primitive church the setting of the christological interpretation of the servant passages is in the proof from Scripture. The situation after the death of Jesus necessitates a proof that the crucifixion is divinely planned. Usually Is. 53 is taken to be so well known that a general reference to Scripture is enough, but the passage is quoted in Acts 8:32-33, and details of Jesus' life are found in Is. 42:1ff.; 53, along with a prophecy of the unbelief of Israel in Is. 53:7, and of the apostolic mission in Rom. 15:21.

b. Primitive Christology. Many christological predicates are based on Isaiah, e.g., *pais* itself, *huiós, amnós, arnion, eklektós, agapētós,* and *díkaios,* and perhaps the description of Jesus as *hilasmós* (1 Jn. 2:2) and *paráklētos* (2:1). Various formulas also derive from Isaiah, e.g., the *hypér* formula, *(para)didónai,* and the phrase *aírein tḗn hamartían* (or *anaphérein hamartías*).

c. Liturgy. The "many" (*pollṓn*) of the eucharistic sayings points to the servant passages (Mk. 14:24), and the liturgical formula *diá Iēsoú toú paidós soú* lives on with great tenacity in the eucharistic prayer and doxology. The hymn of Phil. 2:6ff. extols Jesus as the servant and draws on the Hebrew text in vv. 6-9 (cf. especially the harsh phrase *heautón ekénōsen* [v. 7] as an exact rendering of Is. 53:12). The contrast between humiliation and exaltation, too, plainly reflects Is. 53. The song of Simeon in Lk. 2:29ff. takes up Is. 49:6 and applies it to Jesus.

d. Exhortation. Is. 53 plays an important role in exhortation. Jesus as the servant is a model of ministry (Mk. 10:45), unselfishness (Phil. 2:5ff.), innocent and voluntary suffering (1 Pet. 2:21ff.), and humility (1 Clem. 16.1ff.). In particular, he is an example for the martyr to follow (Ignatius *Ephesians* 10.3). No phase of early Christian life does not bear the stamp of Servant Christology.

III. Does Jesus See Himself as the Servant of Isaiah? The Gospels say so (cf. Mk. 9:12; 9:31; 10:33; 14:8, 24, 61; 15:5; Mt. 26:2; Lk. 24:7, etc.). If there are indications that the present form of some of these statements comes in part from the community, there are points in the texts that forbid their dismissal as inauthentic. Jesus is forced by the situation to expect a violent death (cf. the charges of blasphemy and sabbath-breaking, the need to seek safety in flight, and the examples of the fate of the prophets and of the Baptist). If Jesus expected a violent death, he must have reflected on its purpose, and it is natural that he should have found it in the contemporary concept of the atoning power of death. Since Is. 40ff. obviously affects his sense of mission, the references to Is. 53 fit into the framework of his ministry. Five considerations support the antiquity of the relevant sayings. First, they do not show any plain influence of the LXX. Second, the intimations of the passion and glorification are general and not colored by the actual events of the crucifixion and resurrection. Third, the sayings are firmly anchored in the context (cf. especially Mk. 8:31; 14:8; Lk. 22:37; Mk. 9:12). Fourth, the use of the passive for God's action, which is a later Jewish mode of speech, is a token of the personal style of Jesus, and it occurs in Mk. 9:31 in a saying that has an archaic ring because of its conciseness, its enigmatic character, and its wordplay. Fifth, Is. 53 plays a role in the eucharistic sayings (Mk. 14:24), which in their form in the Gospels (as distinct from Paul in 1 Cor. 11:23ff.) are shown by many Semitic features to belong to the bedrock of the tradition. If Jesus rarely refers Is. 53 to himself, and never in the material peculiar to Matthew and Luke, this is probably because it is only in his teaching of the disciples that he declares himself to be the Servant who has the divinely ordained task of dying vicariously for the many who have come under divine judgment. It is as he goes to death willingly, innocently, and patiently in accordance with the will of God that his death has unlimited atoning power. The life that he pours out is life from God and with God.

[J. JEREMIAS, V, 677-717]

---

pálai [earlier, long ago], *palaiós* [old, ancient] *palaiótēs* [aged, obsolete], *palaióō* [to make old]

---

pálai. This word has such senses as "earlier," "before," "once upon a time," "long since," and "for a long time." It occurs seven times in the NT, for "just before" in Mk. 15:44; 2 Cor. 12:19, much "earlier" in 2 Pet. 1:9, "long ago" in Mt. 11:21; Lk. 10:13; Heb. 1:1; Jude 4.

palaiós.

1. This word means "old" with such nuances as "past," "ancient," "antiquated," and "venerable" (usually *archaíos* in secular Greek); *kainós* and *néos* are antonyms. In Paul *palaiós* has greater theological force than *archaíos*.

2. The LXX uses *palaiós* for various Hebrew terms, but unlike the verb *palaióō*, which denotes the uselessness of worn-out things, and figuratively the transitoriness of creaturely life (cf. Ps. 32:3; Gen. 8:12; Job 21:13; Is. 65:22), it has no theological significance.

3. In the Synoptic tradition *palaiós* occurs in Mk. 2:21-22 and parallels; Lk. 5:36ff.; 5:39; Mt. 13:52 in the sharp antithesis of old and new. In Mk. 2:21-22 Jesus points out the incompatibility of old and new in proverbial sayings. The meaning depends on whether the sayings refer more strictly to the question at issue or more generally to the total mission of Jesus. The latter is more likely; his message is something completely new, although the new is also a fulfilment of the old (Mt. 5:17). Lk. 5:39 seems to contradict what precedes, but in context it is a warning against overvaluing the old. Mt. 13:52 is probably to be interpreted along the lines of 5:17, since the parables in Mt. 13 all deal with the new thing that Jesus presents.

4. Paul, too, sets the old over against the new. Indeed, in 1 Cor. 5:6ff. the old leaven is evil, the reference being to the old life of sin. The antithesis of the old and the new man in Rom. 6:6; Col. 3:9; Eph. 4:22 is along similar lines. The old, crucified with Christ (Rom. 6), is incompatible with the new, and is thus to be put off and to give place to the new (Col. 3:9; Eph. 4:22). Vices mark the old man, but the new is renewed in God's image (Col. 3:5ff.). One may see here an allusion to baptism (cf. Gal. 3:27-28). The law brings no renewal, and its covenant is thus the old one (2 Cor. 3:14) which is the letter that kills. Christ has brought the new covenant of righteousness which replaces it. The old covenant, however, is still a covenant of God.

5. 1 John mentions the old commandment and the new but in a different way, for the old commandment here is that which Christians have already heard (cf. Jn. 13:34-35), and there is thus no antithesis between the two (1 Jn. 2:7).

769

palaiótēs. This rare word means "aged" or "what is dated." It occurs in the NT only in Rom. 7:6, where the service which consists only in observance of the written code is outmoded and must give way to service in the power of the Spirit.

palaióō. This word means "to make old," "to declare to be obsolete." Important in the LXX, it occurs in the NT in Heb. 1:11 (quoting Ps. 102:25) and Lk. 12:33, but is theologically significant only in Heb. 8:13, which argues that God, by setting up the new covenant, has declared the old to be outdated, so that it is ready to disappear. We thus have here an antithesis similar to that of Jesus and Paul.

[H. SEESEMANN, V, 717-20]

---

pálē [wrestling, conflict]

---

pálē means "wrestling," but Greek tragedy prepares for it the broader sense of "conflict," and Philo uses it figuratively for the wrestling of the ascetic. It occurs in the NT only in Eph. 6:12, which gives Christian warfare an eschatological dimension as part of the great final battle that has begun and is intensifying. Christian wrestling is with demonic forces, and the reward is deliverance in the judgment (cf. also 1 Th. 5:8; Rom. 6:13; 13:12).   [H. GREEVEN, V, 721]
→ *panoplía*

palingenesía → *gínomai*

---

panḗgyris [festal gathering]

---

panḗgyris means "gathering of the people," especially cultic (cf. in the LXX Hos. 2:13; 9:5). The only NT instance is in Heb. 12:22, where it is probably in apposition to "myriads of angels" and means "festal assembly." For such an assembly in the NT, cf. Rev. 4.   [H. SEESEMANN, V, 722]

panoplía → *hóplon*

---

panourgía [cunning, craftiness],   *panoúrgos* [cunning, crafty]

A. Nonbiblical Usage.
1. The group denotes "ability," but when it expresses all-around human ability there is the suggestion of a false and presumptuous self-evaluation.
2. The limited positive use is secondary and comes only after centuries of negative use in which the sense is "capable of anything." A piece of wood befitting the *panoúrgos* is not magical wood but the gallows. The group is used for wily animals. The reason why the positive aspect is poorly developed is that the sense of human limitation stands in the way. The negative use rests on the assumption that those who have the secret of success will use it unscrupulously.

B. The LXX and Philo.
1. The Hebrew original means "cunning" but in Proverbs it may also mean "prudent." Since the LXX uses the group mostly in Proverbs, it tends to take on a more

positive sense. Fear of God confers practical wisdom and this implies the ability to do things successfully. The *huiós panoúrgos* is a model of obedience in Prov. 13:1. Sirach follows the same pattern. *panourgía* is good if based on wisdom, otherwise not.

2. Philo once uses *panourgía* for what might be "skill," but even here the sense is bad, as the context shows (*Allegorical Interpretation of Laws* 2.106-07). Humans may have *panourgía*, but their use of it has evil results. One may see from Gen. 3 that it has a satanic background, and it comes at the head of Philo's list of vices (*On the Sacrifices of Abel and Cain* 32).

C. The NT and Early Church.

1. The NT uses the group negatively. "Cunning" is the meaning in Lk. 20:23, 2 Cor. 12:16, and probably 2 Cor. 4:2. In the quotation in 1 Cor. 3:19 Paul differs from the LXX, perhaps on the basis of the Hebrew, or by recollection of Job 5:12. The NT thus follows the usual sense, but with a suggestion of satanic *panourgía* and with a feeling that the group has a self-righteous ring.

2. In Hermas *Visions* 3.3.1 Hermas is called *panoúrgos* in a warning against ulterior motives. [O. BAUERNFEIND, V, 722-27]

pantokrátōr → *krátos*

---

pará [from, beside, before, etc.]

A. With the Genitive (Ablative).

1. Spatially the sense in such cases is "out of," "from beside," "from."

2. The word then denotes authorship: "from." In this sense it comes a. after verbs of asking, demanding, etc. (cf. Mt. 20:20), or verbs of taking, receiving, or buying (cf. Mt. 18:19; Mk. 12:2; Eph. 6:8). Another use b. is with verbs in the passive to denote the doer or logical subject (cf. Lk. 1:45; Jn. 1:6). We also find it c. in movements that stress the starting point or actions that stress the doer (cf. Mt. 14:43; Lk. 2:1; 8:49). Important here are the coming of the Son from the Father (Jn. 6:46) and the procession of the Spirit (15:26). We then find it d. in various prepositional expressions, e.g., Rom. 11:37, where the covenant is willed by God, Mk. 5:26, where the reference is to what the woman has, and Mk. 3:21, where the relatives of Jesus (or perhaps even the disciples) are indicated.

B. With the Dative (Locative).

1. Spatially, *pará* in such constructions is used a. with things for "beside," or "by" (cf. Jn. 19:25), and b. with persons to denote proximity, as in Lk. 9:47, being at home or in a household (1 Cor. 16:2; Lk. 19:7), and presence, fellowship, or sphere of influence (Jn. 14:17, 23; 1 Cor. 7:24).

2. Forensically *pará* is used for appearance "before" a judge (2 Pet. 2:11).

3. Figuratively the term indicates presence with someone who makes an evaluation (Rom. 2:13), or favor with someone (God in Lk. 1:30, men in 2:52), or a quality (cf. God's omnipotence in Mt. 19:26, his impartiality in Rom. 2:11, human faith in Mt. 8:10), or inner relationship (Mt. 21:25).

C. With the Accusative.

1. Spatially *pará* in such constructions means a. "toward" (Mt. 15:10) and b. "beside," "by" (Lk. 7:38; Mt. 13:1) or "along," "by" (Mt. 4:18).

2. Comparatively, *pará* expresses a. preference ("before"; cf. Lk. 13:2), comparison ("more than," "than"; cf. Lk. 3:13; 1 Cor. 3:11 [with "other"]), and exclusion ("except," "in place of"; cf. Rom. 1:25, where idolatry does not lie alongside true worship but takes its place).

3. Denoting difference, *pará* means a. "by so much" (cf. Lk. 5:7) and "less" (2 Cor. 11:24).

4. Adversatively the sense is "without regard for," "in spite of," "against"; cf. Heb. 11:11; Rom. 1:26 (contrary to nature); 11:24 (by divine intervention); 4:18 (against hope); Acts 18:13 (contrary to the law).

5. Causally, the meaning is "because of," "on account of," as in 1 Cor. 12:15-16, where one member cannot say it is not of the body because it is not another member.

[E. H. RIESENFELD, V, 727-36]

---

parabaínō [to transgress], *parábasis* [transgression], *parabátēs* [transgressor], *aparábatos* [unchangeable], *hyperbaínō* [to transgress]

---

parabaínō.

1. This verb means a. "to go beside" (intransitive), b. "to overstep," "transgress" (transitive), and c. "to pass over," "let pass," "let slip" (transitive). In the papyri the original spatial sense is rare and the most common use is for disregarding statutes, contracts, wills, etc., or breaking one's word. A religious use parallels the legal use.

2. The LXX applies the term to the violation of God's commandments and ordinances, e.g., Ex. 32:8: "turning aside from the right way" (cf. also Dt. 9:12). In Is. 66:24 God calls backsliders *hoi parabebēkótes en emoí*. Other expressions are transgressing God's word (Num. 14:41) or covenant (Josh. 7:11) and turning aside from his commandments (Dt. 17:20). There is no fixed original for the LXX rendering. Various Hebrew words are used which denote aberration, rebellion, apostasy, etc.

3. Josephus follows the usage of the LXX either with reference to breaking the divine law and commandments or harming the state (the political order).

4. Philo stresses the penalty for transgressing laws. In two instances he refers to violation of the laws of marriage, i.e., by remarriage after divorce and by adultery (*On the Special Laws* 3.30.61).

5. The word is rare in the NT, where sin is a demonic force and not just transgression of the law. In Acts 1:25 the use suggests that Judas by withdrawing from his apostolic office has incurred guilt. In Mt. 15:2-3 the double use brings into sharp relief the battle of Jesus against Pharisaic piety. Transgression is sin where it is against God's commandment. Even observance of human tradition may be transgression if the tradition obscures the pure and original will of God and turns it into its opposite. In 2 Jn. 9 the reading *parabaínō* is explanatory. Those who do not abide but go ahead (or beyond) are guilty of transgression.

parábasis. This word means "striding to and fro," "stepping over," "transgressing," "violating" (cf. in the LXX Ps. 101:3). In the NT it denotes sin in relation to the law. In Rom. 2:23 the Jew dishonors God by transgressing the law, and in 4:15 the law brings wrath because there is transgression only where there is law. Between Adam and Moses there is sin but no *parábasis* because the law is not yet given. In Gal. 3:19 the law is given to show that evil deeds are transgressions of God's will. In 1 Tim. 2:14 Eve is deceived first and becomes a transgressor by violating God's prohibition.

In Heb. 2:2 every transgression of the law carries a due penalty, and in 9:15 Christ's death serves to remit the transgressions committed under the old covenant, i.e., the acts of disobedience against God's law that have brought Israel into guilt against God.

parabátēs. In secular Greek this word usually means a "companion" or "helper" and only rarely a "transgressor." In military usage it denotes the warrior who stands in a chariot beside the charioteer or the foot soldier set among the cavalry to seize and mount horses whose riders have fallen. The papyri, Josephus, and Philo do not use the term. In the NT Paul uses it for a transgressor of God's commands. Thus in Rom. 2:25, 27 Gentiles may rightly accuse Jews of being themselves transgressors, and in Gal. 2:18, refuting the suggestion that Christ is made an agent of sin, Paul argues that by setting up the law again he would make himself a transgressor, for transgression arises only under the dominion of law. Jms. 2:9 shows that respecting persons is transgression of the law, and 2:11 makes the point that even by breaking a single commandment one becomes a transgressor of the law.

aparábatos.
1. This rare word usually means "unchangeable," "immutable" (cf. the stars).
2. In law it thus comes to mean "valid," "unalterable," "inviolable."
3. In the NT Heb. 7:24 says that Christ has an eternal and imperishable priesthood, not just in the sense that it cannot be transferred to anyone else, but in the sense of "unchangeable."

hyperbaínō.
1. This word means "to step over," "to exceed a limit," "to transgress," and "to overlook." In the papyri we find it for a share that "falls" to someone. Another expression is "to pass over in speech," i.e., to be silent.
2. The LXX uses the word for crossing a threshold (1 Sam. 5:5), climbing over palisades (4 Macc. 3:12), leaping over a wall (2 Sam. 22:30), stepping over a boundary (Job 24:2), passing in a race (2 Sam. 18:23). It also means "to surpass" (3 Macc. 6:24). A theological sense is "to overlook" (Job 9:11), and even "to forgive" (Mic. 7:18).
3. Philo uses the word frequently for "to disregard" and "to cross the limits" (e.g., of selfishness, of truth, or of nature).
4. The only NT instance is in 1 Th. 4:6. If the word has no object here, the sense is "to sin," but if it goes with "his brother" like "wrong," then it means "to overreach," "to defraud." The latter is more likely in the general context.

[J. SCHNEIDER, V, 736-44]

---

parabolḗ [comparison, parable]

A. Secular Greek.
1. This word has the following senses: "setting beside," "standing beside," "aberration," and "division." In rhetoric it means "similitude," "parable."
2. Rhetoric distinguishes between the comparison, the metaphor, the metaphor which has passed into common use, the simile, the allegory, and the parable. The latter compares two things from different fields in order to elucidate the unfamiliar by means of the familiar.
3. Epic poetry makes great use of similitudes because of their illustrative power

and evocative content. Gnomic poetry likes them, and so does Plato, who draws on human life or myth for illustrations. The Stoic-Cynic diatribe also uses illustrations, often in answer to objections. Aristotle thinks examples from history are more valuable than parables, but points out that the latter, as distinct from fables, take their material from real life. The effectiveness of comparisons, he says, rests on the ability to see analogy, and it is better that discerning minds should grasp the point of comparison independently. Parable and allegory often merge into one another.

B. The OT, LXX, and Later Judaism.

1. In the LXX *parabolē* is mostly a rendering of *māshāl*, which indicates likeness. At first the *mashal* is a proverb (1 Sam. 10:12); we find it in the phrase "to become a proverb or byword" (Is. 14:4). In Wisdom writings it is the wise saying and comprises examples from life, rules of prudence and courtesy, vocational advice, moral admonitions, and religious directions. Many proverbs use the comparative "as" (Prov. 25:11ff.; 26:18-19). Comparison is also made by juxtaposition (15:16; 16:8). But parallelism is predominant. Since sages love veiled expressions, *parabolē* and *aínigma* ("riddle") are often synonymous. In Ps. 78:2 the *mashal* is a didactic poem that seeks to solve the riddle of the people's history. Another form of *mashal* is the developed comparison or similitude (cf. 2 Sam. 12:1ff.; Judg. 9:8ff.). The prophets find parables helpful, either constructing them (Is. 28:23ff.) or receiving them in visions (Am. 7:8). The best known is the parable of the vineyard in Is. 5. The OT parable in this sense is a complete story whose meaning is hidden and may be either discerned independently or disclosed by the prophet. In Ezekiel the *mashal* is a word of divine revelation (Ezek. 17:2; 24:3); another word is needed to interpret it (17:11ff.; 24:6ff.). In Ps. 49:4 the psalmist speaks as a prophet who has received from God a word that explains the strange prosperity of the wicked. Parabolic actions are also performed by the prophets. As a rendering of *māshāl*, *parabolē* takes on a richer content that carries over into the NT.

2. In apocalyptic, similitudes are means of giving eschatological instruction. Earthly events clarify heavenly events. Visions of heavenly and future mysteries (judgment, resurrection, abodes of the blessed, etc.) are also parables.

3. The Palestinian rabbis use parables that are close to those of the Gospels. They may have the form of short sayings or they may be longer fables, allegories, or stories. The rabbis use the term *māshāl* impartially for pure or mixed similitudes and allegories. The aim is usually to establish or explain a statement, often polemically. Eschatological parables are rare. A short introductory formula marks off the parable from the general context, as in the NT. The point of comparison may be stated in the final sentence. Some parables have two climaxes, which causes complications. The parables are meant to elucidate, but they have also an oracular quality.

C. The NT.

1. Usage. In the NT *parabolē* occurs 45 times in the Gospels and twice in Hebrews, while *paroimía* occurs three times in John and once in 2 Peter. The use is the same as that of *māshāl–parabolē* in the OT and the rabbis. In the Gospels the *parabolē* is a short saying combined with a comparison, a proverbial saying, or, in most instances, a parable in the usual sense. In Hebrews it is a "type" or "counterpart."

2. Definition and Form of NT Parables. More than a metaphor (Mt. 16:6) or simile (10:16), the parable is a similitude which uses evident truth from a known field (nature or human life) to convey new truth in an unknown (the kingdom, the nature and action of God). In the stricter sense parables are more developed similes or metaphors (Mt.

13:31-32; 18:12ff.). They derive their power from the obvious general truth that is used. But then many parables take the form of stories with secondary details in which a single experience constitutes the known truth (Mk. 4:3ff.). In other cases we have stories in which the truth is presented without figurative garb (Lk. 10:30ff.; 12:16ff.; 16:19ff.; 18:9ff.). Jesus takes his material from nature (Mk. 4:26ff.) or Palestinian life. He uses ordinary occurrences (the leaven), typical incidents (sowing seed), and exceptional circumstances (the workers in the vineyard). He uses stock metaphors but these do not become allegories, although some parables (Mk. 12:1ff.) are close to allegories. Current happenings might be used. While the tendency of expositors to allegorize parables was a mistake, some parables have more than one climax, and the stories are organisms, so that several points of comparison might arise (e.g., the sower and different soils). One must also avoid generalizing, for Jesus is not illustrating general truths but preaching the kingdom of God. The connecting statement, then, lies in a living context within the theme of Jesus' preaching. In form the parables are like those of the rabbis. They begin with a brief introductory formula. An (*amḗn*) *légō hymín* often gives emphasis to the point. The parables may or may not include an application and sometimes end with a question. The application may be antithetical (Lk. 12:40, 56). The final aim is to clarify but not without demanding response from the hearers.

3. The Question of Transmission. The fidelity of transmission seems to be very high. The parables bear the imprint of Jesus' thought and style, and are true to the Palestinian setting. Comparison of the different versions shows that there may be secondary additions, and the community may have adapted for believers some parables that were originally addressed to opponents (cf. Mt. 18:12ff.; Lk. 12:58-59). Allegory tends to invade eschatological parables (cf. Lk. 14:16 and Mt. 22:2), although allegorical features may well have been original. The question of authenticity is particularly urgent when interpretations are given (Mk. 4:13ff.; Mt. 13:36ff.). The disciples ask for these interpretations because of the oracular nature of the parables (cf. Mk. 4:34). Some exegetes believe that allegorical elements and stylistic peculiarities in the interpretations suggest a community setting.

4. The Meaning and Purpose of the Parables in Jesus' Preaching. Mk. 4:33-34 says that Jesus makes much use of parables because the people is slow to understand. Jesus has come at a critical hour and seeks to evoke the right response (Lk. 12:54ff.). As a prophet, he has to be clear. The parables carry their own message, but they presuppose listeners who will accompany the speaker and grasp the point of comparison. Those who do not have the spiritual power to do this, or who reject the revelation of God, will be sifted out by parables. If Jesus uses parables as an aid to understanding, they also serve as veils where there is unbelief. This raises the question of Mk. 4:11, which with its *hína* suggests that parables deliberately conceal the truth with a view to hardening and judgment. On a critical understanding, this is a later construction which ascribes the unbelief of Israel to the prior counsel of God that Jesus fulfils by using parables. On a conservative view, the saying reflects the experience of Jesus as he proclaims the actualization in himself of the divine plan of salvation but meets with the two responses of faith and unbelief; his sayings are light and salvation to disciples but darkness and judgment to the unresponsive masses who hear the same words but do not perceive their truth, and thus come under the prophecy of Is. 6:9-10.

5. The Message of the Parables. The parables deal with the kingdom of God, God's nature and work, and human destiny. While rabbinic parables expound the law, the parables of Jesus are mostly eschatological (although not apocalyptic). Most of Jesus' parables are interwoven into a didactic context. Some, however, are not bound to a theme, but seek by veiled speech to stir the audience to find the statement behind the veil (Mk. 12:1ff.). As regards the kingdom, the parables stress its imminence and sudden coming (Mk. 13:28-29; Mt. 24:43-44). The old aeon has gone (Mk. 2:21-22), demons must yield (3:27), an invitation to enter the kingdom is issued (2:17). The kingdom will grow (4:31-32) and permeate the world (Mt. 13:33). Decision is demanded (Mt. 6:24), the end will entail separation (13:24ff.), those who seek earthly security are fools (Lk. 12:16ff.), and the unfruitful are under threat (13:6ff.). Watchfulness is required (Mt. 25:1ff.). Only doers will stand in the judgment (Mt. 7:24ff.), and the kingdom will reverse all earthly values (Lk. 16:19ff.). As regards God's nature and action, he is like a loving father (Mt. 7:9ff.; Lk. 15:11ff.), a kind and righteous judge (Lk. 18:1ff.), and a more than generous employer (Mt. 20:1ff.). As regards human destiny, self-examination (Lk. 14:28ff.) and prudent action (16:1ff.) are demanded. Disciples have no claims (Lk. 17:7ff.), share the fate of their master (Mt. 10:24-25), and must shine out like a city on a hill (Mt. 5:14). Integrity (Mt. 15:10ff.), humility (Lk. 18:9ff.), gratitude (Lk. 7:36ff.), and a readiness to forgive (Mt. 18:23ff.) are incumbent on them. The love that God requires recognizes no human limits (Lk. 10:30ff.).

6. *Figurative Language in Paul, James, and Revelation.* Paul does not use the word *parabolē* but draws comparisons from human life, e.g., armor, leaven, milk, the temple, the mirror. In more extended comparisons he refers to the legal status of the married woman, to believers as a crop, to the Christian life as a contest, to the community as a bodily organism, to resurrection bodies as seed and plant. James, too, is rich in figures but uses no true parables. Revelation, after the apocalyptic manner, makes copious use of visions, allegories, and symbols, but not parables.

D. The Apostolic Fathers. *parabolē* occurs twice in Barnabas in allegorical interpretation of the OT (cf. 6.10 and Ex. 33:1ff., and 17.2). The word here means a saying with an allegorical sense, a mysterious intimation of the divinely ordained future. Hermas uses *parabolaí* in the title of the third part. The first five *parabolaí* are extended comparisons that are built on current metaphors and accompanied by partly parabolic and partly allegorical interpretations with interwoven admonitions. In 6–10 the *parabolaí* are visions which impart divine revelations in figures of speech, and explanations are again given.   [F. HAUCK, V, 744-61]

---

parangéllō [to give orders, command], **parangelía** [order, command]

A. General Greek Usage. This group has to do with "intimation" in various senses, the only one of which to occur in the NT, with much modification, is that of "order" or "direction." While *parangéllein* denotes transmission of the command, *keleúein* has the actual command in view.

B. Hellenistic Jewish Usage.
1. The LXX does not use the noun but has the verb for military orders, summons to an assembly (1 Sam. 10:17), and official proclamations (2 Chr. 36:22).
2. Philo uses the verb for God's commands, and also has the nouns *parángelma* and *parangelía* for precepts, legal statutes, and demands.

C. NT Usage.
1. The Synoptics use *parangéllein* for "to command," but only with Jesus as subject. Thus he instructs the disciples (Mt. 10:5), commands the spirits to depart (Lk. 8:29), orders the cleansed leper (5:14), tells the crowd to be seated (Mk. 8:6). Luke shows a liking for the word.

2. The verb is fairly common in Acts. Jesus commands the disciples in 1:4, and has told them to preach in 10:42. In Christ's name Paul commands the spirit to depart in 16:18. Various other commands are those of the authorities in 4:18, of the magistrates in 16:23, of Lysias in 23:22.

3. Paul alone uses the noun as well as the verb. Timothy is to charge false teachers in 1 Tim. 1:3; the aim of the charge (v. 5) is love. What the Lord commands is the supreme authority (1 Cor. 7:10), but this authority stands behind Paul's own commands (1 Th. 4:2; 2 Th. 3:12). In 1 Timothy *parangéllein* is enjoined on Timothy; he is to charge false teachers, widows, and the rich (1:3-4; 5:7; 6:17). This charge is laid on him in Christ's name. *parangéllein* is thus traced back to God's saving work in Christ.

[D. SCHMITZ, V, 761-65]

parágō → *agōgḗ*; *paradeigmatízō* → *deíknymi*

---

parádeisos [paradise]

A. History of the Word.
1. This is a loanword from a Persian term meaning "enclosure" or "park." The Greeks first use it for the parks of Persian kings. In the LXX the garden of Gen. 2–3 is God's "park" and *parádeisos* becomes a technical religious term.

2. Hebrew and Aramaic also adopt the word but use it only in the secular sense.

B. Paradise in Later Judaism.
1. The First Age. Statements about paradise begin with Gen. 2–3, which offers rich material for embroidery.

2. The Last Age. Hope develops for a final age of bliss, and this hope uses the paradise motif (Ezek. 36:35). There is indeed an expected return of the original paradise in apocalyptic, which by means of the belief in resurrection offers assurance that all the righteous will share its delights.

3. Present Hiddenness of Paradise. If the paradise of the first age is to return, it still exists in hidden form. It is the present home of the righteous; Sheol is the abode of the wicked. Suggested locations are on earth, on a high mountain reaching up to heaven, or in heaven. The delights of the intermediate and eschatological paradise merge into one another.

4. The Identity of Paradise. While there are references to the first paradise, the last paradise, and the intermediate paradise, these are not three entities but one and the same garden of God.

C. The NT.
1. The First, Hidden, and Last Paradise. The term *parádeisos* occurs in the NT only in Lk. 23:43; 2 Cor. 12:4; Rev. 2:7. It is not used for the garden, but the paradisal state is implied in Rom. 3:23; 5:12; Mt. 19:8. The concealed paradise is the intermediate abode of the redeemed in Lk. 23:43. Other NT terms for the intermediate state are table fellowship with Abraham (Lk. 16:23), being with the Lord (2 Cor. 5:8) or Christ (Phil. 1:23), and the heavenly kingdom (2 Tim. 4:18). In Mk. 13:27 the

dead will assemble in the heavenly world. The final paradise is mentioned in Rev. 2:7, for all the victor sayings have an eschatological thrust, and the fruit of the tree of life is a privilege of the last paradise (cf. Jerusalem in 22:1-2, Jerusalem being the center of the renewed earth).

2. *Paul's Rapture.* In 2 Cor. 12:4 Paul refers to his rapture to the abode of the righteous departed. He does so with great reserve, and it is not certain that paradise is the same as the third heaven of v. 3. The visions of the Lord are visions given by the Lord, not visions of Christ among the departed.

3. *Fellowship with Christ.* Jesus' answer to the prayer of the penitent thief is that he will be with him in paradise (Lk. 23:43). This is the hidden intermediate paradise, but the eschatological "today" points to the dawn of the day of salvation. Paradise is opened to the worst of penitent sinners by fellowship with the Messiah. Fellowship with Christ is the distinctive Christian characteristic of the intermediate state (cf. Acts 7:59; 2 Cor. 5:8; Phil. 1:23; 2 Tim. 4:18; Jn. 12:26; Rev. 7:9ff.). This replaces speculation about paradisal delights.

4. *Paradise and Hades.* The NT says that Jesus enters paradise (Lk. 23:43) and offers his blood in the heavenly sanctuary (Heb. 7:26-27; cf. also Jn. 3:14; 8:28). Yet it also refers to his sojourn in *hádēs* and perhaps to redemptive work there (cf. Rom. 10:7; Acts 2:27; 1 Pet. 3:19-20). Both conceptions express the same assurance of faith in the unique atoning efficacy of Christ's work, but from different angles.

5. *Jesus Restores Paradise.* In Rev. 2:7 it is Jesus who gives the fruit of paradise to the victors. But the NT goes further, for Jesus has already restored paradise by his coming. Thus in Mt. 11:5 his word and work fulfil Is. 35:5-6, and in Mk. 10:2-3 he reimposes the divine will in paradise (cf. also Mk. 1:13; 7:37) and in John his offering of the symbols of paradise in the bread and water of life. The NT makes only sparing use of the term, probably because of the danger of the intrusion of fantastic ideas, as in the inauthentic saying reported by Papias.   [J. JEREMIAS, V, 765-73]

→ *hádēs*

paradídōmi, parádosis → *dídōmi; parádoxos* → *dokéō; parazēlóō* → *zḗlos;*
parathḗkē → *títhēmi; paraitéomai* → *aitéō*

---

parakaléō [to exhort, comfort],   **paráklēsis** [exhortation, comfort]

A. Common Greek Usage.

1. These two words have a wide range of meaning, the first sense being that of "calling to" either literally or with such nuances as calling for aid, inviting, and summoning.

2. A second sense is that of "beseeching," e.g., calling on the gods in prayer, or, from a superior to an inferior, proposing.

3. A third sense is that of "exhorting" or "encouraging," and even on occasion of "winning over" for a plan.

4. The final sense is that of "comforting," mostly in the form of giving exhortation or encouragement in times of sorrow. This is not a common use.

B. Greek Judaism.

1. *Hebrew Equivalents and Their Influence.* In the LXX the words are used for 15 Hebrew terms and also occur in free renderings. Mostly, however, they are used for

nāḥam, and this makes "comfort" the main sense, especially in bereavement (Gen. 24:67). The verb in particular also refers to the comfort that God gives his people under judgment, or individuals in temptation.

2. *The Group in the LXX with No Hebrew Original.* Where there is no Hebrew original, the sense of comfort is almost completely absent, and instead we have such senses as exhortation, encouragement, strengthening, reassuring, proposing, and inviting.

3. *The Extracanonical Writings.* Outside the biblical sphere we seldom find the special LXX use, and such meanings as asking, admonishing, beseeching, etc. predominate. Thus we find "to invite" in Philo and "to invoke" God in prayer in Josephus. Only in the Testaments of the Twelve Patriarchs and 4 Esdras is the idea of comfort more commonly present, whether with God's comfort in view or the comforting of Zion in her mourning.   [O. Schmitz, V, 773-79]

C. Comfort and Comforters in Nonbiblical Antiquity.

I. Comfort and Admonition. The group contains an imperative element ("to admonish") that is accompanied by the indicative ("to console"). A theoretical distinction is made between them but they come together in practice. Exhortation is a form of comfort with a view to overcoming or setting aside grief.

II. Comforters. Antiquity works out different forms of comfort for the elderly, the dying, the bereaved, the separated, exiles, and the victims of injustice or handicaps. All have the duty of offering comfort. The dying give it in parting words, and the dead in writings in which they figure. Mourners try to console themselves in the same way as they console others. They may read works of consolation, and rational considerations have a consoling effect, as does the recounting of one's troubles.

III. Ways and Means of Comfort. The ways of giving comfort are personal presence, visits, letters, and consolatory writings. Professional comforters are also available. Means of comfort are philosophical teachings, religious teachings and practices, e.g., prayer and the mysteries, and such things as music, diversions, sleep, and even wine.

IV. Reasons for Comfort.

1. *Epicurus.* Among reasons for comfort the Epicureans suggest that death is the absolute end, so that there is no reason to grieve for the dead. The true comfort is life itself, i.e., the remembrance that each day might be the last, and therefore the receiving and using of each hour as a gift.

2. *Common Reasons.* Among reasons for comfort commonly adduced are the recollection of past happiness, the consideration of good things still remaining, the thought of the duration of the universe but also of its corruptibility, compared to which individual suffering is petty, and the thought of the universality of death, which overtakes great as well as small.

3. *The Thought of Immortality.* The main basis of comfort in antiquity is the idea of the immortality of the soul. The good are not dead; death is the birth of never-ending life, a returning home. On this view life itself is an exile, with the body as a prison or burden, and death a joyous liberation. One should thus dwell on the better hereafter to which the dead have gone and in which they enjoy a heavenly reward and the fellowship of the blessed gods. The mysteries especially nurture this view. In general, the gods themselves are not comforters. They fix the time of death and will not abandon those who are under their protection, but their function in antiquity is not to console, and the ancients have more fear of their envy than trust in their friendship. For all the appeals to the thought of a better hereafter, many of the state-

ments to this effect have a note of uncertainty and unreality. A profound lack of hope characterizes the world of antiquity. The dead are called blessed whether they live on or cease to be. Transitoriness as a source of consolation is cold comfort. The pessimistic principle that life is evil and death a release testifies to a hopeless sense of meaninglessness. Early death in particular suggests the futility of birth. Cynical notes are heard when the dead are summoned up to give the information that all that is said about the world to come is false. Various symbols, e.g., the broken column, the extinguished torch, and the flawed rose express the hopelessness of antiquity. Even the noblest consolation ends in capitulation to the majesty of death. Pagan antiquity shows "classically" how little our own insights and resources can help us when we encounter the forces that make life a realm of suffering   [G. STÄHLIN, V, 779-88]

D. Comfort and Comfortlessness in the OT.

I. Human Comfort.

1. Bearers. Relatives and friends are called upon to give comfort in the OT (Job 2:11), but also those more distant (cf. 2 Sam. 10:2). It is an honor to be asked to console the mourning (Job 29:25). Some may do it badly (16:2), but a true comforter is like a king among his troops (29:25).

2. Means. Visits are customary, and bread and wine are brought (Jer. 16:5, 7). Wine is a particular solace in trouble (Gen. 5:29; cf. Prov. 31:6-7).

3. Self-comforting. Often comforters counsel self-consolation. Sirach advises that mourning be brief, for nothing can be altered and lamentation is harmful.

II. Divine Comfort.

1. Comfortlessness. There is no true comfort apart from God. The Psalms express human comfortlessness (69:20; 77:2). Lamentations (1:2, 9, 16) and Ecclesiastes (4:1) mention it too. Such desolation is finally a divine judgment (Is. 51:19).

2. Comfort. God's proper work is to comfort. He turns desolation into consolation for individuals (Ps. 23:4) and the people (Is. 54:11ff.). The great promise to Israel is that of Is. 40:1ff. The time of salvation is the time of God's comfort when he will make of ruins a *parádeisos* (51:3).

3. Metaphors. The metaphors of the shepherd (Is. 40:11) and mother (66:13) describe God's comfort. His people find consolation at his breast (66:11) and on his knees (66:12).

4. Mediators. God channels his comfort through mediators, e.g., his word (Ps. 119), Scripture (2 Macc. 5:19), wisdom (Wis. 8:9), and among humans the prophets, who both judge and comfort (cf. Ezek. 4ff. and 33ff.; Jer. 31:18ff.), and especially the servant (Is. 61:2).

E. Human and Divine Comfort in Judaism.

I. Human Comfort.

1. Occasions. Comfort is given to bereaved relatives, to the teachers of those who die young, and to those who are conscience-stricken.

2. Duty. The duty of comforting falls on close relatives, teachers, colleagues, pupils, neighbors, etc. To give comfort is a good work and a following of God, who himself comforts mourners.

3. Forms. The main forms are visits and letters. Books close with words of consolation and blessing.

4. Reasons. The reasons are partly the same as in the pagan world and partly biblical and Jewish.

5. Presuppositions. Knowledge of Scripture and experience of comfort confer the ability to comfort.

6. Self-comforting. Judaism cultivates the ideal of self-comforting.

II. Divine Comfort. With the OT Judaism extols God as the only true comforter. Hellenistic Judaism thinks God has planted a native hope in humanity, but Palestinian Judaism refers to such mediators of comfort as the word of promise, the prophets, the angels, and the Messiah. "Comfort" becomes a comprehensive term for the messianic salvation (Is. 40:1ff.). The consolation of Israel is the messianic hope, and Menachem (Comforter) becomes a name for the Messiah.

[O. SCHMITZ–G. STÄHLIN, V, 788-93]

F. The Words in the NT. In the NT *parakaléō* and *paráklēsis,* which do not occur in the Johannine works or James, receive their main content from the NT event of salvation. Sometimes, of course, we also find the ordinary use (cf. especially Acts, e.g., 8:31; 9:38; 16:39; 28:14, 20, etc.). In other cases there is movement toward a specific use, e.g., when people ask Jesus for help. A general use for comfort occurs in Acts 20:12; 1 Th. 3:7; 2 Cor. 2:7, but this is on the basis of the gospel, and in the main the NT uses the words specifically for address with the three nuances of asking for help, exhorting, and comforting.

1. Asking for Help. This is a common use in the Synoptics when people turn to Jesus for help, e.g., in Mt. 8:5; Lk. 7:4; Mk. 5:18; 6:56; 1:40; 8:22. This asking is urgent beseeching. A similar use in Mt. 26:53 is for calling on God for help; Jesus does not avail himself of this open possibility.

2. Exhorting. This is a common use in Acts and Paul. It implies speaking in God's name and with the Spirit's power. Evangelistic entreaty is the point in 2 Cor. 5:20, but with a note of authority. Proclamation is also *paráklēsis* in 1 Th. 2:3 (cf. Acts 9:31; 2:40; Lk. 3:18). What is meant is the proclaiming of salvation as also a claim on the will and action of the hearers. Often admonition to those already won is at issue (cf. Heb. 13:22; 1 Pet. 5:12; Jude 3; Phil. 2:1; Rom. 12:1, etc.). This admonition is "in Christ," or "by his name," or "by his meekness and gentleness," or "by the mercy of God" (cf. Phil. 2:1; 1 Cor. 1:10; 2 Cor. 10:1; Rom. 12:1). It rests on the saving work of God in Christ and is an inherent part of the apostolic ministry (1 Tim. 5:1; Tit. 2:6). The Holy Spirit is at work in it, and it is almost a function of prophecy (cf. 1 Cor. 14:3, 31; Acts 15:28, 31). Barnabas can give pastoral help as one who is filled with the Spirit (Acts 11:24). Accompanying words show that the admonition is not sharp, polemical, or critical, even though it is urgent and serious. The fact that comfort can be another meaning points in the same direction.

3. Comforting. It is in Paul and Hebrews that *parakaleín* denotes the comfort that God brings through his present and future salvation. Heb. 6:18 and 12:5 relate this comfort to exhortation and encouragement. Rom. 15:4 shows that it comes through Scripture and bases it on the divine constancy. This constancy is that of the divine love displayed in Christ (2 Th. 2:16-17). Paul is time and again concerned to comfort the churches in their afflictions (cf. Col. 2:2; 4:8). He himself is comforted by the kindness of Philemon (Phlm. 7). The good news about the Thessalonian church also comforts him (1 Th. 3:7). The same applies to the good news from Corinth (2 Cor. 7:6).

4. Human and Divine Comfort. Comfort is given by human agents but is real comfort only as it comes from God. God is the God of all comfort (2 Cor. 1:3-4) who makes the fellowship of suffering a fellowship of comfort (1:5ff.). While comfort derives from present salvation, it stands in the light of future deliverance, and is thus linked to both *sōtēría* and *elpís* (cf. 2 Th. 2:16; Rom. 15:4). Enjoying the divine comfort, the Corinthians are to forgive and console the one who wronged Paul (2 Cor. 2:7). Events as well as words bring comfort (2 Cor. 7:6). But the final comfort (Mt. 5:4) is the eschatological act of God which reaches into the present so that those who mourn are already blessed. Those who look for the consolation of Israel (Lk. 2:25) are awaiting messianic salvation (Is. 40:1ff.). The comfort of present salvation is set in the light of the coming consummation when God will remove all suffering by his glorious presence (Rev. 21:3ff.). For this reason it is eternal comfort and good hope (2 Th. 2:16).

5. Conclusion. The NT makes good use of the wealth of meaning in the terms *parakaleín* and *paráklēsis.* The sense "to call in" fades into the background. "To ask" occurs mainly for requests addressed to Jesus during his earthly ministry. The meaning "exhortation" comes into use both for missionary proclamation and pastoral admonition. The sense of "comfort" occurs in connection with salvation history (on an OT basis). In this sense the terms express God's aid to the churches in present affliction on the basis of the saving work of Christ and with a view to final deliverance. Asking thus presupposes that God's salvation is manifested in Jesus, exhorting that it is effected by the Spirit, and comfort that it will finally be consummated by the Father. The words relate, then, to the saving work of the triune God which leads the needy as suppliants to the Son, which is preached as exhortation in the power of the Spirit, and which carries with it already the eternal comfort of the Father.   [O. SCHMITZ, V, 793-99]
→ *paramythéomai*

parákeimai → *keímai*

---

paráklētos [advocate, helper]

A. The Linguistic Problem.

1. Use Outside the NT.

a. In Greek the verbal adjective *paráklētos* has first a passive sense, i.e., "called in to help." From this develops the sense of a "helper in court" (though not an advocate or professional adviser).

b. The LXX does not use *paráklētos,* though two other OT versions (A and Θ) have it for Job's "comforters." Josephus uses *aparáklētos* and *dysparáklētos* in a passive sense.

c. The rabbis have *paráklētos* as a loanword and use it for an advocate before God. Conversion and good works are great advocates in the judgment.

d. Philo also employs *paráklētos* for an advocate. Those who speak on behalf of accused persons are *paráklētoi,* and God's love, intercessions, and good works are *paráklētoi* before God. The symbolic adornment of the high priest's garment is his advocate in his atoning ministry in the temple.

e. In the early church, apart from NT influence, Did. 5.2 refers to advocates who help only the rich. Eusebius *Ecclesiastical History* 5.1.10 mentions an Epagathos who is the *paráklētos* of the persecuted brethren before the governor. In general, then, *paráklētos* means a helper in court who might speak on behalf of those who are accused. Only in one instance do we find the sense of "comforter."

2. The Meaning in the NT. The limited NT use does not make any consistent impression. In 1 Jn. 2:1 Christ as *paráklētos* is plainly the "advocate" who represents the sinning believer in the Father's court. In Jn. 16:7ff. the idea of a trial is again present, but here the Spirit is the disciple's counsellor in relation to the world, and the context (16:7, 13ff.; 15:26; 14:16-17, 26) might suggest the broader sense of "helper." The meaning "comforter," although adopted in some renderings, does not fit any of the passages. In the early church the Greek fathers take Jesus to be a *paráklētos* in the sense of "advocate," Origen bringing in the idea of Christ's intercessory work. As regards the Spirit, the earliest sense is again "advocate," but some fathers then come to think of the Spirit as the "comforter," the Johannine discourses being designed, they think, to comfort the disciples on Jesus' departure. The Latin fathers use both *advocatus* and *consolator,* and so do Latin translations when they do not keep the Greek (*paracletus* or *paraclitus*).

B. The Religious Background.
1. The Helper.
a. Mandaean Writings. Some trace the origin of the use of *paráklētos* in the Johannine works back to the concept of heavenly helpers. We find many such helpers in the Mandaean literature. The term is an elastic one, but it is linked especially to the revealer.

b. The Odes of Solomon. These also speak of a heavenly helper but with reference to God himself. Parallels to the concept in John may be seen, especially in such Mandaean ideas as sending from above, imparting instruction, leading to salvation, and confirming in moral conduct, but the thought of the legal advocate does not occur, and the plurality of helpers contrasts with the two of John, Jesus and the Spirit. Again, neither in the Mandaean writings nor in the Odes is *paráklētos* a title.

2. The Advocate.
a. The OT. The origin of the Johannine use has also been sought in the concept of the advocate. This is important in the OT. The patriarchs (Gen. 18:23ff.) and prophets (Jer. 14:7ff.) intercede with God for others who are guilty or afflicted. The function of such people is also to declare God's will. A somewhat higher advocate is that of Job in Job 33:23 (cf. 5:1; 16:19ff.; 19:25ff.). This is the friend in heaven who not only serves as an advocate in the divine court but also gives correction and summons to repentance. For a similar use cf. Zech. 1:12; 3:1ff.

b. The Apocrypha and Pseudepigrapha. In these writings we again find the idea of advocacy, e.g., that of the prophets, the righteous, those who fear God, and the interceding angels, who can both prosecute and defend, and who also teach and advise those who are committed to their care.

c. The Rabbis. Here again the idea of the heavenly advocate is common. The law, sacrifices, and good works have this function along with the righteous, interceding angels, and the Spirit, who both pleads with God for grace for Israel and reminds Israel of its duty toward God.

d. The NT. The concept of the advocate familiar in the OT and Judaism is obviously present in 1 Jn. 2:1. The OT and Judaism also offer many parallels for the view of the Spirit in Jn. 14ff., e.g., as authoritative teacher (14:26), witness to revelation (15:26), and speaker at the trial of the world by God (16:8ff.). The idea that the advocacy takes place both in heaven and on earth is also common to the OT and Judaism. On balance it seems that the NT usage is more closely linked to the "advocate" concept of the OT than to the "helper" concept of the Mandaean world.

C. The NT Concept.

1. The first clear idea linked with *parákletos* in the NT is that of the advocate at God's bar in heaven. In place of the many advocates Christians now recognize only the one, Jesus Christ. He is our intercessor at God's right hand (Rom. 8:34). He places his incorruptible life in the service of his people (Heb. 7:25). He not only claims the office of judge but also promises to be the defender of those who confess him (Mt. 10:32-33). The Christian idea of an eschatological paraclete goes back to Jesus himself.

2. More richly developed, and difficult to define, is the idea in John of a Paraclete working in and for the disciples. First Jesus is such (14:16), then the Spirit, who, completing the work of Jesus, leads the disciples into all truth (14:26), witnesses to Jesus (15:26), and convicts the world (16:8ff.). This work is similar to that of the OT advocate and links up with descriptions of the Spirit's ministry elsewhere in the NT (Rom. 8:26-27; Mk. 13:11; Lk. 13:6ff.). The Greek term may well go back to the term used by Jesus himself in his mother tongue. In translation the many secondary senses rule out any single equivalent. If we are to avoid "Paraclete," the basic thought is that of "Advocate" but the more general "Supporter" or "Helper" is perhaps the best rendering.   [J. BEHM, V, 800-814]

parakoḗ → akoúō; parakolouthéō → akolouthéō; parakoúō → akoúō

---

parakýptō [to stoop to see, look into]

---

1. This word means "I stoop to see." It applies to a quick, stolen glance. A verb of seeing may be added, but this is unusual.

2. The word occurs eight times in the LXX. The passive is used for the difficult Hebrew of 1 Kgs. 6:4. Elsewhere the idea is that of looking out of a window (Gen. 26:8) or into a window (Sir. 14:23).

3. In Jn. 20:5 the beloved disciple looks into the tomb through the low entrance. The glance is not necessarily a fleeting one (cf. 20:11). A figurative use occurs in Jms. 1:25, where again more than a fleeting glance is at issue. In 1 Pet. 1:12 inquisitive peeping might be the point unless there is a desire for genuine perception.

[W. MICHAELIS, V, 814-16]

paralambánō → lambánō; paraménō → ménō

---

paramythéomai [to admonish, console], **paramythía** [comfort], **paramýthion** [comfort]

A. Meaning.

1. Structure and Basic Meaning. Made up from *pará* ("toward") and *mythéomai* ("to speak"), *paramythéomai* has the basic sense "to speak to someone in a friendly way." With reference to what ought to be done, it develops the sense "to admonish," with reference to what has been done, the sense "to console."

2. "To Admonish." Nuances of this sense are "to urge," "to win over," "to spur on," "to encourage," "to persuade," and "to convince."

3. "To Console." Nuances of this sense are "to cheer," "to refresh" or "tend" (plants), "to mitigate" or "soothe," "to lessen" (shocks), "to resolve" or "explain" (a contradiction), "to excuse," "to appease," "to pacify," and "to satisfy" or "atone."

4. Special Meanings of the Nouns. The main sense of the nouns is "comfort," but they may also denote "means of comfort," "sign of comfort," and in the financial world "compensation," "interest," "pension," or "tip."

B. The Group in the OT. The group does not occur in translation of the Hebrew but only in books in which the LXX is the original. The idea is usually that of encouraging, soothing, comforting, or refreshing.

C. The Group in the NT.

1. Usage. There are only six instances in the NT, two in John and four in Paul. Since the reference in Jn. 11:19, 31 is to Jewish practice, and John does not use *parakaléō*, there is no word in John for Christian *paramythía*. In Paul *paramythéomai* is subsidiary to the more important *parakaléō* (cf. 1 Th. 2:12; 5:14; 1 Cor. 14:3; Phil. 2:1). Since both terms combine admonition and comfort, it is hard to draw any clear distinction between them. In both the unity of admonition and comfort is rooted in the gospel with its dialectical relationship of imperative and indicative. The only possible difference is that *paramythéomai* is not used directly for God's comfort or for eschatological comfort, but always for comfort in the earthly sphere.

2. Comfort and Comforters.

a. Traditional Rites and the Comfort of Jesus. In John the reference is to the typical Jewish visit of condolence (11:19, 31). Comforters stay as close as possible to the bereaved and speak words or perform acts of sorrow and consolation. Jesus as the true comforter uses traditional forms of speech in Mk. 5:36; Lk. 7:13; Jn. 11:23, but he also gives the true comfort of action by breaking the power of sickness and death. Two other Jewish customs, i.e., the letter of condolence and ending a book with a word of consolation, find expression in the NT in 2 Cor. 1ff. and Mt. 28.

b. Recipients. The recipients of comfort in the NT are all who sorrow, the sick and prisoners (Mt. 25:36, 43), and orphans and widows (Jms. 1:27). Usually *paramythéomai* has the church or its members in view (1 Cor. 14:3; Phil. 2:1; 1 Th. 2:12; 5:14).

c. Bearers. First the prophets bring comfort (1 Cor. 14:3). Giving comfort is part of their office. Paul also sees it as part of his apostolic ministry (1 Th. 2:11-12). It has a strongly personal character (cf. also Col. 1:28). Mutual consolation seems to be the point in 1 Th. 5:14. The same applies to Phil. 2:1, where the love might be that of God or Christ, but is probably the mutual love of the brethren. The fellowship of suffering is a fellowship of consolation. Above all earthly comforters, of course, stands the heavenly comforter who is the source of all earthly comfort (2 Cor. 1:3).

d. The Chief NT Motif. In the NT the name of Christ is the main reason for comfort. All thoughts of comfort are oriented to Christ. The OT offers comfort as it is read in the light of Christ. The comfort of the Father and the Spirit relates to the divine work in Christ. Comfort for death lies in the promise of resurrection that is grounded in Christ. Comfort in persecution lies in the fact that it is for Christ's sake and means fellowship in the suffering of Christ (2 Cor. 1:5; 1 Pet. 4:13). The content of NT prophecy is the revelation of the mystery of Christ, the power of Christian comfort lies in the love of Christ (Phil. 2:1), and apostolic comfort rests on God's calling believers into the kingdom and glory of Christ (1 Th. 2:12).

→ *parakaléō, paráklēsis*   [G. STÄHLIN, V, 816-23]

paranoméō, paranomía → *nómos; parapikraínō, parapikrasmós* → *pikrós; parapíptō, paráptōma* → *píptō; paratēréō, paratḗrēsis* → *tēréō; paratíthēmi* → *títhēmi; páreimi* → *parousía*

> *pareiságō* [to bring in secretly],   *pareísaktos* [brought in secretly]

---

pareiságō has the neutral sense "to bring forward," "to present," but often with the suggestion of something unlawful or furtive, e.g., "to introduce strange gods." The term does not occur in the LXX, Philo, or Josephus. In the one NT instance in 2 Pet. 2:1 the false teachers are unlawfully and secretly bringing in their destructive heresies (cf. Jude 4, where they insinuate themselves). The verbal adjective *pareísaktos* in Gal. 2:4 has the same emphasis. The term is a rare one and denotes someone who has wormed his way in and is at work where he does not belong. In Gal. 2:4 it is a disparaging term for opponents of the Gentile mission.   [W. MICHAELIS, V, 824-26]

pareisérchomai → *érchomai; parepídēmos* → *dḗmos; parérchomai* → *érchomai; páresis* → *aphíēmi*

> *parthénos* [young woman, virgin]

A. Nonbiblical and Non-Jewish Use.
1. Usage. Of uncertain origin, *parthénos* means a "mature young woman." According to context the stress may be on sex, age, or status. By a process of narrowing down the more general sense yields to the more specific one of "virgin," with a stress on freshness, or on physical or spiritual purity.

2. The Virgin in Religion.

a. Cultic Honoring of the Divine Virgin. In relation to female deities there is a multiple use. Artemis is strictly *parthénos* but has varied functions as, e.g., the giver of fertility, the mistress of law, and the guardian of oaths. Virgin sacrifices are especially powerful because of the combination of freshness and innocence. The same combination lies behind the worship of virgin deities. Athene is an example, for although she has some maternal characteristics, she epitomizes the chaste and unapproachable maiden of nonsexual origin. Thus the term *parthénos* suggests the immutable, the self-sufficient, and the self-contained in a kind of mythicizing of autarchy.

b. The Virgin as the Mother of the Divine Child. In religion we find many references to the virgin mother of the divine child, but it is not always clear whether the idea is that of a virgin in the strict physical sense, of a woman still in the bloom of youth, or of a virgin in the sense of unapproachable character. Again, what is meant by conception is open to debate, since deities come in many forms, although usually by natural processes, and there seems to be no thought of parthenogenesis in the strict sense.

3. Virginity in Cultic Practice and Magic. Various motifs are at work in the imposing of celibacy on priests, priestesses, and magicians, whether permanently or temporarily. Virginity is thought to convey special power, priestesses are viewed as married to the gods, and ritual purity is a consideration (or freedom from demotic infection). In the use of virgin girls or boys in magic, the special power of virginity is the point.

B. The OT and Judaism.
1. The Mother of Immanuel. The word *'almâ* occurs nine times in the OT. Three times it means an unmarried woman (Gen. 24:43; Ex. 2:8; probably Ps. 68:25). This also seems to be the sense in Ps. 46:1; 1 Chr. 15:20; Cant. 1:3. The meaning is uncertain in Prov. 30:19, but the reference is probably to a girl who has just reached maturity. The same applies to Is. 7:14. Questions regarding Is. 7:14 are whether the

woman is an individual or represents all the women pregnant at the time in Israel, whether Immanuel is an individual or a representative name, and whether honey and milk are the food of deliverance or of judgment. In context the name Immanuel obviously signifies salvation beyond the immediate judgment, and Immanuel seems to be the child, not of the prophet's wife, but of an unknown woman. The father is not named because the child stands under God's protection and is under God's commission to bring salvation. In its immediate reference the verse carries no thought of a divine child, of divine conception, or of parthenogenesis.

2. *The Meaning of parthénos in the LXX.* As the usual rendering of Heb. *bᵉṯûlâ*, *parthénos* means "girl" in many instances, with chastity implied. A stress on virginity occurs in Lev. 21:13-14; Dt. 22:23, 28; 2 Sam. 13:2. When used with place names, the thought is that of not being forced, or, in the case of Israel, of nonpollution with idolatry. Only twice is *parthénos* used for *'almâ*. Although the LXX gives to *parthénos* a stronger emphasis on virginity, it may be used for the young woman who is raped in Gen. 34:3, and on purely lexical grounds one cannot say for certain that it means "virgin" in Is. 7:14, where it might simply denote a woman who is inviolate up to the moment of conception. On the other hand, the use of *neánis* in other renderings may well be polemical, and on the basis of LXX usage the translator of Is. 7:14 could well have had a nonsexual origin in view for Immanuel.

3. *The Allegorical Use in Philo.* Philo allegorizes the supernatural conceptions of the OT. For him Sarah etc. represent virtues. The soul has been corrupted by sensual things, but God makes it *parthénos* again by freeing it from desire, thus befitting it for converse with himself.

C. *parthénos* in the NT.

1. *General Use.* This use may be seen in Mt. 25:1ff. The daughters of Philip in Acts 21:9 are probably called *parthénoi* (adjective) in the sense of "unmarried."

2. *The Virginity of Mary.* Mary's virginity prior to Jesus' birth is not for ascetic reasons (cf. Mt. 1:23; Lk. 1:27). The virgin birth does not disparage marriage, and the idea of Mary's perpetual virginity is a later one. The virgin birth is by a natural process and is not meant to explain either the deity, the sinlessness, or the power of Jesus. In Luke the birth of Jesus plainly differs from that of the Baptist. Mary conceives a son by the creative act of God (1:27, 34). Mt. 1:18, 20 says that the generation is by the Holy Spirit, but in the sense of a new work of creation (cf. Gen. 1:2) rather than a divine begetting. The idea of a sacred marriage is wholly absent. The lack of other NT references to the virgin birth (e.g., in Paul or John) may be explained in different ways, e.g., its acceptance as self-evident, concentration on other matters, or in some cases ignorance on the question. Allusions, as in Jn. 1:13-14; Rom. 1:3; Heb. 7:3, are only indirect.

3. *The Ascetic Sense.* The word *parthénos* seems to have an ascetic sense in 1 Cor. 7:25, 28, 34, 36ff. Some see here a reference to women who have set up house with men so as to be economically independent. The literal sense is also possible in Rev. 14:4.

4. *The Figurative Use.* This is the more likely use in Rev. 14:4 (cf. the use of *pórnē* for the world). The redeemed have remained pure when tempted to fall into idolatry or licentiousness. The community is *parthénos* in 2 Cor. 11:2 as the bride of Christ. The word here signifies exclusive commitment. Paul has affianced the church to Christ and watches over it so that he may present it for marriage at the parousia.

[G. DELLING, V, 826-37]

paríēmi → *aphíēmi*

---

parístēmi [to place, approach],   **paristánō** [to place, approach]

A. Nonbiblical Greek. From the NT standpoint the following are the most important secular senses of these words: "to present," "to place," "to bring," "to offer," "to demonstrate," "to set up," "to make ready," "to make," "to approach," "to assist," "to wait on," "to help," "to stand by," "to be on hand" (cf. also "to happen").

B. The LXX. In the LXX the words have many nuances within the basic meaning. The usual thoughts are those of being present and helping. The religious sense rests on the practice at royal courts, where service implies dignity but also dependence. We thus read of angels and natural forces (Job 1:6; Zech. 6:5), but also of priests and Levites (Dt. 10:8), of prophets (1 Kgs. 17:1), and of the whole people standing in the presence or service of God. God himself stands with Moses in Ex. 34:5, and he is at the right hand of the needy in Ps. 109:31.   [G. BERTRAM, V, 837-39]

C. The NT.

1. The ordinary senses "to place at the disposal" (Acts 23:24), "to furnish" (Mt. 26:53), "to show" (Acts 1:3), and "to prove" (Acts 24:13) occur in the NT.

2. Intransitively one also finds "to approach" (Acts 9:39), "to stand by" (Jn. 18:22), "to assist" (2 Tim. 4:17), "to be present" (Mk. 15:39).

3. The senses "to place or stand at the disposal" and "to serve" have some theological significance. The angel in Lk. 1:19 waits on God. Christians must set their members in the service of God and not of sin (Rom. 6:12-13). Food will not bring us before God (1 Cor. 8:8). God will present believers before his throne (2 Cor. 4:14). Paul will present the church as a bride (2 Cor. 11:2). Christ himself will present the church to himself (Eph. 5:27). We are all to stand before God's judgment seat (Rom. 14:10). Paul is presented before the governor and must appear before Caesar (Acts 23:33; 27:24). In all these instances we have analogies to court ceremonial or legal procedure. A cultic setting is presupposed when Jesus is presented in the temple in Lk. 2:22 (cf. Ex. 13:2, 12ff.). In Lk. 17:14 the cleansed lepers are to show themselves to the priests, and this thought may underlie Col. 1:22, 28 and 2 Tim. 2:15. Bringing offerings lies behind the exhortation to believers to present their bodies as living sacrifices in Rom. 12:1.

D. The Apostolic Fathers. Interesting phrases in the apostolic fathers may be found in 1 Clem. 35.10, Hermas *Similitudes* 8.4.1, and 1 Clem. 23.4.

         [B. REICKE, V, 839-41]

---

pároikos [resident alien],   **paroikía** [resident alien],   **paroikéō** [to live as a resident alien]

A. Secular Greek. *pároikos* means a. "neighboring," "neighbor," and b. "noncitizen," "resident alien." *paroikeín* means a. "to dwell beside" and b. "to be a resident alien."

B. The OT.

1. paroikía and paroikéō.

a. The OT uses the noun to denote the state, position, or fate of a resident alien (Ps. 119:54). The reference is usually to Israel or its members. "Exile" is the sense in Ezr. 2:1.

b. The verb means "to live as a resident alien." It may refer to non-Israelites (cf. 2 Sam. 4:3; Is. 16:4), but usually refers to the patriarchs (Gen. 12:10; 17:8; 26:3; 35:27; 47:4) and Israelites (Judg. 17:7ff.; Ruth 1:1; 2 Kgs. 8:1-2). Residence in the promised land is an alien residence relative to God but also brings alien residence to an end (Ps. 78:55). A nontechnical use occurs in Ps. 61:4 (dwelling with God), though the idea of life on earth as a sojourning lies in the background.

2. *Israel and the pároikos*. The *pároikos* is the resident alien who is accepted by Israel (which was itself a *pároikos* in Egypt) but is excluded from certain cultic rights and duties (cf. Ex. 12:45; Lev. 22:10, though cf. also Dt. 14:21). Resident aliens do have rights (e.g., asylum in Num. 35:15) and must be helped if poor (Lev. 25:35; cf. 25:6). If aliens become proselytes, their cultic rights and obligations are extended (cf. Ex. 12:49). A full equation of citizens and resident aliens is promised in Ezek. 47:22-23. In general, resident aliens are sacrosanct as guests, and in view of their weak position enjoy divine protection. They are not totally outside the covenant community but ought to seek fuller entry by circumcision.

3. *The People of Israel as pároikos*. Israelites, too, may be resident aliens; cf. Moses in Midian (Ex. 2:22) and Israel in Egypt. Israel views its alien residence in Egypt not just as a historical fact but also as an occasion for theological reflection. In God's sight all peoples are resident aliens (cf. Is. 19). This does not cancel out possession of the land but it is a reminder that there must be humility before God. The prophets, proclaiming the impending destruction of the nation, point out that there can be no appeal to land or temple. God will not be tied to the land (Ezek. 8; Jer. 14:8-9). The people have received it and live in it only as *pároikoi* (1 Chr. 29:15; Ps. 119:19). The land truly belongs to God, and the people are his servants in it with the status of resident aliens. Yet God is also the owner of the whole world and creates and posits all human relations. Before his claim to total ownership the distinctions of human law between residents, proselytes, resident aliens, and full aliens lose their final force (cf. linguistically the overlapping of stranger and sojourner in Gen. 23:4; Lev. 25:23; Num. 35:15, and the use of *prosélytos* and *pároikos* for the same Hebrew term).

C. Hellenistic and Rabbinic Judaism.

1. Philo and Josephus.

a. Philo. As more and more Jews came to live in the diaspora, this had a twofold impact on Israel's sense of alien status. In Hellenistic Judaism the historical reference is weakened. Philo uses the *pároikos* group to express the fact that the righteous are strangers on earth. The world is an enemy and the body a tomb, as in contemporary philosophical thinking. The *lógos*, like the soul, is a stranger, as in Gnostic mythology, where the redeemer accepts alien status.

b. Josephus refers to the resident aliens whom Solomon employed for his works of construction (*Antiquities* 8.59).   [K. L. and M. A. Schmidt, V, 841-50]

2. Rabbinic Judaism.

a. Proselyte, God-Fearer, Resident Alien. The rabbis, who develop a stronger historical sense of alien status, distinguish between full proselytes, God-fearers who belong to the wider missionary community in the diaspora, and true resident aliens who live and work in Israel.

b. Duties of Resident Aliens. To make life within the cultic community easier, resident aliens are required to keep the Noachic commands, and especially to avoid idolatry. Amorcan scholars demand a renunciation of paganism.

c. The Historical Orientation. Aliens residing in Israel obviously have to respect the religious customs of the people, but an alien colony in the true sense is possible only after the break-up in A.D. 70. Thus the rabbinic regulations apply properly only to the preexilic situation and have more the force of theory in their own time.

[R. MEYER, V, 850-51]

D. The NT.

a. In the NT *pároikos* occurs four times, *paroikía* twice, and *paroikéō* twice, almost always in quotations from the OT or allusions to it (cf. Acts 7; 13:16ff.; Heb. 11:9, 13).

b. Like ancient Israel, the saints were strangers and sojourners but are now fellow citizens (Eph. 2:19). Again like ancient Israel, they are still resident aliens in another form, i.e., relative to the earth and the *sárx* (1 Pet. 2:11). The church as *ekklēsía* is *paroikía*. It is *ekklēsía* relative to God, *pároikía* relative to the world (cf. Heb. 13:14). Like Israel, it is diaspora in the world (1 Pet. 1:1; Jms. 1:1). As such it has a specific task and burden but also a specific promise and destiny. Its resident status is provisional. Proleptically Christians are *already* fellow citizens even while they are *still* resident aliens, but only because *one day* they will be citizens in the full sense. A term of honor, *paroikía* lays on them the responsibility of befitting conduct (1 Pet. 2:5ff.).

c. A single nontechnical use is perhaps to be found in Lk. 24:18, where the disciples ask the risen Lord if he is the only stranger in Jerusalem (*paroikeís*) not conversant with events. They assume that he must be either a visitor up for the feast or a Jew from abroad living in Jerusalem.

E. The Early Church.
The early church still regards itself as an alien colony (Diog. 5.5). 2 Clem. 5.1 uses *paroikía* in the same way as 1 Peter. Irenaeus calls the churches *paroikíai* (Eusebius *Ecclesiastical History* 5.24.14). This plural becomes a term for the individual congregations (cf. the NT *ekklesíai*), and then *ekklesía* (singular) comes to be used for the whole church, and *paroikíai* for the constituent churches (Lat. *parochiae*; Eng. *parishes*). Strictly, then, the parishes are societies of resident aliens on earth whose true citizenship is in heaven (cf. the verb in Mart. Pol., Introd.; Diog. 6.8).

[K. L. and M. A. SCHMIDT, V, 851-53]

---

paroimía [proverb]

A. Outside the NT.

1. Literally "byword," the *paroimía* is a sentence or proverb summing up what is said. The proverb is a popular, ancient, and familiar saying, expressing common wisdom in pointed form. When based on a typical example, it may be enigmatic to those not conversant with the example. It is less artistic than the maxim or aphorism and less specific than the apophthegm. It is common in speeches and letters, and may also be given poetic form. Drawing often on nature, it has some relation to the fable.

2. The Hebrew term, *māshāl*, is a common one. Only twice in Proverbs and five times in Sirach is *paroimía* used for it. In Prov. 1:1 the term applies to all the sayings that follow. The meaning, then, is wisdom saying (so also Sirach).

3. Philo uses *paroimía* for "proverb." The rabbis make much use of proverbs in elucidation and proof, usually with an introductory formula.

B. The NT.

1. The only NT instance of *paroimía* for "proverb" is in 2 Pet. 2:22, which uses two common sayings in disparagement of the conduct of the heretics. Jn. 4:37 also adduces a popular saying but does not use *paroimía*. The same is true in 1 Cor. 15:33, Gal. 6:7, Acts 26:14, and Tit. 1:12, and many sayings of Jesus reflect current proverbs (cf. Mt. 5:14; 6:21; 7:5, 7, 12; 20:16; Mk. 4:24-25, etc.).

2. John uses *paroimía* three times (10:6; 16:25, 29) but more in the sense of "obscure speech" that needs interpretation. Later, clearer speech about heavenly things will replace this more difficult form of statement, i.e., when Jesus reaches the end of his life's task and tells the disciples that he is going back to the Father (16:29).

[F. HAUCK, V, 854-56]

paromoiázō, parómoios → hómoios

---

paroxýnō [to spur, to stir to anger],   *paroxysmós* [irritation, stimulation]

The verb means "to spur," "to stir to anger," passive "to be provoked, incensed." The noun is rare and means "provocation" or "irritation." In the NT the verb occurs in Acts 17:16, where the meaning is not that Paul is stimulated to preach but that he is honestly angered by the idolatry. Similarly in 1 Cor. 13:5 love does not let itself be provoked—there were many provoking things at Corinth. The noun has the sense of "irritation" in Acts 15:39 when Paul and Barnabas disagree about taking Mark with them. In Heb. 10:24, however, the neutral sense of "stimulating" is the obvious one.

[H. SEESEMANN, V, 857]

parorgízō, parorgismós → orgḗ

---

parousía [presence, coming],   *páreimi* [to be present, come]

A. General Meaning.

1. Presence. páreimi means "to be present" (persons or things). *parousía* denotes "active presence" (e.g., of representatives or troops, in person; cf. 2 Cor. 10:10).

2. Appearing. páreimi also means "to have come," "to come," and *parousía* "arrival."

B. Technical Use.

1. Hellenism.

1. Visit of a Ruler. While the group may be used for the presence of deities, it finds technical use for the visits of rulers or high officials. At first genitives, pronouns, or verbal phrases accompany it in this sense. On the occasion of such visits there are flattering speeches, delicacies to eat, asses for the baggage, street improvements, and wreaths or gifts of money. These are paid for by voluntary contributions or, if necessary, unpopular levies. Under the empire the ceremonies become even more magnificent and visits are marked by new buildings, the institution of holy days, etc. Complaints and requests are customarily addressed to rulers on such visits.

2. parousía of the Gods. In relation to gods the word denotes a helpful appearance.

3. Sacral Meaning in Philosophy. In Plato the word is still a secular one, and it is not prominent in Stoicism, but it acquires a cultic sense in Hermes mysticism and Neo-Platonism. Typical uses are for the invisible presence of the gods at sacrifices and for the appearance of divine fire.

II. OT Presuppositions for the Technical Use in the NT.

1. The Coming of God in Direct Self-Attestation and the Cultus. Since Hebrew is more concrete, it has words for "to be present" and "to come," but not for "presence" or "coming." Theologically we find references to the near coming of the time or end (Lam. 4:18), of evil (Prov. 1:27), or of the day of redemption (Is. 63:4) or recompense (Dt. 32:35). Above all, God comes in self-attestation and at cultic places, there being a close link between these (Gen. 16:13-14; 28:18; 2 Sam. 24:25). The entry of the ark is God's coming (1 Sam. 4:6-7). But God is not tied to places; he may come in dreams (Gen. 20:3), theophanies (18:1ff.), clouds and storms, visions, the quiet breath (1 Kgs. 19:12-13), his word or Spirit (Num. 22:9; 24:2), and with his hand (1 Kgs. 18:46).

2. God's Coming in History. The victory over Sisera is a coming of God (Judg. 5:4-5; cf. Is. 19:1; 30:27). For apostates his coming is terrible (Am. 5:18ff.). He also comes to liberate (Ex. 3:8; Is. 35:2, 4) and to conclude the covenant (Ex. 19:18). The coming of salvation leads to the eschaton.

3. God's Coming as World King. God is lauded as an unparalleled king in Dt. 32:2ff. He is king forever and ever in Ex. 15:18. He will finally assume full kingship (Is. 2:2). His coming as world king will mean the creating of a new heaven and earth (Is. 66:15) and universal peace and joy (Is. 2:2ff.; 65:21ff.; 66:10ff.).

4. The Coming of the Messiah. God's anointed may take his place. As both hero and prince of peace, his main task is to establish peace (Zech. 9:9-10). This coming has a universal sweep and is historical, but with eschatological aspects (Dan. 7:13). In the Psalms the stress is on God's coming, not that of the Messiah.

III. Judaism.

1. Palestinian Judaism.

a. Expectation of God's Coming. Apocalyptic is full of expectation of the imminent end when God will come in full array to rule and judge. The rabbis lay more stress on the coming of the righteous to God but refer at times to God's manifestation as advocate and world ruler in the messianic age.

b. Expectation of the Messiah. Up to A.D. 70 the idea of a coming Messiah or Son of Man is a lively one, but the hope is complex. Other comings are also expected, e.g., Enoch, Elijah, and the priest king. The rabbis expect the Son of David at a time of great affliction and await him with some fear. The cleansing of the people is a precondition of his coming.

2. Hellenistic Judaism.

a. Greek Translations. In the LXX etc. *páreimi* is fairly common for "to come," but is never technical. *parousía* occurs only in works written in Greek. The technical sense is not at first normative but has some impact.

b. Philo. Philo does not use *parousía,* and Hellenistic influences more or less eliminate the idea of a coming of God or the Messiah.

c. Josephus. Josephus uses the verb for God's presence to help and the noun for the Shekinah. He rejects apocalyptic and refers the Son of Man of Daniel to Vespasian, though only in a penultimate sense, for an ultimate ruler will finally establish dominion in Jerusalem.

IV. The Technical Use of the Group in the NT.

1. The Historical Place of the parousía Concept in the NT. In the NT Jesus has come already, but so strong is the hope of his coming in glory that the group is not used for his first coming. There is not a twofold *parousía.* The verb is not a technical term (though it has overtones in Jn. 11:28; 1 Cor. 5:3; 2 Cor. 13:10; cf. also Jn. 7:6; Col.

1:6; Heb. 12:11; 2 Pet. 1:12). For the coming in glory the Synoptists and John use "day of the Lord," the Pastorals use *epipháneia* (cf. also Mt. 24:3; 1 Jn. 2:28; 2 Pet. 1:16; 3:4, 12), and Paul favors *parousía*. The term *parousía* is Hellenistic but its content derives from the OT.

2. *Development of the Concept.*

a. The Synoptic Jesus. Jesus' thinking is permeated with the thought of the *parousía* (Mk. 8:38; 14:63; Mt. 25:1ff.; Lk. 12:35ff.). The concept is present in fully developed form in Mk. 13, which distinguishes between the judgment on Jerusalem and the *parousía,* a space being left for the conversion of the Gentiles. Jesus depicts the *parousía* as imminent (Mk. 9:1; 13:24ff.) but also enjoins perseverance (Mt. 24:13). He attempts no date-setting and divests the *parousía* of its political element, stressing the ethical aspect (Mt. 25:14ff.).

b. The Primitive Community. The word does not occur in Acts but the first community clearly expects the *parousía* (Acts 1:11; 3:20-21; 10:42; 13:33).

c. Paul. Paul's Christology includes preexistence but is still oriented to the future. The word *parousía* is always used with the genitive and refers to men in 1 Cor. 16:17; 2 Cor. 7:6-7, etc., to antichrist in 2 Th. 2:9, and to Christ elsewhere (1 Cor. 15:23; 1 Th. 2:19; 3:13; 4:15; 5:23; 2 Th. 2:1, 8). The expectation in 1 and 2 Thessalonians is both immediate and extended, and the bearing is pastoral. Colorful details are given (1 Th. 4:13ff.; 1 Cor. 15:22ff.). Even in 2 Cor. 5:1ff. there is no interest in the interim period (cf. also Rom. 8:19, 23). Paul realizes he may go to be "with Christ" (Phil. 1:23) but still expects the *parousía* (3:20-21; 4:5).

d. The Pastorals. In 2 Tim. 1:10 *epipháneia* is used for Christ's manifestation in the flesh but the expectation of a coming survives if with a little less emphasis (cf. 1 Tim. 4:1; 2 Tim. 3:1). In Hebrews the main interest is in the past coming and in the believers' entry into rest, but the hope of a future coming persists (9:28; 10:37; 12:26). This will be a second coming in 9:28.

e. James, Peter, and Jude. Jms. 5:7-8 refers to Christ's *parousía.* 1 Peter has a more dynamic view; the decisive manifestation is at hand (1:5, 7, 13). 2 Peter meets the objections of mockers (3:3-4) by adducing God's patience (3:8-9). Believers should wait for and hasten toward the *parousía* of the day of God (or the Lord) (3:12).

f. Revelation. Though it does not use the term, Revelation is full of ardent hope of the *parousía* (cf. 1:1, 3; 22:20). Lofty portrayals are given in 14:14ff. and 19:11ff. The time sequence suggests a double *parousía.*

g. John and 1–3 John. The idea of the *parousía* is present in Jn. 21:22-23 and 1 Jn. 2:28; 3:2. There is a stress on present victory, judgment, and life, but true eschatological expressions are also present (Jn. 6:39, 40, 44; 12:48; 1 Jn. 2:18). We find both realized and unrealized eschatology. The realization is as yet provisional and demands a definitive consummation. If there is more stress on possession, the tension between possession and hope remains.

3. *Theological Summary.* The concept of the *parousía* in the NT defies systematization. Jewish particularism is rejected and the sensual element is minimal, since fellowship with God is the chief concern. Divine transcendence overcomes the antithesis of the present and the future aspects of God's rule. The turning point has already come, and the *parousía* will be a definitive manifestation when God's eternal rule supersedes history. Christ is the resolution of the tension between this world and the next, hope and possession, concealment and manifestation, and faith and sight.

V. Early Christian Writings. The verb plays no important part in earlier writings, though Justin *Dialogue* 54.1 says that Christ will be present at the second *parousía*. The noun often has the secular sense. It has a technical eschatological sense in Diog. 7.6 and Hermas *Similitudes* 5.5.3. Ignatius *Philadelphians* 9.2 uses it for the earthly coming. Justin *Dialogue* 14.8 etc. (and *Apology* 52.3) refer to two *parousíai*, and cf. Irenaeus and Hippolytus. Clement of Alexandria speaks mostly of the earthly *parousía*, but this deeschatologizing is exceptional.   [A. OEPKE, V, 858-71]

→ *epipháneia, érchomai, hḗkō, hēméra, maranathá*

| *parrhēsía* [openness, candor], *parrhēsiázomai* [to speak openly] |

A. The Greek World and Hellenism.

1. The Political Sphere. The term *parrhēsía* is an important one in the political sphere as a presupposition of democracy. It signifies a. the right to say anything, b. an openness to truth, and c. candor.

2. The Private Sphere. Here the main sense is that of frankness or candor. But the bad sense of "impudence" or "insolence" or "shamelessness" also occurs, and when not linked with *lógos* it also means "liberality."

3. The Moral Sphere. Philosophers connect *parrhēsía* with moral rather than political freedom (although the word may also denote shamelessness in the case of those dominated by the passions). Those who have *parrhēsía* (in the good sense) are public figures with cosmopolitan responsibilities.

B. The LXX and Hellenistic Jewish Literature.

1. The word *parrhēsía* is rare in the LXX. It marks free people in Lev. 26:13 and is ascribed to wisdom in Prov. 1:12. *parrhēsía* before God is important in Job 27:9-10 and 22:23ff. (cf. Wis. 5:1-2). It is a virtue of the *díkaios* (see Prov. 13:5) or the *sophós*, and comes to expression in joyful prayer. Another distinctive use in the LXX is for God's own *parrhēsía* (cf. Ps. 94:1, where the meaning is clear, and Ps. 12:5, where the original is uncertain).

2. In Hellenistic Jewish writings, especially Philo and Josephus, *parrhēsía* has the primary sense of "candor," but with a connection to the law and a good conscience in a fusion of Jewish and Hellenistic elements. An important aspect is *parrhēsía* toward God, and God himself is the source of *parrhēsía*.

3. In Ethiopian Enoch *parrhēsía* occurs in an eschatological context when the reference is to the reward of an open standing before God. In antithesis to the shame and anxiety of the wicked, this *parrhēsía* is the confident and joyful freedom of hastening toward God and standing openly in his presence.

C. The NT.

1. The Johannine Writings. In John *parrhēsía* is associated with the work of Jesus. He works publicly, i.e, in the synagogues and temple, not in secret (Jn. 18:20-21; cf. 7:25-26). Yet this openness does not mean open manifestation (cf. 7:10), which begins only with the eschatological event initiated by the ascension (cf. 7:6ff.). Hence the Jews do not understand the public ministry as *parrhēsía* and ask for direct self-attestation (10:24-25). The works give this, but it is grasped only in faith. We see this in 11:11ff., where Jesus has to tell the disciples "plainly" that Lazarus has died. For the moment he speaks in figures, but with his resurrection and the coming of the Spirit he will speak "plainly" (16:25ff.), and in love and faith the disciples will have direct perception. In Mk. 8:32 *parrhēsía* again suggests the open speech that is granted to the disciples, but this openness can still conceal (except for faith), as is apparent in Mk. 8:32-33; cf. 9:32; 10:32. In 1 John *parrhēsía* has the sense of openness toward God (3:21; 5:14), which presupposes a good conscience, faith, and love (3:22-23), and also the gift of the Spirit (v. 24). This *parrhēsía* comes to expression in prayer (5:14-15) that is heard because it is according to God's will. In addition to this present *parrhēsía* there is a future *parrhēsía,* i.e., that of confident standing before the Judge on the ground of the divine love (2:28; 4:17).

2. *Acts.* In Acts we find only a human relation. In 9:27-28; 14:3, etc. the verb has almost the sense "to proclaim," i.e., to speak publicly, whether to Jews, Jews and Gentiles, or Gentiles, whether to the people or their rulers. At issue here is bold and open speaking. But it is also effective speaking (4:13) even though there has been no formal training. The Lord grants the apostles this *parrhēsía,* and he confirms their speech by signs and wonders (4:29-30; 14:3). As may be seen from the example of Apollos, *parrhēsía* as open and eloquent speaking to a hostile world is a charism (18:25-26).

3. *The Pauline Corpus.* Paul, too, stresses apostolic *parrhēsía* in both life (Phil. 1:20) and preaching (Eph. 6:19-20). Openness toward God and men, and in the gospel, is meant (Eph. 3:12; 2 Cor. 3:12; Eph. 6:19-20). The face that is open toward God is also open toward others (2 Cor. 3:7ff.). This open face reflects the Lord's glory in increasing transformation by the Spirit. Openness implies a confident freedom of approach to God (Eph. 3:12). In its human dimension it has the nuance of affection in 2 Cor. 7:4 and authority in Phlm. 8. The ground of *parrhēsía* is faith (1 Tim. 3:13), and it is effected by the Spirit and related to union with Christ (Phil. 1:19-20). Christ himself triumphs "openly" over the powers in Col. 2:15.

4. *Hebrews.* In Hebrews *parrhēsía* has an objective character. It is something one has and must keep as a believer (3:6). It is related to the object of hope. In content it is the freedom of access to God that is given in Christ's blood and grounded in his high-priestly ministry (4:14-15; 10:19). It is preserved by endurance in affliction (10:34ff.) and means confidence before the Judge (4:16).

D. **The Early Church.** The group is an important one in early writings. Diog. 11.2 speaks of the *parrhēsía* of the *lógos* and opposes it to *mystḗrion.* In 1 Clem. 34.1ff. the believer's *parrhēsía* stands in the Lord, is the Lord's gift, demands obedience, and grants participation in the promise by prayer. Of particular significance are the connections with the apostle in apocryphal writings, where the stress is on authority, with the martyr in martyr literature, where the martyr shows it toward persecutors and also has it toward God, and with prayer, e.g., in Origen's *On Prayer,* which points out that calling God Father in the Lord's Prayer expresses a special *parrhēsía.*   [H. SCHLIER, V, 871-86]

---

pás [each, all],   *hápas* [all, everybody]

A. **Linguistic Data in the NT.**

1. pás as Adjective.

a. With Article. *pás* can have different meanings according to its different uses. With the article it may have a predicative position with implicative ("all," "whole"), distributive ("whoever," "all possible"), or elative significance ("all," e.g., knowledge in 1 Cor. 13:2), or it may have an attributive position ("whole," "generally"; cf. Acts 20:18).

b. Without Article. Without the article *pás* may have elative ("full," "total") or distributive significance ("each," "whoever," "whatever," or, in privative phrases, "any" ["without any"] or "none," "nothing" ["not any"]).

2. *pás as Noun.*

a. With Article. With the article *pás* as a noun may have implicative ("all," mostly plural) or summative ("in all," "all together") significance.

b. Without Article. Without the article *pás* may have distributive significance ("each," "all"), or it may be used in adverbial phrases (e.g., "first or last of all," "in every respect," "above all," "in all circumstances," hence "certainly").

3. *hápas.* In Luke *hápas* is sometimes preferred when something impressive is to be said, especially with an implicative meaning and after a consonant, but in the main it is used in exactly the same way as *pás*.

B. Material Aspects.

1. *God as Creator and Ruler of All Things in the OT.* That God is the Creator and Ruler of all things is a basic OT conviction. Totality is expressed by phrases like "heaven and earth" (Gen. 1:1; cf. Ps. 24:1), but the word "all" may also be used (cf. Dt. 10:14; Job 41:3). Depictions of God's omnipotent sway occur in Job 38ff. and Ps. 104, and cf. Jer. 27:5; Dan. 4:32. The human race is a unity prior to Babel (Gen. 9:19; 11:1ff.). The original fellowship with God is broken by the fall and is to be restored by God's saving dealings with Israel (Gen. 12:3; Is. 60). Thus the God of the universe is also the God of Israel but with expectation of a full implementation of his universal sovereignty.   [B. REICKE, V, 886-90]

2. *pás in the LXX.* After *kýrios*, *pás* is the most common theologically significant term in the LXX (6–7,000 instances). In many passages, of course, the use is rhetorical, but in the general context even these instances imply the total claim of God and his word. In the first place the universal God has chosen Israel. Israel must keep all the law, the cultic legislation applies to all the people, and the expiatory rites take away all guilt. All who disobey, and all Israel's foes, fall under God's wrath. Yet Israel's history is a revelation to all peoples. God is the one God over all kingdoms, and his judgments extend to the whole world. God is the Savior in all troubles, all his ways are mercy and truth, his wrath smites all the wicked, but his salvation is for all believers. He knows and sees all things, tries all hearts, and can do all things. Even when a particularism of salvation is present, the belief in God's omnipotence, and in the universal validity of his word and claim, is never lost. A sense of the universal reach of his loving purpose comes out even in passages relating primarily to Israel (cf. 1 Kgs. 8:37ff.).   [G. BERTRAM, V, 890-92]

3. *The World of Greek and Hellenistic Thought.* The Greeks have a developed concept of the universe from early times and seek a basis of unity in, e.g., water, fire, or numbers. This philosophical cosmogony leaves no real place for a personal Creator in the OT sense; even the demiurge is more of a philosophical idea. Pantheistic trends may be seen in the mysteries and Gnosticism. Doxologies similar to those of the OT and NT occur, but these do not presuppose biblical monotheism.

4. *The NT.*

a. In the NT, as in the LXX, *pás* is very common (1,228 times, *hápas* 32). This reflects a liking for the concept of totality resting on the concept of God and joy in salvation. Totality in the NT relates to a specific history of creation and redemption.

NT soteriology is richer than that of the OT. The focus of the NT is on the personal God and personal salvation.

b. For the NT there is only one God and one Lord (1 Cor. 8:6). All creation is God's work. This means that all creatures depend on God (Rom. 9:5; Acts 17:25ff.). They are also ordered to him, not in the sense of a flowing from and to him, but in the sense that restoration of fellowship with him is the goal.

c. That Christ is also Creator rests on OT statements (cf. Ps. 8:6; Prov. 8:22ff.; Gen. 1:1ff.: creation by the Word). All things are both made and made anew by Christ (1 Cor. 8:6). The first creation in the Son points ahead to the new creation in the Son. The firstborn of all creation is the firstborn from the dead. Before all things, and holding all things together, he is the first in all things, and all things are reconciled through him (Col. 1:15ff.). The world, of course, will not recognize its dependence on God. All are in sin (Gal. 3:22) and guilty before God (Rom. 3:19). The original unity of the race is destroyed, and idolatry and corruption result (Rom. 1:18ff.). Only Christ can bring reconciliation (Rom. 7:24-25). To the incarnate Christ God has given all power (Jn. 3:35; 17:2). "All things" in Mt. 11:27 probably includes power as well as knowledge. He has come in humility, but he seizes power with the cross and resurrection (Mt. 28:18) and is now exalted even above angels (Rom. 8:38; Eph. 1:21ff.; Col. 2:10).

d. Since people do not recognize the position of Jesus, mission is needed to actualize it. All flesh is to see God's salvation (Lk. 3:6)—first Israel (Acts 2:36), then the whole world (Mk. 16:15). Then Christ will be all in all (Eph. 1:22-23), all creatures will do him homage (Rev. 5:13), he will make all things new (Rev. 21:5), and he will present his all-embracing kingdom to the Father (1 Cor. 15:24). Until then, all things already belong to Christians (1 Cor. 3:21ff.), sanctified by the word and prayer (1 Tim. 4:4-5).

e. NT proclamation is full of abounding joy at Christ's universality, and this comes to expression in a common use of *pás* (Eph. 1:22-23) which also reflects personal commitment.

f. In many verses, of course, *pás* is used in the NT simply to denote a great number, e.g., "all Jerusalem" in Mt. 2:3, and "all the sick" in 4:24.

[B. Reicke, V, 892-96]

---

páscha [Passover]

páscha is a transcription of the Aramaic. In the NT it may denote a. the seven-day Passover feast, b. the Passover meal, c. the Passover lamb, or d. Easter or the Lord's Supper (cf. Lk. 22:15-16).

1. The Feast. The Passover dates from the exodus; details may be found in Ex. 12. At first a family feast, it is later celebrated at Jerusalem and involves a pilgrimage. The main features of the liturgy are becoming fixed in NT times. In later Judaism the Passover covers the days of unleavened bread as well as the Passover proper. This is the main NT use (Lk. 22:1; Mt. 26:2; Jn. 11:55, etc.; Acts 12:4). Heb. 11:28 refers to the first Passover as an expression of the faith of Moses. The Passover is the setting of many NT stories, e.g., the boy Jesus in the temple (Lk. 2:41ff.), the feeding of the 5,000 (Mk. 6:32ff.), probably the incident mentioned in Lk. 13:1ff., the passion, and the martyrdom of James (Acts 12:1ff.) (cf. also the slaying of James the Lord's brother).

2. The Meal. The meal, which begins after sunset, has to be eaten in Jerusalem and is enframed by a liturgy that includes prayers and psalms. Whether the Last Supper is the actual Passover meal has been debated (cf. Mk. 14:12ff. and Jn. 18:28). Dt. 17:13 shows that there is no objection to the trial being held on the feast day, and many features of the Supper display its paschal character.

3. The Lamb. The NT frequently equates Jesus with the Passover lamb (cf. 1 Cor. 5:7; 1 Pet. 1:19; Jn. 1:29). The sayings of Jesus at the Last Supper probably underlie the equation (Mk. 14:22ff.). In Lk. 22:16 the messianic banquet is a fulfilment of the Passover, in 1 Cor. 5:7-8 the community is the unleavened dough, and in 1 Pet. 1:13ff. the people redeemed by the blood of the spotless lamb sets out on pilgrimage.

4. Easter and the Lord's Supper. The early church takes over the feasts of Passover and Pentecost from Judaism. At first Easter is probably kept on the date of the Jewish celebration, but the paschal vigil replaces the Passover meal and expectation of the parousia replaces expectation of the coming of the Messiah. Later, lights come into use, baptism precedes the eucharist, leavened bread replaces unleavened, and there is more stress on recollection of the passion. In many places, including Rome, the day replaces the date, and after a struggle around A.D. 190 (Eusebius *Ecclesiastical History* 5.23ff.) the Sunday Easter prevails.   [J. JEREMIAS, V, 896-904]

→ *kláō*

---

páschō [to experience, suffer], *pathētós* [subject to suffering], *propáschō* [to suffer before], *sympáschō* [to suffer with], *páthos* [suffering], *páthēma* [suffering], *sympathḗs* [sympathetic], *sympathéō* [to suffer with, sympathize], *kakopathéō* [to suffer misfortune], *synkakopathéō* [to suffer misfortune with], *kakopátheia* [misfortune], *metriopathéō* [to deal gently], *homoiopathḗs* [to have similar feelings], *praüpátheia* [gentleness]

---

páschō.

A. The Greek and Hellenistic World.

1. The basic meaning of *páschō* is "to experience something that comes from outside." At first the "something" is usually bad, and while a neutral use develops, the idea of suffering evil remains so strong that an addition is needed to show that good is meant unless the context is very plain.

2. The forensic use "to suffer punishment" is fairly old, and occurs especially for corporal or capital punishment.

3. Evils suffered are misfortune and disfavor (human or divine). In the case of sickness the idea is that of suffering from it rather than under it. The stress is always on the experience of evil rather than painful feelings. When *páschō* denotes emotions, the reference is more to moods than to sufferings. The group raises the question of suffering, and to this many answers are attempted. Tragedy suggests learning through suffering, Stoicism aims at freedom in its negation (*apátheia*), the Hermetic writings promise redemption from it, at first by initiation and definitively, after death, by deification.

B. The LXX and Judaism.

1. The LXX. The word is rare in the LXX, since the Hebrew has no corresponding term. We find it in Esth. 9:26; Am. 6:6; Zech. 11:5; Ezek. 16:5. The OT, of course, has much to say about suffering in Job, the Psalms, and Is. 53. The term occurs more commonly in the apocryphal works, e.g., for the sufferings of both Israel's enemies and of Israel itself, the former as a punishment, the latter as discipline with a view to salvation. In 2 and 4 Maccabees *páschō* is not a technical term for suffering martyrdom, and does not even have to refer to death. Thus in 2 Macc. 7:18, 32 the reference is a general one to the sufferings of the people, and the sense in 4 Macc. 14:9 is "to undergo."

2. *Philo and Josephus.*

a. Philo uses *páschō* some 150 times, often for suffering evil, but mostly in the sense of passivity as distinct from free action. Sensory impressions are *páschein,* and finally only God is active and everything creaturely is passive, so that even *noús* confers only an illusory freedom.

b. Josephus, too, uses the word a good deal, especially in *Antiquities.* His usage is more general than that of Philo. The main senses are "to experience" and "to suffer punishment" (sometimes death, but this depends on the context).

3. *Pseudepigrapha and Rabbis.*

a. The term is rare in the pseudepigrapha. It may mean "to have an impression" but also denotes "to suffer punishment or afflictions." Present sufferings in Syr. Bar. 78:6 anticipate future punishment, and by the law of compensation are the best guarantee of future felicity.

b. This principle also occurs in the rabbis. The rabbis trace back sufferings to specific sins, and ascribe to them atoning force should they induce repentance. But some sufferings involve no guilt (the chastisements of love) and are tests. The possibility of purification and expiation by suffering is a sign of election. This important insight is often called "passion theology," but this is a dubious term in view of the absence of any word corresponding to *páschō.*

C. The NT.

1. *General.* The word *páschō* occurs 42 times in the NT, mostly with reference to Christ's sufferings and those of his people. It does not occur in OT quotations nor in John, 1–3 John, or Revelation, and Paul uses it only seven times. Some common uses are not found, e.g., as the opposite of verbs of action. In Gal. 3:4 the many things experienced are obviously bad, but the experience is beneficial. In Mt. 27:19 it is unlikely that Pilate's wife suffers punishment; anguish is probably meant. In Mk. 5:26 the sense is simply that the woman has been much doctored. In 1 Cor. 12:26 the idea seems to be that of suffering harm or injury.

2. *The Suffering of Christ.*

a. The Synoptic Gospels and Acts.

(a) In the absolute in Lk. 22:15; 24:26; Acts 1:3; 17:3 *páschō* means "to suffer death." In Lk. 24:26 and Acts 17:3 there is an active nuance. The usage seems to go back to Jesus himself in Lk. 22:15ff.

(b) In a second group (Mk. 8:3; Mt. 16:21; Lk. 9:22; Mk. 9:12; Mt. 17:12; Lk. 17:25) the stress is more passive (cf. Mt. 17:12). We do not have in *pollá patheín* (Mk. 8:31; Lk. 9:22) a master concept. The aim of the phrase is perhaps to show the divine meaning and purpose of what takes place. "Suffering many things" expresses the divine aspect, "being rejected" the human side. Although the Greek renderings do not use *páschō* in Is. 53:4, 11, these verses might well lie behind the NT phrase, with an emphasis on the idea of "bearing" or "enduring." Is. 53 fairly clearly contributes the concept of vicarious and active dying, and if so Jesus may be seen as the active subject of *pollá patheín* as he suffers obediently in discharge of a divine commission. The uniqueness of the passion of Jesus comes out in his use of *páthō* only for his own sufferings, not for those of the prophets (Mt. 5:12), or the Baptist (Mk. 9:12), or his disciples (Mk. 8:34ff.).

b. Hebrews and 1 Peter.

(a) Hebrews uses *patheín* for the passion of Christ in the sense "to die." This is obvious in 13:12, and in 2:18 it is strongly suggested by the statement in 2:9. 5:7, of course, refers to Gethsemane, but 5:8 goes beyond this to Golgotha (cf. Phil. 2:8; Rom. 5:19). In 9:26 the context supports a reference to Christ's death (cf. the "once for all"). Hebrews never uses "for us," but this is implied. The *patheín* of Hebrews is related to the death (2:9, 14, etc.), the blood (9:12, 14), and the cross (12:2).

(b) As in Hebrews, so in 1 Pet. 2:21, 23 the *patheín* of Jesus is his death. The crucifixion is also the point in 4:1. This suffering is "for sins" (3:18) or "for us" (2:21). Stress is laid on its once-for-all character (3:18), on its unity with the resurrection (3:21-22) and glory (1:11), and on its exemplary nature (2:21).

3. The Sufferings of Christians.

a. Acts 9:16. Unlike Jesus himself, the NT writers use *páschein* for the sufferings of believers too. In Acts 9:16 general sufferings are meant if the task in v. 15 is to bear Christ's name "to" Gentiles etc., but specific sufferings if the task is to bear it "before" Gentiles etc. Only the sufferings make the "bearing" possible. This explains the "must" of v. 16. The *patheín* is not a necessary consequence but a validation of the apostle as a chosen vessel (cf. 2 Cor. 11:23ff.). The fact that the suffering is "for the sake of my name" gives it an active character.

b. Paul. Paul normally uses *páschein* with reference to his readers, not himself. In 2 Tim. 1:12 he suffers in the discharge of his high office, but this suffering promotes his work (1:8). Only in 1 Th. 2:14 is Paul's use passive. Phil. 1:29 has an active ring in view of v. 30, where *páschein* is the privilege of the whole community when it is *páschein* "for his sake" (Christ's). This rules out, of course, any soteriological significance, since Christ cannot be the subject of soteriological effort. The *pathḗmata* of Christians count as *pathḗmata* of Christ (2 Cor. 1:5ff.) and have an eschatological goal (cf. 2 Th. 1:5 and the link with glory in Rom. 8:17).

c. 1 Peter. 1 Peter underlines more the exemplary nature of Christ's *páschein,* but in the case of Christians *páschein* does not mean "to die" but covers undeserved punishment by masters or the courts, and possibly abuse, threats, insults, discrimination, etc. (cf. 4:16). The point of the example lies in the unjust nature of the *páschein.* In 3:14 the injustice lies not merely in punishment in spite of the performance of duty but in punishment for doing right. In suffering, Christians are not necessarily participating in Christ's passion but following in his steps (2:21), again with an eschatological orientation (1:6-7; 5:10). In 4:1 there is an allusion to baptismal dying (cf. Rom. 6:7). As Christ accepted God's will in dying, so in baptism Christians cease from sin and will only to live to God (Rom. 6:11). This is the only instance of a transferred use for baptism, and it is made possible only by the use of *patheín* for "to die" and by the teaching of Rom. 6.

D. The Apostolic Fathers. The word *páschō* is a common one in the apostolic fathers. It often means "to die" (Christ or martyrs) (cf. 1 Clem. 6:1-2; Ignatius *Smyrneans* 7.1); *Romans* 4.3; Barn. 5.5, etc. [mostly Christ]; Hermas *Visions* 3.1.9 etc. [martyrs]; Mart. Pol. 17.2 [Christ]). Other senses are "to undergo" in Ignatius *Smyrneans* 2 and "to suffer punishment" in Hermas *Similitudes* 6.3.6.

800

pathētós.

1. This is a verbal adjective of *páschō* and means "open or subject to external impressions" or to *páthē*.

2. The word occurs in the NT only in Acts 26:23. The point of the saying is that Christ has to suffer, and in view of the use of *páschō* in Lk. 24:26; Acts 3:18; 17:3 the reference is clearly to his death, not in the passive sense of "subject to," but in the active one of "ordained for."

3. In the apostolic fathers the only instances are in Ignatius (*Ephesians* 7.2; *To Polycarp* 3.2) with reference to the post- and preexistent Christ, not as the one who entered the world of *páthē,* but as the one who could die.

propáschō. This word means "to be under previous influence" (usually bad), "to suffer before." The one use in the NT is in 1 Th. 2:2, which refers to Paul's prior sufferings in Philippi. As distinct from the parallel reference to shameful treatment, the word has perhaps a more active nuance here.

sympáschō.

1. This word means "to suffer at the same time," "to suffer with," and only very rarely "to sympathize."

2. The only NT instances are in 1 Cor. 12:26; Rom. 8:17. The idea in 1 Cor. 12:26 is not that when one member suffers loss all the members share the loss emotionally but that they all suffer loss too. In Rom. 8:17 the context shows that more than sympathy is at issue. Nor is it the meaning that Christ and Christians share a common suffering. Instead, as Christ has made them heirs and given them a share in heavenly glory, so he has set them in this suffering, so that it is suffering for his sake (Phil. 1:29). As in Christ's case, the glory will come only with the resurrection (Rom. 8:18), i.e., when Christ himself comes in glory (Col. 3:4). Rom. 8:17 shows that *sympáschein* is a presupposition of true fellowship with Christ and hence a condition of future *syndoxasthēnai* (cf. 2 Tim. 2:12).

3. In the apostolic fathers Ignatius *Smyrneans* uses *sympáschein* in the sense "to die with" (Christ). This also might well be the point in Ignatius *Polycarp* 6.1, and it is unquestionably the sense in 9.2. In the only other instance (2 Clem. 4.3) the word means "to sympathize."

páthos.

1. Sharing the history of *páschō,* this noun means "experience," then "misfortune" etc., then "mood," "emotion," "passion," "impulse," also "change," "process," "attribute," and, in rhetoric, "pathos."

2. The LXX uses *páthos* only in works with no Hebrew original.

3. Philo has *páthos* some 400 times, mostly for "emotion." For Philo *hēdonē* is *páthos.* Philo demands *apátheia* or the bridling of *páthē.* Josephus has *páthos* for "misfortune" or "illness." In the Testaments of the Twelve Patriarchs the word means "vice" or "passion." The rabbis have no equivalent term in the sense of "emotion" or "passion."

4. Only Paul uses *páthos* in the NT, the singular in Col. 3:5; 1 Th. 4:5, the plural in Rom. 1:26. The *páthē* of Rom. 1:26 are the vices of homosexuality. The meaning in context in Col. 3:5 is "erotic passion." "Sexual passion" is also the point in 1 Th. 4:5.

5. The apostolic fathers use *páthos* for "adultery" or "bad temper" (Hermas *Mandates* 4.1.6; *Similitudes* 6.5.5). But it also means "suffering" and "death" (Barnabas

and Ignatius), i.e., the passion of Jesus. The stress on the *páthos* of Jesus in Ignatius is part of the original Christian tradition and develops from the use of *pathéō* for "to die."

páthēma.

1. Less common than *páthos,* this means "misfortune," "state of suffering," "sorrow," and occasionally "emotion."

2. It does not occur in the LXX. Philo has it for "sickness," and so does Josephus. But Josephus also has it for cosmic "process" (*Antiquities* 1.156).

3. Always plural in the NT except in Heb. 2:9, it means "passion" or "impulse" in Gal. 5:24; Rom. 7:5, but its main sense is "suffering," e.g., Rom. 8:18; 2 Cor. 1:5ff.; Phil. 3:10; Col. 1:24; 2 Tim. 3:11; Heb. 2:9-10; 1 Pet. 1:11; 4:13.

a. In Gal. 5:24 it embraces the things mentioned in vv. 19-21. The impulses, whose basis is the *sárx,* are crucified in Christians and are thus to be put to death. In Rom. 7:5 life in the flesh means that sinful passions are aroused by the law and work in the members. The phrase *tōn hamartiōn* describes the nature of these passions.

b. In 2 Cor. 1:5 Paul says that he shares in Christ's sufferings, and in v. 6 he says that the readers endure the same sufferings, for in their sufferings, too, they share in those of Christ. Since suffering is an essential part of the faith, it is a grace (Phil. 1:29) and brings blessing to all. In Phil. 3:10-11 the *pathḗmata* of Christ are Christ's own sufferings, but fellowship with these is not just by a passion mysticism but by the actual sufferings that Paul himself endures. The point is not that Christian suffering arises because there has to be analogy, imitation, or continuation of Christ's suffering, but because the way of Christ entails suffering (cf. Acts 9:16; 14:22). In Col. 1:24 a parallel is again seen between the apostle's sufferings and Christ's afflictions. Disciples have to suffer, and therefore the absence of suffering is a lack which has to be made good. The sufferings may be severe, but Rom. 8:18 declares that they are nothing compared to the future glory.

c. In Heb. 2:9 the reference is to the suffering which consists of death. The tautology gives emphasis to this first mention of the death of Jesus, and the singular is an assimilation to the singular *thánatos.* The plural that follows refers to the whole process of the crucifixion (v. 10). In 1 Peter *pathḗmata* (like *patheín*) refers to the death of Christ (1:11). When the author calls himself a *mártys* (witness) of Christ's sufferings in 5:1, the continuation ("partaker of the glory") shows that he has in view sharing in the sufferings and not just eyewitness of the passion.

4. In the early church Ignatius *Smyrneans* 5.1 uses *pathḗmata* for Christian sufferings, 1 Clem. 2.1 uses it for the death of Christ, and Athenagoras *Supplication* 28.4 uses it for "destinies."

sympathḗs, sympathéō.

1. *sympathḗs* means "having the same *páthos*" and hence "sharing the same experience, suffering," etc., and then "having fellow feeling." *sympathéō* means "to suffer with" and hence "to sympathize."

2. *sympathḗs* occurs three times in 4 Maccabees; *sympathéō* occurs only in 4 Macc. 5:25 in the sense "to have the best in view."

3. Philo uses *sympathéō* with mercy in *On the Special Laws* 2.115 and has *sympathḗs* to suggest "fellow feeling," "participation," and "cosmic movement." In Josephus the group means "fellow feeling," "mutual participation," or "sympathy."

4. In the NT *sympathḗs* occurs only in the list in 1 Pet. 3:8, where it denotes understanding participation in the lives of others. In Heb. 4:15 *sympathéō* does not

signify a sympathetic understanding that is ready to condone, but a fellow feeling that derives from full acquaintance with the seriousness of the situation as a result of successfully withstanding temptation. In Heb. 10:34 the compassion on prisoners embraces actual help that is given by both word and deed.

5. In the apostolic fathers Ignatius *Romans* 6.3 uses *sympathéō* in a request for understanding of the author's motives and of his urge for martyrdom.

kakopathéō, synkakopathéō, kakopátheia.

1. *kakopathéō* means "to suffer misfortune," "to be in a sorry situation," or, rarely, "to endure evil." *kakopátheia* means "misfortune," "trouble," "suffering," as well as "enduring suffering," "toil," "exertion."

2. The LXX uses *kakopathéō* in Jon. 14:10 for "to go to pains," and *kakopátheia* in Mal. 1:13 for "trouble." The senses in Philo and Josephus are similar.

3. In the NT the noun occurs only in Jms. 5:10 in the obvious sense of "enduring affliction" rather than mere "affliction." The verb in 5:13 belongs to a new section and refers to the spiritual burden inflicted by misfortune or trouble. In 2 Tim. 2:9 Christian suffering is the point, and in 4:5 the demand is that one should endure suffering. In 2:3 Timothy is not just to sympathize with the apostle in his suffering but to take his share of suffering (cf. 1:8, where suffering is not imposed by the gospel but is for the sake of it).

4. In the apostolic fathers the only use of *kakopathéō* is in 2 Clem. 19.3 for being beset by the afflictions of this world.

metriopathéō.

1. This word denotes moderation in passion.

2. It does not occur in the LXX but Philo has it for the moderate grief of Abraham on Sarah's death, and Josephus extols it in Vespasian and Titus on the conclusion of peace.

3. The only NT instance is in Heb. 5:2, where the high priest's sense of his own weakness and sin results in moderation in dealing with the people's offenses.

4. There are no instances in the apostolic fathers or Apologists.

homoiopathḗs.

1. This word relates to one whose circumstances, feelings, etc. are the same or similar. Wis. 7:3 states that the earth is the same for all, 4 Macc. 12:13 points out that tyrants and their victims have the same feelings, and Philo finds the same feelings and modes of life among animals and humans.

2. There are two instances in the NT. In Acts 14:15 Barnabas and Paul protest that they are humans like those who want to honor them as gods, and in Jms. 5:17 the point is made that we may pray as Elijah did, since he has no superhuman powers but is of the same nature as we are.

3. The Apologists use the term with reference to the incarnate Christ (cf. Justin *Dialogue* 48.3; 57.3).

praüpátheia.

1. This late construct means "gentleness" (cf. Philo *On Abraham* 213).

2. The only NT instance is in the list in 1 Tim. 6:11, where the meaning is not so much "meekness" as "composure" in face of wrongs.

3. Ignatius *Trallians* 8.1 calls it a virtue that believers should acquire.

[W. MICHAELIS, V, 904-39]

> *patássō* [to strike, smite]

The intransitive "to knock loudly" does not occur in the NT. The transitive "to strike" is more common and occurs over 400 times in the LXX, usually for God's "smiting" in judgment. In the NT it is found three times in OT quotations (Acts 7:24; Mk. 14:27; Mt. 26:31). At the arrest of Jesus a disciple "smites" the high priest's slave (Mt. 26:51; Lk. 22:49). The term denotes divine intervention in Acts 12:7 and 12:23. In Rev. 11:6 the two witnesses have power to "smite" the earth in judgment. In Rev. 19:15 (cf. Is. 11:4) the Logos as universal Judge will definitively extirpate all hostility to God on earth.   [H. SEESEMANN, V, 939-40]

> *patéō* [to walk, tread on], *katapatéō* [to trample], *peripatéō* [to walk around], *emperipatéō* [to walk]

A. General Greek Usage.

1. *patéō* means intransitively "to go," "to walk," and transitively "to tread," then in a transferred sense "to tread underfoot," i.e., "to disparage," "maltreat."

2. *katapatéō* means "to trample," "to despise."

3. *peripatéō* means "to walk around," and in a transferred sense "to live."

4. *emperipatéō* is a later term meaning "to walk."   [H. SEESEMANN, V, 940-41]

B. The LXX.

1. In the LXX the terms denote "treading," e.g., on the land to take possession (Dt. 11:24). *peripatein* often denotes a righteous walk or life.

2. Negatively the terms are used for God's judgments, as in the treading of the winepress (Joel 3:13), the trampling of armies (2 Kgs. 7:17), the potter's treading of the clay (Is. 41:25), the treading down of the temple (Is. 63:18), the crushing of lions, adders, etc. (Ps. 91:13). Trampling and deriding are combined in Zech. 12:3. When the wicked do the trampling, their arrogance is implied (Am. 2:7; Ezek. 34:18). The psalmist faces proud enemies who tread him down (Pss. 7:5; 56:1-2; 57:3).

3. *peripatéō* and *emperipatéō* are closely related in the LXX. They denote moving about, e.g., Satan's in Job 1:6-7, God's in Gen. 3:8. Movement expresses life (Ex. 21:19). Idols cannot walk (Ps. 115:7). The religious or ethical walk is sometimes denoted. Wisdom walks in righteousness (Prov. 8:20) and the king has walked in faithfulness (2 Kgs. 20:3). In contrast is walking in darkness in the ethical sense (Is. 59:9). One catches here a hint of the two ways, but more with an indication of the sphere in which life is lived than its goal.   [G. BERTRAM, V, 941-43]

C. The NT.

1. The five NT instances of *patéō* all show LXX influence. In Lk. 10:19 Jesus gives the disciples authority to tread on serpents and scorpions. In Lk. 21:24 Jerusalem will be trodden down by the Gentiles, i.e., plundered, desecrated, and destroyed. The usage in Rev. 11:2 is the same. The figure of treading the winepress for divine judgment occurs in Rev. 14:20; 19:15.

2. *katapatéō* occurs four times for "to tread underfoot" (Mt. 5:13; 7:6; Lk. 8:5; 12:1) and once in a transferred sense for "to despise" (Heb. 10:29).

3. *peripatéō* means first "to walk around" as in Mk. 2:9; Jn. 5:8ff.; Acts 3:6ff. The devil "roams around" in 1 Pet. 5:8. Paul, however, uses the term for the walk of life

on the basis of the LXX. Believers are to walk in the Spirit (Gal. 5:16), to walk worthy of God (1 Th. 2:12) or the Lord (Col. 1:10) or their calling (Eph. 4:1), to walk as children of light (Eph. 5:8). Teaching on the walk of life is given (1 Th. 4:1ff.; Col. 2:6). Those who do not walk as directed are to be avoided (2 Th. 3:6, 11). Faith does not mean social reshuffling but it does mean a changed life (1 Cor. 7:17; Eph. 4:17). Baptism ends the walk in sin (Col. 3:7). It sets in the past walking according to the flesh (Rom. 8:4). Believers still walk *in* the flesh (2 Cor. 10:3), but the flesh is no longer lord. They may now walk in newness of life (Rom. 6:4). This is a walk by faith (2 Cor. 5:7). John uses *peripatein* for ordinary "going" (11:9-10), but in 8:12 it refers to the stance of faith (cf. 12:35; 1 Jn. 1:6-7). Other examples of a figurative use are found in Mk. 7:5; Acts 15:1; 21:21; Heb. 13:9; Rev. 21:24.

4. *emperipatéō* occurs only in 2 Cor. 6:16 (cf. Lev. 26:12), where it refers to God's redeeming presence in the community. [H. SEESEMANN, V, 943-45]

---

patḗr [father], *patrōos* [belonging to the father], *patriá* [from the father, family], *apátōr* [fatherless], *patrikós* [paternal]

---

patḗr.

A. The Indo-European World and Graeco-Roman Antiquity.

I. The Use of patḗr. Of Indo-European origin, and incorporating the childish "pa," *patḗr* means "father" or "forefather," then "initiator," "revered person," "old man," "teacher," etc. The plural means "ancestors," and very occasionally "parents."

II. The Ancient Concept and Its Influence. The term is first genealogical, then legal and sociological for the kindly but severe and authoritative head of the house in a patriarchal order.

III. The Greeks.

1. Head of the House and Teacher. Patriarchal control is found among the Greeks too, modeled on that of Zeus and similar to that of the king. The Stoics regard children as subject to their fathers as elders, benefactors, and superiors. But there is also an emphasis on fatherly love. Fathers are teachers by word and example. Thus Philo states that they should engender and uphold good resolves and brave actions (*On the Special Laws* 2.29).

2. Piety toward the Father. A duty uniformly recognized is that of honoring one's father. To command love of parents is, for the Stoics, superfluous. Parents rank only after the gods. This does not entail ancestor worship. The point is that divine reason comes to expression in human societies, e.g., the family and the state. If conflict arises, however, the good takes precedence over father and mother.

IV. The Roman patria potestas. Roman law vests authority and power in the head of the house. Civil law combines here with sacral law, for the father is also the priest. The father's power continues over all children until his death and embraces slaves as well. It includes disciplinary and penal power, the right to marry and divorce children, and the right to adopt and emancipate. The Roman view affects Greek law, and Jews who are Roman citizens adopt it (cf. Philo *On the Special Laws* 2.227, 233). Relaxation comes only with the Justinian Code.

V. Religious Use of the Father Image.

1. The Indo-Iranian Basis of the Idea of God as Father. Invocation of God as father, i.e., the author of being, is old. It rests on primitive ideas, e.g., the view in India that

805

vegetation arises by conception from heaven and earth. The concept of the divine progenitor spreads in many forms (cf. the ruler as God's son in Egypt).

2. *Zeus as Father and Ruler.* In Homer Zeus is the universal god, the father of all divine and human beings. Patriarchalism, fatherhood, and monarchy meet in this view. If Zeus is not called king, he still rules over all things and is the apotheosis of the head of the house, protecting parental rights. The despotic aspects in Homer's depiction of Zeus perhaps express some revolt against unrestricted paternal authority. His being portrayed in human terms means, however, that he too is subject to fate.

3. *The Father in the Mysteries.* God is commonly called father in the mysteries (cf. Serapis, Mithras, and Helios). The term signifies relationship, and generation by the god attests to his friendship and power to bless. The father god makes initiates both sons and brothers in a spiritual family. The teacher or pastor is also a cultic father in this family, and the office is hereditary or involves a spiritual descent. The priestly father represents the divine father (cf. the priestly role of the earthly head of the house).

VI. *Philosophical and Gnostic Forms of Belief in the Father.*

1. *Father in Plato's Cosmology.* Plato sees in the idea the source of all things. He then gives the father concept cosmological form in the creation myth. God is author and father (*poiētḗs kaí patḗr*). The world is good because its architect is good. Philo makes use of Plato's terms. Neo-Platonism distinguishes between the supreme God and the demiurge. Gnostic systems take a similar view. A common term in cosmological speculation is "the father of all" (*patḗr tṓn hólōn* or *pántōn*).

2. *The Father as Begetter and the Synthesis of King and Father in Stoicism.* Stoicism uses the myth of the sacred marriage of Zeus and Hera and traces back the world to divine begetting (cf. the spermatic *lógoi*). This confers divine sonship on humanity and a share in the divine *lógos*. Only the wise see this, and therefore there is some sense in which God is the father only of the good. The gods want us to be virtuous; hence divine sonship leads to ethical teaching. Later Stoicism stresses God's authority as ruler. As a good king and true father, God grants the powers necessary to struggle against adversity. Zeus as the king of kings is the model for earthly rulers.

3. *The Father Concept in Philo.*

a. Greek Influence. Philo uses the absolute "the Father" for God. He shows the influence of Homer and Plato but also takes up the Stoic idea of generation. The soul is the child of God inasmuch as virtues are begotten in it. The wise are adopted by God as true children. As Father, God cares for his creation and in his fatherly pity grants good gifts to it.

b. Jewish Factors. To express God's authority, Philo prefers *kýrios* or *despótēs* to *basileús*. God has both creative power and royal power. In the *lógos* as the vehicle of his transcendent deity his authority and kindness merge. The *lógos* is the first-begotten of the Father who validates God's fatherly power and ruling authority.

4. *The Father in Hermes Mysticism.* In the confused world of Hermes mysticism the father of all is the one fixed pole. Transcendent, he is related to all things and mystically known. He is father as maker or begetter. Primal man receives light and life from the father and is allowed to create, but falls through mating with nature. As author and father, God is good and embraces all good. He exercises saving rule, fixes human destinies, and has mercy on initiates, who enter into fellowship with him by way of *noús*. Father is the final word of prayer for initiates, but the final goal is absorption into the all.   [G. SCHRENK, V, 945-59]

B. The OT.

1. patḗr and Other Terms for 'āḇ in the OT. In the OT *patḗr* is almost always used for *'āḇ*. Other renderings of *'āḇ* yield no significant results, since we either have adjectival phrases, attempts at greater precision, or softenings.

2. 'āḇ as a Primary Word. *'āḇ* is a primary word connected to no stems, having only one meaning, and with no real synonyms. Suggested relationships to other terms are all questionable (cf. the attempt to read "fear" in Gen. 31:42 as "kinsman" or "ancestor").

3. 'āḇ as a Basic Element in the Family Concept. The socio-legal order of family life determines the Hebrew use of "father." The family is "the father's house." Since "house" here can be a structure, an urban culture is the setting. The father's legal supremacy is in view but the sons' marriages create a clan and dilute this authority as the house becomes a broader community. In this connection the father may be the "forefather," as in the phrase "God of the fathers" (Ex. 3:13). Love and pride and loyalty can prolong the sense of belonging to forefathers (cf. the role of Abraham and David, and the use of "fathers" in Lk. 1:73; Rom. 4:12).

4. Basic Features of Patriarchy. The family laws of Israel give primacy to the father, especially in matters of property and inheritance. At first matriarchal features may also be seen, but the cultus reinforces patriarchy by expecting certain sacral functions from the male head of the clan and limiting the sacral role of women; cf. Judg. 17:10, where the young man is called "father" because he acts as priest, and the later use of the term "father" for the prophet (2 Kgs. 2:12) or official. Dignity and authority are also accorded to the priest, prophet, and official with the use of the term. The father's primacy means that the children belong to his clan and that the sons are heirs unless their mother is a "strange woman" (Judg. 11:2). Fathers may sell daughters as bond servants (Ex. 21:7) and may accuse their children (Gen. 38:24; Dt. 21:18ff.) in their respect for higher law. Fathers play a big role in tribal courts, and are so respected that they must not be cursed or struck (Ex. 21:15, 17). Thus there are no instances of patricide in the OT. The commandment (Ex. 20:12) brings out the impulse behind the law, associating the mother with the father and inculcating a positive norm of conduct. Whether parents deserve this respect is not at issue. The term "father" may set up an ideal when applied to priests, prophets, and officials, but physical fathers are to be honored as such, since they are such by divine ordinance. There is something divine about the father, for there is something fatherly in God.

5. The Father of the Gods. The OT makes sparing use of "father" for God. The three main reasons for this are that the OT expresses trust in more intellectual terms, that the important covenant concept does not fit too well with that of father, and that the father motif is more closely related to myth. Israel does call God Father, as may be seen in theophorous names. But the larger notion of a Father of the gods does not appear in the OT. At most one might quote Dt. 32:8-9, although Dt. 4:19 makes it plain that all things are under the Lord's supreme control. Ps. 82:6-7 refers to "sons of the Most High," and Pss. 29:1 and 89:6 speak about "heavenly beings" without actually calling them God's sons. It is only poetically that the gods may be called "sons of God." Theologically the OT concept of God leaves no place for this mythical conception.

6. Father and Other Terms of Relationship in OT Religion. The idea of God as Father fits in more easily with family than tribal worship, but the community sense of the clan or tribe provides some basis for the wider use of the concept. It is an ancient religious concept that must have been present elsewhere before being adopted by

Israel. Behind the idea lies the sense of generation from a single head and an ultimate beginning in God (although with no hint of ancestor worship). The relationship with God is thus construed along the lines of the relationship to the father, with some diminishing of the sense of distance between Creator and creature, yet not so much as when the deity is thought of as mother, brother, or uncle, since less authority attaches to these figures. It should be noted, too, that the blood relationship suggested by the term father is not thought of literally but metaphorically (for the sake of its emotional content), so that the tradition adopts the concept even if it is misconstrued in periods of apostasy (cf. Jer. 2:26-27). References to the divine begetting (Ezek. 23:4; Gen. 6:4) must be seen in the context of Ps. 90, which does not call God the father of nature but presents him plainly as its sovereign Lord (v. 2) and calls believers his servants rather than his children. Dt. 32 undoubtedly calls God the Father of his people (vv. 6, 18-19), but it does so in order to make the reality of fellowship with God as vivid as possible and to bring out its ethical implications.

7. *Father as a Theophorous Element in the Proper Names of Israel.* The vitality of motifs proper to tribal religions may be seen in a name like Joab ("Yahweh is Father") or Abijah ("Father is Yahweh"). With or without a "my," this is a personal confession, but it also carries a collective sense. God as Head of the blood fellowship is Father to each member. One cannot conclude, however, that kinship provides the basis for the development of the concept of God as Father.

8. *Father as Metaphor.* Israel's belief in God as Father is not to be seen as grounded in myth, for myth does not nurture piety, and Israel always contests an image of God that is simply a heightened human image. Applied to God, the term Father is finally metaphorical. The first point of comparison is the legal authority of the father. If the idea still meets with some resistance, so that the people are called the children of Israel rather than of Yahweh, the sociological position of the father as the one who is a trustworthy and yet a loving authority (cf. Ps. 103:13; Prov. 3:12) gives it enduring strength. Love is an increasingly important element in the use of the term, as may be seen from Hos. 11:1. It is an important element even in the ideology of kingship (cf. 2 Sam. 7:14-15) and thus results in statements like those of Pss. 89:26 and 2:7. Intrinsic to the concept are the greatness and the loving concern of God.

9. *Father as a Concept of Authority.* The element of authority may be seen in the fact that the delight of the Father in the son is more commonly expressed than the joy of the son in the Father. Fatherhood implies a duty of obedience (cf. 2 Kgs. 16:7; Dt. 14:1; Jer. 18:6-7; cf. Is. 64:8). As Creator, God the Father rules and molds his people.

10. *The Universalist Trend in the Designation of God as Father.* Since God is Creator, an extension of the father concept beyond Israel is logical. The Father of Dt. 32:6 creates rather than begets the people and this carries with it the question whether he creates Israel alone (cf. Jer. 3:19; Mal. 2:10). What finally emerges is that paternal feeling is the true motif in the father concept as applied to God (cf. Ps. 73:15; Jer. 31:18ff.; Is. 63:15-16). This has a personal as well as a national reference (Pss. 27:10; 68:5), and at last all reserve is overcome and there can be a full declaration of trust in God as Father (Ps. 89:26; Sir. 51:10). [G. QUELL, V, 959-74]

C. The Father Concept in Later Judaism.

I. The Earthly Father.

1. Piety toward the Father. The rabbis discuss why the father is to be honored first in Ex. 20:12 but the mother in Lev. 19:3 (the LXX and Philo change the order in Leviticus). They think the mother is put first in Leviticus because she advises the child. On the other hand, the father should have more honor because he teaches the law. Rules of proper observance are laid down. Thus fathers should not be contradicted or criticized, and adult children must care for aged parents.

2. *Parents as Instruments and Representatives of God.* Honoring God comes before honoring parents, and this principle can also give precedence to teachers of the law. Yet parents are instruments of divine generation, and therefore honoring parents is honoring God.

3. *The Duties of the Father.* The father must teach his children the law by instruction and example. He may punish children, but the rabbis soften the penalties of Ex. 21:15; Lev. 20:9. Philo and Josephus, however, incline to the Roman view of paternal authority and hence to a severer attitude to punishment.

II. The Fathers in Judaism.

1. *The Concept.* The "fathers" are usually the patriarchs, but the term also embraces the exodus or wilderness generation and outstanding figures of the past. Abraham, Isaac, and Jacob are "fathers of the world," and Abraham, the father of nations, is commonly called "our father Abraham."

2. *The Importance of the Fathers.* The fathers are the rock whence Israel is hewn. They embody tradition and guarantee covenant grace. Their mediated merits blot out later sin and bring pardon in the judgment. They are effective intercessors. God is thus invoked as "our (my) God and the God of our (my) fathers."

III. Father as a Title for Teacher. As a general title of honor, father is a common term for the rabbi. The OT use for the prophet (not the patriarch) is a model for this. The title is often linked with the name of the teacher.

IV. God as Father in Judaism. In Judaism God is often called Father both collectively and individually. Hellenism strengthens this use, but in Israel the accent is less cosmic and genealogical and more national and theocratic. The religious use increases toward the end of the first century A.D.

1. *Distinctions from Greek Cosmology.*

a. Not Cosmic Begetter but National Protector. The most important difference from Greek thinking is that in Judaism God is the Father of the covenant people in a personal relationship. The reference is not to begetting as a principle but to fatherhood as an attitude and as action. God is Lord of the world but as Father he cares for his people. The addition of "our," "your," "my," etc. expresses the personal aspect. For the most part Father is used as a predicate and in address to God.

b. Father and Lord. These terms go together in later Judaism. The combination is prefigured in Mal. 1:6; Sirach, etc. Josephus has *patḗr kaí despótēs,* and "our Father, our King" is a liturgical formula in the synagogue. The conjunction, which Stoicism and Gnosticism also favor, preserves the sense of God's holiness and thus protects the father concept against mawkish weakening.

2. *The Father in the Heavens.* From the end of the first century A.D. this is a common phrase in the Palestinian synagogue. Tradition dates back "Israel and her Father in heaven" to c. A.D. 70. Heaven here is not meant to stress God's remoteness but to distinguish his fatherhood from earthly fatherhood. After A.D. 70 consolation for the loss of political freedom is found by looking to the heavenly Father. The use is collective, but personal versions also occur ("my Father in heaven" etc.). This applies especially but not exclusively in the case of outstanding figures who enjoy an unusually close relationship to God. The phrase "before the Father in heaven" expresses Israel's attitude in prayer.

3. *Invocation of the Father in Prayer.* Jewish Hellenistic writings and synagogue

liturgies show that God is invoked as Father (cf. Is. 63:16; 1 Chr. 29:10 LXX). The form "our Father" is common, but "our Father in heaven" is less so.

4. The Relation to Other Synagogue Names for God and the Limitation in the Understanding of God as Father. The rabbis prefer phrases that denote God's sovereignty, or such terms as the Holy or Merciful One, or substitute terms like the place, the dwelling, or the word. The emphasis is on God's holiness and power rather than his fatherliness. A living sense of fatherly care is uncommon, and the belief in merit tends to rob the term Father of depth and vitality, since legalism restricts fatherly freedom. The materials of true faith in the Father are all present, but the spirit is still to some extent missing.

D. The NT.
I. Father according to the Synoptic Jesus.

1. Honoring the Earthly Father and Its Limits. Jesus unconditionally affirms the fifth commandment (Mk. 10:19) and dismisses the evasions of casuistry (Mk. 7:10ff.). He also shows a tender regard for the parent-child relation (Mk. 5:40; 9:14ff.; Lk. 9:37ff.). Tension arises with Jesus' call to discipleship, for, like marriage (Gen. 2:24), this sets up a new order (Mk. 10:29-30) and demands an eschatological outlook (Mt. 8:21-22), yet does not permit evasion of the commandment. At times the tension may be felt so severely that renunciation of all earthly relationships is entailed (Lk. 14:26), although not in the sense of a vow. The Son of Man tears generations apart (Mk. 13:12), as in Jewish eschatological expectation. On the positive side, however, the gospel does a reconciling work (Lk. 1:17) by healing family disruption and restoring the disobedient.

2. The Religious Use of patēr.

a. The Presupposition of Patriarchy. Patriarchy is the sociological background of the religious use of *patēr*. It is unusual to leave father and trade to follow Jesus (Mt. 4:22). The father orders his sons to work in the vineyard (Mt. 21:28). The father holds and controls the family property (Lk. 15:11ff.). The younger son sins by seeking advance ownership and selfishly leaving his father's house; conversion is returning to the father's fellowship. Being in fellowship with the father is the gift on which all else depends. When Jesus calls God Father, God's lordship is implied in his fatherhood.

b. Invocation of God as "Abba." The NT has preserved the Aramaic term used by Jesus, namely, "Abba." This childish cry is a generalized vocative. An infant sound is confidently applied to God as the simplest term to express his loving attitude. Familiarity is avoided by the setting of the invocation within the kingdom with its demand for submission to God's holy rule.

c. The Father in the Heavens.

(a) Sources. It seems likely that Matthew preserves the original, longer form of this expression (cf. Mk. 11:25). In parallel passages Luke amends it to suit his purpose. Matthew shows that Jesus does not always add "in the heavens," but he presents a true Father theology in a form which stands close to the Palestinian tradition.

(b) Meaning. Distinguishing heaven from earth, the formula suggests sovereignty but also implies perfect fatherhood. The use of "your" or "our" denotes the status of sonship. In the Lord's Prayer the first three petitions express the control of earth by heaven under the divine fatherhood. In Mt. 6:1ff. piety is regulated by the Father. In Mt. 23:9 the heavenly Father normatively fixes the meaning of earthly fatherhood. What the formula always implies is the orientation of earth to heaven, or the control of earth by heaven, under the God who is exalted and yet near.

d. My Father and Your Father.

(a) Sources. The use of "my Father" is limited in Mark but more common in material peculiar to Luke and especially Matthew. In Mark "your Father" occurs only in 11:25. It is more common in Matthew.

(b) Distinction. In Mark and Luke, and material common to Matthew and Luke, "your Father" occurs only in directions to the disciples. Yet the phrase always stands in relation to Jesus. The directions receive their force from the presence of the kingdom in the person of Jesus. The truth of fatherhood is the revelation of the Son. Only through him is it a truth for the disciples.

(c) Christological Confession. Jesus teaches his disciples to pray "our Father," but his own "my Father" expresses a unique relationship. This may be seen already in Lk. 2:49 (cf. 23:34, 46). The use has christological and confessional force in Mt. 16:17; 18:19. The content of this Christology is that the Father reveals himself in the Son, that decision is made relative to him, that the suffering Son is doing the Father's will, that he grants salvation and assurance of acceptance to his followers, and that future consummation is promised.

e. The Absolute *ho patḗr*. The absolute use is uncommon but is found in all strata. On the lips of Jesus it usually occurs with "the Son" or "the Son of Man" in apocalyptic contexts. Dan 7, which expresses the sovereignty of the Father and the commission of the Son, may well be the basis.

f. God the Father of All. Jesus relates God's fatherhood primarily to the privileged nation of Israel, although decision as to Israel's relation to the Father rests on her encounter with the Son (cf. Mt. 21:28ff.; Lk. 15:11ff.). God is the Creator of all (Mt. 5:43ff.) but there is no reference to any general sonship by nature or estate. Disciples encounter the Father in Jesus. Fatherhood is linked to the kingdom and discipleship. It implies the divine lordship.

g. Fatherly Authority and Fatherly Care. The heavenly Father is a model of impartial generosity who expresses his perfection in forgiveness. He combines love with discipline and his greatest gift is his strongest claim (Mt. 6:14-15; Mk. 11:25). Disclosure of the Father replaces legalism and controls conduct with a view to his glory (Mt. 5:16). Solicitude accompanies authority. The Father provides for both earthly needs and final salvation. One may rely on his foresight (Mt. 6:8, 32) and fatherly goodness (Mt. 7:9ff.). He extends assistance in persecution (10:29-30) and does not will that any of his little ones should perish either in time or eternity (Mt. 18:14).

h. Significance for the Disciples.

(a) Christological Form of Belief in the Father. Jesus is totally committed to the Father and his saving purpose and claims no greater power or knowledge than the Father. This comes out in the passion prayer of Mk. 14:36 and the disclaimer of knowledge of the date of the parousia (13:32). The Son's authority is the gift of the Father to be used in the Father's service. The Father reveals the truth concerning the Son (Mt. 16:17). The fellowship of the kingdom is a household fellowship under the Father as Head.

(b) The Cry of Jubilation. The mystery of the Son is an integral part of this cry. The Son's fellowship with the Father gives him his authority and knowledge. The truth about Jesus and the Father takes kerygmatic form here in a way which takes us to the root of the unique sense of Jesus' "my Father."

(c) The Christological Message in Lk. 15:11ff. The christological message in Lk. 15:11ff. is that of the fatherly love that shows mercy meeting true conversion and then seeking to win the elder brother into the circle of blessing. The father's will involves acceptance of his mercy and the joyous feast represents household rejoicing at the restoration of fellowship. The work of Christ is the work whereby the Father unites the righteous and the unrighteous in a new family fellowship by overcoming the legalism of the former and graciously opening the doors to the latter. This work does not make the cross superfluous, for it comes to completion on the cross, where Jesus forgives the thief and prays for the self-righteous. It is on the cross that Jesus fulfils the truth of fatherhood that dominates his ministry.

i. The Unity of Father, King, and Judge.

(a) Father and Judge. In patriarchy fatherly provision and judicial power come together. The Father's will is the norm of judgment (Mt. 7:21ff.; 18:23ff.), and the Son judges in the Father's name (Mt. 25:31ff.).

(b) Father and Ruler. The term "father" includes lordship, but Jesus strengthens this aspect by associating fatherhood and the kingdom. God is seldom called *basileús* in the Gospels but there can be no questioning his lordship. The kingly rule of God is the fatherly rule of grace. Jesus puts an end to any legalistic restriction of such terms as Lord, King, and Judge. The one name Father absorbs and implies others in expression of a trusting simplicity that overcomes both fear of the divine names and their accumulation.

II. patēr in John.

1. Usage. In John *patēr* is used for God some 115 times. The absolute use predominates. We find "your father" only once (20:17), and "our father" and "father in the heavens" not at all.

2. Concept. John does not relate the idea of begetting to the term "father." The Father takes precedence (14:28) in authoritative giving (6:32). The Son knows, obeys, recognizes, and honors him in a harmony of love (10:30). The Son's relation to the Father implies patriarchy. He stays in the Father's house, owns what the Father owns, and can gain a hearing with the Father (8:35; 16:15). He prepares a place for his disciples as members of his Father's household (14:2).

3. Revelation. In John the message of the divine fatherhood relates to revelation. God is not primarily the Father of all but the Father of the Son who reveals him, and who is the Son in a unique sense. In Jn. 1:14, 18 the Father is the Giver of revelation and the Son is the Revealer (cf. 4:21, 24). The Son acts on the Father's commission (5:43). The Father bears witness to him in Scripture (5:37ff.) and gives him as the heavenly bread (6:32). Only as he has always been with the Father can the Son reveal him (1:1, 18). Sending is thus the key. The Father sends the Son to do his work, and it is as he is consecrated and sent that he is manifested as the Son (10:36). "Father" is itself a word of revelation (17:6, 11, 26, 28). It is about the Father that Jesus speaks (16:25). This is no mere verbal concept separate from the saving work of the Son. The work of the Son is the content of witness to the Father (6:41ff.). To know or see the Son is to know or see the Father (14:7ff.). To decide for or against the Son is to decide for or against the Father (8:42). If revelation is the declaration of the Father, the word and work of Jesus fill the term with new and specific content.

4. The Harmony of Father and Son. The union of Father and Son is the core of the message in John. What this means is that the Father loves the Son (3:35). This is no mystical love but is related to the Son's commissioned work. This love has a pretemporal basis and implies mutual knowing and seeing. It is a "being in" but involves action as the Son says and does what the Father wills (5:19; 7:17-18). The works of the Son are the Father's works (10:32, 37-38). The word is the Father's word (14:24). Both works and word attest to both Sender and Sent (10:25). A fellowship of giving produces the act of revelation and comes to fulfilment in the self-giving of the Son as he takes up the cup the Father gives him to drink (18:11) in a union of the Father's love (10:17) and the Son's obedience (10:18). Only when the saving work is done does Jesus make his Father in the true sense the Father of the disciples as well (20:17), for he is the only way to the Father (14:6). The Paraclete works out the new relationship as an abiding gift (14:18ff.), and the disciples are brought into a parallel knowing (10:14-15), loving (15:9-10), union (14:20), and sending (17:18).

5. *The Conflict for the Truth of the Father.* In Jn. 2:16 Jesus accuses the Jews of desecrating the Father's house, but the real issue is Jesus' own relation to the Father (5; 6; 8). Opponents treat Jesus as a mere man and thus demand special validation of his mission (6:42). They appeal to God as their Father (8:41) but fail to recognize the Father and the Son (8:45ff.). Their attitudes and actions show that spiritually their father is the devil (8:42). The battle for the truth of fatherhood is repeated in the "convincing" work of the Paraclete (16:8ff., especially v. 10).

6. *The Father and Prayer.* As suffering intensifies, Jesus increasingly engages in prayer to the Father (11:41-42; 12:27ff.). The unique missionary form of prayer in 11:41-42 states his life's goal. The prayer of 12:27ff. expresses conflict but seeks God's glorifying in a fulfilment of mission. Giving by the Father and the glorifying of the Father are the dominant themes in ch. 17. The disciples have direct access to the Father as they appeal to the Son and agree with him (14:13; 16:23). The absolute *patếr* is the goal of prayer in worship in the Spirit (4:21ff.). The disciples' prayer is the fruit of the Son's completed work of salvation.

III. Father in the Other Apostolic Writings.

1. *The Earthly Father.* The instructions given to fathers in Col. 3:18ff.; Eph. 5:22ff. combine OT and Jewish-Hellenistic elements but give them added depth with the reference to the Lord. The new relationship of faith is the determinative point. Paternal power must not be abused, but obedience pleases the Lord, and education is to be given in the Lord. In Heb. 12:4ff. discipline is right, but only as it evinces loving concern. In a mixed marriage Paul gives the decisive vote to the believing partner inasmuch as the other partner and the children are consecrated by the superior fact of faith. 1 Tim. 5:1-2 enjoins respect for the elderly as though they were fathers.

2. *Men as Fathers in Paul.*

a. Abraham. In Rom. 4:1 Abraham is father as a believer, and this means that all believers are his children. What counts is not blood relationship but a genealogy of faith. He is Israel's father only if she believes as he did.

b. The Apostle. In his relations to the churches Paul thinks in fatherly terms. He refers to birth in 1 Cor. 4:15. Timothy and Titus are children or sons (1 Cor. 4:17; Tit. 1:4; cf. Mark in 1 Pet. 5:13). The father differs from other teachers (1 Cor. 4:15), although he is father only in Christ. A title is not at issue but a living relationship. Both father and child serve the one gospel (cf. Phil. 2:22). Fatherly actions are described in 1 Th. 2:11ff. If there is any model, it is the rabbinic one, not that of the teacher of wisdom or the mystagogue.

3. *God as Father.*

a. The Cry "Abba." Gal. 4:6; Rom. 8:15; 1 Pet. 1:17 and the use of the Lord's Prayer confirm the importance of invoking God as Father. The cry "Abba" is not just liturgical; it is a work of the Spirit of adoption. Paul's doxologies show that a permanent attitude is at stake. The invocation implies the assurance of sonship and inheritance. It marks the end of legalism and servanthood.

b. The Use of *patếr.*

(a) *theós patếr.* This phrase occurs in blessings, salutations, and final greetings, e.g., Gal. 1:3; Rom. 1:7; Phil. 1:2; Eph. 1:2; 6:23. But it never occurs in Paul without mention of the *kýrios*. Omission of the article enhances its effect, and reading the epistles promotes its liturgical use. It has the force of a dogmatic formulation in 2 Pet. 1:17 (cf. Ignatius *Magnesians* 3.1).

(b) *theós ho patḗr*. This lofty confessional phrase occurs only in 1 Cor. 8:6.

(c) *ho theós kaí patḗr*. This is a formula of doxology and thanksgiving in 1 Thessalonians and Galatians. It represents the attitude of prayer in 1 Th. 1:2-3 and is shaped by the implied petition in 3:11. The *kaí* is preferred when a genitive follows, i.e., "God and Father of our Lord Jesus Christ." Here *patḗr toú kyríou* defines *theós*, although probably only "Father" relates to Christ. Statements along these lines contain praise in the style of prayer (2 Cor. 1:3; Eph. 1:3; 1 Pet. 1:3). Solemn force is added in 2 Cor. 11:31. *ho theós kaí patḗr* also occurs in confessional statements in 1 Cor. 15:24; Eph. 4:5-6, and in an admonition in Eph. 5:20. Distinctive phrases are "Father of mercies" in 2 Cor. 1:3 and "Father of glory" in Eph. 1:17. The latter phrase is in apposition to the unusual "God of our Lord Jesus Christ."

(d) *ho patḗr*. In Paul the absolute occurs only in Colossians and Ephesians, which polemically adopt Gnostic terms. Col. 1:12-13 links it with *ho huiós*. Eph. 2:18 shows similarity to John, which also seems to be in conflict with Gnosticism.

(e) *patḗr, theós, huiós, kýrios*. Paul mostly uses *theós* but gives it distinctive content. He uses *patḗr* in prayer and links it to *theós*. *theós* denotes God's power and glory as Creator, *patḗr* his grace and mercy as Redeemer. In 2 Cor. 1:3 "Father of mercy" interprets *theós* as the "God of comfort," while in Eph. 1:17 *patḗr* is defined in terms of *theós* as the Father of glory. Paul reserves *kýrios* for Jesus and he relates *huiós* to *theós* rather than *patḗr*, linking *patḗr* with *kýrios*. God, as the Father of Jesus, is also the Father of believers. Statements about the *kýrios* are more common than those about the *huiós* because Paul proclaims what is given by the Father and the Lord.

c. Content of the Father Concept.

(a) Fatherhood as Lordship. What is said about the Father relates to doxology, prayer, and confession. Fatherhood means sovereignty. His will controls the work of salvation (Gal. 1:4). We owe all things to his power (Eph. 5:20). His gift is a call to sanctification (2 Cor. 6:14ff.). At the parousia we come before him as Judge (1 Th. 3:13). When redeemed, we are put in his kingdom (Col. 1:12-13). At the end the kingdom will be his (1 Cor. 15:24ff.). That the Father is also Ruler is revealed in the fact that he is Father of the *kýrios*, who is also Ruler and Judge. The use of Father for God is controlled by the revelation in Christ. Ditheism is not implied, but it is the Lord who makes possible true belief in the Father.

(b) The Gift of Grace through the Father. The Father dispenses *cháris, agápē, éleos, paráklēsis, eirḗnē* (2 Th. 2:16-17; 2 Cor. 1:3; 1 Pet. 1:3). This is an ongoing part of redemption. Blessing fulfils the counsel of salvation (Eph. 1:3). The cry "Abba" relates to the Father as the Giver of salvation. The Spirit makes us children (Rom. 8:14) and gives us access to the Father (Eph. 2:18). Beloved in God the Father (Jude 1), believers are "in" God the Father by faith.

d. Greek Influences.

(a) The Answer to Belief in the Father of All. In 1 Cor. 8:4ff. confession of the Father is opposed to polytheism. *tá pánta* here is set in the biblical context of creation. God is the author of creation, and through Christ creation and redemption are linked. Paul uses Greek expressions, but he gives them a new sense. In Eph. 2:18ff. the saints, through the Spirit, have rights in God's household. The Father of us all is above, through, and in all. Here OT and Stoic phrases are mixed, but the Stoic phrases receive new content with the reference to the new unity of the redeemed people. A dynamic unity is brought into focus by belief in the Father.

(b) Exceptions. 1 Pet. 1:3 relates "begetting" to the Father. The point here is that he has effected regeneration. Jms. 1:18 also relates regeneration to the Father, but again with a soteriological reference. "Father of lights" in v. 17 may have the stars in view (cf. Philo), but the phrase is an incidental one. Hebrews uses *patḗr* sparingly, but calls God the "Father of spirits" in 12:9 in what seems to be a more general cosmological rather than a soteriological use.

patrṓos.

1. This word means "what belongs to the father or is inherited from the father."

2. In the LXX and Josephus it has the special sense of "what derives from the fathers." It may thus be used with tradition or with God.

3. Josephus prefers *pátrios* in this sense, e.g., for customs, tradition, the land, the language, the constitution, and especially the law.

4. In the NT Paul in Acts 22:3 says that he was brought up in the law of the fathers, while in 24:14 he says that he worships the God of our fathers, and in 28:17 he tells the Jews in Rome that he has done nothing against the customs of the fathers.

patriá.

A. Outside the NT.

1. Meaning. This word, denoting derivation from the father, is used for the family house, tribe, race, nation, or more specifically the family tree.

2. The LXX. The LXX uses the term frequently for "the sept," "the clan," and, in the plural, "nations" (Psalms and Jeremiah). It occurs in the phrase "father's house" and "heads of fathers' houses" (used also for the Levitical divisions in 1 Chr. 24:4).

B. The NT.

1. For "father's house" *patriá* occurs in Lk. 2:4, where it is added to "house" to show that the reference is to descent. In Acts 3:25 "nations" is the sense. This verse displays the liturgical influence of the Psalms with their missionary use of the term (cf. Ps. 96:7).

2. In Eph. 3:14-15 every family is said to be named from the Father. The Father has no *patriaí* in the strict sense but the very term *patriaí* shows that they have their origin in God and are oriented to him. If the family group of the church is included, Israel and the nations are also in view. The heavenly *patriá* is probably that of the angels rather than the perfected community, for Ephesians everywhere relates heaven and earth (cf. 1:10; 3:10). The text does not say directly that God is the prototype reflected in the *patriaí*. The relationship of Creator and creature is in the background, although only in combination with redemption. The *patriaí* are created by him who is the Father of Jesus Christ. God is not the primal Father of all things in the Greek sense, but the revealed Father in Christ who is related to the *patriaí* as such.

apátōr.

A. Outside the NT.

1. Humans. When used of humans, *apátōr* can mean "orphan," "foundling," "bastard," "of unequal parentage," "disinherited," or "of nonnoble or unknown origin." In Judaism converted pagans are said to be "without father," and Judaism also applies the sense of "unnamed" to Esther, who is an orphan in Esth. 2:7.

2. *Deities.* Such deities as Athena, Hephaestus, and Aphrodite are said to be without father or mother. God has no father in Orphic, Gnostic, and mystic works. The point is that he has no origin, or is uncreated.

3. *Philo's Allegorizing.* Philo uses only *amētōr.* Thus Sarah is the motherless principle. This idea rests on allegorical punning and does not imply deification any more than when the high priest is said to be the divine *lógos,* with God as father and *sophía* as mother.

B. The NT. The one NT instance of the word is in Heb. 7:3. This says of Melchizedek that he has no father, mother, nor genealogy. The point is that he does not fall into the sequence of the Levitical priesthood. As the promise precedes the law in Paul, so this priesthood precedes the Levitical priesthood in Hebrews. Similarly, as the reference of the promise is to Christ, so the reference of Melchizedek's priesthood is to the high priesthood of Christ.

patrikós.

1. This word has the sense of "fatherly" or "paternal" with various references, e.g., to rule, command, affection, etc. It is used in the LXX with "house," and *tó patrikón* denotes "patrimony." Jewish Hellenism prefers *patrṓos* to *patrikós* when speaking of the laws or customs of the fathers.

2. There is an inclination to use the term for one's own father in particular. The Gnostics refer it to the regenerate, and Clement of Alexandria uses it for the relation of the Logos to the Father (*Stromateis* 7.2.5.6).

3. Occasionally the reference may be to the fathers, as perhaps in 1 Chr. 7:4 LXX and more clearly in Lev. 25:41 LXX.

4. In Gal. 1:14 *patrikós* denotes the religious inheritance of the father's house (cf. Acts 23:6; Phil. 3:5; 2 Tim. 1:3; Acts 22:3; 26:5).   [G. SCHRENK, V, 974-1022]

---

pachýnō [to make fat, insensitive], *pōróō* [to harden], *(pēróō* [to disable]), *pórōsis* [insensibility], *(pérōsis* [hardness]), *sklērós* [hard], *sklērótēs* [hardness], *sklērotráchēlos* [stiff-necked], *sklērýnō* [to harden]

This group from different stems signifies the "hardening" of unbelievers, of Israel's enemies, of Israel, of Jews against Christians, and finally of Christians. The term "to harden" may have a literal sense but is most commonly used in Scripture in a transferred sense. Luther's practice of bringing the various terms under a common equivalent, which is not followed by other translations, is justified to the extent that the material reference is the same. The LXX tends at times to soften the Hebrew by throwing greater emphasis on human responsibility, but this sharpens the measure of human guilt and misery. Interconnected in the whole complex are the thoughts of hardening and judgment by God on the one side and self-hardening and self-judgment on the other. The hardening is always specific within the history of the elect people, which may also be a history of rejection but is always a history of the divine faithfulness. If the fear of saying either too much or too little produces a kaleidoscope of harsher and softer colors, the basic color is the beautiful one of the divine glory.

pachýnō.

1. Deriving from *pachýs* ("thick"), this word means "to thicken" (medically "to swell").

2. Figuratively it means "to make impervious," "insensitive," as in Mt. 13:15 and Acts 28:27 (both quoting Is. 6:10).

3. In Is. 6:10 the prophet is told to make the people's heart "fat," but the LXX softens this by simply describing the "fattening" or "hardening" as a fact.

pōróō (pēróō), pórōsis (pérōsis).

1. This word group is used medically for the "hardening" or "thickening" of the bone, e.g., in fractures. Hence it may also denote "healing." In a transferred sense it means "to make insensitive."

2. The LXX uses it only in Job 17:7 (for the dimming of the eyes) and Prov. 10:20 A.

3. The verb occurs five times in the NT, usually with the heart in view. The hardening is that of the Jews in Jn. 12:40; Rom. 11:7; 2 Cor. 3:14, and the disciples in Mk. 6:52; 8:17. The verbal noun occurs three times with reference to Jews or Gentiles in Mk. 3:5; Eph. 4:18; Rom. 11:25. God is the author in Jn. 12:40, but God's hardening is also a self-hardening, so that personal responsibility remains and a call can go out for repentance (Ezek. 18:31). Sin and unbelief are the punishment of sin and unbelief, but renewal by God is still a possibility (Is. 6:11ff.). In Rom. 9–11 Paul perceives a partial hardening of Israel, but believing Gentiles may boast only of the divine grace that includes the hope of a conversion of hardened Israel (11:33ff.) both by human decision and sovereign divine act (11:23, 17ff.). Connected with divine hardening is the self-hardening of 2 Cor. 3:14, from which even disciples are not exempt (Mk. 6:52) in their misunderstanding of Jesus' sayings.

4. In most of the above references we find the variant *pēróō*, "to maim," "to wound," and hence "to blind." The verb is found in Mk. 6:17; Jn. 12:40; Rom. 11:7, and *pérōsis* in Mk. 3:5. Ancient translations assume *pēróō* or *pérōsis* in other verses too. But *pōr-* is better attested, and *pēr-*, being more common, is more likely to have been substituted for it.

sklērós.

1. This word means "dry," "arid," "hard," "rough" (cf. "skeleton").

2. It occurs in the NT for "hard" sayings in Jn. 6:60; Jude 15, "contrary" winds in Jms. 3:4, and an "austere" man in Mt. 25:24. The phrase "it is hard for you" occurs in Acts 26:14 (cf. 9:4).

3. Some of the NT passages reflect LXX usage (cf. Jms. 3:4 and Is. 27:8; Mt. 25:24 and Is. 19:4). There are similar parallels in the apostolic fathers.

sklērótēs.

1. This verbal noun, which is rare in classical Greek, occurs four times in the LXX (Dt. 9:27; 2 Sam. 22:6; Is. 4:6; 28:27), and is used physiologically and psychologically by Philo. The only NT instance is in Rom. 2:5, where the hardened and impenitent heart of self-righteous Jews is denoted. In Hermas *Mandates* 5.2.6 we read that the Spirit will not dwell with an evil spirit and with hardness.

sklērotráchēlos. This word, meaning "stiff-necked," is developed by the LXX. It occurs in the NT only in Stephen's address in Acts 7:51. 1 Clem. 53.3 uses it (quoting Dt. 9:13).

sklērýnō.

1. This word, meaning "to harden," is primarily a medical term.

2. The NT uses it figuratively in Acts 19:9; Rom. 9:18; Heb. 3:8, 13, 15; 4:7. It is linked with unbelief in Acts 19:9, God punishes by means of it in Rom. 9:18, but Christians are admonished against it in Heb. 3:8 etc.

3. Rom. 9:18; Heb. 3:8, etc. have in view incidents such as those of Ex. 4:21; 15:23. In the LXX Gentile rulers are hardened, but so are Israel and her kings. The LXX also uses the term with no stress on hardening (cf. the heavy hand of Israel in Judg. 4:24, the hard thing of 2 Kgs. 2:10, the heavy yoke of 2 Chr. 2:10, and the withered grass of Ps. 90:6).

4. The apostolic fathers follow the biblical use for hardening in 1 Clem. 51.3.5 (cf. Barn. 9.5).   [K. L. and M. A. SCHMIDT, V, 1022-31]

→ *sklērokardía* [*kardía*]

> *peíthō* [to convince, persuade], *pepoíthēsis* [trust, confidence], *peithós* [persuasive], *peithṓ* [persuasiveness], *peismonḗ* [persuasion], *peitharchéō* [to obey], *apeithḗs* [disobedient], *apeithéō* [to disobey], *apeítheia* [disobedience]

---

peíthō.

1. The Active (apart from the Perfect).

a. The usual Greek senses of *peíthō* are "to convince," "to persuade," "to seduce," "to corrupt." The present expresses intention, the aorist success.

b. In the LXX *peíthō* is rare and there is no true original. But *pépoitha*, which expresses confidence, is more common. The LXX uses *peíthein* in, e.g., 1 Sam. 24:7 and Jer. 29:8, and more frequently in Maccabees and Tobit.

c. In the NT "to convince" is the most natural sense in Acts 18:4; 28:23, and "to persuade" in Mt. 27:20; Acts 14:19 (with a hint of "seduce"). In Acts 12:20; Mt. 14 "to bribe" is probably meant, though "to pacify" is possible in Mt. 28:14. The meaning is uncertain in 2 Cor. 5:11, where "to win" is possible but "to persuade" is more likely in context. In Gal. 1:10 the sense depends on whether the two questions are parallel. If they are, God is the answer, for it is God's favor that Paul seeks. If they are not, he is asking whom he seeks to persuade with his preaching, and the answer is "men." In this case, the parallel is a material one; Paul pleases God by his efforts to persuade men. In 1 Jn. 3:19 the text is uncertain, and one must ask whether "by this" has a forward or backward reference. The thought is undoubtedly that of reassurance, and the reason is probably given in vv. 20-21, namely, that we have confidence in God whether our hearts condemn us or not.

2. peíthomai.

a. This word has such senses as "to trust," "to be convinced," "to believe," "to follow," and even "to obey."

b. In the LXX it is rare in books with a Hebrew original. In Esth. 4:4 the LXX introduces it to suggest that Mordecai will not be persuaded to stop mourning, and in Prov. 26:25 it brings in the thought of deceit. The ideas of conviction and faith are present in 2 Macc. 9:27; 4 Macc. 5:16, and that of obedience in 3 Macc. 1:11.

c. "To be convinced" is the meaning in Heb. 13:18; Lk. 20:6; Rom. 8:38 (cf. Acts 5:40). "To be won over" makes good sense in Acts 21:14; 23:21, and "to obey" in Heb. 13:17; Jms. 3:3; Rom. 2:8; Gal. 5:7. Only in the last two verses does the term take on theological significance with their stress on "obeying the truth." In such connections "not believing" is the opposite (cf. Acts 28:24). When following false messiahs is the issue, the sense of "being seduced" is present.

3. pépoitha.

a. This term carries the sense of "trust," "reliance," or "confidence."

b. A Hebrew equivalent is *bṭḥ,* which expresses confidence, hope, trust, security, and peace; *pépoitha* is used both for this and for associated terms (some 142 times in all). Trust in God is a basic feature of the OT; there are also warnings against trust in earthly powers.

c. In the NT the strong rely on their armor and the rich on their wealth (Lk. 11:22; Mk. 10:24), but Paul relies on the faithfulness of the church (2 Cor. 2:3; Gal. 5:10) and the obedience of Philemon (Phlm. 21), while the brethren draw confidence from Paul's imprisonment (Phil. 1:14). Christian confidence is that of faith. It is "in the Lord" (Gal. 5:10; Phil. 2:24). It is confidence in God (Phil. 1:6; cf. Heb. 2:13; Mt. 27:43). In the NT, however, confidence in God mostly takes the form of faith and relates to eschatological salvation rather than present situations (as in the Psalms). It is related to obedience and involves the rejection of false confidence (Phil. 3:3-4), which Paul often calls "boasting." Boasting in Christ is the opposite of confidence in the flesh. The apostolic fathers use the term mainly in OT quotations or allusions (1 Clem. 57.7; 58.1; Hermas *Mandates* 9.6; *Similitudes* 9.18.5).

pepoíthēsis. This word means "trust" or "confidence." In 2 Cor. 1:15 Paul is confident that the Corinthians now have some understanding. In 2 Cor. 8:22 his confidence is in the church's readiness regarding the collection. A radical self-confidence is at issue in Phil. 3:4; its opposite is confidence in God (2 Cor. 3:4; cf. 10:2). Eph. 3:12 singles out the element of confidence comprised in faith, *parrhēsía* ("boldness") being synonymous. The apostolic fathers use the term for the confidence of the OT saints (1 Clem. 31.3; 45.8) or of Christians (2 Clem. 6.9); its opposite is the empty confidence of arrogant believers (Hermas *Similitudes* 9.22.3).

peithós, peithṓ. These words occur only in two different readings of 1 Cor. 2:4. The former (an adjective) yields "persuasive words of wisdom," the latter (a noun) "the persuasive art of wisdom." Either way, the sense is that Paul's preaching does not derive its power from rhetorical skill.

peismonḗ. This rare word, not found prior to the NT, occurs only in Gal. 5:8, where it may mean "persuasion" or it may catch up the *peíthesthai* of v. 7 and mean "obedience." Ignatius *Romans* 3.3 says that Christianity is not a matter of persuasion, and Justin *Apology* 53.1 says that the prophecies are adequate for convincing.

peitharchéō. This verb means "to obey." "To pay heed" (Acts 27:21) is the weaker sense, and we find "to obey" rulers in Tit. 3:1, and "to obey God (rather than men)" in Acts 5:29.

apeithḗs. This word means "unworthy of belief," then "disobedient." The Baptist's mission in Lk. 1:17 is to turn the hearts of "the disobedient," false teachers are "disobedient" in Tit. 1:16, believers were once "disobedient" in Tit. 3:3, and Paul was "not disobedient" to the vision in Acts 26:19 (cf. also Rom. 1:30; 2 Tim. 3:2).

apeithéō. This word means "to be disobedient" and is a significant term in the LXX for disobedience to God. In the NT it is used of the wilderness generation in Heb. 3:18, that of the flood in 1 Pet. 3:20, all sinners in Rom. 2:8, and Gentiles in

Heb. 11:31; Rom. 11:30. "To believe" is the opposite in Acts 14:1-2, and unbelief is parallel. We find an absolute use in Acts 14:2; Rom. 15:31; 1 Pet. 2:7. Important phrases are disobeying the word (1 Pet. 2:8), the gospel (4:17), and the Son (Jn. 3:36).

apeítheia. This word means "disobedience." It is used for sin in Rom. 11:32. The disobedience is that of the wilderness generation in Heb. 4:6, 11, the Jews in Rom. 11:30, and all sinners in Rom. 11:32. Sinners are "sons of disobedience" in Eph. 2:2; 5:6. *apeítheia* is the third of the vices personified as virgins in black in Hermas *Similitudes* 9.15.3.   [R. BULTMANN, VI, 1-11]

---

peináō [to hunger, desire avidly],   *(limós* [hunger, famine]*)*

A. The Greek-Hellenistic World.

1. Usage.

a. *peináō* means "to be hungry," or "avidly to desire something."

b. As compared with the noun *hē peína, ho* and *hē limós* expresses a higher degree of want, and figuratively signifies deprivation rather than desire.

2. Attitude to Hunger. Fertility worship is designed to insure nourishment (cf. Israel and Baal). Bad harvests are seen as due to divine anger. Rulers, too, must provide food, and are paid divine honors for so doing. In a well-run state no honest people should go hungry. Philosophy demands that goods should be shared and argues for moderation in food and clothing. Stoicism tries to treat external want as an indifferent matter; if need be, one may escape it by suicide. The later ideal in Neo-Platonism is total abstinence with a view to union with the divine (cf. Christian Gnosticism). In the mysteries the old gods have the new function of serving the hunger for abiding life. Philo adopts the ideal of moderation and the priority of nourishing the soul, but he finds in hunger an unsupportable evil, and extols the fact that through the fall we must provide against it by work.

B. The OT and Judaism.

I. Use. The OT usually refers to hunger, not as the need for food, but as the lack or withdrawal of the fruits of labor. The LXX always has *limós* as the noun (mostly for *rā'āḇ*), but regularly uses the verb *peinán* for *rā'ēḇ*. *peinán* is under the shadow of *limós,* but the two are not coextensive in meaning.

1. limós.

a. This means "acute lack of food," i.e., famine, due to crop failure, drought, war, etc. The OT views it as a divine visitation (Dt. 11:10ff.; 2 Sam. 21:1, etc.), and deliverance is sought from God (1 Kgs. 8:37).

b. *limós* also means "hunger." Here again it is a divine judgment (Dt. 32:23; Ezek. 5:16), both historical and eschatological. With the sword and pestilence, it is a sign of the end, either as imminent (Mt. 24:7) or present judgment (Rev. 6:5-6).

c. Only rarely does the OT use *limós* for extended undernourishment (Is. 5:13; Dt. 28:48). It prefers *peinán* for this.

2. peinán. This term is used for the effects of famine (Gen. 41:55), exhaustion on a campaign or journey (Judg. 8:4-5; Dt. 25:18), or persistent hunger.

II. The OT Interpretation of Hunger. Hunger is proclaimed as a judgment in Is. 5:13; Dt. 28:47-48. Related is the famine of hearing God's word (Am. 8:11). Present hunger is a means of instruction (Dt. 29:5). It teaches the people to receive the necessities of life in the form of the divine promise of salvation (Is. 55:1-2). It is God who satisfies those who languish (Jer. 31:25). The oppressed are sometimes called the hungry (cf. 1 Sam. 2:5; Ps. 107:36ff.). God will meet their needs but also bring hunger on the high and mighty as a sign of rejection (Is. 65:13). Hunger thus becomes a sign of waiting on God, but also a figure of condemnation.

III. Judaism. The pseudepigrapha hold out a promise for poverty, whether as a test, a chastisement, or a criterion of standing before God. The rabbis, however, view it as misfortune. Poverty greatly increases under Herod the Great, and religious groups insure subsistence for their members by mutual aid. After A.D. 70 the strong growth of private and public benevolence sees to it that there is at least sufficient food for the people.

C. *peinán* in the NT.

1. The Synoptic Gospels.

a. The Calling of the Hungry Blessed. The hungry are called blessed in Mt. 5:6; Lk. 6:21. The primary reference is to those who sadly lack the necessities of life and turn to God in their extremity. They are not beggars but believers who seek help from Jesus. Matthew sees in the turning to God a hungering after righteousness, i.e., a readiness that God's will should be done. Luke contrasts the hunger that means salvation with the hunger of rejection. Dives and Lazarus are illustrations (Lk. 16:19ff.). Lazarus is not hungry for the rich man's possessions but seeks only a sufficiency and finally comes to salvation. The rich man's self-sufficient satiety, if it does not become a lack that seeks help in God alone, will finally be a hunger that carries no further promise. Only those who live by God's grace have what is essential to true life (Lk. 15:21ff.; cf. 1:53).

b. Jesus and Hunger. Jesus himself undergoes hunger for his work's sake. In Mt. 4:1-2 he upholds the faith that Israel learns through her desert experiences. Mt. 4:4 (Dt. 8:3) points us to that which comes from God. Jesus lets his disciples pluck ears of corn on the sabbath when they are hungry (Mt. 12:1ff.), not because the hungry have a right to help themselves, but because, having exposed themselves to hunger for his sake, they may receive what he has the right to grant them. Everything is at the disposal of those who are at God's disposal (cf. 1 Cor. 3:22-23). The hunger that stands behind serving God or waiting on God is appeased by Jesus. This is why he feeds the hungry multitudes. Bringing the kingdom, he gives everything necessary to life, and thus puts earthly bread in its true perspective (Mt. 6:33).

c. Teaching. When Jesus, who is hungry, fails to find fruit on the fig tree in Mt. 21:18-19, the point of the enacted parable is that he is hungry for the fruit of righteousness in Israel and proclaims judgment on those in whom he does not find it. In Mt. 25:34ff., however, he promises blessing to those who feed his hungry brethren, for the mercy shown to them is mercy to Jesus himself, who suffered hunger on our behalf. It is in virtue of their association with him that the hungry themselves may be called blessed as co-heirs of the kingdom (Mt. 5:6).

2. The Pauline Epistles. In 1 Cor. 4:6ff. Paul ironically contrasts the Corinthians' supposed fullness of sight with his own hardships as he awaits the consummation in faith. His hunger and thirst are a token of ministry (2 Cor. 11:27). They cannot separate him from Christ (Rom. 8:35). His wants express his dying with Christ and are thus a pledge of participation in the resurrection (2 Cor. 4:7ff.). He is not stoically indifferent to need or plenty, but can affirm both in the light of Christ's death and resurrection (Phil. 4:11ff.).

3. The Johannine Writings. In Jn. 6:35 Jesus fulfils for believers the promise of the age of salvation (Is. 49:10). No earthly bread (Jn. 6:27ff.) can meet the recurrent need for food in the deeper sense. Only the Son who has life in himself can do so by directing the need to its true goal. The desire enclosed in the craving for food is removed and satisfied by faith in him. No dualism is involved, but the spiritual core of the promise is brought out and its comprehensive significance presented. Thus Rev. 7:16-17 promises a future end to hunger. The promise is experienced here only in the harsh dissonance of 1 Cor. 4:6ff. It will be known in physical totality only in the new world of Rev. 21:4ff.   [L. GOPPELT, VI, 12-22]

---

peíra [test, attempt], *peiráō* [to try, test, tempt], *peirázō* [to try, test], *peirasmós* [testing, temptation], *apeírastos* [untried, without temptation], *ekpeirázō* [to try, put to the test]

A. The Terms in Secular Greek.

1. *peiráō* in the active means "to try or strive," "to test," or "to tempt." In the more common middle or passive it means "to put someone to the test," "to test something," or "to know by experience." A rare religious use is for tempting the deity by testing the truth of an oracle.

2. *peirázō,* an uncommon word, also means "to try" or "to test."

3. *ekpeirázō* does not occur in secular Greek, but we find the middle *ekpeiráō* for "to try out" or "to sound someone out."

4. *peíra* means "test," "attempt," or "experience."

5. *peirasmós* is rare in secular Greek. We find it for medical experiments.

6. *apeírastos* does not occur in secular Greek, but *apeíratos* occurs for "what is untried, unknown."

B. The OT and Judaism.

In the LXX we find the ordinary senses (cf. 1 Sam. 17:39), but on a Hebrew basis a religious use develops, partly in relation to divine testing, partly in relation to temptation to transgress God's commands, and partly in relation to the human tempting of God.

1. Human Temptation.

a. The best example of divine testing is in Gen. 22:1ff., where Abraham meets the test. In Ex. 20:20 the law is a test of the people, and Dt. 8:2 views the desert experience as a test. In Judg. 2:22 God tests the people's obedience by not driving out the heathen who are still in the land. Here God uses history to test the people's faith and obedience.

b. The story of the fall describes human temptation that comes, not from God, but from the adversary, who forces Adam and Eve to decide for or against God. Satan also appears in Job 1. The temptation is here allowed by God as a test. Job meets the test because, even in incomprehensible suffering, he is ready to count on God and commit himself to him.

c. There are many references to testing in the Wisdom writings (cf. Sir. 2:1; 33:1), but here the testing is largely educative. All the life of the righteous is a test, and to pass it one should model oneself on Abraham etc.

d. In Dan. 12:10 the last tribulation will be a final testing and sanctifying.

e. The rabbis hold up Abraham as an example. God tests all of us, and due to the evil impulse testing always means peril.

f. Philo so stresses the educative aspect that testing itself is of little account.

g. In the Essene and Qumran writings believers are in a situation of conflict in which there is a constant pressure of temptation to pass over from the side of light to that of darkness.

2. *Tempting God.*

a. The OT offers many instances of human tempting of God. In Ex. 17:2 Moses asks why the complaining people are putting God to the test. Num. 14:22 contains God's judgment on those who put him to the proof. To tempt God is to fail to accept his power or his will to save. It is to challenge him in doubt and unbelief. True love of God rules out the testing of God (Dt. 6:16-17). The strong tradition that one must not tempt God explains the reasoning of Ahaz in Is. 7:12, although in this case the prohibition does not apply, for God offers a sign.

b. Wis. 1:2 shows that faith does not tempt God. Putting God to the test is not belief in him but questioning his power and love.

C. The NT.

I. Secular Use of the Terms. The noun *peíra* means "attempt" in Heb. 11:29 and "experience" in 11:36. The verb *peirázō* means "to examine" in 2 Cor. 13:5; Rev. 2:2 and "to attempt" in Acts 9:26 etc. In Mk. 8:11 the Pharisees "test" Jesus, and in Jn. 6:6 Jesus himself "tests" Philip by asking him how they might feed the multitude.

II. Theological Use of the Terms.

1. Human Temptation.

a. In 1 Cor. 10:13 Paul warns the Corinthians that so far they have come under ordinary human temptations, but he adds the consolation that God will grant the strength to endure whatever may befall them. The warning is probably a general one against too great self-confidence in Corinth. In helping others who fall believers must be humble, lest they also fall (Gal. 6:1).

b. James in 1:13 forbids us to call God the author of temptation. As God cannot be tempted, so he will not tempt others to sin, and is not to be held responsible in any way for sin. It is one's own desire that tempts into sin. In Jms. 1:2-3, however, sufferings for the sake of the gospel are a testing of faith (cf. 1 Peter). James does not suggest that God himself sends sufferings to educate believers, but sufferings should be accepted because they prove faith and produce steadfastness. Jms. 1:12 takes up Mt. 5:4, 10ff. but goes further by promising the crown of life to those who endure trial and stand the test. 1 Pet. 4:12 refers more specifically to the test of persecution, but argues that this should be met with joy because it means participation in the suffering of Christ. In v. 17 suffering is associated with judgment, which begins in God's house.

c. Jesus in Mk. 13 points out that the last time will bring the test both of persecution and of false messianic claims. Rev. 3:10 promises deliverance in the final hour of trial. In 2:10 the church of Smyrna will undergo testing by the *diábolos* and it is thus exhorted to be faithful unto death. As 2 Pet. 2:9 asserts, the Lord can rescue the godly from trial.

d. In the Lord's Prayer (Mt. 6:13; Lk. 11:4) what is at issue is not a test (as in Ps. 139:23) but temptation by ungodly powers, both in the great eschatological tribulations and in all affliction (cf. Lk. 8:13, where those who have no root fall away in time of temptation). In Mk. 14:38 Jesus tells the disciples to watch lest they enter into temptation. He has in view here the weakness of the flesh (cf. 1 Pet. 5:8). Watching involves prayer in the light of our defenselessness against temptation.

e. The NT seldom has the personification *ho peirázōn*. Except in Mk. 4:1ff. we find it only in 1 Th. 3:5. Satan is meant, for *peirázein* is his work (1 Cor. 7:5). "Temptation" or "trial" is a more likely sense than "tempter" in Gal. 4:14. 1 Tim. 6:9 issues a warning to the rich against falling into *peirasmós*; Satan might be in view, but there is no express reference.

2. *Tempting God.* In 1 Cor. 10:9 Paul uses an OT illustration to back up his warning that believers must not "test" or "challenge" God. Heb. 3:8-9 quotes Ps. 95 to the same effect. In Acts 5:9 Peter accuses Ananias and Sapphira of challenging the Spirit by their deceit, for the Spirit sees all things. In 15:10 Peter warns the assembly not to test God by imposing the law on Gentile believers, for by means of the vision God has shown that their freedom from the law is in accordance with his will.

III. The Temptations of Jesus.

1. Hebrews emphasizes that the life of Jesus is one of temptation (2:18; 4:15). He differs from us only in not sinning. The temptation in Gethsemane (5:7ff.) is to disobedience. Opposition is a temptation to give up in 2:18. Perhaps the attacks and questions of, e.g., Mk. 8:11; 12:15, are in view. But the main temptation is to avoid suffering. Because Jesus has victoriously withstood temptation, he can help his people in their temptations.

2. Just after his baptism and before commencing his public ministry, Jesus has an encounter with the *peirázōn,* who tries to deflect him from his mission. Whether the temptations come at the beginning or end of the 40 days, or during their course, makes no difference (cf. Mt. 4:2-3; Mk. 1:13). Jesus is aware of his task and resists efforts to make him disobedient to it. The first temptation is to use his power for purposes out of keeping with his mission, and he resists it by referring to the God who has given him his power. The second temptation is to tempt God by seeking help for selfish reasons and with a false appeal to Scripture; he rejects it as tempting God. The third temptation is the open one to gain world dominion by following Satan instead of God. As in the first two instances, Jesus remains firm, quoting Scripture in confirmation of his exclusive allegiance to God, and refusing to abuse his divine sonship and messianic authority. The only other Synoptic temptation is in Gethsemane, although there is a hint of continued temptation in Lk. 4:13, and cf. 22:28 if "troubles" is not meant, as is more likely. The questions of opponents are testing rather than tempting questions (Mk. 12:13ff. etc.). The words of Peter are perhaps a temptation in Mk. 8:33, since they involve deflection from obedience to Jesus' divine mission. Heb. 5:7 shows that the prayer in Gethsemane is regarded as a prayer in temptation (although *peirasmós* is not used in connection with it). This hour is also one of temptation for the disciples. Jesus himself ratifies the basic decision that he made in Mt. 4:1ff. John only hints at temptation in the life of Jesus (cf. 12:27; 14:30), but the cry of 19:30 suggests victory over opposition.   [H. Seesemann, VI, 23-36]

peismonḗ → *peíthō; pémpō* → *apostéllō*

---

pénēs [poor, needy],   *penichrós* [poor, needy]

---

pénēs.

A. **Secular Greek.** This word, related to *pónos* ("hard work"), denotes a person who must work for a living. Such persons might be relatively well-to-do, even owning slaves, and they are not oppressed or disadvantaged. The ancient Greek nobility finds happiness in wealth, but philosophy seeks value in virtue irrespective of economic conditions. Indeed, the Cynics disdain extreme wealth. For the Stoics *penía* and *ploútos* are matters of indifference. Plutarch sees in *penía* nothing to be ashamed of, and seeks only self-sufficiency with a knowledge of the true good.

B. The OT, LXX, and Philo. The LXX uses *pénēs* for Hebrew terms that denote the economically weak, e.g., day laborers with no patrimony of their own. Since the Hebrew terms merge into one another, and *ptōchós* as well as *pénēs* is used for them, the difference between *pénēs* and *ptōchós* tends to be blurred in the LXX. The law protects the socially weak, the prophets fight against their oppression (Ex. 23:6; Am. 2:6, etc.), and God is their protector (Jer. 20:13 etc.). Later "poor" and "lowly" are terms for the righteous (Pss. 40:17; 70:5, etc.). The Savior King will finally exalt the lowly (Ps. 72:4, 12-13). Proverbial wisdom regards poverty as an evil, but the wise do not seek wealth either (Prov. 10:15; 30:8). To wrong the poor is to despise the Creator (22:16). Riches alone are valueless (Eccl. 6:8). Wisdom and humility make the poor superior to those who are above them socially (4:13-14; 5:7). Philo uses *pénēs* even when the LXX has *ptōchós*. The Jews are *pénētes* after the persecution under Flaccus robs them of their trading capital.

C. The NT. In the NT *pénēs* occurs only in 2 Cor. 9:9 (quoting Ps. 112:9). Giving to the needy is one of the good works for which God makes provision in believers.

penichrós. This word means "very poor," "needy," "wretched." The only LXX instances are in Ex. 22:24 and Prov. 29:7. Lk. 22:2 uses the term for the poor widow (*ptōchḗ* in Mk. 12:42). [F. HAUCK, VI, 37-40]

→ *ptōchós*

---

pénthos [grief, sorrow], *penthéō* [to grieve, sorrow]

A. Greek Usage. *penthéō* means "to mourn," "to grieve," and *pénthos* means "grief" or "sorrow," as well as "painful event or fact"; it is commonly used for mourning for the dead. The Stoics regard *pénthos* as a *páthē* that is to be avoided. Its pointlessness is a common theme in popular philosophy.

B. The LXX and Judaism. The LXX commonly uses *penthéō* and *pénthos* for derivatives of the stem *'bl*. What is denoted is sorrow or lamentation, and especially mourning for the dead, which includes individual sorrow but is also conventional. *pénthos* plays a special role a. in prophecies of disaster (Am. 5:16; Is. 3:26, etc.), b. in descriptions of judgment (Joel 1:9-10; Jer. 14:2; Lam. 2:8), and c. in prophecies of salvation when mourning will end (Is. 61:3; 66:10). Apocalyptic describes the lamentation of Zion and its transformation into joy (4 Esdr. 9:38–10:50).

C. Primitive Christianity. In the NT, too, the words signify sorrow expressed in lamentation, especially mourning for the dead (Mt. 9:15; Rev. 18:7-8). In 1 Cor. 5:2 *pénthos* is passionate grief that leads to action. Only two usages are theologically significant.

a. In Rev. 18 lamentation is part of the divine judgment on Babylon. In Jms. 4:9, too, *pénthos* is God's judgment. The author is weaving a traditional threat into the context of admonition. In 1 Cor. 5:2 *penthein* expresses grief at the shame brought on the church by the case of incest. Grief at sins for which there has been no repentance is also the point in 2 Cor. 12:21 (cf. 1 Clem. 2.6).

b. The blessing of the *penthoúntes* in Mt. 5:4 is to be taken eschatologically. Those who suffer in the present aeon will find comfort in the next. The mourning here is not just sorrow at sin; it is the mourning of those who see this aeon as it is and are not seduced by its charms. Their *penthein* marks them off from the aeon and can hardly fail to include an element of penitent sorrow for sin.   [R. BULTMANN, VI, 40-43]

---

pentēkostē [Pentecost]

A. Secular Use. We find *pentēkostós* from the time of Plato, and the LXX uses it in Lev. 25:10-11 for the Year of Jubilee and in 2 Kgs. 15:23 chronologically. *pentēkostē* occurs from the fourth century B.C. as a technical term in taxation signifying a 2 percent duty on the value of goods, e.g., exports and imports.

B. The OT and Judaism.
I. The OT Feast of Weeks. According to Ex. 34:22 the Feast of Weeks is a harvest festival to mark the gathering of the firstfruits of the wheat harvest. Dt. 16:9 says that it is to begin seven weeks after putting the sickle to the grain. The gifts are to be joyfully offered to God in the designated place. Lev. 23:15 provides further details about the dating and the sacrifices. On the day of the feast all work stops and there is a glad celebration. The only reference elsewhere in the OT is in 2 Chr. 8:13, so this is obviously not a major feast.
II. The Jewish Pentecost.
1. The Date. Judaism fixes the date as the fiftieth day after the Passover, although there is still debate about when to begin the reckoning. Prior to A.D. 70 the Pharisaic view that it should be 50 days after the 16th of Nisan seems to have prevailed. It might thus fall on any day of the week. It is only a one-day feast, although in the dispersion a second day is added because of difficulties in getting the calendar right.
2. As a Harvest Festival. In Judaism Pentecost is still a harvest festival. The Book of Ruth is read and pilgrims take offerings to Jerusalem, where they are met by the priests, and go up to the temple with songs. Two loaves are offered as the firstfruits of the wheat harvest. The numbers attending, however, are far fewer than for the Passover, of which it tends to become an appendage.
3. As a Festival of the Giving of the Law at Sinai. After A.D. 70, when firstfruits can no longer be brought to the temple, Pentecost is linked more closely with the age of Moses and celebrated as a festival of the giving of the law. Jubilees anchors the feast in the story of the patriarchs and thus gives it enhanced significance. The association with the law rests on Ex. 19:1, which puts Israel at Sinai in the third month after the exodus. The account of the giving of the law becomes the reading on the Day of Pentecost, and by the third century A.D. Pentecost is plainly stated to be the day when the law was given. Since there is no evidence that this equation is made in NT days, the idea that the Christian Pentecost is a festival of the new revelation of God has no foundation.

C. The NT.
1. In 1 Cor. 16:8 Paul says that he will stay at Ephesus until Pentecost. He probably has the Jewish feast in mind, as in Acts 20:16, where he wants to be in Jerusalem by Pentecost, possibly to take part, with Jewish Christians, in the Jewish celebration.
2. Luke introduces the story of the Christian Pentecost by linking it to salvation history in the phrase in Acts 2:1: "When the [promised] day of Pentecost had come" (cf. Lk. 9:51). The promise of Jesus in Acts 1:8 is now fulfilled. The account that

follows stresses a. the gift of the Spirit, whose outpouring brings with it the ability to praise (v. 11) and to proclaim (vv. 14ff.), and b. the public birth of the church as a vital community (cf. 2:42ff.). The speaking in tongues (vv. 1ff., 13) offers plain evidence of the Spirit's descent and also serves as a prototype of world mission. The occurrence on the Day of Pentecost means that the Jewish calendar can be worked into the nexus of promise and fulfilment in salvation history.

D. The Early Church. In the early church *pentēkostē* is used for the 50 days of rejoicing that begin with Easter. Since Easter is always kept on Sunday, the seven weeks end on a Sunday too. During this period there are no fasts, prayer is offered standing, catechumens are baptized, and thoughts are directed to the last things, so that *pentēkostē* can be regarded as a sign of the heavenly kingdom, to which Christ has already ascended as the firstfruits of the harvest. Later the last day of the period takes on independent significance and *pentēkostē* comes to be used for it as a day that commemorates the outpouring of the Spirit.   [E. LOHSE, VI, 44-53]

---

perí [around, about, for, etc.]

A. With Genitive.
1. From the spatial sense of "around" there develops the sense of "about."
a. With verbs (a) of speaking, writing, etc., (b) of questioning, complaining, etc., (c) of emotion, and (d) of caring, *perí* means "about," "on account of," or "for."
b. In loose dependence on verbs or nouns, the meaning is "for" or "in respect of."
c. At the beginning of a sentence, *perí* denotes the subject of discussion: "As concerns."
d. In the phrase *tá perí tinos* the reference is to "what concerns someone" (cf. Mk. 5:27; Acts 18:25).
2. As the distinction between *perí* and *hypér* tends to fade, *perí* with the genitive may also mean "on behalf of," "for." In the NT this is a common use in intercession. In Lk. 4:38 people beseech Jesus for Peter's mother-in-law, in Lk. 22:32 Jesus prays for his disciples, in Acts 12:5 the church prays for Peter, in Col. 1:3 Paul prays for the church, and in 4:3 he asks it to pray for him. We also read of striving for others in Col. 2:1, or of Christ's dying for us in 1 Th. 5:10.
3. The phrase *perí hamartías* is a significant one in the NT; it means "for [the remission of] sins." In the LXX this phrase corresponds to the thought of "sin offering." It occurs in relation to the vicarious ministry of the Servant of the Lord in Is. 53:10. A sacrificial sense is obviously present in the NT in Heb. 10:6 (quoting Ps. 40:6), and cf. 5:3; 10:18, 26; 13:11. There is also at least a suggestion of sin offering in Rom. 8:3 and 1 Pet. 3:18.

B. With Accusative.
1. Of place, we find a. the general sense of "round" (Lk. 13:8; Mt. 3:4; Mk. 9:42), and b. "around persons"; cf. the disciples in Mk. 4:10, and Paul's companions in Acts 13:13 (*hoi perí* with the accusative *autón* or *Paúlon*).
2. Of time, to give an approximate time, we find *perí* for "about" (Mt. 20:3).
3. The spatial sense yields the transferred senses a. to be occupied "with" (Lk. 10:40; Acts 19:25), and b. more generally "in respect of" (1 Tim. 6:21); cf. *tá perí eme* ("my situation") in Phil. 2:23.   [E. II. RIESENFELD, VI, 53-56]

periérchomai → *érchomai; perizṓnnymi* → *hóplon; perikátharma* → *katharós; perikeimai* → *keímai; perikephalaía* → *hóplon; perilámpō* → *lámpō; perílypos* → *lýpē; periménō* → *ménō*

---

perioúsios [chosen, special]

---

1. This word means "more than enough." In the papyri we find *ho perioúsios* ("the chosen one") for the married man.

2. The LXX uses the word five times. In Ex. 19:5; Dt. 26:18 the *laós perioúsios* is God's "special possession"; as such it has a duty to avoid idolatry and keep the commandments (Dt. 14:2).

3. The only NT instance is in Tit. 2:4. Christ's work of redemption has created for God a people that is a costly possession or special treasure. The basis is Christ's eschatological work, the orientation is to the final appearing, and the implication is a life that already actualizes the divine promise and command.

[H. PREISKER, VI, 57-58]

peripatéō → *patéō; peripíptō* → *píptō; peripoiéomai* → *poiéō; peripoíēsis* → *poiéō*

---

perisseúō [to be superabundant],   *hyperperisseúō* [to superabound],   *perissós* [superabundant],   *hyperekperissoú* [beyond all measure],   *hyperekperissṓs* [beyond all measure],   *perisseía* [surplus],   *perísseuma* [excess]

---

perisseúō, hyperperisseúō.

A. Outside the NT.

1. Intransitively this word means "to be present overabundantly or to excess," censoriously "to be superfluous," and of persons "to be superior or superabounding." Transitively the sense is "to make overrich," "to provide superabundantly."

2. In the LXX the verb is used personally for "to have more than enough," "to take precedence," or "to increase" (family or progeny).

3. Without using *perisseúō,* the OT suggests that the age of salvation will be one of superabundance (Am. 9:13; Is. 65:17ff.). The rabbis base this hope on Lev. 26:4-5. Later Jewish writings take up the thought with descriptions of great fruitfulness in family, goods, crops, etc., and of a great outpouring of spiritual gifts and blessings, e.g., joy, wisdom, and the Spirit. The loss suffered through the fall will be offset hereby.

B. The NT.

1. Synoptic Gospels and Acts. A secular sense occurs in Mk. 12:44. The plenty of the hired servants in Lk. 15:17 points to the generosity of divine grace. Mt. 13:12 is perhaps a proverb containing the same thought. The messianic feeding of the multitude fulfils and transcends the Mosaic feeding with manna (Mt. 14:20; Lk. 9:17; Jn. 6:12-13). The righteousness required for the kingdom must surpass that of the present masters of piety (Mt. 5:20). The rapid growth of the community (Acts 2:41; 4:4; 6:7; 9:31) bears witness to the work of Christ and the Spirit.

2. Paul. Paul uses the verb and the intensive *hyperperisseúō* in eschatological contexts (Rom. 5:20; Eph. 3:20; 1 Th. 3:10). The new age of salvation is one of abundant blessing in grace and the Spirit. If sin increased through the law, grace is superabundantly greater (Rom. 5:20). The new glory is also superabounding (2 Cor. 3:9). God causes his grace to flow richly on the apostles (Eph. 1:8). Grace increases thanksgiving, which overflows to God's glory (2 Cor. 4:15). Sufferings abound, but so does comfort (*loc. cit.*). God's truth is increased by the disclosure of human unfaithfulness and thus abounds to God's glory (Rom. 3:7). The strong at Corinth gain no advantage by eating meats sacrificed to idols (1 Cor. 8:8), for external things do not count in the kingdom (Rom. 14:17). Deep poverty superabounds in generosity (2 Cor. 8:2). God has richly poured out his grace on the churches, and these superabound for every good work (2 Cor. 9:8). The collection brings many thanksgivings to God (9:12). Material abundance matters no more to Paul than material lack (Phil. 4:12); the gift from Philippi is for him more than abundance (4:18). Spiritual abundance in the churches is Paul's serious missionary concern (Rom. 15:13; 1 Cor. 14:12; 15:58; Phil. 1:9; 1 Th. 3:12; 4:1).

perissós, hyperekperissoú, hyperekperissôs.

1. *perissós,* used of things, means "extraordinary," "unusual," "strange," "overflowing," censoriously "superfluous," "surplus," and of persons "unusual," "noteworthy." The adverb *perissôs* means "unusually."

2. In the LXX *perissós* means "remaining" (Ex. 10:5), "useless" (1 Kgs. 14:19), "extraordinary," "excellent" (Dan. 5:12 Θ). The adverb simply means "very" in, e.g., Dan. 8:9 Θ; Ps. 31:23).

3. The adjective is used only six times in the NT. In Jn. 10:10 it denotes the superabundance of the life that Christ brings. In Mt. 5:37, however, it refers to unnecessary additional assurances. Disciples must do more than others in Mt. 5:47. Paul asks what advantage the Jews have in Rom. 3:1. It is superfluous for Paul to write about the offering in 2 Cor. 9:1. In Mk. 6:61 *ek perissoú* expresses surprise at Christ's works. The adverb is used similarly in 10:26, and the vehemence of enemies comes to expression by means of it in Mt. 27:23; Mk. 15:14; Acts 26:11. The comparative *perissóteros,* a popular substitute for *pleíōn* in the Greek OT, occurs 16 times in the NT. John excels the prophets in Mt. 11:9, love is more important than sacrifice in Mk. 12:23, sham righteousness brings down sharper judgment in Mk. 12:40, Paul wants to spare the sinner too great sorrow in 2 Cor. 2:7, God seeks to display the immutability of his counsel more fully in Heb. 6:17, Paul excels his contemporaries in Gal. 1:14, other apostles in 1 Cor. 15:1, and his opponents (in sufferings) in 2 Cor. 11:23, he behaves with special holiness and sincerity toward the Corinthians (2 Cor. 1:12), has a special love for them (2:4), and has a special desire to see the Thessalonians (1 Th. 2:17).

perisseía. This word, denoting "surplus," is used for the superabundant fullness of the age of salvation in both grace (Rom. 5:17) and joy (2 Cor. 8:2). Paul hopes for unbounded missionary advance when the faith of the Corinthians increases (2 Cor. 10:15). In Jms. 1:21 "exceeding" wickedness rather than "remaining" wickedness is the point.

perísseuma. This word, meaning "excess," occurs in the NT in Mt. 12:34; Lk. 6:45 for that which, abounding in the heart, comes to expression in words. In 2 Cor. 8:13-14 the surplus goods of the Corinthians will make up the lack of the Jerusalem church, and the latter's spiritual surplus will reciprocate. The reference in Mk. 8:8 is to the surplus fragments, which testify to the superabundance of the provision.

[F. HAUCK, VI, 58-63]

---

peristerá [dove],   *trygốn* [turtledove]

A. The Dove in the Ancient World. This word, of disputed etymology, mostly denotes the "house pigeon," but it may also be a general term. Training house pigeons is common in antiquity, probably for religious reasons, for the dove is regarded as a bird of the gods (especially female), either as divine messenger, attribute, or incarnation (cf. the dove goddess). The dove is also a bird of the soul (cf. dove grottos and the use of dovecots as monuments). As a symbol of human conduct in poetry and proverbs, the dove usually stands for chastity, faithfulness, affection, gentleness, and guilelessness, but it may also be connected with garrulity and complaint. Sometimes the dove appears as the bird of misfortune and death.

B. The Dove in the OT and Judaism. The dove appears in the flood story in Gen. 8:8, 12. Later exposition relates the reference in Cant. 2:12 to the Holy Spirit. Philo sees in the dove a symbol of the *lógos,* the *noús,* or *sophía.* The OT finds no place for the idea that the dove is a divine bird but there is perhaps a hint of a connection with the soul in Ps. 84:2-3. Doves are the only birds offered in sacrifice (Lev. 1:14). The dove denotes helplessness in Jer. 48:28 and vacillation in Hos. 7:11. It knows its season in Jer. 8:7, and Israel will return like a flight of pigeons in Hos. 11:11. God will protect his dove in Ps. 74:19, and "my dove" is a term of endearment in Cant. 2:14; 5:2.

C. The Dove in the NT.
1. At the baptism of Jesus the Spirit manifests himself by alighting on Jesus as a dove. This confirms the descent in a powerful symbolic way (cf. the link with the heavenly voice, as in Judaism).
2. Mary offers doves as a sacrifice, thus showing that Jesus belongs to the poor and humble (Lk. 2:24). Sellers of doves are mentioned at the cleansing of the temple; they are either private vendors or official salesmen.
3. The dove symbolizes simplicity in Mt. 10:16. The disciples must meet opposition with the wisdom of serpents, but they still stand under the norm of singleness of eye and purity of heart.

D. The Dove in the Early Church.
1. A combination of biblical references and ancient notions gives the dove rich symbolical power in the early church. The dove is a sign both of the Spirit and of Christ himself (the Logos). The offering of pigeons symbolizes Christ's death. Some heretics take it that the descent of the dove at Christ's baptism shows that only then is there a union of Jesus and Christ.
2. Tertullian contrasts the dove and the serpent in order to show the difference between true Christians and heretics (*Against the Valentinians* 3). He draws a parallel between the nature and housing of doves and those of the church. The dove is also for him a sign of the Holy Spirit.
3. Clement of Alexandria and Origen call believers doves. In Mart. Pol. 16.1 the dove that flies out of the martyr symbolizes the Spirit and is also the bird of the soul.
4. Early Christian literature and art depict the dove of peace, of which Noah's dove is a type, since it signals the end of divine wrath.
5. Among the Manichees the white dove symbolizes God's love, and believers are also white doves, but the Son of Man is no more a real man than the dove at the baptism is a real dove.   [H. GREEVEN, VI, 63-72]

---

peritémnō   [to   circumcise],   *peritomḗ*   [circumcision],   *aperítmētos* [uncircumcised]

A. Nonbiblical Use.

1. Attested from the days of Homer, *peritémnō* means "to cut around," "to make incisions," "to encircle with a view to robbing" (e.g., cattle or lands), and then, as a ritual technical term, "to circumcise."

2. The noun *peritomḗ* means "circumcision."

3. The adjective *aperítmētos* means "unmaimed" or "uncircumcised."

B. The OT.

1. Usage.

a. The OT uses the verb exclusively for "to circumcise" in a literal sense.

b. Similarly the noun *peritomḗ* means "circumcision."

c. The adjective *aperítmētos* means "uncircumcised," usually in a literal sense for Gentiles, but figuratively in Jer. 9:25.

d. The LXX refers more often to circumcision or uncircumcision than the Hebrew.

e. The usage in Philo and Josephus is the same as that of the LXX.

2. Origin, Meaning, and Distribution of the Rite.

a. Performed mostly on males, circumcision serves as a sacrifice of redemption and as a covenant sign. The former significance may be seen in the OT in Lev. 19:23-24, but the latter predominates. Circumcision at birth is the most common form, but circumcision may also be a puberty rite or a marriage rite.

b. The Arab tribes as well as Israel practice circumcision (Gen. 7:23ff.).

3. The OT Tradition.

a. There is a piece of ancient tradition in Ex. 4:24ff., where circumcision is a rite of redemption. Josh. 5:2, 8-9 also rests on ancient tradition. Here circumcision is associated with "rolling off" from Israel the shame of Egypt, i.e., Egypt's scorn for the uncircumcised.

b. In Gen. 17:1ff. circumcision is a covenant sign. It applies to all Abraham's descendants but the covenant is especially with Israel.

c. Jeremiah introduces a figurative use when he talks about the circumcision of the heart (4:4) or ears (6:10). For the people circumcision is little more than sacramental magic. It can be justified only when it is referred to the inner person and the essential relationship with God.

C. Judaism.

1. The Hellenistic Roman Period.

a. Under Antiochus IV attempts are made to prohibit circumcision. It thus becomes a national symbol, either of resistance or of victory. John Hyrcanus I (c. 128 B.C.) imposes mass circumcision and Judaizing. Without circumcision, intimate dealings with Jews are impossible. Even the Herod family prefers to forgo a politically advantageous marriage rather than have an uncircumcised son-in-law.

b. The Hellenistic world finds the ceremony indecorous and perverse. Hadrian even compares it to castration. Philo defends it as hygienically necessary and suitable for a priestly people. It combats sensuality and resists the idea that the power of procreation confers divine likeness. Philo does not mention the covenant significance.

c. The Manual of Discipline 5.5 refers to the circumcising of desire and obduracy. The rite is presupposed, but it is less important as such than its figurative understanding.

831

2. *After the Destruction of the Temple*.

a. After A.D. 70 Pharisaic Rabbinism triumphs. It stresses the literal aspect and banishes the figurative interpretation from official theology.

b. Under Hadrian the equation of circumcision with castration makes it punishable as murder. This perhaps sparks the Bar-Cochba revolt; after a short period of enforcement it is relaxed by Antoninus in A.D. 138.

c. The Tannaites work out the detailed rules for the rite in the second century.

d. The theological significance of circumcision is that it is a precondition, sign, and seal of participation in the covenant with Abraham, and also a sign of confession. It carries with it the covenant blessings of divine protection in this age and divine joys in the messianic age.

D. Primitive Christianity.
1. Usage.

a. The verb is a cultic term in the NT, used literally in Lk. 1:59; Jn. 7:22; Acts 7:8, and figuratively in Col. 2:11 with reference to baptism.

b. The noun *peritomḗ* is used in various senses for "circumcision," e.g., the rite in Jn. 7:22-23, the circumcised in Rom. 3:30, circumcised Christians in Acts 11:2; Gal. 2:12, and Christians as the true Israel in Phil. 3:3.

c. The adjective *aperítmētos* is not used literally in the NT (but cf. Barn. 9.5); it bears a figurative sense in Acts 7:51.

2. The Problem in the Apostolic Period.

a. Circumcision is no problem in the Synoptic tradition. Jesus and his disciples are all circumcised, and while the Baptist implicitly challenges circumcision in Mt. 3:9, Jesus never makes an issue of it.

b. In Jn. 7:22-23 Jesus argues from the lesser (circumcision on the sabbath) to the greater (total healing on the sabbath). The passage shows good knowledge of rabbinic discussions, and in it Jesus accepts the tradition in order to turn it against his opponents.

c. Paul in Rom. 2:28-29 contests the view that physical circumcision alone can bring salvation in this world and the next. He thus follows the line of Jeremiah and the Essenes but without accepting literal circumcision as an essential precondition. For him the only true circumcision is that of the heart which is the Spirit's work and which is identical with redemption by Christ (hence Col. 2:11-12). It follows, then, that the physical sign is unimportant; what counts is being in Christ. Believers are the real circumcision (Phil. 3:3), so that Gentile Christians need not receive circumcision nor Jewish Christians remove its marks (1 Cor. 7:18-19). Jewish Christians from Jerusalem challenge this view in Antioch, but Paul stands firm (cf. Gal. 2:3). The council of Acts 15 declines to make circumcision a condition of fellowship, but does not forbid Jewish Christians to continue the ancient practice.

d. Different courses are taken in the early church. In Barn. 9.1ff. the only valid *peritomḗ* is that of the heart, but Jewish Christians, although excommunicated by the synagogue, remain loyal to their position on physical circumcision.

→ *akrobystía*   [R. MEYER, VI, 72-84]

periphronéō → *kataphronéō*

---

perípsēma [refuse, means of expiation]

A. Meaning outside the NT.

I. Derivation and Development. This word, deriving from *peripsáō,* "to wipe or rub (off)," means "what is wiped off," i.e., refuse or filth, "what wipes off," e.g., bath towel, and "what expiates or religiously cleanses," e.g., the scapegoat.

II. As an Expiatory Sacrifice among the Greeks. The sense "means of expiation" seems to come from the attributing of disasters to some religious impurity that must be laid on a representative of the people. Associated is the concept of the wrath of a deity that has to be placated by a human offering. Those put to death in order to bring cleansing or healing are *pharmakoí.* They are normally young and may be prominent persons but may also be paupers or criminals, i.e., the scum of society (cf. the connection with the meaning "refuse" or "offscouring"). The victims have to volunteer, and the mode of death, e.g., drowning, or stoning outside the city, is designed to guarantee the removal of the impurity. The *perípsēma* personifies deliverance (cf. Acts 13:47; 1 Cor. 1:30), and as an expiation that saves from cultic impurity the term stands closely related to words signifying cleansing and redemption.

III. The Hellenistic and Hellenistic Jewish Use.

1. Used only twice in OT translation, *perípsēma* is first a weaker term for expiation when money is substituted for a threatened life.

2. A second use is for an unworthy subject either in abuse or self-abasement.

B. The NT. In 1 Cor. 4:13 *perípsēma* is almost synonymous with *perikathármata.* It has the double sense of "filth," "offscouring," "rubbish," etc. (as a term of contempt or self-abasement), and of "scapegoat," "expiatory offering," with a strong undertone of scorn. Paul accepts the contempt that is heaped on the apostles by the world, but reinterprets it, for their apparently worthless lives are for the general good. The context shows that behind the term stands the idea of the dregs of society that vicariously suffer death on behalf of all others. Those who are reviled and slandered are a means of blessing and expiation. This thought brings Paul close to the cross (cf. Gal. 6:17; 2 Cor. 4:10-11; 1 Cor. 15:31; Phil. 2:17; Col. 1:24), for it is Christ who is really the (supposed) malefactor who suffers vicarious death, and the apostle, who is the messenger of this atoning act, bears the mark of his crucified Lord.

C. The Apostolic Fathers. The Pauline use influences that of Ignatius with respect to his approaching martyrdom (*Ephesians* 8.1; 18.1). He goes to death for others, not in replacement of Christ's vicarious work, but to spare them persecution in an offering for God (*Romans* 2.2). The sense is more diluted and has no theological implications in Barn. 4.9; 6.5, where it has little more than the force of "your humble servant." This use lives on into the Middle Ages.   [G. STÄHLIN, VI, 84-93]

---

perpereúomai [to boast]

Of contested origin, *perpereúomai* relates to arrogance in speech, being associated with such concepts as loquacity, bluster, bragging, etc. It suggests a literary or rhetorical form of boasting. In 1 Cor. 13:4 it carries such varied nuances as arrogance, pretension, and impotent chatter. Antiquity in general opposes such boasting, but Paul bases its renunciation on the love that makes possible the eschatological life disclosed in faith and hope. Since God has opened up this possibility in Christ, the action of love is presented in personal terms. *We* do not set aside *perpereúesthai* by practice etc., as in Stoicism; love itself sets it aside in us when we take this more excellent way.

[H. BRAUN, VI, 93-95]

---

pétra [rock]

A. Secular Greek and the OT.

1. In secular Greek *pétra* denotes a large "rock," but also a "cliff" or "rocky mountain chain." Figuratively it suggests firmness, immovability, and hardness. *pétros* is more often used for smaller rocks, stones, or pebbles.

2. In the LXX *pétra* means "rock," "cliff," and it occurs as a place name (Judg. 1:36), as a name for God (2 Sam. 22:2), and as a figure for an unbending character (Is. 50:7) or hardened mind (Jer. 5:3).

B. Symbolic Meaning.

In the mythical imagery of the Near East the earth comes up out of the sea like a rock or temple. For Judaism the rock is the holy of holies, which is the center of the earth, the stone that stops up the primal flood, and the gate of paradise. Is. 28 makes use of this concept. The old temple can no longer arrest the Assyrian flood, but God will set up a new one. An echo of the same concept may be caught in Mt. 16:18.

C. The NT.

1. The Literal Sense. The sepulchre is hewn out of a rock in Mk. 15:46. People seek shelter in clefts of the rock in Rev. 6:15-16. The earthquake rends the rocks in Mt. 27:51. Some seed falls on a rocky substratum in Lk. 8:6. The house built on a rock, not on sand, will survive wind and flood in Mt. 7:24ff.

2. The Rock Which Followed. Underlying the statement in 1 Cor. 10:4 is the OT miracle of water gushing out of the rock (Ex. 17; Num. 20). This is given typical significance in rabbinic exposition. The legend arises of a fountain that is with the people in the desert. Paul gives this a messianic turn (cf. Jn. 7:37-38). Christ is a spiritual reality, not an actual rock, but the same Christ acts in history in both the old covenant and the new to sustain his people. The "following" denotes his faithfulness both past and present.

3. Rom. 9:33 and 1 Pet. 2:7-8.

a. Rom. 9:33. Because Israel has rejected salvation by faith, Christ has become for her a rock of offense. Paul here conflates Is. 28:16 and 8:14 in versions closer to the Hebrew than to the LXX. Paradoxically the rock of offense replaces the tested and basic cornerstone. The latter becomes a terrible and invincible thing in face of unbelief. Yet it still bears the gracious invitation and promise of Is. 28:16 with its hope for Israel.

b. 1 Pet. 2:7-8. The author of 1 Peter also uses Is. 8:14 but combines it with Ps. 118:22. The joyous word of Ps. 118:22 at the placing of the keystone over the gate takes on a terrible aspect under the influence of Is. 8:14, in contrast here to Is. 28:16, which is addressed specifically to believers (vv. 6-7).

4. Mt. 16:18. The pun in the Greek text assumes an identity of *pétra* and *Pétros* which is assured only by the Aramaic. Elsewhere in the NT the individual Christian is always *líthos* rather than *pétra* (cf. 1 Pet. 2:5). Strictly only Christ himself is *pétra*. Peter is *pétra* only as he is enclosed within the revelation in Christ. If he himself is *pétra,* it is as Christ has taken him in hand and given him a place in the unique apostolate which is the historical foundation of the church. As Abraham is for the rabbis the rock on which God builds the world, so Peter is the rock on which Christ builds the community of the new covenant.

D. Apostolic Fathers and Apologists. In Barn. 11.5 God is the rock, and in 11.3 God or Christ is the rock that gives water. In Hermas *Similitudes* 9.2ff. Christ is the rock on which the church is built from stones (believers). The rock on which Polycarp builds is Christ (Ignatius *Polycarp* 1.1). Justin makes the same equation (*Dialogue* 113.6; 114.4). The stone knives of Josh. 5:2-3 typify Christ's sayings (*Dialogue* 24.2). The myth of the rock-birth of Mithras is a pagan imitation of Dan. 2:34 (*Dialogue* 70.1).

[O. CULLMANN, VI, 95-99]

Pétros [Peter], *Kēphás* [Cephas]

A. Philological Questions. Except in Jn. 1:42, where it is used to elucidate Aram. *kēphás, Pétros* is used in the NT only as a name for Simon Peter. The Cephas of Gal. 2:11 is obviously the disciple Simon Peter in spite of various attempts to put him among the 70. Symeon, found in the NT only in Acts 15:4, is a common name among the Jews, but the NT mostly adopts the familiar Greek name Simon, which he possibly also bears from the first in addition to Symeon. *Kēphás,* the Aramaic of which *Pétros* is the Greek rendering, is not attested as a proper name. It is mostly used in the NT by Paul (Gal. 1:18; 2:9, 11, 14, etc.), who gives the Aramaic a Greek ending in *-s*. *Pétros* as a masculine form is preferred when a Greek translation is used (Jn. 1:42). *Pétros* establishes itself in the NT, where we find either Simon, Peter, or Simon Peter. The translation supports the view that *Kēphás* is not a proper name, since one does not usually translate proper names.

B. The Person and Place of the Disciple.
1. Biographical Note. Simon, the son of Jona, probably comes from Bethsaida (Jn. 1:44). He is a fisherman who is uneducated by rabbinic and Greek standards (Acts 4:13). He works in partnership with the sons of Zebedee (Lk. 5:10). He later lives in Capernaum, where Jesus visits him. He is married (Mk. 1:29ff.; 1 Cor. 9:5), but accounts of the martyrdom of his wife and children are legendary. He seems to have belonged to the circle of the Baptist's followers (Jn. 1:35ff.).
2. Position. As a disciple, Peter belongs to the inner group around Jesus (Mk. 9:2). He also stands out as a leader (Lk. 5:1ff.). Distinguished by excess of zeal, he tries to come to Jesus on the lake (Mt. 14:28). He acts as spokesman on various occasions (Mt. 18:21; Mk. 8:29ff.). Outsiders come to him (Mt. 17:24), and he goes to prepare the Passover (Lk. 22:8) and is present in the garden (Mk. 14:37). His name stands first in the lists (Mk. 3:16 etc.), and he is sometimes singled out (Mk. 1:36; 16:7). The Synoptists all agree on this, and John recognizes Peter's special position, although displaying a special interest in the beloved disciple (cf. 13:24ff.; 18:16; 20:1ff.; 21).
3. Name-giving. Two problems arise regarding the name Peter, namely, why Jesus always uses Simon, and when the name Peter is given (cf. Mt. 16:18; Mk. 3:16; Jn. 1:42). The name is a nickname in rabbinic style, and is perhaps given earlier and then explained in Mt. 16:18. It cannot refer only to Peter's character but relates to his representative mission as disciple and apostle of Jesus.

C. Peter as the Rock on Which the Church Is Built.

1. The Apostolic Commission apart from Mt. 16:17ff. While Peter does not lead the disciples during the earthly ministry of Jesus, he takes the lead in Jerusalem according to the call of the incarnate Lord and the commission of the risen Lord (Jn. 21:15ff.; 1 Cor. 15:5; Lk. 24:34). Peter is the first eyewitness of the risen Lord in 1 Cor. 15:5, and a specific commission is given in Jn. 21. His prior call is thus confirmed by a postresurrection commission whereby he assumes the first leadership in the church.

2. The Saying Mt. 16:17ff.

a. The Setting. Although the saying occurs only in Matthew, the story occurs in Mark and Luke as well. Mark's is probably the original version. In a crisp and vivid presentation Mark shows how Jesus provokes the question, receives Peter's reply, enjoins silence, foretells his suffering, and rebukes Peter's protests. Matthew prepares the ground in 14:33, but some scholars think that the saying of 16:17ff. breaks the sequence and may be inserted from some other context (cf. Lk. 22:31-32 or Jn. 21:15ff.).

b. Authenticity. The authenticity has been hotly debated. The linguistic character is Semitic. The pun comes out better in Aramaic, which has *kēphâ'* both times. One should also note the phrases bar-Jona and "flesh and blood," the strophic rhythm, and the use of rock for foundation. The usual objection is that Jesus would not talk about establishing a church, but it should be recalled that *ekklēsía* occurs frequently in the LXX and that the messianic task is that of establishing God's people, which is often represented as a house. If it is argued that this building is eschatological, the message of Jesus does not contrast present and future, for the imminent kingdom is present in Jesus himself (Mt. 12:28), and around him he starts establishing God's people with the calling of the 12, whom he then sends out to the lost sheep of Israel. Shepherd, sheep, and flock are all terms associated with the community. The idea of building the temple (Mk. 14:57-58; Jn. 2:19) is also relevant here; the temple not made with hands is the community of faith. Jesus begins building his church in his own ministry, bursts the gates of hell with his death, and gives his people the task of following up the victorious work that he thus initiates. To Peter, the rock, he gives the keys of the kingdom as the mediator of the resurrection. Binding and loosing refer primarily to the remission of sins, although the laying down of precepts may also be included. Jesus himself discharges the primary function of forgiving sins, and he now transmits the same office to Peter, to be shared, of course, with the other disciples (Mt. 18:18).

c. Meaning. By the rock Jesus does not mean the faith of Peter; the parallelism rules this out. Clearly Peter and rock are associated here. Jesus will build his church on the one rock, Peter. Peter is to do a unique work, limited to his own lifetime, on which all future building will be possible. The high-priestly prayer offers a clue to the meaning when it states that future generations will believe through the word of the apostles (Jn. 17:20). The apostles are the foundation (Eph. 1:20; Rev. 21:14) because they bear witness to Christ's death and resurrection. Among the apostles Peter is the first and chief eyewitness.

D. Peter's Leadership and First Missionary Activity.

1. Leadership. Peter assumes leadership in the primitive community in the electing of a twelfth apostle (Acts 1:15), the sermon at Pentecost (2:14), the healing of the lame man (3:1), the defense of the gospel (4:8), the exercise of discipline (5:1ff.), the follow-up in Samaria (8:14ff.), and missionary work in Lydda etc. (9–10). Paul refers to this role of leadership in Gal. 1:18, although James is by now associated with Peter in it.

2. Missionary Activity. After his imprisonment and liberation (Acts 12:17), Peter leaves Jerusalem, where James takes the lead (cf. Acts 15; Gal. 2:9), and apparently gives himself to missionary work. At the council in Acts 15 his work remains more closely tied to Jerusalem than that of Paul. Paul speaks highly of him even when he has to censure him (Gal. 2:11ff.). His link to Jerusalem probably puts him in a delicate situation which accounts for his vacillation at Antioch. 1 Clem. 5 perhaps alludes to this when it speaks of the burdens that he has to bear through envy.

3. Theology. Part of Peter's problem is that he is very close to Paul theologically. He has learned from Jesus that the gospel is for all peoples. By his death Christ has made atonement for all who believe. In his early preaching he identifies Jesus as the Servant of the Lord (Acts 3:13, 26; 4:27, 30) whose vicarious suffering is seen to be necessary in the light of his resurrection (cf. 1 Peter).

D. Later Missionary Activity and Death. Little is recorded about Peter's missionary work. He is linked to three main centers, Antioch, Corinth, and Rome. The claims that he founded the churches at Antioch and Corinth find no support, but he certainly works in Antioch and a stay at Corinth is possible in view of 1 Cor. 1:12. As regards Rome, a ministry there might be inferred from 1 Pet. 5:1; 2 Pet. 1:14, but is can hardly be prior to Paul's letter to the Romans, although Rom. 15:20-21 perhaps relates the founding of the church in Rome to Jewish Christians, and this would make it possible that Peter has at least visited the church there. The greeting in 1 Pet. 5:14, with its reference to Babylon, suggests a Roman origin for this epistle, and if the witnesses of Rev. 11:3ff. are Peter and Paul this passage supports a Roman martyrdom. 1 Clem. 5 certainly gives substance to a Roman martyrdom, for the circumstances apply only in Rome (cf. also Ignatius *Romans* 4.3). In the later second century writers like Irenaeus and Tertullian give more precise form to the tradition of a Roman stay and martyrdom, although it is only in the fourth century that we find reference to his discharging of an episcopal function in Rome. Recent excavations have not yet made possible an identification of his grave. [O. CULLMANN, VI, 100-112]

---

pēgḗ [fountain, spring]

A. Outside the NT.
1. This word means "source of water," i.e., a natural spring. Figuratively it then denotes "tears," and it also finds a more general use for "origin."

2. *pēgḗ* occurs some 100 times in the LXX for various Hebrew terms, some of which are also rendered by *krḗnē,* which means a "well" (cf. also *phréar*). The sources of water mentioned in the OT are usually artificial fountains or wells. The aridity of the country means that there is a need to bore for water and also to conserve it in cisterns. Many springs are mentioned either with or without names, and their importance may be seen from the judgments of Hos. 13ff., the promises of Is. 35:7; 41:18, etc., and the eschatological image of Joel 3:18 (cf. also the use of *pēgḗ* in Jer. 8:23; Cant. 4:12, 15; Prov. 5:16; 10:11). With God himself is the *pēgḗ zōḗs* ("the fountain of life") in Ps. 36:9, and God complains that his people have forsaken him, the fountain of living waters, in Jer. 2:13 (cf. 17:13).

3. Philo uses *pēgḗ* some 150 times, mostly in a transferred sense for "origin" or "cause." When he refers to actual springs, he allegorizes. The divine *lógos* comes

forth from the spring of wisdom, and the grace of God flows from ever living springs, although only for those who thirst after wisdom.

4. Josephus in his use of OT sources mainly follows the original in regard to *pēgế*, sometimes using it synonymously with *phréar*, sometimes distinguishing the two (cf. *Antiquities* 1.246 and 8.154).

B. The NT.

1. The only mention of a specific well in the NT is in Jn. 4:6ff. (*pēgế* in v. 6 and *phréar* in v. 11). This is a true well, not a fountain. Jms. 3:11 has *pēgế* when trying to show how unnatural it is that the same mouth should both bless and curse. In Rev. 8:10 the great star falls on the fountains, rendering the rivers undrinkable even at their source. In Rev. 16:4 the fountains as well as the rivers become blood. In Rev. 14:7 God is the Creator of the fountains of water as well as the seas.

2. The use in Mk. 5:29 is figurative: the flow of blood dries up like a spring. A similar use occurs in 2 Pet. 2:17, which compares false teachers to dried-up springs (cf. Jude 12). In Jn. 4:14 Jesus compares the water that he gives to that which comes from Jacob's well. As well as quenching thirst eternally, this water will become a spring welling up to eternal life. The idea is not that the recipient controls the water, but is brought into eternal life by fellowship with the indwelling Christ. The expression "fountain of [water of] life" is not used here but it occurs in Rev. 21:6 (cf. 7:17; 22:1, 17), where it denotes the consummation that Christ will give at the last day.

[W. MICHAELIS, VI, 112-17]

---

pēlós [clay, mud]

pēlós, denoting a mixture of moisture and dust, has such senses as "morass," "muck," "loam," "clay." The LXX uses it for "mire" in Ps. 69:14 and "clay" in Jer. 18:6. The use is the same in Philo and Josephus. In Rom. 9:21, adopting a common OT image, Paul stresses God's sovereignty by comparing God to the potter and us to the clay. In Jn. 9:6, 11, 14-15 *pēlós* refers to the clay that Jesus makes with spittle and uses to heal the blind man. We do not have here a magical formula, nor, probably, a medical prescription, but there may be a desire to differentiate Jesus from Aesculapius, who advises the use of a similar remedy. The deeper significance of the incident remains.

[K. H. RENGSTORF, VI, 118-19]

---

péra [sack]

1. *péra* is the open sack carried on the left hip by a strap over the right shoulder and used by peasants, shepherds, beggars, and wandering philosophers.

2. The word occurs in the LXX only in Judith. Judith has her slave carry a skin of wine, a jug of oil, and a *péra* with food on her way to the Assyrian camp.

3. Josephus introduces *péra* for the *kádion* of 1 Sam. 17:40, 49, and the rabbis have a similar term for the bag in which they take provisions for journeys.

4. In the NT Mt. 10:10 forbids the disciples to take a *péra*, Lk. 10:4 forbids both purse and *péra*, and Lk. 22:35-36 reverses the ruling. The *péra* here is not the beggar's sack but a bag for provisions. Jesus is teaching the disciples to rely wholly on God's

provision. They are not disappointed in this regard (Lk. 22:35), but Lk. 22:36 reflects a changed situation.

5. In the apostolic fathers the only use is in Hermas (*Visions* 5.1; *Similitudes* 6.2.5) for the shepherd's bag. Tatian among the apologists has *péra* for the sack carried by the wandering philosopher (*Address to the Greeks* 25.1).

→ *ballántion*   [W. MICHAELIS, VI, 119-21]

---

pikrós [bitter], *pikría* [bitterness], *pikraínō* [to embitter], *parapikraínō* [to embitter], *parapikrasmós* [rebellion]

---

pikrós, pikría, pikraínō.

1. *pikrós* originally means "pointed," "sharp" (e.g., arrows), then "penetrating" (e.g., a smell), then "painful" (to the feelings), and "bitter" (to the taste). The sense of bitterness yields such transferred senses as "unpleasant," "unexpected," "painful," "severe," "cruel," "stern," "embittered." *pikría* has the meaning "severity" or "bitterness," *pikraínō* means "to provoke," and the deponent *pikraínomai* means "to become angry, bitter."

2. The LXX uses *pikrós* literally for "bitter" (Ex. 15:23) and figuratively for "soured" (Ruth 1:20) or "cruel" (Hab. 1:6). In Gen. 27:34 *pikrós* makes Esau's voice "shrill" rather than "full of grief." Death is bitter in 1 Sam. 15:32, and fate is grievous in 2 Macc. 6:7. The adverb *pikrós* is linked with crying in Is. 22:4 but suggests "unrestrained" rather than "bitter" tears. The verb *pikraínō* is used only figuratively (cf. Job 27:2). The noun occurs some 30 times. It is a place name in Num. 33:9-10, is combined with poison in Dt. 29:19; 32:32, and denotes grief in Sir. 7:11, bitterness in Ps. 10:7, and God's passing wrath in Is. 28:21, 28.

3. Philo uses *pikrós* literally with reference to bitter water or springs, but is also familiar with the transferred use. Bondage is bitter in *On the Life of Moses* 1.247, and *pikría* heads a list of vices in *On Drunkenness* 223. Josephus calls the Dead Sea bitter in *Jewish War* 4.476, but such things as death and bondage are also bitter (*Antiquities* 6.155; 11.263), and he has *pikrós* for strong agitation, sharp reproaches, strict inquiry, etc. (cf. *Antiquities* 3.13; *Life of Moses* 339; *Jewish War* 2.41).

4. The NT uses *pikrós* literally in Jms. 3:11 for spring water which is bitter or brackish to the taste. The great star in Rev. 8:11 makes the rivers and fountains bitter (*pikraínesthai*). In Rev. 10:9-10 the divine finds the message of God bitter, i.e., painful to proclaim. *pikrós* is used for Peter's weeping in Mt. 26:75; the adverb expresses his utter despair following the denial. In Jms. 3:14 jealousy is bitter. Heb. 12:15 quotes Dt. 29:17 to show what harm the sin of an individual can do in the community. The OT association of poison and bitterness stands behind Peter's saying to Simon Magus in Acts 8:23. Rom. 3:14 quotes Ps. 10:7, and *pikría* heads a short list of vices in Eph. 4:31 (in the sense of resentment). In Col. 3:19 husbands are directed not to be harsh or angry with their wives.

5. In Did. 4.10 masters are not to speak to their slaves in an incensed mood. The word is more common in Hermas in such senses as "ill-humor," "anger," etc.

parapikraínō, parapikrasmós.

1. These words have not been found prior to the LXX, and are late and rare. The verb occurs some 40 times in the LXX, in part for "to provoke" but also, perhaps originally by an oversight, for "to be recalcitrant." The noun occurs only once in Ps.

95:8 for the well which is rendered differently in Ex. 17:7; Num. 20:24; Dt. 32:51. Why this term is chosen is not wholly clear, but it is more likely meant in the sense of "rebellion" than of "bitterness."

2. Heb. 3:8, 15 quotes Ps. 95:8, and then 3:16 uses the verb in a context which obviously shows that the meaning is "to be rebellious," so that the noun, too, has the sense of "obduracy" or "rebellion." Like the LXX, the author no doubt catches an echo of the place name in both *parapikrasmós* and *peirasmós* (3:8).

[W. MICHAELIS, VI, 122-27]

---

pímplēmi [to fill, satisfy], **empímplēmi** [to fill up, satisfy], **plēsmonē̃** [satiety, satisfaction]

---

pímplēmi, empímplēmi.

A. Outside the NT.

1. These two terms both occur in Homer but are not common. The simple form means "to fill" or "to satisfy" and occurs in varied contexts (e.g., the eyes with tears or the soul with vices). The compound means "to fill up" (e.g., a vessel). Other uses are for the fulfilling of wishes or the fulfilling of destiny with death.

2. The LXX prefers the compound to the simple form. In over 100 instances the simple form means "to fill," "to satisfy," or, of time, "to run out," "to end." The compound stands for several Hebrew terms and has many nuances, e.g., "to be filled," "to be satisfied." The sense may be either literal or figurative, and there is some ambivalence when the reference is to God's glory filling the house, for statements to this effect stress both God's gracious coming and the holiness of God which no one can abide. Temporal fulfilment is denoted only in Is. 65:20. In Ps. 103:5 God brings material satisfaction, but the satisfaction has a spiritual aspect in Ps. 63:5. Sexual satisfaction is meant (figuratively) in Ezek. 16:28-29. God satisfies with his grace in Ps. 90:14. Death is insatiable in Hab. 2:5.

B. The NT.

1.a. The simple form is used spatially for "to fill" in Lk. 5:7; Mt. 22:10; 27:48.

b. It denotes reaction to the words and works of Jesus in Lk. 4:28; 6:11; 5:26. Similar responses to the apostles' preaching are denoted in Acts 3:10; 5:17; 13:45; 19:29. Filling by the Spirit occurs only in Luke: first in the infancy stories (Lk. 1:15, 41, 67), and then in Acts with reference to the filling of Christians by the Spirit (Acts 4:8, 31; 13:9). Filling by the Spirit brings the gift of tongues in Acts 2:4. In Acts 9:17 it denotes either becoming a believer, receiving prophetic power, or endowing with apostolic gifts. The usage in Acts combines general Christian endowment with special gifts of the Spirit for preaching etc.

c. In the infancy stories *plēsthē̃nai* denotes the ending of periods, the priest's course in Lk. 2:21, the period for circumcision in 2:21, pregnancy in 1:57; 2:6.

d. OT prophecies come to fulfilment in Lk. 21:22.

2. Whereas the simple form means always "to fill," "to fulfill," the compound in the NT means always "to satisfy," mostly in the passive. Physical satisfaction is at issue in Jn. 6:12. God satisfies the heart in Acts 14:17. Lk. 1:53 (based on Ps. 107:9) relates to the messianic kingdom when want will be removed. Lk. 6:25 refers to those who are satisfied with material things and who are thus excluded from the kingdom.

In Rom. 15:24 Paul wants "to be satisfied with," i.e., "to enjoy," the faith and fellowship of the Roman church.

plēsmonḗ.

A. Usage outside the Greek Bible.

1. General Use. plēsmonḗ first denotes "fullness" in the sense of physical or spiritual satisfaction, but also "over-fullness," "satiety," and "lack of moderation." A second use is for "that which fills," e.g., heavy food, and a derived sense is that of a "great number," "profusion."

2. Philosophical Use. In philosophy the term mostly denotes "satisfaction" with no necessary element of censure. In Philo it plays a role in the attack on an overestimation of physical needs. Hence it usually means "gluttony"; thus the Therapeutae shun it as the enemy of body and soul (*On the Contemplative Life* 37).

B. The Greek OT.
Used 28 times in the LXX, *plēsmonḗ* normally has here the sense of "satisfaction" (e.g., by nourishment in Ex. 16:3, 8, with God's gifts in Dt. 33:23). Yet it may also denote the "satiety" that leads to sin (Hos. 13:6; Is. 65:15). Another usage is for "that which satisfies" (Is. 30:23) and for "fullness" or "profusion" (Jer. 14:22).

C. The NT.
1. In Col. 2:23 the fathers normally equate *sárx* with *sṓma* and thus take *plēsmonḗ* to mean the satisfaction of natural (not sinful) desires. The false teachers do not respect the body and thus deprive it. A more ascetic view taken by some fathers is that to fill the body is to ravage it, or that *sárx* represents the carnal mind, so that that is said to suffice which fleshly care teaches.

2. Modern interpretations tend to take it that the *prós* denotes an effect, that *sárx* is meant in a bad sense, and that *plēsmonḗ* is also negative. Difficulty arises because of the loose syntactical structure; a possible solution is that *ouk en timḗ tini* is an independent statement, and that *lógon . . . sṓmatos* is a subsidiary clause.

3. The context of Col. 2:23 shows that the piety combatted parades an earthly-cosmic glory as distinct from the life that is hid with Christ in God. Precepts that forbid the use of earthly gifts give these undue significance and serve the satisfaction of a selfish desire clothed in the garb of religion. These precepts make a show of wisdom with their promotion of piety, humility, and restraint, but they lack true validity and serve pious self-seeking.   [G. DELLING, VI, 128-34]

---

pínō [to drink], *póma* [drink], *pósis* [drinking], *potón* [drinkable], *pótos* [drinking (party)], *potḗrion* [drinking vessel], *katapínō* [to consume], *potízō* [to cause to drink]

---

pínō.

A. The OT Setting.

1. The Secular Sphere. Drinks to quench thirst are more necessary than food, and as intoxicants they affect personal life more deeply. Water, milk, and wine are the main drinks in Palestine. God shows himself to be the Lord of life by giving or withholding food and drink (cf. the miracles in the wilderness).

2. *The Cultus.*

a. Abstinence. Fasting includes abstinence from drinking (Ex. 34:28). Abstinence from intoxicating drinks is a special form; cf. the Nazirite vow (Num. 6:2ff.; Judg. 13:13-14). Drinks are unclean only when polluted by contact (Lev. 11:34). The mysteries include abstention from drinks in fasting, e.g., when preparing for initiation. The Neo-Pythagoreans refuse wine for ascetic reasons.

b. A Means of Salvation. As part of the covenant meal drinking effects fellowship with God. In the pagan world cultic meals supposedly bring union with the gods. Drinks are also thought to confer potency, to mediate immortality, and to induce ecstasy. In the mysteries eating and drinking are associated with the rites of dedication and have sacramental power. In Gnosticism drinking is a dualistic counterpart of true drinking, i.e., the appropriation of the true life-giving gift by the soul. Philo gives this a moral turn. Earthly drink serves the corruptible body but the heavenly soul seeks the drink of immortality which is virtue (*On the Special Laws* 1.304).

II. The Transferred Sense.

1. *General.* In relation to the ground or to plants, *pínō* means "to suck in," "to absorb." "To drink blood" is a phrase for killing. "To appease desire" and "to accept" what is forced on one are other forms of usage.

2. *The OT.* Theologically important in the OT are the ideas of a. drinking God's cup of judgment, in which drinking represents the fact that those smitten by the judgment bring it on themselves by their bemused acts, and b. taking the salvation that is freely offered by divine grace (Is. 55:1).

3. *Judaism.* In Judaism *pínō* represents taking that which promises life (cf. Prov. 9:5). The rabbis allegorize the drinking of water as receiving the Spirit or studying the law (cf. the phrase "drinking of the water of a scholar"). In the Odes of Solomon knowledge is an overflowing river that supplies the thirsty (11:6ff.).

B. The NT.

1. *Eating and Drinking as Expressions of the Subjection of the World.* In 40 of 70 instances in the NT *pínein* is associated with eating. Eating and drinking are vital functions but as such they may be occasions of sin. Thus those who are content to eat and drink miss the signs of the kingdom (Mt. 24:38; cf. Lk. 14:18ff.; 16:19ff.). Eating and drinking become goals of human striving (Mt. 6:32-33) and objects of anxiety (Mt. 6:31). Security and satisfaction are sought in them (Mt. 6:25). The approach of death simply confirms this attitude (1 Cor. 15:32). Dualism leads to it in another way (1 Cor. 6:13-14). It is a basic expression of paganism (1 Cor. 10:7) but is also a temptation for believers (Mt. 24:49). The frontier between quenching thirst and drunkenness is clearly demarcated only by the community meal (1 Cor. 11:21).

2. *Eating and Drinking as Expressions of the Freedom of Jesus and His Disciples.* By eating and drinking with grateful joy, Jesus and his disciples show their freedom from the world's subjection and also from false protests against it. The Baptist neither eats nor drinks (Mt. 11:18), and Paul refrains from eating and drinking for a period (Acts 9:9), but Jesus and his disciples both eat and drink (Mt. 11:19; Lk. 5:33), for fasting is not suitable for him who brings God's rule, and those who are God's are the free lords of all things (Mk. 2:28; 1 Cor. 3:21ff.; 1 Tim. 4:4; Tit. 1:15). If we seek God's kingdom, God adds what is needed (Mt. 6:31ff.). Eating and drinking are to God's glory (1 Cor. 10:31ff.). Yet the strong in faith should refrain if offense is caused to weaker brethren (Rom. 14:21), especially when pagan libations are at issue (1 Cor. 10:21-22).

3. Eating and Drinking and Salvation History. For Jesus and his disciples, eating and drinking are signs of the coming age of salvation. Table fellowship with Jesus means participation in the kingdom that is present in him, and it secures a place in the consummating banquet (cf. Mk. 2:18-19; 14:22ff.). At the Last Supper Jesus hands the cup to his disciples; it represents his vicarious death on their behalf. By handing out bread and wine, Jesus promises that the table fellowship of his earthly ministry will continue, on the basis of his saving work, until it is consummated in the heavenly banquet. Only when the risen Lord eats and drinks with the disciples for a limited period is there renewal of the table fellowship of the days of the incarnation (Lk. 24:30-31; Jn. 21:13). The sacral meal of Acts 2:42 onward is intelligible only on the basis of Easter and Pentecost. It belongs to the age of the church when the Lord is present as he works in his people through the Spirit. As Paul explains it, the eating and drinking are comparable to the manna and water of the age of Moses (1 Cor. 10:3-4), or to the sacrificial flesh and libations of cultic meals (1 Cor. 10:18ff.), although with no thought of automatic sacramental operation (1 Cor. 10:5ff.). What is involved is encounter with the Lord who offered himself for us. Only if there is partaking in faith, however, does the physical function have the significance of salvation and not of judgment (1 Cor. 11:27ff.). In Jn. 6:26ff. eating and drinking are a spiritual receiving of Christ in his self-offering. In 6:51ff. they are a receiving through partaking of the elements. The statements reflect the vocabulary of Gnosticism and the mysteries, but the reference is to the incarnate, crucified, and ascended Christ who has imparted the Spirit (6:33, 51, 60ff.). Eating and drinking, then, are an encounter with Christ and are to salvation if they express total openness in faith to Christ and his saving work.

4. Figurative Use.

a. Drinking the Cup of Wrath and Suffering. Those who undergo God's judgment drink the cup of wine or of wrath either in the sense of being bemused (Rev. 18:3) or in that of suffering eternal torment (14:10). Drinking the cup of suffering means accepting it (Mk. 10:38-39; Mt. 26:42; Jn. 18:11). This has become a stereotyped phrase in the NT.

b. Drinking the Water of Life. Parallel to eating the bread of life (Jn. 6:35), this phrase (Jn. 4:13-14; 7:37) means receiving Jesus in faith. A Gnostic turn is here given to an OT concept; drinking is to quench the thirst for life. In antithesis to natural drinking, this drinking expresses certain key aspects of faith. Faith receives that which gives life, i.e., Jesus himself, and it results in a corresponding giving forth (Jn. 7:38).

póma, pósis, potón, pótos.

1. Usage. póma means "drink," "beverage," *pósis* means the "act of drinking" or "what one drinks," *potón* means "what is drinkable," and *pótos* means "drinking bout."

2. Material Use in the NT.

a. Legal-Ritual and Ascetic-Dualistic Question. In Heb. 9:10 the OT regulations count only as carnal ordinances for this life. Hence the new covenant sets aside the rules of food and drink. All means of nourishment are pure for the pure in heart (1 Tim. 4:4). No one is to judge regarding food and drink (Col. 2:16). The kingdom of God is not food and drink (Rom. 14:17), although for this very reason the strong in faith must respect the problems of the weak. God's rule unites the heart to God and effects a new creation. Expressing the bodily aspect, food and drink are not indifferent matters (1 Cor. 15:32) but being free from bondage to the form of this world, they are to be practiced in obedience (Rom. 14:21; 1 Cor. 10:31ff.).

b. The Lord's Supper. Israel received spiritual food in the wilderness (1 Cor. 10:2).

This is a type of the last time (10:11). Like the water and manna, the eucharistic food and drink are the gift and vehicle of God's saving work in Christ and offer the possibility of life in faith and obedience. They do not magically confer immortality but demand faith and obedience. In Jn. 6 the true food and drink are set in antithesis to the food that can only maintain physical life (6:31-32). This is not Gnostic dualism but represents the biblical opposition to living materialistically. The food and drink here are not the eucharistic bread and wine but Christ himself in his saving action, i.e., his flesh and blood. Only after the NT period do we begin to find a movement in the direction of magic or the mysteries (Justin *Apology* 1.66).

potérion.

1. Usage. This word, rare in nonbiblical Greek, means "drinking vessel." In a Palestinian home it is the pitcher (usually an earthen bowl) that stands filled on the table. Only once in Ps. 116:13 is the *potérion* a vessel used in the temple ministry, although the word occurs in lists of temple furnishings in nonbiblical Greek.

2. Literal Use. The NT refers to the everyday cup in Mk. 9:41; 7:4. In Lk. 11:39-40; Mt. 23:25-26 the Pharisees go beyond the law by trying to keep the outside of cups free from impurities, but this is hypocrisy, for the cup is clean only if its contents are not the proceeds of greed and avarice. The demand for purity of heart is graphically associated with the demand that the inside of the cup be clean (Lk. 11:39). Thus an everyday illustration pinpoints the need for inward conversion.

3. Figurative Use.

a. Cup of Wrath. This metaphor, found in Revelation, derives from the OT. God hands a cup to those who are under judgment (Ps. 75:8; Is. 51:17). This cup robs them of their senses so that they stagger and fall. It is a cup of stupefaction (Ezek. 23:33) or staggering (Is. 51:17). The cup in the hands of God signifies his control of destiny. As a cup of wrath it denotes his judicial sway (Ps. 75:7-8). Later Judaism adopts the same comparison. The Passover cups are cups of punishment for the nations but of consolation for Israel. Revelation makes its own use of the OT image. In 17:4 Babylon holds a golden cup full of her abominations (cf. Jer. 51:17). Its contents are the wine of the wrath of her fornication (14:8). Babylon, under God, has power to subdue the nations by force and propaganda (Rev. 13), but the eschatological power of God's wrath may be seen in this power. It gives up to antichrist those who are not in the book of life (13:8), and in due course they are the agents of God's wrath to trample down Babylon herself (17:15ff.). God thus gives Babylon the cup of the wine of the fierceness of his wrath, and at the last judgment all who accepted her rule will also drink of the wine of the wrath of God, i.e., final condemnation (14:10). The wine depicts God's active wrath, and the cup depicts the power of his wrathful judgment, whether in its temporary exercise through historical powers or in its definitive manifestation.

b. Cup of Suffering. When the sons of Zebedee ask for a special place in Christ's kingly rule, the reply of Jesus that refers them to his own cup is an intimation of martyrdom, but the question that he puts to them concerns their readiness to accept it. In Gethsemane he himself prays that the cup may pass from him, but after wrestling in prayer he attains to the readiness that is expressed in Jn. 18:11. The cup is not just cruel fate but divine judgment, so that Jesus' shrinking from it is not fear of death but the horror of the Holy One at coming under God's judgment on human sin (Mk. 14:33ff.; Mt. 26:37ff.; Lk. 22:44ff.). On the basis of the cup-sayings of Jesus the cup is a symbol of martyrdom in Mart. Pol. 14.2. The cup of suffering is here decisively defined by Jesus' own drinking of it.

4. *The Supper.*

a. The Eschatological Saying in Lk. 22:17-18. In Lk. 22:17-18 the saying of Mk. 14:25 is linked to a cup. In Mark the phrase "fruit of the vine" shows that it is originally connected with the blessing of a cup, for this phrase occurs in Jewish thanksgivings when wine is drunk, e.g., at the Passover. In Luke the saying relates to the first Passover cup. It is a declaration that this is Jesus' last meal with his disciples prior to the meal of consummation. Jesus himself does not drink, but hands the cup to the disciples, who drink from it, or fill their own cups from it, in a unity of table fellowship that looks ahead to the meal of consummation.

b. The Interpretative Saying. Since the order and the ritual followed at the Last Supper correspond to Jewish practice, there can be no doubt that the cup and saying derive from Jesus himself and are handed down by the Palestinian church. The interpretative saying in Mk. 14:23; 1 Cor. 11:25; Lk. 22:20 refers to the contents, but cup rather than (red) wine is always the term used. The cup reminds those to whom it is given of the cup in God's hand. He who proffers it is the Mediator of God's work of judgment and salvation. Those who receive it are those in whom God is at work in the grace that saves through judgment. The cup itself is the Passover cup of blessing, but materially a reference to God's cup stands behind it.

c. Cup of the Lord and Cup of Demons (1 Cor. 10). In 1 Cor. 10:16ff. Paul refers to the cup of blessing, but the phrase "which we bless" makes the reference a special one to what we receive from the Lord in and with it. This cup means participation in Christ's blood, i.e., committal to him who died for us. It is the Lord's cup inasmuch as it relates us to his efficacious power. Hence believers cannot drink both this cup and that of demons (10:21). This is not because the eucharist differs from the cultic meals of paganism (Justin *Apology* 1.66), but because sacrifices not offered to God are dedicated to demons. Those who drink what is publicly or privately (1 Cor. 8:10; 10:27ff.) poured out to pagan deities fall victim to the rule of demons. They thus belong to another dominion than that of Christ. It is because no one can serve two masters (Mt. 6:24) that one cannot drink both the cup of the Lord and that of demons.

katapinō. Literally this word means "to gulp down," "to swallow" (used either of people or of, e.g., the earth). Figuratively it means "to assimilate," "to overwhelm," or "to consume," "to use up." The LXX often uses the term for destruction, whether by the earth (Ex. 15:12), the depths (Ps. 69:15), the enemy (Hos. 8:8), sinners (Ps. 35:25), or God (Job 8:18). In the absolute it denotes the extinction of human wisdom (Ps. 107:27). Philo refers to the swallowing up of the soul of the foolish by the body or to Balaam being engulfed by the river of folly (*On the Giants* 13; *On the Unchangeableness of God* 181). The NT follows the OT in various ways, combining the literal and figurative senses to suggest hostile destruction by superhuman forces. Thus we find overpowering by darkness or the devil in 1 Pet. 5:8, by hopeless remorse in 2 Cor. 7:9-10, or by God's work of judgment in the case of that which is hostile to him in Heb. 11:29; Rev. 12:6; 2 Cor. 5:4; 1 Cor. 15:54. The Egyptians are swallowed up by the sea in Heb. 11:29, the earth swallows up the river in Rev. 12:6, death is swallowed up by life in 2 Cor. 5:4, and death is swallowed up in victory in 1 Cor. 15:54. Only in the proverbial saying in Mt. 23:24 does the use differ. Here a comparison shows how foolish is the way in which the Pharisees struggle against transgression of the smallest statutes but easily accept nonobservance of the great commandments.

potízō. This word means "to cause or give to drink." In the OT God's *potízein* points to his continuing glory as Creator (Ps. 104:11, 13) and also to his work of salvation and wrath (Pss. 78:15; 60:3). The NT renews the ancient demand that the thirsty should be given drink but on a christological basis (Mk. 9:41; Mt. 25:35; Rom. 12:20). Various motives are seen for giving Jesus to drink on the cross (Mk. 15:36; Jn. 19:29). In 1 Cor. 3:2, 6ff. giving basic instruction in the community is like giving children milk to drink or watering a plant. In Rev. 14:8 Babylon makes the nations drink the wine of her fornication. Drinking of the one Spirit in 1 Cor. 12:13 carries a eucharistic reference.   [L. GOPPELT, VI, 135-60]

---

pipráskō [to sell]

In secular Greek *pipráskō* means literally "to sell," "to sell for a bribe," or "to lease," and figuratively "betrayed," "sold out," "led astray," or "ruined." The NT also uses *pipráskō* literally for "to sell" (Mt. 13:46; 18:25; Acts 2:45, etc.), and the figurative sense appears in Rom. 7:14 to describe the desperate plight of the person "sold under sin."   [H. PREISKER, VI, 160]

---

píptō [to fall], *ptôma* [fall], *ptôsis* [fall], *ekpíptō* [to fall away], *katapíptō* [to fall down], *parapíptō* [to go astray], *paráptōma* [to commit a fault], *peripíptō* [to encounter]

---

píptō.

A. Outside the NT.
1. The basic meaning of *píptō* is "to fall (down)," "to plunge down." From this develop such senses as "to throw oneself down," "to fall (in battle)," "to perish," "to be lost," "to collapse," "to pass away." Moral delinquency is not at issue, but in the papyri a legal sense develops, "to fall under," i.e., "to be counted under."

2. *píptō* occurs over 400 times in the LXX and has the same range of meaning as outside the Bible except that we do not find the legal sense. A hint of the loss of salvation is found only in Prov. 11:28 and Sirach, although the loss suffered as a punishment is more likely misfortune.

3. Philo uses *píptō* for the sin of the *noús* or *psychḗ* but not in the sense "to sin." Josephus uses the term literally for the collapse of buildings, the falling of animals to the ground, the falling of snow, falling down before a ruler, and falling in battle.

B. The NT.
I. Literal Use.
1. General.
a. Common in the NT, *píptō* mostly has a literal sense. It first denotes unintentional falls, e.g., the collapse of walls (Heb. 11:30), houses (Mt. 7:25), or cities (Rev. 16:19); cf. the fall of Babylon (Rev. 14:8; 18:2) as a sign of divine judgment.

b. Another use is for the fall of a stone (Lk. 20:18), the falling of cliffs or hills (Lk. 23:30; Rev. 6:16), or the falling of crumbs (Mt. 15:27) or of seed (Mt. 13:4ff.).

c. A further use is for the falling of stars (Mt. 24:29).

d. Birds fall in Mt. 10:29, while humans may also fall unintentionally (Acts 20:9; Mt. 15:14), and they collapse when suddenly stricken by death (Acts 5:5, 10). On the borders of a figurative use, *pípto* means "to fall" in the sense "to die," "to be killed" (Lk. 21:24).

2. *pípto and proskynéo.* In most instances literal falling down is intentional, either in obeisance to a master (Mt. 18:26) or, with *proskynéo,* in connection with the worship of deity (Mt. 4:9; Acts 10:25; 1 Cor. 14:25; Rom. 4:10), or alone, in face of Jesus, to emphasize a petition, to express gratitude, or to show respect (Mk. 5:22; Lk. 17:16; Jn. 11:32). Jesus himself adopts this attitude in prayer (Mt. 26:39).

II. Figurative Use.

1. *General.* Acts 1:26 adopts the common idea of the lot falling on someone; the idea arose because the lot was originally shaken out of a container. When darkness or fear is said to fall on someone (Acts 13:11; Rev. 11:11), the term suggests a sudden and irresistible happening. The meaning in Lk. 16:17 is "to become null."

2. *Falling as Becoming Guilty.* Although *pípto* in the NT does not mean "to fall" in the sense of committing a specific sin, the NT deepens its use in relation to sin. Thus in Lk. 20:18 falling on the stone involves rejection of Christ's person and claim, in Rom. 11:11 falling means abandonment by God in guilt, and in Rom. 11:22 falling is identical to guilt. *pípto* may also be used for loss of faith and separation from grace (1 Cor. 10:12). At issue here is an apostasy from God or Christ which means disqualification (1 Cor. 9:27). In Rom. 14:4 standing and falling are oriented to the fact that each must answer to the Lord as Judge. The use is absolute in Heb. 4:11; a specific sin is not in view but apostasy. In Rev. 2:5 leaving the first love is the point. In 1 Cor. 13:8 love does not fall in the sense that it does not pass away, unless the idea is that it cannot be defeated, or indeed that it will never resist God's claim (cf. vv. 4ff.).

ptôma. This word means "fall," "plunge," "collapse," "ruin," "corpse," "defeat," and, in the papyri, "windfall." It is used in the LXX for the collapse of a wall, the overturning of a chariot, falling in battle, overthrow, and carcass (Judg. 14:8). Philo uses it for "fall," "tumble," "corpse." The only NT meaning is "dead body"—of an animal in Mt. 24:28, of humans in Mt. 14:12 (the Baptist); Rev. 11:8-9 (the two witnesses); some versions of Mk. 15:45 (Jesus).

ptôsis. This word, meaning "fall," is more common in the LXX than *ptôma* in such senses as the fall of a tree (Ezek. 31:13), falling in battle (Nah. 3:3), and overthrow as a judgment. Josephus uses it for the fall from a roof in *Antiquities* 17.71. In the NT the "collapse" of a house is the point in Mt. 7:27, while "downfall" is meant in Lk. 2:34, i.e., the fate of those to whom Christ is an offense.

ekpípto. This word means "to fall out of or down from," "to make a sortie," "to go forth," "to deviate or digress," "to be cast ashore," "to be expelled," "to be omitted," "to stretch," and "to let slip." It is mostly literal in the LXX for various Hebrew terms; thus it denotes an ax flying from the haft, a chopper slipping from the hand, a star falling from heaven, trees or horns that fall, flowers that fade, and figuratively commands going forth or people who hope in dreams going away empty. Josephus uses it for "to be expelled" and also "to escape." The range of meaning is very great in the ten NT instances. For the literal use one may turn to 1 Pet. 1:24 and Jms. 1:11 (based on Is. 40:7), as well as to Acts 12:7 (the chains falling off). The sense may be literal in Acts 17:32 as well, although, since the boat is already in the water, the idea is probably that of letting it float off, not letting it fall. The sense "to lose" occurs in 2 Pet. 3:17 (with some sense of falling away). "To lose" is also the sense in Gal. 5:4. "To be in vain" is the point in Rom. 9:6: the promise of God to Israel has not failed.

katapíptō. This word means literally "to fall down" (buildings etc.), but it also means "to fall into" (disloyalty etc.), and as a perfect participle it means "lowly." An interesting use in the LXX is for "to succumb" (to oppression, 3 Macc. 2:20). Josephus uses it in a phrase denoting "losing heart" (*Antiquities* 2.336). Only Luke has the word in the literal sense; cf. "to fall down" (Acts 26:14), "to fall down dead" (28:6). The seed in Lk. 8:6 falls on the rock.

parapíptō, paráptōma.

A. The Group outside the NT.
1. The verb has such senses as "to fall beside (or aside)," "to stumble on something," "to be led aside or past," "to be mistaken." The noun means "slip" or "error."
2. In the LXX the verb means "to be in vain" in Esth. 6:10, "to err" in Wis. 6:9, and "to win" in Wis. 12:2; Ezek. 14:13; 15:8; 18:24. The noun generally means a "fault" in the LXX, mostly individual sins before God. The group plays little role in Philo, and Josephus uses only the verb in the general sense "to befall" (*Antiquities* 13.362).

B. The Group in the NT.
1. The verb occurs only in Heb. 6:6, where it means "to commit a fault" rather than "to fall away" but with no specific reference (cf. 10:26).
2. The noun occurs in Mt. 6:14-15; Mk. 11:25. Faults against others are at issue in Mt. 6:14, and against God in v. 15. The repetition brings out the severity of faults against others. The general use in Mk. 11:25 does not specify against whom we offend; offenses against others are also offenses against God. Paul often uses the noun. He has it for Adam's sin in Rom. 5:15, 17 and for the totality of sin in Rom. 5:20 (in distinction from *parábasis* as the transgression of commandments). A similar use occurs in Gal. 6:1, and in Rom. 11:11-12 the *paráptōma* of Israel consists of its rejection of the gospel.

C. The Group in the Apostolic Fathers.
The usage in the apostolic fathers follows that of the NT (cf. 1 Clem. 51.1; Barn. 19.4).

peripíptō. This word means "to come on something by chance," "to be innocently involved in something," "to be overturned"; the noun is used for a "mishap" or "accident." Philo uses the verb for "to fall into" and also "to fall culpably." In Josephus we find the senses "to meet," "to overtake," "to be involved in (danger, misfortune, etc.)," "to fall into the hands," "to fall on one's sword." In Lk. 10:30 the meaning is not so much "to come upon the robbers unawares" as "to fall into their hands unexpectedly." In Acts 27:41 the idea is that of being brought somewhere by chance or unexpectedly. Running into trials unexpectedly is also what is meant in Jms. 1:2. In the apostolic fathers subjection to torments is the point in 1 Clem. 51.2, and the noun means "misfortunes" in 1.1.   [W. MICHAELIS, VI, 161-73]

---

pisteúō [to believe, trust],   *pístis* [faith, trust],   *pistós* [faithful, trusting],
pistóō [to make someone trust],   *ápistos* [faithless, unbelieving],   *apistéō* [to
disbelieve, be unfaithful],   *apistía* [unfaithfulness, unbelief],   *oligópistos* [of
little faith],   *oligopistía* [littleness of faith]

A. Greek Usage.

I. Classical.

1. *pistós*, which is attested first, means a. "trusting" (also with the nuance of
"obedient") and b. "trustworthy," i.e., faithful, reliable.

2. *ápistos* means a. "distrustful" and b. "untrustworthy," "unreliable."

3. *pístis* has the sense of a. "confidence," "certainty," "trust," then
b. "trustworthiness," and c. "guarantee" or "assurance" in the sense of a pledge or
oath with the two nuances of "trustworthiness" and "proof."

4. *pisteúō* means "to trust" (also "to obey"), "to believe" (words), and in the
passive "to enjoy confidence" (cf. the later sense "to confide in").

5. *apisteúō* usually means "to be distrustful" or "not to believe" (words).

6. *apistía* means "untrustworthiness," "unreliability," also "distrust."

7. *pistóō* means "to make someone a *pistós*," i.e., a person bound by a pledge or
contract, and hence reliable. Another sense is to make a person one who trusts.

8. The words in *pist-* do not become religious terms in classical Greek. Faithfulness
to a compact is a religious duty, fidelity is related to piety, and one may trust a deity,
but *pistós* does not refer to a basic relationship with God. At most one finds only
reliance on deities and trust in deities or their utterances.

II. Hellenistic.

1. *Philosophical Discussion.* In the debate with skepticism, philosophy comes to talk
about belief in the gods and its distinctive certainty, which is given by the deity and
is related to piety and general belief in the incorporeal. Conduct is affected by such
belief, which carries with it belief in the soul's immortality, membership in the divine
world, and final judgment.

2. *Religious Propaganda.* Religious propaganda demands belief in the deities that
are proclaimed. The Hermetic writings reflect this terminology, as do the Odes of
Solomon, the papyri, the magical texts, and Celsus.

3. *Stoic Usage.* In older Stoicism *pístis* ("trust") is fitting for the sage. In later
Stoicism *pístis* means "faithfulness" as solidity of character. As God is *pistós,* so we
should be. Primarily faithfulness to self, *pístis* makes possible faithfulness to others.
pístis is religious, not as denoting relationship with deity, but in an actualizing of
the relationship.   [R. BULTMANN, VI, 174-82]

B. The OT Concept.

I. General Remarks.
In the OT a theocentric view prevails. Hence faith is the human
reaction to God's primary action. At first faith is collective, and a wealth of usage
appears only when individuals break free from the collective bond. The prophets give
a new creative impulse to the vocabulary and imagery of faith. The greatest expansion
takes place in the Psalms. Faith and fear are closely related in the OT; although
contradictory, they shade into one another, and together they express the living tension
and polar dynamic of the OT relationship to God. They occur more or less equally.
Among the relevant stems, *'mn* (*pisteúein*) comes only fourth statistically but is perhaps
more important qualitatively. In each case the religious use has secular roots.

II. The Stem 'mn and Related Expressions.

1. Qal. In the qal the stem is used of the mothers, nurses, or attendants of children with the associated ideas of carrying and educating.

2. Niphal. The range is broader in this usage, the translation "firm," "reliable," "secure" being only an approximation. Thus we find the ideas of permanence, devastating effect, correspondence with the facts, and specificity. In the two last instances it is not just a matter of logical connection but of living experience as well. When used of people, e.g., servants, witnesses, messengers, or prophets, what is conveyed is truthfulness, perceptiveness, retentiveness of memory, understanding, and the ability to portray. The qualities vary; the point of intersection is the relationship between the qualities required and those actually present. Religiously, many aspects of God can be comprised under the stem. In Dt. 7:9 the "faithful" God keeps covenant with those who love and obey him. In Is. 49:7 faithfulness is shown in the election of Israel. In 1 Kgs. 8:26; Is. 55:3, etc. God's word comes into force either as promise or threat. The stem may also describe God's commandments or works (Pss. 19:7; 111:7). The material definition depends on the aspect in view, but always present is the thought of that which makes God God. When used of believers the term expresses the attitude to God that is in keeping with God's claim. Totality of disposition, not just a single action, is at issue.

3. When the stem takes the form of a verbal adjective, we are pointed in the same direction (cf. 1 Kgs. 1:36; Num. 5:22; Jer. 28:6; Neh. 8:6; Ps. 41:13). The concept embraces a twofold relation: recognition and acknowledgment of the connection between claim and reality, and the connection between the validity of the claim and its practical consequences for those who accept it.

4. Hiphil. The LXX renders the hiphil 45 times by *pisteúein,* five by *empisteúein,* and once each by *katapisteúein* and *peíthesthai.* The meaning is acknowledgment with all the consequences for both object and subject. Expressed is recognition both of the objective relation of object to reality and of the subjective relation of the believer to the object. Believing a report means taking cognizance of it, accepting its truth, and acting accordingly (Gen. 45:26; Ex. 4:1; 1 Kgs. 10:7, etc.). Trusting in vassals, friends, etc. means recognizing the claims inherent in the terms and the validity of the claims for those who trust (cf. 1 Sam. 27:12; Mic. 7:5; Prov. 26:25; Job 4:18). Behind the word that is believed stands the person who is trusted. As regards God, the first sense is that of saying Amen to God, i.e., acknowledging the relation into which he has entered with us, and setting oneself in that relation. Even when faith is required, God's initiative is thus presupposed. In content the orientation is to the aspect at issue, obedience relating to command, trust and worship to the promise (Dt. 9:23; Gen. 15:6). Yet the totality may also be in view. Thus on God's side his power, love, steadfastness, righteousness, choosing, and demanding might all be covered, namely, everything that makes him God, so that in a covenant context unbelief is tantamount to apostasy. On the human side, faith involves knowledge, will, and feeling, with an element of fear as well, in an attitude of extensive and intensive commitment that embraces the totality of external conduct and inner life. Only with the relation to the OT God is this kind of attitude even a possibility. As Isaiah sees it on the basis of his own experience (6:1ff.), faith in this form, related to the idea of a remnant and a fellowship of faith, stands opposed to political considerations (7:1ff.), earthly security (28:14ff.), and trust in human might (30:15ff.), as a form of existence of those who are bound to God alone and find in this their strength (30:15), their being established

(7:9). Such faith makes both autonomy and idolatry impossible; it also removes all fear of human power (7:1ff.).

5. *'mn and Derivatives*. The stress that Isaiah laid on the word and concept was never lost. We thus see an expansion of the meaning of all the relevant stems to embrace the relationship with God and the whole attitude of a life lived in faith (cf. Hab. 2:4; Jer. 7:28). Also expressed is the idea of the absoluteness and exclusiveness of true religion related to the true God.

6. *The Religious Dynamic*. The covenant, with its idea of the faithfulness of God, seems to have supplied the dynamic for this development. If there is little specific connection of faith with the covenant (cf. Neh. 10:1), its strong link with the relationship to God makes this apparent (Ex. 4:8-9; Num. 14:11; Dt. 1:32; 2 Kgs. 17:14; Ps. 78:22).

III. The Stem bṭḥ.

1. *The State of Security*. This stem first expresses the idea of being in a state of security with either an objective or a subjective emphasis (Judg. 18:7; Is. 32:9ff.). A state rather than a relation is the point. The idea of trust arises only through the thought of basing one's security on someone or something, e.g., work, power, righteousness, riches, chariots, wickedness (usually with a negative judgment). Along these lines, the term may be used without a qualm for trust in idols (Is. 42:17), which the prophets, of course, roundly condemn.

2. *Assurance*. The sense of security yields the more subjective thought of assurance with a strong assimilation to *'mn*. This is especially so in Deuteronomy, Psalms, and Proverbs. In a weaker sense the term may denote the attitude of prayer (Pss. 91:2; 84:12; 25:2, etc.).

3. *Comparison*. As compared with *'mn*, this development involves a shift in basic sense which is due to the growth of monotheistic faith, the influence of the prophets, the religious situation of the exile, the sense of being thrown back on God alone, and the rise of religious individualism. The influence of Isaiah is especially important (cf. Is. 30:15).

IV. The Stem ḥsh.

1. *Seeking Refuge*. This stem undergoes a similar development. What is presupposed is the need of help or protection with a stress on the act of seeking.

2. *Relation to God*. The original sense is apparent when help is sought in God, but more weakly, in liturgical use, the whole relation to God may be covered.

V. The stems qwh, yḥl, ḥkh.

1. *Basic Meaning*. These three stems for hoping or waiting are often equivalent and undergo the same development in relation to faith. The basic sense is that of tautness or tenseness, and what may be expressed is lying in wait, waiting in vain, or lying in a state of painful expectation.

2. *Religious Use*. Religiously the terms express collectively the hope of salvation (Jer. 8:15) and individually the hope of being heard (Ps. 119:81) or helped. God's word and grace are hoped for, and God himself, but mostly along with some concrete expectation (Prov. 20:22). The hope of God's manifestation leads on to the later eschatological hope of a visible establishment of the divine rule.

3. *Isaiah*. In Is. 8:17 (cf. 2 Kgs. 6:33) waiting is a faith which endures in spite of divine judgment and wrath. This waiting is a faith that does not yet see but still believes. The tension is that of a venture of faith in a desperate external situation. Here is not the weak and resigned hope of a perhaps, but the energetic hope of a

nevertheless that arises out of wrestling through to final assurance. The position is much the same in Is. 40:31, which refers the people to the wisdom and power of the hidden God (v. 27). Here hoping in God is a new form of life and energy that makes the impossible possible. The whole of the ensuing prophecy (including ch. 53) is proof of the victorious might of the energy of a faith that is inward master of life's most serious afflictions because it has its roots in the transcendent world.

4. Later References. The Psalms especially use stems of hope in this broader and deeper sense for the whole relationship with God (cf. 42:5, 11; 43:5; 130:5-6). Ps. 119 shows how the various tributaries flow into the one main stream of trust in God—the trust which characterizes the prayers of the righteous.

VI. Summary. In light of the whole development in the OT, one sees that the LXX and NT are right to relate *pisteúein* primarily to the stem *'mn,* which may be quantitatively secondary but is qualitatively so preeminent that it absorbs the other terms, partly because of its formal character, partly because it is closest to the unique relation between God and Israel, and partly because the prophets give it a creative profundity that promotes inner triumph over the catastrophes of history and the afflictions of individual life. Faith in the OT expresses the being and life of the people of God in a vital divine relationship that spans the whole of this form of life and involves a certainty that releases new energies. [A. WEISER, VI, 182-96]

C. Faith in Judaism.

I. The OT Legacy. OT faith corresponds to Gk. *pisteúein* inasmuch as both involve trust in persons and belief in words (including God and his word). The OT term, however, carries a stronger element of acknowledgment and obedience. Thus the divine commandments can be objects of faith (Dt. 9:23), and believing God is acknowledging him as such in a unity of trust, hope, fear, and obedience. This faith has its ground in God's past actions, and has its own relation to the past in the form of faithfulness. But it also relates to the future as an assurance that God will do what he has promised, and to the present as obedience to the commands in demonstration of covenant faithfulness. In the OT faith always bears an essential relationship to the people, individuals being its subjects only as members of the people. As distinct from NT faith, this faith does not plainly cover the problem of death, still leaves some scope for an appeal to piety, and is so fulfilled in history that it is not a radical attitude of desecularization like the peace with God (Rom. 5:1) which is independent of national history and individual destiny in this world.

II. Faith in Judaism.

1. OT Motifs. All the motifs of OT faith appear in Judaism, but with a tendency in the rabbis to put an emphasis on obedience to the law, and a heavier stress on faithfulness in the Apocrypha and pseudepigrapha. Along with trust in God, believing that things are true (e.g., God's word and promises) is inherent in faith. While faith is usually defined by adding the object, the absolute use may also be found. The righteous are the faithful, and they are also believers as distinct from the ungodly or pagans.

2. The Difference from the OT. The main difference from the OT is that faith is no longer to the same degree either faithfulness to God's acts in history or trust in his future acts. It is much more strongly obedience to the law, the role of the present being merely to mediate canonized tradition. In its orientation to divine acts, faith is more one-sidedly either a belief in miracles or a general belief in providence, while hope looks ahead to supernatural events in which salvation is for the righteous and judgment means an individual retribution that is based on fulfilment or nonfulfilment of the divine commands, so that works tend to stand alongside faith, and faith itself may even be viewed as a merit.

III. Philo's Concept of Faith. For Philo faith is primarily belief in the one God and trust in his providence. Its real point is a turning from the transient world to the eternal God. This is a disposition of the soul rather than a response to the word. The influence of Platonism and Stoicism may be seen at these points. The relation to the people and its history is snapped, faith is oriented to pure being, which is finally accessible only to ecstasy, and in the last resort faith seems to be more a relation to the self than it is to God.

D. The *pístis* Group in the NT.

I. Formal Considerations.

1. pisteúō. Formally in the NT, as in Greek usage, *pisteúō* denotes reliance, trust, and belief. We find similar constructions to those in the Greek world. Semitic usage produces some new ones, e.g., with *epí* plus the dative or accusative, or with *en.* Distinctive is the use of *pisteúein* with *eis,* which has the new and strong sense of "believing in" and arises in the context of the church's mission. Another fairly common sense of *pisteúein* is "to entrust or commit oneself" (cf. Lk. 16:11; Jn. 2:24; also in the passive).

2. pístis. As in Greek, this word means "faithfulness" and more commonly (religious) "trust" or "faith," usually in the absolute, but with *eis, prós, epí, en,* and also with an objective genitive.

3. pistós. This word may mean either "faithful" or "trusting." The former sense is usually secular, and no special religious meaning attaches when the reference is to service of God (1 Cor. 4:2 etc.). The situation is different when we read of the loyalty of faith (Rev. 2:10) or of the faithful witness (2:13), but when preaching is *pistós* the idea is simply that it is reliable (and cf. the use in relation to God or Christ, 1 Cor. 10:13; 2 Cor. 1:18; 2 Tim. 2:13). When the idea is "trusting," *pistós* bears the religious sense of "believing."

4. pistóō. This word occurs in the NT only in the passive at 2 Tim.3:14 in the sense "to be made believing (certain)" (cf. 1 Clem. 42:3). In 1 Clem. 15:4, however, the sense is "to remain faithful to. . . ."

5. ápistos. This might mean "faithless" in Lk. 12:46, but the more likely sense is "unbelieving" (cf. more generally Mk. 9:19). In Acts 26:8 the meaning is "unworthy of credence."

6. apistéō. This verb means "to be unfaithful" in Rom. 3:3, "not to believe" in Lk. 24:11, and more technically "to refuse to believe" in Mk. 16:16.

7. apistía. This word means "unfaithfulness" in Rom. 3:3; Heb. 3:12 (closely related to disobedience; cf. Heb. 3:19), "unbelief" in Mk. 6:6, "unbelief" in words in Mk. 16:14, and "unbelief" regarding the Christian message in Rom. 11:20.

8. oligópistos. This word derives from Judaism and occurs only in the Synoptists (Mt. 6:30; 8:26; 14:31; 16:8). *oligopistía* is a variant in Mt. 17:20.

II. General Christian Usage.

1. Continuation of the OT and Jewish Tradition.

a. *pisteúō* as "to believe." In the NT the group becomes a leading one to denote the relationship with God, partly on the OT basis and partly in connection with the Christian mission and its call for faith as a turning to God. The verb is often used for believing God's word, e.g., Scripture (Jn. 2:22), the prophets (Acts 26:27), Moses (Jn. 5:46-47), or what God says through an angel (Lk. 1:20) or the Baptist (Mk.

11:31). Along these lines the NT says that the people should believe Jesus and his words (Jn. 3:34; 5:38).

b. *pisteúō* as "to obey." Heb. 11 stresses that to believe is to obey, as in the OT. Paul in Rom. 1:8; 1 Th. 1:8 (cf. Rom. 15:18; 16:19) shows, too, that believing means obeying. He speaks about the obedience of faith in Rom. 1:5, and cf. 10:3; 2 Cor. 9:13.

c. *pisteúō* as "to trust." This sense is prominent where OT influence is strong, as in Heb. 11, and cf. Mk. 5:36; Acts 3:16; 14:9. A connection with prayer emerges in Mk. 11:22ff.; Jms. 1:6. Paul describes Abraham's faith as trust in God's miracle-working power (Rom. 4:17ff.; cf. also 9:33; 10:11).

d. *pisteúō* as "to hope." The relation between faith and hope is clear in Rom. 4:18 and Heb. 11:13. When hope is directed to what is invisible, it entails trust. Only faith, not sense, can perceive the heavenly reality and grasp the promised future (Heb. 11:1). When *pístis* is specifically faith in Christ, hope is mentioned separately, but such hope contains an element of believing confidence (1 Th. 1:3; 1 Cor. 13:13; 1 Pet. 1:21).

e. Faithfulness. The OT sense of "faithfulness" finds echoes in Heb. 12:1; 13:7; 2 Tim. 4:7; Rev. 2:13; Heb. 11:17; Jms. 1:2-3. This is the point for Paul, too, when he refers negatively to the *apistía* ("unfaithfulness") of Israel in Rom. 3:3. In 1 Cor. 16:13, however, *pístis* is the faith to which one should be faithful.

2. *Specifically Christian Usage.*

a. *pístis* as Acceptance of the Message. Especially when used with *eis*, *pístis* is saving acceptance of Christ's work as proclaimed in the gospel. This includes believing, obeying, trusting, hoping, and being faithful, but it is primarily faith in Christ. For Gentiles, it means conversion to the one God who has brought salvation in and through his Son.

b. The Content of Faith. Paul states the content of faith in Rom. 10:9. It involves acknowledgment of the risen Christ. Faith in Christ means faith in his resurrection, and his resurrection implies his prior death for sin (1 Cor. 15:11; cf. Rom. 4:24; 1 Th. 4:14; Phil. 2:6ff.). Kerygma and faith always go together (cf. Acts 2:22ff.), and the reference is always to Christ and what he has done (cf. Jn. 20:31; 16:27; 14:10; 8:24; Rom. 6:8).

c. Faith as Personal Relation to Christ. Believing *eis* Christ involves a personal relation similar to the relation to God in the OT, although the NT tends to use different constructions for believing in God and in Christ. Acceptance of the gospel is acceptance of Christ as Lord, for Christ and salvation history cannot be severed. Faith accepts the existence of Christ and its significance for the believer. It rests on the message, but as faith in the message it is faith in the person whom the message mediates. The personal aspect comes out in Rom. 10:9, 14; Gal. 2:20; Phil. 1:29; 1 Pet. 1:8.

d. Believing. Faith may be acceptance of the message, as in Acts 20:21, or it may be continuation in believing, as in 1 Cor. 2:5. Since believing is dynamic, it may be weak or strong (Rom. 12:3; 14:1), it may grow (2 Cor. 10:15), it may endure (Col. 1:23), and there may also be references to its fullness (Acts 6:5), practice (1 Th. 1:3), and unity (Eph. 4:13).

e. The Faith. Paul can call the message itself *pístis*. As such, *pístis* is a principle, e.g., in contrast to law (Rom. 3:31; cf. 3:27: the law of faith). Along these lines *pístis* is Christianity either as being a Christian or as the Christian message or teaching (cf. Gal. 6:10; 1:23). Acts 6:7 and Eph. 4:5 offer similar uses, and cf. 1 Tim. 3:9; 4:1, 6. Orthodox doctrine is *pístis* in Jude 3, 20 and 2 Pet. 1:1. The phrases in 1 Tim. 1:2, 4; 2:7; Tit. 1:1, 4; 3:5 are to the same effect.

f. Development of the Use of *pisteúō*. The verb follows much the same pattern as the noun. It usually means "to receive the message," but it may also denote "to be believing," and the participles can have the same force as *pistós,* which is equivalent to "Christian."

3. *Christian Faith and OT Faith.* Faith in the NT is the same as faith in the OT inasmuch as it is belief in God's word, but with the difference that God's deed is now disclosed only in the word. The OT righteous believe in God on the basis of manifested acts, but NT believers believe in God in and with the act of the life, death, and resurrection of Christ as this is known only by gospel proclamation. God's act is here the word, for Jesus is himself God's word. Faith, then, is trust in God's eschatological act in Christ and hope for the consummation of the work that God has thus begun. In the interim it is trust that God will not let believers be confounded but that as they are dead with Christ, so they will be kept until they are also raised with him. Insofar as faith is faithfulness, it is faithfulness to God's saving act in Christ, to the one name in which is salvation (Acts 4:12). The obedience of faith is obedience to the way of salvation in Christ, which includes, of course, turning aside from sin. In every dimension it means a radical reorientation to God that governs all life. Hence faith is the Christian religion and believers are Christians. Yet the stress on Christ is a stress on God, for faith in Christ is faith in God's act in Christ. God meets believers (only) in Christ, in whom all God's fullness dwells. Christ is God's final act embracing already its future and definitive manifestation.

III. pístis and pisteúō in Paul.

1. *Paul and the Common Christian Concept.*

a. Acceptance of the Message. For Paul faith is primarily, not a disposition, but an acceptance of the message related to confession (Rom. 10:9). Faith is a historical, not a psychological, possibility (Gal. 3:25ff.). The event of salvation history is actualized in baptism; faith makes it the believer's. As belief in what the message proclaims, faith recognizes its personal validity. It entails obedience as acceptance of the divine act of both grace and judgment at the cross, which brings understanding both of God and of self, i.e., of the grace of God and of the self under grace. Trust and hope arise within this new understanding.

b. Ways of Believing. Since faith involves confession and obedience, it is a state as well as an act. One can have it (Rom. 14:22), be in it (2 Cor. 13:5), and stand in it (1 Cor. 16:13; cf. 1 Th. 3:8; Rom. 5:2). Yet standing in faith is not static, for faith is under assault and has to establish itself (cf. Rom. 11:20). There are degrees of faith (1 Th. 3:10; 2 Cor. 10:15). A weak faith (Rom. 14:1-2) is related to defective knowledge of right conduct (cf. 14:2, 23). Action must be from faith (Rom. 14:23) according to the measure that each enjoys (12:3). There is a work of faith (1 Th. 1:3); it works by love (Gal. 5:6). This work stands in contrast to the works of the law.

2. *The Contrast with Judaism.*

a. Faith and the Works of the Law. To express the new relation to God, Paul links salvation strictly to faith. Salvation means righteousness, but righteousness is given to faith, not to works. Faith need not be supplemented by works but is a committal to God and his grace. This committal, of course, is an act of will, but one in which a person *is* and does not merely *do.* Faith is the manner of life of those who now live in Christ (Gal. 2:19-20). As a negation of self-will, faith is the supreme act, and as such it is the opposite of works in every sense. It is correlative to grace, which stands in antithesis to works that merit payment. Paul does not oppose the content of works but the manner of their fulfilment. Works do not avail when they are a basis of boasting, i.e., of a claim on God, as in pagan as well as Jewish thinking. What Paul rejects is the attitude of self-assurance before God, or the attempt to attain it. Faith is the true obedience made possible by God's gracious act in Christ.

b. Eschatological Faith. As the surrender of the natural man, determining all conduct, faith is an eschatological attitude made possible by God's eschatological act, i.e., the attitude of the new man. Being in faith, like being in grace or in Christ, means being a new creature (2 Cor. 5:17). The age of grace has ended that of law (Rom. 6:14). The last time has come with faith (Gal. 3:23ff.).

3. *Pauline Faith and Gnosticism.*

a. Orientation to the Future. As an eschatological attitude, faith is not itself fulfilment. Believers are in conflict (Phil. 3:12ff.). It is provisional, like all historical being. It actualizes eschatological being in temporality. Referred back to God's act in Christ, it is also referred forward to the consummation (Rom. 6:8). The past act of God controls the future; hence hope stands alongside faith (cf. 1 Th. 4:14). Faith abides (1 Cor. 13:13), but the present life in faith, not including sight, is provisional (2 Cor. 5:7).

b. Faith and Fear. Since grace is not an infused power, but meets us as the grace of judgment and forgiveness, it never lets us escape the concrete conditions of life. Faith removes the stress of trying to win salvation, but the divine imperative remains, and fear is appropriate as the sense that we do not stand on our own feet and must be careful not to fall in either frivolity or pride (cf. Phil. 2:12; Rom. 11:20). With the confidence of 2 Cor. 3:4 and the boldness of hope of 3:12, Paul knows the fear of the Lord in 5:11, namely, the sense of standing before God (2:17; 4:2).

c. Faith and Historical Existence. Existence in faith is existence in a not yet as well as a no longer (Phil. 3:12ff.). Faith's resolve has abandoned self-confidence but must be sustained by renewal, by a constant forgetting of what is behind. Abandoning self-confidence means renunciation of the urge to possess and committal to grace; there is possession only in Christ.

IV. pisteúō in John.

1. *As Acceptance of the Message.* The noun *pístis* occurs only in 1 Jn. 5:4, but the verb is common in John, and often denotes acceptance of the message, whether with *hóti* clauses, with *eis,* or in the absolute.

2. *With eis and the Dative.* In John believing Jesus or his words is believing in him, for proclaimer and proclaimed are the same as the proclaimed himself meets and speaks with us. The act of God is word, and Jesus is this word-act (Jn. 1:1). Believing in Jesus is the same as coming to him, receiving him, or loving him (1:12; 5:43; 8:42).

3. *Faith and Salvation.* Faith in the word that Jesus proclaims, and that proclaims Jesus, brings salvation (3:18; 5:24). The word for salvation in John is life. What the world calls life is not life; the world is in error (8:44ff.). The world would believe Jesus if he would speak its language and show it a sign, but his sayings and signs are clear only to believers (16:25, 29). If he spoke the truth in the world's way, it would no longer be the truth.

4. *Faith as Renunciation of the World.* The world does not know true life or salvation, and must renounce itself in a turning to what is not seen (Jn. 20:29). People cannot believe when they seek honor from one another in a bid for security (5:44), or when they only want bread that will assure them of bodily life (ch. 6). Faith itself is not a worldly action; it has its roots in the other world as God's gift or act. One must be of God to hear God's voice (8:47). This characterizes faith as a miracle, an act of desecularizing. Believers are no longer of the world (15:19). The world, too, views God

as an object of faith, but it cannot accept the incarnation of the Word (1:14) with its radical concept of desecularizing, not as human soaring up to another world, but by God's free, eschatological act which means judgment for the world but also salvation by revelation and faith. The invisible becomes visible in a way that offends the world (6:42; 7:27; 5:17ff.; 8:28, 58). The divine desecularizing is not a flight from the world but a reversal of the world's values, a turning of believers from evil (17:15), a breaking of the force of the world as a historical entity in which everyone has a share by conduct. Revelation challenges this world and is thus an offense to it. In contrast, faith accepts the divine desecularizing and banishes autonomous human power by grasping the revelation of the word.

5. *Johannine Faith and Pauline Faith.* The inner unity of John and Paul is plain. For neither is faith a good work. For both, however, it is an act with the character of obedience. For both it means renunciation of one's own power or self-achieved righteousness.

6. *Johannine Faith and Gnosticism.* In John, as distinct from Paul, the antithesis is not the Jewish striving for righteousness but the universal worldliness that this represents. The specific antithesis in John is the Christian form of this worldliness, i.e., Gnosticism. John uses Gnostic terms when he speaks about being taken out of the world or passing from death to life, but in the setting of the gospel he turns these phrases against Gnosticism. The believer has life only in faith and not as a possession. Seeing Christ's glory differs from ecstasy, for it comes by seeing the incarnate Lord. Direct vision lies ahead (17:24). Believers are not taken out of the world; they are still exposed to its assaults (17:15; 15:18ff.). Faith cannot break free from the word; it has life only as faith in the word in which alone God's revelation is present.

7. *Faith and Knowledge.* Faith does not set us in a desecularized state. It must abide in the word (8:31), which in turn abides in believers (15:4ff.). Knowledge of the truth comes with abiding (8:32). Knowledge is no rival to faith. The two have the same objects. Each may precede the other, so that they are not just initial and final stages. Knowledge is the knowledge of faith, unlike the mutual knowledge of Father and Son. Only when earthly existence ends will vision replace knowing faith. Then Christ's glory will be seen directly and not under the concealment of the flesh (17:24).

8. *Faith and Love.* If believers can overcome the world only by faith (1 Jn. 5:4), they can demonstrate desecularizing by their conduct as they keep the commandments of Jesus in an obedience and steadfastness of faith (2:3-4; 3:22). The content of the divine commandments corresponds to the unity of faith and love. Faith sees in Jesus the revealer of divine love (Jn. 3:16). Love is engendered by the receiving of this love (15:11ff.) and abiding in it (15:1ff.; cf. also 1 Jn. 2:5, 9ff.; 3:10-11; 4:7ff.). Believers are known to be the disciples of Jesus by their love for one another (Jn. 13:35).

[R. BULTMANN, VI, 197-228]

---

planáō [to go astray, lead astray], *planáomai* [to be deceived, misled], *apoplanáō* [to mislead], *apoplanáomai* [to be misled], *plánē* [wandering, seduction], *plános* [leading astray], *planḗtēs* [wanderer], *plánēs* [wanderer]

A. Classical and Hellenistic Use of the Group.

1. Literal Usage. The idea behind the group is that of "going astray." Wandering is usually denoted, but the group may also be used for the pulsing of the blood through the body and the journeys of merchants. We find wanderers in tragedy, e.g., Io and Oedipus. In the case of Io the lack of a goal has an inner effect in a combination of geographical and spiritual wandering.

II. Transferred Usage.

1. The Verb in Epistemological and Ethical Statements. In a figurative sense the group denotes absence of a goal. Reasons are not always given, but when they are these are more often epistemological than religious.

a. *planáō* and *apoplanáō* can mean "to lead astray" or "to deceive," whether through conduct, speech, or writing. The labyrinth leads astray geographically but obscurity of reality or concepts does so in theoretical or ethical matters. A common Stoic and Neo-Platonic proverb refers to the deceived deceiver.

b. *planáomai* and *apoplanáomai* denote "vacillation" or "irregularity" in speech, action, or conduct. Digression, or making untrue or contradictory statements, may be at issue in speech. Usually "aberration" in judgment is the point, with doubt or hesitation implied. No censure is involved but a summons is issued to right perception and action.

2. Religious and Metaphysical Error.

a. Characters in tragedy are sometimes led into tragic error. Sent by the gods, this aberration leads to an appointed end (cf. Io and Oedipus).

b. Plato refers to the vacillation of the soul when the bodily senses lead it to what is transitory. The wise are saved from this entanglement by turning aside from the world of the senses to that of the ideas. The aberration may thus be a necessary detour on the way to true knowledge.

c. In Plutarch, wandering plays a similar role in the search of Isis, which initiates imitate cultically.

3. The Nouns and Adjectives.

a. *plánē* means "vacillation," "error," with the same range of meanings as the verb. The active sense of "deceit" is rare, and error does not have to imply guilt (the term may even denote an excursus that promotes truth), although confusion is the basis of wickedness in Plato.

b. *planétēs* means "unstable."

c. *plános* as an adjective has both the passive sense of "unstable" and the active sense of "seducing."

d. *plános* as a noun has various senses, e.g., a poetic "digression," the "vacillation" that the soul leaves behind when it renounces sense perception, the "confusion" of comedy, and, with a personal reference, the "conjurer."

B. The Word Group in the LXX.

I. Literal Usage.

a. *planáō* means "to confuse," "to lead astray," "to cause to stagger." One is not to lead the blind astray (Dt. 27:18). Staggering through wine is primarily literal, but with a hint of spiritual vacillation.

b. *planáomai* means "to wander" or "stagger about," e.g., on journeys, in flight, or in judgment. Wandering may be in affliction (Sir. 29:18), and staggering may result from wine (Job 12:25). In the eschaton there will be no more wandering (Is. 35:8). Animals also stray, e.g., the ox (Ex. 23:4), sheep (Dt. 22:1), and young ravens (Job 38:41).

c. *planétēs* is used for the "restless wanderer" (cf. God's judgment on Israel in Hos. 9:17).

d. *planétis* occurs for Job's wife in 2:9.

e. The other terms are used only in a transferred sense.

II. Transferred Usage.

a. *planáō* seldom denotes secular deceiving. Religious seduction, which leads to idolatry, is the work of false prophets and unfaithful rulers (Dt. 13:6; 2 Kgs. 21:9) or of false gods (Hos. 8:6; Am. 2:4). Israel is the object, signs etc. are used (Dt. 13:2-3), and bribes may be the motive (Is. 3:12). God himself may lead astray, e.g., the Gentiles in Job 12:23, the mighty in Job 12:24, lying prophets in Ezek. 14:9, and the people in Is. 63:17.

b. *planáomai* offers a similar usage. Thus Israel strays like sheep in Is. 53:6. If there is little censure in this verse, aberration is usually condemned as wandering from God or transgressing his will (Ezek. 14:11; Ps. 119:110). In the case of Gentiles, this wandering means idolatry (Is. 46:5, 8). In general the LXX uses the whole group in a strong rejection of false prophecy.

c. *apoplanáō* may denote secular deceiving but it may also denote leading into idolatry (2 Chr. 21:11) or offending against God's will (Prov. 7:21). *plánē* as "error" or "seduction" is a general term for Israel's disobedience or idolatry (Ezek. 33:10; Jer. 23:17), or for that of the Gentiles, or for individual sins (Prov. 14:8). *plános* denotes religious error, i.e., idolatry (Jer. 23:32), or the sin of weakness (Job 19:4).

d. Significant in the LXX is the negative judgment expressed in the group, first relative to Israel, then to the Gentiles. Erring is not due to metaphysical dualism but to refusing to hear and obey God. Judgment threatens aberration (Is. 46:8); salvation brings freedom from it (Is. 35:8). Only apocryphal references offer traces of dualism (Sir. 11:16 [variant reading]; Wis. 2:21).

C. Apocalyptic and Hellenistic Mystical Literature.

I. Philo. Philo uses the group both literally and in various senses, e.g., for "imprecision" in speech, "aberration" of sensory perception, "errant vacillation" of the mind, "spiritual aberration" as deviation from the straight path, orientation to the external, contempt for allegorizing, or star worship. Philo's main concern is for aberration in the knowledge of God, which is culpable. Moral defects and idolatry are not so prominent. Sensory perception is inadequate if God is to be known. Aberration is not so much disobedience as bondage to the sensory world.

II. Dualistic Eschatological Use.

1. Seduction by Powers. While apocalyptic and mystical writings often use the group in the classical way, a special thought is that of seduction by spiritual forces, e.g., angels, Azazel, Beliar, unclean demons, evil spirits, the angel of darkness, Satan, the planets, the ungodly aeons, etc. Seduction involves transgression of the law, especially in licentiousness. Alternatively, it means confusion through lack of wisdom. Hopeless entanglement in chaos is one aspect of the soul's wandering; this is presented as a cosmic destiny.

2. The Dualistic Background. Aberration takes place against the background and in the context of metaphysical dualism, e.g., that of light and darkness, truth and error, the world of sense and that of spirit, or mind and chaos.

3. The Eschatological Use.

a. The last things bring confusion, i.e., rumor, terror, and idolatry. Deceivers abound. False prophets seduce by means of winning speech, promises of miracles, and apparent signs. There is only a weak echo of this theme in the rabbis.

b. The last things also end error as the wicked spirits are punished and the Gentiles come to see that idolatry is transgression. Again, the rabbis offer only traces of such ideas, which are formally parallel to the Stoic concept of restoration and Hermetic hopes for the end of aberration.

D. The Word Group in the NT.
I. Literal and Semiliteral Use.

1. Combining in various ways the different uses, the NT employs *planáomai* literally in Heb. 11:38, which refers to those who lose a permanent dwelling for God's sake, thus displaying true faith.

2. Borrowing from the LXX, Mt. 18:12 speaks about the "straying" of a sheep (it is "lost" in Luke's depiction). The passage carries an allusion to backsliders. The straying is culpable but is ended by the mission of Jesus.

3. The same OT metaphor occurs in 1 Pet. 2:25 (cf. Is. 53:6). Christians have ceased to stray and come back to the Shepherd. The state of straying is here less pitiable and more culpable than in Is. 53.

II. Transferred Use.

1. OT and Later Jewish Use. In the NT the categories of error are mostly religious. Thus in Rom. 1:27 the deifying of the creature constitutes the error. Immorality is denoted in Tit. 3:3 and 2 Pet. 2:18. The backsliding of believers is the issue in Heb. 3:10 and Heb. 5:2. In Jms. 5:19-20 the one who wanders from the truth is a sinner. In Mk. 12:24, 27 and Mt. 22:29 the Sadducees err when they deny the resurrection, whether through ignorance of Scripture or of the power of God. In this incident the antithesis between a spiritual and a materialistic view of the resurrection, and the type of argument, correspond to rabbinic discussion and exegesis.

2. The Stoic Use of mḗ planásthe. The warning *mḗ planásthe* in 1 Cor. 6:9; Gal. 6:7; Jms. 1:16; 1 Cor. 15:33 has formal roots in the Stoic diatribe. It almost serves as an interjection or transition. In 1 Cor. 6:9 it precedes a list of vices, in Gal. 6:7 it introduces a warning against mocking God, in Jms. 1:16 it contests the idea that good gifts might not come from God, and in 1 Cor. 15:33 it warns against contesting the resurrection or against the resultant immorality. Popular sayings are adduced in Gal. 6:7 and 1 Cor. 15:33.

3. The Dualistic Use.

a. In Eph. 4:14 *plánē*, as the opposite of growth by pursuit of the truth in love, is marked by craftiness and fickleness. A dualism of error and truth may be seen here.

b. A similar dualism occurs in 1 John, where *plánē* is the opposite of truth as the divine reality, and *planóntes* are either false teachers or those who echo their words by denying sin (1:8-9) or the incarnation (4:2ff.). Ultimately the error is practical (4:6). The false teachers are human but the power of the *kósmos*, the *diábolos*, or the *pneúma tḗs plánēs* lies behind them (4:4; 3:8; 4:6). Having the Spirit and knowing the truth (2:20ff.), believers are proof against the error. The seducing forces have apocalyptic stature (2:18) but have taken the historical form of false teachers.

4. The Eschatological Use.

a. Later Jewish apocalyptic lies behind Mk. 13:5ff. and Mt. 24:4ff., where there are warnings against the false christs or prophets who will come with seductive promises, offer signs, and lead many astray, tempting even the elect. New elements as compared to Jewish models are that the deceivers appeal to Christ (Mk. 13:5), come in his name rather than their own (Mk. 13:6), and seek to lead members of the community away from Christ.

b. Using the same Jewish basis, Revelation presents the seducing powers in more strongly mythical garb and sees them trying to seduce the world rather than believers. The seducer is the dragon, the serpent, the devil, or Satan (12:9), who has fallen from heaven, is chained for a time, is released, and is then destroyed (12:9; 20:3ff.). The second beast is also a seducer, i.e., a seducing prophet who accompanies the first beast, or antichrist. Babylon, too, is a seducing power in 18:23. These forces persecute the community rather than seducing it; their seduction is aimed at the world and leads it into fornication and idolatry (18:3; 13:14-15) by means of false miracles (cf. 13:14) and sorcery (18:23).

c. The phrase "strong delusion" in 2 Th. 2:11, which sums up the phenomena listed in vv. 3-10, unites the apocalyptic motifs, but the context now is the delay in the parousia and the punishment of unbelievers.

5. *The Rationalizing and Moralizing Use.*

a. In 2 Th. 2:11 the seducers of the last time are false teachers of the present age and eschatological apostasy is backsliding into error.

b. In 1 Tim. 4:1 and related passages apostate teachers who follow seducing spirits and are deceived deceivers (2 Tim. 2:13) lead their followers into immorality, hypocrisy, sorcery, avarice, and Gnostic spiritualism (1 Tim. 4:2; 3:13; 6:10; 4:3ff.).

c. In describing false teachers Revelation compares them to Jezebel (2:20), and Jude and 2 Peter refer to Balaam (Jude 11; 2 Pet. 2:15). They are "wandering stars" in Jude 13; this brings out their demonic quality.

6. *The Apostles and Christ as Deceivers.* The apostles are regarded by their opponents as deceivers (2 Cor. 6:8), but Paul firmly denies that his appeal springs from error or deception (1 Th. 2:3). When the rulers refer to the report of the resurrection as the "last deception," they imply that all Christ's work and teaching are a fraud and that he himself is an impostor (Mt. 27:63; cf. Jn. 7:12, 47).

7. *Summary.* The references to charges that Christ and the apostles are deceivers show that the church has not appropriated the group to its own exclusive use, e.g., in opposition to the rabbinic view of the law or the Jewish striving for legal righteousness. At first the NT preserves the Jewish and apocalyptic content of the group and only gradually does it combine it with the Christ event. Everywhere the NT, like the LXX, stresses the culpability of error. God's eschatological work in Christ overcomes this culpable straying, whether in the form of the pre-Christian state or of the seduction and error that threaten believers.

E. Early Church Usage.

1. The Apostolic Fathers.

a. New Material Combinations. In the apostolic fathers individual branches of meaning tend to lose their individuality and extended use produces new material combinations. Thus demons practice seduction in Justin *Dialogue* 7 etc., the Jews are in error in Barn. 2.9, error is the opposite of reason in Justin *Dialogue* 3.3, prayer is made for those who go astray in 1 Clem. 59.4, they are commended to the care of the presbyters in Pol. 6.1, the warning not to err is a warning to cleave to the church and the bishop in Ignatius *Ephesians* 5.2, and the straying of the soul is a rejection of asceticism in 2 Clem. 15.1.

b. New Linguistic Combinations. Along with the new material combinations we find new synonyms for the group which link it with the fall in Diog. 12.3, with offenses (Mk. 4:17) or nonabiding (cf. Jn. 15:7) in Hermas *Mandates* 10.1.5, and with believing myths in 2 Clem. 13.3.

2. *The Later Period.*

a. In the apocryphal Acts the group is set in a more consistently dualistic context and Jesus is presented as the liberator from error. He is a companion in the land of error and he destroys deception even though he is himself called a deceiver.

b. In the Pistis Sophia Jesus turns the powers in the reverse direction so that they are deceived or deluded and can no longer exert their influence. The NT hint of a deluding of rulers (1 Cor. 2:8) is here developed into the concept of a cosmological process.

c. Athanasius in his 39th Festal Letter, quoting Mt. 22:29 and 2 Cor. 11:3, speaks about self-deception, deception, and deceiving with reference to the true scope of the canon, i.e., in a warning against heterodoxy concerning the sources of revelation.

→ *apatáō, ginṓskō, hodós*   [H. BRAUN, VI, 228-53]

> *plássō* [to fashion, form],   *plásma* [figure, fabrication],   *plastós* [formed, fabricated]

---

plássō, plásma.

A. The Greek World.

1. The Verb. plássō and *plássomai* originally relate to the art or craft of "fashioning." They are rarely used of the activity of divine beings, though Hephaistos is said to have fashioned Pandora. Prometheus is later the one who fashions human and other living creatures. The chief deity does not concern itself with *plássein* but gives human beings their reason or soul. Created gods see to the fashioning of bodies, and nature does the fashioning in Aristotle. In other writers *plássein* is used for the training of the body or even its care.

2. The Noun. The word *plásma* has such varied senses as "figure," "forgery," and (literary) "style." It is commonly used for the products of artists or artisans. In magic it is the figure that is made of a person on whom magic is to be exerted. In the Hellenistic period it may denote the body in antithesis to the *psyché.*

B. Judaism.

I. The LXX.

1. The Verb.

a. In the active, God is the subject of the verb 36 times. He forms human and animal beings (Gen. 2:7-8, 19). The righteous confess that he formed them (Job 10:9; Ps. 139:5). He formed the eyes (Ps. 94:9), the breath (Prov. 24:12), the spirit (Zech. 12:1), and the heart (Ps. 33:15). He also formed the earth (Is. 45:18), all things (Jer. 51:19), and summer and spring (Ps. 74:17). He fashions in the election, guidance, and liberation of Israel, both collectively (Is. 43:1) and individually (Jer. 1:5). The use of the verb displays his absolute sovereignty (Job 10:8-9; Ps. 95:5). He can call a prophet or play with Leviathan (Jer. 1:5; Ps. 104:26). He brings salvation and inflicts chastisement (Is. 45:18; Hab. 1:12). He alone understands (Ps. 33:15), perceives (94:9), and revives (2 Macc. 7:23). He alone must teach (Ps. 119:73). Distinctive points are that God's fashioning is historical as well as natural and that it refers to the body as well as the heart or spirit, i.e., to the human totality with no dualistic distinctions.

b. The LXX never speaks neutrally of human *plássein.* The shaping done by the potter either serves to denote God's sovereignty (Is. 29:16) or is mentioned in attacks on idolatry (Wis. 15:8ff.). In Ps. 94:20 *plássein* denotes the harmful action of the unjust judge. The middle in 1 Kgs. 12:33 has to do with the arbitrary rearrangements of the feasts by Jeroboam. God is the implied subject of the passive in Job 34:15 and Ps. 139:16.

2. *The Noun.* The LXX uses *plásma* only six times, e.g., for the human figure in Ps. 103:14, for animals as God's created work in Job 40:19, and for the potter's work in Is. 29:16, especially the idol in Hab. 2:18. Stressed are God's sovereignty over his works in Job 40:19; Is. 29:16, and his pity for them in Ps. 103:14.

II. Philo.

1. *plássō.* Only God is the subject of *plássein* in Philo. It is he who fashions the human species and the human form, although Philo distinguishes between earthly humanity and humanity in the divine likeness, and uses different words for God's fashioning of them. In the middle, Philo uses the term for human inventions in the religious and legal fields. Dualism is pronounced in the passive use (cf. the allegorizing of Ex. 31:2ff.). As in the Greek world, but not the LXX, the passive can also denote "pretense" or "falsity" of word or attitude.

2. *plásma.* The noun has the same nuances as the verb. Mostly it denotes a "fabrication," e.g., in combination with *mýthos,* as for the world conflagration of Stoicism or the Egyptian worship of the bull. As regards his dualism, Philo does not let this interfere with his monotheism by attributing *plássein* to an inferior deity, but it has a marked effect on his anthropology.

III. Hellenistic and Rabbinic Judaism. Judaism accepts the fact that God sovereignly fashions humanity. Rabbinic exegesis makes some play with the two verbs of Gen. 1:27 and 2:7. It also discusses the role of God in relation to the two impulses and the question what earth God used in human creation, e.g., earth from the later site of the altar, or from the four corners of the world.

C. The NT.

1. Paul uses the LXX image of the potter in Rom. 9:20 to stress God's sovereignty. The words refer in the first instance to the potter, but the true subject is God. In Is. 45:9-10 the divine sovereignty brings salvation, but here it means both mercy and judgment with no possibility of appeal.

2. In 1 Tim. 2:13 Adam is said to be formed first, then Eve (cf. 1 Cor. 11:8). The LXX does not actually use the verb in relation to Eve, but Philo and Josephus do. The principle invoked is that the older ranks first; on this ground women are not to teach or have authority over men.

3. The NT does not use the group for God's saving action in history or for his new and spiritual creation, but there is in it no element of dualism, as in Philo.

D. Later Christian Usage.

1. *The Verb.* The LXX influences later Christian use of the verb more than the NT. Features of this use are praise of the Maker (Barn. 2.10), recognition of his benefits (Diog. 10.2), fear of him (Barn. 19.2), and taking his work as a model for doing works of righteousness (1 Clem. 33.8).

2. *The Noun.* Creation in Gen. 1:27 is now seen as a pointer to spiritual renewal by the remission of sins (Barn. 6.12).

plastós. Literally this word means "formed" or "formable." In dualistic works it has the sense of "merely physical." Figuratively it means "fabricated" or "forged." In

2 Pet. 2:3 the *plastoí lógoi* are the claims and teachings of false teachers, which are both speculative and immoral. These *lógoi* are *plastoí* because they lack seriousness and reflect an ethically spurious attitude.   [H. BRAUN, VI, 254-62]

→ *dēmiourgós, hetoimázō, theós, katergázomai, ktízō, poiéō*

---

pleonázō [to increase, abound],   *hyperpleonázō* [to superabound]

A. Outside the NT.

1. The *pléon* in this word first means "too much," with, ethically, a note of censure. Gradually it also takes on the sense of "much." Various things can be too much, e.g., parts of the body, status, or wealth. *hyperpleonázō*, which is very rare, is simply a more intensive form.

2. In ethics the term denotes the opposite of the golden mean. Excess stands opposed to reason or nature (cf. passions in Stoicism). In Philo, as in Stoicism, what is excessive is to be condemned and controlled.

3. In the LXX we find such senses as "to be over," "to have in excess," "to do too much," "to become great," "to increase." The meaning in the transitive is "to make great." Giving the mouth free rein for evil is the point in Ps. 50:19.

B. The NT.

1. Apart from 2 Pet. 1:8 the words are found only in Paul. They occur only in the intransitive and with abstract subjects, usually in the sense "to increase," "to superabound," and sometimes in an eschatological context.

2. In Rom. 5:20 *pleonázō* denotes the effect of the giving of the law, namely, that transgression superabounds and thus displays, not its irrationality as in Stoicism, but its ungodly reality and hence the depth of the human plight. In contrast, the grace of God abounds all the more to offset human wickedness, although this is no reason for continuing in sin. Paul's own work has the increasing extension of grace as its goal (2 Cor. 4:13ff.), for the grace of God has been rich beyond all measure to him (1 Tim. 1:13; cf. Gal. 1:13ff.).

3. If the word has a superlative sense when used of grace, it has the comparative sense of "increasing" when used of love (cf. 1 Th. 3:12; 2 Th. 1:3), with fullness as the goal. In 2 Pet. 1:8 fruit will result when the preceding qualities abound. In Phil. 4:17 Paul, in thanking the church for its gift, states that he wants fruit that will abound to their account.

4. In 2 Cor. 8:15 Paul establishes a principle of equality by liberality (quoting Ex. 16:18). Those who receive much are not to have more but to impart freely to those who have received little.   [G. DELLING, VI, 262-66]

→ *perisseúō*

---

pleonéktēs [covetous (person)],   *pleonektéō* [to covet],   *pleonexía* [covetousness]

A. The Greek Sphere. This group has the meanings a. "having more," b. "receiving more," and c. "wanting more," with a reference to power etc. as well as property. In ethics we find an extension of meaning to "outdoing others," "being superior," "taking precedence," "excelling," or "forging ahead" (at others' expense). In other developments we find such senses as "taking advantage," "taking by force," "violating" (e.g., laws), "greedily desiring" things, and "asserting oneself." In Aristotle *pleonexía* means "covetousness." Antiquity, with its basic ideal of relative equality, tries in different ways to limit excess. It posits the principle of moderation, links this to justice, and thinks covetousness damages the self as well as others, since it is a grasping for more than is ordained for us. There is no *pleonexía* in the divine world, and the checking of wants is a valuable antidote against it. Philosophy teaches the wise to avoid covetousness, and for this reason it should be taught to women as well as men. It is better to suffer wrong than to take advantage of others. Covetousness and avarice figure prominently in lists of vices, and *avaritia* plays a big part in popular Latin philosophy.

B. Jewish Greek Literature.
1. In the LXX the group is used for "(unlawful) gain." Striving for unlawful wealth leads to violence (Jer. 22:17). Ps. 119:36 asks that the heart be inclined to God's testimonies and not to gain. The powerful disregard others' rights in their lust for possessions (2 Macc. 4:50), but wisdom brings riches (Wis. 10:11).
2. The group is more common in other translations than the LXX, and always in the bad sense of material advantage and dishonest gain (e.g., usury and bribery).
3. In the Testaments of the Twelve Patriarchs the group denotes covetousness or taking advantage.
4. The words also have a negative sense in Philo, being used for covetousness, immoderation, violence, violation of human orders, etc.
5. In Pseudo-Phocylides various admonitions bear on the question, e.g., not to cling to money, to give each his own, and to avoid oppressing the poor or receiving stolen property. Love of money is said to be the mother of all evil.

C. The NT.
1. In the NT, where the group occurs mainly in Paul, taking material advantage is the sense everywhere except in 2 Cor. 2:11. Lk. 12:15 warns against increasing material possessions as a means of security. In 1 Th. 4:6 believers are not to wrong other believers; the reference is not to business, nor to the matter of v. 4, but to disputes, which God will decide. In Eph. 4:19 immorality seems to be specifically in view. The *pleonéktēs* is an idolater according to Eph. 5:3 (cf. Mt. 6:24), for covetousness means subjection to an alien power. The community is thus to shun the *pleonéktēs* along with the idolater, reviler, etc. (1 Cor. 5:10-11). The robber is also included here (cf. 6:10), probably because the *pleonéktēs* seizes more by cunning than by force; a sexual sense is unlikely.
2. In 2 Pet. 2:3 false teachers exploit believers for greed (either for money or for power). They are practiced in covetousness (v. 14). Paul himself seems to have had to face a charge of seeking self-enrichment; he defends himself against this in 1 Th. 2:5 and again in 2 Cor. 7:2. In the latter verse a figurative sense is possible (he has kept back nothing), but in the context the reference seems to be similar to that of the question in 12:17-18 (cf. the implied suspicion in 8:20).
3. Corinthian charges perhaps underlie the choice of words in 2 Cor. 9:5, where the point is that the gift, as a gift of love and not of calculation, should be a blessing.
4. In 2 Cor. 2:11 the meaning is "to overpower" or "take advantage of." Satan takes advantage if the community denies forgiveness, e.g., by splitting Paul and the community on the issue and thus disrupting their fellowship.

D. The Apostolic Fathers. Here the group occurs in ethical connections with

reference to coveting the possessions of others and often in lists of vices (cf. Barn. 10.4; Hermas *Similitudes* 6.5.5; Pol. 2.2, etc.). We never find the specialized sense of coveting the spouses of others.   [G. DELLING, VI, 266-74]

---

plḗthos [many, great], *plēthýnō* [to increase, multiply]

---

plḗthos.

A. Nonbiblical Use.

1. General Usage. This word first means "crowd," then the "many." It becomes a term of measurement first in number and then in size, e.g., denoting number, amount, duration, etc. In Plato there is mostly a human reference to a "crowd," to "people," to the "majority," or to the "totality" (in antithesis to the one or the few). When a negative sense is apparent, it is where a judgment is implied, e.g., that most people cannot be philosophers, or that orators must please the crowd. In Aristotle *plḗthos* is synonymous with *dḗmos.* It usually means "the majority" but may also mean the "whole group." A distinction is made between majority and mob rule.

2. The One and the Many in Greek Philosophy. The implied opposite of the many is the one (or the few). Some philosophers argue that plurality would entail many ones, which is impossible, but Plato thinks that the "idea" is contained in the plurality of many individual things. Plurality is thus included in unity.

B. The LXX.

1. In the LXX *plḗthos* mostly means "plurality," "crowd," "totality," "quantity." Adjectivally it signifies "much," "great," "powerful." God's love is abundant in Ps. 106:45 (*katá tó plḗthos*), and so is his righteousness in Is. 63:7. His majesty and kindness are great in Ex. 15:7 and Ps. 145:7. In contrast the people has no great strength (Ps. 33:16) and it cannot rely on its many offerings (Is. 1:11). Stress falls instead on the multitude of its sins (Ps. 5:10), but God promises it descendants as numerous as the sand or stars (Gen. 32:13; Dt. 1:10).

2. In other connections *plḗthos* has such meanings as "numerous," "many," "much," "more . . . than," and "very much."

3. For a different Hebrew term *plḗthos* first denotes "murmuring" or "roaring" and then, from "roaring crowd," it has the transferred sense of "multitude." It is far better adapted to express this, and the implied sense of noise is usually lost in the LXX. Thus in Ezek. 31:2, 18; 32:32 the original seems to have in view the tumult of Egypt, i.e., its pride, but the LXX sees a reference to the host or army.

4. In other passages we find the familiar senses of "numerous," "host," "people," "number," etc., sometimes in misinterpretation of the Hebrew (cf. Ps. 10:25; Mic. 4:13), or on the basis of other readings (Zech. 9:10).

5. In works for which there is no Hebrew original the normal meanings occur, sometimes with distinctions between the leaders (e.g., the elders or priests) and the people, sometimes with emphasis on the people as a whole.

C. The NT.

In the NT, where seven of the 30 instances are in Luke and 17 in Acts, *plḗthos* has the sense of "crowd" with a wide range of meanings (Paul and the Synoptists often have *hoi polloí* in the same sense). Sometimes the "crowd" is distinguished from a smaller group (cf. Acts 6:2, 5; Lk. 1:10). The word may also denote the totality of a group, e.g., in Acts 4:32; 14:4; 15:12. In some cases the majority may be in view, although unanimity as well (cf. Lk. 19:37; 23:1; Acts 25:24). No disparagement is implied in Acts 21:36, but there is a hint of this in 25:24; 2:6. *polý* is added at times by way of strengthening (cf. Lk. 5:6) to indicate the greatness of the number (cf. Jms. 5:20; 1 Pet. 4:8). In Lk. 8:37 "all the people" is a phrase for the "population" of the area. Without the article *plḗthos* may be used adjectivally, as in Jn. 5:3; Lk. 2:13, etc. (cf. *plḗthos* with the article in the sense of "all" in Acts 4:32). "Number" is the sense in Acts 28:3 and probably in Heb. 11:12.

plēthýnō.

1. This word first means "to fill" or (intransitively) "to become full," then "to abound." We find it for the rising of the Nile, for the abundant flow of springs, and more generally for "to increase" or "to become numerous."

2. In the LXX, where it is mostly transitive, the verb has such various meanings as "to increase," "to multiply," "to extend" (borders), "to exalt," "to heap up," etc.

3. In Heb. 6:14 (which quotes Gen. 22:17), the meaning is "to give numerous descendants." In 2 Cor. 9:10 God will bring forth an abundant harvest from the gift. In Acts 6:1 the reference is to the increase in the number of disciples, but in 7:17 the multiplying of the people in Egypt is at issue. The growth of the church is the point in Acts 6:7; 9:31, and in view of 6:7 the increase of the word in 12:24 is probably the increase in the number of believers (cf. *auxánein* in 6:7; 12:24; 19:20). The use in Mt. 24:12 stands in contrast to the passages in Acts, for here wickedness multiplies and consequently love grows cold. In 1 and 2 Peter and Jude the term occurs in salutations; 1 and 2 Peter pray that grace and peace may be multiplied (1:2), and Jude (v. 2) prays that mercy and peace and love may be multiplied. Whether the idea is that of growth or of rich sharing, the wish, which has its roots in Judaism, is certainly that the fullness of the gifts of salvation may be at work in the churches (cf. the references in 1 Pet. 1:2 to sanctification, obedience, and sprinkling).   [G. DELLING, VI, 274-83]

→ *pímplēmi, pleonázō, plēróō*

---

plḗrēs [full, complete], *plēróō* [to fill, complete], *plḗrōma* [fullness], *anaplēróō* [to fill completely], *antanaplēróō* [to complete], *ekplēróō* [to fill up, fulfil], *ekplḗrōsis* [filling, completion], *symplēróō* [to fill with], *plērophoréō* [to bring to fullness], *plērophoría* [supreme fullness]

---

plḗrēs.

1. The meaning of *plḗrēs* is "full," "filled," "manned" (ships), "full of" (e.g., sickness, delusions), "overfull" (cf. divine possession), "satisfied" (figuratively of the soul). Other meanings are "fully covered" (e.g., with fertile soil), "complete" (i.e., wholly filled), and "dense" or "thick" (i.e., fully pressed). "Fully paid" is a meaning in the papyri.

2. In the LXX, as the originals indicate, we find such senses as "satisfied," "intact," "overflowing," "full," "fully covered," and "complete."

3. Philo puts the term to philosophical, ethical, and religious use. Thus God is full of perfect goods or is perfect and complete. Philo refers, too, to the perfect good, e.g., the higher or ideal nature. Creation is complete.

4. The NT uses the term in a transferred sense to denote "rich fullness" (cf. Jn. 1:14, where grace and truth are the content, and the glory of the incarnate word which declares them is manifested). In Acts 6:8 Stephen possesses grace and power from

God in abundant measure (cf. 6:3, 5). This is a permanent endowment, but a special grace is perhaps denoted in 7:55. In Lk. 4:1 Jesus' moving to Galilee (v. 14) is fully under the direction of the Spirit. Acts 13:9 stands in marked contrast to 13:8. The magician has satanic powers, but the Spirit comes on Paul to grant him divine authority. *plḗrēs* means "full" in Mt. 14:20; 15:37; Mk. 8:19, "wholly covered" in Lk. 5:12, and "complete" in Mk. 4:28 and 2 Jn. 8.

plēróō.

A. Nonbiblical Usage. This verb means "to fill," "to man" (ships), "to fill up" (passive), "to fill" in a figurative sense (with emotions, knowledge, etc.), "to satisfy or appease" (demands etc.), "to fulfil" (directions), "to round off or pay in full," "to pay off," "to run its course" (a span of time), "to fulfil" (promises), and "to come to fulfilment" (passive, e.g., of prophecies).

B. LXX Data. In the LXX *plēróō* occurs some 70 times for forms of *mlʾ* and other terms. Literal senses are "to fill" (e.g., with strong drink, or with people), "to fill the hand with offerings" (i.e., to sacrifice), "to be filled" (e.g., rivers with water), "to become full" (the moon), "to be satisfied." Figurative senses are "to fill" (with understanding, confusion, arrogance, etc.), "to fill up," "to satisfy" (desires), "to make or become full" (e.g., divine measures or spans of time), and "to fulfil" (e.g., divine promises).

C. God Fills the World in the OT and Judaism.
1. God knows all things, for he is omnipresent (Jer. 23:24). He sees and hears all things, for he fills heaven and earth. This does not mean that he permeates it materially; it is parallel to his upholding of creation.
2. Philo bases his ethics on the thought of God filling all things. God is distinct from the world. While not embraced by the cosmos, he leaves no part of it empty. He is everywhere at work to preserve it. His omnipresence relates to his self-revelation, but also to his judgment. No one can hide from God. Philo may make paradoxical statements by using philosophical terminology, but plainly he is not thinking of spatial permeation. The divine filling contrasts with the need and emptiness of the world.
3. The rabbis express similar thoughts. The cosmos cannot embrace God. It is by grace that his glory dwells in it. It pleases him to fill heaven and earth, although he himself is in the supreme heaven or above all heavens.

D. The Content of the Word in the NT.
1. Corresponding to the literal sense "to fill" (e.g., a place, Acts 5:28, or a lack, Phil. 4:19), *plēróō* nonliterally has first the sense "to fill with a content." In the active, the subject may be abstract (Jn. 16:6), or it may be Satan (Acts 5:3), or God (Acts 2:28; Rom. 15:13). In the passive God is to be inferred as the one who fills richly (cf. Phil. 1:11; Col. 1:9). He gives knowledge and joy (Acts 13:52) with such fullness that they stamp the whole life and conduct, and claim the whole being, of the recipients. Along similar lines there is a filling with wisdom in Lk. 2:40, with the Spirit in Eph. 5:18 (in contrast to wine), and with comfort in 2 Cor. 7:4. In Eph. 4:10 Christ is the one who, having achieved dominion, dispenses the gifts of grace in fullness (vv. 7ff.). There is no reference here to spatial extension. Eph. 1:23 is to the same effect. "All" means all cosmic beings capable of will and decision, and "in all" means "in every respect" or "through all the forces that are subject to him" (v. 22). In virtue of his universal dominion Christ gives life and power to the whole church. The prayer

of 3:19 is that the recipients may be filled absolutely with God's boundless gifts. In Col. 2:10 there is a play on *plérōma*; the point is either that they have been brought to fullness in Christ's sphere of life or that they are filled absolutely by him as the Giver.

2. A second nonliteral meaning in the NT is "to fulfil a divine demand or claim." Thus (a) in Rom. 13:8; Gal. 5:14 believers fulfil the demand of the law in virtue of their new life in the Spirit (Rom. 8:4, 9-10). The idea is not that love fills up the law as though it were a vessel, but that it meets its norms. In Mt. 5:17 (b) the idea is not simply that of validating the law as distinct from abolishing it. The goal of Jesus' mission is fulfilment. He does not simply affirm the law and the prophets but actualizes the will of God that is declared in them from the standpoint of both promise and demand. An example of such fulfilment may be seen already in Mt. 3:15.

3. A third nonliteral sense in the NT is "to fill up a specific measure." The Jews (a) will fill up their fathers' guilt by crucifying Jesus (Mt. 23:32). The predetermined number of martyrs (b) is completed (Rev. 6:11). Times come to an end (c) (Acts 7:23; 9:23; Lk. 21:24). The thought of the time (*kairós*) being fulfilled in Mk. 1:15 stresses the element of sovereign decision in God rather than impersonal foreordination. The mercy of the living God has brought about a fulfilment that opens the door to faith and forgiveness.

4. Another nonliteral sense in the NT is "to fulfil prophetic sayings." God fulfils his word by actualizing it (Acts 3:18 and cf. 13:27). The NT uses various formulas for the proof from Scripture (cf. Mt. 1:22; Mk. 14:49; Acts 1:16; Lk. 4:21; Jms. 2:23; Jn. 13:18, etc.). The proof is most common in Matthew. In John it relates to details of the passion and especially to the betrayal by Judas (13:18) and rejection by the Jews (12:38). Fulfilment of Is. 53 is the answer to the apparent enigma of the death of Jesus. A final *hína* is important in the Scripture proofs, for it shows that events in Jesus' life are grounded in God's will as the OT declares this. Distinctive of the NT fulfilment is the eschatological content. God's saving will achieves its full measure in the today of the Christ event. The NT concept of fulfilment is summed up in the person of Jesus. Paul has a similar view of OT fulfilment but does not put it in *plēróō* formulas. Lk. 22:16 refers to a fulfilment of the Passover in the future consummation but does not show how. Implied at least is the interrelating of the Passover as a type with the coming redemption as its antitype.

5. A final NT sense is "to complete." With a temporal reference (a) this may mean "to finish" (cf. Lk. 7:1; Acts 13:25). Or it may mean (b) "to perform" (e.g., a divinely given task; cf. Col. 4:17; Acts 14:26; 12:25; Lk. 9:31). Or it may mean (c) "to bring to completion," "to complete," e.g., God's counsel in 2 Th. 1:11, or Paul's joy in Phil. 2:2; in the passive "to become complete," e.g., the Corinthians' obedience in 2 Cor. 10:6. Especially completed or perfected in John is joy, e.g., that of the Baptist in 3:29, that of the recipients of revelation in 15:11 (cf. 1 Jn. 1:4; 2 Jn. 12). Joy is perfected because salvation is effected with the exalting of Jesus. In Jn. 16:24 those who pray for the salvation given in fellowship with Christ have the promise of perfect joy.

plérōma.

A. Outside the NT.

I. Lexical Data.

1. The first sense of *plérōma* is "that which fills," "contents," including, e.g., cargo, crew, population.

2. The idea of what fills yields such senses as "entirety," "mass," "totality," "full measure," "consummation," also "crowd" (of people).

3. We also find the sense "what is filled" for a fully laden ship.

4. A final meaning is "the act of filling."

II. Use in Specific Literary Groups.

1. In the LXX the term mostly has a spatial reference and denotes "content," "fullness," "totality" (cf. "totality" of population or "fullness" of the earth). The sense "act of filling" is perhaps in view in Ex. 35:27; 1 Chr. 29:2.

2. Ignatius uses the term in the sense of "supreme fullness," e.g., of wishes or divine blessing. Justin has the fullness of the earth or sea in mind, and Clement of Alexandria (except in discussing Gnosticism) the means of sustenance.

3. The Hermetic writings have the term in the formal sense of fullness. Thus "God is all and one, for the fullness of all is one and in one."

4. In Christian Gnosticism *plḗrōma* is a technical term for the totality of the 30 aeons. This totality is closest to God but is his product; he stands over it. The *plḗrōma* is the supreme spiritual world from which Jesus comes and into which the spiritual enter. Implied in the use of the term are the fullness and perfection of being. In the plural the aeons are called *plḗrṓmata,* and *plḗrōma* is also used at times for the Gnostics' angelic partners who help to carry them up into the spiritual world.

5. In mystical and Neo-Platonist works *plḗrōma* has the sense of content or totality, e.g., the sum of the qualities that constitute something.

B. The NT.

1. We find the sense "that which fills" in Mk. 6:43; 8:20; 1 Cor. 10:26 (cf. also Mk. 2:21).

2. In measurement (a) we first find the sense "full measure" in various connections, e.g., the number of the Gentiles in Rom. 11:25, full maturity in Eph. 4:13. We then find (b) the sense of "fullness" in, e.g., Rom. 15:29 (blessing), Eph. 3:19 (all God's gifts), Jn. 1:16 (the grace of the incarnate word), Col. 1:19 (the fullness of the divine being in Christ), Col. 2:2-9 (the full deity). The *plḗrōma* statements in Colossians present the full unity of the person and work of God and Christ, yet in such a way that neither distinctness of person nor monotheism is imperiled. The differences between Ephesians and Colossians show that *plḗrōma* is not here a technical term, and the fact that *plḗrēs* or *plēróō* may be used instead supports this conclusion. In part the *plḗrōma* sayings relate to Christ's headship of the church. From him as the bearer of the divine fullness (Col. 1:18ff.) vital powers flow into the church, so that he may be said to fill it.

3. In Eph. 1:23 the church as Christ's body is his fullness as it is thus filled by his mighty working. Eph. 3:19 conveys similar teaching.

4. The "act of filling" is the sense (actively) in Rom. 13:10. Love here is not the sum of the law but the fulfilment of what God demands in it (cf. v. 8). "Act of filling" is also the sense (passively) in Rom. 11:12. When the number of Israel is filled up, the Gentiles will receive the fullness of eschatological consummation. Gal. 4:4 is another example. What is meant is not just that a period has run its course or that an ordained point has been reached, but that time has received its full content with the sending of the Son (cf. Eph. 1:10). God performs his eschatological act with the historical coming of Jesus. God's decree had this fulfilment of the times in view (cf. 1 Cor. 10:11); Eph. 1:9-10 shows it to be grounded in the divine will and purpose.

anaplēróō.

1. This word means "to fill completely," "to fill up," "to complete," "to do completely," "to settle up," "to terminate," and "to appease."

2. In the LXX we find the senses "to insert," "to bring to full measure," "to complete," "to be full," and in the passive "to become full," "to come to an end."

3. In the NT we find the sense "to fill a gap," "to make up for," in 1 Cor. 16:7 and Phil. 2:30. The meaning "to fill up" occurs in 1 Th. 2:16; Judaism augments its sins by opposing the gospel. "To fill a place" is the point in 1 Cor. 14:16. In Gal. 6:2 believers fulfil Christ's law by bearing one another's burdens. The passive in Mt. 13:14 relates to the fulfilment of prophecy by the rejection of Christ's message and work.

antanaplēróō. This rare compound carries the nuance of "adding to," "supplementing," or "mutually augmenting." In the one NT instance in Col. 1:24 the thought is that of a vicarious filling up of the eschatological afflictions laid on the apostle in a wholly realistic fellowship of destiny with Christ on the basis of dying with him (cf. Phil. 3:10).

ekplēróō.
1. This word means a. "to fill" (e.g., to man ships), "to make up," "to furnish" (e.g., a house), "to fill up" (state coffers), "to bring to full measure," b. "to fulfil" (a duty), "to pay" (a debt), passive "to come to fulfilment," c. "to carry out" (a plan or proposal), and d. "to appease."

2. The only NT instance is in Acts 13:33, where Paul says, on the basis of Ps. 2:7, that the good news is that God has fulfilled his promise to the fathers by raising Jesus from the dead (cf. also Lk. 24:7; 1 Cor. 15:4).

ekplḗrōsis.
1. This rare word means "filling," "completion," "perfecting," "satisfaction," "fulfilment."

2. The one NT instance is in Acts 21:26, where Paul gives notice in the temple when the days for purifying the four men will end.

symplēróō.
1. This word means "to fill with," "to fill completely," "to man," "to make complete," and in the passive "to be completed," "to become complete," "to be fulfilled."

2. Only the passive occurs in the NT. Literally the ship is being filled with water in Lk. 8:23. Days are fulfilled (i.e., the time has come) in Lk. 9:51 and Acts 2:1, with a suggestion that God's saving will is carried out in the event of Christ's going to Jerusalem or the descent of the Spirit. What is fulfilled is not just the period up to the event, but the time of the event itself, so that the term has here distinctive theological significance.

plērophoréō.
1. This late compound means "to bring to fullness" in such senses as a. "to fulfil or complete," b. "to satisfy," and c. "to convince" (passive "to come to full certainty").

2. The only LXX instance is in Eccl. 8:10, where the "full" has the sense of being "fully set" on doing evil.

3. In the NT the word means "to fulfil" in 2 Tim. 4:5 (cf. also the passive in 4:17). The meaning in Lk. 1:1 is "to accomplish," but since the reference is to the divine acts of salvation the nuance is that of bringing to fulfilment. Achieving certainty is the point in Rom. 4:21; it is because he is fully convinced that God will do what he promises that Abraham is a model for believers, saving faith being faith in the creative power of God that gives new life in Christ. The same meaning occurs again in Rom. 14:5, where Paul says that whether we observe days or not we should be fully con-

vinced in our own judgment. This may also be the sense in Col. 4:12, but the combination with *téleioi* suggests that the thought is that of being brought to full maturity or completeness.

plērophoría. This word means a. "supreme fullness" and b. "certainty." In the NT it is parallel to power and the Holy Spirit in 1 Th. 2:5 (cf. 1 Cor. 2:4). It is thus one of the terms by which Paul describes the great richness of the divine work in the church's life and mission. In Col. 2:2 (with *ploútos*) it denotes the superabundance of a knowledge of God that is epitomized in Christ as the one in whom God actively reveals himself. In Heb. 6:11 the readers do not lack the zeal that leads to full preservation (or development) of their hope. In Heb. 10:22, however, the reference is to the full assurance of the faith that rests on appropriation of Christ's high-priestly work. Formally, of course, the idea of a full measure is still present.

[G. Delling, VI, 283-311]

---

plēsíon [neighbor]

A. The Greek World. Formed from *plēsíos* ("close by"), *ho plēsíon* is the "neighbor," "the person next to one," then more generally the "fellow human being." The word is a significant one in ethical discussions.   [H. Greeven, VI, 311-12]

B. The OT and LXX.
1. *plesíon* occurs some 225 times in the LXX, sometimes prepositionally, mostly as a noun, often with no Hebrew original, in other instances for various Hebrew terms, the chief of which is *rēa'* (also rendered *phílos* and *allēl-*).

2. Heb. *rēa'* comes from a verb meaning "to have dealings," "to associate." The noun reflects the range of possible dealings from the "friend" of the king to stereotyped use in a phrase like "one another." Thus it covers the friend, lover, companion, neighbor, or fellow human being.

3. Expressed is an encounter which in the OT takes place within the covenant and thus between those who worship the one God and stand under his command. When the term occurs in the legal texts, it has a relatively general character in view of the general validity of the ordinances, so that there is no formal restriction to members of the covenant people. Yet the setting shows that the laws are given specifically to Israel, so that their unequivocal application is to members of the people, with a clear extension only to resident aliens. Thus the use of the term in, e.g., Lev. 19:18, carries both restriction on the one side and extension on the other.

4. With the restriction, voices are heard in Judaism which favor a general extension. The rendering *plēsíon* is one such voice, the more so since it is used in the legal passages. The Hellenistic Jewish tradition, then, joins forces with one stream of Palestinian Judaism which on the basis of belief in the divine likeness demands respect and consideration for all people.   [J. Fichtner, VI, 312-15]

C. *plēsíon* in the NT.
1. Used in the NT only as a noun except in Jn. 4:5, *plēsíon* means "neighbor" and shows strong OT influence; there is allusion to Lev. 19:18 in 12 instances. In his summary of the law (Mk. 12:28ff.; Mt. 22:34ff.), Jesus refers to the command to love one's neighbor as well as God; the unity of the two commands is a distinctive feature in this teaching. Paul finds in the same command the fulfilment of the law (Gal. 5:14)

or the sum of the commandments (Rom. 13:8ff.). James calls it the royal law (2:8). It epitomizes the commandments in the reply to the rich young ruler (Mt. 19:19).

2. The neighbor includes enemies as well as friends (Mt. 5:43ff.). At root, Jesus is here reversing the question. We are not to ask whom to love, for to love is to be a child of God, to be perfect as God is, and hence to love generously and spontaneously.

3. The parable of the Good Samaritan aptly illustrates this reversal. What counts is to be a neighbor to those in need. The neighbor is not generalized here, either into a compatriot or a fellow human being. An element of encounter is suggested by the term. Life itself shows who the neighbor is. The real point is not to define the neighbor but to be a neighbor.

4. In Rom. 15:2; Eph. 4:25; Jms. 4:12 the neighbor is the fellow Christian.

5. While neighbor and brother become virtually synonymous, the apostolic fathers continue to use *plēsíon* (cf. Barn. 19.5; Pol. 3.3).   [H. Greeven, VI, 316-18]

→ *agapáō, adelphós, héteros*

---

ploútos [wealth, riches], *ploúsios* [wealthy, rich], *ploutéō* [to be rich], *ploutízō* [to make rich]

A. Nonbiblical Use.

1. General Data.

a. Linguistic. This group is connected with a root meaning "to flow," which is connected to "to fill." The basic sense, then, is "fullness of goods," and *ploútos* may mean either material wealth or spiritual wealth (of wisdom etc.).

b. Lexical. Lexicography supports the linguistic analysis. Thus *ploútos* means "wealth," *ploúsios* "well-to-do," *ploutéō* "to be or become rich," and *ploutízō* "to make rich."

2. Riches and the Rich in Greek and Hellenistic Thought.

a. The Early Period. In Homer, nobility and wealth are identical. Gain or loss of either is in the hands of the gods. Wealth may consist of property and its products, but happy circumstances are also wealth. In Hesiod, wealth comes through work, which is honorable. But as in Homer, only riches bring virtue and blessing; poverty frays the nerve of life.

2. The Pre-Socratics to Aristotle. The classical period judges wealth from a social standpoint, i.e., that of its effect on the state. The pre-Socratics note that wealth confers no true security, for it is easily lost. Furthermore, the poor may be cultured as well as the rich, and wealth or poverty depends on the individual attitude. Some may decide for technical riches, but others seek the riches of virtue or wisdom. Debate arises whether wealth, poverty, or moderate possessions offer the best security in life. Plato and Aristotle find in riches a means, not an end. By liberating from labor, wealth should be a way to culture. If hereditary, it should promote a striving for justice and a dedication to virtue. Moderate wealth is best; the uncontrolled wealth that finds security in the constant accumulation of material goods leads to political ruin and renders the individual a-social. Plato, unlike Aristotle, keeps to the idea of spiritual as well as material wealth. Wisdom, virtue, and culture are the true riches.

c. The Cynics and Stoics. These groups focus on the individual rather than the state. They stress the inner attitude, but also censure riches because they bring dependence on material things. For the Cynics true wisdom is possible only for the poor. For the Stoics wealth is an indifferent matter, a loan which does not affect one's true nature or destiny. It offers some advantages when properly handled but is easily handled amiss. True wealth consists of wisdom in harmony with the cosmic order.

B. Riches and the Rich in the OT.

1. Linguistic Data. The *ploútos* group occurs some 180 times in the LXX for various Hebrew terms (especially the root '*šr*). It is most common in the Wisdom literature, including Sirach (93 times).

2. The Evaluation of Riches.

a. The Early Period. As the infrequent use of the group shows, the question of riches is not a prominent one in the early period. Wealth consists of flocks, herds, and children. Material possessions come by breeding, dowry, and booty. Wealth is a gift of God and an expression of his blessing (Dt. 28:1ff.).

b. The Prophetic Criticism. Changed social circumstances, especially the development of cities and a plutocracy, bring criticism from the prophets (Is. 10:1ff.; Am. 2:6ff.; Ezek. 22:25ff.; Mic. 2:1ff.). The charge is that they entail forced labor and the depriving of widows etc. of their rights. Wealth is gained by cunning, graft, and violence, and it is contrary to God's will for his elect people (Jer. 5:26-27; Mic. 6:11-12). The rich are ungodly, they will come to ruin with God's judgment on the people, and their riches will be scattered (Is. 5:14; 29:5).

c. The Later Tradition. What the Wisdom literature says about wealth relates to practical experience. The rich have security, friends, and honor (Prov. 10:15; 14:20). Wealth comes through frugality and industry (24:4; Sir. 31:3). But there is also danger in wealth. It easily leads to pride (Prov. 18:10ff.) and to trust in it (Sir. 11:19). One is tempted to use wicked means to attain it (Prov. 28:6). It is impermanent (Eccl. 5:12ff.), carries disadvantages (5:11), and is only a relative good, e.g., compared to health or a good name (cf. Sir. 30:14ff.). Wealth is a divine blessing (Prov. 10:22) and poverty a divine judgment, but it is seen that many who are righteous are poor while the wicked are rich (cf. Pss. 37; 48; 72). In answer, a righteous order is expected (Ps. 37), but meantime there is stress on the impermanence of wealth (Ps. 48), and faith is confident that those who seek God will never suffer real lack (Ps. 34:10).

C. Riches and the Rich in Judaism.

1. The Non-Philonic Tradition. For the Sadducean hierarchy, wealth is still a constituent part of salvation. The Essenes, however, reject earthly riches as a sign of captivity to the passing world and look ahead to an eschatological reversal. Those who combine eschatology and nationalism include wealth in their expectation as a sign and gift. The Pharisees see that riches offer an opportunity for almsgiving and observance of the law, but find in knowledge and keeping of the law the true riches. Riches and poverty are instruments of divine testing: Will the rich be generous, and will the poor accept their lot without complaint? The common denominator in these various thoughts is that God is the only giver of riches and salvation, and that riches carry an obligation toward others. Pervasive, too, is the thought of retribution. Wealth either in this world or the next is a reward for keeping the commandments.

2. Philo. Influenced by Platonic and Stoic thought, Philo regards riches as indifferent. They are transitory and involve danger to the soul, but need not be despised. Philo realizes that God has created material goods to salvation. The main point is to use them with understanding as a loan from God. God himself, however, is the true wealth that can never be lost. The thought persists that this true wealth is earned as a reward rather than received as a free gift.

D. Riches and the Rich in the NT.

1. The Attitude of Jesus to Wealth in Mark and Matthew.

a. In Matthew Jesus abandons the traditional view of riches in favor of one that is wholly theocentric and eschatological. Neither wealth nor poverty is significant in itself (cf. 27:57). The delight in riches (13:22) and the difficulty of salvation for the rich (19:22ff.) simply typify the human situation in which nothing is gained even by winning the world if the soul is lost (6:25ff.), and the anxiety of pagan life stands in marked contrast to seeking righteousness and the kingdom (6:25ff.).

b. The problem of wealth has greater independence in Mark, e.g., in the explanation of the parable of the sower (4:19) and the story of the widow's mite (12:41ff.). Wealth is an obstacle to hearing the message of the kingdom.

2. In Luke. The question of the rich occupies more space in Luke. The setting of the story of the rich young ruler shortly after the parable of the publican (cf. 18:8ff., 18ff.) shows that more than wealth is at issue (cf. the setting of the story of the poor widow, the parable of Dives, and the story of Zacchaeus; 20–21; 16:14ff.; 19:1ff.). The rich, collectively, are opponents of Jesus, for the gospel involves a total reversal of the earthly order (1:53; 14:11, 24). The rich rely on their possessions; riches are thus an obstacle to discipleship (12:19ff.; 18:22-23). The rich should restore what is wrongfully gained (19:8) and give freely with no hope of return (14:12ff.). Separation from riches in discipleship results in much gain in both time and eternity.

3. The Group in Paul. Paul redefines wealth, going back to the basic sense of "fullness of goods." Christ and his work are the true wealth of the community. Christ himself is rich (2 Cor. 8:9). He grants his riches to those who call upon him (Rom. 10:12). God is rich in kindness and glory (Rom. 2:4; 9:23). Christ's word dwells richly in the community (Col. 3:16), which is rich through Christ's poverty (2 Cor. 8:9) and to which God has declared the riches of the glory of the mystery (Col. 1:26). God is rich in mercy and grace (Eph. 1:7; 2:4). The community knows the riches of his glorious inheritance by the Spirit (1:18). The apostle proclaims the unsearchable riches of Christ (3:8). This wealth is poverty to the world (1 Cor. 1:23). The way to it is that of Christ, who, though rich, becomes poor to make the world rich (2 Cor. 8:9). Thus the apostles, being poor, make many rich (6:10). True wealth consists of the love that self-sacrificially follows Jesus, not seeking its own (1 Cor. 13:4ff.), nor bragging about its riches, but trusting the God who supplies all needs according to his riches in glory (Phil. 4:19), and thus ready to give freely to others (2 Cor. 8:1ff.). Material wealth is simply an instrument in the ministry of love; one is to deal with it as though having no dealings with it, for it has no dignity of its own (1 Cor. 7:31).

4. The Other NT Writings. Warnings are given against coveting riches in 1 Tim. 6:9 and against trusting in riches in 6:17ff. Regard for wealth and estate is condemned in Jms. 2:1ff. The rich should boast of their low estate (1:10-11); they are prone to violence (2:6-7), fraud (5:4), and voluptuous living (5:5), and their gold and silver, which rust, will witness against them at the judgment (5:3). The usage of Revelation is similar to that of Paul. The Lamb is worthy to receive riches (5:12). The church at Smyrna is truly rich (2:9), but that at Laodicea, though rich, is really poor and should seek its true wealth by repentance (3:17ff.). The rich of Babylon, who have gained their wealth by wickedness, will fall with their city (18:3ff.). In Heb. 11:25-26 Moses regards abuse for Christ's sake greater riches than the treasures of Egypt.

E. Riches and the Rich in the Postapostolic Period.

1. The Apostolic Fathers. The apostolic fathers follow NT teaching. Barnabas speaks of the rich declarations of God (1.2) and of grace having a rich source in God (1.3). Hermas in *Similitudes* 2.8 shows that wealth is useless as such, and in *Mandates* 8.3 etc. he warns against the luxury to which it leads. Yet wealth is God's gift (Hermas *Similitudes* 1.8). The poor whose prayer is rich toward God should intercede for the rich, who in turn should sustain the poor by material gifts (*Similitudes* 2.4ff.).

2. Clement of Alexandria and Cyprian. Clement in his work on the salvation of the rich teaches the ethical indifference of wealth and poverty; both rich and poor are open to temptation, and neither wealth nor poverty can decide their eternal destiny. The true rich are rich in virtues. Yet riches come from God, and their worth is decided by the use to which they are put, and hence by the attitude of those who have them. Proper use accords with Christ's will and takes the form of service to others. Cyprian, and later Basil of Caesarea, accept this view, but with more stress on avoiding bondage to wealth and the resultant seduction from Christ. The implied tension in the attitude to riches corresponds to the position of Christians as those who are in the world but not of it.   [F. HAUCK and W. KASCH, VI, 318-32]

→ *thēsaurós, mamōnás, pénēs, pleonexía, ptōchós*

---

pneúma [wind, breath, life, Spirit],   *pneumatikós* [spiritual],   *pnéō* [to blow, breathe],   *empnéō* [to breathe in],   *pnoé* [wind, blowing],   *ekpnéō* [to breathe out, die],   *theópneustos* [inspired, God-breathed]

---

pneúma, pneumatikós.

A. *pneúma* in the Greek World.

1. The Meaning of the Term.

1. Wind. From a root denoting vital force acting as a stream of air, *pneúma* first means wind both in its movement and its rarefied materiality. The wind may be stormy, or a normal wind, or a breeze, or even a vapor. It has an effect on climate, health, and character, and is seen as both natural and divine.

2. Breath. A second sense of *pneúma* is breath, inhaled and exhaled in breathing, and ranging from snorting to the fading breath. Poetically *pneúma* denotes the sound that human breath produces by blowing on flutes etc.

3. Life. Breath is a sign of life, and by way of the idea of the breath of life, *pneúma* comes to be used for life or living creature.

4. Soul. As the principle of life, *pneúma* means much the same as *psyché*. Bound to the body in life, it escapes it with the last breath and returns to the ethereal sphere.

5. Transferred Sense of Spirit. In a transferred sense *pneúma* is used for the spirit that blows in interpersonal relations. Thus it may denote the spirit of a city, or the influence of the gods or other people, or various forms of excitement.

6. pneúma and noús. In contrast to *noús* (mind), which resembles the calmer medium of light, *pneúma* (spirit) is a dynamic term suggesting the forceful movement of air that seizes us with elemental power and catches us up into tension or movement.

7. Mantic pneúma. In manticism and mantic poetry, *pneúma* is the spirit that stirs, enthuses, fills, and inspires (cf. priests, poets, and prophets). It may also denote lofty rhetorical speech, the captivating flow of the orator, etc.

8. Divine pneúma. Elemental and uncontrollable, *pneúma* is felt to be divine (e.g., in divine music). But there is in Greek no sense of a personal holy spirit. The divine spirit is immanent.

9. God and pneúma. In Stoicism *pneúma* is a cosmic power or substance, and as such it may be seen as the being or manifestation of deity itself.

10. Non-Greek Development of Meaning. Under Jewish and Christian influence there is a twofold development of meaning. On one side *pneúma* is severed from nature and personified as the active cosmological or soteriological Spirit or God. On the other it is materialized as a demonic magical force that magicians manipulate for good or ill.

II. pneúma in Mythology and Religion.

1. Life-Creating pneúma. On the basis of the connection between wind or breath and generation and life, the idea is widespread that there is conception by wind. This concept may be found in poetry and natural science, and passes into the Stoic theory of *pneúma.* In both Egypt and Greece one reads of the gods begetting life by their breath. The mode of generation distinguishes the divine operation from human conception in accordance with the difference of essence or substantiality.

2. pneúma and Inspiration. The breath of wind or breathing is a form by which higher divine forces impart something of their power either for good or evil. Plato still uses *epípnoia* for inspiration, reserving *pneúma* for natural science. He distinguishes four forms of inspiration corresponding to the four cultural spheres, namely, poetic, mantic, mystic, and erotic.

a. Poetic. When Hesiod is called to be a poet, the Muses breathe into him a divine voice. Socrates ironically refers to his divine gift of poetic speech. A divine force (*pneúma*) lifts the poet above the normal order. Manticism offers a prototype.

b. Manticism. At Delphi Apollo in a kind of sacred marriage fills the woman with divine breath. The *pneúma* sets the Pythia in an ecstatic state which entails physical effects (e.g., streaming hair, panting breath, etc.). Sound effects are associated with the giving of the oracle. The *pneúma* fills the house, and especially the inner being of recipients, carrying them off into the ecstatic sphere, and disclosing hidden things. Uncontrollable, it possesses rather than being possessed, and its theme, content, and source are divine. Mantic inspiration of this kind fills with deity, as Plato puts it, and thus makes people ministering organs of the gods. But it also robs them of understanding, so that their utterances are not their own. The philosopher is needed to assess and interpret the sayings, just as the priests at Delphi clarify the burblings of the Pythia to make them valid oracles. For Plato mantic inspiration is the prototype for poetic inspiration and for the element of enthusiasm in his own philosophy. Plutarch takes up and develops this concept. While rejecting direct inspiration, under Stoic influence he suggests that a natural force acts as the medium of inspiration in poetry and prophecy. This does not lead to irreligion, for the earth and the sun, which bring forth *pneúma,* are for Plutarch divine essences. In Iamblichus divine inspiration or spirit is a pure gift from the gods. Spirit here is more closely associated with light than breath, and *epípnoia* is spiritualized as illumination. While *pneúma* is divine, the deity itself is distinct and more worthy of reverence. Not all people are equally adapted for operations of the *pneúma.* The simpler and younger are more receptive. The intensity and forms of manifestation are as different as the gods (or angels and demons); union with the deity is the supreme form.

III. pneúma in Natural Science and Philosophy. The term *pneúma* does not seem to play much part in earlier physical theories; *aér* and *psyché* are more common terms. Later, of course, the three are equated as the comprehensive life-principle that integrates all things. In medicine *pneúma* is more important. As the air that is taken in with breathing and nourishment, it is a vital and decisive element in health. Distinction is made between the colder external air and the warmer internal air that circulates in the body and has its seat in the heart. For Aristotle *pneúma* is the breath of life that gives soul to varying degrees. In higher creatures outward *pneúma* is added to inner *pneúma*. Both moving and moved, it brings warmth and directs and sustains the body in its movements and experiences. Stoicism makes of this scientific theory a universal principle which explains the whole world in its constitution, unity, tension, and vitality. *pneúma* is here a separate substance that unites fire and air, that is the source and principle of the four elements, that permeates and gives soul to all reality in all its forms, and that is also the basis of individuality in ascending degrees of purity from the inorganic to the organic and finally the human world. Even as the chief organ of the soul, *pneúma* is not a mere principle but a substance, although in rarefied form; the rational *pneúma* is a portion of the most rarefied cosmic divine *pneúma*. It embodies God in the inner being of humanity. *pneúma,* then, is both the vital force and substance that generates and permeates all things, and the rational soul whose functions of guidance and control it executes. In the indissoluble unity of matter, power, life, and form, *pneúma* is ultimately God, who is by nature *pneúma*. Destiny, then, is a pneumatic power, and in religion, myth, and poetry, Zeus is the cosmic *pneúma*. Because Stoicism regards *pneúma* as material, however, Plotinus finds in *psyché* a higher principle; *pneúma* can no more constitute the essence of life than blood. In Hermetic writings *pneúma* belongs to the ethereal sphere, has the form of immaterial light, and forms a bridge between body and soul, enabling the soul both to descend into the world and also to ascend out of it. Whether people are good or evil depends on whether the *psyché* rules the *pneúma* on which it rests or is ruled by it. Here again *pneúma* is matter; it is thus a phenomenon of second rank in the cosmic and human world.

IV. The Greek Concept of pneúma and the NT.

1. In spite of formal parallels, e.g., the idea of *pneúma* as a power, *pneúma* plays only a secondary role in Greek thought as compared to the NT. Belonging to the material world, it is never "spiritual" in the NT sense. As a cosmic factor, it is a vital, impersonal, natural force. It can be the seat or agent of mental and spiritual functions but not their true subject. Stoic monism makes it the essence and power of deity permeating the cosmos, but the saying in Jn. 4:24 offers only a formal parallel. The Apologists and Alexandrians see the difference; God, for them, cannot be material *pneúma*.

2. Even in poetry and manticism *pneúma* is never wholly free from matter. Here, of course, it is something exceptional imparted to the few and bearing an ecstatic character. Again there is a formal parallel to the Holy Spirit and spiritual gifts, but in assessing these the NT avoids the religious vocabulary of secular Greek, coining instead a new and distinctive term like glossolalia.

3. Greek thought has a theoretical interest in the process and nature of *pneúma*. This interest is alien to the NT, which is oriented to the divine content.

4. In medicine, philosophy, and religion, *pneúma* has a mediatorial role on the border between the material and the immaterial. The Holy Spirit plays a similar part,

but the theological presuppositions are totally different. Secular Greek knows no person of the Spirit as a divine entity; *pneúma* is always a thing, not a person.

5. The Greek view can never completely break free from the idea of *pneúma* as a natural phenomenon. In the NT, however, this idea is no longer present when the Spirit is proclaimed as the Spirit of truth who reacts to sin and gives birth to faith in Christ. The fundamental difference between the Greek and NT concepts is that a different God stands behind them. [H. KLEINKNECHT, VI, 332-59]

B. Spirit in the OT.

I. Review of the Term.

1. *rû(a)ḥ in the OT.*

a. Breath, Wind.

(a) Breath of the Mouth. As breath of the mouth, *rû(a)ḥ* means breath (cf. Job 19:17) in such expressions as drawing breath (Job 9:18), gasping for breath (Jer. 2:24), breathing heavily (Job 15:13), the breath of life (Jer. 10:14).

(b) Breath of air. As wind, *rû(a)ḥ* may be a soft wind (Job 4:15), a daily west wind (Gen. 3:8), a strong wind (Is. 32:2), a tearing wind (Ps. 55:8), a hot wind (v. 11). The four winds are the four corners of the earth (Zech. 6:5). Figuratively wind is vanity or futility or deception (Job 6:26); we read of windy knowledge, speech, etc., as well as of vain striving.

b. Human *rû(a)ḥ*.

(a) The Life Principle. *rû(a)ḥ* gives life to the animal or human body (cf. Gen. 7:22). Its entry gives life (Ezek. 37:5-6), its removal means death (Ps. 104:29). Terms used in this connection are reviving, vanishing, languishing, expiring, becoming powerless, etc.

(b) Seat of the Emotions, Intellect, and Will. Emotionally we find such concepts as disquiet, unhappiness, despondency, lack of spirit, impatience, irritation, bad temper, terror, jealousy, arrogance, etc. Intellectually there are references to cleverness, insight into divine mysteries, artistic sense, and planning; negatively to lack of perception, error, and lack of religious or moral insight. Volitionally associated ideas are readiness for things, attitudes of will, courage, forbearance, freedom, longing for God, renewal, and, negatively, unfaithfulness and ungodliness.

(c) Divinely Effected *rû(a)ḥ*. God, the God of spirits (Num. 16:22), gives vital force (Is. 42:5), upholds it (Job 10:12), and takes it away (Ps. 10:29). Life is in his power (Job 12:10). He causes disquiet (2 Kgs. 19:7), gives fervor (Zech. 12:10), grants reason (Job 32:8), and imparts artistic sense (Ex. 28:3). He is behind planning (Jer. 51:1) and may frustrate it (Is. 19:3). He gives or hardens the moral power of the will (Ezek. 11:19; Dt. 2:30). The divine spirit is given with laying on of hands (Dt. 34:9).

c. God's *rû(a)ḥ*.

(a) Effective Divine Power. God's *rû(a)ḥ* gives power to the cherubim (Ezek. 1:12) and Samson (Judg. 13:25), and sets the prophet on his feet (Ezek. 2:2). It induces ecstasy (Num. 11:25), lifts up (1 Kgs. 18:12), snatches away (Ezek. 3:14), gives prophetic speech (Gen. 41:38), grants visions (Ezek. 8:3), endows with the gift of leadership (Judg. 3:10), and is behind human wickedness (Judg. 9:23).

(b) Creative Divine Power. God's power creates life (Ezek. 37:9), injects (37:14), sends (Ps. 104:30), and withdraws it (Job 34:14). It creates the cosmos and life within it (Gen. 1:2; Ps. 33:5). It gives mental abilities, e.g., artistic skill, enlightenment, and wisdom (Ex. 31:3; Dan. 5:14). It gives the gift of prophecy (Mic. 3:8). It equips for kingship (Is. 11:2). It also gives moral qualities, e.g., sanctification (Is. 59:12). It is a power to judge (Is. 4:4) and to save (Is. 32:15). It gives help (Ps. 143:10), shows what is right (Neh. 9:20), and is put in the hearts of the people (Is. 63:11).

(c) God's Inner Nature. *rû(a)ḥ* denotes God's sustaining power (Is. 31:3), omnipresence (Ps. 139:7), wisdom and power (Is. 40:13), command (Is. 34:16), holiness (Is. 63:10), and patience (Mic. 2:7).

(d) Personal Being. *rû(a)ḥ* has a personal aspect in 1 Kgs. 22:21; Ezek. 37:9; perhaps Is. 48:16.

2. *nᵉšāmâ in the OT.*

a. As Breath. This word occurs for strong breathing in Is. 2:22, for God's wrathful breath in Is. 30:33.

b. Human Breath. The reference is to the breath of life in Gen. 7:22, to vital force in Is. 42:5, to living things in Dt. 20:16, to the seat of understanding or inspiration in Job 26:4.

c. God's Breath. Used of God, the term refers (a) to the principle that gives life (Job 33:4) and (b) to that which gives insight (32:8).

3. *'ôḇ in the OT.* This term occurs in the OT with reference to a. the spirits of the dead (Lev. 19:31) and b. those who conjure up such spirits (1 Sam. 28:3, 9).

II. The Spirit of God.

1. God's Spirit represents true power in Is. 31:3. The Spirit changes the desert into paradise in Is. 32:15ff. The power of the Spirit has an ethical character (cf. Is. 30:1). It fashions creatively (Ps. 51:10-11). It works through the servant (Is. 42:1ff.). It perfects the people (Ezek. 36:26-27). It is already at work (Is. 31:3); the transformation of the people takes place through divine judgments in history (Ezek. 11:19; 18:31; 36:26). It both ends and consummates Israel's history. This is not polytheistic power but the personal work of God's will. Divine powers are not habitually present in humanity. People are subject to God's power. Though experienced as God's work, it is inscrutable. Even the prophets do not give precise details of its operation. Its dynamic is plain, but its logic defies analysis.

2. God's Spirit is creative, life-giving power (Gen. 1:2). All life derives from this dynamism (cf. Gen. 2:7). By it God sustains his work (cf. Job 34:14). The Spirit's power is personal. It is no immanent force of nature; nature is de-deified in the OT. God's creative power is free, sovereign, and inscrutable (cf. Gen. 6:3). Its dynamism is known but unsearchable.

3. By the Spirit, God raises up charismatic leaders, e.g., Gideon, Saul, and David (Judg. 6:34; 1 Sam. 11:6; 16:13). The mysterious aspect here finds expression in ecstasy (1 Sam. 10:6). Ecstasy marks the descent of the Spirit on the 70 elders (Num. 11:24ff.). Again we see God's unpredictable and irresistible power. The dynamism is known but the logic is hidden.

4. Similar phenomena occur in other religions, but prophecy lifts the thought of God's *rû(a)ḥ* out of religious and ethical neutrality and sees it as the teleological will and work of personal divine power in creative historical action. God's Spirit expresses his inner nature and presence. Even in judgment God is present as the Lord of history (Hag. 2:5). His is finally a saving action (Zech. 6:1ff.). His Spirit seals his covenant faithfulness (Is. 59:21).

5. The OT even anchors the demonic in the concept of spirits that come from God. Thus God sends an evil spirit in Judg. 9:23 and a lying spirit comes from God in 1 Kgs. 22:19 (cf. Job 1:6ff.). Cosmic spirits are thus deprived of their autonomy.

C. Spirit in Judaism.

I. pneúma in the LXX.

1. The Translation of the Hebrew Terms.

a. The LXX uses *pneúma* 277 times for *rû(a)ḥ*, *ánemos* 52 times, and various other words on occasion.

b. The usual rendering of *nᵉšāmâ* is *pnoḗ*.

c. *engastrímythos* is the normal equivalent of *'ôḇ*.

[F. BAUMGÄRTEL, VI, 359-68]

2. pneúma as Wind. Two references for this sense are Jon. 4:8 and Jer. 4:11.

3. pneúma as Breath of Life.

a. God sends, controls, and withdraws this breath (Job 27:3; Dan. 5:4; Tob. 3:6). One may yield it up but not retrieve it (2 Macc. 12:19; Wis. 16:14).

b. The vital force can retire temporarily (Dan. 10:17) and then return (Judg. 15:19) or be restored (1 Sam. 30:12).

c. The *pneúma* constructs and fills the world as cosmic spirit (Jdt. 16:14). God is the God of spirits (Num. 16:22), but the LXX avoids the dualism of a material and a spiritual world (cf. Is. 31:3).

d. In the last time God gives the *pneúma* as resurrecting power (Ezek. 37:6, 14).

4. pneúma as the Power of Blessing and Punishment. In Is. 11:4 *pneúma* and *lógos* are parallel. God gives a spirit of stupefaction in Is. 29:10. The *pneúma* inspires the teacher of wisdom in Sir. 39:6.

5. pneúma as Spiritual Ability, Resolve, Constitution of Soul. God fills with artistic sense and gives understanding (Ex. 28:3; Job 32:8). He stirs up a will to build (1 Esdr. 2:5). *pneúma* is the seat of the functions of the soul (Wis. 5:3). Fullness of thoughts constrains (Job 32:18). The spirit may lack, or may be given, understanding (Job 20:3; Sus. 45). Courage ebbs (Jdt. 7:19) and flows (1 Macc. 13:7).

6. pneúma as Eschatological Gift. God's Spirit may be one of judgment and burning (Is. 4:4). God can destroy by a breath (Wis. 11:20). His breath of judgment is like a stream in flood (Is. 30:28). It puts the unclean spirit to flight (Zech. 13:2). In the day of salvation the Spirit will bring animals together (Is. 34:16). God will give his people a new spirit (Is. 44:3). He will pour out his Spirit and give a spirit of grace and pity (Joel 2:28; Zech. 12:10). The Spirit will stand in the midst of the people (Hag. 2:5). The servant will bear the Spirit (Is. 42:1). Those who cannot escape the Spirit (Ps. 139:7) but commit their spirits to God (Ps. 31:5) long for messianic salvation (Is. 26:18).

7. pneúma in Ecclesiastes. pneúma is always an anthropological-psychological term in Ecclesiastes. *proaíresis pneúmatos* is the LXX term for vain striving in 1:14; 2:11; 4:4, etc. The same expression occurs in 2:22 for the arbitrariness of the human spirit in its aspirations.

8. pneúma in Wisdom.

a. The Principle of Life. The author of Wisdom thinks God inbreathes or loans the principle of life (15:11, 16). God gives himself to the individual entity, so that while people lose the breath of life at death they gain immortality (5:15).

b. Wisdom. The *pneúma* as wisdom is granted in answer to prayer (7:7). It is a power of clear insight that is oriented to the good. It does not permeate all things or people, but only the prayerful, thoughtful, and morally pure, who may thus be called *pneúmata* (7:23). The *pneúma* that fills the *pneúmata* is superior to all things human, free from care, unlimited in possibility, able to see and hear all things, and uniquely related to God (1:7). As a spirit of discipline, it has no fellowship with evil. Representing God's activity in the world, it has some hypostatic independence, but is still subject to God (9:17). Whether it is material or immaterial is not stated; God is the immaterial God, but he acts in the material world. The *pneúma* shares God's transcendence and yet also his participation in events. The *pneúma* may be equated with the *psyché* on the one side, but it is identical with *sophía* on the other. The author thus perceives a twofold cosmic activity of the *pneúma* which is to the advantage both of the elect and of all humanity.

II. pneúma in Hellenistic Judaism.

1. Philo.

a. *pneúma* in Philo is a term for the higher element of the air, for wind, and for human and animal breath.

b. *pneúma* as the substance of air holds things together; all matter is permeated by it, and by its binding power the earth itself consists.

c. Blood and *pneúma* are the soul's essence. The nonrational soul has blood as its essence; the rational soul, which is distinctively human, has *pneúma*. *pneúma* is the impress of divine power that begets thought.

d. Different is God's *pneúma*. As rational beings, humans receive the divine *pneúma* by inbreathing. The total life of the soul is a divine gift. The refined purity of the mind of heavenly humanity depends on participation in the divine *pneúma* as distinct from the *pneúma* as the impress of divine power (cf. Gen. 1:2; 2:7). Philo's statements about the divine *pneúma* are hampered by his philosophical vocabulary, but for him the influx of the spirit has an ethical character and he maintains the divine transcendence over against Stoic pantheism. At times he calls the *noús* the divine *pneúma*, but only if those who bear it make ethically good decisions. If reason is a genuine impress of the divine *pneúma*, it is the divine *pneúma* only on an ethical basis. If imprecise, the distinction that Philo makes here is a firm one.

e. The Prophetic Spirit. Philo refers to the prophetic spirit but believes that he himself, as an expositor, has the spirit of inspiration like Moses. The prophetic spirit is the supreme divine spirit conferring knowledge that even the *noús* (mind) cannot have in spite of its spiritual endowment. The worlds of rational enlightenment and divine prophecy meet in the sage. Pneumatically permeated rationalism reaches its limit in prophetic ecstasy. The new thing received with the divine *pneúma* points to the world of revelation of a transcendent God. If rational beings receive the divine *pneúma*, they live in the forecourt of a pneumatic reality imparted to the chosen in prophetic ecstasy.

2. Josephus. The usage of Josephus is related to that of the LXX and Philo. *pneúma* is the constitution of the soul or the seat of martial ardor. Saul has an evil spirit. *daimónia* are equated with the *pneúmata* of the wicked dead, and the divine angel and the divine *pneúma* are equated. Josephus normally avoids *pneúma theoú* for the spirit of inspiration. He uses it only when the reference is to the biblical prophets, preferring *pneúma theíon* for present inspiration. Zealots and Essenes prophesy, but they have nothing to do with God's Spirit. In *Antiquities* 1.27 Josephus has *pneúmatos epithéontos* for the Spirit of God of Gen. 1:2; he probably has breath in view, but the Latin rendering (*spiritus dei*) suggests the cosmic Creator-Spirit.

[W. BIEDER, VI, 368-75]

III. rû(a)ḥ in Palestinian Judaism.

1. Wind, Quarter of the World. As in the OT, *rû(a)ḥ* is the common term for "wind." We also find the expression "the four winds"; thus *rû(a)ḥ* can denote "side" or "direction."

2. Angels and Evil Spirits. Beings in the heavenly world can be called spirits, especially in apocalyptic. The elemental spirits are a special class reigning over natural events. The fallen angels, mingling with women, have begotten evil spirits that live on earth. Belief in demons is widespread among religious leaders and scribes as well as the people. Satan and the evil spirits are God's foes seducing or harming people. They arise only in a distortion of God's creation. Thus absolute dualism is avoided, and their activity is integrated into God's rule. In the last time they will be bound and punished.

3. The Deceased. The term spirit also applies to the deceased in graves who may roam the earth at night or may be guests in heaven to overhear divine secrets.

4. The Human Spirit. Later Jewish anthropology strongly underlines the idea of the human spirit.

a. Vocabulary. It is hard to fix distinctions in the terms that denote the human soul. Various words are used, but the soul is one. A relative distinction is made linguistically between the soul as vital force and the soul as it comes down from heaven, but there are many exceptions.

b. The OT Legacy. The OT view of spirit as vital force and the seat of spiritual functions remains the same in Judaism, with an emphasis on the emotional and volitional element, e.g., the proud, rapacious, or humble spirit, the spirit which may be refreshed with joy or given rest. God's spirit finds pleasure in those whose human spirit finds pleasure in him.

c. Spirit and Body. The rabbis develop the distinction between body and soul—the former earthly, the latter heavenly and hence preexistent and immortal. At creation, God already creates a fixed number of souls that are stored up until bodies are ready. These souls are pure and holy and must be returned to heaven pure and holy. The preexistent soul is the spirit that God puts in us. It preserves some independence of the body, as in sleep. After death, it is in a hidden place in heaven or in the realm of the dead awaiting reunion with the body at the resurrection for judgment. The souls of the righteous are kept apart from those of the wicked. At the resurrection, when soul and body are reunited, life is restored either by the returning human spirit or by the Spirit of God.

d. Age of the Ideas of Preexistence and Immortality. These ideas exist quite early in Hellenistic Judaism. The thought of the immortality of the spirit may be found in Palestinian Judaism in Jubilees and Ethiopian Enoch. The Pharisees accept both the soul's immortality and the resurrection. Preexistence, however, is less clearly taught in Palestinian Judaism. The ideas of the soul coming from heaven and of a fixed number of people occur, but these do not necessarily imply preexistence, for which there is firm attestation only from the second century A.D.

e. The Historical Problem. Palestinian as well as Hellenistic Judaism shows Greek influence in its anthropology. On the other hand, the ancient view that the spirit that comes from God is the vital force in humanity remains. The OT legacy thus prevents a complete Hellenizing, especially by ruling out the view that the body is the seat of evil.

5. The Spirit of God.

a. Terminology. In apocryphal and pseudepigraphical writings we find the titles "the Spirit," "God's Spirit," and occasionally "the Holy Spirit." The spirit in us may be called the spirit of God, but the Spirit of God in the strict sense is an entity that is separate from us.

b. The Works of the Spirit.

(a) The OT speaks about a spirit of wisdom, understanding, etc., and increasingly these qualities are seen as works of God's Spirit. Prophecy in particular is a work of the Spirit, and so is a moral life. Knowing all human deeds, the Spirit may accuse in the judgment.

(b) The Spirit finds manifestation in light or sound, but in the rabbis God's Spirit never appears as a dove.

c. The Spirit and the OT. For the rabbis the Spirit is the prophetic Spirit who speaks in the OT. Each book is inspired by the Spirit and hence canonical. In exposition some passages may be ascribed to Israel or other speakers and some directly to the Spirit. Some words may even be said by the Spirit to God. But Scripture as a whole is still inspired by the Spirit.

d. The Spirit and Righteousness. The gift of the Spirit is for the rabbis a reward for righteous conduct which further promotes such conduct. The Spirit turns aside from sinners and will not work in unclean places. At first the Spirit works among the Gentiles (cf. Balaam) but he is then restricted to Israel. Health and strength of body and soul are also conditions for the gift of the Spirit.

e. Past, Future, and Present Endowment with the Spirit.

(a) Great figures of the past, e.g., the prophets, Rebekah, Jacob, the righteous, speak and act under the Spirit's influence. This applies especially to the patriarchs and to those who write Scripture.

(b) In the last time the Messiah will have the Spirit, although the Messiah is not equated with the Spirit. The redeemed righteous will also receive the Spirit, undergoing moral renewal by an alteration of the human spirit which either God or the Spirit effects. On the basis of Ezek. 36:26-27 and 37:14 resurrection by the Spirit is expected.

(c) Although the great age of prophetic inspiration has passed, those who obey the law may receive the Spirit today. Apocalyptic writers speak and write in the Spirit in the names of others, and occasionally there are prophetic experiences. The rabbis do not expect the Spirit as in the past, but they think that a life that pleases God leads to the Spirit, and rabbis at times have visions through the Spirit. Ordination is not viewed as impartation of the Spirit, although later the thesis is advanced that the Spirit is not taken from the wise, i.e., the scribes.

f. The Cosmic Function of the Spirit. The Spirit's function at creation finds a place in Judaism but is secondary in the rabbis to the concept of the Spirit as the agent of prophecy and a gift to the righteous.

g. The Autonomy of the Spirit. The rabbis often speak of the Spirit in personal categories, e.g., speaking, sorrowing, rejoicing, etc. Yet the Spirit is not a separate heavenly being like an angel. He is an objective divine reality encountering us, and as such may also be described in impersonal categories. This reality represents God but is not identical with God. The personal categories derive from the rabbis' love of personification and are always associated with words of Scripture. For all the Spirit's autonomy, the Spirit finally is God's Spirit and comes from God. The Spirit is not a substitute for God's presence nor is the Spirit identical with the Shekinah. Since he comes from God and represents him, his possession means a link with God himself.

h. The Spirit as Advocate. This thought is only weakly attested in Judaism. It occurs clearly only in expositions of Prov. 24:28-29 and in a passage where the *bath qol,* which is a substitute for the Spirit, is called an advocate.

[E. SJÖBERG, VI, 375-89]

D. Development to the Pneumatic Self in Gnosticism.

I. The Dead Sea Scrolls and Their Influence.

1. When the soul is seen as a responsible ego that survives death, the question of its salvation becomes an urgent one, for dealings with the Spirit of God seem to be involved, and speculation arises as to the nature of life after death. In Judaism the idea that the Spirit is the power of ethical goodness becomes increasingly important. Under the impact of Persian dualism, the Spirit as a determinative force is the good for which one has to decide. At Qumran a struggle is seen between the spirit of knowledge and the spirit of darkness. The counsels of the good spirit command various virtues. One must either live by the power of God's Spirit or fall victim to evil. At the same time, the Spirit may be the human spirit embracing both understanding and acts and hence identical with the self.

2. Similar thoughts occur in the Testaments of the Twelve Patriarchs and the Hermetic writings. Contrasted with the good Spirit are evil spirits. These strive for control of people, who are then indwelt by them and do either good or evil. A problem, however, is that the human spirit represents responsible existence before God. A possible solution is to view the human spirit as the spirit that is determined by ethical decision and thus given back to God either corrupt or intact and renewed.

II. Gnosticism.

1. The Problem: The Spirit as Creator of Matter. In contact with Greek thought the creative role of the Spirit in Gen. 1:2 becomes highly significant as Spirit is understood increasingly in terms of substance. If spirit denotes divinely given spiritual existence, Hellenists equate this with the soul that comes from God, is imprisoned in the body, and will return to the heavenly sphere. A parallel thought in Judaism is that of the restoration of paradise, with the associated ideas of a primal and eschatological man, easily construed by Hellenists in terms of the myth of a descending and ascending god, and the identification of believers with the destiny of the god. Put in the language of substance, this means that the original heavenly substance comes into matter to liberate the substance of the human soul. But how, then, can the Spirit be the Creator of matter?

2. The Redemption of the pneúma from Matter. For Gnostics, God is spiritual by nature. Somehow spiritual substance has been bound to matter and must be freed from it. The answer lies in the distinction of *pneúma* from *psyché*. The *pneúma*, which is of the nature of God or Christ, is a seed or spark that Christ gathers up and takes back with him when he consigns body and *psyché* to chaos and commits *pneúma* to God. Redemption is completed with the reassembling of redeemed *pneúmata* into the great spiritual body.

3. Trichotomy. The separation of the *pneúma* from the *psyché* produces a threefold division of humanity. Early triads include *noús, psyché,* and *sóma,* or *theíon, psyché,* and *sóma.* In Judaism the Spirit of God stands over against the human body and soul. Here the idea of a transcendent *pneúma* is decisive. The same idea recurs in Irenaeus, for whom the Spirit of God is the power that resurrects body and soul, although granting perfection by adding spirit.

E. The NT.

I. Mark and Matthew.

1. The Demonic and Anthropological Spirit. Of the 23 *pneúma* sayings in Mark, 14 refer to an unclean spirit or the like. Matthew has "spirits" in 8:14. Anthropologically in Mk. 2:8 and 8:12 *pneúma* is the seat of perceptions and feelings, and in Mt. 27:50

it is the vital force. In Mk. 14:38 the spirit that is willing in contrast to the weak flesh is not a better part. On the basis of Ps. 51:12, it is the Spirit of God that is given to us and that strives against our human weakness.

2. *The Spirit as the Power of God. pneúma* is mostly used in Mark and Matthew for God's power to perform special acts. Not to see God at work in Jesus' exorcisms is to blaspheme against the Spirit (Mk. 3:28ff.). The community finds here an assurance that the Spirit is with it, and hence an enhancement of the seriousness of the decision it demands. Yet the emphasis is on forgiveness; judgment falls only when there is willful defiance that does not want forgiveness. Mt. 12:28 equates the power of the Spirit in exorcisms with the presence of the kingdom (cf. 12:18, where the healings are seen to denote the dawn of the end-time). Mk. 1:12 is to the same effect. As in the OT, the Holy Spirit is the irresistible power of God operative in the salvation event.

3. *General Endowment with the Spirit.* The Spirit is equated with Scripture in Mk. 12:36 and is active in the present in Mk. 13:11, where the Spirit's speaking is a sign of God's help in affliction. Mk. 1:8 mentions a general endowment with the Spirit. The imparting of the Spirit corresponds to eschatological expectation. The addition "and fire" in Mt. 3:11 may suggest judgment, and if so, the Spirit hints perhaps at a stormy wind that scatters the chaff. Yet already in baptism believers undergo a sifting and purifying judgment which is itself deliverance.

4. *Jesus' Endowment with the Spirit.* In Mk. 1:9ff. Jesus' baptism is more than a prophetic call; it depicts the endowment of the Messiah with the Spirit, as attested by the dove and the heavenly voice. God's new age begins, although this beginning involves no conflict with Jesus' prior conception by the Spirit. Jesus is unique in virtue of God's direct work upon him at decisive points. The Hellenistic categories of substance are not used; God himself is at work.

5. *Verses Peculiar to Matthew.* In Mt. 5:3 the reference is not to those who are poor in the Holy Spirit. The dative is one of relation; the blessing rests on those who are not rich in religious knowledge or achievement but who find their sole help in God. In Mt. 28:19 the new feature is the association of the *pneúma* with the name. Once the Lord is associated with God, it is easy to associate the Spirit too. This is not the result of speculation or logical inference. It rests on the fact that God is encountered only where he confronts the community, i.e., in the Son, or in the Spirit in whom there is encounter with the Son.

6. *Jesus' Conception by the Spirit.* Mt. 1:18ff. does not narrate the event but has an angel dispel suspicion about Jesus' conception. As in Luke, the Spirit is God's creative power fashioning the life of this unique child. Popular writings and the exegesis of Is. 7:14 in Hellenistic Judaism form a background, as do many religious parallels. The creative power of the Spirit (cf. the OT) is simply transferred to the process of conception.

7. *Summary.* The paucity of statements about the Spirit in Mark and Matthew is surprising. Yet it supports the fidelity of the tradition. The temptation to portray Jesus as a pneumatic is resisted. He is clearly the bearer of the Spirit, as his power and authority demonstrate. Yet he does not speak much about the Spirit, perhaps because his disciples cannot understand such things until his work is complete. When the community experiences the outpouring of the Spirit that stamps it as the people of the end-time, it realizes that this rests solely on the coming of Jesus and faith in him. Yet it also perceives that to depict Jesus as a pneumatic is to suggest that he makes it the people of the end-time merely as Example or Teacher. The real point is that God meets his people in Jesus. The Spirit-statements stress his uniqueness, his eschatological

status, the direct presence of God in him (cf. Mt. 12:18, 28; Mk. 1:10; 3:29-30; Mt. 1:20). The Spirit is God's power making possible speech and action that are beyond human resources. The phenomena of the Spirit are subordinate to the realization that the messianic age has dawned. They have a christological reference.

II. Luke and Acts.

1. The Relation of the Spirit to Jesus. In Luke and Acts *pneúma* occurs three times more often than in Mark. In Lk. 4:1 Jesus is full of the Spirit, not subject to the Spirit but acting by the Spirit. In 4:18 the Spirit abides on Jesus. In the conception by the Spirit (1:35), the *pneúma* is God's life-giving power, but the result of the act is what counts, namely, that Jesus has the Spirit from the first. If the Spirit is later given at baptism, this does not denote growth but shows that each actualization is a new divine act. Himself having the Spirit, Jesus dispenses the Spirit after the resurrection (24:49). Jesus, then, is not a pneumatic like pneumatics in the church. The Spirit manifests himself for the first time in Jesus, and through Jesus comes to the community (cf. Acts 2:33; 10:14, 19).

2. The Abiding of the Spirit with the Community. The Spirit does not leap on the community and then leave it. He shapes its whole existence, not as a natural possession, but as God's abiding Spirit. Thus the term "full of the Spirit" (Acts 6:3; 11:24) stresses the lasting union, while repeated "filling with the Spirit" retains the dynamic aspect (4:8; 13:9).

3. The Outward Manifestations of the Spirit. At the baptism of Jesus, "in bodily form as a dove" stresses the objectivity of the event. The same applies to the phenomena at Pentecost (Acts 2:1ff.) and the earthquake of Acts 4:31. Glossolalia is also an outward manifestation. The Spirit subordinates physical nature to God by extending his work to this area.

4. The Works of the Spirit. In Lk. 12:10 the Spirit is the power of God in the inspired sayings of the witnesses of Jesus; he is the Spirit of prophecy (cf. 4:23ff.). In Luke healings are not associated with the Spirit but with the name of Jesus, with faith in Jesus, with Jesus himself, with prayer, with bodily contact with apostles, and with the power of Jesus. The Spirit enables disciples to speak with tongues and to prophesy (Acts 2:4; Lk. 1:41, 67). He also grants discerning of the heart (Acts 13:9). Above all he gives power to preaching. Prophesying is *the* work of the Spirit. The eschatological community is a community of prophets. In Acts 5:3, 9 it is hardly likely that we have blasphemy against the Spirit. Perhaps the idea is that the lying is to those who are full of the Spirit (cf. 13:9). A special event takes place in Acts 8:39. Along with prophecy, the Spirit grants other gifts and is also at work in the ethical life of the community. If, as a Hellenist, Luke is interested in the visibility of the Spirit's work, under OT influence he stresses the centrality of prophetic proclamation in this work.

5. The Spirit as a Feature of the Age of the Church. Lk. 11:13 promises the Spirit to those who ask (cf. Mt. 7:11). The Spirit is the absolute gift. The coming of the Spirit is an eschatological event which fulfils the promise of the Spirit to the people of the end-time (cf. Num. 11:29). All the baptized possess the Spirit (Acts 19:2). The Gentiles are included (15:8-9). Endowment with the Spirit goes hand in hand with coming to faith. The outpouring of the Spirit (Acts 2:1ff.) is a renewal of the covenant paralleling in some sense the lawgiving at Sinai. The church age begins, bringing a new speech which all may understand. Yet the Christ event, not the outpouring of the Spirit, is the true eschatological event at the center of time. Hence there can be new outpourings of the Spirit when new steps are taken (cf. 8:17-18; 10:44-45). Again, there may be filling with the Spirit even before the coming of Jesus (Lk. 1–2). At the same time, the Spirit is now given to the church in totality. All God's people are prophets. The Spirit gives believers special gifts enabling them to express their faith in an ongoing history of mission. Luke does not specifically attribute faith, salvation, or obedience to the Spirit. Nor is prayer the Spirit's work. These things precede endowment with the Spirit, which is more specifically an enablement to discharge special tasks. By not attributing the mere existence of the community to the Spirit, Luke reminds it of the task which is indissolubly associated with its existence.

6. *The Reception of the Spirit.* The Spirit comes with baptism in 2:38; 9:17-18; 19:2, but precedes baptism in 10:44ff. Baptism is not, then, a necessary means of obtaining the Spirit. In the case of Apollos and those at Ephesus, the point is not to relate baptism to the Spirit but to show the movement of salvation from the OT by way of the Baptist to the church. Baptism is a self-evident expression of conversion and as such it is related to the imparting of the Spirit. But prayer and faith are the true preparation for reception. In Acts the freedom of the Spirit is to the fore. If baptism is important, the Spirit may come on people before it (10:44) or without it (2:1ff.). Only in 8:14ff. is endowment with the Spirit linked with the apostolic laying on of hands. Here, however, the relationship with Jerusalem may be the important point. As there is a link with Judaism in Lk. 1–2, so believers in new regions are now associated with the existing community. Prophets and apostles come from Jerusalem (11:27; 8:14). Both Jesus and Paul journey to Jerusalem. God's history goes out from Jerusalem and returns to it. The new act of the Spirit relates to previous acts.

7. *Different Meanings of pneúma.* Anthropological use occurs in Lk. 1:48, 80, but with a strong sense of divine power (cf. Acts 17:16). The spirit is the part that survives death in Lk. 8:55. In Lk. 24:37 *pneúma* denotes a shadowy, noncorporeal existence which does not constitute the true I (v. 39).

III. Paul.

1. OT and Hellenistic Strands.

a. The Problem. Thus far the Spirit has been seen as the sign of what is still to come. His outpouring is a prelude to the parousia. His gifts, however, confer power for historical mission. Hellenism finds this a difficult thought, for in its view power means substance. Gnosticism, then, works out the idea that Jesus as the Bearer of the Spirit brings a heavenly substance into the world, attachment to Jesus being attachment to this substantial power. Along these lines the impartation of the Spirit is itself salvation. The role of Jesus is primarily to give instruction. The cross loses its role, and the incarnation becomes a deception of hostile powers.

b. Hellenistic Ideas in Paul. For Paul the cross and resurrection are the great turning point, and life in the Spirit is the life of the new creation: the new existence of the community and not just an added phenomenon. In Rom. 1:3-4 the *pneúma* denotes the heavenly sphere (cf. 1 Tim. 3:16; 1 Pet. 3:18). Jesus is Son of David in the flesh and Son of God in the Spirit. At his resurrection Jesus, already God's Son in v. 3, is designated the Son by entry into the sphere of divine glory, which stands opposed to the earthly sphere. Yet while the relationship of Christ to the Spirit may be formally a statement about his substance (as in Hellenism), materially it is a statement about his power. The Lord's spiritual body embraces all the members (cf. the phrase "in Christ"). The one body is Christ himself (1 Cor. 12:12). It is not just a coming body but the existing body into which believers are baptized. The *en pneúmati* of 1 Cor. 12:13 is probably instrumental ("by one Spirit"). The Lord is equated with the Spirit in 2 Cor. 3:17. The point of the saying is that turning to Jesus is turning to the new covenant in the Spirit and hence the removal of the veil that rests over the old covenant.

To come to Christ is to come into the sphere of the Spirit. The term "Spirit of the Lord" denotes Christ's mode of existence and the power with which he encounters the community. In his powerful action he is equated with the Spirit, in his lordship over it he is differentiated from the Spirit. The union of believers with Christ in his spiritual body comes out plainly in 1 Cor. 6:17. Christ is a life-giving Spirit in 1 Cor. 15:45, and as such he will give believers a spiritual body (v. 44). Union with Christ insures believers of spiritual life, which is life in the community.

c. Primitive Christian Eschatology. Paul differs from Gnosticism by starting with the resurrection. He never speaks of the spiritual substance of the preexistent Lord. The idea of the spiritual body of the risen Lord is simply an aid to understanding. The spiritual body will be given only at the resurrection as a creative act of the risen Lord. No spiritual body underlies the earthly body. Paul's opponents perhaps believe in a spiritual body that will survive death. For Paul, however, our present image is that of the man of dust (v. 49). We are heavenly only in faith in Christ, who one day will make us heavenly in resurrection reality. Paul does not suggest, of course, that the body itself is a continuum, first physical and then spiritual. The body is marked by weakness and corruptibility. Continuity between the physical and the spiritual body is a work of God's creative power. Humanity is first made *of* dust but will then be made *from* heaven. The spiritual body is not made of *pneúma* but controlled by *pneúma*. The terms may be Hellenistic, but the matter is biblical. Similarly, in 1 Cor. 6:14 it is clear that consubstantiality with Christ, which the sexual union seems to express, is not the real point. What counts is that God has raised up Jesus and will raise up believers with him. The body here is not a physical substance; it is distinguished from the stomach (v. 13). The union with Christ, though bodily, is personal, not physical. Rom. 8:11 also starts with the resurrection. The God who raised up Jesus is already at work in believers by the Spirit, and in virtue of the work of the Spirit the righteous will rise again.

d. *pneúma* as a Sign of What Is to Come. If the resurrection and the parousia are decisive, the Spirit is a sign and pledge of what is still to come. The Spirit is the firstfruits (Rom. 8:23) or seal (1 Cor. 1:22). His mighty acts (1 Th. 5:19; Eph. 5:18) are manifestations of his presence. Paul can list tongues, healing, and miracles among these acts (1 Cor. 12). Formally these may resemble the ecstatic phenomena of paganism, but confession of Christ as Lord is a criterion by which to distinguish them (cf. 1 Jn. 4:2 and the ethical test in Mt. 7:16). All Christians are bearers of the Spirit (1 Cor. 14:37). All have gifts—some extraordinary, some not (cf. Rom. 12:7-8). Speaking in tongues has no special importance (1 Cor. 14:5ff.). The criterion of the extraordinary does not apply. The true criterion is confession of Christ and hence the edification of the community.

2. Paul's Interpretation.

a. The Problem. Paul adopts Hellenistic terms that enable him to present the Spirit as representing the new existence in relation to Christ. But he corrects Hellenistic thought along OT lines by showing that salvation is not a human possession. The Spirit represents the new life, for the new creation is present, but there is this new creation and new life only by the decisive event of the cross and resurrection.

b. *pneúma* as the Power of Faith. In 1 Cor. 2:6ff. the Spirit is the power that mediates understanding of the gospel of the cross. The Spirit fixes both the form and content of preaching. The content is formally Gnostic ("the depths of God" in v. 10) but materially it is the very opposite (God's saving work at the cross). The wisdom of God revealed by the Spirit (vv. 7ff.) is foolishness to the nonspiritual (v. 14). The cross divides the old world and the new. If the Spirit is the power that takes us out of the old age, union with the Lord is given, not in pneumatic materiality, but with the knowledge that the Spirit gives of the crucified Lord. The significance of the spiritual body, then, is that of entry into the saving event of the crucifixion and resurrection. Bearers of the Spirit do not live by a new substance but wholly by God's work. The Spirit gives the new life, but not as supplementary miraculous power nor as substantial possession. The new knowledge is supernatural, yet not because it is taught or received ecstatically. The knowledge relates to the act of divine love at the cross, and the miracle is believing that God is for us in Jesus Christ. Hence the Spirit is the Spirit of faith (2 Cor. 4:13). The primary gift is confession of Christ (1 Cor. 12:3). No human merit secures the Spirit (Gal. 3:14). The work of the Spirit lies in ongoing as well as initial faith (Gal. 5:5). The whole life of sonship derives from the Spirit (4:6). Integration both into God's saving event and hence also into the body of Christ is ascribed to the Spirit (1 Cor. 6:11). Being in the Spirit is the same as being in Christ, for the Spirit, as the subjective cause of justification, reveals Christ. The orientation is still to the future. Thus the hope of righteousness (Gal. 5:5), or awareness of the coming redemption (Rom. 8:23), is the gift of the Spirit. The Spirit is no magical power but the power of God for affirmative life. Creating faith, the Spirit is the norm by which faith lives. Thus in Gal. 5:25 the Spirit is the power of God that sustains life, but believers must let their lives be shaped thereby. To live in the Spirit is to renounce the flesh and to be responsive to God and neighbor.

c. Renunciation of the Flesh. The antithesis of Spirit and flesh is that of divine power and human weakness (Gal. 3:2, 5). Living in the Spirit is relying on God's power, not on one's own strength. Worshipping God in the Spirit means having no confidence in the flesh but glorying in Christ (Phil. 3:3). Revelation of God's work by the Spirit demands renunciation of human wisdom (1 Cor. 2:6ff.). Circumcision of the heart in the Spirit sets aside human criteria (Rom. 2:29; cf. 2 Cor. 3:6). Whereas the law uncovers sin, and even incites to it, the Spirit gives the new life of service (Rom. 7:5-6). In Gal. 4:25ff. the two births (by the flesh and the Spirit) represent living by human possibilities and living by divine promise. In Gal. 5:17 believers are not just neutral. The flesh is their own will, but having crucified the flesh they may live and walk by the Spirit. Their life is thus determined by whether they sow to the Spirit or to the flesh (6:8). The liberating norm of the Spirit is that God has done what the law could not do. While the flesh to which one might sow is one's own, the Spirit is a divinely given possibility. To walk in the Spirit (Rom. 8:4-5) is to accept the normative power of God. This implies a decision of faith, although this, too, is God's act. On the basis of God's saving work, those who walk in the Spirit fulfil the law (Rom. 8:4). The antithesis of Spirit and flesh is not a cosmological factor. It arises through God's act in Christ as this is accepted by the Spirit in faith, or rejected.

d. The Spirit as Response to God and Neighbor. The proper act of the Spirit is prayer (Rom. 8:15, 27; Gal. 4:6). The Spirit bears witness to the sonship established in Christ and makes the life of sonship possible. Sonship, however, means service, meeting the demands of the law and not fulfilling the desires of the flesh (Rom. 7:5-6). Loving others is faith at work (Gal. 5:6, 14). Living by Christ, by grace, by the cross, means freedom from the law and freedom for love. The Spirit produces fruit, not works (5:22). But this fruit finds expression in concrete acts, e.g., of worship (1 Cor. 12–14) and love (1 Cor. 13). Love includes all else (Col. 1:8). Yet love relates to faith and is oriented to other gifts. Similarly, when the Spirit sanctifies (Rom. 15:16; 1 Cor. 6:11), this means both that he sets us in God's saving action and that he enables us to live thereby in obedience. He does not destroy individuality (as in Gnosticism) or bring separation from others by knowledge, for knowledge is subordinate to love. The Spirit frees from self and opens up to others, restoring an individuality whereby one may stand before God and live for one's neighbor. The community thus becomes a regulative concept. Spiritual gifts are valuable if they edify, and each has some gift. The Spirit as God's power allows no appeal to wonderful religious potentialities but makes trust in oneself impossible and opens up the self to a life of love. The cross is both the ransom and the call to repentance, i.e., to the shattering of false security. The Spirit is no additional phenomenon. The Spirit is the power of God bringing people to faith in Christ's cross and resurrection, both as a dynamic force and as the basis of a lasting being in Christ. This power determines the new life of faith.

3. The Spirit and Christ. In Rom. 8:1ff. Paul alternates such phrases as the Spirit dwelling in you (v. 9) and Christ being in you (v. 10). This might suggest that the exalted Christ is Spirit, but "in the Spirit" might also be taken instrumentally. Paul's concern, of course, is not to differentiate Christ and the Spirit as persons, but to state in what sphere of power believers live. The *pneúma* in Paul is often impersonal (1 Th. 5:19), and the term may alternate with wisdom or power (1 Cor. 2:4-5). Indeed, the *pneúma* may be the spirit that is given to us. Even if the *pneúma* is said to speak etc., the same is said of wisdom or the flesh. Nevertheless, the Spirit is not an obscure or anonymous force. The Lord is present by the Spirit (cf. 2 Cor. 3:17-18), and God, Christ, and Spirit are associated inasmuch as they encounter believers in the same event (cf. 1 Cor. 12:4ff.). In 2 Cor. 13:13, the genitive could be objective (cf. Phil. 3:10), but the parallels are against this; fellowship with the Spirit (as granted by the Spirit) is the point. The three terms also occur together in Rom. 5:1ff. and Gal. 4:4ff., which show that God's work in the Son or Spirit is always genuinely God's own work. The mode of relationship is not, of course, an issue.

4. The Anthropological pneúma. Since the Holy Spirit affects the whole person and cannot be explained psychologically, Paul adopts popular anthropological ideas quite freely. He uses *pneúma* for psychological functions in 1 Cor. 7:34; 2 Cor. 7:1. It is parallel to *psyché* in Phil. 1:27, denotes the whole person in 2 Cor. 2:13, and is equivalent to "you" in closing greetings (Gal. 6:18; Phil. 4:23). In the last resort, however, the *pneúma* is for Paul the God-given *pneúma* that is alien to us (cf. 1 Cor. 14:14; Rom. 1:9). In 1 Cor. 5:3ff. the *pneúma* seems to be the new I of faith which will be saved if purifying judgment is exercised on the flesh. Paul's *pneúma*, however, is his divinely given authority. The human *pneúma* is not the soul perfected by the Spirit, for it, too, is given by God (Rom. 8:15). The secret of Paul's use lies in the priority of the work of the Holy Spirit and the determination of the believer's existence thereby. The Spirit manifests Christ's saving work and makes responsible acceptance of it possible. Hence *pneúma* denotes both God's Spirit and the innermost being of those who no longer live by the self but by God's being for them.

5. pneumatikós. The *pneumatikoí* are for Paul those who know God's saving work by the Spirit (1 Cor. 2:13-15). The *psychikoí* do not know it and are thus controlled by the spirit of the world. A distinction is made between pneumatic and physical bodies in 1 Cor. 15:44-46. The spiritual know spiritual things (*pneumatiká*; 1 Cor. 2:13; 9:11; Rom. 15:27) in contrast to earthly things, i.e., those pertaining to natural life. Spiritual gifts are called *pneumatiká* in 1 Cor. 14:1. The law, too, is *pneumatikós* (Rom. 7:14). It is the law of God (vv. 22, 25) deriving from the divine world, not the human.

IV. John.

1. The Significance of Eschatology. John strongly proclaims the presence of the salvation that will one day be consummated. He does not depict Jesus as a pneumatic, nor ascribe his words and acts to the Spirit. In Christ one meets the Father himself and not just his gift. The descent of the Spirit in Jn. 1:33 demonstrates but does not effect the divine sonship of Jesus. It is believers who are born of the Spirit in 1:13.

2. pneúma as a Sphere in Antithesis to sárx. pneúma and *sárx* represent the spheres of God and the world in Jn. 3:6; 6:63. *pneúma* is the equivalent of *theós, sárx* of *diábolos* or *kósmos.* God is *pneúma* in 4:24. The eschatological hour has come, but it is a summons to encounter with God in Christ, not a meeting of the substance of God with a similar substance in humanity. To worship God in *pneúma* is not to worship in one's own spirituality but to worship in the world of God and hence of true reality. The true God (1 Jn. 5:20) has entered the world in Christ. True worship is thus oriented to the incarnate Son. To know truth is to know the true God in Jesus (cf. Jn. 8:32; 17:3). "In spirit," then, is equivalent to Paul's "in Christ." No worship is "in spirit" unless it is based on the divine act in Christ.

3. pneúma as Life-giving Power in Antithesis to sárx. In Jn. 3:3ff. *pneúma* is the divine world that is accessible only to those who live in the spirit because they are born of the Spirit. For John life is knowledge (17:3). Christ abolishes the distinction between God and world. The *pneúma* is the world of God as the sphere that controls the new life. Birth of the Spirit is the given realization that in Jesus God has come into the world. This realization is not within human capability. It means renunciation of human possibilities and acceptance of God's gift in faith. The wind (*pneúma*; 3:8) is like the Spirit, but the point is that those who are born of the Spirit are compared to the wind; the world knows nothing of their whence or whither. Although faith leads to love, the world has no criteria by which to measure regeneration by the Spirit. In 6:63 the *sárx* profits nothing but the *pneúma* gives life through Jesus' words. Here (cf. vv. 51ff.) the *sárx* is that of Jesus, which avails only when the *pneúma* grants the realization that life is to be found in it, i.e., when the Spirit shows in the *sárx* of Jesus the glory of the Father. We are not to try to take the external element spiritually (cf. the sacraments), nor to seek life in it alone; we can discern glory and find life only in the Spirit's power. Similarly in 7:38-39 the point is that the Spirit as the water of life will flow into the community in proclamation by word and act, but only after the death of Jesus. In the imparting of the Spirit in Jn. 20:22 the Spirit is the power of proclamation which leads to the knowledge of the true God that means life. The authority of this proclamation is of decisive concern.

4. The Paraclete. As the Spirit of truth (14:17; 15:26; 16:13), the Paraclete represents the world of reality. In him the world of God, present in Jesus, will continue to be present in the word (17:13ff.). He is in the disciples (14:17). The disciples know both him and Jesus (14:17; 16:3), who are both sent by the Father (14:24, 26), teaching and witnessing, yet not speaking about themselves (17:14; 14:26; 8:14; 15:26; 14:10; 16:13). The Paraclete is another Paraclete in whom Jesus comes but who is not Jesus (14:18; 16:7). He abides with believers forever (14:16). He alone truly discloses Jesus to them (14:26), showing that the historical Jesus is the Son and giving force to his words (16:8ff.). While the Spirit's own words are the same as those of Jesus (6:63) and the community (20:22-23), it is thus that he is advocate and supporter. God is *pneúma,* and only those who come to him are in the *pneúma.* But *pneúma* is not a heavenly substance; *pneúma* is the power that gives encounter with God through the knowledge of Christ, the power that is present in the proclamation of the community, shaping the life of the eschatological people of God and in so doing summoning and judging the world.

V. The Rest of the NT.

1. The Pauline Circle.

a. Ephesians. *pneúma* is here the power of growth (3:16), of prayer (6:18), and of revelation (1:17). The Spirit works in Scripture (6:17). The one Spirit is related to the one body of Christ (4:4). An evil *pneúma* works in the lost, and evil spiritual powers rule in the air (2:2; 6:12). The Spirit is a seal in 1:13-14; 4:30, although with no sense of a substance.

b. The Pastorals. Here we have formulas in 1 Tim. 3:16; 2 Tim. 4:22. The prophetic Spirit is at issue in 1 Tim. 4:1. Everyday qualities manifest the work of the Spirit (cf. 2 Tim. 1:7). In Tit. 3:5 the Spirit effects the new birth which means justification and hope. 1 Tim. 4:1 refers to seducing spirits.

2. Hebrews.

In Heb. 12:23 the spirits are the departed. In 1:14 angels are meant. The Spirit who speaks in Scripture is at issue in 3:7; 9:8; 10:15. *pneúma* and *psyché* are distinguished in 4:12. Miracles are works of the Spirit in 2:4; 6:4-5. The Spirit apportions his gifts as he wills (2:4) and offers a foretaste of the coming aeon (6:4-5). He is a sign of eschatological grace in 10:29. In 9:14 Christ offers himself as one who comes from the sphere of the Spirit and who has the Spirit; hence he brings a salvation that lasts beyond the *sárx*. The *diá* ("through") denotes the nature and manner of the sacrifice.

3. The Catholic Epistles.

a. James. The use in Jms. 2:26 is anthropological (body and spirit). Similarly in 4:5 the spirit is the spirit which God has set in us and will require of us.

b. 1 Peter. The Spirit of 1 Pet. 1:11-12 is the prophetic Spirit working in the OT prophets and the apostles. In 1:2 the Spirit is the power of sanctification. The spirit of glory rests on those who are reproached for the name in 4:14. 3:18-19 and 4:6 refer to the spheres in which judgment and deliverance are enacted. In 3:19 the *en hō* probably has the general sense "wherein"; one event of the resurrection is intended. The spirits in prison are the departed, not demons. The dead of 4:6 are probably not the spiritually dead and can hardly be dead Christians. "Judged in the flesh" seems to refer to death as a judgment in the earthly sphere.

c. 2 Peter and Jude. In 2 Pet. 1:21 the Spirit is the prophetic Spirit inspiring canonical Scripture. In Jude 19-20 worldly people are devoid of the Spirit, but believers pray in the Spirit as they also keep themselves in God's love and wait for the mercy of Christ.

d. 1 John. In 1 John the *pneúma* marks the great turning point of the ages; this consists of Christ's abiding in his people (3:24). The Spirit is a gift (4:13). He bears witness (5:6ff.) as the power of proclamation. His testimony to the incarnate Christ opposes the spirit of antichrist (4:2ff.). This is the criterion by which to know his authentic utterances.

4. Revelation.

Unclean demonic forces are *pneúmata* in Rev. 16:13-14; 18:2. The Spirit of prophecy plays a dominant role (19:10). The *pneúma* gives visions and leads off into wonderful regions (17:3; 21:10). In 11:8 *pneumatikós* means "in prophetic speech." The Spirit still speaks (14:13); the one through whom he speaks is immaterial (cf. 2:17; 14:13). The Lord speaks as the Spirit speaks (cf. 2:1, 7, 8, 11). The church calls for its Lord in the power of the Spirit (22:17). The seven spirits are probably the seven archangels; grace and peace go forth from them (1:4); they stand before the throne (4:5); they are sent out over the earth (5:6); they represent the Spirit in all his fullness; they are also parallel to the angels of the churches. If they depict God's work in concrete figures, the work is still God's, and they thus represent God's own action.

F. The Apostolic Fathers.

1. The Gnostic-Substantial Strand. Three dangers develop in the post-NT period. First, Christ tends to be made a spiritual substance. This applies to the preexistent Lord in 2 Clem. 9.5; Hermas *Similitudes* 9.1.1. Even Ignatius sees in Christ a union of the substances of flesh and spirit (*Ephesians* 7.2; *Smyrneans* 3.2-3).

2. The Ecstatic Strand. Second, the Spirit is confused with psychological phenomena (Hermas *Visions* 1.1.3), which may be a reward for special faith (1 Clem. 2.2).

3. The Official Strand. Third, those instituted to office are seen to have the guarantee of endowment by the Spirit (Ignatius *Philadelphians* 7.1-2; 1 Clem. 4.1-2).

pnéō, empnéō.

1. *pnéō* denotes a. the blowing of the wind, b. breathing or snorting, c. wafting forth, and d. full of, or panting for.

2. The first two senses occur in the LXX (cf. the wind in Ps. 148:8 and the breath of God in Is. 40:24). *empnéō* occurs for the inbreathing of the soul in Gen. 2:7.

3. In the NT the blowing of various winds is what is meant in Mt. 7:25; Jn. 6:18; Lk. 12:55; Rev. 7:1. The blowing of the wind denotes the Spirit's work in Jn. 3:8. Only in Acts 9:1 do we have the sense "breathing out" (*empnéō*).

4. The sense "to be fragrant" occurs in Mart. Pol. 15.2 (the scent of the dying martyr is like incense) and Ignatius *Ephesians* 17.1 (the anointed Jesus wafts incorruption on the church as a divine fragrance).

ekpnéō.

This word means "to breathe out," "to blow out," "to flag," "to expire." In the NT it occurs only in Mk. 15:37, 39 with a suggestion of the vital force leaving the body at death. Mt. 27:50; Jn. 19:30; Lk. 23:46 show that the true self may still survive with the handing over of the spirit to God.

pnoḗ.

1. This word means "blowing" (wind or fire), "snorting," "afflation," the "sound" of a wind instrument, e.g., the flute.

2. In the LXX it denotes the stormy wind as God's breath (2 Sam. 22:16). The human spirit is God's inbreathing (Job 27:3). *pnéō* is the human spirit or wisdom in such passages as Prov. 1:23; 11:13; 20:27; 24:12.

3. Philo in *Allegorical Interpretation of Laws* 1.33.42 suggests that *pnoḗ* in Gen. 2:7 signifies the spirit that is created in the divine image.

4. A mighty wind (*pnoḗ*) announces the Spirit's coming in Acts 2:2. The Creator gives the breath of life to all people in 17:25.

theópneustos.

This word is used for the wisdom or dreams that come from God. In the NT it occurs only in 2 Tim. 3:16, where, along with "sacred," it describes the OT writings that have divine authority. In the Hellenistic world the idea of inspiration is common but seldom refers to writings. In Judaism, however, God inscribes the commandments on tablets (Ex. 24:12) and inspires the prophets (Num. 24:2ff.). The law, being taught, dictated, or written directly by God, has supreme authority, but later works, being inspired by God, have a secondary authority. Philo regards all the OT authors as prophets. 2 Tim. 3:16 advances no particular theory of enthusiastic inspiration, uses no comparisons such as that of the flow of air through the flute, and offers no criteria such as the agreement of witnesses, the age of the writing, or the fulfilment of prophecies. The stress is on the work of Scripture.

[E. SCHWEIZER, VI, 389-455]

---

pnígō [to choke, strangle], *apopnígō* [to choke], *sympnígō* [to choke out], *pniktós* [choked, strangled]

---

1. In this group, which comes from tragedy, the compounds are more common but have the same meanings as the simple form: a. "to stifle," b. "to choke," c. "to strangle," "throttle," and d. figuratively "to afflict," "to alarm." In the passive *pnígesthai* often means "to drown." The verbal adjective *pniktós* means "strangled" or "suffocated."

2. The group is rare in the LXX (cf. 1 Sam. 16:14-15; Nah. 2:13).

3. In the NT the swine are drowned (Mk. 5:1ff.), the seed is choked by thorns (Mt. 13:7; Lk. 8:7; Mk. 4:7), i.e., by riches, cares, desires, or pleasures (Mk. 4:13ff.; Mt. 13:22; Lk. 8:14), the wicked servant seizes his fellow servant by the throat (Mt. 18:28), and the crowd almost suffocates Jesus (Lk. 8:42) when he is on his way to raise Jairus' daughter. The use of *pniktón* raises special problems in Acts 15:20, 29; 21:25. It is open to textual challenge, especially in Acts 15. The issue is the prohibiting of certain foods on the basis of Lev. 17:13-14; Dt. 12:16, 23. The OT regulations had been sharpened by the rabbis, but the NT does not use the terms found in the LXX, preferring *pniktón,* which does not occur there. It seems that the practice of eating the flesh of strangled or choked animals falls under the OT prohibition, and since Gentile customs are connected with the cultus they cause particular aversion to Jews, including Jewish Christians. The apostolic decree in its four-membered form is a measure taken against pagan practices. [H. BIETENHARD, VI, 455-58]

---

poiéō [to create, make, do, act], *poíēma* [creation, work, action], *poíēsis* [creating, making, doing], *poiētḗs* [Creator, maker, doer]

A. God's Action as Creator and in Dealings with Humanity.

I. The Greek World and Stoicism.

1. In myths *poiéō* denotes the creative activity of deity. Zeus creates all things, including heaven and the gods. Plato has the term for creating by the chief deity but not for fashioning by the demiurge. God is *ho poiṓn.*

2. The Stoics seldom use the group for their deity. The *lógos ho theós* dwelling in *hýlē* is *tó poioún* for Zeno etc., but later writers do not use the group apart from Epictetus with his more personal view of God as *poiētḗs* or *patḗr.* Stoicism in general is more interested in the permeation of the world by deity and its resultant beauty and harmony.

II. The LXX.

1. The LXX often uses the group for God's creative activity. God created heaven and earth (Gen. 1:1ff.). He created humanity (1:27). He is *ho poiésas* (Prov. 14:31). He is the Creator of the chosen people (Is. 43:1). *poíēsis* denotes either his creating (Ps. 19:2) or his creation (Sir. 16:26).

2. The LXX often uses the terms for God's dealings in history. The *poiḗmata* denote his actions or works (Eccl. 1:14). These take the twofold form of judgment (Num.

14:35; Ezek. 5:10) and salvation (Ex. 13:8). Signs and mighty acts testify to his working (Ex. 15:11; Dt. 11:3).

3. Angels etc. execute God's word (Job 40:19; Ps. 103:20).

III. Rabbinic Judaism. The rabbis often refer to God's creation, e.g., in prayer and thanksgiving. The Qumran writings see in God the creator of the two kinds of spirits. The creation of man and woman by God is an argument against polygamy. Miracles display God's creative work.

IV. Josephus, Philo, and the Hermetic Writings.

1. Josephus uses LXX language with only slight modifications.

2. Philo follows the LXX, but philosophical influence appears in his distinction of terms for various objects of God's work (*plássō* and *poiéō*) and his refusal to see in God the creator of bad impulses. He stresses the ongoing nature of God's action, compares it to begetting, and does not refer to miraculous works. On the other hand, he stresses creation out of nothing. In his view God may obviously be known from his work.

3. In the Hermetic writings the *patḗr* is *poiētḗs*. Generation is parallel to *poieín*. God creates all things; hence the cosmos testifies to the existence of the one Creator. Yet a pantheistic element is present and there is a dualistic strand, for only good things derive from God. In a Gnostic development the *Noús dēmiourgós* is interposed between the supreme God and earthly elements.

V. The NT and Early Christianity.

1. The NT takes it for granted that God is Creator, but seldom uses the *poie-* group. In Acts 4:24; 14:15; Rev. 14:7 God is Creator of heaven and earth (cf. Ex. 20:11). In Mk. 10:6 the indissolubility of marriage rests on the fact that in the beginning God made them male and female. Acts 7:50 quotes Is. 66:2, Acts 17:24 Is. 42:5, and Heb. 1:7 Ps. 104:4. In Heb. 3:2 God is the one who appoints (*poiḗsas*) Jesus. Rom. 9:20 echoes the LXX but Acts 17:26 is more Hellenistic. Heb. 12:27 contrasts what has been made and may be shaken with what cannot be shaken. For Paul God's works of creation guarantee his knowability in principle (Rom. 1–2), but in fact humanity refuses this knowledge. In Heb. 1:2 the Son is the one through whom God made the world; John does not use the group in this connection. The NT uses neither *poiētḗs* nor *poíēsis* for God's creative work.

2. Apart from creation, the group denotes God's judicial and more often his redemptive activity. References to immanent or eschatological judgment occur in Lk. 1:51; 18:7-8; Mt. 18:35; Jude 15. God's saving work is the theme in Lk. 1:68, 72; Heb. 13:21; 8:9. God makes the gospel known to the Gentiles (Acts 15:17), acts through the apostles (14:27), and ends temptation (1 Cor. 10:13). His work surpasses all we can ask or think (Eph. 3:20). He makes all things new (Rev. 21:5). Christians are his *poíēma* (Eph. 2:10). He does what he promises (Rom. 4:21). He finishes what he has begun (1 Th. 5:24). He does signs and wonders (Acts 2:22; 15:12; 19:11). He works out his purpose in Jesus (Eph. 3:11), making him sin at the cross (2 Cor. 5:21) and instituting him Lord (Acts 2:36). The Father works in the words of Jesus (Jn. 5:19-20). Luke likes the group, Paul uses it for God's faithfulness in the Christ event, and John gives it a christological reference. Much of the material derives from the LXX, but John takes Gnostic usage and historicizes it.

3. The NT speaks, too, of the work of supernatural beings, but only negatively and in Revelation. The work of the beasts, the dragon, and the unclean spirits is to instigate war (Rev. 11:7), perform miracles (13:13), persecute the church (12:15), and seduce the world (13:12).

B. Human Work before God.

I. The Greek World and Stoicism.

1. Human Work and Salvation.

a. In Plato other groups are used to express the destiny of the soul in the judgment. What counts is apprehension of the good rather than conduct. *pán poieín* means making every effort, and since conduct according to the idea of the good is natural to humanity, it is attainable. Doing is no problem.

b. Stoicism agrees. Immanent deity coincides with the law by which sages direct their steps and which it is natural for them to follow. Censure arises only in relation to secondary things. Right *poieín* comes when the external that is not in one's power is disregarded. The orientation is to what is in keeping with *phýsis*.

2. Details of Usage. *poieín* is used for making such things as houses, graves, and temples. In Plato it denotes the humbler work of the artisan, but it is also parallel to *prássein*. Things done include good and evil. One may also make war or bring peace. *poieín* can also denote the celebrating of feasts or the producing of fruit by the earth. Other senses are "to suppose," "to spend time," "to bring out," and "to value." A common meaning is "to act." The human *poiētḗs* is the "maker," e.g., of laws, then the "poet." *poíēma* is what is produced either externally or intellectually. It is also "action"; hence *poiḗmata* are "deeds." *poíēsis* is both manual and intellectual activity; it acquires the special sense of "poetry" or "poem."

II. The LXX.

1. Noncommanded Secular poieín. Many LXX references are to secular activity that is not specially commanded, e.g., making cakes (Gen. 18:6), traversing roads (Judg. 17:8), making war (Gen. 14:2), or appointing overseers (1 Macc. 1:51). For the most part this activity is of no theological significance.

2. Noncommanded Secular poieín in Parables. In the LXX *poieín* is rare in parables. The work of the potter illustrates God's sovereignty in Jer. 18:4. As the vessel cannot argue with its *poiḗsas*, so human beings cannot argue with God (Is. 29:16; 45:9).

3. Commanded Secular poieín. Human action is mainly commanded or forbidden. God asks about the *poieín* of Eve and Cain (Gen. 3:13; 4:10). Acts of kings are under divine judgment. God's will lies behind the finding of a bride for Isaac (Gen. 24:66). God commands the making of the ark (Gen. 6:14ff.) and cultic objects, e.g., the altar, the ark, and the sanctuary, for which he gives the necessary skill (Ex. 31). Israel is not to make images (Ex. 20:4). Also commanded is right conduct, e.g., in inheritance (Ex. 21:9) or handling a dangerous ox (21:31).

4. Commanded poieín toward One's Neighbor. Commands and prohibitions apply especially to conduct toward one's neighbor. We first find this in concrete acts, e.g., doing what is right (Gen. 20:13) or showing mercy (Josh. 2:12). Wrong acts may also be denoted; thus Isaac is not to hurt Abimelech (Gen. 26:29). *poieín,* then, may be good, bad, or neutral (Judg. 13:8), but emphasis falls on the doing of good (2 Sam. 2:6; Zech. 7:9; 2 Chr. 9:8), i.e., on the doing of what is right because God expressly demands it.

5. Commanded poieín toward the Law, the Will of God, or Individual Commands.

a. Terminology. In the sense "to do" *poieín* is used with the neuter of the relative pronoun or with relative clauses; in the sense "to execute" it has many objects, e.g., statutes, righteousness, truth; in the sense "to act" we find "in accordance with," e.g., the law. Often we find "all the law or statutes" to express complete obedience. God may demand specific actions, e.g., in the cultus (feasts, sacrifices, etc.). *poieín* may also be used for transgression of God's commandments, doing wrong, committing sins, which may seem right in human eyes but are wrong in God's eyes. Trying to make a name in Gen. 11:4 expresses the arrogance of those who build the tower of Babel. The Canaanites might make Israel sin in Ex. 23:33, and Manasseh sets up soothsayers in 2 Chr. 33:6.

b. Human Work and Salvation. Doing what is commanded underlies the covenant. Jeremiah postulates an eschatological new covenant (31:31ff.) and Isaiah invokes unseen forces to make a highway for God (40:3). But it is by doing the law that there is life (Lev. 18:4-5). Observance is presupposed (15:31). Ezekiel calls for the making of a new heart and spirit (18:31). Only willful sins cannot be expiated (cf. Num. 15:30). Sin occurs, and it involves dependence on God, but God has provided cultic means for dealing with it.

6. *The Doing of Miracles*. Various individuals like Moses, Elijah, and Elisha perform miracles (Ex. 4:17, 30; 2 Kgs. 8:4). They do so as the Lord commands (Ex. 7:6).

7. *poieín as Bringing Forth*. The earth brings forth fruit (Gen. 41:47; Lev. 25:21, etc.).

8. *poíēma, poíēsis, poiētḗs*.

a. *poíēma*. This word denotes human products, works, acts, or deeds in a negative, neutral, or positive sense. It carries a semiskeptical nuance in Ecclesiastes.

b. *poíēsis*. Actively human *poíēsis* is performance, doing, or keeping, and passively it is being made. The meaning "poetry" does not occur.

c. *poiētḗs*. The human *poiētḗs* in 1 Macc. 2:67 is the doer (not the maker) of the law. The meaning "poet" does not occur.

III. Rabbinic and Apocalyptic Judaism. The rabbis have doubts about a doing of the law that will be adequate at the judgment, and the Qumran sect and the Essenes intensify legal observance in answer to the problem. The thought of judgment is a spur to work. Apocalyptists stress the value of confession, and Qumran thinks right conduct is truly possible only with conversion to the sect.

IV. Philo and the Hermetic Writings.

1. *Usage*. Philo finds a link between *légein* and *poieín*. He uses *poieín* in the sense "to work." *poíēsis* and *poiētḗs* are for him poetic terms whereby he shows himself sympathetic to Hellenistic culture.

2. *Human Work and Salvation*. If, for Philo, goodness comes from God, it also coincides with human activity, and faith is a state of soul that does not stand in contrast to works. On the higher level of the *noús*, activity is left behind in the vision of God, and works lose their point. In the Hermetic writings the regenerate are summoned to good works, but regeneration is a regrasping of the innate divine element; because, in regeneration, initiates are no longer identical with their empirical selves, ethical acts are not of real concern. The appeal is not for concrete works but for forsaking death, ignorance, and error. As in Philo, then, the problem of works is bypassed.

3. *Magic*. A special use of *poieín* is for performing magical acts which take place in the name of a specific deity and which involve incantations. *poíēsis* is the term for the performance of these magical acts.

V. The NT.

1. *The Works of Jesus*. As regards Jesus, the main reference is not to the purposes or works of the exalted Lord (cf. Jn. 14:23; Rev. 3:9; 1:6; 3:12), but to the *poieín* of the earthly Jesus. Secular and cultic acts play only a minor role here (cf. Jn. 2:5; Mt. 26:18). The works are mostly acts of power. *poieín* denotes the appointment of the disciples in Mk. 1:7. Jesus is asked to justify his works (Mk. 11:28); in them he is thought to make himself equal to God (Jn. 5:18 etc.). He does the Father's works; this does not express his subordination but the fact that God forces people to decision in

his words and works. His work on the cross makes peace between Jews and Gentiles (Eph. 2:14-15). This is the unique and once-for-all sacrifice for sin (Heb. 1:3; 7:27). He committed no sin (1 Pet. 2:22). His ministry consisted of doing and teaching (Acts 1:1). The stress on doing fences off the teaching from rationalistic misunderstanding and safeguards his historical singularity against ontological dissolution.

2. *Noncommanded Secular poieín*. This type of *poieín* is seldom at issue in the NT. It is ascribed to political figures (Mk. 6:20), opponents (Mk. 15:15), minor characters (Acts 27:18), and disciples (Lk. 5:29). It may be the observing of customs (Mk. 15:8). Often God's will is implied or probable (cf. Jn. 19:23). As regards Christians, the Christ event embraces all their *poieín* (1 Cor. 10:31). As regards Christ himself, and also the church, the authority of God is everywhere dominant. Acts in 17:28 uses *poiētaí* for the poets, but even they are indirectly God's witnesses. *poíēma* and *poíēsis* never denote poetry in the NT.

3. *Noncommanded Secular poieín in Parables*. This type of *poieín* is much more common in the NT than in the LXX; cf. the unjust steward (Lk. 16:3-4), the servant with the talents (Mt. 25:16), making the hair white or black (Mt. 5:36), the rich fool (Lk. 12:17-18), the vinedressers (Mt. 21:36). The parables of the two sons and the servant (Mt. 21:31; Lk. 17:9) are directed against the Pharisees; action is obedience. The parables reflect God's dealings, either directly (Mk. 12:9) or less directly. The equal reward for varied *poieín* (Mt. 20:5, 12, 15) contests the equation of reward and merit and teaches God's sovereign generosity. The servant who does not know what his master is doing contrasts with Jesus himself (Jn. 15:15). The relations between Jesus and common people, which are offensive to religious leaders, lie behind many of the parables depicting God's work.

4. *Commanded Secular poieín*. This type of *poieín* is rare in the NT. Cultically one may adduce Mk. 9:5; Acts 7:40; Rev. 13:14; Heb. 8:5 (Ex. 25:40). The disciples are censured when they obey Jesus in Mk. 11:3, 5, as is Paul in Acts 24:12. Joseph obeys in Mt. 1:24, Peter in Acts 10:33, the disciples in Mt. 21:6, believers in Col. 4:16, and the kings in Rev. 17:16.

5. *Commanded or Forbidden poieín toward One's Neighbor.*

a. Doing Good. Material for this kind of *poieín* is plentiful. Doing good has the sense of showing love in Mt. 5:46-47 etc., of almsgiving in Mt. 6:2-3; Acts 11:30, of preaching freely in 2 Cor. 11:7, of intercession in Rom. 1:9, of establishing joy and peace in Acts 15:3, of making converts in Mt. 23:15; Acts 26:28.

b. Doing Harm. *poieín* is seldom neutral. When the action is negative, it is censured or forbidden, e.g., wrong treatment by believers (Mt. 25:45), sexual offenses (5:32), the harm done by persecution (Mk. 9:13). Good should be done to all people, for the command of love is unconditional and the required obedience is radical.

6. *Commanded poieín toward Jesus*. People meet the earthly Jesus in various ways, positively with cultic correctitude (Lk. 2:27), seeking healing (Mk. 5:32), and showing reverence (Mk. 14:8-9), and negatively with lack of understanding (Jn. 6:15) and enmity, both before (Lk. 6:11) and during the passion (Mk. 15:1 etc.). The exalted Lord is either accepted (Mt. 25:40) or rejected (25:45). Only in the light of Easter is right conduct toward Jesus emphasized as important, and even later it is by way of needy brethren or the community that one acts toward the Lord (Mt. 25:40, 45; Acts 26:10).

7. *Commanded poieín toward the Law, God's Will, and the Proclamation of Jesus.*

a. Terminology. Most of the NT *poieín* passages belong under 7., no matter whether the sense is "to do," "to execute," or "to act." One is to do as God commands, and an account must be rendered to God. Obedience is of paramount importance; faith means involvement (Jn. 7:17). Believers are to do God's will (Eph. 6:6) and bring forth fruit (Mt. 3:8). Sin is not to be committed (Mt. 13:41). There must be agreement between saying (Mt. 7:21) or hearing (Lk. 6:47) and doing, or between the hearer and doer (*poiētēs;* Rom. 2:13).

b. Human Work and Salvation.

(a) The focus on conversion to Jesus raises the question what we must do (Mk. 10:17; Acts 2:37). Jesus answers this question on his own authority, not setting aside the law, but stressing love above cultic observance, emphasizing motivation, and rejecting all claims on God. At one and the same time sharpening the demand, negating merit, and pointing to God's unconditional grace, Jesus both requires and makes possible a true doing of the law.

(b) Developing the same points, Paul contrasts doing law-righteousness with doing faith-righteousness. Only the latter leads to salvation (Rom. 10:5-6; Gal. 3:10, 12). There are no true *poiētaí* of the law (Rom. 2:13); if there were, the work of Christ would not be needed. The demand of the law remains, but the law is now to be done in the obedience of faith. Faith sets life under the law in a new light. This life involves a contradiction between what is willed and what is done (Rom. 7:15, 19). Hence legalism cannot lead to its goal. On the basis of salvation and the Spirit, however, believers may both will and do (Gal. 5:17) in a walk which embraces all the commands of love (1 Cor. 10:31; Phil. 2:14; Col. 3:17). God's gracious Yes is the basis of the Christian life, making it possible for believers, who walk in the Spirit, to do what God wills and they themselves also will.

(c) In John the origin of people determines what they do. Committing sin is a sign of corrupt origin (Jn. 8:34, 41, 44). To do good works one must be a shoot of the true vine (15:5). Coming from the Father, Jesus displays the kind of action required (13:5). His going to the Father enables his followers to do greater works (14:12) as temporal restrictions are removed. In 1 John those who are born of God do naturally what is good (2:29; 3:7ff.). Works are not in tension with salvation but are integrated into it. Love manifests itself in keeping the commandments (5:2). Doing righteousness stands in paradoxical unity with confessing sin (1:8ff.). Prayer is heard when what pleases God is done (3:22).

(d) A relaxing of the tension between faith and works may be seen in Mt. 5:19 and Acts 28:17. The point is made in 1 Tim. 1:13 that Paul acted ignorantly in unbelief when he persecuted Christ. God's mercy brings knowledge, and salvation through Christ makes true fulfilment of the law possible.

c. Cultic Action. Except in relation to OT feasts (Acts 18:21) or in cultic exegesis (Heb. 11:28), cultic action occurs only in the eucharistic formula of 1 Cor. 11:24-25 (cf. Lk. 22:19) and the vow that James tells Paul to undertake (Acts 21:23).

8. *Doing Miracles.* The NT often refers to working signs, wonders, etc. (Mk. 9:39; Jn. 3:2; Acts 6:8). The doers are either individuals (Acts 3:12; 6:8; 8:6) or the disciples or church in general (Mk. 6:30 etc.). The works are done in Jesus' name (Mk. 9:39; Acts 3:12). Jesus continues his work in his followers; the signs testify to his sending by the Father. Miracles as such may be performed by demons too (Acts 19:14); hence they cannot replace true commitment (Mt. 7:22).

9. *poiein as Bringing Forth.* With material objects *poiein* may mean "to do" (Mt. 6:3) or "to bring about" (26:73), but mostly it means "to bring forth" (trees etc., Mt. 3:10; Lk. 13:9; Rev. 22:2; also capital yielding interest, Lk. 19:18). This use is mainly

figurative for the producing of ethical fruits (Mt. 3:10) or the growth of the church (Eph. 4:16).

VI. Early Catholic Use. Certain features call for notice. *poiētḗs* is used for "poet" only with reservations. Developing sacramentalism may be observed in the use with the bread and cup. Asceticism and moralism also increase (cf. Did. 11.11; 1 Clem. 31.2; 2 Clem. 11.7). Pious action is now back in the vicinity of later Jewish casuistry (Did. 6:2; Ignatius *Philadelphians* 8.1).   [H. BRAUN, VI, 458-84]

---

poikílos [various, multicolored],   *polypoíkilos* [most varied]

---

poikílos.
1. This word has the sense of "many-colored" but more often of "various," "manifold."
2. Only the sense "various," "of many kinds" occurs in the NT (cf. Mk. 1:34; Heb. 2:4; 2 Tim. 3:6; Jms. 1:2). In 1 Pet. 4:10 the point is that God's grace manifests itself in many different ways, i.e., in the various charisms (cf. Rom. 12:6ff.; 1 Cor. 12).

polypoíkilos. This stronger form ("most varied") occurs in Eph. 3:10: God's wisdom has shown itself in Christ with boundless variety or richness.
                                                                [H. SEESEMANN, VI, 484-85]

---

poimḗn [shepherd],   *archipoímēn* [chief shepherd],   *poimaínō* [to tend],   *poímnē* [flock],   *poímnion* [flock]

A. The Palestinian Shepherd. Tending flocks and herds is an important part of the Palestinian economy in biblical times. The sheep and cattle have to roam widely, and caring for them is an independent and responsible job that can even involve danger. Owners or their sons may do it (Lk. 15:6; Jn. 10:12), but shepherds are also hired.

B. Transferred Usage.
I. The Ancient Near East.
Shepherd is a common designation for rulers and combines a number of associated tasks or attributes (e.g., in Babylon, Assyria, and Egypt). The gods may also be viewed as shepherds; thus Amun is a strong drover who guards his cattle.
II. The OT.
1. God is early called the Shepherd of Israel who goes before the flock (Ps. 68:7), guides it (Ps. 23:3), leads it to food and water (Ps. 23:2), protects it (Ps. 23:4), and carries its young (Is. 40:11). Embedded in the living piety of believers, the metaphor brings out the fact that the people is sheltered in God.
2. In Jeremiah the term is applied to political and military rulers, but not as a title. The shepherds have proved unfaithful; hence God himself will take up the office and appoint better shepherds (Jer. 3:15; 23:4). He will set up one shepherd who will reunite the people (Ezek. 34:23-24; 37:22, 24). The term thus takes on a messianic significance which undergoes unique development in Zechariah. After the exile bad shepherds bring down judgment, but a shepherd suffers death according to God's will and in so doing ushers in the time of salvation (12:10; 13:1ff.).

C. Later Judaism.

I. Palestinian Judaism.

a. Shepherds are classified by the rabbis as thieves and cheats, and thus lose certain civil rights. Their roving life enables them to steal from the flocks; it is thus forbidden to buy milk, wool, or kids from them.

b. In spite of the bad reputation of shepherds, God is still called Israel's Shepherd, who has led his flock out of Egypt, guides it in the present, and will one day gather it again. Leaders and teachers, e.g., Moses and David, are also called faithful shepherds. In the Damascus Document the leader is a shepherd, and Ps. Sol. 17:40 compares the Messiah to a shepherd.

II. Philo. Philo develops a shepherd typology from the OT stories. The *noús* is a shepherd of irrational powers of the soul, rulers are shepherds, and God is the Shepherd who feeds the world and all that is in it through his *lógos*.

D. The NT.

I. Jesus and Shepherds. The NT does not judge shepherds adversely. They know their sheep (Jn. 10:3), seek lost sheep (Lk. 15:4ff.), and hazard their lives for the flock (Jn. 10:11-12). The shepherd is a figure for God himself (Lk. 15:4ff.). The depiction rests on Jesus' real acquaintance with shepherds and sympathy with their lot.

II. The Nativity Story. Mention of actual shepherds occurs only in the birth story in Lk. 2. Theories explaining their presence are (1) that there is similarity to the story of the child Osiris; (2) that they represent the ideal world; (3) that they represent the sinners for whom the gospel is intended; (4) that they carry a reference to David; and (5) that they are the only ones awake at the time. The probability is that the stall in which Jesus is born belongs to the shepherds, and this is why they are told that as a sign the Savior will be found lying there.

III. The Shepherd as a Picture of God. The NT never calls God a shepherd, and only in the parable of the lost sheep (Lk. 15:4ff.; Mt. 18:12ff.) does the comparison occur. Here God, like the rejoicing shepherd of the parable, takes joy in the forgiveness and restoration of the sinner. The choice of the image reflects vividly the contrast between Jesus' love for sinners and the Pharisees' contempt for them.

IV. Jesus the Good Shepherd.

1. Sayings of Jesus in the Synoptic Gospels.

a. To describe his mission Jesus uses the image of gathering the scattered flock (cf. Mt. 10:6; 15:24; Lk. 19:10 [Ezek. 34]).

b. In Mk. 14:27-28; Mt. 26:31-32 Jesus uses the shepherd comparison in intimation of his death and return (with an allusion to Zech. 13:7). The death of Jesus initiates the scattering of the flock and the testing of the remnant, but it is followed by the gathering of the purified flock under the shepherd's leadership (Zech. 13:7ff.).

c. The nations assemble like a flock at the judgment in Mt. 25:31-32, and the shepherd separates the sheep from the goats.

2. Christological Statements of the Primitive Church. In 1 Pet. 2:25 Christ is the shepherd of souls, providing for his people and watching over them. In Heb. 13:20 he is the "great shepherd," surpassing all who precede him, like Moses. In 1 Pet. 5:4 he is the "chief shepherd" to whom all others must render an account. As the earthly Lord he has pity on the leaderless flock (Mk. 6:34), as the exalted Lord he is the Lamb who leads his people to springs of living water (Rev. 7:17), and as the returning Lord he is the eschatological ruler who rules the nations with an iron rod (Rev. 12:5; 19:15).

3. John 10:1-30.

a. Apart from a possible but hardly probable confusion of order, there are good reasons to treat Jn. 10:1-30 as a unity without critical manipulation.

b. The section 10:1-5 is a simple parable contrasting the shepherd with the thief and the stranger. Unlike the thief he comes through the door, and unlike the stranger he knows his sheep and is known by them. In interpretation Jesus first compares himself to the door (vv. 7ff.) and then to the shepherd (vv. 11ff.). Unlike the hireling, the true shepherd is ready to give his life for the sheep that he knows so intimately (v. 14). Jesus' office as the shepherd extends beyond Israel, thus fulfilling the promise of one flock and one shepherd. The sacrifice of life will be followed by the taking of it again (vv. 17-18).

c. The Palestinian materials and the many Semitisms point to an OT setting. The motifs are in full agreement with the sayings in the Synoptic Gospels. The thought of the shepherd's death as voluntary and vicarious develops an impulse already present in Mk. 14:27-28. No parallels exist in the syncretistic or Gnostic world apart from Mandaean allegories that are clearly based on Jn. 10.

4. Postcanonical Writings and Early Christian Art. In early shepherd statements the didactic element steadily develops as Logos Christology endows Christ with the symbols and features of the Logos shepherd. Yet Christ as teaching shepherd leads people, not to freedom from the reign of the senses, but to eternal truth and salvation. From the third century depictions of the Good Shepherd portray Christ as a radiantly youthful figure who is not simply a guide of souls but the teacher and redeemer who brings salvation.

V. Shepherd as a Term for Congregational Leaders. Only in Eph. 4:11 are congregational leaders called shepherds. The pastors and teachers are a single group of ministers. Shepherd is not yet an established title. Parallel passages are 1 Pet. 5:2; Acts 20:28; Jn. 21:15ff. Only in the last of these is a wider ministry in view. Pastors are to care for the congregation, seek the lost, and combat error. The chief shepherd is an example (1 Pet. 5:3), and he will grant recognition at his coming (v. 4).

E. The Shepherd of Hermas. In this second-century work, the angel of repentance appears in shepherd garb to mediate revelations. Sent by the Most Holy Shepherd Christ (*Visions* 5.2), this shepherd is a teacher and companion of Hermas as he proclaims the revealed message of one repentance for sin after baptism. The idea of a mediating angel shepherd does not come from the NT but possibly from the Hermetic sphere.

poímnē, poímnion.

A. The Palestinian Flock. The term *poímnē* or *poímnion* is used for flocks or herds of sheep or cattle numbering from 20 to over 500. A mixed herd is in view in Mt. 25:32; such herds are common in ancient Palestine. The sheep and goats pasture together but are separated at night because goats are more susceptible to cold. On summer nights several shepherds come together with their flocks and watch over them in open fields. For better protection the flock might be kept in a walled court with the door closed and the shepherds on guard.

B. Flock as a Term for the Community in the OT and Pre-Christian Judaism. The OT describes Israel as the flock of God, the flock of his pasture, the sheep of his pasture, the sheep of his hand or possession (cf. Pss. 95:7; 100:3; Mic. 7:14; also Hos. 4:16; Jer. 13:17; 23:1-2). In Sir. 18:13 and Eth. En. 85ff. the flock will include all nations at the consummation. Ps. Sol. 17:40ff. restricts the flock that the Messiah feeds to Israel, but the reign of the Messiah will extend to the Gentiles too (vv. 30ff.).

C. The Community as the Flock in the NT.

1. OT usage (Israel as God's flock) occurs in Mt. 10:6; 15:24. Jesus goes after the dispersed of the flock in Lk. 19:10 (Ezek. 34:16). He bewails the absence of a shepherd in Mk. 6:34 (Num. 27:17). He has pity on the exhausted flock in Mt. 9:36.

2. In the NT, however, the disciples are mainly the flock as God's eschatological people (Mk. 14:27-28; Mt. 10:16; Lk. 12:32; Jn. 10:1ff.). They are a little flock (Lk. 12:32) but need not fear because they are promised dominion (cf. Dan. 7:27). Threats come from wolves both without (Mt. 10:16) and within (7:15). The flock will be scattered but then regathered (Mk. 14:27-28), and the righteous of all peoples will belong to it (Mt. 26:31-32). In John the flock replaces the missing term *ekklēsía*. Its members know the Good Shepherd, believe in him, hear him, and follow him (Jn. 10). In Jn. 10:26 the meaning might be that only predestined members of the flock can believe, but in the context of v. 24 the point seems to be that the witness that finds a hearing and obedience in Jesus' sheep is neither understood nor believed by his opponents (cf. Mk. 4:11-12). The flock is the community which Jesus assembles from Israel and with which he then associates the children of God among the Gentiles (v. 16). After his death and resurrection the straying sheep (1 Pet. 2:25) that do not belong to the flock (Jn. 10:16), but are scattered children of God (11:52), are gathered into the eschatological flock. Christ's atoning death mediates membership in the community of salvation.

[J. JEREMIAS, VI, 485-502]

---

pólemos [war, conflict],   **poleméō** [to wage war, fight]

A. The Religious Understanding of War in the Greek World and Hellenism.

1. The Problem.

a. Homer and Hesiod. Even before Homer it is felt that divine favor rests on holy wars and that the gods invoked in treaties are displeased when treaties are broken. In Homer war is bound up with the rule of the gods. While there may not be gods of war in the strict sense, Ares is the ideal hero and Athene promotes and rewards martial activity. Hesiod accepts the view that divine counsels stand behind human wars, but war is not for him a natural divinely ordained human activity.

b. Religious Practice. Young Athenians swear their readiness for war in the name of Ares, and troops go into battle with the nickname of Ares on their lips.

c. Critical Reflection. Various views arise as a result of critical reflection. War might be seen as a valid principle of life even though it is without parallel in nature. The true goal of reflection might be seen as the prevention rather than the prosecution of war, since war profits nobody. The Greeks are too realistic to suppose that war is a humble submission to the wisdom of Athene, who steps in to settle things according to the divine will when human counsel fails. Wars are too often due to shortsightedness and unscrupulous self-interest. The view thus arises that war, while it might prevent overpopulation, is an evil in which human wickedness or injustice is always involved. War and evil are thus equated, and war can be averted only when there is a serious resolve to fight inner evil, which has its root in humanity itself.

2. General Attitude to the Political Reality of War. The practical question arises how individuals and individual states can actualize peaceful impulses when their neighbors will not let them. To fight only intellectually evades the question in the eyes of leaders. War is an unavoidable evil. Only a world state can end it. In practice, then, peace is won only from war and is like an island menaced by its floods. Treaties have only limited validity and secure peace only until conditions change. They have to be sworn by higher powers in the hope that these powers will look with displeasure on those who break them.

3. *Expectation of Peace in the First Imperial Period.* The creation of the empire promises peace with the inauguration of a single world state. The inner fight against the evil of war has not been won, but the hope is present that the march of epochs has led, by divine regulation, to a return of the golden age. Augustus has ended war and is thus hailed as a divine figure. The wars that still break out are only the last gasps of the passing order. Treaties no longer need to be confirmed by oaths. Quickly, however, the facts do not bear out this hope. Bad neighbors still challenge the Roman peace. Faith in the divine mission of the ruler fades. Philosophers like Marcus Aurelius, who want nothing to do with war, have to devote much of their energy to campaigns. The soldiers of Probus mutiny when he protests against the majesty of war.

B. The Religious Understanding of War in the OT and Later Judaism.

1. The Tradition.

a. The Holy War. The term "holy war" does not occur in the OT but the reality is present. God protects Israel defensively against invaders by charismatic leaders and personal intervention. Troops assemble voluntarily from the tribes, coming to the help of the Lord (Judg. 5:23), but they prevail, not because of numbers or equipment, but because God is with them to give them courage and confound their foes (Judg. 4:14ff.; 5:2, 9; 7:2ff.; Dt. 20:4; Ex. 15:14ff., etc.). Later, wars are more carefully organized, but the dynamic is the same. The chariots and horsemen of Israel (2 Kgs. 2:12; 13:14) are the people's final defense. The prophets constantly call the people back to their true refuge, not in political or military planning, but in God, and in the distant future they perceive a general attack on Israel that a final holy war will repel (Mic. 4:12). The acquisition of the promised land is understood to be the work of God, but with the ultimate goal of subjection to God in defiance of every idol.

b. God's War against Israel. While God's conflict is primarily with arrogant idolatrous nations, it may also be with Israel herself if Israel reverts to idolatry. God uses foreign peoples in this conflict, and the resultant war might almost be regarded as itself a holy war (Am. 2:14ff.). Already reverses in the past are seen as due to God's withdrawal of his help or even his helping of enemies (Lev. 23:36; Josh. 7:5; 1 Sam. 17:11). Israel always runs the risk, by unfaithfulness, of falling into a hopeless war against the overwhelming strength of God put forth in judgment.

c. Divine and Human Initiatives. Human military initiative is less important in the OT than in Homer. Certain things must be done, but there is confidence that God decides the issue, as at the Red Sea or the fall of Jericho (Ex. 15; Josh. 6).

2. *The Problem.* In the OT many wars can hardly be regarded as holy wars (e.g., those between the tribes). If there is no discussion of the general problem, the main points are clear. Holy wars are directed against human arrogance and idolatry, the holy war against Israel is directed against her unfaithfulness, and other wars are brought on by human sin and are mysteriously integrated into God's overriding plan.

3. *General Attitude to the Political Reality of War.* War in the OT is a normal if undesired reality in human dealings, especially in view of the religious antithesis between Israel and other nations.

4. Expectation of a State of Peace. The hope of a warless future rests on the confidence that although God summons to holy war, he also will usher in a reign of peace (Ps. 46:9; Is. 2:4).

5. Later Judaism.

a. The picture is much the same as in the OT except that the final war has enhanced significance. Those involved will have to be ready for great suffering and sacrifice. Sometimes the final war, or at least the prelude to it, will be fought by believers, but with the guarantee of divine help. Sometimes God or the Messiah is viewed as waging the war directly without human participation, the only role of the righteous being the doing of good works.

b. For Philo the worship of many gods carries the seeds of conflict. One must combat the state of war that exists even in what is called peace. Only a structural change in creation can bring true peace, and only God can bring this about, first by taming the beasts in the human *psyché,* then by ending the war in the animal kingdom, and finally by subduing bloodlessly those who joy in battle.

C. The NT.

1. War in the Events of the Last Time. The NT inherits the concept of a campaign of the Davidic Messiah, but never even dreams of believers being summoned openly to war, not even in the final conflict. Revelation shows how the war that is related to the judgment will overcome war between the millennium and the new heaven and earth. An apparently invincible foe steps forth; but in righteousness (19:11), and executing a heavenly plan, the Word makes war and overthrows the enemy. Unbelievers are unaware of the nearness of this final event, and even believers must be warned about it (cf. 2:16; 14; 16). Rulers, seduced by the authority of the beast, wage war on the prophets, the community, the city, and the Lamb (11:7; 12:17; 20:8-9; 17:14). The second horseman personifies the conflict (6:3-4). Only those who trust in the righteousness of the King of kings can doubt the power of these big battalions.

2. Other References to War. Only Heb. 11:34 construes past events in the light of the divine goal. The idea of holy wars waged by the new community is quite alien to the NT. No discussion arises concerning wars between the OT and the final conflict. Christians are not told to serve as soldiers, nor are soldiers who become Christians told to leave the service. Terms from soldiering are adopted to illustrate the Christian life. This does not mean that honor is paid to war as such. The terms *pólemos* and *poleméō* are never used to describe either literally or figuratively what Christians should do. Indeed, warrings and fightings are incompatible with being a Christian (Jms. 4:2).   [O. BAUERNFEIND, VI, 502-15]

---

pólis [city], *polítēs* [citizen], *politeúomai* [to be a citizen], *politeía* [citizenship, conduct], *políteuma* [commonwealth]

A. Nonbiblical Greek.

1. Lexicography.

1. Of unexplained etymology, *pólis* first means a fortified settlement. With political development, the idea of fortification drops away. Thus Sparta is a complex of four or five open villages. This development makes *pólis* apt to signify a state as distinct from the spatially defined *ásty.* The *pólis* is the ruling center—first a town, then the wider area ruled from it.

2. The _polítēs_ is one who shares in the _pólis,_ i.e., the "citizen" with all the relevant active and passive privileges.

3. _politeúō_ has such meanings as "to be a citizen," "to live or act as such," "to share in government," "to rule," "to prosecute state business." Other senses are "to have business dealings" and the weaker one "to behave."

4. _politeía_ has the meanings "citizenship," "political activity," "constitution," "the state" as such, and "conduct."

5. _políteuma_ has such senses as "political acts," "acts of government departments," "government," "commonwealth," "citizenship," and "foreign colony."

II. Ideal Content. A distinctive phenomenon in antiquity, the _pólis_ draws its significance from the ideal content of the term. The establishment of the _pólis_ leads to culture. This takes place through free union endowed by Zeus with righteousness and piety. Spiritual values develop, and culture is achieved, by freedom under the authority of laws that protect the common welfare. The freedom of the _pólis_ stands opposed to barbarian tyranny. Individuals find true self-development in the common national life. Religious awe encircles state law; the order of state has a religious sanction. The _pólis_ is thus a sacral organization. Its origin is with the supreme God, who is _polioúchos,_ the protector of the state. The tragedy of Greek history is that the reality does not match the ideal. Rational criticism, self-interest, party conflict, mob action, and the cantonal confinement of the state combine to frustrate the achievement of the ideal. The Stoics introduce a wider vision, and Alexander tries to give it political shape in a world kingdom, although for the Stoics it is an ideal fellowship of the wise that does not need legal or social institutions. Indeed, the Stoics use the term _pólis_ for the cosmos itself as a totality that is governed by a single divine law. As history leaves the Greek _pólis_ behind, the concept loses its vitality and falls victim to philosophical spiritualizing.

B. The LXX and Later Judaism.

I. pólis.

1. _Hebrew Originals. pólis_ occurs often in the LXX, usually for '_îr,_ a few times for _qiryâ_ and _qeret._ Heb. '_îr_ embraces any fortified place, e.g., a fortress or even a watchtower. Customarily, however, it is a walled town.

2. _Description of Cities._ Cities are described by name, location, nationality, residents (individuals or clans), and special features, but not by constitution.

3. _Importance of Cities._ Cities in Israel are not important as centers of culture or government. Nor is the city a basic form of the state. In the Near East states are kingdoms. The term _pólis_ is "depoliticized" in the LXX. Cities are important because they can resist aggressors (cf. Jericho in Josh. 6). When Israel conquers Palestine, the cities are quickly rebuilt for the security they seem to offer (Dt. 28:52). Taking a city is hard (cf. Proverbs), but living in it gives a sense of security (10:15). Yet even high walls cannot protect the _pólis_ against God's judgment (Dt. 28:52). The city of Gen. 11 with its lofty tower represents the ungodly arrogance of the human race. Unless the Lord keeps the city, the watchman stays awake in vain (Ps. 126:1).

4. _Jerusalem._ Jerusalem is unique in Israel (Ezek. 7:23). God has set his name there (Dt. 12:5, 11). He has chosen it as the place of worship (2 Chr. 6:38). Prayer is offered toward it (1 Kgs. 8:44). It is the city of God, of the great King, of the Lord (Pss. 46:4; 48:2; Is. 60:14). It is the holy city (Is. 48:2). It symbolizes religious faith and national independence. Yet its people are wicked (Jer. 6:7). Judgment falls on their violence and idolatry (Ezek. 22:2ff.). God still loves it, however, and will finally

establish it (Ps. 87:1-2; Jer. 31:38). His glory leaves it (Ezek. 11:23) but will return, and it will be called the faithful city (Zech. 8:3). National hopes focus on this restoration (Joel 3:17). The OT city thus reaches beyond history to the final change that God will effect.

5. *Jerusalem in the Hope of Later Judaism.* The Prayer of Eighteen Benedictions sustains the hope of a restored Jerusalem as a cultic center. The darker the present situation, the loftier is the hope. Jerusalem is already present in heaven and will be finally manifested. Its temple will be infinitely more glorious than that of the historical city. The wicked will be excluded, and in the thinking of some aliens will also be shut out.

II. *polítēs, politeía, politeúomai, políteuma in the OT.*

1. Except for *polítēs* these words occur only in apocryphal writings (especially 2–4 Maccabees). *polítēs* normally means "neighbor" in the sense of compatriot or coreligionist, with a social and ethical flavoring. Nine of the instances are in 2 Maccabees, one in 3 Maccabees, and only seven elsewhere.

2. *politeía,* too, is a religious and moral concept rather than a political one. It refers mostly to a pious order of life in accordance with the law. Only in 3 Macc. 3:21, 23 does it have the sense of civil rights.

3. *politeúomai* also refers to conduct rather than citizenship. The reference is religious. Religion regulates the life of society and individual behavior within it. The total claim of divine law gives a different character to the society to which Jews belong, and this determines the use of the term.

4. *políteuma* occurs only in 2 Macc. 12:7, where it means "commonwealth."

III. *Josephus and Philo.*

1. Josephus makes rich use of the group, and for him the reference is to such things as the constitution and civil rights. Yet the political sense may yield at times to the more general one of conduct. As a political Hellenist Josephus thinks that Greek terms may help to clarify the alien structure of Israel. Yet he has a keen sense of the differences. Moses established Israel as a theocracy. By using political language, Josephus masks to some extent the religious orientation of political thinking in the OT and Judaism. He sacrifices the eschatological hope of a new Jerusalem for the sake of peace with Rome, applying to Vespasian the oracle of a future world ruler.

2. Philo engages in a spiritualizing transposition. Adam is for him a cosmopolitan. The noetic cosmos is the metropolis of the wise. For world citizens of this type individual states are of lesser worth. Political life is the theater of base passion and degrading dependence. Wisely the Essenes avoid city life. Philo himself lives in Alexandria, advocates democracy as the best constitution, and would like to see philosophers as rulers, but he has no concept of the dignity of the state or of political action. Nor does he share a true eschatological hope. Jerusalem is the holy city but only inasmuch as it represents the cosmos or the soul of the wise. His psychological and ethical cosmopolitanism dissolves history and eschatology.

C. The NT.

I. pólis.

1. *Distribution and Secular Use.* The term *pólis,* which has lost the aura that surrounds it in the Greek world, occurs some 160 times, mostly in the Lucan writings, and especially with a historical or eschatological (Revelation) reference. The term never means "state," for which the NT has king, authorities, etc. When cities are denoted, they are not political organisms. *árchontes* occurs for city officials only

loosely in Acts 16:19. The *pólis* in the NT is an enclosed place of human habitation as distinct from villages, isolated dwellings, or uninhabited places. At times it can also mean "population" (Mt. 8:34). It is not sharply distinguished from *kōmē* (Mk. 1:38; cf. Lk. 4:43). The *pólis* is the walled city and larger center, while the *kōmai* are subordinate towns. Individual cities may be mentioned, as in Mt. 8:33; 21:17; Acts 8:5. Or additions may be made relating the city to a locality (Lk. 4:31), a nation (Mt. 10:5), inhabitants (Acts 19:35), or an individual (Lk. 2:4, 11).

2. *Jerusalem the Holy City.* As in the OT, Jerusalem is the holy or beloved city (Mt. 4:5; 27:53; Rev. 11:2). The reference may be either to the historical or to the heavenly city. The usage reflects Jewish tradition but also points to the importance of Jerusalem for the primitive church. Jerusalem is the Christian center in a religious as well as a practical sense.

3. *The Heavenly Jerusalem.* The historical Jerusalem will be destroyed (Mk. 13:2), so that hope centers on the heavenly and purified Jerusalem that will come to the new earth with the consummation (Rev. 21:10). Law-free Christians already belong to this city that is above (Gal. 4:25-26). The patriarchs seek it as the only city that will endure (Heb. 11:10, 16). Glimpsing it only from afar, they live by faith as pilgrims and strangers on earth (11:14, 16). God has built it for them in heaven (cf. 12:22ff.). Christians look ahead to it, having no abiding city here (13:14). It exists in heaven as the true reality, the city of the fellowship of believers of all ages along with the angelic world. In Rev. 21 this city is prepared as a bride. It is the perfected community of those who bear its name (3:12). Various motifs combine in the image, but these are only metaphors (the walls, the streets of gold, the pure river, the precious stones, etc.) to describe the blessedness of the consummation. Purged of nationalistic features, and opened to believers of all nations, this Jerusalem is not just a replacement for the old one. It inherits the name, but all things are made new. At the same time, the eschatological concept bears no relation to Stoic or Philonic cosmopolitanism. It is still oriented to history.

4. *The Vulgate Translation civitas.* Except in Acts 16:12, 39 the Vulgate always renders *pólis* by *civitas*. This gives the term a political slant which is retained in Augustine's use of it in *The City of God*, where it tends to lose its eschatological and figurative character and becomes a concept of ecclesiastical and philosophical thought.

II. polítēs, politeúomai, politeía, políteuma.

1. There is nothing theological about the four instances of *polítēs* in the NT (Heb. 8:11; Acts 21:39; Lk. 15:15; 19:12ff.). The meaning varies from "compatriot" or "citizen" to "independent inhabitant," but the usage remains within everyday limits.

2. *politeúomai* occurs only in Acts 23:1 and Phil. 1:27. In both cases it refers to conduct that is shaped by religion with no political implications.

3. *politeía,* too, occurs only twice. In Acts 22:28 Paul appeals to his status as a Roman citizen to avoid examination by scourging. In Eph. 2:12 the word refers to the privileged position of Israel. Once excluded, believers now belong, not to the Jewish state, but to the people of God. Having access to God, they share spiritual citizenship with the saints as members of God's household (2:19).

4. *políteuma* occurs only in Phil. 3:20. Exhorting believers to appropriate conduct, Paul tells them that their true homeland is in heaven. On earth (cf. 1 Pet. 2:11) they have no right of domicile; they are not citizens rooted in nature, thought, or interests. The point is not that they are a foreign colony in earthly states, but aliens in the earthly sphere as such. By constitutional right, they belong to the heavenly kingdom of Christ. The kingdom of heaven is their *políteuma.* They should act accordingly.

D. The Apostolic Fathers. The usage here is similar to that of the NT. The everyday sense occurs. In Hermas *Similitudes* 1.1ff. the Christian *pólis* is contrasted with the temporal world. Diog. 5.5 uses *politeía* for "conduct." In Diog. 5.9 *politeú-omai* can mean "to be a citizen," but mostly the term refers to conduct. Used of God in Diog. 10.7, it denotes his reign. The meaning in 1 Clem. 54.4 is that we should conduct ourselves as citizens of God.   [H. STRATHMANN, VI, 516-35]

→ *Siốn, Ierousalḗm*

---

polloí [(the) many]

A. Inclusive Meaning in Judaism.

I. The OT.

1. As Noun.

a. With Article. In Greek *polloí* is used exclusively ("the many" as distinct from "all"), but in the OT it has an inclusive sense, due to the fact that Hebrew has no plural word for "all." This is especially clear when the article occurs (cf. 1 Kgs. 18:25; Is. 53:11; Dan. 9:27).

b. Without Article. Even without the article the use is often inclusive, as in Pss. 109:30; 71:7; Ex. 23:2.

2. As Adjective. Inclusive use of the adjective is found only in the expression "the [whole] host of peoples" (cf. Is. 2:2-4; 52:15).

3. Is. 52:13–53:12. Four instances of the noun and one of the adjective occur in this section (52:14; 53:11, 12; 52:15). While the reference is obscure, there is little doubt that the use is inclusive in every case, as shown by the expression in 52:15, the use of the article in 53:11, 12, the parallel in 53:12, and later interpretation.

II. Postbiblical Judaism.

1. As Noun.

a. With Article. The many Jewish examples confirm the inclusive significance of the use with the article, e.g., in the Qumran writings.

b. Without Article. Without the article, too, we sometimes find an inclusive sense (cf. the use of the Latin *multi* in a comprehensive sense in 4 Esdr. 8:1, 3).

2. As Adjective. Postbiblical Judaism offers further instances of the inclusive sense of the adjective in the phrase "the [whole] host of peoples."

3. Is. 52:13–53:12 in Later Jewish Writings. Ignoring post-Christian exposition, we find that the many who are astonished embrace all kings and mighty men and that the sinless one will die for the ungodly, although whether the ungodly here are Jews, Gentiles, or both is debatable.

B. Inclusive Meaning in the NT.

I. Passages Not Relating to Is. 53.

1. As Noun.

a. With Article. An exclusive sense ("most") may be found in the NT only in Mt. 24:12 and 2 Cor. 2:17. In Rom. 5:15 the meaning and context both support an inclusive sense. Other Pauline instances are Rom. 12:5; 1 Cor. 10:17. Elsewhere cf. Mk. 6:2; 9:26; Heb. 12:15 ("the many" for "the community").

b. Without Article. Parallel passages show that without the article, too, *polloí* may have an inclusive meaning (cf. Mk. 1:32). In Mt. 8:11 the point is that great numbers will come. The *polloí* of Lk. 1:14 are the saved people. In Lk. 2:34-35 some will fall and some will be raised up, but the thoughts of all of them will be disclosed. In Jn. 5:28 an inclusive use is obvious, and both the noun and the adjective of 2 Cor. 1:11 are inclusive. Mt. 20:16 takes the rule of Mk. 10:31 inclusively, but Lk. 13:30 gives it an exclusive application. In Mt. 22:14 we have a formal antithesis between great and small numbers, but materially the many represent the totality; the invitation embraces all, but the choice falls only on the few. Appended to the parable, the statement applies the invitation to both Jews and Gentiles.

2. *As Adjective.* Rom. 4:11 suggests that when Paul quotes Gen. 17:5 in Rom. 4:17 he has all nations in view. As an adjective *polloí* is also inclusive in 2 Cor. 1:11; Heb. 2:10; Lk. 7:47 ("as many as there are").

II. Statements about Jesus' Saving Work.

1. *With Article.* In Rom. 5:15, 19 Paul gives the greatest conceivable breadth to *hoi polloí*, as is shown by the *pántes ánthrōpoi* of v. 18. Christ's obedience, like Adam's disobedience, has an effect on the whole of the human race. In 5:19, then, Paul takes the many of Is. 53:11 inclusively (cf. 5:16 and Jn. 1:29).

2. *Without Article.* The real problem arises in the four passages where there is no article, i.e., Mk. 10:45; 14:24; Rom. 5:16; Heb. 9:28.

a. NT Interpretations. 1 Tim. 2:6 has *pántōn* for the *pollṓn* of Mk. 10:45. We also find *pántes* in Rom. 5:12 and Heb. 2:9. As regards 14:24 the restrictive *hymeís* seems to be the equivalent in 1 Cor. 11:24, but *ho kósmos* is the broader equivalent in Jn. 6:51. In 1 Cor. 11:24, however, the use is liturgical rather than theological, in contrast with 2 Cor. 5:14.

b. The Original Sense.

(a) Age of the Tradition. Mk. 10:45 and 14:24 both have a Semitic character, and the existence of other renderings also suggests a Palestinian original. So does the use of the Hebrew of Is. 53. Semitic usage, especially in Is. 53, is thus the probable basis.

(b) References to Is. 53. All four of the debatable passages are based on Is. 53. Mk. 10:45 rests on Is. 53:10ff., Mk. 14:24, and Heb. 9:28, and Rom. 5:16 on 53:12. The Hebrew is followed in all instances except Heb. 9:28. LXX influence may be discounted in view of the deviations of the LXX from the Hebrew text. Since Paul and John agree with Jewish interpretation in taking the many of Is. 53 inclusively, one may take it that Jesus himself has the same inclusive sense in view in the sayings in Mk. 10:45 and 14:24.

[J. JEREMIAS, VI, 536-46]

---

polylogía [loquacity, verbosity]

1. This word means "loquacity," "volubility," "talkativeness," with a negative ring.

2. The only LXX instance is in Prov. 10:19: In much talking is sin, but material parallels may be found in Is. 1:15; Eccl. 5:1-2; 1 Kgs. 18:26ff.

3. Later Judaism carries warnings against much speaking, but in prayer there is tension between praise of crispness and a preference for length.

4. The only NT example is in Mt. 6:7, where "verbosity" is the point. The saying is parallel to those about almsgiving and prayer, but is not so strictly constructed, and is directed against pagan piety. The much speaking refers either to the enumeration of many deities or to the effort to wear down the gods by repetition. Quantity to the point of verbosity replaces quality. Jesus bases the assurance of being heard, not on the petitioner and the number of words, but on the readiness of the Father to hear.

The Lord's Prayer teaches us to pray for great things in few words; the Father knows the needs even before we ask. [C. MAURER, VI, 545-46]

polypoíkilos → *poikílos; polýs* → *polloí; polýsplanchnos* → *splanchnízomai; póma* → *pínō*

---

ponērós [bad, wicked], **ponēría** [evil, wickedness]

---

ponērós.

A. The Greek World.
I. The Classical Period. This word, from a group denoting poverty or need, has the senses 1. "sorrowful," "unhappy," "laden with care," 2. "bringing trouble," 3. "pitiable," "poor," "unfit," "unattractive," "bad," "unlucky," 4. "unsuccessful," 5. "plebeian," 6. "politically useless," "worthless," and finally 7. "morally reprehensible" with the various nuances.

II. Hellenistic Period. The sense does not undergo much change in Hellenistic usage. We thus find the usual meanings "full of trouble," "useless," "wrong," "harmful," "contrary," and "morally bad," "evil." We also find the idea of the *ponērós daímōn* or *ponērón pneúma,* the latter deriving from LXX influence.

B. The OT and Later Judaism.
I. The LXX and Other OT Translations. ponērós carries the various meanings of the Hebrew original, i.e., "bad" or "worthless" (animals, fruit, land, people), "ill-natured," "unfavorable" (reputation), "prejudicial," "sorrowful" (appearance), "unhappy," "hurtful," "futile," "evil" (words), and "evil" in a more general moral sense (thoughts, the eye, and acts). Acts are evil before God (Gen. 38:7), who decides what is good and evil (Is. 5:20). An absolute use is possible for the wicked person (1 Sam. 25:3) who breaks the law (Dt. 17:7) and is marked by pride (Job 35:12). *ho ponērós* is not yet used for Satan. In contrast to the *ponērós* is the person who seeks God and will be guided by him (Ezek. 11:2). Among the wicked may be men, women, and children (Gen. 13:13; Sir. 25:16; Wis. 3:12). The inner part is evil (Is. 3:9). The organs at the disposal of the evil will and thoughts are also evil (Jer. 23:14). Reference is made to evil in the absolute in 2 Sam. 13:22. For evil before God, see Num. 32:12; Dt. 4:25; evil always stands in antithesis to God and his will even when this is not expressly stated.

II. Later Judaism.
1. Qumran. Here, too, the Hebrew term denotes what is evil in both a general and a moral sense. Enumerations show plainly what is regarded as evil, e.g., abominations in a spirit of fornication and apostasy, and a lack of desire to do good.

2. The Rabbis. The general and moral senses, i.e., what is harmful and what is morally bad, occur among the rabbis too. The two ways depict what is bad and what is good. A bad eye, heart, or companion will lead on to the bad way. God fixes what is bad, and everything bad is contrary to him. Calumniation is a tongue of evil. The evil impulse is directed to earthly, ungodly, and corruptible matters and especially to what runs contrary to the law. This impulse relates to Satan, but Satan is not called the evil one.

III. *Hellenistic Judaism*.

1. *The Pseudepigrapha*. Although the sense of "harmful" occurs in these works, the moral sense predominates, and the idea of evil spirits is now common. These may be moralized (cf. the spirits of desire, excitement, extravagance, and avarice in wine, or covetousness working like an evil spirit).

2. *Philo and Josephus*. Along with the basic senses of "full of trouble" and "detrimental," we find in Josephus the meaning "politically reprehensible" and in Philo the moral sense of "bad." For Philo thinking that focuses on the divine mysteries sets the body in an unfavorable light. The *ponēroí*, in contrast to the *agathoí*, seek only pleasures. The *ponēroí* in a social sense need not be *ponēroí* in the moral sense.

C. The NT.

I. *The Sense of Bad, Harmful, Unserviceable, Useless*.

1. This sense occurs in the NT. Thus the sores in Rev. 16:2 are troublesome, the days of the end-time in Eph. 5:16 are darkened by its woes (unless moral corruption is in view), the day of Eph. 6:13 is a day of distress (whether as an ordinary day, the day of death, the day of judgment, or a day when the devil has special power), and the aeon of Gal. 1:4 is filled with temptation and suffering.

2. In Mt. 7:18 the fruits are "useless" (as distinct from the fruits of the good tree), and in Mt. 18:32; 25:26; 19:22 the servant is no good.

II. *The Moral Sense*.

1. *Adjectival Use*.

a. Persons. Human beings, in contrast to God (Mk. 10:18), are morally bad (Mt. 7:11). They are so in a stronger sense when they oppose God (Mt. 12:34-35). They bring forth evil words from an evil store within (12:35). The generation that wants messianic signs is a wicked one (Mt. 12:39), as its encounter with the word discloses. The term receives its content from decision regarding Jesus, or later the apostolic message (cf. 2 Tim. 3:13). In 2 Th. 3:2 the wicked are those who oppose believers and their faith. Something of a social stigma attaches to the use in Acts 17:5: the "rabble."

b. Things and Concepts. The names of Jesus and his disciples are regarded as evil (cf. Jms. 2:7) by opponents. The evil eye is the covetous one. In Mt. 6:23; Lk. 11:34 the meaning might be "sick" in view of the reference to the body, the ensuing application, and a parallel in Philo, but "evil" is also possible, for the OT and NT assume a close relation between heart and eye, and the idea of the wicked or covetous eye is a common one. In Mt. 15:19 evil thoughts come from within (cf. Mk. 7:21). In Jms. 2:4 the reference is most likely to base motives, e.g., love of fame or money. Insinuations or evil suspicions are meant in 1 Tim. 6:4. In Heb. 3:12 the inner person is evil because of self-willed apostasy (cf. 10:22, where the bad conscience separates from God). Words and deeds can be evil (cf. the boasting of Jms. 4:16, the pre-Christian works of Col. 1:21, or the things done to God's messengers in 2 Tim. 4:18). In Jn. 3:19 the antithesis of light and darkness determines the content of *ponērós* (cf. vv. 20-21). In Jn. 7:7 the works of the world are evil because God does not do them. What is against the gospel is wicked, not just immorality but error and its propagation (2 Jn. 11) and hostile *lógoi* (3 Jn. 11). Wicked works result from rejection of God's salvation. On the lips of Gallio in Acts 18:14, however, the term has the more secular sense of legal wrongdoing punishable by law. The NT often refers to evil spirits (Mt. 12:45; Lk. 11:26). Jesus and the apostles grant release from them (Lk. 7:21; Acts 19:12ff.).

2. *Use as Noun.*

a. Bad People. The *ponēroí* are often the wicked as opposed to the *agathoí* (Mt. 22:10) or *díkaioi* (13:49). The social sense is possible in Mt. 22:10. Mt. 5:45 may be compared with Prov. 15:3. God is kind to both ungrateful and *ponēroí* in Lk. 6:35. At the final separation the *ponēroí* are those who do not meet God's righteous demand (Mt. 13:49). The singular occurs in 1 Cor. 5:13 for one who offends against God's law.

b. The Devil. Since the content of *ponērós* is determined largely by opposition to God's word or will or the message of Jesus, the singular noun may refer to the absolute antithesis, i.e., the devil. There are no models for this, but *ho ponērós* is clearly the devil in Mt. 13:19 and perhaps in Eph. 6:16. The usage possibly develops through a desire not to use the name Satan. It is most common in 1 John (2:13-14; 5:18). The evil one does not touch those who are born of God. In 1 Jn. 3:12 (cf. Jn. 18:37) we might have an abstract use, but Jn. 8:44 suggests a masculine. A masculine is supported in 1 Jn. 5:19 by the antithetical "of God." The devil is the prince of this world in Jn. 12:31; the idea, then, is that the world lies in his power.

c. Evil. Debatable is Mt. 13:38, which contrasts the sons *toú ponēroú* with those of the kingdom. Since the enemy is the devil (v. 39), some argue that "sons of the devil" is meant (cf. 1 Jn. 3:8, 10), but others point out that the antithesis is the kingdom, so that the reference is simply to the wicked. A masculine is to be preferred in Jn. 17:15, although nothing is at stake if the term is taken as a neuter. Hotly contested is Mt. 6:13, which the east has construed as a masculine and the west as a neuter. Mt. 13:19 supports the masculine, but the neuter ("evil") is a more common usage. The petition, then, is probably a request for deliverance from all evil according to Jewish models. The evil in view includes temporal evils but extends beyond these to moral and eschatological evils. In the same way we most likely have a neuter in 2 Th. 3:3, although some see a masculine here too. A masculine is ruled out in Mt. 5:39 by Jms. 4:7; 1 Pet. 5:9 if the devil is in view, but a wicked person is possible (cf. 1 Cor. 5:13). On the other hand, wicked acts are just as likely. In 1 Th. 5:22 the reference is not so much to the appearance of evil as to every kind of evil. In Mt. 5:11 the evil that opponents ascribe to the disciples is the point. The evil in Mt. 9:4 refers to the thoughts of the scribes, and "all these evil things" in Mk. 7:23 summarizes the preceding vices. The plural has a very general sense in Lk. 3:19 (cf. Acts 25:18). In Rom. 12:9 the singular is neuter and what is morally bad is at issue.

ponēría.

A. Classical and Hellenistic Greek. This word has such meanings as "defectiveness," "sickness," "imperfection," and "lack." Morally it means "baseness," "depravity," "intentionally practiced evil will."

B. The OT and Later Judaism. In the LXX the term has such senses as "uselessness," "badness," "ugliness," "displeasure," "misfortune," "trouble," and, morally, "evil" (disposition, plan, will, or acts). The usage of later Judaism is similar; meanings of the equivalent terms range from "imperfection" to "wickedness."

C. Hellenistic Judaism.

1. LXX. In the LXX *ponēría* is an alternative to *kakía,* and only when it has the sense of "misfortune" or "sad mien" in Ecclesiastes is there any distinction. Indeed, even in Ecclesiastes *ponēría* can mean "wickedness" too.

2. Pseudepigrapha. In these works *ponēría* may mean "affliction," "misfortune," but it mostly has the moral sense of "wickedness," and as such it is traced back to Beliar or to evil spirits.

3. Philo and Josephus. ponēría may denote political wrongs for Josephus, but the main sense is moral evil, although Philo prefers *kakía* (as do the Hermetic writings).

D. The NT. The term has a generalized moral sense in the NT (cf. Rom. 1:29; 1 Cor. 5:29). It occurs alongside *kakía* in the list in Mk. 7:22. The plural in Acts 3:26 carries a reference to various kinds of iniquity, and cf. Lk. 11:39. Often there is an association with covetousness (Rom. 1:29; Lk. 11:39: extortion). In Mt. 22:18 *ponēría* is the wicked purpose of the Pharisees. The genitive in Eph. 6:12 characterizes the spiritual forces; it does not describe their origin.

E. The Apostolic Fathers. In the apostolic fathers the moral sense predominates, i.e., "wickedness," "wicked conduct," "baseness" (cf. Hermas *Visions* 3.5.4; 3.6.1; *Similitudes* 9.18.1). The vices in Hermas *Mandates* 8.3 are collectively *ponēríai*. Thus *ponēría* may on the one hand be a collective term for wickedness, while on the other it denotes specific conduct or the disposition that it expresses.

[G. HARDER, VI, 546-66]

---

poreúomai [to go, send], *eisporeúomai* [to go into], *ekporeúomai* [to go out]

---

poreúomai.

A. Nonbiblical Usage.

1. Meaning. The active of *poreúomai* has such senses as "to set in motion," "to convey," "to lead," "to bring," "to send"; the middle means "to go," "to travel," "to journey" (figuratively, but rarely, "to traverse the way of life").

2. Journeys to the Hereafter. In connection with death, the idea of a journey to the hereafter occurs. The land of no return lies in the west, where the sun sets. The way to the abode of the gods lies across a vast waste and a fiery river, although privileged dead are snatched away there at once. The Greeks refer to journeying in Hades and also speak about the western isles of the blest. In poetry some travelers to the underworld return. With the distinction of soul and body, only the immortal soul makes the final journey back to its heavenly home. Judgment decides which course the soul shall take. The idea of the ascent of the soul occurs in the Iranian myth which passes in different forms into Mithraic, Mandaean, Christian, and Jewish thinking. Souls may also travel abroad in dreams or ecstatic rapture, although in the case of ecstasy, which is passive, *poreúomai* does not strictly apply.

B. The LXX and Later Judaism.

1. In the LXX *poreúomai* has the literal sense "to go," "to travel" (cf. Gen. 11:31; 12:4-5; Dt. 1:19), as well as "to wander about" (1 Sam. 23:13) and "to creep" (the serpent in Gen. 3:14). It may have such varied references as to flowing streams, the tossing sea, spreading branches, and the blowing wind. A common closing salutation is: "Go in peace" (1 Sam. 1:17; 2 Sam. 3:21).

2. Deriving from the Hebrew original, the sense "to pass away" is also found (Hos. 13:3; Cant. 2:11; cf. Lam. 4:9).

3. The transferred sense is common in the LXX. Thus conduct is a walking (1 Kgs.

3:14), and the use of "way" or "ways" completes the metaphor (2 Chr. 11:7). The message of the OT is that one should go on God's way, not as a way that leads to God, but as a mode of life that one should live as a member of the covenant people. Various definitions of true or false walking may be given, e.g., in righteousness or truth (Is. 33:15; Prov. 28:6), or in falsehood or confusion (Jer. 23:14; Is. 45:16). Walking in the law of the Lord is contrasted with walking in pagan statutes (Ps. 119:1; Lev. 18:3). Walking in the law is walking in the light (Is. 60:3), for God's countenance shines upon it. The obedient, not trying to evade God's searching glance, are said to walk before God (1 Kgs. 2:4; 8:23; Is. 38:3).

4. The term acquires a theological sense, again on the basis of the Hebrew, when it signifies "to go after" with the nuance "to be subject." Thus Israel is summoned to follow God (1 Kgs. 18:21), and apostasy is following other gods (Dt. 6:14), specifically Baal (Jer. 2:23).

5. In the OT *poreúomai* may also be used in the imperative for sending out on a divine mission. The fact that God himself sends gives this ordinary usage a special content, for those sent thus are bearers of a divine commission (cf. Abraham in Gen. 22:2, Nathan in 2 Sam. 7:5, Elijah in 1 Kgs. 19:15, etc.).

6. As death ends life's journey, it is a "going the way of all the earth" (1 Kgs. 2:2). This is a going with no return (2 Sam. 12:23). The dead are gathered to the fathers in the place of the dead. Later this place is seen as a holding area prior to judgment and resurrection. God does not journey into Hades. The OT refers to the rapture of Enoch (Gen. 5:24) and the ascension of Elijah (2 Kgs. 2:11), but only in later Judaism do we find accounts of heavenly journeys by the heroes of faith or of ascents into heaven or paradise during life with the accompanying disclosure of the secrets of things to come.

7. Philo makes no great use of *poreúomai* and never refers to walking under God's claim. Where he uses the term, it has a moral flavor. The king's highway is for Philo the royal way of virtue and the true middle way. He allegorizes the serpent's creeping (Gen. 3:14), and the interpretation of the name Zilpah as "accompanying mouth" suggests to him that Zilpah should keep her virtue by what she says. The usage of Josephus contains nothing distinctive.

C. The NT.

1. Literal Usage. Used by the NT in the middle and passive, the verb means "to go," "to travel," "to journey" (Lk. 13:33; Acts 9:3). It occurs in parting salutations (Lk. 7:50). It denotes going to a task in Jn. 11:11. Details about the going may be given, e.g., through Galilee (Mk. 9:30), before the sheep (Jn. 10:4), to Israel (Mt. 2:20), after demagogues (Lk. 21:8). Hebraisms are common (Mt. 2:8 etc.).

2. Going to Death. The concept of going to death occurs in the NT. For Jesus this is a divinely appointed way (Lk. 22:22), and Peter expresses a readiness to tread it with Jesus (22:23). At the judgment the wicked are told to depart into eternal fire (Mt. 25:41), and the traitor goes to his own place in Acts 1:25.

3. Imperative Use. The imperative expresses God's sovereign command to Joseph in Mt. 2:20. Jesus in healing power tells the sick man to go home in Lk. 5:24 (cf. Jn. 4:50; Mt. 8:9). He sends out his disciples on their mission in Mt. 10:6-7. An indicative often follows such imperatives (Mt. 2:21; Lk. 5:25, etc.).

4. The Mission of Jesus. The Baptist declares to those who go out to him the message of threatening eschatological judgment. Jesus goes to the people, so that *poreúomai*, while describing his travels, also expresses his mission. At times he goes off to pray or to seek solitude (Lk. 4:42). But he also goes ahead under divine compulsion (Mt. 19:15) even though this be to rejection (Lk. 13:33). His going is a model for his followers (Lk. 9:57-58). He goes out to find his sheep (Mt. 18:12); he goes before his flock to protect and provide for it (Jn. 10:4).

5. *The Apostles.* As itinerants, the disciples carry Jesus' message to the lost sheep of Israel (Mt. 10:6). Mary Magdalene is sent out by the risen Lord to tell of his resurrection (Jn. 20:17). The disciples are then sent out to preach judgment and salvation (Mt. 28:19). Philip is sent to a lonely road (Acts 8:26), Ananias to the persecutor (9:15), and Peter to the Gentiles (10:20). Paul is an indefatigable itinerant (Acts 9:3; 19:21; 22:5, 10, 21).

6. *Transferred Moral and Religious Use.* The NT seldom uses *poreúomai* for the moral or religious walk. One instance is in Lk. 1:6, another in Acts 9:31. References to an ungodly walk occur in 1 Pet. 4:3; Jude 16, 18; 2 Pet. 3:3. Acts 14:16 says that God let all the nations walk in their own ways, probably with a religious nuance.

7. *Parting Discourses.* In Jn. 14:2-3, 12, 28; 16:7, 28 Jesus speaks of going to the Father. He goes on ahead to prepare a place for his disciples (14:2), and at his coming will take them to be with himself (14:3). When he goes, the disciples will do greater works (14:12). His going is his exaltation (14:28). It makes way for the coming of the Paraclete (16:7), completing his own redemptive work (16:28).

8. *The Ascension of Jesus.* In the NT *poreúomai* is used for the ascension in Acts 1:10-11; 1 Pet. 3:22. The ascension differs from the heavenly journey of the soul; it is an ascension of the total person. As an integral part of the exaltation of the resurrection, it leads to the enthronement and dominion of Jesus, and is the presupposition of his coming again in glory (Acts 1:11).

9. *The Descent into Hades.* 1 Pet. 3:19 uses *poreúomai* for the descent into Hades. The location and timing are debated, but the event takes place as part of the complex of crucifixion and resurrection, and the emphasis falls on the proclaiming of the gospel to seducing forces and seduced people. It is a mighty declaration of the victory of Jesus over all opposing forces.

eisporeúomai.

1. This word means "to go in," "to enter."

2. The LXX uses it for entry into a land (Ex. 1:1), a house (Lev. 14:46), and the sanctuary (Ex. 28:30). The expression "going in and out" is a common one (Dt. 28:19). There is a sexual nuance in Gen. 6:4.

3. In the NT the literal use occurs in Mk. 1:21 (Capernaum); 5:40 (the house); Acts 3:2 (the temple), and cf. "going in and out" in Acts 9:28. Figuratively the food that enters the body in Mk. 7:15 cannot make unclean (7:19), desires enter the heart in Mk. 4:19, and one enters God's kingdom in Lk. 18:24.

ekporeúomai.

1. This word means "to go or march out," "to flow out," "to emerge."

2. In the LXX it occurs for "going out" to war, for the "exodus," in the phrase "going out and in," for the "bursting forth" of springs, for "going out" of the sanctuary, for the "going forth" of words from the mouth or of God's word, for the "emerging" of infants from the womb, and for the "breaking out" of wrath.

3. In the NT the term means "to go forth" in Mt. 20:29, "to go out" in Acts 25:4. The people "go out" to John in Mt. 3:5. When the disciples "leave" they are to give testimony against unbelievers in Mk. 6:11. The dead will "emerge" from the tombs in Jn. 5:29. Demons "go out" in Acts 19:12. The word "goes forth" in Mt. 4:4. Words

of grace "go forth" from the mouth of Jesus in Lk. 4:22. Words that "go forth" may also pollute (Mt. 15:11). Vile words, then, should not "go forth" from Christian lips (Eph. 4:29). The Paraclete is the Spirit of truth who "proceeds" from the Father (Jn. 15:26). Many things "break forth" in Revelation, e.g., lightnings (4:5), fire (11:5), fire and brimstone (9:17-18), and unclean spirits (16:14). The word "issues" from the Lord's mouth (1:16), and a river of living water "flows forth" from the throne of God and the Lamb (22:1).   [F. HAUCK and S. SCHULZ, VI, 566-79]

---

pórnē [harlot], *pórnos* [fornicator], *porneía* [prostitution, fornication], *porneúō* [to commit fornication], *ekporneúō* [to live licentiously]

A. The Non-Jewish World.
I. Usage.

1. *pórnē* (from *pérnēmi*, "to sell") literally means "harlot for hire" (Greek harlots were usually slaves).

2. *pórnos* means "whoremonger," then "male prostitute."

3. *porneía* means "licentiousness" or "fornication" (rare in classical Greek).

4. *porneúō* means a. "to prostitute" (passive "to prostitute oneself"), and b. "to commit fornication."

5. *ekporneúō* means "to live licentiously."

II. Extramarital Intercourse.

1. *Cultic Prostitution*. This includes both the single act and a general state. The former is common in Persia. The latter is widespread in cults of mother deities and in Syria and Egypt. Greece rejects it, but it finds an entrance at Corinth and Athens, probably through trade with the Near East.

2. *Secular Prostitution*. Prostitutes are unknown in the Homeric age, but men often have concubines, e.g., female slaves. Prostitution arises with increasing prosperity. Slaves provide a source, as does depriving alien women of civil rights. The professional "friend" becomes a common figure in Greek society, and since intercourse is regarded as just as natural as eating and drinking, extramarital affairs are permitted for husbands. Yet excess is censured, and Plato defends intercourse with harlots only as long as it is secret and causes no offense. Sparta maintains stronger sexual discipline but is also the home of homosexuality. This becomes widespread, lesbianism less so. Among harlots those in brothels form the lowest class, those with some artistic skills a higher group, and independent harlots who can command high prices another higher class.

3. *The Sex Ethics of Stoicism*. Seeking liberation from passion, Stoicism condemns and resists extramarital intercourse, even with female slaves. By unclean acts a person defiles the deity within. Chastity is extolled and adultery regarded as unlawful and infamous.

B. The OT.
I. Usage.

1. The *porneúō* group is mostly used for the root *znh* and has such senses as "to be unfaithful," "to play the harlot." It may be used of the prostitute or of the betrothed or married woman who proves unfaithful.

2. *porneía* means "fornication" (sometimes involving adultery); figuratively it is a term for apostasy as unfaithfulness to God.

3. *pórnē* means "harlot."

4. *pórnos* occurs only in the Apocrypha.

5. *ekporneúō* means "to commit fornication," "to lead into fornication," and figuratively "to turn aside from God and go after other gods."

II. Fornication in the OT. The harlot is a familiar figure in the older histories (cf. Tamar in Gen. 38:15, Rahab in Josh. 2:1; cf. also Judg. 11:1; 16:1; 1 Kgs. 3:16). Social problems promote prostitution (Am. 7:17). Custom protects virgins (Gen. 34:31), but men are allowed some freedom so long as they avoid the wives of others. Sacral prostitution comes in with pagan worship (Jer. 3:2). The prophets combat both the secular and sacral forms (Am. 2:7; Jer. 5:7). The law provides severe penalties for betrothed women who are unfaithful (Dt. 22:21). The priest is not allowed to marry a harlot (Lev. 21:7, 14). No child of fornication may be a member of the covenant people (Dt. 23:3). Prov. 5 warns against the harlot. This is not just a warning against foreign wisdom, nor against foreigners acting as harlots, nor against the wives of others, but against all women, especially from other areas, that are a source of temptation. The repudiation of cultic prostitution goes hand in hand with a condemnation of all forms of *porneía.*

III. Cultic Prostitution in the OT. As noted, cultic prostitution comes into Israel from various pagan cults (cf. 1 Kgs. 14:24). Asa and Jehoshaphat try to end it (1 Kgs. 15:12; 22:47), but it is still there in Hosea's day (4:14). Deuteronomy forbids it (23:17), and Josiah roots it out from the temple (2 Kgs. 23:7). The translators avoid any special term for it, using the more general *pórnē* group or engaging in paraphrase.

IV. Israel's Unfaithfulness as porneía. Hos. 1–3 portrays the unfaithfulness of Israel to God as a form of adultery. Is. 1:21 uses the same image. Jeremiah, rejecting sacral prostitution, also depicts Israel and Judah as unfaithful women who play the harlot with many lovers (3:2). Ezekiel develops the image in extended allegories (16; 23). In a rather different use, Is. 23:15ff. and Nah. 3:1ff. describe Tyre and Nineveh as harlots because they ensnare and seduce people with their commerce and political devices.

C. Later Judaism.

1. Later Judaism shows how the use of *porneía* broadens out to include not only fornication or adultery but incest, sodomy, unlawful marriage, and sexual intercourse in general.

2. Sirach issues warnings against fornicating husbands and unfaithful wives (23:16ff.). Wine and women lead to apostasy (18:30ff.). The Wisdom of Solomon thinks the devising of idols is the source of *porneía* (14:12, 24ff.).

3. The Testaments of the Twelve Patriarchs give various warnings against *porneía.* The first of seven evil spirits is *porneía,* to which women are more subject than men, and which leads to idolatry. In Jubilees Joseph maintains his purity in temptation. Fornication involves paganism and defiles the individual, the family, and the land. Marriage ties with Gentiles are a form of impurity and desecration. The Damascus Document calls licentiousness one of the three nets of Belial. For Qumran it is a mark of the children of darkness, whom the children of light are to shun.

4. Philo views *porneía* as a blot and a disgrace. Allegorically *pórnoi* are polytheists. The honorable woman is *areté,* the dishonorable woman *hēdonḗ.* Josephus as an apologist for his people eliminates or softens references to fornication, e.g., in relation to Rahab or Jephthah's mother.

5. The later rabbis condemn not only extramarital intercouse but also unlawful

marriages, e.g., with women guilty of cohabitation outside marriage. If the illegality comes to light only later, prior intercourse becomes *porneía*. Unnatural forms of intercourse are viewed as licentiousness, but there is some vacillation on the condemnation of husbands who might practice it with their wives. The rabbis commend early marriage as a safeguard against fornication. The Noachic law makes fornication an offense for Gentiles. In this regard fornication becomes with murder and idolatry one of the three chief transgressions, to which blasphemy, judging, and theft are often added.

D. The NT.

I. The Proclamation of Jesus. The NT presupposes the existence of harlots in Palestine and the sinfulness of their trade (Mt. 21:31-32; Lk. 15:30). It also depicts their responsiveness to the message of the Baptist and the invitation of Jesus (Lk. 7:50; Mt. 21:31-32). Jesus proclaims grace and forgiveness to all who repent; the true defilement is within (Mt. 15:18-19), and it is a mark of unbelief. As regards divorce, debate arises concerning Mt. 5:32 and 19:9. In Mk. 10:9; 16:18; 1 Cor. 7:10 Jesus teaches the indissolubility of marriage as God's unconditional will. He thus sets aside the practice based on Dt. 24:1, which stricter schools take to apply to moral offenses, laxer schools to anything objectionable. The problem in Mt. 5:32 and 19:9 is perhaps that Jewish Christians who keep the law are required to divorce adulterous wives and hence cannot be responsible if these contract a new relationship which is from a Christian standpoint itself adulterous. Divorce itself is not conceded. In Jn. 8:41 the Jews claim that they are not born of fornication *(porneía),* but their works show that they are children of the devil rather than of Abraham or God (v. 44).

II. Acts. The only instances of the group in Acts are the three examples of *porneía* in 15:20, 29; 21:15. The apostolic council requires Gentile believers only to avoid four things, of which *porneía* is one (cf. Lev. 17–18). In a simplified version, the prohibitions refer to the three chief sins of idolatry, murder, and fornication, but this is probably secondary.

III. Paul, Hebrews, and James. Paul shows that *porneía* has no part in God's kingdom. The *pórnos* is excluded (1 Cor. 6:9; Eph. 5:5). Idolatry and licentiousness are linked together in 1 Cor. 6:9. The desert generation offers a warning (1 Cor. 10:8, 11). Unnatural sex in the pagan world is an outworking of divine judgment (Rom. 1:18ff.). The church must keep itself pure from such vices (1 Cor. 5:1ff.). Individual *porneía* pollutes the whole church (2 Cor. 12:19ff.). God's will for his people is sanctification (1 Th. 4:3ff.). The Christian is a temple of the Spirit and may not give to a harlot members that belong to Christ (1 Cor. 6:15-16). To do so is to shame both self and the church. Licentiousness is a work of the *sárx,* and is earthly; the Spirit opposes it, and believers are to seek what is above (Gal. 5:19ff.; Col. 3:1ff.). Marriage is a protection against it (1 Cor. 7:2). Serious though fornication is, there is forgiveness for it (1 Cor. 6:11). Thus Rahab is justified by a faith (Heb. 11:31) that shows itself in works (Jms. 2:25).

IV. Revelation. In the letters to Pergamum and Thyatira, the writer of Revelation condemns libertines in the congregations who permit the eating of idol meats and free sex as a demonstration of their superiority (2:14, 20-21). Among pagan sins in the last days Rev. 9:21 mentions sexual indulgence along with idolatry, murder, witchcraft, and theft. In 17–19 *pórnē* and *porneúō* are comprehensive terms for the degeneracy of the world power. Like a city harlot of the day, it bears its name on a headband, and the name declares its nature (17:5). The nations seek its favors (18:3, 9) and ape its customs. Above all, it is *pórnē* as the center of paganism with its harlot-like apostasy from God. The drink that it offers promises pleasure but it is a cup of divine wrath. In contrast to the great harlot is the bride of Christ to which no unclean person belongs (21:27) because she worships God and the Lamb alone. The second death awaits *pórnoi* along with idolaters, murderers, and others (21:8; 22:15).

E. **The Apostolic Fathers.** Hermas *Mandates* 4.1.1 warns against *porneía,* which differs from but also includes adultery (cf. *Mandates* 8.3; 4.1.5). We do not find the transferred use in the apostolic fathers, who abandon the terminology of the OT prophets.   [F. HAUCK and S. SCHULZ, VI, 579-95]

pósis → *pínō*

---

potamós [river],   *potamophórētos* [swept away by a stream],   *Iordánēs* [the Jordan]

---

potamós.

A. **Greek Usage outside the NT.**

1. Secular Greek. The primary sense of *potamós* is "water rushing swiftly by," hence "flowing water," "stream," "river." The ocean that streams around the earth can be called *potamós;* from it derive all seas, rivers, springs, and wells. In Egypt *potamós* with the article denotes the Nile. *potamoí* are early personified as river gods, often depicted as bulls because the noise and tossing of running water remind of bulls. A figurative use occurs, e.g., streams of fire; the idea is that of violent forces that carry things off with them.

2. The LXX. In the LXX *potamós* with the article denotes the Nile. More generally the term suggests water with a lasting flow. This is important relative to the river of paradise in Gen. 2:10ff. and the eschatological river of Ezek. 47:1ff.; Zech. 14:8. The Hebrew term for wadi is not usually rendered by *potamós,* for it denotes the dry streambed rather than the torrent of the rainy season. The idea of lasting fullness controls the figurative use, possibly on the basis of the waters of the Nile (cf. Is. 48:18; Am. 8:8; 9:5). In Dan. 7:19 we have a stream of fire; other apocalyptic passages suggest that this is a feature of divine epiphany. *potamós* is an image of fullness in Sirach (cf. 39:22; 47:14).

3. Philo. Along with the ordinary use, especially for the Nile, Philo has a developed figurative use. Thus the Euphrates signifies divine wisdom, and the *noús* and *lógos* are both associated with *potamós.*

4. Josephus. Along with the river of paradise, Josephus mentions various streams with a steady flow, e.g., the Jordan, Euphrates, Nile, and Arnon. The Jabbok is a *potamós,* but the Kidron *cheimárrous* (wadi) (cf. Jn. 18:1).

B. **The River in the OT and Later Judaism.**

1. The OT. God creates the rivers and is thus their Lord. He can dry them up, even the Nile (Is. 19:5). He can change their water into blood (Ex. 7:14ff.). He fixes their course (Hab. 3:9), and can make them flow even in arid places (Ps. 105:41). They thus join in the chorus of praise to him (Ps. 98:8). River gods are excluded; there are no examples of the worship of water deities in Palestine. No idolatrous notions are associated with fish, although the commandment forbids making images of them. Prior to the conquest river gods might have been worshipped, for the rabbis forbid immolations into seas and rivers, but hard evidence is difficult to come by.

2. The Rabbis.

a. Rivers play an important role in casuistry. Thus salvation from death through the overflowing of a river is a reason for relaxing commands or prohibitions, and the damage done by swollen rivers plays a role.

b. For the rabbis the Euphrates rather than the Jordan is *the* river. Important is the conviction that the Euphrates is the eastern border of the land (Gen. 15:18). Sight of this river in particular leads to benediction of the Creator, and washing in it is said to keep people free of leprosy.

c. Rivers play a big role in rabbinic lustrations, but precautions have to be taken against impurities in the water. At times bathing is for refreshment rather than ritual purification, but there are no references to bathing for healing as prescribed by Greek doctors.

d. Rivers do not figure in proselyte baptism. River water might be used for this (cf. the demand for the washing of the whole body in flowing water), but later practice assumes that it takes place in the special bathhouse, where spring or well water is used.

C. The NT.

1. Ordinary Use.

a. Mt. 3:6 and Mk. 1:5 tell how the masses are baptized by John in the river Jordan, confessing their sins. That the Jordan is a river has importance both in connection with this baptism and as a historical reference. Some textual witnesses omit *potamó,* either because it is regarded as superfluous or because of the specific association of baptism with running water (cf. Did 7.1ff.). The expression *en tō Iordánē potamō* is an unusual one but it reflects, not a dogmatic interest, but the historical circumstance that, unlike proselyte baptism, this baptism takes place in a river, which alone is adequate for the crowds that demand it.

b. In Acts 16:13 Paul and his companions speak at a gathering by a *potamós,* a constant stream close to Philippi. The situation of the meeting place, probably a house, makes possible an observance of the rules of purification, although well water is more correct for this purpose. It may be noted that the ritual bath is permissible on the sabbath.

c. Paul meets dangers from swollen rivers according to 2 Cor. 11:26. The parable in Mt. 7:24ff.; Lk. 6:47ff. describes the force of water; in the rainy season it can sweep down torrentially and carry houses away. The parable is eschatological but it is based on the actuality of the land and its climate and need not be related to the flood or to the woes of the end-time.

2. potamós in Revelation.

a. In Rev. 8:10-11 and 16:4 the *potamoí,* as one part of the world, are ruined as they are turned into wormwood or blood. Without unpolluted rivers life is impossible.

b. The references to the Euphrates in 9:14 and 16:12 adopt OT terms and depict this river as the eastern boundary. When God dries it up, it loses its protective function, and as a result the chosen land will be the theater of the final battle. It may be recalled that the Euphrates serves as the frontier of the Roman empire.

c. In Rev. 12:15 the dragon pours water like a river to sweep away the woman; the use here carries a stress on the element of fullness.

d. The river of the water of life in 22:1 combines the primal river of paradise (Gen. 2:10ff.) with the eschatological temple river of Ezekiel (47:1ff.). The thought of fullness of life is suggested, and the tree of life links up with the similar tree in Gen. 2:9.

God's consummating work both restores and transcends his creative work with new and unrestricted fullness. Apart from Jn. 7:38 there is no precise parallel for the idea of the river of the water of life, although we find references, as at Qumran, to the source of life or the water of life. Older motifs may be adopted, but they are integrated here into the concept of consummated fullness. The sanctuaries of Aesculapius contain sacred springs flowing from under the sanctuary and thus offer some parallel to the depiction of the river as flowing forth from the throne of God and the Lamb. It may be noted that the river does not divide like that of paradise. Here, then, is no mere restoration except at a higher level.

3. *The Saying in Jn. 7:37-38.* On the last day of Tabernacles, with its solemn dispensing of water, Jesus issues the enigmatic saying Jn. 7:37-38. Problems arise regarding the proper division of the verse, its placing, and the use of the formula *hē graphḗ.* In view of the associated Rev. 7:37-38, which also associates the river with the Lamb, it may be noted that Jesus is more the dispenser of the water than its source (cf. also Jn. 4:10). The invitation resembles the ancient invitation to the Passover— an argument for the traditional punctuation. The interpretation in v. 39 is also important. When Jesus has gone, it is the Spirit who makes possible the continuation of his work in and through the disciples. The use of *potamós* suggests that the force and fullness of life will remain unrestrictedly at work; streams of living water will flow out by way of the disciples into the world and will be available for the thirsty who believe. Along these lines one can understand the statement that rivers of living water will flow out of those who drink, although what precise Scripture is in view is still debatable (cf. Is. 12:3; 44:3).

potamophórētos. This word occurs in Egyptian papyri with reference to damage done by the Nile. There is no corresponding term in rabbinic writings, but these often refer to floods and their effects. The one NT instance is in Rev. 12:15. Here the dragon, by sending a stream of water after the woman, seeks to sweep her away like a flood, i.e., to rob her of control of her own destiny.

Iordánēs.
1. The Name and Its Meaning.

a. The Course. The river Jordan rises on Mt. Hermon, flows along the Great Rift Valley, passes through the lake of Galilee, and empties into the Dead Sea about 400 meters below sea level. It is not navigable in its lower reaches but contains fish up to the place where its waters mingle with those of the Dead Sea.

b. The Name. The Greek name is usually *Iordánēs,* but *Iórdanos* also occurs, e.g., in Josephus. Philo and Josephus do not always have the article; the NT does.

c. The Meaning of the Name. Philo links the name with the Hebrew for *katabaínō,* and can thus see in its crossing by Jacob (Gen. 32:11) a type of the overcoming of low spiritual periods. Josephus connects it with Dan, perhaps an early tradition which Jerome later adopts when he says that the meaning is "the river of Dan." Parallel names exist in other areas in Europe and Asia Minor, and this suggests that it is perhaps a general term for a stream which later becomes a proper name. As yet, however, this is merely a conjecture.

2. The Jordan in the OT and Later Judaism.

a. Geographical Position. Num. 34:10ff. fixes the Jordan as the eastern frontier. Although some tribes remain on the far side, the conquest proper begins with the crossing of the Jordan (Josh. 3ff.). The river is a frontier in the NT, and the customs post there brings out its significance as such. In the promise of Gen. 15:18, however, the Jordan is part of the land, and the Euphrates is the eastern border. Scribal materials, then, sometimes group the territory on the far side of the river with Galilee and Judea.

b. Evaluation of the Water. Naaman is cleansed by washing in the Jordan (2 Kgs. 5), and Elisha works another miracle there in 2 Kgs. 6:1ff., but the focus is on the prophet, not on the water as such. Like the OT, later Judaism ascribes no special dignity to the river. Qumran has no particular relation to the river and the Damascus Document does not mention it. The rabbis reject the suitability of its water for certain cultic acts. Theoretically proselyte baptism may be given in it, but there are no records of any actual instances. Below the lake of Galilee access to it is difficult, and the road from Jerusalem to Jericho is a dangerous one in NT times (Lk. 10:30).

3. *The River God Jordan.* The Titus arch in Rome carries a depiction of the Jordan personifying the conquered province, but this is the only known instance of the association of the river with a god on ancient monuments, and the rabbis either do not know the myth or ignore it. Christian art, however, adopts the personification of the Jordan in connection with Joshua, Elijah, and especially Jesus, but with no suggestion, of course, that the river is a god, and probably with a view to making the point that the water of baptism takes the place of the water of Jordan and involves participation with Christ.

4. *The Jordan in the NT and Primitive Christianity.*

a. Survey. *Iordánēs* occurs 15 times in the NT (six in Matthew, four in Mark, two in Luke, and three in John). The references are mostly to the work of the Baptist or to that of Jesus. In general the NT shows great restraint. This is repeated even in the apocryphal gospels, while the apostolic fathers do not mention the river at all, and only Justin among the Apologists does so. It commands no basic interest.

b. The Baptist. Baptism in the Jordan seems to be initiated by the Baptist. He presumably works both east and west of the river, but the data do not enable us to fix the locations with any precision. Indeed, only Matthew and Mark say specifically that he baptized in the river. John does not contest this, but wants to stress that baptism is with water, not especially with that of the Jordan.

c. Jesus and the Jordan. Jesus is among those baptized in the Jordan, but the river is not significant as such. In Luke Jesus' baptism is closely integrated into the Baptist's movement; his prayer, however, expresses his obedient waiting for God's call to begin his own ministry. The Gospel of John, too, sets Jesus at the heart of the Baptist's movement and relates the event to the mission and call of Jesus. In Jesus' later ministry the river Jordan plays no special role. We simply read that people from the Jordan region throng to Jesus (Mt. 4:25) and that he ministers there on the way to Jerusalem (Mt. 19:1; cf. Jn. 3:22ff.; 10:40). The Jordan is not even mentioned in the Zacchaeus incident in Lk. 19:1ff., although this is not due to any desire to separate Jesus' ministry from that of John. The reserve of the NT regarding the river suggests that some principle is at issue regarding what is specifically Christian.

d. Primitive Christianity and the Jordan. Acts does not relate primitive baptismal practice to the Jordan. Neither in Acts 2:37ff., 8:9ff., 8:26ff., nor 10:47-48 can there by any question of baptism in the Jordan. References to the Baptist mention water and repentance, but not the Jordan. The other books do not mention John at all and say nothing about any particular water in relation to baptism. The only requirement for baptism is that there be some kind of water available (Acts 8:36). Such water is in no way linked to that of the Jordan.

e. The Early Church. Justin mentions the Jordan in his *Dialogue with Trypho*, but only in such a way as to show that it is a site of God's working in salvation history

(49.3; 51.2; 88.3.7). Elisha's miracle in 2 Kgs. 6:1ff. becomes a type of water baptism. Jesus' baptism in the Jordan is combined with the idea of a consecration of water by his immersion. Water is important, but not specifically the water of the Jordan. Unlike Did. 7.1-2, Justin makes no plea for the use of flowing water. Some groups seem to have regarded this as important, following Jewish practice and maintaining a closer link with that of John. But these are probably marginal groups. Thus Tertullian (*On Baptism* 4) argues that all water may serve in baptism in virtue of Jesus' baptism. Some liturgies describe all consecrated water as Jordan, and this may have influenced the Mandaeans in their insistence on running water and their mention of the Jordan. But Jewish Christians in Jerusalem are not responsible for the idea that running water, symbolized by the Jordan, is the proper water for Christian baptism. The final question, perhaps, is whether the church baptizes in continuation of John's baptism, or because Jesus was baptized, or because he began his work in connection with his baptism. Where running water is esteemed, there is a closer link to John and hence to the Jordan. In Rom. 6:3ff., however, Paul relates Christian baptism to the death of Jesus as well as his baptism, and Acts connects it with the receiving of the Spirit (10:44ff.). The separation of baptism from the Jordan, like that of the Lord's Supper from the Passover, reflects the understanding of the church as something not merely different but new. Around A.D. 400 some believers are still being baptized in the Jordan but there are also baptisteries in Jerusalem which are decorated with pictures of the baptism of Jesus. What takes place, then, is the same as what took place in Jesus' baptism, whether or not the baptism takes place in the Jordan or in running water similar to it.

[K. H. Rengstorf, VI, 593-623]

potḗrion, potízō, pótos → pínō

---

poús [foot]

A. Secular Greek. This word means human or animal "foot," the "foot" of an artifact, or the "lower end" of something, whether footlike or not. As a foot, it serves as a measure of length. Poetically it expresses movement and hence occurs in phrases denoting involvement or evaluating persons. Address to the feet of the powerful expresses subordination.

B. Comparative Religion. Connected with the idea of power is the belief that the footprints of gods or divine persons can bring about cures. References to worship of the foot of Sarapis may be found. Feet also occur in theophanies, and they are all that may be seen in ascensions. Baring the foot in worship is a common practice. The aim is to put off defiled coverings, to make direct contact with the power of deity, or to avoid magical hindrances caused by knots or ties.

C. The OT and Judaism.
1. The LXX uses *poús* for various Hebrew words meaning "sole," "heel," "hoof," "foot," "step," and "what lies at the foot."
2. The term is used figuratively in connection with people treading a path, i.e., a way of life (cf. *poús* and *psychḗ* as parallels in Ps. 57:6).
3. The foot is a sign of power in Josh. 10:24; 14:9; 2 Sam. 22:39; Ps. 47:3. In contrast, we find a low estimation of the foot in the euphemism in Judg. 3:24.
4. The foot is uncovered for religious reasons in Ex. 3:5; Josh. 5:13ff. There are

no shoes in the list of priestly vestments in Lev. 8. The reason for uncovering the foot in the OT and Judaism is reverent abasement before God.

5. In connection with theophanies we find references to the feet, the footprints, or the footstool of God in, e.g., Pss. 18:9; 77:19; Ex. 24:10. Hab. 3:5 speaks of the treading of God's feet, and Zech. 14:4 says that when God comes on the last day his feet will stand on the Mount of Olives.

D. The NT.

1. Use for the Whole Person. In the NT, which uses *poús* infrequently and sometimes for the leg and not just the foot (Rev. 1:15), the whole person is meant in some cases, e.g., Mt. 4:6; Acts 5:9.

2. Transferred Use. On an OT basis the *poús* may refer to the person who is ready or active (cf. Lk. 1:79 [Is. 59:8]; Heb. 12:13 [Prov. 4:26]; Rom. 10:15 [Is. 52:17]), which has the mission of those who preach salvation in view. The *poús* that gives offense in Mk. 9:45 is partly literal (the foot is the instrument) and partly figurative (the way of life is what really scandalizes).

3. As a Symbol of Power. Only in Revelation do we find the OT use of the foot to denote suppression and subjection (Rev. 3:9). The promise of Rom. 16:20 is that God will crush Satan under believers' feet. Jesus fulfils eschatologically the expectations of Pss. 8:6 and 110:1. Interest focuses, then, not on power plays in politics but on the final conflict. Strength and rule are denoted when the feet of the angel are compared to pillars of fire in Rev. 10:1 and the woman has the moon under her feet in 12:1 (cf. also the bear's feet of the beast in 13:2).

4. Subordination. Respect for the law underlies the expression in Acts 22:3. The apostles represent God when offerings are laid at their feet in Acts 4:35 (cf. 5:10). Shaking the dust off the feet is a judicial gesture in Mk. 6:11. But the authority is that of God or Christ, for Peter will not let Cornelius fall at his feet (Acts 10:25), nor will the angel let the divine fall down to worship him in Rev. 19:10.

5. Veneration of Jesus. No restriction is placed on the veneration of Jesus. The Baptist confesses his unworthiness to unloose his shoes (Mk. 1:7). The divine in Rev. 1:17 falls at his feet. Sometimes the gesture of falling at his feet or grasping them is one of courtesy or respect for the Messiah, but in many instances it is plainly one of worship (cf. Mk. 5:22; 7:25; Mt. 15:30; Jn. 11:32). The majesty of Jesus is seen and he is worshipped as God on his throne is worshipped in Rev. 7:11. Sitting at Jesus' feet may express only readiness to learn and grateful discipleship, but grasping the feet of the risen Lord in Mt. 28:9 is plainly obeisance. The same is true of the washing, anointing, and kissing of the feet of Jesus in Lk. 7:36ff. As the one who forgives sins, Jesus is exalted far above sinners, and it is to his feet (as in theophanies) that worship must be addressed and an offering made (cf. Jn. 11:2; 12:3).

6. The Foot Washing. It is paradoxical that the Lord of glory should wash human feet, but the paradox is the point of the incident. What Jesus does is not to initiate a rite but to interpret his saving work as a self-humbling in the service of others. As an example, this action urges the disciples to discharge a similar mission with the same humility. In 1 Tim. 5:10 washing of the saints' feet by widows is perhaps to be construed along similar lines and may rest on the same tradition.

7. Cultic Uncovering. This is not commanded in the NT and the only reference is in Stephen's speech (Acts 7:33), where he quotes Ex. 3:5.   [K. WEISS, VI, 624-31]

---

prássō [to do], *prágma* [deed, event, task], *pragmateía* [business], *pragmateúomai* [to be occupied with], *diapragmateúomai* [to gain by trading], *práktōr* [bailiff], *práxis* [action, works]

---

prássō.

A. Outside the NT.

I. Secular Greek.

1. Meaning. This word first means a. "to cross," "to traverse," "to advance," then b. "to travel so as to achieve something," c. "to be busy with," "to pursue," d. financially "to demand," "to collect," e. "to do," "to act" (with adverb denoting moral worth or circumstances), and finally f., in magic, "to perform a magical act." A bad sense g. "to betray" appears early in history.

2. Survey. Only rarely is the verb used for acts of deity. Thus Plato uses *poieín* etc. for divine creating, but not *prássein.* The only application to the gods is when divine action is compared to human.

3. Human prássein. As regards human action there is much overlapping with *poieín* but *prássein* denotes the activity rather than the outcome (at least in later Greek). It is thus an apt term in philosophical inquiry which considers human action apart from its content and objects, i.e., the nature and purpose of action. Lack of knowledge rather than capacity lies behind defective action according to a common Greek view. In Epictetus imparted knowledge enables one to perceive and overcome the antithesis between will and act.

II. The LXX. In the LXX *prássein* plays a much smaller role than *poieín,* perhaps because it is too weak to express either divine creating or human action in obedience, and perhaps also because it has too much the sense of business. An ethically negative sense clings to it in Wisdom writings (cf. Prov. 14:17; Job 27:6; 36:21, 23). Only in Maccabees docs it have a positive sense (cf. 2 Macc. 12:43; 4 Macc. 3:20).

III. Philo and Josephus.

1. Philo. Philo refers only once to divine *prássein.* As regards human action, he seeks a harmony of thought, will, and action. Love of God controls piety, but God tends to be equated with nature along Stoic lines. Thus the antithesis of will and action is no serious problem for the sage.

2. Josephus. Josephus often uses both the simple *prássein* and various compounds.

B. The NT.

1. Positive Evaluation. The NT never uses *prássein* for God's work and mostly gives it a negative sense relative to human action. Of the 39 instances, 19 are in Luke and Acts, and 18 in Paul. A positive sense occurs only in Acts 26:20, Rom. 2:25, Phil. 4:9, and Acts 15:29 (either "you will do well" or "it will go well with you"). The use is neutral in Acts 5:35, Rom. 9:11, 2 Cor. 5:10, Acts 26:26, 1 Cor. 9:17, and 1 Th. 4:11. The exacting of money is the issue in Lk. 3:13 and 19:23.

2. Negative Evaluation. The context makes a negative evaluation clear in Acts 19:19. The expression in Acts 16:28 is a singular one (cf. Lk. 22:23). Mitigating circumstances are not the point in Acts 3:17 but the divine forbearance. While *prássein* is synonymous with other verbs of action in Rom. 13:4 and 1 Cor. 5:2, its negative import is apparent in 1 Th. 4:11; Jn. 3:20-21; 5:29. In Rom. 1:32 *prássein* is used for those who are rotting in vices while *poieín* is the term for the willful transgression of

God's command (cf. 2:1ff.). Even in relation to sin *prássein* is less precise and *poieín* more definite. This is perhaps the point in Rom. 7:15, 19 as well. In v. 15 the act that is only a doing is *prássein* but the act that is hated is *poieín*. In v. 19, however, *poieín* denotes the seriousness of the situation in which what is not willed is done, while *prássein* expresses the stupid doing of the evil that is not willed.

3. Acts 26:31 etc. In this context Paul is said not to have done anything worthy of death, in conscious parallelism to the declaration of Jesus' innocence by Pilate (Lk. 23:4, 14-15, 22). In the case of Jesus the declaration does not shift the blame from Pilate to the Jews, for Herod concurs (Lk. 23:14-15), and the execution of an innocent person is the true injustice. Luke's point is rather that God overrules the execution of the innocent Jesus in order to bring salvation to the guilty. Paul, too, becomes God's instrument in Rome by being treated as guilty even though innocent. In contrast, he himself admits that he earlier thought he should do many things against the name of Jesus (Acts 26:9).

C. Apostolic Fathers. The tendency in these authors is to use *prássein* mainly for bad conduct (1 Clem. 35:6; 2 Clem. 4:5; Hermas *Mandates* 3.3).

prágma.
1. This word has the following senses: a. "undertaking," "obligation," "task"; b. "cause," "affair," "phenomenon"; c. "act," "fact," "event"; d. "circumstances," "relations," "situation"; and e. "legal process," "trial."
2. In the LXX the usual sense is "matter," "affair," although "word" is also possible. With reference to God's acts we read of "wondrous things" in Is. 25:1. Indefinitely "something" (or, negatively, "nothing") might be meant. *prágma* denotes "evil" in Lev. 7:21. In the plural, affairs of state are at issue in 2 Macc. 9:24, and other senses are heroic deeds (Jdt. 8:32) and legal affairs (1 Macc. 10:35).
3. In six of eleven NT instances the meaning is the neutral one of "affairs" (Mt. 18:19), "business" (Rom. 16:2), "events" (Lk. 1:1), or "things" (Heb. 6:18; 10:1). In Heb. 11:1 we do not have a subjective genitive, as though unseen things were the proof. Faith, oriented to God, brings assurance regarding the promises. A negative evaluation occurs in Acts 5:4; 2 Cor. 7:11. In 1 Th. 4:6 "business" is possible, as is "lawsuit," but "matter" is the most natural meaning, the content being supplied by what precedes. Christians are not to wrong one another in the matter of sex, and one of the decisive factors in pagan society is thus set under the sanctification that God wills (v. 3). This is not simply a matter of interpersonal relations but of obedience to God (v. 8).
4. Among the apostolic fathers Hermas especially uses the term, mostly in the colorless sense of "thing," "affair," "matter" (*Visions* 3.11.3; *Mandates* 5.2.2).

pragmateía.
1. This word means a. "zealous concern about something," b. "business," "work," "affairs," "duties"; c. "trade"; d. "writing," "treatise."
2. The usual senses occur in the eight LXX instances.
3. In the rabbis we find adoption of the term as a loanword for "business."
4. The only NT occurrence is in 2 Tim. 2:4, where "civilian affairs" is the point. Pay is not the main issue (cf. 1 Cor. 9:7) but turning aside from the various demands of life to prompt and total service of Christ.
5. Only Hermas of the apostolic fathers uses the term, e.g., for "affairs" in *Mandates* 10.1.4 and "business" in *Visions* 3.6.5.

pragmateúomai, diapragmateúomai.

1. *pragmateúomai* is used for "to be occupied with," with reference to affairs of state, literary composition, or business. The only NT instance in Lk. 19:13 obviously relates to trading.

2. *diapragmateúomai* is a more intensive form. In Lk. 19:15, the only NT instance, it signifies the profit gained by trading.

práktōr.

1. This word, originally meaning "avenger," comes to be used for those who execute judgments, exact penalties, or collect taxes, although a more general sense is also possible. The one NT example is in Lk. 12:58, where "bailiff" is the meaning; the parable calls for repentance before the divine decision is made and judgment takes its ineluctable course.

práxis.

1. In secular Greek this word means a. "act" (including the result); b. "action"; c. "individual completed act"; d. "situation," "condition," "destiny"; e. "magical action"; f. "deception"; g. "sexual intercourse."

2. The LXX seldom uses the term, and when it does, it takes it in the ordinary Greek senses. Only in Sir. 35:22 does it have a religious sense, i.e., "works."

3. In Philo it is controlled by the verb. There is no reference to God's *práxis*. For specific acts Philo usually has the plural. He stresses acts more than words, but strongly supports the Stoic unity of word, will, and act.

4. The seven NT instances are by no means uniform, although all tend to carry a derogatory nuance. Acts are "works" in Mt. 16:27. Lk. 23:51 echoes the Stoic unity of word, will, and act. Action or mode of action—not so much the deeds as the inner nature—is the point in Rom. 8:13. Similarly in Col. 3:9 the old nature, which is to be mortified, has already been put off in Christ. In Acts 19:18 there might be a forsaking of wicked acts in general, but in context it seems that "magical practices" are in view. The title of Acts *(práxeis apostólōn)* probably comes from the second century. It hardly accords with Luke's own usage or with his attributing of the church's missionary activity to the exalted Lord and his word rather than to the apostles. The latter emphasis rules out any idea that the "experiences" of the apostles are the theme.

5. In the apostolic fathers *práxis* is most common in Hermas; it refers to human deeds, usually in a bad sense (cf. *Mandates* 4.2.1; *Similitudes* 4.4).

[C. MAURER, VI, 632-44]

praüpátheia → páschō

---

praǘs [gentle, meek], *praǘtēs* [gentleness, meekness]

A. Secular Greek.

1. praǘs. This word means a. "mild" of things, b. "tame" of animals, c. "gentle" or "pleasant" of persons, d. "kindly" or "lenient" of such things as activities or punishments. The adverb *práōs* denotes quiet and friendly composure.

2. praǘtēs. This word means "mild and gentle friendliness." The Greeks value this virtue highly so long as there is compensating strength. Thus rulers should be gentle with their own people and stern with others. Laws should be severe but judges should show leniency. Gentleness is a mark of culture and wisdom if it does not degenerate into self-abasement. It is especially a virtue in women and characterizes female deities.

For Aristotle it is a mean between bad temper and spineless incompetence, between extreme anger and indifference.

B. The LXX and Hellenistic Judaism.

1. The OT. praûs occurs 12 times for various Hebrew terms. Since the Hebrew relates primarily to the social position of a servant or inferior, and thus carries the nuance of humble, *praûs* is never used of God. In the Pentateuch *praûs* is used only in Num. 12:3 for Moses. In Joel 3:10 there is no Hebrew original for *praûs;* the point is that the gentle must become warriors. Zech. 9:9-10 depicts the king of salvation as the king of peace. In Ps. 45:4 *praûtēs* is a quality of the royal hero, and although the group does not occur in Proverbs, Sirach values *praûtēs* as pleasing to God (1:27), an adornment of women (36:23), and an antidote to arrogance (10:28). Since the prophets castigate the wealthy, the lowly come to be seen as the bearers of the promise who keep God's commandments (Zeph. 2:3). A quiet and expectant bearing of destiny that is grounded in God is a mark of piety (cf. Is. 26:6; Pss. 76:9; 37:9ff.).

2. Philo. On the basis of the LXX and Greek ethics, Philo praises God's judicial mildness and depicts Moses as one who moderates passion. The Jews deserve high praise for their meekness in persecution.

3. Josephus. Josephus uses the group for meekness in affliction.

4. Qumran. The Qumran texts demand mildness from members of the sect in accordance with a dualistic view of power which makes gentleness constitutive for the children of light.

C. The NT.

1. Matthew. In accordance with their different emphases in Christology, Mark, Luke, John, and Hebrews never use the group, and Paul uses only the noun. Matthew alone of the Synoptists uses *praûs* (Mt. 5:5; 11:29; 21:5). In 11:25ff. Jesus calls himself *praûs.* His is a lowly mission, and his heart is fixed only on God; for this very reason he can invite with full authority. In 21:5 (cf. Zech. 9:9) he makes a peaceful entry into Jerusalem in sharp contrast to Zealot hopes. In Mt. 5:5 the meek to whom the inheritance is promised are those who acknowledge the great and gracious will of God. The emphasis here is on the future; they will rule with God in the eschaton.

2. Paul. Dealing with the contentious Corinthians, Paul brings to bear the meekness of Christ that has its basis in love (2 Cor. 10:1; 1 Cor. 4:21), not in weakness. *praûtēs* is a gift of the Spirit in Gal. 5:23; it enables the believer to correct others without arrogance (6:1). In Col. 3:12 it is one of the gifts of election, and in Eph. 4:2 it is worthy of Christian calling.

3. Pastoral Epistles. In 2 Tim. 2:25 correcting opponents with gentleness will perhaps bring about their conversion. Tit. 3:2 commends gentleness to all people, and in 1 Pet. 3:16 the defense of the faith should be with gentleness.

4. James. Jms. 1:21 contrasts *praûtēs* with anger (v. 20); it entails a readiness to be taught in the word. The divine wisdom is gentle and peaceable (3:13, 17), and its gentleness will be a mark of the righteous in pleasing contrast to bitterness and contention.

D. Apostolic Fathers. The usage here is much the same as in the NT. The adjective and noun occur in lists or along with other virtues. *praûtēs* is an essential Christian virtue expected in a bishop. Surprisingly, no appeal is made to the example of Jesus.

[F. HAUCK and S. SCHULZ, VI, 644-51]

---

présbys [old, elder], *presbýteros* [older, elder], *presbýtēs* [old man], *sympresbýteros* [fellow elder], *presbytérion* [council of elders], *presbeúō* [to be older, be an ambassador]

---

présbys, presbýteros, sympresbýteros (→ *epískopos*), *presbytérion*.

A. Meaning and Occurrence.

1. *presbýteros,* comparative of *présbys,* means a. "older," or simply "old," with no negative connotations but rather a sense of venerability. It then comes into use b. for presidents, members of various guilds, committees etc., village officials, executive committees of priests, and senior groups of different types. c. In the Jewish and Christian sphere it is often hard to distinguish between the designation of age and the title of office. Age is clearly the point in Gen. 18:11-12 and Jn. 8:9; Acts 2:17. Elsewhere the *presbýteroi* are the bearers of a tradition (Mt. 15:2), and a title is at issue when the reference is to members of governing bodies, as in the nation, the synagogue, or the church.

2. *tó presbytérion,* which occurs in pre-Christian works only in Sus. 50 for the "dignity of elders," occurs in the NT for a. "the Sanhedrin," and b. "the council of elders" in the church (cf. Lk. 22:66; 1 Tim. 4:14). Common in Ignatius, the term signifies for him the council of presbyters, which parallels that of the apostles (*Philadelphians* 5.1) and functions as the bishop's council (8.1).

3. The *sympresbýteros* is the "fellow elder" (1 Pet. 5:5); it becomes a common collegial form used by bishops in addressing presbyters.

B. Elders in Israel and Judah.

1. Elders are presupposed in all strata of the OT. As the heads of large families or clans they are leaders of large units of the people. Yet they lose their original tribal relationship and appear in the OT as representatives of the whole nation along with and under figures like Moses and Joshua. At God's command Moses assembles them to declare to them the approaching exodus and to go with them to Pharaoh (Ex. 3:16, 18). It is they who supervise the Passover and receive God's revelation at Sinai (Ex. 12:21; 19:7). Some of them witness the miracle at Horeb, and 70 see God's glory at the making of the covenant (Ex. 17:5; 24:1). The elders lead the attack on Ai and are specially summoned to the council at Shechem (Josh. 8:10; 24:1). A special group is appointed by God to share the burdens of Moses (Num. 11:16-17, 24-25) and is validated by receiving a portion of Moses' spirit. The rabbis later lay great stress on Ex. 24 and Num. 11. The latter passages form a model for the Sanhedrin and offer support for rabbinic ordination.

2. In the age of the judges and the monarchy elders are leading members of the municipalities who make decisions in political, military, and judicial matters. In addition, elders from the districts or tribes meet for common decisions (1 Sam. 30:26 etc.). It is the elders who bring up the ark in 1 Sam. 4:3, who demand a king in 8:4, whom David wins over in 2 Sam. 5:3, who defect in 17:4, who represent the people in 1 Kgs. 8:1. Their power declines with the rise of a royal bureaucracy, but the king has to turn to them in critical situations or when important decisions must be taken (1 Kgs. 20:7-8; 21:8, 11).

3. Deuteronomy accords the elders specific powers, although only in the local sphere and in company with judges and minor officials. For examples of their functions, see Dt. 19:11ff.; 21:18ff.; 22:13ff. Whereas judges and officials have to be

newly appointed (16:18), the elders are local colleges with limited administrative powers. They are much to the fore in special assemblies (29:9), although not in this case as an official corporation.

4. During and after the exile the elders still play a role both at home and abroad. Local elders plead for Jeremiah in Jer. 26:17, but representative elders in Jerusalem engage in idolatry (Ezek. 8:1). In exile the elders emerge once again as the main leaders in limited self-government. Families are now more important and an aristocracy develops. The elders owe their authority to the special position of the families to which they belong. Thus new terms, e.g., "heads of families," begin to appear. Governors like Nehemiah have considerable difficulty with this new nobility. City elders still play a role (Ezr. 10:7ff.) but these are not identical with the group that Ezra selects in 10:16. As suggested by Neh. 5:17, the trend is toward the establishment of a kind of senate made up of representatives of the leading families in Jerusalem and acting as a centralized college.

5. The beginnings of the council of elders, the Sanhedrin, go back to the Persian period. At first all the members, then only lay members, are called elders; the two other groups are the scribes and the priests, the dominant group. After the fall of Jerusalem the Sanhedrin of Jamnia, composed of 72 elders, takes control, but with no political and only limited judicial power. It consists exclusively of scribes.

6. Elder is a term that is also used for leading older scholars, who may often be members of the Sanhedrin. This use prepares the way for the designation of ordained scholars as elders. It is also reflected in the tradition that 72 elders, i.e., those of good repute and scholarship, translated the OT into Greek.

7. In later Judaism *presbýteroi* is also a term for local authorities and for members of synagogue councils, although it is less common in this sense among dispersion Jews. The use for older people and for notable citizens, e.g., heads of leading families, continues.

C. The Tradition of the Elders in Jesus' Teaching. In the debate of Mk. 7:1ff. Jesus contrasts the commandments of God with the tradition of the elders (7:8). Jesus is not here setting the law as such against its extension, i.e., the Sadducees against the Pharisees. At times he can both amend the law (Mk. 10:1ff.) and use tradition (Mt. 12:11). Nevertheless, the command of God takes precedence over tradition, for, as Mt. 23 shows, tradition often takes the form of a hypocritical exposition that fails to subordinate ceremonial matters to the law of love.

D. Presbyters in the Primitive Christian Community.

1. The First Jerusalem Church. Acts 11:30 refers to elders in the first Jerusalem church. We also read of these elders in Acts 15:2ff. and 21:18; in 15:2ff. they are mentioned along with the apostles. If in 11:30 and 21:18 they obviously represent the congregation like a synagogue council, in 15:2ff. they function (with the apostles) more after the manner of the Sanhedrin. The formation of a body of elders probably takes place as the apostles leave Jerusalem and James assumes the leadership. Its functions are patterned partly after the synagogue council and partly after the Sanhedrin.

2. The Pauline Churches. Paul for the most part refers to leaders of the churches in terms of function rather than office. He enjoins obedience to them but more because of their ministry than their status. The constitutional principle is that of a plurality of gifts. This does not rule out, however, the existence of bishops and deacons (Phil. 1:1).

3. *Presbyteral Development.*

a. James. Jms. 5:14 says that the elders should anoint and pray for the sick. These elders are not just charismatic older believers but officebearers, although obviously with a gift of healing intercession. Since mutual confession and intercession are enjoined in 5:16, the passage does not support the view that these elders are confessors or liturgical leaders.

b. Acts. In Acts 14:23 Paul and Barnabas ordain elders in the Gentile churches. The address of 20:18ff. shows that they are to be overseers and pastors administering the apostles' legacy, following their example, and protecting the people against error. The designation of the elders as bishops in 20:28 (the only use in Acts) is of special interest.

c. 1 Peter. In 1 Pet. 5:1ff. the writer addresses the elders and younger believers as though these were age groups, but obviously the elders are a college of officebearers with a pastoral function. The warnings of vv. 2-3 show that they have charge of the funds and exercise authority. Yet their powers are not autonomous, for they are responsible to Christ, who alone is called *epískopos* (2:25). The dignity of the office may be seen in Peter's self-designation as *sympresbýteros,* for if this modestly sets him alongside them, it also sets them alongside him.

d. The Pastorals. In 1 Tim. 5:1 age is obviously denoted by *presbýteros,* but elsewhere an office is at issue. The *presbytérion* is a college (1 Tim. 4:14). Titus is to ordain *presbýteroi* (1:5), and *presbýteroi* are to be rewarded if they rule well (1 Tim. 5:17) and protected against frivolous charges (5:19). Preaching and teaching are a special function of at least some of the elders (5:17). The bishops and presbyters seem to be much the same (cf. Tit. 1:5, 7ff.). Yet the bishop is always in the singular and the presbyters are always plural (even in Tit. 1:5ff.). Already, then, there may be a tendency for a leading presbyter to take over administrative functions within the presbyteral college—the probable starting point for the later development of the monarchical bishop.

4. *Revelation.*

In Rev. 4:4; 5:6ff., etc. 24 elders surround God's throne. The fact that they sit on thrones (4:4) and are adorned with white robes and crowns (4:4) suggests that they are a heavenly council, yet they have no judicial office but simply discharge a function of worship (4:10; 5:8ff.). Their divine service in heaven accompanies the work of God on earth. Differentiated both from transfigured saints (14:1ff.) and from the angels that surround the throne (5:11), they seem to be closer to the divine throne, and one of them speaks to the divine (5:5; 7:13) and is addressed by him as *kýrios.* Parallels may be seen in 1 Kgs. 22:19; Ps. 89:7; Dan. 7:9-10; Is. 24:23. The number (24) may be influenced by nonbiblical sources (Babylonia and Persia), but one may also think of the 24 classes of priests and Levites in 1 Chr. 24:5 (cf. 25:1). It is unlikely that the picture of a chorus of 24 heavenly presbyters has any bearing on the constitution of the churches of Revelation, in which the prophetic and spiritual aspects are still prominent.

5. *2 and 3 John.*

In 3 John the author, who calls himself "the elder" (2 Jn. 1; 3 Jn. 1), is clearly in conflict with an opponent who contests the authority he has previously enjoyed, and who seems to be acting as a monarchical bishop (vv. 9-10). Here the presbyter cannot simply be an older man, nor is he a local officebearer, but he probably describes himself as elder because of his special position as a bearer of the apostolic tradition.

933

E. The Postapostolic Period and the Early Church.

1. Clement. 1 Clement is close to 1 Peter. It defends elders who for some unspecified reason have been violently deposed by the church at Corinth. The presbyters here are to be honored as older people are (1.3); they constitute a patriarchal college. Within this college are leaders who are called *epískopoi* (44.1.6). The order is divinely instituted, deriving from God by way of Christ and the apostles. It has a cultic ministry, i.e., to present the church's offerings (44.4). The whole ordering of the congregation may thus be compared to that of Israel in the OT (40ff.), and this guarantees the inviolability of the presbyteral office. The deposed elders should be reinstated (57.1).

2. Hermas. While this work allows for general prophesying (*Visions* 3.8.11), it mentions a college of presbyters (including bishops and deacons) with pastoral functions and a high dignity based on their apostolic associations (cf. *Visions* 2.4.2-3; 3.5.1; 3.9.7; *Similitudes* 9.31.5-6). True prophets are marked by humility (*Mandates* 11.8); no conflict arises between them and the presbyters (cf. *Visions* 2.4.3).

3. Ignatius. In Ignatius there is a single bishop and the elders function as his council (*Philadelphians* 8.1). The church must obey them as a spiritual order (*Ephesians* 2.2) but only within a hierarchy culminating in the bishop. The church's unity reflects the divine hierarchy of God, Christ, and the apostles (cf. *Smyrneans* 8.1).

4. Polycarp. The pattern for which Ignatius contends is obviously not the prevailing norm, for in his letter to the Philippians Polycarp refers only to deacons and presbyters (5.2-3). For Polycarp the bishops and elders are virtually the same, as his initial greeting bears witness ("Polycarp and the presbyters with him"). The functions of presbyters include financial administration (11.1-2), discipline, pastoral care, and preaching. If there is any tendency toward the emergence of a single bishop, this is taking place within a presbyterian order.

5. Papias, Irenaeus, Clement of Alexandria, and Origen.

a. Papias. In Papias the term presbyters is used for reliable and revered teachers of the authentic tradition. In his own work he wants to collect and present what he has learned from them. They are not the apostles but their immediate pupils, who are itinerants rather than officebearers in specific churches.

b. Irenaeus. Familiar with the work of Papias, Irenaeus uses *presbýteroi* in a similar sense and states clearly that they are disciples of the apostles (*Against Heresies* 5.5.1). Polycarp is one of them; a disciple of John, he taught the young Irenaeus. These elders sponsor both the acts and sayings of Jesus and the true exposition of Scripture. As distinct from false presbyters, they are in a valid historical and doctrinal succession from the apostles. An equation of these presbyters with the bishops is thus made on apologetic grounds. This is possible because of the clericalizing of what had at first been a freer teaching office.

c. Clement of Alexandria. In Clement the teaching office of the presbyters retains its freer form. The elders here are teachers of an earlier generation who have transmitted the early records and authentic biblical exposition either orally or in writing. They do not have to be pupils of the apostles nor to hold congregational office, which is of no great importance for Clement. An analogy may be seen to the rabbinic teaching succession.

d. Origen. Like Clement, Origen appeals to earlier teachers, but he believes that such teachers should be ordained. He himself seeks ordination and finally achieves it in Caesarea.

6. The Syrian Didascalia and Hippolytan Church Order. In the first of these documents the bishop holds a position of primacy with administrative and sacramental functions, and the presbyters share in this ministry but as the bishop's delegates. In the second document, too, the clergy are graded, the bishop having the right of ordination, but the presbyters, participating in the Spirit, also having authority to baptize and assist at the eucharist.

presbeúō.

1. This word means "to be older or eldest," "to occupy first place" (transitive "to honor"), then "to act as emissary," e.g., in transmitting messages or in negotiations (cf. envoys, imperial legates, business agents). A transferred sense is "to represent."

2. The idea of an envoy occurs in the religious sphere, e.g., in Philo (angels, Moses, etc.), or in Gnostic texts (the Redeemer). In Stoic circles itinerant teachers are seen as God's messengers. Ignatius of Antioch later takes up this idea of envoys carrying divinely authorized messages to the churches (*Philadelphians* 10.1).

3. In 2 Cor. 5:20 Paul calls his own ministry an embassy. God's reconciling of the world to himself has instituted a ministry of reconciliation (5:18-19). This is not just a passing on of the news but part of the total act (v. 19; cf. 6:1). Through the mouth of the ambassador Christ or God himself speaks. The word of reconciliation presents the completed act as a summons or invitation to its appropriation in faith. The focus is on the authority of the message rather than that of the one who conveys it. The *hypér Christoú* of v. 20 shows that the apostles speak in Christ's stead or on his behalf, although with no suggestion that Christ is absent or that the apostles are continuing his work. In Eph. 6:20, unlike 2 Cor. 5:20, Paul is an ambassador for the gospel rather than for Christ. He thus speaks in its favor rather than on its behalf.

presbýtēs. Paul calls himself *presbýtēs* in Phlm. 9, probably in the sense of an older man rather than an ambassador. Pleading for Onesimus, he appeals to Philemon's love, his bonds, his relation to Onesimus, and his age rather than to his authority.

[G. BORNKAMM, VI, 651-83]

---

pró [at, in front of, before]

A. Linguistic Data: *pró* in the NT.

1. Spatially *pró* occurs in such phrases as "at the door(s)" (Acts 12:6; Jms. 5:9), "before the face" (Mt. 11:10), and "before the city" (Acts 14:13).

2. Temporally the meaning is "before," e.g., the flood (Mt. 24:38), the meal (Lk. 11:38), winter (2 Tim. 4:21), the ages (1 Cor. 2:7), all eternity (Jude 25). We also find such expressions as "before you" (Mt. 5:12), "before you ask" (Mt. 6:8), and "before it happened" (Jn. 13:19). The phrase in Acts 12:34 means "before his coming," while "six days from [i.e., before] Passover" is the sense in Jn. 12:1.

3. Metaphorically *pró* expresses preference in Jms. 5:12, and it may suggest protection in Acts 14:13.

B. Biblical Theology: *pró* in Salvation History.

1. The OT. The ideas of primeval time, priority, and antiquity are important in the OT. God is before the world (Ps. 90:2). His majestic eternity embraces the remotest conceivable time. As Lord of history he is Lord of time (Is. 40:28). His eternity is coincident with his power. His wisdom, too, predates the world (Prov. 8:22ff.). His sovereign calling of his people and prophets is before the historical event.

2. The NT. In the NT, too, God's preexistence is linked to his rule of the world and history. He foreordained before all times the sending of the Son and the salvation effected by him. His glory is before all eternity (Jude 25; cf. Jn. 17:5, 24). The Creator Logos is in the beginning with God, although *pró* does not occur in Jn. 1:1ff., nor in Phil. 2:5ff. In Col. 1:17 Christ is before all things; they exist through and to him, so that preexistence and dominion are again seen together. Christ's passion is foreordained (1 Pet. 1:20). Thus priority is given to grace (cf. also 2 Tim. 1:9; Tit. 1:2). The eternal secret is known through the Christ event and the gospel. Believers as the recipients of grace are chosen in Christ before the world's foundation. God foresees and foreordains events, e.g., the name of Mary's child (Lk. 2:21) and human needs (Mt. 6:8); cf. Jesus in Jn. 1:48. Events in salvation history follow a divine plan (Lk. 21:12) whereby we are first prisoners under the law (Gal. 3:23). Evil spirits have an inkling of the plan but think Christ has come before the time (Mt. 8:29). Believers must not judge before the time (1 Cor. 4:5). Some of them are in Christ before others (Rom. 16:7). The prophets and John are forerunners (Mt. 5:12; 11:10). But before Christ are also thieves and robbers (Jn. 10:8) who lead people astray.

3. *The Apostolic Fathers*. Ignatius *Magnesians* 6.1 and 2 Clem. 14.1 mention Christ's preexistence, and Ignatius *Ephesians*, Preface, says that the Ephesian church was foreordained before eternal times to attain to glory.   [B. REICKE, VI, 683-88]

proágō → *agōgḗ*

---

próbaton [sheep],   *probátion* [lamb, sheep]

A. Outside the NT.

1. Domestic sheep are valued for their wool and meat. Tending them is a common occupation in Palestine. They are often used in sacrifice.

2. *próbaton* (also the diminutive *probátion*) is rare in older Greek. It denotes a. a four-footed (domestic) animal, b. a simple person, and c. a fish. The Stoics use it for stupid people, or for those who must be guided by them. References are made to the attachment between shepherds and their sheep.

3. The LXX uses *próbaton* for small cattle, offerings, and booty, as well as for a gift on the manumission of slaves (cf. Gen. 30:38; 22:7; Num. 31:28ff.; Dt. 15:14). The people are sheep (2 Sam. 24:17; Is. 63:11; Num. 27:17), and God is their shepherd (Ps. 100:3) who leads and saves them (Pss. 77:20; 78:52). Moses or the king may act on God's behalf (Ps. 77:20; Jer. 13:10). The sheep suffer severely at the hands of unfaithful shepherds (Ezek. 34:23ff.). On their own they stray (Ps. 119:176; Is. 53:6). The innocent Servant is dumb like a sheep (Is. 53:7). With the restoration, the people will increase like sheep (Ezek. 36:24).

4. The rabbis, too, compare Israel to sheep. Eth. En. 89–90 calls leaders like Moses, David, etc. sheep, and distinguishes between deaf or blind sheep and the white sheep of the holy community whose Lord is God. Philo uses the term literally but also allegorically; thus *noús* is the shepherd of the sheep.

B. The NT.

1. In the NT the literal sense occurs in the illustration in Mt. 12:11, in the parable of Mt. 18:12, in the reference to offerings in Jn. 2:14-15, and in the list of imports in Rev. 18:13.

2. Figuratively Christians were previously lost sheep (1 Pet. 2:21ff.). The sheep

are God's people at the judgment (Mt. 25:32ff.). The Jews wander like lost sheep that need to be led and fed by the shepherd (Mk. 6:34ff.). Jesus sends out his disciples like defenseless sheep (Mt. 10:16). God's hand is behind the smiting of the shepherd and the scattering of the sheep (Mk. 14:27). Wolves may come in sheep's clothing (Mt. 7:15). Jesus is the great Shepherd of the sheep (Heb. 13:20), and under him the apostles care for the flock (Jn. 21:16-17). In Jn. 10:1ff. Jesus calls, knows, precedes, and gives his life for his sheep. On the one side, then, the NT uses the image of sheep for God's ancient people, while on the other it uses it for the new people of God in eschatological affliction and salvation.

C. **The Apostolic Fathers.** In Did. 13.3 the firstfruits of the flock belong to the prophets. In Ignatius *Philadelphians* 2.1 the sheep are to follow the bishop as their shepherd. In Hermas *Similitudes* 6.1.5-6 gamboling sheep signify those who follow their lusts and fall into trouble. In Hermas *Similitudes* 9.1.9, however, sheep resting under the shade are like poor saints sheltered by the bishops and congregations. The term *próbaton* often occurs in quotations (cf. 1 Clem. 16.7; 59.4; Barn. 5.2; 16.5).

[H. PREISKER and S. SCHULZ, VI, 689-92]

proginṓskō, prógnōsis → *ginṓskō; prográphō* → *gráphō; pródromos* → *tréchō; proelpízō* → *élpis; proepangéllomai* → *epangéllō; proetoimázō* → *hétoimos; proeuangelízomai* → *euangelízomai*

---

proéchomai [to have the advantage]

---

1. Outside the NT. Transitively this word means "to hold up," "to hold up one's hands," "to hold up as an excuse," as well as "to have or to have received in advance." Intransitively it means "to stand out," "be prominent," "surpass," "have the advantage over." In the OT it occurs only in an alternative reading in Job 27:6: "stand out in righteousness."

2. In the NT. In the use in Rom. 3:9 there are three possible meanings. First, Paul might be asking: "Do I make excuses?"—but this is unlikely. Second, the point might be: "Are we [the Jews] surpassed?"—but this is awkward. Third, and most simply, Paul is asking: "Have we an advantage?" Having dealt with various arguments in vv. 5ff., Paul asks whether the Jews are any better off, and he rejects the notion. God's promises do not relieve the Jews of the guilt of ch. 2. Only in Rom. 9–11 will the relation between God's promises and Israel's guilt be resolved.

[C. MAURER, VI, 692-93]

proēgéomai → *hēgéomai; próthesis* → *títhēmi*

---

próthymos [ready, willing, eager], *prothymía* [readiness, inclination, eagerness]

---

próthymos.

A. **Outside the NT.**
1. This word means "ready," "willing," "eager," "active," "passionate."
2. In the LXX it carries such senses as "ready," "willing," "resolute," "brave."
3. A parallel use to that of the LXX may be seen at Qumran.
4. Philo uses *próthymos* for "ready" or "courageous," and Josephus has it as an adverb for "willingly" or "eagerly."

B. The NT.

1. In Mt. 26:41 Jesus tells his sleepy disciples that the spirit is *próthymos* but the flesh is weak. The sense is more that of "eager" than "willing." Doubt has been cast on the authenticity of the saying because the antithesis of spirit and flesh seems to be more typical of Paul than Jesus. But the antithesis here is a different one. The point at issue is taking the right way. An inner eagerness is not enough to accomplish this; it runs up against human limitation. The disciples declare their solidarity with Jesus (Mt. 26:35) but they are unable to live up to their good intentions.

2. In Rom. 1:15 Paul expresses his eager resolve to discharge his apostolic office in Rome; he has a sense of obligation to Rome, too, within his apostolic calling (1:5).

C. The Apostolic Fathers. In the apostolic fathers we find the usual senses "ready," "willing," "resolved" (1 Clem. 34.2; Hermas *Mandates* 12.5.1). The adverb *prothýmōs* occurs, sometimes with martyrdom as the goal (Hermas *Similitudes* 9.28.2; cf. Mart. Pol. 8.13).

prothymía.

A. Outside the NT.

1. This word has such varied nuances as "inclination," "readiness," "desire," and "resoluteness." It is common in eulogies.

2. Philo follows the general use. At times the term takes on the sense of "self-awareness" in his works. If one's *prothymía* conflicts with the divine will it is to be rejected.

3. The only LXX instance is in Sir. 45:23 where the word expresses an "initiative" producing "courage" or "resolution" in obedience to God.

4. Josephus uses the word for "inclination," "attraction," "readiness," and also for "impetuosity" in battle.

5. The corresponding term in rabbinic Judaism carries the twofold suggestion of "voluntariness" (in offerings) and "plenty."

6. The idea of voluntariness is also present in the Qumran writings. A willing and cheerful treading of the divine path is denoted.

B. The NT.

1. In Acts 17:11 the Jews at Berea receive the word with "zeal" or "eagerness."

2. In 2 Cor. 8:11-12 and 9:2 Paul hopes for "readiness" on the part of his readers to raise an offering for Jerusalem. It is with such readiness that he himself is organizing it (8:19). Paul clearly wants action, not just agreement, but he has no wish to exert compulsion. He thus uses this term, and associates himself with it, in an effort to promote voluntary compliance in a project which is to God's glory. The "cheerful resolution" that he hopes for cannot be separated as such from being a Christian.

3. In the apostolic fathers the term occurs in 1 Clem. 2.3; Hermas *Similitudes* 5.3.4; Diog. 1.1.   [K. H. RENGSTORF, VI, 694-700]

---

proḯstēmi [to be at the head of, rule, care for]

1. This common word means "to put before," "to present," or, in the intransitive middle, "to go before," "to preside," and figuratively "to surpass," "to lead," "to direct," "to assist," "to protect," "to represent," "to care for," "to sponsor," "to arrange," "to apply oneself to."

2. In the LXX the word is used for various Hebrew terms, and in translation each instance must be considered on its own merits.

3. Only intransitive forms occur in the eight NT instances. The two senses usually involved are "to lead" and "to care for." The reference in Rom. 12:8 is to the special charism of caring for others. The same applies in 1 Th. 5:12. Whether specific offices are at issue is much debated; gift and office are not antithetical in the NT. In 1 Tim. 3:4-5 ruling and caring are closely related. The point in 3:12 is similar: Deacons should be heads of their households but with an emphasis on proper care for them. Again, in 5:17 the elders who rule well are those who exercise a proper care of souls (cf. the preaching and teaching), although this does not exclude their role as leaders. The combination of leading and caring that one may see in NT usage agrees well with the principle of Lk. 22:26 that the leader is to be as one who serves. The use of *prostátis* in Rom. 16:2 offers further illustration of the same point. In Tit. 3:8, 14 we have examples of the sense "to apply oneself to" (i.e., to good works).

4. The senses "to lead" and "to sponsor" are rare in the apostolic fathers. The former occurs in Hermas *Visions* 2.4.3, the latter in Diog. 5.3.

[B. Reicke, VI, 700-703]

prokaléomai → *kaléō; prokatangéllō* → *angelía; prókeimai* →*keímai; prokē-rýssō* → *kḗryx*

---

prokopḗ [progress, advancement],   *prokóptō* [to go forward, make progress]

A. The Word Group in Greek.
1. History and Meaning.

a. This word seems to be originally nautical for "to make headway," "to forge ahead."

b. Transitively it means "to promote," middle "to get on," and then intransitively "to go ahead."

c. The verb and noun are neutral as such (there may be progress in evil), but they usually have a good sense.

d. They thus signify "fortune," "success," "blessing," "distinction" (in rank, honor, etc.), "military success," "progress in healing."

e. *prokopḗ* also denotes moral and spiritual development, cultural progress, or advance in virtue.

f. Antiquity has no sense of the more general progress of humanity or the world; the ideas of cosmic perfection and of eternal becoming and perishing block such a notion.

2. prokopḗ as a Technical Term in Stoicism. In Stoic ethics *prokopḗ* occupies middle ground between good and evil. Older Stoicism still reckons it on the side of imperfection but later Stoicism finds few if any true sages and thus takes a more hopeful view of those in process of development. A natural impulse toward progress is helped by instruction, self-examination, and self-accusation, although there may also be regressions. The perfection toward which there is progress embraces wisdom, virtue, and piety.

B. Progress in the OT.

1. OT thinking is historical and the idea of progress in salvation history is a natural one. The term *prokopḗ* is not used for this, and ideas as to the center and goal of

salvation vary, but there is a common belief that God controls events in a movement from promise to fulfilment. Hence God's history is in a constant flux of election, sending, judgment, and renewal. The human contribution is ambivalent, for while hunanity is under a divine demand to be like God (Lev. 19:2), this very goal, falsely understood, is also the cause of progress in evil (Gen. 3).

2. Directed by the law, the people of God advances toward the goal proclaimed in the past. Yet in the prophets there is also a future orientation. A final goal will vindicate and give meaning to all that has gone before. It will be reached, not by steady progress, but by a new creation.

3. Individual as well as corporate history is in movement. Thus the patriarchs walk before and under God. Resistance to this movement, as in the people as a whole, is set aside only by divine intervention and forgiveness. Wisdom literature portrays wisdom as the beginning of a process (Prov. 1:7; Ps. 111:10) that leads to full personal development. If the OT does not use a general term like *prokopḗ*, this is because each event is taken separately. The late instance of *prokopḗ* in Sir. 51:17 probably has the sense of "blessing."

C. The Group in Hellenistic Judaism.

1. Apart from Sir. 51:17 the LXX has *prokopḗ* only in 2 Maccabees for "military success" (cf. Ps. 45:5). The Testaments of the Twelve Patriarchs, Aristeas, and Josephus use it in the ordinary senses of "progress," "development," "success."

2. In Philo we find a more Stoic usage for individual development. The starting point and impulse are in nature, behind which stands God. Thus, while individuals and their teachers are important, it is only by divine beneficence that the goal is reached. The field of progress is the whole sphere of wisdom and virtue. Philo highly regards those who are making firm and constant progress even though there are still imperfections in them and they rank below the truly wise. He finds examples of the various stages of progress in the OT.

D. The Group in the NT.

1. Linguistic Data.

a. *prokóptō* and *prokopḗ* are Hellenistic rather than intrinsically biblical words. They are rare in the NT (9 instances) and occur only in the Pauline and Lucan material (Gal. 1:14; Rom. 13:12; Phil. 1:12, 25; 1 Tim. 4:15; 2 Tim. 2:16; 3:9, 13; Lk. 2:52).

b. In part the usage is that of everyday speech.

c. There are distant echoes of Hellenistic philosophy in Lk. 2:52; Gal. 1:14; 1 Tim. 4:15.

d. Paul himself seems to have coined the phrases in Phil. 1:12, 25.

2. Individual prokopḗ.

a. The subject in the NT is mostly personal. Exceptions are the night in Rom. 13:12, the gospel in Phil. 1:12, and the faith in 1:25.

b. The personal progress is partly individual and partly corporate. Passages that speak of personal advance (Lk. 2:52; 1 Tim. 4:15; Gal. 1:14) are closest to Hellenism. Thus the phrase in Lk. 2:52 sounds Hellenistic. It might be based on current expressions or on Sir. 51:17, but it has an OT content, for the stress is on spiritual progress and (as in 2:40) the controlling concept is that of favor with God reflected in favor with man. Luke never follows up on the progress of Jesus, and the verse offers no basis for speaking about his growth in self-awareness or his moral development. 1 Tim. 4:15 is relatively closer to the Hellenistic concept. Timothy is to develop the charism of v. 14, giving visible evidence of growth in faith, love, and purity, and devoting himself to preaching and teaching. The progress, however, must take outward form and it is ultimately a matter of divine gift. In Gal. 1:15 (Paul's advance in Judaism) the element of human achievement is stronger as Paul forges ahead in knowledge and observance of the law, but the term has an ironic ring, for this progress is the very opposite of what he now regards as *prokopḗ* (cf. Phil. 1:12, 25; 1 Tim. 4:15); it is closer to the progress in ungodliness of 2 Tim. 2:16 or the going from bad to worse of 2 Tim. 3:13.

3. *The prokopḗ of the Community and the Gospel.* The NT gives the term a distinctive turn relative to the community and the gospel. In Phil. 1:25 the *prokopḗ* might stand alone and denote spiritual advance, or (with joy) it might go with faith and denote advance in faith. Although there is only one saving faith (Eph. 4:5), there are different measures or stages of faith (Mk. 4:24-25; Rom. 12:3), and there may thus be progress in it (Lk. 17:5; 2 Th. 1:3). If Paul stays alive, he may help to promote this progress in faith, although the Spirit, of course, is the ultimate force behind it. If Paul's life serves the *prokopḗ* of faith, his suffering serves that of the gospel in 1:12. As a prisoner he helps to spread the gospel among pagans and to confirm it in Christians, so that there is both outer and inner advance.

4. *The prokopḗ of Heresy.* Over against the gospel, heresy and its teachers also make progress. Nourished by demonic forces, error spreads like a cancer (2 Tim. 2:17). Its power is that of deceit and seduction (3:13). It leads away from God (2:16) to the depth of perdition (3:13). The threefold use of the term in 2 Tim. 2:16–3:13 is perhaps the author's answer to the claim of false teachers that they are progressive theologians. The progress of heresy is part of the multiplying of wickedness (Mt. 24:12) and the eschatological tribulation, but it is not without a limit (2 Tim. 3:9).

5. *The prokopḗ of the Aeons.* Eschatological overtones are plain in Rom. 13:12. The passing of the night signifies the march of time. We are still in the ambivalent period of the already and the not yet. The night is reaching the dark period before the dawn, but it is also almost over; the time has come to wake up. The NT leaves no room here for the thought of human progress. As the history of the world, history has no teleology of its own. Only in the light of the gospel may one see a divinely ordained *prokopḗ*.

E. The Group in the Early Church.

1. *Apostolic Fathers and Apologists.* In these writers there is no specific or theological use. In 2 Clem. 17.3 the exhortation reflects a more legal understanding of the Christian life. In the Apologists the use is mostly everyday (cf. Justin *Dialogue* 11.5). More philosophical usage occurs only in Justin *Dialogue* 2.6. Irenaeus speaks of progress to God (*Against Heresies* 4.11.2) but he contests the view of development held by the Gnostics, who think of themselves as progressives.

2. *Clement of Alexandria.* Clement makes considerable use of both verb and noun, giving the idea broader significance than Philo but also giving it a fuller biblical content as he subjects Stoic and Platonic ideas to the NT. He uses *prokopḗ* for ascent but also for "step" and "highest step," then for "rank in heaven," embracing Christ's exaltation and the angelic hierarchy. For Clement endless progress is a basic principle of creation. Eternal life is eternal progress. The principle embraces all peoples, but God leads to perfection through the Christian faith. The starting point is the desire for change, but the power of true progress is faith. Discipline and instruction further progress, but God is its real giver and Christ supplies the motive power. On the Greek side culture serves progress but the gospel is the proper sphere of ascent, and philosophy must merge into it to achieve its goal. This goal may be variously described as

virtue, the vision of God, immortality, perfection, knowledge, etc. In the long run NT influence is decisive in this view of progress. The progress that Clement finally seeks is progress in perfection and rank in the world to come with its gradations of heavenly destiny.   [G. STÄHLIN, VI, 703-19]

→ *auxánō, perisseúō, plēthýnō, proágō, teleióō*

prókrima → *krínō; prokyróō* → *kyróō; prolambánō* → *lambánō; promartýromai* → *mártys; promerimnáō* → *merimnáō; pronoéō, prónoia* → *noéō; prooráō* → *horáō; proorízō* → *horízō; propáschō* → *páschō*

> *prós* [before, at, near, toward, etc.]

A. With Genitive. The general sense of *prós* is "before." With the genitive it normally expresses going out "from," but in the one use in Acts 27:34 it has the transferred sense of "being essential for" (cf. 1 Clem. 20:10).

B. With Dative.

1. Spatially *prós* with the dative denotes a. place, "before," "at," "by," or "about," and b. direction, "to."

2. Quantitatively it means "besides," but this use does not occur in the NT.

C. With Accusative.

1. Spatially, the common use of *prós* with the accusative, expressing movement toward, occurs a. with an intransitive verb, e.g., going to or entering (but not with a mystical sense; cf. Rev. 3:20; Jn. 7:33); b. with a transitive verb, e.g., sending, bringing, leading, etc., often in the NT with theological significance, e.g., when Jesus on the cross draws people to himself (Jn. 12:32), or when there is access to the Father (Eph. 2:18), or turning to the Lord or to God (2 Cor. 3:16; 1 Th. 1:9), or adherence to idols (1 Cor. 12:2); c. passively with a verb of motion denoting "at" or "by" (cf. Mk. 1:33; 11:4; 14:54; Mt. 3:10), although loosely the same idea may be present without a verb (cf. Mt. 13:56), sometimes with an assumed movement (Mt. 26:18; 2 Cor. 7:12; the formulas in Mk. 2:2; Rom. 15:17; Mt. 27:4); d. with associated verbs of sending and speaking to denote bringing or imparting a message (Mt. 27:19; Mk. 3:31; without the verb of speaking, Acts 10:33).

2. Psychologically, in the sense "to," "toward," *prós* occurs with verbs of speaking to denote "saying something to someone" (e.g., Lk. 1:13; Acts 1:7; with a special reference to God's direct address and hence the assigning of a definite position or task, Rom. 10:21; Heb. 1:8; in the phrase *prós ti,* "with reference to," Lk. 18:1; with verbs of praying or blaspheming; with God or Jesus as object, Acts 8:24; Rev. 13:6); b. with verbs or nouns expressing an attitude, either friendly (2 Cor. 3:4; 2 Tim. 2:24), hostile (Lk. 5:30; Acts 6:1), or neutral (Acts 24:16).

3. Temporally, *prós* with the accusative expresses a. approach to a point in time (Lk. 24:29); b. a period, e.g., "for a while" (Lk. 8:13), "for a few days" (Heb. 12:10), usually with a future reference.

4. Finally, *prós* a. denotes the aim of an action, "with a view to" or even "for the sake of," e.g., Jn. 11:4; Acts 3:10; Rom. 15:2; 1 Cor. 7:35, often with an infinitive, e.g., Mt. 6:1, or elliptically, e.g., Lk. 14:32; Jn. 13:28; b. expresses "attaining or corresponding to" (cf. Lk. 12:47; Mt. 19:8).

5. Consecutively, the use with the accusative denotes "up to" or "so that," e.g.,

"white enough for harvest" in Jn. 4:35, leading "to the satisfaction of the flesh" in Col. 2:23, "to the point of envy" in Jms. 4:5, "resulting in death" in 1 Jn. 5:16, "to the point of lust" in Mt. 5:28. [B. REICKE, VI, 720-25]

proságō, prosagōgḗ → agōgḗ; prosanatíthēmi → anatíthēmi; prosdéomai → déomai; prosdéchomai → déchomai

---

prosdokáō [to wait for, expect], *prosdokía* [expectation]

A. Outside the NT.
1. The word *prosdokáō* means "to wait or look for," "to expect," with some tension of fear and hope. The noun means "expectation" of either good or bad.
2. In the LXX the focus is on God and his acts. Thus it speaks of hoping in God (Ps. 104:27), in his salvation (119:166), in his mercy (Wis. 12:22), in the resurrection (2 Macc. 7:14). But this applies only to the verb; of nine instances of the noun, only Gen. 49:10 and Ps. 119:116 relate to God.

B. The NT.
1.a. In the NT the verb often denotes eschatological hope. Thus in Mt. 11:3 and Lk. 7:19-20 the question is whether Jesus fulfils the messianic hope.
b. In Mt. 24:50; Lk. 12:46; 2 Pet. 3:12ff. the returning Christ is the object of expectation. In 2 Pet. 3:12 and 14 the participles have an indicative and causal character. Waiting for the day of God, believers live holy lives. Hence *prosdokán* is protected against psychological disintegration and oriented to the hope of salvation.
2. In Lk. 21:26 the noun has the Hellenistic sense of "fearful expectation," and in Acts 12:11 it refers to the expectations of the Jewish people on the arrest of Peter.

C. The Apostolic Fathers. Except in Hermas *Visions* 3.11.3 and Diog. 9.2, *prosdokáō* in the apostolic fathers always refers to divine blessings. The noun does not occur. Of the Apologists Justin makes frequent use of the group in connection with OT and NT promises (e.g., *Dialogue* 52.1; 120.3). [C. MAURER, VI, 725-27]

prosérchomai → érchomai; proseúchomai, proseuchḗ → eúchomai

---

prosḗlytos [proselyte]

A. Occurrence. This word has been found only in Jewish and Christian writings, although *epḗlys* and *epēlýtēs* (*epḗlytos*) are found in the same sense in secular Greek.

B. The Alien in the OT. There are two classes of aliens in the OT, visitors (Dt. 14:21) and temporary or permanent residents (Ex. 12:49). The former have no rights and are outside the national and cultic fellowship. The latter are under protection and enjoy personal freedom but have no independent status. Ex. 22:20ff. insures them of God's interest, and Ex. 23:9 appeals to Israel's experience in Egypt. Aliens must keep the sabbath (Ex. 20:10), for, being in the land, they are set in a religious relationship. As the sense of election develops, and hence the distinction from other peoples, resident aliens are drawn into the cultic fellowship. Dt. 5:14; 16:10-11, 13-14 require that they keep the festivals, although they may keep the Passover only if they are circumcised. Aliens, then, are much like later proselytes, except that they have to be resident; hence a sociological difference remains.

C. *prosélytos* in Later Judaism.

1. Hellenistic Judaism. The final development of proselyte as a technical term takes place in dispersion Judaism. This provides a different sociological structure in which Jews live among non-Jews, learn non-Jewish culture, and commence a Jewish mission. The relatively few who fully accept Judaism and are circumcised are called *prosélytoi*. Religiously, but not sociologically, they are like resident aliens. Many more Gentiles accept OT monotheism and keep some parts of the cultic law but are not circumcised; these are God-fearers (*sebómenoi* or *phoboúmenoi tón theón*). Hellenistic Jews regard it as more important that Gentiles should believe in God and follow his ethical commands than that they should be circumcised.

Linguistically 1. the LXX uses *prosélytos* 77 times for the resident alien, in eleven instances using *pároikos,* twice *g(e)ióras,* and once *xénos.*

2. Philo develops the new understanding of the OT term, although he prefers *épēlys* or *epēlýtēs (epélytos)* to the less familiar *prosélytos.* He defines *prosélytos* as one who has left country, relatives, and friends to come under the Jewish constitution. This presupposes circumcision, although Philo stresses the need to circumcise lusts and passions.

3. Josephus avoids *prosélytos,* which his readers would not understand, but he uses other terms for full converts to Judaism as distinct from God-fearers.

4. Jewish inscriptions refer to proselytes, but only in one instance from Palestine. True proselytes may be buried among Jews, having separated themselves from everything Gentile. They are fully integrated into the community and sometimes have new Jewish names. In Italy there are more women than men, for full conversion is easier for women; we also find slaves and adopted children, for whom conversion brings advantages. Restrictive legislation, e.g., under Hadrian, might have affected the distribution. Some inscriptions refer to God-fearers (*theosebés;* Lat. *metuens*).

II. Later Palestinian Judaism. In later Palestinian Judaism the proselyte and the resident alien are much the same; the latter term has lost its sociological sense. Full conversion is more important in Palestine. Those who wish to come over to Judaism must accept the law in its entirety, or they are still Gentiles. Among older proselytes we find such illustrious groups as the Herod family and King Izates of Adiabene and his mother and brother. A certain Simon who played a great role as a guerilla in the first Jewish war was also known as *ho (toú) Gióra*; his father was a proselyte. In the Apocrypha Tob. 1:8 refers to alms that are given to proselytes. The Damascus Document mentions the four orders of priests, Levites, Israelites, and *gerim* (Qumran has only the first three). The *gerim* here are full proselytes, not just resident aliens. As Syr. Bar. 41:4 puts it, they are those who have forsaken their vain life and found refuge beneath God's wings (cf. also 42:5).

III. Rabbinic Judaism.

1. The Term. The rabbis now use the OT term for full Gentile converts to Judaism. Distinction is made between false proselytes, who seek personal advantage, and true proselytes, who become Jews by conviction and keep the whole law (as distinct from those who attend worship and keep the Noachic law).

2. The Attitude. Some rabbis encourage proselytes, others at first treat them with caution. When conversion is made almost impossible under Hadrian they are welcomed, for only those who are sincerely motivated take the risk. Later a less favorable attitude manifests itself again in the view that proselytes delay the coming of the Messiah, or that no more proselytes will be received when the Messiah comes.

3. The Reception. The rite of reception consists of circumcision, baptism, and a sacrifice. Circumcision is the oldest part. The precise age and original meaning and form of baptism are unknown. It is perhaps at first a cultic purification but later it is a fixed public rite of admission involving instruction in the law. The offering lapsed with the destruction of the temple. Rabbis find a basis for the three conditions in the conditions of the Sinai covenant in Ex. 12:48; 24:5; 19:10. When the conditions are fulfilled, converts are regarded as in every respect Jews.

4. Legal Position. Being like newborn children, proselytes cannot be held guilty of Gentile transgressions. Children begotten before conversion cannot be heirs even if they are converted with their parents. Converts may inherit from Gentile fathers so long as no idolatry is involved. The OT laws of incest apply to former Gentile marriages only insofar as Gentile law agrees with them. Women proselytes may not marry priests under the ruling of Lev. 21:13-14, although only on suspicion of fornication, so that the rule does not apply to girls converted under three years of age. Rules providing help for resident aliens (Lev. 19:10) are applied to proselytes.

5. Non-Jews. The rabbis apply to Gentiles who keep the Noachic commands the sociological term that the OT uses for resident aliens. These include the God-fearers, who are sometimes favorably viewed as righteous people who have a share in the world to come. In general, however, the rabbis are not content to have uncircumcised Gentiles as loose adherents. The point is made that they cannot learn the law if they are not already circumcised. They are thus regarded as fully Gentile if they do not take the step of full conversion 12 months after accepting the Noachic law.

D. The NT.

I. prosḗlytos.

1. Of the four NT instances, the first is in Mt. 23:15, where Jesus denounces the legalistic missionary work of the Pharisees, who are not content with loose adherence but make hypocrites by imposing strict legal observance.

2. Acts 2:11 lists proselytes among the dispersion groups present in Jerusalem for the feast. Proselytes and Jews are terms that denote the religious position of those who come from the geographical locations also mentioned.

3. Since in 6:1 *Hellēnistaí* means Jews of Hellenistic origin, Nicolaus as a *prosḗlytos* is distinguished from the other six; he is a convert from paganism who has come to Jerusalem from Antioch.

4. Acts 13:43 lists among those who follow the apostles God-fearing proselytes. This is a unique combination even in Acts and raises the question whether *sebómenoi* or *prosḗlytoi* is the technical term. If the former, *prosḗlytoi* is materially incorrect; if the latter, *sebómenoi* has some such sense as "devout."

II. sebómenoi (phoboúmenoi) tón theón.

1. These phrases occur in Acts—*phoboúmenoi* in the first section, *sebómenoi* in the second. Some Palestinian Christians seem to have thought at first that salvation was only for full Jews (cf. Acts 11:3, where Peter is charged for associating with the *phoboúmenos* Cornelius, and 11:19, where the Palestinian missionaries at first preach only to Jews, although some, who belong to Cyprus and Cyrene, preach to *Héllēnes,* or *sebómenoi,* as well [v. 20]).

2. Paul first preaches in the synagogues to Jews, i.e., full members of the Jewish people by birth or conversion, and *Héllēnes,* i.e., God-fearing Gentiles who attend

Jewish worship (cf. Acts 14:1; 18:4; 19:10; also 13:16, 26; 16:14; 17:17; 18:7; also 17:4). His main success seems to be among the God-fearers. Paul does not demand circumcision, but monotheism is not enough; faith in Christ is necessary to salvation (13:39). The preaching of Christ stirs up Jewish opposition and leads Paul, e.g., in Corinth, to go to God-fearing Gentiles (18:6). The usage in Acts conforms exactly to the existing situation and supports the historicity of the accounts.

[K. G. KUHN, VI, 727-44]

próskairos → *kairós; proskaléō* → *kaléō; proskartaréō, proskartérēsis* → *kar-teréō; prosklēróō* → *klḗros; proskolláō* → *kolláō*

---

proskóptō [to strike, stumble against, give offense], *próskomma* [fall, stone of stumbling], *proskopḗ* [taking or giving offense], *apróskopos* [not taking or giving offense]

A. Usage.

I. proskóptō.

1. Literally, this word means "to strike," "to dash against." Intransitively it means "to stumble against," "bump," "slip," "fall," "suffer harm," "perish."

2. In a transferred sense, *proskóptō* means "to give offense," "to cause displeasure," or "to take offense," "to be annoyed or enraged," "to experience displeasure."

II. próskomma.

1. This noun may denote the result of falling, hence "damage," "wound," "bump," or more generally "hurt," "destruction," "ruin," and morally "fall," "sin."

2. It may also denote a quality as in the phrase "stone of stumbling."

3. Finally, it may indicate a cause of hurt, e.g., an "obstacle," or more generally a cause of ruin, e.g., a "hindrance" to faith, a "temptation" that causes a fall into sin.

III. proskopḗ. This rare verbal noun usually denotes 1. "taking offense," "aversion," "irritation," "antipathy." It may also be used 2. for "cause of falling or taking offense," "reason for antipathy."

IV. apróskopos. This rare and late verbal adjective means 1. "not causing to fall," "not stumbling," "intact," and 2. "not giving offense," "inoffensive," "blameless," "not taking offense" (e.g., a clear conscience).

B. The OT and Judaism.

I. Equivalents. There are various Hebrew equivalents with such senses as "causing to fall," "pushing," "striking," also "falling" or "stumbling."

II. Metaphors. Two metaphors are associated with the group, 1. that of the way, and 2. that of the stone, but the two may also be combined (Prov. 4:12; Lam. 3:9; Mt. 16:23). *proskómmata* are usually harmful obstacles in contrast to the smooth ways of the righteous, but they may also be a mark of the right way (cf. Mt. 7:13-14).

III. Theological Use.

1.a. Often used in connection with the doctrine of retribution, the group denotes idolatry as a stumbling block resulting in destruction.

b. Even apart from idols, falling is a punishment for disobedience. God himself may be the cause of falling (cf. Is. 59:10) as the people does not rely on him. In Prov. 4:19 unrighteous individuals fall in the darkness of their ignorance.

c. Specifically in Is. 8:14 God is a rock of stumbling and a snare, although he is also a rock of refuge, so that the rock depicts both his wrath and his grace just as his action means either salvation or perdition (cf. Ps. 18:25ff.; 1 Cor. 1:23-24).

d. Only outside the canon is the devil a cause of destruction (Test. Reub. 4:7).

e. Only rarely in the Wisdom literature does a nonsupernatural power cause destruction (cf. gold and wine in Sir. 31:7).

2. It is arguable whether the group is used in the LXX for temptation and falling into sin. Is. 29:21 and Sir. 17:25 might be cited in this connection. On the other hand, the Hebrew equivalents in the rabbis often have this sense (cf. also Qumran).

C. The NT.

I. The OT Basis.

1. The NT follows the OT in the form of quotations, e.g., Mt. 4:6; Rom. 9:32-33.

2. It also adopts similar expressions (cf. Rom. 14:13, 21; 1 Cor. 8:9). The main difference in the NT is that unbelief rather than disobedience is now a cause of eternal spiritual perdition, not just temporal destruction. External injury is in view in Mt. 4:6, and cf. the meaning "offense," but spiritual injury is the primary reference in, e.g., Rom. 14:13; 1 Cor. 10:32; 2 Cor. 6:3.

II. Specific NT Use.

1. Jesus and Falling.

a. In Mt. 4:6-7 the tempter fails to mention that the promise is for those who trust in God. He thus seeks to make Jesus into one who tempts God, using the very promise to try to bring about a fall. As a literal fall this would destroy Jesus at the outset. As a spiritual fall, it would be deeper and more fateful than that of Adam.

b. The metaphor of the way is present in Jn. 11:9-10. One does not stumble and fall in the light of day. There is perhaps an allusion here to the approaching passion of Jesus, i.e., his fall into death.

2. Falling in Faith.

a. (a) Humans may be the cause of falling by others. Thus the valid freedom of the strong at Rome and Corinth (Rom. 14:21: 1 Cor. 8:9) can be a stumbling block to the weak, who see in it a compromise with the pagan world. Love, then, demands renunciation of the freedom lest it cause others to fall.

(b) It is a principle for all Christians (1 Cor. 10:32) that they should not give offense either to believers or to those outside. This does not mean simply that they should be pleasant to others. It means that they should do nothing to weaken their faith or to keep them from faith. For himself Paul puts no obstacle in the way of others (2 Cor. 6:3). He tries not to do anything that will bring reproach on the apostolic ministry. His concern is again for the salvation of those among whom he works.

b. Rom. 9:32-33 and 1 Pet. 2:6ff. apply Is. 8:14 and 28:16 to Christ, although in different contexts and combinations. In Romans Israel stumbles on Christ, while in 1 Peter Christ is primarily a precious stone for the elect. Israel stumbles because she has a wrong view of salvation and fails to see in Jesus the Messiah. In 1 Peter the stone supports the building but is a danger to those who stumble over it, so that one must either be built into the divine building or fall on it by taking offense and failing to believe. In both passages Christ has a twofold effect. By means of God's concealed revelation in him, with its justification of the sinner, the summons goes out which leads either to salvation in faith or to perdition in unbelief. God himself has laid the stone and given it this function.

c. In Phil. 1:10 being *apróskopos* is an eschatological goal The meaning might be either "blameless," "without offense for God," or "not falling" (cf. Jude 24). The

947

context suggests that what is in view is much the same as "being saved" in 1 Cor. 1:18. Paul's prayer is that he may not cause the Philippians to stumble on the path of faith, that they might not slip and fall now, and that they will thus stand in the judgment. It is important that this is possible only through Christ or his Spirit, and that if the goal is attained the praise and glory are God's alone.

3. *Offense of Conscience (Rom. 14:20; Acts 24:16)*.

a. In Rom. 14:20 the subject of the section is faith in its relation to conscience. The reference might be to falling in faith, or it might be to giving offense to conscience. If the first view is right, *próskomma* agrees with the *proskóptō* of v. 21. But the second view accords better with the theme of the cleavage between conduct and conscience (cf. v. 23). It is not uncommon for Paul to use the same words, or words of the same group, in two different senses in the same passage (cf. *krínō* in 14:13).

b. The thought of a conscience that takes no offense is clearly present in Acts 24:16 either in the sense of a quiet conscience or an unharmed conscience (cf. 2 Tim. 1:3). Paul's concern for the conscience is apparent in Rom. 14 and 1 Cor. 8; the statement has, then, an authentic ring.

D. The Early Church. The NT use is less prominent in early writings. The thought of stumbling is present in the metaphor of the two ways (cf. Hermas *Mandates* 6.1.3-4; also Justin *Apology* 1.52.10). But the main sense is "(giving) offense" (1 Clem. 21.5), and *apróskopos* is common for "blameless service" (1 Clem. 20:10; cf. 61.1). The focus is more on the threat to the reputation of officebearers than on the threat to the faith of those set under their direction.   [G. STÄHLIN, VI, 745-58]

→ *líthos, pétra, píptō, skándalon*

---

proskynéō [to bow down, worship],   **proskynētḗs** [worshipper]

---

proskynéō.

A. Meaning for the Greeks. Usually connected with the Old High German *Kuss*, although in different ways, *proskynéō* is an ancient term for reverent adoration of the gods, which in the case of chthonic deities would mean stooping to kiss the earth. The Greeks abandon the outward gesture but keep the term for the inner attitude. Later the word takes on a much more general sense expressing love and respect.

B. Jewish Understanding.

1. The LXX uses the term for various words meaning "to bow," "to kiss," "to serve," and "to worship." Most of the instances relate to veneration of the God of Israel or of false gods. *proskynein* may also be directed to angels, to the righteous, to rulers, to the prophets, and to the shade of Samuel (Saul). While it may express regard, it also suggests that those thus honored are in some way God's instruments (cf. Gen. 18:2; 19:1). In Gen. 23:7, 12 observance of the formalities stresses the legality of the purchase. Mordecai's refusal to do *proskýnēsis* to Haman is the focus of the dramatic action in Esther. Obeisance is always intended except later in 4 Macc. 5:12. The LXX prefers the dative or a preposition to the Greek transitive and accusative. This is partly due to the Hebrew, but partly to the fact that transitive kissing is impossible where there is no image of God.

2. Josephus follows the LXX in his use of the term for worship and respect. Yet he tends to restrict *proskynein* to Gentile worship, to avoid the term with a human

reference when speaking of the Jews of his own day, and to use it in relation to the temple and the law in the sense of respect rather than worship (for even the Romans respect the holy place; *Jewish War* 5.402).

3. Philo's usage is mostly secular rather than religious except when he censures the worship of wealth or various forms of idolatry in city life. He accepts *proskyneín* to others as a form of respect but is critical of *proskýnēsis* to the emperor as a contradiction of ancient Roman freedom. He, too, speaks of a *proskyneín* directed to the temple, Scripture, and the Day of Atonement.

4. In rabbinic Judaism *proskýnēsis* is an attitude in prayer (although standing is more customary). It may also be a means of showing respect to rabbis as those who are in a close relation to God because of their study of the law.

C. The NT.

1. The NT uses *proskyneín* only in relation to a divine object. Even Mt. 18:26 is no true exception, for in view of the importance of *proskýnēsis* in Matthew (cf. 8:2; 9:18; 14:33; 15:25; 20:2) the divine king plainly stands behind the king of the parable. Thus when those who seek help from Jesus fall at his feet, this is more than a gesture of respect. The wise men bow in worship (Mt. 2:2, 11). The tempter seeks the worship that belongs to God (4:9-10). The disciples worship Jesus when they begin to grasp his divine sonship (14:33) and when they meet the risen Lord (28:9). The thought of God's transcendence forbids any weakening of the term in the NT. Peter rejects *proskýnēsis* in Acts 10:25-26. Even the angel forbids it in Rev. 19:10. The gesture is expressly mentioned in Acts 10:25.

2. In Jn. 4:20ff. *proskyneín* seems to have a wholly figurative sense. Yet the act of worship stands in the background. What Jesus says is that there is no one place to worship. The concrete act is lifted up into the sphere of spirit and truth which now controls it. This does not mean a total spiritualizing of worship but the possibility of true worship at all times and in all places.

3. The worship of heaven involves repeated *proskýnēsis* (Rev. 4:10; 5:14; 7:11; 11:16; 19:4). Those who fear God (and those who worship the beast!) are also *proskynoúntes* (Rev. 11:1; 13:4). Those who worship Satan will finally bow down at the feet of the angel of the church of Philadelphia (3:9), and all nations shall come and worship God at the last day (15:4).

4. While *proskyneín* is common in the Gospels and Acts, and then again in Revelation, it occurs in the epistles only in Heb. 1:6; 11:21 and 1 Cor 14:25. The last verse offers the only instance of *proskyneín* in the Christian community and it refers along OT lines to the unconditional subjection expressed by an unbeliever. Elsewhere we read of kneeling or raising hands in prayer (Acts 9:40; 1 Tim. 2:8), but the word *proskyneín* does not occur. Being a concrete term, *proskyneín* demands visible majesty. It is thus apposite only when the incarnate Christ is present or when the exalted Lord is again manifested.

D. The Early Church. The data in the apostolic fathers are much the same as in the NT. Mostly the reference is to pagan worship. Veneration of Christ is differentiated from the respect paid to martyrs in Mart. Pol. 17.3. Later the term is given very limited significance. Thus the Council of Nicea in 787 allows *proskýnēsis* to icons but reserves true *latreía* for the divine nature. The Greek accusative reappears alongside the more common dative, but with no consistent difference of sense.

proskynētēs.

1. Outside the NT this term occurs first only on an inscription from the third century A.D.

2. The one NT instance is in Jn. 4:23, where the reference is to "true worshippers, true being defined by "in spirit and truth."   [H. GREEVEN, VI, 758-66]

→ *aspázomai, eúchomai, píptō*

proslambánomai, próslēmpsis → *lambánō; prosménō* → *ménō; prostássō* → *tássō*

---

prósphatos [new], **prosphátōs** [recently]

---

1. Of uncertain etymology, this word means "fresh" (fruit etc.) or "new" (people or events); the adverb means "newly," "lately," "recently."

2. The LXX has the usual senses of "fresh" and "new," but at times with the suggestion of illegitimate (new gods). The adverb means "just," "recently."

3. The NT uses the adjective only in Heb. 10:20 to describe the new way that Christ has opened up through the veil. By Christ's self-offering the community has the right of access to God. This is new compared to the old way into the holy of holies. It is also fresh in quality as compared to dead rites and ceremonies. The way leads via the event of redemption in Christ's life and death. Hence it is by his flesh, which is the very opposite of an obstacle on the way to God. The adverb occurs in Acts 18:2 in the sense of "shortly before."   [C. MAURER, VI, 766-67]

prosphérō, prosphorá → *phérō*

---

prósōpon [face, countenance], **euprosōpéō** [to make a good showing], **prosōpolēmpsía** [partiality], **prosōpolēmptēs** [one who shows partiality], **prosōpolēmptéō** [to show partiality], **aprosōpolēmptōs** [impartially]

---

prósōpon.

A. Greek Usage.

1. Face. The basic sense of *prósōpon* is "face," "countenance." The plural occurs in Homer and the tragedians, but later the singular takes over. Human faces, or at times those of the gods, are at issue, with only occasional exceptions. A wider sense is "personal appearance," "form," "figure." With *katá* "personal presence" is denoted. A figurative use is for a military front or the front of a building.

2. Mask. The mask worn by actors resembles a face and is thus called a *prósōpon.* The role or part is then denoted by the term. Another use is for the anonymous opponent in a dialogue.

3. Person. A further meaning is the person either socially or grammatically or, at a later time, legally.

B. The LXX and Later Jewish Usage.

I. The LXX.

1. Face. Occurring some 850 times or more in the LXX, *prósōpon* first means "face." Falling on the face is an expression of veneration (Gen. 17:3). Seeing a king's face means having an audience. The face of an animal is meant in Ezek. 1:10. "Appearance" is the sense in Gen. 40:7 (of a matter in 2 Sam. 14:20). The *prósōpon* denotes the whole person in 2 Sam. 17:11 (Absalom).

2. *Front Side*. Like the Hebrew original, *prósōpon* may denote "surface" (Gen. 2:6), or "edge" (Eccl. 10:10), or "front" in prepositional phrases signifying movement to or from, e.g., with *apó* (from), *eis* (to or before), *ek* (from), *en* (before), *epí* (on), *katá* (before or over against), *metá* (with), and *pró* (before).

3. *God's Countenance*.

a. Frequently *prósōpon* denotes God's countenance in anthropomorphic expressions. God's lifting his countenance means grace and peace. Prayer is made that his face may shine on Israel (Num. 6:25). Hiding his face denotes withdrawal of grace (Dt. 32:20). In penal wrath God turns his face against sinners (Ps. 34:16). Seeing God's face is a special privilege (Gen. 32:3). Because of God's holiness it involves peril; hence even Moses sees God's glory only from behind (Ex. 32:23). God reveals himself through his word, not through seeing his face.

b. Various cultic expressions use the term. Thus "to see God's face" is to visit the sanctuary; believers seek God's face (Ps. 42:3; Zech. 8:21-22). The accent here is not on seeing God but on assurance of his presence and favor. In Ps. 105:4 seeking God's face is a daily procedure; it is a matter of supreme concern in Ps. 27:8. The holy bread is the bread of the *prósōpon* in 1 Sam. 21:6, i.e., the bread of the presence.

II. Later Judaism.

1. *Philo and Josephus*.

a. For Philo the face is the most important part of the body; it is controlled by the number seven. Philo refers often to God's face. Representing his essential being, it is hidden from us. At times Philo uses *prósōpon* for "person."

b. In Josephus we find the senses "face," "features," "role," and "person."

2. *Pseudepigrapha and Rabbinic Works*. The pseudepigrapha speak of the faces of the righteous shining like the sun as God causes his light to shine on them. Their seventh joy will be to press on to see God's face. The rabbis say that all people see God's face at the hour of death. The wicked see it to receive punishment; the righteous see the face of the Shekinah. To see or greet the face of the Shekinah is also a rabbinic phrase for temple or (later) synagogue worship. Those who pray and study also greet God's face inasmuch as he draws near to them.

C. NT Usage.

1. *Face*. *prósōpon* often means "face" in the NT (cf. Mt. 6:16-17; Acts 16:5; Rev. 4:7). Falling on the face expresses veneration or respect (Mt. 17:6; Lk. 5:12). The faces of the angel (Rev. 10:1) and Jesus (Mt. 17:2) shine like the sun. The face of Moses has a passing radiance (2 Cor. 3:7ff.). For Paul the veil that he puts over it signifies the veil over the OT that conceals its true sense from Israel. Christians, however, see with uncovered face the glory of the Lord and are changed from glory to glory (cf. also 2 Cor. 4:6). Seeing the face means meeting a person in Acts 20:25, and knowing by face denotes personal knowledge in Gal. 1:22. Setting the face in a specific direction announces a firm resolve to follow a particular course. The phrase has great significance for the whole of salvation history in Lk. 9:51. At times the appearance of a person or object may be denoted, e.g., in Jms. 1:23; 1:11; Mt. 16:3.

2. *The Front Side*. As in the LXX *prósōpon* may denote the front, often with prepositions, e.g., *apó* (from, Acts 3:19; 5:4-5), *eis* (before, 2 Cor. 8:24), *en* (in, 2 Cor.

951

2:10; 5:12), *katá* (before, 2 Cor. 10:1, 7), *metá* (with, Acts 2:28), and *pró* (before, Mk. 1:2; Acts 13:24).

3. *God's Countenance*. As OT worshippers "see God's face" when they visit the temple, so Christ in Heb. 9:24 appears before the face of God when he enters the heavenly sanctuary. Angels watching over the little ones always see God's face in Mt. 18:10. In the consummation God's servants will see his face (Rev. 22:4). We now see in a mirror dimly, i.e., imperfectly, but we shall then see face to face, i.e., with perfect vision and knowledge (1 Cor. 13:12).

4. *Person*. This sense occurs in the NT only in 2 Cor. 1:11 ("many persons").

D. Early Church Usage.

1. Apostolic Fathers. No peculiarities occur in these authors. We find the normal meanings "face," "front," and "person," although references to God's countenance are found only in OT quotations, e.g., in 1 Clem. 18.9; 22.6.

2. Christology and Trinitarian Teaching. The word *prósōpon* becomes a crucial one in debates about the person of Christ and the Trinity. The legal sense is not yet important in the early stages, and the term receives its content from the discussions. The fathers realize that the term is an inadequate one, so that what it is meant to express must fix its meaning.

euprosōpéō. This word, meaning "to have a good appearance," occurs in the NT only in Gal. 6:12 for "to make a good showing," "to stand well with others."

prosōpolēmpsía, prosōpolémptēs, prosōpolēmptéō, aprosōpolémptōs.

1. In the OT one finds various phrases that express respectful greeting or reception, e.g., bowing the face, lifting up the face. Out of these arises the idea of showing preference or partiality to certain people. God in contrast respects the face of no one (Dt. 10:17).

2. Following the OT, the NT has different expressions for showing respect of persons, e.g., in Mk. 12:14; Lk. 12:21; Jude 16. God, however, shows no partiality (Gal. 2:6). To express this thought the noun *prosōpolēmpsía* is coined (Rom. 2:11; Eph. 6:9; Col. 3:25; Jms. 2:1). In the judgment Jews and Gentiles are treated alike. Over both employers and employees is a Lord who shows partiality to neither. Sinners will be repaid with no respect of persons. God opens salvation to the Gentiles too (Acts 10:34). Believers must be like God in their treatment of one another, not favoring the rich or despising the poor (Jms. 2:1). To show partiality is to commit sin and to fall under conviction by the law (2:9).

3. The theme is treated by the apostolic fathers in Barn. 19:4; Did. 4.3; Pol. 6.1; 1 Clem. 1.3; Barn. 4.12. [E. LOHSE, VI, 768-80]

protíthēmi → *títhēmi*

---

prophḗtēs [prophet], *prophḗtis* [prophetess], *prophēteúō* [to prophesy], *prophēteía* [prophecy], *prophētikós* [prophetic], *pseudoprophḗtēs* [false prophet]

A. Secular Greek.
I. Linguistic Aspects.

1. The prefix *pro-* causes some ambiguity regarding the precise sense of *prophḗtēs*, but it would seem that the original sense in Greek is "one who proclaims," although soon the idea of "one who predicts" also occurs.

2. The word *prophḗtis* (from the end of the fifth century B.C.) is the feminine form.

3. The verb *prophēteúō* has the twofold sense "to proclaim" and "to be an oracle prophet."

4. *prophēteía* denotes a. "ability to declare the divine will," b. "proclamation," and c. "prophetic office."

5. *prophētikós* means "belonging to a prophet," "prophetic."

6. In the word *pseudoprophḗtēs* the first part can be an object ("prophet of lies") or it may be adjectival ("false prophet").

II. Material Aspects.

1. Oracle Prophets.

a. Although the terms are found only from the fifth century B.C., the reality is much older. Thus compounds like *hypophḗtēs* refer to those who wait to hear the will of the gods declared, and then expound and proclaim it to those seeking advice. The exact process (e.g., the role of priestesses) is not wholly clear, but questions are put and answers are issued as divine decisions or directions relating to specific situations.

b. The Delphic oracle brings the *prophḗtēs* group into specific use. Here the Pythia is stirred to mantic frenzy and then becomes the *prophḗtis* through whom the god speaks. The *prophḗtēs* plays a role too, probably as an interpreter of the words that are uttered ecstatically and enigmatically (cf. Plato). The *prophḗtēs* is not inspired as the Pythia is, but exercises rational discernment. The Pythia probably speaks in words, but the *prophḗtēs* must give these words form and convey them to the person seeking advice. The answers may be in hexameters but are mostly in prose, exclusively so later. The function of the oracle is to preserve standards of conduct, to preserve tradition, and to make a specific application, but the language, making heavy use of metaphors and riddles, is obscure and paradoxical. Apollo, the god of the oracle, may himself be called *Diós prophḗtēs* as the true *mántis* and the spokesman of Zeus.

c. The process in the case of other oracles seems to be essentially the same as at Delphi.

d. A divergent use of the term *prophḗtēs* appears in Lucian in his satire on Alexandros, who calls himself a *prophḗtēs* as a "divine man" who predicts events, heals the sick, etc., and is characterized by outlandish clothing, wild ecstasy, extravagant claims, and a readiness to pass on oracles unasked.

e. Although the same person may be both *prophḗtēs* and *mántis*, the functions denoted by the two terms are different, for the *mántis* offers illumination and the *prophḗtēs* then declares it.

f. Inspiration manticism, which is exercised only by women in Greece but by men in Asia Minor, takes the form of ecstatic possession whereby the soul becomes an agent or zither of the god and reason is lost.

g. In sum, prophets in the Greek world are people who declare things imparted by the gods in direct inspiration or through signs, their task being one of interpretation. Oracle prophets proclaim the will or counsel of the gods in answer to direct questions that cover the whole range of private, political, and cultic life. Human criteria control the selection of oracle prophets, who usually come from higher social classes, and even their inspiration tends to be induced by human initiative. Oracle prophets enjoy high esteem and have official positions, so that they may often be asked to lead delegations etc. In some cases the verb *prophēteúō* may include stating and presenting the question.

2. The Poet as Prophet.

a. In early Greek poetry one finds the belief in a link between the divine Muses and the human poet. The Muses have seen and know all things and give poets the power to portray them. Hesiod regards himself as called by the Muses, who breathe into him a divine voice. Pindar uses the term *prophḗtēs* to denote the link. The poet is a chosen herald of wise sayings, lauding virtues and instructing in them. The Muses play the mantic role and poets the prophetic role. The poet offers himself as a *prophḗtēs* who can mediate divine knowledge. He has a divinely imparted genius that equips him for the task.

b. On occasion the poet may also be a *prophḗtēs* as a spokesman or advocate for other people, expressing public opinion.

3. The Broader Use.

a. The term *prophḗtēs* finds varied religious use for spokesmen who deplore immorality, for the frenzied heralds of Dionysus, for the heralds of the goddess of fate, for grasshoppers as prophets of the Muses, for leaders in cultic purification.

b. In Egypt members of the upper priestly class are given the title *prophḗtēs* in Greek.

c. Officebearers outside the oracle also bear the title on inscriptions.

d. The group finds philosophical use for those who lead inquiries, for spokesmen of *noús,* for those who teach a philosophy, for specialists in science, or for quacks in medicine. *prophḗtis* may denote the study of history, or grammar as exegesis of the poets.

e. In poetry, too, the group comes into varied use for heralds of victors at the games, for the cup at the symposium, for hunger as a warning of the need for food.

4. Summary.

a. The group is a solemn but formal one. It expresses the function of proclaiming and can cover a wide sphere. Yet its primary reference is religious. Historical seers are not *prophḗtai* unless connected with an oracle, and demons or lesser gods may be *prophḗtai* of higher gods. Prophets have a mediatorial role, representing the gods to us and us to the gods. The future aspect of the prefix is a late development.

b. Since the group has a formal character, it can cover a wide sphere, although the religious element is usually clear. The most proper use is in relation to the oracle prophets, but since these have a measure of independence, poets, too, can be called prophets.

c. Because of its solemnity *prophḗtēs* can become a title of office.

d. Because of its formal character the *prophḗtēs* group is a useful one in translation; it can pick up the most diverse contents.   [H. KRÄMER, VI, 781-96]

B. The OT. The picture of prophecy presented by the OT is by no means uniform, and to write a history of OT prophecy is difficult. The difficulty is even linguistic, for the common *nābîʾ* group covers only one side of prophecy. There also seem to be prophetic groups on the one side and independent individual prophets on the other, with only tenuous relationships between them.

I. Derivation of nābîʾ. The derivation of the term is contested, links with Akkadian and Arabic being favored. Whether the term is primarily an active one for "proclaimer" or a passive one for "called" is debatable. The term, however, quickly acquires a fixed usage.

II. The Verb.

1. Older Texts. At first ecstatic features are to the fore (cf. 1 Sam. 10:5-6; 19:18ff.). The Spirit seizes Saul, musical instruments are used, and Saul takes off his clothes. This type of ecstatic prophecy may be found in Egypt too, and in the OT one may recall Balaam (Num. 24:2) and the attempts of the priests of Baal to gain a hearing with cultic dancing and self-mutilation (1 Kgs. 18:26ff.). In 1 Kgs. 22:10-11 we first see the visible aspects and then the speaking.

2. *The Prophetic Books.* In these works the verb occurs only in Amos, Jeremiah, Ezekiel, Joel, and Zechariah. In Amos it denotes authentic speaking prophecy in 3:8; 7:15-16. The later use is similar (cf. Jer. 20:1; 23:16, etc.; Ezek. 6:2; 13:17, etc.; Joel 2:28 [general prophecy]; Zech. 13:2 [cutting off of false prophets]).

3. *The Chronicler.* The verb occurs in 2 Chr. 18:7ff. on the basis of 1 Kgs. 22:8ff. Cf. also 2 Chr. 20:37. In Ezr. 5:1 the verb denotes the work of Haggai and Zechariah. In 1 Chr. 25:1, however, the temple musicians are said to prophesy with their lyres, harps, and cymbals—a distinctive usage.

III. The Noun.

1. *Prophetic Groups.* The history books refer to groups of prophets (1 Kgs. 18–19). Ahab consults these in 1 Kgs. 22. Elisha seems to be head of a prophetic fellowship with locations at Bethel, Jericho, and Gilgal (2 Kgs. 2–9). They meet together, hold common meals, preserve traditions, and live modestly, although they may marry and have their own homes (2 Kgs. 4:1ff.). We do not read of ecstatic features but find crisp oracular pronouncements (2 Kgs. 2:21; 3:16-17) which include political and eschatological sayings. The prophets at times oppose rulers and even anoint successors (cf. 2 Kgs. 9:3). During the later monarchy, however, we no longer read of such groups.

2. *Individuals.* The tradition concerning individuals is complex. Samuel is among the prophets (1 Sam. 19:18ff.) but also stands apart. Elijah is the lone survivor of a prophetic massacre (1 Kgs. 18:22) and, like Elisha, both acts individually and is associated with groups. Later, individuals are to the fore and are of very different types. The common feature is that they speak by God's commission (cf. 1 Sam. 3:19-20; 1 Kgs. 16:7, etc.). In the case of Gad, Jehu, Jonah, Huldah, and the anonymous prophet of 1 Kgs. 20:13ff. the only thing we know is that they come with a word from God (cf. 1 Sam. 22:5; 1 Kgs. 16:1ff.; 2 Kgs. 14:25; 22:14ff.). Gad and especially Nathan have an institutional connection but this does not imply dependence, for Gad proclaims God's judgment on David, and Nathan, although involved in political affairs, rebukes David sharply (2 Sam. 12). At times people may consult prophets (1 Sam. 28:6), but often they come unasked, in many cases with a message of judgment that is directed primarily to the royal house (2 Sam. 12:1ff. etc.), but will also affect all Israel, or in some instances a particular place like Bethel (1 Kgs. 13:2-3). Promises may also be issued (2 Sam. 7; 1 Kgs. 20:13, 28), or answers to prayers (2 Kgs. 20:5-6). Like the prophetic groups, the court prophets seem to have an institutional aspect, but there is no obvious relation between the two forms, and not all prophets fit into either. The connection between prophecy and the cultus is also not wholly clear. Samuel receives his call in the temple (1 Sam. 3), but his position is unusual. Nathan speaks to David about building the temple (2 Sam. 7:1ff.) but is not related to the cultus in any other way. Elijah battles Baal in the cultic sphere but has no official cultic functions. Elisha is consulted on the new moon or sabbath but plays no role in worship. The relationship is positive, but not close.

3. *Transferring of the Term to Earlier Figures.* The OT transfers the term to Abraham in connection with his intercession in Gen. 20:7. Aaron is a prophet for Moses in Ex. 7:1. Miriam prophesies in Ex. 20:1-2 to the accompaniment of timbrels and dancing. Moses is a prophet and more than a prophet (Num. 12:6ff.). A portion of his spirit can cause the 70 elders to prophesy (11:24-25). If there has been none like Moses since according to Dt. 34:10, a successor is promised in 18:15ff.; this prophet will

serve as a mediator and declare God's will to the people. Deborah is also called a prophetess in Judg. 4:4.

4. The Prophetic Books.

a. The writing prophets may be called prophets. Amos rejects the title (7:14), and Isaiah does not use it, but Hosea calls himself a prophet, and the title is common for Jeremiah and Ezekiel. Later in Habakkuk, Haggai, and Zechariah the term occurs both in the titles and within the books. Even Amos does not reject the term in principle, for he uses the verb in 7:15.

b. The prophets sometimes use the term positively for others, usually in the plural and with a reference to the past (cf. Hos. 6:5; 12:11; Jer. 5:13-14; Ezek. 38:17; Am. 2:11-12; 3:7).

c. Yet what is said about other prophets is mostly polemical (cf. Hos. 4:5; Is. 3:1ff.; Mic. 3:5ff.; Jer. 5:31; 6:13-14; 23:14; Zeph. 3:3-4; Ezek. 13:2ff.; Zech. 13:2ff.).

d. The writing prophets thus find themselves in opposition to official prophets, who are often associated with priests, but who have no close connection with the cultus and are, indeed, mentioned along with other national leaders (cf. Jer. 2:26 as well as 6:13 etc.). It is not even conclusive that there is a definite prophetic profession as such.

e. The real difference between the writing prophets and others is not one of terminology but of message (Jer. 14:13-14; 28). A prophet like Jeremiah proclaims a word of judgment that conflicts with the accepted tradition, which has, perhaps, institutional backing. Yet one should recall that Isaiah can also prophesy salvation, so that the distinction is not simply that the message of the writing prophets is always one of disaster. The real issue is that they carry a true word from God which often brings them into conflict with the popular view.

5. The True and False Prophet in Deuteronomy. Dt. 13:2ff. offers the criterion that a prophet who summons the people to idolatry is false. Dt. 18:20 offers the further criterion that a prophet is false if he speaks in the name of other gods. Whether what is proclaimed comes to pass or not is another test in 18:22.

6. The Term in Other Works. In Pss. 51 and 105:15 Nathan and Abraham are called prophets, and Ps. 74:9 complains that there are no longer any prophets. Lam. 2 says that prophets were slain in the sanctuary (v. 20), that the prophets have no vision (v. 9), and that they gave misleading oracles (v. 14). Daniel refers to past prophets (9:6), specifically mentioning Jeremiah (v. 2). Chronicles often speaks of the prophets or refers to individual prophets. Neh. 6 and 9 mention prophets, and Ezr. 5:1-2 calls Haggai and Zechariah prophets. Sir. 36:20-21 prays for the fulfilment of prophecies and the validation of the prophets. Sir. 48:1 refers to Elijah as a prophet and 49:6-7 to Jeremiah. Prophecy does not seem to play as big a role after the exile. The prophets are mostly mentioned in retrospect, and often the writing prophets are in view.

IV. Other Terms.

1. "Man of God" often means the same as prophet (1 Sam. 2:27ff.), particularly when it refers to someone who comes with a word from God. It is common in the Elisha stories and seems to be a title of honor used by others in address or in reference (1 Sam. 9:6ff.; 1 Kgs. 17:18-19). Moses is called a man of God in Dt. 33:1.

2. "Seer" is a term for Samuel in 1 Sam. 9:11, 18-19 (cf. 1 Chr. 9:22 etc.). The text explains that this was an older term for prophet.

3. Another term for "seer" is Gad's title in 2 Sam. 24:11, perhaps denoting his position at court (cf. Am. 7:12).

V. Form and Content of Prophetic Proclamation. The word is the decisive feature of OT prophecy. The prophet must pass on the word that he receives. God sets his word on Jeremiah's lips (Jer. 1:9). When God gives it, he must speak it (1:17). Judgment will fall on those who hamper him (5:13-14). God's word is said to come (2 Sam. 7:4). "Thus says the Lord" is a common prophetic formula (Ex. 4:22; 1 Sam. 10:18; 2 Sam. 7:5; Jeremiah and Ezekiel, but not Hosea, Joel, Jonah, Habakkuk, or Zephaniah). The content is mostly in the first person of God who gives the commission (cf. 2 Sam. 12:11; Am. 6:14, etc.). The saying is usually about an imminent act of salvation or judgment and is thus a promise or a threat. The reference may also be broadly eschatological, often with a messianic element (Jer. 11:1ff.). Threats are mostly directed against the whole people, sometimes against kings, priests, or prophets (2 Sam. 12:7ff.; Am. 7:17). The calamity may be war, exile, etc., or a natural disaster, e.g., famine, earthquake, or plague. The prophets are involuntary instruments of the word that they pass on. They show those whom they address their sin (cf. Jer. 6:27). Rebuke and calamity are closely related. The common charge is disregarding what God thinks right, including especially idolatry, trusting in foreign powers, and cultic abuses. Admonitions and warnings are part of prophecy in an effort to avert judgment (cf. the watchman's office in Ezek. 3:17 etc.). We also find prophetic intercession (Is. 37:1ff.; Jer. 7:16). Forms vary according to the different situations and needs. Thus disputations, legal pronouncements, salvation oracles, and songs may all be found. Visions occur (Is. 6; Jer. 1:4ff.; Ezek. 1ff.; Zech. 1–6; Am. 7:1ff.), but these usually culminate in a word from God. In symbolic acts (Is. 20:1ff. etc.) the prophets are drawn into their proclamation. Their personal lives are affected as they themselves become a sign (cf. Hos. 1; 3; Jer. 16:1ff.; Ezek. 24:15ff.). Personal involvement may take the form of martyrdom (Jer. 37–38; Is. 53).

VI. LXX Usage.

1. The LXX mostly uses *prophḗtēs*, but for "seer" other terms might be used, e.g., *ho blépōn* in 1 Chr. 9:22 or *ho horṓn* in 21:9.

2. Prophetess is always *prophḗtis*.

3. For the late noun "prophecy" *prophēteía* is always used (cf. Neh. 6:12; Ezr. 6:14).

4. As regards the verb forms, the LXX indiscriminately uses *prophēteúō* except in 1 Chr. 25:1-3.

5. An attempt at distinction occurs in Jeremiah with the use of *pseudoprophḗtēs* for those who oppose Jeremiah.   [R. RENDTORFF, VI, 796-812]

C. Judaism in the Hellenistic-Roman Period.

I. Contemporary Prophecy.

1. Nonrabbinic Witness.

a. In Zech. 13:2-3, 4ff. there is a sharp attack on contemporary prophets. On "that day" they will be accused by their parents and will set aside their hairy mantles. In view, perhaps, are ecstatics who wore the prophetic cloak as a guild sign. But the references to Dt. 13:5-6 and Am. 7:14 indicate that oracle-giving priests or cultic prophets might also be under attack.

b. Ps. 74:9 seems to suggest that true prophecy has now come to an end (cf. 1 Macc. 4:38, 46; 9:27; 14:41). Yet the permanent ruins of Ps. 74:3 point us to the destruction of Solomon's temple, so that the temporary silence of the prophets is more likely at issue. If so, the lament has no bearing on postexilic prophecy.

c. The lament of Azariah in Dan. 3:38 LXX also refers to the exilic period.

d. In the Epistle of Baruch prophets seem to be restricted to a canonical period of salvation, although only as "helpers," so that oracles might still be given.

2. 1 Macc. 4:46; 9:27; 14:41. In 1 Macc. 4:46 the stones of the old altar are left until a prophet arises who says what should be done with them. In 9:27 the people is going through a time of affliction such as there had never been since a prophet last appeared. In 14:41 Simon is appointed leader until an authentic prophet arises. From these verses some have argued that 1 Maccabees looks ahead to an eschatological prophet, but others think that the story climaxes with the threefold office of John Hyrcanus as prophet, priest, and king.

3. *The Rabbinic Tradition.* The rabbis restrict legitimate prophecy to a classical period which coincides with the composition of the canon. The Holy Spirit, the Spirit of prophecy, is specifically at work up to the destruction of the temple in 587 B.C., although with some extension to the immediate postexilic period, i.e., that of Haggai, Zechariah, and Malachi as "the latter prophets." After this period the Spirit of prophecy departs and God declares his will directly by the voice from heaven. Josephus adopts a similar schema in which there is movement from the age of prophecy through the present to a future general outpouring of the Spirit. Pharisaic rabbinism relates the prophets specifically to the law, which already contains the salvation history whose stages are actualized according to the divine plan. Thus all later prophecy derives from that of Moses. The prophets are the earliest authorized expositors of the law. Prophets abound, but only those whom the law needs in its self-development have come down to us in writing. As expositors of the law, the prophets are secondary to the law and no different in principle from the wise men whose sayings constitute oral law. The voice from heaven is a valid continuation of the lost Spirit of prophecy. In this whole development a combination of the eruptive work of the Spirit in the prophets with the orderly work of the Spirit in the wise men is achieved. Yet the fusion is not complete, for on the one side some rabbis are hostile to prophecy, while on the other an eschatologically oriented charismatic element, to which Pharisaism contributes, plays a big part in the revolts under Vespasian and Hadrian.

II. Historical Manifestations.

1. *Prophetic Experience in Palestinian Sources.* Dan. 9:1ff., 20ff. describes a pneumatic experience that includes fasting, prayer, mourning, and finally an angelic visitation and a glimpse into the future. In the Qumran exegesis of Hab. 2:2 the prophet is a blind instrument of God who does not know the meaning of his words, but the teacher of righteousness has been granted understanding and brings to light their hidden meaning. In Josephus *Jewish War* 2.159 the Essenes are seers as they study Scripture, engage in purifications, and enter a state of ecstasy in which interpretation of dreams is one form of the pneumatic experience (*Antiquities* 17.345ff.). Josephus *Jewish War* 6.300ff. tells the story of a rough ecstatic (Jesus ben Ananias) whose appearance reminds us of Zech. 13:2ff.

2. *Prophecy in the Light of Alexandrian Theology.* In the Wisdom of Solomon it is wisdom that engenders prophecy in its direction of salvation history. Philo finds in the law the starting point of the salvation event and depicts the patriarchs and Moses as prophets. Moses is a bearer of revelation as ruler, lawgiver, priest, and prophet in one. He rules the people which, with Abraham as its father, is the people of the prophets and a priestly people for all nations. Himself enjoying pneumatic experiences, Philo says that according to Scripture all sages have a prophetic gift. The righteous, too, bear the prophetic Spirit. The way to prophetic experience is that of ecstasy, which involves the four stages of raving, external stimulation, quietness, and divine seizure in which the prophet is a simple organ of the Spirit with no understanding of what is said. The terminology of Plato and the mysteries influences this depiction, but his statements find their basis in Scripture. He attacks a literal understanding of Scripture

mainly because he favors its contemplative consideration under the direction of the invisible spirit who grants spiritual instruction.

3. Seers and Prophets.

a. Various people emerge who claim to be prophets. Thus Josephus *Antiquities* 13.311ff. mentions a famous Essene seer called Simon, 15.373ff. tells the story of the Essene seer Menachem who has a gift of prediction, and 17.345ff. refers to another Simon who foretells the downfall of Archelaus of the house of Herod. Josephus also says that many Essenes have insight into divine things.

b. The Pharisees, too, have their prophets. *Antiquities* 17.43ff. mentions a prophetic group at Herod's court. Josephus himself has a dream in which he learns that an oracle which plays a big role prior to the Jewish War means disaster for Israel. Tradition has it that many rabbis are seers in different ways, e.g., Gamaliel II, Samuel, and Akiba, who in spite of opposition helped to stir up the revolt against Hadrian.

c. Apart from the Essenes and Pharisees there are other prophets of good and evil. Josephus in *Jewish War* 6.286 mentions a Zealot prophet during the temple revolt who proclaims imminent salvation. *Jewish War* 6.300ff. introduces Jesus ben Ananias who in A.D. 62 proclaims disaster to a prosperous Jerusalem, is arrested, and then after being released continues his unsettling ministry until he is himself killed during the siege.

4. The Ruler with the Threefold Office. After the example of Moses there arises in the later postexilic period the priestly ruler who also has a prophetic gift. John Hyrcanus I (135-104 B.C.) is a ruler of this kind. He receives auditions in the temple and can predict the future (*Antiquities* 13.282-83, 300). He is thus an eschatological counterpart of Moses and of the paradisal king; his task is to restore the ideal state to the whole of the human race. Qumran, however, seems to hold the kingly, priestly, and prophetic offices apart. The first two alone are messianic offices, the priest taking precedence over the king. The precise role of the prophet alongside the priest and king is hard to determine.

5. Messianic Prophets. Whereas the charismatic priest-king embodies present salvation, messianic prophets are oriented to the imminent future. They expect a miracle of accreditation that will initiate the new age. Since the new age will bring a reenactment of past salvation events, Moses and Joshua are their models. Josephus *Antiquities* 18.85ff. mentions a Samaritan who plays such a role, 20.97-98 tells the story of Theudas, 20.169ff. refers to an Egyptian prophet, and *Jewish War* 7.437ff. introduces a Zealot in Cyrene who after the Jewish War leads poorer people into the desert in search of signs. As late as the fifth century A.D. there are reports of a messianic movement in Crete in which someone who claims to be Moses stirs up many people to attempt a repetition of the march through the sea to the promised land, but disappears when they are drowned off the coast of Crete.

III. The Apocalyptic Literature. Apocalyptic, which has its roots in Iran, integrates the doctrine of two world epochs into the understanding of salvation history. It also follows the principle of offering history in future form by putting prophecies on the lips of figures from the past. The fact that the writing prophets relate their work to history facilitates this development. At times seers offer their own contemplations and experiences, but by and large these works relate to the prophetic manifestations of the period only by offering a basis for the belief of messianic prophets that they will initiate the new aeon.

IV. The End of Prophecy. There was never a purely prophetic age in Israel, for prophecy always has to contend with opposing trends, and it can also live on in constantly new forms. Yet after the defeat of A.D. 70 rabbinism establishes a new patriarchate on the basis of the law and canon which begins to eliminate other movements and to make the wise men the successors of the prophets. The failure of the revolt under Hadrian brings the final suppression of the charismatic element and the reconstruction of the synagogue under the domination of nomistic rationalism.

[R. Meyer, VI, 812-28]

D. Prophets and Prophecies in the NT.

I. Occurrence and Meaning of the Words.

1. In the NT *prophḗtēs* is easily the most common term of the group. It occurs 144 times, mostly in Matthew, Luke, Acts, and John. The prophet is normally a biblical proclaimer of a divinely inspired message. Apart from Balaam (2 Pet. 2:16), only one Gentile, the Cretan poet in Tit. 1:12, is called a *prophḗtēs*. The biblical prophet can predict the future (cf. Acts 11:28), can know the past (Jn. 4:19), and can look into the heart (Lk. 7:39), but is essentially a proclaimer of the word, not a magician or soothsayer. Since the message of the OT prophets is contained in books, their writings may also be called the prophets.

2. *prophḗtis* occurs in the NT only in Lk. 2:36 (Anna) and Rev. 2:20 (Jezebel), although other women have a prophetic gift (Acts 2:17-18; 21:9; 1 Cor. 11:5).

3. The verb *prophēteúō* is more prominent in Paul (11 of 28 instances). It means a. "to proclaim a divinely imparted message" (1 Cor. 11:4-5), b. "to foretell" (Mk. 7:6; Lk. 1:67), c. "to bring to light something that is hidden" (Mk. 14:65), d. "to teach, admonish, comfort" (1 Cor. 14:3, 31), e. "to glorify God ecstatically" (Acts 10:46-47), f. "to have a prophetic gift" (Acts 21:9), and possibly g. "to act as a prophet" (Mt. 7:22).

4. Of the 19 instances of *prophēteía* seven are in Paul. The word carries the nuances of a. the gift (1 Cor. 12:10), b. the word (1 Cor. 14:6), often as a prediction (Mt. 13:14), c. the authoritative direction (1 Tim. 1:18), and d. the work (Rev. 11:6).

5. The adjective *prophētikós* qualifies *graphaí* in Rom. 16:26 and *lógos* in 2 Pet. 1:19, both times with reference to the OT prophets.

6. Of the eleven instances of *pseudoprophḗtēs* in the NT, three are in Matthew and three in Revelation. The context must decide whether the falsity refers to the claim or the content. Usually the claim is at issue (Mk. 13:22; Mt. 24:24; 1 Jn. 4:1). But in 1 Jn. 4:1ff. the false prophet is also one who proclaims what is false. The same is true in 2 Pet. 2:1. The main stress, however, is on the false claim which will also entail false teaching.

II. The OT Prophets.

1. Various OT prophets are mentioned in the NT, especially Isaiah (Mt. 3:3; Mk. 7:6; Lk. 3:4; Jn. 12:38; Acts 8:28), also Samuel (Acts 13:20), David (Acts 2:30), Enoch (Jude 14), Elisha (Lk. 4:27), Jeremiah (Mt. 2:17), Daniel (Mt. 24:15), and Jonah (Mt. 12:39), with references to Hosea, Amos, Micah, Habakkuk, and Zechariah, and cf. Balaam in 2 Pet. 2:16.

2. The OT prophets are the mouth through which God speaks (Acts 3:21; Mt. 1:22; 2:15). Heb. 1:1 uses *en* rather than *diá,* perhaps to denote God's presence in the prophets, or his speaking with them. In 2 Pet. 1:21 the prophets are involuntary instruments of the Spirit. In 1 Pet. 1:11 the preexistent Christ speaks through them. Mt. 13:35 is perhaps to the same effect, and cf. Jn. 12:38.

3. The prophets write as well as speak (Mt. 2:5; Mk. 1:2; Rom. 1:2, etc.). Hence the writings are also called the prophets (Mk. 1:2). The prophets are combined with the law (or Moses) (Mt. 11:13; Acts 26:22), as well as with the Psalms (Lk. 24:44).

4. The prophets proclaim what is fulfilled in Christ (Rom. 1:2). The *pro-* has here the sense of telling in advance. All prophecy focuses on Christ (Jn. 1:45; Acts 3:24), who fulfils all God's promises (2 Cor. 1:20). They foretell his birth (Mt. 1:23), the return from Egypt (2:15), the work of the Baptist (Mk. 1:2), down to the resurrection (Lk. 18:31ff.), Pentecost (Acts 2:16), the parousia (2 Pet. 3:2), the judgment (Jude 14-15), and the new order (Acts 3:21). Rejection by Israel is also predicted (Mk. 7:6). The passion and resurrection are at the heart of their message (Mt. 26:56; Lk. 24:44ff.). Only God or the Spirit grants the true understanding of prophecy whereby the prophetic promise becomes the apostolic gospel (Rom. 1:1-2). Paul says only what Moses and the prophets foretold (Acts 26:22-23). The prophetic sayings have a reference to their own time (cf. Mt. 2:15 and Hos. 11:1; 2:17-18 and Jer. 31:15; Mk. 7:6 and Is. 29:13), but in the light of the fulfilment the NT sees predictions in their depictions.

5. The prophets do not merely foretell events but are also authorities supporting the truth of the word and work of Jesus (cf. Mk. 11:17; Jn. 6:45). They proclaim forgiveness to all believers in Christ's name (Acts 10:43). They justify the reception of Gentiles into the church (Acts 15:15).

6. The NT often refers to the persecution or execution of the prophets (Lk. 13:33-34; Mt. 23:31; Heb. 11:36-37). The disciples are their heirs in this regard (Mt. 5:12; cf. Jms. 5:10). Mt. 23:34 christianizes an apocryphal wisdom saying, and Acts 7:52 connects the persecution of the prophets with the crucifixion of Jesus.

III. Pre-Christian Prophets.

1. The NT refers to prophets at the beginning of the gospel story. Thus Zacharias utters a prophecy under the inspiration of the Spirit in Lk. 1:67ff.

2. Elizabeth also speaks prophetically in Lk. 1:41-42 and is thus enabled to recognize in Mary the mother of the Messiah.

3. The aged Simeon comes into the temple under the inspiration of the Spirit, having been told that he would see the Lord's Christ; hence he, too, speaks about the infant Jesus prophetically (Lk. 2:25ff.).

4. Anna is expressly called a prophetess in Lk. 2:36. As such, she proclaims Christ as the eschatological Savior (v. 38). Like the others, she is a pious Jew, and all four bear a close relation to the temple, thus denoting a harmony of temple and prophecy in this pre-Christian period.

IV. John the Baptist.

1. John the Baptist is everywhere called a prophet (Mk. 11:32; Mt. 11:9; Lk. 1:76; Jn. 1:25). Jesus, indeed, says that he is more than a prophet (Mt. 11:9).

2. The Synoptists describe his call, appearance, and preaching after the OT model. His call is like that of Jeremiah (Jer. 1:1-2; Lk. 3:1-2). He proclaims judgment and calls for conversion. He confronts the ruler like a true prophet (Mk. 6:17ff.; cf. 1 Sam. 15:10ff.; 2 Sam. 12:1ff.; 1 Kgs. 21:17ff.). He prophesies the mightier one who comes after him (Mk. 1:7-8). His baptism is perhaps a prophetic sign.

3. a. The Baptist has a messianic and eschatological character. This may be seen in Lk. 1:4ff., which shows that his birth and word and work usher in the time of eschatological salvation for the people.

b. His baptizing is the work of an eschatological prophet. It is not a mere rite of purification, nor is it proselyte baptism. It is a once-for-all action for all who will receive eschatological salvation as penitents. By his food and clothing he plainly comes from the desert like Moses, the eschatological redeemer of the old covenant (cf. 1 Cor.

10:1ff.). Jn. 1:25 sees in the baptism a proof of the messianic nature of his ministry; it carries messianic associations for those who question him.

c. Herod, too, fears the Baptist as an eschatological prophet whose coming will shatter the old order. The fact that some people think that he has risen again and is at work in Jesus indicates that they view them as an eschatological deliverer (cf. Mk. 6:14).

d. The statements in Mt. 11:9, 11 confirm the fact that John is more than an ordinary prophet (cf. Lk. 16:16). Mt. 11:13 says that the prophets and the law prophesied until John. This carries the implication that the time of fulfilment has now come, although strictly the meaning might be that they prophesied with reference to John.

e. Other NT verses show that John's special position is that of the precursor of Jesus. He is not himself the Messiah, although some of his disciples perhaps thought so. If John has eschatological significance, it is as the forerunner of the messianic age, the last prophet before the Messiah (cf. Jn. 1:21, 23; Lk. 1:76; Mt. 11:10, 14).

V. Jesus.

1. Jesus is seldom called a prophet in the NT (cf. Mk. 6:15; 8:28; Mt. 21:11, 46; Lk. 7:16; Acts 3:22-23; Jn. 4:19; 6:14). Mostly it is the people that calls him a prophet (Mk. 6:15; Mt. 21:11, etc.), or individuals like the Samaritan woman (Jn. 4:19) and the man born blind (9:17). The disciples see in him a prophet (Lk. 24:19; Acts 3:22). He does not call himself a prophet except perhaps in Lk. 13:33.

2. An ordinary prophet of the time is meant in Mk. 6:15. The Samaritan woman associates prophecy with Jesus' knowledge of her past. Simon the Pharisee thinks Jesus should see that the woman is a sinner if he is a true prophet (Lk. 7:39). He displays such knowledge in the conversation that follows.

3. Some verses compare Jesus to the biblical prophets (Lk. 9:8; Mt. 16:14). Like them he calls for conversion (Mk. 1:15), censures mere externality in worship, and speaks with power (Mt. 7:29). He also performs symbolic actions (Mk. 11:13-14). His passion continues the persecution of the prophets (Lk. 13:33). Yet he is also shown to be superior to the prophets (Mt. 12:41). He brings the new age that they foretold (Lk. 10:24). He fulfils the prophecies.

4. a. Like the OT prophets, Jesus utters promises and threats (Lk. 6:20ff., 24).

b. He has visions, auditions, and ecstatic experiences (Mk. 1:10-11; Lk. 10:18; Jn. 12:28; Lk. 10:21).

c. He scans human thoughts (Mk. 2:5; Lk. 5:22; 6:8; 9:47; Jn. 2:24-25, etc.).

d. He knows future events (Mk. 11:2; 14:13ff.; Mt. 26:21; Mk. 8:31; Lk. 13:33; Jn. 14:29; 16:4, etc.). Even though some scholars contend that details have been added later (e.g., in the passion predictions in Mk. 8:31), the authenticity of prediction by Jesus is beyond dispute.

5. a. Some NT verses depict Jesus as the promised prophet of the last time. Thus Peter and Stephen (Acts 3:22; 7:37) both refer to Dt. 18:15. One might also quote Jn. 6:14; 7:40; Mk. 6:14; Mt. 21:11; Lk. 7:16; 24:19ff.; 1:68, 78.

b. Various stories reflect the idea that Jesus is the prophet of Dt. 18:15 (cf. the birth stories in Mt. 1–2, the 40 days in the wilderness in Mt. 4:2, the reply to the Baptist in Mt. 11:5, the feeding of the crowds in Jn. 6, the teaching of the Sermon on the Mount (in which "But I say" replaces "Thus says the Lord"), and the miracles that follow (Mt. 8–9). In many of these stories and teachings Jesus is set in antithetical typology to Moses; he is the prophet of the last days who brings salvation.

c. As in Judaism, messianic titles and functions merge into one another. Thus Jesus is the kingly as well as the prophetic Messiah in Jn. 6:14-15; Mt. 21:9ff. He is Christ as well as prophet in Acts 3:18ff.

d. If he never calls himself *the* prophet, this is in accord with the messianic secret; he might still have viewed himself as such. The NT probably does not use the term too frequently because Jewish Christians saw him merely as a second Moses. Again, the title prophet does not adequately represent his uniqueness; it thus yields to fuller titles like Son of Man, Lord, and Son of God.

VI. Church Prophets.

1. The Nature of Primitive Christian Prophecy. This prophecy is the utterance of charismatic preachers regarding the divine mysteries (1 Cor. 13:2), God's saving will (Eph. 3:5-6), future events (Acts 21:10-11; Rev. 22:6-7), and contemporary matters (Acts 13:1ff.; 1 Tim. 1:18). The prophets admonish, console, encourage, and censure (cf. 1 Cor. 14:3, 25).

2. Comparison with OT Prophecy. Similarities include the use of actions (Acts 21:10-11), prophetic style (11:11), and visions at calling (cf. Rev. 1:9ff.; 10:8ff.). A main difference is that, while there are some outstanding prophets, all members of the community are now called to prophesy (Acts 2:4, 16ff.; 4:31). Like the OT prophets, NT prophets disclose hidden things (Eph. 3:5) but enjoy less authority, since they are subject to the judgment of their brethren (Mt. 7:16). The divine of Revelation is closest to an OT prophet with his authoritative and decisively significant message (1:2-3; 19:9) which determines the destiny of those who accept or reject it (22:18-19).

3. The Most Important Charisma. Paul prefers prophecy to other gifts (1 Cor. 14:1; cf. 12:28-29; Eph. 4:11). The prophets Barnabas and Silas are leaders of the church (Acts 15:22, 32). The prophets also have a special place in Rev. 11:18; 16:6; 18:24; prophecy is here the revelation and testimony of Jesus Christ. Some prophets may be itinerants (cf. Acts 11:27-28 and 21:10), but this is not a general rule. Even prophecy is transitory (1 Cor. 13:8-9, 12). Paul does not call himself a prophet, although he speaks prophetically (1 Cor. 14:6; cf. Rom. 11:25ff.; 1 Cor. 15:51ff.; 1 Th. 4:13ff.; Acts 20:22-23; 27:22ff.).

4. Ecstasy and Prophecy. The NT never refers to exclusion of the individual ego even though prophecy has ecstatic features (cf. Acts 2:4ff.; 10:44ff.; Rev. 1:10; 4:2). Its chief mark is proclamation of God's word in which the speaker's personhood remains intact (1 Cor. 14). It stays on the sober ground of faith (cf. Rom. 12:6). God gives, and believers make responsible use of the gift.

5. Glossolalia and Prophecy. These two gifts of the Spirit have much in common (Acts 2:4, 17; 19:6). Yet prophecy ranks higher (1 Cor. 14:1ff.). It declares God's counsels openly (1 Cor. 14:5). Both gifts edify, but tongues edify only the speakers, prophecy the whole church (14:2-3). To those outside speakers in tongues seem to be mad, but in prophecy spiritual experience is presented in intelligible speech that all may understand (14:24-25).

6. Prayer and Prophecy. Prayer is a mark of the OT prophets and of Anna, and in the NT, too, prayer and prophecy often go together (Acts 13:1ff.; 1 Cor. 11:4-5; 1 Th. 5:17ff.). Prayer is not a separate charisma; perhaps the prophets lead in prayer (cf. 1 Cor. 14:13ff., where the prophets pray with the mind, and even outsiders may thus join in the Amen).

7. Revelation and Prophecy. Prophecy rests on revelation. Revelation is imparted to the prophet and becomes prophetic proclamation (1 Cor. 14:26ff.). In Revelation we see a transition from prophecy to apocalyptic. Revelation is the Apocalypse of Jesus

Christ, has an apocalyptic theme, and introduces apocalyptic features like the angel, visions, and cryptic numbers. It is also genuine prophecy with its call for repentance (11:3) and its message of admonition and comfort (2–3). The element of prediction, however, is now central.

8. *gnṓsis* and Prophecy. Knowledge and prophecy are both gifts in 1 Cor. 13:8ff., but prophecy rates higher, for it attains to knowledge by inspiration rather than by thought. Furthermore, although both teach, *gnṓsis* is individualistic and easily puffs up (1 Cor. 8:1), whereas prophecy edifies (14:3-4).

9. *Teaching and Prophecy.* Prophets are often mentioned with teachers (Acts 13:1) and they themselves teach (1 Cor. 14:31), but more on the basis of revelations and in specific situations, hence with more freedom.

10. *Evangelism and Prophecy.* Like evangelism, prophecy is proclamation but primarily to believers and for edification (1 Cor. 14:3-4). Yet as evangelism also preserves the community, so prophecy may convict nonbelievers (14:24-25). Whereas evangelism presents the great acts of God, prophecy sets out God's will for the world and the church under the direction of the Spirit.

VII. False Prophets.

1. In the NT the word *pseudoprophḗtēs* covers various kinds of false prophets, e.g., Jewish prophets in Lk. 6:26; 2 Pet. 2:1, the magician in Acts 13:6, and false Christian teachers in 2 Pet. 2:1; 2 Jn. 7; 1 Jn. 2:18 (cf. Jezebel in Rev. 2:20). False prophets are common in the last days (Mt. 24:11). The second beast of Rev. 13:11ff. is at their head.

2. Prophets must be tested, not rationally, but spiritually and charismatically (1 Cor. 12:10) by other prophets (14:29). False prophets may perform miracles (Mk. 13:22; Rev. 13:13). Christological confession forms a test (1 Jn. 4:2-3). So do fruits (Mt. 7:16; cf. Rev. 2:20).

E. Prophets in the Early Church.

I. The OT Prophets.

1. Barnabas often refers to OT prophets in the proof from prophecy, although illumination and love are needed to interpret them (5.6; 6.2ff.). The prophets speak especially of Christ (5.5ff.; 6.6-7) but also of Christians (11.1ff.), who are the holy people of the covenant (14.6ff.).

2. Justin develops the proof from prophecy even more explicitly. Philosophy builds on prophecy and myth imitates it (*Apology* 32; 44.8ff.; 54). The prophetic writings cover the entire OT, all of which relates to Christ, although sometimes obscurely. Later prophets are more precise and expound older prophecies. The Holy Spirit has fully intimated Christ in the prophets, with references to his virgin birth, miracles, entry into Jerusalem, arrest, silence, mocking, crucifixion, death, resurrection, and return (cf. *Apology* and *Dialogue*).

II. Jesus as Prophet. The theme of Jesus as a prophet is most fully developed in the Pseudo-Clementine writings. These present "prophet" as a christological title. Jesus is the prophet of Dt. 18:15 who does signs and wonders like Moses. Sayings and stories from the Gospels are adduced in support of this. In Gnostic style, however, Jesus is the preacher of truth rather than the eschatological deliverer. Although he is unique, the one true prophet predates him, being incarnate in Adam and coming in Abraham, Moses, etc. to bring saving truth to the world.

III. Church Prophets. Prophets are held in high esteem in Did. 13.1ff., where tithes should be paid to them. They may give thanks freely (10.7) and are not to be treated critically unless they prove to be false prophets. They are being replaced, however, by bishops and deacons (15.1-2). Hermas does not call himself a prophet but knows prophets who wait upon the Spirit and speak as the Spirit decides (*Mandates* 11.8-9). In general, prophets gradually become less prominent as charismatic powers fade and false prophets bring discredit on prophecy. Irenaeus claims prophetic gifts but gives priority to the bishops, presbyters, and deacons. Contesting pagan prophecy, Origen quotes OT rather than Christian prophets. Tertullian values Montanist prophets but does not give prophets any very decisive role in the churches. Officebearers and Scripture replace them.

IV. False Prophets. False prophets obviously cause a good deal of trouble. Did. 11.8ff. shows that they are marked by inconsistency of teaching and conduct. Hermas offers moral criteria by which to unmask them (*Mandates* 11.2-3, 12-13). They are bold, ambitious, talkative, etc., offer consultations like soothsayers, take fees, and tell people what they want to hear. The Montanist prophets are regarded as false prophets on the grounds that they produce no miracles, that their prediction of the coming of the new Jerusalem at Pepuza is false, that they prophesy in ecstastic trances, that they accept gifts and adopt an unseemly mode of life, and that Jesus himself said that there would be no more prophets after John. There may be little basis for many of the criticisms, for Tertullian respects the Montanists, they live ascetically, it is generally agreed that they are doctrinally orthodox, and ecstasy is not rejected by the church in principle. With the defeat of Montanism the institutional ministry gains a decisive victory over prophecy.   [G. FRIEDRICH, VI, 828-61]

---

procheirízō [to appoint]

---

1. This verb, developed from the adjective *prócheiros,* means "to hold ready," "to handle," "to prepare," "to appoint" (people).

2. In the LXX the adjective occurs in Prov. 11:3, and the verb is used for "to elect," "to name" (Ex. 4:13).

3. Philo uses the adjective for "close at hand" (ideas etc.). Neither he nor Josephus uses the verb.

4. In the NT Acts has the verb three times. In the accounts of Paul's conversion in 22:14 and 26:16 it means "to choose," "to appoint," "to ordain." It does not carry a sense of foreordination but of appointment to a function. This is also the sense in Acts 3:20, where Peter tells the people that Christ has been appointed for them, i.e., for their restoration, whether with his earthly ministry, resurrection, or return, or from the very beginning.

5. There are no instances of the verb in early Christian writings.

[W. MICHAELIS, VI, 862-64]

---

prṓtos [first], *prṓton* [first, at first], *prōtokathedría* [best seat], *prōtoklisía* [first place], *prōtótokos* [firstborn], *prōtotokeía* [birthright], *prōteúō* [to be first]

---

prṓtos.

1. From Homer *prṓtos* signifies the "first" in space, time, number, or rank.

2. The word occurs in the LXX some 240 times, half in Genesis to Nehemiah, and mostly with reference to number, though also at times rank.

3. Philo uses the term in various connections (e.g., *ho prótos* is the only true God for the sage); in Josephus the term is used for leaders in the tribe, people, or priesthood (e.g., Ezra), as well as for the first in time.

4.a. Although *prótos* occurs over 90 times in the NT, the spatial sense is rare (cf. Heb. 9:2, 6, 8).

b. More common is the meaning "first" in time, number, or sequence (cf. Mk. 14:12; 1 Cor. 16:1). The use for "earlier" or "preceding" is very common (Rev. 2:5; 1 Tim. 5:12). As regards the covenant of Heb. 8:7, 13; 9:1, 15, 18), the opposite is mostly *kainé* or *néa* (*deutéra* only in 8:7). Similarly the new heaven and earth will replace the first in Rev. 21:1. A more common NT antithesis is first and last (*éschatos*). Christ is the first and last in Rev. 1:17; 2:8; he is before and after all time. In Mt. 12:45; 27:64; 2 Pet. 2:20 *prótos* means former and *éschatos* later or last. In 1 Cor. 15:45 the first Adam is not preexistent, and Christ as the second Adam is the present Christ of the resurrection; the former initiated the old humanity, Christ has initiated the new. Although Christ is the second *ánthrōpos*, he is not the second Adam, for as the new Adam he is also the last.

c. The antithesis *prótos/éschatos* may also carry a reference to rank, as in Mt. 20:16 (cf. 19:30). When the disciples squabble about rank, *prótos* is a key word (Mk. 10:44); the opposite may be *doúlos* or *diákonos* as well as *éschatos* (Mk. 9:35). The first commandment of Mk. 12:28 is the same as the great commandment of Mt. 22:36; in this case comparison is made with a second that is like it. Eph. 6:2 (the first commandment with promise) uses *prótē entolé* in a different way. *hoi prótoi* for "leaders" occurs in Mk. 6:21; Lk. 19:47; Acts 13:50.

5. In 2 Clem. 14.1 the preexistent church is *hē ekklēsía hē prótē,* and in Hermas *Mandates* 3.4.1 the archangels are *hoi ángeloi hoi prótoi ktisthéntes.*

próton.

1. As an adverb, this word means "first," "at first," "in the first instance," "before," "earlier"; there are only eight plainly attested instances in the LXX.

2.a. Some of the more than 60 instances in the NT call for special notice. Thus Paul stresses in Rom. 1:16 that, although the gospel is for all who believe, it is for the Jew first (cf. 2:9-10). In 1 Pet. 4:17 judgment comes first upon believers as the household of God.

b. In certain demands of Jesus *próton* indicates priority. Thus we are first to be reconciled (Mt. 5:24), or to pull the beam out of our own eyes (7:5), or to count the cost (Lk. 14:28). In the sequence of eschatological events, Elijah is to come first (Mk. 9:11-12), the Son of Man must be rejected first (Lk. 17:25), and apostasy must first come (2 Th. 2:3). This may well be the sense in Mk. 13:10, where "above all" is also possible. But one should not take the verse out of context as offering a general basis for mission, since in its position between v. 9 and v. 11 it plainly relates to the testimony given to councils and rulers.

c. The sense "above all" is the obvious one in Mt. 6:33, for Jesus is not teaching that we should seek the kingdom first and then other things, but that there should be exclusive orientation to the divine kingdom and righteousness.

prōtokathedría, prōtoklisía.

These words occur together in Mk. 12:39 and parallels; the former also occurs in Lk. 11:43 and the latter in 14:7-8. The terms are rare outside the NT but in context their meaning is clear: "the first place," "the place of honor." Jesus criticizes those who always want to occupy places of honor, and he warns his disciples against self-exaltation in the parables of Lk. 14:8ff.

prōtótokos, prōtotokeía.

A. Outside the NT.

1. *prōtótokos*, "firstborn," is rare outside the Bible and does not occur prior to the LXX. Instead we find *prōtógonos*, which can also mean "first in rank." Of the few nonbiblical examples, many refer to animals.

2.a. There are some 130 instances in the LXX, of which 74 are in the Pentateuch and 29 in 1 Chronicles. The reference may be to animals, to humans and animals together (Ex. 11:5), to humans with *huiós*, or as a noun without *huiós* but with a proper name (cf. Gen. 25:25; 10:15; 22:21).

b. The examples stress the great importance of the firstborn. God has a claim to the firstborn of humans and animals (as well as firstfruits). The firstborn of cattle are brought as offerings. In the family the firstborn take precedence; this is the basis of the later transferred use.

c. As regards the transferred use, the main Hebrew original (*bᵉkôr*) is not connected with terms for giving birth nor with terms for "head" or "chief." Again, a comparison with others is not necessarily suggested, since the first may also be the only one.

d. Ex. 4:22, in calling Israel a firstborn son, is not suggesting that other nations are also God's children but is stressing the fact that it is the object of God's special love. Similarly in Ps. 89:27 the point is the closeness of the king to God. The idea of even a figurative birth is not present, nor is that of a priority in time over other sons. The thought is that of special dearness in God's eyes.

e. The LXX also uses *prōtotokéō*, "to give birth for the first time" (1 Sam. 6:7, 10; Jer. 4:31); *prōtotokeúō*, "to grant the right of a firstborn" (Dt. 21:16); *tá prōtotokeía*, "the right of the firstborn" (Gen. 25:31ff.); cf. *prōtotokía* or *prōtotokeía* (Gen. 25:34).

3. Philo uses *prōtótokos* as both adjective and noun on an OT basis. In one instance Cain is called *prōtótokos* as the first man to come into the world by birth; the idea of firstborn is prominent here. Josephus uses *prōtótokos* for the firstborn of men and cattle. In his version of Josh. 6:26 he uses *prōtos país.*

4. The OT use continues in the pseudepigrapha, where the term denotes the special position of Isaac as Abraham's son, or of Jacob as God's son, or of the seed of Jacob (Israel) as God's firstborn.

5. In the rabbis the term denotes the special position of Israel, the law, Adam, or the Messiah, with a reference either to the special love of God or to the special qualities of those to whom the term applies.

B. The NT.

1. Lk. 2:7 says that Mary gave birth to her firstborn son. Birth is plainly in view here. The statement perhaps stresses the virginity of Mary, and it also prepares the way for vv. 22ff. Of itself it does not necessarily imply that Mary has other children. But it also does not mean *monogenḗs;* indeed, it includes the possibility and expectation that other children will follow.

2. The metaphor of the firstborn among many brethren is used by Paul in Rom. 8:29. In view here is the perfected fellowship with the risen Christ that comes with resurrection on the last day when transfigured believers attain to their inheritance as the brothers and sisters of Christ, who retains his primacy as the firstborn.

3. In Col. 1:18 Christ is the first to rise from the dead, but with a definite primacy as such, as the term "head" and the "that" clause show.

4. In Rev. 1:5, too, the *prōtótokos* signifies not only priority in time but also the primacy of rank that accrues to Jesus with his resurrection.

5. In Col. 1:15 the "for" clause brings out the meaning, namely, that all things owe their creation to Christ's mediation. The point, then, is not that Christ is the first creature. This would demand a stress on the *-tokos* and would also bring birth into conflict with creation. What is stated is Christ's supremacy over creation as its mediator. The term *prōtótokos* is used, then, because of its importance as a word for rank. In spite of v. 4 it does not here denote Christ's special relation to the Father. The twofold use does not necessarily derive from Gnostic ideas of the primal man or the redeemed redeemer. As the mediator of the first creation, Christ is also the mediator of the new creation with his resurrection from the dead (v. 18).

6. Heb. 1:6 perhaps refers to the enthronement of the exalted Christ at his coming. On the other hand, entry into the world seems to fit the incarnation better. In connection with the "son" of v. 2, *prōtótokos* denotes Christ's unique relation of sonship, with a primary although not exclusive reference to his preexistence. The term is not based on the "begotten thee" of the quotation from Ps. 2:7 in v. 5, for Christ is not the firstborn in comparison with the angels. It is probably adopted as a familiar title which is well adapted to bring out Christ's uniqueness.

7. The assembly of the firstborn in Heb. 12:23 is not the company of angels nor the community of Israel but the saved company of Christian believers. How exactly this use fits in with that in the rest of the NT is hard to say. The *prōtótokos* of Rom. 8:29 cannot be transferred to believers, and it is unlikely that the relation to the rest of creation is in view (Jms. 1:18).

prōteúō.

1. This word means "to be first" (in rank), often with a genitive and the person over whom one takes precedence.

2. The LXX uses the term in Esth. 5:11; 2 Macc. 6:18. Other versions have it in Zech. 4:7. Josephus uses *prōteúontes* for "leaders."

3. In Col. 1:18 the subsidiary clause denotes the divine aim, summing up and intensifying what is said in 1:15. As firstborn of all creation, head of the church, and firstborn from the dead, Christ is *prōteúōn* ("preeminent") in everything.

[W. MICHAELIS, VI, 865-82]

> *ptaíō* [to stumble, slip, sin]

1. *ptaíō,* of uncertain etymology, has such senses as "to stumble against," "to collide with," or, in the more usual intransitive, "to stumble," "to fail," "to suffer a reverse," and figuratively "to err," "to sin."

2. In the LXX *ptaíō* has the figurative sense "to slip" in Sir. 37:12. Elsewhere it is used for the defeat of an army, e.g., 1 Sam. 4:2, 10.

3. In Philo it means either "to suffer misfortune" or "to sin."

4. In the five NT instances the main meaning is the figurative one "to slip," "to err," "to sin" (Jms. 2:10; 3:2; 2 Pet. 1:10, though "suffer a reverse" is also possible here). In Rom. 11:11 the basic sense "to stumble" is plain, and there is perhaps a distinction from falling inasmuch as those who merely stumble may regain their balance, but falling has the greater finality of eternal ruin. Such a fall is not the purpose of the stumbling of the Jews.

5. In 1 Clem. 51.1—the one example in the apostolic fathers—forgiveness is sought for what is done amiss through the snares of the adversary.

[K. L. SCHMIDT, VI, 883-84]

pterýgion → *hierós; ptṓma, ptṓsis* → *píptō*

---

ptōchós [poor, destitute], **ptōcheía** [poverty, destitution], **ptōcheúō** [to become (extremely) poor]

A. *ptōchós* in the Greek World.
I. Meaning.
1. *ptōchós* as an adjective means "destitute," "mendicant."
2. *ptōcheúō* in the transitive means "to beg from someone," in the intransitive "to be destitute," "to lead the life of a beggar."
3. *ptōcheía* means "destitution," "begging." It is worthy of note that in distinction from *pénēs,* which refers to those who are poor and have to work for a living, the *ptōchós* group refers to the total poverty which reduces people to begging.
II. View of Poverty. Some beggars are people who will not work and prey on others. But there are also beggars who have lost their property and wander about in great unhappiness. In general, beggars are despised, but small gifts are given to them, and Homer can even say at times that they come from God. The Greeks have no system of poor relief. They protect the rights of orphans and distribute grain to citizens, but the indigent are dependent on the expected generosity of others. Poverty is nowhere commended.

[F. HAUCK, VI, 885-87]

B. The OT.
I. Hebrew Equivalents.
1. The main Hebrew term has the primary sense of dependence, with the more developed implications of lowliness, dispossession, poverty, and, in the religious world, humility or piety. Since the poverty is undeserved, God is regarded especially as the protector of the poor.
2. Another term rendered *ptōchós* in the LXX denotes either physical weakness or wretched status.
3. Another term means "beggar" or "very poor person," but here again with the religious nuance of one who is humble before God, i.e., needy in prayer.
4. Other terms meaning "needy" in a social or economic sense, or "dependent" and "inferior," are also translated *ptōchós,* which occurs some 100 times in the LXX.
II. Attitude to the Poor.
1. In the seminomadic phase there are no sharp distinctions between rich and poor. At the conquest all receive an inheritance but social distinctions in the Canaanite towns exert an influence. The law makes provision for the poor and forbids their oppression. God himself defends them in the courts and restitution ought to be made every seventh year.
2. Economic development during the monarchy brings sharper distinctions and the greater landowners, who also function as judges, reduce many owners of smaller inheritances to poverty. The prophets take up the cause of the poor in the name of God (cf. Am. 2:7; Is. 3:15). They proclaim God's judgment on the wrongdoing of the wealthy (Am. 2:6ff.). The poor are not specially elected but commitment to the law means commitment to those who suffer from its violation.

3. Although Deuteronomy does not use *ptōchós,* it shows that God has given Israel a bountiful land in which all are to have a portion (15:4ff.) and poverty is thus unnecessary. In addition, it offers protective measures to provide for any who become impoverished (15:1ff.; 23:20, 25-26). Unfortunately the laws are not kept, and with the deterioration of the social situation and the final collapse of the state the problem of poverty is increased and perpetuated.

4. In the Psalms the poor are not merely under divine punishment but even more so under divine protection (Pss. 72:2ff.; 132:15). Failure to give the destitute their right is castigated (Ps. 82). The poor turn to God when harried by their enemies (Ps. 9:12), who may be political foes, foreign adversaries, or impersonal forces such as sickness. The poor come to be equated with petitioners, who may not be poor in a financial sense, but who are oppressed in other ways, and thus claim divine protection. The prospect of material aid maintains a link with the literal sense. Thanksgivings are offered when relief is granted.

5. The tragedy of the exile leads to a general collective use of the terms, although more in connection with God's promises, and with no suggestion that God will help because the people is now in some ideal state of poverty. A material reference is still present, and the final solution will be a semieschatological balancing of accounts.

6. The Wisdom literature accepts the social order but links its thoughts on poverty closely to God. Some poverty may be due to laziness or self-indulgence (Prov. 6:6ff.; 21:17). But it is better to be poor and righteous than rich and a liar (19:22). There is sympathy with the poor (14:20; 18:23; Eccl. 9:16). Obligations toward them must not be forgotten (Prov. 22:2). In general, Proverbs tends to have more admonitions for the rich than the poor, and Sirach makes a gentle appeal on their behalf. Job complains that his generosity to the poor receives no recognition (29–30), and that the poor are delivered up to oppressors (24:14), but he holds out hope that God will finally help them (5:15).

C. Later Judaism.

I. Usage.

1. The rabbis know the terms for the poor but make little use of them.

2. Josephus makes more use of the *pénēs* group than the *ptōchós* group, and Philo, who is not concerned about the problem, never uses *ptōchós* at all.

II. The Poor in the Apocrypha and Pseudepigrapha.

1. Some of these works ignore the social situation, while others complain about it but without using *ptōchós* or suggesting an antithesis to the rich.

2. Another group demands pity for the poor, commends generosity, gives examples of it, and considers its rewards.

3. Other works hold out the hope that poverty will vanish in the new aeon. Prior to the end the poor will be in conflict with the rich and will then be set above them. Poverty is threatened for those who follow the harlot Babylon.

4. Yet another group complains violently against the wealthy and interfuses the concepts of poverty and piety.

5. In the Psalms of Solomon (5:2, 11; 10:6, etc.) the poor are considered in relation to God. The term *ptōchós* is used here for various forms of affliction, including material poverty, but in particular it denotes an inner quality. In a martyr theology poverty is integrated into God's dealings in history. The passive mood prevents the development of active movements on behalf of the poor.

III. Qumran.

1. Individuals and groups are called poor in the Qumran literature. God uses them to defeat his enemies. "Community of the poor" becomes a common term for the movement but the use does not enable us to draw any conclusions as to its composition.

2. Members of the community renounce private possessions. There are severe penalties for false statements or for misappropriation of community funds. Property is not wrong in itself; the community is an economic unit, although with its erasing of the distinctions between rich and poor it reflects the life of the coming age when property is left behind. The Damascus Document allows some private property along with common sharing, and the Essenes follow a similar pattern. Philo suggests that the Therapeutae renounce all their goods, but his description is highly rhetorical.

IV. The Poor in Palestinian Judaism.

1. The post-Maccabean age is one of great social tensions, but more settled conditions come with the Herods. The Pharisees grow apart from the masses, among whom extremists find some support. The revolts against Rome bring an ethos of poverty, but wealth increases again and results in social cleavages in which the masses are despised and the poor neglected, although some sectaries continue to glorify them.

2. Legally the poor pay minimum taxes and are also entitled to support (cf. the poor tax based on Dt. 14:29, which is often a dead letter, but which the Pharisees observe as a duty and which becomes more important later). The poor also enjoy traditional gleaning rights.

3. Established custom makes voluntary philanthropy an important source of help for the poor, though it is often abused by beggars. An accepted principle is that, as sin offerings bring atonement for Israel, so does philanthropy for the Gentiles. After the destruction of the temple the latter plays a bigger role for Israel too. Some groups, e.g., the Essenes, make it a duty, food and clothes being given as well as money.

4. After the Jewish War an official system of poor relief comes into effect. The synagogues arrange levies and offerings, provide daily and weekly support, and also set up hospices. But social distinctions remain.

V. The Rabbis. After the exile the rabbis take a negative view of poverty, scorning the modest offerings of the poor and not recognizing in poverty an excuse for not studying the law. Although misfortune might strike anyone, poverty rates as a curse or a punishment. Yet one still finds statements to the effect that the poor are primary objects of the divine mercy.

D. The NT.

I. The Gospels.

1. Mark. In the NT *ptōchós*, not *pénēs*, is the usual term for the poor. Of 31-35 instances, 14-15 are in the Synoptics, and 4-5 in Mark. The use in Mark is literal. Mt. 12:41ff. states that the tiny gift of the poor widow is of more value than the large gifts of the wealthy. In 10:17ff. Jesus challenges the rich landowner to sell his property and give to the poor. In Mk. 14:5, 7 the special circumstances explain what might seem to be a strange rejection of the valid concern of the group around Jesus.

2. Matthew. Mt. 19:21 associates the giving of the ruler's property to the poor with being *téleios*. 26:11 tightens the formulation in Mark but with no change of sense. 11:5 gives special emphasis to the preaching of the gospel to the poor; it stands in correlation to the mission of ch. 10, on which the Baptist must have had information. 5:3 (cf. 5:5)—the first beatitude—lifts the stress from the material to the spiritual sphere.

3. Luke. Lk. 18:22 adds a *pánta* to the demand that the rich young ruler should sell his possessions, and the context implies that a whole class fails to fulfil it. The saying in 7:22 is incorporated into the story. 6:20 might derive from a different source from Mt. 5:3, although the question of priority cannot be settled. The theme of rich and poor plays a role in the Lucan infancy stories. In 4:18 preaching the gospel to the poor has thematic significance. In 14:21, which refers to the eschatological banquet, the poor are invited along with the maimed and blind, and in 14:13 it is these that one should invite to a feast. In 16:19ff. the poor man is the recipient of divine grace and the rich man, by his self-centeredness, is ineluctably alienated from God. In contrast, the rich Zacchaeus, when he meets Jesus, displays extraordinary generosity to the poor. Other passages (6:24-25; 8:14; 12:15ff.; 14:33; 16:10ff.) stress the perils of wealth. There is no primary interest here in the poor as such, but in the salvation of the rich, whom their wealth rivets to this world.

4. *John.* Jn. 12:5-6 ascribes impure motives to Judas' concern for the poor, and this gives a special slant to the reply of Jesus in v. 8. In 13:29 the disciples assume that Judas, who keeps the purse, has been sent out to give the customary Passover alms to the poor.

II. Luke 14ff., Jesus, and the Baptist. Lk. 14ff. refers often to the theme of the rich and the poor and implies a special identification with the poor, widows, sinners, and little people. Lk. 4:18 is to much the same effect, and in Lk. 7:22 (cf. Mt. 11:5) there is emphasis on the fact that the gospel is especially for the poor. Jesus sets himself among the tired and lowly in Mt. 11:28 but will not let himself be tied down to a social principle (Mk. 14:7) or nourish the expectation of fulfilling material expectations. Although *ptōchós* does not occur in the preaching of the Baptist, we find related terms; his message is rich in social overtones, so that a theology of poverty is to some extent present.

III. Paul. Although Paul rarely uses *ptōchos,* and not at all in the context of the removal of distinctions by Christ, the passages in which he does use the term are central. Thus in Gal. 2:10 and Rom. 15:26 he energetically promotes the collection for the poor, or the poor among the Jerusalem saints. This is a voluntary offering, not a tax, but Paul regards it as particularly important. The phrase in Rom. 15:26 may be a term that the Jerusalem church uses for itself. In Gal. 4:9 Paul calls the elemental spirits weak and *ptōchá,* i.e., beggarly. In 2 Cor. 6:3ff., in a series of paradoxes, he points out that the apostles, while materially poor, make many spiritually rich. In 1 Cor. 15:10 *ptōchḗ* is a possible and not implausible reading to describe God's grace to Paul; it was not beggarly. Paul usually seems to have taken over the term *ptōchós* from prior tradition or from an actual situation. He knows the problem of poverty and takes steps to deal with it, but his orientation is too strongly eschatological to let it be a major concern or a subject of theological transvaluation. Thus Paul does not use *ptōchós* as a title for Christians, nor is *ptōcheía* a figurative term for the Christian life.

IV. James. James attacks the rich both inside and outside the church, and opposes to them the humble or the poor. God has chosen the poor in the world to be rich in faith (2:5). The church no longer feels solidarity with the oppressed now that wealthier people are coming into it, and the author protests against dishonoring the poor (2:6).

V. Revelation. In 2:9 the spiritual wealth of the Smyrna church stands in contrast to its material poverty. In 3:17 the supposed spiritual wealth of Laodicea is unmasked as poverty. In 13:16 the rich and poor are the two classes of the materially rich and the materially poor.

VI. The Primitive Community. Rather strangely Acts does not use *ptōchós* when describing the sharing of goods in the Jerusalem church. If Rom. 15:26 contains a title for this church, it suggests the development of a structure that does away with social distinctions, as Acts records. The common meals and the handing over of personal property for administration by the apostles and later by the seven give evidence of a care for the poor that goes far beyond normal synagogue practice, although it is in accord with much Palestinian thinking.

E. The Postapostolic Age.

I. Later Jewish Christianity. The term *Ebiōnaíoi* or *Ebiōnítai (Ebionaei)* becomes a common one in the Jewish Christian sphere, this rendering being preferred to *ptōchoí* even by Jewish Christians. Symmachus in his translation seems to try to dissociate the two concepts, and we find a similar shunning of *ptōchoí* in the Pseudo-Clementines, along with aloofness to the ideal of external poverty.

II. The Apostolic Fathers. Early exhortation commends generosity to the poor (cf. Did. 5.2). The prayers of the poor are efficacious (Hermas *Similitudes* 2.5ff.). The church orders make provision for the poor. Asceticism fosters opposition to property, but argues that lack of desire is true wealth. In an odd twist gifts to martyrs are esteemed more highly than gifts to the poor. Wealth as such is not an evil, only attachment to it (Irenaeus *Against Heresies* 4.30). Poverty indeed may stand in the way of knowledge of God (Clement of Alexandria *Paedagogus* 3.35.1). Almsgiving is stressed, but for the salvation of the giver more than the relief of the poor.

[E. BAMMEL, VI, 888-915]

---

pygmḗ [fist-fight], *pykteúō* [to box]

1. *pygmḗ* means "fight with the fists," "fight," "affray." In Mk. 7:3 the term is textually uncertain; if it is retained, it seems to denote rubbing the palm of one hand with the fist of the other.

2. The verb *pykteúō* means "to box." Paul uses it figuratively in 1 Cor. 9:26 when he says that he does not box as one who beats the air. What Paul has in mind is either a poor boxer who misses his opponent, or a sham boxer who will not face an opponent at all but simply engages in shadow-boxing. Another possibility is that of boxers engaged only in preliminary sparring. In any case, lack of seriousness is the issue. Paul has no time for incompetent or frivolous lunging. He is engaged in a vital contest and he exerts himself to achieve the prize.   [K. L. SCHMIDT, VI, 915-17]

---

pýthōn [spirit of divination]

1. *pýthōn* is the name of the snake that guards the Delphic oracle, and it is also used from the early imperial period for a ventriloquist, through whom, as many think, a god is supposed to speak, and who is thus regarded as a soothsayer. How *pýthōn* comes to be equated with *engastrímythos,* the ventriloquist, is not certain. It may be because the Delphic Pythia, like the ventriloquist, speaks in strange sounds. There is no evidence in first-century imperial Rome for the idea of a spirit of soothsaying.

2. The LXX uses *engastrímythos* for a Hebrew term of uncertain meaning.

3. On the basis of 1 Sam. 28:8 Josephus uses *engastrímythoi* for those who by divination conjure up the spirits of the dead, and for the underlying Hebrew the Vulgate

later uses such terms as *magus, python, pythonicus spiritus* (Lev. 19:31; 2 Sam. 28:3; 9; 2 Chr. 33:6). At first only the LXX links ventriloquism and conjuring up the spirits of the dead; the fathers ask whether the *engastrímythos* can really do this.

4. In Acts 16:16 the "spirit" might be in apposition: a spirit, namely, a *pýthōn*, or named *Pýthōn;* or we might translate the phrase "a pythonian spirit." The point, perhaps, is that *pýthōn* denotes the spirit that speaks through the girl. As a soothsayer-ventriloquist she stands in relation to the demonic. Although many ventriloquists who claim to be prophets are frauds, for this girl ventriloquism is connected with a supposed or authentic gift of divination.

5. In early church writings *pýthōn* is used, not for the ventriloquist, but for the spirit that speaks from him or her. Jerome in Is. 8:20 refers to the unmasking of ventriloquists as python-demons.   [W. FOERSTER, VI, 917-20]

> ### *pýlē* [gate], *pylón* [gateway]

A. The Literal Sense. The *pýlē* is the gate of a city, temple, or prison. The *pylón* is the gateway of a city, temple, house, or complex of houses. In Heb. 13:12 Jesus is said to be crucified outside the gate. This emphasizes the separation from Judaism. The priests have no part in the Christian altar. As the sin offering on the Day of Atonement is burned outside the camp, so Jesus, the sin offering of the new covenant, dies outside the holy city. The execution outside the gate is part of the shame of being numbered among transgressors (Lev. 24:14; Num. 15:35), but it is also an essential aspect of the one true offering for sin.

B. The Narrow Gate of Mt. 7:13-14. Some texts omit *pýlē* from v. 13 as an interpolation from v. 14, but a few also omit it from v. 14, and in view of the parallelism it is best to keep it in both. The link with "way" does not mean that the gate is the entrance to the way or a passage on it. The comparison of entrance into God's kingdom with a gate is a common one in eschatological parlance. The narrowness of the gate and the way indicates the difficulty of entry. Disciples must accept self-sacrifice and suffering if they are to pass through the gate to the eternal city. In Lk. 13:23-24 the image is the different one of the one door (*thýra*) to a banqueting hall which is now open and will soon be shut (v. 25); the lesson, then, is to enter while there is still time.

C. The Gates of Hades in Mt. 16:18. Many peoples in antiquity view the underworld as a land, city, fortress, or prison with strong gates (cf. Babylon, Egypt, and Greece). In the OT we read of the gates of the world of the dead only in Is. 38:10, but cf. the gates of death in Ps. 9:13, or of darkness in Job 38:17, and the bars of the world of the dead in Job 17:16. References to the gates of the world of the dead then occur in Sir. 51:9; Wis. 16:13; Ps. Sol. 16:2; 3 Macc. 5:51. The idea, if not the phrase, is also present in many rabbis. The only NT instance is in the semitism in Mt. 16:18. Here *hádēs* might be the world of the dead, and the thought might then be that the gates cannot withstand either the church's attack to rescue others or the exodus of believers on the descent or resurrection of Jesus. If the phrase is more figurative, the statement might be either that Peter will not die before the parousia, that death has no power over believers, or that believers will not share the fate of the wicked. In context, the most likely meaning is that the gates of Hades stand for the ungodly forces

of the underworld which attack the rock but cannot prevail against it. Later the "gates of Hades" figure especially in references to Christ's descent into Hades, over whose gates he has supreme power (cf. Rev. 1:18).   [J. JEREMIAS, VI, 921-28]
→ *thýra, kleís*

---

pýr [fire], *pyróō* [to burn, set on fire], *pýrōsis* [burning, fiery], *pýrinos* [fiery], *pyrrós* [fiery-red]

---

pýr.

A. The Greek and Hellenistic World.
I. General Usage.
1. Literal. *pýr* is "fire" in its various forms and uses, e.g., for burning, lighting, and warming. Fire is a beneficent and civilizing power but also a destructive and terrifying force. In war it destroys ships, cities, etc., but industrially it serves to purify metals etc.
2. Transferred. Fire denotes violence, irresistibility, desire, and yearning. It figures in various expressions, e.g., "pouring oil on flames," "out of the frying pan into the fire."
II. Philosophy. In philosophy fire is one of the two, four, or five elements. For Heraclitus it is the basic material; the world is the play of fire in various forms of change, namely, from fire to water to earth and back again. In Stoicism all reality is physical. The purest substance is a rational firelike breath that shapes, upholds, and overrules all things. The world is a form of the primal fire in an endless cycle. The soul, as fire, continues after death but returns to the primal fire at the cosmic conflagration.
III. Religion.
1. At first fire is an antidote to evil influences. At death polluted fire is put out and new fire brought. Fire forms a part of various ceremonies, e.g., after birth, before assemblies, etc. In some rites living animals are burned on funeral pyres on hilltops. When cremation establishes itself, the belief persists that fire cannot destroy the soul.
2. In the worship of the gods, Hephaistos and Hestia are associated with the fire of the volcano and the fire of the hearth. Pythagoreans regard the central fire as the hearth of the cosmos, and from the sacred national hearth colonists take fire for the hearth in new settlements. Zeus, Hermes, and Dionysus are also associated in different ways with fire. In theophanies fire is an expression of glory. Fiery phenomena also serve as omens, and descriptions of the underworld contain many references to fire, sometimes with a purifying function.
3. Fire plays a big part in the mysteries in connection with purification before initiation. As a source of light it symbolizes the transfer from darkness to light. In the Roman Bacchanalia raving women fling torches into the Tiber. The fire-god Acon is called the lord of fire and is said to breathe fire, to sow fire, to be strong and joyous in fire, and to be fire-roaring and fire-whirling. For all its destructive aspects, fire is for the most part connected with deity and spirit.
B. Persian Fire Worship. Fire is especially worshipped in Persia. In cosmological dualism fire and the snake represent truth and falsehood. In the human struggle for good conduct, fire is on the good side. Worship is thus paid to it as an embodiment of spiritual divine power. Nothing connected with deformity or death must come into

contact with it; thus corpses are exposed to beasts of prey, which embody the world of the evil spirit. In eschatology fire serves the purpose of final testing. All people will go into molten metal, the righteous coming through unscathed, the wicked suffering. The renewed earth will be a smooth, ice-free plain. At first worship is at a flaming altar in the open, but later a temple of fire comes into use, at whose center is the sacred fire that no human hand must touch or human breath defile, so that the priests who tend it wear mittens and gags and use ritually purified wood. From the sacred hearth new fire is fetched to burn in the houses.

C. The OT, Later Judaism, and Gnosticism.
I. The OT.

1. In the LXX, where it occurs some 490 times, *pýr* usually renders Heb. *'ēš.* Other originals are rare. Some 100 instances occur in works that are only in Greek.

2. *Technical Use.* In everyday use, fire serves in cooking, manufacture, metal work, war, etc. Kindling fires is forbidden on the sabbath (Ex. 35:3). In the cultus the altar fire is kept burning (Lev. 6:2, 6). It alone is to be used for sacrifice (cf. Lev. 10:1). Offering children is strictly forbidden (Lev. 20:2, but cf. 2 Kgs. 16:3; 21:6). Fire is also a means of purification (Lev. 13:52). In nature, lightning is God's fire (Job 1:16; Ex. 9:28). In Am. 7:4 *'ēš* means summer heat or drought. Job 28:5 compares mining to volcanic activity; the reference may be to "firing," i.e., prying hard rocks loose with a fire of wood.

3. *Transferred Use.* Destructive human passions are compared to fire (Prov. 26:20-21; Sir. 28:10-11; Prov. 6:27-28). Fire also represents God's judicial wrath (Jer. 4:4; Ezek. 21:36; Zeph. 1:18; Nah. 1:6; Ps. 79:5). Various thoughts are present, e.g., the forest fire in Jer. 21:14, the fiery oven in Ps. 21:9, the refining fire in Mal. 3:2, lightning in Lam. 1:13. Irresistibility is a primary concept. Escaping great danger is compared to a brand plucked from the burning in Zech. 3:2. Fire expresses dissolution in Mic. 1:4 and purifying in Is. 1:22. Illumination by fire plays only a very small role (cf. Nah. 2:4).

4. *Fire in Relation to God.*

a. Theophany. In most OT theophanies fire represents God's holiness and glory. The fire may be natural (Ex. 19) or it may be the unusual fire of the burning bush (3:2; cf. Judg. 6:21). The pillar of fire represents God's ongoing presence (Ex. 13:21-22). At Horeb God himself is not in the fire (1 Kgs. 19:12); true revelation is by the word. At the call of Isaiah (ch. 6) fire purges unclean lips. In Ezek. 1:28 fire expresses the divine radiance (cf. Dan. 7).

b. A Means of Judgment. God judges by fire and brimstone in Gen. 19:24. Fire and hail form the seventh plague in Ex. 9:24. Fire from God or from heaven is a phrase for judgment in Lev. 10:2; 2 Kgs. 1:10. Fire smites both Israel's enemies (Am. 1:4ff.) and disobedient Israel herself (Am. 2:5). Eschatologically, fire is a sign of the day of the Lord (Joel 2:20), it denotes final destruction (Mal. 3:19), and it stands for eternal punishment (Mal. 3:19).

c. A Sign of Grace. Fire indicates God's gracious acceptance of sacrifices in Gen. 15:17. It plays a role in the taking up of Elijah in 2 Kgs. 2:11. It is a sign of guidance and protection in Ex. 13:21-22 (cf. 2 Kgs. 6:17). It depicts God's final dwelling among his people in Is. 4:5.

d. A Term for God. The description of God as a consuming fire (Dt. 4:24) denotes his majestic being embracing grace and judgment. In the OT fire is viewed theocentrically rather than cosmologically. It expresses God's glory in revelation and judgment.

976

II. Later Judaism.

1. Apocalyptic. In apocalyptic the stars are called fiery bodies, humans are said to be composed of earth, water, air, and fire, the idea of a cosmic conflagration occurs, angels are fiery beings, and fire represents punishment in the world to come.

2. The Rabbis. Some rabbinic works view fire as preexistent, others speak of its creation. Various forms of fire are distinguished, e.g., fever, the fire of Gabriel, and God's fire, along with other ordinary forms. The law is associated with fire, and fire marks its students, so that the fire of hell has no power over them. The place of the dead becomes a place of fire in punishment of the wicked. Sheol is an intermediate stage, Gehinnom the final place of punishment. Punishments in the intermediate place are for purification, and prayers and almsgiving may shorten or alleviate them. All transgressors in Israel as well as the eternally rejected will go through the intermediate place. Various descriptions are given of the intermediate and final fire, e.g., its heat, intensity, duration, etc. Fire characterizes the heavenly world, e.g., the angels and the finger of God.

3. Qumran. The Qumran works also expect a final fiery judgment on God's enemies. Fire denotes affliction, but there is also an eternal fire of hell. Traces of the idea of a cosmic conflagration may be seen.

4. Hellenistic Judaism.

a. Philo adopts the idea of four elements and depicts the nature and cultural significance of fire after the manner of Greek philosophy. Yet he does not equate the human spirit with fire. For him the penal aspect is less important; in the case of Nadab and Abihu the judgment leads to fellowship with God. His stress on God's transcendence protects him from the fire-monism of Stoicism.

b. Josephus uses fire in the literal sense; he also has *pureíon* for "fuel" and *puretós* for "fever."

III. Gnostic Usage.

1. Hermetic Writings. In these works fire denotes the material cosmos, the planetary and demonic sphere, and sensual passion.

2. Coptic Gnostic Works. Here the sublunar world is surrounded by fiery spheres. The ascending soul must pass through the fire zone of the archons. Fiery judgments punish sinners according to their deeds. Along with the baptism of water and the Spirit, there is a baptism of fire.

3. Mandaean Literature. These works contrast living fire and consuming fire. Positively, fire belongs to the victorious and eternal king of light and clothes or crowns his envoys. The soul, too, is living fire. Negatively, consuming or flaming fire is that of material life or judgment. It marks the wicked world, the body, and passion on the one side, eschatological judgment on the other. In one work fire is the root of all things. Visible fire arises out of invisible. Everything material will be dissolved in the final conflagration.

D. The NT.

1. The Earthly Phenomenon. Only rarely does *pýr* denote the earthly phenomenon in the NT. Lightning is meant in Heb. 1:7, heat in Rev. 16:8, everyday fire in Mk. 9:22, a kind of watchfire in Lk. 22:55, a fire for warming in Acts 28:2ff., fire as a means of execution in Heb. 11:34, and as a weapon of war in Rev. 17:16. There is no cultic fire in the NT (but cf. Rev. 8:5).

II. Figurative Use.

1. Fire is a figure of final judgment (cf. the unfruitful tree in Mt. 3:10, chaff in Mt. 3:12, tares in Mt. 13:40, unfruitful branches in Jn. 15:6). Jms. 5:3 interweaves the material and figurative elements more closely. The testing fire of Prov. 17:3 is applied in 1 Pet. 1:7 to the keeping of hope and faith in afflictions, and in Rev. 3:18 to repentance with a view to true riches.

2. The destructive power of the tongue is a fire in Jms. 3:51; it has the force of cosmic conflagration. The context of Lk. 12:49 suggests that the fire of discord is in view.

III. Theological Use.

1. *Theophanies.* Stephen alludes to the fire at the bush in Acts 7:30, and Hebrews refers to the divine self-revelation at Sinai in 12:18ff. When Christ appears to Paul, however, there is only light, not fire (Acts 9:3).

2. *A Means of Judgment.* Fire in temporal judgments occurs only with OT references (cf. Lk. 9:54; 17:26ff.). The NT usually has eschatological fire in view.

a. Fire symbolizes this judgment in Revelation. Fire and hail in 8:7 remind us of the seventh plague. The allusion in 8:8 is to a volcano or a star. The horses of 9:17-18 spew out fire. Divine fire protects the two witnesses in 11:3. In the last days false prophets bring down fire from heaven (13:13). An angel of fire comes forth to execute judgment in 14:18.

b. More directly fire represents the eschatological fire of judgment.

(a) The Baptist portrays judgment in terms of fire in Mt. 3:11.

(b) Jesus perhaps has this fire in mind in the paradox of Mk. 9:49: Those who do not accept God's judgment by self-denial fall victim to the wrath to come (cf. Mt. 10:39; Mk. 10:25ff.). In Lk. 12:49-50 the one who baptizes with the Spirit and fire must first take the way of suffering himself (cf. v. 50). Judgment is already present in and with Jesus; relationship to him decides between alienation from God and fellowship with him.

(c) *pýr* denotes final judgment in the three instances in Paul. In 1 Cor. 3:13 the last judgment will disclose the value of Christian service. Poor work will be burned up, but the workers will be saved "as through fire," i.e., not by purgation but by the skin of their teeth. Combined here are the thoughts of the house on fire, the Lord's coming with fire, purifying fire, and a narrow escape. In 2 Th. 1:7-8 Jesus will come again with fire; this is plainly the fire of judgment. In Rom. 12:20 Paul quotes Prov. 25:21-22 to back up his call for renunciation of revenge. The idea is that we should avenge ourselves by doing good, but the phrase "coals of fire" carries a secondary reference to the final judgment that will come on enemies if they do not react with a change of heart.

(d) In other NT books *pýr* is the fire of final judgment in Heb. 12:29. In Rev. 20:9 God inflicts fiery judgment on Gog and Magog in the last struggle. In 2 Pet. 3:7 a final conflagration will end the present world order as the flood overwhelmed the primal world.

c. In the NT fire is often hellfire.

(a) In the sayings of Jesus *pýr* is the opposite of *basileía* or *zōḗ* (Mt. 13:42; 18:8-9; Mk. 9:43). Mk. 9:49 quotes Is. 66:24, and this verse lies behind the "unquenchable fire" of Mk. 9:43 (cf. the "eternal fire" of Mt. 18:8).

(b) In Jude 7 the inhabitants of Sodom and Gomorrah already suffer hellfire, and in v. 23 the proverbial snatching from the fire denotes saving from hellfire.

(c) In Revelation fire and brimstone denote eternal punishment (14:10). Hell is the abyss in 20:3 and the lake of fire in 19:20; 20:10; 21:8; the imagery may well derive from phenomena at the Dead Sea.

(d) John with its stronger emphasis on present decision does not refer to fire, although a place remains for Christ's return in judgment.

3. *A Sign of Heavenly Glory.* Fire signifies heavenly glory in Rev. 1:9ff.: The eyes of the glorified Jesus are as a flame of fire, and his feet are like bronze refined in a furnace (cf. also 2:18). Angels have feet like pillars of fire in 10:1; this denotes their heavenly glory. Fire also expresses the splendor of heaven when 4:5 equates the seven torches with the seven spirits of God. The crystal sea before God's throne (4:6) is the heavenly counterpart of the molten sea of the temple (1 Kgs. 7:23); it is mingled with fire in 15:2. In Acts 2:3 the comparison with fire indicates the heavenly origin of the descending Spirit. In the main, fire signifies judgment in the NT, but the divine judgment and the divine glory go together. Fire signifies the whole eschatological denouement, whether in hell or in heaven.

E. The Apostolic Fathers.

1. The Biblical Tradition. The apostolic fathers usually follow the biblical tradition, either quoting the Bible (2 Clem. 7.6 etc.) or using fire for the fire of judgment (Ignatius *Ephesians* 16.2) or hellfire (2 Clem. 17:7). Diog. 8.2 contests the Stoic equation of fire and deity in the light of hellfire. Only 2 Clement and Hermas refer to a cosmic conflagration. As in the OT fire may be a temporal judgment (1 Clem. 11:1). Some martyrs are executed by fire, but this fire cannot really harm them (Mart. Pol. 15–16). Fire is a test in Hermas *Visions* 4.3.4; Did. 16.4-5.

II. Alien Influences. The Gnostic opposing of fire and water may be seen in Ignatius *Romans* 7.2. Fire as love of the world or impulse toward matter occurs in Ignatius *Romans* 6.2. Diognetus sees in fire one of the elements. For the most part, however, alien factors are slight compared to the strong biblical impact.

pyróō.

A. The Greek World.

1. This word means a. "to burn," "to destroy with fire," b. "to treat with fire," e.g., "to bake," "to roast," "to smelt," "to smoke out," c. "to make fire" or, passively, "to become fire," and d. "to be hot to the taste," "to suffer heartburn."

2. Figurative senses are "to be incensed" and "to be seized with love."

B. Judaism.

1. In the LXX the literal sense is late. The most common use is for refining metals, hence for divine testing (Is. 1:25) and certifying (2 Sam. 22:31).

2. Philo uses only the passive either literally, "to be glowing with heat," or more often figuratively, "to be inflamed with emotion" (good or bad), e.g., thanksgiving, righteous indignation, zeal, passion. Philo combines the thought of divine testing with the Stoic concept of fiery reason.

3. Josephus uses the verb only in the literal sense "to burn."

4. Qumran refers to the testing of the sect by opposition.

C. The NT.

1. Paul uses the verb only in the figurative and the passive for being inflamed with emotion. In 1 Cor. 7:9 it is better to marry than to burn with desire. In 2 Cor. 11:29 Paul is consumed with sympathy when a member of the church is offended. An attack on the church is an attack on him.

2. The Christian armor of Eph. 6:11ff. includes the shield of faith which can quench the fiery darts of the wicked. The thought is that of the conflict between believers and the hosts of Belial (cf. Qumran).

3. A literal sense occurs in 2 Pet. 3:12 in depiction of the final conflagration.

4. Revelation adopts the OT metaphor of the testing of precious metals. In 3:18 purified gold signifies genuine faith and salvation. This metaphor helps us to understand the expression in 1:15.

D. The Apostolic Fathers. The reference in Mart. Pol. 15.2 is to the metals, not the furnace. Hermas *Visions* 4.3.4 regards the image of testing gold as a call to help in building the tower.

pýrōsis.
1. This word means "burning," "baking," "burning desire," "fever."
2. In Prov. 27:21 it means testing in the fire, and in Am. 4:9 the blasting of crops.
3. Josephus uses it for the punishment of Sodom (*Antiquities* 1.203).
4. In Rev. 18:9 *pýrōsis* denotes the destruction of Babylon by fire. A testing by fire is the point in 1 Pet. 4:12; a link is seen here with the coming revelation of Christ in glory (v. 13).
5. The idea of a future trial by fire is present in Did. 16.5.

pýrinos.
1. This word means "fiery" and occurs for fiery bodies, things that are fiery hot, or, figuratively, great violence.
2. In the LXX, where it is rare, the term denotes the radiance of heavenly phenomena (Ezek. 28:14, 16).
3. The only NT instance is in Rev. 9:17, where the riders wear fiery breastplates, i.e., either the color of fire or engulfed in the fire from their mouths. The description shows that they are destructive demonic beings.

pyrrós.
1. This word means "fiery-red" or "flame-colored." It is used for hair, for the manes of lions etc., for the bloodshot eyes of dogs, and for blushes.
2. The LXX uses the term for the red pottage of Gen. 25:30, the red heifer of Num. 19:2, the water red like blood of 2 Kgs. 3:22, and the red horses of Zech. 1:8.
3. Philo does not use the word but Josephus has it in *Antiquities* 1.34.
4. The colors of the horsemen in Rev. 6:1ff. are based on those of Zechariah. The rider on the red horse causes war and bloodshed. The red color of the fiery dragon of 12:3 signifies his bellicose and bloodthirsty character.
5. In the apostolic fathers 1 Clem. 8:3 is based on Is. 1:18, although the expression in v. 4 is a proverbial one.   [F. LANG, VI, 928-52]

---

pýrgos [tower]

1. *pýrgos* has such senses as a "tower," "fortress," "siege-tower," "castle," "column (of an army)," "high building," and in the papyri "outbuildings."
2. In the LXX the *pýrgos* is usually a "tower," "citadel," "tower on a city wall," or "watchtower."
3. Philo construes the tower of Babel symbolically. Josephus often mentions various

kinds of fortifications. The pseudepigrapha use the term to characterize the sojourning of the patriarchs among the Gentiles. Qumran has a tower and walls, and these are common metaphors in the Scrolls.

4. In the NT the *pýrgos* of the parable in Mk. 12:1 is a field tower (cf. Is. 5:2). The tower of Lk. 13:4 that collapsed must have been of some size. The reference in Lk. 14:28 is probably to a lofty private dwelling, unless "outbuildings" are meant, as often in the papyri.

5. In Barn. 16.5 the tower in context seems to be for flocks. In Hermas the allegories of the tower relate to the church.   [F. MICHAELIS, VI, 953-56]

---

pyréssō [to have a fever], *pyretós* [fever]

1. The word *pyretós* describes the symptom of "fever." Greek medicine distinguishes types of fever, and ascribes them to natural causes. Popular belief thinks gods or demons can both cause and cure fevers.

2. OT words for "fever" also have to do with burning, and some rabbinic statements see in fevers threats of divine judgment. The LXX seldom uses *pyretós* (Dt. 28:22) and never *pyréssō*.

3. The rabbis know the distinctions of Greek medicine and the suggested natural causes and remedies, but they tend to regard fevers as demonically or divinely caused.

4. The NT mentions *pyretós* three times among the sicknesses cured by Jesus or the apostles (Mk. 1:30-31; Jn. 4:52; Acts 28:8). Only Acts 28:8 shows what fever is meant, i.e., feverish dysentery. The Lucan parallel to Mk. 1:30-31 describes the fever as a serious one. Religious forces are associated with the fevers in all three cases, whether in the form of demonic influence or divine punishment. The fevers are thus overcome by the invocation of God or Christ, who, taking on himself the penalty of sin, drives out demons by the finger of God (Lk. 11:20). The healing of fevers demonstrates the dominion of Christ over sin and the devil and is thus a sign that awakens faith (Jn. 4:53-54) in the messianic salvation that he brings (Mt. 11:4-5) and the dawn of God's eschatological rule. The resuming of the daily round in Mk. 1:31 suggests the restoration of the state of creation.   [K. WEISS, VI, 956-59]

---

pôlos [young (ass)]

1. Related to "foal," *pôlos* is used for the young of a horse or ass, then of other animals, e.g., the elephant, camel, swallow, etc., also figuratively boy or girl. *Pôlos* is also a proper name.

2. In the OT the term is used for young asses in Gen. 32:16 (cf. also in parallelism Gen. 49:11 and Zech. 9:9).

3. In later rabbinic tradition, which has various words for the young ass, the bull and ass are messianic images.

4. In Mk. 11:2ff. Jesus enters Jerusalem on a *pôlos* (cf. Gen. 49:11). Lk. 19:30ff. also uses *pôlos*. Mt. 21:2ff. refers to a she-ass and a colt. Jn. 12:15 quotes Zech. 9:9 LXX. The messianic significance of the term is plain.   [O. MICHEL, VI, 959-61]

pōróō, pórōsis → *pýr*

ϱ r

---

rhábbi [rabbi],   **rhabbouní** [master]

A. Judaism.

1. The term *rab* denotes one who holds a respected position, e.g., an official. It is used by an inferior to a superior. Students use it in addressing their teachers, but it may also be used for the Messiah or for God as Lord of the world.

2. The use for teachers goes back to the second century B.C. Students follow their teachers with respectful obedience. When qualified to teach, they themselves are given the title, which the people as a whole also uses. It occurs on many inscriptions from Palestine, Syria, Cyprus, and Italy.

B. The NT.

1. In the NT *rhábbi* occurs only in the Gospels. Mt. 23:7 censures the scribes for desiring the title. The Baptist is called *rhábbi* in Jn. 3:26.

2. Jesus is called *rhábbi* by Peter in Mk. 9:5 and Judas in 14:45. The term *didáskalos* in Mk. 4:38; 9:17, etc. has the same force. John explains the use in 1:38. Jesus is addressed as *rhábbi* in 1:49; 3:2; 4:31; 6:25; 9:2; 11:8. *rhabbouní* in Mk. 10:51 and Jn. 20:16 is an alternative form. The use of *rhábbi* shows that Jesus is viewed as a teacher by his disciples and the people. He differs from an ordinary scribe in that he chooses his own disciples and teaches authoritatively. Since the disciples never become rabbis as Jesus is, he also has a unique status as their *kýrios* (Mt. 8:25; 20:33).

3. As the Palestinian tradition becomes less prominent, *rhábbi* does not occur in other Christian writings.   [E. LOHSE, VI, 961-65]

---

rhábdos [rod, staff, stick],   **rhabdízō** [to strike with a stick],   **rhabdoúchos** [police with clubs]

---

rhábdos.

A. Outside the NT.

I. The Meaning in Greek.

1. This word means "staff," "rod," "stick," "sceptre." It may be used for a riding switch, a magician's rod, an official staff, an angler's rod or pole, a lime twig to catch birds, a metal plate, a stripe in clothes, the shaft of a spear, the shoot of a tree, or a line of poetry.

2. In the LXX the term is used generally for a staff or rod, and specifically for a stick, a shepherd's staff, a staff for walkers or the elderly, a magician's rod, an angel's wand, or a sceptre.

B. The NT.

1. The term is used for a surveyor's measuring rod in Rev. 11:1 (cf. Ezek. 40:3ff.). This verse promises that the community will come through the last time unscathed.

2. The meaning in 1 Cor. 4:21 is the teacher's stick for beating. Since Jewish teachers use straps, the Hellenistic teacher is in view.

3. In Rev. 2:27; 12:5; 19:15 (cf. Ps. 2:9) the reference is to the shepherd's staff, which often has an iron point. The disciple will carry the staff in 2:27, but Christ himself will carry it according to the other two verses.

4. In Mk. 6:8 Jesus allows his disciples to take a traveler's staff (though cf. Mt. 10:10; Lk. 9:3). The staff is normally carried by itinerant teachers, whether Cynics or rabbis, and is necessary on long journeys in the Near East.

5. In Heb. 11:21 the author follows the LXX (Gen. 47:31) and refers to the staff which is a common feature of old age (cf. Greek vases, rabbinic works).

6. Heb. 9:4 speaks of Aaron's rod that buds, but without saying what its prototype is in the heavenly temple. It is mentioned by Philo and Josephus, and is associated with the ark in Jewish works, which say that it was created on the evening of the first sabbath, serves as a sceptre, and will return in the messianic kingdom. In Ignatius *Trallians* 11.2 it becomes the wood of the cross, and in later saga it is a sign of pardoning grace.

7. In Heb. 1:8 Christ holds the sceptre of legitimate divine government.

8. The NT does not mention the magician's rod, but cf. Hermas *Visions* 3.2.4 and the art of the catacombs, which portrays Jesus with a rod when he feeds the crowd and raises the dead.

rhabdízō.
1. This word means "to strike with a stick," "to scourge," "to thresh," "to beat down."

2. The only LXX use is for "to thresh" (Judg. 6:11; Ruth 2:17).

3. Paul uses the term in 2 Cor. 11:25 for his three beatings (cf. Acts 16:22, where the beating is a means of police coercion, is probably public, and is illegal in Paul's case, although he protests against it only later).

rhabdoúchos. This word is used of police with cudgels, referees, supervisors at religious festivals, and ladies accompanying a princess. In Acts 16:35, 38 it refers to the police at Philippi who report to the magistrates and who seem to escort Paul out of the city as a mark of respect. [C. SCHNEIDER, VI, 966-71]

---

rhadioúrgēma [deception, transgression], ***rhadiourgía*** [falsification, wickedness]

The term *rhadiourgós* comes from *rhádios* in the sense of "unburdened," and denotes lack of self-discipline, drifting, ethical carelessness. *rhadioúrgēma* comes into use for deception and then for all kinds of transgressions, while *rhadiourgía* denotes negligence, falsification, wickedness. In Acts 18:14 the proconsul is interested only in vicious crime. In Acts 13:10 the wickedness of Elymas implies a loosening of all moral restraints as a result of his association with the devil in magic and pseudoprophecy. [O. BAUERNFEIND, VI, 972-73]

---

rhaká [blockhead, fool]

1. Derivation. In spite of the double *a,* this term derives from an Aramaic term of abuse. Matthew does not translate it in Mt. 5:22; he is thus writing for readers who speak Greek but will be familiar with the term (probably in Syria).

2. The Aramaic term expresses disparagement accompanied by anger and contempt. Addressed to the foolish, thoughtless, or presumptuous person, it means "blockhead," and is the most common term of abuse in Jesus' day.

3. The structure of Mt. 5:21-22 shows that the reference is to three ascending forms of the same penalty rather than to three courts, and that the sins that are equivalent to murder are all sins of the tongue arranged in a kind of crescendo: Whoso is angry, says "blockhead," or says "fool," deserves to be punished with death, to be condemned to death, to suffer death in hell.

This paradox whereby apparently harmless words are put on a par with murder shows how very serious sins of the tongue are in God's eyes, and it carries a warning against ill feelings that may seem innocuous but poison relationships. Against authenticity it is argued that there is no true crescendo from wrath to insult, but it should be noted that the speech, style, and outlook are all Palestinian and that the teaching accords with Mk. 7:15; Mt. 12:36-37.   [J. JEREMIAS, VI, 973-76]

→ *kenós, mōrós*

---

rhantízō [to sprinkle], **rhantismós** [sprinkling]

A. Meaning in Greek.

1. *rhantízō* is a rare and late form of *rhaínō*, which is used for spraying or sprinkling something on something or something with something.

2. *rhantismós* has not been found in nonbiblical usage.

B. The OT.

I. Linguistic Data.

1. *rhantízō* occurs three times in the OT and *rhaínō* 13 times; *rhaínō* is the preferred cultic term. The more common use is for sprinkling something on something (cf. the Hebrew). Mostly sprinkled are blood, oil, and water, but we also find solids in Prov. 7:17 and righteousness in Is. 45:8.

2. The usual Hebrew original is *nzh,* which is usually rendered *rhaínō,* and means "to sprinkle," "to be sprinkled," or "to cause to sprinkle." For other terms *rhaínō* and compounds have such senses as "to gush out" in Ezek. 36:25, "to pour forth" in Is. 45:8, "to strew" in Prov. 7:17.

3. *rhantismós* occurs only in the expressions "water of sprinkling" or "of cleansing." It stresses the process, whereas the Hebrew stresses the purpose.

II. Material Aspects.

1. The secular uses play only a minor role in the OT (cf. 2 Kgs. 9:33; Is. 63:3; 52:15; Prov. 7:17).

2. The cultic uses predominates. Blood, oil, and water are used in cultic sprinkling, the sanctuary, people, and objects are sprinkled, cleansing and dedication are the purposes, and contact with the dead, making the covenant, offering for sin, and the consecration of priests are the occasions. Water is usually qualified ("of cleansing"), may be mixed with ashes, hyssop, etc., and is used after defilement, e.g., with a dead body, a leper, etc. Oil is used (at times with blood) for consecration. Blood is used at sacrifices as part of the offering, or in purification. The main concept in sprinkling is that of cleansing and expiation, as in Lev. 16 and Num. 19.

3. In Ps. 51:7 a ritual underlies the metaphor (cf. Is. 1:18) but the reference is to purifying by God. In Ezek. 36:25 God's sprinkling signifies his eschatological re-

creation of the people (cf. vv. 26-27). In Is. 45:8 the pouring down of righteousness is an eschatological promise.

4. Though the group is not used in Ex. 24:8, the sprinkling of the blood of the covenant establishes fellowship between the covenant partners and seals the covenant.

C. The NT.

1. The only firmly attested examples in the NT are five in Hebrews and one in 1 Peter. The verb *rhantízō* occurs in Heb. 9:13, 19, 21; 10:22: "to sprinkle something with something." The noun *rhantismós* occurs in Heb. 12:24; 1 Pet. 1:2. "Blood of sprinkling" in Heb. 12:24 is analogous to "water of sprinkling" in the OT.

2. OT cultic use governs the use in the NT. Sprinkling with Christ's blood is compared to OT rites; as expiatory blood it has more force than that of Abel in Heb. 12:24. The reference in Heb. 9:18ff. is to the conclusion of the covenant at Sinai. Christ's blood takes on meaning as the blood of the eternal covenant (13:20) in the light of the Sinai ritual (cf. 9:20). Heb. 9:13-14 has the Day of Atonement in view. The blood of this day can cleanse only the *sárx* in contrast to Christ's blood, which purifies the conscience. Since the blood of the Day of Atonement is not sprinkled on the people, the cleansing ashes of the red heifer are set alongside it in this context. Sprinkling plays an essential role in the NT as in the OT, both for cleansing and for the conclusion of the covenant, but since the sprinkled blood is Christ's the use is figurative and the cleansing is immeasurably superior, for now the heavenly high priest with his own blood purifies his people and brings them into the new and eternal covenant. The second half of Heb. 10:22 shows that baptism is associated with this sprinkling inasmuch as it signifies the granting of participation in the atoning, purifying, and covenant-making power of the blood of Christ.

3. 1 Pet. 1:2 also seems to have baptism in mind (cf. the sanctification by the Spirit and the pledging to obedience, which are here put first; cf. Acts 10:44ff. and the liturgical order). This verse shows that the idea of sprinkling with Christ's blood is not peculiar to Hebrews but is part of an early baptismal tradition.

D. The Apostolic Fathers. The only references in these works are in Barn. 5.1, Barn. 8.1ff. (a typological interpretation of Num. 19), 1 Clem. 18:7 (quoting Ps. 51:1ff.), and Hermas *Similitudes* 9.10.3 (*rhaínō* in the secular sense of "cleaning").

[C.-H. Hunzinger, VI, 976-84]

Rhacháb → Thamár; rhḗma → légō

---

rhíza [root],   *rhizóō* [to cause to take root],   *ekrizóō* [to uproot]

---

rhíza.

1. Secular Greek. This word means literally "root" of a plant, figuratively "foot" of a mountain, historically "founding" of a city, genealogically "origin" or "stem" of a family, cosmologically "origin" of things (i.e., the earth), and psychologically the soul as our "origin."

2. The LXX. In the LXX the word is fairly common but is seldom used for "root" or for such things as the "foot" of a mountain (Jdt. 6:13) or "depths" of the sea (Job 36:30). The phrase "root and branch" occurs in Job 28:9; 31:12. Mostly the use is figurative and refers to the roots of the righteous or the unrighteous with references to firm rootage (Prov. 12:3), good soil (12:12), and ample water (Job 29:19). God has planted Israel in good soil (Is. 5:1ff.; Ps. 80:8ff.). Ezek. 16:3 alludes to the historical origin of Israel. From its root a fallen tree may renew itself (Job 14:7ff.). The abiding root symbolizes the holy remnant (Is. 6:13). Is. 11:1ff. refers to the root of Jesse in a messianic sense. From this house will come the new shoot that will establish the kingdom of righteousness and peace. In v. 1 the genitive is one of apposition, but in v. 10 it is one of origin. Is. 53:2 perhaps carries the same messianic sense, although the traditional LXX rendering compares the proclamation rather than the Servant to a root.

3. *Later Judaism.* The concept of Israel as God's plant is common. The planting goes back to Abraham as its root. Israel is the race of the elect root. God will plant righteous Gentiles in Israel. The idea of the Messiah as the root of Jesse is also common. Some conclude from Is. 11:10 that it is the Gentiles that need the Messiah; Israel has the law. Philo does not refer to the Davidic shoot. For him the metaphor of the root is a stylistic device. Thus the Ten Commandments are the root of individual statutes.

4. *The NT.* Of the 17 NT instances, eight are in the Synoptics, six in Paul, one in Hebrews, and two in Revelation. In Mk. 4:6 and parallels the root that needs good ground is the source of sap for the plant. Mk. 4:17 gives the idea of a personal reference. Mal. 3–4 forms the background of Mt. 3:10 and Lk. 3:9. Israel as God's plant is threatened with complete destruction if she does not repent. In Rom. 11:16ff. the Gentiles are warned not to give up fallen Israel, for the special position of Israel is the premise of all expectation; the branches depend on the root. Israel here is not just Christian Israel. The patriarchs are probably in view in v. 16. As the root, these were chosen with salvation in Christ as the goal. Their holiness embraces all Israel and cannot be cancelled even by Israel's guilt. Against nature, the Gentiles have been grafted in as wild branches, but this process demands and promotes the planting in again of the good branches. Gentiles scorn their own root if they scorn Israel. In Rom. 15:12 Paul quotes Is. 11:10: The root of Jesse is the one in whom the Gentiles hope. Is. 11:10 also lies behind the title "root of David" in Rev. 5:5; 22:16 in the sense of "shoot out of David." Figurative use occurs in 1 Tim. 6:10 when it describes the love of money as the root or origin of all evil. Heb. 12:15 also offers a figurative use (cf. Dt. 29:17 LXX). In this case we have the passive sense of "shoot." The bitter root springs from apostasy from grace, and involves defiling conflict.

5. *The Apostolic Fathers.* Hermas *Similitudes* 9.30.1-2 uses the plural for the "feet" of the mountain, and 9.1.6 compares doubters and nominal believers to plants whose upper parts are still green but whose roots are withered. Pol. 1.2 offers a positive counterpart to 1 Tim. 6:10.

rhizóō.

1. This word means "to cause to take root," or in the passive "to take root."

2. The LXX has the active for unrighteousness and wisdom taking root in Sir. 3:28; 24:12, and the passive with reference to princes in Is. 40:24.

3. Philo speaks of rooted virtue (*Allegorical Interpretation of Laws* 1.45) and the rooted cosmos (*On Noah's Work as a Planter* 11).

4. In the NT Col. 2:7 and Eph. 3:17 refer to the personal rootage of believers. In Christ they find life-giving soil and also their sustaining foundation ("rooted and built up").

ekrizóō. This word, meaning "to uproot," is used literally in Lk. 17:6 and in the parable in Mt. 13:29. The reference in Mt. 15:13 and Jude 12 is to judgment on the Pharisees and false teachers. 1 Clem. 6.4 shows how strife extirpates great peoples, and Hermas *Mandates* 9.9 how doubt uproots faith.   [C. MAURER, VI, 985-91]

---

rhíptō [to throw], **epiríptō** [to throw on], **aporíptō** [to throw oneself]

A. Greek Usage. *rhíptō* means "to throw," "to cast to the ground," "to throw away," "to cast off."

B. OT Usage.

1. Hebrew Terms. *rhíptō* is mostly used for Heb. *šlk* (61 times), for which *aporíptō* is also used 20 times and *epiríptō* 14 times.

2. God's Throwing. God throws stones at Israel's enemies in Josh. 10:11, casts off the people in Jer. 22:26, casts down kings in Is. 14:19, repels or rejects in Jon. 2:4, casts sins behind him in Is. 38:17.

3. Human Throwing. Literally Joseph's brothers cast him in the well in Gen. 37:20, and the dust of the overthrown altars is thrown into the water in Dt. 9:21. Figuratively Jeroboam rejects God in 1 Kgs. 14:9, and the righteous cast their care on God in Ps. 55:22.

C. NT Usage.

1. rhíptō. In Mt. 15:30 the sick are cast at the feet of Jesus, in 27:5 Judas throws the money into the temple, in Lk.4:35 the demon throws the man down when exorcised, in 17:2 those who harm little ones are threatened with destruction, in Acts 22:23 the throwing off of clothes expresses resolve, and in Mt. 9:36 the people are like sheep lying on the ground without a shepherd.

2. epiríptō. 1 Pet. 5:7 echoes Ps. 55:22 but with a reference to the community, which under God's lordship may cast all its care on God.

3. aporíptō. This verb is used intransitively in Acts 27:43: "throw oneself."

D. Apostolic Fathers. Hermas *Visions* 3.2.7 speaks of the throwing away of stones as a symbol of rejection, and *Similitudes* 2.3 uses *rhíptō* to show that the vine can lie on the ground without the elm's support. The exposing of infants is meant in Diog. 5.6. Barn. 4.8 is modeled on Ex. 32:19 (cf. 14.8).   [W. BIEDER, VI, 991-93]

---

rhomphaía [sword]

A. Outside the NT.

1. This word denotes a Thracian weapon, a large javelin, lance, or sword.

2. Uncommon in Greek, the word occurs some 230 times in the LXX, mostly in the sense of "sword" rather than "spear" (cf. Gen. 3:24; 1 Sam. 17:45).

3. Philo is influenced by LXX usage, e.g., in relation to Gen. 3:24. Josephus, too, follows the LXX, and the term also occurs in the pseudepigrapha, although the rabbis do not have it as a loanword, as they do *máchaira* and *xíphos*.

B. The NT.

1. The NT has *máchaira* 27 times but also, under LXX influence, has *rhomphaía* seven times. The aged Simeon in Lk. 2:34-35 looks ahead to the destiny of Jesus which will also bring sorrow to his mother. Ps. 37:15 (rather than Ezek. 14:21) perhaps underlies the saying. Any likeness to Sib. 3.316 is purely formal.

2. The other six instances are in Revelation. The only literal use is in 6:8, where *rhomphaía,* as distinct from *máchaira* in 6:4, perhaps denotes murder. In 1:16; 2:12, 16; 19:15, 21 the sword proceeds from Christ's mouth. With this sword, i.e., his word,

he judges and if necessary punishes the churches. With it he is also the eschatological judge of the nations. Judgment begins at God's house, and although its severity is stressed, the only weapon used is the word.

C. The Apostolic Fathers. The only example in the apostolic fathers is in Barn. 5.13 (quoting Ps. 22:20). Justin uses the term six times in OT quotations.

[W. MICHAELIS, VI, 993-98]

Rhoúth → Thamár

---

rhýomai [to save, protect]

A. Basic Meaning.

1. This word has such senses as "to save," "to protect," "to guard," "to ward off," "to deliver."

2. The LXX uses the word more often than *sṓzō* for Heb. *nṣl* (84 times). It also uses it 12 times for *g'l*, "to release," "to buy back." It is used, too, for other terms meaning "to free," "to redeem," and "to keep."

B. Use.

I. Greek.

1. A first use of the verb in Greek is for keeping or saving by the gods, whether of people or of cities, walls, the land, etc.

2. People, too, offer protection, e.g., princes, warriors, priests, guards, nations. Objects like helmets or walls also protect. But human protection is limited, as indeed is that of the gods in the face of destiny.

II. The OT.

1. *Similarities to Greek Usage.* God's saving and keeping is in many ways parallel to that of the Greek gods. The OT also refers to human deliverers, e.g., Moses, the judges, and the king in 2 Sam. 19:10.

2. *Distinctiveness of OT Usage.* God, however, is not limited by ontological laws as are both mortals and immortals among the Greeks. He saves according to his mercy (Neh. 9:8), for his name's sake (Ps. 79:9), and as he wills. His very name is Deliverer (Is. 63:16). Again, his salvation is not magical but personal. As a salvation in history, it always relates to the community or to individuals as deliverance from situations caused by the hostile intent of others. It means preservation in God's gracious presence; hence faith or trust is demanded on the human side (Ps. 22:4-5). This faith has ethical implications; it goes hand in hand with obedience (cf. Ps. 34:19). Yet God also saves when guilt is confessed (Ps. 39:8). The understanding in terms of will or person tends to expunge the Greek distinction between "protect" and "deliver" and to rule out the use of the term for salvation by things, e.g., walls, weapons, or money, which can be no more than instruments in God's hands.

III. The NT.

1. The word is uncommon in the NT. In the Gospels it occurs only in Mt. 6:13; 27:43; Lk. 1:74, in Paul only three times in Romans, three in 2 Cor. 1:10, and once each in Colossians, 1 Thessalonians, and 2 Thessalonians (cf. also three times in 2 Timothy and two in 2 Peter).

2. The meaning in the NT is always "to save" with God as subject and persons as object. In seven instances there are OT quotations or allusions.

3. The term takes on an eschatological sense in Mt. 6:13; Rom. 11:26; Col. 1:13;

1 Th. 1:10; 2 Tim. 4:18; 2 Pet. 2:9. Salvation is ultimately eternal preservation. Eschatological salvation rests on present deliverance from sin and from the power that rules in this sinful aeon. Prayer is made for final preservation (Mt. 6:13) but with the confidence that God is the Lord who impresses even evil into his service, so that in the very prayer for deliverance evil is overcome by the divinely conferred affirmation of God's will. [W. KASCH, VI, 998-1003]

σ ς

---

sábbaton [the sabbath], *sabbatismós* [sabbath rest], *paraskeuḗ* [day of preparation]

---

sábbaton, paraskeuḗ.

A. The Sabbath in the OT.

1. Origin. The sabbath law is found in Ex. 34:21; 23:12; 20:8ff.; Dt. 5:12ff.; Lev. 23:1ff.; 19:3; 26:2; Ex. 31:12ff.; 35:1ff. Parallels have been found in Babylon, but in connection with the cycle of the moon and as a day of penance. The meaning and content of the OT sabbath are controlled by Israel's faith.

2. The Preexilic Age. The sabbath commandment enjoins absolute rest for all, including servants and animals, on the ground that God made heaven and earth and also redeemed Israel. On the sabbath (and new moon) business stops, offerings are made, feasts are held, and the man of God may be consulted (2 Kgs. 4:23).

3. The Postexilic Period. In the exile circumcision and the sabbath are important marks of distinction (Ezek. 20:12). Sabbath desecration has been a cause of the disaster (20:13). Details about sabbath rest are worked out (cf. Ezek. 45:17; Neh. 13:15ff.). The rules of Ex. 35:3; 16:22ff.; Lev. 24:8 are enforced. Keeping the sabbath holy is pleasing to God (Is. 58:13-14).

4. The Sabbatical Year. The Seventh Year brings remission of all legal and financial obligations, the duty of leaving the land fallow, and the redistribution of property. In the fiftieth year, the Year of Jubilee, slaves are to be freed. It seems unlikely that all these regulations were strictly kept.

B. The Sabbath in Judaism.

1. Development of the Sabbath.

a. Usage. Judaism takes over the sabbath, using the Hebrew or Aramaic term in Palestine and the Greek term *sábbaton* (with *anápausis* as an explanation) in the diaspora. The plural *tá sábbata* may mean one sabbath, several sabbaths, or the whole week (like the Hebrew term). "Seventh day" is also used for the sabbath. The verb *sabbatízein* occurs for keeping the sabbath.

b. The Maccabean Period to the Editing of the Mishnah. The sabbath is a sign of election and grants a foretaste of glory. Even the wicked in Gehenna enjoy respite on it. There is a great reward for observing it. It stands at the heart of the law; hence the Maccabean struggle to keep it, even to the point of refusing to attack enemies on the sabbath. Rules about journeys, driving or rescuing cattle, drawing water, moving vessels, and the like are developed in different circles, although the Pharisees and scribes try to adjust the laws to practical situations. Hellenistic Judaism invests the sabbath with philosophical significance in presenting it to the Gentile world (cf. the cosmological importance of the number seven, or the sabbath as a day for philosophizing).

2. The Prohibition of Work.

a. Jubilees and the Damascus Document. Jubilees lists activities that are forbidden on the sabbath on penalty of death, e.g., preparing food, drawing water, fetching, and carrying. The Damascus Document restricts travel and forbids rescuing from pits, driving cattle, and making sacrifices other than the burnt offering.

b. Rabbinic Works. The rabbis give even more detailed lists of what is prohibited, forty save one tasks in all, but extended by grouping six subsidiary tasks under each main one. The tasks include plowing, threshing, sewing, hunting, writing, carrying, riding, climbing trees, judging. Casuistry fixes what is permissible, e.g., carrying small objects, carrying for minute distances, or carrying shared burdens. In this way a fence is kept around the law but the rules are brought into harmony with practical necessities.

c. Superseding of the Sabbath Law. Inescapable obligations supersede the sabbath law. Thus priests may prepare and sacrifice the burnt offerings. The sabbath may be broken when a person is in mortal danger (cf. self-defense, or helping in grave sickness or childbirth). Circumcision also takes precedence over the sabbath.

3. The Celebration.

a. At Home. All things are made ready the previous day, e.g., the meal or the lamps. Three trumpet blasts herald the sabbath. A meal of dedication introduces the day; at this meal the cup of blessing is followed by a second cup of consecration. As a feast day the sabbath is a day for three meals instead of the usual two; the main meal comes at midday after worship, and guests are often invited. A special blessing closes the day.

b. Worship on the Sabbath. The appointed offerings are made in the temple, more priests being needed than on other days. The change in courses takes place on the sabbath. Synagogue services, including recitation of the Shema, prayer, Scripture readings, and exposition, take place. For public reading, the Pentateuch is divided into sections in one- or three-year cycles. A reading from the prophets concludes the service (sometimes with an exposition).

c. Non-Jewish Views of the Sabbath. In the Roman world Jews are allowed to keep the sabbath unhindered. Some Greek and Latin authors, however, ridicule the sabbath as a day of sloth, or explain it as an unlucky day, or equate it with pagan practices. Yet many Gentiles are impressed by the observance, and God-fearers as well as proselytes join in keeping the sabbath as a day of rest.

4. The Sabbatical Year.

a. Fallow Ground and Remission of Debts. Strict attempts are made to keep the rule of a fallow year, leading to hardship in difficult times. The Romans remit taxes during this seventh year. Remission of debts is less strictly observed, since lenders will advance money only on the condition that they be allowed to collect at any time.

b. The Cosmic Week and Sabbath. Apocalyptic makes much play with the number seven (cf. the 70 weeks of Dan. 9:24ff.). Slav. En. 33:1-2 refers to the seven millennia of world history; the seventh millennium will be a great sabbath and will be followed by the new creation.

C. The Sabbath in the NT.

1. The Jewish Sabbath. NT usage agrees with Jewish usage; the sabbath is *tó sábbaton, hē hēméra toú sabbátou, tá sábbata,* or *hē hebdómē.* Observance is in keeping with what is known from Jewish sources: the body of Jesus is buried prior to the sabbath (Mk. 15:42ff.), plucking ears of grain is forbidden (Mk. 2:23-24), those not in danger of death are not to be helped or healed (Mk. 3:1 etc.), objects are not to be carried (Jn. 5:9-10), travel is restricted (Acts 1:12), priestly work (Mt. 12:4-5) and circumcision (Jn. 7:22-23) are permissible, the sabbath is a day of rest (Lk. 23:56), guests are invited (Lk. 14:1), Scripture is read (Acts 13:15, 27), worship is held in the synagogue (Lk. 4:16ff.), and expositions are given (Acts 13:14-15, 42ff.; 16:13).

2. Jesus and the Sabbath.

a. The Gospel Stories. In Mk. 2–3 conflict arises between Jesus and the Pharisees over the plucking of ears of grain on the sabbath (2:23ff.). Jesus shows from the OT that on occasion the righteous may infringe sabbath rules. In principle human needs are more important than the sabbath (2:27). Jesus is its Lord and decides when the sabbath applies and when it is to be transcended (2:28). Mt. 12:1ff. adds that the sacrifices take precedence over the sabbath commandment, and that in Jesus one who is greater than the temple is present, whose law of mercy or of love (Hos. 6:6) imposes an even more imperious command. A second confrontation then takes place with the healing of Mk. 3:1ff. The rule that healing is permitted only when there is danger of death is obviously broken, but doing good and saving life are imperatives that leave no room for casuistry. Jesus, then, displays his lordship by healing the withered arm. Mt. 12:9ff. presses home the supremacy of human needs by the comparison with helping animals in distress, which some rabbis, although not all, permit even on the sabbath.

b. Lucan Stories. Lk. 13:10ff. and 14:13ff. contain two other stories of sabbath healings. In the former, comparison is made with the feeding of animals, and the story serves to stress the impenitence of Jesus' adversaries (cf. vv. 1-9). In 14:1ff. the story demonstrates yet again the supremacy of human need. The sabbath conflicts in Luke form part of the movement which by way of resistance and rejection leads from an initial synagogue ministry to the Gentile mission.

c. Johannine Stories. Two healings in John lead to sharp controversy. In Jn. 5 the carrying of the bed involves infringement of the prohibition of carrying. Jesus replies by pointing to God's own work on the sabbath, which both Palestinian and Hellenistic Jews accept. Authorized by the Father, Jesus works as God does. Hence the decisive issue is whether Jesus is recognized as the one who has transcendent authority in virtue of his divine sending. The debate continues in 7:19ff., where Jesus appeals to the giving of circumcision on the sabbath. Again, the ultimate issue is the divine sending of Jesus. His work expresses his divine authority (vv. 16-17). In answer to human need, this authority overrides sabbath legislation. Jesus in 9:1ff. breaks the sabbath not only by healing but also by kneading the spittle into clay. To some this shows him to be a sinner, but to others his works prove the contrary. In the healing, Jesus comes as the light of the world (9:5) in encounter with whom decision is made as to who is really blind and who really sees. For those who have eyes to see, God's work is manifest in this granting of sight to blind eyes.

3. The Sabbath in the Churches. Christ rises on the first day of the week (Mk. 16:2; Mt. 28:1), the day of Christian worship (Acts 20:7; 1 Cor. 16:2; cf. Rev. 1:10). Jewish Christians still keep the sabbath (cf. Mt. 24:20), as at first they make offerings in the temple and pay the temple tax (Mt. 5:23; 17:24ff.). Judaizers try to force the same rules on Gentile Christians, but Paul resists them (cf. Gal. 4:8ff.; Rom. 10:4). Among the Colossians a strange syncretism combines keeping the sabbath with angel worship and asceticism in subjection to cosmic forces. In reply, the apostle points out that believers are dead with Christ to all such forces and are thus freed from bondage to them. Neither the supposed necessity of the law to salvation nor the dominion of cosmic powers obliges Christians to keep the sabbath law.

D. The Sabbath and the Early Church.

1. Sabbath and Sunday. The churches observe Sunday as the day of Christ's resurrection (Barn. 15.9; Ignatius *Magnesians* 9.1; Did. 14.1). There is no obligation to keep the sabbath law. Barn. 2.5 shows that the Lord's Day is superior to the sabbath, and although Barn. 15 looks ahead to the seventh millennium as a cosmic sabbath, Christians keep the eighth day as the beginning of the new creation.

2. The Jewish Week. The church takes over the Jewish week, which runs from the first day to the sabbath, and it even uses *sábbaton* or *sábbata* for the week, and calls the sixth day *prosábbaton* and the seventh *sábbaton*. Catechumens bathe on the fifth day, fast on the day of preparation, assemble on the sabbath, and receive baptism early on Easter Day.

3. The Sabbath. Jewish Christians cling to the sabbath, citing its general observance by Jesus, and in some cases combining Gnostic ideas with it. The main body of the church worships on the first day and warns Jewish Christians not to set the sabbath above this day of Christ's resurrection, which unites all believers as a day of joy and jubilation (cf. Justin *Apology* 167.7).

sabbatismós. This uncommon word, not found in the OT, occurs in the NT only in Heb. 4:9. The desert generation did not enter into *katápausis* because of unbelief. Hence the promise of *katápausis*—rest from enemies and from work—is still to be fulfilled. This sabbath rest (*sabbatismós*) which remains for God's people will be the perfect sabbath of heavenly blessing toward which the pilgrim community is moving and which will mean cessation from its own labors. In a hortatory thrust the author warns his readers not to miss this prepared and promised rest by disobedience.

[E. LOHSE, VII, 1-35]

Saddoukaíos [Sadducee]

A. Usage. Based on the Hebrew, this word occurs in the NT and Josephus, always in the plural. Not found outside Jewish and Christian works, it refers to different groups and mostly has a disparaging accent.

B. Sadduceeism in Judaism.

I. Origin of the Term.

1. Zadokites and Sadducees.

a. The term Sadducee comes from Zadok, and thus raises the question of the relation between the Zadokites and Sadducees.

b. Zadok, a ruling priest under David, supports Solomon and becomes high priest. His descendants establish a priestly dynasty which gains strength under Josiah and provides the high priests after the exile, who claim Aaronic descent by way of Ithamar or Phinehas. Sirach refers to Phinehas in his praise of famous men (45:25).

992

c. After 170 B.C. battles for the high priesthood lead to the elimination of the Zadokites, who set up a new center in Egypt.

d. Yet Zadokite traditions remain alive, preserved by groups that are faithful to the law. Thus the Damascus Document presupposes a priestly community with the Zadokites as leaders, and Qumran calls the Zadokites God's chosen priests.

e. A this-worldly eschatology characterizes the Zadokite tradition, so that the concept of resurrection plays little part in it.

f. The Zadokites of the NT period are at odds with the temple government and cannot be simply equated with the Sadducees.

2. Zadok and Boethos.

a. In a rabbinic tradition, Antigonos in the early second century B.C. has two pupils, Zadok and Boethos, who found two sects, the Sadducees and the Boethusians. These look for a temporal reward and thus exclude the resurrection.

b. In A.D. 6/7 Zadok founds the Zealot party with the aim of setting up God's kingdom by eschatological war. Zadok, in legend, becomes the eponymous hero of the Sadducces, who also have a this-worldly eschatology.

c. A certain Joazar ben Boethos opposes Zadok's call for revolt against Rome. In the main the rabbis link the Sadducees with the Boethusians, perhaps because the founder of their dynasty comes from Egypt and possibly has a connection with the Zadokites there; this may well explain the link with Zadok.

3. A Political Group. Before the Maccabean revolt the high priests bring the high priesthood into disrepute by their Hellenizing. Since the Zadokites are identified strongly with this group, the term Zadokite or Sadducee may thus be used for those who favor political compromise, even though this contradicts the true Zadokite tradition preserved in the communities and in Egypt.

II. The Sadducees of Jerusalem.

1. Sadducees and Hasmoneans. The Sadducees are first mentioned by Josephus as a party under Hyrcanus I (135–104 B.C.). Although at first a Pharisee, Hyrcanus goes over to the Sadducees, removing the stigma of illegitimacy by alignment with the priestly aristocracy of "Zadokites," whose particularist eschatology fits in well with the Hasmonean wars of expansion.

2. The Sadducees under Herod and the Romans. When Herod, who favors cooperation with Rome, comes to power, he eliminates the older priestly aristocracy, abolishes the high priesthood for life, and appoints men of his own persuasion to office. The house of Boethos achieves prominence in priestly circles when Simon ben Boethos becomes high priest. In spite of a possible connection with the Egyptian Zadokites, the Boethusians bring the priesthood into disrepute among the righteous with what seems to be their semi-Gentile position. Yet elements within the priesthood maintain the particularist eschatology, attempt to keep the temple state alive, and finally go down with it in the disaster of A.D. 70.

III. Sadduceeism as a Religious Phenomenon.

1. Dogmatics.

a. The Sadducees balance divine and human action synergistically. Good and evil have their origin in the human will, not in divine providence.

b. The Sadducees reject individual survival and future judgment.

c. In particular they deny the resurrection, claiming that it has no clear support in the law.

d. In this regard they defend an older interpretation at a time of dogmatic development which stresses hope for the world to come and thinks in terms of the present and future aeons. In their view the present world is the place of the one encounter with God and the related reward and punishment. This older official position still comes to expression at Qumran, which finds no essential place for the motif of resurrection. The ruling priesthood at Jerusalem regards this teaching as the true orthodoxy, although with the triumph of Pharisaic rabbinism it comes to be presented as heresy and apostasy.

2. *View of the Law.* The Sadducees reject oral law. In so doing they judge more strictly than the Pharisees, whose casuistry adjusts the law to circumstances, but in this way often lessens its rigor in Sadducean eyes. The same distinction may be seen cultically at Tabernacles, when the Sadducees try to block the custom of smiting the earth around the altar with twigs on the seventh day if this day falls on the sabbath. With oral tradition the Pharisees can legalize popular practices whereas the Sadducees with their stricter view of the written law resist them.

C. The Sadducees in the NT.

1. The Synoptic Gospels. The Sadducees are present only on the margin in the NT. In their question in Mk. 12:18ff., in which they show hostility to Jesus, they deny the resurrection. The message of Jesus unavoidably conflicts with the older official teaching that they represent. In Matthew the Sadducees are lumped together with the Pharisees in 3:7; 16:1, 5ff., 11-12 but only in the terms of the common opposition to the Baptist or to Jesus and with no attempt to pinpoint their distinctive teachings.

II. Acts. Acts mentions the Sadducees three times in 4:1ff.; 5:17ff.; 23:6ff. In 4:1ff. they control the politics and theology of the temple, and in particular they oppose the message of resurrection and the eschatological claim of the church. In 5:17ff. they again attack the resurrection but obviously with an eye on apostolic eschatology and its possible political implications. They plainly control the most important ecclesiastical and political offices. In 23:6ff. Paul causes division by raising the issue of the resurrection. When he also refers to angels and spirits, it may be that the popular belief is in view, since other sources do not say that they reject angels altogether. In this case, as the judicial hearing becomes more of an academic debate, the Pharisees rally behind their former pupil. For all the differences, the gospel is closer to the roots of Pharisaic belief than to the official orthodoxy of the Sadducees.

[R. Meyer, VII, 35-54]

→ *Pharisaíos*

---

saínō [to wag, unsettle, flatter]

1. *saínō,* meaning "to wag," is used literally of dogs wagging their tails, and then in transferred usage has such senses as "to fawn," "to greet warmly," "to gladden," "to entice," "to agitate," "to unsettle." The main figurative meaning is "to flatter," but with various nuances.

2. The term does not occur in the LXX but Josephus uses it for "friendly treatment."

3. In the NT the only use is in the passive in 1 Th. 3:3. Two meanings are possible.

(1) The main Greek use favors "to be deluded." In this case Paul's point is that escaping affliction by apostasy is enticing but is still a delusion, since it means the loss of eternal salvation.

(2) The Greek expositors and older translations prefer "to be shaken," and the

papyri and lexicography support what is a more obvious meaning in context. Paul's aim is that believers should not be shaken or unsettled in their faith by assaults.

4. The word does not occur in the apostolic fathers.   [F. LANG, VII, 54-56]

---

sákkos [sackcloth]

A. Origin and Meaning. This word originally means "haircloth," i.e., the coarse fabric, mostly of goats' hair, out of which tents, sails, carpets, etc. are made. The term then comes to be applied to things made of this fabric, especially the "sack," but also "carpet," "sackcloth," "hairnet"; figuratively it refers to a big beard like a sack.

B. Use and Significance of Sackcloth in Antiquity and the OT.
1. In the Semitic world sackcloth is from early days the garb of mourning and penitence. It is also prophetic garb in the OT. Originally perhaps a mere loincloth, it becomes a lower garment fastened with a cord or girdle and worn over the naked body.
2. In mourning it leaves the breast free for beating. Since goats' hair is dark, its color is that of mourning. It is used in the OT both in private mourning (Gen. 37:34) and national mourning (2 Sam. 3:31).
3. In penitence its use seems to derive from Babylon but quickly spreads to Israel. It signifies self-abasement (along with ashes and sometimes self-disfigurement) either before God (2 Kgs. 19:1) or others (1 Kgs. 20:31ff.). It is also worn at night (1 Kgs. 21:27). Personal crises (Ps. 30:11) and times of national emergency (Esth. 4:1-2) or imminent eschatological destruction (Joel 1:13) are occasions for its penitential use. It has become a rite in Neh. 9:1 etc., and its purely formal use comes under prophetic criticism (Is. 58:5). Fasting often accompanies it (Ps. 35:13).
4. For its prophetic use see C.3.

C. The NT.
1. In Rev. 6:12 the dark color of sackcloth explains the use. When the sun is eschatologically darkened (cf. Is. 50:3 etc.), it becomes as black as sackcloth. This darkening, which precedes the parousia in Mk. 13:24ff., is one of the events with which the opening of the next to·the last seal introduces the great day of wrath.
2. *sákkos* is a sign of conversion and penitence in the saying in Mt. 11:21 and Lk. 10:13, whether in the sense of the garment or the penitential mat. Jesus perhaps has Jon. 3:4ff. in mind; but clearly conversion itself, not the external sign, is what matters.
3. The *sákkoi* in which the two prophets of Rev. 11:3 are garbed seem to be modeled on Elijah's clothing in 2 Kgs. 1:8, although this is made of the skin, not the woven hair. The dress suggests that the prophetic message is a threat of judgment and a summons to repentance (cf. the clothing of John in Mk. 1:6).

D. The Post – New Testament Period.
1. In the apostolic fathers and Apologists the use is colored by the OT (cf. 1 Clem. 8.3; Justin *Dialogue* 15.4). Only in Hermas *Mandates* 8.4.1 do we have a working garment.
2. Sackcloth soon becomes part of the practice of penance (cf. Tertullian, Cyprian, and the Council of Toledo in A.D. 400). The roughness symbolizes sorrow and self-

abasement. Sackcloth is also laid over the seriously ill, and in private use it is worn in preparation for death or as the garb of death.

3. The monastic use of sackcloth as permanent dress signifies a life of penitence, although voices are raised against it as a source of vanity and a hindrance to the work monks are commanded to do.

4. Groups of *fratres saccati* and *saccariae* arise, sometimes suspected of heretical teachings. The Byzantine *sákkos* also becomes the ornate purple garb of patriarchs and metropolitans or the black but festive garb worn as a diadem by the emperors and empresses.   [G. STÄHLIN, VII, 56-64]

---

saleúō [to shake],   *sálos* [shaking]

A. Secular Greek. This word is used for the tossing of the sea, the shaking of an earthquake, natural becoming and perishing, political unrest, earthly uncertainty, human vacillation, and physical change. In contrast, Hellenism seeks unshakability in the world to come. Astrological texts refer to eschatological shakings of the earth in political events or natural disasters.

B. The Greek OT. With no fixed Hebrew original, the term in the Greek OT is used for the shaking of the earth, the raging of the sea, human agitation or quaking. God's shaking of the earth, its trembling before him, staggering with strong drink (cf. the cup of staggering), shaking when Jerusalem or Babylon is taken, shaking through confusion or fear of death. In contrast, *saleúō* may be used with the negative to denote unshakable faith or confidence in God, the unshakableness of the earth under God's rule, the unshakableness of figures like Elisha, or the unshakableness of the city of God. The righteous know they will stumble on their own, but they also know that God gives them an unshakableness that keeps them from falling and gives them confidence in spite of the shattering events of nature and history.

C. Philo. The use in Philo is mainly psychological. He defines what is divine as unshakable, e.g., the law, cosmic order, and reason. On the other hand, what is merely human is uncertain and vacillating. Through the movement of the emotions the peace of virtue is attained with the help of wisdom. Grounded in reason, the wise share God's unshakability in contrast to those who are at the mercy of the tossing sea of life. The vibration of the legal statutes, like the harmonious movement of heavenly forces, keeps us attentive.

D. The NT. In Acts 17:13 the verb characterizes the agitators who follow Paul from Thessalonica and stir up the people of Berea. It denotes vacillation in Mt. 21:10; 2 Th. 2:2. The Baptist, however, is not a reed shaken by the wind (Mt. 11:7). In Acts 2:25ff. the reference is to the steadfastness of Christ as crucified and risen Lord. Lk. 6:38 uses *saleúō* in a crescendo to denote the superabundance of the divine gift (pressed down, shaken, and overflowing), while 6:48 points out that the house built on the rock cannot be shaken by the storm and flood. Earthquakes that shake the ground are taken as a sign of answered prayer in Acts 4:31 and 16:26, while eschatological quaking is predicted in Lk. 21:25-26; Heb. 12:26; Revelation. What is made is subject to change; what cannot be shaken remains (1 Cor. 7:27ff.). But this is an eschatological rather than a cosmological hope (cf. Heb. 12:28). Creation stands under the threat of divine shaking, but also under the promise of divine unshakability.

[G. BERTRAM, VII, 65-70]

---

sálpinx [trumpet, trumpet call],   *salpízō* [to sound the trumpet],   *salpistḗs* [trumpeter]

A. The Greek World.

I. Meaning.

1. sálpinx. This word denotes a wind instrument, made of bronze or iron with a mouthpiece of horn, and broadening out to a megaphone, i.e., a "trumpet." The word may also denote the sound made by the instrument, its signal or playing. Other uses are for thunder as a heavenly trumpet sound or for a human speaker as a trumpet.

2. salpízō. This word means "to blow on a trumpet," "to give a trumpet blast or signal," "to blow on an instrument," "to thunder."

3. salpistḗs. This is one form of the word for "trumpeter."

II. Origin and Use.

1. Origin. Trumpets are used from an early date in the Near East (cf. the Persians, Hittites, and Egyptians). The Greeks know them from the time of Homer but not at first as military instruments.

2. The War Trumpet. The trumpet soon finds use in the army for giving signals. It replaces the earlier Spartan flute and Cretan lyre. It passes on signals, fires with courage, terrifies enemies, signals retreat, rallies the scattered, ends battles. In the Roman camp it gives the signal for sleeping, watching, and waking.

3. The Trumpet in Peace. Shepherds use trumpets to gather their flocks. Heralds initiate trials by trumpet sounds. Trumpets silence the people for prayer or summon them to sacrifice. Trumpeters have a place in funerals and triumphs. Trumpet competitions are part of the games. Only a few notes can be played but trumpet playing is an art in view of the strong lungs that it requires.

4. A Musical Instrument. It is doubtful whether the trumpet has much of a role as a musical instrument. The Egyptian trumpets have only two notes. They may give signals and set rhythms but not play real music. Trumpets have a loud and penetrating sound that is sometimes compared to the braying of an ass or roaring of a bull.

B. The OT.

I. Hebrew Equivalents.

1. sálpinx. This word is most often used for a Hebrew term that is better translated as a ram's horn or a horn in general. Trumpet is a more accurate rendering in the case of the cultic instruments of Num. 10:21; 2 Kgs. 11:14; 2 Chr. 5:12-13. This superior instrument then tends to supplant the ram's horn and has an important place in priestly ministry (2 Chr. 29:26ff.). The instrument of Josh. 6:5 seems to be an animal horn; it has a place in Nebuchadnezzar's "orchestra" in Daniel. Another word used in Gen. 4:21 has various senses, e.g., horn, trumpet, signal, or the feast announced by such a signal; it means "horn" in Ex. 19:19, but in Josh. 6:4ff. it denotes, not an instrument, but the material of which the instruments are made. In Lev. 23:24 *sálpinx* is used for a word that really means "noise" (Josh. 6:5) or "alarm" (Num. 10:5). The true reference in Ezek. 7:14 seems to be to blowing rather than to an instrument.

2. salpízō. This word is used for various Hebrew terms in such senses as "to blow an alarm," "to cry," "to draw out a note," "to sound."

3. salpistḗs. This noun does not occur in the OT, which has no special term for those who blow trumpets, e.g., priests in 2 Chr. 29:26; Ezr. 3:10. (For details of the Hebrew terms see *TDNT*, VII, 76-78.)

II. Use and Significance.

1. In War. Horns or trumpets play an important role in war, whether to give warning, to summon to battle, to sound an attack, to frighten enemies, or, religiously, to invoke God's help. The horn also sounds a retreat, announces victory, and dismisses the host.

2. In Peace. Horns or trumpets are used at coronations, at the laying of the temple's foundation, at its dedication, in festal processions, and in solemn self-dedication to God.

3. Cultic Use. The trumpet or horn is sounded at offerings, at the temple dedication, at feasts, at fasts, and at the initiation of the year of release.

4. Theophanies. In both war and peace there is a strict relation to God, but there is a special use of the trumpet at Sinai (Ex. 19:16ff.; cf. Zech. 9:14), where the trumpet seems to denote the inexpressible voice of God.

5. Eschatological Significance. The horn will announce the day of the Lord (Joel 2:1; Zeph. 1:16), the last judgment, and the age of salvation (Is. 27:13; Zeph. 9:14).

6. Musical Instruments. The horn or trumpet is a musical instrument in Babylon in Dan. 3:5ff. and in temple praise in 2 Chr. 5:13; Ps. 150:3. Horns and trumpets do not play melodies but stress the rhythm and strengthen the sound.

C. Judaism.

I. Words. Judaism uses the various OT terms for the horns that are blown at feasts, for priestly trumpets, and for horn instruments in a more general sense.

II. Significance.

1. War Signals. The Qumran scrolls give details about the use of trumpets in war, e.g., to summon to battle, to form ranks, to attack, to pursue, to signal the return home. Different ways of blowing are used for different signals.

2. In Peace. Trumpets are blown to announce fasts in special emergencies, to intimate deaths, and to impose or lift excommunications.

3. Cultic Use. Trumpets signal the opening of the temple, the offering of regular sacrifices, the beginning of the sabbath, the coming of the new moon or the new year. The blowing is an act of prayer and not just a signal. It disposes God to mercy and confuses the adversary.

4. Eschatological Significance. The trumpet proclaims the last time, the return from exile, and the raising of the dead. This last trumpet is blown by the archangel or by God himself.

5. As Musical Instruments. In Judaism the horn and trumpet are not musical instruments like harps or zithers. At most they can only give the signal for striking up a song; they are too loud for musical use.

D. The NT.

I. The Words.

1. sálpinx. This term denotes the instrument (1 Cor. 14:8; Heb. 12:19, etc.), and occasionally the sound or signal (Mt. 24:31; 1 Cor. 15:52; 1 Th. 4:16).

2. salpízō. This word occurs mostly in Revelation.

3. salpistḗs. The only instance is in Rev. 18:22.

II. Significance.

1. In War. Paul uses the metaphor of the military trumpet in 1 Cor. 14:8.

2. On Solemn Occasions. In Mt. 6:2 the use is perhaps figurative ("to blaze abroad") or perhaps an actual practice is in view, e.g., blowing a horn when very generous gifts are given so as to stir up others and to commend the donors in prayer. As Jesus points out, God does not need such reminders, which serve more to bring human glory.

3. *Theophanies and Visions.* In Heb. 12:19 the trumpet sound is an accompanying phenomenon at Sinai. In Rev. 1:10; 4:1 the divine hears a sound like a trumpet, probably the voice of God. The great voice in 1:10 introduces the epistles, and that in 4:1 the visions.

4. *Eschatology.*

a. The trumpet proclaims the last judgment. In Rev. 8–9 the seven trumpets of the seven angels bring successive judgments which aim at conversion (cf. 9:20-21). The series culminates with the proclamation of the divine mystery in 10:7 and the establishment of the dominion of God and Christ in 11:15ff.

b. A trumpet blast gathers the elect in Mt. 24:31.

c. The living are changed and the dead are raised at the sound of the last trumpet in 1 Cor. 15:52, i.e., the eschatological signal which sounds forth when Christ returns (1 Th. 4:16).

5. *As a Musical Instrument.* The trumpet is a musical instrument in the NT only in pagan Babylon, whose trumpeters are silenced with its fall in Rev. 18:22.

[G. Friedrich, VII, 71-88]

Samáreia [Samaria], *Samarítēs* [Samaritan], *Samarítis* [Samaritan woman]

A. The Samaritans in the NT Period.

1. *The Samaritan Religion.* After 27 B.C. Samaria denotes only the territory (which has its own senate) and not the city, which Herod renames *Sebasté*. During the Persian period this territory is detached from Jerusalem and sets up its own cultic center at Gerizim. The Samaritans see in Gerizim the chosen place of worship and accept only the Pentateuch as canonical. They do not believe in the resurrection and do not associate the Messiah with the Davidic house but expect only the prophet like Moses of Dt. 18:15ff. Simon Magus gains quite a following in Samaria in Acts 8:9-10.

2. *Jews and Samaritans.*

a. Up to A.D. 300. Relations fluctuate, being embittered when John Hyrcanus destroys the Gerizim temple and when Samaritans defile the Jerusalem temple, taking a milder turn in the second century A.D., but ending in a complete break in A.D. 300 when the Samaritans are classified as Gentiles.

b. In the Days of Jesus. The days of Jesus are a period of strained relations. The Jews do not accept the patriarchal descent of the Samaritans and question the validity of their worship. They thus exclude them from the cultus and restrict dealings with them, treating them in practice like Gentiles.

B. The Samaritans in the NT.

1. *Hostility between Jews and Samaritans.* The NT reflects the current animosity in Jn. 8:48; Lk. 9:54; 10:37; Jn. 4:9; Lk. 9:53.

2. *Jesus' Attitude.*

a. Jesus accepts the exclusion of Samaritans from the community (Mt. 10:5-6; Lk. 17:18).

b. Yet he rebukes his disciples for their hostility (Lk. 9:55), asks the Samaritan woman for a drink (Jn. 4:7), heals a Samaritan leper (Lk. 17:16), extols a Samaritan for neighborly love (10:30ff.) and gratitude to God (17:11ff.), and preaches to Samaritans (Jn. 4:40ff.). This is not just magnanimity on Jesus' part but proleptically announces the hour of fulfilment when the age of salvation comes and after a first proclamation to Israel a share in God's salvation is offered to the Gentiles too, from whom all uncleanness is taken away with the dawn of God's royal dominion.

3. The Samaritan Mission.

a. In Acts 1:8 the Lord sends out the disciples as witnesses to Samaria. Philip opens the Samaritan mission in 8:5. Perhaps the lasting results are not too strong, for Justin *Apology* 1.26.3 refers to the popularity of Simon's teaching in Samaria. Nevertheless the preaching to Samaria has great significance as the first step in the Gentile mission.

b. Jn. 4:4ff. shows that Jesus himself stands behind the Samaritan mission. It also points to the final goal when the strife about temples ends and religious separation yields to worship of the Father in spirit and in truth.   [J. Jeremias, VII, 88-94]

sandálion → *hóplon*

---

saprós [rotting, decaying],   *sḗpō* [to rot, decay]

---

1. Relating to the process of decay, *sḗpō* means "to cause to decay," or, in the passive, "to decay," "to rot," and figuratively "to perish." *saprós* means "rotting," either literally or figuratively, and the sense of "unpleasant" (even to the ears) is also possible. A person is *saprós* when old, and the same applies to food and drink, which may be better when *saprós* (e.g., ripe cheese). In general, what is *saprós* is "unserviceable" rather than "offensive," but the word may also mean "harmful" or "notorious" (someone's name).

2. In the LXX *sḗpō* means "to destroy" in Job 40:12 and "to rot" in 19:20. *saprós* does not occur in the LXX, Philo, or Josephus.

3. In Jms. 5:2 *sḗpō* has the extended sense "to decay." *saprós* in Eph. 4:29 means "unserviceable." The point in Mt. 13:47ff. is not that the fish are rotting but that they are no good for food. The same applies in Mt. 7:17ff.; 12:33; Lk. 6:43: the trees are useless, and by the same token one should see that false prophets are of no value to the community.

4. Hermas *Similitudes* 2.3-4 uses the terms for the decaying fruit of the vine, 1 Clem. 25.3 speaks of the rotting flesh of the phoenix, and Hermas *Similitudes* 9.6.4 refers to useless stones.   [O. Bauernfeind, VII, 94-97]

---

sárx [flesh, body],   *sarkikós* [fleshly, earthly],   *sárkinos* [fleshly, fleshy]

A. The Greek World.

1. sárx as the Muscular Part of the Body. In older usage *sárx* denotes the flesh of humans, animals, or fish. "Flesh" is often accompanied by "bones" and "blood." As muscle it protects the limbs or bones against cold or heat. The body consists of bones, sinews, flesh, and skin. At first the plural is more common even when *sárx* takes on the more general sense of "body." *sárx* can also mean "meat," but *kréas* is more common for this.

2. The Origin of sárx. sárx supposedly develops out of the four elements, or out of female seed, or perhaps flesh and bone are themselves elements. Plato thinks flesh arises out of blood, while Aristotle seeks its origin in moisture and theorizes that thick blood arises out of flesh.

3. sárx as Body. The use of *sárx* broadens out to include the whole body, especially the physical body, which may be young, aging, or dead. Thus the plural *sárkes* may on occasion signify a corpse.

4. Special Meanings. The inner part of the skin, as dried-up flesh, is also *sárx,* the flesh of fruits is *sárx,* and swellings are *sárkes.* The phrase *eis sárka pēmaínein* means "to hurt to the flesh, i.e., "to the quick."

5. sárkinos. This word has such meanings as "consisting of flesh," "corpulent," and "real" as distinct from imaginary. It can carry the nuance of "corruptible."

6. The Corruptible sárx. In Homer the flesh and bones decay at death but the *thýmos* and *psyché* persist. One must put off all flesh at death. The *noús* may also be the incorruptible part that escapes death. Reference is made to the "alien garb of flesh" or to pure beauty untainted by the flesh (Plato). Plutarch contrasts *sárx* and *psyché* (as well as *sṓma* and *psyché*) as the two elements in humanity, the former perishable and the latter imperishable.

7. sárx as the Seat of Emotions. Stimuli affect the *sárx,* e.g., heat or cold, fear or pity. For Epicurus the *sárx* is the seat of desire. Choices may be made, but in choices the soul heeds the summons of nature. The *sárx* is the seat of sorrow, too, but pleasure surpasses sorrow. True happiness, however, consists of more than the present well-being of the *sárx.*

8. The Influence of Epicurus. In its popularized version Epicureanism supposedly advocates the enthronement of bodily desires. Its opponents, who think that bodily cravings pollute the soul, regard it as a summons to the crudest forms of pleasure. Even Cicero calls the followers of Epicurus voluptuaries. The *sárx,* as the source of uncontrolled sensuality and immoderate gluttony, supposedly makes the freedom of the soul impossible. [E. SCHWEIZER, VII, 98-105]

B. The OT.

1. The most common original for *sárx* in Hebrew is *bāśār,* which may mean flesh in the strict sense (Lev. 13:2ff.) or in the extended sense of the body (Gen. 2:23), which may have collective force (Gen. 6:17; Num. 18:15), which may denote blood relationship (Gen. 2:23), which can be used euphemistically (Ex. 28:42), which may, figuratively, signify external life (Ps. 16:9), inner attitude (Ps. 63:1), or human frailty and impotence (Gen. 6:3), or which can have a metaphorical sense (e.g., Ezek. 11:19; Is. 17:4; cf. also Is. 10:18).

2. A second Hebrew term is *šeʾēr,* which also means flesh in the strict sense (Ex. 21:10), denotes blood relationships (Lev. 18:12-13), and has the transferred sense of our external existence (Prov. 5:11; Ps. 73:26).

3. LXX Translations.

a. For *bāśār* the LXX uses *sárx* 145 times, *kréas* 79, *sṓma* 23, and *chrṓs* 14, with a few other renderings such as *ánthrōpos* in Gen. 6:13. For *šeʾēr* the LXX has *oikeíos* seven times, *sárx* five, and *sṓma* four, and at times such translations as *tá déonta* (Ex. 21:10) or *trápeza* (Ps. 28:20). [F. BAUMGÄRTEL, VII, 105-08]

b. The LXX does not connect *sárx* with sensuality, relates it to circumcision, never uses it for the flesh of sacrifice, and distinguishes the spheres of spirit and flesh (Num. 16:22), although not equating this cosmic dualism with the ethical dualism of Creator and creature, as tends to be the case at times in Judaism.

4. Noncanonical Texts. Common features are the use of *pása sárx* for animals, humans, or both, the reference to the flesh of circumcision, the description of woman as the very flesh of man, and the use of *sárx* for the corruptible body. New points are the use of flesh and blood for human beings and the expression *sṓma sarkós* (cf. Sir. 14:18; 23:17). The *basileús sárkinos* is contrasted with the *basileús tṓn theṓn* in Esth. 4:17. The contrast between *sárx* and *pneúma* continues, and under Hellenistic influence there is a tendency to equate the *sárx* with sinful sexuality or passion. In Sir. 40:8 the *sárx* stamps humans as subject to frailty, sickness, etc., and in Sir. 28:5 the point is perhaps that if man, who is flesh, can restrain his anger, God may be expected to do so too. [E. Schweizer, VII, 108-10]

C. Judaism.
I. Qumran.
1. *General Concept.* The ordinances of the Qumran community are regarded as more efficacious than the flesh of sacrifices. Wicked priests suffer punishment in the flesh. Those smitten in the flesh, i.e., with bodily defects, are excluded from the community.

2. *Term for Person.* The whole person can be flesh, or soul and flesh. The flesh may also denote the true ego.

3. *Collective Use.* Those outside the community are a gathering of flesh (cf. sons of Adam). There are also references to "all flesh" for "all people."

4. *Corruptibility.* Flesh expresses human lowliness and corruptibility in distinction from the Creator. In this respect, i.e., before God, flesh and spirit are on the same level. Yet God's mighty acts are proclaimed to flesh.

5. *Sin.* In some references Qumran relates flesh closely to sin and pride. It evaluates flesh negatively. God has a controversy with flesh, judges it, and gives strength to war against it. God will also expunge evil from the inner part of the flesh of the elect, although here the spirit of evil and the Holy Spirit are opposed rather than flesh and spirit. The elect, however, are exalted above flesh. They belong to the fellowship of the flesh of iniquity, and they may stumble through the sinfulness of the flesh, whose spirit cannot understand the divine mysteries. Yet God pardons them, and does not plant carnal striving in them, or abandon them to the striving of the flesh.

6. *Flesh and Spirit.* Flesh is sometimes neutral, but it also denotes human creatureliness. This is bound up with sinfulness and ignorance, but it does not itself stand in contrast to spirit; instead it is the battleground of conflict between the spirit of evil and the Holy Spirit. Hence flesh does not belong in principle to the ungodly sphere, nor is it the prison of the soul.

II. The Targums.
These works use flesh in much the same way as Qumran. Neutrally the term means "living creatures." It carries a stress on human mortality and creaturely distance from God. It may simply mean humanity but it may also denote sinful and arrogant humanity. It does not seem to be distinguished dualistically from spirit.

III. Talmud and Midrash.
1. Here again flesh denotes human existence either collectively or individually.

2. Whereas the older use of flesh and blood for humanity continues, the term *gup* now comes into use for body or person.

3. This term, which has the basic sense of "hollow" or "cavity," suggests a body that needs to be filled by a soul. Although the concept of unity is unbroken, the emphasis of body now rests on its physical and corruptible side. By nature, then, it differs from the soul—the body deriving from earth and the soul from heaven, the body inclining to sin, the soul to obedience. Yet the expectation of a reuniting of body

and soul, whether for salvation or perdition, keeps popular dualism in check. The soul, when put to test in the body, may start back from it in view of its corruptibility, but it will have to give an account in concert with it at the last judgment.

[R. MEYER, VII, 110-19]

IV. Apocrypha and Pseudepigrapha.

1. LXX usage for the human body, the phrase "all flesh," the connection with circumcision, etc. all continue.

2. The dualism of God and humanity is increasingly linked with that of the world of spirits and that of flesh. Human limitation does not always rest on corporeality, for the angels, too, are sinful, but when angelic sin involves contact with human flesh dualism is evident (cf. Eth. En. 84:4ff.; 15:4ff.). Cf. also the setting aside of flesh at death (102:5, 13-14).

3. Jubilees and later works distinguish the realm of spirit from that of carnal beings. Pure spirits have no bodies. Carnal beings cannot see what spiritual beings see. One can see God only in the spirit.

4. The thought of the resurrection of the body restrains anthropological dualism, but the idea of a spiritual flesh helps to promote the distinction of the spirit or soul from the flesh that encloses it and that is put off at death.

5. At times flesh is linked to sin, and asceticism seeks to curb the body, e.g., vegetarianism or total abstinence from wine, luxury, or sex. Being made of flesh and blood, however, may still be equated with humanity as such, and sin and ignorance traced to seduction by evil spirits.

V. Philo and Josephus.

1. Philo is pulled two ways. In general he takes a negative view of *sárx* as the seat of passion etc., but although he associates the inclination to sin with the *sárx*, he sees that illogical passions are in the soul too, and the right thing is to make responsible choice, not blaming sin on one's carnal side. God, of course, is noncorporeal, and may thus be known only by those who set aside the husk of flesh, which is for the soul a burden or coffin or corpse, and acts as a drag on its spiritual flight to God. The antithesis becomes ethically significant when the soul is content to remain in the flesh and refuses to make the upward flight.

2. In Josephus *sárkes* means animal or human flesh. The *sárx* is vulnerable, and the *psychē* leaves it at death, achieving an unencumbered state.

D. Historical Summary.

1. In Greek thought the concern is the anthropological one of the relation between the different component parts of humanity. Humanity is understood in terms of its nature, i.e., the parts and their conflict, controlling center, distinction, and interrelationship.

2. In the OT the concern is the theological one of the relation of humanity to God. Humanity is understood in terms of its creatureliness, its response to God. The only dualism is that of Creator and creature or obedience and disobedience.

3. In Hellenism humanity belongs to the earthly sphere by destiny rather than by decision, is tied to it during earthly life, and seeks to rise above it through ecstasy and secret formulas.

E. The NT.

1. Synoptic Gospels and Acts.

1. Synoptics. In its use of *sárx* the NT stands under OT influence. Except in OT quotations in Mk. 10:8 and Lk. 3:6, however, the term occurs only three times in

Matthew, Mark, and Luke. In Mt. 16:17 "flesh and blood" denotes humanity in its inability to know God; God is the opposite. In Mk. 14:38 the dualism is only apparent, for the prayer is that *God* will make good the weakness of the flesh. In Lk. 24:39 "flesh and bones" indicates the reality of Christ's resurrection.

2. *Acts.* Apart from the quotations in 2:17, 26 the only instance is in 2:31, which refers to the incorruptibility of the *sárx* of Jesus, but avoids dualism by not repeating the *psyché* of v. 17, using "he" instead.

II. Paul.

1. *sárx as Body.* Though Paul never uses "flesh and bones," he uses *sárx* in the ordinary sense in, e.g., 2 Cor. 12:7 (the thorn in the "flesh"). In 1 Cor. 15:39 *sárx* is the whole physical existence (cf. Gal. 4:13), although in Rom. 6:19 weakness of perception is the point, and in 2 Cor. 7:5 *sárx* embraces inner anxieties as well. The phrase "body and spirit" in 2 Cor. 7:1 is not distinguishing a better and worse part, for both must be cleansed. The "mortal flesh" in 2 Cor. 4:11 is Paul's earthly existence, whose very weakness means life for the churches and thus manifests Christ's risen power. Earthly life is also meant in 2 Cor. 10:3; Gal. 2:20; Phil. 1:22, 24. In it we may die to the law and live for God in faith.

2. *sárx as the Earthly Sphere.* In Rom. 1:3-4 Paul contrasts the sphere of *sárx* with that of heaven or *pneúma*. In this limited and provisional sphere Jesus is the Davidic Messiah, but the decisive thing comes in the sphere of the *pneúma*. In Rom. 9:3 *sárx* denotes an earthly relationship (cf. 4:1; 9:5, 8); this relationship is not evil but is also not decisive. The genitive in 9:8 indicates sphere rather than origin. In 1 Cor. 1:26 wisdom according to the flesh means wisdom according to the categories of this world. There may be wise of this kind in the church, but not many. In Phlm. 16 *sárx* and *kýrios* are linked; Onesimus has a social relationship as well as the more decisive Christian relationship to Philemon. The present aeon or cosmos may be equivalent to *sárx* (cf. 1 Cor. 2:6), but the real antithesis is between God and humanity. God's wisdom is contrasted with that of the *sárx* and God's power with the weapons of the *sárx* (1 Cor. 1:24ff.; 2 Cor. 10:4). Again, God's promise is the opposite of *sárx* (Rom. 9:8). In Christ the divine sphere has invaded the human.

3. *"Flesh and Blood" and "All Flesh."*

a. In Gal. 1:16 "flesh and blood" means humanity but with God as the opposite (cf. Mt. 16:17). The point of the phrase in 1 Cor. 15:50 is not to differentiate a part of us that cannot inherit the kingdom from a part that can, but to show that humanity as a whole cannot inherit the kingdom without transformation. There is perhaps a hint here of human vulnerability to temptation as well as corruption.

b. The phrase "all flesh" occurs in Rom. 3:20; Gal. 2:16; 1 Cor. 1:29 in contexts in which the point is that all humanity stands under divine judgment.

4. *Trust in the sárx.* In Rom. 2:28 Paul contrasts circumcision of the bodily member with that of the heart. But *sárx* takes on a negative aspect because people can see it and boast about it (vv. 23, 27, 29). Gal. 6:12-13 makes a similar point, although in v. 12 the flesh might simply mean the earthly sphere. In Phil. 3:3-4 *sárx* denotes national descent, legal observance, etc. It is not wrong in itself, but only when confidence is put in it instead of in Christ, whose righteousness makes all else loss.

5. *katá sárka with Verb.* In 2 Cor. 10:2-3 earthly life is the meaning; this is wrong only when wrongly oriented to the *sárx* as a norm, which leads to boasting about earthly things (11:18) (cf. the worldly planning of 1:17). In 2 Cor. 5:16 Paul is rejecting judgment from a human standpoint; thus to judge Christ simply as one historical figure among others, as he used to do, is to miss the real point. In Gal. 4:23, 29 birth

katá sárka is birth according to human possibilities in contrast to the promise. This birth has a long-range impact inasmuch as it means walking *katá sárka* (Rom. 8:4) and not according to the Spirit. A basic orientation of all life is obviously at issue.

6. *sárx as the Subject of Sin.* The *sárx* does not work as the Spirit does (Phil. 3:3; Rom. 8:13-14; Gal. 4:23; 5:18). It is the subject of an action only in the shadow of the work of the Spirit. The spheres are not controlling forces as in dualism. Building on the *sárx* or trusting in it is sinful. Yet the *sárx* as norm becomes the *sárx* as power, and there are thus works of the *sárx* (Gal. 5:16, 19; Rom. 13:14). Legal observance, however, is itself a manifestation of the *sárx* (Gal. 3:3; 4:8ff.). Everything human and earthly is *sárx,* and as people trust in *sárx* in this sense, it becomes a power that opposes the working of the Spirit (Gal. 5:13, 17). Subjection to *sárx* is not fate but guilt. A life oriented to it serves it and carries out its thinking. The opposite of the *sárx* is God, who in the form of the Son comes in the likeness of sinful flesh, i.e., in full humanity, and condemns sin in the flesh. Rom. 7:18, 25 might seem to suggest cleavage into *sárx* and *noús,* but the depiction is that of the pre-Christian life in which what is contrasts sharply with what ought to be. Sincere people might wish to serve God but even in so doing they fall into the sin of establishing their own righteousness. Right desires become carnal action, so that only in retrospect can one differentiate the will which opposes the *sárx* but precisely in so doing makes its work responsible and guilty.

7. *Vanquished sárx.* Believers have crucified the *sárx* (Rom. 7:5; 8:8-9; Gal. 5:24). They do not escape corporeality by asceticism etc. (cf. Gal. 2:19-20). They enter a life that in Christ is determined by the relation to God (2:20). Works of the flesh are illogical and call for recommitment. Life is not split up into single acts. It is one *érgon* under one determination, *sárx* or *pneúma.* Believers are no longer building on the *sárx* but on Christ. This is what they are to achieve in the daily practice of the life of faith.

8. *Summary.*

a. Humanity is qualified by the relation to God.

b. Salvation does not lie in a retreat from the physical to the spiritual.

c. Flesh is not a separate and intrinsically bad sphere but becomes bad only with orientation to it either in licentiousness or legalism.

d. The flesh as a wrong disposition away from God seems to become a controlling power.

e. Salvation through Christ means liberation from earthly goals in a life that is lived by God's gift.

III. Colossians, Ephesians, Pastorals.

1. *Colossians.* *sárx* is the external sphere in 2:1, that of human relations in 3:22, and that of physical existence in 1:24. In 2:23 *sárx* denotes those who measure by their own standards and not God's. In 2:13 the Gentiles are in view; their sin comes out in licentiousness (3:5). In 1:22 the body of flesh is Christ's crucified body, but in 2:11 (cf. 2:18) it denotes the body that is to be put off in the circumcision of Christ.

2. *Ephesians.* In 5:31 the wife is a man's own flesh in a union that reflects that of Christ and the church. 2:14 refers to Christ's crucified body. 2:11 shows that the distinction between Jew and Gentile is a provisional one in the earthly sphere. In 2:3 (cf. 2:2) *sárx* has a demonic character. The division into *sárx* and *diánoiai* is surprising, but the latter, too, are corrupt.

3. *Pastorals.* 1 Tim. 3:16 says that Christ's appearing in the earthly sphere is already a mighty saving act.

IV. John.

1. The Gospel. sárx seldom occurs in this work. *pása sárx* in 17:2 is traditional. In 8:15 judgment according to the flesh is blind and ignorant. In 7:27 assessment of Jesus by his known descent yields no adequate understanding. In 3:6 everything human is sárx. sárx is the earthly sphere in which there is no knowledge of God and nothing to save from lostness. Only through unbelief, however, and not through sárx does the world become sinful. In 1:13 sárx is the principle of natural birth and characterizes humanity apart from God. In 1:14 the Logos does not take on sin, nor simply enter the earthly sphere, but takes human form so as to manifest the Father's glory in mighty acts and obedience even to the cross. Only this witness of full commitment, not mere impartation of knowledge, gives rise to faith. In 6:63 the antithesis could be that of 3:6, but, in the light of vv. 51-58, it is more likely that of 8:15. To consider the external appearance of Jesus does not help, for only his preaching is *pneúma* or *zōḗ*. In the eucharist the sárx is not the medicine of immortality. Faith, as it eats the sárx of Jesus, sees that he is the Son who has come in the sárx for the world's salvation, accepts this, and lives by it.

2. The Epistles. In 1 Jn. 4:2 and 2 Jn. 7 the coming in the flesh serves to distinguish true faith from false; the former accepts the humanity as well as the deity. In 1 Jn. 2:16 the warning not to trust in the world becomes a stronger warning against love of it, and the world includes carnal desire, the reference apparently being to sense impressions that stimulate desire.

V. Hebrews. In 5:7 (cf. 2:14) Jesus' earthly existence is denoted, i.e., the whole of his human nature. In 12:9 God as the Lord of the upper world is contrasted with earthly ancestors. The reference in 9:10 (cf. 9:13) is to cultic purity; this symbolizes the earthly sphere and stands in contrast to the inner purity of the heavenly priest. In 10:20 the sárx might be the crucifixion, or Christ's human nature, or the place where the heavenly and earthly spheres meet, but the most likely meaning is that the way to heaven leads believers by Christ's sárx in such a manner that through it they go to the heavenly high priest. Hebrews never links sin to the sárx; the sárx is the provisional earthly sphere under threat of death.

VI. Catholic Epistles.

1. Jms. 5:3 (plural) refers to the consuming of human flesh.

2. 1 Peter follows traditional lines (cf. *pása sárx* in 1:24; 3:18). In 4:1 "in the flesh" echoes 3:18 and signifies the transition from living by the passions to living by God's will. In 3:21 sárx as the external aspect is contrasted with the conscience as in Hebrews.

3. In Jude 7 sárx is "corporeality," the object of a sexual desire that is wicked only in perversion (cf. 2 Pet. 2:10; also v. 18, which has "passions of the flesh" where Jude 16 simply has "passions"). In Jude 6 and 23 sárx seems to be human existence as polluted by sin.

VII. sárkinos, sarkikós. Used of the tables of the heart in 2 Cor. 3:3, this term refers to the inner being in distinction from external legal fulfilment. In Heb. 6:16, however, it denotes the earthly sphere. In 1 Cor. 3:1ff. the readers show by their conduct that they are still of the flesh. In Rom. 7:14 Paul uses the term to describe his pre-Christian state. *sarkikós* in Rom. 15:27 and 1 Cor. 9:11 denotes external things in a neutral sense. It is parallel to *sárkinos* in 1 Cor. 3:1ff., and in 2 Cor. 10:4 it denotes carnal power as distinct from divine. 1 Pet. 2:11 postulates conflict between the soul and the passions of the flesh.

F. The Post–New Testament Period.

1. Apostolic Fathers. While OT influence persists, e.g., in the use of "flesh and blood," or of *sárx* for human life or the earthly life of Jesus, a Hellenistic hierarchy of flesh and soul (or spirit) emerges. This does not necessarily have a dualistic sense, for both are stained, Jesus comes in the flesh, and the flesh has a share in the resurrection. Thus salvation is not the overcoming of the flesh by the spirit but the union of the two. There is in some works a tendency to associate desires more strongly with the flesh, and also a certain ascetic thrust, yet there is no flight from the flesh, which is to be kept like a temple, which becomes immortal through union with the Holy Spirit, and which will finally be raised again.

2. Apocryphal Acts. In these works *sárx* may denote earthly life, but suspicion of the flesh is strong in some cases, e.g., Acts of Thomas.

3. Apologists. *sárx* is in these works an important term for the incarnation. It may also denote external circumcision. Flesh and blood are the principle of natural generation, faith and spirit of divine generation. The idea of the resurrection of the flesh is present. Sexual intercourse is a union of *sárx* and *sárx* in Athenagoras, who also thinks that to serve flesh and blood is to serve earthly desires, and who regards fallen angels as subject to the *sárx* (*Supplication* 24.5; 31.2; 33.2). The resurrection of the flesh forms a bulwark against Hellenistic dualism.

4. Gnosticism. The Gnostics find only a likeness of flesh in the incarnation, although the Gospel of Thomas accepts a full appearance in the flesh. In humans *sárx* is the evil principle, but it plays no great part in early systems and may at times be neutral. Jesus has the true flesh of which ours is a copy, and along these lines there may be resurrection of the flesh. The divine soul is concealed in the flesh for Valentinians, and some works find in redemption a release from the flesh. For the Naassenes the perfect *ánthrōpos* is not *sarkikós* but *pneumatikós,* and among the Manichees the carnal body gives birth to demons and is the root of all evil. In general, however, the negative evaluation of the flesh is not total, and while two-sphere thinking in substantial categories exerts an influence, we do not have a total antithesis to the NT.

[E. SCHWEIZER, VII, 119-51]

---

satanás [Satan]

A. Qumran and Later Jewish Satanology.

1. Qumran. In one place the Scrolls oppose the prince of light to the angel of darkness. Since elsewhere the Scrolls assert God's absolute sovereignty, this cannot imply dualism. The angel of darkness is the same as Belial elsewhere, whom God has created, with whom he is in conflict, who oppresses the righteous, and who will finally be judged. The term *stn* occurs in the Scrolls only three times in obscure connections.

2. Later Judaism. In Jubilees, Ethiopian Enoch, and rabbinic works the devil is still the accuser. The rabbis suggest that the devil is a fallen angel, although Qumran finds no place for this view. The pseudepigrapha play with the story of Gen. 6:1ff. The Testaments of the Twelve Patriarchs poses a choice between the law of God and the work of Belial. Thus free decision replaces the stronger view of election held at Qumran, and this tends to crowd out the figure of Satan. A conviction common to all Judaism is that evil will finally be destroyed.

B. The NT.

1. The Accuser and His Fall. Satan in Lk. 22:31 has a role similar to that found in Job, but Jesus now opposes him with his intercession. In Rev. 12:7ff. Michael fights with Satan. The definitive fall of Satan takes place with the coming of Jesus (cf. Lk. 10:18). This terminates Satan's work of accusation and breaks his power to harm where the power of Jesus is at work. Jn. 12:31 agrees that the ruler of this world is already cast out (or judged, according to 16:11). In general, the NT does not refer to a primal fall of Satan. Thus Jn. 8:44 speaks of lying *from* (rather than *in*) the beginning (cf. 1 Jn. 3:8). Rev. 12:9 equates Satan with the serpent, but the NT does not relate Satan to the angel of death or the evil impulse.

2. Satan Sayings in the Synoptists. Mark and the special Lucan material use *ho satanás*. Elsewhere we find *ho peirázōn, sataná, ho diábolos, ho echthrós,* and *ho ponērós*. At the temptation Jesus gains a decisive victory over Satan's attempt to stop the coming of the kingdom of God. In Mt. 8:33 *sataná* might simply mean "opponent," but the point is that Peter is playing the same role as that played by Satan at the temptation. In Lk. 22:3 Satan enters Judas, but beyond that Satan has little part in the passion except inasmuch as the passion works out the victory at the temptation. In Mk. 3:22ff. the kingdom of evil forms a unit under the headship of Satan, and the possessed are liberated from subjection to this kingdom. In Lk. 13:16 Satan is also behind the woman's sickness (cf. Acts 10:38). Jesus, however, is stronger than the strong man and he binds him by his victory at the temptation, in which the cross and resurrection are already germinally present. In Mt. 13:19 the evil one snatches away the seed that falls along the path, and in Mt. 13:28 an enemy sows weeds among the wheat, so that children of the devil are present in the church (13:38-39), and the need for discipline arises (18:15ff.). No explanation of the origin of Satan is present in the Synoptists but they portray a single force that seeks human destruction and that is broken, although not yet completely eliminated, by the work of Jesus.

3. Satan Sayings in the Epistles. The older epistles usually have *ho satanás ho peirázōn,* or *ho ponērós.* Later epistles also use *ho diábolos,* and Revelation has *ho satanás* and *ho diábolos,* as well as *ho katḗgōr, ho óphis,* and *ho drákōn.* The devil attacks the community by means of persecutions (Rev. 2:10; 1 Pet. 5:8) and especially temptations (1 Th. 1ff.; 1 Cor. 7:5; 2 Cor. 2:11; Eph. 6:11; 1 Tim. 3:7; 2 Tim. 2:26). He may take the form of an angel of light in, e.g., libertinistic ideas (2 Cor. 11:14; cf. Rom. 16:20). Christ's blood, faith, and avoidance are the main defenses against his seduction (Rev. 12:11; Eph. 6:16; 1 Cor. 7:5). Satan may also block journeys (1 Th. 2:18) or cause sickness (Phil. 2:25ff.). In 1 Cor. 5:5, however, his destructive work can be put to saving use (cf. 2 Cor. 12:7). Outside the church his sway continues, so that an apostle's task is to enable people to turn from his power to God (Acts 26:18). At the end he will presumably be destroyed with every rule and authority (1 Cor. 15:24ff.).

4. The Prince of This World in John. John uses *ho diábolos, ho satanás, ho ponērós,* and *ho árchōn toú kósmou* as terms for the devil. The devil determines one's whole being (Jn. 8:44). Indeed, Judas can be called a devil (6:70; cf. Mk. 8:33; Lk. 22:3). 8:44 calls the devil a murderer, a liar, and the father of lies. This verse ignores theories as to Satan's origin. Believers are of God, sinners of the devil (1 Jn. 3:8, 12). The indicative contains an imperative (cf. 5:18), but victory is possible (2:13-14) only in virtue of Christ's intercession (Jn. 17:15).   [W. FOERSTER, VII, 151-63]

C. The Apostolic Fathers.

1. Terms. Various terms are used in these works, e.g., *diábolos, árchōn* (qualified in different ways), *energón, ponērós, antízēlos, báskanos,* and *ánomos.*

2. General Material. The center of concern is salvation. Satan's power has been broken by the event of salvation. Yet he still opposes Christians.

3. The Church. In its unity the church defies Satan (Ignatius *Ephesians* 13.1), but his work may be seen in the breaking of unity (*Trallians* 8.1). External hostility is discerned in Mart. Pol. 17.1.

4. The Martyr. Martyrs wrestle with Satan (Mart. Pol. 3.1). The devil uses the torments of martyrdom to try to break their will and win them over (Ignatius *Romans* 7.1).

5. Individual Christians. Living in the devil's world, Christians must be on guard (Barn. 18.1-2). Satan is the tempter (1 Clem. 51.1). In Hermas he may deceitfully speak truth through false prophets (*Mandates* 11.3), but the main point is that Christians choose between good and evil. Satan achieves power, therefore, in those who lack moral resolution or fail to use the chance given by the angel of repentance (*Mandates* 7.1ff.; 12.4ff.). [K. SCHÄFERDIEK, VII, 163-65]

→ *daímōn, diábolos, echthrós, katégoros, óphis, peíra, ponērós*

---

sbénnymi [to quench]

A. The Greek World.

1. Literal Use.

a. This word means "to quench," passive "to go out"; b. "to suck dry" ("dry up"); c. "to die"; d. "to steam"; and e. in a transferred sense "to still," "damp down," "restrain," or intransitively "to rest," "abate," "die down."

2. Transferred Use. With various references to emotions, influence, strength, attraction, etc. the term means "to calm," "to suppress," or, passively, "to die out," "fade," "wane," "disappear."

B. Hellenistic Judaism.

1. In the LXX (some 45 times) the term is used literally for the quenching of fire or burning objects, figuratively for light or lamps going out, and in a transferred sense for the extinguishing of anger or stilling of emotions.

2. Philo and Josephus use the word similarly.

C. The NT.

1. Literal Use. Mk. 9:48 depicts eternal judgment under the figure of unquenchable fire. In Mt. 25:8 the foolish virgins find that their lamps are going out. Heb. 11:34 alludes to the protection of the three men in Dan. 3:23ff.

2. Figurative Use. Mt. 12:18ff. refers to Jesus the saying of Is. 42:1ff. about not quenching the smoldering wick. In Eph. 6:16 the shield of faith quenches the flaming darts of the evil one; they go out after striking the shield and falling to the ground.

3. Transferred Use. In 1 Th. 5:19 the admonition not to quench the Spirit has reference to the restraint of his manifestations in charisms (cf. v. 20), not to his suppression by impurity or sloth. In the context of a short church order the warning probably does not relate to any particular problem at Thessalonica.

D. Apostolic Fathers. In these works the term occurs only in biblical quotations or echoes. [F. LANG, VII, 165-68]

---

sébomai [reverence, worship], *sebázomai* [to worship], *sébasma* [object of worship], *Sebastós* [His Majesty], *eusebḗs* [pious], *eusébeia* [piety], *eusebéō* [to be pious], *asebḗs* [impious], *asébeia* [impiety], *asebéō* [to get impiously], *semnós* [worthy of respect], *semnótēs* [reverence]

---

sébomai.

A. The Greek World.
1. Homeric Usage. In tune with the sense of the stem ("to fall back before"), Homer first uses this term for "to shrink from." The idea of shrinking from the gods leads to the sense of awe or reverence, first in the general form of respect, then in the more specifically religious form of veneration.

2. Classical and Hellenistic Usage. The meaning "to shrink from" still occurs, but respect is commonly the sense, e.g., for beauty or majesty, for country, parents, the dead, heroes, or benefactors, and, of course, the gods. Relative to the gods, the term takes an active turn and comes to be used not for mere reverence but for worship as a cultic act.

B. The LXX, Pseudepigrapha, Josephus, and Philo.
1. In the few instances in the LXX (cf. Josh. 4:24; Job 1:9; Jon. 1:9), often with no Hebrew original, *sébomai* may be rendered "to fear," but "to serve" is in some cases the best translation (as in Job 1:9).

2. The word is rare in the pseudepigrapha, *phobeísthai* being more common. When used, it expresses worship of the one true God in contrast to false gods.

3. Josephus uses the term for worship either of God or idols, and with an echo of the more general meaning "reverence." The same applies in Philo.

C. The NT.
Mk. 7:7 uses the term when quoting Is. 29:13. It occurs in the accusation of Paul before Gallio in Acts 18:13, and also for the worship of Artemis in 19:27. Six times in Acts the *sebómenoi* are God-fearers (equivalent to *phoboúmenoi,* which would have sounded odd to the Greeks). The term denotes worship of the one true God and indicates that the Gentiles thus styled do not merely honor God but actively worship him.

sebázomai.

1. This word, used for tenses of *sébomai* other than the present, undergoes the same development as *sébomai.*

2. It does not occur in the LXX but means "to worship" in, e.g., Sib. 5.405.

3. In the one NT instance in Rom. 1:25 the parallel *latreúein* shows that it bears the sense of active worship.

sébasma.

1. This term is used for an object of worship, e.g., an idol.

2. In Acts 17:23 it denotes objects of worship, including the altar as that toward which one worships. In 2 Th. 2:4 the reference is again a general one: The man of

lawlessness exalts himself above all that is called God and every object of worship. This might include not only sacred objects but the orders of family, state, and law that are thought to stand under divine protection.

Sebastós.

1. This word, conferred on the emperor as a title in 27 B.C. (Lat.: Augustus), carries the sense of "sacred" or "holy."

2. As a general term the rare Gk. *sebastós* denotes anything to which religious reverence is paid. Used of the emperor, it denotes majesty, but it plays a special role when dead and later living emperors are the objects of worship.

3. In the NT only Festus uses it in Acts 25:21, 25, where it has an official ring. In Acts 27:1 *speíra Sebasté* is a term used elsewhere for auxiliary troops.

eusebḗs, eusébeia, eusebéō.

A. The Greek World.

1. Although these words have a general reference, they usually relate to the gods, as more precise definitions show, and they carry the sense of "piety."

2. In addition to the gods, relatives, rulers, judges, oaths, the law, and the good may all be objects; enjoying divine protection, they must be respected and upheld.

3. Whereas Plato finds piety in serving the gods by doing good, the popular view equates it with cultic worship, although often with some sense of the need for knowledge and an inner attitude of devotion.

4. In the Hellenistic period the main sense is worship, but the term still denotes respect for, e.g., relatives, spouses, or emperors. Philosophers locate true piety in living according to the will of the gods. For Plutarch true piety, as distinct from superstition, expects what is good from the gods. Worship means reverence for what is great and lofty, which is to be equated with the divine. Piety, then, is a virtue, not an unconditional personal commitment, but as awe at the pure and exalted world of divinity, as cultic worship, and as respect for the orders.

B. Judaism.

1. *eusebeín* does not occur in the LXX and is rare in other works. *eusébeia* is found in Is. 11:2; 33:6; Prov. 1:7; Sir. 49:3, and is common in 4 Maccabees. *eusebḗs* occurs eight times in the LXX.

2. In the Epistle of Aristeas *eusébeia* is connected with *dikaiosýnē* and denotes both Gentile respect for the OT God and respectful conduct toward others. It does not relate to the law, but it is a predominant theme in 4 Maccabees, which finds *eusébeia* in worshipping God and serving him by keeping the law.

3. Josephus displays a general usage but also equates *eusébeia* with keeping the law, a main part of which, of course, consists of faith and worship. If Josephus differs from the Greeks by making virtue a part of piety (instead of the reverse), he also regards piety as the cardinal virtue. He avoids speaking of the *phóbos theoú* (the fear of God).

4. In Philo, who uses the group some 200 times, the religious content is dominant. Relative to rulers or parents, the meaning is "to respect," but for the most part *eusébeia* denotes the relation to God. Legal observance is a matter of *eusébeia* but it embraces a true view of God and a turning from the sensory world to the spiritual world of true being. Greek influence emerges in his concept of *eusébeia* as the mean between superstition on the one side and impiety (*asébeia*) on the other.

C. The NT.

1. Except in the Pastorals and 2 Peter, the *euseb-* group never refers in the NT to Christian faith and life. In Acts 3:12 Peter claims no *eusébeia,* Cornelius and his soldier are called *eusebēs* in Acts 10:2, 7, and Paul uses the verb for the worship of the Athenians in Acts 17:23. In this regard the NT follows the OT, sensing that *eusébeia* relates to divinity rather than to God and that it implies a moralistic view of conduct. On such grounds Paul speaks of faith and love rather than piety.

2. In the Pastorals the group denotes a manner of life. Thus the adverbs in Tit. 2:12 refer to conduct relative to self, others, and God. In 1 Tim. 4:7 exercise in *eusébeia* holds out a lasting promise. 1 Tim. 6:11 carries an exhortation to pursue it, but its omission in 2 Tim. 2:22 shows that it is not indispensable like faith or love. Over against the way of life associated with false teaching, *eusébeia* is the godliness that accords with sound teaching (1 Tim. 6:3; Tit. 1:1). False teachers have a form of it but it does not shape their lives, and they use it for gain (2 Tim. 3:5; 1 Tim. 6:5-6), thus missing the gain of true godliness. Christian *eusébeia* is not moralistic, for it is rooted in the Christ event (1 Tim. 3:16). It is not just outward worship, nor a mere concept of God, nor a virtue, nor an ideal. Over against a Gnosticizing asceticism that regards creation as bad and dissolves its orders, true *eusébeia,* born of faith, covers everyday conduct in honoring God as Creator and Redeemer, even though it may expect persecution from the very orders of God which it respects. The term *eusébeia* plays a role here probably because the author hopes that a manner of life that exhibits *eusébeia* will elicit a favorable verdict from non-Christians who set store by it. In this sense it is profitable for this world as well as the next (1 Tim. 4:8). Respect for the orders, however, is now grounded in the will of the Creator who is also Savior (4:10).

3. In 2 Pet. 1:6-7 self-control leads to steadfast waiting for the promises, and this to godliness, and this in turn to brotherly affection and love. In 2:7ff. *eusébeia* is the opposite of an ungodly walk. The plural in 3:11 covers the sum of godly actions. Similarly the singular in 1:3 has the general sense of a godly life, i.e., one that is morally good.

D. The Apostolic Fathers.

1. In 1 Clement *eusébeia* and *eusebēs* (1.3; 11.1; 15.1) describe the life that is lived with an eye on God and which includes trust in him.

2. In 2 Clement there is a tendency to use *eusébeia* as a general term for "piety" or "religion" from the Christian standpoint.

3. The term *theosébeia* (cf. 1 Tim. 2:10) and derivatives incline in the same direction (cf. especially Diog. 1.1; 3.1ff.; 4.5-6; 6.4).

asebēs, asébeia, asebéō.

A. The Greek World.

1. The development of this negative group parallels that of the positive *euseb-* group. Thus the first meaning is the more general one of contempt for established orders.

2. A usage may then be observed that restricts the group to the gods or to the divine sphere. Refusal to worship the city gods, or to fulfil cultic duties, is *asébeia.* Philosophers who reject popular deities are guilty of it in the mind of the people. For Plato *asébeia* embraces unworthy ideas of deity, and for Epictetus the refusal to honor divine gifts or to accept one's divinely ordained lot is *asébeia.*

3. With the decline of the city-state and its official worship, philosophers distinguish between *atheótēs* (denial of the official gods) and *asébeia* (transgression of the ordinances). This distinction is an important one for Christians. Denying the official gods, they rank as *átheoi*, but they need not rank as *asebeís*. For this reason the Pastorals and 1 Peter admonish them to show *eusébeia* by their conduct, and in this way to refute the pagan charge that they are wrongdoers (1 Pet. 2:12).

B. Greek Judaism.

1. The LXX makes common use of the group, especially *asebḗs*. It always denotes action and not just attitude, nor is it restricted to the cultic sphere. Objective fact rather than subjective disposition is at issue (Am. 1:2). All deeds that transgress the law are *asébeiai*. The opposite of *asebḗs* in Proverbs is *díkaios*; a life is either contrary to God and the law or oriented to them. The LXX can make much freer use of the negative *aseb-* group than the *euseb-* group because, whereas the latter is too weak to denote the proper fear of God, the former serves excellently to express the contempt for God and his will that marks the wicked.

2. The group is rare in the pseudepigrapha.

3. Josephus uses the terms fairly often, usually with God as object, and at times with a distinction between *asébeia* and *adikía*.

4. Philo connects denial of God's existence (*atheótēs*) with *asébeia*. He associates *asébeia* with the desire that is the root of all evil. By opposing the *asebḗs* to the *díkaios*, he seems not to distinguish *asébeia* from *adikía*.

C. The NT.

1. The group does not occur in the Synoptic Gospels or Johannine writings, nor in James or Hebrews. There are four instances in Romans. In 1:18 Paul perhaps has offenses against the first and second tables of the law in view, although one should note that the common "all" connects *asébeia* and *adikía*, that the rabbis do not usually distinguish the two tables, and that the *díkē* against which there is offense (*adikía*) is God's righteousness. In Rom. 4:5 the ungodly might be the "irreverent" but are more likely "transgressors." This is clearly the point in 5:6. Rom. 11:26 is a quotation from Is. 59:20.

2. In the Pastorals, 1 Tim. 1:9 materially combines *asebḗs* and *hamartōlós*. The moral and religious consequences of teachings are the point in 2 Tim. 2:16; and in Tit. 2:12, although "irreligion" is probable as the opposite of *eusébeia*, willful transgression of the orders might also be included.

3. In 1 Pet. 4:18 (quoting Prov. 11:31) we find the common combination with *hamartōlós*. In Jude and 2 Peter great sinners of the past are called ungodly (2 Pet. 2:5-6), and false teachers are *asebeís* on account of their lives (and teaching?) (Jude 4, 18; 2 Pet. 2:6; 3:7).

semnós, semnótēs.

A. The Greek World.

1. As an attribute of the gods or divine things, *semnós* means "lofty."

2. Used of objects, it means "majestic," "splendid," "magnificent," and of music, poetry, oratory, etc. "sublime" (although also "proud").

3. *semnós* may denote the inner majesty of things, e.g., the number seven, human position, or deportment. *semnós* is that which evokes *sébesthai* in others. It thus embraces what is majestic or splendid, but only if signs of a higher order may be

detected in it, and if it has an appropriate solemnity or seriousness (although not necessarily severity).

B. The LXX and Judaism.

1. *semnós* and *semnótēs* occur only eleven times in Proverbs and 2 and 4 Maccabees. In Prov. 6:8 and 8:6 the sense is probably "holy" or "sacred" (cf. 2 Maccabees). In 4 Maccabees the term expresses a favorable judgment on martyrs and the law, i.e., "worthy (of God)."

2. In the Epistle of Aristeas we find a use for the law but also a more general sense.

3. The use in Josephus and Philo parallels that in Greek authors. It may be noted, however, that Philo applies the group to God and the law and also to the suprasensory world, but as a human evaluation.

C. The NT.

1. In Phil. 4:8 *semnós* relates to human conduct. Paul, with an eye to outsiders, urges his readers to ponder and practice what is serious and noble and worthy of reverence, although he does not simply accept the judgment of outsiders on what this is.

2. The Pastorals require that the deacon, the deacon's wife, and the older person should be *semnós* (1 Tim. 3:8, 11; Tit. 2:2). The sense is "serious and worthy."

3. *semnótēs* occurs with *eusébeia* in 1 Tim. 2:2 in the sense of serious and worthy conduct. In 1 Tim. 3:4 the point is that children's obedience should be won by an authority that commands respect. In Tit. 2:7 the reference is to the manner and content of the teaching of Titus. With outsiders or opponents in view, it should show gravity or dignity.

D. The Apostolic Fathers.

1. In 1 Clem. 1.3 *semnós* denotes worthy, honorable, and disciplined conduct. This also seems to be the point of the noun in 41.1 (cf. also 7.2; 48.1).

2. A Christian attribute is denoted by the terms in Hermas (cf. *Mandates* 4.3.6; 5.2.8; 6.2.3; *Similitudes* 8.3.8). Everything connected with the world of Christian faith is *semnós,* and *semnótēs* is proper to it.   [W. FOERSTER, VII, 168-96]

---

seíō [to shake, tremble],   *seismós* [shaking, earthquake]

1. *seíō* goes back to a root denoting violent movement. It means "to move to and fro," "to disturb," "to shake." The noun usually means earthquake, the name Poseidon being associated with it. Earthquakes are regarded as bad omens. Philosophers attribute them to congestion of air or the movement of subterranean water. Astrologers relate them to signs of the zodiac and try to make out what they predict. They are commonly thought to accompany or presage theophanies.

2. The OT has vivid depictions of earthquakes, usually in theophanic connections (Ex. 19:18; 1 Kgs. 19:11-12). Earthquakes occur when God marches out to the holy war (Judg. 5:2ff.; Ps. 68:7ff.). The day of the Lord brings a shaking of heaven and earth (Is. 13:1ff.; Ezek. 7:1ff.). In Prov. 30:31 the personified earth shakes because of events that disturb its order.

3. The motif of the shaking of heaven and earth is a common one in later Jewish apocalyptic.

4. In the NT *seíō* has a transferred sense in Mt. 28:4 (the trembling of the guards)

and 21:10 (the people's excitement). *anaseíō* (transitive) means "to stir up" in Mk. 15:11. Cosmic disturbances are at issue in Mt. 27:51; Heb. 12:26; Rev. 6:13. Earthquakes are among the signs of the last time in Mk. 13:8; Mt. 24:7; Lk. 21:11, and Revelation includes them among the terrors of the end in 6:12; 8:5; 11:13, 19; 16:18. Heb. 12:26 contrasts the shaking of the earth alone at Sinai with the final shaking of both heaven and earth. Mt. 8:23 uses *seismós* for the great storm that arises on the lake, perhaps suggesting a parallel with the events of the last time and the ongoing protection of the disciples by Jesus. Matthew also refers to earthquakes accompanying Christ's death and resurrection (27:51, 54; 28:2). These indicate the eschatological significance of Christ's work, and the associated raising of the saints denotes the invading of the realm of the dead by the divine Victor. As shaking (*salythḗnai*) signifies God's answer to prayer in Acts 4:31, so a liberating earthquake is God's response to the prayers and songs of Paul and Silas in 16:25-26.

[G. BORNKAMM, VII, 196-200]

---

sēmeíon [sign, mark], *sēmaínō* [to signify, indicate], *sēmeióō* [to denote, signify], *ásēmos* [insignificant], *epísēmos* [distinguished], *sýssēmon* [signal, standard]

---

sēmeíon.

A. The Greek World.

I. Linguistic Data. sēmeíon develops from *sḗma* and shares with it the sense of "sign" or "mark."

II. Usage.

1. Early Epic.

a. In Homer *sḗma* denotes optical impressions that convey insights, e.g., signs like lightning that indicate the will of Zeus. The signs, which may, of course, be simply pointers, are characterized by prominence and visibility. At first the word contains an active element. *sēmeíon* perhaps develops because of the need for a more abstract term.

b. Acoustic omens come to be included among signs (e.g., thunder), although at first the visible aspect remains strong, as may be seen from the use of *phaínō* for perceiving the sign, and from the continuing emphasis on the clarity of the *sḗma*.

c. The general sense of a mark by which someone or something is recognized makes possible a varied use, e.g., for monuments, finishing posts in races, or identifying marks on the body.

d. Despite divergent use, the sense is uniform. What is meant is an object or circumstance that conveys a perception or insight. The perception may be moral or religious, but the term as such is not intrinsically a religious one.

2. Other Works.

a. Direct Use. In its direct use the *sḗma* or *sēmeíon* may be the symptom of an illness, the scent of an animal, the ensign of a ship, the certifying mark on an animal for sacrifice, the diadem of a ruler, the signet of a ring, the device on a shield, the brand on flocks, etc. *sēmeíon* tends to crowd out *sḗma,* but the latter continues to be used for monuments. In every instance one thing makes possible the correct identification and classification of another.

b. Transferred Use. In the military sphere the *sēmeíon* becomes a command to depart. It is a manifestation of will that impresses itself on others. In the religious sphere the gods give such manifestations of their will, although in this case interpretations must be given. In philosophy *sēmeíon* takes on the sense of demonstration with a logical reference. Everywhere the term is a technical one with a stress on perception and resolve.

c. *sēmeía kaí térata*. At first these terms come together to denote omens that the superstitious perceive in times of crisis. Two things that are not really the same combine in the formula because both are significant in times of human helplessness.

III. Gnosticism. sēmeíon plays no independent role in Gnosticism. In the Hermetic writings it has such varied senses as "constellation," "proof," "mark," and "form in which the nature of a thing comes to expression." The equivalent in Mandaean works simply means "sign," "mark," or "characteristic." Baptism is a "pure sign" or a "sign of life."

B. The Jewish World.

I. The Greek OT.

1. General Material. sēmeíon occurs in the Greek OT some 125 times. The main usage is in the Pentateuch and the prophets. In Ezek. 9:4, 6 *sēmeíon* conveys the sense of the original, as also perhaps in Jer. 6:1. In Num. 21:8-9; Is. 11:12 the reference is to something easily perceived. In some four-fifths of the instances in the canon, however, *sēmeíon* is used for Heb. *'ôt*.

2. 'ôt in the OT.

a. Linguistic Data. The term is of uncertain etymology and meaning. Attempts to link it with an Akkadian *ittu* for "oracular sign," or to construe it commercially as "advice," or to find an original sense of a "fixed time," are all unsuccessful.

b. The Lachish Ostraca. In this military report the term obviously means the "signal" that can be given by some signaling device for the transmission of information.

c. General OT Use. Found some 79 times in the OT, mostly in the Pentateuch, Isaiah, Jeremiah, and Ezekiel, the term often (18 times) goes together with that for "wonders," which always comes second and which occurs alone only in later books.

d. An Object of Sense Perception. The term denotes something that may be perceived, and especially seen. Thus Ps. 86:17 prays for a visible sign of favor. In Gen. 9:12ff. the rainbow is a covenant sign. Num. 14:22 refers to signs done in Egypt. Circumcision is a visible sign in Gen. 17:10ff. So is the blood daubed on the doorposts at the exodus in Ex. 12:7ff. Each tribe has its sign in Num. 2:2. The stones that mark the crossing of the Jordan are visible signs and a lasting memorial in Josh. 4:6ff. Hearing is associated with a sign only in Ex. 4:8, and even here the hearing follows a visible sign that validates Moses and thus gains a hearing for him. The verbs used with *'ôt* stress its visible character (cf. Ex. 10:1-2; Gen. 4:15; Ps. 135:9; 1 Sam. 2:34), and so does the reference to God's hand in connection with the signs in Egypt. The concept is a formal one that derives its more precise sense from the circumstances in which it occurs, whether these be secular or sacral. It does not in itself denote divine revelation, but in its function of indicating, confirming, and promising insight it may be a pointer to revelation.

e. A Means of Confirmation. In some cases the sign does not merely indicate but establishes a certainty not previously present and thus serves to confirm. This is the point in Job 21:29, where experience shows that the doctrine of retribution does not hold water. In Josh. 2:1ff. the sign confirms the oath to Rahab that her family will be saved. In Josh. 4:1ff. (cf. Gen. 9:15) the signs serve as reminders and are thus a basis of confidence. The mark of Cain in Gen. 4:15 serves as a sign of protection rather than a mark of guilt. The expression "to be [as] a sign" (Ex. 13:8; Num. 16:38) makes a similar point. Thus in Ex. 8:18-19 the plague makes it plain to Pharaoh with whom he has to do, although in this instance it has the effect of hardening rather than instructing. In Num. 14:11 faith ought to be the result (cf. also Ex. 4:8). In the OT the sign is an external reality in history that is directed to eyewitnesses and points them to something else with a view to conveying insight, granting confirmation, and evoking decisions that have historical consequences.

f. God's Signs and Wonders. Relative to God's signs and wonders the style takes on almost a hymnic character. The reference is usually to the exodus and the combination is especially common in Deuteronomy. The emphasis in it is on God's action in a revolutionary intervention in human affairs (cf. also Is. 8:18).

g. Symbolical Prophetic Actions. Actions claiming to be signs are common in the prophets. God commands these signs, they presuppose eyewitnesses, they have an intrinsic quality of proclamation, and they acquire force from the prophetic word. Unlike oracular signs, they do not try to read the future but to extract the future from the present.

h. Daniel and the Targums. The Aramaic equivalent occurs three times in Daniel (3:32-33; 6:28) in a way that confirms the general OT use. In the Targums the reference is to the plagues of Egypt and the usage preserves the formal character of the term.

i. Summary. The survey brings to light the formal nature of the Hebrew term that the LXX renders *sēmeíon* and also the tendency of the term to lose its original breadth in the postexilic period.

3. *sēmeíon in the LXX*.

a. Formal Character. Being also formal, *sēmeíon* serves well as an equivalent for the Hebrew, e.g., as a mark, an emblem, a monument, the Passover blood, a covenant sign (the rainbow, circumcision, the sabbath), a prophetic sign, or a divine action. Under Hebrew influence the formal character becomes stricter. This limits the use but increases the interpretative aptness.

b. Interpretatively. In some passages *sēmeíon* adds precision where the Hebrew does not use *'ôt*, e.g., Ex. 7:9; 11:9-10; 2 Chr. 32:24; Is. 11:12; Ezek. 9:4, 6, etc. In Josh. 2:18 the translation uses *sēmeíon* to show why Rahab is to hang out the cord that she is given.

c. *sēmeía kaí térata*. This formula, based on the parallel Hebrew in Deuteronomy, denotes God's wonders in Egypt. It may be noted that Θ drops the verse Dan. 4:2 in which Nebuchadnezzar speaks of signs and wonders to himself, but retains 6:27 (Darius).

II. *Greek Judaism outside the Bible*.

1. *Philo*. Philo follows LXX usage at times (e.g., the mark of Cain or the stars as *sēmeía*). Yet he also uses *sēmeíon* in wider Greek senses, e.g., for symptom or proof. In allegory it has the meaning "pointer." The Bible is for Philo a treasury of *sēmeía*. Miracles, however, play little part in his usage and he uses *sēmeía kaí térata* only traditionally for the wonders in Egypt.

2. *Josephus*. Like Philo, Josephus follows the LXX (e.g., the mark of Cain) but also uses *sēmeía* for military "signals" or "passwords." As a formal term *sēmeíon* can also denote for Josephus something that produces knowledge or certainty by means of impressions, e.g., an experience that carries with it intimations. The *sēmeíon* might be a miracle (a *téras*) but does not have to be. Wishing to protect the wonders in Egypt from a magical understanding, Josephus simply calls them *sēmeía*, not *sēmeía kaí térata*. When God works a *téras*, it is important only as a *sēmeíon* whereby God shows that he is the one and only true God.

3. Apocalyptic. A common idea in later Jewish apocalyptic is that visible cosmic changes will precede the beginning of the end; these are *sēmeía*.

C. Postbiblical Judaism.
I. Dead Sea Scrolls.

1. Biblical Usage. In the Qumran material we find instances of the use of *'ôt* for visible phenomena that serve to confirm or indicate. These range from heavenly luminaries to battle standards (perhaps influenced by Lat. *signum*).

2. A New Sense? In one place the meaning "letter" is possible, but the common "sign" is also a possibility.

II. Rabbinic Literature.

1. Mark. '*ôt* plays only a modest role in the rabbis. It first has the sense of a distinguishing mark or sign, but the term is rare in this sense.

2. Letter. The main use of '*ôt* in the rabbis is for a single letter of the Hebrew alphabet, whose characters reveal God's will and are thus regarded sacrally.

III. sîmān in Rabbinic Usage.

1. General Considerations. This word, which may be a loanword, and is shaped by '*ôt*, tends to replace the latter for "mark" or "sign."

2. Mark. It serves to denote symptoms of an illness, features of a place, characteristics of a person, intimations of the future, signs of God's favor or disfavor, astronomical signs whereby to fix the calendar.

3. Special Use. A special academic use is for a "cue" or "catchword," for a "proof text," or for "n" as a kind of diacritical mark.

D. The NT.
I. General Data.

1. Statistics. In the NT *sēmeíon* occurs some 73 times, ten in Matthew, seven in Mark, ten in Luke, 24 in Johannine works, 13 in Acts 1–15 (mostly plural and nine times with *téras*), eight in Paul, and one in Hebrews.

2. Parallels.

a. *téras.* This word occurs only in the plural with *sēmeía*.

b. *dýnamis.* This occurs with *sēmeía kaí térata* in Acts 2:22; 2 Th. 2:9, but also independently in the plural for miracles, especially in Matthew, but not at all in John (though cf. the verb in Jn. 3:2; 9:16).

c. *érgon.* This word lies alongside *sēmeíon* in John, and one has thus to define the exact relation between them.

3. Preliminary Remarks. On the one side *sēmeíon* occurs with verbs that denote human activity or that objectify it so that one can ask for it, see it, or accept or deny it. On the other side it is from heaven or from God. In two instances (the sign of healing in Acts 4:22 and that of the Son of Man in Mt. 24:30) what is signified is beyond human competence but comes into the human sphere by means of the *sēmeíon*. When a *sēmeíon* occurs in the NT, humans are always involved and there is a pointer to human responsibility, but the variety of possibilities makes classification difficult.

II. The Synoptic Gospels and Acts.

1. Sign or Mark. In the OT phrase that Luke uses in 2:12, the sign demonstrates the truth of the message. Perception of certain data serves a purpose of confirmation. The *sēmeíon* given to the shepherds sets them in motion (v. 15) so that they themselves implicitly become a sign to Mary. In Mt. 26:48 Judas uses the kiss as a sign indicating whom the guard should arrest. In Mt. 24:3 the disciples ask for a sign of Christ's parousia. This does not have to be a miraculous or apocalyptic sign. In itself it simply makes the parousia recognizable. The *sēmeía* in Lk. 21:25 are astronomical signs but even these signs of the parousia are not apocalyptic as such.

2. *The Sign of Jonah.* In Mt. 12:39-40 Jesus applies to himself the sign of Jonah. The point of this obscure statement is that Jonah himself is the sign in the sense that God chooses him and works through him and through his call for repentance. The stress on the person comes out in the added saying that a greater than Jonah is now present (12:41). The sign takes on added significance with Christ's death and resurrection (cf. the future in Lk. 11:30), but in any case Jesus in his prophetic self-portrayal bursts through prophetic categories (cf. also the enigmatic comparatives in Mt. 11:9 and 12:6; Lk. 7:26).

3. *The Demand for a sēmeíon.* The saying in Mt. 12:38ff. is the reply to the demand for a *sēmeíon* (cf. Mt. 16:1; Lk. 23:8). This demand arises primarily in scribal circles and is for one sign, with God as the author, that will convincingly authenticate the ministry of Jesus and refute all doubts concerning him. The Synoptists use *dýnamis*, not *sēmeíon*, for the miracles of Jesus, and it is these *dynámeis* (which opponents attribute to sorcery) that prompt the demand for a sign; for the rabbis, who ground their authority in Scripture, suspect miracles if they are purely human acts that lack a specific divine commission. The demand seems natural inasmuch as Jesus acts in his own power and asserts his freedom from tradition. Yet it is a wrong demand inasmuch as it seeks to impose its own principles on God and is thus an attack on the divine freedom (cf. Lk. 11:29; Mt. 12:39).

4. *The Sign of the Son of Man.* This phrase occurs only in Matthew (24:30), where the sign appears prior to the coming and the gathering of the elect. Although mysterious, it is clearly terrifying and brings the present order to an ineluctable end. Like Rev. 1:7, Mt. 24:30 combines Zech. 12:12, 14 and Dan. 7:13-14, but Revelation puts Daniel first, whereas Matthew puts Zechariah first. Possibly the sign is given so that there may be a last chance to repent. The sign can hardly be the cross, nor the Son of Man himself, but it plainly intimates the imminent parousia.

5. *sēmeíon antilegómenon (Lk. 2:34).* In a passage that has an OT coloring Simeon calls the child Jesus a sign that is spoken against. God posits this sign for the disclosure of inner thoughts as some accept it and others contest it. It is in relation to this sign, therefore, that there is falling and rising in Israel in fulfilment of the messianic mission of Jesus.

6. *Acts.* In Acts 4:16, 22 *sēmeíon* occurs in connection with the healing of the lame man, and in 8:6, 13 (with *dynámeis* in v. 13) it describes the work of Philip. As in the nine instances of *sēmeía kaí térata*, the usage is much the same as in the Synoptics. The works are signs inasmuch as they are evident happenings that point to him in whose name and power they are performed. By them, as by the word, Jesus shows that he is the living Lord whom God himself authenticates. The new feature in Acts is that in the new situation inaugurated by Christ's death and resurrection there is now a chain of *sēmeía*, i.e., of indications that no one can miss. The mighty works are not marvels. They demand interpretation and are thus subordinate to the word (by which faith lives) as obedient and unselfish acts that are done in the power of Jesus and for his sake.

7. *sēmeía kaí térata.* This phrase occurs in Mt. 24:24/Mk. 13:22, nine times in Acts 1-8, three times in Paul, and once in Jn. 4:48.

a. In Mt. 24:24/Mk. 13:22 the doing of *sēmeía kaí térata* is projected into the future as part of the picture of pseudo-messiahs, although this does not rule out their performance by the true Messiah as the promised prophet.

b. In Acts present *sēmeía kaí térata* mark the new age of eschatological redemption as they previously marked the time of Mosaic liberation. Acts 2:19 and 7:36 carry allusions to Joel 2:30 and Ex. 7:3 and typologically demonstrate that the predicted eschatological age has come.

(a) In a first group of *sēmeía kaí térata* references Jesus, Moses, and the apostles all have a place (cf. 6–7).

(b) In a second group the spotlight is on the apostles but in such a way that it moves from Jesus to them, for he it is who is at work in their acts (4:30; 14:3). Where typology is to the fore, the order *térata kaí sēmeía* occurs (cf. 6:8; 7:36), although in view of the common theme it is not wholly clear why this should be so.

III. sēmeíon in the Johannine Writings.

1. General Features.

a. John has *sēmeíon* in the formal sense of "sign" or "pointer" (cf. "portent" in Rev. 12:1, 3, "proof" in Jn. 2:18, "wonderful act" in Rev. 13:13-14).

b. The common reference is to visual perception and the confirmation it gives (cf. Jn. 2:23; 6:14; Rev. 15:11; Jn. 10:32ff.; 14:9ff.).

c. As in the Synoptics, people ask Jesus for a *sēmeíon* (even after the miracle of feeding in 6:1ff.; cf. also 2:18).

d. The phrase *sēmeía kaí térata* occurs in 4:48 in a polemical context, but perhaps echoing again the Mosaic redemption. The point is that now that Jesus is himself present *sēmeía kaí térata* are superfluous and must not be made a basis of faith. Jesus does not have to perform signs and wonders in self-authentication even though he comes as the new Moses; at this point there is perhaps a difference between the type and the antitype. At any rate the resurrection grants the church independence of *sēmeía kaí térata* (cf. 20:29).

2. Distinctive Aspects.

a. In both John and Revelation *sēmeíon* takes over the role of *dýnamis* in the Synoptics. Johannine *sēmeía* are acts related to him who does them (Jn. 3:2). Their quality derives from the quality of their author (9:16). Thus the beast, too, performs great signs but these lead into idolatry (13:13ff.). The many signs of Jesus are distinctly miraculous (2:23; 3:2; 11:47; 12:37), but they bear a messianic character (2:11; 4:54; 6:14) inasmuch as they put an end to disease and want. John does not refer to the curing of lepers or to exorcisms; he mentions *sēmeía* that seem designed to present Jesus as the Messiah.

b. John never calls a saying of Jesus a *sēmeíon*.

c. It is mostly the author (2:11, 23, etc.) or others (3:2; 7:31; 9:16) who use the term *sēmeíon*, Jesus himself only in 6:26. In John, as distinct from the Synoptics, Acts, or the surrounding world, the term is a key one in theological interpretation.

3. sēmeíon and érgon.

a. General. In John the 27 *érga* passages bear a clear relation to the *sēmeía* (cf. 5:20, 36; 6:29; 7:3, 21; 9:3-4; 10:25, etc.). The *érga* are *sēmeía* as God's own *érga* (4:34; 5:36; 9:3-4). Jesus uses *érgon* for what the author calls *sēmeíon*.

b. Sign Character of the *érga*.

(a) Although the *érga* are Jesus' own, he does not call them his. He does them (5:36 etc.) in a unique fellowship with the Father (3:35; 8:19; 12:45; 14:9ff.). He does them only when his hour comes (2:4), but he knows this hour (13:1) and in it does God's own acts (2:1ff.; 6:1ff.; 11:1ff.), i.e., the acts God gives him to do (5:36).

(b) The *érga* are *sēmeía* because as his they serve God's self-revelation. They are not just miracles; they bring a new view of God inasmuch as the Father may be known only through the Son (8:19, 54-55; 14:7). Only Jesus can truly interpret the *sēmeía*, as he does in the revelatory discourses that follow them.

c. The *sēmeía* as God's Witness to the Son. In Jn. 12:37ff. (cf. Is. 53:1) the *sēmeía* are attributed to God. In Jesus human destiny is decided here and now according to God's will. His *érga* have divisive power. Promoting God's self-revelation, they also characterize Jesus as the Son. They are not mere symbols imparting knowledge; reflecting the nature of Jesus, they call for faith, into which, of course, knowledge is integrated.

4. *sēmeíon and Faith.* The aim of the gospel is faith in Jesus as the Christ, God's Son (Jn. 20:31). The *sēmeía* establish faith, but God is the content of this faith, not the *sēmeía*. The *sēmeía* are the Son's revelation of the Father and the Father's confession of the Son. As such they are a basis of faith in God. Although discourses often expound the *sēmeía*, in 2:1ff. and 4:47ff. there is a causal connection between faith and the *sēmeíon*. Encounter with the person of Jesus in the *sēmeíon* leads to seeing or knowing (2:11; 4:53). The added words of revelation confer on the *sēmeía* an enduring power to establish faith, so that they become a permanent part of the divine message. The *sēmeía* neither relate to mere compassion nor to prophetic claims. They are signs that Jesus is the Christ as both Revealer and Revealed. They take precedence over the word so long as Jesus is in the flesh (1:14; 7:39). After Easter the community has the word, and new *sēmeía* are not essential.

5. *sēmeíon and Word.* In John the *sēmeía* point indirectly to the one Jesus really is, while the *lógoi* give direct information. The *lógoi* display the same freedom as the *érga*. They interpret the *sēmeía*; the *sēmeía* confirm the *lógoi*. They both find their unity in the person of him who shows himself to be he who acts and who has the right to say "I am." Whereas in the OT human interpreters say who God is and what he wills and does, in John Jesus himself interprets what he does with reference to himself and the Father (cf. 5:17; 8:25; 11:1ff.).

6. *sēmeíon and dóxa.* The glory of Christ or God is manifested at Cana and in the raising of Lazarus, and the faith of the disciples is linked with this manifestation. Faith arises when it sees the glory in the *sēmeíon* (1:14; 12:37ff.). The glory of Jesus is that of his true being. It is the presupposition of his doing God's work and hence a sign of his preexistence. The glory manifests his omnipotence and impresses the disciples with his majesty. The link with glory shows that for John a *sēmeíon* is no mere symbol. The term is a central one both theologically and christologically. Since it discloses human sin, its anthropological bearing is ethical (9:41). In the *sēmeía* of Jesus the eschatological *krísis* that he brings becomes unmistakable and unavoidable.

7. *sēmeía of the Risen Lord.* The reference in Jn. 20:30-31 is not to the resurrection or the resurrection appearances, for in John these are more directly the work of God, and the issue in Jn. 20 is the self-witness of the risen Lord (vv. 17, 20, 27), not the giving of new *sēmeía*. Nor do we have here a reference to the crucifixion, which in John does not present a sign even though the Father glorifies the Son therein. The "many other signs," then, are the various works that Jesus did from which the author has made a selection; the number as such is unimportant. The "many other things" (not signs) of 21:25 might include the events of ch. 21, but John seems careful not to number the crucifixion and resurrection among the signs.

8. *John's Special Use of sēmeía.*

a. Distinctiveness. The use of *sēmeía* for Jesus' self-manifestation in his works is peculiar to John. It finds a negative counterpart in Revelation with its use of the term for the miracles of the prophet of antichrist.

b. OT Background. The use derives, not from Hellenistic Gnosticism, but from the LXX. Here *sēmeíon* points to the self-declaration of the one God as Israel's God, and it bears a relation to faith on the one side and glory on the other. The works of Jesus are of the same kind as God's works at the exodus. The glory of the works, as in the OT, lies in the manifestation of the divine power. The difference is that the reference is now to Jesus, who unites with God those who unite themselves to him.

c. The Typological Character of Johannine *sēmeía.* John gives the *sēmeía* a typological accent, emphasizing that Jesus is the "prophet" (4:19) and the Passover lamb of eschatological redemption. The *sēmeía* thus have a similar function to the *sēmeía* of the exodus. Yet as Jesus surpasses Moses, so his work surpasses that of Moses. Hence the *sēmeía* acquire enhanced significance. Jesus is a new Moses but he is more, for he acts as God and thereby shows himself to be the Son of God.

IV. The Rest of the NT.

1. Paul.

a. General. Paul uses *sēmeíon* only eight times. *sēmeía kaí térata* occurs in Rom. 15:19; 2 Cor. 12:12; 2 Th. 2:9. The usage is traditional. In the new situation of apostolic witness, the problem of the *sēmeíon* that arises for Jesus now arises for his authorized representatives.

b. Specific. In Rom. 4:11 the meaning is "sign" or "mark," perhaps indicating that circumcision is a covenant sign (cf. the reading *peritomḗn* rather than *peritomḗs*). In 2 Cor. 12:12 the signs of an apostle are visible things that identify an apostle, i.e., the mighty works of the age of redemption. In 1 Cor. 1:22 Paul rejects the Jewish demand that he should prove his claim with signs. In 1 Cor. 14:22 tongues are a sign for unbelievers inasmuch as they make evident to them their unbelief. In 2 Th. 3:17 the *sēmeíon* is a proof of authenticity. It is something visible that confers assurance. Why Paul adds his own greeting as a *sēmeíon* is not immediately clear. In Rom. 15:19 Paul applies *sēmeía kaí térata* to the works that he does as an apostle in the power of the Spirit (cf. 2 Cor. 12:12). In 2 Th. 2:9, however, the parousia of antichrist, aping that of Christ, is accompanied by pretended signs and wonders.

2. Hebrews. Heb. 2:4 uses an expanded form of the *sēmeía kaí térata* formula to describe the things that God does to accredit apostolic preaching and to show the superiority of the gospel to the law. The reference of the *sēmeía kaí térata* is to the credibility of preachers. Their supporting function is rooted in God's will.

E. The Apostolic Fathers. The term is rare in the apostolic fathers, and the few instances conform to ordinary usage. Lot's wife is a sign in 1 Clem. 11.2, the mark on Rahab's house is a sign in 12.7, a verse of Scripture is a pointer in 2 Clem. 15.4, the phenomena of the parousia are proofs in Did. 16.4, the phoenix myth is a sign in 1 Clem. 25.1ff. 1 Clem. 51.5 uses *sēmeía kaí térata* for the wonders in Egypt, and Barn. 5.8 uses the phrase in a typological understanding of the age of Moses relative to that of Jesus. Barn. 12.5 refers the serpent typologically to Jesus as a *sēmeíon.* Did. 16.6 is obscure: The opening of heaven, or the outstretching of the arms of Jesus on the cross, may be the *sēmeíon* intended.

sēmaínō.

A. Greek Use. This word means "to indicate," often in the sense "to order," "to direct." It is used in such senses as "to give a sign or signal," "to signify," "to announce," "to declare," and "to mean."

B. Greek Judaism.
1. *sēmaínō* is used for various Hebrew terms meaning "to impart," "to point," "to intimate," and even "to blow [the trumpet] as a sign."
2. In Philo the term means "to signify," "to represent," "to denote," "to mean" (especially with reference to the deeper signification of the OT).
3. In Josephus the meanings are "to tell," "to notify," "to intimate," "to make known," "to signify," and, with reference to documents, "to seal."

C. The NT.
1. In Acts 25:27 Festus needs to examine Paul further in order that he may be able to "indicate" or "show" what the charges against him are.
2. In Acts 11:28 Agabus "signifies by the Spirit," i.e., foretells, that there will be a famine. In Rev. 1:1 the thought is similar: God gives Jesus the revelation to show his servants what must take place, and Jesus then "makes it known" to John through the angel, i.e., "indicates" or "declares" it.
3. Jn. 12:33; 18:32; 21:19 contain intimations of Jesus concerning the manner of death, first of himself, then of Peter. None of us knows either the time or the manner of death unless God shows it, but Jesus can tell how both he and Peter will die. Hence *sēmaínō* in this context points to his divine dignity even while retaining its purely formal character.

D. The Apostolic Fathers. In these works *sēmaínō* occurs only in some versions of Barn. 15.4, where, in an exposition of Gen. 2:2, it has the sense "to have the deeper meaning" (cf. Philo).

sēmeióō.
1. This word means "to denote," "to signify," "to seal," "to signal," "to mark for oneself," "to diagnose," "to certify."
2. The LXX uses the word only in Ps. 4:6: In God's turning worshippers receive a sign that good things are present for them in God.
3. Philo uses only the middle in such senses as "to characterize," "to show," "to signify," "to get proof."
4. In the NT 2 Th. 3:14 contains the admonition to note those who refuse to obey the apostolic injunctions. The shunning probably applies to spiritual fellowship or common meals, not to everyday matters.
5. 1 Clem. 43.1 uses the word for "to note" with reference to Moses and the *hieraí bíbloi* written by him.

ásēmos.
1. This word means "without *sēma* or characteristic," and takes on such senses as "unstamped," "without emblems," "inarticulate," "obscure," "insignificant," but also "without blemish," i.e., distinguishing mark.
2. In the LXX the meanings are "unimportant" and "insignificant" (Gen. 30:42; Job 42:11).

1023

3. Philo refers to an "insignificant" family, and Josephus speaks of those who are of "obscure or doubtful" lineage.

4. Acts 21:39 has Paul use a common literary device when he calls his native Tarsus "no mean city"; the deliberately restrained description gives the greater emphasis.

epísēmos.

1. This word means "having a distinguishing mark" and takes on such senses as "stamped," "labeled," "showing symptoms."

2. In the LXX it denotes a feast day in Esth. 5:4, an outstanding person in 3 Macc. 6:1, and a generally visible place in 1 Macc. 11:37.

3. Philo uses the word in such senses as "recognizable," "distinguished," "superior," and "clear." In Josephus it means "stamped," "distinguished," "significant," and also "infamous" or "notorious."

4. Rom. 16:7 uses the term in a good sense when it refers to Andronicus and Junias as "significant" or "highly regarded" men in the apostolic circle. In Mt. 27:16, however, Barabbas is outstanding in the bad sense of "notorious." The word is not here a technical one for the leader of a band of Zealots.

5. In the apostolic fathers the word occurs only in the Martyrdom of Polycarp, in which it reflects incipient martyr terminology (3.1) as well as describing Polycarp as an "outstanding" teacher (1i.1).

sýssēmon.

1. This late word has such senses as "signal," "standard," and in the plural "insignia."

2. In the LXX it means "signal" in Judg. 20:38 and "banner" in Is. 5:26.

3. Mk. 14:44 calls Judas' kiss a *sýssēmon,* thus showing that it is a "prearranged sign."

4. The apostolic fathers use the term only once in Ignatius *Smyrneans* 1.2, which gives Is. 5:26 a christological reference.   [K. H. RENGSTORF, VII, 200-269]

→ *eúsēmos*

---

sēmeron [today]

A. Presuppositions in Greek. This word denotes a span of human activity embracing a day up to the evening. It is the time at our disposal, perhaps the last such.

B. Presuppositions in the OT and Judaism.

1. The OT day begins in the evening, and the day is the time of dealings with God. What takes place "today" is from God. On the sabbath believers are bound to "this day." Today means fulfilment, whether in revelation, salvation, or judgment. What is said today, e.g., an oath or covenant, decides what follows. If today is lost, existence is threatened. God's word and today should be commensurate. Today becomes address, and hence looks back to the past and forward to the future. It discloses its truth as the claim to obedience issued by the Lord of history who shows his people what they should do. It is the time of decision between God and his people (cf. Dt. 4:1; 26:17ff.; 30:15ff.).

2. Philo in his use of the term reflects the OT unity between God's word and the reality that is thereby ordained either positively or negatively for us.

3. Josephus, like Philo, uses the term mostly in OT quotations. Apart from the

nontheological use, the term is significant because in it God's revelation seeks expression in Israel's history; his will is proclaimed "today."

C. NT Usage.

1. Nontheological Usage.

a. In Mt. 27:19 Pilate's wife has had a bad dream today; this is an omen for a decisive day, but the immediate sense is the ordinary one. The usual sense is also present in the petition of Mt. 6:11: believers ask today for their daily bread from God. Similarly in 6:30 believers should orient themselves to God's provision today if they are to escape anxiety. In 16:3 the reference is to today's weather, in 21:28 the father asks his son to work today, and in Mk. 14:30 *sḗmeron* is juxtaposed with "this very night" to the extent that the day begins rather than ends with the evening; Mt. 26:34 leaves out *sḗmeron*.

b. In Acts 4:9; 19:40; 20:26; 24:21; 26:2, 29; 27:33 *sḗmeron* is the day when a speaker gives his address. A foolish sense of mastery over one's own time is the point in Jms. 4:13. There is some allegorizing in Lk. 13:31ff.; the *hóti* clause in v. 33 gives the saying theological significance.

c. The emphatic saying in Lk. 23:43 is that of one who is on the point of death; it sets the immediate future in contrast with the present situation.

2. Theological Usage.

a. The style is liturgical in Heb. 13:8. Rom. 11:8 and Mt. 27:8 use a common LXX phrase. The note in Mt. 28:15 points up the emptiness of the explanation. A different judgment is present in Mt. 11:23. Paul stresses the alternative of judgment and promise in 2 Cor. 3:14 (cf. also Lk. 4:21; 5:25; 2:11 for the fulfilment of the promise). Acts 13:33 relates the resurrection to the second psalm. Jesus, who proclaims Scripture to be valid, is himself the fulfilment.

b. Hebrews confirms this point in the enthronement exegesis of 1–2 and the exposition of Ps. 95 in 3–4. Since the "today" of the psalm comes in the time of neither Joshua nor David, it applies to those who, hearing today, hold fast their confession of Jesus as the Son of God and High Priest, for he has united his heavenly rank with his high-priestly sacrifice (cf. 5:5-6), and has thus given the "today" its decisive and definitive theological meaning.

D. Apostolic Fathers. In these works the term occurs some seven or eight times, mostly in quotations. It carries a full stress in the prayer of Mart. Pol. 14.2.

→ *heméra, nýn*   [E. Fuchs, VII, 269-75]

sḗpō → *saprós*

---

sḗs [moth],   *sētóbrōtos* [moth-eaten]

---

1. Various kinds of butterflies or moths are denoted by the noun; the usual reference is to moths in clothes.

2. Is. 51:8 offers the only OT instance with the specific Hebrew original.

3. The moth illustrates feminine malice in Sir. 42:13 and transitoriness in Job 27:18. Prov. 14:30 uses *sḗs*, and Job 13:28 has the adjective ("consumed by moths"). Job 4:19; 27:18; Is. 50:9 also use *sḗs*.

4. Jesus in Mt. 6:19-20; Lk. 12:33 demands renunciation of earthly treasures, which are all threatened by moth, rust, or theft; the emphasis, however, is on orientation to

the true and lasting treasures that are secure from damage or loss. Jms. 5:2 threatens the imminent and ineluctable end of earthly riches with a realism that is enhanced apocalyptically; no efforts can save this kind of wealth.

5. Depicting weak believers, Hermas *Similitudes* 8.1 uses the image of staves that are consumed by moths or small insects. In OT quotations *sēs* also occurs in 1 Clem. 39.5 and Barn. 6.2.   [O. BAUERNFEIND, VII, 275-78]

---

sikários [assassin, dagger-carrier]

1. The Sicarii in Roman Law. From *sicarius*, this word means "dagger-carrier," "assassin." Rome has laws against *sicarii*, i.e., assassins or violent murderers. There are also laws against *latrones*, i.e., armed robbers in bands.

2. The Sicarii in Josephus. Josephus calls the freedom fighters of the Jewish revolt "robbers" and "assassins" (*sikaríous*). The *sicarii* first appear under Felix. They follow Menahem, are partisans in Egypt, and instigate revolt in Cyrene. They seem not to be an organized group but are the guerillas of the Zealot movement. They begin to use the (concealed) dagger when Felix takes harsh measures to crush resistance. During the revolt they use the dagger against Jews who are friendly to the Romans. They are motivated, not by lawlessness or fanaticism, but by zeal for God's honor and the law. They prefer suicide or martyrdom to Roman rule. The Romans defile the land by taxes, coins, statues, and the census; Jews who support them are renegades and no better than Gentiles, and political priests seduce the people into idolatry. By purging out such elements the *sicarii* hope to prepare the land for God's coming and to shield it from God's wrath. They confiscate property, destroy palaces, and burn documents with a view to the overthrow of unrighteous mammon and the inauguration of the jubilee of freedom and equality.

3. The Sicarii in Rabbinic Works. The rabbis use the term in condemnation of the Zealots and their acts of violence, e.g., burning hoarded food and destroying water conduits. They do not mention assassination.

4. The Sicarii in the NT.

a. The tribune in Acts 21:38 suspects that Paul is the Egyptian who has incited to revolt and led 4,000 *sicarii* into the desert. Josephus tells of this event in two accounts that differ in details (*Jewish War* 2.261ff.; *Antiquities* 20.169). Although Josephus does not use the term *sicarii* in these accounts, it is understandable on the lips of a Roman officer, for whom all such freedom fighters rank as *sicarii*.

b. The 40 Jews who plot to assassinate Paul in Acts 23:12ff. might well be *sicarii* seeking to eliminate a false teacher who is also suspected of desecrating the temple.

5. The Sicarii in the Fathers. Hippolytus equates the *sicarii* with the Zealots but mistakenly thinks they are a class of Essenes. Origen also refers to them.

[O. BETZ, VII, 278-82]

Siná [Sinai]

A. The OT and Jewish Tradition.

1. The OT links the Sinai revelation with the exodus. Ex. 19–24 narrates the preparation and the theophany, Ex. 32–34 the people's sin and the destruction and

replacement of the tablets, Ex. 25–31 the giving of cultic ordinances. Sinai, also called Horeb in Deuteronomy, is traditionally associated with Mt. Sinai in the south of the Sinaitic peninsula. The tradition uniformly declares that after the exodus God led his people to Sinai and gave it the law there.

2. Judaism often refers to the event at Sinai and gives expanded descriptions of it. Philo thinks that at Sinai Israel is set in paradisal conditions but it becomes subject to infirmities again with its sin. Later rabbinic tradition concurs. Even the evil impulse is withdrawn and the people again receives the radiance given to Adam in paradise. But the sin of the golden calf intervenes, and the radiance will return only in the messianic age. The law, which also contains oral tradition, is given in all languages, being meant for the Gentiles too. But the Gentiles refuse it; only Israel shapes its life by the divine statutes. Sinai is a high and holy mountain, the place of God's presence (Philo). God will come to it again at the end of the days; as he spoke his word there once, he will speak it again at the eschaton. Sinai links heaven and earth, it will finally be God's throne, it will bear the tree of life, and it will merge with the mountain of paradise (Ethiopian Enoch). Tabor and Carmel will also join with it to be the site of God's sanctuary, according to one rabbinic tradition.

B. The NT.

1. Stephen in Acts 7 refers to the call of Moses in the wilderness of Mt. Sinai (v. 30) and then to his receiving the law at Mt. Sinai (v. 38). This account is in close accord with the historical preaching of Judaism.

2. Paul links Sinai with Hagar in the allegory of Gal. 4:21ff. The equation occurs in the note in v. 25, which is so difficult exegetically that some versions leave out Hagar and simply say that Mt. Sinai is in Arabia. The obvious point is that Hagar signifies Mt. Sinai, and this in turn leads us to present-day Jerusalem. The common term is bondage. The Sinai covenant mediates an enslaving law, but this no longer applies in the Jerusalem which is above, where the children of the free woman live and freedom rules.

C. The Apostolic Fathers. In these works Sinai appears only in OT quotations in Barn. 11.3 and 14.1 and in a reference to the commandments in 15.1. In 14.1 the author claims that, while God gave the covenant at Sinai, the people was unworthy of it on account of its sin. In 15.1 he argues that the sabbath commandment comes to its true fulfilment in the eschatological rest that the church achieves in its observance of the Lord's day.   [E. Lohse, VII, 282-87]

---

sínapi [mustard]

1. Of obscure origin, *sínapi* means "mustard." A derived verb is *sinapízō*, which means "to give a sour look," but medically "to treat with mustard." A *sinapismós* is a "mustard plaster."

2. Mustard is not mentioned in the OT, but later Jewish tradition refers to it. It is grown in the fields, but there is no mention of its medical use. Its seed is proverbially small, but the plant can achieve considerable height, although not on the scale of accounts that are meant to stress the fertility of the land.

3. In the NT *sínapi* occurs in the parable of the grain of mustard seed (Mk. 4:30ff.; Mt. 13:31-32; Lk. 13:18-19) and in the comparison of faith to a grain of mustard seed

(Mt. 17:20; Lk. 17:6). The proverbial smallness figures in both references. Some commentators suggest that the so-called mustard tree might be meant, but *sínapi* is not used for this, and the plentiful growth of the mustard plant fits the sayings well. If the seed of the black mustard is not absolutely the smallest seed, it is extremely small.

a. The saying about the small faith that works miracles comes in three different versions and in different contexts. The grain of mustard seed is used in order to show that the largest promise attaches even to the smallest faith. What counts is simply faith, not the quantity of faith. Faith, looking to God, lets God work, and so the impossible is possible for it. This explains the link with prayer in Mk. 11:23 (cf. Mt. 17:20 in the light of Mk. 9:29).

b. The parable of the grain of mustard seed also comes in different versions. The Marcan version stresses the fact of the contrast between the small seed and the plentiful growth, Lk. 13:18-19 pays more attention to the process, and Mt. 13:31-32 combines the two emphases. Behind the parable is the teaching that the kingdom is already present in Jesus but in hidden and inconspicuous form. This form should not be an offense but a ground of confidence, for in the concealment of God's present work lies the promise of his victorious rule. Having made a beginning, God will carry through his cause to the end.   [C.-H. HUNZINGER, VII, 287-91]

---

siniázō [to sift]

From *siníon*, "sieve," *siniázō* means "to sift." In Lk. 22:31 Satan desires to sift Simon Peter like wheat, but the Lord prays for him, and therefore in spite of his weakness his faith will not be overthrown. The saying is obviously figurative. The sifting is a test of faith (cf. Job 1). Peter will fail (v. 34), but the Lord will uphold and restore him, so that he can then strengthen others.   [E. FUCHS, VII, 291-92]

Sión [Zion],   **Ierousalém** [Jerusalem],   **Hierosólyma** [Jerusalem],   **Hierosolymítēs** [inhabitant of Jerusalem]

A. Zion and Jerusalem in the OT.
I. Occurrence, Etymology, and Meaning.
1. Zion and Related Terms.

a. The word "Zion" occurs in the OT 154 times, sometimes with an addition, e.g., Mount, daughter, sons or daughters, gates, or song. Parallel terms are city of David, Jerusalem, Salem, city of God, holy mountain, sanctuary, and Israel.

b. The etymology is obscure, but as a proper name it is undoubtedly pre-Israelite, and perhaps relates to the nature of the terrain.

c. Originally Zion is a topographical term for the southeast hill of the later city of Jerusalem. After a period of disuse, it then denotes the whole east hill, the whole city, or the northeast hill as the temple hill. A transferred sense occurs in Am. 6:1 where those who are at ease in Zion (the southern capital) are like those who feel secure on the mountain of Samaria (the northern capital).

2. Jerusalem and Related Terms.

a. Jerusalem occurs 660 times in the OT for the Canaanite city, the capital of David and Solomon, the capital of Judah, and the cultic center. Additions are environs, hill, gates, walls, places, inhabitants, daughter(s), prophets, and remnant. Parallel terms are Jebus, city or ridges of the Jebusites, Zion, people, hill of Yahweh Zebaoth, and temple. Combinations include Samaria and Jerusalem (antithetical), house of David and inhabitants of Jerusalem, Jerusalem and all its towns. In apposition we find holy city, holy mountain, and throne of Yahweh.

b. The name comes down in various forms, including an ancient form Ursalem or Urusalim, and also Jerusalajim.

c. The etymology is uncertain.

d. Unlike Zion the term Jerusalem has always applied to the whole settlement.

3. Rare Terms.

a. The name Salem occurs in Ps. 76:2 and Gen. 14:18.

b. In Is. 29:1-2, 7 we find the name Ariel, probably in the sense of Ezek. 43:15-16 ("altar hearth").

4. The Use of Zion and Jerusalem. Zion is less prominent in Ezekiel, Malachi, Ezra, and Nehemiah (cf. also 2 Samuel, 1 and 2 Kings, 1 and 2 Chronicles, Jeremiah, Zechariah, and Canticles). It is more prominent in Psalms and Lamentations. Its most common use is for the city of end-time salvation. It also occurs to denote the royal residence, capital, and cultic center, but only rarely the city of sin and judgment. In the later chapters of Isaiah it is a symbol of the community, in Psalms it is the city of God, the community, and the temple. The name Jerusalem does not concentrate on specific aspects but is used fairly evenly for all aspects.

II. Historical Development of the Significance of Zion and Jerusalem.

1. Early Period. Not favorably placed geographically, Jerusalem owes its rise to historical factors. It is first a city of the Jebusites ruled by its own king. It seems to have been settled prior to the nineteenth century B.C. Melchizedek is the priest-king in Gen. 14:18, and the Amarna Letters contain letters from King Abdi-Hera in the thirteenth century B.C. The city is assigned to Benjamin (Josh. 15:8), but the tribe cannot take it and after the conquest it is an alien city (Judg. 19:11-12) dividing north and south.

2. The Davidic Monarchy to Josiah.

a. When David becomes king of the whole land he sees the need to remove the barrier and captures Jerusalem in a surprise attack (2 Sam. 5:6ff.). He makes it his own city and builds his palace there. He takes over the cultic duties of the previous rulers and makes it the center of worship with Zadok as the officiating priest (at first with Abiathar), the ark as a safeguard against Canaanite intrusions, and the temple as a planned cultic center.

b. Solomon enlarges the city and puts up new public buildings. Set alongside the palace, the temple is associated with the dynasty and functions as a national shrine in which God has his dwelling.

c. After Solomon, national unity is broken, but the Davidic dynasty clings to Jerusalem even though it is close to the border. Work is done on the walls, the water supply is improved under Hezekiah, and the temple continues to play the role assigned to it by Solomon. Sennacherib unexpectedly fails to capture the city in 701 B.C., and Josiah carries through political and religious reforms when the Assyrian empire begins to crumble after 626 B.C. By his conquests he makes Jerusalem a more important capital, and by suppressing local shrines he gives the temple a more truly central place.

3. The Last Kings and the Exile. Babylon destroys the state of Judah but allows Jerusalem to function as a small city-state. Yet the city retains its cultic importance (cf. Jer. 41:5) even though the Babylonians destroy the temple and shake the belief in Zion's invincibility as the place of God's presence. In fact, the importance of the city grows among the exiles (Ps. 137). The sacred site is the focal point for believers, not as the royal residence, but as a spiritual center and the theme of eschatological expectation.

4. The Postexilic Period.

a. Under the Persians the deported leaders return, reestablish the earlier social structure apart from the monarchy, and invest the city with renewed cultic authority. The people now becomes a cultic community and the second temple is more truly the temple of the people rather than of the royal house.

b. Nehemiah establishes Judah as a separate province and rebuilds the walls of the city, which is once again the capital of a larger area. Under Ezra and Nehemiah the population is now almost exclusively Israelite as religious separation is achieved. As the land of the people, Judah, with Jerusalem as its capital, can maintain itself under the Ptolemies in spite of the rash attempt of Antiochus Epiphanes to turn Jerusalem into a Hellenistic *pólis*. Extension over the western hill takes place, and a new wall encloses and defends the expanded territory.

III. Aspects and Meanings of the Terms.

1. Royal Residence and Capital.

a. Often the term Jerusalem, and less often Zion, denotes the political center, e.g., in the Canaanite period, under David, during the monarchy, and again under Nehemiah.

b. In this regard it may be simply the city-state or it may be mentioned along with provincial towns, the whole state of Judah, or both Judah and Israel.

2. Court-Sacral Aspects. As both capital and cultic center Jerusalem plays a part in a developing court theology; cf. the bringing up of the ark, the enthronement and investiture ceremonies, the concept of the divine election of the Davidic dynasty (Ps. 132), and God's choice of Zion. On this basis there is expectation of the stability of the monarchy and material blessing for a righteous people.

3. Symbol of the People or Community.

a. The city symbolizes its inhabitants and may thus speak, suffer, and be saved in an equation with the people or the community (cf. Ps. 79:1-2; Mic. 7:8ff.; Is. 51:17ff.; 46:13).

b. From the time of Jeremiah the city is a symbol of the people or community as such (Jer. 1:3; 4:11; 13:9-10). When Jer. 4:14 summons Jerusalem to repent, the people is in view. The "daughter of Jerusalem" refers partly to the city and partly to the people. In Is. 40:1-2 Jerusalem is God's people in every place and time. The same equation occurs in eschatological expectation (cf. Is. 65:19ff.). This equation of city and people means that none but Israelites should live in it (Neh. 2:20).

4. Seat and City of God.

a. The bringing up of the ark and building of the temple establish Jerusalem or Zion as God's dwelling. The primary reference is perhaps to the holy hill or temple, but the whole city comes to be included. The temple is God's palace side by side with the king's palace (cf. Jer. 8:19). Ps. 9:11 says that God is enthroned in Zion. God has prepared a dwelling to reign there forever (Ex. 15:17-18). He has chosen Zion and causes his name to dwell there (1 Kgs. 11:13, 32, 36; 2 Chr. 7:16; 12:13).

b. To be noted in this development is the extending or transferring of the holy center from the ark to the temple, the temple to the hill, and the hill to the whole city.

Founded on the holy hills, Jerusalem is itself the city of God (Ps. 46:4) or of the great King (48:2); it is the holy city (Is. 48:2; Neh. 11:1).

c. God is thus present in Zion or Jerusalem, even in judgment (Ezek. 9:3; 10:2ff.; 11:22-23). It is there that he now appears (Pss. 68:17; 50:2; Joel 3:16; Am. 1:2). Mt. Zion and Jerusalem are symbols of divine protection (Ps. 125:1-2), and blessing may be pronounced from them (128:5).

d. Judgment may fall on the temple and city (Jer. 26:6ff.; Mic. 3:12), but as God's holy foundation (Is. 14:32-33) it will survive, so that even during the exile the relation between it and the community remains strong. Membership in the temple community has redemptive significance (Is. 56:1ff.), and the temple is to be a center for all nations (56:7). Although distinction may be made between temple and city (Ps. 68:29), the whole city is the temple city (Ps. 48), and Zion is both the site of the cultus and the cultus itself.

5. *The City of Sin and Judgment.*

a. The prophets denounce the city as sinful, ascribing to it, as the capital, the chief blame for the sins of the people (Mic. 1:5). The true sin is that of apostasy and revolt against God (Is. 3:8, 16-17). The idolatrous city is like an unfaithful harlot. Ethical and social sin accompanies religious sin (Mic. 3:10). The very essence of the city is oppression (Jer. 6:6-7); it is a city of blood-guiltiness (Ezek. 22:2-3). There is also the political sin of wooing the great powers (Ezek. 16:23ff.). "This city" is the contemptuous term used for Jerusalem by Jeremiah and Ezekiel. Pagan by origin, the people is worthless by nature (Ezek. 15:6; 16:1ff.). The saving of a remnant brings out the justice of the punishment (14:22).

b. As a city of sin, Jerusalem is also a city of judgment (Is. 29:1ff.; 32:13-14). God will bring it to account (Zeph. 1:12). Babylon is his agent (Ezek. 21:25ff.). The judgment takes the form of war and deportation (Jer. 6:23; Ezek. 12:1ff.). It is pitiless; only radical conversion could avert it (Jer. 4:3-4; 15:5). If the disaster seems incomprehensible in Lamentations, it has been impending for some time (Ps. 137:7).

6. *City of the Age of Eschatological Salvation.*

a. During the exile the prophetic message is that of judgment followed by restoration and final salvation. Lam. 4:22 announces the end of judgment, Is. 40:1ff. offers a message of comfort and return, and Zech. 8:15 promises the future age of salvation.

b. God himself, who does not desert his people (Is. 49:14-15), declares and grants deliverance (Is. 41:27; 46:13). The exile enables him to show his power (Mic. 4:10). The shining of his glory means salvation for Jerusalem in a new creation (Is. 60). God has still chosen Zion (Zech. 3:2), and the building of the second temple presages restoration (Hag. 2:19). God himself returns (Ezek. 43:1ff.), and messengers of joy and peace announce his coming (Is. 52:7ff.). Dwelling again in Zion (Is. 4:5; 30:29; Zech. 2:14), he will inaugurate his eschatological rule (Is. 24:23 etc.). Not merely the Messiah (Zech. 9:9-10) but God himself has his residence there, establishing an acceptable regime (Jer. 3:15), protecting the city, and constituting its inner glory (Zech. 2:9).

c. The city's glory rests wholly on God's saving work (Is. 62; 66:10ff.). Reconstructed with unbelievable magnificence, extending beyond its walls, and open day and night to trade, the new city, as the eschatological capital and religious center, receives new names that God confers and that express his rights (cf. Is. 62:4, 12; Jer. 3:17; 33:16; Ezek. 48:35; Zech. 8:3). The depictions contain human traits, for eschatology deals with historical factors; but God's saving action creates a far more glorious Jerusalem, which forms the starting point for the concept of a heavenly Jerusalem.

d. God washes away the sin of the inhabitants (Is. 4:4). The holy remnant of the redeemed returns to the city (35:10). Hope is held out for a more extensive return from all nations (27:13). The goal of the return is the establishing of a lasting covenant relationship (Jer. 50:5) in divinely imparted faithfulness and righteousness (Zech. 8:8). A new and upright people is born in Zion (Is. 26:2; 66:8), which lives a secure and abundant life (Zech. 8:4-5), enjoys prosperity (2:8), experiences joy (2:4), and pours forth praise and thanksgiving (Is. 12:4ff.).

e. Judgment falls on Babylon and Edom (Jer. 51:24; Obad. 17-18, 21), and the nations that attack Jerusalem will be defeated and destroyed (Is. 17:12ff.; Joel 3:9ff.). It is God who judges the nations and preserves Jerusalem, but in another strand of prophecy God has a saving purpose for the nations too (Is. 18:7; 25:6-7; 45:14). They will go up to the temple and be taught there (Is. 2:2ff.). They will seek God and serve him (Zech. 8:22; 102:22). They will find a home in Jerusalem (Ps. 87:5). Confessing the true God, they will belong to his people and peace will reign (Zech. 2:15; Is. 2:4).

7. Mythical Aspects.

a. Mythical elements, divested of their mythical character, provide metaphors that bring out the significance of Zion, especially the myths of the highest mountain and the water of life (cf. Is. 2:2; Ezek. 47:1ff.; Zech. 14:8).

b. Less common are the ideas of Jerusalem as the navel of the earth (Ezek. 5:5; 38:12), that of the city standing firm in the conflict with chaos (Ps. 46:1ff.), that of its judgment as a paradisal fall (Lam. 2:1), and that of the city as a cosmic tree shading the peoples (Ezek. 17:22ff.).

8. City of Theocracy. In Chronicles, Jerusalem is a theocratic center. God has chosen it, set up the monarchy there, acknowledged the temple, and made the city a holy place to which Gentiles and true believers from the northern state may come. Even now God has thus actualized his rule in and around it.

9. Summary. The special position of Jerusalem expresses humble faith and obedience under God's established or awaited rule but may also be a ground of obstinacy and frivolous self-assurance in which the cry "The temple, the temple" becomes an excuse for evasion of God's demands. The prophets set Jerusalem under the same obligations, threats, and promises as all other cities, for it is God himself who is supreme, and while he may choose Jerusalem and have a future for it, he is not tied to it, but may meet his people at any time or place.   [G. FOHRER, VII, 292-319]

B. Zion and Jerusalem in Postbiblical Judaism.

I. Usage. The Greek of Zion is *Seiōn* or *Siōn*. For Jerusalem the LXX has *Ierousalēm* (*hē* is the article), but the form *Hierosólyma* also occurs, and Hellenistic Jews prefer it because it echoes *hierós*. The use is similar to what one finds in the OT.

II. From the Maccabean Period to A.D. 70. From the days of the Persians Jerusalem plays only a minor political role but achieves increasing importance as the center of worship for all believing Jews. Those impressed by Hellenistic culture try to turn it into a Hellenistic city with a gymnasium and pagan practices. The attempt by Antiochus Epiphanes to replace God with Zeus leads to the Maccabean revolt and the cleansing of the temple. After the capture of the fortress, the restored city becomes the residence of the Hasmoneans, who unite the priesthood with the monarchy and open the door to pagan customs. Pompey takes the city in 63 B.C., even entering the temple. With Roman consent, Herod establishes himself in Jerusalem and undertakes big building projects, e.g., strengthening the fortress, constructing a new palace, and rebuilding the temple. When the Romans transfer rule to the procurators, these reside in Caesarea and pay only occasional visits to Jerusalem. In A.D. 66 the Jews drive the Romans out, but the legions encompass the city and after a long siege capture it in A.D. 70. Titus enters the temple, but it then goes up in flames. The righteous see here a divine visitation.

III. Jerusalem in the Days of Jesus. In the days of Jesus Jerusalem is a large city with a population of not less than 25,000. As a result of Herod's projects it is prosperous. The supreme court, the Sanhedrin, meets there to decide religious questions. Renowned scribes teach the law in Jerusalem, and students come from far and wide to profit from their learning. Many synagogues offer opportunities for worship and for the reading and exposition of the law. The temple lies on Mt. Zion in new splendor. Gentiles may enter the outer court, but then a barrier with an express prohibition sets off the court of women, the court of Israelites, the court of priests, the altar of burnt offering, and the sanctuary.

IV. Jerusalem the Sacred Metropolis. Jews pray three times a day toward Jerusalem. Those who live in the city pray toward the temple. Jews abroad send gifts to the temple. Those who are able go up there for the feasts. Citizens entertain pilgrims without charge. From afar the temple looks like a snow-capped hill. Prayer in the holy place carries a special promise. Even for those who withdraw to the desert Jerusalem is still the elect city. Judgment will fall on unholy priests, but in the age of salvation the temple will be rebuilt in the new Jerusalem as Scripture enjoins.

V. The New Jerusalem. The daily prayer is that God will have mercy on Jerusalem and return to Zion. When the last attack of ungodly powers is repulsed, God will reconstruct the city and it will be the place of eschatological salvation. The new Jerusalem is either the city of David rebuilt with new glory or the preexistent city that is built by God in heaven and comes down with the dawn of a new world. Apocalyptic presents the latter view, but the rabbis favor the former view, whereby God or the Messiah will rebuild the city with great magnificence and greatly enlarge its borders so that it can accommodate the Jews and the many Gentiles who stream into it. The holy vessels and the ark will return to the holy place, the saints will dwell there, and all peoples will come there to worship. Paradise will return with the new Jerusalem.

C. Zion and Jerusalem in the NT.

I. Occurrence and Usage.

1. There are seven instances of *Siốn* in the NT, five in OT quotations, the other two in Heb. 12:22 and Rev. 14:1.

2. Jerusalem is often mentioned in the Gospels and Acts, and sometimes in Paul, Hebrews, and Revelation, but never in the Catholic Epistles. Jerusalem is probably the city on the hill in Mt. 5:14, and it is the holy city in Mt. 4:5; 27:53; Rev. 11:2, the beloved city in Rev. 20:9, and the city of the great king in Mt. 5:35. In most instances the actual city is in view, but the inhabitants may be included, e.g., in Mt. 2:3. Both Greek forms occur. Revelation and Hebrews use only *Ierousalếm,* Paul normally has this form, Luke prefers it, but the other Gospels mostly have *Hierosólyma.*

II. Sayings of Jesus about Jerusalem.

1. Except in references to the passion Jerusalem occurs only three times in Jesus' preaching. In Lk. 10:30 a man goes down from Jerusalem to Jericho. In Lk. 13:4 those on whom the tower falls are not more guilty than others who live in Jerusalem; the summons to all is to repent. In Mt. 5:35 to swear by Jerusalem is to take God's name in vain, for Jerusalem is the city of the great king.

2. The two sayings in Lk. 13:33 and Mt. 23:37ff. deal with martyrdom. It is a

common belief that prophets must suffer in Jerusalem, and Jesus expects his own prophetic passion there, for Jerusalem is the place of decision. The lament probably refers not so much to Jesus' own ministry in the city as to the repeated invitation of God or the divine wisdom. The forsaking of Jerusalem will last until the parousia, when the returning Jesus will be joyfully hailed as the Messiah.

3. Jesus is crucified before the gates of Jerusalem. He predicts his death there in Mk. 8:31; 9:31; 10:32ff. and parallels. Details accord with the apostolic kerygma, and Mt. 16:21 implies that the passion is by divine ordination. The name of Jerusalem does not actually occur in Mk. 9:31 and parallels.

III. Jerusalem in the Four Gospels.

1. Mark. Jerusalem is seldom mentioned in Mark except in the passion predictions and passion story. Its inhabitants go out to listen to the Baptist (Mk. 1:5) and also to Jesus (3:8). Scribes from Jerusalem accuse Jesus of driving out demons with the help of Beelzebul (3:22). Scribes and Pharisees from the city attack him for breaking the law (7:1ff.). Jerusalem is the residence of his bitterest enemies (11:18; 14:1-2). When he dies, the ripping of the temple curtain initiates the divine judgment on the city (15:38).

2. Matthew. Jerusalem occurs in the infancy stories in Matthew. The Wise Men come there, and Herod and the city are startled by their coming (2:1ff.). Jerusalem is the holy city in 4:5. The Son of Man must go there to die (16:21). Jesus has his decisive debate with the scribes (v. 23) and teaches his disciples about the last things there (vv. 24-25). At his death graves open before the gates and dead saints appear to many in the holy city (27:51-52). Judgment will fall on the city for rejecting God's invitation (22:7), but on the last day it will greet the returning Lord with jubilation (23:39).

3. Luke. Giving more emphasis to Jerusalem, Luke begins and ends in the temple (1:5ff.; 24:53). Jesus and the new community fulfil the ancient promises. The intimation to Zechariah takes place in the temple (1:5ff.), where the parents of Jesus also present him (2:24), and Simeon and Anna await redemption (2:38). Jesus goes up to the temple at the age of 12 and is at home there (2:41ff.). He vanquishes the tempter on a pinnacle of the temple (4:9). He debates with scribes and Pharisees from Jerusalem (5:17), and people flock to him from many places, including Jerusalem (6:17). He sets his journey to Jerusalem under the sign of the passion (9:51ff.). His entry brings him to the temple, which he cleanses and uses as a place for teaching (19:45ff.). Jerusalem is destroyed because it does not know what belongs to its peace (19:42ff.). Hence its daughters should weep for themselves and their children (23:28). In and around Jerusalem the risen Lord appears to his disciples (24:13ff.) and commissions them to proclaim his saving death and resurrection. His disciples meet in the temple and praise God there (24:53).

4. John. In John Jerusalem alternates with Galilee as the center of Jesus' ministry. Meeting representatives of the unbelieving cosmos there, he makes it a place for the manifesting of his glory. Various sites receive specific mention, e.g., the pool of Bethesda in 5:2, and the pool of Siloam in 9:7. He teaches in the temple (7:14), and specifically in Solomon's portico (10:22-23). He stays in Bethany with Mary and Martha. At the end he teaches only the disciples, and John does not mention Jerusalem in the passion story. The time has come when the Father is worshipped in neither Gerizim nor Jerusalem (4:23).

IV. Jerusalem and the Primitive Community.

1. The Community in Jerusalem. A group of disciples comes together in the holy city and there the Holy Spirit comes upon it. It inherits the promises of the old covenant as the church of God. When Hellenistic Jews are expelled, they carry the gospel abroad. All believers honor the Jerusalem church under the leadership of Peter and then of James, the Lord's brother. From it messengers and prophets go to other churches (Acts 8:14; 11:22, 27; 15:32). Christians gather there to discuss matters of common concern (Gal. 2:1ff.; Acts 15:1ff.), and missionaries return there after fulfilling their tasks (11:2; 13:13; 19:21; 21:15).

2. *Jerusalem in Paul*. Paul recognizes that the gospel has come from Jerusalem (Rom. 15:19), and that the community there has a right to love and respect. But he has not received his apostleship from the apostles in Jerusalem (Gal. 1:1), nor does he need their confirmation (1:18ff.; 2:1-2). They agree that he should share in the church's mission and arrange the collection (Gal. 2:7ff.). The gifts he brings to Jerusalem are an offering of love, not a tax. Although he does not work in Jerusalem, he describes his ministry as extending from Jerusalem as far around as Illyricum (Rom. 15:19).

3. *Jerusalem in Acts*. The disciples stay in Jerusalem as the Lord commands (Lk. 24:49; Acts 1:4). After the Spirit descends, they preach Christ there (2:36). Many residents and resident aliens receive their message (2:43; 5:16). The rulers oppose them (4:5) but cannot stop the spread of the word (6:7). The community worships in the temple (2:46; 3:1ff.). When the church grows in Judea and Samaria it accepts the leadership of Jerusalem (Acts 8:14ff.; 11:2ff.). Saul persecutes the church in Jerusalem (9:13, 21); he is well known in the city for his exemplary life (26:4). Soon after conversion he comes back to Jerusalem, and Barnabas introduces him to the apostles (9:26ff.). In the temple he receives his commission to go to the Gentiles (22:17-18). He visits Jerusalem as an envoy of the church at Antioch (11:27ff.; 12:25; 15:2, 4). At Ephesus he resolves to go to Jerusalem for Pentecost as a pilgrim (19:21; 20:16, 22). The elders of the church receive him (21:17) but the Jews arrange his arrest (21:27ff.). Since his case cannot be decided in Jerusalem he finally goes to Rome (28:17) and is thus enabled to bear witness in both Jerusalem and Rome as the Lord declares (23:11).

4. *Zion and Jerusalem in Revelation*. In Rev. 14:1 the divine sees the Lamb on Mt. Zion, i.e., the place of eschatological preservation which shelters the 144,000. The city of ch. 11 is clearly Jerusalem. As the theater of Christ's suffering, which is now the seat of blasphemy and obduracy, it comes under God's judgment, although the temple, i.e., God's people, will be saved (11:1).

V. The New Jerusalem.

1. *Paul*. In Gal. 4:21ff. Paul equates the son of the slave with the Sinaitic covenant and present-day Jerusalem, but the son of the free woman with the promise and the Jerusalem above. He adds that the free Jerusalem is our mother. Since the present freedom of believers is at issue, the Jerusalem that is above represents an eschatological salvation that is not just future but has come already.

2. *Hebrews*. In Heb. 12:22 the heavenly mount and the heavenly city are the site of the gathering of angels and the community. The city here is not just the goal of pilgrimage. Believers have come to it already as the place of the new covenant from which they can journey on to the eternal city.

3. *Revelation*. In Rev. 3:12 those who bear the name of God belong to the heavenly Jerusalem which comes down from God to earth (21:10). Paradise will return with this city (22:1ff.). A wealth of images describes it, but it will have no temple (21:22).

D. Zion and Jerusalem in the Early Church.

1. The only two instances in the apostolic fathers are in Barn. 6.2 (quoting Is. 28:16) and 1 Clem. 41.2 (the example of divinely established order).

2. The apocryphal gospels often mention Jerusalem.

3. Theologians apply the allegorical interpretation of the name Jerusalem to the church or believers (cf. Origen). The soul oppressed by evil powers is Jebus (trodden down), but when transformed by divine teaching it is Jerusalem, the city of peace.

4. Clement of Alexandria employs the idea of the Jerusalem above to portray the ideal city in Platonic terms. Gnostic dualism also makes use of the contrast between the lower and upper Jerusalems. The latter belongs to the incorruptible world of light and is wisdom for the Valentinians.   [E. Lohse, VII, 319-38]

---

skándalon [cause of offense, stumbling block],   *skandalízō* [to give offense, cause to stumble]

A. Derivation and Nonbiblical Usage.

1. The original stem has the sense of "springing forward and back," "slamming to," "closing on something," or "trapping," but later the meaning "offense," or "reason for punishment," occurs in the papyri.

2. There are no instances of the verb outside the biblical sphere but *skandalistés* presupposes *skandalízō* in the sense "to set traps."

B. The OT.

I. Hebrew Terms. The LXX uses the group for two sets of Hebrew terms with the different senses of striking or catching in a snare, and slipping or stumbling (with the transferred meaning "occasion of sin").

II. The LXX.

1. *skándalon.* In translation of the Hebrew *próskomma, skólon,* and *skándalon* are used, and by assimilation *skándalon* can mean both "trap" and "stumbling block" or "cause of ruin" either with idols in view or offenses against the law. As a ground of divine punishment *skándalon* can then denote an occasion of sinning or a temptation to sin.

2. *skandalízō.* This verb, which is rare in the LXX, carries the senses "to catch oneself," i.e., "to fall into sin," and in the active (Ps. Sol. 16:7) "to lead astray."

C. Later Translations of the OT.

1. Aquila. Following a rigid principle of translation, Aquila uses *skándalon* for "cause of ruin," *skandalismós* for "disaster," and *skandalízomai* for "to come to hurt."

2. Symmachus. Less rigidly Symmachus, too, uses *skándalon* for "cause of disaster" or "death" (Prov. 29:6; 13:14; 14:27).

3. Theodotion. There is nothing independent in this translation.

C. The NT.

I. Dependence on the OT. Formally and materially NT usage depends on that of the OT. The terms occur in sayings of Jesus, in Paul, and in John. Luke avoids some instances or uses other terms. In Lk. 2:34, although *ptósis* occurs rather than *skándalon,* the NT concept comes to clear expression; the ministry of Jesus can result in death or life, for his person and work will either evoke faith or stir up opposition. Various LXX phrases may be found (cf. Rom. 14:13; 1 Cor. 1:23), and OT allusions and quotations occur (Mt. 13:41; Rom. 11:9). In the NT, as in the OT, the issue in *skándalon* is one's relation to God. The *skándalon* is an obstacle to faith and hence a cause of falling and destruction.

II. Sayings of Jesus.

1. OT Prophecies. In Mt. 13:41 and 24:10 Jesus quotes OT sayings with an eschatological slant (Zeph. 1:3; Dan. 11:41). Mt. 24:10 refers to the final *skandalismós,* and 13:41 to the uprooting of *skándala.* In 13:41 the *skándala* are probably persons who bring ruin by seducing into sin and whose end will come with that of the devil and his hosts. The gathering of the elect (cf. 24:31) is the counterpart of this uprooting.

2. Present skándala.

a. The eschatological apostasy has begun already, for the coming of Jesus has brought *skándala* that accompany the demand for faith. In Mt. 18:7 the coming of *skándala* is inevitable but woes are pronounced on those who participate passively or actively in their coming. They are extremely dangerous, for they involve eternal ruin. They apply to all people but, while unavoidable, they are integrated into God's plan, for history consists of decisions for and against God.

b. In Mt. 16:23 Peter, who has been given a role similar to that of Jesus himself, both foundation stone (1 Cor. 3:11) and rock of offense (Rom. 9:33), becomes a stone of stumbling to Jesus. Opposing human thoughts to the divine will, he acts as an instrument of Satan. Finding the way of Jesus to the cross a *skándalon,* he becomes a *skándalon,* i.e., a personified temptation to turn aside from the will of God.

3. Present skandalismós.

a. Apostasy of the Unstable. When the word of the kingdom is preached, afflictions arise that result in *skandalízesthai* or falling away (Mt. 13:20-21) as a prelude to eschatological *skandalismós.* In this instance people of unstable and superficial character receive the word but their easily kindled enthusiasm just as quickly cools. The apostasy means ruin, so that the *skándalon* which is an occasion of sin is also the cause of destruction.

b. *skandalismós* at Jesus. When reasons are given for *skandalízesthai,* the reference is to Jesus (Mt. 26:31; 33; 13:57). Offense at Jesus is the opposite of faith in him. The disciples take offense and fall at the passion (Mk. 14:27; Mt. 26:31). The sufferings of the Messiah bring panic to his followers and scatter them (cf. Zech. 13:7). Peter falls victim to this *skándalon* in spite of his professed readiness to accept suffering for himself (Mk. 14:29; Mt. 26:33). In the reply to the Baptist Jesus pronounces blessing on those who do not lose confidence in him (Mt. 11:6). The age of salvation is the age of decision. The presence of Jesus may result either in faith or in the missing of faith. A cause of unbelief attaches to his words, even though avoidance of *skandalismós* is the goal. The people of Nazareth, finding a contradiction between his origin and his work, take offense and refuse to believe (Mt. 13:53ff.). Indeed, their unbelief becomes mortal hatred (Lk. 4:28-29). The Pharisees, too, are not just hurt at the attacks of Jesus (Mt. 15:12); they reject his teaching and thereby show that they are not God's plant but blind leading the blind, i.e., unbelievers. The occasions of stumbling are irritation at the freedom of Jesus, annoyance at his distinction between law and tradition, and offense at his person even though, as in the case of the tax (Mt. 17:27), he forgoes his own freedom (cf. Rom. 14:13) so as not to arouse opposition.

c. Not Causing Others to Stumble. Avoiding *skandalismós* is the point in Mk. 9:42. Here the punishment, i.e., eternal perdition, fits the offense, i.e., causing loss of faith and therefore loss of salvation. A similar eschatological light falls on Mk. 9:43ff.; Mt. 5:29-30; 18:8-9. The meaning of *skandalízō* here is "to entice into sin" and therefore to plunge into unbelief and perdition. No price is too high to avoid this; hence the relentless demand of Jesus.

III. Paul.

1. The skándalon of the Gospel. Paul refers first to an unavoidable *skándalon* (Rom. 9:33). Jesus brings salvation but may also be a cause of perdition. 1 Pet. 2:6ff. contains the same thought and uses the same OT quotations. Unbelievers take offense at Jesus and hence he is for them a stone of stumbling. By divine appointment the word serves a twofold function depending on whether its hearers obey or disobey it. An essential mark of faith is that it overcomes the *skándalon* of God's saving work in Christ. As 1 Cor. 1:18ff. shows, the cross is religiously offensive to the Jews, as it is folly to the Greeks. Part of the *skándalon,* of course, is the liberation from the law that it effects (Gal. 5:11). To enforce circumcision is to weaken the *skándalon* by compromise. For the Jews, however, the *skándalon,* foretold in Ps. 69:22, means stumbling but not falling (v. 11). Nor are Christians immune from *skandalízesthai.* In 2 Cor. 11:29 Paul is ready to share the weakness of the weak but he is indignant if any are made to fall.

2. The Danger of Falling. Tensions in the churches are the occasion of *skándalon* (cf. the debates between the strong and the weak in Rom. 14–15 and 1 Cor. 8:1ff.; 10:23ff.). The freedom of those who have fully cast off the past causes offense to those who have not, but it also creates the danger that these will act against their consciences or with wavering faith. In this case the danger is the serious one of an ultimate eschatological fall (Rom. 14:15, 23). The strong with their freedom may destroy the weak and therefore overturn God's work in Christ. Paul, then, sides with the weak even though he shares the faith of the strong (Rom. 15:1).

3. The skándalon of Heresy. False teachers cause both divisions and *skándala,* which are probably temptations to abandon sound doctrine. A similar use of *skándalon* occurs in Rev. 2:14 (cf. also Mt. 13:41), where "to put a stumbling block" recalls Lev. 19:14 and carries the sense of seduction into apostasy and immorality (cf. vv. 15, 20).

IV. John. The noun is semifigurative in 1 Jn. 2:10 ("cause of aberration"). Blindness or darkness is here the presupposition. Where there is love there is light and therefore no reason to go astray and fall. In Jn. 6:61 a crisis of faith is apparent. Lack of understanding causes many disciples to leave Jesus. Only the power of the Spirit illumining the word can overcome the *skandalismós* (v. 63). Peter's confession confirms the truth of this (v. 68). The parting discourses have the aim of keeping the disciples from falling away (Jn. 16:1). Here again the Spirit and his witness will play the crucial role (15:26-27), for the Spirit will enable the disciples to understand the approaching passion, which Jesus himself both intimates and supports with a proof from Scripture (15:18ff.).

D. Patristic Writings. The word group occurs only rarely in the post–NT period. Where it is used, it undergoes psychological and moralistic trivializing.

[G. STÄHLIN, VII, 339-58]

---

skeúos [vessel]

A. Secular Greek.

1. *skeúos,* meaning "vessel" or "container," is used literally for household utensils, agricultural implements, baggage, military equipment, nautical gear, and cultic vessels.

2. In a transferred sense some people are the tools of others, the body is the vessel of the soul, and the *skeúos* is also the reproductive organ.

B. The LXX.

1. Gk. *skeúos* covers much the same field as Heb. $k^e l\hat{\imath}$, being used for it in some 270 of 320 instances and in such senses as vessels, yokes, weapons, baggage, ship's gear, and sacred vessels.

2. In the figurative use, a mark of the OT term is that the human instrument is fragile (Hos. 8:8), that God is radically superior to it (Is. 10:15), and that he shapes it as the potter does his vessel (Jer. 18:1ff.). The meaning in 1 Sam. 21:6 is either "body" or "reproductive organ."

C. Later Judaism.

1. In later Judaism the literal use is similar to that of the OT.

2. In a transferred sense the law is a costly vessel, people are instruments of God or the devil, the body is a vessel for the person, the serpent is a tool of the devil, and the body is a vessel for the soul.

3.a. As regards the use of "vessel" for "woman" it may be noted that harlots are "vessels" in Egyptian Aramaic texts.

b. A similar sexual sense occurs in the rabbinic sphere in which "to use as a vessel" seems to be a euphemism for having sexual intercourse.

c. This may also be the meaning when a widow refuses marriage on the ground that a vessel that has been used for what is holy should not be used for what is profane.

d. The phrase "to make the formless mass of woman a ready or complete vessel" also seems to have marriage in view.

e. In sum, "vessel" means "woman" only in a formal sense but carries the suggestion of "using woman as a vessel" in a sexual sense.

D. The NT.

1. In the NT *skeúos* denotes a vessel that can be carried in Mk. 11:16, a household utensil in Rev. 2:27; Jn. 19:29; Lk. 8:16; Acts 10:11, 16, nautical gear in Acts 27:17, and a liturgical vessel in Heb. 9:21.

2.a. Figuratively *skeúos* occurs in Rom. 9:19ff. The concern in context is with the relations between the old and new covenant peoples; vv. 22ff. bring out the teleological link between the two as God forges them for different ends. The "vessels" denoted here are obviously utensils but the sense of instruments is also to the fore. Although God has perhaps made some vessels for destruction and some for glory, mercy may be seen even in relation to the former, for they are not yet smashed, God's wrath against them brings out his mercy to the latter vessels, and this mercy will finally lead to a fullness of glory. The genitive in "vessels of wrath" is a qualitative one; on and through these vessels God works out his wrath. The line that runs from Esau by way of Pharaoh to disobedient Israel stands in antithesis to that which runs from Isaac by way of Moses to the church, but which includes both Gentiles from the world of Pharaoh and believers from Israel, so that there is no absolute antithesis. Implicit is the thought that even the vessel of wrath may be reshaped into a vessel of mercy.

b. In 2 Tim. 2:20-21 the vessels are evaluated according to both purpose and material. The passage is a summons to purification from error with a view to being a consecrated and useful vessel.

c. Paul himself is a "chosen vessel" in Acts 9:15 (cf. Gal. 1:15-16). He is elected to service and suffering (2 Cor. 11:23ff.). He and his colleagues have the treasure of the gospel in "earthen vessels," i.e., not just their bodies but their whole persons with all their lowliness and frailty (2 Cor. 4:7).

3. The reference in 1 Th. 4:4 may be to the "body," as in Greek thought, or to the "wife," as in the Jewish euphemism. The verb may also mean either "to gain" or "to possess." If the wife is the *skeúos,* then we have an exhortation either to marry as a remedy against fornication or to hold one's wife in esteem. For Paul, who knows both Hebrew and Greek, the most likely meaning is that his readers should know how to live with their wives in sanctification and honor rather than in the lust of passion. Against the rendering of *skeúos* as "body," one may cite the context, the absence in Paul of any concept of the body as the container of the soul, and Paul's lack of interest in an ethics centered on the body. On the other hand, a call for sanctification in marriage is wholly in keeping with both the context and Paul's training (cf. also 1 Cor. 7:2). 1 Pet. 3:7 offers an apt commentary. Linking the marriage relationship to the ordination of both partners to their future inheritance, it gives this relationship its supreme justification and ultimate profundity.

E. Apostolic Fathers. The apostolic fathers use *skeúos* for utensils, for believers as vessels of the Spirit, and for Christ's body and also the land of Jacob as a vessel of the Spirit. 2 Clem. 8.2 summons to repentance in this life on the ground that the potter can refashion vessels only so long as he has not fired them.

[C. MAURER, VII, 358-67]

> *skēnḗ* [tent],   *skḗnos* [tent, body],   *skḗnōma* [tent, temple],   *skēnóō* [to live, dwell],   *episkēnóō* [to take up residence],   *kataskēnóō* [to cause to dwell],   *skēnopegía* [pitching tents, Tabernacles],   *skēnopoiós* [tent-maker]

skēnḗ.

A. Greek Usage. Of uncertain etymology, *skēnḗ* consistently means "tent," although with such nuances as market booth, accommodation in a tent, portable shrine, stage of a theater (originally a framework of pillars with portable walls), cover of a wagon, and cabin on the deck of a ship. The idea of transitoriness is inherent in the term, although later it can have the more general sense of dwelling or lodging.

B. The LXX.

1. *skēnḗ* occurs some 435 times in the OT, mostly for Heb. *'hl.* About two-thirds of the references are to the tent of meeting.

2. The use of tents is common in Israel; cf. Abraham (Gen. 12:8), Jethro (Ex. 18:7), Korah (Num. 16:26-27), and Achan (Josh. 7:21ff.). Nomads (Gen. 4:20), herdsmen (Judg. 6:5), and soldiers (2 Kgs. 7:7-8) live in tents. At Tabernacles living in tents recalls the wilderness period (Lev. 23:42-43).

3. The OT tells us little about the construction of tents. Cedar is mentioned in Cant. 1:5, and we read of pegs (Judg. 4:21) and hangings (Is. 54:2). Pointed tents and matted structures both seem to be in vogue (cf. 2 Sam. 11:11). The structures used at Tabernacles are the latter, i.e., booths or huts of thickly intertwined leaves.

4. The tent of meeting is always called a tent in the OT (*'hl* or *mškn*). Later it perhaps becomes a matted structure, but originally it is the place where one meets God rather than the place where he resides, and *skēnḗ* (or *skḗnōma*) is chosen as the rendering, not because it bears the general sense of dwelling, but because it represents

the original sense of tent, and probably also because the three consonants *skn* also occur in Heb. *mškn*. Yet in time the tabernacle comes to be regarded as the place of God's dwelling and this tends to give to *skēnḗ* more of the sense of a dwelling in this context.

5. A few poetic statements refer to God's dwelling in heaven or on earth as in a *skēnḗ* (cf. Is. 40:22; Ps. 18:11; Job 36:29). In Ps. 27:5 (*skēnḗ*) the idea is that of protection. Ex. 26:30 presupposes a heavenly prototype for the tabernacle, but this does not imply that in heaven God lives in a *skēnḗ*.

6. The idea of living in tents plays no role in eschatology. Ps. 118:15 is not meant eschatologically, and in Hos. 12:9 the point is not the dwelling in tents but the parallel between the wilderness period and the end-time. There is no promise that God himself will tabernacle among his people nor is there any prophecy that the Messiah will dwell in a tent.

C. Nonbiblical Judaism.

1. Philo uses *skēnḗ* in OT connections and in relation to Tabernacles. Allegorically wisdom is a tent in which the wise dwell, and the tent of meeting symbolizes virtue.

2. Josephus, too, uses *skēnḗ* for ordinary tents, in connection with Tabernacles, and as a specific term for the tent of meeting. This is the *prṓtē skēnḗ* compared to Solomon's temple.

3. The pseudepigrapha give evidence of OT influence. Jub. 16:21 mentions Tabernacles, and 1:10 calls the tabernacle (or temple) God's tent. In the Qumran hymns there is reference to God's holy dwelling and the place of his tent, but this seems to be conventional usage.

D. The NT.

1. *skēnḗ* occurs 20 times in the NT, ten of the instances being in Hebrews and eight in Heb. 8–9. In Acts 7:43 (quoting Am. 5:27ff. LXX) the *skēnḗ* is a cultic tent. In Acts 15:16 the rise of the church is the restoration of David's *skēnḗ* according to Am. 9:11-12. Jewish Christians fulfil the first part of the prophecy and Gentile Christians the second. In Acts 4:44 the *skēnḗ* is the tent of witness, carried into Canaan in v. 45. Rev. 15:5 refers to God's temple in heaven (11:19) as "the temple of the tent of witness in heaven."

2. Heb. 8:1-2 distinguishes between the true and heavenly tent and the earthly one. God has pitched the true tent, whereas he ordered but did not himself erect the earthly tent. The heavenly tent is a model for the earthly one, but it also serves its own purpose as a preexistent tent that is eternal in character. The earthly tent in 9:1ff. is twofold; there is an outer and an inner tent, and the way to the inner tent is not yet opened so long as the outer tent still stands (9:8). Similarly the heavenly tent seems to have both an outer and an inner sanctuary, though it is not suggested that God dwells in the heavenly holy of holies. It is through the outer tent that Christ by his blood gains access to the inner tent (9:11-12). What precisely the outer tent is, the author does not say. It is in the light of the exposition in chs. 8–9 that 13:10 refers to those who "serve the tent," i.e., the priests of the OT sanctuary. The fact that Abraham lives in tents (11:9) emphasizes his alien status; the city toward which he moves as a pilgrim is that which God builds.

3. In Rev. 13:6 the beast blasphemes the *skēnḗ* of God. The choice of the word here is probably based on the use of the verb in 7:15, to which corresponds 12:12 with its reference to those who dwell in heaven. These verses help to explain the

combination of temple and tent in 15:5, which catches up the *naós toú theoú* of 11:19 (cf. also 21:3).

4. Lk. 16:9 speaks of eschatological *skēnaí* in the plural. Huts or tents seem to be in contradiction with the idea of permanence. The thought, however, is not that the last age corresponds to the wilderness period, but rather that these are eternal dwellings, with perhaps a suggestion of the indwelling of the divine glory. Peter's proposal to build three *skēnaí* at the transfiguration (Mk. 9:5) obviously has a lengthy stay in view, and since the *skēnaí* are for Jesus, Moses, and Elijah, a messianic or eschatological understanding seems to be present. There is no clear connection with the tent of meeting and only a slight suggestion of Moses' transfiguration on the Mount. Since the booths are not for the disciples, the idea is not that the people of the last time will dwell in tents as in the wilderness. Nor is the proposal related to the idea of God's eschatological tabernacling, nor to that of the Messiah. Moses is a type of the Messiah and Elijah the precursor, but what the proposal expresses seems to be the more general concept of the gracious and abiding presence of God.

5. God dwells in a tent according to Rev. 21:3. Zech. 2:14-15 and Ezek. 37:27 influence this statement, which is not suggesting that in the eschaton there will be a vast heavenly camp with God's tent in the middle, but simply offering a vivid metaphor for God's eternal presence. Emphasis lies on the close relationship between God and his people ("with men," "with them"). The *skēnḗ theoú* is the new Jerusalem or the new heaven and earth (21:1-2). It denotes future eschatological salvation. This prospect is the climax of the history of *skēnḗ* in the NT.

E. The Apostolic Fathers. The term *skēnḗ* occurs three times in 1 Clem. 43 for the OT tent of meeting.

skḗnos.

1. This word means "tent" but is normally used in a transferred sense for a live or dead "body," human or animal.

2. In the LXX it occurs only in Wis. 9:15 for "body."

3. It does not seem to occur in Philo or Josephus.

4. In the NT it occurs only in 2 Cor. 5:1, 4. If it has here the usual sense of "body" rather than "tent," the antithesis of *oikía* and *skḗnos* is lessened. Yet if our present corporeality can be called an *oikía,* this term is neutral as regards durability. Only the eternal, heavenly *oikía* that God builds is a lasting one. Possibly, then, Paul chooses *skḗnos* in order to bring out the corruptibility of the earthly mode of existence. A certain kinship with Gnosticism may perhaps be discerned in the use of *skḗnos,* but if the term bears the normal sense of body this is less pronounced, for the Gnostics prefer *skēnḗ* in their equation of tent and body. The term has no apparent connection with Tabernacles in 2 Cor. 5, nor does it bear an ecclesiological reference.

5. *skḗnos* does not occur in the apostolic fathers.

skḗnōma.

1. This word means "tent," "tentlike dwelling," "temple," and, rarely, "body."

2. It occurs some 80 times in the LXX as a synonym of *skēnḗ* and with no apparent reasons for the choice sometimes of the one and sometimes of the other. The tabernacle and temple are comparatively rarely called *skḗnōma.*

3. Philo does not use *skḗnōma,* but Josephus has it in *Antiquities* 11.187 (cf. Esth. 1:5).

4. The only NT instances are in Acts 7:46 and 2 Pet. 1:13-14. Acts 7:46-47 carries

a hint that Solomon errs by building a solid house for God as distinct from a *skḗnōma*. 2 Pet. 1:13-14 uses the term in the sense of "body," as the verb in v. 14 shows. The expression reminds us of 2 Cor. 5:1, 4 but may simply reflect common usage, especially as 2 Peter, unlike 1 Peter, does not stress the idea of pilgrimage and corruptibility.

5. The only instance in the apostolic fathers is in Diog. 6.8, where "dwelling" or "body" is the sense and the thought of pilgrimage is present.

skēnóō.

1. This word (more commonly *skēnéō*) means "to live or camp in a tent" (or other dwelling), and, transitively, "to pitch or inhabit a tent."

2. The simple form is rare in the LXX compared to the compound *kataskēnóō*.

3. Philo does not have *skēnóō* but Josephus uses it in *On the Life of Moses* 244.

4. In the NT the verb occurs in Jn. 1:14 and several times in Revelation, but never in the literal sense. Rev. 7:15 refers to God's permanent dwelling among the redeemed (cf. 21:3) in abiding and gracious presence. In 13:6, since a tent obviously cannot dwell in a tent, the verb suggests the abiding of God's name and presence. The thought of permanence is also present in 12:12: The redeemed dwell forever in heaven. In Jn. 1:14 the term implies that the earthly stay of the incarnate Logos is an impermanent one between his preexistence and postexistence as the exalted Lord. Yet this is not where the emphasis rests, for the term more specifically shows that what we have here is the presence of the eternal Word in time.

5. *skēnóō* does not occur in the apostolic fathers or Apologists.

episkēnóō.

1. This rare word means "to enter or take up residence in a tent."

2. The only NT use is in 2 Cor. 12:9, where the idea is that the power of Christ enters into, rather than descends upon, the apostle, i.e., resides in him precisely in his human weakness. The combination of the thought of Christ's gracious presence with *epí* (cf. Rev. 7:15) perhaps suggests the rare word.

3. The term occurs neither in the apostolic fathers nor in the Apologists.

kataskēnóō.

1. This uncommon term means "to pitch or enter a tent," "to camp."

2. The word is surprisingly common in the LXX, possibly under the influence of the Hebrew, though the usage is not uniform. It is designed to stress the thought of a longer stay. Secure and lasting dwelling is at issue in, e.g., Num. 14:30; Dt. 33:12; Ps. 16:9; Prov. 1:12. The meaning "cause to dwell" occurs in Ps. 23:2. In Mic. 4:10 living in the country rather than the city is the point. The noun *kataskḗnōsis* occurs six times in the LXX. It refers to the sanctuary in Ezek. 37:27 and means the act of building in 1 Chr. 28:2.

3. Philo equates the tabernacle with wisdom in *Allegorical Interpretation of Laws* 3.46. Josephus uses the term in *Antiquities* 9.34 for Elijah's dwelling in a tent and in 3.202 and 8.106 for God's dwelling in the tent or temple.

4. OT influence fixes the usage in the NT. Acts 2:25ff. quotes Ps. 16:8ff. Hope is not here the place of dwelling but means "as may be hoped." Hence *kataskēnóō* has the absolute sense "to live on," as is fulfilled in the resurrection. In Mk. 4:32 (cf. Dan. 4:12, 21) the idea is that of the birds nesting in the branches rather than simply alighting temporarily on them. Whether there is an allegorical reference to the Gentiles is open to question, but the parable undoubtedly intimates a reign of security and peace.

5. In the apostolic fathers *kataskēnóō* means "to cause to dwell" in Did. 10.2 (God's name at baptism). 1 Clement quotes Prov. 1:33 in 57.7 and 58.1.

skēnopēgía.

1. This word denotes the pitching of a tent or nesting of birds. The verb *skanopagéomai* also occurs in a cultic context for the erection of tents or booths (cf. *skēnopēgéō*).

2. The noun occurs nine times in the LXX, always (except in 2 Maccabees) in connection with Tabernacles. 2 Macc. 1:9, 18 refers to the temple dedication in 164 B.C. and even here there is an analogy to Tabernacles. The LXX use probably derives from the nonbiblical, although this offers no instance of the noun in a cultic context.

3. Josephus plainly connects the noun with Tabernacles (e.g., *Antiquities* 8.123) and an inscription from Cyrenaica (13 B.C.) shows that this is a widespread use.

4. The only NT instance is in Jn. 7:2, where the term denotes the Feast of Tabernacles, as the use in apposition shows. On the middle day of the seven- or eight-day feast Jesus visits the temple (v. 14), and on the great day (the seventh), on which water is dispensed and which forms the true climax, he invites the people to come to him for living water. The account alludes only to the details of the festival. Tabernacles is not of intrinsic theological significance but forms the setting for this visit and the associated teaching of Jesus.

skēnopoiós.

1. This rare word, which combines *skēnḗ* and *poiéō,* generally refers to the pitching of a tent, but it also seems to mean "tent maker," and, since tents are often made of leather, it may mean "leather worker."

2. The only NT instance is in Acts 18:3, where Paul stays with Aquila and Priscilla in Corinth because he works at the same trade. If the trade is that of making tents of goats' hair, Paul is perhaps weaving fabric. But rabbinic scholars do not favor weaving, and it is thus more likely that Paul is a "leather worker," and that as such he is a "tent maker." At any rate, he supports himself so as not to have to depend on the churches (1 Cor. 9).   [W. MICHAELIS, VII, 368-94]

---

skiá [shadow], *aposkíasma* [shadow cast by variation], *episkiázō* [to overshadow]

---

skiá.

A. Greek Usage.

1. This word means "shadow," "shade."

2. In the more common transferred sense it means "shadow" in contrast to "reality" and denotes the worthlessness of things. It is also used for the "shade" of a dead person.

B. The OT.

1. Heb. *ṣēl* usually means "shadow" in the literal sense (Is. 38:8; 32:2; 16:3; Gen. 19:8). Poetically we read of the sheltering shadow of God's wings (Ps. 17:8). The word may also denote human transitoriness (Ps. 102:11).

2. *ṣalmāwet* means "darkness" (Am. 5:8; Job 3:5). Figuratively it denotes distress (Is. 9:1), danger of death (Jer. 2:6), or the world of the dead (Job 10:21-22).

C. The LXX and Later Judaism.

1. The LXX. In the LXX *skiá* occurs some 30 times. It is mostly used for *ṣēl*. At times it means "shadow" in the literal sense (e.g., of the sundial or trees, or evening shadows). But it has mainly a figurative sense, e.g., in the phrase "shadow of death" to which even the righteous are exposed (Job 3:5), into which God can bring us (Job 12:22), but out of which he leads the redeemed (Ps. 107:14). Another figurative use is for the shadow of God's wings (Ps. 57:2), or for the shadow of the Lord's anointed under which the people shall live (Lam. 4:20). *skiá* also bears a positive sense in Ezek. 17:23 and Is. 32:2, which may be messianic.

2. *Philo.* The term usually has a transferred sense in Philo, especially in his development of the concept of original and copy. The *lógos* is God's *skiá* and as such the archetype of other beings. God's works are *skiá* but move us toward the reality. As *skiá*, human work is empty. The world of *skiá* is finally related to that of *sōma* as semblance is to substance. The wording of a statement is *skiá* as distinct from the meaning, which is the reality.

3. *Josephus.* Archelaus in *Jewish War* 2.28, by grasping the reality of rule, makes the emperor the lord, not of things, but of names (*skiá*). In the besieged city in *Jewish War* 6.194 only the shadow of food seems to be available.

4. *Qumran.* In two figurative references oppressors are said to build a fence in the shade (i.e., cause severe distress) and a mythical tree gives shade to the nations.

5. *The Rabbis.* Apart from the literal use, we find human life compared to the shadow of a flying bird, and the advice is given that it is better to eat simply and sit in the shade than to eat dainties and be exposed to creditors.

D. The NT.

1. Synoptic Gospels and Acts. The literal use occurs in Mk. 4:32 (the birds nesting in the shade) and Acts 5:15 (the shadow of Peter). In a transferred sense Mt. 4:13ff. finds Is. 9:1 fulfilled in Jesus' work in Galilee. The land and shadow of death denote the Gentiles to whom the Messiah alone comes with the light of eschatological salvation. Lk. 1:79 uses the phrase "shadow of death" in a similar way. Here there dawns with the Baptist the light that will enlighten those who, alienated from God, live in darkness and are delivered up to death.

2. Colossians. In Col. 2:17 the law is the shadow of future things in contrast to Christ. Since there is no body without shadow, the shadow points to the body. The Hellenistic concept of appearance and reality receives here a typical Pauline development both eschatologically ("future things") and christologically (Christ as the body).

3. Hebrews. Heb. 8:1–10:18 uses the category of heavenly reality and earthly shadow to relativize the OT priesthood by the high-priestly ministry of Christ. Since the law contains only a shadow, it cannot achieve the necessary perfection.

aposkíasma. This word, found only in post-Christian texts, occurs in the NT in Jms. 1:17 with reference to the darkness caused on earth by the movement of heavenly bodies.

episkiázō.

1. This word means "to shade," "to overshadow," "to cast a shadow," "to cover." The use is mostly negative; to overshadow is to obscure. In one instance, Darius' overshadowing of Asia and Europe, political power is at issue.

2. The term is rare in the LXX. In Prov. 18:11 and Ex. 40:34-35 what is suggested is the manifestation of power, and the idea of sheltering occurs in Ps. 91:4.

3. Philo often uses the term, mostly in a transferred sense. Thus the spirit overshadows the senses when awake, desire puts reason in the shade in irrational people, and humans cast a shadow over virtue and truth and the divine glory.

4. In the NT the literal sense occurs in Acts 5:15 (Peter's shadow) and Mk. 9:7 (the cloud at the transfiguration). In Lk. 1:35 the power of the Most High overshadows Mary, denoting divine generation but not describing the mode except in terms of the operation of the Spirit.

5. There are no instances in the apostolic fathers.   [S. SCHULZ, VII, 394-400]

---

skirtáō [to leap]

A. Greek Usage. This word, which first refers to the galloping of young horses, comes to denote restless and undisciplined people, although when used for animals it bears a more favorable sense (cf. the leaping of dogs or gamboling of lambs).

B. Hellenistic Judaism.

1. In the LXX the term describes the restless movement of calves (Joel 1:17), the leaping of released calves (Mal. 4:2), the skipping of mountains like rams (Ps. 114:4), and the jostling of the twins in the womb (Gen. 25:22).

2. Philo uses the term in a parable for an animal that throws off the reins, and Josephus has it for leaping for joy at a successful military stratagem.

C. The NT. The term denotes joy in Lk. 6:23 and joyful movement in 1:41, 44. The movement in the womb is prefigured in Gen. 25:22 and eschatological joy in Mal. 4:2.

D. The Post – NT Period. In Diog. 11.6 the term is a metaphor for joy, but in Hermas *Similitudes* 6.1.6 and 2.3ff. those who give themselves to the world are like sheep leaping on lush pastures.   [G. FITZER, VII, 400-402]

sklērokardía → kardía; sklērós, sklērótēs, sklērotráchēlos, sklērýnō → pachýnō

---

skoliós [crooked]

A. Secular Greek.

1. Used literally of rivers and roads, this term, meaning "winding," "twisted," relates also to the movements of snakes, and may refer, too, to a labyrinth or to ringlets or matted hair.

2. In a transferred sense the term denotes what is "crooked." Deceit spoils things, bondage leads to crooked action, and an ambiguous oracle is *skoliós*.

B. The Greek OT.

1. Of 28 instances of *skoliós* in the OT, 14 are in Proverbs, and three each in Job, Isaiah, and Wisdom of Solomon. The term is used for various Hebrew roots, especially *'qs* and *hpk*.

2. The literal use occurs in Is. 27:1, but the word is poetic in Ps. 125:5 and also in Is. 40:3ff., where the road is uneven rather than crooked (cf. 42:16; 57:14). The free rendering in Hos. 9:8 refers to the nets that are set on the prophet's path.

3. The transferred sense is common in Proverbs. Thus 2:15 warns against crooked paths, which people of little moral worth tread in 28:18. Crookedness is associated with dishonesty in 14:2 and with slander in 10:8. In the main the term in the Greek OT expresses the nature of those who do not walk in the straightness and uprightness that God commands but walk in a cramped and crooked way that merits punishment.

C. The NT.

1. In Lk. 3:5, based on Is. 40:3ff., saving from corruption is the decisive work of God or Christ for which the Baptist prepares by calling for repentance. Carrying an ethical nuance, the term *skoliós* denotes here the social misconduct that has its root in unbelief and that will be set right when the Messiah comes with salvation that all can see.

2. Acts 2:40 and Phil. 2:15 adopt the OT expression "crooked generation" with reference either to contemporary Judaism or to the whole human race. Based on Jesus' own teaching in Mk. 9:19; Mt. 17:17; Lk. 9:41, the phrase describes those among whom believers must live blameless lives and to whom they must bring the light.

3. In 1 Pet. 2:18 the term is perhaps a general ethical concept denoting the perverse master to whom slaves must still show respect. Yet there may also be a specific reference to pagan masters who are still enslaved in idolatry.

D. The Early Church. 1 Clem. 39 quotes Job 4:18, Hermas *Visions* 3.9.1 uses *skoliótēs* as a general term for sin, Barn. 20.1 uses the figure of the crooked way, and Justin *Dialogue* 50.3 quotes Is. 40:3ff.   [G. Bertram, VII, 403-08]

---

skólops [pointed stake, thorn]

1. This rare term denotes a "pointed stake," such as is used in pits or palisades. Being fastened to such a stake is a form of execution; the reference is to crucifixion on a T-shaped cross, or to impaling and exposure on a stake. Corpses are also impaled on stakes as a sign of disgrace.

2. Another meaning in the LXX is a "thorn" or "splinter" on the foot, finger, etc., which doctors remove by plasters or ointments. Spines of palms are used in magic, and demons supposedly put prickles on women's temples. In the OT God blocks the way of Israel with thickets in Hos. 2:8, and oppressors are splinters in the eyes of Israel in Num. 33:55 or thorns in Ezek. 28:24.

3. In 2 Cor. 12:7 Paul is speaking about bodily afflictions, and among these he mentions a *skólops* that God sends, that acts as a messenger of Satan, and that is obviously painful. The idea is not that of a stake to which the apostle is impaled, nor of a barb of depression, e.g., at his failure to win the Jews to Christ, or in reaction from ecstasy. Physical ill-treatment or a physical disability seems to be in view, but there can be no saying what it is. Although it hampers his work, God uses it to keep him from arrogance and to point him to his true strength.

4. Only rarely do Christians use the group with reference to Jesus' execution (cf. Origen *Against Celsus* 2.55.68-69). It lies outside the usage that soon develops in relation to the cross (cf. the paucity of *anastauroún*).   [G. Delling, VII, 409-13]
→ *kolaphízō*

---

skopós [overseer, mark], *skopéō* [to inspect], *kataskopéō* [to spy out, inspect], *katáskopos* [spy, inspector]

skopós.

1. This word has the two senses of "overseer" and "mark" at which one shoots. It is commonly used for a military "guard," "spy," or "scout."

2. It occurs in both the main senses in the LXX (Jer. 6:17; Job 16:12).

3. The only NT instance is in Phil. 3:14. The background is that of the contest in the arena, and the point is that Christians have a mark that is given by the word of the cross. They aim at a future goal, uniting their wills with God's will and in faith pursuing the goal that he sets.

4. The theme of the games is common in the apostolic fathers. We read of the goal of peace in 1 Clem. 19.2, and cf. 63.1. In 2 Clem. 19.1 *skopós* has the sense of "model."

skopéō.

A. **Outside the NT.**

1. This word means "to look at (critically)," "to inspect." It may also mean "to hold up something as a model."

2. The only LXX instances are in Esth. 8:12 LXX and 2 Macc. 4:5.

B. **The NT.**

1. Apart from Lk. 11:35 *skopeín* is peculiar to Paul. In Phil. 3:17 it means "to inspect and hold up as a model." The meaning is less precise in Rom. 16:17: "to take note." In 2 Cor. 4:18 the thought is that of considering things transitory and things eternal with a view to making a critical decision between them. In Gal. 6:1, as we see the faults of others, we must examine ourselves, but in Phil. 2:4 we must have an eye to others as well as ourselves.

2. In Lk. 11:35 the scrutiny in the sphere of the whole person (the *sōma*) has to do with the will and its orientation. We must test whether we are free from stimuli that cloud the glance, for this conveys what the will intends.

C. **The Apostolic Fathers.** 1 Clem. 51.1 contains an interesting instance of *skopeín*.

kataskopéō.

1. This word means "to look around critically" or "to spy out."

2. The LXX prefers *kataskopeúein*.

3. The one NT instance is in Gal. 2:4, where Paul refers to the legalistic believers who, having joined the church to put things right, are wrongly spying out what is to them an intolerable freedom. Since their aim is to reintroduce bondage, their attitude is incompatible with the eschatological gospel of joy.

katáskopos.

1. This word means "spy" or "inspector."

2. It occurs ten times in the LXX for "spy," mostly in Gen. 42:9ff.

3. The only NT instance is in Heb. 11:31 for the spies of Josh. 2:1ff.

[E. FUCHS, VII, 413-18]

---

skorpízō [to scatter, disperse], *diaskorpízō* [to scatter, disperse], *skorpismós* [scattering]

1. *skorpízō* means "to scatter," "to disperse," "to divide."

2. In the LXX it has much the same sense as *diaspeírein* (*diasporá*).

3. It is used in the OT for God's judgment on enemies (2 Sam. 22:15). The Egyptians are scattered according to Wis. 17:3. The judgment on Jerusalem in Ezek. 5:1ff. includes scattering as well as fire and sword. The sheep will be scattered when the shepherd is smitten in Zech. 13:7ff.

4. That Zech. 13:7ff. is understood messianically may be seen in Damasc. 19:7ff.;

the Damascus community equates itself with the scattered sheep. On the basis of Dt. 4:27-28; 28:64 later Judaism regards the dispersion as a divine judgment. Yet God's presence is with the scattered people. A constant prayer is that judgment will be lifted and the people regathered. Philo recalls that those who are dispersed may be bitten by the serpent of lust and passion; he associates the _eskorpisménoi_ with the scorpion (Dt. 8:15). Josephus uses the term for the spreading of rumors, and the rabbis speak of dispersing money to the poor.

5. In Mt. 13:30; Lk. 11:23 Jesus says that those who do not gather with him scatter abroad, i.e., they hinder God's work. He is perhaps referring to undecided and procrastinating hearers. The antithesis of gathering and scattering occurs in rabbinic sayings, and Christ's work is that of gathering in Jn. 11:52. In Mk. 14:27; Mt. 26:31 Jesus relates to himself and his disciples the saying in Zech. 13:7 (cf. Jn. 16:32). Jesus dies, however, in order to gather into one God's dispersed children (Jn. 11:52). The Gentiles are in view here as well as Israel, for all who belong to God's family by faith, and who are now scattered among the nations, are to be gathered. In Jn. 10:1ff. the good shepherd gathers and protects the flock, but the wolf scatters it (cf. Acts 20:29). In Lk. 1:51 God scatters the proud (cf. Ps. 89:10), but in 2 Cor. 9:9 (Ps. 112:9) the righteous distribute generously to the poor. The juxtaposition in Mt. 25:24ff. suggests the scattering of seed, although the reference might be to winnowing. Lk. 15:13 carries the nuance of squandering (cf. 16:1), but the use in Acts 5:37 is military: The followers of Judas the Galilean are scattered.

6. Did. 9.4 refers to the bread scattered on the mountains and then gathered together and made one. Ignatius in _Romans_ 5.3 speaks of the scattering of his bones. Far from being a sign of dereliction, this is a mark of fellowship with Christ.

[O. MICHEL, VII, 418-22]

---

skótos [darkness], _skotía_ [darkness], _skotóō_ [to be darkened], _skotízō_ [to be darkened], _skoteinós_ [dark]

A. Classical Greek.

1. Usage. The word _skótos_ means "obscurity," "darkness." The feminine _skotía_ is Hellenistic. The classical verb is _skotóō,_ and the Hellenistic verb _skotízō._ Both forms occur in the NT but only in the passive.

2. Meaning. Used in both a literal and a transferred sense, _skótos_ denotes darkness experienced as an enveloping sphere that has significance for existence, e.g., by hampering movement or foresight, or causing anxiety or danger. If light means potentiality, going into the dark means death. The realm of the dead is a dark realm. It projects already into the present life. Darkness can take the form of blindness. The transferred senses arise as follows. Subjectively, darkness is (1) secrecy or deception, (2) the obscurity of an object or speaker, or (3) lack of knowledge or insight.

3. Philosophy. Greek epistemology starts with the process of illumination, i.e., the movement from darkness to light. Darkness has no great conceptual significance; it serves only as a foil to light. There is no direct line from what is said about illumination to later dualism.

B. The OT.

1. Background. Brightness and darkness denote salvation and perdition. The natural basis of light is always clear. The sun shines by night in the Egyptian underworld.

Dark ages of crisis are followed by an age of salvation. Creation succeeds primal darkness. How far Iranian dualism, which does not expressly oppose light and darkness, influences Judaism is debatable.

2. *Usage.* The group *ḥšk* dominates the field in Hebrew, and *'pl* has the same sense. The *skot-* group is the consistent rendering of *ḥšk*. The group is most common in the Wisdom writings and some parts of the prophets. The three spheres of use are cosmological, eschatological, and anthropological.

3. *General Features.* Natural darkness, associated with the rhythm of day and night or with the movement of clouds, envelops us (Job 23:17) It describes the human situation (Jer. 13:16). It denotes the range of what is evil or harmful. Darkness of the eyes is sorrow (Lam. 5:17). Darkness expresses captivity (Ps. 107:10ff.) and wickedness (10:7-8). It marks the underworld and the ocean depths as spheres of nonbeing. The realm of the dead is one of darkness and supreme terror (cf. Ps. 88:6; Job 17:12-13).

4. *Specific Features.* God creates light and darkness, and is Lord of both (Is. 45:7). No darkness can hide from him (Job 34:22). He darkens the eyes but also makes darkness bright (Is. 42:16ff.). Darkness is not dark with him (Ps. 139:11-12). It sets forth his sovereignty by expressing his hiddenness (1 Kgs. 8:12), but it is only a penultimate reality.

5. *Cosmology.* Darkness is connected with chaos, and creation begins with light. The stress is not on an original darkness but on its overcoming by God's word of power. Darkness belongs to creation only with the creation of light. It is connected with destruction as creation is with salvation (cf. Is. 45:7).

6. *Eschatology.* Amos proclaims the day of the Lord as a day of darkness (5:20). He has the historical judgment of Israel in view, but the onset of chaos lies behind the metaphor. Yet even this is under God's control (8:9). Darkness describes the "day" in Joel 2:2.

7. *Anthropology.* God sends light to the mind, but darkness smites the wicked and their light is put out (Job 15:22ff.; 18:15ff.). Even in darkness the righteous may hope in God (Ps. 97:11). A broad spiritualized and transferred use develops in Wis. 17:19-20.

C. Judaism.

1. *Usage.* Modifications of OT use include stronger legal thinking, more stress on God's transcendence, and a development of belief in the hereafter and apocalyptic expectation. Darkness is now damnation. A more spatial view of the cosmos finds less place for the rhythm of day and night. Much is said about eschatological darkness, but darkness will finally be destroyed. There are two ways of life, that of light and that of darkness.

2. *Qumran.* At Qumran light and darkness present a dualism of eschatological decision. Two spheres determine our being and destiny. We must decide between them. The sphere determines individual acts. Converts move into the sphere of light, although they then see that the movement is God's work. In this sphere their movement is away from the children of darkness. The present battle is a foretaste of the eschatological conflict which will see the destruction of darkness. The wicked will experience eternal perdition in the fire of dark places. In the Testaments of the Twelve Patriarchs, which belongs to the same milieu, Beliar represents the darkness that God will finally repel. But Wisdom influence may be seen in the Testaments, e.g., in the stronger psychologizing and the closer interweaving of ethical concepts.

3. *Rabbinic Writings.* The word "darkness" is less prominent in these works. The

opposite of light is its absence, and the equation of darkness and wickedness occurs mostly in exegesis.

D. Hellenism and Gnosticism.
1. General Data. Light symbolism now becomes a metaphysics of light. Light is a transcendent sphere and illumination is rapture and divinization. Darkness is not a counterforce but what one leaves behind. The *skótos* group is thus less prominent. It becomes important again only when Gnostics distinguish cosmic light (which is *skoteinón*) from transcendent light.

2. Philo. Philo is of the illumination school. He finds an antithesis, not between light and darkness, but between heavenly and earthly light. He continues the usual transferred use but forges a new product by fusing the OT and Plato.

3. The Hermetic Works. As compared with light, darkness is rare in these writings. Light and darkness are spheres, but light surrounds darkness. Earthly light, however, is not true light. Since darkness is related to the body, salvation means bringing into light by ascent from the body.

4. Odes of Solomon. Humanity is in darkness—both a place and a situation—and its dispelling by light is not a natural but a transcendent possibility.

5. The Mandaeans. In a bewildering medley of ideas the main point is that the soul is lost and only revelation by heavenly envoys can lead it to the world of light. The world is an evil sphere and earthly light stands in the service of this sphere. The world lives by the elements of light within it. Darkness is a force and substance binding us to the dark house of the body. Its children are doomed to destruction and all its works are bad. It does not understand light and fights against it. Only by a call from above is there redemption from it.

6. The Manichees. Here again we find two opposing forces or spheres. Darkness develops by a revolt from below. It finds expression in the sphere of nature. Yet light is superior in quality, as its cosmic bearers show. This superiority finds expression in the work of the envoys of light. The cosmic process, revealed through Mani, is not just a doctrine but a task.

7. Christian Gnosticism. Light depicts transcendent salvation, but darkness is less prominent as its opposite. Where darkness occurs, it is the sphere of lostness represented by its own forces. Redemption is deliverance from the bands of darkness.

E. The NT. *skótos* (in the neuter) is most common, but John prefers *skotía*. *skotízomai* (five times) and *skotóomai* (three) are always passive. The group is used both literally and figuratively but has theological significance only in John.

I. The Synoptics, Acts, and Revelation.
1. Literal Use.
a. An eclipse darkens the sun at the crucifixion (Mk. 15:33). This displays the cosmic significance of the event. It also brings out its depth (cf. the dereliction, which, as a fulfilment of prophecy, is in accordance with the divine will).

b. The underworld is a place of darkness (Mt. 8:12). Its power rules in the passion (Lk. 22:3).

c. Cosmic darkness ushers in the last time (Mk. 13:24); it is a preceding sign in the final period of wickedness. A quotation from Joel 2:28ff. reinforces the picture of the last time in Acts 2:17ff., but the time is now one of epiphany. Darkness also plays a role in Revelation. Thus the stars lose some of their radiance in 8:12, smoke obscures the sun in 9:2, and the kingdom of the beast is darkened in 16:10, leading to a last desperate revolt.

2. *Figurative Use*. Mt. 4:15-16 and Lk. 1:79 adopt the metaphor of Is. 8:23; 9:1-2. By using the Hebrew perfect, not the LXX future, Matthew stresses the fulfilment.

3. *Transferred Use*. What is dark is hidden in Mt. 10:27 (Lk. 12:3-4). The time of Jesus' earthly work is that of concealment, the time of the church that of proclamation. The expression in Mt. 6:22-23 (cf. Lk. 11:34ff.) is paradoxical. The contrast is one of health and sickness, but Matthew also has the evil eye in view, as the context shows. Luke makes the saying an exhortation and changes the final warning into a promise.

II. The Pauline Corpus.

1. *Paul*. The group has no special significance for Paul. Conversion is illumination in analogy to creation (2 Cor. 4:6). Darkness characterizes paganism (Rom. 13:12). We are to set aside its works. Darkness denotes what is hidden and will finally be disclosed (1 Cor. 4:5). Darkness of the heart is a punishment for the perversion of knowledge of God (Rom. 1:21). A dualism of decision occurs in 2 Cor. 6:14.

2. *Colossians and Ephesians*. Darkness has its sphere of power (Col. 1:13). Conversion is again illumination (Eph. 5:8ff.; cf. 1 Pet. 2:9). Believers war with the rulers of this present darkness (Eph. 6:12).

III. John. John presents a theological duality of light and darkness. The greatness of light and its manifestation are the starting point. The world is in darkness (Jn. 8:12), which is a sphere but not a substance. But darkness can neither understand nor resist light. It incurs guilt by trying to fight it. The manifestation of light, not the nature of the world, sets up the situation of decision (3:19). Wickedness actualizes itself in a decision against light. The decision is definitive (cf. 12:46). To walk in darkness is to go astray (12:35). The thrust in 1 Jn. 1:5-6 is ethical. In a practical application of the ontological thesis, there is attack on an enthusiasm that preaches habitual sinlessness. We walk in the light but do not claim sinlessness. A similar ethical concern appears in 2:8ff. If in 1:6 walking in darkness is a reason for breach of fellowship with God, here it is a result. The horizon is not the world but the church in the world. Darkness is disappearing; one can look ahead to the victory of light.

F. The Apostolic Fathers. Ignatius does not use the group, 1 Clem. 36.2 has it for the darkening of the *diánoia,* and Barnabas uses it in characterizing the two ways (5.4; 18.1).   [H. CONZELMANN, VII, 423-45]

---

skýbalon [refuse, dung]

A. The Greek World. Of uncertain etymology, *skýbalon* means literally "dung," "scraps," "refuse." It finds transferred use as "dregs," "filth" to denote what is worthless. The term *skybálisma* is used for "crumbs," *skybalismós* denotes "contempt," *skybaleúein* means "to treat contemptuously," *skybalikós* means "scorned" or "filthy," and *skybalṓdēs* means "waste."

B. Hellenistic Judaism. In the LXX the term occurs only in Sir. 27:4. Philo and Josephus have it only in the literal sense.

C. The NT. The only NT instance is in Phil. 3:8, where Paul evaluates as "refuse" or "dung" all that he has previously regarded as important. The perfect tense in v. 7 relates to his conversion, and the present tenses in v. 8 show that this is his present view. The vulgar term stresses the force of the renunciation he has made for Christ's sake. He does not disown the divine privileges of Israel but unmasks the striving for self-righteousness as a carnal enterprise that stands in antithesis to faith, serves the flesh, and is just as worthless as the *sárx*.   [F. LANG, VII, 445-47]

Skýthēs [Scythian]

1. The Scythians. The Scythians are Iranian nomads who invade Asia Minor about 700 B.C. and thence terrorize the Near East but without establishing any lasting kingdom. Their alliance with Babylon enables the latter to overthrow Assyria.

2. The Scythians in the OT. The OT depicts the Scythian threat in Jer. 4:6; 6:22-23; 5:15; Zeph. 1:2ff., although the equation is not certain. In Gen. 10:3 Ashkenaz (perhaps Ashkuz) may represent the Scythians (cf. Jer. 51:27).

3. The Scythians in the Graeco-Roman World. By colonizing the north shore of the Black Sea the Greeks make contact with the Scythians, whom they regard as a simple and strong people, but also crude, cruel, and uncultured. Later the Scythians represent a slave-type located around the Black Sea. Cicero views them as a good example of barbarians.

4. The Scythians in Later Judaism. The Greek name of Beth-Shan, *Skythópolis*, derives from a Scythian invasion. The Jews, too, abhor the cruelty of the Scythians. Philo, grouping them with the Parthians, says they are no less wild than the Germans. The Egyptians and Scythians represent two different barbarian peoples.

5. The Scythians in the NT. Col. 3:10-11 perhaps contains phrases from a baptismal liturgy which in praise and thanksgiving celebrates the new humanity and its elimination of all distinctions. In the linking of barbarian and Scythian the author is perhaps following traditional usage, or he may have the situation at Colossae in mind. Whether barbarians and Scythians are distinguished or the Scythians are an outstanding example of barbarians is debatable. In any case, baptism overcomes the offense that even Scythians give to natural sensibility.

6. The Scythians in the Apologists. Justin in *Dialogue with Trypho* 28 shows that the new Christian order, which rests on knowledge of God and Christ, enables even rude and immoral peoples like the Scythians and Parthians to be friends of God.

[O. MICHEL, VII, 447-50]

---

skythrōpós [sad-looking]

A. Outside the NT.

1. *skythrōpós* means "serious- or sad-looking" with various nuances, c.g., gloominess, solemnity, embitterment, depression, sorrow, or melancholy.

2. In the OT we find it in Gen. 40:7; Dan. 1:10 Θ, and verb forms occur in Ps. 35:15; Prov. 15:13.

3. Forms of the stem occur in Josephus *Antiquities* 2.19; 11.54; 11.164.

B. In the NT. In Mt. 6:16 the *skythrōpoí* are those who want to appear sad when they fast. Jesus calls them hypocrites because their serious mien makes them seem other than they are, and because they do not turn to the Judge who sees what is hidden. Jesus demands cheerful repentance of his disciples because they find in the Judge a forgiving Father. The two who go to Emmaus are *skythrōpoí* because Jesus seems not to have fulfilled their hopes of deliverance (Lk. 24:17ff.).

[W. BIEDER, VII, 450-51]

---

skṓlēx [worm],   *skōlēkóbrōtos* [worm-eaten]

---

skṓlēx.

A. **The Greek World.** This word means literally "worm," and is also used for the the larvae of insects. In a transferred sense it means "thread," "wave," a "cake" shaped like a worm, and a "heap" of threshed grain.

B. **The OT and Later Judaism.**

1. The OT.

a. Use. The word occurs 18 times in the LXX, nine times in writings only in Greek. The usual Hebrew equivalent can also signify "crimson," since the crushed eggs and bodies of shield-lice constitute a crimson dye (cf. Is. 1:18; Lam. 4:5).

b. Meaning. The *skṓlēx* is sometimes the "worm" in the literal sense (cf. Dt. 28:39; Jon. 4:7). Figuratively the term suggests what is weak or insignificant (Job 25:6; Ps. 22:6).

c. The Worm a Sign of Damnation. This thought is present in Is. 66:24. In the Vale of Hinnom the corpses of apostate Israelites are subject to corruption and burning. That the worm does not die denotes either total destruction or the experience of unending bodily corruption by the soul (cf. Is. 50:11).

2. The Rabbis. The rabbis continue OT usage. Wood with worms in it must not come on the altar. Worms are the human lot in the tomb. Whereas ordinary sinners suffer annihilation of body and soul, very bad ones undergo eternal punishment according to Is. 66:24.

3. Philo and Josephus. The word does not occur in Philo, and Josephus has it only in the literal sense (*Antiquities* 3.30).

4. Qumran. In the Qumran writings the worm denotes human vanity and corruptibility. With dust, it signifies death and the grave. There is no express reference to the worm in connection with eternal damnation.

C. **The NT.** The only NT instance is in Mk. 9:44ff. (quoting Is. 66:24). With *géenna* the term denotes eschatological perdition. As in Is. 66:24 the reference may be either to definitive destruction or to unremitting corruption; the latter is more likely. Worm and fire go together; the former does not suggest the gnawing of conscience, nor the latter physical pain.

D. **The Apostolic Fathers.** The worm symbolizes human pettiness in 1 Clem. 16.15 and eternal perdition in 2 Clem. 7.6. The reference to the worm that emerges from the decaying flesh of the phoenix is a new feature in 1 Clem. 25.3.

skōlēkóbrōtos.

1. Outside the NT. This word means "consumed by worms," "worm-eaten." It has not been found as a medical term but we do find references to people being eaten by worms. Josephus tells how Herod the Great in his last illness suffers from sores in the entrails.

2. In the NT. The one NT instance is in Acts 12:23 with reference to the death of Herod Agrippa, who because of his arrogance is smitten by an angel and "eaten by worms." Josephus in *Antiquities* 19.346ff. speaks of the severe pains that lead to his speedy death.   [F. Lang, VII, 452-57]

---

smýrna [myrrh],   **smyrnízō** [to treat with myrrh]

smýrna.

1. This word means "myrrh," which the Egyptians, Greeks, and Romans use as perfume, medicine, and incense. *mýrra* is an alternative but rare form.

2. In the OT myrrh plays an important role in Ex. 40:23; Ps. 45:8; Cant. 3:6; 4:14; 5:5.

3. In the NT *smýrna* occurs in Mt. 2:11 as one of the gifts brought by the Wise Men, possibly incense. Another instance is in Jn. 19:39, where it is one of the substances in which the body of Jesus is wrapped to prevent rapid decomposition. Those who carry out the burial rites do not expect a speedy resurrection.

smyrnízō. This verb occurs in Mk. 15:23, where the soldiers offer Jesus spiced wine prior to the crucifixion (v. 24). Although Jewish ladies offer wine mixed with frankincense to condemned persons to blunt their self-awareness, it is not clear that the drink of Mk. 15:23 is meant in the same sense (cf. Mt. 27:34).

[W. MICHAELIS, VII, 457-59]

Solomṓn [Solomon]

A. King Solomon in Tradition and Legend. The stories in 1 Kgs. 2–11 refer to the wealth and wisdom of Solomon but also to his foreign marriages, idolatry, and punishment—aspects which are played down in 2 Chr. 1–9. Later accounts magnify his inspiration as poet and author, the magnificence of his court, the range of his knowledge, and his magical powers.

1. Inspiration. 1 Kgs. 4:32 refers to the proverbs and songs of Solomon, and Proverbs, Ecclesiastes, and Canticles are mainly ascribed to him. Later he is accepted as the author of the Psalms of Solomon, and he speaks pseudepigraphically in the Wisdom of Solomon (cf. also the Odes and Testament of Solomon). Josephus in *Antiquities* 8.44-45 refers to the vast range of Solomon's knowledge; he ascribes to him 1,005 books, odes, and songs as well as 3,000 parables and proverbs.

2. Magnificence. Jewish tradition offers staggering numbers for the workers and materials used in building the temple and for its costly furnishings. The same applies to the lavishness of his court. Yet the rabbis blame him for his foreign marriages and for letting his wives engage in idolatry.

3. Wisdom. Legend portrays Solomon as the wisest of rulers. He answers all the riddles of Hiram and the questions of the Queen of Sheba. He controls demons and can cure illnesses. Those who see him in a dream can hope to be wise. His wisdom derives from study of the law. Only Moses surpasses him in knowledge and exposition of the law (cf. Dt. 34:10).

4. Magical Powers. As Solomon has knowledge of the plant and animal kingdoms (1 Kgs. 4:32ff.), he supposedly has astrological learning too, and has demons at his command. In non-Jewish circles, therefore, his name passes into magical use, and his magical skills are widely known and extolled.

B. King Solomon in the NT.

1. Solomon's Temple. There are few references to this in the NT. Stephen says that Solomon was allowed to build God's house (Acts 7:47), and we read of the portico of Solomon—supposedly a part of the original structure—in Jn. 10:23; Acts 3:11; 5:12. Although believers assemble here, we gather from Stephen's speech that they attach no significance to it as a place of true worship; only stiff-necked people tie God down to houses made with hands.

2. *Solomon as the Ancestor of Jesus.* In the genealogy of Matthew Solomon is a link in the chain that leads from Abraham to Jesus. Precisely through the offense of David which produces Solomon, God pushes forward his people's history.

3. *Solomon's Glory and Wisdom.* Jesus refers to the splendor of Solomon in the saying in Mt. 6:29 (cf. Lk. 12:27). Believers need not be anxious, for God clothes even passing flowers in more glorious attire than that of Solomon. The wisdom of Solomon also comes up for comparison in Mt. 12:42 (cf. Lk. 11:31). The Queen of Sheba comes from afar to hear Solomon's wisdom but this impenitent generation will not heed the greater than Solomon who is present, and will have no answer to the Queen's indictment. David's eschatological Son is incomparably superior to his historical son.   [E. LOHSE, VII, 459-65]

| *sophía* [wisdom],   *sophós* [wise],   *sophízō* [to make wise] |

sophía, sophós.

A. The Early Greek Period to Later Philosophical Usage.

1. The Early Period to Socrates. The noun *sophía* derives from the adjective *sophós* and hence always denotes a quality rather than an activity. At first it covers any skill, then suffers restriction to intellectual knowledge, and finally unites the practical and theoretical aspects. Mastery of a skill is the primary meaning in Homer and for some time later. *sophía* is not just the skill itself, but mastery of it, and hence *sophía* is an attribute of the gods and their gift to humanity. The Muses mediate it to poets, who are precursors of the philosophers. The first sages are wise in conduct as well as learning, and their learning embraces practical wisdom, e.g., in political judgment. Under Ionic leadership, however, a new type of sage develops who is devoted to theoretical inquiry. The Sophists contest the knowability of being and reduce wisdom to a power of speech which may be taught, but they go down under the devastating criticism of Socrates, Plato, and Aristotle.

2. Socrates, Plato, and Aristotle. Socrates' wisdom consists of the critical knowledge that autonomous wisdom is no wisdom at all. True wisdom knows being, but humans are not granted this knowledge. For Plato wisdom is acceptance of being. Ignorance brings us under the power of *érōs*. As the idea is divine, wisdom is proper only to God, but philosophy is possible in the power of *érōs*, and through it one may attain to the four virtues, wisdom being the greatest of virtues. Aristotle equates wisdom and philosophy. Wisdom is attainable as the first and most complete form of knowledge, i.e., the knowledge of first causes. Wisdom is a theoretical virtue, not a practical one as in Plato. It contemplates the truth of first causes, not just what results from them.

3. Hellenistic Schools. As individuals become detached from the city-states, a new ideal of the sage develops. Philosophers are often tutors to the sons of the wealthy, preparing them for life in the broadest sense. Stoicism finds wisdom in the harmony of thought and the cosmic order. It is a basic attitude with an ethical connotation. As actualized knowledge, it combines theory and practice. The sage alone has knowledge, is divine by nature, does all things well, possesses all virtues, and is the only truly happy person. The heads of the Stoic school, however, are hesitant to claim that they themselves are sages in this ideal sense.

4. Later Antiquity. Various ideas overlap in later antiquity. In Middle Platonism wisdom is the fulfilment of philosophical approximation to the divine. For Plotinus *sophía* is a vision of the spirit, and it perfects the natural virtues. In a later description *sophía* is knowledge that leads us into light; it takes the form of illumination.

[U. WILCKENS, VII, 465-476]

B. The OT.

I. Terminology. The LXX mostly uses *sophía/sophós* for the Hebrew stem *ḥkm,* of which the verb form occurs 26 times, the adjectival noun form 135 times, and the noun form 147 times, mostly in the Wisdom books, but fairly often in the historical books too, where technical skill or knowledge is usually at issue. In the prophets the terms denote human ability, including the wisdom and magic of surrounding nations. The translation "wise" or "wisdom" is inexact; it catches neither the range nor the precise meaning of the originals, which suggest experienced and competent mastery of life and its various problems. The most common parallels have to do with perception, understanding, or skill, although parallels with uprightness and honesty are also common. The parallels show that action rather than thought is the point. In contrast, folly is a disorder that also finds expression in behavior.

II. Wisdom in the Ancient Near East and the OT.

1. Mesopotamia. While wisdom undergoes special development in the OT, its content may be defined in part by the surrounding world of thought. In Mesopotamia we find no word corresponding to the Hebrew, but an extensive wisdom literature exists. Thus collections of proverbs seek to understand and master life, and other texts deal with ethical questions, impart practical advice, and tackle the problems resulting from an attempt to bring life into accord with a general order. Traditional fables, disputes, and debates are also found. In addition, there is the wisdom that is skill in the fields of cultus and magic.

2. Egypt. Egypt displays an impulse toward a norm of conduct that is defined as truth, rightness, or order, and that obtains in both the heavenly and the earthly spheres. The goal of wisdom is to open the way to this order by the transmission of knowledge. The order itself is unchangeable, and subjection to it is the wisdom which produces mastery and self-control, and brings success in life. On the other hand, offense against it is transgression against God and brings loss. Since cosmic and human order coincide, Egyptian wisdom literature embraces both serial knowledge and instruction for life.

3. Other Nations. Israel knows the wisdom of other nations such as the Canaanites (Ezek. 28:3) and Edomites (Jer. 49:7), but little of this has survived. Prov. 30:1ff. and 31:1ff. both derive from tribes outside Israel.

4. Israel.

a. Since at all cultural stages an attempt is made to order and control life, popular proverbs soon develop which embody and transmit experience (cf. 1 Sam. 24:14; Prov. 11:2; 16:18). Often a second line is added to such proverbs to bring out their practical application (cf. Prov. 25:23; 26:20).

b. In Solomon's reign a school of wisdom develops under the king's leadership (1 Kgs. 4:32-33). This embraces both serial knowledge relating to the plant and animal kingdoms and practical wisdom covering moral and religious conduct. Riddles and fables find a place, too. The prophets are critical of this school, which seems to play an important role in the days of Hezekiah (Prov. 25:1). Thus far wisdom has been mostly a preserve of the establishment, but its base broadens in the time of Jeremiah (cf. 50:35) as wisdom teachers transmit it. The underlying ideal is that of the culture of the whole person who can not merely handle the world but who achieves self-mastery.

c. After the exile the concept is worked out more theologically. Wisdom is a divine principle that issues a summons to the race. Hence all theology is in a sense wisdom thinking.

d. Wisdom is not nationalized and integrated into the people's life. It covers the general human situation and transcends social frontiers. Yet in subordination to Israel's faith it acquires a stronger ethical emphasis and presupposes faith. In keeping with the meaning of the stem, however, it still has a broad practical range.

III. Human Wisdom.

1. Magic and Manticism. In some instances wise men may be magicians, soothsayers, etc. (cf. Gen. 41:8; Is. 44:25; cf. also the astrologers of Esth. 6:13). The wise men of Babylon are a college of such persons (Dan. 2:27; 4:3).

2. Skill and Ability. Wisdom is skill or mastery, even though it be of wickedness (Jer. 4:22). Thus women know laments (Jer. 9:16) and priests the law (8:8-9). Artisans have wisdom in this sense (Ex. 36:8; 1 Chr. 22:15, etc.). The term also covers the art of government (Eccl. 4:13) and judicial ability (1 Kgs. 3:28).

3. Cleverness and Cunning. Animals are adept in self-preservation (Prov. 30:24ff.). The woman who sends Joab to David shows cleverness (2 Sam. 14:2). Political cunning may work adversely for Israel (Ex. 1:10) or for rivals (1 Kgs. 2:6, 9). Wisdom in a bad sense means cunning in the sense of crafty machinations (cf. Dt. 32:5; Job 32:13).

4. Practical Wisdom. Related to prudence, wisdom is practical mastery of life and its situations (cf. Prov. 1:5), whether in wealth or poverty, joy or pain. It knows how to deal with others and how to enjoy life. It recognizes God's rule, knows good and evil, and is aware of the ways of the world.

5. Culture. Wisdom embraces a more general knowledge that covers organic and inorganic nature (1 Kgs. 4:29ff.) as well as the nations and various human types (cf. Gen. 10; Job 24:5ff.). The final goal is finding a secret that will give control as well as knowledge of the world (Job 28). The OT, however, allows little place for cultural wisdom in this wider sense.

6. Rules of Conduct. The concept of wisdom in the OT often has rules of conduct in view (cf. Job 33:33; Prov. 2:2). Possessing knowledge, the wise impart it (Prov. 14:24; 15:2, 7). Fools betray themselves when they try to offer counsel. Instructive words from the heart are like a springing well (16:21ff.; 18:4). Wise people listen to such words (15:12) and may go on to nourish others with their instruction (6:23; 10:17; 13:14; 15:24).

7. Ethical Conduct. Right conduct presupposes understanding, which only reverent seeking can attain. To achieve understanding one must shun such corrupting influences as strong drink, bad company, strange women, unlawful gain, and violent speech (cf. Prov. 23:20-21; 2:12ff., 16ff.; Eccl. 7:7; Job 15:2). The divine law is the source of ethical conduct; it involves uprightness, liberality to the poor, and a right attitude to others in a life governed by wise rules.

8. Piety. Wisdom in the OT may also denote piety, for the wise know God, understand his words and ways, and humbly perceive their sin and the divine lordship. Fear of God is the starting point of true wisdom (Prov. 9:10; Ps. 111:10). It is not itself wisdom but leads to it as a reverence that comes to expression, not in the cultus, but in conduct. Expressing the fear of God in daily life offers valuable insight into life itself. Its correlative is not doing evil (Job 1:1), i.e., its careful avoidance. Wisdom sees that God tests the heart (Prov. 16:2), that he takes pleasure in good and not in evil (11:1), and that he controls human potentialities (16:9, 19; 19:21). It thus comes to put its trust in God (22:19).

9. *Academic Wisdom.* A well-rounded body of wisdom develops with teachers to transmit it. Thus Job 8:8 and Ecclesiastes presuppose a more closed body of teaching (Eccl. 2:12ff.; 8:17). The Preacher has learned from this (1:13, 16) but is also critical of it.

10. *Eschatological Blessing and Apocalyptic Endowment.* In Is. 33:6 wisdom is an eschatological blessing associated with righteousness (v. 5). In Is. 11:2 God's Spirit will fall on the messianic ruler as the Spirit of wisdom etc., imparting strength and understanding beyond the normal human measure. Daniel (2:30; 5:11) has a divinely given wisdom that surpasses ordinary understanding and enables him to know the secrets of the future.

IV. God's Wisdom.

1. *God Has Wisdom.* Only rarely does the OT ascribe wisdom to God. Yet wisdom comes from God (e.g., as a gift to Solomon), and Isaiah in 31:1-2 appeals to the divine wisdom. Later God's wisdom is found in his works (Is. 40:13-14; Job 26:12; 37:16) and acts (Job 11:6). Since God has all knowledge and might, no human understanding can stand against him (Prov. 21:30; Is. 19:11ff.).

2. *God Attains and Creates Wisdom.* a. In Job 28 God alone has found wisdom and used it in creation in the sense of practical mastery. Wisdom here is a quasi-independent entity to which God has access. It has its own reality, although it lies beyond the scope of human inquiry. The idea is similar to the Babylonian or Egyptian concept of an eternal divine wisdom that is proper to the gods.

b. In Prov. 1–9 wisdom plays the part of a teacher or revealer who seeks a dwelling within the race. It precedes creation (8:22ff.) but is created by God as a kind of personal entity. It offers instruction as Preacher (1:20), bride (4:6ff.), companion (6:22), and hostess (9:1). As the figurative depictions show, wisdom here is not just neutral teaching but carries with it a summons. Like a prophet, it authoritatively invites, threatens, and forces to decision. It reveals God's will, and hence we must track it down (2:4), find it (3:13), woo it (4:7), and accept its invitation (4:6ff.). This concept, which incorporates the prophetic element, in no way weakens the basic faith in God himself.

V. The Origin and Source of Wisdom and Knowledge.

1. *Tradition.* In contrast to the situation in Egypt, tradition is only one source of wisdom and knowledge in the OT (cf. Is. 19:11). The friends of Job appeal to tradition. Thus Bildad argues that past generations are superior to one individual or one generation (Job 8:8ff.), and Eliphaz claims that he has received the teaching of the fathers in unperverted form (15:18-19).

2. *Personal Experience.* Experience also gives knowledge, hence respect for older people (Job 12:12). Eliphaz appeals to experience (8:4), and so, too, does Job (21:6). Experience plays a big role in Ecclesiastes (1:13; 16-17, etc.).

3. *Means.* It is by instruction and correction that wisdom is imparted or learned (Prov. 19:20; 21:11). Converse with the wise brings knowledge, but since learning is hard, chastisement may also be necessary (Prov. 8:33).

4. The Gift of God.

a. God endows special people with wisdom in an extraordinary way, e.g., Joseph, Solomon, and Daniel. In this regard one may refer to prophetic inspiration (Jer. 9:11), artistic ability (Ex. 28:3), and nocturnal revelation (Job 4:12ff.). God may give wisdom or hold far from it (Job 11:6; 17:4).

b. According to the concept of the primal man (cf. Ezek. 28:1ff.) the idea of access to the heavenly counsel arises; Eliphaz denies that Job has this kind of wisdom (Job 15:7-8).

c. Elihu claims a knowledge that comes from God by the spirit as the portion that God has given him (Job 32ff.). This resembles the knowledge imparted to the prophets but has a more general application, opening up wisdom to all people irrespective of tradition or experience.

VI. Value, Result, and Criticism.

1. Value and Result. Instruction is valuable (Prov. 18:4) and a teacher profitable (25:12), for wisdom is a supreme treasure (21:20). It offers protection (2:8) and brings success and honor (3:35), for when applied it is strength (21:22). Being directed to a particular result, it might seem to be utilitarian, but the worth and result of good conduct coincide, and the result testifies to God's retributive justice in upholding the order of the world and life. Wisdom stands or falls with the correspondence of act and state, although the innocent may undergo educative suffering and the wicked may seem to prosper for the moment (cf. Job 5:17; 15:20ff.).

2. Criticism. Early criticism focuses on soothsaying and then on clever politics. Ecclesiastes, however, attacks academic wisdom (1:16-17; 2:15). This is helpless when faced by death (2:15). God determines destiny, not pious conduct (8:17). True wisdom is thus to accept life. Job, too, questions the doctrine of retribution. Real understanding comes only from personal encounter with God, and right conduct is resting in God, whose acts are inscrutable but purposeful. Fellowship with God outweighs all else (cf. Job 40:4-5; 42:2-3; Ps. 73:25ff.).   [G. FOHRER, VII, 476-96]

C. Judaism.

1. The LXX. The LXX regularly translates the Hebrew terms by *sophía* and *sophós,* or, in the case of the verb, *sophós eínai* or *gígnesthai.* The Hebrew and Greek traditions overlap, however, only in respect to technical ability. Elsewhere the Hebrew terms are alien to the Greek spirit, e.g., in the juxtaposition of wisdom and the fear of the Lord. In places the translators tend to change the text according to their own intellectual tradition (cf. Prov. 10:14).

2. Wisdom in Hellenistic Judaism.

a. Sirach in general stands within the Hebrew tradition. That which contributes to a devout and happy life constitutes wisdom. New features are the clearer personification of wisdom and the enhancing of its heavenly nature. It is the grace of special revelation to find it.

b. In the Wisdom of Solomon wisdom lives with God. To know wisdom is to attain to it, to be of like nature with it. Wisdom has insight into the secrets of creation, in which it had a hand. Union with wisdom repeats mystically the union of wisdom with God. The knowledge that it mediates is direct revelation, and it brings salvation. Hence one must pray for wisdom.

c. Philo's teaching is similar. Various strands intertwine in him. Wisdom frees us from earthly desire. It is the sphere of the royal way to the sacred *lógos,* i.e., to God. It is itself the way or guide, mediating revelation. It is the divine consort by which one may achieve direct proximity to God. Union with it corresponds to God's union with it. The wise, then, enter into union with God and enjoy the vision of God.

d. In other writings one finds the same idea of preexistent wisdom leading to knowledge of the truth, although wisdom may also be intellectual superiority or a respectable life.

e. For Josephus wisdom is the content of the law, so that only the scribes are wise. This wisdom is the basis of all human wisdom. Those who know and keep the law achieve comprehensive culture and virtue.

3. Jewish Apocalyptic. Apocalyptic contains many wisdom passages. The divine relationship involves keeping the law. The law is equated with wisdom, and its observance is wisdom. Since wisdom is righteousness, the first and basic redemptive gift to the righteous is wisdom. God creates in wisdom, gives the law in wisdom, and grants apocalyptists a glimpse of the mysteries of his wisdom. Wisdom manifests the Son of Man as the just and holy one with whom are wells of wisdom.

4. Qumran. In the Scrolls all things are set in order by the wisdom of the divine knowledge. God's wisdom planned all events from the first. In the wisdom of his glory he has prepared antithetical spirits. He will give the wisdom of heavenly sons to the elect of the good spirit. In the mystery of wisdom he corrects them; they alone are wise and righteous. Wisdom as a special knowledge of God's plan corresponds to the wisdom of keeping the law.

5. Rabbinic Judaism. Among the rabbis wisdom coincides with the law, and wisdom comes through its study, so that the scribes are the wise, and rabbinic teaching is wisdom. Preexistent wisdom is the law. The good things that wisdom confers are fruits of teaching the law. Compared to earthly wisdom, the treasure of the law is inestimable, but even in earthly wisdom the rabbis are sometimes said to surpass the wise of this world.

6. A Wisdom Myth. The idea of wisdom as a heavenly person is often explained only generally as a hypostatizing. In the surrounding world we find similar wisdom deities, but a specific religious influence may be seen in the Jewish sphere. What really happens, then, is perhaps an adaptation of alien myths to the structure of Israel's faith. A common wisdom myth is most apparent in Eth. En. 42, which refers to the descent and reascent of wisdom. Hints of the same idea may be found in Prov. 1:20ff., Sir. 24, and Bar. 3:9ff., although in these texts wisdom, as the law, finds a dwelling in Israel. Essentially alien to Israel's faith, the myth can be adjusted to it only with difficulty. It finds more fruitful soil in Gnosticism.

D. Gnosticism.

1. Odes of Solomon. Throughout Gnosticism *Sophía* plays an essential role and the Sophia myth is one of the few common structural elements in the movement. *Sophía* is of divine nature, has fallen from its high estate, has to be redeemed out of the world, and prototypically plays the role of a redeemer for Gnostics. Goodness has this role in the Odes of Solomon. It comes down, issues its summons, and leads those who heed it from destruction to the ways of truth.

2. Simon. Here *énnoia* is originally in union with the supreme power (Simon), plunges into the depths, and is liberated by the supreme power, thus offering a type of the Gnostics who receive redeeming *gnósis* from Simon.

3. Barbeliognosis and the Gnostics in Irenaeus. Here, too, we read of the fall and reascent of *Sophía*. *Sophía* leaves portions of light captive in the world but works for their redemption, ultimately by sending Christ.

4. The Gnostics in Plotinus. In the system censured by Plotinus we have a fall of the soul and of wisdom with it, and again *Sophía* is redeemed and engages in redemptive activity.

5. Coptic Gnostic Texts. In these texts we read of redemption by Christ in union with the wisdom also redeemed by him. The redeemer is the union of the male *sōtér* and the female *sophía*. In one variant Christ in his saving descent puts on the Father's wisdom and thus descends and reascends unrecognized by the demonic powers.

6. The Valentinians. The Valentinian system has a similar account of the fall and redemption of *Sophía,* which initiate the creation of the world and the redemption of Gnostics from it. The completion of redemption is the full union of redeeming *Sophía* with the redeemed. The marriage of *Sophía* with the Father is hymned in Acts of Thomas 6–7; this marriage symbolizes perfected *gnósis.*

7. Manicheeism. Manichean texts equate Jesus with wisdom, but wisdom is also a term for Mani's doctrine of revelation which as the true wisdom instructs souls and as the wisdom of the living Spirit builds the new heaven. In general, Gnostic wisdom is a heavenly being which loses its heavenly estate, involves humanity in its fall, finds redemption, and redeems the Gnostics by imparting knowledge of human destiny in identity with it. This myth is not only akin to the Jewish wisdom myth but seems to be directly connected with it; its understanding of redemption has roots in the Jewish doctrine of revelation.

E. The NT.

1. Traditional Usage. When Lk. 2:40 says that Jesus grows in wisdom, this reflects OT usage (cf. 1 Sam. 2:26); the reference is to knowledge of the law and a pious mode of life. The same applies to Stephen in Acts 6:3, 10 except that wisdom here finds manifestation in his speech (cf. Lk. 21:15 and Acts 7:10). In Mk. 6:2 Jesus' wisdom causes astonishment. In view is his teaching in the synagogue with charismatic power (cf. Mt. 7:29).

2. The Logia. The two threats in Mt. 23:34ff. and 23:37ff. reflect eschatological wisdom sayings in Jewish apocalyptic. Jesus himself is wisdom here. He has come down preaching and seeking a home; his rejection means destruction. The point is much the same in Mt. 11:16ff. John and Jesus are messengers of wisdom, which will be justified even though the generation treats it capriciously. In Mt. 12:42, too, the Queen of Sheba, who hears Solomon's wisdom, will testify against those who will not hear the wisdom of God in Jesus. The invitation of wisdom perhaps underlies the sayings in Mt. 11:25ff. as well, since knowledge comes by special revelation to babes, and the gift of rest that Jesus offers to the weary is commonly a gift of wisdom. Remarkably, the Revealer is himself the content of revelation, and he calls his own to himself. A distinctive feature is the concealment of revelation from the wise and understanding.

3. Paul.

a. Paul uses traditional language when he calls himself a wise (i.e., skilled) master builder (1 Cor. 3:10), and again when he asks (perhaps with an ironic undertone) whether there is none wise enough to settle disputes in the church (6:5).

b. In Rom. 11:33ff. Paul extols the divine plan of salvation in wisdom terms and with wisdom ideas. The difference is that the divine wisdom must now be related, not to the law, but to Christ, since faith in Christ is the only way of salvation (Rom. 10:4, 9-10).

c. Yet Paul does not make of the gospel a simple word of wisdom as the Corinthians seem to do (cf. 1 Cor. 1:17; 2:1, 4). It is the word of the cross (1:18ff.). At the same time, adopting the language of his critics, Paul describes this word as true wisdom. For the Corinthians, wisdom is apparently not of this aeon but is a blessing of salvation, previously concealed, but now revealed for our eschatological glorification. A form of the wisdom myth lies behind this understanding. Knowing in the descended and exalted Lord the wisdom of God, those who have received revelation have become spiritual and wise, know all things present and future, and are on the far side of judgment in the perfection of the new aeon. Paul deflates this madness, which bypasses the cross, by calling it a worldly wisdom. God has revealed himself only in the folly of the cross which is "wiser" than men (1:25). Christ lives only by the power of God, and similarly believers have no wisdom of their own, but are wise only as they become fools and look to Christ alone for their power and wisdom. God calls fools to himself, and in so doing he confounds the wise. He has chosen things that are not so as to negate things that are. God has made Jesus himself our wisdom, and hence boasting is excluded. The cross makes foolish the wisdom of both Hellenes and scribes. If God invests the world with his wisdom, so that all may know God, the world does not know God through its wisdom (1:21). It is through the foolishness of preaching that God saves believers, the very form of proclamation corresponding to the message (2:1). On this basis, Paul can affirm what the Corinthians say about Christ as the wisdom of God, but only on the basis of the divine initiative at the cross and with firm adherence to the temporal distance of believers relative to the eschaton. Many expositors, of course, refer the wisdom of the world to Greek philosophy, and hence conclude that Paul is here opposing the philosophical and rhetorical presentation of the gospel that would appeal to educated circles in Corinth, not a specific form of Gnosticism and the associated charismatic utterance.

4. Colossians and Ephesians. In Col. 1:9 and Eph. 1:8 growth in Christian knowledge, which includes knowledge of God's will and worthy conduct, is called *sophía*. This wisdom comes by grace (Eph. 1:7). It embraces knowledge of eschatological blessings in Christ (1:17-18). It is understanding of the mystery of Christ, in whom all the treasures of wisdom are hid (Col. 1:26-27). It contrasts with the false *sophía* of Gnostic teachers (cf. 2:8), which is human teaching. In Eph. 3:10 the context demands that the manifold wisdom of God be the divine plan of salvation that is fulfilled with the common entry of Jews and Gentiles into Christ. But perhaps the idea of a hidden and later reascending wisdom shapes the formulation.

5. Revelation. In Rev. 5:12 the slain Lamb is worthy to receive wisdom as one of the eschatological gifts (cf. 7:12). In 13:18 and 17:9 wisdom is esoteric knowledge. Special understanding is needed to reckon the number of the beast and to interpret the vision of 17:1ff. Only confessors can see the meaning and ramification of what is taking place in their day.

6. James. In James wisdom is a morally upright walk (cf. 3:13, 17-18). This wisdom does not lead to strife and disorder but to peace. In this regard, it stands in antithesis to the wisdom sought or taught by opponents. It is not speculative but manifests itself in practical moral results.

7. 2 Peter. 2 Pet. 3:15 says that Paul wrote "according to the wisdom given him"; it thus equates wisdom with apostolic teaching.

F. Apostolic Fathers and Apologists.

1. Sophia Christology. The early church does not develop Sophia Christology, but 1 Clem. 57.3ff. quotes Prov. 1:23ff., Justin *Dialogue* 61.1ff. adduces Prov. 8:21ff. in favor of the preexistence of the Son, and Athenagoras *Supplication* 24.1 has the christological triad of *noús, lógos,* and *sophía.*

2. *Common Christian Usage. sophía* normally denotes blameless conduct or the knowledge of faith. In Barn. 21.5 wisdom is knowing God's statutes, and in 1 Clem. 38.2 it is knowing the divine secrets. True wisdom is only by faith (Justin *Dialogue* 102.4; 1 Clem. 32.4). Tatian *Address to the Greeks* 13.3 finds in Christians, not the Greeks, the proponents of true philosophical wisdom. The word of wisdom shines into the depths of the heart and the understanding (Justin *Dialogue* 121.2).

sophízō.

1. In the active this word means "to make wise," in the middle "to understand."

2. Wisdom dominates the use of the term in the LXX. It can have a negative emphasis, e.g., in Eccl. 7:16. In Ps. 19:7 it is the law that makes wise (cf. 119:98).

3. The use in 2 Tim. 3:14-15 is similar to that in Pss. 19:7 and 119:98. Christian instruction in OT Scripture confers the wisdom that means salvation through faith in Christ and that issues in blameless conduct (vv. 16-17). In the passive in 2 Pet. 1:16 the term is used to characterize errors as cunningly devised myths as distinct from the realities of salvation. Christianity has nothing whatever to do with the insubstantial pseudo-wisdom of heresies. [U. WILCKENS, VII, 496-528]

speírō → spérma

---

spéndomai [to be offered up]

1. *spéndō in the Graeco-Roman World.*

a. The verb *spéndō* is a cultic term for the offering of libations to the gods. Libations are important in the Greek world either alone or with other offerings. They first occur on special occasions, supported by prayer, but later are offered on all occasions. Official public libations are common. To some chthonic deities water or milk is poured out rather than wine. Unmixed wine is offered at the solemn swearing of oaths.

b. From libations at oaths comes the use of the middle for "to conclude a treaty."

c. In a few instances *spéndō* denotes the pouring out of blood in sacrifice.

d. In a transferred sense *spéndō* may be used for the pouring out of tears and lamentations for the dead, or for the shedding of the blood of tyrants, or for the pouring out of melodious sounds on the poet.

e. The Latin word is *libare,* and Roman libations are similar to those of the Greeks.

2. *spéndō in the OT.*

a. The LXX uses the term for the pouring out of drink offerings, with *spondḗ* as the related noun. Israel follows the common practice of offering libations (cf. Jacob at Bethel in Gen. 35:14). In the offerings of Lev. 23:37 and Num. 29:36ff. the libation seems to be independent, but elsewhere it is an appendix to the main offering (Ex. 29:38ff.). Ps. 16:4 refers to libations of blood in connection with some alien cult.

b. A special use is for the expiatory shedding of the blood of animals in sacrificial rites (Ex. 29:12; Lev. 4:7ff.). Related is the shedding of human blood in murder (Gen. 9:6). Violent death may be compared to the offering of a sacrifice (Jer. 11:19). In Is. 53:12 the Servant of the Lord "poured out his soul to death." Denoted here is the vicarious sacrifice which is offered with the voluntary surrender of his life.

3. spéndō in Later Palestinian Judaism.

a. In later Judaism *spéndō* is normatively controlled by the understanding of the cultus. Various accounts either describe or presuppose libations. A spiritualizing trend develops, e.g., in references to the sprinkling of spiritual baptism or the expiatory force of praise or chastisement.

b. Sprinkling of blood plays a great role in the temple rites, at the Passover, and on the Day of Atonement. The pouring out of water is part of the ritual of Tabernacles. A rabbinic saying (probably Zealot) describes the shedding of the blood of the wicked as a sacrifice.

4. Josephus and Philo.

a. Josephus refers to the drink offering and describes the shedding of human blood as a cultic transgression when it takes place in interruption of sacrifices (cf. Lk. 13:1).

b. Philo spiritualizes the sprinkling of blood around the altar; it denotes readiness for total service of God. Hannah's pouring out of her heart signifies the dedication of the mind to God. Since the priest offers the blood of the life-force to God as a drink offering, his ministry typifies the soul in its love for God.

5. spéndomai in the NT. The NT twice uses *spéndō* in the passive, in both instances with reference to Paul's martyrdom (Phil. 2:17; 2 Tim. 4:6). In Phil. 2:17 a cultic act will conclude the apostle's life and work. Enemies may seem to triumph, but the apostle gives his death a sacral meaning. His primary sacrifice is the offering of the Gentiles as believers to God (Rom. 1:9; 15:16). The life of believers is also a cultic ministry (12:1). Paul fulfils his priestly ministry, however, when he is poured out as a libation, possibly, although not necessarily, as a secondary offering alongside the main one (Phil. 2:17). The same thought occurs in the solemn parting words of 2 Tim. 4:6ff., where Paul expresses his readiness to shed his blood as the drink offering is poured out at the foot of the altar. A vivid passion vocabulary thus develops which stresses the dignity and significance of Christian death in cultic terms.

[O. MICHEL, VII, 528-36]

---

spérma [seed], *speírō* [to sow, scatter], *sporá* [sowing, procreation], *spóros* [sowing, seed], *spórimos* [sown]

A. **The Word Group in the Greek World.**

1. spérma. From the time of Homer this word means "seed," whether of plants or animals. In a transferred sense it then means "core" or "basis." In connection with human seed, it comes into poetic use for "scion," "child," "offspring," and along the same lines for "tribe" or "race."

2. speírō. This word means "to sow." In addition to the literal use for sowing seed or fields, we find a figurative use for sowing ideas. Other meanings are "to disseminate," "to disperse," and "to generate," "to beget."

3. sporá. This word first means "sowing," then "seed," also "generation," "progeny," and "child."

4. spóros. This word means "sowing" and poetically "scion" or "child."

5. spórimos. This adjective means "sown," "to be sown," or "adapted to be sown." The noun *tá spórima* occurs for "fields of grain."   [S. SCHULZ, VII, 536-38]

B. **The OT.**

1. LXX Data.

a. *spérma* for "seed," "sowing," or "yield" occurs 217 times in the OT, often in a physical or economic sense. Figuratively the term denotes the organic and purposeful structure of the national body as the "seed" of Abraham. A negative use is for the vitality of corruption, as in Is. 57:3-4. A strong dynamic engenders the wider sense as in Gen. 3:15, and cf. the seed of tears in Ps. 126:5, which presents human destiny in a simple figure of speech. The use of *spérma* for "posterity" in Gen. 7:3; 9:9, etc. is to the same effect.

b. *spóros* is far less common than *spérma*.

c. Even rarer are *sporá* and *spórimos*.

d. The verbs *speírō* and *diaspeírein* occur frequently for the people's dispersion.

2. *Masoretic Data*. In the original text the root *zr'* dominates the picture in the various nuances found for *spérma*. (For details see *TDNT*, VII, 539-40.)

3. *The Seed and Related Motifs in Sayings about God's Work*. In its spiritual use the group communicates the vital force of phenomena by associating them with the biological seed as the basis of organic development. The seed conveys the actuality and seminal force of cultural and sociological entities. While the thrust may be negative (cf. Jer. 4:3), in general the seed motif expresses blessing. Organic force is divine force. As Is. 28:23ff. shows, agricultural work itself depends on God's help (cf. Gen. 8:22). As God has planted trees etc. (Is. 41:19-20; Ps. 104:16), so he has planted his people as a vine (Ps. 80:8ff.; cf. Jer. 2:21; 11:17; Am. 9:15). In general, however, seed sayings simply express the sequence of generations. Only Mal. 2:15 refers to "God's seed," the issue here, of course, being that of a holy seed unadulterated by mixed marriages. Cf. Ezr. 9:2, which perhaps underlies the LXX text of Is. 1:9, the verse which Paul quotes in Rom. 9:29.   [G. Quell, VII, 538-42]

C. Judaism.

1. spérma.

a. Philo. Philo favors the term *spérma* in both the literal and the transferred sense. Vegetable, animal, or human seed is meant when the reference is literal. Figuratively souls arise from divine seed, and we read of the seed of virtue or vice, of thought, of peace, or of hope. Such expressions are related to the Stoic idea of the spermatic *lógos*; the idea of divine seed may also owe something to contacts with Hellenistic mystery wisdom.

b. Qumran. The idea of seed is rare at Qumran. We find references to "sowing," "fruit," and "progeny."

c. The Rabbis. Here again the chief meanings are "seed," "plant," or "offspring."

2. speírō.

a. Philo is fond of this word, which he uses for sowing in both the literal and the transferred sense, e.g., sowing seed or sowing virtue, understanding, noble deeds, etc.

b. In the rabbis the term has such senses as "to sow," "to scatter seed," "to void seed" (the male), and "to fructify."

3. sporá. In Philo this word means "sowing," "seed," "generation," or, transferred, the "seed" of virtue or teaching.

4. spóros. In Philo this word means "seed" or "semen" (also "seed" of virtue).

5. spórimos. This word does not occur in Philo.

D. The NT.

1. spérma.

a. The Synoptists. In the literal sense *spérma* occurs in certain parables and their interpretation for the "seed" of plants (Mt. 13:24, 27, 37-38, 32). The meaning is "offspring" in Mk. 12:19ff. In Lk. 1:55 God has kept his promises to Abraham and his descendants (cf. Acts 3:25; 7:5-6; 13:23).

b. The Johannine Tradition. Christ is David's descendant in Jn. 7:42. The Jews are Abraham's seed in 8:37 (cf. Rev. 12:17 with reference to Christian martyrs). God's seed, i.e., the Spirit, is in believers in 1 Jn. 3:9.

c. Paul. In Paul we read of the seed of plants in 1 Cor. 15:38 and of seed in the sower's hand in 2 Cor. 9:10. Elsewhere the reference is to the seed of Abraham (Rom. 4:13ff.; 9:7), i.e., the Jews, Christ (Gal. 3:16), or the church (Rom. 9:8). Paul also speaks of David's seed in Rom. 1:3 and Isaac's seed in Rom. 9:7.

d. The Pastorals. 2 Tim. 2:8 refers to the descendants of David.

e. Hebrews. Heb. 2:16 refers to Abraham's seed, 11:18 to Isaac's, and 11:11 to human seed in general (unusual in the NT).

2. *speírō*. This word means "to sow" in Mt. 13:3-4, 18-19, 24, 31. It is also literal in Jn. 4:36-37. A transferred sense occurs in Mk. 4:13 (the word) and Mt. 13:19. Paul, too, uses *speírō* in a transferred sense, especially in 1 Cor. 15, where the term is theologically important because it shows how there may be ongoing somatic life through death and resurrection. In 2 Cor. 9:6 *speírō* refers to Christian liberality, and in Gal. 6:7-8 sowing and reaping relate to decision face to face with the gospel; different sowings bring different eschatological harvests. Jms. 3:18 speaks similarly of sowing a harvest of righteousness.

3. *sporá*. This word occurs in the NT only in 1 Pet. 1:23, where it denotes the living and abiding word by which believers are born again.

4. *spóros*. This word, which is not common in the NT, denotes "seed" in Mk. 4:26-27 and 2 Cor. 9:10. It is equated with the word in Lk. 8:11 and with the seed of liberality (for which Paul is appealing) in 2 Cor. 9:10.

5. *spórimos*. The neuter plural occurs for "fields of grain" in Mk. 2:23 and parallels.

E. Apostolic Fathers.
1. *spérma*. The sense "seed" occurs in 1 Clem. 24.5 and "progeny" in 10.4ff. (cf. also "family" in Hermas *Visions* 2.2.2). The angel promises eternal "offspring" to the righteous in Hermas *Similitudes* 9.24.4.

2. *speírō*. This word occurs in the literal sense in 1 Clem. 24.5 and in a transferred sense (sowing bad teaching) in Ignatius *Ephesians* 9.1.

3. *spóros*. This word occurs in the literal sense for sowing seed in 1 Clem. 24.4.

[S. Schulz, VII, 543-47]

> *splánchnon* [compassion], *splanchnízomai* [to have compassion], *eúsplanchnos* [tender-hearted], *polýsplanchnos* [compassionate], *ásplanchnos* [merciless]

A. Greek Usage.
1. *The Noun.* Used mainly in the plural, the noun denotes the "inward parts" of a sacrifice, then the "sacrifice" itself, then the "inward parts" of the body, and finally the "womb" or "loins" (also in a derived sense "children"). In transferred usage the term denotes "impulsive passions" (anger, desire, etc.), then the "seat of feelings or sensibilities." There is, however, no developed transferred use, and in pre-Christian Greek the term does not denote pity or compassion.

2. *The Verb.* The verb means a. "to eat the inner parts" (of an offering) and b. "to use entrails in divination."

3. *The Compounds.* *ásplanchnos* occurs in the sense of "cowardly" ("with no guts")

and *eusplanchnía* in the sense of "boldness." Cf. also *thrasýsplanchnos* for "fearless" and *kakósplanchnos* for "spiritless."

B. Later Jewish Writings.

1. The LXX. The noun and verb are rare in the LXX and seldom have Hebrew equivalents. The verb is used in the sacrificial sense in 2 Macc. 6:8. The noun (plural) means "seat of feelings" in 2 Macc. 9:5-6 (cf. Prov. 26:22; Sir. 30:7). The LXX uses the middle of the verb for "to be merciful" in Prov. 17:5, while the noun denotes natural feelings in 4 Macc. 14:13.

2. Testaments of the Twelve Patriarchs.

a. *splánchna* occurs in these writings for "the center of feelings" or for "noble feelings" (cf. *splánchna eléous* for "loving mercy" in Test. Zeb. 7.3).

b. Once the verb denotes mere emotion but usually it refers to the inner disposition that leads to mercy.

c. *eúsplanchnos* and *eusplanchnía* occur for the human virtue and disposition of "pity" in Test. Sim. 4.4; Benj. 4.1.

d. The originally rather crude term *splanchnía* can thus be applied to God himself (cf. Test. Zeb. 8.2). It characterizes the divine nature relative to God's eschatological acts (Zeb. 9.7). In the Testaments of the Twelve *splánchna, splanchnízomai,* and *eúsplanchnos* replace the LXX *oiktirmoí, oiktírō,* and *oiktírmōn* and offer new renderings for Heb. *raham* etc.

3. Philo and Josephus. Philo mostly uses *splánchna* in a physiological sense, and the same is true of Josephus, in whom the references are often rather bloodthirsty.

C. The NT.

1. splanchnízomai in the Synoptics.

a. The verb occurs in the NT only in the Synoptics. In three parables it denotes human attitudes. Thus in Mt. 18:27 the lord has pity on the servant, in Lk. 15:20 the father has compassion on the prodigal, and in Lk. 10:33 the Samaritan has compassion on the man who has fallen among thieves. In all these instances the term reflects the totality of the divine mercy to which human compassion is a proper response.

b. Elsewhere in the Synoptics the verb has messianic significance, for it is only Jesus who shows compassion, as in Mk. 1:42; 6:34; 8:2; 9:22; Mt. 14:14; 20:34. In each case what we have is not so much the description of a human emotion as a messianic characterization. Cf. also Lk. 7:13.

2. splánchna in Paul. Only the noun occurs in Paul, and he uses it not merely to express natural emotions but as a very forceful term to signify an expression of the total personality at the deepest level. Introduced in very personal passages, it is parallel to *kardía* in 2 Cor. 6:11-12, and to *pneúma* in 2 Cor. 7:13ff. (Titus' deep love for the Corinthians). Twice in Philemon (vv. 7, 20) Paul refers to the refreshing of the *splánchna,* and in v. 12 he says that in Onesimus he is as it were coming in person with a claim for Philemon's love. In Phil. 2:1 *splánchna kaí oiktirmoí* seems to be summing up the three preceding phrases. In context, then, *splánchna* denotes Christian affection and *oiktirmoí* Christian sympathy. Both are essential elements in all Christian dealings. A unique phrase occurs in Phil. 1:8; the reference is to the love or affection which, gripping and moving the whole personality, is possible only in Christ; the genitive "of Christ" denotes the author.

3. The Rest of the NT. Apart from Acts 1:18 ("entrails"), NT usage develops under the influence of Paul or later Judaism. Col. 3:12 refers to a Christian virtue, Lk. 1:78 has God's eschatological mercy in view, and Jms. 5:11 also stands in an eschatological context. In 1 Jn. 3:17 believers are not to close their hearts (the center of compassionate action) to the needy, and cf. the hortatory use of *eúsplanchnos* in Eph. 4:32; 1 Pet. 3:8.

D. The Apostolic Fathers and Early Christian Writings.

1. Only Ignatius *Philadelphians* 10.1 plainly reflects Pauline usage. In 1 Clem. 2.1 *splánchna* denotes the seat of religious conviction. God's mercy in eschatological salvation is the point in 2 Clem. 1.7, and the divine compassion in 1 Clem. 23.1.

2. The eschatological element in Testaments of the Twelve is adopted in Hermas; cf. especially the connection with the summons to repentance (*Similitudes* 8.11.1; 9.14.3).

3. *splánchna* and *eusplanchnía* are divine predicates in Acts of Thomas and Acts of John. The messianic use recurs, but in the latter the apostle has pity in the same way as Jesus in a usage that differs markedly from that of the NT.

[H. KÖSTER, VII, 548-59]

→ *éleos, oiktírō*

---

spoudázō [to make haste, be zealous], **spoudḗ** [haste, zeal], **spoudaíos** [speedy, zealous]

A. Classical and Hellenistic Greek.

1. From *spoudḗ* ("haste"), *spoudázō* means "to make haste" or transitively "to hurry something on," then "to treat seriously or respectfully."

2. *spoudaíos* means "speedy," "diligent," "proficient," "important," "alert," and in a moral sense "noble," "worthy," "good," "upright."

3. *spoudḗ*, from the original sense of "haste," takes on such meanings as "work," "effort," "zeal," "seriousness," "readiness," "dedication."

B. The LXX and Later Judaism.

1. The LXX and Hexapla. The LXX uses *spoudázō* mostly for forms of *bhl* in the sense "to hasten," sometimes (cf. also *spoudḗ*) with the sense of terrified flight. The same constriction of meaning may be seen in the other renderings.

2. Josephus.

a. *spoudázō* in Josephus denotes assiduous interest or engagement.

b. Josephus uses *spoudaíos* for "zealous" or "conscientious."

c. *spoudḗ* has for Josephus the meaning "concern," "piety," "attentiveness," "liking," also "zeal," "effort," "involvement," "dedication," "seriousness," "desire," as well as "haste."

3. Philo. Philo uses *spoudaíos* for what is morally "good" or "upright." *spoudḗ* has in the main an ethical thrust, and the phrase *spoudḗs áxios* denotes what is "worthwhile," "essential," or "important."

C. The NT.

1. *spoudázō* means "to make haste" in 2 Tim. 4:9, 21; Tit. 3:12. It then denotes zealous effort in Gal. 2:10 or 1 Th. 2:17. In Eph. 4:3 Christians must exert themselves to maintain the unity that Christ has achieved for them. In 2 Tim. 2:15 they should do all they can to present themselves as approved. In Heb. 4:11 they must act in such a way as not to be shut out from the rest that God has prepared for them. In 2 Pet. 1:10 they are to secure their calling by their conduct, and in 3:14 they must be zealous

to be found without spot or blemish. At issue in all these references is an actualizing of salvation, a fulfilling of what has been opened up by grace.

2. The adjective *spoudaíos* bears no philosophical coloring. 2 Cor. 8:17 (cf. v. 22) testifies to Titus' God-given zeal in the matter of the collection. The adverb denotes intensive asking in Lk. 7:4 and seeking in 2 Tim. 1:17 (cf. also Tit. 3:13), and Paul uses it in the phrase "as quickly as possible" in Phil. 2:28.

3. In the NT *spoudḗ* first means "haste" (cf. Mk. 6:25; Lk. 1:39). It then means "zeal" or "commitment" in Rom. 8:12; 12:11. It takes on the sense of "zealous concern" in 2 Cor. 7:11; Paul has written sharply in order to provoke this. The Corinthians excel not only in faith, but also in earnestness, i.e., a zeal to perform (2 Cor. 8:7). Zeal (cf. that of Titus in 8:16) is a gift of God. In Heb. 6:11 the readers must show ongoing earnestness in realizing the full assurance of hope. This is part of being a Christian, for believers know who they are and where they are going, and will not lose what they have been given. The use is similar, but with a bigger moral stress, in 2 Pet. 1:5. The zeal here relates to the whole Christian ethos unfolded in vv. 6-10. It relates to the basic orientation of those whose mind is set on the good.

D. The Early Church.

1. *spoudázō* means "to make haste" in, e.g., Ignatius *Ephesians* 1.2; Mart. Pol. 13.2, and "to strive" in Barn. 1.5. But it mostly denotes striving after true Christian conduct (2 Clem. 10.2; Ignatius *Ephesians* 10.2), with the Lord as example, and in Ignatius an ecclesiastical emphasis (*Ephesians* 5.3).

2. *spoudaíos* takes on the sense of concern about knowledge or right conduct in, e.g., Hermas *Visions* 3.1.2 or Ignatius *Polycarp* 3.2.

3. *spoudḗ* is used only adverbially ("in haste" or "with zeal") or with the accusative and infinitive to express attention to something (Mart. Pol. 7.2).

[G. HARDER, VII, 559-68]

> *stásis* [standing, taking a stand]

A. Outside the Bible.

1.a. This word first means "standing," "standing firm or still," "firmness," also "standing" as distinct from sitting.

b. It then means "position," "situation," or "state."

2. Another sense is "taking a stand," especially "rebelling." Along these lines it denotes civil strife, dissension, political unrest, inner strife in the soul, disagreement between groups, or domestic strife.

B. The LXX.
In the LXX *stásis* denotes "what is set up," i.e., a boundary stone, statute, or treaty. It also occurs for the "standing still" of the sun in Josh. 10:13, for "place of rest" in Dt. 28:65, and for "location" in 1 Chr. 28:2. The only instance of *stásis* as (personal) "discord" is in Prov. 17:14.

C. The NT.

1. In Heb. 9:8 the term denotes the continued existence of the old *skēnḗ*.

2. In Mk. 15:7 the meaning is "insurrection" (cf. Lk. 23:19, 25). Acts 19:40 refers to a "commotion" which threatens political security. "Dissension" in the church is the point in Acts 15:2 and a theological "clash" is the issue in 23:7. The reference in

24:5, however, is to more than religious squabbling; Paul is accused of causing "unrest" that threatens the peace between Jews and Romans.

D. The Apostolic Fathers. Only 1 Clement has *stásis*, which he construes as "revolt" as well as "discord." He takes the term from the political sphere. Christianity seeks peace for itself and for all people. The restoration of peace in Corinth is the goal of the epistle.   [G. DELLING, VII, 568-71]

→ *akatastasía, máchē*

---

staurós [cross],   *stauróō* [to crucify],   *anastauróō* [to crucify]

staurós.

A. The Cross and Crucifixion in the NT World.
I. The Meaning of the Word.
1. *staurós* is an upright "stake" such as is used in fences or palisades.
2. The *staurós* is an instrument of torture for serious offenses. It may be a vertical pointed stake, an upright with a cross-beam above it, or a post with an intersecting beam of equal length.
II. The Penalty of Crucifixion.
1. The Persians seem to have invented this form of execution. Alexander the Great and his successors use it, and then the Romans, although not officially for citizens. Josephus mentions mass crucifixions of rebels in Judea.
2. The condemned person carries the cross-beam to the place of execution, is fastened to it with ropes or nails, and is then hoisted on the stake, which is already erected. About the middle of the post a wooden block supports the suspended body. The height of the cross varies. A tablet hung around the victim states the cause of execution, and this is then affixed to the cross. Scourging often precedes crucifixion and the victim is exposed to mockery. Crucifixion takes place publicly, and the body may be left to rot on the cross. The death is extremely slow and agonizing. Constantine ends this form of punishment.
3. Jewish law does not impose crucifixion. Persons stoned are hanged on trees to show that they die accursed by God. Judaism applies this principle to those who are crucified.

B. *staurós* in the NT.
I. The Cross of Jesus. The Synoptics and John tell the story of the crucifixion in narratives that have a kerygmatic and cultic quality. In the background is the thought that Jesus dies as the sacrificial lamb of the new covenant. The events follow current custom. Jewish touches are the stupefying drink in Mk. 15:23 and the taking down of the body of Jesus on the eve of the sabbath (Jn. 19:31). The cross is a post with cross-beam, and Jesus is nailed to it. John ascribes theological significance to the lifting up of Jesus on the cross (3:14; 8:28).
II. The Theology of the Cross.
1. Paul shows the saving significance of the cross. In it, as the lowest stage of humiliation, Jesus completes his obedience and thus does the work of redemption (Phil. 2:8). Human wisdom, which cannot grasp this, robs the cross of its essential content (1 Cor. 1:17). The word of the cross is folly to the lost but the power of God to believers. As the revelation of God's wisdom, it is true wisdom to the perfect

(2:6-7). Christians who spurn the cross by their manner of life are its enemies (Phil. 3:18). Judaizers are trying to avoid persecution for the cross by advocating circumcision (Gal. 6:12). Paul's own sufferings relate to his preaching of the cross, for enforced circumcision and the cross are mutually exclusive. The cross is decisive in salvation history. Abolishing all self-glorying, it is Paul's own glory (Gal. 6:14).

2. The cross is the means of atonement in Col. 1:20 and Eph. 2:16. It is the ground of cosmic reconciliation (Col. 1:20). The blood of Jesus has all-embracing expiatory power. As a sign of his pardoning grace, God has affixed the writ of accusation to the cross (Col. 2:14). By the cross God has brought Jews and Gentiles together in a new humanity and reconciled them to God (Eph. 2:16).

3. Hebrews uses *staurós* only in 12:2, which says that Jesus chose the cross either "instead of" heavenly bliss or "for the sake of" it. The former is perhaps the more natural sense; Jesus renounced the joy that was set before him in order to tread the way of obedience and suffering.

III. The Figurative Use.

1. Jesus demands that his disciples take up their cross and follow him. The saying occurs five times in different contexts (Mk. 8:34 [par. Mt. 16:24; Lk. 9:23]; Mt. 10:38; Lk. 14:27).

2. There is no parallel for the saying among the rabbis. It may be a popular expression arising among the Zealots. Or perhaps Jesus sees in his death a pattern for his followers, who must be ready to suffer and even die for his sake. The saying about the yoke in Mt. 11:29 is possibly connected with the saying about the cross. Carrying the cross to the place of execution suggests an ongoing process. The mark of the cross serves as a confession of Jesus and a seal of belonging to him. In any case, the connection with the denial of self shows that the reference is to a life of dedication which might involve suffering and finally the surrender of life itself.

IV. The Later Use.

1. In Ignatius the cross lifts up believers as living stones in the building of God's temple (*Ephesians* 9.1). It is a trunk which with living force puts forth branches (*Trallians* 11.2). Christians are nailed to it (*Smyrneans* 1.1). Barnabas proves that the crucifixion is necessary from Gen. 14:14; Num. 19:6; Ps. 1:3 (cf. 8.1; 9.8; 11.1). In *Polycarp* the cross testifies to the true corporeality of Christ (7.1). A double cross occurs in Gnostic speculations about the cross, the cross of Golgotha, and a cross of light.

2. In the papyri we find little distinctively Christian use. Once *staurós* means "hardship." In Byzantine times the cross is common in letters. Three crosses serve as marks for the illiterate. The cross also figures as a sign of prayer.

stauróō.

A. Outside the NT.

1. The meaning of *stauróō* is "to put up posts," "to protect by a stockade." The sense "to crucify" is rare.

2. The LXX uses *stauróō* for "to hang on the gallows" (Esth. 7:9). Josephus uses the term in, e.g., *Antiquities* 2.77; 17.295.

B. The NT.

1. In Mt. 20:19 Jesus says that the Son of Man will be crucified, and in Mt. 23:34 he says that God sends prophets, wise men, and scribes, some of whom the Pharisees

crucify. Peter in Acts 2:36 and 4:10 reproaches the people and the Sanhedrin for crucifying Jesus. In 1 Cor. 2:8 Paul says that in shortsighted wisdom the rulers of this world have brought Jesus to the cross, whereby their own power is broken. 2 Cor. 13:4 claims that, whereas Jesus is crucified in weakness, he lives by the power of God. Rev. 11:8 refers to the Lord's crucifixion in the great city which is allegorically called Sodom and Egypt.

2. Theologically significant is the statement in 1 Cor. 1:23 that Paul preaches the crucified Christ, in whom God's power and wisdom are revealed. In form and content his message will proclaim only Christ crucified (2:2). There is no room for factions, for Christ alone was crucified for believers (1:13).

3. In Gal. 3:1 Paul refers to the public portrayal of Christ as the crucified. His focus is on Christ himself, not just the cross. Because of his crucifixion with Christ, he is dead to the law (2:19). By the cross he is crucified to the world and the world to him (6:14). The cross negates the world. It means a renunciation of sin, whose seat is the *sárx* (5:24). Snatched from sin's dominion by God's act, believers say a radical No to sin and walk in newness of life (cf. Rom. 6:4).

C. The Early Church. In early Christian writings *stauróō* is common in the sense "to crucify." Ignatius *Romans* 7.2 echoes Paul. *Trallians* 9.1 affirms the reality of the crucifixion. Justin uses the term in *Dialogue* 85.2; *Apology* 61.13. It also occurs in the famous "Quo vadis?" passage in the Martyrdom of Peter 6.

enastauróō. This verb means "to fence around," "to enclose," but then also "to impale," "to crucify." It occurs in the NT only in Heb. 6:6. Apostates personally align themselves with those who crucify Jesus, and thus crucify him afresh.

[J. SCHNEIDER, VII, 572-84]

> *stégō* [to cover]

A. Linguistic Aspects. This verb comes from a stem meaning "to cover," "to conceal." It is a rare term but persists in both prose and common speech. Its basic meaning is "to keep covered," but this gives it such senses as "to protect," "to ward off," "to hold back," "to resist," "to support." It can also mean "to keep secret," "to keep silent," "to keep a confidence."

B. The Use in Paul. In the NT only Paul uses *stégō*. In 1 Th. 3:1, 5, with no object, it means "to endure." He can no longer bear to leave the Thessalonians alone, and so, unable to come himself, he sends Timothy. In 1 Cor. 9:12 the point is that Paul will put up with anything (i.e., not claiming his rights) rather than obstruct the gospel. Various renderings are suggested for 1 Cor. 13:7. In view of the earlier "bear" the sense "to endure" raises problems, since it seems to be repetitive. "To excuse" is hardly possible, and the middle would be required for the sense "restrains itself." The meaning, then, is perhaps that love "covers" all things. In full self-giving to others, the love that is rooted in God's love keeps silent about unfavorable matters.

[W. KASCH, VII, 585-87]

> *stéllō* [to send, avoid], *diastéllō* [to differentiate, order], *diastolḗ*
> [distinction], *epistéllō* [to send a message], *epistolḗ* [letter], *katastéllō*
> [to restore order], *katastolḗ* [ordered conduct], *systéllō* [to
> shorten], *hypostéllō* [to draw back], *hypostolḗ* [reserve]

stéllō.

1. This word means "to put," "to leave," "to place," "to draw up," and then "to send," "to prepare," "to set out," "to travel." In Plato it usually means "to get ready." In general, it is fairly uncommon.

2. The LXX uses only the middle form, and the term causes difficulties in such texts as Mal. 2:5 and Prov. 31:25.

3. Josephus uses the word mainly for "to send," but the sense of moving is also present, e.g., the moving away of a storm in *Antiquities* 9.213 and the allaying of distress in 5.280.

4. The two NT instances both have the middle. In 2 Th. 3:6 Paul admonishes the church in Christ's name to "hold aloof" from those who live in idleness. Formal excommunication does not seem to be at issue. In 2 Cor. 8:20 Paul explains why he is arranging for others to share responsibility with him for the collection; he is either seeking to "avoid" having any blame attach to him, or, more likely, "taking steps" to see that this does not happen.

diastéllō.

1. This word means "to divide," "to differentiate," "to dissect," "to subdivide," "to define," "to give precise instructions," "to order."

2. The LXX uses the term some 50 times for no less than 22 roots. When the middle occurs, mostly with God as subject, the reference is to definitive directions.

3.a. In the NT five of eight instances are in Mark. Jesus is the subject in these cases, and the term expresses the categorical nature of his prohibitions in 5:43; 7:36 (twice); 9:9, and of his warning in 8:15. The term points to the hidden majesty and power of Jesus in the light of its future manifestation. Matthew has the word only in 16:20, where it is significant in view of the preceding confession of Peter in 16:16.

b. In Acts 15:24 the point is that those who have unsettled the churches by rigorous demands have received no precise instructions from the church's leaders in Jerusalem.

c. In Heb. 12:20 (passive) the reference is to God's strict order at Sinai.

diastolḗ.

1. This uncommon noun takes its meaning from the verb and has such senses as "separation," "division," "incision" (in medicine), "precise exposition," "order," and "punctuation mark" (in grammar).

2. There is no one specific sense in the LXX.

3. In the NT Rom. 3:22 and 10:12 are closely related. The divine event in Christ has ended the "distinction" between Jew and Gentile established by Israel's election. The Jew is equally sinful (3:22), and the Gentile is called to the same faith (10:12). God has set up his all-embracing rule in Christ. In the only other instance in 1 Cor. 14:7 the term has no theological significance; it simply denotes the distinction between musical notes.

epistéllō, *epistolḗ*.

1. The verb *epistéllō* means "to transmit a message," and the noun *epistolḗ* denotes "what is transmitted," usually a "letter."

2. In the NT the few instances of the verb (Acts 15:20; 21:25; Heb. 13:22) suggest the authoritative and almost official nature of the early Christian epistle. The NT epistles bear this character. They speak a definitive word about individuals, humanity, and the Christ event as God's eschatological act. They show that the world cannot escape this word. They thus correspond to prophecy in the OT. 2 Cor. 3:1ff. seems to reflect Paul's conviction that all his epistles are ultimately Christ's. The use in this passage is, of course, figurative. Paul does not need human authorization in the form of letters of recommendation, for the church itself is an epistle that Christ has written through him. The Spirit has written this epistle on the heart. The use of the metaphor shows plainly that with Christ the true apostle has a necessary place in God's work of revelation and reconciliation.

katastéllō, katastolḗ.

1. This verb means "to put in its right place," "to arrange," "to restore order," "to pacify," while the noun means "propriety," "ordered conduct," "action with a view to such conduct," and then "clothing" (as a visible expression of decorum).

2. In the NT the verb occurs only in Acts 19:35-36, where the clerk calms the excited mob at Ephesus. The authority expressed by *katastéllō* differs from that expressed by the use of *katéseisen* when Paul as a witness to Christ brings the crowd to order at Jerusalem in Acts 21:27ff. The noun occurs in the advice to women believers in 1 Tim. 2:9, where Timothy is told to exhort them to adopt either a seemly demeanor or seemly apparel. The context of worship perhaps supports the former rendering, but the use of *stolḗ* for "garment" in the Apologists favors the latter.

systéllō.

1. This word means "to draw together," "to shorten," and figuratively "to humble."

2. The LXX uses the word for "to abase," "to confound," "to overwhelm" (militarily), and "to press closely" (geographically).

3.a. In the NT Paul says in 1 Cor. 7:29 that the time remaining for us is short. The point may be that by Christ's coming God has shortened the time of apocalyptic expectation, or perhaps Paul is simply adapting a popular saying to the imminent expectation of his generation.

b. In Acts 5:6 the young men either "wrap up" the dead Ananias or "catch him up" and "remove" him. The probability is that they wrap him up in his clothes unless they first cover him with a shroud.

hypostéllō.

1. This word means "to draw aside or back," "to retreat," "to withdraw," "to hold back," "to keep away from," "to keep silence," "to conceal."

2. In the LXX the term means "to hide" in Job 13:18, "to shrink from" in Dt. 1:17, and "to hold back" in Hag. 1:10. The sense "to subordinate" occurs in Philo.

3.a. In the NT Paul says in Gal. 2:11-12 that when certain people come from James to Antioch, Peter, who has been eating with the Gentiles, "draws back," or even perhaps "hides."

b. In Acts 20:18ff. Paul stresses to the Ephesians elders (vv. 20, 27) that he has not shrunk or held back from declaring all God's truth to them.

c. Heb. 10:37-38 has the verb in a christological quotation of Hab. 2:4. Believers are committed to confession; there can thus be no confidence or reward if they are guilty of shrinking back or concealment.

hypostolē. This rare word has such senses as "abstinence," "reserve," or "secrecy." The only NT instance is in Heb. 10:39 (cf. v. 37), where, in tension with *pístis*, it denotes "lack of steadfastness" or "unreliability" (cf. 2:1).

[K. H. RENGSTORF, VII, 588-99]

---

stenázō [to groan, sigh], *stenagmós* [groaning, sighing], *systenázō* [to sigh or groan together]

A. The Group outside the NT.

1. *stenázō* means "to sigh," "to groan," *stenagmós* means "sigh" or "sighing," and *systenázō*, which is very rare, means "to sigh or groan with."

2. The group finds no fixed original in the LXX. It is used for sighing or groaning in childbirth (Jer. 4:31) or mortal conflict (Ezek. 26:15), for the dead (Jdt. 14:16), for suffering (Job), at judgment (Ezekiel), at eschatological events (Is. 24:7), and as a sign of penitence (Is. 30:15). God hears it (Ex. 2:24).

3. Philo often uses *stenázō* with *dakrýō* and *klaíō*. He explains that the sighing of the Israelites in bondage (Ex. 2:23) is that of the soul. Conscience causes the soul to sigh at its former misdeeds.

4. Josephus uses the term relative to the fall of Jerusalem (*Jewish War* 6.272).

5. In magic, sighing occurs in, e.g., the conjuring up of dreams.

6. *stenagmós* may be used for the sighs of love.

B. The Group in the NT.

1. In the NT sighing takes place by reason of a state of oppression which causes suffering and from which there is the desire to be free. Thus in 2 Cor. 5:2 existence in the body is a burden, for it is a sign that redemption is not yet complete. Only when we put on the heavenly dwelling will our sighing or groaning cease.

2. In Rom. 8:22ff. there is a triple sighing of creation, Christians, and the Spirit. Through the fall, creation is subject to bondage and hence it sighs or groans until God's children are manifested. Christians also groan as they await the transformation of the earthly body. The Spirit sighs in his intercession for us, which cannot be expressed or grasped in human words, but which God understands. The reference here is not to the Spirit's work in us, e.g., in prayer or tongues, but to intercession on our behalf in the divine sphere where human words are totally inadequate (cf. 2 Cor. 12:4).

3. Elsewhere Heb. 13:17 points out that pastoral work is of value when it is done with joy and not with sighs, Jms. 5:9 tells believers so to act that there will be no reason for sighing at one another, and Mk. 7:34 refers to the prayer-sigh of Jesus when he opens the ears of the deaf man (cf. Jn. 11:41-42). This sigh of Jesus is not part of a magical technique but is a preparatory prayer; the healing itself is by the word. Acts 7:33-34 quotes Ex. 3:7-8 LXX.

C. The Apostolic Fathers.
The terms are rare in these works. Hermas *Visions* 3.9.6 warns the rich so to act that those who suffer want do not sigh. Mart. Pol. 2.2 says that the martyrs do not sigh or groan in their suffering. 1 Clem. 15.6 quotes Ps. 12:5. Later burial inscriptions express the wish that the dead may be far from sighing (cf. Rev. 21:4; Is. 35:10).   [J. SCHNEIDER, VII, 600-603]

---

stenós [narrow],   *stenochōría* [narrow place, affliction],   *stenochōréō* [to confine]

A. Secular Usage. The word *stenós* means "narrow," "thin," "poor," the noun *stenochōría* denotes a "narrow place," and the verb *stenochōréō* means "to confine," "to compress." The ideas of a narrow door and a little trodden way occur in philosophy, e.g., in the difficult ascent to true culture.

B. The Greek OT.

1. The group is none too common in the LXX but we find it in references to a narrow pass or passage, a narrow entry, etc. The Hebrew reference to scanty nourishment in Is. 30:20 is given a figurative sense, i.e., it becomes the bread of affliction. In Jer. 30:7 the LXX construes the Hebrew "time of anxiety" as a *chrónos stenós*, i.e., a time of oppression.

2. The noun, which is rare and has no fixed original, occurs with reference to threats of punishment.

3. The verb, which occurs five times, relates to external straits or oppression. In Is. 28:20 the LXX drops the Hebrew idea of the narrow couch and uses *stenochōroúmenoi* in a transferred sense.

C. The NT.

1. In the NT the word *stenós* occurs in Mt. 7:13-14 and Lk. 13:24 in the figure of the narrow gate or door. In Luke the saying answers the question about the small number of the saved, and it thus has a special urgency; one must strive to enter by the narrow door. In Matthew we find the contrast of a narrow gate and way and a broad gate and way. Many people ignore the warning because they will not accept the authority of Jesus and pass through the narrow gate and tread the narrow way. How narrow the gate is may be seen from the saying in Mk. 10:25. There is no mention of special hazards on the narrow way but the term *stenós*, with its OT associations, suggests that it is also a hard way as distinct from the broad and easy way that so many prefer.

2. In Paul the noun *stenochōría* occurs four times and the verb *stenochōréō* three times. In Rom. 2:8-9 the noun denotes God's judgment as in the OT; the reference is to severe affliction both in this world and the next. In Rom. 8:35 believers are not exempt from afflictions, but these cannot separate them from God. In 2 Cor. 4:8 and 6:4, in a passion piety oriented to Christ, Paul makes the point that he is afflicted but not crushed. In 6:3ff. endurance is the master concept. In the three series of three expressions that follow, *stenochōría* comes in the first. In 2 Cor. 12:10, after a reference to his revelations and then to the thorn in the flesh, *stenochōría* is again at the heart of Paul's passion piety as he speaks of the insults, hardships, persecutions, and calamities that he suffers gladly for Christ's sake. In 2 Cor. 6:12 Paul rejects the charge of narrowness that the Corinthians bring against him. His mouth is open to them and his heart is wide. He thus hopes to overcome their own narrowness of heart, so that they will be equally open to him.   [G. BERTRAM, VII, 604-08]

---

stereós [firm],   *stereóō* [to make firm],   *steréōma* [firmament]

A. Greek Usage. The word *stereós* means "stiff," "tight," "rigid," "hard," "firm," "true," "obstinate." The verb *stereóō* means "to make stiff, firm, strong, or hard." The noun *steréōma* means "what is made firm," "solid body," "basis," "foundation."

B. LXX Use. The word *steréōma* is chosen for the firmament in the creation story; it denotes the solid vault of heaven (cf. Gen. 1; Ezek. 1; 10:1; Ps. 19:2). The verb can then be used for God's establishing of this solid vault (Ps. 33:6). The idea of a celestial refuge occurs in Ps. 18:1. The adjective does not share this cosmological development but remains within the framework of ordinary usage. God visits his people with hard chastisement in Jer. 30:14. Himself firm or constant, he confirms the righteous. He is the rock who summons the people to correction (Hab. 1:12).

C. The Jewish Gnostic View of the World. Later Judaism postulates several firmaments where the prince of this world dwells, through which the Redeemer passes on descending and ascending, whose powers fall down before him, and by way of which disciples or Gnostics also ascend in his train.

D. NT Usage.

1. stereós. In Heb. 5:12, 14 we have the metaphor of "solid" food. Revelation is the food of all believers, but in addition to the first principles (6:1) there is the solid food of a knowledge of Christ's cross and exaltation (12:2). Over against Gnostics who change the hope of the resurrection by spiritualizing, 2 Tim. 2:19 refers to the "firm" foundation of faith. This foundation lies in God, who is *stereós* in himself, who is constant and who makes constant, who gives faithfulness to the community and its members, who holds them fast to their crucified and risen Lord. In 1 Pet. 5:9 believers are to be steadfast in their faith, resisting the devil. The stress here is on faith; the word *stereós* strengthens the exhortation to resist. The term is always positive in the NT.

2. stereóō. In Acts 3:7, 16 the fact that the feet of the lame man become firm hints at a new creation by the author of life (v. 15). Acts 16:5 refers to the inner and outer growth of the churches (cf. 2:41).

3. steréōma. Paul in Col. 2:5 shows concern for the order and firmness of the faith of the Colossians. As the term *táxis* suggests a military division drawn up in ranks, so *steréōma* hints perhaps at a castle or bulwark (cf. 1:23; 2:7). Again faith gives the terms their content. Believers are under assault, but they can stand fast in the stronghold of their faith. Grounded in Christ, they are enabled by faith to stand firm in their conflict with the world.   [G. BERTRAM, VII, 609-14]

---

stéphanos [crown],   *stephanóō* [to crown]

A. The Crown (Wreath) in the Ancient World.

I. Meaning. Connected with *stéphō,* "to encircle," *stéphanos* means "crown" and *stephanóō* "to crown." The crown, as a wreath placed around the head, is a sign of life and fertility, and perhaps also a symbol of light. It has a place in the cultus and supposedly wards off evil. The closed crown is used in magic. The crown expresses joy and honor, but also sorrow. It acknowledges excellence.

II. Nature. The simplest crown consists of a bent twig or of two twigs tied together. Wreaths of grass, leaves, or flowers also occur. The Dionysus cult uses ivy, oak, and acanthus, Neptune and Pan wear wreaths of fig leaves, and Zeus of laurel. Soldiers wear crowns at triumphs, and victors wear laurel or olive wreaths. The myrtle signifies love. Roman magistrates wear gold crowns, and Etruscan crowns, also used at Rome, are of precious stones and golden oak leaves.

III. Use.

1. The Cultus. In cultic acts priests wear various forms of crowns. Aeneas crowns his brow with twigs when he first treads Roman soil and prays. Crowns are placed on sacrifices and altars, and are even offered in sacrifice. Images are crowned when dedicated to cultic use and on the feasts of the gods. The crown expresses reverence; Empedocles takes it as a mark of veneration when crowned.

2. Oracles. Crowns evoke true dreams. The person who delivers the oracle wears a crown. When Creon comes back crowned after consulting the oracle he is hailed as a messenger of joy. Roman frescoes depict crowned prophetesses.

3. Processions and Feasts. Crowning takes place in relation to prayer-processions. On the New Year feast at Rome houses are adorned with crowns or wreaths. Animals are also crowned or garlanded at various feasts.

4. A Sign of Salvation and Protection. Various examples show that crowns are viewed as signs of protection. Thus Tiberius wears a laurel wreath during thunderstorms. Wreaths are put at the entrances to houses. Crowns also serve as a means of power and protection in the invocation of gods or demons in magic.

5. The Mysteries. Mystagogues bear myrtle branches in the Eleusinian mysteries, and neophytes in the Isis mysteries. A crown is handed to the mystagogue in the dedication ceremonies of Mithras.

6. Political Life. Cultic and political life are closely related, hence it is natural that those who hold national office should be crowned. When politicians give orations in Athens they wear wreaths as a sign of immunity. The Roman emperor, his family, the priests, and state officials all wear crowns in processions.

7. The Games. Held in honor of the gods, sporting festivals culminate when the victors, who struggle hard to win, are crowned with wreaths of laurel, olive, or ivy. The herald calls their names, and the names of their fathers and towns, and then hands over the wreaths. The ceremony ends in their homes, which also bear wreaths. In the final rites they offer their wreaths to the deity.

8. The Army. The Spartans put on crowns before doing battle, perhaps in connection with sacrifice and as a sign of protection. In the Roman army the general wears a crown to purify the troops before battle. The goddess of victory is depicted with a crown, and there are crowns for the victors, whether of grass, oak leaves, or laurel. An ancient Roman custom is to offer prisoners for sale with crowns on; this possibly derives from a Germanic practice of sacrificing prisoners.

9. Private Life.

a. A Sign of Joy and Respect. Various examples illustrate the use of the crown or wreath as a mark of joy or respect.

b. Weddings. It is natural that there should be crownings at weddings. Thus we have depictions of brides with crowns, and the guests at the wedding feast also wear crowns.

c. Symposia. Wreaths adorn the participants at banquets and the ensuing symposia, which are held in honor of various gods. The wreaths express festal joy but also serve to cool the head during drinking. Wreaths are also placed on the bowls and vessels and on the walls of the rooms where the feasts are held.

10. The Cult of the Dead. A common custom is to put wreaths on the dead, on the bier, and on the grave. Permanent wreaths are carved on gravestones and funds are set up for regular adornment with wreaths. The wreaths honor the dead but also protect them against demons. Plato hands down an idea that in Hades there will be a symposium for the righteous at which they will be adorned with crowns. The mysteries promise initiates that in the hereafter they will be adorned with crowns and will enjoy the company of the blessed.

B. The OT.

1. Occurrence. In the LXX *stéphanos* and *stephanóō* are used for the Hebrew verb *'tr,* which has the basic sense "to surround," and its derivative (cf. Ps. 5:12; 1 Sam. 23:26). The use, however, is slight compared to what we find outside the OT, for Israel stands under the prohibition of images and therefore of their emblems as well. The silence of the OT confirms the cultic-magical origin of the use of crowns and is a mark of Israel's distinctiveness.

2. Use. In 2 Sam. 12:30 David takes the golden *stéphanos* from the king of Rabbah and puts it on his own head. Esth. 8:15 refers to the crown and mantle that are given to Mordecai. God gives the king a crown in Ps. 21:3 but threatens the proud crown of Ephraim in Is. 23:1, 3. God's servant receives a royal crown in Is. 22:18, 21, and Zech. 6:11 directs that a crown be prepared for Joshua. Various references to crowns may be found in the apocryphal books (cf. 1 Macc. 10:20; 13:37; Sir. 40:4; 45:12). For a reference to the wedding crown, see Cant. 3:11.

3. Figurative Use. God crowns the year with goodness in Ps. 65:11, crowns man with glory and honor in Ps. 8:5, and crowns with protective care in Ps. 103:4. He is himself his people's crown in Is. 28:5, and Israel is his crown in Is. 62:3. The parallelism of Job 19:9 equates crown and glory (cf. Lam. 5:16; Ezek. 21:26-27). A virtuous woman is her husband's crown in Prov. 12:4, gray hair is a crown in 16:31, and grandchildren are a crown in 17:6. Children bear discipline as a crown in 1:9, and wisdom delivers a crown of glory in 4:9. In Wis. 5:16 the righteous receive from God the royal crown of glory and diadem of beauty.

C. Judaism.

1. Use of the Crown. Josephus mentions the victor's crown, and Herod at his death is adorned with a diadem and golden crown. In the Year of Jubilee slaves in Israel are said to wear crowns on their heads as a mark of joy.

2. Figurative Use. The fear of God hands a crown to the Maccabean martyrs, and God is said to give the crown of righteousness to those who act justly and hate evil. The crown of glory is a halo around the head. When Levi is clothed as high priest, a crown is set on his head along with the diadem of priesthood.

3. Apocalyptic. In the Ascension of Isaiah the righteous receive crowns with the appearance of the Messiah (9:9ff.). Crowns are reserved for believers (9:24ff.). Qumran also expects the sons of truth to be led to crowns of glory and robes of splendor. In the rabbis, too, crowns, usually connected with light or glory, serve as eschatological rewards or honors for the righteous.

4. Rabbinic Theology. Rabbinic theology speaks of the three crowns of the law, the priesthood, and the monarchy. The first may be won by all who study the law. One saying rates the crown of a good name above all three. A crown of glory awaits the righteous who endure.

5. Philo. Philo is critical of the games but applies the metaphor of competitors to those who seek and achieve knowledge and are therefore crowned. The victor's crown is the vision of God as insight into the cosmic order. It comes with the victory of the mind over sensual desires.

D. The NT.

1. The Figurative Use in Paul. Like Philo, Paul adopts the metaphor of the games (1 Cor. 9:24ff.; Gal. 2:2; 5:7; Phil. 2:16; 3:12ff.). God grants an imperishable crown

as an eschatological gift to those who train hard and are thus victorious. In 2 Tim.
4:8 the reference is to Paul's own life. As he finishes the course, the Lord, the righteous
Judge, will finally give him the crown of righteousness that is laid up for him. All
who base their lives on the Lord's appearing will similarly receive crowns. Like athletes, they must follow the rules (2:5), conforming their lives to that of Christ (v. 8).
In another sense, the church is Paul's crown with which he comes before the Lord
(Phil. 4:1; 1 Th. 2:19-20). All believers are saved by Christ, but their work is assessed
and judged. Enduring work comes to expression in the church, which is thus Paul's
crown and joy and hope and glory. With this crown, he receives praise and glory from
God, and it is thus a crown of rejoicing.

2. *The Crown of Victory and Life.* In Rev. 2:10 the suffering church of Smyrna has
the promise of a crown of life (cf. Jms. 1:12; 2 Tim. 4:8). As the crown of victory,
this crown has life as its content. It is close to, and perhaps made from, the tree of
life in Rev. 2:7. Christ gives it to those who love him and are faithful to him (cf. 3:11).
In 1 Pet. 5:4 the crown is an imperishable crown of life and light represented as a
halo; the author promises it to pastors who serve in exemplary fashion.

3. *The Crown a Symbol of Divine Honor.* In Rev. 4:4ff. the elders bear golden crowns
which they cast down before God's throne. In 12:1 the woman bears a crown of 12
stars; the dragon with seven diadems seeks to destroy her. The locusts of 9:7 carry
what look like crowns, and the beast of 13:1 bears ten diadems as a sign of his power.
But the Son of Man wears a golden crown in 14:14 and many diadems in 19:12; he
is King of kings and Lord of lords (19:16).

4. *The Crown of Thorns.* The diadems of Rev. 19:12 are the counterpart of the
crown of thorns in Mk. 15:17; Mt. 27:29; Jn. 19:2, 5. This crown, made of a prickly
weed, is a mocking imitation of the crown worn by Roman vassals and is designed to
throw scorn on Jesus as well as to cause pain by scratching. It bears no relation to any
specific Roman festival but is connected with the condemnation of Jesus for his messianic claim. For John the one who is crowned with thorns in apparent defeat is the
true victor (16:33; 19:30; 20:28). As Heb. 2:9 puts it, he is now crowned with glory
and honor because of the suffering of death.

E. The Early Church.

1. *The Martyr's Crown.* The martyr especially bears the crown of victory in the
early church (cf. Mart. Pol. 17.1). The word *coronari* can even mean "to become a
martyr." As Hermas *Similitudes* 8.3.6 says, those who fought with the devil and defeated him are crowned, having suffered for God's law.

2. *The Crown in Gnosticism.* In Gnostic symbolism, Jesus crowns disciples in the
threefold baptism. The Lord is called a crown, and there is reference also to the crown
of truth; the two concepts are plainly related. Sacrificial crowning is spiritualized; the
crown of sacrifice plucked from the tree of life is worn at the sacrificial banquet.

3. *Early Christian Art.* In early Christian art two women crown the apostles Peter
and Paul, Christ hands Vitalis a golden crown, the martyrs carry crowns in their hands
and offer them to Christ, and Christ wears a halo, or a halo with a cross.

4. *The Crown of Thorns in Early Christian Art.* Art depicts the crowning of Jesus by
a soldier, but the crown is the imperial laurel wreath and symbolizes his triumph. The
theme of the passion as a victory is a common one. The crucified Lord is the glorified
Lord who is the believer's crown. Crowns mark the building from which he comes
bearing his cross.

5. *The Wedding Crown.* The wedding crown comes into the church after Constantine and is taken as a sign of victory over lusts.

6. *Rejection of the Non-Christian Use of Crowns.* Tertullian especially contests the use of crowns in his work *De corona.* In his view it is unnatural to wear flowers on the head. The custom is pagan and has no warrant in the Bible. Only God may crown us, the crown being an eschatological gift to believers. Cyprian takes a similar view, and Clement of Alexandria, while comparing the Christian life to a contest, argues against the use of crowns from reason and the repudiation of idolatry.

7. *Later Use of Crowns.* Constantine helps to make the crown more important by combining the cross, the monogram of Christ, and the disc. Crosses with crowns around them are set on imperial vessels. We find depictions of a crowned Lamb, a cross of glory, and Christ receiving crowns.   [W. GRUNDMANN, VII, 615-36]

---

stékō [to stand (firm)],   *hístēmi* [to stand]

---

stékō. This verb is a Hellenistic construct from the perfect of *hístēmi* and forms a substitute for it. It is rare in the LXX but occurs for "to stand still" in Ex. 14:13 and "to stand" in Judg. 16:26 and 1 Kgs. 8:11. In the NT we find it in Mk. 3:31 (Jesus' relatives standing outside), Jn. 1:26 (John's witness to one standing among them), Rev. 12:4 (the dragon standing before the woman), and Mk. 11:25 (standing before God in prayer). But the main use is in Paul, mostly in the imperative. Believers are to stand firm in 1 Cor. 16:13; they do so in faith on the basis of God's promises. Standing in faith is standing in the Lord (Phil. 4:1), for faith looks to the Lord, and he enables it to stand. If believers stand fast, this brings comfort to the apostle (1 Th. 3:7-8). The conditional clause here carries a concealed exhortation. Standing in the Lord gives sustaining power and creates fellowship, i.e., standing in one spirit (Phil. 1:27). Since the Lord grants freedom from sin and legalism, those who trust in him must stand fast in their freedom (Gal. 5:1). 2 Th. 2:15 links these various ideas with its summons to stand firm and hold fast to the traditions that Paul has taught. Finally, of course, believers stand or fall to their own master, i.e., to Christ (Rom. 14:4). For Paul *stékō* suggests that in faith we achieve a standing that is grounded in God, not in the world, and that confers fellowship and freedom. Outside the NT the term does not occur in the apostolic fathers but we find it in apocryphal Acts.

hístēmi.

A. Greek and Hellenistic Usage.
1. In its use for "to stand" this verb forms the opposite of sitting, reclining, or falling, also of moving.

2. The present *hístēmi* means "to stop," "to set up," "to appoint or institute," "to stir up or lift up," and "to place on a scale," "to weigh."

3. The middle means "to stand still," "to remain standing," "to come before," "to stand up," "to arise," and "to begin."

4. The perfect and pluperfect forms mean "to stand" and "to be."

5. The late future and aorist passive share the general meaning.

B. Theological Aspects in the OT.
1. *Usage.* The LXX usage corresponds to the Greek. *hístēmi* transitive means "to stop," "to appoint," or "to weigh" (Gen. 43:9; 1 Sam. 10:19; 1 Kgs. 21:39). *hístamai*

intransitive means "to stand still or erect," "to get up," "to endure" (Gen. 29:35; 1 Sam. 13:34). The perfect and pluperfect mean "to stand" (Gen. 24:13). The passive occurs in, e.g., Job 18:15.

2. With reference to the covenant or word or command of God, the term carries the sense that God has ordained it or established it or given it validity. God establishes the covenant with Noah for all generations (Gen. 9:11-12). He makes a similar covenant with Abraham (17:19) and reminds Moses of this covenant (Ex. 6:4), on which the covenant with Israel rests (Lev. 26:9). The people respond by establishing the covenant themselves as they let it shape their lives (2 Kgs. 23:3). The fact that God confirms the covenant by an oath indicates his self-commitment to it (Gen. 26:3; Jer. 11:5). The words of the covenant are thus inviolable (Dt. 28:69). God will establish his word (1 Kgs. 2:4). This is the psalmist's prayer (Ps. 119:38). God's people establish God's word and statutes by keeping them (2 Kgs. 23:24). God's work, whether in creation or covenant, is grounded in his counsel, which always stands (Is. 46:10), and in fulfilment of which God does not stand still.

3.a. The covenant is the place where God is with his people (cf. Ex. 17:6; 24:10; Ezek. 3:23; Ps. 82:1).

b. Believers also stand before God in the covenant (Gen. 18:22; Dt. 5:5; 1 Kgs. 19:11; Job 37:14). All worship is a coming before God (1 Chr. 23:30; 2 Chr. 29:11). Those who do evil cannot rightly come before God (Jer. 7:10) but sinners may be set before God for judgment (Num. 5:16).

c. The whole congregation comes before God in the sanctuary, and the heavenly hosts stand before him (2 Chr. 18:18).

4. God gives people their standing in deliverance and freedom (2 Sam. 22:34; Pss. 16:12; 30:7). Their wisdom remains (Eccl. 2:9).

C. Judaism.

1. OT concepts continue, e.g., in Sir. 44:20-21. The question of abiding values may be seen in the admonitions of Sir. 37:13; 40:12.

2.a. Taking up the question of what abides, Philo perceives the relativity of movement and standing still; thus the senses deceive us when it seems that the sun or moon stands still, and people may be shaken in convictions in which they think they are stable.

b. God alone stands, and God establishes goodness and gives standing to the righteous.

3. Qumran deals with the same question and argues that those who measure up to God's demands will stand forever, and those who cling to God will stand firm against the scorn of enemies. Yet this is possible only as God's Spirit grants it. Standing takes place as God raises and sets up. The place of standing is before God as God grants mercy and forgives sins. The covenant makes possible a standing that is already present in this life but endures to eternity. The righteous overcome slipping and falling, receive an eternal standing, and may also win standing for others by helping them when they stumble. Standing is by entry into the community in which the covenant with Israel is renewed. Whereas Philo seeks standing through knowledge, Qumran receives it as a gift of grace that rests on the abiding counsel of God.

D. The NT.

1. General Usage.

1. Statistically there are 152 instances of *hístēmi* (with *histánō*), of which 26 are in Luke, 35 in Acts, 16 in Paul, 21 in Matthew, 9 in Mark, 18 in John, and 21 in Revelation. In the general sense of "to set up" or "cause to come," we find *hístēmi*

with persons (Mt. 4:5; Acts 5:27; Jn. 8:3; Acts 6:13; Mk. 9:36) and also with objects (Rom. 3:31; Mt. 26:15; Acts 7:60, where the idea might be that of weighing, but more likely is that of charging or holding against).

2. In the general sense of "to stand," "to stand still," or "to approach," we find *hístamai* with persons (Mt. 20:32; Lk. 6:17; 17:12; 7:38; Acts 10:30; 26:16; Rev. 11:11; 18:17; Jms. 3:2) and also with objects (Lk. 8:44; Acts 8:38).

3. For "stand" we find *héstéka, hestékein* in Jn. 7:37; Lk. 23:10; Mt. 27:47; Acts 5:25. The place of standing may be expressed adverbially (Mt. 12:46-47; Lk. 13:25; 18:13; Rev. 18:10) or prepositionally (Lk. 1:11; Mt. 20:3; Rev. 7:9; Acts 5:23; 7:33; Mt. 13:2; Lk. 5:1; Jn. 20:11).

4. *Passive Forms.* The star is halted in Mt. 2:9, Jesus is set before the governor in Mt. 27:11 (cf. Mk. 13:9), the two on the way to Emmaus stand still (Lk. 24:17), the Pharisee stands self-confidently (Lk. 18:11), and words are confirmed (Mt. 18:17).

II. Theological Aspects of NT Usage.

1. To be able to place someone or something expresses power. God presents his people without blemish (Jude 24). He fixes the time of judgment (Acts 17:31). He has appointed Christ as Judge (Acts 17:31). He places in judgment (Mt. 25:33). He can also cause to stand (Rom. 14:4). Even though people fall, or others judge them, their master can make them stand. They should strive to do so (Lk. 21:36). Standing is oriented to God's act in Christ. Jesus is set on a pinnacle of the temple but he withstands temptation (Mt. 4:5, 11). The church has the authority to put forward an apostolic candidate (Acts 1:23) and to appoint the Seven (6:6)!

2. Paul speaks of the establishing of the law (Rom. 3:31). Seeking faith, the gospel validates the law in its function of convicting of sin and hence of opening the door to forgiveness. As regards the sacrificial cultus, the coming of Jesus invalidates the former covenant but brings into force the new covenant (Heb. 10:9) whereby we may live before God on the ground of Christ's sacrifice.

3. Jesus comes before his disciples as the risen Lord (Jn. 20:19). He stands at the door and waits for it to be opened (Rev. 3:20). Stephen sees him standing at God's right hand (Acts 7:55). This might simply denote his being there, but it might also denote either standing in reverence before the Father, standing to intercede for Stephen, standing to judge his opponents, or standing to welcome Stephen. In the light of 6:15 the last suggestion commends itself.

4. In 2 Tim. 2:19 the divine foundation, on which the church rests, stands firm. In contrast a divided city, house, or kingdom cannot last (Mt. 12:25-26). The church is the pillar and ground of truth (1 Tim. 3:15). Gentile Christians stand fast only through faith (Rom. 11:20). In matters of marriage the main thing is to be firmly established in the heart (1 Cor. 7:36ff.), which is possible through standing in faith; then all decisions are free and secure. Standing firm in faith results in joy (2 Cor. 1:24). It is a standing in the gospel (1 Cor. 15:1). Christ has given us access to the grace in which we stand (Rom. 5:2). We are to stand fast in it (1 Pet. 5:12). We must be on guard against falling (1 Cor. 10:12). Prayer helps us to stand (Col. 4:12). So does all of God's armor (Eph. 6:11). When we withstand, we may stand in the evil day (v. 13). In Acts 26 Paul stands on trial for the hope of the resurrection (v. 6). He once withstood the fulfilment of this hope (v. 9), but Christ appeared and caused him to stand on his feet (v. 16). He thus stands there as a witness to God's fulfilment in Christ of all that the prophets and Moses said would come to pass (v. 22).

[W. GRUNDMANN, VII, 636-53]

---

stērízō [to support, establish], *epistērízō* [to support, rest on],
stērigmós [steadfastness], *astēriktos* [unstable, weak]

A. The Group in Greek.

1. The main sense of the verb *stērízō* is "to support." In figurative use it means "to confirm," politically "to pacify," linguistically "to speak out loud," cosmologically "to fix or secure," anatomically "to gain hold" (an illness), and medically "to strengthen" (of medicines).

2. *epistērízō* means "to support" and in the middle "to rest on."

3. *stērigmós* means "steadfastness," "firmness," "standing still," "sustaining."

4. *astēriktos* means "unsupported," "weak," but also "agile," "lively," "tossing" (a ship).

B. The Group in the OT.

1. *stērízō* finds varied use in the LXX for "to support," "to fix the eyes on," "to plan," and "to strengthen." *epistērízō* means "to rest on," "to be grounded in," or "to be directed to." *stērigmós* does not occur.

2. There is no set Hebrew original for the group, but *smk* is a common equivalent.

C. Judaism.
The Hebrew term becomes a technical one for ordination in later Judaism, and at Qumran it plays a role of some importance for confirming or inward strengthening, especially by God's power.

D. The Group in the NT.

1. *stērízō* means "to fix," "to establish" in Lk. 16:26, and in Lk. 9:51 it denotes the steadfast resolve of Jesus as he sets his face toward Jerusalem. The transferred use is common (cf. Rom. 16:25; 1 Th. 3:13; Lk. 22:32; Rom. 1:11). The strengthening is by God, the Lord, the truth, or others. It may be accomplished, besought, or commanded. It presupposes an assault that threatens faith or zeal. Its aim is impregnability of faith in spite of afflictions. God strengthens the Thessalonians so that they may be blameless at the parousia (1 Th. 3:13). Moral confirmation is the point in 2 Th. 3:3, and preservation from spiritual death in Rev. 3:2. The imparting of a spiritual gift is the means in Rom. 1:11.

2. The compound *epistērízō* in Acts 14:22 and 15:32, 41 adds nothing new.

3. *stērigmós* occurs only in 2 Pet. 3:17, where it denotes perseverance or steadfastness in the truth or in sound teaching (cf. 1:12).

4. *astēriktos* in 2 Pet. 2:14; 3:16 means "unstable." False teachers entice unstable souls, and those who are unstable in their views twist the difficult passages in Paul's epistles.

E. The Apostolic Fathers.
The word *stērízō* occurs in these works for the establishing of heaven (1 Clem. 33.3), the confirming of what is falling (2 Clem. 2.6), and the strengthening of Christians (1 Clem. 13.3). The Lord's commandment (1 Clem. 13.3) and the Spirit of Christ (Ignatius *Philadelphians,* Preface) are the means of strengthening, as is God's almighty will (1 Clem. 8.5). Obedience is the effect (1 Clem. 13.3).   [G. HARDER, VII, 653-57]

---

stígma [mark, brand]

From *stízō,* "to prick," *stígma* means "prick," "point," "mark."

A. The Graeco-Roman World.

1. Owners' marks are branded on cattle. *stígmata* are usually letters burned on the right thigh.

2. People who are branded, e.g., criminals, prisoners of war, slaves, or deserters, are usually regarded as dishonored and are a butt of scorn in comedy. Caligula even has some citizens branded and sent to prison camps. Various devices are tried to remove the brands but without much success. Tattooed signs are placed on army recruits, usually on the hand.

B. The Near East.

1. Cattle are branded in Babylon as a mark of ownership, and rebellious concubines or sons may also be marked as slaves in Babylon.

2. A mark may also denote membership in a tribe or allegiance to a cultic deity. The signs are placed on the knee, wrist, or neck and take various forms. Those bearing the marks of a god are dedicated to service but can also claim protection.

C. The OT.

1. The marking of slaves occurs in Ex. 21:6 with the voluntary acceptance of service.

2. Sacral marking occurs in Is. 44:5. In 49:16 God has a model of the city graven on his hands. The feasts serve as signs and marks (Ex. 13:9ff.). The headplate of the high priest represents a kind of mark (cf. Ex. 28:36), but Lev. 19:28 forbids the marking of the flesh (disobeyed at times; cf. Jer. 16:6).

3. The mark of Cain seems to be a tattooed sign. It does not brand Cain as a murderer but sets him under divine protection (cf. the mark of Ezek. 9:4).

D. Later Judaism.

1. Ps. Sol. 2:6 refers to Pompey's branding of Jewish prisoners. Slaves still bear marks but also carry labels.

2. In 3 Macc. 2:29-30 Ptolemy IV Philopator tries to force pagan brands on Alexandrian Jews. Philo complains that some apostate Jews accept brands; he views the mark of Cain as a symbol of the lasting evil of folly. The rabbis reject tattooing (in contrast to signs that can be erased); they relate it to idolatry. Circumcision is the mark of the covenant people as distinct from pagan *stígmata.*

3. Later Judaism often refers to Ezek. 9:4. Unlike the mark of destruction, it is a sign of protection in affliction, especially that of the end-time. The signs of the cross on some tombs of the NT period probably reflect the influence of Ezek. 9:4. The rabbis do not construe the mark of Cain as a tattooed sign.

E. The NT.
In the NT *stígma* occurs only in Gal. 6:17. Paul perhaps views the marks of Jesus here as protective—a new eschatological sign, which denotes the freedom of grace, as compared to circumcision, which denotes bondage under the law. The marks can hardly be tattooed signs but are almost certainly the scars he has acquired in Christian service (cf. 2 Cor. 4:10; Col. 1:24; Phil. 3:21). These are palpable proof that he suffers with the Lord (Rom. 8:17). Rev. 7:2-3 offers an eschatological exposition of Ezek. 9:4. In 3:12; 14:1; 22:4 the name of God or Christ is the protective sign, but this is not humanly inscribed (unlike the mark of the beast, 13:16-17), for it comes from heaven.

F. Church History.

1. Gnosticism refers to the saving name of the Redeemer as a sign. Normally the use is figurative but some groups seal initiates with a hot iron on the lobe of the right ear—the baptism with fire.

2. The fathers often refer to the marks of slaves to bring out the meaning of Christian appropriation to the Lord in baptism.

3. Later some Christians have the cross or Christ's name tattooed on their wrists or arms, and we also read of the letters IHS being incised on the breast.

4. From the Middle Ages on, various people distinguished for piety and weakened by sickness or abstinence (cf. St. Francis of Assisi) have visibly borne the marks of the nails or spear or the marks of the crown of thorns, the scourging, and the cross-bearing.   [O. Betz, VII, 657-64]

---

stílbō [to shine, glisten]

---

1. The Greek Sphere. The original use of *stílbō* in Homer has to do with the "shining" or "gleaming" of oil. It then relates generally to the glitter of gold, the shining of light or water, or the shining of human beauty.

2. *OT Use.* In the OT the LXX uses the term for the gleaming reflections of various metals (cf. Dan. 10:6; Ezek. 21:15, 20). A common use is for the lightning of the forked sword (Ezek. 21:33). A transferred use occurs in Ps. 7:12.

3. *The NT.* The only NT use is in Mk. 9:3 for the "glistening" of the clothes of Jesus at the transfiguration. The addition "intensely white" clarifies the term (cf. Mt. 17:2). White is the color of light, life, heaven, priesthood, and victory.

4. *The Apostolic Fathers.* Hermas *Similitudes* 9.2.2 uses the word to express supernatural radiance.   [G. Fitzer, VII, 665-66]

---

stoichéō [to be in a series, be in step with], *systoichéō* [to be in a series, correspond], *stoicheíon* [elements, elemental substances]

---

stoichéō.

1. *Outside the NT.* This verb means "to belong to a series," "to be in rank," or, transferred, "to be in agreement," "to come to an agreement," "to remain in agreement."

2. *The NT.* In the NT the word is often taken to have the sense "to walk" (perhaps on the basis of "to be in step with"), but in all the instances it can have the usual sense. Thus in Acts 21:24 the point is to be in the ranks of those who keep the law, in Phil. 3:16 Paul wants his readers to remain in the same thing, in Gal. 6:16 agreement with the rule is at issue, in Rom. 4:12 keeping step is in view, and in Gal. 5:25 the Christian life is one of harmony with the Spirit.

3. *The Early Church.* The saying in Mart. Pol. 22.1 stresses the importance of harmony with the word of Christ, and Clement of Alexandria *Stromateis* 3.66.1 echoes Gal. 6:16.

systoichéō. Giving emphasis to the simple form, this compound means "to be in a series with," "to be in the same ranks." Gal. 4:25 presupposes two antithetical series of concepts: two women, two covenants, Mt. Sinai, and the two Jerusalems. Having equated Hagar with Mt. Sinai, Paul then says that she is in the same series with (i.e., corresponds to) the earthly Jerusalem.

stoicheíon.

A. **Outside the NT.**

1. A first meaning of *stoicheíon* is the "length of a shadow" in calculating time.

2. Another use is for a syllable, i.e., a sound as part of a word, then a basic word. Vowels have special importance, and letters understood as sounds play a special role in some circles.

3. Cosmologically the *stoicheía* are the four elements, Plato's original constituents of the world, the four elements of Stoicism in distinction from the eternal and imperishable *archaí,* the elements which form a basis of brotherhood in Alexandrian Judaism. The use of religious terms tends to divinize the elements, so that in early Christian works (cf. Aristides or Clement of Alexandria) their autonomy is resisted and stress is laid on their creation and their subservience to the *lógos.*

4. Other uses of the word are for the notes of music, for the number one in mathematics, for what is primary, e.g., in education, for first principles, e.g., in geometry or logic, and for the factors which are basic phenomena in dreams.

5. In philosophy, Gnostic speculation, and astrology the stars take on importance as *stoicheía,* whether as visible gods, as creatures that influence earthly events, as features on the heavenly journey, or as bodies that declare the will of the gods.

6. The use of *stoicheíon* alongside *daímōn* and *pneúma* shows that the idea of "stellar spirits" is present.

B. **The NT.**

1. In Gal. 4:3; Col. 2:8, 20 we find the phrase *stoicheía toú kosmoú* (and cf. Gal. 4:9). Outside the NT the term would denote the four elements or the basic materials of the world of which the whole cosmos, and humanity within it, is composed. Only the context can yield any other sense.

2. Gal. 4:3ff., however, seems to number the law among the *stoicheía,* and 4:8-9 seems to include false gods. These references rule out such senses as the cosmic elements, the stars, stellar spirits, or simply spiritual forces. Building on thoughts of his age, Paul is using the term in a new way, describing the *stoicheía* as weak and beggarly. In a transferred sense, the *stoicheía* are the things on which pre-Christian existence rests, especially in pre-Christian religion. These things are impotent; they bring bondage instead of freedom.

3. In Col. 2:6ff. the *stoicheía toú kosmoú* are parallel to the *parádosis tōn anthrṓpōn* (v. 8). Religious ordinances (2:20) are inadequate as a basis of human existence. It is a delusion for Christians to think that such things can sustain them. By dying and rising again with Christ they are freed from this delusion and the bondage it entails.

4. In 2 Pet. 3:10, 12 the reference has to be to the elements (or just possibly the stars). The use of terms and the idea of a final conflagration strongly support "elements" as the true rendering. As v. 12 points out, both the higher and lower elements will be destroyed, including the earth and all its works.

5. The meaning in Heb. 5:12 is obviously "rudiments" or "first principles," with a slightly derogatory nuance in context.   [G. DELLING, VII, 666-87]

---

stolḗ [robe]

1. The Greek World. This word first means "equipping," then "fitting out," and then specifically "dress," either male or female. The *stolḗ* becomes the long and flowing upper garment, and sometimes the special robe of priests and hierophants. Rarely *stolḗ* can mean the act of dressing. Paul's concept of vesting with Christ or the new humanity probably reflects the religious use of robes and religious ceremonies of robing.

2. *The LXX.* *stolḗ* occurs 98 times in the LXX, mostly for "clothing." All kinds of clothing may be denoted, especially the upper garment, but clothing can also have a particular significance (cf. Gen. 41:14, 42). Donning royal garments symbolizes kingship (2 Chr. 18:9). Clothing, then, shows what a person or a person's position is. Wisdom offers a robe of glory (Sir. 6:29, 31) that expresses the heavenly life. God will finally clothe the elect with good things (En. 62:15-16). The priestly robe is a holy one (Ex. 28:2) which goes along with the priesthood (40:13; Num. 20:26). Sprinkling with the blood of the altar sanctifies the priests and their robes (Ex. 29:21). Here again the idea is present that clothing expresses a given status.

3. *The NT.* In the NT *stolḗ* denotes only the upper garment. The robe that the father puts on the returning prodigal marks his restored status as one who was dead and is alive again (Lk. 15:22). Jesus in Mk. 12:38 warns against scribes who go about in long, flowing robes, thus claiming special status and expecting special honor. The white robe of Mk. 16:5 denotes the heavenly being of the messenger and the eschatological revelation contained in the message. The robes of Rev. 6:11 and 7:9 also have an eschatological color. The washing has a passive sense. The wearers have not washed them themselves by martyrdom but they have been washed by Christ (cf. the receiving of the robe of glory in 3:4-5). Entry into the new aeon is a robing with new garments (cf. also 1 Cor. 15:53-54; 2 Cor. 5:3). The garment expresses being, and investing with it expresses the gift of new being.   [U. WILCKENS, VII, 687-91]

---

stóma [mouth]

A. Secular Greek. This word has such varied meanings as the human mouth or face, the animal maw or jaws, the speaker, the speech or word, the opening, entry, or front.

B. Data from Religious History. In Egypt and the Near East the mouth of deity emits the word or breath of life. Phrases like "the word of thy mouth" or "as goes forth from thy mouth" are common. The divine word effects what it says. The gods come forth from the mouth of the primal god, either by utterance or by generation in which the mouth is the organ. The idea of the efficacious word of deity may be extended to the human mouth in expression of the intent of the heart. The mouth of demons goes forth from those who are demonized, and wicked mouths bring harm to people. Charms from the mouth, however, can also pacify the angry person. Cleansing the mouths of newly dedicated idols or of priests and penitents bears witness to the power of the mouth. The mouth of the priest, when used by the deity, has the same force as that of the deity, which it now becomes.

C. The OT.

1. The Hebrew term has much the same sense as *stóma* but is used more clearly and consistently for "word," "command," etc. Various expressions may be noted, e.g., "with one voice" or a "loud voice." Several descriptions also occur, e.g., flattering in Prov. 26:28. Figurative use may be discerned in Ps. 22:21 and Job 36:16,

and also when God says he will take from Bel's mouth what he has swallowed in Jer. 51:44. The simple meaning "entry" occurs in Gen. 4:11.

2. When the reference is to God's mouth, the mouth as the organ of speech is always in view except in Ps. 18:8 and Job 37:2. Poetic style and parallelism determine this use at times, but elsewhere the purpose is perhaps to avoid direct reference to God. Only in Ps. 33:6 does the creative word proceed from God's mouth. Miracles and judgments are uttered in Ps. 105:5 (cf. 1 Chr. 16:12).

3. A common use is for a word or command of God which may be transgressed or resisted (cf. Num. 14:41; 20:24). Fulfilment as well as word is denoted in Is. 11:4.

4. God may also use the human mouth as his own, especially in the case of the prophets (Jer. 15:19). He cleanses or sanctifies the mouth thus used (Is. 6:7; Jer. 1:9). His word is in this mouth and goes forth from it (1 Kgs. 17:24). It is also in the mouth of succeeding generations (Is. 59:21). The law from the priest's mouth is God's word (Mal. 2:7). Even Necho's mouth may be God's (2 Chr. 35:22).

5. Through the mouth the relation to God is effected and proved (Dt. 32:1). The righteous pray that God's word should not depart from their mouth (Ps. 119:43). God's praise is in the mouth of his people (Ps. 8:2). The mouth should speak as the heart thinks (Is. 29:13). The wicked set their mouths against heaven (Ps. 73:9), but the devout seek the ritual cleanness of their mouths (Ezek. 4:14), and ask God to keep guard over them (Ps. 141:3).

D. Judaism.

1. The LXX. The literal *stóma* occurs in the LXX for the Hebrew term, but we also find *rhḗma* when the sense is word or command.

2. The Targums. The Targums disregard the different meanings of the Hebrew and always take it in the sense of saying or word.

3. Rabbinic Texts. The rabbis see no need to interpret the expression "mouth of God." A negative significance attaches to the mouths of idols.

4. Philo. For Philo the mouth of God is a symbol of his word.

5. Qumran. The Qumran literature follows OT usage.

E. The NT. The term *stóma* is none too common in the NT. It denotes the human mouth or animal maw, the give-and-take of dialogue (2 Jn. 12), the mouth as the organ of speech, and in a transferred sense word or speech.

1. Jesus adopts the OT reference to God's mouth in quoting Dt. 8:3. In the Hebrew the point is that the word from God's mouth grants manna, but in the LXX, which uses *rhḗma,* the stress is on the word that confers eternal life.

2. The only mention of the mouth of Jesus in the ordinary sense is in Jn. 19:29. The phrase of Luke in 4:22; 11:54; 22:71 evokes the idea of the majesty of his mouth and of the truth of what it utters (cf. Mt. 5:2). 1 Pet. 2:22 refers Is. 59:3 to Jesus' mouth, and Mt. 13:34-35 refers Ps. 78:2 to it. In Acts 22:14 Paul receives from the mouth of the Just One his election as an apostle. This is the mouth of the risen Lord (cf. Rev. 1:16; 2:16; 19:15, 21). The sword that goes forth from his mouth reminds us of Is. 11:4 (cf. 2 Th. 2:8; Rev. 3:16). Judgment also proceeds from the mouths of the witnesses in Rev. 11:5 and the jaws of the horses in 9:17ff. The dragon sends out water from the mouth to drown the woman (12:15), the beast has a mouth that utters blasphemy (13:5), and foul spirits like frogs hop out of the mouths of the dragon, the beasts, and the false prophets (16:13).

3. God, or the Holy Spirit, speaks through the mouths of the prophets in Lk. 1:70; Acts 1:14; 4:25; the reference is to OT Scripture. God also speaks through the mouths

of NT prophets (Rev. 10:8ff.) and apostles (Acts 15:7). The attack of enemies is directed at the apostle's mouth in Acts 23:2.

4. In the mouths of believers the confession of faith in Christ is a saving one (Rom. 10:8ff. quoting Dt. 30:14). The church is to glorify God with one mouth (Rom. 15:6). Every mouth will finally confess Christ (Phil. 2:11).

5. The mouth is to be kept pure (Eph. 4:29). It is unnatural that the same mouth should praise God and curse others (Jms. 3:10ff.). No lie is in the mouths of the perfected in heaven (Rev. 14:5). Inner purity comes to expression in what the mouth speaks (Col. 3:9ff.). Not what enters the mouth, but what issues from the heart causes defilement. The mouths of the wicked are full of curses and bitterness (Rom. 3:14). Those who honor God with their lips when their hearts are far from him are condemned (Mk. 7:6; cf. 1 Jn. 3:18).   [K. WEISS, VII, 692-701]

→ *prósōpon*

---

strateúomai [to serve in the army], *strateía* [military service], *stratiá* [army], *strateúma* [army division], *stratiṓtēs* [soldier], *systratiṓtēs* [fellow soldier], *stratēgós* [military leader], *stratópedon* [camp], *stratologéō* [to enlist for military service]

A. The Group in Greek.

1. From the basic *stratós,* denoting a camp or army, the first derivative is *strateúō,* "to undertake a campaign," "to serve in the army."

2. We then find *strateía,* meaning "campaign" or "military service."

3. Also found is *stratiá* for "army" or superterrestrial "host."

4. *strateúma* is mostly used for an "army division."

5. The individual on military service is a *strateuómenos,* but *stratiṓtēs* also comes into use. This word can take on adverse connotations when it comes to denote first the professional and then the mercenary, especially among those who favor a citizen army. At the same time professionals prove their worth, and the term is often used in a good sense, as is *systratiṓtēs* for "comrade-in-arms."

6. The *stratēgós* is the "military leader," who may also have high political importance in antiquity. The noun *stratēgía* means "leading the army," "tactics," "the office of general," and "generalship."

7. The *stratópedon* is the site of the *stratós,* i.e., the "camp" or "campsite."

8. The term *stratologéō* means "to enlist for military service."

B. The Group in the OT.

1. The simple *strateúō* occurs in the OT only three times for a Hebrew term (Is. 29:7; Judg. 19:8; 2 Sam. 15:28). It is used in a transferred sense for martyrdom in 4 Macc. 9:24.

2. *stratiá* or *strateía* occurs 22 times for a Hebrew term that denotes cultic as well as military service, so that it carries some sense of the holy war in which the army represents the totality of the people as the people of the one God.

3. *stratópedon* occurs in Jer. 34:1 for military might and in 2-4 Maccabees for camp or army.

4. *stratēgós* is the most common word of the group in the LXX but often means "governor" rather than "general." The prefix *archi-* is sometimes added to yield *archistrátēgos* (cf. Gen. 21:22).

5. The important noun *stratiṓtēs* occurs only once in translation (2 Sam. 23:8) as a variant for the more original *traumatías*. The warrior of ancient Israel is *machḗtḗs* or *polemistḗs*, but 2–4 Maccabees use *stratiṓtēs* more freely, with a reference to Jewish soldiers in 4 Macc. 3:7, 12. In general, the LXX appreciates the distinction between the group and Hebrew ideas and thus makes sparing use of it except where there is no Hebrew control (as in 2–4 Maccabees).

C. The Group in Judaism.
1. Josephus. Having no objections, Josephus uses all the terms that occur in the NT.
2. Philo. Philo, too, uses terms from the group but avoids *stratiṓtēs*, which suggests the Roman legionary. In a military sense he uses the terms more commonly in a transferred sense in theological or psychological statements (e.g., God as leader of the invincible host, the war against desires, or the host of the stars).
3. Qumran. How far the military organization of Qumran is determined by the Greek ethos is hard to say; one might equally think of a use or a shunning of the group in Greek translations of the Scrolls.

D. The Group in the NT.
1. The Apocalyptic Reference. In the *stratópedon* of Titus at the siege of Jerusalem (Lk. 21:20) believers see a fulfilment of Jesus' prediction of wars and rumors of wars prior to the end (Mk. 13:7). They must be ready to suffer but need not participate. The demonic *strateúmata* will destroy a third of the race in Rev. 9:15, but the divine also sees the heavenly *stráteuma* in 19:19 (cf. vv. 14ff.). No earthly *stráteuma* need help this victorious host. What is demanded of believers, as the witnesses of Heb. 11:33ff. testify, is faith, not warlike achievement.
2. The Ordinary Reference. Believers come into contact with Roman soldiers, but do not see in them potential enemies at the human level. Pagan thinking clearly dominates military practice, but all people resist God and not just soldiers (Rev. 13:16-17). Indeed, Christians can learn from the brave and unconditional obedience of soldiers even though their allegiance is an evil one (Mt. 8:5ff.). At the passion soldiers carry out the execution of Jesus but a centurion also confesses him (Mk. 15:39), and if the soldiers divide the clothes and thrust in the spear, their guilt is not thereby stressed. The military watch at the tomb is ready to take a bribe in Mt. 28:12.
3. Lucan Narrative. Only Luke uses *stratēgós, stratópedon,* and *stratiá,* which in Lk. 2:13 is the superterrestrial host in a positive sense, in Acts 7:42 in a negative sense. The *strateuómenoi* who seek the Baptist's advice may be either Jewish or Roman, the *stratiṓtai* of Acts 27:31-32, 42 at first favor Paul and then want to kill him, their centurion overrules Paul and then protects him, the *stratiṓtai* in Acts 12:4, 6, 18; 21:32, 35 behave correctly, the military guards at the freeing of Peter seem to forfeit their lives, the chiliarch sends a considerable *stráteuma* (Acts 23:23ff.) to escort Paul to Caesarea, and the devout centurion Cornelius, who plays such a pivotal role in Acts 10, has a *stratiṓtēs eusebḗs* in his company (v. 7). In general Luke expects soldiers to be just as open to the gospel as others, but he senses a distance between legionaries and believers and thus refrains from using the group in a transferred sense for the Christian life.
4. Paul. Paul takes a different course. In 1 Cor. 9:7 *strateúomai* offers a parallel to his own work; the *strateuómenos* may be mentioned with the vine-dresser or shepherd. In 2 Cor. 10:2ff. Paul does not merely walk but wars, although not in worldly fashion. He has in view a siege which aims to destroy arguments and take thoughts captive. Epaphroditus is a *systratiṓtēs* in Phil. 2:25 and Archippus in Phlm. 2; the term seems

to be a somewhat more complimentary one than *synergós* but bears only a general sense. Except in 1 Cor. 9:7 the group is not really at home in the vocabulary of Paul.

5. *The Pastorals.* The transferred use of the group for Christian conduct is more common in these letters. Leaders are exhorted to *strateúesthai* in 1 Tim. 1:18-19 and 2 Tim. 2:3ff. Life, especially the Christian life, is a *strateía,* a good one controlled by faith and a good conscience in the case of believers (1 Tim. 1:18-19). Timothy is to offer an example. In 2 Tim. 2:3ff. the three comparisons recall 1 Cor. 9:7. Self-denying concentration is the theme. The *stratiṓtēs* exemplifies this plainly. Figuratively, then, Christ's servants bear the same name as his executioners, but the need for "understanding" (v. 7) brings out the difference and the figurative sense is obvious.

6. *The Catholic Epistles.* In 1 Pet. 2:11 the destructive nature of warfare comes to the fore; carnal passions wage war against the soul, and if believers do not withstand them they cannot lead the Gentiles among whom they live to conversion and praise of God. Jms. 4:1 also has the destructive aspect in view, this time in relation to the *strateúesthai* of inner disagreement that leads to wars and fightings as inner tension produces outer conflict.

7. *A Comparison.* To compare the epistles with Luke's narrative is difficult, since the epistles say nothing about actual relations with soldiers. If, however, soldiers here are only the terrible people they are for many Jews, the figurative use of the group makes little sense. There is thus a certain harmony between what we find in Luke and what we find in the epistles.

E. **The Apostolic Fathers.** The group is none too common at first. *stratiá* bears a literal sense in 1 Clem. 51.5 and Ignatius *Romans* 5.1. In 1 Clem. 37.3 Christians obey the Lord as *strateuómenoi* obey the *basileús* and they obey ecclesiastical authorities as soldiers obey their officers. Ignatius *Polycarp* 6.2 echoes 2 Tim. 2:4, but avoids *stratiṓtēs.* The phrase *stratiṓtēs theoú* occurs in Mart. Pol. 4.6 (and cf. 2).

→ *panoplía, pólemos*   [O. Bauernfeind, VII, 701-13]

---

stréphō [to turn], *anastréphō* [to return, overturn], *anastrophḗ* [way of life, conduct], *katastréphō* [to overturn, destroy], *katastrophḗ* [destruction], *diastréphō* [to mislead], *apostréphō* [to turn away], *epistréphō* [to convert, turn to], *epistrophḗ* [attention, conversion], *metastréphō* [to turn, change]

---

stréphō.

1. This word means "to twist, turn, bend, or steer." Education is a turning of the soul to the good, and the moral walk has inner turnings.

2. In the LXX *stréphō* occurs 37 times with a Hebrew original (cf. the changing of Saul in 1 Sam. 10:6, of cursing into blessing in Ps. 30:11, inner conversion in Lam. 1:10, conversion of the people back to God in 1 Kgs. 18:37).

3. In Josephus *Antiquities* 6.153 God does not change his mind. Philo uses *strophḗ* for cosmic processes and changes in human destiny.

4. In the NT *strapheís* is a formula in Luke to introduce sayings of the Lord (cf. 7:9). The word occurs in such sayings three times in Matthew (5:39; 7:6; 18:3). Acts 7:39 (cf. Num. 14:3) refers to the inner turning to Egypt and 7:42 to God's turning from Israel. In Acts 13:46 the apostles turn from Israel to the Gentiles. Water is changed into blood in Rev. 11:6 (cf. Ex. 7:17, 19).

5. There is an occasional use in the early church (cf. the changing of formless

matter in Justin *Apology* 59.1, or the change to matter in Athenagoras *Supplication* 22.6).

anastréphō, anastrophḗ, katastréphō, katastrophḗ.

1. In secular Greek *anastréphō* has such meanings as "to convert," "to bring or come back," "to be occupied with," "to act," "to walk."

2. There is a varied use in the LXX for "to convert," "to come home or back," and "to change."

3. In the NT the word means "to return" in Acts 5:22. It is a variant for *anatrépō* in Jn. 2:15 (overturning the tables). God will return and fulfil the promise to David in Acts 15:16. Conduct is the issue in 2 Cor. 1:12; Eph. 2:3; 4:22; 1 Pet. 1:18; 2 Pet. 2:7, 18; 1 Tim. 3:15; 1 Tim. 4:12. Fear of God shapes the Christian walk (1 Pet. 3:2). The holiness that God demands embraces the whole Christian walk (1:15), including suffering (cf. Heb. 10:33; 13:7). For an eschatological orientation cf. 2 Pet. 3:11.

4. *anastréphō* is the only common compound in the apostolic fathers. It is used both negatively and positively for conduct. Holiness and righteousness of walk are required (1 Clem. 63.3; Did. 3.9). Justin *Apology* 10.2 refers to the walk with God.

diastréphō.

1. This verb means "to twist," "to dislocate," "to confuse." Inner defects lead to confusion of action. Moral corruption is sometimes denoted. Human nature, which is originally good, is twisted by bad teaching, example, etc.

2. The compound occurs 36 times in the OT with no fixed original. Human nature is warped (Dt. 32:5), ways are crooked (Prov. 8:13), Moses and Aaron, and also Elijah, are accused of confusing the people (Ex. 5:4; 1 Kgs. 18:17-18), right is perverted (Mic. 3:9), and those whom God has smitten with confusion cannot make ordinances (Eccl. 7:13; Hebrew text different).

3. The OT controls NT usage. Jesus refers to a perverse as well as a faithless generation in Mt. 17:17; this judgment extends to the whole unbelieving world. Phil. 2:15 quotes the saying in Dt. 32:5 about a crooked and perverse generation. The accusation against Jesus in Lk. 23:2 is the political one that he perverts the people. Paul tells Elymas in Acts 13:10 that he perverts the right ways of God. Acts 20:30 refers to those who speak crooked things (cf. Ezek. 14:5); apostasy is at issue.

4. In the early church the verb is used as in the NT in 1 Clem. 46.3, 9; 47.5. The simile of the potter who can fix a warped vessel so long as it is not yet fired occurs in 2 Clem. 8.2. "To twist the lips (in scorn)" is a phrase in Justin *Dialogue* 101.3 (based on Ps. 22:7).

apostréphō.

1. Secular Greek. This verb means "to turn aside or away from," "to turn back," "to twist words," and, in the middle, "to reject."

2. The OT. The word occurs some 500 times in the OT. Most of the instances are spatial (returning, going home, also repaying). The return from exile has some theological significance, as does turning to Egypt. God can threaten to return Israel to Egypt as a penalty (Dt. 28:68). This will mean apostasy to other gods (Num. 32:15). God's turning aside and the people's falling away coincide (Dt. 31:17). The demand to turn aside from sin initiates renewal (1 Kgs. 8:35). Prayer is made to God not to turn away nor to let the people turn away, but he is also asked to turn aside from his people's sins or to turn aside other peoples. Often his wrath either turns or does not turn to people, and he turns back deeds upon themselves. The verb may also denote inner conversion, especially in Jeremiah (cf. 30:21). In Ezek. 18:21, 24 it is used for both apostasy and conversion in close proximity.

3. Philo and Josephus.

a. Philo rejects as anthropopathic many references to God's turning, but his usage is along OT lines.

b. Josephus warns against turning providence into its opposite by sin, and he says that the Essenes reject joy as sin.

4. The NT. In Mt. 26:52 Jesus orders the disciple to put back the sword into its sheath. Mt. 5:42 refers to lending without return. Lk. 23:14 echoes 23:2. Acts 3:26 says that the work of the Servant is to turn people from sin. The preaching of the kingdom may be resisted, but when it is followed there is divine renewal. Rom. 11:26 quotes Is. 59:20 LXX to the same effect: the Deliverer will turn aside ungodliness from Jacob. This version seems to be a better one than the Hebrew text, which promises the Redeemer to those who turn from sin, for liberation from sin is the decisive act of eschatological salvation. Rejection of the gospel is the point in 2 Tim. 4:4 and Tit. 1:14. The writer is himself repudiated in 2 Tim. 1:15, and there is a warning against rejecting Christ in Heb. 12:25 (cf. 3:1ff.).

5. Early Christianity. The compound is fairly common in early writings but mostly in OT quotations. Justin *Dialogue* 133.5 gives an anthropocentric turn to the theocentric saying in Is. 5:25. Rejection of the needy is a vice in 2 Clem. 15.1; Did. 4.8.

epistréphō, epistrophḗ.

1. Secular Greek. The verb has such varied meanings as "to convert," "to change," "to turn to or against," "to wander," "to walk," "to turn to a matter," "to pay regard to," "to note." The noun means "attention," "returning," "repentance," "conversion," "change of mind."

2. The OT. The compound verb occurs some 579 times in the LXX for various forms of turning (to, from, back, etc.), and religiously for apostasy or conversion. In Is. 6:10 the LXX introduces the idea of conversion for healing. In Jer. 2:27 an apostate people turns its back on God. It turns to the wicked acts of its fathers in 11:10. God is asked to turn again to his people in Ps. 90:13 etc., or to convert his people in Ps. 80:3 etc. National piety becomes individual piety, and this in turn makes a more general application possible (Jer. 18:8; 30:21) as a messianic work of eschatological restoration.

3. Judaism.

a. In the Apocrypha and pseudepigrapha the term is less prominent; it tends to be supplanted by *metanoéō*.

b. Philo allegorizes the turning of Lot's wife or the turning of Moses to God as turning from or to knowledge. He also equates the word with moral improvement or turning to righteousness. The turning of the spirit to itself reflects Hellenistic modes of thought.

c. Only rarely in Josephus does the compound have a religious or ethical sense.

4. The NT.

a. In Jn. 21:20 the verb implies turning aside from Jesus. Spatial movement is the point in Acts 9:40. Concern for the churches finds expression in the returning of Acts 15:36. Physical movement is described in Acts 16:18 but with the suggestion of giving attention to.

b. A transferred sense occurs in Lk. 17:4, i.e., an inner change and consequent renewing of relationship. Falling back into the old servitude is the point in 2 Pet. 2:21 (cf. Gal. 4:9).

c. Is. 6:9-10 is quoted in Mk. 4:12; Mt. 13:15; Jn. 12:40; Acts 28:27. Matthew and Mark explain why Jesus speaks in parables, i.e., so that those who do not truly hear will not understand or turn. In Jn. 12:40 God brings about the hardening that prevents conversion, but Jesus manifests his glory by bringing salvation. In Acts 28:27 the gospel goes to the Gentiles because of the guilty obduracy of Israel.

d. Lk. 1:16-17 refers to the leading back of many in Israel to God. In Lk. 22:32 Jesus prays for Peter, so that after his fall he will turn again and strengthen the brethren. The revelation of the risen Lord brings about the change. Jms. 5:19-20 uses the verb for the restoration of erring brethren. In Acts 3:19 and 26:18ff. it is used with *metanoéō*. In the former the point may be that they should repent and turn to the fact that sin is forgiven, but in the latter turning from and turning to are at issue. Turning from idols is meant in Acts 14:15, and Paul aims at repentance and turning to God in Acts 26:20. Acts 9:35 refers to the converted of Lydda in the Plain of Sharon. To believe and to be converted go together in Acts 11:21 (cf. 15:3, 7, 19). The Thessalonians turn to God from idols in 1 Th. 1:9, and cf. 2 Cor. 3:16, where Paul construes Ex. 34:34 in terms of conversion. In 1 Pet. 2:25 the OT form of expression refers to the bringing of lost sheep to the true Shepherd, i.e., Christ.

5. *Early Christianity.* Various meanings may be found in early writings, e.g., turning aside, turning back, restoring, and converting.

metastréphō. This uncommon verb means "to turn," "to change." In the NT it occurs in Acts 2:20 for the turning of the sun into darkness (quoting Joel 2:31). The only other use is in Gal. 1:7, where Paul's opponents turn the gospel into its opposite.

[G. Bertram, VII, 714-29]

---

strouthíon [sparrow]

1. This diminutive means "sparrow." The poets do not distinguish the sparrow from other small birds, but economically the sparrow is a threat to crops and is regarded as good to eat.

2. The OT equivalent simply means "bird" with no specific reference to the sparrow.

3. Josephus *Jewish War* 5.467 refers to a pool called *Strouthíon* in Jerusalem.

4. The only NT use is in Mt. 10:29ff. and Lk. 12:6-7, which argue that since God cares for a bird that fetches so little when sold, he will care much more for the disciples even though their lives might seem to be just as paltry by human estimation, and are just as exposed to mortal threat. [O. Bauernfeind, VII, 730-32]

---

stýlos [pillar]

A. The Pillar in Antiquity. *stýlos* means "pillar," either in a supporting function or standing free. In a transferred sense it may denote a reliable person.

B. The OT. The *stýlos* is primarily architectural in the LXX (cf. the tabernacle and temple). The pillar of cloud or fire denotes God's directing presence (Ex. 13:21-22), and Jeremiah as an iron pillar is to be a guiding sign (1:18). The *stýlos* is a platform in 2 Kgs. 11:14. Cosmologically *stýlos* suggests the comparison of the universe to a house (Job 9:6 etc.). Wisdom also builds a house (Prov. 9:1). Originally the seven planets are its seven pillars; created by wisdom, they control the world.

C. Rabbinic Statements. Among the rabbis we often find the transferred use, e.g., for Abraham, the righteous, or teachers of the law.

D. The NT. When Paul refers to the "pillars" of the church in Gal. 2:9 the transferred use is apparent but behind the metaphor lies the idea of the church as a building (1 Cor. 3:10ff.; Eph. 2:21; Rev. 3:12). A certain irony emerges in Paul's statement that the three are "reputed" to be pillars, and the agreement of vv. 9-10 shows that they are pillars only of the Jerusalem church and that Paul's apostolate to the Gentiles is no less basic. The thought of the heavenly building is also present in Rev. 3:12. Tried and proved believers are irreversibly integrated into God's kingdom and fitted as pillars into the heavenly building; they belong to the city of God. In 1 Tim. 3:15 the use is slightly different. The cultic community is the house of God and as such it is the pillar and ground of truth. The description in Rev. 10:1 reproduces a familiar feature in OT theophanies (cf. Ex. 13:21-22).   [U. WILCKENS, VII, 732-36]

---

syngenḗs [related to], *syngéneia* [relative, relation]

1. The Group in Greek.

a. The adjective refers to a person of common origin, i.e., belonging to the same family, race, tribe, or people. It can then mean "related" in disposition, "corresponding," "analogous," or "similar."

b. The noun means "relationship" by descent or disposition, then more broadly "analogy" (e.g., between deity and humanity, or ideas and the senses, or the stars and human destiny), whether in philosophy or popular belief.

2. The LXX.

a. The LXX uses the noun some 44 times for "relations," i.e., "relatives."

b. The adjective occurs mostly in the Apocrypha either in the sense of "relative" or as a court title (Persian or Ptolemaic).

3. Judaism.

a. Philo has the noun some 80 times for "relatives," sometimes allegorically. The OT prevents him from developing an unrestricted analogy between deity and humanity. His use of the adjective is similar ("related," "belonging," "corresponding"). Only in a relative sense is humanity *syngenḗs* to God.

b. There is little of note in Josephus. *syngéneia* is rare and mostly means "relationship." *syngenḗs* is very common and usually denotes the "relative" in the narrower sense.

4. The NT. The idea of a relationship between deity and humanity, which is alien to the OT and restricted in Philo, appears in the NT only in the pagan quotation in Acts 17:28, and the *syngenḗs* group has no connections of this kind anywhere in the NT. *syngéneia* means "relatives" in Lk. 1:61; Acts 7:3, 14, and cf. *syngenḗs* in Lk. 1:58; 2:44 and *syngenís* in 1:36. Mk. 6:4 mentions the "kin" of the prophet as well as his country and house. In Lk. 14:12 one is not to invite "kinsfolk" (along with friends, brothers, or rich neighbors). Lk. 21:16 mentions "relatives" and friends as well as parents and brethren. Cornelius summons "kinsfolk" and close friends to listen to Peter in Acts 10:24. "Related" is the sense in Jn. 18:26. Paul uses *syngenḗs* only in Romans. In 9:3 the addition shows that he has fellow Jews in mind. With no addition (16:7, 11, 21) he perhaps means Jewish Christians, for it is unlikely that he has so many relatives in the list or that he is thinking of the tribe of Benjamin, and the use of "my" indicates a smaller group than Christians in general. Another possibility is that he is singling out believers who are especially close to him and thus using *syngenḗs* in much the same sense as *phílos,* especially since all the names do not support the idea that those mentioned are Jewish.

5. *The Apostolic Fathers.* 1 Clem. 10:2-3 uses *syngéneia* and Ignatius *Ephesians* 1.1 has *tó syngenikón érgon* for conduct becoming the community.

[W. MICHAELIS, VII, 736-42]

syngnṓmē → ginṓskō; synkathízō → sýn – metá; synkakopathéō → páschō; synkaléō → kaléō

---

synkalýptō [to conceal, hide]

1. *synkalýptō* means "to conceal fully," or, in the middle, "to hide oneself."
2. It occurs in the LXX for concealing shame (Gen. 9:23), faults (Prov. 26:26), or the soul (Ps. 69:10 [variant reading]), or for "disguising oneself" (1 Sam. 28:8).
3. The only instance in the NT is in the saying of Jesus in Lk. 12:2 (cf. Mt. 10:26). The hidden hypocrisy of the Pharisees will be made so manifest that the disciples need not fear those who can kill only the body. In the Lucan setting the apocalyptic association with the unveiling of the reality of this aeon comes out more strongly than in Matthew.   [W. KASCH, VII, 743]

---

synkleíō [to close, enclose]

1. *synkleíō* has such senses as "to close up together," "to close," "to enclose," "to imprison," "to envelop," "to drive into a corner," "to compel," "to press," "to run out," "to form a circle."
2. In the LXX it represents various Hebrew words and is used for the surrounding desert, enclosed cities, delivering up prisoners etc., hemming in, harassing, and periphrastically "hewing down."
3. The Hebrew verb *sgr,* one of the originals, occurs in the Dead Sea Scrolls for delivering up, closing (e.g., the jaws of lions or the gates of hell), closing in (i.e., punishing) offenders, and closing the door (i.e., excommunicating).
4. In later Judaism other verbs carry such varied senses as ruling, stopping, enclosing, shutting in, wrapping around, and shaping.
5. In the NT the fish are enclosed in the net in Lk. 5:6. In Gal. 3:22-23 Paul says that Scripture shuts up all under sin so that the promise might be given to those who have faith in Christ. Prior to faith there is custody under the law (v. 23). A teleology of history comes to light here. Scripture manifests shutting up under sin, and the law effects this. The eschatological dimension emerges in Rom. 11:32: God has shut up all under disobedience so as to have mercy on all. The figure of the prison is in the background, with the law as its keeper. But protective custody might be the point in view of the positive purpose. God by the law protects the race against self-destruction

until faith is revealed (cf. Gal. 3:24). It is unlikely that Paul has in mind the Gnostic conception of the earthly world as a prison from which the redeemer rescues souls by his descent.

6. In Gnostic thinking the earth is the domain of evil and the descent of the redeemer has the force of a descent into the underworld to open the closed gates of the prison. The idea of the enclosing of the soul in matter occurs in Gnostic works; the female soul is enclosed in matter in which moisture and cold predominate in the composition of the elements. Mandaean works refer to a surrounding ring, an enclosing wall, covered radiance, etc.   [O. MICHEL, VII, 744-47]

synklēronómos → *klḗros; synkoinonéō, synkoinōnós* → *koinós; synkrínō* → *krínō; syzáō* → *sýn – metá*

---

syzētéō [to discuss, debate], *syzḗtēsis* [dispute, debate], *syzētētḗs* [disputant, debater]

---

syzētéō.
1. This word means "to examine with," "to dispute," "to strive."
2. In the NT it means "to discuss" in Mk. 9:10; Lk. 24:15 and "to dispute" in Mk. 8:11; 9:14, 16; 12:28; Lk. 22:23; Acts 6:9; 9:29.
3. In the apostolic fathers "to discuss" occurs in Barn. 4.10, "to dispute" in Ignatius *Smyrneans* 7.1, and "to ponder" in Hermas *Similitudes* 6.1.1.

syzḗtēsis.
1. This noun means "common investigation," "dispute," "debate."
2. It occurs in the NT for "dispute" or "strife" in Acts 15:2, 7; 28:29.

syzētētḗs. This word, meaning "one who investigates or disputes with," occurs only in 1 Cor. 1:20. Having extolled the "folly" of the preaching of the cross which invalidates this world's wisdom, Paul asks ironically where is the scribe and where is the "disputer" or "debater" of this age.   [J. SCHNEIDER, VII, 747-48]

---

sýzygos [companion, partner]

---

1. This uncommon word means "spanned together in a common yoke." It comes into use for the "companion" or "partner," especially where there is a pair or couple, as in marriage.
2. The term does not occur in the LXX.
3. The only NT instance is in Phil. 4:3. Here it could be a proper name, but this is unlikely. Nor does Paul mean his "spouse," since he does not seem to be married during his years of apostleship, and the term *gnḗsios* means "tested" rather than "lawful." He is probably referring to some person with whom he has a particularly close relationship, e.g., Silas. After the NT the sense of "belonging to a pair" is determinative, as in Gnostic works which refer to earth as the *sýzygos* of heaven, or in fathers who relate the Holy Spirit and the Sun of Righteousness, or doing and willing. When the disciples are listed in pairs, Eusebius notes that Matthew puts himself after his *sýzygos* Thomas (*Demonstration of the Gospel* 3.5.84-85).
                               [G. DELLING, VII, 748-50]

syzōopoiéō → *sýn – metá*

sykē [fig tree], *sýkon* [fig], *ólynthos* [late fig], *sykáminos* [mulberry, sycomore fig], *sykomoréa* [sycomore fig], *sykophantéō* [to denounce, extort]

sykē, *sýkon*, *ólynthos*.

1. Linguistic Factors. The *sykē* is the "fig tree," and *sýkon* is the "fig." The LXX distinguishes between the early fig and the (unripe) late fig (*ólynthos*), and also has *sýkōn* for the "fig orchard." In the NT *sykē* occurs 12 times in the Synoptists (also in Jn. 1:48, 50; Jms. 3:12; Rev. 6:13), *sýkon* occurs three times in the Synoptists (also in Jms. 3:12), and *ólynthos* occurs only in Rev. 6:13.

2. The Fig Tree in Palestine.

a. Antiquity. The fig trcc is an ancient and important tree in Palestine and claims special dignity in Judg. 9:7ff. To sit under one's vine and fig tree is to enjoy peace. Figurative use occurs in, e.g., Is. 28:4; Jer. 8:13; Hos. 9:10; Mic. 7:1; Prov. 27:18. The fig tree is the only tree mentioned in Eden (Gen. 3:7).

b. Today. The fig tree is still common in Palestine. Casting its leaves in autumn, it seems very bare, but its big leaves offer shade in summer. The early fruits form in March and are ripe in May. The late figs ripen on the new shoots and are the main crop (August to October).

3.a. The fig tree is of no special importance in Jn. 1:48, 50, where the point of the story is not that Nathanael is under this tree but that Jesus has an inner knowledge of Nathanael that is demonstrated by mentioning a fact that is readily checked, namely, his being under the fig tree.

b. The figure in Mt. 7:16 and Lk. 6:44 combines grapes and figs (as in the OT) in contrast to thorns and thistles. In context it illustrates the saying about the bad tree that cannot bear good fruit with a reference first to words (Lk. 6:45) but mainly to acts (6:46ff.; Mt. 7:21ff.). The saying, which has the character of proverbial wisdom, forms a general rule but carries a sharp edge against opponents whose words and acts betray their evil disposition.

c. Jms. 3:12 recalls Mt. 7:16 but is directed against sins of the tongue. That the same mouth should bless and curse is just as unnatural as that one tree should bear the fruits of another. The comparison is not exact, for the tree does not carry two different fruits, some good and some bad. The point, however, is that the use of the tongue for both good and ill is contrary to nature.

d. In the parable of the unfruitful fig tree in Lk. 13:6ff. Jesus teaches that his summons to repentance offers a final period of grace before judgment strikes.

e. The cursing of the fig tree in Mk. 11:12ff. and Mt. 21:18ff. is the only miracle of judgment in the Synoptists and symbolizes the cursing of unfruitful Israel. In its setting it raises the question whether one might expect to find edible figs (possibly early unripe figs or late figs from the previous season) at the time of the Passover. To deal with this problem various theories have arisen, e.g., that the story is misplaced, or that it is a legend explaining a prominent withered fig tree, or that it rests on a misunderstood saying.

f. The parable of the fig tree in Mk. 13:28-29; Mt. 24:32-33; Lk. 21:29ff. is related to the apocalyptic signs of the end, i.e., future signs of future events. A theory advanced by some scholars is that originally it refers to signs of the kingdom in the works of Jesus (cf. Lk. 12:54ff.), but its present context is plain.

g. Rev. 6:13 compares the stars that plunge from heaven to the *ólynthoi* that the storm shakes from the fig tree (cf. Is. 34:4).

sykáminos, sykomoréa.

1. In Palestine we also find two other trees that are only distantly related to the fig tree, a. the "sycomore fig," a strong-growing tree, planted mainly for wood, whose fruits resemble figs but are of less value, and b. the "mulberry," i.e., the black mulberry whose berries produce a juice used as a dye. The LXX incorrectly uses *sykáminos* for a. but correctly has *tó móron* for the fruit of the mulberry. The correct term for a. is *sykomoréa*.

2. In Lk. 19:4 *sykomoréa* is obviously the "sycomore fig." *sykáminos* in 17:6, however, might be the "mulberry," but in the light of LXX usage it could also be the "sycomore fig," which is especially firm and deeply rooted.

sykophantéō. This word first has the sense "to denounce" and then "to cheat" or "to extort." In Lk. 3:14 and 19:8 it means "to oppress" or "to extort." Its derivation (*sýkon* and *phaínō*) is clear but materially obscure.

[C.-H. HUNZINGER, VII, 751-59]

---

syllambánō [to gather, seize, conceive]

1. This word means "to bring together," "to gather," "to enclose," "to seize," "to snatch," "to arrest," and in a transferred sense "to acquire" (e.g., a language), "to conceive" (ideas), "to help," "to take up the cause of someone."

2. The term occurs in the LXX for different words in the senses "to seize," "to trap," "to capture," and also "to conceive."

3.a. In the NT we find the sense "to catch in a net" in Lk. 5:9 and "to take or arrest" in Mk. 14:48 and Acts 23:27.

b. The sense "to conceive" occurs in Lk. 1:24, 31, 36. The use in Jms. 1:15 makes the point that sin results from human desire (not from God) and that its result is self-destruction. The image of desire as a harlot (v. 14) is unlikely, since the desire is one's own. In contrast is the new life that God wills to give through his word (v. 18). Philo has the same metaphor but with delusion as a result, not the evil deed. In Testaments of the Twelve Patriarchs the fructifying power of evil finally produces sin, but in Jms. 1:15 the desire and the deed are our own. There is an intentional paradox, for birth usually brings life, but this pregnancy issues in death (cf. Gen. 3; Rom. 5:12; 6:21, 23; 7).

c. The sense "to help" (middle) occurs in Lk. 5:7, and in Phil. 4:3 the anonymous yokefellow is asked to help the two women (to concord).

4. In early writings we find the sense "to arrest" in 1 Clem. 12.2 and "to help" in 2 Clem. 17.2.   [G. DELLING, VII, 759-62]

syllypéomai → lýpē; symbasileúō → basileús

---

symbibázō [to hold together, instruct]

A. Outside the Bible. This word means "to bring together," "to reconcile," and in philosophy "to compare," "to infer," "to show," and finally "to expound."

B. The LXX. In the LXX the term bears only the special sense "to teach, to instruct" (in something). The stress is on authoritative direction rather than logical deduction. Teachers include God in Ex. 4:12, his angel in Judg. 13:8, Moses in Ex.

18:16, Aaron in Lev. 10:11, fathers in Dt. 4:9. Subjects are divine orders in Ex. 4, the commandments in Ex. 18, the Sinai revelation in Dt. 4:9-10.

C. The NT.

1. In the NT the term means "to hold together," "to unify" in Col. 2:2, 19; Eph. 4:16. The body is held together by the head, from whom it derives its life. Self-seeking piety severs this conjunction with the head. The church's unity in love and knowledge of salvation in Christ are inseparable.

2.a. In Acts 9:22 the meaning is "to prove"; Paul's spiritual proof that Jesus is the Messiah confounds the Jews in Damascus. Scriptural authority and the continuity of God's saving work are presupposed. For similar terms cf. Acts 17:2-3. A vision leads to the conclusion and decision in Acts 16:10-11.

b. The sense "to instruct" occurs in Acts 19:33; some of the crowd "inform" Alexander. 1 Cor. 2:16 is based on Is. 40:13. To be able to instruct God one must have his mind. The radical difference for believers is that they now have the mind of Christ. By the Spirit they may know the mystery of God's saving work in Christ.

[G. DELLING, VII, 763-66]

symmathētḗs → *manthánō; symmartyréō* → *mártys; symmétochos* → *échō; symmimētḗs* → *miméomai; symmorphízō, sýmmorphos, symmorphóō* → *sýn – metá; sympathéō, sympathḗs, sympáschō* → *páschō; symplēróō* → *plḗrēs; sympnígō* → *pnígō; sympresbýteros* → *présbys; symphérō, sýmphoros* → *phérō; sýmphytos* → *sýn – metá; symphōnéō, symphṓnēsis, symphōnía, sýmphōnos* → *phōnḗ*

---

sýn – metá with the genitive, synapothnḗskō [to die with], **systauróō** [to be crucified with], **syntháptō** [to be buried with], **sýmphytos** [united with], **synegeírō** [to raise up with], **syzáō** [to live with], **syzōopoiéō** [to make alive with], **sympáschō** [to suffer with], **syndoxázō** [to be glorified with], **synklēronómos** [co-heir], **sýmmorphos** [having the same form], **symmorphízō** [to be conformed to], **symbasileúō** [to rule with], **synkathízō** [to cause to sit with]

Greek renderings of the OT have *metá* and the genitive for the important statement: "the Lord is with you," but Paul prefers *sýn* with the dative for Christians' being "with Christ." A number of words with *sýn* bring out the significance of this truth, showing how believers are caught up into the Christ event. This use of *sýn* must be studied along with *metá* and the genitive.

A. The Use of *sýn* and *metá* with the Genitive.

1. Classical Greek and Koine. The use fluctuates over the years. Strictly, *metá* means "among," "between," and first occurs with the dative, accusative, and more rarely the genitive. *sýn* means "together," and with the dative is the most common word for "with" in Homer. Yet *metá* with the genitive may also mean "with" and tends to supplant *sýn* in the time that follows, especially in philosophers, historians, and orators (as distinct from poets). The Koine eliminates the original distinction and *sýn* again becomes more common. With the fading of the dative, however, *sýn* again goes into eclipse, and modern Greek knows only *me(tá)*.

2. The LXX. The LXX usually has *metá* and the genitive. *sýn* is more common only in later works. There is no distinction of meaning, and compounds of which *sýn* is a part are surprisingly used with *metá* and the genitive (Gen. 14:24; 18:16, 23).

3. The NT. The NT use is similar to that of the Koine, and we even find *sýn* with the genitive. *metá* with the genitive (364 times) is more common than *sýn* with the dative (127 times). The *metá* passages are mostly historical, whereas the *sýn* references occur mostly in Luke and Paul. The position of *sýn* is much stronger if one counts the compounds. Paul uses *metá* more than *sýn* (69 times to 37, but cf. 59 compounds with *sýn*), but *sýn* has greater theological significance.

4. The Apostolic Fathers. The Didache, Barnabas, 1 and 2 Clement, and Hermas use only *metá* relative to both persons and things, but Ignatius, Polycarp, and the Martyrdom of Polycarp use *metá* only relative to things, and make more common use of *sýn*. Ignatius and Hermas also employ various compounds with *sýn*, nouns and adjectives as well as verbs.

B. The Range of Meaning of *sýn* and *metá*.

I. sýn.

1. From the basic meaning of "with" in a personal sense, *sýn* first comes to express being or acting together and sharing a common task or destiny.

2. This being or acting together carries the sense of supporting or helping one another, i.e., taking the side of one another.

3. As regards things, the reference is to the things one uses or with which one is equipped, or to the accompanying circumstances of an event or action.

II. metá with the Genitive.

1. Basically *metá* with the genitive means "among," "amidst." Where fellowship with others is at issue, the plural usually follows, for one is "among" many people. Being among animals may also be expressed (Gen. 6:18ff.), and the LXX uses the term for being in a common grave (47:30) or for the union of the living and the dead (Ex. 13:19).

2. *metá* may also denote standing by someone, helping someone.

3. To express the means of accompanying circumstances of help, *metá* has the sense "by means of," "with," or "in connection with."

4. Often an adjectival or adverbial rendering is possible when we find *metá* and the genitive with things, e.g., "strongly armed" for "with armor," or "angrily" for "with anger."

C. *sýn* and *metá* in Statements about the Being Together of God and Humans.

I. The Greek World.

1. The phrase *sýn theō̂* or *sýn theoís* is a common one in the Greek world. It first denotes divine favor. The deities are fickle; fortune smiles only when they are present and do not withdraw. Divine help thus comes to expression in the phrase. Those who fight arrogantly in their own strength, trying to win apart from the gods, will be shattered.

2. Divine help has inward as well as outward effects. Thus Nestor hopes that with divine help (*sýn daímoni*) the words of Patroclus will touch the heart of Achilles, and *sýn theō̂* occurs in formulas denoting the divine inspiration of speech.

3. From poetry and prose the phrase *sýn theō̂* passes into popular speech. We thus find it on many papyri.

II. The Bible.

1. God's Promise.

a. In the OT God gives the promise that he will be with certain people, evoking the response of faith. Examples of this (as distinct from the Greek "with God") are numerous in the historical books (cf. Abraham in Gen. 17:4, Isaac in 26:3, Jacob in

28:15, Moses in Ex. 3:12, Joshua in Josh. 1:5, 9). The promise is unconditional in Jeremiah's call (1:8, 17, 19). It extends to the whole people in Am. 5:14, but the people may forfeit it through sin. On the basis of it the people may be fearless even in face of superior foes (Dt. 20:1, 4). Josh. 7:12 demands purification if God is to stay with his people. Renewal of the promise takes place at the return from exile (Is. 41:10).

b. In the NT Mary receives the same promise in Lk. 1:28; it denotes her gracious election. Paul hears a similar promise from the Lord when in danger at Corinth (Acts 18:9-10). Matthew applies Is. 7:14 to Jesus in 1:23; he is Immanuel (*meth' hēmṓn ho theós*), for in him God's promise becomes a personal reality in history to fulfil the covenant and take away sin (1:21). After the resurrection the risen Lord will be with his disciples to the end of the age (28:20). Between Mt. 1 and Mt. 28 stands Mt. 18:20, where the Lord promises his presence to those who gather in his name (*en mésō autṓn* has here the force of *meth' hymṓn*). John presents the Son in unity with the Father (10:30). The unity of his words and acts with the Father's is that of the Father's fellowship with him (*met' emoú*, 8:29; 16:32). To the disciples he sends the Spirit of truth, who will be with them forever (*meth' hymṓn*, 14:16). Rev. 21:3 depicts the consummation of the promise.

2. *The Response of Faith.*

a. In the OT Jacob makes a response of faith in Gen. 28:20 and Jeremiah in Jer. 20:11. The people responds in Ps. 46:7, 11. Moses depends on God's promise to be with the people (Ex. 33:15-16). Deuteronomy confesses the divine presence (1:30), and cf. David (1 Chr. 22:18) and Solomon (1 Kgs. 8:27).

b. An example of response in the NT occurs in Stephen's speech (Acts 7:9-10). Paul acknowledges God's gracious presence and assistance in his own life (1 Cor. 1:10). This personal confession underlies the apostolic salutation in Paul's (and other) epistles. This occurs in various forms (2 Th. 3:16; 2 Tim. 4:22; Rom. 15:33, etc.), but always with *metá* and the genitive. From these formulas develop the liturgical greeting and response: "The Lord be with you." "And with thy spirit." Behind this salutation lies awareness of the gift of the Spirit in whom the Lord himself is present with the community.

3. *Other Attestations.*

a. The OT often says that God is with people (Ishmael, Joshua, Judah, Solomon, judges, and kings), and that others note his presence (e.g., Abraham, Isaac, Israel, Joshua, etc.).

b. The NT adopts the same phrase in narration and evaluation (cf. the Baptist in Lk. 1:66, or the evaluation of Jesus by Nicodemus in Jn. 3:2 or Peter in Acts 10:38; cf. also the self-confession of Jesus in Jn. 8:29).

4. *The Statement "We with God."* This statement seldom occurs. We find it with "the Lord with you" in 2 Chr. 15:2; God is with those who are with him, i.e., who seek him (cf. Ps. 78:8, 37; 1 Kgs. 11:4 for the opposite). In Ps. 73:23 the psalmist hopes for God's constant support and translation to glory: "I am continually with thee." Ps. 16:11 expresses the same hope that earthly fellowship with God will continue in an eternal fellowship. The LXX construes along similar lines the expression of cultic fellowship in, e.g., Pss. 140:13 and 139:18.

III. Hermas. The Shepherd of Hermas modifies the promise under the impact of ideas of angels and spirit. To strengthen Hermas against bad temper or the devil the power of the Lord (*Mandates* 5.2.1) or the angel of righteousness is with him (6.2.3), and he has the promise of presence and help in his ministry to others (12.3.3). In

Similitudes 9, in connection with the building of the tower, holy spirits are with Hermas. Fashioning after the likeness of God's Son is at issue as in the case of Paul's *sýn Christố*.

D. *sýn Christố* in Paul.

1. Paul's *sýn Christố* is linguistically comparable with Gk. *sýn theố* and *sýn theoís*, but materially it is oriented to eternal eschatological being with Christ and denotes personal coming to Christ and being with him.

a. The LXX understanding of cultic fellowship as eternal fellowship forms a starting point (with some parallels in philosophical and popular ideas of communion with the gods after death).

b. Later Judaism also speaks of eternal fellowship with God.

c. Paul's use of *sýn* makes it plain that the meaning is "together with." Thus Col. 2:5 shows that there may be presence in spirit despite bodily absence. Phil. 2:22 brings out the inner nature of the fellowship with Timothy. In Gal. 3:9 the blessing of believers with Abraham is the point.

2. Paul coins the phrase *sýn Christố* and uses it 12 times. In 1 Th. 4:13–5:11 the "with him" of v. 14 means that deceased believers share his life and glory. The "ever with the Lord" of v. 17 denotes enduring fellowship. In 5:10 living "with him" rests on his dying "for us." Salvation through him (v. 9) comes to fulfilment in fellowship with him.

3. Elsewhere the phrase occurs in Phil. 1:23; 2 Cor. 4:14; 13:4; Rom. 6:8; 8:32. Closest to 1 Thessalonians is 2 Cor. 4:14, which refers to resurrection with Christ and hence to being brought into his presence with other believers. With his own death (Phil. 1:23) Paul attains to "being with Christ." This personal fellowship rules out any concern about the intermediate state. The parallel between Christ's way and that of the church controls 2 Cor. 13:4. As Christ died in weakness but rose in power, so Paul is weak but knows God's power in his ministry, which has, then, an eschatological dimension. This parallelism of destiny finds further development in Romans. In 6:8 dying with Christ rests on his vicarious death and takes effect in renunciation of sin. Posited with it is life with Christ. Christ's vicarious work is again the basis in Rom. 5:12ff. in which the parallelism is seen from the standpoint of Christ as the second Adam. The climax comes in 8:32. Christ's offering for all effects a "with him" that means sharing his victory, dominion, and glory, so that the universe is given to the Christian with him.

4. Four instances in Colossians are along the same lines as Philippians and 2 Corinthians. In baptism those who were dead in sin are made alive with Christ (2:13). Being dead without Christ means being under the dominion of alien forces to which believers die with Christ (2:20). The new life, then, is a resurrection life with Christ (3:3). Having their life in and with Christ, believers will be manifested with him in glory (3:4).

E. Compounds Which Develop the Meaning of *sýn Christố*.

1. Meaning of the Terms.

a. The term *synapothnḗskō* is used for "to die together with" (cf. Mk. 14:31; 2 Cor. 7:3).

b. *systauróō* has the sense "to crucify with" (passive Mt. 27:44; Rom. 6:6; Gal. 2:19).

c. *syntháptō* means "to bury with" (Rom. 6:4).

d. *sýmphytos* carries the sense of "being planted [i.e., united] with" (Rom. 6:5).

e. *synegeírō* means "to help to get up," "to raise up" (Eph. 2:6; Col. 2:12).

f. *syzáō* denotes "living with" (Rom. 6:8; 2 Tim. 2:11).

g. *syzōopoiéō* means "to make alive with" (Col. 2:13).

h. *sympáschō* has the sense of "suffering with" (1 Cor. 12:26; Rom. 8:17).

i. *syndoxázō* means "glorifying with" (Rom. 8:17).

j. *synklēronómos* means "co-heir."

k. *sýmmorphos* denotes similarity of form (Rom. 8:29).

l. *symmorphízō* means "conferring the same form" (Phil. 3:10).

m. *symbasileúō* denotes the sharing of rule (1 Cor. 4:8; 2 Tim. 2:12).

n. *synkathízō* means "setting with another" (Eph. 2:6).

2. *Eschatological Statements in Paul.*

a. By way of justification the goal of *sýn Christō̃* is conformity to Christ's image (cf. Gen. 1:26-27; 2 Cor. 4:4, 6). The term *prōtótokos* insures Christ's uniqueness. Christ is God's image, and by new creation believers are conformed to him. God's purpose in creation thus attains its goal in glorification. Phil. 3:21 shows that this involves transformation. Subject now to death, believers acquire in their corporeality the form of Christ's glorious body. In virtue of union with him, this is effected by his power (Phil. 3:10) by way of an earthly existence that manifests his death and passion (2 Cor. 4:14-15) and thus involves a fellowship of destiny.

b. Baptism is decisively significant in this regard. Like Adam, Christ represents humanity (Rom. 5:12ff.). "Christ for us" underlies "we with Christ." As incorporation into Adam is by the first birth, so incorporation into Christ is by the second birth, denoted by baptism (Rom. 6:1ff.). Baptism acknowledges the dominion that Christ gained by death and resurrection. By vicarious death Christ blots out sin, and baptism means unity with the crucified and risen Christ and hence reconciliation to God. Those who are thus united with him are dead to sin. Previously dead in sin, they are now crucified with Christ, who has borne the curse of the law (Gal. 3:13), and they thus respond by self-appropriation to Christ (Gal. 2:20; Rom. 6:6). As they are now dead to sin, they no longer serve it, for they are alive to God through Christ (Rom. 6:6, 12ff.). Already the new life with Christ finds an expression (2 Cor. 4:7ff.) that will come to consummation in eternal being with Christ (Phil. 3:21). Sharing Christ's resurrection means already the ruling of the present life for God.

c. Control by the Spirit (Rom. 8:4ff.) carries with it sharing with Christ the name and status of son (8:14ff.). This in turn means a common inheritance in the common kingdom of God (8:17). Joint inheritance and joint glorification are two aspects of the same eschatological process in which suffering and glory, death and resurrection, are woven together in Christ in such a way that "with Christ" embraces the totality of the Christian life both now and in eternity.

3. *Colossians and Ephesians.*

a. Col. 2:12ff. reflects Rom. 6:4. In faith those who were dead outside Christ are made alive with him through forgiveness of sin and liberation from cosmic forces. The new and victorious resurrection life is now hidden with Christ in God but will be manifested with him, so that life here and now is a transition to the life which in changed form will finally come forth from the hiddenness of God at the parousia.

b. In Eph. 2:1ff. the merciful God in his grace has given new life to believers with Christ. This present reality has an eschatological dimension, for believers are already set in heavenly places to show forth the riches of divine grace.

4. *The Hymn in 2 Tim. 2:11-12.* Building on the hope of salvation in Christ, the "sure saying" of 2 Tim. 2:11-12 refers to a future living and reigning with Christ

along with the dying with him that baptism denotes and resistance to sin expresses. Polycarp recalls this saying in *Ephesians* 5.2 (cf. also Ignatius *Smyrneans* 4.2).

F. *sýn* and *metá* in Other Christ Sayings in the NT.

1. *sýn* and *metá* describe discipleship. In Lk. 15:11-12 the father reminds the elder son that fellowship with him is what matters (v. 31). Jesus calls the 12 to be with him (Mk. 3:14) right up to the passion (Mt. 26:38) so that they might learn from him and share his ministry. Peter is accused of being with him in Mt. 26:69 and parallels; he has sworn that he will suffer and die with him (26:35). The disciples are with Jesus on his journeys (Lk. 22:14), and the cured demoniac wants to go with him (Mk. 5:18). Peter and John are seen to have been with Jesus in Acts 4:13. Jesus promises the dying thief that he will be with him in paradise (Lk. 23:43). *metá* has a special nuance in John (cf. 6:3; 14:9; 11:16; 15:27). The disciples' being with Jesus is the subject of Jesus' prayer in 17:24. Purification by Jesus is its presupposition in 13:8. 1 John refers to fellowship with the Father and with Christ (1:3). Preaching the word of life establishes fellowship with others (1:6-7). Those who do not recognize this do not continue in the fellowship (2:19).

2. Paul uses *metá* when speaking about the mutual fellowship of believers (Rom. 12:15, 18; 1 Cor. 16:11-12). Christians are not to go to law with one another (1 Cor. 6:6-7) and are to have no fellowship with idols (2 Cor. 6:15-16). In mixed marriages partners must decide about living with one another (1 Cor. 7:12).

3. Revelation has some statements with *metá* that are close to Paul's *sýn Christō* (3:4, 21; 14:1; 17:14; 20:4, 6).

4. *sýn* and *metá* are important in connection with meals, for these create fellowship. Jesus eats with sinners (Mt. 9:10-11). Judas is guilty of a shocking breach of table fellowship (Mk. 14:18). Jesus desires table fellowship (Lk. 22:15) and looks ahead to its eternal restoration (Mt. 26:29). The two who go to Emmaus ask Jesus to stay with them (Lk. 24:29-30). The church finds in the supper a meal of fellowship with the risen Lord that anticipates the final banquet (cf. Rev. 3:20).

5. *metá* is significant in sayings about the second coming and judgment. It relates to the coming in Mk. 8:38; 2 Th. 1:7; Rev. 1:7. This coming is a reckoning with servants in Mt. 18:23. At the judgment various groups arise with others (Mt. 12:41-42). As regards those who die in the Lord, their works follow along with them (Rev. 14:13).

6. Mk. 1:13 says that at the temptation Jesus was with the wild beasts, and angels ministered to him. The animals obviously do not molest him.

7. Mk. 8:27–9:29 develops the thought in the *sýn* sayings of Rom. 8:17. Acts points to the parallels between Christ's death and Stephen's (Lk. 22:69; 23:34, 46; Acts 7:56, 59, 60); at the end of the story Christ receives Stephen, who has been made like him in death and passion. The NT use of *sýn* and *metá* shows plainly that salvation means participation in Christ's destiny, conformity to his likeness, and a being with him in which God binds himself to Christ and hence to all who are his.

[W. Grundmann, VII, 766-97]

---

synagōgḗ [assembly, gathering place, congregation, synagogue], *episynagōgḗ* [assembly, meeting], *archisynágōgos* [ruler of the synagogue], *aposynágōgos* [expelled from the synagogue, excommunicated]

synagōgḗ.

A. Secular Greek.

1. The General Meaning. The basic sense of *synagōgḗ* is that of bringing together or assembling (cf. a gathering of people, a collection of books or letters, the ingathering of harvest, the mustering of troops, the knitting of brows, the drawing in of a sail, and in logic the deduction or demonstration).

2. Societies. Relative to societies, the term usually denotes the periodic meeting. Only rarely is *synagōgḗ* the place of meeting. Often a festal assembly (cultic or otherwise) is denoted, e.g., a feast or even a picnic. Unlike *ekklēsía* (the assembly of free citizens), *synagōgḗ* is not a constitutional term. Conversely *ekklēsía* plays no part in guild life.

B. The LXX.

1. Occurrence. *synagōgḗ* occurs some 200 times in the LXX. It usually translates either *ʿēḏâ* or *qāhāl*. The former is the term for the national, legal, and cultic community of Israel, preferred in Exodus and Leviticus, used exclusively in Numbers, but replaced by *qāhāl* (which has essentially the same meaning) in Deuteronomy, Ezra, Nehemiah, and Chronicles.

2. ekklēsía and synagōgḗ. Like the Hebrew terms, these two words have essentially the same sense. Individual translators seem to prefer either the one or the other. If *synagōgḗ* is mostly found in the Pentateuch, this is perhaps because the translators find here the charter of their synagogal communities. They almost always use it for *ʿēḏâ*.

3. Gathering. The term *synagōgḗ* may have such normal senses as the collecting of taxes, the ingathering of harvest, the heaping up of stones, the gathering of a crowd, the mustering of troops, the swarming of bees, and a great number of people.

4. Assembly. When "assembly" is the point, there is little difference from the secular use. At times the stress may be on assembling for common action, but this is not always the case.

5. The Whole Congregation. *synagōgḗ* is often a term for the congregation, i.e., the whole people of Israel, sometimes with *pása* or *Israḗl*. The people is not as such a religious entity, but often the reference is to the people as it assembles for legal or cultic purposes. The *synagōgḗ* is thus the cultic community engaged in sacred acts or the legal community engaged in judgment. The term bears a strong historical character as the desert community, the community that sees God's wonders and inherits the promises, yet also the eschatological community that is to be gathered from the dispersion.

6. The Individual Congregation. In the Apocrypha the term comes to be used for the local congregation, and the plural is now used for Israel as a whole.

7. The House of Meeting. The LXX never uses *synagōgḗ* for an actual place of meeting, i.e., a building (cf. *parembolḗ* rather than *synagōgḗ* in Num. 17:11).

C. Judaism.

I. Usage.

1. Greek-Speaking Judaism.

a. LXX usage continues in Greek-speaking Judaism either in the secular sense or for the Jewish community, although here with the local congregation in view. Other terms are at first still used for the building.

b. NT Judaism uses *synagōgḗ* for the building, a usage that must have developed in the dispersion. Philo has only one instance of this sense, Josephus has four, and there are also some examples on inscriptions (of uncertain date). Often it is hard to differentiate between the congregation and its place of meeting, since the two go by the same name.

2. *Equivalents*. The rabbis do not use the OT *'ēḏâ* or *qāhāl* for *synagōgḗ* but other Aramaic or Hebrew terms. (For details see *TDNT,* VII, 808-09.)

3. *Qumran*. In the Qumran writings *'ēḏâ* comes into prominence again to denote, not the whole community, but the community as the elect remnant.

II. The Jewish Synagogue.

1. *Origin*. The origin, date, and development of the synagogue are all obscure. It probably arises during the exile or under Ezra due to isolation from the temple and the establishment of the law as the exclusive norm of national life. Testimony to a synagogue outside Israel comes from Egypt in 247–221 B.C. Josephus refers to a synagogue at Antioch under Antiochus Epiphanes, and remains of a synagogue at Delos seem to go back to the first century B.C., to which the oldest inscription in Palestine also belongs.

2. *Spread*. As the Jews spread into many lands, so synagogues are attested for some 150 places throughout the Roman world and into Babylonia and Mesopotamia. Every significant community in Palestine has a synagogue, and larger cities have more than one. Swollen figures say that there are 480 in Jerusalem alone just before its fall. The great number involves strong decentralization.

3. *Founding*. To found and support a synagogue is a task for the congregation, which may be the same as the community in Palestine. With the ark and Scripture, the synagogue belongs to the town, and all Jews may have to contribute to it. Names of donors are inscribed on parts that they have endowed. Sometimes endowments may be very large.

4. *Architecture*.

a. No binding rules exist for architectural style. Theoretically synagogues should be built on the high point of a town, but they are also built over tombs, outside cities, next to other houses, alongside water, and next to Gentile lands in Gentile cities.

b. Mostly synagogues are built with the entrance facing Jerusalem (as prayer is made to Jerusalem). The ark with the law is at the entrance so that the people may face it too. Later it is put in a niche beside the entrance.

c. Details are available for architectural styles in the second century A.D. (especially in Galilee), but nothing is known about the style in NT days. The older Galilean buildings have three naves made by double rows of pillars, galleries (with access from outside) over the side naves, windows at the front and along the side walls, stone seats in ranks along the side walls (sometimes also the back), and a floor of flagged stone. Simpler structures abroad seem to be houses or to have developed out of houses, and this may be true in Palestine in NT days, for in Mk. 6:3; Lk. 13:10ff.; Acts 16:13 the women do not seem to sit in galleries, as they probably do in the basilica-type synagogues.

5. *Furnishings*. All synagogues need scrolls of the OT, which are kept in the special ark. Being sacred, Scripture must be rescued if danger threatens and hidden when no longer usable. A podium with a reading desk is also needed. Other articles include lamps, trumpets, seats, and vessels for washing. Paintings are found in the form of mosaics or murals.

6. *Purpose and Significance*.

a. Teaching the Law. The main purpose of a synagogue is to teach and propagate the law. The traditions, which show how the law applies in practice, must also be transmitted.

b. Relation to the temple. In NT days there is no rivalry between temple and synagogue. After the fall of Jerusalem the synagogue replaces the temple. The adoption of the candelabra and of many liturgical practices from the temple makes this plain. A ministry of the word develops instead of the priestly cultus, the synagogues free worship from geographical bondage to one place, and the laity finds a more important role than in the temple. God is just as present in the synagogue as in the temple, and the synagogue is thus a holy place.

c. Place of Prayer. As the place of the divine presence, the synagogue is the ordained place where the people ought to pray and where an answer is promised.

d. School. In view of the central position of the law, synagogues are also places of teaching and learning. They either serve as schools or contain schoolrooms where children may receive instruction in addition to that given by their parents. Schools may at times be adjacent to the synagogues but they are usually associated. Rabbis, too, study in the synagogues, which Philo calls places where virtues are taught.

e. Council House and Place of Assembly. Synagogues serve as places of assembly for communal discussions and meetings to settle public affairs, make announcements, swear oaths, administer punishments, and execute manumissions.

f. Hospice. As well as offering provision for the poor, synagogues are hospices to put up visiting Jews, especially in Jerusalem during the great feasts.

g. *Aedes sacrae.* Some synagogues are dedicated to civil rulers, and shields, pillars, wreaths, and inscriptions are set up in them in honor of the emperors and to show loyalty to them. In return synagogues have privileges corresponding to *aedes sacrae.* In times of tension this does not always protect them from disrespect and even desecration. Jews regard their synagogues with pride and commitment. Devout Jews visit them daily, rabbis delight to study and teach in them, and attendance is high on sabbaths and feast days. In view of its OT background the term *synagōgḗ* takes on great significance, and the synagogue helps Judaism to survive the disaster of A.D. 70.

D. The NT.

I. Assembly. The term *synagōgḗ* has the sense of "assembly" in the NT only in Acts 13:43 and possibly Jms. 2:2 (a Christian assembly).

II. Congregation. In Acts 9:2 the *synagōgaí* are congregations of the dispersion under the jurisdiction of Jerusalem. Embracing both sexes, they are the sphere in which Christians first appear (18:26; 19:8-9; 22:19). In Rev. 2:9 and 3:9 pseudo-Jews are called a synagogue of Satan; perhaps those who persecute the church are in view. The phrase does not give a negative accent to the synagogue as such. The antithesis is between the synagogue of Satan and the synagogue or *ekklēsía* of God. If the NT prefers *ekklēsía* for the church, this is perhaps because it helps to make a distinction, because synagogue now means primarily the local congregation, because synagogue is more closely tied to the building, and because it focuses on the law rather than on Christ. Furthermore, Gentile circles might well associate *synagōgḗ* with cultic societies and thus be led into a misunderstanding of the church.

III. The Synagogue in the NT.

1. Relation to Jewish Statements.

a. In the NT the term *synagōgḗ* denotes mainly the building with perhaps an implication of the congregation as well. The NT bears witness to synagogues in Capernaum, Nazareth, Jerusalem, Damascus, Pisidian Antioch, Iconium, Thessalonica, Berea, Athens, Corinth, Ephesus, Philippi, and Salamis, and also to various synagogues in Galilee and Judea. The synagogue is an ancient institution (Acts 15:21) and a place of reading, teaching, preaching, prayer, and almsgiving. *proseuchē* occurs only in Acts 16:13.

b. Further points are that Gentiles might build synagogues (Lk. 7:5), that there are seats in them, that healings take place in them, and that sentences are read and scourgings administered in them.

2. *The Attitude of Jesus to the Synagogue.*

a. Jesus often teaches and preaches in synagogues. Even if the geography is loose and the references come in redactional passages, there is no reason to doubt the truth of this. Jesus also eats with sinners, uses an authoritative "I say to you," and proclaims the message of the kingdom. Yet he confronts the people with his teaching in the synagogues (Mk. 1:21ff.; Lk. 4:15; Mt. 9:35). If his healings are mostly outside, he also heals in the synagogues (cf. Mk. 1:21ff.); it is in the synagogue that the first battle between demonic forces and the Holy One of God takes place (Mk. 1:23ff.).

b. Jesus attacks the misuse of the synagogue by the scribes and Pharisees; cf. their ambition and desire for recognition (Mk. 12:39). He does not censure prayer in the synagogue or temple as such, but only prayer that is hypocritically offered for the sake of effect (Mk. 6:5).

c. Attacks on the synagogue as such occur in Mk. 13:9; Mt. 10:17; 23:34; Lk. 12:11; 21:12, where the future persecution of those who confess Christ is in view. The sharpest antithesis is in Mt. 23:34. Discipleship means punishment in the synagogue, but also the opportunity of confession (Lk. 12:11) and witness (Mk. 13:9). The synagogue is treated with some reserve in John (cf. the reduced prominence of the term, the use of *aposynágōgos,* and the polemical edge in Jn. 18:20; Jesus has taught publicly in synagogues and the temple where Jews come together).

3. *The Synagogue in Primitive Christian Mission.* The synagogue is a most important factor in the missionary work in Acts. Paul, who formerly persecutes in the synagogues (Acts 22:19; 26:11), preaches first in the synagogues (Acts 9:19 etc.). By way of them, and the proselytes and God-fearing Gentiles in them, he gathers the churches. Theologically this denotes continuity between Israel and the church in salvation history. Paul gives precedence to Israel, but when rejected he goes to the Gentiles. He does not restrict his work to the synagogues (Acts 14:6ff.), and very quickly the infant church becomes independent of the synagogue either by expulsion or separation (Acts 19:9). In his synagogue preaching Paul's main aim is to show from the OT that Jesus is the Christ (Acts 9:20; 18:5), thus evoking a response either of faith or of rejection and blasphemy (14:1-2; 19:9). There is no suggestion in Acts that he preaches freedom from the law.

IV. Acts 6:9 and Jms. 2:2. Debate continues as to whether the *synagōgē* of Acts 6:9 is a building or a congregation. A rabbinic reference to the sale of "the synagogue of the Alexandrians" supports the former view, but the context favors the latter; conflict is caused by the members. Another dispute is whether Acts 6:9 refers to one synagogue or many. Since there are many synagogues in Jerusalem (cf. Acts 24:12) organized along territorial or social lines, two (or possibly five) synagogues seem to be at issue in Acts 6:9. Jms. 2:2 is the one instance where *synagōgē* is used in a Christian sense, either for the place of meeting or the meeting itself (but not the community; cf. 5:14). The references to coming in and to seating suggest the building, but the place and the meeting merge into one another, and meeting is the more common sense in the apostolic fathers (cf. the Vulgate rendering *conventus*).

E. The Early Church.

1. The secular sense of gathering or collection persists (cf. 1 Clem. 20.6 and Clement of Alexandria *Stromateis* 6.2.1 [collection of books]).

2. In the early church the *synagōgē* is mostly the Jewish building and the use is polemical. Thus in Justin *Dialogue* 16.4 the synagogue is the place where Jews curse Christians and in Jerome *Commentary on Isaiah* 8.21 it is the place where they blaspheme Christ. For Tertullian, then, synagogues are the founts of persecution (*Scorpiace* 10.10). Christians who attend them come under threat of judgment or excommunication (*Apostolic Constitutions* 2.61.1-2; 8.47.65). Chrysosotom goes to extremes in calling synagogues robber caves and comparing them to theaters (*Against the Jews* 1.3ff.). The sad result is that from the fourth century on, Christians attack and destroy synagogues, secure legislation to prevent their repair or rebuilding, and even carry through at times the forcible conversion of synagogues into churches.

3. A new usage in the early church is that *synagōgē* denotes Judaism as a whole in antithesis to the church. Here again the intention is mostly polemical. Jerome has the series "law and gospel, synagogue and church, Jewish and Christian people, Gehenna and kingdom of heaven" (*Commentary on Jeremiah* 5.2), and Augustine equates *ecclesia* with the calling together of men and *synagōgē* with the rounding up of cattle (*Expositions of the Psalms* 81.1).

4. Yet we still find *synagōgē* used for Christian meetings and places of meeting, and even for the church as a whole (cf. Ignatius *Polycarp* 4.2; Irenaeus *Against Heresies* 4.31.1-2 where the two synagogues are the church and the true Judaism of the OT).

episynagōgē.

1. This word, which is rare in secular Greek, has much the same sense as the simple form, i.e., gathering or collecting.

2. The LXX gives the term an eschatological note in 2 Macc. 2:7-8, where it refers to the final gathering of dispersed Israel (cf. also the verb in 1:27).

3. The eschatological orientation persists in the two NT references. Thus in 2 Th. 2:1 *episynagōgē* and *parousía* introduce the eschatological teaching that follows. The object of the *epí* is the returning Lord; it is to meet him that his people is assembled. The sense is harder to fix in Heb. 10:25. The meaning seems to be either the assembled congregation or the assembling, but the cultic character is plain. The point is not leaving the community, but failing to attend its gatherings, which are so necessary in view of the approaching day. The specific reason for the warning is not given. Believers might have been taking part in other gatherings or failing to attend due to pride, fear of persecution, or flagging zeal.

archisynágōgos.

1. This term occurs in connection with pagan cults and guilds. The function of the *archisynágōgos* (who is an official of the god on one inscription) is that of the president (also at times the founder as well) who convenes and leads the assembly.

2. The term has more importance in the Jewish synagogue than the pagan society or guild. The rights of ownership and administration are vested in the congregation, which is the same as the community in Palestine. In purely Jewish communities a board of seven handles synagogue affairs; in mixed communities, or where there is more than one synagogue, a board of three. The officers of the synagogue are the servant and the president. Presidents are highly regarded and are often members of the board. They preside at worship, and see to the erection and care of the building. They are elected for a term and may be reelected. The office often remains in the

same family. Normally each synagogue has only one president; the reference in Acts 13:15 is perhaps to members of the board.

3. The term occurs in the NT only in Mark (5:22, 35, 36, 38) and Luke (Lk. 8:49; 13:14; Acts 13:15; 18:8, 17). The ruler is also the *árchōn* in Lk. 8:41 (cf. v. 49), but cf. Acts 14:2. Named rulers are Jairus, Crispus, and Sosthenes (perhaps the Sosthenes of 1 Cor. 1:1) (Mk. 5:22; Acts 18:8, 17). The duties of rulers are the same as in outside records. Thus the ruler protests in Lk. 13:14, and the rulers ask Paul and Barnabas for a word of exhortation in Acts 13:15.

4. There are only isolated references in the early church. Justin *Dialogue* 137.2 complains that synagogue rulers teach Jews to mock Christ, and Epiphanius *Heresies* 30.18.2 says that Jewish Christians also have synagogue rulers.

aposynágōgos.

1. This term occurs only in John. There are various degrees of discipline in the synagogue, although the distinctions are doubtful in NT times. For various offenses, e.g., opposing teachers, witnessing against Jews in Gentile courts, or spurning the law, a 30-day suspension is imposed which restricts dealings with others and demands certain penitential observances. A sharper suspension, imposed by the court, further restricts contact, but since it is designed to correct and convert, it does not mean permanent exclusion. *aposynágōgos,* however, is complete excommunication, i.e., not just barring of entry to the building or meeting, nor merely exclusion from the local community, but expulsion from the national fellowship. This alone corresponds to Christ's claim and the radical nature of the decision involved. At issue is the fundamental cleavage that issues in anathematizing. As the rabbis put it, heretics are worse than Gentiles. They are shut off from all saving benefits, and true Jews are to have no dealings with them. Jewish Christians fall in this category. The Johannine passage anticipates the relations at the end of the first century A.D. when anathematizing of this type is documented. Qumran, too, imposes irrevocable excommunication as well as temporary suspension, not for errors in belief, but for transgressions of the law and breaches of discipline.

2. In the NT, *aposynágōgos* occurs in Jn. 9:22; 12:42; 16:2. In 9:22 the parents of the blind man are swayed by the threat of excommunication. In 12:42 the fear of expulsion causes many rulers to be secret believers instead of confessors. In 16:2 Jesus warns the disciples that the time will come when they will be put out of the synagogues and even persecuted to death. No mere suspension is in view but total anathematizing and expulsion.   [W. SCHRAGE, VII, 798-852]

synathléō → *athléō; synaichmálōtos* → *aichmálōtos; synakolouthéō* → *akolouthéō; synanákeimai* → *keímai*

---

synanameígnymi [mixing together, intermingling]

---

1. Like the simple form, this compound means "mixing together"; the passive denotes various forms of human "intermingling."

2. In the OT it refers especially to the intermingling with other peoples by which national purity is forfeited (Hos. 7:8); the same is true in Philo.

3. In the NT the only three instances are in 1 Cor. 5:9, 11 and 2 Th. 3:14. In all three it refers to dealings with believers whose conduct compromises the community.

The aim in 1 Cor. 5 (cf. vv. 6ff.) is the avoidance of pollution, while restoration by shaming is the goal in 2 Th. 3:14. The term is not a technical one for association only within the community, and it occurs only in prohibitions. 1 Cor. 5:11 gives precision by adding that believers are not to eat with such people, probably with a eucharistic reference. What the "noting" of 2 Th. 3:14 signifies is not wholly clear, but the breaking off of relations does not rule out fraternal warnings.

[H. GREEVEN, VII, 852-55]

synantilambánomai → *antilambánomai; synapothnḗskō* → *thánatos*

---

synarmologéō [to fit together]

1. This compound has the sense of "joining" or "fitting together."
2. It occurs in the NT in Eph. 2:21, where the church is compared to a temple which has Christ as the cornerstone in whom the structure is joined together. It also occurs in Eph. 4:16. Here the church is a body, and all its parts, with their different ministries and tasks, are mutually joined and knit together, and thus achieve growth in love, as they derive their life from Christ.   [C. MAURER, VII, 855-56]

---

sýndesmos [bond]

A. Secular Usage. The *sýndesmos* is the "middle thing" that serves as a "link," "joint," "loop," or "bond," and in grammar "conjunction." Special meanings are "chain," "cable," or "halter." In Plato the term takes on special significance as the mediation or union that overcomes cosmic dualism. Figuratively for Aristotle it refers to "children" as the bond between father and mother. In rhetoric it may be a "connecting word," and physiologically it is the "joint" or "muscle."

B. The Jewish-Greek Sphere.
1. The term has no special nuance in the LXX but is simply used for "connection," "joint," "yoke," or "bond."
2. In the Epistle of Aristeas 85 it is an architectural feature and in 285 an indissoluble bond.
3. Philo uses the word when allegorizing the four parts of the incense offering as the four elements of water, earth, fire, and air. It is also for him a grammatical term.

C. The NT. The general sense of "bond" occurs in a figurative sense in Acts 8:23: Simon Magus is in the bond of iniquity. The tendon or muscle (figuratively with sinew) is the point in Col. 2:19. Eph. 4:3ff. refers to the "bond" of peace, and Col. 3:14 to love as the "bond" of perfectness. Here the *sýndesmos* brings harmony, as in Plato, but soteriologically rather than cosmologically. No link is documented between either Plato and Gnostic *sýndesmos* teaching or the latter and Ephesians and Colossians. Ephesians and Colossians define mediation as peace, and within the community of faith they find unity in the one God, the one Spirit, and the one faith.

D. The Apostolic Fathers. Barn. 3.3ff. uses the word in a quotation from Is. 58:6ff., and Ignatius *Trallians* 3.1 compares presbyters to the council of God and the band of apostles.   [G. FITZER, VII, 856-59]

syndoxázō → *dokéō; sýndoulos* → *doúlos; synegeírō* → *sýn – metá*

---

synédrion [council, Sanhedrin]

A. Classical and Hellenistic Greek.
1. Secular Greek. This term means "place of assembly," then "session," "council," "governing body."

2. Jewish-Hellenistic Literature.

a. In the LXX the word means "assembly" (cf. Prov. 22:10; 26:26; Ps. 26:4).

b. Philo uses the term in both a literal and a transferred sense (place of rest for the mind or soul).

c. Josephus uses the term for "assembly," "council," "governing body," especially the supreme Jewish council in Jerusalem.

B. The Jewish Sanhedrin.
1. History. Priests and elders govern the postexilic community. Priestly nobles and heads of clans become an aristocratic senate in Jerusalem with the high priest as president. The Hasmoneans curtail the rights of this body. The Pharisees achieve a place in it in 76–67 B.C. The term *synédrion* first appears for it under the Roman governor Gabinius, who sets up five *synédria*. The Jerusalem council regains control of the whole land under Caesar, and *synédrion* comes to be used specifically for the Jerusalem senate. Herod packs the body with supporters, but under the procurators it regains some influence until the disaster of the Jewish war. Later the newly constituted *synédrion* at Jabneh consists only of rabbis and has no political functions.

2. Composition. The Sanhedrin seems to have had 71 members (based on Num. 11:16). The high priest as leader of the people presides. The Sadducean chief priests form a solid faction. Alongside them are the elders, drawn from influential lay families, who are also Sadducean in persuasion. The scribes form a third group whose influence steadily grows so that their agreement is needed in important matters. Both Josephus and the NT usually put the chief priests first when enumerating members. With them we find either scribes, elders, scribes and elders, or Pharisees. Only rarely are the chief priests not mentioned (cf. Mt. 26:57), and at times they may even represent the whole body (Mk. 14:10; Mt. 26:59).

3. Powers. As the supreme council the Sanhedrin governs all secular and religious matters and has the power to try capital cases and impose sentence. Herod takes over de facto control. After A.D. 6 the Sanhedrin has authority only in Judea, and the Roman procurator (based in Caesarea) has governing power. He allows the Sanhedrin to deal only with religious matters and restricts its right to impose the capital sentence to pagan violations of the temple precincts. Yet the Sanhedrin does impose the death penalty in a few other cases, including James the Lord's brother. The Sanhedrin reclaims the right to pass capital sentences on the outbreak of the Jewish war, and the Zealots make gruesome use of this power during their reign of terror.

4. Sanhedrins outside Jerusalem. Little courts patterned on the Sanhedrin have local jurisdiction in Palestine and the dispersion. These courts meet twice a week and claim the right to pass death penalties, although frequent use is discouraged, and in fact the Romans do not permit it. The Essene fellowship exercises its own jurisdiction, and Qumran, too, has its own penal code.

C. The NT.
1. The Gospels.

a. Sayings of Jesus. In Mt. 10:17 Jesus warns his disciples to expect persecution from the sanhedrins, in this case the local courts, to whom they are at first subject.

1115

In Mt. 5:21-22 those who insult others must answer to the Sanhedrin, here the supreme court in Jerusalem. The insulting word is just as bad as the deed of murder that falls under the Sanhedrin's condemnation.

b. Jesus before the Sanhedrin. The Jerusalem Sanhedrin resolves to arrest and execute Jesus when a favorable opportunity comes (Mk. 14:1-2; Jn. 11:47ff.). After the arrest Jesus appears before the hastily summoned chief priests, elders, and scribes (Mk. 14:53), and when the false witnesses fail to make their point, the high priest puts the question which leads to his condemnation for blasphemy (Mk. 14:61ff.). It may be noted that the proceedings at many points do not conform to later rules (cf. the time and place of meeting and the definition of blasphemy), but the Sadducees are not necessarily bound by Pharisaic rulings that are in any case later than the time of Jesus. The only serious problem arises out of the long-standing prohibition of legal proceedings on sabbaths and feast days and the related days of preparation. What probably takes place is that the members of the Sanhedrin, united in hostility to Jesus, hold a brief hearing and then hand Jesus over to Pilate for trial and execution by the Romans as a revolutionary. A prior interrogation also takes place in the house of Annas (Jn. 18:12ff.), but the decisive proceedings are before Pilate, who under pressure cooperates with the Jewish court to secure the elimination of Jesus.

2. *Acts.* In Acts the *synédrion* is the supreme council in Jerusalem whose Sadducean members persecute believers, while the Pharisees are more favorable (cf. 5:17, 34ff.). The Sanhedrin first dismisses Peter and John with a warning (4:5ff.) and then lets them go with a beating and a command to be silent (5:17ff.). The trial of Stephen, however, ends with a riot and stoning (6:8–8:1). When Paul has to answer to the Sanhedrin in 23:1ff., he causes dissension and gains the support of the Pharisees. The Romans protect Paul from any further appearance before the Sanhedrin (23:26ff.). Since he is a Roman citizen, the Sanhedrin must accuse him before the procurator.

D. The Apostolic Fathers. Only Ignatius uses *synédrion,* and in each of the three instances in his epistles it simply means "council" (*Magnesians* 6.1; *Trallians* 3.1; *Philadelphians* 8.1).   [E. LOHSE, VII, 860-71]

syneídesis → *sýnoida; synepimartyréō* → *mártys*

---

synergós [fellow worker, helper],   *synergéō* [to work with, help]

A. The Group in Greek. The word *synergós* means "fellow worker" or "helper," *synergéō* means "to work with," and the more common *synergázomai* refers to the sharing of work or cooperation.

B. The Group in Judaism.

1. The verb and noun occur only four times in the LXX, three of which are in 1 and 2 Maccabees.

2. Philo refers to the cooperation of reason, but also to that of companions, or of all parts of the soul, in sin. The plastic arts help to seduce to idolatry. The human mind does not understand the working together of cosmic forces, and no one can cooperate with God in imparting true knowledge or in the work of creating and preserving the world. Yet Philo seems to suggest that subordinate powers help in the creation of our physical side and its vices.

3. Josephus uses the formula "with God's help," and he says that God was helpful to Jehoshaphat because he was just and pious.

4. A similar synergistic saying occurs in Test. Iss. 3:7-8.

5. There are no real originals in the OT nor do we find much help at Qumran, although here, too, there are synergistic passages.

C. The Group in the NT.

1. In the NT the noun occurs 13 times (always plural), 12 times in Paul and once in 3 Jn. 8. Paul uses it to describe pupils and companions who aid him in his work, adding "in Christ" in Rom. 16:3, 9. He honors his fellow workers by using the term and strengthens their authority. Where he includes himself (2 Cor. 1:24 and cf. Col. 4:11), his point is that they are all God's helpers and are thus workers in God's kingdom. In 1 Cor. 3:9 *synergoí* corresponds to *diákonoi* in 3:5 (cf. 1 Th. 3:2). The verb *synergéō* occurs five times, three in Paul and once each in Jms. 2:22 and Mk. 16:20. In 1 Cor. 16:16 it refers to work on behalf of the church. By preaching the gospel his helpers share with Paul the burden of his ministry of reconciliation. Along the lines of Is. 43:24 they thus share in God's own work. On this ground they can claim obedience but as helpers of the church's joy, not as lords. Rom. 8:28 might seem to be synergistic if taken as the expression of an optimistic philosophy whereby those who love God have the supreme good and hence can suffer no real hurt. In context, however, election is the dominant theme. Human love is the gift and reflection of God's prior love. God, then, is the true subject in v. 28; he helps for good in all things, or turns all things to good, for the called who love him.

2. Jms. 2:22 seems to be refuting misunderstandings of Paul. Faith works together with works; it achieves visibility and hence fulfilment in them.

3. In 3 Jn. 8 the readers, by receiving and aiding itinerant missionaries, become partners in the common ministry by proclaiming the truth.

4. In Mk. 16:20 the absolute genitives describe the Lord's working with the apostles by confirming their message with signs. The verse expresses faith in the Lord's enduring presence and bears witness to the interrelation of word and sign.

D. The Group in Early Christianity. In Hermas *Similitudes* 5.6.6 the *sárx* is the handmaiden of the spirit cooperating in the work of redemption. In Acts of Thomas 24 God's grace works with the apostle's labor. Justin *Dialogue* 142.2 speaks of God's permission and cooperation, and *Apology* 9.4 refers to fatal cooperation in idolatry.

[G. BERTRAM, VII, 871-76]

synérchomai → *érchomai; sýnesis, synetós* → *syníēmi*

---

synéchō [to hold together, enclose, oppress], *synochḗ* [holding together, prison, affliction]

---

synéchō.

1. Greek Usage.

a. This word means first "to hold together," e.g., law upholding the state, or deity the cosmos, or virtues the world.

b. Then we find the meaning "to enclose" or "to lock up," e.g., an army behind walls, or a prisoner, and once for holding one's breath.

c. Another sense is "to oppress," "to overpower," "to rule," e.g., of afflictions, illnesses, emotions, or impulses.

2. The LXX.

a. The term occurs 48 times in the LXX, usually in the three main Greek senses.

b. The main Hebrew equivalent is '*ṣr,* which is mostly rendered *synéchō,* but which normally occurs only in 1 and 2 Samuel, 1 and 2 Kings, and 1 and 2 Chronicles. Usually *synéchō* as a translation means "to enclose," but the Hebrew is rich in nuances which the Greek captures only when restraint is in view.

c. The sense "to hold together" is rare.

d. *synéchō* also represents other Hebrew originals in various senses of enclosing or shutting (up).

e. The meaning "to oppress" occurs only in Job and Wisdom, and once each in Jeremiah and 4 Maccabees, either with no Hebrew original or in very free renderings.

3. *Later Jewish Literature.*

a. In Testaments of the Twelve *synéchō* mostly means "to oppress."

b. Philo often uses the verb for "to hold together" in physiological or cosmological references. Thus he says that invisible forces hold the world together—a view that reflects Stoic influence.

4. *The NT.*

a. Common only in Luke and Acts (nine times), *synéchō* has for Luke the meaning "to close" in Acts 7:57, "to hold prisoner" in Lk. 22:63, and "to surround," "to hem in" in Lk. 8:45 and 19:43.

b. Sickness is said to "oppress" in Lk. 4:38 (cf. Mt. 4:24). A transferred sense ("to be gripped [by fear]") occurs in Lk. 8:37. The meaning "to be claimed or controlled" occurs in Acts 18:5. The love of Christ "controls" or "dominates" Paul in 2 Cor. 5:14, so that he has to live for Christ and not for self. In Phil. 1:23 the thought is perhaps that Paul is governed by two things and hence hemmed in. Lk. 12:50 has caused much debate. The reference to death suggests the translation: "How troubled or pressed I am!" but the saying about fire in v. 49 suggests: "How I am totally governed by this!" The saying expresses Jesus' movement to vicarious death. Like the fire that he has come to kindle, this is the beginning of the new aeon; hence its total claim on him.

5. *The Apostolic Fathers.* Under Hellenistic influence *synéchō* means "to hold together" in 1 Clem. 20.5. In Diog. 6.7, as the soul is enclosed in the body yet holds it together, so it is with Christians in the world. In *Romans* 6.3 Ignatius asks for understanding of what dominates or constrains him in Paul's sense.

synochḗ.

1. *Greek Usage.* The noun *synochḗ* has such meanings as "holding together," "oppression," and "prison." We find it for the "press" of battle and astrologically for cosmic misfortunes (eclipses etc.) and hence for the resultant "anxiety" or "despair."

2. *The LXX.* The word is rare in the LXX, and in Jer. 52:5 and Mic. 4:14 it means "affliction." This is the main sense in later renderings of the Psalms, although once these use the term for "prison."

3. *The NT.* In the NT there are two instances. In 2 Cor. 2:4 Paul is clearly speaking about the "affliction" suffered through hostility at Corinth. In Lk. 21:25 the reference seems to be to the "anxiety" caused by stellar signs that forebode disaster, although believers, of course, need not be afraid, since they know that these signs indicate the closeness of their redemption.

4. The only instance in the apostolic fathers is in Did. 1.5, where the word means "prison" in a free quotation of Mt. 5:25-26.   [H. KÖSTER, VII, 877-87]

syntháptō → *sýn – metá*

---

syníēmi   [to   understand],   *sýnesis*   [understanding],   *synetós*   [under-
standing],   *asýnetos* [not understanding]

A. The Group in Secular Greek.

1. The verb *syníēmi* means "to bring together," "to come to agreement," "to perceive," "to understand."

2. The noun *sýnesis* means "union," "confluence," then "comprehension," "understanding," "discernment," and finally "self-awareness."

3. The adjective *synetós* means "understanding" or "understandable." *asýnetos* for
"not understanding" has at times a moral tinge.

B. The Group in the OT.
The LXX makes much use of the group, especially in
Wisdom writings. The use is similar to that in the Greek world except that understanding is native only to God and hence is a gift for which one must pray (1 Kgs.
3:9; Ps. 119:34). Practical judgment rather than theoretical understanding is the main
concern, its organ is the heart (Is. 6:9-10), and its objects are God's works (Ps. 28:5),
fear (Prov. 2:5), righteousness (2:9), will (Ps. 111:10), and wisdom (Prov. 2:1ff.).
Earlier the appeal for understanding is motivated by a reference to God's will, later
by a reference to the law.

C. The Group in Judaism.

1. Qumran. The Qumran sect seeks understanding in its candidates, but again this
comes from God, to whom alone it is native. The sect experiences election in its
insight into God's acts in history, into predestination, and into the eschatological
sequence. Since understanding God's judgments is a condition of salvation, the law
is an essential theme. The Spirit has an important role in imparting knowledge, but
so, too, does the teacher of righteousness.

2. Rabbinic Writings. The situation is similar in the rabbis but with a slight shift to
more stress on perception and reason.

D. The Group in the NT.

1. Forms of the Verb. With the traditional forms of *-iēmi* we also find the conjugation
in *-ō* with some vacillation in the manuscripts.

2. Theological Significance. The group is not theologically significant and does not
occur in the Johannine material (including Revelation). The OT governs the sense (cf.
the many OT quotations in which the group occurs).

3. The Synoptists.

a. In Mt. 11:25 and Lk. 10:21 *synetós* is parallel to *sophós* in a saying that expresses
the contingent and paradoxical nature of revelation. In Mk. 7:14 the verb simply
denotes understanding. In Mk. 12:33 (cf. v. 30) there is perhaps a slight Hellenistic nuance.

b. In Mk. 4:12 and parallels the term comes in a free rendering of Is. 6:9-10,
whose point is that failure to understand is God's purpose. In the version in Mt.
13:10ff. *syníēmi* achieves great prominence (occurring also in v. 19 and v. 23). If the
emphasis is now on human incapacity rather than divine purpose, the point remains
that understanding is a divine gift and hardening a divine ineluctability.

4. Paul. Paul uses the group in OT quotations and allusions but only a few times
independently. The noun occurs in 1 Cor. 1:19, though here *sophía* is the main term.
In Rom. 1:21 the organ of understanding is the heart, and lack of understanding is
total darkness with moral implications (cf. the "base mind" of 1:28). 2 Cor. 10:12-13

comes with a shorter and a longer (probably more authentic) reading; only the longer includes the group, but the point of the passage does not depend on its presence. If Colossians and Ephesians are Pauline, one should add *sýnesis* in Col. 2:2 (cf. also Eph. 5:7 and 2 Tim. 2:7, where the Lord gives *sýnesis*). In Col. 2:2 the heart is the organ and the divine mystery (defined christologically here, but ecclesiologically in Eph. 3:4) is the object.

E. The Group in the Early Church. The noun has a Stoicizing aspect in 1 Clem. 33.3. Hermas likes the word *sýnesis* and personifies it. Justin and Clement of Alexandria often use the group, but *sýnesis* never achieves the importance of *lógos* or *sophía*.

[H. CONZELMANN, VII, 888-96]

---

synístēmi [to put together],   *synistánō* [to be composed of]

---

1. *synístēmi* has the sense of putting together with the nuances a. "to be composed of," b. "to exist," "to be," c. "to associate," d. "to commend," and e. "to display."

2. In Lk. 9:32 Peter and John see the two men standing with Jesus on the Mount. In 2 Pet. 3:5 the reference is to water in the composition of the earth. Significant theologically is the statement in Col. 1:17 that Christ is before all things and all things consist or have their existence in him. Paul uses the transitive *syniēmi* mostly for "to commend" (cf. Rom. 16:1; 2 Cor. 3:1). His own commendation is his public proclamation of the truth (2 Cor. 4:2) in which he spends himself as the servant of Christ and hence has no self-concern. He will not compare himself with those who commend themselves (2 Cor. 10:12), for it is those whom the Lord commends that are accepted (v. 18). The idea of "presenting" may be seen in 2 Cor. 3:1ff., as well as in Rom. 3:5, where our wickedness serves to show God's truth. Similarly, in Rom. 5:8 God shows and commends his love in Christ's vicarious death. In 2 Cor. 6:4 there is more of the sense "to prove" (cf. 7:11), and this is plainly the meaning in Gal. 2:18, where the proof rests on patent facts. For Paul, acts are determinative in both divine or human judgment. This makes of God's saving act in Christ a miracle that governs his whole understanding of the gospel.

[W. KASCH, VII, 896-98]

---

sýnoida [to be aware, share knowledge],   *syneídēsis* [consciousness, conscience]

A. Secular Greek.

1. sýnoida emautó.

a. *sýnoida* is first of all knowing something with someone.

b. *sýnoida emautó* combines in one the person who knows and the person who shares the knowledge.

c. In philosophy evaluation enters in when people, reflecting on themselves, achieve awareness of their own ignorance in a conflict of knowledge (cf. Socrates, who as the wisest of men realizes his own ignorance).

d. When reflection extends to deeds, conscience arises in the moral sense. The process is still rational, but the matter assessed is now moral. Usually the verdict is negative. The matter assessed is either not given or indicated neutrally. At times it may be stated that there is no awareness of evil, or a positive assertion (rather than self-evaluation) occurs.

e. Thus *sýnoida emautó* comes to be linked with a bad conscience, although self-awareness as such remains a rational process and neither philosophically nor ethically does the conscience have much to do with deity.

2. *syneidós, syneídēsis, sýnesis.*

a. The first two of these terms occur sporadically and with no fixed sense from the fifth to the third century B.C. Often it is debatable whether a moral awareness of bad deeds is at issue, and there is no clear indication that conscience comes from God or is divine.

b. By the first century B.C. *syneidós* and *syneídēsis* frequently denote conscience and almost always in the sense of a bad conscience. *sýneidos* is especially common in Plutarch, who vividly depicts the conscience that shares our knowledge, uncomfortably reminds us of our offenses, and evokes the torments of hell until it is set aside by amendment.

c. The two nouns, which outstrip *sýnesis,* mean much the same thing, although *syneídēsis* can still mean self-consciousness in a nonmoral sense, thus reminding us that the terms relate only secondarily to the phenomenon of the bad conscience.

3. *The Problem of Conscience.*

a. In conscience two egos are in juxtaposition in the same person, knowing and evaluating the same things from different angles, and controlled by two opposing forces, i.e., that of order on the one hand, that of disorder on the other. Conflict begins with the knowledge of past disorder, so that conscience relates more to evaluation of the past than to preparation for the future. Where the stress is ontological, knowledge predominates in self-reflection, but where it is ethical, moral conscience is to the fore. The two strands are historically and materially related.

b. The idea of the Furies reflects moral conscience in ancient Greece, but in the fifth century B.C. humanity becomes its own measure and the moral sense emerges, as seen especially in Euripides.

c. Socratic reflection has to do with knowledge; it points the way to victory over ignorance by awareness of it, but on the basis of sharing in the divine Logos. The Socratic *daimónion* relates to approaching decisions rather than past acts, and hence is not the same as conscience.

d. Stoics seek harmony with their own nature and hence have no conscience in the morally bad sense. Epictetus, however, once equates *syneidós* with the *epítropos,* the divinely appointed overseer of individuals in their moral and intellectual decisions; he thus extends the reach of conscience to the sphere of positive guidance.

e. In Hellenistic philosophy exercises in meditation, designed to promote self-development, include self-examinations which bring the moral conscience into the area of practical deliberation, although not under the terms *syneidós, syneídēsis,* or *conscientia.*

f. Gnosticism solves the problem of conscience by dualistically separating the two egos, putting one in the world of light, the other in that of darkness, and thus opening the door to asceticism, but also libertinism.

g. The secular history of the group is thus complex. Understanding the polarity of the person forms the starting point. This yields the idea of self-consciousness but then in its moral application the sense of the (usually bad) conscience. Since conscience is readily apprehended, popular usage adopts it, but in Greek thinking conscience always includes the idea of self-consciousness. Hence no uniform usage or concept develops.

B. Latin. Cicero and Seneca frequently use the terms *conscius* and *conscientia.* The idea is that of knowing with others, and when this is a knowing with the self,

self-consciousness is the point. If a reference to past deeds arises, the Romans with their strict attachment to duty find it easier to think of a neutral or good conscience. The self-consciousness may act as a witness but is more likely an applauding or dissatisfied spectator. Seneca combines the Stoic watcher with conscience and thus prepares the ground for the elevation of conscience to a norm.

C. The OT.

I. The Hebrew Text.

1. Oddly the OT has no word for conscience. The covenant relation to God governs the people. Knowledge of self comes from God by his word (Ps. 139). This word, which makes responsible action possible, is very close (Dt. 30:14). Good and evil are known by it. Denial of God is folly (Ps. 14:1). Listening to God is self-reflection, and conscience is a willing adherence in the harmony of the I with the divine will.

2. *Inner Discord.* The OT recognizes inner discord (Gen. 42:21; 1 Sam. 24:5; 25:31). It does so on the divine plane of judgment and forgiveness. God's word is decisive in the inner controversy. It condemns but also liberates by pardon and renewal (Ps. 51), by personal and not just cultic cleansing.

II. The LXX.

1. *sýnoida emautố* occurs once in the LXX, and *syneídēsis* three times. The former is a free rendering in Job 27:6. *syneídēsis* is a mistranslation in Eccl. 10:20, and it simply means "knowledge" in the variant reading in Sir. 42:18. A morally bad conscience is at issue in Wis. 17:10. Garbed in legal concepts, it acts as prosecutor and judge.

2. The Hebrew idea of the "clean heart" leads to the development of the notion of a good conscience. This idea plays a bigger role in the LXX than in the MT.

D. Judaism.

1. The Rabbis and Qumran. The rabbis and Qumran have no word for conscience. We find the ideas of the good or bad heart and the good or evil impulse, but beyond the antitheses human unity remains.

2. The Pseudepigrapha. These writings follow the LXX line and make no new contribution. The heart accuses of sin, but there may also be purity of heart.

3. Josephus. For Josephus the verb has an intellectual thrust. Conscience may be bad or good. It is, with God, a witness whom one must fear. As regards *syneídēsis,* it may simply mean "consciousness" or "knowledge," but sometimes it carries the sense of "conscience." With God himself and the law, conscience is for Josephus a witness for resurrection after death.

4. Philo.

a. Usage. Philo uses the middle voice of the verb in the moral sense. *syneídēsis* refers to knowledge of one's acts. The word for conscience is *syneidós.* Unless qualified as pure, this is always a bad conscience.

b. The Task of Conscience. Conscience accuses, threatens, and judges. Yet it also corrects and advises conversion, being placated when heeded.

c. The Theological Context. Conscience is a divinely used spur to conversion from sin. Better to be punished than expelled; the penal function of conscience is positive, for it aims at salvation by the gracious God.

d. The Guiding Function of Conscience. Twice Philo refers to conscience as a guide, but only in connection with the *nóus* and the divine Logos.

e. The Position of Philo. Philo uses popular ideas, learns from philosophy, but is decisively influenced by the OT in his use of *elénchō,* not merely for shaming, censuring, or examining in the Greek sense, but for admonishing and condemning, and in his ascribing to conscience this judicial function, with God behind it as the true accuser and judge. As God works through conscience, its accusatory task is sterner but it is also set in a positive context. Whether Philo is original in this understanding one cannot say, but clearly he combines two types of moral life and thought, that of Hellenism and that of the OT.

E. The NT.

1. General. sýnoida occurs for the guilty knowledge of a second person in Acts 5:2 and with the reflexive pronoun in 1 Cor. 4:4. *syneidós* does not occur but we find *syneídēsis* 31 times, mostly in Paul, although not in the sense of the good or bad conscience.

2. Paul.

a. Eight of the Pauline passages occur in relation to idol meats (1 Cor. 8:7ff.; 10:25ff.). Paul is perhaps adopting here a slogan current in the church in Corinth. The conscience is for him a "self-awareness" that is threatened by the disjunction of willing and knowing or of judgment and action. It is not a detached power of evaluation but the self in its own will and action. In Christ encounter with the one true and gracious God both liberates and commits the conscience in this sense. The liberation is for the weak, who, not yet free from idols, do not enjoy the full freedom of acknowledging their own acknowledgment by the one true God. Commitment is for the strong, who, because Christ died for the weak, should acknowledge weakness and therefore accept the weak. The weak, then, must refrain from anxious questioning and the strong from causing offense. In Rom. 13:5 the formula "for the sake of conscience" could mean (a) to avoid the bad conscience that might ensue, (b) out of duty, or (c) because of the link between the state and God's will. As distinct from 1 Cor. 10, Rom. 13 is urging positive obedience, not under pressure, but in a unity of act and self-awareness. Hence, in the light of v. 6, explanation (c) is to be preferred. Believers are to estimate the state solely as God's servant. 1 Pet. 2:19 is to the same effect.

b. In other passages conscience has a judicial role. In 1 Cor. 4:4 Paul fears no human judgment, only the divine judgment which accepts and liberates him. Hence he glories in the witness of his conscience (2 Cor. 1:12; cf. 1 Jn. 3:19ff.). Because the verdict rests on God's word, the apostle is open to evaluation by the conscience of others (4:2). Conscience has the significance of an oath in Rom. 9:1, but only as governed and confirmed by the Spirit. In Rom. 2:15 the Gentile conscience indicates human responsibility. Conscience has here a judicial function, although it may defend as well as accuse. In general the accusatory role of conscience is weaker in Paul because the law acts as an incomparably sharper accuser, and even the law is set aside by the God who pardons and renews in Christ.

c. For Paul conscience is the central self-consciousness of the knowing and acting person. Various ideas combine in a complex reference to being, act, and knowledge. What holds them together is the new truth that, acknowledged by God in Christ, we can see inner conflicts more sharply yet also set them under the promise of healing.

2. Other Works.

a. The Pastorals. These letters add to *syneídēsis* such words as "good" or "clear." The clear conscience denotes the total standing of the believer. The gospel aims at a good conscience (1 Tim. 1:5-6). Timothy is to hold a good conscience (1:18-19). A corrupt conscience involves discrepancy between confession and action. The connection with faith shows that the good conscience has to do with the new creation which embraces all life, not just with a blameless conscience in a moralistic sense.

b. Hebrews. In Heb. 10:2, 22 the renewing denoted by baptism has no moral or cultic limitation but embraces the whole person in relationship with God.

c. The good conscience is again a formula for the Christian life in 1 Pet. 3:16, 21. 3:21 perhaps embodies a baptismal formula.

d. A new development in these works is the proclamation of a good conscience as the norm in the sense of inner healing and a new existence by God's act in Christ.

F. The Apostolic Fathers. *syneídēsis* is a common term in these works, usually with a qualifying attribute, and with a stronger moralizing thrust (cf. 1 Clem. 1.3; 41.1; Ignatius *Trallians* 7.2; Did. 4:14; Barn. 19.12; Hermas *Mandates* 3.4.

[C. MAURER, VII, 898-919]

synoikodoméō → *oíkos; syntéleia, synteléō* → *télos*

---

syntríbō [to crush, shatter],   *sýntrimma* [destruction, ruin]

A. The Group in the Greek World.

1. Derivation. Of obscure etymology, *tríbos,* from *tríbō,* means a "trodden way," then "intercourse," "circulation."

2. Meaning.

a. Strict Use. *syntríbō* means "to rub together," "to grind," "to crush," "to smash," "to break," "to destroy."

b. Looser Use. Various things, e.g., fear, anxiety, remorse, disappointment, are said to wear people down or shatter them.

B. The Group in the OT.

1. Hebrew Originals.

a. The Root *šbr*. This root occurs some 145 times in the basic sense "to break." In the LXX *syntríbō* corresponds 134 times. The terms overlap, although the Hebrew really means "to break in pieces," the Greek "to crush."

b. Other Roots. More than 30 other roots occur. (For details see *TDNT,* VII, 921.)

c. Other Renderings of *šbr*. Other terms for *šbr* include *apollýō* in Is. 14:25, *erēmóō* in 24:10, *thlíbō* in Lev. 26:26, and *leptýnō* in 2 Chr. 23:17.

2. Important LXX Sayings. Sayings that are important in the NT are Ex. 12:10 (cf. Ps. 34:20); Ps. 46:9 (cf. Hos. 2:20); Is. 57:15; Is. 53:5 A; 66:2 Θ.

C. The Group in the NT.

1. OT Quotations and Expressions. In Mt. 12:20 Jesus has not come to break the bruised reed but to gather sinners to himself; the wretched and oppressed are recipients of the promise. In Lk. 4:18 Jesus applies Is. 61:1 to himself, but probably without the phrase about binding up the brokenhearted, although this aptly describes his work. Only Jn. 19:36 finds significance in the fact that the legs of Jesus are not broken on the cross; this denotes his righteousness (Ps. 34:20) and his correspondence to the Passover lamb. Rom. 3:16 uses Is. 59:7 to describe human sinfulness; *sýntrimma* is both sin and its punishment. The image of smashing Satan in Rom. 16:20 (cf. Gen. 3:15; Ps. 91:13) suggests both present victory over the powers of darkness and the imminent eschatological destruction of Satan. The present triumph is perhaps over the false teachers of v. 17, who are serving Satan. Rev. 2:27 uses the imagery of Ps. 2:9 (cf. Dan. 7:27) to describe the power over the nations that the risen Christ gives to those who overcome and keep his works.

2. *Other Passages*. Mk. 14:3 refers to the breaking of the vessel at the anointing, Mk. 4:5 says that the spirit gives the demoniac the power to break fetters, and in Lk. 9:39 the spirit shatters the boy. In the last two instances Jesus manifests his power over destructive demonic forces.   [G. BERTRAM, VII, 919-25]

synypokrínomai → *hypokrínomai; sýssēmon* → *sēmeíon; sýssōmos* → *sõma; systauróō* → *sýn–metá; systéllō* → *stéllō; systenázō* → *stenázō; systoichéō* → *stoichéō; systratiõtēs* → *strateúomai*

---

spházō [to slaughter, kill],   **sphagḗ** [slaughter, killing]

---

spházō.

A. Secular Usage.

1. Ritual Slaying.

a. Meat Offerings to the Olympian Gods. The word *spházō* means "to slay," "to slaughter," "to kill," "to murder." Strictly it refers to the slaying of animals, especially in sacrifice. Ritual slaying takes place after prayer. Experts do it only when the animals are large or those making the offering are of high rank. Inclination of the head supposedly denotes consent. The ox is struck from behind, the neck is then bent back, the throat is slit, and the blood pours out. Boars may first be stupefied. In the case of smaller animals slaying is by cutting the throat with the neck bent back.

b. *sphágia*. When sacrifices remove curses, or serve as expiation, or the gods or heroes claim the whole animal, the flesh is not eaten and we have *sphágia*. Shedding the blood is now the main point. The neck is deeply cut and the blood is directed to where the special numen reigns. Human beings may be offered as *sphágia* in especially dangerous crises in Greece and Rome.

2. Secular Slaying.

a. Animals. Most slaughtering has ritual connections in antiquity. Domestic slaughtering includes simple ceremonies and the dedicating of parts to the gods. Yet a purely secular use of *spházō* does occur. Indeed, the term is used for the wolf's slaying of its prey.

b. Humans. The term *spházō* serves as a gruesome one for killing, e.g., murder of kin, massacres in war, crimes of passion, and suicide.

B. LXX Usage.

1. Ritual Slaying.

a. Animal Sacrifices. In the LXX *spházō* occurs some 84 times, mostly for *ṭbḥ* and *shṭ*. It is not a technical term but plays an important role relative to animal offerings. A simple form of (illegitimate) offering occurs in 1 Sam. 14:32ff. In early times meat is eaten only in connection with sacrifice. The blood and various parts are set aside for God; atoning power lies in the blood (Lev. 17:11). The head of the house or a servant does the slaying at home; either individuals or cultic personnel may do it in the sanctuaries. The blood ritual at first demands that the beast be slaughtered over the altar so that the blood may flow on it. When centralizing is achieved, the slaughtering is at the entrance to the sanctuary (Lev. 17:3-4). Animals used in purification and not offered to God are slain outside the camp.

b. Human Sacrifices.

(a) To God. In Gen. 22:10 Abraham lifts the knife to slay Isaac, and in 1 Sam. 15:33 Samuel slays the "dedicated" Agag.

(b) To Idols. Accusations of slaughtering children to idols occur in Ezek. 16:17ff.; 23:39; Is. 57:5.

2. *Secular Slaying.*

a. Animals. At first slaughtering is connected with communal offerings, but Dt. 12 allows secular slaughtering, although not the eating of blood.

b. Humans. As in secular Greek, *spházō* in the LXX can denote the violent killing of others, e.g., the slaughter of the priests of Baal in 1 Kgs. 18:40 or the butchering of the righteous in Ps. 37:14.

C. Philo and Josephus.

1. Philo.

a. Philo rarely uses *spházō*, but does have it at times for ritual and secular slaying, including murder.

b. Josephus. Josephus uses *spházō* (also *spháttō*) for ritual slaying and also very commonly for human killing in such senses as hewing down, massacring, and butchering, e.g., defenseless populations. Especially abhorrent is human slaughter in the temple.

D. Rabbinic Writings.

1. The rabbis sometimes use the term "to slay" with no ritual reference, e.g., the butchering of rustled cattle.

2. They also lay down strict rules for correct slaughtering either cultic or noncultic. The main point is that the throat should be slit with a single stroke.

E. The NT.

1. *spházō*, which in the NT occurs only in Johannine works, is a strong term for fratricide (Cain's murder of Abel) in 1 Jn. 3:12.

2. In Rev. 5:6, 9, 12; 13:8 Jesus is the "slaughtered Lamb." With a probable reference to the Passover, this term, in figurative paradox, denotes the extreme nature of the offering and its victorious effect. The blood serves as a ransom in 5:9. In 13:3 the beast with its mortal blow is set in contrast. Historically the assassination of Nero might be in view. In Rev. 6:9 the death of martyrs for the sake of the word is compared to the slaughtering of sacrifices. As the blood flows down the altar, so their souls (which the blood represents) are under the altar. The same mode of speech influences Rev. 18:24, and cf. also the horseman of 6:4, who takes away peace that men should slay one another.

sphagḗ.

1. This word means ritual or secular slaying or slaughtering, the slaying of deer in the hunt, and human slaying. It can also refer to slits or wounds, and in anatomy to the throat.

2. The term occurs 23 times in the LXX for slaying or slaughtering. The image of sheep for slaughter plays a special role (cf. Ps. 44:22; Zech. 11:4, 7, which is directed against those who pitilessly hand over the elect people; Jer. 11:19, where the stress is on the unsuspecting nature of the prophet; Is. 53:7, which states that the servant does not resist or complain; Jer. 12:3, which has the destruction of the wicked in mind).

3. Philo uses *sphagḗ* cultically, militarily, and ethically. He says that nourishment is given to a certain man as to cattle fattening for slaughter. Josephus has an occasional ritual reference but mostly uses the term for human killing, e.g., killing in battle, political murder, and suicide.

4. The Targum on Is. 53 takes the servant messianically but refers the image of the

lamb led to the slaughter to Messiah's judgment on the Gentiles. Ps. 44:22 has great martyrological significance and is also connected with circumcision.

5. Rom. 8:36 uses Ps. 44:22 to describe the situation of the church under external assault. The paradox that the elect community suffers demonstrates rather than negates God's love. In Acts 8:32-33 the eunuch reads Is. 53:7-8 and Philip applies the passage to Jesus. Jms. 5:5 either accuses the rich of feeding on (or for) the day when the poor are slaughtered or warns them that they are feeding on the judgment day when they themselves will be slaughtered.

6. 1 Clem. 16.1ff. quotes the whole of Is. 53:1ff. as an example for the church. Barn. 5.2 quotes Is. 53:5, 7 with reference to salvation by the sprinkling of Christ's blood. Barn. 18.1ff. allegorizes Num. 19: The heifer is Jesus; those who sacrifice it are those who led him to the slaughter.   [O. MICHEL, VII, 925-38]

---

sphragís [seal], *sphragízō* [to seal], *katasphragízō* [to seal up]

A. Seal in the Nonbiblical World.

1. Composition. Using seals, which identify things by a sign, figure, letter, or word, is an ancient custom. The term can denote either the instrument that makes the mark or the impression made. Roll seals or seal cylinders are the oldest form. Cultic or mythical figures are cut in the sheath, and the cylinder is rolled on damp clay. Scarabs or rings with scarabs replace cylinders in Egypt. We then find knobs, cones, and cube seals. Christian seals use symbols like the dove, the fish, and the ship. Seals are usually rolled or impressed on damp loam or clay, which is then dried off or baked. In the case of documents, a little clay is placed on them, and the seal is impressed on the clay.

2. Legal Significance. The seal serves as a legal protection and guarantee. It is thus placed on property, on wills, etc. Laws prohibit the misuse of seals, which owners often break just before death. Seals serve as proof of identity. They also protect houses, graves, etc. against violation. Both testator and witnesses seal wills. In Roman law all six witnesses must break their own seals to open the will, and in South Babylonia beneficiaries signify or seal when the inheritance is divided. Seals also serve as accreditation, e.g., of weights and measures. The seal plays an important public role in government. All authorities have seals. The king's seal confers authorization. In both private and public life holding a seal expresses an element of power.

3. Religious Meaning. From early times seals bear the images of deities. They thus have magical significance, conferring divine protection. The sealing of sacrifices has both cultic and legal significance. Later a stamp duty is paid for sealing. Seals are also placed on chapels when not in use to denote their inviolability. The marking of followers of Dionysus with the ivy leaf is called *sphragízein*.

4. Metaphorical Use. Plato compares the impressions of memory to those made by seals. Aristotle compares the well-articulated sounds of clear voices to sharp impressions made by well-cut seals. In the *Orphic Hymn* 34.26 the creator's seal is said to be stamped on all creation.

B. Seal in the OT.

1. Meaning.

a. The Hebrew equivalent (*ḥtm*) occurs 13 times. *sphragís* also occurs in Ex. 35:22 for "bracelet."

b. The verb *ḥtm* is the main original of the Greek verbs.

2. *Composition.* The roll seal comes to Israel from Babylon and the scarab from Egypt. Various figures along with ancient Hebraic characters occur on the seals. Conic and cube seals are also found in excavation. Seal graving is part of the craft of stone cutting.

3. *Use and Significance.*

a. Although royal seals have not been found in Israel, 1 Kgs. 21:8 mentions their use, and ministers' seals are known. The royal seal would be put on temple doors (cf. the sealing of the lions' den in Dan. 6:18). Joseph has Pharaoh's ring in Gen. 41:42 (cf. Esth. 3:10).

b. Seals make documents legally valid (cf. bills of sale, marriage contracts, the covenant of Neh. 10:1, the book of Is. 29:11).

c. The verb *sphragízō* can also mean engraving stone or metal (cf. Ex. 28:21; 36:21).

d. Since the contents of sealed vessels etc. are inaccessible, the term *sphragízō* takes on the sense "to close" (Sir. 22:27; 42:6) and then "to conceal" (Dan. 8:26).

e. Mixed in the seal are the various motifs of authorization, power, legal validity, inviolability, and closure. The OT thus finds for sealing a rich transferred use (cf. Sir. 17:22; Cant. 8:6; Jer. 22:24; Hag. 2:23).

C. Seal in Judaism.

1. Philo develops the figurative use. The powers around God give form as the seal produces many copies. God's word is the original seal. The incorporeal world is the world of ideas or seals. The verb in Philo can mean "to keep under lock and key," but it can also have the sense "to determine" or "to guarantee," and at times the weaker sense "to confirm."

2. Josephus often refers to the seal in an official sense for authorization. The seal denotes authority or offers protection.

3. Judaism often calls circumcision a seal as a mark impressed in the flesh. As a seal it denotes identity and ownership but also suggests power and protection.

D. Seal in the NT.

1. *The NT apart from Revelation.*

a. The Literal Sense. The group occurs 32 times in the NT, 22 times in Revelation. Only seldom is the reference literal. The tomb of Jesus is sealed in Mt. 27:66, obviously to secure it, though whose seal is used we are not informed. In Rom. 15:28 Paul speaks of handing over the collection under seal, though here the term probably denotes trustworthy transmission (cf. 2 Cor. 8:20-21) rather than literal sealing of the bag.

b. The Transferred Sense. 2 Tim. 2:19 uses *sphragís* in the sense of "inscription." The word of promise and admonition suggests trustworthiness. In 1 Cor. 9:2 the church itself serves to confirm or validate Paul's apostleship. The meaning "to confirm" occurs in Jn. 3:33: Those who receive the witness confirm that God is true. The same thought occurs in Jn. 6:27: The Father confirms his appointment of the Son to give the food of eternal life. In Rom. 4:11 Paul describes circumcision as a seal, not so much of belonging to God as of restoration to fellowship with God by faith. Circumcision does not replace justification but follows and confirms it; it denotes membership in God's justified people. In 2 Cor. 1:22 the sealing of the Spirit refers to God's making believers his inviolable possession. In Eph. 1:13-14 and 4:30 the Spirit is a pledge of the inheritance and hence the seal by which believers are marked and appointed for redemption. There is no specific reference to baptism, and the main idea is that of the marking of those who belong to God.

2. Revelation.

a. Sealing. In Rev. 22:10 the divine is not to seal his prophecy, i.e., keep it secret. In 20:3 the angel seals the abyss for a thousand years. In 10:4 sealing carries the sense of keeping closed or concealing.

b. The Book with Seven Seals. This book reminds us of Roman law with the seal of the testator and six witnesses. The sealed book is a double document. The one NT instance of *katasphragízō* occurs in connection with its sealing in 5:1. Only the Lamb can undo this seal. One seal is broken after the other in 6:1ff., and eschatological events move forward with the breaking of the seals.

c. The Sealed. The second angel in 7:2 and 9:4 has God's seal, and he restrains the four angels of destruction until he seals God's servants (7:3), 12,000 from each tribe (7:4ff.). This sealing marks off the people as God's possession and protects them through the terrible events of the end-time. The seal is a sign with distinctive theological significance. It serves both as a literary image and as a mode of speech among believers. The reality takes shape in the figure.

E. Seal in the Postapostolic Age.

1. "Seal" is rare in the apostolic fathers. 1 Clem. 43 (cf. Num. 17:16ff.) uses the word literally. 2 Clem. 7.6 seems to have the Holy Spirit in view. In Barn. 9.6 circumcision is the seal as a secret sign pointing to Christ. In various "seal" passages in Hermas baptism is called a *sphragís* (*Similitudes* 8.2-3; 9.16.3ff.). This seal, of course, is invisible; hence the motif of eschatological concealment perhaps plays some part. The idea of baptism as a seal then becomes a common one.

2.a. The seal is an important concept in Gnostic writings. Baptism is a seal, with which the eucharist is associated. The baptismal seal follows instruction and grants partial revelations.

b. The Odes of Solomon refers to the sealing of the abyss (24:7) and the sealing of the faces of God's people (8:15). God's plan of salvation is a sealed letter (cf. Acts of Thomas 111). The seal protects Gnostics as they traverse the various zones or aeons.

c. Mandaean works refer to a sealed letter, to baptismal sealing as a protection against demons, and to the seal as a mark whereby to distinguish initiates.

[G. Fitzer, VII, 939-53]

---

schḗma [bearing, form],   *metaschēmatízō* [to change, transform]

schḗma.

A. Usage outside the NT.

1. General. The term *schḗma* denotes the outward structure or form that may be known by the senses. The verb *schēmatízō* refers to decency in human conduct and can easily bear a special reference to clothing.

2. Specific. Specifically *schḗma* has such senses as "bearing," "appearance," "look," "features" (plural), "figure" (transferred in dancing), "constitution," "military formation," "manner of life," "dress," "form" (in rhetoric, grammar, geometry, or astronomy), "sketch," "form of a syllogism," "constellation," in a weak sense "state," "condition," or "manner," and occasionally "semblance," "pretext."

3. The LXX. The only LXX instance is in Is. 3:17 for the proud "bearing" of the noble but degenerate women of Jerusalem.

4. Philo makes rich use of the term with the primary sense of what may be known from outside, e.g., forms, artistic or mathematical figures, forms of speech, also human bearing, disposition, posture, or position. He also uses the word for "distinctive character." Thus at the Passover every house takes on the *schḗma* of a sanctuary.

5. Josephus, too, makes varied use of the term, e.g., for attitude, clothing, outward demeanor, or form.

6. Another use is for "size," e.g., of Jerusalem in Epistle of Aristeas 105.

7. The term occurs as a loanword in rabbinic works.

B. Usage in the NT. The only instances in the NT are in Phil. 2:7 and 1 Cor. 7:31. The point in Phil. 2:7 is that up to the cross Jesus was in the humanity demonstrated by his earthly form. What is meant is his mode of manifestation, i.e., his whole nature and manner as a man. The outward "bearing" that he assumes corresponds to the inner reality. In 1 Cor. 7:31 Paul advises believers to possess material things as though not possessing them, for the distinctive form of this world is perishing.

metaschḗmatízō.

A. The Greek World and Judaism.
1. This word means "to transform, "to alter," "to change the appearance."
2. The only LXX instance is in 4 Macc. 9:22 for the transforming of martyrs at death.
3. Philo uses the verb for "to change into a new form." Josephus has it for changing clothing or disguising as well as transforming.

B. The NT. Paul uses the verb in Phil. 3:21. Believers have the Spirit as an earnest of the consummation, but when Christ comes he will transfigure their present bodies of humiliation into bodies of glory. In 2 Cor. 11:13ff. the verb occurs three times in the middle. Paul's opponents transform themselves into apostles, but since Satan transforms himself into an angel of light, it is no surprise that his servants disguise themselves as servants of righteousness. In 1 Cor. 4:6 the use is literary. Paul does not mean that he is putting things in a figure of speech but that he is expressing the matter in another form, i.e., showing what the attitude of believers should be from the example of Apollos and himself.

C. The Early Church. In Hermas *Visions* 5.1 *schḗma* means "garb," but there is no other instance of either noun or verb in early writings.

[J. Schneider, VII, 954-58]

---

schízō [to split, divide],   *schísma* [split, division]

---

schízō.
1. Secular Greek.
a. This word means literally "to split," "to rend," "to cleave," "to separate" (milk).
b. Less strongly it means "to divide."
c. Rarely it refers figuratively to the division of opinion.
2. The LXX.
a. *schízō* occurs eleven times, mostly for *bqʻ* (normally rendered *rhḗgnymi*).
b. The strong meaning "to rend," "to split," "to tear apart," predominates (cf. Ex. 14:21; Is. 48:21).

c. Compounds include *anaschízō* (ripping up the pregnant, Am. 1:13), *diaschízō* (Wis. 18:23), and *kataschízō* (tearing up the books of the law, 1 Macc. 1:56).

d. *schízō* does not denote division of opinion, but *anaschízō* is used for separating oneself from the ungodly of the people (Num. 16:21).

3. Later Judaism.

a. The verbs translated by *schízō* have little theological significance, but the OT verb *ḥlq* is important for differentiating and also for differing in opinion.

b. Philo seldom uses *schízō*, and when he does it has the weaker sense "to divide." In Josephus the term has its harsher ring: Ahijah rends his mantle as God will rend the kingdom (*Antiquities* 8.207).

4. The NT.

a. In the NT *schízō* occurs nine times in the Gospels for "to split" or "to rend." Thus in Mk. 2:21 the patch tears away from the old cloth; the new thing that Jesus brings demands a new form of life.

b. In Mk. 15:38 the temple veil is rent on the death of Jesus. Probably this is the inner curtain and the tearing represents the end of the old cultus and new access to God by Jesus' death (Heb. 6:19-20; 9:8; 10:19-20).

c. In Mk. 1:10 heaven is torn open at the baptism of Jesus—a motif in eschatological revelation (cf. Is. 64:1).

d. In Jn. 19:24 the soldiers do not divide Jesus' robe, and in Jn. 21:11 the net does not break (cf. Lk. 5:6).

e. In Acts 14:4 and 23:7 (the only two instances outside the Gospels) the reference is to the division of opinion caused by Paul's preaching.

5. The Early Church.

a. An early saying refers to the presence of Christ at the cleaving of wood. In the Gospel of Thomas 77 this suggests pan-Christism, but in its original form the point seems to be that Christ is present with isolated manual workers.

b. In Ignatius *Philadelphians* 3.3 separation from the bishop is parallel to the Gnostic denial of the suffering of the incarnate Lord.

schísma.

1. Secular Greek. This rare term means "what is split," "rift," "rent," "cleft."

2. The LXX. *hē schismḗ* occurs in the LXX in Jon. 2:6 and Is. 2:19, 21 ("clefts").

3. Later Judaism. As with the verb *ḥlq,* the rabbis develop the idea of differences of opinion or controversies (mostly in a bad sense).

4. The NT.

a. In Mk. 2:21 the adding of the patch makes the rent worse.

b. In Jn. 7:43; 9:16; 10:29 the origin, deeds, and words of Jesus cause division among his listeners.

c. The *schísmata* in 1 Cor. 1–4 seem not to be due to doctrinal differences but to attachments to different leaders. They can be overcome only by unity in the body of Christ and mutual subjection and concern. In 1 Cor. 12:25 discord in the human body symbolizes discord in Christ's body.

5. The Apostolic Fathers. In 1 Clem. 2.6; Hermas *Similitudes* 8.9.4 *schísmata* are grouped with debates and rivalries. Love knows no *schísmata* (1 Clem. 49.5). Believers are to avoid them (Did. 4.3). Mountain clefts symbolize contentious people (Hermas *Similitudes* 9.1.7); cf. also splits on branches and cracks in stones (*Similitudes* 8.1.9-10; 9.6.4).   [C. MAURER, VII, 959-64]

---

sōzō [to save],   *sōtēría* [salvation],   *sōtḗr* [Savior],   *sōtḗrios* [saving]

sōzō, sōtēría.

A. The Greek World.

1. Saving. These terms first refer to salvation (human or divine) from serious peril. Curing from illness is another sense. Horses may save in battle, or night may save an army from destruction, good counsel may save ships, etc. Cities, castles, ships, etc. may be saved as well as people. At times protection may be the meaning, and *sōtēría* can have the sense of a "safe return."

2. Keeping. The meaning at times may be that of keeping alive, e.g., pardoning, protecting, keeping from want, keeping a fire going. Other uses are for keeping wine, goods, and even beards, as well as preserving memory.

3. Benefiting. The idea of rescuing from peril disappears when the idea is that of keeping in good health, or benefiting, or when the noun means "well-being," i.e., of a city, country, family, etc.

4. Preserving the Inner Being. A special nuance is when the terms refer to preserving the inner being or nature. In philosophy inner health may be the point or the preservation of one's humanity.

5. Religious Usage. All the nuances occur in religious usage. Thus the gods rescue from the perils of life. Philosophy discusses the preservation of all things from perishing. A demand arises for the preservation of life beyond death. In the Gnostic sphere *gnōsis* supposedly saves from death as it is imparted by revelation. In the mysteries initiates share in the salvation of a mythical divine being from death and thereby attain to a blissful life in the hereafter. A special Syrian belief mentioned in Origen *Against Celsus* 7.9 is that there is salvation from eternal punishment by worship of a divine envoy and faith in him.   [W. FOERSTER, VII, 965-69]

B. The OT.

1. Statistics and Equivalents.

a. In the canon *sōzō* ("to keep," "to save") occurs some three-fifths of the time for *yšʿ* ("to save," "to help," "to free"). *anasōzō* mostly occurs for nouns derived from *plṭ*. *diasōzō* is used especially for *mlṭ* ("to save," "to achieve safety," "to escape"). *sōtēría* ("salvation," "preservation," "protection") is used mostly for derivatives of *yšʿ*.

b. As *sōzō* and *sōtēría* occur mostly for the stem *yšʿ*, so this stem is mostly rendered by *sōzō* and *sōtēría*. The compounds, however, occur for other Hebrew terms, although *sōzō* as well as *diasōzō* commonly renders *mlṭ*.

c. No basic shift of meaning takes place when *sōzō* etc. are used for different Hebrew verbs. Yet the LXX often translates freely (e.g., saving for converting in Is. 10:22; cf. also Zeph. 3:17; Job 20:24; Prov. 10:25; 11:31). Slight shifts might also take place when nouns are translated, as when those who escape become those who are saved (with a more passive emphasis). (For details see *TDNT*, VII, 970-73.)

2. The Stem yšʿ in the OT.

a. Meaning. This verb first means "to be roomy." Bringing into a more spacious place confers the idea of deliverance. A stronger being brings deliverance to the weak or oppressed by superior intervention. Personal relationships are stressed as there is rescue from situations brought about by the hostile intent of others. The nouns comprehend a totality that includes both the deliverance and the ensuing state of salvation.

b. Human Deliverance, Help, and Salvation. The weak need legal or military help (cf. Job 26:2; 5:4; 1 Sam. 11:3). They should cry for help (Judg. 10:12ff.). Those who are strong should be asked to give protection or to secure justice (Is. 37:35; Hos. 13:10). Such a request implies or brings about dependence. The help may come through war (Hos. 1:7) or through legal action (Job 13:16). Military heroes or judges bring deliverance. So do protecting powers. Rulers have the task of helping to justice (2 Sam. 14:4).

c. Limits of Human Deliverance. All salvation that is not divinely validated is limited. Idols and astrologers cannot save (Is. 45:20; 47:13). God, not an angel, rescues from Egypt, brings into the land, and wins victories over enemies (Is. 63:8-9; Ps. 44:3-4; Judg. 7:2, 7). The people must wait on God for salvation (Is. 30:15). It is a sin to reject the God who saves and to seek a king (1 Sam. 10:18-19) or to avenge oneself (25:26ff.). Human intervention is legitimate only if God works in and through it, as in the case of the judges (Judg. 2:18). The God who saves by many or by few (1 Sam. 14:6) must give assurance to a Gideon before he will come forward to help and save (Judg. 6:14ff.).

d. Divine Deliverance, Help, and Salvation. God also helps and saves directly as the one best equipped to intervene or protect or preserve. He is the true hero and king (Pss. 80:2; 44:3-4). Israel conquers through him (Dt. 33:29). He saves and helps her (1 Sam. 11:13). If she is faithful, he promises aid (Num. 10:19). He is the hero who brings victory (Zeph. 3:17). In the Psalms God's help is thus invoked against public or personal foes. He is asked to save against legal attacks, against injustice and violence, against sickness and imprisonment, and against external attacks. There are also references to comprehensive deliverance or salvation. God has established and preserved the people, and its members may thus hope for his help (Ps. 106:4). By forgiveness the garment of salvation replaces their filthy raiment of sin (Is. 61:10; Zech. 3:4-5). They can thus raise the cup of salvation (Ps. 116:13). To the humble who know their littleness, call on God with contrite hearts, and follow his will (Pss. 24:5; 34:6; 119:155), God grants his general help and salvation. Although he denies help to sinners, salvation may at times be from merited judgment. He rescues the oppressed even though they, too, are sinful (Ezek. 34:22), and he frees Israel from all her sins (Ezek. 36:29). Repentance is a prerequisite (Jer. 4:14). The liberation from exile is a form of salvation (Is. 45:17). God alone can effect this (43:11). This redemption points ahead to the final redemption when the age of eschatological salvation dawns (cf. Is. 43:1ff.; 60:16; 63:9). The Hebrew stem covers both the deliverance itself and the salvation that it brings. The eschatological deliverance includes rescue from attacking nations (Zech. 12:7) and the gathering of the dispersed (Is. 43:5ff.). The end-time community will draw on the wells of salvation (Is. 12:3), and all the world can share its salvation (45:22). The messianic ruler, as God's representative, will help Israel so that it may dwell in safety (Jer. 23:6), and he will himself be divinely preserved in the wild eschatological attack of the nations (Zech. 9:9).

3. *Other Stems in the OT.*

a. Nouns of the Stem *plṭ*. Nouns of this stem may denote either the act or the result of escaping, e.g., fugitives or refugees. Usually escape from violent danger is at issue, e.g., death in battle (Judg. 12:5). Religiously God's judgment is a mortal danger that none can escape (Am. 9:1). If a saved remnant lives on, it is only as an object lesson to the exiles (Ezek. 14:12ff.). By God's will and work some do escape divine punishment (Is. 4:2; Ezek. 6:8-9; Neh. 1:2). Even some Gentiles may escape the final judgment in eschatological salvation (Is. 45:20ff.; 66:19).

b. The Verb *mlṭ*. This verb, too, denotes escape from mortal threat and the finding of safety (cf. Judg. 3:29; 1 Sam. 19:10, etc.). David has to protect his life against Saul (1 Sam. 19:11). Escape from invasion (Is. 20:6), or from punishment (Ezek. 17:15), or from custody (2 Sam. 4:6), or from affliction (Job 19:12) may also be meant. Those who trust in God are saved (Ps. 22:5). God saves the innocent (Job 22:30). Escape does not come by trust in horses (Ps. 33:17), in other nations (Is. 20:6), in riches (Job 20:20), or in one's own understanding (Prov. 28:26), but in God (Job 22:30). Transgressors cannot escape (1 Kgs. 19:17; Am. 2:14-15). When God spares the condemned to usher in the eschatological age of salvation, prisoners again escape the oppressor (Is. 49:24-25). In the last time those who call on God's name (Joel 2:32), or whose names are written in the book of life (Dan. 12:1), will be saved.

[G. FOHRER, VII, 970-80]

C. *sōzō* and *sōtēría* in Later Judaism.

1. OT Apocrypha. Where there is no Hebrew original, the terms still refer mostly to human or divine deliverance with a personal reference. Human deliverance is comparatively uncommon; usually what is meant is the deliverance of the righteous by God. The decisive point is not the content of deliverance but the fact that it comes from God. The resurrection brings final salvation when the righteous are delivered from the afflictions and persecutions of earthly life.

2. Qumran. In general the Hebrew terms refer in these works to God's help and deliverance. These are seen in Israel's history and are expected in the conflict of the children of light against the children of darkness. They also apply in the individual struggles of the righteous both past and present. In the last time the divine community is the main object of help, i.e., of definitive salvation. The stress is not on the various emergencies but on the positive fact of God's intervention. Deliverance may be from oppression by the wicked or from temptation, but not from sin and guilt. What counts, however, is the divine help, whether in Israel's past, the community's present, or the final battle.

3. Ethiopian Enoch. In the parts of this work preserved in Greek the terms are mostly eschatological with a reference to God's final salvation in freedom from sin and fulfilment of the OT promises. The content of salvation includes final liberation from persecution and deliverance in the judgment; the opposite is perdition. To be righteous and to repent are ways to eternal salvation.

4. The Testaments of the Twelve. In these writings there are two circles of thought. The one relates to individuals and their temporal and eternal salvation, the other to the community (and sometimes the Gentiles) in the end time. In the first circle individuals attain salvation by prayer and piety along with God's help, while in the other God alone brings salvation for Israel (and the Gentiles).

5. The Psalms of Solomon and 4 Esdras.

a. In the Psalms of Solomon the usage is similar to that in the Testaments of the Twelve. *sōzō* denotes God's intervention in the life of the righteous. In Ps. 10:8 *sōtēría* denotes salvation for Israel.

b. 4 Esdras refers to God's help in Israel's history and to divine preservation in affliction. Salvation includes the end of evil, but since the decision in the judgment is by works, the final destiny is one of preservation in life rather than salvation.

6. Josephus. Josephus uses the group for rescue from death, capture, or destruction. Another common meaning is blessing. Preservation and protection are other senses. God saves Israel and her members from life's perils, needs, and afflictions. Eschatological salvation might be meant in the claim of a Zealot prophet in *Jewish War* 6.285.

7. Rabbinic Works and Hebrew Enoch.

a. In rabbinic works we find both human and divine intervention to help and save. The thought of the deliverance from Egypt leads on to that of eschatological redemption, which also means freedom from the bondage of the nations.

b. The usage in Hebrew Enoch is similar.

8. Philo. For Philo the group has much the same range as in secular Greek. The reference may be to deliverance, preservation, health, or well-being. Religiously God saves from life's dangers and distresses. The *lógos* or reason saves the soul, but the true *sōtḗr* is God; to break free from the passions and to attain to a measure of virtue also helps. God aids in securing liberation from the passions. The content of *sōtēría* is not maintaining one's humanity but acquiring a share in divine forces.

D. The NT.

I. The Saving of Physical Life. As regards physical life, the group in the NT refers only to salvation from acute danger, as in Acts 27:20ff.; Mt. 8:25; 14:30; Mk. 15:30; Jn. 12:27; Heb. 5:7; 11:7; Acts 7:25. In some instances the reference of *sṓzō* is to the healing of the sick (cf. Acts 4:9; 14:9; Jn. 11:12 [ambiguous]; Jms. 5:15).

II. The Theological Sense.

1. The Synoptics.

a. In the healings of Jesus *sṓzō* occurs 16 times and *diasṓzō* twice. Often faith is said to have saved, and the reference is always to the whole person. Clearly, then, the salvation extends to more than the physical sphere. Hence Jesus can tell the sinful woman of Lk. 7:50 that her faith has saved her (cf. also Mt. 8:25).

b. More strictly religious is the use in Lk. 1:68ff., which follows an OT model. In 1:77 the Baptist will give knowledge of salvation in the remission of sins. The explanation of the name of Jesus in Mt. 1:21 makes a similar link. Elsewhere the group is not common in the Synoptists. Mk. 8:35 and parallels refer to the saving and losing of life with an eschatological reference. In Mk. 10:26 being saved is equivalent to entering the kingdom or entering or inheriting life. Mk. 13:13 and parallels speak of deliverance from messianic tribulation. Lk. 13:23 equates salvation with entering the kingdom. In Lk. 19:10 saving and finding take place in the present (cf. 19:9-10). *sōtēría*, then, has both a present reference as finding and a future reference as entering the kingdom.

2. Paul. Paul limits the group to the relationship with God; he uses *rhýomai* for rescue from other perils. What is saved is the whole person or the *pneúma*. Unlike justification or remission or reconciliation, salvation is a future term (1 Cor. 3:15; 5:5; Rom. 13:11; 1 Th. 5:8ff.); it thus has a comprehensive sense. The goal of Paul's work is salvation (Rom. 10:1). Some people may save others (Rom. 11:14; 1 Cor. 9:22). Perishing is the opposite of being saved (1 Cor. 8:11; cf. 1:18). Salvation is salvation from judgment (Rom. 5:9; 1 Cor. 3:15). But positively it is endowment with divine glory that comes with the redemption of the body (Rom. 8:24; Phil. 3:20-21) and conforming to the image of the Son (Rom. 8:29). Righteousness is a parallel concept (Gal. 5:5). Salvation may be future but it also extends into the present (1 Cor. 15:2; 2 Cor. 6:2). Thus in Rom. 8:24 the content is eschatological but the aorist shows that *sōtēría* has come already with the receiving of the gospel.

3. Ephesians and Colossians. In Ephesians the group occurs only in 1:13; 2:5, 8. In 1:13 the reference is to the message of salvation, or the message that saves. In 2:5, 8 the perfect tense is used ("you have been saved") but the consummation has still to come (vv. 6-7).

4. The Pastorals. In 2 Tim. 4:18 salvation is "for the kingdom" rather than entry into it, and in 2:10 it is distinguished from eternal glory. The order in 1 Tim. 2:4 and 2 Tim. 1:9 is surprising; it shows that salvation does not have so strong an eschatological reference (cf. the connection with washing and renewing in Tit. 3:5). Yet the eschatological dimension is clear in 1 Tim. 2:15; 4:16; 2 Tim. 3:15.

5. The Catholic Epistles, Hebrews, and Acts.

a. In 1 Peter believers are kept for salvation, will achieve it, and are to grow into it (1:5, 9; 2:2). It is the gift of eternal glory. The prophets inquired about it (1:10). The verb occurs only in the quotation in 4:18 and in 3:21, where, with a reference to the last judgment, it encloses both a present and a future.

b. In Hebrews the focus is again on the future (cf. 1:14; 10:25). Yet salvation is also present (7:25, where it is immaterial whether *eis tó pantelés* means "wholly" or "forever"). The theological expansion is especially plain in 2:3. The Lord brings salvation by declaring it, but this is a "great salvation" that awaits final consummation. 6:9 offers a cautious formulation; it refers to coming salvation but also embraces the state of the readers that leads to it.

c. James uses only the verb, and except in 5:5 it always denotes final deliverance in the judgment (cf. 4:12).

d. In Acts *sōzō* and *sōtēría* occur 19 times. In 2:21, 40 and 15:1, 11 future salvation is at issue but elsewhere the terms are general ones for Christian salvation. This salvation includes forgiveness (3:19; 5:31; 22:16) but is oriented to the future. An interesting phrase is *hoi sōzómenoi* in 2:47.

e. Jude 5 refers to the exodus, but in v. 3 and v. 23 salvation in the judgment is the issue, the basis being laid for this here and now.

f. The only instance in 2 Peter is in 3:15, which finds salvation in the divine forbearance that allows space for zealous efforts to be found without spot or blemish.

6. The Johannine Writings.

a. In John the only example of *sōtēría* is in the saying in 4:22. The verb occurs in 3:17; 5:34; 10:9; 12:47. The cosmos is to be saved in 3:17; 12:47, the Jews in 5:34, the disciples in 10:9. The idea is that of attaining to life or giving it.

b. Only the noun occurs in Revelation (7:10; 12:10; 19:1). The *sōtēría* is God's, and it carries the OT nuance of victory. The overcomers confess that salvation belongs to God (7:10), a loud voice proclaims that God's salvation has come (12:10), and after the fall of Babylon the voice of the heavenly multitude cries that salvation belongs to God (19:1).

E. The Apostolic Fathers. In 1 Clement *sōzō* means physical well-being or preservation, but a reference to eternal salvation may also be found. The latter sense is most common in 2 Clement. The object is the *psyché* only in Barn. 19.10 and Hermas *Similitudes* 6.1.1; elsewhere it is the person in general. Christ is often the subject, but conduct in 1 Clem. 21.8. We seldom read from what there is salvation; hence the idea of deliverance is less strong. Salvation often carries a present reference, but the thought of coming salvation is also found, especially in Hermas, for whom baptism brings remission but no final certainty.

F. Gnosticism.

1. The basic view of Gnosticism is that a divine particle is trapped in the world of passion and fate. Only a divine intervention can free it. But the term *sōzō* is seldom used for this act.

2. The Valentinians use *sōzō* and *sōtēría* more frequently. They call the Gnostics

sōzómenoi and employ both verb and noun to describe the blessed state of pneumatics and psychics. The latter need saving in the stricter sense of not merely fashioning but transposing from bondage to freedom.

3. The Coptic Gnostics have two equivalents for *sōzō* or *sōtēría,* the one denoting deliverance, the other having the more positive sense of salvation.

4. The Acts of Thomas stresses the dynamic aspect of salvation in relation to the remission of sins and the efficacy of the sacraments.

5. Saving plays a big part in the colorful Mandaean writings. Common ideas are liberation, redemption, deliverance, healing, and blessing. A special relationship is that between death and redemption. Redemption comes with individual death and the end of the world.

G. The Relation between NT *sōtēría* and Later Judaism, the Greek World, and Gnosticism. NT *sōtēría* does not refer to physical health, political liberation, or release from demonic powers. It has to do strictly with the relationship with God, and hence it can be achieved neither by reason nor by contrition. The problem is that of sin, not of the imprisonment of a divine particle in the material world, as in Gnosticism. A call brings salvation, but not the call that awakens the bemused divine self. Nor do sacramental acts bring salvation by initiation into the story of a mythical god, as in the mysteries. The work of Jesus of Nazareth brings salvation from judgment by the forgiveness of sins. All are under judgment, none can escape it unaided, and salvation comes through the word of the cross which is God's power to salvation for all who believe. Only God can save, but hearers can accept or reject the offer and have thus to work out their salvation (Phil. 3:12-13). Salvation is not just future, as in Pharisaic Judaism, nor an enhancement of the present, as at Qumran, nor so strongly present, as in Gnosticism. It is present, for with Christ the new aeon has come and believers are drawn into it as they die and rise again with him. Yet their hope is set on future salvation when their transformation comes, creation is freed, and God's rule over every power is manifested. Negatively salvation is deliverance from wrath, and positively it is the attainment of glory. Either way the message of Christ crucified and risen fixes the content.

sōtḗr.

A. The Greek World.

1. Range of Meaning. This word covers the range of *sōzō* and *sōtēría* but almost always with a personal reference. The *sōtḗr* is either divine or human, and people, not objects, are saved. Salvation involves a dependence (however momentary) of the saved on the savior.

2. Divine Saviors. The gods are *sōtḗres* as they deliver from perils or sicknesses or as they serve as protectors or preservers, e.g., of cities.

3. Human Saviors.

a. The Helper, Saver of Life, Physician. Two points calling for notice are the superiority of saviors to the saved and the lack of any clear distinction between the divine and human worlds in the Greek sphere. Human saviors are those who extend help or protection, those who save the lives of others, and physicians who bring healing.

b. Philosophers. Philosophers often bear the title *sōtḗres* as those who bring help or liberation.

c. Statesmen. Statesmen and rulers are called *sōtḗres,* at first with reference to specific actions, and with suggestions of divinization. In the Roman world the term becomes more common but still relates to specific deeds, does not necessarily imply deification, and may extend to subordinates of the one ultimately responsible, as in the case of Pompey and his legate.

d. *The Hellenistic Ruler Cult.* Under the Ptolemies and Seleucids *sōtér* becomes one of the official royal titles. *sōzō* is the special task of the ruler, and in Egypt it links up with the idea that the ruler is the son of deity. The title is so highly esteemed in Egypt that it is applied to government officials as well.

e. *Emperor Worship.* During the empire *sōtér* becomes more common and the thought of the golden age comes to be associated with it. Yet *sōtér* is not part of the official style of the emperors and is not a technical term for the world savior. In his many travels Hadrian often receives the title of *sōtér* of a particular city (or even individual) to whom he shows favors. The reference in such cases is still to specific acts. Latin equivalents such as *conservator* or *salvator* seldom occur on coins. The use of *sōtér*, then, is much the same as in Greece but with extension due to the greater range of Roman rule.

f. *The Golden Age.* Since the age of Augustus brings a measure of order, peace, security, and prosperity, the emperor is *sōtér* insofar as the term has no specific content, and the regime suggests thoughts of the golden age, causing people to look beyond the emperor to providence or the gods.   [W. FOERSTER, VII, 980-1012]

B. The OT. The LXX always has *sōtér* for the stem *yš'*. It is not a technical term for the judges (cf. only Judg. 3:9, 15), since the LXX emphasizes that it is God who delivers Israel. The LXX seldom uses the term for the kings (cf. 2 Kgs. 13:5), but elsewhere it applies to human helpers or to God as helper. On 16 occasions it is used for Hebrew terms for "help" or "liberation" or "deliverance" where the reference is to God. Only in Zech. 9:9 and Is. 49:6 is there approximation to its use for the Messiah.   [G. FOHRER, VII, 1012-13]

C. Later Judaism.

1. The apocryphal works use *sōtér* only for God as Israel's Savior, e.g., when David fights Goliath (1 Macc. 4:30) or when God saves the Egyptian Jews (3 Macc. 6:29ff.). In Sir. 51:1 God is the Savior from all kinds of dangers.

2. In the Dead Sea Scrolls, Ethiopian Enoch, Jubilees, Slavonic Enoch, Syrian Baruch, and 4 Esdras there is nothing equivalent to *sōtér*. The Testaments of the Twelve uses *sōtér* (Test. Jos. 1:16). In Ps. Sol. 8:33 God is *sōtér* as he protects the righteous, and in 17:3 as the helper of Israel who raises up the King-Messiah. Nowhere is the Messiah *sōtér*.

3. Josephus uses *sōtér* for human deliverers but not for God. The reference is always to specific deeds after the Greek pattern.

4. Among the rabbis the equivalent may be used for God or the Messiah, but there is no evidence that Redeemer or Savior is a current messianic title in NT days.

5. The Sibylline Oracles do not call the inaugurator of the golden age *sōtér* but use the term for God in his deliverance of the righteous, his preservation of all things, and his salvation from the pains of hell (2.27-28; 1.152; 2.344-45).

6. Philo calls God *sōtér* as the Savior of his people, the Preserver of the race, the Upholder of the cosmos, and especially the Helper of the soul.

D. The NT.

1. Occurrence. The NT uses *sōtér* for God in Lk. 1:47 (cf. Jude 25) and six times in the Pastorals. It also uses *sōtér* in Lk. 2:11; Acts 5:31; 13:23; Phil. 3:20; Eph. 5:23;

Jn. 4:42; 1 Jn. 4:14, four times in the Pastorals, and five in 2 Peter. The general restraint and the more common use in the Pastorals need explanation.

2. *The NT apart from the Pastorals and 2 Peter.*

a. In Lk. 2:10-11 the angel specifically addresses the Jewish people and does not use the article. A connection with Lk. 1:69ff. is palpable.

b. Acts 5:31 and 13:23 are directed at Jews and God-fearers. The reference is to messianic hopes but with forgiveness as the content, not political liberation.

c. In Eph. 5:23 the *autós* shows that the author is making a new point. As a model for husbands (vv. 28-29) Christ is *sōtḗr* by sacrificing himself and thus purifying the church so that at the consummation he may display it for himself in glory. The action is a present one but with an eschatological dimension.

d. In Jn. 4:42 the Samaritans represent the world. This verse and 1 Jn. 4:14 are to be seen in relation to Jn. 3:17, which links the verb *sṓzō* and *kósmos*. Christ is Savior of Gentiles as well as Jews.

3. *The Pastorals and 2 Peter.*

a. Six of the ten instances of *sōtḗr* in the Pastorals are in Titus, three in 1 Timothy, and one in 2 Timothy. Six refer to God and four to Christ. Except in 1 Tim. 4:10 it is a title. The general thesis, in opposition to those who contend for a restricted salvation, is that God is the Savior of all, not merely as the Benefactor, but as the Savior whom Christians know and trust. In 1 Tim. 4:10 the meaning might be the broader one of Benefactor (in view of v. 8), but the addition "especially of those who believe" (cf. also 2:3-4) supports the more distinctive sense. When Christ is *sōtḗr,* all the passages apart from Tit. 1:4 offer elucidations: Grace has appeared (2 Tim. 1:10), the appearance of his glory is awaited (Tit. 2:13), the Spirit has been poured forth (3:6-7), he is the incarnate Lord who has abolished death and brought life and immortality to light (2 Tim. 1:10). The phrase "Jesus Christ our Savior" emerges clearly in Tit. 2:13; 3:6 in opposition to some counterposition.

b. In 2 Peter *sōtḗr* applies only to Jesus (1:1, 11; 2:20; 3:2, 18). It alternates with *kýrios* for no obvious reason. Perhaps a taste for solemn statements accounts for its frequent use.

E. **The Apostolic Fathers.** If *sōtḗr* is a common title in the Pastorals and 2 Peter, it is rare in the apostolic fathers. Not found at all in the Didache, Barnabas, or Hermas, it occurs only once in 1 Clement (God), once each in Polycarp, Martyrdom of Polycarp, Diognetus, and 2 Clement, and four times in Ignatius. Mostly there is a strong sense of its material content, but it is not a designation as *kýrios* is, and not even by way of antithesis does it have any contact with *sōtḗr* as part of the style of imperial Rome.

F. **Gnosticism.**

1. Apart from Christian influence *sōtḗr* does not seem to belong to Gnosticism. Of the heads of Gnostic schools only Menander calls himself *sōtḗr.*

2. In Christian Gnosticism the term is plain in Coptic sources. Usually Jesus is the Savior. In reply to disciples' questions, we sometimes read: "The (perfect) *sōtḗr* says." In Apocryphal John Christ is *sōtḗr* as he who gives John a revelation of the heavenly world.

3. In Greek sources the term is none too common. The accounts of Basilides in Irenaeus and Hippolytus contain it four times.

4. In the Acts of Thomas *sōtḗr* seldom occurs in narrative, but it is common in

prayers and preaching, usually with a dependent genitive, e.g., of all, of the whole creation, of souls (164.12; 114.9-10; 159.17).

5. Valentinianism likes to call Jesus *sōtḗr* rather than *kýrios* or even Jesus. Only in this branch of Gnosticism does *sōtḗr* have a firmly established place. The Gnostics mostly follow Christian terminology, and where they use *sōtḗr* they give it a less personal reference. Jesus is *sōtḗr* as the Redeemer who bears a redeeming summons. When the concept goes beyond this, as in Acts of Thomas, a sacramentalism is present that is close to that of the mysteries.

G. The Primitive Christian Use. In primitive Christianity *sṓzō* and *sōtēría* are important terms for salvation. Since Jesus brings this, it is no surprise that he is called *sōtḗr*, the content of the term being fixed by *sṓzō* and *sōtēría*. Restraint in the use of *sōtḗr* may well be due to the risk of confusion with the Jewish hope of a national liberator or with the pagan concept of a political benefactor. The apostolic fathers maintain this restraint. If the Pastorals break it, they relate the term strictly to God, using a Greek term to counter false teachings which belong to the Greek context. Not the title *sōtḗr*, but the content of the *sōtēría* that Jesus brings, raises up Jesus as *sōtḗr* into the divine sphere.

sōtḗrios.

1. In Greek this word has all the range of *sṓzō*. It may be used of the hero, the horse, the sun's rays, water (for fish), reason, etc. in such senses as saving, beneficent, sustaining, beneficial. The noun *tá sōtḗria* means "thanksgiving." As a singular noun, *sōtḗrion* denotes "means of deliverance."   [W. FOERSTER, VII, 1013-22]

2. The LXX uses *sōtḗrion* for "what is beneficial," "deliverance," "festive time," and especially "salvation offering" (Ex. 20ff.; 1–2 Chronicles) in a rendering of Hebrew terms that are sometimes translated "peace offering" and that may carry the sense of the "concluding sacrifice."   [G. FOHRER, VII, 1022-23]

3. In Judaism *tó sōtḗrion* denotes the "salvation offering," the "feast of deliverance," or the "means of deliverance" (cf. Sir. 35:1; 3 Macc. 6:30; Is. 33:20). In the pseudepigrapha "salvation offering" or "salvation" is the meaning. Josephus does not use *tó sōtḗrion* (*toú theoú*), nor does Philo, in the sense of salvation, but we find the adjective *sōtḗrios*.

4. The NT uses the adjective independently in Tit. 2:11 ("bringing salvation"), and in quotations or allusions in Lk. 2:30 (Is. 40:5; cf. Lk. 3:6; Acts 28:28) and Eph. 6:17 (Is. 59:17), where God's salvation seems to be in view, but the LXX leads to the choice of *toú sōtēríou* rather than *tḗs sōtērías*.

5. In the apostolic fathers *tó sōtḗrion* (*theoú*) occurs only in quotations (1 Clem. 15.6; 18.12; 35.12). 1 Clem. 36.1 relates God's salvation to Christ's in a way that clearly reflects LXX influence.   [W. FOERSTER, VII, 1023-24]

---

sṓma [body],   *sōmatikós* [bodily],   *sýssōmos* [belonging to the same body]

A. The Greek World.

1. Up to Plato. Of contested derivation, *sṓma* first occurs in Homer for a dead human or animal body. Use for a living body is attested clearly only from Hesiod. By the fifth century B.C. the term denotes the "trunk" or the whole "body." The body may at times be viewed impersonally, but it can also denote the person. In its limitation, the body is the physical existence that ends with death. As such it is distinct from the soul, without which it has no value. Physical existence is often felt to be an alien affliction, the *sḗma* (tomb) of the soul, the fetter that fate has ordained for humanity. Transmigration associates body and soul more closely, but ecstasy makes possible alienation from the body. The body also calls for censure as the seat of erotic desire. In art the idea of external form is linked to the body; the *sṓma* encounters the eye as a whole defined by its form. Philosophy calls the elements *sṓmata*. Democritus distinguishes the *sṓma* from empty space, while Melissus says that real being has no *sṓma*. In another definition breadth, length, and depth characterize *sṓma*; it must always be "in" a specific place (*tópos*).

2. *Plato to Aristotle.* Plato refers *sṓma* to the human body but also (plural) to the materials used by artists and to the elements. As an integrated totality, the *sṓma* may be the person. As the visible part, it is the object of desire, distinct from the soul, which controls and guides it, and which alone, along with the body, constitutes the living being. The body needs the care of gymnastic instructors and physicians. Unlike the soul, it is mortal. Physical desire leads the soul down. The *sṓma* is a *sḗma* which traps the soul. At death the soul achieves liberation and purification. Yet physical beauty may be a spur to ascent to the idea, and the soul, located in the head, holds the body upright. Body and cosmos stand in relationship. The cosmos is a body that is controlled by the divine soul. Xenophon takes up many of the same thoughts. The *sṓma* is the person, although often as an object of desire. The soul is the guiding force, just as divine reason governs the cosmos. Isocrates extends the body-soul relationship to the state, of which the constitution is the soul. The sense of person continues in later usage, especially in enumeration. Comedy takes up the idea of the ascent of the soul at death. The soul plays the part of helmsman, a good body with a poor soul being comparable to a ship with a poor helmsman. The idea of *sṓma* as substance is also present. Aristotle uses *sṓma* for the trunk or body. In his view the body exists before the soul but the soul is superior. Desire is good but should be restrained, for it is not the supreme good. The soul is a *sṓma* made up of the finest particles, and *sṓma*, even apart from soul, is substance, so that logical argument may be called the *sṓma* of credibility in speech. Bodies are limited. The elements are bodies, and the universe is a body with reason as its soul (cf. also the state). Mathematical bodies are secondary abstractions.

3. *Fourth and Third Centuries.* In the later fourth century *sṓma* means the physically present person, with some stress on corporeality. Epicurus uses *sárx* for *sṓma* in view of his materialistic view of the soul; he thus distinguishes soul from flesh but not from body, and rates the body highly. Stoicism views the soul, located in the heart or head, as the guiding principle. It associates the body, not with extension but with activity and suffering. Sharing these with the body, the soul is in some sense corporeal. To explain the presence of two bodies in the same place, a doctrine of permeation develops. Mental sickness demonstrates the permeation. Yet while the soul is *sṓma*, *sṓma* is still the body as distinct from the soul, and Stoicism maintains the unconditional superiority of the soul over the body. The term *sṓma* may also be used for groups of people, with some distinction later between the limited and the unlimited number. Among other groups regarded as bodies (e.g., an army or chorus) is the assembly (*ekklēsía*). Smaller bodies can make up the larger body. The cosmos is a larger body but also a living entity and as such the perfect *sṓma*. God has created it, and he governs it through the world soul. Middle Stoicism stresses the teleology of the body but also refers at times to the useless and corruptible flesh. In ordinary use

sṓma may mean a slave or may be used in enumeration. *sṓmatopoiéō* denotes the organizing of a people's unity, and *sṓmatoeidés* the unity of history. Astronomers speak of the body of a constellation, grammarians use *sṓma* and *prágma* for the concrete and abstract meanings of words, and scientists regard the body as a compressed molecule that then extends again.

4. From 100 B.C. to A.D. 100. Later Stoicism uses *sṓma* for the human body and for the divine body of heaven. Independent bodies are distinguished from integrated bodies. Latin adopts the word to denote a literary collection. Body and soul suffer together in view of their interpenetration. One may cheerfully leave the prison or fetter of the body at death. Here below we are tied to the body as to an alien corpse or beast of burden. Yet the body bears witness to the wisdom of providence. The cosmos rates as the body of deity. Zeus, the head and center, conceals all things in himself and then causes them to issue forth. All things are in his vast body. Parts of the cosmos rank as members of the body. The supreme God is the world soul and in Stoicism is identical with fate or necessity, although the cosmos may also be presented as a living entity that is governed by divine reason. Human beings are members of the great body that embraces all things. They are also members of the state, a smaller body that reflects the great body. Being composed of many parts, the state resembles a human body, which in Rome has the emperor as its soul or head. Human beings are made up of soul and body, and in true marriage there is unity of the two. Leaders form bodies of supporters, Alexandria as a large city has the rest of Egypt as its body, and the body of the Nile (i.e., its main mass) flows straight. Plutarch uses *sṓma* for the trunk, the body, the person as an object of desire, and the human ego. The elements are *sṓmata. sṓma* is three-dimensional, limited, and spatial. Yet the term can be positive as the visible embodiment of the idea, and body and soul together define humanity. The soul is free in contrast to the evil lusts of the body and should rule over the body. At death the soul parts from the body and achieves true freedom. Some souls are more immersed in the body than others. The idea of totality is still present, e.g., in regard to the body of music as distinct from individual sounds. Some bodies consist of independent parts, others of integrated parts. The cosmos is a perfect body with imperfect members. Plutarch also compares the state to a body.

5. The Post–NT Period. In this period the *sṓma* may still be the corpse, the trunk, or the whole body. Ulcers can be called *sṓmata,* and water, snow, and hail are *sṓmata.* Persons as objects, e.g., slaves, are *sṓmata.* Time may be understood as *sṓma,* but the Stoic view that souls and the gods, too, are *sṓmata* comes under attack. Human beings consist of body and soul, but the body is the lower part that defiles the soul. Even in the body, however, the soul is free. It slips out of the body at death and may even leave it in ecstasy, delirium, dreams, or trances. A phalanx forms a *sṓma,* and the vine as a body loses something when the branches exude sap. Intellectually the body represents a united whole. The cosmos is a body, ruled by divine reason, and both ingenerate and indestructible. Identification of the cosmos with God continues. The state also forms a body, but only later do we find the term with the genitive of the name of a people, and the use of *sṓmátion* for an association is later still.

[E. SCHWEIZER, VII, 1024-44]

B. The OT.

1. Hebrew Equivalents. Various words are rendered by *sṓma* in the LXX, including *bāśār* and *šeʾēr,* which normally mean "flesh," and *gewiyyâ* and *gešēm* (often corpse or carcass). (For details see *TNDT,* VII, 1044-45.)

2. *The LXX Translation.* For the various terms the LXX normally uses *sárx* or *sṓma*, but also at times *nekrós* etc. (For details see *TDNT,* VII, 1045.)

[F. BAUMGÄRTEL, VII, 1044-45]

3. *LXX Works with Hebrew Originals.* There is no fixed LXX rendering for the Hebrew terms. Thus for *bāśār sṓma* replaces *sárx* about one out of seven times, especially when human totality is in view as an object of suffering (Job 7:5). One can make cuttings in the body as in the flesh (Lev. 19:28; 21:5). The sex organ is perhaps meant in Lev. 6:3. For other Hebrew terms the *sṓma* may be the corpse. *sṓma* also denotes the person as an object or with reference to sickness, corruptibility, healing, and resurrection. At times the LXX deviates from the Hebrew (cf. Job 6:4; 33:17, 24). In Prov. 25:20, perhaps through a slip, the *sṓma* is the seat of passion that troubles the heart.

4. *Works Not in the Hebrew Canon.*

a. *sṓma* is used for a healthy or sick body in Sir. 30:14ff., a cursed body in 51:2, a branded body in 3 Macc. 2:29, a corpse in Sir. 38:16. 2 Macc. 7:7 refers to the torment of the body and the torturing of its members. A good name survives the body (Sir. 41:11). A woman's body is the object of desire (Sir. 7:24), and passion burns in the body (23:17).

b. Body and soul constitute the whole person either to make up a third entity or with the soul as the true ego. The righteous hazard both in martyrdom. Both body and *pneúma* come under oppression (4 Macc. 11:11). At times only the body is passive, whereas the soul voluntarily accepts pain. Hence persecutors can attack the body but not the soul, which is God's true gift (4 Macc. 10:4; 13:13).

c. *sṓma* and *psyché* are parallel in Wis. 1:4 but complementary in 8:20. *sophía* is distinct from both, and so is *logismós* in 4 Macc. 1:20ff., although *sṓma* alone is its opposite in 1:35. The *logismós* can and must overcome the *sṓma* when it is subjected to bodily pain (4 Macc. 3:18; 6:7; 10:19-20).

5. The term *sṓma* offers a concept that is not yet developed in Hebrew and hence the translators use it with some hesitation. In the LXX it never refers to an inorganic body, nor to reality as distinct from words, nor to a macro- or microcosmic organism, nor to a city or people. Unlike *sárx,* it does not have the intrinsic character of creatureliness or sin or earthliness. It can denote the person as object (e.g., in enumeration), and it also suggests the human totality with a sense of corporeality, e.g., in pain, sickness, sexuality, death, or resurrection. *sṓma* does not occur in relation to sacrifice or to activity but in relation to God, to others, or to various forces. The person does not stand aloof from the *sṓma*. Soul and body together describe corruptible humanity over against wisdom or reason, but anthropological dualism arises only when soul or reason is set in juxtaposition to the body, e.g., when the body is abandoned to death but the true I survives.

C. Judaism.

1. *Apocrypha and Pseudepigrapha.*

a. *sṓma* denotes a human or animal body, often a corpse. It is also a numerical unit. As a living body it is subject to pain, sickness, death, and self-mortification, but is also an object of care. Its beauty is extolled but it is open to temptation. One commits adultery with it, and yet it is a temple of the Spirit. Distinction is made between body and head or members, and the idea of the body as a microcosm occurs, with the head as heavenly director.

b. Body and soul belong together. God's people are holy in both, and the patriarchs

1143

go up to heaven with both. Both may perish at God's glance. Yet death also separates them—the soul going to heaven, the body to earth. At times we find a trinity of spirit, soul, and body. The soul leaves the body in a trance. The body is like a garment. A new mode of being begins with the new body.

c. Only late instances of the corporate use occur, e.g., the cosmos as a body, the cosmic body of Adam, and the idea of the assuming of Adam's body by the Christ or its taking up to heaven at the resurrection.

2. Philo.

a. Philo uses *sōma* for the human or animal body or corpse. He sees in the *sōma* a totality in which the parts work harmoniously, although usually in a figure of speech for the cosmos or society. Physical union may also be denoted by *sōma*, but this is less important than spiritual union, just as more harm is done to the soul than to the body in adultery.

b. The body has relative importance inasmuch as with the soul it constitutes the person. It must be pure and healthy. The sabbath and fasting serve both body and soul. The body is the soul's house, temple, or brother. Yet the soul remains young when the body ages. The divine *logismós* is a third thing alongside soul and body in the form of *noús* or *pneúma*. Only in virtue of *noús* are people in God's image. Those who live only by body and soul are not authentically human. True humanity lies in noncorporeal *noús*. Only those who withdraw from body to *noús* are capable of vision. Yet the idea is present that the soul itself is really noncorporeal and has come into the body as into an alien land. Thus the *sōma* offers the soul the possibility of choice between alliance with the body or with virtue, which is the true marriage. The body is a tomb or prison, and the soul is bound to it, as a kind of corpse-bearer, during earthly life. Yet ascetics will live for the soul, not the body, and at death the soul will leave the body and return to unity from the duality of soul and body.

c. *diánoia* serves as the head of the soul. The cosmos is a large-scale body that contains all other bodies as members. As the soul dwells in the body and *noús* in the soul, so heaven dwells in earth and God in heaven. The world soul rules the cosmos. The *lógos,* with God as father and wisdom as mother, puts on the cosmos as a garment and holds it together. There is a *noētós kósmos* corresponding to God's thoughts or plan. On the one hand, then, God encompasses all things; on the other the world soul permeates the body and holds it together. Philo also uses body as a metaphor for a city or people.

d. Finally we find in Philo the use of *sōma* for inorganic bodies. Such bodies are objects with shadows. Yet bodies may also be mere wording as distinct from ideas. Over against bodies are incorporeal ideas. These may be present even prior to the bodies they represent; this explains prophecy. God himself is the incorporeal location of incorporeal ideas, a *tópos* not filled by a *sōma*.

e. Philo's view of *sōma* is under strong Greek influence, e.g., in the use for an inorganic body, which is quite alien to the LXX, or in the more emphatic relating of *sōma* to the individual, not to the world or to God. The latter emphasis leads to such ideas as that of the body as a prison for the soul, which is the only essential content, or the notion of a third and transcendent element over against both body and soul which dwells within us but is not as such a human faculty or possibility.

3. Josephus. Josephus uses *sōma* for the strong or weak human body which needs care and exercise, for the corpse, for the slave, and for the whole body as distinct from the *sárx*. Comparisons of a phalanx or country to a body bring out the unity; Jerusalem as capital is like the head of a body, and alienated parties, when reconciled, become a single body. Body and soul are friends in Josephus; hence suicide is especially heinous. If the soul is purified by righteousness, the body may be sanctified by washing. Yet Josephus can also call the soul a divine deposit in the body which leaves the body at death and gains a new body in heaven. Using the body as its instrument, the soul can do a great deal even while chained to it. Yet as the soul returns to God in sleep, so it should seek to be loosed from the body. The body, then, tends to be seen as the abode of the soul, which alone constitutes the true ego.

D. The NT.

I. Books apart from Paul.

1. In these works there are only 51 instances as compared to 91 in Paul, in whom the word acquires its true content. A first meaning is the traditional one of corpse (e.g., the body of Jesus in Mk. 15:43 etc., of an animal in Lk. 17:37, of Moses in Jude 9). A dead *sŏma* can be raised again (Mt. 27:52). Jn. 2:21 relates the temple to the dead and resurrected body of Jesus.

2. The body experiences sickness, healing, etc. (Mk. 5:29) and needs food and clothing (Jms. 2:16). A technical formula occurs in Heb. 10:22.

3. The body is contrasted with the members in Mt. 5:29-30. Yet we have our true life in it as the I from which members may be severed for the good of the whole. If persecutors can kill only the body and not the soul, body and soul together may be cast into hell (Mt. 10:28).

4. Heb. 10:5ff. and 1 Pet. 2:24 refer to the body of Jesus that dies and rises again. A new point is that Jesus offers up his body in sacrifice, not because it counts for little compared to the immortal soul, but in service for others and to accomplish their salvation. This use perhaps rests on the eucharistic saying "This is my body" (Mk. 14:22 and par.). In this context *sŏma* (rather than *sárx*) goes with blood, possibly with the person of Jesus in view, and with a reference to the *sŏma* as that which suffers. Thus the meaning is that Jesus gives himself to his people as the one who dies for them and who concludes the covenant by his death. If a stress later falls on the body as such, body and blood originally denote the whole person of Jesus—body as the I in its totality, blood as the I that suffers death.

5. *somatikós* occurs only in Lk. 3:22 and 1 Tim. 4:8 with an emphasis on corporeality.

II. Paul.

1. Apart from the Concept of the Body of Christ.

a. Generally Accepted Epistles.

(a) Being outside the Body. Paul does not use *sŏma* for corpse or slave or as a complementary term for *psyché* in which the latter is the true ego. Even when he refers to being outside the body (2 Cor. 12:1ff.), he does so only under compulsion and with no intrinsic interest.

(b) Resurrection of the Body: Texts. The future life is bodily in 1 Cor. 15:35ff., but with a new corporeality and not just a new form. In 2 Cor. 5:1ff. we are tested and proved in or by the body but then are at home with the Lord in a new house that comes from God. In Phil. 3:21 the body of glory will replace the body of humiliation in union with Christ. In Rom. 8:11 God will raise up our mortal bodies (cf. 1 Cor. 6:14). Rom. 6:12 shows that we shall share in the resurrection, and 8:11 refers to redemption of the body, not from it.

(c) Resurrection of the Body: Theology. In 1 Cor. 15:35ff. life after death depends on the resurrection but as God's act, not as an ongoing of some part of the I. The same is true in 2 Cor. 5:1ff. and Rom. 6:12; 8:11 (also 1 Cor. 6:14). Awareness of the resurrection of the body implies responsibility regarding present life in the body. In Phil. 3:21 the term *sóma* enables Paul to define as strongly as possible our association with Christ. As participation in Christ's resurrection, the resurrection is a blessing of salvation. The judgment involved in 1 Cor. 3:12ff. is one which condemns or praises the works of those raised up to life.

(d) The Body in Sex Life. The *sóma* is the organ of generation which engages in sex (1 Cor. 7:4) and may be defiled thereby (Rom. 1:24). In sex the body belongs to another (1 Cor. 6:16) but may also be possessed by fornication (6:13). The use of *sóma* rather than *sárx* here shows that the totality of the person is meant.

(e) The Corinthian Spiritualizers. The term *sóma* occurs 56 times in 1 and 2 Corinthians in opposition to a group that stresses the spirit. The *sóma* is the present body (1 Cor. 5:3), which may be hurt or scarred (cf. Gal. 6:17), which must be kept undefiled (1 Cor. 7:34), and which should manifest the life and dying of Jesus (2 Cor. 4:10). The apostle buffets it so as to set it in Christ's service (1 Cor. 9:27).

(f) Indicative and Imperative. In Rom. 12:1 *sóma* appears where imperatives replace indicatives; it is the place of *logiké latreía*. The same is true in Rom. 6:12ff. Christ is magnified in Paul's body in Phil. 1:20. We praise God in the body, the temple of the Spirit (1 Cor. 6:12ff.), which belongs either to God or to sin. In 1 Cor. 6:19 the body is God's because he has bought it back as well as made it. It had become the body of sin or of death (Rom. 6:6; 7:24), and could even be equated with sin (8:13), but in believers it is now a member of Christ and set in his service. Denoting the whole person, *sóma* may be rendered "personality" or "individuality," but such terms miss the relationship to God, sin, and others that is implicit for Paul. The imperatives maintain the totality in which thought, feeling, experience, and action can no longer be sundered.

b. Colossians and Ephesians. In Colossians the body of Christ is predominant. The term *sóma* is neutral in 2:23, and "of sin" is added in 1:22 and 2:11. 2:17 contrasts the body of Christ with the shadow, and hence has the reality in view.

2. *The Body of Christ.*

a. Generally Accepted Epistles.

(a) Given for Us. In Rom. 7:4 (cf. Col. 1:22) the body of Christ is that which is offered up for us on the cross.

(b) Eucharistic Texts. This is also the point in 1 Cor. 11:24 with a stress on the act rather than the substance. The crucified body is present at the eucharist in the blessings that flow therefrom (10:16) and in the claim to lordship that it raises (11:27ff.). The reference to the Lord's body and blood in 11:27 echoes 10:16-17 but has the sense of 8:12: A sin against other believers for whom Christ died is a sin against Christ. Since *sóma* refers to the whole sacrificial act, the *sóma* is not just past. The Lord's exalted body is his crucified body in its ongoing operation.

(c) The Community as the Body of Christ: Figurative Sayings. The community is the body in 1 Cor. 12:27. This fact rules out feelings of inferiority or superiority, since each member needs the others, and all belong together. In Rom. 12:5 the community is a body in Christ. It must live out what it is already in and by him, i.e., by incorporation into the history determined by him.

(d) The Community as the Body of Christ: Stricter Sayings. In 1 Cor. 10:16 fellowship at the Supper is fellowship with Christ; the many are one body. In 6:15 believers are one spirit with Christ as members of Christ; this is what rules out bodily union with others in fornication. In 12:12-13 various renderings are possible but "so Christ" makes sense only if the one body is Christ's (cf. vv. 13, 27). The comparison in Jn. 15:1 offers a parallel. The community achieves unity in the crucified and risen body of Christ.

(e) The Unity of Patriarch and People as a Model. Paul sees in Christ the eschatological Adam (Rom. 5:12ff.; 1 Cor. 15:21-22, 45). Later Judaism links the destiny of the race and eschatological expectation in Adam. Christ as the eschatological Adam is a universalistic variation on this theme. God's deed in Christ is determinative for all who believe in him. This rather than consubstantiality bridges time. All the community's life is shaped by this act. The crucified body in its ongoing work is the risen body, and by integration into this body the community is Christ's body.

(f) Associations of *sōma*. The term *sōma* suggests a true bodily, though not physical, union. Not used in soteriological passages, *sōma* does not denote a fellowship that is more real than justification. It stresses that the unity manifests itself in common life and relationships. We meet others in our corporeality. But since Christ's body is given for us, the term also carries for Paul the thought of the body in which we serve others, or Christ serves them in us.

(g) The Body of Christ and the People of God. At root these two concepts are one; there is merely a shift of categories. Yet the shift of categories is important. The idea of God's people stresses historical development. That of Christ's body stresses the present character of God's saving act, the present union with the risen Lord, and the equality of the ministry of the members. Neither term is conceivable in Paul without the other.

b. Colossians.

(a) Cosmic Understanding. This aspect occurs only in v. 18 in what is perhaps a quotation from a Christian hymn that seeks to allay the cosmic anxieties of the readers. In the hymn Christ replaces wisdom in vv. 15-18, but it is as the head of his body, the church, that he reconciled all things in heaven and on earth (vv. 18-20).

(b) Correction. In v. 22 it is made plain that Christ's body is the crucified body, and in v. 24 this soteriological reference is given an ecclesiological orientation; the body embraces the church rather than the universe (cf. 1:18; 3:15). Cosmic reconciliation comes about through the universal preaching of the gospel (1:6) and the resultant unveiling of the eschatological mystery (1:26). Christ as head is here the controlling member (cf. the LXX and Philo). He has disarmed all opposing forces at the cross (2:10, 14-15), and he so rules the church as his body that it is summoned to obedience and service. In this way the power of growth flows from him to the church and thence to the world. As head, he is also distinct from the body; it must hold fast to him (2:19). The fullness that dwells in Christ is that of God, not of the cosmos (2:19). The *sōmatikōs* in this statement denotes the corporeality in which God encounters us in our world, i.e., the real humanity of Jesus, not a humanity that is a mere cloak for deity.

c. Ephesians.

(a) In Ephesians, as in Colossians, the crucifixion is the decisive saving event (2:14). *sōma* is thus the crucified body in 2:16. It is in the one body that the one new man is created. Unity in the body means unity with others.

(b) The *sōma,* then, is the church in which original aliens and enemies are now united with Israel (2:12ff.; cf. 1:23; 4:4, 12, 15-16; 5:23, 30).

(c) As Christ's body the church is the fullness of him who fills all in all (1:23)— the cosmic dimension. Growth through the preaching of the gospel brings to manifestation what already is (cf. 2:17). The church even bears the message to demonic powers (3:10). Its growth is that of a temple or building as God's dwelling. It permeates the cosmos in the new sense of a penetration that seizes control.

(d) Christ as head stands in contrast with the church but as the one from whom it derives its life and growth (4:16).

(e) In 5:23ff. the concept of the sacred marriage is present but with Christ as the eschatological Adam. The idea of the church as his body parallels the idea of the woman as the man's body (5:28). Gen. 2:24 provides not only the command that underlies the exhortation but also the saving fact on which it rests, the christologically understood indicative that demands the ethical imperative. That Christ is the savior shows that what is at issue is not just traditional superordination but a relation in which life comes to the body from the head.

d. *sýssōmos*. This word, found only in Christian writings, is so unusual that in Eph. 3:6 it catches up 2:16 in an intentional emphasis on the relation to Christ's body.

e. Distinctives. The new problem is that of an alien cosmos. Since the solution does not lie merely in creation-mediation, the universal church comes to the fore rather than the local church with its questions of mutual service. Christ is one with the church but also its head. His body now is the church moving out into the world with the gospel as the answer to cosmic anxiety. In this way Christ permeates the cosmos. This is the eschatological event which discloses the hitherto concealed mystery and fulfils God's plan of salvation.

III. Survey of the Historical Development. An interesting linguistic development comes to a head in Colossians and Ephesians. Hebrew has no special term for body, and Greek-speaking Jews must choose between *sárx* and *sṓma*. Paul adopts *sṓma* as a term for our creatureliness, for the place where we live, believe, and serve. For Paul, however, *sṓma* also means relationship with God and others rather than self-contained individuality. If the community as Christ's body is a self-contained unit, it is so only in mutual service as the body of the crucified Lord. As it grows in the world, in and by it Christ himself penetrates the cosmos. The NT, then, reconstructs the *sṓma* concept by putting it in the service of him who gave his body for the world and who in his body, the church, is still seeking the world.

E. The Post – NT Period.

1. The Apostolic Fathers.

a. *sṓma* means "corpse" in, e.g., Ignatius *Romans* 4.2; Mart. Pol. 17, "living (but weak) body" in Hermas *Visions* 3.11.4, "perishing body" in Hermas *Visions* 3.9.3. It forms a whole in Ignatius *Romans* 5.3. To be without it is demonic (Ignatius *Smyrneans* 2.1). In Mart. Pol. 19.2 the soul is the primary object of Christ's saving work, though there is no disparagement of the body. The soul permeates the whole body in Diog. 6.1ff.; so Christians should permeate society.

b. Pol. 8.1 quotes 1 Pet. 2:24 with reference to the crucified body. Ignatius *Smyrneans* 3.2 presupposes bodily resurrection. 1 Clem. 37.5 applies the metaphor of the body to believers as members (cf. Pol. 11:4; Ignatius *Smyrneans* 11.2). Yet there are few references to the body of Christ even if it is seen as natural that believers have a common body in the church and that the union of Jews and Gentiles is a decisive sign set up by Christ's resurrection. 2 Clem. 14.2ff. calls the living church Christ's *sṓma*; Christ is the *pneúma* and the church the *sárx*. In Ignatius Christ is the new man (*Ephesians* 20.1) and believers are his members (*Trallians* 11.2).

2. *Apologists.*

a. *sṓma* is the "animal body" in Justin *Dialogue* 31.3, the "corpse" in Aristides *Apology* 5.3, the (sick) "body" in Justin *Dialogue* 69.7, which alone ritual washings can affect (14.1). God will resurrect bodies (Justin *Apology* 18.6). God created them (Justin *Dialogue* 62.3), but noncorporeal beings come first (Athenagoras *Supplication* 36.2-3). Soul and body constitute humanity. Christ becomes body, *lógos,* and soul (Justin *Apology* 10.1). Both soul and body come into judgment (8.4). Christologically *sṓma* is less common than *sárx* but it is parallel to blood in the eucharistic sayings (66.3). Composed of the members, it denotes the church (*Dialogue* 42.3), the cosmos (Tatian *Address to the Greeks* 12.2), or God (Athenagoras *Supplication* 8.1).

c. Only Justin *Dialogue* 5.2 uses *sṓma* for an inorganic body.

3. *Gnosticism.*

a. In some Gnostic works the body is neutral. The *noús* may use it as an instrument of knowledge and Christ's resurrection body is perfect. Elsewhere the world is viewed as a corpse and there is a polemic against the bodily resurrection of Jesus. If Adam's body is suitably fashioned, only the *pneúma* enables him to move and makes him a living soul. True humanity, which is immortal, differs from the mortal body, which is its grave. In some systems what is perfect and immortal is separate from the mortal *sṓma,* which is made from the *stoicheía* and is subject to conflict. The Valentinians suppose that the demiurge creates bodies in which souls and heavenly *lógoi* dwell. Jesus has his body from the demiurge but his true essence from wisdom. Other views attribute the soul to the demiurge, the body to the earth, and the *pneúma* to wisdom. In such systems the body is doomed to destruction; baptism alters only the soul. A distinction is also made between *noús* and *sṓma*; authentic humanity is associated only with the *noús,* although not without the possibility of a new and immortal body. The Manichees, too, view the body negatively as the prison of the soul and the essence of desire. The idea of transmigration is a common one. The incarnation causes problems for Gnostics. They try to solve it by dividing up Christ, by attributing to him a psychic body, by denying the reality of the body, or by saying that he comes both with and without the body.

b. Body Embracing the Redeemed. The idea of the cosmic body occurs, but the use for the body of the redeemed is problematical prior to the Manichees. One passage might refer either to the incarnate body or to the resurrection body including the elect as a kind of garment. When Gnostics refer to a gigantic invisible Christ, they have his universal saving significance in view.

c. Summary. In Gnosticism as we know it thus far the idea of the body as a prison of the soul is common, but so is the tendency to view body and soul together as the earthly element in distinction from a divine factor (wisdom), which returns with the redeemer. Wisdom might then be equated with the OT *lógos* and combined with the idea of the supreme God who permeates and controls the cosmic body. It might also be loosely connected with the primal man. Where speculation on the primal man is important, the thought is that real man is trapped in matter, or in the body-soul. This constitutes the fall, which is repeated in the fall of the soul into the body. The real fault is not disobedience but forgetting the divine element. The revealer brings this element to light and thus opens the way to redemption by regeneration. The idea that the saved are a body occurs at most only in the very weakened form in which the divine wisdom that comes in the redeemer is linked to the particles of divine wisdom that humanity still bears.   [E. SCHWEIZER, VII, 1045-94]

---

sōreúō [to heap up],   *episōreúō* [to heap on to]

A. The Greek World.
1. *sōreúō*, a rare word, means "to pile or heap up," either "to pile one thing on another" or "to fill up."
2. The compound *episōreúō* means "to heap on to."

B. Hellenistic Judaism.
1. In the LXX *sōreúō* occurs only in Prov. 25:22 and Jdt. 15:11. *ho sōrós* is more common for a "heap" of stones, a "pile" of fruit, or a burial "mound." In Prov. 25:22 the background may be the custom whereby the guilty carry glowing coals in a brazier on their heads. The idea is plainly that the wise repay evil with good. In Jdt. 15:11 Judith packs the loot in her chariot. The compound does not occur in the LXX, but Σ has it in Job 14:17 (storing up) and Cant. 2:4 (covering).
2. Philo does not use the group but Josephus uses *sōreúō* for the heaping up of bones (*Antiquities* 12.211) or of corpses (*Jewish War* 6.431).

C. The NT.
1. The simple form occurs in the NT only twice. Paul in Rom. 12:20 quotes Prov. 25:21-22. The context shows plainly that the idea is that of vanquishing hostility by love. In 2 Tim. 3:6 we have a transferred sense. False teachers ensnare women who are laden with sins and swayed by desires.
2. The compound occurs in the NT only in 2 Tim. 4:3 in a transferred sense. In the last days people will heap up teachers according to their own liking. The term stresses ironically the superficiality of their desire for knowledge.

D. The Apostolic Fathers. The compound occurs once in Barn. 4.6, which warns the readers not to add new sin by adopting a false view of the covenant.

[F. LANG, VII, 1094-96]

---

sṓphrōn [of sound mind],   *sōphronéō* [to be of sound mind],   *sōphronízō* [to bring someone to his senses],   *sōphronismós* [moderate, self-disciplined], *sōphrosýnē* [moderation, self-control]

---

sṓphrōn, sōphronéō, sōphrosýnē.

A. The Group in Greek.
1. Etymology, Occurrence, and Meaning. sṓphrōn means first "of sound mind." Etymology is of little help in translation. The term has such nuances as "rational" (intellectually sound), "rational" (without illusion), "rational" (purposeful), "moderate," "prudent," "modest," "restrained," and "disciplined."
2. sōphrosýnē. The reference in this word is to a basic attitude that leads to certain modes of conduct. A link with *aidṓs* may be seen. Proper conduct rooted in *aidṓs* is marked by restraint or modesty as distinct from *hýbris*. With *dikaiosýnē, sōphrosýnē* is a leading civic virtue. It has central significance for an aristocratic manner of life. Plato adopts various definitions but the term is broader than all of them. Politically it is the agreement of the three classes as to who should rule and it thus represents restraint. Where it combines with power and reason, we have the best ingredients for a good constitution. For Aristotle it is the mean between license and stupidity. In

Stoicism it is one of the cardinal virtues which by way of Hellenistic Judaism influence the early church. In popular lists of virtues it is a virtue of rulers, of professional people, and of women; it can become the equivalent of chastity.

B. The LXX and Hellenistic Judaism.
1. The group occurs in the LXX only in Greek works or those displaying Hellenistic influence. In Wis. 9:11 it is one of the cardinal virtues that are traced back to wisdom. In 4 Maccabees instruction in the law makes the cardinal virtues possible (cf. 2:16, 18; 3:17, 19).
2. The Testaments of the Twelve gives evidence of Stoic influence in a demand for *sōphronein* that implies ascetic and dualistic tendencies (abstinence, chastity, etc.).
3. Josephus uses the group in the common sense.
4. For Philo *sōphrosýnē* is one of the classical virtues. It is the mean between frivolity and covetousness and battles against lasciviousness. With other virtues it has its origin in paradise. The brazen serpent is *sōphrosýnē*. Those who look on it see God; it thus makes possible the vision of God. With other virtues, it is not just a human attitude, but strictly a divine gift.

C. The NT and Apostolic Fathers.
1. In the NT the group occurs only 14 times (eight in the Pastorals). It is usually of little material significance. In Mk. 5:15, for example, a sign of the healing of the demoniac is that he is in his right mind, and in Acts 26:25 Paul answers the charge of mania by arguing that he speaks sober truth, or true and rational words.
2. Paul makes a play on words in Rom. 12:3 when he tells his readers to think of themselves with sober judgment according to the measure of faith (*sōphronein*, not *hyperphronein*). He expands the thought in 12:16. Christian *sōphrosýnē* is *tapeinophrosýnē* (Phil. 2:3). Paul avoids the term in lists of virtues (cf. 1 Th. 2:10), but in 2 Cor. 5:14 he contrasts the conduct of the pneumatics with *sōphronéō*; sober devotion to others corresponds to ecstasy before God.
3. 1 Pet. 4:7 warns the community not to give way to eschatological frenzy in face of the imminent end of things. To do so is to fall victim to the world. The required moderation is sustained by faith and issues in prayer and love (v. 8). More than the philosophical attitude is thus at issue.
4. The Pastorals use the group to describe Christian life in the world (cf. Tit. 2:12). It occurs in the list of virtues in Tit. 2:2. Faith manifests itself in a proper attitude to the world and its goods (1 Tim. 4:3ff.), i.e., one of moderation and content (1 Tim. 6:6ff.; cf. 2:15). Chastity and self-discipline are the point in Tit. 2:5. *sōphrosýnē* is an important requirement in officebearers (1 Tim. 3:2; Tit. 1:8). Respectability is not the concern, but an avoidance of ecstatic misunderstandings and dualistic tendencies, and the adoption of a proper relation to the world in the light of postponement of the parousia. The apostolic fathers follow a similar pattern.

D. The Early Church. The common equation of *sōphrosýnē* with chastity occurs in Justin *Apology* 14.2; Tatian *Address to the Greeks* 32.2. Justin also uses the group to show the rational character of faith in *Apology* 13.2ff. Prayer for rulers is prayer for their right understanding of Christianity in 17.3. Only a *sōphrōn logismós* can keep Christians from error or apostasy.

sōphronízō.
1. This word means "to bring someone to reason or to duty," but it may also mean "to exhort," "to spur on."

2. Tit. 2:4 asks the older women to spur on the younger to worthy conduct.

3. The passive in Justin *Apology* 1.2 means "to be set right" in respect of a fault and in 2.2 it means "to attain to a morally suitable life."

sōphronismós.

1. This late word means literally "making understanding or wise," then "admonition," also "discretion," "moderation," "discipline."

2. In 2 Tim. 1:7 God has given a spirit of power, love, and *sōphronismós,* which in context denotes a regulated life. The term has a Hellenistic flavor, but it is here understood in terms of the Spirit.   [U. LUCK, VII, 1097-1104]

τ *t*

tágma → *tássō*

---

tapeinós [humble], **tapeinóō** [to humble], **tapeínōsis** [humility],
tapeinóphrōn [humble], **tapeinophrosýnē** [humility]

A. The Greek and Hellenistic World.

1. Derivation and Meaning. Research has yielded no plain results. The basic sense seems to be "low."

2. tapeinós.

a. This word has such senses as "lowly," "mean," "insignificant," "weak," and "poor." It may be used of a city, country, state, or statesman, of a star, a river, goods, influence, etc. The condition may be intrinsic or due to the acts of others.

b. When used of the spiritual or moral state, the term means "lowly" or "servile," usually with the disparaging sense of obsequiousness or submissiveness. Although Socrates teaches that anyone can attain to a high and free disposition, Aristotle argues that whatever prevents the development of virtue makes the spirit *tapeinós.* Epictetus espouses worldly citizenship in spite of differences of status but *tapeinós* is still a negative term for him, denoting pettiness and baseness of disposition.

c. *tapeinós* can express a difficult situation or lowly status, e.g., that of the petitioner. The person who is *tapeinós* easily becomes a flatterer. When abasement is that of wickedness or immoderation, it can have positive meaning but it is not in itself a positive good. The Greeks resist prostration before rulers and the humiliation of children in view of their dislike of abasement.

d. Yet *tapeinós* can sometimes mean "modest" or "obedient" and in this sense be good, e.g., in subjects, soldiers, or children.

e. Oceanus demands that Prometheus be *tapeinós* relative to the gods. The idea is not that he should be humble but that he should adjust himself to them.

3. tapeinóō.

a. This verb means "to make small," "to humiliate," "to weaken."

b. It also takes on the senses "to oppress," "to exploit," "to break the spirit." The idea of self-belittling is abhorrent. Those who disparage themselves simply show how weak and poor they are. A positive sense occurs relative to humbling the self before the gods—a possible explanation of the custom of covering the head in sacrifice and prayer.

4. tapeínōsis. This word means "reduction," e.g., of a swelling, of people by fate (cf. also "depression" of mind).

5. tapeinóphrōn, tapeinophrosýnē.

a. The first of these two terms means "poor-spirited."

b. Epictetus uses the second term (*Dissertationes* 3.24.56) in the sense of a "petty disposition" or "pusillanimity."

6. Meaning of the Derivatives. The derivatives confirm the meaning and the negative usage of *tapeinós,* although they also acquire the sense of obedient integration into a given order and even of subjection to deity.

B. The LXX.

1. Hebrew Originals. In the LXX *tapeinós* and derivatives are more common than in secular Greek. *tapeinós* occurs 67 times and *tapeinóō* 165 times for various Hebrew stems. The prominence of the verb shows that the main reference is to an action rather than a state, and the chief Hebrew originals confirm this. Thus the group *'ānâ* has the basic sense of "stooping," "bowing down," and then "humbling oneself" (or "being humbled" by sickness, poverty, want, etc.). From this we get such senses as humility, modesty, subservience, compliance, and affliction.

2. tapeinóō.

a. This word means "to bow down," "to make low," "to humble."

b. Another sense is "to bend," "to oppress," "to harass," "to weaken," "to destroy," "to force" (also sexually).

c. *tapeinóō emautón* or the middle passive means "to abase oneself," "to cast oneself down." In fasting people humble themselves before God, but the OT never glorifies such self-abasement, stressing instead the humble attitude of the heart (cf. Prov. 25:7; Joel 2:12-13; Is. 58:5ff.).

d. God lays low the mighty and exalts the lowly (1 Sam. 2:7; Ezek. 21:31). This applies both to Israel and to her foes, and also to individuals. Is. 2:11 states the principle. The prophets direct it against Jerusalem and Zion (Is. 3:8). Ps. 75:8 says plainly that the Lord puts down one and lifts up another. Yet while sickness humbles and death brings down to the dust, God does not reject those who humble themselves before him (Pss. 44:25; 51:17). God may humble individuals so as to put them in a right relationship to himself (Ps. 116:6). Hence abasement can mean salvation (Ps. 119:71). The great need is to see God's purpose and find a relation of obedience to the commandment. God abases, but when the humbled repent, the affliction ceases (1 Kgs. 8:35-36).

3. tapeinós.

a. This first means "low," "flat."

b. It then means "bowed down," "small," "base," "insignificant" in a negative sense. God chooses the insignificant for his plans (Judg. 6:15; 1 Sam. 18:23). The *tapeinoí* are those who keep God's statutes (Ps. 119:67). God leaves in Israel a humble and lowly people that seeks his name (Zeph. 3:12).

c. Another meaning is "oppressed," "held down," e.g., by foreign powers or by the wealthy. In this sense poverty and lowliness are related.

d. God, however, exalts those who are outwardly or inwardly oppressed (Pss. 18:27; 34:18). It is God's eternal nature to look on the lowly (Ps. 138:6). He does not despise their prayer (Ps. 102:17). The Messiah will establish right for the meek and pronounce sentence for the oppressed (Is. 11:4). The Lord has made Zion a refuge for the oppressed (Is. 14:32; cf. 25:4). Is. 49:13 speaks similarly. God's covenant of peace is forever with the lowly (54:10-11). He has regard to the humble and contrite in spirit (66:2).

4. tapeínōsis. This word means "humble situation," "lowliness," "sorrow." The lowly or difficult situation might be that of Israel (Dt. 26:7) or of individuals (Gen. 16:11). Ps. 10:14 refers to the *tapeínōsis* brought on by enemies. In Ps. 90:3 it is the destiny of death whose cause is sin (Ps. 25:18). In it God's word leads to life (Ps. 119:153). One should handle with patience those who thus undergo oppression (Prov. 16:19). The Servant undergoes it in Is. 53:8. This is a reason for his exaltation (cf. vv. 7, 10ff.).

5. The Greek and Biblical Understanding. The Greek view of humanity exalts freedom and thus despises subjection. Hence it qualifies *tapeinós* negatively. The Bible sets humanity under God and thus extols obedient service. Hence it gives the *tapeinós* group a positive sense.

C. Judaism.

1. Qumran and Apocalyptic.

a. The Qumran sectaries call themselves the poor, thus stressing their dependence on God and also their election. Their rule demands humility toward one another as well as God. They are also to be humble before the mighty but with concealed hostility.

b. Some passages from the Testaments of the Twelve speak about the abasement that goes with conversion. *tapeínōsis* is the conversion of the heart accompanied by fasting. As subjection to God it must also be shown to priests and to others.

c. Apocalyptic displays a similar spirit. Those who humble themselves receive greater honor. The hearts of the rich convict them as sinners who tread down the lowly. There will finally be an eschatological humbling of the earth by plagues.

2. Rabbinic Writings. The rabbis attach great value to humility. If keeping the law leads to it, it is also needed to attain and retain knowledge of the law. If any become proud of this, God humbles them, but if they repent, he raises them up again. Humility means modesty in relation to others. Long-suffering goes with subjection of heart. The rabbis accuses Christians of pride, but Christians reverse the charge, claiming that rabbinic practice does not accord with theory.

3. Hellenistic Judaism.

a. The Epistle of Aristeas advises travelers to be humble on the twofold ground that God accepts the humble and others are usually gracious to them.

b. Philo uses the group in the Greek sense but also adopts biblical insights. Abasement is an essential transition into God's presence. Persuasion of human pettiness brings appreciation of the divine majesty.

c. Josephus uses the group negatively in the Greek senses of "baseness," "pettiness," "poor-spiritedness," and also in the sense of "abasement" or "humiliation."

D. The NT.

1. Occurrence of the Group in the NT. In the NT *tapeinós* occurs eight times, *tapeinóō* 14, *tapeínōsis* four, *tapeinophrosýnē* seven, and *tapeinóphrōn* once. In all there are 34 instances, 13 of which are in Pauline works, but none in the Johannine material, Mark, Hebrews, Jude, 2 Peter, or the Pastorals.

2. tapeinóō.

a. Lk. 3:5 extends the quotation from Is. 40:3ff.; we see from 1:48, 52 that the saying is taken figuratively.

b. Jesus states that those who exalt themselves will be abased and those who abase themselves will be exalted (Mt. 23:12; Lk. 14:11; 18:14). The form of the saying is Jewish, the OT supplies the content, and the rabbis offer parallels. The future passive conceals the name of God. The placing of the saying (e.g., in Lk. 14:11) shows that humility before God is at issue. In Lk. 18:14 the humility of the publican sets him in a right relation to God. Mt. 18:4 adds the special nuance that abasement before God means becoming a child before him. Jesus does not demand visible self-abasement (cf. Mt. 6:16ff.; Mk. 2:18-19) but a total trust in God that expects everything from him and nothing from self.

c. Paul in 2 Cor. 10:1 faces the accusation that he has a servile disposition because he refuses support from the church. In answer he argues that his self-abasement is for the church's exaltation (11:7). On his coming he fears fresh humiliation unless there be conversion (12:19ff.), not merely through contempt but through the threat to his reputation. In Phil. 4:12-13, however, he knows how to handle abasement as well as abundance through Christ's strengthening. In this regard he follows the Lord who humbled himself and was thus highly exalted (2:7, 9). The reference here is first to a free self-emptying of the divine likeness and then to free obedience even to the death of the cross. At once historical and eschatological, this act is the governing factor in the Christian life.

d. Jms. 4:10, quoting Prov. 3:34 LXX, calls for submission to God and adds the promise of exaltation by him. In context the demanded submission is that of penitence. 1 Pet. 5:5-6, influenced by the same OT verse, calls for the subjection which means putting one's whole trust in the grace of the God who cares for those who humble themselves before him.

3. tapeinós.

a. Close to Lk. 3:5 is 1:52, which refers to God's eschatological work.

b. 1 Pet. 5:5 and Jms. 4:6 quote Prov. 3:34 LXX. They both use *ho theós* to show that the reference is not to Christ. Jms. 1:9 says that the lowly may boast in their exaltation, and the rich in their humiliation, in a reversal of worldly values (cf. Mt. 5:3; 11:5; Lk. 4:18; Jms. 2:5).

c. Applied to Paul in 2 Cor. 10:1, *tapeinós* has the derogatory Greek sense, but Paul makes the OT point that God comforts the humble (7:6). In Rom. 12:16 Paul exhorts to association with the lowly (or possibly to the acceptance of lowly services).

d. In Mt. 11:20 Jesus says that he himself is meek and lowly, not of necessity, but in free dedication to God (in heart), and in service to others (cf. Lk. 22:27; Mt. 20:28) as he gives himself to sinners and the despised.

4. tapeínōsis.

a. Philip in Acts 8:32ff. applies Is. 53:7-8 to Christ and his people as they move through humiliation to exaltation (cf. Lk. 9:22ff.; 12:49-50).

b. In Lk. 1:48 the reference is either to "childlessness" if Elizabeth is meant or "lowliness" if Mary is meant. On the latter view the choice of the humble Mary to give birth to God's Son exemplifies God's eschatological action in history.

c. Paul calls the present body the body of humiliation in Phil. 3:21. The point at issue is its subjection to death, which will be remedied when the body is fashioned afresh after Christ's risen body of glory.

d. In Jms. 1:10 the humiliation of the rich is the subjection to death that brings their affluence to nothing. The eschatological inversion of all things is already at work in the church.

5. *tapeinophrosýnē*.

a. In Phil. 2:4 Paul asks for the humility which takes the form of unselfishness, i.e., concern for the welfare of others. Christ's own self-giving provides the model as God in Christ takes us seriously and acts on our behalf. Only by a similar refraining from self-assertion can members of the church maintain its unity. Paul offers a personal example in Acts 20:19.

b. In Col. 2:18, 23 the term is a concept in the Colossian heresy and it either means "fasting" or "mortification," or else it implies the "inferiority" that leads to the cult of angels. Either way it involves cultic practice, not disposition. In contrast the reference in Col. 3:12 is to the new conduct of Christians toward others. The same applies in Eph. 4:2 with an emphasis on unity.

c. 1 Pet. 5:5 enjoins humility as a readiness for mutual service in the place ordained by God. This stands at the heart of the new Christian life in which the members all live for one another and for God.

6. *tapeinóphrōn*. 1 Pet. 3:8 concludes the detailed directions with the demand that all be of a humble mind. For true Christian fellowship it is essential that there be a humble readiness for service to others (cf. 5:5).

E. The Apostolic Fathers.

1. tapeinós. This term denotes the poor or oppressed in 1 Clem. 59.4. Esther's humility saves the people in 55.6. Barn. 3.3 quotes Is. 58:6-7.

2. tapeinóō. God's abasing and exalting is the theme in 1 Clem. 59.3ff. Barn. 4.4 quotes Dan. 7:24 and 4.5 quotes Dan. 7:7-8.

3. tapeínōsis. 1 Clem. 53.2 refers this term to Moses on the mount.

4. tapeinophronéō. This term denotes self-humbling, renunciation of sin, subjection to Scripture, and in Hermas *Similitudes* 7.6 humble and persevering submission to fasting and affliction.

5. tapeinophrosýnē. This term expresses the disposition in humbling. A lowly mind should mark officebearers (1 Clem. 44.3) and is a presupposition of effectual prayer (Hermas *Visions* 3.10.6).

6. tapeinophrónēsis. In Hermas this new word comes into use for subjection to God's commandments (cf. *Similitudes* 8.7.6).

7. tapeinóphrōn. 1 Clement uses this word as a noun for the humility of the fathers. Other references are Barn. 19.3; Ignatius *Ephesians* 10.2; Hermas *Mandates* 11.8.

8. The Shift in Sense. With the relaxing of eschatological tension humility becomes a disposition that produces penitence rather than an eschatological expectation and a manner of life under Christ's control. Hermas even equates humility with penitence and fasting. Jewish Christian influence and fear of moral decay in society and the church help to explain this decisive change.   [W. Grundmann, VIII, 1-26]

---

tássō [to order, determine],   *tágma* [order, rank],   *anatássō* [to arrange], *apotássō* [to depart],   *diatássō* [to order, direct],   *diatagḗ* [instruction, direction],   *epitagḗ* [command],   *prostássō* [to order, command],   *hypotássō* [to subject],   *hypotagḗ* [subjection],   *anypótaktos* [not subject],   *átaktos* [disordered],   *(atáktōs* [disorderly]) ,   *ataktéō* [to act disorderly]

---

tássō.

1. This word means "to appoint," "to order," with such nuances as "to arrange," "to determine," "to set in place," "to establish," and middle "to fix for oneself."

2. LXX senses are "to appoint," "to prohibit," "to ordain," "to set," "to draw up," and middle "to command," "to make disposition," "to fix," "to turn one's gaze," "to set one's heart," and "to make."

3. In the NT we find "to determine" in Acts 15:2, "to appoint" in 28:23, and "to order" in Mt. 28:16. God orders or appoints (passive voice) in Acts 22:10. Christians are ordained to eternal life in Acts 13:48; conferring of status rather than foreordination is the point. In Rom. 13:1 secular powers are instituted by God and hence have an authorization that believers must respect. The term *exousíai* in this verse is a common one for those in office but can also have the more general sense of authorities or powers. It includes the Roman state but also municipal authorities, with an emphasis on the administration of justice. Ruling powers might promote the pagan cultus, and might also abuse their authority, but they have a divine commission for the task they discharge, and hence they must be respected, as must obligations to them.

4. In the apostolic fathers the verb occurs four times. The stars are ordained by God in 1 Clem. 20.2, the times of cultic practice are set in 1 Clem. 40.1-2, angels are posted on the way of light in Barn. 18.1, and Mart. Pol. 10.2 echoes Rom. 13:1.

tágma.
1. This word usually means "what is fixed" or "ordered" and finds varied use for a set sum, a group, or a position or rank.

2. In the LXX it occurs in the sense of a "unit" (Num. 2:2ff.; 10:14ff.). It represents infantry in 1 Sam. 4:10, and camp is presupposed in 2 Sam. 23:13.

3. In the NT the only instance is in 1 Cor. 15:23, where the most likely meaning is "order," "position," "rank." Christ rises first, then his people at his coming, when they receive a new corporeality. Nothing is said about the rest.

4. In 1 Clem. 37.3; 41.1 we find the same phrase as in 1 Cor. 15:23. *tágma* means "group" in Hermas *Similitudes* 8.5.1ff., and Ignatius *Romans* 5.1 has *stratiōtikón tágma* for a detachment of soldiers.

anatássō. This rare verb means "to order fully," "to arrange." Lk. 1:1ff. refers to the orderly account of the things delivered by eyewitnesses. Putting down in writing necessarily confers order on what is at first oral tradition.

apotássō.
1. This term means "to delegate," "to assign," "to set aside," "to separate," "to part," "to leave," "to renounce."

2. In the LXX it means "to appoint," "to detach," "to separate."

3. The NT uses the middle "to part from" in Acts 18:18, 21; 2 Cor. 2:13, "to depart" in Mk. 6:46. Those who insist on parting from family before becoming disciples are not fit for the kingdom (Lk. 9:61-62). Jesus demands radical renunciation of possessions from intending disciples (Lk. 14:33).

4. In the apostolic fathers the word denotes full separation from wickedness (Hermas *Mandates* 6.2.9; 2 Clem. 6.4) or renunciation of life (Ignatius *Philadelphians* 11.1). In the Apologists Christians leave pagan wisdom (Tatian *Address to the Greeks* 1.3), idols (Justin *Apology* 49.5), and all things worldly (*Dialogue* 119.6).

diatássō.
1. This word means "to order," "to dispose," "to decide," "to establish," "to give directions."

2. The word is rare in the LXX, where it has such senses as "to order," "to arrange," "to allot," "to determine," "to measure," and "to command."

3. In the NT Jesus "directs" in Lk. 8:55, Paul arranges in Acts 20:13, Claudius orders in Acts 18.2, the officer gives instructions in Acts 23:31, the master commands in Lk. 17:9, God gives directions in Acts 7:44, Jesus instructs in Mt. 11:1, the Lord has commanded in 1 Cor. 9:14, and the apostle gives various directions in 1 Cor. 7:17; 11:34; 16:1. The sense is "to direct" in Tit. 1:5 and "to ordain" in Gal. 3:19, where the role of angels suggests that the law does not come directly from God, although God, of course, intends it.

4. In the apostolic fathers Ignatius uses the term relative to his own ordination (*Ephesians* 3.1; *Trallians* 3.3), 1 Clem. 43.1 says that Moses records what is ordained for him, and 1 Clem. 20.6 maintains that the sea does what God has appointed for it. In Diog. 7.2 heaven, earth, and sea are ordained by God.

diatagḗ.

1. This word means "instruction."

2. The only LXX instance is in 2 Esdr. 4:11.

3. In the NT Stephen in Acts 7:53 says that the Jews received the law as directions from angels and hence as God's instructions. In Rom. 13:2 to resist authority is to be in conflict with God's ordinance or appointment. The reference is to persistent resistance or resistance in principle. Not every decree of government is necessarily a divine ordinance.

4. In the apostolic fathers the only instance is in 1 Clem. 20.3, where the heavenly bodies follow their courses by divine "direction."

epitagḗ.

1. This word means "ordinance," "disposition," "order," or "statute."

2. In the LXX it denotes the ordinances of God in Wis. 18:15 and of a ruler in 14:17.

3. In the NT the term occurs only in the Pauline writings and mostly in the phrase *kat' epitagḗn,* which means "by command" or "at the behest." In 1 Cor. 7:25 the Lord's command decides; in contrast Paul's counsel is not by command. In 2 Cor. 8:8 "not by command" stresses the voluntary nature of the offering that Paul is commending. In Rom. 16:26 the proclamation of the mystery is by God's command, and by God's command Paul is entrusted with the preaching of the word (cf. 1 Tim. 1:1). The authority of the pastoral word is the point in Tit. 2:15.

prostássō.

1. This word means "to order," "to command," "to impart an ethical direction or norm" (Stoicism).

2. In the LXX God commands in Lev. 10:1, Moses in Ex. 36:6, rulers in 2 Chr. 31:13.

3. In the NT Peter orders baptism in Acts 10:48, Moses ordained statutes in Mk. 1:44, the angel gives instructions in Mt. 1:24, God has commanded Peter's preaching in Acts 10:33, and God has taken order in Acts 17:26. In the latter verse the reference might be to seasons but is more probably to divisions of years or to epochs. In any case the divine determination testifies to God's providential care and historical supervision.

4. In the apostolic fathers the idea is again that of legitimate commanding, e.g., by the will of God in Ignatius *Polycarp* 8.1, and angel in Hermas *Similitudes* 7.1, God in 1 Clem. 20.11, and the church in 1 Clem. 54.2.

hypotássō.

A. The Greek World.
1. The active form of this verb means "to place under," "to affix," "to subordinate" (passive "to be subject").
2. The middle form means "to subject oneself," "to be subservient," "to submit voluntarily."

B. The LXX.
The verb is not common in the LXX and stands for 13 Hebrew words in the usual senses "to place under," "to subordinate," "to subject," passive "to be subject," and middle "to subject oneself," "to submit," especially to God (Ps. 37:7).

C. The NT.
1. In the NT the term has a wide range of meaning centering on the idea of enforced or voluntary subordination. The active occurs in Rom. 8:20 to express the thought that creation is subjected to futility (cf. 5:12). The other active statements are christological. Quoting Ps. 8:6, 1 Cor. 15:25 says that Christ subjects all things (including death) to himself. Naturally this does not include God, for it is finally God who does the subjecting. Ps. 8:6 also underlies Phil. 3:21. Here Christ does the subjecting; he manifests his unlimited power by transforming the lowly body into the likeness of his glorious body. In Heb. 2:7-8 (cf. again Ps. 8:6) God subjects the world, not to angels, but to the Son, who is superior to the angels. The subjecting has begun but awaits consummation. Eph. 1:22 relates Ps. 8:6 to the enthronement that has already taken place, and with an ecclesiological reference. 1 Pet. 3:22 refers similarly to a subjection that Christ's ascension and session complete. The common use of the verb of Ps. 8:6 shows that this verse holds an important place in the primitive Christian confession.
2. a. The middle denotes enforced submission in Lk. 10:17, 20, but elsewhere voluntary submission is at issue. Thus in Rom. 8:7 the flesh resists submission to God's demand. Pious Judaism resists submission to God's saving work in Rom. 10:3. A play on the active occurs in 1 Cor. 15:28. In his only use of the absolute "the Son," Paul here shows that the Son achieves absolute power only to hand it back to God. All power rightly belongs to God, but to the very limit God has given to "the Son" the precedence that is his due.
b. The middle often occurs in exhortation (cf. submission to God in Jms. 4:7 and to salutary discipline in Heb. 12:9).
c. Lk. 2:51 stresses the subjection of the boy Jesus to his earthly parents. Like the subjection of wives to husbands (Col. 3:18; Eph. 5:21ff.; 1 Pet. 3:1; Tit. 2:5), this is according to a divinely willed order.
d. Also divinely willed is the submission to authorities in Rom. 13:1ff., which acknowledges their legitimacy on the basis of their divine commission to reward good and punish evil. Tit. 3:1 and 1 Pet. 2:13-14 echo this teaching, which possibly rests on the reply of Jesus in Mk. 12:17 and parallels. At issue, of course, is the attitude to government as such rather than specifically the Roman state. Christians do not submit to the state merely because it provides conditions for their life and mission. They and all people owe subjection because government is by divine ordination.
e. Slaves should be subject to their masters, not now because slavery is by divine ordination, but because it is a reality that Christians are in no position to set aside. Among themselves, they can and should set it aside as members of the one family of God (cf. 1 Pet. 2:18; 1 Tim. 6:1-2; Phlm. 16).
f. 1 Pet. 5:5 demands the subjection of the younger to the elder, but also a general

humility corresponding to the mutual subjection of Eph. 5:21. As a witness to unbelievers, Christians should accept submission to all human institutions for the Lord's sake.

g. The general rule in NT exhortation is that there should be mutual readiness to renounce one's own will for others. Even when believers owe secular subjection, this takes on a new aspect and has a new basis with the common subjection to Christ. The demand for mutual subjection shows that Christian *hypotássomai* bears a material relation to Christian *tapeinophrosýnē*.

D. The Early Church. Among the apostolic fathers Ignatius asks for submission to the bishop (and to one another) (*Magnesians* 13.2 etc.). 1 Clem. 57.2 counsels submission to the divinely ordained authorities. The heavens submit to God in 1 Clem. 20.1 (cf. Diog. 7.2). God in love has subjected creation to us (Hermas *Mandates* 12.4.2). Slaves should submit to their masters in godly reverence and fear (Did. 4.10-11). Of the Apologists Justin makes most use of the term, e.g., for God subjecting the earth to us or for the subjecting of enemies or demons to Christ (*Apology* 40.7; *Dialogue* 30.3).

hypotagé.
1. This word means "submission" or "subordination," as well as "slavery."
2. It occurs in the LXX only as a slip in Wis. 18:15A.
3. In the NT it occurs only in the Pauline corpus—for renunciation of initiative in 1 Tim. 2:11, for the submissiveness of children in 1 Tim. 3:4, for readiness to make the collection as a confession of faith in 2 Cor. 9:13, for submission in Gal. 2:5.
4. In the apostolic fathers the noun means unanimous submission to leaders in Ignatius *Ephesians* 2.2. This is based on the submission of members to the body in 1 Clem. 37.5.

anypótaktos.
1. This late term means "not subject," "free," "not subjecting oneself."
2. In the NT it means "not subject" in Heb. 2:8 but "insubordinate" or "refractory" in Tit. 1:6; 1 Tim. 1:9.

átaktos (atáktōs), ataktéō.
1. *átaktos* means "disordered," "disorderly," "undisciplined," "unbridled," "without law or order." *ataktéō* means "to set oneself outside the order," "to evade obligations," "to act without discipline, or irresponsibly."
2. In the NT the adjective occurs in 1 Th. 5:14, the adverb in 2 Th. 3:6, 11, and the verb in 2 Th. 3:7. In 2 Th. 3:7 the reference is not just to laziness but to irresponsibility. Those who will not earn their living are outside the civil order, which embraces believers too. They are also outside the requirements of Christian teaching (v. 6). An undisciplined secular life stands in contradiction with the Christian profession. 1 Th. 5:4 is to the same effect.
3. In the apostolic fathers we find the adjective in Diog. 9.1, which deals with the disorder that God has permitted prior to the saving work of Christ. 1 Clem. 40.2 uses the adverb in showing that we must not perform cultic acts in a disorderly way. The Apologists use only the adjective (Athenagoras *Supplication* 25.3).

[G. DELLING, VII, 27-48]

tekníon, téknon → país

---

télos [end, goal], *teléō* [to carry out, complete], *epiteléō* [to carry out, complete], *synteléō* [to complete, fulfil], *syntéleia* [completion, fulfilment], *pantelḗs* [complete, full], *téleios* [complete, perfect], *teleiótēs* [completeness, perfection], *teleióō* [to complete, perfect], *teleíōsis* [completeness, perfection], *teleiōtḗs* [perfecter]

---

télos.

A. The Greek World.
1. *télos* first means "achievement," "fulfilment," "execution," "success," then "power," "official power," and "office."
2. Another meaning is "completion," "perfection," "final step," "supreme stage," "crown," "goal," "maturity," "result," "conclusion," "end," "cessation." Adverbially the meaning is "finally," "fully," "totally," "unceasingly."
3. *télos* can also mean "obligation."
4. Cultically it denotes an "offering" to the gods or a "celebration" of the "mysterics" or the "fulfilment" of sacrifices.
5. Finally a *télos* may be a "detachment" or "group."

B. The LXX.
1. Used for various Hebrew terms, *télos* means "execution" in 1 Chr. 29:19.
2. It then has such senses as "goal" (Job 23:3), "result" (2 Macc. 5:7), "conclusion" (Eccl. 7:2), "end" (Dan. 9:27). *eis télos* can have such senses as "forever," "completely," "perfectly," "to the limit," *diá télous* denotes "continually," and we find *méchri télous* for "constantly" or "in full measure."
3. *télos* may also mean "tax," "toll," or "tribute" (Num. 31:28).
4. In the headings of many Psalms *eis tó télos* seems to mean "for the cultus" and the reference is thus to an "act" in divine worship.

C. The End in Jewish Apocalyptic.
télos has different senses in apocalyptic according to differing expectations. One use is for the "last time" either as the "latter days" or as a "last epoch" distinct from history in general. This last time will bring the fulfilment of the OT promises. Qumran has the expression "the end of the days." In 4 Esdras the "end" is a culminating time, fixed by God, which embraces great distress, the coming of the Messiah, the judgment, transformation, and salvation. The "end" of this world stands in antithesis to the beginning of the next.

D. The NT.
1. To understand *télos* and *teléō* in the NT one must remember their dynamic character; they denote "fulfilment" (cf. Lk. 22:37).
2. a. Love is the "goal" of instruction in 1 Tim. 1:5, salvation is the "goal" of faith in Christ in 1 Pet. 1:9, and "aim" or "goal" seems to be the point in 1 Cor. 10:11.
   b. In Mt. 26:58 "issue" or "result" is meant (cf. Jms. 5:11; Heb. 6:8). The eschatological "result" or "destiny" is at issue in Rom. 6:21-22 (cf. also Phil. 3:19; 2 Cor. 11:15; 1 Pet. 4:17).
   c. The meaning "end" or "conclusion" is less likely than "fulfilment" in Lk. 22:37. In Rev. 21:6; 22:13 *télos*, with *archḗ*, denotes eternity and majesty. The eschatological end or conclusion is the point in 1 Cor. 15 and Mk. 13. Prepositional phrases have an adverbial character and carry such meanings as "to the end," "fully," "finally," "wholly," and "continually."

d. The sense "cessation" occurs in Heb. 7:3; 2 Cor. 3:13; Lk. 1:33; Mk. 3:26; Rom. 7:4. The narrower context supports this meaning for Rom. 10:4, where the point is that the cross abolishes the possibility of attaining to righteousness by the law.

3. "Tax" or "tribute" is the meaning of *télos* in Mt. 17:25; Rom. 13:7.

4. The meanings "detachment" and "initiatory act" do not occur in the NT.

E. The Apostolic Fathers. In these works the usage is not very specific. We find such senses as "end" (Ignatius *Ephesians* 14.1), "result" (Rom. 6:21-22), "goal" (Rom. 1:1), "last time" (Hermas *Visions* 3.8.9). Adverbial uses are for "finally," "always," "without end," "totally," and "completely."

teléō.

A. Outside the Bible.

1. a. This verb means "to carry out," "to execute."

b. As distinct from promising it means "to fulfil."

c. "To carry out instructions" is another sense.

2. The word also means "to bring to an end."

3. Another meaning is "to fulfil obligations."

4. Cultically the word means "to carry out religious acts," "to sacrifice," "to instal" (as a priest), "to consecrate" (initiates). Philo uses *teléō* both for adopting the worship of false gods and for priestly consecration and initiation into the higher mysteries of knowledge (cf. initiation into the mysteries of government).

B. The LXX. In the LXX *teléō* has such various senses as "to carry through," "to actualize," "to complete," "to conclude," and religiously "to dedicate oneself" (but only to the service of a pagan god).

C. The NT.

1. a. In 2 Cor. 12:9 Christ's power "is truly efficacious" in weakness. Gal. 5:16 forbids "carrying out" a will that is opposed to the Spirit. In Lk. 12:50 the reference is to "accomplishing" the baptism of judgment. "Completed" is the point in Jn. 19:30. "Successfully finishing" is meant in 2 Tim. 4:7. God's wrath is "executed" in the plagues in Rev. 15:1, his plan is "fulfilled" in 10:7, and "ending" or "accomplishing" is the point in 15:8.

b. Divine sayings about the future are "put into effect" in Rev. 17:17 (cf. those about Christ's death in Lk. 22:37).

c. The parents of Jesus "carry out" the rites of purification in Lk. 2:39 (cf. the uncircumcised in Rom. 2:27). Love "fulfils" the royal law in Jms. 2:8ff. (cf. Lev. 19:18).

2. The disciples will not "finish" the list of Israel's cities before the parousia in Mt. 10:23. Jesus "finishes" sets of teaching in Mt. 7:28; 11:1; 13:53; 19:1; 26:1. A divinely appointed time "ends" in Rev. 20:3, 5, 7.

3. The meaning "to pay taxes" occurs in Mt. 17:24; Rom. 13:6.

D. The Apostolic Fathers. Apart from Barn. 7.3 ("fulfilled" type), the word occurs in these works only in Hermas for "to perform," "to carry out," "to complete."

epiteléō.

1. This stronger form of *teléō* has the similar senses "to carry out," "to fulfil," "to execute," "to pay," and "to celebrate."

2. In the LXX we find "to accomplish," "to carry through," "to fulfil," "to end," and "to celebrate" (a feast or a wedding).

3. a. In the NT the meaning "to perform," "to establish" occurs in Heb. 8:5, "to actualize" in 2 Cor. 7:1, "to carry out" or "accomplish" in 2 Cor. 8:11, and "to carry through" in Phil. 1:6.

b. The meaning "to finish" (in contrast to beginning) may be found in Gal. 3:3.

c. Heb. 9:6 refers to priestly functions.

4. "Accomplishing" sacrifices is the meaning in Diog. 3.5, "carrying out" orders (1 Clem. 37.2-3) or cultic acts (40.2-3) also occurs, and "fulfilling" an OT saying (Dt. 32:15) is meant in 1 Clem. 3.1.

syntelḗō.

1. *Nonbiblical Usage.* This word means "to fulfil obligations," "to contribute," "to do together," "to cooperate," "to carry out," "to execute," "to work," "to take place," "to end," "to finish," and "to perform" (sacrifices etc.).

2. *The LXX.* In the LXX we find the senses "to accomplish," "to carry out," "to complete," "to execute," "to end," "to finish," "to put an end to," "to cease," and "to celebrate."

3. *The NT.*

a. A first meaning is "to execute" with such nuances as "to practice" (Lk. 4:13), "to fulfil" (Heb. 8:8), and "to put into effect" (Rom. 9:28).

b. The meaning "to end" or "to come to an end" occurs in Lk. 4:2 and Acts 21:27.

4. *The Apostolic Fathers.* Hermas uses the verb for "to carry out" or "to finish," and Barnabas has it in quotations or with reference to a quotation (15.4; cf. Gen. 2:2).

syntéleia. Outside the Bible this word means "common accomplishment" (also "taxes"), "cooperation," "execution," "completion," "conclusion."

2. In the LXX it has such varied senses as "execution," "totality," "satiety," "fulfilment," "conclusion," "cessation," and "destruction."

3. In Daniel LXX it is a technical term for the eschatological "end" (cf. 11:35; 12:4), though it may also mean "end" in a more general sense (9:26). It is a technical apocalyptic term in the Testaments of the Twelve, sometimes with the thought of completion.

4. Qumran has a reference to the "end" of time.

5. The NT uses the term only in eschatological sayings. In Heb. 9:27 Christ's saving work is the event of the end time. The juxtaposition stresses its definitiveness and perfection. In Matthew the phrase "end of the age" (13:39; 24:3; 28:20) refers to eschatological events that have yet to take place, including the judgment (13:39-40, 49).

6. Of the apostolic fathers only Hermas uses *syntéleia* (the "end"). The Apologist Tatian uses it in the context of resurrection and judgment (*Address to the Greeks* 6.1; 17.1).

pantelḗs.

1. This word refers to full completion and hence has such senses as "full," "complete," "intact," or adverbially "completely," "altogether," "permanently."

2. In the LXX it occurs only in Maccabees for "complete," and as an adverb "totally," "wholly," "fully," or, negatively, "not at all."

3. The NT uses the term only in the adverbial phrase *eis tó pantelḗs.* This means either "fully" or "at all" in Lk. 13:11; the emphasis on being bound favors the latter. The totality of Christ's saving work in Heb. 7:25 means that he is able to save both "forever" and "altogether"; the term has both nuances.

4. The Apologists have *eis tó pantelḗs* for "absolutely" (Tatian *Address to the Greeks* 6.1) and *pantelṓs* for "generally" (Justin *Epitome* 10.8).

téleios.

A. **Outside the Bible**. This adjective means "whole," "unblemished," "full," "perfect," "actualized," "efficacious," "mature," "supreme," and perhaps "dedicated."

B. **The Philosophical Concept of Perfection.**

1. In philosophy *téleios* carries the sense of full humanity with an orientation to what is worthwhile and ethically good. In Plato this entails the attainment of insight by recollection and the resultant achievement of true being. Whereas the perfection of the cosmos is its completeness, the *téleion* in the ethical sphere is intrinsic goodness or the absolute good.

2. In Aristotle perfection is present with right ethical choice, i.e., with the choice for its own sake of the good in an absolute sense.

3. For Stoics that person alone is *téleios* who has all virtues, and that deed alone is *téleios* in which all virtues cooperate.

4. Philo comes under various influences. Academic vision is the perfect good, but divinely given wisdom is the perfect way to God. In the strict sense God himself is the perfect good and the giver of perfect goods. The law means that piety comes though perfect virtue, whose use is happiness, and whose fruitfulness depends on God. The pinnacle of most perfect felicity is God himself. To possess a wholly perfect nature is to be free from passion and desire. The perfect person regards only the ethically beautiful as good, standing between God and humanity, yet not wholly free from error as God is. Taking note of the law is the way to perfectness. The forefathers are perfect, and to the perfect Abraham (after the change of name) God gives the promise of Gen. 22:16-17. Moses is the perfect sage and the most perfect of the prophets; his perfect soul goes directly to God apart from any visible event.

C. **The LXX and Dead Sea Scrolls.**

1. In the LXX *téleios* has such meanings as "unblemished," "undivided" (cf. the obedient heart in 1 Kgs. 8:61; 11:4), "total" (cf. Jer. 13:19).

2. The equivalent terms in the Dead Sea Scrolls have the senses "without defect," "unblemished," "entire," and "undivided."

D. **The NT.**

1. The use in Matthew carries the LXX sense of "whole" or "undivided." Thus the rich young ruler is not yet "undivided" in his obedience to God (19:20). God is undivided in his conduct toward us, and so must we be in our conduct toward him and others (5:48). Our total love should encompass even enemies.

2. The sense "whole" or "complete" also occurs in Jms. 1:4. Those are whole who do the whole work and whose steadfastness works itself out fully. This means looking into the "entire" law of liberty (1:25) and doing it. This law brings liberty with its observance. It finds fulfilment in love but also in self-control, for the whole person bridles the whole body, including the tongue (3:2ff.). What is "whole" and without fault comes from God (1:17). "Full" and "unlimited" love leaves no place for fear (1 Jn. 4:18). This love comes from God (v. 16) in the sending of the Son that removes fear of judgment (v. 10). The command to be "completely" sober in 1 Pet. 1:13 is ethically related and eschatologically grounded.

3. In the Pauline corpus "whole" seems to be the sense in 1 Cor. 13:10. The gifts do not give the full knowledge which is to come. Col. 4:12 refers to the solid position

of those who are "complete" in God's total will. Yet the idea of maturity is also present, as in 1:28, where Paul's aim is to present believers "full-grown" under the direction and in the power of Christ's cross and resurrection. _téleios_ may thus be the opposite of _népios_ etc. (1 Cor. 14:20; cf. Phil. 3:15 and perhaps 1 Cor. 2:6, where the truly mature understand the message of the cross as the wisdom of God). In Rom. 12:2 knowledge of the entire or perfect will of God comes through the renewing of judgment by the Spirit.

4. Heb. 5:14 distinguishes between initial doctrines for _népioi_ and full fare for the mature (_téleioi_) who know God's will and can differentiate good and evil. In 9:11 the heavenly sanctuary is "more perfect" than the provisional temple.

5. The NT never seems to use _téleios_ for a gradual advance to Christian perfection or for a two-graded ideal of ethical perfection. It plainly means "whole" or "entire" in Matthew, Paul, and the Catholic Epistles, and it also has the sense of "mature" in some passages in Paul.

E. The Apostolic Fathers. Here, too, the term has the senses "total," "complete," "full," "supreme," and then "perfect" (cf. fasting in Hermas _Similitudes_ 5.3.6, the church as a perfect temple in Barn. 4.11, Esther in 1 Clem. 55.6, and Christ the "perfect man" in Ignatius _Smyrneans_ 4.2).

teleiótēs.

1. This uncommon term denotes a state of "completeness" and also means "completion."

2. In the LXX it means "wholeness," "integrity," "completeness."

3. a. In the NT Col. 3:14 calls love the bond of "completeness"; it either binds the other virtues into a whole, or gives unity and harmony to the church.

b. In Heb. 6:1 _teleiótēs_ is the "highest stage" of Christian teaching.

4. In the apostolic fathers love has the quality of perfection in 1 Clem. 50.1, and reference is made to the perfection of Moses' love for the people in 1 Clem. 53.5.

teleióō.

1. Nonbiblical Usage. This word means "to make _téleios_" or, in the passive, "to become _téleios_," in such senses as "to complete," "to carry out," "to put into effect," and, passive, "to be completed," "to mature."

2. The LXX. In the LXX we find the senses "to make perfect" (Ezek. 27:11), "to fill (the hands)" (Ex. 29:9, 29, 33, for "to consecrate"), "to complete" (2 Chr. 8:16), and "to conclude" (4 Macc. 7:15).

3. The NT.

a. The sense "to fulfil" occurs in Acts 20:24; Jn. 4:34 (where the aim of Jesus is to accomplish his Father's work); 17:4, etc.

b. In 1 John _teleióō_ denotes the perfection or completeness of God's love, or of Christians in love (4:18). God's love is fully present in those who keep his word (2:5). This love manifests its completeness by removing fear of judgment (4:17). In Jn. 17:23 Jesus prays that his disciples may be wholly one as he is in them and God in him. Scripture comes to completeness or fulfilment in the cross (Jn. 19:28). Faith finds fulfilment in works (Jms. 2:22), as may be seen from the offering of Isaac as a confirmation of the verdict of Gen. 15:6.

c. In Hebrews _teleióō tiná_ means enabling someone to stand before God (cf. the LXX), as in Heb. 7:19; 10:1, 14. Cultic terms here clarify the new order of salvation. The OT priests are inadequate because of their sinfulness and not merely their cultic defects. Jesus is qualified to come before God (5:8-9), not by cleansing, but by proving his obedience. His is an eternal qualification (7:28) which enables him, by his once-for-all high-priestly work, to qualify those whom he represents to come before God (10:14) in the heavenly sanctuary as those whose sins are expiated.

d. In Heb. 11–12 the use is slightly different. The fathers of faith were not made perfect (11:40) in the sense that they did not yet attain to the heavenly city. But through Christ's saving work they now share in the consummation (12:23). Paul says something to the same effect in Phil. 3:12 when he admits that he is not already perfect but still presses on. The thought of fulfilment is present in Lk. 13:32, and cf. the fulfilling of the days of the Passover in 2:43.

e. *teléō* and *teleióō* often have much the same meaning ("to carry through," "to complete"), but *teleióō* has a stronger suggestion of totality, *teléō* of goal or end.

4. *The Apostolic Fathers.* In these works *teleióō* has such senses as "to carry out" (1 Clem. 33.6), "to fulfil" (Hermas *Visions* 4.1.3), "to effect" (Ignatius *Smyrneans* 7.2), "to complete" (Did. 10.5), and, in the passive, "to become perfect" (Did. 16.2).

teleíōsis.

1. Outside the Bible. This word means "actualization," "completion," "conclusion," and "maturing."

2. The LXX. Here we find the senses "execution," "completion," "conclusion," and "maturity."

3. The NT.

a. Mary is blessed in Lk. 1:45 because she believes there will be an execution of God's word.

b. The OT priesthood in Heb. 7:11 does not confer qualification to stand before God. On the basis of LXX usage (cf. *teleióō*) the underlying thought is that of consecration or institution to the priesthood in the sense of cultic qualification. This thought is now given a spiritual application.

4. The Apostolic Fathers. The term does not occur in these works or in the Apologists.

teleiótēs.

1. This rare term denotes one who accomplishes *teleioún.* God is *teleiótēs* both in natural events and in the ministry of the Spirit. The word also applies to those who administer baptism inasmuch as they make the candidate *téleios.*

2. The context supplies the meaning in Heb. 12:2. Jesus gives faith its perfect basis by his high-priestly work and thus completes it. At the same time, he exercises complete faith as demonstrated by his passion.   [G. DELLING, VIII, 49-87]

---

telốnēs [tax collector]

A. Tax Farming in Antiquity.
I. Main Types.

1. Athens. The Greek cities farm out taxes in private agreements between the state and the tax farmers. Laws fix the duties and privileges of the tax farmers but do not specify the methods or demand an audit. The system provides ready cash for the government and reduces officialdom. The problems are that the tax farmers need to impose more taxes in order to make a profit and that they are inclined, if necessary, to resort to illegal practices. Tax farmers also band together to reduce their bids. The tax farmers might be either individuals or companies. Their contract is an annual one but is usually renewed. Backers guarantee the payment and must make good any deficiency. Only when a first instalment is paid may the tax farmers levy taxes, and there are penalties for tardy payment. Tax farming is a lucrative business; in case of war or plague the state might remit the debt if the collection falls short. Employees have the right to search for contraband goods and may lodge complaints against smugglers with the possibility of confiscating their goods.

2. *Ptolemaic Egypt*. Egypt under the Ptolemies adopts tax farming and regulates it by royal legislation. The main difference from Athens is that the state supervises the system in detail. Its officials can calculate the yield more accurately and they probably fix a minimum rate. No large first instalment must be paid, as in Athens, but guarantors are required, who have some share in the profits. The lessees collect the taxes through their agents, whose wages are fixed by law. The tax farmers receive a share of the sum collected and also take over any surplus, although they or their sponsors must also make good any deficit. Only royal officials can distrain goods in the case of those who fail to pay taxes. The main point of the system in Egypt is to guarantee a fixed sum for the state, not to relieve the state of the whole burden or to provide ready cash at the beginning of the fiscal year (as in Athens).

3. *Rome*. Rome develops tax farming for much the same reasons as Athens. With the growth of its possessions, however, a tax-farming class comes into being to handle the large financial transactions. Under Augustus reorganization becomes necessary, and this results in a restriction of the powers of tax-farming corporations. By the second century A.D. imperial officials begin to take over the collection of taxes.

II. Palestine.

1. Tax farming comes into Palestine from at least the time of Ptolemy II Philadelphus (308–246 B.C.). Later, taxes are paid to both Syria and Egypt and leading citizens see to their collection, paying a fixed sum and collecting as they are able.

b. When Pompey conquers Jerusalem in 63 B.C. he imposes a tribute for which the high priests seem to have been responsible. After 57 B.C. there are five taxing districts but a single corporation seems to have contracted with the towns, which pay lump sums that they then have to collect. Caesar reduces taxes in 47 B.C. and in 44 B.C. abolishes the system of farming out taxes to a corporation in Judea.

c. Augustus frees Herod from the tribute to Rome, thus enabling Herod to control his own finances. There are no details about tax collection, but Herod seems not to have used tax farming. Herod Antipas, however, renews the farming system. In NT times direct taxes are not farmed out under the Roman procurator in Judea but indirect taxes (customs etc.) are mostly farmed out, often on a smaller, individual basis.

d. Dues are collected at Gaza, Ascalon, Joppa, and Caesarea, and inland at Jerusalem, Jericho, and Capernaum. Roman officials collect arrears; tax farmers report smugglers and delinquents to them.

III. The Position of Tax Farmers.

1. In General.

a. Since no one pays taxes willingly, people dislike and fear tax farmers. Traders run into problems at toll and customs stations. On long journeys goods are often taxed several times as they pass through various districts.

b. Since tax farmers have to make a profit, they obviously charge more than is legally imposed. They must also protect themselves against fraud. Constant disputes arise, especially as the regulations are not widely known until Nero orders that they should be posted up at every customs house. Travelers must declare what they are carrying but are allowed to bring in personal articles free of duty. The collectors have the right of search and may confiscate dutiable goods not declared. In case of wrongful confiscation double restitution must be paid on timely objection unless a plea of misunderstanding prevails. Simple travelers, however, often do not know the rules or proper channels, and thus become a prey to avaricious tax farmers and their agents. This explains the low esteem in which the latter are held.

2. *Judaism.*

a. The rabbis, regarding tax collectors as people who try to gain money dishonestly, treat them as in a special way unclean.

b. Indeed, they classify them as thieves or robbers.

c. Whereas they view direct taxes as a sign of subjection, they regard indirect taxes, especially tolls, as a form of injustice and chicanery. They thus think that false protestations to tax collectors are legitimate, they deny tax collectors the right to appear as witnesses, and they group both them and their families as gamblers or usurers who, if they wish to "convert," should restore what they have taken illegally where the persons defrauded are known, and contribute the rest of their ill-gotten gains to the common good.

d. A few tax farmers, however, seem to have conducted their business honestly and hence to have earned the respect of their fellow citizens.

B. Jesus and Toll Collectors. *telṓnēs* occurs only in the Synoptics in Mt. 11:18-19 and parallels; 5:46-47; Mk. 2:14ff. and parallels; 10:3; 18:17; 21:31-32; Lk. 3:12-13; 7:29; 15:1; 18:9ff.; 19:2. The noun *telṓnion* occurs only in Mt. 2:14 and parallels. The NT agrees with the rabbis in thinking that tax collectors alienate themselves from God and the people. "Publicans and sinners" are the opposite of the children of the kingdom (cf. Mt. 5:46-47). Tax collectors are notoriously wicked Israelites who may even be grouped with the Gentiles (cf. Mt. 18:15ff.). If the interest of the NT is in their conversion, as in Lk. 18:9ff. and 19:1f., it is as an example of God's miraculous power to bring even the most sinful back to himself. Yet the stress lies on the fact that Jesus seeks them (cf. Mt. 9:36; 10:6; 15:24; Lk. 19:10). Neither the Baptist nor Jesus denies them access to the eschatological community. There is special joy in heaven over the conversion of sinners like them (Mt. 18:13-14; Lk. 15:7, 10). Jesus excludes no specific groups (Mt. 13:24-25). He starts by recognizing all Israel (Lk. 19:9). The summons of the gospel is especially to toll collectors and sinners, and to table fellowship with them. Jesus, indeed, incurs criticism by associating with those whom the people as well as the Pharisees revile (Mt. 11:19). His acceptance of a *telṓnēs* as a disciple must have caused particular offense (Mk. 2:14), followed as it was by a feast attended by many toll collectors and sinners. He also lodges with a chief tax farmer in Jericho (Lk. 19:1ff.). If Zacchaeus promises restitution, Jesus assures him of salvation prior to this commitment. Similarly, he grants the assurance that the publican's prayer for forgiveness is heard by God (Lk. 18:14). He uses the conversion of toll collectors and sinners as a model and a warning (Lk. 15:1ff.; Mt. 20:13ff.). Whereas the Pharisee's prayer has become an extolling of self, that of the publican, which God hears and answers, is a humble plea for mercy. The public acceptance of toll collectors and sinners belongs in the main to the Galilean ministry but there are also striking instances in the later period (Mk. 14:3ff.; Lk. 19:1ff.).   [O. MICHEL, VIII, 88-105]

> *témnō* [to cut], *apotomía* [severity], *apótomos* [severe], *apotómōs*
> [severely], *katatomḗ* [cutting up, mutilation], *orthotoméō* [to cut a straight
> path, teach aright]

témnō. This word, meaning "to cut," does not occur in the NT.

apotomía, apótomos, apotómōs.

1. *apótomos* means "sharply cut," and it then has the more common derived sense of "steep," "inaccessible," and the transferred sense of "sharp," "keen," "exact," "careful," "strict," and even "severe" or "pitiless."

2. *apotomía* occurs only from the Hellenistic period. It means "cutting off," then "difficulty," mostly "strictness" or "severity" (in a good sense as regards the law), and also "hardness" in carrying out a resolve.

B. The LXX and Judaism.

1. Only *apótomos* and *apotómōs* occur in the LXX, and these only in Wisdom. They relate to God's severity in judgment on the wicked. God is like a Father to the righteous but has the severity of a sovereign toward sinners.

2. The noun *apotomía* occurs in Σ with reference to the "cruelty" of Nineveh (Nah. 3:1) and Babylon (Jer. 51:35).

3. Josephus uses *apótomos* for "steep" and also to describe the "harshness" of Herod. Philo uses *apotomía* for "crushing ferocity." The verb *apotémnō* is also common in Josephus.

C. The NT.

1. The adverb *apotómōs* occurs in 2 Cor. 13:10. Paul wants to settle the matter quickly so that he will not have to exert his authority severely, i.e., with the force of judgment (as distinct from the sharp rebuke of Tit. 1:13 that aims at correction).

2. In the NT only Rom. 11:22 uses the noun *apotomía*. As in Wisdom, those who ignore God's kindness come under the threat of his inexorable severity, i.e., in judgment.

D. The Apostolic Fathers. Pol. 6.1 advises presbyters not to use their judicial authority without clemency as though they were tyrants or in anticipation of God's judicial severity.

katatomḗ.

A. Nonbiblical Greek. This word means "incision" or "sectional plane" and occurs mostly in the scientific or technical sphere. The verb *katatémnō*, however, is also used for the cutting up of meat, especially sacrificial meat, and can be used ironically for "to cut into strips," i.e., "to kill" (cf. also "to chop up" with words in the charge against Socrates).

B. The LXX. The noun does not occur in the LXX, but *katatémnō* comes into use for the prohibited slitting of the skin, e.g., in mourning (Is. 15:2); cf. also the use for cultic incisions in A at Jer. 48:37 (Σ *katatomḗ*).

C. The NT. The only NT instance of *katatomḗ* is in Phil. 3:2. Opposing those who press circumcision on believers, Paul is not accusing them of causing "division" but making play on the term *peritomḗ* (circumcision). Their vaunted circumcision is in reality "dissection"—a "mutilation" that the law itself forbids. This ironic play on words, familiar in the diatribe, is perhaps suggested by the common ironic use of the verb *katatémnō* in the Greek world.

orthotoméō.

1. This word occurs in the Greek Bible only at Prov. 3:6; 11:5; 2 Tim. 2:15. Underlying it is the phrase *témnō hodón,* "to lay down a way," "to open a way," "to build a road."

2. The phrase *orthotoméō hodón* has the same sense in Prov. 3:6 and 11:5 (plural). The *ortho-* lays stress on a straight path.

3. In later Jewish writings *orthotoméō* does not occur but other terms convey the idea of the right way, now more closely equated with the commandments.

4. The figurative idea of the way is very pale in the one NT instance of *orthotoméō* in 2 Tim. 2:15. As distinct from those who engage in useless theological chatter, Timothy is to do what is right relative to the word of truth. Other possible meanings, e.g., "to cut," "to handle," or "to deliver," do not fit the context or agree with the parallel expression in Gal. 2:14. The real meaning seems to be that Timothy should speak the word of truth in his conduct, i.e., follow it. When he does this, he need not be ashamed, for, unlike the false teachers, he will present the word legitimately, confirming it in his life.   [H. KÖSTER, VIII, 106-12]

→ *dichotoméō, peritémnō*

---

téras [omen, wonder]

A. Nonbiblical Usage.

1. General. The word *téras* is an ancient one denoting omens, e.g., in the form of natural phenomena or unusual manifestations.

2. Theological.

a. From earliest times *téras* has a theological reference. For Homer Zeus is the author of *térata* such as thunder, the rainbow, or meteorites.

b. Yet the link with Zeus seems to be a secondary harmonizing of awe-kindling phenomena with the Olympian gods.

c. In Homer the *téras* is only for human beings as in their search for the essence of things they experience their dependence on the gods and yet also their closeness to them. The *mántis* is needed to interpret the *téras,* but the *téras* itself may be given in answer to prayer.

3. Trend and Development.

a. Greek thought takes an original experience of the sinister, appropriates it as a means to explain the human situation, and integrates it into the cultus.

b. At a later stage Xenophon mentions dreams as a means of finding the divine will but avoids the term *téras.* When other authors use it, it is usually as a traditional term with no survival of the ancient connotations. In general it takes on negative content and therefore is no longer the right term to present the reality of a divine wonder.

4. sēmeía kaí térata. For this phrase see *sēmeíon.*

B. The OT and Greek Judaism.

1. The LXX.

a. *téras* occurs 46 times in the LXX. In 34 of the 38 instances where there is a Hebrew original, this is *môpēt.*

b. As regards the meaning of the Hebrew term, it is coordinated with the parallel *'ôt* in 18 of 36 passages, and the two together relate to extraordinary phenomena or events together with the impression they make and the knowledge they mediate. The author of these extraordinary manifestations is God, and it is his historical power that they display as he makes decisions for the present that also determine the future. That the two Hebrew terms are not synonymous, but carry different accents, may be seen from a comparison of 2 Kgs. 20:1ff. and 2 Chr. 32:24, 31; the former stresses the sign and the latter the miracle. The revelatory aspect comes out in Ezek. 12:1ff. when the prophet himself becomes a sign for Israel (cf. Ps. 71:7). In Joel 2:30-31 the God who has made heaven and earth gives signs in them to usher in the last time. As Ps. 105:5 shows, it is of the essence of OT signs that in them God reaches the goal of establishing his righteousness.

c. The LXX use of *téras* is governed by the Hebrew. The term denotes something unusual whereby the God who is the Creator and the Lord of events adds a new element to his word of self-manifestation. The emphasis lies on God's action, not on the marvelous aspect, and there is no conceptual abstraction. The translators observe the distinction from *sēmeíon* (cf. Ex. 4:17, 21). The point of *téras* is that it discloses the sovereign being of God in all its uniqueness. The term plays no essential role in works that are Greek in origin. In two of four instances in Wisdom it occurs in the combination *sēmeía kaí térata* (8:8; 10:16). In Wis. 17:14; 19:8, too, the wonderful acts that reveal God are at issue. *téras* does not occur in Maccabees, though God is *teratopoiós* in 2 Macc. 15:21; 3 Macc. 6:32. Greek Judaism perhaps dislikes *téras* (except when combined with *sēmeíon*) because of its pagan associations.

2. Nonbiblical Greek Judaism.

a. Philo. Philo seldom uses *téras,* although *terástios* is more common, and he also uses various derivatives. The connection with what is unusual and terrifying may be seen in his use. Yet the group does not have a negative accent, for God is the author of the *térata* done by Moses. A *sēmeíon* is not necessarily a miracle, but a *téras* is a *sēmeíon* when God stands behind it. The positive sense rests on the *térata* associated with the exodus. The *téras* is a means of revelation. By it Philo shows that Judaism enjoys supreme knowledge of God and the highest form of morality.

b. Josephus. Josephus adopts the traditional use of *téras* for the supernatural. *térata* aid in the knowledge of God, especially in his sovereignty over events. They are sometimes predictive signs indicating the future that God controls. Insight is needed for their correct evaluation and interpretation. Knowledge of Scripture serves best in this regard, for God's *térata* stand in relation to the direction of the history initiated by the exodus.

c. The Pseudepigrapha. The term *téras* plays no significant part in these writings.

d. *sēmeía kaí térata.* In this phrase *térata* is the more important term, inasmuch as it expresses the conviction that the way and goal of God govern all that happens. For Josephus those who ignore signs of the destruction of city and temple refuse faith in God in so doing.

C. Postbiblical Judaism.

1. Qumran. The Dead Sea Scrolls refer only seldom to mighty acts as distinct from signs.

2. The Rabbis. The rabbis practically never use the equivalent Hebrew term.

D. The NT.

1. The Absence of téras Alone. The NT never uses *téras* alone. This is by intent, as may be seen in Acts 2:19, where the author adds an interpretative *kaí sēmeía* to the Hebrew and Greek of Joel 2:30 (cf. 2:22, 43; 6:8; 7:36). This is not because *téras* has become a more colorless term. It is because *téras* does not fit in so well with the aims of proclamation. For the mighty works of Jesus, *dýnamis* serves better to bring out an unambiguous christological interpretation. *téras* might suggest that God does the works and thus restrict the autonomy of Jesus. As regards the works of the apostles, the point is that in them the Spirit continues the work of Jesus, and hence *dýnamis* is better adapted to express the fact that the apostles do the works as the representatives of Jesus.

2. *sēmeía kaí térata—térata kaí sēmeía.* Acts uses both expressions (4:30; 5:12; 14:3; 15:12; 2:19, 22, 43; 6:8; 7:36). Perhaps in *sēmeía kaí térata* the stress is on God's giving a new and specific stamp to the present, whereas in *térata kaí sēmeía* the present stands under the sign of his advance and there is thus an invitation to turn to him, with *dýnamis* as the catchword. Paul, too, uses *dýnamis* in connection with *sēmeía kaí térata* in Rom. 15:19, 2 Cor. 12:12, and even 2 Th. 2:9, where he has the coming of antichrist in view.

E. The Early Church. The apostolic fathers have *sēmeía kaí térata* but never *téras* alone. This is also the case in the apocryphal Acts. The only instance of *téras* in the Apologists is in Athenagoras *Supplication* 20.2, where it is a term taken from ancient epic poetry.   [K. H. RENGSTORF, VIII, 113-26]
→ *sēmeíon*

---

téssares [four], *tétartos* [fourth], *tetartaíos* [fourth (day)], *tesserákonta* [40], *tesserakontaetḗs* [40 (years)]

---

téssares, tétartos, tetartaíos.

A. Four in Antiquity.

1. Linguistic Problems. Differing forms of the term for "four" occur in the Greek dialects (Attic *téttares*, Ionic *tésseres*, Doric *tétores*). The NT perhaps gives evidence of a general intermingling of forms, *tesser-* being preferred on euphonic or rhythmic grounds.

2. The Greek Sphere.

a. On the basis of the four corners, etc., the number four becomes a term for totality. It is only occasionally a sacred number, but it often serves as a round number (cf. the four cardinal virtues, basic emotions, or types of sovereignty).

b. The number frequently has special significance, as in references to the fourth assault, the dangers of the fourth day, the four-day fever, the need for marriage after four years of sexual maturity, the birth of Heracles on the fourth day of the month (cf. also four-year contests).

c. Myths commonly contain the idea of the four ages of the world, and we also read of the four discoveries of Hermes, the four-cornered Hermes pillars, the four-eyed Proserpine, etc.

d. In the Platonic and Pythagorean tradition four is a symbol, but Aristotle stresses the numerical aspect. The four elements play an important role in Mithraism. For the Pythagoreans four is the basis of the decimal system inasmuch as the first four numbers add up to ten. Stress lies elsewhere on the four phases of the moon or the four seasons.

B. Four in the OT and Judaism.

1. The OT.

a. Four is a figure denoting totality in the OT (cf. the four quarters of heaven, the four rivers of paradise, also Dan. 11:4; Ezek. 7:2; Zech. 1:8ff.). Four is important in the theophany of Ezek. 1 (the four living creatures, four faces, and four wheels). There are four phenomena at Elijah's theophany in 1 Kgs. 19:11-12. Four is also important in apocalyptic (cf. Dan. 7:2-3, 6, 17; also 2:31ff.).

b. As a round number, four figures in Zech. 7:1; Judg. 14:15; 2 Kgs. 7:3, and cf. in relation to the ark and tabernacle Ex. 25:12, 26, 34; 26:2, 8, 32.

c. The series three-four, which also occurs in the Greek world, has the sense of a few. It is schematic in proverbs (Am. 1:3, 6, 9; Prov. 30:15, 18, 21, 24, 29).

2. *Judaism.*

a. In rabbinic works four is often a round number, e.g., four categories of penitence or of scholars, or four things for which there are rewards and punishments. The fourth day is the day of demons, and on the fourth day the soul finally leaves the tomb. Qumran has four waters of purification and divides the community fourfold. Eth. En. 22 divides the underworld into four.

b. Philo refers to the four elements. He attributes to Moses the holiness of the number four. Thus on the fourth day God made heaven and the stars. Philo also refers to four main emotions, and for him the most important secret of the number is the tetragrammaton, the divine name.

C. The NT.

1. *General Use.* The use is technical in Mk. 2:3 and Acts 10:11; 11:5. The four anchors of Acts 27:29 are for added safety. Four denotes a short space of time in Jn. 4:35; Acts 10:30. The fourth watch is the dawn in Mk. 6:48. The series of four in 2 Pet. 3:10 and Rev. 5:13 suggests completeness. The four parts of the field in Mk. 4:1ff. contain three that are similar and a fourth that is different. The four days in the tomb in Jn. 11:17 express the irreversibility of death. The fourfold division of Jesus' clothes (Jn. 19:23) corresponds to the number of soldiers in the watch. Fourfold restitution in Lk. 19:8 displays generosity.

2. *Apocalyptic.* Revelation uses the Ezekiel tradition in 4:6, 8; 5:6, 8, etc. The four faces become four animals (4:7), eyes replace the wheels, and the creatures now surround the throne. Rev. 6:1ff. adopts the motif of the four horses, combining it with that of the first four seals (cf. the four destroying angels of 9:14-15). The heavenly city is foursquare (21:16). In Mk. 13:27 the elect are gathered from the four winds.

D. The Early Church. Motifs in the apostolic fathers include the gathering from the four quarters of the earth (Did. 10.5) and the four periods (Hermas *Similitudes* 9.4.3). Irenaeus associates the four Gospels with the four districts of the earth and the need for four pillars (*Against Heresies* 3.11.8). He also characterizes the Gospels as four beasts. Augustine later links the names of the four Evangelists with the beasts (*On the Harmony of the Gospels* 1.6).

tesserákonta, tesserakontaetḗs.

A. 40 in Antiquity.

a. In the Greek world 40 is a round number. 40 years are a long time, 40 days a shorter time.

b. 40 is also the time of maturity. One must be at least 40 to be appointed to certain posts.

c. 40 also denotes specific periods, e.g., the first movement of a child in the womb, the crisis in an illness, and the normal period of pregnancy (7 times 40 days). Pythagoras fasts for 40 days, and we also read of a period of rain for 40 days and of the 40-day period when the Pleiades are not visible.

B. The OT and Judaism.

a. In the OT 40 years are the period of a generation, i.e., when a whole generation is active (cf. the wilderness generation, Ex. 16:35; Dt. 1:3, etc.). David reigns for 40 years in 2 Sam. 5:4-5 (cf. also Solomon in 1 Kgs. 11:42), and the period from the exodus to the temple consists of 480 years.

b. The number 40 also denotes maturity, e.g., the year of marriage or accession (Gen. 25:20; 2 Sam. 2:10). The span of human life consists of 120 years (Gen. 6:3).

c. 40 also serves as a typical round number (cf. the flood in Gen. 7:4, Moses on Sinai in Ex. 24:18, the taunting of Goliath in 1 Sam. 7:16, the time for repentance in Jon. 3:4, Elijah's journey in 1 Kgs. 19:8, the days of impurity in Lev. 12:4, the maximum number of stripes in Dt. 25:3).

2. 40 is a most important number, second only to seven, in later Judaism. 40 days are a typical period in popular medicine and agriculture as well as in relation to biblical incidents (the flood etc.). Reference is made to 40 days of fasting, and 40 years are significant as periods in office. Signs appear 40 years before the destruction of the temple. A rabbinic disciple achieves independence of judgment when reaching 40.

b. 40 also serves as a round number, e.g., in learning or in scourging.

c. In messianic contexts the interim messianic kingdom lasts 40 years. At Qumran 40 years elapse between the Teacher of Righteousness and the coming of the divine kingdom. Apocalyptic attaches 40 days of judgment to the 40-year messianic kingdom. The wilderness years become a messianic type.

C. The NT. 40 serves as a round number in Acts 4:22; 23:13, 21. When Paul is given 40 stripes save one (2 Cor. 11:24), this is the first written instance of the omission of the last stroke. Heb. 3:10, 17 and Acts 13:18 recall God's judging and guiding in the wilderness period. Acts 13:21 seems to ascribe 40 years to Saul. Acts 7:42 gives a negative turn to Am. 5:25. Acts 7:23 refers to the three 40-year periods in the life of Moses. Mk. 1:13 and parallels link the 40-day fast of Jesus to his baptism and thus find in it obedience to his messianic commission. The references to the animals and the angels define the desert as a place of eschatological paradisal peace. We also find Moses typology in Mt. 4:2 (cf. Lk. 4:2-3). The 40 days of appearances to the disciples are the period when the disclosures of the risen Lord elucidate and validate the gospel (Acts 1:3).

D. The Early Church. The apostolic fathers refer only to Moses on Sinai (1 Clem. 53.2). Tertullian mentions the teaching of the risen Lord (*Apology* 21.23). A 40-day fast develops prior to Easter on the model of that of Jesus.

[H. BALZ, VIII, 127-39]

---

tēréō [to watch over, protect], *térēsis* [watch, custody], *paratēréō* [to watch closely, guard], *paratérēsis* [watching, observance], *diatēréō* [to keep, store up], *syntēréō* [to keep in mind, protect]

---

tēréō.

A. Outside the NT.

1. The basic meaning of this word is "to keep in view," "to note," "to watch over"; it takes on such nuances as "to rule," "to observe," "to ward off," "to guard," "to

keep," and in a transferred sense "to see to," "to apply oneself to," "to defend oneself."

2. The word occurs 39 times in the LXX in such senses as "to aim at," "to keep watch," "to pay attention," "to watch over or for," "to keep," "to observe."

3. Philo seldom uses the term. It can mean "to watch over" in Test. Zeb. 4:3, and Josephus uses it for "to hold."

4. Rabbinic parallels denote obedience to the law.

B. The NT.

1. Literal Meaning. Used 60 times in the NT, *tēréō* may have here such literal senses as "to guard" (Acts 12:6; Mt. 27:36), "to keep" (Jn. 2:10; 1 Pet. 1:4), "to retain" (negatively in Jude 6), and "to protect" (1 Cor. 7:37).

2. Transferred Meaning.

a. The sense is "to protect" or "to preserve" in Jn. 17:11-12. So, too, Christ protects his church against temptation in Rev. 3:10. Paul's desire is that the spirits, souls, and bodies of believers may be kept (with an eschatological reference) in 1 Th. 5:23. The called will be kept for the reign of Christ in Jude 1. Christ grants protection against the devil and sin in 1 Jn. 5:18. Keeping aloof from the world is the point in 1 Tim. 5:22 and Jms. 1:27. In Jude 21 the genitive ("of God") expresses God's initiative, the verb our response.

b. With an impersonal object the idea is that of maintaining the essential Christian realities, e.g., faith in 2 Tim. 4:7, the unity of the Spirit in Eph. 4:3, one's garments (i.e., salvation) in Rev. 16:15.

c. A common thought is that of observing or keeping commandments etc.; cf. Mt. 19:17; Acts 15:5; Jn. 9:16 (the sabbath); Mt. 23:3 (scribal teaching); Jms. 2:10 (the royal law); Mt. 28:20 (Jesus' teaching); Jn. 14:15 (Jesus' commandments). The expressions used relative to Christians suggest the existence of a catechetical tradition. This goes back to the teaching of Jesus himself, so that keeping his commands is the same as keeping his word (Jn. 14:23-24). The disciples pass on this word of revelation with a summons to faith and obedience (Jn. 15:20), and keeping it means eternal life (8:51-52). Similar thoughts occur in 1 Jn. 2:3, 4; Rev. 12:17. The Christian life as a fulfilling of God's will is both a prerequisite of answers to prayer and a result of the Spirit's working (1 Jn. 3:22, 24). Love for God finds expression in love for others and keeping the commandments (1 Jn. 5:2-3).

tērēsis.

1. In Greek this word means "attention," "vigilance," "watch," "observation," "preservation," "care," and "custody."

2. In the LXX it occurs only in the Apocrypha for "keeping" or "guarding."

3. In the NT the word means "custody" (or "prison") in Acts 4:3; 5:18 and "keeping" or "fulfilling" God's commandments in 1 Cor. 7:19 (cf. Gal. 5:6; Rom. 14:17).

paratēréō.

1. In Greek this word has such senses as "to observe," "to keep under observation," "to lurk," "to lie in wait," "to pay heed," "to note," "to be on the lookout," "to preserve," "to watch over," and "to keep."

2. In the LXX the verb means "to lurk" in Ps. 37:12 and "to keep in mind" in Ps. 130:3.

3. In other Jewish Greek works one finds the senses "to find by observation," "to wait for observantly," and "to observe" (cultic regulations).

4. In the NT *paratereō* means "to watch" (Jesus) in Mk. 3:2 and "to guard" (the gates) in Acts 9:24. Cultic observance is the point in Gal. 4:10. A relapse into observance of days entails a loss of freedom. Paul may be arguing here against compulsory keeping of the sabbath and OT feasts, but he may also be rejecting the idea of lucky or unlucky days and seasons, for the compound (in the middle) suggests anxious observance in one's own interest.

paratḗrēsis.
1. In Greek this means "watching," "lying in wait," "spying," "attention," "scrutiny," "scientific observation," "self-scrutiny," "self-discipline," "watching over," "keeping" (laws etc.), "observing" (usage), and "maintaining" (obedience).
2. The LXX does not use the term.
3. In the NT it occurs only in Lk. 17:20, where it might have either a temporal or a local reference (observing times or places). These are linked in apocalyptic. The statement that the kingdom is "among you" or "in your midst" suggests, not that the calculation of signs is contrasted with some future incursion of the kingdom, but that the kingdom has already come in Jesus. Some people, however, do not perceive it. Observation of signs cannot show whether the kingdom has come; as it is now at work, God's rule can be grasped only by faith. The messianic expectations of the opponents of Jesus, who are demanding signs, are wholly inadequate in the face of what Jesus effects with his coming among the people.
4. In Diog. 4.5 we find a polemic against the ritual "observance" of Judaism.

diatḗréō. In the NT this word occurs in Lk. 2:51 for "keeping" or "storing up" in the memory. The sense in Acts 15:29 is "to keep oneself," i.e.. "to abstain." Diog. 8:10 says that God keeps his saving plan unchanged up to Christ's coming.

syntḗréō. This word means "to keep" in the memory in Lk. 2:19, "to protect" in Mk. 6:20, "to be preserved" in Mt. 9:17. It means "to think of (and care for)" in Hermas *Mandates* 8.10.   [H. RIESENFELD, VIII, 140-51]

---

títhēmi [to place, lay], *athetéō* [to set aside, annul], *athétēsis* [annulment], *epitíthēmi* [to lay on], *epíthesis* [laying on], *metatíthēmi* [to put in another place], *metáthesis* [change of place], *paratíthēmi* [to present], *parathḗkē* [deposit], (*parakatathḗkē* [deposit]), *protíthēmi* [to set before], *próthesis* [aspiration], *prostíthēmi* [to add to]

---

títhēmi.

A. Secular Greek.
1. The Local Sense.
a. The primary local sense of this word is "to place," "to lay." We thus find it for laying foundations, laying down articles, putting in the hand or before the eyes, putting in one's vote, and interring.
b. Special senses include paying taxes and depositing money.
c. In the military sphere we find several uses, e.g., for camping, siding with, or laying down shields in capitulation.
d. In the games the term denotes the displaying or presenting of prizes.
e. Sacrally it is used for donating gifts to the gods.

f. "To put" in the mind or heart (cf. "to have in mind") is close to the transferred sense.

2. *Transferred Sense.*

a. In the transferred sense we find raising a house, conceiving a child (putting under the girdle), or holding a wedding.

b. Laying down laws etc. is another use.

c. The gods establish ordinances and decrees.

d. Intellectual presupposing or positing offers another field of usage.

e. With a double accusative we find the idea of making someone something, i.e., appointing, marrying, adopting. Along similar lines is the use for making a mock of, or valuing as.

B. The LXX.

1. *Occurrence.* The LXX uses *tithēmi* some 560 times, 260 times for Heb. *šym,* which similarly combines the local and transferred elements.

2. *Meaning.* The OT has much the same meaning as secular Greek, e.g., setting down, erecting, placing, investing, putting on, bringing (gifts), also setting snares, hazarding one's life, taking to heart, appointing, issuing (orders), representing as, or making.

3. In a quarter of the OT references God is the subject in his work of creating, saving, and judging. He sets the stars in the firmament (Gen. 1:17) and sets bounds for the sea (Job 38:10). He makes Abraham the father of many nations (Gen. 17:5-6). He sets his name in specific places (1 Kgs. 9:3). He sets the priest-king's enemies under his feet (Ps. 110:1). He grants life and mercy (Job 10:12). He sets aside tears and sins (Ps. 56:8). He makes idol-manufacturers as nothing (Mic. 1:7). He sets up a wall for Jerusalem (Is. 26:1). Having set Israel in her place (1 Chr. 17:9), he will put her in her own land again (Ezek. 37:14).

C. The NT.

1. *General.*

a. The 101 instances are spread throughout the NT. Often we find the basic local sense, putting a light on a stand (Mk. 4:21), laying out the sick for healing (6:56), serving wine (Jn. 2:10), and laying on hands (Mk. 8:25).

b. Other senses include burying (Mk. 6:29).

c. Financially the term means investing money (Lk. 19:21-22) or setting it aside (1 Cor. 16:2).

d. Figuratively the term means "to set forth" (Mk. 4:30) or "to offer" (1 Cor. 9:18).

2. Peculiar to Luke are such expressions as "to bend the knees" (Lk. 22:41), "to take to heart" or "to intend" (Lk. 1:66; Acts 5:4), "to resolve" (Acts 19:21), and "to lay at the feet" (i.e., "put under the control") (Acts 4:35).

3. Peculiar to John is the expression "to lay down one's life" (10:11). This echoes a Greek expression for "risking one's life" but with a reference to Is. 53:10 which makes the risk into an actual sacrifice (cf. Mk. 10:45).

4. a. Relative to God's action, the NT often quotes Ps. 110:1. In 1 Cor. 15:25 the context shows that the enthronement of Christ and the subjugation of hostile powers take place in time. In Hebrews the exalted position of the Son (1:3) rests on the future subjection of his foes (10:13). Acts 2:33-34 and Mk. 18:19 connect the verse with the ascension (cf. also Col. 3:1). In Mk. 12:35ff. the function of the exalted Lord is denoted by the titles Son of David and Kyrios. Christ is no mere political liberator but the unique and all-embracing Lord.

b. Paul rarely uses *títhēmi* or its compounds. In Rom. 4:17 he quotes Gen. 17:5, where faith is in the God who raises up the promised posterity beyond the bounds of natural procreation. Abraham's election is thus set against the background of the new creation. The same connection appears in 1 Th. 5:9. In Phil. 1:16 and 1 Th. 3:3 the verb denotes the point where divine decision and human existence converge. Divine ordination decides the existence of the members in Christ's body (1 Cor. 12:18, 28). Rom. 9:33 calls Christ the appointed stone of stumbling at which the paths of Israel and the church cross. In 2 Cor. 5:19 the new creation rests on God's reconciling act in Christ's work and the commissioning of the apostles. Divine ordination gives the message its authority. Similarly in 1 Cor. 3:10-11 Paul lays the foundation, but so does God, so that the authorized apostle may be called God's fellow worker (v. 9).

c. In 1 Tim. 1:12 Christ has put Paul in service. In 1 Tim. 2:7 Paul is appointed a herald. The offense of disobedience is ordained in 1 Pet. 2:8, and Sodom and Gomorrah are set as a warning in 2 Pet. 2:6. The Son is appointed heir of all things in Heb. 1:2, and the Servant is appointed a light to the nations in Acts 13:47. The Holy Spirit sets up leaders in Acts 20:28. The Father has fixed the eschatological hour in Acts 1:7.

D. The Apostolic Fathers. Hermas uses the term relative to the fitting and laying of stones in the tower (*Visions* 3.2.7 etc.). Special expressions are bowing the knees (*Visions* 1.1.3), paying heed (*Mandates* 12.4.5), and making mighty (Barn. 6:3). Divine ordination is found in OT quotations (1 Clem. 15.6 etc.). God has set in us the gift of doctrine (Barn. 9.9). He has ordained suffering for believers (Diog. 6.10) and punishment for apostates (1 Clem. 11.1).

atheté̄ō, athétēsis.

1. In secular Greek *atheté̄ō* means "to regard as nought," "to set aside," "to consider invalid," passive "to be struck off," "to break with."

2. The LXX gives the term the sense of willful repudiation, e.g., "to disregard," "to violate" (an oath), "to ignore," "to rebel," "to annul," "to revoke," and intransitively "to act unfaithfully or wickedly," "to be apostate."

3. a. The first NT sense is "to annul," as in Gal. 3:15, where only the testator may annul his will while he is alive, or Gal. 2:21, where Paul does not annul God's grace as Judaizers do by robbing it of its practical force.

b. Violation of God's law or commandment is at issue in Heb. 10:28; Lk. 7:30; Mk. 7:9. Young widows break their first loyalty by remarrying (1 Tim. 5:12), and God brings to nothing the wisdom of the wise (1 Cor. 1:19).

c. The verb also means refusing or rejecting a person (cf. 1 Th. 4:8; Jn. 12:48; Jude 8). *athétēsis* is "abrogation" or "annulment" of the law in Heb. 7:18, of sin in 9:26.

4. The apostolic fathers use the verb for rejecting or despising God, Christ, or Christ's witnesses.

For the *anatíthēmi* group → *anatíthēmi*; for *diatíthēmi* and *diathḗkē* → *diatíthēmi*.

epitíthēmi, epíthesis.

1. In secular Greek the verb means "to lay down," "to set on," "to apply," "to add on," "to give," "to take up." The noun is used for putting up a statue, or putting on a cover, or for an assault.

2. a. The verb is common in the LXX in various senses, e.g., putting on plaster, imposing service or tribute, bringing fire, smearing blood, laying out the showbread,

waving the wave offering, weaving a conspiracy, intending something. Especially common is the expression "to lay on hands," e.g., for consecration to ministry (Num. 8:10), dedication of offerings (Ex. 29:10), imparting blessing or spiritual gifts (Num. 27:18; Gen. 48:17-18), cursing (Lev. 24:14), and once for healing (2 Cor. 5:11).

b. The noun occurs only five times for "conspiracy" in 2 Chr. 25:27, "assault" in 2 Macc. 4:41; 5:5; 14:15, and "wooing" in Ezek. 23:11.

3. a. In the NT the verb is used for laying the sheep on the shoulder in Lk. 15:5, placing on the crown of thorns in Mt. 27:29, putting the title on the cross in Mt. 27:37, laying on blows in Lk. 10:30, imposing a yoke in Acts 15:28, and giving a name in Mk. 3:16-17. In Rev. 22:18 God will "lay" a punishment on those who "add to" the words of the book (a play on the word).

b. In 20 of 40 instances "laying on of hands" is at issue (also *epíthesis* four times). On the one hand Jesus lays on hands to heal (Mk. 5:23 etc.); on the other he lays on hands to bless (Mt. 19:13). Laying on of hands is also connected with imparting the Spirit (Acts 8:17ff.), with ordination for a task (6:6), and with imparting gifts by ordination (1 Tim. 4:14).

4. There is nothing new in the apostolic fathers.

metatíthēmi, metáthesis.

1. In secular Greek the verb means "to bring to, or set in, another place," "to alter," and middle "to change over." The noun means "change of place," "alteration," or "change of mind."

2. The LXX uses the verb for removing boundaries, transplanting peoples, or translating from the earth, as well as for convincing or talking around. The noun denotes "transition" to Greek custom in 2 Macc. 11:24.

3. a. In the NT the verb means "to carry to" in Acts 7:16, "to take up" in Heb. 11:5 (Enoch), "to transform" in Jude 4, "to be done away" in Heb. 7:12, "to fall away" in Gal. 1:6.

b. The noun is used for Enoch's "translation" in Heb. 11:5, the "alteration" of the law in 7:12, and the "metamorphosis" of shaken creation in 12:27.

4. The apostolic fathers use only the verb (cf. the local sense in Barn. 13:5, Enoch's translation in 1 Clem. 9.3, and changing one's mind in Mart. Pol. 11.1).

paratíthēmi, parathḗkē (parakatathḗkē).

1. Secular Greek.

a. This verb means "to set beside or before," "to present."

b. A technical meaning is "to deposit," "to entrust," in the legal sense of leaving an object in another's keeping, with strict penalties for embezzlement. A transferred sense develops out of the technical use.

2. The LXX.

a. The term is used here mostly in the local sense "to serve" (food), "to set forth," "to lay down," "to furnish."

b. The commercial sense "to entrust for safekeeping" occurs, e.g., in Lev. 5:23 (cf. Ex. 22:7ff. for regulations). In Ps. 31:5 the author puts himself under God's protection.

3. Later Judaism. The rabbis supply rulings for goods on deposit. Josephus stresses the need for honesty. Philo speaks about entrusting knowledge and regards the self and all that it has as a trust from God.

4. The NT.

a. The verb occurs 19 times, usually in the literal sense of "laying" food before someone (Mk. 6:41), or "expounding" teaching (Acts 17:3). Jesus commends his spirit to the Father (Lk. 23:46), the persecuted should entrust their lives to a faithful Creator (1 Pet. 4:19), and Paul entrusts the elders to God's abiding faithfulness (Acts 14:23; 20:32).

b. The middle is a commercial term in Lk. 12:48. Along the same lines the faith is a trust in 1 Tim. 1:18 (cf. 2 Tim. 2:2). It is to be kept intact up to the parousia (1 Tim. 6:20). This is to be done with the help of the Spirit and as an act of faith and love (2 Tim. 1:3-4). In 2 Tim. 1:12 the meaning is more probably "what has been entrusted to me" than "what I have entrusted." Christ himself protects this right up to the last day. Not the teaching itself, but he who is its content, insures its continuity. One may thus repulse false teaching without absolutizing tradition.

5. The Apostolic Fathers. In these works there is nothing distinctive about the verb. The noun means entrusted deposit in Hermas *Mandates* 3.2; liars do not return it.

protíthēmi, próthesis.

1. Secular Greek.

a. This word means "to set before" (e.g., food, offerings).

b. It then means "to display, or make known, publicly."

c. Another sense is "to impose (middle "undertake") a task."

d. A final sense is "to prefer," "to put before."

2. The LXX. Here we find such senses as "to collect," "to set out" (the showbread), "to set before the eyes" (God), and "to undertake" (or "purpose").

3. The NT.

a. A reference to the showbread occurs in Mk. 2:26, and cf. also Heb. 9:2, which seems to refer to the bread laid out rather than the act of placing.

b. In Rom. 3:25 the reference might be to God's counsel, i.e., his ordaining of Christ as a means of expiation, but the context seems to demand execution rather than resolve, and hence it is better to think in terms of the public setting forth of Christ as a means of expiation.

c. The verb denotes human resolving in Rom. 1:13 and the noun in Acts 11:23. Paul's "aspiration" is what Timothy observes in 2 Tim. 3:10.

d. Paul gives *próthesis* a new sense when he uses it for the primal decision whereby God initiates his saving work through Christ. In Rom. 8:28 those who love God rest on the basic resolve wherein God's will to bring to final glory is coincident with his will to affirm the community. The content of *próthesis* is God's abiding faithfulness. The goal of foreknowledge and foreordination (vv. 29-30) is the community of the firstborn Son. God is the subject of calling and justification in time, so that on the real basis of the event in Christ Paul can speak already, in prophetic anticipation, of eschatological glorification. In Rom. 9:11 God's purpose in election stands throughout the stories of Esau and Jacob. It is not rigid but freely works out the Yes to Israel in human decisions and by human agents. In Eph. 1:19ff. God's final aim is according to the good pleasure established from the first in Christ. In God's resolve, which comes first both temporally and materially, lies the community's superiority to Gnostic sects. 2 Tim. 1:9 traces salvation and calling to God's eternal purpose and grace in Christ.

4. The Apostolic Fathers. These authors use the verb for undertaking in Hermas *Mandates* 12.3.5 and ordination in Diog. 9.2. *próthesis* means "serving" in 1 Clem. 45.7.

prostíthēmi.

1. In secular Greek this means "to put to," "to add to," "to shut," middle "to attach oneself to," "to win," "to join" (cf. also "to win over").

2. In the LXX we find Hebraizing in many of the references (cf. Gen. 4:2; 25:1). Elsewhere the usage is similar to that of secular Greek.

3. a. There are some Hebraisms in the NT (cf. Lk. 19:11). "Adding to" is the meaning in Mk. 4:24; Heb. 12:19; Lk. 3:20; Mk. 6:27; Mt. 6:33 (unless "give" is the sense here).

b. The idea of "adding" suggests that the law is simply an interlude in Gal. 3:19.

c. The adding of people (to the church) is the point in Acts 2:41, 47; they are added to the Lord in 5:14 and 11:24.

4. In the apostolic fathers we find such senses as "to continue" (Barn. 2.5), "to add" (19.11), "to increase" in sins (Hermas *Visions* 6.1.4) or in righteousness (Did. 11.2).   [C. MAURER, VIII, 152-68]

---

timḗ [honor],   *timáō* [to honor]

A. **Greek and Hellenistic Literature.**

I. Meanings. In general *timḗ* means "worth," "evaluation," "honor," then "price." Specific meanings are "appraisal," "assessment," "honor," "dignity," "honorarium," "honors." Similarly *timáō* means "to value," "to honor," passive "to be deemed worthy of honor." Religiously the honoring of the gods is worship. The Greeks also believe that certain people are honored by the gods, e.g., with wealth, power, etc. *timaí* may be used for offerings, feasts, etc. that honor the gods, or for donations to them. Financially the terms are used for fixing value, appraising, and taxing.

II. The Concept of Honor. timḗ has at first a strong material orientation to possessions, strength, or social influence. Later, moral conduct plays a bigger part. The fact that *timḗ* can also mean "price" upholds the material connection, but *timḗ* as honor increasingly becomes inner worth as distinct from outward esteem. For Aristotle there is no honor without virtue; only on the basis of virtue should outward honor be shown. No honor is enough for perfect virtue, and the person of inner worth is finally above outward honor. In Stoicism inner honor is what counts. The sage, enjoying inward freedom, can live without external honor and can thus be relaxed in relation to it.

B. **Hellenistic Judaism.**

I. The LXX.

1. Hebrew has no exact equivalent for the group but does require the honoring of parents (Ex. 20:12) and of the moral commandments (Gen. 38:23). The LXX uses *timḗ* for 12 Hebrew terms. A first sense is honor, e.g., the honor that must be brought to God, the honor that God gives us, the honor that comes through doing good, the honor that must be shown others. We then find the meaning "price" with such nuances as "payment," "compensation," "evaluation." Other senses are "valuables" and "tax." Finally the term denotes royal dignity or honorable conduct.

2. *timáō* renders six Hebrew terms in such senses as "to honor" (God, kings, parents, the elderly, the poor, loyal slaves, doctors, or the temple), "to appraise," and "to honor with money," i.e., "to reward."

II. Philo. In Philo we find the honoring of God, of parents, the elderly, the sabbath, etc. Philo also uses the term for "dignity," "value," "assessment," "tax." Very typical are combinations that relate inward and outward values.

III. Josephus. In Josephus, the noun (often plural) mostly has such meanings as "honor," "honoring," "veneration" (of God), "dignity" (of the high priest), "distinction," "reward," "recognition," although we also find "price." Special expressions are "to hold in honor," "to come to honor," and "to be highly honored." The verb means "to honor," "to venerate," "to reward," passive "to stand in honor."

C. The NT.

I. *timế*.

1. *Honor.*

a. Rom. 12:10 exhorts Christians to prefer one another in honor, 1 Tim. 6:1 tells slaves to honor their masters lest God's name be defamed, 1 Pet. 3:7 summons men to honor their wives out of loving regard, 1 Th. 4:4 shows that the wife has a claim to honor as God's creation, and Rom. 13:7 asks believers not only to pay taxes to the state but also to give it the fear and respect that are its due.

b. "Recognition" is the sense in Jn. 4:44. The common combination with *dóxa* occurs in christological statements in 2 Pet. 1:17 (the transfiguration) and Heb. 2:7, 9; 3:3. In Heb. 2:7ff. Christ's passion is the presupposition of his crowning with glory and honor (Ps. 8:5ff.), i.e., his institution to high-priestly dignity. Moses has his own honor, but this is far inferior to that of the Son (3:3). In these references *timế* is one part of *dóxa*. Dignity of office is the point in Heb. 5:4. Christians also have *timế* according to 1 Pet. 2:7. They share Christ's honor as living stones built into the spiritual house. In 1 Pet. 1:7 those who prove their faith in affliction will have praise, glory, and honor when Christ comes. In 1 Cor. 12:23-24 believers who have no striking· charisms have equal honor with the rest. In 2 Tim. 2:20-21 some vessels have noble uses, others ignoble; believers must cleanse themselves from error so as to be of noble use. This metaphor carries a suggestion of price or value as well as honor. In Rom. 9:21 the vessel that is made for honor is that to which the use for which it is destined brings honor. In Rom. 2:7, 10 glory, honor, and immortality are the reward at the judgment for doing good in fulfilment of God's will.

2. *Honorarium.* This is perhaps the meaning in 1 Tim. 5:17, unless "honor" be meant.

3. *Col. 2:23.* Paul in this difficult passage is adopting the slogans of his opponents. For them *timế* is perhaps a term denoting election and deification. If so, Paul rejects this kind of *timế*. Other possibilities for *timế* in this passage are "honor" or "value."

4. *Liturgical Use.* Doxological use occurs in 1 Tim. 1:17 and 6:16. Revelation offers more developed doxologies in 4:9, 11; 5:12-13 (to God and the Lamb); 7:12. The church's praise corresponds to these heavenly songs.

5. *Value, Price.* With *dóxa*, *timế* denotes earthly goods in Rev. 21:26. Believers hand over the "proceeds" of sales in Acts 4:34; 5:2-3. The "value" of the books burned at Ephesus is given in Acts 19:19. Acts 7:16 refers to the grave that Abraham bought for a "sum" of money. In 1 Cor. 6:20; 7:23 Christians have been bought with the "price" of Christ's blood.

II. *timáō*.

1. *"To honor."* Jesus presses the commandment to honor parents, criticizing the evasion of financial support in case of need (Mk. 7:10ff.). The honoring of widows in 1 Tim. 5:3 probably includes financial provision as well as respect. Children are to honor their parents in the Lord (Eph. 6:2), and believers are to honor all people, specifically rulers (1 Pet. 2:17). Paul receives many honors, or concretely gifts, after

curing the father of Publius and others on Malta (Acts 28:10). Jesus claims the same honor as is paid to God in Jn. 5:23, for God has commissioned him as eschatological Judge. He himself honors the Father (8:49), and those who serve him will be honored by the Father (12:26), i.e., granted a share in his own glory.

2. *"To value."* Mt. 27:8-9 sees in the purchase of the potter's field a fulfilment of Zech. 11:12-13. The quotation contains both *timáō* ("to assess the value") and *timḗ* ("the sum realized").

D. The Apostolic Fathers. Christians are summoned to honor their teachers (Did. 4.1) and officebearers (1 Clem. 21.6; Ignatius *Smyrneans* 9.1). The congregational office is held in honor (1 Clem. 44.6; cf. Did. 15.2). *timḗ* also denotes the divinely ordained position of the ruler (1 Clem. 61.1). Combination with *dóxa* occurs in 1 Clem. 64 and 65.2.   [J. SCHNEIDER, VIII, 169-80]

---

tolmáō [to dare, presume], *apotolmáō* [to be bold], *tolmētḗs* [presumptuous], *tolmērós* [bold]

A. The Greek World.

1. From a root meaning "to lift," "to carry," *tolmáō* means first "to endure," "to suffer," then "to dare," "to venture," then "to be courageous," "to have the courage," and finally "to make bold," "to presume." In rhetoric we find the phrase "to venture to say."

2. The compound strengthens the sense.

B. The LXX. The term occurs only seven times in the LXX and only twice with Hebrew originals. It has the two meanings "to dare" and "to presume" (3 Macc. 3:21; 2 Macc. 4:2).

C. Philo and Josephus.

1. Philo occasionally uses the term for venturing hypotheses or statements.

2. Josephus makes considerable use of *tolmáō* and related terms for "to have the courage," "to dare," and "to venture." Positive motives behind ventures are courage and warlike passion; negative motives are conceit and wantonness.

D. The NT.

1. The Gospels, Acts, and Jude.

a. *tolmáō* means "to dare" when Joseph takes courage and goes to Pilate to ask for the body of Jesus (Mk. 15:43). He ventures a direct approach.

b. In the negative, no one dare ask Jesus any more questions in Mk. 12:34; they all recognize his supremacy. Faced with the risen Lord, the disciples, too, do not dare ask him who he is (Jn. 21:12). Moses did not dare look closely at the bush (Acts 7:32). Michael does not presume to pass judgment on the devil in Jude 9. In Acts 5:13 the other believers dare not join the apostles, who alone come under arrest (v. 18).

2. Paul.

a. Paul makes lavish use of *tolmáō*, first in the weak sense of "dare," as in Rom. 5:7.

b. "Dare" with the stronger sense of venturing confession or facing up to opponents occurs in Phil. 1:14 and 2 Cor. 10:2. "To dare" with the nuance "to presume" may be found in 2 Cor. 11:21, where Paul's courtesy to opponents carries with it an ironical suggestion of their presumption. Similar irony occurs in 10:12: Paul does not presume to class himself with those who commend themselves.

c. A final use in Paul is for "to be insolent." Believers should not insolently go to law against one another (1 Cor. 6:1), and Paul will not insolently speak about things that Christ has not done through him (Rom. 15:18). In Paul, as in the entire NT, *tolmáō* never denotes the venture of life or of faith. What makes a word or work a venture is danger or propriety. What prevents the venture is recognition of Christ's supremacy or reverence for God.

apotolmáō. This word occurs only in Rom. 10:20 to strengthen the formula.

tolmētḗs. This word relates only to false teachers, whom 2 Pet. 2:10 describes as presumptuous and self-willed (cf. Jude 9).

tolmēróteros. In saying that he has written rather boldly in Rom. 15:15, Paul is simply using an apologetic formula. Behind it lies the conviction that he has something special to say. [G. FITZER, VIII, 181-86]

---

tópos [place]

A. Greek Literature.
1. Simple Use. In common usage this word means a. "territory," "land," "area," "locality," b. "district," "town," "dwelling place," and c. "place" in a very general sense, as in such phrases as "in every place," "in the place in question," "in no place" (nowhere), "on the spot," and "out of place."
2. Special Meanings.
a. In cultic texts *tópos* sometimes means "sanctuary" (the holy place). Later a holy place may be a grave, e.g., of a martyr.
b. Another use is for "someone's place," e.g., a senator's seat, a place at school, one's place in the world. The phrase "in place of" develops out of this sense. So does the transferred sense of "opportunity" or "occasion" (cf. "room for flight," "occasion for tears").
c. In rhetoric, since everything has a place, a *tópos* is what recurs in the same situation (topic). Technically Aristotle first has a "basic element" in view. But the word may then denote various fields of Stoic dialectic.
d. Another meaning is the "place" in a writing.
3. Philosophical, Scientific, and Cosmological Usage. Aristotle starts from the idea of movement from one place to another. There is no empty place; the thought of place is always proper to certain things. When common to several things, it is still defined and not unlimited space. Geographically *tópos* means "position," "territory," or "zone." Cosmological speculation discusses the place in which the cosmos moves. The cosmos has four *tópoi*, namely, heaven, aether, air, and earth. Similarly there are three spheres, the upper one of humanity, the middle one of animals, and the lower one of plants. The soul, too, has three *tópoi* as well as three functions.

B. OT Usage.
1. General. The Hebrew original of *tópos* is *māqôm*, which is almost always translated *tópos*, although *tópos* also occurs frequently for other terms or where there is no original. The Greek and Hebrew largely correspond, but not wholly so.

2. *Linguistic Peculiarities.*

a. Basis. The idea of a "site" or "settlement" is intrinsic to the Hebrew, not that of space or locality.

b. Place Where. This explains the common use for "where," e.g., "the place where his tent was" in Gen. 13:14.

c. The Place. The Hebrew often adds the demonstrative to denote the place meant, often perhaps in the sense of "here" (cf. Dt. 1:31).

d. A close relation comes to expression in the use with a possessive pronoun (cf. Gen. 30:25).

3. *Comparable Meanings.*

The Hebrew may denote a. a "land" or "locality," but always in the singular (cf. Ex. 3:8).

b. Another meaning is "town" or "dwelling place" (cf. Gen. 18:24).

c. The term may also be used for various other places (cf. the campsite in Dt. 1:33, the narrow place in Num. 22:26).

4. *The Promised Land.* The Hebrew term does not come into technical use for the promised land but it may denote the place that God has appointed for his people (Ex. 23:20). Those who are abroad are away from both their people and their own place (2 Sam. 15:19).

5. *Holy Places.*

a. In a cultic sense the term may denote original Canaanite shrines; some of these come into association with faith in God and the promise of the land (cf. Gen. 12:6ff.; 28:11ff.), and are thus appropriated theologically as well as historically.

b. Zion and the Temple. Although Jerusalem, too, must have been an original holy place, the OT gives it significance only as the city of David to which he brings the ark and where he plans the temple. It thus becomes the holy place that God has chosen according to Dt. 12:5, 11 etc. Since God has set his name, and tabernacles, there, the people must destroy all other holy places.

c. This Place. In prophetic warnings "this place" often means Jerusalem but at times the temple is perhaps in view (cf. Jer. 14:13ff.). If judgment falls on the people, land, and city, special significance attaches to the destruction of the temple.

d. Postexilic Usage. The cultic use is now governed by the idea of the sanctity of the place and its precincts. Only the LXX, however, develops the term into a technical one for the holy place. 1–4 Maccabees never call the land *tópos* and only rarely Jerusalem, but they often have "holy place" for the sacred precincts.

6. *Places in Creation.* Another sense, worked out in Wisdom writings, is that of the proper place (cf. Gen. 24:31; Num. 32:1). The place may be large or narrow, or may even cease to exist (1 Sam. 26:13; 2 Kgs. 6:1; Is. 5:8). The place of the wicked denies them when they perish (Job 8:18). Gog comes forth from his place (Ezek. 38:15), and God has his place in heaven (cf. Hos. 5:15) or the temple (1 Chr. 16:27). Humans have their place, but the time comes when it knows them no more (Ps. 103:16). Geographical features also have their place (Ps. 104:8). This may give reassurance (Job 38:12, 19), but it also suggests pointlessness (Eccl. 3:20). God alone knows the place of wisdom (Job 28:12, 20). Wrong may at times stand in the place of right (Eccl. 3:16). But *tópos* is also the opportunity or possibility of being that God has given. There is a place for repentance and also for mercy (Wis. 12:10; Sir. 16:14). God has provided a place—that of repentance and salvation—which is the basis of a life in faith.

C. Later Jewish Usage.

1. The Rabbis. A distinctive rabbinic use is as a term for God.

2. Philo. Philo takes *tópos* a. as a place that a body fills, b. as the divine *lógos* that God has filled with immaterial forces, and c. as God himself inasmuch as he comprehends all things, i.e., in a cosmic sense. God is a place of refuge for all things and provides a place for all creatures. Earthly movement is a change of place. Creatures all have their places, but human beings are at home in all spheres. The soul has left its heavenly place, and the wicked have no place to go. The righteous, however, prepare their souls as a place for God to dwell. Philo, then, spiritualizes the OT understanding with some help from the usage of Greek cosmology.

D. NT Usage.

1. tópos as a General Term for Place.

a. Semitic influence may be seen in John in the use of *tópos* with *hópou* ("there where") (cf. 6:23; 10:40; 11:6). In Lk. 10:32 *tópos* links up the story topographically (cf. 19:5). Adverbial phrases are "everywhere" in 1 Cor. 1:2, "here and there" in Mk. 13:8, and "to another place" in Acts 12:17.

b. To denote a place *tópos* is parallel to *pólis* in Acts 16:2 etc. In the plural a district is suggested (cf. Lk. 4:37). An adjective may describe the place; cf. *érēmos tópos* (Mk. 1:35) for "desert" or "waste place."

c. The name seldom accompanies *tópos,* but *tópos* and Golgotha always go together (Mk. 15:22; Jn. 19:17). Mk. 15:2 and Mt. 27:33 add that the name means the place of a skull, John gives the Greek translation first, and Lk. 23:33 has "the place which is called The Skull." Fixing the site exactly assumes importance in view of the need to establish the historical reality of the crucifixion.

2. Special Senses.

a. Temple. The use of *tópos* for the temple is rare in the NT. We find it in Mt. 24:15 and Jn. 4:20, and most likely in Jn. 11:48, although *tópos* could be the city here. In Acts one might mention 6:13 and 21:28, where Stephen and Paul are accused of attacking the holy place after the manner of OT prophets.

b. The Right Place. Luke uses *tópos* in this sense in 14:9 and Paul in 1 Cor. 14:16. In Acts 1:25 the vacated "place" rather than "office" is the meaning, and Judas goes to the "place" where he really belongs. The transferred sense of "opportunity" suggests itself in Rom. 15:28 and Acts 25:16. In Heb. 12:17 Esau's failure to find opportunity to repent shows that one cannot control repentance at will; the chance to repent comes only as God provides it. Similarly in Heb. 8:7 a divine act establishes the new covenant. Rom. 12:19 demands that we give divine wrath the opportunity to act, but Eph. 4:27 warns against giving place to the devil. In Rev. 6:14 *tópos* has a cosmic reach; every mountain and island will be moved from its place. In Rev. 2:5 the removal of the church's lampstand from its place signifies judgment. In Rev. 12:6 God prepares a place for the woman, who represents the church. She can flee to this place in time of persecution (v. 14). Judgment means that no place remains (cf. 12:8; 20:11) except the place of torment (cf. Lk. 16:28).

c. Place of Scripture. The use for an OT reference occurs only in Lk. 4:17.

E. Apostolic Fathers. The use in these works is much the same as in the NT but with some movement toward the sense of "position" or "office" (cf. 1 Clem. 40.51; 44.5; Ignatius *Smyrneans* 6.1; Ignatius *Polycarp* 1.2; Pol. 11.1), although only in isolated cases.   [H. KÖSTER, VIII, 187-208]

---

trápeza [table, meal]

A. Usage.
1. General Use. This word means "table" and then in a transferred sense "meal," "food."

2. Dining Table. Tables develop out of stands of cloth, leather, wickerwork, or metal on which food is placed. The forms of tables vary according to the posture adopted for eating, e.g., crouching, sitting, or reclining. In Palestine crouching or sitting seems to have been the usual posture, but the rabbis make reclining obligatory for the Passover. One reclines on the left arm and eats chopped-up food with bread and fingers. In the NT only reclining is mentioned, but probably in the weak sense of "sitting down for a meal" in many instances. One cannot always assume that a table is present, although the term for "to recline" can include it even when *trápeza* is not mentioned.

3. Money-Changers' Table. Money changers regularly use tables for their coins and thus come to be called *trapezítai* ("table men").

4. Table for the Showbread. This is the only OT cultic table mentioned in the NT (Heb. 9:2). We read of such a table in 1 Sam. 21:7; 1 Kgs. 6:20; 1 Macc. 1:22. 1 Cor. 10:20 refers to a cultic table in the pagan sphere.

B. Theological Table Sayings.
1. Daily Bread. In Lk. 16:21 and Mk. 7:28 the table represents the supply of daily food; the poor seek nourishment from its superfluity. In Rom. 11:9 the table is a figure of nourishment. What should contribute to life becomes a snare; the law is probably meant (cf. 11:7; 9:31).

2. Table Fellowship. In Lk. 22:21 the expression shows that the traitor belongs to the innermost circle, i.e., those who have table fellowship. Lk. 22:28ff. connects sitting at table with sitting on thrones, i.e., participation in the kingdom (cf. Mt. 19:28). Behind this figure stand the ideas of the royal table and the eschatological banquet. In Acts 6:2 the common sacral meal of the community is at issue. The apostles should minister the word instead of having to see to meals. Meal is also the sense in Acts 16:33-34; the converted jailer sets food before Paul and Silas.

3. The Table of the Lord and the Table of Demons. The table of the Lord is the table or meal which the Lord provides and which lays claim to those who receive it. The table of demons is the sacrificial meal which similarly binds participants (cf. 1 Cor. 10:18), not to the gods, but to the demons that stand behind them. The phrase *trápeza kyríou* finds an OT basis in Mal. 1:7, 12, although Paul is not suggesting that the table is an altar or that the Supper has a sacrificial character. The common feature is not sacrifice but participation and commitment. The *kýrios* and demons offer different things and summon to different dominions; one cannot alternate between them (1 Cor. 10:21-22).

4. Congregational Worship. In the early church worship takes place in houses around everyday tables. Only when the sacramental meal is detached does a special table come into use. In the third century A.D. this table as the place of consecration is called an altar, but it is still an ordinary table. Later the eucharistic table is honored as a holy place, left continuously in one spot, and called either table or altar with appropriate preciser definitions. [L. GOPPELT, VIII, 209-15]

---

treís [three],   ***trís*** [three],   ***trítos*** [third]

A. Three in the Greek and Hellenistic Roman World. Divine triads are common in ancient cults, and threefold utterance or execution supposedly makes valid or definitive. Thus we find threefold oaths, invocations, prayers, etc. Some healing processes last three days. Aristotle thinks the number three is significant in nature. It embraces beginning, middle, and end. There are three dimensions, and time has three aspects. Philo thinks that the soul has three divisions. The right is the mean between two extremes.

B. Three in the OT and LXX. Three seldom has specific importance in the OT. The three sons of Noah are the ancestors of the whole race in Gen. 6:10. Balaam blesses Israel three times in Num. 24:10. The priestly blessing is threefold (Num. 6:24ff.), and we find a threefold crescendo of promise in Hos. 2:21-22 and of action in 1 Kgs. 18:34. Notable threes are David's heroes, the three righteous men of Ezek. 14:14, the three friends of Job, the three friends of Daniel, the three who visited Abraham, and cf. the three flocks of Gen. 29:2. Cultic threes are the three feasts (Ex. 23:14) and the three hours of prayer (Dan. 6:11). Three is a round number in the combination two-three (Job 33:29). Three days are important in Ex. 15:22; 2 Kgs. 2:17; Judg. 14:14; 2 Chr. 20:25; Esth. 4:16; Hos. 6:2; 2 Macc. 5:14. Only in the third generation can Edomites and Egyptians enter the Lord's community (Dt. 23:9). A three-member description of the Spirit's works occurs in Is. 11:2, and threefold utterance emphasizes validity in Is. 6:11.

C. Three in Jewish Literature. John Hyrcanus holds the threefold office of prophet, priest, and king. Three gifts are given for the sake of three persons, water for Miriam, the pillar of cloud for Aaron, and manna for Moses. We find three ranks, but also three nets of Belial and three offenses that God notes. A three-year cycle is worked out for the reading of the law.

D. Three in the NT.
1. a. Strict use occurs in 2 Cor. 11:25; 12:14; 13:1; Gal. 1:18; Mk. 9:5; Rev. 21:13. The third heaven of 2 Cor. 12:2 accords with current ideas. In Lk. 12:52-53 the two-and-three division arises out of the relationships in a Palestinian household. The number 153 in Jn. 21:11 seems to be a triangular number expressing totality.

b. Round numbers are common in Acts (months in 7:20; 19:8; 20:3; 28:11, days in 9:9; 25:1; 28:7, 12, 17).

2. The sayings about Christ's resurrection on the third day stand in obvious relation to Hos. 6:2 (cf. Mk. 8:31; 14:58; Mt. 27:63-64; Jn. 2:19-20; 1 Cor. 15:4), but the events of Easter (the empty tomb and the first appearances) give precision to the number.

3. Ideas of few or many may be connected with the number three. Three years are too long and exhaust the owner's patience in Lk. 13:7, but in Mt. 18:20 "two or three" tells us that the Lord will be present even with the smallest number that meet in his name. Paul limits the speakers in 1 Cor. 14:29, and God sets a term for the work of Jesus in Lk. 13:32.

4. In sayings based on Dt. 19:15 "two or three" stands in antithesis to one. In the three steps of Mt. 18:15ff. the one that starts the process is one of the two or three witnesses needed. Paul refers to the witness of threefold action in 2 Cor. 13:1. 1 Jn. 5:7-8 stresses the agreement of three testimonies. Heb. 10:28 rests on a combination of Dt. 17:6 and Num. 15:30. Lk. 10:36 distinguishes the conduct of the third traveler from that of the other two.

5. Threefold performance or occurrence denotes completeness and hence importance in Acts 10:16, urgency in Mt. 26:44, intensity in 2 Cor. 12:8, long-suffering and obstinacy in Lk. 20:12, definitiveness in Lk. 23:22, totality in Mk. 14:30, penetrating scrutiny in Jn. 21:17, and certainty in 20:19ff.

6. "These three" in 1 Cor. 13:13 is meant comprehensively. The same triad of faith, love, and hope occurs in 1 Th. 1:3 and Col. 1:4ff. Another fixed triad in Paul is God, Lord, and Spirit (1 Cor. 12:4ff.; Eph. 4:4ff.; 2 Cor. 13:13; cf. 2 Jn. 3; Jude 20-21). In context the three are the authors or agents of salvation; this shows that the statements arise out of the matter itself and not by way of speculation. One may compare Father, Son, and Holy Spirit in Mt. 28:19, God, the spirits, and Christ in Rev. 1:4-5, and God, Christ, and the angels in Rev. 3:5. The serpent, beast, and false prophet are an ungodly triad in Rev. 16:13.

7. Three plays a role in parables and stories (cf. the three gifts of Mt. 2:11, the three types of people in Lk. 14:18ff., the three forms of judgment in Mt. 5:22, the three temptations of Mt. 4:1ff., the threefold prediction of the passion in Mk. 8:31; 9:31; 10:33-34. (For a full list see *TDNT,* VIII, 223-25.)

E. **The Apostolic Fathers.** Did. 12.2 limits hospitality to two or three days. The herald declares three times that Polycarp has confessed Christ (Mart. Pol. 12.1). Trine immersion is the rule in Did. 7.3. (For various other triads cf. *TDNT,* VIII, 225.) Father, Son, and Spirit occur in Did. 7.1, God, Christ, and Spirit in 1 Clem. 46.6, Father, Christ, and Holy Spirit in Ignatius *Ephesians* 9.1, and Christ, Father, and Spirit in Ignatius *Magnesians* 13.1-2.   [G. DELLING, VIII, 216-25]

---

tréchō [to run, hasten],   **drómos** [course],   **pródromos** [forerunner]

---

tréchō.

A. **The Greek World.**
1. *Literal Sense.* Literally this word means "to run," "to rush on," "to run through."
2. *Transferred Sense.* A common transferred sense is "to hasten (on)."
3. *The Stadium.* Runners in the Olympic games rank high, and the term has a cultic nuance in this connection. Yet there is also criticism of runners. Plato contends for intellectual achievement, and the Cynics point out that many animals excel men in running. Yet critics like to depict themselves as the true contestants who deserve the crown, even though wreaths in fact are better adapted for goats, which can eat them.

B. **The OT and Later Judaism.**
1. *The LXX.* *tréchō* occurs in Job 41:14 for "to leap," in Gen. 18:7 for "to run," in 2 Kgs. 4:22 for "to ride." In addition to professional runners, there are those who run for everyday reasons, e.g., to bring good news or to save life (2 Sam. 18:19; Prov. 7:23). Elijah runs when the hand of God is on him (1 Kgs. 18:46). Prophets run even when God has not sent them (Jer. 23:21). This may be related to the spreading of the message or we may have the transferred sense of reading with ease. God's word runs swiftly (Ps. 147:15), God seems to run against Job like a warrior (Job 16:14), and sinners run as in battle against God (15:26). Running the way of God's commandments is an emphatic form of walking (Ps. 119:32). The seven martyrs in 4 Macc. 14:5 run the way of immortality by fearlessly hastening to death.
2. *Qumran.* Qumran relates Hab. 2:2 to the Teacher of Righteousness either in the

sense of hastening to spread truth or in that of ready reading of the record. A readiness to run with those who seek righteousness comes to expression. By joining the runners one is lifted out of confusion.

3. *Survey.* Running means prompt obedience, and blessing attends it just as eschatological expectation promotes it. Apart from 4 Macc. 14:5 the texts are not dependent on Hellenistic usage. This verse shows how easy it is to combine the Hellenistic idea with others, but Philo and Josephus do not do this.

C. The NT.

1. *Paul.* The prayer of 2 Th. 3:1 rests on Ps. 147:15. Gal. 2:2 and Phil. 2:16 both refer to running in vain. In Gal. 2:2 Paul has his missionary work in mind, in Phil. 2:16 the reference is more personal but he still thinks of a commissioned running with which others associate. In 1 Cor. 9:24ff. and Phil. 3:12ff. running for a prize is the point. The stress is on preparation and effort, not on defeating rivals. The runner in the arena is thus a model only with qualifications. The use in Rom. 9:16 is unexpected. The statement stresses the normative action of God. Willing and running are not directly connected. The idea seems to be that things do not depend on exerting all the force of will in an effort to win salvation. They do not depend on such brilliant but superfluous achievements as those of runners in the arena.

2. *Other Works.* Forgiving love forces the father to run to meet the prodigal in Lk. 15:20. Why the person runs with the vinegar in Mk. 15:36 is not clear. Running under demonic possession occurs in Mk. 5:6 (cf. Rev. 9:9). The running to the tomb in Jn. 20:4 (cf. Mary in 20:2) has symbolical force, as does the difference in speed. A transferred sense may be found only in Heb. 12:1.

D. Post – NT Writings.
Pol. 9.2 rests on Phil. 2:16. 2 Clem. 7.3 relates the language of the games to conduct. The sense is literal in Mart. Pol. 7.1. Ignatius uses the compound *syntréchō* (cf. Pol. 6.1, where the context does not support an allusion to the games).

drómos.

1. This term means "course" with reference to horses, clouds, journeys, etc. Other senses are "way" and "corridor."

2. In the LXX the use in Eccl. 9:11; 2 Sam. 18:27; Jer. 8:6 is much the same as elsewhere. The phrase in Jer. 23:10 (cf. v. 21) means running with authorization.

3. Philo refers to the *drómos* of nature, the tongue, deliberation, and the eyes of the *psyché.*

4. In the NT reference is made to a course of life that has ended (Acts 13:25) or that will shortly end (20:24; 2 Tim. 4:7). At issue is the content of this life, e.g., the Baptist's work as a herald or Paul's discharge of his commission. In 2 Tim. 4:7 keeping the faith gives a special slant to the athletic allusions.

5. 1 Clem. 6.2 combines faith and the *drómos* more closely by speaking of the course of faith which the martyred women have successfully run, thus winning the imperishable crown of victory. 1 Clem. 20.2 and Diog. 7.2 refer to the course of the cosmos. In Ignatius *Polycarp* 1.2 Polycarp is to prove himself as an athlete by adding to his course.

pródromos.

1. This word, meaning "running before," is used of messengers and also in athletics and sailing (e.g., winds or ships).

2. It is used of early figs in Is. 28:4. Hornets are the forerunners of God's host in Wis. 12:8.

3. In the one NT instance in Heb. 6:20 Christ is our forerunner. The idea is not so much that of an onrushing warrior or an advance ship as of the one who has run the same course and whose successful running makes that of believers possible. The term is part of the vocabulary of edification but fits in well with the priestly and sacral context (cf. 5:5-10; 7:1ff.). [O. BAUERNFEIND, VIII, 226-35]

→ *agón*

trygōn → *peristerá*

---

trōgō [to gnaw, eat]

---

1. Usage.

a. This word means "to gnaw," "to bite," "to chew," "to eat." Later it often replaces *esthíō*.

b. The use in biblical Greek is in accord with this. In the NT the Synoptists prefer *esthíō*, but John generally has *trōgō* (cf. Ps. 41:10 and Jn. 13:18).

2. Theological Meaning in Jn. 6. The usage in Jn. 6:51ff. suggests that the change from *éphagon* in 6:52-53 to *trōgō* in 6:54, 56ff. is merely grammatical alteration, but the change throws light on the intention of the section. From 6:51 onward eating is not just appropriating Jesus' self-offering by faith but receiving it eucharistically. The section consists of proclamation summoning to faith, but the self-offering in word becomes self-offering in the eucharist, and believing hearing becomes believing eating. The uncurtailed incarnation of the Word demands eucharistic reception. Word and sacrament thus belong together. [L. GOPPELT, VIII, 236-37]

---

tynchánō [to obtain, happen], *entynchánō* [to run up against, to approach], *hyperentynchánō* [to intercede for], *énteuxis* [encounter, petition]

---

tynchánō.

A. The Greek World.

1. In Homer the word *tynchánō* develops from the aorist *étychon* (future *teúxomai*).

2. The word mostly means "to hit" a target, then "to do the right thing," "to obtain," and intransitively "to happen." Even when a hit is made, there is an element of good fortune as well as skill.

3. After Homer the accidental element gains in strength, as in the phrase "it so happened."

B. The LXX.

1. *tynchánō* does not fit in easily with any Hebrew original. It occurs in Dt. 19:5 for the chance blow. In Job 17:1 (negative) the grave is the object, and in 7:2 the shadow. In Prov. 30:23 a despised woman finally becomes a wife.

2. *tynchánō* is more common in 2 and 3 Maccabees but has little theological significance.

3. In Is. 65:11 the noun *týchē* denotes a pagan deity. The only other instance of

týchē is in Gen. 30:11. The translators avoid the noun because it stands in more direct antithesis to OT piety. It may stand in Gen. 30:11 because it expresses happiness rather than good luck.

C. Hellenistic Judaism.

1. Philo uses the verb in the phrases "as the matter stands" or "for example." In Josephus it has such senses as "to get" or "to receive."

2. Philo uses the noun quite freely, although he argues that when people speak of *týchē* they should really think of the divine *lógos*. Josephus finds *týchē* indispensable in his apologetic to the Romans.

D. The NT.

1. In 2 Tim. 2:10, Heb. 11:35, and Lk. 20:35, *tynchánō* in the sense "to achieve" or "to obtain" occurs in contexts which show that we cannot win salvation for ourselves. Heb. 8:6, referring to the ministry that Christ has obtained, is to the same effect. In Acts 19:11 and 28:2 the verb denotes unusual events; the reference in 19:11 is to the nature of the healings. In 1 Cor. 15:37, where Paul picks a random instance, the meaning of *ei týchoi* is "for example." In 1 Cor. 14:10 the same phrase suggests an unknown number. The point of *tychón* in 1 Cor. 16:6 is "perhaps"; Paul does not yet know how his plans will work out.

2. The NT makes only sparing use of the verb and does not use the noun at all. This is important theologically; like that of the LXX, the NT message leaves no room for *týchē*.

E. The Apostolic Fathers. God is the object of *tynchánō* in Ignatius *Ephesians* 10.1. The term signifies reaching port in *Smyrneans* 11.3. Vines suffer neglect in Hermas *Mandates* 10.1.5. Intransitively *tynchánō* means *eimí* in Diog. 5.8, and *ei týchoi* means "perhaps" in 2.3.

entynchánō.

A. Outside the NT.

1. This compound means "to run up against," often in a bad sense (e.g., against missiles or crocodiles), but also a good sense (e.g., lighting on a book). In relation to visits it may have the connotation of complaint or intercession.

2. In the LXX (no Hebrew originals) we find the use for "complaint" and "petition."

3. In Jewish Hellenistic works we find the meaning "to encounter" and also such senses as "to approach," "to turn to" (God in prayer), "to raise a complaint," and "to have to do with."

B. The NT. "To approach with a complaint" is the meaning in Rom. 11:2 (cf. Acts 25:24), and "to intercede for" is the point of *hyperentynchánō* in Rom. 8:26-27. Christ is the subject in Rom. 8:34. As in Heb. 7:25, believers have in the Spirit or Christ a heavenly intercessor.

C. The Apostolic Fathers. The compound has little theological significance in these works. It refers to intercession in 1 Clem. 56.1. "To approach" occurs positively in Mart. Pol. 17.2 and negatively in Hermas *Mandates* 10.2.5. "To read" is meant in Diog. 12.1.

énteuxis.

1. This noun has such varied senses as "encounter," "dealings," "conversation," "conduct," and "petition."

2. It means "conversation" in 2 Macc. 4:8.

3. In 1 Tim. 2:1 "intercession" is the fairly obvious sense, while in 1 Tim. 4:4 it means "thanksgiving," perhaps in the sense of "grace" at meals.

4. Hermas uses the term for "prayer" either as petition or more broadly. In 2 Clem. 19.1 it has the force of "address" and in 1 Clem. 63.2 of "concern" (i.e., the letter's concern for peace and unity).   [O. BAUERNFEIND, VIII, 238-45]

---

týpos [mark, type], *antítypos* [copy, antitype], *typikós* [typological], *hypotýpōsis* [model, prototype]

A. Usage.

I. Nonbiblical.

1. týpos. Deriving from *týptō,* "to strike," *týpos* denotes "the impress" of a blow, and then "form" with such nuances as "mark," "mold," and "outline" or "figure."

2. antítypos. This word has the actual smiting in view and takes on such senses as "striking back," "sending back," then "resistant," "inimical," "antitypical," "corresponding," and "reproducing."

3. typikós. This rare adjective means "open to impressions" and "corresponding to type."

4. hypotýpōsis. This word means "model" or "sketch."

II. Judaism.

1. LXX. In the LXX *týpos* means "model" in Ex. 25:40, "idol" in Am. 5:26, "text" in 3 Macc. 3:30, and "example" in 4 Macc. 6:19.

2. Philo. Philo often uses the term in traditional ways.

III. The NT. In the NT we find *týpos* for "mark" in Jn. 20:25, "idol" in Acts 7:43, and "text" in 23:25. Paul has it for "example" but also in the new hermeneutical sense of (OT) "type" (cf. *typikós* in 1 Cor. 10:11 and *antítypos* in 1 Pet. 3:21). In Acts 7:44 and Heb. 8:5 we find the idea of the heavenly original (cf. Ex. 25:40) in contrast to the earthly copy (*antítypos,* Heb. 9:24).

B. Theological Significance in the NT.

1. The Scars in Jn. 20:25. Jn. 20:25 refers to the scars left by the nails (cf. 20:20) in connection with the resurrection appearances. These are marks of identity and serve to establish faith. Doubt demands touching, the Lord offers it, but the disciples do not in fact touch; they believe.

2. Example of the Obedience of Faith.

a. Paul is an example or model to the church in Phil. 3:17 and 2 Th. 3:9. The church is a model in 1 Th. 1:7. The thought here is not that of an ideal but of a model that makes an impress because God has molded it, and that is effective through faith. Word and deed bear witness to the life of faith that summons to faith and is grasped in faith. The more life is molded by the word, the more it becomes a *týpos.* It cannot be imitated, but is lived out in freedom by faith. Officebearers are to be examples in this way (by word and deed) in 1 Tim. 4:12 and 1 Pet. 5:3.

b. The term *hypotýpōsis* expresses the same thought in 1 Tim. 1:16 (Christ's dealings with Paul) and 2 Tim. 1:13 (Paul's own preaching).

3. Teaching as Mold and Norm in Rom. 6:17. The idea of a molded figure applies also in Rom. 6:17. God has handed over believers to a new power, to which he has made them obedient from the heart. The *týpos didachḗs* is not just an outline of teaching here, but an impress that molds their whole conduct, serving therefore as a norm or standard.

4. týpos as a Hermeneutical Term.

a. Events in the wilderness are *týpoi* in 1 Cor. 10:6 (cf. *typikós* in v. 11). The apostle has the events and not just the OT texts in mind. God caused these events both to happen and to be recorded because of their essential similarity to his end-time acts. The likeness is not just external, nor does it rule out difference in view of the eschatological nature of God's present work. But Paul here stresses the basic likeness so as to relate baptism and the Lord's Supper, which the Corinthians misunderstand, to the saving acts of the God who personally met Israel in salvation and judgment. The word *týpoi* might, of course, mean "examples," but the context suggests that it has here the force of "advance presentations" intimating eschatological events. "Types," then, is the best translation.

b. Rom. 5:14 demands the same rendering. In the havoc he wrought, Adam is for Paul a *týpos* through which God intimates the future Adam (Christ) in his work of salvation. Christ corresponds antithetically to Adam and also emulates him. The *týpos* here is the advance presentation, but with a suggestion of the hollow form which makes an opposite impression. The "shadow of what is to come" in Col. 2:17 stands in close analogy.

c. Other terms relating the OT and the NT are *parabolḗ* in Heb. 9:9 and *allēgoroúmena* in Gal. 4:24. But *týpos* proves more adequate and hence the church adopts it in this hermeneutical sense. 1 Pet. 3:21 uses *antítypos* in a similar sense when relating baptism to the flood; baptism is the counterpart.

d. In the apostolic fathers Barnabas and Hermas adopt *týpos* very naturally as a hermeneutical term. Justin defines it in this sense, and the Latin fathers render it by *figura* or *typus*.

e. The underlying thought of correspondence occurs in the OT in, e.g., Hos. 2:17; Jer. 16:14-15; Am. 9:11-12; Is. 11:1ff.; 11:6ff.; 51:3 with reference to the new exodus, the new Davidic kingdom, and the new creation. Cyclic ideas may be seen here, but more decisive are the belief that election reaches its goal in spite of judgment and the confidence that the renewal transcends what has gone before. The continuity of salvation history and its expected consummation control this approach. In apocalyptic and the rabbis the idea of recurrence (either of paradise or of the age of Moses) is stronger, yet the typology still relates to the end time. Jesus emphasizes transcending what precedes (Mt. 12:41-42; Mk. 14:24). By a divine self-offering that surpasses that of the OT the relation to God is definitively healed. Paul develops the typology along similar lines, relating OT phenomena to the situation of the church by explicit comparison or hidden allusion. Though tied to current thought-forms, this is the decisive interpretation of Jesus, the gospel, and the church. In the apostolic fathers typology is either unimportant or it suffers basic change. Thus 1 Clem. 12.7 sees Christ's blood in the scarlet thread. Baranabas proceeds similarly in 7.3ff.; 8.1ff. The new thing here is the focus on external form rather than essential feature. Distortion results as typology becomes, not a spiritual and kerygmatic approach as in Paul, but a hermeneutical device. Yet at its NT core typology is still theologically constitutive for understanding the gospel.

5. týpos as the Heavenly Original (Ex. 25:40).

a. In Ex. 25:40 the heavenly original of the tabernacle is called *týpos*. The underlying thought is that of an analogical relation between heaven and earth. 1 Chr. 28:11-12 transfers the idea to the horizontal plane; David gives Solomon a model. Philo finds a difference in worth between the two sanctuaries along the lines of the world of ideas and sensory phenomena.

b. Acts 7:44 quotes Ex. 25:40 to make the two points (a) that the tabernacle, unlike the temple, is divinely commanded, and (b) that above it is the *týpos* as the place of God's self-proffering in the age of salvation (cf. Mt. 26:61).

c. Heb. 8:5 also quotes Ex. 25:40 and relates it directly to Jesus' saving work. As the true High Priest he enters the heavenly holy of holies with his own blood. The earthly sanctuary, the *antítypos,* goes with the first covenant. The analogous ministry in the heavenly sanctuary is a metaphor from salvation history relating intercession to the enactment of eschatological salvation. In accompanying comparisons the law is a shadow of final expiation, and Israel's disobedience is an illustrative warning. The comparative (*kreíttōn* in 8:6 and *meízōn* in 9:11) expresses an absolute intensifying. Christ's work is new, but it achieves the intentions of what precedes, so that continuity is preserved. The typology of Hebrews overlaps and transcends the ancient cyclic and vertical analogies of the upper world and the lower with its emphasis on the word of revelation in salvation history. The fundamental conviction is that in spite of every setback God's work achieves its goal in new and yet corresponding demonstrations of grace.

d. 1 Clement views the OT records as analogies from which one may read off the lasting cosmic order. Barnabas (6:13) expresses the principles of once-for-all recurrence. For Ignatius (*Magnesians* 6.2) the church is the type of immortality. The Gnostics find in earthly phenomena symbols of the real events. For them, therefore, the earthly church is an antitype of the true church.   [L. GOPPELT, VIII, 246-59]

> ### *týptō* [to strike]

A. Relations and Usage.
I. Relations.

1. *týptō* is one of many NT words for "to strike." The basic sense is "to stupefy with a blow." It then means "to stamp on," "to impress." Later it takes on the more general sense "to strike."

2. The most important OT equivalent in *nkh,* but this is mostly translated *patássō* in the LXX (344 times) and only 26 times *týptō.*

3. The rabbis have an equivalent for the reflexive "to strike oneself."

II. Usage.

1. *týptō* occurs for striking with the hand, fist, or foot, or with a staff, rod, whip, or weapon. It may mean "to strike dead," "to smite an enemy," or "to smite a land with destruction."

2. In a transferred sense it means "to stab" with grief, remorse, the pang of conscience, terror, etc.

3. "To smite oneself" occurs in training for the games and in expression of sorrow.

4. In a transferred sense "to strike oneself" means "to lament," but for this the Attic prefers *kóptomai.*

B. NT Contexts.
I. The Preaching of Jesus. Lk. 6:29 uses *týptō* in a simplified version of Mt. 5:39. In Lk. 12:45 the servant abuses his position by beating the menservants and even the

maidservants. In Mt. 24:51 and parallels the punishment corresponds to the offense of v. 49 but with enhanced severity. The picture of the carousing and striking servant serves to warn those who have special responsibilities in the church against playing the lord in the period prior to the parousia (cf. 2 Cor. 4:5). In Lk. 18:9ff. the tax collector adopts a conventional practice, but the prayer of v. 13 shows that it is a spontaneous expression of conviction of sin and of the desire for grace, and that as such it is the only attitude that can stand before God.

II. The Passion Narrative. In the passion narrative Jesus is twice beaten (Lk. 22:63-64; Mk. 15:19) and the spectators also strike themselves (Lk. 23:48). In the mocking of the blindfolded Jesus in Lk. 22:64 rough handling is part of the game. Even in the wording a relation to Is. 50:6 LXX is plain. The events point the writers to the OT original for their phrasing and presentation. So does the patient acceptance of mockery and smiting by Jesus. Striking him on his thorn-crowned head, the soldiers mock Jesus as king (Mk. 15:18-19). In contrast, those who beat their breasts at the foot of the cross (Lk. 23:48) seem to be uttering an Amen to the confession of the centurion, not merely bewailing Jesus but offering a sign of penitence as in 18:13.

III. Acts. In their resistance to the gospel in Acts the Jews often resort to blows, as in the beating of Sosthenes in 18:17 (cf. the attack on Paul in 23:27ff.). In 23:2 Ananias has Paul struck on the mouth, and Paul in response tells him that God will smite him. God's smiting in judgment takes various forms (Dt. 28:22) but it is usually depicted as a direct mortal blow (Gen. 8:21; Num. 33:4, etc.). Paul perhaps lived to see Ananias struck down in A.D. 66.

IV. Paul. The only NT instance of a transferred use of *týptō* is in 1 Cor. 8:12, where the strong inflict a blow on the conscience of the weak by causing them to act against conscience. The blow is not the resultant pang of conscience but the damage done to faith and hence to the relationship with God.   [G. STÄHLIN, VIII, 260-69]

---

typhlós [blind],   *typhlóō* [to blind]

A. Greek Antiquity and Hellenism.

I. Meaning.

1. The adjective *typhlós* denotes human and animal blindness. It then refers to objects without light or access (cf. blind alleys) and also to what is invisible or concealed.

2. The verb *typhlóō* means "to make blind," "to rob of sight," passive "to go blind," "to be blinded," and less strictly "to render (or be) ineffectual."

II. Literal Blindness.

1. Normally in antiquity blindness means full loss of sight. The blind, deaf, and lame are often mentioned together.

2. Causes of blindness are heredity, animal poison, wounds, accidents, exposure to bright light, etc. Psychological causes are sought in sorrow or tears. Excesses and affronting the gods might also cause blindness.

3. The barbaric custom of blinding others in jealousy, revenge, retribution, or punishment is another cause of blindness. Orestes tries to atone for his incest by self-blinding. Goddesses often inflict blindness as a penalty.

4. The blind walk unsteadily, stretch out their hands for support, use sticks for their feet, and are helped by others, especially relatives. Antigone is an example of devotion

to the blind. Many of the blind are beggars, although a few of the more talented make their mark as musicians, seers, philosophers, even jurists or statesmen.

5. Blindness does not necessarily bring moral betterment and may even augment wickedness. It is thought to enhance mental perception, hence blind seers and sages. Inability to see the world's beauty counts as a grievous blow of fate. Yet philosophers think one should not bewail it but accept it; the real evil is the failure to live the life of the sage with no wants.

6. Although cataracts may be removed and incipient blindness arrested, there are no natural cures for blindness in antiquity. Sight can be restored only by divine intervention. Vespasian and Hadrian are said to have cured blind people as divine agents, but normally the gods restore sight directly when penitence is expressed, some divine condition is met, or petition is made. Usually the return of sight is sudden, but the gods may also use or command medicine or magic as instruments. Aesculapius is of special importance in this area.

III. Comparisons and the Transferred Sense.

1. The unsteady walk of the blind offers a common point of comparison. So do the pain and unalterability of blindness. The thought of the blind leading the blind occurs frequently. A paradoxical proverb is that even the blind can see something that is plain.

2. Metaphorically other bodily members, or acts, or objects may be called blind. We also read of mental or moral blindness. Spiritual blindness can be set in juxtaposition with physical sight.

a. It is a terrible affliction for the mind or the soul to be blind. The whole person may be blind when the field of vision is restricted. Thus all of us are blind regarding the future. Wealth leads to intellectual and moral blindness; it is a poor optician. Lovers are also blind, and love of self blinds us to our faults. In philosophy ignorance is blindness, e.g., ignorance of who we are, why we are here, and what good and evil are. Skeptics, whose wisdom is to know, see, and hear nothing, are blind. There may also be blindness to art, science, and beauty. In Gnosticism those who have not attained to saving knowledge are blind. Ignorance is dream, sleep, and blindness. Woes fall on those who grope around like the blind. The redeemer comes to bring sight to the blind, although full freedom comes only at death with freeing from the body.

b. What blinds can also be called blind, e.g., wealth, or the gods of wealth (Plutos), love (Eros), and war (Ares). Gnostic texts also refer to the blind god or blind evil powers, which are blind in their pride or ignorance.

B. The LXX.

I. Usage.

1. The adjective occurs some 21 times in the LXX, but mostly the word is used as a noun. We find both literal and transferred uses.

2. The verb occurs only three times in the LXX.

II. Literal Use. 1. Causes of blindness in the OT are heredity, striking, blinding, etc. Blindness, mentioned with deafness and lameness, is a severe handicap.

2. Laws protect the blind. If they cannot be priests (Lev. 21:18ff.), they enjoy God's help and are thus to be treated humanely (Lev. 19:14; Dt. 27:18).

3. God as Creator is behind blindness (Ex. 4:11). He threatens it as a penalty for those who reject his word and break his commandments (Dt. 28:28-29). He can also open the eyes of the blind (Ps. 146:8).

III. Transferred Sense.

1. On the day of the Lord people will wander about like the blind, i.e., in anxiety and confusion (Zeph. 1:17). When justice is far off, they grope for the wall like the blind (Is. 59:9-10).

2. In the deliverance from exile God brings forth the blind who have eyes but do not see, i.e., who cannot interpret events (Is. 43:8). To be blind is to be without knowledge (42:19; 56:10).

3. Curing blindness is part of the message of salvation. The reference is partly literal (Is. 35:5) and partly figurative (29:18). The Servant has the task of opening blind eyes (42:7). God himself will be a guide to the blind on the way (42:16). The messenger of Is. 61:1ff. proclaims sight to the blind in the LXX version.

C. Judaism apart from Philo.

I. Usage. Various Hebrew and Aramaic words are used for those born blind or those who go blind in either one eye or both.

II. Literal Sense.

1. Judaism follows the OT closely in relation to blindness. Blindness is a severe affliction, although it may give enhanced spiritual light and greater powers of memory. Laws ameliorate the lot of the blind, protecting them from various ills, but the blind are often beggars.

2. The law frees the blind from various cultic duties and penalties, e.g., attending feasts and scourging. They must not go out with a stick on the sabbath, and others must help them to fulfil some obligations, e.g., purification. The blind may not be witnesses or judges, nor may they divorce their wives or accuse them out of jealousy.

3. Judaism views blindness as a divine punishment, especially for sins with the eye (cf. Samson). In the case of those born blind, the sin is their parents' or else they sin in the womb or God foresees future sin. But the defect also ranks as a wise provision to check the full development of evil impulses.

4. Blindness may also be traced back to demons, or to the tears of sorrowing angels (Isaac), or to seeing God's glory (Abraham). Jacob's blindness is a blessing when Esau marries foreign wives. Cures are not expected unless God intervenes. The messianic age will bring the end of blindness. As God gave the law to a people with no defects, so there will be no defects in the end time. In the eschatological restoration, the Messiah will heal the blind first.

III. Transferred Sense.

1. When Is. 35:5 is taken spiritually, the main hope is that of removing blindness to the law. Yet blindness may also denote ignorance and aberration. Sinners are blind. In the Damascus Document Israel is blind in the sense of being unable to find God without the Teacher of Righteousness.

2. Jewish literature contains few proverbs referring to the blind. When the blind are present, a person with one eye is said to see clearly. A doctor at a distance is called a blind eye.

D. Philo.

1. Philo mostly uses *typhlós* in a transferred sense for moral, philosophical, or spiritual blindness. Comparisons are common, e.g., the partial judge blundering along like the blind without stick or guide, or the wicked groping about at midday like the blind. The crowd follows blind riches or blind *aísthēsis*. To miss the allegorical sense of the OT is blindness. Ordinary people who choose the evil, ugly, or perishable are blind.

2. Philo makes little use of the verb. The blinded in soul perceive only sensory things and regard them as the source of all being.

E. **The NT.**

I. Usage.

1. *typhlós* occurs in the NT some 36 times in the literal and 12 in the transferred sense. Only Mark has it solely in the literal sense. The senses merge in Jn. 9. Paul uses the term only in the metaphor in Rom. 2:19.

2. *typhlóō* occurs three times in the NT in a transferred sense.

II. Literal Sense.

1. The NT mostly uses *typhlós* as a noun with reference to blindness in both eyes.

2. The NT sheds little light on the social, legal, or religious status of the blind. Interest centers on the cure at the physical level. The traditional cry of Mk. 10:47 brings the NT view into sharp focus. Begging is for many blind people the only means of livelihood (Mk. 10:46; Jn. 9:8). The association with the deaf and the lame is traditional. Lk. 14:13 enjoins kindness to the blind. Mt. 12:22 traces back blindness to demons. A curse causes temporary blindness in Acts 13:11; the verse presupposes miraculous healing.

3. The main NT references come in accounts of healing. Features of these accounts are the cry for mercy, the separation of the blind (Mk. 8:23), the use of spittle and washing (Jn. 9), the laying on of hands (Mk. 8:23), the suddenness or difficulty of the cure (Mk. 8:25), and confirmation of the result (10:52). The stress falls on faith and the healing power of the word. The pity of Jesus calls for notice in Mt. 20:34. In Mk. 8:17ff. the dramatic healing of the blind man answers the blindness of the disciples regarding the saying of Jesus in 8:14. With Jesus' other mighty works, the healings of the blind signify the dawn of the age of eschatological salvation in fulfilment of prophetic promise (Mt. 11:5; Lk. 4:18). In Lk. 7:19-20 John's disciples see the blind cured and can thus reassure the Baptist that Jesus is the expected Savior. In Jn. 9 the fact that the man is born blind stresses the greatness of the cure but also suggests that all of us are by nature blind to the light of revelation. The disciples echo a common view when they ask whether the blindness is due to some sin of the parents. When they ask about his own sin, they possibly have in mind some sin in the womb or God's foreseeing of future sin. Jesus points to a differently oriented divine prescience. If the cure shows that Christ is in truth the light of the world (9:5) who has come to bring sight (9:39), it still evokes doubt and strife and rejection (vv. 8-9, 16, 18, 34). Christ makes the blind to see, but he also makes those who see blind (v. 39).

III. Transferred Sense.

1. The blind of Jn. 9:39ff. are those who cannot understand the signs of Jesus, or perceive his divine origin (v. 29), or be led by him out of darkness. Their fault is to think that they see when they are blind. God himself sends this blindness according to Jn. 12:40. In 1 Jn. 2:11 darkness is the force that brings blindness, but only through hatred of the brother and walking in darkness. This kind of blindness is sin.

2. In the saying about "blind leaders of the blind" the reference is to those who judge others without seeing their own sin (Lk. 6:37ff.), but also involved is blindness to God's will and the word of Jesus (Mt. 15:14). The blindness of the scribes and Pharisees is a refrain in the great attack of Mt. 23 (vv. 16, 17, 19, 24, 26). Their blind folly may be seen in their false exposition of the law, which fixes on details and misses essentials. Thinking they are guides of the blind, they are in truth blind guides.

3. In Rom. 2:19 Paul's more general charge against the Jews is that their failure to

do what they say invalidates their claim to be a guide to the blind. In 2 Cor. 4:4 the god of this aeon has blinded the eyes of unbelievers so that they cannot see the light of the gospel. The decision regarding blinding comes with the preaching of the gospel.

4. In 2 Pet. 1:9 it is the unfruitful rather than the ignorant who are blind and shortsighted (cf. vv. 5-6). Rev. 3:17 complains that the Laodicean church thinks it is spiritually rich but is really blind. Only Christ (v. 18) can cure this blindness of self-deception and complacency.

F. The Apostolic Fathers. In these works *typhlós* occurs only in LXX quotations in Barn. 14.7, 9 (Is. 42:6-7; 61:1-2). [W. SCHRAGE, VIII, 270-94]

υ y, u

---

hýbris [arrogance], *hybrízō* [to treat with arrogance], *enybrízō* [to insult], *hybristḗs* [an arrogant person]

A. Greek Usage.

1. The original sense of this group, which is of obscure derivation, is that of invading the sphere of another, with an implication of arrogance. Conveyed is the idea of trespass with overweening force and the infliction of insult, injury, etc. There are warnings against *hýbris,* which is a common fault among the free, but which finally brings destruction to the self or others.

2. Tragedy deals with *hýbris.* It is the scornful right of the mighty. The gods visit it with retribution and hence it plays a big role in the Greek sense of sin. It breeds tyrants, plunges into excess, and entails violation of reverence for the holy. In human relations it means either scorn and contempt or, more actively, hurt and violence.

3. For the historians *hýbris* is an important factor in the course of events. In Herodotus the religious basis is plain; the Persian plan of conquest is in keeping with a fundamental attitude. In Thucydides affluence leads to *hýbris* and punishment follows. Xenophon finds in the decay of Sparta and Athens a judgment on *hýbris.*

4. In legal rhetoric *hýbris* denotes the violence of the rich or the violation of personal rights.

5. Socrates has no sense of arrogance. For Plato *hýbris* is the negative side of *érōs* and an essential force. In young people it leads to attacks on parents and public order. It hits the weakest most severely and results in injustice and destruction. If education brings victory over it, the victory can lead to fresh *hýbris. hýbris* is a power of fate that permeates all areas of life.

6. In Aristotle *hýbris* denotes sexual violation but also scorn, ill-will, arrogance, greed, and offense against the gods. A presumptuous disposition is a general human complaint which the law cannot punish. It raises a political problem; only prudence can achieve the peace that is the goal of politics, but periods of peace also produce transgression.

7. The usual senses continue in the later period, but while *hýbris* retains its emotional force, it often takes on much weaker meanings, and it never becomes a key concept in Greek thinking.

B. The OT.

1. The main Hebrew originals for *hýbris* belong to the *g'h* group denoting loftiness and then pride or arrogance, which are wrong inasmuch as they involve presumptuousness and defiance. God comes to overthrow pride (Am. 6:8). Pomp and careless ease lead to it (Ezek. 16:49-50). A fall ineluctably follows pride (Prov. 16:18). This applies to Israel (Hos. 5:5) no less than its enemies (Jer. 48:29-30). The arrogant encroach on the weak (Jn. 35:12). The righteous hold aloof from them (Prov. 16:19). Zeph. 3:11 promises their overthrow. Since the Greek terms correspond only to the negative side, they can be used only in appropriate passages.

2. Another root is *zyd*, which denotes bubbling or boiling, and which has the force of "impudence" or "insolence" when applied to foreign powers (Jer. 50:29ff.) or to Israel herself (Ezek. 7:10). The group is important in Proverbs for frivolous or contentious conduct (13:10). In Sir. 3:16 arrogance is sin and is thus aimed against God. For this root *hýbris* and related terms occur only six times, in spite of the similarity between the Greek and Hebrew words.

3. Since *hýbris* is so broad, it is hard to fix its limits either over against synonymous Greek words or in relation to Hebrew terms.

4. Other roots connected to *hýbris* denote kicking, despising, unruliness, etc.

5. Only a few instances occur in works available only in Greek. The references are to pride, arrogance, and violence, especially in the Gentiles. Opposing them, God is the one who hates *hýbris* (*mísybris*). (For OT details see *TDNT*, VIII, 299-302.)

C. Judaism.

1. Philo refers to persecutions of the Jews or attacks on them. *hýbris* occurs between men and women or among men or women. It includes infringements, excesses, and boasting, but also legally inflicted dishonoring. It permeates the Gentile world (cf. the games, festivals, and excessive taxation). Affluence breeds it, and the senses lead to it.

2. Josephus finds *hýbris* in OT history (e.g., Cain, Nimrod, and the people of Sodom). It includes disparagement, ignominy, ravishing, encroachment, violence, cruelty, provocation, and shaming. It characterizes those in power, poisons human relations, and explains the fall of Israel and Judah.

3. The Dead Sea Scrolls refer to arrogant people, scoffing priests, and wicked pride.

4. In eschatology *hýbris* is a mark of the kingdom of evil. For the rabbis pride is willful sin and involves denial of God and idolatry. Two aspects of pride are the wicked act of destruction and joy in it.

D. The NT.

1. The group occurs only infrequently in the NT. Paul in Acts 27:10, 21 uses the noun *hýbris* in the sense of "injury" or "loss." Among the sufferings of 2 Cor. 12:10 the *hýbreis* are "difficulties" that he meets with on his travels due to the terrain, the weather, and human hostility.

2. Paul uses the verb in 1 Th. 2:2 with reference to the sufferings and insults that he and Silas undergo at Philippi. The meaning of *hybrízō* here is "to suffer ignominious punishment." The general sense in Acts 14:5 is "to revile or maltreat." In Lk. 11:45 the scribe accuses Jesus of reproaching the leaders with insulting mockery. Rough handling is the point in Mt. 22:6. Jesus himself suffers the fate of the righteous by being shamefully treated according to Lk. 18:32.

3. *hybristés* occurs in the list of vices in Rom. 1:30 for despisers who disrupt relations with both God and their fellows. Paul himself was once a blasphemer, persecutor, and evildoer (1 Tim. 1:13; cf. 1 Cor. 15:9; Gal. 1:13; Acts 9:4-5).

4. Heb. 10:29 uses the compound *enybrízō*. As those who violate Moses' law incur severe punishment, how much more those who spurn God's Son, profane the covenant blood, and do despite to the Spirit of grace. The three statements correspond.

E. The Early Church. 2 Clem. 14.4 echoes Heb. 10:29, while 1 Clem. 59.3 shows the influence of the liturgical usage of Judaism. In Hermas *Similitudes* 6.3.4 the reference is to temporal punishment. The wicked rejection of Christ in Justin *Dialogue* 136.3 is directed against God. Pagans deride their own goods (*Apology* 4.9). Idolatry is mocking God (9.3). Apocryphal works refer to the charge of *hýbris* leveled against Christ. Later *hýbris* is a mark of the despotic ruler who is hostile to God. For Augustine it is the basic sin which causes the fall and from which other sins derive.

[G. BERTRAM, VIII, 295-307]

---

hygiḗs [healthy, sound],   *hygiaínō* [to be healthy, sound]

A. Secular Greek.
1. Meaning. The group has the sense of "healthy" and then more generally "rational," "intelligent," "reliable," and "whole." Health implies a proper balance of the whole and on some views is maintained by a balance of such forces as the moist, dry, cold, hot, bitter, and sweet.

2. Assessment of Health. Health is regarded as the normal state and is highly valued. In philosophy it ranks as one of the goods. Healing is an important craft. All excess damages health. There is a health of soul as well as body, but bodily and spiritual health belong together. Stoicism views bodily health as indifferent. Passion of every kind is sickness, and virtue results from health of soul. Magic associates health with life, but Gnosticism shows little interest in it.

B. The LXX.
1. *hygiaínō* occurs 41 times in the LXX. Health is a divine gift, a part of life, and denotes human well-being.
2. *hygiḗs* occurs ten times in the LXX and denotes healthy or safe (Is. 38:21; Josh. 10:21). The Hellenistic evaluation of health emerges in Sir. 30:14. Physicians and apothecaries work through divinely given means (38:1ff.).

C. Hellenistic Judaism.
1. Josephus mostly uses the group for rational thought and action.
2. Philo believes with the Stoics that if the soul is healthy sickness does little harm, and that the soul is healthy when healthy thoughts overpower passion. The soul's corruption is the basis of all vice. The pillar of the healthy soul is the *noús*.

D. The NT.
1. The NT does not especially value health. Yet Jesus as the victor over sin and suffering restores health by his word (Mk. 5:34; Mt. 12:13; Jn. 5:9; Lk. 5:31). Making the whole man healthy (Jn. 7:23), he liberates for a new life that embraces the body. He transmits the power to heal, or to make whole, to the apostles (Acts 4:10).
2. 3 Jn. 2 uses a Hellenistic epistolary greeting.
3. In 1 Tim. 1:10; 6:3; Tit. 2:8 we find the idea of "sound" teaching or words. The reference is to true teaching, not to teaching that makes whole. This teaching, validated by the apostles, is concerned, not with speculation, but with true, rational, and proper

life in the world. Being "sound in faith" (Tit. 1:13) goes hand in hand with being temperate, serious, and sensible (2:2).

E. Apostolic Fathers. Prayer is made for the "health" of kings and rulers in 1 Clem. 61.1. The tree that represents the law in Hermas *Similitudes* 8.1.3-4 is "sound." So are the stones used in building the church (*Similitudes* 9.8.3). Not keeping the seal of baptism "intact" is the point in *Similitudes* 8.6.3. But the group seldom occurs in these writings.   [U. Luck, VIII, 308-13]

→ *therapeía, iáomai, ischýō, nósos*

---

hýdōr [water]

A. The World of Antiquity.

I. Greek Usage. *hýdōr* is found from Homer in the sense of "water." Derivatives and compounds include "water jug," "to drink water," and "dropsical" (*hydrōpikós*).

II. Meaning.

1. The Flood. Water figures first in human experience as the flood that surrounds and threatens dry land. Many cosmogonies have the world arise out of the primal flood. Distinction is made between the upper and lower waters. The Greeks localize water in the seas but still distinguish between the water that comes from the depths of the earth and the water that falls as rain.

2. The Dispenser of Life. Water also has a life-giving role in human experience. The Greeks regard springs and rivers as divine, and the Egyptians hail the Nile as "the lord of the water that brings greenness." The idea of a "water of life" occurs in Babylonian myth, and Hellenism develops the legend of Alexander's campaign for the water of life that confers immortality.

3. Cleansing. A third use of water is for cleansing. In religion this results in rites of purification, e.g., for cultic qualification. If possible, running water should be used, and sometimes it is consecrated by special rites. Whether ritual cleansing is supposed to wash away sins is highly doubtful.

B. The OT and Jewish World.

1. Usage. The LXX uses *hýdōr* for a Hebrew term (*mayim*) that is partly singular and partly plural. In the Hebrew the term is sometimes added to define springs or channels that may or may not contain water. With place names water means that a body of water is close by (Josh. 11:5, 7; 16:1; Judg. 5:19). Water is a general term for what might be cloud, mist, rain, or dew; spring, stream, canal, pond, lake, or cistern; or simply drinking water.

II. Meaning.

1. Literal Use.

a. Drinking Water and Irrigation. Palestine is poor in water resources; there is no assurance of it for people or plants. Water is thus emphasized along with bread (Ex. 23:25; 1 Sam. 30:11-12). Great importance attaches to wells (Gen. 26:18-19), pitchers (24:14ff.), water pots (1 Sam. 26:11-12), conduits (2 Kgs. 18:17), and troughs (Gen. 30:38). Rain, dew, and watercourses provide for the watering of tillable land. The provision of water in the desert stresses its great importance (Num. 20:24; 27:14, etc.). In the promise of the land the assurance of water is decisive (Dt. 8:7). The prophecy of living streams depicts end-time Israel as an antitype of paradise (Ezek.

47:1ff.; Zech. 14:8). God can both send rain and dry up great rivers (1 Kgs. 18:41ff.; Is. 15:6). It is he who provides the necessities of life (Is. 55:1).

b. The Flood. The earth arises out of chaos as God divides the waters. At the flood the upper and lower waters engulf the earth. God keeps back the flood at the exodus but causes it to overwhelm the pursuing Egyptians. A parallel occurs with the crossing of the Jordan and again when Elijah parts the Jordan (2 Kgs. 2:8). These events declare God's lordship over creation. In rabbinic Judaism the temple rock stops up the lower waters but allows them to flow across the earth. The water ceremonies at Tabernacles make the earth's fertility possible. The paradisal rivers will flow from this place in the age of salvation.

c. Cleansing. Water is offered to guests to wash their feet (Gen. 18:4), and it is also used for washing clothes. Yet it is supremely important in ritual cleansing. Living water should be used for special purifications. Its application is by sprinkling, partial washing, or total washing, whether of the body or of clothes. The entrails of sacrifices should also be washed. Ordained for the holy people, the cleansing rites have symbolical and eschatological significance (cf. Ezek. 36:25; Zech. 13:1; Is. 4:4). Washing to cleanse from blood-guiltiness (Dt. 21:6) is partly ritual and partly figurative. The Pharisees and Essenes develop the OT rites of cleansing into all-embracing systems, e.g., cleansing before meals. From OT washings proselyte baptism arises. Ritual washings seem to have been common at Qumran in the form of bathing. Washing and inner conversion are demanded for total consecration. In a final cleansing God sprinkles the spirit of truth like cleansing water on the elect.

2. *Transferred Usage.*

a. As water quenches thirst and nourishes life, so God is the source of living water (Jer. 2:13), and desire for him is the true thirst (Ps. 42:1). His people is like a flock by the water or a tree by the brook (Pss. 23:2; 1:3). In the last time Israel will be like a watered garden (Is. 58:11). The Qumran community regards its members as trees of life hidden by lofty trees (the wicked). It also speaks of the water of life and the drink of knowledge. Rabbinic Judaism compares the word of the law or of scribes to water. Damascus describes false teaching as lying water.

b. As in the flood, water may symbolize oppression of the nation (Is. 8:6-7) or of individuals (2 Sam. 22:17). The breadth of water is compared to the knowledge of God (Hab. 2:14). Other images are the running off of water (the heart failing for fear), the spilling of water (death), and water bursting the dam (2 Sam. 5:20) and flooding the earth (Is. 30:28).

c. The figure of cleansing occurs mostly with verbs of washing rather than the term "water."

C. The NT.

I. Water Literally and Metaphorically.

1. The Synoptic Tradition.

a. Flood. Jesus displays his divine authority over the flood (Mk. 4:35ff.) when the raging water threatens the disciples. He commands the storm as only God can do, and he summons the disciples to faith. When he walks on the water he does so as God coming to the aid of his people. Peter's walking depicts faith's walking over the flood of evil that engulfs unbelievers (Mk. 6:45ff.; Mt. 14:28ff.; cf. Jn. 21:7).

b. Drinking Water. A cup of cold water is a small gift (Mt. 10:42), but it carries a share in the kingdom (25:40). Those who refuse it will thirst in vain for a drop of water in the world to come (Lk. 16:21ff.).

c. Cleansing Water. The sinful woman displays her devotion by washing Jesus' feet with her tears (Lk. 7:36ff.). Pilate washes his hands (Mt. 27:24-25) to shift guilt from himself to the people. Jesus calls for inner cleansing rather than the outer washing of the hands before meals (Mk. 7:2ff.), which as a human tradition evades the true demand of the law. He himself effects the eschatological cleansing of the heart.

2. *The Johannine Writings*.

a. The Flood in Revelation. The voice of the exalted and victorious Son is as "the sound of many waters" in Rev. 1:15 (cf. 14:2; 19:6). The harlot is enthroned on many waters in 17:1, the waters being the nations. The dragon spews out water in 12:15; depicted here is the church's flight into the wilderness and its deliverance from the flood of oppression.

b. Drinking Water in Revelation and John's Gospel. God smites the earth's drinking water in judgment in Rev. 8:10-11; 14:7; 16:4-5. The redeemed receive the water of life to drink. The Lamb leads them to fountains of the water of life (7:17), God gives drink to the thirsty from the fountain of the water of life (21:6), a river of water of life issues from the throne (22:1), and the thirsty are invited to take the water of life without cost (22:17). In this figurative usage the water represents true life in fellowship with God. In John's Gospel Jesus at the well offers the true water that quenches the thirst for life by giving life (Jn. 4:13-14). The gift that becomes a well of water is his word or Spirit or he himself (8:37; 7:39; 6:56). To drink is to believe (7:38). The living water of 4:10-11; 7:38 is not running water (the traditional sense) but the water that mediates life.

c. Healing and Cleansing Water in John's Gospel. Water has a curative effect in Jn. 5:7, but Jesus' healing as a demonstration of eschatological grace sets aside the natural rules. The washing in the pool in 9:6-7 does not effect the healing; the man regains his sight by coming to him whom God has sent. The symbolism of Jn. 2:1ff. is that Jesus is he who brings salvation. Using water for purification, Jesus replaces with his gift all that the law can offer. The foot-washing signifies what Jesus does for the disciples by his death. Rabbinic disciples have to wash the rabbis' feet, slaves those of their masters, and wives those of their husbands, but Jesus by this act shows that his work of salvation is a service of love that cleanses his people and pledges them to similar mutual service (13:6ff., 12ff.).

3. *2 Pet. 3:5-6*. In the NT only 2 Pet. 3:5-6 refers to the cosmogonic significance of water. By God's word the earth is formed out of and by water, and it is then destroyed by water. The verse uses a Hellenistic idea but replaces emanation with creation by the word. The point of the passage is to draw a parallel between destruction by water and future destruction by fire.

II. *Baptismal Water*.

1. *The Saying of the Baptist*. The saying in Mk. 1:8 and Mt. 3:11 describes the imminent eschatological event as the completion of what has already begun. The initial cleansing mediates forgiveness, the final cleansing will create the new life and abolish all that is against God.

2. *Water Baptism and Spirit Baptism*. Acts 1:5 applies the saying of the Baptist to the receiving of the Spirit (cf. 11:16). The promise of the Spirit marks off Christians from disciples of John (19:1ff.). The uncircumcised who receive the Spirit by hearing in faith cannot be denied water (10:47-48). Water here is the element, not a figurative term for baptism itself; it is not efficacious as such (cf. 2:38). God gives the Spirit through the human action but in orientation to faith and church growth (8:16-17; 11:17). In John the climax of John's baptism is the manifestation of Jesus as the bearer

of the Spirit (1:26-27, 31, 33). 1 John links baptism with death; Christ has come through both water and blood (5:6), and is thus thrice attested by Spirit, water, and blood (5:7-8). Water is efficacious through the Spirit (Jn. 3:5; cf. flesh and blood and the Spirit in 6:53, 63). The blood and water of Jn. 19:34 also recall baptism. In Eph. 5:26 Christ cleanses through the washing as he is at work by the word, i.e., the invocation of his name. Heb. 10:22 associates washing and spiritual cleansing. Baptism replaces previous washings, and Christ's blood sprinkles the heart. It has inner, not outer significance (1 Pet. 3:21).

3. *Water Symbolism.* Christian baptism is compared to a cleansing bath (Eph. 5:26; Heb. 10:22), to the death-dealing and saving flood (1 Pet. 3:20-21), to the sea that divides the saved from the lost (1 Cor. 10:1-2), and to a death from which there is emergence to new life (Rom. 6; cf. 1 Pet. 1:3) in fellowship with God and his people.

D. The Early Church.

1. Water Symbolism. Hermas *Similitudes* 9.16.4ff. compares the church to a tower standing over the primal flood. Barn. 11 relates baptism to drinking water that mediates life. Tertullian *On Baptism* 3ff. calls water, as the first element, the seat of the Spirit. As living creatures come forth from it, so does new life in baptism.

2. Rules about Baptismal Water. As in proselyte baptism, so in John's the candidates probably stand in the water and the Baptist either immerses them or pours water over them. Did. 7.1ff. prescribes running water if possible and trine immersion or pouring. Tertullian thinks it makes no difference what water is used (*On Baptism* 4) in view of its sanctification for the purpose of baptism.

3. Sanctifying. From Ignatius *Ephesians* 18.2 one finds the idea of a sanctifying of the baptismal water. This supposedly empowers it for its special task. Invocation of the Spirit develops in the baptismal liturgy. Tertullian *On Baptism* 4 views the sanctifying as the descent of a heavenly substance but *Apostolic Constitutions* 7.43 prays only that the baptism that follows may have an effect corresponding to the promise.

4. Holy Water. In the fourth century A.D. the sanctifying of the baptismal water merges with a hallowing of the water of lustration, which originally is unconsecrated and largely symbolic. *Apostolic Constitutions* 8.29 offers a dedicatory prayer that seeks for the holy water effective power through Christ to preserve health, cure sickness, drive out demons, and ward off assaults.   [L. GOPPELT, VIII, 314-33]

---

huiós [son],   *huiothesía* [adoption]

A. *huiós* in Greek.
I. Classical Usage.
1. The word occurs in the two forms *huiós* and *hyós*.
2. From Homer *huiós* is a word for "son" alongside *país*. It embraces illegitimate sons and sons-in-law as well as physical sons.
3. The gods have both divine sons and sons by mortal women.
4. The possibility of an extended use occurs in phrases like "son of sorrow."
II. Hellenism.
1. *huiós* occurs in the style of Near Eastern and Egyptian rulers: "son of Helios or Zeus." Augustus styles himself *Divi filius (theoú huiós)*.
2. "Son of the city" etc. is an honorary title for leading citizens.

3. On papyri *huiós* may also denote one who is not a relative but close, e.g., a pupil.

4. Among the Stoics the idea of divine sonship is suggested by the doctrine of the unity of the human race.

5. a. A question arises whether the description of Jesus as the *huiós toú theoú* is linked with the Hellenistic idea of the *theíos anér* (divine man). Homer uses *theíos* to describe heroes, but this is a mark of epic style. In classical Greek *theíos* means "pious" or "extraordinary," but carries no sacral connotation.

b. We find the idea of divine charisma in some personages, but not with any clear-cut concept of divine descent.

c. The son formula occurs relative to Simon Magus and other Gnostics, but we know these claims only from Christian polemic.

d. In pre-Christian times *theíos anér* is not a fixed expression, and *theíos* usually has predicative significance and does not necessarily imply strict divine sonship. The only mortals who are sons of gods are doctors as descendants of Aesculapius (a functional use), rulers, Gnostics in Christian polemic, and some philosophers. Usage does not support any firm association between divine sonship and *theíos*.

[W. von Martitz, VIII, 334-40]

B. Old Testament.

1. Linguistic Data. The Hebrew term for "son" is *bēn,* and the Aramaic, with a shift from *n* to *r,* is *bar.*

2. Physical Descendants and Relatives.

a. The primary meaning of *bēn* or *bar* is "son," but the terms may also denote other degrees of relationship, e.g., brother, grandson, or cousin. We also find a use for the offspring of animals, the shoots of trees, and sparks as the offshoots of fire.

b. Mostly the terms serve to denote personal status. By relating people to their fathers or ancestors they put them in the organic context of a family or tribe.

c. A genealogical sense leads to the desire for many sons (Dt. 28:4ff.; Ps. 127:3ff.). Jeremiah commands the exiles to have children as an expression of the divine promise of life (29:6). Sons insure the future and are the crown of the aged (Prov. 17:6; 23:24-25). The wicked have no sons or lose them (Num. 27:1ff.; 2 Chr. 21:17). David regards his many sons as a gift from God (1 Chr. 28:5).

d. The son is under his father's authority. The firstborn has privileges (Gen. 43:33; Dt. 21:17) but may forfeit them (Gen. 35:22; 25:29ff.); the father may prefer, or God elect, a younger son instead (cf. Gen. 37:3; 1 Sam. 16:12). Parents must bring up sons, instructing (Prov. 1:8; Dt. 6:9; Ex. 10:2) and chastising them (Prov. 13:1) as needed. Sons owe moral duties to their parents (Prov. 1:8, 4:1; 6:20, etc.). They have responsibility for the debts and offenses of their fathers (2 Kgs. 4:1; Josh. 7:24-25), but with some limitation (cf. Dt. 24:16). If God visits the sins of parents on their children (Ex. 20:5), this does not abrogate personal responsibility (Ezek. 18:1ff.). Tensions may arise between fathers and sons (cf. Gen. 27; 34).

e. Certain sons like Isaac and Jacob have special significance as heirs of the divine promise. The sons of Hosea and Isaiah (Hos. 1; Is. 7:3; 8:1ff.) play a symbolical role (cf. also Is. 7:10ff.).

f. Adoption confers equality with physical sons. The OT has legitimation rites that serve this purpose; cf. Gen. 30:3 and perhaps Ruth 4:16-17 (where Naomi recognizes the child of Boaz and Ruth as the rightful heir of her dead son).

3. Association.

a. In the plural *bēn* may carry the sense of "young men" or "children" (Prov. 7:7; Gen. 3:16). It may also be used for members of a group or for students etc. for whom the speaker is a father.

b. In Zech. 4:14 Joshua and Zerubbabel are "sons of oil," i.e., anointed ones; the term "sons" expresses their relationship to the anointing oil.

4. Relationship.

a. In a weaker sense *bēn* or *bar* expresses membership in a collective society.

b. This may be a people, country, or place.

c. It may also be a vocational guild or a class of people (e.g., resident aliens).

d. Another use is to denote the sharing of a quality (courage etc.) or fate (captivity).

e. Finally, the terms are used to express belonging to a time or age (cf. Jon. 4:10; Ex. 12:5; Lev. 12:6; Gen. 7:6).

5. Relationship to God.

a. The OT uses *bēn* or *bar* for beings that belong to the divine world but never with the term Yahweh (cf. Gen. 6:2, 4; Job 1:6; Dan. 3:25; Pss. 82:1; 89:5). The idea is that of a pantheon under the sovereignty of God. Yahweh is Judge in the heavenly council. The heavenly beings are totally subject to God and his will (Job 1:6ff.). There is no strict father-son relationship such as one finds in surrounding cults. If divine beings, including the gods of other nations, exist under the supreme God, they have no independent power and simply constitute a heavenly court.

b. In 2 Sam. 7:14; Pss. 2:7; 89:26-27 the king is called God's son, but this cannot be meant in a physical sense. God will play the role of a father to the Davidic dynasty (2 Sam. 7:14-15). He will give the Davidic king both legitimacy and a share in his kingly rule. Ps. 89 offers a poetic paraphrase of the divine legitimation of the Davidic dynasty. The king of Judah has here the privilege of a firstborn. He does not claim deity but uses his divine legitimation as a ground on which to seek help. Ps. 2:7 recalls the divine legitimation by enthronement. God's declaration may well be part of the ritual. It takes the form of acknowledgment (as of the child of a concubine). The ruler is not a divine son by nature, nor does he enter the divine sphere by enthronement. He is recognized as a son by divine resolve and hence shares the divine authority and inheritance. A legal sonship replaces the physical sonship of Egyptian thinking.

c. More commonly Israel is God's son, his firstborn (Ex. 4:22), his dear child (Jer. 31:20), his favored one (3:19). The people are God's children (Dt. 14:1) whom the wife Israel (Hos. 2:4) or Jerusalem (Ezek. 16:20) has borne. They may thus call God "our Father" (Is. 63:16; 64:7; Mal. 2:10). Israel and the Israelites are equally God's son or sons, although only the righteous are so in Ps. 73:15 and the priests in Mal. 1:6. God acts toward Israel as both father and mother (Dt. 1:31; Is. 66:13). The relationship is not a natural one and may be dissolved. On the one side it stresses distance (cf. Mal. 1:6; Dt. 8:5). God has a legal claim to Israel, and it owes him duties in response for care. On the other side the relation stresses intimacy. God deals with Israel in kindness and love. It may thus appeal to his mercy (Is. 63:15-16). Even when it disappoints him by its sin, he still admonishes it to return to a loving Father (Jer. 3:14, 22) and promises that he will again receive its members as sons (Hos. 2:1). It is, of course, by God's free resolve and not by physical generation that Israel is God's son, and when it proves disobedient to God the term "son" becomes in the prophets an expression for sinful and guilty Israel (cf. Is. 1:2ff.; 30:1, 9).

d. Personal names with "father" or "brother" show that individuals may be seen in a father-son relation to God. There are no similar names with "son" in the OT, but perhaps the use of "shoot" in 1 Chr. 7:17; Ezr. 10:35 serves this purpose.

C. Judaism.

I. Hellenistic Judaism.

1. The LXX.

a. The LXX usually has *huiós* for *bēn* (*bar*), and less commonly *téknon* and *paidíon*. No solid conclusion can be drawn from the use of other terms than *huiós* in, e.g., Ex. 4:23 and Hos. 11:1.   [G. FOHRER, VIII, 340-54]

b. Special phrases are "beloved son" in Gen. 22:2, and "sons of wisdom" (Sir. 4:11), of "captivity" (1 Esdr. 7:11ff.), of "Adam" (Sir. 40:1); of "the covenant" (Ps. Sol. 17:15), and of "aliens" (1 Macc. 3:45).

c. Wis. 9:7 and Ps. Sol. 17:27 adopt the OT phrase "sons of God" for Israel. The whole nation is God's son in Wis. 18:13, but not every Israelite is a son of God (Sir. 51:10). After death the righteous dwell among God's sons (Wis. 5:5).

d. In the LXX the king is God's son in Ps. 110:3, the angels are God's sons in Dt. 32:43, and Israel is the firstborn son in Ex. 4:22. In general, however, there is some hesitation about the use of the title "son of God."

2. Josephus. Josephus does not use "son of God," although he views God as the Father and Lord of Israel and the Creator of all people. He restates 2 Sam. 7:14 (*Antiquities* 7.93) in such a way as to rule out any mythical idea of divine sonship.

3. Philo. Philo accepts God as the Father of all; the cosmos is his "younger son." Individually only doers of good are God's sons. The sons of Israel should seek to be sons of the firstborn *lógos*. The wise are adoptive sons of God by a second birth. Nevertheless, the title "man of God" is more appropriate. Philo upholds the differentiation of God and man but comes near to divinizing Moses. The *lógos* is God's firstborn son as the force that creates and sustains the world and as the sinless mediator. Hellenistic Judaism uses "son of God" more freely than Palestinian Judaism. Yet it does not equate the son of God with the *theíos anér* either as a Hellenistic charismatic or as a biblical man of God through whom God works miracles.

[E. SCHWEIZER, VIII, 354-57]

II. Palestinian Judaism.

1. Duties of the Son. Sons are circumcised on the eighth day, learn the law from their fathers, and assume responsibility in their thirteenth year. They must honor and respect their parents, merely inviting them to see any errors, and making expiation for them the first year after death. Since sons learn from fathers, students view their teachers as fathers and owe them the same respect. Teachers are fathers for the world to come and not just for this world. The rabbis set stages for the various periods of life. Thus the learning of Scripture comes at five years, practice at thirteen, marriage at eighteen, work at twenty, maturity at thirty, age at sixty, and old age at seventy. In the father's house study of Scripture and its legal exposition are the primary duty.

2. Relationship. As in the OT the term "son" often denotes relationship, e.g., to a city or society or to the covenant. Common phrases are "sons of the world" and "sons of the world to come." Qumran uses "sons of light and darkness," "sons of the truth, righteousness, and grace," and "sons of iniquity, guilt, and Belial."

3. Sons of God. Israel ranks as the son, the firstborn, or the only son of God, and Israelites are God's sons. Divine sonship is grounded in the law and demands its study and observance. The righteous in particular are God's sons; he protects them and punishes those who mistreat them.

4. The Messiah as God's Son. Postbiblical Judaism does not forget the promise of a royal anointed one called God's son, but treats the phrase "son of God" cautiously so as to avoid ideas of physical descent. "Son of God" is not a messianic title and references occur only in connection with promises such as that of Ps. 2:7 and 2 Sam. 7:10ff. Qumran takes these messianically but offers no precise exposition. Reservations become stronger when Christians call Jesus "Son of God." Thus 2 Sam. 7:14 is no longer taken messianically and Ps. 2:7 is reduced to a mere comparison. The rabbis also stress God's uniqueness and deny that he can have a son.

[E. LOHSE, VIII, 357-62]

D. The NT.

I. huiós without Reference to God.

1. Jesus as the Son of Mary and Joseph. Jesus is Mary's son in Mt. 1:21ff.; Lk. 1:31. In the genealogies legal descent is at issue. In Mk. 6:3 "son of Mary" is probably used because Joseph is dead. The point in Mt. 13:55 is that the people do not sense the true mystery of the origin of Jesus. The son of Rev. 12:5 seems to be the son of the community.

2. Father and Son in Illustration of God's Care for Believers. God deals with believers as his sons in Mt. 7:9 and Heb. 12:5ff. Believers are sons of the king in Mt. 17:25-26 but may retain synagogal fellowship in this freedom.

3. High Estimation of the Son. Hostility of fathers and sons marks the horror of eschatological tribulation (Lk. 12:53). Serious discipleship means not loving sons or daughters more than Jesus (Mt. 10:37). Jesus shows his compassion by raising the widow's only son (Lk. 7:22). On some readings Lk. 14:5 puts the son before the ox to show the urgency of rescue even on the sabbath.

4. The Transferred Sense. In Jn. 19:26 Jesus makes the favorite disciple Mary's son.

5. Sons of Abraham and Israel. In Lk. 15:21ff. only the word of forgiveness makes the prodigal a true son. Being a son of Abraham is the essential thing in salvation in Lk. 19:9. God's election decides this (Gal. 3:7; 4:22ff.). Mt. 27:9, Lk. 1:16, and 2 Cor. 3:7ff. refer to pre-Christian Israel.

6. huiós for Student. Jesus calls students "sons" of the Pharisees in Mt. 12:27 (cf. Paul in Acts 23:6). Mark is Peter's son in 1 Pet. 5:13.

7. Relationship. NT phrases are "sons of the kingdom" (Mt. 8:12), "of peace" (Lk. 10:6), "of light" (Lk. 16:8), "of the resurrection" (Lk. 20:36), "of this aeon" (Lk. 16:8), "of the wicked one" (Mt. 13:38), "of the devil" (Acts 13:10), "of disobedience" (Eph. 2:2), and "of perdition" (Jn. 17:12); cf. also "sons of the bride chamber" (Mk. 2:19) and "of thunder" (Mk. 3:17).

II. Jesus as the Son of God in the Tradition.

1. Jesus. Jesus seldom uses "Son of God" for himself, though scoffers accuse him of doing so in Mt. 27:43. He works out more by his life and teaching than the title as such can ever say. He distinguishes, however, between God as "my Father" and God as "your Father," thus setting himself in a unique relationship to God.

2. The Davidic Son of God.

a. The Regency of the Exalted. In Rom. 1:3-4 Jesus is the son of David who after Easter is granted eternal dominion as messianic King of the community. In this verse "Son of God" denotes a function.

b. Resurrection as Son of God. In Acts 13:33 Jesus is raised as the Son. The resurrection is central here. It means victory over death and the beginning of the royal dominion of the Son with God's unique act of intervention.

c. The Baptism of Jesus. The statement at the baptism comes in an eschatological setting and fulfils expectation of the Davidic Son of God. The good pleasure of God denotes election to the office of eschatological King, and Jesus' ministry is thus understood as the regency promised to David's house and executed by God's commission.

d. Separation to the Kingdom. In Col. 1:12ff. the church is taken out of the world and set in the kingdom of God's beloved Son. Remission of sins delivers believers from the power of darkness and sets them under the rule of the exalted Lord. The terminology resembles that of Qumran.

e. The Transfiguration. Here again one sees a link between the institution of Jesus as end-time King and his designation as Son of God.

f. Ps. 110. Mk. 12:35ff. relates the rule of the Son of David to the session at God's right hand (cf. also Heb. 1:5ff.). Heb. 5:5-6 combines Ps. 2:7 with Ps. 110:4 in order to forge a link with the important high-priestly motif.

3. The Eschatological Role of the Son of God and the Absolute ho huiós.

a. The Link with Son of Man Christology. 1 Th. 1:10 presents the eschatological role of the Son of God in connection with Christ's atoning death and resurrection. Paul is perhaps adapting here an original Son of Man saying. Rev. 2:18 describes the Son of God in the same way as the one like a son of man in 1:13ff. Here again, then, an original Son of Man saying is perhaps transferred to the exalted Son of God. Conversely Mk. 14:62 links the Son of Man with Ps. 110:1, and cf. the link between Ps. 8:6 and Ps. 110:1 in 1 Cor. 15:25ff.; Eph. 1:20ff.

b. 1 Cor. 15:28. *ho huiós* occurs in this verse in an apocalyptic context. The term safeguards against a Christology that forgets the consummation, avoids a unitarian concept of God, and yet steers clear of a doctrine of two Gods by giving the Son his place within the one divine glory.

c. Mk. 13:32. In this verse the parousia is again central and the Son is subordinate to the Father in his earthly work, for while he brings about the meeting of God and the world he does not know the time of the consummation. The title "Son" is not the primary point of the saying and perhaps relates to the title "Son of Man" (cf. Lk. 12:8; Mt. 13:41; Jn. 1:51 for references to the Son of Man and angels together).

d. Mt. 11:27. This verse associates the Son and the Father. The reference is not so much to mutual knowledge as to the election and acknowledgment of the Son, to whom the Father has given all power, and hence to the work of the Son for the acknowledgment of the Father in the world. The stress is on the unique mediatorial position of the Son in his function of representing God in the world.

e. Johannine Passages. The apocalyptic basis of the absolute *ho huiós* may be seen in Jn. 3:5 and 5:19ff. In the Son one sees the Father, so that faith in him is faith in the Father. Jn. 8:35-36 contrasts the transitory stay of the slave with the permanent residence of the son (cf. Heb. 3:5-6; Gal. 4:7; Rom. 8:15ff.).

4. The Sending of the Preexistent Son of God. In Gal. 4:4-5; Jn. 3:17; 1 Jn. 4:9 we find the phrase "God sent his Son," with a *hína* clause to express the saving mission of the Son. As such the term "send" does not have to mean preexistence (God also sent the prophets), but in Paul and John a developed Christology may be presupposed. As God sent wisdom or the Spirit, so he sends the preexistent Son whose closeness to God constitutes his significance as distinct from angels or prophets. The categories are such as we find in Hellenistic Judaism but with a new historical singularity and eschatological urgency. They are thus more temporal than spatial.

5. The Miraculously Born and Miracle-Working Son of God.

a. The Virgin Birth. Lk. 1:35 links the annunciation to *huiós theoú*. The saying explains the title in terms of the power of the Spirit while relating the divine Son to the stem of David. There are no true parallels for this usage.

b. The Miracle Worker. The demon addresses Jesus as "Son of the Most High God" in Mk. 5:7. The cries in 1:24 show that the root idea may be that of the OT charismatic (possibly associated with the *theíos anér*); expectation of a Messiah who drives out demons helps to complete the picture.

c. The Temptation. Satan's questions presuppose the manifestation of God's Son by mighty acts. Jesus himself, however, rejects a divine sonship that manifests itself along the lines suggested.

6. The Suffering Righteous as Son of God. In Mt. 27:43 the chief priests mock Jesus in the words of Ps. 22:8 for regarding himself as the Son of God along the lines of the suffering righteous of Wis. 2:18, i.e., the servant who trusts God and is exalted among his sons after suffering ignominious death. The general point here is that suffering and sonship are not incompatible.

III. Jesus' Divine Sonship in the NT Writers.

1. Mark. Mk. 1:11 adopts the title "Son of God" and thus presents the divine dimension of the work of Jesus. The demons know him as the Son in 1:24, God manifests his sonship to the three in 9:7, Jesus links the sonship and the passion in 12:1ff., he relates it to the coming exaltation in 14:61, and the centurion confesses it in 15:39. Mark, then, finds in the title the mystery of Jesus but only insofar as Jesus manifests himself as Son of God in the passion, death, and exaltation of the Son of Man.

2. Matthew. In Matthew the divine sonship lies hidden under his suffering as the righteous one (cf. 3:15, 17; 21:39; 27:40). Jesus is the Son as he fulfils Israel's destiny (2:15). Discipleship leads to confession of Jesus as God's Son (14:33; 16:16). 17:5 repeats 3:17 and thus strengthens the disciples and illustrates the promise. 11:27 presents the Son as the Revealer of all mysteries. Finally, 28:19 associates Father, Son, and Holy Spirit.

3. Luke and Acts. The title "Son of God" characterizes Paul's preaching in Acts 9:20. The term Christ explains Son of God in Lk. 4:41. Lk. 22:69-70 connects divine sonship with session at God's right hand. In 23:47 Luke is perhaps preventing pagan misunderstanding by avoiding "Son of God." Luke omits Mk. 13:32. Lk. 1:32-33 takes up the tradition of a Davidic Son of God but relates it to Christ's rule over the church. In 1:35 conception by the Spirit underlies Jesus' description as the Son of God. Jesus is no mere man elevated to deity after the pagan model. His election reaches back to his birth and preexistence. While there is no biological or metaphysical concern, Luke finds it important to stress that the birth of Jesus rests on God's act and thus testifies to his unique election and sonship.

4. Paul.

a. Apocalyptic Passages. Paul in 1 Th. 1:10 plainly takes the Son of God concept from the apocalyptic Son of Man tradition. Final honor belongs to the Father but not apart from the unique dignity of the Son (1 Cor. 15:28; Phil. 2:11). Metaphysical equality is not Paul's concern.

b. The Sending of God's Son. Paul adopts and reconstructs the traditional pattern in Gal. 4:4-5; Rom. 8:3-4. In Galatians the sending of the Son is unique and is related strictly to the incarnation and the death for sinners. Romans stresses the judicial destruction of sin in the flesh of Jesus. The Son who is sent is connected with God's acts in Israel's history. He is the heir of Abraham who overcomes the curse of the law, vindicating it without entailing our eternal death.

c. The Suffering Son. Paul descries the sonship in Christ's suffering in Rom. 5:10; 8:32; Gal. 2:20. "Son" describes the bond of love between God and Jesus and hence the greatness of the sacrifice. The title relates, not so much to preexistence, but to the wonder of the saving act. It is grounded in Christ's passion rather than his exaltation and kingship.

d. Other References. In Rom. 1:3, 9 the Son is the content of the gospel and implies Christ's uniqueness. In Rom. 8:29 and Gal. 4:6 the root of the designation lies in the resurrection and related apocalyptic expectation.

5. *John.*

a. Eschatological Passages and the Absolute *ho huiós.* Jn. 3:35-36 brings out the love of the Father and the Son and the apocalyptic endowment of the Son with power; hence the demand for faith and obedience. In 5:19ff. the Father meets us in the Son. The greater works of resurrection relate to the present awakening to faith. 6:40 plainly has an eschatological background. The reference is to the enduring will of the Father by which we may have eternal life through the Son. In 1 Jn. 2:22ff. one cannot have the Father without the Son. It is thus fatal to lose the Son (2 Jn. 9). The absolute *ho huiós* occurs in the sending formula in 1 Jn. 4:14.

b. The Sending of God's Son. John presupposes preexistence but finds the uniqueness in the greatness of God's love (Jn. 3:16). The sending formula points ahead to the cross (vv. 14-15). The giving of the Son means eternal life (3:17; 1 Jn. 4:9). The claim to sonship, which involves sending to do the Father's works, brings on the death of Jesus (10:36ff.). By the sending come faith and deliverance from judgment. Salvation is being in the Son (1 Jn. 5:20), which is being in the truth and not in evil.

c. The Son as the Content of Confession. For John the Son whom God sends is also the King of Israel and the Christ (Jn. 1:49; 11:27). The formulation in 3:19 stresses his uniqueness. Like the Hellenistic charismatic, he performs miracles but his titles are different. 1 Jn. 4:15 and 5:5 repeat Jn. 20:31, though without the Christ title. Believing in God and believing in the Son are the same (1 Jn. 5:10). Eternal life is in the Son (5:11). The Son is the content of God's witness (5:9), and believers confess the Son (2:22-23); they have fellowship with the Father and with "his" Son (1:3).

d. Sonship in John. In John sonship presupposes an essential unity of Father and Son. This has its basis in their mutual love whereby the Father wills and gives, and the Son hears and obeys. Manifested in the acts of Jesus, it is grounded in the depths of the divine being and hence implies Christ's preexistence (cf. Jn. 8:56), although the emphasis does not lie here but on the unity of love.

6. *Other Writings.*

a. Hebrews refers to the exalting of the Son of David to eternal rule. The name Son implies a divine dignity even above that of angels (Heb. 1:5 quoting Ps. 110:1). The Son is also the High Priest in 4:14; 5:5; 7:28. In this way the passion and the sonship come together. The special position of Melchizedek serves to bring out Christ's uniqueness as Son and High Priest; it is dangerous to reject so great a Deliverer.

b. 2 Pet. 1:17, referring to Mk. 9:7, finds dignity and majesty in the title.

c. Revelation uses "Son of God" only in 2:18 on the basis of Ps. 2:7. As the Lord of earthly rulers the Son is close to Jewish models but only as the faithful witness who freed us from sins by his blood (1:5).

IV. Human Sons of God.

1. Apart from Paul. In the NT the sonship of Jesus is determinative. God is a common Father but not all are his sons; hints that they are so by creation occur only in Lk. 3:38 and Acts 17:28. In Mt. 5:45 the righteous are God's sons on the basis of God's fatherly love that makes obedience possible. But in Lk. 6:35 this finds actualization only eschatologically. In Lk. 20:36 the sons of the resurrection are beings in the heavenly sphere immune from death and corruption. Yet by liberation from the law, disciples of Jesus are already a company of free sons in Mt. 17:25-26. Eschatological life as a son means sharing Christ's apocalyptic lordship in Rev. 2:26-27. In Jn. 1:12 there is already a present sonship by the authority granted in the Logos, i.e., the incarnate Lord. Yet John reserves *huiós* for Christ and uses *tékna* for believers as those who are born of God. Heb. 2:10-11 shows that believers become sons only as the Son calls them his brethren.

2. Paul. In Rom. 9:26 (quoting Hos. 2:1) Paul finds the divine sonship of the eschaton fulfilled in the community. Those who are in Christ are heirs with him (Gal. 3:28-29). The Son has been sent to break the power of the law and to give life and sonship through his vicarious death (Gal. 4:5-6). In this sonship they cry "Abba, Father" (Rom. 8:15). They are no longer slaves, but free (Gal. 4:7). Yet their manifestation as sons comes only with the eschaton (Rom. 8:19). The spirit of sonship is the Spirit of the Son (Gal. 4:6). Christ is God's image, and believers are fashioned in his likeness (Rom. 8:29) by a new creation that begins already yet awaits its full consummation. [E. SCHWEIZER, VIII, 363-92]

E. Early Christian Literature.

1. Survey.

a. 1 Clement never uses *huiós theoú* but it is presupposed in 36.4-5.

b. The Didache uses the baptismal formula in 7.1, 3 and cf. 16.4.

c. Ignatius uses *huiós theoú* several times (cf. *Ephesians* 4.2; 20.2; *Magnesians* 8.2). It is plainly a current title (cf. also Pol. 12.2 and Mart. Pol. 17.3).

d. In Barnabas the title has a solid place but is not especially significant (cf. 5.9; 7.2; 12.10).

e. *huiós theoú* is common in Hermas (especially *Similitudes* 9) but in different connections and often with imprecise content.

f. The apocryphal gospels are familiar with the title but it is hard to date and interpret the references.

g. The Coptic Gospel of Thomas has the term only indirectly ("Son of the living One"); the Father here is primal light and the Son is the Revealer.

h. The Gospel of Peter uses the phrase in a naive way and on the basis of the canonical Gospels.

i. With Justin and Irenaeus theological reflection begins.

2. Meaning. In 1 Clement ideas of preexistence and subordination seem to be determinative. For Ignatius Christ's sonship is central and involves true deity, although with an antidocetic stress on his coming in the flesh. In Barnabas Christ is the preexistent Son who was active in creation and who took flesh for our salvation. In Hermas the title is an inalienable if obscure constituent of the faith. Justin finds Logos more significant. The Logos, begotten as Son with no loss to the Father, is also God. In this way Justin maintains the deity of the Son without imperiling monotheism. Irenaeus, too, identifies Son and Logos but with a primary emphasis on the incarnation and hence on the Very Man and Very God in a Word-flesh Christology.

[W. SCHNEEMELCHER, VIII, 392-97]

huiothesía.

1. The Greek World.

a. Legal Presuppositions. This late word means "adoption as a child." In ancient Greece adoption is often informal but public. It is a way of meeting the absence of heirs, available only for citizens of legitimate descent, and carrying no change of name for those adopted. When associated with a will, adoption usually includes the duty of providing for the adopting parents.

b. Religious Presuppositions. In Greek there are no instances of a transferred use, but in myth Heracles is adopted by Hera in a mock birth to confer legitimacy on him after his apotheosis.

2. Judaism. The LXX does not use the term, but Philo has it for the relation of the wise to God.

3. The NT. In the NT only Paul uses the term. His aim is to show that the sonship of believers is not a natural one but is conferred by divine act. The term might refer either to the act or to the result. In Rom. 9:4, relating to Israel, adoption is associated with the covenant and the promises. It means freeing from the law in Gal. 4:5. In Rom. 8:15 freedom comes with the spirit of "sonship" in virtue of Christ's all-transforming act. Eph. 1:5 traces it back to God's foreordination and thus leaves no room for boasting. In Rom. 8:23 the adoption is future; this teaches us that we always need God, but also that his purpose does not change.   [E. SCHWEIZER, VIII, 397-99]

→ *país, patér*

---

ho huiós toú anthrópou [the Son of Man]

A. The Linguistic Problem.

1. This NT expression is an Aramaism in which there stands behind *ánthrōpos* a general concept that is then individualized.

2. In Hebrew the indeterminate form occurs 93 times in Ezekiel as God's address to the prophet and also another 14 times, always in a poetic or lofty context as a term for man.

3. The Hebrew term does not occur in rabbinic Hebrew.

4. The Aramaic is found from the eighth century for "someone," and it then has the general sense of "man" or the individual sense of "somebody." The various expressions for man or son of man are common in the Aramaic of the time of Jesus in both collective and individual senses.

5. The NT *ho huiós toú anthrópou* is the literal rendering of an ambivalent Aramaic expression. In apocalyptic contexts this can bear a messianic sense but only approximates a title. Except in Jn. 5:27, however, the Gospels use the Greek in a messianic sense as distinct from the simple *ánthrōpos*. This may well be an interpretation in passages like Mk. 2:10; Mt. 8:20; 11:19; 12:32, although conversely the Aramaic might have had a messianic sense in Mt. 9:8 ("to men"; cf. v. 6). Deliberate interpretation is possibly present in 1 Tim. 2:5; Heb. 2:6; 1 Cor. 15:21; Rom. 5:15. The Aramaic can have a typical as well as a messianic sense—another possibility in Mk.

2:10; Mt. 8:20; 11:19; 12:32. Other sayings, however, permit only a reference to Jesus, and more than the meaning "I" is obviously at issue, as the church perceives when it fixes a messianic interpretation with its *ho huiós toú anthrṓpou*.

B. The Historical Problem.
I. Impossibility of an Israelite Genealogy.
1. General. The "Son of Man" attracts the attributes of God (Dan. 7:13; 4 Esdr. 13:3ff.); this is possible only if he is a heavenly being and not just an earthly Messiah. The author of Daniel seems to have taken over his imagery from outside and not inherited or invented it. An alien tradition seems also to be present in 4 Esdras and Ethiopian Enoch.
2. OT Concepts.
a. Ezekiel. In Ezekiel the term "son of man" applies to the prophet. Similarities to Jesus lie in his humanity and his solidarity with the people. Yet in the case of Ezekiel suffering is no essential part of his creaturely lowliness, and he does not in any strict sense represent or embody the people.
b. Ps. 80. In Ps. 80:15, 17 Israel is a man at God's right hand, a son of man whom God has made strong for himself. But the collective sense is by no means certain, and we may have here a prayer for the strengthening of a king to bring salvation to the people.
c. Personification of Israel. Personification of Israel takes place, but only on the basis of given concepts, and with no implication of the transcendence or judicial work of the Son of Man.
3. Results. One has thus to seek a non-Israelite background for the concept, although the figure will not derive from this, nor will one will be able to explain its significance in either Jewish apocalyptic or the NT in the light of it.
II. Non-Israelite Background.
1. Untenable Hypotheses.
a. Iran. One cannot explain the apocalyptic Son of Man as a Judaized form of Gayomart of Iran.
b. Babylonia. Only if the Son of Man was originally a second Adam can one associate him with the Babylonian Adapa, who has no eschatological, judicial, or redemptive function.
c. Egypt. Nor is there much support for the view that the Ancient of Days is the Egyptian sun-god and the Son of Man his successor.
d. Judaism. Rabbinic speculations about a glorified Adam are protological even if they manifest a soteriological concern, and this Adam is heavenly only in the sense of cosmic, not as the one who comes from heaven. Philo's heavenly man has a macrocosmic character and cosmological function as distinct from the eschatological and judicial character and function of the Son of Man. Wisdom speculation links up with the idea of the Son of Man inasmuch as wisdom manifests the Son or the Son has wisdom, but there is no equation of the two.
e. Gnosticism. Gnostic derivation usually presupposes common kinship with other sources, although more precise theories try to trace a development of the Gnostic *ánthrōpos* (the heavenly or primal man) by way of Judaism. Intellectually the Gnostic primal man originates in the microcosm-macrocosm idea which relates cosmic and human structure. Gnosticism then spiritualizes primal man as a universal *plérōma*, or as a central hypostasis within this *plérōma*, or as both. As a hypostasis he is the chief and best part of the macrocosm and microcosm, or of the cosmic and human soul, as

the heavenly man in the cosmos and the inner man in the outer man. In Gnostic systems the two best parts become detached, and an earthly prophet representing or incarnating the cosmic soul comes to men in order to achieve reconciliation. This involves a mythological or at least a docetic view of the prophet and an understanding of redemption in the categories of a revelation of the identity of the inner soul and of its reuniting with the cosmic soul. Fundamentally this view of the Gnostic *ánthrōpos* bears no relation to the apocalyptic Son of Man. The personification may be due to common hypostatic thinking, but the Jewish Son of Man plays an eschatological role, has a judicial function, redeems by acquitting, does not stand in natural union with the cosmos, is announced by prophetic and apocalyptic writers, and has no mission of descent and reascent. Arguments relating John more closely to Gnosticism appeal to preexistence, descent, and reascent in John, but John shows no acquaintance with Gnostic cosmology or anthropology, e.g., the idea of a collective soul plunged into darkness. The parallelism of *ánthrōpos* and wisdom or word in Jewish tradition explains the ideas of preexistence, descent, and reascent in John, and if the Gnostic redeemer is also judge this may well be due to Christian influence.

2. *A Possible Hypothesis (Canaan).* Another possible hypothesis is that Canaan (cf. Ras Shamra) provides the background for the Son of Man in Daniel (cf. the fourth beast and the chaos dragon, the Son of Man and Baal, the Ancient of Days and El). The details, however, do not correspond, and OT monotheism modifies the adopted nexus of motifs. Thus God embraces in himself the predicates of various Canaanite deities.

3. *Bearing on Interpretation.* The discussion warns us against overstressing the human form of the Son of Man. Jewish apocalyptic has developed its own figure and not just taken over a heavenly *macroanthropos* or archetypal primal man. This Jewish figure bears a messianic reference and hence Son of Man can become a title. Different groups ascribe to the figure different functions, and heterogeneous traditions and related speculations affect the presentation.

III. Jewish Apocalyptic.

1. Dan. 7.

a. The Vision. Within the general vision Dan. 7:9ff. offers a little apocalypse in which the Ancient of Days sits on the throne, and the one like the Son of Man is brought to him, and is given eternal dominion. The happening is in the heavenly world and the coming with the clouds denotes the superhuman majesty of the one like the Son of Man. The "like" shows that there is no exact equation with earthly humanity. The coming after the beasts represents the coming, not of archetypal man, but of the eschaton itself after the rule of the beast-powers. Earthly empires yield to the eschatological dominion of the one like the Son of Man. He symbolizes this dominion rather than any specific group or kingdom. In this way he suggests messianic ideas.

b. The Interpretation. In the interpretation the one like the Son of Man is the representative of God's entourage who in the end time exercises power in place of earthly rulers. The saints of the Most High are Jews who remain loyal to the ancient traditions. Hence the one like the Son of Man represents the true Israel that will replace the empires. He has a saving eschatological function.

2. Ethiopian Enoch.

a. Usage and Interpretation. In Ethiopian Enoch the Son of Man figures only in 37–71. Again the term "man" describes the appearance of the heavenly being and is not as such a messianic title. The alternation of three forms of expression makes this plain. In all three the heavenly one in human form ejects and destroys earthly rulers because of their revolt against God. He is preexistent and will be manifested by God to the saints. His word will be mighty before the Lord of spirits. Looking like a man, he is with the Head of Days, reveals what is hidden, avenges the righteous, and is the light of the nations and hope of the afflicted. Chosen by the Lord of spirits, he appears before him, the Spirit is poured out upon him, righteousness rules in his days, and he sits on the throne of glory. The descriptions insure the messianic significance of the figure with their combination of salvation and judgment, but they do not make Son of Man a messianic title. He is not a personification of Israel, does not mediate creation, is not God's image nor a prototype of humanity, and while associated with the Servant of Is. 53 undergoes no passion.

b. The Exaltation of Enoch. The third similitude includes an exaltation of Enoch as the Son of Man. This implies neither incarnation nor provisional mystical identity but simply the institution of Enoch into the office and function of the eschatological Son of Man. The idea perhaps originates with a group which makes Enoch its hero and whose head takes the name of Enoch. Taking over existing Son of Man eschatology, it assumes that its master is the future Son of Man and ruler and judge of the world.

3. *The Sixth Vision of 4 Esdras.* In 4 Esdras we find a Son of Man eschatology, a messianic eschatology, and a third eschatology in which God himself brings the end. The Son of Man in the sixth vision is preexistent, comes from Zion at a time of strife, destroys and punishes the nations, and protects and gathers Israel. Associated with the Son of Man are Enoch, Moses, and Elijah, and the Son of Man emerges as the national leader of Israel, although not without messianic features of lowliness conferred by the title of servant.

4. *Synoptic Data.* Allusions to Dan. 7 occur on the lips of Jesus. The tradition in Ethiopian Enoch has little influence, and the political Son of Man of 4 Esdras, which may not predate the NT, bears no relation to Son of Man Christology. Jewish apocalyptic, then, does little to shape the concept of the Son of Man in the NT. This concept forms a fourth source of thinking in this area along with those mentioned in 1-3. It derives from the application of the term Son of Man to Jesus himself, whether by Jesus or by his community.

5. *Son of Man Expectation and Jewish Messianology.* Son of Man eschatology stands in tension with expectations of a kingly, priestly, or exalted Messiah, or of the return of figures like Elijah and Moses, or of salvation apart from any specific savior. Only individual groups expect a transcendent Son of Man. Yet Judaism in general identifies the Son of Man of Dan. 7:13-14, or the Son of the clouds, as the glorious and powerful Messiah who has still to come, but who has not come in Christ either crucified or coming again (cf. Trypho in Justin *Dialogue* 32.1).

C. The Son of Man in the NT.
I. Synoptic Gospels.
1. Jesus' Preaching.

a. (a) Jesus calls himself "man" three times, and first in Mk. 2:1ff., where he meets the objection that God alone can forgive sins.

(b) He is "man" again in Mt. 11:18-19, where a comparison and contrast with the Baptist is the point, and the evidence supports an original Son of Man in Aramaic.

(c) "Man" also seems to be the thrust in Mt. 8:20 and parallels. Expositions of this saying include a contrast with animals, a stress on humanity as compared with the Son of God, and a reference to the concealment of the Son of Man. Yet discipleship, and the homelessness that it demands, seem to be the main issue. Those who follow Jesus must be prepared for the fact that although even animals have dens a "man such as he" has nowhere to lay his head.

b. (a) Eight sayings of Jesus yield a self-contained apocalyptic picture, the first of which is found in Mt. 24:27 and parallels. Here the Son of Man will shine like lightning so that none can miss him. The saying plainly replaces a political Messiah with a bringer of eschatological salvation.

(b) Mt. 24:37 and parallels express the element of suddenness or surprise. The comparison with Noah suggests that the Son of Man has the office of judgment. The need, then, is to be prepared for his coming, as is confirmed by Lk. 21:34ff.

(c) Lk. 18:8 goes hand in hand with 18:6. Will the Son of Man, at his coming, find that people have responded to his message in faith and are petitioning God as the widow did the unjust judge? Lk. 17:24 carries the same message as an intimation, and Lk. 21:36 as a demand.

(d) Before the council in Lk. 22:69 Jesus says that the Son of Man sits in judgment at the right hand of power (with some allusion to Ps. 110:1). The saying is a veiled confession and refers to majesty rather than exaltation.

(e) Mt. 10:23 limits the disciples' mission to Israel. The point may be either that the disciples must make haste or that the last hour is hastening on. But the saying may also be a promise that persecution will end. It fits in with other sayings that expect the coming, whether to earth or in heaven. Various explanations have been advanced for the sign, e.g., a phenomenon of light, the Son of Man himself, or the banner around which his people will rally.

(f) These dominical sayings form a basis for later messianological statements and offer a fourth tradition independent of Dan. 7 etc. It is unlikely that charismatics in Jewish Christian circles formulate them, since statements directly in Jesus' name are unknown, the charismatic period and that of the independence of the Palestinian churches end too quickly, and after Easter the resurrection comes to the fore as the dawn of the new age.

c. There are four group parallels to Son of Man statements. In the first one may place Lk. 22:27, in the second Mk. 3:28-29, in the third Mt. 10:32-33, and in the fourth Mk. 9:9, 31, etc. With these sayings Jesus' proclamation of the Son of Man achieves completeness. He is not just a preacher of repentance, a second Amos or Baptist. By his passion he confers forgiveness of sins and achieves a perfecting whereby those who confess him may share his glory.

d. Whether Jesus thinks of himself directly as the apocalyptic Son of Man is hard to say for certain in view of the Palestinian refusal to make explicit identifications. In Jesus' prophetic preaching he can easily relate his work and God's rule, for prophetic preaching sets up such a relation in regard to present and future, or present person and future event. Direct identification, however, destroys the dynamic element in the relation and robs the preaching of its prophetic character. Jesus brings the eschatological future into the present in statements about his perfecting, in his proclamation of God's kingdom, and in his intimation of the Son of Man. These parallels may not be equated expressly but they are not mutually exclusive. Jesus' eschatological role begins with his preaching of the kingdom. In this role he is associated with the Son of Man and is thus neither a rabbi nor a community member reflecting on the group leader, even if it is difficult to equate him directly with the Son of Man or the day of the Son of Man with God's rule. Since the Son of Man sayings are primarily addressed to the disciples, they come at first in less public preaching. But the apocalyptic Son of Man symbolizes Jesus' assurance of perfecting while perhaps carrying an ambivalent messianic and nonmessianic meaning. The association with the passion does not have to imply a link between the Son of Man and the Servant of the Lord but may develop out of a unique extension of the sufferings of various individuals in Israel on behalf of the people as a whole.

2. *The Oral Tradition.*

a. First Stage. (a) In the light of Easter and the prospect of Christ's return the original Son of Man sayings are related to the return and bear a clear messianic sense relative to the earthly ministry.

(b) Mt. 10:32-33 assumes fuller significance as confession of Jesus is seen to be decisive for future pardon or condemnation.

(c) According to the saying about speaking against the Son of Man and blaspheming the Spirit, it is also perceived that with Jesus comes an offer of forgiveness but that rejection of this offer leaves no further room for remission.

(d) A "for my sake" appropriately supplements the last beatitude in Mt. 5:11.

b. Second Stage. (a) The title Son of Man finds a place in prophetic (Mk. 9:31; 8:31; 10:33; 9:9) and situational (Mk. 14:41; 14:21; Lk. 22:48) intimations of the passion. If Jesus himself perhaps put the statements in the first person, the correct basis of the title is that it is he who brings together the concept of the Son of Man and his own perfecting through violent death and passion (cf. Mt. 23:37ff.; also Mk. 2:19-20; 10:38; Lk. 12:49-50). Messianic majesty and lowliness meet in Jesus to produce the gospel of the suffering Son of Man. The simple passion prediction in Mk. 9:31 stresses the divine action. Mk. 8:31ff. emphasizes the necessary fulfilment of Scripture. A more detailed prediction of the sufferings comes in Mk. 10:33-34. Mk. 9:9 relates the transfiguration to the glory of the resurrection and the resultant disclosure of the messiahship. Mk. 14:41 develops a basic theological saying; the betrayal is the time of the handing over to sinners of him whom God has appointed for the work of perfecting. In Mk. 14:21 the betrayal is again the issue. The term Son of Man adds weight to an emphatic I (cf. the "me" and "with me" of v. 18). The "going" is that of the Son of Man who is destined to die as he is now to be delivered up to his enemies. The saying in Lk. 22:48 does not supplement the story of the arrest but is an expression, not of reproach, blame, or warning, but of sorrow on the part of Jesus. Here again Son of Man is equivalent to a "me," as in Lk. 22:21.

(b) The title Son of Man also finds a place in eschatological and "I" sayings of Jesus. The Son of Man confesses every confessor (Lk. 12:8) and denies every denier (Mk. 8:38) at the judgment. It is thus that he judges. In Mt. 19:28 the Son of Man sits on his glorious throne of judgment and rewards those who leave all for his sake; this is to take place in the new world. In Mk. 10:45 the second half elucidates the first and the term Son of Man corresponds to the "I" of Lk. 22:27. Jesus as Son of Man offers an example of service as the principle of discipleship. Lk. 6:22 has "for the Son of Man's sake" rather than "for my sake" (Mt. 5:11) in the last beatitude.

c. Third Stage. (a) An important saying is that about the sign of Jonah in Lk. 11:30. The basic point is that the generation seeks a sign, that it will be given no sign, but that the sign of Jonah will be given it. When the parousia of the risen Jesus grants the sign of messianic accreditation, which may be perceived directly, it will be too late to accept this as a validation of his preaching.

(b) Mk. 13:26 cites Dan. 7:13, thereby relating the intimation of the end to Son of Man prediction and supporting it with a biblical reference.

(c) Lk. 17:22 has the sufferings of the disciples as its theme. The day of the Son of Man is not visible in such a way that one can adjust one's conduct to it. Since the kingdom comes suddenly, one should be ready even though not knowing when the hour will strike.

(d) In Mt. 24:43-44 the coming of the Son of Man is like that of a burglar for which a prudent householder should be prepared. Cf. 1 Th. 5:2, 4 and 2 Pet. 3:10 for the same comparison to a thief, although the Son of Man is not now himself the thief.

(e) The story in Mk. 2:23ff. concludes with the saying that the Son of Man is lord of the sabbath. Not just human need, but the authority of Jesus as Son of Man decides the proper attitude to the sabbath, which is "made for man," not "man for the sabbath" (v. 27).

(f) In Lk. 12:10 rejection of Jesus in his earthly life is not so serious as rejection of the Spirit of the exalted Lord subsequent to the resurrection.

(g) Mt. 12:32 paraphrases the same saying.

(h) Lk. 19:10 at the end of the story of Zacchaeus reminds us of Mk. 2:17 and Mt. 15:24 ("I" sayings).

3. *Literary Tradition.*

a. Mark and the Lucan Source. (a) Mk. 14:62 carries an allusion to Dan. 7:13 (cf. Mk. 13:26). Here is a full confession of messiahship which focuses on its proclamation and hence on disclosure of Jesus' majesty to the whole world. Earlier proclamations of majesty occur in the forgiving of sins and the assuming of authority over the sabbath (Mk. 2:10, 28). The sayings in 8:31 etc. establish the theology of the suffering Son of Man wherein the suffering necessarily precedes his resurrection and the manifestation of his glory (cf. 9:9, 12). The execution of the Baptist (Elijah) does not render the passion of the Son of Man superfluous (cf. vv. 11-12). In Mk. 10:45 it is as the Son of Man that Jesus gives his life as a ransom for many. The saying brings out the depth of the service that Jesus renders and makes it paradigmatic for the self-humbling which he demands of the disciples. The betrayal saying in Mk. 14:21 sets in juxtaposition "that man" and "the Son of Man" and in so doing adds weight to the threat and stresses the dignity of the Son of Man. After 14:41 the passion itself is depicted and there is no further need for the title. In Mk. 8:38 the coming of the Son of Man is clearly the return of Jesus to the earth (cf. the coming of the kingdom in power in 9:1). The main interest of Mark, however, is in the suffering Son of Man, as the treatment and the order both show. Since the suffering of Jesus is also his perfecting, no alternative of lowliness and glory arises.

(b) The Lucan source includes six sayings in which Son of Man is a present self-designation on the part of Jesus. All are addressed to a mixed audience. Ten sayings about the coming Son of Man are addressed to the disciples (apart from 22:69 to the Sanhedrin). The saying about Jonah in 11:30 is addressed to the crowds.

b. Luke. Luke does not use the Son of Man title independently but is faithful to Mark and his special source.

c. Matthew. In Matthew we find Son of Man sayings from Mark, from the logia, and from a special source, whether in unaltered form or with variations. The Son of Man, equated with Jesus, preaches on earth, suffers vicariously, is exalted as Lord of the church, will come again as final Judge, and rules over the new aeon in the kingdom of God.

II. The Later Apocalyptic Tradition.

1. Acts 7:56. Stephen here cries out that he sees the Son of Man standing at God's right hand. The references to heaven, to God's glory, and to Jesus in v. 55 introduce the saying. The standing is unusual. Is it in order to welcome Stephen, to bear witness to him, to minister to God, or to come forth in judgment or salvation as God does (cf. Ass. Mos. 10:3; Is. 14:22; Ps. 3:7)? Another possibility is simply that "standing (upright)" denotes "living."

2. *Rev. 1:13; 14:14.* These two visions introduce Christ with descriptions based on Dan. 7:13. The coming one is the Lord who is already present, and in keeping with the integration of messianic statements Son of Man sayings are transferred to the Son of God.

3. *Heb. 2:6.* Hebrews refers various OT sayings to Christ (Pss. 2:7; 104:4, etc.). Stress falls on the ruling power of Christ in an apocalyptic use of Ps. 8. Here the majesty of man, which is limited by God's power, becomes the majesty of the Son of Man who is paradoxically lowly.

III. John.

1. The Son of Man sayings in John reproduce and reinterpret the apocalyptic sense. In 5:17ff. v. 27 takes up Dan. 7:13. In context the judgment is the reaching of a judicial decision through the present preaching of Jesus. In 9:35 the confession of Jesus as Son of Man implies added dignity as compared to his recognition as a prophet (v. 17) authorized by God (v. 33); the title is a messianic one. In 6:27 the Son of Man/Revealer gives the bread of life, and again, as we see from v. 53 with its solemn introduction, he does so as the suffering Son of Man by giving himself. Significant here is the implication that Jesus is not just a heavenly being but a real man with a real body whom God has commissioned (v. 27).

2. The other Son of Man sayings all refer to the descent and the exaltation of Jesus. In 3:13ff. the lifting up refers to the cross, so that we have a counterpart to the passion sayings (cf. 12:32-33). The combining of Son of Man and exaltation is a declaration of faith for which apocalyptic prepares the ground and which the ascension confirms by relating exaltation to ascent into the transcendent world. 8:28 and 12:34 testify to the same connection between the Son of Man and lifting up. The secondary sense of crucified is present in 8:28. Jesus is already Son of Man, but his judicial function comes into effect only with his exaltation. In 12:34 the opponents fail to grasp the point that the Son of Man must be lifted up as Jesus says. The ascension into heaven causes similar problems for the disciples in 6:62. The ascent presupposes preexistence and the identification of the earthly Jesus as the Son of Man of apocalyptic tradition. Glorification is the theme in 12:23 and 13:31-32. In 12:31 glorifying by enthronement accompanies a form of passion prediction. In 13:31-32 exaltation again comes by death and passion, and the meaning of Son of Man is assimilated to the more general concept of Son. The first Son of Man saying in 1:51 catches up many of the previous nuances. The anticipation of future revelation is here a transposition into proleptic epiphany (cf. Mk. 1:10-11). The basis lies in Jacob's vision (Gen. 28:12), and the verse testifies to the fellowship of both the heavenly and earthly Son of Man with the Father, to the ministry of angels to the Son of Man in heaven and on earth, to the judicial mandate of the Son of Man in the eschaton, and to his present and future epiphany.

3. Possibly in John the Son of Man bears some analogy to the Logos of the prologue. If so, then it is necessary to say that the Word became flesh, paradoxical though it may sound, for to say that the Word became man would be tautological, and simply to say that the Word came down would be too vague. The incarnation of the Logos and the earthly walk of the Son of Man express a new fact by which our redemption or rejection is decided.

IV. Reformulation.

1. Christ as the Second Adam.

a. 1 Cor. 15:21, 27-28, 45ff. In 1 Cor. 15 and Rom. 5 Christ might be an eschatological primal man, but more likely we have a christological interpretation of Adam. 1 Cor. 15:27 offers a christological reading of Ps. 8. The man by whom resurrection comes stands in contrast with the man by whom death comes (v. 21). Christ is the pneumatic-heavenly man, Adam the psychical-earthly man. The equation of Christ with the pneumatic-heavenly man is due to his life-giving function, his exaltation, and his heavenly nature as an apocalyptic figure. Although ontically second, Adam is chronologically first; Christ as Son of Man is the Coming One.

b. Rom. 5:12ff. In Rom. 5:12ff. Christ in contrast to Adam is the "one man Jesus Christ" in v. 15 and "one man" in vv. 17ff. The Christology in this passage does not rest on Son of Man messianology, but the term "man" can have prototypical significance. Christ as the prototype of a new humanity becomes the antitype of Adam. He is thus more of an eschatological and prototypical Son of Man than an apocalyptic Son of Man. Only incidentally does the term "man" suggest the latter.

2. Christ as Eikṓn and Sṓma. Christ is the *eikṓn* of God in 2 Cor. 4:4; Col. 1:15, and as such he is preexistent in the same way as the Logos. He is also the mediator of creation. As cosmic Anthropos, he fills the universe, is set above it as head, and in his eschatological function redeems it.

D. The Early Church.

I. Jewish Christianity. According to Hegesippus in Eusebius *Ecclesiastical History* 2.23.3ff., James, the Lord's brother, describes Christ in terms of an eschatological and soteriological Son of Man. In the Pseudo-Clementines the true Prophet of Judaism comes to rest on or in Jesus as Son of Man. This title describes only his majesty as the earthly Jesus, Christ being the title for his eschatological function.

II. Christian Gnosticism.

1. Sources. In Gnostic and semi-Gnostic texts Son of Man sometimes occurs for the macrocosmic primal man who acts in creation and redemption in a varied fusion of Christology with *anthrṓpos*-aeon speculation.

2. General. Since the term "Son of Man" is taken genealogically, the redemptive function of the Son of Man results in ascribing a soteriological role to his progenitor, the upper Anthropos.

III. Debates about Christ's Human Nature. In christological discussion the title "Son of Man" comes to denote Christ's humanity as distinct from his deity (cf. Ignatius *Ephesians* 20.2; Justin *Dialogue* 100.3). Irenaeus argues that the Son of God becomes the Son of Man for our salvation (*Against Heresies* 3.10.2 etc.). In Tertullian *Against Marcion* 4.10 the "man" of whom Jesus is the son is the virgin. Eusebius *Ecclesiastical History* 1.2.26 relates Dan. 7:13 to the Logos who was with God and who is Son of Man in virtue of the incarnation. Chrysostom *Homily on John* 27.1 (on 3:13) states that Jesus calls his whole self the Son of Man in terms of its lowlier essence. Augustine *Sermon* 121.5 (on Jn. 1:10ff.) offers the common formulation that the Son of God became the Son of Man so that we sons of men might become the sons of God.

[C. COLPE, VIII, 400-477]

---

huiós Dauíd [son of David]

A. David and the Son of David in Judaism.
1. King David. In Judaism David receives God's grace and promise as one of the righteous of Israel. He is renowned as a musician and warrior and also as one who always gives glory to God. A model ruler and an example of virtuous conduct, he finds forgiveness for his sins, although as a man of blood he is not allowed to build the temple. The rabbis extol him for his study of the law and his leading of Israel. They excuse his taking the showbread on the ground of mortal peril. They suggest that he either did not really sin with Bathsheba or did so only by divine foreordination. They ascribe all the psalms to him, endow him with great intercessory power, and refer to the manifestation of monotheism in his day by which many proselytes are added to Israel.
2. The Messiah of David's Lineage. Judaism links the promise of 2 Sam. 7:12ff. to the hope of an anointed ruler who will free the people and bring it renown. The title Son of David (Ps. Sol. 17:21) comes into common use. The expected ruler, not identified with the Hasmoneans, will throw off alien dominion, purge the city, subdue the Gentiles, and establish righteousness. Sometimes he is simply called David. Messianic expectation varies, for some circles await a preexistent Deliverer or even God himself and others expect a messianic high priest. The dominant view, however, is that a Messiah of the lineage of David will, by God's commission, execute deliverance for the people after the pattern of the historical David.

B. The NT.
I. King David.
1. David as God's Servant. David, son of Jesse and father of Solomon, is one of the righteous of Israel and a servant of God (Lk. 1:69; Acts 4:25). Belonging to Bethlehem, he is a witness of faith (Heb. 11:32) who sings God's praise and as God's voice predicts future salvation (Heb. 4:7; Mk. 12:36-37).
2. David as a Prophet of Christ. In the Psalms David makes it plain that the promises refer to the Christ (cf. Mk. 12:36; Acts 2:27ff.). The promises made to him find their fulfilment in Jesus (Acts 13:34ff.).
3. David as a Type of Christ. As God's servant and Israel's king David is a type as well as a prophet of the Messiah. The coming kingdom is that of "our father David" (Mk. 11:10). God honors the promise made to David by giving Israel a Savior who is of David's seed (Acts 13:23).
II. Christ of David's Lineage.
1. The Davidic Sonship. That Christ is indeed of David's seed forms part of the Christian confession in Rom. 1:3-4 and 2 Tim. 2:8. Implied is not only his Davidic descent but also the messianic nature of his mission in fulfilment of OT promise. His dignity as risen Lord, of course, far transcends the glory of his Davidic lineage.
2. Christ as David's Son and Lord. The problem of Mk. 12:35ff.—how Christ can be David's Son and also David's Lord—implies no repudiation of Davidic descent. Christ is David's son as the earthly Jesus and David's Lord as the risen Christ (cf. Rom. 1:3-4). The "Son of David" refers to the earthly ministry, "Lord" (cf. Ps. 110:1) to the exaltation.
3. Son of David in the Gospels.
a. In Mk. 10:47-48 the blind man, by addressing Jesus as Son of David, expresses hope for messianic deliverance.

b. Lk. 1:32 states that God will give Jesus the throne of his father David, 1:69 says that God has raised up a horn of salvation in the house of his servant David, 1:27 mentions the Davidic lineage of Joseph, 2:1ff. places the birth of Jesus in the city of David, and 3:31 lists David in the genealogy of Jesus.

c. Mt. 1:1 calls Jesus the son of David, 1:17 gives David a prominent role in the genealogy, 9:27 and 15:22 use the title Son of David in stories of healing, 12:23 has the crowd asking whether Jesus can be the Son of David, 21:9, 15 contain the greeting "Hosanna to the Son of David," and 22:41ff. shows that he who is the Son of David in his earthly work is also the Lord, the Son of God, to whom all power is given (28:18).

d. In Jn. 7:41-42 doubters question the messiahship of Jesus on the ground that he is from Galilee, whereas the Christ descends from David and comes from Bethlehem.

4. *The Davidic Sonship in Revelation*. In Rev. 5:5; 22:16 Christ is the "root of David," and in 3:7 he holds the "key of David." As the awaited messianic ruler, he has the key to the messianic banquet. God's promise of salvation finds fulfilment in the crucified, risen, and ascended Christ.

C. The Postapostolic Age.

1. David. Most of the references to David in early Christian writings call him the singer of Israel and the prophet of Christ; there is little interest in the events of his life except occasionally by way of example (cf. Justin *Dialogue* 141.4).

2. Son of David. The early church uses "Son of David" as a christological title but with reference to Christ's Davidic descent (cf. Ignatius *Ephesians* 20.2), which is by way of his mother (18.2; Justin *Dialogue* 45.4). Jesus belongs to the house of David both on his mother's side and also on that of his foster father Joseph.

[E. LOHSE, VIII, 478-88]

> *hýmnos* [song of praise, hymn], *hymnéō* [to sing praise], *psállō* [to play, sing praise], *psalmós* [playing, song of praise, psalm]

A. The Greek Sphere.

I. Usage.

1. Homer and Pindar use *hýmnos* in the sense of "song." The reference in later use may be to either text or melody. Mostly religious songs come to be denoted.

2. *hymnéō* means first "to sing a song" of praise, then "to praise the gods in choral song," then more generally "to praise," with "to affirm" and "to recite" as other possible senses.

3. *psállō* first seems to mean "to touch," then it takes on the sense "to pluck" (a string), and finally it means "to play" (an instrument).

4. *psalmós* means "plucking," then "playing" (a stringed instrument).

II. Greek Hymns. Tragedies contain hymns to the gods sung by the choruses, and inscriptions record cultic songs. Various references occur to choirs, and some hymns are shared by soloists and choirs. Hymns often follow a similar structure: invocation, praise of the birth and acts of the deity, and prayer for his or her coming. Hymns to alien deities sometimes contain self-revelation in I-sayings. The term *hýmnos* may also denote more general praise of a deity in rhythmic prose.

B. The OT and Judaism.

I. Word Groups.

1. *hýmnos* occurs several times in the LXX for different Hebrew words (cf. Pss. 40:3; 119:171; 53 and 54 [titles]; 72:20; Is. 42:10); it means "song of praise."

2. Most LXX instances of *hymnéō* are in Dan. 3 (36 times).

3. *psállō* occurs some 50 times for "to play a stringed instrument" (mostly in Psalms, 1 Samuel, and 2 Kings). The idea of a song of praise is often suggested (Pss. 9:11; 30:4; with "to the name," 7:17; 9:2; with "to thee," Ps. 57:9).

4. *psalmós* occurs over 50 times in psalm titles and also for "taunting song" in Lam. 3:14, "playing on a stringed instrument" in Lam. 5:14, "stringed instrument" in Ps. 81:2, and "song accompanied by a stringed instrument" in Ps. 95:2; cf. also the instrument in Ps. 71:22 ("lyre").

II. The Songs of the OT and Judaism.

1. Ps. 136, an example of an OT psalm, begins with a call for praise, recounts God's acts in creation and the exodus, and then closes with a fresh summons to praise. The refrain in each verse is probably sung by a second choir or by the congregation. It recurs in Ps. 118:1ff. In Ps. 148 creation is central; all God's works are summoned to praise him. The structure of Dan. 3:59ff. is similar. The song in 1 Chr. 16:8ff. extols God's acts for his people.

2. The singing of psalms is connected with sacrifices as well as prayer (cf. 2 Macc. 1:30; 1 Macc. 4:54). Psalms are set for each day. e.g., Ps. 24 for Sunday.

3. Josephus calls the psalms *hýmnoi,* Ex. 15 is for him an *ōdḗ,* Dt. 32 a *poíēsis.* The Levites sing *hýmnoi* to God, and *ōdḗ* or *hýmnos* is used for David's compositions.

4. 4 Macc. 18:15 states that the father in the diaspora teaches the psalms to his sons, and in Test. Job 14 there is reference to accompaniments on the *kithára.*

5. Philo often uses *hýmnos* for the OT Psalms, and he says expressly that they are sung. Temple worship includes hymns, prayers, and offerings. The best thing one can "conceive" is a hymn to the Father of all. Two choirs may sing antiphonally or together, and Philo also mentions a leader. When individuals sing either new or older songs, the rest join in the refrains.

6. Judaism composes many songs in the second and first centuries B.C., as we now see from Qumran. The coins of the Bar Cochba revolt depict stringed instruments. Depictions of Tabernacles refer to stringed instruments and to the singing of the Levites and of persons of outstanding piety.

C. The NT.

I. The Word Group.

1. *hýmnos* occurs only in Col. 3:16 and Eph. 5:19. Christ's word lives in the church's songs to God, which extol from the heart his saving work (Col. 3:16). In Eph. 5:19 praise is addressed to the Lord with God's saving work again as the theme. Emphasis is given in v. 19 by the verbs "singing and making melody" (cf. Ps. 27:6). *psállontes* does not now denote literally playing on a stringed instrument, and the psalms, hymns, and spiritual songs hardly refer to different kinds of texts. In 1 Cor. 14:26 *psalmós* is a Christian song which the individual sings at worship.

2. In Heb. 2:12 *hymnéō* is used for Christ's praise of God, but in Acts 16:25 it perhaps refers to a song, and singing recitation of the second part of the Hallel (Ps. 114ff.) is the meaning in Mk. 14:26; Mt. 26:30.

3. Rom. 15:9 interprets the *psállō* of Ps. 18:49 by *doxázō* in biblical support of Gentile praise of God's mercy. Jms. 5:13 uses *psállō* for grateful praise of Christ.

4. Acts 13:13 uses *psalmós* for the OT Psalms, and cf. Lk. 24:44; 20:42; Acts 1:20. The Psalms are authoritative in Acts 13:33 (cf. Lk. 20:42). For other uses of *psalmós* see 1 Cor. 14:26; Col. 3:16; Eph. 5:19.

II. The Songs of Primitive Christianity. Attempts have been made to distinguish Christian hymns in the NT but these are hypothetical in the absence of clearly discernible laws. The Magnificat and Benedictus are in Jewish style. Eph. 5:14 and 1 Tim. 3:16 are in fixed form but are not necessarily fragments of songs. Phil. 2:6ff. seems to be a pre-Pauline song, and Col. 1:15ff. may be a hymn that the author has taken over and augmented. Elements of songs are perhaps worked over in 1 Pet. 2:21ff., and the songlike portions of Revelation (11:17-18; 15:3-4) show what form Christian hymns might take. Yet the mere presence of lofty speech or integrated structure does not have to denote a hymn.

D. The Early Church.

1. The Word Group in the Apologists. Justin *Apology* 13.2 uses *hýmnos*, and *hymnéō* occurs in OT quotations (cf. *Dialogue* 106.1). Only Justin *Dialogue* uses *psállō* and *psalmós*, the latter almost always for OT Psalms. In the apostolic fathers only the quotation in Barn. 6:16 contains *psállō*, and the *hymnéō* group does not occur.

2. Early Songs. Ignatius *Romans* 2.2 presupposes a common song of the church, and Ignatius supposedly introduces antiphonal singing to Antioch. Acts of John 94–95 preserves a Gnostic hymn, and cf. Acts of Thomas 6–7. Clement of Alexandria *Paedagogus* 3.101.3 contains the first Christian hymn in Greek versification. The first Christian song with notes is in Papyrus Oxyrhynchus XV.1786 (3rd cent. A.D.). There is opposition to nonbiblical hymns, but they develop in the East in the form of biblical odes, which are included in Greek MSS of the Bible from the fifth century A.D.

→ *ádō, ainéō, doxázō, megalýnō, exomologéomai* [G. DELLING, VIII, 489-503]

---

hypágō [to go away]

1. This word means "to lead under," "to lead from under," "to lead," "to lead astray," in the middle "to subdue," "to put oneself at the disposal," and in the perfect passive "to devote oneself." Intransitively it means "to withdraw," "to go away," "to journey to," "to go to," and it is common in the imperative for "go away," "be off."

2. The term is rare in the LXX. The transitive occurs only in Ex. 14:21, and in the passive in 4 Macc. 4:13; the intransitive may be found only in Jer. 36:19 and Tobit.

3. a. The NT uses only the intransitive, and *hypágō* does not occur in Paul, Hebrews, or Acts, or in the Catholic Epistles except in Jms. 2:16 and 1 Jn. 2:11. In the Synoptics it never occurs in all three at the same place, Matthew and Luke alone never have it in common, and Mark and Luke only in Mk. 11:2 and parallel.

b. The Synoptics mostly use it in imperatives, e.g., 17 times in Matthew and 12 in Mark. Other imperatives follow seven times in Matthew and four in Mark. The prior imperative gives point and weight to the command. When *hýpage* precedes the answer to a request, it shows that the cure depends on Jesus' word and calls for trust in this word. In the last temptation Jesus signals his victory by ordering Satan to depart (Mt. 4:9ff.). In Mk. 8:33, however, the command puts Peter in his proper place. In Mk. 14:21 the *hypágō* denotes the going up of the Son of Man to his death.

c. The word is common in John, but with a second imperative only in 4:16; 9:7. Mostly the reference is to the going or going away of Jesus (cf. 7:33; 8:14, 21-22, etc.). Misunderstanding arises in 7:33-34. Even the disciples do not see at first that the going is to God (13:33; 14:4-5). The puzzle is solved in 16:27ff. Like many words in John, *hypágō* has a multiple sense; death as well as ascension is in view. *hypágō* corresponds to the coming of Jesus; if we know whence Jesus comes, we also know whither he goes. The going shows that he has fulfilled his divine commission. His future coming also corresponds to his going (14:28).

4. The verb plays no special role in early Christian writings. Did. 1.4 carries an allusion to Mt. 5:41. Hermas uses it with another imperative in *Visions* 3.1.7. Justin *Dialogue* 76.5 is based on Mt. 25:41. In Clement of Alexandria the aim of the law is to "lead" us to righteousness (*Stromateis* 3.46.1), and we may be "led" to faith (4.73.5), "brought" to tears (*Paedagogus* 2.56.3), or "seduced" to wickedness (*Stromateis* 2.83.3).   [G. DELLING, VIII, 504-06]

→ *poreúomai*

hypakoḗ, hypakoúō → *akoúō; hypantáō, hypántēsis* → *katantáō*

---

hypér [over, for, in the place of]

A. With Genitive.

1. Over, Beyond. The local sense of "over" or "beyond" is common in classical Greek, but it yields to the widespread transferred use in the Hellenistic age.

2. a. With the sense of protection the closest meaning to the spatial sense is "for," "on behalf or in defense of." Cf. in the NT Mk. 9:40; Phil. 1:7; 1 Cor. 4:6.

b. After terms of dedication the meaning is "for." Thus the high priest is appointed and offers for the people in Heb. 5:1; 9:7. Aquila and Priscilla are ready to hazard their lives for Paul in Rom. 16:4 (cf. 9:3; 2 Cor. 12:15; Eph. 3:1). Christ's death is for others in Rom. 5:8; 1 Th. 5:10; 2 Cor. 5:15; 1 Pet. 3:18, etc. Paul develops the saving significance of Christ's death with the help of typology in Gal. 3:13 and 2 Cor. 5:21. Jesus in his death vicariously takes the curse for us, and thus secures our liberation from the law. In this context *hypér* has the sense of "in our favor" but also "in our place or stead." God has made the sinless one the sin-bearer, and hence his reconciling death brings it about that believers share the righteousness of God. Typical combinations are with the verb *(para)dídomi,* as in Rom. 8:32. One might also quote the combinations in Heb. 2:9; 6:20; 1 Pet. 2:21; Jn. 11:50ff.; 18:14. The words of institution at the Last Supper perhaps underlie these formulations (cf. 1 Cor. 11:24; Lk. 22:19; Mk. 14:24). With the symbolism of the action, the *hypér* saying interprets Christ's death as the saving act which is to benefit God's people and through them all humanity. Behind this interpretation one may discern Is. 53:11-12 and the sacrificial concepts of the OT. The negative fact of death becomes a positive event with fruitful results for others. Hence the eucharistic sayings take catechetical, typological, and theological form (cf. Eph. 5:2; 1 Cor. 5:7; Jn. 11:50). Christians, too, accept suffering and death on behalf of others (2 Cor. 12:15) in a parallel between Christology and discipleship (1 Jn. 3:16). The death of Christ is also "for (the expiation of) sins" (1 Cor. 15:3; Gal. 1:4; cf. Is. 53:5). There is alternation with *perí* in this regard (cf. Heb. 5:1). Heb. 9:7 combines the ideas of offering for a person (the high priest for himself) and for the errors of the people.

3. In Place Of. Often "on behalf of" carries an implication of "in place of," "in the name of." It is hard to avoid this sense in 1 Cor. 15:29, and this is the obvious meaning in Phlm. 13. In 2 Cor. 5:14-15 Paul plays on the double sense of *hypér*. Christ's death is first "in our place," but it is then "on our behalf" or "for our sake" at the end of v. 15. The representative sense occurs in 2 Cor. 5:20. Christ himself issues the call through his authorized apostle.

4. *With Reference To.* The weaker sense "with reference to," "as concerns," "for the sake of," occurs in various expressions (cf. Eph. 6:19-20; Rom. 1:5; 15:8). With a genitive of person and verbs of asking or praying, the meaning is simply "for," e.g., Mt. 5:44; Rom. 8:27. "About" or "with reference to" occurs with persons in, e.g., Jn. 1:30, and also with abstract concepts (cf. 2 Th. 2:1) ("concerning the coming of Christ").

5. *On Account Of.* When Christians suffer hardship because of their faith, *hypér* is used as in Phil. 1:29; 2 Th. 1:5; Acts 9:16. A similar use is in expressions of praise and thanksgiving (cf. 1 Cor. 10:30; Eph. 5:20; Rom. 15:9), and also to specify the reason for prayer, as in 2 Cor. 12:8.

B. With Accusative.
1. In the NT the spatial sense occurs in the transferred sense of "more than," "above measure," or "over" (cf. Eph. 1:22; 1 Cor. 10:13; 4:6; 2 Cor. 12:6).

2. After comparatives *hypér* simply means "than" (cf. Heb. 4:12; Lk. 16:8; 2 Cor. 12:13; Lk. 6:40; Phil. 2:9; Phlm. 16; Eph. 3:20; Mt. 10:37; Gal. 1:14).

C. As Adverb. The NT rarely makes adverbial use of prepositions, but there is one instance with *hypér* in 2 Cor. 11:23: "I am (a servant of Christ) in greater measure," i.e., a "better one" (*hypér egó*).   [H. RIESENFELD, VIII, 507-16]

> *hyperauxánō* [to grow abundantly],   *auxánō* [to grow]

1. The rare word *hyperauxánō* means "to grow to the limit," or in the middle passive, "to attain great power," "to achieve the highest position." *auxánō* means "to bring to growth," "to promote," "to raise one's position," or intransitive "to grow," "to rise in repute or power," "to increase."

2. The LXX does not use the compound but has the simple form for "to become fruitful," "to make fruitful," "to make great," "to grow."

3. The NT uses the compound only in 2 Th. 1:3. The idea of growth in creation stands behind the use of the simple form. The language of the parables (cf. Mk. 4:3ff.) underlies its figurative employment in, e.g., Col. 1:6ff.; 2 Cor. 9:10; 1 Cor. 3:6-7, which stresses the fact that God alone can produce decisive growth. Natural human growth plays a part in 1 Pet. 2:2; Col. 2:19 (the church derives its growing life from its Head); Eph. 4:15-16 (the growing is "to" Christ as well as "from" Christ). In Eph. 4:16 the metaphor of physical growth merges into that of the growing building in which God dwells in, with, and by the Spirit.

The figurative background is less evident when Paul speaks about the growth of faith (2 Cor. 10:15); in 2 Th. 1:3 he gives thanks because this growth is so abundant (*hyperauxánei*). Increase of influence or authority is the point in Jn. 3:30.

4. The compound does not occur in the apostolic fathers, but 1 Clem. 33.6 quotes Gen. 1:28, Hermas *Visions* 1.1.6 says that God multiplies creatures for the church's sake, and Did. 16.4 speaks about the increase of wickedness (cf. Mt. 23:12).

                                                          [G. DELLING, VIII, 517-19]

hyperbaínō → *parabaínō*

> *hyperbállō* [to go beyond, surpass],   *hyperballóntōs* [exceedingly, immeasurably],   *hyperbolé* [excess, beyond measure]

1. This verb, having an original sense of "to throw beyond," means "to go beyond," "to stand out," "to excel," or, censoriously, "to transgress the proper measure." The noun means "excess" or "supreme stage or measure."

2. The LXX uses the group only in Greek writings (cf. the verb in Sir. 25:11; 2 Macc. 4:24, and the noun, adverbially, in 4 Macc. 3:18). Philo uses the participle for "going beyond," "surpassing," and the noun for "supreme measure."

3. In the NT the group occurs only in the Pauline corpus. In Eph. 3:19 Christ's love surpasses comprehension, in Eph. 2:7 "immeasurable" tops another word of fullness, and in Eph. 1:19 the word outbids *mégethos*. Combination with *dýnamis* occurs in 2 Cor. 4:15, and with *cháris* in 9:14. The glory of the new order is all-surpassing or beyond comparison in 2 Cor. 3:10; the term also occurs in connection with Paul's suffering in 11:23. The noun is often found in the phrase for "exceedingly" or "beyond measure," e.g., Rom. 7:13. A double use stresses the lack of comparison between present affliction and eternal glory in 2 Cor. 4:17. The mode of life described in 1 Cor. 13:1ff. far surpasses a life controlled by the charisms (1 Cor. 12:31). In Gal. 1:13 Paul uses the expression to describe the intensity of his former persecuting activity. In ministry supreme power belongs to God alone (2 Cor. 4:7). In 2 Cor. 12:7 Paul is restrained lest he be too elated by the abundance of revelations granted to him.

4. The apostolic fathers use only the participle of the verb (cf. 1 Clem. 19.2; Diog. 9.2; Ignatius *Ephesians* 19.2 ["superabounding"]). The noun denotes the high measure of goodness achieved in love of enemies (2 Clem. 13.4).

[G. DELLING, VIII, 520-22]

hyperekperissoú, hyperekperissôs → *perisseúō; hyperekteínō* → *ekteínō; hyperentynchánō* → *tynchánō*

> *hyperéchō* [to surpass, exceed],   *hyperochḗ* [power, prominence]

1. This verb means "to hold over," "to tower," "to surpass," "to amount to more," "to stand out." The noun denotes "position" or "power."

2. The LXX uses the verb only for "to surpass" (cf. Ex. 26:13) or intransitively for "to take precedence" (Gen. 25:23; 39:9).

3. In the NT the verb has only a transferred sense. God's salvation "exceeds" what we can grasp or think (Phil. 4:7). Paul's knowledge of Christ as Lord is supreme (2:8). He does not preach in lofty words of wisdom (1 Cor. 2:1). In humility believers reckon that others excel themselves (Phil. 2:3). In 1 Pet. 2:13 the king is the supreme ruler. The authorities are those who are supreme in Rom. 13:1. The church prays for those in a position of rule in 1 Tim. 2:2.

4. In the apostolic fathers Hermas *Similitudes* 9.6.1 uses the verb literally, and *Similitudes* 9.28.3-4 in a transferred sense. "Taking precedence" is the point in Barn. 13.2. The noun occurs only adverbially in the phrase *kath' hyperokḗn* (cf. 1 Clem. 57.2). In the Apologists we find "to excel" in Athenagoras *Supplication* 23.1 and "surplus" in 6.1.   [G. DELLING, VIII, 523-24]

---

hyperéphanos [arrogant, proud], **hyperēphanía** [arrogance, pride]

A. Secular Usage. *hyperéphanos* means "outstanding," "distinguished," but both the adjective and the associated noun may also be used censoriously to denote arrogance or boasting.

B. The Greek OT. In the Greek OT the words occur mostly in Psalms and the Wisdom literature. God is against pride in Prov. 3:34. The righteous prays that God will destroy the proud in Ps. 94:2. Maccabees characterizes Gentiles and foreign rulers as "insolent" (1 Macc. 1:21; 2 Macc. 9:4, etc.). The enemies of the righteous are arrogant (Ps. 17:10 etc.). Prov. 13:10 warns against the evil result of an arrogant attitude.

C. Hellenistic Judaism. Hellenistic Judaism adopts the OT development of the concept. Arrogance derives from a spirit of error or from Satan. It is a mark of the great peoples of history. God himself punishes it. Josephus refers to the arrogance of Nero in *Jewish War* 3.1. Self-control guards against pride (Epistle of Aristeas 211), and a recognition of human equality protects kings against it (263).

D. The NT. The NT, which makes a sparing use of the terms, follows OT usage. Paul puts *hyperéphanos* in the list of pagan vices in Rom. 1:30. The three terms "insolent," "arrogant," and "boastful" go together. "Boastful" precedes "arrogant" in 2 Tim. 3:2; the two terms describe different aspects of pride. In Mk. 7:22 "arrogance" comes between "blasphemy" and "folly." It contrasts with proper submission to God and involves a haughty disdain for others. In Lk. 1:51 God scatters the proud in their imaginings, topples the mighty, and exalts the lowly. 1 Pet. 5:5 enjoins humility to others. The arrogant, thinking they need no forgiveness, run up against God's opposition, but grace is given to the humble.

E. Early Church Usage. Christ is an example of humility in 1 Clem. 16.2 and insolence is rejected in 30.1. Christians must resist arrogance, for it is contrary to love (49.5). It is one of the sins on the way to death (Did. 2.6; cf. Barn. 20.1). Similar warnings against it appear in Hermas *Mandates* 6.2.5 and Ignatius *Ephesians* 5.3. Tatian *Address to the Greeks* 3.1 calls Heraclitus "arrogant."

[G. BERTRAM, VIII, 525-29]

hypernikáō → nikáō; hyperperisseúō, hyperperissós → perisseúō; hyperpleonázō → pleonázō; hypékoos → akoúō

---

hypērétēs [assistant, servant], **hypēreteō** [to assist, serve]

A. Nonbiblical Usage.

1. Classical Greek and Hellenism. The term *hypērétēs* first occurs with reference to Hermes, the messenger of the gods. It denotes one who does the will of Zeus and has his authority behind him. Further instances reinforce the sense of one who serves a higher will. This higher will need not be that of the gods; we thus find the term in the military, medical, commercial, or legal sphere, e.g., for medical assistants, or for those who carry out judicial sentences. In religions cultic assistants are described by the term, and in personal relations *hypērétēs* denotes one who unselfishly helps to secure something for a friend. Service that accepts subordination is always at issue, but a measure of power may also be involved in the discharge of the imposed mission or function. The *hypērétēs* differs from a *doúlos,* however, for the *hypērétēs* is free and may claim a due reward for the service rendered. As distinct from *diákonos* or *therápōn, hypērétēs* carries the emphasis of learning what is to be done from the superior, and doing it with no prejudice to personal dignity or worth.

2. *The Linguistic Problem.* Traditionally the group has been related to *erétēs* ("rower") and explained as "underrower." But historically there are not two levels of rowers, and while rowers have a superior it is not rowing that makes a person *hypērétēs,* but acting under direction. It is possible, then, that *hypērétēs* is of different linguistic origin, or, if not, that the original root suggests steering rather than rowing. Thus in a boat with a crew of two the *hypērétēs* would take orders from the helmsman. Hence the term would contain the idea of the one who must follow orders, but as a free person, not as a slave.

B. Hellenistic Judaism.

1. The LXX, Apocrypha, and Pseudepigrapha.

a. The group plays little role in the Greek Bible. In Prov. 14:35 we have a reference to the *hypērétēs* who is to carry out orders in the proper way, in Dan. 3:46 Θ "servants of the king" execute royal commands, and in Job 1:3 *hypēresía* is used for Job's servants. A fuller use occurs only in the Greek Wisdom of Solomon.

b. The pseudepigrapha offer many examples of the group, and these are in accord with nonbiblical usage, whether in the military, legal, cultic, or even the demonic sphere (the assistants of Beliar in Testaments of the Twelve).

2. Philo. Philo gives the terms a personal reference, with God, rulers, ordinary people, or even bodily organs as controlling subjects. The stress is again on compliance with lawful instructions. When Joseph styles himself *hypērétēs* and *diákonos* for his family, *hypērétēs* refers to his function as God's assistant, and *diákonos* to the service he renders the family (*On Joseph* 241).

3. Josephus. In Josephus the usage is governed by the idea of helping someone. Moses, Levites, etc. are God's assistants, and we also read of royal officials, of agents, and of members of a bodyguard. Jacob helps his mother when she prepares the meal that will win him the birthright. A *doúlos* can act as *hypērétēs,* but intrinsically the *hypērétēs* can accept or refuse the commission. The functional character of the activity distinguishes the *hypērétēs* from the *diákonos* or *therápōn.*

4. Palestinian Judaism. Since the OT offers no models, it is hard to find exact equivalents in Palestinian Judaism. Temple assistants (probably Levites) play something of the role of the *hypērétēs,* but the Hebrew stem may suggest a directive rather than supporting role. The root *sms* is perhaps closer with its implication of assistance in specific situations and its interest in the correct functioning of certain relations and obligations.

C. The NT.

1. Usage.

a. The group is comparatively rare in the NT, and *hypēresía* does not occur at all. Luke–Acts and John have the most examples with nine each.

b. *hypērétēs,* as in classical and Hellenistic Greek, has the general sense of "assistant carrying out the will of another."

c. Thus in Mt. 6:25-26 the *hypērétēs* is the servant of the court who executes its sentence, and who in so doing carries a warning of eschatological judgment unless there is timely conversion. Lk. 12:58 uses *práktōr* instead because the offender is a debtor who cannot pay. In Lk. 4:16ff. a liturgical assistant receives back from Jesus the scroll of Isaiah from which he has just read. Various authorities have assistants or officers in Mt. 26:58; Jn. 7:32; 18:12; Acts 5:22. The officers of the Sanhedrin seem to differ from Levites serving as temple police (Jn. 7:30; 8:20; Acts 4:3) even though a similar function may come within their more general duties. In Acts 13:36; 20:34; 24:23 the verb carries the sense of helping others to carry out their wishes and meet their needs. Passages like Phil. 2:25; 4:18 (Epaphroditus as *leitourgós tḗs chreías mou*) show what is meant.

2. *Difficult Passages.*

a. Acts 13:5. John Mark as the *hypērétēs* of Barnabas and Paul meets their needs and carries out their wishes in the discharge of their apostolic mission.

b. Jn. 18:36. The meaning here may be that Jesus is not the kind of king who has *hypērétai* that will fight, or that he has *hypērétai* but in a kingdom that permits no fighting. The disciples can be *hypērétai* as well as friends; as friends they are close to their king, but as *hypērétai* they work with him to achieve his goals. The term for "fight," of course, need not involve bloody conflict; the verse may refer to the passivity of the disciples by divine counsel, although in the context of vv. 33ff. the statement seems strongly to suggest that Jesus aims at no political crown.

c. 1 Cor. 4:1. Paul and Apollos are executive organs of Christ. Their work finds its basis in God's plan as this is manifested in Christ. That they are servants (and stewards) protects them against criticism and even self-criticism. Epictetus calls the Cynic both *hypērétēs* and *oikonómos,* but Paul in his association of the terms probably follows Lk. 12:42.

d. Acts 26:16. As Christ's servant, Paul is also his witness; the second term defines the first more closely. The stress is on the task that the Lord has laid on him. The mention of obedience in v. 19 brings out the controlling role of *hypērétēs* in v. 16.

e. Lk. 1:2. The ministers of the word in Lk. 1:2 are those who assist the writer in his task; they are obviously the same as the eyewitnesses. The use of the term shows that they are not propagandists for their own views. It also establishes continuity between the preaching of Jesus and the written history.

D. The Early Church. The apostolic fathers add nothing new in their use of either noun or verb. The *hypērétēs* is the serving official (Diog. 7.2), and the verb may denote the ministry of a deacon (Ignatius *Philadelphians* 11.1). In Justin *Apology* 1.14.1 the noun (used with *doúlos*) has the sense of the free servant receiving and carrying out orders. [K. H. Rengstorf, VIII, 530-44]

→ *diakonéō, doúlos, therapeía*

---

hýpnos [sleep], *aphypnóō* [to fall asleep], *enýpnion* [dream], *enypniázomai* [to dream], *éxypnos* [awake], *exypnízō* [to wake up]

A. The Greeks.

1. *Origin, Meaning, and Use of the Stem hypn-.* Deriving from a basic *supnos,* this word means "sleep," and the phrase *en hýpnō* ("during sleep") produces *enýpnion* as a term for "dream." *agrypnéō* means "to sleep in the open," then "to watch."

2. *Sleep as a Natural Process.* Natural sleep is described as sweet, kindly, etc. It rules over all, is taken as a gift, overpowers people, especially when tired with wine,

and is enjoyed. Phrases are "at the time of the first sleep" and "shortly after going to sleep." Dreams during sleep are a locus of revelation. A special mixture of wine induces sleep.

3. The Scientific View. At first sleep is explained as a relaxing of energy, as a loss of warmth, or as a withdrawing of blood, and hence as a transitional stage to death. Later observation refutes the last theory. Light or heavy sleep during sickness determines the severity of the sickness. Too much sleep is bad. Aristotle perceives a basic phenomenon of animal life in the alternation of waking and sleep.

4. Disparagement of Sleep. Disparagement of sleep appears early. Sleep is a metaphor for the conduct of fools. In it the *noús* loses contact with the world and the individual is shut up in the self. Sleep impairs thought and signifies weakness. Sleepers are as good as dead. We should cut down on sleep. It robs us of half of life on the Stoic view, and it belongs to the material world.

5. Sleep and Death. Philosophy stresses the nearness of sleep to death, although only rarely is sleep a euphemism for death prior to the Hellenistic period. Later we often read of the sleep of death. This sleep is sweet. It means end and dissolution, but the belief is also present that it brings redemption from the body, enabling the true self to mount up to heaven.

6. The God Hypnos. There is a god Hypnos as well as a god Thanatos, although often with a link between them, e.g., as twins. This god can put even Zeus to sleep. Sailors invoke him, and he imparts revelations in sleep. He is a rival of Hermes, who brings sleep but is not sleep personified.

B. The LXX and Judaism.

1. The group occurs fairly frequently in the LXX, mainly for the root *yšn*. The Hebrew differentiates the dream more sharply from sleep than does the Greek. *hýpnos* is a euphemism for coitus in Wis. 4:6. Revelatory sleep occurs in Gen. 28:10ff.; 1 Kgs. 3:5. Dreams may carry a divine message (Gen. 20:3; 40:9, etc.), but they may also be equated with false prophecy (Jer. 23:25). The stem is linked to sloth in Prov. 6:4 and to sin in Judg. 16:14. It depicts eschatological destruction in Is. 29:7-8 (and cf. the sleep of death in Jer. 51:39). The fool is in large measure a sleeper (Sir. 22:9).

2. The spirit of sleep in Test. Reub. 3:1, 7 may be the spirit of creation or possibly the spirit of death or error. The idea of the eschatological sleep of death occurs in Eth. En. 49:3. The state between death and the eschaton is sleep, and resurrection is a waking from sleep. Sleep is also a figure for the time of this aeon. Dreams convey revelation during sleep.

3. Philo finds in sleep a natural process, but it also characterizes those who are far from knowledge. One must repel it as an enemy; faith resembles waking out of a deep sleep. Philo never uses sleep for death, but the two are close.

4. Josephus refers to natural sleep. He accepts the dream revelations of the OT. The soul parts from the body in sleep. Sleep is a prototype of death.

C. The NT.

1. The stem *hypn-* refers to the natural process or state of sleep in Mt. 1:24; Lk. 8:23 (Jesus asleep in the boat); Acts 16:27 (the jailor is jolted awake out of sleep).

2. The NT finds no great place for dreams, so that *enýpnion* and *enypniázomai* occur only in Acts 2:17 (quoting Joel 2:28) and Jude 8 (which briefly denounces opponents as dreamers, i.e., not as visionaries, but as blind to the truth).

3. In Lk. 9:32 the disciples on the Mount of Transfiguration are heavy with sleep. This phrase stresses the contrast between Jesus and the disciples, explains their

confusion after the experience, and anticipates what happens in Gethsemane. The sleep motif is prominent in Acts 20:9ff. Rom. 13:11-12 uses awaking from sleep as a metaphor for casting off bondage to the old aeon (cf. the parallels in Judaism and Hellenism). As in 1 Th. 5:4ff., the call is not merely to watch but to renounce attachment to the world. The command to watch (with *agrypnéō*) occurs in Mk. 13:33; Lk. 21:36; Eph. 6:18. In 2 Cor. 6:5; 11:27 Paul's watchings are his unremitting labors.

4. The sleep of death figures in Jn. 11:11ff. The illness of Lazarus will not lead to death (v. 4). Implied in v. 11 is the deeper background of actual death which is only an apparent reality face to face with Jesus. When the disciples fail to understand (v. 12), distinction is made between the sleep of death and "the rest which is sleep" (v. 13). The verses proclaim the basic impotence of death in the light of the resurrection.

D. The Early Church and Gnosticism. The noun does not occur in the apostolic fathers, and the verb only in 1 Clem. 26:2 (quoting Ps. 3:3: the sleep of death). The images of sleep and awaking occur relative to the resurrection. Among compounds we find *agrypnía* (watchful care) in Barn. 21.7. Apocryphal works refer to Jesus' steering of the boat during sleep, to drunkenness with sleep, and to the sleep of death. In Gnosticism sleep is ignorance and oblivion. It symbolizes bondage to the world. To sleep is to be in the sphere of death. More generally we also find the idea that in view of the resurrection death is merely sleep during the time up to the resurrection.

→ *egeírō, katheúdō, ónar, hórama*   [H. BALZ, VIII, 545-56]

hypogrammós → *gráphō; hypódeigma* → *deíknymi; hypodéō, hypódēma* → *hóplon*

---

hypódikos [accountable]

1. Secular Greek. This word means "guilty," "culpable," "accountable," "subject to trial."

2. Judaism.

a. The term does not occur in the LXX; we are accountable to God, not to *díkē*.

b. Philo uses the word for accountability in various connections.

c. Josephus also has it in the sense of "subject to punishment."

d. It is hard to find any exact rabbinic equivalent but we do find the ideas of financial accountability and penal liability.

3. The NT. In the NT the term occurs only in Rom. 3:19, where it applies to accused persons who cannot refute the charges leveled against them. Since Jews no less than Gentiles are in this position, all fall under God's condemnation apart from the new right that God establishes for them in Christ.

4. The early Christian writers do not use the word.   [C. MAURER, VIII, 557-58]

---

hypokrínomai [to play the hypocrite], **synypokrínomai** [to join in playing the hypocrite], **hypókrisis** [hypocrisy], **hypokritḗs** [hypocrite], **anypókritos** [without hypocrisy]

A. Classical and Hellenistic Greek.

1. Original Meaning.

a. The verb *hypokrínomai* first means "to explain," also, rarely, "to answer."

b. *hypókrisis* can mean "answer," but *hypokritḗs* means "actor," probably as one who interprets a poet, depicting by his whole conduct the role assigned.

2. *Recitation and Acting*. Declamation is essential in acting; hence elocution is an important part of rhetoric. For Aristotle, it is the doctrine of linguistic expression. The art of speaking is a specialized skill both on the stage and in the marketplace. Demosthenes achieves success when he takes lessons from an actor. *hypókrisis* embraces the delivery of a speech, including mime and gesture.

3. *Transferred Meaning*. Human life comes to be compared to the stage, and conduct to the task of the actor (cf. Plato, and especially the Stoics). The noble person can play any part assigned with no loss of inner stability. Negatively, the stage is a sham world and actors are deceivers. Hence *hypókrisis* takes on the sense of "pretense" or "pretext." But additions are needed to show whether the group has a positive, negative, or neutral sense. Only under Christian influence does the negative sense prevail in the Byzantine period.

B. Dispersion Judaism.

1. *The LXX*. Already in the LXX the terms take on a negative sense (cf. 2 Macc. 5:25; 6:21; 4 Macc. 6:12ff.). Fear of God and hypocrisy are opposites in Sir. 1:28ff. The righteous who sin are hypocrites (Ps. 12:2). *hypókrisis* has the character of sin (Job 34:30). The *hypokrités* and the sinner are equated.

2. *Philo and Josephus*.

a. In Philo, too, the sense is mostly negative. *hypókrisis* as concealment of the truth or dissembling is a worse evil than death.

b. For Josephus *hypokrínomai* is more a matter of strategy. As one may see from the story of Joseph, this may be for a good end (*Antiquities* 2.160). But *hypókrisis* also means false appearance, and the *hypokrités* is a "hypocrite" (*Jewish War* 2.586-87).

3. *The Historical Problem*. Since Judaism uses the group almost exclusively in a bad sense, not so much for hypocrisy as for the deception that characterizes evil as apostasy against God, a question arises how this identification comes about. The answer possibly lies in Testaments of the Twelve, which opposes truth and deception: wickedness is deception, and deceit is satanic and ungodly. Qumran sees a similar antithesis between truth and falsehood. The idea, then, is that the bad person, who ought to be good, is in disguise when acting wickedly. This dissembling is deception, and as such opposition to God's truth.

C. The NT.

1. *The Synoptic Tradition*. As in the LXX, the group has a bad sense in the Synoptists. Jesus calls his opponents *hypokritaí* because they cannot discern "this time" (Lk. 12:54ff.), i.e., because they are in self-contradiction in their evaluations. A similar self-contradiction arises regarding what is permissible on the sabbath (13:15-16), or regarding their own faults and those of others (Mt. 7:3ff.), or regarding the outward and inward worship of God (Mk. 7:8). The jarring contradiction between precept and practice gives rise to the charge in Mt. 23:13ff. A pious appearance and a distortion of proportion conceal the failure to do God's will. In contrast, the disciples must achieve a greater righteousness (Mt. 5:20), showing a concern for integrity rather than status (6:2ff.). Sham will result in ruin (6:2ff.; 24:51). It comes to expression in the attempt to entrap Jesus while supposedly raising serious questions (cf. Mk. 12:15).

2. *Paul*. Paul uses the group in Gal. 2:13. When Peter changes his practice on the arrival of envoys from Jerusalem, he is not just trying to deceive the envoys, nor acting in contradiction with himself; he is falling away from the truth of the gospel, which, with the doctrine of justification by faith, implies equality of Jew and Gentile.

3. *The Pastorals*. In 1 Tim. 4:2 the term conveys the sense of evildoer or apostate.

The sayings of the false teachers are deceitful, for they contradict the truth of God (cf. 6:5; 2 Tim. 3:8). This is *hypókrisis*.

D. The Apostolic Fathers. Hermas uses *hypokritaí* for false teachers in *Similitudes* 8.6.5. Did. 8.1 calls the Jews *hypokritaí*. *hypókrisis* is apostasy from God. But it is also dissembling (cf. Pol. 6.3; Hermas *Visions* 3.6.1). As a summary term for any kind of pretense or deception, *hypókrisis* occurs in lists of vices (Did. 2.6; Barn. 20.1; Hermas *Mandates* 8.3).

anypókritos.

1. This word occurs first in the LXX in Wis. 5:18; 18:15. Describing God's eschatological salvation, it denotes unfeigned simplicity.

2. In the NT the term becomes a fixed attribute of *agápē* (cf. Rom. 12:9; 2 Cor. 6:6-7). In the latter passage, the idea in context seems to be that the unfeigned simplicity of God should also mark the neighborly love of believers. Where this is not so, there is not just an assumed love but a wicked failure to correspond to God's own attitude, and hence a conflict with the truth of God. In 1 Pet. 1:22 sincere love is from the heart; it rests on new birth of the word of God. 1 Tim. 1:5 teaches similarly that the goal is a love that issues from a pure heart and sincere faith. Those who hold office must be models, and Timothy himself has had a sincere faith from childhood (2 Tim. 1:5). Such faith is both inwardly sincere and outwardly orthodox. Jms. 3:17 opposes to the demonic wisdom of false teachers the pure wisdom that is marked by no insincerity. In contrast, heresy is also immoral; it is "hypocrisy."

3. In 2 Clem. 12.2-3 the author understands the supposed dominical saying that "two are one" as a structural description of the virtue of truthfulness.

[U. WILCKENS, VIII, 559-71]

---

hypóstasis [being, essence, reality]

A. Greek Usage.

1. Preliminary. Formed as a verbal noun from *hyphístēmi*, *hypóstasis* reflects some of the meanings of the intransitive and middle *hyphístamai*, namely, "support," "concealment," "deposit or sediment," "existence or reality," and, technically, "lease." The use is mostly specialized in the early period. The philosophical use grows out of an earlier scientific use, and the later range of meaning hardly goes beyond the scientific and philosophical senses.

2. Medical and Scientific Use. In medicine *hypóstasis* rarely means "support," e.g., a hip as a support for the body. More common is the use for "sediment," e.g., for urine. The word can also denote fluid or solid excrement. More generally anything that settles is *hypóstasis* (cf. curds, or the slimy bottom of stagnant water, or the deposit of moist air, or any kind of residue).

3. Philosophical Use.

a. Stoicism. Stoicism first brings the term into philosophy to denote what has come into being or attained reality. In contrast to *ousía*, which is eternal being as such, *hypóstasis* is real being as this is manifested in individual phenomena. Because being is primal matter, its coming into existence may be viewed as a physical process, and thus *hypóstasis* offers itself as a suitable term for the resultant reality. The distinction from *ousía*, however, is only a theoretical and not a practical one. *ousía* exists in its actualization, *hypóstasis* is *ousía* in its actuality. *hypóstasis* is not the real, concrete phenomenon as such but the reality behind it.

b. Peripatus. Dependence on Stoicism is evident in the Peripatetic use. There is reality only in individual things; these have essence and reality in themselves.

c. Middle Platonism. References here are few, but in Albinus *hypóstasis* denotes the actualization of the ground of being relative to the intelligible world.

d. Neo-Platonism. Neo-Platonic development has no significance for biblical usage but is important later. *hypóstasis* now bears no relation to matter. As a term for the actuality derived from the one, it is synonymous with *ousía*. While deriving from ultimate being, it also has ultimate being. This understanding lies behind the use in the later doctrine of the Trinity.

4. *General Usage*. Denoting the reality behind appearance, *hypóstasis* can have such general senses as "plan," "purpose," "concern," or "basic conception." The fundamental reality of time, which is the "instant," is also its *hypóstasis*. In other contexts the term simply means "presence" or "existence."

5. *Special Meanings*.

a. Astrology. In this sphere *hypóstasis* means the reality of life present in the constellations at the hour of birth.

b. Papyri. In the papyri *hypóstasis* finds a special use for "lease" or "aggregate of deeds of ownership," and consequently "possession" on the basis of such deeds.

B. Judaism.

1. *The LXX*. The noun occurs some 20 times in the LXX for 12 Hebrew terms, and the verb *hyphístēmi* occurs somewhat more often in the sense "to endure." The meaning of *hypóstasis* seems to be "movable property" in Dt. 11:6, "immovable property" in Job 22:20, "basis of power" in Ezek. 26:11, "reality" that gives a firm guarantee in Ruth 1:12; Ps. 39:7, "life plan" in Ps. 139:15, "plan" in Jer. 23:22, and "counsel" in Ezek. 19:5; Dt. 1:12. LXX usage thus conforms to Greek. *hypóstasis* is the underlying reality behind things, often as a plan or purpose, or as that which, enclosed in God, endures.

2. *Apocrypha and Pseudepigrapha*. The term is rare in these works; it occurs in such senses as "basis," "power," "plan," or "purpose."

3. *Philo and Josephus*.

a. Philo uses both noun and verb in theological and philosophical contexts. The verb denotes real existing, and Philo has the noun in the expression "intelligible reality," which stands in contrast to what may be known by sensory perception or the seeing of figures. Elsewhere *hypóstasis* means "real existence."

b. The noun is rare in Josephus. He uses it for distinctive reality in *Against Apion* 1.1, and for the invisible reality that lies behind the endurance of the martyrs in *Antiquities* 18.24.

C. The NT.

1. *Paul*. Two of the five NT instances of *hypóstasis* are in Paul. In 2 Cor. 9:2ff. Paul does not want his boasting about the collection at Corinth to be found empty. But his concern in v. 4 is not so much that his boasting might be exposed as that his "plan" or "project" might be frustrated by Achaia's unreadiness. The same sense is plain in 2 Cor. 11:17, where, in a foolish comparison, he speaks of a "purpose" of boasting that is forced upon him. The rendering "confidence" or "assurance" gives rise to many difficulties and has little outside support.

2. *Hebrews*. The other three instances of *hypóstasis* are all in Hebrews. The usage

is simplest in 1:3, where the term is parallel to *dóxa* and relates to God's essence. "Transcendent reality" is perhaps closest to what is meant. Christ as Son reflects God's glory and bears the impress of this reality. In 11:1 the rendering "assurance" has gained much support since Melanchthon commended it to Luther, but this introduces an untenable subjective element. The parallel term *élenchos* is an objective one that denotes "demonstration" rather than "conviction," i.e., the proof of things one cannot see. Similarly, *hypóstasis* is the "reality" of the things hoped for, which have a transcendent quality. The terms define the character of transcendent future things, and the verse boldly equates faith with the reality and demonstration of these things. Only the work of Jesus and faith as participation in this work are not subject to the corruptibility of what is shadowy and prototypical. The statement in 3:14 is along similar lines. The reference is not a subjective one to our first confidence but an objective one to the basic reality on which the faith of believers rests since Christ is the very presence of the reality of God which they now share. Clinging to the first reality as it comes with the preaching of salvation in Christ does, of course, mean having confidence to the end in the reality of God, but *hypóstasis* itself denotes, not the confidence, but the divine reality that contrasts with everything shadowy and prototypical and that is paradoxically present in Jesus and possessed by the community in faith.

D. Further Christian Usage. After the NT *hypóstasis* occurs again only with Tatian, who uses it for God's absolute reality as this is manifested in the cosmos, for the reality which lies behind existence and which is visible only to God, for the reality of demons or the elements, or for the realities of nature permeating the elements. In Gnostic texts *hypóstasis* is the hidden spiritual reality of pneumatics which suffers no damage even in the midst of the material world. In another text *hypóstasis* is the reality of earthly existence which the redeemed use until they enter eternal life. From the usage in Tatian and the Gnostics no straight line can be drawn to the later theological usage, which must be related to contemporary philosophical development.

[H. KÖSTER, VIII, 572-89]

hypostéllō, hypostolé → *stéllō; hypotagé, hypotássō* → *tássō; hypotýpōsis* → *týpos*

---

hypōpiázō [to strike on the face, treat roughly]

1. This verb means "to strike on the face" with resultant disfigurement, then figuratively "to defame," "to castigate" (with words).
2. The LXX has only the noun *hypópion* for "blow in the face," "contusion."
3. In the NT the sense might be literal in Lk. 18:5, but a transferred meaning is much more likely: either "lest she finally expose me in a public scene," or "lest she wear me out completely by her persistent coming." In 1 Cor. 9:26-27 Paul is using athletic metaphors for his work. He does not box as one who beats the air but pommels and subdues his body. The expression is figurative. He is not subjecting himself to ascetic exercises but subjecting his body to the demands of ministry (cf. Rom. 8:13), gaining strength from the hardships to which this exposes him and which God overrules for good (2 Cor. 12:7ff.).   [K. WEISS, VIII, 590-91]

> *hýsteros* [later, last], *hýsteron* [later, finally], *hysteréō* [to come too late, lack], *aphysteréō* [to withhold], *hystérēma* [need, want], *hystérēsis* [need, want]

A. Secular Greek.

1. *hýsteros* has the basic sense of "what is behind or after" (cf. *ex hystérou* for "later" and *hoi hýsteroi* for "descendants"). In a transferred sense the term may also denote what is of lesser worth. It also finds a use in logic and astrology.

2. *hýsteron* has such senses as "secondly," "after," "later," "too late," and "finally."

3. *hysteréō* means "to come after or too late," and it then takes on such senses as "to be wanting," "to be behind," and, in the active, "to lack."

4. The nouns *hystérēma* and *hystérēsis*, which are very rare, have the meanings "want," "need," "what is missing."

B. The LXX.

1. *hýsteros* (14 times) and *hýsteron* (15) always have the sense of "after," "later," but the idea of deficiency is predominant in the case of *hysteréō* (cf. Eccl. 6:2; 9:8; Cant. 7:3; Ps. 23:1; Sir. 51:24). The thought of coming too late and hence not attaining occurs in Sir. 11:11-12. The meaning of *hysteréō* in Job 36:17 is "to remain far off," i.e., "to avoid."

2. *hystérēma* (six times) always means "lack" (cf. Judg. 18:10; Eccl. 1:15), "want," or "need" (Ps. 34:10).

C. The NT.

1. hýsteros, hýsteron.

a. The adjective means "the last-named" in Mt. 21:31, and the reference is to the "last" times in 1 Tim. 4:1, i.e., the future prophetic times when error, debate, and apostasy will plague the church (cf. 2 Tim. 3:1; 2 Pet. 3:3; Jude 18 with 2 Pet. 2:1; 1 Jn. 2:18 with 4:1).

b. The adverb has a comparative sense in Mt. 21:30, 32 ("afterward"). The thrust is eschatological in Heb. 12:11: The present time is that of the exercise of faith, the eschatological future will bring salvation as its fruit. In Jn. 13:36 the probable reference is not to a future martyrdom of Peter, as Peter supposes (v. 37), but to the radical abrogation of earthly discipleship with the death of Jesus, and hence to presence with the exalted Lord (cf. 14:1ff.). The superlative occurs mostly in Matthew (cf. 4:2; 21:37; 22:27; 26:60), but Mark has it in 16:14.

2. hysteréō.

a. The basic sense "to come too late," "to fail to attain," which occurs twice in Heb. 4:1, contains an eschatological warning not to miss attainment of the promise through lack of faith. 12:15 warns against failing to attain to God's grace by not maintaining peace and pursuing sanctification (v. 14). Paul sums up the discussion in Rom. 1:18–3:20 by saying that all of us fall short of God's glory (v. 23) and are thus dependent on the justifying grace which through Christ's work makes good the loss and achieves our glorification (cf. 5:2; 8:17-18, 29-30; 9:23; 1 Th. 2:12).

b. With reference to circumstances, *hysteréō* means "to lack." Jesus tells the rich young ruler what is the one thing he lacks for entry into life (Mk. 10:21). In Mt. 19:20 the ruler himself asks what he still lacks, i.e., in the sense of something that needs to be added rather than in that of absolute lack. The point in Jn. 2:3 is probably that the wine is finished rather than that there is a lack of it.

c. The most common sense in the NT is "to be in want." This is the prodigal's plight in Lk. 15:14. Jesus asks the returning disciples whether they were ever in want in Lk. 22:35. Paul thanks God that the Corinthians lack no spiritual gift in 1 Cor. 1:7; this emphasis is in material contrast with the theological ambitions of the Corinthian pneumatics in 4:8. As regards idol meats, believers suffer no lack if they do not eat; hence the strong should not harry or offend the weak by their freedom. Paul knows how to have enough and how to be in want (Phil. 4:12). He is ready to suffer want in Corinth rather than be a burden to the church (2 Cor. 11:9). Heb. 11:37 describes the plight of the fathers as they await the eschatological fulfilment of the divine promise in Christ.

d. The meaning "to come after, behind" occurs in 2 Cor. 11:5; 12:11: Paul is not behind other apostles. In 1 Cor. 12:24 God has given greater honor to the inferior part (i.e., that which comes behind) so that there should be no discord, but all the members should care for one another.

3. *aphysteréō.* This verb occurs in the NT only in Jms. 5:4 for "to withhold."

4. *hystérēma, hystérēsis.* In Mk. 12:44 Jesus lauds the poor widow for giving out of her "want," i.e., her poverty. In 2 Cor. 8:14 Paul encourages the collection so that Gentile abundance should supply the "want" or poverty of the Jerusalem saints and thus lead to thanksgiving (9:12-13). Paul's "needs" in 2 Cor. 11:9 are supplied by the Macedonian church (cf. 1 Cor. 16:17; Phil. 2:30). Paul's joy when his "needs" are met is not because of the needs but because of the sharing and the love that it expresses (Phil. 4:10ff.). He himself hopes to supply the teaching that the faith of the Thessalonians needs by coming to them (1 Th. 3:10). By his sufferings he enters into the sufferings of Christ, who is now exalted above earthly suffering as the Head of the church (Col. 1:24).

D. Early Writings.

1. Early Church Writings.

a. The adverb has a temporal sense in Papias (Eusebius *Ecclesiastical History* 3.39.15).

b. The verb means "to lack something" in Diog. 5.13; Ignatius *Ephesians* 5.2, and "to be in want," "to be poor" in Did. 11.12; Barn. 10.3.

c. *hystérēma* means "what is lacking" in 1 Clem. 38.2 and "lack" in Hermas *Visions* 3.2.2; *Similitudes* 6.3.4. Clement of Alexandria *Fragment* 46 excludes all *hysterein* from the future kingdom, and for a christological statement cf. *Stromateis* 8.9.29.5.

2. *Gnosticism.* The terms *hysteréō* and *hystérēma* are important in Christian Gnosticism as denoting what is of lesser worth outside the original divine *plérōma.* Thus lower wisdom is an inferior power. As *hystérēma* is a result of ignorance, the attainment of *gnósis* remedies it. Gnostics flee the place of *hystérēma* and strive back up to the one (cf. Irenaeus *Against Heresies* 1.11.2; 16.2; 18.4; 21.4).

[U. WILCKENS, VIII, 592-601]

---

hýpsos [height], *hypsóō* [to lift up, exalt], *hyperypsóō* [to raise to the highest position], *hýpsōma* [height], *hýpsistos* [highest]

---

hýpsos.

A. Nonbiblical Greek. *hýpsos* has reference to the dimension of height. It can be a "high place," a "summit"; it also means "height," "highness" (in a title), and it has such senses as "sublimity," "climax," "nobility."

B. The Greek OT. The use of the term is manifold in the LXX, whether to express height, to denote a high place or position, exaltation by God, human pride, or the loftiness of heaven or of God.

C. Judaism.
1. The idea of rapture on high occurs in Slav. En. 3, and the height of the third heaven comes to expression in Test. Levi 2:8. Josephus *Antiquities* 8.126 speaks of the infinite height and greatness of bliss.
2. Philo refers to the highest stage in the knowledge of God, to sublimity of style (e.g., Moses), and to the difference between true and false *hýpsos*.

D. The NT. Rev. 21:6 gives the height of the heavenly city. Eph. 4:8-9 refers to the ascension of Christ. Christ comes from above and returns triumphantly to his home on high (cf. Ps. 68:18). In Lk. 1:78; 24:49 "on high" is almost a term for God (cf. also Acts 1:8). In Jms. 1:9 the sense is that of exaltation in rank. The poor, in contrast to the rich, are lifted up on high by God.

E. Early Christianity. The usage here is similar to that of the Bible (cf. 1 Clem. 36:2; Ignatius *Ephesians* 9.1; Barn. 20.1; Did. 5.1; Diog. 7.2).

hypsóō, hyperypsóō.

A. Nonbiblical Greek. The late and rare *hypsóō* means "to lift up," "to exalt," in both literal and transferred senses.

B. The Greek OT. The word is common in the LXX with reference to the exaltation of God, joyful exaltation by God, the exaltation which on the presupposition of abasement means glorification (cf. Is. 52:13), and arbitrary and arrogant self-exaltation (Hos. 13:6).

C. Judaism. Ps. Sol. 1:5 bewails the exaltation (i.e., arrogance) of sinners, Test. Jos. 1:7 develops the theme of abasement and exaltation, Qumran refers to the exaltation of resurrection, of a remnant in the community, of Michael over heavenly beings, and of Israel over the nations.

D. The NT.
1. The OT motif of exalting the humble and abasing the proud occurs in Mt. 23:12; Lk. 14:11; 18:14. True exaltation is God's work (Lk. 1:52; Jms. 4:10; 1 Pet. 5:6). Being made worthy to receive the gospel and Christ's glory is the church's exaltation (2 Cor. 11:7). Exaltation is blessing (Mt. 11:23) and has an eschatological reference (Phil. 2:5ff.).
2. Phil. 2:9 speaks about Christ's exaltation. His obedience to death is humiliation; in resurrection he is raised to the highest position (*hyperypsóō*). For all its ethical implications, the statement is soteriological and eschatological. Paul preaches Christ crucified as the Lord of glory (1 Cor. 2:2) who speaks to him on high and sets him in the same tension of abasement and exaltation (2 Cor. 12:1ff.).
3. In Heb. 1:3 Christ, having suffered, is at the right hand of the majesty on high, exalted above the heavens.
4. In Acts 2:33 the risen Christ is set at God's right hand in the place of rule. This is the presupposition of the outpouring of the Spirit. In 5:31 the exalted Savior grants repentance and forgiveness of sins to Israel.
5. In Jn. 3:14; 8:28; 12:32, 34 Jesus is exalted both on the cross and up to heaven.

Those who believe in the exalted Son of Man have life (3:14-15). Death is the presupposition of parting from the earthly sphere and transfiguration. But *hypsóō* also denotes the form of death. Those who lift Jesus up on the cross exalt him as Ruler and Judge. His exaltation makes the discipleship of the cross constitutive for believers. Jesus' exalting is also his perfecting (19:30). He does not set up an earthly kingdom, but by his resurrection and ascension is exalted to his heavenly home.

6. The exaltation of Jesus embraces resurrection, reception, ascent, enthronement, and royal dominion. It is the climax of his earthly abasement and the presupposition of his coming in glory. It is not so much a change of place as institution to power and glory both on earth and in heaven. The transfiguration anticipates this future glory and the empty tomb points to it. Exaltation is a basic concept in all Christology, especially as the resurrection forms a corrective to any docetic evaporation.

E. Early Christianity. The apostolic fathers sometimes use *hypsóō* for human arrogance (Did. 3.9). We find it in OT quotations only in Justin. In Acts of Thomas elevation is a presupposition of the vision of Christ. Inscriptions follow John in giving "to exalt" the sense of "to glorify."

hýpsōma.
1. *The Nonbiblical Sphere.* This rare and late word means "eminence," "high place," and in astrology "culmination."
2. *The LXX and Hellenistic Judaism.* LXX uses are for "arrogance," "lifting up," and the "high places." Philo says that the Decalogue is fashioned in the height of heaven.
3. *The NT.* The only NT instances are in Rom. 8:39 and 2 Cor. 10:5. In Rom. 8:39 Paul asserts that the "height" of creation cannot separate us from the love of Christ, who has pierced this sphere and subjected it to himself. In 2 Cor. 10:5 Paul uses the image of a "fortress with high towers" for the attitude which proudly resists the true knowledge of God but which the apostle overcomes with the gospel.
4. *Early Christianity.* Acts of John 23 echoes Paul's usage in Rom. 8:39.

hýpsistos.

A. Nonbiblical Greek. This word means "highest," "loftiest." It is used for the highest peaks, but also for Zeus as the most high god, or for Mithra as the most high.

B. 'elyôn in Semitic Usage. Possibly on a Canaanite (Jebusite?) basis, the OT designates God the Most High (cf. Gen. 14:19ff.; 2 Sam. 24:17). With a focus on Zion, the name expresses eschatological hopes. As a title of majesty, it refers to God as the one who dwells on high, always in poetry except in Gen. 14. Qumran refers to knowledge of the Most High and calls its members the saints of the Most High.

C. hýpsistos in the LXX. *hýpsistos* is mostly a term for God in the LXX; it serves as the equivalent for the divine title *'elyôn,* and also for other Hebrew terms whose point is that God is the Lord on high. In Sirach *hýpsistos* is the most common term for God after *Kýrios.* It is used only for Israel's God and as a proper name. In a phrase like *theós hýpsistos* it is a noun in apposition.

D. hýpsistos in Judaism. Most High becomes a favorite term for God in Hellenistic Judaism. It brings together the OT title for God and the Greek concept of the chief god. Whereas in the OT the Most High denotes the one God on high, *hýpsistos* in Hellenistic Judaism becomes an apologetic term for the supreme God, although not in a syncretistic sense.

E. The NT.

1. The formula "in the highest" occurs in Lk. 2:14 (the Christmas story) and in Mt. 21:9; Mk. 11:10; Lk. 19:38 (the story of the triumphal entry). In the entry story we have an invocation of God, and in Lk. 2:14 the parallelism counterbalances glory for God on high with salvation for humanity on earth.

2. *hýpsistos* is used nine times in the NT as a term for God. In Lk. 1:32, 35 Mary's child will be called the Son of the Most High, and in 1:76 the forerunner is the prophet of the Most High. A demon calls Jesus the Son of the Most High in Mk. 5:7; Lk. 8:28, and the girl greets Paul as a servant of God the Most High in Acts 16:17. Most High is a term for God in Lk. 6:35, and the name stresses the divine transcendence in Acts 7:48. The description in Heb. 7:1 simply repeats Gen. 14:18. In general, *hýpsistos* as a divine name is on the margin of the NT tradition whether as an expression of sublimity, a term of transcendence, or a traditional title.

F. Early Christianity. Apart from liturgical use under OT influence, *hýpsistos* finds little place in the early church (for examples cf. 1 Clem. 29:2; Ignatius *Romans*, Introduction; Justin *Apology* 33.5). Apocryphal Acts ascribe the title to the exalted Lord (cf. Acts of Thomas 48). Christ is the *Kýrios* and *hýpsistos* of the community.

[G. BERTRAM, VIII, 602-20]

φ *ph*

---

phaínō [to shine, appear], *phanerós* [visible, evident], *phaneróō* [to reveal, show], *phanérōsis* [revelation, appearance], *phantázō* [to appear], *phántasma* [ghost], *emphanízō* [to show, appear], *epiphaínō* [to show, appear], *epiphanḗs* [visible, magnificent], *epipháneia* [appearance]

---

phaínō.

1. This word means "to manifest, "to show," intransitively "to shine," "to light up," "to become visible," "to appear." In philosophy the reference of the word is to sense perception.

2. In the NT the active occurs only intransitively, e.g., the shining of the sun (Rev. 1:6), of the sun and moon (21:23), of a lamp (Jn. 5:35), or of the day or night (Rev. 8:12). A figurative use may be seen in Jn. 1:5. *phaínomai* is more common for "to shine," "to light up" (cf. the star in Mt. 2:7, stars in Phil. 2:15, lightning in Mt. 24:23, the lamp in Rev. 18:23), or for "to appear," "to be manifest" (Jms. 4:14), "to occur" (Mt. 9:33), "to show oneself" (Mt. 13:26; Rom. 7:13). The subjects comprise eschatological manifestation (Mt. 24:30), dream phenomena (Mt. 1:20), and the appearances of the risen Lord (Mk. 16:9). An impersonal sense is "to strike" or "look" (Mk. 14:64), and cf. "to look as though" in Mt. 23:27-28 and "to give the appearance" in Mt. 6:16. A distinction between the visible and the invisible may be seen in Heb. 11:3.

phanerós.

1. This adjective means "visible," "manifest," "outstanding," "public."
2. In the NT Rom. 2:28 has in view what is "visible" outwardly. What is "evident"

is the point in Rom. 1:19; Gal. 5:19; 1 Tim. 4:15. 1 Jn. 3:10 carries the nuance of what is "made manifest" (cf. Mk. 4:22; Lk. 8:17; Mk. 6:14), eschatologically so in 1 Cor. 3:13. The adverb *phanerós* means "publicly" in Mk. 1:45; Jn. 7:10, and "plainly" in Acts 10:3.

phaneróō.

A. Outside the NT. This rare verb means "to make visible," or in the passive "to become visible."

B. The NT.

1. Common in the NT, *phaneróō* refers to the disclosure of the hidden meaning of parables in the proverbial saying in Mk. 4:22.

2. In Paul *phaneróō* is a synonym of *apokalýptō* (Rom. 1:17 and 3:21). Except in 1 Cor. 4:5 and Rom. 1:19 ("to make visible") the point is revelation in the gospel. Rom. 3:21 refers to the once-for-all revelation of justification in Christ. In 2 Corinthians *phaneróō* is perhaps a term of Paul's opponents that he adopts. He uses it for God's revelation in his preaching (2 Cor. 2:14) and life (4:10-11). Although eschatologically qualified, this is definitive.

3. Revelation takes place in proclamation in Col. 1:25-26. Light categories occur in Eph. 5:13-14, and concealment is the opposite in Col. 3:3-4. The bearers of revelation mediate salvation (cf. also 2 Tim. 1:10; Tit. 1:2-3). Past revelation in Christ is at issue in 1 Pet. 3:16 (cf. 1 Pet. 1:18ff.).

4. *phaneróō* is common in John (*gnōrízō* is synonymous). Jesus "discloses before all eyes" (Jn. 7:4-5) God's reality, name, and works. All Jesus' work is revelation. Indirectly God's reality is also revealed in the witness of the Baptist (1:31). The appearances of the risen Lord are at issue in 21:1, 14. Jesus reveals God's love in 1 Jn. 4:9. The goal is life (1:2; 4:9). Revelation is the content of the word of life, which includes proclamation. Future revelation is the reference in 2:28 and 3:2.

5. The two instances in Rev. 3:18 have no theological significance (cf. also the use in the hymn in 15:4).

C. The Apostolic Fathers. For Ignatius revelation breaks the eternal silence and is fulfilled in Christ (*Ephesians* 19.1-2). The heavenly *ekklēsía* is revealed in Christ's flesh (5.31-32). God through Christ has revealed the truth and heavenly life according to 2 Clem. 20.5. Barn. 5.6, 9 refers to revelation in the flesh (cf. 6.7, 9, 14). The OT revelation prophesies it (2.4). In Hermas *phaneróō* denotes the revelation of a vision and the appearance of the shepherd (*Visions* 3.1.2; *Similitudes* 2.1). Diog. 8.11 speaks of the revelation of divine mercy in Christ after the exposing of human sin (9.2).

phanérōsis.

1. This word means "revelation," "appearance."

2. In 1 Cor. 12:7 it is the revelation imparted by the Spirit and consisting of the charisms listed in vv. 8ff. It entails acts in which the Spirit manifests himself. In the only other NT instance in 2 Cor. 4:2 Paul describes true proclamation as a manifestation of the truth in contrast to the falsification of God's word by his opponents.

phantázō, phántasma.

1. In the middle or passive, the verb often means "to appear" with reference to unusual phenomena. This is the sense in Heb. 12:21 ("the sight").

2. The noun, meaning "phenomenon," is often used for dream appearances or apparitions. It means "ghost" in Mk. 6:49.

emphanízō.

1. This word means "to make visible," "to demonstrate," "to set forth," "to declare," and in the active and middle "to appear."

2. In the NT it means "to show" in Acts 23:22 and Heb. 11:14. The appearing of the dead is at issue in Mt. 27:53. A twofold sense is apparent in Jn. 14:21ff. where Judas has a resurrection appearance in mind but Jesus is speaking about his self-revelation in believers when he and the Father come to reside in them. Heb. 9:24 is perhaps using a cultic or legal expression when it refers to the exalted Christ appearing before God for us.

epiphaínō, epiphanḗs, epipháneia.

A. Classical and Hellenistic Greek.

1. The verb means "to show," "to show oneself," "to appear," the adjective means "visible," "magnificent," and the noun means "appearance" in various senses (e.g., a geometrical "surface," the "appearance" of an enemy, the "front" of an army, or the "renown" of famous people). The group has religious significance with reference to the intervention of the gods to bring divine help. The word thus comes to denote "divine assistance." The Ptolemies adopt the title *theós epiphanḗs*.

2. In the LXX we find the verb for "to shine" in Dt. 33:2 and for God's appearing in Gen. 35:7. The adjective means "splendid" in Esth. 5:1. The most common use of the group is for mighty demonstrations of aid (cf. 2 Sam. 7:23; 2 Macc. 2:21; 1 Chr. 17:21; 2 Macc. 15:34; 3 Macc. 2:19).

3. Josephus uses *epipháneia* for "fame" but mostly for "helpful intervention." The verb means "to appear" and the adjective "magnificent." Philo uses the noun for "appearance," "renown," "splendor," and "geometrical surface," the adjective for "splendid," "distinguished," and the verb for "to appear."

B. The NT.

1. In the NT *epiphaínō* in the intransitive means "to show oneself," "to appear" (the stars in Acts 27:20). God intervenes to help in the metaphor of Lk. 1:79. The grace of God has appeared to salvation in the Christ event (Tit. 2:11; cf. 3:4).

2. The adjective characterizes the day of the Lord in Acts 2:20 ("manifest").

3. The noun is a religious term in the NT. It refers to Christ's future eschatological appearing in 2 Th. 2:8; 1 Tim. 6:14; 2 Tim. 4:1; Tit. 2:13, and to Jesus' earthly appearing as an eschatological manifestation of grace in 2 Tim. 1:9-10 (cf. also perhaps 4:8).   [R. BULTMANN and D. LÜHRMANN, IX, 1-10]

Pharisaíos [Pharisee]

A. Phariseeism in Judaism.

I. Usage. A common term in the NT and Josephus, usually in the plural, *Pharisaíos* transcribes an Aramaic word denoting "separated." The Hebrew equivalent, whose root can have both positive and negative nuances, is very rare and does not cover all aspects of Pharisaism. Contemporaries (but not the Pharisees themselves) seem to use it in a derogatory sense for "sectaries."

II. Pharisaism to the Fall of the Jerusalem Hierarchy.

1. The Origin. The beginnings of Pharisaism are obscure but seem to reach back into the second century B.C.

Possible precursors are a. the Chasidim. The sources, which are sparse, suggest that this group originates under Antiochus Epiphanes (cf. 1 Macc. 2:42). It forms an opposition movement prior to the Maccabean revolt. Its first target is the Jerusalem establishment that is departing from the law. Its main aim seems to be to champion and observe the law within the hierarchy. It thus thinks of itself as the true Israel.

An origin might also be sought b. in the Perushim, whose concern is separation by the law, primarily priestly separation by the sacral law with a view to the cultic validity of priestly acts, but then by extension the sanctification of the people by the everyday application of the law. The Pharisees, of course, are concerned about inner and not merely outer separation, but a priestly movement with holiness as its goal may well have contributed to Pharisaism, particularly in the case of Pharisaic priests. The decisive factor, however, is the ideal of everyday sanctification by the law, as may be seen in the lay dominance that belongs to the very structure of Pharisaism and the denial of any prominence to priests as such.

2. *The Pharisaic Societies.* Although we have no real data for the B.C. period, it seems that the Pharisees form societies which are oriented to sanctification and distinguished from the rest of Judaism by specific rules. Only on the basis of some such organization can the Pharisees resist the Hasmoneans, and rabbinic references confirm a corporate existence according to rule.

In this regard we find a. the term Chabura, a general term for "union" which suggests the formation of Pharisaic societies.

We also find b. the term Chaberim for members who accept the society statutes.

A third term c. is Chaberuth for the obligations that members accept. These might vary over the years and in different groups but they always include the payment of tithes and the everyday application of sacral law, although with distinction between those who accept only tithing and those who accept full sanctification after a prior course of instruction and the satisfactory passing of a test. The societies are small groups who regard themselves as the true Israel in distinction from the masses who reject the ideal of actualizing sacral law in everyday life, no matter what may be their culture or status. Political, economic, and social factors, however, rule out the sharp restriction of everyday dealings with the masses which is the Pharisaic ideal.

3. *Pharisaic Wisdom and Learning.*

a. The Chakamim. Pharisaism provides fruitful soil for learning. In postexilic times secular wisdom makes a significant agreement with Israel's faith. It leads believers to see in the law an order of life as well as a plan of salvation. The teachers of wisdom, the chakamim, are aristocrats of the spirit ranking immediately after the priestly and social aristocracy. In the democratic Pharisaic societies they quickly assume positions of leadership. Here they develop, not the doctrine of God, but the themes of anthropology, soteriology, and eschatology which relate believers to both this world and the next. Under their guidance a new faith-world develops which forms the background of the NT. The tension which this development causes with the sacred text of the OT poses a necessary task for scholars which produces scribal learning.

b. The Soferim. This term covers a broad range from literate persons, elementary teachers, secretaries, and temple scribes to students and expositors of the law. When the fusion of law and wisdom takes place, the soferim become virtually identical with the chakamim with the special task of interpreting the law in the light of the new development. Naturally the soferim do not have to be Pharisees. They exist prior to the Pharisaic movement, and there are always non-Pharisaic scribes. Nevertheless, since the Pharisees are diligent students of the law who seek to apply it in everyday life, they inevitably have need of soferim to guide their thought and practice.

4. The Pharisees as a Party.

a. The Hasmoneans. Pharisaism is essentially a trend or movement, and it remains such in the diaspora. In Palestine, however, its concern for legitimacy entails its development as a party, probably as early as the reign of Hyrcanus I (134 B.C.). Opposing the Hasmoneans, the Pharisees seek to replace them with an Aaronite high-priestly family. To this end they even seem to have invoked the aid of the Seleucid Demetrius III Eukairus, but after a brief success they suffer severely at the hands of Jannai when the Syrians withdraw. Under Salome Alexandra (76-67 B.C.) they achieve power and brutally suppress their opponents; the rabbis depict this reign as one of great prosperity. The death of the queen breaks their hegemony, but they retain minority representation on the council. In the ensuing dynastic struggles the Pharisees now seek the end of the prince-priesthood as an invalid innovation. Rejecting the hierocracy, they can lead a religious life without political dependence. They can thus advise the surrender of Jerusalem to Herod I, and after Herod's victory in 37 B.C. they not only survive but maintain the respect of the people (in contrast to Herod).

b. From Herod to the Destruction of the Temple. Herod accepts and even favors the Pharisees, taking care not to wound their religious scruples. In line with their anti-Hasmonean policy, they never champion nationalistic resistance movements aiming at eschatological salvation. They become enmeshed in various palace intrigues, however, and after Herod's death and the banishment of Archelaus, when the Sadducees regain control, they no longer play a normative role. Yet their scribes remain popular as they legalize popular customs and beliefs, and the aristocracy does not attempt any forceful measures against them.

c. The Zealots. Different trends may be seen in Pharisaism, often sharply divided. Thus the Zealots emerge as a radical or particularist wing of Pharisaism under Judas the Galilean, who is distinguished by a love of freedom and an acknowledgment of God alone as Lord. The Zealots quickly attain a following, for they have a predominantly religious rather than political program, and Judas unites scribal learning with his ability as a leader. If on the one side he is the messianic heir-apparent, on the other he is a chakam who seeks the victory of the law and hence eternal freedom in the form of the rule of God. The older Pharisaism resists the Zealot movement but cannot prevent the intrusion of Zealot trains of thought and aspirations.

d. Zadokite Criticism. Qumran shows that Pharisaism is opposed by the older orthodoxy in respect of its detailed rulings and also of its whole interpretation of the law. What is contested is not the applying of the law to life but the placing of Pharisaic rulings as a fence around the law and the resultant according to oral tradition of equal validity with the law and consequent immunity from criticism. The ideal of Pharisaism is a detailed ordering of life which will protect believers against mortal sin and produce fellowship with God through every change and chance of life. The Damascus Document is a Zadokite work which attacks the idea of a fence around the law on the ground that it involves transgression of the law and imposes too heavy burdens on the people by way of false exposition. Similarly Qumran accuses Pharisaism of dissolving the law by scribal misdirection and evasion. An example of such an evasion is the arrangement whereby Hillel supposedly permits a loan to be required even in the year of remission, thereby adopting into sacral law a secular practice which virtually annuls the law.

III. The Victory of Pharisaism.

1. The Fall of the Hierocracy. Except under Salome Alexandra the Pharisees have the role of a minority up to A.D. 70. Their great period comes only with the fall of the hierocracy. When the capture of Jerusalem shatters the Sadducean ideal, Pharisaism provides the direction needed for reconstruction. Politically independent, it nurtures community life in the synagogue. The failure of the Zealots clears the way for more moderate leaders such as Jochanan ben Zakkai. Jabneh with its chakamim, which plays no part in the revolt, forms a center for reorganization.

2. The Reconstruction.

a. Religio-Social Change. The chakamim can now apply more fully their own concepts. They enjoy the support of the eastern diaspora. A new court is set up in which the scribes have final authority. The Jabneh academy supplies the leaders, so that power passes from an aristocracy to men of religious and intellectual quality who after a long period of preparation qualify for ordination as rabbis.

b. Inner Reorganization. In inner reorganization the first task is to give the community a uniform basis in religious law. A voice from heaven settles the old dispute between Hillel and Shammai in favor of the former. Excommunication falls on dissenting groups like the Sadducees and Essenes, and full separation from the Samaritans takes place. Pharisaic Hillelites ultimately prevail in Galilee and the dispersion. Steps are taken to suppress speculation, to fix the canon, and to standardize speech, writing, and liturgy. The chakamim had tried to fix the canon earlier, but they now achieve the threefold canon of law, prophets, and writings in debate with the Sadducees, Samaritans, and Jewish Christians. They also standardize the text and achieve a new and more literal translation into Greek. As regards law, they adopt and revise cultic law, make use of written as well as oral tradition, and establish the threefold principle of majority decision, local custom, and normative authority. Exegesis seeks to establish the unity of the written law and oral tradition; rules borrowed from Hellenistic hermeneutics aid in this task, although these conflict with the older and simpler rules illustrated in the expository work of Qumran. An eschatological element remains that anticipates the restoration of the temple and the dawn of the kingdom. The reconstruction is so thorough that it is hard today to gain even a general picture of Judaism prior to the fall of the hierocracy.

IV. Summary. Prior to A.D. 70 Judaism is a multiform phenomenon; after A.D. 70 we see the triumph of one movement with Pharisaism. This movement, previously a minority, acquires such force as to make its impress on worldwide Judaism as a whole. Only much later will opposition arise against it, and even this opposition cannot decisively alter the totality of the new rabbinic Judaism.   [R. Meyer, IX, 11-35]

B. The NT.

I. The Synoptic Tradition.

1. The Historical Problem. The NT mentions the Pharisees some 98 or 101 times, mostly in the Synoptics. The Pharisees oppose the Baptist in Mt. 3:7ff. and are a contending party against Jesus in Mk. 10:1ff.; 12:13ff. Quite early they resolve on his death (Mk. 3:6). They incur in return the sharp criticism of Jesus (Mk. 7; Mt. 25). In some sense they represent Judaism as a whole in this regard. Yet the picture is not uniform, for Jesus has friendly relations with many Pharisees (cf. Lk. 7:36; 13:31ff.; Mk. 12:34). Furthermore, the Pharisees, who have little real power, play only a minor role in the actual passion story.

2. Other Parties. Other groups as well as the Pharisees oppose Jesus (cf. the references to the Pharisees and Sadducees in Mt. 16:6, to the leaven of the Pharisees and Herod in Mk. 8:15, and to the question of the Sadducees in Mt. 22:34).

b. We also find mention of the chief priests and elders along with the Pharisees (cf. Mk. 12:1ff.; Mt. 21:23, 45).

c. Frequently the scribes figure in the accounts, and while many scribes are Pharisees, the two groups are not identical (cf. Lk. 11:37ff., 45ff.; Mk. 7:5; Lk. 5:21). In exegetical questions the scribes probably play a leading role, and only incidentally are some of them Pharisees (cf. Mk. 12:35; Mt. 22:41).

d. Mark refers to the Herodians in 3:6; 12:13. These are perhaps political adherents of Herod Antipas, although little is known about them or about their connection with the Pharisees. Matthew and Luke omit the references in view of their lack of interest in the group or its lack of any further relevance.

3. Opposition to the Pharisaic Understanding.

a. The opposition of Jesus to the Pharisees is directed against their legal piety and the resultant practice of the law. Jesus accepts the law (Mt. 5:17) and even gives it a sharper interpretation (5:21ff.). Love of God and neighbor is his criterion, not the law itself or oral tradition. In proclaiming God's will Jesus implicitly sets himself above the law and opposes the oral tradition of Pharisaism (Mk. 7:8-9, 13). Emphasizing detailed rules means abrogating essential demands. Hence the legal practice of Pharisaism amounts to hypocrisy (Mt. 6:1ff.).

b. Rules whereby Pharisaism claims to be the true Israel arouse the particular opposition of Jesus, e.g., strict sabbatarianism (Mk. 2:23ff.), tithing (Lk. 18:12), fasting (Mk. 2:18ff.), and purifyings (Mk. 7:1ff.). What Jesus seeks is inner, not outer purity (Mk. 7:15).

c. The separation of the Pharisees from the people is also a cause of conflict in view of Jesus' mingling with publicans and sinners. Since he himself enjoys table fellowship with the Pharisees (Lk. 7:36), he incurs heavy criticism on this point (Mk. 2:15ff.), but in return he opposes his saving mission to Pharisaic legalism. Indeed, in the parable of Lk. 18:9ff. he sets aside the subjectively honest concern of the Pharisees to fulfil the law in favor of those who expect nothing from their own works but everything from the divine mercy.

d. Mt. 5:18-19, of course, maintains the infallible validity of the law. The directions in Mt. 23:2-3 do not in themselves contest Pharisaic authority. The attack in Mt. 23:3, 23 is on Pharisaic practice rather than the Pharisaic ideal. The door is thus left open for Jewish Christians to achieve a true Pharisaic legitimacy while rejecting Pharisaic Judaism and even adopting elements from Zadokite criticism.

II. John's Gospel. In John, too, the Pharisees oppose the Baptist (1:19), collide with Jesus over observance of the sabbath (5:1ff.), and resolve to put Jesus to death (7:32). Yet "the Jews" as a whole are more prominent in John (i.e., the intellectual and religious leaders), the Pharisees are now in closer contact with the chief priests (7:32; 11:47), and little account is taken of the distinction between the scribes and Pharisees (cf. Jn. 9). The separation of the Pharisees from the people still plays a role (7:49), but there is no collective judgment on the Pharisees, and in Nicodemus Jn. 3:1-2 portrays a sympathetic Pharisee (cf. 12:42).

III. Acts and Paul.

1. In Acts the Pharisees play no special role in opposition either to Jesus (2:23) or to the infant church (4:1: the Sadducees and priests). Indeed, Gamaliel advocates a tolerant attitude to the church (5:34ff.), and for party reasons the Pharisees on the council defend Paul's innocence (23:6ff.).

2. Paul himself is brought up as a Pharisee (Acts 26:4-5) and studies under Gamaliel (22:3). He alludes to his zeal in striving to fulfil the Pharisaic ideal (Gal. 1:13-14; Phil. 3:5-6). For him, however, this Pharisaic past is of no importance (Phil. 3:7). He nowhere opposes Pharisaism as such. The theological conflict between Christ and legalism subsumes the historical conflict.

C. **Early Christian Writings.** The sharp rift between Judaism and Christianity means that the Pharisees tend to fade from the picture. The apostolic writings do not mention them. Other works follow the NT tradition. Justin uses the fixed phrase "Pharisees and scribes" (*Dialogue* 51.2; 76.7). Christian Gnostic texts also reflect hostility to the Pharisees. Irenaeus *Against Heresies* 4.12.1 claims that Jesus attacks only the Pharisaic law, not the law as such. Jewish Christianity (Pseudo-Clementine *Recognitions* 1.54.7), however, accepts the authority of the scribes and Pharisees but not their practice (cf. Mt. 23:2-3, 13). The Woes apply to hypocritical Pharisees, not to Pharisees as such (Pseudo-Clementine *Homilies* 11.29.1-2). Jewish Christians are finally the true Pharisees.   [H. F. WEISS, IX, 35-48]

→ *katharós, krýptō, nómos, prophḗtēs, Samáreia, Saddoukaíos*

---

phátnē [manger]

A. **Greek Usage.** *phátnē*, meaning "manger" or "feeding trough," occurs in the spheres of animal husbandry and veterinary science. The extended sense of "stall" is less common. In a transferred sense the word is used for the digestive organs, "trough" suggests a parasitic life, and we also find a use for the "hollow" of the mouth, the "cavity" in teeth, and the "star cluster." The word has no specific religious significance.

B. **The OT and Rabbinic Judaism.**
1. The LXX uses the word for "feeding trough" in Is. 1:3; Job 39:9; Prov. 14:4. "Stall" is a possible sense in Is. 1:3 and Prov. 14:4, but it is likely only in 2 Chr. 32:38; stalls are uncommon in Palestine apart from the royal stables.
2. The rabbis use the Hebrew equivalent mostly for "manger" or "feeding trough." Special rules apply for feeding on the sabbath, e.g., for the size of the trough. Since humans and animals live close together, the sense "stall" is less common. In exposition of Is. 1:3 knowing the master's crib is not taken messianically but is related to knowing the law.

C. **Historical Witness.** Archaeology has discovered feeding troughs in Ahab's stables at Megiddo. We also find pictures of mangers. In the Hellenistic period larger estates have cave-stalls, but on small farms there are feeding places in the main room, troughs outside, or annexed stalls. Cattle and sheep may also be sheltered in folds or caves.

D. **The NT.**
1. In the NT *phátnē* occurs only four times in Luke. In Lk. 13:15 Jesus refers to the practice, dictated by necessity, of loosing cattle from their stalls and leading them to water on the sabbath. If this is permissible for animals, surely the relief of human suffering is even more permissible.
2. The other three instances occur in Lk. 2:1ff. in connection with the birth of Jesus (v. 7), the promise of the angels (v. 12), and the adoration of the shepherds

(v. 16). The theme is clearly an important one, and the meaning is obviously "manger," whether in a stall, in the open, or in a cave. The shepherd setting in the city of David proclaims the birth of the Davidic Messiah. The manger contrasts the lowly birth of the world's Redeemer with the glory of Augustus as the present ruler of the world (2:1, 11, 14). It also prefigures the humility and suffering of the Son of God and Man who has nowhere to lay his head (Lk. 9:58).

E. The Early Church. The manger tradition combines with a cave tradition in the early church (cf. Origen *Against Celsus* 1.51). After Helena's pilgrimage a church is built at the traditional site of the crib and cave (ca. A.D. 330). The late Pseudo-Matthew places the birth in a cave, puts Mary in a stall, has her lay the child in a crib, and then describes the entry into Bethlehem. The ox and ass come into the story on the basis of Is. 1:3 and Hab. 3:2 LXX; they occur in depictions from the middle of the fourth century.   [M. HENGEL, IX, 49-55]

---

phérō [to bring, carry], *anaphérō* [to bear, take up], *diaphérō* [to carry through], *tá diaphéronta* [what matters], *diáphoros* [different], *(adiáphoron* [indifferent]*)*, *eisphérō* [to bring in, carry in], *prosphérō* [to offer], *prosphorá* [offering, sacrifice], *symphérō* [to profit], *sýmphoros* [profitable], *phóros* [tribute], *phoréō* [to wear, bear], *phortíon* [load, burden], *phortízō* [to load, burden]

---

phérō (→ aírō).

1. Secular Literature. From a root meaning "to carry," then "to bring forth," *phérō* has the senses a. "to bring," "to lead," "to go," b. "to bring forth," "to express," "to convey," c. "to issue" (a complaint, accusation, etc.), d. "to bring" (gifts), "express" (thanks), or "show" (a favor), e. "to bear or bring forth," f. "to bear or endure" (afflictions), and g. "to rule."

2. The LXX. The LXX uses the term mostly for "to present," e.g., offerings, at times in the sense "to sacrifice." Other uses are for carrying burdens, bringing gifts, paying tribute, enduring sufferings, and bearing responsibility (Moses in Num. 11:14). "To blow" (the wind) is the sense in Is. 64:5.

3. Josephus. In Josephus the word means "to bring" and intransitively "to lead," middle or passive "to be moved" (cf. also "to ride").

4. The NT.

a. In the sense "to bring" the sick etc. are fetched to Jesus (Mk. 1:32; 2:3, etc.) or to Peter (Acts 5:6). Peter will be "led off" to martyrdom (Jn. 21:18). Intransitively the middle denotes the onrushing wind in Acts 2:2, and in the passive the ship is driven by the storm in 27:15, 17. Heb. 6:1 invites believers to "press on," and 2 Pet. 1:21 says that the prophets were "impelled" by the Spirit.

b. The "bringing" of the gospel is the point in 2 Jn. 10, and in 2 Pet. 1:17-18 the voice "comes" to Jesus, while prophecy does not "come" by human will in 1:21.

c. The term is a legal one in Jn. 18:29 and Acts 25:18 (cf. 2 Pet. 2:11). In Heb. 9:16 proof of the death of the testator must be "adduced" to bring the *diathḗkē* into effect.

d. In 1 Pet. 1:13 grace is "offered" to believers at the parousia. The kings will "bring" their glory in Rev. 21:24 and offer it to God and the Lamb. Believers "bring" their possessions to the apostles to be used for the common good (Acts 4:34, 37; 5:2).

e. Lk. 23:26 refers to Simon's "bearing" of the cross.

f. "Bearing fruit" is at issue in Mt. 7:18; Mk. 4:8; Jn. 15:2, 4. The fruit is that of discipleship or of the word. It is the fruit of Christ's death in Jn. 12:24.

g. The sense of "enduring" occurs in Heb. 12:20 and 13:13. God "bears" with the objects of his wrath in Rom. 9:22; this toleration does not restrict his judgment but enables him to show his glory in mercy.

h. "To uphold" or "to rule" is the sense in Heb. 1:3, where the Son upholds by his word of power the universe that is created through him (v. 2).

5. *The Apostolic Fathers.* In these works we find the senses "to offer," "to bear fruit," "to bear suffering," and "to be impelled" (cf. Barn. 2.5; Hermas *Similitudes* 2.3-4; 1 Clem. 45.5; Hermas *Similitudes* 6.5.7).

anaphérō.

1. *Secular Literature.* This compound has two main senses in accordance with the force of *ana-* as either "up" or "back." To the first group belong such meanings as "to lift up," "to bear."

2. *The LXX.* In the LXX *anaphérō* is a technical term for "to offer," "to sacrifice." It is also used for bringing a matter before someone (Ex. 18:19). In the sense "to bear suffering or guilt" (i.e., for others, Is. 53:11-12), the word may have the force of "to do away," "to expiate."

3. *The NT.*

a. Jesus takes the disciples up the mountain in Mt. 17:1, and he himself is taken up (the ascension) in some versions of Lk. 24:51.

b. "To offer sacrifices" is the sense in Heb. 7:27; 13:15; Jms. 2:21; 1 Pet. 2:5. Christ's once-for-all offering has abolished the Levitical sacrifices in Heb. 7:21. The offering of Isaac is a work of faith in Jms. 2:21. 1 Pet. 2:5 refers to the spiritual offering of the whole person to God. 1 Pet. 2:24 interprets Is. 53:12 LXX as Christ's bearing of sin on the cross in his self-offering for sin (cf. Heb. 9:26, 28).

4. *The Apostolic Fathers.* The term is used in these works for "bringing" or "presenting" to God, e.g., prayers in Barn. 12.7, believers in Ignatius *Ephesians* 9.1.

diaphérō, tá diaphéronta, diáphoros (adiáphoron)

1. *Secular Literature.*

a. In secular works *diaphérō* has such varied senses as "to transmit," "to spread," "to drive," intransitively "to stand out," "to fall behind," impersonally "it matters," "it is of interest or importance."

b. *tá diaphéronta* means either "marks of difference" or "interests."

c. *diáphoros* has the force of "different," "varied," "outstanding," or, negatively, "unwelcome."

d. Aristotle uses *adiáphoron* for the integrity of a substance in its external form or for the similarity of members of a species. For the Cynics and Stoics it is the middle sphere between virtue and vice, i.e., the ethically indifferent.

2. *The LXX.*

a. We find the verb in the LXX in the senses "to transmit," "to scatter," "to spread," "to differentiate oneself," and, in the passive, "to be divided, estranged."

b. The adjective in Lev. 19:19 and Dt. 22:9 renders a Hebrew term signifying "of two kinds."

c. Dan. 7:7 uses the adverb *diaphórōs* for "differently" in a bad sense.

3. *Josephus.* In Josephus the verb means "to be driven or scattered" or "to differentiate oneself," and the adjective means "different."

4. The NT.

a. In the NT the verb means "to carry through" in Mk. 11:16, "to drift" in Acts 27:27, "to be spread" in Acts 13:49, "to differ" in 1 Cor. 15:41, "to be better" in Mt. 6:26, and "to be of no account" in Gal. 2:6.

b. *tá diaphéronta* occurs in Rom. 2:18 and Phil. 1:10 with reference to what is essential either in fulfilling the law or in the Christian life.

c. In Rom. 12:6 the adjective means "different" rather than "superior" (cf. 1 Cor. 12). The term has a negative ring in Heb. 9:10: The ablutions are ineffectual for all their multiplicity.

5. The Apostolic Fathers. "To carry through" is the sense in Hermas *Similitudes* 9.4.1, and "to differ" in Diog. 3.5. 1 Clem. 36.2 quotes Heb. 1:4.

eisphérō.

1. This word means "to carry or bring in," "to convey."

2. The LXX uses it for bringing offerings into the sanctuary.

3. In the NT we brought nothing into the world (1 Tim. 6:7), the sick man is brought into the house (Lk. 5:17-18), disciples will be haled before the courts (Lk. 12:11), blood is brought into the sanctuary (Heb. 13:11), and we pray not to be brought into temptation, or not to cause it to happen (Mt. 6:13).

4. In Hermas *Similitudes* 8.6.5 the compound corresponds to the simple form in 2 Jn. 10.

prosphérō (→ *thýō, proságō*).

A. Secular Literature. This word has such senses as "to bring to," "to set before" (middle "to take," "to enjoy"), "to bring," "to offer," and (passive) "to encounter."

B. Jewish Hellenistic Literature.

1. In the LXX *prosphérō* is mostly a sacrificial term for bringing offerings, for presenting at the altar, or for sacrificing.

2. Josephus uses the word both in the general sense "to bring" or "to serve" (food or drink) and in the sacrificial sense "to offer."

3. Philo uses the term for "to bring" and (middle) "to take" (food and drink).

C. The NT.

1. In Mt. 4:24; 8:16, etc. the sick are brought to Jesus, in Lk. 23:14 Jesus is handed over to the Sanhedrin, and in Mk. 10:13 and parallels children are brought to Jesus.

2 Money is brought in Mt. 22:19, and vinegar handed to Jesus in Lk. 23:36.

3. Heb. 12:7 refers to God's dealings with his sons.

4.a. Cultically Jesus tells the cured leper to make the prescribed offering in Mk. 1:44, and in Mt. 5:23-24 he counsels reconciliation before making an offering. He thus makes the offering for cleansing a witness to his own mission and he gives the sacrificial system a norm in the commandment of love.

b. Paul follows the norm of Jesus in Acts 21:26 when he undertakes the offering and in so doing attempts reconciliation with his Jewish brethren. Stephen, however, echoes prophetic criticism of the cultus in Acts 7:42, and Jn. 16:2 makes the sharper criticism that killing Jesus' disciples will be regarded as offering God service.

c. Hebrews uses the sacrificial theology of the OT as witness to Christ. Jesus offers only once (10:12), offers himself (9:4; 10:10), by his sacrifice sanctifies once and for all (10:10), and ministers on the basis of a new and better covenant (8:6). Yet the old offerings prefigure his perfect offering (10:1) and he shares with Aaron a divinely instituted high-priestly ministry (5:1ff.), albeit of a different order. His unique offering makes all other offerings superfluous apart from that of praise (13:15), which, after the model of Abel and Abraham (11:4, 17), is made in faith.

D. The Apostolic Fathers. The apostolic fathers almost always use the term for "to sacrifice." They find in the OT offerings either examples (1 Clem. 10.7) or types (Barn. 7.3, 5). Did. 14 sees in the eucharist a fulfilment of Mal. 1:11 (cf. 1 Clem. 44.4). Diog. 3.3 has pagan sacrifices in view.

prosphorá.
1. This word has various meanings, including "sacrifice" (as gift or act).
2. In the NT it denotes Levitical offerings in Heb. 10:5, Christ's sacrifice in Heb. 10:10, and the offering of pagans won for or by the gospel in Rom. 15:16.
3. In the apostolic fathers Barn. 2.4ff. rejects *prosphoraí* as superfluous but 1 Clem. 40.2ff. uses the OT order as a model and Mart. Pol. 14.1 compares the martyr to a choice offering.

symphérō, sýmphoros.

A. The Group in Greek.
I. Meaning.
1. symphérō. This word has such varied meanings as "to gather," "to bring," "to be of use, service, or advantage," "to assist," "to suit," "to agree," "to yield or turn to," "to unite," "to correspond," "to be like," "to be construed with" (in grammar), and, in the passive, "to happen."
2. sýmphoros. This word means "accompanying," "suiting," or "useful."
3. Synonyms. The *ōpheléō* group gives the idea of advantage more of the sense of help, but there is little difference of sense in the case of *lysiteléō*.
II. Philosophical Discussion.
1. The Pre-Socratics. The synonyms are interchangeable in the philosophical discussion of what is useful. Nothing clear-cut emerges in pre-Socratic fragments, but belligerence diverts attention from the useful, the sense of what is useful forges an alliance against animals, and hedonistic ideas of the useful may be discerned.
2. The Sophists. The Sophists teach the relative nature of the useful. The stronger find it in following natural law, the weaker in the curtailments imposed by the laws of the state.
3. Socrates. Opposing the Sophists, Socrates virtually equates the useful and the good. The useful bears a final reference to society, i.e., the *pólis,* and can be equated concretely with laws. It also applies in discussion of the afterlife.
4. Post-Socratic Philosophy.
a. Aristotle, too, equates the useful and the good.
b. Historians laud various deeds as useful for a given polis.
c. Stoicism is close to Socrates. Ultimately the useful is what promotes piety. Since individuals are world citizens, individual and general profit coincide. Failure to see this brings meaningless conflict. The good and the useful are identical, but only where there is free self-determination.
d. For Epicurus the useful is what serves the ethical goal of *hēdonḗ*; it is thus the criterion of striving toward this goal, e.g., by promoting fellowship.

B. The OT. In Is. 48:17 God's teaching is of profit, but in 1 Sam. 12:21; Is. 44:9-10 false gods are useless, as are lying speeches in Jer. 7:8, false prophets in

23:32, the magicians of Babylon in Is. 47:12, and unlawful possessions in Prov. 10:2. The wicked ask what good it is to pray to God in Job 21:15, Prov. 11:4 considers profit in the day of wrath, and Eliphaz accuses Job of unprofitable talk in Job 15:3 and thinks the wise are profitable only to themselves and not to God in 22:2-3.

C. Judaism.

1. The LXX uses *symphéron* and *sýmphoron* for various Hebrew terms denoting what is good, suitable, or profitable (cf. Dt. 23:7; Prov. 19:10; Esth. 3:8; 2 Macc. 4:5).

2. Philo's usage falls within the sphere of philosophy, especially Stoicism.

3. Josephus uses the group for "bringing together" and also for what is of use or advantage, always in a secular sense.

4. Qumran uses the corresponding root only in the rendering of Is. 48:17.

5. The Testaments of the Twelve calls profitable both the conduct of the righteous and what God gives them.

6. Rabbinic texts contain terms denoting profit, advantage, or success, e.g., in business, claims, or petitions. Discussion arises as to which of two courses or of two evils is better or more advantageous. The profit in view is the avoidance of judgment, as when it is said that it would have been better for the wicked to have been born blind. Better shame in this world than the loss of salvation in the next!

D. The NT.

I. Usage.

1. *symphérō* means "to bring together" only in Acts 19:19. It means "to profit" in 1 Cor. 6:12; 2 Cor. 8:10; Mt. 15:29; 19:10; Jn. 18:14, etc.

2. *tó sýmphoron* for "profit," "advantage" occurs in 1 Cor. 7:35; 10:33.

II. Meaning.

1. In Mt. 5:29-30 the loss of one member that incites to sin is better than the destruction of the whole person. In this case the profit is entrance into life. The same applies in Mt. 18:6, where drowning is better for the seducers of little ones than eternal perdition.

2. In Jn. 11:50ff. Caiaphas perceives profit in Christ's death, although without realizing that this profit is the gathering of God's scattered children, a process that reaches its goal only in the heavenly world (14:3; 17:24). In Jn. 16:7ff. Christ's departure profits the present life of believers through the sending of the Spirit.

3. Paul uses the group for what profits the spiritual life. Fornication as union with the body of a harlot is inimical to union with Christ, and hence does not profit (1 Cor. 6:12). As regards marriage, Paul seeks what is profitable both for individuals and for the church (1 Cor. 7:35). He himself seeks the advantage of others (1 Cor. 10:33). He speaks hesitantly about visions because there is no good in boasting (2 Cor. 12:1). What edifies is profitable (1 Cor. 10:23; 12:7). The collection as a demonstration of love is of profit (2 Cor. 8:10). Paul preaches all the things that are profitable (Acts 20:20). Profit lies, not in promotion of the *pólis* or the cosmos, nor in what serves the national theocracy, but in what builds up the church, whose *políteuma* is in heaven (Phil. 3:20).

4. Heb. 12:10 describes present sufferings as a divine discipline that is for our good, whether in present perfecting or, as is more likely, in eternal participation in God's holiness.

E. The Apostolic Fathers. Ignatius finds profit in that which leads to eternal fellowship with Christ (*Romans* 5.3). Barnabas finds what is profitable in moral perfection (4.12) or in eternal life (4.10). Hermas commends as profitable the words of the old lady (*Visions* 1.3.3), a walk according to the commandments (*Similitudes* 6.1.3), and delight in good works (*Similitudes* 6.5.7), since these things serve the attainment of life. The profit of an upright life is at issue in *Mandates* 6.1.3ff.

phóros.

A. Outside the NT.
1. Literally this word means "carrying or bringing," then "tribute," "tax," "dues," "payment," and in the papyri "lease," "rent," or "hire."
2. Hebrew equivalents mean "gift," then "tribute," "tax."
3. The rabbis have various terms for levies, tributes, taxes, etc.
4. The LXX mostly uses *phóros* for "tribute" (2 Chr. 36:3) or "forced labor" (Judg. 1:29ff.).
5. Philo contrasts taxes for the priests with the *phóroi* paid to secular authorities.
6. Josephus uses *phóros* or *phóroi* for tribute paid to foreign rulers.

B. The NT.
1. In Rom. 13:6-7, Lk. 20:22, and Mk. 12:14 *phóros* means "tribute" paid to a foreign ruler. At issue is a land tax or poll tax as distinct from a toll or business tax (*télē*). The *phóros* poses for Jews the alternative of loyalty or treason to God as the only Lord. This is what confronts Jesus with a dilemma in Mk. 12:13ff. and parallels. The Pharisees support payment, the Zealots oppose it, but Jesus lifts the problem onto another plane. He abandons God's claim in the restricted sense but raises it again in an unrestricted sense, anchoring the answer in eschatological fulfilment of the kingdom, and leaving it to responsible individual decision to fill out today the content of giving to God the things that are his.
2. In Lk. 23:2 Jesus is accused of inciting the people not to pay the *phóros*, but Pilate's declaration of Jesus' innocence exposes the charge as false. The accusation shows that the point of the question in 20:20 is to entrap Jesus.
3. Although we know nothing of the detailed situation of the church in Rome when Paul wrote Rom. 13, we may assume that believers there have adopted a latently negative attitude to the state. Yet they pay taxes without demur (v. 6), and on this basis Paul exhorts to obedience, pointing out that rulers fulfil a divinely given function. The requirement in v. 7 should not be seen as the climax of the passage. It is repeated in a general form in v. 8; the essential Christian obligation is that of showing respect and displaying love. This obligation sets the duty to authorities within the larger duty to all people, and especially to fellow believers.

phoréō.
1. This word, expressing continuous action, means "to carry forward," or "to keep carrying" (e.g., water from the well, or food to animals). It is used particularly, however, for wearing clothes, carrying weapons, and habitual standing. In the absolute it means "to endure."
2. The term is rare in the LXX. Wisdom is carried on the tongue in Prov. 3:16, and destruction in the mouth in 16:26.
3. Josephus uses the word for wearing clothes and for what is customary.
4. In the NT the authorities bear the sword in Rom. 13:4, clothes are worn in Mt. 11:8, Jesus wears the crown of thorns and a purple robe in Jn. 19:5, and the bearing of the image of the earthly and heavenly man is the point in 1 Cor. 15:49.
5. In 1 Clem. 5.6 Paul carries fetters, and in Hermas *Similitudes* 9.13ff. there is

reference to bearing the name or power of the Son of God, or of the names and garments of virgins and their spirits (representing Christian virtues).

phortíon.

1. This word has such senses as "freight," "lading," "burden," "goods," and a child in the womb. "Burdening" with cares, sickness, etc. is another sense.

2. The OT equivalent *šḥd* has such senses as "bearing," "burden," "tribute," "toll," or "trouble."

3. The LXX uses *phortíon* for "burden" (Is. 46:1), "burden of sin" (Ps. 38:4), the "burden" one person is for another (Job 7:20), and "load" (of wood) (Judg. 9:48-49).

4. The rabbis use the Hebrew in various ways for "bearing," "business," "occupation," "burden," "obligation," or "duty."

5. In the NT ship's "cargo" is the meaning in Acts 27:10. In Mt. 23:4 Jesus chides the scribes and Pharisees for imposing overheavy burdens with their interpretation of the law, which leads people away from God by substituting ritualistic requirements for the real concerns of justice, mercy, and faith, i.e., a right relationship to others and to God. In contrast, Jesus himself promises rest to those who accept his light *phortíon* (Mt. 11:28ff.), i.e., the discipleship which means fellowship with himself and unity with the will of God. In Gal. 6:5 Paul probably has in view much the same thing as in 2 Cor. 10:12ff. and 1 Cor. 3:10ff., where he speaks about the task or work that is entrusted to each and that each must accomplish in the power of God. The same thought is present in Rom. 14:12. The negative image of the load or burden is appropriate in view of accountability in the judgment.

phortízō.

1. This word means "to load on a ship," then "to ship," and in a transferred sense "to burden (oneself) with."

2. The LXX has the word in Ezek. 16:33 for "to present with," i.e., to load with gifts.

3. In the NT Jesus in Lk. 11:46 accuses the lawyers of loading the people with burdens, i.e., with legal demands. In Mt. 11:28 he invites the heavy-laden to come to himself for rest. Liberation from burdens of all kinds is part of his eschatological message, but release from the burdens of scribal piety is especially in view. Mt. 12 offers illustrations of liberation from various troubles in spite of legalistic Pharisaic opposition.   [K. WEISS, IX, 56-87]

---

phtháno [to precede, arrive at],   **prophtháno** [to come before, do before]

---

1. Secular Greek. This common verb means "to come, do, or be first," "to overtake." The comparative element fades out to yield the sense "to reach." The compound is a stronger form.

2. Hellenistic Judaism.

a. The LXX uses *phtháno* for a Hebrew term meaning "to show oneself ready," "to do quickly," "to accomplish." In the absolute the word means "to attain," "to reach," "to come to." *prophtháno* means "to come before" (Ps. 17:13) or "to meet" (Job 30:27).

b. In Philo we find the weaker sense "to attain to" or "to come before." "To come before" is the usual sense in Josephus.

3. The NT.

a. The original sense occurs in the NT only in 1 Th. 4:15 ("to precede"). The compound follows ancient usage in Mt. 17:25.

b. The meaning "to arrive at" occurs in 1 Th. 2:16; Rom. 9:31; Phil. 3:16; 2 Cor. 10:14. Paul has reached the Corinthians with the gospel, we are to hold fast what we have attained, Israel has not attained what it sought, and as the Jews oppose the gospel God's wrath has come upon them at last (or totally). In Mt. 12:28 Jesus' expelling of demons by the Spirit means that God's kingdom has come; it is present in his person.

4. Apostolic Fathers. 2 Clem. 8:2 uses the compound in the sense "to do before."

[G. FITZER, IX, 88-92]

---

phtheírō [to destroy, corrupt], *phthorá* [destruction, corruption], *phthartós* [perishable], *áphthartos* [imperishable], *aphtharsía* [imperishability], *aphthoría* [soundness], *diaphtheírō* [to destroy, corrupt], *diaphthorá* [destruction, corruption], *kataphtheírō* [to destroy, corrupt]

A. The Greek World.

I. General Usage.

1. *phtheírō* means "to destroy," middle and passive "to perish." It is often used for "to kill" ("to be killed"), but may also mean "to languish" (e.g., in prison). Economic ruin may also be in view. In curses the meaning may be "be damned" or more weakly "be off." Another sense is "to spoil" (e.g., milk). The loss of food or of animals may sometimes be denoted.

2. *phthorá* means "destruction," "death," "shipwreck," etc.

3. A moral sense is "to lead astray," "to ruin," "to seduce," "to corrupt," "to bribe."

4. In various combinations *diaphtheírō* means "to frustrate" or "to weaken."

II. Philosophical Usage.

1. *Older Philosophy.* Greek philosophy opposes perishing to becoming. The cosmos abides, the parts are subject to corruption. Or else the elements abide, while forms are perishable. The concern is to find what is permanent in the flux of nature.

2. *Aristotle.* For Aristotle the corruptible and incorruptible condition one another. *ousía* as such has no share in becoming or perishing, but *ousíai* do, and *archaí* (principles or elements) are preceded by prior *archaí*. Distinctions arise in the concepts of perishing and change. In nature *phthorá* (death) comes through lack of heat or of blood, and *áphthartos* in this connection means "long-lived." Ethically *phtheírō* is the opposite of *sṓzō* ("to uphold").

3. *Later Hellenistic Period.* The antonyms *phthartón–áphtharton* increasingly acquire a religious rather than a natural or ontological sense in a contrast of the divine world and the earthly. What is immutable does not lie in the cosmos, in its principles, or elements, or abiding relations, but in what transcends it, although Plutarch can still call the atoms or the all incorruptible.

B. The OT and Judaism.

I. The OT. In the LXX *phtheírō* is the rendering of Heb. *šḥt,* which carries the various senses of corruption, e.g., decay, destruction, depravity, or disfigurement (Jer. 13:7; 48:18; Ex. 32:7; Is. 52:14). Other equivalents mean "to dry out" (Judg. 16:7), "to fade" (Is. 24:4), and "to leave empty" (Is. 32:6).

II. Palestinian Judaism.

1. *Qumran.* The Qumran scrolls use such phrases as the snares, waves, arrows, or gates of destruction. The destruction of a land may be meant but also eternal destruction, and, of course, moral corruption.

2. *Talmudic and Midrashic Writings.* In these works we find various words meaning "to ruin," "to mar," "to destroy," "to take by force," "to wrong," "to injure," "to wound," or, in the case of the nouns, "pit," "moral ruin," "injury," "damage," "destruction," "mutilation," and "destruction."

III. Hellenistic Judaism.

1. *The Greek OT.* For the Hebrew terms the LXX uses the *phtheirō* group with reference to killing, to blemishes in offerings, to destruction, to the pit, to moral corruption, to overthrow, to laying waste, and to fading or sinking down exhausted.

2. *Josephus.* In Josephus the group signifies "to kill," "to drive off," "to perish," or, as a noun, "bloodshed," "massacre," "destruction," "harm," "annihilating defeat." In the moral field the term denotes "seduction," "bribery," or "moral corruption" in general.

3. *Philo.* In Philo we find references to corruptibility as well as to killing or destruction. The cosmos falls victim to corruption, but the eternal is incorruptible. Only God can guarantee our preservation. The world of becoming and perishing stands in antithesis to the inner incorruptible world of God's making. When the soul has the vision of what is incorruptible it finds release from temporal and inauthentic things. Virtues enjoy immortality, the life of virtue and wisdom is immortal, the good is immortal, and Abraham enjoys immortality after death. Philo also uses the group for moral corruption.

4. *Other Works.* In the Testaments of the Twelve we find the normal use for "destruction" or "moral corruption." Humans are mortal (2 Macc. 7:16), as are life's goods (Test. Benj. 6:2) and idols (Wis. 14:8), but God's Spirit is immortal (Wis. 12:1), and so is the light shed by the law (18:4). To keep the commandments is an assurance of immortality (6:18-19), and the victory of martyrs is immortality (4 Macc. 17:12).

C. The NT.

1. *Real Sense.* Rev. 11:18 uses *diaphtheirō* for destruction by God's judgment (cf. *phtheirō* in 1 Cor. 3:17). The destruction of ships is the point in Rev. 8:9 and of clothes in Lk. 12:33. To ruin economically is perhaps Paul's ironical point in 2 Cor. 7:2. In the metaphor in 1 Cor. 3:17 he has in mind the destruction of the temple, not inner corruption. Foods are destined for destruction in Col. 2:22, and as irrational animals are born to be destroyed in 2 Pet. 2:12, so false teachers will perish in the judgment (rather than in their conduct). "Decay" is the sense in the quotation from Ps. 16 in Acts 2:27, 31; 13:34ff.

2. *Moral and Religious Sense.* 1 Cor. 15:33 quotes Menander, and in 2 Cor. 11:3 the allusion to Eve shows that the thoughts of the Corinthians are subject to perversion. A corrupt mind is the point in 1 Tim. 6:5; 2 Tim. 3:8, and the "old man" is corrupt or degenerate in Eph. 4:22. Rev. 11:18 refers to those who corrupt or seduce the human race (cf. the harlot of 19:2). In Tit. 2:7 what is in view is not impregnability against false teaching, nor doctrine safeguarded by the truth, but the character of Titus as one who is not, and cannot be, corrupted.

3. *Ideal Sense.* The group often has human corruptibility in view. The outward man experiences the process of dying in 2 Cor. 4:16. Humanity is mortal (Rom. 1:23), its

goals are mortal (1 Cor. 9:25), and it needs a new mode of being (2 Cor. 15:53) which is made possible, not by corruptible means, but by the indestructible blood of Christ (1 Pet. 1:18). Over against perishable seed stands the imperishable word of God by which believers are born anew (1 Pet. 1:23). What is corruptible is subject to futility (Rom. 8:20-21); in contrast stands freedom from decay and the glorious liberty of God's children. But corruptibility also corresponds to the *sárx,* and not just to flesh and blood. In distinction from "life," it thus means "eternal destruction" (Gal. 1:8). Moral failure means corruption but also falling under the spell of corruptibility (2 Pet. 1:4; 2:19). The dead will rise incorruptible (1 Cor. 15:52). God is immortal (1 Tim. 1:17), and so is the Christian inheritance (1 Pet. 1:4). A quiet spirit is an imperishable jewel (1 Pet. 3:4). In Eph. 6:24 incorruptibility and grace characterize the new life if *aphtharsía* goes with *cháris,* but if it goes with Christ or those who love him it denotes the new mode of being, and if it has a general reference it simply means "in eternity." With "life" *aphtharsía* marks the future eternal life that Christ has brought into a corruptible world (2 Tim. 1:10). As an eschatological blessing it will be manifested with the parousia (1 Cor. 15:42, 50, 53-54). It is to be sought here (Rom. 2:7) but remains hidden until Christ comes.

D. The Early Church. The antithesis of the corruptible–incorruptible plays a bigger part in the early church under growing Hellenistic influence. Diog. 2.4-5 opposes the designation of corruptible things as gods, and 9.2 says that Christ alone is incorruptible. The natural heart is corruptible in Barn. 16.7. *tá phthartá* are perishable goods, and *phthorá* is corruptibility (Ignatius *Romans* 7.3). Christ, the true temple, and the *agápē* are imperishable (Diog. 9.2; Barn. 16.9; Ignatius *Romans* 7.3). So is the crown of victory (Mart. Pol. 17.1). Christ leads to immortality (2 Clem. 20.5), which comes already through the gospel (Ignatius *Ephesians* 17.1; *Philadelphians* 9.2; Mart. Pol. 14.2). [G. HARDER, IX, 93-106]

philágathos → *agathós; philadelphía, philádelphos* → *adelphós*

---

philanthrōpía [hospitality], *philanthrōpós* [benevolently, kindly]

A. The Greek World.
1. Occurrence and Meaning. Found from the fifth century B.C., this group at first denotes friendly relations, especially of the gods or rulers etc. to those under them, then more generally, and with such nuances as "hospitality," "clemency," "usefulness," and "tip" or "present."

2. The Greek-Hellenistic World. Primarily deities are *philánthrōpoi,* then rulers and outstanding people. *philanthrōpía* is a virtue in popular ethics and later in philosophical ethics. Human *philanthrōpía* imitates that of the gods and is demanded of rulers. Julian regards it as the typical quality of the Hellenes and Romans and requires it of officials and pagan priests. It takes the form of clemency in punishment and aid in distress.

B. The LXX and Hellenistic Judaism.
1. In the LXX the word occurs in apocryphal works with the same senses as in the Greek and Hellenistic tradition (cf. 2 Macc. 9:27; Wis. 12:19).

2. The Epistle of Aristeas argues that rulers can practice it only in obedience to God (208).

3. Josephus calls the generous conduct of the Romans *philanthrōpía (Antiquities* 12.124). He also refers to God's *philanthrōpía* (16.42).

4. Philo integrates the virtue into his thinking (*On Virtues* 51). The friend of God must also be a *philanthrōpos* (*On the Decalogue* 110). *philanthrōpía* embraces enemies, slaves, animals, and even plants, as well as compatriots. It determines God's own actions in creation and in Israel's history (*On the Creation of the World* 81; *On the Life of Moses* 1.198).

C. The NT. The group is marginal in the NT. The centurion acts *philanthrōpōs* when he lets Paul visit friends in Sidon (Acts 27:3), and the inhabitants of Malta show *philanthrōpía* (aid or hospitality) after the shipwreck (28:2). God's *philanthrōpía* comes to expression in the Christ event (Tit. 3:4), i.e., in regeneration and renewal by the Spirit through Christ. God is no remote and alien God but has condescended to us and placed our life under the concrete obedience that issues in right conduct to others (vv. 1ff.).

D. The Early Church. The early writers also hesitate to make much use of the group. Justin *Dialogue* 47 refers to the *philanthrōpía* of God (cf. Diog. 9.2). Acts of Thomas 170 calls Christ *philánthrōpos*. Clement of Alexandria and Origen begin to use the group more freely both for the work of God or Christ and for Christian conduct.

→ *philoxenía, philóxenos* [U. Luck, IX, 107-12]

---

philéō [to love, kiss], *kataphiléō* [to kiss], *phílēma* [kiss], *phílos* [friend], *phílē* [female friend], *philía* [friendship, love]

---

philéō, kataphiléō, phílēma.

A. Common Greek Usage.

1. With Personal Object.

a. The stem *phil-* is of uncertain etymology but carries the sense of "related." Hence *philéō* means "to treat somebody as one of one's own people." It is used for the love of spouses, of parents and children, of employers and servants, of friends, and of gods and those favored by them.

b. With reference to gods and friends it often has the concrete sense "to help," "to care for," "to entertain."

c. It can also denote sexual love.

d. It often approximates *agapáō* in meaning and use but is more common than *agapáō* in secular Greek (not in the LXX or NT) and has more of the sense "to love" in distinction from "to like," although the verbs are often interchangeable and in the NT *agapáō* is the warmer and deeper term.

2. With Neuter Object. With a neuter object the sense of *philéō* is "to like," "to value."

3. With Infinitive. Common phrases are "to like doing" and "to be accustomed to doing."

4. philéō ("To Kiss"), kataphiléō, phílēma.

a. Usage. Unlike *agapáō*, *philéō* can be used for acts of affection, e.g., fondling and especially kissing. Increasingly *kataphiléō* is used when the meaning is "to kiss," and from Aeschylus to the NT the noun for "kiss" is always *phílēma*.

b. The Kiss in Antiquity.

(a) The animistic idea of conveying the soul perhaps underlies kissing on the mouth or nose. But the aim of knowing and enjoying the related person by scent may also play a role.

(b) Kisses are for relatives, rulers, and those one loves. The primary intent is not erotic. Respect as well as affection is shown by the kiss. To kiss the ruler is a privilege; the ruler's kiss is a supreme honor. Later we find the erotic kiss, including the widespread homosexual kiss.

(c) Kisses are on the mouth, hands, and feet, also on the cheeks, forehead, eyes, and shoulders. As a mark of respect the kiss is usually on the hands or feet. The kiss on the mouth becomes prominent only with the erotic kiss.

(d) Occasions of kissing are greeting, parting, reconciling, making contracts, etc. The kiss signals entry into a fraternity. In the mysteries the initiate kisses the mystagogue. Kissing is common in the games; there is even a kissing contest, and kisses are sometimes given as prizes.

(e) With pleasure in kissing we find warnings against excess and against the danger of demonic infection or cultic defilement.

(f) Cultic kisses are important (cf. the kissing of images, divine kissing as a means of healing, kissing substitutes, e.g., the earth in front of idols rather than the idols, blowing kisses to stellar deities or as a hasty sign of reverence when passing shrines or tombs).

B. The LXX.
I. Usage.

1. In the LXX *philéō,* which is less common than *agapáō,* is mostly used for *'hb.* In meaning it is very similar to *agapáō.* "To like" with a neuter object occurs six times (e.g., Gen. 27:4; Hos. 3:1; Prov. 21:17), and "to like to do" once (Is. 56:10). With a personal object *philéō* can sometimes mean "to prefer" (Gen. 37:4) and is used five times for sensual love (cf. Tob. 6:15; Lam. 1:2).

2. For "to kiss" *philéō* and *kataphiléō* are used for *nšq.* The noun *phílēma* occurs for the kiss of the beloved in Cant. 1:2 and the treacherous kiss of the enemy in Prov. 27:6.

II. The Kiss in the OT and Judaism.

1. The transmission of soul-breath by kissing seems to be the point in Gen. 2:7; 2 Kgs. 4:34 (cf. also the kiss at the consecration of the king in 1 Sam. 10:1).

2. Relatives kiss in Gen. 31:28; 50:1; 2 Sam. 14:33; Gen. 33:4; 29:11; Ex. 18:7, etc. The kiss of respect occurs in 2 Sam. 19:40.

3. The kiss on the lips becomes the true kiss (cf. Prov. 24:26), but the kiss of honor is a kiss on the hands or feet (although in the OT it is the nations, not Israel, that are to kiss the feet of the Lord, Ps. 2:11).

4. Kissing is common in salutations and at partings (Gen. 29:11; 31:28). It is also a sign of reconciliation (33:4), ratifies an adoption (48:10), and is given in blessing (27:26-27).

5. The kisses of harlots are rejected (Prov. 7:13), and so are erotic kisses in general; the praise of the erotic kiss in Cant. 1:2 is acceptable to the rabbis only when the work is allegorized.

6. The OT has nothing comparable to cultic kisses. In Judaism the kiss of God brings death (on the basis of a misunderstanding of Dt. 34:5). God's kiss is the easiest form of death among the 903 forms distinguished by the rabbis.

C. The NT.
I. "To Love."

1. *With Neuter Object and Infinitive.* Like the LXX, the NT prefers *agapáō* to *philéō.* Only John makes a more theological use of *philéō. philéō* is never used for love of

God, and neither it nor *agapáō* ever denotes erotic love. The use of *philéō* is mostly in stereotyped expressions. With a neuter object we find it only in Mt. 23:6-7, and an infinitive follows in 23:7. The passage serves to characterize the complacency and ambition of the scribes and Pharisees (cf. Lk. 20:46; 11:43).

2. *With Personal Object.*

a. The Synoptists. The only instance is in Mt. 10:37, where the meaning is "to prefer." Placing love for himself above love for relatives, Jesus claims the super-abundance of love that is due to God (cf. Lk. 14:26).

b. John.

(a) In Jn. 15:19 the basic sense "to love what is one's own" is plain. The love of Jesus for his own (*idioi*) corresponds to the world's love for its own, for what belongs to it (*idion*). In Jn. 12:25 Jesus demands an uncompromising renunciation of self-love (cf. Lk. 17:33; Mt. 10:39; Mk. 8:35). Although love of self may serve as a criterion for love of neighbor (Mk. 12:31), denial of self is a presupposition of salvation. In the context of Jn. 12:24 it may take the form of forfeiture of life. In Jn. 11:3, 36 love of friends is the point, but Lazarus is specially chosen and he is called "our friend" rather than "my friend" (11:11).

(b) A special form of friendship is the love of Jesus for the beloved disciples. *philéō* denotes this love only in Jn. 20:2; *agapáō* is used in 13:23; 19:26; 21:7, 10. The idea of choice is evident here. Lying close to Jesus' breast at table expresses unique intimacy (13:25). This friend is the supreme disciple as Jesus is the supreme Son (cf. Jn. 1:18). Both are primary witnesses—the disciple to Jesus, Jesus to the Father (cf. 19:35; 21:7, 24). The beloved disciple is also the supreme brother, so that Jesus entrusts his mother to him (20:7). He takes precedence even over Peter in reaching the empty tomb (20:4) and then in believing (20:8). Jn. 21:24 identifies the beloved disciple as the author of chs. 1–20, and tradition has equated him with John the son of Zebedee (who is not mentioned by name in John), although other candidates are Lazarus (cf. 11:3), the rich young ruler (Mk. 10:21), the timid disciple of Mk. 14:51-52, Paul, or the so-called elder John. Some scholars have seen in the beloved disciple the ideal believer or witness, a projection of the author and his community into the history of Jesus, an embodiment of Gentile Christianity, or a representative of prophetic ministry over against Peter's pastoral ministry. But a specific disciple is clearly in view, although the circumlocutions prevent us from identifying him with any certainty. In the figure of the beloved disciple the gospel claims that its presentation is the abiding form of the gospel with Christ's own validation, especially in relation to the decisive events of the crucifixion and resurrection.

(c) In Jn. 16:27 the disciples meet Jesus' demand that they should love him by believing in him, and to their love for Jesus corresponds the reciprocal love of the Father for them. There is perhaps some distinction here from God's general love for the world in Jn. 3:16. Yet God's love of the disciples may also be expressed by *agapáō* (cf. 14:21, 23), just as *philéō* and *agapáō* may both denote the Father's love of the Son (5:20; 3:35, etc.). Only *agapáō*, however, is used for Jesus' love of the disciples (13:1), their love of one another (13:34), and Jesus' love of the Father (14:31). John nowhere refers to the disciples' love of the Father.

(d) Alternation between *agapáō* and *philéō* occurs in Jn. 21:15ff. Some exegetes think that Peter is grieved because Jesus uses *philéō* the third time (21:17), but the words are mostly synonymous in John, and Peter is more likely grieved because Jesus asks for a third time. Jesus demands that Peter love him "more than these" (v. 15) because he has for him a special commission, which is threefold like the threefold denial and the threefold affirmation of a special love. The exceptional love corresponds in some sense to the love of Jesus for the beloved disciple and underlies Peter's twofold discipleship in his pastoral office and his death.

c. The Rest of the NT.

(a) In 1 Cor. 16:22 Paul seems to be using a fixed liturgical formula connected with the eucharist. Grace is only for those who confess their love for the Lord by word and deed, i.e., in a total orientation of faith to him. An epistolary formula occurs in Tit. 3:15 but with a Christian significance imparted by "in the faith" and a certain exclusiveness suggested by the "us." Love for the apostle is the bond that unites the churches in a special way.

(b) In Rev. 3:19 the exalted Lord uses an OT phrase (Prov. 3:12 LXX): His chastening love (cf. 1 Cor. 11:32) is no other than God's own love. The background is not so much that of the friend of God who finds fulfilment of fellowship in the common meal but that of the parental love that manifests itself to the erring child in correction that leads to repentance. Another current formula may well be present in Rev. 22:15, where we have a concluding phrase that characterizes the prior concepts in an absolute antithesis to the love of God (cf. the parallel ideas in Jn. 3:19; 1 Jn. 2:15; Jms. 4:4).

II. The Kiss in the NT.

1. Manner and Occasion. The NT does not mention the erotic kiss, nor the kiss between close relatives except in Lk. 15:20, but we find the greeting kiss in Lk. 7:45; 15:20; perhaps 22:47, the parting kiss in Acts 20:37, and the kiss of honor in Lk. 7:38, 45; perhaps 22:47-48. The kiss is a mark of penitence in Lk. 7:44ff., of reconciliation in Lk. 15:20, and of gratitude in Acts 20:37, and we find a liturgical kiss in 1 Th. 5:26; 1 Cor. 16:20; 2 Cor. 13:12; Rom. 16:16. Before the eucharist the kiss confirms and actualizes the unity of the church as the eschatological family of God; it also points ahead to the eschatological consummation, to the future fellowship of the perfected.

2. The Kiss of Judas. In Mk. 14:44-45 the kiss of Judas is obviously a sign of recognition. Whether it is actually given is left an open question in Lk. 22:47-48. Betrayal by one of the Twelve with a kiss is a fulfilment of prophecy in Jn. 13:18; 17:12 (cf. Mk. 14:18). The kiss is perhaps a kiss of greeting or a kiss of brotherhood; but it is perhaps also a kiss of feigned love and respect, open to severe condemnation as a misuse of the sign of affection.

D. The Post–NT Period.

1. The Early Church.

1. In spite of ascetic tendencies the kiss is still common in the early church between relatives and married couples, and Hermas *Similitudes* 9.11.4 finds a special use for the erotic kiss (cf. also 9.15.2).

2.a. More important is the cultic kiss. Justin mentions the eucharistic kiss in *Apology* 65.2. Tertullian attaches great significance to the kiss of peace as a sign of reconciliation (*De oratione* 18). For Cyril of Jerusalem and Chrysostom it is a sign of the unity of the body. In the west it comes immediately before communion and it is called either the kiss of peace or simply the peace. Yet objections to the kiss arise early, especially pagan suspicion and the danger of erotic perversion (Athenagoras *Supplication* 32). Hence Clement of Alexandria in *Paedagogus* 3.81.2ff. demands a mystical kiss in which the mouth remains closed. From the third century the sexes are separated for the kiss (*Apostolic Constitutions* 2.57.17), and then the clergy and laity (8.11.9).

b. The liturgical kiss occurs twice in baptism, first as the kiss of the bishop pronouncing the reconciliation and acceptance of the candidates, then as the kiss whereby the newly baptized grant their new brothers and sisters a share in the imparted grace and power of peace.

c. Many liturgies include the kiss of peace in the consecration of a bishop, a priest, or a monk.

d. We also read of the kiss at the burial of the dead.

e. The kiss occurs, too, in the honoring of martyrs. Believers kiss them in prison, especially kissing their wounds or their chains, and they kiss one another before execution. We also read of the kissing of their graves, their relics, and the thresholds of their churches.

f. Among substitute kisses we find the kissing of doorposts and altars. Kissing altars is important since they point to Christ. Cf. also the kissing of icons, the cup, and the book of the gospel. In the west we find the kissing tablet which the priest hands communicants to kiss.

II. Gnosticism. In Gnosticism the kiss is a favorite symbol for union with the redeemer and the reception of immortal life thereby. The sacrament of the bridal chamber is the supreme sacrament and the mutual kiss is the means of mystical conception. Important kisses are Jesus' kissing of Mary Magdalene, his kissing of his heavenly twin, and the kiss on Mani's entry into the realm of light.

phílos, phílē, philía.

A. Nonbiblical Antiquity.

I. Meaning of the Words.

1. phílos.

a. This word means "friend," "loved one," "lover," "client."

b. *hetaíros* is a more or less interchangeable term.

c. Another related term is *ídios.*

d. The *syngenés* may also be identical with the *phílos,* since relatives and friends form the closest living circle. The two words may also be related in a transferred sense. Popular usage prefers to link *phílos* with individual degrees of close relationship, parents and brethren.

e. The common idea of friends of the king brings a close connection to *sýmboulos* ("counselor").

f. *phílos* is close to *sýmmachos* for nations in alliance.

g. Since the whole *phil-* group can denote hospitality, we often find *phílos* with *xénos,* the "stranger."

2. phílē. This word means "dearest," "beloved," sometimes with an erotic nuance, but also at times for a female friend. *Phílē* is a proper name which is used for Aphrodite, for *hetaerae,* and also for honorable women. Finally, we find *phílē* as a political title.

3. philía.

a. This word means "love" or "friendship" with the same broad range of meaning as *phílos.* The strongest ties of *philía* are love of parents, brothers and sisters, or spouse.

b. The term also denotes erotic love, both heterosexual and homosexual.

c. Friendship is commonly the sense, with such nuances as a "pleasant relationship" and "hospitality."

d. In politics the word means "alliance."

e. In a transferred sense it means "harmony" as a principle of unity.

f. *Philía* becomes a proper name, e.g., for Isis.

g. Special meanings are friendship with animals (either positive or negative), the kiss as a sign of loving fellowship, and *philía* as a formal address or title.

II. Friendship in Antiquity.

1. Antiquity writes a great deal about friendship both in special works and in sections of larger works.

2. There are various proverbs about friendship. The motif of *koinōnía* is common, the idea of "one soul" is attributed to Aristotle, and the friend counts as one's other self.

3. We find groups of friends, but personal friendship is the heart of the matter for the Greeks. Hence the pair is the true ideal (cf. Achilles and Patroclus, or Orestes and Pylades). Partly historical and partly fictional accounts of pairs of friends are passed down, usually with one of the pair more active or older than the other. The supreme duty of the friend is that of self-sacrifice for the other even to the point of death.

B. The OT and Judaism.

I. Usage.

1. philos. In the OT *philos* renders various Hebrew terms but only in 70 out of some 180 cases is there an original. Meanings range from "personal friend" by way of "friend of the family" and "best man" to "client" or "political supporter," as well as "friend of the king." Related terms are *adelphós, hetaíros, plēsíon, sýmboulos,* and *sýmmachos.*

b. Philo's usage is much the same.

2. philía. Having Hebrew equivalents only in Proverbs (5:19; 10:12; 7:18; 15:17; 17:9; 27:5), this term may denote either erotic love (Prov. 5:19; 7:18) or political friendship (1 Macc. 8:1; 2 Macc. 4:11). From *philía, philiázō* is a word that the LXX also uses in the senses "to be, act as, or become a friend."

II. Friendship in the OT and Judaism.

1. The paucity of Hebrew originals for the group shows that the Greek view of friendship is an alien one in the OT world.

2. Yet the story of David and Jonathan ranks with the great accounts of friendship in antiquity. A pact seals the friendship (1 Sam. 8:3-4), Jonathan hands over his cloak and weapons, the pact applies to their children (2 Sam. 21:7), the two love one another as their own life (1 Sam. 18:1), and the story ends with a lament that is a song in praise of friendship (2 Sam. 1:26). Yet the Hebrew has no true term for the relationship, and even the LXX does not use *philía.*

3. Many friendship sayings occur in Proverbs and Sirach. Most of these take the form of warnings (cf. Sir. 6:8ff.). Many people protest friendship, but true friends are few. Only those who fear God are capable of friendship and will have true friends (Sir. 6:16-17). Political friendships occur (cf. 2 Chr. 19:2; 20:37), and there is reference to a friend of the king in 1 Chr. 27:33 (cf. 1 Kgs. 4:5). In a transferred sense we read of friendship with wisdom (Wis. 8:18).

4. The rabbis apply the concept to the relation between teachers and students of the law. *koinōnía* is a mark of Qumran (cf. the extolling of friendship among the Essenes in Josephus *Jewish War* 2.119), but although the community achieves a high degree of communal life (the sharing of lodging, food, knowledge, talents, and work), the strict ranking seems to militate against true friendship.

5. Philo speaks about friendship with God. The patriarchs are examples, but all the righteous may be called God's friends. Philo also finds a pair of human friends in

Moses and Joshua, and he believes that human friendship is pleasing to God. God, the refuge of friendship, does not despise its rights (*Every Good Man Is Free* 44).

C. The NT.

1. Usage. phílos occurs 28 times in the NT, *phílē* and *philía* once each. The main use is in the Lucan and Johannine writings. *phílos* occurs in Mt. 11:19; Jms. 2:23; 4:4, and the one instance of *philía* is in Jms. 4:4.

2.a. Of the 18 instances of *phílos*, 17 are in Luke (also the one instance of *phílē*). Jesus, however, is never *phílos* except in the taunt of 7:34. Mostly the use is the common one found in secular circles. People who are close are in view in Lk. 14:12; 15:6. "Boon-companion" is the point in 7:34. "Personal friend" is meant in Lk. 11:5, 8; 23:12, "guest" in Lk. 11:6, and one of a circle in 7:6; Acts 10:24.

b. The rule of Lk. 14:12 conflicts with the conventions of antiquity by rejecting the principle of reciprocity (cf. Mt. 5:46-47). Jesus breaks down the wall of an exclusiveness of fellowship and love. In Lk. 14:12 friendship and table fellowship are correlative (cf. 15:6, 9, 29). The fact that Jesus eats with publicans and sinners is the basis of the charge that he is their boon-companion (7:34). In fact, he loves sinners and is loved by them, as the washing of his feet, the kiss, and the anointing show (7:37ff.). Hospitality expresses the relation between friendship and table fellowship, as in Lk. 11:5ff. where *phílos* has almost the sense of "good neighbor" in vv. 5, 8 and of "guest" in v. 6. The friend as neighbor and host must be available for a friend.

c. Joy stands closely related to friendship (cf. Lk. 15:6, 9, 29). Yet friends must be ready, too, for service, concern, and self-sacrifice (11:5ff.). Friends may expect help from one another even when it is inconvenient. Again, friends want to share great experiences (Acts 10:24). Asiarchs, who are Paul's friends, intervene to save him at Ephesus (Acts 19:31). Only here and in Acts 27:3 do we hear of Paul's friends; he himself never uses *phílos*, but prefers *adelphós* or *téknon*. The friends of Paul in 27:3 are not his hosts or personal friends but Christians who care for him. The term "friends" for believers is not peculiar to Luke but occurs in John too (cf. 11:11; 15:13ff.). It seems to be a term used by the first disciples, who as the friends of Jesus and of one another are also the new friends of God and members of his family. If the term drops out of usage, it comes to expression in the life of the primitive church as depicted in Acts 2:44ff.

d. In the final tribulation friends will turn into enemies in an eschatological version of the common experience of the unreliability of friends.

e. Jesus calls his disciples friends in Lk. 12:4. This could be court style but more likely belongs to the imagery of the family of God. Here is not a friendship of equals but that of the Master and his pupils as he teaches them concerning their future tasks and destiny (cf. Jn. 14:26).

f. Certain parables suggest that God is a friend; cf. Lk. 11:5ff.; 14:11 (God as the host at the eschatological banquet); 16:9 (we are to win God as a friend; cf. vv. 5-7); Mt. 11:19 and parallels (Jesus' love for sinners as an enacted parable expressing the message that God is the friend of sinners).

3. Johannine Writings. John uses *phílos* for "best man" in 3:29 to express the close relationship yet also the subordination of the Baptist to Jesus. The link with joy comes out here and with table fellowship in 12:1ff. (cf. Lk. 10:38ff.). Lazarus is "our friend" in Jn. 11:11. The disciples are friends of Jesus by his free choice (15:13ff.). He remains the Lord, but his commands are commands of love (vv. 14ff.) which he himself fulfils (v. 10). The disciples must show a similar love even to the point of self-offering in death (v. 13). In this regard a rule of friendship serves the NT thought of vicariousness in first a soteriological and then a hortatory sense. 3 John closes with the mutual salutations of friends (v. 15), i.e., fellow believers who are friends by relationship to Jesus. *phílos* is a political term in Jn. 19:12. Association with the court title is present, but the charge expresses a judgment on Pilate's relation to the emperor rather than his stripping of the title.

4. *James.* In Jms. 4:4 to seek the friendship of the world is to become an enemy of God. Abraham is the friend of God in 2:23. The OT rather than Greek or Egyptian usage underlies the description. The link with Gen. 15:6 relates "friend of God" to "just by faith," the passive "is called" implies that it is God who gives the title, and the aorist suggests a specific event in Abraham's life. If the works as an expression of faith have a bearing on the title, the emphasis is on the fact that Abraham is one who is loved and chosen by God, and therefore called his friend.

D. The Post – NT Period.

I. The Early Church.

1. Although the group is little used in this period, we find it in NT quotations even where the NT uses *agapáō* (cf. Did. 1.3; Ignatius *Polycarp* 2.1; 2 Clem. 6.5). The Gospel of Peter 2.3 presents Joseph of Arimathea as a friend of Pilate as well as Jesus.

2. Abraham is commonly referred to as the friend of God (cf. 1 Clem. 10.1; 17.2; Pseudo-Clementine *Homilies* 18.13). Moses, too, is God's friend, and those with whom God is well pleased are his children and friends (Aphrahat in *Homilies* 17.3). True Gnostics, martyrs, and ascetics also receive the title of God's friends (Clement of Alexandria, Tertullian, and Augustine).

3. Apocryphal writings take up the idea that disciples are friends of Jesus (cf. Martyrdom of Peter 10; Acts of John 113).

4. Pagan friendships pose special dangers according to Hermas *Mandates* 10.1.4. Christians forge new friendships with one another based on their union with Christ (cf. Paulinus of Nola and St. Felix).

5. Hermas *Similitudes* 5.2.6ff. depicts the heavenly original of a circle of friends with God as ruler at the center. The friends are the archangels to whom creation is committed and who will perfect the church (*Similitudes* 5.4.1).

II. Gnosticism. Conversations between the redeemer and the redeemed reflect a special vocabulary of friendship, as in Manichean hymns. At issue is the reciprocity of love in mystical union. [G. STÄHLIN, IX, 113-71]

→ *agapáō, adelphós, aspázomai, hetaíros, xénos, plēsíon, proskynéō, syngenḗs*

philḗdonos → *hēdonḗ; philoxenía, philóxenos* → *xénos*

---

philosophía [philosophy], *philósophos* [philosopher]

A. Usage outside the Bible.

1. To Sophism. These words are late constructs. The *philo-* denotes willing intercourse with people, zealous handling of affairs, or active striving toward a goal. The question of the basis of all things arises in the sixth century B.C., and varied experience and observation are linked to the acquiring of knowledge. The Sophists use *philosophéō* for methodical research and reflection in ethics. The *philósophos* is one who, unable to reach true knowledge, achieves practical insight by external study.

Since the presentation of things is important, rhetoric forms a good part of *philosophía*. It attempts to show the truth of things by etymology or logic.

2. *Plato and Aristotle.*

a. In showing by way of transmigration that humanity is part of the immutable being of ideas, Plato uses the *philosoph-* group to denote a basic possibility of life. Change comes in dialogical encounter with the *philósophos,* who is capable of instruction, and is therefore a reorientation. The Platonic school thus takes on the character of a living fellowship. Fundamental is the link between striving for truth and educational and political action.

b. Aristotle uses *philosophéō* for systematic efforts to understand the world, especially by sensory perception. The aim is to reduce phenomena to principles and hence to achieve knowledge of eternal and unmoved being. *philosophía* is both knowledge as a whole and the individual discipline. The science devoted to the unmoved mover is the *prótē philosophía*. Physics, dealing with sensory phenomena, is the *deutéra philosophía*. Aristotle has no comprehensive system that assigns a place to each branch of learning, but he lays a foundation that enables Hellenistic metaphysics both to seek a concept for the unity of the world and to bring all reality within the range of its investigations.

3. *The Hellenistic Period.*

a. Various schools develop with sharp debates between their representatives, who form the educated class in the state and a special group in politics. With the older Academicians and Peripatetics, Epicurus heads one important school. He makes sensory perception the measure of knowledge. His system banishes superstition and produces a hedonistic ethics. Passionless *hēdonḗ* is achieved in a school united in *philía*. Excessive emotion that might bring about disorders is to be avoided. Although deity is spiritualized, the Epicureans still find a place for the cultus.

b. Zeno establishes Stoicism in Athens ca. 301 B.C. The action of a principle on matter explains becoming. Logic, physics, and ethics are the main fields of inquiry. The goal is progress in right conduct. The term *philósophos* is not a common one; it is used for those who work in the three areas of philosophy, or for the ideal Stoic sage.

c. Poseidonius gives philosophy the task of probing the basic causes of things. Individual disciplines describe reality, and philosophy utilizes their results to work out the principles or nexus of being. If philosophy is viewed as a living creature, physics is the flesh and blood, logic the sinews, and ethics the soul. Life in the cosmos shares in the divine spirit. This is especially true of human rationality. Union with the divine gives rise to primal religion. As the union dissolves, acquired religions develop, though these owe their force to primal religion. The poet, artist, lawgiver, and philosopher are all interpreters of immortal nature, but the philosopher is the best.

d. With the rise of the empire Rome becomes the center of philosophical debate. Seneca does not agree that arts and crafts are products of philosophy. As Stoic concentration on lifestyle intensifies, philosophy is viewed increasingly as the right way of living. It is a message of salvation for the soul with moral perfection as the goal. In polytheism one may see an expression of the operation of the universal *lógos* in natural forces. Demons are manifestations of cosmic life, and the *daimónion* plays a role in personal destiny. As Stoics and Epicureans both seek liberation from stress by education in the art of living, but in different ways, they become bitter rivals.

e. Middle Platonism is eclectic. The goal of philosophy is to achieve likeness to God, which stands related to moral action. Philosophy is also defined as a practicing of death.

4. The Group in Relation to Eastern Wisdom and Religion. Alexander's campaigns introduce the Greeks to eastern wisdom, which reminds them of Greek philosophy. The Druids and Chaldeans are also seen to relate their lives to wisdom, and the Jews are *philósophoi* for Clearchus. The Hermetic writings contain a fusion of Greek philosophy with wisdom or mythology which links salvation to knowledge. True philosophy is contemplation and piety with an orientation to knowledge of God. Alchemy also uses the group. The philosopher, having insight into the secrets of nature, can bring about transmutations. As an expert in such processes, he shapes his life in a manner suited to his exalted position.

B. Hellenistic Judaism.

1. The LXX. In the LXX the group occurs only in Daniel and 4 Maccabees. The magicians and enchanters of Dan. 1:20 are *sóphoi kaí philósophoi.* 4 Maccabees links the martyr principle to the Stoic teaching that reason is the mistress of impulse. The Jewish religion teaches three cardinal virtues, and the death of Eleazar demonstrates its philosophical authenticity (5:23-24; 7:9-10).

2. The Epistle of Aristeas. This work stresses the recognition of Jewish wisdom by representatives of Hellenistic learning (200-201). The Jewish envoys reflect philosophical insights with practical living as the main concern (207). Only those who know God can achieve this (256). The law deserves a place in the library at Alexandria inasmuch as it meets Hellenistic criteria (30-31).

3. Philo compares and relates philosophical knowledge and biblical wisdom. Philosophical exegesis elucidates the biblical tradition, which in turn corrects what philosophy teaches. General culture is a prerequisite of virtue, but it is subject to wisdom, and to glorify God is the goal of wisdom. Knowledge begins with sensory perception and leads by contemplation of the cosmos to worship of the Creator. Wisdom forms the link between the Hellenistic tradition and the biblical tradition. Only revelation can bring us to the final stage of knowledge. By revelation Moses stands on the pinnacle of philosophy.

4. Josephus. Josephus makes no great use of the group. He quotes philosophers, applies the terms to barbarian sages, regards the Greeks as pupils of the Jews, and finds Jewish superiority in the general possibility of faith in God in Israel. At times he uses the group for Jewish instruction and he also describes as philosophical schools the religio-political groupings of the Jewish people, comparing the Essenes to the Pythagoreans and the Pharisees to the Stoics.

C. Rabbinic Judaism.

The rabbis describe as philosophers the representatives of the philosophical schools, accomplished orators, and royal advisers. They also adopt certain insights and comparisons from popular Greek philosophy. But they are conscious of Jewish superiority and reject motifs that are alien to their own system of instruction. Thus in various debates a representative philosopher challenges Israel's faith with a polemical question or thesis, but is repulsed with a wisdom-like answer. Tradition and succession are built up in rabbinism as in the Greek schools.

D. The NT.

1. On the basis of the LXX various concepts pass with the Greek language into the NT. Thus we find the thought-forms of physics in Jn. 1:1ff., and expressions from philosophical anthropology and ethics in Rom. 1:20, 28; 1 Cor. 11:13ff.; Jms. 3:3ff. Yet the NT uses such concepts or expressions only as they contribute to the presentation, elucidation, or establishment of the gospel. The central theme of God's escha-

tological action in fulfilment of his goal for Israel and the world is neither related to philosophy nor dependent on it. Indeed, it calls the goal of philosophy in question and contradicts it with Semitic concepts that are an irrevocable part of its message.

2. The only NT instance of *philosophía* is in Col. 2:8. What Paul has in view here is not philosophy in general but the teaching of a syncretistic religious group that claims special insight into God, Christ, astral powers, and creation, that imposes a set of rules on its members, and that bases the authority of its message on its age or esoteric nature. The group itself probably argues that its teaching is *philosophía*; hence Paul's use of the term and his equation of it with "empty deceit." For Paul himself the gospel is not *philosophía* but a distinctive form of *sophía*.

3. Acts 17:18 records an encounter between Paul and the Epicureans and Stoics. The wording suggests that the former respond with disparagement, the latter with interest. *spermológos* has the sense of "pseudo-philosopher" and carries the implication that the philosophical schools are the mediators of true instruction. The Stoics, however, seek universal fellowship and aim to honor all deities; they are thus more open to Paul as the preacher of a Near Eastern cult. The address in vv. 22ff. points out that veneration of the gods is incompatible with the nature and works of the one true God. It takes the form, not of a debate, but of a criticism of pagan worship and a call for repentance.

E. Gnosticism. The group plays no part in later Gnosticism. In Acts of Thomas 139 *philosophía* is a Christian virtue; as love of God's wisdom it stands in contrast to human wisdom.

F. Apologists. The Apologists use the group to assert their claim to truth. They contrast the wisdom of God with philosophical babbling (Theophilus *To Autolycus* 2.15). Philosophy is essential to understanding (Justin *Dialogue* 2.3). Governed by Christ the Logos, Christians are the true philosophers (*Apology* 46). Along these lines the group seems to offer an apt basis for mediating the gospel in educated circles.

[O. MICHEL, IX, 172-88]

---

phobéō [to fear, reverence],   *phobéomai* [to be afraid],   *phóbos* [fear],   *déos* [fear, awe]

A. The Greeks.

1. Derivation, Meaning, and History of the Group. Basic to the group is the primary verb *phébomai,* "to flee." As an emotion develops from the action, being startled and running away suggest "fear." The older word for "fear" is *déos.* This is "apprehension," while *phóbos* is "fright" or "panic."

2. General Usage. In ordinary use the group has the nuances of "flight," "fright," "apprehension," "anxiety," and "awe."

3. The God Phóbos. In Greek superstition *Phóbos* is a powerful deity, the son of Ares, and a god of war. Sparta has a temple to *Phóbos.* He is depicted in a fear-inspiring form that actualizes the god of terror presented by Homer.

4. Evaluation of Fear.

a. Ordinary Speech. Since fear brings oppression and anxiety, absence of fear is worth seeking, as proverbial sayings show. The characters in tragedy are filled with a dread of fate and the unknown future that is comparable to the terror of a helpless animal. Choral songs that suck the audience into the action express the fear. If Aristotle sees a purging here, the poets themselves are more concerned about the ineluctability of destiny. Fear is also an important motive in exhortation. It is an unavoidable basis of respect for both human and divine authorities. To repudiate fear is to promote anarchy. Epiphanies of divine power evoke a fear that calming self-declarations of deity then allay. Outstanding personages can evoke the same reaction. In ordinary use, then, fear may be rejected or it may be accepted as inescapable in the face of certain structures of dependence and force. The meaning covers anxiety and respect as well as fear or terror.

b. Philosophy. From its origins, philosophy discusses fear. The pre-Socratics sharply criticize emotional fear. Talk about fear of God is invented to frighten people. Aristotle differentiates this fear, which has physiological relations, from proper awe or reverence. As in Socrates and Plato, it is caused by a threat to existence, which can cause pity when we see it in others. The Stoics define fear psychologically as an irrational emotion that we should resist. A true relation to God as author and father frees us from emotional fear of God, fear of tyrants is nonsensical since we need fear only what we do to ourselves, and fear of death is childish. The Epicureans, too, condemn fear of the future and of death. Yet fear has some place in philosophy. Thus Plato teaches fear of wrongdoing, and he thinks fear of God is natural in education. Plutarch argues that fear of God and fear of death are unavoidable; even Epicurus has to admit that death usually means pain, and rejection of a true fear of God results in the false fear of superstition. In general, philosophy agrees in rejecting emotional fear, but when *phóbos* has the sense of awe or reverence it regards these as imperative and unavoidable reactions to the claim of authorities and especially of the gods.

[H. BALZ, IX, 189-97]

B. The OT.

I. Occurrence and Equivalents.

1. In most cases in the OT *phobéomai* is used for the stem *yr'*, "to be afraid," "to have in honor." In seven instances it is used for *phd*, "to quake." We also find it for various other terms, and it occurs without an original in apocryphal works.

2. *phóbos* is the equivalent noun for the same stems in the sense of "fear" or "quaking," and so, too, is *phoberós* (*phoberós*) for "feared" or "terrible" ("terribly").

3. *déos* occurs only in 2 Maccabees.

4. The two chief Hebrew stems are mostly rendered by the *phob-* group.

II. The Stem yr' in the OT.

1. Meaning.

a. Originally meaning "to tremble," the verb of the group means "to fear" or, more weakly, "to honor."

b. The noun has the sense of "fear" but mostly signifies "respect."

2. Human Fear. Humans are the main subjects of fear in the OT (cf. Isaac in Gen. 26:7, David in 1 Sam. 21:13, the Aramaeans in 2 Sam. 10:19). The reasons for fear are war, death, enslavement, loss of a wife or child, disaster, or a place. Individuals like Goliath occasion fear, as do wild beasts, the desert, or the sea. The fearful are excluded from the army (Dt. 20:8); the death penalty is a deterrent (13:11). Trust in God brings freedom from fear, which is a promised eschatological blessing in Is. 54:14. Fear arises in the presence of those who stand in a special relation to God, like Moses in Ex. 34:30, Joshua in Josh. 4:14, or Samuel in 1 Sam. 12:18. Lev. 19:30 demands fear of the sanctuary.

3. *Fear of God.*

a. God can be a threat (Is. 8:12-13), for his acts are terrible (Dt. 4:34), and so is God himself (Ex. 15:11) or his day (Joel 2:11).

b. Fear of God takes the form of reverent and submissive recognition in trust and obedience. Hence those who fear God are reliable (Ex. 18:21). Fear of God results from hearing the law (Dt. 4:10). It is the same as serving God or treading his way (Dt. 6:13; 8:6). Fear of God is more than an attitude; it is observance of moral and cultic demands. It thus excludes fear of the punishment that overtakes those who do not fear God (Dt. 6:13ff.).

c. By hearkening to wisdom one comes to understand the fear of God (Prov. 2:5). This fear is integral to a purposeful life that is pleasing to God, and as such it is the beginning of wisdom (Prov. 1:7; Ps. 111:10). It has a moral orientation as the avoidance of evil (Ps. 34:11) or the hatred of sin (Prov. 23:17). It brings wealth, honor, and life (Prov. 22:4). It promotes confidence and is a refuge (14:26).

d. A special group in the Psalms consists of those who fear God, lauding his name (Ps. 22:22-23), hoping in him (147:11), and sacrificing in the temple (66:16). God looks on these people (33:18) and has pity on them (103:13). They are the righteous in the congregation (145:19; 115:11; cf. Mal. 3:16).

e. In Pss. 1:2; 19:7ff.; 119:33ff. the stress is on the fact that those who fear God faithfully observe the law.

4. *The Formula "Fear Not."*

This formula occurs 75 times in the OT and is spoken in reassurance by God, by those commissioned by him, or simply by one person to another. It has a place in the oracle of salvation in Is. 41:10, 13-14, and counteracts terror in theophanies in Ex. 20:20; Dan. 12:19.

III. *The Stem phd in the OT.*

1. *Linguistic Aspects.*

a. The original sense of the verb of this stem is "to quake," "to tremble."

b. The noun denotes "trembling" or "fear," and only rarely "respect" (2 Chr. 19:7, and perhaps Ps. 36:1).

2. *Material Aspects.*

a. Found mostly in later works, the stem has the sense of anxious uncertainty or disquiet (Dt. 28:65ff.). Calamitous situations cause panic (cf. the terrors of the night in Ps. 91:4 or fear of battle in Job 39:22).

b. The stem can also denote fear at God's acts (Is. 19:16-17) or word (Jer. 36:16). God himself as well as his acts can evoke terror.

c. In Gen. 31:42, 53 "Fear of Isaac" is a divine name. The meaning seems to be that God is the object of Isaac's reverence; "kinsman" is the sense of *pahad* here.

IV. *The Apocrypha.*

The situation in the Apocrypha is much the same as in the OT. We find fear of war, disaster, supernatural events, and also fear of God in the religious, legal, or cultic sense. In the Epistle of Jeremiah and 4 Maccabees fear is the antithesis of obedience; Stoic influence may be seen in the way that 4 Maccabees contrasts fear of death with obedience, while the Epistle of Jeremiah tries to ward off apostasy by showing that idols are not gods and that therefore one need not fear them.

[G. WANKE, IX, 197-205]

C. Palestinian and Hellenistic Judaism.

1. *The Pseudepigrapha.*

The Testaments of the Twelve develops the theme of the fear of the Lord. This fear is seated in the heart, leads to love, means renouncing Satan and avoiding evil, and confers a wisdom that one can never lose. Other works state that fear of God produces respect for parents, is the beginning of all good things, and differs from the fear (e.g., of death) that perverts the heart.

b. More common in apocalyptic is fear at epiphanies. The righteous will die, but they need not fear sinners or enemies, for God comforts them by revealing future salvation. Sinners do not fear the Lord, but the last judgment will plunge them into terror. Even the righteous will be afraid in the divine judgment, but sevenfold joy awaits them.

2. *Qumran.* The righteous at Qumran are aware of being among those who fear God. There is terror at the judgment, and God is terrible in his acts. The children of the light have no reason to be afraid in battle.

3. *Rabbinic Writings.* Fear of God is basic for the righteous. It includes fear of sin and stands related to love of God, which is rated higher. Among Gentiles we find a group of God-fearers (*sebómenoi*) who venerate the God of Israel but do not accept circumcision (cf. *phoboúmenoi* in 2 Chr. 5:6 LXX).

4. *Philo and Josephus.*

a. Although Philo adopts the OT concept of the fear of God, he stresses the fact that God is an antidote to fear and finds in love rather than fear the main motive for the righteous. Fear, however, has a place in education.

b. Josephus uses the group for "fear" (in war, or of death or punishment), "anxiety," and "reverence," and uses *déos* in much the same way. He adopts Hellenistic terms (e.g., *deisidaimonía*) rather than the *phob-* group for fear of God.

D. The NT.

1. *General Usage.* The NT uses the group some 158 times (*phobéomai* 95 times, *phóbos* 47). The main examples are in the Gospels and Acts, although Paul makes common use of the noun. With an infinitive the verb means "to be afraid to . . ." and, with *mḗ*, "to be afraid that. . . ." The fear may be that of individuals or of the whole people. Mostly the concepts are traditional. The NT opposes all hampering anxiety but relates fear of God to faith as total trust.

2. *The Epiphany of the Kingdom and Fear.*

a. The incomprehensible nature of Jesus' mighty acts arouses fear in the spectators and in those affected, e.g., at the stilling of the storm in Mk. 4:41, the curing of the demoniac in 5:15, the raising of the young man at Nain in Lk. 7:16. In the infancy stories fear comes on those to whom the angel appears (1:12) or who experience a divine miracle (1:65). Fear plays an important role at the transfiguration, whether at entry into the cloud (Lk. 9:34), at hearing the voice (Mt. 17:6), or at the whole incident as a divine epiphany (Mk. 9:6). This fear differs from dread at visions (Rev. 11:11) or the terror of the wicked at the eschaton (Lk. 21:26). It is like the fear of the church in its experiences of salvation (Acts 2:43; 5:5; 19:17). It rules out ordinary fear but arouses fear of him who can cast into hell (Lk. 12:4-5).

b. News of the resurrection causes fear and astonishment (Mk. 16:8). This reaction might be the real climax of Mark, but fear and silence hardly seem to be fitting as the final word of the gospel, for surely the postresurrection life does not stand under the sign of fear. What the women fear is not the resurrection itself but the empty tomb and the strange message of the angel. Mt. 28:8 adds the element of joy to the fear, and Lk. 24:22 refers only to astonishment and joy.

c. The summons "Fear not" occurs in the Gospels too. Jairus is not to be anxious in Mk. 5:36, the disciples receive reassurance in 6:50, the three at the transfiguration are enabled to look up in Mt. 17:7, the women's fear gives way to proclamation and faith in 28:10, those whom the angels visit in the infancy stories are told not to fear in Lk. 1:13, 30; 2:10, and Peter and Paul (in a vision) are told the same thing by the Lord in a context of discipleship and service (Lk. 5:10; Acts 18:9).

3. *The Fear of God in Formulas.* Luke likes the formula "to fear God" (cf. 1:50; 18:2; 23:40). Acts uses *phoboúmenos(oi)* five times (10:2; 22, 35; 13:16, 26; *seboúmenos[oi]* six times) for Gentile adherents to the Jewish faith. These "God-fearers" form the starting point for the Gentile mission in Acts 10 (and cf. Paul's practice in ch. 13).

4. *Faith and Fear.* Like Jesus, Paul shows that fear can be an essential part of faith even though faith rules out anxiety. Believers are to fear the divine judgment (Rom. 11:20). But they need not fear an uncertain state after death (2 Cor. 5:6ff.). Paul knows fear because of the human weakness of his preaching (1 Cor. 2:3-4; cf. 2 Cor. 7:15). The self-sacrifice of Christ makes possible only an attitude of humble acceptance of God's will (in fear and trembling; Phil. 2:12). There is no anxiety in this fear, for it is that of God's children (Rom. 8:15). They need fear neither suffering nor death (1 Pet. 3:14; Heb. 2:15), for Christ has freed them from the bondage of death and they know that God helps them in all things (Heb. 13:6). Nevertheless, they fear and reverence God as the holy God in both grace and wrath; they are to worship him with reverence and awe (*metá eulabeías kaí déous*) (Heb. 12:28).

5. *Fear in Exhortation.* Paul refers to fear of punishment by the authorities in Rom. 13:3. Recognition of their divine function, however, makes fear unnecessary (vv. 3ff.). The work of love comes to terms with the valid claims of the authorities and hence rules out fear. Those who are born of God, knowing that God will not punish them, no longer know any fear (1 Jn. 4:17-18). They have a confidence that means an open relationship to both God and others. Fear is a basis of action in Acts 9:31. With holiness and prayer, it characterizes those who are freed from their futile ways (1 Pet. 1:17). It liberates from human intimidation (3:6), although there must still be fear of defilement (Jude 23). Fear as respect still has a place in human relationships (1 Pet. 2:18; 3:2; Eph. 6:5; Col. 3:22) but only on the basis of fear of God (1 Pet. 2:17). All believers are finally to be subject to one another in the fear of Christ (Eph. 5:21). Precisely because reverence is due to Christ, the point of all these admonitions lies in the demand for a pure, patient, and gentle heart (Col. 3:22; Eph. 6:5; 1 Pet. 3:2, 4).

E. The Early Church and Gnosticism.

1. *The Early Church.* The group is a favorite one in the apostolic fathers. We increasingly find the fear of God in formulas (Barn. 10.10-11; Did. 4.9). Fear of God banishes other fears (2 Clem. 4.4) but not fear of judgment (Ignatius *Ephesians* 11.1) or fear of Satan's works (Hermas *Mandates* 7.3). After faith, fear is a decisive work (Hermas *Mandates* 8.89), a fruit of the Spirit (Barn. 11.11), that helps us resist evil (Hermas *Mandates* 12.2.4). Fear as respect plays a role in relationships, e.g., of children to parents (Pol. 4.2) or subjects to rulers (Barn. 19.5). Clement of Alexandria finds a logical place for fear in *Stromateis* 2.7.32.1ff. True fear is a response to God's commands (4.3.9.5ff.). *phóbos* checks licentiousness and *déos* frees us from bad impulses (2.8.39.1ff.). Tertullian relates fear to penitence (*On Penitence* 2.1-2; 5.3-4; 6.14ff.).

2. *Gnosticism.* The Hermetic writings contain a personification of *Phóbos*. In Christian Gnosticism Adam takes over the original fear of primal man. The corporeal elements arise from *phóbos,* and *phóbos* also passes into psychic things. We also read of a demon of fear that is nourished on matter and creates passion. Echoes of the

biblical motif of fear of God also occur, yet the righteous who stand against wickedness need not tremble, for knowledge of redemption liberates them from fear.

[H. BALZ, IX, 205-19]

phoréō, phóros, phortízō, phortíon → *phérō*

---

phrḗn [mind, understanding], *áphrōn* [foolish], *aphrosýnē* [folly], *phronéō* [to think], *phrónēma* [thought], *phrónēsis* [thinking], *phrónimos* [thoughtful]

A. The Greek-Hellenistic World.

1. History and Oldest Sense. *phrḗn,* or plural *phrénes,* means "diaphragm," regarded as the seat of mental and spiritual activity, then "mind" or "understanding." The compounds reflect the intellectual focus, *phronéō* usually means "to think" or "to plan," and the nouns *phrónēma* and *phrónēsis* mean "thought," "thinking," or "reason."

2. From Homer to the Classical Period. Homer refers to the possibilities of a sound or sick development of the mind. Aeschylus uses *phrḗn* for the "disposition"; this may be arrogant or rational. *aphrosýnē* is a term for "youthful folly," while *áphrōn* means "out of one's mind." *phronéō* occurs for "to have understanding" but also "to intend," and we find *phrónēsis* for divine "counsel" and *phrónēma* for human "pride" or "arrogance."

3. phrónēsis and Cognates in Philosophy.

a. Plato uses *phrḗn* in the physical sense and also for the inner person. The soul has *phrónēsis* ("receptivity") prior to being in us. *sophía* differs from the more practical *phrónēsis,* but the two are also interchangeable. *phrónēsis* is the right state of the intellect and the source of virtue. Education is admonition in *phrónēsis* and truth. *phrónēsis* is the chief virtue. All culture is linked to it. It is a divine gift that should guide lawgivers and that directs the mind to immortality. *phrónēma* is the disposition, the intellectual and spiritual attitude, or self-confidence, which may produce arrogance if based on physical fitness alone.

b. Aristotle uses *phrḗn* only in quotations. *phronéō* as the ability to comprehend belongs only to the few. *phrónēsis* is God's gift; it is moral insight or knowledge leading to a virtuous life. As practical acumen it differs from theoretical wisdom.

c. In Stoicism the three other cardinal virtues proceed from *phrónēsis* or *sophía.* Since philosophy and virtue are one, *phrónēsis* is integral to philosophy.

d. In Neo-Platonism *phrónēsis* is an emanation ruled by *noús.* The rational soul is beautiful. Regard for *noús* is *phrónēsis.* *phrónēsis* is the intellectual activity of an individual soul related to a body. By a later tradition labor and training precede *phrónēsis* (cf. the discussion of *phýsis, máthēsis,* and virtue in Plato).

e. In popular usage we find the term on magical papyri, in Gnostic texts, and in a legal context (for "competence").

B. The OT.

1. Reason, Insight, and Cleverness. There is no single Hebrew original for the group. The LXX uses only the plural *phrénes,* which occurs seven times in Proverbs (*phrónēsis* in 9:16). *phrónimos* has a negative accent in Gen. 3:1 (cf. *phrónēsis* for presumptuous cleverness in Job 5:13). Wisdom in government is the point in Ezek. 28:4 (cf. 1 Kgs. 3; Wis. 7:7; also Is. 44:28 LXX). *phronéō* and *phrónēsis* occur in the negative with reference to idol worship in Is. 44:18-19.

2. Negative Expressions. Vaunting human reason is folly (*áphrōn, aphrosýnē*). The *áphrōn* is the fool (who denies God) in the Psalms. In Proverbs *áphrōn* refers to the simple or inexperienced person. *phrónimos* occurs in Prov. 14:17, and *aphrosýnē* is used for "misdeed" in Judg. 20:6.

3. Theological and Ethical Significance. God's *phrónēsis* is unsearchable (Is. 40:28). By it he has set up the world. It is parallel to his power and wisdom. In us *phrónēsis*, which is from God, goes with *sophía* and *aísthēsis* ("understanding, wisdom, and knowledge"). The three constitute a unity as practical wisdom with a religious slant. *phrónēsis* is the principle of creation, and God gives us a share in it. In Sirach *phrónēsis*, with wisdom, is subordinate to the fear of God. Wisdom puts *phrónēsis* under *sophía*, but both are hypostases, and with wisdom *phrónēsis* is an architect of the universe. 4 Macc. 1:2 makes *phrónēsis* the chief virtue. 1 and 2 Maccabees use the group for perception, disposition, but also arrogance. In 4 Macc. 7:17 lack of understanding means lack of control of the impulses.

C. Judaism.

1. Qumran. The Hebrew terms behind *phrónēsis* occur in the Qumran writings for the divine insight or wisdom that God has also given to us. Those outside the community are fools or simpletons. Wisdom and folly do battle in the heart. Various terms are used for planning evil, for plotting, for aberration, for trickery, and for leading astray. The gifts of knowledge combine with humility and mercy to differentiate members of the community from outsiders. Knowledge is an outworking of salvation with an eschatological hope for the destruction of folly.

2. Hellenistic Judaism.

a. Pseudepigrapha. In older works the occurrence of the group is haphazard and rare. The Epistle of Aristeas 124 uses *phrónēsis* in an imprecise sense for "understanding." Test. Naph. 2:8 says that God has made the heart for understanding. The sin of Shechem is folly in Test. Levi 7:2-3. Sib. 5.366 echoes Gen. 3:1, and Greek En. 32:3 alludes to the tree of knowledge in Gen. 2:9, 17.

b. Philo. For Philo God has the fullness of *phrónēsis*. He dispenses it to the race. The river Phison represents *phrónēsis*. Humanity comprises both *phrónēsis* and its opposite *aphrosýnē*. As practical wisdom, *phrónēsis* is a virtuous mean. It is the eye of the soul and imperishable in the species. In education fear is needed against *aphrosýnē*, but unless one sees that God alone is wise our own *phrónēsis* is arrogance. *aphrosýnē* is poison, sickness, or drunkenness. God is the Lord of fools, admonishing or destroying them. Polytheism leads to atheism among the irrational.

c. Josephus. *phrénes* is for Josephus a parallel term to *noús*. The soul has lost its rational understanding. *áphrōn* and *aphrosýnē* denote youthful folly or lack of restraint. *phronéō* has to do with the disposition and occurs in expressions meaning "to lose heart," "to plan on," or "to think arrogantly." *phrónēsis*, a divine gift, refers to right thinking oriented to God. It is practical wisdom. *phrónēma* means much the same but with more stress on action; it sometimes means "courage," but it also denotes "arrogance." *phrónimos*, meaning "rational," "clever," or "prudent," is rare.

d. Rabbinic Use. The area in rabbinic works that corresponds to the Greek group is controlled by the idea of wisdom or understanding with a moral reference.

D. The NT.

1. phrénes. To prefer tongues, according to 1 Cor. 14:20, is to be childish. The Corinthians should use reason and press on to maturity.

1278

2. *áphrōn, aphrosýnē*.

a. The Synoptists. In Lk. 11:40 Jesus challenges the Pharisees. In their concern for ritual purity and neglect of moral purity they are fools even though they think of themselves as correctors of the foolish (Rom. 2:20). Implied is the charge that they do not truly know God. In Lk. 12:20 the folly of the rich farmer is that he does not reckon with God and thus lulls himself into false security. Folly is one of the vices that issues from within in Mk. 7:21-22. The arrangement seems to be arbitrary, but *aphrosýnē* perhaps comes at the end as the chief or basic sin.

b. Paul. In Rom. 2:20 Paul is expressing the Jewish standpoint. He docs not pronounce judgment in 1 Cor. 15:36, but makes a rhetorical appeal for understanding. Self-criticism comes to expression in 2 Cor. 11–12. To meet his opponents Paul sets himself on the plane of carnal boasting. Since the clever Corinthians have submitted to the claims of fools, Paul, speaking foolishly, will surpass them all (11:16ff.). He does so by boasting of his sufferings. Here, then, is no folly but truth (12:6). In Eph. 5:17 *aphrosýnē* is foolish or careless conduct on the part of believers. Its opposite is understanding God's will; this will is that by good conduct they should silence the ignorance of foolish people (1 Pet. 2:15).

3. *phronéō, phrónēma*.

a. Mark, Matthew, and Acts. In Mk. 8:33 and parallels Jesus sharply rebukes Peter; he can grasp only human thoughts with a focus on earthly life. In Acts 28:22 the Jewish leaders want Paul to state his own views regarding the new "sect."

b. Paul. In Phil. 3:19 Paul refers to those whose minds are set on earthly things (in contrast cf. vv. 14-15; Col. 3:1-2). Rom. 11:20 warns the church against arrogance. Believers are not to be wise in their own conceits (11:25; 12:17) but are to associate with the lowly. Rom. 12:3 counsels sober aspiration. We are not to aim so high that we miss the goal. Paul's goal in Phil. 2:2 is a common mind, for which confession of Christ is the norm (2:5), in a fellowship that Christ himself has instituted (cf. 4:2). With this mind believers will reject any other message (Gal. 5:10). A like mind is also the theme in 2 Cor. 13:11 and Rom. 15:5. "Observance" is the meaning of *phronéō* in Rom. 14:6. We are not to observe rules but to make responsible judgments. Maturity means setting aside childish reasoning (1 Cor. 13:11). In Phil. 1:7; 4:10 *phronéō hypér* or *epí* carries the thought of "concern" in both thought and act.

4. *phrónēsis*. In Lk. 1:17, in a liturgical context, the forerunner's task is to bring back the disobedient to the manner of thought and conduct of the just. Eph. 1:8 also has a liturgical ring; God has graciously endowed us with wisdom and understanding whereby we know the mystery of his will.

5. *phrónimos*.

a. Matthew and Luke. In Mt. 7:24 the doer of the word is like a wise or prudent builder, although the motif of prudence is secondary here. In Mt. 25:1ff. wisdom is preparedness, for everything depends on encounter with the Lord. Cunning in the sense of cleverly resolute action in a hopeless situation is the point in Lk. 16:8. In these parables *phrónimos* applies to those who have grasped their eschatological position. Mt. 10:16 is perhaps a proverbial saying; it carries some allusion to Gen. 3:1.

b. Paul. Paul uses *phrónimos* along with *phronéō* in Rom. 11:25 and 12:20. He employs *phrónimoi* dialectically in 1 Cor. 4:10. In 1 Cor. 10:15 he presupposes a power of judgment, but in 14:20 this is the subject of an admonition, and the use is ironical in 2 Cor. 11:19.

E. The Apostolic Fathers and Apologists.

1. The disputes at Corinth in 1 Clement are between the wise and arrogant fools; the author (cf. also 2 Clement) counsels humility and concord. Ignatius *Magnesians* 3.1 demands an understanding attitude. Idolatry is folly in Diog. 3.3. In Hermas *Mandates* 3.4 *phronéō* relates to right thinking, but the author deplores the lack of understanding in himself and others (*Visions* 5.4; *Similitudes* 9.22.2-3). Baptism confers a common mind in a unity of faith and love (*Similitudes* 9.17.2).

2. Aristides *Apology* 8.1; 14.1 thinks that the wise among pagans are fools. Justin *Dialogue* 5.4-5 refers to the folly of souls (in opposition to Plato). Opposing false gods, Athenagoras (*Supplication* 22.5) quotes the equation of Athene and *phrónēsis*.

3. Gnosticism includes *phrónēsis* in its mythological constructions. It is part of a series that includes *noús, lógos,* etc., or *cháris, sýnesis,* etc. In opposition to Gnosticism the Epistle of the Apostles 43ff. puts knowledge and understanding among the foolish virgins; the five wise virgins are faith, love, grace, peace, and hope.

4. In official usage *phrónēsis* is a form of episcopal address (*prudentia* in Latin).

[G. BERTRAM, IX, 220-35]

> *phylássō* [to protect, watch],   *phylakḗ* [watch, prison]

phylássō.

A. Nonbiblical Greek.

1. Homer to Aristotle. From *phýlax* ("watchman"), the verb *phylássō* means "to protect," "to watch," "to guard," "to care for," "to note," "to observe," "to keep," in the middle "to be on guard," and intransitively "to be awake."

2. Hellenistic Usage. The term finds a use for guard duty, also for God's keeping, for keeping deposited goods, and in legal contracts.

B. The OT and Judaism.

1. The LXX.

a. *phylássō* occurs 471 times for *šmr* and 379 times for *nṣr.*

b. In the middle it can express the required attitude to the covenant (Ex. 19:5) and to cultic laws etc. In Judg. 2:22 etc. it means "keeping to" God's ways. We also find "keeping" knowledge, truth, righteousness, peace, etc. (Mal. 2:7; Is. 26:2-3).

c. The verb expresses God's attitude too; God observes, guard, protects, etc. (Job 13:27; 10:14). He cares for animals and men (Job 39:1; Jer. 5:24). He is the Guardian or Watcher (Pss. 12:7; 17:1, etc.). He watches over Israel (Ps. 121:4), keeps the city (127:1), and watches over aliens, the poor, the righteous, etc. (146:9; 97:10). He keeps his covenant (1 Kgs. 3:6) and maintains truth (Ps. 146:6). He spares the wicked for the evil day (Prov. 16:9). Yet he does not keep his wrath forever (Jer. 3:5).

2. Qumran. Qumran stresses the keeping of the law etc., maintaining faithfulness, and keeping oaths, but in the background is God who keeps his covenant and thus preserves the righteous.

3. Philo and Josephus.

a. Keeping in mind is the goal for Philo on the basis of Gen. 4:9 and Num. 8:26.

b. Josephus repeats Dt. 22:5 in *Antiquities* 4.301. The Essenes call for observing rights and for keeping oneself from unholy gain. Keeping the law etc. is important for Josephus. His people must protect customs and maintain piety. Politically and militarily the verb is used for keeping treaties, as well as for protecting, besieging, occupying, and holding captive.

4. Apocrypha and Pseudepigrapha. Here we find the familiar ideas of keeping truth, of preserving one's heritage, and of God's upholding (of the kingly power of Judah).

5. The Rabbinic Tradition. The rabbis both guard the law and observe it. The patriarchs are thought to have kept the whole law.

C. The NT.

1. The Gospels and Acts. In Mk. 10:20 and parallels the verb expresses the legal piety of the rich young ruler. Jesus in Lk. 11:28 blesses those who hear the word and keep it (cf. 8:21). Hearing and observing are christologically oriented in Jn. 12:47. Not to keep Christ's words means judgment (cf. doing the truth in 3:21; 1 Jn. 1:6). In Acts 7:53 Stephen accuses his hearers of not keeping the law. Paul is challenged to show himself to be living in observance of the law in Acts 21:24, and in 16:4 he delivers the rulings of the council so that they may be observed (in the preciser sense of "keeping from"; cf. 15:20). In Lk. 4:10 Satan tempts Jesus to claim the protection of Ps. 91:11. In Jn. 17:12 he himself keeps those whom the Father has given him. In Jn. 12:25 those who sacrifice their lives will keep them to eternal life.

2. The Epistles. In Rom. 2:26 Gentile observance of the statutes of the law reverses the relation between Jews and Gentiles in view of Jewish nonobservance. In Gal. 6:13 Paul's opponents are zealous for the law but do not keep it. The author of 1 Timothy asks for observance of his directions in 5:21 and for keeping of the faith in 6:20. Believers are to keep themselves from idols (1 Jn. 5:21). God will keep against evil (2 Th. 3:3) or keep from falling (Jude 24). Noah became a preacher of righteousness as God kept him (2 Pet. 3:5). The secular senses of guarding or holding captive occur in, e.g., Lk. 11:21; 8:29; Acts 12:4.

D. Early Christianity. We find the sense "to keep" in Justin *Dialogue* 46.1ff. True death is "reserved" for the wicked in Diog. 10.7, and Diog. 7.2 refers to the observance of cosmic order. "To guard oneself" is the point in Justin *Apology* 14.1. Did. 4.13 demands preservation of the church's tradition (cf. Barn. 19.1).

phylakḗ.

A. Outside the Bible.

1. *phylakḗ* means a. "watching" or "protection," b. "guard," "post," or "watch," c. "watchtower," "guardpost," d. "prison," e. "night watch," and f. "attention."

2. The planets are heavenly watchers or guardposts blocking access to heaven. They are inhabited by demons and serve as places of punishment. A rather different notion is that of heavenly guardians that help the soul in its ascent out of the prison of the body.

B. The LXX and Judaism.

1. In the LXX, where there is no single Hebrew original, we find the senses "watch," "watchtower," "maintenance," and "observance."

2. The astral idea of heavenly "guardhouses" is present in Bar. 3:34, and cf. the stars or starry spirits as "watchers" (Dan. 4:14).

3. The Epistle of Aristeas 125 calls wise and righteous persons the "protection" of the monarchy, and Philo refers to the "preservation" of laws, customs, or virtues, to the "prison" of the passions, and to the sacrifice of bodies for the "protection" of the law.

C. The NT.

1. Lk. 2:8 uses a cultic phrase in a secular way; the shepherds keep "watch" over their flock.

2. Where *phylakē* means "night watch" in comparisons, the sense is literal, but the reference is eschatological (cf. Mt. 24:43). Mk. 6:48 (the "fourth watch") perhaps carries an eschatological hint as well.

3. In all other NT instances *phylakē* means "prison" (cf. Lk. 23:19; Mk. 6:17; Acts 5:18ff.; 12:4ff.; 16:23ff.). Like the righteous of the OT, the disciples often suffer imprisonment. Peter is ready to accept it in Lk. 22:33, Jesus predicts it in 21:12, it is almost a formula for Paul in 2 Cor. 6:5; 11:23, and visiting those in prison is a duty in Mt. 25:36ff. A hint of eschatological punishment is present in Mt. 5:25; 18:30. *phylakē* is the place of departed spirits in 1 Pet. 3:19, Babylon is the prison of unclean spirits in Rev. 18:2, and Satan is temporarily released from his prison in Rev. 20:7.

[G. Bertram, IX, 236-44]

---

phylē [tribe]

A. Secular Greek.

1. This word denotes a group bound together by common descent, and then the subdivision of a people, e.g., a tribe or family.

2. *phylaí* are subdivisions in the Ionic and Doric spheres, traditionally four in the Ionic sphere and three in the Doric. The original element of blood relationship disappears and the main distinctions are sacral, military, and administrative. The troops enrolled in the subdivisions can also be called *phylaí*. The *phylaí* are integrated into the city-states; the *dēmoi* are smaller districts. *tribus* is the Latin equivalent.

3. In the Egyptian priesthood the *phylaí* are divisions or classes performing their ministry in turn.

B. The LXX.

1. In the LXX *phylē*, which renders three main Hebrew terms, becomes a fixed term in the tribal system. The family or clan is the *dēmos, patría,* or *syngéneia*. In some instances the *phylē* may be a group outside Israel (cf. Gen. 10:5; 36:40).

2.a. The tribes take on historical concreteness with the conquest. They are related by common descent and common leadership. Inwardly they consist of clans and families. The number 12 remains even though Manasseh emerges as a separate tribe and Simeon tends to merge into Judah. The electing God shapes their cultic and legal life.

b. The covenant at Shechem in Josh. 24 knits the tribes into an amphictyony and pledges them to loyalty to God and to certain cultic, legal, and military requirements. The holy war unites the tribes politically, and the annual swearing of the covenant oath keeps Canaanite cults in some subjection. Philistine pressure produces a more unified state that reduces tribal autonomy. David provides a cultic center at Jerusalem, and Solomon's new districts coincide only formally with the older tribal structure.

c. Trust in God's faithfulness nourishes the hope of a new future for the 12 tribes. Elijah at Carmel makes his altar of 12 stones (1 Kgs. 18:31). The Servant of Is. 49:6 will reestablish the tribes. Ezekiel names the gates of the new Jerusalem after the 12 tribes (48:30ff.). God sees all the tribes (Zech. 9:1), they are his possession (Is. 63:17), and he will restore them (Sir. 36:10).

C. Later Judaism.

1. In the pseudepigrapha the number 12 plays a role in the reference to 72 translators of the OT and also in the design of the Testaments of the Twelve. Prayers are offered for the regathering of Israel. Apocalyptists expect the Messiah to accomplish this.

2. Palestinian Judaism discusses the tribes in connection with cultic and jurisdictional matters. It expresses a hope for the return of the ten tribes.

3. Qumran refers to the future restoration of the 12 tribes.

4. Philo has little interest in the historical tribes, but he points out that Levi is the priestly tribe because of its zeal regarding the golden calf, and the number 12 is significant for him as a perfect number.

5. Josephus follows the historical records. He mentions vast numbers of the ten tribes settled by the Euphrates. He also uses *phylé* for Arab tribes.

D. The NT.

1. *phylé* occurs 31 times in the NT (21 times in Revelation). Four persons are said to belong to tribes: King Saul and Paul to Benjamin, Anna to Asher, and Jesus to Judah (Acts 13:21; Rom. 11:1; Lk. 2:36; Mt. 1:1; Rom. 1:3; Mk. 10:47-48; Rev. 5:5; Heb. 7:13-14).

2. At the judgment the disciples will play the role assigned to the elders, but they will judge the 12 tribes, not the Gentiles (Mt. 19:28). The gates of the new Jerusalem will bear the names of the 12 tribes (Rev. 21:12). In the end time God will preserve 12,000 of each tribe (7:4ff.). The precedence given to Judah and the omission of Dan suggest that the reference is to the new community of Jews and Gentiles. In Jms. 1:1 the Jewish dispersion might be meant, but since the author is a Christian and is dealing with misunderstandings of justification by faith, the tribes here are probably the new people of God in which OT expectations find their fulfilment and which is also a dispersion on the march to the final consummation.

3. In an eschatological context the Gentile peoples bewail the return of the Son of Man in Mt. 24:30; Rev. 1:7. The Gentile world from which the redeemed are sealed in Rev. 5:9 consists of *phylaí* as well as tongues, peoples, and nations. The overcomers of 7:9 are from the same world, the bodies of the two witnesses confront it in 11:9, it is delivered up to the beast in 13:7, but it also has the offer of the gospel in 14:6.

E. The Apostolic Fathers.
NT themes find an echo in 1 Clem. 43.2 (the 12 tribes), Barn. 8.3 (the apostles), Hermas *Similitudes* 9.17 (the new people of God), and 2 Clem. 10.1 (the nations, Gen. 12:3). [C. MAURER, IX, 245-50]

---

phýsis [nature], *physikós* [natural], *physikôs* [naturally]

A. Greek Literature.

1. Etymology and Basic Sense.

a. From a root *bhū*, meaning "to become," *phýsis* has the original sense of "form" or "nature," but also "budding," "growth," or "development," first in relation to plants, then animals and people.

b. In Homer and Pindar it denotes "external form."

c. The sense "birth" or "origin" occurs in pre-Socratic philosophy, and from this we have *phýsei* for "physical descent."

d. The later adjective *physikós* means "natural."

2. Nature and Constitution.

a. The nature and qualities of people are often called *phýsis*, as is the "inner nature" or "manner" or "character" (cf. also the "true nature" in contrast to acts). In the absolute *phýsis* also means "creature," and among plants it has the sense of "kind" (cf. also "types" of animals or even political constitutions, and "features" of the soul).

b. The inner "constitution" of things is their *phýsis*. The *phýsis* of water or of a sickness or a person is its "proper nature." A person's "temperament" is also that person's *phýsis*. Aristotle defines the *phýsis* of a thing as the end product of its development.

c. *phýsis* may often be used for what is human as distinct from what is nonhuman. Within humanity the nature of the male is distinguished from that of the female. The term also expresses the limitation and vulnerability of human existence. In contrast, that which transcends human weakness shares in the divine nature. Some deities are so by their true nature, others by human positing, e.g., by the divinizing of worthy rulers.

3. True Nature and Universal Nature.

a. Philosophy considers ontological questions from the twofold standpoint of the true nature of things and the origin of all being. The pre-Socratics examine the true nature of things—not personified universal nature, but true being in distinction from appearance.

b. Plato contests the validity of calling the material world *phýsis*, for, if *phýsis* is the primal origin of all things, then the soul is *phýsis*. In general, however, Plato avoids the term for higher stages of being. By *phýsis* he means primarily the "true being" or "idea" of a thing.

c. Aristotle tries to achieve a unified definition by discussing what is involved in the two main senses of origin and constitution. His analysis leads him to the two concepts of "essence" and "primal force." The order of nature allows no operation of supernatural forces; anything against its normal operation is miracle. Nature is an autonomous force that allows no disorder, that adapts things to their ends, that has utility and beauty, and that constantly invents new things. The ideal form that is the origin and goal of movement is in indissoluble union with both divine essence and phenomenal nature.

d. In Hellenism we find an equation of *phýsis* as universal nature with deity (cf. both Stoicism and Epicureanism). The supreme God creates *Phýsis* by his word, and *Phýsis* plays a decisive role in creation. In the Gnostic sphere a distinction arises between two "natures," that of heaven, sun, light, or day on the one side, that of earth, moon, darkness, and night on the other.

4. Nature and Ethics.

a. The antithesis of nature and law exerts a great influence on Greek thought. *phýsis* has to do with natural constitution, *nómos* with environment. The Sophists stress the utility of laws, although some younger Sophists reject *nómos* in the name of nature, which has an element of the necessary as distinct from what is arbitrary and conventional.

b. Among the pre-Socratics education combines with aptitude, but it is valued more highly than natural talent. Plato, however, does not build on *phýsis*, for what is right by nature may well be prejudicial to good education. Aristotle regards *phýsis* as the presupposition of ethical action but not its standard. Virtues do not arise by nature but as we act according to the understanding that is made possible by *lógos*.

c. *phýsin échei* can have the weaker sense "it is natural," and we also find *katá phýsin* and *pará phýsin* ("according to" or "against nature"). These phrases occur in the ethical sphere, especially with a reference to sexual matters (e.g., pederasty).

5. *Nature as a Cosmic and Vital Principle in Stoicism.*

a. God, World, and Nature. Stoicism tries to overcome the antitheses of nature and reason. Nature is not just necessity but permeates the universe. It is both divine principle and primal matter. It is not opposed to *téchnē* but does all things artistically and purposefully.

b. Humanity as *lógos* and *phýsis*. The *télos* formula enables Stoicism to unite humanity with universal divine nature. Agreement with nature comes with appropriation of one's own *lógos*. We receive the *lógos* by nature, and it belongs to our nature that we can get what is good only by contributing to the general good.

c. *katá* and *pará phýsin*. For the Stoics *katá phýsin* summarizes the *télos* formula. Action *katá phýsin* aims at the full development of the self and perfect insight into nature. Health is *katá phýsin* at the primary level, while sound common sense tells us what is *katá phýsin* at the ethical level. The given order is often in fact the standard; thus it is *pará phýsin* ("against nature") to live with someone who is legally married to a third party.

d. The older Stoics do not use the phrase "natural law." Greek-speaking Stoics find it hard to combine the two terms *phýsis* and *nómos*. Cicero, however, uses *lex naturae* or *naturalis,* and Philo uses *nómos physéōs*. For the Greeks, *phýsis* is a final court. Since it can be known only rationally, it is open to discussion, along with its norms, but since it forms a causal nexus, it rules out human freedom except as free concurrence with nature (as in Stoicism) or as abandonment of the natural world (as in Gnosticism). Only the OT and NT belief in nature as God's creation can give significance to the concept of natural law (as in the Christian Apologists), for only in this context is there relationship with both the divine Creator and the divine Lawgiver as the ultimate critical authority.

B. Jewish Literature.

1. *The LXX and Pseudepigrapha.* There is no Hebrew original for *phýsis* and the term is rare. It occurs a few times in 3 and 4 Maccabees and Wisdom, and *phýsis* and *physikós* also occur in Testaments of the Twelve. In these works we find the usual senses "nature," "species," "aptitude," "universal nature" (contrasted with both law and reason in 4 Maccabees), and "physical nature." Wis. 13:1 says that the Gentiles are ignorant of God "by nature" (cf. in contrast Rom. 1:19ff.), and Test. Naph. 3:4-5 refers to the "natural order" that the "watchers" of Gen. 6:1ff. and the Sodomites pervert (cf. Rom. 1:18ff.).

2. *Philo.*

a. God and Universal Nature. A central concept for Philo, *phýsis* unites for him certain decisive elements in Greek thought and the OT. He describes nature as the creator and sustainer of all things, and hence furnishes it with divine predicates. As talent it is the basis of the learning to whose pinnacle God leads. It permeates the visible world and molds water and earth to produce the human form. Nature has given humanity the *lógos* which makes it social and civilized. It makes all people equal and free. As itself the world of visible things, it is distinct from God and its riches are inferior to those of wisdom. Visible nature consisting of matter contrasts with noetic nature, to which humanity, with its share of *noús*, belongs.

b. Nature and Law. The law of nature is the constitution of the cosmos when this is viewed as a city. This natural law is the OT law by which God made the world and cares for it. The true cosmopolitan acts according to the will of nature, i.e., the OT law (cf. Abraham). Individual laws are laws of nature; sexual aberrations violate natural law. Humanity has seven natural capacities (sexual potency, speech, and the five senses). The origin of evil lies in *páthos,* which is against nature.

3. *Josephus.* The word *phýsis* is common in Josephus. Topographically it denotes the setting or configuration of places. Other uses are for the "nature" of things, the "natural state," the "type," "true being," or "character." In the absolute, *phýsis* denotes "human nature" (usually in a bad sense). The divine nature differs from ours, which is also mortal. In some passages nature is an independent force; it makes certain areas beautiful, or commands paternal love in animals. Death is a law of nature, but so, too, is the desire to live. To deny burial is to violate the laws of nature. Sexual processes are according to nature, but not sexual lapses or physical deformity.

C. The NT.

1. *General.* The NT makes little use of *phýsis.* In this respect it makes the same theological decision as the OT, excluding natural theology.

2. *Pauline Usage.*

a. Paul uses *katá* and *pará phýsin* in Rom. 11:21, 24 in his comparison with the olive into which, contrary to their nature, branches of wild olive are grafted. The point here is that branches which do not belong to the tree by nature have no advantage over those that do. God can the more easily graft the latter back in again. In Rom. 2:27 the Gentiles are "by nature" the foreskin. Although unconverted, by their fulfilment of the law they will accuse Jews who have the law but do not fulfil it. The reference in Gal. 2:15 is to those who are Jews "by nature," i.e., by descent, but who realize that justification is now by faith.

b. Gal. 4:8 speaks about bondage to things that "by nature" are no gods. Paul probably refers to the elements here rather than specifically to the divinized natural forces of the Greeks. Acceptance of the law means a return to slavery under the cosmic elements. These elements are no gods; they have no essential divine qualities. In 1 Cor. 11:14 nature is personified as a teacher; it reminds us of what is seemly. There is no thought here of nature as a divine creator, and the example used is a common one in popular philosophy. In Rom. 1:18ff. Paul uses the common *pará phýsin* for perversions that are "against nature" and that are substituted for "natural" relations (with the usual sexual reference). In Rom. 2:1ff. Paul brings the Jews under the judgment that falls on the whole race. They have precedence only in judgment. Their superiority through possession of the law is challenged by the fact that Gentiles who do not have the law do it "by nature" (2:14) and are thus a law to themselves. Paul is not here appealing to nature as a court equal to God. Nor is he trying to show that the Gentiles have a share in the blessings of salvation. He is simply contesting the soteriological boasting of the Jews on the basis of possession of the law. The other side of the same coin in Eph. 2:3 is that Jewish Christians as well as Gentiles were by nature children of wrath, i.e., subject to the fall and divine judgment.

3. *The Rest of the NT.*

a. In a common comparison Jms. 3:7 uses *phýsis* twice, first for "kind" (of beasts), then for "human nature." 2 Pet. 1:4 presupposes the distinction between our weak mortal nature and the divine essence. The idea of participation in the divine nature possibly comes from Gnosticism but it is integrated here with future expectation.

b. 2 Pet. 2:12 uses *physikós* and the parallel Jude 10 has the adverb *physikós.* Jude 10 is arguing that the false teachers, who are probably claiming redemption from nature, are destroyed by things that they know only naturally and irrationally. 2 Pet. 2:12 carries a similar comparison. Those who claim to have knowledge are in fact like irrational animals, creatures of instinct.

D. Early Christian Writings.
1. Apostolic Fathers. In Barn. 10.7 *phýsis* has the sense of "gender," while Ignatius *Ephesians* 1:1 refers to the true "nature" of Christians (cf. also *Trallians* 1.1).

2. Apologists. In Justin *Apology* 10.6 *phýsis* is "human nature." The power to distinguish good and evil is proper to our "nature" in *Apology,* Appendix 7.6. Justin *Dialogue* 45.3-4 equates the law with what is good "by nature," and in *Apology,* Appendix 2.4 Justin says that a dissolute life is "against nature." Paganism is absurd in its mythology, for there can be no single *phýsis* of the gods if they are in conflict (Aristides *Apology* 13.5-6).

3. Apocryphal Acts. Some of these works use *phýsis* frequently in such senses as the "natural world," "nature," "true essence" (e.g., of humanity or of individuals), and "proper nature" (cf. also the hidden nature of the devil).

4. Gnosticism. The Valentinians divide souls into those that are good and those that are evil "by nature." Pneumatics belong to the "divine nature"; the "nature" of the devil is not of the truth. The terms *katá* and *pará phýsin* also play a role.

[H. KÖSTER, IX, 251-77]

---

phōnḗ [sound, speech, voice],   *phōnéō* [to make a sound, speak],   *symphōnéō* [to be in harmony with],   *sýmphōnos* [harmonious],   *symphōnía* [harmony], *symphṓnēsis* [agreement]

---

phōnḗ.

A. The Greek World.
1. *phōnḗ* is the audible "sound" made by living creatures in the throat. It thus denotes the cry of the animal or song of the bird.

2. The main use, however, is for articulate human speech. *phōnḗ* is both the "voice" and the "sound" made by it. It is often a loud voice, but may denote any speaking or crying.

3. Greek has no special word for speech. *phōnḗ*, then, serves to denote the "faculty of speech" or the "speech" of a people.

4. A single statement or declaration can also be called *phōnḗ* (cf. also a message or a testamentary disposition).

5. *phōnḗ* is also the "voice" of deity either as organ or utterance. The divine voice of Zeus has numinous force. God shows himself through the voice. The shrine is the place where the divine voice goes forth. The Delphic Pythia mediates the divine voice. Socrates appeals to the divine voice as a directing force. The saying of a divine voice supposedly lies behind the legal order.

B. The OT.
1. *phōnḗ* is normally the rendering of Heb. *qôl,* which has the primary sense of "noise" (cf. the roar of water, swish of rain, rolling of an earthquake, sound of steps, trampling of horses, whistling of whips, noise of a camp, rustling of wings, crackling of fire, grinding of millstones, sound of horns, etc.).

2. *qôl* also denotes the sound made by animals, e.g., sheep, cattle, horses, lions, birds, turtledoves, or snakes.

3. *qôl* is especially the sound of the human voice in such senses as crying, lamenting, rejoicing, etc. One utters the voice, or lifts it up, or raises it, or speaks with a loud or high voice, or a lovely voice. The voice is individual and enables us to know the speaker. In dealings with God *qôl* may denote "petition" or "complaint," or it may take the form of praise, thanksgiving, etc., and it may may be loud or fervent.

4. In Ps. 19 day and night declare God's praise, although their voice is not heard. The cries of the seraphim cause the lintels to shake in Is. 6:3-4. The voice of the angel in Dan. 10:6 is like the noise of a crowd. A voice from heaven declares judgment in Dan. 4:28. The prophet hears a voice in Is. 40:3, 6. In general, however, there are few OT references to angelic voices.

5. God's self-revelation takes audible form; he is heard, though not seen. *qôl* refers to God in some 50 of 560 instances. God speaks to Moses. The thunder is his voice (cf. Ps. 29). His voice chases the primal waters (Ps. 104:7). It frightens Israel's foes (1 Sam. 7:10). The prophets refer to God's word, but not to his voice except in Is. 6:8; Ezek. 1:28-29. Their emphasis is on the message, not the sound. In Ex. 19:16ff. the sounds herald God's coming, but again the reference is not just to noise but to an intelligible voice. God causes his voice to be heard so as to instruct Israel (Dt. 4:36). By his *qôl* God declares his will for the people (5:25-26). 1 Kgs. 19 distinguishes the theophany and the voice. The people must hearken to God's voice, which comes as a summons in the form of the word, so that hearkening to the voice is keeping the law (Dt. 4:30; 8:20, etc.). This is the epitome of worship (Josh. 24:24) and obedience (Jer. 3:13), and it decides Israel's weal or woe (Dt. 8:20). Personified wisdom also actualizes God's voice (Prov. 1:20; 8:1; cf. Is. 18:23). The Servant of Is. 42:1ff. does not cry or lift up his voice.

C. Palestinian Judaism.

I. Apocalyptic Writings.

1. Noise and Sound. In these works *qôl* is used at times for the roaring of waters, the fuming of enemies, the noise of clouds, the sound of a host, or the sounding of horns.

2. Human Voice. *qôl* is more important as a human voice praising, sighing, laughing, or praying. Speech is a miracle of creation and the last time will bring miraculous phenomena of speech. Abel's soul lifts up its voice so that it is heard in heaven.

3. Angelic Voice. The angels praise God with one voice, heavenly voices laud human faithfulness, Michael speaks with God's voice, the voices of the heavenly hosts are raised in a cry of battle, the voice of one like the Son of Man causes foes to melt away, and the demons hearken to the voice of Mastema.

4. God's Voice. God's voice was heard in the past and is expected in the future. Angels control the voices of thunder. True Israelites hear God's voice. As Moses was its interpreter, so is the teacher of the Qumran sect. OT figures hear a voice from heaven whose author is God. God will speak to the high priest of the end time at his institution. A mighty voice will announce the last judgment.

II. Rabbinic Judaism.

1. Noise and Sound. *qôl* may be any noise or sound, e.g., that of a door opening, of children playing, etc. Three noises not heard are the sound of the sun, that of the city of Rome, and that of a departing soul.

2. Human Voice. *qôl* denotes the individual human voice in prayer, rejoicing, etc.

A loud voice is unseemly in prayer, but the "Hear, O Israel" is to be recited out loud. *qôl* can also mean "rumor" or "report," and in a transferred sense we read of the voice of a scroll. Elijah will come before the Messiah and cause his voice to be heard in proclamation of God's glory.

3. *Thunder.* The voices of thunder come from God and serve as a universal declaration, e.g., on the death of a rabbi or the coming of the Messiah.

4. *God's Voice at Sinai.* Some rabbis think that God spoke directly to Israel at Sinai and not by a voice from heaven. Stress falls on the power and range of God's voice. The plural is taken by some to mean that the voice splits into 70 voices corresponding to the 70 languages of the earth, so that each people can hear it in its own tongue.

5. *Heavenly Voice.* After the second temple is destroyed there arises the idea that a voice from heaven replaces the prophets. The rabbis do not view this as a continuation of the older revelation, but apocalyptic and Josephus make less distinction; the belief in oracles has an impact. As distinct from the gift of the Spirit, the *bath qôl* sets up no lasting relationship with God. It can come to Gentiles too. It usually comes from heaven, and God is the speaker, often with accompanying phenomena such as thunder. Its task is to announce a judgment which is not in itself compelling or according to the common view. It may be a call to repentance, a cry of disaster, or an accusation. It often applies to individuals, either condemning the wicked or acknowledging the righteous. It plays a role in earlier periods when there is no prophecy. It can take the form of a chance human voice, e.g., a child reciting Scripture. To rabbis it may censure lack of interest or decide a difficult case. It often uses a text, applying the word to a specific situation or explaining a difficult OT saying.

D. Hellenistic Judaism.

1. *The LXX.* The LXX follows the OT use of *qôl* and almost always renders it by *phōnḗ*. The revelation of God is almost exclusively by the word; the LXX often translates passages that speak of seeing God in such a way that the element of vision drops out (cf. Ex. 24:9ff.; Job 19:25ff.). The plural *phōnaí* occurs in Ex. 9:24 (claps of thunder) but the singular *phōnḗ* in 20:18.

2. *Aristobulus.* Aristobulus guards against anthropomorphism by understanding God's voice as operation rather than spoken word (cf. creation as divine words). The Greeks follow Moses when speaking of God's voice relative to the cosmic structure.

3. *Josephus.* Josephus uses *phōnḗ* for "speech." For him the idea of God's voice expresses God's distance from us; the voice is not God himself (cf. Moses at the bush). The idea of the *bath qôl* occurs when Josephus refers to voices in the temple, e.g., before the outbreak of the Jewish war.

4. *Philo.* Philo uses *phōnḗ* for the audible "utterance" of living creatures. He reflects on the human voice. It serves to exalt the Creator and is an instrument of reason. The divine Spirit uses the human voice, which alone is articulate, as a medium. *phōnḗ* also means "language" for Philo. The race has one language prior to Babel. Philo stresses the miracle of the divine voice, which he differentiates from the thunder at Sinai. Strictly the process of revelation is inward, for God's voice is uniquely spiritual. It takes a visible form as light, but this depiction simply stresses its objectivity; the true speaking and receiving take a psychological and ethical form. The trumpet sound makes the law-giving at Sinai universal, but revelation applies only to Israel, which "sees being without voice and by the soul alone" (*On the Giants* 52; cf. *On the Migration of Abraham* 38).

E. The NT.

1. Noise and Sound. In the NT, under OT influence, *phōnḗ* often means "noise" or "sound," e.g., the rolling of wheels in Rev. 9:9, the grinding of millstones in 18:22, the noise of the crowd in 19:1, the rushing of the wind in Jn. 3:8, the melody of instruments in 1 Cor. 14:7, the sound of words in Lk. 1:44, the cry of grief in Mt. 2:18.

2. Human Voice. Rhoda knows Peter by his voice in Acts 12:14, the sheep know the shepherd's voice in Jn. 10:3-4, the best man rejoices at the bridegroom's voice in Jn. 3:29, Paul wants to use another tone of voice in Gal. 4:20, the Baptist is the voice in the wilderness in Mk. 1:3, and Rachel's voice laments in Mt. 2:18 etc. We find such expressions as raising the voice, crying, e.g., for mercy, and speaking haughtily (Rev. 13:5).

3. Loud Voice. The martyrs cry with a loud voice in Rev. 6:10, the angels praise God with a loud voice in 5:12, and voices are compared to lions (10:3), trumpets (1:10), waters (1:15), and thunder (Jn. 12:29-30). The loud cry of Jesus in Mk. 15:37 perhaps has the force of an epiphany (cf. also Mt. 27:50; Lk. 23:46). The shout of Acts 12:22 leads to God's judgment on Herod. Unclean spirits cry with a loud voice in Mk. 1:26; Acts 8:7. Paul heals with a loud voice in Acts 14:10, and Jesus raises Lazarus with a loud voice in Jn. 11:43 (cf. 5:28-29). A voice speaks to Paul on the Damascus road in Acts 9:4 (cf. v. 7).

4. Cry, Word, Confession, Speech. phōnḗ may take the form of a "cry" (cf. Acts 19:34), a "word" (2 Pet. 1:17), a "confession" (Acts 24:21), or "speech" (2 Pet. 2:16).

5. God's Voice. The NT refers to God's speaking as the OT does. The seven thunders reply to the mighty angel in Rev. 10:3. The Son of Man utters a word of revelation in 1:10ff. The Sinai theophany finds an end-time parallel here. Acts 2 is also reminiscent of Sinai. The gospel of God's great acts in Christ now replaces the law. Jn. 5:37 resists any claim based on Dt. 4:12. Revelation reaches its climax with the coming of the Logos. Those who hear his voice move out of the sphere of death into that of eternal life (cf. 5:25, 28). To hear the shepherd's voice is to know and follow him (10:27). In this regard there are no national limits. All who are of the truth hear Jesus' voice (18:37). Yet it is possible to hear the voice, as to hear the sound of the wind, without knowing where it comes from or where it is going (3:8; cf. 8:14). Heb. 12:18ff. offers another comparison with Sinai. At the end God will shake heaven as well as earth. Everything created will be changed, but what cannot be shaken will remain. Heb. 1:1ff. finds in the word of the Son a climax to the word of the prophets (cf. also 2:2). Now that God has spoken through the Son, the great "today" has come in which God's voice sounds forth in the church's preaching, which ends with the sabbath of the eschaton.

6. The Heavenly Voice. Heavenly voices are common in Revelation (10:8; 11:12, etc.). They come from the sanctuary, throne, or altar, and are uttered by the beasts or the Son of Man in the form of commands, charges, or assertions. Acts enhances the sense of God's transcendence by references to the voice from heaven (7:31; 10:13ff.; 11:9). At Jesus' baptism a voice from heaven confirms his messiahship. God is the speaker, and the address is directly to Jesus (Mk. 1:11). At the transfiguration the voice from the cloud transfers authority to Jesus (Mk. 9:7). In 2 Pet. 1:16ff. this voice guarantees the truth of the apostolic message. In Jn. 12:20ff. a voice from heaven confirms the glorifying of God's name. This voice is for the sake of the people, not of Jesus himself (v. 30), but the people does not understand it (v. 29). Revelation does not come by a direct voice from heaven.

F. Gnosticism.

1. In Gnostic thinking the "call" plays a considerable role. First it is the human call for redemption, or the call of the oppressed.

2. Then in many forms we find the supraterrestrial call that brings redemption. Thus we have the voice of a dove, the heavenly voice, the voice of the redeemer, or the voice of the heavenly man. The voice comes from the upper kingdom, from on high, from concealment, or from outside. The voice is bright, sublime, wonderful, soft, or pure. The call may come through emissaries, helpers, the shepherd, the fisherman, etc. The heavenly messenger can bear the name Call. The first, great, or sacred call is Christ. A first duty is to hear the call in faith, then to pass it on. The call is an awakening out of sleep, and it insures the return of the soul to its heavenly home unless one turns aside from it in sin. The call, then, has much the same function as the OT law or as the Holy Spirit.

3. We also read of an opposing call of wicked forces which is rebellious or vain. The call can take form, e.g., in the planets or signs of the zodiac.

G. The Early Church.

Ignatius uses the metaphor of a choir in *Ephesians* 4.2. He himself mediates God's voice in *Philadelphians* 7.1. Mart. Pol. 9.1 mentions a voice from heaven. Barn. 9.2 makes eternal life dependent on hearing the voice of the Son. In Justin *phōnē* is "spoken word" in *Dialogue* 131.2 and "speech" in *Apology* 31.1. The prophets proclaim God's *phōnē* in *Dialogue* 119.6. Christ calls out of the wicked world in 119.5. OT quotations are *phōnaí* in 21.1. Papias values the living voice, i.e., oral tradition (Eusebius *Ecclesiastical History* 3.39.4).

phōnéō.

1. The Greek World. phōnéō denotes the producing of a sound or noise, usually by living creatures, and especially by people in such senses as "to speak," "to sing," "to address," "to call to," "to reply to," "to invoke," "to order (someone) to," "to speak about something," or "to tell something."

2. Hellenistic Judaism.

a. *phōnéō* is rare in the LXX. We find it for the pealing of trumpets (Am. 3:6), the cries of animals (Is. 38:14), and various kinds of speaking (Ps. 115:5; Is. 8:19) or crying (4 Macc. 15:21).

b. Philo uses *phōnéō* for "to lift up the voice," "to speak openly." In a transferred sense it expresses for him the capturing of the senses by visible objects.

3. The NT.

a. *phōnéō* in the NT means loud speaking, calling, or crying, whether by humans, angels, or demons. In Lk. 8:54 it denotes the word of power which raises the dead. In Luke and John it may also have the force of "to summon" (cf. Lk. 16:2; Jn. 2:9). In Mk. 15:35 the onlookers think Jesus is calling for the eschatological deliverer, while in Mk. 10:49 a turning point comes for the blind man when Jesus calls him with a mighty eschatological summons (cf. Jn. 1:48; 11:28). Those whom the shepherd calls by name know that they are his (10:3). In Jn. 11:43 the calling of Lazarus from the tomb is equivalent to raising him from the dead (12:17). In Lk. 14:12 the meaning is "to invite," and "to name" or "address as" is the point in Jn. 13:13.

b. The "crowing" of the cock is meant in Mk. 14:30; Mt. 26:34; Lk. 22:24. Since the cock crows between midnight and 3 a.m., the third watch is *alektorophōnía*, "the time of the crowing of the cock."

4. The Apostolic Fathers. This word does not occur in these works.

symphōnéō, sýmphōnos, symphōnía, symphônēsis.

A. The Greek World.

1. symphōnéō.

a. This verb means "to agree or be in harmony with." It is used for musical harmony, and also for the fitting together of stones in a building.

b. The word also has a more common transferred sense for the agreement of, e.g., texts or opinions.

c. A further sense is "to reach agreement," "to come to terms," in treaties and especially contracts. In a bad sense the term may also mean "to conspire."

2. sýmphōnos.

a. This word means "harmonious," "consonant," mostly in a transferred sense, e.g., with reference to movements, statements, records, or partners.

b. *tó sýmphōnon* means "agreement," "arrangement."

c. The adverb *symphónōs* also occurs.

d. In a passive sense *sýmphōnos* means "arranged."

3. symphōnía.

a. This word first denotes the "harmony" of sounds.

b. We then find it for a musical instrument or an orchestra.

c. In a transferred sense it is the "harmony" of thought and life, or the "agreement" of theory and facts, or inner "harmony" of the self, or the "harmony" of beautiful soul and body.

d. Commercially it has the sense of "contract."

B. The OT and Judaism.

1. In the LXX *symphōnéō* is used for concerted planning, conspiring, agreeing, or corresponding. *symphōnía* occurs only in 4 Macc. 14:3 for the "concord" of the seven brothers.

2. In Dan. 3:5, 15 Θ we find the term for a musical instrument. In this sense Aramaic adopts it as a loanword, possibly for a double flute or a bagpipe.

3. Philo uses *symphōnía* for musical harmony.

4. Josephus uses the verb for the agreement of historical accounts, for the attempt to reach a common concept of God, and for the harmony of thought and life achieved by the Jewish people on the basis of the law.

5. Apocalyptic shows a concern for the harmonious order of the world. The law, which also shapes the social order, is what leads Judaism to this sense of harmony.

C. The NT.

1. In the NT *symphōnéō* means "to correspond," "to be at one," "to agree." In Lk. 5:36 the new cloth does not fit in with the old. In Acts 15:15, however, the words of Scripture agree with eschatological events on the mission field. The common content of prayer is at issue in Mt. 18:19; God's assent follows the disciples' agreement. Agreement in a wicked plan is what Peter has in mind in his charge against Sapphira in Acts 5:9. An oral agreement about wages is meant in the parable in Mt. 20:2, 13.

2. The phrase *ek symphónou,* which occurs in contracts, expresses in 1 Cor. 7:15 the consent of the two partners in accordance with v. 4.

3. The elder brother hears *symphōnía* in Lk. 15:25, i.e., "music," possibly that of the flute, although "song" and the "bagpipe" have also been suggested.

D. The Early Church.

1. Ignatius uses the group to depict the unity of the church in *Ephesians* 4.1-2.

2. Gnosticism uses *symphōnéō* and *sýmphōnos* to express the agreement of the

heavenly aeons or the agreement of the Son of Man with Sophia. Lack of agreement, e.g., between Sophia and Spirit, brings disaster.   [O. Betz, IX, 278-309]

---

phṓs [light],   *phōtízō* [to shine, make known],   *phōtismós* [shining, illumination],   *phōteinós* [light, clear],   *phōsphóros* [bearing light, morning star],   *phōstḗr* [gleam],   *epiphaúskō* [to shine forth],   *epiphōskō* [to shine forth]

A. The Group in Greek.

1. Usage.

a. *phṓs,* meaning "light," occurs from Homer, but the derivatives arc late.

b. *phōtízō* means "to shine" or "to illumine," and in a transferred sense "to make known."

c. *phōtismós* means "shining"; it is rare.

d. *phōstḗr,* also rare, means "gleam."

e. *phōsphóros* means "bringing morning light," or as a noun "morning star."

f. *phōteinós* means "light" or in a transferred sense "clear."

g. *epiphaúskō* and *epiphóskō,* both rare and late, mean "to shine forth."

2. Meaning. phṓs, used in both a literal and a transferred sense, has the meanings "daylight," "sunlight," "brightness," "shining," and "lamp." Light is both a medium and object of sight. It enables us to grasp and master the world; to see it is life. Light brings freedom, deliverance, and hope. It is thus an object of praise. It denotes what is publicly known. It accompanies divine manifestations. The light of knowledge brings illumination.

3. Light and Illumination in Philosophy.

a. The pre-Socratics treat light simply as a physical phenomenon, but Parmenides speaks of the way to truth as a way to light, i.e., to being, or to God.

b. Early dualism refers to primal chaos or night but does not develop the antithesis of light and darkness.

c. Light and darkness are among the ten antithetical principles for the Pythagoreans.

d. Plato develops a metaphysics of light. True being is light, there is an ascent to light, ideas are light, knowledge gives light to being, light and truth correspond. Illumination for Plato is ontological; in inquiry one understands oneself in the light of the disclosure of the object.

e. Aristotle compares the activity of the *noús* to light. If for Plato things are light, for Aristotle the *noús* illumines them.

4. Light in the Cultᵘ. In the cult of the dead light drives out demons. New light is hailed in the mysteries. Light is at first epiphany rather than personal illumination. Later, interest focuses on the goal with the idea of a mystical ascent to light.

B. The Group in the OT.

1. Background. The primary reference in the Near Eastern world is to the light of day, but sun, light, salvation, and life soon come into association, and the predicates of light are also transferred to bearers other than the sun. In Iran we find spheres of brightness and darkness but no early development of the antithesis. Later, light and darkness play an important role; they dominate the Mandaean writings.

2. Usage. The group *'wr,* used both literally and in a transferred sense, is the main one for light. From it we find the verb "to shine," "to cause to shine," and the noun "daylight" or "starlight," the "light" that characterizes natural and spiritual life. Of the 200 instances of the root, 137 are rendered by *phōs* and cognates. Light is not so much an object of sight in the OT, nor does it have attributes. The transferred use presupposes movement in a space that may be a sphere of light or darkness, with both salvation and perdition as possibilities, but with an orientation to salvation.

3. *General.* Light is experienced brightness, the sphere of natural life. Earthly light neither derives from transcendent light nor is contrasted with it. Radiance surrounds God, but God's glory is not light. God is our light (Ps. 27:1), and he causes his light to shine (Job 37:3). But light denotes relation, not being. It is a term for true life or salvation (cf. Ps. 36:9). To see it is to live (Job 3:16). Salvation is to be in the light, and light and joy go together (Ps. 97:11). Theophany is the theme in Job 37:15, and creation in Is. 45:7. Praise (Ps. 104:2), prayer (43:3), and teaching (Prov. 4:18) are all related to it.

4. *God.* God is Lord of light and darkness (Am. 5:8). Light is his sphere (Ps. 104:2). He has created, but may also interrupt, the order of day and night (cf. Josh. 10:12-13). Light is God in action (Ps. 44:3). His face shines (4:6). He is manifested in the cloud that sends forth light (Job 37:15) or in the pillar of fire (Ps. 78:14). No darkness can hide from him (Ps. 139:11-12). He is resplendent (Is. 42:16ff.), and he brings what is hidden to light (Job 12:22).

5. *The World.* God has created the world. Is. 45:7 associates cosmology and soteriology by linking light and darkness with salvation and perdition. Gen. 1 refers to creation by the word and distinguishes light from light-bearers as God first creates light and then the sun, moon, and stars to carry it, and to establish the rhythm of day and night.

6. *Eschatology.* The expectation is that God's coming day will be a day of light (though cf. Am. 5:18). The beginning may be dark, but then light will shine for Israel (Is. 30:26; Zech. 14:6-7). God will be its eternal light (Is. 60:1ff.).

7. *Anthropology.* Wisdom is compared to light (Eccl. 2:13). It excels folly as light does darkness (8:1). The law is light (Ps. 19:8). Light is already present (56:13), but is also coming (112:4). The wise are enlightened; the law is their light (119:105). They go in the light (Prov. 4:18), or with a light (Job 29:3). They pray for light (Ps. 4:6).

C. Judaism.

1. *General.* Judaism, like the OT, uses the terms in the fields of cosmology, eschatology, and ethics. Light is the brightness of the world, salvation, and wisdom. God causes his light to shine, or gives light, through wisdom or the law. Salvation is now more individual, and there is a sharper duality as the light of the law comes into contrast with the darkness of Adam. Jub. 2:2ff. depicts creation more spatially and statically. Slav. En. 25ff. attaches more importance to the stars and to the annual rather than the daily rhythm. The idea of primal light arises. Eschatologically the element of time becomes more important, and a transcendent world of light, of full and eternal brightness, stands over against the present world of darkness. The law, as light, also confronts darkness. Light and darkness thus become moral qualities.

2. *Special Features.* Note should be taken of the idea of wisdom as primal light (Wis. 7:29-30), the use of Greek philosophy in exposition of Gen. 1 (Aristobulus in Eusebius *Preparation for the Gospel* 13.12.9-10), and the development of a cosmological conversion idiom.

3. Qumran.

a. The dualism of eschatological decision dominates the Scrolls. There may be some Iranian influence here, but the cosmology is strongly monotheistic. Light and darkness are spheres but also paths. The children of light, who are marked by confession of sin, thanksgiving, and the doing of works of light, are at enmity with the children of darkness in an anticipation of the final conflict.

b. The Testaments of the Twelve is more Hellenistic. The light of the law or of knowledge or righteousness is to the fore. Being precedes works; one can do the works of light only when already in the light (Test. Naph. 2:10).

4. Rabbinic Literature. The rabbis use light for the law, for the age of salvation, for the Messiah, for God, for the righteous, for the temple, for the works of the righteous, and for the human soul.

D. Hellenism and Gnosticism.

1. General. Along classical lines, light is still what is grasped philosophically or speculatively, but in Hellenistic fashion it is now also the reality of saving power or the sphere of salvation. There is no consistent development. The world may be compared to light, the mysteries speak of illumination, and the idea of a transcendent world of brightness is present. As regards salvation, light is both a sphere and a substance (cf. the concept of the light-soul). Illumination is ascent and change. The main contrast is between divine light and earthly or human light. Darkness is the sphere one leaves behind in a movement to illumination. This is deification; it brings knowledge by translation into a transcendent substance.

2. Philo. Philo belongs to the illumination group. The antithesis for him is between heavenly and earthly light. The divine world, as light, is the presupposition of earthly light and also of the possibility of the vision of light in mystical ascent. God is the source of purest radiance, prior to every archetype. The *lógos,* a middle being, is also light. Intelligible light is its *eikōn.* Transcendence receives added emphasis. The *lógos* is the enlightening power in conversion. One can reach light only through light. If divine light is too strong for human vision, the divine *pneúma* impels the human *noús* and makes new vision possible in self-transcendence. By the world of ideas the royal way leads to the vision of God. If deification threatens, Philo guards against this by insisting on revelation and on the linking of light to the law. Philo also uses the vocabulary of conversion; this is for him a transition from darkness to light.

3. Gnosticism. Two types may be distinguished. In the one darkness is an emanation from light by weakening or a fall; in the other preexistent darkness revolts against the world of light. Only in the latter, Iranian, type is there a stricter dualism. In the former, which is more common, the orientation is to light and redemption, as one sees in the liturgies. Darkness has importance only as the whence of redemption. In Gnosticism light is the formless space of the world. It is also the self of the redeemed. Illumination is the kindling of the spark of light imprisoned in darkness or matter. It is transformation in light, or deification. Redemption is the ascent of the redeemed to light. Light and life are identical; both are transcendent.

4. Corpus Hermeticum. Darkness is bracketed here by light; it comes from it alone. Light is both sphere and substance. Earthly light and divine light stand in antithesis. Light mediates between God and humanity. Light and life are a primal unity. In knowledge we find our origin in light and the way back to it. Illumination is the presupposition, and this means deification, anticipated already in ecstasy, and worked out to some degree in the asceticism which signifies regeneration from self-alienation. The redeemed are awakened by a call, but only the illuminated can be awakened.

5. *The Mandaeans*. Mandaean writings combine the two main types, so that the data are not uniform. The main points are that light is transcendent, that it is identical with deity, that it differs totally from earthly brightness, that it is the living power in creation, that even in the present dark house we live by it and it is our true being, that redemption comes through an envoy from the kingdom of light, that his revelation is illumination, that it brings a call to awakening, that this call imparts knowledge of present lostness but also of origin in light, that the redeemed are to clothe themselves with light, and that light is finally victorious.

6. *Manicheeism*. In this system the visible light of sun and moon is true light. Duality arises as two primal spheres confront one another in absolute antithesis. As in cosmology, so in psychology and ethics the conflict is absolute; there are no gradations of good and evil, and total separation is both necessary and possible. Although darkness actively resists light, the triumph of the latter is certain, for light is at one with itself, whereas darkness is inwardly divided. Soteriology takes both a mythical and an existential form. The point of the dualism is decision based on the prior derivation of the self from light. It is by preaching that separation or redemption takes place, and the elect actualize the separation in ethical action.

7. *Odes of Solomon*. In this work light is the place of the redeemed. There is a walk or ascent to it. It is also the essence of the redeemed, put on like a garment. It is transcendent and banishes darkness. As revelation, it goes hand in hand with knowledge, truth, and life. Radiance marks both redeemer and redeemed.

8. *Christian Gnosticism*. This movement contributes nothing new. It simply offers variations on old themes, sometimes in Gnostic versions of NT sayings. The dualism can be strong, but light is primary. Light is God and his world. God is in pure light. Light is indescribable, infinite, etc. Salvation is illumination in a transition from darkness to light. Knowledge is knowledge of the self as a being of light. Redemption is the release of the particle of light from the bonds of darkness.

E. The NT.

I. Occurrence. The noun *phốs* is the most common term, *phōtízō* occurs 11 times, *phōtismós* in 2 Cor. 4:4, 6, *phōteinós* in Mk. 6:22 and parallels and 17:5, *phōstḗr* in Phil. 2:15; Rev. 21:11; *phōsphóros* in 2 Pet. 1:19, *epiphaúskō* in Eph. 5:14, and *epiphṓskō* in Mt. 28:1; Lk. 23:54. Only *phốs* is theologically significant.

II. Synoptic Gospels and Acts.

1. Literal. Sometimes we have a literal use, as at the epiphany in Mt. 17:5. Light from heaven shines in Acts 9:3; 22:6, 9, 11; 26:13. Fire in Mk. 14:54, a lamp in Lk. 8:16, and a torch in Acts 16:29 are bearers of light. God is the Father of lights (the stars) in Jms. 1:17. Mt. 6:23 has in view the source of light as a figure of inner light.

2. Figurative. Mt. 4:16 quotes Is. 8:23-24 with a reference to both the teaching and the person of Jesus. The OT describes persons as light in Is. 42:6; 49:6, and in the NT cf. Lk. 2:32; Acts 13:47. Jesus is the light of the world in Jn. 8:12; 12:35. In Mt. 5:14ff. both the disciples and their works serve as light; one cannot abstract the one from the other.

3. Transferred. Light signifies openness in Mt. 10:27 and parallels. What Jesus teaches privately, the disciples will declare openly. Christ proclaims light in Acts 26:23. Conversion means moving from darkness to light in Eph. 5:8; 1 Pet. 2:9. Believers are children of light in Lk. 16:8; Jn. 12:36; 1 Th. 5:5; Eph. 5:8. The context gives the sense in each case; in Lk. 16:8 the contrast is with the children of this aeon (not of darkness) (cf. Lk. 20:34).

III. The Pauline Corpus.

1. Paul. Paul follows Jewish usage in a mostly eschatological context. The last day will bring to light what is hidden (1 Cor. 4:5; cf. 2 Cor. 5:10). The Jewish view controls Rom. 2:19; Paul turns it against itself. The lord of darkness and angels of light are in conflict in 2 Cor. 11:14; the former uses the stratagem of appearing as one of the latter. Phil. 2:15 depicts eschatological life as an illumining that is already present (cf. 1 Th. 5:5). Rev. 13:12 bases the appeal on the imminence of the day, which should motivate a replacement of the works of darkness with the armor of light. In 2 Cor. 4:4ff. Paul relates creation and conversion. Conversion is an eschatological new creation. The link with knowledge and shining shows that a process or movement is in view. The exhortation is dualistic in 2 Cor. 6:14ff., which aims to show that believers can have no fellowship with the wicked.

2. Colossians and Ephesians. These epistles reflect current usage. Thus *phôs* in Col. 1:12 is the transcendent sphere depicted as Christ's kingdom. The style is that of conversion with an element of realized eschatology inasmuch as the deliverance is already effected (yet not to the exclusion of the transcendence of the sphere nor of upward movement to it, 3:1ff.). Eph. 5:8ff. adopts the style of eschatological light-exhortation within a schema of once (*skótos*) and now (*phôs*). The terms sound Gnostic, but *phôs* is a sphere, not a substance, the idea of new creation is present, "in the Lord" should be noted, and the basis is the Pauline relation between indicative and imperative. If illumination constitutes the transition, it is the capacity for active knowledge. Eph. 3:9 takes up the concept of a mystery that God now makes people see through preaching. The content of the mystery is the economy of salvation. Eph. 5:14, using the rare *epiphaúskō,* quotes from an unknown source; if the saying has a Gnostic ring, Ephesians gives it an ethical thrust.

3. The Pastorals. In 2 Tim. 1:10 Christ has not merely shown the mystery but effectively manifested it (*phōtízō*).

IV. Johannine Writings.

1. The Gospel. Since the OT alone hardly seems adequate to explain the use of light and darkness by John, scholars have proposed various other historical backgrounds, e.g., Philo, Stoicism, Platonism, Gnosticism, and Qumran. As regards motifs, dualism is too simple to play an expository role, for there are different forms of dualism. John can use *phôs* in the literal sense, e.g., for the light of the lamp in 5:35, or for brightness in 3:20-21. Vacillation between the literal and the figurative is present in 12:35-36, where the brightness of the day signifies the presence of revelation or of the Revealer. Illumination here makes movement possible, but it is restricted to the time of Jesus or of the church's preaching. Revelation, then, is once-for-all and urgently demands decision. We must believe in the light so as to become its children (12:36). The equation of light with the Revealer rules out metaphysical and cosmological speculation. Knowledge of light is faith focused on him who is the light of the world (8:12). Whether the ego is subject or predicate, the statement is meant to be literal; Jesus is the true light, and the article denotes the exclusiveness of revelation. The same statement in 9:5 indicates the temporal nature of the revelation, and in 12:46 it formulates the goal. In distinction from Qumran the statement allows of no sphere of light independent of the Revealer. In Jn. 1:1ff. light comes into association with life and the Logos. The life was the light of men, and the Logos was the (true) light. The predicate of v. 4 becomes the subject of v. 5. The verb *phaínō* expresses the work of light and the verb *phōtízō* in v. 9 its effect. These verbs, unlike those of v. 4 and vv. 6ff., are in the present tense. The Logos came into history but the revelation endures. The word "true" bears an exclusive sense (v. 9). This light alone is really light. Notwithstanding Gnostic parallels, the meaning is nonmythological. This comes out in 3:19. The manifestation of light is judgment; it brings a cleavage between faith and unbelief. A prior human decision is taken in favor of evil. People hate the light. Revelation brings to light what they really are. When the light appears, those whose works are evil love the darkness, but those who do what is true come to the light.

2. *1 John.* This work uses only the noun, and only in 1:5, 7 and 2:8ff. The main thesis is that God is light (1:5); light defines his nature. The statement has a hortatory aim. Fellowship with God is a walk in light, i.e., in truth and love. Part of this walk is confession of sins. In 2:8ff. this walk is possible because the true light now shines— true now in distinction from false. The dispelling of darkness means that love is now possible as the ontic ground of fellowship with God. *phṓs* defines both the conduct of believers (1:5ff.) and their relation to God (2:8ff.).

V. The Rest of the NT.

1. *Hebrews.* Hebrews uses *phōtízō* twice with reference to the beginning of the Christian life as illumination (6:4; 10:32). The word is not here a technical term for baptismal illumination.

2. *James.* Jms. 1:17-18 refers to God as the "Father of lights." The reference is probably to the stars, with an apocalyptic ring. In itself cosmological, the expression is linked with a soteriological saying.

3. *1 Peter.* 1 Pet. 2:9 is an example of a conversion saying. The apocalyptic motif of the brightness of the end time finds a parallel in Rev. 18:1 (cf. 21:23; 22:5).

F. The Early Church.

1. *Apostolic Fathers.* The words for light play no great part in these works. Some OT quotations occur, as in 1 Clem. 16.12. OT usage continues in 1 Clem. 36.2. Light is linked with life and knowledge in 1 Clem. 59.2. Jesus is light in Diog. 9.6. Ignatius *Romans* addresses the community as enlightened. Barn. 18.1 contrasts the ways of light and darkness (cf. life and death in Did. 1ff.).

2. *Baptism as phōtismós.* Justin develops the technical use of *phōtismós* (illumination) for baptism (*Apology* 61.12; *Dialogue* 122.5). Baptism is *phṓtisma* in Clement of Alexandria *Paedagogus* 1.6.26.2. Clement offers a different explanation from that of Justin, who refers to the light that Christian teaching brings to the understanding.

[H. CONZELMANN, IX, 310-58]

χ *ch*

---

chaírō [to rejoice], *chará* [joy], *synchaírō* [to rejoice with], *cháris* [grace], *charízomai* [to give freely], *charitóō* [to bestow favor, bless], *acháristos* [ungrateful], *chárisma* [gift], *eucharistéō* [to show favor, give thanks], *eucharistía* [gratitude, thanksgiving], *eucháristos* [grateful, thankful]

---

chaírō, chará, synchaírō.

A. Secular Greek.

1. Usage.

a. As a phenomenon or feeling, "joy" is a culmination of being that raises no problems as such and that strains beyond itself.

b. *chaírō* means "to rejoice," "to be merry." *chaíre* serves as a morning greeting. It is above all a greeting to the gods and is a stereotyped ending to hymns. The verb is also an epistolary formula in greetings from sender to recipient.

c. *chará* means "rejoicing," "joy," "merriness."

2. Philosophy.

a. Philosophy reflects on joy. For Plato it is much the same as *hēdonḗ*.

b. *hēdonḗ* almost completely replaces it in Aristotle with little distinction.

c. For the Stoics *chará* is a special instance of *hēdonḗ*. Since the Stoics regard emotions as defective judgment of the *lógos*, they tend to view *chará* negatively. But they mitigate this verdict by classifying it as a "good mood" of the soul rather than an emotion (*páthē*).

3. Religious Connection. Hellenism uses *chará* for festal joy. It takes on an eschatological character in expectations of a world savior.

B. The OT.
In the OT the experience and expression of joy are close, as the terms for joy (usually *śmḥ*) and its expression show. Joy expresses the whole person and aims at sharing, as in festal joy. God's work of salvation is a chief occasion (Pss. 5:11; 9:2; 16:9, etc.). The law is an object in Ps. 119:14, the word of God in Jer. 15:16. Joy is a reward for faithfulness to the law in Is. 65:13-14. There is joy at weddings (Jer. 25:10) and at harvest (Is. 9:2). God himself rejoices (Is. 65:19), and thanksgiving demands joy (Dt. 16:13ff.). Feasts offer occasions for joy before God (Dt. 2:7). Hymnal jubilation expresses devotion to God (Joel 2:21). In accordance with its inner intention, OT joy culminates in eschatology (Pss. 14:7; 126:2; Is. 9:2; 12:6, etc.). High points in the prophets carry the call: *chaíre* (Zeph. 3:14ff.; Joel 2:21ff.; Zech. 9:9-10).

C. Judaism.

1. Qumran. At Qumran we find the OT motifs of joy in God, of God's own joy, and of eschatological joy. The elect can rejoice in spite of present suffering because they know that they are in God's hand.

2. Rabbinic Writings. Here, too, we find festal joy, which God gives and into which it is a duty to enter. Joy is joy before God. The meal is part of the joyful festival. A significant thought is that of perfect future joy.

3. Philo. The group is a significant one in Philo. He relates joy to religious "intoxication." Joy is a supreme "good mood." It is the opposite of fear. Isaac is its OT symbol. God is the giver of joy, and its objects are health, freedom, honor, the good, the beautiful, and worship. While joy is a "good mood" Philo does not view it in Stoic fashion as a self-achieved harmony of soul. Joy is native to God alone; we find it only in God. It comes with virtue and wisdom. But this is possible only on the presupposition that by way of the *lógos* God himself is the giver.

D. The NT.

1. Usage. In the NT *chaírō* is the secular term and *agalliáomai* the religious term, but the two may be synonymous (cf. Rev. 19:7), and they are associated, e.g., in

Mt. 5:12; 1 Pet. 4:13. The participle means "full of joy" in Lk. 19:6. Various constructions are used, e.g., accusative, dative, *epí* with dative, *diá* with accusative, *en*, *hóti*, and participle. The greeting with *chaírein* occurs only in Acts 15:23; 23:26; Jms. 1:1. The greeting *chaíre* (Mk. 15:18; Mt. 26:49; 27:29; Jn. 19:3) may mean "rejoice" rather than "greetings" in Lk. 1:28, where *kecharitōménē* ("favored one") gives it special significance. The meanings of both verb and noun are to be sought in the contexts in which they are used.

2. *The Synoptics and 1 Peter.* The group is common only in Luke, which refers to joy at finding what is lost (15:5ff.), at one's name being written in heaven (10:20), at the coming of the Savior (1:14), and at the acts of Jesus (13:17). The mood of the people is one of joy in 18:43, as is that of the disciples after the ascension in 24:52. There is joy at epiphany in Mt. 2:10. Even trials are an occasion of joy (Jms. 1:2). Suffering is a testing of faith (1 Pet. 1:6-7) with a christological basis (2:20ff.; 4:12ff.). One should not just rejoice "in" suffering but "at" suffering (Acts 5:41). Already in Mt. 5:11-12 Jesus forges a link between joy and persecution. The hope of future glory adds an eschatological dimension in 1 Pet. 4:12ff. Heb. 10:32ff. presents another version of the same tradition that one should suffer with joy for faith's sake and with the hope of imminent deliverance.

3. *The Pauline Corpus.*

a. For Paul *chará* is the joy of faith (Phil. 1:25) and a fruit of the Spirit (Gal. 5:22). God's kingdom is joy (Rom. 14:17). Joy and hope are related (Rom. 12:12). Its opposite is affliction (cf. Rom. 5:1ff.). Joy actualizes freedom and takes shape in fellowship (12:15). Paul wants to come with joy (15:32). Joy is reciprocal (Phil. 2:28-29). Joy is in God (1 Th. 3:9) or in the Lord (Phil. 3:1). In the relation between Paul and the church, joy is eschatological; the church will be his joy (1 Th. 2:19). The mood of Philippians is one of joy (1:4). This is joy at the preaching of Christ (1:18). It is future joy experienced as joy in the present (4:1). As the joy of faith it includes a readiness for martyrdom (1:25). This joy maintains itself in face of affliction (2 Cor. 7:4ff.). Paul himself, like the Lord, is an example in this regard (1 Th. 1:6). Paul's apostolic authority works for the joy of the church (2 Cor. 1:24). He rejoices in his own weakness when it means the church's strength (13:9).

b. There is nothing new in later works. *chaírō* occurs in Col. 1:24; 2:5, and *chará* in Col. 1:11; 2 Tim. 1:4. The most important aspect is that of joy in suffering.

4. *The Johannine Writings.* Jn. 4:36 adopts the image of harvest joy and Jn. 3:29 that of wedding joy. The time of joy has come with Jesus. The Baptist's joy is fulfilled because its object is now present. In 8:56 *chaírō* is the anticipation, *agalliáomai* the fulfilment. "Perfect joy" is the climax (15:11; 16:24; 17:13; 1 Jn. 1:4; 2 Jn. 12). The disciples should rejoice at Jesus' death, for it means exaltation. Jesus does not censure the disciples' sorrow but shows how the resurrection turns it into *chará* (16:20ff.). The association with peace brings out the eschatological nature of joy (14:27). In 15:11 the joy is Jesus' joy in his people. If keeping the commandments is the occasion of joy, there is no legalism here. Love is not the way to attain eschatological life but the leading of this life. The world rejoices at the sorrow of the disciples, thinking it has triumphed by destroying Jesus, but this victory is only for the moment (16:20). By promise the church has already moved on from sorrow to joy. The world's hostility remains (15:18-19), but this very fact shows that joy cannot be lost. Its perfection rests on its lack of any perceptible ground from the world's standpoint. In practice, joy is the possibility of prayer, which brings its fulfilment (16:24).

E. The Apostolic Fathers. God rejoices in the good works of creation, and believers should also rejoice in good works (1 Clem. 33.7-8). Joy is a reward for excess works (Hermas *Similitudes* 5.3.3).

F. Gnosticism. Gnosticism refers to joy at the vision of God. Joy is now a constituent part of human nature. Joy is in the Lord, the saints rejoice from the heart, the gospel of truth is joy, there is for the Mandaeans a great day of joy, and the Manichees speak of an ascent into the *aér* of joy.

cháris, charízomai, charitóō, acháristos.

A. Secular Greek.
1. Usage.
a. *cháris* is what delights. It may be a state causing or accompanying joy. It is joyous being or "charm," the element of delight in the beautiful, the favor shown by fortune, i.e., what is pleasing in it. As a mood *cháris* means "sympathy" or "kindness," with a reference to the pleasure that is caused. In certain expressions the idea of "thanks" is brought out, and *cháris* with the genitive has the sense of "for the sake of," "out of consideration for." Aeschylus uses *cháris* for the "favor" of the gods, but *cháris* is not a central religious or philosophical term. In Plato it has the meanings "good pleasure," "goodwill," "favor," "pleasure," "what pleases," and "thanks." Stoicism stresses the disposition, but the aesthetic aspect persists even in ethics.
b. The verb *charízomai* means "to show pleasure" or "to show oneself to be pleasant," and in the passive, especially the perfect, "to be agreeable."
c. *charitóō* has not been found prior to Sir. 18:17.
d. *acháristos* means "without charm" or "ungrateful."
2. Hellenism.
a. In Hellenism *cháris* becomes a fixed term for the "favor" shown by rulers, with such nuances as "gracious disposition" or "gracious gift." *cháris* may also be ascribed to other dignitaries. Philosophy discusses the "grace" and "wrath" of the gods. The Epicureans deny these; the Stoics accept grace but not wrath. In recipients, *cháris* denotes "thanks."
b. In a second development Hellenism stresses the power in *cháris*. This power, which comes from the world above, appears in the divine man and expresses itself in magic. [H. CONZELMANN, IX, 359-76]

B. The OT.
1. ḥnn and Derivatives.
a. The LXX uses *cháris* especially for Heb. *ḥēn,* which seems to derive from the widespread verbal stem *ḥnn,* found in Ancient Babylon, Akkadian, and Assyrian, and also in Ugaritic, Aramaic, Syriac, and Arabic.
b. The verbal stem denotes a gracious disposition that finds expression in a gracious action (cf. Gen. 33:5; Ps. 119:29). The construction with accusative of person brings out the thrust, namely, gracious address to another. We find an impersonal object only marginally, as in Ps. 102:14. What is in view is the process whereby one who has something turns graciously to another who is in need. Initially the term is not theological. It may be used for having pity on the poor (Prov. 14:31) or the defenseless (Dt. 7:2). More weakly it may simply denote friendly speech (Prov. 26:25).
c. Yet the main OT development relates to God, who is the subject in 41 of 56 instances; 26 in the Psalms, which call on God to hear prayer (4:1), to heal (6:2), to

redeem (26:11), to set up (41:10), to pardon (51:1), and to strengthen (86:16) in the corresponding needs. Appeal is made in these prayers to the love of God or to his word or covenant. The Aaronic blessing (Num. 6:25) invokes the gracious will of God as God has pledged it in the covenant. Yet God's graciousness is a free gift (Ex. 33:19). Judgment is often mentioned alongside it, as in Am. 5:15, where graciousness to a remnant is all that may be hoped for. The liturgical formula "gracious and merciful," one of the rare adjectival predications of God, relates to the acts of God rather than specifically to his being.

d. One of the verbs derived from the stem carries the sense "to request" or "to beseech," directed either to people (Gen. 42:21; 2 Kgs. 1:13), or to God (Dt. 3:23; 1 Kgs. 8:33).

e. In the case of nouns, the reference again might be to requests directed to others (Jer. 37:20) or to God (Ps. 28:2), or it might be to "mercy," e.g., that of the conqueror for the conquered (Josh. 11:20) or that of God for his people (Ezr. 9:8).

f. In the case of *ḥēn,* in analogy to showing no favor in Jer. 16:13, one might expect the same thought in, e.g., Gen. 39:21; Ex. 3:21; Ps. 84:11; Prov. 3:34. In fact, however, *ḥēn* undergoes a different development; the reference is to the favor that God gives along with other favors, i.e., their "gracefulness" or "attractiveness" or "worth" which causes others to be favorably disposed. In the *ḥēn* that God gives there is thus reflected, not the relation between giver and recipient, but the relation between the recipient and a third person.

g. This relation emerges clearly in the very common phrase "to find grace in the eyes" of another, whether the other be another person or God. Thus Noah found grace in the eyes of the Lord in Gen. 6:8 and Moses in Ex. 33:12, while Jacob seeks favor in Esau's eyes in Gen. 32:5 and Joseph finds favor in Potiphar's house in Gen. 39:4.

h. In the Psalms *ḥēn* does not occur in the context of petition but refers to the "grace" that God gives in Ps. 84:11 and to "grace" on the lips of the bridegroom in Ps. 45:2. In Proverbs, where the term is more common, it has the same sense, although in Ecclesiastes the favor that comes to a person is meant (9:11; 10:12). In general, *ḥēn* thus becomes a term that qualifies the recipient, with a certain aesthetic accent in many cases (cf. Zech. 4:7). The meaning is closer to that of the verbal stem in Zech. 12:10, where mercy and supplication are poured out in place of an original hardness. But for the most part *ḥēn* fails to supply the noun corresponding to verbs of the stem. It thus opens the door to another term which the LXX usually renders *éleos,* the noun related to *eleéō,* its translation of *ḥnn.* This term is *ḥeseḏ.*

2. *ḥeseḏ.*

a. The term *ḥeseḏ* demands treatment here, partly because of the connection made by its translation as *éleos,* partly because of its later merging with *ḥēn,* and partly also because the later translators relate it to *cháris.* Debate continues as to the precise meaning of *ḥeseḏ.* One school relates it to right or duty and sees a basic connection with the covenant. Another school finds in it simple kindliness both as will and act. The truth, perhaps, is that it expresses spontaneous goodness, or grace, in a specific relationship or in ongoing fellowship (cf. Gen. 19:19; 47:29; 1 Sam. 20:8; 2 Sam. 16:17). The primary sphere of *ḥeseḏ* seems to be that of relationships among humans. It then comes into the vicinity of covenant statements either as the presupposition of a covenant or as its expression. Here the element of duty emerges; constancy and loyalty are native to it.

b. The word then acquires its distinctive OT sense in relation to God. In Ex. 20:5-6 God is jealous for his rights but shows covenant grace to thousands of those who love him and keep his commandments. Here grace is converted into act, and the "thousands" shows that it is incomparably stronger than wrath. Grace often occurs in the context of forgiveness (Ex. 30:7 etc.) and along with an express reference to the covenant (Dt. 7:9). Mercy accompanies it in Ex. 34:6 etc., and faithfulness in Dt. 7:9 etc. The Psalms develop the divine aspect with 127 of the 237 instances, only three of which refer to *hesed* among humans. Invoking it, the Psalms beseech God to hear (Ps. 119:149), to save (109:26), to redeem (44:26), to give life (119:88), and to forgive (25:7). Thanks are given for expressions of it (5:7; 106:45). Accounts are given of various instances (94:18; 21:7; 59:10, etc.). Parallels are salvation (13:5), mercy (25:6), righteousness (36:10), redemption (130:7), and faithfulness (36:5). Miracles are connected with it (107:8), and joy and praise arise at it (31:7; 138:2). The earth is full of it (33:5), it reaches to heaven (36:5), it endures forever (89:2), and if death seems to limit it (88:11), it is better than life itself (63:3). God sends it, it comes, it meets and follows us (57:3; 59:10; 85:10; 23:6), and we must remember, consider, and wait for it (106:7; 48:9; 33:18). Praise of it takes liturgical form (107; 136; 1 Chr. 16:34; Jer. 33:11). In its sphere, God's people show it to one another (Gen. 24:49; Ruth 1:8; 3:10).

c. Among the prophets, Hosea, Jeremiah, and Isaiah (40ff.), who speak most of the covenant, are rich in references to *hesed*. A new element here, however, is that of human *hesed* toward God (Hos. 4:1; 6:4). What is meant is Israel's covenant conduct, i.e., spontaneous love of God. Jeremiah refers to this in 2:2. It is possible only as God's own gracious gift (Hos. 2:19-20). Is. 55:3, appealing to the covenant of grace with David, stresses the character of *hesed* as salvation. In Is. 40:6, however, there is an approximation to the meaning of *hēn,* the reference being to the collapse of human glory (cf. Esth. 2:9, 17).

d. In general one may state that *hesed* plays the role of a substitute noun for the *hnn* group. The only difference is that it stresses free kindness within a specific relationship and does not necessarily express the movement of the stronger to the weaker or poorer. The social relationship controls the content, so that when it is oriented to a covenant, the particular understanding of the covenant fixes the sense.

e. The derived adjective occurs especially in the Psalms. Often here God is in view as the active giver of grace. With a human reference the use may be passive for the recipients of divine grace or active for those who themselves show faithfulness. A covenant context is apparent in Ps. 50:5.   [W. ZIMMERLI, IX, 376-87]

C. Judaism.
1. Qumran and the Testaments of the Twelve.

a. *hsd* is dominant in the Qumran writings. Closely connected with mercy and righteousness, it is a basic term for God's dealings. The righteous rely on it, they extol God's fullness of it, and it proves itself in times of trouble.

b. The use in the Testaments of the Twelve is of little significance.

2. Rabbinic Writings. In the rabbis the verb *hnn* means "to be favorable," and the noun *hsd* signifies "favor" or "attractiveness." The central problem is the relation between grace and works. Grace arises where there are no works, and the stress falls on the freedom of the divine giving. Yet the concept of grace remains caught in the schema of the law, i.e., the principle of act and reward.

3. The LXX.

a. *cháris* translates *hēn* rather than *hesed* and usually denotes "attractiveness" or "favor" with God or others. It is not a theological term.

b. *charízomai* occurs only in Sirach and Maccabees and means "to give."

4. *Philo.* Some development may be seen in Philo, for whom Hannah symbolizes *cháris,* and who views *chárites* as God's gifts and *cháris* as the power behind them. The content of *cháris* derives from the understanding of God as Creator and Preserver, always in an active sense. In one sense *cháris* is the human endowment at creation. In relation to salvation, Philo has no doctrine of merit but he also thinks that *cháris* is only for the righteous. He demands a struggle for virtue but also a confession that virtue is God's achievement and not ours. Recognition of sin and need forms the essential starting point. Over against this stands the greatness of grace. Those who are pious in the sense of self-renunciation are impelled by divine forces and may thus attain to virtue.

D. The NT. The noun *cháris* does not occur in Matthew, Mark, or 1 and 3 John, in John it occurs only in 1:14ff., and in 1 Thessalonians and Philemon only in salutations. *charízomai* is found only in Luke and Paul, and *charitóō* only in Lk. 1:28 and Eph. 1:6. The preposition *chárin* is not very common in the NT (in contrast to the Koine). The OT *hēn* offers little guidance, and *heseḏ* points us to *éleos* rather than *cháris.*

1. *Luke.*

a. The secular sense may be seen in Acts 24:27; 25:3, 9, and more positively in Acts 2:47; 4:33.

b. OT influence may be seen in the religious use in Lk. 1:30; Acts 7:46; 7:10; Lk. 2:40, 52; 6:32ff.

c. *cháris* characterizes the good news in Lk. 4:22; Acts 14:3. It depicts the Spirit-filled man in Acts 6:8. Its overruling may be seen in the church's growth in Acts 11:23. There is commendation to divine grace in Acts 14:26; 15:40. Acts 15:11 has a Pauline ring but in a context of exhortation.

d. As regards *charízomai,* Barabbas is freed as a favor to the people in Acts 3:14, but Paul asks not to be handed over as a favor to them in 25:11 (cf. v. 16). God grants Paul the lives of those who travel with him in 27:24. Luke summarizes the work of Jesus in Lk. 7:21 (cf. 4:22), and Lk. 7:42-43 is also typically Lucan.

e. *charitóō* ("to show grace," "to bless") occurs in the NT only in connection with divine *cháris* (Lk. 1:28).

f. *acháristos* means "ungrateful" in Lk. 6:35. It derives its force from *cháris* in vv. 32ff.

2. *Paul.*

a. A central concept in Paul, *cháris* has a special place in his greetings (Rom. 1:7 etc.; 1 Th. 5:28 etc.). It echoes the familiar *chaírein,* but comes into association with peace in a liturgical formula that forms a constituent part of the letter.

b. Distinctively *cháris* in Paul expounds the structure of the salvation event. The basic thought is that of free giving. In view is not just a quality in God but its actualization at the cross (Gal. 2:21) and its proclamation in the gospel. We are saved by grace alone. It is shown to sinners (Rom. 3:23-24), and it is the totality of salvation (2 Cor. 6:1) that all believers have (1 Cor. 1:4). To the "grace alone" embodied in Christ corresponds the "faith alone" of believers (Rom. 3:24ff.) that rules out the law as a way of salvation (4:16). *cháris* and *pístis* together are in antithesis to *nómos* (law). Grace is the basis of justification and is also manifested in it (5:20-21). Hence grace is in some sense a state (5:2), although one is always called into it (Gal. 1:6), and it is always a gift on which one has no claim. Grace is sufficient (1 Cor. 1:29). One neither needs more nor will get more. It carries an element of assurance, but not of false security, thus leaving no place for boasting (1 Cor. 1:29; cf. Gal. 5:4).

c. The work of grace in overcoming sin displays its power (Rom. 5:20-21). It differs from sin structurally, for it comes, not as destiny, but as free election (11:5-6). It finds actualization in the church, e.g., in Paul's collection (2 Cor. 8). Its goal is every good work (9:8), and in this regard it poses a demand (6:1), yet in such a way as to make compliance possible. To think that grace means libertinism is only pseudo-logic; Paul dismisses the mere suggestion in Rom. 6:1.

d. Paul's apostolic office is a special grace in Rom. 1:23 etc. It is given to him (12:3), and its discharge is grace (2 Cor. 1:12), e.g., in visiting a church (v. 15).

e. The verb *charízomai* has for Paul the sense "to give." The context gives it a soteriological nuance in Rom. 8:32, and the sense is close to that of the noun in 1 Cor. 2:12. Suffering is a gift in Phil. 1:28-29, and the institution of Jesus as *kýrios* rewards his obedience in Phil. 2:9.

3. *Colossians, Ephesians, the Pastorals, Hebrews, 1 and 2 Peter, and James.*

a. In Col. 1:6 *cháris* means the gospel. "Charm" is perhaps the sense in Col. 4:6. In Eph. 1:6-7 *cháris* is the divine "favor" shown in Christ. 2:5ff. is distinctively Pauline. So, too, is 3:2, 7-8. The combination with "given" in 4:7, 29 is stereotyped. The verb *charízomai* means "to forgive" in Col. 3:13 (cf. Eph. 4:32). Believers are to forgive one another on the basis of the Lord's forgiveness (cf. also 2:13). *charitóo* means "to bless" in 1:6.

b. In the Pastorals "thanks" is the meaning of *cháris* in 1 Tim. 1:12 and the "grace" of office in 2 Tim. 2:1. 2 Tim. 1:9 contrasts grace and works in a context of epiphany (cf. Tit. 2:11). Terms like goodness and mercy are equivalents in Tit. 3:4ff. Again we have the contrast with works, but with a reference to grace in baptism (vv. 5ff.). *cháris* replaces hope in the triad in 1 Tim. 1:14.

c. Hebrews uses *cháris* and *éleos* in 4:16 (cf. 1 Tim. 1:2). Christ embodies grace, and one receives it at God's throne (7:25). Christ suffers by the grace of God in 2:9. Christ's death (or blood) comes into association with the covenant and grace in 10:29. The antithesis of grace and meats is part of the antithesis of the covenants in 13:9. One must not fall short of grace in 12:15.

d. In 1 Peter suffering is understood as grace (2:19-20). 2 Pet. 3:18 relates *cháris* to *gnósis*. The precise sense of "giving more grace" in Jms. 4:6 is not clear.

4. *John.* The group is rare in Johannine works. *cháris* occurs in the greetings in 2 Jn. 3 and Rev. 1:4; 22:21. In Jn. 1:14, 16-17 grace denotes the result of the revelation of the Logos in antithesis to the law and in combination with truth and fullness, which help to give it its distinctive significance.

E. The Apostolic Fathers. The formulas in Barn. 21.9; Pol. 14.2, etc. adopt the NT salutation. Normal use for "thanks," "favor," and "reward" may be seen in, e.g., Did. 1.3. If *cháris* is the reading in Did. 10.6, salvation, or the Lord himself, is meant. Grace is the result of salvation in 1 Clement; the Christian state is the yoke of grace (16.17), and one may attain to grace by right conduct (20.2-3). Grace is a power at work in the church in Ignatius *Smyrneans* 9.2. It is salvation (*Ephesians* 11.1), or God's will (*Romans* 1.2), and a motif in the summons to unity (*Ephesians* 20.2). Ignatius trusts in God's grace (*Philadelphians* 8.1), and he views his martyrdom as grace (*Romans* 6.2). The verb *charízomai* denotes God's giving in the sacrament in Did. 10.3 (cf. *charitóō* in Hermas *Similitudes* 9.24.3).

F. Gnosticism. *cháris* is not a basic term in Gnosticism. It occurs as a power, sometimes hypostatized. It is also a gift, e.g., in the Marcosite eucharist. Coptic Gnosticism speculates about the grace of light that comes forth through the first mystery. From Christ as light *cháris* is one of four great lights, and elsewhere it is one of three aeons.

chárisma.

A. Usage. This rare and late verbal noun of *charízomai* denotes the result of *cháris* as an action, i.e., "proof of favor," "benefit," or "gift."

B. The LXX and Judaism. Ps. 31:21 Θ has *chárisma* for *ḥeseḏ* (LXX *éleos*), and the term occurs in Sir. 7:33 (Cod. S) and 38:30 (B) for "favor." Philo uses it in much the same sense as *cháris* (*Allegorical Interpretation of Laws* 3.78).

C. The NT.

1. General. Paul uses the word in Romans, 1 and 2 Corinthians, and the Pastorals. He relates it to *cháris* and *pneúma* in soteriological contexts. It occurs in the prefaces to Romans and 1 and 2 Corinthians, and takes shape as gifts in Rom. 12:6 and 1 Cor. 12:11. Linked to *eucharistéō*, it also has an eschatological orientation. The present is eschatologically determined by *cháris* as the age of the Spirit. The gift is present but its possession is provisional (1 Cor. 1:8). The whole gift of salvation is *chárisma* (2 Cor. 1:11; cf. Rom. 5:15-16). The sense is more formal in Rom. 6:23 and Rom. 1:11, where Paul has a spiritual gift to impart. An individualizing element emerges in 1 Cor. 7:7. The fact that all have their own gifts means that celibacy is not imposed as a law.

2. charísmata.

a. In 1 Cor. 12ff. and Rom. 12 the *charísmata* are operations of the Spirit at worship, notably tongues and prophecy. The Corinthians stress tongues, but Paul shows the ambivalence of ecstasy, makes confession of the *kýrios* the norm, argues that God gives individual gifts for the church's upbuilding, views these as future possession in provisional form, and finds a *chárisma* in everything that edifies. The two triads in vv. 4ff. do not mean that the gifts are the Spirit's, the services the Lord's, and the operations God's. We simply have three different descriptions of the work of the one Spirit (v. 11); these descriptions bring out the unity in multiplicity. The operations are supernatural but not magical; one can cultivate the gifts (12:31). Only to a certain degree can one define and distinguish the *charísmata*. The inclusion of acts of ministry forbids the distinction between charismatics and officebearers or between office/law on the one side and Spirit on the other. The Spirit himself posits law.

b. Ordination confers the *chárisma* of office in 1 Tim. 4:14; 2 Tim. 1:6. In 1 Pet. 4:10 any act of service in love is *chárisma*. Endowment with the Spirit is here virtually a quality.

D. The Early Church. Formalizing may be seen in Did. 1.5. 1 Clem. 38.1 includes the gifts of the Creator. Justin argues that the gifts have passed from Judaism to Christianity (*Dialogue* 88.1). Irenaeus *Against Heresies* 5.6.1 finds in them the divine power of the church.

eucharistéō, eucharistía, eucháristos.

A. Secular Greek.

1. Usage.

a. We first find *eucháristos* in the senses "pleasant" and "graceful." *eucharistéō* means "to show a favor," but this imposes a duty of gratitude and the meaning "to be thankful" or "to give thanks" develops. We also find the sense "to pray."

b. *eucharistía* is common on inscriptions and means "gratitude" or "giving thanks."

c. *eucháristos* has the senses "pleasant," "grateful," and "beneficent."

2. *Meaning.*

a. The Greek world holds thanksgiving in high esteem. With the ordinary use we find a public use (gratitude to rulers) and a religious use (thanksgiving to the gods for blessings). Thanks are also a constituent part of letters.

b. Compounds in *eu-* are slow to appear and late. Epictetus speaks of *tó eucháriston* as a basic ethical attitude. He stresses the duty of giving thanks to God.

B. Judaism.

a. Hebrew has no equivalent term but thanks come to expression in the OT in the thank offering and the song of thanksgiving, both collective and individual. Except for *eucháristos* in Prov. 11:16, the group occurs only in apocryphal works, where it signifies thanks to others or to God (2 Macc. 12:31; 10:7). For epistolary style cf. 2 Macc. 1:10-11. 2 Macc. 1:11ff. offers a prototype for Paul's salutations.

b. In Judaism thanks are given for food and drink and for good news. Thanksgiving will never cease.

c. In Philo the central theme is thanks to God as inward veneration. This is an obligation for gifts received. But it is not a human achievement and has no goal beyond itself.

C. The NT.

1. Gospels, Acts, and Revelation.

a. We find a secular use of the verb in Lk. 17:16 and of the noun in Acts 24:3.

b. The verb denotes thanksgiving in general in Jn. 11:41; Acts 28:15; Rev. 11:17 and grace at meals in Mk. 8:6; Jn. 6:11; Acts 27:35. *eulogéō* is a synonym (cf. Mk. 8:6 and 6:41).

c. Jewish practice explains the use at the Last Supper. Both terms occur in Mk. 14:22-23 and Mt. 26:26-27. Paul has *eucharistéō* at the blessing of the bread in 1 Cor. 11:24, and Luke has it in 22:17, 19. *eulogéō* is perhaps closer to the Jewish blessing, but the use in translation of Hebrew or Aramaic terms is random.

2. Paul.

a. Most prominent in Paul is the epistolary use. Paul makes the thanksgiving part of the content; it may even introduce the principal theme, although in the main the prefaces constitute sections of their own. The chief forms are the verb with two or three participles (1 Th. 1:2ff.; Phil. 1:3ff.; Phlm. 4ff.) or the verb with *hóti* (1 Cor. 1:4-5; Rom. 1:8).

b. Formal use also occurs in 1 Cor. 1:14 and Rom. 16:4, and for grace at meals cf. 1 Cor. 10:30. Thanks are due to the Creator in Rom. 1:21. One sees the liturgical setting in 1 Cor. 14:16-17. God's act is the presupposition of the summons to *eucharistía* either in general exhortation (1 Th. 5:18) or in the special form of the collection (2 Cor. 9:11). The aim is the increase of God's glory (v. 12). Christ is the mediator of thanksgiving but not the recipient in Rom. 1:8.

3. Colossians, Ephesians, and the Pastorals. Thanksgiving goes with joy and confession in Col. 1:12, although confession does not have here a technical sense. A christological basis may be seen in Col. 2:7, and we have general exhortation in 3:15. Prayer is the proper mode of eschatological vigilance in 4:2. The two streams of petition and thanksgiving figure in 1 Tim. 2:1. 1 Tim. 4:3 attacks the Gnostic demand for asceticism by pointing to grace at meals. This practice rests on belief in God the

Creator. Thanksgiving expresses an attitude toward God and is the condition of enjoyment.

D. The Early Church.

a. Epistolary use occurs in, e.g., Ignatius *Philadelphians* 6.3; *Ephesians* 21.1, and there is a call to prayer in Hermas *Similitudes* 7.5; 1 Clem. 28.2, 4.

b. The eucharistic use in Did. 9–10; Ignatius *Ephesians* 13.1; Justin *Apology* 1.65 is of special interest. In Did. 9.1ff. it covers the prayer of thanksgiving, the elements, and the whole action (Did. 9.1, 5). A technical use develops (cf. Ignatius *Ephesians* 13.1). *eucharistía* comes to denote the sacrifice of *eucharistía* (cf. Justin *Apology* 1.13.1-2; *Dialogue* 117.2).   [H. CONZELMANN, IX, 387-415]

---

cháragma [mark, stamp]

A. The Greek World.

1. This word denotes an engraved, etched, branded, or inscribed "mark" or "sign." It can be used for an "inscription" or a "stamp," e.g., the imperial stamp on decrees. The impress on coins gives it the more general sense of "money."

2. The word does not occur in the LXX, though we find *charássō*, "to inscribe," in Sir. 50:27.

3. In Rev. 13:11ff. the second beast demands cultic recognition of the image of the first. The mark which is required in vv. 16-17 probably indicates the religious totalitarianism of emperor worship. Marking is common in antiquity (cf. slaves, and the branding of devotees with the marks of deities). The number 666 may well be a cipher for Nero; we thus have a confrontation between the claim of the emperor with his mark and the claim of Christ with his seal (Rev. 7:1ff.). The angel threatens with eschatological judgment all who bear the *cháragma* of the beast (14:9, 11; cf. 16:2; 19:20). Those who do not bear it have the role of eschatological judges (20:4). A different sense is apparent in Acts 17:29, where "handiwork" is meant. What we make cannot resemble deity, but we ourselves are God's offspring and are thus close to him (vv. 27-28).   [U. WILCKENS, IX, 416-17]

---

charaktḗr [impress, image, characteristic feature]

A. The Greek World. This word has first the meaning "die" (in minting) and then such further senses as "image," "impress," "coinage," "money," "stamp," "seal," "sign," "copy," and "letter." A special development is for the "typical feature(s)" of an individual or nation. This produces the idea of "moral character," but other uses are for the "distinctiveness" of a language, the "style" of a writer, or a "type" of philosophy.

B. Judaism.

1. In the LXX *charaktḗr* denotes a "scar" in Lev. 13:28, the "likeness" impressed by parents on children in 4 Macc. 15:4, and the "characteristic features" of Hellenistic culture in 2 Macc. 4:10.

2. In Josephus we find the senses "feature," "individuality," and "letter."

3. Philo uses the figure of the seal. The soul is like wax on which perceptions make

both good and bad impressions. The image of God is not a physical impress (*charaktḗr*) but extends only to the *noús*. Yet the soul has received a divine impress (*charaktḗr*) whereby it may know God. In the process of imaging the prototype inserts itself into the image and hence *eikṓn* and *charaktḗr* statements tend to merge. In self-impartation—God to *lógos* and *lógos* to us—the *eikṓn* is like the die impressing its stamp on wax.

C. **The NT.** The only NT use is in Heb. 1:3. The two statements in this verse correspond to what is said in v. 2. Viewing Christ's exaltation and preexistence, they hymn his eternal nature. As God's glory and hypostasis are synonymous, Christ both reflects the glory and bears the impress of the nature. It is by the Son that God is represented and acts. The Son as God's image and impress both contains God's glory and discloses it. As Ruler of the cosmos, he sustains all things by his mighty word, by his humiliation and exaltation he has become for us the cause of eternal salvation, and by the way of discipleship God leads those who trust in him as his children in glory (2:10). The Son's character as image is the essential presupposition of all his saving work. Unlike Philo, with whom there is linguistic similarity, Hebrews does not work out the soteriological significance of the concepts merely in terms of the knowledge of God. It is the humiliated and exalted Christ who bears the very stamp of God's nature.

D. **The Apostolic Fathers.** 1 Clem. 33.4 expounds Gen. 1:26-27 in a way that makes the man made in God's image the impress of the image, which is itself the original. Ignatius *Magnesians* 5.2 uses the figure of the coins to differentiate those who belong to Christ from the children of the world. The "character" that believers receive through Christ is participation in his sufferings as the presupposition of participation in his life. In Ignatius *Trallians,* Introduction "after the manner" expresses a sense of difference from the apostles.

E. **Gnosticism.** In Gnostic works *charaktḗr* tends to be associated with corporeality, so that the original spheres are featureless. Nevertheless, the emanations of primal being may have their own *charaktḗres*. The *charaktḗres* give form to matter but fall into the hands of the demiurge. The firmament prevents further *charaktḗres* from being dragged down from the upper world into darkness.   [G. KELBER, IX, 418-23]

---

cheír [hand],   *cheiragōgéō* [to lead by the hand],   *cheiragōgós* [one who leads by the hand],   *cheirógraphon* [hand-written document],   *cheiropoíētos* [made with human hands],   *acheiropoíētos* [not made with human hands], *cheirotonéō* [to raise the hands, select]

---

cheír.

A. **Greek Usage.**
1. The Human Hand.
a. Aristotle attaches great importance to the hand. It is the instrument of movement and action. It controls implements. Since it exerts the power of the arm, the arm may also be called the *cheír.* Various expressions such as "with the hand" or "to take (or have) in hand" describe acts performed by the hand. We take others by the hand or greet them with a handshake. The hand may also be raised in attack or defense (cf. the terms for hand-to-hand fighting).

b. The gods protect or intervene with the hand, and lay on their hands to bless, heal, or save. Wonder-workers mediate healing power by the laying on of hands.

2. *Transferred Sense*. Various uses develop, e.g., for the right side or the left, for power, for work as that which is done by the hands, for handwriting, and for a handful or troop.

B. The OT and Judaism.

1. *The Human Hand*. The usual Hebrew term for "hand" is *yāḏ*, although there are other words such as *kap* for "palm." Since hands are used in work, what we make is the work of our hands (Dt. 28:12). The hand can stand for the person (Ex. 19:13). The stronger right hand imparts the richer blessing (Gen. 48:14). The right hand is the place of honor (Ps. 110:1). The hand gives and receives, and a handshake seals a bargain (2 Kgs. 10:15; Ex. 17:18). The hand on the mouth expresses silence (Job 21:5). Clapping the hands is a sign of joy (Ezek. 25:6). Hands are lifted up for prayer or oaths (Ps. 28:2; Ex. 6:8), stretched forth hands signify resolution (Num. 15:30), and filling the hands denotes investiture (Ex. 28:41).

b. The OT laws of ritual cleanness apply to the hands. Cleanness or uncleanness can be transferred by objects that touch them. Hence one must wash the hands after handling the Scriptures.

2. *Transferred Sense*. The Hebrew word can express direction, power, or an object (e.g., a socket or signpost) that projects the hand. One may send, order, or speak by the hand of someone, e.g., God by the hand of the prophets (1 Sam. 28:15; Ezek. 38:17).

3. *God's Hand*.

a. The OT often refers to God's hand in creation or history. Thus God lays his hand on people, stretches it out, and creates and redeems by it. He brings Israel out of Egypt with a strong hand. Both creation and redemption are extolled as the work of his hand. His hand comes into the lives of individuals (cf. 1 Kgs. 18:46). It seizes Jeremiah and Ezekiel for their prophetic tasks (Jer. 15:17; Ezek. 1:3).

b. Qumran follows the OT in speaking about God's hand. In particular the hand of God gives victory over enemies and it offers comfort in prayer.

c. Hellenistic Judaism, however, seldom refers to God's hand. Avoiding anthropomorphisms, it prefers to speak about God's power.

d. The rabbis, too, exercise great restraint in this area. At the Exodus, the idea that Israel goes out with lifted hand replaces the OT statement that it is taken out by God's hand.

4. *Laying On of Hands*.

a. In blessing, hands are laid on others to impart the blessing (Gen. 48:14). The laying on of hands may also transfer power (2 Kgs. 13:16). In the OT and the rabbis, however, we never read of the laying on of hands for healing.

b. The law orders that the hand be laid on the heads of various animals at offerings (Lev. 1:4; 8:22; 4:4). The high priest on the Day of Atonement puts his hand on the scapegoat and drives it into the desert (16:21). In the case of the offerings, the thought seems to be one of identification, in the case of the scapegoat it is one of transfer.

c. Laying on of hands institutes into office. In Joshua's case it transfers the needed power (Num. 27:21ff.). The rabbis work out a ceremony of once-for-all ordination by laying on of hands in the presence of witnesses. This ceremony adds another link to the chain of tradition extending back to Moses, and qualifies the new rabbi to deliver his own judgments.

C. The NT.

1. The Human Hand. Work is done with the hand in 1 Th. 4:11. The hand is an instrument of the will, e.g., for plucking ears of grain, or holding the plow. One gives the hand, beckons with it, stretches it out, carries things in it, etc. Rings are set on the hand (Lk. 15:22). The hand may wither (Mk. 3:1). A mark on the hand denotes ownership (Rev. 13:16). Hands can hang down (Heb. 12:12) or may be lifted in blessing (Lk. 24:50) or prayer (1 Tim. 2:8). God is not to be worshipped with human hands (Acts 17:25). Ritual washings are prescribed for the hands (Mk. 7:2). With the hand one dips in the common dish (Mt. 26:23). Paul writes a greeting with his own hand at the end of dictated letters (1 Cor. 16:21; 2 Th. 3:17; Col. 4:18).

2. Transferred Sense.

a. *cheír* often means power in the NT (cf. Mk. 9:31; Lk. 1:71; 2 Cor. 11:33; Jn. 3:35).

b. After a preposition *cheír* strengthens the preposition but loses its own sense. Thus *diá cheirós* means "through" (Mk. 6:2) and *en cheirí* "by" (Gal. 3:19).

3. God's Hand. The NT refers to God's hand only when adducing OT sayings or following OT usage (Lk. 23:46; Rom. 10:21). God's hand executed creation (Acts 7:50). It acts in history (Lk. 1:66; Acts 13:11). To fall into the hands of God is a fearful thing (Heb. 10:31).

4. Laying On of Hands.

a. As in the healings of antiquity, NT healing often involves the laying on of hands. Jairus asks Jesus to lay his hands on his daughter (Mk. 5:23). Jesus lays hands on the blind man in Mk. 9:27, and on the woman in Lk. 13:13. He takes Peter's mother-in-law by the hand in Mk. 1:31, touches the leper in 1:41, lays hands on the sick man in Lk. 14:4, and heals by laying on of hands in Mk. 6:5. The apostles continue this healing ministry (Mk. 16:18; Acts 3:7; 5:12, 15; 19:11; 28:8). If power is thus transferred by contact, there is no magical practice, for the decisive elements are the mighty word of Jesus and the faith that is put in him. The word is not tied to the means of transfer (cf. Mt. 8:8, 13; Jn. 4:50ff.).

b. Hands are imposed in blessing (cf. the children in Mt. 19:13). Laying on of hands serves as a visible sign of the imparting of the Spirit at baptism (Acts 8:17). Only with their acceptance by the apostles do Samaritan believers become full members of the one church (cf. also the disciples of the Baptist in 19:6).

c. Laying on of hands accompanies institution to office (cf. the ordination of the Seven in Acts 6:6 and the commissioning of Paul and Barnabas in 13:1ff.). The Spirit plays an important role in the selection, and prayer is an essential part of the installation. The divine *chárisma* is imparted to Timothy (1 Tim. 1:18; 4:14) with the laying on of hands, although the gift itself is God's (2 Tim. 1:6) and it is given by prophetic utterance (1 Tim. 4:14). The apostle seems to ordain along with presbyter assistants. There is no reference to a consecrating power placed in the hands of individuals. God's will and call govern the ordination by which authorization and equipment come. Timothy himself must assume responsibility for further ordinations. The warning in 1 Tim. 5:22 is directed against overhasty ordinations, unless the reception of penitent sinners is the issue.

D. The Apostolic Fathers.

1. Several passages refer to the human hand in the usual manner, e.g., Did. 4.6.
2. In a transferred sense *cheír* again means power (1 Clem. 55.5), and we find *en*

cheirí for to have "in hand," and *hypó cheíra* for "on every occasion" (Hermas *Visions* 3.10.7).

3. In OT references, or passages modeled on the OT, God's hand is mentioned, e.g., creation as the work of his hand, or his hand intervening to save or punish.

4. Only Barn. 13.5 refers to the laying on of hands (Jacob blessing Ephraim in Gen. 48:14).

cheiragōgéō, cheiragōgós.

1. The verb *cheiragōgéō* means "to lead by the hand."

2. In the NT both verb and noun express the helplessness of the blind. Paul's companions lead him by the hand in Acts 9:8; 22:11, and the sorcerer in 13:11 has to look for people to lead him by the hand.

cheirógraphon.

1. A document is written in one's own hand as a proof of obligation, e.g., a note of indebtedness.

2. The meaning in Col. 2:14, then, is a "promissory note." God cancels the bond that lies to our charge. This bond is not a compact with the devil, as in some patristic exegesis. It is the debt that we have incurred with God. The forgiveness of sins (v. 13) through identification with Christ in his vicarious death and resurrection means that this note is cancelled; God has set it aside and nailed it to the cross.

cheiropoíētos, acheiropoíētos.

1. These words mean "made (or not made) with human hands." The LXX describes idols as "made with hands" in Is. 46:6.

2. The NT contrasts what is made by human hands with God's work. Mk. 14:48 refers to a temple not made with hands. Acts 7:48 stresses that God does not dwell in temples made with hands. Heb. 9:11, 24 contrasts the heavenly sanctuary with the earthly temple. Eph. 2:11 shows that circumcision is not decisive, since it is done by human hands. Col. 2:11 refers to the circumcision that is made without hands, i.e., that of Christ, whereby his people are buried and raised again with him. The heavenly house of 2 Cor. 5:1 is not made with hands. After death, God will have ready for us the new dwelling with which we shall be clothed.

cheirotonéō.

1. Raising the hand expresses agreement, and hence *cheirotonéō* first means "to vote for." Other meanings that develop are "to select" and "to nominate." *cheirotonía* in the LXX means "pointing with the finger" in Is. 58:9 (cf. Barn. 3.5).

2. 2 Cor. 8:19 uses the verb in the sense "to select." Paul refers to the person who has been "chosen" to accompany him in the matter of the collection. In Acts 14:23 Paul and Barnabas "nominate" the elders and then institute them into their work with prayer and fasting.   [E. LOHSE, IX, 424-37]

→ *brachíōn, dáktylos, dexiós*

Cheroubín [cherubim]

1. The OT cherubim guard Eden (Gen. 3:24), are on the mount of God (Ezek. 28:14ff.), carry God's throne chariot (10:1ff.), and serve as God's throne (1 Sam. 4:4). God rides on them (Ps. 18:10) and meets his people from between them (Ex. 25:22). They receive mention along with the ark (1 Sam. 4:4), and representations of them

conceal its cover with their wings (Ex. 25:18ff.). They stand facing one another at both ends of the mercy seat (Ex. 25:19).

2. Judaism regards them as a class of the heavenly host around God's throne. From the name the rabbis infer that they are like boys in shape, but Philo relates the name to knowledge and insight, and Josephus refers to winged creatures. Magical papyri use the name in efforts to achieve magical effects.

3. The only NT reference to the cherubim is in Heb. 9:5. This passage is describing the earthly sanctuary, and along with the ark of the covenant (v. 4) it mentions the cherubim of glory that stand over the mercy seat and overshadow it with out-spread wings.   [E. LOHSE, IX, 438-39]

---

chḗra [widow]

A. **Common Greek Usage.** This word, meaning "widow," derives from a root meaning "forsaken," and it may thus refer to any woman living without a husband. Later we also find *chḗros* for "widower." The verbs *chēróō* and *chēreúō* mean "to make a widow" and "to become a widow," and we also find the derived noun *chēreía*, "widowhood."

B. **The Widow outside the NT.**
I. The Pagan World.
1. Women dread the fate of becoming widows. Widows must either return to their own family, take a subordinate position in their husbands' family, remarry, or seek death. Many cultures frown on their remarriage. Those who do remarry lose cultic privileges and other rights. When Augustus orders the remarriage of widows as a means of repopulation, the decree arouses much criticism. Judaism takes a more relaxed view, e.g., in the Levirate law. Having lost their normal protector, widows come under social and economic oppression. Orphans are grouped with them in this regard. We find many accusations against their exploitation, e.g., when they are sold for debt. Pericles praises war widows, however, and wealthy widows often control considerable power and property after the achievement of some feminine liberation in early Hellenism.

2. Appeals for the helping of widows and orphans are also common. The gods of the Near East (e.g., Amon-Re in Egypt) are concerned about their plight. An Athenian law makes some provision for them, but in the world of Greece and Rome the gods show less concern for widows or the poor. The military welfare fund for the sick, orphans, and parents does not include widows, and restrictions apply to their rights of inheritance.

II. The OT.
1. The LXX. The LXX uses *chḗra* mainly for "widow," although "woman without a husband" is the sense in, e.g., 2 Sam. 20:3. *chēreía* occurs in Is. 54:4, *chēreúō* in Jdt. 8:4, *chēreusis* ("widow's weeds") in Gen. 38:14, 19.

2. The Widow in the OT. The fate of the widow is bewailed (Ex. 22:25). Widowhood may indeed be a divine penalty (Ex. 22:22ff.). Widows are associated with others who are disadvantaged, e.g., orphans, aliens, or day laborers. They suffer wrongs (Is. 10:2) or loss of rights (1:23). They are held in low esteem (54:4); cf. their special clothes (Gen. 38:14). Like harlots or divorcées, they may not marry the high priest (Lev. 21:14), or, in the program of Ezek. 44:22, any priest at all unless they are the widows of priests.

3. Benevolence to Widows in the OT. Some widows enjoy high regard (cf. Gen. 38), and the OT enjoins all the righteous to be kind to widows. God is their refuge, and he helps them to their rights (Ps. 146:9; Dt. 10:18). He threatens judgment on those who wrong them and promises blessing to those who assist them (Ex. 22:21ff.; Jer. 7:6). He witnesses in their favor (1 Kgs. 17:20). The supreme disaster is when he no longer pities them (Is. 9:16). Their vows are valid (Num. 30:10), they have a share of the tithe (Dt. 14:29), they may glean (24:19ff.), they participate in feasts (16:11), their clothes may not be taken as a pledge (24:17), and incidentally Levirate marriage grants them some protection (25:5ff.).

III. The Widow in Judaism. Judaism takes up the same motifs as the OT. Widows suffer oppression, but God defends them, adopts them, hears their prayers, and judges on their behalf. Various laws assist them, e.g., the right to live in the house and on the estate of the late husband, the right to keep money in the temple, and the right to a share of tithes and war booty. For Philo the *chḗra* of God is, allegorically, the soul apart from God.

C. The NT

1. Mark. In Mk. 12:40 and parallels Jesus takes up the prophetic condemnation of injustices done to widows. Scribes who ostensibly are helping widows to their rights charge so highly that the widows lose their possessions. Jesus thus comes forward as their true advocate. In contrast to avaricious scribes and the ostentatious rich is the poor widow of Mk. 12:41ff. who shows her trusting devotion by giving her whole living, meager though this is.

2. Luke. The widow's conduct in Lk. 18:2ff. provides an illustration of persistent and confident prayer. The issue is a financial one, and the judge, not wishing to alienate her powerful adversary, defers the case. But the woman's pertinacity prevails. In Lk. 4:25-26 the example of one of the elect widows of the OT releases God's messengers from obligations to their own obdurate people. In Lk. 7:11ff. the stress is on the loss of the only remaining protector of the widow of Nain and hence on the messianic trait of Jesus' compassion for her. Early in Luke we find alongside the virgin Mary and Simeon the charismatic widow Anna (2:36ff.), who refrains for a whole lifetime from any remarriage, who engages in constant prayer and fasting, who is a prophetess, and who as a privileged witness of the infant Jesus serves as a model for the witness of women in the church (cf. Lk. 18:3ff.). The church itself makes provision for widows in Acts 6:1. Many Jews of the dispersion retire to Jerusalem and leave widows there. Since the Palestinian believers administer the common funds, they tend to neglect Hellenist widows as tension develops between the native group and the dispersion element; hence the intervention of the apostles and the appointment of the Seven. Tabitha is an example of a concern for widows that is either individual or perhaps collective if the church commissions her for the purpose (cf. Acts 9:36ff.). Mention of *chḗrai* along with the *hágioi* (v. 41) suggests that the *chḗrai* might already be viewed as a special class, and that the raising of Tabitha takes place in their favor (cf. Lk. 4:26; 7:11ff.).

3. Paul. Paul offers counsel to the unmarried and widows in 1 Cor. 7:8-9 (cf. 39-40). In his view they should remain unmarried unless their sexual drive, stronger in young widows (cf. 1 Tim. 5:6ff.), demands remarriage. Those who can remain unmarried have a special *chárisma* (7:7) like Paul himself, and a special blessing attaches to them for following this better course.

4. Pastorals.

a. The Widow in the Family Unit. An early order for widows may be found in 1 Tim. 5:3ff. This order does not accept widows for service in the church or for the church's care if they have tasks, or may be cared for, within the family. Expositors differ as to whether it is the widows who are to look after the children and grandchildren, or the children and grandchildren who are to look after the widows. Possibly both views are right and mutual obligations are at issue. Widows must not neglect their immediate duties, nor relatives their duties toward them, in favor of duties to the church and its care for widows.

b. Younger Widows. Younger widows, too, have immediate tasks, and easily fall victim to frivolity or sensuality. If they are entrusted with a widow's office in the church, and subsequently remarry, they will break their primary loyalty to Christ. In the discharge of their duties, they also run the risk of becoming idlers and gossips and thus of bringing disrepute on the church. It is better, then, that they should remarry (5:14) and thus assume duties that will leave them less chance of getting into mischief.

c. "True" Widows. Those who are "really" widows are to be honored and supported (vv. 3ff.). These are women who are truly on their own and have resolved not to remarry (v. 5). They trust in God alone, give themselves to prayer night and day (cf. 1 Th. 3:10), and undertake various tasks on behalf of the church (v. 10).

d. Ministry. "True" widows are selected for service in the church (v. 9). This is implied by the "enrollment" of vv. 9, 11. Qualifications for selection are that they have no family (v. 5), give proof of good works (v. 10), be at least 60 years old (v. 9), have had only one husband (v. 9), and have no desire to remarry (v. 11). Whether the reference to one husband refers to remarriage after the death of a first husband or to remarriage after divorce is debated. Jesus allows the former but not the latter (Mk. 12:24ff.; 10:12). Paul leaves the former open in principle (Rom. 7:2-3). Lk. 2:36-37 extols the widow who has married only once. The tasks of widows include prayer, duties corresponding to those of a wife, and probably the training of younger women as enjoined on the *presbýtides* in Tit. 2:3ff. Wealthy widows might also have had charge of house churches (cf. Lydia, Mary the mother of Mark, Chloe, and Nympha in Col. 4:15). Relatives are to provide for widows where possible. The church assumes responsibility where there is no one else to do so (1 Tim. 5:16).

5. James.

Jms. 1:27 equates active concern for widows with pure service of God.

6. The Widow Figuratively.

In Lk. 18:2ff. the widow is a figure of God's eschatological people, which may expect an answer to believing supplication for final vindication. In Rev. 18:7 the harlot Babylon—representing Rome—compares herself to a queen and not a widow. But there will soon be a reversal of roles. The oppressed widow will be a royal bride (21:2) and haughty Babylon will be a diseased widow. The imagery combines the two motifs of God's people as bride and the city as a woman. The two cities of Jerusalem and Babylon stand for the two human peoples— the people *with* God, the bride, and the people *without* God, the widow. The church, which replaces OT Israel, now resembles a woman without a husband, as did Israel during the exile. But at the parousia it will be the bride that meets the heavenly Bridegroom (22:17).

D. The Widow in the Early Church.

1. Biblical Allusions. In early writings we find many biblical quotations and allusions (1 Clem. 8.4; Justin *Apology* 44.3, etc.). Examples of true widowhood are given (cf. *Apostolic Constitutions* 3.7.6, 8). Barn. 20.2 associates widows and orphans, Pol. 6.1

widows and the poor, and Ignatius *Smyrneans* 6.2 widows and the oppressed. Barn. 20.2 complains about the ill-treatment of widows. Hermas *Mandates* 8.10 commends the helping of widows as a work of love that is pleasing to God. Generosity to widows expresses thanksgiving to God. The rich who have no compassion on widows and orphans suffer torments in hell.

2. *Care for Widows*. Church orders arrange care for widows and the sick. Churches like Rome and Antioch provide daily support for hundreds of widows. Homes are set up for them. The bishops keep lists, and gifts are made through the bishops (cf. Ignatius *Polycarp* 4.1; *Apostolic Constitutions* 2.25.2). The presbyters and especially the deacons help (Hermas *Similitudes* 9.26.2). Wealthy lay members provide meals. At worship widows have special places alongside matrons. The deacons must not accept gifts from evildoers nor turn their ministry to self-enrichment. Older women receive preference over younger widows who might support themselves. Under Constantine laws provide tax concessions and legal aid for widows, and the care of widows and orphans shifts to the state.

3. *Rules for Widows*. Widows must not teach, gossip, or seek gain. They are to stay at home and pray. They must not drink too much wine nor laugh too much, and if they have property they should use it on behalf of the poor. Tertullian argues that they ought not to remarry but use their widowhood as an occasion for continence. They might enter into spiritual marriage with widowers to keep house for them. Normally younger widows are allowed to remarry once, but need must not be allowed to force them into it, and ascetic trends later lead to legislation against remarriage.

4. *Widows as an Institution*. An institution of widows develops, although whether they are ranked as ordained ministers is debatable. To be accepted widows must go through a time of testing, must have been married only once, must have led blameless lives and cared well for their families, and must be of a certain (variable) age. When appointed church widows, they take a vow not to remarry and are accountable to God for keeping it. In later orders there are to be only three church widows in a congregation. Some references group them with the bishops, presbyters, and deacons; others not. Ignatius *Smyrneans* 13.1 mentions virgins who are called widows, perhaps because there are not enough real widows. Women deacons, or deaconesses, have some precedence over widows because they have functions of supervision and direction, but they are often selected from among virgins or widows. We thus read of widows who are deaconesses, although even later the two groups are not identical. The tasks of widows include prayer, caring for the sick, visiting prisoners, showing hospitality to traveling preachers, and teaching women catechumens and Christian girls. Because of their work in the church they are highly honored, have a special place at worship on the left behind the presbyters (as deacons are on the right behind the bishop), receive communion after the deacons and before subdeacons, etc. Yet by the end of the early period the order disappears. It perhaps finds a new form in the monastic orders for women, for nuns take up many of the duties that widows originally discharge.

→ *orphanós*   [G. STÄHLIN, IX, 440-65]

---

chiliás [a thousand],   *chílioi* [a thousand]

A. Greek Usage. The term *chílioi* (a "thousand") occurs from the time of Homer. In combinations it may precede or follow. With it collective words are often singular, e.g., "a thousand horse." *chili-* is a common prefix. The *chiliétēs* is the period of the soul's journey in Plato, and the *chilíarchos* is the leader of a thousand men. Multiples take the appropriate number in front, e.g., *dischílioi* for "2,000." The word *chiliás* denotes a "thousand," and the plural *chiliádes* may signify a large number beyond computation.

B. The OT and Judaism.

1. In the LXX *chiliás* for a "thousand" occurs over 250 times. It is common in lists of numbers (e.g., Num. 1:21). The plural often denotes vast numbers, e.g., in Ex. 20:6; Dan. 7:10. *chílioi* is less common.

2. Jewish apocalyptic often refers to the innumerable host of angels (Eth. En. 14:22; 40:1). The righteous will bring forth thousands of children (10:17) and vines will produce wine a thousandfold (10:19; cf. Syr. Bar. 29:5). The idea of a cosmic week results in the theory that the world will last 7,000 years and then the eighth millennium will initiate the new aeon (cf. Slav. En. 33:1). Another view is that the world will last 6,000 years—2,000 without the law, 2,000 with it, and 2,000 as the age of the Messiah. Some compute the age of the Messiah as one of a thousand years, however, while others think it will last for 7,000 years (Is. 62:5).

3. At Qumran the number 1,000 is important in the military organization of the community, with leaders for each group of a thousand. Those who keep the commandments have the promise of life for a thousand generations (Dan. 7:9).

4. Josephus follows the Greek world in his use of the terms.

C. The NT.

1. The NT often uses *chílioi* or *chiliás* in references to numbers, as in 2 Pet. 3:8 (Ps. 90:4) or Mk. 5:13. 3,000 are added to the church in Acts 2:41, and about 5,000 in 4:4. Jesus feeds 5,000 men in Mk. 6:44 and 4,000 in 8:9. Acts 21:38 says that 4,000 followed the Egyptian rebel leader into the desert. Paul in Rom. 11:4 refers to the 7,000 who do not bow the knee to Baal (1 Kgs. 19:18). 1 Cor. 10:8 points to the 23,000 who fall in the wilderness. Lk. 14:31 asks whether a king will with 10,000 men challenge one who has 20,000.

2. In Revelation numbers have mysterious significance. Rev. 5:11 refers to the thousands of thousands who praise God, and 7:4ff. to the 12 times 12,000 of the sealed, who, representing the 12 tribes, comprise the whole people of God. In 11:3 and 12:6 we read of 1,260 days (42 months or three and a half years). This half of seven years is the period of acutest affliction. In the earthquake that follows, 7,000 will be killed (11:13). The thousands who accompany the Lamb in 14:1, 3 will enjoy eschatological preservation, but the last judgment will be so terrible that blood will flow as high as a horse's bridle for 1,600 stadia. The new Jerusalem will be 12,000 stadia in length, breadth, and height (21:16).

3. In Rev. 20 the devil will be bound and the saints will reign with Christ for a thousand years (vv. 2, 6). Satan will then be loosed, a decisive battle will ensue, the last judgment comes, and the new world of God begins (vv. 7ff.; 21–22). The idea of a millennial kingdom fuses the hope of a restoration of the Davidic monarchy with expectation of an eschatological aeon. Revelation proclaims Jesus as both Messiah-King and Son of Man, and thus relates all eschatological hope to him. It adopts the number 1,000 for the intermediate reign in accordance with the schema of 6,000 years of world history, a sabbath of 1,000 years, and then the initiation of the new heaven and earth. The author holds out to the suffering witnesses of Jesus the consoling prospect that they will rise again for the millennium even prior to the general resurrection, the last judgment, and the new creation.

D. The Apostolic Fathers. The number 1,000 occurs in these works only in 1 Clement and Barnabas. 1 Clem. 34.6 adduces Dan. 7:10 (cf. also 1 Clem. 43.5), and Barn. 15.4 refers to Ps. 90:4.   [E. LOHSE, IX, 466-71]

chliarós → *zéō*

---

choïkós [made of earth, earthy]

A. The Greek World. This is a new term that is possible only on the basis of Gen. 2:7 LXX. Primal heroes are earthborn (*gēgenés*), and human beings are formed from the earth (*pēlós*), but *choïkós* does not occur prior to Paul.

B. The OT.
1. Gen. 2:7 says that God made man of dust from the earth and blew into him the breath of life. Dust is the more common term (*'āpār*). We are raised from dust (Job 8:19), are always dust (Gen. 3:19), will return to dust (Ps. 22:29), and without the Spirit are only dust (Ps. 104:29). Dust is thus a term for the dead (30:9), and the fact that we are dust shows our frailty (103:14). We are also earth (*'ªdāmâ*). Taken from it, we return to it (Gen. 3:19; Ps. 146:4) and sleep in the dust of the earth (Dan. 12:2). Another OT parallel is "clay" (*hōmer*, Job 33:6; Is. 64:7).

2. The LXX does not use *choïkós* but has instead such terms as *pēlós, choús, chōma*, and *gḗ. gēgeneís* describes all people in Ps. 49:2, especially as mortal (Prov. 2:18) (but only Gentiles in Jer. 32:20).

C. Judaism.
1. Apocalyptic distinguishes the spheres of spirit and flesh as heavenly and earthly. Dwellers on earth can know only what is earthly, which is corruptible but will one day be changed. God created the dust, so that sin is due to Adam's fall, not to his being made of dust.

2. Our being made of dust underscores our limitation and even our impurity in the Qumran texts. But God's Spirit has joined this dust. Although we shall return to dust, God has an eternal destiny for this dust. Of other terms, clay is more important than earth. As dust, we have fallen victim to sin, but God shows his power by lifting up the dead from the dust into the community. There is no anthropological antithesis of spirit and dust (or flesh) in the Qumran works.

3. a. Philo does not use *choïkós*, but we see the full range of its meaning in his use of *choús*. We are made of dust and are thus earthborn. The earthly is the fleshly. The children of earth give the earthbound *noús* a fleshly nature. Only the descending breath of God's deity makes the vision of God possible. The soul's foot is on the ground, its head reaches up to heaven. The soul may thus oppose God or fill itself with heavenly knowledge. In the latter case it stands opposed to dust or body. But the *noús* is our true being. It is equated with heaven, while the bodily is equated with earth. The soul of the wicked is concerned with earth. What is ungodly is earthly. The body is in exile in Egypt. The royal way leads up to heaven. Purified souls mount up from the earthly body, the rest sink back to earth.

b. In Gen. 2:7 Philo is primarily concerned with the inbreathed *pneúma*. This is the image of God's power and the substance of the *psychḗ*. As the soul of the soul, it is distinct from the fleshly soul. Only in the *noús* is man the image of God, or a copy of the higher *lógos*, the true image. The body of the man of Gen. 2:7 is *choús*, his *psyché* is *pneúma*. Yet he is more glorious in body and soul than all his progeny. In sum, the higher *lógos* is God's image, the human *noús* is its copy, and earthly man is a further copy.

c. We thus have two classes of people—those who live by *logismós* in virtue of the Spirit, and those who live by blood and carnal desire. The *noús* holds a middle position with possibilities of going either way. The dualism is an ethical one; it results from the equation of wisdom and the divine Spirit (*pneúma*). The first man of Gen. 1:26-27 is the idea of man, i.e., wisdom, *lógos,* or *pneúma*. The man of Gen. 2:7 is the earthly man who has become *psyché*.

4. In Judaism, then, dust denotes limitation and mortality. We must admit that we are dust, for this moves God to pity. The fact that we are God's work also stresses our fragility compared to God. For Philo the earthly man is of lesser worth than the heavenly man. Dust is what we must flee as evil.

D. The NT. 1 Cor. 15:47ff. calls the first man *choïkós* on the basis of Gen. 2:7. In contrast stands the second man from heaven, Christ. Each founds a race—the one race earthly, the other heavenly. The differences from Philo are that the second man is now the heavenly one, that there is a christological reference, and that the opposite of the earthly man comes as a gift. Paul lays no stress on the distinction between created and uncreated. What counts is an Adam/Christ theology related to a Son of Man Christology. The resurrection qualifies Christ as the heavenly man. As *choïkós* we differ from what the risen Christ already is, and what we will one day be through him. As in the rabbis, Paul brings the Spirit of Ezek. 37:14 into some juxtaposition with the Spirit of Gen. 2:7.

E. Gnosticism. Simon Magus equates the world-creating *eikón* with the Spirit. Many Gnostics differentiate image and similitude, although in different ways. What is *choïkós* is linked with the lower creation in contrast to the new creation. Valentinus has three classes: the *choïkoí, psychikoí,* and *pneumatikoí*. We also read of a fleshly aeon, an aeon of the soul, and the coming aeon. Some souls are cast back into bodies in judgment. Non-Christian Gnosticism does not use *choïkós,* but we find references to the material body, the distinction of *psyché* and *noús,* and some use of *gēgeneís* in connection with drunkenness and sleep. [E. SCHWEIZER, IX, 472-79]

---

chrḗma [matter, money], *chrēmatízō* [to handle a matter, impart a revelation], *chrēmatismós* [money making, answer]

---

chrḗma.
1. Related to *chrḗ* ("necessity"), *chrḗma* means "matter," "affair," "amount," "sum" (of money), and in the plural "objects of value," "wealth," or "capital."

2. In the LXX it occurs for various Hebrew terms in the senses "money," "riches," "booty."

3. In the NT it means "sum of money" in Acts 4:37 and "wealth" or "possessions" in the plural in Mt. 19:22; Mk. 10:22-23. Simon Magus brings "money" in the hope of acquiring the divine gift (Acts 8:18), and Felix expects Paul to secure his release by giving him "money" (Acts 24:26). Not riches as such, but trust in them and their unworthy use come under NT criticism.

4. The only instance in the apostolic fathers is in Hermas *Similitudes* 2.5, which refers to the joint operation of the goods of the rich and the prayers of the poor.

chrēmatízō.

1. This word means "to handle a matter." It has this sense in political and economic contexts. It may also mean "to be active or to appear as this or that," e.g., as ruler.

2. In the LXX it corresponds to the Hebrew for "to speak" in Jer. 26:2, or "to declare a revelation" in 29:23; 30:2.

3. a. In the NT the verb denotes divine instruction by revelation. An order is implied in Mt. 2:12, 22; Acts 10:22. Moses is told how to make the tabernacle in Heb. 8:5. Noah receives instruction about unseen things, and accepts this as a warning, in Heb. 11:7. Simple impartation is the point in Lk. 2:26. Moses gives instruction (on earth) in Heb. 12:25, but the stress here lies on the greater instruction that comes with Jesus from heaven.

b. In Acts 11:26 the disciples appear for the first time as Christians (i.e., are called such), and in Rom. 7:3 the wife who lives with another while her husband is still alive is publicly reckoned an adulteress.

chrēmatismós.

1. This word means "money making," then official "answer" or "decree," also divine "answer" or "direction."

2. In the LXX it has the secular meaning "dispatch" and the religious meaning "oracle" (Is. 13:1). It is the name of a people in Gen. 25:14.

3. In the NT it occurs only in Rom. 11:4. The meaning is "answer." Elijah has been pleading with God against Israel (v. 2), and Paul asks: "But what is God's reply to him?", and he then quotes 1 Kgs. 19:18 to show that God has kept himself a remnant. Elijah is here a man of God receiving revelation.

4. 1 Clem. 17.5 calls God's utterance to Moses from the burning bush a *chrēmatismós,* i.e., a "divine instruction" imparting to Moses his task.

[B. REICKE, IX, 480-82]

> *chrēstós* [good, kind],   *chrēstótēs* [goodness, kindness],   *chrēsteúomai* [to be kind, loving],   *chrēstología* ["friendly" speech]

chrēstós.

A. Greek Usage.

1. This word has the basic sense of "excellent," "useful," "good of its kind." Nuances include "orderly," "healthy" (of food), "propitious" (offerings), "serious" (a wound or bite), "good" (experiences), and as noun "benefit" or "fortune."

2. When used of people the term means "worthy," "decent," "honest," morally "upright" or "good." The term may thus be used for a "good" character or disposition, or for someone who is "good" at a particular task. Other meanings are "kind," "gentle," "clement," "good-hearted," and even "simple." An ironical address is *chrēsté,* "my dear fellow."

3. We sometimes find *Chrēstós* as a proper name.

4. Only rarely does *chrēstós* describe the gods, for the term often arouses disdain and is thus thought to be incompatible with the majesty of deity.

B. The LXX and Judaism.

1. The LXX.

a. The LXX uses *chrēstós* for various Hebrew terms in the senses "excellent," "genuine," or "costly."

b. With reference to people it means "good," "serviceable," "kind," "benevolent."

c. Since the OT more readily associates majesty and condescension, it commonly uses *chrēstós* for God (Ps. 106:1; Jer. 33:11) or his name (Ps. 52:9) or mercy (Ps. 69:16). One can hope and trust in the Lord who is good (34:8). God is good and upright (25:8; cf. Dt. 32:4). Yet the severity that God shows in the law is the presupposition of this goodness; his ordinances are good (119:41, cf. 65ff.).

2. *Philo.* Philo uses *chrēstós* in the senses "serviceable," "helpful," and "good." He relates it to the goodness of God that the righteous seek to follow. Rulers are "gracious," and "friendly" or "kind" is implied when God is called *chrēstós*.

3. *Josephus.* In Josephus the term means "morally good" but also has the nuances "kind," "gentle," "benevolent," "considerate," and "well disposed."

C. The NT.

1. Secular use occurs in the NT in the proverbial saying in Lk. 5:39 and in the quotation in 1 Cor. 15:33 ("good morals").

2. God is "kind" even to the ungrateful and selfish in Lk. 6:35; he seeks and saves the lost (Lk. 15). The fullness of the divine kindness also lies behind the statement of Jesus that his yoke is "easy" in Mt. 11:30. In Rom. 2:4 Paul has *tó chrēstón* as a noun to describe the divine kindness which allows space for repentance, but which the impenitent disdain and hence store up wrath for themselves. What is meant is God's gracious restraint in face of his people's sins prior to Christ. *chrēstótēs* is used interchangeably in Rom. 2:4, and it occurs again in 11:22 with reference to God's gracious act in Christ. As Paul sees it, kindness constantly characterizes God, but this kindness finds particular expression and completion in his saving work in and through Christ. The continuity of God's kindness may also be seen in 1 Pet. 2:3, which applies Ps. 34:8 to Christ: "You have tasted the kindness of the Lord."

3. Eph. 4:32 takes up the saying of Christ in Lk. 6:35-36 and shows the implications of God's gracious action for the mutual relationships of believers.

D. Early Christian Literature.

1. 1 Clem. 14.3-4 demands mutual kindness with an appeal to Prov. 2:21. If God's work as Creator is here in view, Diog. 8.8 plainly refers to his saving work in Christ.

2. As the names Christ and Christian suggest, Christ is *chrēstós* and Christians are *chrēstoí* for Justin in *Apology* 4.1. A Marcionite inscription substitutes *Chrēstós* for *Christós.* This is a rejection of the OT *christós,* but the referring of OT quotations to Christ (e.g., Ps. 34:8) suggests it.

chrēstótēs.

1. *Secular Greek.* This noun has such senses as a. "honesty," "respectability," "worthiness," and b. "kindness," "friendliness," "clemency." Negatively it denotes a false "pliability" or "softness" toward evil.

2. *The LXX and Judaism.*

a. The LXX uses the term for "piety" or "clemency" but also for God's "kindly disposition or action," or for the "benefits" he confers.

b. Psalms of Solomon often uses the word for the "goodness" of God and the plenitude of his gifts.

c. Philo puts it in the list of virtues, although negatively it can take the form of "indulgence." God's dealings are motivated by it; he prefers forgiveness to punishment.

d. Josephus uses the word for God's "grace" and "magnanimity," but mostly he refers it to outstanding human figures in such senses as "piety," "hospitality" (Abraham), and "benevolence" (David).

3. The NT.

a. The word is a human attribute in Rom. 3:12 (quoting Ps. 14:1).

b. In Rom. 2:4 and 11:22 it denotes God's gracious attitude to sinners either before Christ or in and through Christ. In Tit. 3:4ff. the fullness of salvation in Christ elucidates it. Eschatological consummation forms its content in Eph. 2:7. *chrēstótēs*, then, is an equivalent of *cháris*. It implies that God's work in Christ is appropriate to his nature. In this work he acts, and is manifested, as the one he is by nature.

c. Used in lists of virtues, the term has a richer sense than in parallel Stoic lists. The experience of the love of God that is manifested in Christ and shed abroad by the Spirit works itself out as *chrēstótēs* toward others. *chrēstótēs* is a fruit of the Spirit in Gal. 5:22, it is again associated with the Spirit in 2 Cor. 6:6, and it is based on the similar attitude of the Lord in Col. 3:12.

4. The Apostolic Fathers.

Diog. 9.1ff.; 10.4 relates God's *chrēstótēs* to his saving work in Christ and more generally to his fatherly acts as Creator, Sustainer, Redeemer, and Consummator. 1 Clem. 9.1 asks for submission to the divine *chrēstótēs*, 2 Clem. 15.5 relates it to the promise of Is. 58:9, and in 19.1 it is the goal of Christian striving. Ignatius *Magnesians* 10.1 finds it specifically in the salvation effected by Christ's resurrection.

chrēsteúomai.

1. This word is first found in Ps. Sol. 9:6 for God's proofs of grace to those who call upon him.

2. Paul uses the verb in 1 Cor. 13:4 to describe the work of love as an actualizing of *chrēstótēs*.

3. 1 Clem. 13.2 derives kindly conduct to others from the divine goodness, which is a basis of the demand for it in 14.3.

chrēstología. This word occurs only in Rom. 16:18, where Paul shows that the "friendly speeches and fine words" by which the readers are wooed are simply a mask for deceitful purposes.   [K. WEISS, IX, 483-92]

→ *éleos, epieíkeia, makrothymía, philanthrōpía*

---

chríō [to anoint],   *christós* [Christ, Messiah, Anointed One],   *antíchristos* [antichrist],   *chrísma* [anointing],   *christianós* [the Christian]

A. General Usage.

1. *chríō*, found in Homer and then in the tragic dramatists, means "to rub," "to stroke," or, with oils etc., "to smear," "to anoint." Use varies, so that we find the oiling of weapons, their smearing with poison, the rubbing of birds' wings with pitch, whitewashing or painting, and rubbing with a garment, as well as anointing after bathing, or the anointing of the sick or the dead.

2. *christós* means "smeared on," "anointed," and as a noun (*tó christón*) "ointment." It never relates to persons in the nonbiblical sphere.

3. *chrísma* (also *chríma*) means "what is rubbed on," i.e., "ointment," "whitewash." Medically it denotes a "healing ointment."   [W. GRUNDMANN, IX, 493-96]

B. The OT.

1. General Data. Anointing, the rubbing of the body with grease or oil, is meant to promote physical well-being. Legal anointing by pouring oil over the head supposedly confers strength or majesty. The Hittites anoint their kings, in Egypt the king anoints high officials, the vassal princes of Syria and Canaan are anointed, and priesthood is at times associated with anointing.

II. The Act of Anointing in the OT.

1. The Verb. The verb "to anoint" occurs some 69 times in various forms and expressions.

2. Royal Anointing.

a. Survey. The most common form of anointing in the OT is that of the king. Anointing is part of the ritual of enthronement and is the most distinctive individual act. Saul, David, and Solomon are all anointed, and among later kings we read of Joash, Jehoahaz, and Jehu (cf. also Hazael and the general reference in Judg. 9:7ff.). God does the anointing in Ps. 45:7.

b. Characteristics. The men of Judah anoint David (2 Sam. 2:7), then the elders of Israel representing the people (5:3). David authorizes the anointing of Solomon (1 Kgs. 1:34ff.), which Zadok (and Nathan) perform. Anointing is solidly attested only for Judah. By means of it the people give the king his authority. It is carried out by pouring oil on the head from a horn (1 Sam. 16:13) or other vessel (10:1). God himself may anoint or command the anointing (9:16; 10:1; 16:3). This fact denotes legitimacy in God's eyes. When the anointing refers to neighboring kings, the point is that God directs the destinies of other nations as well. Anointing by God implies authorization and a specific commission whereby the king now represents the people. Whether anointing is common in Northern Israel may be doubted. Even in Judah it seems to be unusual. Saul and David are the first kings, Absalom sets himself up as a rival king, Solomon has only a tenuous claim, the enthronement of Joash breaks the tyranny of Athaliah, and Jehoahaz becomes king in a threatening international situation. It is possible, then, that anointing takes place only in special circumstances.

3. Other Officebearers.

a. The High Priest. The OT does not tell us much about the anointing of the high priest. Its meaning is disputed; some view it as a rite of purification, others as a rite of empowering inasmuch as the high priest becomes the successor of the Davidic dynasty. In Zech. 4:14 we have both an authorized ruler and an authorized high priest. When these are called sons of oil, the element of holiness, i.e., of separation to God, is of great importance.

b. The Priests. The idea of dedication and purification lies behind the extension of anointing to all priests.

c. Prophets. In spite of 1 Kgs. 19:16 anointing of prophets is never the rule. In Is. 61:1 God himself anoints for a particular task, probably by conferring the Spirit.

d. Objects. Jacob consecrates a pillar by anointing in Gen. 28:18. We also read of the anointing of the altars (Ex. 29:36), the tabernacle (30:26), the ark (30:26), the laver (40:11), and all objects relating to the altar (40:10).

III. The Noun.

1. Occurrence. The noun "the anointed" occurs 38 times in the OT, always with reference to persons. Kings are "the anointed" some 30 times. The high priest is "the anointed" six times, and the fathers are so twice.

2. The King.

a. Survey. Saul is most commonly called "the Lord's anointed." Apart from Saul, only Davidic kings bear the title (except in Is. 45:1).

b. Saul. Since anointing is most common in Judah and for Davidic kings, it is surprising that Saul mostly frequently bears the title "the Lord's anointed." The divine anointing that confers divine authorization and protection is the theological principle behind the usage. Even though God's anointing is by means of Samuel (1 Sam. 9:16), it insures validity before God and hence the inviolability of the king's person.

c. David. The Davidic references confirm this (cf. 1 Sam. 16:1ff.). Anointing signifies divine election. With it the Spirit comes on David. The title thus denotes a special relationship with God. Ps. 89:20, 38 brings out the significance of the election of David for his successors. Ps. 132:10 prays that God for David's sake will not abandon his anointed. Nathan's promise to David in 2 Sam. 7:11, 16 lies behind these sayings.

d. The Davidic King. The title is used for David's successors as an appeal to God in times of trouble (cf. Ps. 89:38; Lam. 4:20; perhaps Hab. 3:13). Yet there is solid hope for the future (cf. Ps. 2). The anointed enjoys a majesty and supremacy which are not yet a full reality but which God will establish in the near future (cf. 1 Sam. 2:10; Pss. 84:9; 132:17). The anointed belongs to God and is thus under his protection (Ps. 2:2). Yet he also belongs to the people (Ps. 28:8). He thus occupies a mediating position like the priest or prophet. Passages that refer to God's anointed are not directly messianic or eschatological, but a messianic or eschatological understanding is implicit in many of them.

e. Cyrus as the Lord's Anointed. Is. 45:1 shows that the title may be used even where there is no rite of anointing and where a ruler of an alien faith and people is intended. The point here is that God gives Cyrus a definite mission that relates to Israel's redemption. In this regard he replaces the impotent Davidic dynasty. As salvation is expected from the kingly rule of the anointed, hope focuses on the Persian king who steps into the breach. The expression is a bold and isolated one.

f. The Fathers. Ps. 105:15 uses "anointed ones" for the fathers, probably to stress their inviolability under God's protection. The idea, perhaps, is that the fathers are initial kingly or prophetic (cf. Gen. 20:7) figures.

4. *The High Priest.* Although the term is used attributively in Lev. 4:3ff.; 6:15, it has the force of a title and plainly refers to the high priest. It is an indefinite noun in Dan. 9:25-26. At the end of the specified period, an anointed one will come, and after 62 weeks (years) an anointed one is removed. If there are immediate references here, it is hard to say what they are.

IV. Messianic Ideas in Israel.

1. *Royal Psalms.* The development of messianic ideas brings us into a debatable area. Possibly the royal psalms bear witness already to such development in Judah. One element in them is an oracle addressed to the king, perhaps by cultic prophets, and promising salvation and the manifestation of God's supremacy in universal rule. Since Judah does not in fact exercise rule of this kind, the statements offer a prolepsis of what ought to be and will finally come to pass.

2. *Is. 9:5-6.* The point here is the accession of a new Davidic ruler but with the eschatological implication (v. 6) of an indefinite reign of perfect salvation. The final Davidic king will be God's representative on earth.

3. *Jeremiah and Ezekiel.* Jer. 23:5-6 awaits the ideal of a wise and righteous ruler of David's line bearing the name "The Lord our righteousness." Ezek. 34:23-24 and 37:22ff. also look for the coming of a second David.

4. *Postexilic Period.*

a. Haggai. With the return from exile the messianic hope is strong. Hag. 2:20ff. looks on Zerubbabel as a signet ring and hence as a guarantee of God's mighty and saving presence and an accreditation of his promise. Zerubbabel is a representative of God, the true ruler.

b. Zechariah. In the visions of two anointed ones, the high priest and ruler, the giving of a crown seems to relate Zerubbabel to the messianic king of the end time (4:1ff.; 6:9ff.). Close association between priest and king marks these passages. Zerubbabel himself does not fulfil messianic expectation, and v. 13 points to a future ruler who will be both priest and king.

c. Older Prophets. Some scholars regard as postexilic additions such passages as Is. 11:1, which contrasts the glory of the messianic shoot with the present impotence of David's house; Ezek. 17:22ff., which has the birth of the Messiah in view; and Mic. 5:1ff., which links the Messiah to Bethlehem. In Is. 11:1ff. the Spirit is closely related to the Messiah, endowing him with piety, wisdom, and righteousness, and making possible a reign of divine power, dignity, and greatness. Yet humility and peace also characterize the messianic ruler in Zech. 9:9-10. His dominion will be universal (Is. 11:1) and will mean the regaining of paradise (11:6ff.) and the ending of the final affliction (16:4-5). Jer. 33:15ff. again associates the priesthood with the Davidic monarchy.

d. Difficult Passages. Passages like Am. 9:11-12; Hos. 3:5; Mic. 4:8; Is. 32:1; Jer. 30:9 are hard to interpret; they seem to imply the restoration of the Davidic dynasty.

5. *Problems of Messianism*. There is unquestionably a messianic movement, but it is hard to trace in detail. Problems include the relation of Josiah and Nehemiah to it, its extent, its connection with other trends, and its prominence at different periods.

[F. HESSE, IX, 496-509]

C. Messianic Ideas in Later Judaism.

I. Linguistic Aspects. In later sources we find "the anointed" with the definite article, and also "my Messiah" and the "Messiah of righteousness." But Messiah without the article also occurs and is virtually a proper name. "The Lord's anointed" is used only for royal figures, but the OT prophets, and also (at Qumran) the eschatological high priest and prophet, are described as anointed.

II. The LXX. The LXX nearly always uses *chríō* for the normal Hebrew verb. Other words of the group are *chrísis, chrísma* (cf. Dan. 9:26), and *christós*. The LXX renderings of Num. 24:7 and 24:17 imply expectation of a messianic king. The LXX brings in the group in Am. 4:13; 2 Sam. 3:39; 2 Chr. 36:1. In its reading of Ezek. 43:3 its use of *chríō* changes God's leaving of the temple into his return to it.

[A. S. VAN DER WOUDE, IX, 509-10]

III. Apocrypha and Pseudepigrapha.

1. *Sirach*. Moses anoints Aaron in Sir. 45:15, Samuel anoints princes in 46:13, and cf. 48:8. There is no express eschatological reference, but stress falls on the eternal character of the high priesthood and monarchy (cf. 45:15ff.).

2. *Testaments of the Twelve*. Test. Jud. 21:1ff. subjects the monarchy to the priesthood. Test. Reub. 6:8 seems to be saying that the priesthood of Levi will last until the end times when the high priest Christ will come. Test. Levi uses *christós* for priestly figures in 17:2-3. Test. Jud. 24:1 quotes Num. 24:17 and seems to be from a Christian source. Test. Levi 18 also betrays Christian influence with its reference to a new and ideal priest who is also a king and whose work transcends human ideas.

3. *Psalms of Solomon*. This work uses *christós* four times, always with additions. In 18:5 the anointed one acts on God's commission and in God's power. In 18:7 he bears

the rod and is full of wisdom, righteousness, and power. In ch. 17 he is a king of David's house, will do God's will in Israel, and will establish universal rule.

4. *Ethiopian Enoch.* "Anointed one" occurs twice in the Similitudes (48:10; 52:4). "Son of Man" and "elect of God" seem to be parallel expressions. The Messiah is the ideal future ruler in an apocalyptic framework.

5. *Syriac Baruch and 4 Esdras.* These later works (1st cent. A.D.) use "the anointed" in the absolute for a royal figure of the end time. With the Messiah comes victory over the nations and the reign of peace and supernatural plenty. The messianic period finally merges into the time of general resurrection. In 4 Esdr. 7:28-29 the resurrection comes only after the death of the Messiah and seven days of primal silence. The "servant" of ch. 13 has many messianic features. An important term in these works is "revelation," which at times presupposes preexistence. The "servant" has preexistence with God in 4 Esdr. 7:28; 13:26, and the Messiah is kept with God in 12:32. Since the focus is on God's acts, the national redeemer and heavenly liberator are fundamentally the same.

6. *Sibyllines.* These works do not use "the anointed," but features of OT expectation may be seen (cf. 788ff. and Is. 11:6ff.).

7. *Pseudo-Philo.* This work refers to the anointing of Phinehas by God at Shiloh and to the anointing of David by Samuel. The people anoints Samuel in ch. 51.7, and there is reference to a royal figure in 5.6 (with an allusion to 1 Sam. 2:10).

8. *Apocalypse of Abraham.* The redeemer of ch. 31 is "my elect" and holds an essential place in God's future and final action.   [M. DE JONGE, IX, 511-17]

IV. Qumran.

1. *Two Messianic Figures.* The Qumran community expects at the end of the days a messianic high priest of the house of Levi and a messianic king of the house of Judah, i.e., the Messiah of Aaron and the Messiah of Israel.

2. *The Kingly Messiah.* This Messiah is a shoot of David and a prince of the community, once perhaps called Messiah in the absolute.

3. *The Eschatological High Priest.* This Messiah is mentioned first, takes precedence in the council, has a dominant role in the eschatological war, and discharges a teaching function, giving new end-time directions.

4. *The Two Messiahs.* The two Messiahs, God's final instruments, are expected on the basis of God's eternal covenants with Phinehas and David. They embody the ideal future of legitimate priesthood and monarchy. The priestly interest of the community comes out in the superiority of the high priest, but a strong political interest also emerges in the hope of a theocratic order. The final orientation is to God's age of righteousness; hence both Messiahs are subject to God.

5. *The Teacher of Righteousness.* This figure, who founds or consolidates the community, is not himself messianic, nor does the community await his return in the end time. The community gives him high esteem and trust, but does not think of him as the Messiah or even as the prophet like Moses.

6. *Precedence of the High Priest.* The texts do not support the view that either earlier or later the community looks for only one Messiah. It follows the tradition reflected in Zech. 4:14; Sirach; Testaments of the Twelve. Its giving of precedence to the high priest is in keeping with priestly Zadok ideas.

[A. S. VAN DER WOUDE, IX, 517-20]

V. Philo and Josephus.

1. Philo. In *On Rewards and Punishments* 95 Philo refers to a redeemer (on the basis of Num. 24:7 LXX), but mainly as a representative of the saints triumphing in God's strength.

2. Josephus. Josephus does not use the term "messiah" for those who lay claim to royal or prophetic office in the first century A.D. When he goes over to the Romans, he makes Vespasian the central figure in his biblically inspired expectation for the future. He is thus a strong opponent of other forms of messianism.

[M. DE JONGE, IX, 520-21]

VI. Rabbinic Writings.

1. Prayers. The Palestinian recension of the Eighteen Benedictions contains a petition for mercy on "the monarchy of the house of David, the Messiah of thy righteousness." The date is disputed, and the stress is on the dynasty rather than an individual figure. Elsewhere we find prayer for "the shoot of David thy servant," or for "the sprouting of a horn for David thy servant." We also find prayers (which may be later) for the kingdom of the Messiah and the redemption of the people. In their hope for an independent state, such prayers may well reflect popular expectation at the time of Jesus (cf. Acts 1:6).

2. The Mishnah. The only reference here is an incidental one, which may be an addition. This paucity of material is hard to explain; it can hardly be due to a polemic against Christianity or to the fading of messianic expectation, but probably reflects concentration on the law and opposition to the false hopes raised by the Zealots and apocalyptic groups.

3. Simon bar Koseba. Akiba hails Simon as the promised Messiah (on the basis of Num. 24:17) even though he is not of David's line. Some rabbis disagree, but many among both scholars and people follow Akiba's example. Although a high priest is mentioned, the prince now takes the lead. The incident shows that even into the second century A.D. messianic ideas are not fixed.

4. Justin's Dialogue. In this work Trypho the Jew refers to the general messianic hope of his people but criticizes the Christian exalting of Messiah to deity. Elijah will manifest the Messiah, who will come forth in glory, fulfil the law, and in spite of suffering vindicate himself as the Messiah (cf. 89.1; 48–49; 110.1; 67.2; 36.1).

5. Targums. These works set the messianic kingdom before the resurrection and last judgment. Of the house of David, the Messiah is hidden for a time, but God will initiate the new age by enabling him to defeat all enemies, to establish peace, to bring forgiveness to Israel, and to regather the dispersed people. As a prophet and teacher of the law, he observes it, makes the people hear it, and renews the covenant between God and the people. During his righteous rule the temple will be rebuilt and miracles, including resurrections, will occur.

6. Talmudic Literature and Midrashim. These works often mention the Messiah and his functions and qualities. They embody, in embellished form, the same traditions as the Targums. The Messiah's name is created before the world. A time of affliction precedes his coming. His age differs both from this aeon and from that of the resurrection and last judgment, although there is no unanimity on these points. At times the Messiah is David, but usually he is David's son. Conversion and obedience will prepare the way for his coming, although there will also be apostasy when he comes. The rabbis reject calculations of the time of his coming. Elijah will announce it. The nations will band together to resist him, but after a time he will defeat them, and his (ninth) empire will precede the tenth empire, the kingdom of God. The Messiah is both a righteous king and a teacher of the law. His reign is one of abundance and peace. The temple will be built again, but sin will cease, so that only thank offerings will be given. Only later does the idea of paradise regained find general acceptance. The Messiah is no divine figure, and his kingdom will end with the attack of Gog and Magog. God is the true author of his people's liberation and glorification.

7. *The Messiah ben Joseph.* A few references to this figure occur from the second century A.D. He is a military leader who gains victories, establishes peace for 40 years, is then killed (although his death has no expiatory significance), and thus makes way for the Messiah ben David, who finally conquers Israel's foes. The concept of the Messiah ben Joseph seems to go back to older ideas and shows how complex messianic expectation must have been at the time of Jesus.

[A. S. VAN DER WOUDE, IX, 521-27]

D. The Christ Statements of the NT.

I. Occurrence of christós. Only the Lucan writings use the OT *christós kyríou* (or *autoú*). The absolute is common. Paul often uses *christós* without the article (cf. *en* or *sýn Christō̄*, or *diá Christoú*). With Jesus, the absolute produces the title *ho Christós Iēsoús*, which for Gentiles becomes the name *Iēsoús Christós* or *Christós Iēsoús*. With this, *ho kýrios* is also used. In all, *christós* occurs 529 times in the NT (379 times in Paul). There are only seven instances in Mark, 12 in Luke, 17 in Matthew, and 19 in John. *Christianoí* for "believers" derives from *christós.*

II. Synoptic Gospels and Acts.

1. Mark.

a. In the mocking demand of Mk. 15:32, Christ and king of Israel are in apposition (cf. 15:26). Jesus is crucified as a messianic pretender, and the onlookers deride him as such. He confesses his messiahship in answer to the question of 14:61. Here *ho christós* is equated with the Son of the Blessed, and also with the Son of Man in Jesus' reply. It is as the Son of God that Jesus is the Messiah, and as such he is also the Son of Man.

b. In Mk. 8:27ff. Peter calls Jesus the Messiah, whereas the people simply regards him as a prophet. Jesus answers with his teaching about the Son of Man who must suffer many things. Peter's opposition rests on human ideas which cannot combine messiahship and suffering. But Jesus thinks the thoughts of God. His sense of his messiahship and messianic mission does not follow traditional patterns. He has a different understanding which he believes to be consonant with God's own thinking and purpose.

c. In Mk. 12:35 and parallels Jesus raises the question, not to affirm or reject his messiahship, but to pose the difficulty that arises when the Messiah's Davidic sonship is related to Ps. 110:1. The implied answer is that the decisive aspect is the divine thought and act.

d. Mk. 13:21-22 contains a warning against false claims to messiahship. The warning presupposes the messiahship of Jesus.

e. According to Mk. 9:41 the disciples hold a special position by belonging to the Messiah—*christós* is used without the article here, as also in some versions of Mk. 1:34 (cf. 1:24; 3:11; 5:7 for parallels).

2. Matthew.

a. In 16:20 Jesus tells his disciples to keep his messiahship secret; his acceptance of Peter's confession is plainly implied. In 24:5 the expansion brings assimilation to

24:23. The scoffers at the foot of the cross in 26:68 adopt the confession before the Sanhedrin in 26:64, and Pilate uses the Jewish title in 27:17, 22.

b. The statement in 1:16 shows that Jesus is the Messiah by Davidic descent and as the offshoot of Abraham, that he belongs to Israel, and that he comes as King at the end of the period that extends "to the Christ" (1:17). In v. 18 we then have a transition to his virgin birth and his ordination as Savior and Immanuel. The birth at Bethlehem completes the circle (2:1ff.). The works of 11:4ff. are "deeds of the Christ" (v. 2); with the Scriptures they bear witness to the hidden messiahship. In his attack on the scribes Jesus also claims that he as Christ is their one master. By his teaching and authority (7:28-29; 9:33) he exercises his messianic dominion.

3. Luke.

a. With the absolute *ho christós* (20:41; 22:67) Luke also uses "the Christ of God" (9:20). The "of God" shows by whom he is anointed and to whom he belongs. Before the high priest Jesus refuses to say whether he is the Christ but he affirms his divine sonship (22:67ff.). The title occurs in the accusation before Pilate (23:2), and the scoffers mock at his claim to be the Christ of God, the Chosen One (23:35). The impenitent thief joins in the mockery (v. 39).

b. In the infancy stories the angel proclaims Jesus as Savior, Christ, and Lord (2:11). The eternal King of 1:31ff. is the royal Messiah of David's house and also the Lord of Gentile believers. Simeon hails the infant Jesus as the Lord's Christ (2:26) who brings peace and salvation. The Messiah is also the Son of God in 1:32; 4:41. In 4:18 Jesus quotes Is. 61:1 to show that he is the Messiah as the recipient of the Spirit by whom he is conceived and who is given to him at his baptism.

c. In 24:26 Jesus explains to the two disciples why the Christ had to suffer. This is the Lord's own understanding. In prophetic action, the way through the cross to glory brings it to fulfilment. The crucifixion and resurrection give the picture of the Messiah its decisive shape.

4. Acts.

a. In Acts 4:27 the holy servant of God is said to be anointed by him. Peter tells Cornelius that God anointed Jesus (10:38). As Lord and Christ (2:36) Jesus is the one who is risen (v. 31) but who was also crucified (3:18). Conversion to this Christ brings remission of sins (3:19) and is the presupposition of the actualizing of eschatological salvation with his return. God has appointed Jesus as the Christ (3:20), and heaven must receive him until the time of consummation. The eschatological prophet is the royal Messiah—all according to Scripture (vv. 22ff.). When the apostles preach and teach Jesus as the Christ they have the whole of his person and work in view (5:42; cf. 8:5, 12). Baptism into his name is the saving event of a transfer to his possession (2:38); Christians are those who call on the name of the Lord (2:21) and believe in the Lord Jesus Christ (11:17; cf. 16:31; 20:21). Preaching about the kingdom of God goes hand in hand with teaching about the Lord Jesus Christ (28:31). Jesus Christ is the content of the message; he is also the power of healing (4:10; 9:34).

b. Paul in 17:23 presents the new understanding of the Messiah with proofs from the OT. Jesus fully meets this understanding (v. 3).

c. The disciples come to be called *Christianoí* in Antioch (11:26). This word denotes adherents of Christ. Probably non-Christians use it first, assuming that *Christós* is a proper name, and treating his followers as a mystery fellowship. Paul by his preaching of Christ (11:26) perhaps helps to promote the usage, which rapidly spreads to other places.

5. *Gospel Titles*. Mk. 1:1 and Mt. 1:1 use the title *Iēsoús Christós*. *Christós* has here become a second name attached to the personal name Jesus.

6. *The Messiah in the History of Jesus and the Synoptic Tradition*. Jesus does not seem openly to claim messiahship even though he exercises eschatological authority as healer, prophet, and teacher. In Mark his concealed messiahship shapes his history, although the secret is more that of the Son of Man than of the Messiah. The reason for the secret is that the current understanding cannot express his authoritative work. Messiahship needs to be related to his history and reinterpreted accordingly. The Gospels repeat the restraint of Jesus, for what happens to him shows how people try to adapt him to their ideas and are disappointed when he treats Satan as his true foe, seeks to serve rather than to rule, and finds his victory in suffering and death. Yet even though Jesus forbids equation with the Messiah as currently expected, messiahship is still associated with him in the new form impressed upon it by his history, i.e., by his anointing with the Spirit, his special relation to God, and his authoritative lordship of service. For Christians, Jesus is no earthly Messiah on whom religious, national, and political hopes are set. He is Conqueror of the death which he suffers for his people. Having entered God's eternity, he frees them from their sin and will come again in glory. The concept of the Son of Man and the predicates of divine sonship fill out the picture. He is thus able to unite in one the characteristics of the messianic King, the messianic High Priest, and the Prophet like Moses, so that what Josephus finds in Hyrcanus comes to fulfilment in Jesus.

III. Paul's Epistles.

1. Usage.

a. Easter has related Israel's expectation to Jesus; God has accredited Jesus as the Messiah. The designation *christós* thus becomes a name; *christós* is Jesus.

b. Paul uses *christós* in the absolute, sometimes with and sometimes without the article, but with no difference of sense. Whether Paul says *ho Christós* or *Christós*, he has the uniqueness of Jesus in view. *Christós* without the article is more common.

c. Paul also uses both *Christós Iēsoús* and *Iēsoús Christós*; often the textual witness is equivocal. He tends to use the double form at significant points, e.g., in salutations, at the end of sections, and in vital statements. *Christós* serves as a second proper name but also confers the dignity of the title, especially when it comes first. Paul himself comes to see that the crucified Jesus is indeed the Messiah as the power of God (1 Cor. 1:24), but Gentiles tend to see *Christós* mainly as a second name, although not without some sense of its significance as a title. Paul himself avoids simply using the two titles *kýrios* and *Christós* together without adding the name of Jesus. For him the term *Christós* has especially the force of Savior. Jesus Christ means Jesus the Savior.

2. The Chief Epistles: The Christ and Christ.

a. A common formula in Paul is "the gospel of Christ" (Rom. 15:19; 1 Cor. 9:12), i.e., the good news whose content and source is Christ. This is also the gospel of his glory (2 Cor. 4:4), the witness of Christ (1 Cor. 1:6) or the gospel of God (Rom. 1:1). It leads on to such phrases as preaching Christ (Phil. 1:15ff.). Paul takes over the gospel from the churches (1 Cor. 15:3ff.). Its content is Christ dead, risen, and exalted for us. Paul, who has first found in the cross an offense, speaks plainly of the crucifixion, since it is for us that Christ is accursed, and the cross is thus a declaration of the love of God (Rom. 5:5-6; 8:35). The resurrection is also linked with *Christós*. As the risen Lord, he guides eschatological events to their consummation. As the Lord of the living and the dead, who is the paschal lamb (1 Cor. 5:7) and purchase price of redemption (6:20), Christ confers freedom but also imposes responsibility (cf. Rom. 15:3). Freedom from the law means being under the law of Christ (1 Cor. 9:21), but not in such a way that additional demands negate his saving and liberating work (Gal. 5:1ff.). Christ as the image of God (2 Cor. 4:4) fashions his people into his likeness (cf. Gal. 3:26-27). The glory of God shines in his face and brings the light of new creation (2 Cor. 4:6; 5:17ff.). The power in all this is that of Christ, so that one may gladly boast of one's own weakness (2 Cor. 12:9). The love of Christ controls those who belong to him (2 Cor. 5:14ff.). In this love one has a new knowledge of his reconciling work which amounts to a new creation (v. 17). This new creation is grounded in the reconciliation that God has effected through Christ (vv. 18ff.). God was in Christ, so that he is the mediator of salvation, God's representative to us. The apostles now beseech people on Christ's behalf to be reconciled to God. In so doing they suffer for him (Phil. 1:29). For Paul, Christ is thus the one who achieves victory through defeat. He finds all this presented in OT Scripture (1 Cor. 15:3ff.). Christ will come again as Judge (2 Cor. 5:10), but the focus is on his love (Gal. 2:20), or grace (1:6), or meekness and gentleness (2 Cor. 10:1), or steadfastness (2 Th. 3:5), or truth (2 Cor. 11:10)—qualities which the historical Jesus displays.

b. The people of Christ belongs to him by baptism as death and resurrection with him (Gal. 2:19-20). Their aim is to magnify him (Phil. 1:20). His thinking should control them (1 Cor. 2:16). Christ is in them (Rom. 8:10). They have his Spirit (8:9), who is the Spirit of God that raised Christ Jesus from the dead (8:11). This Spirit makes them God's children (8:17) and imitators of Christ (1 Cor. 11:1) in the renunciation of self-pleasing (Rom. 15:3) and the receiving of the weak (v. 7). His people are his body (1 Cor. 12:12). Christ is the body and they, being in him, are the members. As such they cannot belong to a harlot (6:15) or to Beliar (2 Cor. 6:15). They partake of the body and blood of Christ in the Lord's Supper (1 Cor. 10:16). Christ is also the head (1 Cor. 11:3). In this sense, he is supreme, and his people are under obligation to him (2 Cor. 10:5). If slaves, they are his freedmen; if free, they are his slaves (1 Cor. 7:22). The churches of Christ (Rom. 16:16) are his bride (2 Cor. 11:2) or epistle (3:3). Paul by his work has a part in Christ's triumph as he spreads the fragrance of the knowledge of him in every place (2:14-15). The task of the apostles is to proclaim the good news of which he is the content (1 Cor. 1:17). False apostles pretend to be apostles of Christ (2 Cor. 11:13). Christ speaks through the true apostle (13:3). If the apostles are his glory (2 Cor. 8:23), they are also his slaves (Gal. 1:10). They are in Christ (12:1-2) and Christ's stewards (1 Cor. 4:1). Their work is Christ's (cf. Phil. 2:30). Those who serve Christ are acceptable to God (Rom. 14:18). Paul will give up everything to gain Christ (Phil. 3:8). Yet he is also ready to be cut off from Christ for Israel's sake (Rom. 9:3). In answer to a Christ party at Corinth, he shows that Christ died for all (1 Cor. 1:12-13). All enjoy freedom by allegiance to him (3:21ff.).

c. Paul often uses prepositions with "Christ" to express relationship to the field of force that his saving work establishes. Baptism brings us "into Christ" (cf. Rom. 16:5). We are then "with Christ" (Phil. 1:23). God does the work "through Christ" (cf. 2 Cor. 1:5); this gives us confidence in God (3:4). Being "in Christ" expresses the operation of salvation in the field of force that Christ sets up. Gal. 2:17 refers to the event and reception of salvation, 1 Cor. 4:15 to the work, Gal. 1:22 to the saved community, and 2 Cor. 12:2 to the members. In this field of force all events are spiritually caused and ordained by God through Christ.

3. The Chief Epistles: Jesus Christ and Christ Jesus.

a. The common "Christ Jesus" implies knowledge of Christ as the bringer of salvation who is called Jesus. It stands strongly related to *ho Christós* or *Christós* (cf. Gal. 3:27 and Rom. 6:3). Jesus Christ is the author of thanksgiving or of the fruit of righteousness (Rom. 1:8; Phil. 1:11). He has been appointed judge (Rom. 2:16). Paul's apostleship is from him (Gal. 1:1) in an act of divine grace (1:15). *en Christō Iēsoú* has the same force as *en Christō* (cf. Gal. 2:4, 17; 1 Cor. 1:4-5; Rom. 3:24; Phil. 3:14, etc.). Members of the church are sanctified in Christ Jesus (1 Cor. 1:2). Their boasting is in Christ Jesus (Phil. 1:26). Paul is the father of believers in Christ Jesus (1 Cor. 4:15).

b. Various formulations show the kinship of *(ho) Christós* and Christ Jesus or Jesus Christ, e.g., in relation to the cross (1 Cor. 1:7; Gal. 3:1), or the resurrection (Rom. 6:4; 8:11), or his grace (Gal. 1:6; Rom. 5:15), or revelation (Gal. 1:16, 12). Christ Jesus is common in statements about faith, for faith focuses on his saving work and yet he is also its author. Believers are Christ's but also belong to Christ Jesus (1 Cor. 15:23; Gal. 5:24). Jesus Christ, or Christ, is in them (2 Cor. 13:5; Rom. 8:10). Paul is an apostle of Christ Jesus but refers also to the apostles of Christ (1 Cor. 1:1; 2 Cor. 11:13). Plainly the Christ, Christ, Christ Jesus, and Jesus Christ all have the same force.

4. Lord Jesus Christ and the (Our) Lord Jesus Christ. Lord Jesus (1 Cor. 12:3) becomes Lord Jesus Christ in Phil. 2:6ff., where Christ bears in context the sense of messianic Savior. Paul preaches Christ Jesus the Lord (2 Cor. 4:5; cf. Rom. 14:7ff.). Divinely commissioned, Christ is our wisdom etc. (1 Cor. 1:30). His sonship and lordship embrace both earthly and eternal modes (Rom. 1:3-4). As there is one God, so there is one Lord, Jesus Christ (1 Cor. 8:6). Through him are all things, e.g., the grace and peace of the salutations (Rom. 1:7; Gal. 1:3, etc.). Those who have God as Father have Jesus Christ as Lord. The full "Lord Jesus Christ" is important in salutations and in statements like that in 1 Cor. 15:31 or in the baptismal formula of 1 Cor. 1:2. God is confessed as the Father of our Lord Jesus Christ in Rom. 15:6. 1 Cor. 1 heaps up references to Christ Jesus etc. in order to point the church to its true basis and to show that its Christ and Lord is Jesus. 1 Th. 1:3 refers to the hope that is based on our Lord Jesus Christ, and 1 Th. 5:23 speaks about his parousia.

5. Christ's Significance. Paul relates Christ to Adam as well as David. Christ is the author of a new humanity (1 Cor. 15:47-48). As a servant of both circumcised and uncircumcised (Rom. 15:8, 18), he has universal and not just national significance.

6. chríō in 2 Cor. 1:21-22. Paul uses *chríō* only of believers in the baptismal formula of 2 Cor. 1:21-22. The three aorists here refer to the act of God which accomplishes the establishing. The *chríō* perhaps embraces also the sealing and giving of the Spirit. Its sense is transferred; it denotes the appropriating to Christ that baptism signifies and seals, that the Spirit renders efficacious, and that God himself confirms.

7. Colossians and Ephesians. In debate with Gnostic ideas, *Christós* is a leading concept in these two epistles. Christ is a historical figure; his mystery is disclosed in his work and preached in the gospel. The mystery is "Christ in you, the hope of glory" (Col. 1:27). It is in faith, not ecstasy, that Christ is thus present. The mystery of Christ is also the mystery of the church (Eph. 5:32). All knowledge and wisdom are hidden in Christ (Col. 2:2-3). The fullness of the Godhead dwells in him (2:9). He is the Head of all dominion (2:10). Forgiveness through him brings full salvation (1:12ff.). The goal is complete human maturity in him (1:28). He grants access to God to both Jews and Gentiles (Eph. 2:18). The Gentiles who were far from him are now "in" him (2:12-13). Making peace, he is the Savior and Head of the community. He discharges his lordship over the church by serving it (5:22ff.) in a relation that provides a model for that of husbands and wives. The church is his body (Col. 1:24). The reality of God is present with him (2:17). His word is to dwell in his people richly and his peace is to rule in their hearts (3:15-16). God is his Father (1:3). His grace is with those who truly love him (Eph. 6:24). His love for them surpasses knowledge (3:19). His gifts bring his work to believers (4:7) by way of his ministers (4:11-12), by whom he initiates a process of growth to steadfast maturity in truth and love (4:13ff.). Faith works itself out in a life shaped by it (Col. 2:6), i.e., in mutual forgiveness (Eph. 4:32), service of Christ (3:24), and dying and rising with him (3:1ff.). The term "Christ" embraces the cross and resurrection; those who trust in him are taken up into this twofold event. The Father of our Lord Jesus Christ has conferred spiritual blessings on us in him (Eph. 1:3ff.). Christ is elect and beloved (1:6); his salvation means sonship and redemption. Salvation is foreordained in him (1:11). The power of God set forth in his resurrection grants to believers the assurance of protection and eschatological consummation. Prayer is made for his indwelling (3:17) and for knowledge of his love (3:19). Illumination comes through him (5:14). He comes from the Creator God, is one with him, reveals his purpose, and leads creation back to him (Col. 1:15ff.).

8. The Pastorals.

a. The Pastorals contain confessional sections that mostly use "Christ Jesus." In 1 Tim. 1:15 remission of sins is through his cross and resurrection. 1 Tim. 6:13 refers directly to the passion. In 2 Tim. 1:9-10 God granted us grace in Christ Jesus from eternity but has now manifested it. The abolition of death most likely carries a reference to his own death. Tit. 2:13 speaks about the blessed hope of his appearing, but again with a look at his atoning death (v. 14). Tit. 4:6 refers to the pouring out of the regenerating and renewing Spirit through him.

b. Christ Jesus our Lord occurs in salutations (1 Tim. 1:2), and Paul is an apostle of Christ Jesus in 1 Tim. 1:1. Timothy is his servant in 1 Tim. 4:6, and his good soldier in 2 Tim. 2:3. Faith, love, and salvation are in him (1 Tim. 1:14; 2 Tim. 2:10), and so are grace and a godly life (2 Tim. 2:1; 3:12). Paul is a model appointed by him (1 Tim. 1:12), for in him Jesus Christ has displayed his patience (1:16). Christ occurs alone only in 1 Tim. 5:11. Elsewhere Christ is linked with Jesus, and God and Christ Jesus are so coordinated that God plainly acts in him and he himself acts on God's behalf.

IV. 1 Peter, Hebrews, James, Jude, and 2 Peter.

1. 1 Peter. Like Paul, 1 Peter uses *Christós, ho Christós,* and *Iēsoús Christós.* At the heart of the epistle stands the confession of 3:18ff. Christ brings salvation and access to God by his victorious cross, resurrection, and exaltation. His saving death brings remission, and his resurrection is the ground of regeneration (1:2-3). He manifests his invisible glory (1:7), and links promise and fulfilment (1:11). His passion and glorification serve as a model (2:21ff.; 3:18). A good walk and the acceptance of suffering sanctify Christ in the heart (3:15). Trust in him brings confidence in God (1:21), and new birth is by him as the Word of God (1:23). The author is an apostle of Jesus Christ (1:1) and a witness of the sufferings of Christ (5:1). His readers love Christ though they have not seen him (1:8). Peace is the author's wish for all who are in Christ (5:14).

2. Hebrews. In Hebrews Jesus Christ is the eternal Son and High Priest who as the pioneer of salvation brings many sons to glory (2:10). The term *Christós* occurs between 3:6 and 9:28 and *Iēsoús Christós* from 10:10 to 13:21, but with no discernible distinction. Heb. 1:8-9 relates Ps. 45:6-7 to Christ. God has appointed him (5:5). His people is under him (3:6). He has won this people for himself (9:11-12) through his blood (v. 14). His exaltation (v. 24) and his parousia (v. 28) are also vital elements in his work. The term *Christós* is still firmly related to his passion, his exaltation, and his church. The formula *diá Christoú* occurs (13:21), but not *en Christō̌*. A basic affirmation that sets the readers in solid fellowship with their teachers is that Jesus Christ is the same yesterday, today, and forever (13:8).

3. *James, Jude, and 2 Peter.*

a. In James *Iēsoús Christós* occurs in 1:1 (the author is his servant) and in 2:1(the reference is to faith in our Lord Jesus Christ in his glory).

b. Jude calls himself a servant of Jesus Christ (v. 1) and addresses those who are kept for him (v. 2). He refers to the apostles of our Lord Jesus Christ (v. 17), but also to those who deny our only Master and Lord, Jesus Christ (v. 4). Believers wait for the mercy of Christ (v. 21). The work closes with an ascription of praise to God through Jesus Christ our Lord (v. 25).

c. 2 Peter. The author is a servant and apostle of Jesus Christ (1:1), he greets those who stand in the righteousness of our Savior Jesus Christ (1:1), and he prays for the knowledge of our Lord Jesus Christ (1:8). This knowledge relates to his power and coming (1:16). The author has received a revelation from our Lord Jesus Christ (1:14). His wish for his readers is that they may enjoy an entrance into the eternal kingdom of our Lord and Savior Jesus Christ (1:11). For the most part *Christós* has here the force of a proper name.

V. The Johannine Writings.

1. The Gospel.

a. Jesus is the Revealer through whom believers receive life. The Messiah is one of the predicates that shed light on this fact (1:41ff.; 4:25).

b. The incarnate Logos is Jesus Christ (1:17). Contrasted with Moses, he brings grace and truth. Eternal life (17:3) is knowledge of the only true God and of Jesus Christ whom he has sent. In these passages the use of Christ characterizes Jesus as the Revealer who brings salvation.

c. The Baptist denies that he is the Messiah (1:20), and Andrew claims that he has found the Messiah in Jesus (1:41; cf. 1:45, 49). The Messiah here is the kingly Messiah, Son of God and Son of Man (cf. 1:51), who has a special endowment of the Spirit (1:33). The aim of the gospel is to lead to faith that Jesus is the Christ, the Son of God (20:31), who acts in unity with the Father, who has come into the world to do so (cf. 11:27), and who by so doing gives life (5:21, 26). The Samaritan woman also sees in Jesus the Messiah (4:29), but she can do this only because Jesus reveals himself to her (4:25-26). Jewish leaders object to his connection with Nazareth and his open origin (7:26-27). In reply, Jesus points to his true origin with the Father (7:28-29). His coming from Galilee conceals his Davidic birth at Bethlehem (7:41-42). Only the power and content of his sayings show that he is truly the Christ. The final objection of his crucifixion remains (12:34). In his answer Jesus points to the limited duration of his earthly work (12:35-36). He also testifies to the eternal work of the glorified Lord (12:31-32; 14:12ff.).

d. Since Jesus does not plainly disclose his messiahship, the people asks him for a direct answer (10:24). Jesus in reply refers to his word, which only faith receives (v. 25). He is the Messiah as the Shepherd who leads his people, whose voice they obey, who gives them life, whose power, grounded in his unity with God, is superior to death (12:31-32). He is the Messiah as God's Son (1:49; 11:27)—a reason for offense (5:18; 10:31ff.). As Son of God and Messiah, he is the Revealer who in revealing grants life by way of his passion and exaltation.

2. *The Epistles.*

a. Christ. Divine sonship takes precedence here too (cf. 1 Jn. 1:3; 3:23; 5:5-6). Titular use of *christós* occurs in 1 Jn. 2:22; 5:1. Awareness of Christ as a predicate is a factor in the name combinations. As Son of God, Jesus is from the beginning (1 Jn. 1:1). He has come in history as a man (vv. 1ff.). The witnesses have fellowship with the Father and with his Son Jesus Christ, and they pass on this fellowship (v. 3). Jesus Christ is an advocate for sinners (2:1). The requirement is faith in his name and mutual love (3:23; 2 Jn. 9). He is God, and hence his messianic work is God's own work (1 Jn. 1:7-8; 2:1; 3:8; 5:18ff.). From him and the Father come grace, mercy, and peace in truth and love (2 Jn. 3). Opponents, possibly Ebionites but more likely docetic Gnostics, deny that Jesus is the Christ (1 Jn. 2:22; cf. 5:5). In answer the author points to the one Jesus Christ who is Son of God (5:5-6). In 5:6 Jesus Christ is not just a double name; it firmly associates the historical Jesus and the heavenly Christ.

b. Antichrist. Those who confess the sonship and messiahship of Christ by the Spirit (1 Jn. 4:15; 2:22; 4:2) are born of God (5:1), but those who contest them are antichrists (2:22) controlled by the spirit of antichrist (4:2). In 2:18 and 4:3 antichrist is a coming apocalyptic figure, the opponent of Christ whose power increases prior to the end but who is finally judged and destroyed. This figure, however, is already at work in false teachers (antichrists) who come from within the community and whose appearance shows that the last hour is near (1 Jn. 2:18; cf. 4:3; 2 Jn. 7).

c. *chrísma.* The "anointing" of the Spirit enables believers to resist false teaching by imparting clarity of faith and judgment. *chrísma* here is not "anointing oil" but an instructive power that remains in the church and makes it independent of an official teaching office. The term reminds us of the Messiah's anointing by the Spirit and of the close relation between the Son and sons by way of reception of the Spirit.

3. *Revelation.*

a. John calls his work the revelation of Jesus Christ, bears witness to the testimony of Jesus Christ, and wishes grace and peace from Jesus Christ, who is the faithful witness (1:1ff.) by reason of his loving work for us in his death and resurrection. Only in this passage in Revelation do we find *Iēsoús Christós.* The usage plainly denotes an awareness of his significance as the bringer of salvation.

b. In four other verses *ho christós* is used as a title. In 11:15 and 12:10 Christ assumes dominion at the side of God. As intercessor, he replaces the accuser in 12:10. In 20:4, 6 those who overcome reign with Christ and are priests of God and of Christ in the millennial reign. In Revelation Christ is Ruler. He protects and cares for his people and has dominion over all other powers. He won this dominion by his death, and God has conferred it. It is a priestly rule which is now hidden but will be manifest in the millennium, which will be followed by the final aeon when God is all in all (21:1ff.; 22:1ff.).

E. *The Early Church.*

1. *Ignatius.*

a. Christ and Jesus Christ. Ignatius mostly uses the full form *Iēsoús Christós* (*Ephesians* 14.2; *Romans* 4.1, etc. are exceptions). (Our) Lord Jesus Christ is rare. Ignatius makes good use of the *en* formula (*Trallians* 1.1 etc.) with Christ Jesus, Jesus Christ, the power, faith, etc. of Jesus Christ, and the love of God the Father and the Lord Jesus Christ. He links Christ firmly to his cross and resurrection (*Ephesians* 9.1 etc.)

and also speaks about his love (*Trallians* 6.1). Ignatius coordinates Christ and God; Christ is our God (cf. *Ephesians* 8.2; *Trallians* 7.1, etc.), our Savior (*Philadelphians* 9.2), etc. In large measure *Christós* has lost its true sense in Ignatius, so that he has to find new ways to express who Jesus Christ is.

b. Confessional Formulas and Statements. Ignatius adopts various confessional formulas, as in *Ephesians* 7.2; 18.2; *Magnesians* 6.1. He also develops statements of his own based on earlier models (cf. *Magnesians* 8.2 and *Romans* 8.2).

c. Christ and the Church. Ignatius stresses the link between Christ and the church but with a more institutional body in view (*Smyrneans* 8.2). The church's relation to Christ parallels Christ's to the Father (*Ephesians* 5.1). Ignatius finds a close connection between Jesus Christ, the bishop's office, and the apostolic witness (*Trallians* 7.1).

d. *Christianós* and *Christianismós*. Ignatius often uses *Christianós* for a believer; one must be this in reality and not in name only (*Magnesians* 4). *Christianismós* also occurs for being a Christian, for the Christian lifestyle (*Magnesians* 10.3), or for discipleship (10.1). Ignatius also uses such other terms as *christophóros*, *christónomos*, and *christomathía*.

2. *Polycarp and Martyrdom of Polycarp.*

a. In Polycarp we find the full form "our Lord Jesus Christ," a link with Savior, and coordination with God.

b. The Martyrdom of Polycarp also uses the full form. Polycarp knows the significance of the Messiah as the bringer of salvation but has to explain the term to pagans. In 10.1 he calls himself *Christianós,* and his enemies call him the father of the Christians in 12.2 (cf. also the phrase in 3.2).

3. *The Didache.* This work mostly uses *kýrios* for Jesus. *Iēsoús Christós* occurs only in the formula in 9.4. We also find *Christianós* once in 12.4.

4. *Barnabas.* In this work Jesus is Christ on the basis of OT quotations (Ps. 110:1 in 12.10), but we find *Christós* with Jesus only in 2.6.

5. *1 Clement.* This work shows awareness of the messianic significance of Jesus in 42.1-2. A confessional formula underlies 49.6 (cf. 2.1 with reference to the resurrection). A connection with the church may be seen in 44.3 etc. *en Christṓ* occurs in 1.2; 21.8, etc., and *en Christṓ Iēsoú* in 32.4; 38.1, but *en* formulas usually include nouns that express Christian lifestyle and conduct.

6. *2 Clement.* This work relates *Christós* to Savior on the basis of the passion. Those whose lives are shaped by Christ are the church, his body. In the union of flesh and spirit the church is the flesh and Christ the Spirit. The work does not use the full formula "our Lord Jesus Christ"; it does have the simple name Jesus and the designation *kýrios.*

7. *Diognetus.* This work does not use *Christós,* but *Christianós* is common as the author describes Christians as those who love though they are hated, who are the soul of the world, etc. (2.6; 6.1ff.). A new style is forged to describe who Jesus Christ is (7.4-5), but the term Son appears (9.2, 4; 10.2).

8. *Summary.* The survey shows that there is still some awareness that *Christós* denotes messiahship and is linked with the cross and resurrection as the salvation event. In many circles, however, *Christós* is now merely a name, and other words, especially *sōtḗr,* have to be used to bring out the content of the term, i.e., that Christ is the bringer of salvation. We thus find many notable attempts to express who Christ is for the early church.   [W. GRUNDMANN, IX, 527-80]

→ *aleíphō, mýron*

---

chrónos [time, period of time]

A. The Greek World.

I. Lexical Data.

1. This word has first the general sense of "time" or "the course of time" or "the passage of time."

2. a. It then means a "section" of time.

b. A related sense is a "measure" or "span" of time, a "limited time."

3. A further meaning is a "point of time," a "date."

II. Time in Greek Philosophy.

1. Philosophy asks whether time is unending, whether the corruptibility of the universe means its finitude, whether the reality of time is bound up with the movement of the cosmos, whether it is a reality at all. Whereas for some thinkers time is what gives order to eternal flux, and time is infinite, for others (e.g., the Sophist Antiphon) it has no real significance. For the Eleatics, being is a connected whole in the now, and Zeno concludes that, since there is no real movement, time does not really exist.

2. For Plato time is the moving image of eternity. It arises and perishes with the heavens. True being does not belong to time. The original is eternal; only the copy was and is and is to come.

3. Aristotle stresses that the all is eternal. Time exists only in terms of movement or change, i.e., as earlier or later. The peripatetic Strato argues that to be in time is not to be encircled by it. Time measures duration; day and night are not part of it. Epicurus thinks that time simply accompanies days and nights.

4. Stoicism relates time to movement. Nothing happens without it. It is also infinite. Yet it does not truly exist. The present exists, but one side of it still belongs to the past, another belongs already to the future.

5. The Sceptics claim that the concept of time yields no objectively solid insight. Time is neither limited nor endless, created nor uncreated, divisible nor indivisible. The concept is unserviceable.

6. Philo regards the creation of time as important. God's existence is eternity, not time. Eternity is the original of time, which arises only with the cosmos. Time is an interval of cosmic movement. It comes into being through the cosmos, not vice versa. Days and months arise with the ordered courses of the sun and moon, and with these also comes number.

7. Plutarch agrees with Plato that only the eternal has true being and that time comes with the cosmos as something moved and hence as impermanent.

8. Plotinus also traces time to the rise of the world. The world soul makes itself temporal by creating the perceptible world. It subjects this world to time. Time is the life of the world soul in movement from one form to another. It will end when this activity ceases. Like the world soul, it is everywhere. The cosmos strives ceaselessly toward the real being of eternity. The courses of the heavenly bodies measure time. By giving precedence to eternity, this line of thinking escapes the bondage to time that follows when time is viewed as unending and only the visible world is taken into account (Aristotle).

B. Time in Judaism.

I. The LXX.

1. Hebrew Terms. *chrónos* is not very common in the LXX. It is mostly used for the word "day" when this denotes a period of time, e.g., the "time" of a ruler's reign,

1337

a "lifetime," the "age" of someone. Another use is for "delay" in Dan. 2:16, and the sense of "time" occurs in Sir. 43:6 LXX. The meaning in Job 14:13 is a "set time." The LXX also uses it for the numbering of the reign in Dan. 5:26 (a free rendering).

2. *Works with No Hebrew Text.* Some contact with current ideas occurs in Hellenistic works. Solomon has knowledge of the times in Wis. 7:17ff., i.e., time's rise, extension, and cessation. Wisdom knows periods of time in advance, i.e., historical processes (8:8). 2 Macc. 1:22 refers to the passage of time, Wis. 2:4 to its course, Wis. 7:2 to a span, 2 Macc. 4:23 to all time, 2 Macc. 12:15 to an epoch, and Tob. 14:4 to a specific time.

II. Nonbiblical Judaism.

1. *Testaments of the Twelve.* In this work *chrónos* means a "period of time," a "certain time," a "point in time," or an "indefinite time."

2. *Qumran.*

a. The first meaning in the Scrolls is a "period of time." Each time has its own order. "This time" is the time of the separation of the community. The elect of the time are the sect.

b. A genitive is often added to characterize a period, e.g., the time of wrath, of transgression, of judgment, of devastation, of grace, of divine glory, or of salvation. We also find references to "all times" or "all eternal times." God sets times, e.g., for wickedness, or appoints times, e.g., for new creation.

c. Another use is for a "point of time." A particular event may fix the point, e.g., the time of harvest, or more generally of visitation, of penitence, or of judgment. The set time of God's intervention is contrasted with the times of darkness; today is God's time.

III. Time in Judaism. Jewish history fixes events in time and hence presupposes in some sense a linear view. Thus the OT coordinates successive events (1 Kgs. 6:1 etc.), and later works follow suit. Josephus dates the flood etc. from Adam, and he synchronizes his references with the number of years from the exodus, the migration of Abraham, and the flood (cf. *Antiquities* 1.82; 8.61). Jubilees connects its dating with the religious calendar. Qumran relates time to a yearly calendar. God has fixed the times for powers and events. In particular, Judaism perceives two aeons. Negative and positive epochs follow one another even within the one aeon. The relation between God and Israel is decisive in their assessment. Thus the ages of Moses, David, and Josiah are positive ones. Divine foreordination fixes their coming and duration. Hence the times are God's times. As Lord of history, God is also Lord of time (cf. Is. 41:2ff.; 45:1ff.; Ezr. 1:1-2). He is thus independent of it. Acting by thought and command, he does not need time (cf. Ps. 33:9). The six days of Gen. 1 indicate the orderliness of the world. Whether there is a true concept of eternity in references to numberless times may be debated.

C. The NT.

I. Lexical Data. In the NT *chrónos* mostly means "span of time" (cf. Acts 1:21). This may be indefinite (1 Cor. 16:7). The absolute *chrónon* means "time" in Acts 19:22. "Span" seems to be the sense in Mt. 2:7, 16, and we find "set time" in Acts 1:7, "delay" in Rev. 2:21, "term" in Lk. 1:57, and "point of time" in Acts 1:6. The word is relatively more common in 1 Peter (four times) and Acts (17).

II. Specific Sayings. The NT makes no basic statements about time. Rev. 10:6 does not mean that time ends, but that judgment will be delayed no longer. Rev. 6:11 ("a little longer") points to imminent eschatological expectation. Believers must wait in view of the delay (Mt. 25:5; 24:48). God has established the times (Acts 1:7); detailed information about them is not available. Yet Jesus has been manifested at the end of the times (1 Pet. 1:20; cf. Gal. 4:4: Time reaches its fullness with the Son's coming). The last time of Jude 18 is the time immediately before the end. For believers it is "the rest of the time in the flesh" and must be lived in a different way from "the time that is past" (1 Pet. 4:2-3). It is a time of exile (1:17). In 2 Tim. 1:9-10 the gracious work of God that is actualized in Christ is already given to us "before eternal times." The apostolic message manifests the hope of eternal life which God promised "ages ago" (Tit. 1:2-3). In Christ we have the revelation of the mystery which was not disclosed "in eternal times"; the implication here again is that it was conceived ages ago by God but only now made known (Rom. 16:25). Heb. 4:7 refers to the spacing of time within the OT revelation; David's saying comes long after Num. 14:22-23.

D. The Apostolic Fathers. In these works we find such expressions as a "stretch of time," a "short time," a "length of time," a "set time" (cf. Hermas *Similitudes* 5.5.3; 2 Clem. 19.3; Hermas *Similitudes* 7.2; Mart. Pol. 22.3; Did. 16.2). More generally we read of "every time" (Did. 14.3), of "earlier times" (Hermas *Similitudes* 9.20.4), or of "our times" (Mart. Pol. 16.2). The *polloí chrónoi* of 1 Clem. 44.3 embrace only a few decades, but those of 42.5 cover the period from Is. 60:17. The *anagraphás tṓn chrónōn* in 1 Clem. 25.5 are "chronicles" (of pagan priests).

→ *aiṓn, nýn, hṓra, kairós*   [G. DELLING, IX, 581-93]

ψ *ps*

psállō, psalmós → *hýmnos; pseudádelphos* → *adelphós; pseudapóstolos* → *apostéllō; pseudodidáskalos* → *didáskō; pseudómartys, pseudomartyréō, pseudomartyría* → *mártys; pseudoprophḗtēs* → *prophḗtēs*

---

pseúdos [lie, falsehood], *pseúdomai* [to lie], *pseudḗs* [false], *pseúsma* [lie, falsehood], *pseústēs* [liar], *apseudḗs* [true], *ápseustos* [truthful]

A. Secular Greek.
1. Usage. Of uncertain derivation, this group has the basic sense of "false" in various contexts. The active verb means "to deceive," passive "to be deceived" or "to deceive oneself," and intransitive "to lie." The noun *pseúdos* means "what is untrue," "deceit," "falsehood." The adjective *pseudḗs* means "deceiving," "untrue," the adverb "falsely." *apseudḗs* means "true" and may be used either for those who do not deceive or for those who are not deceived. The *pseústēs* is the "liar," and *pseúsma* means "untruth," "deception," or "lie."
2. Meaning. In philosophical discussion lying is not just the opposite of truth. It carries the sense both of untruth as nonbeing and of untruth as error. Lying is ethically wrong in virtue of the divinely protected order of the world which links right and truth. The worst lie is perjury. Calumniation is also wrong because it deprives its victim of dignity and honor. The gods may deceive. Indeed, all superiors have a certain freedom to lie, and social or political lies are acceptable. So is deceit in art. In tragedy

deceit and cunning bring about just punishment. Historians, however, contrast the truth of their accounts with the fictions of poets. They often give assurances of their reliability in their prefaces.

3. The Group in Philosophy. Two lines of investigation develop: a. into what is true or false in logic, and b. into what is true (or truthful) and false in ethics. Basic is the understanding of truth in equation with reality. For Aristotle perception is true, but thinking may be in error. Truthfulness is the point in ethics. Opinions may be true or false without being good or bad.

B. The OT.

1. Usage. The LXX uses the group for three main Hebrew equivalents meaning "to lie," "to deceive," "to feign," "to belie oneself," "to deny," and "to give false witness." *pseúdomai* is used for a verb meaning "to hide" in Job 6:10; 27:11.

2. Meaning. Legally perjury is the worst offense (Ex. 20:16), but slander is also a legal matter (Ps. 15:3). God, who protects what is right, hates lying (Prov. 6:16ff.). Wisdom condemns lying on the ground that it is folly (Prov. 17:7), but it allows lies of necessity (cf. Gen. 12:13; Jer. 38:24ff.). Hos. 7:1ff. gives prophetic intensity to the attack on lying. Religiously we find unfaithfulness to God, apostasy to false gods, and false prophets. Idol worship denies God (Job 31:28). Idols are deceitful (Is. 44:20). False prophecy is particularly reprehensible because it appeals to God (Ezek. 13:6-7), although God himself may send a lying spirit (1 Kgs. 22:22-23). The age of salvation will end the deception of false prophecy (Zech. 13:2ff.). Ezek. 13:19 shows the inner relation between false prophecy and apostasy. Jeremiah works out criteria of differentiation (14:14-15; 20:6; 23:17ff.).

C. Judaism.

1. Qumran. Qumran relates truth and falsehood dualistically to two spheres, that of salvation and that of perdition. Eschatology combines with decision. The Testaments of the Twelve also has a concept of decision, but here it is more individualistic.

2. Rabbinic Works. These works obviously condemn lying, but contain nothing distinctive.

3. Philo. Philo often links *pseudés* with *dóxa* (opinion). Pagans have false notions about God, idols, etc. He places lying in lists of vices, but within the exposition of the law.

D. The NT.

1. Synoptic Gospels and Acts. The verb occurs in these works only in Mt. 5:11 and Acts 5:3-4, and the noun and adjective only in Acts 6:13. In Mt. 5:11 the verb is in the absolute. This beatitude alone is compound and in the second person. Acts 5:3-4 comes within the sphere of sacral law. The offense against the church is an offense against the Spirit and brings down the judgment of God.

2. Paul.

a. Paul uses *pseúdomai* negatively as a catchword in the solemn affirmation of Rom. 9:1. The parallel references to Christ, conscience, and the Holy Spirit give the protestation its force. In Rom. 1:25 humanity sins by exchanging the truth of God for a lie; it is through humanity itself that sin gains entry (5:12). When God's truth is manifested, all people are shown to be liars (3:4). To see the character of God's work as grace and irrevocable word is to perceive the self-evident absurdity of the objection of v. 3.

b. In Tit. 1:2 God never lies. Deceptive signs and wonders, however, accompany antichrist (2 Th. 2:9, 11). The group also occurs in the exhortation of Col. 3:9 and various admonitions in Eph. 4:25; 1 Tim. 1:9-10 (cf. Jms. 3:14).

3. John.

a. Truth is a leading concept in John, but an antithesis comes only with Jn. 8:44-45, where falsehood has a personal representative, who again has children. Lying here is an active contesting of the truth, i.e., unbelief. On the one side we have God and Christ, on the other the father of lies and Christ's opponents. Murderer and liar go together (as do truth and life) in 14:6.

b. God is light, and hence we should do the truth in fellowship (1 Jn. 1:6; 2:4; 4:20). Lying denies the confession (2:21-22). The liar manifests antichrist. Confession includes admission of sin; refusing to admit it is the same as opposing God's truth and thus treating God as a liar (1:10; 5:10).

c. Revelation attacks those who falsely claim to be Jews (3:9) and also false prophets (2:2). The 144,000 do not lie (14:5), and lying receives emphasis as the last of the things excluded from the eschatological city (21:27; cf. 22:14-15).

E. The Early Church. Truthfulness is a divine gift and the attack on it is theft in Hermas *Mandates* 3.2. Antitheses bring out the nuances of unfaithfulness and hypocrisy. *pseúdos* is personified in Hermas *Similitudes* 9.15.3, and *pseudés* means "perjury" in Barn. 2.8. Falsehood is not prominent in Gnosticism, and although the Mandaeans heavily stress truth, they say little about lying.   [H. CONZELMANN, IX, 594-603]

pseudóchristos → *chríō*

---

psḗphos [pebble, vote], *psēphízō* [to calculate, reckon], *sympsēphízō* [to reckon], *(katapsēphízomai* [to resolve, condemn]), *synkatapsēphízomai* [to be chosen]

A. Normal Greek Usage.

1. psḗphos. This word means "little stone," "pebble," "dressed stone," or "stone" used in mosaics or board games. The plural, for "stones" used in counting, can denote "account." Other uses for small stones are in astrology, soothsaying, and especially voting. The latter use leads to the meaning "vote" or "voice," then "opinion," and in the legal sphere "voting" and "verdict."

2. psēphízō, sympsēphízō, (katapsēphízomai), synkatapsēphízomai.

a. *psēphízō* means "to count" or "calculate" with stones, in a transferred sense "to reach a verdict," and middle "to vote with a stone," "to vote," "to resolve."

b. *sympsēphízō,* an uncommon word, means "to reckon up," "to agree on."

c. *katapsēphízomai* means "to pronounce guilty" or "to resolve," middle "to be condemned."

B. The LXX and Hellenistic Judaism.

1. The LXX.

a. We find *psḗphos* in Lam. 3:16 for "little stone" and in Ex. 4:25 for the sharp stone used for cutting the foreskin. The plural in Sir. 18:10 is used for little stones in the sand. The sense of "voting stone" occurs in 4 Macc. 15:26.

b. *psēphízō* is a variant in 1 Kgs. 3:8; 8:5 for "counting." *sympsēphízō* occurs in Jer. 49:20 Cod. AQ for "counting" (sheep).

2. *Josephus*.

a. Josephus uses *psḗphos* for "resolve" or "vote."

b. *psēphízomai* in Josephus means "to resolve" or "to reckon."

c. *katapsēphízomai* has the meaning "to condemn."

3. *Philo*.

a. Philo uses *psḗphos* for "pronouncement" or "verdict." Pronouncements may be just and legal or unjust and illegal.

b. *psēphízomai* has in Philo the sense "to decree" or "to resolve."

c. *katapsēphízomai* means "to condemn."

C. The NT and Apostolic Fathers.

1. Paul in Acts 26:10 says that he gave his "voice" against believers, i.e., condemned them.

2. The white stone of Rev. 2:17 may have been an amulet. It serves to ward off evil forces. The color denotes its new and distinctive character or category.

3. In Lk. 14:28 *psēphízō* means "to reckon." As the builder should count the cost before starting, so disciples should consider their resources. They must also consider the cost of the required renunciation. "Reckon" is also the meaning of *sympsēphízō* in Acts 19:19 when those who had burned their books of magic valued them and found they came to a very high sum.

4. The number of the beast is counted in Rev. 13:18. Numerical value is ascribed to the letters, and the total is 666. One interpretation of this number is that it is the sum of the numbers 1 to 36, and that 36 is the sum of the numbers 1 to 8. In Gnosticism the number 8, the ogdoad, is identical to *sophía,* so that Gnostic wisdom might be the enemy. Others arrive at the emperor Domitian.

5. *katapsēphízomai* in Acts 1:26 seems to indicate that Matthias is officially given a place with the eleven.

6. *sympsēphízō* means "to reckon," "to add up," "to calculate" in Hermas *Visions* 3.1.4.   [G. BRAUMANN, IX, 604-07]

---

psychḗ [life, soul], *psychikós* [natural, physical], *anápsyxis* [relief, refreshing], *anapsýchō* [to revive, refresh], *dípsychos* [double-minded], *oligópsychos* [of little spirit]

A. The Greek World.

1. Homer. In Homer *sṓma* is the dead body, words like *mélea* are used for the living organism, and *psychḗ* is the vital force that resides in the members and finds expression in the breath. Hazarded in battle, the *psychḗ* leaves a person at death, goes to the underworld, leads a shadowy existence there, and may appear in dreams. The real self becomes food for beasts or in a few cases goes to the gods. The *psychḗ* has nothing to do with mental or spiritual functions. Terms like *nóos, kardía,* or *thymós* are used to denote such functions. Bodily parts are their agents. But the *nóos,* which one bears in the breast or which a god has put there, becomes a permanent and integral part of the person. A varied psychological vocabulary develops, but there is no master concept of soul.

2. Older and Classical Usage. psychḗ becomes a master concept in the sixth century B.C. The idea of retribution helps to bring this about. The *psychḗ* in the underworld assures continuity between this world and the next. The *psychḗ,* then, is the epitome of the individual. The *sṓma* (body) comes to be seen as the *sḗma* (tomb) of the soul.

Transmigration of the soul also finds supporters (Pythagoras). After 500 B.C. the *psychḗ* represents the essential core embracing thought, will, and emotion and not sharing the body's dissolution. The soul is not limited by space. It has a self-expanding *lógos*. Communication between souls is possible. The soul's autonomy and higher worth are taken for granted. Moral instruction is a training of the soul for virtue. Medicine accepts the division of body and soul; the *psychḗ* is the self, or the seat of moral and spiritual qualities.

3. Plato.

a. Plato starts with the position of Socrates that we are to be judged by the state of the soul. But there may be conflict between resolve based on insight and spontaneous impulses that also originate in the soul.

b. Different parts of the soul have different ontological value. The aim is to insure for *logistikón* its due control over other parts. Moral struggle is a flight from the world of sense and an approximation to intelligible being.

c. In its dominant part the soul is preexistent and immortal; it belongs to transcendent being.

d. The state is a larger model of the soul. So, too, is the cosmos. As life means movement, movement is proper to the soul as it is to the living organism of the cosmos.

4. Post-Platonic Philosophy.

a. Constitution of the Soul. For the Peripatetics the immaterial soul is the principle of the form, life, and activity of the total organism. For the Epicureans and Stoics the soul is made of finer matter. The individual soul is a broken off part of the world soul and will be reunited with it at death.

b. Division of the Soul. Plato's trichotomy is the starting point of later views. A common division is into rational, irrational, and vegetative spheres. The power of thought has the highest worth; the understanding should control the alogical domain. For Middle Platonism the soul derives from *noús* but has powers that enable it to work on matter; the *noús* affects the *psychḗ*, and the *psychḗ* the *sṓma*. On this view the *noús* is the innermost core. Demons are *psychaí* without bodies, not purely noetic beings. Neo-Pythagoreans see two souls. They equate the logical soul with the *noús*, while the alogical soul is the garment that it puts on in its descent through the spheres. In sum, the *psychḗ*, in distinction from the *noús*, undergoes a certain devaluation, since it cannot denote pure spirituality. Medicine is interested in the organic relation of intellectual functions but differs as to the corporeality of the soul, arguing both for and against it from the fact that a corpse seems to be heavier than a living body.

5. Popular Ideas. In popular thinking the *psychḗ* is the impalpable essential core of a person, the agent of thought, will, and emotion, the quintessence of human life. The soul embraces the conscience. The book of dreams presupposes that souls can go abroad during sleep and that they go to bliss or punishment after death. Freedom is freedom of soul; astrology promises such freedom. In various expressions *psychḗ* can denote "life," e.g., to hazard one's *psychḗ*, and the phrase *pása psychḗ* means "everyone."

B. OT Anthropology.

1. nepeš.

a. Breath. The Hebrew term which *psychḗ* renders is a fluid and dynamic one which it is hard both to define and to translate. The root means "to breathe" in a physical sense. Breathing is a decisive mark of the living creature; its cessation means the end of life. The root thus comes to denote "life" or "living creature." In a localization, the meaning may be "neck" or "throat." Departure of the breath is a metaphor for death. The alternation of breathing (cf. the use of the verb in Ex. 23:12; 31:17) corresponds to the fluid nature of the terms life and death in the OT. Life and death are two worlds that do not admit of sharp differentiation. Sickness and anxiety, which constrict the breath, are manifestations of the world of death.

b. Blood. Basic to both breath and blood is the idea of the living organism. Every form of life disappears when these leave the body. Gen. 9:4 finds the life in the blood, and Lev. 17:11 sees in blood the seat of the life (cf. also Dt. 12:23). There is no concept here of a blood-soul; the obvious thought is that of vital force.

c. Person. *nepeš* denotes the total person, what he or she is. Gen. 2:7 expresses this truth, although more in relation to the external aspect than to the modalities of life. What is meant is the person comprised in corporeal identity. Yet the total personality, the ego, is also involved. The noun can thus become a synonym of the personal pronoun (Gen. 27:25; Jer. 3:11).

d. Corpse and Tomb. The accent on the person leads to the use for a lifeless corpse (cf. Num. 6:6; 19:13; Lev. 19:28). The reference is to the dead person prior to final dissolution. Outside the Bible a use for "tomb" develops on the basis that the individual is in some sense present after death. In the Bible, however, the *nepeš* never exists independently of the individual, and the word is never used for an inhabitant of the underworld.

e. Will. The term expresses movement as well as form. The orientation may be to such elemental realities as hunger and thirst or to yearning for God. It embraces various parts of the organism, which can thus be used as synonyms for *nepeš*. It arises in relation to sex in Gen. 34:3, hatred in Ps. 27:12, pain and sorrow in 1 Sam. 1:10, the will in Gen. 23:8, and striving for God in Is. 26:9; Ps. 63:1, etc. The vocative in Ps. 42:5 etc. is a kind of question to the self, which rises to its full intensity before God, and relaxes when the goal is reached (Ps. 131:2).

2. *Flesh and Body.*

a. Flesh. The term "flesh" stands in some antithesis to *nepeš* and may also denote the whole person. It often has a very material sense for flesh that is eaten. "All flesh" is a phrase for all living things. Used later with blood, it denotes what is human as distinct from divine. It can denote the male organ (e.g., Ezek. 23:20; Ex. 28:42). But when used for the whole person it may also be synonymous with *nepeš* (Pss. 84:2; 119:120). In itself, however, it relates to human weakness and transitoriness (Gen. 6:3). Trust in the flesh is no help (Jer. 17:5). The flesh finally becomes the evil principle that opposes God, but this is never so in the OT, in which, as an organism that receives its life from the spirit, it may be connected with praise of God and longing for him. One should not corrupt the way of the flesh on earth (Gen. 6:12). Flesh becomes the antithesis of soul and spirit only in Wis. 8:19; 9:15.

b. Bones. Flesh undergoes total destruction at death. The bones endure longest, hence they receive special care (2 Kgs. 13:20), they are connected with the hope of rising again (Ezek. 37), they may be said to be joyful in God (Ps. 35:9-10), their breaking expresses the violence of an assault (Is. 38:7), and they can also denote true being or innermost substance (Ex. 24:10; Gen. 7:13; Ezek. 24:2).

3. *Parts of the Body as the Seat of Life.*

a. The Head. In the OT the totality may be concentrated in a part as life is seen in its manifestation or movement. Thus the head may be the focus, e.g., when hands are laid on it in blessing (Gen. 48:14), or punishment is called down on it (Josh. 2:19), or it is entrusted to someone (1 Sam. 28:2), or its white hairs go down to Sheol (Gen. 48:38), or it is the seat of knowledge (Dan. 2:28).

b. The Face. The face acts as a focus as it expresses various emotions or as its features denote envy (the eyes), arrogance (the forehead), pride (the neck), or anger (the nose).

c. The Hand. The hand (or palm or finger) is that which takes up a matter and executes it. It expresses the will and the means to carry it out. To give power is to "strengthen the hands" (Judg. 9:24).

d. The Foot. The foot also expresses strength (cf. standing on one's feet or planting the foot on an enemy's neck). But the foot may also slip or stumble or be caught in a net (Ps. 94:18; Job 12:5; 9:15).

e. Inner Organs. As emotions like grief and joy affect the liver, heart, etc., these inner organs come to be viewed as their seat (cf. Pss. 44:26; 64:6; 16:7; Gen. 35:11; Job 31:20; Lam. 2:11).

4. *The Heart.* The heart holds a special place as the most common anthropological term (850 instances). Although localized exactly, it denotes the totality in its inner worth. Like breathing, it has an ebb and flow. But its cessation does not mean death (1 Sam. 25), since it has more than a physical sense. It is the point where impressions meet (1 Sam. 1:8; Ps. 13:2). It comes close to conscience (1 Sam. 25:31). It directs the ways of life as the place where God's statutes are written. The insane have no heart (cf. Gen. 31:20), and wine and harlotry take the heart away (Hos. 4:11). The heart differentiates humans from animals, whose hearts are purely physical (Dan. 4:13). It forms plans that produce action. By nature it is not pure (Ps. 101:4) but inclines to falsehood and pride (Pss. 12:2; 131:1). It may become fat or hard (Is. 6:10; Ezek. 11:19). God tests it (Ps. 17:3), knows it (Ps. 33:15), purifies it, and unites it with himself (1 Kgs. 8:61). A new creation begins in it (Lev. 26:41; Ezek. 11:19; 36:26).

5. *The Spirit.*

a. Origin of the Concept. Without *rû(a)ḥ* there is no life, and the source of life is outside us. The word means "wind" or "breath." Breath, being fleeting, can denote vanity (Job 16:3), but it is also life-giving (Gen. 8:1 etc.). As wind denotes the breath of God, it loses its physical aspect and signifies invisible power (cf. Is. 31:3).

b. Outworking in People. As divine power the Spirit comes on certain people and enables them to do mighty deeds (Judg. 13:25) or to prophesy (1 Sam. 10:6). The Messiah has the Spirit in special measure (Is. 11). There are also other spirits which God may use but which oppose him (1 Sam. 16:14). *rû(a)ḥ* is a condition of *nepeš* and regulates its force (cf. Judg. 15:19; 1 Kgs. 10:5).

c. Creative Activity. In Ps. 104:29; Num. 16:22; 27:16 the Spirit is the creative power of life. In us it may thus express intensity of feeling (cf. 1 Sam. 1:15; Hos. 4:12; Num. 5:14). The phrase "to awaken the spirit" expresses its stimulative role (Hag. 1:14).

d. Relation to *nepeš* and Heart. In spite of parallels, a distinction remains between "spirit" and both *nepeš* and heart, although spirit and heart are virtually identical in Ezek. 11:5 and Jer. 3:17. Later one may discern a tendency to psychologize "spirit" (cf. Dt. 2:30). Yet there is no separate anthropology, nor do we find the concept of becoming a spirit when the body decays.

e. Flesh and Spirit. The OT sets these in antithesis in, e.g., Gen. 6:1ff.; Is. 31:3, but only in the sense of human weakness and divine strength. In view of creation, the two are not irreconcilable except when flesh trusts in self instead of God (Jer. 17:5ff.). The eschatological age will erase all tensions, yet not by replacing flesh with spirit. Although spirit finds a religious use in, e.g., Pss. 31:5; 34:18, etc., heart is more common in such contexts. OT anthropology views people less according to their nature and more in their relation to God.

6. Relational Character of OT Anthropology.

a. In principle OT anthropology differs little from that of surrounding nations. It is God who gives it its distinctive coherence. The one God as Creator and also as Lord of history gives a unity of structure and thrust to what is said about his human creatures. Before the living God, the individual is a responsible person.

b. This person is always seen in a totality that finds expression, not in the antithetical concepts of body and soul, but in the complementary ones of body and life.

c. The OT never views the person as an abstraction but always as a historical individual or the member of a historical people. The name expresses the personal being and history.

d. Life is not just the movement from birth to death but stands under constant threat and finds a counterthrust in contact with the source of life. Life is breathing which is dependent on the divine breath and in which both the manner of breathing and the quality of the air breathed are important. When God ceases to breathe into a person, life stops.

e. Life depends, then, on the relation of the human image to the divine original and the task that this implies. We are truly alive only in the situation of choice in which we fulfil what we are.

[E. Jacob, IX, 608-31]

C. Judaism.

I. Hellenistic Judaism.

1. LXX. In works with a Hebrew original *psychē* mostly translates *nepeš* either as: vital force or as seat of the mind or spirit (cf. Num. 35:11; Dt. 11:18). The idea of the soul as an essential core, however, is alien to the OT, which posits no antithesis of body and soul. In Is. 10:18 the expression "soul and body" denotes the total person with no thought of antithesis. Ps. 16:10 means that God will keep the author alive; only the LXX suggests that the soul will spend some time in the underworld, but that God will not leave it there. When the LXX uses *psychē* for living people, however, this fits in well with Hebrew usage (cf. Ex. 16:16).

2. Apocalyptic and Pseudepigraphical Works. These works attest to the conceptual differentiation of body and soul, as in Greek thought. The soul may denote the person, as in Hebrew, but it is also the inner person, the moral or spiritual self, which parts from the body and lives on at death, either with God or in hell or the underworld. The soul is the sphere of human responsibility. Magicians can steal souls, which can leave the body for a time. At the resurrection, however, body and soul will be reunited.

3. LXX (Greek Works).

a. Greek thought dominates Wisdom. Soul and body are in antithesis, the body is a burden, well-being of soul is all-important, the soul lives on after death. On the other hand, the soul is not divine. The whole person is in God's image, and the *pneúma* has to be imparted by God.

b. 4 Maccabees reproduces popular philosophical psychology. Platonic trichotomy appears in 3:2ff., in 14:6 the soul is the center of consciousness and feeling, and in 15:25 it is the organ of intellectual functions.

4. Aristeas and Josephus. The Epistle of Aristeas uses the expression "save the soul" for "save the life." Elsewhere it ascribes purity, as a matter of the mind, to the soul rather than the body. Josephus uses a differentiated psychological terminology.

5. Philo. Philo knows the division of the soul into various parts. The divine *pneúma* is for him the *noús* or *logismós* of the soul which cures it of the passions. Only the highest part of the human soul has union with God. Yet all its parts share in the rise of sin. Angels and demons are *psychaí,* and the world has a *psychē* as a living organism governed by rational laws.   [A. DIHLE, IX, 632-35]

II. Palestinian Judaism.

1. *nepeš* denotes the vital element, the breath, or the ego. In Qumran texts it is often equivalent to "life." It is not the soul as a distinct part, but the whole person living in responsibility. In many references it simply means the self.

2. The rabbis continue the OT use for "life" but also, under Hellenistic influence, see some antithesis between body and soul. The soul dwells like a guest in the body and gives strength to keep the law, receiving power from heaven for this purpose. In some statements the soul is preexistent. Yet the rabbis do not disparage the body or abandon personal unity. If the soul leaves the body at death, the two come together at the resurrection, and both are responsible before God.   [E. LOHSE, IX, 635-37]

D. The NT.

I. The Gospels and Acts.

1. Natural and Physical Life.

a. General. In Acts 20:10 the *psychē* is the life, in 27:22 there will be no loss of life, in 27:10 no lives will be lost, and in Mt. 6:25 the life needs nourishment.

b. Giving of Life. When Jesus says that he gives his *psychē* as a ransom for many, what he means is the life bound up with flesh and blood, along with the individual ego (Mk. 10:45). Jn. 10:11ff. uses *tithénai* for giving the *psychē*; this word can mean "to risk" as well as "to give." The disciples can sacrifice their lives too, but only Jesus can take his life again. In Acts 15:26 *paradídōmi* suggests the hazarding of resources; it does not have to imply martyrdom. Rev. 12:11 refers to those who do not love their *psychē* unto death, and in Acts 20:24 Paul does not hold his life dear. In Lk. 14:26 *psychē* embraces everything that makes up the earthly life that one must hate for Jesus' sake.

c. Seeking, Killing, and Saving Life. In Mt. 2:20 the child's foes seek his life (*psychē*). In Lk. 12:20 God requires the life of the rich farmer. The decision in Mk. 3:4ff. is between saving life and taking it. The earthly life is taken so seriously that leaving it sick is tantamount to robbing it of all that makes it worthwhile. Life here is not just a formal concept but has content as the full life that God intends at creation. Yet this means finally a life that is lived in God's service, so that the degree of physical health is a subsidiary matter. Thus in Lk. 9:55-56 the Son of Man has come to protect physical life, but more than this is plainly in view, as may be seen in Lk. 19:10, where seeking and saving go hand in hand with the summons to faith. The call to faith is a call to the true life that God intends; salvation is salvation from anything that hinders this, whether it be sickness or unbelief.

2. The Whole Person. If *psychē* means "physical life," what is at issue is not the phenomenon as such, but the life manifested in individuals. Thus *pása psychē* means "everybody" in Acts 2:43, but with an individualizing thrust (3:23). Mt. 11:29 promises rest to the souls of all who come to Jesus. The expression rests on Jer. 6:16 and carries the implication of the human self that lives before God and must give account to him. Hence the rest is not that of liberation from the body. It is attained in acts of physical obedience to God, for the physical life that God gives cannot be separated from the life with God that takes shape in prayer, praise, and doing God's will.

3. The Place of Feeling.

a. The Influence of Others. Paul's enemies poison the *psychaí* of the Gentiles in Acts 14:2. The *psychaí* of the brethren in Antioch are unsettled in 15:24. The *psyché* can thus be swayed by others. Jesus holds the *psyché* of the people in suspense in Jn. 10:24; it might tilt either to faith or to unbelief. On the positive side, Paul and Barnabas strengthen the *psychaí* of the disciples in Acts 14:22.

b. Experiences of Joy, Sorrow, and Love. Active decision is at issue when God's *psyché* takes pleasure in his servant in Mt. 12:18. The *psyché* of Lk. 12:19 hopes to enjoy physical and psychological pleasures on the basis of a radical decision. In Lk. 1:46 the *psyché* is the subject of praise of God; the presence of *pneúma* shows that this is God's gift and work. The *psyché* may also be the locus of sorrow, as in Mk. 14:34 (cf. Ps. 42:5). Mk. 12:30 demands love with all the *psyché*; the word is close to strength of will in this context (cf. Mt. 22:37). Yet its omission in Mk. 12:33 shows that it is not supremely important or distinctive (cf. Acts 4:32). The sword of sorrow pierces the *psyché* in Lk. 2:35.

c. Heart. When the soul is said in OT fashion to praise and love God, the meaning is very close to that of heart. The question arises whether the praise and love of God are a response to the influence of God as other movements of the soul are responses to other influences.

4. True Life.

a. Jesus. In Mk. 8:35; Mt. 10:39; Lk. 17:33; Jn. 12:25 we have the saying that those who would save their *psyché* will lose it, and those who lose it will save it. The primary reference might be to physical life, but in the sense of the true and full life that the Creator intends, and therefore with a broader scope than that of life on earth. Since true life means the liberation of openness to God and neighbor, it differs from the stringent asceticism that the similar rabbinic saying commends.

b. Mark. In the context of Mk. 8:31ff. the saying stresses the fact that the giving of life is possible only by following him who gave his life for all. True life thus finds a new center, and it is more explicitly a life lived according to God's purpose and therefore in his presence. God will preserve this life even if the loss of physical life is entailed. Death is not a frontier that makes the truth of God untrue. Resurrection finally actualizes the receiving of life as a gift from God. Only orientation to Jesus and the gospel can lead to this.

c. Matthew. In Mt. 10:39 the verb "find" suggests that the *psyché* is not given already but that one attains to it only when ready to lose it.

d. Luke. Lk. 17:33 seems to be using LXX expressions, but the eschatological context makes it likely that the original sense of *psyché* here is "eternal life," which we lose if, like Lot's wife, we cannot detach ourselves from the present life.

e. John. Jn. 12:25 relates primarily to Jesus himself (cf. v. 24), but with a glance at the disciples too (v. 26). The contrasting of "in this world" with "for eternal life" shows that the reference is to both earthly and eternal life, but not in sharp distinction. There is no magical change, for the believer already has *psyché*. Nor is the *psyché* an immortal soul; it is the life which God gives, and which by our attitude to God takes on a mortal or eternal character. Life is kept for eternity only by its sacrifice and in constant living by God's gift.

f. Life That Survives Death. True life is life that is given by God and lived before him. It is the self lived in the body, yet not consisting of health or wealth, but as the gift of God that death cannot limit.

5. The Supreme Good. In Mk. 8:35-36 (cf. Ps. 49:7-8), the supreme good is the true life that is lived before God by following Jesus. To live life merely as a natural phenomenon is to miss it. *psyché* is physical life as that which expresses the self (cf. Lk. 9:25), but in the faithfulness of God it also applies beyond physical life (cf. v. 38). The coming of the Son of Man will show whether the orientation is to the cosmos or to God. The *psyché* is not a substance that survives death; it is life from God and in fellowship with God that comes to fulfilment through the judgment.

6. *psyché in Contrast to the Body*. Mt. 10:28 presents God as the one who can cast both body and *psyché* into Gehenna. The saying posits the unity of the two and negates the idea of the soul's immortality. Persecutors cannot affect the true life by putting an end to physical life, which is threatened already by sickness and other hazards. God alone controls the *psyché*, and for those who have true life with him he prepares a new body, just as he destroys both the body and *psyché* of those who do not have true life with him.

7. *The psyché after Death in Luke*.

a. Lk. 12:4-5; 9:25; Acts 2:31. These sayings omit the references to the *psyché* in Gehenna or Hades. The emphasis is on the corporeality of the resurrection as distinct from the Hellenistic survival of the soul. The weighty role of judgment in the call to repentance demands the resurrection of both the just and the unjust (Acts 24:15).

b. Lk. 12:20. This statement simply means that the rich farmer will die, although there is perhaps a suggestion that the *psyché* is a loan that God now demands back from him.

c. Lk. 21:19. This might refer to the preservation of earthly life but after v. 16 true and authentic life is probably meant, i.e., eternal life, although not in the sense of an immortal soul after the Greek fashion.

II. Paul.

1. *Natural Life and True Life*. Paul makes sparing use of *psyché*. He speaks about the attempt on Elijah's life in Rom. 11:3, refers to Epaphroditus hazarding his life in Phil. 2:30, and says that he and his helpers will give their lives (i.e., their time and energy as well as physical life) for the church in 1 Th. 2:8 (cf. Rom. 16:4). In 2 Cor. 12:15 he is ready to spend and be spent for the *psychaí* of his readers, i.e., that they might know the authentic life that comes from God and is lived responsibly before him.

2. *Person*. Paul has the individual person in mind in Rom. 2:9 and 13:1. In 2 Cor. 1:23 (cf. the *pneúma* of Rom. 1:9) he means the self that is aware of responsibility to God.

3. *mía psyché*. In Phil. 12:27, as a parallel to *hén pneúma*, this term lays more stress on the task that is to be achieved. *pneúma* may be parallel to *psyché* in the believer, but there is no thought of a soul regenerated by the Spirit and detached from the body. The *psyché* is physical life, or person, or the moral and spiritual person; Paul never assesses it negatively.

4. *Colossians and Ephesians*. *psyché* bears a neutral sense in Col. 3:23; Eph. 6:6. Even in opposition to the Colossian heresy Paul does not develop a doctrine of the soul. He conducts the debate in terms of Christology, not anthropology.

5. *Secularity of Usage*. Paul never uses *psyché* for the life that survives death. He sees eternal life wholly as a divine gift on the basis of a new creative act. It is future and heavenly. There is continuity with the earthly life, but this lies wholly with God, and is better denoted by *pneúma* than *psyché*.

III. Hebrews. The *psychaí* that grow weary in Heb. 12:3 are probably the normal forces of believers. The *psychaí* of 13:17, however, are the members described with reference to their spiritual lives. Leaders bear special responsibility for the *psyché*, for

1349

which they must give account at the judgment. What is meant is the whole person, or possibly the life before God. 10:39 has the latter in view; the preservation of this life means its attainment of the consummation through judgment and resurrection. Spiritual existence is also the point in 6:19. This stands under threat, but it has solid hope because Jesus has already entered the inner shrine behind the curtain. In 4:12 the word pierces both soul and spirit rather than dividing them. The verse does not teach trichotomy; it relates both soul and spirit to the inner person to which the word can penetrate.

IV. The Catholic Epistles.

1. John. 3 Jn. 2 distinguishes between general health and health of soul. *psyché* is the true life before God that can be sound even in physical ill-health. Body and soul are not set in express antithesis, for the hope is that the two will be in harmony.

2. James. In 1:21 salvation embraces eschatological salvation and thus the *psyché* is the life before God that comes to fulfilment in the resurrection. The same applies in 5:20, where *thánatos* may be either death or condemnation or both. The *psyché* is the true life before God that is saved through the judgment that threatens it with death.

3. 1 Peter. In 3:20 we simply have a number, although with a hint of preservation by and for God. In 1:19 the *psyché* is the individual life or person; its salvation is the eschatological goal of faith, but already on earth it is purified by obedience for love (v. 22). In 4:19 the *psyché* might be the physical life, but in context it seems to refer to the life which the Creator takes into his keeping hands through death and fashions anew. Christ in 2:25 shepherds the faith-life of believers. In 2:11 *psyché* is the life that is given by God and lived before him. Carnal desires war against it, so that we have here an antithesis of *psyché* and *sárx* (similar to Paul's antithesis of *pneúma* and *sárx*). The *psyché* is not unconditionally good, nor is it summoned to asceticism, but it must so live in the earthly sphere as to be at home in the heavenly sphere.

4. 2 Peter. In 2:8, 14 *psyché* is the person, living responsibly, distinguishing between good and evil, and hence exposed to temptation. In itself it is neutral; *dikaía* and *astériktos* qualify it positively or negatively.

V. Revelation.

1. Physical Life. Rev. 16:3 uses *pása psyché* with *zōés* for "every living creature" (i.e., in the sea; cf. 8:9). "Life" is the meaning in 12:11—the life that the martyrs loved not even unto death.

2. Person. As in the OT, *psyché* means "person" in 18:13. The addition *anthrópōn* shows that the use is not just numerical; the phrase expresses horror at the traffic in slaves, who are also human persons.

3. Life after Death. This sense is clearest in 6:9. The *psychaí* here are those that await God's righteous judgment prior to the resurrection. They are martyrs who enjoy self-awareness, may be seen in their white garments, but do not yet have the full life that comes with the new corporeality of the resurrection. In 20:4 the *psychaí* have attained to the final state after the first resurrection, so that obviously *psyché* does not denote merely a provisional, noncorporeal state but embraces the whole person living in eschatological salvation.

VI. NT Usage in Distinction from pneúma.

1. psyché often denotes physical life. *pneúma* may be used for this too, but whereas the *psyché* can be persecuted and slain, one can only hand back the *pneúma* to God. Only *psyché*, then, can refer to the purely natural life that can reach an end (cf. the contrast in 1 Cor. 15:45).

2. psyché is always individual life, or the whole person, often as the locus of joy and sorrow or love and hate. In contrast *pneúma* for the human totality represents a special aspect, i.e., God's gift, and never characterizes either unbelievers or ethically negative impulses. *psychē* can be the locus of faith, but as such it is interesting for Paul only inasmuch as God can use psychological faculties. Proclamation and edification take place through the *pneúma*.

3. *psychē* is authentic life only as God gives it and one receives it from him. Whereas the problem with *pneúma* is that it tends to be seen as the inner spiritual life that we are given, the problem with *psychē* is that it tends to be restricted to the physical sphere instead of embracing within this sphere the gift of God that transcends death.

4. As God's faithfulness does not end with death (cf. Ps. 49), so *psychē* comes to signify a life that death does not extinguish. Later this is specifically the religious life that one must nurture as a gift, which implies responsibility. The continuity of the life of faith and the resurrection life does not reside in the divine indwelling but in the divine faithfulness. *pneúma*, too, can denote the departed believer, but in this context both terms refer, not to a surviving part, but to the total life given by God and lived out before him: a bodily but not a fleshly life. John develops *psychē* to express the continuity, but Paul prefers *pneúma*, which stresses the continuity of the divine activity.

5. The NT does not use *psychē* as a term for life in an intermediate state. Rev. 6:9 does not have this sense, nor does 2 Cor. 5:3, and at most Mt. 10:28 is debatable. Paul is wisely content to know that the dead are with Christ (Phil. 1:23).

[E. Schweizer, IX, 637-56]

E. Gnosticism.

1. Gnostic texts vary considerably in teaching and usage. A common feature is the view that the human self is part of the transcendent world that is entangled in this cosmos. The revealer discloses its true origin and frees it for a return home. In some texts the self is called the soul, and we find the corresponding pairs light/darkness, good/evil, spirit/matter, and soul/body.

2. Gnostics who use *psychē* view it as the inner human core in a cosmos fashioned by pneumatic particles but sharply differentiated from the good world of light, to which only the *pneúma* belongs. The threefold structuring (*pneúma, psychē, sṓma*) follows the philosophical model, but the union of the soul with matter is not now an act of the self-unfolding *noús* but involves alienation of the pneumatic particle. Natural and moral laws enslave the pneumatic self and keep it from entering the *plérōma*. The *psychē* is the disputed area of redemption; it is good only insofar as it takes *pneúma* into itself.

3. The psychological terminology varies widely in detail. Valentinians refer to two souls. Others contrast *psychē* with *noús, pneúma*, or *lógos*. Redemption applies strictly to the *pneúma*, but the *psychē* may be included. For Basilides the *psychē* is a bird, the *pneúma* its wings that enable it to soar. Popular Gnosticism uses the terms with no great exactitude.

4. a. Trichotomy. The Nag Hammadi texts give evidence of trichotomy, e.g., in speaking of the pneumatic, psychical, and earthly Adam, or the threefold resurrection of spirit, soul, and flesh.

b. Varied Use of *psychē*. Nag Hammadi texts also use *psychē* in different ways. A basic distinction is between the cosmic and supercosmic soul. The latter is the *pneúma*, which is redeemed by its bridegroom, the life-giving Spirit. Another distinction is between immortal and mortal souls. The *psychē*, however, is usually the cosmic soul, which stands between the spirit and the body and may incline one way or the other; negative evaluation of this soul is common, and it cannot be redeemed without the *pneúma*.

c. The Soul's Destiny. The descent and reascent of the soul are described in various categories; its redemption is the great theme of Gnostic texts. Everything depends on whether the *pneúma* of life gains control over it. Some souls are pure and some are punished. The redeemer sent by the Father gives new life to the soul, frees it, and thus makes its reascent possible. Saved souls are in the ogdoad and sing praise in silence.

[K.-W. Tröger, IX, 656-60]

psychikós.

1. *The Greek World.* This term is common in religious and philosophical speech and then enters ordinary usage as the adjective of *psychē̆*. In 2 Macc. 4:37 *psychikós* means "from the heart" or "very much" in intensification of a verb of emotion; Greek usually has *ek psychḗs* for this. In one instance *psychikós* also has the sense "brave" or "manly."

[A. Dihle, IX, 661]

2. *Judaism.* The only instance is in 4 Macc. 1:32, but an important relation develops to *choïkós* (cf. 1 Cor. 15:46ff.) (cf. also in this connection *sarkikós* and *pneumatikós*). In Philo the soul is the earthly component. Whereas reason is neutral, the irrational impulses of the soul seduce us and bring us to grief. A negative estimation stands behind Philo's statements.

3. *The NT.*

a. 1 Cor. 15:44ff. *psychē̆* is ambiguous in the NT. It may denote either the true life that God gives or ordinary life that belongs to everyone. In the latter case the Spirit stands in sharp antithesis. Only when the Spirit is imparted either in time or eschatologically does that which is *psychikós* cease to be purely earthly. In 1 Cor. 15:44ff. Paul views impartation as eschatological. What is *psychikós* is not sinful as such but it is corruptible. Over against it is the risen Christ as life-giving Spirit. Our heavenly pneumatic being is still future. It is given to us only as God's promise in Christ to faith. Continuity between what is *psychikós* and *pneumatikós* lies in the faithfulness of God through Christ. We shall bear the image of the heavenly, not as ourselves life-giving spirit, but as spiritual body, for Christ alone is Creator Spirit.

b. 1 Cor. 2:14. Here again *psychikós* means natural humanity without the eschatological gift of the *pneúma*. If the unbeliever is *psychikós,* the believer who makes no progress is *sarkikós*. Being *psychikós* is not a higher stage, then, but it also does not involve the same censure. The *psychikós* becomes a *sarkikós* when confessing faith but remaining set on what is earthly, i.e., the *sárx*.

c. Jms. 3:15. In this verse *psychikós* describes what is earthly and closed to God's world. In this case, however, demonic influence is involved and disorder results.

d. Jude 19. What is *psychikós* is equated here with what is ungodly. Without the Spirit's aid the person who is *psychikós* will be the victim of desire and will cause division.

[E. Schweizer, IX, 661-63]

anapsýchō.

1. The basic sense of this word is "to cool or refresh with a breath" or "to dry out." In medicine treating a wound with fresh air is meant. The transferred use for "restoration" or "refreshment" either physical or spiritual is very old.

[A. Dihle, IX, 663-64]

2. In the LXX "to refresh oneself" means "to regain strength" (Ex. 23:12; Judg. 15:19; 2 Sam. 16:14; Ps. 39:13).

3. In the LXX the verb is always intransitive, but in the NT it is transitive in 2 Tim. 1:16 in the sense either of attending to the needs of Paul in prison or of bringing spiritual encouragement, or possibly both. [E. SCHWEIZER, IX, 664]

anápsyxis.
1. This word means "cooling," "drying out," "refreshing," "alleviation," "relief," or "rest." [A. DIHLE, IX, 664]
2. The only NT instance is in Acts 3:20. The "times of refreshing" are the eschatological age of salvation which comes with Israel's repentance. The context is one of admonition. To the large number of Jews already converted will be added believing Gentiles. The parousia will thus bring the perfecting of Israel.
[E. SCHWEIZER, IX, 664-65]

dípsychos. This term (Jms. 1:8; 4:8) denotes the "divided" person. Behind it lies the OT thought of the divided heart (cf. Dt. 29:17; Ezek. 14:3ff.). Hermas is fond of the word and of the derived *dipsychía*. [E. SCHWEIZER, IX, 665]

oligópsychos.
1. This rare word means "faint-hearted," perhaps on the basis of physical weakness (cf. *oligopsychía*, meaning "short breath").
2. Along with the related verb and noun the term occurs in the LXX with the nuances "despondent," "cross," "impatient," "exhausted." "Faint-hearted" or "anxious" occurs only in Sir. 4:9, and "short-tempered" seems to be the point in Prov. 14:29. The normal use is for "despondent" in a religious sense (Is. 25:5; 35:4).
[G. BERTRAM, IX, 666]
3. In 1 Th. 5:14 the term suggests weakness of faith and may be compared with *sýmpsychos* in Phil. 2:2, *isópsychos* in 2:20, and *eupsychô* in 2:19 (but not *ápsychos* for a "lifeless" musical instrument in 1 Cor. 14:7). The reference is to inner spiritual vigor (or the lack of it) in relation to the task that God has set.
[E. SCHWEIZER, IX, 666]

psychrós → *zéō*

ω   *Ō*

Ō → *Alpha and Omega*; *ōdḗ* → *adō*

ōdín [birthpang],   **ōdínō** [to suffer birthpangs]

A. Secular Greek. Of uncertain derivation, *ōdínō* means "to suffer birthpangs" and *ōdínes* are "birthpangs." Homer uses the term figuratively for the sudden and violent pain of wounds. Plato relates the group to Socrates' work as a midwife of knowledge. Aristotle reserves it for the natural process of birth. Plotinus finds for it both a cosmological and a psychological application. The emanation of lower hypostases is like a painful birth. In mythology the goddesses of fate are present at birth and rule over the pangs, which may be the cause of death. *ōdís* may denote the result of the pangs, i.e., "fruit" or "child."

B. The LXX. The LXX introduces more subjective terms for the pains of childbirth and uses *ōdínō* and *ōdínes* for Hebrew terms that denote pregnancy as such. When Hebrew employs the metaphor of childbirth, the reference is more to the convulsive trembling than to the pain, and at issue are the anxiety and distress caused by war, affliction, or divine judgment. In Isaiah the concept expressed by *ōdínō* is that of national birth or rebirth (cf. 45:10; 51:1-2; 54:1ff.). The image of travail points beyond itself as even in judgment there is expectation of new salvation. As God takes out of the natural womb (Ps. 22:9), so he takes out of the womb of suffering and death; he will not finally destroy (Jer. 17:7; Jon. 4:11).

C. Judaism.

1. Qumran, Ethiopian Enoch, and 4 Esdras. Qumran compares the sufferings of the poet to those of a woman in travail, but it is unclear who the woman or her child or children represent. The only sure point is that end-time sufferings are in view. The community lives under pressures that are a prelude to the messianic age. Eth. En. 62:4 refers to birthpangs in face of final judgment, and 4 Esdr. 4:42 uses the metaphor for the new birth of resurrection.

2. Philo. Philo expounds the OT birth stories allegorically. The soul receives the seed of divine wisdom, falls into labor, and bears a sound mind. If it tries to bear without God's blessing, the result is a miscarriage or the birth of what is bad. The one soul may bear either Abel or Cain. Wisdom receives God's seed and gives birth to the sons of God, i.e., the world.

3. Josephus. Josephus uses *ōdínes* only on an OT basis for pregnancy or labor.

4. The Rabbinic Tradition. Many rabbis find the metaphor of travail in Ps. 18:4. Connected is the idea of the woes of the Messiah or the birthpangs of the messianic age, namely, unrest, war, plague, and famine. Study of the law and works of love afford protection against these afflictions.

D. The NT. 1 Th. 5:3 adopts the metaphor and uses the singular either collectively or with reference to the first and sudden pang. The point here is that destruction will unexpectedly overtake those who live in self-security. Afflictions will usher in the end time in Mk. 13:8, although when they occur one must not overhastily expect the end. Mt. 24:8 relates "beginning of sorrows" to all the eschatological woes that precede the new birth of the world; they indicate the imminence of the time of salvation. In Rom. 8:22 the afflictions are a cosmic event. All creation waits for the new birth of the world, the coming into being of a new heaven and a new earth. In Gal. 4:27 Paul quotes Is. 54:1: The woman who does not bear has many children, i.e., believers, through God's gracious miracle. Yet in 4:19 members of the church come to faith only through Paul's painful efforts on their behalf, which are like the pangs of labor. Rev. 12:2 offers the sign of the pregnant woman who cries out in her pain. Acts 2:24 refers to the new birth of the resurrection. The abyss cannot hold Christ any more than the womb can hold the child; God helps it to end the pains with the release of the Redeemer. The christological orientation fits in with the general picture of birthpangs as a sign both of end and of renewing, and therefore as an admonition and warning to the church.

E. The Apostolic Fathers and Apologists. In these works the OT and NT influence is limited to a few quotations that are handled in stereotyped fashion (cf. Pol. 1.2; 2 Clem. 2.1-2; Justin *Apology* 53.5; *Dialogue* 85.8-9 etc.).

→ *lýpē, odýnē, páschō*   [G. BERTRAM, IX, 667-74]

---

hṓra [hour]

A. **Nonbiblical Usage.**

1. This word first means a "right, fixed, or favorable time," e.g., for sowing, marrying, etc. It may then be the "customary time" or a "set" or "appointed time."

2. A special use is for the "best" time. This may be the time of greatest bodily fitness, i.e., the "bloom of youth."

3. We then get the sense of "short stretch of time," or "hour" (cf. the "hour" of death, but also the last "moment").

B. **The LXX.** In the LXX we find the usual senses "fixed time," "time," "usual time," "appointed time," "short period of time." The meaning "hour" occurs only in works with no Hebrew original. The idea of imminence sometimes occurs (cf. *pró hōras*, "prematurely," or *katá tḗn hōran taútēn*, "now").

C. **The NT.**

1. In the NT we find "set time" in Lk. 14:17 (cf. the "hour" of prayer in Acts 3:1). In Rev. 9:15 a specific "hour" is set for an apocalyptic event. The hour may be an "hour of judgment" (14:7), an "hour to reap" (14:15), or an "hour of trial" (3:10). The content of the hour of Jn. 12:27 gives it special significance as "this hour"; "hour" can stand for the content (Mk. 14:35). The "hour" of dawn is the time to awake out of sleep and to act with vigilance (Rom. 13:11-12).

2. The expression *hōra tinós* denotes the time for human suffering or action. "Her hour" is the hour when a woman is to bear her child in Jn. 16:21. Similarly Jesus fulfils the requirement of the hour that God has set for him, e.g., when he goes to the cross in 13:1. He knows that "his hour" has not yet come (7:30; 8:20). The thought is that of obedience to the divine will and purpose (cf. 2:4). Negatively the hour may be that of his opponents (16:4; cf. Lk. 22:53).

3. With "my time has come" we also find "the time has come," i.e., God's appointed time (Jn. 17:1; Mk. 14:41). In Lk. 22:14 the reference is to the time for the Passover ("when the hour [of the Passover] came").

4. In Jn. 4:21, 23; 5:25, 28; 16:2, 25 the phrase "the time will come" intimates future events. "And now is" in 4:23 (cf. 16:32) shows that something is just at hand. *eschátē hōra* is the "end time."

5. *hōra* can also denote a fixed time (cf. "from that time" in Mt. 9:22, or "in that moment" in 8:13, or "instantly" in Acts 16:18). God will give the right words "at the time" of trial (Mk. 13:11).

6. No one knows the day or hour of the parousia, not even the Son (Mk. 13:32). In this context "hour" may be simply a section of the day or night; it is not necessarily a twelfth part of the day. The Son comes unexpectedly; this is the point in Mt. 12:44. We do not know the day or hour of the bridegroom's coming (25:13), nor when the thief comes (24:43). Watchfulness is thus demanded (Mk. 13:33ff.).

7. A strict "hour" is the meaning in Jn. 11:9. Except in Mt. 20:3, 5-6 the Synoptic Gospels give specific times only for the events of the passion (Mk. 15:25, 33-34; cf. Jn. 19:14). Jn. 1:39 and 4:52-53 give the times for particular reasons. Details of time also occur in Acts 10:3, 30; 23:23. Acts 5:7 and 19:34 mention periods of hours. Lk. 22:59 refers to a short time of about an hour. Contrast with "forever" occurs in Phlm. 15, and *mían hōran* means "for a short time" in Rev. 17:12.

D. **The Apostolic Fathers.** In these works we find the meanings 1. "a set time"

(Pol. 7.1); 2. an "hour" with specific content (Mart. Pol. 14.2); 3. the twelfth part of a day (Hermas *Visions* 3.1.2); 4. a "short time" in contrast to eternal life (Mart. Pol. 2.3); 5. (in the plural) a period of hours (Mart. Pol. 7.3); and 6. a "period of time" (Hermas *Similitudes* 6.4.4). [G. DELLING, IX, 675-81]

→ *kairós, chrónos*

---

hōsanná [hosanna]

---

1. This word is usually seen as a transliteration of the Hebrew expression *hôšî-'â(-n)nā'*, which is a cry for help (Ps. 118:25), which with the Hallel Psalms (113–118) comes into liturgical use, which, accompanied by the waving of branches at Tabernacles, then becomes a shout of jubilation in the solemn procession around the altar of burnt offering, and which echoes the messianic hope inasmuch as Ps. 118 sometimes finds a messianic interpretation.

2. The NT uses the term in the story of the entry into Jerusalem. The "blessed is he . . ." of Ps. 118:25 occurs with it in Mk. 11:9-10, and v. 10 brings out its messianic significance. The repetition of *hōsanná* points to the fulfilment of the messianic hope in Jesus. Luke omits the *hōsanná*, which Gentile readers would not understand, but has "peace on earth and glory in the highest" (cf. 2:14). Matthew retains the double *hōsanná* in shorter form (21:9). In a later repetition he emphasizes the "Son of David" (v. 15). When the authorities object, Jesus defends the cries of the children on the basis of Ps. 8:2; children are a model of true discipleship. In John the cry is the same as in Mark (Jn. 12:13); the addition "the King of Israel" shows precisely that "he who comes" is the Messiah.

3. As a liturgical cry *hōsanná* quickly finds a place in Christian worship (Did. 10.6). The church probably adopts it from the liturgical tradition of Judaism. It bears a christological and eschatological character (cf. Eusebius *Ecclesiastical History* 2.23.13-14, where it occurs in the story of the martyrdom of James, the Lord's brother). The Gentile church, however, is not familiar with its original meaning, as may be seen from the explanation given by Clement of Alexandria in *Paedagogus* 1.5.12.5. [E. LOHSE, IX, 682-84]

ōtárion, ōtíon → *oús*